YEARBOOK OF THE
UNITED NATIONS
1971

Volume 25

YEARBOOK
OF THE
UNITED
NATIONS
1971

Volume 25

Office of Public Information
United Nations, New York

14978

UNITED NATIONS PUBLICATION

SALES NO.: E.73.I.1

Manufactured in the United States of America

Foreword

At a time when the United Nations is approaching its goal of full universality of membership, and when its work affects virtually all human activities, the role of the *Yearbook of the United Nations* is more important than ever.

The *Yearbook* provides an authoritative and concise account of these activities. But it is not only valuable as a work of historical record; it provides us with the opportunity to evaluate the performance of the world organization and to give us guidance for the future.

The United Nations urgently needs an informed public if it is to succeed in its many tasks, and the *Yearbook* plays an important role in this process. It is used as the standard publication on the annual work of the United Nations, and it enables all who are interested in that work—and particularly diplomats, government officials, scholars, teachers and journalists—to have full and accurate information, easily obtained.

Those who study the *Yearbook* see quickly how the work of the United Nations has changed and expanded since its foundation in 1946. But despite the movement of the world organization into new fields of activity not anticipated by its founders, the essential objectives have not changed. These are the restoration and establishment of lasting peace; the elimination of injustice and oppression; and the eradication of human suffering and misery in all its forms.

These goals are eternal. The *Yearbook of the United Nations* describes how the world organization is endeavouring to achieve them, and to create a real international partnership between nations.

KURT WALDHEIM
Secretary-General

Contents

Part One: *The United Nations*

POLITICAL AND SECURITY QUESTIONS

ECONOMIC AND SOCIAL QUESTIONS

QUESTIONS RELATING TO TRUST AND NON-SELF-GOVERNING TERRITORIES AND THE DECLARATION ON GRANTING INDEPENDENCE

LEGAL QUESTIONS

ADMINISTRATIVE AND BUDGETARY QUESTIONS

Part Two: *The inter-governmental organizations related to the United Nations*

Appendices

Indices

LIST OF ABBREVIATIONS

ACABQ	Advisory Committee on Administrative and Budgetary Questions
ACC	Administrative Committee on Co-ordination
CPC	Committee for Programme and Co-ordination
ECA	Economic Commission for Africa
ECAFE	Economic Commission for Asia and the Far East
ECE	Economic Commission for Europe
ECLA	Economic Commission for Latin America
FAO	Food and Agriculture Organization of the United Nations
GATT	General Agreement on Tariffs and Trade
IAEA	International Atomic Energy Agency
ICAO	International Civil Aviation Organization
ICITO	Interim Commission for the International Trade Organization
ICJ	International Court of Justice
ICSAB	International Civil Service Advisory Board
IDA	International Development Association
IFC	International Finance Corporation
ILO	International Labour Organisation
IMCO	Inter-Governmental Maritime Consultative Organization
ISMAC	Israel-Syria Mixed Armistice Commission
ITU	International Telecommunication Union
IUOTO	International Union of Official Travel Organizations
NGO	Non-Governmental Organization
OAS	Organization of American States
OAU	Organization of African Unity
OPEX	United Nations Programme for Provision of Operational, Executive and Administrative Personnel
UNCTAD	United Nations Conference on Trade and Development
UNCURK	United Nations Commission for the Unification and Rehabilitation of Korea
UNDP	United Nations Development Programme
UNEF	United Nations Emergency Force
UNEPRO	United Nations East Pakistan Relief Operation
UNESCO	United Nations Educational, Scientific and Cultural Organization
UNESOB	United Nations Economic and Social Office at Beirut (Lebanon)
UNFICYP	United Nations Peace-keeping Force in Cyprus
UNHCR	United Nations High Commissioner for Refugees (Office of)
UNICEF	United Nations Children's Fund
UNIDO	United Nations Industrial Development Organization
UNITAR	United Nations Institute for Training and Research
UNMOGIP	United Nations Military Observer Group for India and Pakistan
UNRWA	United Nations Relief and Works Agency for Palestine Refugees in the Near East
UNTSO	United Nations Truce Supervision Organization in Palestine
UPU	Universal Postal Union
WFP	World Food Programme
WHO	World Health Organization
WMO	World Meteorological Organization
WWW	World Weather Watch
Y.U.N.	*Yearbook of the United Nations*

EXPLANATORY NOTE ON DOCUMENTS

To assist readers who wish to make a more detailed study of subjects discussed in Part One of this *Yearbook of the United Nations,* documentary references are provided at the end of each chapter and sub-chapter. These references give the symbols and titles of documents of the principal organs of the United Nations dealing with the subject concerned, records of voting and texts of adopted resolutions. Also listed are the numbers of the meetings of the various organs at which the subject dealt with was discussed. These meeting numbers indicate the relevant discussion records.

For those unfamiliar with United Nations documentation, the following information may serve as a guide to the principal document symbols:

A/- refers to documents of the General Assembly. A/C.- documents are those of six of its Main Committees, e.g., A/C.1/- is a document of the First Committee, A/C.2/L.- a document of the Second Committee, the "L" denoting limited circulation. The symbol for documents of the seventh Main Committee of the Assembly, the Special Political Committee, is A/SPC/-. A/AC.- documents are those of *ad hoc* bodies of the Assembly, e.g., A/AC.105/- refers to a document of the Assembly's Committee on the Peaceful Uses of Outer Space.

E/- refers to documents of the Economic and Social Council. E/AC.- and E/C.- documents are those of Committees of the Council, e.g., E/AC.6/- refers to a document of the Economic Committee, and E/C.2/- to a document of the Council Committee on Non-Governmental Organizations. E/CN.- documents are those of the Commissions of the Council, each of which also has its own number. E/ICEF/- indicates documents of the United Nations Children's Fund (UNICEF).

S/- refers to documents of the Security Council.

T/- refers to documents of the Trusteeship Council.

DC/- refers to documents of the Disarmament Commission.

DP/- refers to documents of the United Nations Development Programme.

ID/- refers to documents of the United Nations Industrial Development Organization.

TD/B/- refers to documents of the Trade and Development Board of the United Nations Conference on Trade and Development.

U.N.P. designates United Nations sales publications.

Full titles are given for documents of the International Court of Justice.

PART ONE

The United Nations

Political and security questions

Disarmament and related matters

Among the collateral measures of disarmament and arms control discussed in 1971, two questions received particular attention both in the Conference of the Committee on Disarmament and in the General Assembly. These questions were the banning of underground nuclear weapon tests and the prohibition and destruction of chemical and bacteriological (biological) weapons. There was also considerable discussion during the year of the methods and procedures to be followed in future disarmament negotiations, including a proposal for a world disarmament conference.

The Conference of the Committee on Disarmament met at Geneva, Switzerland, from late February to mid-May and then from the end of June to the end of September. In its report to the twenty-sixth session of the General Assembly (which opened on 21 September 1971), the Conference submitted a special report on its deliberations on a treaty banning underground nuclear weapon tests. Also, it transmitted with its report a draft convention on the prohibition of the development, production and stockpiling of bacteriological (biological) and toxin weapons and on their destruction for the Assembly to examine.

The General Assembly considered this draft convention and, on 16 December 1971, commended it in a resolution (for details, see pp. 15-21). The General Assembly also adopted 13 other resolutions concerning various disarmament measures. Three of them dealt with general and complete disarmament (for details, see pp. 12-15).

Another two resolutions were concerned with chemical and bacteriological (biological) weapons (for details, see pp. 15-22). Three resolutions were concerned with the suspension of nuclear and thermonuclear tests (for details, see pp. 22-26). The balance of the Assembly's resolutions on disarmament pertained to: ratification by nuclear-weapon States of Additional Protocol II of the Treaty for the Prohibition of Nuclear Weapons in Latin America (see pp. 26-27); nuclear explosions for peaceful purposes (see pp. 28-29); the economic and social consequences of the armaments race (see pp. 29-30); the convening of a world disarmament conference (see pp. 30-33); and the declaration of the Indian Ocean as a zone of peace (see pp. 33-35).

The Conference of the Committee on Disarmament

During 1971, the Conference of the Committee on Disarmament (CCD) held two sessions at Geneva, Switzerland, the first from 23 February to 13 May and the second from 29 June to 30 September.

The following States continued to participate in the work of the Conference: Argentina, Brazil, Bulgaria, Burma, Canada, Czechoslovakia, Egypt, Ethiopia, Hungary, India, Italy, Japan, Mexico, Mongolia, Morocco, the Netherlands, Nigeria, Pakistan, Poland, Romania, Sweden, the USSR, the United Kingdom, the United States and Yugoslavia. As in previous years, France did not participate.

On 1 October 1971, the Committee submitted its report to the General Assembly.

The Committee reported that CCD had continued work on the following measures in the field of disarmament: (1) further effective measures relating to the cessation of the nuclear arms race at an early date and to nuclear disarmament; (2) non-nuclear measures; (3) other collateral measures; and (4) general and complete disarmament under strict and effective international control.

As requested by the General Assembly on 7 December 1970,[1] the Committee also submitted to the Assembly a special report on the results of its deliberations on a treaty banning underground nuclear weapon tests.

Further, the Committee reported that, keeping in mind the recommendations of the General Assembly, CCD had continued its efforts to achieve progress on all aspects of the problem of elimination of chemical and bacteriological (biological) weapons. The text of a draft convention on the prohibition of the development, production and stockpiling of bacteriological (biological) and toxin weapons and on their destruction was attached to the Committee's report.

[1]See Y.U.N., 1970, pp. 31-32, text of resolution 2663B(XXV).

Nuclear disarmament

Special report on treaty banning underground nuclear weapon tests

A number of possible approaches towards progress on the question of drafting a treaty banning underground nuclear weapon tests were presented in CCD. However, the basic difference between the principal parties concerning the means of controlling a ban on underground nuclear tests persisted.

The USSR and those Committee members supporting its position restated the view that a reliable control did not represent any real difficulty and could be achieved without on-site inspections.

Most of the 12 members of the Committee who described themselves as non-aligned (Argentina, Brazil, Burma, Egypt, Ethiopia, India, Mexico, Morocco, Nigeria, Pakistan, Sweden and Yugoslavia) as well as a number of others, including Canada, Italy, Japan and the Netherlands, agreed that obstacles to an adequate verification of underground tests had so diminished that only a political decision was necessary for an immediate underground test ban.

However, the United States, supported by the United Kingdom, expressed continued belief that adequate verification required on-site inspections.

Several specific recommendations were made by members of the Committee regarding a comprehensive test ban agreement. (A comprehensive test ban treaty would extend to underground tests the existing ban on tests in all other environments.)

Sweden submitted a working paper with suggestions as to possible provisions of a treaty banning underground nuclear weapon tests. This was a revised version of a Swedish proposal made to CCD in 1969.[2] The revised treaty would provide for: (1) the prohibition, after a phasing-out period to be specified in a protocol to the treaty, of all underground nuclear weapon tests or other underground nuclear explosions, with the exception of explosions for peaceful purposes; (2) explosions for peaceful purposes which could be carried out in conformity with a second protocol annexed to the treaty; and (3) co-operation of the parties in the full implementation of the treaty, in an effective exchange of seismological data—as specified in a third protocol attached to the treaty—and in the clarification of all events pertaining to the subject of the treaty.

As in the 1969 Swedish draft treaty, each party would be entitled: (1) to make inquiries and to receive information in reply; (2) to invite inspection on its own territory in a manner it prescribed; (3) to propose suitable methods of clarification if it deemed the information made available to it inadequate; and (4) to bring to the attention of the Security Council and other parties the fact that it deemed a party to have failed to co-operate in the fullest clarification of a particular event. A new article would provide for a review conference.

In submitting the new proposal, Sweden expressed the hope it would contribute to more specific negotiations on a comprehensive test ban without binding any member to any specific wording.

A memorandum on a comprehensive test ban treaty was jointly submitted by Burma, Egypt, Ethiopia, Mexico, Morocco, Nigeria, Pakistan, Sweden and Yugoslavia. The authors of the memorandum pointed out, *inter alia*, that as yet not all nuclear-weapon States had adhered to the partial test ban Treaty (the Treaty Banning Nuclear Weapon Tests in the Atmosphere, in Outer Space and under Water, signed in Moscow, USSR, on 5 August 1963[3]) and that tests still continued in the atmosphere and underground. They believed that scientific progress had taken place in the field of seismology so that the verification problem could be resolved on the basis of national means of detection, supplemented and improved upon by international co-operation and procedures. Such measures, coupled with a withdrawal clause and provisions for review conferences, should ensure the required deterrence level against clandestine testing.

They also felt that peaceful application of nuclear explosives needed to be regulated, with an important role to be played by the International Atomic Energy Agency. The partial test ban treaty and a treaty banning underground tests, they stated, should be adhered to by all nuclear-weapon States. The testing nuclear-weapon States should give priority to a treaty banning underground tests and should take an active and constructive part in working it out. The nuclear-weapon States were requested to submit urgently their own proposals so that purposeful negotiations could be immediately undertaken.

Pakistan submitted a proposal on the relationship between nuclear weapons and peaceful nuclear explosive devices. Pakistan proposed that an underground test ban treaty include two specific provisions in this regard: for the nuclear-weapon States the proposed treaty would prohibit all underground nuclear weapon tests, but permit explosions for peaceful purposes in conformity with an international agreement to be negotiated separately; for the non-nuclear-weapon States all underground nuclear explosions would be prohibited.

Several specific problems connected with the underground test ban were discussed by the Committee.

[2]See Y.U.N., 1969, pp. 4-5, for details.
[3]See Y.U.N., 1963, pp. 124-26 and 137-40.

On the question of verification, CCD members felt that progress during the last several years in the means of detecting and identifying underground tests was narrowing the differences that had so far persisted on the verification issue. Mexico suggested that renewed consideration be given to the role of automatic seismic stations ("black boxes") for verification. This had been proposed in 1962.[4] The USSR, however, expressed doubts that resumed discussion of this proposal would lead to progress.

In this context, international co-operation in the exchange of seismic data, improvement of worldwide seismological capabilities, and further study of detection and identification of underground nuclear tests were also discussed.

A number of Committee members dealt with the question of banning underground tests above a certain threshold (i.e. above a specified level on the Richter scale used to measure the magnitude of earthquakes) and of adopting certain interim measures pending achievement of a comprehensive ban.

Canada and Japan supported a United Kingdom suggestion that, pending a comprehensive test ban, tests above a certain magnitude should be banned.

Several members opposed this suggestion. The USSR stated that the idea of a threshold ban was based on the assumption that some tests were not identifiable by national means, which was not acceptable to the USSR.

Czechoslovakia, Egypt, Ethiopia, the Netherlands and Sweden expressed doubts on the desirability of a threshold treaty.

Canada suggested that pending a total ban on underground testing, certain transitional or confidence-building measures should be considered that would reduce underground testing and represent progress towards a comprehensive ban. Canada outlined the following steps: (1) measures to help develop seismological techniques through (a) advance notification of the details of planned underground explosions and (b) undertakings to co-operate in the use, development and improvement of monitoring facilities; (2) measures to reduce testing and its harmful effects through (a) undertaking to reduce testing, beginning with large explosions, and (b) consideration of measures against environmental risks.

Italy, Japan, the Netherlands and Sweden supported the suggestion for transitional measures.

The USSR, on the other hand, maintained that partial or transitional measures would not be helpful in achieving a comprehensive test ban. Moreover, the publication of underground nuclear testing programmes would facilitate the acquisition of information by military services of other States, but would not help in the solution of halting underground nuclear tests.

Mongolia felt that suggestions for a partial solution had questionable political and technical aspects and could delay a comprehensive solution.

With regard to the type of international instrument to be used for a ban on underground tests, Canada, the Netherlands, Sweden and the USSR favoured a treaty independent from the partial test ban Treaty.

Sweden considered it unwise to try to achieve the desired comprehensive test ban by renegotiating the partial test ban Treaty, as that might open questions now settled by a treaty binding on more than 100 parties.

Pakistan suggested that the ban on underground tests could be a protocol to the partial test ban Treaty. Sweden agreed, but stressed that a protocol should not affect the provisions of the Treaty.

Concluding its special report to the General Assembly, CCD stated that it would continue negotiations on this matter as a priority item, taking into consideration the various proposals put forward during its 1971 session.

Other aspects of nuclear disarmament

Other matters relating to nuclear disarmament on which CCD members expressed views were the bilateral negotiations between the USSR and the United States on the limitation of strategic armaments (the Strategic Arms Limitation Talks, known as SALT); nuclear-free zones; prohibition of the use of nuclear weapons; a cut-off in the production of fissionable material for weapon purposes; and implementation of the Treaty on the Non-Proliferation of Nuclear Weapons[5] (which came into force on 5 March 1970), including a safeguards system of the International Atomic Energy Agency.

Question of chemical and bacteriological (biological) weapons

During 1971, CCD continued work on the problem of the elimination of chemical and bacteriological (biological) weapons. The Committee had before it various proposals, namely: the revised draft convention on the prohibition of biological methods of warfare, submitted in 1970 by the United Kingdom; and the revised draft convention on the prohibition of the development, production and stockpiling of chemical and bacteriological (biological) weapons and on the destruction of such weapons, submitted in 1970 by Bulgaria, the Byelorussian SSR, Czechoslovakia,

[4]See Y.U.N., 1962, p. 12.
[5]See Y.U.N., 1968, pp. 17-19, for text of Treaty.

Hungary, Mongolia, Poland, Romania, the Ukrainian SSR and the USSR; as well as other working papers and suggestions put forward in CCD and in the First Committee of the General Assembly (at its 1970 session).[6]

The Assembly, on 7 December 1970,[7] had taken note of these proposals. The General Assembly had also commended the basic approach to the solution of the problem of chemical and biological weapons, suggested in a joint memorandum submitted on 25 August 1970 to CCD by 12 members, according to which both chemical and bacteriological weapons should continue to be dealt with together, and verification should be based on a combination of appropriate national and international measures.

At the beginning of the Committee's session, efforts were aimed at a comprehensive solution of the problem of chemical and biological weapons, an approach supported by the great majority of members. The USSR and the other sponsors of the revised draft convention on chemical and bacteriological weapons maintained that their draft was a sound basis for an agreement.

Argentina, Brazil, Egypt, Ethiopia, India, Mexico, Morocco, Nigeria, Sweden and Yugoslavia felt that efforts in 1971 should be concentrated on reaching agreement on a ban on all chemical and biological weapons, in pursuance of the approach commended by the General Assembly in 1970.

The United States maintained that there was no prospect for early progress on the basis of a comprehensive approach. However, the United States felt it was possible to reach agreement on biological weapons without delay.

The United Kingdom was prepared to consider chemical and biological weapons together, but noted that the deliberations during the previous year had shown that the solution to the problem of verification of a ban on chemical weapons was still remote.

On 16 March 1971, Sweden submitted a working paper containing an outline of a model for a comprehensive agreement prohibiting chemical and biological means of warfare. Sweden proposed that the agreement should not include prohibitory rules against the use of chemical and biological weapons, since use had been dealt with in the 1925 Geneva Protocol for the Prohibition of the Use in War of Asphyxiating, Poisonous or Other Gases, and of Bacteriological Methods of Warfare; instead, it should contain an obligation not to develop, test, produce, stockpile or transfer those weapons or agents.

Verification should be based on a complaints procedure which would comprise a system of successive steps, including consultations, various fact-finding measures and, as a final step, lodging of complaints with the United Nations Security Council. More specific verification procedures would be concentrated on various categories of agents and on ways of destruction and disposal of existing stocks of chemical and bacteriological weapons, which would comprise international or a combination of national and international control measures.

On 30 March 1971, Bulgaria, Czechoslovakia, Hungary, Mongolia, Poland, Romania and the USSR introduced a draft convention on the prohibition of the development, production and stockpiling of bacteriological (biological) weapons and toxins and on their destruction. The draft text they submitted was also sponsored by two non-members of CCD: the Byelorussian SSR and the Ukrainian SSR.

According to this text, which consisted of a preamble and 14 articles, all States parties: would undertake not to develop, produce, stockpile or otherwise acquire microbiological or other biological weapons or toxins and means of their delivery; would destroy them within a period of three months; and would take all necessary legislative and administrative measures to implement the provisions of the convention. Also, they would be able to lodge a complaint with the United Nations Security Council in case of violations of the provisions by other parties. Further, a conference of States parties would be held five years after the entry of the convention into force, to review its operation.

Introducing the draft convention, the sponsors stressed that their position regarding the need to achieve the complete prohibition and elimination of chemical and bacteriological (biological) weapons remained unchanged. The new draft convention on bacteriological weapons, they said, was a compromise in a situation where the negative attitude of some Western powers made an agreement on the comprehensive prohibition of chemical and bacteriological weapons unlikely. The prohibition of bacteriological and toxin weapons would be a first step towards achieving the complete prohibition of chemical and bacteriological weapons.

Argentina, Brazil, Egypt, India, Italy, Morocco, the Netherlands, Nigeria, Pakistan, the United Kingdom and the United States welcomed the new draft convention as a positive step forward and hoped that the acceptance of the principle of a gradual approach to the prohibition of chemical and bacteriological weapons would be a basis for the preparation of a draft convention to be submitted to the twenty-sixth session of the General Assembly, due to open on 21 September 1971.

[6] See Y.U.N., 1970, pp. 5-7 and 22-26.
[7] *Ibid.*, p. 27, text of resolution 2662 (XXV).

Mexico, Sweden and Yugoslavia, on the other hand, criticized an agreement limited only to bacteriological (biological) weapons and toxins. They considered it to be only a marginal measure, since they felt there was little likelihood those weapons would ever be used. These members urged immediate negotiations on a comprehensive ban on both chemical and bacteriological weapons.

The discussion on the draft convention indicated differences on several specific questions. Among these were the following: whether to restate the ban on the use of biological weapons already covered by the 1925 Geneva Protocol; the legal formulation of the provisions concerning the international responsibility of the parties for implementation of the convention; the formulation of the undertaking to continue negotiations on the prohibition of chemical weapons; and the possible role of the United Nations Secretary-General in the complaints procedure in case of suspected violation of the convention.

On 5 August 1971, two separate but identical drafts of a convention on the prohibition of the development, production and stockpiling of bacteriological (biological) and toxin weapons and on their destruction were submitted. One was a revised version of the text proposed on 30 March by Bulgaria, Czechoslovakia, Hungary, Mongolia, Poland, Romania and the USSR and sponsored also by the Byelorussian SSR and the Ukrainian SSR. The second draft was sponsored by the United States.

The identical draft conventions contained a preamble and 14 articles.

By the preamble the parties would express their determination to achieve effective progress towards general and complete disarmament and their conviction that the prohibition of the development, production and stockpiling of bacteriological (biological) weapons and toxins intended for use as weapons, and their elimination, would facilitate the achievement of general and complete disarmament. Also, they would express their desire to exclude completely the possibility of bacteriological (biological) agents and toxins being used as weapons and their conviction of the immense importance and urgent necessity of eliminating from the arsenals of States such dangerous weapons of mass destruction as weapons using bacteriological (biological) agents and toxins.

Further, by the preamble, States parties would express their desire to contribute to the strengthening of confidence between peoples and the general improvement of the international atmosphere. They would express their belief that scientific discoveries in the field of bacteriology (biology) must be used solely for peaceful purposes, yet recognize, nevertheless, that in the absence of appropriate prohibitions the development of scientific knowledge throughout the world would increase the risk of the use of bacteriological methods of warfare.

Convinced that such use would be repugnant to the conscience of mankind and that no effort should be spared to minimize this risk, they would recognize the important significance of the 1925 Geneva Protocol to mitigating the horrors of war. States parties, reaffirming their adherence to the purposes and principles of that Protocol and calling on all States to comply strictly with them, and recalling General Assembly resolutions on the subject, would express their conviction that an agreement on the prohibition of bacteriological (biological) and toxin weapons would facilitate progress towards agreement on effective measures to prohibit the development, production and stockpiling of chemical weapons, on which negotiations would be continued.

Article I provided for an undertaking not to develop, produce, stockpile or otherwise acquire or retain biological agents or toxins that had no justification for prophylactic or other peaceful purposes, as well as weapons and means of delivery designed to use such agents or toxins for hostile purposes or in armed conflict.

Article II provided for the destruction or diversion to peaceful purposes within an agreed period of time of these agents, weapons, toxins and means of delivery.

Article III prohibited any transfers of these objects.

Article IV provided that States parties would take necessary measures to prohibit and prevent any activity prohibited under the convention on their territory or under their jurisdiction or control anywhere.

Article V dealt with consultation and co-operation among parties in implementing the convention.

Article VI dealt with the complaints procedure in the case of violation of the convention, i.e. States parties might lodge a complaint with the Security Council and would undertake to co-operate in any Security Council investigations.

Article VII provided that nothing in the convention should be interpreted as in any way limiting or detracting from the obligations assumed under the Geneva Protocol of 17 June 1925 for the Prohibition of the Use in War of Asphyxiating, Poisonous or Other Gases, and of Bacteriological Methods of Warfare.

Article VIII provided for an undertaking to conduct negotiations with a view to prohibiting chemical weapons.

Article IX dealt with international co-operation in peaceful uses of bacteriological (biological) agents and toxins.

Article X dealt with amendments to the convention, and article XI provided for the convening of a conference to review the operation of the convention.

Article XII contained a withdrawal clause. Articles XIII and XIV dealt with signatures and ratifications, authentic languages and depositary Governments of the convention.

Introducing the revised draft convention, the USSR said that the text reflected the opinions expressed by a number of CCD members. Thus, it recognized the significance of the 1925 Geneva Protocol and reaffirmed adherence to its purposes and principles. Due to different views as to whether the Protocol established a universally recognized rule of international law or whether it was obligatory only to its parties, no provisions were included in the draft reaffirming or refuting any of the above concepts. The sponsors of the draft text, however, continued to consider the prohibition of the use of all chemical and biological weapons as a universally recognized rule of international law. Prohibition of the use of biological weapons was not included in the draft, the USSR representative continued, because it was already codified by the Geneva Protocol. An important objective of the draft convention was to ensure the complete prohibition and elimination of chemical weapons and therefore the terms of the draft obliged States parties to conduct negotiations to this end.

The review conference provided for in the draft, he further explained, would examine also the implementation of provisions relating to the prohibition of chemical weapons. The draft convention was based on a combination of international and national safeguards against possible infringements.

The USSR representative pointed out that States parties would be obliged to adopt necessary measures for the implementation of the convention within their respective territories or under their jurisdiction or control anywhere; parties would undertake to consult and co-operate in solving problems arising from the implementation of the convention. The sponsors felt that the procedure permitting the lodging of a complaint with the Security Council ensured an objective investigation and the adoption of effective measures to suppress possible violations of the convention.

The United States said that the new parallel draft conventions were based primarily on the draft text submitted on 30 March, but owed much also to the United Kingdom's previous draft convention. While the prohibition of biological and toxin weapons would not solve the problem of chemical and biological weapons completely, it would control the deadliest and most indiscriminate weapons. Although biological weapons had never been used in hostilities their possible use caused widespread concern, since a potential existed for developing biological weapons against which there was no effective defence.

The United States representative said the draft convention would in no way detract from continued efforts to ban chemical weapons as well. It would also strengthen the Geneva Protocol. The inclusion of a ban on toxins would significantly broaden the scope of this first agreement in the field of chemical and bacteriological (biological) weapons. The United States was determined to find solutions to the difficult problem of verifying the ban on chemical weapons. It was not prepared, however, to support any formulation disregarding the problems of effective control in the field of chemical weapons.

Almost all the Committee members welcomed the submission of the two identical draft conventions as a suitable basis for negotiations on a broadly acceptable draft to be submitted to the twenty-sixth (1971) session of the General Assembly. Comments and suggestions for modifications were made orally by several members and written amendments were submitted jointly by 11 powers—Brazil, Burma, Egypt, Ethiopia, India, Mexico, Morocco, Nigeria, Pakistan, Sweden and Yugoslavia—and individually by Mexico and Morocco.

The 11-power amendments contained a number of suggestions dealing with preambular paragraphs of the two identical draft conventions. The amendments were designed to reflect the common basic approach of the sponsors that a link be maintained in respect of the prohibition of chemical and bacteriological weapons. A new preambular paragraph was also suggested: this would affirm the principle that a substantial portion of the savings derived from disarmament measures should be devoted to promoting economic and social development, particularly in the developing countries.

Also proposed was the addition of a new paragraph to article V (dealing with co-operation in implementing the convention) by which the consultation and co-operation provided for might also be undertaken through appropriate international procedures within the framework of the United Nations and in accordance with its Charter.

A revision of the article dealing with future negotiations on chemical weapons was proposed in order to strengthen the undertaking to continue negotiations in good faith with a view to reaching early agreement on the prohibition of these weapons.

Finally, an addition to the provision dealing with the peaceful uses of bacteriological agents and toxins was proposed, by which States parties to the convention should co-operate in contributing to the further development and application of scientific discoveries in the field of bacteriology for prevention of disease, or for other peaceful purposes.

Mexico suggested that a new article be inserted, providing that States parties undertake to refrain, pending an agreement on the prohibition of chemical weapons, from any further development, production or stockpiling for weapons purposes of highly toxic chemical agents, which would be listed in a protocol to the convention.

Morocco proposed, *inter alia:* that the international community should be notified, through the Secretary-General of the United Nations, of the destruction of biological and toxin agents as provided for in the convention; and also that a new article be added providing for humanitarian assistance to a party to the convention which requested it and was exposed, in violation of the convention, to dangers resulting from biological agents or toxins intended for military purposes.

Hungary, Mongolia and Poland submitted a working paper containing a draft Security Council resolution, by which the Council would: declare its readiness to consider immediately any complaints lodged under the draft convention; take all necessary measures to investigate; inform States parties of the results; and call on all States parties to co-operate for these purposes.

During the ensuing discussion, the sponsors of the 11-power amendments to the identical draft conventions stressed the necessity that a solid link be established between the ban on biological weapons and the ban on chemical weapons.

Canada, Japan, the Netherlands and the United Kingdom felt that the convention should prohibit the use of biological weapons, as well as their production. On the other hand, the USSR and the other sponsors of the draft convention it had introduced, as well as Egypt, India, Mexico, Morocco, Pakistan, Yugoslavia and others, considered the question of the use of biological weapons to be solved by the 1925 Geneva Protocol. They believed that the inclusion of a prohibition of the use of biological weapons might bring negative results and might, particularly, be misused for misinterpretation of the Protocol.

Argentina and Yugoslavia stressed the importance of the proposal to include in the preamble a provision that a substantial portion of the savings from disarmament should be devoted to promoting economic and social development, particularly in the developing countries.

Canada and Morocco proposed that notification be given to depositary Governments regarding the implementation of the provisions of article II, which provided for destruction or diversion to peaceful purposes of all agents, toxins and so forth

covered by the convention. The USSR declared its willingness to notify all parties of the destruction of biological weapons on the basis of reciprocity. The United States also announced its readiness to notify all parties on the implementation of this obligation and invited other States to follow this procedure.

On 28 September 1971, a revised draft convention on the prohibition of the development, production and stockpiling of bacteriological (biological) and toxin weapons and on their destruction, consisting of a preamble and 15 articles, was submitted. It was sponsored by Bulgaria, Canada, Czechoslovakia, Hungary, Italy, Mongolia, the Netherlands, Poland, Romania, the USSR, the United Kingdom and the United States.

The principal revisions in the newly revised draft convention were the following.

The preambular paragraphs referring to the significance of the 1925 Geneva Protocol and reaffirming the adherence of States parties to the principles and objectives of that Protocol were given prominence.

The phrase "never in any circumstances" was added to the undertaking in article I by which States parties agreed not to develop, produce, stockpile or retain bacteriological (biological) weapons or toxins.

The phrase "whatever their origin or method of production" was added to the reference to toxins in this same article, thus, the sponsors noted, broadening the definition of toxins. An exclusion from the ban of agents or toxins for "protective" purposes was also added.

The undertaking of States parties to consult with one another, set forth in article V, was further defined to include consultations and co-operation through appropriate international procedures within the framework of the United Nations and in accordance with its Charter.

A new article was added (article VII) by which States parties undertook to provide or support assistance, in accordance with the United Nations Charter, to any party requesting it, if the Security Council decided that such party had been exposed to danger as a result of violation of the convention.

The article providing for co-operation for peaceful purposes was expanded to include an undertaking by States parties to co-operate individually, or together with other States or international organizations, in the further development and application of scientific discoveries in the field of bacteriology (biology) for prevention of disease or for other peaceful purposes.

The USSR and the United States stressed that the new text resulted from the constructive discussion of previous drafts and careful study of all proposed amendments; it therefore seemed fair to consider it as a product of the entire

Conference. The main modification in the new text was the strengthening of the link between the biological weapons convention and the prohibition of chemical weapons.

The USSR and the United States commented also on the provisions dealing with the strengthening of the 1925 Geneva Protocol, and they called attention to the broad definition of toxins, which excluded the possibility of interpreting article I as prohibiting only certain types of toxins, and to the time-limit for the destruction of all biological weapons.

Members generally expressed satisfaction with the consensus achieved. The draft convention was annexed to the report of CCD to the General Assembly and members expressed the hope that it would be commended by the Assembly and opened for signature at an early date.

(The Convention was commended by the General Assembly on 16 December 1971 with the adoption of resolution 2826(XXVI). For text, see pp. 19-21).

Simultaneously with the negotiations on the draft convention on the prohibition and destruction of bacteriological (biological) and toxin weapons, negotiations continued in CCD on the prohibition of chemical weapons.

In addition to the proposals described above, papers on various aspects of the question were submitted by Canada, Italy, the Netherlands, Sweden and the United States.

On 28 September 1971, a joint memorandum on the prohibition of the development, production and stockpiling of chemical weapons and on their destruction was submitted by 12 powers: Argentina, Brazil, Burma, Egypt, Ethiopia, India, Mexico, Morocco, Nigeria, Pakistan, Sweden and Yugoslavia.

Recalling the memorandum they had submitted in 1970[8] and the General Assembly's resolution of 7 December 1970[9] outlining the basic approach to the prohibition of chemical and bacteriological weapons, they set forth several elements on which they believed further negotiations on the prohibition of chemical weapons should be based. These were: an obligation to prohibit the development, production, stockpiling, acquisition and retention of chemical weapons and their means of delivery; an undertaking not to assist any State or group of States in the prohibited activities; an undertaking to destroy or convert to peaceful uses all chemical weapons and means of delivery; an undertaking to disband special forces for using chemical weapons; solution of the problem of verification in accordance with the suggestions contained in the 12-power joint memorandum submitted in 1970; an understanding that any future agreement on the prohibition of chemical weapons would not limit or detract from the obligations under the 1925 Geneva Protocol; a provision that the prohibition of chemical weapons should not hamper peaceful utilization of chemical agents or hinder the economic or technological development of States parties; an undertaking to facilitate the exchange of materials and information for the use of chemical agents for peaceful purposes; and a recognition of the principle that a substantial part of the savings from disarmament should be devoted to economic and social development, particularly of the developing countries.

Other collateral measures

The Conference of the Committee on Disarmament (CCD) was informed by Hungary, Japan, Mongolia, the USSR and the United Kingdom of their ratifications of the Treaty on the Prohibition of the Emplacement of Nuclear Weapons and Other Weapons of Mass Destruction on the Sea-Bed and the Ocean Floor and in the Subsoil Thereof.[10]

Other questions raised in CCD included: conventional arms control, a European security conference and the freezing and reduction of military budgets.

General and complete disarmament

Taking into account the General Assembly's resolution of 7 December 1970 urging the Conference of the Committee on Disarmament (CCD) to try to accelerate the achievement of disarmament,[11] discussions on the question of general and complete disarmament were continued in CCD in 1971.

Mexico recommended that special attention be given to the comprehensive programme of disarmament which it, together with Ireland, Morocco, Pakistan, Sweden and Yugoslavia, had submitted to the General Assembly on 1 December 1970.[12]

India suggested that an appropriate balance should be maintained among measures to prevent armament, measures to limit armament and measures of disarmament. Also, India felt that it would be useful for the USSR and the United States to submit revisions of the draft treaties on general and complete disarmament which they had respectively submitted in 1962.[13] Furthermore, India observed that the 1961 United States/USSR Joint Statement of Agreed Principles for Disarmament Negotiations[14] should form a basis for concrete work in the Committee and that the general order of the Committee's priorities

[8]*Ibid.*, p. 6.
[9]See footnote 6.
[10]See Y.U.N., 1970, pp. 18-19, for text of Treaty.
[11]*Ibid.*, p. 21, text of resolution 2661 C (XXV).
[12]*Ibid.*, pp. 15-16.
[13]See Y.U.N., 1962, pp. 6-9.
[14]See Y.U.N., 1961, pp. 10-11.

should be on the lines suggested in the declaration on disarmament issued by the Third Conference of Heads of State or Government of Non-Aligned Countries, held at Lusaka, Zambia, in September 1970.

Hungary felt that when dealing with general and complete disarmament, the Committee should pay special attention to the 1961 United States/ USSR Joint Statement of Agreed Principles for Disarmament Negotiations. Bulgaria, Hungary, Mongolia, Romania and the USSR were among other members declaring their readiness to continue efforts to achieve a positive solution of the problem of general and complete disarmament.

Italy suggested the establishment of a small working group to examine the principles of an organic programme of disarmament and proposed that CCD resume work on the problem of general and complete disarmament as the main item on its agenda for its next session in 1972.

Romania maintained that progress towards general disarmament could best be achieved by starting negotiations for the drafting of a treaty and suggested that official and informal meetings of the Committee be devoted to a thorough study of all aspects of this problem.

Argentina, Canada, Egypt, Japan, Mongolia, Pakistan and Romania pointed out the desirability of participation in disarmament negotiations by all militarily important States, including all nuclear-weapon States.

DOCUMENTARY REFERENCES

A/8457 (DC/234). Report of Conference of Committee on Disarmament (CCD) (for period 23 February–30 September 1971). (Annex C: Text of working papers and other CCD documents; Annex D: List of verbatim records of meetings of CCD.)

A/8457 (DC/234), Annex A. Draft convention on prohibition of development, production and stockpiling of bacteriological (biological) and toxin weapons and on their destruction.
A/8457 (DC/234), Chapter III. Special report on question of a treaty banning underground nuclear weapon tests.

Consideration of disarmament questions by the General Assembly

Eight disarmament items were on the agenda of the twenty-sixth session of the General Assembly, which opened on 21 September 1971. These included six items placed on the agenda by virtue of decisions taken by the Assembly in 1970. They were: the question of general and complete disarmament; the question of chemical and bacteriological (biological) weapons; the urgent need for suspension of nuclear and thermonuclear tests; the establishment, within the framework of the International Atomic Energy Agency (IAEA), of an international service for nuclear explosions for peaceful purposes under appropriate international control; the question of signature and ratification of Additional Protocol II of the Treaty for the Prohibition of Nuclear Weapons in Latin America (Treaty of Tlatelolco); and the economic and social consequences of the armaments race and its extremely harmful effects on world peace and security.

The question of convening a world disarmament conference was proposed for the agenda by the USSR, while an item suggesting an Assembly declaration of the Indian Ocean as a zone of peace was proposed for inclusion by Ceylon and the United Republic of Tanzania.

The Assembly decided to defer to its 1972 session items concerning the implementation of the results of the Conference of Non-Nuclear-Weapon States and a report from IAEA in this connexion. These had been placed on the provisional agenda by 1970 Assembly decisions on these subjects.

All of the agenda items, with the exception of that concerning a world disarmament conference, were discussed mainly in the Assembly's First Committee. The proposed world disarmament conference was discussed in plenary meetings.

The First Committee held a general debate on the seven items together, and then considered separately draft resolutions relating to each item. These discussions were conducted at meetings held between 11 November and 10 December 1971.

The Assembly adopted a total of 14 resolutions on these disarmament questions.

Three of them dealt with the question of general and complete disarmament, including the attainment of general and complete disarmament, the application of safeguards to nuclear material and means of informing public opinion.

Three resolutions had to do with the question of chemical and bacteriological (biological) weapons; these included one resolution commending the Convention on the Prohibition of the Development, Production and Stockpiling of Bacteriological (Biological) and Toxin Weapons and on Their Destruction and requesting early signature and ratification, and two resolutions urging action to prohibit chemical weapons.

Three other resolutions dealt with the suspension of nuclear and thermonuclear tests.

The subjects of the five remaining resolutions were: ratification by nuclear-weapon States of Additional Protocol II of the Treaty of Tlatelolco (by which those States would, among other things, respect the denuclearized status of Latin America); establishment of an international service for nuclear explosions for peaceful purposes; the economic and social consequences of the armaments race; the question of a world disarmament conference; and the declaration of the Indian Ocean as a zone of peace.

For details of these decisions, see the following sections.

General and complete disarmament

Discussion of the question of general and complete disarmament at the 1971 session of the General Assembly took place mainly in the Assembly's First Committee. A wide range of topics was covered, including: the question of progress towards general and complete disarmament; nuclear and conventional disarmament; the Treaty on the Non-Proliferation of Nuclear Weapons;[15] and expert reports and studies on disarmament.

The Committee had before it, in addition to the report of the Conference of the Committee on Disarmament: a letter dated 23 June 1971 from the Permanent Representative of the USSR to the Secretary-General transmitting a statement of the Government of the USSR concerning its proposal for convening a conference of the five nuclear-weapon powers; a letter from the Permanent Representative of Czechoslovakia to the Secretary-General concerning a conference on nuclear disarmament; and a letter from the Minister of Foreign Affairs of the German Democratic Republic addressed to the Chairman of the First Committee on the question of general and complete disarmament.

Progress towards general
and complete disarmament

Several Committee Members, including the USSR, the United Kingdom and the United States, maintained that the ultimate goal of general and complete disarmament should continue to be approached through pragmatic and limited agreements. Others believed that too much attention had been given to partial and collateral measures, which, they felt, had failed to bring the final goal any nearer.

India, the Philippines and Yugoslavia supported the view that there should be a thorough review and redefinition of the question of general and complete disarmament. They also recommended bringing up to date the United States and the USSR 1962 draft treaties on general and complete disarmament[16] which, together with the United States/USSR Joint Statement of Agreed Principles for Disarmament Negotiations of September 1961,[17] could serve as the basis for renewed negotiations.

Concern over the continuing momentum of the nuclear arms race was expressed by many speakers in the First Committee; it was urged that nuclear disarmament be given the highest priority in international negotiations. Several representatives, including those of China, Hungary, Mongolia, Pakistan, Poland and Romania, regarded the prohibition of the use of nuclear weapons as an important measure which would facilitate further progress in the field. Japan and Yugoslavia mentioned the importance of discontinuing the production of weapons-grade fissionable materials.

Several Members spoke favourably of the Strategic Arms Limitation Talks (known as SALT) between the USSR and the United States, particularly of a joint statement of May 1971 and agreements announced in September 1971 on measures to reduce the risk of nuclear war and to improve the direct telecommunication link between the United States and the USSR. A number of Members—including Brazil, Ireland and Pakistan—expressed dissatisfaction, however, with the slow pace of those negotiations and concern that an agreement at SALT would include only quantitative limitations and would not halt the qualitative arms race.

A few Members, including Indonesia and the United States, stressed that increased attention should be given to controlling conventional armaments, and especially conventional arms deliveries to the developing countries.

On 16 December 1971, the Assembly reaffirmed the responsibility of the United Nations in the attainment of general and complete disarmament and urged the Conference of the Committee on Disarmament (CCD) to resume its efforts on the question of general and complete disarmament along the lines set forth in the Assembly's resolution of 7 December 1970.[18] The Assembly also asked CCD to report to it in 1972 on the results of its efforts.

These Assembly decisions were embodied in resolution 2825 B (XXVI), adopted by a recorded vote of 105 to 0, with 4 abstentions. The text was approved by the First Committee on 8 December by 92 votes to 0, with 1 abstention, on the basis of a proposal sponsored by Denmark, Ethiopia, Gha-

[15]See Y.U.N., 1968, pp. 17-19, for text of Treaty.
[16]See Y.U.N., 1962, pp. 6-9.
[17]See Y.U.N., 1961, pp. 10-11.
[18]See Y.U.N., 1970, p. 21, text of resolution 2661 C (XXV).

na, Ireland, Italy, Malta, Morocco, the Philippines, Sweden, Uruguay and Yugoslavia.

(For text of resolution, see DOCUMENTARY REFERENCES below.)

Application of safeguards to nuclear material

Many Members commended the International Atomic Energy Agency (IAEA) for its elaboration of a safeguards system, as specified in article III of the Treaty on the Non-Proliferation of Nuclear Weapons.[19] Malta, however, believed that new methods of uranium enrichment posed a threat to the Treaty. Although the General Assembly, by a decision of 7 December 1970,[20] had called upon IAEA to pay attention to safeguard procedures for new techniques of uranium enrichment, Malta was disappointed with the rate of progress cited in the annual report of IAEA covering the period from 1 July 1970 to 30 June 1971.

Malta accordingly proposed that the General Assembly once again request that IAEA devote attention to safeguards applicable to new methods of uranium enrichment. This the Assembly did on 16 December 1971 with the adoption, by 89 votes to 0, with 17 abstentions, of resolution 2825 A (XXVI).

By this resolution, the Assembly expressed its confidence in the ability of IAEA to meet, without delay, the obligations likely to be placed upon it in respect of the application of safeguards to nuclear material in all types of civil nuclear facilities, including uranium enrichment plants.

The draft resolution proposed by Malta was approved by the First Committee on 8 December by a roll-call vote of 76 to 0, with 17 abstentions. (For text of resolution, see DOCUMENTARY REFERENCES below.)

Informing public opinion

By another decision taken on 16 December 1971, the General Assembly, considering that public opinion should be adequately informed about the problems of the arms race and of disarmament so that it might influence the strengthening of disarmament efforts: (1) affirmed the value of holding conferences of experts from various countries on the problem of the arms race; (2) supported the practice of requesting the Secretary-General to prepare, with the assistance of consultant experts, reports on concrete questions relating to disarmament; (3) declared that progress towards general and complete disarmament would be promoted if universities and academic institutions in all countries were to study the problems of the arms race; and (4) asked the Secretary-General to bring this resolution to the attention of all Member States and the United Nations Educational, Scientific and Cultural Organization with a view to its wide publication.

The text was adopted by the General Assembly by a recorded vote of 110 to 0. It was approved by the First Committee on 8 December by 94 votes to 0, with 2 abstentions, on the basis of a proposal sponsored by Ireland, Mexico, Morocco, Pakistan and the Philippines. (For text of resolution, see DOCUMENTARY REFERENCES below.)

---

[19]See footnote 15.
[20]See Y.U.N., 1970, p. 20, text of resolution 2661 B (XXV).

DOCUMENTARY REFERENCES

General Assembly—26th session
General Committee, meeting 191.
First Committee, meetings 1803, 1827-1843, 1845, 1846.
Plenary meetings 1937, 1939, 2022.

A/8328 (S/10236). Letter of 23 June 1971 from USSR.
A/8337 (S/10252). Letter of 6 July 1971 from Czechoslovakia.
A/8384. Note of 1 November 1971 by Secretary-General (transmitting 15th report of International Atomic Energy Agency for year ending 30 June 1971).
A/8401. Report of Secretary-General on work of the Organization, 16 June 1970–15 June 1971, Part One, Chapter IV A.
A/8401/Add.1. Introduction to report of Secretary-General, September 1971: Part One, Chapter IV: Part Two, Chapter II.
A/8429. Resolutions adopted by General Assembly during its 26th session, 21 September–22 December 1971. Decisions, p. 19.
A/8457 (DC/234). Report of CCD (covering period 23 February–30 September 1971).
A/8500. First report of General Committee.
A/C.1/1018. Letter of 9 November 1971 from German Democratic Republic.

Progress towards general and complete disarmament
A/C.1/L.589 and Corr.1. Denmark, Ethiopia, Ghana, Ireland, Italy, Malta, Mexico, Morocco, Philippines, Sweden, Uruguay, Yugoslavia: draft resolution, approved by First Committee on 8 December 1971, meeting 1846, by 92 votes to 0, with 1 abstention.
A/8573. Report of First Committee, draft resolution B.

RESOLUTION 2825 B (XXVI), as recommended by First Committee, A/8573, adopted by Assembly on 16 December 1971, meeting 2022, by recorded vote of 105 to 0, with 4 abstentions, as follows:

In favour: Afghanistan, Algeria, Australia, Austria, Bahrain, Belgium, Brazil, Bulgaria, Burma, Burundi, Byelorussian SSR, Cameroon, Canada, Central African Republic, Ceylon, Chad, Chile, Colombia, Congo, Costa Rica, Cuba, Cyprus, Czechoslovakia, Dahomey, Denmark, Dominican Republic, Ecuador, Egypt, Equatorial Guinea, Ethiopia, Fiji, Finland, Ghana, Greece, Guatemala, Guinea, Guyana, Honduras, Hungary, Iceland, India, Indonesia, Iran, Ireland, Israel, Italy, Ivory Coast, Jamaica, Japan, Jordan, Kenya, Khmer Republic, Kuwait, Laos, Lebanon, Lesotho, Liberia, Libyan Arab Republic, Luxembourg, Madagascar, Malaysia, Mali, Malta, Mauritania, Mexico, Mongolia, Morocco, Nepal, Netherlands, New Zealand, Nicaragua, Nigeria, Norway, Pakistan, Paraguay, People's Democratic Republic of Yemen, Peru, Philippines, Poland, Portugal, Romania, Rwanda, Saudi Arabia, Singapore, Somalia, South

Africa, Spain, Sweden, Thailand, Togo, Trinidad and Tobago, Tunisia, Turkey, Uganda, Ukrainian SSR, USSR, United Kingdom, United Republic of Tanzania, United States, Uruguay, Venezuela, Yemen, Yugoslavia, Zaire, Zambia.

Against: None.

Abstaining: France, Qatar, Senegal, Upper Volta.*

*Subsequently Upper Volta advised the Secretariat that it had intended to vote in favour.

The General Assembly,

Recalling its resolutions 1722(XVI) of 20 December 1961 and 2602 E (XXIV) of 16 December 1969,

Further recalling its resolution 2661 C (XXV) of 7 December 1970, in which it urged the Conference of the Committee on Disarmament to make more intensive efforts to bring about a faster pace towards the achievement of disarmament measures, expressed its appreciation of the important and constructive documents and views submitted at the Conference of the Committee on Disarmament, and recommended to the Conference that it take into account in its further work and its negotiations the comprehensive programme of disarmament as well as other documents presented on the same subject,

Considering that it has declared the decade of the 1970s as the Disarmament Decade,

Taking into account the proposals, suggestions and views put forward in the General Assembly and in the Conference of the Committee on Disarmament,

1. *Reaffirms* the responsibility of the United Nations in the fundamental goal of the attainment of general and complete disarmament;

2. *Urges* the Conference of the Committee on Disarmament, at its next session, to resume its efforts on the question of general and complete disarmament along the lines set forth in General Assembly resolution 2661 C (XXV);

3. *Requests* the Conference of the Committee on Disarmament to report to the General Assembly at its twenty-seventh session on the results of these efforts.

Application of safeguards to nuclear material

A/C.1/L.588. Malta: draft resolution, approved by First Committee on 8 December 1971, meeting 1846, by roll-call vote of 76 to 0, with 17 abstentions, as follows:

In favour: Australia, Austria, Barbados, Belgium, Bulgaria, Burma, Burundi, Byelorussian SSR, Cameroon, Canada, Ceylon, Chile, Costa Rica, Cyprus, Czechoslovakia, Denmark, Egypt, El Salvador, Ethiopia, Finland, Ghana, Greece, Guyana, Honduras, Hungary, Iceland, Indonesia, Iran, Ireland, Italy, Ivory Coast, Jamaica, Japan, Kenya, Khmer Republic, Lebanon, Liberia, Libyan Arab Republic, Madagascar, Malaysia, Malta, Mauritius, Mexico, Mongolia, Morocco, Nepal, Netherlands, New Zealand, Nicaragua, Niger, Nigeria, Norway, Pakistan, Panama, Philippines, Poland, Portugal, Saudi Arabia, Singapore, South Africa, Sudan, Swaziland, Sweden, Thailand, Togo, Trinidad and Tobago, Tunisia, Turkey, Uganda, Ukrainian SSR, USSR, United Kingdom, United States, Uruguay, Yemen, Yugoslavia.

Against: None.

Abstaining: Algeria, Argentina, Brazil, Central African Republic, Colombia, Congo, France, India, Israel, Kuwait, Peru, Romania, Senegal, Spain, United Republic of Tanzania, Venezuela, Zambia.

A/8573. Report of First Committee, draft resolution A.

RESOLUTION 2825 A (XXVI), as recommended by First Committee, A/8573, adopted by Assembly on 16 December 1971, meeting 2022, by 89 votes to 0, with 17 abstentions.

The General Assembly,

Recalling its resolution 2661 B (XXV) of 7 December 1970,

Noting with appreciation the report of the International Atomic Energy Agency,

Noting with satisfaction the success of the International Atomic Energy Agency in drawing up detailed guidelines for the structure and content of agreements between the Agency and States required in connexion with the Treaty on the Non-Proliferation of Nuclear Weapons,

Noting that the procedures embodied in such agreements are applicable to all stages of the nuclear fuel cycle and are to be concentrated on those stages involving the production, processing, use or storage of nuclear material from which nuclear weapons or other nuclear explosive devices could readily be made,

Noting from the report of the International Atomic Energy Agency that detailed safeguards procedures with respect to nuclear enrichment plants, including those employing new techniques of uranium enrichment, have still to be elaborated and applied,

1. *Expresses its confidence* in the ability of the International Atomic Energy Agency to meet, without delay, the obligations likely to be placed upon it in respect of the application of safeguards to nuclear material in all types of civil nuclear facilities, including uranium enrichment plants;

2. *Requests* the International Atomic Energy Agency to include in its annual report to the General Assembly full information on the progress of its work on the application of safeguards in connexion with the Treaty on the Non-Proliferation of Nuclear Weapons, including safeguards on nuclear material in uranium enrichment plants using both existing and new techniques.

Informing public opinion

A/C.1/L.591 and Rev.1. Ireland, Mexico, Morocco, Pakistan, Philippines: draft resolution and revision, approved by First Committee on 8 December 1971, meeting 1846, by 94 votes to 0, with 2 abstentions.

A/8573. Report of First Committee, draft resolution C.

RESOLUTION 2825 C (XXVI), as recommended by First Committee, A/8573, adopted by Assembly on 16 December 1971, meeting 2022, by recorded vote of 110 to 0, as follows:

In favour: Algeria, Argentina, Australia, Austria, Bahrain, Belgium, Bhutan, Brazil, Bulgaria, Burma, Burundi, Byelorussian SSR, Cameroon, Canada, Central African Republic, Ceylon, Chad, Chile, Colombia, Congo, Costa Rica, Cuba, Cyprus, Czechoslovakia, Dahomey, Denmark, Dominican Republic, Ecuador, Egypt, Equatorial Guinea, Fiji, Finland, France, Ghana, Greece, Guatemala, Guinea, Guyana, Honduras, Hungary, Iceland, India, Indonesia, Iran, Ireland, Israel, Italy, Ivory Coast, Jamaica, Japan, Jordan, Kenya, Khmer Republic, Kuwait, Laos, Lebanon, Lesotho, Liberia, Libyan Arab Republic, Luxembourg, Madagascar, Malaysia, Mali, Malta, Mauritania, Mexico, Mongolia, Morocco, Nepal, Netherlands, New Zealand, Nicaragua, Nigeria, Norway, Pakistan, Panama, Paraguay, People's Democratic Republic of Yemen, Peru, Philippines, Poland, Portugal, Qatar, Romania, Rwanda, Saudi Arabia, Senegal, Singapore, Somalia, South Africa, Spain, Sweden, Thailand, Togo, Trinidad and Tobago, Tunisia, Turkey, Uganda, Ukrainian SSR, USSR, United Kingdom, United Republic of Tanzania, United States, Upper Volta, Uruguay, Venezuela, Yemen, Yugoslavia, Zaire, Zambia.

Against: None.

The General Assembly,

Recalling its resolution 1149(XII) of 14 November 1957 on collective action to inform and enlighten the peoples of the world as to the dangers of the armaments race, and particularly as to the destructive effects of modern weapons,

Recalling its resolution 2602 E (XXIV) of 16 December 1969, in which it declared the decade of the 1970s as a Disarmament Decade and requested the Secretary-General and Governments to publicize the Decade by all appropriate means at their disposal,

Recalling its resolution 2661 C (XXV) of 7 December 1970 which dealt, *inter alia*, with the comprehensive programme of disarmament,

Considering that public opinion should be adequately informed about the problems of the arms race and of disarmament so that it might bring its influence to bear on the strengthening of disarmament efforts,

1. *Affirms* the value of holding conferences of experts and scientists from various countries on the problems of the arms race and disarmament;

2. *Expresses its support* for the practice of requesting the Secretary-General to prepare, with the assistance of consultant experts, authoritative reports on concrete questions relating to the arms race and disarmament;

3. *Declares* that progress would be promoted towards general and complete disarmament if universities and academic institutes in all countries were to establish continuing courses and seminars to study problems of the arms race;

4. *Requests* the Secretary-General to bring the present resolution to the attention of all Member States and to the attention of the United Nations Educational Scientific and Cultural Organization with a view to its wide publication and dissemination.

Question of chemical and bacteriological (biological) weapons

In dealing with the question of chemical and bacteriological (biological) weapons at its 1971 session, the General Assembly's First Committee had before it the report of the Conference of the Committee on Disarmament to which was annexed the text of the draft convention on the prohibition of the development, production and stockpiling of bacteriological (biological) and toxin weapons and on their destruction. In the course of the debate in the First Committee, a majority of States gave general support to the draft convention and welcomed it as the first measure of genuine disarmament, providing for the elimination of one type of weapons of mass destruction. Satisfaction was also widely expressed over the fact that the draft convention was the result of compromise, reflecting the views and suggestions of many States.

At the same time, however, a number of Members expressed disappointment that it had not proved possible to achieve a joint prohibition of chemical and bacteriological (biological) weapons.

Many, including Belgium, Brazil, Czechoslovakia, Finland, Ghana, India, the Ivory Coast, Lebanon, Malta, Pakistan, Poland, Sweden, the USSR, the United Kingdom, the United States and Uruguay, stressed the inseparable link between the prohibition of bacteriological (biological) weapons and of chemical weapons and underlined the significance of the relevant provisions of the draft convention in this regard.

On 16 December 1971, the Assembly adopted a resolution by which it commended the Convention on the Prohibition of the Development, Production and Stockpiling of Bacteriological (Biological) and Toxin Weapons and on Their Destruction, and requested the depositary Governments to open it for signature and ratification at the earliest possible date. At the same time, it expressed hope for the widest possible adherence to the Convention.

By the preamble of this resolution, the Assembly, among other things, made the following points. It expressed its conviction of the importance and urgency of eliminating from the arsenals of States such dangerous weapons of mass destruction as those using chemical or bacteriological (biological) agents. The Assembly recognized the important significance of the Protocol for the Prohibition of the Use in War of Asphyxiating, Poisonous or Other Gases, and of Bacteriological Methods of Warfare, signed at Geneva, Switzerland, on 17 June 1925, and expressed its awareness also of the contribution the Geneva Protocol had already made and continued to make to mitigating the horrors of war.

The Assembly noted that the Convention on the prohibition and destruction of bacteriological weapons provided for the parties to reaffirm their adherence to the principles and objectives of the 1925 Geneva Protocol and to comply strictly with them. It further noted that nothing in the Convention should be interpreted as in any way limiting or detracting from the obligations assumed by any State under the Geneva Protocol.

The Assembly expressed its determination to exclude completely the possibility of bacteriological (biological) agents or toxins being used as weapons. It recognized that an agreement on the prohibition of bacteriological (biological) and toxin weapons represented a first possible step towards the achievement of agreement on effective measures also for the prohibition of the development, production and stockpiling of chemical weapons.

Further, the Assembly noted that the Convention contained an affirmation of the recognized objective of effective prohibition of chemical weapons and, to this end, an undertaking to continue negotiations in good faith.

The Assembly also made the observation that the implementation of measures in the field of disarmament should release substantial additional resources, which should promote economic and social development, particularly in developing countries.

These Assembly decisions were set forth in resolution 2826(XXVI), which was adopted by a recorded vote of 110 to 0, with 1 abstention. The text of the resolution was approved by the First Committee by acclamation on 8 December.

The resolution was sponsored in the First Committee by the following States: Afghanistan, Argentina, Australia, Austria, Belgium, Bulgaria, the Byelorussian SSR, Canada, Costa Rica, Czechoslovakia, Denmark, the Dominican Republic, Finland, Greece, Honduras, Hungary, Iceland, Iran, Jamaica, Japan, Jordan, Lebanon, Lesotho, Liberia, Madagascar, Malaysia, Mongolia, Nepal, the Netherlands, Nicaragua, Norway, Poland, Romania, Rwanda, Singapore, Tunisia, Turkey, the Ukrainian SSR, the USSR, the United Kingdom, the United States, Yemen and Zaire.

(For texts of the resolution and the Convention, see DOCUMENTARY REFERENCES below.)

During the First Committee's discussion of the draft resolution and the draft Convention, a 16-power amendment was submitted calling for the insertion, in the preamble of the resolution, of a paragraph by which the General Assembly would affirm the principle that a substantial portion of the savings derived from disarmament should be devoted to promoting economic and social development in the developing countries.

A provision to this effect was included in a revised version of the draft resolution and the amendment was then withdrawn. Sponsors of this amendment were Argentina, Barbados, Brazil, Burma, Cameroon, Egypt, Ethiopia, Guinea, India, Indonesia, Morocco, Nigeria, Pakistan, the Philippines, Yemen and Yugoslavia.

Most Members shared the view that the Convention did not detract from the obligations resulting from the 1925 Geneva Protocol, but on the contrary strengthened it. The USSR and the United States observed that the phrasing of article I of the Convention (". . . never in any circumstances to develop, produce, stockpile or otherwise acquire or retain . . .") made it clear that it would apply equally in times of peace and war—and thus rendered inapplicable, as far as the use of biological weapons was concerned, the reservations of many parties to the Geneva Protocol, by which they retained the right to use weapons covered by the Protocol under certain circumstances.

The Netherlands, Nigeria and Morocco welcomed this interpretation. Belgium announced that it intended to study the possibility of abandoning the reservations it made in ratifying the Protocol, after the entry into force of the Convention.

The USSR and the United States expressed their respective interpretations of the provision of article I permitting the retention of biological agents and toxins for "prophylactic, protective or other peaceful purposes." The USSR said that this provision was not a loop-hole in the Convention, since it referred to the use of such agents for peaceful purposes. Both States stressed that possession of biological agents and toxins for weapon purposes, on the theory that such weapons were for "defensive" warfare, retaliation or deterrence, was not permitted by the Convention.

On the verification aspects, most Members shared the view that the complaints procedure set forth in the Convention was based on an appropriate combination of national and international means, and they welcomed the specific role assigned to the Security Council.

Sweden, supported by Austria, Brazil, Pakistan and Turkey, requested some guarantees against the possible use of the veto by the Security Council's permanent members and felt that the complaint provisions could not be interpreted in such a way as to enable the permanent members to enjoy discriminatory protection.

France disagreed with the verification and complaints procedures, feeling they were not sufficient.

Australia, Brazil, Ceylon and Turkey suggested that the Secretary-General would provide a better medium than the Security Council for the investigation of complaints.

Before the First Committee voted on the draft resolution commending the draft Convention, Sweden formally stated its view that: (1) the Convention was to be entered into by all States on the basis of equality; (2) article VI (concerning complaints procedure) would not be utilized by the permanent members of the Security Council in such a manner as to prevent the investigation of complaints; (3) under article V (concerning consultation and co-operation) a clarification of complaints could take place; (4) appropriate international procedures within the framework of the United Nations should be used for investigation, i.e. any appropriate organ or officer of the United Nations could be used in gathering necessary information, on the basis of which the Security Council would then discuss the matter and take a decision; (5) a kind of investigation should thus in fact take place before the matter was dealt with by the Security Council; and (6) all factual evidence available would be presented to the Council, the consideration of which was a procedural matter, where a majority vote applied.

The USSR stated that, concerning the procedure for taking decisions under article VI (complaints procedure), as in other matters, the Security Council should act in strict accordance with the provisions of the United Nations Charter.

A number of representatives, particularly those from the developing countries, expressed dissatisfaction during the early part of the First Committee discussion that the draft Convention did not include acknowledgement of the principle that a substantial proportion of savings derived from disarmament should be devoted to the promotion of economic and social development, particularly in developing countries. Subsequently, these Members expressed satisfaction with the inclusion

Article I

arty to this Convention undertakes never in any
develop, produce, stockpile or otherwise acquire

r other biological agents, or toxins whatever their
of production, of types and in quantities that have
for prophylactic, protective or other peaceful

, equipment or means of delivery designed to use
toxins for hostile purposes or in armed conflict.

Article II

Party to this Convention undertakes to destroy, or to
eful purposes, as soon as possible but not later than
after the entry into force of the Convention, all agents,
ons, equipment and means of delivery specified in
e Convention, which are in its possession or under its
r control. In implementing the provisions of this article
ry safety precautions shall be observed to protect
and the environment.

Article III

ate Party to this Convention undertakes not to transfer to
nt whatsoever, directly or indirectly, and not in any way
encourage or induce any State, group of States or
al organizations to manufacture or otherwise acquire
e agents, toxins, weapons, equipment or means of
pecified in article I of the Convention.

Article IV

State Party to this Convention shall, in accordance with its
ional processes, take any necessary measures to prohibit
vent the development, production, stockpiling, acquisition
tion of the agents, toxins, weapons, equipment and means
very specified in article I of the Convention, within the
of such State, under its jurisdiction or under its control
ere.

Article V

States Parties to this Convention undertake to consult one
er and to co-operate in solving any problems which may arise
ation to the objective of, or in the application of the provisions
e Convention. Consultation and co-operation pursuant to this
e may also be undertaken through appropriate international
edures within the framework of the United Nations and in
rdance with its Charter.

Article VI

. Any State Party to this Convention which finds that any other
ate Party is acting in breach of obligations deriving from the
ovisions of the Convention may lodge a complaint with the
curity Council of the United Nations. Such a complaint should
clude all possible evidence confirming its validity, as well as a
quest for its consideration by the Security Council.

2. Each State Party to this Convention undertakes to
o-operate in carrying out any investigation which the Security
Council may initiate, in accordance with the provisions of the
Charter of the United Nations, on the basis of the complaint
received by the Council. The Security Council shall inform the
States Parties to the Convention of the results of the investigation.

Article VII

Each State Party to this Convention undertakes to provide or support assistance, in accordance with the United Nations Charter, to any Party to the Convention which so requests, if the Security Council decides that such Party has been exposed to danger as a result of violation of the Convention.

Article VIII

Nothing in this Convention shall be interpreted as in any way limiting or detracting from the obligations assumed by any State under the Protocol for the Prohibition of the Use in War of Asphyxiating, Poisonous or Other Gases, and of Bacteriological Methods of Warfare, signed at Geneva on 17 June 1925.

Article IX

Each State Party to this Convention affirms the recognized objective of effective prohibition of chemical weapons and, to this end, undertakes to continue negotiations in good faith with a view to reaching early agreement on effective measures for the prohibition of their development, production and stockpiling and for their destruction, and on appropriate measures concerning equipment and means of delivery specifically designed for the production or use of chemical agents for weapons purposes.

Article X

1. The States Parties to this Convention undertake to facilitate, and have the right to participate in, the fullest possible exchange of equipment, materials and scientific and technological information for the use of bacteriological (biological) agents and toxins for peaceful purposes. Parties to the Convention in a position to do so shall also co-operate in contributing individually or together with other States or international organizations to the further development and application of scientific discoveries in the field of bacteriology (biology) for the prevention of disease, or for other peaceful purposes.

2. This Convention shall be implemented in a manner designed to avoid hampering the economic or technological development of States Parties to the Convention or international co-operation in the field of peaceful bacteriological (biological) activities, including the international exchange of bacteriological (biological) agents and toxins and equipment for the processing, use or production of bacteriological (biological) agents and toxins for peaceful purposes in accordance with the provisions of the Convention.

Article XI

Any State Party may propose amendments to this Convention. Amendments shall enter into force for each State Party accepting the amendments upon their acceptance by a majority of the States Parties to the Convention and thereafter for each remaining State Party on the date of acceptance by it.

Article XII

Five years after the entry into force of this Convention, or earlier if it is requested by a majority of Parties to the Convention by submitting a proposal to this effect to the Depositary Governments, a conference of States Parties to the Convention shall be held at Geneva, Switzerland, to review the operation of the Convention, with a view to assuring that the purposes of the preamble and the provisions of the Convention, including the provisions concerning negotiations on chemical weapons, are being realized. Such review shall take into account any new scientific and technological developments relevant to the Convention.

Article XIII

1. This Convention shall be of unlimited duration.

2. Each State Party to this Convention shall in exercising its national sovereignty have the right to withdraw from the Convention if it decides that extraordinary events, related to the subject-matter of the Convention, have jeopardized the supreme interests of its country. It shall give notice of such withdrawal to all other States Parties to the Convention and to the United Nations Security Council three months in advance. Such notice shall include a statement of the extraordinary events it regards as having jeopardized its supreme interests.

Article XIV

1. This Convention shall be open to all States for signature. Any State which does not sign the Convention before its entry into force in accordance with paragraph 3 of this article may accede to it at any time.

2. This Convention shall be subject to ratification by signatory States. Instruments of ratification and instruments of accession shall be deposited with the Governments of the Union of Soviet Socialist Republics, the United Kingdom of Great Britain and Northern Ireland and the United States of America, which are hereby designated the Depositary Governments.

3. This Convention shall enter into force after the deposit of instruments of ratification by twenty-two Governments, including

of this principle in the preamble of the Assembly's resolution commending the Convention.

During the First Committee's consideration, various other proposals were made by Members. Thus, Mexico submitted a proposal suggesting inclusion of an additional article in the draft Convention providing that, pending the agreement on chemical weapons referred to in the draft Convention, the States parties would undertake to refrain from further development, production or stockpiling for weapons purposes of those chemical agents which, because of their high toxicity, had the highest lethal effects. Those agents would be listed in a protocol annexed to the Convention.

In this connexion, 14 Members—Colombia, Costa Rica, Ecuador, Ethiopia, Ghana, Ireland, Malta, Mexico, Morocco, Peru, Sweden, the United Republic of Tanzania, Uruguay and Venezuela—submitted a draft resolution by which the General Assembly, noting that the Convention contained an undertaking to negotiate in good faith on measures to prohibit chemical weapons and that it was desirable to adopt measures of a preliminary nature immediately, would urge all States to undertake, pending agreement on the complete prohibition of chemical weapons and their destruction, to refrain from any further development, production or stockpiling of those chemical agents for weapons purposes which because of their degree of toxicity had the highest lethal effects and were not usable for peaceful purposes.

On 8 December 1971, the First Committee approved the draft resolution by a roll-call vote of 96 to 0, with 11 abstentions. Before the vote, the Chairman of the First Committee drew the Committee's attention to the fact that no action was called for on the proposal submitted by Mexico to amend the draft Convention in view of the substance of the draft resolution.

On 16 December, the General Assembly adopted the text recommended by the First Committee by a recorded vote of 101 to 0, with 10 abstentions, as resolution 2827 B (XXVI).

(For text of resolution, see DOCUMENTARY REFERENCES below.)

Another aspect of the question of prohibition of chemical weapons led to the submission in the First Committee of two draft resolutions dealing with negotiations on chemical weapons.

The first of these, a 38-power text, proposed by its operative part that the General Assembly would: (1) request the Conference of the Committee on Disarmament (CCD) to continue consideration of the problem of chemical methods of warfare with a view to reaching early agreement on the prohibition and elimination of chemical weapons; (2) request CCD to take into account in its further work (*a*) the views expressed in the 12-power memorandum submitted on 28 September 1971 to CCD (see page 10), and (*b*) other proposals, working papers and views put forward in CCD and in the First Committee; (3) urge Governments to take all steps to contribute to a successful outcome of the negotiations for prohibition of chemical weapons; (4) reaffirm its resolution of 5 December 1966[21] and call anew for the strict observance by all States of the principles and objectives of the 1925 Geneva Protocol; (5) invite all States that had not already done so to accede to or ratify the Protocol; and (6) request CCD to report to the 1972 session of the General Assembly.

This text was sponsored by the following 38 Members: Afghanistan, Australia, Austria, Belgium, Bulgaria, the Byelorussian SSR, Canada, Costa Rica, Czechoslovakia, Denmark, El Salvador, Finland, Honduras, Hungary, Iceland, Italy, Japan, Jordan, Kuwait, Lebanon, Liberia, Madagascar, Malaysia, Malta, Mongolia, Nepal, the Netherlands, New Zealand, Nicaragua, Norway, Poland, Rwanda, the Syrian Arab Republic, Tunisia, the Ukrainian SSR, the USSR, the United Kingdom and the United States.

The second draft resolution—a 30-power text—provided by its operative part that the General Assembly would, among other things: (1) take note of (*a*) the provisions of the Convention on the prohibition and destruction of bacteriological weapons concerning the determination to continue negotiations aimed at early agreement on the prohibition of chemical weapons, (*b*) the 12-power memorandum submitted on 28 September 1971 to CCD, and (*c*) other proposals, working papers and views put forward in CCD and in the First Committee on the question; (2) request CCD to proceed with negotiations, as a high priority item, on the prohibition and elimination of chemical weapons; (3) further request CCD to be guided in its negotiations by the elements contained in the 12-power memorandum of 28 September and also to take into account other views expressed in CCD and the First Committee; (4) urge all States to take all measures to facilitate early agreement on effective measures for the prohibition and destruction of chemical weapons; (5) call anew for the strict observance by all States of the 1925 Geneva Protocol and invite accessions and ratifications thereto; and (6) request CCD to report on this question to the 1972 session of the General Assembly.

The sponsors of the 30-power draft were Argentina, Barbados, Brazil, Burma, Burundi, Ceylon, Chile, Cyprus, Egypt, Ethiopia, Guinea, Guyana, India, Indonesia, Iran, Kuwait, Morocco, Nigeria, Pakistan, Panama, Peru, Sierra Leone,

[21]See Y.U.N., 1966, p. 27, text of resolution 2162 B (XXI).

Somalia, Sudan, Sweden, Uganda, the United Republic of Tanzania, Yemen, Yugoslavia and Zambia.

The above two draft resolutions were later replaced by a 63-power text which the First Committee approved by acclamation on 8 December 1971. On 16 December, the Assembly adopted the text recommended by the First Committee by a recorded vote of 110 to 0, with 1 abstention, as its resolution 2827 A (XXVI).

By the preamble to this resolution, the Assembly among other things made the following observations. It recalled its resolution of 7 December 1970 by which it had commended a basic approach for reaching an effective solution to the problem of chemical and bacteriological (biological) methods of warfare[22] and expressed its conviction of the importance and urgency of eliminating such dangerous weapons of mass destruction as those using chemical or bacteriological agents.

The Assembly also expressed its conviction that the Convention on the prohibition and destruction of bacteriological weapons was a first possible step towards the achievement of early agreement on the effective prohibition of chemical weapons. It recalled that it had repeatedly condemned all action contrary to the 1925 Geneva Protocol prohibiting use of bacteriological methods of warfare and noted that the Convention on bacteriological weapons provided for parties to reaffirm their adherence to the principles and objectives of that Protocol.

By the operative part of the resolution, the Assembly noted with satisfaction that the Convention on bacteriological weapons contained an affirmation of the recognized objective of effective prohibition of chemical weapons and an undertaking to negotiate in good faith to this end. The Assembly asked CCD to continue, as a matter of high priority, its negotiations with a view to reaching early agreement on effective measures for the prohibition of the development, production and stockpiling of chemical weapons and for their elimination from the arsenals of all States. It

also asked CCD to take into account in its further work: (*a*) the elements contained in the 12-power memorandum submitted to CCD on 28 September 1971 (see page 10), and (*b*) other proposals and views put forward in CCD and in the First Committee.

The Assembly urged Governments to take all steps that might contribute to a successful outcome of the CCD negotiations and that could facilitate early agreement on effective measures to prohibit chemical weapons. It then reaffirmed its resolution of 5 December 1966[23] (which called for strict observance of and accession to the 1925 Geneva Protocol) and called anew for strict observance of the principles and objectives of the Geneva Protocol. The Assembly invited all States which had not already done so to accede to or ratify the Protocol.

The Assembly also asked CCD to report on the results of the negotiations to the 1972 Assembly session and asked the Secretary-General to transmit to CCD all relevant First Committee records.

(For text of resolution, see DOCUMENTARY REFERENCES below.)

The 63 sponsors of resolution 2728 A (XXVI) were Afghanistan, Argentina, Australia, Austria, Barbados, Belgium, Brazil, Bulgaria, Burma, Burundi, the Byelorussian SSR, Canada, Ceylon, Chile, Costa Rica, Cyprus, Czechoslovakia, Denmark, Egypt, El Salvador, Ethiopia, Finland, Guyana, Honduras, Hungary, Iceland, India, Indonesia, Iran, Italy, Japan, Jordan, Kuwait, Lebanon, Lesotho, Liberia, Madagascar, Malaysia, Malta, Mexico, Mongolia, Morocco, Nepal, the Netherlands, New Zealand, Nicaragua, Nigeria, Norway, Pakistan, Peru, Poland, Rwanda, Singapore, Sweden, the Syrian Arab Republic, Tunisia, Uganda, the Ukrainian SSR, the USSR, the United Kingdom, the United States, Yemen and Yugoslavia.

---

[22]See Y.U.N., 1970, p. 27, text of resolution 2662(XXV).
[23]See footnote 21.

DOCUMENTARY REFERENCES

General Assembly—26th session
First Committee, meetings 1803, 1827-1843, 1845-1847.
Plenary meetings 1939, 2022.

A/8457 (DC/234). Report of CCD (covering period 23 February–30 September 1971).
A/8457 (DC/234), Annex A: Draft convention on prohibition of development, production and stockpiling of bacteriological (biological) and toxin weapons and on their destruction.
A/C.1/L.578 and Corr.1. Mexico: working paper containing proposal for inclusion of additional article in draft convention in Annex A of A/8457 (DC/234).
A/C.1/L.579. Afghanistan, Australia, Austria, Belgium, Bulgaria, Byelorussian SSR, Canada, Costa Rica, Czechoslovakia,

Denmark, Dominican Republic, Finland, Greece, Honduras, Hungary, Iceland, Iran, Jamaica, Japan, Jordan, Lebanon, Liberia, Madagascar, Malaysia, Mongolia, Nepal, Netherlands, Nicaragua, Norway, Poland, Rwanda, Somalia, Tunisia, Turkey, Ukrainian SSR, USSR, United Kingdom, United States, Zaire: draft resolution and annex (A/8457, Annex A).
A/C.1/L.579/Rev.1. Afghanistan, Argentina, Australia, Austria, Belgium, Bulgaria, Byelorussian SSR, Canada, Costa Rica, Czechoslovakia, Denmark, Dominican Republic, Finland, Greece, Honduras, Hungary, Iceland, Iran, Jamaica, Japan, Jordan, Lebanon, Lesotho, Liberia, Madagascar, Malaysia, Mongolia, Nepal, Netherlands, Nicaragua, Norway, Poland, Romania, Rwanda, Singapore, Tunisia, Turkey, Ukrainian SSR, USSR, United Kingdom, United States, Yemen, Zaire: revised

---

draft resolution and annex (A/8457, Annex A), approved unanimously (by acclamation) by First Committee on 8 December 1971, meeting 1846.
A/C.1/L.582. Argentina, Barbados, Brazil, Burma, Cameroon, Egypt, Ethiopia, Guinea, India, Indonesia, Morocco, Nigeria, Pakistan, Philippines, Yemen, Yugoslavia: amendment to 39-power draft resolution, A/C.1/L.579.
A/8574. Report of First Committee, draft resolution I.

RESOLUTION 2826 (XXVI), as recommended by First Committee, A/8574, adopted by Assembly on 16 December 1971, meeting 2022, by recorded vote of 110 to 0, with 1 abstention, as follows:

In favour: Afghanistan, Algeria, Argentina, Australia, Austria, Bahrain, Belgium, Bhutan, Brazil, Bulgaria, Burma, Burundi, Byelorussian SSR, Cameroon, Canada, Central African Republic, Ceylon, Chad, Chile, Colombia, Congo, Costa Rica, Cuba, Cyprus, Czechoslovakia, Dahomey, Denmark, Dominican Republic, Ecuador, Egypt, Equatorial Guinea, Ethiopia, Fiji, Finland, Ghana, Greece, Guatemala, Guinea, Guyana, Honduras, Hungary, Iceland, India, Indonesia, Iran, Ireland, Israel, Italy, Ivory Coast, Jamaica, Japan, Jordan, Kenya, Khmer Republic, Kuwait, Laos, Lesotho, Liberia, Libyan Arab Republic, Luxembourg, Madagascar, Malaysia, Mali, Malta, Mauritania, Mexico, Mongolia, Morocco, Nepal, Netherlands, New Zealand, Nicaragua, Nigeria, Norway, Pakistan, Panama, Paraguay, People's Democratic Republic of Yemen, Peru, Philippines, Poland, Portugal, Qatar, Romania, Rwanda, Saudi Arabia, Senegal, Singapore, Somalia, South Africa, Spain, Sweden, Thailand, Togo, Trinidad and Tobago, Tunisia, Turkey, Uganda, Ukrainian SSR, USSR, United Kingdom, United Republic of Tanzania, United States, Upper Volta, Uruguay, Venezuela, Yemen, Yugoslavia, Zaire, Zambia.
Against: None.
Abstaining: France.

The General Assembly,

Recalling its resolution 2662(XXV) of 7 December 1970,

Convinced of the importance and urgency of eliminating from the arsenals of States, through effective measures, such dangerous weapons of mass destruction as those using chemical or bacteriological (biological) agents,

Having considered the report of the Conference of the Committee on Disarmament dated 6 October 1971, and being appreciative of its work on the draft Convention on the Prohibition of the Development, Production and Stockpiling of Bacteriological (Biological) and Toxin Weapons and on Their Destruction, annexed to the report,

Recognizing the important significance of the Protocol for the Prohibition of the Use in War of Asphyxiating, Poisonous or Other Gases, and of Bacteriological Methods of Warfare, signed at Geneva on 17 June 1925, and conscious also of the contribution which the said Protocol has already made, and continues to make, to mitigating the horrors of war,

Noting that the Convention on the Prohibition of the Development, Production and Stockpiling of Bacteriological (Biological) and Toxin Weapons and on Their Destruction provides for the parties to reaffirm their adherence to the principles and objectives of that Protocol and to call upon all States to comply strictly with them,

Further noting that nothing in the Convention shall be interpreted as in any way limiting or detracting from the obligations assumed by any State under the Geneva Protocol,

Determined, for the sake of all mankind, to exclude completely the possibility of bacteriological (biological) agents and toxins being used as weapons,

Recognizing that an agreement on the prohibition of bacteriological (biological) and toxin weapons represents a first possible step towards the achievement of agreement on effective measures also for the prohibition of the development, production and stockpiling of chemical weapons,

Noting that the Convention contains an affirmation of the

recognized o[...]
and, to this e[...]
faith with a [...]
measures for t[...]
stockpiling and [...]
concerning equi[...]
for the product[...]
purposes,

Convinced that [...]
disarmament sho[...]
which should prom[...]
larly in the developir[...]

Convinced that th[...]
of the purposes and [...]

1. *Commends* th[...]
Development, Produ[...]
(Biological) and Toxin [...]
of which is annexed to t[...]

2. *Requests* the dep[...]
tion for signature and rati[...]

3. *Expresses* the ho[...]
the Convention.

**Convention on the Prohib[...]
tion and Stockpiling of Bac[...]
Weapons and [...]**

The States Parties to this Co[...]

Determined to act with a vi[...]
towards general and comple[...]
prohibition and elimination of [...]
destruction, and convinced that th[...]
production and stockpiling of [...]
(biological) weapons and their [...]
measures, will facilitate the achievo[...]
disarmament under strict and effecti[...]

Recognizing the important signifi[...]
Prohibition of the Use in War of Aspl[...]
Gases, and of Bacteriological Met[...]
Geneva on 17 June 1925, and consc[...]
which the said Protocol has already ma[...]
to mitigating the horrors of war,

Reaffirming their adherence to the p[...]
that Protocol and calling upon all Stat[...]
them,

Recalling that the General Assembly [...]
repeatedly condemned all actions contra[...]
objectives of the Geneva Protocol of 17 Jur[...]

Desiring to contribute to the strengt[...]
between peoples and the general improvem[...]
atmosphere,

Desiring also to contribute to the realizatio[...]
principles of the Charter of the United Nations,[...]

Convinced of the importance and urgency[...]
the arsenals of States, through effective[...]
dangerous weapons of mass destruction as th[...]
or bacteriological (biological) agents,

Recognizing that an agreement on the prohi[...]
logical (biological) and toxin weapons represen[...]
step towards the achievement of agreement on ef[...]
also for the prohibition of the development,[...]
stockpiling of chemical weapons, and determin[...]
negotiations to that end,

Determined, for the sake of all mankind, to exclu[...]
the possibility of bacteriological (biological) agen[...]
being used as weapons,

Convinced that such use would be repugnant to th[...]
of mankind and that no effort should be spared to n[...]
risk,

Have agreed as follows:

20

Each State P[...]
circumstances t[...]
or retain:

(1) Microbial[...]
origin or metho[...]
no justificatio[...]
purposes;

(2) Weapon[...]
such agents o[...]

Each State[...]
divert to pea[...]
nine months[...]
toxins, wea[...]
article I of th[...]
jurisdiction[...]
all necessa[...]
populations[...]

Each St[...]
any recip[...]
to assist,[...]
internatio[...]
any of t[...]
delivery [...]

Each[...]
constitu[...]
and pre[...]
or refer[...]
of deli[...]
territor[...]
anywh[...]

Th[...]
anoth[...]
in re[...]
of, tl[...]
artic[...]
prod[...]
acc[...]

St[...]
pr[...]
S[...]
ir[...]
r[...]

the Governments designated as Depositaries of the Convention.

4. For States whose instruments of ratification or accession are deposited subsequent to the entry into force of this Convention, it shall enter into force on the date of the deposit of their instruments of ratification or accession.

5. The Depositary Governments shall promptly inform all signatory and acceding States of the date of each signature, the date of deposit of each instrument of ratification or of accession and the date of the entry into force of this Convention, and of the receipt of other notices.

6. This Convention shall be registered by the Depositary Governments pursuant to Article 102 of the Charter of the United Nations.

Article XV

This Convention, the Chinese, English, French, Russian and Spanish texts of which are equally authentic, shall be deposited in the archives of the Depositary Governments. Duly certified copies of the Convention shall be transmitted by the Depositary Governments to the Governments of the signatory and acceding States.

IN WITNESS WHEREOF the undersigned, duly authorized, have signed this Convention.

DONE in triplicate, at ......, this ...... day of ......, ...

A/C.1/L.592 and Rev.1. Colombia, Costa Rica, Ecuador, Ethiopia, Ghana, Ireland, Malta, Mexico, Morocco, Peru, Sweden, United Republic of Tanzania, Uruguay, Venezuela: draft resolution and revision, approved by First Committee on 8 December 1971, meeting 1846, by roll-call vote of 96 to 0, with 11 abstentions, as follows:

In favour: Afghanistan, Algeria, Argentina, Australia, Austria, Barbados, Bhutan, Brazil, Bulgaria, Burma, Burundi, Byelorussian SSR, Cameroon, Central African Republic, Ceylon, Chile, Colombia, Congo, Costa Rica, Cuba, Cyprus, Czechoslovakia, Denmark, Dominican Republic, Ecuador, Egypt, El Salvador, Ethiopia, Fiji, Finland, Ghana, Guinea, Guyana, Haiti, Honduras, Hungary, Iceland, India, Indonesia, Iran, Ireland, Israel, Ivory Coast, Jamaica, Japan, Jordan, Kenya, Khmer Republic, Kuwait, Lebanon, Lesotho, Liberia, Libyan Arab Republic, Madagascar, Malaysia, Mali, Malta, Mauritius, Mexico, Mongolia, Morocco, Nepal, New Zealand, Nicaragua, Niger, Nigeria, Norway, Pakistan, Panama, Peru, Philippines, Poland, Portugal, Saudi Arabia, Senegal, Singapore, Somalia, South Africa, Spain, Sudan, Swaziland, Sweden, Thailand, Togo, Trinidad and Tobago, Tunisia, Uganda, Ukrainian SSR, USSR, United Republic of Tanzania, Uruguay, Venezuela, Yemen, Yugoslavia, Zaire, Zambia.

Against: None.

Abstaining: Belgium, Canada, France, Greece, Italy, Malawi, Netherlands, Romania, Turkey, United Kingdom, United States.

A/8574. Report of First Committee, draft resolution II B.

RESOLUTION 2827 B (XXVI), as recommended by First Committee, A/8574, adopted by Assembly on 16 December 1971, meeting 2022, by recorded vote of 101 to 0, with 10 abstentions, as follows:

In favour: Algeria, Argentina, Australia, Austria, Bahrain, Bhutan, Brazil, Bulgaria, Burma, Burundi, Byelorussian SSR, Cameroon, Central African Republic, Ceylon, Chad, Chile, Colombia, Congo, Costa Rica, Cuba, Cyprus, Czechoslovakia, Dahomey, Denmark, Dominican Republic, Ecuador, Egypt, Equatorial Guinea, Ethiopia, Fiji, Finland, Ghana, Guatemala, Guinea, Guyana, Honduras, Hungary, Iceland, India, Indonesia, Iran, Ireland, Israel, Ivory Coast, Jamaica, Japan, Jordan, Kenya, Khmer Republic, Kuwait, Laos, Lebanon, Lesotho, Liberia, Libyan Arab Republic, Madagascar, Malaysia, Mali, Malta, Mauritania, Mexico, Mongolia, Morocco, Nepal, Netherlands, New Zealand, Nicaragua, Nigeria, Norway, Pakistan, Panama, Paraguay, People's Democratic Republic of Yemen, Peru, Philippines, Poland, Portugal, Qatar, Rwanda, Saudi Arabia, Senegal, Singapore, Somalia, South Africa, Spain,

Sweden, Thailand, Togo, Trinidad and Tobago, Tunisia, Uganda, Ukrainian SSR, USSR, United Republic of Tanzania, Upper Volta, Uruguay, Venezuela, Yemen, Yugoslavia, Zaire, Zambia.

Against: None.

Abstaining: Belgium, Canada, France, Greece, Italy, Luxembourg, Romania, Turkey, United Kingdom, United States.

The General Assembly,

Noting that the Convention on the Prohibition of the Development, Production and Stockpiling of Bacteriological (Biological) and Toxin Weapons and on Their Destruction contains an undertaking to continue negotiations in good faith with a view to reaching early agreement on effective measures for the prohibition of the development, production and stockpiling of chemical weapons and for their destruction,

Believing that it is most desirable that some measures of a preliminary nature be adopted immediately,

Urges all States to undertake, pending agreement on the complete prohibition of the development, production and stockpiling of chemical weapons and their destruction, to refrain from any further development, production or stockpiling of those chemical agents for weapons purposes which, because of their degree of toxicity, have the highest lethal effects and are not usable for peaceful purposes.

A/C.1/L.580. Afghanistan, Australia, Austria, Belgium, Bulgaria, Byelorussian SSR, Canada, Costa Rica, Czechoslovakia, Denmark, El Salvador, Finland, Honduras, Hungary, Iceland, Italy, Japan, Jordan, Kuwait, Lebanon, Liberia, Madagascar, Malaysia, Malta, Mongolia, Nepal, Netherlands, New Zealand, Nicaragua, Norway, Poland, Rwanda, Syrian Arab Republic, Tunisia, Ukrainian SSR, USSR, United Kingdom, United States: draft resolution.

A/C.1/L.581. Argentina, Barbados, Brazil, Burma, Burundi, Ceylon, Chile, Cyprus, Egypt, Ethiopia, Guinea, Guyana, India, Indonesia, Iran, Kuwait, Morocco, Nigeria, Pakistan, Panama, Peru, Sierra Leone, Somalia, Sudan, Sweden, Uganda, United Republic of Tanzania, Yemen, Yugoslavia, Zambia: draft resolution.

A/C.1/L.596. Afghanistan, Argentina, Australia, Austria, Barbados, Belgium, Brazil, Bulgaria, Burma, Burundi, Byelorussian SSR, Canada, Ceylon, Chile, Costa Rica, Cyprus, Czechoslovakia, Denmark, Egypt, El Salvador, Ethiopia, Finland, Guyana, Honduras, Hungary, Iceland, India, Indonesia, Iran, Italy, Japan, Jordan, Kuwait, Lebanon, Lesotho, Liberia, Madagascar, Malaysia, Malta, Mexico, Mongolia, Morocco, Nepal, Netherlands, New Zealand, Nicaragua, Nigeria, Norway, Pakistan, Peru, Poland, Rwanda, Singapore, Sweden, Syrian Arab Republic, Tunisia, Uganda, Ukrainian SSR, USSR, United Kingdom, United States, Yemen, Yugoslavia: draft resolution, approved unanimously (by acclamation) by First Committee on 8 December 1971, meeting 1846.

A/8574. Report of First Committee, draft resolution II A.

RESOLUTION 2827 A (XXVI), as recommended by First Committee, A/8574, adopted by Assembly on 16 December 1971, meeting 2022, by recorded vote of 110 to 0, with 1 abstention, as follows:

In favour: Afghanistan, Algeria, Argentina, Australia, Austria, Bahrain, Belgium, Bhutan, Brazil, Burma, Burundi, Byelorussian SSR, Cameroon, Canada, Central African Republic, Ceylon, Chad, Chile, Colombia, Congo, Costa Rica, Cuba, Cyprus, Czechoslovakia, Dahomey, Denmark, Dominican Republic, Ecuador, Egypt, Equatorial Guinea, Ethiopia, Fiji, Finland, Ghana, Greece, Guatemala, Guinea, Guyana, Honduras, Hungary, Iceland, India, Indonesia, Iran, Ireland, Israel, Italy, Ivory Coast, Jamaica, Japan, Jordan, Kenya, Khmer Republic, Kuwait, Laos, Lebanon, Lesotho, Liberia, Libyan Arab Republic, Luxembourg, Madagascar, Malaysia, Mali, Malta, Mauritania, Mexico, Mongolia, Morocco, Nepal, Netherlands, New Zealand, Nicaragua, Nigeria, Norway, Pakistan, Panama, Paraguay, People's Democratic Republic of Yemen, Peru,

Philippines, Poland, Portugal, Qatar, Romania, Rwanda, Saudi Arabia, Senegal, Singapore, Somalia, South Africa, Spain, Sweden, Thailand, Togo, Trinidad and Tobago, Tunisia, Turkey, Uganda, Ukrainian SSR, USSR, United Kingdom, United Republic of Tanzania, United States, Upper Volta, Uruguay, Venezuela, Yemen, Yugoslavia, Zaire, Zambia.

Against: None.

Abstaining: France.

The General Assembly,

Recalling its resolution 2454 A (XXIII) of 20 December 1968, its resolution 2603 B (XXIV) of 16 December 1969, and in particular its resolution 2662(XXV) of 7 December 1970 in which it stressed that the prospects for international peace and security, as well as the achievement of the goal of general and complete disarmament under effective international control, would be enhanced if the development, production and stockpiling of chemical and bacteriological (biological) agents for purposes of war were to end and if those agents were eliminated from all military arsenals, and commended the following basic approach for reaching an effective solution to the problem of chemical and bacteriological (biological) methods of warfare:

(a) It is urgent and important to reach agreement on the problem of chemical and bacteriological (biological) methods of warfare,

(b) Both chemical and bacteriological (biological) weapons should continue to be dealt with together in taking steps towards the prohibition of their development, production and stockpiling and their effective elimination from the arsenals of all States,

(c) The issue of verification is important in the field of chemical and bacteriological (biological) weapons, and verification should be based on a combination of appropriate national and international measures, which would complement and supplement each other, thereby providing an acceptable system that would ensure the effective implementation of the prohibition,

Convinced of the importance and urgency of eliminating from the arsenals of States, through effective measures, such dangerous weapons of mass destruction as those using chemical or bacteriological (biological) agents,

Having considered the report of the Conference of the Committee on Disarmament, in particular its work on the draft Convention on the Prohibition of the Development, Production and Stockpiling of Bacteriological (Biological) and Toxin Weapons and on Their Destruction and its efforts towards reaching early agreement also on the elimination of chemical weapons,

Convinced that the Convention on the Prohibition of the Development, Production and Stockpiling of Bacteriological (Biological) and Toxin Weapons and on Their Destruction is a first possible step towards the achievement of early agreement on the effective prohibition of the development, production and stockpiling of chemical weapons and on the elimination of such weapons from military arsenals of all States, and determined to continue negotiations to this end,

Recalling that the General Assembly has repeatedly condemned all actions contrary to the principles and objectives of the Protocol for the Prohibition of the Use in War of Asphyxiating, Poisonous or Other Gases, and of Bacteriological Methods of Warfare, signed at Geneva on 17 June 1925,

Noting that the Convention provides for the parties to reaffirm their adherence to the principles and objectives of that Protocol and to call upon all States to comply strictly with them,

1. *Notes with satisfaction* that the Convention on the Prohibition of the Development, Production and Stockpiling of Bacteriological (Biological) and Toxin Weapons and on Their Destruction contains an affirmation of the recognized objective of effective prohibition of chemical weapons and, to this end, an undertaking to continue negotiations in good faith with a view to reaching early agreement on effective measures for the prohibition of their development, production and stockpiling and for their destruction, and on appropriate measures concerning equipment and means of delivery specifically designed for the production or use of chemical agents for weapons purposes;

2. *Requests* the Conference of the Committee on Disarmament to continue, as a matter of high priority, its negotiations with a view to reaching early agreement on effective measures for the prohibition of the development, production and stockpiling of chemical weapons and for their elimination from the arsenals of all States;

3. *Also requests* the Conference of the Committee on Disarmament to take into account in its further work:

(a) The elements contained in the joint memorandum on the prohibition of the development, production and stockpiling of chemical weapons and on their destruction, submitted on 28 September 1971 to the Conference by Argentina, Brazil, Burma, Egypt, Ethiopia, India, Mexico, Morocco, Nigeria, Pakistan, Sweden and Yugoslavia;

(b) Other proposals, suggestions, working papers and expert views put forward in the Conference and in the First Committee;

4. *Urges* Governments to take all steps that may contribute to a successful outcome of the negotiations of the Conference of the Committee on Disarmament and that could facilitate early agreement on effective measures for the prohibition of the development, production and stockpiling of chemical weapons and the elimination of such weapons from the arsenals of all States;

5. *Reaffirms* its resolution 2162 B (XXI) of 5 December 1966 and calls anew for the strict observance by all States of the principles and objectives of the Protocol for the Prohibition of the Use in War of Asphyxiating, Poisonous or Other Gases, and of Bacteriological Methods of Warfare;

6. *Invites* all States that have not already done so to accede to or ratify the Protocol;

7. *Requests* the Conference of the Committee on Disarmament to submit a report on the results achieved to the General Assembly at its twenty-seventh session;

8. *Requests* the Secretary-General to transmit to the Conference of the Committee on Disarmament all documents and records of the First Committee relating to questions connected with the problem of chemical and bacteriological (biological) methods of warfare.

Suspension of nuclear and thermonuclear tests

The urgent need for suspension of nuclear and thermonuclear tests was discussed at the 1971 session of the General Assembly during the disarmament debate in the Assembly's First Committee.

Many Member States, including in particular Canada, Mexico and Sweden, expressed disappointment and impatience with the continuing lack of progress towards a comprehensive test ban to fulfil the commitments contained in the Treaty Banning Nuclear Weapon Tests in the Atmosphere, in Outer Space and under Water (the partial test ban Treaty) signed in Moscow, USSR, on 5 August 1963, and in the Treaty on the Non-Proliferation of Nuclear Weapons. [24]

Denmark, Ecuador, Indonesia, Mexico and the Netherlands expressed the view that the failure of the testing powers to accept such a comprehensive ban was in fact undermining the effectiveness of those two key Treaties. Canada, as well as Mexico, Sweden and Yugoslavia, deplored the failure of the major nuclear powers to undertake serious

[24]See Y.U.N., 1968, pp. 17-19, for text of Treaty.

negotiations or to submit specific proposals on a comprehensive test ban treaty, without which no treaty was possible.

Mexico and others maintained that the current lessening of mutual distrust between the super-powers, together with the significant progress realized in recent years on the verification problem, had created a new situation favourable to achievement of a comprehensive treaty and requiring the setting of a deadline for its realization.

The United States and several other Members stressed the view that there was a continuing need for on-site inspections to ensure adequate verification of such a treaty. The majority of Members disagreed with this view. A number of them, including Denmark, Finland, Mexico, Pakistan, Sweden and Yugoslavia, stated that such inspections were either unnecessary or of marginal importance. Austria, Iran and the Netherlands were among those expressing the view that in light of recent substantial progress in verification technology the risks of minor violations of a treaty would be less than the risks to the world of continued unrestricted testing.

Canada, Denmark, Ireland and Norway believed that the verification problem had at least been reduced to manageable proportions.

Virtually all Members agreed that negotiations for the early achievement of a comprehensive treaty should be given highest priority. There was some support for a partial approach, such as a threshold treaty banning tests above a certain agreed magnitude (i.e. above a specified level on the Richter scale used to measure the magnitude of earthquakes), provided that such a measure was accompanied by a moratorium on all tests.

A Canadian proposal for immediate "measures of restraint" on the part of the testing powers pending early realization of a full test ban received support, but it was emphasized that such measures must be purely provisional and transitory. Brazil, the Byelorussian SSR and India specifically opposed any partial approach, while the United Kingdom and the United States opposed immediate measures of restraint on the ground that they would have to be unilateral and would arouse false hopes.

The United Kingdom, the United States and others also opposed the setting of a deadline for achievement of a treaty as inappropriate and unrealistic.

China, opposing the draft resolutions proposed in connexion with this item, stressed that its development of nuclear weapons was purely in self-defence and that it had consistently supported the complete prohibition and destruction of nuclear weapons. In this connexion, several Members stressed the need for the participation of all nuclear powers in negotiations for a comprehensive test ban.

On 16 December 1971, the General Assembly adopted three resolutions concerning the suspension of nuclear and thermonuclear testing.

By the first of these—resolution 2828 A (XXVI) —the Assembly reiterated solemnly and most emphatically its condemnation of all nuclear weapon tests and urged the Governments of the nuclear-weapon States to halt all such tests at the earliest possible date and, in any case, not later than 5 August 1973. In taking this decision, the Assembly expressed its conviction that whatever might be the differences on the question of verification, there was no valid reason to delay the conclusion of a comprehensive test ban.

The Assembly also asked the Secretary-General to transmit the resolution to the nuclear-weapon States and to inform the Assembly at its 1972 session of any measures taken in implementation.

The General Assembly adopted this resolution by a recorded vote of 74 to 2, with 36 abstentions, on the recommendation of the First Committee, which approved the text by a roll-call vote of 66 to 2, with 39 abstentions, on 9 December 1971.

The sponsors of the text in the First Committee were Chile, Colombia, Costa Rica, Ecuador, Ghana, Guatemala, Honduras, Mexico, Panama, Peru, the United Republic of Tanzania, and Uruguay.

(For text of resolution, see DOCUMENTARY REFERENCES below.)

By the second resolution, adopted on 16 December 1971, the General Assembly: (1) appealed to the nuclear powers to desist from carrying out further nuclear tests of any kind; (2) urged all nuclear powers to reach agreement on a cessation of tests without delay; and (3) requested the nuclear powers not to deploy nuclear weapons of mass destruction. By the preamble to this resolution, the Assembly called attention to the health and other hazards arising from nuclear testing.

The Assembly adopted this resolution— 2828 B (XXVI)—by a recorded vote of 71 to 2, with 38 abstentions. The First Committee approved the text on 9 December by a vote of 49 to 2, with 51 abstentions, acting on a proposal by Saudi Arabia.

(For text of resolution, see DOCUMENTARY REFERENCES below.)

In its third decision on this question, the Assembly stressed anew the urgency of bringing to a halt all nuclear weapon testing in all environments by all States. The Assembly urged all States to adhere without delay to the Treaty Banning Nuclear Weapon Tests in the Atmosphere, in Outer Space and under Water and meanwhile to refrain from testing in the environments covered by that Treaty. It called on all Governments conducting nuclear weapon tests, particularly those of parties to the partial test ban Treaty, immediately to undertake unilateral or negotiated measures of restraint to suspend testing or reduce the size and number of tests, pending the early entry into force of a comprehensive ban.

The Assembly also urged Governments to develop and use more effectively existing capabilities for seismological identification of underground tests in order to facilitate the monitoring of a comprehensive test ban.

It asked the Conference of the Committee on Disarmament (CCD) to give highest priority to an underground test ban treaty and asked testing Governments, in particular, to take an active and constructive part in developing in CCD specific proposals for such a ban.

Finally, the Assembly expressed the hope that these efforts would enable all States to sign in the near future a treaty banning underground tests.

The text of this resolution was proposed in the First Committee by 16 Members, namely: Australia, Austria, Belgium, Canada, Denmark, Ethiopia, Finland, Ghana, Iran, Ireland, Japan, Morocco, the Netherlands, Nigeria, Norway and Sweden.

Two amendments were proposed by New Zealand. By one, an amendment to the preamble, the Assembly would note with regret that some States continued nuclear testing in the atmosphere; by the other, the Assembly, in the operative part, would call on all States to refrain from testing in the environments covered by the partial test ban Treaty.

On 9 December 1971, the First Committee approved the New Zealand amendments by a roll-call vote of 53 to 3, with 49 abstentions. The draft resolution as a whole, as amended, was then adopted by a roll-call vote of 82 to 2, with 22 abstentions.

On 16 December, the General Assembly, after separate roll-call votes approving the phrases added as a result of the New Zealand amendments, adopted the resolution as a whole by a recorded vote of 91 to 2, with 21 abstentions, as resolution 2828 C (XXVI).

The preambular amendment was approved by 49 votes to 5, with 62 abstentions. The amendment to the operative paragraph was approved by 55 votes to 5, with 57 abstentions.

(For text of resolution, see DOCUMENTARY REFERENCES below.)

DOCUMENTARY REFERENCES

General Assembly—26th session
First Committee, meetings 1803, 1827-1843, 1845-1848.
Plenary meetings 1939, 2022.

A/8457 (DC/234). Report of CCD (covering period 23 February–30 September 1971).
A/C.1/L.584. Chile, Colombia, Costa Rica, Ecuador, Ghana, Guatemala, Honduras, Mexico, Panama, Peru, United Republic of Tanzania, Uruguay: draft resolution, approved by First Committee on 9 December 1971, meeting 1847, by roll-call vote of 66 to 2, with 39 abstentions, as follows:

In favour: Afghanistan, Argentina, Austria, Bhutan, Brazil, Burma, Burundi, Cameroon, Canada, Ceylon, Chile, Colombia, Costa Rica, Cyprus, Denmark, Dominican Republic, Ecuador, Egypt, El Salvador, Ethiopia, Fiji, Ghana, Guatemala, Guyana, Haiti, Honduras, Iceland, India, Indonesia, Iran, Ireland, Israel, Ivory Coast, Jamaica, Jordan, Kenya, Kuwait, Lebanon, Liberia, Libyan Arab Republic, Malaysia, Malta, Mexico, Morocco, Nepal, New Zealand, Niger, Nigeria, Norway, Panama, Peru, Rwanda, Saudi Arabia, Singapore, Sudan, Swaziland, Sweden, Tunisia, Uganda, United Republic of Tanzania, Upper Volta, Uruguay, Venezuela, Yemen, Yugoslavia, Zambia.
Against: Albania, China.
Abstaining: Algeria, Australia, Belgium, Bulgaria, Byelorussian SSR, Central African Republic, Congo, Cuba, Czechoslovakia, Equatorial Guinea, Finland, France, Gabon, Greece, Hungary, Italy, Japan, Khmer Republic, Madagascar, Mali, Mauritius, Mongolia, Netherlands, Pakistan, Philippines, Poland, Portugal, Romania, Senegal, South Africa, Spain, Thailand, Togo, Turkey, Ukrainian SSR, USSR, United Kingdom, United States, Zaire.

A/8575. Report of First Committee, draft resolution A.

RESOLUTION 2828 A (XXVI), as recommended by First Commit-

tee, A/8575, adopted by Assembly on 16 December 1971, meeting 2022, by recorded vote of 74 to 2, with 36 abstentions, as follows:

In favour: Afghanistan, Argentina, Austria, Bahrain, Bhutan, Brazil, Burma, Burundi, Cameroon, Ceylon, Chad, Chile, Colombia, Costa Rica, Cyprus, Dahomey, Denmark, Dominican Republic, Ecuador, Egypt, El Salvador, Equatorial Guinea, Ethiopia, Fiji, Ghana, Guatemala, Guyana, Honduras, Iceland, India, Indonesia, Iran, Ireland, Israel, Ivory Coast, Jamaica, Jordan, Kenya, Kuwait, Laos, Lebanon, Lesotho, Liberia, Libyan Arab Republic, Malaysia, Mali, Malta, Mexico, Morocco, Nepal, New Zealand, Nigeria, Norway, Paraguay, Peru, Qatar, Rwanda, Saudi Arabia, Senegal, Singapore, Somalia, Sweden, Togo, Trinidad and Tobago, Tunisia, Uganda, United Republic of Tanzania, Upper Volta, Uruguay, Venezuela, Yemen, Yugoslavia, Zaire, Zambia.
Against: Albania, China.
Abstaining: Algeria, Australia, Belgium, Bulgaria, Byelorussian SSR, Canada,* Central African Republic, Congo, Cuba, Czechoslovakia, Finland, France, Greece, Guinea, Hungary, Italy, Japan, Khmer Republic, Luxembourg, Madagascar, Mongolia, Netherlands, Pakistan, People's Democratic Republic of Yemen, Philippines, Poland, Portugal, Romania, South Africa, Spain, Thailand, Turkey, Ukrainian SSR, USSR, United Kingdom, United States.

*Subsequently Canada advised the Secretariat that it had intended to vote in favour.

The General Assembly,
Viewing with the utmost apprehension the harmful consequences of nuclear weapon tests for the acceleration of the arms race and for the health of present and future generations of mankind,
Fully conscious that world opinion has, over the years,

demanded the immediate and complete cessation of all nuclear weapon tests in all environments,

Recalling that the item on the question of a comprehensive test ban has been included in the agenda of the General Assembly every year since 1957,

Deploring the fact that the General Assembly has not yet succeeded in its aim of achieving a comprehensive test ban, despite eighteen successive resolutions on the subject,

Noting with regret that all States have not yet adhered to the Treaty Banning Nuclear Weapon Tests in the Atmosphere, in Outer Space and under Water, signed in Moscow on 5 August 1963,

Deploring the fact that the determination expressed by the original parties to that Treaty to continue negotiations to achieve the discontinuance of all test explosions of nuclear weapons for all time has not so far produced the desired results,

Noting with special concern that the continuation of nuclear weapon tests in the atmosphere is a source of growing pollution and that the number and magnitude of underground tests have increased at an alarming rate since 1963,

Having considered the special report submitted by the Conference of the Committee on Disarmament in response to General Assembly resolution 2663 B (XXV) of 7 December 1970,

Recalling its resolution 1762 A (XVII) of 6 November 1962, whereby all nuclear weapon tests, without exception, were condemned,

Convinced that, whatever may be the differences on the question of verification, there is no valid reason for delaying the conclusion of a comprehensive test ban of the nature contemplated in the preamble to the Treaty Banning Nuclear Weapon Tests in the Atmosphere, in Outer Space and under Water,

1. *Reiterates solemnly and most emphatically* its condemnation of all nuclear weapon tests;

2. *Urges* the Governments of nuclear-weapon States to bring to a halt all nuclear weapon tests at the earliest possible date and, in any case, not later than 5 August 1973;

3. *Requests* the Secretary-General to transmit the present resolution to the nuclear-weapon States and to inform the General Assembly at its twenty-seventh session of any measures they have taken to implement it.

A/C.1/L.583 and Rev.1. Saudi Arabia: draft resolution and revision, approved by First Committee on 9 December 1971, meeting 1847, by 49 votes to 2, with 51 abstentions.
A/8575. Report of First Committee, draft resolution B.

RESOLUTION 2828 B (XXVI), as recommended by First Committee, A/8575, adopted by Assembly on 16 December 1971, meeting 2022, by recorded vote of 71 to 2, with 38 abstentions, as follows:

In favour: Afghanistan, Bahrain, Bhutan, Bulgaria, Burundi, Byelorussian SSR, Cameroon, Canada,* Central African Republic, Chad, Colombia, Costa Rica, Cuba, Cyprus, Czechoslovakia, Dahomey, Dominican Republic, Ecuador, El Salvador, Fiji, Ghana, Guatemala, Guyana, Hungary, Indonesia, Iran, Ireland, Ivory Coast, Jamaica, Japan, Jordan, Kenya, Khmer Republic, Kuwait, Laos, Lebanon, Lesotho, Liberia, Libyan Arab Republic, Malaysia, Mexico, Mongolia, Morocco, Nepal, New Zealand, Nicaragua, Nigeria, Pakistan, Paraguay, People's Democratic Republic of Yemen, Philippines, Poland, Qatar, Romania, Rwanda, Saudi Arabia, Singapore, Somalia, Thailand, Togo, Trinidad and Tobago, Tunisia, Turkey, Ukrainian SSR, USSR, Upper Volta, Uruguay, Venezuela, Yemen, Zaire, Zambia.

Against: Albania, China.

Abstaining: Algeria, Argentina, Australia, Austria, Belgium, Brazil, Burma, Ceylon, Chile, Congo, Denmark, Equatorial Guinea, Ethiopia, Finland, France, Greece, Guinea, Honduras, India, Israel, Italy, Luxembourg, Madagascar, Mali, Malta, Netherlands, Norway, Peru, Portugal, Senegal, South Africa, Spain, Sweden, Uganda, United Kingdom, United Republic of Tanzania, United States, Yugoslavia.

*Subsequently Canada advised the Secretariat that it had intended to abstain.

The General Assembly,

Noting that one of the first steps in the strengthening of international security is to dissipate world-wide fears that nuclear, thermonuclear and other weapons of mass destruction may be used by miscalculation in what could appear to be a desperate situation,

Considering that for the last few years the United Nations has been preoccupied with finding ways and means of diminishing the pollution of the earth's atmosphere,

Noting that scientists have been unanimous in the conclusion that the fall-out from nuclear tests is injurious to human and animal life and that such fall-out may poison the earth's atmosphere for many decades to come,

Taking into account that underground nuclear and thermonuclear tests may not only create serious health hazards but may also cause as yet undetermined injury to humans and animals of the region where such tests are conducted,

Recognizing that there already exist sufficient nuclear, thermonuclear and other lethal weapons of mass destruction in the arsenals of certain Powers to decimate the world's population and possibly render the earth uninhabitable,

1. *Appeals* to the nuclear Powers to desist from carrying out further nuclear and thermonuclear tests, whether underground, under water or in the earth's atmosphere;

2. *Urges* the nuclear Powers to reach an agreement without delay on the cessation of all nuclear and thermonuclear tests;

3. *Reassures* the peoples of the world that the United Nations will continue to raise its voice against nuclear and thermonuclear tests of any kind and earnestly requests the nuclear Powers not to deploy such weapons of mass destruction.

A/C.1/L.585. Australia, Austria, Belgium, Canada, Denmark, Ethiopia, Finland, Ghana, Iran, Ireland, Japan, Morocco, Netherlands, Nigeria, Norway, Sweden: draft resolution, as amended by New Zealand, A/C.1/L.595, approved by First Committee on 9 December 1971, meeting 1847, by roll-call vote of 82 to 2, with 22 abstentions, as follows:

In favour: Afghanistan, Australia, Austria, Belgium, Bhutan, Burma, Burundi, Cameroon, Canada, Central African Republic, Colombia, Costa Rica, Cyprus, Denmark, Dominican Republic, Ecuador, Egypt, El Salvador, Ethiopia, Fiji, Finland, Gabon, Ghana, Greece, Guatemala, Guyana, Haiti, Honduras, Iceland, Indonesia, Iran, Ireland, Israel, Italy, Ivory Coast, Jamaica, Japan, Jordan, Kenya, Khmer Republic, Kuwait, Lebanon, Liberia, Madagascar, Malaysia, Mali, Malta, Mexico, Morocco, Nepal, Netherlands, New Zealand, Niger, Nigeria, Norway, Pakistan, Panama, Philippines, Portugal, Rwanda, Saudi Arabia, Senegal, Singapore, Somalia, South Africa, Spain, Sudan, Swaziland, Sweden, Thailand, Togo, Tunisia, Turkey, Uganda, United Republic of Tanzania, Upper Volta, Uruguay, Venezuela, Yemen, Yugoslavia, Zaire, Zambia.

Against: Albania, China.

Abstaining: Algeria, Argentina, Brazil, Bulgaria, Byelorussian SSR, Ceylon, Chile, Congo, Cuba, Czechoslovakia, France, Hungary, India, Libyan Arab Republic, Mongolia, Peru, Poland, Romania, Ukrainian SSR, USSR, United Kingdom, United States.

A/C.1/L.595. New Zealand: amendments to 16-power draft resolution, A/C.1/L.585.
A/8575. Report of First Committee, draft resolution C.

RESOLUTION 2828 C (XXVI), as recommended by First Committee, A/8575, adopted by Assembly on 16 December 1971, meeting 2022, by recorded vote of 91 to 2, with 21 abstentions, as follows:

In favour: Afghanistan, Australia, Austria, Bahrain, Belgium, Bhutan, Bolivia, Burma, Burundi, Cameroon, Canada, Central African Republic, Chad, Colombia, Costa Rica, Cyprus,

Dahomey, Denmark, Dominican Republic, Ecuador, Egypt, El Salvador, Equatorial Guinea, Ethiopia, Fiji, Ghana, Greece, Guatemala, Guyana, Haiti, Honduras, Iceland, Indonesia, Iran, Ireland, Italy, Ivory Coast, Jamaica, Japan, Jordan, Kenya, Khmer Republic, Kuwait, Laos, Lebanon, Lesotho, Liberia, Libyan Arab Republic, Luxembourg, Madagascar, Malaysia, Mali, Malta, Mauritania, Mexico, Morocco, Nepal, Netherlands, New Zealand, Nicaragua, Nigeria, Norway, Pakistan, Panama, Paraguay, People's Democratic Republic of Yemen, Philippines, Portugal, Qatar, Rwanda, Saudi Arabia, Senegal, Singapore, Somalia, South Africa, Spain, Sweden, Thailand, Togo, Trinidad and Tobago, Tunisia, Turkey, Uganda, United Republic of Tanzania, Upper Volta, Uruguay, Venezuela, Yemen, Yugoslavia, Zaire, Zambia.

Against: Albania, China.

Abstaining: Algeria, Argentina, Brazil, Bulgaria, Byelorussian SSR, Ceylon, Chile, Congo, Cuba, Czechoslovakia, France, Guinea, Hungary, India, Mongolia, Poland, Romania, Ukrainian SSR, USSR, United Kingdom, United States.

The General Assembly,

Recognizing the urgent need for the cessation of nuclear and thermonuclear weapon tests, including those carried out underground,

Recalling that this subject has been included in the agenda of the General Assembly every year since 1957,

Recalling in particular its resolutions 914(X) of 16 December 1955, 1762(XVII) of 6 November 1962, 1910(XVIII) of 27 November 1963, 2032(XX) of 3 December 1965, 2163(XXI) of 5 December 1966, 2343(XXII) of 19 December 1967, 2455(XXIII) of 20 December 1968, 2604(XXIV) of 16 December 1969 and 2663(XXV) of 7 December 1970,

Expressing serious concern that the objectives of those resolutions have not been fulfilled,

Noting with regret that all States have not yet adhered to the Treaty Banning Nuclear Weapon Tests in the Atmosphere, in Outer Space and under Water, signed in Moscow on 5 August 1963, and that some continue to test in the atmosphere,

Taking into account the determination expressed by the parties to that Treaty to continue negotiations to achieve the discontinuance of all test explosions of nuclear weapons for all time,

Noting the appeal for progress on this issue made by the Secretary-General in the introduction to his report on the work of the Organization,

Noting with special concern that nuclear weapon tests in the atmosphere and underground are continuing,

Having considered the special report submitted by the Conference of the Committee on Disarmament in response to General Assembly resolution 2663 B (XXV),

1. *Stresses anew* the urgency of bringing to a halt all nuclear weapon testing in all environments by all States;

2. *Urges* all States that have not yet done so to adhere without further delay to the Treaty Banning Nuclear Weapon Tests in the Atmosphere, in Outer Space and under Water and meanwhile to refrain from testing in the environments covered by that Treaty;

3. *Calls upon* all Governments that have been conducting nuclear weapon tests, particularly those of parties to the Treaty Banning Nuclear Weapon Tests in the Atmosphere, in Outer Space and under Water, immediately to undertake unilateral or negotiated measures of restraint that would suspend nuclear weapon testing or limit or reduce the size and number of nuclear weapon tests, pending the early entry into force of a comprehensive ban on all nuclear weapon tests in all environments by all States;

4. *Urges* Governments to take all possible measures to develop further, and to use more effectively, existing capabilities for the seismological identification of underground nuclear tests, in order to facilitate the monitoring of a comprehensive test ban;

5. *Requests* the Conference of the Committee on Disarmament to continue, as a matter of high priority, its deliberations on a treaty banning underground nuclear weapon tests, taking into account the suggestions already made in the Conference as well as the views expressed at the current session of the General Assembly;

6. *Requests particularly* Governments that have been carrying out nuclear tests to take an active and constructive part in developing in the Conference of the Committee on Disarmament, or in any successor body, specific proposals for an underground test ban treaty;

7. *Expresses the hope* that these efforts will enable all States to sign, in the near future, a treaty banning underground nuclear weapon tests.

Treaty for the Prohibition of Nuclear Weapons in Latin America

On 16 December 1971, the General Assembly once again urged nuclear-weapon States that had not done so to sign and ratify the Protocol (Additional Protocol II) to the Treaty for the Prohibition of Nuclear Weapons in Latin America (Treaty of Tlatelolco) which called for nuclear-weapon powers to undertake to respect the denuclearized status of Latin America and also to undertake not to use or threaten to use nuclear weapons against the parties to the Treaty.

In addition, the Assembly noted with satisfaction that the United States had become a party to the Protocol on 12 May 1971, as had the United Kingdom in 1969.

It reaffirmed its conviction that, for the maximum effectiveness of any treaty establishing a nuclear-weapon-free zone, the co-operation of the nuclear-weapon States was necessary and should take the form of commitments that were legally binding.

The Assembly deplored the lack of response by the other nuclear-weapon States to its urgent

appeals and decided to take up the question again at its 1972 session.

The Assembly's decisions were embodied in resolution 2830(XXVI), adopted by 101 votes to 0, with 12 abstentions, on the recommendation of its First Committee, which had approved the text on 10 December by 85 votes to 0, with 10 abstentions. (For text of resolution, see DOCUMENTARY REFERENCES below.)

The text was sponsored in the First Committee by Bolivia, Brazil, Colombia, Costa Rica, the Dominican Republic, Ecuador, El Salvador, Guatemala, Honduras, Jamaica, Mexico, the Netherlands, Nicaragua, Panama, Paraguay, Peru, Uruguay and Venezuela.

When considering this item, the First Committee had before it an exchange of letters between the USSR and Mexico, a note by the Secretary-General on the subject and a communication from the United States reporting its ratification of Additional Protocol II of the Treaty of Tlatelolco, subject to understandings and declarations.

The debate reflected wide support for the position of most Latin American countries that adherence to and ratification of Additional Protocol II by all nuclear-weapon States was necessary for its effectiveness and viability.

Mexico, strongly urging ratification of Additional Protocol II by all nuclear powers, maintained that China could now become a party to the Protocol since its previous opposition had been on the ground that China had been denied its legal rights in the United Nations.[25]

Mexico also stressed that France, which had always been sympathetic to the Treaty, had had ample time to study it, and that the USSR should now sign the Protocol instead of laying down unilateral conditions.

China said that the declaration which it had made—before the Treaty of Tlatelolco was signed —that it would never be the first to use nuclear weapons constituted the best support for the good wishes of many countries for the establishment of nuclear-free and peace zones. For such zones to be effective, China considered, it was necessary that the USSR and the United States pledge not to be the first to use nuclear weapons, to dismantle their bases on the territories of other countries, not to stockpile weapons and station nuclear-armed troops on territories of other countries and immediately to stop their aggression, interference, control and subversion against other countries.

France stated that it intended to do nothing that would infringe upon the principle of denuclearization.

The USSR stressed that it favoured nuclear-free zones of all types, including that of Latin America. With respect to the Treaty of Tlatelolco, however, the USSR wondered to what extent the Treaty ensured the prohibition of nuclear weapons in Latin America, or ensured that the territory of States parties would remain denuclearized regions. In the opinion of the USSR, the Treaty contained certain provisions which did not correspond to this objective.

The USSR reiterated that it was ready to assume a commitment to respect the status of Mexico as a totally denuclearized zone, subject to the same commitment being made by other nuclear powers. It would take similar action towards other Latin American countries that made their territory completely nuclear-free.

[25]On 25 October 1971, the General Assembly, in adopting resolution 2758(XXVI), decided, *inter alia*, "to restore all its rights to the People's Republic of China and to recognize the representatives of its Government as the only legitimate representatives of China to the United Nations, and to expel forthwith the representatives of Chiang Kai-shek from the place which they unlawfully occupy at the United Nations and in all the organizations related to it." (See page 136.)

DOCUMENTARY REFERENCES

General Assembly—26th session
First Committee, meetings 1803, 1827-1843, 1845-1848.
Plenary meetings 1939, 2022.

A/8336/Rev.1 (S/10250/Rev.1). Letter of 28 June 1971 from USSR (transmitting letter of 23 June 1971 containing reply of 4 January 1971 from Supreme Soviet of USSR to Senate of Mexico regarding signature and ratification of Additional Protocol II of Treaty for Prohibition of Nuclear Weapons in Latin America (Treaty of Tlatelolco)).
A/8346 (S/10275). Letter of 22 July 1971 from Mexico (transmitting memorandum summarizing some basic facts concerning Treaty for Prohibition of Nuclear Weapons in Latin America and Additional Protocol II).
A/8435 and Add.1. Notes of 28 September and 8 December 1971 by Secretary-General.
A/8560. Note verbale of 23 November 1971 from United States (transmitting Department of State document reporting ratification by United States of Additional Protocol II).
A/C.1/L.587. Bolivia, Brazil, Colombia, Costa Rica, Dominican Republic, Ecuador, El Salvador, Guatemala, Honduras, Jamaica, Mexico, Netherlands, Nicaragua, Panama, Paraguay, Peru, Uruguay, Venezuela: draft resolution, approved by First Committee on 10 December 1971, meeting 1848, by 85 votes to 0, with 10 abstentions.
A/8582. Report of First Committee.

RESOLUTION 2830(XXVI), as recommended by First Committee, A/8582, adopted by Assembly on 16 December 1971, meeting 2022, by 101 votes to 0, with 12 abstentions.

The General Assembly,
Recalling its resolutions 1911(XVIII) of 27 November 1963, 2286(XXII) of 5 December 1967, 2456 B (XXIII) of 20 December 1968 and 2666(XXV) of 7 December 1970,
Recalling in particular that in its resolution 2286(XXII) it declared

that the Treaty for the Prohibition of Nuclear Weapons in Latin America (Treaty of Tlatelolco) constituted an event of historic significance in the efforts to prevent the proliferation of nuclear weapons and to promote international peace and security and that in its resolution 2666(XXV) it repeated the appeals which on two previous occasions it had addressed to the nuclear-weapon States to sign and ratify Additional Protocol II of the Treaty as soon as possible and urged them to avoid further delay in the fulfilment of such appeals,

1. *Reaffirms its conviction* that, for the maximum effectiveness of any treaty establishing a nuclear-weapon-free zone, the co-operation of the nuclear-weapon States is necessary and that such co-operation should take the form of commitments likewise undertaken in a formal international instrument which is legally binding, such as a treaty, convention or protocol;

2. *Notes with satisfaction* that the United States of America deposited its instrument of ratification of Additional Protocol II of the Treaty for the Prohibition of Nuclear Weapons in Latin America on 12 May 1971, thus becoming a State party to the Protocol, as the United Kingdom of Great Britain and Northern Ireland has been since 11 December 1969;

3. *Deplores* the fact that the other nuclear-weapon States have not yet heeded the urgent appeals which the General Assembly has made in three different resolutions and urges them once again to sign and ratify without further delay Additional Protocol II of the Treaty for the Prohibition of Nuclear Weapons in Latin America;

4. *Decides* to include in the provisional agenda of its twenty-seventh session an item entitled "Implementation of General Assembly resolution 2830(XXVI) concerning the signature and ratification of Additional Protocol II of the Treaty for the Prohibition of Nuclear Weapons in Latin America (Treaty of Tlatelolco)";

5. *Requests* the Secretary-General to transmit the present resolution to the nuclear-weapon States and to inform the General Assembly at its twenty-seventh session of any measure adopted by them in order to implement it.

International service for nuclear explosions for peaceful purposes

At its 1971 session, the General Assembly took up again the question of the establishment, within the framework of the International Atomic Energy Agency (IAEA), of an international service for nuclear explosions for peaceful purposes under appropriate international control.

In the debate in the Assembly's First Committee on this question, the United States expressed satisfaction with the significant progress achieved in the past year by IAEA and supported further studies by the Agency on the establishment of an international service for nuclear explosions for peaceful purposes. Similar views were expressed by Austria, Czechoslovakia, Malta, Nigeria and the United Kingdom.

The importance of an international service for nuclear explosions for peaceful purposes for the future success of the Treaty on the Non-Proliferation of Nuclear Weapons[26] was emphasized by several Members, including Belgium, Ireland and New Zealand. Others, including Argentina and India, felt that such a service should be made independent of the non-proliferation Treaty and that all members of IAEA, regardless of whether or not they were parties to the Treaty on the Non-Proliferation of Nuclear Weapons, should have access to the benefits of an international service for nuclear explosions for peaceful purposes.

(Article V of the Treaty on the Non-Proliferation of Nuclear Weapons provides that non-nuclear-weapon States which are parties to the Treaty will be able to obtain benefits from any peaceful applications of nuclear explosions, pursuant to a special international agreement, through an appropriate international body.[27])

Pakistan, while agreeing that IAEA could not discriminate between its members, argued for the establishment of a special body within IAEA to implement article V of the non-proliferation Treaty and maintained that there must be a clear relation between the service for nuclear explosions for peaceful purposes and a comprehensive test ban. Accordingly, nuclear-weapon States should be permitted to carry out nuclear explosions for peaceful purposes on their own behalf as well as for others, but non-nuclear-weapon States should not be permitted to conduct nuclear explosions of any kind.

Brazil argued that a comprehensive test ban should include provisions that assured the development of nuclear explosions for peaceful purposes, while the Netherlands and New Zealand took the view that a test ban must not be delayed on account of negotiations concerning nuclear explosions for peaceful purposes.

On 16 December 1971, the General Assembly adopted a resolution setting forth its decision on the question. Noting that IAEA, in accordance with its statute, was an appropriate body to exercise the functions of an international service for nuclear explosions for peaceful purposes, the Assembly commended IAEA for its intensive work on problems in connexion with nuclear explosions for peaceful purposes. It requested IAEA to continue its activities in this field and to study ways and means of establishing within its framework a service for nuclear explosions for peaceful purposes under appropriate international controls. Finally it invited the Director-General of IAEA to submit, in his annual report to the General Assembly, information on further developments.

This resolution—2829(XXVI)—was adopted by 103 votes to 0, with 9 abstentions, on the recommendation of the First Committee, which had approved it on 10 December by 83 votes to 0, with 7 abstentions. The text was sponsored in the First Committee by Austria, Belgium, Canada, Denmark, Japan and Mexico. (For text of resolution, see DOCUMENTARY REFERENCES below.)

---

[26]See Y.U.N., 1968, pp. 17-19, for text of Treaty.

[27]Article V of the non-proliferation Treaty reads: Each Party to the Treaty undertakes to take appropriate measures to ensure that, in accordance with this Treaty, under appropriate international observation and through appropriate international procedures, potential benefits from any peaceful applications of nuclear explosions will be made available to non-nuclear-weapon States Party to the Treaty on a non-discriminatory basis and that the charge to such Parties for the explosive devices used will be as low as possible and exclude any charge for research and development. Non-nuclear-weapon States Party to the Treaty shall be able to obtain such benefits, pursuant to a special international agreement or agreements, through an appropriate international body with adequate representation of non-nuclear-weapon States. Negotiations on this subject shall commence as soon as possible after the Treaty enters into force. Non-nuclear-weapon States Party to the Treaty so desiring may also obtain such benefits pursuant to bilateral agreements.

DOCUMENTARY REFERENCES

General Assembly—26th session
First Committee, meetings 1803, 1827-1843, 1845-1848.
Plenary meetings 1939, 2022.

A/8384. Note of 1 November 1971 by Secretary-General (transmitting 15th report of International Atomic Energy Agency for year ending 30 June 1971, paras. 94, 95).
A/C.1/L.594. Austria, Belgium, Canada, Denmark, Japan, Mexico: draft resolution, approved by First Committee on 10 December

1971, meeting 1848, by 83 votes to 0, with 7 abstentions.
A/8581. Report of First Committee.

RESOLUTION 2829(XXVI), as recommended by First Committee, A/8581, adopted by Assembly on 16 December 1971, meeting 2022, by 103 votes to 0, with 9 abstentions.

The General Assembly,
Recalling its resolution 2665(XXV) of 7 December 1970,

Having considered the report of the International Atomic Energy Agency on the establishment, within its framework, of an international service for nuclear explosions for peaceful purposes under appropriate international control,

Noting with satisfaction that the International Atomic Energy Agency has demonstrated its efficiency with regard to promoting co-operation in the peaceful uses of nuclear energy,

Noting further that the International Atomic Energy Agency, in accordance with its statute, is an appropriate organ to exercise the functions of an international service for nuclear explosions for peaceful purposes, taking into account the relevant provisions of the Treaty on the Non-Proliferation of Nuclear Weapons,

1. *Commends* the International Atomic Energy Agency for its intensive work on problems in connexion with nuclear explosions for peaceful purposes;

2. *Requests* the International Atomic Energy Agency to continue its activities in this field and to study ways and means of establishing, within its framework, an international service for nuclear explosions for peaceful purposes under appropriate international control;

3. *Invites* the Director-General of the International Atomic Energy Agency to submit, in his annual report to the General Assembly, information on further developments and on the progress made in this regard.

Economic and social consequences of the armaments race

As requested by the General Assembly on 7 December 1970,[28] a group of consultant experts were appointed by the Secretary-General to prepare a report on the economic and social consequences of the arms race and of military expenditures. They held three working sessions during 1971.

In a unanimous report, the experts concluded that: (1) the sooner a substantial reduction in military expenditures and the halt of the arms race were achieved, the faster would be the progress towards the goal of general and complete disarmament; (2) all countries, regardless of their size or stage of development, shared the responsibility to help achieve this goal; (3) achievement of this goal would help the social and economic development of all countries and would increase the possibilities of providing additional aid to developing countries; and (4) the Secretary-General should keep the facts concerning the arms race under periodic review.

At the 1971 session of the General Assembly, the experts' report was considered by the Assembly's First Committee. Many representatives who spoke on the subject felt that the report provided significant information and data on the economic and social aspects of the arms race and that the report should be given as wide publicity as possible. Stressing the importance of the report's conclusions, they deemed it desirable to have it brought up to date periodically.

Others did not agree. Australia found the report too general. Belgium said that since the financial burden of armaments came first from conventional weapons, closer attention should be given to controlling and reducing conventional arsenals.

Brazil and Venezuela contended that the report was exceedingly brief and lacked a sufficiently scientific approach to the problems; they also felt that the report should have dealt primarily with the nuclear aspects of the arms race. Due to the report's shortcomings, they believed it would be premature to give it wide publicity.

On 16 December 1971, the General Assembly adopted a resolution embodying its decisions on the report. Welcoming the report with satisfaction, the Assembly requested the Secretary-General to give it the widest possible publicity and recommended that all Governments, specialized agencies, inter-governmental, national and non-governmental organizations use their facilities to make the report widely known. The Assembly further recommended that the conclusions of the report be taken into account in future disarmament negotiations. It called upon all States to intensify their efforts during the Disarmament Decade (the 1970s) to promote negotiations on current disarmament problems.

The resolution—2831(XXVI)—was adopted by 111 votes to 1, with 3 abstentions, on the recommendation of the First Committee, which had approved the text on 10 December by 94 votes to 0, with 6 abstentions. The Committee, at the request of Indonesia, voted separately on the operative paragraph requesting the widest possible publicity, approving it by 86 votes to 1, with 9 abstentions.

The resolution was sponsored in the First Committee by Austria, Bulgaria, Canada, Chile, Cyprus, Denmark, Ethiopia, Finland, France, India, Iran, Ireland, Italy, Japan, Lebanon, Madagascar, Malaysia, Malta, Mexico, Morocco, the Netherlands, Norway, Pakistan, Romania, Rwanda, Singapore, Tunisia and Yugoslavia.

(For text of resolution, see DOCUMENTARY REFERENCES below.)

[28]See Y.U.N., 1970, p. 41, text of resolution 2667(XXV).

DOCUMENTARY REFERENCES

General Assembly—26th session
First Committee, meetings 1803, 1827-1843, 1845-1848.
Fifth Committee, meeting 1484.
Plenary meetings 1939, 2022.

Economic and Social Consequences of the Arms Race and of Military Expenditures. Report of the Secretary-General (A/8469/Rev.1). U.N.P. Sales No.: E.72.IX.16.
A/8469/Add.1. Economic and social consequences of armaments

race and its extremely harmful effects on world peace and security. Addendum to report of Secretary-General (containing replies received from Governments).

A/C.1/L.593. Austria, Bulgaria, Canada, Chile, Cyprus, Denmark, Ethiopia, Finland, France, India, Iran, Ireland, Italy, Japan, Lebanon, Madagascar, Malaysia, Malta, Mexico, Morocco, Netherlands, Norway, Pakistan, Romania, Rwanda, Singapore, Tunisia, Yugoslavia: draft resolution, approved by First Committee on 10 December 1971, meeting 1848, by 94 votes to 0, with 6 abstentions.

A/C.1/L.597, A/C.5/1419, A/8603. Administrative and financial implications of draft resolution recommended by First Committee in A/8583. Statements by Secretary-General and report of Fifth Committee.

A/8583. Report of First Committee.

RESOLUTION 2831(XXVI), as recommended by First Committee, A/8583, adopted by Assembly on 16 December 1971, meeting 2022, by 111 votes to 1, with 3 abstentions.

The General Assembly,

Concerned about the ever spiralling arms race and military expenditures, which constitute a heavy burden for all peoples and have extremely harmful effects on world peace and security,

Deeply convinced that the common aspirations of mankind for peace, security and progress require the urgent cessation of the arms race, particularly of the nuclear arms race, and the reduction of military expenditures, as well as the adoption of effective measures leading towards general and complete disarmament,

Considering that a halt in the arms race and a significant reduction of military expenditures would promote the economic and social development of all countries and would increase the possibilities of providing additional resources to developing countries,

Recalling its resolution 2667(XXV) of 7 December 1970, in which it requested the Secretary-General to prepare, with the assistance of qualified consultant experts appointed by him a report on the economic and social consequences of the arms race and of military expenditures,

1. *Welcomes with satisfaction* the report of the Secretary-General on the economic and social consequences of the arms race and of military expenditures and expresses the hope that it will help to focus future disarmament negotiations on nuclear disarmament and on the goal of general and complete disarmament under effective international control;

2. *Extends its thanks* to the Secretary-General and to the consultant experts as well as to the Governments and international organizations that have rendered assistance in the preparation of the report;

3. *Requests* the Secretary-General to arrange for the reproduction of the report as a United Nations publication and to give it the widest possible publicity in as many languages as is considered desirable and practicable;

4. *Recommends* to all Governments the widest possible distribution of the report so as to acquaint public opinion in their countries with its contents, and invites the specialized agencies as well as intergovernmental, national and non-governmental organizations to use their facilities to make the report widely known;

5. *Recommends* that the conclusions of the report of the Secretary-General on the economic and social consequences of the arms race and of military expenditures should be taken into account in future disarmament negotiations;

6. *Calls upon* all States to intensify their efforts during the Disarmament Decade with a view to promoting negotiations on effective measures for the cessation of the nuclear arms race at the earliest possible date and for nuclear disarmament, as well as on a treaty on general and complete disarmament under strict and effective international control;

7. *Decides* to keep the item entitled "Economic and social consequences of the armaments race and its extremely harmful effects on world peace and security" under constant review and to place it on the provisional agenda of its twenty-eighth session.

World disarmament conference

At its 1971 session, the General Assembly discussed the question of convening a world disarmament conference. It did so on the proposal of the USSR.

In an explanatory memorandum accompanying its proposal, the USSR referred to a proposal it had made in June 1971 for a conference of the five nuclear-weapon powers to deal with the problem of nuclear disarmament. The USSR stressed that the course of events had made it desirable to encourage more active efforts by all countries in the world, both nuclear and non-nuclear, to solve the problems relating to disarmament. The participation at a world disarmament conference of all States possessing significant armed forces and armaments would be of special importance. The USSR suggested that the conference could consider the whole complex of problems relating to disarmament, with regard to both nuclear and conventional armaments; primary attention could be devoted to the questions of prohibiting and eliminating nuclear weapons if the majority of the participants in the conference should so desire.

The General Assembly considered the question in plenary meetings.

When it began its discussion, the Assembly had before it a draft resolution sponsored by the USSR, and later also by Rwanda.

By this proposal, the General Assembly would: (1) proclaim the urgent necessity of intensifying the efforts of States in the field of disarmament; (2) express the conviction that the convening of a world disarmament conference to consider the whole range of disarmament problems, especially the prohibition and elimination of nuclear weapons, was a matter of expediency and urgency; (3) call upon all States to contribute to the preparation and early convening of such a conference by holding the necessary bilateral and multilateral consultations; (4) call upon all nuclear-weapon States to discharge their special responsibility for the solution of nuclear disarmament questions and to promote the success of the conference by every means, including joint action to establish the prerequisites for reaching agreement on these questions; (5) request the Conference of the Committee on Disarmament (CCD) to make further efforts to work out measures for the curtailment of the arms race and for disarmament, which would also contribute to the success of the conference; (6) deem it desirable that agreement should be reached among States before the end of 1972 on an actual date for convening the conference and on its agenda; and (7) decide to include the item "United Nations assistance in the convening of a world disarmament conference" in the provisional agenda of its 1972 session.

Early in the general discussion, the USSR suggested initially that such a conference should be held outside the framework of the United Nations, so that all States might take part in it, irrespective of whether or not they were Members of the United Nations. The conference, the USSR stated, would in no way detract from the importance of the existing forums and channels for disarmament negotiations, including CCD, and might become a permanent international forum, active for a long time and meeting every two or three years.

The USSR also renewed its proposal of June 1971 for convening a conference of the five nuclear powers, to complement the world disarmament conference.

On 3 November 1971, acting on a proposal of Mexico, the Assembly decided to postpone general debate on the question in order to allow for the arrival of the delegation of the People's Republic of China.[29] The debate resumed on 16 November 1971.

The majority of Members favoured the convening of a world disarmament conference, though they did not necessarily agree with the specific terms proposed by the USSR. Many Members held that the conference should be organized within the United Nations framework, not outside of it. Doubts were also expressed as to the need to create a permanent or recurring conference at that particular time.

Egypt proposed that if the General Assembly endorsed the idea of a world disarmament conference, it might request the Secretary-General to obtain the opinions of all States on the modalities of the conference, particularly its time, place, agenda, level of representation, and its relationship with the United Nations. The Secretary-General might also consult with the five permanent members of the Security Council, as well as States outside the United Nations. On the basis of those consultations, the Secretary-General might submit a report to the next session of the General Assembly.

Most Members supported the Egyptian suggestions, especially with regard to the need for a distinct agenda before convening the conference.

There was general agreement that such a conference should be held within the framework of the United Nations and that it should have universal participation. Canada said that appropriate provisions might be made by the United Nations for participation not only by non-Member States, but also by non-governmental organiza-

tions, private institutions, and individuals with a demonstrated interest in disarmament.

France said it would favour a conference of the five nuclear powers so that they might set an example on disarmament. Stating that such a five-power conference seemed improbable at present, France expressed support for the plan for a world disarmament conference, feeling that it could provide an opportunity to explore, define and better elucidate the desired political and technological conditions necessary for disarmament.

The United States, while believing that the question of a world disarmament conference deserved careful consideration, suggested that such a conference could not be expected to have the required characteristics of serious disarmament negotiations. Progress on reversing the arms race was likely to be reached through concrete agreements among States and not through convening large and unwieldy conferences. The United States, moreover, saw no reason for establishing more disarmament machinery outside the United Nations framework.

The United Kingdom believed that thorough preparations were needed for a world disarmament conference, including extensive consultations among States. It feared that the proposed conference would be too unwieldy to negotiate treaties and agreements and would tend to become a debating society. The United Kingdom was willing to consider the proposal most carefully and take part in any negotiations likely to bring effective disarmament nearer. It would not, however, want to do away with existing and proved negotiating forums. The aim should be for new measures on disarmament, rather than the creation of new organizations.

China said that there were at least two prerequisites for a world disarmament conference, namely: (1) that the two super-powers pledge not to be the first to use nuclear weapons at any time or in any circumstances and particularly undertake not to use nuclear weapons against non-nuclear countries or nuclear-free zones; and (2) that each withdraw to their own countries all forces stationed abroad and dismantle all military bases on foreign soil.

As to nuclear-free zones, China observed that, to free those zones truly from the threat of nuclear war, it was necessary first of all for the nuclear countries to guarantee that they would not use nuclear weapons against those countries and zones

[29]On 25 October 1971, the General Assembly, in adopting resolution 2758(XXVI), decided, *inter alia*, "to restore all its rights to the People's Republic of China and to recognize the representatives of its Government as the only legitimate representatives of China to the United Nations, and to expel forthwith the representatives of Chiang Kai-shek from the place which they unlawfully occupy at the United Nations and in all the organizations related to it." (See page 136.)

and would withdraw all their nuclear forces and dismantle all their nuclear bases and nuclear installations from those zones.

China said that it was compelled to develop nuclear weapons because it was under nuclear threat by the two super-powers, and it did so entirely for the purpose of defence and for breaking the imperialist nuclear monopoly and finally eliminating nuclear weapons.

China declared that the partial test ban Treaty (the Treaty Banning Nuclear Weapon Tests in the Atmosphere, in Outer Space and under Water, signed in Moscow, USSR, on 5 August 1963) and the Treaty on the Non-Proliferation of Nuclear Weapons (approved by the General Assembly on 12 June 1968)[30] were a camouflage for nuclear arms expansion by the two super-powers, a means for consolidating their nuclear monopoly. China could never agree to those Treaties.

China declared, in addition, that it would not participate in so-called nuclear disarmament talks among the nuclear powers behind the backs of the non-nuclear countries.

The position of China was further delineated in a letter of 24 November 1971 addressed to the Secretary-General. In that letter, China stated that it could not accept the USSR proposal for a conference of the five nuclear powers. It reaffirmed its position in favour of complete prohibition and destruction of nuclear weapons, adding that it would never be the first to use nuclear weapons and that it favoured a summit conference of all countries of the world to discuss these questions and, as the first step, to reach agreement on the non-use of nuclear weapons.

During the Assembly's debate on the proposal for a world disarmament conference, China made the point that it had consistently stood for the convening of a world conference to discuss the question of the complete prohibition and thorough destruction of nuclear weapons. In the opinion of China's representative, the USSR proposal for convening a world disarmament conference neither set out a clear aim nor put forward practical steps for its attainment. He accordingly proposed that the USSR draft resolution on the question not be put to a vote at that session of the General Assembly.

Responding to various points raised in the debate, the USSR said it welcomed the constructive proposals made by Egypt on the practical steps that should be taken towards preparing for a world disarmament conference and was willing to accept them. The USSR also agreed that a world disarmament conference take place within the United Nations framework and not outside of it.

The USSR representative expressed regret at the negativism of China in regard to the USSR proposal and deplored what he termed "the Sino-American duet of negativism" which, he said, struck a discordant note when compared with the views of the overwhelming majority of Assembly Members.

The USSR could not pass over the Chinese attempt to distort its position, the USSR representative added, citing USSR efforts of previous years for general and complete disarmament, for nuclear disarmament, the establishment of nuclear-free zones, the elimination of foreign military bases on foreign soil, and for the convening of a world disarmament conference. The forces of imperialism had prevented the attainment of those objectives, the representative declared, and the Chinese proposal not to vote on the USSR proposal for convening a world disarmament conference was the best possible gift China could make to the imperialists.

In a subsequent exchange of views, the representative of China declared, among other things, that the USSR had carried out aggression, subversion, control and interference against other countries and was practising social imperialism.

The USSR representative countered that the USSR had never threatened anyone and would never do so. China, he said, was seeking to establish itself as the hegemonical leader of the third world and was apparently attempting to use the third world as an arm for its true objectives, namely as a spring-board to become a "super super-power."

On 16 December, after it was announced that the text sponsored by Rwanda and the USSR would not be pressed to a vote, the Assembly adopted by acclamation a text sponsored by 30 Members.

The Assembly thereby expressed the conviction that it was most desirable to take immediate steps in order that careful consideration be given to the convening, following adequate preparation, of a world disarmament conference open to all States.

The Assembly invited all States to communicate to the Secretary-General, before 31 August 1972, their views and suggestions on any relevant questions relating to a world disarmament conference, in particular the following: (a) main objectives; (b) provisional agenda; (c) site favoured; (d) date and contemplated duration; (e) procedures to be adopted for carrying out the preparatory work; and (f) relationship to the United Nations.

The Secretary-General was asked to submit a report to the General Assembly in 1972 containing the views and suggestions communicated to him.

Finally, the Assembly decided to include on the provisional agenda of its 1972 session an item entitled "World Disarmament Conference."

The decisions to this effect were embodied in

[30]See Y.U.N., 1968, pp. 17-19, for text of Treaty.

resolution 2833(XXVI). (For text, see DOCUMEN-TARY REFERENCES below.)

The sponsors of the resolution were Algeria, Austria, Bulgaria, Ceylon, Chile, Congo, Cyprus, Ecuador, Egypt, Ethiopia, Guinea, Hungary, Indonesia, Iran, Iraq, Jamaica, Malaysia, Mali, Mexico, Morocco, Nepal, the People's Democratic Republic of Yemen, Peru, Poland, Romania, Rwanda, Somalia, the Syrian Arab Republic, the United Arab Emirates and Yugoslavia.

In explanation of its vote before the vote was taken, China said that as a necessary prerequisite for such a conference, the nuclear powers should openly undertake the obligation: not to be the first to use nuclear weapons and not to use them against non-nuclear States or zones; and to withdraw all their forces from nuclear bases outside their territory. On that understanding, China would vote in favour of the text.

The USSR said, in this connexion, that it had put forward a draft convention on the prohibition of nuclear weapons as long ago as 1967. In addition, it had repeatedly proposed withdrawal of nuclear weapons and means of their delivery from abroad, as well as prohibition of nuclear bomber flights beyond national frontiers and limitation of the movements of nuclear missile submarines. China, the USSR said, spoke in favour of disarmament, but in deeds did everything possible to prevent its attainment. As a vivid illustration, China was not a party to any of the disarmament treaties and continued to conduct nuclear weapon tests in the atmosphere.

DOCUMENTARY REFERENCES

General Assembly—26th session
General Committee, meeting 193.
Plenary meetings 1978, 1985, 1987, 1989, 1990, 1992, 1994-1996, 2022.

A/8328 (S/10236). Letter of 23 June 1971 from USSR.
A/8337 (S/10252). Letter of 6 July 1971 from Czechoslovakia (transmitting statement of 24 June 1971).
A/8452. Letter of 1 October 1971 from USSR (transmitting letter and statement of Government of German Democratic Republic).
A/8491. Letter of 6 September 1971 from USSR (request for inclusion in agenda of item entitled: "World Disarmament Conference").
A/8500. First report of General Committee.
A/8536 (S/10397). Letter of 24 November 1971 from China (transmitting statement of 30 July 1971).
A/8539. Letter of 29 November 1971 from Hungary (transmitting message to Assembly adopted by Disarmament Committee of World Peace Council at Moscow, USSR, 30-31 October 1971).
A/L.631 and Corr.1 and Add.1. Rwanda and USSR: draft resolution.
A/L.659 and Add.1. Algeria, Austria, Bulgaria, Ceylon, Chile, Congo, Cyprus, Ecuador, Egypt, Ethiopia, Guinea, Hungary, Indonesia, Iran, Iraq, Jamaica, Malaysia, Mali, Mexico, Morocco, Nepal, People's Democratic Republic of Yemen, Peru, Poland, Romania, Rwanda, Somalia, Syrian Arab Republic, United Arab Emirates, Yugoslavia: draft resolution.

RESOLUTION 2833(XXVI), as proposed by 30 powers, A/L.659, adopted by acclamation by Assembly on 16 December 1971, meeting 2022.

The General Assembly,
Conscious of the responsibility of the United Nations under the Charter for disarmament and the consolidation of peace,
Convinced that all peoples of the world have a vital interest in the success of disarmament negotiations,
Believing that it is imperative that all States exert further efforts for the adoption of effective measures of disarmament and, more particularly, nuclear disarmament,
Believing also that a world disarmament conference could promote and facilitate the realization of such aims,
1. *Expresses the conviction* that it is most desirable to take immediate steps in order that careful consideration be given to the convening, following adequate preparation, of a world disarmament conference open to all States;
2. *Invites* all States to communicate to the Secretary-General, before 31 August 1972, their views and suggestions on any relevant questions relating to a world disarmament conference, in particular the following:
  (a) Main objectives;
  (b) Provisional agenda;
  (c) Site favoured;
  (d) Date and contemplated duration;
  (e) Procedures to be adopted for carrying out the preparatory work;
  (f) Relationship to the United Nations;
3. *Requests* the Secretary-General to submit to the General Assembly at its twenty-seventh session a report containing the views and suggestions communicated to him;
4. *Decides* to include in the provisional agenda of its twenty-seventh session an item entitled "World Disarmament Conference."

Declaration of the Indian Ocean as a zone of peace

Among the disarmament questions before the General Assembly at its 1971 session was a proposal by Ceylon and the United Republic of Tanzania that the Assembly declare the Indian Ocean as a zone of peace.

Explaining the proposal, the sponsors called on the United Nations to make the entire high seas of the Indian Ocean an international domain, subject to international regulation and responsibility, and to declare that area a zone of peace from which armaments, offensive and defensive, as well as military installations would be excluded. A draft resolution to this effect was placed before the Assembly's First Committee by Burundi, Ceylon, India, Iran, Iraq, Kenya, Somalia, Swaziland, Uganda, the United Republic of Tanzania, Yemen, Yugoslavia and Zambia.

By the operative part of the 13-power text, the General Assembly would, among other things: (1) declare the Indian Ocean, within limits to be determined, to be a zone of peace; (2) call upon the great powers to enter into consultations with the littoral States of the Indian Ocean with a view to halting the further expansion of their military presence in the Indian Ocean and eliminating from the area all bases, military installations, nuclear weapons and weapons of mass destruction, and any manifestation of great-power military presence conceived in the context of great-power rivalry; (3) call upon the littoral and hinterland States of the Indian Ocean, the permanent members of the Security Council and other major maritime users of the Indian Ocean to enter into consultations with a view to implementing the declaration and ensuring that: (a) warships and military aircraft would not use the Indian Ocean for any threat or use of force against any of its littoral or hinterland States; (b) subject to the foregoing and to the norms and principles of international law, the right to free and unimpeded use of the zone by all nations was unaffected; and (c) arrangements were made to give effect to any international agreement ultimately reached on the question.

Although the proposal received wide support from Members, several States, in particular the major maritime users of the Indian Ocean such as France, Japan, the USSR, the United Kingdom and the United States, expressed reservations.

Ceylon and other sponsors insisted that the draft resolution merely commended the principle of a peace zone and urged consultations on the specific means of realizing that principle, but several representatives held that the resolution itself, particularly the second and third operative

paragraphs which called for consultations to halt great-power military presence in the area and to ensure no naval or air threat against littoral or hinterland States, predetermined the results of those consultations.

Some Members, including France and the USSR, stressed that no resolution should undermine recognized principles of international law dealing with freedom of the seas.

On 10 December 1971, the First Committee, after voting separately on three operative paragraphs, approved the draft text by a roll-call vote of 50 to 0, with 49 abstentions. The first operative paragraph, declaring the area a zone of peace, was voted on separately and was approved by 47 votes to 0, with 46 abstentions. The second and third operative paragraphs taken together were approved by a roll-call vote of 43 to 0, with 55 abstentions.

At a plenary meeting of the Assembly on 16 December, separate votes were again taken on the same three operative paragraphs. The first operative paragraph, declaring the Indian Ocean a zone of peace, was adopted by a recorded vote of 60 to 0, with 55 abstentions. The second and third operative paragraphs taken together were adopted by a recorded vote of 52 to 0, with 63 abstentions. The text as a whole was then adopted by a recorded vote of 61 to 0, with 55 abstentions, as resolution 2832(XXVI).

(For text of resolution, see DOCUMENTARY REFERENCES below.)

DOCUMENTARY REFERENCES

General Assembly—26th session
General Committee, meeting 194.
First Committee, meetings 1803, 1827-1843, 1845-1849.
Plenary meetings 1959, 2022.

A/8492 and Add.1. Letter of 1 October 1971 from Ceylon and United Republic of Tanzania (request for inclusion in agenda of item entitled: "Declaration of the Indian Ocean as a zone of peace").
A/8500/Add.1. Second report of General Committee.
A/C.1/1012/Add.1. Letter of 8 October 1971 from President of General Assembly to Chairman of First Committee.
A/C.1/L.590. Burundi, Ceylon, Iran, Iraq, Kenya, Somalia, Swaziland, Uganda, United Republic of Tanzania, Yemen, Zambia: draft resolution.
A/C.1/L.590/Rev.1,2. Burundi, Ceylon, India, Iran, Iraq, Kenya, Somalia, Swaziland, Uganda, United Republic of Tanzania, Yemen, Yugoslavia, Zambia: revised draft resolution, approved by First Committee on 10 December 1971, meeting 1849, by roll-call vote to 50 to 0, with 49 abstentions, as follows:

In favour: Afghanistan, Algeria, Bhutan, Burma, Burundi, Cameroon, Ceylon, China, Colombia, Congo, Cyprus, Egypt, El Salvador, Ethiopia, Ghana, Guinea, Guyana, Iceland, India, Indonesia, Iran, Iraq, Japan, Kenya, Khmer Republic, Kuwait, Lebanon, Libyan Arab Republic, Malaysia, Malta, Mexico, Morocco, Nepal, Nicaragua, Nigeria, Pakistan, Qatar, Romania, Somalia, Sudan, Swaziland, Sweden, Trinidad and Tobago,

Tunisia. Uganda, United Arab Emirates, United Republic of Tanzania, Yemen, Yugoslavia, Zambia.
Against: None.
Abstaining: Argentina, Australia, Austria, Belgium, Brazil, Bulgaria, Byelorussian SSR, Canada, Central African Republic, Chile, Cuba, Czechoslovakia, Denmark, Fiji, Finland, France, Greece, Honduras, Hungary, Ireland, Israel, Italy, Ivory Coast, Jamaica, Liberia, Madagascar, Malawi, Mongolia, Netherlands, New Zealand, Norway, Peru, Philippines, Poland, Portugal, Rwanda, Senegal, Singapore, South Africa, Spain, Thailand, Turkey, Ukrainian SSR, USSR, United Kingdom, United States, Upper Volta, Venezuela, Zaire.

A/8584. Report of First Committee.

RESOLUTION 2832(XXVI), as recommended by First Committee, A/8584, adopted by Assembly on 16 December 1971, meeting 2022, by recorded vote of 61 to 0, with 55 abstentions, as follows:

In favour: Afghanistan, Algeria, Bhutan, Burma, Burundi, Cameroon, Ceylon, Chad, China, Colombia, Congo, Costa Rica, Cyprus, Egypt, El Salvador, Equatorial Guinea, Ethiopia, Ghana, Guinea, Guyana, Iceland, India, Indonesia, Iran, Japan, Jordan, Kenya, Khmer Republic, Kuwait, Laos, Lebanon, Liberia, Libyan Arab Republic, Malaysia, Mali, Malta, Mauritania, Mexico, Morocco, Nepal, Nicaragua,* Nigeria, Pakistan, Panama, Qatar, Romania, Saudi Arabia, Somalia, Sudan, Swaziland, Sweden,

Syrian Arab Republic, Togo, Trinidad and Tobago, Tunisia, Uganda, United Republic of Tanzania, Uruguay, Yemen, Yugoslavia, Zambia.

Against: None.

Abstaining: Argentina, Australia, Austria, Belgium, Bolivia, Brazil, Bulgaria, Byelorussian SSR, Canada, Central African Republic, Chile, Cuba, Czechoslovakia, Dahomey, Denmark, Dominican Republic, Fiji, Finland, France, Greece, Guatemala, Haiti, Honduras, Hungary, Ireland, Israel, Italy, Ivory Coast, Jamaica, Lesotho, Luxembourg, Madagascar, Mongolia, Netherlands, New Zealand, Norway, People's Democratic Republic of Yemen, Peru, Philippines, Poland, Portugal, Rwanda, Senegal, Singapore, South Africa, Spain, Thailand, Turkey, Ukrainian SSR, USSR, United Kingdom, United States, Upper Volta, Venezuela, Zaire.

*Subsequently, Nicaragua advised the Secretariat that it had intended to abstain.

The General Assembly,

Conscious of the determination of the peoples of the littoral and hinterland States of the Indian Ocean to preserve their independence, sovereignty and territorial integrity, and to resolve their political, economic and social problems under conditions of peace and tranquillity,

Recalling the Declaration of the Third Conference of Heads of State or Government of Non-Aligned Countries, held at Lusaka from 8 to 10 September 1970, calling upon all States to consider and respect the Indian Ocean as a zone of peace from which great Power rivalries and competition as well as bases conceived in the context of such rivalries and competition should be excluded, and declaring that the area should also be free of nuclear weapons,

Convinced of the desirability of ensuring the maintenance of such conditions in the Indian Ocean area by means other than military alliances, as such alliances entail financial and other obligations that call for the diversion of the limited resources of the States of the area from the more compelling and productive task of economic and social reconstruction and could further involve them in the rivalries of power blocs in a manner prejudicial to their independence and freedom of action, thereby increasing international tensions,

Concerned at recent developments that portend the extension of the arms race into the Indian Ocean area, thereby posing a serious threat to the maintenance of such conditions in the area,

Convinced that the establishment of a zone of peace in the Indian Ocean would contribute towards arresting such develop-

ments, relaxing international tensions and strengthening international peace and security,

Convinced further that the establishment of a zone of peace in an extensive geographical area in one region could have a beneficial influence on the establishment of permanent universal peace based on equal rights and justice for all, in accordance with the purposes and principles of the Charter of the United Nations,

1. *Solemnly declares* that the Indian Ocean, within limits to be determined, together with the air space above and the ocean floor subjacent thereto, is hereby designated for all time as a zone of peace;

2. *Calls upon* the great Powers, in conformity with this Declaration, to enter into immediate consultations with the littoral States of the Indian Ocean with a view to:

(a) Halting the further escalation and expansion of their military presence in the Indian Ocean;

(b) Eliminating from the Indian Ocean all bases, military installations and logistical supply facilities, the disposition of nuclear weapons and weapons of mass destruction and any manifestation of great Poer military presence in the Indian Ocean conceived in the context of great Power rivalry;

3. *Calls upon* the littoral and hinterland States of the Indian Ocean, the permanent members of the Security Council and other major maritime users of the Indian Ocean, in pursuit of the objective of establishing a system of universal collective security without military alliances and strengthening international security through regional and other co-operation, to enter into consultations with a view to the implementation of this Declaration and such action as may be necessary to ensure that:

(a) Warships and military aircraft may not use the Indian Ocean for any threat or use of force against the sovereignty, territorial integrity and independence of any littoral or hinterland State of the Indian Ocean in contravention of the purposes and principles of the Charter of the United Nations;

(b) Subject to the foregoing and to the norms and principles of international law, the right to free and unimpeded use of the zone by the vessels of all nations is unaffected;

(c) Appropriate arrangements are made to give effect to any international agreement that may ultimately be reached for the maintenance of the Indian Ocean as a zone of peace;

4. *Requests* the Secretary-General to report to the General Assembly at its twenty-seventh session on the progress that has been made with regard to the implementation of this Declaration;

5. *Decides* to include in the provisional agenda of its twenty-seventh session an item entitled "Declaration of the Indian Ocean as a zone of peace."

Chapter II

Strengthening of international security

In 1971, the General Assembly considered proposals for giving effect to the Declaration on the Strengthening of International Security which it had adopted on 16 December 1970.[1]

Background material for the discussions included a report by the Secretary-General requested by the Assembly in 1970.

The Secretary-General reported that he had sent the text of the Declaration to United Nations Member States asking for information on any steps taken to strengthen international security. By 3 November 1971, 37 replies had been received.

Presenting his own observations in the introduc-

tion to the report, the Secretary-General expressed the view that there were signs testifying to the potential of the Declaration. The recently concluded four-power negotiations concerning West Berlin had opened the door to the solution of outstanding European problems as well as to further *détente*, the prospects for the reduction of armed forces and armaments were brighter and the Strategic Arms Limitation Talks appeared to have gathered momentum.

However, the Secretary-General observed, the

[1]See Y.U.N., 1970, pp. 105-7, text of resolution 2723(XXV).

world situation continued to be fraught with grave dangers. Peace was yet to come in Indo-China. The situation in East Pakistan and in the Middle East threatened international peace and security, and dangerous colonial tensions and *apartheid* still survived in Africa. All these factors, the Secretary-General said, called for a rededication by States to the standards of international morality set out in the United Nations Charter and for the implementation of the provisions of the Declaration.

At the Assembly's 1971 session, the question of implementing the Declaration was discussed at 21 meetings of the Assembly's First Committee.

In addition to the Secretary-General's report, the First Committee had before it: (*a*) a communication from the German Democratic Republic to the Chairman of the First Committee transmitting a Government statement on the question of strengthening international security; and (*b*) a declaration and communiqué issued by the meeting of Foreign Ministers of the countries of the Association of South East Asian Nations (Indonesia, Malaysia, the Philippines, Singapore and Thailand), held at Kuala Lumpur, Malaysia, on 27 November 1971, relating to peace and security in the south-east Asian region.

Five draft resolutions were presented during the course of the First Committee's discussions. One of these, submitted by Saudi Arabia, was withdrawn and later resubmitted for consideration in the discussion on the agenda item dealing with the urgent need for suspending nuclear and thermonuclear tests (see pp. 22-26).

The first text submitted was sponsored by the following eight Members: Bulgaria, the Byelorussian SSR, Czechoslovakia, Hungary, Mongolia, Poland, the Ukrainian SSR and the USSR.

By the preambular part of this text the General Assembly would, *inter alia:* (*a*) emphasize the urgency of adopting specific measures in order to fulfil the primary task of the United Nations, which was the maintenance of international peace and security; (*b*) reaffirm that the strengthening of international security required of all States coordinated action making full use of United Nations capabilities to suppress immediately and firmly any acts of aggression and international arbitrariness; and (*c*) express its deep concern over the continued military conflicts and acts of aggression in different parts of the world, which engendered tensions and threats to world peace.

By the operative part of this text, the General Assembly would, *inter alia:* (1) declare that continued tensions and threats to world peace derived from flagrant violations of the Charter and from the non-implementation of the provisions of the Declaration on the Strengthening of International Security; (2) condemn States that continued to resort to coercive acts which deprived peoples of

their inalienable rights to self-determination, freedom and independence, obstructed the full implementation of the United Nations decisions on the elimination of colonialism and racism and threatened the sovereignty of newly independent States; (3) urgently appeal to all States to take immediate and effective measures to implement the provisions of the Declaration and to renounce the use or threat of force in settling controversial issues; and (4) request the Secretary-General to report to it in 1972 on the implementation of the Declaration.

A second draft resolution was sponsored by the following 21 States: Argentina, Barbados, Bolivia, Brazil, Colombia, Costa Rica, the Dominican Republic, Ecuador, El Salvador, Guatemala, Guyana, Haiti, Honduras, Jamaica, Nicaragua, Panama, Paraguay, Peru, Trinidad and Tobago, Uruguay and Venezuela.

By the preamble to this text the General Assembly would, *inter alia:* (*a*) affirm that the effective implementation of the Declaration required the strengthening of the United Nations machinery for international peace and security, disarmament, economic development and social progress; (*b*) express awareness that the strengthening of international security was a continuous process involving the interaction of international measures at the multilateral and bilateral levels; (*c*) recognize that however important the measures adopted individually by States might be, they must be complemented by collective measures adopted by the competent organs of the United Nations in order to ensure the complete fulfilment of the aims and purposes of the Declaration; (*d*) express its conviction of the need for systematic and continuous action for the promotion of respect for, and the effective exercise of, fundamental human rights and freedoms, and for the implementation of the General Assembly's resolution of 14 December 1960 (containing the Declaration on the Granting of Independence to Colonial Countries and Peoples)[2] and for strict compliance with the Assembly's resolution of 21 December 1965 (on the inadmissibility of intervention in the domestic affairs of States);[3] and (*e*) express its awareness of the importance for strengthening international security of peace-keeping operations and operations for the restoration of peace.

By the operative part of this text, the General Assembly would:

(1) solemnly reaffirm that all the provisions of the Declaration on the Strengthening of International Security must be fully respected and implemented by all Member States in their

---

[2]See Y.U.N., 1960, pp. 49-50, resolution 1514(XV), containing text of Declaration.
[3]See Y.U.N., 1965, pp. 94-95, text of resolution 2131(XX).

international relations, in accordance with the purposes and principles of the Charter;

(2) declare that appropriate measures must be adopted to establish a system of collective economic security designed to promote the sustained development of national economies along with efforts towards general and complete disarmament under effective international control and the strengthening of a political system of collective security;

(3) declare further that the strengthening of international security demanded universal respect for fundamental human rights and freedoms and elimination of all manifestations of colonialism;

(4) decide to undertake a broad review of all aspects of the question of peace-keeping operations in order to develop an early definition of that concept, to establish appropriate and effective machinery capable of maintaining or restoring peace and to determine appropriate guidelines for its application;

(5) invite the Security Council to give priority to the consideration of appropriate means and procedures for ensuring the strict and full implementation of its resolutions relating to international peace and security;

(6) invite all Member States, in particular the more developed countries, to adopt all appropriate measures to normalize the financial situation of the United Nations and to provide it with the means of achieving its goals effectively and carrying out its programmes, in particular those relating to the implementation of the Declaration;

(7) request a report from the Secretary-General and indicate the scope of the report; and

(8) place the item on the provisional agenda of its 1972 session.

The third draft text before the First Committee was sponsored by the following 45 States: Afghanistan, Algeria, Barbados, Burundi, Cameroon, Ceylon, Chile, the Congo, Cyprus, Egypt, Equatorial Guinea, Ethiopia, Ghana, Guinea, Guyana, India, Indonesia, Jamaica, Jordan, Kenya, the Khmer Republic, Kuwait, Laos, Lebanon, Lesotho, the Libyan Arab Republic, Malaysia, Mali, Malta, Mauritius, Morocco, Nepal, Nigeria, Senegal, Sierra Leone, Singapore, Somalia, Swaziland, Trinidad and Tobago, Tunisia, Uganda, the United Republic of Tanzania, Yemen, Yugoslavia and Zambia.

By the preamble to this 45-power draft text the General Assembly would *inter alia*: (*a*) note some positive results achieved in the reduction of tension and in the strengthening of peace and security and promoting co-operation among States, bearing in mind that regional efforts to achieve security should be an integral part of universal security of nations; (*b*) express its conviction that the lack of substantial progress in solving long-standing questions and problems such as those of economic development and independence, disarmament, colonialism, *apartheid* and racial discrimination, which burdened the international community, was a constant source of unequal relations and threats to the security of nations; and (*c*) emphasize that the provisions in the Declaration needed to be implemented for the strengthening of international security and the independence and sovereignty of all States through co-ordinated action, making full use of United Nations capabilities, including the implementation of the provisions of Chapter VII of the United Nations Charter.[4]

By the operative part of the draft resolution, the General Assembly would:

(1) urgently appeal to all States to take effective measures to implement all parts of the Declaration;

(2) call upon all States to contribute towards resolving the existing crises in accordance with the Charter, United Nations resolutions, and the Declaration;

(3) call upon all States to respect the territorial integrity of every State, to renounce the threat or use of force and to observe fully the principles that the territory of a State should not be the object of forcible military occupation and that the acquisition of territories by force was inadmissible;

(4) declare that coercive acts depriving peoples of their inalienable rights to self-determination, freedom and independence, the non-implementation of United Nations resolutions, including those against colonialism, racialism and *apartheid*, serious and systematic violations of human rights and fundamental freedoms, and economic and social discrimination constituted a threat to international peace and security;

(5) declare that any measure, threat, pressure or reprisal directed against any State while exercising its inalienable right to permanent sovereignty over its natural resources constituted a violation of the obligation of Member States to ensure international co-operation, as well as an inadmissible economic coercion against the State so affected;

(6) urge the implementation of the provision of the resolution on the Second United Nations Development Decade calling for general and complete disarmament in order to facilitate the redirection of resources employed in the production of armaments towards social and economic development, especially in the developing countries;

(7) call for an early agreement on guidelines for peace-keeping operations and on a definition of aggression;

[4]For text of Chapter VII of the Charter, see APPENDIX II.

(8) urge all States to respect human rights and fundamental freedoms and reaffirm that the elimination of the violation of those rights was essential to the strengthening of international security; and

(9) ask the Secretary-General to report to it in 1972 on the implementation of the Declaration.

Yet another text, sponsored by 57 States, was approved by the First Committee, having been given priority in the voting, and later adopted at a plenary meeting of the General Assembly on 21 December 1971 as resolution 2880(XXVI).

By the preamble of the resolution, the General Assembly, *inter alia,* noted that some positive results conducive to the strengthening of international peace and security had been achieved through negotiations and co-operation among States. It expressed its conviction that bilateral and regional efforts towards achieving international security should be strictly in accordance with the purposes and principles of the United Nations and that such efforts should be complemented by collective measures adopted by the competent organs of the United Nations, in order to ensure the complete implementation of the Declaration on the Strengthening of International Security.

The Assembly expressed deep concern at the persistence of armed conflicts and other situations resulting therefrom which threatened international peace and security. It emphasized that the Declaration, which constituted an organic whole, needed to be implemented in its entirety, through the full use of United Nations machinery and capabilities, including those provided for in Chapters VI and VII of the United Nations Charter[5] and the dispatch of special missions by the Security Council.

By still another part of the preamble, the Assembly expressed its conviction that the lack of substantial progress in solving issues relating to international peace and security, economic development and independence, disarmament, colonialism, *apartheid* and racial discrimination, human rights and fundamental freedoms was a constant source of tension and a threat to the security of nations.

By the operative part of the resolution, the General Assembly took the following decisions.

It solemnly reaffirmed all the principles and provisions contained in the Declaration on the Strengthening of International Security and strongly appealed to all States to implement the Declaration in its entirety. It called upon all States to help resolve existing conflicts and situations likely to endanger international peace and security, in accordance with the purposes and principles of the United Nations Charter and the Declaration.

The Assembly also called upon all States to respect the national unity, political independence and territorial integrity of every State, to refrain from the threat or use of force and to observe fully the principles that the territory of a State should not be the object of military occupation resulting from the use of force in violation of the Charter and that the acquisition of territories by force was inadmissible.

Also, the Assembly declared that the termination of coercive acts which deprived peoples of their inalienable rights to self-determination, freedom and independence, the implementation of relevant United Nations resolutions concerning colonialism, racialism and *apartheid,* and the elimination of serious and systematic violations of human rights and fundamental freedoms were essential elements for the strengthening of international peace and security.

The Assembly invited the Security Council to consider all appropriate means and procedures for ensuring the strict and full implementation of its resolutions relating to international peace and security. It urged early undertaking of a broad review of all aspects of the concept of peace-keeping operations in order to determine appropriate guidelines for its application and to establish machinery capable of preserving and restoring peace. Further, the Assembly called for an early agreement on the definition of aggression.

It declared that in view of the close connexion between the strengthening of international security, disarmament and development, the United Nations should evolve a concept of collective economic security designed to promote sustained development and expansion of national economies. In this connexion, the Assembly affirmed that a substantial portion of the savings derived from disarmament measures should be devoted to economic and social development, particularly in the developing countries.

In addition, the Assembly declared that any measure or pressure directed against any State while exercising its sovereign right freely to dispose of its natural resources constituted a flagrant violation of the principles of self-determination of peoples and non-intervention.

The Assembly invited all Member States, in particular the more developed countries, to adopt all appropriate measures to normalize the financial situation of the United Nations and to provide it with the means of effectively achieving its goals.

Finally, the Assembly asked the Secretary-General to report to it in 1972 on measures taken in pursuance of the Declaration, and decided to place the item on the provisional agenda of its 1972 session.

The Assembly adopted the 57-power text by a

[5]For texts of Chapters VI and VII of the Charter, see APPENDIX II.

recorded vote of 96 to 1, with 16 abstentions, as its resolution 2880(XXVI).

It acted on the basis of a text approved by the First Committee, by a roll-call vote of 71 to 1, with 14 abstentions, on 17 December. The sponsors of the other draft resolutions did not press their texts to a vote.

(For text of resolution, see DOCUMENTARY REFERENCES below.)

The 57 sponsors of resolution 2880(XXVI) in the First Committee were Afghanistan, Algeria, Argentina, Bolivia, Brazil, Burundi, Ceylon, Chile, Colombia, Costa Rica, Cyprus, the Dominican Republic, Ecuador, El Salvador, Equatorial Guinea, Ethiopia, Ghana, Guatemala, Guinea, Guyana, Haiti, Honduras, India, Indonesia, Jamaica, Kenya, Kuwait, Laos, Lesotho, Liberia, the Libyan Arab Republic, Malaysia, Mali, Malta, Mauritius, Mexico, Morocco, Nepal, Nicaragua, Nigeria, Panama, Paraguay, Peru, the Philippines, Romania, Rwanda, Senegal, Sierra Leone, Singapore, Swaziland, Trinidad and Tobago, Uganda, the United Republic of Tanzania, Uruguay, Venezuela, Yugoslavia and Zambia.

In the debate preceding approval of the 57-power text by the First Committee, various Members expressed their views on the approaches to the question represented by the several draft resolutions.

The USSR and other supporters of the eight-power text stressed the need for a collective effort by all States to adopt concrete measures of implementation and to remove all impediments to effective operation of the Declaration. They cited the preparation of a draft convention on the prohibition and elimination of bacteriological (biological) weapons by the Conference of the Committee on Disarmament as an example of such an effort.

The sponsors and others, such as Cuba, advocated, *inter alia*, the adoption of a resolution embodying various provisions which in the present international situation deserved to be emphasized. In order to establish the renunciation of the threat or use of force as a strictly respected principle of international relations, they urged that the General Assembly should once again appeal to all States to take urgent and effective measures to implement the Declaration and should denounce States that violated its provisions.

In support of the eight-power text, reference was made to the need to solve a number of serious problems facing the world community, such as: extinguishing the hotbeds of war in Indo-China and the Middle East; paving the way for the peaceful reunification of Korea; liquidating the remnants of colonialism; eradicating racism and *apartheid*; taking steps to achieve an appropriate political settlement of the crisis in East Pakistan;

assisting in the creation of proper conditions for economic progress compatible with the requirements of individual States; halting the arms race; and establishing an effective system of peace-keeping operations under the authority of the Security Council.

During the First Committee's discussion, several Members observed that tensions in Europe had eased and that the climate was more favourable than before for convening a European conference on security and co-operation with the participation of the United States and Canada. Among those sharing such views were Austria, Bulgaria, Finland, Ireland, Romania and the USSR.

In this connexion, supporters of the eight-power text stressed the importance of regional and bilateral agreements in implementing the Declaration.

Several States, including Australia, Belgium, France, Ireland, Japan, the United Kingdom and the United States, expressed opposition to the eight-power draft resolution. They believed that the objective of strengthening international security could better be served by constructive action on the various specific items relating to international security already on the agenda of the current Assembly session rather than by adopting a resolution which, in their opinion, could have the effect of watering down the Declaration. These States emphasized the comprehensiveness of the Declaration and called for a reaffirmation of its provisions.

Brazil, Ecuador, Peru, Venezuela and other sponsors of the 21-power draft resolution felt that the Declaration should be considered as an organic whole and should not be fragmented in order to meet immediate or circumstantial interests.

They argued that the Declaration was not a mere duplication of the Charter, but rested on its philosophy and developed its juridical and political doctrines, thus seeking to ensure its coherent and progressive expansion.

In view of the close relationship between security, disarmament and economic development, they stressed the need to adopt appropriate measures for establishing a system of collective economic security and for channelling into development the resources saved through disarmament. Among the concrete steps which they urged were the formulation of a generally accepted definition of peace-keeping machinery that could maintain or restore peace, the consideration by the Security Council of appropriate means and procedures for ensuring strict implementation of its resolutions, and the adoption by Member States, in particular by developed countries, of appropriate measures to solve the grave financial crisis of the United Nations.

The following were among the points made in

support of the draft text sponsored by 45 powers.

Peace could not be divided into political, economic, social or cultural components in the vain hope of solving one without tackling the others. Many positive developments had taken place since the adoption of the Declaration, such as the restoration of the lawful rights of the People's Republic of China, increasing use by the Security Council of new methods of resolving disputes—including the appointment of special missions—and regional progress towards strengthening security.

Nevertheless, much more remained to be done, supporters of the 45-power text noted. Cited in particular were the many problems of Asian and African peoples.

It was also stressed that questions arising from colonial oppression, non-implementation of United Nations resolutions against colonialism, racism and *apartheid*, systematic violations of human rights and fundamental freedoms and the widening economic gap between developed and developing countries called for a continuing effort to strengthen international security and to enhance the powers of the United Nations in that field.

Among those expressing views to this effect were Algeria, India, Indonesia, Lebanon, Senegal, Yugoslavia and Zambia.

They and other sponsors of the 45-power text also felt that the need for an early agreement on general and complete disarmament was urgent and they called for effective measures to redirect to the economic development of developing countries the resources employed in the production of armaments.

They also called for clear recognition of the inalienable right of every State to permanent sovereignty over its natural resources and for ensuring respect for the principle of the territorial integrity of States.

The 57-power text was introduced by the representatives of Venezuela and Zambia who said that their text was the result of negotiations—between the sponsors of the 21-power and the 45-power texts—to work out a text that would receive the broadest support and would reflect as widely as possible the views of the various Member States.

DOCUMENTARY REFERENCES

General Assembly—26th session
First Committee, meetings 1804-1818, 1827-1829, 1835, 1856, 1857.
Plenary meeting 2029.

A/8401. Report of Secretary-General on work of the Organization, 16 June 1970–15 June 1971, Part One, Chapter IV L.
A/8401/Add.1. Introduction to report of Secretary-General, September 1971, Part Two, Chapter I, paras. 162-169.
A/8402. Report of Security Council, 16 June 1970–15 June 1971, Chapter 21.
A/8431 and Add.1-5. Implementation of Declaration on Strengthening of International Security. Report of Secretary-General.
A/C.1/1015. Letter of 24 September 1971 from Minister of Foreign Affairs of German Democratic Republic to Chairman of First Committee (transmitting statement of 7 September 1971 from Government of German Democratic Republic).
A/C.1/1019. Letter of 29 November 1971 from Indonesia, Malaysia, Philippines, Singapore and Thailand (transmitting declaration and joint communiqué issued by Meeting of Foreign Ministers of Association of South East Asian Nations, Kuala Lumpur, Malaysia, 27 November 1971).
A/C.1/L.566. Bulgaria, Byelorussian SSR, Czechoslovakia, Hungary, Mongolia, Poland, Ukrainian SSR, USSR: draft resolution.
A/C.1/L.567. Saudi Arabia: draft resolution.
A/C.1/L.573 and Rev.2. Argentina, Barbados, Bolivia, Brazil, Colombia, Costa Rica, Dominican Republic, Ecuador, El Salvador, Guatemala, Guyana, Haiti, Honduras, Jamaica, Nicaragua, Panama, Paraguay, Peru, Trinidad and Tobago, Uruguay, Venezuela: draft resolution and revision.
A/C.1/L.577. Afghanistan, Algeria, Barbados, Burundi, Cameroon, Ceylon, Chile, Congo, Cyprus, Egypt, Equatorial Guinea, Ethiopia, Ghana, Guinea, Guyana, India, Indonesia, Jamaica, Jordan, Kenya, Khmer Republic, Kuwait, Laos, Lebanon, Lesotho, Libyan Arab Republic, Malaysia, Mali, Malta, Mauritius, Morocco, Nepal, Nigeria, Senegal, Sierra Leone, Singapore, Somalia, Swaziland, Trinidad and Tobago, Tunisia, Uganda, United Republic of Tanzania, Yemen, Yugoslavia, Zambia: draft resolution.

A/C.1/L.604 and Corr.1. Afghanistan, Algeria, Argentina, Bolivia, Brazil, Burundi, Ceylon, Chile, Colombia, Costa Rica, Cyprus, Dominican Republic, Ecuador, El Salvador, Equatorial Guinea, Ethiopia, Ghana, Guatemala, Guinea, Guyana, Haiti, Honduras, India, Indonesia, Jamaica, Kenya, Kuwait, Laos, Lesotho, Liberia, Libyan Arab Republic, Malaysia, Mali, Malta, Mauritius, Mexico, Morocco, Nepal, Nicaragua, Nigeria, Panama, Paraguay, Peru, Philippines, Romania, Rwanda, Senegal, Sierra Leone, Singapore, Swaziland, Trinidad and Tobago, Uganda, United Republic of Tanzania, Uruguay, Venezuela, Yugoslavia, Zambia: draft resolution, as orally revised by sponsors, approved by First Committee on 17 December 1971, meeting 1857, by roll-call vote of 71 to 1, with 14 abstentions, as follows:

In favour: Afghanistan, Algeria, Argentina, Austria, Bolivia, Brazil, Bulgaria, Burundi, Byelorussian SSR, Ceylon, Chile, Costa Rica, Cuba, Cyprus, Czechoslovakia, Denmark, Egypt, Ethiopia, Finland, Ghana, Greece, Guatemala, Guinea, Haiti, Honduras, Hungary, Iceland, India, Indonesia, Iran, Iraq, Jamaica, Kenya, Khmer Republic, Kuwait, Laos, Lebanon, Liberia, Libyan Arab Republic, Madagascar, Malaysia, Malta, Mauritius, Mexico, Mongolia, Nepal, Nigeria, Norway, Pakistan, Peru, Philippines, Poland, Romania, Senegal, Singapore, Spain, Sudan, Sweden, Trinidad and Tobago, Turkey, Uganda, Ukrainian SSR, USSR, United Republic of Tanzania, Upper Volta, Uruguay, Venezuela, Yemen, Yugoslavia, Zaire, Zambia.
Against: South Africa.
Abstaining: Australia, Belgium, Canada, France, Ireland, Israel, Ivory Coast, Japan, Luxembourg, Netherlands, New Zealand, Portugal, United Kingdom, United States.

A/8626. Report of First Committee.

RESOLUTION 2880(XXVI), as recommended by First Committee, A/8626, adopted by Assembly on 21 December 1971, meeting 2029, by recorded vote of 96 to 1, with 16 abstentions.

In favour: Afghanistan, Algeria, Argentina, Austria, Bahrain, Bhutan, Brazil, Bulgaria, Burundi, Byelorussian SSR, Cameroon, Central African Republic, Chile, Colombia, Congo, Costa Rica, Cuba, Cyprus, Czechoslovakia, Dahomey, Denmark, Dominican Republic, Ecuador, Egypt, El Salvador, Equatorial Guinea, Ethiopia, Fiji, Finland, Gabon, Gambia, Ghana, Greece, Guatemala, Guinea, Honduras, Hungary, Iceland, India, Indonesia, Iran, Iraq, Jamaica, Jordan, Kenya, Khmer Republic, Kuwait, Laos, Lebanon, Lesotho, Liberia, Libyan Arab Republic, Madagascar, Malaysia, Mali, Malta, Mauritania, Mexico, Mongolia, Morocco, Nepal, Nicaragua, Nigeria, Norway, Pakistan, Panama, Paraguay, People's Democratic Republic of Yemen, Peru, Philippines, Poland, Romania, Rwanda, Saudi Arabia, Senegal, Sierra Leone, Singapore, Somalia, Spain, Sudan, Sweden, Togo, Trinidad and Tobago, Turkey, Uganda, Ukrainian SSR, USSR, United Arab Emirates, United Republic of Tanzania, Upper Volta, Uruguay, Venezuela, Yemen, Yugoslavia, Zaire, Zambia.

Against: South Africa.

Abstaining: Australia, Belgium, Canada, France, Ireland, Israel, Italy, Ivory Coast, Japan, Luxembourg, Netherlands, New Zealand, Portugal, Swaziland, United Kingdom, United States.

The General Assembly,

Bearing in mind the Declaration on the Strengthening of International Security contained in General Assembly resolution 2734(XXV) of 16 December 1970,

Noting that some positive results conducive to the strengthening of international peace and security have been achieved through negotiations and co-operation among States,

Convinced that bilateral and regional efforts towards achieving international security should be strictly in accordance with the purposes and principles of the United Nations,

Convinced further that such efforts should be complemented by collective measures adopted by the competent organs of the United Nations, in order to ensure the complete implementation of the Declaration,

Deeply concerned at the persistence of armed conflicts and other situations resulting therefrom which threaten international peace and security,

Convinced that the United Nations, as a centre for harmonizing the actions of nations, bears the responsibility for promoting, through all its principal and subsidiary organs, full respect for the Preamble and the purposes and principles of the Charter of the United Nations,

Emphasizing that the Declaration, which constitutes an organic whole, needs to be implemented in its entirety, through the full use of United Nations machinery and capabilities, including those provided for in Chapters VI and VII of the Charter and the dispatch of special missions by the Security Council,

Expressing its conviction that the lack of substantial progress in solving issues relating to international peace and security, economic development and independence, disarmament, colonialism, *apartheid* and racial discrimination, human rights and fundamental freedoms is a constant source of tension and a threat to the security of nations,

Convinced that a broad exchange of views on the question of the strengthening of international security, undertaken annually, will make it possible to review the changing international situation and to seek areas of negotiation and agreement, thereby helping to improve the prospects for peace and international security,

Believing that the achievement of universality in the United Nations, in accordance with the Charter, would increase the effectiveness of the Organization in the strengthening of international peace and security,

Taking note of the report of the Secretary-General and having considered the item entitled "Implementation of the Declaration on the Strengthening of International Security,"

1. *Solemnly reaffirms* all the principles and provisions contained in the Declaration on the Strengthening of International Security and strongly appeals to all States to take effective measures to implement the Declaration in its entirety;

2. *Calls upon* all States to contribute towards resolving existing conflicts and situations likely to endanger international peace and security, in accordance with the purposes and principles of the Charter of the United Nations and in keeping with the Declaration;

3. *Calls upon* all States to respect the national unity, political independence and territorial integrity of every State, to refrain from the threat or use of force and to observe fully the principle that the territory of a State shall not be the object of military occupation resulting from the use of force in violation of the Charter and the principle that the acquisition of territories by force is inadmissible;

4. *Declares* that the termination of coercive acts which deprive peoples of their inalienable rights to self-determination, freedom and independence, the implementation of relevant United Nations resolutions concerning colonialism, racialism and *apartheid*, and the elimination of serious and systematic violations of human rights and fundamental freedoms, which should be respected by all States, are essential elements for the strengthening of international peace and security;

5. *Invites* the Security Council to consider all appropriate means and procedures for ensuring the strict and full implementation of its resolutions relating to international peace and security;

6. *Urges* the early undertaking of a broad review of all aspects of the concept of peace-keeping operations in order to determine, in accordance with the Charter, appropriate guidelines for its application and to establish appropriate and effective machinery capable of preserving and restoring peace;

7. *Calls* for an early agreement on the definition of aggression, which would assist the United Nations in its fundamental task of maintaining international peace and security;

8. *Declares* that, in view of the close connexion between the strengthening of international security, disarmament and development, the United Nations should evolve a concept of collective economic security designed to promote the sustained development and expansion of national economies and, moreover, affirms that a substantial portion of the savings derived from measures in the field of disarmament should be devoted to promoting economic and social development, particularly in the developing countries;

9. *Declares* that any measure or pressure directed against any State while exercising its sovereign right freely to dispose of its natural resources constitutes a flagrant violation of the principles of self-determination of peoples and non-intervention, as set forth in the Charter, which, if pursued, could constitute a threat to international peace and security;

10. *Invites* all Member States, in particular the more developed countries, to adopt all appropriate measures to normalize the financial situation of the United Nations and to provide it with the means of effectively achieving its goals;

11. *Requests* the Secretary-General to submit to the General Assembly at its twenty-seventh session a report on measures adopted in pursuance of the Declaration, containing, *inter alia:*

(a) An introduction by the Secretary-General regarding events within the context of the implementation of the Declaration;

(b) Communications from Member States relating to the implementation of the Declaration;

(c) Relevant information on compliance with the provisions of the Declaration by United Nations organs and other international bodies;

12. *Decides* to include in the provisional agenda of its twenty-seventh session an item entitled "Implementation of the Declaration on the Strengthening of International Security."

Other documents

S/10091/Rev.1. Letter of 25 January 1971 from Secretary-General to President of Security Council (transmitting excerpts of Declaration on Strengthening of International Security (resolution 2734(XXV))).

A/8639 (S/10464). Letter of 20 December 1971 from Poland (transmitting resolution on security and co-operation in Europe, adopted by Sixth Polish United Workers' Party Congress).

A/8642 (S/10469). Letter of 15 December 1971 from Bulgaria,

Czechoslovakia, Hungary, Poland, Romania and USSR (transmitting communiqué issued by Conference of Foreign Ministers of States Parties to Treaty of Warsaw, Warsaw, Poland, 1 December 1971).

Chapter III

Review of the question of peace-keeping operations

Various aspects of the question of peace-keeping operations were considered in 1971 by the General Assembly and by its 33-member Special Committee on Peace-keeping Operations, set up by an Assembly decision of 18 February 1965.[1]

Consideration by Special Committee

The Special Committee on Peace-keeping Operations held four meetings between 1 April and 3 December 1971.

On 1 April 1971, the Special Committee agreed that its Working Group should meet to deal with the problems related to its study of United Nations military observer missions. (In 1968, the Working Group had decided upon the study of observer missions as a first model in its programme of work. In 1969, it had agreed on the outline for an eight-chapter study, known as Model I, and had completed five of the eight chapters. In 1970, the Working Group had been unable to make further progress.)

In May and December 1971, the Special Committee discussed reports from the Working Group. In both reports, the Group stated it had not been able to achieve any further progress on basic issues.

A number of concrete proposals were examined, the Working Group reported, but it had not developed them to the point where they could form the basis of negotiations. The Group also considered certain proposals made by Brazil and Kuwait on arrangements for the financing of peace-keeping operations.[2] However, the Group concluded that in the absence of progress on basic political issues, it would not be productive to pursue those proposals.

The Working Group stated it had also continued its discussion aimed at finding a common position on issues of command and control of United Nations military observers authorized by the Security Council. However, it was unable to achieve progress; nor had it been able to agree on Model II, dealing with peace-keeping operations on a broader scale.

The difficulties confronting the Working Group, the report concluded, were unlikely to be overcome without thorough, detailed negotiation,

for which purpose the methods and procedures of the Group continued to be appropriate.

Reporting to the General Assembly on 3 December 1971, the Special Committee expressed regret it had been unable to fulfil the mandate entrusted to it. In its discussion of the Working Group's report, some Special Committee members, among them Brazil, had been critical of the methods and procedures of the Working Group, especially of what they regarded as the exclusion of some members of the Special Committee from the informal consultations.

Other members, among them Canada, Czechoslovakia and the USSR, had stated that the difficulties faced by the Working Group were not of a procedural nature; it would take more time to find agreed solutions.

Regarding the composition of the Special Committee, some of its members, it was reported, had suggested at the Committee's meeting on 1 December 1971 that since four permanent members of the Security Council were already members of the Special Committee (France, the USSR, the United Kingdom, and the United States), China should also become a Committee member.

The Special Committee believed that it would be better to look to the future and to make a renewed collective effort to break the deadlock.

In the introduction to his annual report to the General Assembly on the work of the Organization covering the period 16 June 1970 to 15 June 1971, the Secretary-General stated that in the continued absence of a consensus among the great powers on controversial issues, such as the respective roles of the Security Council and the Secretary-General in the management of peace-keeping operations and the financing of those operations, it was hardly surprising that no further progress had been made. The Secretary-General believed that agreement on future guidelines for all aspects of United Nations peace-keeping would contribute enormously to the effective functioning of the Organization.

The Secretary-General also believed that the basic ingredients for an agreed solution of the

[1]See Y.U.N., 1964, p. 59, text of resolution 2006(XIX).
[2]See Y.U.N., 1970, pp. 87-88.

peace-keeping problem could be found in the documents of the Working Group of the Special Committee on Peace-keeping Operations. The missing ingredient was the required degree of political accommodation by the principal members of the Special Committee. He suggested that perhaps the time had come to study once again the manner in which the Military Staff Committee might function in co-operation with the Security Council and the Secretary-General with respect to peace-keeping operations.

The Secretary-General concluded that he felt compelled to suggest that if no appreciable progress were made in the near future, the question of peace-keeping operations should be considered at a periodic meeting of the Security Council.

Consideration by General Assembly

At the General Assembly's twenty-sixth session, which opened on 21 September 1971, the report of the Special Committee on Peace-keeping Operations was referred for consideration to the Assembly's Special Political Committee.

The speakers in the debate generally regretted the lack of progress and urged renewed efforts to find a solution.

Some speakers, among them Cyprus, Greece, Liberia, Madagascar and Turkey, commented on the importance of the peace-keeping functions of the United Nations. Liberia and Madagascar felt the Special Committee had not failed. Liberia noted that the Special Committee had to resolve delicate matters involving political decisions which gave rise to considerations of national interest.

Greece and Turkey considered that the United Nations Peace-keeping Force in Cyprus had done outstanding work and said no efforts should be spared to strengthen the peace-keeping capabilities of the United Nations. Cyprus felt the lessons of the peace-keeping operation in Cyprus could usefully be borne in mind in the work of the Special Committee.

A number of Member States expressed strong reservations about the work of the Special Committee on Peace-keeping Operations. Thus, in the opinion of Brazil, it would not have made any difference—in terms of its mandate—if the Special Committee had not met. Brazil felt that the Special Committee and its Working Group had disregarded the instructions given by the General Assembly in 1970.[3]

El Salvador commented, in this connexion, that the Special Committee had not indicated the reasons for the lack of progress, and had not specified the obstacles hampering it. If, in 1972, the same situation should prevail, it would be appropriate to reconsider the composition of the Committee.

Ireland considered that the work of the Special Committee to date had not had any impact on the problem. The Committee had had very few meetings and had not shown the required sense of urgency.

Venezuela felt it was time for the Assembly to take steps to modify activities which consisted in considering an almost non-existent report. The dissolution of the Special Committee was not desirable, but the Assembly should ask it to make radical changes in its working methods to allow for the participation of all its members.

Brazil, El Salvador, Iran, Italy, Turkey, Venezuela and Yugoslavia felt that the Special Committee should either be enlarged or its composition changed.

Yugoslavia said that the current stalemate reflected more than the usual difficulties in formulating a concept on a complex matter. The Special Committee was paralysed; it experienced an institutional crisis. Yugoslavia felt that enlargement of the Committee's membership would enhance its capacity to deal effectively with the main issues.

Yugoslavia, as well as Italy and Turkey, urged that the People's Republic of China should become a member of the Special Committee and its Working Group.

In the opinion of the United States there were few, if any, issues before the Organization as important as peace-keeping. The United States regretted that due to a lack of agreement on the principal issues, there had been no progress during the past year, but it hoped that a renewed collective effort would be made to break the deadlock. The United States said it did not favour any particular formula and was not rigid or doctrinaire in details. It held, as did many other Members, that while the Security Council was ultimately responsible for peace-keeping, effective management required that the executive authority of the Secretary-General must not be impaired. In the opinion of the United States, the key to the problem was not machinery but political will.

The United Kingdom said the current procedures of the Special Committee seemed to allow discussions on the main issues, but determination to use those procedures seemed less evident. The problems encountered by the Special Committee were negotiable; the important thing was to search unremittingly for a solution. The United Kingdom felt that everyone should be constantly ready to re-examine, in the light of changes in the international situation, the difficulties that hampered negotiations.

France said that on the basis of several fundamental considerations it was convinced there

[3]See Y.U.N., 1970, pp. 89-90, text of resolution 2670(XXV).

was some hope of success, despite the difficulties.

First, it was generally recognized that making the United Nations effective in the field of peace-keeping should be given the highest priority. Second, the lack of progress which was being discussed was not due, in France's view, to a lack of political will. Nor was recognition of the fundamental political and doctrinal differences among the permanent members of the Security Council —whose role was all important—a confession of failure. It must be unequivocally decided which authority would be responsible for negotiating and supervising peace-keeping operations. These were basic questions which involved an interpretation of the United Nations Charter.

In the opinion of France, the powers of the Security Council with regard to observation missions or investigative missions should not be confined to the mere authorizing of such missions.

France was convinced that fidelity to the Articles of the Charter would make it possible to work out answers to the basic questions of peace-keeping, which were and would continue to be of an institutional nature. The working procedures instituted by the Special Committee provided a context that seemed most appropriate for bringing about agreement among the major powers.

The USSR noted with regret the lack of substantive progress in the work of the Special Committee, and fully appreciated the dissatisfaction of Members with the situation. However, the USSR felt it was wrong to be pessimistic.

There were two distinct points of view with regard to the United Nations peace-keeping operations, the USSR said. One group of countries attempted to maintain obsolete practices which bypassed the Security Council and were not in keeping with the Charter of the United Nations. Another group of countries, including the USSR, insisted that the basic provisions of the Charter should be respected and that the Security Council and its subsidiary organs should remain responsible for the direction and control of peace-keeping operations.

The USSR, during informal consultations in the past year, had submitted detailed proposals, calling for the provision of assistance by the Security Council on military matters through the Military Staff Committee or through an *ad hoc* subsidiary body of the Council established pursuant to Article 29 of the Charter (which provides that the Security Council may establish such subsidiary organs as it deems necessary for the performance of its functions). These proposals provided the basis for agreement on guidelines for peace-keeping operations. It was essential, the USSR stated, to expedite the work on establishing such guidelines.

Czechoslovakia considered that there was no

alternative but to continue the work and try to bring it to a successful end; the Special Committee and its Working Group were suitable instruments for that purpose.

Poland suggested that one of the difficulties facing this endeavour was that certain powers were accustomed to considering peace-keeping as a means of attaining their unilateral political goals.

Japan shared the regret expressed by the Secretary-General at the continuing impasse in reaching agreement, even on Model I. It placed high value on past peace-keeping operations and believed that if a new conflict arose, despite the constitutional problems involved, the Security Council would establish appropriate peace-keeping machinery on a voluntary basis. Instead of acting on such an *ad hoc* basis, Japan believed it would be better to establish adequate machinery and arrangements on a stable basis. To explore that possibility was one of the most important aspects of the Special Committee's work.

Ghana considered that the maintenance of peace was a collective responsibility. If the great powers could not reach an agreement, or a consensus, on the roles of the Security Council and the Secretary-General in the conduct and financing of peace-keeping, and if the Special Committee could not produce a more satisfactory report to the Assembly's twenty-seventh session in 1972, the whole question—currently the Special Committee's assignment—should be taken over by the General Assembly.

Some Members suggested new approaches. Madagascar believed the placing of observers in an area of conflict should be subject to special agreements between the Secretary-General and the countries concerned. Observers should not be withdrawn without the express authorization of the Security Council, or of the General Assembly meeting in extraordinary session.

Morocco suggested circulation of a questionnaire asking for the views of all Member States on modalities, concept and financing of peace-keeping operations; the replies could be considered by either the Special Committee or an *ad hoc* body which would report to the Assembly.

Zambia suggested that the Special Committee should work out rules and procedures on peace-keeping operations and submit them to the 1972 session of the Assembly; if necessary, the Committee should be enlarged to include Member States in areas where peace and security were threatened.

The Byelorussian SSR suggested that important documents adopted at the twenty-fifth session of the General Assembly in 1970, especially the Declaration on the Strengthening of International Security, set forth a practical programme.

Some Members, among them Cyprus, Ireland,

Japan, Kenya and Zambia, raised the question of financing peace-keeping operations. Kenya maintained that peace-keeping operations should be financed collectively by all Member States. Zambia suggested the creation of an emergency fund from the regular budget of the Organization, while Japan appealed to all Members for voluntary contributions.

On 17 December 1971, the General Assembly recommended that in order to expedite progress and to enable the Special Committee on Peace-keeping Operations to hold a more frequent exchange of views on the question the Working Group should submit reports to the Special Committee at intervals of not more than three months. In so doing, the Assembly took particular note of the view expressed by the Special Committee on the need for a renewed collective effort to break the deadlock.

Stressing the importance of achieving agreed guidelines to enhance the effectiveness of United Nations peace-keeping operations in conformity with the Charter, the Assembly urged the Special Committee to accelerate its work.

The Assembly also asked Member States to make available to the Special Committee before 15 March 1972 any views or suggestions to help the work of that body, which was to study such views and suggestions. Members contributing such views, as well as other interested Members, would be invited to participate.

Finally, the Assembly asked the Special Committee to report to it in 1972 on the progress it had achieved.

These Assembly decisions were embodied in resolution 2835(XXVI) adopted by 86 votes to 0, with 2 abstentions. The text was recommended to the Assembly by the Special Political Committee, which approved it on 10 December 1971 by 70 votes to 0, with 2 abstentions. The text was sponsored by Belgium, Cyprus, Denmark, Greece and New Zealand.

(For text of resolution, see DOCUMENTARY REFERENCES below.)

DOCUMENTARY REFERENCES

Special Committee on Peace-keeping Operations, meetings 49-52.

General Assembly—26th session
Special Political Committee, meetings 794-797.
Plenary meeting 2023.

A/8401. Report of Secretary-General on work of the Organization, 16 June 1970–15 June 1971, Part One, Chapter III.
A/8401/Add.1. Introduction to report of Secretary-General, September 1971, Part Two, paras. 170-176.
A/8550. Comprehensive review of whole question of peace-keeping operations in all their aspects. Report of Special Committee on Peace-keeping Operations.
A/SPC/L.234. Belgium, Cyprus, Denmark, Greece, New Zealand: draft resolution, as orally amended by Liberia and Mali, modified by USSR, approved by Special Political Committee on 10 December 1971, meeting 797, by 70 votes to 0, with 2 abstentions.
A/8597. Report of Special Political Committee.

RESOLUTION 2835(XXVI), as recommended by Special Political Committee, A/8597, adopted by Assembly on 17 December 1971, meeting 2023, by 86 votes to 0, with 2 abstentions.

The General Assembly,
Recalling its resolutions 2006(XIX) of 18 February 1965, 2053 A (XX) of 15 December 1965, 2249(S-V) of 23 May 1967, 2308(XXII) of 13 December 1967, 2451(XXIII) of 19 December 1968 and 2670(XXV) of 8 December 1970,
Having received and examined the report of the Special Committee on Peace-keeping Operations of 3 December 1971,

Noting with regret that the mandate entrusted to the Special Committee has not as yet been fulfilled,
Conscious, nevertheless, that the problems with which the Special Committee has been faced are of a fundamental nature and require close and thorough consideration to which any Member of the United Nations may usefully contribute,
Bearing in mind the concern of Member States in the present dangerous international situation over the need to reach an early agreement for carrying out United Nations peace-keeping operations consistent with the Charter of the United Nations,
1. *Takes note* of the report of the Special Committee on Peace-keeping Operations, in particular paragraph 14 of the report;
2. *Recommends* that, in order to expedite progress and to enable the Special Committee to hold a more frequent exchange of views on the question, its Working Group should submit reports at intervals of not more than three months;
3. *Stresses* the importance of achieving agreed guidelines to enhance the effectiveness of United Nations peace-keeping operations in conformity with the Charter and to this end urges the Special Committee to accelerate its work;
4. *Requests* Member States to make available to the Special Committee before 15 March 1972 any views or suggestions which they may wish to submit to help the work of the Special Committee;
5. *Requests* the Special Committee, taking into account the progress made by its Working Group at that time, to study the views and suggestions received from Member States and to arrange for further discussion at meetings in which those delegations that had contributed views and suggestions, as well as other interested delegations, would be invited to participate;
6. *Requests* the Special Committee to report to the General Assembly at its twenty-seventh session on the progress it has achieved.

Chapter IV

Question of promoting the peaceful uses of the sea-bed and the ocean floor

Report of Sea-Bed Committee

The Committee on the Peaceful Uses of the Sea-Bed and the Ocean Floor beyond the Limits of National Jurisdiction (Sea-Bed Committee) held two sessions at Geneva, Switzerland, in 1971, from 12 to 26 March and from 19 July to 27 August. The Committee also met at United Nations Headquarters in New York on 14, 15 and 22 October to complete its report to the twenty-sixth (1971) session of the General Assembly.

In its report to the General Assembly, the Sea-Bed Committee set forth the results of its efforts to carry out the mandates given it by the Assembly's decisions of 17 December 1970.[1]

The Sea-Bed Committee established three sub-committees of the whole and agreed on the organization of its work as follows.

Sub-Committee I was to prepare draft treaty articles embodying the international régime—including an international machinery—for the area (the sea-bed and ocean floor, and the subsoil thereof, beyond the limits of national jurisdiction) and its resources on the basis of the Declaration of Principles Governing the Sea-Bed and the Ocean Floor, and the Subsoil Thereof, beyond the Limits of National Jurisdiction[2] and taking into account the economic implications resulting from the exploitation of the resources of the area as well as the needs and problems of land-locked countries.

Sub-Committee II was to prepare a comprehensive list of subjects and issues relating to the law of the sea, including those concerning the régimes of the high seas, the continental shelf, the territorial sea (including the question of its breadth and the question of international straits) and contiguous zone, fishing and conservation of the living resources of the high seas (including the question of the preferential rights of coastal States), and to prepare draft treaty articles thereon.

Sub-Committee III was to deal with the preservation of the marine environment (including, *inter alia*, the prevention of pollution) and scientific research, and to prepare draft treaty articles thereon.

The Sea-Bed Committee reserved to itself the precise definition of the area of the sea-bed and ocean floor as well as the question of priority of certain subjects.

Before the Committee were reports requested by the General Assembly on the possible impact of sea-bed mineral production in the area beyond national jurisdiction on world markets, with special reference to the problems of developing countries, and a study on the question of free access to the sea of land-locked countries and of the special problems of land-locked countries relating to the exploration and exploitation of the resources of the sea-bed.

By the terms of an agreement reached on 27 August 1971, the Sea-Bed Committee decided that the question of the international régime should receive a certain priority.

Also, the main Committee would not reach a decision on the final recommendation with regard to limits of national jurisdiction until the recommendations of Sub-Committee II on the precise definition of the area had been received.

Various proposals in the form of draft conventions, draft treaty articles, working papers and draft lists of subjects and issues were submitted to the Sea-Bed Committee during 1971. These were annexed to the Committee's report to the General Assembly.

Certain broad questions, the Committee's report noted, had been the subject of comment in almost every intervention in the general debate. These questions might be taken as: the relationship between existing law and the problems requiring consideration and resolution by the Conference on the Law of the Sea scheduled by the General Assembly for 1973;[3] the identification of particular interests of States, as well as of categories of States, and of the international community as such; and suggestions regarding possible means of reconciliation of divergent interests and needs.

The Sea-Bed Committee recognized the need to bear in mind, in an account of its general debate, the Assembly's statement that problems of ocean space were closely interrelated and needed to be considered as a whole.[4]

The Committee's report gave an account of different attitudes regarding the 1958 Geneva Conventions on the law of the sea[5] and other existing law and regarding the basis on which rights of States were founded. It listed special circumstances and interests as well as specific problems of States and of the international community interests, mentioned in the debates. It also described suggestions put forward as means

[1]See Y.U.N., 1970, pp. 79-83, texts of resolutions 2750 A-C(XXV).
[2]See Y.U.N., 1970, pp. 78-79, text of resolution 2749(XXV) containing the Declaration of Principles.
[3]*Ibid.*, pp. 81-83, text of resolution 2750 C (XXV).
[4]*Ibid.*
[5]See Y.U.N., 1958, pp. 377-81.

for an over-all accommodation of the interests involved.

Regarding the subjects allocated to Sub-Committee I, the report presented a summary of the philosophy or basic approach of proposals for an international sea-bed régime presented by Canada, by France, by Malta, by Poland, by the USSR, by the United Kingdom, by the United Republic of Tanzania, by the United States, and by the following two groups of States: Afghanistan, Austria, Belgium, Hungary, Nepal, the Netherlands and Singapore; and Chile, Colombia, Ecuador, El Salvador, Guatemala, Guyana, Jamaica, Mexico, Panama, Peru, Trinidad and Tobago, Uruguay and Venezuela.

The major topics of the debate in Sub-Committee I were briefly described. They included: the scope and nature of the international régime; the instrument by which the régime should be established; the question of the precise definition of the area; the orderly development of the marine environment; the relationship between the international régime and the rights of the coastal States; the international régime and the question of the freedom of the high seas and the traditional uses of the sea; the scope and functions of the international machinery; organs of the international machinery; the relationship of the international machinery to the United Nations system; the international machinery and regional arrangements; transitional arrangements; sharing by all States in the benefits to be derived from the development of the resources of the area; economic implications resulting from exploitation of the resources of the international sea-bed area; and special problems of land-locked countries.

Another section of the Sea-Bed Committee's report described the work carried out by its Sub-Committee II, which began preparation of a comprehensive list of subjects and issues relating to the law of the sea. The preparation of the list was to be undertaken with some flexibility, so that the inclusion of a particular subject or issue should not prejudice the position of any member, and the list was not to prejudge the order of priority for consideration of the subjects and issues.

Various proposals by Committee members pertaining to a comprehensive list of subjects and issues were cited, as were draft treaty articles submitted by the United States on the territorial sea, straits and fisheries and a draft ocean space treaty submitted by Malta.

Summarizing the work of Sub-Committee III, the report noted the topics dealt with under the general subjects of preservation of the marine environment, including prevention of pollution, and scientific research. These were: the nature of the instruments or articles that might be established; the scope of the application of such

instruments or articles; the nature of the problems involved; the kinds of data needed; the problems of co-ordination with other bodies; and the problems involved in the study of and preparation of articles or instruments covering scientific research.

Also referred to were: a proposal by Norway and Canada on preliminary measures to prevent and control marine pollution; and debates in Sub-Committee III on a proposal for a statement expressing anxious concern on atmospheric nuclear tests conducted in 1971 in the Pacific.

Consideration by General Assembly

The question of promoting the peaceful uses of the sea-bed and ocean floor was discussed by the General Assembly, later in 1971, mainly in the Assembly's First Committee.

The First Committee considered the item at nine meetings held from 2 to 16 December 1971.

In a statement on the work of the Sea-Bed Committee, its Chairman said a fundamental principle had been accepted by the majority—that the problems of ocean space were closely inter-related and formed a unit that should be considered as a whole.

The Committee, he continued, had considered three main categories of issues: first, the identification of the interests of individual States and groups of States on the one hand and of the international community as a whole on the other; second, the methods of reconciling those often divergent interests; and third, the need for a critical review of what some States considered to be the existing law and feasible ways and means of modifying that law to accommodate the current needs and aspirations of all States, particularly developing States.

The Chairman also described trends which had become evident in the discussions and the group interests which had emerged in reference to such factors as geography or the degree of economic development in which a State found itself.

The First Committee's discussions were largely procedural and concerned the questions of enlargement of the membership of the Sea-Bed Committee and venue of its 1972 sessions. However, a number of First Committee Members not members of the Sea-Bed Committee made substantive statements. Among them were Fiji, Portugal and Zambia.

On 21 December 1971, the General Assembly, among other things, noted with satisfaction the encouraging progress of the preparatory work of the Sea-Bed Committee towards a comprehensive conference on the law of the sea, in conformity with its mandate of 17 December 1970,[6] in

_____
[6]See footnote 1.

particular with regard to the elaboration of the international régime and machinery for the sea-bed and the ocean floor beyond the limits of national jurisdiction.

The Assembly also noted that the Sea-Bed Committee had examined, among other things, a study of possible methods and criteria for sharing benefits derived from the exploitation of the resources of the area.

The Assembly decided to add to the membership of the Sea-Bed Committee China and four other members to be appointed by the Chairman of the First Committee in consultation with regional groups, with due regard to the interests of under-represented groups.

The Assembly decided the Sea-Bed Committee should hold two sessions, one in New York during March and April and one in Geneva during July and August 1972.

These Assembly decisions were embodied in resolution 2881(XXVI), adopted by a recorded vote of 123 to 0. The Assembly amended the text,

which had been recommended to it by the First Committee, to provide for the addition of China and four (rather than three) other members. This amendment, sponsored by Norway, was adopted by a recorded vote of 55 to 7, with 58 abstentions. (For text of resolution, see DOCUMENTARY REFERENCES below.)

The text recommended by the First Committee was approved by that body on 16 December by a roll-call vote of 97 to 0. The text was sponsored by the following 27 Members: Algeria, Argentina, Australia, Brazil, Canada, Chile, Colombia, Ecuador, Greece, Iceland, Indonesia, Iran, Kenya, Kuwait, Malaysia, Mauritius, Morocco, Peru, the Philippines, Spain, Thailand, Trinidad and Tobago, Tunisia, the United Republic of Tanzania, Uruguay, Venezuela and Yugoslavia.

In the First Committee a number of amendments to the 27-power text dealt with questions of venue for the 1972 sessions of the Sea-Bed Committee and with its enlargement.

DOCUMENTARY REFERENCES

General Assembly—26th session
First Committee, meetings 1843, 1844, 1849-1855.
Fifth Committee, meeting 1488.
Plenary meetings 2029, 2031.

A/8401. Report of Secretary-General on work of the Organization, 16 June 1970–15 June 1971: Part One, Chapter IV D; Part Four, Chapter IV M.
A/8401/Add.1. Introduction to report of Secretary-General, September 1971, paras. 212-216.
A/8421. Report of Committee on Peaceful Uses of Sea-Bed and Ocean Floor beyond Limits of National Jurisdiction. (Annex VII: List of documents of Committee.)
A/C.1/L.586. Algeria, Argentina, Brazil, Colombia, Ecuador, Iceland, Indonesia, Kenya, Malaysia, Mauritius, Peru, Philippines, Thailand, Trinidad and Tobago, United Republic of Tanzania, Venezuela, Yugoslavia: draft resolution.
A/C.1/L.586/Rev.1. Algeria, Argentina, Australia, Brazil, Canada, Chile, Colombia, Ecuador, Greece, Iceland, Indonesia, Iran, Kenya, Kuwait, Malaysia, Mauritius, Morocco, Peru, Philippines, Spain, Thailand, Trinidad and Tobago, Tunisia, United Republic of Tanzania, Uruguay, Venezuela, Yugoslavia: revised draft resolution, as further orally revised by sponsors and as amended by 2 powers (A/C.1/L.599/Rev.1), as orally sub-amended by Ceylon and as sub-amended by Jamaica (A/C.1/L.601) and by Japan (A/C.1/L.603), approved by First Committee on 16 December 1971, meeting 1855, by roll-call vote of 97 to 0, as follows:

In favour: Afghanistan, Algeria, Argentina, Australia, Austria, Barbados, Bolivia, Brazil, Bulgaria, Burma, Burundi, Byelorussian SSR, Canada, Ceylon, Chile, China, Colombia, Congo, Costa Rica, Cuba, Cyprus, Czechoslovakia, Denmark, Dominican Republic, Ecuador, Egypt, Ethiopia, Fiji, Finland, France, Ghana, Greece, Guatemala, Guyana, Haiti, Honduras, Hungary, Iceland, India, Indonesia, Iran, Iraq, Ireland, Israel, Italy, Ivory Coast, Jamaica, Japan, Kenya, Khmer Republic, Kuwait, Laos, Lebanon, Liberia, Libyan Arab Republic, Madagascar, Malaysia, Mali, Mauritania, Mexico, Mongolia, Morocco, Nepal, Netherlands, New Zealand, Nicaragua, Nigeria, Norway, Paraguay, Peru, Philippines, Poland, Portugal, Romania, Rwanda, Senegal, Singapore, Somalia, South Africa, Spain, Sudan, Sweden, Thailand, Trinidad and Tobago, Tunisia, Turkey, Uganda,

Ukrainian SSR, USSR, United Kingdom, United Republic of Tanzania, United States, Uruguay, Venezuela, Yemen, Yugoslavia, Zambia.
Against: None.

A/C.1/L.598 and Add.1, A/C.5/1425, A/8627. Administrative and financial implications of draft resolution recommended by First Committee in A/8623. Statements by Secretary-General and report of Fifth Committee.
A/C.1/L.599. Sweden: amendment to 27-power revised draft resolution, A/C.1/L.586/Rev.1.
A/C.1/L.599/Rev.1. Sweden and Zambia: revised amendment to 27-power revised draft resolution, A/C.1/L.586/Rev.1.
A/C.1/L.600. Afghanistan, Bolivia, Liberia, Nepal, Paraguay, Singapore, Ukrainian SSR: amendment to 27-power revised draft resolution, A/C.1/L.586/Rev.1.
A/C.1/L.601. Jamaica: sub-amendment to Swedish amendment, A/C.1/L.599.
A/C.1/L.602. Cameroon: sub-amendment to Swedish amendment, A/C.1/L.599.
A/C.1/L.602/Rev.1. Cameroon: revised sub-amendment to 2-power revised amendment, A/C.1/L.599/Rev.1.
A/C.1/L.603. Japan: amendments to 27-power revised draft resolution, A/C.1/L.586/Rev.1.
A/L.670. Norway: amendment to draft resolution recommended by First Committee in A/8623.
A/8623. Report of First Committee.

RESOLUTION 2881(XXVI), as recommended by First Committee, A/8623, as amended by Norway, A/L.670, adopted by Assembly on 21 December 1971, meeting 2029, by recorded vote of 123 to 0, as follows:

In favour: Afghanistan, Algeria, Argentina, Australia, Austria, Bahrain, Barbados, Belgium, Bhutan, Bolivia, Brazil, Bulgaria, Burma, Burundi, Byelorussian SSR, Cameroon, Canada, Central African Republic, Ceylon, Chad, Chile, China, Colombia, Congo, Costa Rica, Cuba, Cyprus, Czechoslovakia, Dahomey, Denmark, Dominican Republic, Ecuador, Egypt, El Salvador, Equatorial Guinea, Ethiopia, Fiji, Finland, France, Gabon, Ghana, Greece, Guatemala, Guinea, Guyana, Honduras, Hungary, Iceland, India, Indonesia, Iran, Iraq, Ireland, Israel, Italy, Ivory Coast, Jamaica, Japan, Jordan, Kenya, Khmer

the damage is due to its fault or the fault of persons for whom it is responsible.

Article IV

1. In the event of damage being caused elsewhere than on the surface of the earth to a space object of one launching State or to persons or property on board such a space object by a space object of another launching State, and of damage thereby being caused to a third State or to its natural or juridical persons, the first two States shall be jointly and severally liable to the third State, to the extent indicated by the following:

(*a*) If the damage has been caused to the third State on the surface of the earth or to aircraft in flight, their liability to the third State shall be absolute;

(*b*) If the damage has been caused to a space object of the third State or to persons or property on board that space object elsewhere than on the surface of the earth, their liability to the third State shall be based on the fault of either of the first two States or on the fault of persons for whom either is responsible.

2. In all cases of joint and several liability referred to in paragraph 1 of this article, the burden of compensation for the damage shall be apportioned between the first two States in accordance with the extent to which they were at fault; if the extent of the fault of each of these States cannot be established, the burden of compensation shall be apportioned equally between them. Such apportionment shall be without prejudice to the right of the third State to seek the entire compensation due under this Convention from any or all of the launching States which are jointly and severally liable.

Article V

1. Whenever two or more States jointly launch a space object, they shall be jointly and severally liable for any damage caused.

2. A launching State which has paid compensation for damage shall have the right to present a claim for indemnification to other participants in the joint launching. The participants in a joint launching may conclude agreements regarding the apportioning among themselves of the financial obligation in respect of which they are jointly and severally liable. Such agreements shall be without prejudice to the right of a State sustaining damage to seek the entire compensation due under this Convention from any or all of the launching States which are jointly and severally liable.

3. A State from whose territory or facility a space object is launched shall be regarded as a participant in a joint launching.

Article VI

1. Subject to the provisions of paragraph 2 of this article exoneration from absolute liability shall be granted to the extent that a launching State establishes that the damage has resulted either wholly or partially from gross negligence or from an act or omission done with intent to cause damage on the part of a claimant State or of natural or juridical persons it represents.

2. No exoneration whatever shall be granted in cases where the damage has resulted from activities conducted by a launching State which are not in conformity with international law including, in particular, the Charter of the United Nations and the Treaty on Principles Governing the Activities of States in the Exploration and Use of Outer Space, including the Moon and Other Celestial Bodies.

Article VII

The provisions of this Convention shall not apply to damage caused by a space object of a launching State to:

(*a*) Nationals of that launching State;

(*b*) Foreign nationals during such time as they are participating in the operation of that space object from the time of its launching or at any stage thereafter until its descent, or during such time as they are in the immediate vicinity of a planned launching or recovery area as the result of an invitation by that launching State.

Article VIII

1. A State which suffers damage, or whose natural or juridical persons suffer damage, may present to a launching State a claim for compensation for such damage.

2. If the State of nationality has not presented a claim, another State may, in respect of damage sustained in its territory by any natural or juridical person, present a claim to a launching State.

3. If neither the State of nationality nor the State in whose territory the damage was sustained has presented a claim or notified its intention of presenting a claim, another State may, in respect of damage sustained by its permanent residents, present a claim to a launching State.

Article IX

A claim for compensation for damage shall be presented to a launching State through diplomatic channels. If a State does not maintain diplomatic relations with the launching State concerned, it may request another State to present its claim to that launching State or otherwise represent its interests under this Convention. It may also present its claim through the Secretary-General of the United Nations, provided the claimant State and the launching State are both Members of the United Nations.

Article X

1. A claim for compensation for damage may be presented to a launching State not later than one year following the date of the occurrence of the damage or the identification of the launching State which is liable.

2. If, however, a State does not know of the occurrence of the damage or has not been able to identify the launching State which is liable, it may present a claim within one year following the date on which it learned of the aforementioned facts; however, this period shall in no event exceed one year following the date on which the State could reasonably be expected to have learned of the facts through the exercise of due diligence.

3. The time-limits specified in paragraphs 1 and 2 of this article shall apply even if the full extent of the damage may not be known. In this event, however, the claimant State shall be entitled to revise the claim and submit additional documentation after the expiration of such time-limits until one year after the full extent of the damage is known.

Article XI

1. Presentation of a claim to a launching State for compensation for damage under this Convention shall not require the prior exhaustion of any local remedies which may be available to a claimant State or to natural or juridical persons it represents.

2. Nothing in this Convention shall prevent a State, or natural or juridical persons it might represent, from pursuing a claim in the courts or administrative tribunals or agencies of a launching State. A State shall not, however, be entitled to present a claim under this Convention in respect of the same damage for which a claim is being pursued in the courts or administrative tribunals or agencies of a launching State or under another international agreement which is binding on the States concerned.

Article XII

The compensation which the launching State shall be liable to pay for damage under this Convention shall be determined in accordance with international law and the principles of justice and equity, in order to provide such reparation in respect of the damage as will restore the person, natural or juridical, State or international organization on whose behalf the claim is presented to the condition which would have existed if the damage had not occurred.

Article XIII

Unless the claimant State and the State from which compensation is due under this Convention agree on another form of compensation, the compensation shall be paid in the currency of the claimant State or, if that State so requests, in the currency of the State from which compensation is due.

Article XIV

If no settlement of a claim is arrived at through diplomatic negotiations as provided for in article IX, within one year from the date on which the claimant State notifies the launching State that it has submitted the documentation of its claim, the parties concerned shall establish a Claims Commission at the request of either party.

Article XV

1. The Claims Commission shall be composed of three members: one appointed by the claimant State, one appointed by the launching State and the third member, the Chairman, to be chosen by both parties jointly. Each party shall make its appointment within two months of the request for the establishment of the Claims Commission.

2. If no agreement is reached on the choice of the Chairman within four months of the request for the establishment of the Commission, either party may request the Secretary-General of the United Nations to appoint the Chairman within a further period of two months.

Article XVI

1. If one of the parties does not make its appointment within the stipulated period, the Chairman shall, at the request of the other party, constitute a single-member Claims Commission.

2. Any vacancy which may arise in the Commission for whatever reason shall be filled by the same procedure adopted for the original appointment.

3. The Commission shall determine its own procedure.

4. The Commission shall determine the place or places where it shall sit and all other administrative matters.

5. Except in the case of decisions and awards by a single-member Commission, all decisions and awards of the Commission shall be by majority vote.

Article XVII

No increase in the membership of the Claims Commission shall take place by reason of two or more claimant States or launching States being joined in any one proceeding before the Commission. The claimant States so joined shall collectively appoint one member of the Commission in the same manner and subject to the same conditions as would be the case for a single claimant State. When two or more launching States are so joined, they shall collectively appoint one member of the Commission in the same way. If the claimant States or the launching States do not make the appointment within the stipulated period, the Chairman shall constitute a single-member Commission.

Article XVIII

The Claims Commission shall decide the merits of the claim for compensation and determine the amount of compensation payable, if any.

Article XIX

1. The Claims Commission shall act in accordance with the provisions of article XII.

2. The decision of the Commission shall be final and binding if the parties have so agreed; otherwise the Commission shall render a final and recommendatory award, which the parties shall consider in good faith. The Commission shall state the reasons for its decision or award.

3. The Commission shall give its decision or award as promptly as possible and no later than one year from the date of its establishment, unless an extension of this period is found necessary by the Commission.

4. The Commission shall make its decision or award public. It shall deliver a certified copy of its decision or award to each of the parties and to the Secretary-General of the United Nations.

Article XX

The expenses in regard to the Claims Commission shall be borne equally by the parties, unless otherwise decided by the Commission.

Article XXI

If the damage caused by a space object presents a large-scale danger to human life or seriously interferes with the living conditions of the population or the functioning of vital centres, the States Parties, and in particular the launching State, shall examine the possibility of rendering appropriate and rapid assistance to the State which has suffered the damage, when it so requests. However, nothing in this article shall affect the rights or obligations of the States Parties under this Convention.

Article XXII

1. In this Convention, with the exception of articles XXIV to XXVII, references to States shall be deemed to apply to any international intergovernmental organization which conducts space activities if the organization declares its acceptance of the rights and obligations provided for in this Convention and if a majority of the States members of the organization are States Parties to this Convention and to the Treaty on Principles Governing the Activities of States in the Exploration and Use of Outer Space, including the Moon and Other Celestial Bodies.

2. States members of any such organization which are States Parties to this Convention shall take all appropriate steps to ensure that the organization makes a declaration in accordance with the preceding paragraph.

3. If an international intergovernmental organization is liable for damage by virtue of the provisions of this Convention, that organization and those of its members which are States Parties to this Convention shall be jointly and severally liable; provided, however, that:

(a) Any claim for compensation in respect of such damage shall be first presented to the organization;

(b) Only where the organization has not paid, within a period of six months, any sum agreed or determined to be due as compensation for such damage, may the claimant State invoke the liability of the members which are States Parties to this Convention for the payment of that sum.

4. Any claim, pursuant to the provisions of this Convention, for compensation in respect of damage caused to an organization which has made a declaration in accordance with paragraph 1 of this article shall be presented by a State member of the organization which is a State Party to this Convention.

Article XXIII

1. The provisions of this Convention shall not affect other international agreements in force in so far as relations between the States Parties to such agreements are concerned.

2. No provision of this Convention shall prevent States from concluding international agreements reaffirming, supplementing or extending its provisions.

Article XXIV

1. This Convention shall be open to all States for signature. Any State which does not sign this Convention before its entry into force in accordance with paragraph 3 of this article may accede to it at any time.

2. This Convention shall be subject to ratification by signatory States. Instruments of ratification and instruments of accession shall be deposited with the Governments of the Union of Soviet Socialist Republics, the United Kingdom of Great Britain and Northern Ireland and the United States of America, which are hereby designated the Depositary Governments.

3. This Convention shall enter into force on the deposit of the fifth instrument of ratification.

4. For States whose instruments of ratification or accession are deposited subsequent to the entry into force of this Convention, it shall enter into force on the date of the deposit of their instruments of ratification or accession.

5. The Depositary Governments shall promptly inform all signatory and acceding States of the date of each signature, the date of deposit of each instrument of ratification of and accession to this Convention, the date of its entry into force and other notices.

6. This Convention shall be registered by the Depositary Governments pursuant to Article 102 of the Charter of the United Nations.

Article XXV

Any State Party to this Convention may propose amendments to this Convention. Amendments shall enter into force for each State Party to the Convention accepting the amendments upon their acceptance by a majority of the States Parties to the Convention and thereafter for each remaining State Party to the Convention on the date of acceptance by it.

Article XXVI

Ten years after the entry into force of this Convention, the question of the review of this Convention shall be included in the provisional agenda of the United Nations General Assembly in order to consider, in the light of past application of the Convention, whether it requires revision. However, at any time after the Convention has been in force for five years, and at the request of one third of the States Parties to the Convention, and with the concurrence of the majority of the States Parties, a conference of the States Parties shall be convened to review this Convention.

Article XXVII

Any State Party to this Convention may give notice of its withdrawal from the Convention one year after its entry into force by written notification to the Depositary Governments. Such withdrawal shall take effect one year from the date of receipt of this notification.

Article XXVIII

This Convention, of which the Chinese, English, French, Russian and Spanish texts are equally authentic, shall be deposited in the archives of the Depositary Governments. Duly certified copies of this Convention shall be transmitted by the Depositary Governments to the Governments of the signatory and acceding States.

IN WITNESS WHEREOF the undersigned, duly authorized, have signed this Convention.

DONE in triplicate, at the cities of London, Moscow and Washington, this ...... day of ...., one thousand nine hundred and ....

PREPARATION OF AN INTERNATIONAL
TREATY CONCERNING THE MOON

A/8391 and Corr.1. Letter of 27 May 1971 from USSR (request for inclusion in agenda of item entitled: "Preparation of an international treaty concerning the Moon").

A/C.1/1017. Letter of 24 September 1971 from Minister of Foreign Affairs of German Democratic Republic to Chairman of First Committee.

A/C.1/L.568. USSR: draft treaty concerning Moon.

A/C.1/L.572. Austria, Belgium, Bulgaria, Czechoslovakia, Hungary, India, Mongolia, Poland, Romania, Sierra Leone, Sweden, USSR: draft resolution, approved unanimously by First Committee on 11 November 1971, meeting 1826.

A/8529. Report of First Committee.

RESOLUTION 2779(XXVI), as recommended by First Committee, A/8529, adopted unanimously by Assembly on 29 November 1971, meeting 1998.

The General Assembly,

Recalling its resolution 2222(XXI) of 19 December 1966 stressing the importance of international co-operation in the field of activities in the peaceful exploration and use of outer space, including the Moon and other celestial bodies, and the importance of developing the rule of law in this new area of human endeavour,

Reaffirming the common interest of all mankind in furthering the peaceful exploration and use of outer space for the benefit of all States and for the development of friendly relations and mutual understanding among them,

Taking into account the advances made in recent years in the exploration of outer space, including those resulting from extensive lunar research programmes on the basis of modern science and technology,

Bearing in mind the interest of all mankind in the exploration and utilization of the Moon exclusively for peaceful purposes and in preventing the Moon from becoming a scene of international conflict,

Prompted by the consideration that the Moon, as the only natural satellite of the earth, has an important role to play in the conquest of outer space and that it should be used with due regard to the interests of present and future generations,

Desiring to further the elaboration of specific rules of international law to govern the activities of States on the Moon on the basis of the Charter of the United Nations and the Treaty on Principles Governing the Activities of States in the Exploration and Use of Outer Space, including the Moon and Other Celestial Bodies, as a means of further developing a sound legal basis for such activities,

Considering that special rules should also govern activities in the use of all natural resources and substances of the Moon and other celestial bodies,

1. *Takes note* of the draft treaty concerning the Moon submitted to the General Assembly by the delegation of the Union of Soviet Socialist Republics;

2. *Requests* the Committee on the Peaceful Uses of Outer Space and its Legal Sub-Committee to consider, as a matter of priority, the question of the elaboration of a draft international treaty concerning the Moon in accordance with the recommendations contained in paragraph 38 of the report of the Committee and to report thereon to the General Assembly at its twenty-seventh session.

Scientific and technical aspects of the peaceful uses of outer space

In 1971, various scientific and technical aspects of the peaceful uses of outer space were considered by the General Assembly and its Committee on the Peaceful Uses of Outer Space and the latter's Scientific and Technical Sub-Committee. (For details on discussion of the legal aspects of the peaceful uses of outer space, see above.)

Among several Assembly decisions concerning international co-operation in the uses of outer space was one by which the Assembly welcomed the establishment and convening of a Working Group on Remote Sensing of the Earth by Satellites. The Assembly shared the view of its Committee on Outer Space that technological developments in remote sensing of the earth could contribute to the economic development of all countries.

In endorsing the report of the Committee on Outer Space, the Assembly invited States that had not yet done so to consider ratifying or acceding to the Treaty on Principles Governing the Activities of States in the Exploration and Use of Outer Space, including the Moon and Other Celestial Bodies[2] and the Agreement on the Rescue of Astronauts, the Return of Astronauts and the Return of Objects Launched into Outer Space.[3]

The Assembly also reiterated the importance of the goal of making satellite communications available to States on a world-wide and non-discriminatory basis.

Details of these and other decisions are described below.

[2]See Y.U.N., 1966, pp. 41-43, for text of Treaty.
[3]See Y.U.N., 1967, pp. 34-35, for text of Agreement.

Reports of the Sub-Committee and the Committee on Peaceful Uses of Outer Space

The Scientific and Technical Sub-Committee of the Committee on the Peaceful Uses of Outer Space met from 6 to 15 July 1971.

Special attention was given by the Sub-Committee to: convening a working group on remote sensing of the earth by satellites; practical applications of space technology, including the holding of United Nations–sponsored technical panels on this subject; assessment of the needs of developing countries in practical applications of space technology and the ability of the United Nations to meet those needs; exchange of information on national and international space activities; education and training, including national fellowship programmes sponsored by the United Nations; international sounding rocket facilities sponsored by the United Nations; and the participation of the International Astronautical Federation in future meetings of the Sub-Committee.

On the question of remote earth-resources surveying techniques, the Scientific and Technical Sub-Committee decided to establish and convene a Working Group on Remote Sensing of the Earth by Satellites.

The Sub-Committee believed that the objective of a study of the use of satellites for remote sensing of earth resources should be to promote the optimum use of this space application, including the monitoring of the total earth environment for the benefit of individual States and the international community, taking into account the sovereign rights of States and the provisions of the Treaty governing activities in outer space.

The Committee on the Peaceful Uses of Outer Space, at meetings held from 1 to 10 September 1971, welcomed the decision of the Scientific and Technical Sub-Committee to convene the Working Group on Remote Sensing of the Earth by Satellites, and looked forward to the initiation of the Group's substantive work, scheduled for 1972.

To finance the programme of international co-operation for promoting the practical applications of space technology, the Committee on Outer Space asked the Secretary-General to take steps to allocate to the United Nations budget for 1972 an additional sum not exceeding $70,000.

The Committee took note of the various measures taken by the World Meteorological Organization (WMO) to discover ways and means to mitigate the harmful effects of tropical storms and to remove or minimize their destructive potential. The Committee also welcomed various specific activities of the United Nations Educational, Scientific and Cultural Organization (UNESCO) and International Telecommunication Union (ITU).

The Committee on Outer Space noted that France had extended an invitation to United Nations–sponsored technical panels to observe work on space technology applications being carried out by France's National Space Research Centre. Japan's intention to invite a panel to meet on satellite broadcasting for education was also noted.

The Committee also welcomed decisions of France, India and the United Kingdom to offer training opportunities in space technology and its practical application, and in satellite communications technology.

The Committee on Outer Space recommended to the General Assembly that it continue to grant United Nations sponsorship to the Thumba Equatorial Rocket Launching Station in India and the Mar del Plata Rocket Launching Station in Argentina.

Observer status at future meetings of the Scientific and Technical Sub-Committee was granted to the International Astronautical Federation.

Consideration by the General Assembly

The General Assembly considered the recommendations of its Committee on the Peaceful Uses of Outer Space during its twenty-sixth session, which opened on 21 September 1971.

International co-operation in the peaceful uses of outer space

On 29 November 1971, the General Assembly reiterated the importance of the goal of making satellite communications available to States on a world-wide and non-discriminatory basis, and it took note of agreements relating to space communications recently concluded between a number of States. It noted that ITU had allocated frequencies and adopted administrative procedures for all kinds of space communications.

The Assembly endorsed continuation and development of the programme for promoting practical applications of space technology taking into account the needs of developing countries.

The Assembly welcomed efforts by Member States in exchanging information, co-operating in research, and providing education and training. It also welcomed their efforts to keep the Committee on Outer Space fully informed of their space activities.

Approving the continued sponsorship by the United Nations of rocket launching stations in Argentina and India, the Assembly expressed satisfaction with the work carried out at those ranges.

Among other things, the Assembly noted the activities of WMO, in particular those directed towards discovering ways and means of mitigating the harmful effects and destructive potential of tropical storms.

These were among decisions embodied in resolution 2776(XXVI), adopted unanimously by the Assembly on the recommendation of its First Committee, which had unanimously approved the text on 11 November 1971. The draft text was proposed by Australia, Austria, Belgium, Canada, France, Hungary, Iran, Italy, Japan, Lebanon, Liberia, Morocco, Poland, Romania, Sierra Leone, Sweden, the USSR, the United Kingdom and the United States. (For text of resolution, see DOCU-MENTARY REFERENCES below.)

Earth resources surveying by satellites

Also on 29 November 1971, the Assembly asked the Committee on Outer Space to bring about early initiation of the substantive work of the Working Group on Remote Sensing of the Earth by Satellites, stating that the potential benefits from technological developments in remote sensing of the earth from space platforms could be extremely meaningful for the economic development of all countries, especially the developing countries, and for the preservation of the global environment.

The Assembly asked Member States to submit information on their national and co-operative international activities in this field to the Working Group, and it endorsed a request by the Outer Space Committee's Scientific and Technical Sub-Committee that the Working Group solicit views on the matter from appropriate United Nations

bodies and other international organizations. It also asked the Secretary-General to provide the Working Group with his comments on the subject.

These were among decisions set forth in resolution 2778(XXVI), adopted unanimously on the recommendation of the First Committee, which had approved the text unanimously on 11 November 1971, on a proposal by Argentina, Australia, Austria, Belgium, Bulgaria, Canada, France, India, Iran, Italy, Japan, Hungary, Mexico, Morocco, Poland, Sierra Leone, Sweden, the USSR, the United Kingdom and the United States. (For text of resolution, see DOCUMENTARY REFERENCES below.)

In the course of the discussion in the First Committee, many Members, including Canada, France, Italy and Sweden, pledged active participation in the work of the Working Group.

Although they welcomed the convening of the Working Group, some Members cautioned that while the technological feasibility of remote sensing was assured, its social, economic, legal and political implications must be carefully assessed before further action at the international level could be contemplated. Argentina, Brazil, Chile, Egypt, Ghana, the Ukrainian SSR and Yugoslavia in this connexion stressed the importance of proper regard for the sovereignty of the countries over whose territory such remote surveying is to be conducted.

Some speakers, including those representing Argentina, Canada, Egypt and the Ukrainian SSR, urged early development of a legal régime to govern international activities in the field.

DOCUMENTARY REFERENCES

General Assembly—26th session
First Committee, meetings 1819-1826.
Fifth Committee, meeting 1462.
Plenary meeting 1998.

A/8401. Report of Secretary-General on work of the Organization, 16 June 1970–15 June 1971, Part One, Chapter IV C.
A/8401/Add.1. Introduction to report of Secretary-General, September 1971, Part Two, Chapter III, paras. 205-211.
A/8420. Report of Committee on Peaceful Uses of Outer Space. (Chapter II A: Report of Scientific and Technical Sub-Committee on its 8th session, 6-15 July 1971.)

INTERNATIONAL CO-OPERATION IN
THE PEACEFUL USES OF OUTER SPACE
A/C.1/L.569 and Corr.1. Australia, Austria, Belgium, Canada, France, Hungary, Iran, Italy, Japan, Lebanon, Liberia, Morocco, Poland, Romania, Sierra Leone, Sweden, USSR, United Kingdom, United States: draft resolution, approved unanimously by First Committee on 11 November 1971, meeting 1826.
A/C.1/L.575. Administrative and financial implications of 19-power draft resolution, A/C.1/L.569. Statement by Secretary-General.
A/C.5/1402, A/8535. Administrative and financial implications of draft resolutions I and III in A/8528. Statement by Secretary-General and report of Fifth Committee.
A/8528. Report of First Committee, draft resolution I.

RESOLUTION 2776(XXVI), as recommended by First Committee, A/8528, adopted unanimously by Assembly on 29 November 1971, meeting 1998.

The General Assembly,
Recalling its resolution 2733(XXV) of 16 December 1970,
Having considered the report of the Committee on the Peaceful Uses of Outer Space,
Reaffirming the common interest of mankind in furthering the exploration and use of outer space for peaceful purposes,
Continuing to believe that the benefits deriving from space exploration can be extended to States at all stages of economic and scientific development if Member States conduct their space programmes in a manner designed to promote maximum international co-operation, including the widest possible exchange of information in this field,
Convinced of the need for continued international efforts to promote practical applications of space technology,
1. *Endorses* the report of the Committee on the Peaceful Uses of Outer Space;
2. *Invites* States which have not yet become parties to the Treaty on Principles Governing the Activities of States in the Exploration and Use of Outer Space, including the Moon and Other Celestial Bodies, and the Agreement on the Rescue of Astronauts, the Return of Astronauts and the Return of Objects Launched into Outer Space to give early consideration to ratifying or acceding to those agreements so that they may have the broadest possible effect;

3. *Reiterates* the importance of the goal of making satellite communications available to States on a world-wide and non-discriminatory basis, as expressed in General Assembly resolution 1721 D (XVI) of 20 December 1961;

4. *Takes note* of the agreements relating to space communications recently concluded between a number of States and of the desirability of keeping the United Nations currently informed concerning activities and developments in this field;

5. *Notes* the action taken by the International Telecommunication Union, through the World Administrative Radio Conference for Space Telecommunications held in June and July 1971, to allocate frequencies and to adopt administrative procedures for all kinds of space communications, and recommends that the Union and its specialized bodies, as well as the members of the Union, should apply these provisions with a view to promoting the use of space communications for the benefit of all countries in accordance with the relevant resolutions of the General Assembly;

6. *Welcomes* the progress achieved by the Committee on the Peaceful Uses of Outer Space in its efforts to encourage international programmes to promote practical applications of space technology for the benefit of all countries and commends to the attention of Member States, specialized agencies and interested United Nations bodies the programme contained in the report of the Scientific and Technical Sub-Committee of the Committee;

7. *Takes note with appreciation* of the valuable work carried out by the Secretary-General within the framework of the programme for promoting the application of space technology in accordance with the relevant recommendations of the Committee on the Peaceful Uses of Outer Space and resolutions of the General Assembly;

8. *Endorses* the resolution contained in paragraph 15 of the report of the Committee on the Peaceful Uses of Outer Space and recommends the continuation and development of the programme for promoting the practical applications of space technology taking into account the needs of the developing countries;

9. *Welcomes* the efforts of a number of Member States to share with other interested Member States the practical benefits that may be derived from programmes in space technology;

10. *Welcomes* the progress achieved in international co-operation among Member States in space research and exploration, including the exchange and analysis of lunar material on a broad international basis and studies of the development of compatible rendezvous and docking systems for manned spacecraft;

11. *Welcomes also* the action of a number of States and of the Food and Agriculture Organization of the United Nations in promoting international co-operation in education and training in the peaceful uses of outer space and endorses the appeal made to other States by the Committee on the Peaceful Uses of Outer Space for similar contributions to international education and training in this field;

12. *Approves* continuing sponsorship by the United Nations of the Thumba Equatorial Rocket Launching Station in India and the CELPA Mar del Plata Station in Argentina, expresses its satisfaction at the work being carried out at these ranges in relation to the use of sounding rocket facilities for international co-operation and training in the peaceful and scientific exploration of outer space, and recommends that Member States continue to give consideration to the use of these facilities for appropriate space research activities;

13. *Welcomes* the efforts of Member States to keep the Committee on the Peaceful Uses of Outer Space fully informed of their space activities and invites all Member States to do so;

14. *Notes* that in accordance with General Assembly resolution 1721 B (XVI) of 20 December 1961, the Secretary-General continues to maintain a public registry of objects launched into orbit or beyond on the basis of information furnished by Member States;

15. *Takes note with appreciation* of the activities of the World Meteorological Organization during the past year, as reported to the Committee on the Peaceful Uses of Outer Space, in particular the measures taken in implementation of General Assembly resolution 2733 D (XXV) recommending that the World Meteorological Organization mobilize technical resources in order to discover ways and means of mitigating the harmful effects and destructive potential of tropical storms;

16. *Takes note* of the programmes currently being undertaken by the United Nations Educational, Scientific and Cultural Organization and the International Telecommunication Union in satellite broadcasting for the purpose of contributing to the advancement of education and training, and draws attention to the fact that questions relating to the legal implications of space communications are also on the agenda of the Legal Sub-Committee of the Committee on the Peaceful Uses of Outer Space, with which the two agencies should co-ordinate their activities in this field;

17. *Requests* the specialized agencies and the International Atomic Energy Agency to continue, as appropriate, to provide the Committee on the Peaceful Uses of Outer Space with progress reports on their work relating to the peaceful uses of outer space and to examine and report to the Committee on the particular problems which arise or may arise from the use of outer space in the fields within their competence and which should, in their opinion, be brought to the attention of the Committee;

18. *Endorses* the recommendations contained in paragraph 38 of the report of the Committee on the Peaceful Uses of Outer Space concerning the future work of its Legal Sub-Committee;

19. *Requests* the Committee on the Peaceful Uses of Outer Space to continue its work as set out in the present resolution and in previous resolutions of the General Assembly and to report to the Assembly at its twenty-seventh session.

EARTH RESOURCES SURVEYING BY SATELLITES

A/C.1/L.571. Argentina, Australia, Austria, Belgium, Bulgaria, Canada, France, India, Iran, Italy, Japan, Hungary, Mexico, Morocco, Poland, Sierra Leone, Sweden, USSR, United Kingdom, United States: draft resolution, approved unanimously by First Committee on 11 November 1971, meeting 1826.

A/C.1/L.576. Administrative and financial implications of 20-power draft resolution, A/C.1/L.571.

A/C.5/1402, A/8535. Administrative and financial implications of draft resolutions I and III in A/8528. Statement by Secretary-General and report of Fifth Committee.

A/8528. Report of First Committee, draft resolution III.

RESOLUTION 2778(XXVI), as recommended by First Committee, A/8528, adopted unanimously by Assembly on 29 November 1971, meeting 1998.

The General Assembly,

Recalling its resolution 2733 C (XXV) of 16 December 1970 in which it requested the Scientific and Technical Sub-Committee of the Committee on the Peaceful Uses of Outer Space, as authorized by the Committee, to determine at what time and in what specific frame of reference a working group on earth resources surveying, with special reference to satellites, should be convened,

Welcoming the decision of the Sub-Committee at its eighth session to establish and convene a Working Group on Remote Sensing of the Earth by Satellites,

Sharing the view expressed by the Committee on the Peaceful Uses of Outer Space in the report on its fourteenth session that the potential benefits from technological developments in remote sensing of the earth from space platforms could be extremely meaningful for the economic development of all countries, especially the developing countries, and for the preservation of the global environment,

Noting that the Working Group on Remote Sensing of the Earth by Satellites held a first organizational meeting in connexion with the fourteenth session of the Committee on the Peaceful Uses of Outer Space,

Looking forward to the early initiation of the substantive work of the Working Group, keeping in mind that experiments to test the feasibility of remote sensing of the earth from space platforms are scheduled to begin early in 1972,

Expressing confidence that in discharging its responsibility the Working Group would seek to promote the optimum utilization of this space application for the benefit of individual States and of the international community,

1. *Requests* Member States to submit information on their national and co-operative international activities in this field, as well as comments and working papers, through the Secretary-General to the Working Group on Remote Sensing of the Earth by Satellites;

2. *Endorses* the request of the Scientific and Technical Sub-Committee that the Working Group solicit the views of appropriate United Nations bodies and specialized agencies, and other relevant international organizations;

3. *Requests* the Secretary-General to provide the Working Group with his comments on this subject and to submit working papers on matters falling within the terms of reference of the Group;

4. *Requests* the Committee on the Peaceful Uses of Outer Space and its Scientific and Technical Sub-Committee to bring about the early initiation of the Working Group's substantive work and to keep the General Assembly informed in a comprehensive fashion on the progress of its work.

Other documents

Space Activities and Resources. A Review of the Activities and Resources of the United Nations, of its Specialized Agencies and of Other Competent International Bodies relating to the Peaceful Uses of Outer Space. U.N.P. Sales No.: E.72.I.11.

Registration of space launchings

In 1971, United Nations Member States launching objects into orbit around the earth or further into space continued to supply information on space launchings to the United Nations in accordance with a General Assembly resolution of 20 December 1961.[4] Eighteen notifications were received during the year and distributed as documents of the Assembly's Committee on the Peaceful Uses of Outer Space. (Notifications included objects launched during the latter part of 1970, as well as during 1971.)

The United Kingdom registered the launching of one space vehicle during the period. Japan registered the launching of two space vehicles. The USSR registered the launchings of 76 space vehicles. The United States submitted information on 37 launchings, which covered functional and non-functional objects placed into orbit around the earth and into heliocentric and selenocentric orbits.

[4]See Y.U.N., 1961, p. 35, text of resolution 1721 B (XVI).

DOCUMENTARY REFERENCES

A/AC.105/INF.225, 226 and Corr.1, 227-237, 238 and Rev.1, 239-242. Information furnished in conformity with General Assembly resolution 1721 B (XVI) by States launching objects into orbit or beyond (Japan, USSR, United Kingdom, United States).

Chapter VI

Questions concerning the uses of atomic energy

The effects of atomic radiation

The United Nations Scientific Committee on the Effects of Atomic Radiation held its twenty-first session at New York from 14 to 23 June 1971.

On the basis of reviews prepared by the United Nations Secretariat, the Scientific Committee discussed recent information on genetic effects of radiation, induction of cancer by radiation, effects of radiation on the immune response, medical and occupational exposure, and environmental radiation.

It expressed its intention of preparing for submission to the General Assembly, in 1972, a report dealing with such evaluations of risk as the Committee might make after considering these subjects.

The Committee also considered a basic paper on radiation problems prepared on its behalf for and submitted to the secretariat of the United Nations Conference on the Human Environment. (See pp. 307-13.)

On 29 November 1971, when the General Assembly considered the annual report of the United Nations Scientific Committee on the Effects of Atomic Radiation, it commended the Scientific Committee for the contributions it had made to wider knowledge and understanding of the levels and effects of atomic radiation and for its contribution to the United Nations Conference on the Human Environment.

The Assembly also expressed appreciation for the response to the Scientific Committee's request for data on releases of radioactivity into the environment resulting from peaceful uses of nuclear energy and radio-isotopes.

The Assembly welcomed the continuing collaboration between the Scientific Committee and the International Atomic Energy Agency, the specialized agencies, and the non-governmental organizations concerned.

These were among decisions set forth in resolution 2773(XXVI), adopted unanimously by the Assembly on the recommendation of its Special Political Committee, which had unani-mously approved the text on 15 October 1971. The text was sponsored in the Special Political Committee by Argentina, Australia, Belgium, Brazil, Canada, Czechoslovakia, Egypt, Fiji, France, India, Indonesia, Japan, Mexico, Morocco, New Zealand, Sweden, the USSR, the United Kingdom and the United States. (For text of resolution, see DOCUMENTARY REFERENCES below.)

In the course of the Special Political Committee's discussion, Jordan submitted and later withdrew an amendment by which the Assembly would have called upon all Member States to provide full disclosure to the Scientific Committee on the effects of radiation on man and the environment, and the genetic effects of radiation in any region of the world, wherever atomic research and production was carried out.

DOCUMENTARY REFERENCES

General Assembly—26th session
Special Political Committee, meetings 755, 756.
Plenary meeting 1997.

A/8401. Report of Secretary-General on work of the Organization, 16 June 1970–15 June 1971, Part One, Chapter IV B.
A/8334. Report of United Nations Scientific Committee on Effects of Atomic Radiation.
A/SPC/L.203 and Rev.1. Argentina, Australia, Belgium, Brazil, Canada, Czechoslovakia, Egypt, Fiji, France, India, Indonesia, Japan, Mexico, Morocco, New Zealand, Sweden, USSR, United Kingdom, United States: draft resolution and revision, approved unanimously by Special Political Committee on 15 October 1971, meeting 756.
A/SPC/L.204. Jordan: amendment to 19-power draft resolution, A/SPC/L.203.
A/8484. Report of Special Political Committee.

RESOLUTION 2773(XXVI), as recommended by Special Political Committee, A/8484, adopted unanimously by Assembly on 29 November 1971, meeting 1997.

The General Assembly,
Recalling its resolution 913(X) of 3 December 1955, which established the United Nations Scientific Committee on the Effects of Atomic Radiation, and its subsequent resolutions,
Reaffirming the desirability of the Scientific Committee continuing its work,
Concerned about the potentially harmful effects on present and future generations resulting from the levels of radiation to which man is exposed,
Conscious of the continued need for compiling information about atomic radiation and for analysing its effects on man and his environment,
Noting the intention of the Scientific Committee to include in its report to the General Assembly, at its twenty-seventh session, the subjects of genetic effects of radiation, induction of cancer by radiation, effects of radiation on the immune response, population doses from medical and occupational exposure and environmental radiation,
1. *Notes with appreciation* the report adopted by the United Nations Scientific Committee on the Effects of Atomic Radiation at its twenty-first session;
2. *Commends* the Scientific Committee for the valuable contributions it has made since its inception to wider knowledge and understanding of the levels and effects of atomic radiation;
3. *Requests* the Scientific Committee to continue its work, including its co-ordinating activities, to increase knowledge of levels and effects of atomic radiation from all sources;
4. *Notes* the intention of the Scientific Committee to hold its twenty-second session in March 1972;
5. *Expresses its appreciation* for the valuable response to the Scientific Committee's request for data on releases of radio-activity into the environment from peaceful uses of nuclear energy and radio-isotopes;
6. *Draws attention* to the Scientific Committee's statement that further information of the same nature, if received before the end of the year, would be of great value in the preparation of its report to the General Assembly at its twenty-seventh session;
7. *Welcomes* the continuing collaboration between the Scientific Committee and the International Atomic Energy Agency, the specialized agencies and the non-governmental organizations concerned, which is essential to the Committee's work;
8. *Commends* the Scientific Committee for its contribution to the United Nations Conference on the Human Environment, takes note of the basic paper that on its behalf has been prepared for, and submitted to, the secretariat of the Conference, and recommends that the relevant experience of the Committee should be fully utilized in the further preparations for the Conference;
9. *Requests* the Secretary-General to continue to provide the Scientific Committee with the assistance necessary for the conduct of its work and for the dissemination of its findings to the public.

Fourth International Conference on the Peaceful Uses of Atomic Energy

The Fourth International Conference on the Peaceful Uses of Atomic Energy was held in Geneva, Switzerland, from 6 to 16 September 1971.

Eighty-four States, nine specialized agencies, eight inter-governmental organizations, and 16 non-governmental organizations participated in the Conference. Observers included representatives of institutions, universities and industries, as well as individuals. The various public officials, economists, planners and technologists who attended totalled 1,816 representatives and advisers and 2,154 observers.

The Conference focused particularly on the

rapid rise of nuclear power as a major source of energy in the world, confirming that nuclear energy already played a significant role in electricity generation and that it was expected to account for about a quarter of the total installed capacity by 1985 and about half by the year 2000.

Conference participants also studied the possible global effects of the anticipated increase in power production and the problems of radioactive waste disposal up to the year 2000.

The Conference reviewed safety standards and regulations and proposals for international agreements in this respect.

Several meetings at the Conference were devoted to an examination of operating experiences with currently established nuclear reactor types, namely pressurized or boiling light-water reactors, carbon dioxide–cooled graphite reactors, and heavy-water reactors. Special attention was given to the role of small nuclear power reactors to meet the needs of developing countries. Another important aspect of the deliberations of the Conference was the future development of fission reactors, including high-temperature helium-cooled reactors, as well as breeder reactors.

Participants also discussed the integrated planning of power programmes to obtain the optimum balance between hydroplants, fossil-fuel plants and nuclear plants. The economic management of nuclear fuels was also considered.

The Conference took up the question of the development of systems for the safeguarding of peaceful nuclear materials to reduce the danger that such materials could be diverted to military purposes.

Conference participants heard reports of progress on nuclear fusion, the uses of nuclear explosions for peaceful purposes and the applications of radio-isotopes and radiation in agriculture, hydrology, medicine and industry.

The education and training of scientists and engineers in the nuclear field in the framework of the general technological development of a country was also discussed.

Other topics covered included the ecological aspects and public understanding of nuclear power and the introduction of nuclear power into developing countries.

The proceedings of the Conference were to be published by the International Atomic Energy Agency, jointly with the United Nations, for distribution to all Governments and organizations which participated in the Conference.

At the twenty-sixth session of the General Assembly, which opened on 21 September 1971, a report of the Secretary-General on the Conference was circulated to United Nations Member States.

On 22 September 1971, the General Committee of the General Assembly decided to recommend to the Assembly that the item on the Fourth International Conference on the Peaceful Uses of Atomic Energy be deleted from the Assembly's agenda. On 24 September, the Assembly approved the General Committee's recommendation.

DOCUMENTARY REFERENCES

General Assembly—26th session
General Committee, meeting 191.
Plenary meeting 1937.

A/8487. Report of Secretary-General.
A/8500. First report of General Committee.
Peaceful Uses of Atomic Energy. Proceedings of the Fourth International Conference on the Peaceful Uses of Atomic Energy, jointly sponsored by United Nations and IAEA, Geneva, Switzerland, 6-16 September 1971 (in 15 volumes). U.N.P. Sales Nos: E.72.IX.1-15.
  Vol. 1: Opening and closing speeches; special talks; world energy needs and resources, and the role of nuclear energy; national and international organizations; narrative of the exhibits.
  Vol. 2: Performance of nuclear plants; costing of nuclear plants; fuel management.
  Vol. 3: Safety aspects of nuclear plants; legal aspects of nuclear energy.
  Vol. 4: Integration of nuclear plants in electrical networks; integrated planning of nuclear industry; fuel materials
  technology.
  Vol. 5: Breeder and advanced converter reactors.
  Vol. 6: Small and medium power reactors; desalination and agro-industrial complexes; role of research reactors; impact of nuclear energy in developing countries.
  Vol. 7: Advanced energy concepts: peaceful nuclear explosions; special applications, including ship propulsion; controlled thermonuclear reactions; application of transuranium isotopes.
  Vol. 8: Uranium and thorium ore resources; fuel fabrication and reprocessing.
  Vol. 9: Isotope enrichment; fuel cycles; safeguards.
  Vol. 10: Effects of irradiation on fuels and materials.
  Vol. 11: Health physics and radiation protection; radioactive waste management; the environment and public acceptance.
  Vol. 12: Nuclear methods in food production; education and training, and public information.
  Vol. 13: Medical applications; radiation biology.
  Vol. 14: Applications of nuclear techniques in industry and natural resources.
  Vol. 15: Indexes and lists.

Annual report of the International Atomic Energy Agency

The annual report of the International Atomic Energy Agency (IAEA) for 1970-1971 was discussed by the General Assembly at its twenty-sixth session, which opened on 21 September 1971.

The Director-General of IAEA, in introducing the report to the Assembly, stated that a significant event of the previous year had been the successful completion by IAEA's Safeguards Committee of the formulation of the content and structure of the safeguard agreements that non-nuclear-weapon States parties to the Treaty on the Non-Proliferation of Nuclear Weapons[1] were required to conclude with the Agency. He noted in this connexion that only four States had ratified the non-proliferation Treaty during the preceding year.

During the previous two years, he said, there had been improvement in IAEA's technical assistance programme; the target for voluntary contributions had been increased from $2 million in 1970 to $3 million in 1972. The increasing number of projects that the Agency was executing on behalf of the United Nations Development Programme reflected a growing interest and capability of developing countries in carrying out larger projects in the nuclear energy field.

The Director-General stated that IAEA was continuing its series of technical meetings on the subject of peaceful nuclear explosives. He also commented on the Fourth International Conference on the Peaceful Uses of Atomic Energy (see above).

In the course of the discussion in the General Assembly, Members commended the work of IAEA's Safeguards Committee and the efforts of the Agency towards a cleaner human environment. Favourable comments were made on the increased target for voluntary contributions destined for technical assistance. Some Members expressed the view that IAEA was the appropriate body to take on the role of the international service for nuclear explosions for peaceful purposes under the terms of the non-proliferation Treaty.

Speakers in the discussion included the representatives of Australia, Austria, Canada, Czechoslovakia, Denmark, France, Ireland, Japan, Mexico, the Netherlands, Pakistan, Poland, Romania, South Africa, the USSR and the United States.

On 8 November 1971, the Assembly took note of IAEA's annual report, commended the work being undertaken by the Agency to meet its safeguards responsibilities, and noted its appreciation of the role IAEA was playing in the peaceful application of nuclear energy. The Assembly invited the Agency to study the records of the 1971 session of the Assembly relating to IAEA's activities and to take them into account in its future work.

These were among decisions set forth in resolution 2763(XXVI), adopted, without vote, on the basis of a proposal by Ceylon, Czechoslovakia and the Netherlands. (For text, see DOCUMENTARY REFERENCES below.)

(For additional information on the work of IAEA, see PART TWO, CHAPTER I, of this volume. See also pages 13 and 28-29, which contain information, respectively, on General Assembly decisions taken within the context of the disarmament debate on the activities of IAEA with regard to safeguards and the establishment within the framework of IAEA of an international service for nuclear explosions for peaceful purposes.)

[1] See Y.U.N., 1968, pp. 17-19, for text of Treaty.

DOCUMENTARY REFERENCES

General Assembly—26th session
Plenary meeting 1979.

A/8384. Note by Secretary-General (transmitting 15th annual report of International Atomic Energy Agency, consisting of annual report of Board of Governors to General Conference covering period 1 July 1970–30 June 1971).

A/L.642/Rev.1. Ceylon, Czechoslovakia, Netherlands: draft resolution.

RESOLUTION 2763 (XXVI), as proposed by 3 powers, A/L.642/Rev.1, adopted without vote by Assembly on 8 November 1971, meeting 1979.

The General Assembly,
Having received the report of the International Atomic Energy Agency to the General Assembly for the year 1970/1971,
Aware that the statement of the Director-General of the International Atomic Energy Agency of 8 November 1971 brings up to date major developments since the report was published,
  1. *Takes note* of the report of the International Atomic Energy Agency;
  2. *Appreciates* the constructive role that the International Atomic Energy Agency is playing in the peaceful application of nuclear energy for the welfare of Member States;
  3. *Commends* the work being undertaken by the International Atomic Energy Agency to meet its safeguards responsibilities;
  4. *Further commends* the co-operation of the International Atomic Energy Agency with the United Nations in organizing the Fourth International Conference on the Peaceful Uses of Atomic Energy, held at Geneva from 6 to 16 September 1971;
  5. *Requests* the Secretary-General to transmit to the Director-General of the International Atomic Energy Agency the records of the twenty-sixth session of the General Assembly relating to the Agency's activities;
  6. *Invites* the International Atomic Energy Agency to take these records into account in its future work.

Chapter VII

Questions relating to Africa

Matters concerning South Africa's *apartheid* policies

During 1971, the question of the *apartheid* policies of the Government of South Africa were again considered by various United Nations organs. The Security Council did not meet on the question, but it received a number of communications, particularly relating to the arms embargo against South Africa and alleging that certain countries were furnishing arms to South Africa in violation of resolutions of the Council and General Assembly.

During the year, the General Assembly's enlarged 16-member Special Committee on *Apartheid* again considered various aspects of the question and submitted its report and recommendations to the Assembly and the Security Council in October. The Commission on Human Rights and the Economic and Social Council also examined aspects of the question and made several recommendations to the Assembly.

At its twenty-sixth session, which opened on 21 September 1971, the General Assembly considered the reports and recommendations before it and adopted a number of resolutions on various aspects of the *apartheid* question. On 9 November, it first adopted—as a matter of urgency—a resolution on the repression and maltreatment of opponents of *apartheid* in South Africa, and among other things asked the Special Committee on *Apartheid* to prepare a special report on the subject.

On 29 November, the Assembly adopted a resolution by which, among other things, it deplored the actions of Governments which had provided or allowed companies to provide assistance for the build-up of South African military and police forces. It declared that the arms embargo against South Africa made no distinction between arms for external defence and arms for internal repression and called for full implementation of the arms embargo against South Africa.

By another decision, the Assembly expressed its conviction of the special role education should play in efforts to eliminate *apartheid* and asked the United Nations Educational, Scientific and Cultural Organization (UNESCO) to prepare an educational kit on racial discrimination and *apartheid* in southern Africa for possible adaptation by national UNESCO commissions and for distribution to institutions of learning.

The Assembly endorsed the Special Commit-

tee's work programme for 1972 and authorized it, within budgetary limitations, to participate in international conferences on *apartheid* and to consult with organizations engaged in the campaign against *apartheid*.

With regard to *apartheid* in sports, the Assembly urged all States to promote adherence to the Olympic principle of non-discrimination and to encourage their sports organizations to withhold support from sporting events organized in violation of that principle. The South African Government was condemned for its actions in enforcing racial discrimination and segregation in sports.

The General Assembly again condemned the establishment of Bantu homelands (Bantustans) and the forcible removal of the African people of South Africa and Namibia to such areas as a violation of their inalienable rights. The Assembly considered that the establishment of Bantustans was designed to consolidate and perpetuate domination by a white minority and the dispossession and exploitation of the African and other non-white people of South Africa and Namibia. It declared that the United Nations would continue to encourage and promote a solution to the situation in South Africa through the full application of human rights and fundamental freedoms, including political rights, to all the inhabitants regardless of race, colour or creed.

By another decision, the Assembly expressed concern over the explosive situation in South Africa and in southern Africa as a whole resulting from the inhuman and aggressive policies of *apartheid* pursued by the South African Government. It condemned the continued and increasing co-operation of certain States and foreign economic interests with South Africa in military, economic and other fields, and appealed to Governments, organizations and individuals to assist the national movement of the oppressed people of South Africa in their legitimate struggle. The Assembly also, among other things, recommended that the Security Council consider urgently the situation in South Africa and in southern Africa as a whole with a view to adopting effective measures against South Africa.

Another resolution adopted by the General Assembly had to do with the dissemination of information about *apartheid*. By it, the Assembly among other things asked the Secretary-General to intensify information activities with a view to promoting national and international action for the elimination of *apartheid*. The Special Committee on *Apartheid* was asked to take steps to promote the establishment of national committees against *apartheid*.

Also, the General Assembly, by a resolution concerning trade union activities against *apartheid*, appealed to all national and international trade union organizations to intensify their action against *apartheid* by discouraging the emigration of skilled workers to South Africa, by taking action on infringements of trade union rights and the persecution of trade unionists in South Africa, by exerting maximum pressure on foreign interests which were profiting from discrimination against non-white workers in South Africa, and by co-operating with other organizations engaged in the international campaign against *apartheid*.

The General Assembly, by another decision, appealed to States, organizations and individuals for generous contributions to the United Nations Trust Fund for South Africa to meet increasing needs, and asked the Secretary-General to intensify the dissemination of information on the need for relief and assistance to persons persecuted under repressive and discriminatory legislation in South Africa, Namibia and Southern Rhodesia.

The Assembly also adopted a resolution relating to the credentials of the representatives of South Africa.

The Assembly at its twenty-sixth session also adopted resolutions concerning: the elimination of all forms of racial discrimination; the question of a draft convention on the suppression and punishment of *apartheid*; the importance of the right to self-determination; and the co-operation of the specialized agencies and international institutions in implementing the 1960 Declaration on the Granting of Independence to Colonial Countries and Peoples.

These and other decisions of United Nations organs with regard to the *apartheid* question are described in the sections that follow.

Political and related developments

Communications to Security Council

During 1971, the Security Council, which did not meet on the question of South Africa's *apartheid* policies during the year, received a number of communications particularly relating to the arms embargo against South Africa and containing allegations that certain countries were furnishing arms to South Africa in violation of the Council's resolution of 23 July 1970,[1] the General Assembly's resolution of 13 October 1970,[2] and earlier resolutions of these bodies.

During February and March, the Security Council received communications relating to a decision announced on 22 February 1971 by the United Kingdom that it would grant export licences for helicopters and spare parts to South Africa under the terms of the Simonstown Agreement of 1955 (contained in an exchange of letters of 30 June 1955 between the two Governments).

On 24 February, the Executive Secretary of the Organization of African Unity (OAU) transmitted the text of a memorandum stating among other things that a study of the so-called Simonstown Agreement showed clearly that the United Kingdom had no obligation to sell any more military equipment to South Africa. The Agreement—concluded before the achievement of independence by most African States—was anachronistic and had little current validity. Any revitalization of the Agreement, accompanied by the breach of the arms embargo against South Africa, could only be regarded by the independent African States as an unfriendly and hostile act.

On 1 March, the President of the United Nations Council for Namibia transmitted a statement by the Council that the United Kingdom's decision was contrary to Security Council resolutions calling on all States to refrain from selling arms and ammunition to South Africa.

On 5 March, the Chairman of the Special Committee on the Situation with regard to the Implementation of the Declaration on the Granting of Independence to Colonial Countries and Peoples transmitted the text of a consensus adopted by the Special Committee on 4 March deploring the United Kingdom's decision which, the Special Committee said, would have serious repercussions throughout the whole of southern Africa.

The United Kingdom transmitted on 23 March the text of the Opinion of the Law Officers of The Crown for England and Wales on the extent of the existing legal obligations of the United Kingdom arising under the Simonstown Agreement of 1955. It was maintained that the Agreement was still valid and remained in force and that, contrary to the OAU memorandum, the United Kingdom had certain legal obligations subsisting under it.

In a letter dated 7 May 1971, the Chairman of the Special Committee on *Apartheid* transmitted a note concerning implementation of the arms

[1]See Y.U.N., 1970, pp. 146-147, text of resolution 282(1970).
[2]*Ibid.*, p. 148, text of resolution 2624(XXV).

embargo against South Africa, and the text of a communiqué issued by the Special Committee about the resumption of arms sales to South Africa by the United Kingdom. The United Kingdom's decision to accord export licences for helicopters and spare parts to South Africa was viewed by the Special Committee as a breach of relevant Security Council resolutions and of its international obligations under the United Nations Charter.

The letter went on to say that information concerning the involvement of the United Kingdom had been more readily available than that of other countries because of the public and political controversy it had created. In the case of France—currently the main supplier of arms—Belgium, the Federal Republic of Germany, Israel, Switzerland, the United States and others, information had been restricted, so that the amount of coverage given in the note to the collaboration of those countries did not necessarily reflect the full extent to which they were involved in the arms trade.

Subsequent communications to the Security Council from Israel, Belgium, the United States, the Federal Republic of Germany and Switzerland replied to allegations contained in the report of the Special Committee.

On 23 September, the text of a consensus—adopted on 13 September by a joint meeting of the Special Committee on *Apartheid,* the Special Committee on the Situation with regard to the Implementation of the Declaration on the Granting of Independence to Colonial Countries and Peoples and the United Nations Council for Namibia—was transmitted to the Security Council.

Report of Special Committee on *Apartheid*

The General Assembly's Special Committee on *Apartheid* submitted its report to the Security Council and the Assembly on 11 October 1971. The report reviewed the Special Committee's work during 1971 and new developments in South Africa since the previous report. It also contained the Special Committee's conclusions and recommendations for consideration by the Assembly and the Council.

The Special Committee held a special session in New York from 22 to 24 March in connexion with the observance of both the International Day for the Elimination of Racial Discrimination—21 March—and the International Year for Action to Combat Racism and Racial Discrimination, proclaimed for 1971.

The meeting in observance of the International Day was attended by representatives of Member States, the specialized agencies and the Organization of African Unity (OAU). Statements were made by the Secretary-General, the President of the twenty-fifth (1970) session of the General Assembly, the President of the Security Council and the Chairmen of the Committee of Trustees of the United Nations Trust Fund for South Africa and the Special Committee. The meeting closed with a silent tribute to the memory of the victims of Sharpeville and all who had fallen victim to racial persecution and racial injustice.

Attending the meetings in connexion with the observance of the International Year were, among others, representatives of the specialized agencies and OAU, representatives of international non-governmental organizations active against *apartheid,* and representatives of liberation movements.

In accordance with a request by the General Assembly, the Special Committee sent a mission to Europe and Africa to consult with the specialized agencies and various regional organizations and non-governmental organizations on means to promote further concerted international action against *apartheid.* Between 3 and 26 June, the three-member mission visited Dublin (Ireland), London (United Kingdom), Brussels (Belgium), Geneva (Switzerland), Paris (France), Yaoundé (Cameroon) and Addis Ababa (Ethiopia) and held 34 meetings for consultations with specialized agencies, OAU, liberation movements, anti-*apartheid* movements and other organizations. It attended a United Nations seminar on racial discrimination held at Yaoundé in June and its members also attended as observers the Assembly of Heads of State and Government of OAU in Addis Ababa on 24 June.

In its report, the Special Committee expressed its concern that South Africa had continued its efforts to suppress all protests against its *apartheid* policy by repressive measures which violated all principles of law. A significant development in the past year had been the application of such repressive measures against churchmen who had criticized *apartheid* or assisted its victims. The Anglican Dean of Johannesburg, the Very Reverend G. A. ffrench-Beytagh, had been detained in January and subsequently put on trial under the notorious Terrorism Act. Threats had been directed against churches and against student and other organizations.

The Special Committee reported that South Africa had continued its military build-up: the defence budget for 1971-1972 reached a record figure of $443.1 million, an increase of 18 per cent over the previous year. The Special Committee noted that South Africa had been able to obtain military equipment—as well as assistance for local manufacture of such equipment—from other countries despite the arms embargo called for by the Security Council.

The Special Committee stated that South Africa had been obliged to make certain adjustments and concessions in its policies and practices because of international and internal opposition, and economic and other difficulties. However, the discrimination laws, the implementation of the "Bantustans" policy and the relegation of Africans to reservoirs of cheap labour, as well as other measures, remained unchanged. In the face of the defiant intransigence of the South African régime, the international community was left with no other choice but to intensify its efforts to isolate that régime and to provide assistance to the oppressed people of South Africa and their movement for liberation.

In the framework of the International Year for Action to Combat Racism and Racial Discrimination, the Special Committee recommended that the General Assembly adopt a declaration on the elimination of *apartheid,* stressing the grave concern of the international community over the situation in South Africa and restating the essential elements of a solution in accordance with the United Nations Charter. Such a declaration would help counteract the propaganda and manoeuvres of the South African régime and its friends, and would represent a programme of action for the opponents of racism everywhere.

The Special Committee deplored the fact that the arms embargo called for by the Security Council in its resolution 282(1970) of 23 July 1970[3] had not yet been implemented by certain States, which were supplying additional equipment and technical assistance to the South African Government for its military build-up. The attitudes and actions of those powers constituted an encouragement to the South African régime in its defiance of the United Nations and in its pursuit of the inhuman policy of *apartheid.* The Special Committee reiterated that it was essential that the Security Council declare that the arms embargo against South Africa was mandatory.

The Special Committee also drew attention to the continued and increasing collaboration by some Governments and private enterprises with the South African régime and South African companies in violation of repeated recommendations of the General Assembly. It recommended that such activities be condemned, and suggested that reports on continued collaboration by Governments and private enterprises with South Africa be prepared and published periodically.

In order to ensure the provision of greater assistance to the national movement of the oppressed people of South Africa, the Special Committee recommended that the General Assembly welcome the establishment of the OAU Assistance Fund for the Struggle against Colonialism and *Apartheid,* and appealed for contributions by Governments, organizations and individuals to the Fund or directly to liberation movements.

The Special Committee also recommended that

the United Nations should greatly increase its information activities on *apartheid,* and it suggested certain specific measures in that regard.

Also suggested by the Special Committee were measures that specialized agencies might take in their respective fields in the campaign against *apartheid.* It also felt that the establishment of national committees against *apartheid* in all countries would greatly contribute to the campaign.

The Special Committee expressed satisfaction at the response in many countries to the appeals of the General Assembly and the Special Committee for the boycott of racially selected South African sports teams. In connexion with the observance of the International Year for Action to Combat Racism and Racial Discrimination, the Special Committee recommended that the Assembly adopt a declaration against racism in national and international sports—inviting Governments, sports organizations and the public to pledge to combat racial discrimination in sports and not to patronize any sporting events in which teams selected on the basis of racial discrimination participated.

With regard to refugees from South Africa, the Special Committee recommended that the General Assembly issue an appeal to all Member States, especially African countries and those neighbouring South Africa, to assist South African refugees to obtain travel documents, education and training and suitable employment.

The Special Committee emphasized again the need to consider the problem of *apartheid* in its wider context in southern Africa, where the South African régime had become the bastion of racism and colonialism. A thorough study of the interrelationships of the problems of southern Africa should be made and a plan formulated for more effective international action to secure the elimination of *apartheid* and colonialism in the area.

Decisions of Human Rights Commission and of Economic and Social Council

Decisions of Commission

At its meetings in February and March 1971, the Commission on Human Rights took a number of decisions having to do with *apartheid.*

By one of these, the Commission approved the text of a resolution on policies of *apartheid* and racial discrimination which it recommended for adoption by the Economic and Social Council. (See below for action by the Council. See also pp. 405-6.)

On the question of racial discrimination in the political, economic, social and cultural spheres, the Commission approved a text also for adoption by

---

[3]See footnote 1.

the Economic and Social Council. (See below for Council action, and pp. 411-12.)

Another resolution recommended by the Commission for adoption by the Economic and Social Council was one having to do with the question of slavery and the slave trade in all their practices and manifestations, including the slavery-like practices of *apartheid* and colonialism. (See below for action by the Council, and page 434.)

The Human Rights Commission also adopted a text relating to the implementation of United Nations resolutions on the right of peoples under colonial and alien domination to self-determination. This text was proposed for adoption by the Economic and Social Council and it contained the text of a resolution which the Council would ask the General Assembly to adopt. (For decisions by the Council and the Assembly, see below. See also pp. 420-24.)

The Human Rights Commission also adopted a resolution on the report of its *Ad Hoc* Working Group of Experts in which, among other things, it stated that it looked forward to receiving the text of a study concerning the question of *apartheid* (which had been declared a crime against humanity) from the point of view of international penal law. The study had been requested by the Commission in 1970.[4]

Decisions of Economic and Social Council

On 21 May 1971, the Economic and Social Council adopted resolution 1591(L) on the policies of *apartheid* and racial discrimination. Among other things, the Council:

(1) requested the Security Council to find means of enforcing its own resolutions, by which all United Nations Members were called upon not to supply arms to South Africa, and of effectively implementing the pertinent resolutions of the General Assembly;

(2) urged States and, in particular, the major trading partners of South Africa to apply fully the resolutions concerning *apartheid* adopted by the General Assembly, the Security Council and other United Nations organs;

(3) invited the specialized agencies—and especially the financial institutions—to follow towards South Africa a policy in conformity with those resolutions;

(4) invited all States to strengthen and expand their programmes of assistance to the victims of *apartheid* and to respond as promptly as possible to the Assembly's appeal for substantial contributions to the United Nations Trust Fund for South Africa;

(5) invited all States to undertake, with the assistance of non-governmental organizations—including workers, religious, social and professional organizations, universities, youth and civic groups

and national women's organizations, where appropriate—an educational programme designed to acquaint the public of each country and territory with the evil consequences of the policy of *apartheid*;

(6) also invited non-governmental organizations in consultative status with special interest in the elimination of racism and racial discrimination, independent of any action being undertaken by States, to mount a regular and constant campaign against *apartheid* both at the national and international levels and to report their endeavours and progress biennially to the Council;

(7) appealed to all humanitarian organizations, and to the International Committee of the Red Cross in particular, to take an active role in assisting the victims of *apartheid,* especially those who were detained or imprisoned;

(8) urged the General Assembly to provide funds on the scale required to combat effectively the propaganda undertaken by South Africa by which that country sought to defend and justify the policy of *apartheid*; and

(9) invited the Secretary-General to make special efforts, utilizing the existing information services available to the United Nations, to alert world public opinion, and particularly that of countries trading with South Africa, to the recommendations made by various United Nations bodies on the subject of *apartheid,* in order to facilitate compliance by Governments with those recommendations.

(For further details, see pp. 405-6.)

Also on 21 May, the Council adopted resolution 1588(L), on racial discrimination in the political, economic, social and cultural spheres, by which it recommended that certain actions be taken against racial discrimination, particularly during 1971—designated as the International Year for Action to Combat Racism and Racial Discrimination. (For details, see pp. 411-12.)

On the question of slavery and the slave trade in all their practices and manifestations, including the slavery-like practices of *apartheid* and colonialism, the Economic and Social Council on 21 May adopted resolution 1593(L). (For details, see page 434.)

The Council adopted another resolution (1599(L)) on the same date on the report of the *Ad Hoc* Working Group of Experts in connexion with allegations regarding infringements of trade union rights in southern Africa. (For details, see pp. 434-35.)

Also approved by the Council on 21 May was a resolution (1592(L)) by which it recommended that the General Assembly adopt a draft resolution

[4]See Y.U.N., 1970, p. 514.

on the implementation of United Nations resolutions relating to the right of peoples under colonial and alien domination to self-determination. This text was adopted later in 1971 by the General Assembly as its resolution 2787(XXVI). (For details, see page 420.)

Consideration by General Assembly

General aspects

An item relating to the policies of *apartheid* of the Government of the Republic of South Africa was included in the agenda of the twenty-sixth (1971) session of the General Assembly on the recommendation of the Assembly's General Committee.

During the discussion regarding the adoption of the agenda, the representative of South Africa reaffirmed his Government's reservations with regard to the inscription in the agenda and the eventual consideration of the item. The Assembly, however, approved the inclusion of the item in the agenda, allocating it to the Special Political Committee.

The Rapporteur of the Special Committee on *Apartheid*, introducing the Special Committee's report, said it had been hoped that during the International Year for Action to Combat Racism and Racial Discrimination efforts would be made to develop wider awareness of the dangers of racism, and particularly *apartheid*, resulting in more effective national and international measures. However, the deteriorating situation in South Africa had continued to belie that hope. All appeals, decisions and suggestions by various United Nations organs for a peaceful and equitable solution to the problem had only strengthened the South African racist régime in its intransigence and defiance of world public opinion.

The Special Committee on *Apartheid* had, he pointed out, documented the evidence of continued violations of the arms embargo by various countries, and it was hoped that the General Assembly and the Security Council would give thorough and urgent consideration to the matter and take the necessary decisions to secure full implementation of the embargo.

Military and economic support of the South African Government had, he went on, encouraged it to intensify its application of callous *apartheid* measures, and the ensuing racial bitterness and resolute opposition and resistance to them had further intensified the danger of violent conflict. In the year under review, repressive measures had increased in severity and had been more widely applied. The Special Committee on *Apartheid* was gravely concerned about the people who had been gaoled under South Africa's numerous security laws, especially since at least 15 persons were known to have died while in arbitrary detention, including one detained in 1971.

The Rapporteur deplored the fact that the South African Government had continued its relentless assault on the fundamental human rights of "non-white" South Africans and had caused them untold misery and hardship. In 1971, thousands of Africans and Indians had been uprooted from their homes and communities and systematically forced into "resettlement camps," which lacked the most rudimentary facilities, in areas which could barely provide even a meagre livelihood. The Special Committee on *Apartheid*, he said, was convinced that there could be no peaceful and just solution within the framework of Bantustans and *apartheid* institutions which confined Africans to one eighth of the land.

The Rapporteur said the Special Committee was convinced that the situation in South Africa constituted a serious and ever-growing threat to international peace and security and required the prompt application of decisive mandatory sanctions and related economic measures. Special emphasis should be given to the need for greater assistance by States and organizations to the oppressed people of South Africa in their legitimate struggle for freedom. The need for vigorous and diversified information programmes on the evils and dangers of *apartheid* was greater than ever before. At the end of the International Year for Action to Combat Racism and Racial Discrimination, efforts to implement concrete and realistic action should be redoubled. The report of the Special Committee on *Apartheid* outlined various measures for the elimination of *apartheid* provided, he stressed, that the international community was willing to make the necessary effort.

The Chairman of the Special Committee on *Apartheid* said that despite the arms embargo imposed by the Security Council, South Africa had continued to obtain military equipment, technical assistance and licences for the manufacture of arms from many States. Countries which supplied South Africa with arms continued to maintain their fraudulent distinction between arms for internal repression and arms for external security, and to pretend ignorance of the fact that aircraft or helicopters supplied for so-called non-military purposes could easily be converted for military use.

South Africa, he continued, had felt the need to guard against further isolation by initiating its new so-called outward policy of dialogue with African States. Those States should be warned that in return for South African financial aid and technical assistance, they could only expect a new colonial relationship. By providing new markets for South African manufactured goods they would reinforce the industrial system built on *apartheid*, and by entering into a dialogue with South Africa they were contributing to that country's efforts to undermine the international campaign against *apartheid*. Such a dialogue, he stressed, would not restore to the non-white people of South Africa their political, social and economic rights.

The Chairman stressed that the international campaign to isolate South Africa must be pursued until the South African Government showed its willingness to carry out the kind of consultation within South Africa called for by the Security Council's Group of Experts in 1964,[5] or the kind of dialogue called for by the Organization of African Unity (OAU) in the Lusaka Manifesto of 1969.[6]

The Chairman further emphasized that national and international trade unions could play an important role in the campaign against *apartheid* by effectively discouraging the immigration of skilled workers to South Africa, by conducting a vigorous campaign to end the persecution of trade unionists in South Africa and by bringing pressure to bear on investors in the Western countries.

He went on to say that there was heartening evidence of the strength of the anti-*apartheid* movements in many countries. The boycotts of all-white South African teams by a number of international and national sports associations had had measurable repercussions in South Africa, where many sportsmen were demanding an end to racism in sport for fear of total international isolation. It would be a tremendous contribution to the International Year for Action to Combat Racism and Racial Discrimination if Governments followed the moral lead given by so many of their peoples and took action to complete the boycott of *apartheid* in sports.

The Chairman pointed out that in their resolutions and decisions various United Nations bodies had stressed the need for the widest possible dissemination of information on the evils and dangers of colonialism, *apartheid* and racial discrimination in southern Africa, and on United Nations efforts to eradicate such phenomena.

The Special Political Committee first took up a proposal—eventually sponsored by 56 Member States—on the question of the ill-treatment and torture of political prisoners and others detained or in police custody in South Africa for their anti-*apartheid* activities. The Special Political Committee approved the text, as revised by the sponsors, by a roll-call vote of 98 to 1, with 2 abstentions, on 3 November 1971, and recommended its adoption by the General Assembly as an interim measure and as a matter of urgency. The Assembly adopted it on 9 November by a recorded vote of 109 to 2, as its resolution 2764(XXVI).

By this text, the Assembly among other things expressed grave concern at continuing reports of ill-treatment and torture of opponents of *apartheid* in detention in South Africa and at the deaths of several detainees during interrogation. It also noted the recent deportations, bannings, detentions and trials of a number of religious leaders in South Africa for their opposition to *apartheid* and assistance to victims of that inhuman policy.

By the operative paragraphs of the text, the Assembly:

(1) expressed grave indignation and concern over any and every act of maltreatment and torture of opponents of *apartheid* in South Africa and the increased persecution of religious leaders opposed to that policy;

(2) again called upon all States to do everything in their power to promote the cause of justice for all people in South Africa and to exert their influence to secure: (*a*) the repeal of all legislation designed to give effect to the oppressive policies of *apartheid* and all legislation designed to persecute and suppress the rights of those opposed to such policies; (*b*) the liberation of all persons imprisoned or detained for their opposition to *apartheid*; and (*c*) the removal of orders against those banned or banished for their opposition to *apartheid*;

(3) appealed to national and international associations of jurists to take all appropriate steps in support of the purposes of the present resolution;

(4) urged all religious organizations to continue and intensify their efforts for the elimination of *apartheid* and racial discrimination;

(5) requested the Special Committee on *Apartheid* to prepare a special report on all known cases of maltreatment and torture of prisoners in South Africa, together with any other information pertinent to those cases;

(6) invited all organizations and individuals with knowledge of such cases to provide the Special Committee with all available information;

(7) asked the Secretary-General: (*a*) to bring the present resolution to the attention of Governments, organizations and anti-*apartheid* movements, including religious organizations and associations of jurists; (*b*) to publicize, through the Unit on *Apartheid* of the United Nations Secretariat and the United Nations Office of Public Information, all available information on the maltreatment and torture of prisoners and detainees in South Africa and the persecution of opponents of *apartheid*, including religious leaders; and (*c*) to assist the Special Committee in preparing the report requested and publicize it as widely as possible.

[5]See Y.U.N., 1964, pp. 107-9.
[6]See Y.U.N., 1969, pp. 147-52.

The resolution was sponsored by Afghanistan, Algeria, Barbados, Burundi, Cameroon, Chile, the Congo, Cyprus, Denmark, Egypt, Ethiopia, Finland, Ghana, Guinea, Guyana, Hungary, Iceland, India, Indonesia, Ireland, Jamaica, Jordan, Iran, Kenya, Kuwait, Liberia, the Libyan Arab Republic, Malaysia, Mali, Mauritania, Mongolia, Morocco, Nepal, Nigeria, Norway, Pakistan, the Philippines, Rwanda, Senegal, Sierra Leone, Singapore, Somalia, Sudan, Sweden, the Syrian Arab Republic, Togo, Trinidad and Tobago, Tunisia, Uganda, the Ukrainian SSR, the United Republic of Tanzania, Upper Volta, Yemen, Yugoslavia, Zaire and Zambia.

Introducing the draft resolution in the Special Political Committee, the representative of Somalia said it reflected the concern and indignation aroused by recent events in South Africa. He and many other speakers deplored the death of Ahmed Timol while under detention in Johannesburg, and the arrest and conviction of the Anglican Dean of Johannesburg, the Very Reverend G. A. ffrench-Beytagh. The representative of Nigeria hoped the resolution could be adopted unanimously in order to express the concern felt at the inhuman policies of the South African Government. Zambia, a sponsor, deplored the increased sufferings of non-whites in police custody and prison in South Africa, the petty nature of the offences for which they were being imprisoned, the appalling conditions to which anti-*apartheid* fighters were being subjected, and the arrogant attitude of the South African Government towards efforts to end *apartheid*.

(For text of resolution 2764(XXVI), see DOCUMENTARY REFERENCES below.)

Following the approval of the resolution concerning maltreatment and torture of opponents of *apartheid*, the Special Political Committee returned to a general discussion of South Africa's *apartheid* policies, which were again deplored by a majority of speakers.

Many Members commended the efforts of the Special Committee on *Apartheid* in gathering information concerning South Africa's repressive policies and endorsed the conclusions and recommendations contained in the Special Committee's report. It was noted that the dangers of *apartheid* were spreading beyond South Africa, whose authorities were using their increased military power to extend the inhuman practice of *apartheid* to other territories, to suppress national liberation movements throughout the African continent and to threaten the sovereignty of independent African States. It was the duty of all Member States of the United Nations to adopt the necessary measures to curb the South African racists.

Many speakers condemned the economic and military co-operation of major Western powers with South African authorities. By giving military and economic assistance to South Africa those powers were grossly violating United Nations resolutions. Any money channelled into Pretoria helped to fortify *apartheid* and every delivery of arms served to encourage its military ventures. It was the opinion of many speakers that South Africa's trading partners and those who violated the arms embargo were largely responsible for the ineffectiveness of United Nations decisions. It was again stressed that the United Nations must consider mandatory measures to control a situation that might spark unprecedented violence.

Most Members emphasized the importance of spreading information on the evils of *apartheid* and of eliciting the support of people in all parts of the world. The Special Committee on *Apartheid* was urged to continue and intensify dissemination of information about those countries that were co-operating with the Pretoria racist régime and on the evils and atrocities committed by the South African racists. Also stressed was the need for publicizing United Nations decisions on *apartheid*.

Many Members emphasized the importance of co-ordinating the efforts of anti-*apartheid* and national liberation movements in their struggle against *apartheid*. A number pledged their Governments' material and moral support to those struggling against the system of racial oppression.

The general debate on the *apartheid* question resulted in the adoption, on 29 November, of nine additional resolutions by the General Assembly. One of these—resolution 2774(XXVI)—dealt with the United Nations Trust Fund for South Africa and is described in another section of this chapter (see pp. 86-88). The others are described below.

By the first resolution—2775 A (XXVI)—the Assembly among other things expressed grave concern at the continued build-up of South African military and police forces and noted that South Africa continued to receive military equipment—and technical and other assistance for the manufacture of such equipment—from certain Member States in contravention of the arms embargo.

After reaffirming its resolution of 13 October 1970,[7] the Assembly declared that the arms embargo against South Africa made no distinction between arms for external defence and arms for internal repression, and deplored the actions of those Governments which had provided, or allowed companies registered in their countries to provide, assistance for the build-up of the military and police forces.

The Assembly called upon all Governments to implement fully the arms embargo against South

[7]See footnote 2.

Africa and urgently appealed to all national and international organizations to discourage and denounce all military collaboration with South Africa and ensure implementation of Security Council resolutions on the arms embargo.

The Security Council was invited to consider the situation in the light of the reports and communications addressed to it by the Special Committee on *Apartheid* and of the present resolution, with a view to securing full implementation of the Council's resolution of 23 July 1970.[8]

Finally, the Assembly asked the Special Committee on *Apartheid* to undertake a comprehensive study of the military collaboration with, and military assistance to, South Africa by Governments and private enterprises and to report thereon to the Assembly at its 1972 session.

The resolution was adopted by the General Assembly by a recorded vote of 107 to 2, with 5 abstentions, on the recommendation of the Special Political Committee, which approved it, as amended by Sierra Leone, on 15 November by a roll-call vote of 87 to 1, with 6 abstentions.

(For text of resolution 2775A(XXVI), see DOCUMENTARY REFERENCES below.)

The sponsors of the resolution were Afghanistan, Algeria, Burundi, Cameroon, Colombia, the Congo, Cyprus, Czechoslovakia, Egypt, Ethiopia, the Gambia, Ghana, Guatemala, Guinea, Guyana Hungary, India, Indonesia, Kenya, Liberia, the Libyan Arab Republic, Malaysia, Mali, Mauritania, Mongolia, Morocco, Nepal, Nigeria, Pakistan, the People's Democratic Republic of Yemen, the Philippines, Rwanda, Senegal, Sierra Leone, Singapore, Somalia, Sudan, the Syrian Arab Republic, Togo, Tunisia, Uganda, the Ukrainian SSR, the United Republic of Tanzania, Upper Volta, Yemen, Yugoslavia and Zambia.

The next resolution adopted by the Assembly—2775 B (XXVI)—concerned educational material on *apartheid*. The text, which was twice revised, was approved in the Special Political Committee on 15 November by a roll-call vote of 97 to 0, with 2 abstentions, and adopted by the Assembly on 29 November by a recorded vote of 112 to 1, with 3 abstentions. It was sponsored by Afghanistan, Algeria, Burundi, Cameroon, Chile, Colombia, the Congo, Costa Rica, Denmark, Egypt, Ethiopia, the Gambia, Ghana, Guatemala, Guinea, Guyana, Hungary, Iceland, India, Indonesia, Iran, Ireland, Jamaica, Kenya, Liberia, the Libyan Arab Republic, Madagascar, Malaysia, Mali, Mauritania, Morocco, Nepal, New Zealand, Niger, Nigeria, Norway, Pakistan, the People's Democratic Republic of Yemen, the Philippines, Rwanda, Senegal, Sierra Leone, Singapore, Somalia, Sudan, Sweden, the Syrian Arab Republic, Togo, Trinidad and Tobago, Tunisia, Uganda, the Ukrainian SSR, the United Republic of

Tanzania, Upper Volta, Uruguay, Venezuela, Yemen, Yugoslavia and Zambia.

By this resolution, the General Assembly among other things considered that the International Year for Action to Combat Racism and Racial Discrimination should be the occasion to add new emphasis to efforts to enlighten the international community about the evils of *apartheid* and racial discrimination in South Africa. It was convinced of the special role education should play in international efforts to eliminate *apartheid* and other forms of racial discrimination.

By the operative parts of the text, the Assembly commended the proposal of the Special Committee on *Apartheid* for the preparation of an educational kit on racial discrimination and *apartheid* in southern Africa, and it asked the United Nations Educational, Scientific and Cultural Organization (UNESCO) to prepare such a kit for possible adaptation by national UNESCO commissions and for distribution to institutions of learning.

The Assembly also asked UNESCO to consider the production of films and audio-visual material on *apartheid,* with special reference to its adverse effects on education, science and culture, and invited all concerned to co-operate with UNESCO to ensure the widest possible use of the material prepared.

(For text of resolution 2775 B (XXVI), see DOCUMENTARY REFERENCES below.)

By another resolution adopted on 29 November—2775 C (XXVI)—the General Assembly endorsed the programme of work of the Special Committee on *Apartheid* contained in its report and authorized it, within the budgetary provisions to be made for this purpose: (a) to send representatives or delegations, as appropriate, to international conferences dealing with the problem of *apartheid* and (b) to hold consultations with experts and with representatives of the oppressed people of South Africa, as well as anti-*apartheid* movements and non-governmental organizations concerned with the campaign against *apartheid*.

The Assembly adopted this text by a recorded vote of 108 to 1, with 5 abstentions, on the recommendation of the Special Political Committee, which approved it, as revised, on 15 November, by 89 votes to 0, with 4 abstentions. It was sponsored by Afghanistan, Algeria, Cameroon, the Congo, Egypt, the Gambia, Ghana, Guinea, Hungary, India, Indonesia, Kenya, Liberia, the Libyan Arab Republic, Madagascar, Malaysia, Mali, Mauritania, Morocco, Nepal, Niger, Nigeria, Pakistan, the People's Democratic Republic of Yemen, the Philippines, Senegal, Sierra Leone,

---

[8]See footnote 1.

Singapore, Somalia, Sudan, the Syrian Arab Republic, Trinidad and Tobago, Tunisia, Uganda, the Ukrainian SSR, the United Republic of Tanzania, Yemen and Zambia.

(For text of resolution 2775 C (XXVI), see DOCUMENTARY REFERENCES below.)

Another resolution adopted on 29 November by the General Assembly—2775 D (XXVI)—had to do with the question of *apartheid* in sports. After recalling its requests to all States and national and international sports organizations to suspend exchanges of sporting events with South African teams selected under *apartheid* policies, the Assembly declared its unqualified support of the Olympic principle that no discrimination be allowed on the grounds of race, religion or political affiliation, and affirmed that merit should be the sole criterion for participation in sports activities.

The Assembly then called upon all national and international sports organizations to uphold the Olympic principle of non-discrimination and to discourage and deny support to sporting events organized in violation of that principle. It also called upon individual sportsmen to refuse to participate in any sports activity in which there was an official policy of racial discrimination or *apartheid* in the field of sports.

By this text, the Assembly then urged all States to promote adherence to the Olympic principle of non-discrimination and to encourage their sports organizations to withhold support from sporting events organized in violation of that principle. National and international sports organizations and the public were asked to deny any form of recognition to any sports activity from which persons were debarred or in which they were subjected to any discrimination on the basis of race, religion or political affiliation.

The General Assembly then condemned the actions of the South African Government in enforcing racial discrimination and segregation in sports.

Some national and international sports organizations, the Assembly noted with regret, had continued exchanges with teams from South Africa selected for international competition on the basis of competition closed to otherwise qualified sportsmen solely on the basis of their race, colour, descent or national or ethnic origin.

The Assembly commended those international and national sports organizations that had supported the international campaign against *apartheid* in sports, and requested all States to urge their national sports organizations to act in accordance with the present resolution. It asked the Secretary-General to bring the resolution to the attention of international sports organizations, to keep the Special Committee on *Apartheid* informed as to its

implementation and to report on the matter to the Assembly at its 1972 session.

The resolution was adopted by the General Assembly by a recorded vote of 106 to 2, with 7 abstentions, on the recommendation of the Special Political Committee, which approved it on 15 November by a roll-call vote of 91 to 0, with 8 abstentions. The text was sponsored by Afghanistan, Algeria, Burundi, Cameroon, the Congo, Cyprus, Egypt, Ethiopia, the Gambia, Ghana, Guatemala, Guinea, Guyana, Hungary, India, Indonesia, Iran, Kenya, Liberia, the Libyan Arab Republic, Malaysia, Mali, Mauritania, Mongolia, Morocco, Nepal, Niger, Nigeria, Pakistan, the People's Democratic Republic of Yemen, the Philippines, Rwanda, Senegal, Sierra Leone, Singapore, Somalia, Sudan, the Syrian Arab Republic, Togo, Trinidad and Tobago, Tunisia, Uganda, the Ukrainian SSR, the United Republic of Tanzania, Upper Volta, Uruguay, Yemen, Yugoslavia and Zambia.

(For text of resolution 2775 D (XXVI), see DOCUMENTARY REFERENCES below.)

In connexion with the question of the establishment of Bantustans, the General Assembly on 29 November adopted resolution 2775 E (XXVI) by a recorded vote of 110 to 2, with 2 abstentions. It had been approved in the Special Political Committee on 15 November—as revised to take into account amendments by Egypt, by Ghana and by Sierra Leone—by a roll-call vote of 99 to 1, with 3 abstentions.

The General Assembly thereby noted, in the preambular part of the text, that South Africa, while treating its white inhabitants—irrespective of their national origin—as constituting one nation, sought artificially to divide the African people into "nations" according to their tribal origins and justified the establishment of non-contiguous Bantu homelands (Bantustans) on that basis. The Assembly recognized that the real purpose of the establishment of Bantustans was to divide the Africans, setting one tribe against the other with a view to weakening the African front in its struggle for its inalienable and just rights.

After recalling previous resolutions on South Africa's *apartheid* policies, the Assembly noted further that under those resolutions crimes against humanity were committed when enslavement, deportation and other inhuman acts were enforced against any civilian population on political, racial or religious grounds. It also noted that many African communities had been uprooted and that large numbers of Africans had been forcibly removed from their homes in pursuance of the policies of *apartheid*.

The Assembly considered that the establishment of Bantustans and other measures adopted by South Africa in pursuance of *apartheid* were designed to consolidate and perpetuate domination by a white minority and the dispossession and exploitation of the African and other non-white people of South Africa, as well as of Namibia.

By the operative parts of the text, the Assembly:

(1) again condemned the establishment by South Africa of Bantustans and the forcible removal of the African people of South Africa and Namibia to those areas as a violation of their inalienable rights, contrary to the principles of self-determination and prejudicial to the territorial integrity of the countries and the unity of their peoples;

(2) declared that the United Nations would continue to encourage and promote a solution to the situation in South Africa through the full application of human rights and fundamental freedoms, including political rights, to all the inhabitants of the territory of South Africa as a whole, regardless of race, colour or creed; and

(3) decided to keep the situation in South Africa constantly under review.

(For text of resolution 2775 E (XXVI), see DOCUMENTARY REFERENCES below.)

The text was sponsored by Afghanistan, Algeria, Bulgaria, Burundi, Cameroon, the Congo, Cyprus, Czechoslovakia, Egypt, Ethiopia, the Gambia, Ghana, Guinea, Guyana, Hungary, India, Indonesia, Kenya, the Libyan Arab Republic, Malaysia, Mali, Mauritania, Mongolia, Morocco, Nepal, Niger, Nigeria, Pakistan, the People's Democratic Republic of Yemen, the Philippines, Rwanda, Senegal, Sierra Leone, Singapore, Somalia, Sudan, the Syrian Arab Republic, Togo, Trinidad and Tobago, Uganda, the Ukrainian SSR, the United Republic of Tanzania, Upper Volta, Yemen, Yugoslavia and Zambia.

Another resolution—2775 F (XXVI)—adopted by the General Assembly on 29 November concerned the situation in South Africa resulting from the policies of *apartheid.*

In the preambular part of the resolution, the Assembly among other things considered that the United Nations organs concerned should adopt a concerted and co-ordinated approach to the inter-related problems of southern Africa. It was gravely concerned over the explosive situation in South Africa and in southern Africa as a whole resulting from the inhuman and aggressive policies of *apartheid* pursued by the South African Government. The United Nations and Member States, the Assembly considered, should intensify their efforts to solve the situation in accordance with the Charter and the Declaration on the Granting of Independence to Colonial Countries and Peoples.

By the operative parts of the text, the Assembly reaffirmed its resolution 2671(XXV) of 8 December 1970 (which dealt, in several parts, with aspects of the *apartheid* question).[9] It then commended all States, organizations and individuals struggling against *apartheid* and racial discrimination, especially in South Africa.

The Assembly declared that the current tactics of the racist Government of South Africa in pursuance of its so-called "outward policy" were designed primarily to obtain acquiescence in its racial policies, to confuse world public opinion, to counter international isolation, to hinder assistance to the liberation movements by the international community and to consolidate white minority rule in southern Africa.

The Assembly condemned the continued and increasing co-operation of certain States and foreign economic interests with South Africa in military, economic, political and other fields, as such co-operation encouraged the South African Government in the pursuit of its inhuman policies.

By this text, the Assembly also reaffirmed the legitimacy of the struggle of the oppressed people of South Africa to eliminate, by all means at their disposal, *apartheid,* racial discrimination and similar ideologies and to attain majority rule in the country as a whole, based on universal adult suffrage. It appealed to Governments, the specialized agencies, national and international organizations and individuals to provide every assistance—directly or through the OAU Assistance Fund for the Struggle against Colonialism and *Apartheid*—to the national movement of the oppressed people of South Africa in their legitimate struggle.

The Assembly reaffirmed the determination of the United Nations to intensify its efforts to remedy the grave situation in southern Africa and to ensure the achievement of the legitimate rights of all the inhabitants of that area, irrespective of race, colour or creed.

All States were asked by the Assembly to take more effective action for the elimination of *apartheid* in the light of previous resolutions of the Assembly and the Security Council. They were also asked to take steps to dissuade their nationals from emigrating to South Africa so long as the South African Government pursued policies of *apartheid.*

The Assembly commended the activities of States, organizations and individuals engaged in dissuading economic interests from increasing collaboration with South Africa and profiting from racial discrimination and exploitation of African and other non-white workers.

The Special Committee on *Apartheid* was asked to arrange—in consultation with the Secretary-General—for the preparation of special studies on

---

[9]See Y.U.N., 1970, pp. 149-53, texts of resolutions 2671 A-D and F (XXV), and p. 156, text of resolution 2671 E (XXV).

apartheid and its international repercussions and for publication of a periodic bulletin on the collaboration of Governments and private enterprises with the South African régime and South African companies.

The Assembly also asked the Special Committee on *Apartheid* to continue its close co-operation with other United Nations bodies concerned with *apartheid*, racial discrimination and colonialism in southern Africa, with a view to co-ordinated action to find ways and means of eliminating those evils.

It was again recommended by the Assembly that the Security Council consider urgently the situation in South Africa and in southern Africa as a whole, with a view to the adoption of effective measures against South Africa, including those under Chapter VII of the United Nations Charter.[10]

Finally, the Secretary-General was asked to report on the implementation of the present resolution to the Assembly at its 1972 session.

(For text of resolution 2775 F(XXVI), see DOCUMENTARY REFERENCES below.)

The General Assembly adopted the text by a recorded vote of 86 to 6, with 22 abstentions, on the recommendation of the Special Political Committee, which approved it on 15 November—as revised to take into account amendments by Cameroon, by Lebanon and by Sierra Leone—by a roll-call vote of 76 to 6, with 21 abstentions. The text was sponsored by Afghanistan, Algeria, Burundi, Cameroon, the Congo, Egypt, Ethiopia, Guinea, India, Kenya, Kuwait, the Libyan Arab Republic, Mali, Mauritania, Nepal, Nigeria, Pakistan, the People's Democratic Republic of Yemen, Somalia, Sudan, the Syrian Arab Republic, Togo, Uganda, the United Republic of Tanzania, Yemen, Yugoslavia and Zambia.

Another resolution adopted by the General Assembly on 29 November—2775 G(XXVI)—had to do with the dissemination of information about *apartheid*. The text, as amended by Sierra Leone, was approved in the Special Political Committee on 16 November by 82 votes to 1, with 5 abstentions. The Assembly adopted it by a recorded vote of 108 to 2, with 6 abstentions.

By this text, the Assembly among other things recognized the importance of the widest dissemination of information on the evils and dangers of *apartheid*, and of United Nations efforts for the elimination of *apartheid*, in order to secure increasing support of world public opinion. By the operative paragraphs, the Assembly:

(1) requested the Secretary-General, in conformity with the relevant parts of his report on the review and reappraisal of United Nations information policies and activities and in compliance with recommendations of the Special Committee on *Apartheid*, to intensify information activities with a view to promoting national and international action for the elimination of *apartheid;*

(2) requested the Secretary-General to ascertain the needs and to take into account the recommendations of the General Assembly bodies concerned with the problems of southern Africa in intensifying information activities on those problems;

(3) invited Governments, specialized agencies and regional organizations, as well as non-governmental organizations, information media and educational institutions, to co-operate with the United Nations in disseminating information on *apartheid;*

(4) invited the specialized agencies to contribute to the campaign against *apartheid* in the light of the relevant recommendations of the report of the Special Committee on *Apartheid;*

(5) requested the Special Committee on *Apartheid*, in consultation with non-governmental organizations concerned with the campaign against *apartheid*, to take appropriate steps, where necessary, to promote the establishment of national committees against *apartheid;*

(6) appealed to Governments and organizations to make voluntary contributions to enable the Organization of African Unity (OAU) to acquire equipment for recording and distributing information on *apartheid* through various broadcasting facilities and to lend their co-operation to OAU in preparing and disseminating radio broadcasts on *apartheid;* and

(7) requested the Secretary-General to submit a detailed report to the Assembly at its 1972 session on the implementation of the present resolution and on means of securing adequate publicity for United Nations efforts against *apartheid* in the light of recommendations by the General Assembly bodies concerned.

(For text of resolution 2775 G(XXVI), see DOCUMENTARY REFERENCES below.)

The text was sponsored by Afghanistan, Algeria, the Congo, Cyprus, Egypt, Ethiopia, the Gambia, Ghana, Guinea, India, Indonesia, Jamaica, Kenya, the Libyan Arab Republic, Malaysia, Mali, Mauritania, Morocco, Nepal, Niger, Nigeria, Pakistan, the People's Democratic Republic of Yemen, the Philippines, Senegal, Sierra Leone, Singapore, Somalia, Sudan, the Syrian Arab Republic, Togo, Trinidad and Tobago, Uganda, the United Republic of Tanzania, Yugoslavia and Zambia.

Finally, the General Assembly adopted a resolution—2775 H(XXVI)—concerning trade union activities against *apartheid*.

After noting the report of the Special Committee on *Apartheid* concerning ways and means of

---

[10]For text of Chapter VII of the Charter, see APPENDIX II.

promoting concerted action against *apartheid* by the trade union movements, the Assembly appealed to all national and international trade union organizations to intensify their action against *apartheid*, in particular by: (*a*) discouraging the emigration of skilled workers to South Africa; (*b*) taking appropriate action in connexion with the infringements of trade union rights and the persecution of trade unionists in South Africa; (*c*) exerting maximum pressure on foreign economic and financial interests which were profiting from racial discrimination against non-white workers in South Africa, in order to persuade them to cease such exploitation; and (*d*) co-operating with other organizations engaged in the international campaign against *apartheid*.

The Assembly also decided to give further consideration at its 1972 session to a proposed international trade union conference.

The Special Committee on *Apartheid* was requested and authorized by the Assembly to send a mission to hold consultative meetings, if possible, with the workers' representatives to the fifty-seventh (1972) session of the International Labour Conference, to consider lines of action which the trade union movement might take against *apartheid*—including the holding of an international trade union conference—and to invite representatives of international and regional trade union federations to those consultative meetings.

Finally, the Assembly requested the International Labour Organisation and invited the workers' representatives to lend their co-operation to the Special Committee on *Apartheid* in preparing and holding the consultative meetings.

The resolution was adopted by the General Assembly on 29 November by a recorded vote of 104 to 1, with 9 abstentions, on the recommendation of the Special Political Committee, which approved it on 16 November by a roll-call vote of 92 to 0, with 10 abstentions. The text was sponsored by Algeria, Chile, the Congo, Guinea, Hungary, India, Indonesia, the Libyan Arab Republic, Malaysia, Mali, Mauritania, Mongolia, Morocco, Nepal, Nigeria, Pakistan, the People's Democratic Republic of Yemen, Singapore, Somalia, Sudan, the Syrian Arab Republic, Trinidad and Tobago, the United Republic of Tanzania, and Zambia.

(For text of resolution 2775 H (XXVI), see DOCUMENTARY REFERENCES below. For further details about the question of trade union rights, see pp. 434-36.)

Other General Assembly decisions

At its 1971 session, the General Assembly adopted a number of other resolutions having a bearing on the question of *apartheid* and racial discrimination. These are described briefly below.

ELIMINATION OF ALL FORMS
OF RACIAL DISCRIMINATION

In a four-part resolution (2784(XXVI)) on the elimination of all forms of racial discrimination, the General Assembly requested the President of the Assembly to forward to all heads of State or Government of each State a message containing specific recommendations to be taken to ensure the continuation of the campaign against racial discrimination, bearing in mind that the International Year for Action to Combat Racism and Racial Discrimination should be considered as the opening year for a full decade of vigorous struggle against the evil of racial discrimination.

The Secretary-General was asked to submit a report based on replies from Governments to the message, and the Economic and Social Council was asked to request the Commission on Human Rights to submit suggestions for launching continued international action to combat racism on the basis of a "Decade for vigorous and continued mobilization against racism and racial discrimination in all its forms."

By a second part of the resolution, the General Assembly, after reaffirming that *apartheid* was a crime against humanity, called for increased and continued moral and material support to all peoples struggling for their liberation, self-determination and the elimination of all forms of racial discrimination. The Economic and Social Council was invited to ask the Human Rights Commission to make recommendations for the further elaboration of international instruments to deal with crimes against humanity, particularly those arising from the policies of *apartheid*. All Governments continuing to supply arms to the Pretoria régime in violation of relevant resolutions of the Assembly and the Security Council were strongly condemned.

By the third part of the resolution the Assembly among other things called upon all the trading partners of South Africa to abstain from any action encouraging the continued violation of the International Convention on the Elimination of All Forms of Racial Discrimination by South Africa and the illegal régime in Southern Rhodesia, and to use their influence to ensure the eradication of the policies of *apartheid* and racial discrimination in the international territory of Namibia and Southern Rhodesia.

The Assembly invited the Economic and Social Council to ask the Human Rights Commission to continue its comprehensive studies of policies and practices of racial discrimination, taking into account in particular discrimination against peoples of African origin in all countries, and to report to the Assembly not later than in 1973 with recommendations for combating such policies and practices.

Finally, the Assembly, by the fourth part of the resolution, decided to consider the matter again at its session in 1972.

Annexed to the resolution was the text of the President's message to heads of State or Government.

These decisions were embodied in resolution 2784(XXVI), adopted on 6 December 1971. (For details and text of resolution, see pp. 398-400 and 402-4.)

IMPORTANCE OF THE RIGHT TO SELF-DETERMINATION

In a resolution adopted on 6 December 1971 on the importance of the universal realization of the right of peoples to self-determination and of the speedy granting of independence to colonial countries and peoples for the effective guarantee and observance of human rights, the General Assembly among other things expressed the belief that the main objectives and principles of international protection of human rights could not be effectively implemented while some States—particularly Portugal and South Africa—pursued the imperialist policy of colonialism, used force against independent African States and developing countries and peoples fighting for self-determination, and supported régimes that were applying the criminal policy of racism and *apartheid.*

(For details and text of resolution 2787(XXVI), see pp. 420-22 and 423-24.)

CO-OPERATION OF SPECIALIZED AGENCIES

Among the provisions of a resolution on implementation of the Declaration on the Granting of Independence to Colonial Countries and Peoples by the specialized agencies and the international institutions associated with the United Nations were two which related to South Africa. The General Assembly thereby requested the specialized agencies and other organizations within the United Nations system to discontinue all collaboration with the Governments of Portugal and South Africa, as well as with the illegal régime in Southern Rhodesia, in accordance with the relevant resolutions of the Assembly and of the Security Council relating to colonial territories in southern Africa.

The Assembly also urged the specialized agencies and other organizations in the United Nations system—in particular the International Bank for Reconstruction and Development and the International Monetary Fund—to take all necessary measures to withhold financial, economic, technical and other assistance from Portugal and South Africa until they renounced their policies of racial discrimination and colonial domination.

These decisions were among those embodied in resolution 2874(XXVI), which the Assembly adopted on 20 December 1971. (For details and text of resolution, see pp. 526-27 and 528-29.)

DRAFT CONVENTION ON SUPPRESSION
AND PUNISHMENT OF *APARTHEID*

By another decision, the General Assembly among other things invited the Secretary-General to transmit to the Commission on Human Rights the text of a draft convention on the suppression and punishment of the crime of *apartheid* (submitted in the Assembly's Third (Social, Humanitarian and Cultural) Committee by Guinea and the USSR), so that the Commission and the Economic and Social Council—in co-operation with the Special Committee on *Apartheid*—could submit a text to the Assembly at its 1972 session.

In doing so, the Assembly recognized that the conclusion of such a convention would be an important contribution to the struggle against *apartheid,* racism, economic exploitation, colonial domination and foreign occupation.

The Assembly took these decisions when it adopted resolution 2786(XXVI) on 6 December 1971. (For details and text of resolution, see pp. 406-7 and 408.)

Credentials

At the meeting of the Credentials Committee on 17 December 1971, the representative of Somalia noted that the General Assembly had in 1970 approved the first report of the Credentials Committee except with regard to the credentials of the representatives of the Government of South Africa.[11] He stated that the credentials of those representatives should again be singled out for special consideration by the Assembly. He was supported by Liberia, Mongolia and the USSR.

The French representative said the question was not political but a simple one of whether or not the credentials of representatives emanated from their Governments.

The representative of Colombia emphasized that rule 27 of the General Assembly's rules of procedure[12] called only for the Credentials Committee to pronounce itself on whether the credentials had been submitted in due form. In his opinion—and aside from his country's abhorrence of colonialism and racial discrimination—the Committee could not assume prerogatives properly belonging, under the United Nations Charter, to the General Assembly and the Security Council.

Somalia emphasized that South Africa's membership in the United Nations was not in question.

---

[11]See Y.U.N., 1970, pp. 143-45.
[12]Rule 27 of the Assembly's rules of procedure states: "The credentials of representatives and the names of members of a delegation shall be submitted to the Secretary-General if possible not less than one week before the opening of the session. The credentials shall be issued either by the Head of the State or Government or by the Minister for Foreign Affairs."

The question was that South Africa's whole posture towards the Organization had been changing since 1948; today its application for membership would be rejected since it did not follow the principles of the Charter. Somalia could not endorse as valid the credentials of the representatives of South Africa. The examination of credentials could not be reduced to the mere verification of a piece of paper.

The United States stressed that rule 27 laid down purely technical requirements for the verification of credentials and recalled that the Committee had in the past rejected similar attempts to exclude representatives of Member States.

A proposal by Somalia that the credentials of the representatives of South Africa should be reported upon separately and that the Committee should not pronounce itself on the acceptability of those credentials was rejected by 5 votes to 4.

The Committee eventually recommended—by a vote of 5 to 2, with 2 abstentions—that the Assembly adopt a draft resolution approving the report of the Credentials Committee.

At a plenary meeting of the Assembly on 20 December, a Somali amendment to the draft, by which the Assembly would approve the report of the Credentials Committee "except with regard to the credentials of the representatives of South Africa," was adopted by the Assembly by a vote of 60 to 36, with 22 abstentions. The draft resolution submitted by the Credentials Committee, as thus amended, was then adopted by the Assembly by a vote of 103 to 1, with 16 abstentions, as resolution 2862(XXVI). The Assembly thereby approved the report of the Credentials Committee except with regard to the credentials of the representatives of South Africa.

(For text of resolution 2862(XXVI), see DOCU-MENTARY REFERENCES below.)

The representative of Somalia said that his reason for challenging the credentials of the South African representatives was based on the fact that the issuing authority—the so-called Government of South Africa—represented only a small minority group; it did not represent the 15 million Bantus, or the 500,000 Asians, or the 1.5 million Coloured people, who together made up over 70 per cent of the population.

Educational and Training Programme for Southern Africa

During 1971, a total of 191 South African students were studying abroad in 21 countries on scholarships granted under the United Nations Educational and Training Programme for Southern Africa, established by the Assembly in 1967.

Applications received from South Africans during the period 1 November 1970 to 8 October 1971 totalled 248. Forty-seven new awards were granted and 144 were extended.

The General Assembly reviewed the programme at its 1971 session and, among other things, urgently appealed to all States, organizations and individuals to make generous contributions to the trust fund for the Programme so that it might not only be continued but also strengthened and expanded.

(For additional information about the Educational and Training Programme for Southern Africa and the decisions of the Assembly thereon, see pp. 123-25.)

DOCUMENTARY REFERENCES

Communications to Security Council

S/10092. Report of 3 February 1971 of Secretary-General in pursuance of Security Council resolution 282(1970) of 23 July 1970 concerning question of *apartheid.*

S/10132. Letter of 24 February 1971 from Executive Secretary of Organization of African Unity (OAU) at United Nations (transmitting memorandum on Simonstown Agreement prepared by OAU).

S/10143. Letter of 1 March 1971 from President of United Nations Council for Namibia.

S/10147. Letter of 5 March 1971 from Chairman of Special Committee on Situation with regard to Implementation of Declaration on Granting of Independence to Colonial Countries and Peoples (transmitting text of consensus adopted by Special Committee on 4 March 1971, meeting 782).

S/10162. Letter of 23 March 1971 from United Kingdom (transmitting text of Opinion of Law Officers of The Crown for England and Wales on extent of existing legal obligations of Her Majesty's Government, arising under Simonstown Agreements of 1955).

S/10190. Letter of 7 May 1971 from Chairman of Special Committee on *Apartheid* (transmitting notes of 16 March, 9 April and 6 May 1971 and communiqué of 24 February 1971).

S/10195. Letter of 14 May 1971 from Israel.

S/10201. Letter of 19 May 1971 from Belgium.

S/10202. Letter of 20 May 1971 from Vice-Chairman of Special Committee on *Apartheid* (transmitting addendum to note of 16 March 1971).

S/10211. Note of 27 May 1971 by President of Security Council (transmitting letter of 26 May 1971 from Permanent Observer of Federal Republic of Germany).

S/10212. Letter of 25 May 1971 from United States.

S/10243. Letter of 25 June 1971 from Secretary-General (transmitting relevant text of Economic and Social Council resolution 1591(L)).

S/10272. Letter of 13 July 1971 from Executive Secretary of OAU at United Nations (transmitting resolutions adopted by 8th Assembly of Heads of State and Government of OAU).

S/10311. Note of 8 September 1971 by President of Security Council (transmitting letter of 8 September 1971 from Acting Permanent Observer of Switzerland).

S/10331. Letter of 23 September 1971 from Chairman of 9th meeting of Joint Meeting of Special Committee on *Apartheid,* Special Committee on Situation with regard to Implementation of Declaration on Granting of Independence to Colonial Countries and Peoples and United Nations Council for Namibia (transmitting consensus adopted by Joint Meeting on 13 September 1971).

S/10354. Letter of 6 October 1971 from Chairman of Special Committee on *Apartheid*.

S/10366 and Corr.1 (A/8422/Rev.1). Report of 8 October 1971 of Special Committee on *Apartheid*.

Reports of Special Committee on Apartheid

A/8422/Rev.1 (S/10366 and Corr.1). Report of Special Committee on *Apartheid*. (Chapter I E: Commemoration of International Day for Elimination of Racial Discrimination; Annex III: List of documents of Special Committee.)

A/8515/Rev.1. Ways and means of promoting concerted action against *apartheid* by trade union movement. Report of Special Committee on *Apartheid*.

Consideration by General Assembly

GENERAL ASPECTS

General Assembly—26th session
Special Political Committee, meetings 757-780.
Fifth Committee, meeting 1462.
Plenary meetings 1939, 1981, 1997.

A/8401. Report of Secretary-General on work of the Organization, 16 June 1970–15 June 1971, Part One, Chapter IV E.

A/8401/Add.1. Introduction to report of Secretary-General, September 1971, Part Two, Chapter VII.

A/8402. Report of Security Council, 16 June 1970–15 June 1971, Chapter 5.

A/8403. Report of Economic and Social Council on work of its 50th and 51st sessions, Chapter XVII C.

A/8422/Rev.1. Report of Special Committee on *Apartheid*.

A/8467. Report of Secretary-General.

A/SPC/L.205. Afghanistan, Algeria, Barbados, Burma, Burundi, Cameroon, Chile, Congo, Cyprus, Egypt, Ethiopia, Ghana, Guinea, Hungary, India, Indonesia, Kenya, Liberia, Libyan Arab Republic, Malaysia, Mali, Mauritania, Mongolia, Morocco, Nepal, Nigeria, Philippines, Rwanda, Senegal, Sierra Leone, Singapore, Somalia, Sudan, Syrian Arab Republic, Togo, Trinidad and Tobago, Tunisia, Uganda, Ukrainian SSR, United Republic of Tanzania, Upper Volta, Yugoslavia, Zambia: draft resolution.

A/SPC/L.205/Rev.1. Afghanistan, Algeria, Barbados, Burundi, Cameroon, Chile, Congo, Cyprus, Denmark, Egypt, Ethiopia, Finland, Ghana, Guinea, Guyana, Hungary, Iceland, India, Indonesia, Ireland, Jamaica, Jordan, Iran, Kenya, Kuwait, Liberia, Libyan Arab Republic, Malaysia, Mali, Mauritania, Mongolia, Morocco, Nepal, Nigeria, Norway, Pakistan, Philippines, Rwanda, Senegal, Sierra Leone, Singapore, Somalia, Sudan, Sweden, Syrian Arab Republic, Togo, Trinidad and Tobago, Tunisia, Uganda, Ukrainian SSR, United Republic of Tanzania, Upper Volta, Yemen, Yugoslavia, Zaire, Zambia: revised draft resolution, as further orally revised by sponsors, approved by Special Political Committee on 3 November 1971, meeting 766, by roll-call vote of 98 to 1, with 2 abstentions:

In favour: Afghanistan, Algeria, Argentina, Australia, Austria, Belgium, Bulgaria, Burma, Burundi, Byelorussian SSR, Cameroon, Canada, Central African Republic, Chile, Colombia, Congo, Costa Rica, Cuba, Cyprus, Czechoslovakia, Denmark, Ecuador, Egypt, El Salvador, Ethiopia, Finland, France, Ghana, Greece, Guinea, Guyana, Honduras, Hungary, India, Indonesia, Iran, Iraq, Ireland, Israel, Italy, Ivory Coast, Jamaica, Japan, Jordan, Kenya, Khmer Republic, Kuwait, Laos, Lebanon, Lesotho, Liberia, Libyan Arab Republic, Madagascar, Malaysia, Mali, Mauritania, Mexico, Mongolia, Morocco, Nepal, Netherlands, New Zealand, Nigeria, Norway, Pakistan, Peru, Philippines, Poland, Romania, Rwanda, Saudi Arabia, Senegal, Sierra Leone, Singapore, Somalia, Spain, Sudan, Swaziland, Sweden, Syrian Arab Republic, Thailand, Togo, Trinidad and Tobago, Tunisia, Turkey, Uganda, Ukrainian SSR, USSR, United Kingdom, United Republic of Tanzania, United States,

Upper Volta, Uruguay, Venezuela, Yemen, Yugoslavia, Zaire, Zambia.

Against: Portugal.

Abstaining: Brazil, Malawi.

A/SPC/146. Resolution adopted by Special Political Committee on 3 November 1971, meeting 766.

A/8504. Report of Special Political Committee (part I).

RESOLUTION 2764(XXVI), as recommended by Special Political Committee, A/8504, adopted by Assembly on 9 November 1971, meeting 1981, by recorded vote of 109 to 2, as follows:

In favour: Afghanistan, Algeria, Argentina, Australia, Austria, Belgium, Bolivia, Botswana, Brazil, Bulgaria, Burma, Burundi, Byelorussian SSR, Cameroon, Canada, Central African Republic, Ceylon, Chile, Colombia, Congo, Costa Rica, Cuba, Cyprus, Czechoslovakia, Dahomey, Denmark, Ecuador, Egypt, El Salvador, Equatorial Guinea, Ethiopia, Fiji, Finland, France, Gambia, Ghana, Greece, Guinea, Guyana, Haiti, Honduras, Hungary, Iceland, India, Indonesia, Iran, Iraq, Ireland, Israel, Italy, Ivory Coast, Jamaica, Japan, Jordan, Kenya, Khmer Republic, Kuwait, Laos, Lebanon, Lesotho, Liberia, Libyan Arab Republic, Luxembourg, Madagascar, Malaysia, Mali, Mauritius, Mexico, Mongolia, Morocco, Nepal, Netherlands, New Zealand, Nigeria, Norway, Oman, Pakistan, Panama, People's Democratic Republic of Yemen, Philippines, Poland, Romania, Senegal, Sierra Leone, Singapore, Somalia, Spain, Sudan, Swaziland, Sweden, Syrian Arab Republic, Thailand, Togo, Trinidad and Tobago, Tunisia, Turkey, Uganda, Ukrainian SSR, USSR, United Kingdom, United Republic of Tanzania, United States, Upper Volta, Uruguay, Venezuela, Yemen, Yugoslavia, Zaire, Zambia.

Against: Portugal, South Africa.

The General Assembly,

Recalling its resolution 2627(XXV) of 24 October 1970, strongly condemning the evil policy of *apartheid* as a crime against the conscience and dignity of mankind,

Further recalling its resolutions calling for the liberation of persons persecuted in South Africa for their opposition to *apartheid* and condemning the maltreatment and torture of prisoners and persons in police custody,

Taking note of the reports of the Special Committee on *Apartheid* and the *Ad Hoc* Working Group of Experts on the treatment of political prisoners in South Africa, established under resolution 2(XXIII) of the Commission on Human Rights of 6 March 1967,

Gravely concerned at continuing reports of ill-treatment and torture of opponents of *apartheid* in detention in South Africa and at the deaths of several detainees during interrogation,

Noting also the recent deportations, bannings, detentions and trials of a number of religious leaders in South Africa for their opposition to *apartheid* and assistance to victims of that inhuman policy,

1. *Expresses its grave indignation and concern* over any and every act of maltreatment and torture of opponents of *apartheid* in South Africa and the increased persecution of religious leaders opposed to that policy;

2. *Again calls upon* all States to do everything in their power to promote the cause of justice for all people in South Africa and, to that end, to exert their influence to secure:

(a) The repeal of all legislation designed to give effect to the oppressive policies of *apartheid* and all legislation designed to persecute and suppress the rights of those who are opposed to such policies;

(b) The liberation of all persons imprisoned or detained for their opposition to *apartheid*;

(c) The removal of orders against those banned or banished for their opposition to *apartheid*;

3. *Appeals* to national and international associations of jurists to take all appropriate steps in support of the purposes of the present resolution;

4. *Urges* all religious organizations to continue and intensify their efforts for the elimination of *apartheid* and racial discrimination;

5. *Requests* the Special Committee on *Apartheid* to prepare a special report on all known cases of maltreatment and torture of prisoners in South Africa, together with any other information pertinent to those cases;

6. *Invites* all organizations and individuals that may have knowledge of such cases to provide all available information to the Special Committee on *Apartheid*;

7. *Requests* the Secretary-General:

(a) To bring the present resolution to the attention of Governments, national and international organizations and anti-*apartheid* movements, including religious organizations and associations of jurists;

(b) To publicize, through the Unit on *Apartheid* and the Office of Public Information, all available information on the maltreatment and torture of prisoners and detainees in South Africa and the persecution of opponents of *apartheid*, including religious leaders;

(c) To provide necessary services and assistance to the Special Committee on *Apartheid* in the preparation of the report requested in paragraph 5 above and to publicize the report as widely as possible.

A/SPC/145 (S/10354). Letter of 6 October 1971 from Chairman of Special Committee on *Apartheid*.

A/SPC/L.208. Afghanistan, Algeria, Burundi, Cameroon, Colombia, Congo, Cyprus, Czechoslovakia, Egypt, Ethiopia, Gambia, Ghana, Guatemala, Guinea, Guyana, Hungary, India, Indonesia, Kenya, Liberia, Libyan Arab Republic, Malaysia, Mali, Mauritania, Mongolia, Morocco, Nepal, Nigeria, Pakistan, People's Democratic Republic of Yemen, Philippines, Rwanda, Senegal, Sierra Leone, Singapore, Somalia, Sudan, Syrian Arab Republic, Togo, Tunisia, Uganda, Ukrainian SSR, United Republic of Tanzania, Upper Volta, Yemen, Yugoslavia, Zambia: draft resolution, as amended by Sierra Leone, A/SPC/L.217, approved by Special Political Committee on 15 November 1971, meeting 778, by roll-call vote of 87 to 1, with 6 abstentions, as follows:

In favour: Afghanistan, Algeria, Argentina, Austria, Botswana, Brazil, Bulgaria, Burma, Burundi, Byelorussian SSR, Cameroon, Canada, Central African Republic, Ceylon, Chile, Colombia, Congo, Costa Rica, Cuba, Cyprus, Czechoslovakia, Denmark, Ecuador, Egypt, El Salvador, Ethiopia, Finland, Gambia, Ghana, Greece, Guatemala, Guinea, Guyana, Hungary, India, Indonesia, Iran, Iraq, Ireland, Israel, Italy, Ivory Coast, Jamaica, Japan, Kenya, Kuwait, Lebanon, Liberia, Libyan Arab Republic, Luxembourg, Malaysia, Mali, Mauritania, Mexico, Mongolia, Morocco, Nepal, Netherlands, Nigeria, Norway, People's Democratic Republic of Yemen, Peru , Philippines, Poland, Romania, Rwanda, Saudi Arabia, Senegal, Sierra Leone, Somalia, Spain, Sudan, Sweden, Syrian Arab Republic, Thailand, Togo, Trinidad and Tobago, Tunisia, Turkey, Ukrainian SSR, USSR, Upper Volta, Venezuela, Yemen, Yugoslavia, Zaire, Zambia.

Against: Portugal.

Abstaining: Australia, Belgium, France, New Zealand, United Kingdom, United States.

A/SPC/L.217. Sierra Leone: amendment to 47-power draft resolution, A/SPC/L.208.

A/8504/Add.1. Report of Special Political Committee (part II), draft resolution II A.

RESOLUTION 2775 A(XXVI), as recommended by Special Political Committee, A/8504/Add.1, adopted by Assembly on 29 November 1971, meeting 1997, by recorded vote of 107 to 2, with 5 abstentions, as follows:

In favour: Afghanistan, Albania, Algeria, Argentina, Austria, Bahrain, Barbados, Belgium, Bolivia, Botswana, Brazil, Bulgaria, Burma, Burundi, Byelorussian SSR, Cameroon, Canada, Central African Republic, Chad, Chile, China, Colombia, Congo,

Costa Rica, Cuba, Cyprus, Czechoslovakia, Dahomey, Denmark, Ecuador, Egypt, El Salvador, Equatorial Guinea, Ethiopia, Fiji, Finland, Gabon, Gambia, Ghana, Greece, Guatemala, Guinea, Guyana, Haiti, Honduras, Hungary, India, Indonesia, Iran, Iraq, Ireland, Israel, Italy, Ivory Coast, Jamaica, Japan, Jordan, Kenya, Khmer Republic, Kuwait, Libyan Arab Republic, Luxembourg, Madagascar, Malaysia, Mali, Mauritania, Mauritius, Mongolia, Morocco, Nepal, Netherlands, New Zealand, Niger, Nigeria, Norway, Panama, Paraguay, People's Democratic Republic of Yemen, Peru, Philippines, Poland, Qatar, Romania, Rwanda, Saudi Arabia, Senegal, Sierra Leone, Singapore, Somalia, Spain, Sudan, Sweden, Syrian Arab Republic, Thailand, Togo, Trinidad and Tobago, Tunisia, Turkey, Uganda, Ukrainian SSR, USSR, United Republic of Tanzania, Upper Volta, Uruguay, Venezuela, Yugoslavia, Zambia.

Against: Portugal, South Africa.

Abstaining: Australia, France, Malawi, United Kingdom, United States.

The General Assembly,

Taking note of the report of the Special Committee on *Apartheid* and the letter dated 6 October 1971 from the Chairman of the Special Committee to the President of the General Assembly,

Recalling its resolution 2624(XXV) of 13 October 1970 calling upon all States to take immediate steps to implement fully the provisions of Security Council resolution 282(1970) of 23 July 1970 to strengthen the arms embargo against South Africa,

Gravely concerned at the continued build-up of the South African military and police forces,

Noting that South Africa continues to receive military equipment, and technical and other assistance for the manufacture of such equipment, from certain Member States in contravention of the arms embargo,

1. *Reaffirms* its resolution 2624(XXV);

2. *Declares* that the arms embargo against South Africa makes no distinction between arms for external defence and arms for internal repression;

3. *Deplores* the actions of those Governments which, in contravention of the arms embargo, have provided or have allowed companies registered in their countries to provide assistance for the build-up of the military and police forces in South Africa;

4. *Calls upon* all Governments to implement fully the arms embargo against South Africa;

5. *Urgently appeals* to all national and international organizations to discourage and denounce all military collaboration with South Africa and to ensure the implementation of the Security Council resolutions on the arms embargo against South Africa;

6. *Invites* the Security Council to consider the situation in the light of the reports and communications addressed to it by the Special Committee on *Apartheid* and of the present resolution, with a view to securing the full implementation by all States of Council resolution 282(1970);

7. *Requests* the Special Committee on *Apartheid* to undertake a comprehensive study of the military collaboration with, and military assistance to, South Africa by Governments and private enterprises and to submit a report thereon to the General Assembly at its twenty-seventh session.

A/SPC/L.209. Afghanistan, Algeria, Burundi, Cameroon, Chile, Colombia, Congo, Denmark, Egypt, Ethiopia, Gambia, Ghana, Guatemala, Guinea, India, Indonesia, Iran, Ireland, Kenya, Libyan Arab Republic, Madagascar, Malaysia, Mali, Nepal, Nigeria, Norway, Pakistan, People's Democratic Republic of Yemen, Philippines, Senegal, Sierra Leone, Somalia, Sudan, Sweden, Syrian Arab Republic, Togo, Trinidad and Tobago, Tunisia, United Republic of Tanzania, Upper Volta, Uruguay, Venezuela, Yemen, Yugoslavia, Zambia: draft resolution.

A/SPC/L.209/Rev.1. Afghanistan, Algeria, Burundi, Cameroon, Chile, Colombia, Congo, Costa Rica, Denmark, Egypt, Ethiopia, Gambia, Ghana, Guatemala, Guinea, Guyana, Hungary, India, Indonesia, Iran, Ireland, Kenya, Liberia, Libyan Arab Republic, Madagascar, Malaysia, Mali, Mauritania, Morocco, Nepal, New

Zealand, Niger, Nigeria, Norway, Pakistan, People's Democratic Republic of Yemen, Philippines, Senegal, Sierra Leone, Singapore, Somalia, Sudan, Sweden, Syrian Arab Republic, Togo, Trinidad and Tobago, Tunisia, Uganda, Ukrainian SSR, United Republic of Tanzania, Upper Volta, Uruguay, Venezuela, Yemen, Yugoslavia, Zambia: revised draft resolution.

A/SPC/L.209/Rev.2. Revised draft resolution, sponsored by above 56 powers and by Iceland, Jamaica and Rwanda, approved by Special Political Committee on 15 November 1971, meeting 778, by roll-call vote of 97 to 0, with 2 abstentions, as follows:

In favour: Afghanistan, Algeria, Argentina, Australia, Austria, Belgium, Botswana, Brazil, Bulgaria, Burma, Burundi, Byelorussian SSR, Cameroon, Canada, Central African Republic, Ceylon, Chile, Colombia, Congo, Costa Rica, Cuba, Cyprus, Czechoslovakia, Denmark, Ecuador, Egypt, El Salvador, Ethiopia, Finland, France, Gambia, Ghana, Greece, Guatemala, Guinea, Guyana, Hungary, Iceland, India, Indonesia, Iran, Iraq, Ireland, Israel, Italy, Ivory Coast, Jamaica, Japan, Kenya, Kuwait, Lebanon, Liberia, Libyan Arab Republic, Luxembourg, Madagascar, Malaysia, Mali, Mauritania, Mexico, Mongolia, Morocco, Nepal, Netherlands, New Zealand, Nicaragua, Nigeria, Norway, People's Democratic Republic of Yemen, Peru, Philippines, Poland, Romania, Rwanda, Saudi Arabia, Senegal, Sierra Leone, Singapore, Somalia, Spain, Sudan, Swaziland, Sweden, Syrian Arab Republic, Thailand, Togo, Trinidad and Tobago, Tunisia, Turkey, Ukrainian SSR, USSR, United States, Upper Volta, Venezuela, Yemen, Yugoslavia, Zaire, Zambia.

Against: None.

Abstaining: Portugal, United Kingdom.

A/8504/Add.1. Report of Special Political Committee (part II), draft resolution II B.

RESOLUTION 2775B(XXVI), as recommended by Special Political Committee, A/8504/Add.1, adopted by Assembly on 29 November 1971, meeting 1997, by recorded of 112 to 1, with 3 abstentions, as follows:

In favour: Afghanistan, Albania, Algeria, Argentina, Australia, Austria, Bahrain, Barbados, Belgium, Bolivia, Botswana, Brazil, Bulgaria, Burma, Burundi, Byelorussian SSR, Cameroon, Canada, Central African Republic, Chad, Chile, China, Colombia, Congo, Costa Rica, Cuba, Cyprus, Czechoslovakia, Dahomey, Denmark, Dominican Republic, Ecuador, Egypt, El Salvador, Equatorial Guinea, Ethiopia, Fiji, Finland, France, Gabon, Gambia, Ghana, Greece, Guatemala, Guinea, Guyana, Haiti, Honduras, Hungary, India, Indonesia, Iran, Iraq, Ireland, Israel, Italy, Ivory Coast, Jamaica, Japan, Jordan, Kenya, Khmer Republic, Kuwait, Libyan Arab Republic, Luxembourg, Madagascar, Malaysia, Mali, Mauritania, Mauritius, Mongolia, Morocco, Nepal, Netherlands, New Zealand, Niger, Nigeria, Norway, Panama, Paraguay, People's Democratic Republic of Yemen, Peru, Philippines, Poland, Qatar, Romania, Rwanda, Saudi Arabia, Senegal, Sierra Leone, Singapore, Somalia, Spain, Sudan, Swaziland, Sweden, Syrian Arab Republic, Thailand, Togo, Trinidad and Tobago, Tunisia, Turkey, Uganda, Ukrainian SSR, USSR, United Republic of Tanzania, United States, Upper Volta, Uruguay, Venezuela, Yugoslavia, Zambia.

Against: South Africa.

Abstaining: Malawi, Portugal, United Kingdom.

The General Assembly,

Considering that the International Year for Action to Combat Racism and Racial Discrimination should be the occasion to add new emphasis to efforts to enlighten the international community about the evils of *apartheid* and racial discrimination in South Africa and about the role of the United Nations in this cause,

Convinced of the special role that education should play in international efforts to eliminate *apartheid* and other forms of racial discrimination,

Considering the important role of the United Nations Educational, Scientific and Cultural Organization in such a cause,

Commending the activities of the United Nations Educational, Scientific and Cultural Organization in disseminating information on *apartheid*, with special reference to its effects on education, science and culture,

Taking note of the report of the Special Committee on Apartheid, in particular the account of its consultations with anti-*apartheid* movements and with the United Nations Educational, Scientific and Cultural Organization concerning the need for the preparation of an educational kit on southern Africa,

Noting with satisfaction the growing interest among educational and other institutions in educational material to enlighten their students on the evils of *apartheid* and racial discrimination,

1. *Commends* the proposal for the preparation of an educational kit on racial discrimination and *apartheid* in southern Africa;

2. *Requests* the United Nations Educational, Scientific and Cultural Organization to prepare such an educational kit for possible adaptation by national commissions of that organization and for distribution to institutions of learning;

3. *Further requests* the United Nations Educational, Scientific and Cultural Organization to consider the production of films and audio-visual material on *apartheid*, with special reference to its adverse effects on education, science and culture;

4. *Invites* all concerned to lend their full co-operation to the United Nations Educational, Scientific and Cultural Organization to ensure the widest possible use of the material prepared by that organization.

A/SPC/L.210. Afghanistan, Algeria, Cameroon, Congo, Egypt, Gambia, Ghana, Guinea, Hungary, India, Indonesia, Kenya, Liberia, Libyan Arab Republic, Madagascar, Malaysia, Mali, Mauritania, Morocco, Nepal, Niger, Nigeria, Pakistan, People's Democratic Republic of Yemen, Philippines, Senegal, Sierra Leone, Singapore, Somalia, Sudan, Syrian Arab Republic, Trinidad and Tobago, Tunisia, Uganda, Ukrainian SSR, United Republic of Tanzania, Yemen, Zambia: draft resolution, approved by Special Political Committee on 15 November 1971, meeting 778, by 89 votes to 0, with 4 abstentions.

A/SPC/L.216. Administrative and financial implications of 38-power draft resolution, A/SPC/L.210. Statement by Secretary-General.

A/C.5/1403, A/8408/Add.12, A/8534. Administrative and financial implications of draft resolutions II C, II G and II H recommended by Special Political Committee in A/8504/Add.1. Statement by Secretary-General and reports of Advisory Committee on Administrative and Budgetary Questions (ACABQ) and Fifth Committee.

A/8504/Add.1. Report of Special Political Committee (part II), draft resolution II C.

RESOLUTION 2775C(XXVI), as recommended by Special Political Committee, A/8504/Add.1, adopted by Assembly on 29 November 1971, meeting 1997, by recorded vote of 108 to 1, with 5 abstentions, as follows:

In favour: Afghanistan, Albania, Algeria, Argentina, Australia, Austria, Bahrain, Barbados, Belgium, Bolivia, Botswana, Brazil, Bulgaria, Burma, Burundi, Byelorussian SSR, Cameroon, Canada, Central African Republic, Chad, Chile, China, Colombia, Congo, Costa Rica, Cuba, Cyprus, Czechoslovakia, Dahomey, Denmark, Ecuador, Egypt, El Salvador, Equatorial Guinea, Ethiopia, Fiji, Finland, Gabon, Gambia, Ghana, Greece, Guatemala, Guinea, Guyana, Haiti, Honduras, Hungary, India, Indonesia, Iran, Iraq, Ireland, Israel, Italy, Ivory Coast, Jamaica, Japan, Jordan, Kenya, Khmer Republic, Kuwait, Luxembourg, Madagascar, Malaysia, Mali, Mauritania, Mauritius, Mongolia, Morocco, Nepal, Netherlands, New Zealand, Niger, Nigeria, Norway, Panama, Paraguay, People's Democratic Republic of Yemen, Peru, Philippines, Poland, Qatar, Romania, Rwanda, Saudi Arabia, Senegal, Sierra Leone, Singapore, Somalia, Spain, Sudan, Swaziland, Sweden, Syrian Arab Republic, Thailand, Togo, Trinidad and Tobago, Tunisia, Turkey, Uganda, Ukrainian SSR, USSR, United Republic of Tanzania, Upper Volta, Uruguay, Venezuela, Yugoslavia, Zambia.

Against: South Africa.

Abstaining: France, Malawi, Portugal, United Kingdom, United States.

The General Assembly,
Noting with appreciation the work of the Special Committee on *Apartheid* in pursuance of General Assembly resolution 2671(XXV) of 8 December 1970,
Considering that further efforts should be made to intensify the international campaign against *apartheid*,
Endorsing the programme of work of the Special Committee on *Apartheid* contained in its report,
Authorizes the Special Committee on *Apartheid*, within the budgetary provisions to be made for this purpose:
(a) To send representatives or delegations, as appropriate, to international conferences dealing with the problem of *apartheid*;
(b) To hold consultations with experts and representatives of the oppressed people of South Africa, as well as anti-*apartheid* movements and non-governmental organizations concerned with the campaign against *apartheid*.

A/SPC/L.211. Afghanistan, Algeria, Burundi, Cameroon, Congo, Cyprus, Egypt, Ethiopia, Gambia, Ghana, Guatemala, Guinea, Guyana, Hungary, India, Indonesia, Iran, Kenya, Liberia, Libyan Arab Republic, Malaysia, Mali, Mauritania, Mongolia, Morocco, Nepal, Niger, Nigeria, Pakistan, People's Democratic Republic of Yemen, Philippines, Rwanda, Senegal, Sierra Leone, Singapore, Somalia, Sudan, Syrian Arab Republic, Togo, Trinidad and Tobago, Tunisia, Uganda, Ukrainian SSR, United Republic of Tanzania, Upper Volta, Uruguay, Yemen, Yugoslavia, Zambia: draft resolution, approved by Special Political Committee on 15 November 1971, meeting 778, by roll-call vote of 91 to 0, with 8 abstentions, as follows:

In favour: Afghanistan, Algeria, Argentina, Austria, Belgium, Botswana, Brazil, Bulgaria, Burma, Burundi, Byelorussian SSR, Cameroon, Canada, Ceylon, Chile, Colombia, Congo, Costa Rica, Cuba, Cyprus, Czechoslovakia, Denmark, Ecuador, Egypt, El Salvador, Ethiopia, Finland, Gambia, Ghana, Guatemala, Guinea, Guyana, Hungary, Iceland, India, Indonesia, Iran, Iraq, Ireland, Israel, Italy, Ivory Coast, Japan, Kenya, Kuwait, Lebanon, Liberia, Libyan Arab Republic, Luxembourg, Malaysia, Mali, Mauritania, Mexico, Mongolia, Morocco, Nepal, Netherlands, Nicaragua, Nigeria, Norway, People's Democratic Republic of Yemen, Peru, Philippines, Poland, Romania, Rwanda, Saudi Arabia, Senegal, Sierra Leone, Singapore, Somalia, Spain, Sudan, Swaziland, Sweden, Syrian Arab Republic, Thailand, Togo, Trinidad and Tobago, Tunisia, Turkey, Ukrainian SSR, USSR, United States, Upper Volta, Venezuela, Yemen, Yugoslavia, Zaire, Zambia.
Against: None.
Abstaining: Australia, Central African Republic, France, Greece, Madagascar, New Zealand, Portugal, United Kingdom.

A/8504/Add.1. Report of Special Political Committee (part II), draft resolution II D.

RESOLUTION 2775D(XXVI), as recommended by Special Political Committee, A/8504/Add.1, adopted by Assembly on 29 November 1971, meeting 1997, by recorded vote of 106 to 2, with 7 abstentions, as follows:

In favour: Afghanistan, Albania, Algeria, Argentina, Austria, Bahrain, Barbados, Belgium, Bolivia, Botswana, Brazil, Bulgaria, Burma, Burundi, Byelorussian SSR, Cameroon, Canada, Chad, Chile, China, Colombia, Congo, Costa Rica, Cuba, Cyprus, Czechoslovakia, Dahomey, Denmark, Dominican Republic, Ecuador, Egypt, El Salvador, Equatorial Guinea, Ethiopia, Finland, Gabon, Gambia, Ghana, Guatemala, Guinea, Guyana, Haiti, Honduras, Hungary, India, Indonesia, Iran, Iraq, Ireland, Israel, Italy, Ivory Coast, Jamaica, Japan, Jordan, Kenya, Khmer Republic, Kuwait, Libyan Arab Republic, Luxembourg, Malaysia, Mali, Mauritania, Mauritius, Mongolia, Morocco, Nepal, Netherlands, Niger, Nigeria, Norway, Pakistan, Panama, Paraguay,

People's Democratic Republic of Yemen, Peru, Philippines, Poland, Qatar, Romania, Rwanda, Saudi Arabia, Senegal, Sierra Leone, Singapore, Somalia, Spain, Sudan, Swaziland, Sweden, Syrian Arab Republic, Thailand, Togo, Trinidad and Tobago, Tunisia, Turkey, Uganda, Ukrainian SSR, USSR, United Republic of Tanzania, United States, Upper Volta, Uruguay, Venezuela, Yugoslavia, Zambia.
Against: Malawi, South Africa.
Abstaining: Australia, Central African Republic, Greece, Madagascar, New Zealand, Portugal, United Kingdom.

The General Assembly,
Recalling that Member States have pledged themselves, under Article 1 of the Charter of the United Nations, to promote and encourage respect for human rights and for fundamental freedoms for all without distinction as to race, sex, language or religion,
Recalling further its request to all States and national and international sports organizations to suspend exchanges of sporting events with South African teams selected under *apartheid* policies,
Bearing in mind that 1971 was designated as the International Year for Action to Combat Racism and Racial Discrimination, to be observed in the name of the ever-growing struggle against racial discrimination in all its forms and manifestations and in the name of international solidarity with those struggling against racism,
1. *Declares* its unqualified support of the Olympic principle that no discrimination be allowed on the grounds of race, religion or political affiliation;
2. *Affirms* that merit should be the sole criterion for participation in sports activities;
3. *Solemnly calls upon* all national and international sports organizations to uphold the Olympic principle of non-discrimination and to discourage and deny support to sporting events organized in violation of this principle;
4. *Calls upon* individual sportsmen to refuse to participate in any sports activity in a country in which there is an official policy of racial discrimination or *apartheid* in the field of sports;
5. *Urges* all States to promote adherence to the Olympic principle of non-discrimination and to encourage their sports organizations to withhold support from sporting events organized in violation of this principle;
6. *Requests* national and international sports organizations and the public to deny any form of recognition to any sports activity from which persons are debarred or in which they are subjected to any discrimination on the basis of race, religion or political affiliation;
7. *Condemns* the actions of the Government of South Africa in enforcing racial discrimination and segregation in sports;
8. *Notes with regret* that some national and international sports organizations have continued exchanges with teams from South Africa that have been selected for international competition on the basis of competition closed to otherwise qualified sportsmen solely on the basis of their race, colour, descent or national or ethnic origin;
9. *Commends* those international and national sports organizations that have supported the international campaign against *apartheid* in sports;
10. *Requests* all States to urge their national sports organizations to act in accordance with the present resolution;
11. *Requests* the Secretary-General:
(a) To bring the present resolution to the attention of international sports organizations;
(b) To keep the Special Committee on *Apartheid* informed on the implementation of the present resolution;
(c) To submit a report on this matter to the General Assembly at its twenty-seventh session.

A/SPC/L.212. Afghanistan, Algeria, Cameroon, Congo, Cyprus, Czechoslovakia, Egypt, Ethiopia, Gambia, Ghana, Guinea, Guyana, Hungary, India, Indonesia, Kenya, Libyan Arab Republic, Malaysia, Mali, Mauritania, Mongolia, Morocco, Nepal, Niger, Nigeria, Pakistan, People's Democratic Republic of Yemen, Rwanda, Senegal, Sierra Leone, Singapore, Somalia,

Sudan, Syrian Arab Republic, Togo, Trinidad and Tobago, Uganda, Ukrainian SSR, United Republic of Tanzania, Upper Volta, Yemen, Yugoslavia, Zambia: draft resolution.

A/SPC/L.212/Rev.1. Revised draft resolution, sponsored by above 43 powers and by Bulgaria, Burundi and the Philippines, as further amended by Ghana (A/SPC/L.215) and Sierra Leone (A/SPC/L.218), approved by Special Political Committee on 15 November 1971, meeting 779, by roll-call vote of 99 to 1, with 3 abstentions, as follows:

In favour: Afghanistan, Algeria, Argentina, Austria, Botswana, Brazil, Bulgaria, Burma, Burundi, Byelorussian SSR, Cameroon, Canada, Central African Republic, Ceylon, Chile, Colombia, Congo, Cuba, Cyprus, Czechoslovakia, Denmark, Ecuador, Egypt, El Salvador, Ethiopia, Finland, France, Gambia, Ghana, Greece, Guatemala, Guinea, Guyana, Honduras, Hungary, Iceland, India, Indonesia, Iran, Iraq, Ireland, Israel, Italy, Ivory Coast, Jamaica, Japan, Jordan, Kenya, Khmer Republic, Kuwait, Lebanon, Liberia, Libyan Arab Republic, Luxembourg, Madagascar, Malaysia, Mauritania, Mexico, Mongolia, Morocco, Nepal, Netherlands, New Zealand, Nicaragua, Niger, Nigeria, Norway, Pakistan, People's Democratic Republic of Yemen, Philippines, Poland, Romania, Rwanda, Saudi Arabia, Senegal, Sierra Leone, Singapore, Somalia, Spain, Sudan, Swaziland, Sweden, Syrian Arab Republic, Thailand, Togo, Trinidad and Tobago, Tunisia, Turkey, Uganda, Ukrainian SSR, USSR, United Republic of Tanzania, United States, Upper Volta, Venezuela, Yemen, Yugoslavia, Zaire, Zambia.

Against: Portugal.

Abstaining: Australia, Belgium, United Kingdom.

A/SPC/L.215. Ghana: amendment to 43-power draft resolution, A/SPC/L.212.

A/SPC/L.218. Sierra Leone: amendment to 43-power draft resolution, A/SPC/L.212.

A/8504/Add.1. Report of Special Political Committee (part II), draft resolution II E.

RESOLUTION 2775 E (XXVI), as recommended by Special Political Committee, A/8504/Add.1, adopted by Assembly on 29 November 1971, meeting 1997, by recorded vote of 110 to 2, with 2 abstentions, as follows:

In favour: Afghanistan, Albania, Algeria, Argentina, Australia, Austria, Bahrain, Barbados, Belgium, Bolivia, Botswana, Brazil, Bulgaria, Burma, Burundi, Byelorussian SSR, Cameroon, Canada, Central African Republic, Chile, China, Colombia, Congo, Costa Rica, Cuba, Cyprus, Czechoslovakia, Dahomey, Denmark, Dominican Republic, Ecuador, Egypt, El Salvador, Equatorial Guinea, Ethiopia, Fiji, Finland, Gabon, Gambia, Ghana, Greece, Guatemala, Guinea, Guyana, Haiti, Honduras, Hungary, India, Indonesia, Iran, Iraq, Ireland, Israel, Italy, Ivory Coast, Jamaica, Japan, Jordan, Kenya, Khmer Republic, Kuwait, Libyan Arab Republic, Luxembourg, Madagascar, Malaysia, Mali, Mauritania, Mauritius, Mongolia, Morocco, Nepal, Netherlands, New Zealand, Niger, Nigeria, Norway, Pakistan, Panama, Paraguay, People's Democratic Republic of Yemen, Peru, Philippines, Poland, Qatar, Romania, Rwanda, Saudi Arabia, Senegal, Sierra Leone, Singapore, Somalia, Spain, Sudan, Sweden, Syrian Arab Republic, Thailand, Togo, Trinidad and Tobago, Tunisia, Turkey, Uganda, Ukrainian SSR, USSR, United Republic of Tanzania, United States, Upper Volta, Uruguay, Venezuela, Yugoslavia, Zambia.

Against: Portugal, South Africa.

Abstaining: France, United Kingdom.

The General Assembly,

Recalling its resolution 103(I) of 19 November 1946 declaring that it is in the higher interests of humanity to put an immediate end to racial persecution and discrimination, and its resolution 395(V) of 2 December 1950, in which the General Assembly considered that a policy of "racial segregation" (*apartheid*) is necessarily based on doctrines of racial discrimination,

Recalling further its resolution 616B(VII) of 5 December 1952 declaring that in a multiracial society harmony and respect for human rights and freedoms and the peaceful development of a unified community are best assured when patterns of legislation and practice are directed towards ensuring equality before the law of all persons regardless of race, creed or colour, and when economic, social, cultural and political participation of all racial groups is on a basis of equality,

Noting that the Government of South Africa, while treating the white inhabitants of that country, irrespective of their national origins, as constituting one nation, seeks artificially to divide the African people into "nations" according to their tribal origins and justifies the establishment of non-contiguous Bantu homelands (Bantustans) on that basis,

Recognizing that the real purpose of the establishment of Bantustans is to divide the Africans, setting one tribe against the other with a view to weakening the African front in its struggle for its inalienable and just rights,

Having regard to the subsequent resolutions adopted by the General Assembly and the Security Council on the policies of *apartheid* of the Government of South Africa, and in particular General Assembly resolution 2671(XXV) of 8 December 1970,

Recalling its resolution 95(I) of 11 December 1946, in which it affirmed the principles of international law recognized by the Charter of the International Military Tribunal, Nuremberg, and the judgement of the Tribunal,

Bearing in mind the obligations of all States under international law, the Charter of the United Nations, the human rights principles and the Geneva Conventions of 12 August 1949,

Noting further that under the aforementioned resolution crimes against humanity are committed when enslavement, deportation and other inhuman acts are enforced against any civilian population on political, racial or religious grounds,

Noting that many African communities have been uprooted and that large numbers of Africans have been forcibly removed from their homes in pursuance of the policies of *apartheid,*

Considering that the establishment of Bantustans and other measures adopted by the Government of South Africa in pursuance of *apartheid* are designed to consolidate and perpetuate domination by a white minority and the dispossession and exploitation of the African and other non-white people of South Africa, as well as of Namibia,

1. *Again condemns* the establishment by the Government of South Africa of Bantu homelands (Bantustans) and the forcible removal of the African people of South Africa and Namibia to those areas as a violation of their inalienable rights, contrary to the principle of self-determination and prejudicial to the territorial integrity of the countries and the unity of their peoples;

2. *Declares* that the United Nations will continue to encourage and promote a solution to the situation in South Africa through the full application of human rights and fundamental freedoms, including political rights, to all inhabitants of the territory of South Africa as a whole, regardless of race, colour or creed;

3. *Decides* to keep the situation in South Africa constantly under review.

A/8388. Report of Secretary-General (transmitting consensus adopted on 13 September 1971 by joint meeting of Special Committee on *Apartheid,* Special Committee on Situation with regard to Implementation of Declaration on Granting Independence to Colonial Countries and Peoples and United Nations Council for Namibia).

A/SPC/L.214. Afghanistan, Algeria, Burundi, Cameroon, Congo, Egypt, Ethiopia, Guinea, India, Kenya, Kuwait, Libyan Arab Republic, Mali, Mauritania, Nepal, Nigeria, Pakistan, People's Democratic Republic of Yemen, Somalia, Sudan, Syrian Arab Republic, Togo, Uganda, Yemen, Yugoslavia, Zambia: draft resolution.

A/SPC/L.214/Rev.1. Revised draft resolution, sponsored by above 26 powers and by United Republic of Tanzania, as orally amended by Lebanon, approved by Special Political Committee on 15 November 1971, meeting 779, by roll-call vote of 76 to 6, with 21 abstentions, as follows:

In favour: Afghanistan, Algeria, Botswana, Brazil, Bulgaria, Burma, Burundi, Byelorussian SSR, Cameroon, Ceylon, Chile, Colombia, Congo, Costa Rica, Cuba, Cyprus, Czechoslovakia, Ecuador, Egypt, Ethiopia, Gambia, Ghana, Greece, Guinea, Guyana, Hungary, Iceland, India, Indonesia, Iran, Iraq, Ireland, Israel, Jamaica, Jordan, Kenya, Kuwait, Lebanon, Liberia, Libyan Arab Republic, Malaysia, Mali, Mauritania, Mexico, Mongolia, Morocco, Nepal, Niger, Nigeria, Pakistan, People's Democratic Republic of Yemen, Philippines, Poland, Romania, Rwanda, Saudi Arabia, Sierra Leone, Singapore, Somalia, Sudan, Syrian Arab Republic, Thailand, Togo, Trinidad and Tobago, Tunisia, Turkey, Uganda, Ukrainian SSR, USSR, United Republic of Tanzania, Upper Volta, Venezuela, Yemen, Yugoslavia, Zaire, Zambia.

Against: Australia, Belgium, France, Portugal, United Kingdom, United States.

Abstaining: Argentina, Austria, Canada, Central African Republic, Denmark, El Salvador, Finland, Guatemala, Honduras, Italy, Ivory Coast, Japan, Luxembourg, Madagascar, Malawi, Netherlands, New Zealand, Nicaragua, Norway, Spain, Sweden.

A/SPC L.220. Sierra Leone: amendments to 26-power draft resolution, A/SPC/L.214.

A/SPC/L.221. Cameroon: amendment to 26-power draft resolution, A/SPC/L.214.

A/8504/Add.1. Report of Special Political Committee (part II), draft resolution II F.

RESOLUTION 2775 F (XXVI), as recommended by Special Political Committee, A/8504/Add.1, adopted by Assembly on 29 November 1971, meeting 1997, by recorded vote of 86 to 6, with 22 abstentions, as follows:

In favour: Afghanistan, Albania, Algeria, Bahrain, Barbados, Bolivia, Botswana, Brazil, Bulgaria, Burma, Burundi, Byelorussian SSR, Cameroon, Chad, Chile, China, Colombia, Congo, Costa Rica, Cuba, Cyprus, Czechoslovakia, Dahomey, Ecuador, Egypt, Equatorial Guinea, Ethiopia, Gabon, Gambia, Ghana, Greece, Guinea, Guyana, Haiti, Hungary, India, Indonesia, Iran, Iraq, Ireland, Israel, Jamaica, Jordan, Kenya, Kuwait, Libyan Arab Republic, Malaysia, Mali, Mauritania, Mauritius, Mongolia, Morocco, Nepal, Niger, Nigeria, Pakistan, Panama, Paraguay, People's Democratic Republic of Yemen, Peru, Philippines, Poland, Qatar, Romania, Rwanda, Saudi Arabia, Senegal, Sierra Leone, Singapore, Somalia, Sudan, Syrian Arab Republic, Thailand, Togo, Trinidad and Tobago, Tunisia, Turkey, Uganda, Ukrainian SSR, USSR, United Republic of Tanzania, Upper Volta, Uruguay, Venezuela, Yugoslavia, Zambia.

Against: Australia, France, Portugal, South Africa, United Kingdom, United States.

Abstaining: Argentina, Austria, Belgium, Canada, Central African Republic, Denmark, Dominican Republic, El Salvador, Finland, Guatemala, Honduras, Italy, Ivory Coast, Japan, Luxembourg, Madagascar, Malawi, Netherlands, New Zealand, Norway, Spain, Sweden.

The General Assembly,

Recalling its resolutions and those of the Security Council on the question of *apartheid*,

Taking note of the report of the Special Committee on *Apartheid*,

Taking note of Economic and Social Council resolution 1591(L) of 21 May 1971,

Taking note also of the report of the Secretary-General on the joint meeting of the Special Committee on *Apartheid*, the Special Committee on the Situation with regard to the Implementation of the Declaration on the Granting of Independence to Colonial Countries and Peoples and the United Nations Council for Namibia, convened by him in pursuance of General Assembly resolution 2671 F (XXV) of 8 December 1970, and the consensus adopted by the joint meeting, which is annexed to that report,

Considering that the United Nations organs concerned should adopt a concerted and co-ordinated approach to the interrelated problems of southern Africa,

Gravely concerned over the explosive situation in South Africa and in southern Africa as a whole resulting from the inhuman and aggressive policies of *apartheid* pursued by the Government of South Africa,

Considering that the United Nations and Member States should intensify their efforts to solve the situation in South Africa in accordance with the principles of the Charter of the United Nations and the Declaration on the Granting of Independence to Colonial Countries and Peoples,

1. *Reaffirms* its resolution 2671(XXV);

2. *Commends* all States, organizations and individuals struggling against *apartheid* and racial discrimination, especially in South Africa;

3. *Declares* that the present tactics of the racist Government of South Africa in pursuance of its so-called "outward policy" are designed primarily to obtain acquiescence in its racial policies, to confuse world public opinion, to counter international isolation, to hinder assistance to the liberation movements by the international community and to consolidate white minority rule in southern Africa;

4. *Condemns* the continued and increasing co-operation of certain States and foreign economic interests with South Africa in the military, economic, political and other fields, as such co-operation encourages the Government of South Africa in the pursuit of its inhuman policies;

5. *Reaffirms* the legitimacy of the struggle of the oppressed people of South Africa to eliminate, by all means at their disposal, *apartheid*, racial discrimination and similar ideologies and to attain majority rule in the country as a whole, based on universal adult suffrage;

6. *Appeals* to Governments, the specialized agencies, national and international organizations and individuals to provide every assistance, directly or through the Assistance Fund for the Struggle against Colonialism and *Apartheid* of the Organization of African Unity, to the national movement of the oppressed people of South Africa in their legitimate struggle;

7. *Reaffirms* the determination of the United Nations to intensify its efforts to remedy the grave situation in southern Africa and to ensure the achievement of the legitimate rights of all the inhabitants of that area, irrespective of race, colour or creed;

8. *Requests* all States to take more effective action for the elimination of *apartheid* in the light of the recommendations contained in the previous resolutions of the General Assembly and the Security Council;

9. *Requests* all States to take steps to dissuade their nationals from emigrating to South Africa so long as the Government of South Africa pursues the policies of *apartheid*;

10. *Commends* the activities of States, organizations and individuals engaged in dissuading economic interests from increasing collaboration with South Africa and profiting from racial discrimination and exploitation of African and other non-white workers;

11. *Requests* the Special Committee on *Apartheid* to arrange, in consultation with the Secretary-General, for the preparation of special studies on *apartheid* and its international repercussions and for the publication of a periodic bulletin on the collaboration of Governments and private enterprises with the South African régime and South African companies;

12. *Requests* the Special Committee on *Apartheid* to continue its close co-operation with other United Nations bodies concerned with *apartheid*, racial discrimination and colonialism in southern Africa with a view to co-ordinated action to find ways and means of eliminating those evils;

13. *Again recommends* that the Security Council should consider urgently the situation in South Africa and in southern Africa as a whole with a view to the adoption of effective measures against South Africa, including those under Chapter VII of the Charter of the United Nations;

14. *Requests* the Secretary-General to submit a report on the

implementation of the present resolution to the General Assembly at its twenty-seventh session.

A/SPC/L.213. Afghanistan, Algeria, Congo, Cyprus, Egypt, Ethiopia, Gambia, Ghana, Guinea, India, Indonesia, Jamaica, Kenya, Libyan Arab Republic, Malaysia, Mali, Mauritania, Morocco, Nepal, Niger, Nigeria, Pakistan, People's Democratic Republic of Yemen, Philippines, Senegal, Sierra Leone, Singapore, Somalia, Sudan, Syrian Arab Republic, Togo, Trinidad and Tobago, Uganda, United Republic of Tanzania, Yugoslavia, Zambia: draft resolution, as amended by Sierra Leone, A/SPC/L.219, approved by Special Political Committee on 16 November 1971, meeting 780, by 82 votes to 1, with 5 abstentions.

A/SPC/L.219. Sierra Leone: amendment to 36-power draft resolution, A/SPC/L.213.

A/SPC/L.224. Administrative and financial implications of 36-power draft resolution, A/SPC/L.213.

A/C.5/1403, A/8408/Add.12, A/8534. Administrative and financial implications of draft resolutions II C, II G and II H recommended by Special Political Committee in A/8504/Add.1. Statement by Secretary-General and reports of ACABQ and Fifth Committee.

A/8504/Add.1. Report of Special Political Committee (part II), draft resolution II G.

RESOLUTION 2775 G (XXVI), as recommended by Special Political Committee, A/8504/Add.1, adopted by Assembly on 29 November 1971, meeting 780, by recorded vote of 108 to 2, with 6 abstentions, as follows:

In favour: Afghanistan, Albania, Algeria, Argentina, Australia, Austria, Bahrain, Barbados, Belgium, Bolivia, Botswana, Brazil, Bulgaria, Burma, Burundi, Byelorussian SSR, Cameroon, Central African Republic, Chad, Chile, China, Colombia, Congo, Costa Rica, Cuba, Cyprus, Czechoslovakia, Dahomey, Denmark, Dominican Republic, Ecuador, Egypt, El Salvador, Equatorial Guinea, Ethiopia, Fiji, Finland, Gabon, Gambia, Ghana, Greece, Guatemala, Guinea, Guyana, Haiti, Honduras, Hungary, India, Indonesia, Iran, Iraq, Ireland, Israel, Italy, Ivory Coast, Jamaica, Japan, Jordan, Kenya, Khmer Republic, Kuwait, Libyan Arab Republic, Luxembourg, Madagascar, Malaysia, Mali, Mauritania, Mauritius, Mongolia, Morocco, Nepal, New Zealand, Niger, Nigeria, Norway, Pakistan, Panama, Paraguay, People's Democratic Republic of Yemen, Peru, Philippines, Poland, Qatar, Romania, Rwanda, Saudi Arabia, Senegal, Sierra Leone, Singapore, Somalia, Spain, Sudan, Swaziland, Sweden, Syrian Arab Republic, Thailand, Togo, Trinidad and Tobago, Tunisia, Uganda, Ukrainian SSR, USSR, United Republic of Tanzania, Upper Volta, Uruguay, Venezuela, Yugoslavia, Zambia.

Against: Portugal, South Africa.

Abstaining: Canada, France, Malawi, Netherlands, United Kingdom, United States.

The General Assembly,

Considering that the United Nations has a vital role in promoting national and international action for the elimination of *apartheid*,

Recognizing the importance of the widest dissemination of information on the evils and dangers of *apartheid*, and of United Nations efforts for the elimination of *apartheid*, in order to secure increasing support of world public opinion for such action,

Noting the report of the Secretary-General on the review and reappraisal of United Nations information policies and activities, analysing the relationship of United Nations public information activities to the achievement of the substantive goals of the United Nations, including the elimination of *apartheid*, racial discrimination and colonialism, and stressing the need, within the principles of universality and objectivity, of a United Nations information programme more directly geared to the support of these goals,

Recalling its resolution 2671 C (XXV) of 8 December 1970,

Taking note of the report of the Secretary-General and the recommendations contained in the report of the Special Commit-

tee on *Apartheid* concerning the dissemination of information on *apartheid*,

Taking note also of the consensus adopted by the joint meeting of the Special Committee on *Apartheid*, the Special Committee on the Situation with regard to the Implementation of the Declaration on the Granting of Independence to Colonial Countries and Peoples and the United Nations Council for Namibia, in particular the request that the Secretary-General consider appropriate arrangements for intensifying and co-ordinating research, information and publicity on southern Africa and the recommendation that the presiding officers of the three bodies or their representatives should advise the Secretary-General from time to time,

Welcoming the increasing co-operation between the United Nations and the Organization of African Unity in disseminating information on *apartheid*,

1. *Requests* the Secretary-General, in conformity with the conclusions set forth in paragraphs 52 and 57 of his report on the review and reappraisal of United Nations information policies and activities, and in compliance with the recommendations contained in paragraphs 274 to 278, 289 and 290 of the report of the Special Committee on *Apartheid*, to intensify information activities with a view to promoting national and international action for the elimination of *apartheid*;

2. *Requests* the Secretary-General to ascertain the needs and to take into account the recommendations of the General Assembly bodies concerned with the problems of southern Africa in intensifying information activities on those problems;

3. *Invites* Governments, specialized agencies and regional organizations, as well as non-governmental organizations, information media and educational institutions, to co-operate with the United Nations in disseminating information on *apartheid*;

4. *Invites* the specialized agencies to contribute to the campaign against *apartheid* in the light of the recommendations contained in paragraphs 282 to 284 of the report of the Special Committee on *Apartheid*;

5. *Requests* the Special Committee on *Apartheid*, in consultation with non-governmental organizations concerned with the campaign against *apartheid*, to take appropriate steps, where necessary, to promote the establishment of national committees against *apartheid*;

6. *Appeals* to Governments and organizations to make voluntary contributions to enable the Organization of African Unity to acquire equipment for recording and distributing information on *apartheid* through various broadcasting facilities and to lend their co-operation to the Organization of African Unity in preparing and disseminating radio broadcasts on *apartheid*;

7. *Requests* the Secretary-General to submit a detailed report to the General Assembly at its twenty-seventh session on the implementation of the present resolution and on means of ensuring adequate publicity for United Nations efforts against *apartheid* in the light of recommendations by the General Assembly bodies concerned.

A/8515/Rev.1. Ways and means of promoting concerted action against *apartheid* by trade union movement. Report of Special Committee on *Apartheid*.

A/SPC/L.222. Algeria, Chile, Congo, Guinea, Hungary, India, Indonesia, Libyan Arab Republic, Malaysia, Mali, Mauritania, Mongolia, Morocco, Nepal, Nigeria, Pakistan, People's Democratic Republic of Yemen, Singapore, Somalia, Sudan, Syrian Arab Republic, Trinidad and Tobago, United Republic of Tanzania, Zambia: draft resolution, approved by Special Political Committee on 16 November 1971, meeting 780, by roll-call vote of 92 to 0, with 10 abstentions, as follows:

In favour: Afghanistan, Albania, Algeria, Austria, Brazil, Bulgaria, Burma, Byelorussian SSR, Cameroon, Central African Republic, Ceylon, Chile, China, Colombia, Congo, Costa Rica, Cuba, Cyprus, Czechoslovakia, Denmark, Ecuador, Egypt, El Salvador, Ethiopia, Finland, Gambia, Ghana, Guatemala, Guinea, Guyana, Honduras, Hungary, Iceland, India, Indonesia, Iran, Iraq, Ireland, Israel, Italy, Ivory Coast, Jamaica, Japan, Jordan, Kenya, Khmer Republic, Kuwait, Lebanon, Liberia,

Libyan Arab Republic, Madagascar, Malaysia, Mali, Mauritania, Mauritius, Mexico, Mongolia, Morocco, Nepal, Netherlands, New Zealand, Nigeria, Norway, Pakistan, People's Democratic Republic of Yemen, Peru, Philippines, Poland, Romania, Saudi Arabia, Senegal, Sierra Leone, Singapore, Somalia, Sudan, Sweden, Syrian Arab Republic, Thailand, Trinidad and Tobago, Tunisia, Turkey, Uganda, Ukrainian SSR, USSR, United Republic of Tanzania, United States, Upper Volta, Venezuela, Yemen, Yugoslavia, Zaire, Zambia.

Against: None.

Abstaining: Argentina, Australia, Belgium, Canada, France, Greece, Malawi, Portugal, Spain, United Kingdom.

A/SPC/L.223. Administrative and financial implication of 24-power draft resolution, A/SPC/L.222. Statement by Secretary-General.

A/C.5/1403, A/8408/Add.12, A/8534. Administrative and financial implications of draft resolutions II C, II G and II H recommended by Special Political Committee in A/8504/Add.1. Statement by Secretary-General and reports of ACABQ and Fifth Committee.

A/8504/Add.1. Report of Special Political Committee (part II), draft resolution II H.

RESOLUTION 2775H(XXVI), as recommended by Special Political Committee, A/8504/Add.1. adopted by Assembly on 29 November 1971, meeting 1997, by recorded vote of 104 to 1, with 9 abstentions, as follows:

In favour: Afghanistan, Albania, Algeria, Austria, Bahrain, Barbados, Belgium, Bolivia, Brazil, Bulgaria, Burma, Burundi, Byelorussian SSR, Cameroon, Central African Republic, Chad, Chile, China, Colombia, Congo, Costa Rica, Cuba, Cyprus, Czechoslovakia, Dahomey, Denmark, Dominican Republic, Ecuador, Egypt, El Salvador, Equatorial Guinea, Ethiopia, Finland, Gabon, Gambia, Ghana, Guatemala, Guinea, Guyana, Haiti, Honduras, Hungary, India, Indonesia, Iran, Iraq, Ireland, Israel, Italy, Ivory Coast, Jamaica, Japan, Jordan, Kenya, Khmer Republic, Kuwait, Libyan Arab Republic, Luxembourg, Madagascar, Malaysia, Mali, Mauritania, Mauritius, Mongolia, Morocco, Nepal, Netherlands, New Zealand, Niger, Nigeria, Norway, Pakistan, Panama, Paraguay, People's Democratic Republic of Yemen, Peru, Philippines, Poland, Qatar, Romania, Rwanda, Saudi Arabia, Senegal, Sierra Leone, Singapore, Somalia, Sudan, Sweden, Syrian Arab Republic, Thailand, Togo, Trinidad and Tobago, Tunisia, Turkey, Uganda, Ukrainian SSR, USSR, United Republic of Tanzania, United States, Upper Volta, Uruguay, Venezuela, Yugoslavia, Zambia.

Against: South Africa.

Abstaining: Argentina, Australia, Canada, France, Greece, Malawi, Portugal, Spain, United Kingdom.

The General Assembly,

Recalling its resolution 2671 D(XXV) of 8 December 1970,

Noting the opposition of the international trade union movement to *apartheid* and racial discrimination,

Convinced of the need to promote concerted action by the trade union movement at the national and international levels in the campaign against *apartheid,*

Noting that the question of *apartheid* will be before the International Labour Conference at its fifty-seventh session, to be held at Geneva in June 1972,

Taking note of the report of the Special Committee on *Apartheid* concerning ways and means of promoting concerted action against *apartheid* by the trade union movements,

1. *Appeals* to all national and international trade union organizations to intensify their action against *apartheid,* in particular by:

(a) Discouraging the emigration of skilled workers to South Africa;

(b) Taking appropriate action in connexion with the infringements of trade union rights and the persecution of trade unionists in South Africa;

(c) Exerting maximum pressure on foreign economic and financial interests which are profiting from racial discrimination against non-white workers in South Africa, in order to persuade them to cease such exploitation;

(d) Co-operating with other organizations engaged in the international campaign against *apartheid;*

2. *Decides* to give further consideration to the proposed international trade union conference at its twenty-seventh session;

3. *Requests and authorizes* the Special Committee on *Apartheid* to send a mission to hold consultative meetings, if possible, with the workers' representatives to the fifty-seventh session of the International Labour Conference, to consider lines of action which the trade union movement may take against *apartheid,* including the holding of the international trade union conference, and to invite representatives of international and regional trade union federations to those consultative meetings;

4. *Requests* the International Labour Organisation and invites the workers' representatives to lend their co-operation to the Special Committee on *Apartheid* in preparing and holding the consultative meetings.

Credentials

General Assembly—26th session
Credentials Committee, meeting 56.
Plenary meetings 1934, 2025, 2027.

A/8625. Report of Credentials Committee, containing draft resolution suggested by Chairman and adopted by Committee on 17 December 1971, meeting 56, by 5 votes to 2, with 2 abstentions.

A/L.666. Somalia: Amendment to draft resolution submitted by Credentials Committee in A/8625, adopted by Assembly on 20 December 1971, meeting 2027, by recorded vote of 60 to 36, with 22 abstentions, as follows:

In favour: Afghanistan, Albania, Algeria, Bulgaria, Burundi, Byelorussian SSR, Cameroon, Chad, China, Congo, Cuba, Czechoslovakia, Dahomey, Ecuador, Egypt, Equatorial Guinea, Ethiopia, Ghana, Guinea, Guyana, Hungary, India, Indonesia, Iraq, Jamaica, Kenya, Kuwait, Liberia, Libyan Arab Republic, Malaysia, Mali, Mauritania, Mongolia, Morocco, Niger, Nigeria, Oman, Pakistan, People's Democratic Republic of Yemen, Philippines, Poland, Qatar, Romania, Rwanda, Senegal, Sierra Leone, Somalia, Syrian Arab Republic, Togo, Trinidad and Tobago, Tunisia, Uganda, Ukrainian SSR, USSR, United Arab Emirates, United Republic of Tanzania, Upper Volta, Yemen, Yugoslavia, Zambia.

Against: Australia, Austria, Belgium, Bolivia, Brazil, Canada, Colombia, Costa Rica, Denmark, El Salvador, Finland, France, Greece, Honduras, Iceland, Iran, Ireland, Israel, Italy, Luxembourg, Malawi, Malta, Mexico, Netherlands, New Zealand, Nicaragua, Norway, Paraguay, Portugal, South Africa, Spain, Sweden, United Kingdom, United States, Uruguay, Venezuela.

Abstaining: Argentina,* Barbados, Botswana, Burma, Central African Republic, Ceylon, Chile, Cyprus, Dominican Republic, Fiji, Guatemala, Ivory Coast, Japan, Laos, Lebanon, Lesotho, Nepal, Panama, Peru, Singapore, Thailand, Turkey.

*Subsequently Argentina advised the Secretariat that it had intended to vote against.

RESOLUTION 2862(XXVI), as recommended by Credentials Committee, A/8625, and as amended by Somalia, A/L.666, adopted by Assembly on 20 December 1971, meeting 2027, by recorded vote of 103 to 1, with 16 abstentions, as follows:

In favour: Afghanistan, Albania, Algeria, Austria, Belgium, Bolivia, Botswana, Brazil, Bulgaria, Burma, Burundi, Byelorussian SSR, Cameroon, Canada, Ceylon, Chad, Chile, China, Colombia, Congo, Cuba, Cyprus, Czechoslovakia, Dahomey, Denmark, Dominican Republic, Ecuador, Egypt, El Salvador, Equatorial Guinea, Ethiopia, Finland, France, Ghana, Guinea,

Guyana, Hungary, Iceland, India, Indonesia, Iran, Iraq, Israel, Italy, Ivory Coast, Jamaica, Japan, Jordan, Kenya, Khmer Republic, Kuwait, Laos, Lebanon, Liberia, Libyan Arab Republic, Luxembourg, Malaysia, Mali, Malta, Mauritania, Mexico, Mongolia, Morocco, Netherlands, New Zealand, Nicaragua, Niger, Nigeria, Norway, Oman, Pakistan, Panama, Paraguay, People's Democratic Republic of Yemen, Peru, Philippines, Poland, Qatar, Romania, Rwanda, Senegal, Sierra Leone, Singapore, Somalia, Spain, Sudan, Sweden, Syrian Arab Republic, Thailand, Togo, Trinidad and Tobago, Tunisia, Turkey, Uganda, Ukrainian SSR, USSR, United Arab Emirates, United Republic of Tanzania, United States, Upper Volta, Yemen, Yugoslavia, Zambia.

Against: South Africa.

Abstaining: Argentina, Australia, Barbados, Central African Republic, Costa Rica, Fiji, Greece, Honduras, Ireland, Lesotho, Malawi, Nepal, Portugal, United Kingdom, Uruguay, Venezuela.

The General Assembly

Approves the report of the Credentials Committee, except with regard to the credentials of the representatives of South Africa.

Other documents

Basic Facts on the Republic of South Africa and the Policy of Apartheid. U.N.P. Sales No.: E.72.II.K.10.

United Nations Trust Fund for South Africa

Reports of Secretary-General and Committee of Trustees

In a report to the General Assembly on 15 October 1971, the Secretary-General and the Committee of Trustees of the United Nations Trust Fund for South Africa said that in the year since the last report, the Fund had received contributions from 19 Governments totalling $287,518. Pledges from five Governments were outstanding.

In accordance with decisions of the Committee of Trustees, four grants—totalling $280,000—were made from the Fund during the period under review. Total contributions to the Trust Fund since its inception in 1965 amounted to $1,369,263 and the total of grants made from it was $1,280,400. The Fund—which is made up of voluntary contributions from States, organizations and individuals—is used for grants to voluntary organizations, Governments of host countries of refugees from South Africa, and other bodies. The grants provide: (a) legal assistance to persons persecuted under the repressive and discriminatory legislation of South Africa; (b) relief to such persons and their dependants; (c) education of such persons and their dependants; and (d) relief for refugees from South Africa.

On 8 December 1970, the General Assembly authorized the Committee of Trustees of the Fund to decide on grants from the Fund to voluntary organizations engaged in providing relief and assistance to persons persecuted under repressive and discriminatory legislation in Namibia and Southern Rhodesia and to their families, to the extent that additional voluntary contributions were received for that purpose.[13] The Committee of Trustees reported that France, Ireland and Sweden had specifically indicated that their contributions could be used for grants for the above-mentioned purpose.

The Committee of Trustees also noted with concern that during the year a large number of persons had been detained in South Africa, and a number of trials had been conducted, under

repressive legislation such as the Terrorism Act and the Suppression of Communism Act. The needs for legal assistance and relief to families—within the Trust Fund's terms of reference—had greatly increased.

The Committee hoped that generous contributions would be forthcoming to meet the pressing needs. It also hoped that efforts would be redoubled to persuade the South African Government to refrain from hindering humanitarian assistance to victims of repressive legislation. It stressed the importance of intensifying the dissemination of information on the continued repression of opponents of *apartheid* and the increasing hardships faced by the victims of repression and their families. The dissemination of such information would—taking into account the expanded mandate of the Trust Fund—help to encourage Governments, organizations and individuals to contribute to the Fund and to voluntary organizations engaged in assistance to victims of *apartheid*.

Consideration by General Assembly

At the General Assembly's 1971 session, the report of the Secretary-General and the Committee of Trustees of the United Nations Trust Fund for South Africa was discussed mainly in the Assembly's Special Political Committee.

The Chairman of the Committee of Trustees told the Special Political Committee that the Trust Fund had enjoyed virtually unanimous support in the General Assembly and had been commended by the Organization of African Unity and by numerous non-governmental organizations concerned with the situation in South Africa. Fifty-five Member States had so far contributed to the Fund. During 1971—which had special significance as the International Year for Action to Combat Racism and Racial Discrimination—the Trust Fund had received somewhat greater contributions. While expressing appreciation to the donor

[13]See Y.U.N., 1970, p. 156, text of resolution 2671 E(XXV).

Governments for their generous contributions, the Chairman appealed for a substantial increase in the number of contributing Governments. The Committee of Trustees hoped that all Governments would consider making annual contributions even if, for economic or other reasons, they were able to contribute only a token amount.

The Chairman stressed that the present level of contributions was still far below the minimum needs because the scope of the Trust Fund had been expanded to cover Namibia and Southern Rhodesia and because of recent developments in South Africa. A large number of persons had been detained in February and March 1971 under the Terrorism Act, and several trials had taken place under that Act and other legislation during the year. People released after serving long terms of imprisonment had been subjected to banning orders or removed to "resettlement camps" and continued to require assistance. The South African Government, moreover, appeared to be intent on hindering humanitarian assistance to the victims of repression.

On 29 November 1971, the General Assembly among other things expressed its appreciation to the Governments, organizations and individuals that had contributed to the Trust Fund and again appealed to all States, to governmental or non-governmental organizations and to individuals for generous contributions to the Trust Fund to enable it to meet the increasing needs. The Assembly further appealed for generous direct contributions to voluntary organizations engaged in providing relief and assistance to persons persecuted under repressive legislation in South Africa, Namibia and Southern Rhodesia.

The Assembly authorized the Committee of Trustees to send a representative away from Headquarters (in New York) to hold informative discussions, as necessary, with the voluntary organizations concerned, particularly those receiving grants from the Trust Fund. The Secretary-General was asked to take appropriate steps to intensify the dissemination of information on the need for relief and assistance to persons persecuted under repressive and discriminatory legislation in South Africa, Namibia and Southern Rhodesia.

The Assembly took these decisions when it adopted resolution 2774(XXVI) by a recorded vote of 110 to 1, with 1 abstention. The text was adopted on the recommendation of the Special Political Committee, which approved it, as revised, on 11 November, by 102 votes to 0, with 1 abstention.

The text was sponsored in the Special Political Committee by Austria, Brazil, Cameroon, Chile, Colombia, the Congo, Cyprus, Denmark, Egypt, Finland, Ghana, Guinea, Iceland, India, Indonesia, Iran, Jamaica, Kenya, Liberia, Mali, Mauritania, Morocco, Nigeria, Norway, Pakistan, the People's Democratic Republic of Yemen, Rwanda, Somalia, Sudan, Sweden, Tunisia, Turkey, Uganda, the United Republic of Tanzania, Yemen, Yugoslavia and Zambia.

(For text of resolution 2774(XXVI), see DOCUMENTARY REFERENCES below.)

Total contributions from Governments in 1971 were as follows:

Country	Amount (in U.S. dollars)
Austria	5,000
Belgium	20,149
Bulgaria	1,000
Cyprus	242
Denmark	66,796
Finland	25,000
France	20,000
Ghana	1,000
Ireland	2,750
Jamaica	840
Japan	20,000
Khmer Republic	1,000
Liberia	1,000
Morocco	3,972
Norway	35,000
Pakistan	3,000
Saudi Arabia	2,400
Sweden	77,369
Yugoslavia	1,000

DOCUMENTARY REFERENCES

General Assembly—26th session
Special Political Committee, meetings 757-776.
Plenary meeting 1997.

A/8468. Report of Secretary-General. (Annex: Report of Committee of Trustees of United Nations Trust Fund for South Africa.)
A/SPC/L.206. Austria, Ceylon, Chile, Cyprus, Denmark, Finland, Ghana, Iceland, India, Kenya, Liberia, Mali, Morocco, Nigeria, Norway, Pakistan, Somalia, Sweden, Uganda, United Republic of Tanzania, Yugoslavia, Zambia: draft resolution.
A/SPC/L.206/Rev.1. Austria, Brazil, Cameroon, Chile, Colombia, Congo, Cyprus, Denmark, Egypt, Finland, Ghana, Guinea, Iceland, India, Indonesia, Iran, Jamaica, Kenya, Liberia, Mali, Mauritania, Morocco, Nigeria, Norway, Pakistan, People's Democratic Republic of Yemen, Rwanda, Somalia, Sudan, Sweden, Tunisia, Turkey, Uganda, United Republic of Tanzania, Yemen, Yugoslavia, Zambia: revised draft resolution, approved by Special Political Committee on 11 November 1971, meeting 776, by 102 votes to 0, with 1 abstention.
A/SPC/L.207. Administrative and financial implications of 22-power draft resolution, A/SPC/L.206.
A/8504/Add.1. Report of Special Political Committee (part II), draft resolution I.

RESOLUTION 2774(XXVI), as recommended by Special Political Committee, A/8504/Add.1, adopted by Assembly on 29 November 1971, meeting 1997, by recorded vote of 110 to 1, with 1 abstention, as follows:

In favour: Afghanistan, Albania, Algeria, Argentina, Australia, Austria, Bahrain, Barbados, Belgium, Bolivia, Botswana, Brazil, Bulgaria, Burma, Burundi, Byelorussian SSR, Cameroon,

Canada, Central African Republic, Chad, Chile, China, Colombia, Congo, Cuba, Cyprus, Dahomey, Denmark, Dominican Republic, Ecuador, Egypt, El Salvador, Equatorial Guinea, Ethiopia, Finland, France, Gabon, Gambia, Ghana, Greece, Guatemala, Guinea, Guyana, Haiti, Honduras, Hungary, India, Indonesia, Iran, Iraq, Ireland, Israel, Italy, Ivory Coast, Jamaica, Japan, Jordan, Kenya, Khmer Republic, Kuwait, Libyan Arab Republic, Luxembourg, Madagascar, Malawi, Malaysia, Mali, Mauritania, Mauritius, Mongolia, Morocco, Nepal, Netherlands, New Zealand, Niger, Nigeria, Norway, Panama, Paraguay, People's Democratic Republic of Yemen, Peru, Philippines, Poland, Qatar, Romania, Rwanda, Saudi Arabia, Senegal, Sierra Leone, Singapore, Somalia, Spain, Sudan, Sweden, Syrian Arab Republic, Thailand, Togo, Trinidad and Tobago, Tunisia, Turkey, Uganda, Ukrainian SSR, USSR, United Kingdom, United Republic of Tanzania, United States, Upper Volta, Uruguay, Venezuela, Yugoslavia, Zambia.

Against: South Africa.

Abstaining: Portugal.

The General Assembly,

Recalling its resolution 2671 E (XXV) of 8 December 1970 concerning the United Nations Trust Fund for South Africa,

Taking note with appreciation of the report of the Secretary-General, to which is annexed the report of the Committee of Trustees of the United Nations Trust Fund for South Africa,

Conscious of the continuing need for humanitarian assistance to persons persecuted under repressive and discriminatory legislation in South Africa, as well as in Namibia and Southern Rhodesia, and to their families,

Concerned at the actions of the South African Government in persecuting persons engaged in providing humanitarian assistance to victims of *apartheid,*

1. *Expresses its appreciation* to the Governments, organizations and individuals that have contributed to the United Nations Trust Fund for South Africa;

2. *Again appeals* to all States, to governmental or non-governmental organizations and to individuals for generous contributions to the Trust Fund in order to enable it to meet the increasing needs;

3. *Further appeals* for generous direct contributions to voluntary organizations engaged in providing relief and assistance to persons persecuted under repressive and discriminatory legislation in South Africa, Namibia and Southern Rhodesia;

4. *Authorizes* the Committee of Trustees of the United Nations Trust Fund for South Africa to send a representative away from Headquarters to hold informative discussions, as necessary, with the voluntary organizations concerned, particularly those receiving grants from the Trust Fund;

5. *Requests* the Secretary-General to take appropriate steps to intensify the dissemination of information on the need for relief and assistance to persons persecuted under repressive and discriminatory legislation in South Africa, Namibia and Southern Rhodesia.

The situation in Southern Rhodesia

The situation in Southern Rhodesia continued to receive consideration in 1971 by the Security Council, the General Assembly and the Assembly's Special Committee on the Situation with regard to the Implementation of the Declaration on the Granting of Independence to Colonial Countries and Peoples, as well as by the Commission on Human Rights and the Economic and Social Council.

These bodies were concerned with bringing to an end the illegal white minority régime of Ian Smith—which had unilaterally declared its independence from the United Kingdom on 11 November 1965—and with enabling the African people of the territory to exercise their basic human rights, particularly their inalienable right to freedom and independence in accordance with the Declaration on the Granting of Independence to Colonial Countries and Peoples adopted by the General Assembly in 1960.[14]

Also under consideration was the implementation of the various decisions of the Security Council calling for sanctions against the illegal régime in Southern Rhodesia, particularly Security Council resolution 253(1968) of 29 May 1968,[15] by which the Council had, among other things, imposed more extensive mandatory economic sanctions against the illegal régime and emphasized the need for withdrawal of all consular and trade representation in Southern Rhodesia.

The Security Council met in November and December to consider the question of Southern Rhodesia in the light of the proposals for a settlement agreed upon between the illegal régime and the United Kingdom Government; a draft resolution sponsored by four African and Asian States failed to be adopted owing to the negative vote of the United Kingdom, a permanent member of the Council.

The General Assembly's Special Committee on the implementation of the Declaration on granting independence to colonial countries and peoples adopted, on 30 April, a resolution concerning Southern Rhodesia's participation in the XXth Olympic Games. On 2 July, it adopted a resolution concerning the continuation of talks between the United Kingdom and the illegal régime and, on 24 August, it adopted a resolution on aspects of the question of Southern Rhodesia as a whole.

The General Assembly, at its twenty-sixth session later in 1971, adopted four resolutions on the question. By the first, adopted on 16 November, it called on the United States to prevent the importation of chrome into the United States from Southern Rhodesia. By the second, adopted on 22 November, among other things it reaffirmed the principle that there should be no independence before majority rule in Southern Rhodesia and affirmed that any settlement must be worked out with the participation of the nationalist leaders of Zimbabwe (Southern Rhodesia) and endorsed freely by the people.

A third resolution, adopted by the Assembly on

---

[14]See Y.U.N., 1960, pp. 49-50, resolution 1514(XV), containing text of Declaration.

[15]See Y.U.N., 1968, pp. 152-54, text of resolution 253(1968).

10 December, laid down a number of provisions on the general aspects of the situation in Southern Rhodesia.

On 20 December, the Assembly adopted a fourth resolution by which, among other things, it rejected the proposals for a settlement agreed upon by the United Kingdom and the racist minority régime as constituting a flagrant violation of the inalienable right of the Zimbabwe people to self-determination and independence.

Details of these and other related decisions on Southern Rhodesia are described in the sections below.

Communications and reports to Security Council (January–November 1971)

On 16 June 1971, the Committee established in pursuance of Security Council resolution 253(1968) of 29 May 1968[16] submitted its fourth report to the Council, covering its work since the submission of its third report on 15 June 1970.

The report said that, as a result of consultations, it had been agreed that as of 1 October 1970 the Committee would be enlarged to include all members of the Security Council. Since then, the Committee had held 29 meetings at which it had continued examination of 36 cases of suspected violations of the provisions of the resolution of 29 May 1968, listed in its previous report, and considered 40 new cases brought to the Committee's attention, as well as information about attempts to evade the sanctions against Southern Rhodesia. The Committee had also considered certain procedural issues in connexion with its future work, as well as other questions such as: consular and other representation in Southern Rhodesia; representation of the illegal régime in other countries; delegations and groups entering or leaving Southern Rhodesia; airlines operating to and from Southern Rhodesia; and immigration to and tourism in that territory.

Annexes attached to the report contained factual accounts of the cases carried over from previous reports, as well as new cases, of transactions conducted with or without the knowledge of reporting Governments, and two studies—one on the automobile industry in Southern Rhodesia and the other on imports of ammonia into Southern Rhodesia as a basic element for fertilizers.

In an addendum to the report, issued on 13 July, further annexes were published showing statistics of imports of all commodities from Southern Rhodesia, exports of all commodities to Southern Rhodesia and trade in commodities.

The Committee said it had noted that there were several commodities in which there appeared to be considerable trade with Southern Rhodesia in contravention of the resolution of 29 May 1968, in spite of the efforts being made by reporting Governments. Certain goods apparently destined for Southern Rhodesia were being declared as destined for neighbouring countries in southern and eastern Africa, and goods exported from Southern Rhodesia were being imported into or allowed transit through countries on the basis of fraudulent or accommodation documents.

The Committee drew the Council's attention to four specific cases in which it had found that commercial transactions had been conducted with Southern Rhodesia. In one such case, concerning the sale of an aircraft to Air Rhodesia by the Middle East Airlines via an intermediary in Mozambique, the Government of Lebanon had informed the Committee that the transaction had been conducted without its knowledge. In the three other cases, which concerned imports of Southern Rhodesian graphite into the Federal Republic of Germany, meat into Switzerland and exports of wheat from Australia to Southern Rhodesia, the Governments concerned had acknowledged that those operations had been conducted with their knowledge and consent. Australia had explained that because wheat was a basic foodstuff of the people of Southern Rhodesia, its export thereto was a humanitarian action permitted under the provisions of the resolution of 29 May 1968.

In four letters between 2 July and 6 October, the Chairman or Acting Chairman of the Special Committee on the Situation with regard to the Implementation of the Declaration on the Granting of Independence to Colonial Countries and Peoples transmitted the texts of three resolutions concerning the situation in Southern Rhodesia adopted by the Special Committee at meetings on 2 July, 24 August, 9 September, and two consensuses adopted on 6 October. (For further details, see below.)

On 8 November, the Chairman of the African group of States at the United Nations transmitted the text of a statement by the group concerning action taken by the United States Congress on 4 November to allow Southern Rhodesian chrome ore to be imported into the United States in contravention of the Security Council's resolution of 29 May 1968. The African group said the decision, if implemented, would undermine the basis for State responsibility for mandatory sanctions imposed by the Security Council, and it asked the Secretary-General to use his good offices to draw the attention of the United States Government to the effect of such violation.

Consideration by Special Committee

The General Assembly's Special Committee on the Situation with regard to the Implementation of

[16]*Ibid.*

the Declaration on the Granting of Independence to Colonial Countries and Peoples considered the question of Southern Rhodesia at meetings held between 4 March and 6 October 1971.

The Special Committee heard one petitioner, Abdul S. Minty, Honorary Secretary of the Anti-*Apartheid* Movement in the United Kingdom, whose statement concerned territories in southern Africa in general. During May 1971, an *ad hoc* group of the Special Committee—established for the purpose of maintaining contact with representatives of national liberation movements from colonial territories in Africa—also heard the views of two representatives of national liberation movements of Southern Rhodesia: N. M. Shamuyarira, Secretary of External Affairs of the Zimbabwe African National Union (ZANU), and G. B. Nyandoro, National Secretary of the Zimbabwe African People's Union (ZAPU).

Mr. Minty said that Southern Rhodesia had become a virtual colony of South Africa, which provided it with both financial and military support. Armed units from South Africa had been operating in Southern Rhodesia for some years. South Africa was also providing military and economic assistance to the Portuguese authorities in Angola and Mozambique, resulting in a military alliance between the three white régimes against African freedom. Mr. Minty said that many Western countries with increasing economic investments in southern Africa were committed to maintaining this alliance to protect their investments and were therefore largely responsible for the perpetuation of the iniquitous situation in the area.

The petitioner also said that the commitment of Western Governments to peaceful change in southern Africa was a distortion of that noble idea in order to maintain the *status quo*.

The representatives of the liberation movements from Southern Rhodesia told the *ad hoc* group that economic sanctions against the illegal régime would never achieve the desired results unless they were extended to cover South Africa and Portugal, backed by the use of force and strictly enforced. The petitioners said that although the policy of sanctions had failed so far to achieve its chief purpose, it had nevertheless succeeded in increasing the political and moral isolation of the illegal régime.

The petitioners also expressed their opposition to the holding of discussions between the United Kingdom Government and the illegal régime. Discussions concerning the future political status of the territory should, they said, be held between the United Kingdom Government and the representatives of political parties in Zimbabwe favouring majority rule. The petitioners also expressed disapproval of the five principles

formulated by the United Kingdom as a basis for settlement which, they said, did not envisage the establishment of majority rule on the basis of "one man, one vote" prior to independence.

On 4 March 1971, the Special Committee adopted a consensus by which, among other things, it deplored the decision of the United Kingdom Government to proceed with the sale to South Africa of a number of helicopters and spare parts for military equipment despite the provisions of Security Council resolutions. The consensus further stated that because of the close co-operation existing between South Africa, Portugal and the illegal régime in Southern Rhodesia, the decision of the United Kingdom Government would inevitably increase the capacity and efforts of those authorities to suppress the struggle of the peoples of southern Africa for freedom and independence. The Special Committee urged all States, without exception, to desist forthwith from such sales or supplies.

During the debate, members expressed deep concern over new developments in the territory, including: the eviction of the Tangwena people from their traditional home; the coming into force of the so-called Republican Constitution; and the steps taken by the illegal régime to entrench further an *apartheid* system by means of the "Property Owners (Residential Protection) Bill."

Committee members agreed that the situation in Southern Rhodesia had continued to deteriorate; it was pointed out that despite international condemnation and efforts by the United Nations the illegal régime had consolidated its position. Sweden noted that in spite of the failure to oust the illegal régime, some positive results of United Nations efforts could be seen, namely, that no Member State had accorded recognition to the illegal régime, thus leaving it in political isolation.

Most speakers—including Ethiopia, Iran, the USSR and the United Republic of Tanzania—agreed that the United Kingdom had the primary responsibility for bringing an end to the illegal situation in Southern Rhodesia and had failed to take effective action to end the rebellion and hand over political power to the African majority. They said that the original decision of the United Kingdom Government not to use force to overthrow the illegal regime was the principal cause of the present situation.

Most members of the Special Committee held that the sanctions imposed by the Security Council had so far been ineffective. Afghanistan, Ethiopia, India, Iran, Iraq, the Syrian Arab Republic and the United Republic of Tanzania, among others, felt that the refusal of South Africa and Portugal to comply with the sanctions imposed by the United Nations and their continuing support of and aid to the illegal régime were the main factors accounting for the régime's economic survival. Poland and the USSR, among others, felt that many Western countries, including the United Kingdom, were also guilty of undermining sanctions by continuing to invest in Southern Rhodesia. Afghanistan, Bulgaria, Ethiopia, India, Trinidad and Tobago, and the United Republic of Tanzania called for the tightening of sanctions against Southern Rhodesia and the extension of mandatory sanctions to Portugal and South Africa.

Ecuador and Venezuela felt that the Special Committee should urge the Security Council to adopt stronger sanctions against Southern Rhodesia and that Member States should practise strict compliance with those sanctions in force. Sweden felt that the sanctions already imposed against Southern Rhodesia had had a noticeable effect on the territory's economy and should not be regarded as a total failure.

The representatives of Bulgaria, Ethiopia, India and Venezuela held that moral and material assistance to the Zimbabwe national liberation movements should be increased to enable those groups to wage their legitimate struggle for freedom and independence.

The United Republic of Tanzania, supported by Bulgaria and the Syrian Arab Republic among others, proposed that the Special Committee should establish a sub-committee to study ways and means by which the specialized agencies could give assistance to liberation movements and cease all collaboration with those States that hindered the process of decolonization. The same sub-committee could also consult with the liberation movements for this purpose.

Many members—including Bulgaria, Ecuador, Ethiopia, India, Iraq, Poland and the United Republic of Tanzania—agreed that the United Kingdom Government should discontinue all negotiations with the minority régime and instead deal directly with representatives of the African people.

On 30 April, the Special Committee unanimously adopted a resolution concerning the XXth Olympic Games scheduled for 1972. It was sponsored by Afghanistan, Bulgaria, Ecuador, Ethiopia, Fiji, India, Iran, Iraq, Madagascar, Mali, Poland, Sierra Leone, Sweden, the Syrian Arab Republic, Trinidad and Tobago, the USSR, the United Republic of Tanzania, Venezuela and Yugoslavia.

By this, the Special Committee among other things deplored the International Olympic Committee's continued recognition of the so-called National Olympic Committee of Rhodesia and the invitation extended to the national Committee to participate in the Olympic Games at Munich, Federal Republic of Germany; it also urged the International Olympic Committee to suspend the so-called National Olympic Committee from its membership, asked the Organizing Committee of the XXth Olympic Games to annul its invitation and called upon all States to comply fully with the relevant Security Council resolutions and to work for the full implementation of the present resolution.

In a consensus concerning the same subject adopted on 6 October, the Special Committee noted with deep regret the decision of the International Olympic Committee to permit the participation in the XXth Olympic Games of the so-called National Olympic Committee of Rhodesia; having considered that this decision contravened the aims and purposes of the relevant Security Council decisions, the Special Committee requested all States to take steps ensuring the exclusion of the so-called National Olympic Committee of Rhodesia from participation in the Games and to refrain from any action which might confer a semblance of legitimacy on the illegal racist minority régime in Southern Rhodesia.

On 21 June, the Special Committee, at the suggestion of Ethiopia, considered the question of Southern Rhodesia in the light of the dispatch by the United Kingdom Government of a special envoy to continue consultations with the illegal racist minority régime in Southern Rhodesia. On 2 July, the Special Committee adopted a resolution on this aspect of the question, sponsored by Afghanistan, Bulgaria, Ethiopia, India, Poland, Sierra Leone, the Syrian Arab Republic, the United Republic of Tanzania, and Yugoslavia. The vote, by roll call, was 18 to 0, with 2 abstentions (Fiji and Sweden).

By this resolution, the Special Committee: condemned the continued failure and refusal of the United Kingdom Government to take effective measures to put an end to the illegal régime and called on that Government to take such measures without further delay; reaffirmed that any attempt to negotiate the future of Zimbabwe with the illegal racist minority régime on the basis of independence without majority rule would be contrary to the provisions of the General Assembly's resolution of 14 December 1960[17] (containing the Declaration on the Granting of Independence to Colonial Countries and Peoples); and called once again on the United Kingdom to enter into consultations without further delay with the representatives of political parties of Zimbabwe favouring majority rule, in order to transfer power to the Zimbabwe people on the basis of free elections by universal adult suffrage and of majority rule, in accordance with the relevant United Nations resolutions. The Special Committee also recommended that the Security Council

---

[17]See footnote 14.

urgently consider the possibility of taking further measures under the United Nations Charter, as envisaged in the relevant resolutions adopted by the General Assembly during its twenty-fifth (1970) session.

In explanation of vote, Fiji said it could neither condemn nor deplore the talks in advance, and it hoped that they might result in some satisfactory solution. It regretted, however, that the United Kingdom Government was not in simultaneous consultation with the leaders of the African majority. For these reasons, Fiji, although agreeing with a substantial portion of the resolution, abstained from voting.

On 24 August, the Special Committee—by a roll-call vote of 18 to 0, with 2 abstentions (Fiji and Sweden)—adopted a third resolution on the question of Southern Rhodesia, sponsored by Afghanistan, Ethiopia, India, Iraq, Sierra Leone, the Syrian Arab Republic, the United Republic of Tanzania, and Yugoslavia.

By this, the Special Committee among other things:

(1) reaffirmed the inalienable right of the people of Zimbabwe to freedom and independence in conformity with the provisions of the General Assembly's resolution of 14 December 1960 (containing the Declaration on the granting of independence), and the legitimacy of their struggle by all necessary means at their disposal to attain that right;

(2) condemned the failure and refusal of the United Kingdom to take effective measures to bring down the illegal régime in Southern Rhodesia and to transfer power to the people of Zimbabwe on the basis of universal adult suffrage and majority rule, in accordance with the relevant resolutions of the General Assembly, and called upon the United Kingdom to take such measures, including the use of force, without further delay in fulfilling its responsibility as administering power;

(3) deplored the failure of the United Kingdom to co-operate with the Special Committee by rejecting the Special Committee's invitation to participate in its consideration of the question of Southern Rhodesia, and called upon the United Kingdom Government to co-operate with and assist the Special Committee in the discharge of its mandate;

(4) condemned the policies of South Africa, Portugal and other Governments which continued to have political, economic, military or other relations with the illegal régime in Southern Rhodesia in defiance of the relevant United Nations resolutions and contrary to their Charter obligations, and called on them to cease forthwith all such relations and, in particular, to interrupt any existing means of transportation to and from Southern Rhodesia;

(5) condemned the continued presence and intervention of South African forces in Southern Rhodesia in violation of the Security Council's resolution of 18 March 1970,[18] and called upon the administering power to ensure the immediate expulsion of all such forces and the release of freedom fighters detained by the illegal régime;

(6) called upon the United Kingdom Government, in view of the armed conflict in the territory and the inhuman treatment of prisoners, to ensure the application to that situation of the 1949 Geneva Conventions relative to the treatment of prisoners of war and to the protection of civilian persons in time of war;

(7) called upon all States, the specialized agencies and other international organizations within the United Nations system to extend, with the co-operation of the Organization of African Unity (OAU), all moral and material assistance to the people of Zimbabwe in their struggle to attain freedom and independence;

(8) strongly urged all States to comply with the sanctions adopted by the Security Council in order to bring about the isolation of the illegal régime in Southern Rhodesia in all aspects; and

(9) drew the Security Council's attention to the urgent need to widen the scope of the sanctions against the illegal régime by declaring mandatory all the measures envisaged under Article 41 of the United Nations Charter,[19] as well as to the need to consider imposing sanctions against South Africa and Portugal in view of their refusal to implement the relevant Security Council resolutions.

On 9 September, the Special Committee—by a roll-call vote of 17 to 0, with 1 abstention (Sweden)—adopted a resolution covering aspects of the situation in common in Southern Rhodesia, Namibia and the territories under Portuguese administration. The resolution was sponsored by Afghanistan, Ethiopia, India, Iraq, Mali, Sierra Leone, the Syrian Arab Republic, Trinidad and Tobago, the United Republic of Tanzania, and Yugoslavia.

By this, the Special Committee among other things:

(1) reaffirmed the legitimate right of the peoples in Southern Rhodesia, Namibia and territories under Portuguese domination to struggle by all necessary means at their disposal against colonial authorities, and the obligation of Member States to render all necessary moral and material assistance to those peoples;

(2) condemned the increasing collaboration between Portugal, South Africa and the illegal régime in Southern Rhodesia;

---

[18]See Y.U.N., 1970, pp. 181-83, text of resolution 277(1970).
[19]For text of Article 41 of the Charter, see APPENDIX II.

(3) urged all States, in consultation with OAU, to increase their financial and material assistance to the peoples of those territories;

(4) requested all States to discontinue all collaboration with the Governments of Portugal and South Africa, as well as with the illegal régime; and

(5) drew the Security Council's attention to the urgent need to take effective measures to put an end to the grave situation created by the continued defiance of their Charter obligations by the Governments concerned.

By a consensus adopted on 6 October, the Special Committee noted with concern the decision of the United States Senate which would permit the importation of chrome into the United States from Southern Rhodesia and thus violate the sanctions being applied by the Security Council. The Committee urged the United States Government to take the necessary measures to prevent the enactment of such legislation.

Decisions of Human Rights Commission and of Economic and Social Council

At its meetings in February and March 1971, the Commission on Human Rights again considered the question of the violation of human rights and fundamental freedoms, including policies of racial discrimination and segregation and of *apartheid,* in all countries, with particular reference to colonial and other dependent countries and territories.

On 8 March, it endorsed the observations, conclusions and recommendations of its *Ad Hoc* Working Group of Experts, which had conducted an investigation into, among other things, the question of capital punishment in southern Africa; the treatment of political prisoners and captured freedom fighters in southern Africa; the condition of Africans in the so-called native reserves and transit camps in South Africa, Namibia and Southern Rhodesia; and grave manifestations of colonialism and racial discrimination in Namibia, Southern Rhodesia and the African territories under Portuguese administration.

The Human Rights Commission decided that the *Ad Hoc* Working Group should continue to survey developments in those areas, with particular reference to grave manifestations of colonialism and racial discrimination present in the situation prevailing in Namibia, Southern Rhodesia, Angola, Mozambique and Guinea (Bissau), resulting from the actions of the illegal South African régime in Namibia, the illegal minority régime in Southern Rhodesia and the Portuguese régime in Angola, Mozambique and Guinea (Bissau). The Commission asked the Group to remain active and vigilant in its observation of colonial and racially discriminatory practices in Africa and bring to the Commission's attention any new developments in the field. (See also pp. 405-6.)

The Economic and Social Council, at its session in April–May 1971, acting on a recommendation of the Human Rights Commission, approved a resolution (1592(L)) by which it recommended that the General Assembly adopt a resolution relating to the right of peoples under colonial and alien domination to self-determination. The text was adopted later in 1971 by the Assembly as its resolution 2787(XXVI). (For details, see pp. 420-22.)

The Council also adopted a resolution (1599(L)) concerning allegations regarding infringements of trade union rights in southern Africa by which, among other things, it called on the United Kingdom to fulfil its responsibility to put an immediate end to discrimination and repression against African workers and trade unionists in Southern Rhodesia. It also asked the *Ad Hoc* Working Group of Experts established by the Human Rights Commission to investigate thoroughly the system of recruitment of African workers in Namibia, Southern Rhodesia and the territories under Portuguese domination. (For details, see pp. 434-36.)

Consideration by Security Council (November–December 1971)

In a letter dated 24 November 1971, the United Kingdom representative requested—in connexion with the situation in Southern Rhodesia—that a meeting of the Security Council be convened on 25 November so that he could inform the Council about the recent discussions his Government's Secretary of State for Foreign and Commonwealth Affairs had had in Salisbury, Southern Rhodesia.

The question was considered by the Council at meetings held between 25 November and 30 December, during which the representatives of Algeria, Ghana, India, Kenya, Nigeria, Saudi Arabia, Uganda, the United Republic of Tanzania, and Zambia were invited, at their request, to participate in the discussion without the right to vote.

At the Council's meeting on 25 November, the United Kingdom representative said that while the settlement of the problem of Southern Rhodesia was primarily a matter for the United Kingdom Government, it had always been recognized that the question was one of legitimate and continuing concern to the world community. For that reason, his Government considered it right to inform the Security Council that agreement had been reached between the United Kingdom Foreign Secretary, Sir Alec Douglas-Home, and Ian Smith in Salisbury, on 24 November, on proposals for a settlement of the Southern Rhodesian problem. He emphasized that the fact that agreement had been reached on certain proposals did not in itself represent any change in the existing situation; it was a first step only. Finality would not be reached until the people of Rhodesia as a whole had had a full and free opportunity to demonstrate whether the proposals were acceptable to them.

The United Kingdom representative went on to say that the proposals—which had been accepted by the British Cabinet—were based upon the five principles to which the United Kingdom had consistently adhered. These were that in any settlement: (i) the principle and intention of unimpeded progress to majority rule would have to be maintained and guaranteed; (ii) there would also have to be guarantees against retrogressive amendment of the Constitution; (iii) there would have to be immediate improvement in the political status of the African population; (iv) there would have to be progress towards ending racial discrimination; and (v) the British Government would need to be satisfied that any basis proposed for independence was acceptable to the people of Rhodesia as a whole.

The proposals, he stressed, would depend for their implementation on their acceptance by the people of Southern Rhodesia as a whole. The United Kingdom Government would appoint a commission, headed by Lord Pearce, to ascertain from all sections of the population their views on the acceptability of the proposals and to report thereon to the British Government. The commission would, among other things, visit the main centres of population, councils in the rural areas and traditional meeting places in the tribal trust lands. The test of acceptability would be a full, free and fair ascertainment—under the direct control of the British Government, not of the Rhodesians.

The United Kingdom representative then turned to the central part of the proposals—the constitutional arrangements—which he described in detail and termed as vital in connexion with the principle of unimpeded progress towards majority rule. They constituted, he said, a real and substantial change in direction away from the existing state of affairs as embodied in the 1969 Constitution.

An important element in the proposals, he went on, was the new Declaration of Rights, which would afford protection to the fundamental rights and freedoms of the individual and confer, for any person who claimed that its provisions had been contravened, a right of access to the High Court to obtain redress.

Other main constitutional provisions, the United Kingdom representative continued, related to amendment of the Constitution. Also provided for was a review of existing legislation through an independent commission to examine the problem of racial discrimination. Other provisions would

have a direct bearing on the status and rights of the Africans concerning land and development, which would include a development programme assisted by the British Government to increase significantly education and job opportunities for Africans.

The main thrust of the agreed proposals was to be the advancement of the Africans in education and in social, economic and political matters. Acceptance of the proposals by the people of Southern Rhodesia as a whole was a *sine qua non* of the whole exercise, the United Kingdom representative stressed.

He said that the proposals presented an acceptable alternative to the *status quo* and a healthy reversal of an unhealthy trend. The cloud of growing racial discrimination was creeping northwards and seemed bound to turn Southern Rhodesia into a satellite of the *apartheid* system unless it was halted and reversed.

In conclusion, the representative of the United Kingdom said that only if the Rhodesian people accepted the proposals, and if the British Government was fully satisfied that the Rhodesian Government had enacted the necessary legislation and taken the necessary steps to give effect to the proposals, would the final section of the proposals—which envisaged the conferring of legal independence on Southern Rhodesia and the lifting of sanctions—come into effect. Until that stage was reached, the situation would remain unchanged and all existing measures would remain in force.

The USSR representative asserted that the talks had been conducted with an illegal racist régime, already universally condemned as such by the United Nations, and had resulted in an agreement concluded without the knowledge or participation of the people of Zimbabwe. The talks were conducted contrary to the direct appeals of the General Assembly and contrary to appeals not to have anything to do with the unlawful régime and not to have talks with it concerning the future of the Zimbabwe people.

It was clear, he went on to say, that the purpose of the proposals was to maintain for an indefinitely long time the existing racist order prevailing in Southern Rhodesia. The United Kingdom promised a long-term educational programme for Africans to prepare them for more rapid political progress. But, he said, this was a further manifestation of the colonialist thesis that Africans were not ready for independence, a thesis that had long ago been condemned. The attainment of independence by many African countries and the presence of their representatives in the United Nations had amply refuted it. Zimbabwe, too, had capable political leaders who were well prepared to manage the affairs of their country by themselves;

however, they were imprisoned, without trial, for many years, including Joshua Nkomo, the leader of the Zimbabwe African People's Union (ZAPU) and the Reverend Ndabaningi Sithole, the leader of the Zimbabwe African National Union (ZANU).

The USSR representative said the Security Council could not overlook the fact that the visit of the United Kingdom Foreign Secretary to the Southern Rhodesian racists had coincided with the action by the United States Congress to repeal the embargo on the purchase by United States monopolies of chrome from Southern Rhodesia. It was clear that attempts were being made to rescue the unlawful régime in Southern Rhodesia, to support the Portuguese colonial system and the racist system of South Africa, with a view to strengthening and maintaining in southern Africa a bastion of imperialism, colonialism and racism. This was required, he said, to prevent at all costs the progress of the national liberation movement in southern Africa and the implementation there of the 1960 Declaration on the Granting of Independence to Colonial Countries and Peoples.

The USSR representative proposed that the leaders of ZAPU and ZANU, Mr. Nkomo and Mr. Sithole, be invited to appear before the Security Council and give it their appraisal of the proposals. At a meeting on 2 December, acting on this USSR proposal, which was supported by Somalia, the Security Council decided without objection to invite Messrs. Nkomo and Sithole to participate in the discussion. Subsequently, in a note dated 23 December, the President of the Council said he had addressed a letter to the United Kingdom representative on 2 December expressing the hope that the United Kingdom, as administering authority of the territory, would take the appropriate steps to ensure compliance with the Council's decision. In a reply dated 21 December, the United Kingdom representative informed him that Mr. Nkomo was in detention and Mr. Sithole was serving a prison sentence in Southern Rhodesia. His Government regretted that in the circumstances it was not in a position to require the Rhodesian authorities to allow either Mr. Nkomo or Mr. Sithole to come to New York.

Commenting on the note from the President, several Council members expressed their disappointment at the United Kingdom reply; the USSR representative in particular said that the reply was not even an argument but a simple declaration of the refusal on the part of the United Kingdom to implement a decision of the Security Council, to which the Council should not reconcile itself.

On the question of the importation of chrome ore from Southern Rhodesia, the United States representative denied that there had been any connivance between the United States and the United Kingdom concerning Southern Rhodesia, adding that the action of the United States Congress was not supported by the United States Government but reflected concern about the ineffectiveness of the sanctions. The United States was not currently buying chrome ore from Southern Rhodesia but someone else was doing so, he said. The United States had not violated the sanctions.

The representative of Burundi wondered whether the proposed electoral system might not be too complicated for the people of Southern Rhodesia to pronounce themselves on, since they had always been denied accession to independence on the ground that they lacked the necessary scholastic training to participate in a referendum. He also asked why the leader of the rebel régime sought discretionary powers with regard to the release of political detainees or the return of exiles; Burundi considered that all who had sought to lead Southern Rhodesia to independence should be freed, and all political exiles should be unconditionally repatriated.

Burundi's representative also asked for clarification as to what assurance there was that the development aid promised by the United Kingdom would not be diverted to other purposes. He also wanted to know what the duration of the rebel régime and of the transitional system under the agreement would be.

The Syrian Arab Republic's representative asked about the length of time it would take for parity to be achieved. If the test of acceptability should prove negative, how did the United Kingdom intend to discharge its responsibility as administering power, he asked. Would it leave the Smith régime full freedom of action by saying that the proposals had been rejected?

The representative of the United Republic of Tanzania stressed that the United Kingdom bore ultimate responsibility for Southern Rhodesia and for the actions of the Southern Rhodesian Government. The United Kingdom had now decided to legalize the usurpation of power by the Smith régime and its interpretation of events was, at best, an apology for its own inaction and, at worst, a clumsy justification for its treachery, double standards and perhaps pre-planned impotence to control those events.

The Africans of Zimbabwe, he continued, had rejected in advance any settlement outside the principle of majority rule. Neither his Government, nor Africa, nor the rest of the international community had ever accepted the so-called five principles as the basis of a settlement. He charged that the so-called settlement favoured white oppression and domination in Southern Rhodesia and was in flagrant negation of the principles of freedom, human equality, justice and democracy.

The representative of Somalia asked whether the United Kingdom intended to publish the texts of representations made to the British Foreign Secretary by African political leaders during the Salisbury talks, and whether the United Kingdom, if it intended to go ahead with the test of acceptability, would ensure a full, free and fair conduct of the test by removing the apparatus of the police State which existed in the territory, tyrannizing the African people and depriving them of their liberty. He also suggested that the proposed Declaration of Rights should be examined and evaluated by United Nations legal experts.

On 1 December, the United Kingdom transmitted the text of a White Paper entitled "Rhodesia: Proposals for a Settlement," containing the proposals he had described on 25 November.

The representative of Somalia said that neither the goals nor the special involvement of the United Nations with regard to Southern Rhodesia had been taken into account in the negotiations preceding the proposals or in the proposals themselves. The United Nations should be closely associated with any initiative aimed at a settlement of the problem, not after but before the fact. Instead, it was being asked to accept a bilateral proposal worked out not with all the people of the territory but with the rebel régime. Furthermore, it was a proposal drawn up within the existing framework of minority privilege and racial discrimination against the African population—a framework long ago rejected by the United Nations.

In the proposals, he pointed out, progress towards majority rule was impeded at every stage; the guarantees against retrogressive amendment of the Constitution were completely unsatisfactory; improvement in the political status of the African population, far from being immediate, depended on an incalculable factor—the economic progress of the African majority; there were no firm guarantees of progress towards ending racial discrimination; and the modalities for determining the acceptability of the proposals by the people as a whole left much to be desired.

The representative of Somalia also noted that the new proposals were to be set within the framework of the blatantly racist Constitution of 1969, to which not only the United Nations but the United Kingdom had refused to accord legal recognition. Voter rolls were to remain segregated. Qualifications of candidates remained unchanged—a significant omission considering that the existing Constitution provided that anyone who had been detained or restricted for six months could not be a candidate for five years thereafter. The result of this would be that the majority of the African leaders would be eliminated from political life at a time when their experience and dedication were most needed. The infamous Land Tenure Act had been retained—a giant step towards the South African model of *apartheid.*

Somalia felt strongly, he said, that the proposals did not represent sufficient grounds for the United Kingdom to claim that it had done everything possible to fulfil its responsibilities towards the people of Southern Rhodesia. To grant independence while a white racist minority régime still held all the reins of power was to betray the African majority and give, finally, the powerful minority the opportunity to entrench its power, privileges and prejudices. Consequently, he urged the United Kingdom to continue to act in concert with the world community and on the basis of the objectives set and established by the United Nations.

However, since the agreement had already been signed and since the United Kingdom intended at all costs to set in motion the machinery for a test of acceptability, he put forward, as a second line of approach, proposals to ensure that the consultation with the people of Southern Rhodesia was valid and fully understood.

He suggested, first, that the period of the test should be long enough to enable a largely illiterate and rural African population to understand the proposals by means of a thorough educational campaign; second, that during that critical period the apparatus of the police State should be removed, maintenance of public order taken over by the United Kingdom and normal political activity, including activity by African political parties, permitted; third, that all political prisoners, detainees and restrictees should be released in order to participate in the educational campaign for their people; fourth, that the initial contribution of the United Kingdom to African education be applied immediately and specifically to adult education on the political issues involved in the settlement; and, last, that the United Kingdom arrange for a team of United Nations observers to observe preparations for and the actual exercise of the test of acceptability.

The Saudi Arabian spokesman suggested that the United Nations Educational, Scientific and Cultural Organization might institute an educational programme on human rights for all the inhabitants of Southern Rhodesia or that the United Nations might set up a fund to encourage a programme of civil disobedience and boycott in the territory.

The Zambian representative said his Government had concluded that the proposals would indefinitely postpone African majority rule in Southern Rhodesia. Messages smuggled out of the territory from Mr. Nkomo and Mr. Sithole had, he said, requested the Zambian delegation to report to the Security Council those leaders' total rejection of the agreement.

Ghana's representative disputed the United Kingdom's claim that it was unable to use force against the rebel régime, a method it had employed in several of its former colonies. Ghana feared that the new proposals would not only diminish the hopes of the Zimbabwe people but lead to frustration and despair and thus constitute an invitation to violence and revolution. Ghana appealed to the United Nations to maintain and strengthen the sanctions, extend them to Portugal and South Africa and reject any independence for Southern Rhodesia not based on majority rule. Otherwise, the United Nations would be faced with yet another *apartheid*-ridden minority régime within its ranks.

The representative of Kenya said that the new proposals were totally unacceptable and constituted a shameful betrayal of the Zimbabwe people and a flagrant violation of United Nations resolutions and the United Nations Charter. The United Kingdom's negotiations with the rebel régime had been held in total disregard of the principles laid down in resolutions of the Security Council and the General Assembly.

The United Kingdom representative, responding to some of the questions put to him during the debate and saying that he awaited instructions regarding others, confirmed his Government's intention to go ahead with the conduct of the test of acceptability, but said it was impossible to answer the hypothetical question as to what the United Kingdom would do if the proposals were rejected. He said that 97 African representatives, including Mr. Nkomo, had had consultations with the United Kingdom Foreign Secretary during his stay in Salisbury. As for the written or other communications received during those contacts, he said they were confidential and could not be made available to the Council without the consent of those who had submitted them.

With regard to guarantees concerning the development funds to be provided by his Government, he said that comprehensive discussions would be undertaken with the Rhodesians about the programme before any projects were selected or money disbursed. As to the suggestion that United Nations legal experts compare the proposed new Declaration of Rights with relevant United Nations instruments, he said that that would depend on the outcome of the usual consultations among the members and on further instructions from his Government; in his view, it would be more meaningful for such an examination, if carried out, to include a comparison with the provisions for the protection of human rights embodied in the legal systems of Member States—a comparison with what actually existed elsewhere and not just with an ideal situation.

The spokesman for China said that the essence of the question of Southern Rhodesia was the Zimbabwe people's struggle against foreign colonialist rule and for national independence. The colonialist authorities of Southern Rhodesia, with the connivance and support of imperialism, colonialism and neo-colonialism, had become unbridled in enforcing their fascist rule of the South African type over the people of Zimbabwe and had intensified their suppression of the struggle of the Zimbabwe people for national independence.

These colonialist authorities, he went on, had stepped up their military, economic and political collusion with the South African and Portuguese colonialists in carrying out threats and plotting various schemes of subversion and aggression against African countries, thus posing a grave menace to the independent African States and peoples. The so-called proposal for a settlement of the question of Southern Rhodesia which the British Government had contrived with the Smith régime behind the backs of the African people was, in fact, "a big fraud."

The Chinese representative maintained that as a result of the prolonged, brutal rule and plunder by foreign colonialists, the Zimbabwe people were poor and backward economically. The experience of the African and Asian countries proved, he said, that without political independence it was impossible to achieve economic independence. As long as colonialist rule and plunder existed, development of the national economy was impossible. How many people in Zimbabwe could possibly meet the economic and educational qualifications as stipulated in the proposals, he asked.

The proposals were aimed at legalizing fascist and racist rule over the Zimbabwe people, he added, and at enabling the colonialists and neo-colonialists openly to cancel the sanctions against the colonialist authorities of Southern Rhodesia. The Chinese Government and people totally rejected this fraud devised by the British Government and the colonialist authorities of Southern Rhodesia, and firmly supported the Zimbabwe people and other African countries and peoples in their just struggle against colonialist rule in Southern Rhodesia and for national independence.

Sierra Leone deplored the fact that the proposed constitutional arrangements were based on the illegal 1969 Constitution. It was apprehensive about the sincerity of the rebel regime's intentions to implement the terms of the proposals—in particular, the promised educational advancement of the Africans, changes in the Land Tenure Act, the ending of racial discrimination, and guarantees against retrogressive amendment of the Constitution. Sierra Leone also regretted that the proposals had been negotiated without the active participation of the African leaders of Zimbabwe.

Argentina noted that the responsibility of the United Kingdom for Southern Rhodesia had repeatedly been emphasized by the General Assembly and the Security Council and believed that the burden of that responsibility had motivated the United Kingdom to seek a negotiated solution to the difficult and reprehensible situation created by the Ian Smith régime. It was clear that the United Kingdom had taken a decision not to impose an agreement on the population of Southern Rhodesia. However, Argentina had fundamental objections about the system of voting and representation and about the long and indefinite period required to fulfil the terms of the agreement.

Nicaragua expressed the hope that the United Kingdom would continue its efforts to contribute to a solution consistent with the principles of the Charter and with the will of the people of Southern Rhodesia.

The Japanese representative said his Government recognized the primary responsibility and obligation of the United Kingdom to restore constitutional government in Southern Rhodesia and to ensure that the African majority enjoyed all political and economic rights. Japan, he said, had consistently supported the principle of majority rule in Southern Rhodesia on the basis of universal suffrage, though it did not subscribe to the view that the United Kingdom should use force to bring down the Smith régime and establish majority rule.

In Japan's view, he continued, the proposals did not seem to guarantee majority rule in the near future, and assumed the good faith of the current régime or a similar successor régime as the only guarantee for implementation. The proposals, if implemented in full, might help to improve the status of the African people and help to halt the deteriorating trend. But it was vitally important that the test of acceptability was conducted justly and fairly and the genuine will of the African population ascertained. Japan therefore strongly supported the suggestion that United Nations observers participate in carrying out the test of acceptability.

The spokesman for Poland said the question of Southern Rhodesia involved fundamental principles and decisions of the United Nations, but the administering power had consistently and deliberately pursued a course contrary to them and to the interests of the Zimbabwe people. First, there was the principle of the right to self-determination and independence contained in the Charter, developed by the General Assembly and reaffirmed by the Security Council; but the proposals elaborated by the United Kingdom and the Smith régime had already been rejected as a violation of that right of the Zimbabwe people by the Assembly, by the representatives of the African States in the Council and by the African leaders of Zimbabwe themselves. Instead of conducting talks with representatives of 5 million people, the United Kingdom had consulted only with the rebel régime, openly aiming at the recognition of its independent status.

The Polish representative went on to say that the United Nations sanctions had not been effective because of large-scale and wilful violations—the violators being protected in the Security Council by some of its permanent members. The erosion of sanctions was now being adduced as justification for the possible lifting of those sanctions.

Finally, he emphasized that the United Kingdom bore the primary responsibility for enabling the people of Southern Rhodesia to achieve self-determination and independence; the proposals for a settlement certainly did not provide for that. The United Nations and the Security Council could not become a party to an act of colonial and racist entrenchment, to a "deal" that was dooming an African people to many years of racist enslavement.

Italy's representative observed that the process of decolonization had halted at the borders of Southern Rhodesia, where a handful of settlers—defying the metropolitan power—had established their domination over millions of Africans. Italy, he said, had unconditionally supported the Security Council's measures to bring the Salisbury régime to an end, but even though the sanctions had had some results, they had not, unfortunately, brought the régime to its knees. Indeed, the sanctions were perhaps slowing down progress towards nationhood and self-determination for the territory when they cut off the people mainly concerned from all contacts with the outside world.

The Italian representative felt that the proposals, whatever their shortcomings, had been submitted to try to overcome the present deadlock and create conditions that might help improve the situation of the Africans and lead them towards self-determination. However unsatisfactory it might seem, the test of acceptability was the first concrete approach to the real problems involved. The test must be performed under fair and democratic conditions, and Italy felt, further, that the United Kingdom should try to associate the United Nations more closely with the conduct of the test.

The French representative said that the new proposals, whatever their inadequacies, had the merit of ending the *status quo* and offering the people of Southern Rhodesia the possibility of setting in motion a machinery that could and must transform their insitutions. France did not want to prejudge the test of acceptability but to await its results.

Uganda's spokesman said he found the proposals for a settlement to be unworkable, meaningless, inadequate as to guarantees and otherwise prejudicial to the interests of the majority of the people of Southern Rhodesia. The only test of acceptability in the colonial history of the United Kingdom had been by universal franchise, through an electoral process tested for almost 350 years; he did not understand why Southern Rhodesia should be exempted from that process.

He went on to say that the same régime that had violated the Constitution and passed discriminatory laws was to sit in judgement on the application of the Declaration of Rights; there was no assurance that those provisions would be faithfully implemented. Moreover, he said, Uganda could not understand why the United Kingdom declined to use force against Southern Rhodesia, after having done so in several of its former colonies. He urged the United Kingdom to listen to members of its own Parliament, to public opinion and to the Security Council, and accept modifications to the proposals that would not allow the legitimization of a rebellion.

Nigeria's representative said that the proposals for an agreement were tantamount to an endorsement by the United Kingdom Government of the perpetual subjugation of the black people of Southern Rhodesia by the white minority.

The United Nations, he said, should not be an accomplice to this attempt at abandoning the Zimbabwe people to bondage. If the United Kingdom would not use force to meet a situation which was currently out of hand, at least it should not put obstacles in the way of the Zimbabwe people by aiding and abetting the illegal régime of Ian Smith.

India said that over the years discussion in the Council had been characterized by a number of fictions: first, that the United Kingdom was responsible for the administration, defence and external relations of Southern Rhodesia but had neither the administrative machinery nor the power to enforce any decision on Southern Rhodesia or its rebel régime; second, that no British Government could be expected to use force against its kith and kin; and, third, that sanctions could bring down the Smith régime without being extended to South Africa, South West Africa [Namibia] and the Portuguese colonies. It would be of great advantage for a British Government to have the United Nations underwrite its decisions, but those decisions seemed to have been taken without regard for what the Security Council and the United Nations might or might not have

recommended or decided about the territory.

In India's view, the Pearce commission would have an impossible task in ascertaining the genuine wishes of the people of Southern Rhodesia under a state of emergency: the police State intact, recognized political leaders detained, the major political parties banned, and all channels of communication—radio and television included—available only to the parties in Parliament. India felt that for the United Nations to be associated with such an exercise would give respectability to the suppression and oppression of the black people of Southern Rhodesia and was therefore not appropriate. Sanctions should be strengthened and compulsorily applied; this would neither bring down the Smith régime nor introduce majority rule, but it would prove that international opinion would in no way be a party to giving respectability or recognition to that régime.

The representative of Algeria, who said he was speaking as one of three African countries carrying a mandate from the Organization of African Unity to follow the Security Council's debates on Southern Rhodesia, urged the Council to reject the proposals for an agreement as not complying with the principles laid down by the Council for a solution of the problem of Southern Rhodesia.

The spokesman for Belgium said that scrupulous implementation of sanctions had resulted for Belgium in the loss of important traditional markets. Belgium appreciated the initiative taken by the United Kingdom, which would introduce a thaw in the political situation in the territory. The state of stagnation and paralysis there was becoming more and more dangerous, since it led towards the creation of a new citadel of racism and intolerance. It was for the Security Council to take note of the United Kingdom's programme of action; it would be dangerous for the Council to arrogate to itself the right to dictate or impose a political settlement behind the back of the administering power. It should follow closely the implementation of the test of acceptability and the results and possible recommendations of the Pearce commission.

The representative of the United Kingdom said that some Council members sought an ideal solution of the problem; his Government had to take account of the harsh realities of the situation and the limitations on its effective power. He suggested six propositions by which the Council should be guided: first, that the position of the Africans in Southern Rhodesia was not yet as bleak as in South Africa but it had deteriorated in the past six years and might well lead to the degradation and misery of *apartheid;* second, that barring military intervention, the United Kingdom—even with the support of the United Nations—could not physically impose its will; third, that an agreed settlement was therefore the only way to avert the danger; fourth, that some details of the agreed proposals might be open to criticism and were not ideal; fifth, the proposals, however, if accepted, would bring about a change of direction and could lead towards majority rule in a multiracial society and a prosperous and expanding economy; and, sixth, the final word on the proposals must rest with the Rhodesians themselves—their views would be ascertained in an open, impartial and painstaking process of consultation.

On 30 December, the representative of Somalia formally introduced the text of a draft resolution which he had previously circulated as a working paper. The draft was sponsored also by Burundi, Sierra Leone and the Syrian Arab Republic.

By the preambular parts of this draft text, the Security Council—having considered the proposals for a settlement—would among other things note that the proposals, agreed upon by the United Kingdom and the rebel régime in Southern Rhodesia on the political and constitutional future of the territory, had not been negotiated in consultation with the accredited political leaders of the majority of the people of Southern Rhodesia.

The Council would then take note of the General Assembly's resolution of 20 December 1971 (2877(XXVI); for text, see DOCUMENTARY REFERENCES below) and reaffirm its own resolution of 17 November 1970[20] by which the Council called upon the United Kingdom, as administering power in the discharge of its responsibility, to take urgent and effective measures to bring to an end the illegal rebellion in Southern Rhodesia and enable the people to exercise their right to self-determination, in accordance with the Charter and in conformity with the objectives of the Assembly's resolution 1514(XV) of 14 December 1960.[21]

Mindful of the conditions necessary to permit the free expression of the right to self-determination, the Council would then recall its resolution of 6 May 1965[22] by which it endorsed the General Assembly's request to the United Kingdom to obtain: (a) the release of all political prisoners, detainees and restrictees; (b) the repeal of all repressive and discriminatory legislation, and in particular the Law and Order (Maintenance) Act and the Land Apportionment Act; and (c) the removal of all restrictions on political activity and the establishment of full democratic freedom and equality of political rights.

By the final preamblular part of the draft text, the Council would recognize, without prejudice to the primary role of the administering power, the special responsibilities of the United Nations towards the people of Southern Rhodesia in securing their inalienable rights.

By the operative parts of the draft resolution, the Security Council would:

(1) decide that the terms of these proposals did not fulfil the conditions necessary to ensure that all the people of Southern Rhodesia would be able to exercise freely and equally their right to self-determination;

(2) reject the "proposals for a settlement," as they did not guarantee the inalienable rights of the majority of the people of Southern Rhodesia;

(3) consider that the principle of universal adult suffrage for the people of Southern Rhodesia, without regard to colour or race, must be the basis for any constitutional and political arrangements for the territory;

(4) urge the United Kingdom, pursuant to paragraph (3) above, not to accord any form of recognition to an independent State of Southern Rhodesia which was not based on majority rule or on the will of the majority as determined by universal adult suffrage;

(5) call on the United Kingdom to ensure that in any exercise to ascertain the wishes of the people of Southern Rhodesia as to their political future, the procedure to be followed would be by secret referendum on the basis of one man, one vote, without regard to race or colour or to educational, property or income considerations;

(6) further call on the United Kingdom, after having ensured the establishment of conditions under which all the people of Southern Rhodesia would be able to exercise freely and equally their right to self-determination on the basis of paragraphs (3) and (5) above, to facilitate the participation of a United Nations team of observers during the preparation for, and in the actual conduct of, any exercise to ascertain the wishes of the people of Southern Rhodesia as to their political future;

(7) decide to continue with the imposition of political, diplomatic and economic sanctions on Southern Rhodesia until the rebellious régime in that territory was brought to an end; and

(8) request the United Kingdom Government not to transfer under any circumstances to its colony of Southern Rhodesia, as at present governed, any of the powers or attributes of sovereignty, but to promote the country's attainment of independence by a democratic system of government in accordance with the aspirations of the majority of the population.

When voting took place, on the same day, Somalia asked for separate votes on certain paragraphs.

The second preambular paragraph—by which

[20]See Y.U.N., 1970, pp. 183-84, text of resolution 288(1970).
[21]See footnote 14.
[22]See Y.U.N., 1965, pp. 128-29, text of resolution 202(1965).

the Council would note that the proposals for a settlement had not been negotiated in consultation with the accredited political leaders of the majority of the people of Southern Rhodesia—was adopted by 10 votes to 0, with 5 abstentions (Belgium, France, Italy, the United Kingdom and the United States).

The preambular paragraph by which the Council would state it was mindful of the conditions necessary to permit the free expression of the right to self-determination was adopted by 14 votes to 0, with 1 abstention (the United Kingdom).

The third operative paragraph—dealing with the principle of universal adult suffrage as the only basis for any constitutional and political arrangements for the territory—was adopted by 14 votes to 0, with 1 abstention (the United Kingdom).

The fourth operative paragraph—by which the Council would urge the United Kingdom not to accord recognition which was not based on majority rule or the will of the majority as determined by universal adult suffrage—was adopted by 10 votes to 0, with 5 abstentions (Belgium, France, Italy, the United Kingdom and the United States).

The fifth operative paragraph—by which the Council would call on the United Kingdom to ensure that the procedure to be followed in ascertaining the wishes of the people of the territory would be by secret referendum on the basis of one man, one vote, without regard to considerations of race, colour, education, property or income—was adopted by 10 votes to 0, with 5 abstentions (Belgium, France, Italy, the United Kingdom and the United States).

The draft resolution as a whole received 9 votes in favour to 1 against (the United Kingdom), with 5 abstentions (Belgium, France, Italy, Japan and the United States), and was not adopted owing to the negative vote of a permanent member of the Security Council.

Communications (December 1971)

By a letter of 6 December 1971 to the Secretary-General, the representative of the USSR transmitted the text of a statement of the Telegraphic Agency of the Soviet Union (TASS), dated 3 December, concerning the United Kingdom announcement that an agreement had been reached between London and Salisbury on "settling the constitutional conflict." This action, the statement said, was a direct infringement of the Zimbabwe people's inalienable rights and an open challenge to the African peoples and world public opinion.

By a letter of 29 December 1971 to the Secretary-General, the Nigerian representative transmitted the text of a statement made on 23 December by the Nigerian Commissioner for External Affairs rejecting the agreed proposals for a settlement in Southern Rhodesia and, among other things, urging: (*a*) effective United Nations intervention in Zimbabwe; (*b*) the immediate introduction of a constitution providing for majority rule under the supervision of a United Nations commission; (*c*) arrangement for massive international aid for economic reconstruction and educational development of Zimbabwe's African population; and (*d*) a United Nations guarantee of the territorial integrity of the new independent Zimbabwe.

Consideration by General Assembly

At its twenty-sixth session, which opened on 21 September 1971, the General Assembly referred the question of Southern Rhodesia to its Fourth Committee, which decided to consider the item together with the questions of Namibia and the territories under Portuguese administration. It decided to hold a general debate covering all three items, it being understood that individual draft resolutions on the items would be considered separately after the conclusion of the general debate and the hearing of petitioners. On this basis, the Fourth Committee considered the question of Southern Rhodesia at meetings held between 11 October and 16 December 1971. The General Assembly eventually adopted four resolutions on the question.

During its meetings, the Fourth Committee heard statements by Romesh Chandra, Lucio Luzzatto, Emilson Randriamihasinoro and Nicolai Voshinin of the World Peace Council; I. B. Tabata, President of the Unity Movement of South Africa; and the Reverend Michael Scott, International League for the Rights of Man.

In the course of the general debate on the question of colonial territories in southern Africa, Members agreed that the situation in Southern Rhodesia was deteriorating and that the illegal régime was persisting in its oppression of the people of Zimbabwe. The majority of speakers expressed the belief that the situation in Southern Rhodesia remained unsolved principally because of the failure of the United Kingdom, which as the administering power had the primary responsibility for bringing the rebellion to an end, to take effective action to bring down the illegal régime. This lack of action on the part of the United Kingdom was giving the illegal régime time to entrench itself and to increase its oppression of the African people.

Also stressed by many speakers was the failure of the sanctions policy imposed by the United Nations to bring down the illegal régime. This was felt to be a result of the open breach of sanctions by South Africa and Portugal, as well as the failure of other States, in particular the Western powers, to comply strictly with the provisions of Security Council resolutions governing sanctions. Therefore, it was said, although the sanctions policy was now in its sixth year, Southern Rhodesian trade continued to increase.

Trinidad and Tobago pointed out that, by maintaining normal trading relations with Southern Rhodesia, South Africa and Portugal had made it possible for the illegal régime to continue to export minerals and tobacco, either by buying the goods themselves and re-exporting them or by providing misleading certificates of origin. This "unholy alliance" between the three white régimes of southern Africa was being further consolidated by extensive military and police co-operation. Collaboration was reported between South African police forces and the security police of Southern Rhodesia against African freedom fighters. It was clear that this military bloc, which was being established to ensure the survival of white minority rule, could not have been created without the support of certain Western business interests and international finance corporations.

The representative of the Byelorussian SSR said that the sanctions were being ignored by Western powers, including the Federal Republic of Germany, Japan, the United Kingdom and the United States, which were carrying on trade with Southern Rhodesia through South Africa and Portugal.

The USSR—among others—felt that the support given by the Western powers to the illegal régime, as well as to Portugal and South Africa, was dictated by economic interests which had enormous investments in southern Africa and derived fabulous profits from the exploitation of its natural and human resources. The only way of rendering sanctions fully effective would be by extending them to South Africa and Portugal, to bring about their total political and economic isolation and to cut off all sources of assistance and supplies of weapons. Unfortunately, the United Kingdom and the United States—which had economic interests in southern Africa—had vetoed such proposals in the Security Council.

Sweden said that no matter how frustrating the results of sanctions had been so far, they had kept the illegal régime in political isolation and should not only be continued but strengthened. The means enumerated in Article 41 of the United Nations Charter[23] had not been exhausted and the sanctions could be widened to comprise further measures provided for in that Article.

Support for strengthening the sanctions policy and its scrupulous application was also expressed by Afghanistan, Ethiopia, Ghana, Jamaica, Mauritania, Nepal, Nigeria, Pakistan, Poland, Sudan and Turkey.

Iran said that sanctions could not be regarded as a substitute for the administering power's responsibility to introduce constitutional government in Southern Rhodesia on the basis of majority rule.

In Ghana's view, sanctions would be effective only if they were comprehensive, mandatory, properly supervised and extended to cover South Africa and Portugal. Since such sanctions were not being instituted, it would seem that the use of force or the threat of force should be reconsidered. Support for the use of force was also expressed by Egypt, Nepal, Pakistan, Sudan and Uganda, among others.

Brazil and Japan considered that the immediate problem of the United Nations was to find a solution to the problem of Southern Rhodesia without the use of force.

The representatives of Cameroon, Egypt, India, Indonesia, Mongolia, Morocco, Pakistan, Sierra Leone and Yugoslavia, among others, expressed the fear that, in view of the illegal régime's outspoken opposition to majority rule, any settlement arrived at between the illegal régime and the administering power would continue to deny the Africans of Southern Rhodesia their inalienable right to self-determination and independence.

India stressed that any negotiations undertaken by the administering power should be with the true representatives of the people of Zimbabwe and not with the illegal régime, which had shown no intention of instituting majority rule in Southern Rhodesia.

Jamaica, Nepal, Sierra Leone and Uganda, among others, said they could not accept independence for Southern Rhodesia under the present régime, and would condemn any settlement which granted independence before majority rule was established.

Ecuador and others said that any talks between the United Kingdom and the illegal régime were in violation of General Assembly resolutions on Southern Rhodesia which called for a severance of all relationships with that régime. India, Indonesia, Iran and Morocco held that negotiations between the United Kingdom and the illegal régime on any basis other than the principle of majority rule prior to independence gave the impression of tacit recognition of that régime and should be rejected.

Chile, Iceland, India, Mali, Nigeria, and the Syrian Arab Republic stressed the need for all Member States to give material and moral assistance to the national liberation movements of Zimbabwe to enable the African people themselves to achieve their legitimate rights.

On 10 November, the United Kingdom representative drew attention to a statement by the

[23]For text of Article 41 of the Charter, see APPENDIX II

United Kingdom Foreign Secretary on 9 November in which he announced his intention to hold talks in Southern Rhodesia. In that statement, he had said that any basis for settlement would have to be ·consistent with the five principles to which the United Kingdom adhered (see p. 94) and that, if agreement was reached, the United Kingdom Government would have to satisfy itself that the terms were fully understood by the Southern Rhodesian people as a whole and acceptable to them. The United Kingdom Government was firmly convinced that a settlement based on the five principles would offer the means of enabling Southern Rhodesia to embark peacefully on a new phase of its development which would be in the best interests of all the people of Southern Rhodesia.

The United Republic of Tanzania, supported by Egypt, Somalia, Sudan and Zambia, rejected the five principles as being a formula that would satisfy the interests of the white minority and betray the Zimbabwe people. The real intention of the United Kingdom Government, he said, was to make peace with the rebels by disregarding the rights of the Zimbabwe people and thereby to save face on the international scene. He made a final appeal to the administering power to give up negotiating with the illegal régime and to recognize the right of the African majority to self-determination.

Following the general debate, a draft resolution was put forward in the Fourth Committee, eventually sponsored by the following 23 Member States: Burundi, Cameroon, the Congo, Ethiopia, Ghana, India, Indonesia, Iraq, Liberia, Mali, Mongolia, Nigeria, Pakistan, the People's Democratic Republic of Yemen, the Philippines, Sudan, the Syrian Arab Republic, Togo, Uganda, the United Republic of Tanzania, Upper Volta, Yugoslavia and Zambia.

On 11 November, the draft resolution, as revised by the sponsors, was approved by the Fourth Committee by a roll-call vote of 93 to 2, with 12 abstentions. On 16 November, the General Assembly adopted the text—as amended by Ghana on behalf of the sponsors—by a roll-call vote of 106 to 2, with 13 abstentions, as resolution 2765(XXVI).

By the preambular paragraphs to this text, the Assembly—after recalling previous resolutions adopted on the question of Southern Rhodesia—expressed its grave concern at the recent decision of the United States Congress which, if confirmed, would permit the importation of chrome into the United States from Southern Rhodesia and thus constitute a serious violation of the Security Council resolutions imposing sanctions against the illegal régime in Southern Rhodesia.

By the operative part of this text, the Assembly:

(1) called upon the United States Government to take the necessary measures—in compliance with Security Council resolutions concerning sanctions and bearing in mind its obligations under Article 25 of the Charter[24]—to prevent the importation of chrome into the United States from Southern Rhodesia;

(2) asked the United States to inform the Assembly at its current session of the action taken or envisaged in implementing the present resolution;

(3) asked the President of the Assembly to draw the attention of the United States Government to the urgent need for implementing the resolution;

(4) reminded all Member States of their obligations under the Charter to comply fully with the Security Council's decisions on mandatory sanctions against the illegal régime in Southern Rhodesia; and

(5) decided to keep this and other aspects of the question under continuous review.

(For text of resolution 2765(XXVI), see DOCUMENTARY REFERENCES below.)

Prior to the vote on the 23-power draft resolution in the Fourth Committee, the representative of the United States categorically rejected the allegation that his Government had been guilty of sanction-breaking. Except for one instance—which had occurred before the imposition of sanctions—the United States had not imported any chrome from Southern Rhodesia since 1965. However, the latest report of the Security Council's Committee on sanctions indicated that Southern Rhodesia was exporting more chrome than in 1965, which meant that other countries whose names were not mentioned in the draft resolution must certainly have violated sanctions. His Government would continue to adhere to the sanctions and report to the Committee on sanctions in due course on legislation adopted by the United States and its possible effect on the sanctions programme. Since Congress had not completed its examination of the bill referred to in the draft resolution, the United States would not take part in the vote.

The spokesmen for Austria, Belgium, Brazil, France, Greece and the United Kingdom said that adoption of the draft resolution would be an encroachment on the responsibilities and competence of the Security Council and its Committee on sanctions, which were the proper bodies to consider alleged violations of sanctions. They would therefore abstain from voting. The representative of Italy said the draft resolution amounted to interference in the law-making processes of a Member State and was thus contrary

[24]For text of Article 25 of the Charter, see APPENDIX II.

to the Charter. The Netherlands representative said it was not the Fourth Committee's place to exert pressure on the United States Government, which thus far had always supported the sanctions programme.

A second resolution on the question of Southern Rhodesia was approved by the Fourth Committee on 19 November by a roll-call vote of 99 to 3, with 10 abstentions. It was sponsored by the following 31 Member States: Algeria, Barbados, Burundi, Cameroon, Chad, the Congo, Ethiopia, Ghana, Guinea, Guyana, Iraq, Jamaica, Kenya, Lesotho, Liberia, Mali, Mauritania, Niger, Nigeria, Pakistan, the People's Democratic Republic of Yemen, Rwanda, Senegal, Sierra Leone, Sudan, the Syrian Arab Republic, Uganda, the United Republic of Tanzania, Yugoslavia, Zaire and Zambia.

The General Assembly adopted the text on 22 November by a roll-call vote of 102 to 3, with 9 abstentions, as resolution 2769(XXVI).

By the preambular part of this resolution, the General Assembly among other things noted the statement made in the House of Commons on 9 November 1971 by the United Kingdom Foreign Secretary announcing his Government's decision to hold the talks that were currently under way in Salisbury with the illegal racist minority régime.

By the operative paragraphs, the General Assembly: (1) reaffirmed the principle that there should be no independence before majority rule in Southern Rhodesia; (2) affirmed that any settlement relating to the future of that territory must be worked out with the fullest participation of all nationalist leaders representing the majority of the people of Zimbabwe and must be endorsed freely by the people; and (3) decided to keep the situation in the territory under review.

(For text of resolution 2769(XXVI), see DOCU-MENTARY REFERENCES below.)

On 24 November, a third draft resolution was approved by the Fourth Committee by a roll-call vote of 89 to 10, with 13 abstentions. It was sponsored by the following 34 Member States: Afghanistan, Algeria, Burma, Burundi, Cameroon, Chad, the Congo, Egypt, Ethiopia, the Gambia, Ghana, Guinea, India, Indonesia, Iraq, Kenya, the Khmer Republic, the Libyan Arab Republic, Mali, Mauritania, Mongolia, Niger, Nigeria, Pakistan, the People's Democratic Republic of Yemen, Somalia, Sudan, the Syrian Arab Republic, Tunisia, Uganda, the United Republic of Tanzania, Yugoslavia, Zaire and Zambia.

The General Assembly adopted the text on 10 December by a recorded vote of 91 to 9, with 12 abstentions, as resolution 2796(XXVI).

By the preambular part of this text, the General Assembly among other things expressed its grave concern at the further deterioration of the situation in Southern Rhodesia—which the Securi-ty Council had reaffirmed as constituting a threat to international peace and security—resulting from the failure and refusal of the United Kingdom to put an end to the illegal racist minority régime, and from the racialist and repressive policies pursued by that régime in violation of the relevant United Nations resolutions.

It also expressed deep concern about the continued presence of South African forces in the territory, which constituted a threat to the sovereignty and territorial integrity of neighbouring African States, and deplored the continued collaboration of certain States—in particular South Africa and Portugal—with the illegal régime, thereby seriously obstructing the efforts of the international community to put an end to that régime.

It also noted that the United Kingdom, as the administering power, had the primary responsibility for putting an end to the rebellion of the British settlers who organized the illegal régime and for transferring effective power to the people of Zimbabwe on the basis of the principle of majority rule.

It further deplored the intransigent attitude of the United Kingdom, which persisted in refusing to co-operate with the Special Committee on the Situation with regard to the Implementation of the Declaration on the Granting of Independence to Colonial Countries and Peoples in the discharge of the mandate entrusted to it by the General Assembly, and noted with deep regret the decision of the International Olympic Committee to permit the so-called National Olympic Committee of Rhodesia to participate in the XXth Olympic Games.

By the operative paragraphs of the resolution, the General Assembly:

(1) reaffirmed the inalienable right of the people of Zimbabwe to self-determination, freedom and independence and the legitimacy of their struggle to secure by all the means at their disposal the enjoyment of that right as set forth in the Charter and in conformity with the General Assembly's resolution of 14 December 1960;[25]

(2) strongly deplored the continued refusal of the United Kingdom to take effective measures to bring down the illegal racist minority régime in Southern Rhodesia and to transfer power without any delay to the people of Zimbabwe on the basis of majority rule, in accordance with the relevant resolutions of the General Assembly, and called upon that Government to take such measures without further delay;

(3) condemned the continued intervention and presence of South African armed forces in

[25]See Y.U.N., 1960, pp. 49-50, text of resolution 1514(XV).

Southern Rhodesia in violation of Security Council resolutions, and called upon the administering power to ensure the immediate expulsion of all such forces;

(4) condemned the policies of those Governments—particularly South Africa and Portugal—which continued to maintain political, economic, military and other relations with the illegal régime, in contravention of the relevant United Nations resolutions and contrary to their obligations under the Charter, and called upon those Governments to cease forthwith all such relations;

(5) reaffirmed its conviction that the sanctions would not put an end to the illegal régime unless they were comprehensive, mandatory, effectively supervised, enforced and complied with by all States, particularly by South Africa and Portugal;

(6) strongly urged all States to take more stringent measures to prevent any circumvention by individuals and corporate bodies of the sanctions prescribed by the Security Council, and to refrain from any action which might confer a semblance of legitimacy on the illegal régime;

(7) strongly deplored the imprisonment and detention of Zimbabwe freedom fighters by the illegal régime, and called upon the administering power to effect their immediate and unconditional release;

(8) called upon all States to take all appropriate steps to ensure the exclusion of the so-called National Olympic Committee of Rhodesia from participating in the XXth Olympic Games;

(9) called upon all States, the specialized agencies and other organizations within the United Nations system—in consultation with the Organization of African Unity—to extend all moral and material assistance to the people of Zimbabwe;

(10) called upon the United Kingdom—in view of the armed conflict in the territory and the inhuman treatment of prisoners—to ensure the application to that situation of the 1949 Geneva Conventions relative to the treatment of prisoners of war and to the protection of civilian persons in time of war;

(11) called upon the United Kingdom to report on the implementation of the present resolution to the Special Committee and to the twenty-seventh (1972) session of the General Assembly;

(12) drew the attention of the Security Council—in view of the gravity of the situation arising from the further intensification of repressive activities against the Zimbabwe people—to the urgent necessity of taking further steps to ensure the full and strict compliance by all States with the Council's decisions, in accordance with Article 25 of the Charter, and to the need to widen the scope of the sanctions against the illegal racist minority

régime and to impose sanctions against South Africa and Portugal, whose Governments persisted in their refusal to carry out the mandatory decisions of the Council;

(13) asked the Secretary-General to report to the Assembly in 1972 on the implementation of the present resolution; and

(14) asked the Special Committee to keep the situation in the territory under review.

(For text of resolution 2796(XXVI), see DOCUMENTARY REFERENCES below.)

On 16 December, the Fourth Committee approved—by a roll-call vote of 78 to 8, with 21 abstentions—a fourth draft resolution on the question of Southern Rhodesia, sponsored by the following 34 Member States: Afghanistan, Algeria, Barbados, Burundi, Cameroon, Chad, the Congo, Egypt, Equatorial Guinea, Ethiopia, the Gambia, Guinea, Guyana, Jamaica, Kenya, the Libyan Arab Republic, Mali, Mauritania, Mongolia, Nigeria, the People's Democratic Republic of Yemen, Rwanda, Saudi Arabia, Sierra Leone, Somalia, Sudan, the Syrian Arab Republic, Togo, Trinidad and Tobago, Uganda, the United Republic of Tanzania, Yugoslavia, Zaire and Zambia.

On 20 December, the General Assembly, by a roll-call vote of 94 to 8, with 22 abstentions, adopted the text as resolution 2877(XXVI).

By the preambular part of this text, the Assembly among other things expressed its grave concern at the "proposals for a settlement" which, if implemented, would entrench the rule of the racist minority régime in Southern Rhodesia and perpetuate the enslavement of the African people of Zimbabwe. After observing that the proposals had been agreed upon without the participation of the representatives of the African people of Zimbabwe, the Assembly, by the operative paragraphs of the text:

(1) rejected the "proposals for a settlement" agreed upon by the United Kingdom and the racist minority régime in Salisbury as constituting a flagrant violation of the inalienable right of the African people of Zimbabwe to self-determination and independence;

(2) reaffirmed that no settlement which did not conform strictly to the principle of "no independence before majority rule" on the basis of one man, one vote, would be acceptable;

(3) invited the Security Council, when examining the question of Southern Rhodesia, to consider taking appropriate measures—in accordance with relevant Charter provisions—to enable the Zimbabwe people to exercise freely and without further delay their inalienable right to self-determination and independence;

(4) welcomed the Security Council's decision of 2 December 1971 to invite Messrs. Nkomo and Sithole, the leaders of ZAPU and ZANU, to appear

before the Council to express their views about the future status of the territory, and called on the United Kingdom, as the administering power, to comply with that decision; and

(5) called upon all States to adhere strictly to the relevant provisions of resolutions of the Assembly and the Security Council on the question of Southern Rhodesia, and in particular to observe the Council's resolutions imposing sanctions against the racist minority régime.

(For text of resolution 2877(XXVI), see DOCU-MENTARY REFERENCES below.)

Other General Assembly decisions

At its twenty-sixth session, the General Assembly took a number of other decisions bearing upon general and specific aspects of the situation in Southern Rhodesia. These are described briefly below.

DECLARATION ON GRANTING INDEPENDENCE

On 20 December, the General Assembly adopted two resolutions on the implementation of the 1960 Declaration on the Granting of Independence to Colonial Countries and Peoples.

By one of these (2878(XXVI)), the Assembly among other things reaffirmed that the continuation of colonialism in all its forms and manifestations—including racism, *apartheid* and activities of foreign economic and other interests, as well as the waging of colonial wars to suppress national liberation movements in southern Africa—was incompatible with the Charter, the Universal Declaration of Human Rights and the Declaration on the granting of independence and posed a threat to international peace and security.

The Assembly also reaffirmed its recognition of the legitimacy of the struggle of colonial peoples to exercise their right to self-determination and independence by all the necessary means at their disposal, and noted with satisfaction the progress made by national liberation movements, both through their struggle and through reconstruction programmes.

All States and the specialized agencies and other organizations were urged by the Assembly to provide moral and material assistance to all peoples struggling for their freedom and independence in the colonial territories. States were asked to withhold assistance of any kind from Portugal, from South Africa and from the illegal régime in Southern Rhodesia until they renounced their policy of colonial domination and racial discrimination; the colonial powers were asked to withdraw their military bases and installations immediately from colonial territories.

The Special Committee on the Situation with regard to the Implementation of the Declaration on the Granting of Independence to Colonial Countries and Peoples was asked by the Assembly to make concrete suggestions which might assist the Security Council in considering appropriate measures regarding developments in colonial territories likely to threaten international peace and security, and to undertake a special study on the compliance of Member States with the Declaration and other relevant resolutions on decolonization, particularly those relating to the territories under Portuguese domination, Namibia and Southern Rhodesia. (See also pp. 518-20.)

By another resolution (2874(XXVI)), on implementation of the Declaration on granting independence by the specialized agencies and international institutions associated with the United Nations, the General Assembly among other things reaffirmed that recognition by United Nations bodies of the legitimacy of the struggle of colonial peoples to achieve freedom and independence entailed the extension of all necessary moral and material assistance to national liberation movements, and reiterated its appeal to the specialized agencies and other United Nations organizations to render all such assistance possible to the peoples in Africa struggling for their liberation from colonial rule and to work out —with the co-operation of the Organization of African Unity (OAU) and, through it, of the national liberation movements—concrete programmes for assisting the peoples of Southern Rhodesia, Namibia and the territories under Portuguese administration.

The Assembly also asked the specialized agencies and other organizations to discontinue all collaboration with Portugal and South Africa, as well as with the illegal régime in Southern Rhodesia, and invited those organizations to continue to examine, in consultation with OAU, the participation of representatives of the national liberation movements in conferences, seminars and other regional meetings. (See also pp. 526-27.)

IMPORTANCE OF THE RIGHT
TO SELF-DETERMINATION

On 6 December, the General Assembly adopted a resolution (2787(XXVI)) on the importance of the universal realization of the right of peoples to self-determination, which had been recommended by the Commission on Human Rights and the Economic and Social Council.

By this text, the Assembly among other things: confirmed the legality of the peoples' struggle for self-determination and liberation from colonial and foreign domination and alien subjugation, notably in southern Africa, and in particular that of the peoples of Zimbabwe and other territories; called upon all States to give political, moral and material assistance to peoples struggling for liberation, self-determination and independence;

and condemned the colonial and usurping powers that were suppressing the right of peoples to self-determination and hampering the liquidation of the last hotbeds of colonialism and racism. The Assembly also resolved to devote constant attention to the question of flagrant large-scale violations of human rights and fundamental freedoms resulting from the denial to peoples under colonial and foreign domination of their right to self-determination. (See also pp. 420-22.)

FOREIGN ECONOMIC INTERESTS

On 20 December, the General Assembly adopted a resolution (2873(XXVI)) on the activities of foreign economic and other interests impeding the implementation of the Declaration on the Granting of Independence to Colonial Countries and Peoples in Southern Rhodesia, Namibia and territories under Portuguese domination and in all other territories under colonial domination, and efforts to eliminate colonialism, *apartheid* and racial discrimination in southern Africa.

By this, the Assembly among other things reaffirmed the inalienable right of the peoples of dependent territories to self-determination and independence and to the enjoyment of the natural resources of their territories, as well as their right to dispose of those resources in their best interests, and affirmed that foreign economic, financial and other interests operating in the colonial territories of Southern Rhodesia, Namibia and those under Portuguese domination constituted a major obstacle to political independence and to the enjoyment of the natural resources of those territories by the indigenous inhabitants.

Further, the Assembly reiterated its declaration that any administering power, by depriving colonial peoples of the exercise of their rights or by subordinating them to foreign economic and financial interests, violated the obligations it had assumed under the United Nations Charter. It also condemned the current activities and operating methods of those foreign economic and other interests which were designed to perpetuate the subjugation of dependent peoples, and deplored the support given by colonial powers and other States to those foreign economic and other interests engaged in exploiting the natural and human resources of the territories without regard to the welfare of the indigenous peoples, thus violating their political, economic and social rights.

The Assembly also called upon administering powers to abolish every discriminatory and unjust wage system which prevailed in the territories under their administration and to apply a uniform system of wages to all inhabitants. It called upon the colonial powers and States concerned whose companies and nationals were engaged in enterprises detrimental to the interests of the inhabitants of those territories to take measures to put an end to such enterprises and to prevent new investments which ran counter to the interests of the inhabitants. All States were asked to take effective measures to end the supply of funds and other forms of assistance, including military equipment, to those régimes which used such assistance to repress the national liberation movements. (See also pp. 532-34.)

ELIMINATION OF RACIAL DISCRIMINATION

On 6 December, the General Assembly adopted a four-part resolution (2784(XXVI)) on the elimination of all forms of racial discrimination.

By this text, the Assembly among other things called upon all trading partners of South Africa to abstain from encouraging South Africa and the illegal régime in Southern Rhodesia to continue to violate the International Convention on the Elimination of All Forms of Racial Discrimination and to use their influence to eradicate *apartheid* and racial discrimination in Namibia and Southern Rhodesia. The Assembly also called upon the United Kingdom, as the administering power, to adopt all necessary measures, including the use of force, to end the racist and illegal régime of Ian Smith.

Annexed to the resolution was a message from the President of the General Assembly to the heads of State or Government, which made the following points, among others:

(a) the racist Government of South Africa and the illegal régime in Southern Rhodesia had blatantly continued to pursue policies of racial discrimination and *apartheid;*

(b) the racist Government of South Africa continued to effect an extensive arms build-up, threatening the independent African States opposed to its racist policies, as well as those peoples struggling against the racial and inhuman policies in southern Africa;

(c) racist policies in southern Africa had been permitted to expand through the continued existence and operation of the white racist minority régime in Southern Rhodesia because of the deliberate ineffectiveness of measures so far taken by the United Kingdom;

(d) the racist Governments in southern Africa had been further strengthened through the maintenance by many States of political, commercial, military, economic, social and other relations with them, and through an unholy alliance between South Africa, Portugal and Southern Rhodesia established to suppress the struggle of the peoples of that region and to silence the cry of Africa against racism, *apartheid,* economic exploitation and colonial domination.

It was recommended in the message that the following measures be taken, among others, in connexion with and as a continuation of the International Year for Action to Combat Racism and Racial Discrimination: continuation of open moral support and the increasing of material aid to the peoples struggling against racial discrimination and *apartheid*; termination of all relations with the South African Government and all other racist régimes; and the repeal of all laws and regulations contributing to the maintenance and propagation of racial discrimination. (See also pp. 398-400.)

HUMAN RIGHTS IN ARMED CONFLICTS

In a resolution (2852(XXVI)) adopted on 20 December, on respect for human rights in armed conflicts, the General Assembly among other things reaffirmed that persons participating in resistance movements and freedom fighters in southern Africa and in territories under colonial and alien domination and foreign occupation struggling for their liberation and self-determination should, in case of arrest, be treated as prisoners of war in accordance with the principles of the Hague Convention of 1907 and the Geneva Conventions of 1949. The Assembly also drew attention to the need to evolve norms designed to increase the protection of persons struggling

against colonial and alien domination, foreign occupation and racist régimes. (See also pp. 424-26.)

Educational and Training Programme for Southern Africa

Under the United Nations Educational and Training Programme for Southern Africa, established by the General Assembly in 1967, 454 applications from Southern Rhodesia were received during the period from 1 November 1970 to 8 October 1971. Fifty-six new awards were made and 55 were extended. There were 111 Southern Rhodesians studying abroad in 14 countries.

On 20 December 1971, the General Assembly adopted a resolution (2875(XXVI)) by which, among other things, it decided to appropriate $100,000 from the United Nations regular budget for the financial year 1972 to ensure continuity of the Programme, pending receipt of adequate voluntary contributions.

(For additional information about the Educational and Training Programme for Southern Africa, see pp. 123-25.)

DOCUMENTARY REFERENCES

*Communications and reports to Security Council
(January-November 1971)*

S/10229 and Add.1 and 2 and Corr.1. Fourth report, dated 16 June 1971, of Committee established in pursuance of Security Council resolution 253(1968) of 29 May 1968, and addenda dated 16 June and 13 July 1971.
S/10229 Add.2, Annex III. Table on trade in commodities annexed to 4th report.
S/10249 and Corr.1, S/10298, S/10312. Letters of 2 July, 25 August and 10 September 1971 from Chairman of Special Committee on Situation with regard to Implementation of Declaration on Granting of Independence to Colonial Countries and Peoples (transmitting text of resolutions adopted by Special Committee on 2 July, 24 August and 9 September 1971, respectively).
S/10355. Letter of 6 October 1971 from Acting Chairman of Special Committee on Situation with regard to Implementation of Declaration on Granting of Independence to Colonial Countries and Peoples (transmitting text of two consensuses adopted by Special Committee on 6 October 1971).
S/10385. Letter of 8 November 1971 from Upper Volta (transmitting statement adopted on 5 November 1971 by African group).

Consideration by Special Committee

Special Committee on Situation with regard to Implementation of Declaration on Granting of Independence to Colonial Countries and Peoples, meetings 782, 784-791, 793, 795, 796, 802-803, 806, 807, 813, 814, 817-820, 824, 825, 828.

A/8423/Rev.1, Vol. II. Report of Special Committee (covering its work during 1971), Chapter VI. (Section B: Decisions of Special Committee; Section D: Further decisions of Special Committee.)
A/8423/Rev.1, Vol. II, Chapter V. Meetings in Africa of *Ad Hoc* Group of Special Committee. (Section B: Decisions of Special Committee.)

*Consideration by Security Council
(November-December 1971)*

Security Council, meetings 1601-1605, 1609, 1622, 1623.

S/10229 and Add.1,2. Fourth report, dated 16 June 1971, of Committee established in pursuance of Security Council resolution 253(1968) of 29 May 1968, and addenda dated 16 June and 13 July 1971.
S/10396. Letter of 24 November 1971 from United Kingdom (request to convene Council).
S/10398-S/10400, S/10404. Letters of 25, 29 and 30 November 1971 from Saudi Arabia, United Republic of Tanzania, Kenya and Zambia (requests to participate in Council's discussion).
S/10405. Letter of 1 December 1971 from United Kingdom (transmitting text of White Paper entitled: "Rhodesia: Proposals for a Settlement").
S/10407. Letter of 2 December 1971 from Ghana (request to participate in Council's discussion).
S/10408. Interim report dated 3 December 1971 of Committee established in pursuance of Security Council resolution 253(1968) of 29 May 1968.
S/10427 (A/8551). Letter of 6 December 1971 from USSR (transmitting TASS statement of 3 December 1971).
S/10470. Note of 23 December 1971 by President of Security Council.
S/10478. Letter of 29 December 1971 from Uganda (request to participate in Council's discussion).
S/10481 (A/8650). Letter of 29 December 1971 from Nigeria (transmitting statement of 23 December 1971 by Nigerian Commissioner for External Affairs).
S/10482-S/10484. Letters of 29 and 30 December 1971 from Nigeria, Algeria and India (requests to participate in Council's discussion).
S/10489. Burundi, Sierra Leone, Somalia, Syrian Arab Republic: draft resolution, rejected by Council on 30 December 1971, meeting 1623, by vote of 9 in favour (Argentina, Burundi, China,

Nicaragua, Poland, Sierra Leone, Somalia, Syrian Arab Republic, USSR) to 1 against (United Kingdom), with 5 abstentions (Belgium, France, Italy, Japan, United States).

Consideration by General Assembly

General Assembly—26th session
Fourth Committee, meetings 1923-1926, 1928-1949, 1951-1959. 1963, 1965, 1970-1972.
Plenary meetings 1984, 1991, 2012, 2028.

A/8401. Report of Secretary-General on work of the Organization, 16 June 1970–15 June 1971: Part One, Chapter IV G; Part Two, Chapter I B 1.

A/8401 Add.1. Introduction to report of Secretary-General, September 1971: Part One, Chapter V, para. 60; Part Two, Chapter VIII, para. 300.

A/8402. Report of Security Council, 16 June 1970–15 June 1971, Chapter 4.

A/8423/Rev.1, Vol. II. Report of Special Committee on Situation with regard to Implementation of Declaration on Granting of Independence to Colonial Countries and Peoples (covering its work during 1971), Chapters V and VI.

A/8551 (S/10427). Letter of 6 December 1971 from USSR (transmitting TASS statement of 3 December 1971).

A/8650 (S/10481). Letter of 29 December 1971 from Nigeria (transmitting statement of 23 December 1971 by Nigerian Commissioner for External Affairs).

A/C.4/736 and Add.1. Questions of Namibia, territories under Portuguese administration and Southern Rhodesia: requests for hearing.

A/C.4/741. Question of Southern Rhodesia: request for hearing.

A/C.4/L.988. Burundi, Cameroon, Congo, Ethiopia, Ghana, India, Indonesia, Iraq, Liberia, Mali, Mongolia, Nigeria, Pakistan, People's Democratic Republic of Yemen, Philippines, Sudan, Syrian Arab Republic, Uganda, United Republic of Tanzania, Upper Volta, Yugoslavia, Zambia: draft resolution.

A/C.4/L.988/Rev.1. Revised draft resolution, sponsored by above 22 powers and Togo, approved by Fourth Committee on 11 November 1971, meeting 1948, by roll-call vote of 93 to 2, with 12 abstentions, as follows:

In favour: Afghanistan, Algeria, Argentina, Australia, Barbados, Bulgaria, Burma, Burundi, Byelorussian SSR, Cameroon, Central African Republic, Ceylon, Chile, Colombia, Congo, Costa Rica, Cuba, Czechoslovakia, Dahomey, Denmark, Ecuador, Egypt, Equatorial Guinea, Ethiopia, Fiji, Finland, Gabon, Gambia, Ghana, Guinea, Guyana, Haiti, Hungary, Iceland, India, Indonesia, Iran, Iraq, Ireland, Ivory Coast, Jamaica, Japan, Jordan, Kenya, Kuwait, Lebanon, Lesotho, Liberia, Libyan Arab Republic, Madagascar, Malaysia, Mali, Mauritania, Mauritius, Mexico, Mongolia, Nepal, New Zealand, Niger, Nigeria, Norway, Pakistan, People's Democratic Republic of Yemen, Peru, Philippines, Poland, Romania, Saudi Arabia, Senegal, Sierra Leone, Singapore, Somalia, Spain, Sudan, Swaziland, Sweden, Syrian Arab Republic, Thailand, Togo, Trinidad and Tobago, Tunisia, Turkey, Uganda, Ukrainian SSR, USSR, United Republic of Tanzania, Upper Volta, Uruguay, Venezuela, Yemen, Yugoslavia, Zaire, Zambia.
Against: Portugal, South Africa.
Abstaining: Austria, Belgium, Brazil, Canada, Dominican Republic, France, Greece, Guatemala, Italy, Luxembourg, Netherlands, United Kingdom.

A/C.4/L.989. Draft report of Fourth Committee (part I).
A/L.643. Ghana: amendment to draft resolution recommended by Fourth Committee in A/8518.
A/8518. Report of Fourth Committee (part I).

RESOLUTION 2765(XXVI), as recommended by Fourth Committee, A/8518, and as amended by Ghana, A/L.643, adopted by Assembly on 16 November 1971, meeting 1984, by roll-call vote of 106 to 2, with 13 abstentions, as follows:

In favour: Afghanistan, Albania, Algeria, Argentina, Australia, Austria, Bahrain, Barbados, Botswana, Bulgaria, Burma, Burundi, Byelorussian SSR, Cameroon, Central African Republic, Ceylon, Chad, Chile, China, Colombia, Congo, Cuba, Cyprus, Czechoslovakia, Dahomey, Denmark, Ecuador, Egypt, Equatorial Guinea, Ethiopia, Fiji, Finland, Gabon, Gambia, Ghana, Guinea, Guyana, Haiti, Honduras, Hungary, Iceland, India, Indonesia, Iran, Iraq, Ireland, Ivory Coast, Jamaica, Japan, Jordan, Kenya, Kuwait, Laos, Lebanon, Lesotho, Liberia, Libyan Arab Republic, Madagascar, Malaysia, Mali, Malta, Mauritania, Mexico, Mongolia, Morocco, Nepal, New Zealand, Niger, Nigeria, Norway, Oman, Pakistan, Panama, Paraguay, People's Democratic Republic of Yemen, Peru, Philippines, Poland, Romania, Rwanda, Saudi Arabia, Senegal, Sierra Leone, Singapore, Somalia, Spain, Sudan, Swaziland, Sweden, Syrian Arab Republic, Thailand, Togo, Trinidad and Tobago, Tunisia, Turkey, Uganda, Ukrainian SSR, USSR, United Republic of Tanzania, Upper Volta, Uruguay, Venezuela, Yemen, Yugoslavia, Zaire, Zambia.
Against: Portugal, South Africa.
Abstaining: Belgium, Brazil, Canada, Dominican Republic, El Salvador, France, Greece, Guatemala, Italy, Luxembourg, Malawi, Netherlands, United Kingdom.

The General Assembly,

Having considered the question of Southern Rhodesia,

Recalling its resolution 1514(XV) of 14 December 1960, containing the Declaration on the Granting of Independence to Colonial Countries and Peoples, and its resolution 2621(XXV) of 12 October 1970, containing the programme of action for the full implementation of the Declaration,

Recalling also the relevant resolutions of the Security Council, particularly its resolution 232(1966) of 16 December 1966, 253(1968) of 29 May 1968, 277(1970) of 18 March 1970 and 288(1970) of 17 November 1970,

Recalling further all previous resolutions concerning the question of Southern Rhodesia adopted by the General Assembly and the Special Committee on the Situation with regard to the Implementation of the Declaration on the Granting of Independence to Colonial Countries and Peoples, and also the consensus adopted by the Special Committee at its 828th meeting, on 6 October 1971,

Expressing its grave concern at the recent decision taken by the Congress of the United States of America which, if confirmed, would permit the importation of chrome into the United States from Southern Rhodesia and thus would constitute a serious violation of the above-mentioned Security Council resolutions imposing sanctions against the illegal régime in Southern Rhodesia,

1. *Calls upon* the Government of the United States of America to take the necessary measures, in compliance with the relevant provisions of Security Council resolutions 253(1968), 277(1970) and 288(1970) and bearing in mind its obligations under Article 25 of the Charter of the United Nations, to prevent the importation of chrome into the United States from Southern Rhodesia;

2. *Requests* the Government of the United States to inform the General Assembly at its current session of the action taken or envisaged in the implementation of the present resolution;

3. *Requests* the President of the General Assembly to draw the attention of the Government of the United States to the urgent need for the implementation of the present resolution;

4. *Reminds* all Member States of their obligations under the Charter to comply fully with the decisions of the Security Council on mandatory sanctions against the illegal régime in Southern Rhodesia;

5. *Decides* to keep this and other aspects of the question under continuous review.

A/C.4/L.990. Algeria, Burundi, Cameroon, Chad, Congo, Ethiopia, Ghana, Guinea, Iraq, Jamaica, Kenya, Niger, Nigeria, Pakistan, People's Democratic Republic of Yemen, Senegal, Sudan, Syrian Arab Republic, United Republic of Tanzania, Yugoslavia, Zaire, Zambia: draft resolution.

A/C.4/L.990/Rev.1. Algeria, Barbados, Burundi, Cameroon,

Chad, Congo, Ethiopia, Ghana, Guinea, Guyana, Iraq, Jamaica, Kenya, Lesotho, Liberia, Mali, Mauritania, Niger, Nigeria, Pakistan, People's Democratic Republic of Yemen, Rwanda, Senegal, Sierra Leone, Sudan, Syrian Arab Republic, Uganda, United Republic of Tanzania, Yugoslavia, Zaire, Zambia: revised draft resolution, approved by Fourth Committee on 19 November 1971, meeting 1952, by roll-call vote of 99 to 3, with 10 abstentions, as follows:

In favour: Afghanistan, Algeria, Argentina, Austria, Bahrain, Barbados, Botswana, Brazil, Bulgaria, Burma, Burundi, Byelorussian SSR, Cameroon, Central African Republic, Ceylon, Chad, Chile, Colombia, Costa Rica, Cuba, Cyprus, Czechoslovakia, Denmark, Ecuador, Egypt, Equatorial Guinea, Ethiopia, Finland, Gambia, Ghana, Greece, Guatemala, Guinea, Guyana, Haiti, Honduras, Hungary, Iceland, India, Indonesia, Iran, Iraq, Ireland, Israel, Ivory Coast, Jamaica, Japan, Jordan, Kenya, Khmer Republic, Kuwait, Lesotho, Liberia, Libyan Arab Republic, Madagascar, Malaysia, Mali, Mauritania, Mauritius, Mexico, Mongolia, Morocco, Nepal, Nicaragua, Niger, Nigeria, Norway, Pakistan, People's Democratic Republic of Yemen, Peru, Philippines, Poland, Qatar, Romania, Rwanda, Senegal, Sierra Leone, Singapore, Somalia, Spain, Sudan, Swaziland, Sweden, Syrian Arab Republic, Thailand, Togo, Trinidad and Tobago, Tunisia, Turkey, Uganda, Ukrainian SSR, USSR, United Republic of Tanzania, Upper Volta, Uruguay, Venezuela, Yugoslavia, Zaire, Zambia.

Against: Portugal, South Africa, United Kingdom.

Abstaining: Australia, Belgium, Canada, France, Italy, Luxembourg, Malawi, Netherlands, New Zealand, United States.

A/8518/Add.1. Report of Fourth Committee (part II).

RESOLUTION 2769(XXVI), as recommended by Fourth Committee, A/8518/Add.1, adopted by Assembly on 22 November 1971, meeting 1991, by roll-call vote of 102 to 3, with 9 abstentions, as follows:

In favour: Afghanistan, Albania, Algeria, Argentina, Austria, Bahrain, Barbados, Bhutan, Bolivia, ·Brazil, Bulgaria, Burma, Byelorussian SSR, Cameroon, Central African Republic, Ceylon, Chad, Chile, China, Colombia, Costa Rica, Cuba, Cyprus, Czechoslovakia, Dahomey, Denmark, Dominican Republic, Ecuador, Egypt, Ethiopia, Finland, Gabon, Gambia, Ghana, Greece, Guatemala, Guinea, Guyana, Haiti, Honduras, Hungary, Iceland, India, Indonesia, Iran, Iraq, Ireland, Israel, Ivory Coast, Jamaica, Japan, Jordan, Khmer Republic, Kuwait, Lebanon, Lesotho, Liberia, Libyan Arab Republic, Madagascar, Malaysia, Mali, Mauritania, Mexico, Mongolia, Morocco, Nepal, Nicaragua, Niger, Nigeria, Norway, Pakistan, Panama, Paraguay, Peru, Philippines, Poland, Qatar, Romania, Saudi Arabia, Senegal, Sierra Leone, Singapore, Somalia, Spain, Sudan, Swaziland, Sweden, Syrian Arab Republic, Thailand, Togo, Trinidad and Tobago, Tunisia, Turkey, Ukrainian SSR, USSR, United Republic of Tanzania, Upper Volta, Uruguay, Venezuela, Yugoslavia, Zaire, Zambia.

Against: Portugal, South Africa, United Kingdom.

Abstaining: Australia, Belgium, Canada, France, Italy, Luxembourg, Netherlands, New Zealand, United States.

The General Assembly,

Having considered the question of Southern Rhodesia,

Recalling its resolution 1514(XV) of 14 December 1960 and all other relevant resolutions of the General Assembly and the Security Council on the question of Southern Rhodesia,

Having noted the statement made in the House of Commons on Tuesday, 9 November 1971, by the Secretary of State for Foreign and Commonwealth Affairs of the United Kingdom of Great Britain and Northern Ireland, announcing his Government's decision to hold the talks that are currently under way in Salisbury with the illegal racist minority régime,

1. *Reaffirms* the principle that there should be no independence before majority rule in Southern Rhodesia;

2. *Affirms* that any settlement relating to the future of that Territory must be worked out with the fullest participation of all nationalist leaders representing the majority of the people of Zimbabwe and must be endorsed freely by the people;

3. *Decides* to keep the situation in the Territory under review.

A/C.4/736/Add.1. Questions of Namibia, Territories under Portuguese administration and Southern Rhodesia: request for hearing.

A/C.4/L.991. Afghanistan, Algeria, Burma, Burundi, Cameroon, Chad, Congo, Egypt, Ethiopia, Gambia, Ghana, Guinea, India, Indonesia, Iraq, Kenya, Khmer Republic, Libyan Arab Republic, Mali, Mauritania, Mongolia, Niger, Nigeria, Pakistan, People's Democratic Republic of Yemen, Somalia, Sudan, Syrian Arab Republic, Tunisia, Uganda, United Republic of Tanzania, Yugoslavia, Zaire, Zambia: draft resolution, approved by Fourth Committee on 24 November 1971, meeting 1955, by roll-call vote of 89 to 10, with 13 abstentions, as follows:

In favour: Afghanistan, Algeria, Argentina, Barbados, Botswana, Bulgaria, Burma, Burundi, Byelorussian SSR, Cameroon, Central African Republic, Ceylon, Chad, Chile, Colombia, Congo, Costa Rica, Cuba, Czechoslovakia, Dahomey, Ecuador, Egypt, Equatorial Guinea, Ethiopia, Gabon, Gambia, Ghana, Greece, Guatemala, Guinea, Guyana, Honduras, Hungary, Iceland, India, Indonesia, Iran, Iraq, Israel, Ivory Coast, Jamaica, Japan, Jordan, Kenya, Khmer Republic, Kuwait, Lebanon, Liberia, Libyan Arab Republic, Madagascar, Malaysia, Mali, Mauritania, Mexico, Mongolia, Morocco, Nepal, Nicaragua, Niger, Nigeria, Pakistan, Panama, People's Democratic Republic of Yemen, Peru, Philippines, Poland, Romania, Saudi Arabia, Sierra Leone, Singapore, Somalia, Sudan, Syrian Arab Republic, Thailand, Togo, Trinidad and Tobago, Tunisia, Turkey, Uganda, Ukrainian SSR, USSR, United Republic of Tanzania, Upper Volta, Uruguay, Venezuela, Yemen, Yugoslavia, Zaire, Zambia.

Against: Australia, Belgium, France, Luxembourg, Netherlands, New Zealand, Portugal, South Africa, United Kingdom, United States.

Abstaining: Austria, Brazil, Canada, Denmark, Fiji, Finland, Ireland, Italy, Lesotho, Malawi, Norway, Spain, Sweden.

A/8518/Add.2. Report of Fourth Committee (part III).

RESOLUTION 2796(XXVI), as recommended by Fourth Committee, A/8518/Add.2, adopted by Assembly on 10 December 1971, meeting 2012, by recorded vote of 91 to 9, with 12 abstentions, as follows:

In favour: Afghanistan, Algeria, Argentina, Bahrain, Barbados, Botswana, Bulgaria, Burma, Burundi, Byelorussian SSR, Cameroon, Central African Republic, Ceylon, Chad, Chile, Colombia, Congo, Cuba, Cyprus, Czechoslovakia, Dahomey, Dominican Republic, Ecuador, Egypt, El Salvador, Equatorial Guinea, Ethiopia, Finland,* Gabon, Gambia, Ghana, Greece, Guatemala, Guyana, Haiti, Honduras, Hungary, Iceland, India, Indonesia, Iran, Iraq, Israel, Ivory Coast, Jamaica, Japan, Jordan, Kenya, Khmer Republic, Kuwait, Laos, Lebanon, Liberia, Libyan Arab Republic, Madagascar, Malaysia, Mali, Mauritania, Mexico, Mongolia, Nepal, Nicaragua, Niger, Nigeria, Oman, People's Democratic Republic of Yemen, Peru, Philippines, Poland, Qatar, Romania, Saudi Arabia, Senegal, Singapore, Somalia, Sudan, Togo, Trinidad and Tobago, Tunisia, Turkey, Uganda, Ukrainian SSR, USSR, United Republic of Tanzania, Upper Volta, Uruguay, Venezuela, Yemen, Yugoslavia, Zaire, Zambia.

Against: Australia, Belgium, France, Netherlands, New Zealand, Portugal, South Africa, United Kingdom, United States.

Abstaining: Austria, Brazil, Canada, Denmark, Fiji, Ireland, Italy, Lesotho, Malawi, Norway, Spain, Sweden.

*Subsequently, Finland advised the Secretariat that it had intended to abstain.

The General Assembly,

Having considered the question of Southern Rhodesia,

Having examined the relevant chapters of the report of the Special Committee on the Situation with regard to the Implementation of the Declaration on the Granting of Independence to Colonial Countries and Peoples,

Bearing in mind the views expressed by representatives of national liberation movements,

Having heard the statement of the petitioner,

Recalling its resolution 1514(XV) of 14 December 1960, containing the Declaration on the Granting of Independence to Colonial Countries and Peoples, and its resolution 2621(XXV) of 12 October 1970, containing the programme of action for the full implementation of the Declaration,

Recalling further all previous resolutions concerning the question of Southern Rhodesia adopted by the General Assembly and the Special Committee,

Recalling also the relevant resolutions of the Security Council, particularly its resolutions 232(1966) of 16 December 1966, 253(1968) of 29 May 1968, 277(1970) of 18 March 1970 and 288(1970) of 17 November 1970,

Gravely concerned at the further deterioration of the situation in Southern Rhodesia, which the Security Council has reaffirmed as constituting a threat to international peace and security, resulting from the failure and refusal of the Government of the United Kingdom of Great Britain and Northern Ireland to put an end to the illegal racist minority régime in that Territory and from the racialist and repressive policies pursued by that régime in violation of the relevant resolutions and decisions of the United Nations,

Deeply concerned at the continued presence of South African forces in the Territory, which constitutes a threat to the sovereignty and territorial integrity of neighbouring African States,

Deploring that certain States, in particular South Africa and Portugal, continue to collaborate with the illegal racist minority régime in violation of the relevant resolutions of the General Assembly and the Security Council, contrary to their specific obligation under Article 25 of the Charter of the United Nations, thereby seriously obstructing the efforts of the international community to put an end to that régime,

Bearing in mind that the Government of the United Kingdom, as the administering Power, has the primary responsibility for putting an end to the rebellion of British settlers who organized the illegal racist régime and for transferring effective power to the people of Zimbabwe on the basis of the principle of majority rule,

Deploring the intransigent attitude of the Government of the United Kingdom, as the administering Power, which, in contravention of the provisions of the relevant resolutions of the General Assembly and the Special Committee, persists in its refusal to co-operate with the Special Committee in the discharge of the mandate entrusted to it by the General Assembly,

Noting with deep regret the decision of the International Olympic Committee to permit the participation in the XXth Olympic Games of the so-called National Olympic Committee of Rhodesia,

1. *Reaffirms* the inalienable right of the people of Zimbabwe to self-determination, freedom and independence and the legitimacy of their struggle to secure by all the means at their disposal the enjoyment of that right as set forth in the Charter of the United Nations and in conformity with the objectives of General Assembly resolution 1514(XV);

2. *Strongly deplores* the continued refusal of the Government of the United Kingdom of Great Britain and Northern Ireland to take effective measures to bring down the illegal racist minority régime in Southern Rhodesia and to transfer power without any delay to the people of Zimbabwe on the basis of the principle of majority rule, in accordance with the relevant resolutions of the General Assembly, and calls upon that Government to take such measures without further delay in fulfilment of its responsibility as the administering Power;

3. *Condemns* the continued intervention and presence of South African armed forces in Southern Rhodesia in violation of Security Council resolutions 277(1970) and 288(1970), and calls upon the administering Power to ensure the immediate expulsion of all such forces;

4. *Condemns* the policies of those Governments, particularly the Governments of South Africa and Portugal, which continue to maintain political, economic, military and other relations with the illegal racist minority régime, in contravention of the relevant resolutions of the United Nations and contrary to their obligations under the Charter, and calls upon those Governments to cease forthwith all such relations;

5. *Reaffirms its conviction* that the sanctions will not put an end to the illegal racist minority régime unless they are comprehensive, mandatory, effectively supervised, enforced and complied with by all States, particularly by South Africa and Portugal;

6. *Strongly urges* all States to take more stringent measures in order to prevent any circumvention by all individuals and bodies corporate of their nationality, or under their jurisdiction, of the sanctions prescribed by the Security Council, and to refrain from any action which might confer a semblance of legitimacy on the illegal racist minority régime;

7. *Strongly deplores* the imprisonment and detention of freedom fighters of Zimbabwe by the illegal racist minority régime and calls upon the administering Power to effect the immediate and unconditional release of those persons;

8. *Calls upon* all States to take all appropriate steps to ensure the exclusion of the so-called National Olympic Committee of Rhodesia from participating in the XXth Olympic Games and requests the Secretary-General to draw the attention of the President of the International Olympic Committee to the relevant provisions of Security Council resolution 253(1968) for appropriate action;

9. *Calls upon* all States, the specialized agencies and other organizations within the United Nations system, in consultation with the Organization of African Unity, to extend all moral and material assistance to the people of Zimbabwe;

10. *Calls upon* the Government of the United Kingdom, in view of the armed conflict in the Territory and the inhuman treatment of prisoners, to ensure the application to that situation of the Geneva Convention relative to the Treatment of Prisoners of War and the Geneva Convention relative to the Protection of Civilian Persons in Time of War, both dated 12 August 1949;

11. *Calls upon* the Government of the United Kingdom to report on the implementation of the present resolution to the Special Committee on the Situation with regard to the Implementation of the Declaration on the Granting of Independence to Colonial Countries and Peoples and to the General Assembly at its twenty-seventh session;

12. *Draws the attention* of the Security Council, in view of the gravity of the situation arising from the further intensification of repressive activities against the people of Zimbabwe, to the urgent necessity of taking further steps to ensure the full and strict compliance by all States with the decisions of the Council, in accordance with Article 25 of the Charter, and to the need to widen the scope of the sanctions against the illegal racist minority régime and to impose sanctions against South Africa and Portugal, whose Governments persist in their refusal to carry out the mandatory decisions of the Council;

13. *Requests* the Secretary-General to report to the General Assembly at its twenty-seventh session on the implementation of the present resolution;

14. *Requests* the Special Committee to keep the situation in the Territory under review.

A/C.4/L.1012. Afghanistan, Algeria, Barbados, Burundi, Cameroon, Chad, Congo, Egypt, Equatorial Guinea, Ethiopia, Gambia, Guinea, Guyana, Jamaica, Kenya, Libyan Arab Republic, Mali, Mauritania, Mongolia, Nigeria, People's Democratic Republic of Yemen, Rwanda, Saudi Arabia, Sierra Leone, Somalia, Sudan, Syrian Arab Republic, Togo, Trinidad and Tobago, Uganda, United Republic of Tanzania, Yugoslavia, Zaire, Zambia: draft resolution, approved by Fourth Committee on 16 December 1971, meeting 1971, by roll-call vote of 78 to 8, with 21 abstentions, as follows:

In favour: Afghanistan, Albania, Algeria, Barbados, Botswana, Bulgaria, Burma, Burundi, Byelorussian SSR, Cameroon,

Central African Republic, Ceylon, Chad, Chile, Congo, Cuba, Czechoslovakia, Ecuador, Egypt, Equatorial Guinea, Ethiopia, Gambia, Ghana, Guatemala, Guinea, Guyana, Honduras, Hungary, Iceland, India, Indonesia, Iran, Iraq, Israel, Ivory Coast, Jamaica, Jordan, Kenya, Kuwait, Lebanon, Liberia, Libyan Arab Republic, Madagascar, Malaysia, Mali, Mexico, Mongolia, Morocco, Nepal, Nigeria, Peru, Philippines, Poland, Romania, Rwanda, Saudi Arabia, Senegal, Singapore, Somalia, Spain, Sudan, Swaziland, Syrian Arab Republic, Thailand, Togo, Trinidad and Tobago, Tunisia, Turkey, Uganda, Ukrainian SSR, USSR, United Republic of Tanzania, Upper Volta, Venezuela, Yemen, Yugoslavia, Zaire, Zambia.

Against: Australia, France, Luxembourg, Netherlands, New Zealand, Portugal, South Africa, United Kingdom.

Abstaining: Argentina, Austria, Belgium, Brazil, Canada, Colombia, Costa Rica, Denmark, Dominican Republic, Fiji, Finland, Greece, Ireland, Italy, Japan, Malawi, Nicaragua, Norway, Sweden, United States, Uruguay.

A/8518/Add.3. Report of Fourth Committee (part IV).

RESOLUTION 2877(XXVI), as recommended by Fourth Committee, A/8518/Add.3, adopted by Assembly on 20 December 1971, meeting 2028, by roll-call vote of 94 to 8, with 22 abstentions, as follows:

In favour: Afghanistan, Albania, Algeria, Bahrain, Barbados, Botswana, Bulgaria, Burma, Burundi, Byelorussian SSR, Cameroon, Central African Republic, Ceylon, Chad, Chile, Colombia, Congo, Cuba, Cyprus, Czechoslovakia, Dahomey, Ecuador, Egypt, El Salvador, Equatorial Guinea, Ethiopia, Gambia, Ghana, Guatemala, Guinea, Guyana, Haiti, Honduras, Hungary, India, Indonesia, Iran, Iraq, Israel, Ivory Coast, Jordan, Kenya, Khmer Republic, Kuwait, Laos, Lebanon, Lesotho, Liberia, Libyan Arab Republic, Madagascar, Malaysia, Mali, Malta, Mauritania, Mexico, Mongolia, Morocco, Nepal, Niger, Nigeria, Oman, Pakistan, People's Democratic Republic of Yemen, Peru, Philippines, Poland, Romania, Rwanda, Saudi Arabia, Senegal, Sierra Leone, Singapore, Somalia, Spain, Sudan, Swaziland, Syrian Arab Republic, Thailand, Togo, Trinidad and Tobago, Tunisia, Turkey, Uganda, Ukrainian SSR, USSR, United Arab Emirates, United Republic of Tanzania, Upper Volta, Venezuela, Yemen, Yugoslavia, Zaire, Zambia.

Against: Australia, France, Luxembourg, Netherlands, New Zealand, Portugal, South Africa, United Kingdom.

Abstaining: Argentina, Austria, Belgium, Brazil, Canada, Costa Rica, Denmark, Dominican Republic, Fiji, Finland, Greece, Ireland, Italy, Japan, Malawi, Nicaragua, Norway, Panama, Paraguay, Sweden, United States, Uruguay.

The General Assembly,

Having heard the statement by the representative of the Government of the United Kingdom of Great Britain and Northern Ireland concerning the "proposals for a settlement" agreed upon between that Government and the racist minority régime in Salisbury,

Recalling its resolution 1514(XV) of 14 December 1960, containing the Declaration on the Granting of Independence to Colonial Countries and Peoples, and its resolution 2621(XXV) of 12 October 1970, containing the programme of action for the full implementation of the Declaration,

Recalling further all previous resolutions concerning the question of Southern Rhodesia adopted by the General Assembly and the Special Committee on the Situation with regard to the Implementation of the Declaration on the Granting of Independence to Colonial Countries and Peoples,

Recalling also its resolution 2769(XXVI) of 22 November 1971, in particular paragraphs 1 and 2 thereof,

Gravely concerned at the "proposals for a settlement" which, if implemented, will entrench the rule of the racist minority régime in Southern Rhodesia and will perpetuate the enslavement of the African people of Zimbabwe,

Deeply conscious that the "proposals for a settlement" were agreed upon without the participation of the representatives of the African people of Zimbabwe,

1. *Rejects* the "proposals for a settlement" agreed upon by the Government of the United Kingdom of Great Britain and Northern Ireland and the racist minority régime in Salisbury as constituting a flagrant violation of the inalienable right of the African people of Zimbabwe to self-determination and independence as provided for in General Assembly resolution 1514(XV);

2. *Reaffirms* that no settlement which does not conform strictly to the principle of "no independence before majority rule" on the basis of one man, one vote, will be acceptable;

3. *Invites* the Security Council, when examining the question of Southern Rhodesia, to consider taking appropriate measures, in accordance with the relevant provisions of the Charter of the United Nations, in order to enable the people of Zimbabwe to exercise freely and without further delay their inalienable right to self-determination and independence;

4. *Welcomes* the decision by the Security Council on 2 December 1971 to invite Mr. Joshua Nkomo and the Reverend Ndabaningi Sithole, the respective leaders of the Zimbabwe African People's Union and the Zimbabwe African National Union, to appear before the Council to express their views concerning the future status of the Territory, and calls upon the Government of the United Kingdom, as the administering Power, to comply with that decision;

5. *Calls upon* all States to adhere strictly to the relevant provisions of the resolutions of the General Assembly and the Security Council on the question of Southern Rhodesia, and in particular to observe the resolutions of the Council imposing sanctions against the racist minority régime.

The question of Namibia

During 1971, United Nations bodies again considered the question of Namibia. The International Court of Justice delivered an advisory opinion on the question in response to a 1970 Security Council request for an opinion as to the legal consequences for States of South Africa's continued presence in Namibia. Decisions on the territory were also taken by the Council, the General Assembly and the Assembly's Special Committee on the Situation with regard to the Implementation of the [1960] Declaration on the Granting of Independence to Colonial Countries and Peoples. The United Nations Council for Namibia reported to the General Assembly on its activities, and aspects of the question were again taken up by the Commission on Human Rights and the Economic and Social Council.

The International Court of Justice delivered its advisory opinion on 21 June 1971 and stated among other things that, the continued presence of South Africa in Namibia being illegal, South Africa was under obligation to withdraw its administration immediately and thus put an end to its occupation of the territory. United Nations Member States were under obligation to recognize the illegality of South Africa's presence in Namibia and the invalidity of its acts on behalf of or concerning the territory. States were under obligation to refrain from any acts or dealings with South Africa implying recognition of the legality of or support for South Africa's presence or administration. The Court also said it was incumbent upon States not Members of the United Nations to give assistance in the action taken by the United Nations with regard to Namibia.

On 20 October, the Security Council adopted a four-power resolution by which, among other things, it agreed with the Court's opinion and called on States to refrain from actions pertaining to Namibia contrary to the views expressed by the Court. The Council called once again on South Africa to withdraw from the territory and declared that any further refusal to do so could create conditions detrimental to the maintenance of peace and security in the region.

The Security Council's *Ad Hoc* Sub-Committee on Namibia, set up by the Council in 1970, was asked to continue its work and to study appropriate measures for fulfilling the responsibilities of the United Nations towards Namibia. It was also asked to review all treaties and agreements which were contrary to the present resolution in order to ascertain whether States had entered into agreements which recognized South Africa's authority over Namibia.

The Special Committee on implementation of the Declaration on granting independence, in a consensus adopted on 2 September, noted among other things that South Africa had not only continued its illegal occupation of Namibia but had persisted in the application of the criminal policies of *apartheid*. The Special Committee condemned the support South Africa received from its allies in pursuit of its policies of economic exploitation of the Namibians, and called on the Governments concerned to withdraw such support. By a resolution adopted on 9 September, the Special Committee asked all States to increase their assistance to the peoples of Namibia, Southern Rhodesia and the territories under Portuguese administration and to discontinue collaboration with the Governments of Portugal and South Africa.

The United Nations Council for Namibia, in its sixth report to the General Assembly, described its activities during the year and said that South Africa had continued to defy the United Nations with regard to Namibia and that the situation had further deteriorated. South Africa had increasingly applied its *apartheid* policy to the territory, had continued its military repression and had pursued policies aimed at fragmenting and annexing the territory.

At its twenty-sixth session later in 1971, the General Assembly on 20 December adopted a resolution by which among other things it reaffirmed the legitimacy of the struggle of the Namibian people, condemned South Africa for its refusal to withdraw and welcomed the advisory opinion of the International Court of Justice. States were called upon, among other things, to refrain from all relations, economic or otherwise, with South Africa, where those relations concerned Namibia. The United Nations Council for Namibia was asked to represent Namibia whenever that was required and to assume responsibility for the urgent establishment of a co-ordinated programme of technical and financial assistance to Namibia.

In another resolution adopted on 20 December, the Assembly decided among other things to allocate $50,000 to the United Nations Fund for Namibia from the United Nations regular budget for 1972, and authorized the Secretary-General to appeal to Governments for voluntary contributions to the Fund.

(For details about these and other decisions taken during 1971 concerning Namibia, see pp. 546-64.)

Complaint by Zambia against South Africa

By a letter dated 6 October 1971, addressed to the President of the Security Council, Zambia requested a meeting of the Council to consider a series of incidents and violations of the sovereignty, air space and territorial integrity of Zambia by South Africa, including, on 5 October 1971, an alleged crossing by South African forces into Zambian territory from the Caprivi Strip of Namibia.

Forty-eight United Nations Member States supported Zambia's request. In doing so, they declared that the latest armed incursion by South African military authorities constituted a serious threat not only to the sovereignty and territorial integrity of Zambia but to the peace and security of the region.

The Council met to consider the complaint by Zambia on 8, 11 and 12 October 1971.

At their request, Zambia and South Africa, as well as Guinea, India, Kenya, Nigeria, Pakistan, the United Republic of Tanzania, and Yugoslavia, participated in the Security Council debate without the right to vote.

The representative of Zambia stated that on 5 October 1971, units of the South African army had entered Zambia illegally at Katima Mulilo, allegedly pursuing freedom fighters operating in the Caprivi Strip. The South African forces spent some time inside Zambia before retreating to their military base at the Caprivi Strip, he said.

The representative of Zambia then cited 23 other occasions since 1968 on which, he said, South Africa had violated Zambia's territorial integrity. These violations had occurred because Zambia bordered Namibia, believed in a policy of non-racialism, opposed the so-called dialogue with South Africa, rejected white supremacy and supported the right to self-determination of the peoples of southern Africa and Guinea (Bissau).

South Africa was feeling the pressure of the liberation movements and was letting off steam on Zambia, the representative continued. Zambia, however, accepted no responsibility for the activities of the Namibian freedom fighters inside Namibia. Zambia considered that it was in a state of undeclared war with South Africa and other white minority régimes, which formed an unholy alliance. The root cause of Zambia's deep-seated differences with South Africa was *apartheid*. Furthermore, Zambia had consistently opposed South Africa's policy of creating client States.

After unsuccessful attempts to destroy the unity of Zambia by financing reactionary opposition parties inside the country, South Africa had initiated direct military action. The Security Council must take appropriate measures to prevent a racial war and guarantee the freedom, independence and security of small and weak States, the Zambian representative held.

The Minister for Foreign Affairs of South Africa, replying to the charges by Zambia, said that incidents had indeed occurred in the Caprivi Strip on 4 and 5 October 1971. On 4 October, four members of the South African police force were injured by a landmine explosion; on the following day, a landmine killed a South African police officer investigating the earlier incident. The trail of four persons had been found leading from the direction of the Zambian border to the location of the landmines and back.

The Prime Minister of South Africa, who had repeatedly and publicly warned that his country would not tolerate attacks on its people or the people of South West Africa, had stated that steps were being taken to pursue the culprits and that the pursuers would defend themselves if attacked. In fact, however, South African police had not crossed the Zambian border but had followed the trail to where it disappeared within the area of the Caprivi Strip. At no time was the Zambian border violated, South Africa's Foreign Minister stated.

Instances of unauthorized border crossings had occurred in the past, but both sides had been responsible, he added. Between November 1969 and July 1971, Zambia had violated South West African air space on 12 occasions. More serious was the infiltration of armed bands across the border from Zambia into the Caprivi Strip to cause violence. These bands operated from camps situated in Zambia and received the support of the Zambian Government, which had not responded to South Africa's request that it take measures to prevent such incursions.

South Africa wanted to avoid border incidents, the Foreign Minister said, but in cases of incursions by terrorists it did not compromise, for it had a duty to protect its citizens and would do everything in its power to prevent such acts or to apprehend the culprits.

During the debate, some Council members held that South Africa had not provided evidence against Zambia's charges but instead had confirmed South Africa's militant intentions.

South Africa had admitted violating the territorial integrity of Zambia, Sierra Leone said; it only denied having done so on the date specified by Zambia.

India and Pakistan commented that South Africa had invoked the right of pursuit into foreign territory.

South Africa had no evidence that Zambia had anything to do with the laying of mines, the Nigerian representative held; the incident had been used as a pretext for terrorizing the Zambian population in the hope that Zambia would change its anti-*apartheid* policy.

Somalia stated that news of the illegal incursion by South African forces had been widely reported in the international press. South Africa had established a large military presence in Namibia, employing arms supplied by some Member States despite an embargo, and was attempting to force Zambia to give up its support of the principle of self-determination.

The USSR said that South Africa was using the international territory of Namibia as a platform for launching aggression; it had constructed bases, air strips and a missile system in the Caprivi area, from which it organized subversive activities against Zambia.

A number of Council members expressed the view that acts of aggression by South Africa represented a challenge to the United Nations, and specifically to the Security Council. They held that conciliatory attitudes of some permanent members of the Council contributed to South Africa's position. Among those holding this view were Guinea, Kenya, Nigeria, the USSR, the United Republic of Tanzania, and Yugoslavia.

Guinea, Pakistan, Poland, the United Republic of Tanzania, and Yugoslavia, among others, stated that there was a co-ordinated plan by South Africa and Portugal against Zambia and other independent African States.

Some members—among them Burundi, India,

Nigeria, Somalia and the United Republic of Tanzania—raised the question of the Namibian resistance and the African freedom fighters. They held that since South Africa continued to occupy Namibia, its population had no choice but to resort to armed struggle. India felt that the Council should declare that the struggle for liberation from colonialism and against a racist, minority régime was legitimate.

On 8 October 1971, Burundi, Sierra Leone, Somalia and the Syrian Arab Republic introduced a draft resolution by which the Council would, among other things, condemn the violations of the sovereignty, air space and territorial integrity of Zambia by South Africa, and call upon South Africa to respect fully the sovereignty and territorial integrity of Zambia and to desist forthwith from any violation thereof.

On 12 October, the representative of Somalia introduced a revised version of the draft—co-sponsored by Burundi and Sierra Leone—which, he said, took into account the various positions of Council members. This text was adopted unanimously on the same date as resolution 300(1971).

By this resolution, the Council (a) bearing in mind that all Member States must refrain in their relations from the threat or use of force against the territorial integrity or political independence of any State, (b) conscious that the Council had the responsibility to take efficient collective measures to prevent and eliminate threats to peace and security, and (c) concerned at the situation on the Zambia-Namibia border, in the vicinity of the Caprivi Strip, took the following action.

It (1) reiterated that any violation of the sovereignty and territorial integrity of a Member State was contrary to the United Nations Charter; (2) called upon South Africa to respect fully the sovereignty and territorial integrity of Zambia; and (3) declared that, in the event that South

Africa violated the sovereignty or territorial integrity of Zambia, the Security Council would meet again to examine the situation further in accordance with the relevant provisions of the Charter.

Following adoption of the resolution, the United States representative said that the statements made to the Council by Zambia and South Africa were not fully consistent and had left some questions open. However, it was clear that there was concern that similar incidents might occur in future. The United States had supported the resolution in the hope that it would encourage the parties concerned to exercise restraint. The representative also reaffirmed United States support for the General Assembly's decision of 27 October 1966[26] as well as the advisory opinion by the International Court of Justice that South Africa's presence in Namibia was illegal.

Italy noted that although it had voted for the resolution because of the tension prevailing in the area, it would have preferred a more concise, sober resolution adhering more closely to the information provided to the Council.

France felt that the resolution was firm and measured and had achieved the desired objective: the Council had stressed its determination to preserve the sovereignty and territorial integrity of a Member State, which constituted an assurance for Zambia.

The representative of Zambia said that in giving South Africa such a mild reprimand, the Security Council had set a dangerous precedent which would not give comfort to Zambia or to other small and weak States in Africa and the rest of the world. However, Zambia welcomed the resolution in a spirit of compromise as the minimum action the Council could take under the circumstances.

[26]See Y.U.N., 1966, pp. 605-6, text of resolution 2145(XXI).

DOCUMENTARY REFERENCES

Security Council, meetings 1590-1592.

S/10352. Letter of 6 October 1971 from Zambia (request to convene Council).
S/10357-S/10361, S/10363. Letters of 7 and 8 October 1971 from United Republic of Tanzania, Zambia, Nigeria, South Africa, Kenya, Guinea (requests to participate in Council's discussion).
S/10364. Letter of 7 October 1971 from Algeria, Barbados, Botswana, Burundi, Cameroon, Central African Republic, Chad, Congo, Dahomey, Egypt, Equatorial Guinea, Ethiopia, Gabon, Gambia, Ghana, Guinea, Guyana, India, Ivory Coast, Jamaica, Kenya, Liberia, Libyan Arab Republic, Madagascar, Malaysia, Mali, Mauritania, Mauritius, Morocco, Niger, Nigeria, Pakistan, Rwanda, Senegal, Sierra Leone, Somalia, Sudan, Syrian Arab Republic, Togo, Trinidad and Tobago, Tunisia, Uganda, United Republic of Tanzania, Upper Volta, Yugoslavia, Zaire, Zambia.
S/10365. Burundi, Sierra Leone, Somalia, Syrian Arab Republic: draft resolution.
S/10365/Rev.1. Burundi, Sierra Leone, Somalia: revised draft resolution.

S/10367. Letter of 8 October 1971 from Yugoslavia (request to participate in Council's discussion).
S/10368. Letter of 11 October from Lesotho (supporting request to convene Council).
S/10370, S/10371. Letters of 11 October 1971 from India and Pakistan (request to participate in Council's discussion).

RESOLUTION 300(1971), as submitted by 3 powers, S/10365/Rev.1, adopted unanimously by Council on 12 October 1971, meeting 1592.

The Security Council,
Having received the letter of the Permanent Representative of Zambia contained in document S/10352 and also the letter from forty-seven Member States contained in document S/10364,
Taking note of the statement of the Permanent Representative of Zambia concerning violations of the sovereignty, air space and territorial integrity of Zambia by South Africa,
Taking note of the statement of the Minister for Foreign Affairs of the Republic of South Africa,

Bearing in mind that all Member States must refrain in their relations from the threat or use of force against the territorial integrity or political independence of any State,
Conscious that it has the responsibility to take efficient collective measures to prevent and eliminate threats to peace and security,
Concerned by the situation on the borders of Zambia and Namibia, in the vicinity of the Caprivi Strip,
1. *Reiterates* that any violation of the sovereignty and territorial integrity of a Member State is contrary to the Charter of the United Nations;
2. *Calls upon* South Africa to respect fully the sovereignty and territorial integrity of Zambia;
3. *Further declares* that, in the event of South Africa violating the sovereignty or territorial integrity of Zambia, the Security Council will meet again to examine the situation further in accordance with the relevant provisions of the Charter.

Relations between African States and Portugal

Complaints by Senegal against Portugal

By three letters to the President of the Security Council, dated 27 April, 16 June and 6 July 1971, the representative of Senegal charged Portuguese armed forces stationed in Guinea (Bissau) with attacking Senegalese frontier villages, laying mines and explosive devices in Senegalese territory and violating Senegalese air space. In the last of these letters, Senegal requested an urgent meeting of the Security Council.

By a letter dated 10 July 1971, addressed to the President of the Council, Portugal rejected the Senegalese charges; expressed regret that Senegal had requested a meeting of the Council without first seeking to ascertain, through direct contact with Portugal, the truth of the charges; and asserted that Senegal had not presented sufficient evidence to substantiate them.

Both Portugal and Senegal were suffering from the terrorist activities of the *Partido Africano da Independência de Guiné e Cabo Verde* (PAIGC), a subversive group which enjoyed special privileges from the Government of Senegal and which was responsible for all the problems in the frontier areas, Portugal said. Senegal should seek its remedy by maintaining order within its own territory.

By a letter dated 12 July 1971, addressed to the President of the Security Council, 37 African States supported Senegal's request for a meeting of the Council; they called on the Council to take measures to ensure that Portugal halt its flagrant acts of aggression and grant self-determination and independence to its colonies, in accordance with the 1960 Declaration on the Granting of Independence to Colonial Countries and Peoples.[27]

The Council considered the Senegalese complaint at four meetings held from 12 to 15 July. At their request, Senegal, Guinea, Mali, Mauritania, Mauritius, Sudan, Togo and Zambia participated in the debate, without the right to vote.

The Minister for Foreign Affairs of Senegal stated that the latest acts of Portuguese aggression were part of a long series of violations of the territorial integrity of Senegal and were closely linked with Portuguese repression of the nationalist movements in Guinea (Bissau). Portuguese violence had recently escalated and taken a new form in the laying of anti-tank and anti-personnel mines on Senegalese territory. Senegal was asking the Council to take effective measures against Portugal in terms of its resolution of 9 December 1969, which declared that, in the event of failure by Portugal to desist forthwith from violating the sovereignty and territorial integrity of Senegal, the Council would meet to consider other measures.[28]

Representatives of African countries drew attention to a resolution adopted by the Council of Ministers of the Organization of African Unity on 8 December 1970, which declared that the presence of Portuguese colonialism on the African continent was a serious threat to the peace and security of independent African States. Stating that it was no longer sufficient merely to condemn Portugal, they called for vigorous measures by the Security Council.

The representative of Somalia said that the Security Council should use to the full its investigative powers under Article 34 of the United Nations Charter,[29] so that any action it deemed necessary might be undertaken on a sound and informed basis.

A draft resolution sponsored by Burundi, Japan, Sierra Leone, Somalia and the Syrian Arab Republic was placed before the Council. By its operative part, the Security Council would: (1) demand that Portugal stop immediately any acts of violence and destruction in Senegalese territory and respect the sovereignty, territorial integrity and security of Senegal; (2) condemn Portuguese acts of violence and destruction perpetrated against Senegal since 1963; (3) condemn the unlawful laying of anti-tank and anti-personnel mines in Senegalese territory; and (4) request the President of the Security Council and the Secretary-General to send to the spot, as a matter of urgency, a special mission of members of the Security Council, assisted by their military experts, to carry out an inquiry into the facts of which the Council had been informed, to examine the situation along the border between Guinea (Bis-

[27]See Y.U.N., 1960, pp. 49-50, text of resolution 1514(XV), containing the Declaration.
[28]See Y.U.N., 1969, p. 144, text of resolution 273(1969).
[29]For text of Article 34 of the Charter, see APPENDIX II.

sau) and Senegal and to report to the Council, making any recommendations aimed at guaranteeing peace and security in that region.

At the request of the United States representative, a separate vote was taken on the operative paragraph dealing with the special mission. The United States said that while it strongly regretted the continuing acts of violence complained of, the draft contained certain determinations of guilt before the proposed special mission embarked on its inquiry. Therefore, while supporting the proposal to send a special mission to the region, the United States would abstain from voting on the draft resolution as a whole.

The paragraph was put to the vote and adopted unanimously.

The draft resolution as a whole was then adopted by a vote of 13 to 0, with 2 abstentions, as resolution 294(1971). (For text of resolution, see DOCUMENTARY REFERENCES below.)

In explanation of vote, the United Kingdom stated that it had abstained because Portugal had denied responsibility for the incidents, and therefore, in the absence of an investigation, some parts of the resolution went too far in condemning Portugal.

On 21 July 1971, the President of the Security Council and the Secretary-General announced that the Special Mission of the Security Council would be composed of Nicaragua (Chairman), Belgium, Burundi, Japan, Poland and the Syrian Arab Republic.

On 24 July, in response to a request by the Chairman of the Special Mission to the Governments of Senegal and Portugal to extend to the Mission all necessary facilities, Portugal stated that it had been unjustifiably condemned by the Security Council without any evidence having been advanced in support of Senegal's charges. It could not collaborate with the Mission, as that would presuppose an acceptance of a condemnation which it had repudiated. As proof of its goodwill, however, it was renewing its proposal that a commission for controlling the Luso-Senegalese frontier be set up, consisting of Portuguese and Senegalese representatives and presided over by an impartial person.

On 16 September 1971, the Special Mission submitted its report to the Security Council. The report described the inquiries which the Mission had conducted in the frontier area, its consultations with the Senegalese authorities and its interview with the Secretary-General of PAIGC. The Mission deplored the Portuguese Government's lack of co-operation, which had prevented it from implementing fully its mandate.

The Special Mission concluded that it was clear that Senegalese foreign policy was aimed at avoiding any engagement with Portuguese forces

other than for reasons of defence, and that the recurrent armed attacks against Senegal had caused considerable loss of life and material damage and created a climate of insecurity and instability which posed a threat to peace and security in the region.

Since the Special Mission had been refused access to Guinea (Bissau), some information was lacking. But all the evidence of acts of violence and destruction found by the Mission had been along the frontier between Senegal and Guinea (Bissau), an area in which PAIGC was not engaged in any military activity. The indications were such as to designate the Portuguese authorities in Guinea (Bissau) as responsible, the report concluded.

The Special Mission recommended that the Security Council should ensure the prerequisites for eliminating the causes of tension in the region and creating an atmosphere of peace and security, namely (a) respect for the sovereignty and territorial integrity of Senegal; (b) the immediate cessation of acts of violence and destruction against Senegal; (c) as regards Guinea (Bissau), respect for the principle of self-determination and independence and the exercise of the right deriving from that principle without further delay.

The Mission recommended that the Council take all necessary steps to ensure that Portugal respect and fully implement these recommendations.

The Special Mission further recommended that the Council remain informed of the matter and that its President and the Secretary-General keep the situation under review. Finally, it recommended that the Secretary-General report to the Council on the question within six months.

The report of the Special Mission was considered at four meetings of the Security Council held between 29 September and 24 November 1971.

Also before the Council was a letter dated 29 September 1971 to the President of the Security Council by which Portugal categorically rejected the conclusions of the Special Mission as wholly in contradiction with the facts and with the words of PAIGC's Secretary-General, who made no secret of the fact that PAIGC was engaged in warlike acts of violence.

The authorities in Portuguese Guinea were only exercising their right of legitimate self-defence under Article 51 of the United Nations Charter,[30] Portugal stated. Nevertheless, Portugal asserted that it remained ready to seek a formula capable of establishing a climate of *détente*. In this context, it reported that an accord had been reached between the Foreign Ministers of Portugal and Senegal regarding the setting up of a control commission for the frontier, but that Senegal had failed to

---

[30]For text of Article 51 of the Charter, see APPENDIX II.

implement the measures that had been agreed upon.

Also before the Council was a letter of 15 November 1971, addressed to the Council President, by which Senegal asserted that further incidents had occurred on the frontier between Senegal and Guinea (Bissau) on 30 October and on the night of 3-4 November 1971.

Senegal, Guinea, Mali, Mauritania, Mauritius, Sudan, Togo and Zambia were invited once again to participate, without vote, in the Council's deliberations.

Several representatives commended the Special Mission for the manner in which it had performed its task.

The USSR expressed the hope that the Council would continue the practice of sending Security Council missions to carry out investigations on the spot which would mark a return to the practical working methods envisaged for the Council in the Charter and in the Council's rules of procedure.

Senegal expressed its gratitude to the members of the Special Mission for the objectivity and impartiality with which they had approached their task.

Portugal's letter of 29 September 1971, the Senegalese representative said, was designed to create a diversion by suggesting that Senegal had informed the Council of the dispute after having come to an agreement with Portugal. There had been a meeting in May 1971 between the Foreign Ministers of Senegal and Portugal, at the latter's request, but no positive decision had been reached; nor had Senegal accepted the establishment of a joint control commission, the representative stated. He felt that the Council could not consider measures against Portugal without taking into account the deep-rooted causes underlying the climate of chronic insecurity in the region.

Some members of the Council—including Poland, Sierra Leone, Somalia, the Syrian Arab Republic and the USSR—held that the report of the Special Mission had clearly established the responsibility of the Portuguese authorities in Guinea (Bissau) for the attacks on Senegal, and were the consequence of Portugal's denial to the people of Guinea (Bissau) of their right to self-determination and independence; these States called for the Council to take effective measures to end Portugal's aggressive actions, which threatened the independence and sovereignty of Senegal and other African States.

Somalia said that another round of condemnations and appeals would have no effect unless Portugal was convinced that the Council would take coercive action; he suggested that it call for an arms embargo against Portugal so long as colonial wars continued in Africa.

The USSR said that the security and independence of African States could be strengthened only if a speedy end was put to colonial wars in Africa and all peoples were granted independence in accordance with the United Nations Declaration on the Granting of Independence to Colonial Countries and Peoples.

France noted that the Special Mission had attempted to prepare a report that was as accurate, complete and objective as possible. The report had indicated that the various incidents described originated in Guinea (Bissau). Since Portugal was responsible for peace and order in that territory, it was to Portugal that the Council must turn to put an end to the acts of violence and destruction.

Japan said that the recommendations of the report were well balanced and if implemented fully would eliminate the causes of tension in the region.

On 24 November 1971, the Council proceeded to vote on a draft resolution sponsored by Burundi, Sierra Leone and Somalia. The text had been revised by the sponsors to incorporate changes resulting from consultations with other members of the Council.

By a vote of 14 to 0, with 1 abstention, the Council adopted the text as its resolution 302(1971).

The Council thereby: expressed its appreciation for the work of the Special Mission and noted with satisfaction its recommendations; reaffirmed the provisions of its resolution (294(1971)) of 15 July 1971; and strongly deplored the Portuguese Government's lack of co-operation with the Mission.

The Council then called upon Portugal: to take immediate effective measures (*a*) so that the sovereignty and territorial integrity of Senegal be fully respected, and (*b*) to prevent acts of violence and destruction against the territory and people of Senegal; to respect fully the inalienable right to self-determination and independence of the people of Guinea (Bissau); and to take without further delay the necessary measures so that this inalienable right could be exercised.

The President of the Security Council and the Secretary-General were asked to keep the question under review and to report on the implementation of the present resolution to the Council within six months.

In the event of failure by Portugal to comply with the provisions of the resolution, the Council would meet to consider necessary initiatives and steps.

(For text of resolution, see DOCUMENTARY REFERENCES below.)

Before the adoption of the resolution, the United States deplored Portugal's lack of co-operation with the Special Mission, which made it impossible for the Mission to implement fully its mandate. The Mission had carefully pointed out the hearsay nature of much of the evidence and had not determined responsibility for the mine-laying incidents, the United States noted. The draft resolution, however, made no effort to reflect those aspects of the report, nor did it take into account the role which the use of sanctuaries by insurgent groups played in creating border tensions. The United States therefore abstained in the vote.

The United Kingdom said that it supported the resolution since it was along the same lines as the report and its recommendations.

Speaking after the vote, China said that, in view of the defiant attitude of the Portuguese colonialists, the Council should harbour no illusions as to the actual result of the resolution just adopted. China resolutely supported the just struggle of the peoples of Guinea (Bissau), Angola and Mozambique for national independence and sovereignty.

The USSR said that in its view the resolution adopted was a weak and ineffective one.

Complaints by Guinea and Portugal

Communications

In a series of letters addressed to the President of the Security Council between 16 February and 12 March 1971, Portugal and Guinea exchanged charges regarding an overflight of Guinea (Bissau), armed attacks against the frontiers of Guinea, and terrorist attacks against Portuguese populations.

Consideration by Security Council

On 3 August 1971, the Permanent Representative of Guinea to the United Nations addressed a letter to the President of the Security Council stating that on 2 August the Intelligence Service of Guinea had intercepted conversations between overseas marine units and two other headquarters units of the Portuguese colonial army discussing an imminent military aggression by Portugal against Guinea. The letter requested an immediate meeting of the Security Council to consider this imminent threat to international peace and security.

The Security Council met on the same day to consider the complaint by Guinea.

Guinea was invited to participate in the Council's deliberations, without the right to vote.

The representative of Guinea stated that for 12 years Guinea had been the victim of daily and permanent acts of aggression, which had been brought to the attention of the Security Council. He recalled that the Special Mission dispatched to Guinea by the Security Council in connexion with the Portuguese attack on 22 November 1970 had found incontrovertible evidence of Portuguese

acts of aggression; on the basis of the Mission's report, the Council, on 8 December 1970, had strongly condemned Portugal for its invasion of Guinea.[31]

Portugal, however, had continued its aggressive policies against Guinea, the representative held. It was Guinea's fate that its borders were contiguous with those of the colonial enclave Guinea (Bissau), which Portugal was determined to keep under its colonial domination in spite of the Declaration on the Granting of Independence to Colonial Countries and Peoples,[32] which was designed to put an end to colonialism. Guinea had come before the Security Council out of an awareness that the peace, security and territorial integrity of every country had to be safeguarded by the Council. It had confidence in the Council with respect to all decisions it might consider appropriate and effective to safeguard Guinea's territorial integrity, peace and security.

During discussion, the representatives of Somalia and the Syrian Arab Republic held that the threat of imminent attack by Portugal against Guinea should be taken seriously by the Security Council because of the history of continued aggression by Portugal against Guinea.

The USSR said that in its view the Council was obliged to take urgent measures to avert the implementation of the aggressive plans of the Portuguese colonists, who enjoyed the support of the imperialist forces in their fight against the African States and the national liberation movements.

Burundi, Sierra Leone, Somalia and the Syrian Arab Republic introduced a draft resolution, which was unanimously adopted by the Security Council as its resolution 295(1971).

The Council thereby: (1) affirmed that the territorial integrity and political independence of Guinea must be respected; (2) decided to send a special mission of three members of the Security Council to Guinea to consult with the authorities and report on the situation immediately; (3) decided that the special mission be appointed after consultation between the Council President and the Secretary-General; and (4) decided to maintain the matter on its agenda.

On 26 August 1971, the Council approved a consensus statement by which it agreed that the Special Mission be composed of two members instead of three, and that it proceed to Conakry, Guinea, to consult the Government of Guinea on its complaint and report back to the Council as soon as possible. It was subsequently announced that the Special Mission would be composed of the representatives of Argentina and the Syrian Arab

[31]See Y.U.N., 1970, p. 193, text of resolution 290(1970).
[32]See footnote 27.

Republic, who would be accompanied by a staff from the Secretariat.

On 29 August 1971, the mission left New York for Conakry; it remained in Guinea from 30 August to 2 September 1971.

On 29 September 1971, the Security Council met to consider the report of the Special Mission.

The Special Mission reported that it had held meetings with the President of Guinea and with a government delegation and had visited various localities in Guinea. As evidence of the alleged planned Portuguese invasion of Guinea, the Mission had been shown: a map containing a plan of attack on Guinea, together with an explanatory note; the depositions of prisoners accused of plotting against the State in collusion with foreign powers; the text of a telegraphic message between two dissident elements which had been intercepted by the Guinean authorities; and a collection of military uniforms identical to those of the Guinean army, made in Guinea (Bissau) but bearing the inscription of the *Partido Africano da Independência da Guiné e Cabo Verde* (PAIGC), which, it was said, were to be used by the attackers in order to create confusion in the Guinean ranks.

The Council also had before it a letter dated 29 September 1971 from Portugal, stating that a perusal of the report of the Special Mission made it clear that the Mission had found no evidence to support Guinea's charges.

During discussion, the representative of Guinea stated that the report was a faithful record of observed facts which clearly indicated the continuing threat Portugal posed to a small African country.

The representatives of Somalia held that the report was a factual one, containing neither an assessment of the facts or charges made nor any recommendations. However, the evidence of the report bore out the contention that unless the United Nations resolved to do something about the Portuguese colonial territories in Africa, the peace and security of certain parts of Africa would always be threatened.

Sierra Leone said that it was clear from the report that there was a planned invasion of Guinea, and that it was essential that the Council try once and for all to eliminate the root cause of the disease: Portugal's belief that it could continue to be an imperialistic nation.

The USSR held that the Security Council should pay due attention to the report and seriously ponder what specific practical measures it should take to ensure peace and security in Africa.

It was agreed that the Council would consider the question further after members had had time to study the report of the Special Mission.

On 19 November 1971, the Permanent Representative of the Ivory Coast to the United Nations addressed a letter to the President of the Security Council by which the Ivory Coast categorically denied any allegations or inferences made by Guinean authorities in their statements to members of the Special Mission to the effect that the Ivory Coast might be implicated in plotting to overthrow the Guinean régime, through such acts as allowing the establishment on its territory of training camps for subversion and bases of operation for commandos and mercenary forces.

On 30 November 1971, the Council approved the text of a consensus among members regarding the question. The Council thereby agreed that it was evident from the report of the Special Mission that there was continuing concern in Guinea regarding the possibility of renewed acts against the country's territorial integrity and political independence, similar to those which led to the events of November 1970. In this respect, the view had been expressed by Guinea that action should be taken by the Security Council to prevent Portugal from violating the territorial integrity and political independence of Guinea.

The Council further agreed that it was clear that the failure by Portugal to apply the principle of self-determination, including the right to independence, in Guinea (Bissau) was having an unsettling effect on conditions in the area.

The Security Council, having taken note with appreciation of the report of the Special Mission and of the representations made by Guinea, reiterated the affirmation expressed in its resolution of 3 August 1971 (295(1971)) that the territorial integrity and political independence of Guinea must be respected.

During the discussion on 30 November, the representative of Somalia expressed the view that the consensus did not go as far as it should have; nonetheless, Somalia supported it because it reflected basic agreement among Council members that Guinea was under threat of aggression from Portugal and reaffirmed that Guinea's territorial integrity and political independence must be respected.

The United Kingdom commented that while it fully endorsed the principle of self-determination, including the right to independence, for all non-self-governing territories, it considered that responsibility for its implementation and timing rested with the administering power.

The representative of China stated that countless facts showed that the colonialist policies followed by Portugal were aimed not only at subverting the Government of Guinea but at suppressing the national liberation movement in Africa. The Guinean people were fighting not only for their own independence but for that of other African States.

In the opinion of Poland and the USSR, the

aggressive imperialist policies of Portugal towards Guinea clearly demonstrated that so long as colonialist régimes, with their military forces and bases, remained in Africa, the political independence and security of African States would always be threatened. The USSR said that the Council should adopt all possible measures to protect the political independence and territorial integrity of Guinea and other African States from the aggressive acts of Portuguese colonizers.

Burundi and Sierra Leone held that the Council should take appropriate action to prevent Portugal from carrying out acts which threatened the sovereignty and independence of Guinea.

Complaint by Zambia against Portugal

On 15 June 1971, Zambia addressed a letter to the Secretary-General seeking, through his good offices, to apprise members of the Security Council of the serious situation that had arisen from actions of the Portuguese authorities, who since January 1971 had virtually blockaded the flow of all categories of Zambian imports and were holding them in the Portuguese-controlled seaports of Beira, Nacala and Lourenço Marques in Mozambique and Lobito in Angola.

Among the blockaded imports was maize, the main staple diet of the people of Zambia. Owing to adverse weather conditions, the importation of slightly over 2 million bags was required for the period July 1970–June 1971. In view of the situation, Zambia had had to import from various countries an additional quantity of maize to replace the stocks held by Portuguese port authorities, incurring even greater costs in having it transported via non-traditional routes. For the 1971-1972 period, Zambia needed to import 1.5 million bags.

Zambia stated that it could not afford the unnecessary loss of foreign exchange through actions taken against its imports in traditional ports and countries of transit.

In seeking to apprise members of the Security Council of the situation, Zambia wished to draw their attention to the special circumstances affecting its geographical position, as duly recognized by the Council by its resolutions of 29 May 1968 and 18 March 1970.[33] Zambia deeply regretted that notwithstanding those resolutions, it had not received any assistance of the nature envisaged by the Security Council.

[33]See Y.U.N., 1968, p. 153, text of resolution 253(1968), operative para. 15; and Y.U.N., 1970, p. 182, text of resolution 277(1970), operative para. 16.

DOCUMENTARY REFERENCES

Complaints by Senegal against Portugal

Security Council, meetings 1569–1572.

S/10182. Letter of 27 April 1971 from Senegal.
S/10191. Letter of 10 May 1971 from Guinea.
S/10227. Letter of 16 June 1971 from Senegal.
S/10251. Letter of 6 July 1971 from Senegal (containing, *inter alia*, request to convene Council and to participate in Council's discussion).
S/10255. Letter of 10 July 1971 from Portugal.
S/10258. Letter of 12 July 1971 from Guinea (request to participate in Council's discussion).
S/10259 and Add.1,2. Letter of 12 July 1971 from Algeria, Botswana, Burundi, Cameroon, Central African Republic, Chad, Congo, Egypt, Equatorial Guinea, Ethiopia, Gabon, Ghana, Guinea, Ivory Coast, Kenya, Lesotho, Liberia, Libyan Arab Republic, Madagascar, Mali, Mauritania, Mauritius, Niger, Nigeria, Rwanda, Senegal, Sierra Leone, Somalia, Sudan, Swaziland, Togo, Tunisia, Uganda, United Republic of Tanzania, Upper Volta, Zaire and Zambia (supporting request to convene Council).
S/10260-S/10265. Letters of 12 and 13 July 1971 from Mali, Mauritania, Sudan, Togo, Mauritius and Zambia (requests to participate in Council's discussion).
S/10266. Burundi, Japan, Sierra Leone, Somalia, Syrian Arab Republic: draft resolution.

RESOLUTION 294(1971), as proposed by 5 powers, S/10266, adopted by Council on 15 July 1971, meeting 1572, by 13 votes to 0, with 2 abstentions (United Kingdom, United States).

The Security Council,
Taking note of the complaints by Senegal against Portugal contained in documents S/10182 and S/10251,
Taking note of the letter of the Chargé d'affaires ad interim of Portugal,
Having heard the statement of the Minister for Foreign Affairs of Senegal,
Bearing in mind that all States Members of the United Nations must refrain in their international relations from the threat or use of force against the territorial integrity or political independence of any State, or in any other manner inconsistent with the purpose of the United Nations,
Conscious of its duty to take effective collective measures for the prevention and removal of threats to international peace and security and for the suppression of acts of aggression,
Disturbed by the increasingly serious situation created by acts of violence perpetrated by the Portuguese armed forces against Senegal since the adoption of Security Council resolution 273(1969) of 9 December 1969,
Deeply distressed by the repeated laying of mines in Senegalese territory,
Gravely concerned that incidents of this nature, by threatening the sovereignty and territorial integrity of Senegal, might endanger international peace and security,
Bearing in mind its resolutions 178(1963) of 24 April 1963, 204(1965) of 19 May 1965 and 273(1969) of 9 December 1969,
Having taken note of the report of the *Ad Hoc* Working Group of Experts of the Commission on Human Rights concerning Portuguese acts of violence in Senegalese territory,
Noting that Portugal has not complied with the provisions of paragraph 2 of resolution 273(1969),
1. *Demands* that the Government of Portugal should stop immediately any acts of violence and destruction in Senegalese territory and respect the sovereignty, territorial integrity and security of Senegal;
2. *Condemns* the acts of violence and destruction perpetrated since 1963 by the Portuguese armed forces of Guinea (Bissau) against the population and villages of Senegal;
3. *Condemns* the unlawful laying of anti-tank and anti-personnel mines in Senegalese territory;

4. *Requests* the President of the Security Council and the Secretary-General to send to the spot, as a matter of urgency, a special mission of members of the Council assisted by their military experts to carry out an inquiry into the facts of which the Council has been informed, to examine the situation along the border between Guinea (Bissau) and Senegal and to report to the Council, making any recommendations aimed at guaranteeing peace and security in this region.

S/10274. Report of 21 July 1971 by President of Security Council and Secretary-General.
S/10284. Letter of 6 August 1971 from Portugal (transmitting letter of 24 July 1971 from Portugal to Chairman of Special Mission established under Security Council resolution 294(1971)).

Security Council, meetings 1586, 1599–1601.

S/10308 and Corr.1. Report of 16 September 1971 of Special Mission of Security Council established under resolution 294(1971).
S/10342. Letter of 28 September 1971 from Senegal (request to participate in Council's discussion).
S/10343. Letter of 29 September 1971 from Portugal.
S/10388 and Corr.1. Letter of 15 November 1971 from Senegal.
S/10395. Burundi, Sierra Leone, Somalia: draft resolution.

RESOLUTION 302(1971), as proposed by 3 powers, S/10395, as orally amended by sponsors and by Argentina, adopted by Council on 24 November 1971, meeting 1601, by 14 votes to 0, with 1 abstention (United States).

The Security Council,
Considering the complaints by Senegal against Portugal contained in documents S/10182 and S/10251,
Recalling its resolutions 178(1963) of 24 April 1963, 204(1965) of 19 May 1965 and 273(1969) of 9 December 1969,
Having considered the report of the Special Mission of the Security Council established in accordance with resolution 294(1971) of 15 July 1971,
Deeply concerned at the climate of insecurity and instability, fraught with a threat to peace and security in the region,
Affirming the need to ensure the prerequisites for eliminating the causes of tension in the region and creating an atmosphere of trust, peace and security, as recommended by the Special Mission in its report,
1. *Expresses its appreciation* for the work accomplished by the Special Mission of the Security Council established under resolution 294(1971);
2. *Takes note with satisfaction* of the recommendations of the Special Mission contained in paragraph 128 of its report;
3. *Reaffirms* the provisions of its resolution 294(1971) condemning the acts of violence and destruction perpetrated since 1963 by the Portuguese armed forces of Guinea (Bissau) against the population and villages of Senegal;
4. *Strongly deplores* the lack of co-operation with the Special Mission on the part of the Portuguese Government, which prevented the Special Mission from implementing fully the mandate given to it under paragraph 4 of resolution 294(1971);
5. *Calls upon* the Government of Portugal to take immediate effective measures:
(a) So that the sovereignty and territorial integrity of Senegal shall be fully respected;
(b) To prevent acts of violence and destruction against the territory and the people of Senegal, in order to contribute to the safeguarding of peace and security in the region;
6. *Calls upon* the Government of Portugal to respect fully the inalienable right to self-determination and independence of the people of Guinea (Bissau);
7. *Calls upon* the Government of Portugal to take without further delay the necessary measures, so that this inalienable right of the people of Guinea (Bissau) shall be exercised;

8. *Requests* the President of the Security Council and the Secretary-General to keep this question under review and report on the implementation of the present resolution to the Council within an appropriate period and at the latest within six months;
9. *Declares* that, in the event of failure by Portugal to comply with the provisions of the present resolution, the Security Council will meet to consider the initiatives and steps that the situation requires;
10. *Decides* to remain seized of the question.

A/8402. Report of Security Council, 16 June 1970–15 June 1971, Chapter 12.

Complaints by Guinea and Portugal

Security Council, meetings 1573, 1576.

S/10118. Letter of 16 February 1971 from Portugal.
S/10125, S/10145. Letters of 17 February and 4 March 1971 from Guinea.
S/10156. Letter of 12 March 1971 from Portugal.
S/10180 and Add.1. Replies of Governments to Secretary-General's note verbale of 18 December 1970 transmitting text of Security Council resolution 290(1970). Note by Secretary-General.
S/10280. Letter of 3 August 1971 from Guinea (request to convene Council).
S/10281. Burundi, Sierra Leone, Somalia, Syrian Arab Republic: draft resolution.
S/10282. Letter of 3 August 1971 from Guinea (request to participate in Council's discussion).

RESOLUTION 295(1971), as submitted by 4 powers, S/10281, as orally revised by sponsors in consultation with Council members, adopted unanimously by Council on 3 August 1971, meeting 1573.

The Security Council,
Taking note of the letter addressed to the President of the Security Council by the Permanent Representative of Guinea,
Having heard the statement of the Permanent Representative of Guinea,
Bearing in mind that all States Members of the United Nations must refrain in their international relations from the threat or use of force against the territorial integrity or political independence of any State, or in any other manner inconsistent with the purposes of the United Nations,
1. *Affirms* that the territorial integrity and political independence of the Republic of Guinea must be respected;
2. *Decides* to send a special mission of three members of the Security Council to Guinea to consult with the authorities and to report on the situation immediately;
3. *Decides* that this special mission be appointed after consultation between the President of the Security Council and the Secretary-General;
4. *Decides* to maintain the matter on its agenda.

S/10283, S/10287. Letters of 4 and 12 August 1971 from Guinea.
S/10299. Note of 26 August 1971 by President of Security Council and Secretary-General.
S/INF/27. Resolutions and decisions of Security Council, 1971. Decision, p. 4: consensus, approved by Council on 26 August 1971, meeting 1576.

"It is the consensus of the Security Council that the Special Mission called for in resolution 295(1971) should be composed of two members of the Council instead of three. The Special Mission will proceed to Conakry to consult the Government of the Republic of Guinea on its complaint and will report back to the Council as soon as possible."

Security Council, meetings 1586, 1603.

S/10309/Rev.1. Report of Security Council Special Mission to Republic of Guinea established under resolution 295(1971).
S/10344. Letter of 29 September 1971 from Portugal.
S/10393. Letter of 19 November from Ivory Coast.
S/INF/27. Resolutions and decisions of Security Council, 1971. Decision, p. 5: consensus, approved by Council on 30 November 1971, meeting 1603.

"It will be recalled that on 3 August the Security Council decided to dispatch a Special Mission to the Republic of Guinea. The Special Mission, consisting of the representative of Syria, Ambassador George J. Tomeh, and the deputy representative of Argentina, Minister Julio César Carasales, visited Guinea from 30 August to 2 September 1971 and held extensive consultations with officials of the Government of Guinea.
"In those consultations, the Guinean authorities co-operated fully with the Special Mission and extended to it all the facilities necessary for the successful achievement of its task.
"Upon its return to New York and in accordance with its terms of reference, the Special Mission submitted its report to the Security Council, circulated as document S/10309. The Council began its first examination of the report of the Special Mission at its 1586th meeting on 29 September 1971.
"It is evident from this report that there is continuing concern in

Guinea regarding the possibility of renewed acts against that country's territorial integrity and political independence similar to those which led to the events of November 1970. In this respect, the view has been expressed by the Government of Guinea that action should be taken by the Security Council to prevent Portugal from violating the territorial integrity and political independence of Guinea.
"It is also clear that the failure by Portugal to apply the principle of self-determination, including the right to independence, in Guinea (Bissau) is having an unsettling effect on conditions in the area.
"The Security Council, having taken note with appreciation of the report of the Special Mission and the representations made by the Government of Guinea, reiterates paragraph 1 of resolution 295(1971) which 'affirms that the territorial integrity and political independence of the Republic of Guinea must be respected'."

A/8401. Report of Secretary-General on work of the Organization, 16 June 1970–15 June 1971, Part One, Chapter IV H.
A/8402. Report of Security Council, 16 June 1970–15 June 1971, Chapter 7.

Complaint by Zambia against Portugal
S/10225. Letter of 15 June 1971 from Zambia.
A/8402. Report of Security Council, 16 June 1970–15 June 1971, Chapter 14.

United Nations Educational and Training Programme for Southern Africa

The United Nations Educational and Training Programme for Southern Africa continued during 1970-1971 to grant scholarships for education and training to persons from Namibia, South Africa, Southern Rhodesia and the territories under Portuguese administration.

Reporting to the General Assembly at its 1971 session on the progress of the Programme, the Secretary-General stated that during the period from 1 November 1970 to 8 December 1971, 25 States had pledged $689,036. Total contributions to the Programme since its establishment in 1967 had amounted to $1,937,282 as at 8 December 1971. (The target originally envisaged for the period 1968-1970 was $3 million.)

During 1970-1971, 938 applications for training were received, 175 new awards were granted, and 381 awards were renewed. The majority of those who held scholarships were at educational institutions in Africa. Also during the year, 13 States offered scholarships.

The Advisory Committee on the Programme, established by the General Assembly in 1968, held four meetings in 1971 at which it discussed ways of expanding and strengthening the Programme and questions concerning the United Nations Fund for Namibia. (See pp. 556-57.)

On 20 December 1971, the General Assembly, noting that the voluntary contributions received in the period from 1968 to 1971 had fallen far short of the original three-year target, urgently ap-

pealed to all States, organizations and individuals to make generous contributions to the trust fund for the Programme so that it might not only be continued but also strengthened and expanded.

The Assembly decided that, as a transitional measure, provision should be made under the regular budget of the United Nations for the financial year 1972 for an amount of $100,000 to ensure continuity of the Programme pending the receipt of adequate voluntary contributions.

The Assembly also took note with approval of the efforts made to strengthen co-operation between the Programme and the United Nations High Commissioner for Refugees, the specialized agencies and the Organization of African Unity, and hoped that those efforts would be continued with a view to further co-ordination of their activities in the field of education and training for persons from the territories concerned.

These decisions were set forth in resolution 2875(XXVI), adopted by a recorded vote of 121 to 2, on the recommendation of the Assembly's Fourth Committee, which had approved the text on 14 December 1971, by 90 votes to 2, on a proposal by Cameroon, Egypt, Equatorial Guinea, Finland, Ghana, India, the Ivory Coast, Kenya, Liberia, Nigeria, Norway, Senegal, Sweden, Tunisia, the United Republic of Tanzania, Yugoslavia and Zambia. (For text of resolution, see DOCUMENTARY REFERENCES below.)

Table I. United Nations Educational and Training Programme for Southern Africa: applications and awards

(1 November 1970–8 October 1971)

	Applications received	New awards	Awards extended	Current scholarship holders
Namibia	31	14	53	67
South Africa	248	47	144	191
Southern Rhodesia	454	56	55	111
Territories under Portuguese administration	205	58	129	187
Total	938	175	381	556

Table II. Contributions pledged to the United Nations Educational and Training Programme for Southern Africa

(1 November 1970–8 December 1971)

Country	Pledge (in U.S. dollars)
Barbados	500
Burma	1,000
Canada	50,000
Cyprus	478
Denmark	99,906
Federal Republic of Germany	85,000
Finland	30,000
France	100,000
Ghana	1,530
Greece	3,500
India	1,500
Indonesia	1,000
Iran	3,000
Iraq	1,500
Ireland	5,000
Japan	20,000
Kenya	2,002
Khmer Republic	1,000
Malaysia	1,000
Norway	75,000
Philippines	1,000
Sierra Leone	120
Sweden	80,000
United Kingdom	120,000
Yugoslavia	5,000
Total	689,036

DOCUMENTARY REFERENCES

General Assembly—26th session
Fourth Committee, meetings 1953, 1956–1958, 1960, 1962–1968.
Fifth Committee, meeting 1487.
Plenary meeting 2028.

A/8401. Report of Secretary-General on work of the Organization, 16 June 1970–15 June 1971, Part Two, Chapter I C 6.
A/8485 and Add.1,2. Report of Secretary-General (covering period 1 November 1970–8 December 1971).
A/C.4/L.1001. Cameroon, Egypt, Equatorial Guinea, Finland, Ghana, India, Ivory Coast, Kenya, Liberia, Nigeria, Norway, Senegal, Sweden, Tunisia, United Republic of Tanzania, Yugoslavia, Zambia: draft resolution, approved by Fourth Committee on 14 December 1971, meeting 1968, by 90 votes to 2.
A/C.4/L.1003, A/C.5/1424, A/8634. Administrative and financial implications of draft resolution recommended by Fourth Committee in A/8621. Statements by Secretary-General and report of Fifth Committee.
A/8621. Report of Fourth Committee.

RESOLUTION 2875(XXVI), as recommended by Fourth Committee, A/8621, adopted by Assembly on 20 December 1971, meeting 2028, by recorded vote of 121 to 2, as follows:

In favour: Afghanistan, Algeria, Argentina, Australia, Austria, Bahrain, Barbados, Belgium, Botswana, Brazil, Bulgaria, Burma, Burundi, Byelorussian SSR, Cameroon, Canada, Central African Republic, Ceylon, Chad, Chile, Colombia, Congo, Costa Rica, Cuba, Cyprus, Czechoslovakia, Dahomey, Denmark, Dominican Republic, Ecuador, Egypt, El Salvador, Equatorial Guinea, Ethiopia, Fiji, Finland, France, Gambia, Ghana, Greece, Guatemala, Guinea, Guyana, Haiti, Honduras, Hungary, Iceland, India, Indonesia, Iran, Ireland, Israel, Italy, Ivory Coast, Jamaica, Japan, Jordan, Kenya, Khmer Republic, Kuwait, Laos, Lebanon, Lesotho, Liberia, Libyan Arab Republic, Luxembourg, Madagascar, Malawi, Malaysia, Mali, Malta, Mauritania, Mexico, Mongolia, Morocco, Nepal, Netherlands, New Zealand, Nicaragua, Niger, Nigeria, Norway, Oman, Pakistan, Panama, Paraguay, People's Democratic Republic of Yemen, Peru, Philippines, Poland, Romania, Rwanda, Saudi Arabia, Senegal, Sierra Leone, Singapore, Somalia, Spain, Sudan, Swaziland, Sweden, Syrian Arab Republic, Thailand, Togo, Trinidad and Tobago, Tunisia, Turkey, Uganda, Ukrainian SSR, USSR, United Arab Emirates, United Kingdom, United Republic of Tanzania, United States, Upper Volta, Uruguay, Venezuela, Yemen, Yugoslavia,

Zaire, Zambia.
Against: Portugal, South Africa.

The General Assembly,

Recalling its resolution 2349(XXII) of 19 December 1967, whereby it established an integrated educational and training programme for Namibians, South Africans, Southern Rhodesians and persons from Territories under Portuguese administration,

Taking note of the report of the Secretary-General on the United Nations Educational and Training Programme for Southern Africa,

Recalling its decision, contained in paragraph 7 of resolution 2349(XXII), that the Programme should be financed from a trust fund made up of voluntary contributions,

Further recalling that, by paragraph 8 of resolution 2349(XXII), it authorized the Secretary-General to appeal to States Members of the United Nations or members of specialized agencies for funds to achieve a target of $U.S.3 million in the period from 1968 to 1970,

Noting that the voluntary contributions received in the four-year period from 1968 to 1971 have fallen far short of the original three-year target,

Noting further that such funds as have been made available have been expended annually to provide assistance in the form of individual awards to persons from the Territories concerned to further their education and that, consequently, additional funds are required if the Programme is to continue in operation,

Expressing its firm conviction that the provision of assistance for the education and training of persons from the Territories concerned is as essential as ever and should not only continue, but also be expanded,

1. *Expresses its appreciation* to all those who have made voluntary contributions to the United Nations Educational and Training Programme for Southern Africa since its inception;

2. *Urgently appeals* to all States, organizations and individuals to make generous contributions to the trust fund for the Programme so that it might not only be continued, but also strengthened and expanded;

3. *Decides* that, as a further transitional measure, provision shall be made, under section 12 of the regular budget of the United Nations for the financial year 1972, for an amount of $100,000 to ensure continuity of the Programme pending the receipt of adequate voluntary contributions;

4. *Expresses its appreciation* to the Secretary-General and to the members of the Advisory Committee on the United Nations Educational and Training Programme for Southern Africa, established in pursuance of paragraph 2 of General Assembly

resolution 2431(XXIII) of 18 December 1968, for the work they have accomplished during the period under review in connexion with the Programme;

5. *Takes note with approval* of the efforts made during the period under review to strengthen co-operation between the Programme and the United Nations High Commissioner for Refugees, the specialized agencies and the Organization of African Unity, and hopes that these efforts will be continued with a view to further co-ordination of their activities in the field of education and training for persons from the Territories concerned;

6. *Requests* the Secretary-General to report to the General Assembly at its twenty-seventh session on the progress of the Programme.

Co-operation between the United Nations and the Organization of African Unity

On 15 November 1971, the representatives of 36 African States requested the inclusion in the agenda of the General Assembly's current session of an item entitled: "Co-operation between the United Nations and the Organization of African Unity: holding of meetings of the Security Council in an African capital."

In an explanatory memorandum these States recalled that the item on co-operation between the two bodies had been included in the agenda of the Assembly's 1965, 1966, 1967 and 1969 sessions. They also recalled that the Assembly of Heads of State and Government of the Organization of African Unity (OAU) had, at its eighth session, at Addis Ababa, Ethiopia, in June 1971, adopted a resolution requesting the convening early in 1972 of a special session of the Security Council, in an African member country of OAU, devoted solely to the measures to be taken with a view to implementing the various Security Council and General Assembly resolutions on decolonization, the struggle against *apartheid* and racial discrimination in Africa.

The Assembly took up the item in plenary meetings. At the same time it considered a report by the Secretary-General on co-operation between the United Nations and OAU since 1 November 1967, the date of his last report. The report covered the following major topics: representation at meetings; technical co-operation offered by United Nations bodies at the request of OAU; co-operation between OAU and the Economic Commission for Africa; and co-operation with respect to the situation in southern Africa.

On 20 December 1971, the General Assembly invited the Security Council to consider the OAU request to hold meetings of the Council in an African capital.

The Assembly took note with satisfaction of the Secretary-General's report and asked him to continue his efforts to intensify co-operation between the United Nations and OAU. It invited the specialized agencies and other United Nations organizations, particularly the United Nations Development Programme, to continue their co-operation with OAU.

These decisions were embodied in resolution 2863(XXVI), adopted by 113 votes to 2, on the basis of a text proposed by the following 41 Members: Algeria, Botswana, Burundi, Cameroon, the Central African Republic, Chad, the Congo, Dahomey, Egypt, Equatorial Guinea, Ethiopia, Gabon, the Gambia, Ghana, Guinea, the Ivory Coast, Kenya, Lesotho, Liberia, the Libyan Arab Republic, Madagascar, Malawi, Mali, Mauritania, Mauritius, Morocco, Niger, Nigeria, Rwanda, Senegal, Sierra Leone, Somalia, Sudan, Swaziland, Togo, Tunisia, Uganda, the United Republic of Tanzania, Upper Volta, Zaire and Zambia. (For text of resolution, see DOCUMENTARY REFERENCES below.)

DOCUMENTARY REFERENCES

General Assembly—26th session
General Committee, meeting 196.
Fifth Committee, meeting 1487.
Plenary meetings 1990, 2025, 2027.

A/8386. Co-operation between United Nations and Organization of African Unity (OAU). Report of Secretary-General.
A/8494 and Corr.1 and Add.1. Letter of 15 November 1971 from Algeria, Botswana, Burundi, Cameroon, Central African Republic, Chad, Congo, Dahomey, Egypt, Equatorial Guinea, Ethiopia, Gabon, Gambia, Ghana, Guinea, Ivory Coast, Kenya, Liberia, Libyan Arab Republic, Madagascar, Mali, Mauritania, Morocco, Niger, Nigeria, Senegal, Sierra Leone, Sudan, Swaziland, Togo, Tunisia, Uganda, United Republic of Tanzania, Upper Volta, Zaire, Zambia (request for inclusion in agenda of item entitled: "Co-operation between the United Nations and the Organization of African Unity: holding of meetings of the Security Council in an African capital").
A/8500/Add.3. Fourth report of General Committee.
A/L.653. Algeria, Botswana, Burundi, Cameroon, Central African Republic, Chad, Congo, Dahomey, Egypt, Equatorial Guinea, Ethiopia, Gabon, Gambia, Ghana, Guinea, Ivory Coast, Kenya, Lesotho, Liberia, Libyan Arab Republic, Madagascar, Malawi, Mali, Mauritania, Mauritius, Morocco, Niger, Nigeria, Rwanda, Senegal, Sierra Leone, Somalia, Sudan, Swaziland, Togo, Tunisia, Uganda, United Republic of Tanzania, Upper Volta, Zaire, Zambia: draft resolution.
A/C.5/1427, A/8631. Administrative and financial implications of 41-power draft resolution, A/L.653. Statement by Secretary-General and report of Fifth Committee.

RESOLUTION 2863(XXVI), as proposed by 41 powers, A/L.653, adopted by Assembly on 20 December 1971, meeting 2027, by 113 votes to 2.

The General Assembly,

Taking note of the request by thirty-six African States for the holding early in the year 1972, in an African country member of the Organization of African Unity, of meetings of the Security Council devoted solely to the measures to be taken with a view to implementing the various resolutions of the Security Council and the General Assembly on decolonization, the struggle against *apartheid* and racial discrimination in Africa,

Taking note of the statement made by the Chairman of the Organization of African Unity before the General Assembly on 24 September 1971,

Recalling its resolutions 2011(XX) of 11 October 1965, 2193(XXI) of 15 December 1966 and 2505(XXIV) of 20 November 1969 on co-operation between the United Nations and the Organization of African Unity,

Noting with satisfaction the increased co-operation between the Organization of African Unity and the United Nations, the specialized agencies and other organizations within the United Nations system, especially in their efforts to solve the grave situation in southern Africa,

1. *Takes note with satisfaction* of the report of the Secretary-General on co-operation between the United Nations and the Organization of African Unity;

2. *Invites* the Security Council to consider the request of the Organization of African Unity concerning the holding of meetings of the Council in an African capital;

3. *Requests* the Secretary-General to continue his efforts to intensify co-operation between the United Nations and the Organization of African Unity in accordance with the relevant resolutions of the General Assembly;

4. *Invites* the specialized agencies and other organizations concerned within the United Nations system, particularly the United Nations Development Programme, to continue their co-operation with the Organization of African Unity;

5. *Decides* to include in the provisional agenda of its twenty-seventh session the question of co-operation between the United Nations and the Organization of African Unity.

Other documents

S/10272. Letter of 13 July 1971 from Executive Secretary of Organization of African Unity (OAU) to United Nations (transmitting resolutions adopted by 8th Assembly of Heads of State and Government of OAU).

S/10477. Letter of 23 December 1971 from Guinea.

S/10480. Letter of 29 December 1971 from Secretary-General (transmitting text of resolution 2863(XXVI)).

Chapter VIII

Questions relating to Asia and the Far East

Representation of China in the United Nations

Consideration by General Assembly

On 25 October 1971, the General Assembly decided "to restore all its rights to the People's Republic of China and to recognize the representatives of its Government as the only legitimate representatives of China to the United Nations, and to expel forthwith the representatives of Chiang Kai-shek from the place which they unlawfully occupy at the United Nations and in all the organizations related to it."

The question of the "Restoration of the lawful rights of the People's Republic of China in the United Nations" was placed on the Assembly's provisional agenda at the request of the following 17 Members: Albania, Algeria, the Congo, Cuba, Guinea, Iraq, Mali, Mauritania, the People's Democratic Republic of Yemen, Romania, Somalia, Sudan, the Syrian Arab Republic, the United Republic of Tanzania, Yemen, Yugoslavia and Zambia. Their request was dated 15 July 1971.

A second item entitled "The representation of China in the United Nations" was also put on the Assembly's provisional agenda at the request, presented on 17 August 1971, of the United States.

On 22 September 1971, in the Assembly's General Committee, the United States proposed that the two items be combined into a single one under the title "Question of China." This proposal, however, was rejected by 12 votes to 9, with 3 abstentions.

In an explanatory memorandum accompanying their request of 15 July 1971, the 17 States observed that for years they had protested against the hostile and discriminatory policy followed by several Governments with regard to the lawful Government of China, the sole genuine representative of the Chinese people. The existence of the People's Republic of China, they declared, was a reality which could not be changed to suit the myth of a so-called "Republic of China," fabricated out of a portion of Chinese territory. The unlawful authorities installed in the island of Taiwan, claiming to represent China, remained there only because of the permanent presence of United States armed forces.

No important international problems, they added, could be solved without the participation of the People's Republic of China. It was in the fundamental interest of the United Nations to restore promptly to the People's Republic of China its seat in the Organization, thus putting an end to a grave injustice and to an unacceptable and dangerous situation which had been perpetuated in order to fulfil a policy increasingly repudiated. This meant the immediate expulsion of the representatives of the Chiang Kai-shek régime from the seat which it unlawfully occupied in the United Nations and its affiliated bodies.

In the explanatory memorandum accompanying its request of 17 August 1971, the United States said that, in dealing with the problem of the representation of China, the United Nations should take cognizance of the existence of both the People's Republic of China and the Republic of China; it should reflect that incontestable reality in the manner in which it made provision for China's representation. The United Nations should not be required to take a position on the respective conflicting claims of the People's Republic of China or the Republic of China pending a peaceful resolution of the matter as called for by the United Nations Charter. Thus, the memorandum added, the People's Republic of China should be represented and at the same time provision should be made to ensure that the Republic of China was not deprived of its representation. To succeed in its peace-keeping role and in advancing the well-being of mankind, the United Nations should deal with the question of the representation of China in such a just and realistic manner.

In a letter of 15 October 1971 the representatives of 22 States—Albania, Algeria, Burma, Ceylon, the Congo, Cuba, Equatorial Guinea, Guinea, Iraq, Mali, Mauritania, Nepal, Pakistan, the People's Democratic Republic of Yemen, Romania, Somalia, Sudan, the Syrian Arab Republic, the United Republic of Tanzania, Yemen, Yugoslavia and Zambia—requested the Secretary-General to distribute, as an official Assembly document, a statement of the Ministry of Foreign Affairs of the People's Republic of China dated 20 August 1971. In this statement, made in response to the United States letter of 17 August 1971 and its accompanying explanatory memorandum, the Ministry of Foreign Affairs declared that the United States proposal was a blatant exposure of the Nixon Government's scheme of creating "two Chinas" in the United Nations. There was only one China, the People's Republic of China. Taiwan, it added, was an inalienable part of Chinese territory and a province of China, which had already returned to the motherland after the Second World War.

For over 20 years, the statement continued, the United States Government had arbitrarily inserted in the United Nations the Chiang Kai-shek clique—which had long been repudiated by the Chinese people—to usurp the seat of the People's Republic of China. The relationship between the Chinese people and the Chiang Kai-shek clique

was entirely China's internal affair. The United States was plotting to separate Taiwan from China and was wildly attempting to force Members of the United Nations to submit to its will.

The Chinese Government declared that the Chinese people and Government firmly opposed "two Chinas," "one China, one Taiwan" or any similar absurdities, as well as the fallacy that "the status of Taiwan remains to be determined" and the scheme of creating "an independent Taiwan." Should any such situation or any other similar situation occur in the United Nations, the Government of the People's Republic of China would have absolutely nothing to do with the United Nations.

The statement further called for the immediate expulsion of the representatives of Chiang Kai-shek from the United Nations and all its organs and for the restoration of all the legitimate rights of the People's Republic of China in the Organization.

Discussion in the Assembly took place at 12 plenary meetings between 18 and 26 October 1971, with 73 Members taking part in the debate.

At the beginning of the debate, the General Assembly had before it three draft resolutions.

The first draft resolution, submitted on 25 September 1971, was sponsored by the following 23 States, including the 17 States which had joined in placing the question on the agenda: Albania, Algeria, Burma, Ceylon, the Congo, Cuba, Equatorial Guinea, Guinea, Iraq, Mali, Mauritania, Nepal, Pakistan, the People's Democratic Republic of Yemen, Romania, Sierra Leone, Somalia, Sudan, the Syrian Arab Republic, the United Republic of Tanzania, Yemen, Yugoslavia and Zambia.

By the preambular paragraphs of this draft, the Assembly would recall Charter principles, make the point that restoration of the lawful rights of the People's Republic of China was essential both for the protection of the Charter and for the cause the United Nations must serve under the Charter, and recognize that the representatives of the People's Republic of China were the only lawful representatives of China to the United Nations and that the People's Republic of China was one of the five permanent members of the Security Council.

By the operative paragraph of the text, the General Assembly would decide to restore to the People's Republic of China all its rights, to recognize the representatives of its Government as the only legitimate representatives of China to the United Nations and to expel forthwith the representatives of Chiang Kai-shek from the seat which they unlawfully occupied in the United Nations and in all the organizations related to it.

The second draft resolution, submitted on 29

September 1971, was sponsored by the following 22 States: Australia, Bolivia, Colombia, Costa Rica, the Dominican Republic, El Salvador, Fiji, the Gambia, Guatemala, Haiti, Honduras, Japan, Lesotho, Liberia, Mauritius, New Zealand, Nicaragua, the Philippines, Swaziland, Thailand, the United States and Uruguay.

By this text the General Assembly, recalling the provisions of the United Nations Charter, would have the Assembly decide that any proposal in the General Assembly which would result in depriving the Republic of China of representation in the United Nations was an important question under Article 18 of the Charter.[1]

The third draft resolution, also submitted on 29 September, was sponsored by 19 States, namely: Australia, Bolivia, Chad, Costa Rica, the Dominican Republic, Fiji, the Gambia, Haiti, Honduras, Japan, Lesotho, Liberia, Mauritius, New Zealand, the Philippines, Swaziland, Thailand, the United States and Uruguay.

By the preamble to this text, the General Assembly would note that since the founding of the United Nations fundamental changes had occurred in China. It would take into account the existing factual situation and then note that the Republic of China had been continuously represented as a Member of the United Nations since 1945. It would express its belief that the People's Republic of China should be represented in the United Nations, recall that according to the Charter the United Nations was established to be a centre for harmonizing the actions of nations, and finally express its belief that an equitable resolution of the problem of the representation of China should be sought in the light of the above considerations and without prejudice to the eventual settlement of the conflicting claims involved.

By the operative part of the draft resolution, the General Assembly would: (1) affirm the right of representation of the People's Republic of China and recommend that it be seated as one of the five permanent members of the Security Council; (2) affirm the continued right of representation of the Republic of China; and (3) recommend that all United Nations bodies and the specialized agencies take into account the provisions of this resolution in deciding the question of Chinese representation.

During the debate four more draft resolutions were submitted to the Assembly, one by Saudi Arabia and three by Tunisia.

Saudi Arabia, expressing the view that the whole question revolved around the right of self-determination and that the Assembly had neither the right nor the power to compel the people of Taiwan to merge with the mainland, also introduced amendments to the 23-power text.

The representative of Tunisia said that as a result of developments since 1949 the Republic of China had acquired rights which were now challenged. If the Republic of China had to free China's seat for the People's Republic of China, that should not prejudge the future of Formosa which—in accordance with the right of self-determination—might wish to be represented in the United Nations as a separate entity. Such a possibility should not be rejected out of hand. To facilitate the solution to that problem, the Tunisian delegation had submitted three separate proposals.

The Saudi Arabian draft resolution, by its preamble, among other things would have the General Assembly: affirm that no State nor any coalition of Member States had the right under the Charter to divest any people of its own right to self-determination; consider that the Republic of China, "i.e. the people of the island of Taiwan," constituted a separate political entity; recognize that it was economically viable; and consider that any decision which disposed of the right of a people to self-determination against its will would lead to suppression and conflict while one of the main purposes of the United Nations was to maintain international peace.

By its operative provisions, the Saudi Arabian draft text would have the Assembly decide that the People's Republic of China should assume its rightful place in the United Nations and be seated as one of the five permanent members of the Security Council and that it should also be represented in all the organizations related to the United Nations. At the same time, the Republic of China, "i.e. the people of the island of Taiwan," should retain its seat in the United Nations and in all the organizations related to it until its people were enabled by plebiscite or referendum under the auspices of the United Nations to declare themselves on the following three options: (i) continued independence as a sovereign State with a neutral status defined by a treaty recorded by the United Nations; (ii) confederation with the People's Republic of China, the terms to be negotiated by the two parties concerned; or (iii) federation with the People's Republic of China, subject to protocols negotiated by both parties.

The Saudi Arabian text would also have the Assembly appeal to the magnanimity of both the People's Republic of China and the Republic of China, "i.e. the people of the island of Taiwan," to consider the proposed options as a basis for, if not a final solution to, a political dispute among Asian brothers.

By the first Tunisian draft resolution, the Assembly, considering the urgent need for partici-

---

[1]For text of Article 18 of the Charter, see APPENDIX II.

pation of the People's Republic of China in the work of the United Nations, in a spirit of universality, would invite the People's Republic of China to arrange to be represented by duly accredited representatives in the General Assembly and the different organs of the United Nations, including the Security Council.

By the second Tunisian proposal, the Assembly, noting that the People's Republic of China did not exercise its sovereignty over the island of Formosa and considering that the Republic of China currently occupied the seat of China in the different organs of the United Nations and represented, in fact, only the island of Formosa, would invite the delegation of the Republic of China, subject to any resolution or to any international agreement affecting the *status quo* in Formosa, to continue to sit under the name of Formosa in the General Assembly and the other organs of the United Nations, with the exception of the Security Council.

By the third Tunisian draft text, which was to apply if the Assembly took no decision on the item "Restoration of the lawful rights of the People's Republic of China in the United Nations," the Assembly would decide to include the item in the provisional agenda of its 1972 session. It would also request the Secretary-General, in consultation with the Assembly President and the Security Council President, to make inquiries of the parties concerned, either directly or through an *ad hoc* mission, with a view to seeking a solution to the problem of the representation of China in the United Nations and to submit a report on the subject to the General Assembly in 1972.

By the Saudi Arabian amendments to the 23-power draft resolution, the Assembly would among other things decide to restore all the rights to which the People's Republic of China was entitled at the United Nations and to recognize the representatives of its Government as the sole legitimate representatives of the whole territory over which the People's Republic of China exercised full authority, and to notify the representatives of the Republic of China that they represented only the people of the country over which their Government ruled both *de jure* and *de facto* and that, as such, the Government might retain its seat at the United Nations, taking into account that no people should be denied the right of self-determination. This text was proposed to replace the provision in the 23-power proposal whereby the Assembly would decide to restore to the People's Republic of China all its rights, to recognize the representatives of its Government as the only legitimate representatives of China to the United Nations and to expel forthwith the representatives of Chiang Kai-shek from the place which they unlawfully occupied at the United Nations and in all the organizations related to it.

By another Saudi Arabian amendment the Assembly would recommend that the People's Republic of China should also occupy its seat in all the organizations related to the United Nations.

These amendments were not pressed to a vote following rejection by roll-call votes of two Saudi Arabian preambular amendments. By these the Assembly would: (i) observe that the restoration of the lawful rights of the People's Republic of China was essential for the observance of the purposes and principles of the United Nations Charter and the role the Charter should play in harmonizing the international policies of Member States, rather than essential both for the protection of the Charter and for the cause which the United Nations must serve under the Charter; and (ii) recognize that the People's Republic of China should "assume its seat as" rather than "is" one of the five permanent members of the Security Council.

Introducing the 23-power draft resolution, the representative of Albania said that the United States, with its persistent anti-Chinese policy, had managed—through various procedural devices and by misleading a number of States—to impose its position upon the Assembly and to prevent the will of the majority of its Members from being heeded. Further to delay the restoration of the lawful rights of the People's Republic of China in the Organization, the United States was now embarking upon a new manoeuvre in proposing the so-called question of "The representation of China in the United Nations." The thesis of a dual representation for China was absurd, the Albanian representative added. The question before the Assembly was the representation of a State which was already a Member of the United Nations. To settle such a question only a simple majority vote of the Assembly was necessary. The restoration of the lawful rights of the People's Republic of China in the United Nations unconditionally required, as an absolutely indispensable step, the immediate expulsion of the representatives of the Chiang Kai-shek clique, Albania declared.

The representative of Algeria, speaking to the 23-power text, declared that during the period when Peking was unjustly kept out of the United Nations, the Taipeh régime had continued illegally to hold a mandate in the United Nations institutions in the name of the Chinese people as a whole. During the same period, no one had ever claimed that there were two Chinese States. To recognize that the Government of the People's Republic of China was lawfully entitled to that mandate did not therefore imply the eviction of a Member State but the eviction of the representatives of a dissident minority régime. The question of retaining Taiwan's representatives in the

United Nations must be viewed as the admission of a new Member, Algeria continued. Formosa, which had never had the status of Member of the United Nations, could not have a seat except through the regular procedure of admission. Yet the problem of Taiwan's dissidence was a Chinese internal affair. The United Nations could not, without violating one of the fundamental principles of the Charter, embark upon a discussion of a subject which in fact bore on China's territorial integrity and independence.

The representative of the United States, speaking on behalf of the co-sponsors of the 19-power and 22-power draft resolutions, said it had become increasingly clear that the pattern followed in the United Nations in the past was no longer sufficient. The time had arrived to find a way to welcome the People's Republic of China into the United Nations, but with due regard for realism, justice and the purposes and principles of the Organization. It must be a way which would avoid the unacceptable route of expelling a law-abiding and faithful Member of the United Nations. The United States had set out to develop such a proposal and had consulted with nearly the whole membership. It had gone ahead in the belief that this year ought to be the year of decision and that the decision must be realistic and just. It was in this spirit and with the help of many Governments that the United States had shaped an alternative to the 23-power proposal.

In essence, the United States representative added, the 19-power proposal recommended that the People's Republic of China take over China's place as a permanent member of the Security Council and provided representation both for the People's Republic and for the Republic of China in the General Assembly.

The sponsors believed this proposal was a realistic, pragmatic and equitable solution to the problem. Moreover, while achieving these things the 19-power draft resolution was carefully written in order to avoid any prejudice to related matters: Member States were not asked to alter their recognition policies or bilateral relations. The proposal did not take either a two-Chinas position or a one China–one Taiwan position, or in any other way seek to dismember China. On the contrary, it expressly stated in the preamble that a solution should be sought without prejudice to a future settlement. Voting in favour of expulsion would be voting against universality and thus undermining the very foundation of the United Nations.

For that reason, the United States and other Members had proposed a second draft resolution requiring that any proposal having the effect of depriving the Republic of China of representation must obtain a two-thirds majority to be adopted.

The representative of the United States moved that the General Assembly vote first on the text calling for the two-thirds majority requirement.

The spokesman of the Republic of China said that his country had earned its place in the United Nations by virtue of its contribution to peace and freedom during the Second World War. During the war years, the Republic of China lost a major portion of its territory and was cut off in its land and sea communications with other parts of Asia, yet no one questioned the right of that Government to speak and sit on behalf of the Chinese people at international conferences. The present Government represented in the United Nations was the very same that participated in the founding of the United Nations. There had been no break in the continuity of its leadership, institutions or policy. Its legal status had not in any way changed, even though the communists had been in occupation of the Chinese mainland since 1949. The Chinese communist régime, which had never had the moral consent of the Chinese people, could in no way be regarded as the representative of the great Chinese nation.

The whole purpose of the 23-power draft resolution, he added, was to help Peiping obtain the expulsion of the Republic of China from the United Nations. This was a matter of the utmost seriousness with far-reaching implications for all Members of the Organization. One of the express conditions laid in the Charter for the expulsion of a Member State was the persistent violation of its provisions. Unlike the Government of the Republic of China, which had seriously assumed its obligations under the Charter, the Chinese communist régime had negated all the basic Charter principles. It was difficult to understand how a régime bent on reshaping the world by force of arms could contribute to the cause of international peace. Peiping's interest in the United Nations stemmed primarily from a desire to broaden the scope of its aggressive activity and to transform the Organization into an instrument of its own policy. It could wreck the United Nations, as it had torn asunder the much-vaunted monolithic unity of international communism. It would be a tragic and irreparable mistake if the Assembly bowed to the demands of those who would replace the membership of the Republic of China by the communist régime in Peiping.

A number of Members, among them Australia, Dahomey, Japan, Malawi, New Zealand and Nicaragua, felt that the question before the Assembly was how the representation of the People's Republic of China could be achieved without doing violence to the Charter and without ignoring the realities of the prevailing international situation.

They maintained that the 23-power proposal

contained an unreasonable, peremptory demand, punitive in substance and intent. The expulsion or exclusion against its will of a peace-loving Member that effectively controlled a territory with a viable system of its own would be contrary to the very spirit of harmony and friendship between nations, they said. It would both contravene the Charter and set a dangerous precedent. Since the word "expel" was clearly written into the 23-power draft resolution, the application of Article 18 of the Charter[2] listing expulsion as an important question was in order. The 19-power draft resolution, on the other hand, merely accepted, without prejudice to the eventual settlement of the claims, the fact that for the time being there were two Chinese Governments, but refrained from embracing the idea of two Chinas. By adopting it, they argued, the United Nations would open the path to reconciliation and peaceful dialogue, thus promoting peace and stability in Asia.

Members who spoke in opposition to the draft resolution calling for a two-thirds majority and that calling for seating of both the People's Republic of China and the Republic of China included Ceylon, Chile, Cuba, France, Hungary, Mali, Norway, Sierra Leone, Uganda, the USSR and the United Kingdom.

They made the point, among other things, that the precise issue of the restoration of the lawful rights of the People's Republic of China in the United Nations did not imply a question of admission or expulsion. Rather, the issue was one of credentials. The vacating of the seat of China by the Chiang Kai-shek régime was a legal, logical consequence of the restoration of the lawful rights of the People's Republic of China. Moreover, Taiwan had never been a Member State of the United Nations. There was only one Chinese State that was entitled to a seat at the United Nations. To have an additional seat would require as a prior condition the creation of a second Chinese State which would have to apply for membership under the Charter.

Mali commented that a vote for the two resolutions would create a precedent which far from finding a solution to the problem of divided countries could foster parcellization of the States of the third world, many of which were looking for final boundaries conforming to their national identity. Cuba said that foreign intervention which had sought to segregate a province from the territory of China could never be a valid justification to accord to that territory, separated by force, any national character or any sovereignty.

Supporters of the 23-power draft resolution maintained that this proposal was the only one which took into account the rights and the reality of the People's Republic of China, for the People's Republic of China was clearly the only Chinese

Government empowered to exercise responsibility in the Assembly and the Security Council. The proposal for dual representation was contrary to the Charter, would only create obstacles and delay an event whose inevitability had been made apparent by the diplomatic initiatives under way. To fail to support that draft would be to disavow the vast efforts at rapprochement which had grown since last year and to assail the unity and the rights of China. It would be to refuse to see the world as it was, with China.

Other Members, including Argentina, Laos, Malta and Spain, among others, felt that since both the People's Republic of China and the Republic of China agreed that there was only one China, the question of the retention in or removal from the Organization of the representatives of the Republic of China should be left to the Chinese people themselves. They indicated that the guiding principles in their votes on the various proposals would be the principles of universality and of non-intervention in internal affairs.

On 25 October, the General Assembly proceeded to vote on the proposals before it, after rejecting by 56 votes to 53, with 19 abstentions, a motion by Saudi Arabia for postponement of the voting.

The General Assembly adopted by a roll-call vote of 61 to 53, with 15 abstentions, a motion by the United States that priority be given in the voting to the 22-power draft resolution calling for a two-thirds majority on any proposal depriving the Republic of China of representation in the United Nations.[3]

The Assembly then rejected the 22-power draft resolution by a roll-call vote of 59 against to 55 in favour, with 15 abstentions.

Following this vote, Tunisia withdrew the three draft resolutions it had submitted, stating it would vote for the 23-power text. The representative of Tunisia said that the texts had been submitted in anticipation of the adoption of a decision affirming

[2]*Ibid.*
[3]The roll-call vote was as follows:
In favour: Argentina, Australia, Bahrain, Barbados, Belgium, Bolivia, Brazil, Central African Republic, Chad, China, Colombia, Costa Rica, Dahomey, Dominican Republic, El Savador, Fiji, Gabon, Gambia, Ghana, Greece, Guatemala, Haiti, Honduras, Indonesia, Ireland, Israel, Italy, Ivory Coast, Jamaica, Japan, Jordan, Khmer Republic, Lebanon, Lesotho, Liberia, Luxembourg, Madagascar, Malawi, Mauritius, Mexico, Morocco, Netherlands, New Zealand, Nicaragua, Niger, Panama, Paraguay, Philippines, Portugal, Rwanda, Saudi Arabia, South Africa, Spain, Swaziland, Thailand, Tunisia, United States, Upper Volta, Uruguay, Venezuela, Zaire.
Against: Afghanistan, Albania, Algeria, Bhutan, Bulgaria, Burma, Burundi, Byelorussian SSR, Cameroon, Canada, Ceylon, Chile, Congo, Cuba, Czechoslovakia, Denmark, Egypt, Equatorial Guinea, Ethiopia, Finland, France, Guinea, Guyana, Hungary, Iceland, India, Iraq, Kuwait, Libyan Arab Republic, Mali, Mauritania, Mongolia, Nepal, Nigeria, Norway, Pakistan, People's Democratic Republic of Yemen, Peru, Poland, Romania, Sierra Leone, Somalia, Sudan, Sweden, Syrian Arab Republic, Uganda, Ukrainian SSR, USSR, United Kingdom, United Republic of Tanzania, Yemen, Yugoslavia, Zambia.
Abstaining: Austria, Botswana, Cyprus, Ecuador, Iran, Kenya, Laos, Malaysia, Malta, Qatar, Senegal, Singapore, Togo, Trinidad and Tobago, Turkey.

the two-thirds majority. Since the Assembly did not adopt such a decision, Tunisia would withdraw its draft resolutions which had been intended to provide for an Assembly invitation to the People's Republic of China.

After the first two Saudi Arabian amendments were rejected by roll-call vote, the representative of Saudi Arabia stated that the remainder need not be put to a vote. Neither did he wish to press to a vote the draft resolution he had submitted.

The Assembly then voted on a United States motion for a separate vote on the provision in the 23-power proposal whereby the Assembly would expel forthwith the representatives of Chiang Kai-shek from the place which they unlawfully occupied at the United Nations and in all the organizations related to it. The United States motion was defeated by a recorded vote of 61 against to 51 in favour, with 16 abstentions.

Thereupon, the representative of China, speaking on a point of order, made a declaration to the following effect: The rejection of the 22-power draft resolution calling for a two-thirds majority was a flagrant violation of the United Nations Charter which governed the expulsion of Member States. The delegation of the Republic of China had decided not to take part in any further proceedings of the General Assembly.

The Assembly then adopted the 23-power text, by a roll-call vote of 76 to 35, with 17 abstentions, as resolution 2758(XXVI). It did not proceed to a vote on the 19-power draft text.

By this action, the General Assembly, recalling the principles of the Charter and considering that the restoration of the lawful rights of the People's Republic of China was essential both for the protection of the Charter and for the cause that the United Nations must serve under the Charter, recognized that the representatives of the Government of the People's Republic of China were the only lawful representatives of China to the United Nations and that the People's Republic of China was one of the five permanent members of the Security Council. It accordingly decided to restore all its rights to the People's Republic of China and to recognize the representatives of its Government as the only legitimate representatives of China to the United Nations, and to expel forthwith the representatives of Chiang Kai-shek from the place which they unlawfully occupied at the United Nations and in all the organizations related to it. (For text of resolution, see DOCUMENTARY REFERENCES below.)

On 26 October 1971, the General Assembly decided that in view of its adoption of resolution 2758(XXVI), it would not consider the agenda item entitled "The representation of China in the United Nations."

Discussion in Security Council concerning representation of China

At a meeting of the Security Council held on 9 February 1971, the representative of Somalia, speaking on a point of order, placed on record his Government's strong objections "to acceptance of the credentials of the representative who, since December 1962, has been occupying the seat reserved for the true representative of the Government of the State of China." These credentials, he continued, had been issued by the régime of Chiang Kai-shek which had been ousted from authority by the Chinese people 21 years previously. The refusal to allow the representatives of the People's Republic of China—the effective Government—to occupy the seat of the State of China was, in his delegation's view, tantamount to nullifying China's membership in the United Nations. It was obvious that the State of China could not exercise its membership unless it was properly represented. China's exclusion, he added, had been sparked by the ideological factor in the cold-war struggle supported by cold-war power politics. Demands for a more realistic approach to the question had, however, been continually increasing. Somalia expressed the hope that the Security Council would respond to that call for reason and realism and for a just solution to the problem of the representation of the great State of China.

In support, France, Poland, the Syrian Arab Republic and the USSR also made the point that only the representatives of the People's Republic of China were entitled to the Chinese seat in the United Nations.

Italy shared the reservations expressed by previous speakers on the representation of China in the United Nations.

The representative of China said that the question raised by Somalia was not a question of credentials but that of the representation of the Republic of China on the Security Council. Such a question was a political one of far-reaching consequences. The Republic of China was specifically mentioned in Article 23 of the United Nations Charter[4] as one of the five permanent members of the Security Council. Its representation on the Council was not a matter that concerned members of the Council alone; it was a matter in which all Member States of the United Nations had an interest. It would therefore be in the interest of the proper functioning of the United Nations as a whole and in the interest of the sanctity and integrity of the Charter that the Security Council not engage in any substantive debate on the question of China's representation.

[4]For text of Article 23 of the Charter, see APPENDIX II.

The United States representative said that the credentials of the representative of China, as well as those of all other representatives at the Council's table, had fully satisfied the provisions of the pertinent rule of procedure of the Security Council. With regard to the broad question of Chinese representation in the United Nations, he added, the Security Council was manifestly not the organ in which such a question, which concerned every single Member of the United Nations, could be properly dealt with. He recalled that the General Assembly, by a resolution it adopted on 14 December 1950,[5] had noted that the Assembly was the organ in which consideration could best be given to the views of all Member States in matters affecting the functioning of the Organization as a whole, and had recommended that when any such question arose it should be considered by the General Assembly.

After the General Assembly's decision of 25 October 1971, at a Security Council meeting held on 23 November 1971 the President of the Council and the other representatives made statements welcoming the representatives of the People's Republic of China, who were attending a meeting of the Security Council for the first time. The representative of China made a statement in reply.

Developments in specialized agencies consequent upon General Assembly decision

On 26 October 1971, the Secretary-General transmitted to the executive heads of all the organizations of the United Nations system the text of the General Assembly's resolution (2758(XXVI)) of 25 October 1971 by which it had decided to restore to the People's Republic of China all its rights and to recognize its representatives as the only legitimate representatives of China to the United Nations, and to expel forthwith the representatives of Chiang Kai-shek from the place which they unlawfully occupied at the United Nations and in all the organizations related to it.

The Secretary-General requested the executive heads to keep him informed of any relevant action taken within their respective organizations.

The Secretary-General also drew the attention of the organizations in the United Nations system to the General Assembly's resolution (396(V)) of 14 December 1950 on recognition by the United Nations of the representation of a Member State, by which the Assembly had recommended that it should consider issues involving representation and that the attitude adopted by the General Assembly or its Interim Committee concerning any such question should be taken into account in other organs of the United Nations and in the specialized agencies.[6]

International Labour Organisation

The question of "Representation of China in the International Labour Organisation: communication and request from the Secretary-General of the United Nations" was added to the agenda of the November 1971 session of the Governing Body of the International Labour Office in accordance with the terms of the Agreement between the United Nations and the International Labour Organisation (ILO), which provides that ILO should arrange for the submission, as soon as possible, to the Governing Body, the Conference or such other organs of ILO as might be appropriate of all formal recommendations which the General Assembly might make to it.

On 16 November 1971, the Governing Body, by 35 votes to 10, with 2 abstentions, rejected the operative paragraph of a draft resolution moved by the United States Government requesting the Director-General to refer the General Assembly resolution (2758(XXVI)) of 25 October 1971 to the next session of the General Conference of ILO. By 35 votes to 10, with 3 abstentions, the Governing Body decided, upon a proposal by the Workers' Group, to take a decision immediately. The Governing Body then adopted, by 36 votes to 3, with 8 abstentions, a decision as proposed by the Workers' Group to recognize the Government of the People's Republic of China as the representative Government of China.

Food and Agriculture Organization

At its November 1971 session, the Council of the Food and Agriculture Organization (FAO) was informed of the United Nations General Assembly's resolution of 25 October 1971 concerning the representation of China.

The FAO Director-General indicated, in this context, that in view of the fact that the Government of the Republic of China had withdrawn from the agency in 1951, the question presented itself in FAO in a different way from that in other agencies in which China was currently a member. Recalling similar approaches to other Governments recommended by the Council in the past, the Director-General sought the Council's guidance as to the question whether an approach should be made to ascertain whether the Government of the People's Republic of China would wish to seek membership in FAO.

The Council, on 2 November 1971, decided to authorize the Director-General to invite the People's Republic of China to seek formal membership in the organization and, if it so requested, to attend the sixteenth (November 1971) session of

[5]See Y.U.N., 1950, p. 435, text of resolution 396(V).
[6]*Ibid.*

the governing Conference of the organization.

On the same date, the Director-General sent a cable to the Prime Minister of the Government of the People's Republic of China conveying an invitation for the People's Republic of China to seek formal membership in the organization, and also, if it so requested, to attend the sixteenth session of the Conference.

On 23 November 1971, the Director-General informed the Conference that he had received a reply from the Acting Foreign Minister of the People's Republic of China. The Director-General noted that while no reference was made in this reply to formal membership in FAO, there was reason to believe that China would be interested in resuming its place in the organization.

The Director-General added that he had been advised that it would be legally possible for the People's Republic of China to resume, without being formally re-admitted, the seat of China if it wished, since the notice of withdrawal given in 1951 by the Government of the "Republic of China" emanated from a Government whose right to represent the State of China had already at that time been formally contested. This notice of withdrawal would not be held against the Government of the People's Republic of China, which had no part in it and which had now been recognized as being the legitimate representative of China. This Government had indeed not been in a position to exercise, since the time of its establishment in 1949, its membership rights in FAO and had been prevented from making its contribution to the achievement of the aims of the organization. Even if the People's Republic of China had wished in the past to take its place in FAO, it might be assumed that it would not have been recognized as the legitimate representative of China in view of the position taken by the General Assembly of the United Nations.

The Director-General added that under the present circumstances the Government of the People's Republic of China should not, in his personal view, be deprived of the possibility of availing itself of the rights deriving from original membership in the organization. As a consequence, it would be permissible for the People's Republic of China to resume its place in FAO without any special formality.

On 25 November 1971, by 68 votes to 0, with 3 abstentions, the Conference adopted a resolution whereby it authorized the Director-General, when the People's Republic of China manifested the wish to resume its place in the organization, to take all appropriate measures to bring into effect the resumption by China of its place in the organization. It also authorized the Director-General to take all necessary measures concerning financial questions, taking into account any action that might be taken by the United Nations in this respect and after consultation with the competent organs of FAO, and requested the Director-General to transmit the text of the resolution to the Government of the People's Republic of China.

United Nations Educational, Scientific and Cultural Organization

On receipt of the Secretary-General's communication, the Director-General of the United Nations Educational, Scientific and Cultural Organization (UNESCO) drew the attention of that agency's Executive Board to the United Nations General Assembly's decision of 25 October 1971 concerning the representation of China. The Executive Board, which was then in session, decided by 30 votes to 0, with 1 abstention, to add a new item to its agenda entitled "Participation of China in the execution of the programme."

Following consideration of various draft resolutions, the Executive Board—on 29 October 1971—decided, by 25 votes to 2, with 5 abstentions, that from that day onwards the Government of the People's Republic of China was the only legitimate representative of China in UNESCO. The Director-General was invited to act accordingly.

World Health Organization

On 11 November 1971, the Director-General of the World Health Organization (WHO) sent to all WHO members the communication from the Secretary-General of the United Nations concerning the General Assembly's decision of 25 October 1971 on the representation of China. He also informed them that as a consequence of the decision taken by the General Assembly, the question of the representation of China in WHO would be proposed for inclusion in the provisional agenda of the 1972 World Health Assembly, as well as included in the agenda of the January 1972 session of the Executive Board.

International Bank for Reconstruction and Development, International Finance Corporation and International Development Association

On 26 October 1971, the President of the International Bank for Reconstruction and Development acknowledged receipt of the Secretary-General's communication concerning the United Nations General Assembly's decision of 25 October 1971 on the representation of China and informed him that the communication had been brought to the attention of the Executive Directors of the International Bank.

International Monetary Fund

On 26 October 1971, the Managing Director of the International Monetary Fund acknowledged receipt of the Secretary-General's communication concerning the General Assembly's decision of 25 October 1971 on the representation of China and informed him that the communication had been brought to the attention of the Executive Directors of the Fund.

International Civil Aviation Organization

The President of the Council of the International Civil Aviation Organization (ICAO) and the Secretary-General of ICAO brought to the attention of the Council the texts of the General Assembly's decision of 25 October 1971 on the representation of China and its decision of 14 December 1950,[7] together with relevant constitutional and historical background information.

On 19 November 1971, the ICAO Council decided, for the matters within its competence, to recognize the representatives of the Government of the People's Republic of China to the International Civil Aviation Organization and it requested the Secretary-General of ICAO immediately to communicate these decisions to all contracting States.

International Telecommunication Union

On 29 October 1971, the Secretary-General of the International Telecomunication Union (ITU) formally transmitted the communication from the Secretary-General of the United Nations concerning the General Assembly's decision of 25 October 1971 on the representation of China to the Chairman of the ITU Administrative Council. Copies of that communication were sent to all the other members of the Council.

World Meteorological Organization

On 26 November 1971, the Secretary-General of the World Meteorological Organization (WMO) drew the attention of all its member States to the United Nations General Assembly's decision of 25 October 1971 on the representation of China and its decision of 14 December 1950.[8] The Secretary-General also informed WMO members that, in consultation with the President and members of the Executive Committee of WMO, it had been decided that the matter should be referred to those WMO members which were States and that a vote by correspondence should be conducted in order to decide upon the application of the United Nations decision within WMO. It was requested that the voting slip be returned not later than 24 February 1972, that being the end of the 90-day period prescribed for such votes.

International Atomic Energy Agency

On 9 December 1971, the Board of Governors of the International Atomic Energy Agency (IAEA) adopted a resolution entitled "Representation of China in the Agency" by which it recognized that the Government of the People's Republic of China was the the only Government which had the right to represent China in IAEA.

The resolution was adopted by 13 votes to 6, with 5 abstentions.

General Agreement on Tariffs and Trade

On 16 November 1971, at the opening of the twenty-seventh session of the Contracting Parties to the General Agreement on Tariffs and Trade (GATT), the Chairman drew attention to the General Assembly's decision of 25 October 1971 on the representation of China and recalled that in 1965, in reaching their decision to accede to the request from the "Republic of China" that it be represented by observers at sessions of the Contracting Parties, the Contracting Parties had agreed to follow decisions of the United Nations on essentially political matters.

The Chairman added that it would be logical for the Contracting Parties to rely in this case likewise on the decision taken by the United Nations and to decide accordingly that the Republic of China should no longer have observer status at sessions of the Contracting Parties. After a short debate, the Chairman noted that no request for a vote had been made and declared that there was a consensus for adoption of the views he expressed.

[7] *Ibid.*
[8] *Ibid.*

DOCUMENTARY REFERENCES

Consideration by General Assembly

General Assembly—26th session
General Committee, meeting 191.
Plenary meetings 1937, 1966-1977, 1982, 1983.

A/8392. Letter of 15 July 1971 from Albania, Algeria, Congo, Cuba, Guinea, Iraq, Mali, Mauritania, People's Democratic Republic of Yemen, Romania, Somalia, Sudan, Syrian Arab Republic, United Republic of Tanzania, Yemen, Yugoslavia and Zambia (request for inclusion in agenda of item entitled: "Restoration of the lawful rights of the People's Republic of China in the United Nations").

A/8401. Report of Secretary-General on work of the Organization, 16 June 1970–15 June 1971, Part One, Chapter IV I.
A/8401/Add.1. Introduction to report of Secretary-General, September 1971, Part One, Chapter VIII.
A/8442. Letter of 17 August 1971 from United States (request for inclusion in agenda of item entitled: "The representation of China in the United Nations").
A/8470. Letter of 15 October 1971 from Albania, Algeria, Burma, Ceylon, Congo, Cuba, Equatorial Guinea, Guinea, Iraq, Mali, Mauritania, Nepal, Pakistan, People's Democratic Republic of Yemen, Romania, Somalia, Sudan, Syrian Arab Republic, United Republic of Tanzania, Yemen, Yugoslavia and Zambia (request for distribution as official document of statement dated

20 August 1971 of Ministry for Foreign Affairs of People's Republic of China).

APPROVAL OF ITEMS FOR AGENDA

A/8500. Organization of 26th regular session of General Assembly, adoption of agenda and allocation of items. First report of General Committee. [*Item 93:* Restoration of the lawful rights of the People's Republic of China in the United Nations (provisional agenda item 101), approved without vote for inclusion in agenda by Assembly on 24 September 1971, meeting 1937; *item 96:* The representation of China in the United Nations (provisional agenda item 105), approved for inclusion in agenda by Assembly on 24 September 1971, meeting 1937, by roll-call vote of 65 to 47, with 15 abstentions, as follows:

In favour: Argentina, Australia, Bahrain, Barbados, Belgium, Bolivia, Botswana, Brazil, Central African Republic, China, Colombia, Costa Rica, Cyprus, Dahomey, Dominican Republic, Ecuador, El Salvador, Fiji, Gabon, Gambia, Greece, Guatemala, Haiti, Honduras, Indonesia, Ireland, Israel, Italy, Ivory Coast, Jamaica, Japan, Jordan, Kenya, Khmer Republic, Lebanon, Lesotho, Liberia, Luxembourg, Madagascar, Malawi, Malta, Mexico, Netherlands, New Zealand, Nicaragua, Niger, Panama, Paraguay, Philippines, Portugal, Qatar, Rwanda, Saudi Arabia, South Africa, Spain, Swaziland, Thailand, Tunisia, Turkey, Uganda, United States, Upper Volta, Uruguay, Venezuela, Zaire.

Against: Afghanistan, Albania, Algeria, Bhutan, Bulgaria, Burma, Byelorussian SSR, Cameroon, Ceylon, Chile, Congo, Cuba, Czechoslovakia, Denmark, Egypt, Equatorial Guinea, Ethiopia, Finland, Guinea, Guyana, Hungary, Iceland, India, Iraq, Libyan Arab Republic, Mali, Mauritania, Mongolia, Nepal, Nigeria, Norway, Pakistan, People's Democratic Republic of Yemen, Peru, Poland, Romania, Sierra Leone, Somalia, Sudan, Sweden, Syrian Arab Republic, Ukrainian SSR, USSR, United Republic of Tanzania, Yemen, Yugoslavia, Zambia.

Abstaining: Austria, Burundi, Canada, France, Ghana, Iran, Kuwait, Laos, Malaysia, Mauritius, Morocco, Senegal, Singapore, Trinidad and Tobago, United Kingdom.]

A/8501 and Add.1-5. Agenda of 26th regular session of General Assembly, adopted by Assembly on 24 September 1971, meeting 1939 (items 93 and 96).

DECISIONS OF GENERAL ASSEMBLY

A/L.630 and Corr.1 and Add.1,2. Albania, Algeria, Burma, Ceylon, Congo, Cuba, Equatorial Guinea, Guinea, Iraq, Mali, Mauritania, Nepal, Pakistan, People's Democratic Republic of Yemen, Romania, Sierra Leone, Somalia, Sudan, Syrian Arab Republic, United Republic of Tanzania, Yemen, Yugoslavia, Zambia: draft resolution.

A/L.637. Saudi Arabia: amendments to 23-power draft resolution, A/L.630.

RESOLUTION 2758(XXVI), as proposed by 23 powers, A/L.630, adopted by Assembly on 25 October 1971, meeting 1976, by roll-call vote of 76 to 35, with 17 abstentions, as follows:

In favour: Afghanistan, Albania, Algeria, Austria, Belgium, Bhutan, Botswana, Bulgaria, Burma, Burundi, Byelorussian SSR, Cameroon, Canada, Ceylon, Chile, Congo, Cuba, Czechoslovakia, Denmark, Ecuador, Egypt, Equatorial Guinea, Ethiopia, Finland, France, Ghana, Guinea, Guyana, Hungary, Iceland, India, Iran, Iraq, Ireland, Israel, Italy, Kenya, Kuwait, Laos, Libyan Arab Republic, Malaysia, Mali, Mauritania, Mexico, Mongolia, Morocco, Nepal, Netherlands, Nigeria, Norway, Pakistan, People's Democratic Republic of Yemen, Peru, Poland, Portugal, Romania, Rwanda, Senegal, Sierra Leone, Singapore, Somalia, Sudan, Sweden, Syrian Arab Republic, Togo, Trinidad and Tobago, Tunisia, Turkey, Uganda, Ukrainian SSR, USSR, United Kingdom, United Republic of Tanzania, Yemen, Yugoslavia, Zambia.

Against: Australia, Bolivia, Brazil, Central African Republic, Chad, Costa Rica, Dahomey, Dominican Republic, El Salvador, Gabon, Gambia, Guatemala, Haiti, Honduras, Ivory Coast, Japan, Khmer Republic, Lesotho, Liberia, Madagascar, Malawi, Malta, New Zealand, Nicaragua, Niger, Paraguay, Philippines, Saudi Arabia, South Africa, Swaziland, United States, Upper Volta, Uruguay, Venezuela, Zaire.

Abstaining: Argentina, Bahrain, Barbados, Colombia, Cyprus, Fiji, Greece, Indonesia, Jamaica, Jordan, Lebanon, Luxembourg, Mauritius, Panama, Qatar, Spain, Thailand.

The General Assembly,

Recalling the principles of the Charter of the United Nations,

Considering that the restoration of the lawful rights of the People's Republic of China is essential both for the protection of the Charter of the United Nations and for the cause that the United Nations must serve under the Charter,

Recognizing that the representatives of the Government of the People's Republic of China are the only lawful representatives of China to the United Nations and that the People's Republic of China is one of the five permanent members of the Security Council,

Decides to restore all its rights to the People's Republic of China and to recognize the representatives of its Government as the only legitimate representatives of China to the United Nations, and to expel forthwith the representatives of Chiang Kai-shek from the place which they unlawfully occupy at the United Nations and in all the organizations related to it.

A/L.632 and Add.1,2. Australia, Bolivia, Colombia, Costa Rica, Dominican Republic, El Salvador, Fiji, Gambia, Guatemala, Haiti, Honduras, Japan, Lesotho, Liberia, Mauritius, New Zealand, Nicaragua, Philippines, Swaziland, Thailand, United States, Uruguay: draft resolution, rejected by Assembly on 25 October 1971, meeting 1976, by roll-call vote of 55 in favour to 59 against, with 15 abstentions, as follows:

In favour: Argentina, Australia, Bahrain, Barbados, Bolivia, Brazil, Central African Republic, Chad, China, Colombia, Costa Rica, Dahomey, Dominican Republic, El Salvador, Fiji, Gabon, Gambia, Ghana, Greece, Guatemala, Haiti, Honduras, Indonesia, Israel, Ivory Coast, Jamaica, Japan, Jordan, Khmer Republic, Lebanon, Lesotho, Liberia, Luxembourg, Madagascar, Malawi, Mauritius, Mexico, New Zealand, Nicaragua, Niger, Panama, Paraguay, Philippines, Portugal, Rwanda, Saudi Arabia, South Africa, Spain, Swaziland, Thailand, United States, Upper Volta, Uruguay, Venezuela, Zaire.

Against: Afghanistan, Albania, Algeria, Bhutan, Bulgaria, Burma, Burundi, Byelorussian SSR, Cameroon, Canada, Ceylon, Chile, Congo, Cuba, Czechoslovakia, Denmark, Ecuador, Egypt, Equatorial Guinea, Ethiopia, Finland, France, Guinea, Guyana, Hungary, Iceland, India, Iraq, Ireland, Kenya, Kuwait, Libyan Arab Republic, Malaysia, Mali, Mauritania, Mongolia, Nepal, Nigeria, Norway, Pakistan, People's Democratic Republic of Yemen, Peru, Poland, Romania, Sierra Leone, Singapore, Somalia, Sudan, Sweden, Syrian Arab Republic, Trinidad and Tobago, Uganda, Ukrainian SSR, USSR, United Kingdom, United Republic of Tanzania, Yemen, Yugoslavia, Zambia.

Abstaining: Austria, Belgium, Botswana, Cyprus, Iran, Italy, Laos, Malta, Morocco, Netherlands, Qatar, Senegal, Togo, Tunisia, Turkey.

A/L.633 and Add.1,2. Australia, Bolivia, Chad, Costa Rica, Dominican Republic, Fiji, Gambia, Haiti, Honduras, Japan, Lesotho, Liberia, Mauritius, New Zealand, Philippines, Swaziland, Thailand, United States, Uruguay: draft resolution.

A/L.634 and Add.1. Australia, Colombia, Costa Rica, Dominican Republic, El Salvador, Fiji, Gambia, Guatemala, Haiti, Honduras, Japan, Lesotho, Liberia, Mauritius, New Zealand, Nicaragua, Philippines, Swaziland, Thailand, United States, Uruguay: draft resolution [text identical to draft resolution A/L.632].

A/L.635 and Add.1. Australia, Chad, Costa Rica, Dominican Republic, Fiji, Gambia, Haiti, Honduras, Japan, Lesotho, Liberia, Mauritius, New Zealand, Philippines, Swaziland, Thailand, United States, Uruguay: draft resolution [text identical to draft resolution A/L.633].
A/L.638. Saudi Arabia: draft resolution.
A/L.639. Tunisia: draft resolution.
A/L.640. Tunisia: draft resolution.
A/L.641. Tunisia: draft resolution.
A/8429. Resolutions adopted by General Assembly during its 26th session, 21 September–22 December 1971. Other decisions, p. 21.

Discussion in other United Nations organs in 1971

Security Council, meetings 1565, 1599.

S/10378. Letter of 26 October 1971 from Secretary-General to President of Security Council (transmitting General Assembly resolution 2758(XXVI)).
S/10382. Report of 2 November 1971 by Secretary-General to President of Security Council concerning credentials of representative of People's Republic of China on Security Council.

Trusteeship Council, 38th session, meeting 1385.

The situation in the India-Pakistan subcontinent

Humanitarian assistance activities

Immediately after the outbreak of civil strife in East Pakistan in March 1971, the Secretary-General expressed his concern over the situation to the President of Pakistan and thereafter remained in continuous touch with the Governments of Pakistan and India, both through their Permanent Representatives to the United Nations and through other contacts. It soon became clear that international assistance on an unprecedented scale was urgently needed, both for the relief of the distressed people in East Pakistan and for aid to the refugees who had gone to India.

Humanitarian effort for relief of refugees from East Pakistan

The United Nations humanitarian effort for the relief of East Pakistan refugees in India was initiated by the Secretary-General following a request for assistance addressed to him on 23 April 1971 by the Government of India. The Secretary-General agreed to the request and, after consultation with specialized agencies through the inter-agency Administrative Committee on Co-ordination, designated the United Nations High Commissioner for Refugees as the focal point for the co-ordination of assistance from all the organizations and programmes of the United Nations system.

A three-man team, designated by the High Commissioner, visited India from 7 to 19 May 1971 to assess the nature and magnitude of the needs of the refugees and to discuss with officials of the Government of India modalities of assistance. During this period, initial assistance was provided in India by the World Food Programme (WFP) and the United Nations Children's Fund (UNICEF) from their resources available on the spot.

On 19 May 1971, the Secretary-General launched an appeal to Governments, inter-governmental and non-governmental organizations and private sources to help meet the urgent needs for humanitarian assistance to relieve the plight of the refugees. The Indian Government had indicated that massive external assistance of the order of $175 million for six months would be required on an emergency basis to provide clothing, shelter, medical supplies and other essential items. In his appeal, the Secretary-General stated that the solution of the problem lay in the voluntary repatriation of the displaced persons at the earliest possible time.

Revised estimates based on 8 million refugees in camps were compiled in October 1971, at which time India foresaw a requirement of $558 million. A new appeal to Governments for funds was thus made by the High Commissioner in October.

The number of East Pakistan refugees in India was questioned by the Government of Pakistan, which, in mid-September, cited figures in the vicinity of 2 million as having left East Pakistan since the disturbances of March 1971.

At a meeting of the Economic and Social Council held on 16 July 1971, the High Commissioner reported that the co-ordinating mechanism which had been set up at the focal point was designed: (a) to mobilize and secure international support and contributions; (b) to arrange for the procurement of supplies in a co-ordinated manner and for delivery of the supplies to India; and (c) to maintain close liaison with the Government of India. Those functions were carried out in close association with UNICEF, WFP, the Food and Agriculture Organization (FAO), the World Health Organization (WHO) and the League of Red Cross Societies. The execution of the actual relief operations, however, remained the responsibility of the Indian Government. A representative of the focal point was stationed in Delhi, India; he acted as principal contact with the Government and co-ordinated the activities of the various United Nations agencies and programmes in the field.

The High Commissioner also reported on his activities as focal point at a meeting of the General Assembly's Third (Social, Humanitarian and Cultural) Committee on 18 November 1971. The Assembly's action on the matter is described below.

United Nations East Pakistan Relief Operation (UNEPRO)

By a letter dated 22 April 1971 to the President of Pakistan, the Secretary-General expressed deep concern at the situation in East Pakistan and offered to the Government of Pakistan, on behalf of the United Nations family of organizations, all possible assistance to help it in its task of providing urgently needed relief to the population of East Pakistan. While he scrupulously observed the provisions of Article 2, paragraph 7, of the United Nations Charter,[9] the Secretary-General said he was also deeply conscious of the responsibility of the United Nations, within the framework of international economic and social co-operation, to help promote and ensure human well-being and humanitarian principles.

Replying on 3 May 1971, Pakistan's President Yahya Khan welcomed the Secretary-General's generous offer but added that reports of heavy casualties and destruction were exaggerated and that any international assistance would be administered by Pakistan's relief agencies.

Pakistan's preliminary estimates of its requirements for such assistance were communicated to the Secretary-General on 22 May by the Permanent Representative of Pakistan. These listed food import requirements amounting to 250,000 tons of food grains and 100,000 tons of edible oils, in addition to assistance in the acquisition of 30 coastal craft and 500 land vehicles. It was indicated that the Pakistan Government would be prepared to associate UNICEF and WFP personnel in the planning and organization of relief, and that it would be willing to receive a representative of the Secretary-General to work out the modalities of United Nations humanitarian assistance.

On 28 May, the Secretary-General announced that the Assistant Secretary-General for Inter-Agency Affairs, Ismat T. Kittani, would travel to Pakistan for consultations, as suggested by the Pakistan Government. In discussions with the President of Pakistan, the latter indicated to Mr. Kittani that he shared the Secretary-General's concern that the United Nations must be in a position to assure the international community, and donors in particular, that all relief assistance would reach its intended destination—the people of East Pakistan. Bahgat A. El-Tawil, appointed by the Secretary-General as his representative in East Pakistan, arrived in Dacca on 7 June to co-ordinate assistance from and through United Nations agencies and programmes.

On 16 June, the Secretary-General appealed to Governments, inter-governmental and non-governmental organizations and private sources to contribute in cash and in kind to the United Nations humanitarian effort in East Pakistan.

On 15 July 1971, the Secretary-General repeated his appeal and issued a comprehensive review of the relief needs of East Pakistan. He indicated that $28.2 million in assistance by and through the United Nations system would be required to meet initial needs. These included the charter of minibulkers and river craft, purchase of trucks and other vehicles, cloth for clothing and blankets, tents and medical supplies, and establishment of a $10 million fund for grants to returning refugees and other affected persons. Subsequent surveys by the United Nations East Pakistan relief operation indicated that the people of East Pakistan would face a food gap of up to 200,000 tons a month starting in September 1971 and continuing into the second quarter of 1972.

In view of the increasing scope of United Nations humanitarian activities in the area, the Secretary-General on 24 August appointed Paul-Marc Henry to take charge at Headquarters of the United Nations East Pakistan Relief Operation (UNEPRO).

On 15 October, the Secretary-General reported that, in response to his appeals, 15 Governments had pledged $10.4 million in cash and $73.3 million in kind for the United Nations relief effort in East Pakistan. Those figures included, in addition to the relief activities of the various organizations and programmes of the United Nations system, relief contributions made directly to East Pakistan by certain Governments and placed under the auspices of the United Nations.

An agreed statement of "conditions for the effective discharge of the functions of UNEPRO" was formalized by an exchange of letters between the Secretary-General and the Permanent Representative of Pakistan dated 15 and 16 November 1971. The agreement specified: that UNEPRO personnel and associated personnel would enjoy freedom of access and movement to and in East Pakistan, subject to temporary restrictions for security reasons, as well as the unrestricted right of communication; that the Government of Pakistan would ensure the security and safety of such personnel; and that UNEPRO property and relief supplies would not be diverted to any purposes incompatible with the strictly humanitarian functions of UNEPRO.

Consideration by Economic and Social Council

The various humanitarian efforts of the United Nations described above were undertaken by the

---

[9]Article 2, para. 7, of the Charter states: "Nothing contained in the present Charter shall authorize the United Nations to intervene in matters which are essentially within the domestic jurisdiction of any state or shall require the Members to submit such matters to settlement under the present Charter; but this principle shall not prejudice the application of enforcement measures under Chapter VII."

Secretary-General on an emergency basis, without the backing of resolutions of the deliberative organs of the United Nations. However, the Secretary-General's actions were discussed by the Economic and Social Council at a meeting held on 16 July 1971. The United Nations High Commissioner for Refugees, in his capacity as focal point, gave the Council a detailed account of his activities on behalf of the displaced persons in India. The Assistant Secretary-General for Inter-Agency Affairs reported on the humanitarian operation in East Pakistan. After the discussion, the President of the Council made a statement expressing full support of the Secretary-General's actions in the face of the emergency in the subcontinent.

Question of voluntary repatriation of refugees

From the beginning of the United Nations humanitarian actions in India and Pakistan, it was recognized that the solution of the problem lay in the voluntary repatriation of the East Pakistan refugees, as specified by the Secretary-General in his appeal of 19 May 1971. That view was supported by both India and Pakistan. Accordingly, the United Nations High Commissioner for Refugees entered into contact with the Government of Pakistan soon after the relief operation was started in India. On 21 and 24 May, the President of Pakistan appealed to the refugees to return home, where their safety would be ensured, and he repeated those appeals on several subsequent occasions.

Following a visit by the High Commissioner to Islamabad, Pakistan, in June 1971, it was agreed that he would provide assistance to Pakistan in arranging the return and rehabilitation of the refugees and that a representative of the High Commissioner would be stationed at Dacca with a small team to maintain contact with the local authorities in East Pakistan. Their work was closely co-ordinated with that of UNEPRO through the Secretary-General's representative in Dacca.

In July 1971, the Secretary-General reported that efforts to bring about the repatriation of refugees had so far been unavailing. Since issuance of the appeal by the Pakistan President for the return of the refugees, only an insignificant number had done so. On 19 July, the Secretary-General submitted to the Governments of India and Pakistan a proposal aimed at facilitating the process of voluntary repatriation of refugees by stationing on both sides of the border a limited number of representatives of the United Nations High Commissioner for Refugees. The Government of Pakistan accepted the Secretary-General's suggestion but the Government of India did not, on the grounds that India was not preventing the refugees from returning to East Pakistan and that the exodus from that area was continuing.

Consideration by General Assembly

In the introduction to his annual report on the work of the Organization, for the period 16 June 1970 to 15 June 1971, the Secretary-General informed the General Assembly, at its session which opened on 21 Spetember 1971, of the various aspects of the problems arising from the recent events in East Pakistan, which had resulted in the flight of millions of people to the bordering State of India, imposing an intolerable burden upon the resources of that country. International assistance on an unprecedented scale was urgently needed, both for the relief of the distressed people in East Pakistan and for aid to the East Pakistan refugees in India. Moreover, humanitarian relief needs were increasing, hampered by the lack of substantial progress towards a political solution based on reconciliation and the respect of humanitarian principles. This in turn affected law, order and public administration, especially in Pakistan; serious food shortages were an imminent danger. Political, economic and social factors had produced a series of vicious circles which largely frustrated the efforts of the authorities concerned and of the international community to deal with the vast humanitarian problems involved.

The programmes established by the Secretary-General for humanitarian assistance to the refugees in India and to the people in East Pakistan were considered by the General Assembly in connexion with the agenda item entitled "Report of the United Nations High Commissioner for Refugees."

Most of the Assembly's discussions on the matter took place in the Third (Social, Humanitarian and Cultural) Committee.

On 18 November 1971, the High Commissioner for Refugees reported to the Third Committee on his activities as focal point for aid to the refugees. The High Commissioner said that the situation was growing worse, that suffering was increasing and that the gap between resources and needs was growing, despite the generosity of the international community and the remarkable relief efforts of the Government of India. He therefore appealed for massive additional international assistance.

The High Commissioner emphasized that voluntary repatriation was the only viable solution, supported in principle by both Governments. However, this could not be implemented unless the host country and the country of origin arrived at an agreement, which was not yet the case. The refugees would only return in significant numbers when they were convinced that real peace and security prevailed in their country.

The representative of Pakistan expressed his Government's appreciation of the assistance given, because it was meant for its own nationals and because Pakistan was at the centre of the tragedy.

His Government had made repeated appeals to the refugees to return to their homes, and it had implemented a number of measures to encourage them to do so, including giving assurances that their property would be returned and that they would not be subject to reprisals. The co-operation of the Indian Government was essential in making the refugees' return possible. As for the need to arrive at a political solution to resolve the internal crisis, the objective should be attained before the end of the year, but the nature of the solution was the sole responsibility of the Government of Pakistan.

The representative of India endorsed the description of the situation given by the High Commissioner. Referring to the burdens placed on India in consequence of the events in Pakistan, he noted that the Consortium of the International Bank for Reconstruction and Development, meeting in Paris, France, on 26 October 1971, had estimated that the cost of relief operations for the refugees for the financial year ending March 1972 would amount to $700 million. Emergency relief must lead to voluntary repatriation, which was the only possible lasting solution. India, which was looking after millions of Pakistan refugees on behalf of the international community, could not allow that situation to continue indefinitely. There was no appreciable progress towards political reconciliation, the principal cause being gross violation of basic human rights amounting to genocide, with the object of stifling the democratically expressed wishes of a people. India considered that the problem had to be solved in East Pakistan by the Pakistan Government and that it must not be transformed into a dispute between India and Pakistan.

On 18 November, the Third Committee heard a statement by the Assistant Secretary-General in charge of UNEPRO, who explained that the food gap in East Pakistan for 1971/1972 was estimated at 3 million tons, which would involve import shipments of 200,000 tons monthly between August and December 1971. The United Nations relief operation had chartered minibulkers and other craft and had arranged to provide over 1,000 trucks to overcome transport difficulties caused in part by the recent events which had disrupted the railway network. All transport operating directly or indirectly under United Nations auspices were clearly identified with United Nations markings and inscriptions so as to leave no doubt concerning their purely humanitarian functions.

While it was true that the Pakistan Government had guaranteed freedom of access for UNEPRO to any part of East Pakistan, the exercise of that freedom depended on uncontrollable factors such as the intensification of military pressure in the border areas and the continuing breakdown of communications and transport. The situation in this regard was rapidly reaching a critical stage in which the Secretary-General might no longer be in a position to guarantee that all the relief supplies would reach those for whom they were intended. While UNEPRO was a purely humanitarian operation, its effectiveness depended upon the situation in East Pakistan. As a matter of policy, everything had been done to avoid involvement in the political situation in the area. If, despite these efforts, opposition to UNEPRO were to develop, the situation would make the humanitarian relief operation impossible.

During the debate, several Members voiced their concern at the disastrous situation in the subcontinent concerning the influx of refugees into India and the distress of the population of East Pakistan. Several speakers drew attention to the deteriorating security and political situation, as well as to the serious danger of war between India and Pakistan which would inevitably aggravate the suffering of the people. They expressed appreciation of the efforts of the Secretary-General and of the High Commissioner for Refugees, and indicated that the solution of the problem must eventually be found in the voluntary repatriation of the displaced persons. A number of representatives urged their colleagues to avoid introducing political considerations in the discussion of purely humanitarian problems.

The representative of Pakistan, referring to certain press reports, denied that any pattern of misbehaviour by Pakistan soldiers in East Pakistan had been confirmed. He questioned the theory, which he said had been invented by India, that an influx of refugees constituted aggression against the country that harboured them, and he noted that under international law such countries were required to prevent political activities by refugees that might endanger law and order in their country of origin. Pakistan was prepared to engage in conversations with India and the United Nations concerning repatriation.

The representative of the United States praised the Government of India for its efforts on behalf of the refugees and the Government of Pakistan for its attempt to facilitate the return of the refugees by establishing special camps for their reception. He appealed to both Governments to take all possible measures to facilitate the humanitarian role of the United Nations.

France felt it was essential to arrive at a peaceful solution of the political problem, which was the only way to put an end to the suffering of the population.

The United Kingdom believed that the Third Committee should concern itself solely with the humanitarian aspects of the question of the East

Pakistan refugees. While it was clear that the causes of the problem were political and that a political solution would have to be found, it was not the job of the Third Committee to find that solution. The United Kingdom supported the United Nations humanitarian activities for the refugees and would continue to play its role in that endeavour.

Expressing concern at the situation in the subcontinent, the USSR considered that problems such as those afflicting Pakistan must be solved peacefully, since repression harmed the country's vital interests. The inalienable rights of the people of East Pakistan must be recognized. The USSR hoped that everything would be done to maintain peace in the region.

India stated that humanitarian action could not be a substitute for a political reconciliation between the Government of Pakistan and the people of East Pakistan. The refugees had fled because of political persecution, not because of food shortages. India had never advocated the secession of East Pakistan, and if the territorial integrity of Pakistan was in jeopardy, it was due to the actions of that country's Government.

China said that the question of East Pakistan was an internal affair which could only be settled by the people of Pakistan. The so-called question of refugees had come about as a result of interference in Pakistan's internal affairs by a country which was continuing subversive activities against Pakistan and obstructing the return of the refugees. Similar tactics had been used against China in past years in relation to Tibet.

The Netherlands, New Zealand and Sweden submitted a draft resolution by which the Assembly would appeal to Pakistan and India to act to promote voluntary repatriation of refugees and would request the Secretary-General and the High Commissioner to continue their efforts to co-ordinate international assistance and to ensure that it was used to the maximum advantage to relieve the suffering of the refugees in India and of the people in East Pakistan.

Amendments to this draft resolution were proposed by Nigeria, by Saudi Arabia and by Somalia. By these amendments, the Assembly among other things would urge all Member States to help bring about speedy and voluntary repatriation of the refugees, and endorse the Secretary-General's designation of the High Commissioner for Refugees as focal point to co-ordinate assistance and the Secretary-General's initiative in establishing UNEPRO. The amendments were accepted by the sponsors and the final amended version of the text was unanimously approved by the Third Committee on 22 November 1971.

The representative of Tunisia proposed that the President of the General Assembly should be asked to make a statement voicing the concern of the international community, calling on Governments and organizations to assist the Secretary-General and the High Commissioner in their meritorious action, and stating that the only solution was the safe return of the refugees to their homes. This proposal was subsequently resubmitted as a draft resolution and was unanimously approved by the Third Committee on 22 November 1971.

At the meeting of the Third Committee on 22 November, the representatives of Pakistan and India referred to reports of severe clashes involving their armed forces, but gave differing interpretations as to the origin of the incidents.

The representative of Pakistan also said India was using the problem of the refugees as a political and military weapon in order to disrupt Pakistan's territorial integrity and cause the United Nations to interfere in Pakistan's internal affairs. No Member State could abdicate its right to arrange its own political life and it was not for others to judge whether Pakistan had restored the climate of confidence which would induce the displaced persons to return to their homes.

The representative of India stated that the consequences of the activities of the military régime of Pakistan threatened India's national life and posed a serious threat to its security, which obliged his country to take all necessary defensive measures. The fact that India was not an interested party was borne out by the insistence of the representative of Pakistan that the whole situation was an internal affair of that country. The problem could be solved only by peaceful negotiations between the military leaders of West Pakistan and the elected leaders of East Bengal; the release of Sheikh Mujibur Rahman should be the first step towards the opening of such negotiations.

The two texts recommended by the Third Committee were adopted without a vote by the General Assembly on 6 December 1971 as a two-part resolution (2790(XXVI)).

By the preamble to the first part of the resolution, the Assembly among other things expressed deep concern at the magnitude of the human suffering to which the crisis in East Pakistan had given rise and at its possible consequences. Concern was also expressed at the heavy burden imposed on India and at the disturbing influence of the general situation on the process of economic and social development in the area. The Assembly therefore noted with appreciation the prompt and generous response of the international community to the needs that had arisen from the crisis, including the efforts of non-governmental organizations to raise funds for the relief of the suffering. It recognized that voluntary repatriation was the only satisfactory solution to the refugee problem, but could be brought about only if a climate of confidence was created. In addition, the Assembly stated its conviction that further large-scale international assistance was required to meet the needs of the refugees in India and of the people in East Pakistan.

By the operative paragraphs of the first part of the resolution, the Assembly: (1) expressed profound sympathy with those who had suffered from the situation in the area; (2) endorsed the designation by the Secretary-General of the United Nations High Commissioner for Refugees to be the focal point for the co-ordination of assistance to East Pakistan refugees in India from and through the United Nations system, as well as the Secretary-General's initiative in establishing UNEPRO; (3) requested the Secretary-General and the High Commissioner to continue their efforts to co-ordinate international assistance and to ensure that it was used to the maximum advantage to relieve the suffering of the refugees in India and of the people in East Pakistan; (4) appealed to Governments, inter-governmental agencies and non-governmental organizations to intensify their efforts to assist directly or indirectly, with the collaboration of the Governments concerned, in relieving the suffering of the refugees in India and of the people in East Pakistan; and (5) urged all Member States in accordance with the purposes and principles of the Charter of the United Nations to intensify their efforts to bring about conditions necessary for the speedy and voluntary repatriation of the refugees to their homes.

By the second part of its resolution, the Assembly, aware of the urgency and extreme seriousness of the situation of the refugees, which was assuming dangerous proportions, recommended that the President of the General Assembly make a statement indicating:

(*a*) the concern of the international community, which had seldom been confronted with a refugee problem of such enormous dimensions as that of the refugees from East Pakistan in India;

(*b*) that the voluntary participation of Governments and organizations should be continued and intensified with a view to assisting the Secretary-General and his representative, and the United Nations High Commissioner for Refugees acting as the focal point, in their meritorious humanitarian action for the relief of the suffering of the refugees and of the population of East Pakistan;

(*c*) that the only solution to this grave refugee problem was the safe return of the refugees to their homes and that this required a favourable climate which all persons of goodwill should work to bring about in a spirit of respect for the principles of the Charter of the United Nations.

(For full text of both parts of resolution, see DOCUMENTARY REFERENCES below.)

Implementation of Assembly resolution

Immediately following the adoption of the resolution, the President of the Assembly stated that he would give effect to the Assembly's request contained in the second part of the resolution. The two resolutions, he continued, indicated the strong conviction of the international community that the humanitarian aspects of the serious situation in the subcontinent should not be forgotten and that international assistance should be further intensified. He noted that political and other aspects of the problem were being discussed in another organ of the United Nations and appealed to Member States to continue to support the humanitarian actions of the United Nations.

A statement by the Secretary-General was then read to the Assembly by the Under-Secretary-General for General Assembly Affairs. The statement noted that the Secretary-General's initiative to relieve the plight of the victims of the events in the subcontinent had now been endorsed by the Assembly and that he and the High Commissioner for Refugees had been requested to continue their efforts. The United Nations East Pakistan Relief Operation (UNEPRO) had developed the capacity to provide approximately 200,000 tons of food commodities monthly for the relief of the distressed population of East Pakistan, and to co-ordinate distribution to the local supply depots. Pledges and payments amounting to approximately $100 million in cash and in kind had been received from a number of Governments.

However, with the outbreak of large-scale hostilities between India and Pakistan on 3 December 1971, the humanitarian activities of the United Nations in East Pakistan had had to be suspended, since it was impossible to move supplies in a situation of active hostilities and there was no practical possibility of ensuring the reasonable safety of the international staff. Nor was he then in a position to assure the donors that the relief supplies would reach those for whom they were intended. The Secretary-General added in this connexion that he planned to evacuate the remaining personnel of UNEPRO, but that the necessary arrangements were being made for the United Nations to be in a position to resume its humanitarian operations in the area as soon as conditions permitted. Meanwhile, the High Commissioner for Refugees was continuing his efforts as focal point.

Towards the end of December 1971, the name of the operation was changed to United Nations Relief Operation in Dacca.

DOCUMENTARY REFERENCES

Economic and Social Council—51st session
Plenary meetings 1779, 1783, 1799.

E/L.1433. Letter of 16 June 1971 from USSR.

General Assembly—26th session
Third Committee, meetings 1876-1880.
Plenary meeting 2001.

A/8401/Add.1. Introduction to report of Secretary-General on work of the Organization, September 1971: Part Two, Chapter I, paras. 177-191; Chapter IX, para. 323.
A/C.3/L.1885. Netherlands, New Zealand, Sweden: draft resolution, as amended by Nigeria (A/C.3/L.1891, as orally revised) and as orally amended by Somalia and by sponsors, approved unanimously by Third Committee on 22 November 1971, meeting 1879.
A/C.3/L.1890. Saudi Arabia: amendment to 3-power draft resolution, A/C.3/L.1885.
A/C.3/L.1891. Nigeria: proposals and amendments to 3-power draft resolution, A/C.3/L.1885.
A/8544. Report of Third Committee (on report of United Nations High Commissioner for Refugees (UNHCR)), draft resolution II A.

RESOLUTION 2790A(XXVI), as recommended by Third Committee, A/8544, adopted without vote by Assembly on 6 December 1971, meeting 2001.

The General Assembly,
Noting the report of the United Nations High Commissioner for Refugees on his activities as the focal point in co-ordinating international relief assistance for refugees from East Pakistan in India,
Noting also the report of the Secretary-General on the United Nations programme of relief assistance to the people of East Pakistan,
Wishing to pay a tribute to the Secretary-General and the High Commissioner, and to their staffs, for the work they have done under difficult conditions,
Deeply concerned at the magnitude of the human suffering to which the crisis in East Pakistan has given rise and at its possible consequences,
Concerned also at the heavy burden imposed on India and at the disturbing influence of the general situation on the process of economic and social development in the area,
Noting with appreciation the prompt and generous response of the international community to the needs that have arisen from the crisis, including the efforts of non-governmental organizations to raise funds for the relief of the suffering,
Recognizing that voluntary repatriation is the only satisfactory solution to the refugee problem and that this is fully accepted by all concerned,
Believing that the voluntary repatriation of the refugees can be brought about only if a climate of confidence is created,
Convinced that further large-scale international assistance is required to meet the needs of the refugees in India and of the people of East Pakistan,
1. *Expresses its profound sympathy* with those who have suffered from the situation in the area;
2. *Endorses* the designation by the Secretary-General of the United Nations High Commissioner for Refugees to be the focal point for the co-ordination of assistance to East Pakistan refugees in India, from and through the United Nations system, as well as the Secretary-General's initiative in establishing the United Nations East Pakistan relief operation;
3. *Requests* the Secretary-General and the High Commissioner to continue their efforts to co-ordinate international assistance and to ensure that it is used to the maximum advantage to relieve the suffering of the refugees in India and of the people of East Pakistan;
4. *Appeals* to Governments, intergovernmental agencies and non-governmental organizations to intensify their efforts to assist directly or indirectly, with the collaboration of the Governments concerned, in relieving the suffering of the refugees in India and of the people of East Pakistan;
5. *Urges* all Member States in accordance with the purposes and principles of the Charter of the United Nations to intensify their efforts to bring about conditions necessary for the speedy and voluntary repatriation of the refugees to their homes.

A/C.3/L.1887 and Rev.1. Tunisia: draft recommendation to President of General Assembly on report of UNHCR.
A/C.3/L.1887/Rev.2. Tunisia: draft proposal, approved unanimously by Third Committee on 22 November 1971, meeting 1879.
A/8544. Report of Third Committee (on report of UNHCR), draft resolution II B.

RESOLUTION 2790B(XXVI), as recommended by Third Committee, A/8544, adopted without vote by Assembly on 6 December 1971, meeting 2001.

The General Assembly,
Recognizing the large-scale efforts undertaken for humanitarian reasons to meet the unprecedented problems confronting the international community,
Aware of the urgency and extreme seriousness of the situation of the refugees, which is assuming dangerous proportions,
Recommends that the President of the General Assembly should make a statement indicating:
(a) The concern of the international community, which has seldom been confronted with a refugee problem of such enormous dimensions as that of the refugees from East Pakistan in India;
(b) That the voluntary participation of Governments and organizations should be continued and intensified with a view to assisting the Secretary-General and his representative, and the United Nations High Commissioner for Refugees acting as the focal point, in their meritorious humanitarian action for the relief of the suffering of the refugees and of the population of East Pakistan;
(c) That the only solution to this grave refugee problem is the safe return of the refugees to their homes and that this requires a favourable climate which all persons of goodwill should work to bring about in a spirit of respect for the principles of the Charter of the United Nations.

A/8640 (S/10466). Report of 21 December 1971 of Secretary-General concerning implementation of General Assembly resolution 2790(XXVI) and Security Council resolution 307(1971).
A/8701 and Corr.1. Report of Secretary-General on work of the Organization, 16 June 1971–15 June 1972, Part One, Chapter IV P.

Political and security aspects

Communications concerning India-Pakistan question

In January and February 1971, India and Pakistan each addressed two letters to the President of the Security Council, continuing their correspondence of previous years regarding the State of Jammu and Kashmir. The Permanent Representative of Pakistan complained of repressive actions by the Government of India in that State, and emphasized that the status of Jammu and Kashmir remained to be determined in accordance with resolutions of the Security Council.

The Permanent Representative of India contended that since the State had become an integral part of India by virtue of its accession in 1947, the issues raised by Pakistan concerned matters of domestic jurisdiction. His Government would not discuss such matters with any other country or in the United Nations, though it was prepared to discuss bilaterally with Pakistan the question of Pakistan's illegal occupation of part of the State.

In reply, Pakistan restated its position concerning the international character of the question of the status of Jammu and Kashmir and its readiness to co-operate with any effort to resolve the problem in accordance with the wishes of the people of that State.

In another series of five letters between 13 February and 2 September 1971, the two Permanent Representatives expressed their views on the subject of the hijacking of an Indian plane to Pakistan on 30 January 1971 and the subsequent prohibition by India of the overflight of Pakistan aircraft.

The Permanent Representative of Pakistan claimed that India's action violated several international aviation agreements and was an act of belligerence. His Government deplored the hijacking and disapproved of such acts despite the fact that it appeared to be a desperate act arising from conditions of repression in Jammu and Kashmir. There was no obligation for Pakistan to compensate India for the loss of the aircraft or to extradite the hijackers who, as citizens of Jammu and Kashmir, were not Indian nationals.

The Permanent Representative of India rejected Pakistan's disclaimer of responsibility for the hijacking; he contended that the Pakistan authorities had made no effort to disarm the hijackers and had aided and encouraged them, as part of Pakistan's policy of confrontation with India. The prohibition of Pakistan overflights had been imposed as a protection against further hijackings. The situation, however, was amenable to settlement through bilateral negotiations.

Developments prior to
Security Council consideration

Following the outbreak of civil strife in East Pakistan in March 1971, two United Nations humanitarian programmes in the subcontinent were established by the Secretary-General and commenced operations during the spring and summer of 1971 (see section above). Meanwhile, the situation in the region was undergoing a steady deterioration in almost all aspects. Border clashes, clandestine raids and acts of sabotage were becoming more frequent.

In a memorandum dated 20 July 1971 to the President of the Security Council, the Secretary-General indicated that in East Pakistan international and governmental efforts to cope with the humanitarian problem were increasingly hampered by the lack of substantial progress towards a political reconciliation and the consequent effect on law, order and public administration. Reconciliation, an improved political atmosphere and the success of relief efforts were indispensable prerequisites for the return of any large proportion of the refugees from India. There was a danger that serious food shortages and even famine would soon add to the suffering of the population unless conditions could be improved to the point where a large-scale relief programme could be effective. The situation was thus one in which political, economic and social factors had produced a series of vicious circles largely frustrating the efforts of the authorities concerned and of the international community to deal with the vast humanitarian problems involved. For these reasons, and having in mind the deep preoccupation of the members of the Security Council and many other Members of the Organization with developments in the area, the Secretary-General said he had taken the unusual step of reporting to the President of the Council on this question, which was not on the Council's agenda.

After a brief account of the actions he had taken in pursuance of his responsibilities relating to humanitarian questions, the Secretary-General indicated that the problem could have serious repercussions in the context of the long-standing differences between India and Pakistan and otherwise. A conflict between the principles of the territorial integrity of States and of self-determination was involved, which had often before given rise to strife. The Secretary-General expressed deep concern about the possible consequences of the situation, not only in the humanitarian sense but also as a potential threat to peace and security and for its bearing on the future of the United Nations as an effective instrument for international co-operation and action. While not suggesting precise courses of action, the Secretary-General believed that the United Nations, with its long experience in peace-keeping and its varied resources for conciliation and persuasion, should now play a more forthright role to avert further deterioration of the situation. The Security Council, he said, was in a position to consider what measures might be taken; such consideration might take place formally or informally, in public or in private. The Secretary-General observed that his memorandum was meant to provide a basis for discussions on this matter.

The Secretary-General later reported to the Council that he had used his good offices in various ways in connexion with the situation in the subcontinent. Thus, he had addressed a letter to the President of Pakistan concerning the case of Sheikh Mujibur Rahman, who was being detained in West Pakistan, and on 10 August 1971 he had issued a statement indicating that while the matter was within the competence of Pakistan, it was also of extraordinary interest and concern in many quarters. The Secretary-General felt that any developments concerning Sheikh Mujibur's fate would inevitably have repercussions outside Pakistan.

On 20 October 1971, with the situation continuing to worsen along the borders of East Pakistan and amid reports of growing tension on the border between West Pakistan and India, the Secretary-General said that he had addressed identical messages to the heads of the Governments of India and Pakistan in which he had expressed increasing anxiety that the situation might give rise to open hostilities, which might pose a threat to the wider peace. Despite the sincere desire of both Governments to avoid a senseless war, feelings were running high and even a small incident could lead to wider conflict. He referred in this regard to the efforts of the Chief Military Observer of the United Nations Military Observer Group in India and Pakistan (UNMOGIP) to ease tensions and prevent military escalation along the cease-fire line in Jammu and Kashmir. There was of course no comparable United Nations mechanism on the borders of East Pakistan and on the frontier between India and West Pakistan. In this potentially very dangerous situation, the Secretary-General offered his good offices to both sides with a view to avoiding any development that might lead to disaster.

The Secretary-General reported that the President of Pakistan replied to his message on 22 October, suggesting withdrawal of troops to a mutually agreed safe distance along both sides of the India-Pakistan borders. United Nations observers should oversee the withdrawals and supervise the maintenance of peace. He welcomed the Secretary-General's offer of good offices, assured him of his full co-operation, and suggested that he visit India and Pakistan to seek a settlement of differences.

Replying to the Secretary-General on 16 November 1971, the Prime Minister of India stated that the military authorities of Pakistan were pursuing a deliberate policy of suppression in East Bengal, causing a continuing large-scale flight of the people from that area into India, thus placing intolerable political and social burdens on India. The problem, which involved the rights and the fate of the people of East Bengal, could only be resolved by peaceful negotiations between the military rulers of West Pakistan and the elected leaders of East Bengal. Only in this manner could the flow of refugees into India be reversed and the threat to India's security relieved. The Prime Minister said that Pakistan had sought to divert attention from the situation in East Bengal by projecting the issue as an India-Pakistan dispute, and she accused Pakistan of initiating large-scale armed conflict with India. The measures taken by India were entirely defensive. The Secretary-General's offer of good offices could play a significant role, the Prime Minister of India continued. Whatever efforts he could make to bring about a political settlement in East Bengal which met the declared wishes of the people there would be welcome. If the Secretary-General viewed the problem in perspective, he would have India's support in his initiatives.

The Secretary-General reported that he had replied to the Prime Minister of India on 22 November, making it clear that he could not under the United Nations Charter ignore a potential threat to international peace and security such as now seemed to exist in the subcontinent. He noted that his offer of good offices had been made in the context of his memorandum of 20 July 1971 to the President of the Security Council, which took into account those aspects of the situation mentioned in the Prime Minister's letter. However, under the circumstances, there did not seem to be a basis for the exercise of his good offices since this would require the consent and co-operation of both parties.

On 23 November, the President of Pakistan informed the Secretary-General that Indian armed forces were maintaining pressure along Pakistan's eastern borders. The Pakistan armed forces had been under orders to exercise strict restraint, but they must now meet the Indian military offensive with all the force at their command. The President said that the situation was fast reaching a point of no return, but the Secretary-General's personal initiative could still avert a catastrophe.

In replying to the President of Pakistan on 26 November, the Secretary-General indicated his conclusion that he had gone, for the moment, as far as his authority under the United Nations Charter permitted him to go, but that he would remain in touch with the representatives of Pakistan and India concerning ways in which the United Nations might prove able to assist in preserving the peace.

On 29 November, the Secretary-General further reported, the Permanent Representative of Pakistan had conveyed to the Secretary-General a message from his President stating that Indian armed forces were carrying out large-scale attacks along the borders of East Pakistan. He requested the Secretary-General to station a force of United Nations observers on the Pakistan side of the border immediately.

On the same day, the Secretary-General, who had kept the President of the Security Council continuously informed of his offer of good offices and the reactions to it, transmitted to the President of the Council a copy of the message of 29 November from the President of Pakistan. The Secretary-General noted that the stationing of observers as requested would require authorization by the Security Council. He felt that in the light of its primary responsibility under the Charter for the maintenance of international peace and security, the Council should give serious consideration to the situation prevailing in the subcontinent.

On 3 December, in the light of reports of a further grave deterioration in the situation along the border of East Pakistan and elsewhere in the subcontinent, the Secretary-General reported to the Security Council on the efforts he had made thus far in regard to the problem. He stated his conviction that the situation constituted a threat to international peace and security and pointed out that the President of the Council had been kept informed of the Secretary-General's efforts under the broad terms of Article 99 of the Charter.[10] The Secretary-General felt that an initiative on this matter in the Council could best be taken by the parties or by the members of the Security Council themselves.

On 4 December 1971, the Secretary-General reported to the Council his receipt of two additional messages, an oral one of 3 December from the Prime Minister of India and a written one of the same date from the President of Pakistan. Both messages reported the spread of armed hostilities between the two countries and charged aggressive actions on the part of the other State.

In further reports of 4, 5 and 6 December, the Secretary-General made information available to the Council regarding the situation along the cease-fire line in the State of Jammu and Kashmir, based on reports from UNMOGIP. That was the only part of the subcontinent where the United Nations had observation machinery, the Secretary-General pointed out. The Chief Military Observer of UNMOGIP had awarded over-all violations to both India and Pakistan as from 21 October for breaches of the Karachi Agreement of 1949[11] and in certain cases systematic non-observance of it. On 3 December, the Chief Military Observer had reported that hostilities along the cease-fire line had commenced and that he had instructed the military observers to remain at their stations.

Consideration by Security Council between 4 and 6 December 1971

On 4 December 1971, the representatives of Argentina, Belgium, Burundi, Italy, Japan, Nicaragua, Somalia, the United Kingdom and the United States requested an immediate meeting of the Council to consider the deteriorating situation which had led to armed clashes between India and Pakistan.

The Council met on the same day. It decided to place the item on its agenda, together with the reports of the Secretary-General, and invited the representatives of India and Pakistan to participate in the debate without the right to vote.

The Council had also before it a letter dated 4 December from the representative of India, transmitting a letter of the same date from Justice Abu Sayeed Chowdhury requesting that he be allowed to make a statement on behalf of the people and government of Bangladesh. The USSR representative proposed that the representatives of Bangladesh be given a hearing, but, after a procedural discussion, the President ruled, without objection, that the Council should defer consideration of that issue.

Opening the debate, the representative of Pakistan said that India had not only launched aggression on the territory of Pakistan but had openly demanded that Pakistan dismember itself. The situation before the Council involved not only Pakistan but all States in danger of being overrun by larger, more powerful, predatory neighbours. If the Council failed to suppress the aggression, the Charter of the United Nations would have been shattered. Pakistan's eastern province had been under a massive, unprovoked attack since 21 November by India's regular troops, tanks and aircraft.

He stated that in the fighting that had preceded and culminated in the full-scale war on 3 December, Pakistan had been the victim of acts of sabotage and terrorism, as well as armed incursions by bands organized by India. It was for the Security Council to find the means to make India desist from its war of aggression. Political, economic, strategic, social or ideological considerations could not be invoked by one State to justify interference in the internal affairs of, or aggression against, another State. Only those means devised by the Security Council which were consistent with Pakistan's independence, sovereignty and territorial integrity and with the principle of non-intervention in the domestic affairs of Member States would command his Government's support and co-operation.

[10]For text of Article 99 of the Charter, see APPENDIX II.
[11]See Y.U.N., 1948-49, pp. 279-83.

The representative of India said that the problem before the Council had a long history and was essentially one between West Pakistan and the people of Bangladesh. Therefore, without the participation of representatives of the people of Bangladesh it was impossible to obtain a proper perspective of the problem.

He read to the Council a passage from a report by the Secretary-General dated 4 December on the situation along the cease-fire line in Jammu and Kashmir, which gave details of military action along the line on 3 December. The Indian representative stated that the whole picture was that of a build-up for military action. It was not India, he said, which was breaking up Pakistan; it was Pakistan which was breaking up itself and in the process creating aggression against India. Ten million people had gone to India as refugees. That was surely a kind of aggression and had subjected India to intolerable social, financial and administrative pressures.

The representative of India said that, after having failed totally to suppress what Pakistan called the Bengali rebellion, Pakistan had made an effort to internationalize the problem, to make it into an Indo-Pakistan dispute in the hope that people would forget what the Pakistan army was doing in East Pakistan. But the refugees were still coming, and India could not take any more; their conditions were already intolerable.

India, he said, wished to give a very serious warning to the Security Council that it would not be a party to any solution arrived at without the participation of the people of East Bengal and which would mean continuation of that people's oppression. The question of a cease-fire was not one between India and Pakistan but between the Pakistan army and the people of Bangladesh.

The United States representative said that a state of open hostilities existed between India and Pakistan and that there was a grave threat to the peace and stability of Asia. The United States had proposed that both sides should withdraw their military forces from the border, and the Secretary-General had offered his good offices towards resolving the grave situation in South Asia, but India had not accepted either proposal. The United Nations should now call upon India and Pakistan to agree to an immediate cease-fire and the immediate withdrawal of forces from foreign territories, so as to create suitable conditions for progress towards a political solution.

The United States representative concluded by introducing a draft resolution.

By this proposed text, the Council, convinced that the hostilities on the India-Pakistan border constituted an immediate threat to international peace and security, would: (1) call for an immedi-ate cessation of hostilities; (2) call for immediate withdrawal of armed forces to their respective territories; (3) authorize the Secretary-General, at the request of either Government, to place observers along the India-Pakistan borders to report on the implementation of the cease-fire and troop withdrawals; (4) call upon both Governments to exert their best efforts towards creation of a climate conducive to the voluntary return of refugees to East Pakistan; (5) call upon all States to refrain from any action that would endanger the peace in that area; (6) invite the two Governments to respond affirmatively to the Secretary-General's offer of good offices; and (7) request the Secretary-General to report on implementation.

The representatives of Argentina, Belgium, Burundi, France, Italy, Japan, Sierra Leone, Somalia, the Syrian Arab Republic and the United Kingdom all called for an immediate end to the hostilities; most of them added a demand for the withdrawal of armed forces. Some of the speakers expressed views to the following effect: each side should respect the other's territorial integrity; the human suffering must be alleviated; there should be an immediate cease-fire supervised by the United Nations; conditions, including political conditions in East Pakistan, should be created which would permit the early voluntary return of the refugees; and an eventual over-all solution of the problem was necessary.

Belgium, Italy and Japan also submitted a resolution. By this text, the Council, gravely concerned at the hostilities between India and Pakistan which constituted an immediate threat to international peace and security, would: (1) call for an immediate cease-fire; (2) urge the Governments concerned, in accordance with Charter principles, to bring about conditions necessary for speedy and voluntary repatriation of the millions of refugees; (3) call for full co-operation with the Secretary-General in relieving the distress of refugees; (4) request the Secretary-General to keep it informed; and (5) decide to follow the situation closely.

The representative of China said that the Government of India had openly dispatched troops to invade East Pakistan. This had given rise to a large-scale armed conflict and aggravated tension in the India-Pakistan subcontinent and in Asia as a whole. The Council should condemn India's aggression, which had been launched with the support of social imperialism, and should demand that India immediately and unconditionally withdraw all its armed forces from Pakistan.

The representative of the USSR said that the situation in East Pakistan was a result of the actions of the Pakistan military authorities. Because of the application of force and terror against the people of East Pakistan, millions of people had been compelled to leave their homeland, forsake their property, flee to a neighbouring country—India—and become political refugees. The representative of Pakistan had officially acknowledged that there was a serious domestic crisis in his country and that the crisis had acquired an international character. The Security Council should deal with the root cause of the crisis.

The USSR subsequently introduced a draft resolution by which the Council would: (1) call for a political settlement in East Pakistan that would inevitably result in a cessation of hostilities; and (2) call upon the Government of Pakistan to take measures to cease all acts of violence by Pakistan forces in East Pakistan which had led to deterioration of the situation.

The representative of Poland said that the source of the conflict could not be liquidated and peace restored except through a political settlement in East Pakistan that would take into account the will of the people of East Bengal.

Also placed before the Council at its first meeting on the question was a draft resolution sponsored by Argentina, Burundi, Nicaragua, Sierra Leone and Somalia. By the preamble to this text, the Council among other things would express grave concern at the outbreak of hostilities along the India-Pakistan border, and its conviction that they represented an immediate threat to international peace and security. It would also recognize the need to deal subsequently with the issues that had given rise to the hostilities and the need to take preliminary measures to bring about an immediate cease-fire.

By the operative part of the text, the Council would call upon India and Pakistan to take measures for an immediate cease-fire and withdrawal of their armed forces to their own sides of the border and ask the Secretary-General to keep the Council informed.

At the same meeting, which continued into 5 December, the Council voted on the United States draft resolution. It was not adopted owing to the negative vote of a permanent member of the Council. The text received 11 votes in favour to 2 against (Poland and the USSR), with 2 abstentions (France and the United Kingdom).

Later on 5 December 1971, when the Council next met, the representatives of Tunisia and Saudi Arabia were invited, at their request, to participate in the discussion without the right to vote.

The representative of the USSR again urged that the Council extend an invitation to a representative of Bangladesh to participate in the debate. Argentina, China, India, Italy, Pakistan, Poland and the USSR spoke on the issue. With the consent of the USSR representative, the question was adjourned to a later date for further consultations.

The representative of the USSR also circulated a statement of the Telegraphic Agency of the Soviet Union (TASS) which, he stated, set out the position of the USSR on the situation. The statement warned against the dangerous course followed by Pakistan which had given rise to serious events in direct proximity to the USSR border.

A draft resolution was introduced by China. By the preamble to this draft text, the Security Council would note that India had launched large-scale attacks on Pakistan, thus gravely undermining peace in the Indo-Pakistan subcontinent and strongly condemn the Indian Government's acts of creating a so-called Bangladesh and of subverting, dismembering and committing aggression against Pakistan. By the operative section of the text, the Council would call for withdrawal of Indian and Pakistan armed forces, cessation of hostilities and support for the Pakistan people in their just struggle to resist Indian aggression. The Council would also ask the Secretary-General to report to it on implementation.

Speaking in support of his proposal, the representative of China said that a cease-fire in place, without withdrawals, would constitute an encouragement of aggression.

The representative of Tunisia said that the Security Council should give an order, or at least make an appeal, for an immediate cease-fire. He felt that the voluntary repatriation of refugees was the best and indeed the only solution to the problem, and that a climate of confidence was necessary to that end. The representative of Saudi Arabia proposed a meeting of Asian chiefs of State to seek an acceptable end to the conflict.

An eight-power draft resolution—sponsored by Argentina, Belgium, Burundi, Italy, Japan, Nicaragua, Sierra Leone and Somalia—was introduced to replace the earlier three-power text put forward by Belgium, Italy and Japan and the five-power text proposed by Argentina, Burundi, Nicaragua, Sierra Leone and Somalia.

By the preamble to this eight-power draft, the Security Council among other things would: (*a*) express grave concern that hostilities had broken out between India and Pakistan which constituted an immediate threat to international peace and security; (*b*) recognize the need to deal appropriately at a subsequent stage, within the framework of the United Nations Charter, with the issues which had given rise to the hostilities; (*c*) express conviction that an early political solution would be necessary for the restoration of conditions of normalcy and the return of refugees to their homes; (*d*) recall those provisions of the United Nations Charter and the United Nations Declaration on the Strengthening of International Security of 16 December 1970, which dealt in particular with the necessity to refrain from the threat or use of force against the territorial integrity and political independence of a State, respect for the sovereignty of States and the right of people to determine their own destinies, and the need to use the methods provided for in the Charter to solve disputes;[12] and (*e*) recognize the need to take immediate measures to bring about immediate cessation of hostilities and withdrawal of armed forces.

By the operative part of the draft resolution, the Security Council would: (1) call for an immediate cease-fire and withdrawal of armed forces to their own territories; (2) urge intensified efforts to bring about conditions necessary for the voluntary return of the refugees to their homes; (3) call on States to help the Secretary-General aid the refugees; (4) ask the Secretary-General to report on implementation; and (5) decide to follow the situation closely.

Later in the meeting on 5 December, the Council voted on the USSR draft resolution. This received 2 votes in favour, 1 against and 12 abstentions; lacking the required majority, it was therefore not adopted. (See DOCUMENTARY REFERENCES below for voting details.)

The Council then voted on the eight-power draft resolution, which received 11 votes in favour, 2 against and 2 abstentions; it was not adopted because of the negative vote of a permanent member of the Council (the USSR). (See DOCU-MENTARY REFERENCES below for voting details.)

The representative of France, deploring the failure of the Council to act, recalled the attempts of the Secretary-General in July 1971 to draw the Council's attention to the situation, and referred to the efforts of the representatives of France and Italy, when they served as Presidents of the Council, to have the matter considered. He explained his abstention on the eight-power resolution on the grounds that it had no chance of adoption, and he urged further consultations in the Council.

The United Kingdom representative, expressing views similar to those of France, supported the suggestion for adjournment to continue consultations.

The representatives of China and the USSR, and the representatives of India and the United States, exchanged differing opinions on the situation and on the positions of their respective Governments.

Later on 5 December 1971, Belgium, Italy, Japan, Nicaragua and Sierra Leone circulated a new draft resolution. Expressing grave concern at the outbreak of hostilities, which constituted an immediate threat to international peace and security, the Council would thereby call as a first step for an immediate cease-fire, request the Secretary-General to keep the Council informed of the implementation of the resolution and decide to continue to discuss the further measures to be taken to restore peace in the area.

When the Council met again on 6 December, Tunisia appealed for a cease-fire and withdrawal of troops. The representative of Nicaragua said that if the Security Council was paralysed because of the veto, the General Assembly could take action.

The representative of France informed the Council that, in co-operation with the United Kingdom, he had drawn up a text, based on the draft proposed on 4 December by Belgium, Italy, and Japan, calling as a first step for a cease-fire, cessation of all military activity and mutual disengagement. Because of objections by some Council members, this proposal by France and the United Kingdom would not be submitted; thus peace was defeated, the United Nations had again failed, and arms would decide the issue.

The representative of the USSR said that the five-power draft resolution (that submitted by Belgium, Italy, Japan, Nicaragua and Sierra Leone) dealt only with a cease-fire in the military action undertaken by Pakistan against India. But this question was inseparably bound with that of the recognition by Pakistan of the will of the East Pakistan people as expressed by their elected representatives. He submitted amendments to the five-power resolution to this end.

Italy then announced the withdrawal of the five-power resolution, which was no longer up to date and had no chance of being adopted.

The representative of India read a statement made that day (6 December) before Parliament by his Prime Minister, announcing India's recognition of the People's Republic of Bangladesh. He said that India was not in the same category as Pakistan and could not accept any decision or resolution which equated the two nations, failed to take account of the views of the representatives of Bangladesh, and did not go to the root cause of the problem in the subcontinent.

The representative of Pakistan said that the problem in the subcontinent was brought about by India's subversion, support of armed secession, armed intervention and aggression. He stated that military action by his country was in response to armed attacks by India. The question was whether the Council would legitimize that so-called reality, perpetuate occupation and guarantee the fruits of aggression and the illegal use of force.

The representative of China said that India with the support of the USSR had created the

---

[12]See APPENDIX II, below, text of Article 2, para. 4, of the United Nations Charter; also Y.U.N., 1970, pp. 105-7, resolution 2734(XXV) (especially operative paras. 4-6), containing text of Declaration on the Strengthening of International Security.

Bangladesh Government in order to dismember Pakistan.

The representative of Somalia said that the principle of withdrawal of enemy troops from the territory of another country could not be subject to negotiation. It was not for any other State to impose a political solution on East Pakistan by military means. The time had come to transfer the question to the General Assembly, as provided for in the Assembly's "Uniting for Peace" resolution (377 A (V)) of 3 November 1950.[13] He introduced a draft resolution, also sponsored by Argentina, Burundi, Japan, Nicaragua and Sierra Leone, by which the Council, taking into account that the lack of unanimity of its permanent members had prevented it from exercising its primary responsibility for the maintenance of international peace and security, would decide to refer the question before it to the twenty-sixth session of the General Assembly (then meeting) as provided for by the Assembly's resolution of 3 November 1950.

Also on 6 December 1971, the representative of the USSR introduced a draft resolution. By this, the Council, expressing grave concern at the hostilities between India and Pakistan which constituted an immediate threat to international peace and security, would: (1) call for an immediate cease-fire and (2) simultaneously call for effective action by Pakistan towards a political settlement in East Pakistan giving immediate recognition to the will of the population of East Pakistan as expressed in the elections of December 1970; (3) declare that the first two operative provisions constituted a single whole; (4) ask the Secretary-General to report on implementation; and (5) decide to continue to discuss measures needed to restore peace in the area.

The USSR representative disputed suggestions that the USSR controlled the actions of India and criticized the proposal to refer the matter to the General Assembly.

The representative of the United States deplored the fact that the veto of a permanent member had rendered the Council unable to act in the face of a clear and present danger to the peace of the world.

The representative of Poland said that the USSR proposal would deal with the root of the evil.

The representative of Pakistan said that if the secessionist elements in East Pakistan were prepared to repudiate secession, there might still be a way out of the difficulty.

The representative of India said that his country had faced aggression from a neighbour four times, and was threatened again. It faced mortal danger through the annihilation of 75 million people at its doorstep. This could not fail to overwhelm India and India could not tolerate it.

France and the United Kingdom said that they were unable to support the proposal for referring the question to the General Assembly because they had doubts that this procedure would promote a solution.

After the President announced his understanding that the Chinese and USSR draft resolutions were not to be pressed to a vote, the Council voted on the six-power text proposed by Argentina, Burundi, Japan, Nicaragua, Sierra Leone and Somalia, adopting it as resolution 303(1971). The vote was 11 in favour to 0 opposed, with 4 abstentions. The Council thereby decided to refer the question before it to the General Assembly at its current session.

(For text of resolution and voting details, see DOCUMENTARY REFERENCES below.)

Consideration by General Assembly

The General Assembly took up the question referred to it by the Security Council at two plenary meetings held on 7 December 1971.

Before the Assembly was a draft resolution sponsored eventually by the following 34 Members: Algeria, Argentina, Brazil, Burundi, Cameroon, Chad, Colombia, Costa Rica, Ecuador, Ghana, Guatemala, Haiti, Honduras, Indonesia, Italy, the Ivory Coast, Japan, Jordan, Liberia, the Libyan Arab Republic, Morocco, the Netherlands, Nicaragua, Panama, Paraguay, Sierra Leone, Somalia, Spain, Sudan, Tunisia, Uruguay, Yemen, Zaire and Zambia.

Introducing this proposal, Argentina called for continued efforts by the General Assembly or the Security Council to work out a political solution for the problem confronting India and Pakistan.

The 34-power text, as revised during the debate, was adopted by the Assembly on 7 December 1971 by a vote of 104 to 11, with 10 abstentions, as resolution 2793(XXVI).

By the preamble to this resolution, the Assembly expressed grave concern that hostilities had broken out between India and Pakistan, which constituted an immediate threat to international peace and security. It recognized the need to deal appropriately at a subsequent stage, within the framework of the United Nations Charter, with the issues which had given rise to the hostilities, and expressed conviction that an early political solution would be necessary for the restoration of conditions of normalcy in the area of conflict and for the return of the refugees to their homes. The Assembly also recalled provisions of the Charter, particularly those of Article 2, paragraph 4 (calling on Members to refrain from the threat or use of force against the territorial integrity or political independence of any State), and certain specific

---

[13]See Y.U.N., 1950, pp. 193-95, text of resolution 377 A (V).

provisions of the 1970 Declaration on the Strengthening of International Security.[14] The Assembly recognized the need to take immediate measures for a cessation of hostilities and withdrawal of armed forces to their own territories and, finally, recalled its Charter responsibilities and the provisions of its "Uniting for Peace" resolution of 3 November 1950.[15]

By the operative part of the resolution which it adopted on 7 December 1971, the Assembly called upon India and Pakistan to take forthwith all measures for an immediate cease-fire and withdrawal of armed forces to their own territories. It urged intensified efforts to bring about, speedily and in accordance with Charter purposes and principles, conditions necessary for the voluntary return of the East Pakistan refugees to their homes.

In addition, the Assembly called for the full co-operation of all States with the Secretary-General in aiding the refugees and urged that every effort be made to safeguard the lives and well-being of the civilian population in the area of conflict. It asked the Secretary-General to keep it and the Security Council informed on implementation, and decided to follow the question closely and to meet again should the situation so demand. Finally, it called upon the Security Council to take appropriate action in the light of this resolution.

(For full text of resolution, see DOCUMENTARY REFERENCES below.)

A second draft resolution, put forward by the USSR, was not put to the vote. By this text, the Assembly, gravely concerned that hostilities had broken out between India and Pakistan which constituted an immediate threat to international peace and security, would: (1) call on all parties concerned forthwith, as a first step, for an immediate cease-fire; and (2) call upon Pakistan simultaneously to take effective action towards a political settlement in East Pakistan, giving immediate recognition to the will of the East Pakistan population as expressed in the elections of December 1970. The Assembly would, in addition, declare that the provisions set forth under (1) and (2) above constituted a single whole. It would request the Secretary-General to keep the Security Council and General Assembly informed on implementation and call upon the Security Council to take appropriate measures in the light of this resolution.

During the debate, the Secretary-General said that since March 1971 he had taken a number of humanitarian initiatives in an attempt to mitigate the consequences of the situation in East Pakistan. He appealed to all the parties to the conflict to take every possible measure to spare the lives of the innocent civilian population, to observe the terms of the four Geneva Conventions of 12 August 1949 (relative to the treatment of prisoners of war; the wounded and sick in armed forces in the field; the wounded, sick and shipwrecked forces at sea; and the protection of civilian persons in time of war) and to do their utmost to ensure that the current developments did not give rise to yet another senseless sacrifice of human lives on a vast scale. He had instructed his representative in Dacca to examine urgently, in full co-operation with the International Red Cross, what practical measures could be taken to that end.

The representative of India said that his country had made repeated attempts over many months to inform international opinion of the developing dangers of the situation. As early as 30 March 1971, he had circulated a note stating that the events in East Pakistan had caused human suffering on such a large scale as to cease to be a matter of domestic concern to Pakistan, and urging the international community to take suitable action. India could not ignore what was happening just across the border and the effect on its national integrity, amounting to civil aggression against India. When Pakistan found it could not impose its military solution in Bangladesh, it had sought to create a confrontation with India and launched armed attacks against India. Bangladesh was a reality and could no longer be considered a part of Pakistan. India had recognized the People's Republic of Bangladesh. Any withdrawal of troops had to include the withdrawal of Pakistan occupation troops from Bangladesh. Any cessation of hostilities had to be simultaneous with the release of the leader of Bangladesh, Sheikh Mujibur Rahman.

The representative of Pakistan said that the issue involved all States that wanted freedom from the fear of aggression. Today it was Pakistan that was fighting armed aggression; tomorrow it might be any other State. The three causes of the current situation were India's invasion of Pakistan territory, India's armed interference in Pakistan's internal affairs and India's publicly avowed goal of breaking up Pakistan. Pakistan had initiated or accepted every proposal to settle the situation and avoid hostilities. The fact was beyond challenge that India had caused and aggravated Pakistan's internal crisis and then used that crisis as a pretext for aggression against Pakistan. Aggression should be condemned. The USSR draft resolution would have Pakistan sign away its national integrity, he said.

In the view of the United States representative, the Assembly's task was to bring the influence of the United Nations to bear in order to restore conditions of peace essential for a political

[14]See footnote 12.
[15]See footnote 13.

settlement. He urged prompt action by the Assembly to save lives and restore peace.

The representative of China maintained that India was committing aggression and that the USSR was behind the aggression. The United Nations should not repeat the mistakes of the League of Nations but should act to condemn India's aggression, support Pakistan, and call for an immediate cease-fire and withdrawal as well as military disengagement and peaceful settlement of the disputes between India and Pakistan.

The USSR representative contended that Pakistan had launched an attack on India in order to solve its domestic problem. A cease-fire between India and Pakistan would only give Pakistan the right to continue its terror campaign against the East Pakistan population. The Assembly should face realities and deal with the root causes of the problem. He also criticized the Chinese representative's attacks on the USSR, and denied that the USSR posed a threat to China.

The representatives of the United Kingdom and France felt that the passage of neither draft resolution would contribute to a settlement and that consultations should be pursued in the Security Council.

The representative of Chile hoped that the principles of the various drafts could be combined so as to make possible a consensus.

Most Members participating in the Assembly's debate spoke in favour of an immediate cease-fire and withdrawal of the troops of both India and Pakistan to their own territories; most of them regretted the failure of the Security Council to fulfil its responsibilities and argued that one country's internal difficulties should not be used as a pretext for intervention from outside.

A number of Members argued that a peaceful resolution of the conflict depended on a political settlement in East Pakistan based on the will of the people of that area as expressed by their representatives.

Others considered that while a political settlement in East Pakistan was necessary in order to create conditions that would make possible the voluntary repatriation of the refugees, the United Nations immediate response must still be to bring the fighting to an end. The point was made by some Members that the fighting must end not only between India and Pakistan but also between West Pakistan troops and East Bengalis. There was disagreement, however, as to the order in which these events should take place. Some felt that West Pakistan troops should withdraw from the province; others maintained that the integrity of Pakistan should be upheld.

In addition, some Members spoke in favour of a United Nations observer mission to be installed on both sides of the East Pakistan frontier.

Reports and communications

On 7 December 1971, the Secretary-General reported to the General Assembly and the Security Council on his efforts to evacuate 46 staff members of the United Nations East Pakistan Relief Operation (UNEPRO) and some 240 other international personnel from Dacca. Non-essential United Nations personnel had been evacuated earlier, some of them to Singapore where a staging area for the operation was set up. Since Dacca could only be reached by air, one aircraft was made available by the Canadian Government, another was chartered commercially, and with the co-operation of the Indian and Pakistan authorities temporary cease-fires were arranged around and on the approaches to the Dacca airport. However, attempts to reach Dacca on 6 and 7 December were unsuccessful owing to difficulties relating to the timing and observance of the cease-fires.

A later report by the Secretary-General, circulated on 21 December 1971, indicated that after a third unsuccessful attempt on 11 December, an evacuation was carried out on 12 December by British aircraft under arrangements made by the United Kingdom Government in co-operation with the United Nations. Among 437 personnel evacuated there were 10 United Nations officials, but in response to the decision of the Secretary-General to maintain a United Nations presence in Dacca for humanitarian purposes, a group of 37 officials headed by Paul-Marc Henry volunteered to remain. Together with representatives of the International Red Cross, this group assisted in taking practical measures, including the establishment of safe havens for evacuee groups, to help ensure observance of the Geneva Conventions of 1949 and to avoid the loss of lives, as indicated by the Secretary-General at the meeting of the General Assembly on 7 December. With the co-operation of the Indian and Pakistan authorities, four neutral zones were eventually established in Dacca under United Nations and Red Cross protection.

Between 7 and 18 December 1971, the Secretary-General issued another series of reports to the General Assembly and the Security Council on the situation along the cease-fire line in Jammu and Kashmir, based on information supplied by the United Nations Military Observer Group in India and Pakistan (UNMOGIP). The reports gave an account of hostilities in the several sectors, with incursions across the cease-fire line in various places by both sides. The Chief Military Observer noted, however, that his reports did not cover all military activities in the UNMOGIP area of responsibility, since military observers as a rule had had to limit their observations to the immediate areas of their stations. At 1930 hours on 17 December, he said, a cease-fire announced by the two Governments involved had gone into effect in the area.

Meanwhile, the Secretary-General had communicated the text of the General Assembly's resolution (2793(XXVI)) of 7 December 1971 to the Governments of India and Pakistan immediately after its adoption.

The representative of Pakistan responded by a letter dated 9 December informing the Secretary-General that his Government had decided to accept the call for an immediate cease-fire and withdrawal of troops contained in the resolution, and expressing the hope that United Nations observers would be stationed on both sides of the border to supervise the cease-fire and withdrawals.

On 12 December, the representative of the United States wrote to the President of the Security Council that despite the resolution of the General Assembly, the war on the subcontinent continued to rage unabated. One of the parties, Pakistan, had accepted the resolution. The other party, India, had not yet done so. He therefore requested the immediate convening of a meeting of the Council to end this threat to world peace.

On the same day, the representative of India responded to the General Assembly's resolution, stating in a letter to the Secretary-General that there could be a cease-fire and withdrawal of Indian forces if the rulers of West Pakistan withdrew their forces from Bangladesh and reached a peaceful settlement with those who now owed allegiance to the duly constituted Government of Bangladesh. India felt aggrieved that in calling for a cease-fire the United Nations made no distinction between the aggressor and its victims; it was Pakistan that had launched the aggression against India.

Further consideration by Security Council (12-21 December 1971)

Following the request of the United States, the Security Council, between 12 and 21 December 1971, held a second series of meetings on the situation in the subcontinent. Representatives expressed substantially the same positions as during the earlier meetings, and a number of draft resolutions were introduced, as described below.

At the meeting of 12 December, the representative of the United States recalled his Government's efforts to move matters to the conference table rather than the battlefield, including submitting a proposal to the Prime Minister of India during her visit to Washington in November that Pakistan was willing to make an initial unilateral withdrawal of troops, provided it was assured of subsequent reciprocal steps by India. The Indian Government had also been informed that the Pakistan Government was prepared to meet with appropriate representatives designated by Sheikh Mujibur Rahman.

India, the United States representative continued, had responded by publicly calling on Pakistan to pull its forces out of its own territory of East Pakistan. With the support of USSR vetoes, India had prevented the Security Council from acting. The Council had the responsibility to demand immediate compliance by India with the Assembly's resolution. It should also insist that India give a clear and unequivocal assurance that it did not intend to annex Pakistan territory or change the *status quo* in Kashmir contrary to United Nations resolutions. The United States representative submitted a draft resolution intended to give effect to these views.

By the preamble to the United States text as later revised, the Security Council, among other things would: (*a*) note that Pakistan had accepted a cease-fire and withdrawal of forces as set forth by the General Assembly in its resolution of 7 December 1971 and regret that India had not yet done so; (*b*) express grave concern at the continued hostilities, which constituted an immediate threat to international peace and security; (*c*) recognize the need to deal appropriately at a subsequent stage with the issues which had given rise to the hostilities; (*d*) express conviction that an early political solution would be necessary for the restoration of conditions of normalcy and the return of refugees to their homes; (*e*) keep in mind provisions of the Charter and of the Declaration on the Strengthening of International Security dealing with, among other things, the obligation of States to refrain from the threat or use of force against the territorial integrity or political independence of any State; (*f*) recognize the need for immediate action to end hostilities and effect withdrawal of forces; and (*g*) keep in mind the Security Council's responsibilities under the Charter.

By the operative paragraphs of the United States text, the Council would: (1) call upon India and Pakistan to take forthwith all measures for an immediate cease-fire and withdrawal of armed forces to their own side of the borders; (2) urge intensified efforts to bring about—in accordance with Charter purposes and principles—conditions necessary for the voluntary return of the East Pakistan refugees to their homes; (3) call on States to co-operate in aiding the refugees; (4) call on all parties concerned to safeguard the lives and well-being of the civilian population in the area; (5) request the Secretary-General to keep the Council informed; and (6) decide to remain seized of the matter and meet again as circumstances warranted.

The Foreign Minister of India said that the solution of the problem suggested by the General Assembly was unrealistic and took no account of the immediate problems confronting the people of

India and of Bangladesh. It was after Pakistan's massive attacks and military provocations against India that the latter had decided to move into Bangladesh and to repel Pakistan aggression in the west. India's recognition of Bangladesh was necessary to provide a proper basis for the presence of Indian armed forces in order to assist the Bangladesh freedom fighters, and to make clear that the entry of those forces into Bangladesh was not motivated by any intention of territorial aggrandizement, either in Bangladesh or in West Pakistan. Pakistan had sought to make the United Nations a party to the repression of the people of Bangladesh. India would co-operate with the United Nations in any realistic effort to deal with the root cause of the problem, and would be willing to discuss a cease-fire or withdrawals which would ensure the freedoms of the people of Bangladesh, but India would not be deflected from the vital task of ensuring its own territorial integrity and security. Any solution, moreover, must take account of the views of the Government of Bangladesh.

The Deputy Prime Minister and Foreign Minister of Pakistan said that while his Government admitted that it had made serious mistakes, it was now fighting for a cause that affected all States, namely, that every State had a right to remain independent, sovereign and free and not to be dismembered by force by a more powerful country. If Pakistan were dismembered, the germs of dismemberment would spread. There should be friendship and coexistence with India, but if a secessionist Bangladesh were imposed on Pakistan by force, there would be a Bangladesh everywhere soon in Africa, Asia and Europe. The real trouble on the subcontinent, he maintained, had begun when the India-USSR treaty was concluded for offensive purposes on 9 August 1971. Pakistan thus had had to face India supported by the power, resources and technology of the USSR. But Pakistan would not abandon its friendship with China. It would fight to retain East Bengal.

When the Council met on 13 December, the USSR again suggested that the representative of Bangladesh be heard by the Council. Following a discussion, the President ruled without challenge that he could not admit the participation in the debate of the representative of a State which had, in his mind, not yet satisfied the necessary criteria of existence and recognition. The USSR did not press for a vote on inviting the same person to participate as an individual.

Speaking to the United States proposal, the USSR said it still avoided the issue of a political settlement in East Pakistan. He criticized China for seeking to exacerbate the political crisis in that area for Chinese chauvinist ends.

The representative of Poland said that the conflict was basically within East Pakistan and therefore must be resolved in conformity with the wishes of the population of East Pakistan.

The Foreign Minister of India said that his country had no claims to the territory of West Pakistan or of Bangladesh and would consider the proposals for a cease-fire and withdrawals in the wake of a political settlement in the East acceptable to the elected representatives of Bangladesh. As for Kashmir, that area was under massive attack by Pakistan armed forces across the cease-fire line.

On 13 December 1971, the Security Council voted on the revised United States text. It received 11 votes in favour, 2 against (Poland and the USSR), and 2 abstentions (France and the United Kingdom), but was not adopted owing to the negative vote of a permanent member of the Council.

The representative of the United States said that the statement by the Indian Foreign Minister provided no clear-cut answers on whether India intended to destroy the Pakistan army in the West or take part of Pakistan-controlled Kashmir.

The Deputy Prime Minister and Foreign Minister of Pakistan said that his country would spare no effort in achieving a peaceful settlement of its internal problems consistent with the will of its people and its territorial integrity, provided it was free from foreign pressure.

Later on 13 December 1971, a draft resolution sponsored by Italy and Japan was put before the Council.

By the preamble to this text, the Council, keeping in mind the Security Council's responsibilities under the Charter, would, among other things: (a) note the Assembly's resolution of 7 December 1971, note with appreciation Pakistan's reply and note further India's reply; (b) express grave concern that hostilities continued, which constituted an immediate threat to international peace and security; (c) recognize the need to deal with the issues which had given rise to the hostilities and that a lasting solution must be based on a political settlement in Pakistan which respected the rights and interests of its people; (d) recall certain provisions of the Declaration on the Strengthening of International Security; and (e) recognize the need to take immediate measures to end hostilities and secure withdrawal of armed forces.

By the operative provisions of the two-power proposal, the Security Council would: (1) call on Member States to refrain from any action or threat of action likely to worsen the situation in the Indo-Pakistan subcontinent or to endanger international peace; (2) call on all parties concerned to take forthwith, as a first step, all measures for an immediate cease-fire and cessation of all hostilities; (3) urge India and Pakistan to disengage and withdraw so as to end the confrontation and return to normalcy; (4) call for immediate steps for a comprehensive political settlement; (5) call on States to co-operate with the Secretary-General in aiding the East Pakistan refugees; (6) call on all parties concerned to safeguard the lives and well-being of the civilian population in the area and to ensure full observance of all the Geneva Conventions of 1949; (7) decide to appoint, with the consent of India and Pakistan, a committee composed of three Security Council members to assist them in bringing about normalcy in the area of conflict; (8) ask the Secretary-General to keep the Council informed; and (9) decide to remain seized of the matter.

On 15 December 1971, the President appealed to the Security Council members to reach a positive decision as soon as possible because the situation in the subcontinent was deteriorating and innocent lives were being lost.

The Deputy Prime Minister and Foreign Minister of Pakistan declared that the Security Council had failed shamefully: it had procrastinated, it had failed to end aggression and it had denied justice to Pakistan. He said he was leaving the Council because he would not be a party to legalizing aggression and military occupation.

The representative of Tunisia, who had been invited to participate in the debate without the right to vote, said that the population of East Pakistan should exercise its democratic rights within the framework of Pakistan.

At a meeting held on the night of 15 December 1971, the representative of China said that the three USSR vetoes were cast with the aim of marking time so as to shield India in its occupation of East Pakistan. The object was to strengthen the USSR position in its confrontation with another super-power in the Middle East.

The representative of Ceylon, who participated in the discussion without the right to vote, urged a cease-fire, negotiations between the Government of Pakistan and the leaders of East Pakistan, and subsequent withdrawal of forces; if the result were a withdrawal of Pakistan from East Pakistan, this should be done with honour and dignity.

The representative of the USSR said that power in East Pakistan must be transferred to the elected representatives of the people of that land. He rebutted the criticism of the USSR position voiced by the representative of China.

A draft resolution was put before the Council by Poland. By this, as subsequently revised, the Council, gravely concerned over the military conflict on the Indian subcontinent which constituted an immediate threat to international peace and security and having heard the Indian Foreign Minister and Pakistan's Deputy Prime Minister, would set forth a schedule for: transfer of authority over East Pakistan to those elected in December 1970; a cease-fire; withdrawal of Pakistan troops as well as West Pakistan civilian personnel, followed by Indian withdrawal from East Pakistan; a voluntary return to their homes, under United Nations supervision, of people from East Pakistan to the West and vice versa; and negotiations between India and Pakistan.

The representative of Pakistan deplored the suggestion of Ceylon that East Pakistan should be allowed to secede. He also asserted that the Polish draft resolution would have Pakistan withdraw from East Pakistan, where a transfer of power would then be effected under Indian occupation.

Poland's spokesman responded that under his proposal power in East Pakistan would be transferred to representatives who had been elected in 1970 without duress. The Polish draft resolution provided for the withdrawal of Indian troops as well.

The representative of Argentina pointed out that the General Assembly, by the terms of its resolution of 7 December 1971, might resume its consideration of the question. He felt the provision to this effect would be relevant if the Council did not reach a decision and that the Assembly debate would fix responsibility.

The Syrian Arab Republic then proposed a draft resolution by which the Council, expressing grave concern at the situation in the India-Pakistan subcontinent which was an immediate threat to peace, and noting the General Assembly resolution of 7 December, would: (1) urge Pakistan to release all political prisoners so that the elected representatives of East Pakistan could resume their mandate; (2) decide on an immediate cease-fire and withdrawal of forces to their own sides of the border and of the cease-fire line in Jammu and Kashmir; and (3) request the Secretary-General to appoint a special representative to supervise the above operations and assist in a settlement between the Government of Pakistan and the elected representatives of East Pakistan and in establishing the conditions for a voluntary return of refugees and the normalizing of relations between India and Pakistan.

Also presented to the Council was a draft resolution sponsored by France and the United Kingdom.

By the preamble to this text, the Security Council would: (a) express grave concern at the situation in South Asia, which constituted a threat to international peace and security; (b) keep in mind its responsibilities under the United Nations Charter; (c) recognize the urgent need to deal effectively with the basic causes of the current conflict and that any lasting solution must include a political settlement that respected the fundamental rights and interests of the people; (d) indicate deep distress at the enormity of human suffering that had occurred and resulted in the wholesale displacement of millions of people from East Pakistan; and (*e*) express grave concern that measures should be taken to preserve human life and observe the 1949 Geneva Conventions.

By the operative part of the text put forward by France and the United Kingdom, the Security Council would: (1) call for an immediate cease-fire to remain in effect until disengagement leading to withdrawal of forces had taken effect; (2) call for the conclusion of a comprehensive political settlement in accordance with the wishes of the people concerned as declared through their elected and acknowledged representatives; (3) call on Member States to refrain from action which might aggravate the situation; (4) call on all concerned to protect human life and to observe the 1949 Geneva Conventions as regards protection of the wounded and sick, prisoners of war and the civilian population; (5) call for full international assistance in relief of the suffering of the refugees and in their return home; (6) invite the Secretary-General to appoint a special representative to lend his good offices, in particular for the solution of humanitarian problems; (7) ask the Secretary-General to report to the Council on implementation.

Next, the USSR introduced a draft resolution. By this, the Council, gravely concerned by the conflict in the Indo-Pakistan subcontinent which was an immediate threat to international peace and security, would: (1) call for an immediate cease-fire; (2) call for the simultaneous conclusion of a political settlement in accordance with the wishes of the people of East Pakistan, as declared through their already elected representatives; (3) call on all concerned to take all measures necessary to preserve human life and to observe the 1949 Geneva Conventions; (4) request the Secretary-General to report on implementation; and (5) decide to continue to discuss the further measures to be taken to restore peace in the whole area.

Italy announced the Italian-Japanese draft resolution would not be pressed to a vote.

On 16 December, the representative of China circulated a statement by his Government charging that India was seeking to destroy Pakistan so as to become a sub-super-power that would assist the USSR in committing aggression against Asia.

When the Council met on that day, the representative of India read the text of a statement by his Prime Minister to the effect that, as the Pakistan armed forces had surrendered in Bangladesh and Bangladesh was free, it was pointless to continue the conflict. India, which had no territorial ambitions, had ordered its armed forces to cease fire on the western front at 2000 hours (India Standard Time) on 17 December.

The representative of Saudi Arabia said that owing to the policies of the great powers which paid no heed to the cause of peace and justice, the United Nations had been reduced to a shadow and consultations in the Council to a farce. Secession brought about by intervention from outside was not self-determination. He suggested negotiations in another Asian country between India and Pakistan, as well as talks between East and West Pakistan.

The representative of Somalia asked what proposals India had in mind for withdrawing its armed forces from East and West Pakistan.

The Foreign Minister of India said that his Government's answer to this question was on record, but that its proposal for a cease-fire should have priority now.

At a second meeting on 16 December 1971, the USSR said that, in the light of India's decision to cease fire on both the eastern and western fronts, the draft resolutions submitted earlier had lost their point. It therefore withdrew its own text submitted on 15 December, and introduced a new USSR draft resolution.

By the new text, the Council, for the purpose of restoration of peace on the Indostan subcontinent, would: (1) welcome the cessation of hostilities in East Pakistan and express the hope that the cease-fire would be observed by both sides which would guarantee transfer of power there to the elected representatives of the people and appropriate settlement of problems related to the conflict; (2) call for an immediate cease-fire in the West; and (3) call on Member States to refrain from any action which would impede normalization of the situation in the Indostan subcontinent.

The representative of the United States also introduced a new draft resolution, co-sponsored by Japan. By this text as subsequently revised, the Council, gravely concerned with the situation in the India-Pakistan subcontinent which constituted an immediate threat to peace and security, and noting the General Assembly's resolution of 7 December 1971 and the statement of the Indian Foreign Minister that India had no territorial ambitions, would: (1) demand strict observance of the cease-fire followed by disengagement and leading to prompt withdrawal of armed forces from all occupied territories; (2) call on Member States to refrain from aggravating the situation; (3) call on all concerned to take all measures necessary to preserve human life and to observe the 1949 Geneva Conventions; (4) call for international aid to relieve suffering and help refugees return to their homes; (5) invite the Secretary-General to appoint a special representative to lend his good offices in solving humanitarian problems; (6) ask the Secretary-General to keep the Council informed on implementation; and (7) decide to discuss further measures to restore peace to the area.

The Council met again on 21 December 1971. The President announced that agreement had been reached on a compromise resolution sponsored by the following six members: Argentina, Burundi, Japan, Nicaragua, Sierra Leone and Somalia.

The six-power resolution was adopted by the Council by 13 votes to 0, with 2 abstentions (Poland and the USSR), as resolution 307(1971).

By the preamble to the resolution, the Council, having discussed the grave situation in the subcontinent, which remained a threat to international peace and security, noted the General Assembly's resolution of 7 December 1971, the replies and statements relating to the cease-fire by India and Pakistan and the fact that a cease-fire prevailed. It then, by the operative part of the resolution: (1) demanded that a cessation of all hostilities in all areas of conflict remain in effect until withdrawals took place, as soon as practicable, of all armed forces to their respective territories and to positions which fully respected the cease-fire line in Jammu and Kashmir supervised by the United Nations Military Observer Group in India and Pakistan (UNMOGIP); (2) called upon all Member States to refrain from any action which might aggravate the situation; (3) called upon all those concerned to take all measures necessary to preserve human life and for the observance of the Geneva Conventions of 1949; (4) called for international assistance in the relief of suffering and the rehabilitation of refugees and their return in safety and dignity to their homes; (5) authorized the Secretary-General to appoint, if necessary, a special representative to lend his good offices for the solution of humanitarian problems; (6) requested the Secretary-General to keep the Council informed without delay on developments relating to the implementation of the resolution; (7) decided to remain actively seized of the matter.

Prior to the vote, the President of the Council, referring to the provision of the text calling for observance of the the 1949 Geneva Conventions, mentioned rumours of the danger of retaliatory action in Dacca.

Following the vote, Somalia made a statement on behalf of the sponsors of the six-power text in explanation of certain aspects of the resolution, emphasizing in particular that India and Pakistan had subscribed to it in general. It was understood that in the eastern theatre, foreign troops were to be withdrawn as soon as practicable, while in the western theatre there was to be disengagement leading without delay to withdrawals. India's disclaimer of territorial ambitions was noted by the sponsors, who further considered that in implementing the resolution, the parties might make any mutually acceptable arrangement or adjustment.

In explanation of his vote, the representative of the Syrian Arab Republic, while supporting the resolution, voiced serious reservations over the fact that it deferred withdrawals to the uncertain future. He appealed to the parties to stop individual or collective reprisals.

The representative of China said that, although he had voted in favour of the draft, he was highly dissatisfied with it because it did not condemn the open aggression against and dismemberment of a sovereign State by the Indian expansionists with the support of the USSR Government.

The USSR and Poland said that the resolution contained provisions with which they could not agree, notably the reference to the General Assembly's resolution (2793(XXVI)) of 7 December 1971. Consequently, they had abstained in the voting although they noted the merits of certain provisions of the resolution just adopted, especially the ones dealing with the cease-fire, withdrawals and humanitarian measures.

The representative of the USSR also drew attention to a statement of 18 December issued by his Ministry of Foreign Affairs, welcoming the cessation of hostilities which created the conditions for a normal transfer of power to the elected representatives of the people of East Pakistan.

The representative of Pakistan said that the Council had failed signally in dealing with the situation in accordance with the principles of the United Nations Charter. Pakistan had been subjected to open and unconcealed aggression and the Council had failed to prevent or stop the blatant breach of the peace. An untold number of lives had been lost and the Council had done nothing to save them. The resolution as adopted was weak. This would cause reappraisal of the Council's relevance to issues of war and peace.

The Pakistan representative defined his Government's understanding that Indian troops were to withdraw from East and West Pakistan territory alike. The United Nations, he said, could not violate the territorial integrity of a Member State. Consequently it was precluded from according even implicit recognition to the result of any attempt to dismember Pakistan. Also, the cease-fire line in Jammu and Kashmir remained as established by the Karachi Agreement of 1949.[16] He said that acts of genocide were being carried out in East Pakistan since the fall of Dacca on 13 December. Lastly, the resolution did not embody any amicable settlement of the conflict between the two parties.

The Foreign Minister of India questioned the relevance of the reference in the adopted resolu-

[16]See footnote 11.

tion to the General Assembly's resolution of 7 December 1971 and regretted that the Council's resolution ignored the existence of Bangladesh and of the Bangladesh Government. The Indian armed forces would withdraw from Bangladesh as soon as practicable, but their presence there was necessary for such purposes as the protection of Pakistan troops who had surrendered and for prevention of reprisals and the like. Pakistan no longer had the right to keep any troops in Bangladesh, and any attempt by Pakistan to enter Bangladesh by force would create a threat to peace and security and could endanger stability again. As for the western theatre, the international frontier between India and Pakistan was well defined, but during the hostilities certain areas of India and Pakistan had come under the control of the opposing forces. India accepted the principle of withdrawals and wished to negotiate and settle the matter with Pakistan as early as possible. The State of Jammu and Kashmir was an integral part of India. However, in order to avoid bloodshed, India had respected the cease-fire line supervised by UNMOGIP. There was a need to make some adjustments in the cease-fire line, a subject that India would discuss and settle with Pakistan. India had no territorial ambitions and would like a similar declaration from Pakistan.

The representative of Pakistan rejected the contention of the Foreign Minister of India that Pakistan had no right to keep troops in so-called Bangladesh. East Pakistan was an integral part of the territory of Pakistan, and the juridical status and the inalienable rights of the people of Pakistan could not be altered in any manner by an act of aggression and military occupation. The withdrawal of occupying armed forces could not be conditional upon negotiations. It was only after withdrawal that negotiations could really take place. As for the statement of the Indian representative regarding territorial ambitions, Pakistan had no territorial claims on Indian territory but did not consider Jammu and Kashmir to be part of India; it was disputed territory whose future would be settled by agreement under the aegis of the Security Council.

Reports and communications to Security Council (December 1971)

On 21 December, shortly after the adoption of Security Council resolution 307(1971), the Secretary-General issued a report on the implementation of that resolution and of General Assembly resolution 2790(XXVI) of 6 December 1971 dealing with aid to East Pakistan refugees. Referring to efforts to reactivate the relief operation in the area, he stated that United Nations personnel in Dacca would be strengthened and as soon as possible would reassess the requirements for international assistance in the light of the changed situation. Significant amounts of supplies which had been diverted to nearby staging areas when the hostilities broke out made possible a prompt response to the needs of the distressed population. United Nations Children's Fund and World Food Programme shipments were *en route.* It was anticipated that the United Nations High Commissioner for Refugees in his capacity as focal point (for co-ordination of United Nations assistance to East Pakistan refugees), as well as the United Nations Relief Operation in Dacca (UNROD), would henceforward assign high priority in their work to the repatriation from India and the resettlement of refugees.

The Secretary-General reported United Nations losses sustained during the hostilities, including the death of two captains and the wounding of four other crew members of vessels transporting humanitarian supplies under United Nations auspices. The Secretary-General also indicated that he was giving serious consideration to the provision in the Security Council's resolution of 21 December concerning the appointment of a special representative to lend his good offices for the solution of humanitarian problems.

In a report of 22 December, the Secretary-General, on the basis of information from UNMOGIP, reported on the observance in Jammu and Kashmir of the cease-fire as called for by the resolution. The situation along the cease-fire line in Jammu and Kashmir was generally quiet. The Secretary-General said he was in no position to report on the observance of the cease-fire in other areas of the subcontinent, since the United Nations had no military observation machinery outside Jammu and Kashmir. The Chief Military Observer was endeavouring to return the functioning of UNMOGIP to normal.

Addenda to the report were issued on 29 December 1971 and 4 January 1972; the latter indicated that the cease-fire in Jammu and Kashmir appeared relatively stable.

On 21 December 1971, the representative of Pakistan circulated an appeal from President Zulfikar Ali Bhutto to the heads of State of the members of the Security Council, drawing attention to reports of mass murders and other atrocities in areas of Pakistan under Indian military occupation. The appeal suggested an immediate approach to India to stop the violence and comply with humanitarian principles.

The representative of China on 24 and again on 28 December, in letters to the President of the Security Council, similarly referred to persecution and massacres of the Pakistan people being carried out by Indian troops and East Pakistan rebels under their command. He asked the President of the Security Council to request the Secretary-General to issue an immediate report on the implementation of the relevant portions of the Council's resolution of 21 December 1971.

On 25 December 1971, the Secretary-General reported that, in accordance with the terms of the Security Council's resolution of 21 December and in the light of developments in the subcontinent, he had appointed Vittorio Winspeare Guicciardi as his special representative for humanitarian good offices and had asked him to proceed to the subcontinent immediately.

On 27 December, the Foreign Secretary of Pakistan replied to a letter of 22 December of the Secretary-General conveying the text of the Security Council resolution of 21 December. He noted the Security Council's demand for a cessation of hostilities and stated that only the cessation of aggression by India in East Pakistan and in all other areas of conflict could restore peace in the subcontinent.

Complaints of cease-fire violations by Indian and Pakistan armed forces in Jammu and Kashmir and along the international border to the south were received by the Secretary-General from the Pakistan and Indian representatives on 23 and 30 December, respectively.

In a letter of 30 December 1971, the representative of Pakistan stated that his Government on 27 December had initiated discussions with Sheikh Mujibur Rahman.

On 31 December 1971, Pakistan conveyed to the Secretary-General its concern over reports of official Indian statements that trials of high government and civilian officials of the East Pakistan Government, as well as of certain prisoners of war, were contemplated by the "Bangladesh authorities." Such action would constitute a flagrant violation of the Geneva Conventions of 1949 and of the Security Council's resolution of 21 December, Pakistan declared. India was the sole "detaining power" with respect to the prisoners of war, and was also the "occupying power" with respect to civilians. Pakistan requested the intervention of the Secretary-General in this matter, as well as action through his special representative.

DOCUMENTARY REFERENCES

*Communications concerning
India-Pakistan question*

COMMUNICATIONS TO SECURITY COUNCIL
(1 JANUARY–2 SEPTEMBER 1971)

S/10084. Letter of 21 January 1971 from Pakistan.
S/10094, S/10100. Letters of 28 January and 2 February 1971 from India.
S/10102, S/10116. Letters of 5 and 13 February 1971 from Pakistan.
S/10171. Letter of 8 April 1971 from India.
S/10193. Letter of 10 May 1971 from Pakistan.
S/10273. Letter of 20 July 1971 from India.
S/10304. Letter of 2 September 1971 from Pakistan.

*Decisions of Security Council
and General Assembly*

SECURITY COUNCIL DECISION OF 6 DECEMBER 1971

Security Council, meetings 1606-1608.

S/10380, S/10383, S/10390. Letters of 29 October and 4 and 16 November 1971 from Pakistan.
S/10410 and Add.1. Report of 3 December 1971 of Secretary-General, and addendum.
S/10411. Letter of 4 December 1971 from Argentina, Belgium, Burundi, Italy, Japan, Nicaragua, Somalia, United Kingdom and United States (request to convene Council).
S/10412 and Add.1,2. Report of 4 December 1971 by Secretary-General on situation along cease-fire line in Kashmir, and addenda.
S/10413. Letter of 4 December 1971 from Tunisia (supporting request to convene Council).
S/10414. Letter of 4 December 1971 from Tunisia (request to participate in Council's discussion).
S/10415. Letter of 4 December 1971 from India (transmitting letter of 4 December 1971 from "Leader, Bangladesh delegation").
S/10416. United States: draft resolution, rejected by Council,
having received the negative vote of a permanent member, on 4 December 1971, meeting 1606, by vote of 11 in favour (Argentina, Belgium, Burundi, China, Italy, Japan, Nicaragua, Sierra Leone, Somalia, Syrian Arab Republic, United States) to 2 against (Poland, USSR), with 2 abstentions (France, United Kingdom).
S/10417. Belgium, Italy, Japan: draft resolution.
S/10418. USSR: draft resolution, rejected by Council on 5 December 1971, meeting 1607, by vote of 2 in favour (Poland, USSR) to 1 against (China), with 12 abstentions (Argentina, Belgium, Burundi, France, Italy, Japan, Nicaragua, Sierra Leone, Somalia, Syrian Arab Republic, United Kingdom, United States).
S/10419. Argentina, Burundi, Nicaragua, Sierra Leone, Somalia: draft resolution.
S/10421. China: draft resolution.
S/10422. Letter of 5 December 1971 from USSR (transmitting TASS statement of 5 December 1971).
S/10423. Argentina, Belgium, Italy, Japan, Nicaragua, Sierra Leone, Somalia: draft resolution, rejected by Council, having received the negative vote of a permanent member, on 5 December 1971, meeting 1607, by vote of 11 in favour (Argentina, Belgium, Burundi, China, Italy, Japan, Nicaragua, Sierra Leone, Somalia, Syrian Arab Republic, United States) to 2 against (Poland, USSR), with 2 abstentions (France, United Kingdom).
S/10424. Letter of 5 December 1971 from Saudi Arabia (request to participate in Council's discussion).
S/10425. Belgium, Italy, Japan, Nicaragua, Sierra Leone: draft resolution.
S/10426 and Rev.1. USSR: amendment and revised amendment to 5-power draft resolution, S/10425.
S/10428. USSR: draft resolution.
S/10429. Argentina, Burundi, Japan, Nicaragua, Sierra Leone, Somalia: draft resolution.

RESOLUTION 303(1971), as proposed by 6 powers, S/10429, adopted by Council on 6 December 1971, meeting 1608, by 11 votes to 0, with 4 abstentions (France, Poland, USSR, United Kingdom).

The Security Council,

Having considered the item on the agenda of its 1606th meeting, as contained in document S/Agenda/1606,*

Taking into account that the lack of unanimity of its permanent members at the 1606th and 1607th meetings of the Security Council has prevented it from exercising its primary responsibility for the maintenance of international peace and security,

Decides to refer the question contained in document S/Agenda/1606 to the General Assembly at its twenty-sixth session, as provided for in Assembly resolution 377 A (V) of 3 November 1950.

*The item on the agenda of the Council (S/Agenda/1606) read as follows:

"(a) Letter dated 4 December 1971 from the Permanent Representatives of Argentina, Belgium, Burundi, Italy, Japan, Nicaragua, Somalia, the United Kingdom of Great Britain and Northern Ireland and the United States of America addressed to the President of the Security Council (S/10411);

"(b) Report of the Secretary-General (S/10410)."

REPORTS OF SECRETARY-GENERAL OF 7 DECEMBER 1971

S/10432 and Add.1-11 (A/8556 and Add.1-11). Report of 7 December 1971 of Secretary-General on situation along cease-fire line in Kashmir, and addenda.

S/10433 (A/8557). Report of 7 December 1971 of Secretary-General on his efforts to evacuate United Nations and other international personnel from Dacca.

CONSIDERATION BY GENERAL ASSEMBLY

General Assembly—26th session
Plenary meetings 2002, 2003, 2031.

A/8401/Add.1. Introduction to report of Secretary-General on work of the Organization, September 1971, paras. 177-191.

A/8402. Report of Security Council, 16 June 1970–15 June 1971, Chapter 15.

A/8555. Letter of 6 December 1971 from President of Security Council (transmitting text of Security Council resolution 303(1971)).

A/L.647 and Rev.1. Algeria, Argentina, Brazil, Burundi, Cameroon, Chad, Colombia, Costa Rica, Ecuador, Ghana, Guatemala, Haiti, Honduras, Indonesia, Italy, Ivory Coast, Japan, Jordan, Liberia, Libyan Arab Republic, Morocco, Netherlands, Nicaragua, Panama, Paraguay, Sierra Leone, Somalia, Spain, Sudan, Tunisia, Uruguay, Yemen, Zaire, Zambia: draft resolution and revision.

A/L.648. USSR: draft resolution.

RESOLUTION 2793(XXVI), as proposed by 34 powers, A/L.647/Rev.1, adopted by Assembly on 7 December 1971, meeting 2003, by roll-call vote of 104 to 11, with 10 abstentions, as follows:

In favour: Albania, Algeria, Argentina, Australia, Austria, Bahrain, Barbados, Belgium, Bolivia, Botswana, Brazil, Burundi, Cameroon, Canada, Central African Republic, Ceylon, Chad, China, Colombia, Congo, Costa Rica, Cyprus, Dahomey, Dominican Republic, Ecuador, Egypt, El Salvador, Ethiopia, Fiji, Finland, Gabon, Gambia, Ghana, Greece, Guatemala, Guyana, Haiti, Honduras, Iceland, Indonesia, Iran, Iraq, Ireland, Israel, Italy, Ivory Coast, Jamaica, Japan, Jordan, Kenya, Khmer Republic, Kuwait, Laos, Lebanon, Liberia, Libyan Arab Republic, Luxembourg, Madagascar, Malaysia, Mali, Malta, Mauritania, Mexico, Morocco, Netherlands, New Zealand, Nicaragua, Niger, Nigeria, Norway, Pakistan, Panama, Paraguay, People's Democratic Republic of Yemen, Peru, Philippines, Portugal, Qatar, Romania, Rwanda, Saudi Arabia, Sierra Leone, Somalia, South Africa, Spain, Sudan, Swaziland, Sweden, Syrian Arab Republic, Thailand, Togo, Trinidad and Tobago, Tunisia, Turkey, Uganda, United Republic of Tanzania, United States, Upper Volta, Uruguay, Venezuela, Yemen, Yugoslavia, Zaire, Zambia.

Against: Bhutan, Bulgaria, Byelorussian SSR, Cuba, Czechoslovakia, Hungary, India, Mongolia, Poland, Ukrainian SSR, USSR.

Abstaining: Afghanistan, Chile, Denmark, France, Malawi, Nepal, Oman, Senegal, Singapore, United Kingdom.

The General Assembly,

Noting the reports of the Secretary-General of 3 and 4 December 1971 and the letter from the President of the Security Council transmitting the text of Council resolution 303(1971) of 6 December 1971,

Gravely concerned that hostilities have broken out between India and Pakistan which constitute an immediate threat to international peace and security,

Recognizing the need to deal appropriately at a subsequent stage, within the framework of the Charter of the United Nations, with the issues which have given rise to the hostilities,

Convinced that an early political solution would be necessary for the restoration of conditions of normalcy in the area of conflict and for the return of the refugees to their homes,

Mindful of the provisions of the Charter, in particular of Article 2, paragraph 4,

Recalling the Declaration on the Strengthening of International Security, particularly paragraphs 4, 5 and 6,

Recognizing further the need to take immediate measures to bring about an immediate cessation of hostilities between India and Pakistan and effect a withdrawal of their armed forces to their own side of the India-Pakistan borders,

Mindful of the purposes and principles of the Charter and of the General Assembly's responsibilities under the relevant provisions of the Charter and of Assembly resolution 377 A (V) of 3 November 1950,

1. *Calls upon* the Governments of India and Pakistan to take forthwith all measures for an immediate cease-fire and withdrawal of their armed forces on the territory of the other to their own side of the India-Pakistan borders;

2. *Urges* that efforts be intensified in order to bring about, speedily and in accordance with the purposes and principles of the Charter of the United Nations, conditions necessary for the voluntary return of the East Pakistan refugees to their homes;

3. *Calls* for the full co-operation of all States with the Secretary-General for rendering assistance to and relieving the distress of those refugees;

4. *Urges* that every effort be made to safeguard the lives and well-being of the civilian population in the area of conflict;

5. *Requests* the Secretary-General to keep the General Assembly and the Security Council promptly and currently informed on the implementation of the present resolution;

6. *Decides* to follow the question closely and to meet again should the situation so demand;

7. *Calls upon* the Security Council to take appropriate action in the light of the present resolution.

A/8556 and Add.1-11 (S/10432 and Add.1-11). Report of 7 December 1971 of Secretary-General on situation along cease-fire line in Kashmir, and addenda.

A/8557 (S/10433). Report of 7 December 1971 of Secretary-General on his efforts to evacuate United Nations and other international personnel from Dacca.

A/8567 (S/10440). Letter of 9 December 1971 from Pakistan.

A/8580 (S/10445). Letter of 12 December 1971 from India.

A/8587 (S/10452). Note verbale of 13 December 1971 from Pakistan.

A/8614 (S/10460). Letter of 16 December 1971 from Libyan Arab Republic.

A/8637/Rev.1 (S/10463/Rev.1). Letter of 18 December 1971 from USSR.

A/8640 (S/10466). Report of 21 December 1971 of Secretary-General concerning implementation of General Assembly resolution 2790(XXVI) and Security Council resolution 307(1971).

A/8641 (S/10468). Letter of 21 December 1971 from Pakistan.

A/8644 (S/10485), A/8645 (S/10486). Notes verbales of 15 and 16 December 1971 from Pakistan.

A/8429. Resolutions adopted by General Assembly during its 26th session, 21 September–22 December 1971. Other decisions, p. 21.

SECURITY COUNCIL DECISION OF 21 DECEMBER 1971

Security Council meetings 1611, 1613-1617, 1621.

S/10432 and Add.1-11 (A/8556 and Add.1-11). Report of 7 December 1971 of Secretary-General on situation along cease-fire line in Kashmir, and addenda.

S/10440 (A/8567). Letter of 9 December 1971 from Pakistan.

S/10444. Letter of 12 December 1971 from United States (request to convene Council).

S/10445 (A/8580). Letter of 12 December 1971 from India.

S/10446 and Rev.1. United States: draft resolution and revision, rejected by Council, having received the negative vote of a permanent member, on 13 December 1971, meeting 1613, by vote of 11 in favour (Argentina, Belgium, Burundi, China, Italy, Japan, Nicaragua, Sierra Leone, Somalia, Syrian Arab Republic, United States) to 2 against (Poland, USSR), with 2 abstentions (France, United Kingdom).

S/10451. Italy and Japan: draft resolution.

S/10452 (A/8587). Note verbale of 13 December 1971 from Pakistan.

S/10453 and Rev.1. Poland: draft resolution and revision.

S/10454. Letter of 15 December 1971 from Ceylon (request to participate in Council's discussion).

S/10455. France and United Kingdom: draft resolution.

S/10456. Syrian Arab Republic: draft resolution.

S/10457, S/10458. USSR: draft resolutions.

S/10459 and Rev.1. Japan and United States: draft resolution and revision.

S/10460 (A/8614). Letter of 16 December 1971 from Libyan Arab Republic.

S/10461. Letter of 16 December 1971 from China.

S/10463/Rev.1 (A/8637/Rev.1). Letter of 18 December 1971 from USSR.

S/10465. Argentina, Burundi, Japan, Nicaragua, Sierra Leone, Somalia: draft resolution.

RESOLUTION 307(1971), as proposed by 6 powers, S/10465, adopted by Council on 21 December 1971, meeting 1621, by 13 votes to 0, with 2 abstentions (Poland, USSR).

The Security Council,

Having discussed the grave situation in the subcontinent, which remains a threat to international peace and security,

Noting General Assembly resolution 2793(XXVI) of 7 December 1971,

Noting the reply of the Government of Pakistan on 9 December 1971,

Noting the reply of the Government of India on 12 December 1971,

Having heard the statements of the Deputy Prime Minister of Pakistan and the Foreign Minister of India,

Noting further the statement made at the 1616th meeting of the Security Council by the Foreign Minister of India containing a unilateral declaration of a cease-fire in the western theatre,

Noting Pakistan's agreement to the cease-fire in the western theatre with effect from 17 December 1971,

Noting that consequently a cease-fire and a cessation of hostilities prevail,

1. *Demands* that a durable cease-fire and cessation of all hostilities in all areas of conflict be strictly observed and remain in effect until withdrawals take place, as soon as practicable, of all armed forces to their respective territories and to positions which fully respect the cease-fire line in Jammu and Kashmir supervised by the United Nations Military Observer Group in India and Pakistan;

2. *Calls upon* all Member States to refrain from any action which may aggravate the situation in the subcontinent or endanger international peace;

3. *Calls upon* all those concerned to take all measures necessary to preserve human life and for the observance of the Geneva Conventions of 1949 and to apply in full their provisions as regards the protection of the wounded and sick, prisoners of war and civilian population;

4. *Calls for* international assistance in the relief of suffering and the rehabilitation of refugees and their return in safety and dignity to their homes, and for full co-operation with the Secretary-General to that effect;

5. *Authorizes* the Secretary-General to appoint if necessary a special representative to lend his good offices for the solution of humanitarian problems;

6. *Requests* the Secretary-General to keep the Council informed without delay on developments relating to the implementation of the present resolution;

7. *Decides* to remain seized of the matter and to keep it under active consideration.

Reports and communications to
Security Council (December 1971)

REPORTS OF SECRETARY-GENERAL

S/10466 (A/8640). Report of 21 December 1971 of Secretary-General concerning implementation of General Assembly resolution 2790(XXVI) and Security Council resolution 307(1971).

S/10467 and Add.1,2. Report of 22 December 1971 of Secretary-General on implementation of Security Council resolution 307(1971).

S/10473. Report of 25 December 1971 of Secretary-General concerning implementation of Security Council resolution 307(1971).

COMMUNICATIONS TO SECURITY COUNCIL

S/10468 (A/8641), S/10472. Letters of 21 and 23 December 1971 from Pakistan.

S/10474. Letter of 24 December 1971 from China.

S/10475. Letter of 27 December 1971 from Pakistan.

S/10476. Letter of 28 December 1971 from China.

S/10485 (A/8644), S/10486 (A/8645). Notes verbales of 15 and 16 December 1971 from Pakistan.

S/10487. Letter of 30 December 1971 from Pakistan.

S/10488. Letter of 30 December 1971 from India.

S/10490. Letter of 31 December 1971 from Pakistan.

S/10493, S/10497. Letters of 3 and 7 January 1972 from India.

Questions pertaining to Korea

In response to a General Assembly request of 7 December 1970,[17] the United Nations Commission for the Unification and Rehabilitation of Korea (UNCURK) submitted a report to the Secretary-General covering the period 14 August 1970 to 4 August 1971. The Assembly had asked UNCURK to keep it informed on the situation in the area and on the results of its efforts through regular reports.

The Commission stated in the report that while there was a noticeable decrease in the number of incidents along the demilitarized zone, the Republic of Korea had reported some 20 significant

[17] See Y.U.N., 1970, pp. 211-12, text of resolution 2668(XXV).

incidents south of the military demarcation line in the demilitarized zone, as well as engagements with North Korean agents in the rear areas of the Republic of Korea.

The report noted that the question of Korean reunification had featured prominently during the 1971 presidential and parliamentary elections in the Republic of Korea; President Park Chung Hee of the Republic of Korea had stated that he was giving serious consideration to approaches other than political and diplomatic, such as steps of a humanitarian nature, for easing tensions between North and South Korea, and had also declared that if the North Korean régime recognized United Nations competence, authority and objectives with respect to the Korean problem his Government would not be opposed to the presence of a representative of the Democratic People's Republic of Korea at United Nations deliberations on that question.

The Commission recalled that on 12 April 1971, the Foreign Minister of the Democratic People's Republic of Korea had announced a peaceful unification programme which suggested, *inter alia*, the following points as a means of achieving the unification of Korea;

(1) withdrawal of United States forces from South Korea;

(2) reduction of forces in North and South Korea to 100,000 or less each after that withdrawal;

(3) abolition of all "subordinate treaties and agreements" concluded by South Korea;

(4) establishment of a unified central government through free North-South general elections on a democratic basis, without outside interference, following United States withdrawal;

(5) guarantee of freedom of political activity for the North-South general elections for all persons and organizations throughout Korea and release of all political prisoners in South Korea;

(6) establishment of a North-South confederation, as a transitional measure while retaining the two differing social systems intact, if need be, prior to complete unification; or, if South Korea did not accept establishment of a unified democratic government through free North-South general elections, organization of a supreme national committee of both sides for mutual co-operation was suggested;

(7) promotion of trade and economic co-operation, as well as scientific, cultural, social and personal contacts between the people of both parts of Korea, or alternatively, in lieu of a confederation, establishment of a North-South economic committee for economic co-operation independently of the political problems for the time being;

(8) convocation of a political consultative meeting of both sides including all political parties and organizations at any given time and place.

The Commission further noted that the eight-point programme of the Democratic People's

Republic of Korea also formally proposed that "the representatives of political parties, public organizations and individual persons in North and South Korea sit together at Panmunjom or in a third country at any time to have a heart-to-heart consultation with each other."

Notwithstanding such moves by both sides, UNCURK stated, no real and meaningful progress had been made with respect to Korean unification. While the Government of the Republic of Korea had consistently co-operated with and accepted United Nations authority and General Assembly resolutions, the Democratic People's Republic of Korea had, on the other hand, consistently denied United Nations competence and authority to deal with the Korean question.

During August 1971, three separate items relating to Korea were proposed for the agenda of the General Assembly, whose twenty-sixth session was due to open on 21 September 1971. One item entitled "Withdrawal of United States and all other foreign forces occupying South Korea under the flag of the United Nations" was jointly proposed by the following 19 States: Algeria, Bulgaria, the Byelorussian SSR, the Congo, Cuba, Czechoslovakia, Guinea, Hungary, Iraq, Mauritania, Mongolia, the People's Democratic Republic of Yemen, Poland, Romania, Somalia, Sudan, the Syrian Arab Republic, the Ukrainian SSR and the USSR. An explanatory memorandum accompanying the proposal stated that the occupation of South Korea by foreign troops and their continued provocative acts against the Democratic People's Republic of Korea hindered peaceful Korean unification by the Korean people themselves and constituted a grave threat to peace in the whole region of the Far East. The memorandum also expressed support for the eight-point programme of peaceful unification proposed by the Democratic People's Republic of Korea.

A second item entitled "Dissolution of the United Nations Commission for the Unification and Rehabilitation of Korea" was proposed by the same 19 States and Mali.

An explanatory memorandum accompanying this proposal stated that the illegally established Commission served only United States interests in Korea and was a major obstacle to Korean unification, which was a domestic matter which should be solved by means of direct negotiations between the two parties in Korea.

Finally, the Secretary-General proposed the inclusion in the agenda of an item entitled "Question of Korea: report of the United Nations Commission for the Unification and Rehabilitation of Korea."

An explanatory memorandum stated that his request was in compliance with a communication dated 5 August 1971 from the Chairman of

UNCURK who, in transmitting the UNCURK report, had requested that it be transmitted to the General Assembly for its consideration should an item on the Korean question be included in the provisional agenda of the twenty-sixth (1971) session.

On 23 September 1971, the General Committee considered the requests for the inclusion of the three items in the agenda. On a proposal by the United Kingdom, the General Committee decided by a vote of 13 in favour to 9 against, with 2 abstentions, that the consideration of these three items should be deferred at the twenty-sixth (1971) session and that the items should be placed on the provisional agenda of the twenty-seventh (1972) session for consideration by the General Assembly at that session. The General Assembly discussed this recommendation of the General Committee at two plenary meetings.

Speaking against the recommendation of the General Committee were the following Members, among others: Albania, Algeria, Czechoslovakia, Guinea, Mali, Mongolia, Sierra Leone, Somalia, the USSR and the United Republic of Tanzania. Their arguments included the following.

The maintenance of foreign troops on Korean soil, the numerous acts of provocation against the Democratic People's Republic of Korea, a peace-loving State, and the escalation of military preparations in South Korea created an extremely serious situation and were converting the Far East region into one of the most dangerous hotbeds of war. UNCURK was an instrument of United States aggressive policies intervening in the internal affairs of the Korean people in the interests of outside forces.

While the first contact between the two Red Cross Societies of Korea, initiated by the Democratic People's Republic of Korea, was a promising event, these Members felt that if such contacts between North and South Koreans were to be facilitated, discussion at the current session was essential and representatives of both North and South Korea should be invited to participate.

Members supporting the General Committee's recommendation to include the item on Korea in the provisional agenda of the twenty-seventh (1972) session argued that consideration of the items should be deferred in view of the unprecedented significance of the talks recently begun between the two Red Cross Societies in Korea.

A debate at the current session was bound to have adverse and unhealthy effects on the atmosphere surrounding the talks. They maintained that if, prior to the twenty-seventh session in 1972, progress were made in dealing with the humanitarian aspects of the Korean problem, the atmosphere would be greatly improved for consideration by the General Assembly of the question of Korea at that session.

Speakers who shared this view included the representatives of Australia, Canada, Costa Rica, New Zealand, Saudi Arabia, Thailand, the United Kingdom and the United States.

On 25 September 1971, the General Assembly in three separate votes approved the General Committee's recommendation to defer consideration of the three Korean items at the 1971 session and to include them in the provisional agenda of the twenty-seventh (1972) session.

The voting was as follows:

–on the recommendation concerning the item entitled "Withdrawal of United States and all other foreign forces occupying South Korea under the flag of the United Nations," 68 in favour to 28 against, with 22 abstentions (by roll-call);

–on the recommendation concerning the item entitled "Dissolution of the United Nations Commission for the Unification and Rehabilitation of Korea," 68 in favour to 25 against, with 22 abstentions;

–on the recommendation concerning the item entitled "Question of Korea: report of the United Nations Commission for the Unification and Rehabilitation of Korea," 70 in favour to 21 against, with 23 abstentions.

DOCUMENTARY REFERENCES

General Assembly—26th session
General Committee, meetings 192, 193.
Plenary meeting 1938, 1939.

A/8401. Report of Secretary-General on work of the Organization, 16 June 1970–15 June 1971, Part One, Chapter IV J.
A/8402. Report of Security Council, 16 June 1970–15 June 1971, Chapter 16.
A/8427. Report of UNCURK (covering period 14 August 1970–4 August 1971).
A/8443 and Add.1. Letter of 21 August 1971 from Mongolia, and letter of 26 August 1971 from Algeria, Bulgaria, Byelorussian SSR, Congo, Cuba, Czechoslovakia, Guinea, Hungary, Iraq, Mauritania, People's Democratic Republic of Yemen, Poland, Romania, Somalia, Sudan, Syrian Arab Republic, Ukrainian

SSR and USSR (request for inclusion in agenda of item entitled: "Withdrawal of United States and all other foreign forces occupying South Korea under the flag of the United Nations").
A/8444 and Add.1,2. Letter of 21 August 1971 from Mongolia, and letters of 26 August 1971 from Algeria, Bulgaria, Byelorussian SSR, Congo, Cuba, Czechoslovakia, Guinea, Hungary, Iraq, Mali, Mauritania, People's Democratic Republic of Yemen, Poland, Romania, Somalia, Sudan, Syrian Arab Republic, Ukrainian SSR, and USSR (request for inclusion in agenda of item entitled: "Dissolution of the United Nations Commission for the Unification and Rehabilitation of Korea").
A/8445. Note by Secretary-General dated 23 August 1971 (proposal for inclusion in agenda of item entitled: "Question of Korea: report of the United Nations Commission for the Unification and Rehabilitation of Korea").

A/BUR/177 and Corr.1. Organization of 26th regular session of General Assembly, adoption of agenda and allocation of items. Memorandum by Secretary-General (containing draft provisional agenda).
A/8500. First report of General Committee, paragraph 18.

[*Item 106 of draft agenda* (Withdrawal of United States and all other foreign forces occupying South Korea under the flag of the United Nations), *item 107 of draft agenda* (Dissolution of the United Nations Commission for the Unification and Rehabilitation of Korea) and *item 108 of draft agenda* (Question of Korea: report of the United Nations Commission for the Unification and Rehabilitation of Korea) recommended for inclusion in provisional agenda of Assembly's 27th session by General Committee on 23 September 1971, meeting 193, by 13 votes to 9, with 2 abstentions.

Draft agenda items 106, 107 and 108 approved for inclusion in agenda of 27th session by General Assembly on 25 September 1971, meeting 1939, as follows:

(a) Item 106, by roll-call vote of 68 to 28, with 22 abstentions, as follows:

In favour: Argentina, Australia, Barbados, Belgium, Bolivia, Botswana, Brazil, Canada, Central African Republic, Chad, China, Colombia, Costa Rica, Dahomey, Denmark, Dominican Republic, Ecuador, El Salvador, Fiji, France, Gabon, Gambia, Ghana, Greece, Guatemala, Guyana, Haiti, Honduras, Iceland, Ireland, Italy, Ivory Coast, Jamaica, Japan, Jordan, Khmer Republic, Laos, Lesotho, Liberia, Luxembourg, Madagascar, Malawi, Malaysia, Malta, Mauritius, Morocco, Netherlands, New Zealand, Nicaragua, Niger, Norway, Panama, Paraguay, Peru, Philippines, Saudi Arabia, South Africa, Spain, Swaziland, Thailand, Togo, Turkey, United Kingdom, United States, Upper Volta, Uruguay, Venezuela, Zaire.

Against: Albania, Algeria, Bulgaria, Burundi, Byelorussian SSR, Chile, Congo, Cuba, Czechoslovakia, Egypt, Equatorial Guinea, Guinea, Hungary, India, Iraq, Libyan Arab Republic, Mali, Mauritania, Mongolia, People's Democratic Republic of Yemen, Poland, Romania, Sierra Leone, Somalia, Ukrainian SSR, USSR, United Republic of Tanzania, Yugoslavia.

Abstaining: Afghanistan, Austria, Bahrain, Burma, Cameroon, Ceylon, Cyprus, Ethiopia, Finland, Indonesia, Iran, Kuwait, Lebanon, Mexico, Nepal, Pakistan, Rwanda, Senegal, Singapore, Sweden, Tunisia, Uganda.

(b) Item 107, by 68 votes to 25, with 22 abstentions;
(c) Item 108, by 70 votes to 21, with 23 abstentions.]

A/8429. Resolutions adopted by General Assembly during its 26th session, 21 September–22 December 1971. Other decisions, p. 19.

Communications concerning the situation in and around the Viet-Nam area

During 1971, a number of communications were addressed to the President of the Security Council or to the Secretary-General which dealt with various aspects of the situation in and around the area of Viet-Nam.

Eight of these dealt largely with the subject of the military operations undertaken in Laos during February-March 1971 by units of the armed forces of the United States and the Republic of Viet-Nam. (For further details, see below.)

One of the other communications, from the USSR, transmitted the text of a statement on developments throughout Indo-China and other international problems. This was issued jointly in Hanoi, Democratic Republic of Viet-Nam, on 7 October 1971, by the President of the Presidium of the USSR Supreme Soviet and the First Secretary of the Central Committee of the Workers' Party of Viet-Nam, on behalf of the Governments of the USSR and the Democratic Republic of Viet-Nam. (For further details, see below.)

On 8 February 1971, the Permanent Observer of the Republic of Viet-Nam to the United Nations transmitted to the President of the Security Council the text of a message from the President of the Republic to "the people, soldiers and cadres on the operations carried out on 8 February 1971 by the armed forces of the Republic of Viet-Nam on Laotian territory."

The President stated that he had ordered the armed forces to attack North Viet-Namese bases situated on Laotian territory along the Viet-Nam/Laos border in an operation limited in both time and space, with the clear and unique objective of disrupting the supply and infiltration network of the North Viet-Namese troops situated in Laotian territory and used to launch attacks against the Republic of Viet-Nam. The President added that the Republic of Viet-Nam had always respected and continued to respect the independence, neutrality and sovereignty of Laos, had no territorial ambition whatsoever and had never interfered, and would never interfere, in the internal politics of Laos. He pledged that when the military operation ended, the armed forces of the Republic of Viet-Nam would withdraw completely from Laotian territory.

Also on 8 February 1971, the United States transmitted a statement by the official press spokesman of the United States Department of State. This noted that the Republic of Viet-Nam had announced that elements of its armed forces had crossed into enemy-occupied territory of Laos to attack North Viet-Namese forces and military supplies assembled in sanctuaries located close to the border of South Viet-Nam. The United States military command in Saigon had announced the limits of the United States military participation.

The United States Government said it continued to favour the neutrality of Laos and the restoration of the situation contemplated by the 1962 Geneva Agreement (Declaration on the neutrality of Laos, and Protocol, signed at Geneva, Switzerland, on 23 July 1962) by which all foreign forces would be withdrawn from Laos territory, which could be accomplished through a new Indo-China conference as proposed by President Richard M. Nixon.

On 11 February 1971, the representative of the

USSR transmitted a statement issued by the Telegraphic Agency of the Soviet Union (TASS) on 4 February 1971 on the situation in Indo-China. According to the TASS statement, the situation in Indo-China had recently become decidedly more complicated, inasmuch as large numbers of Saigon ground forces with United States air support had invaded Laos, and United States aircraft, including B-52 heavy bombers, were carrying out mass air raids over Laotian territory. These acts constituted an act of aggression, a further direct violation of the United Nations Charter, a blatant outrage against the principles of international law and a further violation of the Geneva Agreement, to which the United States was a party.

Similar charges, made by the Bulgarian news agency, the Czechoslovak Government, the Mongolian parliament and the Mongolian news agency were transmitted in February and March by the representatives of the Governments concerned.

Also, the representative of Poland, on 13 February 1971, transmitted an unofficial translation of an aide-mémoire which his Government had addressed on 12 February to the Co-Chairmen of the International Conference on the Settlement of the Laotian Question at Geneva.

This condemned United States intervention in Laos as contrary to the Geneva Agreement of 1962, and stated, *inter alia*, that the Polish Government, as a member of the International Commission for Supervision and Control in Laos, was appealing to the Co-Chairmen of the Geneva Conference on Laos to use their utmost influence to prevent the United States from escalating military operations in Indo-China and to induce it to refrain from any further aggression against Laos.

By a letter dated 26 February 1971, the USSR representative transmitted a declaration of his Government condemning United States intervention in Laos as being in violation of standards of international law and the provisions of the United Nations Charter. The declaration emphasized that, in the view of the USSR, the main prerequisite for a settlement of the Indo-China problem was the cessation of United States aggression and *de facto* recognition of the essentially inalienable national right of the peoples of the area to settle their own fate without foreign interference, in accordance with proposals of the Provisional Revolutionary Government of the Republic of South Viet-Nam made on 17 September 1970, which were supported by the Government of the Democratic Republic of Viet-Nam, as well as the proposals of the National United Front of Cambodia and the Patriotic Front of Laos.

On 30 November 1971, the USSR representative transmitted the text of a statement—issued jointly in Hanoi on 7 October 1971 by a visiting Party-Government delegation of the USSR and senior representatives of the Government of the Democratic Republic of Viet-Nam—which dealt with the subject of future friendly co-operation between the Governments of the USSR and the Democratic Republic of Viet-Nam, and with the situation in Viet-Nam and on the Indo-Chinese peninsula created by the United States aggression.

The USSR among other things pledged its continuing support on the military, political and diplomatic fronts for the struggle of the Viet-Namese people against the United States.

Both parties also urged that the United States end the war of aggression, withdraw all its troops from South Viet-Nam and dismantle its military bases there, and cease its support of the present régime in Saigon in accordance with the seven-point proposals of the Provisional Revolutionary Government of the Republic of South Viet-Nam which, it was stated, provided a fair and reasonable basis for settling the Viet-Namese question.

Complaints by the Khmer Republic

During 1971, the Government of the Khmer Republic addressed 19 communications to the President of the Security Council alleging numerous violations of its sovereignty and territorial integrity by armed units of "Viet-Cong and North Viet-Namese forces."

The most frequent complaints related to armed incursions into its territory, attacks upon Khmer military posts, clashes with Khmer defence forces and the occupation of several points in the country. As a result of those attacks, it was stated, scores of Khmer nationals, both military and civilian, including women and children as well as Buddhist monks, were reported to have been killed, several were missing and hundreds of buildings had been set on fire and destroyed.

One letter charged that the Viet-Cong–North Viet-Namese forces had used poison gas shells in their attacks against Kompong Thom province. In some of the letters it was reported that many of the weapons captured by Khmer forces were of Chinese manufacture.

In most of its communications, the Government of the Khmer Republic declared its firm protest against "the illegal and permanent occupation" of Khmer territory, and the savage attacks committed by the "Viet-Cong–North Viet-Namese forces" against a neutral and peace-loving country in flagrant violation of the Charter of the United Nations, international law and the 1954 Geneva Agreements.

These criminal attacks, the Khmer Republic stated, revealed the annexationist aims of the "Viet-Cong–North Viet-Namese communist imperialists" and represented a dangerous threat to peace and security, not only in the Khmer Republic but throughout South-East Asia. The Government of the Khmer Republic held the

Government of the Democratic Republic of Viet-Nam and the so-called Provisional Revolutionary Government of South Viet-Nam entirely responsible for all the very serious consequences resulting from that situation. It reserved the right to take any necessary action to defend the country's independence, neutrality, sovereignty and territorial integrity.

Statement by Secretary-General

In the introduction to his annual report to the General Assembly on the work of the Organization for the period 16 June 1970 to 15 June 1971, the Secretary-General, expressing concern with the situation in Indo-China, stated that the conflict in the peninsula constituted a direct challenge to the principles and authority of the Organization. Moreover, it diverted the energies and the technical and financial capacity of some of the world's most powerful nations towards the barren task of advancing or consolidating so-called zones of influence.

Noting that the absence of the People's Republic of China and both parts of Viet-Nam from the Organization had largely deprived the parties themselves of United Nations channels of communication and the world community of the means of exerting a mediatory role, the Secretary-General said he had made it clear to the parties involved that the Organization and the Secretary-General were ready to use their best efforts in the service of peace in the area.

Referring to the United States decision to halt bombings, the opening of Paris talks and the withdrawal of important contingents of foreign troops from Viet-Nam as encouraging elements, the Secretary-General noted that, despite these steps, the war was still raging on the peninsula.

Could an end to that tragic situation be seriously expected, he asked, as long as the peoples of the area were not allowed to attempt to reconcile their differences and to express freely their wishes without any interference from outside powers? He expressed the hope that it would soon be possible for all trends of opinion in Viet-Nam to participate in the elaboration of decisions at the national level and for political discussions to be substituted for armed confrontations between factions.

A lasting settlement, the Secretary-General believed, would undoubtedly have to take into account a political reality which was also one of the reasons for the conflict, namely the community of language, civilization and interest and the close kinship between North and South Viet-Nam.

Another distressing factor in the situation in Indo-China, the Secretary-General commented, was the extension of the conflict to two neighbouring countries—Laos and Cambodia (the Khmer Republic)—which had become battlefields where soldiers of foreign countries confronted each other.

No solution to the Laotian conflict, the Secretary-General observed, would be found as long as the bombing lasted and as long as Laos was denied the actual exercise of sovereignty over parts of its territory. It was high time for the international community, and particularly for those powers which had signed the Geneva agreements on Laos, to fulfil the responsibilities they had accepted at that time. Furthermore, no strategic or other outside interests could justify the current afflictions of the people of Cambodia. Cambodia as well as the other countries of Indo-China, he added, should be free from foreign intervention and should be allowed to live in peace.

DOCUMENTARY REFERENCES

S/10104. Note of 8 February 1971 by President of Security Council (transmitting note verbale containing message of 8 February 1971 of President of Republic of Viet-Nam).

S/10106. Letter of 8 February 1971 from United States (transmitting statement issued 8 February 1971 by official spokesman of Department of State).

S/10115. Letter of 11 February 1971 from USSR (transmitting TASS statement of 4 February 1971).

S/10117. Letter of 13 February 1971 from Poland (transmitting aide-mémoire of 12 February 1971 from Government of Poland to Co-Chairmen of Geneva Conference on Laos).

S/10120. Letter of 12 February 1971 from Bulgaria (transmitting Bulgarian Telegraph Agency statement).

S/10134. Letter of 26 February 1971 from USSR (transmitting Declaration of 25 February 1971).

S/10150. Letter of 5 March 1971 from Czechoslovakia (transmitting statement of 25 February 1971).

S/10164/Rev.1. Letter of 26 March 1971 from Mongolia (transmitting statement of 12 February 1971 of 4th session of Great National Khural of Mongolia).

S/10406. Letter of 30 November 1971 from USSR (transmitting joint statement of 7 October 1971 of USSR and Democratic Republic of Viet-Nam).

A/8402. Report of Security Council, 16 June 1970–15 June 1971, Chapter 18.

Complaints by the Khmer Republic

S/10077, S/10093, S/10095, S/10099. Letters of 7, 26, 27, and 28 January 1971 from Khmer Republic.

S/10114, S/10122, S/10131. Letters of 9, 16 and 23 February 1971 from Khmer Republic.

S/10137, S/10153. Letters of 1 and 9 March 1971 from Khmer Republic.

S/10183. Letter of 27 April 1971 from Khmer Republic.

S/10186, S/10192, S/10198, S/10206. Letters of 5, 10, 14 and 20 May 1971 from Khmer Republic.

S/10221. Letter of 9 June 1971 from Khmer Republic.

S/10248. Letter of 1 July 1971 from Khmer Republic.

S/10302. Letter of 23 August 1971 from Khmer Republic.

S/10349. Letter of 27 September 1971 from Khmer Republic.

S/10450. Letter of 8 December 1971 from Khmer Republic.

A/8402. Report of Security Council, Chapter 17.

Statement by Secretary-General

A/8401/Add.1. Introduction to report of Secretary-General on work of the Organization, September 1971, Part One, Chapter III.

Chapter IX

The situation in the Middle East

During 1971, efforts continued in the search for a peaceful settlement of the Middle East problem. The Secretary-General reported on the activities of his Special Representative to the Middle East, Ambassador Gunnar V. Jarring—in particular, Ambassador Jarring's renewed efforts to carry out the mandate entrusted to him by the Security Council in its resolution of 22 November 1967.[1]

At its twenty-sixth session, which opened on 21 September 1971, the General Assembly again discussed the situation in the Middle East, and on 13 December adopted a resolution sponsored by 21 States. By this, the Assembly among other things reaffirmed the principle that the acquisition of territories by force was inadmissible and that territories thus occupied must be restored. It also reaffirmed that the establishment of peace in the Middle East should include application of the following two principles—which had been set forth in the Security Council's resolution of 22 November 1967—namely: (a) withdrawal of Israeli armed forces from territories occupied in the 1967 conflict; and (b) termination of all claims or states of belligerency and respect for and acknowledgement of the sovereignty, territorial integrity and political independence of every State in the area and its right to live in peace within secure and recognized boundaries free from threats or acts of force.

The Assembly also asked the Secretary-General to take measures to reactivate Ambassador Jarring's mission and invited the parties to the conflict to co-operate with the Special Representative in working out practical measures to: guarantee freedom of navigation through international waterways in the area; achieve a just settlement of the refugee problem; and guarantee the territorial inviolability and political independence of every State in the area. The Security Council was asked to consider, if necessary, making arrangements under the relevant Articles of the United Nations Charter with regard to the implementation of its resolution of 22 November 1967.

Also during 1971, communications and reports concerning the status of the cease-fire between Israel on the one hand, and Egypt, Jordan, Lebanon and the Syrian Arab Republic on the other, were received by the Security Council which, owing to the relative quiet in the area, was not convened to consider that aspect of the question.

The Council did, however, meet to consider charges by Jordan that Israel was adopting measures to change the character and status of the City of Jerusalem. On 25 September, the Council adopted a resolution by which among other things it urgently called on Israel to rescind all previous measures and to take no further steps in the occupied section of Jerusalem tending to change the status of the City or prejudicing the rights of its inhabitants or the interests of the international community.

The question of the treatment of the civilian population of the Arab territories occupied by Israel was again considered by the Commission on Human Rights and the General Assembly, both of which took decisions based on the findings of the three-member Special Committee to Investigate Israeli Practices Affecting the Human Rights of the Population of the Occupied Territories.

Details of these and other related matters are described in the sections that follow.

[1]See Y.U.N., 1967, pp. 257-58, text of resolution 242(1967).

Search for a peaceful settlement of the Middle East problem

Reports by Secretary-General

In a report dated 30 November 1971, the Secretary-General gave a comprehensive review of the activities of his Special Representative to the Middle East, Ambassador Gunnar V. Jarring, since January 1971.

The Special Representative, the report stated, had resumed his discussions with the parties early in January and had received memoranda from them elaborating their positions. Israel had presented papers containing its views on the "essentials of peace," and Egypt and Jordan had subsequently presented papers containing their views on the implementation of the Security Council's resolution of 22 November 1967.[2]

The Secretary-General said he had noted with growing concern that each side had been insisting that the other make certain commitments before the formulation of provisions for a peace settlement. Israel had insisted that Egypt should give specific, direct and reciprocal commitments that it would be ready to enter into a peace agreement and to make various undertakings within the framework of the resolution of 22 November

[2]*Ibid.*

1967. When agreement was reached on those points, it would then be possible to discuss others, including the refugee problem.

Egypt, the Secretary-General said, had continued to regard the resolution of 22 November 1967 as containing provisions to be implemented by the parties, and for its part had once again expressed its readiness to carry out its obligations under the resolution, provided that Israel did likewise. Egypt had held, however, that Israel persisted in its refusal to implement the resolution, since it would not commit itself to withdraw from all Arab territories occupied in June 1967. Furthermore, according to Egypt, Israel had not committed itself to implementing the United Nations resolutions relevant to a just settlement of the refugee problem.

The Secretary-General added that the papers received by Ambassador Jarring from Israel and Jordan relating to peace between those two countries showed a similar divergence of views. Israel had stressed that Jordan should enter into a peace agreement specifying each party's direct and reciprocal obligations; Jordan emphasized the inadmissibility of the acquisition of territory by war and held that an Israeli commitment to evacuate all occupied territories was an essential first step towards peace.

At that stage of the talks, the Secretary-General said, his Special Representative had reached the conclusion, which he shared, that the only possibility of breaking the deadlock arising from the differing views of Israel and Egypt as to the priority to be given to commitments and undertakings was for him to seek from each side the parallel and simultaneous commitments that seemed to be the inevitable prerequisites of an eventual peace settlement. It should thereafter be possible to formulate at once the terms of a peace agreement, not only for those topics covered by the commitments but with equal priority for other topics, in particular the refugee problem.

Thus, in identical aides-mémoires to Egypt and Israel on 8 February, Ambassador Jarring requested them to make certain prior commitments. His initiative was presented on the basis that the commitments should be made simultaneously and reciprocally and subject to the eventual satisfactory determination of all other aspects of a peace settlement, including in particular a just settlement of the refugee problem. Israel would commit itself to withdraw its forces from occupied Egyptian territory to the former international boundary between Egypt and the British Mandate of Palestine. Egypt would commit itself to enter into a peace agreement with Israel and to make explicitly therein to Israel, on a reciprocal basis, various undertakings and acknowledgements arising directly and indirectly from the Security Council's resolution adopted on 22 November 1967.

On 15 February, Egypt indicated that it would accept the specific commitments requested of it, as well as other commitments arising directly or indirectly from the resolution. It would also be ready to enter into a peace agreement with Israel if Israel would give commitments covering its own obligations under the resolution, including commitments for the withdrawal of its armed forces from Sinai and the Gaza Strip and for the achievement of a just settlement of the refugee problem in accordance with United Nations resolutions.

On 17 February, the Special Representative informed Israel of Egypt's reply to his aide-mémoire. On 26 February, Israel, without specific reference to the commitments which the Special Representative had sought from that Government, stated that it viewed favourably Egypt's expression of readiness to enter into a peace agreement with Israel, and reiterated that it was prepared for meaningful negotiations on all subjects relevant to a peace agreement. Israel considered that both parties, having presented their basic positions, should now pursue detailed and concrete negotiations without prior conditions.

On the question of withdrawal, on which the Special Representative had sought a commitment from Israel, the Israeli position was that it would give an undertaking to withdraw from the Israeli-Egyptian cease-fire line to secure, recognized and agreed boundaries to be established in the peace agreement; it would not withdraw to the lines existing prior to June 1967.

On 28 February, Ambassador Jarring informed Egypt of the contents of the Israeli communication. Egypt held that it was improper for the Israeli authorities to have responded to Egypt's reply, which had been addressed to Ambassador Jarring and which would have full effect only if the Israeli authorities gave the commitment requested of them by Ambassador Jarring.

The Secretary-General reported that he had then stated that the problems to be settled had been more clearly identified and that on some points there was general agreement. He had also noted with satisfaction the positive reply given by Egypt to Ambassador Jarring's initiative. However, Israel had not so far responded to the request of the Special Representative that it should give a commitment on withdrawal to the international boundary of Egypt. In view of that, the Secretary-General had appealed to Israel to respond favourably to Ambassador Jarring's initiative. He also appealed to the parties to withhold fire and maintain the quiet which had prevailed in the area since August 1970. Israel had then indicated its willingness to continue to observe the cease-fire on a basis of reciprocity. However, the

President of Egypt had declared on 7 March that his Government was no longer committed to a cease-fire.

The Secretary-General said that on 11 March Israel had informed Ambassador Jarring that it was awaiting Egypt's reaction to Israel's invitation to enter into detailed and concrete discussions. Egypt maintained that it was still awaiting an Israeli reply to Ambassador Jarring's aide-mémoire.

Subsequently, the Secretary-General reported, the talks under Ambassador Jarring's auspices had lapsed. He had therefore resumed his post as Ambassador of Sweden to the USSR on 25 March. Although he returned to Headquarters from 5 to 12 May and from 21 September to 27 October, and had held certain consultations elsewhere, he had found himself faced with the same deadlock and with no possibility of actively pursuing his mission.

During much of this time, the Secretary-General noted, the promotion of agreement between the parties was the object of two separate initiatives —first, an effort by the United States to promote an interim agreement providing for the reopening of the Suez Canal, which had not, so far, achieved any positive results. The second initiative was a mission of inquiry being conducted by certain African Heads of State on behalf of the Organization of African Unity (OAU). Both initiatives were described by the sponsors as designed to facilitate the resumption of Ambassador Jarring's mission. While they were being pursued, they obviously constituted an additional reason for him not to take personal initiatives.

In the introduction to his annual report to the General Assembly, the Secretary-General said that if the impasse in the search for a peaceful settlement in the Middle East persisted, there could be little doubt that new fighting would break out sooner or later. The parties had taken advantage of the current lull to strengthen considerably their military capabilities and any new round of fighting would be more violent and dangerous than previous ones. There was always the danger, he added, that it might not be possible to limit it to the present antagonists and to the confines of the Middle East.

The Secretary-General believed that the only way to forestall such a disastrous eventuality was to intensify the search for a peaceful and agreed settlement. The Security Council's cease-fire resolutions of June 1967[3] and its resolution of 22 November 1967, if implemented simultaneously and fully, should provide the framework for achieving such a settlement.

He went on to say that Ambassador Jarring had clearly defined the minimum conditions required to move the peace talks ahead and, until those conditions were met, it was hard to see what else he could do to further his efforts. Steps to ensure that those conditions were met had to be taken by the parties concerned and, failing that, by the Security Council itself or by the States Members of the United Nations—particularly the permanent members of the Security Council, both because of their special responsibility within the United Nations and their influence on the parties concerned.

Communications from Israel and Egypt relating to OAU proposals

On 9 December 1971, Israel transmitted to the Secretary-General the text of Israel's reply to proposals made by the Committee of Ten African Heads of State of the Organization of African Unity (OAU). Israel stated that it agreed: (*a*) to resume negotiations without prior conditions under the auspices of Ambassador Jarring within the terms of the Security Council's resolution of 22 November 1967; (*b*) to work out a Suez Canal agreement, the details of which would be negotiated and agreed; (*c*) that secure and recognized boundaries should be determined by negotiations between the parties and embodied in the peace agreement; (*d*) that in addition to the determination of agreed, secure and recognized boundaries, further arrangements for ensuring security could be negotiated; (*e*) that the terms of withdrawal to the boundaries negotiated and agreed should be embodied in the peace treaty; and (*f*) that the question of Sharm el Sheikh would be included in the peace negotiations as specified in point (*c*) above. In accordance with the Security Council's resolution, free navigation in all international waterways, such as the Suez Canal and the Strait of Tiran, for all ships and cargoes, including those of Israel, would be provided for in the peace agreement.

On 10 December 1971, Egypt transmitted to the Secretary-General the text of a memorandum submitted to the Chairman of the Sub-Committee of four African Heads of State in response to the proposals submitted by the OAU Committee of Ten. The memorandum stated that Egypt:

(1) agreed to hold indirect negotiations under the auspices of Ambassador Jarring for the implementation of the Security Council's resolution of 22 November 1967 in all its parts;

(2) was ready to undertake the required arrangements for reopening the Suez Canal in return for the first stage of Israeli withdrawal on condition that Israel responded positively to Ambassador Jarring's aide-mémoire of 8 February;

---

[3]See Y.U.N., 1967, p. 189, texts of resolution 233(1967) of 6 June and resolution 234(1967) of 7 June 1967, and p. 190, texts of resolution 235(1967) of 9 June and resolution 236(1967) of 11 June 1967.

(3) agreed that secure and recognized boundaries should be embodied in the peace agreement, based on the withdrawal of Israeli forces to the lines of 5 June 1967 and in conformity with the borders specified in Ambassador Jarring's initiative, which underlined the necessity of the withdrawal of Israeli forces to Egypt's international borders;

(4) accepted as guarantees for peace: (a) United Nations guarantees; (b) establishment of demilitarized zones astride the borders; and (c) stationing of international forces at some strategic points; and

(5) accepted the stationing of international forces in Sharm el Sheikh to guarantee the freedom of navigation in the Strait of Tiran.

Consideration by General Assembly

On 25 September 1971, the General Assembly included the item "The situation in the Middle East" in its agenda and discussed it at plenary meetings held between 3 and 14 December.

Opening the debate, the Minister for Foreign Affairs of Egypt stated that his Government asked the General Assembly to consider Israel's continued aggression and expansionist policy—the emergence of a colonial power invoking military conquest as a means of territorial expansion. The expulsion of inhabitants of the occupied territories, the destruction of villages, houses and refugee camps and the establishment of Israeli colonies were examples of such policy.

The Security Council's resolution of 22 November 1967[4] had, he said, clearly emphasized the inadmissibility of the acquisition of territory by force. That principle—which was based on the United Nations Charter—should apply fully to all the occupied territories and could not be fragmented. Israel had not only refused to implement the resolution but had also attempted to distort its provisions. Thus, it had selected a particular phrase referring to "secure and recognized boundaries" and used the words to try to justify its policy of territorial expansion. But, he stressed, the resolution referred to all States in the area and not only to Israel. Security could rest only on respect for territorial integrity, political independence and sovereignty. It could be reinforced by a system of guarantees under the auspices of the Security Council, but Israel had rejected all proposals on security measures.

Outlining the initiatives and endeavours of the past four years to carry out the peaceful settlement embodied in the Security Council's resolution, including the mission of the African Heads of State, the Egyptian Foreign Minister declared that Israel had employed manoeuvres, delaying tactics and slogans to undermine every opportunity for a peaceful settlement. The latest of such

tactics was its declaration that it was ready to resume talks with Ambassador Jarring without pre-conditions. Were there any pre-conditions in the Jarring memorandum of 8 February 1971? If Israel considered itself bound by the Charter, by the Security Council's resolution, by the principle of the inadmissibility of acquisition of territory by force, and by the rules and norms of international legal order, then there were no pre-conditions whatsoever in the memorandum.

The Egyptian Foreign Minister went on to say that opposition to Israel's colonial policy was universal. However, in the case of the United States there was a basic contradiction between that country's declared commitment to support the territorial integrity of all the States in the Middle East and its policy of providing military and economic aid to Israel. Nothing had enabled Israel to evade its obligations more than its reliance on United States support. By its aggression against three Arab States and by its failure to meet its obligations under the resolution of 22 November 1967, Israel had violated the United Nations Charter. The enforcement measures of Chapter VII of the Charter[5] were specifically envisaged to meet such a situation.

The Minister for Foreign Affairs of Israel said that the urgent task was to strengthen the cease-fire, to begin detailed and concrete negotiations, and to show directions in which a final peace could be approached. The Middle East was in turmoil largely because the Arab Governments had never had a true perception of Israel's purpose or identity. Contrary to Egypt's assertion that Israel was an expansionist, imperialist country imposing its power on the Arab world, his country, the Foreign Minister said, was a small nation fighting for its own peace, freedom and security. Since the war of June 1967, Egypt had refused to meet Israel at the conference table and had declined all negotiations except on condition that its terms be accepted in advance. Israel, on the other hand, had sought negotiation, agreement and peace with Egypt. Maintenance of the cease-fire was the essential condition for progress towards peace.

He went on to say that Egypt had refused to co-operate with the United States in seeking a Suez Canal agreement, although the opening of the Canal, with a withdrawal of Israeli forces to an agreed distance from the cease-fire lines, would carry tangible advantages to Egypt and would weaken Israel's position strategically. Israel was prepared to make those concessions, provided that compensating conditions for its security were ensured. Israel would undertake that the Canal

---

[4]See footnote 1.
[5]For text of Chapter VII of the Charter, see APPENDIX II.

agreement would not affect or annul the agreement of August 1970, by which Israel and Egypt would hold discussions under Ambassador Jarring's auspices in conformity with his mandate under the Security Council's resolution of 22 November 1967 to promote agreement on a final settlement. When agreement on a final boundary had been reached in the peace settlement, Israeli forces would withdraw to it. Israel's position was fully in accordance with international law, with the established precedents of peace-making and with the Security Council's resolution.

The Israeli Foreign Minister said that, with regard to Ambassador Jarring's aide-mémoire of 8 February 1971, the assertion that Egypt had made a positive response while Israel had given a negative reply, or none at all, was not true. Egypt had replied to nearly all the points in Ambassador Jarring's aide-mémoire not with a straightforward acceptance but with a counter-proposal. The Egyptian reply differed from the Jarring memorandum on many positions. Israel had also replied to Ambassador Jarring's proposals, sometimes in general acceptance and in some cases with counter-proposals. Its reply was in full accord with the Charter and with the Security Council's resolution. Each party was within its right in stating its basic position in its reply. Now that the parties had done that, they should pursue their negotiations in a detailed and concrete manner, without prior conditions and with a view to concluding a peace agreement.

Israel, he said, had also welcomed the initiative taken by the African Heads of State and had replied positively to their proposals aimed at resolving the deadlock without prior surrender of its position by either party. The main virtue of the proposals was that they placed the renewal of Ambassador Jarring's mission strictly within the terms of the resolution of 22 November 1967 and did not attempt to specify the conclusions which the negotiations should reach.

The Minister for Foreign Affairs of Senegal said that the purpose of the OAU mission had been to establish contacts with the parties in order to help towards the resumption of Ambassador Jarring's mission. The main concern of OAU was the implementation of the Security Council's resolution of 22 November 1967.

At the talks with the parties, he said, some positive elements had emerged: Egypt had accepted the resumption of negotiations under Ambassador Jarring and it had maintained its proposal for an interim Suez Canal agreement to enable the Special Representative to establish a time-table for implementing the resolution. Israel, for its part, had confirmed its acceptance of the resolution and, although it preferred direct negotiations, was prepared to undertake indirect negotiations through Ambassador Jarring. Israel had also agreed to the conclusion of an interim agreement on the reopening of the Suez Canal, provided that such agreement was not linked to the resolution.

The remaining obstacles, the Foreign Minister of Senegal said, were the withdrawal of Israeli troops and the concept of secure and recognized boundaries, which Israel based on security considerations. He pointed out that no State could invoke security reasons to seize or annex territories of other States. That principle, he added, should be reaffirmed in order to enable Ambassador Jarring to resume his mission.

The representative of China said that the essence of the Middle East question was the aggression of Israeli zionism against the Palestinians and other Arab peoples, with the support of the United States. It was because of the arms provided by the United States to Israel that the Palestinian people and other Arab countries had failed in their efforts to recover the lost territories.

Under the control and manipulation of the super-powers, he said, the United Nations had also ignored the just demands of the Palestinians and other Arab peoples and had adopted resolutions that were unjust to the Arabs and in contravention of the Charter. Also, the two super-powers were taking advantage of the temporary difficulties facing the Palestinians and other Arab peoples to make political deals in their contention for important strategic points and oil resources and the division of spheres of influence in the Middle East at the expense of the national rights and territorial integrity and sovereignty of the Arab peoples. That was why the question had remained unsolved for so long.

The theory of so-called secure boundaries advanced by Israel, he said, was only an excuse to perpetuate the occupation of the territories seized; to accept it would be tantamount to recognizing as legal the aggression and expansion of Israeli zionism.

China maintained that Israel must withdraw from the Arab territories it had occupied and that the legitimate rights of the Palestinians to return to their homeland and to national existence must be restored.

The USSR representative maintained that the key to the restoration of peace in the Middle East was the withdrawal of Israeli forces from Arab territories. The United Nations had taken a definite stand against Israeli occupation by the Security Council's resolution of 22 November 1967, by the General Assembly's 1970 Declaration on the Strengthening of International Security[6]

---

[6]See Y.U.N., 1970, pp. 105-7, resolution 2734(XXV) of 16 December 1970, containing text of Declaration.

and by the Assembly's resolution of 4 November 1970 on the situation in the Middle East,[7] Israel had defied those decisions and, with the support of the United States, had paralysed Ambassador Jarring's mission.

Moreover, he went on to say, the United States had blocked the work of the consultative meetings of the permanent members of the Security Council on the Middle East, making it impossible to reach any agreed decision. It had instead undertaken a one-sided uncalled-for mediation that had proved a total fiasco. It was time to return to the collective diplomacy of the United Nations through the Jarring mission, with consultations by the permanent members and the participation of the Security Council and the General Assembly in a Middle East settlement.

The USSR believed that the General Assembly could effectively contribute to a solution of the problem if it displayed determination to curb the aggressor and called upon the United States not to play the role of mediator. The USSR was prepared to participate, together with other States, in establishing international guarantees for a political settlement and for security in the Middle East.

The United States representative said his country had supported all United Nations efforts to find a solution to the Arab-Israeli conflict; it favoured a peaceful settlement based on agreement among the parties within the framework of the provisions and principles of the Security Council's resolution of 22 November 1967. Unfortunately, efforts towards an over-all peace settlement had not produced the results which had been hoped for.

The most promising avenue of progress since February 1971, he said, had been the possibility of an agreement on interim measures, involving partial Israeli withdrawal from Sinai and a reopening of the Suez Canal as a step towards final peace. Both Egypt and Israel, on their own initiative, had expressed interest in that concept and both had asked the United States to assist them in pursuing negotiations towards that end. However, a major difficulty had been that the parties had sought to introduce into the context of an interim agreement concepts which logically belonged in an over-all settlement. The merits of an interim agreement were precisely that it offered a prospect for practical on-the-ground progress, while leaving some of the most difficult problems for further negotiations at a subsequent stage.

The United States spokesman added that although the negotiations on an interim agreement were in suspense—temporarily, he believed—his Government would review the situation after the General Assembly's debate had been concluded. Both sides had put forward positive ideas; both sides held firmly to key points; both

sides would be required to make adjustments if an interim agreement was indeed to be achieved.

The basic problem, he stressed, was to find ways to help both sides overcome the deep suspicion and distrust they felt towards each other.

The United States representative commended the mission undertaken by the OAU Committee of Ten to promote a narrowing of the differences between the parties.

The spokesman for the United Kingdom said that virtually all Member States, including the main parties to the conflict, agreed that any Middle East settlement should be based on the Security Council's resolution of 22 November 1967; disagreement arose as to the means to achieve that end. His Government had wholeheartedly supported the three main attempts made over the past year to bring about a settlement in accordance with the Council's resolution. It believed that an interim agreement on the reopening of the Suez Canal, if successfully concluded, would result in a certain deconfrontation that might pave the way for a comprehensive settlement. The OAU mission was also a valuable initiative, as it was intended to move the Jarring mission out of the present impasse. Finally, the most important development in Ambassador Jarring's mission had been his initiative of 8 February.

In this connexion, the United Kingdom representative noted that Israel, in its response, had clearly indicated that its main concern was not with territory but with security. If Israel were able, in the context of the correspondence with Ambassador Jarring, to say that it had no desire to incorporate any Egyptian territory into the State of Israel, that might constitute the response which Ambassador Jarring needed to resume the search for a peaceful settlement.

The United Kingdom, he said, believed that dialogue must supplant confrontation; he hoped that, at an early stage after the resumption of Ambassador Jarring's mission, it would be possible to arrange some closer form of contact between the Egyptian and Israeli Governments to agree on the basis of a settlement. A similar procedure might then be followed in the case of the other parties concerned.

The representative of France said that the first obstacle to peace in the Middle East resulted from the scope and multiplicity of problems which could be resolved only in the framework of an over-all settlement. That was the essence of the Security Council's resolution of 22 November 1967: peace could be lastingly established only if the settlement dealt with all the problems and applied to all the countries concerned.

[7]*Ibid.*, p. 261, text of resolution 2628 (XXV).

A second obstacle, he said, resulted from the interpretation of the concept of withdrawal in relation to commitments to peace, a question that must be settled in accordance with the principle of the inadmissibility of the acquisition of territory by war. Since the right of conquest was excluded, he added, borders must coincide—except for minor, agreed-upon rectifications—with the borders and lines existing prior to the 1967 conflict. Respect for those borders, ensured by the peace agreement, would be strengthened by political and military measures taken by the parties, as well as by international guarantees.

The third obstacle, according to the French representative, resulted from deep divergences concerning the solution to the painful problem of the Palestinian people. Without a solution to that problem, any settlement negotiated by the States concerned might, in the long run, be jeopardized.

France, he concluded, believed that the General Assembly could make a useful contribution to a peaceful settlement in the Middle East by reaffirming the necessary principles, by inviting the parties to comply with them, and by supporting the efforts of Ambassador Jarring and encouraging him to pursue his task.

Representatives of Arab States said that the moral aspects and legal implications of the Middle East problem had been debated exhaustively in the United Nations and many resolutions had been adopted; but the time had come for the General Assembly to take concrete action to end Israel's occupation of Arab territories and to ensure respect for the inalienable rights of the Palestinians.

Several Arab Members, in particular Algeria, Iraq and the People's Democratic Republic of Yemen, maintained that any political solution to the problem of Palestine that was based on the Security Council's resolution of 22 November 1967 would not be practical; that resolution had addressed itself only to the situation created by the Israeli aggression of June 1967. The Algerian representative said that the alleged equilibrium of the resolution rested, above all, on a flagrant injustice to the Palestinians and constituted a vexing and dangerous precedent for future aggression.

Saudi Arabia stated that even if the conflict between Israel and the three Arab neighbouring States were to be solved, the core of the problem would remain. Israel was a foreign body in the region and the zionists were usurping colonialists. Peace could be achieved only if Israel's domination ceased and a democratic State established in which both Jews and Arabs could live together.

Many Arab spokesmen deplored United States military assistance to Israel which, they believed, had helped Israel in its aggression and its continued defiance of United Nations decisions.

The majority of speakers, including representatives from Africa, Asia and Eastern Europe, shared the view that the General Assembly should demand a positive and definitive answer from Israel to Ambassador Jarring's aide-mémoire of 8 February 1971 concerning the complete withdrawal of Israeli forces from the occupied Arab territories.

Many Members praised the OAU mission for its conciliation efforts and felt that the Security Council's resolution of 22 November 1967 provided the basis for a political solution. They felt that Ambassador Jarring's mission should be reactivated and that the parties should co-operate in good faith to seek a peaceful settlement.

On 13 December, the General Assembly adopted—by a recorded vote of 79 to 7, with 36 abstentions—a draft resolution sponsored by the following 21 Members: Afghanistan, Cameroon, the Congo, Cyprus, Equatorial Guinea, Ethiopia, Guinea, India, Indonesia, Iran, Malaysia, Mali, Mauritania, Mauritius, Nigeria, Pakistan, Somalia, Spain, the United Republic of Tanzania, Yugoslavia and Zambia. It was revised by the sponsors during the course of the debate to take into account amendments by Belgium, France, Italy, Luxembourg, the Netherlands and the United Kingdom.

By the preambular part of this text, the General Assembly among other things expressed its deep concern at the continuation of the grave situation prevailing in the Middle East, particularly since the conflict of June 1967, which constituted a serious threat to international peace and security. The Assembly said it was convinced that the Security Council's resolution of 22 November 1967 should be implemented immediately in all its parts in order to achieve a just and lasting peace in the Middle East in which every State in the area could live in security. It expressed grave concern at the continuation of Israel's occupation of the Arab territories since 5 June 1967.

By the operative part of the text, the Assembly:

(1) reaffirmed that the acquisition of territories by force was inadmissible and that, consequently, territories thus occupied must be restored;

(2) reaffirmed that the establishment of a just and lasting peace in the Middle East should include the application of both the following principles: (*a*) withdrawal of Israeli armed forces from territories occupied in the recent conflict; and (*b*) termination of all claims or states of belligerency and respect for and acknowledgement of the sovereignty, territorial integrity and political independence of every State in the area and its right to live in peace within secure and recognized boundaries free from threats or acts of force;

(3) requested the Secretary-General to take the necessary measures to reactivate the mission of his Special Representative to the Middle East in order to promote agreement and assist efforts to reach a peace agreement as envisaged in the Special Representative's aide-mémoire of 8 February 1971;

(4) expressed its full support for all the efforts of the Special Representative to implement the Security Council's resolution of 22 November 1967;

(5) noted with appreciation the positive reply given by Egypt to the Special Representative's initiative for establishing a just and lasting peace in the Middle East;

(6) called upon Israel to respond favourably to the Special Representative's peace initiative;

(7) further invited the parties to the Middle East conflict to give their full co-operation to the Special Representative in order to work out practical measures for: (a) guaranteeing freedom of navigation through international waterways in the area; (b) achieving a just settlement of the refugee problem; and (c) guaranteeing the territorial inviolability and political independence of every State in the area;

(8) requested the Secretary-General to report to the Security Council and to the General Assembly, as appropriate, on the progress made by the Special Representative in the implementation of the Security Council's resolution of 22 November 1967 and of the present resolution; and

(9) requested the Security Council to consider, if necessary, making arrangements, under the relevant Articles of the United Nations Charter, with regard to the implementation of its 1967 resolution.

The Assembly adopted this text as its resolution 2799(XXVI).

(For full text of resolution, see DOCUMENTARY REFERENCES below.)

Two other draft resolutions and several amendments to the 21-power text were before the Assembly and were either voted on and rejected or withdrawn.

One of these, a text proposed by Barbados and Ghana, was withdrawn following adoption of the 21-power text. By this, the Assembly among other things would have:

(1) expressed its support for the following proposals submitted by the OAU Committee of African Heads of State for consideration by the parties: (a) resumption of indirect negotiations under Ambassador Jarring's auspices and within the terms of the Security Council's resolution of 22 November 1967; (b) an interim agreement for the opening of the Suez Canal and the stationing—on the eastern bank of the Canal—of United Nations forces between the Egyptian and Israeli lines; (c)

determination of "secure and recognized boundaries" in the peace agreement; (d) a solution to security problems to be found within the guarantee of the United Nations, in the creation of demilitarized zones, and in the presence of international forces at some strategic points; (e) embodiment in the peace agreement of the terms of withdrawal from occupied territories; and (f) a guarantee of freedom of navigation of all ships through the Strait of Tiran by the stationing of international forces at Sharm el Sheikh;

(2) taken note of the response of the parties to the aforesaid proposals;

(3) called on the Secretary-General to reactivate the mission of his Special Representative in pursuance of the Security Council's resolution of 22 November 1967; and

(4) called on the parties to resume immediately the conversations under the auspices of the Special Representative with a view to concluding a peace agreement.

The other draft resolution, orginally submitted by Costa Rica, Haiti and Uruguay, was subsequently submitted in a revised version by Costa Rica, El Salvador, Haiti and Uruguay. It was rejected by the Assembly on 13 December by a recorded vote of 56 to 18, with 47 abstentions.

By the operative part of this proposal, the Assembly would have:

(1) expressed its gratitude for the efforts of the Secretary-General's Special Representative and of the Committee of African Heads of State of OAU to achieve peace in the Middle East;

(2) requested the Special Representative to redouble his efforts to induce the belligerent parties to renew negotiations through him;

(3) requested the parties to agree to renew negotiations through the Special Representative and to do their utmost to make possible the agreements necessary for the implementation of the Security Council's resolution of 22 November 1967 taken as a single whole;

(4) urged the parties to study carefully and with determination the conciliation proposals of OAU, which might constitute practical measures conducive to the implementation of the resolution of 22 November 1967 in all its provisions and hence to a just and lasting peace for the region;

(5) appealed to all Member States to help to create an atmosphere favourable to a peaceful, just and definitive solution; and

(6) decided to retain the item entitled "The situation in the Middle East" on its agenda until a peaceful, just and definitive settlement had been achieved.

Among the amendments submitted to the 21-power text and rejected by the Assembly were two by Barbados and Ghana, which would have added a new preambular paragraph by which the

Assembly would express its appreciation to the Special Representative for his efforts to bring about a peace agreement, and would have substituted parts of their own draft resolution for certain operative paragraphs of the 21-power text.

Amendments proposed by Senegal and rejected by the Assembly would have deleted the phrase —in the first operative paragraph of the 21-power text—stipulating that territories occupied by force must be restored. Also, among other things, a new operative paragraph would have noted with satisfaction the replies given by Egypt and Israel to the Committee of African Heads of State and considered the replies sufficiently positive to make possible a resumption of the Special Representative's mission. Senegal also proposed deletion of the paragraph in the 21-power draft by which the Security Council would be asked to consider, if necessary, making arrangements under the relevant Articles of the United Nations Charter to ensure the implementation of its resolution of 22 November 1967.

Prior to the vote, the representative of Canada said he could not conscientiously support any of the texts as being a realistic and forward-looking basis for renewed peace talks. What was needed, he said, was a substantial display by the parties of readiness to move forward from the fixed positions which had been at the root of the long-standing impasse. The framework for a peaceful settlement, and ample machinery for elaborating its terms, remained intact and at the parties' disposal in the form of the Security Council's resolution of 22 November 1967 and the Jarring mission. In Canada's view, there was no valid reason why the process of forging agreement should not be resumed in the wake of the Assembly's debate.

The Chinese representative said he would abstain in the vote on the 21-power text as it failed to condemn United States imperialism for its support of Israeli zionist aggression against the Arab countries and peoples, and failed to mention that the just national rights of the Palestinian people must be restored.

The United States representative said he would abstain from voting on all three texts. While agreeing with much of the revised 21-power text, the United States felt that that text would alter the balance of the Security Council's resolution of 22 November 1967. The United States attached great importance to strict adherence to that basic document, he added, on which his Government's hopes for a peaceful settlement in the Middle East were based. The General Assembly could not by itself resolve the differences Ambassador Jarring had been unable to overcome, and the United States representative feared that the 21-power text might delay rather than promote the engagement of the parties in productive negotiations.

DOCUMENTARY REFERENCES

Communications to Security Council

S/10070 and Add.1,2. Report of 4 January 1971 of Secretary-General on activities of Special Representative to Middle East, and addenda.

S/10083. Letter of 20 January 1971 from Egypt (enclosing aide-mémoire of 15 January 1971 to Special Representative of Secretary-General).

S/10089. Letter of 25 January 1971 from Jordan (enclosing statement submitted to Special Representative of Secretary-General).

S/10098. Letter of 2 February 1971 from Egypt (enclosing aide-mémoire of 1 February 1971 to Special Representative of Secretary-General).

S/10403 (A/8541). Report of 30 November 1971 of Secretary-General on activities of his Special Representative to Middle East.

S/10438 (A/8566). Letter of 9 December 1971 from Israel (transmitting reply of 28 November 1971 to proposals by Committee of 10 of OAU).

S/10443 (A/8576). Letter of 10 December 1971 from Egypt (enclosing memorandum to Chairman of Sub-Committee of 4 African Heads of State).

Consideration by General Assembly

General Assembly—26th session
Plenary meetings 1999-2002, 2004, 2006, 2008-2010, 2012-2017.

A/8272 (S/10075). Letter of 8 January 1971 from Egypt and Jordan.
A/8281 (S/10123). Letter of 17 February 1971 from Jordan.

A/8282 and Add.1,2 (S/10124 and Add.1,2). Report of 18 February 1971 of Secretary-General, under Security Council resolutions 252(1968), 267(1969) and 271(1969) and General Assembly resolution 2254(ES-V), and addenda.

A/8283 (S/10126), A/8284 (S/10127). Letters of 18 and 19 February 1971 from Israel.

A/8286 and Corr.1 (S/10130 and Corr.1). Letter of 22 February 1971 from Egypt and Jordan.

A/8288 (S/10136). Letter of 28 February 1971 from USSR.

A/8289 (S/10138). Letter of 1 March 1971 from Israel.

A/8290 (S/10139). Letter of 2 March 1971 from Jordan.

A/8291 (S/10140). Letter of 2 March 1971 from Syrian Arab Republic.

A/8292 (S/10141). Letter of 2 March 1971 from Egypt.

A/8294 and Corr.1 (S/10144 and Corr.1). Letter of 4 March 1971 from Bulgaria.

A/8295 (S/10146). Letter of 5 March 1971 from Israel.

A/8296 (A/10149). Letter of 8 March 1971 from Jordan.

A/8297 (S/10152). Letter of 9 March 1971 from Egypt, Indonesia, Jordan, Pakistan, Saudi Arabia, Somalia and Tunisia (transmitting letter of 22 February 1971 from International Moslem Organizations).

A/8298 (S/10154). Note verbale of 11 March 1971 from Iran.

A/8300 (S/10158). Letter of 16 March 1971 from Israel.

A/8301 (S/10159). Letter of 15 March 1971 from Spain.

A/8302 (S/10160). Letter of 19 March 1971 from Israel.

A/8303 (S/10163). Letter of 23 March 1971 from Spain.

A/8305 (S/10167). Letter of 29 March 1971 from Israel.

A/8306 (S/10168). Letter of 30 March 1071 from Spain.

A/8307 (S/10169). Letter of 1 April 1971 from Jordan.

A/8310 (S/10188). Letter of 6 May 1971 from Iraq (transmitting letter of 28 April 1971 from Grand Rabbi of Jewish Community in Iraq).

A/8318 (S/10215). Letter of 1 June 1971 from Syrian Arab Republic.

A/8323 and Corr.1 (S/10220 and Corr.1). Letter of 10 June 1971 from Israel.

A/8356 (S/10290). Letter of 13 August 1971 from Syrian Arab Republic.

A/8401. Report of Secretary-General on work of the Organization, 16 June 1970–15 June 1971, Part One, Chapter I.

A/8401/Add.1. Introduction to report of Secretary-General, September 1971, Part Two, Chapter IV, paras. 217-229.

A/8402. Report of Security Council, 16 June 1970–15 June 1971, Chapter 2.

A/8541 (S/10403). Report of 30 November 1971 of Secretary-General on activities of his Special Representative to Middle East.

A/8566 (S/10438). Letter of 9 December 1971 from Israel (transmitting reply fo 28 November 1971 to proposals by Committee of 10 of OAU).

A/8576 (S/10443). Letter of 10 December 1971 from Egypt (enclosing memorandum to Chairman of Sub-Committee of 4 African Heads of State).

A/8586. Letter of 11 December 1971 from Egypt (transmitting telegram of 7 December 1971 from German Democratic Republic).

A/L.650 and Corr.1 and Add.1,2 and Rev.1. Afghanistan, Cameroon, Congo, Cyprus, Equatorial Guinea, Ethiopia, Guinea, India, Indonesia, Iran, Malaysia, Mali, Mauritania, Mauritius, Nigeria, Pakistan, Somalia, Spain, United Republic of Tanzania, Yugoslavia, Zambia: draft resolution and revision.

A/L.651 and Add.1. Barbados and Ghana: draft resolution.

A/L.652 and Add.1. Costa Rica, Haiti and Uruguay: draft resolution.

A/L.652/Rev.1. Costa Rica, El Salvador, Haiti, Uruguay: revised draft resolution, rejected by Assembly on 13 December 1971, meeting 2016, by recorded vote of 18 in favour to 56 against, with 47 abstentions, as follows:

In favour: Barbados, Bolivia, Botswana, Costa Rica, Dominican Republic, El Salvador, Haiti, Israel, Kenya, Khmer Republic, Lesotho, Liberia, Mdagascar, Malawi, New Zealand, Nicaragua, Senegal, Uruguay.

Against: Afghanistan, Albania, Bahrain, Bulgaria, Burma, Burundi, Byelorussian SSR, Cameroon, Ceylon, Chad, China, Congo, Cuba, Cyprus, Czechoslovakia, Egypt, Equatorial Guinea, France, Gambia, Guinea, Hungary, India, Indonesia, Iran, Iraq, Jordan, Kuwait, Lebanon, Libyan Arab Republic, Malaysia, Mali, Mauritania, Mongolia, Nigeria, Oman, Pakistan, People's Democratic Republic of Yemen, Poland, Qatar, Romania, Saudi Arabia, Somalia, Spain, Sudan, Syrian Arab Republic, Togo, Tunisia, Turkey, Uganda, Ukrainian SSR, USSR, United Arab Emirates, United Republic of Tanzania, Yemen, Yugoslavia, Zambia.

Abstaining: Argentina, Australia, Austria, Belgium, Brazil, Canada, Central African Republic, Chile, Colombia, Denmark, Ethiopia, Fiji, Finland, Gabon, Ghana, Greece, Guyana, Honduras, Iceland, Ireland, Italy, Ivory Coast, Jamaica, Japan, Laos, Luxembourg, Malta, Mexico, Nepal, Netherlands, Niger, Norway, Panama, Paraguay, Peru, Rwanda, Sierra Leone, Singapore, Swaziland, Sweden, Thailand, Trinidad and Tobago, United Kingdom, United States, Upper Volta, Venezuela, Zaire.

A/L.655 and Add.1. Barbados and Ghana: amendments to 21-power draft resolution, A/L.650.

A/L.656. Senegal: amendments to 21-power draft resolution, A/L.650.

A/L.657. Belgium, France, Italy, Luxembourg, Netherlands, United Kingdom: amendments to 21-power draft resolution, A/L.650.

RESOLUTION 2799(XXVI), as proposed by 21 powers, A/L.650/Rev.1, adopted by Assembly on 13 December 1971, meeting 2016, by recorded vote of 79 to 7, with 36 abstentions:

In favour: Afghanistan, Argentina, Austria, Bahrain, Belgium, Bulgaria, Burma, Burundi, Byelorussian SSR, Cameroon, Ceylon, Chad, Chile, Colombia, Congo, Cuba, Cyprus, Czechoslovakia, Egypt, Equatorial Guinea, Ethiopia, Finland, France, Gambia, Greece, Guinea, Guyana, Hungary, India, Indonesia, Iran, Ireland, Italy, Jamaica, Japan, Jordan, Kenya, Kuwait, Laos, Lebanon, Luxembourg, Malaysia, Mali, Malta, Mauritania, Mexico, Mongolia, Nepal, Netherlands, Niger, Nigeria, Norway, Oman, Pakistan, Peru, Poland, Qatar, Romania, Rwanda, Saudi Arabia, Sierra Leone, Somalia, Spain, Sudan, Thailand, Togo, Trinidad and Tobago, Tunisia, Turkey, Uganda, Ukrainian SSR, USSR, United Arab Emirates, United Kingdom, United Republic of Tanzania, Venezuela, Yemen, Yugoslavia, Zambia.

Against: Costa Rica, Dominican Republic, El Salvador, Haiti, Israel, Nicaragua, Uruguay.

Abstaining: Algeria, Australia, Barbados, Bolivia, Botswana, Brazil, Canada, Central African Republic, China, Dahomey, Denmark, Ecuador, Fiji, Gabon, Ghana, Honduras, Iceland, Ivory Coast, Khmer Republic, Lesotho, Liberia, Libyan Arab Republic, Madagascar, Malawi, Morocco, New Zealand, Panama, Paraguay, People's Democratic Republic of Yemen, Senegal, Singapore, Sweden, Syrian Arab Republic, United States, Upper Volta, Zaire.

The General Assembly,

Deeply concerned at the continuation of the grave situation prevailing in the Middle East, particularly since the conflict of June 1967, which constitutes a serious threat to international peace and security,

Convinced that Security Council resolution 242(1967) of 22 November 1967 should be implemented immediately in all its parts in order to achieve a just and lasting peace in the Middle East in which every State in the area can live in security,

Determined that the territory of a State shall not be the object of occupation or acquisition by another State resulting from the threat or use of force, which is contrary to the Charter of the United Nations and to the principles enshrined in Security Council resolution 242(1967) as well as in the Declaration on the Strengthening of International Security adopted by the General Assembly on 16 December 1970,

Expressing its appreciation of the efforts of the Committee of African Heads of State undertaken in pursuance of the resolution adopted on 23 June 1971 by the Assembly of Heads of State and Government of the Organization of African Unity at its eighth ordinary session,

Gravely concerned at the continuation of Israel's occupation of the Arab territories since 5 June 1967,

Having considered the item entitled "The situation in the Middle East,"

1. *Reaffirms* that the acquisition of territories by force is inadmissible and that, consequently, territories thus occupied must be restored;

2. *Reaffirms* that the establishment of a just and lasting peace in the Middle East should include the application of both the following principles:

(a) Withdrawal of Israeli armed forces from territories occupied in the recent conflict;

(b) Termination of all claims or states of belligerency, and respect for and acknowledgement of the sovereignty, territorial integrity and political independence of every State in the area and its right to live in peace within secure and recognized boundaries free from threats or acts of force;

3. *Requests* the Secretary-General to take the necessary measures to reactivate the mission of the Special Representative of the Secretary-General to the Middle East in order to promote agreement and assist efforts to reach a peace agreement as envisaged in the Special Representative's aide-mémoire of 8 February 1971;

4. *Expresses its full support* for all the efforts of the Special Representative to implement Security Council resolution 242(1967);

5. *Notes with appreciation* the positive reply given by Egypt to the Special Representative's initiative for establishing a just and lasting peace in the Middle East;

6. *Calls upon* Israel to respond favourably to the Special Representative's peace initiative;

7. *Further invites* the parties to the Middle East conflict to give their full co-operation to the Special Representative in order to work out practical measures for:

(a) Guaranteeing freedom of navigation through international waterways in the area;

(b) Achieving a just settlement of the refugee problem;

(c) Guaranteeing the territorial inviolability and political independence of every State in the area;

8. *Requests* the Secretary-General to report to the Security Council and to the General Assembly, as appropriate, on the progress made by the Special Representative in the implementation of Security Council resolution 242(1967) and of the present resolution;

9. *Requests* the Security Council to consider, if necessary, making arrangements, under the relevant Articles of the Charter of the United Nations, with regard to the implementation of resolution 242(1967).

The status of the cease-fire

Israel-Jordan sector

During 1971, the situation along the Israel-Jordan cease-fire line remained quiet. No complaints were submitted by either country regarding any cease-fire violation, nor did the Security Council meet to consider any complaint in that connexion.

Communications concerning Israel and Egypt

From 1 January to 10 March 1971, the Suez Canal sector was quiet. Reports on the situation there issued by the Secretary-General on 11 January and 2 and 22 February related mainly to the relocation or reopening of United Nations observation posts in the area.

On 10 March, the Secretary-General reported that the situation in the Suez Canal sector had been quiet since 8 August 1970, although during that period there had been a number of flights by both Egyptian and Israeli jet aircraft over the sector. He felt that in the circumstances it was advisable to resume the practice of reporting to the Security Council concerning the Suez Canal sector which had prevailed before 8 August 1970. The Secretary-General hoped that his reports might be helpful during a period when the maintenance of quiet was crucial to efforts to find a peaceful settlement in the whole area. He then reported that although there had been no ground activity in the Suez Canal sector, Israeli aircraft and one unidentified aircraft had crossed the Canal from east to west and that Israeli overflights had been confirmed by several United Nations observation posts.

Supplemental information issued by the Secretary-General between 19 March and 31 December, on the basis of reports received from the Chief of Staff of the United Nations Truce Supervision Organization in Palestine (UNTSO), reported little or no ground activity, but noted that from time to time there were reports of some aerial activity involving flights by both Egyptian and Israeli aircraft over the sector. On occasion, these flights had taken place over the positions of one party or the other, and charges and countercharges of cease-fire violations were filed with UNTSO.

Complaints by Israel and Lebanon

On 15 January 1971, Lebanon said that helicopter-borne Israeli armed units had attacked the village of Sarafand located some 43 kilometres north of Lebanon's southern border and, after having been engaged by Lebanese armed forces, had withdrawn at three o'clock that morning. The Israeli authorities had attempted to justify their action by alleging that, on 2 January, six *fedayeen* coming by boat from that village had landed just south of Lebanon's border and that five of them had been captured. However, investigation by Lebanese authorities had established that Israel had engineered the whole plan. Thus, Israel had first initiated an incident and then used it as a pretext for military action against Lebanon.

Israel stated on 19 January that since 30 December there had been a further intensification of sabotage raids and shelling attacks on Israeli villages carried out from bases inside Lebanon. In all their activities, the terrorists had full support and encouragement from the Lebanese Government. As for the complaint made by Lebanon in its letter of 15 January, Israel said that on 2 January five raiders coming from the Lebanese harbour of Sarafand, which served as a base of operation against Israel, had attempted to land in northern Israel but had been captured. During the night of 14/15 January, an Israeli unit had acted to disable that terrorist base and, in the ensuing encounter, had killed 10 saboteurs and wounded many others. Six Israeli soldiers had been injured. Thus, Israel's action had not been against a civilian village, as alleged by Lebanon.

On 5 February, Lebanon stated that on 1 February Israeli patrols had crossed the Lebanese border and attacked villages in southern Lebanon, blown up some houses and abducted some civilians in another premeditated encroachment upon the sovereignty and territorial integrity of Lebanon.

On 8 April, Lebanon charged that on 5 April Israeli patrols, in violation of the Armistice Agreement and in defiance of relevant United Nations resolutions, had crossed the border at three points and had blown up several houses in three different villages.

On 12 April, Israel drew the attention of the Security Council to the intensification of attacks committed against it from Lebanese territory and stated that, between 11 March and 10 April, 19 such attacks had been carried out against Israeli villages by terror organizations from bases in Lebanon, compelling Israel to take measures in self-defence to protect the lives and property of its citizens.

In communications dated 16 and 23 June, 1 July, 10 August, and 4 and 20 September 1971, Lebanon submitted complaints that on several occasions Israel had used artillery and mortars to shell border villages in southern Lebanon and had crossed the border at several points to destroy Lebanese houses, civilian property and crops. Many civilians had been killed, wounded or abducted. Lebanon charged also that these new acts of aggression were aimed at disturbing peace and security in southern Lebanon, and at undermining all efforts to establish a just and lasting peace in the Middle East. Lebanon protested Israel's violation of Lebanon's sovereignty and territorial integrity, its disregard of the United Nations Charter and its disrespect for the pertinent Security Council resolutions.

Israel submitted counter-complaints on 21 and 30 June, 12 August, and 7 and 24 September that terror squads coming from Lebanese territory had attacked civilian installations and villages in Israeli territory on several occasions, causing casualties and property damage. The letters stated that it was a matter of common knowledge that bases from which acts of aggression were launched against Israel were located on Lebanese territory and that those acts had taken place with the knowledge and consent of the Government of Lebanon, as indicated by several press reports and official statements in Lebanon. Israel, which had the right to defend and protect its territory and citizens, pursued a policy based on the reciprocal observance of the cease-fire, which entailed the obligation of Lebanon to prevent armed attacks from its territory against Israel.

Complaints by Israel and the Syrian Arab Republic

On 7 January 1971, the Secretary-General circulated a report received from the Chief of Staff of the United Nations Truce Supervision Organization in Palestine (UNTSO) regarding an incident that had taken place at United Nations Observation Post Four in the Israel-Syria sector. At 2305 hours GMT on 2 January, United Nations military observers had been held up in their living-caravan by three persons carrying sub-machine guns of an unidentified type. Before leaving, 20 minutes later, the intruders had taken a number of items from the caravan and had ripped the radio

communication set. Subsequently, the Chairman of the Israel-Syria Mixed Armistice Commission (ISMAC) had reported the incident to the Syrian delegate, who had promised to inform the Syrian authorities.

An inquiry conducted by UNTSO on 3 January, the report continued, had failed to establish the identity of the intruders and the UNTSO findings had been communicated to the authorities of both countries with the request that they provide the results of their inquiries.

On 5 January, Israel had reported that a search conducted on 3 January at the site of the post had revealed tracks of three persons wearing regular Syrian boots leading towards Syrian territory. The Israeli investigators had found some of the items that had been taken from the United Nations caravan. On the following day, the Syrian authorities had informed ISMAC that, as a consequence of their investigations, they could assure the Commission unreservedly that the intruders had not been members of the Syrian regular army. The Chief of Staff of UNTSO reported that, despite inquiries conducted into the incident, it appeared that the identity of the intruders could not be established.

In forwarding the report to the Security Council, the Secretary-General expressed his concern about that type of incident and warned against the serious implications it could entail for the cease-fire observation operation in the sector. The United Nations observers, he added, did not carry arms and depended for their safety on their special status and on the protection provided by the parties to the cease-fire. The Secretary-General concluded by appealing to all concerned to take all possible measures to prevent a recurrence of such incidents.

In a letter dated 18 January, the Syrian Government denied a charge broadcast by Radio Israel to the effect that on the night of 2/3 January, three Syrian regular soldiers had entered United Nations Observation Post Four and stolen some items.

In a letter dated 25 January, Israel stated that an investigation carried out by Israeli authorities following the raid on the observation post had revealed that tracks of three persons wearing regular Syrian boots had led investigators towards Syrian territory. Those findings had been transmitted to the United Nations observers and had been published in the report of 7 January. As the Syrian lines were well guarded by a network of military positions, Israel's letter added, no armed elements could operate from within the Syrian military zone without the knowledge of the Syrian authorities. Syrian responsibility for all violations of United Nations observation posts by elements operating from behind its lines was clearly evident.

In a letter dated 26 January, the Syrian Arab

Republic stated that the "investigation" carried out by Israel and its allegation that the Syrian Government had been responsible for all violations of United Nations observation posts were one-sided and constituted an attempt to distort facts. Furthermore, the report of 7 January referred to by Israel had denied the Israeli allegation and had, in fact, concluded that the identity of the armed intruders could not be established.

In a series of reports issued in late June and early July, the Chief of Staff of UNTSO stated that Israeli forces had crossed the limits of the Israeli forward defended localities and, after having penetrated about 800 to 1,000 metres inside Syrian territory, recrossed the cease-fire line. On 22 July, the Chief of Staff reported that the Israeli Liaison Officer had objected to those reports as incorrect. Following verification inquiries conducted by UNTSO into the Israeli complaint, the general conclusion was that although verbal and documentary evidence confirmed the accuracy of the observers' reports, no physical evidence could be found of the reported incursions.

During 1971, the Secretary-General continued to issue reports containing supplemental information he received from the UNTSO Chief of Staff relating to sporadic firing incidents that took place in the Israel-Syria sector and to some aerial activity. The Chief of Staff included in his reports complaints submitted by both Israel and the Syrian Arab Republic to the Chairman of ISMAC regarding cease-fire violations. In their complaints, the parties requested that necessary measures be taken to prevent future violations.

DOCUMENTARY REFERENCES

Communications concerning Israel and Egypt
S/7930/Add.1043. Supplemental information received by Secretary-General, dated 11 January 1971.
S/7930/Add.1066, 1085. Supplemental information received by Secretary-General, dated 2 and 22 February 1971.
S/7930/Add.1104, 1111, 1115, 1117, 1120, 1128, 1130. Supplemental information received by Secretary-General, dated 10, 16, 19, 20, 22 and 30 March 1971.
S/7930/Add.1134, 1138, 1144, 1153, 1154, 1162, 1164, 1166, 1168. Supplemental information received by Secretary-General, dated 2, 6, 11, 19, 20 and 26-29 April 1971.
S/7930/Add.1174, 1179, 1182, 1186, 1188. Supplemental information received by Secretary-General, dated 4, 8, 10, 13, and 15 May 1971.
S/7930/Add.1209, 1211, 1220, 1227, 1230, 1232, 1235, 1238. Supplemental information received by Secretary-General, dated 3, 5, 14, 21, 23, 24 and 28 June 1971.
S/7930/Add.1244, 1250, 1252, 1256, 1257, 1259, 1262, 1264, 1268, 1270, 1277, 1281. Supplemental information received by Secretary-General, dated 1, 7, 9, 12-15, 17, 19, 21, 27 and 29 July 1971.
S/7930/Add.1286, 1289, 1292, 1294 and Corr.1, 1300, 1307, 1311, 1314, 1315, 1319, 1320 and Corr.1, 1321, 1325. Supplemental information received by Secretary-General, dated 2, 4, 6, 9, 12, 18, 23, 24, 27, 28, 30 and 31 August 1971.
S/7930/Add.1329, 1331, 1334, 1337, 1341, 1344, 1348, 1351-1353, 1363. Supplemental information received by Secretary-General, dated 3, 6, 8, 12, 13, 16, 18, 20 and 27 September 1971.
S/7930/Add.1368, 1375, 1378, 1381, 1386, 1388, 1390, 1393, 1397, 1400, 1407. Supplemental information received by Secretary-General, dated 1, 7, 9, 11, 15, 16, 18, 20, 22, 25 and 30 October 1971.
S/7930/Add.1414, 1416, 1422, 1426, 1437, 1441. Supplemental information received by Secretary-General, dated 5, 8, 11, 15, 24 and 29 November 1971.
S/7930/Add.1451, 1459. Supplemental information received by Secretary-General, dated 8 and 20 December 1971.

Complaints by Israel and Lebanon
S/10078. Letter of 15 January 1971 from Lebanon.
S/10081. Letter of 19 January 1971 from Israel.
S/10101, S/10172 and Corr.1. Letters of 5 February and 8 April 1971 from Lebanon.
S/10175. Letter of 12 April 1971 from Israel.
S/10226. Letter of 16 June 1971 from Lebanon.
S/10231. Letter of 21 June 1971 from Israel.

S/10235. Letter of 23 June 1971 from Lebanon.
S/10244. Letter of 30 June 1971 from Israel.
S/10247, S/10286. Letters of 1 July and 10 August 1971 from Lebanon.
S/10289. Letter of 12 August 1971 from Israel.
S/10305. Letter of 4 September 1971 from Lebanon.
S/10307. Letter of 7 September 1971 from Israel.
S/10329. Letter of 20 September 1971 from Lebanon.
S/10335. Letter of 24 September 1971 from Israel.

Complaints by Israel and the Syrian Arab Republic
S/7930/Add.1031-1042, 1044-1062. Supplemental information received by Secretary-General, dated 2, 4-9, 11-16, 18-23 and 25-30 January 1971.
S/7930/Add.1063-1065, 1067-1084, 1086-1092. Supplemental information received by Secretary-General, dated 1-6, 8-13, 15-20 and 22-27 February 1971.
S/7930/Add.1093-1103, 1105-1109, 1110 and Corr.1, 1112-1114, 1116, 1118, 1119, 1121-1127, 1129, 1131. Supplemental information received by Secretary-General, dated 1-6, 8-13, 15-20, 22-27 and 29-31 March 1971.
S/7930/Add.1132, 1133, 1135-1137, 1139-1143, 1145-1152, 1155-1161, 1163, 1165, 1167, 1169. Supplemental information received by Secretary-General, dated 1-3, 5-10, 12, 13, 15-17, 19-24 and 26-30 April 1971.
S/7930/Add.1170, 1171 and Corr.1, 1172, 1173, 1175-1178, 1180, 1181, 1183-1185, 1187, 1189-1205. Supplemental information received by Secretary-General dated 1, 3-8, 10-15, 17-22 and 24-31 May 1971.
S/7930/Add.1206-1208, 1210, 1212-1219, 1221-1226, 1228, 1229, 1231, 1233, 1234, 1236, 1237, 1239-1242. Supplemental information received by Secretary-General, dated 1-5, 7, 8, 10-12, 14-19, 21-26 and 28-30 June 1971.
S/7930/Add.1243, 1245-1249, 1251, 1253-1255, 1258, 1260, 1261, 1263, 1265-1267, 1269, 1271-1276, 1278-1280, 1282, 1283. Supplemental information received by Secretary-General, dated 1-3, 5, 7, 9, 10, 12-17, 19-24 and 26-31 July 1971.
S/7930/Add.1284, 1285, 1287, 1288, 1290, 1291, 1293, 1295-1299, 1301-1306, 1308-1310, 1312, 1313, 1316-1318, 1322-1324. Supplemental information received by Secretary-General, dated 2-7, 9-14, 16-21, 23, 25, 27, 30 and 31 August 1971.
S/7930/Add.1326-1328, 1330, 1332, 1333, 1335, 1336, 1338-1340, 1342, 1343, 1345-1347, 1349, 1350 and Corr.1, 1354-1362, 1364-1366. Supplemental information received by Secretary-General, dated 1-4, 6-11, 13-18, 20-25 and 27-30 September 1971.

S/7930/Add.1367, 1369-1374, 1376, 1377, 1379, 1380, 1382-1385, 1387, 1389, 1391, 1392, 1394-1396, 1398, 1399, 1401-1404, 1405 and Corr.1, 1406. Supplemental information received by Secretary-General, dated 1, 2, 4-9, 11-16, 18-23 and 25-30 October 1971.
S/7930/Add.1408-1413, 1415, 1417-1421, 1423-1425, 1427-1436, 1438-1440, 1442-1444. Supplemental information

received by Secretary-General, dated 1-6, 8-13, 15-20, 22-27, 29 and 30 November 1971.
S/7930/Add.1445-1450, 1452-1458, 1460-1470. Supplemental information received by Secretary-General, December 1971.
S/10080. Letter of 18 January 1971 from Syrian Arab Republic.
S/10088. Letter of 25 January 1971 from Israel.
S/10090. Letter of 26 January 1971 from Syrian Arab Republic.

The situation in and around Jerusalem and its Holy Places

During 1971, the Security Council and the Secretary-General received a number of communications relating to the status of the City of Jerusalem. The Arab countries in general and Jordan in particular protested the changes in the status of the City, charging that Israel had violated United Nations resolutions in this regard. Israel, for its part, denied the charges. The Secretary-General reported several times during the year on the subject; the Security Council met at the request of Jordan to discuss the matter and on 25 September adopted resolution 298 (1971). (For details, see below.)

Communications and reports

On 8 January 1971, Jordan and Egypt, in a joint letter to the Secretary-General, protested Israeli measures to change the character of the City of Jerusalem and drew attention to a so-called master plan for Jerusalem, which called for an additional 200,000 Jewish people to be settled within five years in the occupied lands in and around the City.

In another letter, dated 17 February, Jordan said that according to information it had received, Israeli authorities had bulldozed parts of the premises of Government House—the headquarters of the United Nations Truce Supervision Organization in Palestine (UNTSO)—situated in no man's land in Jerusalem. It requested a report by the Secretary-General on that violation, in accordance with the Security Council's resolutions of 21 May 1968[8] and 3 July 1969.[9]

On 18 February, Israel declared that United Nations headquarters in Jerusalem had in no way been affected by development activities being undertaken in the City to meet urgent housing needs of the population. In another letter, dated 19 February, Israel stated that in fact it was Jordan that had violated and occupied the compound of United Nations headquarters in Jerusalem on 5 June 1967, and it recalled that the Secretary-General had reported on that issue to the Security Council at its meeting on that day.

On 18 February, the Secretary-General, in accordance with previous resolutions of the Security Council and the General Assembly, submitted a report concerning Jerusalem that included texts of notes by him to Israel, and Israel's replies thereto.

In a note to Israel of 10 December 1970, the Secretary-General reported, he had referred to reports concerning a master plan for an area within and outside the Old City walls in which the Government House area had been classified as a residential area, with land to be set aside for hotels. Representatives of UNTSO had approached Israeli authorities on the matter and had been informed that the plan in question had not yet been made public. The Israeli authorities gave no reply as to whether the plan affected the Government House premises.

In order to meet his responsibilities to the Security Council and the General Assembly in connexion with the status of the City of Jerusalem, the Secretary-General asked for detailed information on and a copy of the reported master plan. He also underscored the importance he attached to the status of the United Nations premises at Government House and sought clarification from Israel as to whether the plan envisaged any development affecting those premises, both as to their current limits and those in effect before June 1967.[10]

In a reply dated 8 January 1971, the Secretary-General reported, Israel had indicated that its position with regard to Government House continued to be the same as had been indicated by Israel in June and August 1967 and that no changes were contemplated in the arrangements made then.

On 26 January, the Secretary-General reported, he had again requested a copy of the reported master plan for Jerusalem, together with detailed information thereon.

Also on 26 January, in a note dealing with the United Nations Government House premises, the Secretary-General said that in so far as the assurances proffered by Israel on 8 January did not safeguard the right of the United Nations to possession of the whole of its Government House premises as constituted on 5 June 1967, they did not cover the obligations of the Secretary-General in the matter.

He went on to say that he had been informed by UNTSO that on 3 January a bulldozer had begun

[8] See Y.U.N., 1968, pp. 264-65, text of resolution 252 (1968).
[9] See Y.U.N., 1969, p. 220, text of resolution 267 (1969).
[10] For background information see Y.U.N., 1967, pp. 174-89 and p. 237.

working within the perimeter of the Government House premises as constituted on 5 June 1967. This activity, coinciding with recent press reports about a project to erect housing units and other buildings in the area, indicated a further and serious violation of the inviolability of United Nations premises under the United Nations Charter and the Convention on the Privileges and Immunities of the United Nations. In view of the irreparable physical change to the premises which the work currently being undertaken might bring about, the Secretary-General, while reserving the right of the United Nations to claim compensation for any ensuing loss or damage, requested that the work be suspended.

The Secretary-General said he continued to maintain that there was no basis for any curtailment of United Nations rights to Government House as constituted on 5 June 1967. Accordingly, in the exercise of his responsibility in the matter, he requested the unreserved return to the United Nations of the remainder of its Government House premises.

In his report, the Secretary-General noted that no reply had been received from Israel to the above two notes.

On 22 February, Jordan and Egypt drew attention to Israel's continued confiscation of Arab land and property and the construction of Israeli settlements, housing, hotels and industrial projects, in violation of General Assembly and Security Council resolutions. The letter added that according to Israeli press reports, Israel was planning to build 3,000 housing units as well as 13 buildings on confiscated Arab land in east Jerusalem, and that Arab inhabitants of that area were being evacuated to be replaced by Jewish families. Those measures appeared to be a prelude to the so-called master plan for Jerusalem, which envisaged the construction of a total of 35,000 units on confiscated private and public Arab lands, designed to accommodate 122,000 new Jewish immigrants in order to make Jerusalem "a Jewish city."

The so-called master plan for Jerusalem, the letter went on, continued to draw sharp criticism from the international community, for it purported to change the demographic situation and character not only of Jerusalem but also of the villages and hills around the City, extending to the towns of Ramallah in the north and Bethlehem in the south.

On 1 March, Israel replied that Jewish and Arab lands alike had been expropriated, without any discrimination, for public development and housing and that some Arab and Jewish owners had already received full compensation. With regard to the existence of a master plan for Jerusalem, Israel said, the preparation of a development plan

for any city was a customary procedure of modern urban development throughout the world and the municipal authorities of Jerusalem were doing their best in that direction through consultations with world-renowned experts.

In further protests about alleged confiscation of Arab property by Israel, Jordan informed the Secretary-General on 2 and 8 March that, according to an Israeli press report, Israeli authorities had issued an order transferring the shares of the Electricity Company of the District of Jerusalem—which belonged to the Jordanian municipality—to the Israeli municipality.

By a letter of 5 March, Israel replied that in order to ensure the continuity and operation of electrical service to the people of Jerusalem it was necessary to change the status of certain elements of the public ownership of those services. However, no change had taken place in the ownership status of private persons, Arabs or others.

By a letter dated 2 March, the Syrian Arab Republic recalled that the Secretary-General, in two notes reproduced in his report of 18 February, had asked Israel for information on and a copy of the master plan for Jerusalem. United Nations Members desirous of maintaining the rule of law had been awaiting Israel's replies. Instead, according to press reports Israel had continued to implement its master plan in Jerusalem, including work being carried out within United Nations premises. The Government and people of the Syrian Arab Republic could not keep silent on the fate of the Holy City of Jerusalem, which was being turned into a "zionist exhibition."

By a letter dated 9 March, Egypt, Indonesia, Jordan, Pakistan, Saudi Arabia, Somalia and Tunisia transmitted to the Secretary-General the text of a resolution on the question of Jerusalem adopted by the International Moslem Organizations, which had met at Mecca, Saudi Arabia, from 11 to 15 February 1971. The resolution urged that efforts be continued for the liquidation of all traces of Israeli aggressions, supported the Palestinian commandos, and called for an end to the continuance of inhuman zionist aggression, in order to save the Holy City of Jerusalem from Judaization and the Arab citizens of the Holy City from becoming refugees.

On 16 March, Israel said in reply that the letter from the seven powers contained allegations that were misleading and reflected the belligerent policies pursued by the Arab States against Israel. In spite of the abnormal conditions in the region and the security problems caused by the belligerent policies of the Arabs, the Moslem institutions in Jerusalem and its Moslem residents and visitors enjoyed the liberty and facilities to pursue their normal activities. Israel rejected the accusation that it was "Judaizing" Jerusalem, the very City in which the Jewish ethos was so deeply marked and where Jews had constituted the majority of the population for generations. Israel treated with reverence all that was related to the Holy Places of all faiths and had made great efforts to ensure their improvement and safety.

On 15 March, Spain stated that Israel's continued occupation of Jerusalem could not justify certain measures of assimilation designed to change the true nature and alter the status of the City. The relevant Security Council resolutions should be strictly complied with.

On 19 March, Israel replied that Spain's letter was one more expression of its pro-Arab policy and denied that Israel had taken any measures of assimilation in Jerusalem.

Spain said on 23 March that Israel had been taking advantage of its occupation of Jerusalem in order to alter the status and character of that City, in clear violation of the relevant United Nations resolutions.

On 29 March, Israel replied that Spain had omitted to mention the aggressions against Jerusalem by Jordan and Egypt and the uprooting of the Jewish quarter and Jewish institutions from the Holy City during the Jordanian occupation. While ignoring those facts, Spain had continued to pursue a pro-Arab policy in Middle East matters.

In its reply on 30 March, Spain noted that Israel had not cited examples of any violations by Jordan or Egypt of United Nations resolutions in so far as they related to the character and status of Jerusalem. Spain was concerned over Israel's attempt to change the true nature of Jerusalem and to alter its status in violation of United Nations resolutions.

On 1 April, Jordan drew attention to reported excavations by Israel in the areas adjacent to the southern and western walls of Haram Esh-Sharif, which were endangering the Al Aqsa Mosque, the Moslem Museum and the El-Fakhariyya Minaret. There were also reports that Israel was planning to enact a law confining the Moslem Holy Places in the Haram Esh-Sharif area to Al Aqsa and the Dome of the Rock mosques, placing the Plaza of Haram Esh-Sharif and other religious and cultural places, which were held sacred by Moslems all over the world, outside the designation of Holy Places and at the mercy of future illegal Israeli regulations and excavations. Israel's excavations and the contemplated legislation violated the Hague Convention for the Protection of Cultural Property in the Event of Armed Conflict, of 14 May 1954. They were also contrary to the resolution adopted on 10 October 1962 by the Executive Board of the United Nations Educational, Scientific and Cultural Organization with regard to cultural properties, particularly in the Old City of Jerusalem, which called on Israel among other things to desist from

any archaeological excavations, transfer of cultural properties or any changes in their cultural and historical character.

On 20 April, the Secretary-General issued an addendum to his report of 18 February, containing a further exchange of communications with Israel concerning the status of Jerusalem and United Nations headquarters there. Israel, he said, had replied to his notes of 26 January by a note dated 8 March, in which Israel stated that its position remained as it had been conveyed in various communications on the subject. At the same time, it wished to record reservations to the various legal and other considerations advanced by the Secretary-General, particularly to claims of the United Nations to the occupancy and possession of the whole of the premises of Government House.

In his reply, on 12 April, the Secretary-General had said that, presumably because of the reservations referred to in its note of 8 March, Israel had neither provided a copy of the reported Jerusalem master plan nor any information about it. He also noted that Israel's reply contained neither a direct response to his request to return the whole of the United Nations premises at Government House as constituted on 5 June 1967, nor any precise information on the exact terms of the reservations which Israel held with regard to that request. Furthermore, the reservations in Israel's note had been raised for the first time and had not been mentioned when part of the Government House premises had been returned to the United Nations. In fact, in its letter of 22 August 1967, Israel had not indicated any reservations, although the Secretary-General had expressly preserved the rights of the United Nations to the occupancy and possession of the whole of Government House as constituted when UNTSO was forced to evacuate it on 5 June 1967. He further observed that it was in reliance on the preservation of those United Nations rights that he had authorized the return of UNTSO staff to a lesser area.

The Secretary-General went on to say that, as Israel's reservations related in part to legal considerations, one way of resolving any differences would be to resort to the procedure for settlement provided for in the Convention on the Privileges and Immunities of the United Nations. In view of Israel's current work within and bordering upon Government House property and the absence of a direct reply to the specific requests contained in his note of 26 January 1971, the Secretary-General was constrained to reiterate his request for the unreserved return to the United Nations of the remainder of its Government House premises.

On 1 June, the Syrian Arab Republic transmitted the text of an appeal made by the spiritual leaders of the Christian community of the Syrian Arab Republic, drawing to the attention of the Christians of the world the illegal measures taken by Israeli authorities in order to "zionize" the City of Jerusalem and to expel its Christian and Moslem inhabitants in violation of United Nations resolutions. In a reply dated 10 June, Israel stated that the 80,000 Arabs then visiting Israeli-held territories and Jerusalem did not seem to give much credence to the Syrian charges.

Further to his reports of 18 February and 20 April, the Secretary-General on 20 August issued another report, containing a further exchange of communications with Israel on the subject of the United Nations premises at Government House in Jerusalem.

The Secretary-General said that on 18 August Israel had informed him that, while it reserved its position as recorded in the 1967 exchange of letters, no changes were contemplated with regard to the situation ensuing from that exchange. On 19 August, the Secretary-General had replied that he had understood Israel's letter to mean that Israel, having already discontinued all construction and other work within the area of the United Nations premises at Government House as constituted on 5 June 1967, would refrain from re-initiating such construction or other work within the area until the difference of opinion reflected in the 1967 exchange of letters had been satisfactorily resolved. If that understanding was incorrect, the Secretary-General reiterated that one way of resolving any differences would be to resort to the procedure for settlement laid down in the Convention on the Privileges and Immunities of the United Nations.

Consideration by Security Council (September 1971)

On 13 September 1971, Jordan requested an urgent meeting of the Security Council to consider Israel's illegal actions in Jerusalem in defiance of Security Council resolutions which—among other things—called on Israel to rescind measures already taken and to desist from further action tending to change the status of Jerusalem. Jordan charged that, contrary to those resolutions and in spite of local and international objections, Israel had continued its illegal and unilateral measures to change the character of the City and its environs; the situation thus created was a direct threat to the character of the City and the surrounding suburbs and villages, to the lives and destiny of its people and to international peace and security.

The Security Council held four meetings on the question, between 16 and 25 September. The representatives of Egypt, Israel, Jordan, Lebanon, Mali, Morocco, Saudi Arabia and Tunisia were invited, at their request, to participate in the discussion in the Council without the right to vote.

The representative of Jordan said that the measures taken by Israel in Jerusalem were designed to change the status and character of the Holy City and, at the same time, aimed at preventing the conclusion of a just and peaceful settlement of the Middle East conflict, in the hope that the cease-fire lines would ultimately become Israel's new borders. Israel was contemplating new legislation to extend the borders of Jerusalem to include, by annexation, three Arab towns and 27 villages, over and above what had already been unilaterally and illegally annexed in June 1967. Furthermore, Israeli attempts to enact a law were reported which would confine Moslem Holy Places in the Haram Esh-Sharif area to Al Aqsa and the Dome of the Rock mosques.

The Jordanian representative went on to say that many General Assembly and Security Council resolutions had deplored measures of annexation and called on Israel to rescind such measures and to desist from taking action which would alter the status of Jerusalem. However, Israel had shown contempt for those resolutions and still refused to supply the Secretary-General with any details or satisfactory information on the master plan for Jerusalem which envisaged, among other things, development affecting the United Nations premises at Government House. Israel's determination to Judaize Arab Jerusalem had been manifested in legislative, fiscal and urban measures which were imposing on the City an increasingly special character at the expense of the non-Jewish population. In the light of Israel's disregard of General Assembly and Security Council resolutions, and to ensure Israel's respect for them, he urged that the Council invoke whatever sanctions it deemed fit under Chapter VII of the United Nations Charter.[11]

Israel's spokesman said that Jordan's complaint was a manoeuvre to divert attention from its own internal difficulties. Jordan, which had invaded Jerusalem in 1948 and seized its eastern sector, was now trying to infringe the City's right to normal existence and development. The General Assembly and the Security Council had displayed singular disinterest in Jerusalem's welfare at the most trying and crucial moments. Now that the City was united, the Security Council was being mobilized in an attempt to retard progress and to stifle growth.

With regard to construction work in the City, he noted that city planning was a normal and indispensable element in the development of any city. Building activities in the eastern sector of Jerusalem constituted slum clearance, the reconstruction of the Jewish quarter, the Hebrew

[11] For text of Chapter VII of the Charter, see APPENDIX II.

University campus and the Hadassah Hospital, and the erection of new housing for Arab and Jewish residents who had been living in slums. In order to accommodate the growth of the City's population—Jewish as well as Arab—land had been acquired and landowners, both Arabs and Jews, were being fully compensated. Contrary to Jordanian allegations, there was no master plan. However, in view of the universal interest in the City, the Mayor of Jerusalem had invited an international group of outstanding individuals to form an advisory board to aid the municipality of Jerusalem. The Israeli authorities, he concluded, had ensured and would ensure the sanctity of the Holy Places, freedom of access to them and the jurisdiction of the various religious communities over them.

The spokesmen for Egypt, Lebanon, Morocco, Saudi Arabia and Tunisia supported Jordan's complaint and maintained that the Council, in the face of Israel's defiance, should put an end to that defiance and take any necessary further steps to implement its resolutions, including the application of Chapter VII of the Charter. Morocco hoped that the Council would decide to dispatch a representative or a mission to determine whether or not Israel was complying with the resolutions adopted on Jerusalem. Saudi Arabia urged the Council to bear in mind that no matter what Israel's contention might be, the fact remained that hundreds of millions in the Arab or Moslem world would not concede that 2 million zionists should have sovereignty over Jerusalem.

The representative of Mali noted that the question of Jerusalem was only one of many aspects of the Middle East conflict; any measure infringing relevant United Nations resolutions would hinder negotiations for a peaceful settlement.

The USSR representative said that the resolutions of the Security Council and General Assembly condemning Israel's annexation of the Arab part of Jerusalem were in accordance with the principles of international law based on the inadmissibility of acquiring territory through war. Israel's defiant and negative attitude towards United Nations decisions showed its expansionist and aggressive policy towards the Arab world. Israel's measures in Jerusalem were aimed at changing the Arab nature of the Old City by expelling Arab inhabitants, destroying Arab houses and imposing Israeli settlements in the Arab section.

It was clear, he said, that Israel's plans were intended to undermine the peaceful political settlement envisaged in the Security Council's resolution of 22 November 1967.[12] Therefore, the Council was duty bound to take more decisive action to compel Israel to respect the will of the international community. He felt that the demand to apply Chapter VII of the Charter against Israel was justifiable, and supported the suggestion to dispatch a special mission to Jerusalem.

Belgium's representative said that at a time when it was still possible to reach a negotiated solution, it was advisable to avoid any discussion which might vitiate attempts made in that respect. Belgium, he said, hoped that the Council would adopt a resolution calling on Israel to abrogate measures aimed at changing the status of Jerusalem, and he suggested that the Secretary-General should submit a report showing how measures taken by Israel violated previous resolutions of the Security Council and the Hague conventions on the laws of war.

The spokesman for France said that a review of events since 1967 showed that Israel was pursuing a policy designed to integrate the Arab city totally and permanently within an administratively unified Jerusalem. No one could deny that such measures might soon lead to an irreversible situation. Israel's policy of annexation was in formal contradiction to United Nations resolutions and violated the rules of international law and the Charter. Israel's policy of *fait accompli* increased the resentment of the parties concerned, aggravated the tension in the Middle East and jeopardized the chances of a peaceful settlement which the international community had tried so hard to achieve.

The representative of Argentina believed that the concern of the world over Jerusalem was fully justified because of its historical importance to three religious faiths. Until the status of the City could be defined on the basis of respect for historic and religious interests, innovation should not take place there. Israel must adjust its conduct to the requirements of United Nations resolutions and the Security Council must once again reaffirm its position on Jerusalem.

The Polish representative said that developments in Jerusalem were a part of Israel's over-all aggressive policy of military occupation of territories seized as a result of aggression and consolidating such territorial conquests by creating *faits accomplis*. He urged the Security Council to study the question in the context of its illegality according to the principles of international law, bearing in mind Israel's attitude and actions in disregard of the will of the international community. The Council, he said, should not only reaffirm previous resolutions on the matter but should also consider all measures necessary to ensure their implementation.

In Italy's view, the future of Jerusalem should be determined in accordance with the pertinent

[12] See Y.U.N. 1967, pp. 257-58, text of resolution 242(1967).

resolutions of the United Nations and not through unilateral actions. Israel's measures in the occupied section of Jerusalem were inconsistent with the provisions of international law governing rights and obligations of an occupying power. In particular, the Geneva Convention relative to the Protection of Civilian Persons in Time of War, of 12 August 1949, was, in Italy's opinion, fully applicable to the occupied sections of Jerusalem.

In his capacity as representative of Japan, the President of the Council stated that the Council's resolution of 22 November 1967 had clearly emphasized the inadmissibility of the acquisition of territory by war, a principle which applied also to the situation of Jerusalem. He said that Japan deplored Israel's failure to grant the Secretary-General a detailed description of the so-called master plan and reiterated Japan's position on the desirability of an international régime for the City. He favoured the idea of designating a mission of investigation which would report to the Council on conditions in Jerusalem.

Burundi's representative said that the status of Jerusalem called for respect from all parties concerned, who should do nothing that might in any way contribute to making the situation in the area more dangerous. Burundi believed that the responsibility of the Council lay in re-establishing an atmosphere conducive to prayer and meditation in the Holy City; the United Nations should devise ways of convincing Israel to rescind its decisions concerning the City, including measures for annexation that might become irreversible.

Sierra Leone believed that peace in the Middle East could only be achieved by Israel's withdrawal from the occupied territories in accordance with the Council's resolution of 22 November 1967. Relying on its military power, Israel had rejected a peaceful settlement and had continued its defiance of the international will. Furthermore, it had been taking measures to change the status of the Holy City without any consideration for the feelings of Christians and Moslems throughout the world. If that policy was not ended, the dreadful result would be an intensification of hostility involving Moslems, Jews and Christians alike.

The representative of Somalia said that in occupied Jerusalem, as in other areas of occupied Arab territory, Israel was following its classic policy of expropriation followed by colonization, of creating *faits accomplis* in complete disregard of humanitarian principles or principles of international law. Furthermore, Israel's approach was clearly to make Israeli national interest the sole determining factor of the administration of the City. The administrative and legislative measures taken by Israel in Jerusalem violated numerous United Nations resolutions and had undoubtedly hindered a political settlement of the Middle East problem. The Security Council, he stressed, was duty bound to adopt more effective measures and, to take the United Nations one step forward in meeting its responsibilities in that regard, he submitted a draft resolution.

By the preambular part of the Somali draft, the Council would, among other things, recall its own and the General Assembly's earlier resolutions concerning measures and actions by Israel designed to change the status of the Israeli-occupied section of Jerusalem and would reaffirm the principle that acquisition of territory by military conquest was inadmissible.

The Council would also note with concern the non-compliance by Israel with the relevant resolutions and would note further that since their adoption Israel had taken further measures designed to change the status and character of the occupied section of Jerusalem.

By the operative part of the draft text, the Council would:

(1) reaffirm its resolutions of 21 May 1968[13] and 3 July 1969;[14]

(2) deplore the failure of Israel to respect the previous resolutions adopted by the United Nations concerning measures and actions by Israel purporting to affect the status of the City;

(3) confirm in the clearest possible terms that all legislative and administrative actions taken by Israel to change the status of the City, including expropriation of land and properties, transfer of populations, and legislation aimed at the incorporation of the occupied section, were totally invalid and could not change that status;

(4) urgently call upon Israel to take no further steps in the occupied section of Jerusalem which might purport to change the status of the City, or which would prejudice the rights of the inhabitants and the interests of the international community, or a just and lasting peace;

(5) request the Secretary-General, in consultation with the President of the Security Council and using such instrumentalities as he might choose, including a representative or a mission, to report to the Security Council as appropriate and in any event within 60 days on the implementation of the resolution.

The Syrian Arab Republic submitted four amendments to the Somali draft resolution. By the first of these, in the fourth operative paragraph, Israel would be called upon to rescind all previous measures and actions, as well as to take no further steps purporting to change the status of the City.

This amendment was adopted by the Council by 13 votes to 0, with 2 abstentions (Nicaragua and the United States).

[13] See footnote 8.
[14] See footnote 9.

Three other Syrian amendments were withdrawn as a result of appeals by several members. These would have amended the fifth operative paragraph so that the Council would ask the Secretary-General, in consultation with the President of the Security Council and using such instrumentalities as they [rather than he] might choose, including a representative or a mission, to report to the Council as appropriate and in any event within 30 [rather than 60] days on the implementation of the resolution. A new operative paragraph would have been added by which the Council would decide to reconvene without delay to consider the report referred to in the fifth operative paragraph and what further action should be taken under the Charter.

In submitting its amendments, the Syrian Arab Republic said that the Council should have started at the place where the issue was left after the adoption of its resolution of 3 July 1969, to which Israel had never responded. The opposition expressed by many members to Israel's violations of international law and of various United Nations resolutions should have been reflected in a resolution more responsive to the obligations of the Council, which should call upon Member States to recognize the illegality of Israel's actions in Jerusalem and to refrain from giving any form of assistance to Israel. The final step would be the application of sanctions according to Chapter VII of the Charter.

The Council voted separately on the fifth operative paragraph of the Somali text at the request of the USSR and adopted it by 12 votes to 0, with 3 abstentions (Poland, the Syrian Arab Republic and the USSR).

The draft resolution, as amended by the Syrian Arab Republic, was then adopted, on 25 September, by 14 votes to 0, with 1 abstention (the Syrian Arab Republic), as resolution 298(1971).

(For text of resolution, see DOCUMENTARY REFERENCES below.)

Subsequent report of Secretary-General

In pursuance of the Security Council's resolution of 25 September 1971, the Secretary-General on 19 November reported that he had consulted with the President of the Council in September on the implementation of the resolution. He had then informed Israel that he intended to nominate a mission of three members of the Council to enable him to report to the Council as requested. He had in mind as members of the mission the representatives of Argentina, Italy and Sierra Leone, whose Governments had signified their willingness to serve. He had reminded Israel that under the terms of the resolution he had a 60-day limit for reporting and therefore was bound to report within that period. On 28 October, he had again

drawn Israel's attention to the fact that he would appreciate receiving its comments as soon as possible.

On 11 November, the President of the Council and the Secretary-General orally conveyed to the representative of Israel their concern over the absence of a reply. On 15 November, Israel transmitted a letter containing its views concerning the paragraph of the resolution calling on Israel to rescind all previous measures and actions and take no further steps in the occupied section of Jerusalem which might purport to change the status of the City or prejudice the rights of the inhabitants, the interest of the international community or a just and lasting peace. However, the letter did not touch upon the question of Israel's response to the Secretary-General's proposal for a mission to Jerusalem to enable him to discharge his mandate.

On 16 November, the Secretary-General, after noting that Israel's reply had not referred to the question of a mission, indicated to Israel that since the time-limit for his report would expire on 24 November, he had no alternative but to submit his report to the Security Council without taking any further action to activate the three-member mission.

Consequently, he then informed the Council that he had had no means of obtaining first-hand information in fulfilment of his reporting responsibilities. After careful consideration of the Council's resolution he and the President of the Council had concluded that the best way to fulfil those responsibilities was through a mission of three members of the Council, for which the co-operation of Israel would obviously be required; however, Israel had not indicated willingness to comply with the Council's resolution. In the light of Israel's failure to abide by the Council's decision, he had been unable to fulfil his mandate under the resolution of 25 September.

The Secretary-General annexed to his report his exchange of letters with Israel. In its letter of 15 November, Israel pointed out that the restoration of the status of Jerusalem prior to 1967 would involve rescinding the unity, peace and sanctity of the City in order to restore division and conflict. Israel considered it inconceivable that the majority of the Security Council would wish to restore such a situation.

Concerning the suggestion that Israel was planning action to annul the heterogeneous character of the population, Israel gave assurances that the proportions of different ethnic population groups in the City were not expected to change.

As for the interests of the international community, Israel reaffirmed that the protection of the Holy Places was ensured by law and that there was freedom to visit and pray at the Holy Places of the three great faiths. It was Israel's policy to promote the rights of Jerusalem's inhabitants in order to advance the interests of the international community and thus to contribute to the promotion of a just and lasting peace.

DOCUMENTARY REFERENCES

Communications and reports

S/10075 (A/8272). Letter of 8 January 1971 from Egypt and Jordan.

S/10123 (A/8281). Letter of 17 February 1971 from Jordan.

S/10124 and Add.1,2 (A/8282 and Add.1,2). Report of 18 February 1971 of Secretary-General, under Security Council resolutions 252(1968), 267(1969) and 271(1969) and General Assembly resolution 2254 (ES-V), and addenda.

S/10126 (A/8283), S/10127 (A/8284). Letters of 18 and 19 February 1971 from Israel.

S/10130 and Corr.1 (A/8286 and Corr.1). Letter of 22 February 1971 from Egypt and Jordan.

S/10138 (A/8289). Letter of 1 March 1971 from Israel.

S/10139 (A/8290). Letter of 2 March from Jordan.

S/10140 (A/8291). Letter of 2 March 1971 from Syrian Arab Republic.

S/10146 (A/8295). Letter of 5 March 1971 from Israel.

S/10149 (A/8296). Letter of 8 March 1971 from Jordan.

S/10152 (A/8297). Letter of 9 March 1971 from Egypt, Indonesia, Jordan, Pakistan, Saudi Arabia, Somalia and Tunisia (transmitting letter of 22 February 1971 from International Moslem Organizations).

S/10158 (A/8300). Letter of 16 March 1971 from Israel.

S/10159 (A/8301). Letter of 15 March 1971 from Spain.

S/10160 (A/8302). Letter of 19 March 1971 from Israel.

S/10163 (A/8303). Letter of 23 March 1971 from Spain.

S/10167 (A/8305). Letter of 29 March 1971 from Israel.

S/10168 (A/8306). Letter of 30 March 1971 from Spain.

S/10169 (A/8307). Letter of 1 April 1971 from Jordan.

S/10215 (A/8318). Letter of 1 June 1971 from Syrian Arab Republic.

S/10220 and Corr.1 (A/8323 and Corr.1). Letter of 10 June 1971 from Israel.

Consideration by Security Council (September 1971)

Security Council, meetings 1579-1582.

S/10313. Letter of 13 September 1971 from Jordan (request to convene Council).

S/10314, S/10317, S/10319, S/10321-S/10325. Letters of 13-17 September 1971 from Jordan, Egypt, Israel, Mali, Lebanon, Morocco, Saudi Arabia, Tunisia (requests to participate in Council's discussion).

S/10337. Somalia: draft resolution.

S/10338 and Rev.1. Syrian Arab Republic: amendments and revised amendments to Somali draft resolution, S/10337.

RESOLUTION 298(1971), as proposed by Somalia, S/10337, and as amended by Syrian Arab Republic, S/10338/Rev.1, adopted by Council on 25 September 1971, meeting 1582, by 14 votes to 0, with 1 abstention (Syrian Arab Republic).

The Security Council,

Recalling its resolutions 252(1968) of 21 May 1968 and 267(1969) of 3 July 1969 and the earlier General Assembly resolutions 2253(ES-V) and 2254(ES-V) of 4 and 14 July 1967 concerning measures and actions by Israel designed to change the status of the Israeli-occupied section of Jerusalem,

Having considered the letter of the Permanent Representative of Jordan on the situation in Jerusalem and the reports of the Secretary-General, and having heard the statements of the parties concerned on the question,

Reaffirming the principle that acquisition of territory by military conquest is inadmissible,

Noting with concern the non-compliance by Israel with the above-mentioned resolutions,

Noting with concern also that since the adoption of the above-mentioned resolutions Israel has taken further measures designed to change the status and character of the occupied section of Jerusalem,

1. *Reaffirms* its resolutions 252(1968) and 267(1969);

2. *Deplores* the failure of Israel to respect the previous resolutions adopted by the United Nations concerning measures and actions by Israel purporting to affect the status of the City of Jerusalem;

3. *Confirms* in the clearest possible terms that all legislative and administrative actions taken by Israel to change the status of the City of Jerusalem, including expropriation of land and properties, transfer of populations and legislation aimed at the incorporation of the occupied section, are totally invalid and cannot change that status;

4. *Urgently calls upon* Israel to rescind all previous measures and actions and to take no further steps in the occupied section of Jerusalem which may purport to change the status of the City or which would prejudice the rights of the inhabitants and the interests of the international community, or a just and lasting peace;

5. *Requests* the Secretary-General, in consultation with the President of the Security Council and using such instrumentalities as he may choose, including a representative or a mission, to report to the Council as appropriate and in any event within sixty days on the implementation of the present resolution.

S/10392. Report of 19 November 1971 of Secretary-General, under Council resolution 298(1971) of 25 September 1971.

The treatment of the civilian population in Israeli-occupied territories and related matters

During 1971, the question of the human rights of the civilian population of the Israeli-occupied territories was again considered by United Nations bodies.

The Security Council and the Secretary-General received a number of communications from Arab countries alleging violations of human rights in the territories, and Israeli replies thereto. The Council did not meet on the question during the year.

The first (1970) report of the Special Committee to Investigate Israeli Practices Affecting the Human Rights of the Population of the Occupied Territories, which had been considered by the General Assembly at its twenty-fifth (1970) session,[15] was also taken up by the Commission on Human Rights at its 1971 session. Among other

---

[15]See Y.U.N., 1970, pp. 523-26.

things, the Commission—basing itself on the recommendations and conclusions contained in the Special Committee's report—condemned Israel's continued violations of human rights in the occupied territories, including policies aimed at changing the status of those territories. The Commission deplored certain specific policies and practices of Israel, and called on it among other things to comply fully with its obligations under the fourth Geneva Convention, of 12 August 1949, having to do with the protection of civilian persons in time of war.

In its second report and a supplementary report thereto issued later in 1971, the Special Committee noted that certain policies and practices found to exist in the occupied territories had been continued, in some instances on an even wider scale than before. The Special Committee also noted that the International Committee of the Red Cross (ICRC) had expressed its willingness under certain conditions to assume the role of a protecting power under the Geneva Conventions of 1949, after concluding that all tasks falling to a protecting power under the Conventions could be considered humanitarian functions.

The General Assembly, by a resolution (2851(XXVI)) adopted on 20 December 1971, noted this ICRC decision with satisfaction. It called upon Israel to rescind all measures and desist from all policies such as annexation of any part of the occupied Arab territories, establishment of Israeli settlements on those territories, and other practices. The Assembly also asked the Special Committee to continue its work, consulting as appropriate with ICRC. Israel was called upon to co-operate with the Special Committee and facilitate its entry into the occupied territories so that it could perform its functions.

Details of these and other related matters are to be found in the sections that follow.

Communications

During 1971, the President of the Security Council and the Secretary-General received a number of communications concerning the treatment of the civilian population in territories occupied by Israel. The Arab States complained about Israel's policies in these territories, alleging the arrest, detention, dispossession and expulsion of civilians and confiscation or expropriation of Arab lands. Israel rejected the Arab charges.

In two letters dated 8 January, Jordan complained of arbitrary and continued expulsion by Israel of Arab inhabitants of the Gaza Strip and the West Bank of Jordan and said that such measures constituted a link in the chain of Israel's policy to replace the indigenous population with alien elements who settled on confiscated or sequestered Arab land.

On 8 February, Egypt charged that Israel had committed acts of repression and indiscriminate attacks against the civilian population in Sinai and the Gaza Strip. On 9 February, Israel rejected the charges as unfounded and unsubstantiated and reiterated that its policy was to ensure normal life and development for all the inhabitants under its control, including those of the Gaza area and Sinai, despite the efforts of Arab terrorist organizations to make life intolerable for the local populations.

On 10 February, the representatives of 14 Arab States charged that Israel was intensifying its oppressive measures against the Palestinians in the Gaza Strip by imposing long and intolerable curfews in several areas. Moreover, several thousand Arab inhabitants had been arrested and taken to detention areas in the Sinai Desert, where they had suffered cruel interrogation and inhuman punishment. Israel rejected those charges on 11 February and stated that the repetition of allegations by the 14 Arab States had not brought those allegations nearer reality.

By a letter dated 12 February, Jordan and Lebanon transmitted a report that 10 Israeli soldiers had been tried for unjustified violence in the Gaza Strip and that three officers had been reprimanded for having failed to quell excesses committed by soldiers belonging to their unit.

In a reply dated 19 February, Israel said that the Arab Governments, particularly Jordan and Lebanon, had been directly responsible for the acts of terror and murder carried out in the Gaza area because they allowed the existence of bases on their territory from which terrorist operations had been carried out. The Israeli Government had no choice but to take measures to ensure the safety, welfare and security of the population of the Gaza area and to maintain public order there.

On 26 February, Jordan stated that Israel, in violation of the Geneva Conventions of 1949 and in disregard of United Nations resolutions, had arbitrarily confiscated lands and carried out mass transfers of the population within the occupied territories. The Israeli Military Governor had informed leaders of villages north of Ramallah that Israel intended to confiscate lands with the aim of resettling a number of Palestinian refugees from the Gaza area. On 26 March, Jordan said that between 8 December 1970 and 24 February 1971, 111 Arab inhabitants from the Gaza Strip and the West Bank of Jordan had been forcibly expelled and deported to the East Bank of Jordan under inhuman conditions.

On 3 March, Israel denied Jordan's allegation of 26 February that confiscation or expropriation of lands had occurred in the villages cited by Jordan and said that it had no intention of taking such steps in the future.

On 21 May, Jordan charged that Israel continued to intimidate, harass and suppress the inhabitants of the occupied territories, confiscating their property and deporting them in great numbers to the East Bank of Jordan. On 25 May, Israel replied that because of its policy to ensure the safety, welfare and security of the inhabitants of the areas referred to in the Jordanian letter, it had taken steps to prevent terrorism and to hinder individuals engaged in terrorist activities from disturbing peace in those areas.

On 28 May, the Syrian Arab Republic stated that in violation of relevant United Nations resolutions and of the 1949 Geneva Convention relative to the Protection of Civilian Persons in Time of War, Israel had continued its policy of colonizing Arab lands with intensive settlement, the demolition of Syrian towns and villages in the Golan Heights and the forcible eviction of the inhabitants from that area.

On 8 June, the Syrian Arab Republic further stated that, according to reports published by competent organizations, Israel had been barring the distribution by the International Committee of the Red Cross (ICRC) of medicaments to the population in occupied territories. That report had been confirmed by a resolution adopted by the twenty-fourth World Health Assembly of the World Health Organization (WHO) on 18 May, which had drawn attention to Israel's violation of the basic human rights of the refugees, displaced persons and inhabitants of the occupied territories, constituting a severe impediment to their health, and had called upon Israel to refrain from any interference with the activities of ICRC in the occupied territories.

On 10 June, Israel replied that the charges contained in the Syrian letters only reflected the belligerent attitude of the Syrian Arab Republic towards Israel and towards the peace-making efforts under the auspices of the Secretary-General's Special Representative to the Middle East, Ambassador Gunnar V. Jarring. With regard to the resolution of the World Health Assembly accusing Israel of barring the distribution of medicaments, Israel denied the charge and stated that the resolution had been adopted by only 43 member States; the majority of WHO's membership had dissociated itself from the text. The charge had also been denied by ICRC in a letter to WHO.

Replying on 15 June, the Syrian Arab Republic said that Israel's policy of lawlessness had been condemned or deplored in no less than 39 United Nations resolutions since 14 June 1967. On 15 March 1971, the Commission on Human Rights had condemned Israel for its continued violations of human rights in the occupied territories, including its policies aimed at changing the status of those territories. Moreover, since 1 July 1970, the Chief of Staff of the United Nations Truce Supervision Organization in Palestine had reported numerous acts of aggression invariably committed by Israel against the Syrian Arab Republic. Unable to reject any of the facts brought to the attention of the Security Council concerning its activities in the occupied Golan Heights, Israel had sought to veil its war crimes and crimes against humanity by referring to Arab resistance to Israeli occupation in the West Bank of Jordan. In citing a letter from ICRC to refute the resolution of the World Health Assembly, Israel had ignored the fact that the ICRC letter had not contested the paragraph of the resolution drawing Israel's attention to the violations of basic human rights of the refugees, displaced persons and inhabitants of the occupied territories that constituted a serious impediment to their health.

On 17 June, Israel stated that the Syrian Arab Republic's reply was a reflection of its warfare against the rights of the Jewish people to equality with other nations. The Syrian Arab Republic had rejected the Security Council's resolution of 22 November 1967[16] calling for peace with Israel, had refused to participate in the peace-making efforts of Ambassador Jarring, had continued to wage terror warfare against Israel and had cruelly oppressed the Jewish community of the Syrian Arab Republic.

With regard to the resolution of the Human Rights Commission alleging violations of human rights in Israeli-controlled territory, Israel pointed out that the majority of Commission members had refused to support that resolution and that only representatives of Arab, Soviet and Moslem States and their traditional followers had voted for it. Such resolutions, Israel added, clearly demonstrated the impossibility of dealing with the Middle East situation equitably and effectively by means of United Nations resolutions not based on agreement of the parties to the conflict.

In a letter dated 20 July regarding the activities of the Special Committee to Investigate Israeli Practices Affecting the Human Rights of the Population of the Occupied Territories, Israel noted that the Special Committee continued to serve as a tool of Arab propaganda, dissipating United Nations funds on visits to Arab capitals and disseminating falsehoods regarding the situation in Israeli-held territories. The letter quoted from a statement by the Israeli Minister for Foreign Affairs to the effect that the Special Committee was gathering false testimony on Israel's alleged misdeeds against its Arab inhabitants, but that the hundreds of visitors to Israel were the best eyewitnesses to the true picture.

---

[16]See Y.U.N., 1967, pp. 257–58, text of resolution 242 (1967).

In a letter dated 16 August, Egypt drew attention to the deteriorating situation in occupied Gaza as a result of Israel's systematic campaigns to terrorize and coerce the area's lawful inhabitants. The Israeli occupation forces, the letter said, were resorting to forcible expulsion in order to depopulate the area—a process aimed at changing the demographic structure of the occupied Arab territories with a view to annexing them. The United Nations was urged to take the necessary steps to end Israel's breaches of law, morality and international peace and security.

In a letter dated 19 August, Israel replied that a campaign of indiscriminate terror in the Gaza area had been instigated and supported by Egypt and other Arab States, whose main victims had been local Arab inhabitants. The aim was to spread violence and insecurity and to keep the Arab population in conditions of misery and congestion created during the Egyptian occupation. Consequently, Israel had been compelled to take measures to ensure safety and security in the refugee camps, requiring the construction of access roads within the camps and involving in certain cases the demolition of houses. Alternate housing had been provided and the evacuees had been given compensation for any expenses incurred.

On 18 September, Egypt transmitted the text of a telegram to the Secretary-General from the Executive Committee of the Palestine Liberation Organization concerning the situation in Gaza resulting from Israeli acts of terror, harassment, mass imprisonment, deportation and displacement of its people.

Decision of Human Rights Commission

The 1970 report of the Special Committee to Investigate Israeli Practices Affecting the Human Rights of the Population of the Occupied Territories, which had been considered by the General Assembly at its twenty-fifth (1970) session,[17] was also studied by the Commission on Human Rights at its twenty-seventh (1971) session. On 15 March, the Commission adopted a resolution based on the recommendations and conclusions contained in the 1970 report.

Among other things, the Commission condemned Israel's continued violations of human rights in the occupied territories, including policies aimed at changing the status of the territories, and condemned specifically the following policies and practices of Israel: (*a*) denial of the right of the refugees and displaced persons to return to their homes; (*b*) resort to collective punishment; (*c*) the deportation and expulsion of the citizens of the occupied territories; (*d*) arbitrary arrest and detention of the citizens of the occupied territo-

ries; (*e*) ill-treatment and torture of prisoners; (*f*) destruction and demolition of villages, town quarters, houses, and confiscation and expropriation of property; (*g*) evacuation and transfer of sections of the population of the occupied territories; and (*h*) transfer of parts of its own civilian population into the occupied territories.

The Commission strongly deplored Israel's policies in the occupied territories aimed at placing the population in a general state of repression, fear and deprivation, and particularly deplored: (*a*) requisition of hospitals and their transformation into police stations; (*b*) abrogation of the national laws and interference with the judicial system; and (*c*) refusal to allow use of the textbooks approved by the United Nations Educational, Scientific and Cultural Organization for schools in the occupied territories, and the insistence on forcing upon school children an alien system of education.

The Commission again called upon Israel: to comply fully with its obligations under the fourth Geneva Convention of 1949 (having to do with the protection of civilian persons in time of war); to enable forthwith the refugees and displaced persons to return to their homes; and to heed and implement the many resolutions adopted by United Nations organs and the specialized agencies for the safeguarding of human rights in the occupied territories.

The Commission reaffirmed that all measures taken by Israel to colonize the occupied territories, including occupied Jerusalem, were completely null and void and declared that Israel's continued and increasing violations of the human rights of the population of the occupied territories—and its deliberate and persistent refusal to abide by its legal obligations under the United Nations Charter, international law, and the fourth Geneva Convention of 1949—indicated the necessity of collective action on the part of the international community to ensure respect for the human rights of the population of the occupied territories.

The International Committee of the Red Cross was urged by the Commission to co-operate with United Nations organs, and particularly with the Special Committee to Investigate Israeli Practices Affecting the Human Rights of the Population of the Occupied Territories in the fulfilment of its task to ensure the safeguarding of the human rights of the population of the occupied territories, and to inform the Human Rights Commission at its 1972 session of the steps taken. The Secretary-General was asked to give wide publicity to United Nations documents dealing with the violations of human rights in the occupied territories, and in particular to the report of the

[17]See footnote 15.

Special Committee, and to use United Nations information media in disseminating information on the conditions of the population of the occupied territories, the refugees and displaced persons.

Reports of the Special Committee in 1971

The Special Committee to Investigate Israeli Practices Affecting the Human Rights of the Population of the Occupied Territories carried out further investigations from 7 to 16 July 1971. It held meetings in Amman (Jordan), Beirut (Lebanon), Geneva (Switzerland) and New York; 49 witnesses were heard and written evidence was received. Its second report was issued on 5 October 1971 and a supplementary report on 10 December.

The Special Committee noted that since the presentation of its first report in 1970 certain policies and practices found to exist in the occupied territories had been continued, in some instances on an even wider scale than before, especially with regard to the policy of encouraging the movement of Israeli settlers into settlements in the occupied territories.

The practice of deporting civilians from the occupied territories had continued unabated, the Special Committee reported, and it recorded its grave concern that this practice, together with the policy of establishing settlements in the occupied territories, seemed calculated to eliminate an identifiable Palestinian community altogether from those territories.

For these reasons, the Special Committee reiterated the recommendations it had made in 1970: that the States whose territory was occupied by Israel appoint immediately either a neutral State or States, or an international organization offering all guarantees of impartiality and effectiveness, to safeguard the human rights of the population of the occupied territories; that suitable arrangements be made for the proper representation of the interests of the large population in the occupied territories which had not been given the opportunity of exercising the right of self-determination; and that a neutral State or international organization be nominated by Israel and be associated in this arrangement.

The Special Committee further recommended that the State or States or international organization duly nominated under this arrangement might be authorized to undertake the following activities: (*a*) to secure the scrupulous implementation of the provisions relating to human rights contained in the third and fourth Geneva Conventions of 12 August 1949 (the third Convention having to do with the treatment of prisoners of war, the fourth Convention with the treatment of civilian persons in time of war), and particularly to

investigate allegations of violations of the human rights provisions of these Conventions or of other applicable international instruments; (*b*) to ensure that the population of the occupied territories was treated in accordance with the applicable law; and (*c*) to report on its work to the States concerned and to the General Assembly.

In its supplementary report issued on 10 December, the Special Committee took note of a statement that had been made by the International Committee of the Red Cross (ICRC) to the effect that it was willing under certain conditions to assume the role of a protecting power under the Geneva Conventions. The Special Committee noted that ICRC had expressed its readiness to assume these functions after giving careful consideration to the question of the reinforcement of the implementation of the existing Geneva Conventions and arriving at the conclusion that all tasks falling to a protecting power under the Conventions could be considered humanitarian functions.

The Special Committee therefore modified its original recommendations and recommended that the General Assembly might: (*a*) request the Secretary-General to inform the parties concerned of ICRC's readiness to take upon itself all the functions envisaged for protecting powers in the Geneva Conventions and to invite them to avail themselves of the services of ICRC in dealing with the application of the provisions of the Geneva Conventions in the occupied territories in the Middle East; (*b*) request ICRC to consider the need for keeping the United Nations fully informed, through the Secretary-General, of its activities as a protecting power, in addition to reporting to the parties concerned; and (*c*) reconsider the mandate of the Special Committee as to whether or not there was need for the continuation of its activities once ICRC began in fact to function as a protecting power.

Consideration by General Assembly

On 20 December 1971, at its twenty-sixth session, the General Assembly adopted a resolution (2851(XXVI)) on the 1971 reports of the Special Committee to Investigate Israeli Practices Affecting the Human Rights of the Population of the Occupied Territories.

By the preambular parts of this text, the Assembly among other things expressed its grave concern about the violations of the human rights of the inhabitants of the occupied territories. The Assembly considered that the system of investigation and protection was essential for ensuring effective implementation of international instruments, such as the 1949 (fourth) Geneva Convention relative to the Protection of Civilian Persons in Time of War, and regretted that the relevant provisions of that Convention had not been implemented by the Israeli authorities. The Assembly also recalled that States parties to that Convention had undertaken not only to respect but also to ensure respect for the Convention in all circumstances.

The Assembly then noted with satisfaction that the International Committee of the Red Cross (ICRC) had concluded that all tasks falling to a protecting power under the 1949 Geneva Conventions could be considered humanitarian functions and ICRC had declared itself ready to assume all the functions envisaged for protecting powers in the Conventions.

By the operative part of the text, the Assembly among other things strongly called upon Israel to rescind forthwith all measures and to desist from all policies and practices such as: (a) the annexation of any part of the occupied Arab territories; (b) the establishment of Israeli settlements on those territories and the transfer of parts of Israel's civilian population into the occupied territory; (c) the destruction and demolition of villages, quarters and houses and the confiscation and expropriation of property; (d) the evacuation, transfer, deportation and expulsion of the inhabitants of the occupied Arab territories; (e) the denial of the right of the refugees and displaced persons to return to their homes; (f) the ill-treatment and torture of prisoners and detainees; and (g) collective punishment.

The Assembly then called upon Israel to permit all persons who had fled from the occupied territories or had been deported or expelled therefrom to return to their homes. It reaffirmed that all measures taken by Israel to settle the occupied territories, including occupied Jerusalem, were completely null and void.

Israel was called on by the Assembly to comply fully with its obligations under the fourth Geneva Convention of 1949, and States parties to the Convention were asked to do their utmost to ensure that Israel respected and fulfilled such obligations.

The Assembly asked the Special Committee—pending the early termination of Israeli occupation of Arab territories—to continue its work and to consult as appropriate with ICRC to ensure the safeguarding of the welfare and human rights of the population of the occupied territories. It urged Israel to co-operate with the Special Committee and to facilitate its entry into the occupied territories so that it could perform its functions.

The resolution was adopted on the recommendation of the Assembly's Special Political Committee, which approved it on 16 December by a roll-call vote of 48 to 16, with 42 abstentions, on the basis of a proposal by Mali and Mauritania. Amendments proposed by Indonesia and Nigeria

were accepted by the sponsors. The resolution was adopted by the Assembly on 20 December by a recorded vote of 53 to 20, with 46 abstentions, as resolution 2851(XXVI).

(For text of resolution and voting details, see DOCUMENTARY REFERENCES below.)

During the debate, the Chairman of the Special Committee to Investigate Israeli Practices Affecting the Human Rights of the Population of the Occupied Territories informed the Special Political Committee that Israel had continued to refuse to receive the Special Committee—nor had it furnished the evidence which it claimed to have in rebuttal of allegations made before the Special Committee.

The Special Committee, he stressed, had sought to discharge its duty by separating the humanitarian aspects of the problem from political and other considerations. It was not the purpose of the Special Committee to indict any of the parties to the conflict, but to verify the true nature of Israel's policies and practices as they affected the human rights of the population of the occupied territories.

In the Special Committee's view, he said, the most important development since the adoption of its second report had been the statement of ICRC that it was ready to assume the functions envisaged for protecting powers in the 1949 Geneva Conventions. In view of the fact that Israel had allowed ICRC to function within the occupied territories, it was desirable and even urgent that arrangements be made to enable ICRC to begin forthwith to exercise the functions of a protecting power in the occupied territories.

Spokesmen for the Arab States—including Algeria, Egypt, Iran, Iraq, Jordan, Kuwait, Lebanon, the Libyan Arab Republic, Morocco, Sudan, the Syrian Arab Republic, Tunisia and Yemen —commended the Special Committee for its report, which they considered objective and impartial, and condemned Israel for persisting in its categorical refusal to co-operate with the Special Committee or allow it to visit the occupied territories.

Iran, among others, found the report alarming in its description of mass expulsions, the demolition of whole villages and unnecessary sufferings inflicted on a population which, in a single generation, had been subjected to the consequences of three wars. Jordan, Sudan and others deplored the fact that Israel, while continuing to defy United Nations resolutions and pursuing its systematic policy of colonization, resorted to all kinds of manoeuvres to obstruct the humanitarian missions of the United Nations. It was clear that Israel intended to transform the military occupation into a permanent condition. The plight of the Palestinians and the Arab population of the

Israeli-occupied territories was of concern not only to the Arab people but to the whole of mankind.

Many Members, including Czechoslovakia, India, Mali, Poland, Sudan, the Syrian Arab Republic, Turkey and the USSR, shared the view of the Special Committee that the fundamental violation of the human rights of the Arab population of the occupied territories lay in the very fact of occupation, and that the most effective way of safeguarding the human rights of the population was to end the occupation itself.

The USSR representative said that for four and a half years Israel had committed outrages in the Arab lands it had illegally seized; the facts showed that there was almost no article of the Universal Declaration of Human Rights or the fourth Geneva Convention of 1949 which the Israeli aggressor had not violated. It was the duty of the United Nations to condemn Israel's actions and call upon it to end its policy of aggression and expansionism, to withdraw its troops from the occupied Arab territories and to implement United Nations decisions relating to a peaceful political settlement in the Middle East. The USSR, he said, pursued a consistent policy of providing broad assistance to the Arab Governments so they could defend their legitimate national rights and interests.

Turkey stated that it could not condone the acquisition of territorial and political advantage through the use of force. It could not tolerate the measures taken by Israel with a view to changing the status of Jerusalem or the other occupied territories by means of a *fait accompli*. Furthermore, the rights of several thousands of innocent persons living under military occupation should be a matter of prime concern; pending the final settlement, a way should be found to alleviate their suffering.

The spokesman for Israel said that the eagerness of the Special Committee to serve as a tool of Arab propaganda was even more obvious than in its earlier report. The current report was politically oriented, ignoring or misrepresenting the facts and full of tendentious suggestions and proposals. The language of the Special Committee's terms of reference had predetermined the conclusions the Special Committee was expected to reach and had completely ignored the problem of discrimination and violation of human rights in Jewish communities in Arab lands, especially since 1967. None of the three States serving on the Special Committee maintained diplomatic relations with Israel and all had espoused the Arab cause. In those circumstances, he said, it was obvious that Israel had not found it possible to extend its co-operation to the Special Committee or engage in a debate on the details of the "evidence" adduced before it or the conclusions reached by it.

After giving details of Israeli administration in the occupied territories, the Israeli representative said that the present administration would come to an end when final boundaries were established. In the meantime, Israel was doing its utmost to administer the territories in a liberal and enlightened manner, by respecting the human rights of the inhabitants and promoting their welfare. Israel had no desire to exploit or assimilate the population of the territories or change their way of life. Approval of the Special Committee's report would, he said, serve the purposes of Arab propaganda, exacerbate artificial hatred and obstruct peace-making efforts.

The Byelorussian SSR drew a parallel between what it described as the policies of racial and national superiority pursued by South Africa and by Israel: Israel was pursuing a policy similar to the policy of Bantustans in South Africa. It had among other things set up internment camps in which not just individuals but whole families were detained. While the opponents of *apartheid* were persecuted and maltreated in South Africa, similar persecution existed in the Israeli-occupied territories. Just as South Africa continued to receive arms and technical assistance in spite of Security Council and General Assembly resolutions, Israel, too, benefited from the co-operation of certain Western countries. Not only did South African racism and Israeli zionism have many features in common, but the attitudes of the imperialist powers towards them were identical.

The representative of Mali believed that Israel's policy, far from ensuring the security that country sought, served only to aggravate the violence around it and would lead the Middle East and the world to disaster. He hoped that ICRC's decision to assume the functions of a protecting power under the Geneva Conventions would help to ensure the full implementation in the occupied territories of all the provisions of the international instruments concerning respect for human rights.

India's spokesman said that the problem of the Arab refugees and their return to their homes and the question of investigating Israeli practices affecting human rights could not be separated from the basic question of the illegal occupation of Arab territories by Israel. Israel was again trying to divert the Assembly's attention from the disturbing evidence produced by the Special Committee. He wondered how Israel could refuse to co-operate with the Special Committee and, at the same time, challenge its source of information. India, he said, rejected all Israeli excuses for not withdrawing from the territories occupied as a result of the 1967 aggression and thought that the Special Committee should continue its work so that the Israeli practices would continue to be exposed.

The United States believed that any approach to

the problem must take into account any evidence that violations of human rights had occurred on both sides of the Arab-Israeli conflict. It had opposed the establishment of the Special Committee because its investigations were to be restricted to the inhabitants of the Israeli-occupied territories while ignoring the condition of Jewish minorities in certain States in the area of conflict. The application of human rights principles was

universal and the United States saw no reason to limit the commitment of the General Assembly to one group of people. It could not support extension of the Special Committee's mandate.

During the debate, in accordance with the practice established at previous sessions, the Special Political Committee heard a statement by a representative of the "Palestine Arab delegation."

DOCUMENTARY REFERENCES

Communications

S/10073 (A/8270), S/10074 (A/8271). Letters of 8 January 1971 from Jordan.

S/10075 (A/8272). Letter of 8 January from Egypt and Jordan.

S/10105. Letter of 8 February 1971 from Egypt.

S/10107. Letter of 9 February 1971 from Israel.

S/10111. Letter of 10 February 1971 from Algeria, Egypt, Iraq, Jordan, Kuwait, Lebanon, Libyan Arab Republic, Morocco, People's Democratic Republic of Yemen, Saudi Arabia, Sudan, Syrian Arab Republic, Tunisia and Yemen.

S/10113. Letter of 11 February 1971 from Israel.

S/10119 (A/8280). Letter of 12 February 1971 from Jordan and Lebanon.

S/10128 (A/8285). Letter of 19 February 1971 from Israel.

S/10133 (A/8287). Letter of 26 February 1971 from Jordan.

S/10142 (A/8293). Letter of 3 March 1971 from Israel.

S/10155 (A/8299), S/10165 (A/8304), S/10203 (A/8315). Letters of 12 and 26 March and 21 May 1971 from Jordan.

S/10210 (A/8316). Letter of 25 May 1971 from Israel.

S/10213 (A/8317), S/10219 (A/8321). Letters of 28 May and 8 June 1971 from Syrian Arab Republic.

S/10220 and Corr.1 (A/8323 and Corr.1). Letter of 10 June 1971 from Israel.

S/10224 (A/8324). Letter of 15 June 1971 from Syrian Arab Republic.

S/10228 (A/8325). Letter of 17 June 1971 from Israel.

S/10232 (A/8326). Letter of 21 June 1971 from Syrian Arab Republic.

S/10234 (A/8327). Letter of 23 June 1971 from Israel.

S/10238 and Corr.1 (A/8329 and Corr.1). Letter of 25 June 1971 from Syrian Arab Republic.

S/10256 (A/8335). Letter of 25 June 1971 from Iraq.

S/10270 (A/8343), S/10271 (A/8344). Letters of 20 and 21 July 1971 from Israel.

S/10272. Letter of 13 July 1971 from Executive Secretary of Organization of African Unity (OAU) to United Nations (transmitting resolutions adopted by 8th Assembly of Heads of State and Government of OAU).

S/10278 (A/8347). Letter of 30 July 1971 from Iraq.

S/10293 (A/8357). Letter of 16 August 1971 from Egypt.

S/10295 (A/8363). Letter of 19 August 1971 from Israel.

S/10328 (A/8395). Letter of 18 September 1971 from Egypt (transmitting telegram of 17 September 1971 from Executive Committee of Palestine Liberation Organization).

Decision of Human Rights Commission

E/4949. Report of Commission on Human Rights on its 27th session, 22 February–26 March 1971, Geneva, Switzerland, Chapters IV and XIX (resolution 9(XXVII)).

E/L.1395. Note of 5 May 1971 by Secretary-General (transmitting communication from International Committee of Red Cross).

Consideration by General Assembly

General Assembly—26th session
Special Political Committee, meetings 798–803.
Fifth Committee, meeting 1488.
Plenary meeting 2027.

A/8270 (S/10073), A/8271 (S/10074). Letters of 8 January 1971 from Jordan.

A/8272 (S/10075). Letter of 8 January 1971 from Egypt and Jordan.

A/8279. Letter of 11 February 1971 from Jordan (transmitting letter of 10 February 1971 from Algeria, Egypt, Iraq, Jordan, Kuwait, Lebanon, Libyan Arab Republic, Morocco, People's Democratic Republic of Yemen, Saudi Arabia, Sudan, Syrian Arab Republic, Tunisia and Yemen (S/10111)).

A/8280 (S/10119). Letter of 12 February 1971 from Jordan and Lebanon.

A/8285 (S/10128). Letter of 19 February 1971 from Israel.

A/8287 (S/10133). Letter of 26 February 1971 from Jordan.

A/8293 (S/10142). Letter of 3 March 1971 from Israel.

A/8299 (S/10155), A/8304 (S/10165), A/8315 (S/10203). Letters of 12 and 26 March and 21 May 1971 from Jordan.

A/8316 (S/10210). Letter of 25 May 1971 from Israel.

A/8317 (S/10213), A/8321 (S/10219). Letters of 28 May and 8 June 1971 from Syrian Arab Republic.

A/8323 and Corr.1 (S/10220 and Corr.1). Letter of 10 June 1971 from Israel.

A/8324 (S/10224). Letter of 15 June 1971 from Syrian Arab Republic.

A/8325 (S/10228). Letter of 17 June 1971 from Israel.

A/8326 (S/10232). Letter of 21 June 1971 from Syrian Arab Republic.

A/8327 (S/10234). Letter of 23 June 1971 from Israel.

A/8329 and Corr.1 (S/10238 and Corr.1). Letter of 25 June 1971 from Syrian Arab Republic.

A/8335 (S/10256). Letter of 25 June 1971 from Iraq.

A/8343 (S/10270), A/8344 (S/10271). Letters of 20 and 21 July 1971 from Israel.

A/8347 (S/10278). Letter of 30 July 1971 from Iraq.

A/8357 (S/10293). Letter of 16 August 1971 from Egypt.

A/8363 (S/10295). Letter of 19 August 1971 from Israel.

A/8365 (S/10300). Letter of 25 August 1971 from Syrian Arab Republic.

A/8389 and Corr.1,2 and Add.1 and Add.1/Corr.1,2. Report of Special Committee to Investigate Israeli Practices Affecting Human Rights of Population of Occupied Territories. Note by Secretary-General, and addendum.

A/8395 (S/10328). Letter of 18 September 1971 from Egypt (transmitting telegram of 17 September 1971 from Executive Committee of Palestine Liberation Organization).

A/8401. Report of Secretary-General on work of the Organization, 16 June 1970–15 June 1971, Part One, Chapter I D.

A/8402. Report of Security Council, 16 June 1970–15 June 1971, Chapter 2 B.

A/8472. Letter of 15 October 1971 from Israel.

A/8478. Letter of 21 October 1971 from Jordan.

A/SPC/149. Letter of 22 October 1971 from Afghanistan, Indonesia, Pakistan and Saudi Arabia (request for hearing of "Palestine Arab delegation").

A/SPC/L.235. Mali and Mauritania: draft resolution, as revised by Nigeria (A/SPC/L.237, as orally amended), and as orally amended by sponsors and by Indonesia, approved by Special Political Committee on 16 December 1971, meeting 803, by roll-call vote of 48 to 16, with 42 abstentions, as follows:

In favour: Afghanistan, Algeria, Bahrain, Bulgaria, Burundi, Byelorussian SSR, Ceylon, Congo, Cuba, Cyprus, Czechoslovakia, Egypt, Greece, Guinea, Hungary, India, Indonesia, Iran, Iraq, Jordan, Kuwait, Lebanon, Libyan Arab Republic, Malaysia, Mali, Mauritania, Mongolia, Morocco, Nigeria, Oman, People's Democratic Republic of Yemen, Poland, Qatar, Romania, Saudi Arabia, Somalia, Spain, Sudan, Syrian Arab Republic, Tunisia, Turkey, Ukrainian SSR, USSR, United Arab Emirates, United Republic of Tanzania, Yemen, Yugoslavia, Zambia.

Against: Barbados, Belgium, Canada, Costa Rica, Dominican Republic, El Salvador, Guatemala, Haiti, Israel, Liberia, Luxembourg, Malawi, Nicaragua, United States, Uruguay, Zaire.

Abstaining: Argentina, Australia, Austria, Bolivia, Botswana, Brazil, Central African Republic, Chile, Colombia, Dahomey, Denmark, Ecuador, Ethiopia, Finland, France, Ghana, Guyana, Honduras, Iceland, Ireland, Italy, Ivory Coast, Jamaica, Japan, Kenya, Lesotho, Madagascar, Mexico, Netherlands, New Zealand, Norway, Peru, Philippines, Portugal, Rwanda, Singapore, Swaziland, Sweden, Uganda, United Kingdom, Upper Volta, Venezuela.

A/SPC/L.236, A/C.5/1426, A/8636. Administrative and financial implications of draft resolution recommended by Special Political Committee in A/8630. Statements by Secretary-General and report of Fifth Committee.

A/SPC/L.237. Nigeria: amendments to 2-power draft resolution, A/SPC/L.235.

A/8630. Report of Special Political Committee.

RESOLUTION 2851(XXVI), as recommended by Special Political Committee, A/8630, adopted by Assembly on 20 December 1971, meeting 2027, by recorded vote of 53 to 20, with 46 abstentions, as follows:

In favour: Afghanistan, Algeria, Bahrain, Bulgaria, Burundi, Byelorussian SSR, Ceylon, Congo, Cuba, Cyprus, Czechoslovakia, Egypt, Equatorial Guinea, Greece, Guinea, Hungary, India, Indonesia, Iran, Iraq, Jordan, Kuwait, Lebanon, Libyan Arab Republic, Malaysia, Mali, Mauritania, Mongolia, Morocco, Niger, Nigeria, Oman, Pakistan, People's Democratic Republic of Yemen, Poland, Qatar, Romania, Saudi Arabia, Senegal, Somalia, Spain, Sudan, Syrian Arab Republic, Togo, Tunisia, Turkey, Ukrainian SSR, USSR, United Arab Emirates, United Republic of Tanzania, Yemen, Yugoslavia, Zambia.

Against: Barbados, Bolivia, Canada, Costa Rica, Dominican Republic, El Salvador, Gambia, Guatemala, Haiti, Israel, Lesotho, Liberia, Madagascar, Malawi, Nicaragua, Paraguay, Swaziland, United States, Uruguay, Zaire.

Abstaining: Argentina, Australia, Austria, Belgium, Botswana, Brazil, Burma, Cameroon, Central African Republic, Chad, Chile, Colombia, Dahomey, Denmark, Ecuador, Ethiopia, Finland, France, Ghana, Guyana, Honduras, Ireland, Italy, Ivory Coast, Jamaica, Japan, Kenya, Luxembourg, Malta, Mexico, Netherlands, New Zealand, Norway, Peru, Philippines, Portugal, Rwanda, Sierra Leone, Singapore, Sweden, Thailand, Trinidad and Tobago, Uganda, United Kingdom, Upper Volta, Venezuela.

The General Assembly,

Guided by the purposes and principles of the Charter of the United Nations,

Bearing in mind the provisions and principles of the Universal Declaration of Human Rights, as well as the provisions of the Geneva Convention relative to the Protection of Civilian Persons in Time of War, of 12 August 1949,

Recalling Security Council resolutions 237(1967) of 14 June 1967 and 259(1968) of 27 September 1968, as well as other pertinent resolutions of the United Nations,

Having considered the report of the Special Committee to Investigate Israeli Practices Affecting the Human Rights of the Population of the Occupied Territories,

Gravely concerned about the violations of the human rights of the inhabitants of the occupied territories,

Considering that the system of investigation and protection is essential for ensuring effective implementation of the international instruments, such as the aforementioned Geneva Convention of 12 August 1949, which provide for respect for human rights in armed conflicts,

Noting with regret that the relevant provisions of that Convention have not been implemented by the Israeli authorities,

Recalling that, in accordance with article 1 of that Convention, the States parties have undertaken not only to respect but also to ensure respect for the Convention in all circumstances,

Noting with satisfaction that the International Committee of the Red Cross, after giving careful consideration to the question of the reinforcement of the implementation of the Geneva Conventions of 12 August 1949, has arrived at the conclusion that all tasks falling to a protecting Power under those Conventions could be considered humanitarian functions and that the International Committee of the Red Cross has declared itself ready to assume all the functions envisaged for protecting Powers in the Conventions,

1. *Commends* the Special Committee to Investigate Israeli Practices Affecting the Human Rights of the Population of the Occupied Territories and its members for their efforts in performing the task assigned to them;

2. *Strongly calls upon* Israel to rescind forthwith all measures and to desist from all policies and practices such as:

(a) The annexation of any part of the occupied Arab territories;

(b) The establishment of Israeli settlements on those territories and the transfer of parts of its civilian population into the occupied territory;

(c) The destruction and demolition of villages, quarters and houses and the confiscation and expropriation of property;

(d) The evacuation, transfer, deportation and expulsion of the inhabitants of the occupied Arab territories;

(e) The denial of the right of the refugees and displaced persons to return to their homes;

(f) The ill-treatment and torture of prisoners and detainees;

(g) Collective punishment;

3. *Calls upon* the Government of Israel to permit all persons who have fled the occupied territories or have been deported or expelled therefrom to return to their homes;

4. *Reaffirms* that all measures taken by Israel to settle the occupied territories, including occupied Jerusalem, are completely null and void;

5. *Calls upon* the Government of Israel to comply fully with its obligations under the Geneva Convention relative to the Protection of Civilian Persons in Time of War, of 12 August 1949;

6. *Requests* the Special Committee, pending the early termination of Israeli occupation of Arab territories, to continue its work and to consult as appropriate with the International Committee of the Red Cross in order to ensure the safeguarding of the welfare and human rights of the population of the occupied territories;

7. *Urges* the Government of Israel to co-operate with the Special Committee and to facilitate its entry into the occupied territories in order to enable it to perform the functions entrusted to it by the General Assembly;

8. *Requests* the Secretary-General to provide the Special Committee with all the necessary facilities for the continued performance of its tasks;

9. *Requests* all States parties to the Geneva Convention of 12 August 1949 to do their utmost to ensure that Israel respects and fulfils its obligations under that Convention;

10. *Requests* the Special Committee to report to the Secretary-General as soon as possible and whenever the need arises thereafter;

11. *Decides* to include in the provisional agenda of its twenty-seventh session an item entitled "Report (or reports) of the Special Committee to Investigate Israeli Practices Affecting the Human Rights of the Population of the Occupied Territories."

Other matters relevant to the Middle East situation

Interference with international civil aviation

By a letter dated 8 October 1971, Israel transmitted the text of a letter it had addressed on 30 September to the International Civil Aviation Organization (ICAO) in which it was stated that, between 23 August and 3 September 1971, two Arab terrorists had attempted to bring about the destruction in flight of an aircraft belonging to El Al, the national airline of Israel. It was Israel's belief that further acts of sabotage were contemplated and it therefore urged ICAO to take the necessary measures to prevent the recurrence of acts of violence against international civil aviation that jeopardized the safety of persons and property, gravely affected the operations of the international air services and undermined public confidence in the safety of civil aviation.

Other communications

Several communications were received by the Secretary-General during the year—for transmittal to the Security Council—concerning the situation in the Middle East.

By a letter dated 28 February 1971, the USSR transmitted the text of a statement of the USSR Government concerning the situation in the Middle East. The statement noted that on 21 February Israel had said that it refused to commit itself to withdrawal from the occupied territories of Arab States, in particular from the territory of Egypt, thus showing its unwillingness to assume a part of the commitments required for a political settlement in accordance with the Security Council's resolution of 22 November 1967.[18]

On 4 March, Bulgaria transmitted the text of a statement, issued by the Bulgarian Ministry for Foreign Affairs, in which it was stated that Egypt's readiness to conclude a peace treaty with Israel and Egypt's constructive proposals provided a basis for a political solution of the Middle East crisis. However, Israel's rejection of those proposals and its refusal to withdraw its troops from occupied Arab territories had shown that Israel was persisting in its policy of aggression and its defiance of the relevant United Nations resolutions.

By a note dated 11 March, Iran transmitted the text of a statement issued by the Iranian Government in which, among other things, it reiterated its position that the withdrawal of Israeli forces from occupied territories was an essential factor for the establishment of peace in the Middle East. It welcomed the positive attitude taken by Egypt towards implementation of the Security Council's resolution of 22 November 1967 and hoped that Israel would reciprocate by taking positive steps in

the direction of peace and regional tranquillity so that an agreement might be reached. It warned that if Israel were to persist in maintaining its negative attitude, Iran would have no alternative but to condemn such an attitude.

By a letter dated 6 May, Iraq transmitted the text of a letter addressed to the Secretary-General by the Grand Rabbi of the Jewish community in Iraq, which stated that Israel had been waging a vicious campaign against Iraq and its Jewish citizens. The Grand Rabbi maintained that there was a vast difference between zionism—a political and racial ideology—and Judaism, one of the world's major religions. Zionism had all too often done Judaism and its followers a disservice by distorting its conceptions and history and by resorting to violence against Iraqi Jews, in order to force them to emigrate to Israel. Zionism could never change the loyalty to Iraq of Jewish Iraqi citizens by involving them in the whirlpool of dual allegiance.

On 13 July, the Executive Secretary of the Organization of African Unity (OAU) transmitted among others the texts of resolutions adopted by the Assembly of African Heads of State and Government at its eighth session held at Addis Ababa, Ethiopia, from 21 to 23 June 1971. Among other things, OAU called for immediate withdrawal of Israeli forces from all Arab territories and expressed its full support for the Special Representative of the United Nations Secretary-General in his efforts to implement the Security Council's resolution of 22 November 1967.

In a letter dated 13 August, the Syrian Arab Republic referred to a reported decision by the International Bank for Reconstruction and Development to grant Israel a loan of $30 million to expand its highway network. The loan must shock every United Nations Member having a minimum of respect for the Organization and its specialized agencies, the letter said. It was all the more shocking in view of Israel's disregard and defiance of all the United Nations resolutions adopted on the Arab-Israeli conflict. Moreover, Israel took by force in 1948 more than $2,000 million worth of Arab property in Palestine, and thousands of millions of American dollars had since poured into Israel, giving the settlers a status of privileged social, economic and technological development in relation to the region as a whole. Even after Israel's third aggressive war against the Arabs in 1967, United States military and economic assistance had run into the thousands of millions of dollars, in spite of severe indictments of Israel by

---

[18]See Y.U.N., 1967, pp. 257–58, text of resolution 242(1967).

the United Nations and by its specialized agencies.

On 24 August, Israel drew attention to a joint declaration made in Damascus, Syrian Arab Republic, on 20 August 1971 by the Presidents of Egypt, the Libyan Arab Republic and the Syrian Arab Republic to mark the signing by the three States of the Constitution of the Federation of Arab Republics. The declaration stated among other things: "There will be no peace or negotiation with the Zionist enemy." Israel charged that the declaration was a flagrant breach of the United Nations Charter and a defiant negation of the obligation to reach a just and lasting peace in the Middle East through agreement between Israel and the Arab States, as called for by the Security Council's resolution of 22 November 1967.

On 11 December 1971, Egypt forwarded a telegram to the President of the General Assembly from the Minister of Foreign Affairs of the German Democratic Republic stating that responsibility for the failure of efforts to bring about a just and lasting peace in the Middle East rested with Israel and the imperialist circles backing it. The German Democratic Republic advocated a settlement based on the Security Council's resolution of 22 November 1967, and considered that the complete withdrawal of Israeli troops from Arab territories occupied in 1967, recognition of the sovereignty, territorial integrity and political independence of the Arab States, and

respect for the legitimate rights of their respective peoples were pre-conditions for the creation of a stable peace in the Middle East.

Decision by General Assembly on right to self-determination

On 6 December 1971, the General Assembly adopted resolution 2787(XXVI) on the importance of the universal realization of the right of peoples to self-determination and of the speedy granting of independence to colonial countries and peoples for the effective guarantee and observance of human rights.

By this, the Assembly among other things reaffirmed the inalienable rights of all peoples, and in particular those of Zimbabwe, Namibia, the Portuguese territories in Africa and the Palestinian people, to freedom, equality and self-determination, and the legitimacy of their struggles to restore those rights.

The Assembly also confirmed the legality of the peoples' struggle for self-determination and liberation from colonial and foreign domination and alien subjugation, in particular that of the peoples of Zimbabwe, Namibia and the Portuguese territories in Africa, as well as of the Palestinian people, by all available means consistent with the United Nations Charter.

(See also pp. 421-22.)

DOCUMENTARY REFERENCES

Interference with international civil aviation
S/10362. Letter of 8 October 1971 from Israel (enclosing letter of 30 September 1971 to Council of International Civil Aviation Organization).
A/8401. Report of Secretary-General on work of the Organization, 16 June 1970–15 June 1971, Part Four, Chapter IV D.
A/8401/Add.1. Introduction to report of Secretary-General, Part Two, Chapter IX, paras. 311-312.
A/8402. Report of Security Council, 16 June 1970–15 June 1971, Chapter 9.

Other communications
S/10136 (A/8288). Letter of 28 February 1971 from USSR.
S/10141 (A/8292). Letter of 2 March 1971 from Egypt (transmitting excerpts from statement of 4 February 1971 by President of Egypt).

S/10144 and Corr.1 (A/8294 and Corr.1). Letter of 4 March 1971 from Bulgaria.
S/10154 (A/8298). Note verbale of 11 March 1971 from Iran.
S/10188 (A/8310). Letter of 6 May 1971 from Iraq (transmitting letter of 28 April 1971 from Grand Rabbi of Jewish community in Iraq).
S/10272. Letter of 13 July 1971 from Executive Secretary of Organization of African Unity (OAU) to United Nations (transmitting resolutions adopted by 8th Assembly of Heads of State and Government of OAU).
S/10290 (A/8356). Letter of 13 August 1971 from Syrian Arab Republic.
S/10297. Letter of 24 August 1971 from Israel.
A/8586. Letter of 11 December 1971 from Egypt (transmitting telegram of 7 December 1971 from German Democratic Republic).

Chapter X

Assistance to refugees in the Near East

During 1971, the United Nations Relief and Works Agency for Palestine Refugees in the Near East (UNRWA) maintained its programmes of assistance to Palestine refugees in Jordan, the West

Bank, Lebanon, the Syrian Arab Republic and the Gaza Strip. It continued to face a grave financial crisis, despite the efforts of the Working Group on the Financing of UNRWA, which had been established during the twenty-fifth session of the General Assembly in 1970.[1] The Working Group succeeded in reducing the Agency's 1971 deficit from $5.5 million to $2.4 million, but a deficit of $6 million was expected for 1972.

On 1 January 1971, the Director-General of the United Nations Educational, Scientific and Cultural Organization (UNESCO) launched an appeal on behalf of the UNRWA/UNESCO education and training programme; by the end of the year, the appeal had produced over $1.1 million in cash and in kind. Additional income was also raised through the efforts of the Working Group, notably a $1.3 million emergency contribution of foodstuffs from the World Food Programme. In May, the World Health Assembly requested the Director-General of the World Health Organization (WHO) to expand the organization's health programme for refugees and displaced persons in the Middle East to the amount of $1 million from contributions outside the regular budget.

Also in May, the Economic and Social Council called for increased support for UNRWA from organizations of the United Nations system.

In December, the General Assembly extended the mandate of the Agency until 30 June 1975 and extended the mandate of the Working Group for one year.

The Assembly also, among other decisions: reaffirmed that full respect for the inalienable rights of the people of Palestine was an indispensable element in the establishment of a just and lasting peace in the Middle East; called once more upon Israel to take immediate and effective steps for the return of persons who had fled the occupied areas since the outbreak of hostilities in 1967; and called upon Israel to desist from further destruction of refugee shelters and the removal of refugees, to return the refugees concerned to their camps and to provide adequate shelters for them.

Sir John Rennie (United Kingdom) succeeded Laurence Michelmore (United States) as Commissioner-General of UNRWA, taking office on 15 May 1971.

Activities in 1971

The number of refugees registered with UNRWA in 1971 rose to 1,487,096, an increase of 3 per cent over 1970.

More than 834,000 rations were issued monthly. Verification procedures removed from the ration rolls a large number of absentees and previously unreported dead whose rations were re-allocated, mainly to children who had not been receiving rations because of ration ceilings. The Agency also distributed monthly rations to 214,000 displaced persons and 40,000 displaced refugee children in east Jordan, against repayment by the Jordanian Government.

The Agency continued to provide preventive and curative medical services for eligible refugees, in co-operation with WHO. Expenditures on health services rose to $6.6 million in 1971. In addition, UNRWA continued its emergency and regular supplementary feeding programmes for vulnerable groups, particularly children, at an approximate annual cost of $2.7 million.

Expenditure on education increased to $22.6 million in 1971, nearly 47 per cent of the Agency's total expenditure.

In the 1971/72 school year, 257,000 children were enrolled in the schools run jointly by UNRWA and UNESCO, an increase of 15,000 over 1970/71. Over 50 per cent of the pupils were attending classes on a shift basis, despite the construction of 150 new schoolrooms during the year.

Protracted negotiations between UNESCO and the Governments concerned regarding textbooks for Agency schools resulted in the delivery of large quantities of badly needed books to the West Bank and Gaza.

Using funds donated specifically for the purpose, the Agency added more places in its training centres, bringing the total number of students to 2,544 in vocational and 1,031 in teacher-training sections. Since 1954, more than 15,000 trainees had been graduated from Agency centres.

The Agency's operations were again affected by political tensions. In July and August 1971, the demolition by Israeli military authorities, for security reasons, of the shelters of about 2,400 families in three refugee camps in the Gaza Strip displaced about 15,000 persons; of these, about 2,150 accepted accommodation at El Arish outside the Gaza Strip, a smaller number went to the West Bank and more than 12,000 found housing, improvised shelters or doubled up with others.

In Lebanon, a number of buildings in camps continued to be occupied by Palestinian organizations, despite representations to the Government.

Economically, the situation remained very depressed in east Jordan, where refugees and displaced persons formed nearly half the population. In the West Bank, the economy continued to recover, providing more opportunities for employment.

With the aid of funds provided by special contributions, a start was made towards the replacement of tents by concrete-block shelters in four emergency camps in the Syrian Arab Republic.

Decisions by Economic and Social Council

At its April-May 1971 session, the Economic and Social Council, recognizing the acute financial situation of the United Nations Relief and Works Agency for Palestine Refugees in the Near East

---

[1]See Y.U.N., 1970, p. 280, text of resolution 2656(XXV) of 7 December 1970.

(UNRWA), considered the need for emergency assistance to Palestine refugees.

On 3 May 1971, after welcoming the efforts made by various organizations of the United Nations family to provide emergency aid or to maintain existing services, the Council requested the Secretary-General and the heads of the specialized agencies, the United Nations Children's Fund and the United Nations Development Programme, as well as non-governmental organizations concerned, to continue to consider appropriate ways and means of rendering all possible assistance to the Palestine refugees. It also asked all organizations of the United Nations system to include in their annual reports information on possible current and future assistance to UNRWA and on activities of benefit to the Palestine refugees, in order to lessen the financial burden of the Agency.

These Council decisions were set forth in resolution 1565(L), based on a text proposed by Ghana and Norway and adopted unanimously.

(For text of resolution, see DOCUMENTARY REFERENCES below.)

Consideration by General Assembly

When the situation of refugees in the Near East was considered by the General Assembly in 1971, the subject was referred to the Special Political Committee, which discussed it at 13 meetings held from 17 November to 2 December 1971.

Prior to the opening of the debate, the President of the General Assembly and the Secretary-General made a joint appeal for funds to ensure continuation of UNRWA's assistance to refugees. They noted that the Agency would require $6 million more in 1972 than in 1971 if it was to maintain its services at their current level, and that any reduction of services would not only aggravate the misery of the refugees but increase the tensions in the area.

Reports before Special Political Committee

In its consideration of the situation of refugees in the Near East, the Special Political Committee had before it: (1) the annual report of the Commissioner-General of UNRWA; (2) a report of the Secretary-General concerning displaced persons who had fled the Israel-occupied territories since the 1967 hostilities; (3) a special report of the Commissioner-General on the condition of Palestine refugees in the Gaza Strip; and (4) a report of the Working Group on the Financing of UNRWA. A summary of these reports follows.

REPORT OF COMMISSIONER-GENERAL

In his annual report to the General Assembly, covering the period from 1 July 1970 to 30 June 1971, the Commissioner-General of UNRWA stated

that the Agency's regular programmes of assistance were being carried out amid continuing uncertainty about UNRWA's ability to maintain its essential programmes.

The Commissioner-General expressed the hope that concern for the Agency's future had generated wider understanding of the plight of the Palestine refugees and of the nature of the Agency's operations. With regard to the latter, he noted that UNRWA provided services in, rather than administered, refugee camps (in which only 40 per cent of the registered refugees lived); that the camps were not extraterritorial areas under United Nations jurisdiction; that the refugees were free to move in and out; and that responsibility for the maintenance of law and order rested not with the Agency but with the Government of the host countries of Jordan, Lebanon and the Syrian Arab Republic, and with the Government of Israel, as the occupying power, in the occupied territories of the West Bank and Gaza.

The emphasis on the Agency's relief operations, the Commissioner-General continued, tended to obscure its constructive programmes of education and training, which in 1971 accounted for about 47 per cent of expenditure and which formed the foundation for individual rehabilitation as well as contributed to economic and social development in many Arab countries.

The report noted that the Agency's operations had been disrupted by violence on several occasions during the period under review. In east Jordan, UNRWA's services had been suspended for 10 days in September 1970 during the fighting between Jordanian Government forces and Palestine *fedayeen;*[2] in all, 13 Agency employees had been killed and the Agency had suffered damages amounting to about $524,000.

In the Gaza Strip, the Agency's operations were affected by the security measures taken by the Israeli authorities in January 1971, following persisting violence in which both Arabs and Israelis had lost their lives.

With regard to UNRWA's financial situation, the report noted that thanks to the response by Governments and others to appeals made by the Working Group on UNRWA financing, by the Secretary-General and by the Director-General of the United Nations Educational, Scientific and Cultural Organization (UNESCO), the deficit of the Agency was reduced from about $5.5 million to $2.4 million as at 30 June 1971. However, an estimated deficit of $6 million was expected for 1972 on an expenditure budget of more than $51 million. The deficit was attributed to growing costs for education, set against a less rapidly increasing income and a declining capital reserve.

[2] See Y.U.N., 1970, p. 270.

In conclusion, the Commissioner-General noted that the need for the Agency's regular programmes continued to be felt by the refugees and acknowledged by authorities in all areas of operation. Nevertheless, the threat to the maintenance of Agency programmes had not receded. An assurance of adequate financing was required if the General Assembly decided that the Agency should continue on its current lines and with its current programmes.

REPORT OF SECRETARY-GENERAL

In a report prepared in response to a General Assembly request, the Secretary–General stated that he had asked Israel to inform him of steps it had taken to implement the Assembly's decision of 8 December 1970 concerning displaced persons who had fled the Israel–occupied territories since the 1967 hostilities.[3]

In its reply, dated 23 August 1971, Israel stated that the extent and rapidity of the return of the persons concerned were inevitably affected by the political and security conditions in the area. Arab Governments continued to encourage and assist acts of terrorism and violence; moreover, permits for the return of displaced persons had been used for the purpose of infiltrating terrorists, saboteurs and espionage agents. In these conditions, Israel could not agree to repatriation on a large scale. Pending a peace settlement, Israel continued to seek to reconcile the return of displaced persons with its responsibility for the welfare and security of the local population and the security of the State itself. It also continued to facilitate the return of persons displaced in the June 1967 hostilities in co-operation with Arab authorities in the area and in the context of family reunion and hardship cases, Israel asserted.

SPECIAL REPORT OF COMMISSIONER-GENERAL

The Commissioner-General of UNRWA submitted a special report on the effect on Palestine refugees of operations carried out in July and August 1971 by Israeli military authorities in the Gaza Strip.

The Commissioner-General stated that as a result of the demolition of shelters in refugee camps, almost 15,000 persons had been displaced. He reported that UNRWA had formally protested the action being taken by the Israeli authorities and had asked that a halt be called to the operations and steps taken to provide adequate shelter within the Gaza Strip for those who had lost their homes.

In transmitting the report to the General Assembly, the Secretary-General stated that he had urgently requested Israel to undertake promptly all measures necessary to ensure the immediate cessation of the destruction of refugee homes in the Gaza Strip and to halt the removal of the refugees to places outside the Strip. He had also requested Israel to provide adequate housing within the Gaza Strip for those displaced as a result of the operations.

In a letter of 28 September 1971, Israel replied that the measures taken in the refugee camps of the Gaza area had been aimed at putting an end to the acts of terror directed against the local Arab population. Because of overcrowding, the congested layout of houses and other circumstances, the refugee camps offered convenient conditions for terror operations which, in the period June 1967 to June 1971, had resulted in 219 Arab residents of the Gaza area being killed and 1,314 wounded, it was stated. To ensure safety in the camps, Israel had constructed roads, involving in certain places the demolition of dwellings. However, in all cases alternative housing of at least equal standard had been provided, or the cost of moving into new accommodations had been covered. Israel had informed the United Nations that those who had moved to housing available at El Arish and who wished to return to the Gaza area would be able to do so as soon as housing facilities were available.

As a result of the above measures, terror activities in the Gaza area, including activities aimed at Arab refugees, had drastically diminished, it was stated.

Subsequently, in a supplementary report, the Commissioner-General of UNRWA stated that 14,704 persons had been affected by the demolition, that the Agency had submitted to Israel a claim for compensation amounting to about $400,000, and that the Agency was continuing to provide services to those refugees whose dwellings had been demolished and who had remained in the Gaza Strip.

REPORT OF WORKING GROUP
ON FINANCING OF UNRWA

The Working Group on the Financing of UNRWA submitted a report prepared in compliance with a General Assembly decision of 7 December 1970.[4]

At its meetings in 1971, the Working Group examined ways and means of obtaining additional contributions for UNRWA and broadening the base of its support.

In February 1971, the Chairman of the Working Group contacted all the regional groups within the United Nations and explained to them the Agency's grave budgetary crisis and its need for additional contributions in cash or in kind.The Organization of African Unity, the League of Arab States and the Organization of American States were also contacted.

---

[3]See Y.U.N., 1970, p. 283, text of resolution 2672 D (XXV).
[4]See footnote 1.

The Chairman also visited the refugee camps. The host countries subsequently endorsed the efforts of the Working Group and reaffirmed that they were unable to accept any reduction in UNRWA's relief, health and education services.

As the result of approaches made to agencies of the United Nations system, to individual Governments and to non-governmental and other sources, several new or additional contributions were obtained, including up to $2 million in emergency food aid from the World Food Programme.

The Working Group concluded that it would be necessary to maintain the activities of UNRWA in the immediate years to come, that the system of financing by voluntary contributions should be continued and that extraordinary measures were required to maintain UNRWA's activities at their current level.

Concerning the financing of UNRWA activities for 1972, the Working Group recommended, among other things: that an urgent appeal be made to non-contributing Governments to contribute, and that special efforts be made both to identify specific projects or areas of activity in which other agencies of the United Nations family could assist UNRWA and to obtain voluntary contributions from non-governmental sources.

With regard to financing UNRWA activities after 1972, the Working Group recommended a basic reappraisal of the Agency's operations to establish them on a more secure foundation. It also suggested that consideration be given to the establishment of a high-level international committee of philanthropists in each potential donor country, and to the issuing of special UNRWA or United Nations stamps, proceeds from the sale of which would be channelled to the Agency.

The Working Group recommended that its own mandate be extended for one year.

General Assembly discussion

In presenting his annual report to the Special Political Committee, the Commissioner-General of the United Nations Relief and Works Agency for Palestine Refugees in the Near East (UNRWA) stated that the financial crisis of the Agency, which had been temporarily deferred by the establishment of the Working Group on the Financing of UNRWA had not receded and presented an immediate threat to the Agency's programmes and to the welfare of the refugees.

Since 1959, the Commissioner-General said, the resolutions of the General Assembly had tended to take UNRWA programmes for granted and had not offered guidance on their scope. It had been assumed that the same programmes could be maintained despite higher costs and greater numbers of refugees; the Working Group's report must cast doubt on any such assumption in regard to 1972.

The Agency's doubt about its future was deepened by its awareness of the impasse reached in the implementation of the Security Council's resolution of 22 November 1967.[5] The need for UNRWA's services would continue so long as there was no peace settlement in the Middle East which included a just solution of the refugee problem; yet there was no guarantee that the necessary funds would be available.

The Commissioner-General then reviewed the services provided by the Agency and noted that the scope for effective savings was limited. He asked Committee Members earnestly to consider the desirability of concerted action to preserve intact the UNRWA programme.

The representative of Lebanon, speaking on behalf of the host countries, stated that despite the efforts of the Working Group on the Financing of UNRWA, the future operations of the Agency were far from being assured. It had been recognized that a collapse of operations or even reductions in relief, health and educational services would have ominous effects on the refugees and on the over-all situation in the Middle East.

The financial crisis with which UNRWA was faced was not the only obstacle involved, the Lebanese representative continued, for Israel had taken measures to make the situation even more difficult. It had prevented the distribution of textbooks in the UNRWA/UNESCO and privately run schools in the occupied territories; it had detained 36 of the Agency's staff in the Gaza Strip without pressing any criminal charges; during the summer of 1971, it had subjected the refugees in the Gaza Strip to untold sufferings in violation of the Geneva Convention of 1949 (relative to the protection of civilians in time of war).

Most seriously, Israel had refused to co-operate in the implementation of United Nations resolutions. It continued to disregard United Nations resolutions regarding the refugees displaced as a result of the 1967 hostilities, and ignored the General Assembly's resolution of 11 December 1948 calling for either repatriation or compensation of the refugees.[6]

Replying to suggestions that the Arab Governments should assume greater responsibility in caring for the refugees, Lebanon stated that the Arab Governments alone could not bear this burden because they were already facing the complex problems of development, which were constantly aggravated by Israeli aggression and expansionism. Despite their difficulties, the Arab countries had provided the Palestinians with as much humanitarian assistance as possible. Arab contributions to UNRWA had increased every year; in 1970-1971, they amounted to about $23.5 million.

Some 43 per cent of refugees were not dependent on UNRWA, whose expenses and activities constituted the minimal expression of the international community's responsibility towards the refugees. Thus the Arab countries would continue to oppose any attempt to reduce those services.

The representative of Israel stated that the solution of the problem of the Palestinian Arab refugees must be reconciled with the safeguarding of the rights and sovereignty of Israel. The Security Council had put the refugee problem in its proper context in its resolution 242(1967),[7] which made the solution one of the interdependent elements of peace agreements to be negotiated between Israel and the Arab Governments, he continued. It was regrettable that the parties had not yet entered into such negotiations.

Since 1948, the Arab States had used the refugees as a political and military weapon to undermine Israel's independence, the Israeli representative stated; the events in Gaza in 1971 had shown that refugee camps could continue to serve as centres for terrorist activities. Nevertheless, the Israeli Government had shown that it was prepared to take considerable security risks for the sake of the refugees; since 1967, it had granted permits for the return of more than 38,000 West Bank and Gaza inhabitants.

Over the years, Israel said, it had offered to participate in any programme to assist the resettlement of the refugees in the Arab world, to place the refugee question at the top of any peace negotiations and to pay compensation before the conclusion of peace agreements. The Arab Governments had turned down all such offers.

Since 1967, about 40 per cent of all refugees registered with UNRWA had been living in areas administered by Israel, the Israeli representative noted. Israel had evidenced its willingness to co-operate with the Agency, subject only to considerations of military security. Since 1967, conditions had improved, and security measures had been further relaxed.

With regard to the textbook issue, the representative said that Israel had objected to the use, in United Nations–supported schools, of books containing derogatory passages on Jews and Israel. However, out of 118 textbooks submitted by UNESCO to Israel, only seven remained contestable.

Israel noted that in the past four years, its contribution to UNRWA had amounted to more than $3.5 million, in addition to services it provided directly to refugees and general services for the population of the administered areas as a whole, half of whose inhabitants were refugees.

During the discussion, many speakers praised the work of UNRWA and expressed concern regarding the threatened reduction of its services to refugees, particularly in education.

A number of Members stated that if the Agency was to continue its programmes at the current level, a substantial increase in contributions was necessary. The United States, among others, appealed to countries which had not contributed to UNRWA to do so, and to those which had contributed to increase their contributions.

Czechoslovakia and the USSR said that they would continue to provide bilateral aid to the Arab States.

China said that it would, as in the past, give the Palestinian people aid and assistance through bilateral arrangements.

Egypt, among others, noted that if the United Nations resolutions calling for the return of the refugees to their homes were implemented, a good part of the Agency's deficit would be eliminated. India held that responsibility for the refugees rested with the State which forced them to flee rather than the State which was assisting them.

Many Members supported the conclusions and recommendations of the Working Group on the Financing of UNRWA. Some hoped that as a result of the Working Group's efforts, the United Nations specialized agencies would increase their contributions. Norway and Sweden mentioned in particular the need for contributions in kind. Kuwait, however, questioned the Working Group's recommendation that the Agency continue to be supported by voluntary contributions; nor were the other proposals put forward by the Working Group very imaginative or likely to be fruitful, Kuwait felt.

Many representatives said that the solution of the refugee problem was to be found in the implementation of the relevant United Nations resolutions.

Some members—including Belgium, Greece, Japan, Romania and the United States—held that the problem of the refugees was inextricably linked to issues that divided Israel and the Arab States and could be resolved only as part of an over-all Middle East settlement in accordance with the Security Council's resolution of 22 November 1967.[8]

Representatives of Arab countries considered

[7]See footnote 5.
[8]By resolution 242(1967), the Security Council affirmed, among other things, that the establishment of a just and lasting peace in the Middle East should include both (i) the withdrawal of Israeli armed forces from territories occupied in the conflict of June 1967; and (ii) the termination of all claims or states of belligerency and respect for and acknowledgement of the sovereignty, territorial integrity and political independence of every State in the area and their right to live in peace within secure and recognized boundaries free from threats or acts of force. (See Y.U.N., 1967, pp. 257-58.)

that the refugee problem was the result of Israel's disregard of past United Nations resolutions. Kuwait was among those maintaining that the return of the refugees could not be made contingent on peace between Israel and its Arab neighbours. Jordan said that the right of the Palestine refugees to return to their homes was a fundamental human right. Others stated that the Agency's financial problem would not exist if Palestinian properties and assets which had been usurped by Israel were returned to the legitimate owners.

Many representatives, recalling that in its resolution of 8 December 1970 the General Assembly had recognized the right of the people of Palestine to self-determination,[9] held that respect for the inalienable rights of the people of Palestine was an indispensable element in the establishment of a just and lasting peace in the Middle East. Thus, the representative of Tunisia supported the idea that the only way to ensure a lasting peace in the Middle East was to enable the Palestinian people to build a united Palestine where all could live in peace and equality. The representative of the Syrian Arab Republic called for the reactivation of the United Nations Conciliation Commission for Palestine. Poland asserted that the struggle waged by the Arab people of Palestine would receive support from all progressive peoples in the world.

China held that the only possible lasting and effective solution to the so-called question of Palestine refugees was the restoration of the Palestinian people's national rights. In recent years, the struggle against zionism had become an important element of the Arab liberation movement and of the world struggle against colonialism and imperialism. Victory belonged to the Palestinians and the Arab peoples, the Chinese representative said.

In accordance with decisions taken by the Committee on 18 and 24 November 1971, respectively, spokesmen for the "Palestine Arab delegation" and the Palestine Liberation Organization participated in the discussion. The spokesmen reiterated the right of the Palestinian people to self-determination, and asserted that the Palestine liberation movement would continue its struggle to promote a just and lasting peace in the region and to establish a popular democratic State of Palestine.

Six draft resolutions on the question of the refugees in the Middle East were introduced in the Special Political Committee. On 1 December 1971, the Committee approved all six drafts, and they were subsequently adopted by the General Assembly on 6 December.

By the first of these, the Assembly recognized that the financial situation of the United Nations

Relief and Works Agency for Palestine Refugees in the Near East (UNRWA) continued to be acute, and emphasized the urgent need for extraordinary efforts and exceptional measures in order to maintain, at least at their current level, the activities of the Agency.

The Assembly then, among other things, approved the report of the Working Group on the Financing of UNRWA and extended its mandate for one year. The Working Group was asked to submit a comprehensive report on all aspects of the financing of the Agency to the Assembly at its 1972 session.

The Assembly also supported the joint appeal by its President and the Secretary-General to Governments to join in the collective effort to solve the financial crisis of UNRWA, and endorsed the request of the Economic and Social Council, made on 3 May 1971, that the Secretary–General, the heads of the specialized agencies, the United Nations Children's Fund and the United Nations Development Programme, and the non-governmental organizations concerned, continue to consider appropriate ways and means of rendering all possible assistance to the Palestine refugees.

These decisions by the Assembly were set forth in resolution 2791(XXVI), adopted by a vote of 114 to 0, with 2 abstentions. The text was based on a proposal by Belgium, Denmark, Finland, Greece, Iran and Sweden, as amended by the United States, and was approved without objection by the Special Political Committee.

(For text of resolution, see DOCUMENTARY REFERENCES below.)

By another decision, the Assembly noted with deep regret that the repatriation or compensation of the refugees as provided for by its resolution 194(III) of 11 December 1948[10] had not been effected and that no substantial progress had been made towards the reintegration of refugees, either by repatriation or resettlement. The Assembly requested the United Nations Conciliation Commission for Palestine to report on the implementation of resolution 194(III) by no later than 1 October 1972.

The Assembly also directed attention to the continuing critical financial position of UNRWA, and called upon all Governments to make the most generous efforts possible to meet the Agency's anticipated needs.

The Assembly decided to extend the mandate of UNRWA until 30 June 1975, without prejudice to the provisions of its resolution 194(III).

These decisions were set forth in resolution 2792 A (XXVI), adopted by a vote of 112 to 0, with 3 abstentions. The text, approved without objec-

[9]See Y.U.N., 1970, pp. 282-83, text of resolution 2672 C (XXV).
[10]See footnote 6.

tion by the Special Political Committee, was based on a draft sponsored by the United States, and incorporated an amendment submitted by Denmark.

(For text of resolution, see DOCUMENTARY REFERENCES below.).

The Assembly also expressed its concern about the continued human suffering resulting from the June 1967 hostilities in the Middle East. It endorsed the efforts of the Commissioner-General of UNRWA to continue to provide humanitarian assistance, as far as practicable, on an emergency basis and as a temporary measure, to other persons in the area who were displaced as a result of the 1967 hostilities, and appealed to all Governments and to organizations and individuals to contribute generously for this purpose to UNRWA and to other inter-governmental and non-governmental organizations concerned.

The Assembly took these decisions in adopting resolution 2792 B (XXVI), by a vote of 113 to 0, with 1 abstention. The text was based on a proposal by 19 States: Afghanistan, Austria, Belgium, Canada, Chile, Denmark, Finland, Ghana, Greece, India, Iran, Ireland, Italy, Japan, Nigeria, Norway, Sweden, Turkey and Yugoslavia. It was approved without objection by the Special Political Committee.

(For text of resolution, see DOCUMENTARY REFERENCES below.)

In another action, the General Assembly took note of the special report and supplement thereto of the Commissioner-General of UNRWA on the effect on Palestine refugees of operations carried out by Israeli military authorities in the Gaza Strip.

The Assembly deplored the destruction of refugee shelters and the forcible removal of their occupants to other places, including places outside the Gaza Strip, which it declared in contravention of the 1949 Geneva Convention relative to the Protection of Civilian Persons in Time of War and of the Assembly's decision of 9 December 1970[11] concerning the protection of civilian populations in armed conflicts.

The Assembly called upon Israel: (1) to desist from further destruction of refugee shelters and removal of refugees from their current places of residence; and (2) to take immediate and effective steps for the return of the refugees concerned to the camps from which they were removed and to provide adequate shelters for their accommodation.

The Secretary-General was requested to report no later than the opening date of the Assembly's 1972 session on Israel's compliance with the above provisions.

This Assembly action was embodied in resolution 2792 C (XXVI), which was adopted by a recorded vote of 79 to 4, with 35 abstentions. The text was based on a proposal by Afghanistan, Indonesia, Malaysia, Mali, Pakistan, Senegal and Somalia, and was approved by the Special Political Committee by a roll-call vote of 66 to 4, with 32 abstentions.

(For text of resolution, see DOCUMENTARY REFERENCES below.)

In treating another aspect of the refugee problem, the Assembly observed that the problem of the Palestinian Arab refugees had arisen from the denial of their inalienable rights under the United Nations Charter and the Universal Declaration of Human Rights.

The Assembly then: (1) recognized that the people of Palestine were entitled to equal rights and self-determination, in accordance with the Charter; (2) expressed its grave concern that the people of Palestine had not been permitted to enjoy their inalienable rights and to exercise their right to self-determination; and (3) declared that full respect for the inalienable rights of the people of Palestine was an indispensable element in the establishment of a just and lasting peace in the Middle East.

The Assembly took these decisions in adopting resolution 2792 D (XXVI), by a roll-call vote of 53 to 23, with 43 abstentions. The draft—approved by the Special Political Committee by a roll-call vote of 46 to 20, with 36 abstentions—was based on a text sponsored by Afghanistan, Guinea, Indonesia, Malaysia, Mali, Pakistan, Senegal, Somalia and Yugoslavia.

(For text of resolution, see DOCUMENTARY REFERENCES below.)

By yet another decision on the refugee problem, the General Assembly made the point that the plight of the displaced inhabitants continued since they had not yet returned to their homes and camps, and expressed its grave concern that the displaced inhabitants had not been able to return in accordance with earlier Assembly resolutions. It then called once more upon Israel to take immediately and without any further delay effective steps for the return of the displaced inhabitants. Finally, it requested the Secretary-General to report to the Assembly on the implementation of this resolution.

The Assembly took this action in adopting resolution 2792 E (XXVI), by a roll-call vote of 88 to 3, with 28 abstentions. Afghanistan, Indonesia, Malaysia, Mali, Pakistan, Senegal, Somalia and Yugoslavia sponsored the text, which was approved by the Special Political Committee by a roll-call vote of 75 to 2, with 25 abstentions.

(For text of resolution, see DOCUMENTARY REFERENCES below.)

---

[11]See Y.U.N., 1970, pp. 542-43, text of resolution 2675(XXV).

Pledges and payments for 1971

For the calendar year 1971, 62 countries and territories pledged the equivalent of $43,683,086 towards UNRWA's budget. As at 31 December 1971, the equivalent of $33,306,111 had been received in payment of these pledges. In addition, contributions were received from non-governmental organizations, private individuals and business corporations.

Pledges and contributions to UNRWA for year ending 31 December 1971

(Showing equivalent in U.S. dollars of pledges and contributions in cash, kind and services)

Pledging Government	Pledge	Contribution Received
Abu Dhabi	110,000[a]	110,000
Argentina	125,000	—
Australia	213,014	68,440[b]
Austria	20,000	20,000
Bahrain	10,000[a]	10,000
Belgium	506,762	20,694
Canada	1,330,150	1,330,150
Ceylon	1,000	1,000
Chile	2,000[c]	1,000
China	30,000	30,000
Cyprus	731[a]	731
Denmark	714,612	646,112
Dubai	20,000[a]	20,000
Federal Republic of Germany	3,475,889[a]	3,475,889
Finland	197,500[a]	197,500
France	1,445,348	296,808
Gaza Authorities	88,728	88,728
Ghana	3,500	—
Greece	16,000	16,000
Holy See	2,500	—
Iceland	10,000	10,000
India	15,333[a]	—
Iran	23,030[a]	18,030
Iraq	125,000[a]	125,000
Ireland	60,000	60,000
Israel	454,030	454,030
Italy	187,921	15,952

Pledging Government	Pledge	Contribution Received
Japan	550,000	550,000
Jordan	194,607	194,607
Kuwait	400,000[a]	400,000
Lebanon	50,810	50,810
Liberia	5,000	—
Libyan Arab Republic	250,000[a]	250,000
Luxembourg	4,000	4,000
Malaysia	1,500	1,500
Monaco	180	180
Morocco	76,442[a]	76,442
Netherlands	176,471	176,471
New Zealand	69,172	69,172
Niger	450	—
Nigeria	5,600	5,600
Norway	600,696[a]	600,696
Oman	10,000	10,000
Pakistan	20,969	20,969
Panama	500	—
Qatar	32,000[a]	32,000
Republic of Korea	5,000	5,000
Republic of Viet-Nam	3,000	3,000
Romania	5,555[a]	—
Saudi Arabia	297,000	—
Singapore	1,000	1,000
Spain	782,513	782,513
Sudan	2,870	2,870
Sweden	2,449,864[a]	2,449,864
Switzerland	877,671	845,621
Syrian Arab Republic	88,145	60,060
Trinidad and Tobago	1,500	1,500
Tunisia	5,000	5,000
Turkey	15,000	15,000
United Kingdom	4,512,000[a]	4,512,000
United States	22,980,523[d]	15,144,172
Yugoslavia	20,000	20,000

[a] Includes a contribution in response to an appeal by the Director-General of UNESCO.

[b] The remainder of the Australian Government's pledge, which was deposited in UNRWA's procurement account for the purchase of supplies in Australia, had not yet been utilized.

[c] Includes $1,000 pledged for 1970.

[d] Since the United States fiscal year ends in June, the amount shown as a pledge is the allocation by UNRWA to its 1971 programme of half the United States contribution for its fiscal year 1970/71 and half for 1971/72. The contribution shown is the amount received against this allocation in 1971 (excluding payments received in 1971 and allocated by UNRWA to its 1970 programme). Also includes special contributions for 1971 totalling $780,523.

DOCUMENTARY REFERENCES

Economic and Social Council—50th session
Plenary meeting 1747.

E/L.1387. Ghana and Norway: draft resolution.

RESOLUTION 1565(L), as proposed by 2 powers, E/L.1387, and as orally amended by Sudan, by United Kingdom and by sponsors, adopted unanimously by Council on 3 May 1971, meeting 1747.

The Economic and Social Council,
Recognizing the acute financial situation of the United Nations Relief and Works Agency for Palestine Refugees in the Near East which endangers the minimum services provided to Palestine refugees,
Recalling General Assembly resolutions 2656(XXV) of 7 December 1970 and 2672B(XXV) of 8 December 1970,
Recalling further General Assembly resolution 2728(XXV) of 15 December 1970 by which the Assembly approved the report of the Working Group on the Financing of the United Nations Relief and Works Agency for Palestine Refugees in the Near East and endorsed the Working Group's recommendations, thereby, *inter alia,* urging all organizations of the United Nations system to study ways by which they might assist the Agency or undertake activities helpful to the refugees which would lessen the financial burden of

the Agency, to the maximum extent possible,
Noting with appreciation the efforts made so far by the Working Group with regard to the organizations of the United Nations system in soliciting increased assistance to the Palestine refugees,
Noting also with appreciation the assistance already offered by some organizations within the United Nations system in response to those efforts, in recognizing that, especially in cases of emergency, concern for human welfare requires an extra interagency solidarity,
Being convinced, however, that further contributions and assistance for the benefit of the Palestine refugees are urgently needed,
1. *Welcomes* in particular the decisions already taken under the World Food Programme to provide emergency food aid up to $2 million;
2. *Welcomes also* the contacts initiated with the International Labour Organisation and the World Health Organization with a view to obtaining services to the maximum extent possible;
3. *Welcomes further* the positive steps taken by the Director-General of the United Nations Educational, Scientific and Cultural Organization in launching an appeal for funds to maintain the educational services for Palestine refugees and the encouraging results obtained so far;
4. *Expresses the hope* for an early implementation of the above-mentioned decisions, particularly of paragraph 3 of General

Assembly resolution 2672B(XXV), as well as manifestations of concrete results of the above-mentioned contacts and steps in accordance with constitutional procedures;

5. *Requests* the Secretary-General of the United Nations, the executive heads of specialized agencies, the Executive Director of the United Nations Children's Fund and the Administrator of the United Nations Development Programme as well as the non-governmental organizations concerned to continue to consider appropriate ways and means of rendering all possible assistance to the Palestine refugees;

6. *Requests further* all organizations of the United Nations system to include in their annual reports information on their possible present and future assistance to the United Nations Relief and Works Agency for Palestine Refugees in the Near East and on their activities that benefit the Palestine refugees, and thus lessen the financial burden of the Agency.

General Assembly—26th session
Special Political Committee, meetings 754, 781-793.
Ad Hoc Committee of General Assembly for Announcement of Voluntary Contributions to United Nations Relief and Works Agency for Palestine Refugees in Near East (UNRWA), meeting 1.
Fifth Committee, meeting 1470.
Plenary meeting 2001.

A/8366. Report of 27 August 1971 of Secretary-General.
A/8383 and Add.1. Notes of 17 September and 23 November 1971 by Secretary-General (transmitting special report, and supplement, of Commissioner-General of UNRWA on effect on Palestine refugees of operations carried out in July and August 1971 by Israeli military authorities in Gaza Strip).
A/8401. Report of Secretary-General on work of the Organization, 16 June 1970–15 June 1971, Part One, Chapter IV K.
A/8403. Report of Economic and Social Council on work of its 50th and 51st sessions, Chapter XVIII D.
A/8413. Report of Commissioner-General of UNRWA (for period 1 July 1970–30 June 1971).
A/8432. Letter of 28 September 1971 from Israel.
A/8476 and Corr.1. Report of Working Group on Financing of UNRWA.
A/8526. Joint appeal of 17 November 1971 by President of General Assembly and Secretary-General.
A/SPC/147. Letter of 22 October 1971 from Afghanistan, Indonesia, Pakistan and Saudi Arabia (requesting hearing for "Palestine Arab delegation").
A/SPC/148. Letter of 23 November 1971 from Afghanistan, Albania, Algeria, Bahrain, Bulgaria, Byelorussian SSR, China, Congo, Cuba, Cyprus, Czechoslovakia, Egypt, Guinea, Hungary, India, Indonesia, Iraq, Jordan, Kuwait, Lebanon, Libyan Arab Republic, Malaysia, Mali, Mauritania, Mongolia, Morocco, Oman, Pakistan, People's Democratic Republic of Yemen, Poland, Qatar, Romania, Saudi Arabia, Somalia, Sudan, Syrian Arab Republic, Tunisia, Ukrainian SSR, USSR, Yemen and Yugoslavia (requesting hearing for delegation of Palestine Liberation Organization).
A/SPC/L.228. Belgium, Denmark, Sweden: draft resolution.
A/SPC/L.228/Rev.1. Belgium, Denmark, Finland, Greece, Iran, Sweden: revised draft resolution, as amended by United States, A/SPC/L.233, approved without objection by Special Political Committee on 1 December 1971, meeting 791.
A/SPC/L.229, A/C.5/1411, A/8548. Administrative and financial implications of draft resolution I recommended by Special Political Committee in A/8547. Statements by Secretary-General and report of Fifth Committee.
A/SPC/L.233. United States: amendment to 6-power draft resolution, A/SPC/L.228/Rev.1.
A/8547. Report of Special Political Committee, draft resolution I.

RESOLUTION 2791(XXVI), as recommended by Special Political Committee, A/8547, adopted by Assembly on 6 December 1971, meeting 2001, by 114 votes to 0, with 2 abstentions.

The General Assembly,
Recalling its resolutions 2656(XXV) of 7 December 1970 and 2728(XXV) of 15 December 1970,
Having considered the report of the Working Group on the Financing of the United Nations Relief and Works Agency for Palestine Refugees in the Near East,
Taking into account the annual report of the Commissioner-General of the United Nations Relief and Works Agency for Palestine Refugees in the Near East, covering the period from 1 July 1970 to 30 June 1971,
Taking note of the joint appeal made by the President of the General Assembly and the Secretary-General on 17 November 1971,
Recognizing with grave concern that the financial situation of the United Nations Relief and Works Agency for Palestine Refugees in the Near East continues to be acute, thereby imminently endangering the already minimum services being provided to Palestine refugees,
Emphasizing the urgent need for extraordinary efforts and exceptional measures in order to maintain, at least at their present level, the activities of the United Nations Relief and Works Agency for Palestine Refugees in the Near East,
1. *Commends* the Working Group on the Financing of the United Nations Relief and Works Agency for Palestine Refugees in the Near East for its work and approves its report, drawing special attention to the conclusions and recommendations contained in chapter V of that report;
2. *Requests* the Working Group to continue its work for one year in accordance with the provisions of its previous mandate and, as appropriate, to pursue urgently with Governments, both bilaterally and on a regional basis, with specialized agencies and other organizations within the United Nations system, and with other organizations and individuals concerned, the implementation of the recommendations approved by the General Assembly in the present resolution, as well as the implementation of other resolutions relating to the mandate of the Working Group;
3. *Endorses* Economic and Social Council resolution 1565(L) of 3 May 1971, and in particular urges serious consideration and early implementation of paragraph 5 of that resolution;
4. *Supports* the joint appeal made by the President of the General Assembly and the Secretary-General to Governments to join in the collective effort to solve the financial crisis of the United Nations Relief and Works Agency for Palestine Refugees in the Near East;
5. *Requests* the Working Group, after consultation with all concerned, in particular the Secretary-General and the Commissioner-General of the United Nations Relief and Works Agency for Palestine Refugees in the Near East, and taking into account the views expressed in the course of the debate during the twenty-fifth and twenty-sixth sessions of the General Assembly relevant to the mandate of the Working Group, to prepare and submit a comprehensive report on all aspects of the financing of the Agency to the General Assembly at its twenty-seventh session;
6. *Requests* the Secretary-General to provide the necessary services and assistance to the Working Group for the conduct of its work.

A/SPC/L.225 and Rev.1 and Rev.1/Corr.1. United States: draft resolution and revision, approved without objection by Special Political Committee on 1 December 1971, meeting 792.
A/SPC/L.227. Denmark: amendment to United States draft resolution, A/SPC/L.225.
A/8547. Report of Special Political Committee, draft resolution II A.

RESOLUTION 2792A(XXVI), as recommended by Special Political Committee, A/8547, adopted by Assembly on 6 December 1971, meeting 2001, by 112 votes to 0, with 3 abstentions.

The General Assembly,
Recalling its resolution 2672A(XXV) of 8 December 1970 and all previous resolutions mentioned therein, including resolution 194(III) of 11 December 1948,

Taking note of the annual report of the Commissioner-General of the United Nations Relief and Works Agency for Palestine Refugees in the Near East, covering the period from 1 July 1970 to 30 June 1971,

Taking note also of the joint appeal made by the President of the General Assembly and the Secretary-General on 17 November 1971,

1. *Notes with deep regret* that the repatriation or compensation of the refugees as provided for in paragraph 11 of General Assembly resolution 194(III) has not been effected, that no substantial progress has been made in the programme endorsed by the Assembly in paragraph 2 of resolution 513(VI) for the reintegration of refugees either by repatriation or resettlement and that, therefore, the situation of the refugees continues to be a matter of serious concern;

2. *Expresses its sincere appreciation* to Mr. Laurence Michelmore, on the occasion of his resignation as Commissioner-General of the United Nations Relief and Works Agency for Palestine Refugees in the Near East, for his efficient administration of the Agency during the past seven years and for his dedicated service to the welfare of the refugees;

3. *Expresses its thanks* to the Commissioner-General and to the staff of the United Nations Relief and Works Agency for Palestine Refugees in the Near East for their continued faithful efforts to provide essential services for the Palestine refugees, and to the specialized agencies and private organizations for their valuable work in assisting the refugees;

4. *Notes with regret* that the United Nations Conciliation Commission for Palestine was unable to find a means of achieving progress in the implementation of paragraph 11 of General Assembly resolution 194(III), and requests the Commission to exert continued efforts towards the implementation thereof and to report thereon as appropriate, but not later than 1 October 1972;

5. *Directs attention* to the continuing critical financial position of the United Nations Relief and Works Agency for Palestine Refugees in the Near East, as outlined in the Commissioner-General's report;

6. *Notes with concern* that, despite the commendable and successful efforts of the Commissioner-General to collect additional contributions to help relieve the serious budget deficit of the past year, contributions to the United Nations Relief and Works Agency for Palestine Refugees in the Near East continue to fall short of the funds needed to cover essential budget requirements;

7. *Calls upon* all Governments as a matter of urgency to make the most generous efforts possible to meet the anticipated needs of the United Nations Relief and Works Agency for Palestine Refugees in the Near East, particularly in the light of the budgetary deficit projected in the Commissioner-General's report, and therefore urges non-contributing Governments to contribute and contributing Governments to consider increasing their contributions;

8. *Decides* to extend until 30 June 1975, without prejudice to the provisions of paragraph 11 of General Assembly resolution 194(III), the mandate of the United Nations Relief and Works Agency for Palestine Refugees in the Near East.

A/SPC/L.226. Afghanistan, Austria, Belgium, Canada, Chile, Denmark, Finland, Ghana, Greece, India, Iran, Ireland, Italy, Japan, Nigeria, Norway, Sweden, Turkey, Yugoslavia: draft resolution, approved without objection by Special Political Committee on 1 December 1971, meeting 792.

A/8547. Report of Special Political Committee, draft resolution II B.

RESOLUTION 2792B(XXVI), as recommended by Special Political Committee, A/8547, adopted by Assembly on 6 December 1971, meeting 2001, by 113 votes to 0, with 1 abstention.

The General Assembly,

Recalling its resolutions 2252(ES-V) of 4 July 1967, 2341B(XXII) of 19 December 1967, 2452C(XXIII) of 19 December 1968, 2535C(XXIV) of 10 December 1969 and 2672B(XXV) of 8 December 1970,

Taking note of the annual report of the Commissioner-General of the United Nations Relief and Works Agency for Palestine Refugees in the Near East, covering the period from 1 July 1970 to 30 June 1971,

Taking note also of the joint appeal made by the President of the General Assembly and the Secretary-General,

Concerned about the continued human suffering resulting from the June 1967 hostilities in the Middle East,

1. *Reaffirms* its resolutions 2252(ES-V), 2341B(XXII), 2452C(XXIII), 2535C(XXIV) and 2672B(XXV);

2. *Endorses*, bearing in mind the objectives of those resolutions, the efforts of the Commissioner-General of the United Nations Relief and Works Agency for Palestine Refugees in the Near East to continue to provide humanitarian assistance, as far as practicable, on an emergency basis and as a temporary measure, to other persons in the area who are at present displaced and in serious need of continued assistance as a result of the June 1967 hostilities;

3. *Strongly appeals* to all Governments and to organizations and individuals to contribute generously for the above purposes to the United Nations Relief and Works Agency for Palestine Refugees in the Near East and to the other intergovernmental and non-governmental organizations concerned.

A/SPC/L.230 and Rev.1. Afghanistan, Indonesia, Malaysia, Mali, Pakistan, Senegal, Somalia: draft resolution and revision, approved by Special Political Committee on 1 December 1971, meeting 792, by roll-call vote of 66 to 4, with 32 abstentions, as follows:

In favour: Afghanistan, Albania, Algeria, Australia, Austria, Bahrain, Belgium, Bulgaria, Burundi, Byelorussian SSR, Ceylon, China, Cuba, Cyprus, Czechoslovakia, Denmark, Egypt, Finland, France, Greece, Guinea, Hungary, Iceland, India, Indonesia, Iran, Iraq, Ireland, Italy, Japan, Jordan, Kuwait, Lebanon, Libyan Arab Republic, Luxembourg, Malaysia, Mali, Mexico, Mongolia, Morocco, Nepal, Netherlands, New Zealand, Norway, Pakistan, People's Democratic Republic of Yemen, Poland, Romania, Rwanda, Saudi Arabia, Senegal, Somalia, Spain, Sudan, Sweden, Syrian Arab Republic, Togo, Trinidad and Tobago, Tunisia, Turkey, Ukrainian SSR, USSR, United Kingdom, United Republic of Tanzania, Yemen, Yugoslavia.

Against: Dominican Republic, Ecuador, Haiti, Israel.

Abstaining: Barbados, Bolivia, Brazil, Canada, Chad, Chile, Colombia, Costa Rica, El Salvador, Ethiopia, Ghana, Guatemala, Guyana, Ivory Coast, Jamaica, Kenya, Lesotho, Liberia, Madagascar, Malawi, Nicaragua, Nigeria, Peru, Philippines, Portugal, Singapore, Swaziland, Uganda, United States, Upper Volta, Uruguay, Venezuela.

A/8547. Report of Special Political Committee, draft resolution IIC.

RESOLUTION 2792C(XXVI), as recommended by Special Political Committee, A/8547, adopted by Assembly on 6 December 1971, meeting 2001, by recorded vote of 79 to 4, with 35 abstentions, as follows:

In favour: Afghanistan, Albania, Algeria, Australia, Austria, Bahrain, Belgium, Bulgaria, Burma, Burundi, Byelorussian SSR, Cameroon, Ceylon, China, Cuba, Cyprus, Czechoslovakia, Denmark, Egypt, Equatorial Guinea, Ethiopia, Finland, France, Greece, Guinea, Hungary, Iceland, India, Indonesia, Iran, Iraq, Ireland, Italy, Japan, Jordan, Kenya, Kuwait, Lebanon, Libyan Arab Republic, Luxembourg, Madagascar, Malaysia, Mali, Malta, Mauritania, Mexico, Mongolia, Morocco, Nepal, Netherlands, New Zealand, Niger, Nigeria, Norway, Oman, Pakistan, People's Democratic Republic of Yemen, Poland, Qatar, Romania, Saudi Arabia, Senegal, Somalia, Spain, Sudan, Sweden, Syrian Arab Republic, Thailand, Togo, Trinidad and Tobago, Tunisia, Turkey, Ukrainian SSR, USSR, United Kingdom, United Republic of Tanzania, Yemen, Yugoslavia, Zambia.

Against: Costa Rica, Ecuador, Guatemala, Israel.

Abstaining: Argentina, Barbados, Botswana, Brazil, Canada,

Central African Republic, Chad, Chile, Dahomey, Dominican Republic, El Salvador, Gabon, Ghana, Guyana, Honduras, Ivory Coast, Jamaica, Laos, Lesotho, Liberia, Malawi, Nicaragua, Panama, Paraguay, Peru, Philippines, Portugal, Singapore, Swaziland, Uganda, United States, Upper Volta, Uruguay, Venezuela, Zaire.

The General Assembly,

Having considered the special report of the Commissioner-General of the United Nations Relief and Works Agency for Palestine Refugees in the Near East on the effect on Palestine refugees of recent operations carried out by the Israeli military authorities in the Gaza Strip, and the supplement thereto,

Noting that both the Secretary-General and the Commissioner-General of the United Nations Relief and Works Agency for Palestine Refugees in the Near East have expressed great concern about the effect on Palestine refugees of these operations, in which shelters in refugee camps were demolished and about 15,000 persons displaced, some of them to places outside the Gaza Strip,

Recalling Commission on Human Rights resolution 10(XXVI) of 23 March 1970, in which the Commission deplored all policies and action aiming at the deportation of the Palestinian refugees from the occupied Gaza Strip and called upon Israel to desist forthwith from deporting the Palestinian civilians from the Gaza Strip,

1. *Declares* that the destruction of refugee shelters and the forcible removal of their occupants to other places, including places outside the Gaza Strip, contravene articles 49 and 53 of the Geneva Convention relative to the Protection of Civilian Persons in Time of War of 12 August 1949 as well as paragraph 7 of General Assembly resolution 2675(XXV) of 9 December 1970 entitled "Basic principles for the protection of civilian populations in armed conflicts";

2. *Deplores* these actions by Israel;

3. *Calls upon* Israel to desist from further destruction of refugee shelters and from further removal of refugees from their present places of residence;

4. *Calls upon* Israel to take immediate and effective steps for the return of the refugees concerned to the camps from which they were removed and to provide adequate shelters for their accommodation;

5. *Requests* the Secretary-General, after consulting with the Commissioner-General of the United Nations Relief and Works Agency for Palestine Refugees in the Near East, to report as soon as possible and whenever appropriate thereafter, but in any case not later than the opening date of the twenty-seventh session of the General Assembly, on Israel's compliance with the provisions of paragraph 3 and on implementation of the provisions of paragraph 4 of the present resolution.

A/SPC/L.231. Afghanistan, Guinea, Indonesia, Malaysia, Mali, Pakistan, Senegal, Somalia, Yugoslavia; draft resolution, approved by Special Political Committee on 1 December 1971, meeting 792, by roll-call vote of 46 to 20, with 36 abstentions, as follows:

In favour: Afghanistan, Albania, Algeria, Bahrain, Bulgaria, Byelorussian SSR, Ceylon, Chile, China, Cuba, Cyprus, Czechoslovakia, Egypt, Greece, Guinea, Hungary, India, Indonesia, Iran, Iraq, Japan, Jordan, Kuwait, Lebanon, Libyan Arab Republic, Malaysia, Mali, Mongolia, Morocco, Pakistan, People's Democratic Republic of Yemen, Poland, Romania, Saudi Arabia, Senegal, Somalia, Spain, Sudan, Syrian Arab Republic, Tunisia, Turkey, Ukrainian SSR, USSR, United Republic of Tanzania, Yemen, Yugoslavia.

Against: Belgium, Bolivia, Canada, Colombia, Costa Rica, Denmark, Dominican Republic, Ecuador, El Salvador, Guatemala, Haiti, Israel, Italy, Liberia, Luxembourg, Malawi, Netherlands, New Zealand, United States, Uruguay.

Abstaining: Australia, Austria, Barbados, Brazil, Burundi, Chad, Ethiopia, Finland, France, Ghana, Guyana, Iceland, Ireland, Ivory Coast, Jamaica, Kenya, Lesotho, Madagascar, Mexico, Nepal, Nicaragua, Nigeria, Norway, Peru, Philippines, Portugal, Rwanda, Singapore, Swaziland, Sweden, Togo,

Trinidad and Tobago, Uganda, United Kingdom, Upper Volta, Venezuela.

A/8547. Report of Special Political Committee, draft resolution II D.

RESOLUTION 2792 D (XXVI), as recommended by Special Political Committee, A/8547, adopted by Assembly on 6 December 1971, meeting 2001, by roll-call vote of 53 to 23, with 43 abstentions, as follows:

In favour: Afghanistan, Albania, Algeria, Bahrain, Bulgaria, Byelorussian SSR, Cameroon, Ceylon, Chile, China, Cuba, Cyprus, Czechoslovakia, Egypt, Equatorial Guinea, Greece, Guinea, Hungary, India, Indonesia, Iran, Iraq, Japan, Jordan, Kuwait, Lebanon, Libyan Arab Republic, Malaysia, Mali, Mauritania, Mongolia, Morocco, Niger, Oman, Pakistan, People's Democratic Republic of Yemen, Poland, Qatar, Romania, Saudi Arabia, Senegal, Somalia, Spain, Sudan, Syrian Arab Republic, Tunisia, Turkey, Ukrainian SSR, USSR, United Republic of Tanzania, Yemen, Yugoslavia, Zambia.

Against: Barbados, Belgium, Canada, Colombia, Costa Rica, Denmark, Dominican Republic, Ecuador, El Salvador, Guatemala, Honduras, Israel, Italy, Liberia, Luxembourg, Madagascar, Malawi, Netherlands, New Zealand, Nicaragua, Swaziland, United States, Uruguay.

Abstaining: Argentina, Australia, Austria, Botswana, Brazil, Burma, Burundi, Central African Republic, Chad, Dahomey, Ethiopia, Finland, France, Gabon, Ghana, Guyana, Iceland, Ireland, Ivory Coast, Jamaica, Kenya, Laos, Lesotho, Malta, Mexico, Nepal, Nigeria, Norway, Panama, Paraguay, Peru, Philippines, Portugal, Singapore, Sweden, Thailand, Togo, Trinidad and Tobago, Uganda, United Kingdom, Upper Volta, Venezuela, Zaire.

The General Assembly,

Recognizing that the problem of the Palestinian Arab refugees has arisen from the denial of their inalienable rights under the Charter of the United Nations and the Universal Declaration of Human Rights,

Recalling its resolution 2535 B (XXIV) of 10 December 1969, in which it reaffirmed the inalienable rights of the people of Palestine, its resolution 2672 C (XXV) of 8 December 1970, in which it recognized that the people of Palestine are entitled to equal rights and self-determination in accordance with the Charter, and its resolution 2649(XXV) of 30 November 1970, in which it recognized that the people of Palestine are entitled to the right of self-determination,

Bearing in mind the principle of equal rights and self-determination of peoples enshrined in Articles 1 and 55 of the Charter and more recently reaffirmed in the Declaration on Principles of International Law concerning Friendly Relations and Co-operation among States in accordance with the Charter of the United Nations and the Declaration on the Strengthening of International Security,

1. *Recognizes* that the people of Palestine are entitled to equal rights and self-determination, in accordance with the Charter of the United Nations;

2. *Expresses its grave concern* that the people of Palestine have not been permitted to enjoy their inalienable rights and to exercise their right to self-determination;

3. *Declares* that full respect for the inalienable rights of the people of Palestine is an indispensable element in the establishment of a just and lasting peace in the Middle East.

A/SPC/L.232 and Rev.1. Afghanistan, Indonesia, Malaysia, Mali, Pakistan, Senegal, Somalia, Yugoslavia: draft resolution and revision, approved by Special Political Committee on 1 December 1971, meeting 792, by roll-call vote of 75 to 2, with 25 abstentions, as follows:

In favour: Afghanistan, Albania, Algeria, Australia, Austria, Bahrain, Belgium, Bulgaria, Burundi, Byelorussian SSR, Canada, Ceylon, Chile, China, Cuba, Cyprus, Czechoslovakia, Denmark, Egypt, Finland, France, Greece, Guinea, Guyana,

Hungary, Iceland, India, Indonesia, Iran, Iraq, Ireland, Italy, Japan, Jordan, Kuwait, Lebanon, Liberia, Libyan Arab Republic, Luxembourg, Malaysia, Mali, Mexico, Mongolia, Morocco, Nepal, Netherlands, New Zealand, Norway, Pakistan, People's Democratic Republic of Yemen, Philippines, Poland, Romania, Rwanda, Saudi Arabia, Senegal, Singapore, Somalia, Spain, Sudan, Sweden, Syrian Arab Republic, Togo, Trinidad and Tobago, Tunisia, Turkey, Ukrainian SSR, USSR, United Kingdom, United Republic of Tanzania, United States, Upper Volta, Venezuela, Yemen, Yugoslavia.

Against: Israel, Malawi.

Abstaining: Barbados, Bolivia, Brazil, Chad, Colombia, Costa Rica, Dominican Republic, Ecuador, El Salvador, Ethiopia, Ghana, Guatemala, Haiti, Ivory Coast, Jamaica, Kenya, Lesotho, Madagascar, Nicaragua, Nigeria, Peru, Portugal, Swaziland, Uganda, Uruguay.

A/8547. Report of Special Political Committee, draft resolution II E.

RESOLUTION 2792E(XXVI), as recommended by Special Political Committee, A/8547, adopted by Assembly on 6 December 1971, meeting 2001, by roll-call vote of 88 to 3, with 28 abstentions.

In favour: Afghanistan, Albania, Algeria, Australia, Austria, Bahrain, Belgium, Bulgaria, Burma, Burundi, Byelorussian SSR, Cameroon, Canada, Ceylon, Chad, Chile, China, Cuba, Cyprus, Czechoslovakia, Denmark, Egypt, Equatorial Guinea, Ethiopia, Finland, France, Greece, Guinea, Guyana, Hungary, India, Indonesia, Iran, Iraq, Ireland, Italy, Japan, Jordan, Kuwait, Lebanon, Liberia, Libyan Arab Republic, Luxembourg, Madagascar, Malaysia, Mali, Malta, Mauritania, Mexico, Mongolia, Morocco, Nepal, Netherlands, New Zealand, Niger, Nigeria, Norway, Oman, Pakistan, People's Democratic Republic of Yemen, Peru, Philippines, Poland, Qatar, Romania, Saudi Arabia, Senegal, Singapore, Somalia, Spain, Sudan, Sweden, Syrian Arab Republic, Thailand, Togo, Trinidad and Tobago, Tunisia, Turkey, Ukrainian SSR, USSR, United Kingdom, United Republic of Tanzania, United States, Upper Volta, Venezuela, Yemen, Yugoslavia, Zambia.

Against: Costa Rica, Guatemala, Israel.

Abstaining: Argentina, Barbados, Botswana, Brazil, Central African Republic, Colombia, Dahomey, Dominican Republic, Ecuador, El Salvador, Gabon, Ghana, Honduras,* Iceland, Ivory Coast, Jamaica, Kenya, Laos, Lesotho, Malawi, Nicaragua, Panama, Paraguay, Portugal, Swaziland, Uganda, Uruguay, Zaire.

*Subsequently Honduras advised the Secretariat that it had intended to vote in favour.

The General Assembly,

Recalling Security Council resolution 237(1967) of 14 June 1967,

Recalling also its resolutions 2252(ES-V) of 4 July 1967, 2452A(XXIII) of 19 December 1968, 2535B(XXIV) of 10 December 1969 and 2672D(XXV) of 8 December 1970, calling upon the Government of Israel to take effective and immediate steps for the return without delay of those inhabitants who had fled the areas since the outbreak of hostilities,

Having considered the report of the Secretary-General of 27 August 1971 concerning the implementation of resolution 2672D(XXV),

Gravely concerned about the plight of the displaced inhabitants,

Convinced that the plight of the displaced inhabitants could be relieved by their speedy return to their homes and to the camps which they formerly occupied,

Emphasizing the imperative of giving effect to its resolutions for relieving the plight of the displaced inhabitants,

1. *Considers* that the plight of the displaced inhabitants continues since they have not yet returned to their homes and camps;

2. *Expresses its grave concern* that the displaced inhabitants have not been able to return in accordance with the above-mentioned resolutions;

3. *Calls once more upon* the Government of Israel to take immediately and without any further delay effective steps for the return of the displaced inhabitants;

4. *Requests* the Secretary-General to follow the implementation of the present resolution and to report thereon to the General Assembly.

Chapter XI

Other questions relating to the Middle East

Matters concerning the islands of Abu Musa, Greater Tunb and Lesser Tunb

On 3 December 1971, the representatives of Algeria, Iraq, the Libyan Arab Republic and the People's Democratic Republic of Yemen requested an urgent meeting of the Security Council to consider the situation in the Arabian Gulf area arising from the occupation by Iran on 30 November 1971 of the islands of Abu Musa, the Greater Tunb and the Lesser Tunb.

On 9 December 1971, the Security Council included the letter from those representatives in its agenda and invited them as well as the representatives of Iran, Kuwait and the United Arab Emirates, at their request, to participate in the discussion without the right to vote.

The representative of Iraq told the Security Council that on 30 November 1971 his Government had received a cable from the Ruler of Ras al Khaimah stating that the islands of the Greater Tunb and the Lesser Tunb in the Arabian Gulf had been occupied and that in the process four local policemen had been killed and two wounded. The two islands, the cable added, had always been part of Ras al Khaimah. Therefore the Iranian occupation was an aggression against all Arab people.

Stating that the occupation of the islands was a flagrant violation of the United Nations Charter, the representative of Iraq charged that the invasion was the latest step in a policy of expansion by Iran and a demonstration of collusion between Iran and the United Kingdom. He rejected Iran's "historical" claim to the islands which, he said, had always been inhabited by Arab people, and rejected also the theory of a "power vacuum," which he said was a colonial and imperialistic concept. Referring to the argument that the islands were of strategic importance to Iran, he pointed out that the islands were of strategic importance to other littoral States in the Gulf, most of which were major oil-producing countries.

The Iraqi representative also said that the United Kingdom was committed, under treaties with the rulers of the Trucial States, to preserve the territorial integrity of the States concerned; it should be condemned for not living up to those obligations.

Kuwait, observing that it was concerned with the stability and security of the Gulf after the withdrawal of British troops by the end of 1971, said it had made many efforts to assist the Emirates of the area to form a federation. That federation was, however, blocked by Iran which made its acceptance of that development conditional on its possession of the Arab islands of the Greater and the Lesser Tunb and Abu Musa.

The stability of the Gulf area had been disrupted, Kuwait's representative said, and the security of the Emirates encroached upon. Therefore, it was incumbent upon the Security Council to call on Iran to withdraw its troops from the Arab islands immediately.

Algeria observed that the three islands occupied by Iran were part of the federation of the United Arab Emirates which had just joined the United Nations, Therefore, the matter could not be settled by agreement between Iran and the United Kingdom, but should be discussed among all the parties concerned. Iran's military action had violated the United Nations Charter and should be condemned by the Security Council.

The representative of the People's Democratic Republic of Yemen maintained that the discussion of the islands concerned the entire Arabian Gulf because the islands were extensions of the Arab mainland. The representative put the responsibility for Iran's recent aggression on the United Kingdom, because under the prevailing treaties, he said, the United Kingdom had full authority in that territory until the end of 1971. The Council

should demand the withdrawal of Iranian troops.

The representative of Iran said that at a time when the flames of war were rapidly spreading in South-East Asia, the Council was convened not to discuss real acts of war but the wanton and fanciful preoccupations of a few. He rejected the charges made by the previous speakers against Iran as baseless, and said that the question was essentially a domestic matter.

The term "Arabian Gulf" used by the representative of Iraq, he noted, was a misrepresentation of facts, because the area from the most ancient times had been called the "Persian Gulf." Iran's position in the area of the Gulf was one based on creating conditions for peace and security for all the littoral States, which should work together in a spirit of friendship and co-operation.

Iran did not entertain any expansionist ambitions and had a policy based on settling disputes by peaceful means, as shown by its action the previous year in the case of Bahrain which had been acclaimed by the Security Council.

With regard to the islands of Abu Musa and the Greater and the Lesser Tunb, the representative of Iran recalled that Iran had tried to find a peaceful settlement, although there was no doubt that the islands belonged to Iran as shown in maps hundreds of years old. There had been reported threats by Iraq and the Libyan Arab Republic to send troops to the islands; however, Iran would not allow any violation of its sovereignty on its territory.

The representative of the United Kingdom recalled that on 1 March 1971 his Government's Foreign Secretary had declared that the existing treaties between the United Kingdom and Bahrain, Qatar and the seven Trucial States, would be terminated and British forces withdrawn by the end of 1971. In taking that decision, he added, his Government's primary concern was to see stability preserved in the area through a federation of the States and the settlement of outstanding territorial differences—which mainly concerned conflicting claims by the Arab States and Iran to certain islands in the Gulf.

With regard to the conflicting claims, he said that the island of Abu Musa, administered by the Ruler of Sharjah and having a population of 800, had been the subject of an agreement between that ruler and Iran. Concerning the Greater and the Lesser Tunb, the United Kingdom had made it known that it could not protect the two islands if agreement was not reached by the time of withdrawal.

The ending of the United Kingdom's special position and responsibilities in the Gulf, he noted, had meant the striking of a balance between the conflicting claims of neighbouring States and the taking into account of realities. While agreed solutions to all problems could have been better, it was not for lack of trying.

The representative of the Libyan Arab Republic felt that from past deliberations of the Security Council it could be seen that big powers could do anything they wished while small ones were powerless. Moreover, other States with the support of a big power took liberties in violation of the Charter of the United Nations. Iran's occupation of the islands with the complicity of the British was an example.

The representative of the United Arab Emirates observed that the action of Iran in using force to settle a territorial dispute arising out of a claim—which he felt was untenable both historically and juridically—was not only contrary to the Charter but was incompatible with the traditional friendship between the Arab and Iranian peoples.

Iran, which claimed that the islands were Iranian, had failed to produce any convincing evidence in support of that claim. Those islands, in the opinion of the United Arab Emirates, were Arab and always had been, and the British had recognized them as such. However, Iran had chosen the method of force to settle its claims although thousands of Iranians lived and worked in the United Arab Emirates; the two countries should have friendly neighbourly relations.

The representative expressed his country's hope that Iran would reconsider its position regarding the islands and would find it possible to settle the matter in a way that befitted neighbours.

Somalia said that the statements made in the Council led to the conclusion that the parties in the dispute before the Council were all concerned with the well-being of the people of the region. This was a reason to settle the dispute amicably so that peace, security and stability could reign in the area.

In dealing with such sensitive matters, Somalia continued, the Council must always act in strict conformity with the letter and spirit of the United Nations Charter. While Chapter VI of the Charter provided for the peaceful settlement of disputes, it would be precipitate at that stage to recommend any recourse under Article 36,[1] as some States friendly to both the complainants and Iran were attempting to bring both sides together. Somalia therefore suggested that the Council defer consideration of the matter to a later date to allow sufficient time for quiet diplomacy. In case the third-party efforts should fail, the Council could resume consideration of the complaint.

The Council agreed to the proposed course without objection.

[1]For text of Chapter VI of the Charter, including Article 36, see APPENDIX II.

DOCUMENTARY REFERENCES

Security Council, meeting 1610.

S/10409. Letter of 3 December 1971 from Algeria, Iraq, Libyan Arab Republic and People's Democratic Republic of Yemen (request to convene Council and participate in discussion).
S/10431. Letter of 6 December 1971 from Kuwait (request to participate in Council's discussion).

S/10434. Letter of 7 December 1971 from Iraq (transmitting cable of 30 November 1971 from Ruler of Ras al Khaimah).
S/10436, S/10437, S/10439. Letters of 9 December 1971 from Iran, People's Democratic Republic of Yemen and United Arab Emirates (requests to participate in Council's discussion).
S/INF/27. Resolutions and decisions of Security Council, 1971. Decisions, p. 11.

The question of Oman

Consideration by Special Committee

The General Assembly's Special Committee on the Situation with regard to the Implementation of the Declaration on the Granting of Independence to Colonial Countries and Peoples took up the question of Oman on 17 September 1971.

The Special Committee took into account the General Assembly's request of 14 December 1970[2] to follow closely developments regarding the colonial situation in the territory and to report thereon in 1971.

On a proposal of the Chairman, the Special Committee, having followed recent developments concerning Oman and having noted that the Security Council had under consideration the application of the Sultanate of Oman for membership in the United Nations, decided to suspend consideration of the question pending such action

as the Assembly might wish to take in that connexion at its 1971 session, due to open on 21 September 1971.

Consideration by General Assembly

On 6 October 1971, on the proposal of Iraq, the General Assembly's Fourth Committee decided to give priority to the question of Oman.

Iraq also submitted the text of a draft consensus on the item which the Committee approved without objection.

By the consensus the Fourth Committee, noting that the Security Council on 30 September 1971 had recommended to the General Assembly that Oman be admitted to membership in the United Nations, recommended that the Assembly decide

[2]See Y.U.N., 1970, pp. 289-90, text of resolution 2702(XXV).

to conclude consideration of the item by taking note with satisfaction that Oman had achieved the goals set forth in the Charter of the United Nations and in the Declaration on the Granting of Independence to Colonial Countries and Peoples (contained in the Assembly's resolution of 14 December 1960)[3] and by extending to the Government and the people of Oman its best wishes for peace and prosperity in the future.

At a plenary meeting on 7 October 1971, the Assembly considered the text recommended by the Fourth Committee.

Explaining his vote before the vote was taken, the representative of the People's Democratic Republic of Yemen stated that, with due respect to the Fourth Committee, his delegation was astonished to see it suddenly change its position and

cede to the allegation that Oman had achieved the goals set forth in the Charter and the Declaration on the granting of independence. In fact, he said, Oman had not achieved such goals and was still under colonial rule. No independence had been declared and British political and military presence had not been eliminated.

The People's Democratic Republic of Yemen maintained its view, expressed on several occasions, and would vote against the Fourth Committee's recommendation.

The consensus was adopted by a recorded vote of 115 to 2, with 1 abstention.

(For text of the consensus, see DOCUMENTARY REFERENCES below.) (See also pp. 219-20.)

[3]See Y.U.N., 1960, pp. 49-50, text of resolution 1514(XV).

DOCUMENTARY REFERENCES

Special Committee on Situation with regard to Implementation of Declaration on Granting of Independence to Colonial Countries and Peoples, meeting 827.

General Assembly—26th session
General Committee, meeting 191.
Fourth Committee, meeting 1920.
Plenary meeting 1957.

A/8401. Report of Secretary-General on work of the Organization, 16 June 1970–15 June 1971, Part Two, Chapter I B 8.
A/8423/Rev.1. Report of Special Committee on Situation with regard to Implementation of Declaration on Granting of Independence to Colonial Countries and Peoples (covering its work during 1971), Chapter XIII.
A/C.4/L.987. Draft consensus, submitted by Iraq, approved without objection by Fourth Committee on 6 October 1971, meeting 1920.
A/8456. Report of Fourth Committee, draft consensus.
A/8429. Resolutions adopted by General Assembly during its 26th session, 21 September–22 December 1971. Other decisions, p. 112: Consensus, adopted by Assembly on 7 October 1971, meeting 1957, by recorded vote of 115 to 2, with 1 abstention, as follows:

In favour: Afghanistan, Albania, Algeria, Argentina, Australia, Austria, Bahrain, Barbados, Belgium, Bhutan, Brazil, Bulgaria, Burma, Burundi, Byelorussian SSR, Cameroon, Canada, Central African Republic, Ceylon, Chad, Chile, China, Costa Rica, Cyprus, Czechoslovakia, Dahomey, Denmark, Dominican Republic, Ecuador, Egypt, El Salvador, Ethiopia, Fiji, Finland,

France, Gabon, Gambia, Ghana, Greece, Guatemala, Guinea, Guyana, Haiti, Honduras, Hungary, Iceland, India, Indonesia, Iran, Iraq, Ireland, Italy, Ivory Coast, Jamaica, Japan, Jordan, Kenya, Khmer Republic, Kuwait, Lebanon, Lesotho, Liberia, Libyan Arab Republic, Luxembourg, Madagascar, Malawi, Malaysia, Mali, Malta, Mauritania, Mauritius, Mexico, Mongolia, Morocco, Nepal, Netherlands, New Zealand, Nicaragua, Niger, Nigeria, Norway, Pakistan, Paraguay, Peru, Philippines, Poland, Portugal, Qatar, Romania, Senegal, Sierra Leone, Singapore, Somalia, South Africa, Spain, Sudan, Swaziland, Sweden, Syrian Arab Republic, Thailand, Togo, Trinidad and Tobago, Tunisia, Turkey, Uganda, Ukrainian SSR, USSR, United Republic of Tanzania, United States, Upper Volta, Uruguay, Venezuela, Yemen, Yugoslavia, Zambia.
Against: Cuba, People's Democratic Republic of Yemen.
Abstaining: Saudi Arabia.

"The General Assembly, having examined the chapter of the report of the Special Committee on the Situation with regard to the Implementation of the Declaration on the Granting of Independence to Colonial Countries and Peoples concerning the question of Oman, and noting that the Security Council in its resolution 299(1971) of 30 September 1971 has recommended to the General Assembly that Oman be admitted to membership in the United Nations, decides to conclude consideration of the item entitled 'Question of Oman' by taking note with satisfaction that Oman has achieved the goals set forth in the Charter of the United Nations and the Declaration on the Granting of Independence to Colonial Countries and Peoples and by extending to the Government and the people of Oman its best wishes for peace and prosperity in the future."

Chapter XII

The situation in Cyprus

During 1971, the Secretary-General submitted two reports to the Security Council on the United Nations operation in Cyprus. On the basis of the Secretary-General's recommendation, the Council, noting the consent of the Government of Cyprus,

on each occasion (26 May and 13 December) unanimously decided to extend the stationing of the United Nations Peace-keeping Force in Cyprus (UNFICYP) for an additional period of six months.

Major-General Dewan Prem Chand continued to command the United Nations Peace-keeping Force in Cyprus (UNFICYP) in 1971. Bibiano F. Osorio-Tafall continued as the Secretary-General's Special Representative in Cyprus.

On 10 and 19 April 1971, the Permanent Representative of Turkey to the United Nations transmitted letters from Fazil Kuchuk, Vice-President of Cyprus, addressed to the Secretary-General. The Vice-President drew attention to statements by Archbishop Makarios, President of Cyprus, and by Greek Cypriot cabinet ministers in which, he said, they had stressed their adherence to the policy of *enosis* (union of Cyprus with Greece); such statements caused grave concern among the Turkish Cypriot community and could only have the object of undermining inter-communal talks.

In letters dated 3 and 6 May 1971, addressed to the Secretary-General, the Permanent Representative of Cyprus to the United Nations —protesting, respectively, Turkish statements which he asserted revealed Turkey's aims of territorial expansion over Cyprus, and the letters of the Vice-President of Cyprus—stated that the Government of Cyprus had decided to exert every effort to solve the problem of Cyprus on the basis of a sovereign, independent and unitary State.

In further letters, dated 12 and 18 May 1971, Turkey stated, among other things, that there was overwhelming evidence of the Greek Cypriot administration's participation in the implementation of the *enosis* policy and that the Greek Cypriots had chosen to misrepresent the Turkish community's defence of its vested rights and interests in order to justify their uncompromising and aggressive attitude.

Consideration by Security Council (May 1971)

In his report to the Security Council on the United Nations operation in Cyprus for the period 2 December 1970 to 19 May 1971, the Secretary-General said that there had been little improvement in the situation and no indication of progress towards a negotiated solution of the underlying problems of the island. On the contrary, the tendency on the part of spokesmen for both the Government of Cyprus and the Turkish Cypriot community to adopt uncompromising attitudes in their public statements had resulted in an aggravation of tension.

The best interest of all the parties lay in continuing inter-communal talks, the Secretary-General felt. Leaders of all parties should publicly restate their determination to solve the problem of Cyprus on the basis of an independent and unitary State.

In recommending the extension of the United Nations Peace-keeping Force in Cyprus (UNFICYP) until 15 December 1971, the Secretary-General stated that a further reduction of the Force had been considered, but it had become clear that despite the negative budgetary situation, any sizable reduction would be inadvisable in the current situation. He expressed the hope that the Security Council would consider undertaking a comprehensive review of the problem, including constructive alternatives to the current arrangements.

The Security Council discussed the Secretary-General's report on 26 May 1971. As on previous occasions, the representatives of Cyprus, Greece and Turkey participated in the discussion, without the right to vote.

The representative of Cyprus noted that there had been increased agricultural, communal and economic co-operation between the Greek Cypriot and Turkish Cypriot communities. However, the Turkish Cypriot leadership had rejected UNFICYP proposals regarding deconfrontation and had intensified military preparations.

The inter-communal talks had been stalled for nearly 30 months on the question of local government, the representative continued. The Cypriot Government had made all possible concessions in order to reach an accommodation, but the Turkish Cypriot proposals threatened the very existence of the State. He expressed the hope that the Turkish Cypriot side would join in an effort to reach a peaceful and lasting solution on the basis of an independent, unitary State.

The representative of Turkey said that if the inter-communal talks had not made substantial progress, it was because of mistrust between the two communities, the result of the Greek Cypriot community's openly expressed policy of *enosis*. The Turkish community's demands for the restoration of its constitutional rights and interests had been labelled as divisionist by the Greek Cypriots in order to conceal an ultimate political objective: the abrogation of the independence of the Turkish community. The Turkish Government once again stated its willingness to work for a just solution of the problem that would safeguard the independence of Cyprus and the rights and interests of the two communities, within the framework established at the inception of the State.

The Greek representative said he wished to note the constructive role of the Cypriot Government in taking measures to ensure a return to normalcy. Greece agreed with the Secretary-General that the inter-communal talks were the best way to reach an agreed settlement and reiterated its desire to see both parties live together in an independent, sovereign and unified State.

As the result of prior consultations, the Security Council had before it the text of a draft resolution by which it would extend the mandate of UNFICYP for a further period of six months, ending 15 December 1971, in the expectation that by then sufficient progress towards a final solution would make possible a withdrawal or substantial reduction in the size of Force.

The text was unanimously adopted on 26 May 1971 as resolution 293(1971). (For text of resolution, see DOCUMENTARY REFERENCES below.)

A number of Security Council members—including Italy, Japan, Somalia, the United Kingdom and the United States—noted that they had voted for a further extension of the UNFICYP mandate because they felt the presence of the Force had helped to preserve calm in the island. Italy added that its support of UNFICYP was consistent with its views on the necessity of increasing the peace-keeping ability of the Organization. The United States held that without UNFICYP's presence, a threat to international peace could develop in Cyprus.

Certain positive aspects of the situation on Cyprus were noted, including the reduced number of incidents and the increased economic co-operation between the two communities. At the same time, members expressed regret at the lack of progress in the inter-communal talks and in efforts towards normalization.

Some Council members also expressed concern about the prolonged stay of UNFICYP on the island. The United Kingdom, while approving the stabilizing role of the Force, said that UNFICYP should not remain in Cyprus indefinitely. France, noting that UNFICYP had been able to maintain the fragile *status quo* but had failed to achieve peace, expressed the view that the quasi-automatic renewals of the mandate ran counter to the interests of the United Nations and of the Cypriots themselves. Argentina, Japan and the Syrian Arab Republic also felt that the prolongation of the Force should not serve as a pretext for deferring a final settlement.

Poland and the USSR held that the seven-year presence of the Force in the island, even under the aegis of the United Nations, could not be considered normal and should not be regarded as a model for other such operations.

A number of Council members—including France, Italy, Japan, the USSR, the United Kingdom and the United States—believed that the inter-communal talks represented the only way to surmount the difficulties between the parties.

Other views expressed included the concern of some members—Italy and the Syrian Arab Republic, for example—that the precarious situation in Cyprus might develop into a new crisis englobing the eastern Mediterranean. The USSR said that the question of Cyprus must be settled without any outside interference, and that the complete independence of the island would require the withdrawal of all foreign forces and the elimination of all foreign military bases.

With regard to financial matters, the United States noted that it had pledged up to 40 per cent of UNFICYP costs; it was fully prepared to play its part, the United States said, but the interests of other States in preserving the peace on Cyprus should be reflected in their financial support of the operation.

On 26 May 1971, the Permanent Representative of Turkey to the United Nations transmitted a letter from the Vice-President of Cyprus protesting the detention of Turkish Cypriot officials by Greek Cypriot police.

On 21 June 1971, the Permanent Representative of Cyprus drew the Secretary-General's attention to statements by Turkey's President and by its Foreign Minister that, he said, represented a threat to the independence and sovereignty of Cyprus and indicated Turkey's imperialist designs for territorial expansion over the island.

On 24 June, the representative of Turkey denied the allegations of Cyprus.

Security Council consideration (December 1971)

In his twentieth report on the United Nations peace-keeping operation in Cyprus, covering the period 20 May to 30 November 1971, the Secretary-General stated that the preceding six months had been marked by a deterioration of the situation. Tensions between the two communities had noticeably increased and there had been a number of inter-communal incidents, some of them serious. The United Nations Force had been able to achieve only limited progress in the normalization of conditions and none in the fields of freedom of movement and deconfrontation. While the Cypriot Government had continued to co-operate with UNFICYP in most cases, the Turkish Cypriot leadership had been reluctant to extend the same measure of co-operation as in the past, the Secretary-General reported.

He had reached the conclusion, the Secretary-General continued, that the inter-communal talks had reached an impasse which could not be overcome without new impetus. He had therefore suggested that his Special Representative in Cyprus be included in the talks and that the Greek and Turkish Governments each delegate a constitutional expert to attend the talks in an advisory capacity.

The Secretary-General also felt that it would be appropriate and desirable for the Security Council to become more actively involved in assisting the parties in the search for a solution.

The Secretary-General recommended a further six months' extension of the mandate of UNFICYP, until 15 June 1972.

In making this recommendation, the Secretary-General again expressed concern at the lack of sound and effective arrangements for the financing of the Force; the deficit of UNFICYP had reached $16.4 million, he reported.

On 13 December 1971, when the Security Council met to discuss the Secretary-General's report, it had before it, as a result of prior consultations, a draft resolution by which the Security Council would extend UNFICYP for a further six-month period ending 15 June 1972, in the expectation that by then sufficient progress towards a final solution would make possible a withdrawal or substantial reduction in the size of the Force.

The draft resolution was adopted unanimously as resolution 305(1971). (For text of resolution, see DOCUMENTARY REFERENCES below.)

China did not participate in the voting. It stated that it regarded the Cyprus question as one left over from imperialist colonial rule and maintained that such questions should be settled in a reasonable way by the countries concerned through consultation on an equal footing.

As on previous occasions, the representatives of Cyprus, Greece and Turkey participated in the debate, without the right to vote.

The representative of Cyprus noted that despite various efforts and the adoption of resolutions, a peaceful solution to the problem of Cyprus still had not been found.

Cyprus had expressed reservations on the Secretary-General's suggestion concerning the participation of Greek and Turkish experts in the inter-communal talks, since it had been established that the talks would be between the Cypriots themselves. However, Cyprus would accept the proposal as an indication of its desire to explore all ways for progress, and would also welcome the participation of the Secretary-General's Special Representative in the talks.

If this new effort failed, Cyprus would support the Secretary-General's proposal that the Security Council become more actively involved in efforts to reach a settlement.

The representative of Turkey, in supporting the extension of the UNFICYP mandate, expressed the view that the deterioration of the situation on the island was particularly due to an upsurge of the pro-*enosis* campaign of the Greek Cypriots; this had increased the sensitivity of the Turkish Cypriots to their security requirements.

The inter-communal talks still provided some ground for optimism, the Turkish representative said, and he was confident that the continuation of contacts with the Secretary-General by the parties

concerned would soon produce a consensus upon which the talks could be resumed.

The Greek representative expressed satisfaction that, in general, calm had reigned in Cyprus for the preceding six months, but regretted that the stagnation in the inter-communal talks had resulted in a hardening of positions. Greece shared the Secretary-General's desire to see the inter-communal talks renewed and made more effective, and for this reason, supported the Secretary-General's suggestions concerning the participation in the talks of his Special Representative and of expert legal advisers from Greece and Turkey. Greece hoped that the Security Council would support this proposal.

During discussion in the Council, some members—including Burundi, Nicaragua and the Syrian Arab Republic—felt that the calm prevailing in Cyprus should be broadened into a climate of reconciliation.

Other members expressed concern at the Secretary-General's report of increased tension between the Greek and Turkish communities on the island.

France held that setbacks in the search for a solution had led to frustration and a heightening of tension. Italy felt that the situation might worsen unless precautionary measures were taken and progress towards a solution was achieved. Sierra Leone said that after eight years of United Nations peace-keeping and the expenditure of more than a hundred million dollars, a solution was not in sight; the Greek Cypriots' fears of partition and the Turkish Cypriots' of *enosis* were understandable, but they had to be allayed if a peaceful settlement was to be attained.

The United States regretted the deterioration in the situation and the apparent trend towards aggressiveness and non-co-operation.

The USSR considered that the Cyprus problem should be settled peacefully, on the basis of freedom, independence and territorial integrity. It was against any attempts to infringe the sovereignty of Cyprus. Poland and the USSR called for the elimination of all foreign influences and military bases from Cyprus.

A number of States—including Belgium, Italy, Poland, Sierra Leone, the Syrian Arab Republic, the USSR, the United Kingdom and the United States—reiterated their belief that the best hope for breaking the current deadlock lay in the reactivation of the inter-communal talks. Belgium, France, Japan, the United Kingdom and the United States, among others, supported the Secretary-General's initiatives in this regard, including his proposal that his Special Representative in Cyprus be included in any reactivated talks.

The USSR shared the Secretary-General's view that the Security Council should play a more active role in the search for a solution; it felt that the time had come for the Council once again to study all the possibilities for a settlement of the situation which would lead to a withdrawal of United Nations troops from the island.

The United Kingdom felt that it would be premature for the Council to take any action, since the local talks still provided hope for progress.

Somalia said that it would not be appropriate for the Council to take any initiative until the proposals of the Secretary-General concerning the inter-communal talks had been given the chance to succeed. If after some months the Secretary–General could not report any progress, the Council should consider new measures to solve the problem. In any solution, Cyprus had to retain its independence and territorial integrity.

Several Council members commented on the fact that this was the twentieth time that the Security Council had decided to extend the mandate of UNFICYP. Japan felt that there was justifiable criticism directed against the apparently indefinite perpetuation of the mandate.

The United Kingdom observed that its accept-

ance of the burden of support for UNFICYP in men and money could not be taken for granted, and that there was a growing belief that it was high time that the problem was solved.

The USSR said it continued to take the view that the operation must not go on indefinitely; the very stationing of foreign troops on the territory of an independent sovereign State could only be a short-term measure.

With regard to financing, the United States associated itself with the Secretary-General's statement in his report that the financial burden of UNFICYP had been borne by a limited number of Governments. The United States held that the financial burden of the operation should be collective, and it appealed to members to contribute their share. It also noted that it was consulting other interested Governments on ways to end the deficit.

At the end of the discussion, the President of the Council appealed to the parties to reactivate the talks in accordance with the suggestions made by the Secretary-General.

The United Nations Peace-keeping Force in Cyprus

(Contingents by country of origin, as at 31 December 1971)

Military		Civilian Police	
Austria (Hospital Unit)	56	Australia	38
Canada	585	Austria	49
Denmark	296	Denmark	41
Finland	288	Sweden	40
Ireland	391	Total	168
Sweden	286	Grand total	3,119
United Kingdom	1,049		
Total	2,951		

The financing of the United Nations peace-keeping operation in Cyprus

The following table lists pledges to the UNFICYP Special Account for the period 27 March 1964 to 15 June 1972.

Government	Total pledges (in U.S. dollar equivalents)
Australia	1,519,875
Austria	1,240,000
Belgium	1,747,889
Botswana	500
Cyprus	717,589
Denmark	2,085,000[a]
Federal Republic of Germany	11,000,000
Finland	525,000[a]
Ghana	21,667
Greece	10,150,000
Guyana	5,020
Iceland	14,000
Iran	30,000
Ireland	50,000
Israel	26,500
Italy	3,459,039
Ivory Coast	60,000
Jamaica	17,800
Japan	740,000
Khmer Republic	600
Laos	1,500
Lebanon	1,597
Liberia	10,155
Libyan Arab Republic	30,000
Luxembourg	45,000
Malawi	5,590
Malaysia	7,500
Malta	1,820
Mauritania	2,041
Morocco	20,000
Nepal	400
Netherlands	921,000
New Zealand	42,000
Niger	2,041
Nigeria	10,800
Norway	1,989,741
Pakistan	17,800
Philippines	4,000
Republic of Korea	16,000
Republic of Viet-Nam	4,000
Sierra Leone	21,650
Singapore	4,500
Sweden	3,160,000[a]
Switzerland	1,703,333
Thailand	2,500
Trinidad and Tobago	2,400
Turkey	1,839,253
United Kingdom	30,125,481[ab]
United Republic of Tanzania	7,000
United States	59,300,000[c]

Government	**Total pledges** *(in U.S. dollar equivalents)*
Venezuela	3,000
Zaire	30,000
Zambia	38,000
Total	132,780,581

a Payment was to be made by means of an offset against Government's claims for reimbursement of its costs.

b Maximum amount pledged.

cMaximum amount pledged. The ultimate contribution of the United States was to be dependent upon the contributions which might be made by other Governments.

DOCUMENTARY REFERENCES

Communications for period 1 January to 26 May 1971

S/10082. Letter of 18 January 1971 from Secretary-General to Governments containing further appeal for voluntary contributions for financing of United Nations Peace-keeping Force in Cyprus (UNFICYP).

S/10174, S/10179. Letters of 10 and 19 April 1971 from Turkey.

S/10185 and Corr.1, S/10187. Letters of 3 and 6 May 1971 from Cyprus.

S/10194, S/10200. Letters of 12 and 18 May 1971 from Turkey.

Consideration by Security Council (May 1971)

Security Council, meetings 1567, 1568.

S/10199 and Corr.1. Report of 20 May 1971 by Secretary-General on UNFICYP (for period 2 December 1970–19 May 1971).

S/10204, S/10207, S/10208. Letters of 24 and 25 May 1971 from Greece, Turkey and Cyprus (requests to participate in Council's discussion).

S/10209. Draft resolution.

RESOLUTION 293(1971), as prepared following consultations among Council members, S/10209, adopted unanimously by Council on 26 May 1971, meeting 1567.

The Security Council,

Noting from the report of the Secretary-General of 20 May 1971 that in the present circumstances the United Nations Peace-keeping Force in Cyprus is still needed if peace is to be maintained in the island,

Noting that the Government of Cyprus has agreed that in view of the prevailing conditions in the island it is necessary to continue the Force beyond 15 June 1971,

Noting also from the report the conditions prevailing in the island,

1. *Reaffirms* its resolutions 186(1964) of 4 March, 187(1964) of 13 March, 192(1964) of 20 June, 193(1964) of 9 August, 194(1964) of 25 September and 198(1964) of 18 December 1964, 201(1965) of 19 March, 206(1965) of 15 June, 207(1965) of 10 August and 219(1965) of 17 December 1965, 220(1966) of 16 March, 222(1966) of 16 June and 231(1966) of 15 December 1966, 238(1967) of 19 June and 244(1967) of 22 December 1967, 247(1968) of 18 March, 254(1968) of 18 June and 261(1968) of 10 December 1968, 266(1969) of 10 June and 274(1969) of 11 December 1969, and 281(1970) of 9 June and 291(1970) of 10 December 1970, and the consensus expressed by the President at the 1143rd meeting on 11 August 1964 and at the 1383rd meeting on 25 November 1967;

2. *Urges* the parties concerned to act with the utmost restraint and to continue determined co-operative efforts to achieve the objectives of the Security Council, by availing themselves in a constructive manner of the present auspicious climate and opportunities;

3. *Extends* once more the stationing in Cyprus of the United Nations Peace-keeping Force, established under Security Council resolution 186(1964), for a further period ending 15 December 1971, in the expectation that by then sufficient progress towards a final solution will make possible a withdrawal or substantial reduction of the Force.

Communications for period 26 May to 13 December 1971

S/10217. Letter of 26 May 1971 from Turkey.

S/10230. Letter of 21 June 1971 from Cyprus.

S/10239. Letter of 24 June 1971 from Turkey.

S/10268/Rev.1. Letter of 14 July 1971 from Secretary-General to Governments containing further appeal for voluntary contributions for financing of UNFICYP.

Security Council consideration (December 1971)

Security Council, meetings 1612, 1613.

S/10401. Report of 30 November 1971 by Secretary-General on UNFICYP (for period 20 May–30 November 1971).

S/10441. Draft resolution.

S/10447-S/10449. Letters of 10 and 13 December 1971 from Turkey, Cyprus and Greece (requests to participate in Council's discussion).

RESOLUTION 305(1971), as prepared following consultations among Council members, S/10441, adopted by Council on 13 December 1971, meeting 1612, by 14 votes to 0 (China did not participate in voting).

The Security Council,

Noting from the report of the Secretary-General of 30 November 1971 that in the present circumstances the United Nations Peace-keeping Force in Cyprus is still needed if peace is to be maintained in the island,

Noting that the Government of Cyprus has agreed that in view of the prevailing conditions in the island it is necessary to continue the Force beyond 15 December 1971,

Noting also from the report the conditions prevailing in the island,

1. *Reaffirms* its resolutions 186(1964) of 4 March, 187(1964) of 13 March, 192(1964) of 20 June, 193(1964) of 9 August, 194(1964) of 25 September and 198(1964) of 18 December 1964, 201(1965) of 19 March, 206(1965) of 15 June, 207(1965) of 10 August and 219(1965) of 17 December 1965, 220(1966) of 16 March, 222(1966) of 16 June and 231(1966) of 15 December 1966, 238(1967) of 19 June and 244(1967) of 22 December 1967, 247(1968) of 18 March, 254(1968) of 18 June and 261(1968) of 10 December 1968, 266(1969) of 10 June and 274(1969) of 11 December 1969, 281(1970) of 9 June and 291(1970) of 10 December 1970, and 293(1971) of 26 May 1971, and the consensus expressed by the President at the 1143rd meeting on 11 August 1964 and at the 1383rd meeting on 25 November 1967;

2. *Urges* the parties concerned to act with the utmost restraint and to continue and accelerate determined co-operative efforts to achieve the objectives of the Security Council, by availing themselves in a constructive manner of the present auspicious climate and opportunities;

3. *Extends* once more the stationing in Cyprus of the United Nations Peace-keeping Force, established under Security Council resolution 186(1964), for a further period ending 15 June 1972, in the expectation that by then sufficient progress towards a final solution will make possible a withdrawal or substantial reduction of the Force.

Other documents

A/8401 and Corr.1. Report of Secretary-General on work of the Organization, 16 June 1970–15 June 1971, Part One, Chapter II.

A/8401/Add.1. Introduction to report of Secretary-General, September 1971, Part Two, Chapter IV, paras. 230-235.

A/8402. Report of Security Council, 16 June 1970–15 June 1971, Chapter 6.

Chapter XIII

Questions relating to the organs of the United Nations and the membership of the United Nations

Appointment of the Secretary-General

After three closed meetings—held on 17, 20 and 21 December 1971—on the question of its recommendation for the appointment of a Secretary-General of the United Nations to replace Secretary-General U Thant, whose term of office expired 31 December 1971, the Security Council unanimously adopted a resolution recommending to the General Assembly that Kurt Waldheim be appointed Secretary-General.

On 22 December, the General Assembly adopted by acclamation a resolution (2903(XXVI)) appointing Mr. Waldheim for a five-year term of office as Secretary-General, from 1 January 1972 to 31 December 1976.

(For text of resolution, see DOCUMENTARY REFERENCES below.)

Salary and retirement allowance of the Secretary-General

On 29 November 1971, the General Assembly made certain changes in the salary and the retirement allowance of the Secretary-General of the United Nations.

Noting that the base salary of the Secretary-General had remained unchanged since 1 January 1968 at $31,600 net ($50,000 gross) per annum, while other United Nations salaries had been rising, the Assembly decided to increase, as from 1 December 1971, the Secretary-General's annual salary to $37,850 net ($62,500 gross) per annum. It also set his annual retirement allowance as one half of his gross salary after completion of a full term of office, with a schedule of smaller allowances for lesser periods.

At the same time, the Assembly established certain benefits for the widow and minor children of a Secretary-General who died in office or while receiving a retirement allowance. The widow's benefit was set at one half the retirement allowance of the Secretary-General. In addition, provision was made for benefits to the Secretary-General or his survivors, as the case might be, to be paid in the event of death, injury or illness of the Secretary-General attributable to the performance of official duties on behalf of the United Nations.

The Assembly took these decisions in adopting resolution 2772(XXVI) by 95 votes to 0, with 8 abstentions, on the recommendation of its Fifth (Administrative and Budgetary) Committee, which approved the text on 23 November by 68 votes to 0, with 7 abstentions.

(For text of resolution, see pp. 633-34.)

(See also p. 632.)

DOCUMENTARY REFERENCES

Appointment of Secretary-General

Security Council, meetings 1618–1620.

S/PV.1618–1620. Official communiqués of Security Council meetings 1618–1620 (held in private).

RESOLUTION 306(1971), adopted unanimously by Council by secret ballot on 21 December 1971, meeting 1620.

The Security Council,
Having considered the question of the recommendation for the appointment of the Secretary-General of the United Nations,
Recommends to the General Assembly that Mr. Kurt Waldheim be appointed Secretary-General of the United Nations.

General Assembly—26th session
Plenary meeting 2031.

A/8496. Letter of 21 December 1971 from President of Security Council to President of General Assembly (transmitting Council resolution 306(1971)).

A/L.671 and Rev.1. Argentina, Belgium, Burundi, China, France, Italy, Japan, Nicaragua, Poland, Sierra Leone, Somalia, Syrian Arab Republic, USSR, United Kingdom, United States: draft resolution and revision.

RESOLUTION 2903(XXVI), as proposed by 15 Security Council members, A/L.671/Rev.1, adopted by acclamation by Assembly on 22 December 1971, meeting 2031.

The General Assembly,
Acting in accordance with the recommendation contained in Security Council resolution 306(1971) of 21 December 1971,
Appoints Mr. Kurt Waldheim Secretary-General of the United Nations for a term of office beginning on 1 January 1972 and ending on 31 December 1976.

Salary and retirement allowance of the Secretary-General

General Assembly—26th session
Fifth Committee, meetings 1440, 1446, 1460.
Plenary meeting 1997.

A/8408/Add.9. Tenth report of Advisory Committee on Administrative and Budgetary Questions (ACABQ) on budget estimates for 1972. (Annex: Financial implications of 29-power draft resolution, A/C.5/L.1062/Rev.1. Report of Controller.)

A/C.5/L.1062. Afghanistan, Chile, Colombia, Costa Rica, India, Italy, Ivory Coast, Kuwait, Libyan Arab Republic, Mexico, Nicaragua, Niger, Pakistan, Peru, Poland, Somalia, Sudan: draft resolution.

A/C.5/L.1062/Rev.1. Afghanistan, Algeria, Barbados, Chile, Colombia, Costa Rica, Cyprus, Denmark, Ecuador, India, Indonesia, Iran, Ireland, Italy, Ivory Coast, Kuwait, Lebanon, Libyan Arab Republic, Mexico, Nicaragua, Niger, Nigeria, Pakistan, Peru, Poland, Somalia, Sudan, Tunisia, Yugoslavia: revised draft resolution, as amended by ACABQ (A/8408/Add.9, para. 12), approved by Fifth Committee on 23 November 1971, meeting 1460, by 68 votes to 0, with 7 abstentions.

A/8531. Report of Fifth Committee (part I).

RESOLUTION 2772(XXVI), as recommended by Fifth Committee, A/8531, adopted by Assembly on 29 November 1971, meeting 1997, by 95 votes to 0, with 8 abstentions.

[For text of resolution, see pp. 633-34.]

Admission of new Members

In 1971, Bahrain, Bhutan, Oman, Qatar and the United Arab Emirates were admitted to United Nations membership. Their admission increased the number of United Nations Member States to 132.

The admission of all five Members was unanimously recommended by the Security Council. At plenary meetings of the General Assembly, the resolution of admission of Bhutan was adopted without a vote, of Bahrain by a vote of 119 to 0, of Qatar by 126 to 1, of Oman by 117 votes in favour to 1 against, with 2 abstentions, and of the United Arab Emirates by 93 in favour to 1 against.

The following table indicates the dates of United Nations action:

Applicant	Date of Recommendation of Council	Date of Admission by Assembly
Bhutan	10 February 1971	21 September 1971
Bahrain	18 August 1971	21 September 1971
Qatar	15 September 1971	21 September 1971
Oman	30 September 1971	7 October 1971
United Arab Emirates	8 December 1971	9 December 1971

(For texts of resolutions, see DOCUMENTARY REFERENCES below.)

DOCUMENTARY REFERENCES

Admission of Bhutan

Security Council, meetings 1565, 1566.

S/10050. Letter of 10 December 1970 from Bhutan.
S/10109. Report of Security Council Committee on Admission of New Members concerning application of Bhutan for membership in United Nations.
S/10110, S/10112. Letters of 9 and 10 February 1971 from India and Pakistan (request to participate in Council's discussion).

RESOLUTION 292(1971), as proposed by Council Committee on Admission of New Members, S/10109, recommending to General Assembly that Bhutan be admitted to membership in United Nations, adopted unanimously by Council on 10 February 1971, meeting 1566.

General Assembly—26th session
Plenary meeting 1934.

A/8275. Note by Secretary-General (transmitting letter of 10 December from Bhutan (S/10050)).
A/8278. Letter of 10 February 1971 from President of Security Council.
A/8401. Report of Secretary-General on work of the Organization, 16 June 1970–15 June 1971, Part One, Chapter IV O.
A/8402. Report of Security Council, 16 June 1970–15 June 1971, Chapter 8 B.
A/L.627 and Add.1. Afghanistan, Argentina, Australia, Austria, Belgium, Burundi, Canada, Ceylon, Cyprus, Czechoslovakia, Egypt, Ethiopia, Fiji, Ghana, Guyana, India, Indonesia, Iran, Jamaica, Japan, Kenya, Malaysia, Malta, Mauritius, Mexico, Mongolia, Nepal, Netherlands, New Zealand, Nicaragua, Nigeria, Pakistan, Peru, Philippines, Poland, Sierra Leone, Singapore, Somalia, Spain, Syrian Arab Republic, Thailand, Trinidad and Tobago, Turkey, United Kingdom, Yugoslavia: draft resolution.

RESOLUTION 2751(XXVI), as proposed by 45 powers, A/L.627, adopted without vote by Assembly on 21 September 1971, meeting 1934.

The General Assembly,
Having received the recommendation of the Security Council of 10 February 1971 that Bhutan should be admitted to membership in the United Nations,
Having considered the application for membership of Bhutan,
Decides to admit Bhutan to membership in the United Nations.

Admission of Bahrain

Security Council, meetings 1574, 1575.

S/10291. Letter of 15 August 1971 from Bahrain.
S/10294. Report of Security Council Committee on Admission of New Members concerning applications of Oman and Bahrain for membership in United Nations.

RESOLUTION 296(1971), as recommended by Council Committee on Admission of New Members, S/10294, as orally amended by Syrian Arab Republic, adopted unanimously by Council on 18 August 1971, meeting 1575.

The Security Council,
Having examined the application of Bahrain for admission to the United Nations,
Welcomes the application of Bahrain and recommends to the General Assembly that Bahrain be admitted to membership in the United Nations.

General Assembly—26th session
Plenary meeting 1934.

A/8358. Note by Secretary-General (transmitting letter of 15 August 1971 from Bahrain (S/10291)).
A/8359. Letter of 18 August 1971 from President of Security Council.
A/L.628. Afghanistan, Algeria, Burundi, Ceylon, Cyprus, Egypt, India, Indonesia, Iran, Iraq, Jordan, Kuwait, Lebanon, Libyan Arab Republic, Malaysia, Mali, Mauritania, Mauritius, Mongolia, Morocco, Pakistan, Saudi Arabia, Somalia, Sudan, Syrian Arab Republic, Thailand, Tunisia, Turkey, Yemen: draft resolution.

RESOLUTION 2752(XXVI), as proposed by 29 powers, A/L.628, adopted by Assembly on 21 September 1971, meeting 1934, by recorded vote of 119 to 0, as follows:

In favour: Afghanistan, Albania, Algeria, Argentina, Australia, Austria, Barbados, Belgium, Bhutan, Bolivia, Botswana, Brazil, Bulgaria, Burma, Burundi, Byelorussian SSR, Cameroon, Canada, Central African Republic, Ceylon, Chad, Chile, China, Colombia, Congo, Costa Rica, Cuba, Cyprus, Czechoslovakia, Dahomey, Denmark, Dominican Republic, Ecuador, Egypt, El Salvador, Equatorial Guinea, Ethiopia, Fiji, Finland, France, Gabon, Gambia, Ghana, Greece, Guatemala, Guinea, Guyana, Haiti, Honduras, Hungary, Iceland, India, Indonesia, Iran, Iraq, Ireland, Italy, Ivory Coast, Jamaica, Japan, Jordan, Kenya, Khmer Republic, Kuwait, Laos, Lebanon, Lesotho, Liberia, Libyan Arab Republic, Luxembourg, Madagascar, Malawi, Malaysia, Mali, Malta, Mauritania, Mauritius, Mongolia, Morocco, Nepal, Netherlands, New Zealand, Nicaragua, Niger, Nigeria, Norway, Panama, Paraguay, Philippines, Poland, Portugal, Romania, Rwanda, Saudi Arabia, Senegal, Sierra Leone, Somalia, South Africa, Spain, Sudan, Sweden, Syrian Arab Republic, Togo, Trinidad and Tobago, Tunisia, Turkey, Uganda, Ukrainian SSR, USSR, United Kingdom, United Republic of Tanzania, United States, Upper Volta, Uruguay, Venezuela, Yemen, Yugoslavia, Zaire, Zambia.
Against:* None.

*Subsequently, Pakistan stated that, due to apparent mechanical error, its vote in favour was not recorded.

The General Assembly,
Having received the recommendation of the Security Council of 18 August 1971 that Bahrain should be admitted to membership in the United Nations,
Having considered the application for membership of Bahrain,
Decides to admit Bahrain to membership in the United Nations.

Admission of Qatar

Security Council, meetings 1577, 1578.

S/10306. Letter of 4 September 1971 from Qatar.
S/10316. Letter of 13 September from People's Democratic Republic of Yemen (request to participate in Council's discussion).
S/10318. Report of Security Council Committee on Admission of New Members concerning application of Qatar for membership in United Nations.

RESOLUTION 297(1971), as proposed by Council Committee on Admission of New Members, S/10318, recommending to General Assembly that Qatar be admitted to membership in United Nations, adopted unanimously by Council on 15 September 1971, meeting 1578.

General Assembly—26th session
Plenary meeting 1934.

A/8373. Note by Secretary-General (transmitting letter of 4 September 1971 from Qatar (S/10306)).

A/8381. Letter of 15 September 1971 from President of Security Council.
A/L.629. Afghanistan, Algeria, Burundi, Ceylon, Cyprus, Egypt, India, Indonesia, Iran, Iraq, Jordan, Kuwait, Lebanon, Libyan Arab Republic, Malaysia, Mali, Mauritania, Mauritius, Mongolia, Morocco, Pakistan, Saudi Arabia, Somalia, Sudan, Syrian Arab Republic, Thailand, Tunisia, Turkey, Yemen: draft resolution.

RESOLUTION 2753(XXVI), as proposed by 29 powers, A/L.629, adopted by Assembly on 21 September 1971, meeting 1934, by recorded vote of 126 to 1, as follows:

In favour: Afghanistan, Albania, Algeria, Argentina, Australia, Austria, Bahrain, Barbados, Belgium, Bhutan, Bolivia, Botswana, Brazil, Bulgaria, Burma, Burundi, Byelorussian SSR, Cameroon, Canada, Central African Republic, Ceylon, Chad, Chile, China, Colombia, Congo, Costa Rica, Cuba, Cyprus, Czechoslovakia, Dahomey, Denmark, Dominican Republic, Ecuador, Egypt, El Salvador, Equatorial Guinea, Ethiopia, Fiji, Finland, France, Gabon, Gambia, Ghana, Greece, Guatemala, Guinea, Guyana, Haiti, Honduras, Hungary, Iceland, India, Indonesia, Iran, Iraq, Ireland, Italy, Ivory Coast, Jamaica, Japan, Jordan, Kenya, Khmer Republic, Kuwait, Laos, Lebanon, Lesotho, Liberia, Libyan Arab Republic, Luxembourg, Madagascar, Malawi, Malaysia, Mali, Malta, Mauritania, Mauritius, Mexico, Mongolia, Morocco, Nepal, Netherlands, New Zealand, Nicaragua, Niger, Nigeria, Norway, Pakistan, Panama, Paraguay, Peru, Philippines, Poland, Portugal, Romania, Rwanda, Saudi Arabia, Senegal, Sierra Leone, Singapore, Somalia, South Africa, Spain, Sudan, Swaziland, Sweden, Syrian Arab Republic, Thailand, Togo, Trinidad and Tobago, Tunisia, Turkey, Uganda, Ukrainian SSR, USSR, United Kingdom, United Republic of Tanzania, United States, Upper Volta, Uruguay, Venezuela, Yemen, Yugoslavia, Zaire, Zambia.
Against: People's Democratic Republic of Yemen.

The General Assembly,
Having received the recommendation of the Security Council of 15 September 1971 that Qatar should be admitted to membership in the United Nations,
Having considered the application for membership of Qatar,
Decides to admit Qatar to membership in the United Nations.

Admission of Oman

Security Council, meetings 1574, 1575, 1587.

S/10216. Letter of 24 May 1971 from Oman.
S/10294. Report of Security Council Committee on Admission of New Members concerning applications of Oman and Bahrain for membership in United Nations.
S/10345. Report of Security Council Committee on Admission of New Members concerning application of Oman for membership in United Nations.
S/10348. Letter of 30 September 1971 from People's Democratic Republic of Yemen (request to participate in Council's discussion).

RESOLUTION 299(1971), as proposed by Council Committee on Admission of New Members, S/10345, recommending to General Assembly that Oman be admitted to membership in United Nations, adopted unanimously by Council on 30 September 1971, meeting 1587.

General Assembly—26th session
Plenary meeting 1957.

A/8320. Note by Secretary-General (transmitting letter of 24 May 1971 from Oman (S/10216)).
A/8402. Report of Security Council, 16 June 1970–15 June 1971, Chapter 8 C.
A/8449. Letter of 30 September 1971 from President of Security Council.

A/L.636 and Add.1. Afghanistan, Algeria, Bahrain, Burundi, Ceylon, Cyprus, Egypt, Guinea, India, Indonesia, Iran, Iraq, Japan, Jordan, Kuwait, Lebanon, Libyan Arab Republic, Madagascar, Malaysia, Mali, Mauritania, Mauritius, Morocco, Nepal, Pakistan, Philippines, Qatar, Sierra Leone, Somalia, Sudan, Syrian Arab Republic, Thailand, Tunisia, Turkey, Yemen, Zambia: draft resolution.

RESOLUTION 2754(XXVI), as proposed by 36 powers, A/L.636, adopted by Assembly on 7 October 1971, meeting 1957, by recorded vote of 117 to 1, with 2 abstentions, as follows:

In favour: Afghanistan, Albania, Algeria, Argentina, Australia, Austria, Bahrain, Barbados, Belgium, Bhutan, Brazil, Bulgaria, Burma, Burundi, Byelorussian SSR, Cameroon, Canada, Central African Republic, Ceylon, Chad, Chile, Congo, Costa Rica, Cyprus, Czechoslovakia, Dahomey, Denmark, Dominican Republic, Ecuador, Egypt, El Salvador, Equatorial Guinea, Ethiopia, Fiji, Finland, France, Gabon, Gambia, Ghana, Greece, Guatemala, Guinea, Guyana, Haiti, Honduras, Hungary, Iceland, India, Indonesia, Iran, Iraq, Ireland, Italy, Ivory Coast, Jamaica, Japan, Jordan, Kenya, Khmer Republic, Kuwait, Lebanon, Lesotho, Liberia, Libyan Arab Republic, Luxembourg, Madagascar, Malawi, Malaysia, Mali, Malta, Mauritania, Mauritius, Mexico, Mongolia, Morocco, Nepal, Netherlands, New Zealand, Nicaragua, Niger, Nigeria, Norway, Pakistan, Paraguay, Peru, Philippines, Poland, Portugal, Qatar, Romania, Senegal, Sierra Leone, Singapore, Somalia, South Africa, Spain, Sudan, Swaziland, Sweden, Syrian Arab Republic, Thailand, Togo, Trinidad and Tobago, Tunisia, Turkey, Uganda, Ukrainian SSR, USSR, United Kingdom, United Republic of Tanzania, United States, Upper Volta, Uruguay, Venezuela, Yemen, Yugoslavia, Zambia.
Against: People's Democratic Republic of Yemen.
Abstaining: Cuba, Saudi Arabia.

The General Assembly,
Having received the recommendation of the Security Council of 30 September 1971 that Oman should be admitted to membership in the United Nations,
Having considered the application for membership of Oman,
Decides to admit Oman to membership in the United Nations.

Admission of United Arab Emirates

Security Council, meetings 1608, 1609.

S/10420. Letter of 2 December 1971 from United Arab Emirates.
S/10430. Report of Security Council Committee on Admission of New Members concerning application of United Arab Emirates for membership in United Nations.

RESOLUTION 304(1971), as proposed by Council Committee on Admission of New Members, S/10430, recommending to General Assembly that United Arab Emirates be admitted to membership in United Nations, adopted unanimously by Council on 8 December 1971, meeting 1609.

General Assembly—26th session
Plenary meeting 2007.

A/8553. Note by Secretary-General (transmitting letter of 2 December 1971 from United Arab Emirates (S/10420)).
A/8561. Letter of 8 December 1971 from President of Security Council.
A/L.649. Afghanistan, Algeria, Bahrain, Burundi, Ceylon, Cyprus, Egypt, India, Indonesia, Japan, Jordan, Kuwait, Lebanon, Lesotho, Libyan Arab Republic, Madagascar, Malaysia, Mali, Mauritania, Morocco, Nepal, Niger, Nigeria, Oman, Pakistan, Philippines, Qatar, Rwanda, Senegal, Sierra Leone, Somalia, Sudan, Syrian Arab Republic, Thailand, Tunisia, Turkey, Yemen, Zambia: draft resolution.

RESOLUTION 2794(XXVI), as proposed by 38 powers, A/L.649, adopted by Assembly on 9 December 1971, meeting 2007, by recorded vote of 93 to 1, as follows:

In favour: Afghanistan, Albania, Algeria, Argentina, Australia, Austria, Bahrain, Barbados, Belgium, Brazil, Bulgaria, Burma, Burundi, Byelorussian SSR, Cameroon, Canada, Chad, Chile, China, Costa Rica, Denmark, Ecuador, El Salvador, Equatorial Guinea, Ethiopia, Fiji, Finland, France, Gabon, Ghana, Greece, Guatemala, Guyana, Honduras, Hungary, India, Indonesia, Iran, Ireland, Italy, Ivory Coast, Jamaica, Japan, Jordan, Kenya, Khmer Republic, Kuwait, Laos, Lebanon, Lesotho, Liberia, Libyan Arab Republic, Luxembourg, Madagascar, Malawi, Malaysia, Mauritania, Mexico, Mongolia, Nepal, Netherlands, Norway, Oman, Pakistan, Paraguay, Philippines, Poland, Portugal, Qatar, Romania, Singapore, Somalia, South Africa, Spain, Sudan, Sweden, Syrian Arab Republic, Thailand, Togo, Trinidad and Tobago, Tunisia, Turkey, Ukrainian SSR, USSR, United Kingdom, United States, Upper Volta, Uruguay, Venezuela, Yemen, Yugoslavia, Zaire, Zambia.
Against: People's Democratic Republic of Yemen.

The General Assembly,
Having received the recommendation of the Security Council of 8 December 1971 that the United Arab Emirates should be admitted to membership in the United Nations,
Having considered the application for membership of the United Arab Emirates,
Decides to admit the United Arab Emirates to membership in the United Nations.

Chapter XIV

Other political and security questions

Twenty-fifth anniversary of the United Nations

At its twenty-sixth session, which opened on 21 September 1971, the General Assembly had before it the final report of its Committee for the Twenty-fifth Anniversary of the United Nations, which had been established on 31 October 1969.[1]

On 26 November 1971, without adopting a resolution, the Assembly took note of the final report of the Committee.

[1]See Y.U.N., 1969, pp. 258-59, text of resolution 2499 A (XXIV).

Among the highlights of the twenty-fifth anniversary celebrations to which the report referred were the commemorative session of the General Assembly held at United Nations Headquarters from 14 to 24 October 1970, the meeting commemorating the signing of the United Nations Charter, held in San Francisco (United States) on 26 June 1970, and the World Youth Assembly, which met at United Nations Headquarters in July 1970.[2]

The report also referred to commemorative stamps and medals issued to mark the anniversary, awards for long service presented to staff members, and commemorative ceremonies held at various United Nations offices, by the specialized

agencies and at national levels by many countries.

At its commemorative session, the report noted, the General Assembly adopted several major declarations, including the Declaration on the Occasion of the Twenty-fifth Anniversary of the United Nations.[3]

The Committee's report also noted that public information activities connected with the anniversary were varied and were devised in such a way as to involve all media, as well as non-governmental organizations and other groups interested in the work of the United Nations.

[2]See Y.U.N., 1970, pp. 107-18, for details of the anniversary celebrations.
[3]See Y.U.N., 1970, pp. 116-17, text of resolution 2627(XXV).

DOCUMENTARY REFERENCES

General Assembly—26th session
Committee for Twenty-fifth Anniversary of United Nations, meetings 46-52.
Plenary meeting 1996.

A/8401/Add.1. Introduction to report of Secretary-General on work

of the Organization, September 1971, Part Two, Chapter I, paras. 154-161.
A/8425. Report of Committee for Twenty-fifth Anniversary of United Nations.
A/8429. Resolutions adopted by General Assembly during its 26th session, 21 September–22 December 1971. Decisions, p. 20.

Peace research

At its 1971 session, the General Assembly, at the suggestion of Belgium, discussed the question of scientific work on peace research.

At a plenary meeting on 14 December 1971, the Assembly asked the Secretary-General to prepare every other year an informative report on scientific works produced by national and international, governmental and non-governmental, public and private institutions working in the field of peace research. The Assembly invited Governments and institutions to provide information in this connexion, and it asked the United Nations Institute for Training and Research and specialized agencies active in the field of peace research to assist in the

drafting of the report to the General Assembly.

In taking this decision, the Assembly observed that scientific research on the problems of war and peace had expanded, and considered it desirable to bring this work to the notice of the international community.

These Assembly decisions were set forth in resolution 2817(XXVI), adopted by 59 votes to 7, with 3 abstentions, on the basis of a proposal by Belgium, Burundi, Canada, Denmark, Finland, Ghana, Indonesia, Iran, Ireland, Lebanon, Mexico, the Netherlands, Norway, Romania and Yugoslavia. (For text of resolution, see DOCUMENTARY REFERENCES below.)

DOCUMENTARY REFERENCES

General Assembly—26th session
Fifth Committee, meeting 1474.
Plenary meeting 2018.

A/8394. Letter of 21 July 1971 from Belgium (request for inclusion in Assembly's agenda of item entitled: "Scientific work on peace research").
A/L.645 and Add.1,2. Belgium, Burundi, Canada, Denmark, Finland, Ghana, Indonesia, Iran, Ireland, Lebanon, Mexico, Netherlands, Norway, Romania, Yugoslavia: draft resolution.
A/C.5/1412, A/8408/Add.17, A/8554. Administrative and financial implications of 15-power draft resolution, A/L.645. Statement by Secretary-General and reports of Advisory Committee on Administrative and Budgetary Questions and Fifth Committee.

RESOLUTION 2817(XXVI), as proposed by 15 powers, A/L.645,

adopted by Assembly on 14 December 1971, meeting 2018, by 59 votes to 7, with 3 abstentions.

The General Assembly,
Considering that the fundamental purpose of the United Nations is to save mankind from the scourge of war and to maintain international peace and security,
Considering that scientific research on the problems of war and peace has expanded and that many national and international institutions have made them the subject of their studies,
Noting with interest the work undertaken in this field by the United Nations Educational, Scientific and Cultural Organization and the United Nations Institute for Training and Research,
Conscious of the importance that States attach to the study of the means and recourses to implement the relevant provisions of the Charter of the United Nations in order to build peace, security and co-operation in the world,

Considering it desirable to bring to the notice of the international community the work done in the field of peace research by national and international institutions and to promote on a permanent basis, in the light of the purposes and principles of the Charter, a recording of the studies devoted to this subject,

1. *Requests* the Secretary-General to prepare every other year an informative report on scientific works produced by national and international, governmental and non-governmental, public and private institutions in the field of peace research;

2. *Invites* the Governments of Member States and the institutions referred to in paragraph 1 above to provide the Secretary-General, to the best of their ability and competence, with all the information he may require;

3. *Requests* the United Nations Institute for Training and Research and those specialized agencies which are active in the field of peace research to lend their assistance in the drafting of the report referred to above;

4. *Requests* the Secretary-General to submit to the General Assembly, at the beginning of its twenty-eighth session, the first report prepared under paragraph 1 above.

Proposal by Cuba concerning Puerto Rico

In a letter dated 17 August 1971 to the Secretary-General, Cuba requested the inclusion of an item entitled "The colonial case of Puerto Rico" in the provisional agenda of the 1971 session of the General Assembly. Attached to the letter was an explanatory memorandum stating that the people of Puerto Rico had an inalienable right to independence and that the United Nations had the unavoidable duty to take all necessary steps to ensure that those people achieved the full exercise of their national rights.

On 24 September 1971, the General Assembly decided, by a roll-call vote of 57 to 26, with 38 abstentions, not to include the item on its agenda. It did so on the recommendation of its General Committee, which had taken its decision on the matter on 23 September by 10 votes to 5, with 8 abstentions.

DOCUMENTARY REFERENCES

General Assembly—26th session
General Committee, meeting 192.
Plenary meetings 1937, 1938.

A/8441. Letter of 17 August 1971 from Cuba (request for inclusion in agenda of item entitled: "The colonial case of Puerto Rico").
A/8441/Add.1. Letter of 20 August 1971 from Cuba.
A/8500. First report of General Committee, para. 17, recommendation, adopted by Assembly on 24 September 1971, meeting 1938, by roll-call vote of 57 to 26, with 38 abstentions, as follows:

In favour: Afghanistan, Australia, Austria, Belgium, Botswana, Brazil, Canada, Ceylon, China, Colombia, Costa Rica, Denmark, Ethiopia, Fiji, Finland, France, Ghana, Greece, Guatemala, Haiti, Honduras, Iceland, Iran, Israel, Italy, Ivory Coast, Japan, Jordan, Kenya, Khmer Republic, Lebanon, Lesotho, Liberia, Luxembourg, Madagascar, Malawi, Malaysia, Malta, Morocco, Netherlands, New Zealand, Nicaragua, Niger, Nigeria, Norway, Paraguay, Philippines, Portugal, Qatar,* South Africa, Sweden, Thailand, Turkey, United Kingdom, United States, Uruguay, Zaire.

Against: Albania, Algeria, Bulgaria, Byelorussian SSR, Chile, Congo, Cuba, Czechoslovakia, Ecuador, Equatorial Guinea, Guinea, Hungary, Iraq, Libyan Arab Republic, Mali, Mongolia, People's Democratic Republic of Yemen, Poland, Romania, Sierra Leone, Somalia, Syrian Arab Republic, Ukrainian SSR, USSR, United Republic of Tanzania, Zambia.

Abstaining: Argentina, Bahrain, Barbados, Bolivia, Burma, Burundi, Cameroon, Central African Republic, Chad, Cyprus, Dahomey, Egypt, El Salvador, Gabon, Gambia, Guyana, India, Indonesia, Ireland, Jamaica, Kuwait, Laos, Mauritius, Mexico, Nepal, Panama, Peru, Rwanda, Saudi Arabia, Senegal, Singapore, Togo, Trinidad and Tobago, Tunisia, Uganda, Upper Volta, Venezuela, Yugoslavia.

*Subsequently, Qatar advised the Secretariat that it had intended to vote against.

Proclamation of United Nations Day as an international holiday

Believing that the anniversary of the United Nations should be an occasion for Governments and peoples to reaffirm their faith in the purposes and principles of the Charter of the United Nations, the General Assembly, on 6 December 1971, declared that 24 October—United Nations Day—should be an international holiday. It recommended that the day should be observed as a public holiday by all States Members of the United Nations.

The Assembly took this action with the adoption of resolution 2782(XXVI), by 63 votes to 6, with 32 abstentions, on the basis of a text sponsored by Barbados, Burundi, Cyprus, Greece, Guyana, the Khmer Republic, Liberia, Mauritius, the Philippines, Swaziland, Yugoslavia and Zambia. (For text of resolution, see DOCUMENTARY REFERENCES below.)

The question was discussed at a plenary meeting at the suggestion of Zambia.

DOCUMENTARY REFERENCES

General Assembly—26th session
Plenary meeting 2000.

A/8393. Letter of 20 July 1971 from Zambia (request for inclusion in agenda of item entitled: "Proclamation of United Nations Day as an international holiday").
A/L.646 and Add.1,2. Barbados, Burundi, Cyprus, Greece, Guyana, Khmer Republic, Liberia, Mauritius, Philippines, Swazi-

land, Yugoslavia and Zambia: twelve-power draft resolution.

RESOLUTION 2782 (XXVI), as proposed by 12 powers, A/L.646, adopted by Assembly on 6 December 1971, meeting 2000, by 63 votes to 6, with 32 abstentions.

The General Assembly,
Conscious of the need to enhance the purposes and principles of the Charter of the United Nations,

Mindful that in its resolution 168(II) of 31 October 1947 the General Assembly declared 24 October, the anniversary of the coming into force of the Charter, as "United Nations Day,"
Believing that the anniversary of the United Nations should be an occasion for Governments and peoples to reaffirm their faith in the purposes and principles of the Charter,
Declares that 24 October, United Nations Day, shall be an international holiday and recommends that it should be observed as a public holiday by all States Members of the United Nations.

Communication concerning the foreign relations of Malta

By a letter dated 30 June 1971 to the President of the Security Council, the Acting Permanent Representative of Malta transmitted the text of a statement by his Government concerning its relations with the British Government, the United States and the North Atlantic Treaty Organization (NATO).

The statement denied accusations appearing in the foreign press of the unilateral abrogation of the 1964 Defense Agreement. According to the statement, that Agreement was no longer in being.

Although the Maltese Government could have ordered the withdrawal of all British forces from

Malta, the statement went on, it had preferred not to do so, in order for Britain to be given an opportunity for new arrangements to be properly discussed.

The statement declared that the position of NATO was that it had "provisional and limited permission, which should have led to some form of arrangements that were never concluded."

It was also noted in the statement that there was no treaty or agreement between Malta and the United States giving the American Sixth Fleet the right to take shelter in Maltese harbours and that visits by it were not in the interests of Malta.

DOCUMENTARY REFERENCES

S/10246. Letter of 30 June 1971 from Malta.

Report of Security Council

On 20 December 1971, when it took note of the report of the Security Council to the General Assembly for the period from 16 June 1970 to 15 June 1971, the General Assembly asked the Secretary-General to suggest ways and means of enhancing the effectiveness of the Security Council in accordance with the principles and provisions of the Charter of the United Nations. In doing so, he was asked by the Assembly to give due consid-

eration to the views of interested Governments.

The Assembly took this decision in adopting resolution 2864(XXVI), by 76 votes to 10, with 24 abstentions, on a proposal of Belgium, Burundi and Tunisia. Tunisia suggested the addition of the request to the Secretary-General.

(For text of resolution, see DOCUMENTARY REFERENCES below.)

DOCUMENTARY REFERENCES

General Assembly—26th session
Plenary meetings 2024, 2027.

A/8402. Report of Security Council, 16 June 1970–15 June 1971.
A/L.654. Belgium and Burundi: draft resolution.
A/L.654/Rev.1. Belgium, Burundi, Tunisia: revised draft resolution.
A/L.664. Tunisia: amendment to draft resolution, A/L.654.

RESOLUTION 2864(XXVI), as proposed by 3 powers, A/L.654/Rev.1, adopted by Assembly on 20 December 1971, meeting 2027, by 76 votes to 10, with 24 abstentions.

The General Assembly
1. *Takes note* of the report of the Security Council to the General Assembly covering the period from 16 June 1970 to 15 June 1971;
2. *Requests* the Secretary-General to present in his report to the General Assembly at its twenty-seventh session, due consideration having been given to the views of interested Governments, suggestions concerning ways and means of enhancing the effectiveness of the Security Council in accordance with the principles and provisions of the Charter of the United Nations.

Economic and social questions

Chapter I

The Second United Nations Development Decade

On 1 January 1971, the Second United Nations Development Decade began. The Decade had been proclaimed by the General Assembly on 24 October 1970, at which time an International Development Strategy for the Decade was adopted.[1]

During 1971, the General Assembly, the Economic and Social Council and other United Nations bodies took up the question of the periodic review and appraisal of progress in implementing the Strategy. Many bodies within or related to the United Nations system were called upon to contribute to this appraisal. Governments and organizations concerned within the United Nations system were also urged to conduct

programmes for the dissemination of information on the objectives and policies of the Strategy.

Identifying the least developed among the developing countries was also a concern during the year, and in this connexion the Assembly approved a list of hard core least developed countries.

Problems of long-term development planning were also taken up by the Economic and Social Council and other bodies during 1971.

Details of these and other questions are presented in the sections that follow.

[1]See Y.U.N., 1970, pp. 319-29, text of resolution 2626(XXV), in which the Strategy was embodied.

International Development Strategy

Having adopted the International Development Strategy for the Second United Nations Development Decade in October 1970,[2] the General Assembly turned its attention during 1971 to the question of periodic review and appraisal of progress in implementing the Strategy. This question was also discussed by the Economic and Social Council and other concerned bodies.

Decisions taken by the General Assembly and the Economic and Social Council in 1971 provided for the first over-all review and appraisal of progress to be undertaken in 1973 by the Assembly, through the Council, with the aid of the Committee for Development Planning.

The work on the over-all review and appraisal of progress was to be aided by similar work carried out by the organizations of the United Nations system in their areas of competence. The regional economic commissions and the United Nations Economic and Social Office at Beirut were given, in accordance with the International Development Strategy, the main responsibility for appraisals at the regional level. (See pp. 346-49.)

Similarly, the United Nations Conference on Trade and Development (UNCTAD), the United Nations Industrial Development Organization (UNIDO) and the specialized agencies were to continue to review progress in their respective sectors.

The Advisory Committee on the Application of Science and Technology to Development was commended for the activities which culminated in the World Plan of Action for the Application of Science and Technology to Development; the World Plan was seen as an adjunct to the International Development Strategy. (See pp. 316-17.)

According to the International Development Strategy, appraisals of progress at the national level were to be conducted by individual Governments. In 1971, Governments were called upon by the General Assembly to co-operate in the review and appraisal by the international community and in the mobilizing of public opinion in favour of the objectives and policies for the Second Development Decade.

In addition, the role of non-governmental organizations in contributing to the International Development Strategy was emphasized by the Economic and Social Council. (See p. 447.)

Reports before Council and Assembly

The Economic and Social Council had before it at its mid-1971 session the United Nations Secretariat's study entitled *World Economic Survey, 1969–1970*, and subtitled *The Developing Countries*

[2]See Y.U.N., 1970, pp. 319-29, text of resolution 2626(XXV).

in the 1960s: The Problem of Appraising Progress.
The study examined the methodological problems
involved in measuring progress in the developing
countries, reviewed available data and suggested
ways in which those might be used to throw light
on the economic and social progress of the 1960s.

The study dealt with: the production of goods
and services and the ways in which that might be
measured; the ways in which what had been
produced was used; the question of economic
balance both within individual countries and
between one country and the rest of the world;
and the external environment (the more advanced
countries) and how it related to the situation of
developing countries.

The Council and the Assembly also had before
them the report of the Council's Committee for
Development Planning on its seventh session, held
from 22 March to 1 April 1971. The report
contained, among other things, a series of suggestions and recommendations relating to the character and functions of a system of evaluation of
progress, the information required for such an
evaluation and recommendations concerning the
least developed countries. (See p. 232.)

Another document before the Council and
Assembly in 1971 was a report of the Secretary-
General outlining the details of a system of over-all
appraisal of progress. The report emphasized that
such a system must take into account the distinctive roles of appraisals at both global and other
levels called for by the Assembly, as well as the
intimate links between those appraisals.

The report gave attention to those elements
before turning to questions relating to the
mechanics and preparation of over-all appraisals.
It dealt with the timing, information requirements
and institutional arrangements for the appraisals.

Decisions of Economic and Social Council

Review and appraisal

On 30 July 1971, the Economic and Social
Council recommended to the General Assembly
that it take note with appreciation of the report of
the Secretary-General on a system of over-all
review and appraisal of the objectives and policies
of the International Development Strategy as
generally providing a sound initial basis for such a
system.

The Council took this decision without adopting
a resolution, on the basis of a proposal by the
United States.

System of appraisal

Also on 30 July 1971, the Council, aware of the
different levels of review and appraisal that were
to be carried out by Governments and the United
Nations system, decided to establish a committee

of the Council on review and appraisal, composed
of 54 members to be elected in 1972, in accordance
with the geographical distribution of seats in the
Council. This Committee was to enable the
Council to discharge its review and appraisal
responsibilities.

The Council also decided to review in 1974 the
machinery for over-all review and appraisal.

The inter-governmental bodies of the specialized agencies and of other organizations of the
United Nations system, in particular the Trade
and Development Board of UNCTAD and the
Industrial Development Board of UNIDO, were
asked to consider adequate procedures for the
review and appraisal of the policy measures and
the goals and objectives of the International
Development Strategy falling within their competence and to report thereon to the General
Assembly through the Council.

Finally, the Council asked the Committee for
Development Planning to assist the Committee on
Review and Appraisal by reviewing all relevant
material concerning the over-all progress made in
implementing the Strategy and by conveying to
that Committee its comments and recommendations.

These decisions were embodied in Council
resolution 1621 C (LI), adopted by a roll-call vote
of 18 to 5, with 4 abstentions, on the basis of a
proposal by Ghana, Haiti, Indonesia, Italy, Jamaica, Kenya, Lebanon, Madagascar, Malaysia, New
Zealand, Niger, Norway, Sudan, Tunisia, the
United States and Zaire. (For text, see DOCUMEN-
TARY REFERENCES below.)

This resolution having to do with a system of
appraisal was one part of a three-part resolution
on various measures to improve the organization
of the work of the Council. Part A had to do with
enlargement of the Council's membership (see pp.
468-69); part B had to do with institutional
arrangements for science and technology (see pp.
315-16).

During the discussion of machinery for appraisal, the Council also considered a draft resolution
proposed by Greece. By it, the Council would have
deferred decisions on questions concerning structural reforms and review and appraisal of the
International Development Strategy to a later
session in 1971, and would have called upon
Governments to continue active consultations with
the objective of reaching final decisions at that
later session. This draft text was rejected on 30
July 1971 by a roll-call vote of 17 to 8, with 2
abstentions.

Suggested amendments to the text that was
ultimately adopted, proposed by Brazil, Ceylon
and Uruguay and by Yugoslavia, were all rejected
on 30 July 1971.

By one of the proposed amendments, suggested

by Brazil, Ceylon and Uruguay, the paragraphs on the establishment of a committee on review and appraisal and a review in 1974 of machinery for appraisal would have been replaced by a paragraph recommending to the Assembly that it take a final decision on the matter at its 1971 session, taking into account all relevant elements. This proposal was rejected by a roll-call vote of 16 to 5, with 6 abstentions.

The Yugoslav amendment, which was rejected by 18 votes to 5, with 4 abstentions, would have made the Council's decision to establish a committee subject to the final decision of the General Assembly.

No action was taken on a draft resolution proposed by Brazil, Ceylon, Haiti, Uruguay and Yugoslavia and amendments thereto proposed by Norway and the United States that had been transmitted for consideration to the Council by its Economic Committee.

By this draft text, the Council would have requested various organizations of the United Nations system to consider procedures for review and appraisal, would have expressed its readiness to contribute to the review and appraisal, and would have recommended that the General Assembly consider and take a final decision on the matter in 1971.

Committee for Development Planning

By decisions taken on 30 July 1971 concerning the Committee for Development Planning, the Economic and Social Council took note with appreciation of the Committee's report containing, *inter alia*, its views and recommendations on aspects of its work relating to over-all appraisals of progress during the Second Development Decade and on the formulation of a strategy against mass poverty as part of the work on appraisals.

The Council assigned to the Committee for Development Planning, in addition to its current functions, the task of preparing comments and recommendations that could help the Council in discharging its responsibility with regard to the biennial over-all appraisal of progress in implementing the International Development Strategy.

To permit the Committee to carry out its tasks efficiently, the Council decided: *(a)* to enlarge the membership of the Committee, with effect from 1 January 1972, from 18 to 24; *(b)* to provide for an additional session of the Committee in each of the years of biennial over-all appraisal; *(c)* to permit the Committee to continue the practice of holding meetings of its working groups; and *(d)* to authorize the Committee to commission research on selected topics considered important for making appraisals of progress.

These were among the decisions embodied in resolution 1625(LI), adopted unanimously on the

basis of a text transmitted to the Council by its Economic Committee on 26 July 1971. The text had been proposed in the Economic Committee by Indonesia and Kenya. The Committee did not vote on the text. (For text of resolution, see DOCUMENTARY REFERENCES below.)

On 30 July 1971, in a decision taken without adopting a resolution, the Council recommended that two of the members of the enlarged Committee for Development Planning be specialists in the social aspects of development.

Science and technology

The Economic and Social Council, on 30 July 1971, requested the Secretary-General and the organizations of the United Nations system to ensure that the reports and studies prepared for periodic appraisals of progress during the Second Development Decade brought out clearly, in accordance with the provisions of the International Development Strategy, the application of science and technology to the development of various sectors of the economies of developing countries.

That decision was taken by the adoption of resolution 1626(LI). (For text, see p. 321.)

Decisions of General Assembly

Review and appraisal

On 14 December 1971, the General Assembly, in taking note of the report of the Secretary-General on a system of over-all review and appraisal of the objectives and policies of the International Development Strategy for the Second United Nations Development Decade, expressed its conviction that the appropriate discharge of the function of over-all review and appraisal required the adoption of comprehensive guidelines.

In that connexion, the Assembly reiterated that the International Development Strategy should be viewed in a dynamic context involving continuing review to ensure its effective implementation and adaptation in the light of new developments.

The Assembly expressed its conviction that the review and appraisal exercises at the sectoral level by UNCTAD and by UNIDO should be conducted by their respective inter-governmental bodies with a view to seeking new areas of agreement and widening the existing ones in the context of the Strategy.

The Assembly also reaffirmed its responsibility for carrying out, through the Economic and Social Council, the over-all review and appraisal of the progress in implementing the policy measures and the realization of the goals and objectives of the Strategy.

It resolved that:

(a) Review and appraisal at all levels should be

informed by the common purpose of assessing the manner in which the operation of the International Development Strategy had contributed to economic growth and social progress with a view to identifying shortfalls in the achievement of the goals and objectives of the Second United Nations Development Decade, and the factors which accounted for them, and also to recommending positive measures, including new goals and policies as needed;

(b) The scope of that exercise should be sufficiently wide to ensure that, in addition to assessing the extent to which the operation of the Strategy had promoted the growth and progress of the developing countries, the contribution which the developed countries had made to global economic development should also be assessed.

It was decided that the Committee for Development Planning would prepare comments and recommendations relating to the over-all review and appraisal to be undertaken every two years and to a major mid-term review in 1975. The measures set out in the Council's decision of 30 July 1971 concerning the Committee for Development Planning (see above) were endorsed by the Assembly.

The Assembly requested competent secretariats at the sectoral and regional levels to co-operate with the Committee for Development Planning in the fulfilment of its task, and it invited UNCTAD, UNIDO, the specialized agencies, the regional economic commissions and the United Nations Economic and Social Office at Beirut to integrate their review activities with the preparatory work for review and appraisal.

Governments were called upon to extend their co-operation for the success of this international endeavour.

Finally, the Assembly decided that, at the sessions of the Assembly at which the biennial over-all appraisal took place, the work of its Second (Economic and Financial) Committee should be organized so as to ensure sufficient time for in-depth consideration of the Council's report on over-all review and appraisal together with the reports of the main bodies of the United Nations having responsibilities for sectoral review and appraisal.

These decisions were embodied in resolution 2801(XXVI) which was adopted, without objection, on the recommendation of the Assembly's Second Committee. The Committee had approved the text, without vote, on 29 November 1971 on the basis of a revised draft text proposed by Bhutan, Brazil, Burundi, Cameroon, Ceylon, Chad, Cyprus, Egypt, Ethiopia, Honduras, India, Indonesia, Iraq, Kuwait, Lebanon, Lesotho, Liberia, Madagascar, Malaysia, Mali, Nepal, Niger, Nigeria, Paraguay, the Philippines, Rwanda, Su-

dan, Swaziland, the Syrian Arab Republic, Tunisia, Turkey, the United States, Upper Volta, Uruguay, Yemen and Yugoslavia. (For text of resolution, see DOCUMENTARY REFERENCES below.)

During the discussion of the draft text of the resolution in the Second Committee, a number of amendments proposed orally, and, in the case of a proposal by Ghana (later withdrawn) in written form, were taken into account in revisions.

Mobilization of public opinion

On 14 December 1971, the General Assembly adopted a resolution on the dissemination of information and the mobilization of public opinion relative to the review and appraisal of progress in the implementation of the International Development Strategy[3] for the Second United Nations Development Decade.

The mobilization of public opinion, the Assembly thereby noted, was an essential component of the Strategy.

It recognized that, through the intensive dissemination of information on the objectives and policy measures of the Strategy both in developed and in developing countries, a favourable world public opinion would be achieved that would help promote and ensure the implementation of the goals and measures set forth in the Strategy.

Recalling its decision of 13 December 1969[4] on the mobilization of public opinion and the Second Development Decade, the Assembly took note of the administrative arrangements for the Centre for Economic and Social Information which the Secretary-General had made in pursuance of that decision.

In order to make policy-makers and peoples conscious of the tasks and objectives to be pursued during the Second Development Decade, the Assembly stated, there must be full and effective use of the resources available in the United Nations system for this particular endeavour, as well as the support and co-operation of Governments.

A favourable public opinion at the national, regional and global levels, the Assembly was convinced, could have a persuasive influence and could provide dynamism to the review and appraisal of the progress achieved in the implementation of the Strategy.

The Assembly welcomed a statement by the Secretary-General on the need to intensify efforts to achieve the objectives set forth in the Assembly's decision of 13 December 1969 on disseminating information and mobilizing public opinion to help

[3]See Y.U.N., 1970, pp. 319-29, General Assembly resolution 2626(XXV) for text of Strategy, and paragraph 84 of that text relating to mobilization of public opinion.
[4]See Y.U.N., 1969, pp. 289-90, text of resolution 2567(XXIV).

achieve the goals and objectives of the Second Development Decade.

Governments and the organizations concerned within the United Nations system were urged by the Assembly to conduct, in co-ordination with the Secretary-General, campaigns for the dissemination of information on the objectives and policy measures, as well as to the progress achieved and the shortfalls, of the International Development Strategy, and also for the promotion of those objectives and measures.

The decisions to this effect were embodied in resolution 2800(XXVI), adopted by a recorded vote of 100 to 0, with 8 abstentions. The Assembly acted on the recommendation of the Second Committee, which approved the text of the resolution on 29 November 1971 by a vote of 71 to 0, with 17 abstentions, on the basis of a proposal by Argentina, Chile, Colombia, the Dominican Republic, Ecuador, Nicaragua, the Philippines, Uruguay and Zaire. (For text of resolution, see DOCUMENTARY REFERENCES below.)

The wording of the preambular paragraph noting the Secretary-General's arrangements for the Centre for Economic and Social Information was that proposed by India in the course of the Second Committee's discussion. Rejected by 32 votes to 28, with 24 abstentions, was an amendment by Jordan to delete the reference in the resolution whereby the Assembly would take note of the administrative arrangements for the Centre for Economic and Social Information.

Social aspects

By a decision taken by the Assembly on 22 November 1971, Governments of developed countries were urged to fulfil their obligation to implement the International Development Strategy, and in particular to attain the targets for trade, financial resources and the transfer of science and technology for the development of developing countries embodied in the Strategy—and where possible to exceed those targets—which was essential to the amelioration of the world social situation.

The decision was among those embodied in resolution 2771(XXVI) on the world social situation. (For text of resolution, see pp. 366-67.)

DOCUMENTARY REFERENCES

Reports before Council and Assembly
World Economic Survey, 1969–1970: The Developing Countries in the 1960s: The Problem of Appraising Progress (E/4942). U.N.P. Sales No.: E.71.II.C.I.

E/4990. Report of Committee for Development Planning on its 7th session, 22 March–1 April 1971, Geneva, Switzerland, Chapter I.

E/5000 and Add.1, Add.2 and Corr.1, Add.3–5, Add.6 and Corr.1, Add.7. Views of Governments on system of over-all appraisal of progress in implementing International Development Strategy. Note by Secretary-General.

E/5040. Second United Nations Development Decade: system of over-all review and appraisal of objectives and policies of International Development Strategy. Report of Secretary-General.

Decisions of Economic and Social Council

Economic and Social Council—51st session
Economic Committee, meetings 529, 530, 532, 533, 539.
Plenary meetings 1773–1782, 1794–1799.

REVIEW AND APPRAISAL
E/5040. Report of Secretary-General.
E/L.1457. United States: draft decision.
E/5073. Resolutions adopted by Economic and Social Council during its 51st session, 5–30 July 1971. Other decisions, p. 10.

SYSTEM OF APPRAISAL
E/AC.6/L.427 and Rev.1. Brazil, Ceylon, Haiti, Uruguay, Yugoslavia: draft resolution and revision, transmitted for consideration to Economic and Social Council by Economic Committee on 26 July 1971, meeting 539.
E/AC.6/L.437. Norway and United States: amendments to 5-power draft resolution, E/AC.6/L.427/Rev.1.
E/AC.6/L.437/Add.1. Administrative and financial implications of 2-power amendments (E/AC.6/L.437) to 5-power draft resolution (E/AC.6/L.427/Rev.1).
E/5059. Report of Economic Committee, draft resolution I, amendments II and Annex A.

E/L.1451. Ghana, Haiti, Indonesia, Italy, Jamaica, Kenya, Lebanon, Madagascar, Malaysia, New Zealand, Niger, Norway, Sudan, Tunisia, United States, Zaire: draft resolution, part C.
E/L.1451/Add.1. Administrative and financial implications of 16-power draft resolution, E/L.1451. Statement by Secretary-General.
E/L.1454. Brazil, Ceylon, Uruguay: amendments to part C of 16-power draft resolution, E/L.1451.
E/L.1455. Yugoslavia: amendment to part C of 16-power draft resolution, E/L.1451.
E/L.1458. Greece: draft resolution.

RESOLUTION 1621 C (LI), as proposed by 16 powers, E/L.1451, part C, as orally revised by sponsors, adopted by Council on 30 July 1971, meeting 1798, by roll-call vote of 18 to 5, with 4 abstentions, as follows:

In favour: France, Ghana, Haiti, Indonesia, Italy, Jamaica, Kenya, Lebanon, Madagascar, Malaysia, New Zealand, Niger, Norway, Sudan, Tunisia, United Kingdom, United States, Zaire.
Against: Brazil, Ceylon, Peru, Uruguay, Yugoslavia.
Abstaining: Greece, Hungary, Pakistan, USSR.

Draft resolution, as a whole (including parts A and B),* adopted by Council on 30 July 1971, meeting 1798, by roll-call vote of 17 to 7, with 3 abstentions, as follows:

In favour: Ghana, Haiti, Indonesia, Italy, Jamaica, Kenya, Lebanon, Madagascar, Malaysia, New Zealand, Niger, Norway, Pakistan, Sudan, Tunisia, United States, Zaire.
Against: Brazil, Ceylon, Hungary, Peru, USSR, Uruguay, Yugoslavia.
Abstaining: France, Greece, United Kingdom.

*For texts, roll-call votes and supporting documentation for parts A and B of resolution 1621(LI), which dealt with enlargement of the membership of the Economic and Social Council and with institutional arrangements for science and technology, respectively, see pp. 468-69 and 319-20.

The Economic and Social Council,

Noting that paragraph 83 of the International Development Strategy for the Second United Nations Development Decade, approved by the General Assembly in resolution 2626(XXV) of 24 October 1970, provides for an over-all appraisal by the General Assembly, through the Economic and Social Council, of the progress in the implementation of the policy measures and the attainment of the goals and objectives embodied in the Strategy,

Recalling its resolution 1556 B (XLIX) of 31 July 1970, in which the Council expressed its readiness to assume responsibility for assisting the General Assembly in the task of the over-all review and appraisal of progress in the implementation of the Strategy,

Aware of the different levels of review and appraisal that are going to be carried out by Governments and the United Nations system,

1. *Decides* to establish a committee of the Council on review and appraisal, composed of 54 members to be elected at the fifty-second session, in accordance with the present geographical distribution of seats in the Council, to enable the Council to discharge the responsibilities entrusted to it by the General Assembly, in accordance with the Council's functions under the Charter of the United Nations, to assist the General Assembly in the over-all review and appraisal of the Second United Nations Development Decade, as provided for in General Assembly resolution 2626(XXV), in particular in paragraph 83;

2. *Decides further* to review at its fifty-seventh session the machinery for over-all review and appraisal in the light of the implementation of the provisions of operative paragraph 1 of resolution 1621 A (LI) above and the provisions of its resolution 1623(LI) of 30 July 1971;

3. *Requests* the intergovernmental bodies of the specialized agencies and of other organizations of the United Nations system, in particular the Trade and Development Board of the United Nations Conference on Trade and Development and the Industrial Development Board of the United Nations Industrial Development Organization, to consider adequate procedures for the review and appraisal of the policy measures and the goals and objectives of the International Development Strategy falling within their competence and to report thereon to the General Assembly, through the Economic and Social Council;

4. *Requests* the Committee for Development Planning to assist the Committee on Review and Appraisal by reviewing all relevant material concerning the over-all progress made in implementing the International Development Strategy, and by conveying to that Committee its comments and recommendations.

COMMITTEE FOR DEVELOPMENT PLANNING

E/4990. Report of Committee for Development Planning on its 7th session, Chapter I.

E/AC.6/L.429. Indonesia and Kenya: draft resolution, orally amended by sponsors, transmitted for consideration to Economic and Social Council by Economic Committee on 26 July 1971, meeting 539.

E/AC.6/L.429/Add.1. Administrative and financial implications of 2-power draft resolution, E/AC.6/L.429.

E/5059. Report of Economic Committee, draft resolution III and Annex B.

RESOLUTION 1625(LI), as transmitted by Economic Committee, E/5059, adopted unanimously by Council on 30 July 1971, meeting 1799.

The Economic and Social Council,

Recalling its resolution 1079 (XXXIX) of 28 July 1965, which, *inter alia,* provided for the appointment of the members of the group of experts subsequently named as the Committee for Development Planning and set forth the functions of the group,

Bearing in mind General Assembly resolution 2626(XXV) of 24 October 1970, which, *inter alia,* calls for comments and recommendations, within the framework of a specific mandate, by the Committee for Development Planning relating to the progress during the Second United Nations Development Decade that could be drawn upon for the over-all appraisal of progress in implementing the International Development Strategy for the Decade, to be made biennially by the General Assembly through the Council,

Recognizing that the Committee for Development Planning has provided valuable expertise to the United Nations for use in the formulation and implementation of national development plans, as well as in the preparation at the technical level of the action programme for the Second Development Decade,

Aware that the International Development Strategy serves as a focus for the formulation and execution of appropriate national development strategies and for the harmonization of national and international measures to accelerate the development of developing countries and that these fields will continue to require the close attention of experts,

Further bearing in mind the finding of the Committee for Development Planning in its report on its seventh session that its membership should be enlarged so that it may have a larger pool of experience at its disposal for performing its functions adequately,

1. *Takes note with appreciation* of the report of the Committee for Development Planning on its seventh session, containing, *inter alia,* the views and recommendations of the Committee on aspects of its work relating to over-all appraisals of progress during the Second United Nations Development Decade and on the formulation of a strategy against mass poverty as part of the work on appraisals of progress;

2. *Assigns* to the Committee for Development Planning, in addition to its current functions, the task of preparing comments and recommendations that could help the Council in discharging its responsibility to the General Assembly relating to biennial over-all appraisals of progress in implementing the International Development Strategy, as envisaged in paragraph 36 of the report of the Committee and the relevant paragraphs of the report of the Secretary-General;

3. *Decides* in order to permit the Committee for Development Planning to carry out its tasks efficiently:

(*a*) To enlarge, with effect from 1 January 1972, the membership of the Committee from 18 to 24;

(*b*) To provide for an additional session of the Committee in each of the years of biennial over-all appraisal;

(*c*) To permit the Committee to continue its existing practice of holding meetings of its working groups;

(*d*) To authorize the Committee to commission research work on selected topics considered important for making appraisals of progress;

4. *Expresses the hope* that the organizations of the United Nations system will continue to offer co-operation and assistance to the Committee for Development Planning in performing its expanded functions;

5. *Requests* the Secretary-General to continue to furnish to the Committee for Development Planning the necessary help through the appropriate work undertaken by both the staff of the Secretariat and the consultants to the Secretariat appointed for specific research assignments.

E/5073. Resolutions adopted by Economic and Social Council during its 51st session, 5-30 July 1971. Other decisions, pp. 10-11 (Membership of Committee for Development Planning).

Decisions of General Assembly

REVIEW AND APPRAISAL

General Assembly—26th session

Second Committee, meetings 1409–1412, 1415, 1416, 1418, 1421, 1423.

Fifth Committee, meeting 1456.

Plenary meeting 2017.

A/8380. World social situation. Note by Secretary-General (transmitting *1970 Report on the World Social Situation*).

A/8387 and Rev.1. Note by Secretary-General.

A/8401. Report of Secretary-General on work of the Organization, 16 June 1970–15 June 1971, Part Three, Chapter II B.

A/8403. Report of Economic and Social Council on work of its 50th and 51st sessions, Chapter V.

A/8415/Rev.1. Report of Trade and Development Board, 14 October 1970–21 September 1971, Part Three, Annex I (resolution 81(XI)).

A/C.2/L.1182. Bhutan, Brazil, Burundi, Cameroon, Ceylon, Chad, Egypt, India, Iraq, Kuwait, Lebanon, Lesotho, Liberia, Madagascar, Mali, Nepal, Niger, Nigeria, Paraguay, Rwanda, Sudan, Swaziland, Syrian Arab Republic, Tunisia, Turkey, Upper Volta, Uruguay, Yemen: draft resolution.

A/C.2/L.1182/Rev.1. Revised draft resolution, sponsored by above 28 powers and by Ethiopia, Honduras, Philippines and Yugoslavia.

A/C.2/L.1182/Rev.2. Bhutan, Brazil, Burundi, Cameroon, Ceylon, Chad, Cyprus, Egypt, Ethiopia, Honduras, India, Indonesia, Iraq, Kuwait, Lebanon, Lesotho, Liberia, Madagascar, Malaysia, Mali, Nepal, Niger, Nigeria, Paraguay, Philippines, Rwanda, Sudan, Swaziland, Syrian Arab Republic, Tunisia, Turkey, United States, Upper Volta, Uruguay, Yemen, Yugoslavia: revised draft resolution, approved without vote by Second Committee on 29 November 1971, meeting 1423.

A/C.2/L.1189. Ghana: amendments to 32-power revised draft resolution, A/C.2/L.1182/Rev.1.

A/8559. Report of Second Committee, draft resolution II.

RESOLUTION 2801 (XXVI), as recommended by Second Committee, A/8559, adopted without objection by Assembly on 14 December 1971, meeting 2017.

The General Assembly,

Recalling its resolution 2626 (XXV) of 24 October 1970, containing the International Development Strategy for the Second United Nations Development Decade, and in particular paragraphs 79 to 83 thereof,

Recalling also its resolution 2641(XXV) of 19 November 1970, in which it requested the Secretary-General to submit a report to the General Assembly at its twenty-sixth session outlining the details of the system of over-all review and appraisal of the progress in implementing the International Development Strategy to enable the Assembly to take a final decision on the matter,

Taking note of Economic and Social Council resolutions 1621 C (LI) and 1625(LI) of 30 July 1971,

Taking note also of Trade and Development Board resolution 81(XI) of 17 September 1971,

Reiterating that the International Development Strategy should be viewed in a dynamic context involving continuing review to ensure its effective implementation and adaptation in the light of new developments,

Convinced that the review and appraisal exercises at the sectoral level by the United Nations Conference on Trade and Development and the United Nations Industrial Development Organization should be conducted by their respective intergovernmental bodies with a view to seeking new areas of agreement and widening the existing ones in the context of the International Development Strategy,

1. *Takes note* of the report of the Secretary-General on a system of over-all review and appraisal of the objectives and policies of the International Development Strategy for the Second United Nations Development Decade;

2. *Expresses its conviction* that the appropriate discharge of the function of over-all review and appraisal requires the adoption of comprehensive guidelines for this purpose;

3. *Reaffirms* its responsibility for carrying out, through the Economic and Social Council, the over-all review and appraisal of the progress in implementing the policy measures and the realization of the goals and objectives of the International Development Strategy;

4. *Resolves* that:

(a) Review and appraisal at all levels should be informed by the common purpose of assessing the manner in which the operation of the International Development Strategy has contributed to economic growth and social progress with a view to identifying shortfalls in the achievement of the goals and objectives of the Second United Nations Development Decade, and the factors which account for them, and also to recommending positive measures, including new goals and policies as needed;

(b) The scope of the exercise should be sufficiently wide to ensure that, in addition to assessing the extent to which the operation of the International Development Strategy has promoted the growth and progress of the developing countries, the contribution which the developed countries have made to global economic development should also be assessed;

5. *Decides* that the Committee for Development Planning, in the light of the purpose and scope explained above, will prepare, at the expert level, comments and recommendations relating to the over-all review and appraisal which is to be undertaken every two years and to the major mid-term review in 1975;

6. *Endorses* the measures set out in Economic and Social Council resolution 1625(LI) to enable the Committee for Development Planning to assist the Council in discharging its responsibilities to the General Assembly in respect of the over-all review and appraisal;

7. *Requests* competent secretariats at the sectoral and regional levels to co-operate with the Committee for Development Planning in the fulfilment of its task by collecting, processing and making available the necessary data and information;

8. *Invites* the United Nations Conference on Trade and Development, the United Nations Industrial Development Organization, the specialized agencies, the regional economic commissions and the United Nations Economic and Social Office at Beirut to integrate their review activities with the preparatory work for the over-all review and appraisal so as to avoid unnecessary duplication in this field;

9. *Calls upon* Governments to extend their co-operation for the success of this important international endeavour;

10. *Decides* that, at the sessions of the General Assembly at which the biennial over-all appraisal takes place, the work of the Second Committee shall be organized in such a manner as to ensure sufficient time for in-depth consideration of the Economic and Social Council's report on over-all review and appraisal together with the reports of the main bodies of the United Nations having responsibilities for sectoral review and appraisal.

MOBILIZATION OF PUBLIC OPINION

A/C.2/L.1152. Uruguay: draft resolution.

A/C.2/L.1152/Rev.1,2. Chile, Colombia, Dominican Republic, Ecuador, Nicaragua, Philippines, Uruguay, Zaire: revised draft resolution.

A/C.2/L.1152/Rev.3. Argentina, Chile, Columbia, Dominican Republic, Ecuador, Nicaragua, Philippines, Uruguay, Zaire: revised draft resolution, approved by Second Committee on 29 November 1971, meeting 1423, by 71 votes to 0, with 17 abstentions.

A/C.2/L.1196. India: amendments to 8-power revised draft resolution, A/C.2/L.1152/Rev.2.

A/C.2/L.1201. Jordan: amendment to 9-power revised draft resolution, A/C.2/L.1152/Rev.3.

A/8559. Report of Second Committee, draft resolution I.

RESOLUTION 2800 (XXVI), as recommended by Second Committee, A/8559, adopted by Assembly on 14 December 1971, meeting 2017, by recorded vote of 100 to 0, with 8 abstentions, as follows:

In favour: Afghanistan, Algeria, Argentina, Australia, Austria, Bahrain, Belgium, Bolivia, Brazil, Burma, Burundi, Cameroon, Canada, Central African Republic, Chile, Colombia, Costa Rica, Cuba, Cyprus, Dahomey, Denmark, Dominican Republic, Ecuador, Egypt, El Salvador, Ethiopia, Fiji, Finland, France, Gabon, Ghana, Greece, Guatemala, Guinea, Guyana, Honduras, India, Indonesia, Iran, Ireland, Israel, Italy, Jamaica, Japan, Jordan, Kenya, Khmer Republic, Kuwait, Laos, Lebanon, Liberia, Libyan Arab Republic, Luxembourg, Madagascar, Malawi, Malaysia, Mali, Malta, Mauritania, Mexico, Morocco, Nepal, Netherlands, New Zealand, Nicaragua, Niger, Nigeria, Norway, Oman, Panama, Paraguay, People's Democratic

Republic of Yemen, Portugal, Qatar, Romania, Rwanda, Senegal, Sierra Leone, Singapore, Somalia, South Africa, Spain, Sudan, Swaziland, Sweden, Thailand, Togo, Trinidad and Tobago, Tunisia, Turkey, Uganda, United Kingdom, United States, Upper Volta, Uruguay, Venezuela, Yemen, Yugoslavia, Zaire, Zambia.

Against: None.

Abstaining: Bulgaria, Byelorussian SSR, Czechoslovakia, Hungary, Mongolia, Poland, Ukrainian SSR, USSR.

The General Assembly,

Recalling Economic and Social Council resolution 1357(XLV) of 2 August 1968 on the mobilization of public opinion in developed and developing countries regarding the Second United Nations Development Decade,

Recalling also its resolution 2567(XXIV) of 13 December 1969 on the mobilization of public opinion and taking note of the administrative arrangements for the Centre for Economic and Social Information which the Secretary-General has made in pursuance of that resolution,

Bearing in mind paragraph 84 of the International Development Strategy for the Second United Nations Development Decade, contained in resolution 2626 (XXV) of 24 October 1970, on the mobilization of public opinion, which is an essential component of the Strategy,

Recognizing that through the intensive dissemination of the objectives and policy measures of the International Development Strategy in both developed and developing countries a favourable world public opinion will be achieved that will help promote and ensure the implementation of the goals and measures set forth in the Strategy,

Realizing that in order to make policy-makers and peoples conscious of the tasks and objectives to be pursued during the Second United Nations Development Decade there must be full and effective utilization of the resources available in the United Nations system for this particular endeavour, as well as the support and co-operation of Governments,

Convinced that a favourable public opinion at the national, regional and global levels can have a persuasive influence and can provide dynamism to the review and appraisal of the progress achieved in the implementation of the objectives and policies of the International Development Strategy,

1. *Welcomes* the statement of the Secretary-General that efforts to achieve the objectives set forth in General Assembly resolution 2567(XXIV), relating to the dissemination of information and the mobilization of public opinion with regard to the progress in the implementation of the goals and objectives of the Second United Nations Development Decade, should be intensified;

2. *Urges* Governments and the organizations concerned within the United Nations system to conduct, in co-ordination with the Secretary-General, such campaigns as they may deem appropriate for the dissemination of information relative to the objectives and policy measures, as well as to the progress achieved and the shortfalls, within the framework of the International Development Strategy for the Second United Nations Development Decade, and also for the promotion of those objectives and measures.

Identification of least developed countries

In 1971, both the General Assembly and the Economic and Social Council took decisions on the identification of the least developed among the developing countries. Before those bodies in their discussions were a number of reports by Committees which themselves had considered questions concerning the least developed countries.

Reports before Council and Assembly

The Committee for Development Planning, reporting on its seventh session, held from 22 March to 1 April 1971, outlined the characteristics of the least developed among the developing countries, the identification of them on the basis of a set of criteria, and special measures that might be taken in favour of them in terms of technical co-operation, financial assistance and international trade and regional co-operation.

In the light of its deliberations, the Committee for Development Planning suggested that the following countries could be classified among the least developed of the developing countries: Afghanistan, Bhutan, Botswana, Burundi, Chad, Dahomey, Ethiopia, Guinea, Haiti, Laos, Lesotho, Malawi, Maldives, Mali, Nepal, Niger, Rwanda, Sikkim, Somalia, Sudan, Uganda, the United Republic of Tanzania, Upper Volta, Western Samoa and Yemen.

The Trade and Development Board of the United Nations Conference on Trade and Development (UNCTAD) also took up the question of the least developed countries in 1971, at its eleventh session, held from 24 August to 21 September. (See page 277.) The basis of its discussions was a report prepared by the *Ad Hoc* Group of Experts on special measures in favour of the least developed among the developing countries, which had been established in 1970 by UNCTAD.

The report reviewed progress with regard to the issue, discussed the identification of least developed countries and outlined basic policy issues and a framework for action.

Decision of Council

On 30 July 1971, the Economic and Social Council, believing it vital to reach an agreement at an early date on a list of the least developed countries so that special measures could be initiated in their favour at the very beginning of the Second United Nations Development Decade, requested the General Assembly to take a decision at its 1971 session concerning an agreed list of the least developed countries, on the basis of the report of the Committee for Development Planning and reports by the UNCTAD Trade and Development Board.

It was recommended that the Secretary-General and the organizations concerned in the United Nations system should continue to examine, as part of the work on the review and appraisal of progress during the Second Development Decade, the economic and social advancement of the least developed countries, keeping in view the possibility of modifications in the list of those countries at the time of the comprehensive mid-term appraisal in 1975.

These decisions were embodied in Council resolution 1628(LI), adopted, unanimously, as recommended by the Economic Committee, which had approved the text unanimously on 26 July 1971, on a proposal of Sudan. (For text of resolution, see DOCUMENTARY REFERENCES below.)

Decisions of Assembly

At its twenty-sixth session, which opened on 21 September 1971, the General Assembly took up the question of the identification of the least developed among the developing countries.

On 18 November 1971, the General Assembly, mindful of the varying stages of economic development among the developing countries, approved the list of hard core least developed countries contained in the report of the Committee for Development Planning.

In this connexion, the Assembly observed that the criteria used for the identification of the hard core least developed among the developing countries needed to be reviewed and refined and that there was a lack of necessary comparative data in most developing countries.

The Assembly asked the Economic and Social Council to instruct the Committee for Development Planning to continue, in close collaboration with UNCTAD, the review of criteria for the identification of the least developed countries, keeping in view the possibility of modifications in the list of those countries as early as possible.

The Assembly commended the request of the UNCTAD Trade and Development Board that the Secretary-General of UNCTAD work out a detailed action-oriented programme, within UNCTAD, for the implementation of the relevant provisions of the International Development Strategy for the Second United Nations Development Decade[5] in favour of the least developed countries. (See also page 277.) Other organs and programmes of the United Nations were requested to initiate similar programmes, within their fields of competence.

The international organizations within the United Nations system were further requested to take fully into account the special needs of the least developed countries when formulating their programmes or selecting the projects they financed.

These decisions were embodied in resolution 2768 (XXVI), adopted, as amended in a plenary meeting, by 106 votes to 0, on the recommendation of the Assembly's Second (Economic and Financial) Committee.

The Committee approved the text on 11 November 1971, by 116 votes to 0, with 4 abstentions, on a proposal of Afghanistan, Burundi, Ceylon, Chad, Egypt, Ethiopia, France, India, Iran, Lesotho, Malaysia, Mali, Nepal, Niger, Rwanda, Sudan, the Syrian Arab Republic, Uganda, the United Kingdom, the United Republic of Tanzania, Upper Volta, Yemen and Yugoslavia, as amended by Kenya. (For text, see DOCUMENTARY REFERENCES below.)

In a plenary meeting on 18 November 1971, a proposal was presented by the 23 powers that had sponsored the draft text in the Second Committee. By it, they suggested that the recommended text be amended to note that the criteria used for the identification of the hard core least developed countries "needed to be reviewed and refined." (The wording approved by the Committee, on the basis of an amendment proposed by Kenya, had stated that the criteria were "far from adequate.") This 23-power amendment was adopted by 106 votes to 0.

A number of amendments had been proposed in the Committee. All were put to the vote on 18 November 1971. Amendments proposed by Uruguay and by Kenya were incorporated into a revised version of the draft resolution. Others—by Pakistan and by Bolivia, Ecuador, El Salvador and Guatemala—were withdrawn.

Of the remaining amendments submitted, only one was accepted. This was a proposal by Kenya to add the paragraphs to the text by which the Assembly would observe that the criteria used for the identification of the least developed countries were far from being adequate and that there was a lack of necessary comparative data in most developing countries. This proposal was adopted by a roll-call vote of 37 to 31, with 50 abstentions.

Amendments proposed by Colombia, to add paragraphs requesting that special measures taken in favour of the least developed countries would be supplementary to the general measures applicable to all developing countries and would not result in injury or prejudice to the interests of other developing countries, were rejected by a roll-call vote of 35 to 34, with 46 abstentions.

An amendment proposed by Madagascar, to add a paragraph requesting the Economic and Social Council to refine the existing criteria with a view to drawing up a list of countries that were relatively disadvantaged, was rejected by a roll-call vote of 39 to 27, with 51 abstentions.

A proposal by Kenya to add a paragraph requesting the Council to consider according appropriate treatment to all developing countries, on a sliding scale, was rejected by a roll-call vote of 51 to 13, with 56 abstentions.

A Guatemalan proposal to describe the list of hard core countries as "provisional" was rejected by a roll-call vote of 37 to 31, with 52 abstentions.

An amendment proposed by Australia, Bolivia, Ecuador, El Salvador, Guatemala and Trinidad and Tobago was rejected by a roll-call vote of 43 to 32, with 45 abstentions. In the paragraph on

[5]See Y.U.N., 1970, pp. 319-29, text of resolution 2626(XXV).

review by the Committee for Development Planning of criteria for identification, this amendment would have added an instruction to work on criteria for relatively disadvantaged countries in the context of a geographic region.

In another decision, taken on 14 December 1971 and dealing with the capacity of the United Nations development system, the Assembly acted again on the question of the least developed countries.

It requested the United Nations Development Programme to establish and implement special programmes in the field of identification and optimum utilization of the natural resources of the least developed countries and to exempt those countries from the payment of local costs as long as required by their special situation.

In this connexion, the Assembly expressed awareness of the significance and impact of sub-regional, regional and inter-regional projects on the harmonious and accelerated development of developing regions and countries, particularly the least developed among them, and also of the urgent necessity to improve the absorptive capacity of those countries, through appropriate financial and technical assistance.

These decisions were among those embodied in Assembly resolution 2814(XXVI). (For text, see pp. 251-52.)

DOCUMENTARY REFERENCES

Reports before Council and Assembly
Special Measures in Favour of the Least Developed among the Developing Countries. Report of the Ad Hoc Group of Experts on special measures in favour of the least developed among the developing countries (TD/B/349/Rev.1). U.N.P. Sales No.: E.71.II.D.11.
E/4990. Report of Committee for Development Planning on its 7th session, Geneva, Switzerland, 22 March–1 April 1971, Chapter II, and Annex II (list of documents).
E/5038. Report of Committee for Programme and Co-ordination on its 9th Session, 24 May–14 June 1971, Chapter VIII D.
A/8415/Rev.1. Report of Trade and Development Board, 14 October 1970–21 September 1971, Part Three, Chapter VII and Annex I (resolution 82(XI)).
A/8459. Report of Secretary-General.

Economic and Social Council—51st session
Economic Committee, meetings 534, 539.
Plenary meeting 1799.

E/4990. Report of Committee for Development Planning on its 7th session, Chapter II B.
E/5038. Report of Committee for Programme and Co-ordination on its 9th session, Chapter VIII D.
E/AC.6/L.435. Sudan: draft resolution, as orally revised by sponsor, approved unanimously by Economic Committee on 26 July 1971, meeting 539.
E/5061. Report of Economic Committee.

RESOLUTION 1628 (LI), as recommended by Economic Committee, E/5061, adopted unanimously by Council on 30 July 1971, meeting 1799.

The Economic and Social Council,
Recalling General Assembly resolution 2724 (XXV) of 15 December 1970, which, *inter alia*, affirmed the urgency of identifying the least developed among the developing countries, in order to enable such countries to benefit as early as possible from the special measures adopted in the various forms, particularly those incorporated in the International Development Strategy for the Second United Nations Development Decade,
Recognizing that significant work, designed to help intergovernmental organs in identifying the least developed among the developing countries, has been carried out at the technical level by organizations of the United Nations system in response to General Assembly resolutions 2564(XXIV) of 13 December 1969 and 2724 (XXV), resolution 24(II) of the United Nations Conference on Trade and Development of 26 March 1968 and resolution 68(X) of the Trade and Development Board of 16 September 1970,
Believing that it is vital to reach an agreement at an early date on a list of the least developed among the developing countries, so

that special measures can be initiated in their favour at the very beginning of the Second United Nations Development Decade,
1. *Commends* the Committee for Development Planning for its technical work reflected in chapter II of its report on its seventh session, which helps to identify, on the basis of a set of criteria, the least developed among the developing countries and to formulate special measures in their favour;
2. *Requests* the General Assembly to take a decision at its twenty-sixth session concerning an agreed list of the least developed among the developing countries on the basis of the aforementioned work of the Committee and the reports to be submitted to the Assembly at its twenty-sixth session by the Trade and Development Board through the Economic and Social Council and by the Secretary-General;
3. *Recommends* that the Secretary-General and the organizations concerned in the United Nations system, including the regional economic commissions and the United Nations Economic and Social Office at Beirut, should continue to examine, as part of the work on the review and appraisal of progress during the Second United Nations Development Decade, the economic and social advancement of the least developed among the developing countries, keeping in view the possibility of modifications in the list of those countries at the time of the comprehensive mid-term appraisal in 1975.

General Assembly—26th session
Second Committee, meetings 1399-1404.
Plenary meeting 1988.

A/8403. Report of Economic and Social Council on work of its 50th and 51st sessions, Chapter VI.
A/8415/Rev.1. Report of Trade and Development Board, 14 October 1970–21 September 1971, Part Three, Chapter VII and Annex I (resolution 82(XI)).
A/8459. Report of Secretary-General.
A/C.2/L.1168. Chad, Rwanda, Sudan, Syrian Arab Republic, Yugoslavia: draft resolution.
A/C.2/L.1168/Rev.1,2. Afghanistan, Burundi, Ceylon, Chad, Egypt, Ethiopia, France, India, Iran, Lesotho, Malaysia, Mali, Nepal, Niger, Rwanda, Sudan, Syrian Arab Republic, Uganda, United Kingdom, United Republic of Tanzania, Upper Volta, Yemen, Yugoslavia: revised draft resolution, as amended by Kenya (A/C.2/L.1173/Rev.1, para. 1), approved by Second Committee on 11 November 1971, meeting 1403, by 116 votes to 0, with 4 abstentions.
A/C.2/L.1169. Colombia: amendment to 23-power revised draft resolution, A/C.2/L.1168/Rev.1.
A/C.2/L.1169/Rev.1. Colombia: revised amendments to 23-power revised draft resolution, A/C.2/L.1168/Rev.2.
A/C.2/L.1170. Pakistan: amendment to 23-power revised draft resolution, A/C.2/L.1168/Rev.1.

A/C.2/L.1171 and Rev.1. Madagascar: amendment and revised amendment to 23-power revised draft resolutions, A/C.2/L.1168/Rev.1,2.

A/C.2/L.1172. Uruguay: amendment to 23-power revised draft resolution, A/C.2/L.1168/Rev.1.

A/C.2/L.1173 and Rev.1. Kenya: amendments and revised amendments to 23-power revised draft resolutions, A/C.2/L.1168/Rev.1,2.

A/C.2/L.1174. Bolivia, Ecuador, El Salvador, Guatemala: amendment to 23-power revised draft resolution, A/C.2/L.1168/Rev.2.

A/C.2/L.1175. Guatemala: amendment to 23-power revised draft resolution, A/C.2/L.1168/Rev.2.

A/C.2/L.1176. Australia, Bolivia, Ecuador, El Salvador, Guatemala, Trinidad and Tobago: amendment to 23-power revised draft resolution, A/C.2/L.1168/Rev.2.

A/L.644. Afghanistan, Burundi, Ceylon, Chad, Egypt, Ethiopia, France, India, Iran, Lesotho, Malaysia, Mali, Nepal, Niger, Rwanda, Sudan, Syrian Arab Republic, Uganda, United Kingdom, United Republic of Tanzania, Upper Volta, Yemen, Yugoslavia: amendment to draft resolution recommended by Second Committee in A/8521.

A/8521. Report of Second Committee.

RESOLUTION 2768 (XXVI), as recommended by Second Committee, A/8521, and as amended by 23 powers, A/L.644, adopted by Assembly on 18 November 1971, meeting 1988, by 106 votes to 0.

The General Assembly,

Recalling its resolution 2626(XXV) of 24 October 1970, in which it provided a separate section in the International Development Strategy for the Second United Nations Development Decade on special measures in favour of the least developed among the developing countries to enhance their capacity to benefit fully and equitably from the policy measures of the Decade,

Further recalling its resolution 2724(XXV) of 15 December 1970, in which it affirmed the urgency of identifying the least developed among the developing countries in order to enable those countries to benefit as early as possible from the special measures in their favour adopted in the various forums,

Considering that the criteria used so far for the identification of the hard core least developed among the developing countries need to be reviewed and refined,

Further considering that there is a lack of necessary comparative data in most developing countries,

Mindful of the varying stages of economic development among the developing countries as a whole,

1. *Commends* the report of the Committee for Development Planning on its seventh session and that of the *Ad Hoc* Group of Experts on special measures in favour of the least developed among the developing countries of the United Nations Conference on Trade and Development;

2. *Takes note* of Economic and Social Council resolution 1628(LI) of 30 July 1971;

3. *Takes note also* of Trade and Development Board resolution 82 (XI) of 18 September 1971;

4. *Approves* the list of hard core least developed countries contained in paragraph 66 of the report of the Committee for Development Planning on its seventh session;

5. *Requests* the Economic and Social Council to instruct the Committee for Development Planning to continue, in close collaboration with the United Nations Conference on Trade and Development, the review of criteria now being used, as well as any other criteria which may in due course be deemed appropriate for the identification of the least developed countries, keeping in view the possibility of modifications in the list of those countries as early as possible;

6. *Commends* the request of the Trade and Development Board in resolution 82(XI) that the Secretary-General of the United Nations Conference on Trade and Development work out a detailed and comprehensive action-oriented programme, within the competence of the Conference, for the implementation of the relevant provisions of the International Development Strategy for the Second United Nations Development Decade in favour of the least developed countries;

7. *Requests* other organs and programmes of the United Nations, including the United Nations Development Programme and the United Nations Industrial Development Organization, to initiate, as appropriate, similar action-oriented programmes, within their respective fields of competence, in favour of the least developed countries;

8. *Further requests* the international organizations within the United Nations system to take fully into account the special needs of the least developed among the developing countries when formulating their programmes of activities or selecting the projects they finance;

9. *Requests* the Secretary-General to include information on the implementation of paragraphs 6, 7 and 8 above in the reports to be submitted by him under paragraph 83 of General Assembly resolution 2626(XXV).

Development planning

Problems of development planning were discussed by the Economic and Social Council at its mid-1971 session, on the basis of a report by the Committee for Development Planning and a progress report by the Secretary-General on development planning advisory services.

The main concern of the Committee for Development Planning at its seventh session, held at Geneva, Switzerland, from 22 March to 1 April 1971, was aspects of long-term planning at national and international levels and its implications for world development, drawing upon the European experience. The Committee also discussed appraisal of progress during the Second United Nations Development Decade (see page 226) and questions relating to the least developed among developing countries (see page 232).

In its discussion of the rationale and methods of long-term plans and studies, the Committee discussed the elements of uncertainty inherent in long-term planning and choices of objectives and growth patterns. It also studied the key aspects of industrialization and foreign trade, including questions of choices between labour-intensive and capital-intensive patterns or between patterns involving trade substitution and those involving trade expansion.

The Committee also discussed measures to be taken to combat mass poverty, most fundamentally a rapid expansion of employment opportunities.

During the discussion in the Economic and Social Council of the report of the Committee for Development Planning, it was agreed that elements of uncertainty were inherent in the formulation of long-term plans—examples were that scientific discoveries and technological applications could bring about far-reaching changes, consumer habits could change very substantially over a long period of time, and the safeguarding of the environment could become a major goal of society.

It was pointed out that in drawing up long-term plans the developed countries should take into account the need for enlarging their markets for the exports of developing countries. Support was expressed for the Committee's suggestion that the role of international corporations in influencing the shape of developing economies needed to be investigated, and it was noted that the problems of the transfer of technology to developing countries were already receiving attention within the United Nations system.

On 30 July 1971, the Council (without adopting a resolution) took note of the examination of the European experience in long-term planning and its relevance for developing countries contained in the report of the Committee for Development Planning.

In another decision concerning the Committee, the Council took note with appreciation of the Committee's report on its seventh session. This decision was one of several embodied in resolution 1625(LI), adopted on 30 July 1971. (For text, see p. 230.)

DOCUMENTARY REFERENCES

Economic and Social Council—51st session
Economic Committee, meeting 537.
Plenary meeting 1799.

E/4990. Report of Committee for Development Planning on its 7th session, 22 March–1 April 1971, Geneva, Switzerland, Chapters III and IV.
E/5034 and Corr.1. Development planning and projections. Development planning advisory services. Progress report of Secretary-General.
E/5062. Report of Economic Committee.
E/5073. Resolutions adopted by Economic and Social Council during its 51st session, 5-30 July 1971. Other decisions, p. 11.

Other documents
A/8401. Report of Secretary-General on work of the Organization, 16 June 1970–15 June 1971, Part Three, Chapter II C 1.
A/8403. Report of Economic and Social Council on work of its 50th and 51st sessions, Chapter X D.
Journal of Development Planning, No. 2. U.N.P. Sales No.: E.70.II.A.1; *No.3.* U.N.P. Sales No.: E.71.II.A.19 and corrigendum; *No.4.* U.N.P. Sales No.: E.72.II.A.2.
ST/TAO/SER.C/133. Development Prospects and Planning for the Coming Decade (with special reference to Asia). Report of the Fifth Inter-regional Seminar on Development Planning, Bangkok, Thailand, 15-26 September 1969.

Chapter II

The world economic situation

In 1971, both the General Assembly and the Economic and Social Council took decisions concerning the international monetary situation.

The Economic and Social Council, in July and October 1971, among other things called upon Members of the United Nations to take measures to remedy monetary imbalances.

Later in the year, at its twenty-sixth session, which opened on 21 September 1971, the Assembly recommended a number of measures as guidelines in the reform of the international monetary order. Among other things, it called upon the developed market economy countries to take immediate measures to eliminate the state of uncertainty due to the international monetary crisis.

Background material before the Economic and Social Council included a report by the Secretary-General reviewing the salient features of the world economy, 1970-1971, and covering developments in world production and trade and developments in the developed market economy countries, the centrally planned economy countries and the developing countries.

The Council also considered regional surveys for Africa, Asia and the Far East, Europe, and Latin America and special studies on selected development problems in various countries in the Middle East.

Details of the decisions of the Assembly and the Economic and Social Council are given in the following sections.

International monetary situation

Decisions by Economic and Social Council

At its July 1971 session, the Economic and Social Council discussed international economic and social policy.

In this connexion, the Managing Director of the International Monetary Fund observed that the international monetary system could not function unless countries kept in mind two basic principles: the need to take steps to maintain or restore balance in their international payments, and the importance of taking into account the effects of any steps they might take to improve their internal economic situation.

On 30 July 1971, the Council called upon Members of the United Nations and members of the specialized agencies, individually and collectively, to take positive and co-ordinated fiscal and monetary measures to remedy such imbalances as might exist or from time to time occur within the international monetary system, and to improve the working of that system.

The Council also invited the International Monetary Fund to accord the highest priority to seeking long-term improvements of a kind which would be of benefit to developed and developing countries alike, and in that connexion to consult with and seek, in accordance with established procedures, the co-operation of the Secretariat of the United Nations, the International Bank for Reconstruction and Development and other appropriate organizations.

These were among decisions embodied in Council resolution 1627(LI), adopted by 25 votes to 0, with 2 abstentions, on the basis of a text proposed by Greece, Indonesia, Jamaica, Kenya, Malaysia and Sudan. (For text of resolution, see DOCUMENTARY REFERENCES below.)

The Managing Director of the Fund also addressed the Council on 27 October 1971 and introduced the report of the Fund for 1970-1971

After having studied that report and the statement of the Managing Director, the Council, on 29 October 1971, expressed grave concern at the serious disarray in the international monetary situation and affirmed its conviction that a satisfactory solution to the crisis could be found and recurrent crises avoided if all Members of the United Nations, the International Monetary Fund and other international organizations concerned acted in the sense expressed in the Council's resolution of 30 July 1971.

The Council further affirmed that all members of the Fund should be given the opportunity to participate fully and from the outset in consultations and negotiations leading to international monetary reform.

These Council decisions were included in resolution 1652(LI), adopted by 16 votes to 0, with 6 abstentions, on the basis of a proposal by Ceylon, Kenya, Madagascar and Tunisia. (For text of resolution, see DOCUMENTARY REFERENCES below.)

Decisions by General Assembly

At its twenty-sixth session, which opened on 21 September 1971, the General Assembly discussed the international monetary situation and adopted resolutions on long-term and short-term fiscal measures.

On 14 December 1971, by the preamble to the first of these resolutions, the Assembly recognized that the international monetary crisis was the result of an imbalance among the developed market economy countries and had severely undermined the international monetary system, and that the restrictions imposed on international trade by some developed market economy countries to resolve their payment imbalances were particularly prejudicial to the economies of the developing countries.

The Assembly recorded its apprehension that the situation could degenerate into a trade war among the developed market economy countries. It stressed that as a general principle, balance-of-payments difficulties among developed market economy countries should not be used as a justification for the adoption of measures that restricted the trade of developing countries, delayed the liberalization of trade by developed countries or resulted in a reduction in the flow of development assistance to developing countries.

The uncertainty surrounding the international monetary situation, the Assembly considered, warranted immediate and urgent action. It was convinced that it was completely unacceptable for a small group of countries, acting outside the framework of the International Monetary Fund, to take decisions that were vital to the future of the international monetary system and that were of concern to the entire world community.

By the operative paragraphs, the Assembly recommended that any reform of the international monetary system must be geared to a more dynamic concept of world trade based on a recognition of the emerging trade requirements of the developing countries, must create conditions appropriate for a continuing expansion of world trade, and must facilitate, *inter alia,* the transfer of additional development financing to developing countries, in line with the objectives of the International Development Strategy.[1]

[1]See Y.U.N., 1970, pp. 319-29, text of resolution 2626(XXV).

As a preliminary measure, the Assembly urged the elimination of restrictive measures adopted in the context of the international monetary crisis that adversely affected the developing countries.

It called upon all developed countries that had not already done so to proceed with the implementation of the Generalized System of Preferences, as provided for in the International Development Strategy.

Finally, it resolved that the following considerations and guidelines, among others, should be taken into account in the reform of the international monetary order:

(a) The full participation of all interested countries in the process of decision-making with a view to achieving a steady, uninterrupted expansion of commercial and financial flows, especially those of the developing countries;

(b) The restoration and strengthening of the operation and authority of the International Monetary Fund in all matters of concern to the international community as a means of protecting the interests of all countries, especially those of the developing countries;

(c) The establishment of a satisfactory structure of exchange rates maintained within narrow margins;

(d) Adequate provision for the creation of additional international liquidity, through truly collective international action, in line with the requirements of an expanding world economy and the special needs of developing countries and with such safeguards as would ensure that the total supply of international liquidity was not unduly influenced by the balance-of-payments position of any single country or group of countries;

(e) The creation of a link between Special Drawing Rights and additional resources for financing development as an integral part of the new international monetary system;

(f) The establishment of a permanent system of guarantees against exchange losses affecting the reserves of developing countries, combined with the elaboration of appropriate measures to compensate developing countries against the involuntary losses they had suffered because of currency speculations in certain currencies in developed countries;

(g) The introduction of appropriate provisions in the Articles of Agreement of the International Monetary Fund which would increase the voting power of the developing countries.

These decisions were embodied in resolution 2806(XXVI), adopted by 82 votes to 11, with 15 abstentions, on the recommendation of the Assembly's Second (Economic and Financial) Committee, which approved the text (after a series of votes on individual paragraphs) on 7 December 1971, by a roll-call vote of 69 to 12, with 17 abstentions.

The Second Committee's text was proposed by the following 90 Members: Afghanistan, Algeria, Argentina, Bahrain, Barbados, Bhutan, Bolivia, Botswana, Brazil, Burma, Burundi, Cameroon, the Central African Republic, Ceylon, Chad, Chile, Colombia, the Congo, Costa Rica, Cyprus, Dahomey, the Dominican Republic, Ecuador, Egypt, El Salvador, Equatorial Guinea, Ethiopia, Fiji, Gabon, Gambia, Ghana, Guatemala, Guinea, Guyana, Haiti, Honduras, India, Indonesia, Iran, Iraq, the Ivory Coast, Jamaica, Jordan, Kenya, the Khmer Republic, Kuwait, Laos, Lebanon, Lesotho, Liberia, the Libyan Arab Republic, Malawi, Malaysia, Mali, Mauritania, Mauritius, Mexico, Morocco, Nepal, Nicaragua, Niger, Nigeria, Pakistan, Panama, Paraguay, the People's Democratic Republic of Yemen, Peru, the Philippines, Qatar, Rwanda, Saudi Arabia, Sierra Leone, Singapore, Somalia, Sudan, Swaziland, the Syrian Arab Republic, Thailand, Togo, Trinidad and Tobago, Tunisia, Uganda, the United Republic of Tanzania, Upper Volta, Uruguay, Venezuela, Yemen, Yugoslavia, Zaire and Zambia.

(For text of resolution, see DOCUMENTARY REFERENCES below.)

In the course of the Committee's discussion, Italy proposed an amendment to the draft resolution which would have deleted the idea of the restoration of the operation of the International Monetary Fund from the sub-paragraph that had to do with the restoration and strengthening of the operation of the International Monetary Fund. On 7 December 1971, the Italian amendment was rejected by 68 votes to 20, with 6 abstentions.

By another resolution also adopted on 14 December 1971, the Assembly took a number of decisions on immediate measures to eliminate the state of uncertainty resulting from the international monetary crisis.

The Assembly called upon the developed market economy countries to take immediate measures to reverse the restraints on international trade, such as import surcharges, and on the level of assistance to the developing countries, and, as an urgent measure, to arrange the realignment of their currencies, taking into account the interests of the developing countries, so as to remove the state of uncertainty and eliminate the adverse consequences that had resulted therefrom.

In so doing, the Assembly recognized that the international monetary crisis was the result of an imbalance among the developed market economy countries that had undermined the world monetary system and adversely affected the prospects for trade and development of the developing countries.

The Assembly expressed deep concern lest further delay in reaching a solution should result in retaliatory protectionist measures among the developed market economy countries, which would precipitate a general recession in the world economy and thus threaten the realization of the objectives of the Second United Nations Development Decade.

These decisions were embodied in resolution 2808(XXVI), adopted by 78 votes to 1, with 31 abstentions, on the recommendation of the Assembly's Second Committee, which approved the text on 10 December 1971, by 52 votes to 2, with 31 abstentions, on the basis of a proposal by Kuwait, Nigeria, Pakistan, and Sudan. (For text, see DOCUMENTARY REFERENCES below.)

During the preceding discussions in the Second Committee, Peru, in introducing the 90-power text, said that the developing countries were asking for full participation on the basis of equality with other members of the international community in any prior consultations and decision-making in the reform of the world trade and monetary system; they felt that developed countries ought not take unilaterally any decisions that directly or indirectly affected the social and economic development of developing countries. The sponsors of the resolution (in suggesting guidelines for reform) Peru added, were not asking the developed countries to adopt the proposed guidelines but merely to take them into account in the eventual reform of the international monetary system.

A similar view was presented by Pakistan, which introduced the four-power text on immediate measures to eliminate the state of uncertainty. Noting that the upheaval in monetary and trade relations among the developed countries had repercussions on the economies of the developing countries, he said that the developing countries were therefore interested in having the major parties reach an agreement as soon as possible.

The USSR representative felt that both draft resolutions correctly stated that the monetary crisis was disastrous for the developing countries. He was pleased to see that the sponsors of the text had recognized that the international monetary crisis was the result of imbalances among the market economy countries and thus, indirectly, of the action of the capitalist countries. He stressed the need to reform the International Monetary Fund, whose incapacity to solve problems and tendency to serve the interests of a small group of countries had been proved.

Several Members—among them Australia, Canada, France, Japan, New Zealand and the United Kingdom—believed that the wording of the 90-power text appeared to be not a global resolution but a statement by developing countries about their special preoccupations.

The Netherlands, while recognizing that the consequences of long-term decisions with regard to monetary reform were too serious for developing countries not to be allowed to participate from the beginning in the studies, discussions and negotiations in that field, felt that the proposal in the 90-power text that the Assembly should endorse certain conclusions without further study was manifestly unreasonable and unacceptable.

Several Members—including Denmark, France, the Netherlands, New Zealand and the United Kingdom—in explaining their negative votes on the 90-power text stated that it had been clear that the sponsors of that proposal had been unwilling to negotiate on a text dealing with complex problems of extreme importance.

A recurrent objection to the four-power text, voiced primarily by those who had opposed it in the vote, was that it duplicated the 90-power text. Supporters of both texts, however, argued that the crisis called for immediate and effective measures.

(For information on action by the United Nations Conference on Trade and Development concerning monetary reform, see pp. 271-72.)

DOCUMENTARY REFERENCES

Economic and Social Council—51st session
Plenary meetings 1773-1782, 1793, 1799, 1800, 1801, 1805.

World Economic Survey, 1971. Current Economic Developments (E/5144). U.N.P. Sales No.: E.72.II.C.2.
A Survey of Economic Conditions in Africa, 1970 (Part I). U.N.P. Sales No.: E.71.II.K.9; (Part II). U.N.P. Sales No.: E.72.II.K.5.
E/5004. General discussion of international economic and social policy. Economic conditions in Africa, 1970. Summary.
Economic Survey of Europe in 1970. Part II: The European Economy in 1970. U.N.P. Sales No.: E.71.II.E.5.
E/5007. Economic survey of Europe in 1970. Summary.
Economic Survey of Latin America, 1970. U.N.P. Sales No.: E.72.II.G.1.
E/5009. Economic survey of Latin America, 1970. Summary.
Studies on Selected Development Problems in Various Countries in the Middle East, 1971. U.N.P. Sales No.: E.71.II.C.2.
E/5010. Studies on selected development problems in various countries in Middle East, 1971. Summary.

Economic Survey of Asia and the Far East, 1970. U.N.P. Sales No.: E.71.II.F.1; 1971. U.N.P. Sales No.: E.72.II.F.1.
E/5016. Economic survey of Asia and Far East, 1970. Summary.
E/5036 and Add.1-3. Review of salient features of world economy, 1970–1971. Report of Secretary-General.
E/L.1432. Indonesia, Jamaica, Kenya. Malaysia: draft resolution.
E/L.1432/Rev.1. Greece, Indonesia, Jamaica, Kenya, Malaysia, Sudan: revised draft resolution.

RESOLUTION 1627(LI), as proposed by 6 powers, E/L.1432/Rev.1, as orally amended by sponsors, adopted by Council on 30 July 1971, meeting 1799, by 25 votes to 0, with 2 abstentions.

The Economic and Social Council,
Considering the spirit and objectives of the Charter of the United Nations relating to economic and social development in a changing world,
Noting that it is imperative that States Members of the United

Nations co-operate to enable the international community to achieve the goals and objectives of the International Development Strategy for the Second United Nations Development Decade,

Concerned that international monetary instability and inflation and stagnation occurring together can frustrate efforts to promote world trade, economic growth and development,

Taking note of the views expressed in the Council by the Managing Director of the International Monetary Fund on this matter on 6 July 1971, and noting in particular that there is considerable scope for better international monetary policy co-ordination,

Further noting the observations and concern of members of the Council as expressed during its fifty-first session,

1. *Calls upon* States Members of the United Nations and members of the specialized agencies, individually and collectively, to take positive and co-ordinated fiscal and monetary measures to remedy such imbalances as may exist or from time to time occur within the international monetary system, and to improve the working of that system;

2. *Invites* the International Monetary Fund to accord the highest priority to seeking long-term improvements of a kind which would be of benefit to developed and developing countries alike, and in this connexion to consult with and seek, in accordance with established procedures, the co-operation of the Secretariat of the United Nations, the International Bank for Reconstruction and Development and other appropriate organizations.

E/5075. Note by Secretary-General (transmitting summary of annual report of International Monetary Fund for fiscal year ended 30 April 1971).

E/L.1466. Ceylon, Kenya, Madagascar, Tunisia: draft resolution.

RESOLUTION 1652(LI), as proposed by 4 powers, E/L.1466, and as orally amended by Ceylon and orally sub-amended by France, adopted by Council on 29 October 1971, meeting 1805, by 16 votes to 0, with 6 abstentions.

The Economic and Social Council,

Having studied the report of the International Monetary Fund,

Having heard the statement of the Managing Director of the International Monetary Fund in the Council on 27 October 1971,

Taking note of Trade and Development Board resolution 84(XI) of 20 September 1971,

1. *Expresses grave concern* at the serious disarray in the international monetary situation and, in particular, its effects on the economic and social progress of the developing countries;

2. *Affirms its conviction* that a satisfactory solution to the present crisis can be found, and recurrent crises avoided, if all States Members of the United Nations, the International Monetary Fund and other international organizations concerned act in the sense expressed in resolution 1627(LI) of the Council of 30 July 1971;

3. *Notes with satisfaction* resolution 26.9 of 1 October 1971 adopted at the twenty-sixth annual meeting of the Board of Governors of the International Monetary Fund and expresses the hope that this forms the initial basis for an early and satisfactory solution to the present crisis, which would take into account the interests of all Member States and, in particular, those of the developing countries;

4. *Affirms* that all member States of the International Monetary Fund should be given the opportunity to participate fully and from the outset in consultations and negotiations leading to international monetary reform;

5. *Urges* States Members of the United Nations to co-operate with the International Monetary Fund in the search for equitable solutions that would facilitate the achievement of the goals and objectives of the International Development Strategy for the Second United Nations Development Decade.

General Assembly—26th session
Second Committee, meetings 1369-1382, 1398, 1425, 1431, 1433, 1434, 1439, 1441.

Plenary meeting 2017.

A/8401. Report of Secretary-General on work of the Organization, 16 June 1970–15 June 1971, Part Three, Chapter II A 1.

A/8403. Report of Economic and Social Council on work of its 50th and 51st sessions, Chapter III.

A/C.2/L.1166. Letter of 22 October 1971 from Peru to Chairman of Second Committee.

A/C.2/L.1199. Afghanistan, Algeria, Argentina, Bahrain, Barbados, Bhutan, Bolivia, Botswana, Brazil, Burma, Burundi, Cameroon, Central African Republic, Ceylon, Chad, Chile, Colombia, Congo, Costa Rica, Cyprus, Dahomey, Dominican Republic, Ecuador, Egypt, El Salvador, Equatorial Guinea, Ethiopia, Gabon, Gambia, Ghana, Guatemala, Guinea, Guyana, Haiti, Honduras, India, Indonesia, Iran, Iraq, Ivory Coast, Jamaica, Jordan, Kenya, Khmer Republic, Kuwait, Laos, Lebanon, Lesotho, Liberia, Libyan Arab Republic, Madagascar, Malawi, Malaysia, Mali, Mauritania, Mauritius, Mexico, Morocco, Nepal, Nicaragua, Niger, Nigeria, Pakistan, Panama, Paraguay, People's Democratic Republic of Yemen, Peru, Philippines, Qatar, Rwanda, Saudi Arabia, Sierra Leone, Singapore, Somalia, Sudan, Swaziland, Syrian Arab Republic, Thailand, Togo, Trinidad and Tobago, Tunisia, Uganda, United Republic of Tanzania, Upper Volta, Uruguay, Venezuela, Yemen, Yugoslavia, Zaire, Zambia: draft resolution.

A/C.2/L.1199/Rev.1. Revised draft resolution, sponsored by above 90 powers, excluding Madagascar, and subsequently co-sponsored also by Fiji, approved by Second Committee on 7 December 1971, meeting 1434, by roll-call vote of 69 to 12, with 17 abstentions, as follows:

In favour: Afghanistan, Algeria, Argentina, Bahrain, Barbados, Bolivia, Brazil, Burma, Cameroon, Central African Republic, Ceylon, Chile, Colombia, Congo, Costa Rica, Cuba, Cyprus, Dahomey, Ecuador, Egypt, El Salvador, Ethiopia, Fiji, Ghana, Greece, Guatemala, Honduras, India, Indonesia, Iran, Iraq, Ivory Coast, Jamaica, Kenya, Khmer Republic, Kuwait, Laos, Lebanon, Libyan Arab Republic, Madagascar, Malaysia, Mali, Mexico, Nepal, Nicaragua, Nigeria, Panama, Paraguay, Peru, Philippines, Qatar, Romania, Rwanda, Saudi Arabia, Senegal, Singapore, Sudan, Swaziland, Thailand, Togo, Trinidad and Tobago, Tunisia, Turkey, Upper Volta, Uruguay, Venezuela, Yugoslavia, Zaire, Zambia.

Against: Australia, Belgium, Canada, Denmark, Finland, Ireland, Japan, New Zealand, Norway, Sweden, United Kingdom, United States.

Abstaining: Austria, Bulgaria, Byelorussian SSR, Czechoslovakia, France, Hungary, Iceland, Israel, Italy, Mongolia, Netherlands, Poland, Portugal, South Africa, Spain, Ukrainian SSR, USSR.

A/C.2/L.1216. Italy: amendment to 90-power revised draft resolution, A/C.2/L.1199/Rev.1.

A/8578. Report of Second Committee (Part I) (on report of Economic and Social Council), draft resolution V.

RESOLUTION 2806(XXVI), as recommended by Second Committee, A/8578, adopted by Assembly on 14 December 1971, meeting 2017, by 82 votes to 11, with 15 abstentions.

The General Assembly,

Recalling Economic and Social Council resolutions 1627(LI) of 30 July 1971 and 1652(LI) of 29 October 1971 regarding the international monetary situation,

Recognizing that the current international monetary crisis is the result of an imbalance among the developed market economy countries and has severely undermined the international monetary system, adversely affecting the international environment and prospects for the trade and development of the developing countries,

Recognizing further that the restrictions imposed on international trade by some developed market economy countries to resolve their payment imbalances are particularly prejudicial to the economies of the developing countries,

Apprehending that the present situation could degenerate into a trade war among the developed market economy countries which would have disastrous effects on all countries, especially the developing countries,

Stressing that as a general principle balance-of-payments difficulties among developed market economy countries should not be used as a justification for the adoption of any measures which restrict the trade of developing countries, delay the liberalization of trade by developed countries in favour of developing countries or result in a reduction in the flow of development assistance to these countries,

Considering that the uncertainty surrounding the international monetary situation warrants immediate and urgent action in order to eliminate the adverse consequences it has already created for the whole world, especially for the developing countries,

Convinced that it is completely unacceptable for a small group of countries, acting outside the framework of the International Monetary Fund, to take decisions which are vital to the future of the international monetary system and which are of concern to the entire world community,

1. *Recommends* that any reform of the international monetary system must be geared to a more dynamic concept of world trade based on a recognition of the emerging trade requirements of the developing countries, must create conditions appropriate for a continuing expansion of world trade, taking into account especially the needs of the developing countries, and must facilitate, inter alia, the transfer of additional development financing to developing countries, in line with the objectives and commitments of the International Development Strategy for the Second United Nations Development Decade, contained in General Assembly resolution 2626(XXV) of 24 October 1970;

2. *Urges* as a preliminary measure the elimination of all restrictive measures adopted in the context of the international monetary crisis which adversely affect the developing countries;

3. *Calls upon* all developed countries which have not already done so to proceed with the implementation of the Generalized System of Preferences in favour of developing countries in 1971, as provided for in paragraph 32 of the International Development Strategy;

4. *Resolves* that the following considerations and guidelines, among others, should be taken into account in the reform of the international monetary order:

(a) The full participation of all interested countries in the process of decision-making with a view to achieving a steady, uninterrupted expansion of commercial and financial flows, especially those of the developing countries;

(b) The restoration and strengthening of the operation and authority of the International Monetary Fund in all matters of concern to the international community as a means of protecting the interests of all countries, especially those of the developing countries;

(c) The establishment of a satisfactory structure of exchange rates maintained within narrow margins;

(d) Adequate provision for the creation of additional international liquidity, through truly collective international action, in line with the requirements of an expanding world economy and the special needs of developing countries and with such safeguards as will ensure that the total supply of international liquidity is not unduly influenced by the balance-of-payments position of any single country or group of countries;

(e) The creation of a link between Special Drawing Rights and

additional resources for financing development as an integral part of the new international monetary system;

(f) The establishment of a permanent system of guarantees against exchange losses affecting the reserves of developing countries, combined with the elaboration of appropriate measures to compensate developing countries against the involuntary losses they have suffered because of currency speculations in certain currencies in developed countries;

(g) The introduction of appropriate provisions in the Articles of Agreement of the International Monetary Fund which would increase the voting power of the developing countries.

A/8415/Rev.1. United Nations Conference on Trade and Development. Report of Trade and Development Board, 14 October 1970–21 September 1971, Part Three, Annex I (resolution 84(XI)).

A/C.2/L.1206 and Rev.I,2. Kuwait, Nigeria, Pakistan, Sudan: draft resolution and revisions, approved by Second Committee on 10 December 1971, meeting 1441, by 52 votes to 2, with 31 abstentions.

A/8578. Report of Second Committee (Part I) (on report of Economic and Social Council), draft resolution VII.

RESOLUTION 2808(XXVI), as recommended by Second Committee, A/8578, adopted by Assembly on 14 December 1971, meeting 2017, by 78 votes to 1, with 31 abstentions.

The General Assembly,

Recognizing that the current international monetary crisis is the result of an imbalance among the developed market economy countries that has undermined the world monetary system and adversely affected the prospects for trade and development of the developing countries,

Taking note of Trade and Development Board resolution 84 (XI) of 20 September 1971,

Taking note further of resolution 26.9 of 1 October 1971 adopted by the Board of Governors of the International Monetary Fund at its twenty–sixth annual meeting,

Recalling Economic and Social Council resolutions 1627(LI) of 30 July 1971 and 1652(LI) of 29 October 1971 regarding the international monetary situation,

Recalling further its resolution 2806(XXVI) of 14 December 1971 on the international monetary situation,

Deeply concerned lest further delay in reaching a solution should result in retaliatory protectionist measures among the developed market economy countries, which would precipitate a general recession in the world economy and thus threaten the realization of the objectives of the Second United Nations Development Decade,

Calls upon the developed market economy countries to take immediate measures to reverse the recent restraints on international trade, such as import surcharges, and on the level of assistance to the developing countries and, as an urgent measure, to arrange the realignment of their currencies, taking into account the interests of the developing countries, so as to remove the prevailing state of uncertainty and eliminate the adverse consequences which have resulted therefrom pending the indispensable reform to be adopted as early as possible with the full participation of the developing countries.

Other documents
Income Distribution in Latin America. U.N.P. Sales No.: E.71.II.G.2.

Report of the International Monetary Fund

The report of the International Monetary Fund for the fiscal year ended 30 June 1971 was considered by the Economic and Social Council in October and November 1971.

The Managing Director of the Fund, introducing the report, observed that despite exchange rate action taken by five European countries in May 1971, the international payments situation had remained precarious, largely because of the continuing deficit in the United States balance of payments.

On 15 August 1971, he said, the United States authorities had taken wide-ranging measures which could seriously disrupt trade and currency relations within the international community.

When the Governors representing the 118 member countries of the Fund had met in September 1971 at Washington, D.C., he said, a consensus had emerged on some important issues. The Governors had unanimously called upon all members to collaborate with the Fund and with each other in establishing a satisfactory structure of exchange rates and in facilitating resumption of the orderly conduct of the Fund's operations.

Members had also been called upon to collaborate in efforts to reduce restrictive trade and exchange practices and to establish satisfactory arrangements for the settlement of international transactions.

The Managing Director reported that the Executive Directors of the Fund had been requested to report to the Board of Governors without delay on the measures that were necessary or desirable for the improvement or reform of the international monetary system.

Such improvement or reform over the long term, he said, would involve measures relating both to the effectiveness of the international adjustment process and to improvement in control over the volume of international liquidity; in that context, it had been thought that the Special Drawing Rights could in time become the main asset in which countries would hold their reserves.

The Council took note with appreciation of the report of the International Monetary Fund, in adopting resolution 1647(LI).

DOCUMENTARY REFERENCES

Economic and Social Council—51st session
Plenary meetings 1800, 1801, 1805.

E/5075. Note by Secretary-General (transmitting summary of annual report of International Monetary Fund for fiscal year ended 30 April 1971).

RESOLUTION 1647(LI), as proposed by Council President, taking note with appreciation of report of International Monetary Fund, adopted without objection by Council on 27 October 1971, meeting 1801.

A/8403/Add.1. Addendum to report of Economic and Social Council, resumed 51st session, Chapter II A.

Chapter III

United Nations operational activities for development

The United Nations Development Programme

The United Nations Development Programme (UNDP), financed by voluntary contributions of Governments, continued in 1971 as the largest multilateral source of technical and pre-investment assistance in the world.

The Programme provides Governments of developing countries, at their request, with technical and pre-investment assistance aimed at helping them:

— in carrying out survey and feasibility studies to determine the economic potential and plan the productive use of natural resources such as soil, rivers, forests and minerals;

— in establishing and strengthening permanent educational and training institutes;

— in creating and expanding research centres for the development and application of modern technology;

— in supplying technical, training and advisory services to help build the economic and social infrastructure necessary for development.

The Programme came into existence on 1 January 1966, following a General Assembly decision of 22 November 1965[1] to combine two existing assistance programmes of the United Nations: the Expanded Programme of Technical Assistance and the United Nations Special Fund. The former, established in 1950, provided short-term technical advisory services, fellowships to nationals of developing countries for study abroad, and equipment for demonstration and training purposes. The Special Fund, established in 1959, focused on large-scale pre-investment projects designed to assist developing countries in

[1]See Y.U.N., 1965, pp. 273–75, text of resolution 2029 (XX).

widening their productive capabilities, making more effective use of their human and natural resources and attracting investment capital.

In 1970, the UNDP Governing Council reviewed an extensive study that had been made of the United Nations development system and adopted many of the principles and guidelines proposed for strengthening it. These reforms were subsequently endorsed by the Economic and Social Council and approved by the General Assembly.[2]

Among other things, they called for the elimination of the distinction between the Special Fund and Technical Assistance components of UNDP and the introduction of country programming. By the end of 1971, 19 UNDP country programmes had been drawn up for approval by the UNDP Governing Council in 1972.

[2]See Y.U.N., 1970, pp. 350-55, text of resolution 2688(XXV) of 11 December 1970.

Activities in 1971 under the United Nations Development Programme

In 1971, the first year of the Second United Nations Development Decade, the United Nations Development Programme (UNDP) provided a record level of assistance to developing countries. During the year, 4,807 technical co-operation projects were being implemented, assistance to 196 large-scale and 1,297 small-scale projects was approved, and some 640 field projects were completed.

The year also saw the introduction of a revised system of programming, in accordance with the reforms approved by the General Assembly in 1970.[3] Under the new country programming arrangements, the distinction between Special Fund and Technical Assistance projects was to be eliminated by 1 January 1972.

In 1971, Governments of 19 countries, assisted by the staff of UNDP and the participating organizations, formulated the first UNDP country programmes for approval by the Governing Council at its January 1972 session.

Each of the 19 Governments identified the sectoral development objectives against which it envisaged the need for external assistance in general, and UNDP assistance in particular, and established a preliminary list of specific projects to be continued or approved over a period of years. This forward planning of UNDP assistance was carried out in the context of the country's national development plan or programme and within the framework of an indicative planning figure, proposed by the UNDP Administrator and approved by the Governing Council, of UNDP resources estimated as being reasonably likely to be available to the country for five years beginning in January 1972.

Projects approved in 1971

During 1971, the UNDP Governing Council approved 196 large-scale (Special Fund component) projects and 1,297 small-scale (Technical Assistance component) projects.

Of the large-scale projects approved during the year, 167 were country projects, 24 were regional and four, inter-regional; and one global project was approved, for the study of the implications of the "green revolution."

Of the $203.4 million earmarked for large-scale projects, 43 per cent went to projects in agriculture, an increase of 30 per cent over 1970. Industry accounted for 17.4 per cent of the new earmarkings and public utilities for 15.7 per cent. There was a fivefold increase in the funds set aside for multi-sector projects, which rose to 14.2 per cent of earmarkings in 1971. Funds for education and science amounted to 8.4 per cent of the total for large-scale projects.

The distribution of funds for large-scale projects by region was as follows: Africa, 30 per cent; the Americas, 22.5 per cent; Asia and the Far East, 19.8 per cent; Europe, the Mediterranean and the Middle East, 26 per cent. For inter-regional and global projects, funds totalled 1.5 per cent.

The United Nations, the International Labour Organisation (ILO) and the Food and Agriculture Organization (FAO) assumed responsibility for executing 57 per cent of the projects. The World Health Organization (WHO) and the International Bank for Reconstruction and Development, and, to a lesser degree, the Inter-Governmental Maritime Consultative Organization (IMCO) and the International Atomic Energy Agency (IAEA) each had a larger number of projects to execute than in 1970. Two projects were to be executed by UNDP.

A total of 10 investment feasibility studies, costing $1,336,490, were authorized by the UNDP Administrator in 1971. These were to assist Afghanistan, Iceland and Peru and five countries in Africa—Burundi, Chad, Liberia, Rwanda and Senegal. Six of the studies were entrusted to the International Bank for execution, and one each to FAO, the International Civil Aviation Organization, UNDP and the International Development Bank.

Of the 1,297 small-scale projects approved during 1971—62 more than in 1970—1,206 (or 93 per cent) were country projects, 58 were regional and 33, inter-regional.

[3]See Y.U.N., 1970, pp. 350–55, text of resolution 2688(XXV) of 11 December 1970.

The United Nations was assigned the largest number of projects for execution (376). The other organizations given responsibility for the implementation of a substantial number of projects were: FAO (25); the United Nations Educational, Scientific and Cultural Organization (UNESCO) (158); the United Nations Industrial Development Organization (UNIDO) (141); and ILO (125).

1971 field activities

During 1971, a total of 4,807 projects were being implemented by UNDP in 137 countries and territories of the developing world. This involved an outlay of some $245 million ($189 million for Special Fund component projects and $56 million for Technical Assistance component projects) of resources voluntarily contributed by Governments; this figure compared with expenditures of some $207 million in 1970 and $177 million in 1969, an increase of 39 per cent over a three-year period. An additional $280 million in cash or in kind came from recipient Governments.

The distribution of UNDP projects being implemented in 1971—by executing agency, geographical region and economic and social sector—is shown in the following table.

1971 Expenditures
(in millions of U.S. dollars)

Participating and Executing Agency	Special Fund Component	Technical Assistance Component
United Nations	31.3	10.8
International Labour Organisation (ILO)	24.2	6.7
Food and Agriculture Organization (FAO)	70.8	12.3
United Nations Educational, Scientific and Cultural Organization (UNESCO)	25.2	8.8
International Civil Aviation Organization (ICAO)	2.9	2.1
World Health Organization (WHO)	6.2	5.7
International Bank for Reconstruction and Development	9.5	—
Universal Postal Union (UPU)	0.5	0.5
International Telecommunication Union (ITU)	4.4	2.1
World Meteorological Organization (WMO)	4.4	1.3
Inter-Governmental Maritime Consultative Organization (IMCO)	0.1	0.2
International Atomic Energy Agency (IAEA)	0.7	1.0
United Nations Industrial Development Organization (UNIDO)	6.5	2.8
United Nations Conference on Trade and Development (UNCTAD)	0.5	1.4
Asian Development Bank	1.1	—

Participating and Executing Agency	Special Fund Component	Technical Assistance Component
International Development Bank	0.2	—
United Nations Development Programme (UNDP)	0.6	0.3
Region		
Africa	60.8	17.5
The Americas	38.1	12.3
Asia and the Far East	46.6	13.5
Europe, Mediterranean and the Middle East	41.2	8.4
Inter-regional	2.3	4.3
Economic and Social Sector		
Agriculture	68.2	12.9
Industry	42.7	7.1
Public utilities	30.8	7.0
Housing, building and physical planning	3.0	0.7
Multi-sector	14.5	5.3
Health	1.7	5.5
Education and science	18.6	8.7
Social welfare	0.7	3.0
Public administration and other services	8.9	5.8

Of the projects under implementation, 4,349 were country projects (86 per cent of total expenditures), 342 were regional projects (11.5 per cent), 114, inter-regional projects (2.7 per cent) and two, global projects (0.1 per cent of expenditures).

Project expenditures were highest in Africa, which accounted for 32 per cent of the total, while those in the Americas amounted to 21 per cent, in Asia and the Far East to 25 per cent, and in Europe, the Mediterranean and Middle East to 20 per cent.

Sectorally, agriculture accounted for 33 per cent of the expenditures, industry for 20.3 per cent, public utilities for 15.4 per cent, and education and science for 11.1 per cent.

Four organizations—FAO, the United Nations, UNESCO and ILO—executed 71 per cent of all operational projects and spent 78 per cent of all the monies expended on UNDP-financed project inputs. As in previous years, the largest number of operational projects (1,114) were carried out by FAO, which spent $83.1 million, or 34 per cent of UNDP expenditures.

The United Nations, with 1,085 projects, accounted for 17.2 per cent of the total expenditures; UNESCO, with 686 projects, for 13.9 per cent; and ILO, with 539 projects, for 12.6 per cent.

A total of 10,139 experts belonging to 111 nationalities served in various UNDP-assisted projects during the year. Of these, 38 per cent were from France, the United Kingdom and the United States. The developing countries furnished 29 per cent of the experts; India was the principal source among this group of countries, providing 4.2 per cent of the total number of experts.

Technical Assistance component projects financed 4,465 fellowships during 1971 to enable nationals of developing countries to study or train abroad; 2,650 fellowships were awarded to national personnel appointed to Special Fund-assisted projects. Asia and the Far East received the largest number of fellowships—2,027, or 28.5 per cent.

The majority of fellowships were awarded for study or training in the industrially advanced countries, principally France, the United Kingdom and the United States, which together received 27 per cent of the fellows. The Federal Republic of Germany, Italy, Switzerland and the USSR also received a large number of fellows.

A growing number—46.7 per cent—of fellowship placements were made in countries which were recipients of UNDP aid. Also, some fellows attended regional and inter-regional seminars in the less developed countries.

Project equipment ordered during 1971 totalled $40.9 million in value, an increase of 19 per cent over 1970. Some 73 per cent of the total orders were placed with 10 industrially advanced countries. Major orders in 1971 included laboratory, agricultural and communications equipment, tools and motor vehicles. Orders for computers increased more than fivefold over 1970.

During 1971, field work was completed on 113 large-scale (Special Fund component) projects. This brought the cumulative number of projects completed in the field during 1959–1971 to 549, or 38 per cent of the large-scale projects approved by the Governing Council. An estimated 525 small-scale (Technical Assistance component) projects were also completed during the year.

Investment commitments resulting directly from large-scale projects exceeded $1,200 million in 1971, bringing over-all follow-up investment commitments to $5,800 million.

Provision of operational, executive and administrative personnel

Under the scheme for the provision of operational, executive and administrative personnel in the field of public administration, experts are appointed on a temporary basis as officials of the Governments being assisted, although they remain in the employ of the United Nations or the specialized agencies participating in the scheme. The United Nations, or the agency concerned, recruits the experts for service with Governments and supplements the salaries paid by Governments when they are too low to attract experts of the required calibre. The experts are responsible for training nationals to take over from them as rapidly and as completely as possible.

In 1971, the Technical Assistance component of UNDP financed 184 operational experts who worked in the following 47 countries and territories: Antigua, the Bahamas, Barbados, Botswana, British Honduras, the Cayman Islands, Chad, Cyprus, Equatorial Guinea, Ethiopia, Gambia, Ghana, Guinea, Guyana, Haiti, Iran, Ivory Coast, Jamaica, Kenya, Lesotho, Liberia, the Libyan Arab Republic, Malawi, Malaysia, Mali, Malta, Morocco, Nepal, the Netherlands Antilles, Niger, Nigeria, the Republic of Viet-Nam, Sierra Leone, Singapore, Somalia, Sudan, Swaziland, the Syrian Arab Republic, Tonga, Trinidad and Tobago, Uganda, the United Republic of Tanzania, West Irian, Western Samoa, Yemen, Zaire and Zambia.

Extra-budgetary operations

In 1971, as in previous years, the United Nations and its related agencies carried out some technical aid projects on the basis of extra-budgetary financing, that is with funds other than those provided under the assessed budgets of those organizations or under allocations for the Technical Assistance component of UNDP.

In 1971, the trust funds in which the Administrator of UNDP participated at the request of the Secretary-General of the United Nations included the following: (1) the United Nations Fund for Population Activities (see pp. 356-57); (2) the Special Industrial Services (SIS) Trust Fund, administered jointly by the UNDP Administrator and the Executive Director of UNIDO (see page 288); (3) the Fund of the United Nations for the Development of West Irian (see below); (4) the United Nations Capital Development Fund (see pp. 302-3); (5) the United Nations Volunteers (see below); (6) the Funds-in-Trust Programme for the Republic of Zaire, which in 1971 totalled $2,303,398; (7) the Swedish Trust Fund for Lesotho and Swaziland, which in 1971 totalled $1,160,000; and (8) the United Nations Korean Reconstruction Agency, whose residual assets as at the end of the year stood at $20,888.

The United Nations Fund for the Development of West Irian (FUNDWI), the largest funds-in-trust programme administered by UNDP, was financed from the $30 million pledged by the Government of the Netherlands and an approximately equivalent amount in local currency made available by the Government of Indonesia.

Seventy-two international personnel (of 24 nationalities) were on duty in West Irian in 1971, of whom 64 were project personnel.

Sixty-six counterpart personnel had completed or were in the process of completing fellowship training and travel grants financed by FUNDWI.

By the end of 1971, equipment and supplies estimated at a value of $7,350,000 had been either delivered or were *en route* to West Irian.

The West Irian Joint Development Foundation was formally inaugurated on 14 May 1971 in Djajapura. The Foundation, a small loan agency for which FUNDWI pledged $4 million and the Government of Indonesia an equal amount in local currency, was set up to encourage the development of transportation, export earning projects, agricultural processing, and fishing, through equity investment or concessional low-interest loans, and management and technical advice.

The United Nations Volunteers programme (UNV) established by the General Assembly on 7 December 1970,[4] completed its first year of operation in 1971. By the end of the year, formal requests for the services of more than 110 United

Nations Volunteers to work in various UNDP-assisted projects had been received from Governments of developing countries, and about 10 Volunteers had begun their respective assignments, serving in Chad, Niger and Yemen.

Contributions to the Special Voluntary Fund established to support the activities of the Volunteers programme were pledged by Cyprus, Denmark, the Holy See, India, Iran, Iraq, Laos, Lebanon, Morocco, Switzerland, Togo, Turkey and the United States. A number of non-governmental and private sources also contributed to the Fund. As at 1 December 1971, total pledges amounted to $256,955.

[4]See Y.U.N., 1970, pp. 356-57, text of resolution 2659(XXV).

Finances of the United Nations Development Programme

Programmes assisted by the United Nations Development Programme (UNDP) are financed by voluntary contributions of countries which are Members of the United Nations and/or the specialized agencies and the International Atomic Energy Agency.

In 1971, 126 Governments pledged contributions to UNDP totalling the equivalent of $240,589,769. In addition, cash counterpart contributions from recipient Governments amounted to $9,831,132, and programme costs payable in local currency by recipient Governments totalled $9,546,703. Within the total resources available and earmarkings of funds authorized by the Governing Council, allocations were issued by the Administrator totalling $288.8 million, including $27.4 million for the UNDP administrative and programme support costs budget.

Expenditures in 1971 totalled $317.1 million, including costs of Technical Assistance contingencies, costs of preparatory assistance to Governments, pre-project activities for Special Fund component project requests, the Special Industrial Services (SIS) programme, investment feasibility studies, and administrative and programme support of UNDP and the participating and executing agencies.

A summary statement of expenditures for 1971 from UNDP resources is shown below.

	Special Fund	Technical Assistance	Total
	(in millions of U.S. dollars)		
Project costs	196.9	64.5	261.4
Overhead costs	19.2	9.1	28.3
Sub-total	216.1	73.6	289.7
UNDP administrative and programme support costs budget			27.4
Total			317.1

Special Fund projects

In 1971, the UNDP Governing Council approved earmarkings from UNDP resources totalling $203,786,100 to finance 196 Special Fund component projects approved at the eleventh and twelfth sessions of the Governing Council. An additional amount of $159,877 was earmarked to cover costs of preparatory assistance missions not resulting in approved projects. After deduction of an amount of $2,207,673 of earmarkings surrendered in respect of completed and cancelled projects, the net earmarkings for 1971 amounted to $201,738,304.

Allocations issued by the UNDP Administrator in 1971 to cover project costs and pre-project activities, including preparatory assistance missions, totalled $181.5 million.

Technical Assistance projects

At its eleventh session, the Governing Council approved earmarkings from UNDP resources totalling $78,705,966 to cover the following costs of the Technical Assistance component projects in 1971: $57,316,000 for projects to be approved by the UNDP Administrator against country targets; $12,504,000 for inter-country projects; and $8,885,966 for overhead costs of the participating and executing agencies. As a result of decisions taken by the Council at its twelfth session, this last figure was increased to $9,108,115.

Allocations issued by the Administrator for country and inter-country projects and overhead costs of the participating and executing agencies totalled $77,780,490.

Revolving Fund

At its June 1970 session, the Governing Council approved a level of $14 million for the UNDP

Revolving Fund for the financing of Technical Assistance component contingency projects, Special Fund component preparatory activities, investment-oriented feasibility studies, projects of the Special Industrial Services type and activities of an urgent nature arising from emergency situations.

Allocations issued totalled $12,213,326 as at 31 December 1971. Of this amount, $1,522,799 was for Technical Assistance component contingencies; $3,487,647 for Special Industrial Services activities; $366,430 for investment feasibility studies; $4,346,200 for Special Fund component pre-project activities; and $2,490,250 for Special Fund preparatory assistance missions.

The unallocated balance of the Revolving Fund as at 31 December 1971 amounted to $1,786,674. This amount was to be surrendered to the UNDP account, since by decision of the Governing Council the Revolving Fund was to be replaced as of 1 January 1972 by a Programme Reserve, set up to meet unforeseen needs, to finance projects of the Special Industrial Services type, to finance unanticipated projects or phases and to meet other purposes as might be determined from time to time by the Governing Council. The 1972 level of the Programme Reserve was set at $9 million.

Contributions pledged for 1972

At the Pledging Conference held in New York on 1 November 1971, 119 Governments announced contributions to UNDP for 1972 totalling the equivalent of $172.7 million. Additional contributions subsequently announced by 12 Governments brought the total pledges to $269,862,073, as at 31 May 1972. These contributions brought to $2,377,301,438 the cumulative amount of all Government contributions to UNDP and its predecessor programmes.

CONTRIBUTIONS PLEDGED TO UNITED NATIONS DEVELOPMENT PROGRAMME FOR 1972
(As at 31 May 1972)

Country	Amount (In U.S. dollars)	Country	Amount (In U.S. dollars)	Country	Amount (In U.S. dollars)
Afghanistan	130,000	Finland	3,500,000	Malaysia	100,000
Albania	4,348	France	5,923,622	Maldives	1,000
Algeria	310,000	Gabon	43,165	Mali	10,000
Argentina	850,000	Gambia	3,120	Malta	8,400
Australia	2,000,000	Ghana	260,000	Mauritania	15,000
Austria	1,800,000	Greece	400,000	Mauritius	3,500
Bahrain	10,000	Guatemala	27,000	Mexico	500,000
Barbados	15,000	Guyana	105,000	Monaco	4,319
Belgium	3,796,095	Haiti	1,000	Mongolia	13,000
Bolivia	30,000	Holy See	5,000	Morocco	268,240
Botswana	8,000	Honduras	7,500	Nauru	575
Brazil	1,300,000	Hungary	126,674	Nepal	23,000
Bulgaria	88,000	Iceland	45,455	Netherlands	13,750,000
Burma	100,000	India	3,750,000	New Zealand	714,626
Byelorussian SSR	164,034	Indonesia	120,000	Nicaragua	28,000
Cameroon	34,222	Iran	1,000,000	Niger	25,180
Canada	18,000,000	Iraq	300,000	Nigeria	140,000
Central African Republic	4,317	Ireland	285,000	Norway	10,055,780
Ceylon	180,000	Israel	218,000	Oman	50,000
Chile	320,000	Italy	3,500,000	Pakistan	1,067,000
Colombia	400,000	Ivory Coast	90,000	Panama	115,000
Congo	7,194	Jamaica	100,000	Paraguay	3,048
Costa Rica	10,000	Japan	8,000,000	People's Democratic	
Cuba	100,000	Jordan	54,102	Republic of Yemen	1,650
Cyprus	23,316	Kenya	90,000	Peru	200,000
Czechoslovakia	761,773	Khmer Republic	21,622	Philippines	500,000
Denmark	20,741,758	Kuwait	350,000	Poland	630,000
Dominican Republic	18,000	Laos	13,000	Qatar	200,000
Ecuador	133,000	Lebanon	123,006	Republic of Korea	220,000
Egypt	459,982	Lesotho	10,000	Republic of Viet-Nam	22,000
El Salvador	15,000	Liberia	75,000	Romania	221,833
Equatorial Guinea	2,121	Libyan Arab Republic	310,000	Rwanda	7,320
Ethiopia	95,000	Luxembourg	45,455	Saudi Arabia	350,000
Federal Republic of Germany	15,028,036	Madagascar	24,490	Senegal	70,000
Fiji	10,000	Malawi	10,000	Sierra Leone	75,000

Country	Amount (In U.S. dollars)	Country	Amount (In U.S. dollars)	Country	Amount (In U.S. dollars)
Singapore	100,000	Trinidad and Tobago	90,000	Uruguay	179,500
Somalia	4,141	Tunisia	180,000	Venezuela	920,000
Spain	475,000	Turkey	663,000	Western Samoa	1,440
Sudan	170,000	Uganda	28,011	Yemen	2,300
Swaziland	5,601	Ukrainian SSR	407,117	Yugoslavia	908,589
Sweden	26,000,000	USSR	3,256,936	Zaire	200,000
Switzerland	4,250,000	United Kingdom	20,154,848	Zambia	109,000
Syrian Arab Republic	26,178	United Republic of Tanzania	84,034		
Thailand	355,500	United States	86,000,000	Total	269,862,073
Togo	6,000	Upper Volta	5,000		

DOCUMENTARY REFERENCES

A/8350. Financial reports and accounts for financial year ended 31 December 1970 and reports of Board of Auditors. Report of Advisory Committee on Administrative and Budgetary Questions, Section B.

A/8407/Add.1. United Nations Development Programme (UNDP). Financial reports and accounts for year ended 31 December 1970 and report of Board of Auditors.

A/8643. Operational activities for development. Budget estimates for administrative and programme support services of UNDP for year 1972. Report of Advisory Committee on Administrative and Budgetary Questions (ACABQ).

E/4954 and Corr.1. Report of Governing Council of UNDP on its 11th session, 14 January–2 February 1971, Chapter V and Annexes II-IV.

E/5043/Rev.1. Report of Governing Council of UNDP on its 12th session, Santiago, Chile, 7-23 June 1971, Chapter V and Annex III.

1971 Pledging Conference

1971 United Nations Pledging Conference on UNDP and United Nations Capital Development Fund, meetings 1 and 2 (A/CONF.53/SR.1-2).

A/CONF.53/1. Final Act of 1971 United Nations Pledging Conference on UNDP and United Nations Capital Development Fund.

Decisions of Governing Council, Economic and Social Council and General Assembly

During 1971, the Governing Council of the United Nations Development Programme (UNDP) held its eleventh session from 14 January to 2 February in New York, and its twelfth session from 7 to 23 June in Santiago, Chile. The decisions of the Governing Council, and of the Economic and Social Council and the General Assembly, on various aspects of UNDP activities are described below.

Capacity of the United Nations development system

In 1971, the UNDP Governing Council took a number of steps to implement the decisions taken by the General Assembly on 11 December 1970 on the capacity of the United Nations development system.[5]

At its eleventh session, the Governing Council approved a major reorganization of the UNDP administration, along the lines proposed in 1970 in Sir Robert Jackson's "A Study of the Capacity of the United Nations Development System."[6] Four regional bureaux were established: for Africa; Asia and the Far East; Latin America; and Europe, the Mediterranean and the Middle East. Each bureau was to be headed by an Assistant Administrator and to be responsible for the administration of UNDP programmes and projects in its respective region, including appraisal, implementation, evaluation and follow-up.

The Governing Council also approved the establishment of the Planning Bureau to carry out long-term planning, programme analysis, research and over-all evaluation of the Programme.

In a related action, the Council authorized the UNDP Administrator to delegate to UNDP Resident Representatives authority to approve projects costing up to $100,000.

With regard to the question of resources, the Governing Council noted the Administrator's call for a doubling of financial contributions to UNDP by 1975. The Governing Council urged Governments to increase their contributions to enable the Programme to assist them in achieving the aims of the Second United Nations Development Decade. The Council also approved indicative planning figures proposed by the Administrator for countries receiving assistance from UNDP, and established a Programme Reserve of $9 million to meet urgent and unforeseen needs.

The Council approved the establishment of a Management Information System at UNDP Headquarters and the participation of UNDP in the International Computing Centre.

Later in the year, at its twelfth session, the Council reviewed the progress in the preparation of country programmes. It was noted that the Governing Council would be considering the first

[5]See Y.U.N., 1970, pp. 350-55, text of resolution 2688(XXV) of 11 December 1970.
[6]See Y.U.N., 1970, p. 345.

group of country programmes at its thirteenth (January 1972) session. The Council also examined criteria to be used in calculating indicative planning figures for recipient countries.

Also, the Council: reviewed the role of the Inter-Agency Consultative Board under the country programming system; decided to consider further the question of an Advisory Panel on Programme Policy; reviewed the role of UNDP in promoting follow-up investment; and discussed the importance of recruiting high-calibre personnel for development assistance.

At its 1971 session, the General Assembly expressed its satisfaction with the steps taken by the UNDP Governing Council to implement the reforms called for by the Assembly on 11 December 1970.

The Assembly reaffirmed the authority of the Governing Council of UNDP, under the guidance of the General Assembly and the Economic and Social Council, as the main policy-formulating body of the Programme.

Among other things, the Assembly then requested the Governing Council: (1) to study, within the framework of the review of criteria for the indicative planning figures, ways and means of eliminating inequities due to historical circumstances, including those suffered by countries whose indicative planning figures were already committed to ongoing projects; (2) to consider ways and means of improving the procedures for global, inter-regional, regional and sub-regional projects in order to make them fully compatible with the country programmes of the region or area concerned; (3) to study ways of promoting a greater number of global projects in the context of the implementation of the objectives of the International Development Strategy for the Second Development Decade in the field of science and technology, emphasizing, among other things, the development of industry, agriculture and natural resources; (4) to prepare the omnibus statute of the Programme in such a way that it would incorporate new matters or procedures agreed upon by the Governing Council in 1972, as well as keep the flexibility necessary for future adaptation to changing situations; (5) to establish and implement special programmes in the identification and optimum utilization of the natural resources of the least developed among the developing countries, and to exempt those countries from the payment of local costs as long as required by their special situation; and (6) to define at the earliest opportunity the scope of the activities of the Inter-Agency Consultative Board.

Finally, the Assembly expressed the hope that increased contributions to UNDP would make it possible to enlarge substantially the resources available for the Programme, taking especially into account the interests and needs of the least developed among the developing countries.

These decisions by the Assembly were set forth in resolution 2814(XXVI), which was adopted on 14 December 1971 by a vote of 101 to 2, with 12 abstentions. This action was taken on the recommendation of the Second (Economic and Financial) Committee, which approved the text on 15 November 1971 by a vote of 88 to 2, with 10 abstentions. (For text of resolution, see DOCUMENTARY REFERENCES below.)

The text was based on a draft ultimately sponsored by the following 20 States: Afghanistan, Brazil, Burundi, Chile, Colombia, Cuba, Ecuador, Egypt, Guinea, Iraq, Kenya, Kuwait, the Libyan Arab Republic, Mali, Mauritania, Peru, the United Republic of Tanzania, Upper Volta, Uruguay and Venezuela.

Prior to the vote on the text, the Committee voted on and rejected a series of amendments submitted by the United Kingdom, and an amendment submitted by the Netherlands.

The Committee approved in a separate vote the provision requesting UNDP, in collaboration with the Committee on Natural Resources, to establish and implement special programmes in the field of the identification and optimum utilization of the natural resources of the least developed among the developing countries and to exempt them from the payment of local costs as long as required by their special situation.

Financial contributions to UNDP

Several decisions concerning the financing of UNDP were taken by the Economic and Social Council and the General Assembly during 1971.

On 26 July 1971, the Economic and Social Council, noting that the high expectations of an increase in resources as a result of the improvement in the capacity of the United Nations development system were not being fulfilled, expressed concern that the 9.6 per cent per annum increase in over-all resources for the period 1972–1976, the figure on which the UNDP Governing Council had based indicative planning figures, would result in the stagnation of the Programme at its present level in real terms. At that rate of increase, eight to 10 years would be required to double the current level of resources.

The Council: (1) requested the UNDP Governing Council to review at the first possible opportunity the planning estimates on which the indicative planning figures it had approved were based, in order to attain the goal of the doubling of the resources of the Programme during the coming five years; and (2) urged Governments to increase their financial contributions to the Programme so as to enable it to use as fully as possible its improved capacity to assist developing countries in reaching the objectives of the Second United Nations Development Decade.

These decisions by the Council were set forth in resolution 1615(LI), which was adopted by a roll-call vote of 17 to 4, with 6 abstentions. The text was based on a draft sponsored by Brazil, as orally amended. (For text, see DOCUMENTARY REFERENCES below.)

On 14 December 1971, the General Assembly endorsed the Economic and Social Council resolution of 26 July 1971. It did so after (*a*) considering the need for a fundamental and speedy strengthening of operational activities for development of the United Nations system in such a manner as to enable UNDP to carry, by 1976, a total programme of a least $1,000 million; (*b*) considering the need for a substantial increase in the financial resources of UNDP so as to enable it to utilize as fully as possible its improved capacity; and (*c*) bearing in mind that planning estimates and procedures of UNDP would take into account, among other things, the rate of growth of delivery capacity already existing in the system in terms of field programmes.

This decision of the Assembly was set forth in resolution 2811(XXVI), which was adopted, by a vote of 82 to 5, with 24 abstentions, on the recommendation of the Second Committee. The text, based on a proposal by Brazil, Chile, India, Madagascar, Pakistan, Tunisia and Yugoslavia, was approved by the Second Committee on 19 October 1971 by a recorded vote of 81 to 5, with 25 abstentions.

(For text, see DOCUMENTARY REFERENCES below.)

United Nations Volunteers programme

During 1971, the United Nations Volunteers programme was reviewed by the UNDP Governing Council, the Economic and Social Council and the General Assembly. The United Nations Volunteers, an international corp of volunteer workers for development, was established by the General Assembly on 7 December 1970[7] and came into being on 1 January 1971.

At its 1971 sessions, the UNDP Governing Council had before it two progress reports on the Volunteers programme prepared by the UNDP Administrator. The reports included proposals concerning the programme's financing, staffing and recruitment. At its eleventh session, the Governing Council approved the proposals in principle and requested the Administrator to report to it in detail at its thirteenth (January 1972) session on the experience gained from the operation of the Volunteers programme.

At its mid-1971 session, the Economic and Social Council had before it a report by the Secretary-General on the United Nations Volunteers programme. The report listed the steps that had been taken to implement the programme, including the establishment of a central co-ordinating office in New York and a liaison office in Geneva, Switzerland, the signing of an agreement with several international volunteer organizations, and the carrying out of negotiations with recipient countries. It was felt that the programme stood a fair chance of success, provided the Governments and agencies concerned with development continued to lend their support.

On 23 July 1971 the Council took note of the Secretary-General's report and transmitted it to the General Assembly. The Council did so by adopting without a vote resolution 1614(LI), as suggested by the Council President.

In a further decision on the Volunteers programme, the Council, among other things: requested all specialized agencies and volunteer organizations concerned to co-ordinate all volunteer activities within the United Nations-assisted projects with the Co-ordinator of the United Nations Volunteers; and urged Governments, international organizations and voluntary agencies to contribute to the Special Fund for United Nations Volunteers in order to meet the external cost of Volunteers from developing countries and to make the programme truly universal in scope.

This action was taken with the adoption of resolution 1618(LI), on 27 July 1971, by a vote of 23 to 0, with 4 abstentions. The text was based on a proposal by Kenya, Lebanon and Pakistan. (For text, see DOCUMENTARY REFERENCES below.)

The General Assembly also acted with regard to the Volunteers programme at its 1971 session.

The Assembly requested the Administrator and the Governing Council of UNDP to continue to assist in the promotion of the United Nations Volunteers programme, particularly in overcoming the financial difficulties which tended to inhibit its growth; and reaffirmed its conviction that United Nations Volunteers should not be sent to countries without the explicit request and approval of the recipient Governments concerned.

The Assembly asked all specialized agencies and other organizations in the United Nations system to channel all requests for Volunteers in development projects executed by them through the United Nations Volunteers programme and to co-ordinate all volunteer activities within United Nations-assisted projects with the Co-ordinator of the programme.

It also invited United Nations and specialized agencies Member States, international organizations, voluntary agencies and individuals to contribute in every way possible to the Special Voluntary Fund for the United Nations Volunteers.

[7]See Y.U.N., 1970, pp. 356-57, text of resolution 2659 (XXV).

These decisions were set forth in resolution 2810(XXVI), which was adopted by a vote of 100 to 0, with 13 abstentions, on 14 December 1971. This action was taken on the recommendation of the Second Committee, which had approved the text on 19 October 1971 by a vote of 93 to 0, with 18 abstentions.

The text was based on a proposal by Denmark, Greece, Iran, Kenya, Lebanon, Lesotho, Malaysia, Morocco, Pakistan, the Philippines, Togo, Turkey, the United States, Uruguay and Yemen. (For text of resolution, see DOCUMENTARY REFERENCES below.)

Other decisions

In another decision concerning the United Nations Development Programme, the Economic and Social Council acted to encourage projects in industrial development in developing countries.

The Council requested the UNDP Governing Council to instruct the Programme's Administrator: (1) to give special attention to requests in the field of industrial development submitted by the developing countries, in particular the least developed countries, including requests for industrial technological development and industrial pilot projects; and (2) to present to the Governing Council annually at its mid-year session a comprehensive progress report on the preparation, approval and implementation of projects in the field of industrial development.

These decisions were set forth in resolution 1617(LI), which was adopted unanimously. The text was based on a proposal sponsored by Brazil, Haiti, Hungary, Kenya, Pakistan, Sudan, the USSR and Yugoslavia. (For text, see DOCUMENTARY REFERENCES below.)

DOCUMENTARY REFERENCES

Capacity of the United Nations
development system

DECISIONS OF GOVERNING COUNCIL
E/4954 and Corr.1. Report of Governing Council of United Nations Development Programme (UNDP) on its 11th session, 14 January–2 February 1971, Chapter III.
E/5043/Rev.1. Report of Governing Council of UNDP on its fifth session, Santiago, Chile, 7-23 June 1971, Chapter III.

DECISIONS OF GENERAL ASSEMBLY

General Assembly—26th session
Second Committee, meetings 1385-1391, 1393, 1397-1399, 1404, 1407, 1408.
Plenary meeting 2017.

A/8399. Operational activities for development. Note by Secretary-General.
A/8403. Report of Economic and Social Council on work of its 50th and 51st sessions, Chapter VIII A.
A/C.2/L.1149. Statement by Administrator of UNDP in Second Committee on 14 October 1971, meeting 1385.
A/C.2/L.1154. Brazil, Chile, Colombia, Cuba, Kenya, Kuwait, Libyan Arab Republic, Peru, Uruguay, Venezuela: draft resolution.
A/C.2/L.1154/Rev.1-4. Afghanistan, Brazil, Chile, Colombia, Cuba, Ecuador, Guinea, Iraq, Kenya, Kuwait, Libyan Arab Republic, Mauritania, Peru, Uruguay, Venezuela: revised draft resolution.
A/C.2/L.1154/Rev.5. Revised draft resolution, sponsored by above 15 powers and by Burundi, Egypt, Mali, United Republic of Tanzania and Upper Volta, approved by Second Committee on 15 November 1971, meeting 1408, by 88 votes to 2, with 10 abstentions.
A/C.2/L.1155. Cuba, Kenya, Kuwait, Libyan Arab Republic, Venezuela: amendments to 10-power draft resolution, A/C.2/L.1154.
A/C.2/L.1157. Mauritania: amendments to 10-power draft resolution, A/C.2/L.1154.
A/C.2/L.1158. Philippines: amendment to 10-power draft resolution, A/C.2/L.1154.
A/C.2/L.1158/Rev.1. Philippines: revised amendment to 15-power revised draft resolution, A/C.2/L.1154/Rev.2.
A/C.2/L.1159. Trinidad and Tobago: amendments to 10-power draft resolution, A/C.2/L.1154.

A/C.2/L.1159/Rev.1. Trinidad and Tobago: revised amendments to 15-power revised draft resolution, A/C.2/L.1154/Rev.2.
A/C.2/L.1161. Barbados: amendments to 10-power draft resolution, A/C.2/L.1154.
A/C.2/L.1161/Rev.1. Barbados: revised amendments to 15-power revised draft resolution, A/C.2/L.1154/Rev.2.
A/C.2/L.1162. United Kingdom: amendments to 15-power revised draft resolution, A/C.2/L.1154/Rev.1.
A/C.2/L.1162/Rev.1. United Kingdom: revised amendments to 15-power revised draft resolution, A/C.2/L.1154/Rev.3.
A/C.2/L.1163. Norway: amendments to 15-power revised draft resolution, A/C.2/L.1154/Rev.1.
A/C.2/L.1164. Netherlands: amendments to 15-power revised draft resolution, A/C.2/L.1154/Rev.1.
A/C.2/L.1164/Rev.1. Netherlands: revised amendments to 15-power revised draft resolution, A/C.2/L.1154/Rev.3.
A/C.2/L.1167. Egypt: amendments to 15-power revised draft resolution, A/C.2/L.1154/Rev.3.
A/8563. Report of Second Committee, draft resolution VI.

RESOLUTION 2814(XXVI), as recommended by Second Committee, A/8563, adopted by Assembly on 14 December 1971, meeting 2017, by 101 votes to 2, with 12 abstentions.

The General Assembly,
Considering the need for the United Nations Development Programme to keep abreast of the increasing requirements of the developing countries in the context of the implementation of the International Development Strategy for the Second United Nations Development Decade, contained in General Assembly resolution 2626(XXV) of 24 October 1970,
Mindful of the fact that the challenges of development require the continuous adaptation, improvement and updating of the United Nations system for development assistance,
Expressing its satisfaction with the steps taken by the Governing Council of the United Nations Development Programme during its eleventh and twelfth sessions to implement the reforms incorporated in General Assembly resolution 2688(XXV) of 11 December 1970 on the capacity of the United Nations development system,
Aware of the significance and impact of subregional, regional and interregional projects on the harmonious and accelerated development of developing regions and countries, particularly the least developed among them,
Bearing in mind that the Governing Council of the United Nations Development Programme, in the decision taken at its

262nd meeting, has agreed that additional regional bureaux may be established when appropriate in order to meet the needs of the various geographical areas,

Cognizant of the fact that global projects have a special significance in terms of transfer as well as creation of technology in conditions especially adapted to the specific needs and requirements of the developing countries,

Bearing in mind also the need to maximize the capacity of the United Nations development system through the most efficient and rational utilization of all its components,

Recalling the decisions taken by the Governing Council of the United Nations Development Programme at its eleventh and twelfth sessions on the criteria to be followed in calculating indicative planning figures as reflected in paragraph 71 (*h*) of the report on its eleventh session and paragraph 84 of the report on its twelfth session,

Conscious of the fact that industrial development constitutes one of the essential features of development policies and planning at every stage of development,

Conscious also of the equally essential role of agricultural, pastoral, artisanal, tourism and mining development, as well as natural resources development in general, for a fully integrated and independent economy,

Stressing the importance it attaches to the developing countries themselves determining the priorities they attach to each sector of their economies, in accordance with paragraphs 5 and 22 of the annex to General Assembly resolution 2688(XXV),

Aware of the urgent necessity to improve the absorptive capacity of the least developed among the developing countries through appropriate financial and technical assistance,

1. *Reaffirms* the authority of the Governing Council of the United Nations Development Programme, under the guidance of the General Assembly and the Economic and Social Council, as the main policy-formulating body of the Programme from which the Administrator would receive the necessary directives for the general planning of the activities of the Programme, and commends the Governing Council for the guidance given to the Administrator in adapting the machinery of the Programme to the new demands made upon it, as reflected in the decision of the Governing Council adopted at its 262nd meeting on the organization, methods and general procedures of the Programme;

2. *Requests* the Governing Council of the United Nations Development Programme to study, within the framework of the review of criteria for the indicative planning figures at its fourteenth session, ways and means of eliminating inequities due to historical circumstances, including those suffered by countries whose indicative planning figures are already committed to ongoing projects as a result of their special circumstances;

3. *Stresses* the importance it attaches to the regional bureaux of the United Nations Development Programme and to their operative capacity through direct access to the Administrator of the Programme as essential elements for the fulfilment of the objectives of the Programme;

4. *Calls upon* the Governing Council of the United Nations Development Programme to consider, within the framework of the comprehensive review to be undertaken at its fourteenth session, ways and means of improving the procedures for global, interregional, regional and subregional projects—in accordance with paragraphs 21, 22 and 23 of the annex to General Assembly resolution 2688(XXV)—in order to make them fully compatible with the country programmes of the region or area concerned while according equitable emphasis to the interests and priorities of all developing countries, in particular the least developed among them, members of the regional economic commissions and of the United Nations Economic and Social Office at Beirut;

5. *Requests* the Governing Council of the United Nations Development Programme to study the possible ways of promoting, within the present proportional allocation of resources, in accordance with paragraphs 25 and 26 of the annex to General Assembly resolution 2688(XXV), a greater number of global projects in the context of the implementation of the objectives of the International Development Strategy for the Second United Nations Development Decade in the field of science and technology, with emphasis on industrial development and agricul-

tural, pastoral, artisanal, tourism and mining development, as well as natural resources development in general;

6. *Also stresses* that the Governing Council of the United Nations Development Programme should prepare the omnibus statute of the Programme in such a way that it incorporates any new matter or procedures that might be agreed upon at its thirteenth and fourteenth sessions and, at the same time, keeps the flexibility necessary for the future adaptation of the Programme to changing situations;

7. *Requests* the United Nations Development Programme:

(a) To establish and implement, in collaboration with the Committee on Natural Resources, special programmes in the field of the identification and optimum utilization of the natural resources of the least developed among the developing countries;

(b) To exempt the least developed among the developing countries from the payment of local costs as long as required by their special situation;

8. *Further stresses* that the scope of the activities of the Inter-Agency Consultative Board must correspond to its functions of interagency consultations and co-ordination at the secretariat level and should be defined accordingly by the Governing Council of the United Nations Development Programme at the earliest possible opportunity, in the light of paragraph 65 of the annex to General Assembly resolution 2688(XXV);

9. *Endorses* Economic and Social Council resolution 1617(LI) of 27 July 1971 on projects in the field of industrial development;

10. *Expresses the hope* that increased contributions to the United Nations Development Programme will make it possible to enlarge substantially the resources available for the Programme, taking especially into account the interests and needs of the least developed among the developing countries.

Financial contributions to UNDP

Economic and Social Council—51st session
Plenary meetings 1788, 1791.

E/4954 and Corr.1. Report of Governing Council of UNDP on its 11th session, 14 January–2 February 1971, Chapter III B and Annex V.
E/L.1447 and Corr.1. Brazil: draft resolution.

RESOLUTION 1615(LI) as proposed by Brazil, E/L.1447, as orally revised by sponsor and by Lebanon, adopted by Council on 26 July 1971, meeting 1791, by roll-call vote of 17 to 4, with 6 abstentions, as follows:

In favour: Brazil, Ceylon, Ghana, Haiti, Indonesia, Jamaica, Kenya, Lebanon, Madagascar, Malaysia, Niger, Pakistan, Peru, Sudan, Tunisia, Uruguay, Yugoslavia.
Against: France, Italy, United Kingdom, United States.
Abstaining: Greece, Hungary, New Zealand, Norway, USSR, Zaire.

The Economic and Social Council,

Noting that the high expectations of an increase in resources as a result of the improvement in the capacity of the United Nations development system are not being fulfilled,

Considering that the provision for a growth of 9.6 per cent per annum over the next five years in the over-all resources for establishing indicative planning figures constitutes a departure from the provisions concerning the United Nations Development Programme approved by the General Assembly in its resolution 2688(XXV) of 11 December 1970, which considered the rate of growth in the resources of the Programme during the past few years as only one of the bases and the minimum to be taken into account for calculating future rates of growth,

Further noting with concern that, with a 9.6 per cent per annum increase, the over-all increase in contributions during the next five years will be less than 60 per cent and that, at this rate, eight to ten years might be required to double the current level of resources,

Recognizing that one of the serious consequences of a 9.6 per cent growth in contributions would be a decline in the rate of increase in the expenditures for field programmes from 16 per cent during the last five years to less than 10 per cent during the next five years, which would imply that even the present capacity of the United Nations development system will remain unused,

Considering further that if allowance is made for increase in the cost of the Programme, a 9.6 per cent per annum growth in contributions will result in the stagnation of the Programme at its present level in real terms,

Believing that the provision in the indicative planning figures for only 9.6 per cent growth in resources is a source of concern when viewed in the context of the Administrator's statement that a doubling of the programme by 1975 is a realistic goal and when Governments have accepted the provision within the framework of the International Development Strategy for the Second United Nations Development Decade, to make available an increasing proportion of their assistance in the form of official financial transfers,

1. *Requests* the Governing Council of the United Nations Development Programme to review at the first possible opportunity the planning estimates on which the indicative planning figures as approved by it were based, in order to attain the goal of the doubling of the resources of the Programme during the next five years, thus imparting a real meaning to the concept of country programming on a long-term dynamic basis;

2. *Urges* Governments to increase their financial contributions to the Programme, so as to enable it to use as fully as possible its improved capacity to assist developing countries in reaching the objectives of the Second United Nations Development Decade.

General Assembly—26th session
Second Committee, meetings 1385-1390, 1392.
Plenary meeting 2017.

A/8399. Note by Secretary-General.
A/C.2/L.1149. Statement by Administrator of UNDP in Second Committee on 14 October 1971, meeting 1385.
A/C.2/L.1150. Brazil, Chile, India, Madagascar, Pakistan, Tunisia, Yugoslavia: draft resolution, approved by Second Committee on 19 October 1971, meeting 1392, by recorded vote of 81 to 5, with 25 abstentions, as follows:

In favour: Afghanistan, Algeria, Bahrain, Barbados, Bhutan, Bolivia, Brazil, Burma, Burundi, Cameroon, Central African Republic, Ceylon, Chad, Chile, China, Colombia, Cuba, Cyprus, Dahomey, Dominican Republic, Ecuador, Egypt, El Salvador, Ethiopia, Ghana, Guatemala, Guinea, Guyana, Honduras, India, Indonesia, Iran, Iraq, Israel, Ivory Coast, Jamaica, Jordan, Kenya, Kuwait, Lebanon, Lesotho, Liberia, Libyan Arab Republic, Madagascar, Malaysia, Mali, Malta, Mauritania, Mexico, Mongolia, Morocco, Nepal, Nicaragua, Nigeria, Pakistan, Panama, Philippines, Romania, Rwanda, Saudi Arabia, Senegal, Sierra Leone, Singapore, Sudan, Swaziland, Sweden, Syrian Arab Republic, Thailand, Togo, Trinidad and Tobago, Tunisia, Turkey, Uganda, United Republic of Tanzania, Upper Volta, Uruguay, Venezuela, Yemen, Yugoslavia, Zaire, Zambia.

Against: Australia, Canada, Japan, United Kingdom, United States.

Abstaining: Argentina, Austria, Belgium, Bulgaria, Byelorussian SSR, Czechoslovakia, Denmark, Fiji, Finland, France, Greece, Hungary, Iceland, Ireland, Italy, Khmer Republic, Netherlands, New Zealand, Norway, Poland, Portugal, South Africa, Spain, Ukrainian SSR, USSR.

A/8563. Report of Second Committee, draft resolution III.

RESOLUTION 2811 (XXVI), as recommended by Second Committee, A/8563, adopted by Assembly on 14 December 1971, meeting 2017, by 82 votes to 5, with 24 abstentions.

The General Assembly,
Considering the need for a fundamental and speedy strengthening of operational activities for development of the United Nations system in such a manner as to enable the United Nations Development Programme to carry, by 1976, a total programme of at least $1,000 million,

Considering further the need for a substantial increase in the financial resources of the United Nations Development Programme so as to enable it to utilize as fully as possible its improved capacity,

Bearing in mind that planning estimates and procedures of the United Nations Development Programme will take into account, *inter alia,* the rate of growth of delivery capacity already existing in the system in terms of field programmes,

Endorses Economic and Social Council resolution 1615(LI) of 26 July 1971.

United Nations Volunteers programme

Economic and Social Council—51st session
Plenary meetings 1788-1790, 1792.

E/4954 and Corr.1. Report of Governing Council of UNDP on its 11th session, 14 January–2 February 1971, Chapter IV.
E/5028. Report of Secretary-General.
E/5043/Rev.1. Report of Governing Council of UNDP on its 12th session, Santiago, Chile, 7-23 June 1971, Chapter VII.

RESOLUTION 1614 (LI), as suggested by Council President, taking note of report of Secretary-General on United Nations Volunteers programme and transmitting it to General Assembly at its 26th session, adopted without vote by Council on 23 July 1971, meeting 1790.

E/L.1446. Pakistan: draft resolution.
E/L.1446/Rev.1. Kenya, Lebanon, Pakistan: revised draft resolution.

RESOLUTION 1618 (LI), as proposed by 3 powers, E/L.1446/Rev.1, and as further orally revised by sponsors, adopted by Council on 27 July 1971, meeting 1792, by 23 votes to 0, with 4 abstentions.

The Economic and Social Council,
Recalling with appreciation the initiative taken by the Government of Iran for the creation of an international corps of volunteers,

Further recalling General Assembly resolution 2659(XXV) of 7 December 1970, which established the United Nations Volunteers programme,

Noting the report of the Secretary-General,

Welcoming the appointment of the Co-ordinator of the United Nations Volunteers,

Regretting that so far no substantial contributions to the Special Fund for United Nations Volunteers, established under operative paragraph 4 of General Assembly resolution 2659 (XXV), have been received,

1. *Commends* the efforts of the Administrator of the United Nations Development Programme and the Co-ordinator of the United Nations Volunteers in initiating the programme;

2. *Requests* all the specialized agencies and volunteer organizations concerned to co-ordinate all volunteer activities within the United Nations-assisted projects with the Co-ordinator of the United Nations Volunteers;

3. *Urges* Governments, international organizations and voluntary agencies, especially those who are in a position to do so, to contribute to the Special Fund for United Nations Volunteers, in order to meet the external costs of Volunteers from developing countries and to make the programme truly universal in scope.

General Assembly—26th session
Second Committee, meetings 1385-1392.
Plenary meeting 2017.

A/8399. Note by Secretary-General, part D.
A/8401. Report of Secretary-General on work of the Organization, 16 June 1970–15 June 1971, Part III, Chapter VI B 2.
A/8403. Report of Economic and Social Council on work of its 50th and 51st sessions, Chapter VIII D.
A/C.2/L.1145 and Rev.1. Denmark, Greece, Iran, Kenya, Lebanon, Lesotho, Malaysia, Morocco, Pakistan, Philippines, Togo,

Turkey, United States, Uruguay, Yemen: draft resolution and revision, as further orally revised by sponsors, approved by Second Committee on 19 October 1971, meeting 1391, by 93 votes to 0, with 18 abstentions.
A/8563. Report of Second Committee, draft resolution II.

RESOLUTION 2810(XXVI), as recommended by Second Committee, A/8563, adopted by Assembly on 14 December 1971, meeting 2017, by 100 votes to 0, with 13 abstentions.

The General Assembly,
Recalling its resolution 2659(XXV) of 7 December 1970 establishing the United Nations Volunteers programme within the existing framework of the United Nations system,
Taking note of Economic and Social Council resolution 1618(LI) of 27 July 1971 and also the report of the Governing Council of the United Nations Development Programme on its twelfth session,
Noting with appreciation the statement of the Co-ordinator of the United Nations Volunteers programme,
Reaffirming its conviction that the active participation of the younger generation in all aspects of social and economic life constitutes an important additional source of trained manpower in the over-all development efforts, thus ensuring the increased effectiveness of collective efforts necessary for a better society,
1. *Takes note* of the report of the Secretary-General on the United Nations Volunteers programme, which was submitted in accordance with General Assembly resolution 2659(XXV);
2. *Requests* the Administrator of the United Nations Development Programme, as well as the Governing Council of the Programme, to continue to assist in the promotion of the United Nations Volunteers programme, particularly in overcoming the question of financial difficulties which tend to inhibit the growth of this programme;
3. *Reaffirms* its conviction that United Nations Volunteers should not be sent to countries without the explicit request and approval of the recipient Governments concerned;
4. *Requests* all the specialized agencies and other organizations in the United Nations system to channel all requests for volunteers in development projects executed by them through the United Nations Volunteers programme and to co-ordinate all volunteer activities within United Nations-assisted projects with the Co-ordinator of the programme;
5. *Invites* Governments of States Members of the United Nations or members of specialized agencies, international organizations, voluntary agencies and individuals to contribute in every way possible to the Special Voluntary Fund for the United Nations Volunteers;
6. *Requests* the Secretary-General and the Administrator of the United Nations Development Programme to report, through the Governing Council and the Economic and Social Council, to the General Assembly at its twenty-seventh session on the progress made in the implementation of Assembly resolution 2659 (XXV).

Other decisions

INDUSTRIAL DEVELOPMENT PROJECTS

Economic and Social Council—51st session
Plenary meetings 1788-1790, 1792.

E/L.1444. Brazil, Kenya, Pakistan, USSR, Yugoslavia: draft decision.
E/L.1444/Rev.1 Brazil, Haiti, Hungary, Kenya, Pakistan, Sudan, USSR, Yugoslavia: draft resolution.
E/L.1448. Madagascar: amendment to 5-power draft decision, E/L.1444.
E/L.1449. United Kingdom and United States: amendments to 5-power draft decision, E/L.1444.

RESOLUTION 1617(LI), as proposed by 8 powers, E/L.1444/Rev.1, as further orally revised by sponsors, adopted unanimously by Council on 27 July 1971, meeting 1792.

The Economic and Social Council,

Considering that industrial development constitutes one of the basic features of an integrated and comprehensive development to which all countries are entitled for the achievement of economic independence and well-being,
Considering further that the United Nations Industrial Development Organization and the United Nations Development Programme have an essential role to play in assisting developing countries, in all stages of development, to acquire the necessary industrial technical capabilities as defined by their own development plans,
Taking into account the need to impart more dynamism and speed to the processing of requests for assistance in the field of industrial development,
1. *Requests* the Governing Council of the United Nations Development Programme to instruct the Administrator of the Programme:
(a) To give, in accordance with the priorities assigned by the developing countries, special attention to requests submitted by them, and in particular to those of the least developed among them, in the field of industrial development, including requests for industrial technological development and industrial pilot projects;
(b) To present to the Governing Council at its summer session each year a comprehensive progress report on the preparation, approval and implementation of projects in the field of industrial development;
2. *Further requests* the Governing Council to give during its summer session each year due consideration to the report referred to above.

ENLARGEMENT OF MEMBERSHIP OF UNDP GOVERNING COUNCIL

General Assembly—26th session
Second Committee, meetings 1385-1390, 1395, 1397-1399, 1404-1407.
Plenary meeting 2017.

A/C.2/L.1146. Afghanistan, Argentina, Bolivia, Brazil, Chile, Colombia, Congo, Ghana, Indonesia, Iran, Kenya, Malaysia, Nigeria, Peru, Philippines, Sudan, Swaziland, Thailand, Yugoslavia, Zaire: draft resolution.
A/C.2/L.1146/Rev.1. Afghanistan, Congo, Ghana, Indonesia, Iran, Kenya, Lebanon, Malaysia, Nigeria, Philippines, Sudan, Swaziland, Thailand, Yugoslavia, Zaire: revised draft resolution.
A/C.2/L.1146/Rev.2. Afghanistan, Congo, Ghana, Indonesia, Iran, Kenya, Malaysia, Nigeria, Philippines, Sudan, Swaziland, Thailand, Tunisia, Yemen, Yugoslavia, Zaire: revised draft resolution, approved by Second Committee on 12 November 1971, meeting 1406, by roll-call vote of 74 to 7, with 29 abstentions, as follows:

In favour: Afghanistan, Algeria, Australia, Austria, Belgium, Burma, Burundi, Cameroon, Congo, Cuba, Denmark, Egypt, Equatorial Guinea, Ethiopia, Finland, France, Ghana, Greece, Guinea, Iceland, India, Indonesia, Iran, Iraq, Ireland, Italy, Ivory Coast, Japan, Jordan, Kenya, Khmer Republic, Kuwait, Laos, Lebanon, Lesotho, Liberia, Libyan Arab Republic, Luxembourg, Madagascar, Malaysia, Mali, Mauritania, Morocco, Nepal, Netherlands, New Zealand, Niger, Nigeria, Norway, Pakistan, People's Democratic Republic of Yemen, Philippines, Portugal, Rwanda, Saudi Arabia, Senegal, Sierra Leone, Singapore, Spain, Sudan, Swaziland, Sweden, Syrian Arab Republic, Thailand, Togo, Tunisia, Turkey, Uganda, United Republic of Tanzania, Upper Volta, Yemen, Yugoslavia, Zaire, Zambia.
Against: Argentina, Canada, Malta, Panama, Paraguay, Peru, United States.
Abstaining: Barbados, Bolivia, Brazil, Bulgaria, Byelorussian SSR, Chile, Colombia, Czechoslovakia, Dominican Republic, Ecuador, El Salvador, Guatemala, Guyana, Honduras, Hungary, Israel, Jamaica, Mexico, Mongolia, Nicaragua, Poland, Romania, South Africa, Trinidad and Tobago, Ukrainian SSR, USSR, United Kingdom, Uruguay, Venezuela.

A/C.2/L.1153. United Kingdom: amendments to 20-power draft resolution, A/C.2/L.1146.

A/C.2/L.1160. Barbados: amendments to 20-power draft resolution, A/C.2/L.1146.

A/C.2/L.1177. Argentina, Bolivia, Colombia, Jamaica, Peru, Venezuela: amendment to 16-power revised draft resolution, A/C.2/L.1146/Rev.2.

A/C.2/L.1178. Algeria, Bulgaria, Byelorussian SSR, Cuba, Czechoslovakia, Egypt, Hungary, Mongolia, People's Democratic Republic of Yemen, Poland, Romania, Ukrainian SSR, USSR: amendment to 16-power revised draft resolution, A/C.2/L.1146/Rev.2.

A/C.2/L.1179. Canada: amendment to 16-power revised draft resolution, A/C.2/L.1146/Rev.2.

A/L.658. Philippines: amendment to draft resolution V recommended by Second Committee in A/8563.

A/8563. Report of Second Committee, draft resolution V.

RESOLUTION 2813 (XXVI), as recommended by Second Committee, A/8563, as amended by Philippines, A/L.658, adopted by Assembly on 14 December 1971, meeting 2017, by recorded vote of 86 to 2, with 25 abstentions, as follows:

In favour: Afghanistan, Algeria, Australia, Austria, Bahrain, Belgium, Brazil,* Burma, Burundi, Cameroon, Central African Republic, Chile, Colombia, Congo, Costa Rica, Cuba, Cyprus, Dahomey, Denmark, Egypt, Ethiopia, Fiji, Finland, France, Gabon, Ghana, Greece, Guatemala, Guinea, Honduras, Iceland, India, Indonesia, Iran, Ireland, Israel, Italy, Ivory Coast, Japan, Jordan, Kenya, Khmer Republic, Kuwait, Laos, Lebanon, Liberia, Libyan Arab Republic, Luxembourg, Madagascar, Malawi, Malaysia, Mali, Mauritania, Morocco, Nepal, Netherlands, New Zealand, Niger, Nigeria, Norway, Oman, Panama, People's Democratic Republic of Yemen, Philippines, Portugal, Qatar, Rwanda, Senegal, Sierra Leone, Singapore, Somalia, Spain, Sudan, Swaziland, Sweden, Thailand, Togo, Tunisia, Turkey, Uganda, United Republic of Tanzania, Upper Volta, Yemen, Yugoslavia, Zaire, Zambia.

Against: Canada, United States.

Abstaining: Argentina, Bolivia, Bulgaria, Byelorussian SSR, Czechoslovakia, Ecuador, El Salvador, Guyana, Hungary, Jamaica, Malta, Mexico, Mongolia, Nicaragua, Paraguay, Peru, Poland, Romania, South Africa, Trinidad and Tobago, Ukrainian SSR, USSR, United Kingdom, Uruguay, Venezuela.

*Subsequently, Brazil advised the Secretariat that it had intended to abstain.

The General Assembly,

Having considered the reports of the Governing Council of the United Nations Development Programme, in particular the report on its twelfth session,

Bearing in mind its resolution 2626(XXV) of 24 October 1970 containing the International Development Strategy for the Second United Nations Development Decade,

Realizing the important role that the United Nations Development Programme has to play in the achievement of the goals, objectives and policy measures of the International Development Strategy,

Recalling its resolution 2688(XXV) of 11 December 1970 on the capacity of the United Nations development system,

Recalling further its resolution 2029(XX) of 22 November 1965 consolidating the Special Fund and the Expanded Programme of Technical Assistance in the United Nations Development Programme, particularly the annex thereto concerning the composition of the Governing Council of the United Nations Development Programme, which was to consist of thirty-seven members,

Convinced that a strengthened and expanded United Nations Development Programme and the prospect of its handling, by 1975, resources double that of present resources necessitate the increased participation of Member States in the work of the Governing Council,

Convinced further that a larger membership of the Governing Council would make the Council more representative of both developed and developing countries,

Aware that since the United Nations Development Programme

was established in 1965 a number of new States have been admitted to membership in the United Nations,

1. *Decides* to enlarge the membership of the Governing Council of the United Nations Development Programme to forty-eight members to be elected from among States Members of the United Nations or members of specialized agencies or of the International Atomic Energy Agency, subject to the following conditions:

(*a*) Twenty-seven seats shall be filled by developing countries, allocated as follows:

(i) Eleven seats for African States;

(ii) Nine seats for Asian States and Yugoslavia;

(iii) Seven seats for Latin American States;

(*b*) Twenty-one seats shall be filled by economically more advanced countries, allocated as follows:

(i) Seventeen seats for Western European and other States;

(ii) Four seats for Eastern European States;

(*c*) The composition of seats in each group should at all times give due expression to adequate subregional representation;

(*d*) Elections to these forty-eight seats shall be for a term of three years and retiring members shall be eligible for re-election;

2. *Requests* the Economic and Social Council to elect, at its resumed fifty-first session, the additional eleven members of the Governing Council.

Economic and Social Council—51st session
Plenary Meeting 1808.

E/5043/Rev.1. Report of Governing Council of UNDP on its 12th session, Santiago, Chile, 7–23 June 1971, Annex V.

E/5073/Add.1. Resolutions adopted by Economic and Social Council at its resumed 51st session. Other decisions, p. 4.

REPORTS OF GOVERNING COUNCIL

Economic and Social Council—51st session
Plenary meetings 1788-1790.

E/4954 and Corr.1. Report of Governing Council of UNDP on its 11th session, 14 January–2 February 1971.

E/5043/Rev.1. Report of Governing Council of UNDP on its 12th session, Santiago, Chile, 7–23 June 1971.

RESOLUTION 1613(LI), as suggested by Council President, taking note of reports of Governing Council of UNDP on its 11th and 12th sessions, adopted without vote by Council on 23 July 1971, meeting 1790.

General Assembly—26th session
Second Committee, meetings 1385-1390.
Plenary meeting 2017.

A/8563. Report of Second Committee, draft resolution I, as suggested by Committee Chairman, approved without objection by Committee on 18 October 1971, meeting 1390.

RESOLUTION 2809(XXVI), as recommended by Second Committee, A/8563, taking note with appreciation of reports of Governing Council of UNDP on its 11th and 12th sessions, adopted without objection on 14 December 1971, meeting 2017.

APPOINTMENT OF ADMINISTRATOR

General Assembly—26th session
Plenary meeting 2017.

A/8475. Note by Secretary-General.

A/8429. Resolutions adopted by General Assembly during its 26th session, 21 September–22 December 1971. Decisions, p. 21.

Other documents

A/8401. Report of Secretary-General on work of the Organization, 16 June 1970–15 June 1971, Part III, Chapter VI A-C.

Pre-Investment News. Issued monthly, January-December 1971.

Pre-Investment Assistance Provided in 1971 Under the Special Fund Component
of the United Nations Development Programme

Country or Territory	Total Expenditures (in thousands of U.S. dollars)	Number of Experts	Number of Fellowships	Value of Equipment Provided (in thousands of U.S. dollars)	Country or Territory	Total Expenditures (in thousands of U.S. dollars)	Number of Experts	Number of Fellowships	Value of Equipment Provided (in thousands of U.S. dollars)
Afghanistan	2,575	101	62	304	Kenya	2,997	130	27	278
Algeria	3,562	218	51	719	Khmer Republic	655	36	16	60
Argentina	2,231	80	37	520	Kuwait	359	19	4	33
Australia	—	—	—	—	Laos	—	5	10	—
Barbados	—	7	4	—	Lebanon	1,194	56	20	186
Bolivia	2,113	59	6	436	Lesotho	1,156	28	2	123
Botswana	637	29	3	110	Liberia	1,297	56	3	179
Brazil	3,302	135	32	534	Libyan Arab				
Bulgaria	858	64	65	291	Republic	1,125	45	17	67
Burma	582	7	8	164	Madagascar	2,453	105	23	492
Burundi	1,797	77	13	298	Malawi	435	25	12	133
Cameroon	1,753	69	17	228	Malaysia	2,380	92	35	483
Central African					Mali	1,791	86	52	292
Republic	1,346	41	7	293	Malta	232	17	3	13
Ceylon	1,460	67	30	165	Mauritania	820	22	14	177
Chad	223	17	6	50	Mauritius	503	34	4	77
Chile	5,253	104	38	1,718	Mexico	2,274	75	29	630
China	824	25	49	172	Mongolia	1,818	34	4	980
Colombia	2,660	105	61	636	Morocco	2,701	125	18	334
Congo	1,718	62	12	321	Nepal	1,688	124	35	283
Costa Rica	450	19	14	76	Netherlands				
Cuba	1,173	36	17	442	Antilles	48	—	8	—
Cyprus	1,231	69	12	218	New Caledonia	59	2	—	4
Czechoslovakia	195	9	8	4	New Zealand	—	—	1	—
Dahomey	693	25	23	302	Nicaragua	422	26	11	57
Dominican					Niger	1,520	62	15	323
Republic	1,056	40	10	248	Nigeria	3,076	131	29	585
Ecuador	929	37	18	230	Pacific Islands,				
Egypt	3,793	126	66	1,328	Trust Territory of	—	—	2	—
El Salvador	878	22	14	213	Pakistan	3,660	81	46	498
Ethiopia	3,200	157	41	517	Panama	1,472	55	9	160
Fiji	439	27	8	42	Papua				
Gabon	890	20	6	204	New Guinea	400	14	1	25
Gambia	—	—	5	—	Paraguay	598	32	11	81
Ghana	2,204	77	32	291	People's Democratic				
Greece	1,572	68	21	150	Republic of Yemen	1,192	41	35	207
Guatemala	176	7	11	16	Peru	2,600	103	21	464
Guinea	2,131	78	6	474	Philippines	2,879	104	52	574
Guyana	271	7	5	25	Poland	902	20	68	435
Haiti	376	23	6	69	Qatar	54	2	—	—
Honduras	535	24	7	81	Republic of				
Hong Kong	—	—	5	—	Korea	2,656	109	63	623
Hungary	376	35	26	139	Republic of				
India	6,044	159	101	2,778	Viet-Nam	859	18	17	286
Indonesia	3,633	307	57	900	Romania	1,027	75	44	112
Iran	3,469	138	36	471	Rwanda	1,212	34	12	144
Iraq	2,846	120	55	496	Saudi Arabia	1,071	78	9	132
Ireland	24	—	—	9	Senegal	1,809	99	7	151
Israel	569	21	17	246	Sierra Leone	917	36	11	74
Ivory Coast	2,432	153	25	465	Singapore	2,239	65	29	655
Jamaica	1,248	56	14	261	Solomon Islands				
Japan	197	15	13	12	(British)	103	3	—	24
Jordan	1,886	43	10	899	Somalia	1,483	52	12	161

Country or Territory	Total Expenditures (in thousands of U.S. dollars)	Number of Experts	Number of Fellowships	Value of Equipment Provided (in thousands of U.S. dollars)	Country or Territory	Total Expenditures (in thousands of U.S. dollars)	Number of Experts	Number of Fellowships	Value of Equipment Provided (in thousands of U.S. dollars)
Spain	1,526	116	23	333	Uruguay	460	17	10	59
Sudan	2,439	74	36	652	Venezuela	1,542	89	28	25
Surinam	339	12	2	168	West Irian	—	10	—	—
Swaziland	102	17	2	4	Western Samoa	341	23	6	83
Syrian Arab					Yemen	837	95	8	123
Republic	1,423	65	19	399	Yugoslavia	942	58	49	224
Thailand	2,650	91	205	331	Zaire	4,054	110	21	474
Togo	1,767	63	27	600	Zambia	2,280	97	23	236
Tonga	—	—	1	—					
Trinidad and					Regional, inter-				
Tobago	423	14	5	62	regional and global				
Tunisia	2,526	156	39	452	projects	22,353	509	—	3,205
Turkey	3,616	120	35	867	Not specified	—	—	9	—
Uganda	1,090	52	23	127	Total*	189,057	7,441	2,650	38,004
United Republic									
of Tanzania	1,639	83	41	231					
Upper Volta	762	29	7	189	*Totals may not equal sums of items because of rounding.				

United Nations programmes of technical co-operation

The term "United Nations programmes of technical co-operation" is used in a collective sense to describe the broad range of activities carried out by the United Nations in developing countries. These activities are financed under both the regular budget of the United Nations and the United Nations Development Programme (UNDP), a co-operative undertaking of the United Nations and its related agencies which is financed from voluntary contributions by Governments.

Activities in 1971

During 1971, obligations for the United Nations programmes of technical co-operation were $60.9 million, as compared with $55.3 million in 1970 and $47.9 million in 1969.

The expenditures in 1971 under various programmes were as follows:

(1) "regular programme" allocations, that is, financed from the regular budget of the United Nations—$5.7 million;

(2) allocations from the Technical Assistance component of UNDP—$13.4 million;

(3) projects under the UNDP Special Fund component for which the United Nations served as executing agency—$35.3 million;

(4) extra-budgetary sources (including the United Nations Educational and Training Programme for Southern Africa and programmes financed from the United Nations Fund for Population Activities and the Fund of the United Nations for

the Development of West Irian)—$6.5 million.

Under the regular programme, regional and inter-regional activities accounted for 63.2 per cent of expenditures in 1971, as compared with 52.8 per cent in 1970 and 51.2 per cent in 1969. Under all programmes—the regular programme, the Technical Assistance component of UNDP and other programmes—regional and inter-regional activities accounted for 31.6 per cent of expenditures in 1971, as compared with 27.2 per cent in 1970 and 29.9 per cent in 1969.

The total number of experts, excluding those working on Special Fund component projects was 1,393, as compared with 1,241 in 1970. The number of experts working on Special Fund component projects totalled 943 in 1971, compared with 977 in 1970. During the year, 1,052 experts received their initial appointments.

The number of fellowships awarded in 1971 totalled 2,043, as compared with 2,344 in 1970. This included Special Fund fellowships (which totalled 753 in 1971), as well as those awarded under the United Nations Educational and Training Programme for Southern Africa (territories under Portuguese administration, Namibia, South Africa and Southern Rhodesia).

The two tables below show the number of experts and fellowships provided during 1971 and the technical co-operation expenditures by field of activity under the United Nations regular programme, UNDP and funds-in-trust.

EXPERTS AND FELLOWSHIPS PROVIDED BY THE UNITED NATIONS IN 1971
(E = Experts; F = Fellowships)

Field of Activity	Regular Programme		UNDP Technical Assistance Component		UNDP Special Fund Component		Funds-in-Trust	
	E	F	E	F	E	F	E	F
Economic surveys and policies	33	1	24	9	33	21	3	—
Economic planning and projections	23	7	93	27	76	133	13	—
Natural resources development and power	33	6	162	60	403	235	67	1
Trade promotion and marketing	9	7	93	55	102	4	2	—
Fiscal and financial matters	9	7	82	35	17	6	1	—
Statistics	14	14	69	137	40	200	20	7
Transport and communications	5	1	26	12	19	8	28	8
Legal	—	—	5	3	1	—	1	19
Social development	34	25	77	22	20	17	23	8
Population	4	18	6	15	19	2	105	38
Housing, building and planning	31	11	91	24	101	45	34	—
Public administration	60	43	86	54	112	82	8	4
Human rights	16	64	—	—	—	—	—	—
Narcotic drugs control	—	46	3	3	—	—	—	—
Special training programmes	—	—	—	—	—	—	—	499
Total	271	250	817	456	943	753	305	584

UNITED NATIONS TECHNICAL CO-OPERATION EXPENDITURES IN 1971
(in U.S. dollars)

Field of Activity	Regular Programme	UNDP Technical Assistance Component	UNDP Special Fund Component	Funds-in-Trust	Total
Development planning, projections and policies	1,038,686	2,354,206	4,733,145	160,495	8,286,532
Public finance and financial institutions	201,304	1,191,950	757,011	34,945	2,185,210
Resources and transport	801,469	3,608,366	20,488,534	2,706,962	27,605,331
Statistics	459,348	1,346,922	1,244,114	426,447	3,476,831
International trade	257,528	1,582,493	857,250	77,413	2,774,684
Legal	—	74,988	—	18,340	93,328
Social development	667,574	852,164	517,978	343,241	2,380,957
Population	150,531	103,558	439,745	1,681,874	2,375,708
Housing, building and planning	585,896	1,048,142	3,204,483	408,186	5,246,707
Public administration	883,546	1,245,999	3,088,699	104,817	5,323,061
Narcotic drugs control	100,351	26,668	—	—	127,019
Human rights activities	261,184	—	—	62,434	323,618
United Nations Educational and Training Programme for Southern Africa	130,000	3,761	—	498,501	632,262
International law	51,525	2,314	—	1,284	55,123
Natural disasters	89,688	—	—	—	89,688
Total	5,678,630	13,441,531	35,330,959	6,524,939	60,976,059

Provision of operational assistance personnel

During 1971, under projects administered by the United Nations for the provision of operational assistance personnel, 64 officers filled posts in the following 27 countries and territories: Botswana, Ethiopia, Ghana, Guyana, Haiti, the Ivory Coast, Jamaica, Kenya, Lesotho, Malawi, Malaysia, Malta, Nepal, Niger, Nigeria, the People's Democratic Republic of Yemen, the Republic of Viet-Nam, Sierra Leone, Somalia, Sudan, Swaziland, the Syrian Arab Republic, Trinidad and Tobago,

Uganda, the United Republic of Tanzania, Yemen and Zambia.

Public administration

The Economic and Social Council and the General Assembly took several decisions concerning the public administration programme of the United Nations during the Second United Nations Development Decade.

At its April-May 1971 session, the Economic and Social Council reviewed the Secretary-General's proposed objectives and programmes in public administration for the Second Development Decade, the work programme of the United Nations Public Administration Division for the period 1971-1975 and the recommendations thereon of the Second Meeting of Experts on the United Nations Programme in Public Administration, held in January 1971 at United Nations Headquarters, New York.

On 6 May 1971, the Council: (1) called the attention of Member States to the importance of measures to increase administrative capability for development and of incorporating such measures in development plans; (2) endorsed the Secretary-General's proposed objectives and programmes in public administration for the Second United Nations Development Decade as constituting the basis for a co-ordinated international programme in public administration and recommended that it be taken into account by the governing bodies of all organizations in the United Nations system and interested non-governmental organizations when they were programming activities in that field; (3) approved the Secretary-General's proposed 1971-1975 work programme for the Public Administration Division, subject to the proposed changes and views of the Committee for Programme and Co-ordination; (4) invited the Secretary-General to undertake preparations for the Third Meeting of Experts in 1975 to review the United Nations public administration programme and to contribute to the mid-term review of progress in implementing the relevant provisions of the International Development Strategy for the Second Development Decade; and (5) requested the Secretary-General to ensure that the United Nations Public Administration Division and the public administration units of the regional economic commissions and of the United Nations Economic and Social Office at Beirut should have the necessary staff to implement fully their work programme.

These decisions were set forth in resolution 1567(L), adopted by a vote of 22 to 0, with 2 abstentions. The text was based on a proposal by Kenya, Pakistan, Sudan, Tunisia and Yugoslavia. (For text of resolution, see DOCUMENTARY REFERENCES below.)

At its 1971 session, the General Assembly drew the attention of Member States to the importance of measures to increase administrative capability for economic and social development, the desirability of making such measures an integral part of development plans at all levels, and the need for such measures to be adequate to enable Governments, individually and collectively, to achieve the aims of the Second Development Decade.

After taking note of the existence of the African Training and Research Centre in Administration for Development and of the forthcoming entry into service of the Asian Centre of Development Administration, the Centre of the Arab Organization for Administrative Sciences and the Latin American Centre of Administration for Development, the Assembly: (a) endorsed the objectives of the regional centres of administration for development to increase the administrative capability and efficiency of the developing countries in order to speed up the process of economic and social development, and (b) invited the UNDP Governing Council to provide the centres with the necessary technical and financial support.

These actions by the Assembly were taken with the adoption of resolution 2845(XXVI) on 20 December 1971. The resolution was adopted, without objection, on the recommendation of the Second (Economic and Financial) Committee.

The text, approved without objection by the Second Committee on 13 December 1971, was based on a proposal by the following 36 States: Algeria, Bahrain, Bolivia, Chile, Colombia, Costa Rica, the Dominican Republic, Ecuador, Egypt, El Salvador, Guatemala, Guyana, Honduras, Iran, Iraq, Jamaica, Jordan, Kuwait, Lebanon, the Libyan Arab Republic, Morocco, Nicaragua, Nigeria, Panama, Paraguay, the People's Democratic Republic of Yemen, Peru, the Philippines, Spain, Sudan, the Syrian Arab Republic, Trinidad and Tobago, Tunisia, Uruguay, Venezuela and Yemen.

(For text of resolution, see DOCUMENTARY REFERENCES below.)

Budget appropriations

The budget appropriations for the United Nations for the financial year 1972, approved by the General Assembly on 22 December 1971 (see pp. 644-45, text of resolution 2899 A (XXVI)), included an appropriation of $8,733,000 for the regular programme of technical co-operation. Of this amount, $1,825,000 was appropriated for regional and sub-regional advisory services, and $5,408,000 for programmes in economic development, social development and public administration, human rights advisory services and narcotic drugs control. The sum also included $1.5 million for activities in the field of industrial development to be undertaken by the United Nations Industrial Development Organization (see pp. 288-98.)

A recommendation concerning the budget for the United Nations regular programme of technical assistance was contained in an Economic and Social Council resolution of 20 July 1971. The Council recommended that the allocation for 1972 be maintained at the current level of $5,408,000, and that the programme be concentrated on country programmes in the least developed of the developing countries, as well as on regional and sub-regional programmes of special interest to those countries. The resolution (1601 (LI)) dealt primarily with regional and sub-regional advisory services.

(For text of resolution, see p. 348.)

On 14 December 1971, the General Assembly acted on this Council recommendation, deciding that the United Nations budget for the regular programme of technical assistance should be maintained for 1972 at its current level of $5,408,000 and that its operations should be concentrated as suggested by the Council.

This Assembly decision was embodied in resolution 2803(XXVI), which dealt mainly with the establishment of a separate section in the United Nations budget to provide for a unified system of regional and sub-regional advisory services earmarked for the operations of the regional economic commissions and the United Nations Economic and Social Office at Beirut.

(For text of resolution, see p. 349.)

DOCUMENTARY REFERENCES

Decisions of Economic and Social Council and General Assembly

PUBLIC ADMINISTRATION

Economic and Social Council—50th session
Plenary meetings 1748-1750, 1753.

Public Administration in the Second United Nations Development Decade. Report of the Second Meeting of Experts, 16–26 January 1971 (ST/TAO/M/57). U.N.P. Sales No.: E.71.II.H.3.
E/4950. Public administration in Second United Nations Development Decade. Report of Secretary-General.
E/4950/Add.1. Note by Secretary-General (circulating report of 2nd Meeting of Experts on United Nations Programme in Public Administration (ST/TAO/M/57)).
E/4989. Report of Committee for Programme and Co-ordination on its 8th session, 22 March–8 April 1971, Chapter VI B.
E/L.1392. Kenya, Sudan, Yugoslavia: draft resolution.
E/L.1329/Rev.1. Kenya, Pakistan, Sudan, Tunisia, Yugoslavia: revised draft resolution.

RESOLUTION 1567(L), as proposed by 5 powers, E/L.1392/Rev.1, as further orally amended by sponsors, adopted by Council on 6 May 1971, meeting 1753, by 22 votes to 0, with 2 abstentions.

The Economic and Social Council,
Recalling its resolution 1199(XLII) of 24 May 1967 and General Assembly resolution 2561(XXIV) of 13 December 1969,
Having reviewed the Secretary-General's proposed objectives and programmes in public administration for the Second United Nations Development Decade, the work programme of the Public Administration Division for the period 1971-1975 and the recommendations thereon of the Second Meeting of Experts on the United Nations Programme in Public Administration as summarized in the report of the Secretary-General entitled "Public administration in the Second United Nations Development Decade," and also the relevant section of the report of the Committee for Programme and Co-ordination on its eighth session,
Stressing the important role of public administration in accelerating economic and social development of the developing countries and in realizing the goals and objectives of the Second United Nations Development Decade,
Considering that the United Nations could particularly assist developing countries in the field of public administration because of its ability to draw upon the experience of countries in various regions having different administrative systems, and should therefore be able to respond promptly, effectively and in a co-ordinated way to requests of Governments for assistance,

1. *Calls the attention* of Member States to the importance of measures to increase administrative capability for economic and social development, to the advisability of having such measures form an integral part of development plans at all levels, as appropriate, and to the need for such measures to be adequate to enable Governments individually and collectively to achieve the goals of the Second United Nations Development Decade;
2. *Endorses* the Secretary-General's proposed objectives and programmes in public administration for the Second United Nations Development Decade as constituting the basis for a co-ordinated international programme in public administration and recommends that it be taken into account by the governing bodies of all organizations in the United Nations system and interested non-governmental organizations when they are programming activities in this field;
3. *Approves* the Secretary-General's proposed work programme of the Public Administration Division for the period 1971-1975, subject to the proposed changes and views of the Committee for Programme and Co-ordination;
4. *Invites* the Secretary-General to undertake preparations for the Third Meeting of Experts in 1975 to review the United Nations public administration programme, taking into account the programmes of other organizations of the United Nations system in this field, and to contribute to the mid-term review of progress in implementing the relevant provisions of the International Development Strategy for the Second United Nations Development Decade;
5. *Requests* the Secretary-General, with due regard to paragraphs 25 and 58 of the report of the Committee for Programme and Co-ordination on its eighth session, to ensure that the Public Administration Division at Headquarters and the public administration units of the regional economic commissions and of the United Nations Economic and Social Office at Beirut shall have the necessary staff to implement fully their work programmes.

General Assembly—26th session
Second Committee, meetings 1370-1382, 1438, 1444.
Plenary meeting 2026.

A/8401. Report of Secretary-General on work of the Organization, 16 June 1970–15 June 1971, Part III, Chapter II C 3.
A/8403. Report of Economic and Social Council on work of its 50th and 51st sessions, Chapter X A.
A/C.2/260. Note by Secretary-General.
A/C.2/L.1194 and Rev.1. Algeria, Bahrain, Bolivia, Chile, Colombia, Costa Rica, Dominican Republic, Ecuador, Egypt, El Salvador, Guatemala, Guyana, Honduras, Iran, Iraq, Jamaica, Jordan, Kuwait, Lebanon, Libyan Arab Republic, Morocco, Nicaragua, Nigeria, Panama, Paraguay, People's Democratic Republic of Yemen, Peru, Philippines, Spain, Sudan, Syrian Arab Republic, Trinidad and Tobago, Tunisia, Uruguay,

Venezuela, Yemen: draft resolution and revision, approved without objection by Second Committee on 13 December 1971, meeting 1444.

A/8578/Add.1. Report of Second Committee (part II) (on report of Economic and Social Council), draft resolution VIII.

RESOLUTION 2845(XXVI), as recommended by Second Committee, adopted without objection by Assembly on 20 December 1971, meeting 2026.

The General Assembly,

Taking into account its previous resolutions on the role of public administration in economic and social development, particularly resolutions 723(VIII) of 23 October 1953, 1024(XI) of 21 December 1956, 1256(XIII) of 14 November 1958, 1530(XV) of 15 December 1960, 1710(XVI) of 19 December 1961 and 2561(XXIV) of 13 December 1969,

Recalling Economic and Social Council resolutions 1199(XLII) of 24 May 1967 and 1567(L) of 6 May 1971,

Emphasizing the importance of improving public administration in order to speed up the economic and social development of the developing countries and to achieve the aims and objectives of the Second United Nations Development Decade,

Considering, therefore, that the measures needed to increase the capability and efficiency of public administration in the developing countries are indispensable for the formulation and implementation of economic and social development plans and programmes,

Recognizing the importance for developing countries of the establishment and entry into service of regional centres of administration for development, the purpose of which is to co-operate with Governments in increasing their administrative capability for the implementation of their economic and social development programmes,

Noting the existence of the African Training and Research Centre in Administration for Development and the forthcoming entry into service of the Asian Centre of Development Administration, the Centre of the Arab Organization for Administrative Sciences and the Latin American Centre of Administration for Development,

Recognizing the prompt and effective co-operation given by the United Nations Development Programme for the establishment and operation of the regional centres in Asia and Africa,

1. *Draws the attention* of Member States to the importance of measures to increase administrative capability for economic and social development, the desirability of making such measures an integral part of development plans at all levels, as appropriate, and the need for such measures to be adequate to enable Governments, individually and collectively, to achieve the aims of the Second United Nations Development Decade;

2. *Takes note* of the report of the Second Meeting of Experts on the United Nations Programme in Public Administration;

3. *Endorses* the objectives of the regional centres of administration for development to increase the administrative capability and efficiency of the developing countries in order to speed up the process of economic and social development;

4. *Invites* the Governing Council of the United Nations Development Programme to provide the technical and financial co-operation necessary for the establishment and operation of the Latin American Centre of Administration for Development and the Centre of the Arab Organization for Administrative Sciences in the same way in which it supported the regional centres in Africa and Asia, and further invites it to continue to provide the necessary assistance to the regional centres in Africa and Asia.

Other documents

Administrative Aspects of Urbanization (ST/TAO/M/51). U.N.P. Sales No.: E.71.II.H.1.

Training of Public Service Trainers. Report on a Pilot Course, St. Augustine, Trinidad, 10 August–18 September 1970 (ST/TAO/M/60). U.N.P. Sales No.: E.72.II.H.2.

Pre-investment and technical aid received and provided during 1971 through the United Nations and related agencies

The following table, based on data compiled by the United Nations Development Programme (UNDP), shows the type of aid received and provided during 1971 through the United Nations and its related agencies under both components of UNDP and under the regular technical assistance programmes of the United Nations and agencies that are financed from their respective regular budgets.

The listings and regional groupings used follow those used by the United Nations Development Programme.

Country, territory or region	Total project expenditure[a] (in thousands of U.S.$)		No. of experts[b]				No. of fellowships[c]				Equipment for UNDP projects[d] (in thousands of U.S.$)	
			By country of assignment		By nationality		By nationality		By host country		Re-ceived by	Sup-plied by
	UNDP[e]	Reg. Prog.[f]	UNDP	Reg. Prog.[f]	UNDP	Reg. Prog.[f]	UNDP	Reg. Prog.[f]	UNDP	Reg. Prog.[f]		
Afghanistan	3,211	940	134	31	3	2	103	56	—	—	362	59
Albania	33	38	—	3	—	—	17	6	—	—	16	—
Algeria	4,252	300	283	20	4	—	91	31	9	16	779	11
American Samoa	—	4	—	—	—	—	—	2	—	—	—	—
Angola	—	—	—	—	—	—	—	1	—	—	—	—
Antigua	52	19	3	—	—	—	3	5	—	—	—	—
Argentina	2,675	259	129	10	153	35	101	52	141	62	527	172
Australia	—	29	—	—	246	33	4	15	103	47	—	230
Austria	—	27	—	—	64	17	—	34	75	63	—	258
Bahamas	110	3	9	1	—	—	5	3	—	—	—	—
Bahrain	—	29	—	1	—	—	4	13	—	—	—	—
Barbados	130	17	21	2	4	1	17	6	11	1	—	6

Country, territory or region	Total project expenditure[a] (in thousands of U.S.$)		No. of experts[b]				No. of fellowships[c]				Equipment for UNDP projects[d] (in thousands of U.S.$)	
			By country of assignment		By nationality		By nationality		By host country		Re-ceived by	Sup-plied by
	UNDP[e]	Reg. Prog[f]	UNDP	Reg. Prog[f]	UNDP	Reg. Prog[f]	UNDP	Reg. Prog[f]	UNDP	Reg. Prog[f]		
Belgium	—	24	—	—	338	42	—	16	85	86	—	258
Bermuda	—	—	—	—	—	—	1	1	—	—	—	—
Bolivia	2,647	188	94	12	27	12	71	36	1	1	483	238
Botswana	869	55	46	2	—	—	24	11	—	—	126	1
Brazil	3,951	794	192	26	59	13	77	75	28	67	557	46
British Honduras	70	36	4	2	—	—	4	4	—	—	17	—
Brunei	30	7	1	1	—	—	—	3	—	—	—	—
Bulgaria	894	57	64	1	39	3	118	45	7	18	291	4
Burma	1,162	413	37	8	6	4	31	138	—	109	274	—
Burundi	2,219	238	95	7	11	1	41	27	—	—	319	63
Byelorussian SSR	—	11	—	—	2	—	—	—	—	—	—	—
Cameroon	2,196	210	88	5	6	3	61	27	40	43	265	35
Canada	—	25	—	—	297	61	—	3	204	77	—	595
Cayman Islands	44	—	4	—	—	—	1	1	—	—	3	—
Central African Republic	1,646	134	55	2	—	—	33	32	2	3	301	34
Ceylon	1,953	504	98	27	50	12	85	142	9	72	174	6
Chad	681	169	41	6	—	—	32	30	3	—	67	63
Chile	5,624	234	134	8	148	56	148	51	199	80	1,720	44
China	1,108	245	44	12	44	20	87	50	32	38	190	11
Colombia	3,049	133	132	9	58	32	116	37	47	72	638	22
Comoro Islands	24	27	1	1	—	—	—	1	—	—	—	—
Congo	1,933	169	78	3	1	1	40	33	2	111	325	79
Cook Islands	3	6	—	—	—	—	1	2	—	—	—	—
Costa Rica	709	116	44	8	19	9	53	16	18	31	79	—
Cuba	1,466	209	56	11	10	1	82	45	—	5	565	—
Cyprus	1,371	98	80	3	12	1	23	24	15	3	218	49
Czechoslovakia	228	51	9	—	153	38	28	37	80	84	5	48
Dahomey	1,086	279	44	6	3	4	68	79	7	—	305	9
Denmark	—	19	—	—	140	29	—	19	60	130	—	1,237
Dominica	61	—	6	—	4	—	5	2	—	—	—	—
Dominican Republic	1,517	167	64	10	2	—	30	23	—	2	251	15
Ecuador	1,428	205	67	14	28	8	73	34	22	1	239	363
Egypt	4,498	517	165	21	199	43	150	157	180	150	1,429	95
El Salvador	1,165	200	41	11	7	1	44	32	4	2	213	182
Equatorial Guinea	368	104	44	7	—	—	4	2	—	—	18	—
Ethiopia	3,930	715	194	22	3	3	75	30	176	21	520	109
Federal Republic of Germany	—	24	—	—	392	49	—	21	235	155	—	3,571
Fiji	587	62	33	1	—	—	22	16	5	13	48	32
Finland	—	16	—	—	37	6	—	26	20	47	—	175
France	—	29	1	—	1,284	181	—	25	545	483	—	2,367
French Polynesia	—	7	—	—	—	—	1	2	—	—	—	—
Gabon	1,054	174	31	9	—	—	26	41	10	32	206	14
Gambia	157	7	9	—	1	1	22	5	1	5	14	—
Ghana	2,686	196	98	8	10	3	94	26	26	6	323	34
Gilbert and Ellice Islands	98	22	1	2	—	—	—	4	—	—	—	—
Greece	1,811	66	89	7	36	13	55	39	5	—	155	10
Grenada	56	25	3	1	—	—	5	3	—	—	—	—
Guam	—	2	—	—	—	—	—	2	—	—	—	—
Guatemala	398	152	23	9	6	5	64	26	4	24	20	4
Guinea	2,332	152	89	5	2	1	13	8	2	—	484	67
Guyana	487	128	25	7	4	2	25	16	3	1	26	6
Haiti	693	157	39	14	45	11	18	9	—	—	92	6
Honduras	815	174	43	11	1	2	39	26	13	1	81	15
Hong Kong	54	30	4	—	—	—	13	14	—	17	—	15
Hungary	425	99	36	7	100	11	54	48	5	24	167	5
Iceland	9	26	—	2	29	1	4	3	2	2	—	—
India	7,645	1,603	249	66	427	71	314	345	197	409	3,112	20
Indonesia	4,445	1,014	352	37	74	11	164	252	60	163	945	32
Iran	4,398	370	208	13	12	20	104	123	43	162	481	761

Country, territory or region	Total project expenditure[a] (in thousands of U.S.$)		No. of experts[b]				No. of fellowships[c]				Equipment for UNDP projects[d] (in thousands of U.S.$)	
			By country of assignment		By nationality		By nationality		By host country		Received by	Supplied by
	UNDP[e]	Reg. Prog.[f]	UNDP	Reg. Prog.[f]	UNDP	Reg. Prog.[f]	UNDP	Reg. Prog.[f]	UNDP	Reg. Prog.[f]		
Iraq	3,354	496	147	22	24	4	125	69	22	4	524	41
Ireland	24	13	—	—	41	8	—	16	5	7	9	3
Israel	688	151	36	7	102	16	44	41	84	16	246	251
Italy	—	23	2	—	266	44	1	28	276	195	—	1,773
Ivory Coast	2,798	108	177	3	3	—	55	36	53	38	504	218
Jamaica	1,512	159	78	12	11	5	36	35	55	74	271	97
Japan	197	53	16	—	249	24	26	26	216	82	12	2,749
Jordan	2,092	165	58	1	31	14	63	56	—	3	942	90
Kenya	3,676	456	170	17	7	—	90	31	127	18	301	235
Khmer Republic	1,204	281	62	13	1	—	41	13	—	1	104	22
Kuwait	417	52	22	3	—	—	15	14	12	2	33	24
Laos	509	273	30	13	1	—	39	12	3	—	37	12
Lebanon	1,489	148	76	5	26	16	49	33	248	93	208	89
Lesotho	1,384	85	49	2	—	1	14	10	—	—	127	9
Liberia	1,661	212	80	7	—	4	26	20	—	3	206	99
Libyan Arab Republic	1,465	111	67	6	—	—	33	55	11	—	85	3
Luxembourg	—	4	—	2	4	1	—	5	2	2	—	—
Madagascar	2,867	137	133	5	4	—	51	44	43	6	596	215
Malawi	685	200	35	9	1	—	61	12	1	—	135	69
Malaysia	2,836	655	129	28	10	2	75	37	48	52	483	59
Maldives	42	81	3	3	—	—	—	4	—	—	6	—
Mali	2,248	333	104	9	3	2	93	49	14	18	316	86
Malta	393	20	30	1	—	1	8	6	12	1	14	—
Mauritania	1,052	157	33	7	—	—	29	3	—	1	207	59
Mauritius	816	153	53	5	4	4	22	25	4	—	83	35
Mexico	2,673	320	99	22	24	15	120	73	282	66	645	37
Monaco	—	—	—	—	—	—	—	2	1	—	—	—
Mongolia	1,974	295	45	13	—	—	30	41	—	—	994	3
Montserrat	14	—	2	—	—	—	4	1	—	—	—	—
Morocco	3,221	313	161	14	6	—	43	51	82	25	344	33
Nauru	—	—	—	—	—	—	1	—	—	—	—	—
Nepal	2,455	651	161	23	1	5	75	128	—	68	316	39
Netherlands	—	9	—	—	341	36	—	26	168	134	—	974
Netherlands Antilles	108	3	5	—	—	—	14	3	—	—	—	—
New Caledonia	59	—	2	—	—	—	—	3	—	21	4	9
New Hebrides	51	83	2	4	—	—	—	8	—	—	15	—
New Zealand	—	32	—	—	104	19	5	14	19	63	—	54
Nicaragua	713	161	46	6	—	1	35	16	4	—	64	33
Niger	1,813	151	77	7	—	—	32	25	2	1	359	83
Nigeria	4,520	804	217	34	19	10	83	72	60	127	609	90
Niue	—	2	—	—	—	—	—	2	—	—	—	—
Norway	—	11	—	—	130	15	—	12	51	39	—	1,321
Oman	—	—	—	—	—	—	1	—	—	—	—	—
Pacific Islands, Trust Territory of	—	72	—	—	—	—	3	22	—	—	—	—
Pakistan	4,506	861	137	24	56	18	110	75	17	23	525	9
Panama	1,741	112	79	4	7	4	38	17	17	8	166	44
Papua New Guinea	529	102	24	8	—	—	12	15	—	1	25	—
Paraguay	943	78	53	4	5	4	35	22	1	—	98	11
People's Democratic Republic of Yemen	1,484	322	54	6	1	1	68	34	—	—	237	64
Peru	3,226	201	149	17	51	20	77	32	26	42	482	74
Philippines	3,600	432	133	22	54	34	147	102	103	175	625	46
Poland	1,001	89	39	4	110	27	152	91	83	77	458	121
Portugal	—	—	—	—	18	3	—	5	1	—	—	—
Puerto Rico	—	—	—	—	—	—	—	—	11	58	—	—
Qatar	54	49	2	2	—	—	3	7	—	—	—	—
Republic of Korea	2,833	443	122	19	9	7	107	54	16	58	623	21
Republic of Viet-Nam	1,107	516	32	23	18	5	37	339	3	312	286	2
Reunion	—	2	—	—	—	—	—	5	—	—	—	—
Romania	1,102	110	77	1	30	9	112	64	9	31	142	16

Country, territory or region	Total project expenditure[a] (in thousands of U.S.$)		No. of experts[b]				No. of fellowships[c]				Equipment for UNDP projects[d] (in thousands of U.S.$)	
			By country of assignment		By nationality		By nationality		By host country		Re-ceived by	Sup-plied by
	UNDP[e]	Reg. Prog.[f]	UNDP	Reg. Prog.[f]	UNDP	Reg. Prog.[f]	UNDP	Reg. Prog.[f]	UNDP	Reg. Prog.[f]		
Rwanda	1,585	198	50	8	—	—	41	23	—	11	168	46
Ryukyu Islands	—	89	—	4	—	—	—	15	—	—	—	—
St. Kitts-Nevis-Anguilla	42	—	5	—	—	—	2	2	—	—	—	—
St. Lucia	49	—	3	—	—	—	6	7	—	—	—	2
St. Vincent	51	—	3	—	—	—	5	—	—	—	—	—
Saudi Arabia	1,325	229	95	11	—	—	35	13	—	1	—	7
Senegal	2,107	326	113	12	6	3	43	41	169	82	189	167
Seychelles	—	31	—	1	—	—	—	—	—	—	—	—
Sierra Leone	1,213	233	53	8	4	3	34	25	—	—	80	14
Singapore	2,466	299	87	16	2	2	55	51	32	51	657	194
Solomon Islands	180	81	7	3	—	—	1	11	—	—	24	—
Somalia	2,088	494	82	25	1	1	45	37	—	1	181	35
South Africa	—	—	—	—	5	—	—	1	—	—	—	94
Southern Rhodesia	—	—	—	—	3	—	5	—	—	—	—	—
Spain	1,601	27	129	—	131	20	50	30	92	26	334	196
Sudan	2,756	679	100	25	20	7	121	76	5	39	655	34
Surinam	380	27	15	2	—	—	3	—	4	—	169	29
Swaziland	424	60	45	3	—	—	24	15	—	—	49	27
Sweden	—	20	—	—	247	33	—	22	109	157	—	1,141
Switzerland	—	16	—	—	169	26	2	14	409	270	—	1,489
Syrian Arab Republic	1,851	408	90	11	44	10	79	82	1	12	443	33
Thailand	3,275	773	131	33	9	3	318	183	412	126	365	67
Togo	2,143	408	81	11	6	2	65	81	15	76	641	32
Tonga	35	38	2	2	—	—	2	6	—	—	—	—
Tortola	20	—	—	—	—	—	—	—	—	—	—	—
Trinidad and Tobago	617	64	25	4	10	5	22	20	50	9	63	58
Tunisia	2,952	285	182	9	19	3	93	28	103	8	457	43
Turkey	4,324	236	155	14	22	7	131	56	22	8	945	23
Turks and Caicos Islands	7	—	2	—	—	—	1	—	—	—	—	—
Uganda	1,675	245	81	11	3	—	67	54	24	20	135	93
Ukrainian SSR	—	16	—	—	—	—	—	—	—	—	—	—
USSR	—	52	—	—	193	37	—	27	315	206	—	452
United Kingdom	—	22	—	—	1,567	258	19	29	970	777	—	5,072
United Republic of Tanzania	2,430	345	120	13	3	5	107	47	49	9	292	87
United States	—	57	1	6	1,035	291	—	19	867	550	—	9,242
Upper Volta	1,298	194	57	5	—	1	39	25	3	49	236	46
Uruguay	637	200	30	11	37	8	51	16	15	9	62	27
Venezuela	1,918	270	124	15	15	13	61	56	11	85	30	2
Virgin Islands (U.K.)	—	—	3	—	—	—	2	—	—	—	—	—
Western Samoa	554	145	35	7	—	—	13	11	—	1	85	20
West Indies	—	83	1	7	—	—	—	—	—	—	—	—
West Irian	—	—	10	—	—	—	—	—	—	—	—	—
Yemen	1,316	449	127	24	1	—	31	57	—	—	182	61
Yugoslavia	1,270	92	90	2	201	35	75	45	47	49	324	19
Zaire	4,718	1,009	135	51	2	—	63	49	40	4	502	29
Zambia	2,905	254	142	10	1	1	50	18	35	3	236	85
Stateless	—	—	—	—	11	3	—	—	—	—	—	—
Not specified	—	—	—	—	—	—	26	2	—	5	—	1,105
Country Total	209,898	31,762	9,653	1,313	—	—	—	—	—	—	37,400	—
Africa	11,027	3,171	339	101	—	—	—	—	—	—	1,733	—
Americas	8,563	2,793	311	154	—	—	—	—	—	—	1,143	—
Asia and the Far East	6,992	2,733	239	153	—	—	—	—	—	—	429	—
Europe, Mediterranean and Middle East	1,886	1,567	23	106	—	—	—	—	—	—	107	—
Inter-regional	6,555	3,584	260	274	—	—	—	—	—	—	1,107	—
Global	139	—	8	—	—	—	—	—	—	—	36	—
Regional Total	35,162	13,848	1,180	788	—	—	—	—	—	—	4,555	—
Grand Total	245,060	45,610	10,833	2,101	10,139	2,029	7,115	5,904	8,727	7,528	41,955	40,869

[a]Totals have been rounded.

[b]The totals for experts by country of assignment are somewhat higher than the totals shown by nationality because a number of individual experts had more than one country of assignment.

[c]The totals for fellowships by host country are somewhat higher than the totals shown by nationality because some fellowship awards called for study in two or more countries.

[d]The figures given under the heading "Supplied by" are based on orders placed in the various countries during the course of 1971, whereas the figures given under the heading "Received by" refer to estimated expenditure within the year (as do the figures for "Total project expenditure"). Consequently, the totals of the two equipment columns do not correspond exactly.

[e]Data exclude agency overhead costs.

[f]Refers to technical assistance activities, other than those carried out under UNDP, which were financed from regular budgetary resources of other organizations of the United Nations system.

World Food Programme

The World Food Programme (WFP), a joint undertaking of the United Nations and the Food and Agriculture Organization of the United Nations (FAO), continued during 1971 to provide food aid to developing countries to assist them in carrying out development projects while combating malnutrition; the Programme also continued to meet emergency food needs.

As at the end of 1970, Governments had pledged contributions to WFP for the period 1971-1972, in the form of food commodities, cash and services, to a value of $216.1 million. During 1971, Governments made new pledges of $11.6 million, bringing the total in contributions for 1971-1972 to $227.7 million; of this amount, however, only $212.2 million was available due to a matching clause in the United States pledge. (For table on pledges for 1971-1972, see pp. 267-68.)

As at the end of 1971, the total in pledges made available to WFP since its inception in 1963 stood at $743.7 million.

In addition, a number of Governments channelled through WFP food grains which they had undertaken to contribute to developing countries under the Food Aid Convention of 1967. During 1971, $7.8 million worth of food grains, together with $1.8 million in cash for transport and administration, was thus made available to the Programme. This brought the total contributions to the Programme under the 1967 Food Aid Convention to $51.5 million. (For table on Food Aid Convention contributions for 1970-1971, see pp. 268-69.)

Sweden announced its intention to channel through the Programme its entire contribution of 35,000 tons of food grains under the Food Aid Convention of 1971.

Activities in 1971

During 1971, 14 projects for economic and social development were approved by the WFP Intergovernmental Committee, and 30 projects were approved by the Programme's Executive Director. These projects entailed commitments of $93 million, as compared with commitments of $227 million in 1970, $324 million in 1969 and $177 million in 1968. The decrease in commitments in 1971 reflected the fact that the Programme's reserves were being used to implement ongoing projects; the volume of disbursement on ongoing projects totalled $46.4 million in 1968, $71.8 million in 1969, $126.1 million in 1970 and $114.1 million in 1971. New commitments were undertaken mainly on the basis of conservative estimates of future contributions. (For table on commitments approved during 1971, see p. 269.)

During 1971, WFP concluded agreements for the implementation of 56 development projects, of which 21 related to projects approved during the same year.

Development projects assisted by WFP during 1971 included the feeding of mothers and young children; nutritional education; feeding of primary and secondary school students, university students and student and volunteer workers; feeding of hospital patients; hospital development; livestock improvement; dairy development; soil conservation; land reclamation and development, including the settlement of refugees, afforestation, and the construction of dikes, dams and roads; self-help housing; the construction of community facilities through mutual help schemes; and the establishment of food reserves.

In appraising requests and evaluating projects, WFP drew on the staff and resources of the United Nations and FAO, as well as on the International Labour Organisation, the United Nations Educational, Scientific and Cultural Organization and the World Health Organization. In several cases, these organizations, through the United Nations Development Programme or on their own, provided technical co-operation to recipient Governments in the execution of projects for which WFP furnished food aid. Assistance in WFP projects was also provided by the United Nations Children's Fund and the Office of the United Nations High Commissioner for Refugees. The Programme co-operated on a number of projects with the International Bank for Reconstruction and Development and with the regional development banks. In several cases, WFP's activities were co-ordinated with those of bilateral government-to-government programmes or with development activities of non-governmental organizations.

As in previous years, the $10 million of the Programme's resources annually reserved for use by the Director-General of FAO for emergency aid proved inadequate and was increased by the Intergovernmental Committee to $18 million. Thus in 1971, the FAO Director-General approved 28 allocations, totalling $18 million, for emergency aid in 23 countries. The largest of these allocations, $3.1 million, went to assist refugees in India, where WFP co-operated with other United Nations organizations in the efforts co-ordinated by the United Nations High Commissioner for Refugees. The Programme also took part in the United Nations East Pakistan Relief Operations, for which a WFP emergency allocation of $1.5 million was made available.

At its March-April 1971 session, the WFP Intergovernmental Committee heard an appeal by the Chairman of the Working Group on the Financing of the United Nations Relief and Works Agency for Palestine Refugees in the Near East (UNRWA), concerning the need for WFP assistance to the Palestine refugees, in view of the financial difficulties of UNRWA. The Committee endorsed the intention of the Director-General of FAO to make an emergency allocation, if requested by a Government in the area. Subsequently, at the request of Jordan, an allocation of $2 million was made for aid to Palestine refugees in that country.

Other large emergency operations in 1971 served to alleviate the effects of drought in Afghanistan ($2 million), Iraq ($1.3 million), Kenya ($0.8 million), Mauritania ($1 million) and Senegal ($0.6 million); $0.6 million was provided for earthquake relief in Chile.

At its March-April 1971 session, the Intergovernmental Committee considered a proposal by the Netherlands for the establishment of an emergency food supply scheme, which would enable WFP to arrange with donor countries to ship promptly the food commodities required in emergency situations. The Committee accepted the proposal in principle and requested its Executive Director to explore the matter further.

Consideration by Economic and Social Council

The Economic and Social Council considered the work of the World Food Programme in July and October 1971.

At its July 1971 session, the Council had before it the ninth annual report of the WFP Intergovernmental Committee. The report covered the Committee's eighteenth and nineteenth sessions, held respectively from 2 to 6 November 1970 and from 29 March to 6 April 1971, as well as WFP's activities in support of economic and social development projects and its relief operations during the period April 1970 to April 1971.

At its March-April 1971 session, the Intergovernmental Committee had carried out the review of the Programme which, pursuant to a General Assembly resolution of 20 December 1965,[8] was to precede each biennial pledging conference, and considered the pledging target to be recommended for 1973-1974. The Committee adopted a draft resolution, for submission to the General Assembly through the Economic and Social Council, calling for continuation of the Programme and for the convening of a pledging conference early in 1972. However, the Committee felt unable to recommend a target figure for 1973-1974 as it lacked the necessary information, including the extent to which the target for 1971-1972, which was substantially under-subscribed at the time, would be met. The Committee therefore decided to defer the matter to its October 1971 session.

On 30 July 1971, the Economic and Social Council, acting on the recommendation of its Economic Committee but without adopting a resolution, took note of the ninth annual report of the Intergovernmental Committee of the World Food Programme and deferred until later in the year a decision on the pledging target for 1973-1974.

Subsequently, the Intergovernmental Committee recommended a target of $340 million for 1973-1974. The Committee took into account, on the one hand, that the 1971-1972 target of $300 million had not been met and, on the other, that the needs of developing countries justified a higher target.

On 29 October 1971, the Council decided, as proposed by the WFP Intergovernmental Committee, to submit to the General Assembly a draft resolution containing this pledging target and to urge States Members of the United Nations and members and associate members of FAO to prepare for the announcement of pledges at a pledging conference to be held early in 1972.

These decisions by the Council were set forth in resolution 1650(LI), which was adopted without objection. (For text of resolution, see DOCUMENTARY REFERENCES below.)

During the discussion preceding this decision, some representatives expressed doubt that the $340 million target figure was realistic. Other Members noted that with the current rate of participation, the multilateral character of the Programme was diminished and the target of $600 million, which it was hoped to reach by the end of the Second United Nations Development Decade, would be unattainable.

[8]See Y.U.N., 1965, pp. 308-9, text of resolution 2095(XX).

Consideration by General Assembly

At its 1971 session, the General Assembly considered the draft resolution on the review and continuation of the World Food Programme proposed by the Economic and Social Council. This draft was endorsed by the Second (Economic and Financial) Committee on 2 December and adopted by the Assembly on 14 December 1971, in both cases without discussion or objection.

The Assembly thereby recognized the necessity for the World Food Programme to continue its action in providing multilateral food aid as a form of capital investment and for meeting emergency food needs. It then: established a target of voluntary contributions of $340 million for 1973-1974, of which not less than one third should be in cash and services; expressed the hope that these resources would be augmented by substantial contributions from additional sources; urged States Members of the United Nations and members and associate members of FAO to make every effort towards attainment of the target; requested the Secretary-General, in co-operation with the Director-General of FAO, to convene early in 1972 a pledging conference for this purpose at United Nations Headquarters; and decided that, subject to further review, the next pledging conference for the World Food Programme should be convened, at the latest, early in 1974, with a view to reaching the target to be recommended by the General Assembly and the Conference of FAO at that time.

These decisions by the Assembly were set forth in resolution 2805(XXVI). (For text of resolution, see DOCUMENTARY REFERENCES below.)

On 22 December 1971, the Secretary-General and the Director-General of FAO, in accordance with the Assembly's resolution, announced that the fourth WFP pledging conference would be convened on 31 January 1972.

STATEMENT OF PLEDGES TO THE WORLD FOOD PROGRAMME FOR 1971–1972
RECEIVED AS AT 31 DECEMBER 1971
(in U.S. dollar equivalents)

Contributor	Contributions			
	Commodities	*Cash*	*Services*	*Total*
Algeria	—	30,000	—	30,000
Australia	1,320,000	330,000	—	1,650,000
Austria	1,350,000	150,000	—	1,500,000
Barbados	—	5,000	—	5,000
Belgium	280,000	130,152	—	410,152
Botswana	2,000	—	—	2,000
Brazil	250,000	—	—	250,000
Canada	23,400,000	6,600,000	—	30,000,000
Ceylon	126,050	—	—	126,050
Chile	—	14,000	—	14,000[a]
Colombia	150,000	—	—	150,000
Cuba	385,000	—	—	385,000
Cyprus	—	2,500	—	2,500
Denmark	10,000,000	5,000,000	—	15,000,000
Dominican Republic	—	5,000	—	5,000
Ecuador	—	1,600	—	1,600
Egypt	100,000	—	—	100,000
European Economic Community	1,350,000	—	—	1,350,000
Federal Republic of Germany	5,980,049	2,897,855	—	8,877,904
Finland	2,588,780	264,344	—	2,853,124[a]
Gabon	—	1,799	—	1,799
Ghana	30,000	—	—	30,000
Greece	170,000	—	—	170,000
Hungary	80,000	—	—	80,000
India	666,667	333,333	—	1,000,000
Indonesia	50,000	—	—	50,000
Iraq	80,000	40,000	—	120,000
Ireland	660,067	325,003	—	985,070
Israel	6,667	3,333	—	10,000
Italy	—	1,000,000	—	1,000,000[b]
Jamaica	—	10,000	—	10,000
Japan	940,000	470,000	—	1,410,000
Kenya	—	2,802	—	2,802
Khmer Republic	—	1,000	—	1,000

Contributor	Contributions Commodities	Cash	Services	Total
Laos	—	833	—	833
Lebanon	—	5,000	—	5,000
Liberia	—	6,000	—	6,000
Libyan Arab Republic	—	10,000	—	10,000
Luxembourg	—	18,761	—	18,761
Madagascar	—	1,799	—	1,799
Malaysia	6,601	4,950	—	11,551
Malawi	—	2,808	—	2,808
Malta	—	1,000	—	1,000
Mexico	250,000	100,000	—	350,000
Nepal	—	1,000	—	1,000
Netherlands	7,628,072	3,148,148	—	10,776,220
New Zealand	470,430	241,657	—	712,087
Niger	—	7,194	—	7,194
Norway	6,067,945	1,673,222	—	7,741,167
Pakistan	172,800	—	—	172,800
Peru	69,284	—	—	69,284
Philippines	—	108,889	—	108,889
Republic of Korea	—	8,000	—	8,000
Republic of Viet-Nam	—	1,000	—	1,000
Saudi Arabia	40,000	—	—	40,000
Senegal	—	3,597	—	3,597
Sierra Leone	—	2,400	—	2,400
Somalia	2,000	—	—	2,000
Sweden	5,625,000	3,375,000	—	9,000,000
Switzerland	843,882	401,145	—	1,245,027
Syrian Arab Republic	23,810	—	—	23,810
Thailand	60,000	—	—	60,000
Trinidad and Tobago	—	5,000	—	5,000
Tunisia	7,500	11,500	—	19,000
Turkey	150,000	—	—	150,000
United Kingdom	2,408,953	1,344,335	—	3,753,288
United Republic of Tanzania	35,014	—	—	35,014
United States	85,000,000[c]	3,000,000	37,000,000[d]	125,000,000
Upper Volta	—	1,799	—	1,799
Uruguay	10,000	—	—	10,000 [a]
Venezuela	100,000	—	—	100,000
Yugoslavia	180,000	—	—	180,000
Zambia	—	2,500	—	2,500

[a]For 1971 only.

[b]Subject to parliamentary approval.

[c]The United States pledged up to $85 million in commodities on the condition that the United States contribution would not exceed 50 per cent of the total contribution of all Governments in commodities and cash used for the purchase of commodities.

[d]The United States was also prepared to furnish shipping services to transport all of the commodities it provided. The value of this service was estimated at $37 million for the $85 million worth of commodities.

1967 FOOD AID CONVENTION CONTRIBUTIONS TO THE WORLD FOOD PROGRAMME
FOR CROP YEAR 1970–1971
(As at 31 December 1971)

Country	Commodities (in U.S. dollars)	Cash (in U.S. dollars)	Country	Commodities (in U.S. dollars)	Cash (in U.S. dollars)
Australia	500,000	100,000	Netherlands	1,334,899	300,353
Belgium	317,834	63,560	Norway	890,000	222,500
Denmark	430,000	86,000	Sweden	3,432,602	772,300
European Economic Community	572,100	114,420	Switzerland	762,800	152,560
Federal Republic of Germany	1,271,334	254,240	United Kingdom	4,296,207	965,646
Finland	889,934	200,340	Total	14,697,710	3,231,919

PROJECTS FOR FOOD AID FOR DEVELOPMENT
(Approved in period 1 January–31 December 1971)
(in U.S. dollars)

	WFP food cost	WFP total cost		WFP food cost	WFP total cost
Africa			**Asia and Far East (cont.)**		
Algeria	4,539,700	5,453,900	Indonesia	1,367,600	2,289,000
Egypt (2 projects)	8,037,600	11,165,700	Iran	2,369,800	3,125,000
Botswana	6,836,800	8,809,100	Nepal (3 projects)	2,348,900	3,610,600
Burundi	378,700	587,400	Pakistan (3 projects)	2,168,300	2,769,000
Gambia	430,000	619,000	Philippines	262,300	347,700
Ghana	89,400	127,300	**Europe**		
Liberia	957,100	1,219,200			
Madagascar	105,000	135,500	Hungary	662,100	902,600
Malawi	421,800	643,600	**Latin America and Caribbean**		
Mauritania	664,500	889,600			
Mauritius	667,600	908,500	Bolivia	1,944,200	2,615,700
Niger	83,300	171,700	Chile	535,500	718,600
Nigeria	107,800	164,300	Costa Rica	749,600	973,300
Somalia (3 projects)	1,656,300	2,465,000	Dominica	62,500	85,200
Sudan	1,460,100	2,278,000	Ecuador	1,015,500	1,347,000
Uganda	744,000	932,000	Jamaica	61,700	85,300
United Republic of Tanzania	312,000	489,000	Nicaragua	442,500	670,000
Zaire	320,400	435,300	Venezuela	5,469,900	6,922,400
Zambia	212,200	364,800	**Middle East**		
Asia and Far East			People's Democratic Republic of Yemen	2,255,800	2,974,200
Afghanistan (2 projects)	790,400	1,772,900	Yemen	1,786,100	2,773,000

DOCUMENTARY REFERENCES

Economic and Social Council—50th session
Plenary meeting 1772.

E/L.1385. Consideration of provisional agenda for 51st session. Note by Secretary-General.

Economic and Social Council—51st session
Economic Committee, meeting 536.
Plenary meetings 1793, 1805.

E/5022. Note by Secretary-General (transmitting 9th annual report, covering period 16 April 1970–6 April 1971, of United Nations/FAO Intergovernmental Committee of World Food Programme (WFP), on its 18th and 19th sessions).
E/5057. Report of Economic Committee.
E/5073. Resolutions adopted by Economic and Social Council during its 51st session, 5-30 July 1971. Other decisions, p. 16.

E/L.1462 and Add.1. WFP: pledging target for 1973-1974. Note by Secretary-General (reproducing text of draft resolutions proposed by Intergovernmental Committee of WFP at its 19th session for adoption by Council and by General Assembly) and addendum.

RESOLUTION 1650(LI), as recommended by Intergovernmental Committee of WFP, E/L.1462 and Add.1, adopted without objection by Council on 29 October 1971, meeting 1805.

The Economic and Social Council,
Having considered the ninth annual report of the United Nations/FAO Intergovernmental Committee of the World Food Programme,
Noting the comments of the Intergovernmental Committee and its recommendation concerning the target for voluntary contributions to the Programme for the period 1973-1974,
Recalling General Assembly resolutions 2462(XXIII) of 20 December 1968 and 2682 (XXV) of 11 December 1970, in which the Assembly recognized the experience gained by the World Food Programme in the field of multilateral food aid,
1. *Submits* for consideration and approval of the General Assembly the draft resolution set forth below:

[For text, see General Assembly resolution 2805(XXVI) below.]

2. *Urges* States Members of the United Nations and members and associate members of the Food and Agriculture Organization of the United Nations to undertake the necessary preparation for the announcement of pledges at the Fifth Pledging Conference for the World Food Programme.

E/5050 and Corr.1. International food aid: procedures for assessing requirements and assuring availability of supplies. Report of Director-General of FAO prepared in response to General Assembly resolution 2462(XXIII).

General Assembly—26th session
Second Committee, meetings 1370-1382, 1426, 1427.
Plenary meeting 2017.

A/8401. Report of Secretary-General on work of the Organization, 16 June 1970–15 June 1971, Part Three, Chapter VI D.
A/8403. Report of Economic and Social Council on work of its 50th and 51st sessions, Chapter VIII E.
A/8403/Add.1. Addendum to report of Economic and Social Council, resumed 51st session, Chapter IV.
A/C.2/267. Note by Secretary-General, attaching text of resolution 1650(LI) adopted by Economic and Social Council, approved without objection by Second Committee on 2 December 1971, meeting 1427.
A/8578. Report of Second Committee (part I) (on report of Economic and Social Council), section IV and draft resolution IV.

RESOLUTION 2805(XXVI), as recommended by Second Committee, A/8578, adopted without objection by Assembly on 14 December 1971, meeting 2017.

The General Assembly,

Recalling the provisions of its resolution 2095(XX) of 20 December 1965 under which the World Food Programme is to be reviewed before each pledging conference,

Recalling the provisions contained in paragraph 5 of its resolution 2527(XXIV) of 5 December 1969 whereby, subject to the review mentioned above, the next pledging conference should be convened, at the latest, early in 1972, at which time Governments should be invited to pledge contributions for 1973 and 1974 with a view to reaching such a target as may then be recommended by the General Assembly and by the Conference of the Food and Agriculture Organization of the United Nations,

Noting that the review of the Programme was undertaken by the United Nations/FAO Intergovernmental Committee of the World Food Programme at its nineteenth session and by the Economic and Social Council at its fifty-first session,

Having considered Economic and Social Council resolution 1650(LI) of 29 October 1971, as well as the recommendation contained in the report of the Intergovernmental Committee,

Recognizing the value of multilateral food aid as implemented by the World Food Programme since its inception and the necessity for continuing its action both as a form of capital investment and for meeting emergency food needs,

1. *Establishes* for the two years 1973 and 1974 a target for voluntary contributions to the World Food Programme of $340 million, of which not less than one third should be in cash and services, and expresses the hope that such resources will be augmented by substantial additional contributions from other sources in recognition of the prospective volume of sound project requests and the capacity of the Programme to operate at a higher level;

2. *Urges* States Members of the United Nations and States members or associate members of the Food and Agriculture Organization of the United Nations to make every effort to ensure the full attainment of the target;

3. *Requests* the Secretary-General, in co-operation with the Director-General of the Food and Agriculture Organization of the United Nations, to convene a pledging conference for this purpose at United Nations Headquarters early in 1972;

4. *Decides* that, subject to the review provided for in General Assembly resolution 2095(XX), the next pledging conference at which Governments should be invited to pledge contributions for 1975 and 1976 with a view to reaching such a target as may then be recommended by the General Assembly and by the Conference of the Food and Agriculture Organization, should be convened, at the latest, early in 1974.

Elections

Economic and Social Council—50th session
Plenary meetings 1737, 1770.

E/L.1365. Election of 4 members of United Nations/FAO Intergovernmental Committee of WFP. Note by Secretary-General.

E/L.1374. Note by Secretary-General.

E/5044. Resolutions adopted by Economic and Social Council during its 50th session. Other decisions, pp. 28-29.

Chapter IV

Trade and development

In 1971, the inflation and monetary instability which marked the year were accompanied by a much reduced rate of growth of output in developed market economy countries. This posed a serious threat to the growth of exports from developing countries and to the terms of trade of those countries. Both the General Assembly and the Trade and Development Board of the United Nations Conference on Trade and Development (UNCTAD) took decisions concerning these monetary questions.

One of the Trade and Development Board's main tasks in 1971 was to prepare for the work of the third session of UNCTAD, scheduled to open at Santiago, Chile, on 11 April 1972. The Board approved a provisional agenda covering virtually all the issues within the competence of UNCTAD.

In preparation for the session at Santiago, a number of inter-governmental meetings took place: the Second Ministerial Meeting of the Group of Seventy-seven Developing Countries (at the time comprising more than 90 countries), held at Lima, Peru, from 25 October to 7 November 1971; regional meetings of the African, Asian and Latin American members of the Group of Seventy-seven held at Addis Ababa, Ethiopia, Bangkok, Thailand, and Lima, respectively; meetings of the countries members of the Organisation for Economic Co-operation and Development; and meetings of the centrally planned economy countries of Eastern Europe, under the auspices of the Council for Mutual Economic Assistance.

During 1971, the generalized system of non-discriminatory and non-reciprocal preferences for the exports of developing countries to the markets of developed countries began to be implemented. Efforts were made to negotiate an agreement on cocoa and to improve the competitive position of natural products.

Technical assistance in the field of international trade and invisible transactions continued to be extended by UNCTAD, and a work programme was approved for UNCTAD's Inter-governmental Group on Transfer of Technology.

Details of these and other matters are given in the sections that follow.

Questions of financing related to trade

During 1971, the General Assembly, the Trade and Development Board of the United Nations Conference on Trade and Development (UNCTAD) and its Committee on Invisibles and Financing related to Trade discussed matters relating to financing for trade and development in the light of the International Development Strategy for the Second United Nations Development Decade,[1] and relevant decisions of UNCTAD bodies.

Among the questions examined were: the flow of financial resources to developing countries, the liberalization of terms and conditions of assistance, the mobilization of domestic resources by developing countries, and international monetary issues.

On the question of the flow of financial resources to developing countries, the Committee, at its December 1971 session, had before it several reports. The reports noted, *inter alia,* the relative lack of progress towards attainment of the targets laid down in the Strategy with regard to the transfer of financial resources from the developed to the developing countries and the increased outflow of financial resources from developing countries in the form of remittances of profits and payments on account of amortization and interest.

The problems of developing countries experiencing a shortfall in their export earnings were examined on several occasions by the Board and the Committee. The International Bank for Reconstruction and Development, which had been requested to work out details of a scheme of supplementary financing and to assess its probable cost, informed the Board, at the latter's August-September 1971 session, that it had decided to defer further detailed studies of such a scheme because of the lack of any reasonable prospect of obtaining funds for it.

At the December 1971 meeting of the Committee on Invisibles and Financing related to Trade, developing countries members of UNCTAD repeated in a joint statement an invitation to the Bank to report on the scheme to the third session of UNCTAD, due to be held in 1972.

The Committee also had before it documents related to the evaluation of the economic effects of private foreign investment in developing countries. On the question of the mobilization of domestic resources by developing countries, the Committee requested the UNCTAD secretariat to continue to recommend appropriate measures.

A secretariat study on the debt problems of developing countries estimated that the pressure of the debt problem might increase during the 1970s and that a larger number of developing countries might be faced with difficult situations than in the 1960s. The study discussed a series of remedial measures.

Another document examined various developments relating to terms and conditions of assistance and noted that, whereas progress had been made in certain areas, significant advances had yet to be achieved on other issues, particularly on a generalized agreement on untying of aid.

In a decision taken on 14 December 1971, the General Assembly expressed its concern at the debt situation and urged competent international financial institutions and the creditor countries to give sympathetic consideration to requests from developing countries in need of rescheduling, refinancing or consolidation of their debts, and to examine ways of better adapting the conditions and terms of financial aid to the situation of individual countries. The Assembly also invited competent international organizations to identify urgently the appropriate policies to be pursued for long-term avoidance of debt crises. The Assembly's decision was embodied in resolution 2807 (XXVI). (For text of resolution, see page 301.)

One possible means of alleviating the terms of lending—namely, a multilateral interest equalization fund—was discussed by the Trade and Development Board at its August-September 1971 session. Under this scheme, the International Bank would borrow resources in capital markets and re-lend them to developing countries at lower rates of interest. The difference in the rates would be covered by a fund made up of contributions from developed countries.

International monetary issues

By a resolution adopted at its August-September 1971 session, the Trade and Development Board expressed concern at the effects of the international monetary crisis on world trade and development and called for the participation of all countries, including the developing countries, in consultations and negotiations on the reform of the international monetary system.

The Board also called upon the Secretary-General of UNCTAD to engage in urgent consultations with the Managing Director of the International Monetary Fund with a view to ensuring that the interests of all and particularly of developing countries were taken fully into account in any further evolution of the international monetary system. In addition, the Board asked the Secretary-General to carry out studies on the impact of the current international monetary situation on world trade and development, especially on that of the developing countries, and on the elements which should contribute to the necessary reform of the international monetary system.

[1]See Y. U. N., 1970, pp. 319–29, text of resolution 2626 (XXV).

In pursuance of the Board's request, a secretariat study on the monetary crisis was presented to the December 1971 session of the Committee on Invisibles and Financing related to Trade. The study pointed out that the crisis created both an opportunity for a basic reconsideration of international monetary arrangements and a means of providing for the needs of countries that had so far not played any significant role in the consultations and negotiations relating to international monetary issues.

Also, the study examined the various alternative systems available to the international community and pointed out the advantages of linking additional creation of reserves (Special Drawing Rights) with development assistance.

According to the study, such a link would stimulate world trade, assist the developed countries to attain the trade surpluses they were seeking and enable resources to be transferred to developing countries. A secretariat study presented earlier to the Board had examined in detail various aspects of the proposal to establish a link between the creation of reserves and development assistance.

At the same session of the Committee, the Secretary-General of UNCTAD reported on his consultations with the Managing Director of the International Monetary Fund. In a joint declaration, developing countries members of UNCTAD expressed their desire to participate in the consultations on the international monetary situation and expressed their intention to set up an inter-governmental group to this end. In another declaration, they invited the Managing Director of the Fund to submit a report to the third session of UNCTAD on a link between the creation of Special Drawing Rights and additional development assistance.

On 14 December 1971, the General Assembly took a number of decisions concerning the international monetary situation. These were embodied in resolutions 2806(XXVI) and 2808(XXVI).

Among other things, the Assembly recommended that any reform of the international monetary system must be geared to a more dynamic concept of world trade based on a recognition of the emerging trade requirements of the developing countries. It also urged as a preliminary measure the elimination of all restrictive measures adopted in the context of the international monetary crisis which adversely affected the developing countries. (See pp. 240-241 for the text of resolution 2806(XXVI).)

In a related decision on immediate measures to eliminate the state of uncertainty resulting from the international monetary crisis, the General Assembly called upon the developed market economy countries to take immediate measures to reverse the recent restraints on international trade and to arrange the realignment of their currencies. (See page 241 for the text of resolution 2808(XXVI).)

DOCUMENTARY REFERENCES

The Measurement of Development Effort. U. N. P. Sales No.: E.71.II.D.4.
Debt Problems of Developing Countries. Report by UNCTAD Secretariat. U. N. P. Sales No.: E.72.II.D.12.
TD/B/395 (TD/B/C.3/105). Report of Committee on Invisibles and Financing related to Trade on its 5th session, Geneva, Switzerland, 1–14 December 1971. (Annex VII: List of documents issued for 5th session.)

A/8401 and Corr.I. Report of Secretary-General on work of the Organization, 16 June 1970–15 June 1971, Part Three, Chapter IV D and E.
A/8415/Rev.I. Report of Trade and Development Board, 14 October 1970–21 September 1971: Part One, Chapter VI C 3 and 4; Part Three, Chapters III and IV F, and Annexes I (resolution 84(XI)) and II.

Commodity questions

Much of 1971 was devoted by the Trade and Development Board to preparation for the third session of the United Nations Conference on Trade and Development (UNCTAD), scheduled to open on 11 April 1972, at Santiago, Chile.

Efforts were continued towards the negotiation of an international agreement on cocoa. The International Wheat Agreement, 1971, was negotiated under UNCTAD auspices in January-February 1971.

More emphasis was given to work on commodity diversification, and studies were continued on the problems of natural products facing competition from synthetics and other substitutes.

Conferences, meetings and agreements in 1971

Committee on Commodities

The sixth session of the Committee on Commodities, held at Geneva, Switzerland, from 5 to 16 July 1971, concentrated mainly on diversification, marketing and distribution systems, and international action on particular commodities.

After considering the report of the Advisory Committee on diversification, the Committee on Commodities requested the secretariat to pursue its work on diversification on the basis of selected commodities and countries. It also called for reports to be prepared, before the third session of

UNCTAD, on possible international action to solve urgent structural problems in specific fields of the commodity sector, on technical and financial assistance for diversification and on facilities available for harmonizing diversification programmes.

The Committee on Commodities also asked the secretariat to prepare, in co-operation with other international organizations concerned, a pilot study in depth of the marketing and distribution system for cocoa.

The Committee reviewed the international commodity situation and outlook as well as international action on cocoa, oilseeds, oils and fats, rubber, tobacco, rice, temperate-zone products, iron ore, manganese ore, phosphates, tin and tungsten.

Also, the Committee adopted a recommendation (subject to reservation by certain developed market economy countries) requesting the Secretary-General of UNCTAD to accelerate his discussions with Governments, with a view to reaching an early decision on holding formal inter-governmental consultations on phosphates.

Permanent Group on Synthetics and Substitutes

The fifth session of the Permanent Group on Synthetics and Substitutes (a subsidiary body of the Committee on Commodities) was held in Geneva from 28 June to 3 July 1971. Special attention was given to UNCTAD's current survey of research and development efforts and the special problems related to natural products.

The Permanent Group took note of two reports on research and development: one on cotton and the other on hides, skins and leather.

The Permanent Group also recommended to the Secretary-General of UNCTAD that an expert group be convened to give further consideration to the UNCTAD survey of research and development efforts on hides, skins and leather and that the proposed Group assess the urgent needs for expanded international action.

Advisory Committee to Board and to Committee on Commodities

The sixth session of the Advisory Committee to the UNCTAD Trade and Development Board and to the Committee on Commodities—held 22 March to 2 April 1971—devoted itself entirely to the problems of diversification.

In its report, the Advisory Committee underlined the need for each developing country to adopt a diversification strategy appropriate to its own circumstances and stressed that the Governments of developed countries could greatly facilitate diversification in developing countries by improving access to their markets for both agricultural and industrial products. It was noted that the international agencies could play a particularly important role in assisting the harmonization of national diversification programmes and the expansion of research and development for natural products facing competition from synthetics.

Trade and Development Board

The provisional agenda for the third session of UNCTAD (scheduled to open on 11 April 1972 at Santiago, Chile), as approved by the Trade and Development Board, included the following items on commodity problems and policies: (*a*) access to markets and pricing policy, including international price stabilization measures and mechanisms; marketing and distribution systems of primary commodities; (*b*) competitiveness of natural resources; and (*c*) diversification.

Consultations on individual commodities

Cocoa

The Secretary-General of UNCTAD held separate consultations with cocoa producing and consuming countries in May and June 1971. In the light of these and earlier discussions, the secretariat prepared a document dealing with the economic provisions of a new draft cocoa agreement. On 20 September 1971, the Trade and Development Board asked the Secretary-General of UNCTAD to take all appropriate steps towards the convening of a negotiating conference on cocoa as soon as possible. It further requested Governments to do their utmost to ensure that an international cocoa agreement was concluded as soon as possible.

In response to these requests, the document on economic provisions of a new cocoa agreement was considered during consultations held in Geneva from 22 September to 1 October 1971.

Later in the year, in connexion with decisions taken concerning the third (1972) session of UNCTAD, the General Assembly expressed the view that the conclusion of an international cocoa agreement as soon as possible would be of great importance and would contribute to the success of the third session of UNCTAD. This decision was embodied in resolution 2820(XXVI), adopted on 16 December 1971. (See pp. 283-84 for text of resolution.)

Hard fibres

The Consultative Sub-Committee of the Food and Agriculture Organization Study Group on Hard Fibres met in May 1971 and agreed on new quotas and on indicative target prices. Consequently, informal arrangements for hard fibres that were in operation in 1968 and 1969 were again in force.

Sugar

The fifth session of the International Sugar Council, which had been held in November 1970, established the initial export quotas for 1971.

At the sixth session of the International Sugar Council, held in March 1971, a procedure was adopted to review the operation of the international agreement concerning this commodity. In addition, the International Sugar Organization made representations to the European Economic Community, drawing attention to concern about the effects that an enlarged Community might have on the access to markets of sugar from exporting countries.

Tea

In April 1971, the standing Exporters Group met and an earlier decision on the global quota for tea for 1971 was confirmed. Individual country quotas and the principles of a long-term agreement were also discussed during 1971.

Tin

The Fourth International Tin Agreement went into operation on 1 July 1971 for a period of five years.

Wheat

The United Nations Wheat Conference, which was held under UNCTAD auspices in Geneva from 18 January to 20 February 1971, adopted the text of the International Wheat Agreement, 1971, consisting of the Wheat Trade Convention and the Food Aid Convention.

The Wheat Trade Convention contained no price provisions but did provide for continued international co-operation and consultations on wheat and for the examination, at an appropriate time, of the questions of prices and related rights and obligations, with a view to renegotiating the Convention when a successful outcome seemed likely. The duration of both conventions was to be three years, except in the event of an earlier renegotiation of the Wheat Trade Convention.

Other commodity matters

On 20 September 1971, the Trade and Development Board took decisions concerning commodity problems and policies. It asked the Secretary-General of UNCTAD to prepare, in co-operation with the commodity bodies concerned and for submission to the third (1972) session of UNCTAD, a study on the effectiveness of existing international commodity agreements, with a view to suggesting measures designed to maximize possible benefits from those agreements to all participating countries, especially the developing countries.

Also on 20 September 1971, the Board asked the Secretary-General of UNCTAD to prepare a factual study, to be submitted to the third session of UNCTAD, on developments in the terms of trade over the longer term, paying special attention to the situation of the developing countries, particularly the least developed among them.

DOCUMENTARY REFERENCES

TD/B/348 (TD/B/C.1/113). Report of Advisory Committee to Trade and Development Board and to Committee on Commodities on its 6th session, Geneva, Switzerland, 22 March–2 April 1971.

TD/B/366 (TD/B/C.1/112). Report of Permanent Group on Synthetics and Substitutes on its 5th session, Geneva, Switzerland, 28 June–3 July 1971. (Annex II: List of documents issued for 5th session.)

TD/B/370 (TD/B/C.1/119). Report of Committee on Commodities on its 6th session, Geneva, Switzerland, 5–16 July 1971. (Annex I: Decision 5(VI) and recommendation 6(VI) adopted by Committee at its 6th session; Annex IV: List of documents issued for 6th session.)

United Nations Wheat Conference, 1971. U.N.P. Sales No.: E.71.II.D.10.

A/8401. Report of Secretary-General on work of the Organization, 16 June 1970–15 June 1971, Part Three, Chapter IV B.

A/8403/Add.1. Addendum to report of Economic and Social Council, resumed 51st session, Chapter III.

A/8415/Rev.1. Report of Trade and Development Board, 14 October 1970–21 September 1971: Part One, Chapter VI C 1; Part Three, Chapter IV A and Annex I (resolution 85(XI)).

Other commodity matters

A/8415/Rev.1. Report of Trade and Development Board, 14 October 1970–21 September 1971: Part Three, Chapter IV A and Annex I (resolution 86(XI)), and other decision taken by Board during its 11th session, p. 213 (Study on developments in terms of trade over longer term).

Questions pertaining to manufactures

During 1971, the United Nations Conference on Trade and Development (UNCTAD) continued its efforts to promote and diversify the exports of manufactures and semi-manufactures produced in developing countries. Through its Committee on Manufactures, which held its fifth session from 3 to 14 May 1971, UNCTAD was also concerned with questions of restrictive business practices, tariff and non-tariff barriers as well as export policies.

An emphasis in 1971 was on the implementation of the generalized system of non-reciprocal and non-discriminatory preferences for exports of products originating in developing countries and destined for markets in developed countries. In this connexion, special attention was given to the liberalization of non-tariff barriers and to appropriate adjustment assistance measures by the developed countries.

The identification of restrictive business practices affecting exports of developing countries and appropriate remedial measures were studied. Research continued on export policies for the expansion and diversification of trade in manufactures and semi-manufactures.

Preferential arrangements

In pursuance of a provision of the Agreed Conclusions adopted by the Special Committee on Preferences in 1970[2] the preference-giving countries, Contracting Parties to the General Agreement on Tariffs and Trade (GATT), obtained a waiver of their obligations under GATT for a period of 10 years, permitting them to accord preferential treatment to products originating in developing countries and territories.

Subsequently the European Economic Community implemented its scheme of generalized preferences on 1 July 1971. Schemes of Japan and Norway were implemented on 1 August 1971 and 1 October 1971, respectively. Czechoslovakia, Denmark, Finland, Hungary, Sweden and the United Kingdom were to put into effect their schemes on 1 January 1972. Austria and Switzerland indicated they would implement their schemes early in 1972.

When, in October 1970, the Trade and Development Board agreed that UNCTAD had the responsibility for the review of the implementation of the generalized system of preferences, as outlined in the Agreed Conclusions of the Special Committee on Preferences, no decision was taken on the appropriate body within UNCTAD to carry out this work.

On 17 September 1971, the Board decided again to postpone this decision for a period not beyond the thirteenth session of the Board, due to be held in 1973, and, pending this decision, the existence of the Special Committee on Preferences was to be extended.

The Governing Council of the United Nations Development Programme (UNDP), at its June 1971 session, approved a Special Fund project on training and advisory services on the generalized system of preferences, which would be carried out by UNCTAD in co-operation with other appropriate bodies. The purpose of the three-year project was to assist developing countries to derive maximum benefits from the generalized system of preferences.

On 16 December 1971, the General Assembly among other things urged UNCTAD at its third session (which was scheduled to open on 11 April 1972 at Santiago, Chile) to appeal to all preference-giving countries which had not yet done so to implement their offers under the generalized system of preferences in favour of the developing countries; and to pursue efforts in a dynamic context for further improvements of these preferential arrangements. This decision was among those embodied in resolution 2820(XXVI). (For text, see pp. 283-84.)

Tariff reclassification

At its May 1971 session, the Committee on Manufactures considered a note on tariff reclassification prepared by the UNCTAD secretariat in collaboration with the Customs Co-operation Council. This report contained a list of hand-made and handicraft products that did not appear to be included in the various preferential offers under the generalized system of preferences. The Committee reiterated its request to the Customs Co-operation Council to expedite the technical study of hand-made and handicraft products in order to develop criteria for their identification and distinction from machine-made counterparts.

Non-tariff barriers

With the progressive lowering of tariffs, non-tariff barriers were found to have become the principal instrument for restricting imports. In the light of developments tending to widen the application of such barriers, efforts towards their liberalization became an important concern of UNCTAD.

Among the measures for liberalization under consideration in UNCTAD were: effective adherence to a standstill on the raising or establishment of non-tariff barriers; measures for the reduction and removal of quantitative restrictions and related non-tariff barriers; and advanced liberalization of quantitative restrictions affecting exports of developing countries.

The Committee on Manufactures, at its May 1971 session, reviewed progress made in the field of non-tariff barriers and adjustment assistance, on the basis of reports submitted by the secretariat.

A proposal recommending the establishment of an *ad hoc* inter-governmental group to carry out consultations and negotiations on non-tariff barriers was considered, as was another concerning the secretariat's work on non-tariff barriers, giving special attention to barriers of concern to developing countries.

The Committee on Manufactures took note of these proposals and referred them to the Trade and Development Board, at the same time requesting the UNCTAD secretariat to continue its work on non-tariff barriers. It was recommended that this work be carried out in co-operation with GATT.

The Trade and Development Board, at its

---

[2]See Y.U.N., 1970, pp. 378–79.

August-September 1971 session, in turn referred the proposals raised in the Committee for consideration at the third (1972) session of UNCTAD.

Restrictive business practices

The first substantive report on the question of restrictive business practices was considered by the Committee on Manufactures at its May 1971 session. The report presented the legal aspects and facts about restrictive business practices in relation to the export interests of the developing countries. In particular, it dealt with import and export cartels, agreements on standards, and restrictions on export activity in licensing agreements with firms in developing countries. Following consideration of the report, the Committee gave the secretariat a broad and flexible mandate to continue its work on the subject.

Export policies

Also at the May 1971 session of the Committee on Manufactures, it was noted that in future country studies the UNCTAD secretariat would give priority to the least developed among the developing countries and that, in addition to short- and medium-term export prospects, the secretariat would take into account long-term prospects for exports.

With regard to international sub-contracting, the Committee agreed that this activity could be a valuable means of assisting the expansion and diversification of exports from developing countries, as well as an effective vehicle for the transfer of technology to developing countries. Intensive studies would be carried out in this area by UNCTAD in co-operation with other bodies.

(See also pp. 286-87 and 299-300.)

DOCUMENTARY REFERENCES

Restrictive Business Practices. Interim Report by the UNCTAD Secretariat. U.N.P. Sales No.: E.72.II.D.10.

TD/B/352 (TD/B/C.2/112). Report of Committee on Manufactures on its 5th session, Geneva, Switzerland, 3–14 May 1971. (Annex I: Decision 1(V) and conclusion 2(V) of Committee; Annex VIII: List of documents issued for 5th session.)

A/8401. Report of Secretary-General on work of the Organization, 16 June 1970–15 June 1971: Part Three, Chapter IV C.

A/8415/Rev.1. Report of Trade and Development Board, 14 October 1970–21 September 1971: Part One, Chapters IV and VI C 2; Part Three, Chapters IV B and C and IX A, and Annexes I (resolution 80(XI)) and III.

Questions pertaining to invisibles, including shipping

The Committee on Shipping of the United Nations Conference on Trade and Development (UNCTAD), at its March-April 1971 session, considered questions relating to current and long-term trends of shipping problems, consultation in shipping, technological progress in shipping, the development of ports, and financial assistance for the acquisition of ships by developing countries.

On trends of shipping problems, the Committee on Shipping urged members of UNCTAD to continue their efforts to give effect to UNCTAD resolutions by inviting their shipowners to reduce maritime transport costs and freight rates, taking into account the special needs of the least developed countries and the land-locked developing countries. The UNCTAD secretariat was asked to study the question.

The Committee on Shipping, in another decision, recommended that a study be undertaken on the economic implications, in particular for developing countries, of a proposed convention on the international combined transport of goods.

Considering that adequate data on port operations was essential for the efficient working of ports, the Committee recommended that the United Nations regional economic commissions be invited to support requests for assistance through the United Nations Development Programme for the implementation of recommended methods of selection, collection and presentation of port data.

The Committee on Shipping also took note of the report of the Working Group on International Shipping Legislation and of decisions taken by the Group, at its February 1971 session, on bills of lading and on a programme of work on liner conference practices.

At its August 1971 session, the Committee on Shipping increased the membership of the Working Group from 33 to 38 and elected the members.

Among the principal publications issued in 1971 on shipping and ports were: *Review of Maritime Transport; Unitization of Cargo;* and *Port Statistics.*

Insurance and tourism

Insurance and tourism were considered at the fifth session of the Committee on Invisibles and Financing related to Trade (held in December 1971).

The Committee discussed various measures designed to strengthen the national insurance markets of the developing countries and to reduce their insurance costs. On tourism, it examined steps for encouraging travel to the developing countries.

DOCUMENTARY REFERENCES

TD/B/347 (TD/B/C.4/89). Report of Committee on Shipping on first part of its 5th session, Geneva, Switzerland, 22 March–3 April 1971. (Annex I: Resolutions adopted and decisions taken by Committee during first part of 5th session; Annex IX: List of documents issued for 5th session.)

TD/B/377 (TD/B/C.4/91). Report of Committee on Shipping on 2nd part of its 5th session, Geneva, Switzerland, 31 August 1971. (Annex II: List of documents issued for 2nd part of 5th session.)

TD/B/395 (TD/B/C.3/105). Report of Committee on Invisibles and Financing related to Trade on its 5th session, Geneva, Switzerland, 1–14 December 1971. (Annex I: Texts of draft resolutions relating to insurance and tourism submitted during 5th session; Annex VIII: List of documents issued for 5th session.)

A/8401. Report of Secretary-General on work of the Organization, 16 June 1970–15 June 1971, Part Three, Chapter IV E.

A/8415/Rev. 1. Report of Trade and Development Board, 14 October 1970–21 September 1971: Part One, Chapter VI C 3; Part Three, Chapters IV D and IX A.

Publications

Port Statistics. Selection, Collection and Presentation of Port Information and Statistics. Manual prepared by UNCTAD secretariat. U.N.P. Sales No.: E.72.II.D.1.

Unitization of Cargo. U.N.P. Sales No.: E.71.II.D.2.

Review of Maritime Transport, 1970. U.N.P. Sales No.: E.71.II.D.8.

Insurance Legislation and Supervision in Developing Countries. U.N.P. Sales No.: E.72.II.D.4 and corrigendum and addendum.

Questions pertaining to the development of trade relations

Least developed countries

The Group of Experts convened by the Secretary-General of the United Nations Conference on Trade and Development (UNCTAD) to consider the question of special measures in favour of the least developed among the developing countries met at Geneva, Switzerland, from 26 April to 5 May 1971, and prepared a report which was considered by the Trade and Development Board of UNCTAD at its August-September 1971 session.

On 18 September 1971, the Board approved, without prejudice to future consideration, the list of countries identified as the hard core least developed by the Group of Experts and by the Committee for Development Planning.

At the same time, the Board requested the Secretary-General of UNCTAD to work out a detailed and comprehensive action-oriented programme, within UNCTAD's competence, in favour of the least developed countries, and to present it to the third session of UNCTAD due to open on 11 April 1972, at Santiago, Chile.

The Board also invited the Secretary-General of UNCTAD to appoint a group of experts to assist him in the preparation of this action programme. The expert group met in Geneva from 13 to 21 December 1971.

On 30 July 1971, the Economic and Social Council asked the General Assembly to take a decision at its 1971 session on an agreed list of least developed countries on the basis of the relevant reports to be submitted to it by the Committee for Development Planning and by the UNCTAD Trade and Development Board. This was among decisions contained in resolution 1628(LI). (For text of resolution, see p. 234.)

At its twenty-sixth session, which opened on 21 September 1971, the General Assembly approved the list of hard core least developed countries and called for the review of criteria for identification keeping in view the possibility of modifications of the list as early as possible.

The Assembly took note of the action-oriented programme to be prepared by the Secretary-General of UNCTAD, and requested other organs and programmes of the United Nations to initiate, as appropriate, similar programmes within their respective fields of competence. These decisions were among those embodied in resolution 2768(XXVI). (For text, see p. 235.)

In a related decision, the Assembly urged the adoption of a comprehensive action-oriented programme in favour of the least developed countries at the third (1972) session of UNCTAD. (See pp. 283-84, text of resolution 2820(XXVI)).

Land-locked countries

At its August-September 1971 session, the Trade and Development Board considered the special problems of the land-locked countries, and requested the Secretary-General of UNCTAD to prepare a comprehensive action programme, within the competence of UNCTAD, in favour of the land-locked developing countries, and to present it to the third (1972) session of UNCTAD.

Later in the year—on 16 December 1971—the General Assembly urged the adoption at the third session of UNCTAD of a comprehensive action programme in favour of the land-locked developing countries. This decision was embodied in resolution 2820(XXVI). (For text of resolution, see pp. 283-84.)

Trade promotion: International Trade Centre

In 1971, the International Trade Centre, jointly administered by UNCTAD and by the Contracting Parties to the General Agreement on Tariffs and Trade, completed its fourth year of operation.

The Centre offered trade promotion assistance to developing countries by providing information on export markets, assisting in the development of export promotion and marketing organizations and services, and helping in the training of specialized personnel.

(For further information on the International Trade Centre, see pp. 286-87.)

Trade expansion, economic co-operation and integration among developing countries

In 1971, the activities of the UNCTAD secretariat in the field of trade expansion, economic co-operation and regional integration among developing countries included, in addition to research and technical assistance programmes, the preparation of documentation for UNCTAD's third session.

Research studies on the following matters were completed: the expansion of agricultural trade in groupings of developing countries; industrial integration systems; and the institutional aspects of regional integration in developing countries.

The following studies were in preparation: the effects of reverse preferences and other discriminatory arrangements on trade among developing countries, regional economic integration, and regional integration and the generalized system of preferences.

In the field of technical assistance, sectoral reports on economic co-operation between the member countries of the Association of South-East Asian Nations were completed. Continued assistance was extended to the East African Community, the Caribbean Free Trade Association, the Regional Co-operation for Development (embracing Iran, Pakistan and Turkey) and the South Pacific Commission.

New activities included, among others: support for the new phase of integration of the Central African Customs and Economic Union; assistance to the Central American Common Market for the preparation of a study which would serve as a basis for the Market's restructuring, and to Ecuador, one of the less developed members of the Latin American Free Trade Association, for the formulation of foreign trade and industrial development policy and an export promotion programme; and the preparation of a technical assistance project for the regional integration programme of the Andean Group.

The Trade Negotiations Committee of Developing Countries, jointly serviced by the Contracting Parties to the General Agreement on Tariffs and Trade (GATT) and UNCTAD, concluded successfully a first round of negotiations. The results were embodied in a Protocol and a consolidated schedule of concessions to be applied among the 16 participating countries—two of which were not Contracting Parties to GATT. The Contracting Parties had granted a waiver to participating countries allowing the implementation of the tariff concessions exchanged during the negotiations.

As part of the preparation for the third session of UNCTAD, the secretariat prepared three separate studies on: the main problems of trade expansion

and economic integration among developing countries; the support of the centrally planned economy countries of Eastern Europe to economic co-operation among developing countries; and the role of multinational development institutions in economic integration.

The Trade and Development Board, at its March 1971 session, invited all member Governments of UNCTAD to act on the conclusions of the report of the Inter-governmental Group which met in 1970, recommending that the main Committees of the Board take account of relevant matters contained in that report and welcoming the measures taken by member countries of the Organisation for Economic Co-operation and Development.

Trade relations among countries with different economic and social systems

In 1971, the United Nations Conference on Trade and Development (UNCTAD) continued to deal with the problems of trade relations among countries having different economic and social systems, on the basis of guidelines accepted at the UNCTAD session held at New Delhi, India, in 1968.

The Trade and Development Board, at its August-September 1971 session, considered the results attained and the possible ways for their implementation.

Concerning trade between the centrally planned economy countries of Eastern Europe and the developing countries, the Board observed an increase and further diversification, particularly in respect of increasing imports of manufactures from the developing countries. East-West trade was expanding at an appreciable rate as a result of diminishing obstacles and rising industrial specialization. The centrally planned economy countries of Eastern Europe continued to give active support to preferential measures applied to imports of manufactures from the developing countries.

By a decision of 16 December 1971, the General Assembly urged UNCTAD at its third (1972) session to review the progress achieved since its second (1968) session in promoting trade relations among countries having different economic and social systems. This decision was among those embodied in resolution 2820(XXVI). (For text, see pp. 283-84.)

International trade law

During its August-September 1971 session, the Trade and Development Board asked the Secretary-General of UNCTAD to convey to the General Assembly the comments made during the session on the report of the United Nations Commission on International Trade Law. The Board also expressed satisfaction with the co-ordination of the work programmes of the Commission and of the UNCTAD Working Group on International Shipping Legislation.

(For further information on the Commission on International Trade Law, see pp. 595-96.)

DOCUMENTARY REFERENCES

Least developed countries
Special Measures in Favour of the Least Developed among the Developing Countries. Report of the Ad Hoc Group of Experts on special measures in favour of the least developed among the developing countries, Geneva, Switzerland, 26 April–5 May 1971 (TD/B/349/Rev.1). U.N.P. Sales No.: E.71.II.D.11.
A/8415/Rev.1. Report of Trade and Development Board, 14 October 1970–21 September 1971, Part Three, Chapter VII and Annex I (resolution 82(XI)).

Land-locked countries
A/8415/Rev.1. Report of Trade and Development Board, 14 October 1970–21 September 1971, Part Three, Chapter VIII and Annex I (Other decisions taken by Board during its 11th session), p. 213.

Trade promotion:
International Trade Centre
A/8415/Rev.1. Report of Trade and Development Board, 14 October 1970–21 September 1971, Part One, Chapter III.

Trade expansion, economic co-operation
and integration among developing countries
A/8415/Rev.1. Report of Trade and Development Board, 14 October 1970–21 September 1971, Part One, Chapters I and VI C 6, and Annex I (resolution 77(X)).
Current Problems of Economic Integration. Fiscal compensation and the distribution of benefits in economic groupings of developing countries. U.N.P. Sales No.: E.71.II.D.6.
A/8401. Report of Secretary-General on work of the Organization, 16 June 1970–15 June 1971, Part Three, Chapter IV F.

Trade relations among countries
with different economic and social systems
A/8415/Rev.1. Report of Trade and Development Board, 14 October 1970–21 September 1971: Part One, Chapter VI C 5; Part Three, Chapter V.

International trade law
A/8415/Rev.1. Report of Trade and Development Board, 14 October 1970–21 September 1971, Part Three, Chapter IX B.

Technical assistance and related activities

Technical assistance

During 1971, the United Nations Conference on Trade and Development (UNCTAD), as a participating agency of the United Nations Development Programme (UNDP), continued its operational role in developing technical assistance in the field of international trade and invisible transactions.

The technical assistance activities of UNCTAD encompassed these main areas: export promotion and marketing; trade expansion and economic integration; shipping and ports; and insurance and re-insurance.

The projects took the form of providing advisory services to Governments, granting fellowships for study or observation abroad and organizing training courses and seminars on specialized subjects, including symposia for Government officials, particularly in export promotion and trade policy.

Projects on export promotion included market surveys for specific products of developing countries in foreign markets. Export promotion continued to receive the primary emphasis in UNCTAD's technical assistance, substantive support being carried out by the International Trade Centre, jointly administered by UNCTAD and the Contracting Parties to the General Agreement on Tariffs and Trade (GATT). (See pp. 286-87.)

Such activities were funded by extra budgetary resources obtained from UNDP, and the United Nations Regular Programme of Technical Co-operation. As at 30 June 1971, the UNCTAD programme included projects to a value of $2,546,800 for 1971, and $4,540,700 for 1972.

Technical assistance was also provided by UNCTAD through inter-regional advisers. The UNDP Governing Council, at its June 1971 session, approved a large-scale project involving advisory services and training of Government officials on an inter-regional basis to assist developing countries in benefiting from the generalized system of preferences. More than a million dollars for a period of three years was earmarked for this purpose.

Transfer of technology

The 45-member Inter-governmental Group on Transfer of Technology of UNCTAD, set up by the Trade and Development Board in 1970,[3] held its first session from 14 to 21 June 1971.

The Group unanimously agreed on a comprehensive work programme, covering four main areas which fell directly within the competence of UNCTAD and two other areas where UNCTAD's contribution would be to supplement the activities of various international agencies and organizations.

The main areas to be covered were: channels and mechanisms for the transfer; costs of the transfer; access to technology; trade and the transfer of technology.

The two other areas were: the substitution of domestic for imported technology and the choice of technology.

The Trade and Development Board, at its August-September 1971 session, took note of the Group's report.

[3]See Y.U.N., 1970, p. 390.

At its twenty-sixth session, which opened on 21 September 1971, the General Assembly also took up the question of the transfer of technology.

On 16 December 1971, the Assembly welcomed the comprehensive programme of work adopted by the Inter-governmental Group on Transfer of Technology. In this connexion it noted that unless decisive action was taken at all levels for a more rapid transfer of adequate technology to the developing countries, the growing rate of technological development in the world would contribute to widening further the technological gap between developed and developing countries.

The Assembly recommended that UNCTAD at its third session, due to open on 11 April 1972, seek agreement on action, to be carried out as part of the International Development Strategy for the Second United Nations Development Decade,[4] to facilitate the adequate transfer of technology to developing countries and to create the necessary infrastructure for the technological development of developing countries.

International financing organizations, in particular the United Nations Development Programme, the International Bank for Reconstruc-tion and Development and the regional development banks, were urged to give high priority to economic assistance to meet the needs of developing countries in the field of technology, particularly in connexion with the development of a basic infrastructure.

Finally, the Assembly recommended that in all action related to the transfer of operative technology referred to in these decisions, special consideration should be given to the stage of development and special position of the least developed countries.

These decisions were embodied in resolution 2821(XXVI), adopted, without objection, on the recommendation of the Assembly's Second (Economic and Financial) Committee, which had approved without objection, on 7 December 1971, a revised text sponsored by Brazil, Chile, India, Nicaragua, Peru, the Philippines, Romania, Sudan, Uganda, Uruguay, Venezuela and Yugoslavia.

(For text of resolution, see DOCUMENTARY REFERENCES below.)

[4]See Y.U.N., 1970, pp. 319–29, text of resolution 2626(XXV).

DOCUMENTARY REFERENCES

Technical assistance
A/8401. Report of Secretary-General on work of the Organization, 16 June 1970–15 June 1971, Part Three, Chapter IV G.
A/8415/Rev.1. Report of Trade and Development Board, 14 October 1970–21 September 1971, Part Three, Chapter IX A.

Transfer of technology
TD/B/365. Report of Inter-governmental Group on Transfer of Technology on its organizational (first) session, Geneva, Switzerland, 14–21 June 1971.
Transfer of Operative Technology at the Enterprise Level. Report of an Inter-regional Expert Group on its Meeting held in New York from 21 to 26 June 1971. U.N.P. Sales No.: E.72.II.A.1.

General Assembly—26th session
Second Committee, meetings 1414–1421, 1424, 1429–1432.
Plenary meeting 2021.

A/8403/Add.1. Addendum to report of Economic and Social Council, resumed 51st session, Chapter III.
A/8415/Rev.1. Report of Trade and Development Board, 14 October 1970–21 September 1971: Part One, Chapter V; Part Two; Part Three, Chapter IV E.
A/C.2/270 and Corr.1. Letter of 12 November 1971 from Peru (transmitting Declaration and Principles of Action Programme adopted at Lima, Peru, on 7 November 1971, by 2nd Ministerial Meeting of Group of 77 Developing Countries (TD/143)).
A/C.2/L.1198. Brazil, Chile, Peru, Philippines, Romania, Sudan, Uganda, Uruguay, Venezuela, Yugoslavia: draft resolution.
A/C.2/L.1198/Rev.1. Brazil, Chile, India, Nicaragua, Peru, Philippines, Romania, Sudan, Uganda, Uruguay, Venezuela, Yugoslavia; revised draft resolution, as orally revised by sponsors, approved without objection by Second Committee on 7 December 1971, meeting 1432.
A/8558. Report of Second Committee, draft resolution II.

RESOLUTION 2821(XXVI), as recommended by Second Commit-tee, A/8558, adopted without objection by Assembly on 16 December 1971, meeting 2021.

The General Assembly,
Recalling its resolution 2658(XXV) of 7 December 1970, concerning the role of modern science and technology in the development of nations and the need to strengthen economic and technico-scientific co-operation among States, and its resolution 2726(XXV) of 15 December 1970 on the transfer of technology, including know-how and patents,
Having considered the report of the Trade and Development Board on its eleventh session,
Conscious of the fact that, unless decisive action is taken at all levels, especially at the international level, for a more rapid transfer of adequate technology to the developing countries, the growing rate of technological development in the world will contribute to widening further the technological gap between developed and developing countries, particularly the least developed among them,
1. *Welcomes* the unanimous adoption by the Intergovernmental Group on Transfer of Technology of the United Nations Conference on Trade and Development—at its first session, devoted to organizational matters—of a comprehensive programme of work, in the field of the transfer of operative technology to the developing countries, to be pursued on a continuing basis;
2. *Reiterates* the request made in its resolution 2726(XXV) that the States members of the United Nations Conference on Trade and Development give their fullest support to the Intergovernmental Group on Transfer of Technology, and expresses the hope that the three remaining vacancies in the Group will be filled from among States given in list B of the annex to General Assembly resolution 1995(XIX) of 30 December 1964 before it holds its first substantive session;
3. *Recommends* that the United Nations Conference on Trade and Development at its third session should seek agreement on action, to be carried out as an integral part of the International Development Strategy for the Second United Nations Develop-

ment Decade, contained in General Assembly resolution 2626(XXV) of 24 October 1970, within its field of competence, to facilitate the adequate transfer of technology to developing countries on reasonable terms and conditions and to create the necessary infrastructure for the technological development of developing countries, including the transfer of specifications of the raw materials and technological processes utilized in production;

4. *Urges* international financing organizations and programmes, in particular the United Nations Development Programme, the International Bank for Reconstruction and Development and regional development banks, to give high priority to economic assistance, according to the priorities established by developing countries, to meet their needs in the field of technology, particularly in connexion with the development of a basic infrastructure, including the training of personnel and the establishment or strengthening of extension services for the application of technology to production units, and taking into consideration the need to reduce the effective cost involved in the transfer of operative technology to developing countries;

5. *Recommends* that in all action related to the transfer of operative technology referred to in paragraphs 3 and 4 above special consideration shall be given to the stage of development and special position of the least developed countries.

Role of the United Nations Conference on Trade and Development in Second United Nations Development Decade

The General Assembly, in adopting the International Development Strategy for the Second United Nations Development Decade, on 24 October 1970, included a provision whereby the United Nations Conference on Trade and Development (UNCTAD) would continue to review progress in its fields of competence.[5]

On 27 August 1971, the Secretary-General of UNCTAD invited member Governments of UNCTAD to provide information needed in determining UNCTAD's role in achieving the purposes of the International Development Strategy. It noted, in this connexion, that since the Second Development Decade had only begun, indications of progress in conformity with the Strategy would largely involve indications of actions envisaged or planned.

On 17 September 1971, the Trade and Development Board reaffirmed UNCTAD's responsibility within its fields of competence for: (a) reviewing the progress made in implementation of the measures contained in the International Development Strategy; (b) reaching agreement in more specific terms on issues which had not been fully resolved; (c) seeking new areas of agreement and widening existing ones; and (d) evolving new concepts and seeking agreement on additional measures.

The Board also requested the third session of UNCTAD (due to open on 11 April 1972) to consider adequate procedures and mechanisms necessary for the review and appraisal of the objectives and measures of the International Development Strategy falling within UNCTAD's competence.

Prior to the Board's action, the Economic and Social Council took certain decisions concerning the machinery for review and appraisal of the policy measures and the goals and objectives of the International Development Strategy. The Council, on 30 July 1971, among other things called upon the Trade and Development Board of UNCTAD, among other bodies, to consider adequate procedures for such review and appraisal. This Council action was embodied in resolution 1621C(LI). (See pp. 229-30 for text of resolution.)

At its twenty-sixth session, which opened on 21 September 1971, the General Assembly also considered the question of review and appraisal of the objectives and policies of the International Development Strategy. On 14 December 1971, the Assembly among other decisions invited the UNCTAD Trade and Development Board and other bodies to integrate their review activities with the preparatory work for the over-all review and appraisal so as to avoid unnecessary duplication. This Assembly decision was embodied in resolution 2801(XXVI). (See page 231 for text of resolution.)

On 16 December, the Assembly, in adopting resolution 2820(XXVI), reaffirmed the essential role of UNCTAD in the review and appraisal of progress in the implementation of the Strategy and invited UNCTAD at its third (1972) session to provide general guidelines for the establishment by the Trade and Development Board of procedures and mechanisms for this review and appraisal, including appropriate institutional arrangements. (See pp. 283-84 for text of resolution.)

(For further details about the Second United Nations Development Decade, see pp. 225-36.)

---

[5]See Y.U.N., 1970, pp. 319–29, text of resolution 2626(XXV), para. 82.

DOCUMENTARY REFERENCES

A/8415/Rev.1. Report of Trade and Development Board, 14 October 1970–21 September 1971: Part One, Annex IV; Part Three, Chapters I and XI H and Annexes I (resolution 81(XI)) and V.

Third session of the United Nations Conference on Trade and Development

During 1971, the General Assembly and the Trade and Development Board of the United Nations Conference on Trade and Development (UNCTAD) considered the question of the third session of UNCTAD, due to be held in April-May 1972.

In accordance with an Assembly decision of 30 December 1964,[6] by which UNCTAD was established, UNCTAD was expected to convene a conference at intervals of not more than three years. Its second session was held at New Delhi, India, in 1968.[7]

On 5 March 1971, the Trade and Development Board recommended to the General Assembly that the third session of UNCTAD be held at Santiago, Chile. By a Board decision of 6 March, the Secretary-General of UNCTAD was requested to pursue his consultations with member Governments with a view to submitting by July 1971 a draft provisional agenda for consideration by the Board.

The Board approved a provisional agenda for the Conference on 18 September 1971. The agenda covered the wide range of topics that fall within the competence of UNCTAD: trends in world trade, the international monetary situation, special problems of the least developed countries, export promotion, commodity problems, questions relating to manufactures, financial resources for development, shipping, trade expansion, trade relations among countries with different economic and social systems, the transfer of technology, and other subjects.

The General Assembly, on 16 December 1971, took a number of decisions concerning the third session of UNCTAD.

Noting with concern that the monetary crisis and trends towards intensification of protectionism might threaten the very basis of international economic co-operation and have a negative impact on the vital trade and development interests of developing countries, the Assembly expressed the view that the third session of UNCTAD provided a fresh opportunity to make a collective and determined endeavour to correct the adverse situation confronting the developing countries.

The Assembly accepted the invitation of the Government of Chile to hold the third session of UNCTAD at Santiago, from 11 April to 19 May 1972.

The Assembly urged UNCTAD to adopt at its third session comprehensive action-oriented programmes incorporating special measures in favour of the least developed countries and the land-locked developing countries. The Assembly expressed the view that the conclusion of an international cocoa agreement as soon as possible would be of great importance and would contribute to the success of the third session of UNCTAD.

Member States were urged in their preparations for the session to give serious consideration to the Declaration and Principles of the Action Programme adopted at an October-November 1971 meeting of the Group of Seventy-seven Developing Countries, which contained proposals aimed at solving through international co-operation the problems of trade and development of developing countries.

The Assembly also urged UNCTAD at its third session to appeal to preference-giving countries that had not yet done so to implement their offers under the generalized system of preferences in favour of developing countries, and to pursue efforts for further improvements of these preferential arrangements.

The Assembly agreed that the third session of UNCTAD should undertake a comprehensive review of its institutional arrangements with a view to improving the efficiency of its operations and strengthening its role as a centre for the initiation of action for the negotiation and adoption of multilateral legal instruments in the field of trade.

The Assembly reaffirmed the essential role of UNCTAD to review and appraise the progress achieved in the implementation of the International Development Strategy of the Second United Nations Development Decade,[8] to seek new areas of agreement and to evolve new concepts or additional measures.

The Conference at its third session was invited: to provide general guidelines for the establishment by the Trade and Development Board of adequate procedures and mechanisms for assessing progress in the implementation of the policy measures within its fields of competence; to make the institutional machinery of UNCTAD fully oriented towards the implementation of the relevant provisions of the International Development Strategy and, to this end, to promote consultations aimed at enabling member States to make a more effective contribution to the achievement of the Strategy's goals and objectives; and to give consideration to such reforms of the fundamental provisions of the 1964 Assembly decision establishing UNCTAD as to promote further evolution in the continuing machinery and in the method of work of UNCTAD designed to increase its effectiveness.

Finally, the Assembly decided to consider the results of the third session of UNCTAD in 1972.

These decisions were embodied in the Assembly's resolution 2820(XXVI), adopted, unanimously, on the recommendation of the Assembly's

[6]See Y.U.N., 1964, pp. 210–14, text of resolution 1995(XIX).
[7]See Y.U.N., 1968, pp. 368–85.
[8]See Y.U.N., 1970, pp. 319–29, text of resolution 2626(XXV).

Second (Economic and Financial) Committee. The Committee unanimously approved, on 6 December, a revised text proposed by Afghanistan, Algeria, Brazil, Ceylon, Chad, Chile, Colombia, the Congo, the Dominican Republic, Ecuador, Egypt, Ethiopia, Ghana, Honduras, Indonesia, Laos, Malaysia, Mali, Nepal, Nigeria, Pakistan, Peru, the Philippines, Romania, Rwanda, Sudan, the Syrian Arab Republic, Thailand, Trinidad and Tobago, Uganda, the United Republic of Tanzania, Upper Volta, Venezuela and Yugoslavia. (For text of resolution, see DOCUMENTARY REFERENCES below.)

A number of amendments, both oral and written, proposed by Colombia, by Kenya, by Madagascar, Rwanda and Senegal, and by the Netherlands were withdrawn after they had been taken into account in a revision of the text.

In the Second Committee, a separate vote was requested by Australia on the paragraph having to do with UNCTAD undertaking a comprehensive review of its institutional arrangements; the paragraph was adopted by 90 votes to 0, with 5 abstentions.

Japan requested a separate vote on the paragraph inviting UNCTAD to give consideration to such reforms of the 1964 Assembly decision establishing UNCTAD as to promote further evolution in the continuing machinery of UNCTAD; this paragraph was adopted by 82 votes to 0, with 17 abstentions.

DOCUMENTARY REFERENCES

General Assembly—26th session
Second Committee, meetings 1414–1421, 1424, 1429–1431.
Fifth Committee, meetings 1463, 1464, 1482, 1483.
Plenary meeting 2021.

A/8401. Report of Secretary-General on work of the Organization, 16 June 1970–15 June 1971, Part Three, Chapter IV I.
A/8403/Add.1. Addendum to report of Economic and Social Council, resumed 51st session, Chapter III.
A/8415/Rev.1. Report of Trade and Development Board, 14 October 1970–21 September 1971: Part One, Chapter II and Annex I (decision 76(X)), other decisions taken by Board during 2nd part of its 10th session, p. 66, and Annex III; Part Three, Chapter II and Annex I (resolution 83(XI)), and other decisions taken by Board during 11th session, p. 215.
A/C.2/270 and Corr.1. Letter of 12 November 1971 from Peru (transmitting Declaration and Principles of Action Programme adopted at Lima, Peru, on 7 November 1971 by Ministerial Meeting of Group of 77 Developing Countries).
A/C.2/L.1197. Afghanistan, Brazil, Chile, Egypt, Ethiopia, Ghana, Malaysia, Nigeria, Pakistan, Peru, Philippines, Romania, Sudan, Thailand, Trinidad and Tobago, Upper Volta, Venezuela, Yugoslavia: draft resolution.
A/C.2/L.1197/Rev.1. Revised draft resolution, sponsored by above 18 sponsors and by Ceylon, Congo, Ecuador, Indonesia and Uganda.
A/C.2/L.1197/Rev.2. Afghanistan, Algeria, Brazil, Ceylon, Chad, Chile, Colombia, Congo, Dominican Republic, Ecuador, Egypt, Ethiopia, Ghana, Honduras, Indonesia, Laos, Malaysia, Mali, Nepal, Nigeria, Pakistan, Peru, Philippines, Romania, Rwanda, Sudan, Syrian Arab Republic, Thailand, Trinidad and Tobago, Uganda, United Republic of Tanzania, Upper Volta, Venezuela, Yugoslavia: revised draft resolution, as orally amended by sponsors, approved by Second Committee on 6 December 1971, meeting 1430, unanimously (102–0).
A/C.2/L.1205. Madagascar, Rwanda, Senegal: amendment to 23-power revised draft resolution, A/C.2/L.1197/Rev.1.
A/C.5/1414 and Corr.1, A/8408/Add.23, A/8599. Administrative and financial implications of draft resolution I recommended by Second Committee in A/8558. Statement by Secretary-General and reports of Advisory Committee on Administrative and Budgetary Questions and Fifth Committee.
A/8558. Report of Second Committee, draft resolution I.

RESOLUTION 2820(XXVI), as recommended by Second Committee, A/8558, adopted unanimously by Assembly on 16 December 1971, meeting 2021.

The General Assembly,
Recalling:

(a) Resolution 2570(XXIV) of 13 December 1969, in which it suggested that the United Nations Conference on Trade and Development at its third session should consider ways and means of implementing the measures agreed upon within the continuing machinery and seek new areas of agreement in the dynamic context of the Second United Nations Development Decade,

(b) Resolution 2626(XXV) of 24 October 1970, by which it proclaimed the Second United Nations Development Decade and adopted the International Development Strategy for the Decade, in which Governments subscribed to the goals and objectives of the Decade and resolved to take the necessary policy measures to translate them into reality,

(c) Resolution 2725(XXV) of 15 December 1970, in which the attention of the Conference at its third session, in pursuing the functions falling within its competence and its role in the implementation of the International Development Strategy, is drawn to the importance of:

  (i) Reviewing the progress made in implementation of the policy measures as agreed upon,
  (ii) Reaching agreement in more specific terms on issues which have not been fully resolved,
  (iii) Seeking new areas of agreement and widening existing ones,
  (iv) Evolving new concepts and seeking agreement on additional measures,

Recalling also:
(a) Resolution 1995(XIX) of 30 December 1964, in which it expressed the intention to seek advice from the United Nations Conference on Trade and Development before making changes in the fundamental provisions thereof,

(b) Resolution 2570(XXIV), in which it expressed the view that the Trade and Development Board, while making a fuller and more effective utilization of the improved machinery and methods of work of the Conference, in accordance with Board decision 45(VII) of 21 September 1968 and General Assembly resolution 2402(XXIII) of 13 December 1968, should, at the same time, keep the question of further improvement in the institutional machinery of the Conference constantly under review and from time to time make such suggestions as may enable the continuing machinery to discharge the responsibility entrusted to it,

(c) Resolution 2725(XXV), in which it requested the Trade and Development Board to give consideration, in accordance with General Assembly resolution 1995(XIX) and Board decision 45(VII), to such reforms of the fundamental provisions of that resolution as to promote further evolution in the institutional arrangements of the Conference, in its continuing machinery and in its method of work, designed to increase its effectiveness, and to put forward concrete suggestions for its improvement with a view to enabling the Conference to make specific recommendations for consideration by the General Assembly,

Recalling further that in resolution 2626(XXV) of 24 October 1970, containing the International Development Strategy, in particular paragraph 82 thereof, as well as in resolution 2641(XXV) of 19 November 1970, it requested the United Nations Conference on Trade and Development to continue to review progress towards achieving the goals and objectives of the Second United Nations Development Decade in its fields of competence, according to the procedures already established and to be adapted as necessary,

Taking note of Trade and Development Board resolution 81(XI) of 17 September 1971, in which the Board reaffirmed the responsibility of the United Nations Conference on Trade and Development in the context of the review and appraisal process of the International Development Strategy and requested the Conference at its third session to consider adequate procedures and mechanisms for the review and appraisal of the objectives and policy measures of the Strategy falling within its competence,

Having considered the annual report of the Trade and Development Board for the period from 14 October 1970 to 21 September 1971,

Noting with deep concern that the present international monetary crisis and trends towards intensification of protectionism may threaten the very basis of international economic co-operation at the outset of the Second United Nations Development Decade and have a negative impact on the vital trade and development interests of developing countries,

Expressing the view that the forthcoming third session of the Conference provides a fresh opportunity to make a collective and determined endeavour to correct effectively the adverse situation confronting the developing countries,

Noting with interest the Declaration and Principles of the Action Programme adopted at Lima on 7 November 1971 by the Second Ministerial Meeting of the Group of Seventy-seven Developing Countries and submitted to the General Assembly at its twenty-sixth session, containing concrete proposals on the various issues to be considered by the Conference at its third session,

I

1. *Takes note with satisfaction* of the report of the Trade and Development Board on its activities between 14 October 1970 and 21 September 1971, in particular of the decisions taken by the Board at its eleventh session on various aspects of the preparatory work for the third session of the United Nations Conference on Trade and Development, and endorses the work programme established by the Board at its eleventh session;

2. *Accepts with appreciation* the invitation of the Government of Chile to hold the third session of the United Nations Conference on Trade and Development at Santiago, from 11 April to 19 May 1972;

3. *Urges* Member States to make maximum efforts, in their further preparations for the third session and during the deliberations of the United Nations Conference on Trade and Development, to ensure its success and, to this end, to give serious consideration to the Declaration and Principles of the Action Programme adopted at Lima by the Second Ministerial Meeting of the Group of Seventy-seven Developing Countries, which contain concrete and specific proposals aimed at solving through international co-operation the urgent problems of trade and development of developing countries as well as other proposals which may be put forward by other countries or groups of countries;

4. *Also urges* the United Nations Conference on Trade and Development at its third session to adopt comprehensive action-oriented programmes incorporating special measures in favour of both the least developed among developing countries and the land-locked developing countries;

5. *Expresses the view* that the conclusion of an international cocoa agreement as soon as possible would be of great importance and would contribute to the success of the third session of the United Nations Conference on Trade and Development, as stated in Trade and Development Board resolution 85(XI) of 20 September 1971;

6. *Urges* the United Nations Conference on Trade and Development at its third session to review the progress achieved since its second session in promoting trade relations among countries having different economic and social systems, bearing in mind Conference resolution 15(II) of 25 March 1968;

7. *Also urges* the United Nations Conference on Trade and Development at its third session:

(a) To appeal to preference-giving countries which have not yet done so to implement their offers under the generalized system of preferences in favour of developing countries;

(b) To pursue efforts in a dynamic context for further improvements of these preferential arrangements, bearing in mind the agreed conclusions contained in the annex to Trade and Development Board decision 75(S-IV) of 13 October 1970, *inter alia*, that developing countries sharing their existing tariff advantages with the rest of the developing countries as a result of the implementation of the generalized system of preferences will not be adversely affected;

8. *Requests* the Secretary-General of the United Nations Conference on Trade and Development to undertake further consultations with the Governments of States members of the Conference and with appropriate international organizations, with a view to contributing to the success of the Conference;

II

1. *Agrees* that the United Nations Conference on Trade and Development at its third session should undertake a comprehensive review of its institutional arrangements with a view to improving the efficiency of its operations, strengthening its role as a centre for the initiation of action—where appropriate in co-operation with the competent organs of the United Nations—for the negotiation and adoption of multilateral legal instruments in the field of trade, bearing in mind that the task of negotiation, including exploration, consultation and agreement on solutions, is a single process, with due regard to the adequacy of the existing organs of negotiation and without duplication of their activities, thus enabling the Conference to fulfil its basic objectives as set forth in General Assembly resolution 1995(XIX);

2. *Reaffirms* the essential role of the United Nations Conference on Trade and Development to review and appraise the progress achieved in the implementation of the International Development Strategy within its field of competence and to seek new areas of agreement and the widening of existing ones as well as to evolve new concepts and seek agreement on additional measures as envisaged in the Strategy;

3. *Invites* the United Nations Conference on Trade and Development at its third session:

(a) To provide general guidelines for the establishment by the Trade and Development Board of adequate procedures and mechanisms for defining and keeping under constant review the indicators and other data necessary for assessing the progress in the implementation of the policy measures within the field of competence of the Conference;

(b) To make the institutional machinery of the Conference fully oriented towards the implementation of the relevant provisions of the International Development Strategy, and particularly to this end to promote consultations aimed at enabling member States to make a fuller and more effective contribution to the achievement of the goals and objectives thereof;

(c) To give consideration to such reforms of the fundamental provisions of General Assembly resolution 1995(XIX) as to promote further evolution in the continuing machinery and in the method of work of the Conference designed to increase its effectiveness;

III

Decides to consider at its twenty-seventh session, as a matter of high priority, the results of the third session of the United Nations Conference on Trade and Development.

Organizational questions

Improvement of institutional machinery

At its August-September 1971 session, the Trade and Development Board of the United Nations Conference on Trade and Development (UNCTAD) discussed reviewing the institutional arrangements of UNCTAD and took note of the views expressed on the subject. The President suggested that these views might serve as a basis for the consideration of this question at the third session of UNCTAD, due to open on 11 April 1972.

In taking decisions on the third session of UNCTAD, the General Assembly expressed the view that the Trade and Development Board should keep the question of further improvement in the institutional machinery of UNCTAD constantly under review and from time to time make such suggestions as might enable the continuing machinery to discharge the responsibility entrusted to it.

The General Assembly also agreed that UNCTAD at its third session should undertake a comprehensive review of its institutional arrangements, with a view to improving the efficiency of its operations and strengthening its role as a centre for the initiation of action for the negotiation and adoption of multilateral legal instruments in the field of trade. It also invited UNCTAD at its third session: to provide guidelines for the establishment by the Trade and Development Board of

adequate measures and mechanisms for defining and keeping under constant review the indicators and other data necessary for assessing the progress in the implementation of the policy measures within the fields of competence of UNCTAD; to make the institutional machinery of UNCTAD fully oriented towards the implementation of the relevant provisions of the International Development Strategy; and to give consideration to such reforms as to promote further evolution in the continuing machinery and method of work of UNCTAD designed to increase its effectiveness.

These were among decisions embodied in resolution 2820(XXVI), adopted by the Assembly on 16 December 1971. (For text, see pp. 283-84.)

Other questions

Among other organizational questions that the Trade and Development Board took up in 1971 was the designation and classification of non-governmental organizations. The following three organizations were included in the list of non-governmental organizations enabled to participate in the deliberations of the Committee on Shipping: the International Federation of Forwarding Agents Associations; the International Shipowners Association; and the National Shippers Councils of Europe (Plenary).

DOCUMENTARY REFERENCES

Improvement of institutional machinery
A/8415/Rev.1. Report of Trade and Development Board, 14 October 1970–21 September 1971: Part One, Chapter VI A and B, Chapter VIII and Annex V; Part Three, Chapter X B and C and Chapter XI.

Report of Trade and Development Board

Economic and Social Council—51st session
Plenary meeting 1804.

E/5076 and Add.1, 2. Notes by Secretary-General (transmitting Parts One, Two and Three of report of Trade and Development Board, 14 October 1970–21 September 1971 (A/8415/Rev.1)).

RESOLUTION 1649 (LI), as suggested by Council President, adopted without objection by Council on 29 October 1971, meeting 1804.

The Economic and Social Council,
Having considered the annual report of the Trade and Development Board,
1. *Transmits* that report to the General Assembly;
2. *Draws the attention* of the General Assembly to the comments and observations on the subject made in the Council at its 1804th meeting.

General Assembly—26th session
Second Committee, meetings 1414-1421, 1424, 1429-1431.
Fifth Committee, meetings 1463, 1464, 1482, 1483.
Plenary meeting 2021.

A/8415/Rev.1. United Nations Conference on Trade and Development. Report of Trade and Development Board, 14 October 1970–21 September 1971. Part One: Report of Trade and Development Board on 2nd part of its 10th session, Geneva, Switzerland, 1–9 March 1971; Part Two: Report of Trade and Development Board on 3rd part of its 10th session, Geneva, 24 May 1971; Part Three: Report of Trade and Development Board on its 11th session, Geneva, 24 August–21 September 1971.

A/8433. Confirmation of appointment of Secretary-General of UNCTAD. Note by Secretary-General.

RESOLUTION 2820(XXVI), as recommended by Second Committee (A/8558, draft resolution I), adopted unanimously by Assembly on 16 December 1971, meeting 2021.

[For text of resolution and supporting documentation, see section above on THIRD SESSION OF UNITED NATIONS CONFERENCE ON TRADE AND DEVELOPMENT.]

A/8429. Resolutions adopted by General Assembly during its 26th session, 21 September–22 December 1971. Other decisions, p. 20.

Other questions
A/8415/Rev.1. Report of Trade and Development Board, 14 October 1970–21 September 1971: Part One, Chapter VI C 7–9 and Annex I (resolution 78(X)), and other decisions taken by Board during 2nd part of its 10th session; Part Two, Chapter I; Part Three, Chapters VI and X A and Annex I (resolutions 79(XI) and 87(XI)), and other decisions taken by Board during its 11th session.

Other documents
TD/B/331. Resolutions and decisions of Trade and Development
    Board, 10th session, 26 August–24 September 1970, 1–9

March and 24 May 1971, held in 3 parts, at Geneva, Switzerland.
TD/B/386. Resolutions and decisions of Trade and Development
    Board, 11th session, 24 August–21 September 1971.

Chapter V

The International Trade Centre

Decision by Economic and Social Council

During the discussion of United Nations export promotion efforts at its July 1971 session, the Economic and Social Council had before it a report by the Secretary-General which outlined efforts in the field of production for exports, export promotion and marketing, strengthening national and multinational export promotion institutions and training of personnel for export promotion. The Council took a number of decisions on export promotion matters.

On 27 July 1971, the Council, recognizing that the International Trade Centre, jointly administered by the United Nations Conference on Trade and Development (UNCTAD) and by the General Agreement on Tariffs and Trade (GATT), had emerged as the focal point for technical assistance and co-operation activities for export promotion within the United Nations family, urged developed countries to give their full support to the regional export promotion centres as well as to the International Trade Centre and other organizations participating in the United Nations export promotion programme.

The Council recognized that the increasing requirements of developing countries for United Nations assistance in the field of export promotion and development made it necessary that the level of resources for the programme be increased. It also noted that a lack of financial resources had impeded the efficient working of the regional export promotion centres of the regional economic commissions.

In this connexion, the Council noted its belief that the implementation of the generalized system of preferences would open new export opportunities for the developing countries.

The Secretary-General was asked to continue to prepare periodic reports on United Nations export promotion and development efforts and to study the feasibility of establishing a United Nations export development fund.

These were among decisions embodied in resolution 1620(LI), adopted by 18 votes to 2, with 6 abstentions, on the recommendation of the Council's Economic Committee, which approved the text on 23 July 1971 by 11 votes to 3, with 5 abstentions, on the basis of a proposal by Brazil, Indonesia, Malaysia, Pakistan and Yugoslavia. (For text, see DOCUMENTARY REFERENCES below.)

Activities in 1971

During 1971, the fourth year of operation of the International Trade Centre, developing countries were assisted by the provision of information and counsel on export markets and strategies, help in developing export promotion and marketing organizations and help in training specialized personnel. Such assistance continued to be channelled through four main services: the Trade Promotion Advisory Service, the Training Service, the Market Research Service and the Export Promotion Techniques Research Service, supported by a documentation and a publishing service.

The Trade Promotion Advisory Service was responsible in 1971 for the provision of assistance to 53 developing countries in the form of 10 country programmes, 60 technical assistance assignments and 60 fact-finding and programming missions. The Service also organized five symposia in developing countries. The multinational product promotion unit operated projects on tea, oilseeds, oils and fats, tropical timber, cotton, hard fibres, wine, natural rubber and sugar.

In 1971, the Training Service developed and presented training courses, seminars and workshops for export promotion and market personnel and business executives from developing countries. The 21 programmes organized and implemented in 1971 were attended by over 300 trade officials and export executives from 46 developing countries.

The Market Research Service, providing trade and marketing information to developing countries, completed in 1971 major surveys on grade beef, citrus juices, rice and handicrafts. It also completed country projects on sugar (Cuba), engineering products (India), miscellaneous manufactures (Pakistan), handicrafts (Jamaica), and potassium chloride (Ethiopia). Some 500 trade inquiries were answered during the year.

The Export Promotion Techniques Research Service, which continued to carry out research into export promotion techniques that could be applied by both the public and private sectors in developing countries, published in 1971 four issues of the Centre's regular trade promotion journal, the *International Trade Forum*, as well as the following publications: *Handbook on Exporting to the Socialist Countries of Eastern Europe; Handbook on Export Promotion by Private Sector Organizations; and Directory of National and Regional Trade and Economic Journals.*

In 1971, the International Trade Centre had a total regular staff of 46 professionals and 62 general service personnel. This number included 10 professional and 28 general service staff located in the GATT secretariat providing administrative and linguistic services. Additional staff financed from overheads or seconded by developed countries brought the total to 58 professionals and 74 general service personnel.

The Centre's regular budget (used for the maintenance of the base staff and services) in 1971 amounted to $1,469,800. Operational assistance programmes were financed primarily by United Nations Development Programme funds and voluntary country contributions, amounting in 1971 to $1,800,000.

(See also pp. 277-79, 300 and 758-62.)

DOCUMENTARY REFERENCES

Economic and Social Council—51st session
Economic Committee, meetings 527, 528, 536.
Plenary meetings 1773, 1793.

E/4940 and Corr.1. Regional co-operation. United Nations export promotion efforts. Report of Secretary-General.
E/5039. Report of meetings of executive secretaries of regional economic commissions held in 1971 (New York, 27–29 January 1971; Geneva, Switzerland, 28–30 June and 3 July 1971), Chapter VI.
E/L.1419. Regional co-operation. Note by Secretary-General.
E/AC.6/L.430 and Rev.1. Brazil, Indonesia, Malaysia, Pakistan, Yugoslavia: draft resolution and revision, approved by Economic Committee on 23 July 1971, meeting 536, by 11 votes to 3, with 5 abstentions.
E/5058. Report of Economic Committee.

RESOLUTION 1620(LI), as recommended by Economic Committee, E/5058, adopted by Council on 27 July 1971, meeting 1793, by 18 votes to 2, with 6 abstentions.

The Economic and Social Council,
Recalling its resolutions 1362(XLV) of 2 August 1968 and 1464(XLVII) of 28 October 1969,
Recalling further paragraph 36 of the International Development Strategy, which calls for effective international assistance for the developing countries' trade promotion efforts,
Noting with appreciation the Secretary-General's second report on United Nations export promotion efforts,
Recognizing that the increasing requirements of developing countries for United Nations assistance in the field of export promotion and development make it necessary that the level of resources from budgetary and extra-budgetary sources for this programme be accordingly increased, in order to contribute to the attainment of the objectives of the Second United Nations Development Decade relating to the trade expansion of developing countries,
Recognizing further, in this respect, that the UNCTAD/GATT International Trade Centre has emerged as the focal point for technical assistance and co-operation activities for export promotion within the United Nations family,
Believing that the implementation of the generalized system of preferences will open new export opportunities for the developing countries,
Noting that the lack of financial resources has impeded the efficient working of the regional export promotion centres of the regional economic commissions,
Considering the need for additional financial resources to be placed at the disposal of the regional economic commissions, to allow them to establish and operate the regional export promotion centres,
1. *Urges* developed countries to give their full support to the regional export promotion centres, as well as to the UNCTAD/GATT International Trade Centre and other agencies and organizations participating in the United Nations export promotion programme, and to make contributions commensurate with the increasing requirements of the developing countries in the field of export promotion during the Second United Nations Development Decade;
2. *Requests* the Secretary-General of the United Nations to continue to prepare periodic reports on United Nations export promotion and development efforts, to be submitted to the Council on a biennial basis, after a substantive examination by the Trade and Development Board, as provided for in Council resolution 1464(XLVII);
3. *Further requests* the Secretary-General of the United Nations to study, in consultation with the Secretary-General of the United Nations Conference on Trade and Development, the feasibility of establishing a United Nations export development fund, in order to assist all the developing countries in their export promotion and development efforts and also in taking full advantage of the generalized system of preferences, and to report on this matter to the Council, through the Trade and Development Board, as early as possible.

Other documents
A/8401. Report of Secretary-General on work of the Organization, 16 June 1970–15 June 1971, Part Three, Chapter IV H.
A/8403. Report of Economic and Social Council on work of its 50th and 51st sessions, Chapter XIII C.
A/8415/Rev.1. Report of Trade and Development Board, 14 October 1970–21 September 1971, Part Three, Chapter X D.
A/C.5/1362. Budget estimates for financial year 1972. Joint UNCTAD/GATT International Trade Centre (ITC). Note by Secretary-General (transmitting report of Secretary-General of UNCTAD and Director-General of GATT on ITC budget estimates for financial year 1972 (ITC/AG/17)).
ITC/AG/16 and Corr.1. Report of Joint UNCTAD/GATT Advisory Group on ITC on its 4th session, Geneva, Switzerland, 12–16 January 1971.
ITC/AG/19. Financial report of Director-General of GATT on 1970 accounts of ITC and report of external auditor thereon.
ITC/AG/20. Evaluation of market research service of ITC.
ITC/AG/21. Work programme of ITC, its budgetary requirements for 1973 and planning estimates for 1974.
ITC/AG/22. Report of Technical Committee of Joint UNCTAD/GATT Advisory group on ITC on its 5th session.

Chapter VI

Industrial development

The United Nations Industrial Development Organization (UNIDO) completed its fifth full year of operations in 1971. During the year, the work of the organization was reviewed by the Special International Conference convened by the United Nations. The Conference made a number of recommendations concerning UNIDO's future activities, organizational structure and financing. These were subsequently endorsed by the General Assembly.

In 1971, UNIDO provided increased technical assistance for industrial purposes under a number of programmes. Special attention was given to the problems of industrialization in the least developed among developing countries and to programmes to facilitate the transfer of technology from developed to developing countries.

A number of meetings, seminars, workshops and training programmes were held during the year.

Activities in 1971

In 1971, technical assistance was provided by the United Nations Industrial Development Organization (UNIDO) to 111 countries and to 10 regions or groups under the following programmes: the Special Fund and Technical Assistance components of the United Nations Development Programme (UNDP); the Special Industrial Services programme (SIS); the United Nations regular programme of technical assistance; the UNIDO General Trust Fund, formed from voluntary contributions by Governments; funds-in-trust provided by Governments for specific purposes; and the regular budget of UNIDO.

The breakdown of expenditures during 1971 was as follows:

	Expenditure (in U.S. dollars)
UNDP/Special Fund component	6,700,000
UNDP/Technical Assistance component	3,000,000
Special Industrial Services (SIS)	4,400,000
UNIDO General Trust Fund	800,000
Funds-in-trust	600,000
United Nations regular programme of technical assistance	1,500,000
Overhead funds*	1,100,000
UNIDO regular budget	12,300,000
Total	30,400,000

*Funds which UNIDO, as participating and executing agency, received from UNDP for managing field projects.

As a participating and executing agency of the United Nations Development Programme, the United Nations Industrial Development Organization was responsible for the execution of 70 long-term projects financed from the Special Fund component in 1971, including 15 new projects allocated during the year. The value of these projects was approximately $122 million, of which $50 million was in UNDP allocations and $72 million was in Government counterpart contributions.

In addition, UNIDO assisted in the implementation of projects executed by other agencies, including the International Labour Organisation and the Food and Agriculture Organization of the United Nations.

The Special Industrial Services (SIS) programme, financed by UNDP, provides emergency assistance through simplified procedures. In 1971, expenditures reached $4.4 million, as against $3 million in 1970. The number of projects approved was 339, compared with 297 in 1970, bringing the total number of projects approved to 1,156, with a value of approximately $18 million.

As in previous years, about two thirds of the 1971 SIS projects were in the form of direct advisory assistance related to specific industrial enterprises or to development policies and problems; the remaining projects were exploratory and pre-feasibility missions.

A total of 787 UNIDO experts served in the field during 1971, of whom 328 were associated with SIS projects; the experts were drawn from 35 developing and 20 developed countries. Fellowships were awarded to 532 persons, including nationals of 70 developing countries, by the organization.

The breakdown of UNIDO assistance in 1971 by region was as follows: Africa, 34.3 per cent; Asia and the Far East, 19.9 per cent; the Americas, 18.8 per cent; and Europe and the Middle East, 16.6 per cent. Inter-regional projects accounted for 10.4 per cent of expenditures.

Table I, below, shows UNIDO expenditures for direct technical assistance projects and for support activities (programmes of study, meetings and research).

Table II lists the number of experts received and provided, fellowships awarded and cost of equipment provided, by country and territory, during 1971.

Table I. UNIDO expenditures in 1971 on technical assistance and support activities

(In thousands of U.S. dollars)

Type of activity	Technical Assistance	Support Activities	Type of activity	Technical Assistance	Support Activities
Engineering industries	1,873.8	324.3	Industrial information	232.0	363.7
Metallurgical industries	1,294.0	134.8	Management and consulting services	1,317.9	192.7
Construction and building materials industries	526.9	67.2	Small-scale industries and related activities	1,766.0	253.3
Chemical, pharmaceutical and pulp and paper industries	702.6	178.4	Industrial training	797.2	230.0
Fertilizer, pesticide and petrochemical industries	1,401.7	278.0	Industrial programming and project planning	2,199.8	374.9
Light industries	1,698.4	326.9	Industrial policies and financing	371.4	529.0
Industrial branch reports and across-the-board techniques	296.4	149.9	Promotion of export-oriented industries	452.9	223.3
Industrial administration	13.6	50.9	Industrial surveys	403.1	263.0
Industrial institutions	1,623.3	262.4	Total	16,971.0	4,202.7

Table II. Countries and territories aided by UNIDO in 1971

Country or Territory	No. of Experts Received	No. of Experts Provided*	Fellow-ships Awarded	Operational Cost of Equipment Provided (in U.S. dollars)	Country or Territory	No. of Experts Received	No. of Experts Provided*	Fellow-ships Awarded	Operational Cost of Equipment Provided (in U.S. dollars)
Afghanistan	2	—	1	60,600	Lesotho	1	—	1	18,700
Albania	—	—	—	4,400	Liberia	1	—	—	10,000
Algeria	19	1	4	219,300	Libyan Arab Republic	1	—	—	15,800
Argentina	15	4	6	166,100	Madagascar	7	—	3	148,000
Bahamas	1	—	—	—	Malawi	—	—	3	6,000
Barbados	1	—	1	8,500	Malaysia	9	—	—	106,100
Bolivia	10	—	2	315,700	Mali	4	—	4	104,300
Botswana	—	—	—	2,000	Malta	—	—	—	3,400
Brazil	16	4	2	733,900	Mauritania	1	—	—	25,000
Brunei	1	—	—	24,000	Mauritius	11	—	—	88,500
Bulgaria	7	2	24	122,200	Mexico	5	2	2	36,400
Burma	3	—	—	29,000	Mongolia	7	—	8	119,500
Burundi	2	—	1	55,400	Morocco	5	—	—	93,400
Cameroon	7	—	—	94,500	Nepal	10	1	3	78,200
Central African Republic	4	—	2	18,600	Nicaragua	5	—	—	25,000
Ceylon	7	5	2	69,700	Niger	3	—	2	56,200
Chad	8	—	—	25,100	Nigeria	8	—	4	158,900
Chile	9	9	2	260,000	Pakistan	15	2	7	453,000
China	7	4	—	—	Panama	3	—	—	11,000
Colombia	10	1	9	235,900	Papua New Guinea	3	—	—	10,000
Congo	2	—	—	46,000	Paraguay	10	—	2	129,300
Costa Rica	8	1	1	54,200	People's Democratic Republic of Yemen	3	—	1	45,000
Cuba	10	1	6	82,300	Peru	7	—	—	183,300
Cyprus	10	—	1	96,400	Philippines	10	2	8	111,200
Czechoslovakia	—	14	7	28,800	Poland	—	11	88	165,700
Dahomey	4	—	4	71,300	Qatar	4	—	—	17,000
Dominican Republic	6	—	—	86,000	Republic of Korea	4	—	6	114,500
Ecuador	4	1	1	59,200	Republic of Viet-Nam	1	2	2	26,000
Egypt	49	28	12	652,600	Romania	1	7	32	373,100
El Salvador	5	—	—	99,000	Rwanda	8	—	6	791,000
Ethiopia	9	—	—	131,200	Saudi Arabia	10	—	—	169,400
Fiji	5	—	—	86,800	Senegal	7	—	7	227,000
Gabon	4	—	1	82,000	Sierra Leone	—	—	—	3,100
Gambia	2	—	1	51,400	Singapore	—	—	2	78,900
Ghana	10	—	3	462,500	Somalia	7	—	—	100,100
Greece	1	1	1	131,900	Spain	2	12	—	39,000
Guatemala	1	1	—	5,000	Sudan	12	1	9	430,200
Guinea	—	—	2	33,200	Surinam	—	—	—	2,000
Guyana	—	—	1	—	Swaziland	4	—	—	53,600
Haiti	2	—	—	18,000	Syrian Arab Republic	15	3	6	—
Honduras	3	—	—	16,000	Thailand	17	—	39	302,900
Hong Kong	—	—	—	6,100	Togo	5	—	1	148,300
Hungary	1	13	16	19,800	Trinidad and Tobago	5	—	3	159,700
Iceland	3	—	—	16,000	Tunisia	18	—	18	288,300
India	19	72	48	476,400	Turkey	19	1	14	315,100
Indonesia	16	1	9	202,200	Uganda	9	—	4	144,500
Iran	29	2	7	548,500	United Republic of Tanzania	16	—	3	153,900
Iraq	11	1	3	143,400	Upper Volta	6	—	-	63,000
Israel	10	6	12	270,400	Uruguay	2	—	9	37,400
Ivory Coast	3	—	2	89,400	Venezuela	7	—	1	62,800
Jamaica	11	—	—	117,200	Western Samoa	1	—	—	3,000
Jordan	4	2	4	169,400	Yemen	2	—	2	27,900
Kenya	5	—	—	140,600	Yugoslavia	22	34	21	407,100
Khmer Republic	1	—	2	18,500	Zaire	8	—	3	106,800
Kuwait	3	—	—	50,600	Zambia	7	—	2	106,000
Laos	6	—	2	23,700					
Lebanon	10	3	—	52,100					

Group and Regional Technical Aid	No. of Experts Received	Fellow-ships Awarded	Operational Cost of Equipment Provided (in U.S. dollars)	Group and Regional Technical Aid	No. of Experts Received	Fellow-ships Awarded	Operational Cost of Equipment Provided (in U.S. dollars)
East African Community (Kenya, United Republic of Tanzania, Uganda)	10	1	205,900	Organization of the Senegal Riparian States	—	—	24,100
Industrial Development Centre for Arab States	—	2	—	Maghreb countries	2	2	—
Common Organization of the African, Malagasy and Mauritian States	—	—	3,000	Africa	3	—	242,500
				Latin America	7	—	251,600
				Asia and the Far East	7	—	189,500
				Europe and the Middle East	1	—	412,000
				Inter-regional	13		1,924,000

*Experts were also provided by the following countries: Australia (12 experts), Austria (21), Belgium (31), Canada (7), Denmark (14), the Federal Republic of Germany (46), Finland (10), France (68), Ireland (11), Italy (18), Japan (11), the Netherlands (15), New Zealand (6), Norway (13), Sweden (40), Switzerland (14), the USSR (16), the United Kingdom (127), and the United States (81).

Assistance to least developed countries

Operational activities of UNIDO in the least developed of the developing countries amounted to $2.6 million during 1971. The organization was the executing agency for four UNDP projects in least developed countries, as follows: the construction of a pyrethrum plant in Rwanda; the creation of an industrial research institute in Sudan; a small-scale industries development programme in Uganda; and an industrial studies and development centre at Dar es Salaam, United Republic of Tanzania.

Under other programmes, work was in progress in 18 more of the 25 countries identified as least developed: Afghanistan, Botswana, Burundi, Chad, Dahomey, Ethiopia, Guinea, Haiti, Laos, Lesotho, Malawi, Mali, Nepal, Niger, Somalia, Upper Volta, Western Samoa and Yemen. The projects were in such fields as: planning and programming for development, the establishment of industrial estates, small- and medium-scale industries, building materials, management and training, metallurgy and metal-working, repair and maintenance, product adaptation for exports, food processing, agricultural machinery, tools and implements, textiles, leather and its products, fertilizers, chemicals and petrochemicals, utilization of natural resources and standardization.

Industrial services and institutions

Essential services which can be provided institutionally include industrial administration, legislation, patents and licensing, research, standardization, promotion, information, training and management. In 1971, UNIDO continued its programmes of co-operation with developing countries in this respect.

The possibility was examined of setting up an industrial administration training centre for developing countries. A group of experts meeting in 1971 recommended setting up national or regional semi-commercial centres to provide consultancy services for management. Programmes of co-operation with regional and inter-regional professional and business organizations and a programme with universities to improve industrial management were initiated, the latter in collaboration with the United Nations Educational, Scientific and Cultural Organization.

Collection and dissemination of information continued. The industrial inquiry service for individuals and institutions from developing and developed countries was enlarged, and an advisory service on supply of industrial equipment was established.

Policies and programming

The activities of UNIDO relating to the economic and financial aspects of the industrialization process in developing countries are carried out at country, regional, sub-regional and international levels.

Surveys of national industrial policies continued with examinations of the policies of Cuba and the Republic of Korea. A seminar on selected policy aspects was held in Beirut, Lebanon.

Increasing interest was shown in efforts to link industry in the advanced and developing countries through sub-contracting work to be undertaken in developing countries. In an effort to promote exports, reciprocal visits were arranged by buyers from developed countries and manufacturers from developing countries.

Training programmes to assist in raising levels of production were held in several countries. These included a training programme in Belgium for industrial representatives from English-speaking developing countries, a seminar in Turkey on the utilization of excess capacity and a training programme in India on food processing.

Transfer of technology and industrial information

Special emphasis continued to be given by UNIDO to activities relating to the application of new technology to the developing countries.

During the year, 15 in-plant training programmes for engineers from developing countries were offered in co-operation with Governments and industrial establishments in both developed and developing countries.

A number of meetings concerned with the transfer of technology were held during the year. These included: a second inter-regional fertilizer symposium, held in the Ukrainian SSR and in

India, attended by 130 experts; a seminar on the development of the leather and leather products industry in developing countries, held in Vienna, Austria, with 25 African participants and 50 observers from industrialized countries; an inter-regional seminar on industrial processing of rice, held in India and attended by 200 participants from 25 countries; a workshop on the creation and transfer of metallurgical know-how, also held in India; and a regional seminar on machine tools in the developing countries of Europe and the Middle East, which took place in Bulgaria. Other meetings of experts were held on subjects such as electronic components and packaging.

Under the SIS programme, the number of projects involving transfer of technology rose to 1,700.

Collaboration with technological research institutes, information centres and specialists was increased to make the UNIDO information advisory service more responsive to the needs of developing countries. Co-operative work with the United Nations and other bodies also developed, including participation in the first meeting of the Intergovernmental Group on Transfer of Technology, sponsored by the United Nations Conference on Trade and Development.

Future programme and structure of UNIDO

Special International Conference of UNIDO

The Special International Conference of the United Nations Industrial Development Organization (UNIDO) was convened in accordance with a General Assembly decision of 19 November 1970,[1] following a recommendation of the Industrial Development Board. The Conference, held in Vienna, Austria, from 1 to 8 June 1971, was attended by representatives of 106 member States and of a number of United Nations bodies, specialized agencies and inter-governmental and non-governmental organizations.

The Conference adopted a resolution representing a consensus of the views expressed, and including recommendations on three aspects of the organization: (1) long-range strategy and orientation of activities, (2) organizational structure and (3) financing.

With regard to the future orientation of UNIDO's programmes, the Conference recommended that operational activities be geared to the varying needs of individual developing countries and groupings, bearing in mind their diverse resources, markets and levels of growth.

It also recommended that particular emphasis be placed on: the promotion of industries that would have a multiplier effect in other fields; the transfer and adaptation of technology; the collection and dissemination of industrial information;

and the training of technical and skilled personnel.

The Conference recommended that at the country level the operational activities of UNIDO be co-ordinated within the framework of the country programming procedures of the United Nations Development Programme (UNDP) and with the activities of other United Nations agencies and organizations. Specific measures should be undertaken, in co-operation with the United Nations Conference on Trade and Development and the regional economic commissions, to help developing countries take full advantage of the Generalized System of Preferences for manufactured and semi-manufactured products. It was also recommended that UNIDO promote co-operation between the industrial and commercial interests of the developed and developing countries, including both public and private sectors, in conformity with the policies of the Governments concerned.

The Conference urged that UNIDO pay special attention to the recruitment of highly qualified experts from both developed and developing countries. The establishment of industrial estates and industrial pilot projects, the promotion of multinational industrial projects and the development of industries related to agriculture were also favoured.

The Conference recommended that the United Nations General Assembly request the Secretary-General to appoint a small group of high-level experts to formulate the long-range strategy for the activities of UNIDO.

It was further proposed that the Executive Director of UNIDO take measures to achieve the most purposeful use of UNIDO resources. The Conference agreed that the main emphasis in UNIDO's programmes should be: on aiding the developing countries in their industrial development as the basis for social and economic development and economic independence; and on identifying obstacles to such progress and proposing measures to overcome them, including assistance to developing countries.

The Conference also suggested that UNIDO: (1) seek ways and means of co-operation with international, regional and sub-regional financing institutions, as well as with UNDP, to follow up technical assistance projects that required capital investment; (2) bear in mind the effects of industrial pollution on the human environment; and (3) upon request, advise member States on industrial development plans, policies and specific targets directed towards achieving the goals of the Second United Nations Development Decade.

With regard to organizational structure, the Conference recommended that the General Assembly at its 1971 session: (1) decide to convene a

---

[1]See Y.U.N., 1970, pp. 417-18, text of resolution 2638(XXV).

general conference of UNIDO in 1974 or 1975 to review the progress achieved during the first half of the Second Development Decade; and (2) consider establishing regional and sub-regional offices of UNIDO. Also, the Conference asked UNDP to make available resources to increase the number of industrial development field advisers.

The Industrial Development Board was requested to establish a permanent committee to evaluate semi-annually the results of UNIDO secretariat activities and to provide guidelines for the implementation of Board decisions.

The Board was requested to ask the Executive Director of UNIDO to strengthen the services within the secretariat relating to the transfer and adaptation of industrial technology, including industrial information.

The Executive Director was also asked to establish closer contacts with the regional economic commissions and the United Nations Economic and Social Office at Beirut, which in turn were requested to consult with UNIDO when preparing their programmes of industrial development.

On the question of financing, the Conference considered that UNDP should continue to be the main source of financing for UNIDO's operational activities, and requested the UNDP Governing Council to facilitate measures to ensure an increase in the level of UNDP funds allocated for industrial development.

The Conference felt that the Board should have more influence in budgetary matters, and asked that it hold an annual exchange of views on the budget estimates which hitherto had been submitted to it by the Secretary-General for information before presentation to the General Assembly for approval.

In particular, the Conference urged UNDP to make available the necessary additional resources if demonstrated needs rose above the annual expenditure level of $2 million set by the UNDP Governing Council in 1969.

Finally, the General Assembly was asked to increase UNIDO's share in the United Nations regular programme of technical assistance, and member States were asked to make larger voluntary contributions through the annual pledging conferences.

Observations, reservations or expressions of dissent on the above consensus resolution were registered by a number of Governments or groups of Governments. These related principally to the organizational structure of UNIDO. Among them was a proposal by the Group of Seventy-seven Developing Countries that the General Assembly be asked to transform UNIDO into a specialized agency in the near future, with sufficient resources and full financial and administrative autonomy, and, pending such transformation, to give the

organization administrative and financial autonomy, including an independent geographical quota system in the recruitment of personnel.

Decisions of Economic and Social Council

The report of the Special International Conference of UNIDO was before the Economic and Social Council at its mid-1971 session.

On 30 July 1971, the Council took note of the report of the Conference and transmitted it, together with the comments of Council members, to the General Assembly at its 1971 session. The Council took this decision by adopting, without a vote, resolution 1635(LI), as recommended by its Economic Committee.

The text, based on a proposal by Ghana and Indonesia, as orally amended by Sudan, Brazil and the sponsors, was approved without a vote by the Economic Committee on 26 July 1971.

Decisions of General Assembly

The General Assembly considered the report of the Special International Conference of UNIDO at its 1971 session.

On 16 December 1971, the General Assembly endorsed the consensus resolution on the long-range strategy, structure and financing of UNIDO, adopted by the Special International Conference and took note of the Conference's report.

Among other things, the Assembly requested the Secretary-General to take immediate action to appoint a small group of high-level experts to formulate the long-range strategy for the activities of UNIDO, in accordance with the guidelines set out in the consensus resolution; requested the Industrial Development Board to propose the necessary measures for convening another general conference of UNIDO in 1974 or 1975; and recommended that the Industrial Development Board take action to set up a permanent committee of the Board to evaluate secretariat activities and provide guidelines for implementing Board decisions.

The Assembly considered it desirable that UNIDO should have greater autonomy in administrative matters, including the recruitment of personnel and the management of its publications programme.

The Governing Council of UNDP was urged to plan the level of its programme reserve in such a way that a minimum of $2 million might be retained annually for financing the Special Industrial Services (SIS) programme of UNIDO.

The Assembly decided to set up an *Ad Hoc* Committee on Co-operation between UNDP and UNIDO, to examine in detail all aspects of co-operation between the two organizations, especially those related to the formulation, appraisal and approval of industrial projects, and to report thereon to the General Assembly at its 1972 session. The Secretary-General was requested to convene the *Ad Hoc* Committee at an early date.

The Assembly called upon UNIDO, in co-operation with the United Nations Conference on Trade and Development and with the regional economic commissions and the United Nations Economic and Social Office at Beirut, to assist the developing countries to take full advantage of the Generalized System of Preferences for manufactures and semi-manufactures.

It invited the Executive Director of UNIDO to review the organization and structure of the secretariat with a view to adapting it to the changing needs of the work programme in the light of the International Development Strategy.

Among other things, the Assembly also recommended that, as part of the preparatory work for the next general conference of UNIDO, the Industrial Development Board keep under consideration the proposals submitted to the Special International Conference of UNIDO on such changes and improvements as might be necessary to meet fully the growing needs in the field of industrial development.

These decisions by the Assembly were set forth in resolution 2823(XXVI), which was adopted, by a vote of 114 to 0, on the recommendation of the Second (Economic and Financial) Committee.

In both the Committee meeting and the plenary meeting separate votes were taken on provisions calling for the establishment and convening of an *Ad Hoc* Committee on Co-operation between UNDP and UNIDO, and recommending that the Industrial Development Board keep under consideration the changes and improvements that had been proposed to the Special International Conference.

The resolution as a whole was approved by the Second Committee on 7 December 1971, by a vote of 97 to 0.

The text was based on a proposal sponsored in the Second Committee by Bolivia, Brazil, Chile, Colombia, Ghana, Iran, Kuwait, Nigeria, Panama, Peru, the Philippines, Sudan, Upper Volta, Uruguay and Venezuela. The Committee rejected an amendment which would have replaced the establishment of an *Ad Hoc* Committee on Co-operation by a request that the executive heads of UNDP and UNIDO jointly examine all aspects of co-operation. The amendment had been sponsored by Canada, Denmark, Finland, Greece, Iceland, Norway, Sweden, the United Kingdom and the United States. (For text of resolution, see DOCUMENTARY REFERENCES below.)

Programme decisions

Decisions of Industrial Development Board

At its fifth session, held in Vienna, Austria, from 24 to 28 May and on 8 June 1971, the Industrial

Development Board approved the report of its Working Group on Programme and Co-ordination covering UNIDO's activities in 1970, 1971 and 1972. Also before the Board were reports on the role of co-operatives in industrial development and on the use of computers and computer techniques for industrial development, and a note on progress in implementing previous Board recommendations on field operations.

The Board adopted a resolution which reaffirmed the importance of the Special Industrial Services (SIS) programme. The Board requested the UNDP Governing Council to increase in 1971 the annual expenditure level of $2 million and the programming level of $4 million, set by the Governing Council in 1969, in order to meet the growing number of requests for assistance from developing countries. Both UNIDO and UNDP were requested to make a constant effort to accelerate the examination of the requests and the relevant approval procedures.

Decisions of Economic and Social Council

At its July 1971 session, the Economic and Social Council took several decisions—embodied in resolution 1617(LI)—concerning UNDP projects in the field of industrial development.

The Council requested the Governing Council of UNDP to instruct the Administrator of the Programme: (*a*) to give, in accordance with the priorities assigned by the developing countries, special attention to requests submitted by them in the field of industrial development, including requests for industrial technological development and industrial pilot projects; and (*b*) to present to the Governing Council at each mid-year session a comprehensive progress report on the preparation, approval and implementation of projects in the field of industrial development.

(For text of Economic and Social Council resolution 1617(LI), see p. 254.)

Also at its mid-1971 session, the Economic and Social Council had before it a report prepared by the Secretary-General on the role of the United Nations in training technical personnel for the accelerated industrialization of developing countries. The report, prepared in accordance with a General Assembly request of 5 December 1969,[2] noted that a great deal had been done during the First United Nations Development Decade to improve training of technical personnel for the accelerated development of the developing countries. Despite this progress, however, existing systems and programmes were insufficient to meet present and future demand: provisional estimates suggested that for the developing countries alone, some 30 million skilled workers, foremen, techni-

---

[2]See Y.U.N., 1969, pp. 358-59, text of resolution 2528 (XXIV).

cians, engineers and managers would have to be given initial training by the end of the 1970s. It was felt that in addition to increasing the effectiveness and, if necessary, the reorientation of existing institutions, special attention would have to be devoted to achieving rapid improvement and expansion of non-institutional training during the 1970s. The report concluded that close co-operation must be maintained among all responsible for education, technical and commercial training and management development, and that the developing countries must recognize that the training of technical personnel was essential to the achievement of accelerated industrialization.

The report contained a number of recommendations for extending technical training, with special reference to planning, policy-making, general education, institutional and non-institutional training, continuing education and training, training abroad, special training techniques and social aspects of training.

On 30 July 1971, the Council, without adopting a resolution, took note of the report of the Secretary-General on the role of the United Nations in training national technical personnel for the accelerated industrialization of the developing countries. It took this action on the recommendation of its Economic Committee.

The relation of science and technology to industrial development was also discussed by the Economic and Social Council at its July 1971 session.

On 30 July, the Council—with the adoption of resolution 1636(LI)—took several decisions on the subject, including the following. It requested UNIDO, among other organizations, to promote the application of the recommendations contained in the report of the Advisory Committee on the Application of Science and Technology to Development for the period April 1970 to April 1971 (see pp. 314 and 316).

It further recommended that UNIDO, the International Labour Organisation, the United Nations Conference on Trade and Development and the Food and Agriculture Organization of the United Nations study ways in which reliable information on known alternative technologies for selected major industries of interest to developing countries could best be furnished systematically to Governments, enterprises and industrial consultants.

It recommended that UNDP, the International Bank for Reconstruction and Development, the regional development banks and other sources of financial and other assistance give favourable consideration to requests from Governments desirous of strengthening their capability for plant and product design. Also, the Council recommended to Governments that more attention be given to matters relating to higher engineering education and managerial training activities.

(For text of resolution 1636(LI), see p. 321.)

Other matters

Membership of UNIDO

At its 1971 session, the Industrial Development Board took note of the General Assembly's decision of 19 November 1970 to include Fiji in the list of States eligible for membership in the Industrial Development Board.[3]

On 16 December 1971, the General Assembly decided to include Bahrain, Bhutan, Oman, Qatar and the United Arab Emirates in list A of the annex to its resolution of 17 November 1966,[4] making these States eligible for membership in the Industrial Development Board.

This decision was set forth in resolution 2824 (XXVI), which was adopted, without objection, on the recommendation of the Second Committee. The text, approved without vote by the Second Committee on 7 December 1971, was suggested by the Committee Chairman; it was subsequently orally amended by the General Assembly President. (For text of resolution, see DOCUMENTARY REFERENCES below.)

Report of Industrial Development Board

The report of the Industrial Development Board on its fifth (1971) session was considered by the Economic and Social Council at its mid-1971 session. On 30 July 1971, the Council took note of the report and transmitted it to the General Assembly, together with comments of Council members; it did so by adopting, without vote, resolution 1634(LI), as recommended by its Economic Committee. The text was based on a proposal by Ghana and Indonesia, as orally amended by Sudan, Brazil and the sponsors, and was approved without vote by the Economic Committee on 26 July 1971.

On 16 December 1971, with the adoption of resolution 2823(XXVI), which was concerned with the work of UNIDO, the General Assembly among other things took note of the 1971 report of the Industrial Development Board. (For text of resolution 2823 (XXVI), see below, pp. 296-97.)

UNIDO Pledging Conference

At the fourth annual United Nations Pledging Conference on UNIDO, held at United Nations Headquarters, New York, on 26 October 1971, 69 Governments pledged contributions totalling $1,943,611. Subsequent pledges by eight countries brought total pledges to $2,054,959 for 1972 (as at

---

[3]See Y.U.N., 1970, p. 418, text of resolution 2637 (XXV).
[4]See Y.U.N., 1966, p. 302-6, text of resolution 2152 (XXI).

31 May 1972). (For 1972 pledges, by country, see table below.)

Total voluntary contributions pledged to UNIDO

since the establishment of the General Trust Fund in 1968 reached $8,928,296 as at 31 December 1971.

Contributions pledged to the United Nations Industrial Development Organization for 1972

(As at 31 May 1972)

Country	Amount (in U.S. dollar equivalents)	Country	Amount (in U.S. dollar equivalents)	Country	Amount (in U.S. dollar equivalents)
Afghanistan	1,000	India	50,000	Philippines	20,000
Algeria	10,000	Indonesia	25,000	Poland	54,348
Argentina	30,000	Iran	50,000	Qatar	15,000
Austria	15,000	Iraq	12,500	Republic of Korea	11,000
Barbados	1,000	Israel	10,000	Republic of Viet-Nam	1,000
Bolivia	3,025	Italy	300,000	Romania	33,333
Brazil	15,000	Ivory Coast	5,396	Rwanda	1,500
Bulgaria	12,500	Jamaica	4,000	Saudi Arabia	10,000
Burma	1,000	Kenya	4,000	Singapore	1,000
Central African Republic	396	Kuwait	30,000	Sudan	10,000
		Laos	1,200	Syrian Arab Republic	3,000
Chile	5,000	Lebanon	4,747	Thailand	10,000
Colombia	4,000	Liberia	3,000	Togo	2,248
Congo	7,000	Lesotho	1,000	Trinidad and Tobago	5,000
Costa Rica	2,000	Malaysia	2,000	Tunisia	5,000
Cuba	20,000	Mali	2,703	Turkey	3,571
Cyprus	1,044	Malta	480	Uganda	500
Czechoslovakia	173,130	Mauritania	2,000	USSR	603,136
Egypt	109,246	Mauritius	250	United Republic of Tanzania	2,002
Fiji	1,000	Mexico	10,000	Upper Volta	5,000
France	53,257	Mongolia	1,500	Uruguay	5,000
Gabon	8,993	Morocco	10,827	Venezuela	20,089
Gambia	495	Nigeria	7,000	Yugoslavia	100,000
Ghana	14,700	Pakistan	40,000	Zaire	1,000
Greece	6,000	Peru	12,000	Zambia	1,000
Guyana	1,000	People's Democratic Republic of Yemen	600		
Hungary	36,193				

DOCUMENTARY REFERENCES

Future programme and structure of UNIDO

SPECIAL INTERNATIONAL CONFERENCE OF UNIDO

A/8341/Rev.1. Note by Secretary-General (transmitting report of Special International Conference of United Nations Industrial Development Organization (UNIDO) (ID/SCU/4/Rev.1), Vienna, Austria, 1-8 June 1971). (Chapter II A: Resolution of consensus on long-range strategy, structure and financing of UNIDO.)

Economic and Social Council—51st session
Economic Committee, meetings 538, 539.
Plenary meeting 1799.

E/5041. Note by Secretary-General (transmitting report of Industrial Development Board on work of its 5th session, Vienna, Austria, 24-28 May and 8 June 1971 (A/8416 and Corr.1)). Chapter VII: Special International Conference of UNIDO; and Annex III.

E/5042 and Corr.1,2. Note by Secretary-General (transmitting report of Special International Conference of UNIDO (A/8341/Rev.1)).

E/5064. Report of Economic Committee, draft resolution II, as orally proposed by Ghana and Indonesia, and as orally amended by Sudan, Brazil and sponsors, approved without vote by Economic Committee on 26 July 1971, meeting 539.

RESOLUTION 1635(LI), as recommended by Economic Committee, E/5064, taking note of report of Special International Conference of UNIDO and transmitting report, together with comments of delegations, to General Assembly at its 26th session, adopted without vote by Council on 30 July 1971, meeting 1799.

General Assembly—26th session
Second Committee, meetings 1411–1413, 1417, 1418, 1421, 1428, 1429, 1431, 1432.
Fifth Committee, meeting 1483.
Plenary meeting 2021.

A/8341/Rev.1. Note by Secretary-General (transmitting report of Special International Conference of UNIDO).

A/8341/Add.1. Administrative and financial implications of decision of Special International Conference of UNIDO. Statement by Secretary-General.

A/8385. Note by Secretary-General, Section B.

A/8401. Report of Secretary-General on work of the Organization, 16 June 1970–15 June 1971, Part Three, Chapter V A.

A/8403. Report of Economic and Social Council on work of its 50th and 51st sessions, Chapter XIV B.

A/8416 and Corr.1. Report of Industrial Development Board on work of its 5th session, Vienna, Austria, 24-28 May and 8 June 1971, Chapter VII and Annex III.

A/C.2/L.1183. Brazil, Chile, Panama, Peru, Philippines, Venezuela: draft resolution.

A/C.2/L.1183/Rev.1. Revised draft resolution, sponsored by above 6 powers and by Bolivia, Colombia and Uruguay.

A/C.2/L.1183/Rev.2,3. Revised draft resolution, sponsored by above 9 powers and by Ghana.

A/C.2/L.1183/Rev.4,5. Bolivia, Brazil, Chile, Colombia, Ghana, Iran, Kuwait, Nigeria, Panama, Peru, Philippines, Sudan, Upper Volta, Uruguay, Venezuela: revised draft resolution, approved by Second Committee on 7 December 1971, meeting 1432, by 97 votes to 0.

A/C.2/L.1186. Nigeria: amendments to 6-power draft resolution, A/C.2/L.1183.

A/C.2/L.1188. Kuwait and Syrian Arab Republic: amendment to 9-power revised draft resolution, A/C.2/L.1183/Rev.1.

A/C.2 L.1191, A/C.5/1415, A/8408/Add.22, A/8602. Administrative and financial implications of draft resolution I recommended by Second Committee in A/8562. Statements by Secretary-General and reports of Advisory Committee on Administrative and Budgetary Questions and Fifth Committee.

A/C.2/L.1192. Sweden: amendment to 9-power revised draft resolution, A/C.2/L.1183/Rev.1.

A/C.2/L.1207. Canada, Denmark, Finland, Greece, Iceland, Norway, Sweden, United Kingdom, United States: amendment to 15-power revised draft resolution, A/C.2/L.1183/Rev.4.

A/8562 and Corr.1. Report of Second Committee, draft resolution I.

RESOLUTION 2823(XXVI), as recommended by Second Committee, A/8562, adopted by Assembly on 16 December 1971, meeting 2021, by 114 votes to 0.

The General Assembly,

Recalling its resolution 2638(XXV) of 19 November 1970, in which it convened the Special International Conference of the United Nations Industrial Development Organization to deal with the long-range strategy and orientation of that organization's activities, including its role in the Second United Nations Development Decade and the transfer and adaptation of technology for the industrial development of the developing countries, the organizational structure of the United Nations Industrial Development Organization and questions of its financing,

Bearing in mind the leading role of industrialization in the economic and social progress of the developing countries, as well as the central role and the responsibility of the United Nations Industrial Development Organization in reviewing and promoting the co-ordination of all activities of the United Nations system in the field of industrial development, as established in paragraph 27 of General Assembly resolution 2152(XXI) of 17 November 1966,

Convinced that the successful achievement of the tasks assigned to the United Nations Industrial Development Organization in the field of promoting the industrialization of the developing countries, in connexion with the International Development Strategy for the Second United Nations Development Decade, contained in General Assembly resolution 2626 (XXV) of 24 October 1970, is only possible if the efforts and resources of that organization and the resources of other appropriate organizations of the United Nations system entrusted with the financing of industrial development are concentrated on priorities indicated in a clearly defined long-term strategy for its activities,

Taking note of Economic and Social Council resolution 1635(LI) of 30 July 1971, by which the Council transmitted the report of the Special International Conference of the United Nations Industrial Development Organization, together with the comments of delegations, to the General Assembly at its twenty-sixth session,

Taking note of the report of the Industrial Development Board on the work of its fifth session,

1. *Endorses* the resolution of consensus on long-range strategy, structure and financing of the United Nations Industrial Development Organization, adopted by the Special International Conference of the United Nations Industrial Development Organization on 8 June 1971, and takes note of the report of the Conference and the views of Member States contained in it, as well as of the corrigendum to the report and the views expressed thereon;

2. *Commends* the guidelines contained in section I of the resolution as an adequate framework for drafting the long-range strategy of the activities of the United Nations Industrial Development Organization;

3. *Requests* the Secretary-General to take immediate action to appoint a small group of high-level experts from the various geographical groups, chosen in consultation with their respective Governments, to carry out the important task of formulating, in accordance with the guidelines set out in section I of the above-mentioned resolution, bearing in mind the one referring to special consideration of the industrialization needs of the least developed among the developing countries, the long-range strategy for the activities of the United Nations Industrial

Development Organization, and to submit their final report to the Industrial Development Board as soon as possible and, at any rate, in time for consideration at its seventh session;

4. *Requests* the Industrial Development Board to propose to the General Assembly, in due time, the necessary measures for convening another general conference of the United Nations Industrial Development Organization in 1974 or 1975, as appropriate, and to make recommendations for a provisional agenda, keeping in mind the need to review the progress of industrialization during the Second United Nations Development Decade;

5. *Recommends* that the Industrial Development Board, at its sixth session, should take action in accordance with section II, paragraph 9, of the resolution of consensus and set up as its subsidiary organ a permanent committee of the Board with the terms of reference established therein;

6. *Considers* it desirable that the United Nations Industrial Development Organization should have greater autonomy in administrative matters, including the recruitment of personnel and management of its publications programme;

7. *Expresses its satisfaction* at the initiative taken by the Economic and Social Council, in its resolution 1617(LI) of 27 July 1971, to ensure that special attention should be given by the Administrator of the United Nations Development Programme, in accordance with the priorities assigned by the developing countries, to the requests for assistance made in the field of industrial development, in particular by the least developed among the developing countries, and including industrial technological development and industrial pilot projects;

8. *Urges* the Governing Council of the United Nations Development Programme to plan the level of its programme reserve in such a way that a minimum of $2 million may be retained annually for financing the Special Industrial Services programme, and that additional resources be provided in the light of future requirements based on demonstrated needs;

9. *Requests* the Administrator of the United Nations Development Programme to give, among the global projects mentioned in paragraphs 21 to 26 of the consensus adopted on 30 June 1970 by the Governing Council of the Programme at its tenth session, particular attention to projects within the sphere of industrial technological development;

10. *Invites* the Executive Director of the United Nations Industrial Development Organization to extend full co-operation to regional industrial conferences held at the ministerial or other levels under the auspices of the regional economic commissions and the United Nations Economic and Social Office at Beirut in order to facilitate greater regional co-ordination of industrial development policies;

11. *Decides* to set up an *Ad Hoc* Committee on Co-operation between the United Nations Development Programme and the United Nations Industrial Development Organization composed of those Member States whose representatives are serving as officers of the Governing Council of the Programme and the Industrial Development Board to examine in detail, in consultation with the Administrator of the United Nations Development Programme and the Executive Director of the United Nations Industrial Development Organization, all aspects of co-operation between the two organizations, especially those related to the formulation, appraisal and approval of industrial projects, and to submit a report thereon to the General Assembly at its twenty-seventh session, through the Economic and Social Council, together with the comments of the Governing Council of the Programme and those of the Industrial Development Board;

12. *Requests* the Secretary-General to convene the *Ad Hoc* Committee at an early date in New York and to extend to it all the necessary facilities and assistance;

13. *Calls upon* the United Nations Industrial Development Organization, in co-operation with the United Nations Conference on Trade and Development and with the regional economic commissions and the United Nations Economic and Social Office at Beirut, to assist the developing countries, especially the least developed among them, to take full advantage of the benefits of the generalized system of preferences for manufactures and semi-manufactures;

14. *Invites* the Executive Director of the United Nations Industrial Development Organization to review the organization and the structure of its secretariat, with a view to adapting it to the changing needs of the work programme in the light of the International Development Strategy and, in particular, to the needs for effective implementation of the operational activities of the organization, and to submit appropriate reports and proposals thereon to the Industrial Development Board;

15. *Recommends* that, as part of the preparatory work for the next general conference of the United Nations Industrial Development Organization, the Industrial Development Board should keep under consideration the proposals submitted to the Special International Conference on such changes and improvements as might be necessary, pursuant to paragraph 37 of General Assembly resolution 2152(XXI), in order to meet fully the growing needs in the field of industrial development.

Programme decisions

DECISIONS OF INDUSTRIAL DEVELOPMENT BOARD
A/8416 and Corr.1. Report of Industrial Development Board on work of its 5th session, Vienna, Austria, 24-28 May and 8 June 1971, Chapters II and IV B and Annex IV (resolution 30(V)).

DECISIONS OF ECONOMIC AND SOCIAL COUNCIL

**Training national technical personnel
for accelerated industrialization**

Economic and Social Council—51st session
Economic Committee, meetings 538, 539.
Plenary meeting 1799.

E/5024 and Corr.1. Role of United Nations in training national technical personnel for accelerated industrialization of developing countries. Report of Secretary-General.
E/5024/Summary. Summary of report of Secretary-General.
E/5024/Add.1. Supplementary paper by International Labour Organisation.
E/5024/Add.2. Supplementary paper by United Nations Educational, Scientific and Cultural Organization.
E/5064. Report of Economic Committee, draft decision III.
E/5073. Resolutions adopted by Economic and Social Council during its 51st session, 5-30 July 1971. Other decisions, p. 11.
A/8403. Report of Economic and Social Council on work of its 50th and 51st sessions, Chapter XIV C.

MEMBERSHIP OF UNIDO

General Assembly—26th session
Second Committee, meeting 1432.
Plenary meeting 2021.

A/8416 and Corr.1. Report of Industrial Development Board on work of its 5th session, Vienna, Austria, 24-28 May and 8 June 1971, Chapter VIII C.
A/8562. Report of Second Committee, draft resolution II, as suggested by Committee Chairman, approved without vote by Second Committee on 7 December 1971, meeting 1432.

RESOLUTION 2824(XXVI), as recommended by Second Committee, A/8562, as orally amended by Assembly President, adopted without objection by Assembly on 16 December 1971, meeting 2021.

The General Assembly,
Recalling section II, paragraph 4, of its resolution 2152(XXI) of 17 November 1966 on the United Nations Industrial Development Organization,
Decides to include Bahrain, Bhutan, Oman, Qatar and the United Arab Emirates in list A of the annex to its resolution 2152(XXI).

REPORT OF INDUSTRIAL DEVELOPMENT BOARD

Economic and Social Council—51st session
Economic Committee, meetings 538, 539.
Plenary meeting 1799.

E/5041. Note by Secretary-General (transmitting report of Industrial Development Board on its 5th session, Vienna, Austria, 24-28 May and 8 June 1971 (A/8416 and Corr.1)).
E/5064. Report of Economic Committee, draft resolution I, as orally proposed by Ghana and Indonesia, and as orally amended by Sudan, Brazil and sponsors, approved without vote by Economic Committee on 26 July 1971, meeting 539.

RESOLUTION 1634(LI), as recommended by Economic Committee, E/5064, taking note of report of Industrial Development Board on its 5th session and transmitting report, together with comments of delegations, to General Assembly at its 26th session, adopted without vote by Council on 30 July 1971, meeting 1799.

General Assembly—26th session
Second Committee, meetings 1411–1413, 1417, 1418, 1421, 1428, 1429, 1431, 1432.
Fifth Committee, meeting 1483.
Plenary meeting 2021.

A/8401. Report of Secretary-General on work of the Organization, 16 June 1970–15 June 1971, Part Three, Chapter V.
A/8403. Report of Economic and Social Council on work of its 50th and 51st sessions, Chapter XIV A.
A/8416 and Corr.1. Report of Industrial Development Board on work of its 5th session, Vienna, Austria, 24-28 May and 8 June 1971. (Chapter V: Pre-session documentation submitted by secretariat to Industrial Development Board.)

RESOLUTION 2823(XXVI), as recommended by Second Committee (A/8562, draft resolution I), adopted by Assembly on 16 December 1971, meeting 2021, by 114 votes to 0.

[For text of resolution and supporting documentation, see section above on SPECIAL INTERNATIONAL CONFERENCE OF UNIDO.]

UNIDO Pledging Conference

1971 United Nations Pledging Conference on UNIDO, meetings 1, 2 (A/CONF.54/SR.1-2 and Corr.1).

A/CONF.54/1/Rev.1. 1971 United Nations Pledging Conference on UNIDO. Final Act.
A/CONF.54/2. Contributions pledged to UNIDO for year 1972 as at 31 May 1972. Memorandum by Secretary-General.

Other documents

Industrial Implementation Systems: No. 1. Programming and Control of Implementation of Industrial Projects in Developing Countries. U.N.P. Sales No.: E.70.II.B.18.
Guide to Industrial Directories. U.N.P. Sales No.: E/F/S/70.II.B.20.
Production of Prefabricated Wooden Houses. U.N.P. Sales No.: E.71.II.B.13.
Perspectives for Industrial Development in the Second United Nations Development Decade. The Textile Industry. U.N.P. Sales No.: E.71.II.B.14 and erratum.
Industrial Development Survey, Vol. III. U.N.P. Sales No.: E.71.II.B.15.
Maintenance and Repair in Developing Countries. Report of the Symposium Held in Duisburg, Federal Republic of Germany, 10-17 November 1970. U.N.P. Sales No.: E.71.II.B.16.
Selected Aspects of Industrial Policy. Report and Proceedings of Inter-regional Seminar, Beirut, Lebanon, 4–15 January 1971. U.N.P. Sales No.: E.71.II.B.17.
Manual on the Establishment of Industrial Joint-Venture Agreements in Developing Countries. U.N.P. Sales No.: E.71.II.B.23.

Organization and Administration of Industrial Services for Asia and the Middle East. Report of Seminar Held in Tashkent, Uzbek SSR, USSR, 12–24 October 1970. U.N.P. Sales No.: E.71.II.B.20.

Industrial Research Institutes. Guidelines for Evaluation. U.N.P. Sales No.: E.71.II.B.22.

Industrialization and Productivity Bulletin No. 16. U.N.P. Sales No.: E.70.II.B.31; *No. 17.* U.N.P. Sales No.: E.71.II.B.8; *No. 18.* U.N.P. Sales No.: E.71.II.B.19.

Profiles of Manufacturing Establishments, Vol. II. Industrial Planning and Programming Series, No. 5. U.N.P. Sales No.:

E.68.II.B.13; *Vol. III, No. 6.* U.N.P. Sales No.: E.71.II.B.12.

Fertilizer Demand and Supply Projections to 1980 for South America, Mexico and Central America. Fertilizer Industry Series, Monograph No. 6. U.N.P. Sales No.: E.71.II.B.9.

Guidelines for the Production and Marketing of Acrylic Sheet in Developing Countries. Petrochemical Industry Series, Monograph No. 6. U.N.P. Sales No.: E.71.II.B.21.

Industrial Development Abstracts, Nos.1 and 2, 1971 (UNIDO/LIB/Ser.B/1 and erratum).

Rules of Procedure of the Industrial Development Board, January 1972. U.N.P. Sales No.: E.72.II.B.14.

Chapter VII
The financing of economic development

Various issues relating to the financing of economic development were discussed by United Nations bodies in 1971. Among other things, the promotion of foreign investment, export credits and development financing, tax reform, and budget policy and management were considered by the Economic and Social Council, which took decisions on these questions.

The General Assembly adopted resolutions on the burden of debt servicing and the Capital Development Fund.

These and other matters are described in the following pages. Various other aspects of financing economic development were considered in 1971 by the United Nations Conference on Trade and Development (see pp. 271-72).

Capital assistance to developing countries

Promotion of private foreign investment

On 30 July 1971, the Economic and Social Council noted the report on the Panel on Foreign Investment in Latin America, which had been convened at Medellín, Colombia, from 8 to 11 June 1970, and it welcomed the offer of the Government of Japan to act as host to a world-wide panel on foreign investment, to be held at Tokyo from 29 November to 2 December 1971.

In this connexion, the Council recognized that a thorough and continued review of the conditions, forms and effects of private foreign investment should help to bring about a greater inflow of capital into developing countries.

It invited the Secretary-General to pursue with the Governments of Member States and the international organizations concerned arrangements for other panels and technical assistance activities for the promotion of foreign investment in developing countries, and it requested him to report to the Council in 1972 on progress in the matter.

These decisions were embodied in resolution 1629(LI), adopted, without vote, on the recommendation of the Council's Economic Committee, which approved the text without vote on 21 July 1971 on a proposal of Indonesia, Jamaica, Kenya

and Zaire. (For text, see DOCUMENTARY REFERENCES below.)

The Tokyo Panel discussed: the impact of foreign investment on developing countries in the context of national development priorities; forms of foreign investment, including contractual arrangements; and the transfer of technology through private foreign investment.

The findings and recommendations of the Tokyo Panel, together with the Secretary-General's proposals on the implementation of these recommendations, were to be submitted to the Council in 1972.

The question of private foreign investment against the background of the world monetary crisis was also discussed at the third annual session of the joint International Chamber of Commerce, United Nations and General Agreement on Tariffs and Trade Economic Consultative Committee, held in Geneva, Switzerland, on 9 and 10 December 1971. In addition to international payments and trade, the Economic Consultative Committee discussed the transfer of technology and the human environment.

Problems and issues relating to the transfer of technology were also reviewed by the Inter-regional Expert Group on the Transfer of Operative Technology at the Enterprise Level, which was established by the United Nations Conference on Trade and Development in 1970. The Expert Group met in New York from 21 to 26 June 1971. It was comprised of experts from 10 developed and 11 developing countries and 41 observers, and included representatives of international business, the academic community and interested United Nations agencies. (See also pp. 279-80.)

The Expert Group stressed the need for advisory services and for the continuation of case studies on operative technology at the country and sectoral levels. It also recommended integrated technological strategies for developing countries, with the assistance of the United Nations, and studies of industrial property legislation and administration. The report of the Expert Group was to be submitted to the Economic and Social Council in 1972.

Burden of debt servicing

On 14 December 1971, the General Assembly took a number of decisions having to do with the increasing burden of debt services.

It noted with concern that the attainment and maintenance of an adequate rate of economic growth in a number of developing countries was threatened by the burden of increasing debt service repayments; and that this burden was compounded by the stagnation in the net flow of external assistance from some donor countries and the effects of the deterioration in terms of trade for many developing countries.

The Assembly considered: that debt relief could be an appropriate and effective means of increasing the net flow of resources to developing countries experiencing serious debt service problems; that one of the important causes of the frequent debt crises was the unfavourable terms and conditions on which some financial resources had been provided to the developing countries; that the proportion of official development assistance in the gross resource transfers to the developing countries had also contributed to the burden of debt servicing; and that the inappropriate use of export credit financing had been in some cases another cause of the burden.

Competent international financial and credit institutions and the creditor countries concerned were urged to give sympathetic consideration to requests from those developing countries in need of the rescheduling, refinancing or consolidation of their debts, with appropriate grace and amortization periods and reasonable rates of interest.

The Assembly invited competent international organizations, in particular the International Bank for Reconstruction and Development, the International Monetary Fund and the United Nations Conference on Trade and Development, to identify urgently the appropriate policies to be pursued by debtors and creditors for long-term avoidance of debt crises.

International financial and credit institutions and contributing countries were further invited to examine ways of better adapting the conditions and terms on which they provided financial aid to the situation of individual countries.

The Assembly urged developing countries with potential shortages of foreign exchange to take due account of that situation in their use of external credits and to improve as rapidly as possible their statistics on foreign borrowings.

These decisions were embodied in resolution 2807(XXVI), adopted, by 99 votes to 0, with 11 abstentions, on the recommendation of the Second (Economic and Financial) Committee, which approved the text on 9 December 1971 by 81 votes to 0, with 17 abstentions, on the basis of a proposal by Canada, Ghana, the Netherlands, New Zealand, Pakistan, Peru and Tunisia. (For text of resolution see DOCUMENTARY REFERENCES below.)

During the discussion in the Second Committee, amendments proposed by Canada, Chile and the United States were incorporated in the final text.

Export credits and development financing

At its July 1971 meetings, the Economic and Social Council considered reports by the Secretary-General on the establishment and operation of multinational export credit insurance schemes, the refinancing of short-term export credits granted by developing countries, and export credit and export promotion in developing countries. It also had before it the report of the first Interregional Seminar on Export Credit Insurance and Export Credit Financing, held at Belgrade, Yugoslavia, from 28 September to 7 October 1970.

On 30 July 1971, after taking note of the various reports, the Council invited the Secretary-General to convene late in 1972 two inter-governmental working groups of interested Member States: the first to deal with various aspects of arrangements for a multinational export credit insurance scheme; the second to deal with the harmonization of the terms of financing export credits for engineering and similar capital goods and related services in developing countries.

The Secretary-General was invited to further expand within the technical assistance programmes the share devoted in this field to advisory services, training programmes and similar activities, including the convening of an inter-regional seminar on export credit insurance and export credit financing in 1973.

The Council stressed the need for active support by the Secretary-General of initiatives towards the establishment of sub-regional or regional schemes for the association of export credit financing institutions in developing countries, in co-operation with the relevant regional and inter-regional organizations.

These decisions were among those embodied in resolution 1630(LI), adopted, without vote, on the recommendation of the Economic Committee, which approved the text without objection on 22 July 1971, on a proposal of Jamaica and Yugoslavia. (For text of resolution, see DOCUMENTARY REFERENCES below.)

Export promotion activities

The Secretary-General submitted the second report on United Nations export promotion efforts to the July 1971 session of the Economic and Social Council.

After considering the report, the Council recognized that the level of United Nations assistance in the field of export promotion and development would need to be augmented in order to assist developing countries attain the objectives of trade expansion set for the Second United Nations Development Decade.

It urged developed countries to give their full support to the regional export promotion centres established by the regional economic commissions as well as to the International Trade Centre (jointly administered by the United Nations Conference on Trade and Development (UNCTAD) and by the General Agreement on Tariffs and Trade (GATT)) and to other agencies and organizations participating in the United Nations export promotion programme. (For text of resolution 1620(LI), in which these and other decisions were embodied, see p. 287.)

During 1971, the regional economic commissions, the United Nations Economic and Social Office at Beirut, the Food and Agriculture Organization, the International Labour Organisation, GATT, UNCTAD, the United Nations Development Programme and the United Nations Industrial Development Organization participated in the United Nations export promotion programme, which was established in 1969.

Programmes of assistance, which included training seminars for officials from developing countries concerned with export promotion and development, were held in all the developing regions with the assistance of the International Trade Centre. The Centre emerged as the focal point for technical assistance and co-operation activities for export promotion within the United Nations system. (See pp. 286-87.)

Tax treaties between developed and developing countries

The third meeting of the Expert Group on Tax Treaties between Developing and Developed Countries, held in Geneva, Switzerland, from 25 October to 5 November 1971, had as its purpose the promotion of the flow of foreign investment and the increase of substantial revenues from the international sector through guidelines for international tax agreements.

Comprehensive guidelines were formulated for the tax treatment of royalties and shipping profits, on the basis of reports submitted by the Secretary-General on those questions.

Investment assistance programmes and tax incentives in developing countries, and their effects on tax revenue, were discussed on the basis of documentation provided by the Secretary-General on the inter-relationship between the tax systems of certain capital exporting countries and those of developing countries and on double taxation relief provisions of capital exporting countries.

More than 40 replies had been received from Governments in response to a questionnaire prepared by the Secretary-General on international tax evasion and avoidance. The Expert Group reviewed the conclusions drawn from these replies as well as a series of studies prepared by the Secretary-General on international income tax evasion, international tax havens, and fiscal fraud.

The Expert Group's report was to be submitted to the Economic and Social Council in 1972.

DOCUMENTARY REFERENCES

Promotion of private foreign investment

Economic and Social Council—51st session
Economic Committee, meeting 534.
Plenary meeting 1799.

Panel on Foreign Investment in Latin America, Medellín, Colombia, 8–11 June 1970. U.N.P. Sales No.: E.71.II.A.14.
Panel on Foreign Investment in Developing Countries, Tokyo, Japan, 29 November–2 December 1971. U.N.P. Sales No.: E.72.II.A.9.
Transfer of Operative Technology at the Enterprise Level. Report of an Interregional Expert Group on its Meeting held in New York from 21 to 26 June 1971. U.N.P. Sales No.: E.72.II.A.1.
E/4996. Fiscal and financial matters. Promotion of private foreign investment in developing countries for development financing. Report of Secretary-General.
E/AC.6/L.431. Indonesia, Jamaica, Kenya, Zaire: draft resolution, approved without vote by Economic Committee on 21 July 1971, meeting 534.
E/5060. Report of Economic Committee.

RESOLUTION 1629(LI), as recommended by Economic Committee, E/5060, adopted without vote by Council on 30 July 1971, meeting 1799.

The Economic and Social Council,
Recalling the International Development Strategy for the Second United Nations Development Decade, and in particular paragraph 50 thereof on foreign investment,

Recalling also its resolution 1451(XLVII) of 8 August 1969 on the promotion of private foreign investment in developing countries,

Noting with satisfaction the report on the Regional Panel on Foreign Investment in Latin America organized by the United Nations at Medellín from 8 to 11 June 1970, in co-operation with regional organizations and with the generous assistance of the Government of Colombia,

Recognizing that a thorough and continued review of the conditions, forms and effects of foreign investment should help to bring about a greater inflow of capital into developing countries,

Bearing in mind the Secretary-General's report on the promotion of private foreign investment in developing countries for development financing,

1. *Invites* the Secretary-General to pursue with the Governments of Member States and the international organizations concerned arrangements for other panels and technical assistance activities for the promotion of foreign investment in developing countries;

2. *Welcomes* the generous offer by the Government of Japan to act as host to a world-wide panel on foreign investment, at Tokyo, from 29 November to 2 December 1971;

3. *Requests* the Secretary-General to report to the Council at its fifty-third session on the progress in this matter.

Burden of debt servicing

General Assembly—26th session
Second Committee, meetings 1369-1382, 1408, 1437, 1438.
Plenary meeting 2017.

A/C.2/L.1165. Ghana, Pakistan, Peru, Tunisia: draft resolution.
A/C.2/L.1165/Rev.1. Canada, Ghana, Netherlands, New Zealand, Pakistan, Peru, Tunisia: revised draft resolution, as orally amended by United States and by sponsors, approved by Second Committee on 9 December 1971, meeting 1438, by 81 votes to 0, with 17 abstentions.
A/C.2/L.1180. Canada: amendments to 4-power draft resolution, A/C.2/L.1165.
A/C.2/L.1209. Chile: amendment to 7-power revised draft resolution, A/C.2/L.1165/Rev.1.
A/8578. Report of Second Committee (part I) (on report of Economic and Social Council), draft resolution VI.

RESOLUTION 2807(XXVI), as recommended by Second Committee, A/8578, adopted by Assembly on 14 December 1971, meeting 2017, by 99 votes to 0, with 11 abstentions.

The General Assembly,

Noting with concern that the attainment and maintenance of an adequate rate of economic growth in a number of developing countries is threatened by the burden of increasing debt service repayments,

Noting also that this burden is further compounded as a result of the current stagnation in the net flow of external assistance from some donor countries,

Noting further that the adverse effects of the deterioration in terms of trade for many developing countries are contributing to the aggravation of this burden,

Considering that debt relief can be an appropriate and effective means of increasing the net flow of resources to those developing countries experiencing serious debt service problems,

Considering that one of the important causes of the frequent debt crises is the unfavourable terms and conditions on which some financial resources have been provided, and continue to be provided, to the developing countries,

Considering that the present proportion of official development assistance in the gross resource transfers to the developing countries has also contributed to the burden of debt servicing,

Considering also that the inappropriate use of export credit financing has been in some cases another cause of the burden of debt servicing,

Recalling the recommendations contained in annex A.IV.5 of the

Final Act of the United Nations Conference on Trade and Development, as well as decision 29(II) of 28 March 1968 of the Conference,

Further recalling its resolutions 2170(XXI) of 6 December 1966 and 2415(XXIII) of 17 December 1968 and Economic and Social Council resolution 1183(XLI) of 5 August 1966,

Reiterating the provisions of paragraph 48 of the International Development Strategy for the Second United Nations Development Decade, contained in General Assembly resolution 2626(XXV) of 24 October 1970, regarding the policy measures required to forestall and alleviate the effects of debt crises,

1. *Urges* the competent international financial and credit institutions, and the creditor countries concerned, to give sympathetic consideration to requests from those developing countries which, in view of their situation, are in need of the rescheduling, refinancing or consolidation of their debts, with appropriate periods of grace and amortization and reasonable rates of interest;

2. *Invites* competent international organizations, in particular the International Bank for Reconstruction and Development, the International Monetary Fund and the United Nations Conference on Trade and Development, to identify urgently the appropriate policies to be pursued by debtors and creditors for long-term avoidance of debt crises;

3. *Further invites* international financial and credit institutions and contributing countries to examine ways of better adapting the conditions and terms on which they provide financial aid to the situation of individual countries, bearing in mind United Nations Conference on Trade and Development decision 29(II);

4. *Urges also* those developing countries with current or medium-term potential shortages of foreign exchange to take due account of this situation in their use of external credits;

5. *Further urges* developing countries to improve as rapidly as possible their statistics on foreign borrowings in order to provide both themselves and creditor countries with complete and up-to-date information on the time-profile of their debt-servicing obligations, and urges the developed countries and appropriate international institutions, on request, to assist developing countries to this end;

6. *Requests* that it should be kept informed of any progress made in relation to the recommendations set forth in the present resolution.

Export credits and development financing

Economic and Social Council—51st session
Economic Committee, meeting 535.
Plenary meeting 1799.

ST/TAO/SER.C/129. Report of First Interregional Seminar on Export Credit Insurance and Export Credit Financing, Belgrade, Yugoslavia, 28 September–7 October 1970.
E/4834. Export credits and export promotion in developing countries. Practical considerations relating to establishment and operation of multinational export credit insurance schemes. Report of Secretary-General.
E/4992. Export credit and export promotion in developing countries. Refinancing of short-term export credits granted by developing countries. Report of Secretary-General.
E/5011 and Corr.1. Export credit and export promotion in developing countries. Report of Secretary-General.
E/AC.6/L.428. Jamaica and Yugoslavia: draft resolution, as orally revised by sponsors, approved without objection by Economic Committee on 22 July 1971, meeting 535.
E/5060/Add.I. Report of Economic Committee.

RESOLUTION 1630(LI), as recommended by Economic Committee, E/5060/Add.1, adopted without vote by Council on 30 July 1971, meeting 1799.

The Economic and Social Council,

Recalling its resolutions 1358(XLV) of 2 August 1968 and 1452(XLVII) of 8 August 1969,

Recalling paragraph 36 of the International Development Strategy for the Second United Nations Development Decade,

Reaffirming the importance of the actual and potential role of export credit as an instrument for the promotion of exports from the developing countries and stressing the need for effective international co-operation for that purpose,

Having considered the reports of the Secretary-General entitled "Practical considerations relating to the establishment and operation of multinational export credit insurance schemes" and "Refinancing of short-term export credits granted by developing countries," the report of the first Interregional Seminar on Export Credit Insurance and Export Credit Financing, held at Belgrade from 28 September to 7 October 1970, and the report of the Secretary-General on export credit and export promotion in developing countries,

1. *Takes note with interest* of the report of the Interregional Seminar on Export Credit Insurance and Export Credit Financing and of the observations of the Secretary-General on the conclusions and suggestions of the Seminar;

2. *Takes note* of the report of the Secretary-General on the refinancing of short-term export credits granted by developing countries and invites the Secretary-General to revise the report, in the light of the discussion in the Council, for submission at its fifty-third session after consultations with appropriate specialized agencies, and also to make a final report available to the Trade and Development Board of the United Nations Conference on Trade and Development for its substantive consideration;

3. *Invites* the Secretary-General to convene late in 1972 two intergovernmental working groups of interested Member States:

(*a*) The first to deal with the various aspects of arrangements for a multinational export credit insurance scheme at the subregional or regional level among developing countries or with the co-operation of developing countries;

(*b*) The second to deal with the harmonization of the terms of financing export credits for engineering and similar capital goods and related services in developing countries;

4. *Invites* the Secretary-General to further expand within the technical assistance programmes the share devoted in this field to advisory services, training programmes and similar activities, including the convening of an interregional seminar on export credit insurance and export credit financing in 1973;

5. *Emphasizes* the need for active support by the Secretary-General of initiatives towards the establishment of subregional or regional schemes for the association of export credit financing institutions in developing countries, in co-operation with the relevant regional and interregional organizations;

6. *Invites* the Secretary-General to report to the Council at its fifty-fifth session on the findings and recommendations of the intergovernmental working groups.

A/8403. Report of Economic and Social Council on work of its 50th and 51st sessions, Chapter IX B.

Tax treaties between developed and developing countries

Tax Treaties between Developed and Developing Countries. Second Report (E/4936). U.N.P. Sales No.: E.71.XVI.2.

Interaction between the French Tax System and Those of Developing Countries (ST/ECA/149). U.N.P. Sales No.: E.71.XVI.3.

International Tax Agreement, Vol. IX, Supplement No. 24. U.N.P. Sales No.: E.72.XVI.1.

Tax Treatment of Private Investment in Developing Countries by the United Kingdom of Great Britain and Northern Ireland (ST/ECA/163). U.N.P. Sales No.: E.72.XVI.2.

Taxation of Private Investments in Developing Countries by the Federal Republic of Germany (ST/ECA/164). U.N.P. Sales No.: E.72.XVI.3.

United Nations Capital Development Fund

The United Nations Capital Development Fund was discussed during 1971 by the Governing Council of the United Nations Development Programme (UNDP), by the Economic and Social Council in the course of its discussion of the report of the Governing Council, and by the General Assembly.

On 14 December 1971, the General Assembly decided again to preserve the original functions of the Capital Development Fund, as outlined by the Assembly in a decision of 13 December 1966,[1] this time until 31 December 1972.

The Assembly stressed the urgent need to make the Fund fully operational as soon as possible, and expressed regret that it was not possible for the Governing Council of UNDP to achieve positive results on the subject during 1971.

United Nations Member States were urged to continue the search for practical means of implementing the objectives of the Fund. Hope was expressed that a report to be presented by the Administrator to the Governing Council of UNDP in 1972 would make possible, on the basis of suggestions received from Member States, the beginning of the effective operation of the Fund.

The Secretary-General was asked to invite Member States to contribute separately, at the same pledging conference, to UNDP and to the Capital Development Fund. The Assembly also appealed to Member States, and in particular to developed countries, to provide substantial contributions to the Fund so as to make it fully operational and more effective. These decisions were embodied in resolution 2812(XXVI), adopted by 82 votes to 8, with 22 abstentions, on the recommendation of the Assembly's Second (Economic and Financial) Committee, which approved the text on 19 October 1971 by a recorded vote of 75 to 7, with 24 abstentions, on a proposal by Brazil, Ceylon, Chile, Egypt, India, Jamaica, Pakistan, Tunisia, Upper Volta and Yugoslavia.

(For text of resolution, see DOCUMENTARY REFERENCES below.)

Pledging Conference

The 1971 Pledging Conference for the United Nations Capital Development Fund was convened by the Secretary-General on 1 November 1971. Pledges for 1972 amounting to $853,258 were made at the Conference and later. (See table below.)

As at 1 March 1972, the resources of the Fund totalled the equivalent of $5,255,250.

[1] See Y.U.N., 1966, pp. 288-91, text of resolution 2186(XXI).

Pledges of contributions to Capital Development Fund for 1972

(As at 1 March 1972)

Country	Contribution (in U.S. dollar equivalent)	Country	Contribution (in U.S. dollar equivalent)
Algeria	20,000	Khmer Republic	1,000
Argentina	30,000	Laos	1,000
Bolivia	3,000	Liberia	10,000
Brazil	20,000	Mauritius	1,994
Cameroon	35,000	Morocco	9,960
Ceylon	20,000	Niger	25,180
Chile	10,000	Nigeria	7,000
Colombia	1,000	Pakistan	200,000
Cuba	20,000	Philippines	10,000
Cyprus	750	Qatar	15,000
Dominican Republic	5,000	Republic of Viet-Nam	1,000
Egypt	40,000	Trinidad and Tobago	2,474
Ghana	29,400	Tunisia	1,500
Greece	3,000	Yugoslavia	300,000
Iran	10,000	Zaire	7,000
Iraq	10,000	Total	853,258
Jamaica	3,000		

DOCUMENTARY REFERENCES

General Assembly—26th session
Second Committee, meetings 1390-1392.
Plenary meeting 2017.

E/4954. Report of Governing Council of United Nations Development Programme (UNDP) on its 11th session, 14 January–2 February 1971, Chapter VIII.

E/5043/Rev.1. Report of Governing Council of UNDP on its 12th session, 7–23 June 1971, Chapter IX.

A/8399. Operational activities for development. Note by Secretary-General, part B.

A/8401. Report of Secretary-General on work of the Organization, 16 June 1970–15 June 1971, Part Three, Chapter VI B 4.

A/8403. Report of Economic and Social Council on work of its 50th and 51st sessions, Chapter VIII B.

A/C.2/L.1151. Brazil, Ceylon, Chile, Egypt, India, Jamaica, Pakistan, Tunisia, Upper Volta, Yugoslavia: draft resolution, as orally amended by Zambia, approved by Second Committee on 19 October 1971, meeting 1392, by recorded vote of 75 to 7, with 24 abstentions, as follows:

In favour: Afghanistan, Algeria, Argentina, Bahrain, Barbados, Bhutan, Bolivia, Brazil, Burma, Burundi, Cameroon, Central African Republic, Ceylon, Chile, China, Colombia, Cuba, Cyprus, Dahomey, Dominican Republic, Ecuador, Egypt, Ethiopia, Ghana, Greece, Guinea, Guyana, Honduras, India, Indonesia, Iran, Iraq, Israel, Ivory Coast, Jamaica, Jordan, Kenya, Kuwait, Lebanon, Lesotho, Liberia, Libyan Arab Republic, Madagascar, Malawi, Malaysia, Mali, Mauritania, Mexico, Morocco, Nepal, Nicaragua, Nigeria, Pakistan, Panama, Peru, Philippines, Rwanda, Senegal, Sierra Leone, Singapore, Sudan, Swaziland, Syrian Arab Republic, Thailand, Togo, Trinidad and Tobago, Tunisia, Turkey, Uganda, Upper Volta, Uruguay, Venezuela, Yugoslavia, Zaire, Zambia.

Against: Australia, Belgium, Canada, France, Japan, United Kingdom, United States.

Abstaining: Austria, Bulgaria, Byelorussian SSR, Czechoslovakia, Denmark, Finland, Hungary, Iceland, Ireland, Italy, Khmer Republic, Mongolia, Netherlands,* New Zealand, Norway, Poland, Portugal, Romania, Saudi Arabia, South Africa, Spain, Sweden, Ukrainian SSR, USSR.

*Subsequently, the Netherlands said it had intended to vote in favour of the draft resolution.

A/8563. Report of Second Committee (on operational activities for development), draft resolution IV.

RESOLUTION 2812(XXVI), as recommended by Second Committee, A/8563, adopted by Assembly on 14 December 1971, meeting 2017, by 82 votes to 8, with 22 abstentions.

The General Assembly,

Recalling its resolutions 2186(XXI) of 13 December 1966, 2321(XXII) of 15 December 1967 and 2525(XXIV) of 5 December 1969,

Recalling further its resolution 2690(XXV) of 11 December 1970, in which it decided to continue the provisional arrangements for the operation of the United Nations Capital Development Fund and requested the Governing Council of the United Nations Development Programme to consider, taking into account the observations made by Member States, all possibilities for reaching the objectives of the Fund,

Stressing the urgent need to make the Fund fully operational as soon as possible, within the framework of the expanded United Nations activities in the field of development assistance,

Mindful of the fact that the International Development Strategy for the Second United Nations Development Decade, contained in General Assembly resolution 2626(XXV) of 24 October 1970, calls for the opening up of new avenues of international co-operation for development,

Regretting that it was not possible for the Governing Council of the United Nations Development Programme at its eleventh and twelfth sessions to achieve positive results on the subject,

1. *Reaffirms* its resolution 2690(XXV) and urges Member States to continue the search for practical means of implementing the objectives of the United Nations Capital Development Fund;

2. *Expresses the hope* that the report to be presented by the Administrator to the Governing Council of the United Nations Development Programme at its thirteenth session will make possible, on the basis of suggestions received from Member States, the beginning of the effective operation of the United Nations Capital Development Fund;

3. *Decides* to preserve the original functions of the United Nations Capital Development Fund until 31 December 1972, in accordance with the measures set forth in paragraph 1 of General Assembly resolution 2321(XXII);

4. *Requests* the Secretary-General to invite Member States to contribute separately, at the same pledging conference, to the United Nations Development Programme and to the United Nations Capital Development Fund;

5. *Appeals* to Member States, and in particular to developed countries, to provide substantial contributions to the United Nations Capital Development Fund so as to make it fully operational and more effective.

Pledging Conference

1971 United Nations Pledging Conference on United Nations Development Programme and United Nations Capital Development Fund, meetings 1 and 2 (A/CONF.53/SR.1-2).

A/CONF.51/2. Contributions pledged to United Nations Capital Development Fund for year 1971, as at 15 April 1971. Memorandum by Secretary-General.
A/CONF.53/1. Final Act of 1971 United Nations Pledging Conference on UNDP and Capital Development Fund.

Other aspects of financing economic development

Tax reform planning

Before the Economic and Social Council at its July 1971 session were several studies and reports pertaining to tax reform planning.

One was a study on taxation, mobilization of resources, and income distribution in developing countries, prepared by the Secretary-General. It examined the global relationship between taxation and the mobilization of domestic financial resources. In preparing this, studies had been undertaken on sales taxes, income taxes, tax incentives, land taxation and income distribution and on Ecuador, Greece, Iraq, Mali, Pakistan and Uganda.

The Council also considered a report of the Expert Group on Tax Reform Planning and a summary of that report by the Secretary-General. The Expert Group made a number of recommendations on the role of the United Nations in tax reform planning and suggested further research in urban taxation, agricultural taxation and improved techniques of analysis and administration.

On 30 July 1971, the Council noted the Secretary-General's report on taxation, mobilization of resources and income distribution in developing countries.

Conscious of the need to increase private and public national savings in the developing countries, the Council recognized that an increase in total savings was essential to accelerate the rate of development in the developing countries.

The Secretary-General was invited to undertake a study on the most suitable ways and means of promoting the mobilization of financial resources for the developing countries in an appropriate framework, within which an effort would be made: (*a*) to consider and evaluate the programmes and activities of United Nations bodies and specialized agencies with regard to the mobilization of national and external financial resources, and propose to the Council measures for improving them; (*b*) to study problems relating to the mobilization of resources; and (*c*) to examine certain questions relating to the mobilization of financial resources submitted by the Council or the executive heads of the specialized agencies.

Among other things, the Council also requested the Secretary-General, the regional economic commissions and the United Nations Economic and Social Office at Beirut to continue their technical assistance activities relating to the mobilization of financial resources, in co-operation with the International Bank for Reconstruction and Development, the International Monetary Fund, other agencies and the Governments concerned.

These decisions were embodied in resolution 1631(LI), adopted by 16 votes to 2, with 8 abstentions, on the recommendation of the Council's Economic Committee, which approved the text on 23 July 1971 by 15 votes to 2, with 7 abstentions, on a proposal by Niger, as orally amended. (For text of resolution, see DOCUMENTARY REFERENCES below.)

Also on 30 July 1971, the Council requested the Secretary-General, in consultation with the International Monetary Fund and any other interested organization, to formulate and undertake a programme of work based on the report of the Expert Group on Tax Reform Planning and the views expressed by the Council, particularly with a view to creating capacity for tax planning in developing countries through the organization of training programmes and for exchange of experiences at the regional and sub-regional levels, paying attention to the need to take account of local situations in various developing countries.

The United Nations Development Programme was invited, within its country programming procedures, to extend the fullest support possible for training and technical assistance activities in this area.

These were among decisions embodied in resolution 1632(LI), adopted, without vote, on the recommendation of the Economic Committee, which approved the text without objection on 23 July 1971, on a proposal of Brazil, Ghana and Kenya, as orally amended. (For text of resolution, see DOCUMENTARY REFERENCES below.)

Budget policy and management

At its July 1971 session, the Economic and Social Council considered a report of the United Nations Interregional Seminar on Government Accounting and Financial Management, held at Beirut, Lebanon, in December 1969. It also had before it a progress report on the subject by the Secretary-General.

On 30 July 1971, the Council requested the Secretary-General to continue to undertake work on techniques of budget policy and management in developing countries, and to undertake studies on the financing of investment enterprises, whether State-owned or with State participation, in developing countries, with a view to assisting them to improve their financial management practices and to play a greater role in the development process.

The United Nations Development Programme, within its inter-country and country programming procedures, was invited to continue to support inter-regional seminars and technical assistance requests from developing countries in this area.

These were among decisions embodied in the Council's resolution 1633(LI), adopted, without vote, on the recommendation of the Economic Committee, which approved the text without vote on 23 July 1971, on a proposal by Ghana, Kenya and Tunisia, as orally amended. (For text of resolution, see DOCUMENTARY REFERENCES below.)

DOCUMENTARY REFERENCES

Tax reform planning

Economic and Social Council—51st session
Economic Committee, meetings 535-537.
Plenary meeting 1799.

Report of the Expert Group on Tax Reform Planning, Headquarters, 8-12 September 1970. U.N.P. Sales No.: E.71.XVI.1.
E/4988 and Corr.1, E/4988 (Summary). Fiscal and financial matters. Tax reform planning. Taxation, mobilization of resources and income distribution in developing countries. Report of Secretary-General.
E/5002. Fiscal and financial matters. Tax reform planning. Note by Secretary-General.
E/AC.6/L.432. Niger: draft resolution, as orally amended by Ceylon, France, Italy, Tunisia and by sponsor, approved by Economic Committee on 23 July 1971, meeting 537, by 15 votes to 2, with 7 abstentions.
E/5060/Add.2. Report of Economic Committee, draft resolution I.

RESOLUTION 1631 (LI), as recommended by Economic Committee, E/5060/Add.2, adopted by Council on 30 July 1971, meeting 1799, by 16 votes to 2, with 8 abstentions.

The Economic and Social Council,
Recalling its resolution 1271(XLIII) of 4 August 1967 on tax reform planning and General Assembly resolution 2562(XXIV) of 13 December 1969 on the same question,
Bearing in mind the recommendations of the Expert Group on Tax Reform Planning,
Noting the work programme of the Secretariat concerning foreign private investments and, in particular, the interest aroused by regional and international symposia on foreign investments,
Conscious of the need to increase private and public national savings in the developing countries,
Recognizing that an increase in total savings is essential to accelerate the rate of development in the developing countries,
1. *Notes with satisfaction* the Secretary-General's report on taxation, mobilization of resources and income distribution in developing countries;
2. *Invites* the Secretary-General to undertake a study on the most suitable ways and means of promoting the mobilization of financial resources for the developing countries in an appropriate framework, within which an effort would be made:
(a) To consider and evaluate the programmes and activities of United Nations bodies and specialized agencies regarding the mobilization of national and external financial resources, and propose to the Council measures for improving them;
(b) To study problems relating to the mobilization of resources at the subregional, regional and international levels;
(c) To examine certain questions relating to the mobilization of financial resources submitted by the Council or the executive heads of the specialized agencies;
3. *Requests* the Secretary-General to submit a further report to the Council at its fifty-fifth session;

4. *Requests* the Secretary-General, the regional economic commissions and the United Nations Economic and Social Office at Beirut to continue their technical assistance activities relating to the mobilization of financial resources, in co-operation with the International Bank for Reconstruction and Development, the International Monetary Fund, the specialized agencies and the Governments concerned.

E/AC.6/L.433. Brazil, Ghana, Kenya: draft resolution, as orally amended by USSR and by sponsors, approved without objection by Economic Committee on 23 July 1971, meeting 537.
E/5060/Add.2. Report of Economic Committee, draft resolution II.

RESOLUTION 1632 (LI), as recommended by Economic Committee, E/5060/Add.2, adopted without vote by Council on 30 July 1971, meeting 1799.

The Economic and Social Council,
Recalling its resolution 1271(XLIII) of 4 August 1967 on tax reform planning,
Having examined the report of the Expert Group on Tax Reform Planning,
Convinced that long-term continuous and dynamic tax planning is essential for development,
1. *Appreciates* the note by the Secretary-General on tax reform planning;
2. *Notes with appreciation* the general findings and views expressed by the Expert Group on Tax Reform Planning in its report;
3. *Requests* the Secretary-General, in consultation with the International Monetary Fund and any other interested organization, to formulate and undertake a programme of work in this area based on the report of the Expert Group and the views expressed by the Council, particularly with a view to creating capacity for tax planning in developing countries through the organization of training programmes and for exchange of experiences at the regional and subregional levels, paying attention to the need to take account of local situations in various developing countries;
4. *Invites* the United Nations Development Programme, within its country programming procedures, to extend the fullest support possible for training and technical assistance activities in this area.

A/8401. Report of Secretary-General on work of the Organization, 16 June 1970–15 June 1971, Part Three, Chapter II C 4.
A/8403. Report of Economic and Social Council on work of its 50th and 51st sessions, Chapter IX C.

Budget policy and management

Economic and Social Council—51st session
Economic Committee, meeting 537.
Plenary meeting 1799.

ST/TAO/SER.C/117. Report of the United Nations Interregional

Seminar on Government Accounting and Financial Management, Beirut, Lebanon, 8-19 December 1969.

E/4999. Progress report of Secretary-General.

E/AC.6/L.434. Ghana, Kenya, Tunisia: draft resolution, as orally amended by sponsors and by Italy and United Kingdom, approved without vote by Economic Committee on 23 July 1971, meeting 537.

E/5060/Add.3. Report of Economic Committee.

RESOLUTION 1633 (LI), as recommended by Economic Committee, E/5060/Add.3, adopted without vote by Council on 30 July 1971, meeting 1799.

The Economic and Social Council,

Having considered the report of the United Nations Interregional Seminar on Government Accounting and Financial Management,

Recognizing the importance of good government budgetary systems for the efficient management of public sector programmes and for the implementation of development plans,

Aware of the potential contribution which efficient enterprises, whether State-owned or with State participation, can make towards the pace of development,

Recalling its resolution 1360(XLV) of 2 August 1968 on this subject,

1. *Takes note with appreciation* of the progress made by the secretariat in this area;

2. *Requests* the Secretary-General to continue to undertake work on techniques of budget policy and management in developing countries;

3. *Further requests* the Secretary-General to undertake studies on the financing of investment of enterprises whether State-owned or with State participation, in developing countries, with a view to assisting them to improve their financial management practices and to play a greater role in the development process;

4. *Invites* the United Nations Development Programme, within its inter-country and country programming procedures, to continue to support inter-regional seminars and technical assistance requests from developing countries in this area;

5. *Further invites* the Secretary-General to submit periodically to the Council progress reports on the work in this area.

A/8403. Reports of Economic and Social Council on work of its 50th and 51st sessions, Chapter IX D.

Reports of International Bank for Reconstruction and Development, International Development Association and International Finance Corporation

The annual reports for the fiscal year ended 30 June 1971 of the International Bank for Reconstruction and Development and its affiliates, the International Finance Corporation (IFC) and the International Development Association (IDA) —which together are known as the World Bank Group—were considered by the Economic and Social Council at meetings held in October 1971.

Introducing the reports, the President of the Bank observed that the Group was operating at a high level of activity, meeting and in some cases surpassing the goals set for the 1968-1973 period.

In the fiscal year ended 30 June 1971, the Group had made loans, credits and investments amounting to the equivalent of $2,600 million, as against $2,300 million in 1970 and $1,900 million in 1969. In order to finance disbursements and increase liquidity, the Bank had borrowed nearly $1,400 million in 1971.

There had been fresh departures in the Group's policies and practices: for the first time it had made loans or investments for agricultural research, paramedical education, an institution created exclusively to develop a capital market, farmer-training mobile units, a company to finance hotel construction and a pollution-control project.

The President went on to observe that most countries of the third world, even those where the symptoms of overpopulation were not yet fully evident, should give population planning a much higher priority in their development programmes. There was a need for development policies aimed at greater employment and greater equality of income distributions, and there was a challenge to ensure that the benefits of the so-called green revolution accrued to the small farmers as well as to the wealthier farmers, he said.

The President of the Bank stated that in his view the world community now had the best opportunity it had had since the Bretton Woods Conference to take a memorable step forward in the realm of international economic relations. It was the fear of an adverse balance-of-payments position, even a temporary one, that lay behind the inequitable attitude of the high-income countries towards the developing countries, he said.

On 28 October 1971, by resolution 1648(LI), the Council took note with appreciation of the reports. It took this action on the proposal of its President.

DOCUMENTARY REFERENCES

Economic and Social Council—51st session
Plenary meetings 1802, 1803.

E/5074. Note by Secretary-General (transmitting summaries of 1971 annual reports of International Bank for Reconstruction and Development (Bank), International Development Association (IDA) and International Finance Corporation (IFC)).

RESOLUTION 1648 (LI), as proposed by Council President, taking note with appreciation of report of Bank and IDA and of report of IFC, adopted by Council without objection on 28 October 1971, meeting 1803.

A/8403/Add.1. Addendum to report of Economic and Social Council, resumed 51st session, Chapter II B.

Chapter VIII

Development and environment

During 1971, the Economic and Social Council and the General Assembly took several decisions concerning development and the environment, with particular reference to the United Nations Conference on the Human Environment, to be held in Stockholm, Sweden, in June 1972. The Preparatory Committee for the Conference held two sessions during 1971.

Work of Preparatory Committee

The Preparatory Committee for the United Nations Conference on the Human Environment held its second session in Geneva, Switzerland, from 8 to 19 February 1971, and its third session in New York from 13 to 24 September 1971.

At its second session, the Preparatory Committee drew up a provisional agenda for the Conference, covering six main subjects: the planning and management of human settlements for environmental quality; environmental aspects of natural resources management; identification and control of pollutants and nuisances of broad international significance; educational, informational, social and cultural aspects of environmental issues; development and environment; and the international organizational implications of action proposals made by the Conference.

The Preparatory Committee established an inter-governmental working group to prepare a draft declaration on the human environment, for submission to the Committee at its third session. There was general agreement among Committee members that the declaration should be inspirational, concise and readily understandable by the general public, so as to effectively stimulate public awareness and participation in the protection of the environment.

Four other inter-governmental working groups were also established, dealing with marine pollution, soils, monitoring or surveillance, and conservation.

Among other things, the Preparatory Committee also discussed the need for the wide participation of developing countries in the Conference and approved measures taken by the Secretary-General in this regard.

At its third session, the Preparatory Committee considered a draft preamble and fundamental principles for the declaration on the human environment, prepared by the inter-governmental working group. The Committee requested the working group, if possible, to present a final draft to its fourth (January 1972) session.

The Committee also: approved draft rules of procedure for the Conference; reviewed regional meetings that had been organized on development and the environment for the purpose of facilitating the participation of developing countries in the Conference; and agreed that inter-governmental organizations that had previously participated in United Nations conferences and non-governmental organizations with a direct interest in environmental questions should be invited to participate on an observer basis in the Conference.

Decision of Economic and Social Council

At its mid-1971 session, the Economic and Social Council considered the report of the Preparatory Committee for the United Nations Conference on the Human Environment on its second session.

On 20 July 1971, the Council, without adopting a resolution, took note with appreciation of the report and, in the light of the importance of the subject, decided to transmit the summary records of its Co-ordination Committee's discussion on the item to the General Assembly at its 1971 session, and to the Preparatory Committee at its third session.

Decisions of General Assembly

At its 1971 session, the General Assembly took a number of decisions concerning development and the environment. Serving as a basis for discussion was a report by the Secretary-General of the United Nations Conference on the Human Environment.

The Assembly also had before it the following communications concerning the Conference:

(1) a letter dated 14 April 1971 from the Permanent Representative of the USSR to the United Nations, addressed to the Secretary-General of the United Nations, stating that a questionnaire prepared by the Secretariat in connexion with the Secretary-General's report on the Declaration on the Human Environment was sent to Governments of a number of States not Members of the Organization; the letter declared that this was a departure from the principle contained in the recommendation of the Preparatory Committee and expressed the hope that the Secretary-General would take the necessary steps to ensure that only Member Governments were consulted in this manner;

(2) a note verbale dated 7 May 1971 from the Secretary-General, addressed to the Permanent Representative of the USSR, stating that he would seek the advice of the Preparatory Committee in regard to the above-mentioned report, and,

pending such advice, would not issue further addenda to the report except as they were limited to replies from States Members of the United Nations; and

(3) a letter dated 8 October 1971 from the Permanent Representative of Czechoslovakia to the United Nations, addressed to the Secretary-General, transmitting a statement of the Government of the German Democratic Republic expressing its readiness to participate in the United Nations Conference on the Human Environment.

On 20 December 1971, the Assembly set forth its main decisions on the Conference with the adoption of resolution 2849(XXVI).

By the preamble, the Assembly among other things reaffirmed the importance, urgency and universality of environmental problems and observed that the rational management of the environment was of fundamental importance for the future of mankind.

Expressing its awareness that the environmental problems generated by under-development posed a serious threat to the developing countries, the Assembly was convinced that the solution of those problems depended, in large measure, on integrated comprehensive development, including industrial development based on advanced technologies and the rational management of natural resources. It observed that pollution of world-wide impact was caused primarily by some highly developed countries and therefore responsibility for financing corrective measures fell upon those countries.

The Assembly recognized the importance of bilateral and multilateral co-operation in solving environmental problems and the need for additional technical assistance and financing to enable developing countries to incorporate environmental consideration in their development planning. While recognizing the right of each country to formulate its own national policies on the environment in accordance with its own particular situation, the Assembly stressed that the exercise of such rights should take due consideration of their possible effects on other countries.

By the first operative paragraph of the resolution, the Assembly urged the international community and the organizations of the United Nations system to strengthen international co-operation in the fields of environment, rational management of natural resources and preservation of adequate ecological balance.

The Assembly then took a number of decisions concerning the United Nations Conference on the Human Environment.

It reaffirmed the importance for the Conference to take fully into account the interests of the developing countries, and in this context endorsed the view expressed by the Second Ministerial Meeting of the Group of Seventy-seven Developing Countries (adopted at Lima, Peru, on 7 November 1971).

The Assembly stressed that the action plan and the action proposals to be submitted to the Conference must, *inter alia*: (a) respect the exercise of sovereignty over natural resources and the right of each country to exploit its own resources in such a manner as to avoid producing harmful effects on other countries; (b) recognize that no environmental policy should adversely affect the present or future development of the developing countries; (c) recognize further that the burden of the environmental policies of the developed countries could not be transferred to the developing countries; (d) respect the sovereign right of each country to plan its own economy and formulate environmental policies in accordance with its own local conditions in such a manner as to avoid producing harmful effects on other countries; and (e) avoid any adverse effects of environmental policies and measures on the economy of the developing countries in all spheres, including international trade, international development assistance and the transfer of technology.

The action plan and action proposals should also include measures: (a) to promote programmes of training, applied research and exchange of information on environmental problems; (b) to provide additional technical assistance and financial resources, beyond the targets indicated in the International Development Strategy, to enable developing countries to implement needed environmental policies; (c) to give special attention to the environmental problems of the land-locked and least developed among the developing countries; (d) to promote assistance programmes for developing countries to solve their environmental problems originating in the problems of under-development itself; (e) to study environmental effects of marine pollution on coastal countries; and (f) to promote international co-operation to control adverse ecological effects caused by activities in all spheres.

The Assembly stressed the necessity of prohibiting the production and use of nuclear, chemical and biological weapons and of ensuring their early destruction, and urged States possessing nuclear weapons to put an end to testing.

The Assembly urged international co-operation in the field of the environment, taking into account the need for increased technical and financial assistance to the developing countries. It felt that it would be advisable for international financial institutions to consider the increase in volume and softening of terms of their economic assistance to the developing countries for the planning and implementation of projects with environmental implications which those countries deemed desirable. The Assembly also requested the Secretary-General to submit a report to the Conference on a scheme of voluntary contributions to provide additional financing by the developed countries to the developing countries for environmental purposes.

The Secretary-General of the United Nations Conference on Trade and Development was requested to submit to that Conference at its 1972 session a study on the effects of environmental policies of developed countries which might adversely affect the present and future development possibilities of developing countries by means of, *inter alia*: (*a*) a decrease in the flow of international development assistance and deterioration of its terms and conditions; and (*b*) creation of additional trade barriers such as the new non-tariff measures.

Finally, the Assembly reiterated the primary importance of independent economic and social development as the main objective of international co-operation, in the interests of the welfare of mankind and the peace and security of the world.

The Assembly requested that the provisions embodied in the preambular and operative parts of its resolution be fully reflected in the documents prepared for the Conference on the Human Environment.

The above resolution was adopted by a recorded vote of 85 to 2, with 34 abstentions, on the recommendation of the Second (Economic and Financial) Committee. The Committee approved the text on 8 December 1971 by a roll-call vote of 62 to 4, with 31 abstentions.

The text was based on a proposal by 38 States—Afghanistan, Algeria, Argentina, Bahrain, Brazil, Burundi, the Central African Republic, Ceylon, Colombia, the Congo, Costa Rica, Ecuador, Egypt, Ethiopia, Guatemala, Guinea, Guyana, Iraq, Kuwait, Mali, Mauritania, Mexico, Nepal, Niger, Nigeria, Panama, Peru, Rwanda, Saudi Arabia, Sudan, Swaziland, the Syrian Arab Republic, the United Republic of Tanzania, Upper Volta, Uruguay, Yemen, Yugoslavia and Zaire—as orally revised by the sponsors and orally amended by Spain, by Ghana, and by Ghana, Iran and Tunisia, and as amended by Venezuela and orally sub-amended by Cuba.

(For text of resolution, see DOCUMENTARY REFERENCES below.)

Prior to the vote on the draft resolution, the Second Committee voted on a series of amendments that had been submitted to it; 14 of these were rejected and 2 were approved. The Committee also approved in separate votes the provisions or wording of four operative paragraphs.

Also on 20 December 1971, the General Assembly took several other decisions concerning the Conference on the Human Environment.

The Assembly noted various measures that had been taken in preparation for the Conference, and expressed its appreciation for the assistance provided by Governments, organizations of the United Nations system and other inter-governmental and non-governmental organizations.

The Assembly then approved the provisional agenda and the draft rules of procedure for the Conference, as submitted by the Preparatory Committee for the Conference.

The Assembly asked the Secretary-General to invite States Members of the United Nations or members of specialized agencies or of the International Atomic Energy Agency (IAEA), as well as representatives of the specialized agencies and of IAEA, to participate in the Conference. The Assembly further requested the Secretary-General to invite other inter-governmental and non-governmental organizations to be represented by observers at the Conference on the basis of criteria recommended by the Preparatory Committee.

The Secretary-General was also asked to conclude the preparations for the Conference and to circulate in advance the following documents: (*a*) a draft declaration on the human environment; (*b*) a draft action plan; (*c*) such other draft proposals as might be ready for consideration by the Conference; and (*d*) draft proposals for organizational and financial arrangements needed within the United Nations system for work in the environmental field. The Conference was requested to consider the drafts submitted to it and to take such appropriate action as it desired.

Finally, the Assembly requested the Secretary-General to report on the results of the Conference to the General Assembly at its 1972 session and to make the necessary arrangements for the follow-up work to be undertaken after the Conference.

These decisions were set forth in resolution 2850(XXVI), which was adopted, by a recorded vote of 104 to 9, with 7 abstentions, on the recommendation of the Second Committee. (For text of resolution, see DOCUMENTARY REFERENCES below.)

The Assembly rejected several amendments to the text submitted by the Second Committee. Amendments sponsored by Bulgaria, the Byelorussian SSR, Czechoslovakia, Hungary, Mongolia, Poland, the Ukrainian SSR and the USSR would have added to the text a new provision by which the Assembly would decide, modifying its decision of 15 December 1969,[1] to convene the United Nations Conference on the Human Environment in 1973 (rather than 1972), and would also have had the Assembly decide to settle at its 1972 session the question of participants in the Confer-

---

[1]See Y.U.N., 1969, pp. 392–93, text of resolution 2581(XXIV).

ence. These amendments were rejected by a recorded vote of 70 to 17, with 29 abstentions.

An amendment sponsored by Algeria, India, the People's Democratic Republic of Yemen, Romania and Yugoslavia would have had the Assembly request the Secretary-General to invite "other interested States"—as well as States Members of the United Nations or members of the specialized agencies or of IAEA—to participate in the Conference. This amendment was rejected by a recorded vote of 57 to 43, with 20 abstentions.

The text, approved by the Second Committee on 9 December 1971 by a vote of 94 to 8, with 7 abstentions, was based on a proposal put forward by the following 34 States: Argentina, Austria, Canada, Costa Rica, Dahomey, Denmark, Finland, Ghana, Guinea, Iceland, India, Indonesia, Iran, Ireland, Italy, Ivory Coast, Japan, Liberia, Madagascar, Malaysia, Mexico, the Netherlands, Nicaragua, Nigeria, Norway, the Philippines, Singapore, Sudan, Sweden, Thailand, Togo, Turkey, Uruguay and Zambia, as orally amended by the sponsors and by Brazil.

Prior to voting on the draft, the Second Committee approved, by a vote of 64 to 21, with 20 abstentions, a 12-power amendment which added to the text a provision by which the Assembly requested the Secretary-General to invite States Members of the United Nations or members of specialized agencies and the International Atomic Energy Agency to participate in the Conference.

It rejected, by a roll-call vote of 53 to 34, with 22 abstentions, a 16-power sub-amendment to the above amendment which would have inserted the words "and other interested States" after the words "the International Atomic Energy Agency."

The 12-power amendment was sponsored by: Australia, the Dominican Republic, France, Italy, Lesotho, New Zealand, Niger, Rwanda, Swaziland, the United Kingdom, the United States and Zaire.

The 16-power sub-amendment had been proposed by: Bulgaria, the Byelorussian SSR, Cuba, Czechoslovakia, Egypt, Hungary, Guinea, India, Mongolia, Poland, Romania, Somalia, the Syrian Arab Republic, the Ukrainian SSR, the USSR and Yugoslavia.

DOCUMENTARY REFERENCES

A/CONF.48/PC.9. Report of Preparatory Committee for United Nations Conference on Human Environment on its 2nd session, 8–19 February 1971, Geneva, Switzerland.
A/CONF.48/PC.13. Report of Preparatory Committee for United Nations Conference on Human Environment on its 3rd session, 13–24 September 1971, Headquarters, New York.

Decisions of Economic and Social Council

Economic and Social Council—51st session
Co-ordination Committee, meetings 412-416.
Plenary meeting 1785.

E/4991. Note by Secretary-General (transmitting report of Preparatory Committee for United Nations Conference on Human Environment on its 2nd session).
E/4991/Add.1. Note by Secretary-General.
E/5012 (Part I). Development and co-ordination of activities of organizations within United Nations system. Report of Administrative Committee on Co-ordination, Chapter I C.
E/5039. Report of meetings of executive secretaries of regional economic commissions held in 1971 (New York, 27-29 January 1971; Geneva, Switzerland, 28–30 June and 3 July 1971), Chapter IX.
E/L.1427. Letter of 5 July 1971 from Hungary (transmitting letter of 5 July 1971 from German Democratic Republic to President of Economic and Social Council).
E/5052. Report of Co-ordination Committee.
E/5073. Resolutions adopted by Economic and Social Council at its 51st session, 5–30 July 1971. Other decisions, p. 27.

Decisions of General Assembly

General Assembly—26th session
Second Committee, meetings 1422-1428, 1435, 1436, 1438, 1439.
Fifth Committee, meetings 1486, 1487.
Plenary meeting 2026.

A/8308. Letter of 14 April 1971 from Permanent Representative of USSR addressed to United Nations Secretary-General.
A/8309. Note verbale of 7 May 1971 from Secretary-General to Permanent Representative of USSR.
A/8401. Report of Secretary-General on work of the Organization, 16 June 1970–15 June 1971: Part Three, Chapter VII D; Part Four, Chapter IV P.
A/8401/Add.1. Introduction to report of Secretary-General, September 1971, paras. 331-334.
A/8403. Report of Economic and Social Council on work of its 50th and 51st sessions, Chapter X!.
A/8509 and Add.1. Report of Secretary-General.
A/C.2/269. Letter of 8 October 1971 from Czechoslovakia (transmitting statement of 7 September 1971 of Government of German Democratic Republic).
A/C.2/L.1185. Brazil, Egypt, Iraq, Kuwait, Peru, Sudan, Upper Volta, Uruguay, Yugoslavia: draft resolution.
A/C.2/L.1185/Rev.1. Afghanistan, Algeria, Bahrain, Brazil, Colombia, Egypt, Guinea, Guyana, Iraq, Kuwait, Mali, Nepal, Niger, Nigeria, Panama, Peru, Saudi Arabia, Sudan, Upper Volta, Uruguay, Yemen, Yugoslavia, Zaire: revised draft resolution.
A/C.2/L.1185/Rev.2. Afghanistan, Algeria, Argentina, Bahrain, Brazil, Burundi, Central African Republic, Ceylon, Colombia, Congo, Costa Rica, Ecuador, Egypt, Ethiopia, Guatemala, Guinea, Guyana, Iraq, Kuwait, Mali, Mauritania, Mexico, Nepal, Niger, Nigeria, Panama, Peru, Rwanda, Saudi Arabia, Sudan, Swaziland, Syrian Arab Republic, United Republic of Tanzania, Upper Volta, Uruguay, Yemen, Yugoslavia, Zaire: revised draft resolution, as orally revised by sponsors and as orally amended by Spain, by Ghana, and by Ghana, Iran and Tunisia, and as amended by Venezuela (A/C.2/L.1213, as orally sub-amended by Cuba), approved by Second Committee on 8 December 1971, meeting 1436, by roll-call vote of 62 to 4, with 31 abstentions, as follows:

In favour: Afghanistan, Algeria, Argentina, Bolivia, Brazil, Burma, Cameroon, Central African Republic, Ceylon, Chile, Colombia, Congo, Costa Rica, Cuba, Cyprus, Dahomey, Dominican Republic, Ecuador, Egypt, El Salvador, Equatorial Guinea, Ethiopia, Fiji, Guatemala, Guyana, Honduras, India, Indonesia, Iran, Iraq, Ivory Coast, Jamaica, Kenya, Kuwait,

Libyan Arab Republic, Madagascar, Malawi, Mali, Mexico, Nigeria, Pakistan, Peru, Philippines, Romania, Rwanda, Saudi Arabia, Senegal, Sudan, Swaziland, Syrian Arab Republic, Thailand, Togo, Tunisia, Turkey, Uganda, Upper Volta, Uruguay, Venezuela, Yemen, Yugoslavia, Zaire, Zambia.

Against: Australia, Belgium, United Kingdom, United States.

Abstaining: Austria, Bulgaria, Byelorussian SSR, Canada, Czechoslovakia, Denmark, Finland, France, Ghana, Greece, Hungary, Iceland, Ireland, Israel, Italy, Japan, Liberia, Malta, Mongolia, Netherlands, New Zealand, Norway, Poland, Portugal, Sierra Leone, Singapore, Spain, Sweden, Trinidad and Tobago, Ukrainian SSR, USSR.

A/C.2/L.1213. Venezuela: amendments to 38-power revised draft resolution, A/C.2/L.1185/Rev.2.

A/C.2/L.1214. Australia and United Kingdom: amendments to 38-power revised draft resolution, A/C.2/L.1185/Rev.2.

A/8577. Report of Second Committee, draft resolution I.

RESOLUTION 2849(XXVI), as recommended by Second Committee, A/8577, adopted by Assembly on 20 December 1971, meeting 2026, by recorded vote of 85 to 2, with 34 abstentions, as follows:

In favour: Afghanistan, Algeria, Argentina, Bahrain, Bolivia, Botswana, Brazil, Burma, Burundi, Cameroon, Central African Republic, Ceylon, Chad, Chile, Colombia, Congo, Costa Rica, Cuba, Cyprus, Dahomey, Dominican Republic, Ecuador, Egypt, El Salvador, Equatorial Guinea, Ethiopia, Gabon, Guatemala, Guinea, Guyana, Haiti, Honduras, India, Indonesia, Iran, Iraq, Ivory Coast, Jamaica, Jordan, Kenya, Kuwait, Laos, Lebanon, Lesotho, Libyan Arab Republic, Madagascar, Malaysia, Mali, Mauritania, Mexico, Morocco, Nepal, Nicaragua, Niger, Nigeria, Oman, Pakistan, Panama, Paraguay, People's Democratic Republic of Yemen, Peru, Philippines, Romania, Rwanda, Saudi Arabia, Senegal, Somalia, Sudan, Swaziland, Syrian Arab Republic, Thailand, Togo, Trinidad and Tobago, Tunisia, Turkey, Uganda, United Arab Emirates, United Republic of Tanzania, Upper Volta, Uruguay, Venezuela, Yemen, Yugoslavia, Zaire, Zambia.

Against: United Kingdom, United States.

Abstaining: Australia, Austria, Belgium, Bulgaria, Byelorussian SSR, Canada, Czechoslovakia, Denmark, Finland, France, Ghana, Greece, Hungary, Iceland, Ireland, Israel, Italy, Japan, Liberia, Luxembourg, Malawi, Malta, Mongolia, Netherlands, New Zealand, Norway, Poland, Portugal, Singapore, South Africa, Spain, Sweden, Ukrainian SSR, USSR.

The General Assembly,

Recalling its resolutions 2398(XXIII) of 3 December 1968, 2581(XXIV) of 15 December 1969 and 2657(XXV) of 7 December 1970,

Expressing satisfaction for the efforts made and the results already achieved towards planning action to be taken by the United Nations system in the field of the environment in a manner compatible with the priorities and interests of the developing countries,

Taking note with appreciation, in particular, of the work done by the regional seminars on development and environment, held under the auspices of the Economic Commission for Asia and the Far East, the Economic Commission for Africa, the Economic Commission for Latin America and the United Nations Economic and Social Office at Beirut, as well as by the Panel of Experts on Development and the Environment,

Conscious of the significance of the results achieved in the Symposium on Problems relating to Environment, convened at Prague by the Economic Commission for Europe, for a better understanding of environmental problems,

Fully conscious of the importance, urgency and universality of environmental problems,

Aware that the rational management of the environment is of fundamental importance for the future of mankind,

Convinced that development plans should be compatible with a sound ecology and that adequate environmental conditions can best be ensured by the promotion of development, both at the national and international levels,

Fully aware that the environmental problems generated by the condition of under-development pose a serious threat to the developing countries,

Cognizant that, aside from environmental disturbances provoked by human settlements and ecological problems related to nature itself, pollution of world-wide impact is being caused primarily by some highly developed countries, as a consequence of their own high level of improperly planned and inadequately co-ordinated industrial activities, and that, therefore, the main responsibility for the financing of corrective measures falls upon those countries,

Convinced that most of the environmental problems existing in developing countries are caused by their lack of economic resources for dealing with such problems as the improvement of unfavourable natural areas or the rehabilitation of environmental conditions that have deteriorated through the application of improper methods and technologies,

Conscious that the main objective of developing countries is integrated and rational development, including industrial development based on advanced and adequate technologies, and that such development represents at the present stage the best possible solution for most of the environmental problems in the developing countries,

Conscious further that the quality of human life in the developing countries also depends, in large measure, on the solution of environmental problems which have their origin in nature and which are the product of under-development itself, within the general framework of development planning and the rational management of natural resources,

Emphasizing that, notwithstanding the general principles that might be agreed upon by the international community, criteria and minimal standards of preservation of the environment as a general rule will have to be defined at the national level and, in all cases, will have to reflect conditions and systems of values prevailing in each country, avoiding where necessary the use of norms valid in advanced countries, which may prove inadequate and of unwarranted social cost for the developing countries,

Stressing that each country has the right to formulate, in accordance with its own particular situation and in full enjoyment of its national sovereignty, its own national policies on the human environment, including criteria for the evaluation of projects,

Stressing further that in the exercise of such right and in the implementation of such policies due account must be taken of the need to avoid producing harmful effects on other countries,

Recognizing the importance of bilateral and multilateral co-operation in solving environmental problems,

Aware of the fact that a greater amount of scientific and technical knowledge than at present available would provide a more adequate basis for the satisfactory comprehension and evaluation of environmental problems in general, and that, therefore, international co-operation in this field is of paramount importance,

Convinced that rational planning procedures at both the national and the regional levels constitute an essential tool for an adequate equilibrium between the needs of development and the preservation and enhancement of the environment,

Bearing in mind the need for developed countries to provide additional technical assistance and financing, beyond the targets indicated in the International Development Strategy for the Second United Nations Development Decade, contained in General Assembly resolution 2626(XXV) of 24 October 1970, and without affecting adversely their programmes of assistance in other spheres, to enable developing countries to enforce those new and additional measures that might be envisaged as a means of protecting and enhancing the environment,

Considering that environmental conditions can be adversely affected by activities conducted by States beyond the limits of their national jurisdiction, including the sea, the sea-bed, the ocean floor and the atmosphere, particularly by the testing of nuclear weapons, with harmful effects for other States,

Considering further that various aspects of marine pollution and related matters will also be dealt with at the forthcoming United Nations Conference on the Law of the Sea and Inter-Governmental Maritime Consultative Organization Conference on Marine Pollution,

1. *Urges* the international community and the organizations of the United Nations system to strengthen international co-operation in the fields of environment, rational utilization of natural resources and preservation of adequate ecological balance;

2. *Requests* the Secretary-General, the Preparatory Committee for the United Nations Conference on the Human Environment and the other bodies established to advise and assist the Secretary-General in the preparations for the Conference to ensure that in the exercise of their responsibilities the documentation to be submitted to participating States and, in particular, the action plan and the action proposals for each of the main subject areas, as well as the draft Declaration on the Human Environment, be elaborated in such a manner as to take into full account the provisions embodied in the preamble and in the operative paragraphs of the present resolution;

3. *Reaffirms* that it is important for the United Nations Conference on the Human Environment to take fully into account the interests of the developing countries and, in this context, endorses the views expressed in part three, section A.VII, of the Declaration and Principles of the Action Programme adopted at Lima on 7 November 1971 by the Second Ministerial Meeting of the Group of Seventy-seven Developing Countries;

4. *Stresses* that both the action plan and the action proposals to be submitted to the United Nations Conference on the Human Environment must, *inter alia*:

(a) Respect fully the exercise of permanent sovereignty over natural resources, as well as the right of each country to exploit its own resources in accordance with its own priorities and needs and in such a manner as to avoid producing harmful effects on other countries;

(b) Recognize that no environmental policy should adversely affect the present or future development possibilities of the developing countries;

(c) Recognize further that the burden of the environmental policies of the developed countries cannot be transferred, directly or indirectly, to the developing countries;

(d) Respect fully the sovereign right of each country to plan its own economy, to define its own priorities, to determine its own environmental standards and criteria, to evaluate its own social costs of production, and to formulate its own environmental policies, in the full understanding that environmental action must be defined basically at the national level, in accordance with locally prevailing conditions and in such a manner as to avoid producing harmful effects on other countries;

(e) Avoid any adverse effects of environmental policies and measures on the economy of the developing countries in all spheres, including international trade, international development assistance and the transfer of technology;

5. *Further stresses* that the action plan and the action proposals should include measures:

(a) To promote programmes of training, applied research and exchange of information, with the objective of amplifying and disseminating knowledge of questions pertaining to the preservation and improvement of environmental conditions, to an adequate relationship between environmental policies and development policies, and to the question of comparative costs of different technologies in relation to the environment;

(b) To provide additional technical assistance and financial resources, beyond the targets indicated in the International Development Strategy, to enable developing countries to enforce those measures and policies acceptable to them in such a manner as to ensure that no action is defined or proposed without the proper means of implementation;

(c) To give special attention to the particular problems and

conditions of the environment of the land-locked and least developed among the developing countries;

(d) To promote programmes designed to assist developing countries, at their request, in solving environmental problems which have their origin in nature itself, which are the direct consequence of under-development and which particularly affect the living conditions of the population of developing countries;

(e) To study with special attention the environmental problems and conditions of the countries with coastlines particularly exposed to the risks of marine pollution;

(f) To promote international co-operation in order to prevent, eliminate or at least adequately reduce and effectively control adverse ecological effects resulting from activities conducted in all spheres, in such a way that due account will be taken of the interests of all States;

6. *Urges* the States possessing nuclear weapons to put an end to the testing of those weapons in all spheres and, also in the context of measures designed to improve environmental conditions on a world-wide basis, stresses the necessity of prohibiting the production and use of nuclear, chemical and biological weapons, and of ensuring their early destruction;

7. *Further urges* Member States, the United Nations system and other international organizations which deal with ecological problems to plan international co-operation in the field of the environment, taking into particular account the need for increased technical and financial assistance to the developing countries to help them improve their ecological conditions, both in rural and urban areas;

8. *Indicates* the advisability of the international financial institutions being enabled, without affecting adversely their operations in other spheres, to consider favourably the increase in the volume and the softening of the terms of their economic assistance to the developing countries for the planning and implementation of projects which, in the exclusive judgement of those countries, might be desirable and which, in their view, might be justifiable on environmental terms;

9. *Requests* the Secretary-General to submit a report to the United Nations Conference on the Human Environment, after ascertaining the views of Member States, on a scheme of voluntary contributions which would provide additional financing by the developed countries to the developing countries for environmental puposes, beyond the resources already contemplated in the International Development Strategy;

10. *Requests* the Secretary-General of the United Nations Conference on Trade and Development to prepare a comprehensive study, to be submitted to the Conference at its third session on the effects of environmental policies of developed countries which might adversely affect the present or future development possibilities of developing countries, by means of, *inter alia*:

(a) A decrease in the flow of international development assistance and a deterioration of its terms and conditions;

(b) A further deterioration in the trading prospects of developing countries by the creation of additional obstacles, such as the new non-tariff measures, which might lead to a new type of protectionism;

11. *Reiterates* the primacy of independent economic and social development as the main and paramount objective of international co-operation, in the interests of the welfare of mankind and of peace and world security.

A/C.2/L.1195. Argentina, Austria, Canada, Costa Rica, Dahomey, Denmark, Finland, Ghana, Guinea, Iceland, India, Indonesia, Iran, Ireland, Italy, Ivory Coast, Japan, Liberia, Madagascar, Malaysia, Mexico, Netherlands, Nicaragua, Nigeria, Norway, Philippines, Singapore, Sudan, Sweden, Thailand, Togo, Turkey, Uruguay, Zambia: draft resolution, as orally amended by sponsors and by Brazil, and as amended by 12 powers, A/C.2/L.1202, approved by Second Committee on 9 December 1971, meeting 1438, by 94 votes to 8, with 7 abstentions.

A/C.2/L.1202. Australia, Dominican Republic, France, Italy, Lesotho, New Zealand, Niger, Rwanda, Swaziland, United Kingdom, United States, Zaire: amendment to 34-power draft resolution, A/C.2/L.1195.

A/C.2/L.1212. Bulgaria, Byelorussian SSR, Cuba, Czechoslovakia, Egypt, Hungary, Guinea, India, Mongolia, Poland, Romania, Somalia, Syrian Arab Republic, Ukrainian SSR, USSR, Yugoslavia: sub-amendment to 12-power amendment, A/C.2/L.1202.

A/C.2/L.1215. Brazil: amendments to 34-power draft resolution, A/C.2/L.1195.

A/C.5/1416 and Corr.1, A/8408/Add.26, A/8601. Administrative and financial implications of draft resolution II recommended by Second Committee in A/8577. Statement of Secretary-General and reports of Advisory Committee on Administrative and Budgetary Questions and Fifth Committee.

A/L.661. Bulgaria, Byelorussian SSR, Czechoslovakia, Hungary, Mongolia, Poland, Ukrainian SSR, USSR: amendments to draft resolution II recommended by Second Committee in A/8577.

A/L.665. Algeria, India, People's Democratic Republic of Yemen, Romania, Yugoslavia: amendment to draft resolution II recommended by Second Committee in A/8577.

A/8577. Report of Second Committee, draft resolution II.

RESOLUTION 2850(XXVI), as recommended by Second Committee, A/8577, adopted by Assembly on 20 December 1971, meeting 2026, by recorded vote of 104 to 9, with 7 abstentions, as follows:

In favour: Afghanistan, Algeria, Argentina, Australia, Austria, Bahrain, Belgium, Bolivia, Botswana, Brazil, Burma, Burundi, Cameroon, Canada, Central African Republic, Ceylon, Chad, Colombia, Costa Rica, Cyprus, Dahomey, Denmark, Dominican Republic, Ecuador, Egypt, El Salvador, Equatorial Guinea, Ethiopia, Finland, France, Gabon, Ghana, Greece, Guatemala, Guyana, Haiti, Honduras, Iceland, Indonesia, Iran, Iraq, Ireland, Israel, Italy, Ivory Coast, Japan, Jordan, Kenya, Kuwait, Laos, Lebanon, Lesotho, Liberia, Libyan Arab Republic, Luxembourg, Madagascar, Malawi, Malaysia, Mali, Malta, Mauritania, Mexico, Morocco, Nepal, Netherlands, New Zealand, Nicaragua, Niger, Nigeria, Norway, Pakistan, Panama, Paraguay, People's Democratic Republic of Yemen, Peru, Philippines, Portugal, Rwanda, Saudi Arabia, Senegal, Singapore, Somalia, South Africa, Spain, Sudan, Swaziland, Sweden, Syrian Arab Republic, Thailand, Togo, Trinidad and Tobago, Tunisia, Turkey, Uganda, United Arab Emirates, United Kingdom, United Republic of Tanzania, United States, Upper Volta, Uruguay, Venezuela, Yemen, Zaire, Zambia.

Against: Bulgaria, Byelorussian SSR, Congo, Czechoslovakia, Hungary, Mongolia, Poland, Ukrainian SSR, USSR.

Abstaining: Chile, Cuba, Guinea, India, Jamaica, Romania, Yugoslavia.

The General Assembly,

Recalling its resolutions 2398(XXIII) of 3 December 1968, 2581(XXIV) of 15 December 1969 and 2657(XXV) of 7 December 1970 on the preparations for the United Nations Conference on the Human Environment,

Having noted with appreciation the report of the Secretary-General called for in resolution 2657(XXV),

Having considered chapter XI of the report of the Economic and Social Council and the relevant summary records,

Taking note of the reports of the Preparatory Committee for the United Nations Conference on the Human Environment on its second and third sessions,

Recognizing the important contributions to the preparations for the Conference made by the intergovernmental working groups on the declaration on the human environment, marine pollution, soils, monitoring or surveillance, and conservation,

Taking note with satisfaction of the steps that have been taken through which the concerns of developing countries have been increasingly reflected in the preparations for the Conference, such as the meeting of the Panel of Experts on Development and the Environment, held at Founex, Switzerland, in June 1971, the four regional seminars on development and environment organized by the Economic Commission for Africa, the Economic Commission for Asia and the Far East, the Economic Commission for Latin America and the United Nations Economic and Social Office at Beirut, and the meeting of scientists from developing countries organized by the Scientific Committee on Problems of the Environment of the International Council of Scientific Unions at Canberra,

Taking into account the important contribution to the preparations for the Conference made by the Symposium on Problems relating to Environment, held at Prague in May 1971, by the Economic Commission for Europe,

Recognizing the importance of ensuring that the global efforts in the field of the human environment be supplemented and made more effective by agreements at the regional or subregional levels,

Taking note with appreciation of the assistance lent to the preparations for the Conference by Governments, organizations of the United Nations system, other intergovernmental and non-governmental organizations, including youth organizations,

Taking into account the views expressed during its twenty-sixth session,

1. *Approves* the provisional agenda for the United Nations Conference on the Human Environment as formulated in the report of the Secretary-General on the basis of the recommendations of the Preparatory Committee for the United Nations Conference on the Human Environment;

2. *Approves* the draft rules of procedure for the Conference submitted by the Preparatory Committee and recommends them for adoption by the Conference;

3. *Requests* the Secretary-General to invite States Members of the United Nations or members of specialized agencies or of the International Atomic Energy Agency to participate in the Conference;

4. *Requests* the Secretary-General to invite representatives of the specialized agencies and the International Atomic Energy Agency to participate in the Conference;

5. *Requests* the Secretary-General to invite other intergovernmental and non-governmental organizations to be represented by observers at the Conference on the basis of the criteria recommended by the Preparatory Committee;

6. *Requests* the Secretary-General to conclude the preparations for the Conference and to circulate the following documents in advance of the Conference:

(a) A draft declaration on the human environment;

(b) A draft action plan, constituting a blueprint for international co-operation to protect and enhance the present and future quality of the environment for human life and well-being;

(c) Such other draft proposals as may be ready for consideration by the Conference;

(d) Draft proposals for organizational and financial arrangements needed to pursue effectively the work of the United Nations system of organizations in the environmental field;

7. *Requests* the Conference to consider the drafts submitted to it and to take such appropriate action as it desires;

8. *Requests* the Secretary-General to report on the results of the Conference to the General Assembly at its twenty-seventh session and also to transmit his report to the Economic and Social Council;

9. *Requests* the Secretary-General to make the necessary arrangements for the work that will have to be undertaken after the Conference, pending consideration of the recommendations of the Conference by the General Assembly at its twenty-seventh session.

Chapter IX

The application of science and technology to development

Questions relating to science and technology continued to receive attention from the General Assembly and the Economic and Social Council during 1971.

The Assembly took action on such subjects as the human environment, population, the peaceful uses of atomic energy, and the increase and use of edible protein. (Information on these matters is contained in other chapters of this volume.) It also took a decision on the application of computer technology.

During 1971, the Economic and Social Council considered, among other things, reports on the work during 1970–1971 of its Advisory Committee on the Application of Science and Technology to Development; computer technology; future institutional arrangements for science and technology; and progress in applying science and technology during the Second United Nations Development Decade.

The Advisory Committee's regional groups for Africa, Asia, Europe and Latin America met during the year. The group for Europe devoted its meeting primarily to the preparation for a joint meeting of the Advisory Committee and a group of European scientists and directors of research. The other regional groups discussed the regional proposals for the World Plan of Action for the Application of Science and Technology to Development.

Details of these and other matters follow.

Reports of Advisory Committee

The Advisory Committee on the Application of Science and Technology to Development held two sessions in 1971, its fourteenth from 16 to 25 February and its fifteenth from 15 to 26 November.

At the February session, the Advisory Committee adopted a report on the World Plan of Action for the Application of Science and Technology to Development, and reports on technologies appropriate for industrial development and effective provision and use of industrial research.

Other items considered by the Advisory Committee at that session included the transfer of technology to developing countries, the population problem, collaboration between scientists of developed and developing countries, the protein problem confronting the developing countries, the role of modern science and technology in reducing the impact of natural disasters on mankind, the role of science and technology in the development of nations, and global research projects for the solution of problems relating to development.

At the November session, the Advisory Committee strongly urged all relevant bodies within the United Nations family, national Governments and the scientific community in general to give careful consideration to the targets and proposals contained in the World Plan of Action, which in July 1971 had been considered by the Economic and Social Council. (See section below.) It also approved a report on science and technology and problems of population growth in developing countries.

A draft report on space technology for development, prepared by a group of consultants in close co-operation with the Committee on the Peaceful Uses of Outer Space, was commended by the Advisory Committee; and a report on the role of science and technology in reducing the impact of natural disasters on mankind was adopted. (See also pp. 473-79.)

The Advisory Committee also discussed technology and employment, problems of the human environment, collaboration between scientists of developed and developing countries, the role of modern science and technology in the development of nations, a systems approach to development, the nature of scientific community, and the creation of basic technology and research facilities for natural resources development.

On 19 and 20 November 1971, the Advisory Committee met with a selected group of 20 European scientists and directors of research to discuss international links between research and development institutions and industries of developing and developed countries. A list of priority areas for co-operative research was agreed upon.

Decisions of Economic and Social Council

Application of computer technology

A report by the Secretary-General on international co-operation with a view to the use of computers and computation techniques for development was before the Economic and Social Council at its May 1971 session. The report dealt with computer technology programmes for developing countries and with barriers and incentives relating to computer technology.

In the report, it was concluded that education and training for the application of computers for the purpose of accelerating the process of economic and social development must receive first priority; that each developing country needed a broad national policy, consistent with its national goals, on the application of computer technology; that international co-operation needed to be increased in activities relating to the application of computer technology for development; and that computer technology would increase in importance in the developing countries in the 1970s and its diffusion and application could make a significant contribution towards accelerating the rate of the economic and social development of those countries.

On 14 May 1971, the Council requested the Secretary-General to circulate the report widely to the Governments of Member States and to international governmental and non-governmental organizations interested in the application of computer technology to development, so as to elicit their comments on the conclusions and recommendations in the report. Another report on the subject was requested, for submission in 1972.

The United Nations Development Programme (UNDP) was invited to consider granting to developing countries suitable assistance for the application of computer technology to development, while Governments were urged to assist the Secretary-General in promoting international co-operation in this field.

These decisions were embodied in resolution 1571(L) which the Council adopted unanimously, on the basis of a proposal by France, Lebanon, Madagascar, Norway, Tunisia and Yugoslavia. (For text of resolution, see DOCUMENTARY REFERENCES below.)

Future institutional arrangements

After having decided, on 21 May 1971, to postpone consideration of the matter, the Economic and Social Council considered the question of institutional arrangements for science and technology at its July 1971 session.

The Council took no action on a number of proposals submitted at its April-May 1971 session by Brazil, Kenya, Sudan and Yugoslavia, by France, and by the United States.

On 30 July 1971, the Council decided to establish a Standing Committee of the Council composed of 54 members, to be elected in accordance with the geographical distribution of seats in the Council, to provide policy guidance and make recommendations on matters relating to the application of science and technology to development; the Committee was to report to the General Assembly through the Council.

The Secretary-General was requested to submit a report to the Council early in 1972 on the possible terms of reference of the Standing Committee. The Council also decided to maintain the Advisory Committee on the Application of Science and Technology to Development. The

terms of office of the members were to be three years and could be renewed.

In addition to its tasks under its terms of reference, the Advisory Committee was to furnish expertise to the Standing Committee as required. The Council further decided to review at its fifty-seventh (1974) session the institutional arrangements for science and technology in the light of the implementation of its resolutions on this matter.

Finally, the Council reiterated the view that any institutional arrangements in the field of science and technology could only be meaningful if adequate resources were made available for tackling major problem areas.

These were among decisions embodied in resolution 1621 B (LI) which the Council adopted on 30 July 1971, by a roll-call vote of 19 to 5, with 3 abstentions, on the basis of a proposal by Ghana, Haiti, Indonesia, Italy, Jamaica, Kenya, Lebanon, Madagascar, Malaysia, New Zealand, Niger, Norway, Sudan, Tunisia, the United States and Zaire.

(For text of resolution, see DOCUMENTARY REFERENCES below.)

This resolution on institutional arrangements for science and technology was one part of a three-part resolution on measures to improve the organization of the work of the Council. Part A dealt with enlargement of the Council's membership (see page 466); part C with machinery for review and appraisal of the International Development Strategy for the Second United Nations Development Decade (see page 226).

During the discussion of institutional arrangements for science and technology, the Council also considered a draft resolution proposed by Greece. By it, the Council would have deferred the adoption of decisions on questions concerning structural reforms as well as institutional arrangements for science and technology to a later date in 1971 and would have called upon all Governments to continue active consultations with the objective of reaching final decisions at that later date. This draft resolution was rejected on 30 July 1971 by a roll-call vote of 17 to 8, with 2 abstentions.

Suggested amendments to the text that was ultimately adopted, proposed by Brazil, Uruguay and Yugoslavia, were all rejected on 30 July 1971.

One of the amendments, which would have had the effect of replacing the paragraph on the establishment of a 54-member Standing Committee of the Council by a paragraph deciding to establish a Special Committee composed of the 27 members of the Council and 27 other Members, was rejected by a roll-call vote of 18 to 5, with 4 abstentions.

Other amendments (one of which would have had the Secretary-General report back to the Council in 1971 rather than 1972) were rejected by a roll-call vote of 18 to 5, with 4 abstentions.

In a related decision, taken on 20 December 1971, the Council decided to postpone until its organizational meetings in 1972 the appointment of members of the Advisory Committee on the Application of Science and Technology to Development. This decision was taken without the adoption of a resolution.

Decision on report of Advisory Committee

The Council, at its July 1971 session, noted the report of the Advisory Committee on the Application of Science and Technology to Development on its work from 16 April 1970 to 15 April 1971. Among the subjects covered in the report were: the question of global research projects; the transfer of technology; collaboration between scientists of developed and developing countries; and the World Plan of Action for the application of science and technology to development.

On 30 July 1971, the Council welcomed the Committee's continuing emphasis on the transfer of technology to developing countries and its collaboration with the United Nations Conference on Trade and Development (UNCTAD), the United Nations Industrial Development Organization (UNIDO), and other United Nations bodies in that field.

The Council requested the United Nations Educational, Scientific and Cultural Organization (UNESCO) to consider the Committee's recommendations to proceed with a survey of research institutions and laboratories in developed countries which had been concerned with research problems of developing countries, and to implement the Committee's recommendations concerning bilateral links between research institutions of developed and developing countries.

These decisions were embodied in Council resolution 1637(LI) which was adopted unanimously, on the recommendation of its Co-ordination Committee; on 27 July 1971 the Committee had approved without a vote the draft text, submitted by Norway. (For text of resolution, see DOCUMENTARY REFERENCES below.)

The World Plan of Action

The Council considered the report on the World Plan of Action for the Application of Science and Technology to Development at its July 1971 session.

The report, prepared by the Advisory Committee on the Application of Science and Technology to Development in close association with the specialized agencies, the International Atomic Energy Agency (IAEA), and a number of other inter-governmental as well as non-governmental organizations, was intended to provide a framework for some of the principal efforts of the

United Nations organizations in the application of science and technology during the Second United Nations Development Decade.

The first part of the report listed priority areas in which the Advisory Committee considered that science and technology could make a major impact.

Priority areas for research were: high-yielding varieties of staple foods, edible protein, fish, pest and vector control, tropical hardwood and fibres, groundwater, desalination, arid land, natural disasters warning systems, indigenous building and construction materials, industrial research and design, schistosomiasis, and human fertility.

Priority areas for the application of existing knowledge were: storage and preservation of agricultural products, control of livestock diseases, human diseases control, housing construction methods, glass and ceramics, improvement and strengthening of science and technology teaching in secondary schools, industrial extension, and natural resources.

The third priority was the building up of an indigenous science and technology capacity.

The second part of the report contained more detailed proposals for a wider range of areas.

On 30 July 1971, the Council noted that the Plan was an important adjunct to the International Development Strategy for the Second Development Decade.

In view of its inability to study the Plan adequately at its July 1971 session, the Council decided to consider it in more detail in 1972 and recommended that the General Assembly defer any in-depth consideration of the Plan until 1972.

The Council called on Member Governments to consider carefully the World Plan, and called on various inter-governmental bodies to study the World Plan and to bear in mind the ideas proposed in it in developing their programmes. The regional economic commissions were requested to consider the proposals contained in the Plan in the light of the needs of the countries in each of the regions, with a view to preparing specific plans of action for each region.

These recommendations were embodied in resolution 1638(LI) which the Council adopted, unanimously, on the recommendation of its Co-ordination Committee. The draft text was approved by the Committee without a vote, on 27 July 1971, on the basis of a proposal by France and the United States, revised to include suggestions by Brazil, Norway and the USSR. (For text of resolution, see DOCUMENTARY REFERENCES below.)

Progress in applying science and technology during Second United Nations Development Decade

On 30 July 1971, the Economic and Social Council requested the Secretary-General and the organizations of the United Nations system to ensure that the reports and studies prepared for periodic appraisals of progress during the Second United Nations Development Decade brought out clearly, in accordance with the provisions of the International Development Strategy,[1] the application of science and technology to the development of various sectors of the economies of developing countries.

In this connexion, the Council noted the goals and objectives of the International Development Strategy and the special problems of developing countries, and it noted further the special measures to be taken in favour of the least developed and the land-locked developing countries.

It expressed its conviction that the application of science and technology to development constituted one of the ways in which economic and social development in developing countries could be promoted, and that there was a need for monitoring the performance of these countries in respect of the various elements of the Strategy.

These decisions were embodied in resolution 1626(LI), adopted by the Council without vote on the basis of a proposal by Kenya transmitted to the Council by its Economic Committee on 26 July 1971. The Committee did not vote on the text.

(For text of resolution, see DOCUMENTARY REFERENCES below.)

(For information on the Second Development Decade, see pp. 225-36.)

Technology and industrial development

Before the Economic and Social Council at its July 1971 session were: a report on technologies appropriate for industrial development and a report on the effectiveness of existing industrial research organizations in developing countries, both prepared by the Council's Advisory Committee on the Application of Science and Technology to Development.

On 30 July 1971, the Council commended the reports to the attention of Governments; the specialized agencies concerned and the regional economic commissions were requested to consider the reports in relation to their own activities. At the same time, the Advisory Committee was requested to continue its consideration of appropriate technology for other sectors of the economy.

The Council recommended that UNCTAD, UNIDO, the International Labour Organisation and the Food and Agriculture Organization study in close collaboration ways in which reliable information on known alternative technologies for selected major industries of interest to developing countries could best be furnished in a systematic way to Governments, enterprises and industrial consultants.

It recommended that UNDP, the International Bank for Reconstruction and Development, the regional development banks and other sources of financial and other assistance give favourable consideration to requests from Governments of developing countries desirous of strengthening their capability for plant and product design.

The Council further recommended to Governments that more attention be given to matters relating to higher engineering education and managerial training activities, referred to in the report.

These decisions were embodied in resolution 1636(LI) which the Council adopted, unanimously, on the recommendation of its Co-ordination Committee. On 27 July 1971, the Co-ordination Committee had approved unanimously the text, which had been proposed by the Advisory Committee on the Application of Science and Technology to Development, as amended at the suggestion of France to include an expression of appreciation to the Advisory Committee. (For text of resolution, see DOCUMENTARY REFERENCES below.)

Reports on scientific co-operation

Also at its July 1971 session, the Council had before it a progress report by the Secretary-General concerning a study on the role of modern science and technology in the development of nations.

On 30 July, the Council took note of the progress report, expressing the wish that an effort be made to shorten and simplify it; and endorsed the recommendation of the Advisory Committee on the Application of Science and Technology to Development that the proposed study not be encyclopaedic in character but limited and well-defined in scope and essentially forward-looking. Member States, specialized agencies, IAEA and other organs of the United Nations system were called on to contribute to the preparation of the Secretary-General's study.

The Council expressed the wish that UNESCO examine, in agreement with the Secretary-General, the possibility of combining the study to be prepared by the Secretary-General with a revised edition of the study by UNESCO entitled *Current Trends in Scientific Research*, which had originally been published in 1961.

The Secretary-General and UNESCO were invited to take all necessary steps to promote the preparation of these studies, and the Secretary-General was asked to report regularly on the progress of the work.

These decisions were embodied in resolution 1639(LI) which was adopted, unanimously, by the

[1]See Y.U.N., 1970, pp. 319-29, text of resolution 2626(XXV).

Council on the recommendation of its Co-ordination Committee, as orally amended by France.

The Committee had approved the text without objection on 27 July 1971, on the basis of a proposal by France, Kenya, Niger, Norway, Tunisia, the United States and Yugoslavia. (For text of resolution, see DOCUMENTARY REFERENCES below.)

In the Council, a proposal by France to describe the character of the proposed study as essentially forward-looking was adopted.

Decision of General Assembly

Computer technology

At its twenty-sixth session, which opened on 21 September 1971, the General Assembly took up the question of computer technology and considered a report by the Secretary-General on the application of computer technology for development which had earlier been considered by the Economic and Social Council. (See section above.)

On 14 December 1971, the Assembly took note with interest of the conclusions and recommendations contained in the report and urged Governments to give particular attention to the application of computer technology, consistent with their national goals. It invited them to encourage broader bilateral and multilateral co-operation in this field and to explore new ways and means of intensifying this co-operation.

In this connexion, the Assembly expressed its conviction that the use of electronic computers and computation techniques might make an important contribution to accelerating the progress of vital economic and social sectors. It also observed that the United Nations system should take new measures with a view to supporting the efforts being undertaken by States in carrying out their tasks relating to the use of computers in accelerating the process of economic and social development.

The Assembly invited all relevant bodies to stimulate the application of computer technology to development along the lines outlined in the report.

The United Nations Development Programme, in particular, was invited to envisage providing the developing countries with suitable assistance in the field of computer technology. Finally, the Secretary-General was asked to prepare an up-dated report on the subject to be considered by the Council and the Assembly in 1972.

These decisions were embodied in resolution 2804(XXVI), adopted, without objection, on the recommendation of the Assembly's Second (Economic and Financial) Committee, which approved the text by acclamation on 21 October 1971, on the basis of a proposal by Argentina, Austria, Bulgaria, Canada, Chile, Czechoslovakia, France, Iran, Jamaica, Lebanon, Madagascar, Malaysia, Nigeria, Peru, the Philippines, Poland, Romania, Tunisia, Upper Volta, Uruguay and Yugoslavia. (For text of resolution, see DOCUMENTARY REFERENCES below.)

DOCUMENTARY REFERENCES

Reports of Advisory Committee
E/4970. Eighth report of Advisory Committee on Application of Science and Technology to Development, March 1971 (for period 16 April 1970–15 April 1971, containing review of work of Committee's 14th session, 16-25 February 1971).
E/5131 and Corr.1. Ninth report of Advisory Committee on Application of Science and Technology to Development, May 1972 (for period 16 April 1971–15 April 1972, containing review of work of Committee's 15th (15-25 November 1971, Geneva, Switzerland) and 16th (5-13 April 1972, New York) sessions).
The Role of Science and Technology in Reducing the Impact of Natural Disasters on Mankind. Report of the Advisory Committee on the Application of Science and Technology to Development (ST/ECA/157 and Corr.1). U.N.P. Sales No.: E.72.II.A.8 and corrigendum.

Decisions of Economic and Social Council

APPLICATION OF COMPUTER TECHNOLOGY

Economic and Social Council—50th session
Plenary meetings 1753, 1755, 1756, 1763.

The Application of Computer Technology for Development. Report of the Secretary-General (E/4800). U.N.P. Sales No.: E.71.II.A.1.
E/4800/Summary. Application of computer technology for development (Summary).

E/L.1410. France, Lebanon, Madagascar, Norway, Tunisia, Yugoslavia: draft resolution.

RESOLUTION 1571(L), as proposed by 6 powers, E/L.1410, as orally revised by sponsors, adopted unanimously by Council on 14 May 1971, meeting 1763.

The Economic and Social Council,
Considering General Assembly resolution 2458(XXIII) of 20 December 1968 concerning the role of computer technology in development,
Recalling that during the Second United Nations Development Decade the application of science and technology should make a vital contribution to the economic and social advancement of all countries, particularly the developing countries, and that computer technology is destined to play a leading role in this process,
Noting with satisfaction the result of the action taken by the organizations in the United Nations system to strengthen co-operation among Member States as regards the application of science and technology to development,
Realizing, however, that the application of computer technology to development for which there is still very wide scope for international co-operation, requires considerable efforts by all Member States and particularly by the developing countries,
Having considered the report of the Secretary-General entitled *The Application of Computer Technology for Development,* prepared in pursuance of General Assembly resolution 2458(XXIII),
Noting that the report, which is the first comprehensive study of

this important question in the United Nations, still does not cover all aspects of the question, particularly as regards data concerning the developing countries,

1. *Takes note* with interest of the report of the Secretary-General;

2. *Requests* the Secretary-General to circulate the report widely to the Governments of Member States and to international governmental and non-governmental organizations interested in the application of computer technology to development, so as to elicit their comments on the conclusions and recommendations in the report;

3. *Further requests* the Secretary-General, in consultation with the Advisory Committee on the Application of Science and Technology to Development and with the assistance of the specialized agencies concerned, in particular the United Nations Educational, Scientific and Cultural Organization aided by the Intergovernmental Bureau for Informatics, to prepare for the fifty-third session of the Council another report on this subject, which should take into account the discussion of the current report in the Council and in the General Assembly and the comments made on it by the Governments and organizations consulted;

4. *Invites* the United Nations Development Programme to consider granting to developing countries, at their request and with the help of the specialized agencies concerned, suitable assistance for the application of computer technology to development;

5. *Urges* the Governments of Member States, the specialized agencies and the International Atomic Energy Agency, and the other international organizations concerned to help the Secretary-General to promote international co-operation among Member States in the application of computer technology to development.

FUTURE INSTITUTIONAL ARRANGEMENTS

Economic and Social Council—50th session
Plenary meetings 1752-1754, 1756, 1766, 1767, 1772.

E/4959. Future institutional arrangements for science and technology. Note by Secretary-General.
E/4989. Report of Committee for Programme and Co-ordination (CPC) on its 8th session, 22 March–8 April 1971, Chapter VII.
E/L.1400. Brazil, Kenya, Sudan, Yugoslavia: draft resolution.
E/L.1407. United States: draft resolution.
E/L.1407/Add.1. Administrative and financial implications of United States draft resolution, E/L.1407. Statement by Secretary-General.
E/L.1420. France: draft resolution.
E/L.1420/Add.1. Administrative and financial implications of French draft resolution, E/L.1420. Statement by Secretary-General.
E/5044. Resolutions adopted by Economic and Social Council during its 50th session, 11–13 January and 26 April–21 May 1971. Decisions, p. 15.

Economic and Social Council—51st session
Plenary meetings 1794-1798, 1808.

E/5012 (Part I). Development and co-ordination of activities of organizations within United Nations system. Report of Administrative Committee on Co-ordination (ACC), Chapter I B.
E/5045. Development and co-ordination of activities of organizations within United Nations system. Report of Chairmen of CPC and ACC on joint meetings, Section 2.
E/L.1451. Ghana, Haiti, Indonesia, Italy, Jamaica, Kenya, Lebanon, Madagascar, Malaysia, New Zealand, Niger, Norway, Sudan, Tunisia, United States, Zaire: draft resolution, part B.
E/L.1451/Add.1. Administrative and financial implications of 16-power draft resolution, E/L.1451. Statement by Secretary-General.
E/L.1458. Greece: draft resolution.
E/L.1459. Brazil, Uruguay, Yugoslavia: amendments to part B of 16-power draft resolution, E/L.1451.

RESOLUTION 1621 B (LI), as proposed by 16 powers, E/L.1451, part B, as orally amended by sponsors, adopted by Council on

30 July 1971, meeting 1798, by roll-call vote of 19 to 5, with 3 abstentions, as follows:

In favour: France, Ghana, Haiti, Indonesia, Italy, Jamaica, Kenya, Lebanon, Madagascar, Malaysia, Niger, Norway, New Zealand, Pakistan, Sudan, Tunisia, United Kingdom, United States, Zaire.
Against: Brazil, Ceylon, Peru, Uruguay, Yugoslavia.
Abstaining: Greece, Hungary, USSR.

Draft resolution, as a whole (including parts A and C),* adopted by Council on 30 July 1971, meeting 1798, by roll-call vote of 17 to 7, with 3 abstentions, as follows:

In favour: Ghana, Haiti, Indonesia, Italy, Jamaica, Kenya, Lebanon, Madagascar, Malaysia, New Zealand, Niger, Norway, Pakistan, Sudan, Tunisia, United States, Zaire.
Against: Brazil, Ceylon, Hungary, Peru, USSR, Uruguay, Yugoslavia.
Abstaining: France, Greece, United Kingdom.

*For texts, roll-call votes and supporting documentation for parts A and C of resolution 1621(LI), which dealt with enlargement of the membership of the Economic and Social Council and with the system of over-all appraisal of progress in implementing the International Development Strategy for the Second United Nations Development Decade, respectively, see pp. 468-69 and 229-30.

The Economic and Social Council,
Recalling its resolution 1454(XLVII) of 8 August 1969 and 1544(XLIX) of 30 July 1970, and in particular paragraph 4 of the latter, on future institutional arrangements for science and technology,
Recognizing the ever-growing role of the application of science and technology in the resolution of economic and social problems of the developing countries,
Recognizing further that the United Nations system urgently needs an adequate institutional framework to ensure the increasing application of science and technology to development and to eliminate any existing institutional gaps among the bodies and organizations of the United Nations system dealing with specific scientific and technological problems,
Noting with satisfaction the establishment by the Trade and Development Board, in its resolution 74(X) of 18 September 1970, of an intergovernmental group on the transfer of operative technology,

1. *Decides* to establish a standing committee of the Council composed of 54 members, to be elected in accordance with the present geographical distribution of seats in the Council, to provide policy guidance and make recommendations on matters relating to the application of science and technology to development and to report to the General Assembly, through the Council;

2. *Decides further* to review at its fifty-seventh session the institutional arrangements for science and technology in the light of the implementation of the provisions contained in operative paragraph 1 of resolution 1621 A (LI) above and of the provisions of its resolution 1623(LI) of 30 July 1971;

3. *Requests* the Secretary-General to submit a report to the Council at its fifty-second session on the possible terms of reference of the Standing Committee referred to in paragraph 1 above, taking into account the specific competence of the United Nations Conference on Trade and Development, the United Nations Industrial Development Organization, the specialized agencies and the International Atomic Energy Agency and of the intersessional organs of the General Assembly, and the need for co-ordination between them and the Standing Committee;

4. *Decides further* to maintain the Advisory Committee on the Application of Science and Technology to Development, with a membership of 24, to be appointed in the manner laid down in Council resolution 980 A (XXXVI) of 1 August 1963, that the term of office of the members shall be three years and can be renewed, that the Advisory Committee is to furnish expertise to the Standing Committee, in addition to its terms of reference as set forth in that resolution and that it may receive such instructions from the

Standing Committee as will be necessary to provide it with scientific, technological, and innovative advice and ideas in this field;

5. *Reiterates* the view that any institutional arrangements in the field of science and technology can only be meaningful if adequate resources are made available for tackling major problem areas, in accordance with the relevant provisions of the International Development Strategy for the Second United Nations Development Decade.

E/5073 and Corr.1. Resolutions adopted by Economic and Social Council during its 51st session, 5-30 July 1971. Other decisions, p. 13.

E/5073/Add.1. Resolutions adopted by Economic and Social Council during its resumed 51st session, 27-29 October, 23 and 30 November and 20 December 1971. Other decisions, p. 4.

A/8403. Report of Economic and Social Council on work of its 50th and 51st sessions, Chapter XII B.

A/8403/Add.1. Addendum to report of Economic and Social Council, resumed 51st session, Chapter VIII.

DECISION ON REPORT OF ADVISORY COMMITTEE

Economic and Social Council—51st session
Co-ordination Committee, meetings 420, 433.
Plenary meeting 1799.

E/4970. Eighth report of Advisory Committee on Application of Science and Technology to Development, March 1971 (for period 16 April 1970–15 April 1971).

E/AC.24/L.416. Norway: draft resolution, approved without vote by Co-ordination Committee on 27 July 1971, meeting 433.

E/5068. Report of Co-ordination Committee, draft resolution I.

RESOLUTION 1637(LI), as recommended by Co-ordination Committee, E/5068, adopted unanimously by Council on 30 July 1971, meeting 1799.

The Economic and Social Council
1. *Notes with appreciation* the eighth report of the Advisory Committee on the Application of Science and Technology to Development;

2. *Welcomes* the Committee's continuing emphasis on the importance of the transfer of technology to developing countries and its collaboration with the United Nations Conference on Trade and Development, the United Nations Industrial Development Organization and other United Nations bodies in this field;

3. *Requests* the United Nations Educational, Scientific and Cultural Organization to consider the Committee's recommendations to proceed with a survey of research institutions and laboratories in developed countries which have been concerned with research on problems of developing countries, and to implement the Committee's recommendations concerning bilateral links between research institutions of developed and developing countries.

A/8403. Report of Economic and Social Council on work of its 50th and 51st sessions, Chapter XII A.

A/8401 and Corr.1. Report of Secretary-General on work of the Organization, 16 June 1970–15 June 1971, Part Three, Chapter II C 5.

THE WORLD PLAN OF ACTION

Economic and Social Council—51st session
Co-ordination Committee, meetings 425, 426, 432, 433.
Plenary meeting 1799.

World Plan of Action for the Application of Science and Technology to Development (E/4962/Rev.1 and Corr.1). U.N.P. Sales No.: E.71.II.A.18 and corrigendum.

E/4970. Eighth report of Advisory Committee on Application of Science and Technology to Development, March 1971, Chapter II, paras. 8-13, and Chapter III, para. 48 (c).

E/AC.24/L.413 and Rev.1. France and United States: draft resolution and revision, adopted without vote by Co-ordination Committee on 27 July 1971, meeting 433.

E/5068. Report of Co-ordination Committee, draft resolution II.

RESOLUTION 1638(LI), as recommended by Co-ordination Committee, E/5068, adopted unanimously by Council on 30 July 1971, meeting 1799.

The Economic and Social Council,
Considering that the General Assembly, in the International Development Strategy for the Second United Nations Development Decade, has stressed the need for greater efforts in the application of science and technology to development,

Considering further that the Advisory Committee on the Application of Science and Technology to Development, in response to General Assembly resolutions 1944(XVIII) of 11 December 1963 and 2318(XXII) of 15 December 1967 and to Council resolution 1155(XLI) of 5 August 1966, and with the assistance of the regional economic commissions, the specialized agencies, the International Atomic Energy Agency and other organizations of the United Nations, has prepared and proposed the World Plan of Action for the Application of Science and Technology to Development,

1. *Commends* the Advisory Committee on the Application of Science and Technology to Development, the Secretariat, the specialized agencies and the International Atomic Energy Agency for the activities which have culminated in the World Plan of Action for the Application of Science and Technology to Development, and for the stimulating ideas contained in volume I;

2. *Notes with great interest* the World Plan of Action as an important adjunct to the International Development Strategy for the Second United Nations Development Decade;

3. *Decides,* in view of its inability to study adequately the World Plan of Action at its fifty-first session and in the light of its continuing importance and dynamic nature, to consider it in more detail at its fifty-second and fifty-third sessions;

4. *Recommends* that the Secretary-General solicit, prior to 1 February 1972, the views of all concerned, so that appropriate follow-up action can be taken, and that the General Assembly defer any in-depth consideration of the World Plan of Action until its twenty-seventh session;

5. *Calls on* Governments of Member States to consider carefully the World Plan of Action, and to bear in mind its ideas where appropriate, when considering their bilateral programmes of aid to developing countries;

6. *Further calls on* the United Nations Conference on Trade and Development, the United Nations Industrial Development Organization, the governing bodies of the specialized agencies, in particular of the International Bank for Reconstruction and Development, and those of the International Atomic Energy Agency and other intergovernmental bodies, and more especially the United Nations Development Programme in connexion with global projects, to study the World Plan of Action and to bear in mind the ideas proposed in it in developing their own programmes;

7. *Requests* the regional economic commissions to consider the proposals contained in the World Plan of Action in the light of the needs of the countries in each of the regions, with a view to preparing specific plans of action for each region.

A/8403. Report of Economic and Social Council on work of its 50th and 51st sessions, Chapter XII C.

PROGRESS IN APPLYING SCIENCE AND TECHNOLOGY
DURING SECOND UNITED NATIONS DEVELOPMENT DECADE

Economic and Social Council—51st session
Economic Committee, meetings 529, 530, 532, 533, 539.
Plenary meetings 1773-1782, 1794-1799.

E/4990. Report of Committee for Development Planning on its 7th session, 22 March–1 April 1971, Geneva, Switzerland.

E/5000 and Add.1, Add.2 and Corr.1, Add. 3-5, Add.6 and Corr.1, Add.7. Views of Governments on system of over-all appraisal of progress in implementing International Development Strategy. Note by Secretary-General and addenda.

E/5040. Report of Secretary-General, para. 36.

E/AC.6/L.436. Kenya: draft resolution, transmitted for consideration to Economic and Social Council by Economic Committee on 26 July 1971, meeting 539.

E/5059. Report of Economic Committee, draft resolution IV.

RESOLUTION 1626(LI), as transmitted by Economic Committee, E/5059, adopted without vote by Council on 30 July 1971, meeting 1799.

The Economic and Social Council,

Taking note of the goals and objectives of the International Development Strategy and the special problems of the developing countries in this regard,

Noting further the special measures to be taken in favour of the least developed among the developing countries and the land-locked developing countries,

Aware of the growing scientific and technological gap between the developed and the developing countries,

Convinced that the application of science and technology to development constitutes one of the ways in which economic and social development in developing countries, including the least developed among them and those that are land-locked, can be promoted,

Further convinced of the need for monitoring the performance of these countries in respect of the various elements of the International Development Strategy,

Requests the Secretary-General and the organizations of the United Nations system to ensure that the reports and studies prepared for periodic appraisals of progress during the Second United Nations Development Decade bring out clearly, in accordance with the provisions of the International Development Strategy, the application of science and technology to the development of various sectors of the economies of developing countries.

TECHNOLOGY AND INDUSTRIAL DEVELOPMENT

Economic and Social Council—51st session
Co-ordination Committee, meetings 428-430, 433.
Plenary meeting 1799.

Appropriate Technology and Research for Industrial Development. Report of the Advisory Committee on the Application of Science and Technology to Development on two aspects of industrial growth (ST/ECA/152). U.N.P. Sales No.:E.72.II.A.3.

E/4960. Science and technology in relation to industrial development. Factors affecting effectiveness of existing industrial research organizations in developing countries. Report of Advisory Committee on Application of Science and Technology to Development.

E/4967. Technologies appropriate for industrial development. Report of Advisory Committee.

E/4967, Annex. Draft resolution submitted by Advisory Committee for action by Economic and Social Council, as orally amended by France and by Co-ordination Committee Chairman, approved unanimously by Co-ordination Committee on 26 July 1971, meeting 430, and further amended by Committee, as orally proposed by Chairman, on 27 July 1971, meeting 433.

E/4970. Eighth report of Advisory Committee, March 1971, Chapter II, paras. 16-19, and Chapter III, para. 48 (*d*), (*e*).

E/5066. Report of Co-ordination Committee.

RESOLUTION 1636(LI), as recommended by Co-ordination Committee, E/5066, adopted unanimously by Council on 30 July 1971, meeting 1799.

The Economic and Social Council

1. *Congratulates* the Advisory Committee on the Application of Science and Technology to Development on its reports on technologies appropriate for industrial development and on factors affecting the effectiveness of existing industrial research organizations in developing countries, commends them to the attention of Governments of all Member States and invites them to have its recommendations considered and, where appropriate, implemented by scientific, technical and management bodies concerned with industry in their countries and to report on the steps taken to encourage such consideration and implementation;

2. *Requests* the specialized agencies concerned and the regional economic commissions to consider the reports in relation to their own activities, including arrangements to promote the exchange of information between the developing countries on their experience in the field of appropriate technology and product and plant design, and to report to the Council on the steps taken on the matters covered by the reports;

3. *Requests* the Advisory Committee to continue its consideration of appropriate technology for other sectors of the economy, in addition to the industrial sector;

4. *Recommends* that the United Nations Industrial Development Organization, the International Labour Organisation, the United Nations Conference on Trade and Development and the Food and Agriculture Organization of the United Nations study in close collaboration ways in which reliable information—which should include relevant data on the requirements for capital, labour, raw materials and other factors of production—on known alternative technologies for selected major industries of interest to developing countries could best be furnished in a systematic way to Governments, enterprises and industrial consultants;

5. *Recommends* to the United Nations Development Programme, the International Bank for Reconstruction and Development and its affiliates, the regional development banks and other sources of financial and other assistance, that favourable consideration should be given to requests from Governments of the developing countries that are desirous of strengthening their capability for plant and product design, including the establishment of design centres, information services and other appropriate institutions and the training of personnel;

6. *Recommends* to Governments of States Members of the United Nations and members of the specialized agencies and the International Atomic Energy Agency that more attention should be given to the matters referred to in the report within the framework of their higher engineering education and managerial training activities and asks the United Nations Industrial Development Organization, the International Labour Organisation and the United Nations Educational, Scientific and Cultural Organization to promote the application of the above recommendations in their contacts with Governments of their Member States.

A/8403. Report of Economic and Social Council on work of its 50th and 51st sessions, Chapter XIV D.

REPORTS ON SCIENTIFIC CO-OPERATION

Economic and Social Council—51st session
Co-ordination Committee, meetings 421, 423, 432, 433.
Plenary meeting 1799.

E/4970. Eighth report of Advisory Committee on Application of Science and Technology to Development, March 1971, Chapter II, paras. 36-38.

E/5019. Role of modern science and technology in development of nations and need to strengthen economic and technico-scientific co-operation among States. Progress report of Secretary-General.

E/AC.24/L.412. France, Kenya, Niger, Norway, Tunisia, United States, Yugoslavia: draft resolution, as orally amended by sponsors, approved without objection by Co-ordination Committee on 27 July 1971, meeting 433.

E/5068. Report of Co-ordination Committee, draft resolution III.

RESOLUTION 1639(LI), as recommended by Co-ordination Committee and as orally amended by France, adopted unanimously by Council on 30 July 1971, meeting 1799.

The Economic and Social Council,

Having considered the progress report of the Secretary-General and the eighth report of the Advisory Committee on the Application of Science and Technology to Development,

Conscious of the fact that the purpose, conception and planning of the revised edition of the study entitled *Current Trends in Scientific Research,* published in 1961 pursuant to General Assembly resolution 1260(XIII) of 14 November 1958, currently being prepared by the United Nations Educational, Scientific and Cultural Organization, are similar in many respects to those of the study requested of the Secretary-General in operative paragraph 8 of General Assembly resolution 2658(XXV) of 7 December 1970,

1. *Takes note with appreciation* of the draft outline submitted by the Secretary-General in the annex to his progress report, expressing at the same time the wish that an effort be made to shorten and simplify that outline;

2. *Endorses* the recommendation of the Advisory Committee on the Application of Science and Technology to Development that the proposed study should not be encyclopaedic in character, but limited and well defined in scope and essentially forward-looking;

3. *Calls again* on the Governments of Member States, the specialized agencies, in particular the United Nations Educational, Scientific and Cultural Organization and the World Health Organization and the International Atomic Energy Agency, and the other organs of the United Nations system concerned, to contribute to the preparation of the study requested in paragraph 8 of General Assembly resolution 2658(XXV);

4. *Invites* the Secretary-General and the United Nations Educational, Scientific and Cultural Organization to take all the necessary steps to promote the preparation of these studies;

5. *Expresses the wish* that the United Nations Educational, Scientific and Cultural Organization should examine, in agreement with the Secretary-General, the possibility of combining these studies, as is eminently desirable, in a single publication;

6. *Requests* the Secretary-General to report to the Council and to the General Assembly on the result of these exchanges of views and to keep the Council, the General Assembly and the Advisory Committee regularly informed of the progress of the preparatory work.

A/8403. Report of Economic and Social Council on work of its 50th and 51st sessions, Chapter XII D.

Decision of General Assembly

COMPUTER TECHNOLOGY

General Assembly—26th session
Second Committee, meetings 1370-1382, 1396.
Plenary meeting 2017.

A/8403. Report of Economic and Social Council on work of its 50th and 51st sessions, Chapter XII F.
The Application of Computer Technology for Development. Report of the Secretary-General (E/4800). U.N.P. Sales No.: E.71.II.A.1.
Report of the Interregional Seminar on Electronic Data Processing in Government, Bratislava, Czechoslovakia, 22-30 November 1971. Vol. I: Report and technical papers. U.N.P. Sales No.: E.72.II.H.3.
A/C.2/262. Questions relating to science and technology. Note by Secretary-General.
A/C.2/L.1156. Argentina, Austria, Bulgaria, Canada, Chile, Czechoslovakia, France, Iran, Jamaica, Lebanon, Madagascar, Malaysia, Nigeria, Peru, Philippines, Poland, Romania, Tunisia, Upper Volta, Uruguay, Yugoslavia: draft resolution, as orally revised by sponsors, approved by acclamation by Second Committee on 21 October 1971, meeting 1396.
A/8578. Report of Second Committee (part I) (on report of Economic and Social Council), draft resolution III.

RESOLUTION 2804(XXVI), as recommended by Second Committee, A/8578, adopted without objection by Assembly on 14 December 1971, meeting 2017.

The General Assembly,

Recognizing the need for strengthening international co-operation with a view to facilitating the access of all peoples to the achievements of modern science and technology in order to accelerate their progress and to enable the technological gap to be significantly reduced,

Noting that, in accordance with the International Development Strategy for the Second United Nations Development Decade, contained in General Assembly resolution 2626(XXV) of 24 October 1970, the developing and the developed countries and competent international organizations will draw up and implement a programme in the field of science and technology for promoting the transfer of technology to developing countries,

Convinced that the utilization, on a world-wide scale, of electronic computers and computation techniques may make an important contribution to accelerating the progress of vital economic and social sectors,

Recalling its resolution 2458(XXIII) of 20 December 1968 on international co-operation with a view to the use of computers and computation techniques for development,

Recalling also Economic and Social Council resolution 1571(L) of 14 May 1971,

Considering that the United Nations system should take new measures with a view to supporting the efforts being undertaken by States in carrying out their tasks relating to the use of computers in accelerating the process of economic and social development,

Bearing in mind the report of the Secretary-General entitled *The Application of Computer Technology for Development,* prepared in pursuance of General Assembly resolution 2458(XXIII),

1. *Takes note with interest* of the conclusions and recommendations contained in the report of the Secretary-General, among which are those relating to the need for each developing country to draw up a broad national policy on the application of computer technology, to education and training for the application of computers to accelerate the process of economic and social development, to the increase of international co-operation in this field and to the establishment of an international advisory board on the application of computer technology to development, and believes that the early implementation of the recommendations will assist Member States, especially the developing countries, in obtaining the maximum benefits from the achievements of modern science and technology;

2. *Urges* Governments to give particular attention to the application of computer technology, consistent with their national goals, and invites them to encourage, in accordance with the principles of the Charter of the United Nations, broader bilateral and multilateral co-operation in this field and to explore new ways and means of intensifying this co-operation;

3. *Expresses its appreciation* to the organizations of the United Nations system as well as to the various intergovernmental and other bodies concerned which assisted in the preparation of the Secretary-General's report for their co-operation and invites all relevant bodies in their ongoing programmes to stimulate, under sound and realistic conditions, the application of computer technology to development along the lines outlined in the Secretary-General's report;

4. *Invites* in particular the United Nations Development Programme to envisage providing the developing countries, at their request, with suitable assistance in the field of computer technology;

5. *Requests* the Secretary-General to prepare, on the basis of his present report and in accordance with the envisaged modalities of paragraph 3 of Economic and Social Council resolution 1571(L), an up-dated report on the application of computer technology to development and decides to re-examine this question at its twenty-seventh session, taking into account the recommendations the Council will adopt at its fifty-third session, with a view to making further progress in this field.

Chapter X

The use and development of natural (non-agricultural) resources

During 1971, the Committee on Natural Resources established by the Economic and Social Council on 27 July 1970,[1] held its first session. A number of issues taken up by that Committee were the subjects of Council decisions; these are described below.

The United Nations continued its operational activities in the fields of energy, mineral and water resources development, and cartography. During the year, it was the executing agency for 109 projects; in addition, it administered the visits of over 115 experts in various countries.

Its operational activities during the year led, among other things, to the discovery of uranium, phosphate and iron deposits and to potential geothermal fields. Other operational activities concentrated on institution building projects and on the provision of technical advisory services, particularly on matters concerning mineral and petroleum development agreements and mining and petroleum legislation.

Operational activities

The United Nations continued to provide assistance for the development of non-agricultural natural resources during 1971. Projects under the United Nations Development Programme (UNDP) in the fields of cartography, energy, and mineral and water resources were in operation in the following countries: Afghanistan, Argentina, Bolivia, Burma, Burundi, Cameroon, the Central African Republic, Ceylon, Chile, Colombia, Costa Rica, Dahomey, Ecuador, El Salvador, Egypt, Ethiopia, Gabon, Gambia, Greece, Guatemala, Guinea, Guyana, Honduras, India, Indonesia, Iran, Israel, the Ivory Coast, Jamaica, Jordan, the Khmer Republic, Kuwait, Lesotho, Liberia, Madagascar, Mali, Malawi, Mauritania, Morocco, Nicaragua, Niger, Pakistan, Panama, Paraguay, the Philippines, Poland, Rwanda, Senegal, Sierra Leone, Somalia, Sudan, Togo, Tunisia, Turkey, the United Republic of Tanzania, Upper Volta, Yugoslavia, Zaire and Zambia.

Technical assistance was also provided in the form of individual advisory experts to the following countries: Afghanistan, Argentina, Bolivia, Burma, Burundi, Cameroon, the Central African Republic, Ceylon, Chad, Chile, China, Colombia, Dahomey, the Dominican Republic, Ecuador, Egypt, El Salvador, Equatorial Guinea, Fiji, Gambia, Ghana, Guatemala, Guyana, Haiti, India, Israel, Iraq, Jamaica, Laos, Lebanon, Lesotho, Madagascar, Mali, Malta, Mauritius, Morocco, Nepal, Niger, the People's Democratic Republic of Yemen, Peru, Saudi Arabia, Sierra Leone, Somalia, Sudan, Swaziland, Syria, Togo, Trinidad and Tobago, Tunisia, Turkey, Uganda, the United Republic of Tanzania, Venezuela, Yemen, Yugoslavia and Zambia.

The following seminars and meetings of experts were convened during 1971: Inter-regional Seminar on Photogrammetric Techniques (Zurich, Switzerland, 15 March–3 April); Inter-regional Seminar on the Development of Mineral Resources of the Continental Shelf (Port-of-Spain, Trinidad and Tobago, 5-16 April); Inter-regional Seminar on the Development and Utilization of Natural Gas (Moscow, USSR, 12-28 October); Inter-regional Seminar on Rural Electrification (New Delhi, India, 2-7 December); Ad Hoc Group of Experts on Geographical Names (New York, United States, 2-12 February); Ad Hoc Group of Experts on Projection of Demand and Supply of Crude Petroleum and Products (New York, 9-18 March); Ad Hoc Group of Experts on New Geological Concepts as Applied to Exploration for Mineral Deposits (New York, 29 April–7 May); Second Session of the Panel of Experts on Water Resources Development Policies (Delft, Netherlands, 30 August–4 September); Ad Hoc Group of Experts on Projections and Planning of United Nations Activities in Cartography for the Second Development Decade (New York, 8-19 November).

Report of Committee on Natural Resources

The Committee on Natural Resources, established by the Economic and Social Council by a decision of 27 July 1970,[2] held its first session at United Nations Headquarters, New York, from 22 February to 10 March 1971.

In its report, the Committee made a number of recommendations on the programming and implementation of United Nations projects in the development of natural resources. In particular, it recommended setting up natural resources advisory services, and it discussed the establishment of a revolving fund for natural resources exploration, data collection and dissemination, natural resources satellites and permanent sovereignty over natural resources.

[1]See Y.U.N., 1970, pp. 459–460, text of resolution 1535(XLIX).
[2]Ibid.

The Committee for Programme and Co-ordination considered the report of the Committee on Natural Resources at its March-April 1971 meetings. While noting the indecisiveness of portions of the report, the Committee endorsed the decision to recommend the creation of natural resources advisory services and requested that the Secretary-General take into account the comments, views and criticisms made concerning the different work programme proposals.

On 18 May 1971, the Economic and Social Council took a series of decisions relating to recommendations of the Committee on Natural Resources.

It did this by adopting resolution 1572(L), which was in seven parts. The resolution as a whole was adopted by a roll-call vote of 21 to 0, with 6 abstentions, on the basis of a proposal by Jamaica, Kenya, Pakistan, Sudan, Yugoslavia and Zaire.

The individual sections of the resolution, described below, were voted on individually.

Sessions of the Committee

The Council agreed that the Committee should meet and report to the Council at least once every other year and that the second session of the Committee should be convened early in 1972. (Later, on 30 July 1971, the Council decided to accept Kenya's invitation to hold the second session at Nairobi from 31 January to 11 February 1972.)

These decisions were embodied in resolution 1572 A (L), adopted by a roll-call vote of 21 to 2, with 4 abstentions. (For text, see DOCUMENTARY REFERENCES below.)

Special natural resources advisory services

By the second part of resolution 1572(L), adopted on 18 May 1971, the Council approved the establishment of special natural resources advisory services and recommended that the United Nations Secretariat and UNDP work out arrangements to ensure the harmonious functioning of such services. It requested the Governing Council of UNDP to consider the matter and to offer its comments to the Council by July 1971.

The Council recommended that the concept of special advisory services be broadened to include experts who might be made available by Member States on a short-term, non-reimbursable basis, and it requested the Secretary-General to invite Members interested in providing experts to submit rosters of such experts as soon as possible.

Finally, the Secretary-General was asked to report to the Committee on Natural Resources at its 1972 session on the progress made in the establishment of the special natural resources advisory services.

These decisions were embodied in resolution

1572 B (L), adopted by a roll-call vote of 21 to 5, with 1 abstention. (For text, see DOCUMENTARY REFERENCES below.)

Among the amendments proposed by New Zealand to this text was one by which the Governing Council of UNDP would be asked to offer its comments to the Economic and Social Council in July 1971. This amendment was adopted on 18 May 1971 by 16 votes to 6, with 3 abstentions.

Later in the year, on 27 July 1971, the Council again took decisions concerning special natural resources advisory services.

Among other things, it welcomed a proposal of the Governing Council of UNDP for a joint study, by the Secretary-General and the Administrator of UNDP, of short-term special advisory services in other fields or of various separate advisory services, all based on the principle of speedy action in response to Government requests, efficiency in using all existing high-level expertise and in minimizing costs to developing countries, and full consultation with the Governments involved in each case.

The Council also urged all the parties to whom the implementation of its resolution of 18 May 1971 had been assigned to implement forthwith the provisions on advisory services.

These were among decisions embodied in resolution 1616(LI), adopted by a roll-call vote of 16 to 1, with 4 abstentions, on a proposal of Indonesia, Jamaica, Kenya, Pakistan, Yugoslavia and Zaire. (For text of resolution, see DOCUMENTARY REFERENCES below.)

Amendments proposed by France and by the United States were taken into account in the final revision of the draft text.

Revolving fund for natural resources exploration

In another part of its resolution of 18 May 1971, the Council recognized the urgent need to expand natural resources exploration in the developing countries and endorsed the decision of the Committee on Natural Resources to set up an inter-governmental working group to consider the detailed administrative, institutional and financial aspects of the proposal, together with alternative proposals, with a view to working out a scheme that would enable the activities of the United Nations development system in the field of natural resources exploration to be extended and intensified.

These decisions were embodied in resolution 1572 C (L), adopted by a roll-call vote of 22 to 4, with 1 abstention. (For text, see DOCUMENTARY REFERENCES below.)

The inter-governmental group thus set up held meetings in October and November 1971 to fulfil its mandate concerning the proposed revolving fund and produced an interim report. The central idea of the proposed fund was to share among countries subscribing to its principles the benefits arising out of successes and discoveries by projects financed by the fund.

International water conference

Recognizing that water was a limiting factor in development processes, especially in developing countries, the Economic and Social Council recalled a proposal by the Secretary-General to convene an international water conference in 1975 to exchange experience on water resources development and water use, review new technologies and stimulate greater international co-operation in the field of water.

The Council also recalled an offer by the Government of Argentina to host the conference.

It requested the Secretary-General to prepare, after ascertaining the views of Governments of Member States and of relevant bodies within the United Nations system, a report containing the views expressed on the desirability of and possible topics for the conference and to submit it to the 1972 session of the Committee on Natural Resources.

These decisions were embodied in resolution 1572 D (L), adopted by a roll-call vote of 26 to 0, with 1 abstention. (For text, see DOCUMENTARY REFERENCES below.)

Amendments proposed by Brazil and the USSR were adopted on 18 May 1971 by a vote of 16 to 7, with 1 abstention. The first of the two-power amendments provided for the paragraph in which the Secretary-General was requested to prepare a report. This amendment replaced paragraphs that would have had the Secretary-General convene, if necessary, a group of experts to assist and advise him on the objectives and purposes of the conference. The other amendment had the effect of deleting a paragraph that would have urged the Committee on Natural Resources to consider water resources development as one of the priority items at its 1972 session.

Studies requested by Committee

Also on 18 May 1971, the Council endorsed requests by the Committee on Natural Resources for studies on such other natural resources as atmospheric and biological resources, on non-agricultural uses of land, and on the operational activities of the United Nations system in the field of natural resources development.

The Council asked the Secretary-General to give all possible help to the Committee in the preparation of these studies, bearing in mind the Committee's request that information be given on the activities of all organizations within the United Nations system; and called upon all the regional economic commissions, UNDP, the specialized agencies, the International Atomic Energy Agency and other concerned bodies for co-operation in the preparation of the studies.

These decisions were embodied in resolution 1572 E (L), adopted by a roll-call vote of 23 to 2, with 2 abstentions. (For text, see DOCUMENTARY REFERENCES below.)

Work programme of Committee

The Council, recalling the central programming role envisaged for the Committee on Natural Resources and noting that the Committee had been unable to formulate an integrated work programme during its first (1971) session, recommended, as a matter of priority, that the Committee plan and undertake its future work in such a manner as to ensure that short-term and medium-term work programmes were formulated and subjected to continuous review.

The Council further recommended that the Secretary-General, after appropriate consultations with all concerned within the United Nations system, submit a draft short-term and medium-term work programme, with a full explanation of the financial implications, to the 1972 session of the Committee on Natural Resources.

In this respect, the Council endorsed the wishes of the Committee for Programme and Co-ordination regarding the drafting of the work programme in the field of natural resources.

These decisions were embodied in resolution 1572 F (L), adopted by a roll-call vote of 25 to 0, with 2 abstentions. (For text of resolution, see DOCUMENTARY REFERENCES below.)

Amendments to this part of resolution 1572(L) were proposed by Brazil and the USSR, by New Zealand, and by the United States.

The two-power amendment, by which the paragraph was added endorsing the wish of the Committee for Programme and Co-ordination, was adopted by 16 votes to 7, with 1 abstention.

The New Zealand amendment, which would have had the effect of recommending as a "first" matter of priority (rather than a "matter of priority") that the Committee plan its future work so as to ensure that its programmes were subjected to a process of review, was rejected by a vote of 8 to 7, with 10 abstentions.

The United States amendment, which was adopted by 10 votes to 6, with 9 abstentions, added the phrase "with a full explanation of the financial implications" in the paragraph having to do with the Secretary-General submitting a draft programme to the 1972 session of the Committee.

Permanent sovereignty over natural resources

In the final part of the seven-part resolution, the Council endorsed measures and actions concerning permanent sovereignty over natural resources of developing countries that had been recommended by the Committee on Natural Resources in its report. (These concerned mainly the outline for a periodic report by the Committee on the advantages derived from the exercise by developing countries of permanent sovereignty over their natural resources.)

The Council's endorsement was embodied in resolution 1572 G (L), adopted by a roll-call vote of 22 to 2, with 3 abstentions. (For text, see DOCUMENTARY REFERENCES below.)

Uses of the marine environment

Mineral resources of the sea

Before the Economic and Social Council at its July 1971 session, when it was discussing the resources of the sea and marine affairs in general, were three reports by the Secretary-General on: prevention and control of marine pollution; long-term and expanded programme of oceanic research; and mineral resources of the sea.

On 30 July 1971, the Council, expressing awareness of the fast-growing economic importance of the off-shore mineral potential and its increasing contribution to the economies of developing countries, requested the Secretary-General to pursue his programme of education and training in the field of marine mineral resources and related issues.

Governments of Member States were asked to consider the possibility of offering host facilities for the convening of seminars and training courses in this field.

These decisions were embodied in resolution 1641(LI), adopted by the Council without vote, on the recommendation of its Co-ordination Committee, which approved the draft without vote on 27 July 1971, on a proposal of Jamaica. (For text of resolution, see DOCUMENTARY REFERENCES below.)

In a related decision, also taken on 30 July 1971, the Council took note with appreciation of the reports by the Secretary-General on marine science (oceanic research), the mineral resources of the sea, and marine pollution, and it endorsed the proposal that continuing efforts should be made to disseminate information on mineral resources of the sea and that a programme of seminars and training courses for the benefit of

the developing countries should be implemented.

Among other things, the Council also decided that the report on the prevention and control of marine pollution be transmitted to the General Assembly at its 1972 session.

These decisions were taken without the adoption of a resolution.

(See also pp. 46-49 and 307-13.)

Creation of an inter-governmental sea service

At the request of Malta, the General Assembly discussed at its 1971 session the need for the creation of an inter-governmental sea service as the operational arm of the United Nations system in ocean space. The purpose of such a service was for the United Nations system to have available and operate vessels and other facilities to make possible training and/or scientific programmes related to ocean space.

On 20 December 1971, the General Assembly decided to refer the question for further consideration to the Committee on the Peaceful Uses of the Sea-Bed and the Ocean Floor beyond the Limits of National Jurisdiction.

The Assembly asked the Committee to report to it on the question through the Economic and Social Council.

These decisions were embodied in resolution 2846(XXVI), which the Assembly adopted, by 106 votes to 0, with 8 abstentions, on the recommendation of its Second (Economic and Financial) Committee. The Committee approved the text on 13 December 1971 by 46 votes to 14, with 25 abstentions, on the basis of a proposal by Norway. (For text of resolution, see DOCUMENTARY REFERENCES below.)

During the discussion in the Second Committee, Malta proposed a draft resolution by which, among other things, the General Assembly would have requested the Secretary-General to seek the views of Members and of organizations within the United Nations system on the concept of an inter-governmental sea service which would have the objectives of making available vessels for use by the United Nations system and providing shipboard training for persons, particularly from developing countries, in trades related to the seas.

Malta did not press its proposal to the vote.

(See also pp. 46-49.)

DOCUMENTARY REFERENCES

Economic and Social Council—50th session
Plenary meetings 1758, 1762, 1764, 1766.

Report of Committee on Natural Resources
E/4969. Report of Committee on Natural Resources on its first session, 22 February–10 March 1971. (Annex VI: List of documents before Committee.)
E/4989. Report of Committee for Programme and Co-ordination

on its 8th session, 22 March–8 April 1971, Chapter VI, Section C.
E/L.1411. Jamaica, Kenya, Pakistan, Sudan, Yugoslavia, Zaire: draft resolution.

RESOLUTION 1572 A-G (L), as proposed by 6 powers, E/L.1411, as amended, adopted by Economic and Social Council on 18 May 1971, meeting 1766, by roll-call vote of 21 to 0, with 6 abstentions, as follows:

In favour: Ceylon, France, Ghana, Haiti, Indonesia, Italy, Jamaica, Kenya, Lebanon, Madagascar, Malaysia, New Zealand, Niger, Norway, Pakistan, Peru, Sudan, Tunisia, Uruguay, Yugoslavia, Zaire.
Against: None.
Abstaining: Brazil, Greece, Hungary, USSR, United Kingdom, United States.

[For text of resolution and additional documentation, see parts A through G below.]

SESSIONS OF THE COMMITTEE
E/L.1411. Jamaica, Kenya, Pakistan, Sudan, Yugoslavia, Zaire: draft resolution, part A.

RESOLUTION 1572 A (L), as proposed by 6 powers, E/L.1411, adopted by Council on 18 May 1971, meeting 1766, by roll-call vote of 21 to 2, with 4 abstentions, as follows:

In favour: Brazil, Ceylon, Ghana, Haiti, Indonesia, Italy, Jamaica, Kenya, Lebanon, Madagascar, Malaysia, New Zealand, Niger, Norway, Pakistan, Peru, Sudan, Tunisia, Uruguay, Yugoslavia, Zaire.
Against: Hungary, USSR.
Abstaining: France, Greece, United Kingdom, United States.

A

The Economic and Social Council,
Recalling its resolution 1535(XLIX) of 27 July 1970 by which it established the Committee on Natural Resources,
1. *Takes note* of the report of the Committee on Natural Resources on its first session;
2. *Agrees* that the Committee on Natural Resources meet and report to the Council at least once every other year;
3. *Agrees further* that, subject to determination of specific date and venue in conjunction with the calendar of conferences, the second session of the Committee be convened in the early part of 1972.

SPECIAL NATURAL RESOURCES ADVISORY SERVICES
E/L.1411. Jamaica, Kenya, Pakistan, Sudan, Yugoslavia, Zaire: draft resolution, part B.
E/L.1414. New Zealand: amendments to parts B and F of 6-power draft resolution, E/L.1411.

RESOLUTION 1572 B (L), as proposed by 6 powers, E/L.1411, and as amended by New Zealand (E/L.1414, para. 2) adopted by Council on 18 May 1971, meeting 1766, by roll-call vote of 21 to 5, with 1 abstention, as follows:

In favour: Brazil, Ceylon, France, Ghana, Haiti, Indonesia, Italy, Jamaica, Kenya, Lebanon, Madagascar, Malaysia, New Zealand, Niger, Pakistan, Peru, Sudan, Tunisia, Uruguay, Yugoslavia, Zaire.
Against: Greece, Hungary, USSR, United Kingdom, United States.
Abstaining: Norway.

B

The Economic and Social Council,
Recalling paragraph 4(b) of its resolution 1535(XLIX) of 27 July 1970 and the subsequent proposal of the Secretary-General,
Having taken into account the specific recommendations of the Committee on Natural Resources on this subject, contained in paragraphs 107 and 108 of its report on its first session,
1. *Approves* the establishment of special natural resources advisory services;
2. *Recommends* that the Secretariat of the United Nations and the United Nations Development Programme work out arrangements to ensure the harmonious functioning of such services;
3. *Requests* the Governing Council of the United Nations Development Programme to consider these arrangements at its

twelfth session with a view to offering its comments to the Economic and Social Council at its fifty-first session;
4. *Recommends further* that the concept of the special advisory services be broadened, as suggested in the report of the Committee on Natural Resources, to include experts who may be made available by Member States on a short-term, non-reimbursable basis;
5. *Requests* the Secretary-General to invite Member States interested in providing experts for the special advisory services set up under the provisions of paragraph 2 above to submit rosters of such experts to the Secretary-General as soon as possible;
6. *Further requests* the Secretary-General to report to the Committee on Natural Resources, at its second session, on the progress made in the establishment and operations of the special natural resources advisory services.

Economic and Social Council—51st session
Plenary meetings 1788-1792.

DP/L.191. Report on arrangements between United Nations and United Nations Development Programme (UNDP) about special natural resources advisory services. Joint report by Secretary-General and Administrator.
E/5043/Rev.1. Report of Governing Council of UNDP on its 12th session, 7–23 June 1971, Santiago, Chile, Chapter VIII, paras. 250–259.
E/L.1439 and Rev.1,2. Indonesia, Jamaica, Kenya, Pakistan, Yugoslavia and Zaire: draft resolution and revisions.
E/L.1445. United States: amendments to 6-power draft resolution, E/L.1439.
E/L.1450. France: amendments to 6-power revised draft resolution, E/L.1439/Rev.1.

RESOLUTION 1616(LI), as proposed by 6 powers, E/L.1439/Rev.2, adopted by Council on 27 July 1971, meeting 1792, by roll-call vote of 16 to 1, with 4 abstentions, as follows:

In favour: Brazil, France, Ghana, Greece, Haiti, Indonesia, Italy, Kenya, Lebanon, Madagascar, Malaysia, New Zealand, Niger, Pakistan, Sudan, Yugoslavia.
Against: United Kingdom.
Abstaining: Hungary, Norway, USSR, United States.

The Economic and Social Council,
Recalling the terms of reference of the Committee on Natural Resources established under Council resolution 1535(XLIX) of 27 July 1970, stating *inter alia* that the Committee on Natural Resources should be responsible for the establishment of guidelines for the provision and for the improvement and strengthening of advisory services to the Governments of Member States, to be made available at their request, for the planning, development and utilization of their natural resources,
Recalling further Council resolution 1572 B (L) of 18 May 1971, which approved the establishment of special natural resources advisory services and requested the Secretary-General to report to the Committee on Natural Resources, at its second session, on the progress made in the establishment and operations of the special natural resources advisory services,
Welcoming the joint report by the Secretary-General and the Administrator of the United Nations Development Programme on the arrangements between the United Nations and the Programme about the special natural resources advisory services,
Convinced that the speedy implementation of Council resolution 1572 B (L) is desirable,
1. *Urges* all the parties to whom the implementation of Council resolution 1572 B (L) has been assigned, to implement forthwith all provisions of the resolution as stipulated, taking into account, when appropriate, the results of the joint study referred to in paragraph 2 below;
2. *Welcomes* the proposal of the Governing Council of the United Nations Development Programme for a joint study, by the Secretary-General and the Administrator of the Programme, of short-term special advisory services in other fields or of various separate advisory services, based on the principles of speedy

action in response to Government requests, of efficiency in using all existing high-level expertise and in minimizing costs to developing countries, and of full consultation with the Governments involved in each case.

Economic and Social Council—50th session
Plenary meetings 1758, 1762, 1764, 1766.

E/4969. Report of Committee on Natural Resources on its first session, 22 February–10 March 1971.
E/4989. Report of Committee for Programme and Co-ordination on its 8th session, 22 March–8 April 1971, Chapter VI C.

FUND FOR NATURAL RESOURCES EXPLORATION
E/L.1399 and Add.1. Letters of 6 April and 30 July 1971 from Kenya.
E/L.1411. Jamaica, Kenya, Pakistan, Sudan, Yugoslavia, Zaire: draft resolution, part C.
E/L.1411/Add.1. Administrative and financial implications of parts C and D of 6-power draft resolution, E/L.1411. Statement by Secretary-General.

RESOLUTION 1572C (L), as proposed by 6 powers, E/L.1411, adopted by Council on 18 May 1971, meeting 1766, by roll-call vote of 22 to 4, with 1 abstention, as follows:

In favour: Ceylon, France, Ghana, Haiti, Indonesia, Italy, Jamaica, Kenya, Lebanon, Madagascar, Malaysia, New Zealand, Niger, Norway, Pakistan, Peru, Sudan, Tunisia, United States, Uruguay, Yugoslavia, Zaire.
Against: Greece, Hungary, USSR, United Kingdom.
Abstaining: Brazil.

C

The Economic and Social Council,
Recognizing the urgent need to expand natural resources exploration in the developing countries,
Taking note of the proposal by the Secretary-General,
Endorses the decision of the Committee on Natural Resources to set up an intergovernmental working group to consider the detailed administrative, institutional and financial aspects of the proposal, together with alternative proposals with a view to working out a scheme which would enable the activities of the United Nations development system in the field of natural resources exploration to be extended and intensified.

INTERNATIONAL WATER CONFERENCE
E/L.1411. Jamaica, Kenya, Pakistan, Sudan, Yugoslavia, Zaire: draft resolution, part D.
E/L.1411/Add.1. Administrative and financial implications of parts C and D of 6-power draft resolution, E/L.1411. Statement by Secretary-General.
E/L.1413. Brazil and USSR: amendments to parts D and F of 6-power draft resolution, E/L.1411.

RESOLUTION 1572D (L), as proposed by 6 powers, E/L.1411, and as orally amended by Lebanon and by sponsors, and as amended by 2 powers (E/L.1413, paras. 1 and 2), adopted by Council on 18 May 1971, meeting 1766, by roll-call vote of 26 to 0, with 1 abstention, as follows:

In favour: Ceylon, France, Ghana, Greece, Haiti, Hungary, Indonesia, Italy, Jamaica, Kenya, Lebanon, Madagascar, Malaysia, New Zealand, Niger, Norway, Pakistan, Peru, Sudan, Tunisia, USSR, United Kingdom, United States, Uruguay, Yugoslavia, Zaire.
Against: None.
Abstaining: Brazil.

D

The Economic and Social Council,
Recognizing that water is a limiting factor in the economic and social development processes, especially in the developing countries,
Recalling the Secretary-General's proposal to convene an international water conference in 1975 in order, *inter alia,* to exchange experience on water resource development and water use, review new technologies and stimulate greater international co-operation in the field of water,
Recalling further the offer made by the Government of Argentina to host the international water conference,
Requests the Secretary-General to prepare, after ascertaining the views of Governments of Member States, of the Food and Agriculture Organization of the United Nations, the United Nations Educational, Scientific and Cultural Organization, the World Health Organization, the World Meteorological Organization, regional bodies and other interested organizations within the United Nations system, a consolidated document containing the views expressed on the desirability and possible topics for the international water conference, such a document to be submitted to the Committee on Natural Resources at its second session.

STUDIES REQUESTED BY COMMITTEE
E/L.1411. Jamaica, Kenya, Pakistan, Sudan, Yugoslavia, Zaire: draft resolution, part E.

RESOLUTION 1572E (L), as proposed by 6 powers, E/L.1411, adopted by Council on 18 May 1971, meeting 1766, by roll-call vote of 23 to 2, with 2 abstentions, as follows:

In favour: Brazil, Ceylon, France, Ghana, Greece, Haiti, Indonesia, Italy, Jamaica, Kenya, Lebanon, Madagascar, Malaysia, New Zealand, Niger, Norway, Pakistan, Peru, Sudan, Tunisia, Uruguay, Yugoslavia, Zaire.
Against: Hungary, USSR.
Abstaining: United Kingdom, United States.

E

The Economic and Social Council,
Considering that the Committee on Natural Resources has to deal with the development of all aspects of natural resources, giving special emphasis to the development of water, energy and mineral resources,
1. *Endorses* the requests made by the Committee on Natural Resources for studies as set out in paragraphs 94 and 98 of its report on its first session;
2. *Requests* the Secretary-General, within existing means, to give all possible assistance to the Committee in the preparation of the studies, bearing in mind the Committee's request that information be given on the activities of all organizations within the United Nations system;
3. *Calls on* the secretariats of all regional economic commissions, the United Nations Development Programme, the specialized agencies, the International Atomic Energy Agency and other bodies concerned to co-operate, where appropriate, with the Secretary-General in the preparation of the studies.

WORK PROGRAMME OF COMMITTEE
E/L.1411. Jamaica, Kenya, Pakistan, Sudan, Yugoslavia, Zaire: draft resolution, part F.
E/L.1413. Brazil and USSR: amendments to parts D and F of 6-power draft resolution, E/L.1411.
E/L.1414. New Zealand: amendments to parts B and F of 6-power draft resolution, E/L.1411.
E/L.1415. United States: amendment to part F of 6-power draft resolution, E/L.1411.

RESOLUTION 1572F (L), as proposed by 6 powers, E/L.1411, and as amended by 2 powers (E/L.1413, para. 3) and by United States (E/L.1415), adopted by Council on 18 May 1971, meeting 1766, by roll-call vote of 25 to 0, with 2 abstentions, as follows:

In favour: Brazil, Ceylon, Ghana, Haiti, Hungary, Indonesia, Italy, Jamaica, Kenya, Lebanon, Madagascar, Malaysia, New Zealand, Niger, Norway, Pakistan, Peru, Sudan, Tunisia, USSR,

United Kingdom, United States, Uruguay, Yugoslavia, Zaire.
Against: None.
Abstaining: France, Greece.

F

The Economic and Social Council,
Recalling the central programming role envisaged for the Committee on Natural Resources in the field of natural resources, particularly with regard to the development of water, energy and mineral resources,
Noting that the Committee on Natural Resources was unable to formulate an integrated work programme during its first session,
Taking into account the recommendations of the Committee for Programme and Co-ordination at its eighth session relating to the elaboration of a work programme by the Committee on Natural Resources,
1. *Recommends*, as a matter of priority, that the Committee on Natural Resources plan and undertake its future work in such a manner as to ensure that short-term and medium-term work programmes are formulated and subjected to a continuous process of review, taking into account the merits of each specific proposal;
2. *Recommends further* that the Secretary-General submit a draft short-term and medium-term work programme, with a full explanation of the financial implications, after appropriate consultations with all concerned within the United Nations system, to the Committee on Natural Resources at its second session;
3. *Endorses* the wish expressed by the Committee for Programme and Co-ordination in relation to the drafting of the work programme for 1972 in the field of natural resources.

PERMANENT SOVEREIGNTY OVER NATURAL RESOURCES
E/L.1411. Jamaica, Kenya, Pakistan, Sudan, Yugoslavia, Zaire: draft resolution, part G.

RESOLUTION 1572 G (L), as proposed by 6 powers, E/L.1411, adopted by Council on 18 May 1971, meeting 1766, by roll-call vote of 22 to 2, with 3 abstentions, as follows:

In favour: Brazil, Ceylon, Ghana, Haiti, Hungary, Indonesia, Italy, Jamaica, Kenya, Lebanon, Madagascar, Malaysia, Niger, Norway, Pakistan, Peru, Sudan, Tunisia, USSR, Uruguay, Yugoslavia, Zaire.
Against: United Kingdom, United States.
Abstaining: France, Greece, New Zealand.

G

The Economic and Social Council,
Recalling General Assembly resolution 2692(XXV) of 11 December 1970,
Taking into account paragraphs 129 to 134 of the report of the Committee on Natural Resources on its first session regarding permanent sovereignty over natural resources of developing countries,
Endorses the measures and actions recommended by the Committee on Natural Resources in paragraphs 131 to 134 of its report.

Uses of the marine environment

MINERAL RESOURCES OF THE SEA

Economic and Social Council—51st session
Co-ordination Committee, meetings 430-433.
Plenary meeting 1799.

E/4973 and Corr.1. The sea. Mineral resources of the sea. Report of Secretary-General.
E/4973/Summary. Summary of report of Secretary-General.
E/5003. The sea. Prevention and control of marine pollution. Report of Secretary-General.
E/5017. The sea. Marine science. Long-term and expanded

programme of oceanic research. Progress report of Secretary-General.
E/AC.24/L.411. Jamaica: draft resolution, approved without vote by Co-ordination Committee on 27 July 1971, meeting 432.
E/AC.24/L.415. Draft decision, suggested by Chairman of Co-ordination Committee.
E/5065. Report of Co-ordination Committee.

RESOLUTION 1641 (LI), as recommended by Co-ordination Committee, E/5065, adopted without vote by Council on 30 July 1971, meeting 1799.

The Economic and Social Council,
Recalling General Assembly resolution 2414(XXIII) of 17 December 1968, which stressed the need for extending technical assistance to Member States in relation to the development of mineral resources of their continental shelf areas and called upon the Secretary-General to pursue the task of collecting and disseminating available information regarding the mineral and other resources of the sea-bed and ocean floor,
Recalling resolution 2.342 of the sixteenth session of the General Conference of the United Nations Educational, Scientific and Cultural Organization, in which member States were invited to request assistance from the United Nations Development Programme authorities in organizing training courses and providing fellowships for education and training in aspects of marine science and its technology related to the investigation and exploration of the sea-bed,
Recalling also Council resolution 1380(XLV) of 2 August 1968 on the resources of the sea,
Aware of the fast growing economic importance of the off-shore mineral potential and its increasing contribution to the economies of developing countries,
Mindful of the manifold and interrelated ongoing activities within the United Nations system in relation to the marine environment and of the pressing need to expand the dissemination of relevant information and the training of personnel in the developing countries,
Taking note with appreciation of the reports on the sea submitted by the Secretary-General, and in particular of his report on the mineral resources of the sea,
Noting the success of the United Nations Interregional Seminar on the Development of the Mineral Resources of the Continental Shelf, held in April 1971 in Trinidad and Tobago,
1. *Requests* the Secretary-General to pursue his programme of education and training in the field of marine mineral resources and related issues;
2. *Calls upon* the Secretary-General and the Administrator of the United Nations Development Programme to extend their support to this programme, in co-operation with the specialized agencies and organizations concerned;
3. *Appeals* to the Governments of Member States to consider the possibility of offering host facilities for the convening of seminars and training courses in this field.

E/5073. Resolutions adopted by Economic and Social Council during its 51st session, 5-30 July 1971. Other decisions, p. 28.

CREATION OF INTER-GOVERNMENTAL SEA SERVICE

General Assembly—26th session
Second Committee, meetings 1417, 1444.
Plenary meeting 2026.

A/8401. Report of Secretary-General on work of the Organization, 16 June 1970–15 June 1971, Part Three, Chapter II E 2.
A/8403. Report of Economic and Social Council on work of its 50th and 51st sessions, Chapters VII A and VIII A, paras. 206-215.
A/C.2/271. Letter of 16 November 1971 from Malta (transmitting memorandum prepared in co-operation with University of Santa Clara on need for creation of inter-governmental sea service).
A/C.2/L.1193 and Rev.1. Malta: draft resolution and revision.
A/C.2/L.1218 and Rev.1. Administrative and financial implications of Maltese draft resolution, A/C.2/L.1193/Rev.1. Statement and

revised statement by Secretary-General of the United Nations. A/8578/Add.1. Report of Second Committee (part II) (on report of Economic and Social Council), draft resolution IX, as orally proposed by Norway and as orally revised by sponsor and by Malta, approved by Second Committee on 13 December 1971, meeting 1444, by 46 votes to 14, with 25 abstentions.

RESOLUTION 2846(XXVI) as recommended by Second Committee, A/8578/Add.1, adopted by Assembly on 20 December 1971, meeting 2026, by 106 votes to 0, with 8 abstentions.

The General Assembly,
Having given preliminary consideration to the question of the creation of an intergovernmental sea service,

1. *Decides* to refer this question for further consideration to the Committee on the Peaceful Uses of the Sea-Bed and the Ocean Floor beyond the Limits of National Jurisdiction at its session to be held in July and August 1972;
2. *Requests* the Committee to report on this question to the General Assembly through the Economic and Social Council.

Other documents
A/8401. Report of Secretary-General on work of the Organization, 16 June 1970–15 June 1971, Part Three, Chapter II E 1.
A/8403. Report of Economic and Social Council on work of its 50th and 51st sessions, Chapters VII A and VIII A, paras. 206-215.
Natural Resources Forum, Vol. I, No. 1. U.N.P. Sales No.: E/F/S.71.II.A.13.

Chapter XI

Statistical developments

Activities in 1971

The International Computing Centre (ICC), Geneva, Switzerland, began operations in March 1971, with the United Nations, the United Nations Development Programme (UNDP) and the World Health Organization as the initial participants. Various existing data bases were being prepared at ICC, Geneva; copies of all data bases of the Statistical Office of the United Nations were available there, as well as in New York, thus facilitating access to information by all users, including government agencies.

Long-term statistical centres, both national and international, set up in Africa and Asia and aided by the United Nations, continued to operate in 1971 in Cameroon, Ghana, the Ivory Coast, Japan, Morocco, Uganda and the United Republic of Tanzania.

An African Census Programme, financed by the United Nations Fund for Population Activities (UNFPA), was established. It provided for seven regional advisers (concerned with demographic statistics, sampling and data processing), country experts and the financing of imported equipment and even local costs, as appropriate, in order to assist the countries of Africa in developing or improving their demographic statistics. A similar Latin American Census Programme was set up, also financed by UNFPA.

In January 1971, the Governing Council of UNDP approved a project to assist the Government of Mongolia in establishing a national computer centre which would pave the way for gradually computerizing data at the enterprise, sectoral and national levels and for improving the quality, range and speed of operational, scientific and technical information.

During 1971, the Statistical Office of the United Nations continued to collect and publish statistics showing the main economic and social characteristics of the world as a whole, its regions and the individual countries. These included data on external trade, production and prices, transport, energy, national economic accounts, population, vital statistics and migration.

(For details on publications, see DOCUMENTARY REFERENCES below.)

Decisions of Economic and Social Council

On 30 April 1971, the Economic and Social Council, recognizing the important role of vital statistics as a primary source of national data for achieving purposes associated with economic and social development, requested the Secretary-General to publish the "Principles and recommendations for a vital statistics system," adopted by its Statistical Commission in 1970 with a view to improving vital statistics,[1] and to distribute them widely to States Members of the United Nations or of the specialized agencies and to bodies associated with the United Nations. The Secretary-General was also asked to assist developing countries in the implementation of these principles and recommendations.

These were among decisions embodied in resolution 1564(L), adopted unanimously by the Council, on the basis of a text submitted by the Statistical Commission as amended by Brazil, Pakistan, Sudan and Yugoslavia. (For text of resolution, see DOCUMENTARY REFERENCES below.)

On 3 May 1971, the Economic and Social Council also took a number of decisions with a view to improving the co-ordination of work in the field of statistics.

[1] See Y.U.N., 1970, p. 440, decisions of Statistical Commission.

Recognizing the importance of reliable and complete statistical data for socio-economic analyses, particularly as regarding the monitoring of progress achieved in the Second United Nations Development Decade, the Council asked the Statistical Commission to assign high priority in its work programme to the task of assisting the Council in the co-ordination of activities of United Nations organs and agencies in the statistical field. The ultimate goal of the work of the Commission and the United Nations in this respect, the Council considered, should be the achievement of an integrated system in the collection, data processing and dissemination of international statistics, particularly in the context of the policy measures and objectives of the Second Development Decade.

The Council also asked the regional United Nations bodies concerned, the specialized agencies, the United Nations Conference on Trade and Development and the United Nations Industrial Development Organization to continue to co-oper-ate fully with the Commission. The Council, further, emphasized the importance for United Nations Member States to seek improved procedures for ensuring that statistical matters at the national level were dealt with in a co-ordinated manner.

Among other things, the Council asked the Secretary-General to undertake, in co-operation with the specialized agencies and in the context of the United Nations Development Programme, concerted action to assist the developing countries in strengthening their statistical systems as the basis for their development plans and the evaluation of their economic and social progress.

These were among the decisions embodied in resolution 1566(L), adopted unanimously by the Council, on the basis of a text submitted by Hungary, Lebanon, Pakistan, Sudan, Tunisia and the USSR and orally amended by France. (For text of resolution, see DOCUMENTARY REFERENCES below.)

DOCUMENTARY REFERENCES

Economic and Social Council—50th session
Plenary meetings 1740, 1741, 1744, 1746, 1747.

E/4938. Report of Statistical Commission on its 16th session, Geneva, Switzerland, 5-15 October 1970.
E/4989. Report of Committee for Programme and Co-ordination on its 8th session, 22 March–8 April 1971, Chapter VI A.
E/L.1372. Note by Secretary-General.
E/5044. Resolutions adopted by Economic and Social Council during its 50th session. Decisions, p. 14.

Vital statistics system
E/4938. Report of Statistical Commission, Chapter IX A.
E/4938. Chapter XV. Draft resolution recommended for action by Economic and Social Council.
E/L.1386. Brazil, Pakistan, Sudan, Yugoslavia: amendments to draft resolution recommended by Commission in E/4938.

RESOLUTION 1564(L), as recommended by Statistical Commission, E/4938, and as amended by 4 powers, E/L.1386, adopted unanimously by Council on 30 April 1971, meeting 1744.

The Economic and Social Council,
Noting that the Statistical Commission, at its sixteenth session, adopted a set of principles and recommendations for the improvement of vital statistics,
Recalling that paragraph 78 of the International Development Strategy for the Second United Nations Development Decade, adopted by the General Assembly in resolution 2626(XXV) of 24 October 1970, provides that developing countries will, as appropriate, establish or strengthen their planning mechanisms, including statistical services, for formulating and implementing their national development plans during the Decade,
Also recalling General Assembly resolution 1710(XVI) of 19 December 1961 on the United Nations Development Decade, in which the Assembly requested the Secretary-General to develop proposals for the intensification of action in the fields of economic and social development with particular reference to the need to review facilities for the collection, collation, analysis and dissemination of statistical and other information required for charting economic and social development and for providing a constant measurement of progress towards the objectives of the Decade,
Further recalling its resolution 1307(XLIV) of 31 May 1968, in which the Council requested the Secretary-General to undertake a World Programme for the Improvement of Vital Statistics,

Recognizing the important role of vital statistics as a primary source of national data for achieving the above-mentioned purposes,
1. *Requests* the Secretary-General to publish the "Principles and recommendations for a vital statistics system" in English, French, Russian and Spanish and to distribute them widely to States Members of the United Nations or members of specialized agencies, to regional economic commissions and other appropriate regional bodies, and to specialized agencies;
2. *Further requests* the Secretary-General to give assistance to developing countries in the implementation of these principles and recommendations by mobilizing all available resources, both international and bilateral, to help in the very large task of assisting those countries to develop, improve and maintain civil registers of vital events and to use these registers for statistical purposes as well as other sources of vital statistics as provided in the World Programme for the Improvement of Vital Statistics.

Co-ordination of work in field of statistics
E/4938. Report of Statistical Commission, Chapter IV.
E/L.1389. Hungary, Pakistan, Tunisia, USSR: draft resolution.
E/L.1389/Rev.1. Hungary, Lebanon, Pakistan, Sudan, Tunisia, USSR: revised draft resolution.

RESOLUTION 1566(L) as proposed by 6 powers E/L.1389/Rev.1, and as orally amended by France, adopted unanimously by Council on 3 May 1971, meeting 1747.

The Economic and Social Council,
Recognizing the importance of reliable and complete statistical data for socio-economic analysis, particularly as regards the monitoring of progress achieved under the Second United Nations Development Decade,
Bearing in mind the current expansion of activities of the United Nations and the specialized agencies in the statistical field,
Noting the interest which the Committee for Programme and Co-ordination, the Statistical Commission and the Administrative Committee on Co-ordination have demonstrated in the co-ordination and integration of statistical activities of the various organs and agencies in the United Nations system,
Further noting the necessity to avoid deficiencies, parallelism and duplication in this field as suggested in the report of the Statistical Commission on its sixteenth session,
Taking note of the Statistical Commission's intention to make a

critical review of the strategy of statistical activities, as well as the basic ideas underlying such a review,

Reaffirming its resolution 8(I) of 16 February 1946 concerning the establishment of the Statistical Commission, as amended by resolution 8(II) of 21 June 1946, which indicated that the Commission shall assist the Council:

(a) In promoting the development of national statistics and the improvement of their comparability,

(b) In the co-ordination of the statistical work of the specialized agencies,

(c) In the development of the central statistical services of the Secretariat,

(d) In advising the organs of the United Nations on general questions relating to the collection, analysis and dissemination of statistical information,

(e) In promoting the improvement of statistics and statistical methods generally,

1. *Requests* the Statistical Commission to assign high priority in its work programme to the task of assisting the Council in the co-ordination of activities of United Nations organs and agencies in the statistical field;

2. *Considers* that the ultimate goal of the work of the Statistical Commission and that of the Department of Economic and Social Affairs in this respect should be the achievement of an integrated system in the collection, data processing and dissemination of international statistics by the organs and agencies of the United Nations system with special regard to the requirements of reviewing and appraising economic and social progress, particularly in the context of the policy measures and objectives of the Second United Nations Development Decade, taking into account the needs of the developing countries;

3. *Requests* the specialized agencies, the regional economic commissions, the United Nations Economic and Social Office at Beirut, the United Nations Conference on Trade and Development and the United Nations Industrial Development Organization to continue to co-operate fully with the Statistical Commission in their efforts to carry out these tasks and to regard them as of first importance in co-ordinating their work programmes, especially long-term programmes, and also work in new directions;

4. *Emphasizes* the importance for Member States to seek improved procedures for ensuring that statistical matters at the national level were dealt with in a co-ordinated manner;

5. *Recognizes* the interest of the Statistical Commission and the Statistical Office in matters related to the use of computers in the United Nations system and draws attention to this field where further co-ordination is likely to be most required;

6. *Requests* the Secretary-General to undertake, in co-operation with the specialized agencies and in the context of the United Nations Development Programme, concerted action to assist the developing countries in strengthening their statistical systems as the basis for their development plans and the evaluation of their economic and social progress;

7. *Requests* the Secretary-General, in co-operation with the United Nations system of organizations, to submit to the Economic and Social Council at its fifty-second session, through the Committee for Programme and Co-ordination, a report on the existing technical assistance of the United Nations system of organizations to the developing countries as well as on the steps envisaged to assist those countries in improving their statistical services with a view to meeting the requirements of the Second United Nations Development Decade.

A/8403. Report of Economic and Social Council on work of its 50th and 51st sessions, Chapter X B.

Publications
Monthly Bulletin of Statistics, Vol. XXV, Nos. 1-12 (January-December 1971).

Population and Vital Statistics Report. Statistical Papers, Series A, Vol. XXIII, Nos. 1,2,3,4 (data available as at 1 January, 1 April, 1 July, 1 October 1971).

1970 World Trade Annual (5 vols.) and *Supplement* (5 vols.). Data supplied by Statistical Office of United Nations; published commercially by Walker and Company (720 Fifth Avenue, New York, N.Y. 10019).

Commodity Trade Statistics. Statistical Papers, Series D. Vol. XIV (1964 data), *No. 27; Vol. XV* (1965 data), *No. 30; Vol. XVI* (1966 data), *No. 37; Vol. XIX* (1969 data), *No. 37; Vol. XX* (1970 data), *Nos. 19-42.*

Demographic Yearbook 1971. U.N.P. Sales No.: E/F.72.XIII.1.

Retail Price Comparisons for International Salary Determination. U.N.P. Sales No.: E.71.XVII.9.

Basic Principles of the System of Balances of the National Economy. U.N.P. Sales No.: E.71.XVII.10.

Classification by Broad Economic Categories. U.N.P. Sales No.: E.71.XVII.12.

Recommendations for the 1973 World Programme of Industrial Statistics. Part I: General Statistical Objectives; Part II: List of Selected Products and Materials. U.N.P. Sales Nos.: E.71.XVII.13 and E.71.XVII.16.

Classification of Commodities by Industrial Origin. Links between the Standard International Trade Classification and the International Standard Industrial Classification. U.N.P. Sales No.: E.71.XVII.15.

Statistical Yearbook, 1971. U.N.P. Sales No.: E/F.72.XVII.1.

Price Movements of Basic Commodities in International Trade: 1950-1970. U.N.P. Sales No.: E.72.XVII.2.

Yearbook of National Accounts Statistics, 1970. Vol. I: Individual Country Data; Vol. II: International Tables. U.N.P. Sales Nos.: E.72.XVII.3, Vol.I, and E.72.XVII.3, Vol. II.

The Growth of World Industry, 1970 Edition. Vol. I: General Industrial Statistics, 1960-1969 (ST/STAT/SER.P/8, Vol.I); Vol. II: Commodity Production Data, 1961-1970 (ST/STAT/SER. P/8, Vol. II). U.N.P. Sales Nos.: E/F.72.XVII.4 and E.72.XVII.9.

A Short Manual on Sampling. Vol. I: Elements of Sample Survey Theory. U.N.P. Sales No.: E.72.XVII.5.

Chapter XII

Regional economic activities

The Economic Commission for Europe (ECE)

The Economic Commission for Europe (ECE) continued during 1971 to pursue the following priority objectives: (1) to help develop international trade and inter-governmental trade co-operation; (2) to assist Governments in economic policy planning and programming; (3) to promote inter-governmental co-operation on scientific and technological problems of economic significance;

and (4) to assist Governments in their efforts to improve environmental conditions.

These objectives were pursued through the implementation of the programmes of work and priorities adopted by the Commission and by its principal subsidiary bodies.

At its twenty-sixth session, held from 19 to 30 April 1971, the Commission approved its programme of work and priorities for 1971-1972 and its long-term programme of work for 1972-1976. The Commission also took decisions on the following subjects: chemical industries; application of modern mathematical-economic methods and computer techniques to economic research; energy problems; standardization; automation; mechanical and electrical engineering; foreign trade; industrial, scientific and technological co-operation; problems of the environment, including air pollution; and long-term economic trends in the ECE region.

The following activities in these fields were carried out in 1971 by the Commission and its subsidiary bodies.

Activities in 1971

Trade

The Committee on the Development of Trade examined practical measures which could be taken to remove obstacles to and promote diversification of East-West trade. In so doing, the Committee took into account the work of an informal meeting of trade experts on problems arising in general economic policy and trade policy.

The Committee decided to transform its group of experts on the simplification and standardization of external trade documents into a working party on the facilitation of international trade procedures; the working party was to seek to facilitate international trade and transport through the rationalization of trade procedures, notably by developing a uniform system of codes for use in automatic processing and transmission of trade data.

The Committee also reached decisions concerning industrial co-operation, trade promotion, marketing and business contacts and trade problems of less industrialized ECE countries.

Scientific and technological co-operation

The Commission established a new principal subsidiary body of Senior Advisers to ECE Governments on Science and Technology and approved short- and long-term programmes of work in the field of scientific and technological co-operation. The first session of these Senior Advisers was scheduled to be held in December 1972; preparations were also made to convene seminars and prepare reports on such subjects as the effective

application of science and technology in industry; incentives to and problems arising in the transfer of technology among ECE countries; means of improving the design and international compatibility of systems and services of technological information relevant to the innovation process; and criteria for the choice of projects suitable for co-operative international research.

Projections and programming

In 1971, the Senior Economic Advisers to ECE Governments considered the broad topic of investment in human resources and manpower planning. The Advisers recommended that a review be made of long-term trends in the structure of the economies of the ECE region, including structural trends in the manufacturing industry, the social implications of economic development, the economic aspects of environmental policy and the impact of technological progress.

Energy

The work of ECE on general energy policies was carried forward at a meeting of government experts on model building in the energy sectors. Preparations were also made for a symposium on energy models, to be held in the USSR in 1973.

The Committee on Electric Power continued its studies on the long-term prospects for the electric power industry; the interconnexion between electric power transmission networks of Eastern and Western European countries; and policy and technical problems arising with regard to thermal-, hydro- and nuclear-power stations. A group of experts was established to examine environmental problems related to electric power production. A symposium on the automation of dispatching centres with a view to the rational utilization of electric power systems was held in France, and a study tour was undertaken of electric power stations in Greece.

The Coal Committee examined the coal market situation in Europe in 1970 and continued its study of problems of coal production and utilization.

The Committee on Gas continued its studies on economic problems arising from the use, distribution, transport and storage of gas; the estimate of natural gas resources; economic problems arising as a result of exploitation of gas fields; and methods of forecasting the demand for gas. It also conducted its regular annual analysis of the gas situation in Europe, including gas market prospects.

Steel

In addition to preparing its annual review of the steel market, the Steel Committee continued to study the production and use of steel tubes; the distribution and marketing of steel products; and long-term prospects for steel production, consumption and trade.

A seminar on air and water pollution arising in the iron and steel industry was held in Leningrad, USSR, in August 1971. A study tour was made of the Romanian steel industry.

Automation

A seminar on the use of computers as an aid to management was held in October 1971, and preparations were made for a seminar on numerically controlled machine tools, to be held in 1972. Work was started on the establishment of a statistical framework for assessing the economic impact of automation.

Inland transport

The Inland Transport Committee continued its work in the fields of motor transport, inland waterways and container traffic, with particular emphasis on the removal of trade barriers and the protection of life and property.

The number of regulations for the safety and environmental standards of motor vehicle construction was raised to 28. Work went forward on the development of recommendations on the standardization of technical requirements in inland waterway vessels. A draft convention on the safety of containers was prepared for the World Conference on International Container Transport, to be held in Geneva, Switzerland, in November 1972, under the auspices of the United Nations and the Inter-Governmental Maritime Consultative Organization.

The revision of the European Agreement concerning the International Carriage of Dangerous Goods by Road, in harmony with the revision of the corresponding railway regulations, continued, and steps were taken towards the preparation of a similar agreement on inland waterway transport. Proposals were made for a new all-European agreement on a system of road markings. A draft convention on the contract for carriage of passengers and luggage by road was studied, and preparations were made for the revision of a similar contract for goods carried by road and for a new convention on the liability of inland shipowners. The results of studies on the economic and technical aspects of specialized container shipping and lighter-aboard-ship operation on inland waterway transport were examined.

Environment and pollution

A symposium on problems relating to the environment was held from 3 to 10 May 1971 in Prague, Czechoslovakia, followed by a study tour of the regions of Ostrava (Czechoslovakia) and Katowice (Poland). (The proceedings of the symposium were published by ECE in November 1971.) On the basis of the discussions at the symposium, an inquiry was carried out among ECE Governments regarding the inter-governmental exchange of environmental information.

Preparations were made for the first meeting of a new ECE subsidiary body, the Senior Advisers to ECE Governments on Environmental Problems.

Studies were initiated on the methodology for assessing the economic effects of air pollution. Preparations were made for a meeting of a new working party on air pollution, and for a seminar on the control of emissions from the non-ferrous metallurgical industries, both to be held in 1972.

Housing, building and planning

The Committee on Housing, Building and Planning sponsored a seminar on non-profit housing, held in Bulgaria in October 1971.

The Committee continued its work on various aspects of the following problems, among others: methods of estimating housing needs; financing of housing; modernization of building; urban transport; planning in rural areas; urban and regional research; the economics of urban renewal; construction and planning statistics; the evolution of the concept of housing; and the decision-making process in housing, building and planning.

Water

A seminar on water problems in southern European countries was held in Zagreb, Yugoslavia, in October 1971. The conclusions of the seminar were to be submitted to the Committee on Water Problems at its 1972 session.

Work continued on the preparation of a manual on the compilation of balances of water resources and needs and on a number of specialized studies in the field of water management and water pollution control.

Statistics

At its 1971 session, the Conference of European Statisticians continued work on the development of integrated statistical systems in the economic, social and demographic fields; the preparation of standard classifications; the formulation of programmes for promoting the development and comparability of national data in numerous subjects, especially the priority areas of ECE's work; the exchange of experience in the use of computers for statistical purposes; and the co-ordination of international statistical work in the countries of the ECE region.

Agriculture

The Committee on Agricultural Problems reviewed the situation of agriculture and agricultural trade, as a whole and by major commodity. The Committee also discussed a study on the marketing of fruit and vegetables.

An ECE report on governmental measures aimed at promoting beef production, a topic of special interest to the less developed ECE countries, was discussed at an *ad hoc* expert meeting.

Timber

Developments in the market for forest products were reviewed by the Timber Committee in 1971. A symposium on forest operations in mountainous regions was held in Krasnodar, USSR, in August-September 1971.

The study group on methods and organization of forest work met in March and April 1971, and the study group on vocational training and prevention of accidents in forest work met in December 1971.

Decisions of Economic and Social Council

At its mid-July 1971 session, the Economic and Social Council considered the activities and future programme of work of ECE.

On 20 July, the Economic and Social Council took note of the annual report of ECE, of the views expressed during the discussion and of the resolutions and other decisions adopted during the twenty-sixth session of the Commission, and endorsed ECE's programme of work and priorities.

These decisions were set forth in Council resolution 1602(LI), which was adopted by the Council, without objection, on the recommendation of its Economic Committee. The text was based on a draft submitted by ECE and was approved without vote by the Economic Committee on 14 July 1971. (For text of resolution, see DOCUMENTARY REFERENCES below.)

Also on 20 July 1971, the Economic and Social Council acted on the question of the admission of the Swiss Confederation to ECE. The Council noted the desire of the Swiss Confederation, which had participated since 1947 in the work of ECE, to accept the responsibilities of membership in the Commission. Accordingly, the Council decided to change ECE's terms of reference by adding the Swiss Confederation to the list of members of the Commission, on condition that the State offer itself as a candidate and agree to pay each year an equitable contribution.

The above decisions were set forth in resolution 1600(LI), adopted by the Council, without objection, on the recommendation of its Economic Committee. The text was based on a proposal put forward by France, Ghana, Greece, Italy, Lebanon, New Zealand, Norway, the United Kingdom and Yugoslavia, as orally amended by Hungary, and was approved unanimously by the Economic Committee on 13 July 1971. (For text of resolution, see DOCUMENTARY REFERENCES below.)

DOCUMENTARY REFERENCES

Economic and Social Council—51st session
Economic Committee, meetings 523-526.
Plenary meetings 1773, 1777, 1785.

E/5001. Annual report of Economic Commission for Europe (ECE) (25 April 1970–30 April 1971).
E/5001/Summary. Summary of annual report of ECE.
E/5039. Report of meetings of executive secretaries of regional economic commissions held in 1971 (New York, 27–29 January 1971; Geneva, Switzerland, 28–30 June and 3 July 1971).
E/L.1427. Letter of 5 July 1971 from Hungary (transmitting letter of 5 July 1971 from German Democratic Republic to President of Economic and Social Council).
E/L.1453. Letter of 23 July 1971 from France, United Kingdom and United States to President of Economic and Social Council.
E/AC.6/L.422. France, Ghana, Greece, Italy, Lebanon, New Zealand, Norway, United Kingdom, Yugoslavia: draft resolution, as orally amended by Hungary, approved unanimously by Economic Committee on 13 July 1971, meeting 524.
E/5054 and Corr.1. Report of Economic Committee, draft resolution I.

RESOLUTION 1600(LI), as recommended by Economic Committee, E/5054 and Corr.I, adopted without objection by Council on 20 July 1971, meeting 1785.

The Economic and Social Council,
Considering that the Swiss Confederation has participated since 1947 in the work of the Economic Commission for Europe in consultative status and that it now wishes to be able to make a more positive contribution to the activities of the Commission by accepting the responsibilities inherent in the status of members,

1. *Decides* to change paragraph 7 of the Economic Commission for Europe's terms of reference by adding the Swiss Confederation to the list of members of this Commission, on condition that this State offers itself as a candidate and agrees to pay each year an equitable contribution, the total amount of which will be determined periodically by the General Assembly in accordance with the procedure established by the Assembly in similar cases;
2. *Invites* the Secretary-General to enter into the consultations and to take the steps necessary for the Swiss Confederation and the General Assembly to reach agreement on the contribution which this State will be required to make to the United Nations budget.

E/5001, Part IV. Draft resolution submitted by ECE for action by Economic and Social Council, approved without vote by Economic Committee on 14 July 1971, meeting 526.
E/5054 and Corr.1. Report of Economic Committee, draft resolution III.

RESOLUTION 1602(LI), as recommended by Economic Committee, E/5054, adopted without objection by Council on 20 July 1971, meeting 1785.

The Economic and Social Council
1. *Takes note* of the annual report of the Economic Commission for Europe for the period 25 April 1970 to 30 April 1971, of the views expressed during the discussion, and the resolutions and the other decisions adopted by the Commission during its twenty-sixth session;
2. *Endorses* the programme of work and priorities contained in the report.

Other documents

A/8401. Report of Secretary-General on work of the Organization, 16 June 1970–15 June 1971, Part Three, Chapter III A.

A/8403. Report of Economic and Social Council on work of its 50th and 51st sessions, Chapter XIII A.

E/5136. Annual report of ECE (1 May 1971–28 April 1972).

ECE Symposium on Problems Relating to Environment. Proceedings and documentation of the Symposium organized by ECE and held from 2 to 15 May 1971 in Prague, Czechoslovakia, with a study tour to the region of Ostrava, Czechoslovakia, and Katowice, Poland. U.N.P. Sales No.: E.71.II.E.6.

Investment in Human Resources and Manpower Planning. Papers presented to the Eighth Session of Senior Economic Advisers to ECE Governments, Geneva, Switzerland, November 1970. U.N.P. Sales No.: E.71.II.E.11.

Statistics of World Trade in Steel, 1970. U.N.P. Sales No.: E.71.II.E.12.

Guide for Use in Drawing Up Contracts relating to the International Transfer of Know-how in the Engineering Industry. U.N.P. Sales No.: E.70.II.E.15.

Quarterly Bulletin of Coal Statistics for Europe, Vol. XX, Nos. 1-4.

Quarterly Bulletin of Steel Statistics for Europe, 1971, Vol. XXII, Nos. 1-4.

Timber Bulletin for Europe. Vol. XXIII, Supplement 2: Annual forest products market review (Parts II and III); *Supplement 3:* Changing structure of the forest products trade and industry in Europe; *Supplement 4:* Survey of trends in the wood-based panel sector, Vols. I and II; *Supplement 5:* Papers presented to the Symposium on the Production and Industrial Utilization of Eucalyptus; *Supplement 6:* Review of European forest products market.

Annual Bulletin of General Energy Statistics for Europe, Vol. III, 1970. U.N.P. Sales No.: E/F/R.72.II.E.6.

Annual Bulletin of Coal Statistics for Europe, Vol. IV, 1969. U.N.P. Sales No.: E/F/R.70.II.E.8; *Vol. V, 1970.* U.N.P. Sales No.: E/F/R.71.II.E.8; *Vol. VI, 1971.* U.N.P. Sales No.: E/F/R.72.II.E.9.

Annual Bulletin of Electric Energy Statistics for Europe, Vol. XVI, 1970. U.N.P. Sales No.: E/F/R.71.II.E.9.

Annual Bulletin of Transport Statistics for Europe, Vol. XXII, 1970. U.N.P. Sales No.: E/F/R.71.II.E.10 and addendum.

Annual Bulletin of Housing and Building Statistics for Europe, Vol. XV, 1971. U.N.P. Sales No.: E/F/R.72.II.E.4.

Annual Bulletin of Gas Statistics for Europe, Vol. XVII, 1971. U.N.P. Sales No.: E/F/R.72.II.E.10.

Economic Bulletin for Europe, Vol. 23, No. 1. U.N.P. Sales No.: E.72.II.E.2 and corr.; *No. 2.* U.N.P. Sales No.:E.72.II.E.7.

MIMEOGRAPHED SALES PUBLICATIONS

Problems in the Design and Operation of Thermal Power Stations, Vol. X. 70.II.E/Mim.22.

Symposium on the Automation of Mining Operations, Hombourg, France, April 1970: Proceedings. 70.II.E/Mim.24.

Proceedings of the Seminar on the Protection of Ground and Surface Waters against Pollution by Crude Oil and Oil Products, Geneva, Switzerland, December 1969, Vols. I and II. 70.II.E/Mim.30.

Rural Electrification, Vol. XIII. 71.II.E/Mim.1.

Problems and Methods of Compiling Regional Statistics. Proceedings of United Nations European Seminar on Regional Statistics, Warsaw, Poland, September-October 1969. 71.II.E/Mim.2.

Methodological Problems of International Comparison of Levels of Labour Productivity in Industry. 71.II.E/Mim.3.

Statistics of Road Traffic Accidents in Europe, 1969. E/-F/R/71.II.E/Mim.4.

Symposium on the Use of Electronic Computers in the Coal Industry, Prague, Czechoslovakia, October 1970: Proceedings. 71.II.E/Mim.5.

Bulletin of Statistics on World Trade in Engineering Products, 1969. 71.II.E/Mim.6.

European Standards Recommended by the Working Party on Standardization of Perishable Foodstuffs: Raspberries. F.71.II.E/Mim.7.

Prices of Agricultural Products and Fertilizers in Europe, 1969/70. 71.II.E/Mim.8.

Agricultural Mechanization: Mechanical Equipment for Field Drainage and Ditching. 71.II.E/Mim.9.

Report on the Proceedings of the Seminar on Progressive Methods of Design Organization and Management in Building, Moscow, USSR, October 1970, Vols. I and II. 71.II.E/Mim.10.

Agricultural Trade in Europe: Principal Trends from 1960 to 1969. 71.II.E/Mim.11.

Problems Relating to Iron and Steel Scrap. 71.II.E/Mim.12.

Review of the Agricultural Situation in Europe at the End of 1970. Vols. I and II. 71.II.E/Mim.13.

The Economic Commission for Asia and the Far East (ECAFE)

In 1971, the Economic Commission for Asia and the Far East (ECAFE), seeking to bring about the goal of economic growth combined with social justice, as called for at its 1971 session, continued or initiated various programmes to spur regional development during the Second United Nations Development Decade.

The membership of ECAFE rose to 30 full members, with the admission of Bhutan, Nauru and Tonga, and to five associate members, with the addition of the British Solomon Islands Protectorate.

Activities in 1971

Development strategy

At its twenty-seventh session, held in Manila, the Philippines, from 20 to 30 April 1971, the Economic Commission for Asia and the Far East reviewed social and economic development in the region during the First United Nations Develop-

ment Decade and discussed ways of strengthening ECAFE's contribution to the implementation of the International Development Strategy of the Second Development Decade.[1]

The Commission noted the finding of the *Economic Survey of Asia and the Far East, 1970* that, during the 1960s, most developing ECAFE countries had achieved the targeted annual growth rate of 5 per cent; it was felt that growth rates of 6 to 7 per cent should be feasible for those countries during the Second Development Decade. The Commission expressed concern, however, that despite a satisfactory rate of economic growth, the region continued to face great income disparities, unemployment, poor living conditions and inadequate social progress, all of which were causing widespread discontent. The Commission reiterated that economic growth must be accompanied by

[1]See Y.U.N., 1970, pp. 319-29, text of resolution 2626(XXV) of 24 October 1970, setting forth the International Development Strategy.

qualitative, structural and institutional changes in society, to achieve a better blend of economic growth and social justice. Among other points raised by the Commission were the need for regional economic co-operation, for increased assistance from the developed countries and for a constructive partnership between private foreign investors and the recipient developing countries.

Trade and payments

The ECAFE Inter-Governmental Committee on Trade Expansion met for the first time during 1971 and agreed to launch an Asian trade expansion programme, aimed at countering the declining Asian share in world trade.

Various meetings held under ECAFE auspices during the year discussed the establishment of a regional shippers' council, steps for pooling cargo and centralizing loading points and development of a multinational export credit insurance scheme to aid exports promotion. A grant of $33,000 was made by the Government of Norway to assist the work of the Centre for Shipping Information and Advisory Services.

A training course on customs administration was sponsored in co-operation with the United Nations Conference on Trade and Development (UNCTAD).

The ECAFE Trade Promotion Centre, operated in co-operation with UNCTAD and the General Agreement on Tariffs and Trade, held an export promotion and international marketing course.

Industry and natural resources

The South-East Asia Iron and Steel Institute was formally inaugurated in Singapore in March 1971. The Institute—designed to help member countries develop and improve iron and steel industries through regional co-operation and advanced technology—grew out of recommendations of an ECAFE-sponsored mission.

The Commission undertook a study of steel industry development possibilities in the Lower Mekong Basin countries, an assessment of the industrialization potential of east and south Asian developing countries, and a study of a proposed Asian handicraft centre in the Philippines.

An ECAFE seminar on development and environment urged the incorporation of environmental concerns into national development plans and the establishment of an Asian environment council.

Surveys were carried out in the waters of the Java Sea, and off Malaysia and Indonesia, under an ECAFE committee for the co-ordination of joint prospecting for mineral resources in Asian off-shore areas.

Commodities

In 1971, three countries—India, Indonesia and Malaysia—signed an agreement to set up a Pepper Community; the agreement called for the promotion and co-ordination of all activities relating to the pepper economy.

The Asian Coconut Community—set up in 1969 to promote and co-ordinate activities of the coconut industry—established permanent headquarters in Djakarta, Indonesia.

Both Communities were inaugurated under the auspices of the Economic Commission for Asia and the Far East.

Commodity studies on major Asian products were undertaken by the Commission.

Transport and communication

The Commission continued to seek ways to meet the need for national, sub-regional and regional shipping services; solve urban traffic problems; close gaps in the Trans-Asian railway network; and develop the region's postal services.

Field missions on transport problems visited Afghanistan, Ceylon, Laos and Thailand.

Field work on a feasibility survey for an Asian telecommunication network was completed in the 12 participating countries. The interim report included proposals in such priority areas as system specifications, operating methods, switching and interconnexions, signalling, tariffs and traffic evaluation.

Water resources

Studies completed by ECAFE during 1971 revealed that recurrent damage caused by typhoons and other storms was a serious drain on the economy of the region: a loss of $9,300 million was sustained during the years 1961-1970.

The seven-nation inter-governmental Typhoon Committee of ECAFE held its fourth session in 1971 and studied plans for improving meteorological facilities for flood forecasting.

Flood control planning was also a main subject of the roving seminar on water resources development, which visited 12 Asian countries. An expert on computer analysis of hydrological data and computer planning of water resources visited five countries.

Statistics

The Asian Statistical Institute offered its first general course, attended by 32 fellows, and its first advanced course, attended by 16; the fellows were drawn from 15 ECAFE countries.

During the year, ECAFE published the *Statistical Yearbook for Asia and the Far East, 1970*, providing regional and country-by-country data for 1959-1969; the quarterly *Statistical Indicators in ECAFE Countries*, giving month-by-month demographic and economic trends analysis; and the *Quarterly Bulletin of Statistics for Asia and the Far East*.

Population

The first survey of demographic research and training facilities in the ECAFE region was completed and was to be published in early 1972. The survey covered governmental, academic and non-governmental population activities.

Seminars were held on evaluating family planning programmes and data, the ecological implications of rural and urban population growth and the inter-relation between population and manpower problems; a training course was offered on the use of computers in fertility research.

Social development

The Commission continued to stress the need for balanced economic and social development.

Two sub-regional workshops on advanced training in social welfare planning and plan implementation for key social welfare personnel considered ways to ensure that national development plans would be responsive to the people's needs, that social welfare and social development would be fully integrated into these plans, and that social development would contribute effectively to national progress.

As part of its expanding activities in the field of youth, the Commission conducted a survey of training programmes for youth workers in the ECAFE region, and appointed a consultant on youth to the secretariat staff.

Agriculture

Among the agricultural problems studied by ECAFE in 1971 were the impact on international trade of increased cereal production in the region, and the need for international consultations to adjust the trade and production policies of countries in the region.

An expert group meeting on intra-regional trade in rice and cereals and harmonization of national plans recommended further development of a proposed special Asian rice trade scheme.

Public administration

Preparations advanced for an Asian Centre for Development Administration, following approval in June 1971 of a joint financing plan by the United Nations Development Programme (UNDP) and participating Governments.

An ECAFE country mission to Ceylon inaugurated a new programme to develop national systems to administer development plans.

Mekong river development

The $30 million Nam Ngum dam and the Nam Dong dam and power station, both in Laos, and the Lam Dom Noi dam and power station in Thailand were completed during 1971. Work progressed on the $25 million Prek Thnot power and irrigation project in the Khmer Republic, and on the Nam Phrom hydroelectric project in Thailand.

An agreement was signed between the Mekong Committee, UNDP, and the International Bank for Reconstruction and Development for the execution of a pioneer agricultural programme; under the programme, 5,000 to 10,000 hectare farms would be set up for detailed study of such subjects as livestock development, rain-fed crop improvement, irrigation development and flood control.

Asian Highway

The planned 60,452 kilometre east-west route linking all the countries of Asia was nearly completed by the end of 1971. The Asian Highway Co-ordinating Committee was considering the possibility of including the road networks of Bhutan, Brunei, China and Mongolia within the scope of the Highway.

A third Asian Highway Motor Rally, in the western sector, was proposed for 1973.

Training

By the end of 1971, the Asian Institute for Economic Development and Planning had trained more than 1,400 fellows from some 25 countries of the ECAFE region.

The Netherlands Government was financing a fellowship programme for advanced training of specialists within the region, a move aimed at halting the "brain drain" process.

Consideration by Economic and Social Council

At its July 1971 session, the Economic and Social Council considered the annual report of the Economic Commission for Asia and the Far East, covering the period 28 April 1970 to 30 April 1971. On 20 July 1971, the Council took note of the report and endorsed the Commission's programme of work and priorities.

This decision by the Council was set forth in resolution 1606(LI), which was adopted, without objection, on the recommendation of the Economic Committee. The text was based on a draft submitted by ECAFE and approved without vote by the Economic Committee on 14 July 1971. (For text, see DOCUMENTARY REFERENCES below.)

Also on 20 July 1971, the Council approved the recommendations of ECAFE that the geographical scope of the Commission be extended to permit Nauru and Tonga to be admitted as members, and the British Solomon Islands Protectorate as an associate member, of the Commission. These decisions by the Council were set forth, respectively, in resolutions 1605(LI), 1604(LI) and 1603(LI), each of which was adopted, without objection, on the recommendation of the Economic Committee.

The three resolutions had been approved without vote by the Economic Committee on 14 July 1971; the texts were based on drafts submitted by ECAFE. (For texts, see DOCUMENTARY REFERENCES below.)

DOCUMENTARY REFERENCES

Economic and Social Council—51st session
Economic Committee, meetings 523-526.
Plenary meetings 1773, 1777, 1785.

E/5020. Annual report of ECAFE, 28 April 1970–30 April 1971.
E/5020/Summary. Summary of annual report of ECAFE.
E/5020/Add.1. Administrative and financial implications of draft resolutions recommended by ECAFE in E/5020. Note by Secretary-General.
E/5020, Part IV, para. 493. First draft resolution submitted by ECAFE for action by Economic and Social Council, approved without vote by Economic Committee on 14 July 1971, meeting 526.
E/5039. Report of meetings of executive secretaries of regional economic commissions held in 1971 (New York, 27-29 January 1971; Geneva, Switzerland, 28-30 June and 3 July 1971).
E/5054 and Corr.1. Report of Economic Committee, draft resolution IV.

RESOLUTION 1603(LI), as recommended by Economic Committee, E/5054, adopted without objection by Council on 20 July 1971, meeting 1785.

The Economic and Social Council,
Taking note of the recommendation of the Economic Commission for Asia and the Far East with regard to the request of the Government of the United Kingdom of Great Britain and Northern Ireland for the inclusion of the British Solomon Islands Protectorate within the geographical scope of the Commission and the admission of the Protectorate as an associate member,
1. *Approves* the recommendation of the Economic Commission for Asia and the Far East that the British Solomon Islands Protectorate be included in the geographical scope of the Commission and admitted as an associate member of the Commission;
2. *Decides* to amend paragraphs 2 and 4 of the terms of reference of the Commission accordingly.

E/5020, Part IV, para. 493. Second draft resolution submitted by ECAFE for action by Economic and Social Council approved without vote by Economic Committee on 14 July 1971, meeting 526.
E/5054 and Corr.1. Report of Economic Committee, draft resolution V.

RESOLUTION 1604(LI), as recommended by Economic Committee, E/5054, adopted without objection by Council on 20 July 1971, meeting 1785.

The Economic and Social Council,
Taking note of the recommendation of the Economic Commission for Asia and the Far East with regard to the request of the Kingdom of Tonga that it be included within the geographical scope of the Commission and admitted as a member of the Commission,
1. *Approves* the recommendation of the Economic Commission for Asia and the Far East that the Kingdom of Tonga be included in the geographical scope of the Commission and admitted as a member of the Commission;
2. *Decides* to amend paragraphs 2 and 3 of the terms of reference of the Commission accordingly.

E/5020, Part IV, para. 493. Third draft resolution submitted by ECAFE for action by Economic and Social Council, approved without vote by Economic Committee on 14 July 1971, meeting 526.
E/5054 and Corr.1. Report of Economic Committee, draft resolution VI.

RESOLUTION 1605(LI), as recommended by Economic Committee, E/5054, adopted without objection by Council on 20 July 1971, meeting 1785.

The Economic and Social Council,
Taking note of the recommendation of the Economic Commission for Asia and the Far East with regard to the request of the Republic of Nauru that it be included within the geographical scope of the Commission and admitted as a member of the Commission,
1. *Approves* the recommendation of the Economic Commission for Asia and the Far East that the Republic of Nauru be included in the geographical scope of the Commission and admitted as a member of the Commission;
2. *Decides* to amend paragraphs 2 and 3 of the terms of reference of the Commission accordingly.

E/5020, Part IV, para. 493. Fourth draft resolution submitted by ECAFE for action by Economic and Social Council, approved without vote by Economic Committee on 14 July 1971, meeting 526.
E/5054 and Corr.1. Report of Economic Committee, draft resolution VII.

RESOLUTION 1606(LI), as recommended by Economic Committee, E/5054, adopted without objection by Council on 20 July 1971, meeting 1785.

The Economic and Social Council,
Taking note of the annual report of the Economic Commission for Asia and the Far East for the period 28 April 1970 to 30 April 1971 and of the recommendations and resolutions contained in parts II and III of that report,
Endorses the programme of work and priorities contained in part V of that report.

Other documents
A/8401. Report of Secretary-General on work of the Organization, 16 June 1970–15 June 1971, Part Three, Chapter III B.
A/8403. Report of Economic and Social Council on work of its 50th and 51st sessions, Chapter XIII A.
E/5134. Annual report of ECAFE (1 May 1971–27 March 1972).
Statistical Yearbook for Asia and the Far East, 1970. U.N.P. Sales No.: E/F.71.II.F.3.
Stratigraphic Correlation between Sedimentary Basins of the ECAFE Region (2nd vol.) (Report of Second Special Working Group and related documents, together with articles submitted at the Fourth Symposium on the Development of Petroleum Resources of Asia and the Far East, Canberra, Australia, October-November 1969). Mineral Resources Development Series, No. 36. U.N.P. Sales No.: E.71.II.F.9.
Proceedings of the Second Symposium on the Development of Deltaic Areas. Water Resources Series, No. 39. U.N.P. Sales No.: E.71.II.F.10.
Proceedings of the Ninth Session of the Regional Conference on Water Resources Development in Asia and the Far East, Bangkok, Thailand, 28 September–5 October 1970. Water Resources Series No. 40. U.N.P. Sales No.: E.72.II.F.20.
Asian Industrial Development News, No. 6, 1970. Special Issue: Second Asian Conference on Industrialization. U.N.P. Sales No.: E.71.II.F.11; *No. 7, 1971.* U.N.P. Sales No.: E.71.II.F.17; *No. 8, 1971.* U.N.P. Sales No.: E.72.II.F.9.
Manual on Traffic Surveys. U.N.P. Sales No.: E.71.II.F.13.
Trade and Monetary Co-operation in Asia and the Far East. Regional Economic Co-operation Series, No. 7. U.N.P. Sales No.: E.71.II.F.16.
Proceedings of the Second Asian Conference on Industrialization,

Vol. I (Report of the Second Asian Conference on Industrialization). U.N.P. Sales No.: E.71.II.F.18.

Foreign Trade Statistics of Asia and the Far East, Vol. VI, Series A, Nos. 1-2. U.N.P. Sales No.: E.71.II.F.4; Series B, No. 2. U.N.P. Sales No.: E.71.II.F.20.

Regional Economic Co-operation in Asia and the Far East: Report of the Meeting of the Council of Ministers for Asian Economic Co-operation (4th session). Regional Economic Co-operation Series, No. 8. U.N.P. Sales No.: E.71.II.F.21.

Quarterly Bulletin of Statistics for Asia and the Far East, Vol. I, No. 1, September 1971. U.N.P. Sales No.: E.71.II.F.22; Vol. I, No. 2, December 1971. U.N.P. Sales No. E.72.II.F.22.

Economic Survey of Asia and the Far East, 1971 (also issued as the Economic Bulletin for Asia and the Far East, Vol. XXII, No. 4). U.N.P. Sales No.: E.72.II.F.1.

Fertility Studies in the ECAFE Region. A Bibliography of Books, Papers and Reference Materials. Asian Population Studies Series, No. 6. U.N.P. Sales No.: E.72.II.F.3.

Guidelines for Statistics on Children and Youth (Provisional). U.N.P. Sales No.: E.72.II.F.4.

Select Annotated Bibliography on Social Aspects of Development Planning. U.N.P. Sales No.: E.72.II.F.6.

Report of the Working Party on Social Development (8-15 December 1970) and Report of the Expert Group on Social Development (30 November—5 December 1970). U.N.P. Sales No.: E.72.II.F.7.

Social Development in Asia—Retrospect and Prospect. U.N.P. Sales No.: E.72.II.F.8.

Transport and Communications Bulletin for Asia and the Far East, No. 47. U.N.P. Sales No.: E.72.II.F.13.

Economic Bulletin for Asia and the Far East, Vol. XXII, No. 1/2, June/September 1971. U.N.P. Sales No.: E.72.II.F.15.

Electric Power in Asia and the Far East, 1969. U.N.P. Sales No.: E.72.II.F.18. and corrigendum.

Small Industry Bulletin for Asia and the Far East, No. 9. U.N.P. Sales No.: E/F.72.II.F.19.

Boiler Codes in the ECAFE Region: Suggested Guidelines for the Operation, Care and Inspection of Boilers. U.N.P. Sales No.: E.72.II.F.21.

The Economic Commission for Latin America (ECLA)

In 1971, the Economic Commission for Latin America (ECLA) examined in some detail the application to the region during the Second United Nations Development Decade of the International Development Strategy.[2] Recommendations were made to the Governments of member developing countries and the secretariat was given new responsibilities for evaluating the economic and social progress of the region.

The Commission continued its activities in the field of trade policy and export promotion, especially in connexion with Latin American participation in the third (1972) session of the United Nations Conference on Trade and Development (UNCTAD). Also during the year, ECLA intensified its programmes for the exchange of documentation and information, as well as its assistance to regional and sub-regional integration movements in Latin America.

Activities in 1971

Economic Trends

At its fourteenth session, held from 27 April to 8 May 1971, the Economic Commission for Latin America reviewed economic trends in Latin America in 1970 and during the First United Nations Development Decade, and formulated guidelines for future action.

The 1970 *Economic Survey of Latin America*, published in 1971, indicated that in 1970 the growth rate of the gross domestic product was more than 6.5 per cent (as against 6.4 per cent in 1969 and 6.1 per cent in 1968), while exports increased by about 10 per cent and imports by 8.5 per cent. The share of gross domestic investment (19.5 per cent of the product in 1970) represented an increase in absolute terms, with a relative increase in public investment.

During the 1960s, the gross domestic product grew by 5.4 per cent annually, or at the same rate as the world economy. There was little change in the relative importance of the main sectors—the slight decline in the agricultural product was offset by a corresponding increase in manufacturing—although in the structure of employment there was a greater decline in the agricultural sector and a sharp rise in the service sector.

Exports rose by 5.5 per cent annually during the 1960s, compared with 8.8 per cent for world exports; there was no change in the average rate of 5.5 per cent a year for imports, which had remained stable for the past 20 years. The terms of trade continued to deteriorate for the region as a whole, with sharp variations in which the gains of some countries were more than offset by the losses of others.

It was generally agreed during discussions at the 1971 session of the Commission that economic and social development in Latin America during the 1960s, the First United Nations Development Decade, represented an improvement over the previous decade, although there were still serious problems such as unemployment and sectoral and regional disequilibria.

Moreover, some ECLA members felt that it had not been possible to meet the pressing need to raise the standard of living of the majority of people.

Also stressed was Latin America's increasing dependence and vulnerability with respect to other countries, and the widening financial and technological gap between it and the developed countries. In this respect, it was noted that the balance-of-payments deficit on current accounts

[2]See Y.U.N., 1970, pp. 319-29, text of resolution 2626(XXV) of 24 October 1970, setting forth the International Development Strategy.

had increased, and that there had been a sharp rise in net payments of profits and interest on foreign investment. The total external debt had risen from $2,213 million in 1950 to $6,631 million in 1960 and $16,432 million in 1968.

International Development Strategy

When the Commission discussed the International Development Strategy at its 1971 session, the questions before it included: the specific activities within the context of the Strategy which Latin American countries and ECLA should carry out in the near future; and the establishment of a system for appraising progress during the Second Development Decade. The Commission adopted five resolutions dealing with various aspects of the Second Development Decade activities. It also established a committee of high-level government experts to serve as a forum for analysing the factors connected with the achievement and appraisal of the objectives of the International Development Strategy.

Among other recommendations, the commission asked the ECLA secretariat, in its studies on the Strategy, to give high priority to the questions to be discussed at the third UNCTAD session, in view of the importance of UNCTAD as a major forum for the discussion of concerted action by the developing and developed countries.

Meetings, seminars and training

As in earlier years, ECLA provided training courses during 1971 for high-level officials. A trade policy course was attended by 22 government officials from 15 Latin American countries; an export promotion course was attended by 19 officials from the public and private sectors of four countries.

Within its export promotion programme, ECLA organized a meeting of experts from Latin America and other parts of the world, held from 26 July to 4 August 1971. The meeting explored ways of increasing the volume of exports of manufactures and provided an opportunity for comparing the experiences of a number of countries, including industrialized countries.

A seminar for executives in the industrial sector was attended by representatives from 16 countries of the region. The seminar, held in conjunction with the United Nations Industrial Development Organization (UNIDO), examined methods for speeding up industrial development in the Latin American countries.

In preparation for the 1972 United Nations Conference on the Human Environment, a regional seminar was held in Mexico City, Mexico, from 6 to 11 September 1971. The seminar provided an opportunity for an exchange of information on problems common to all countries

of the region, such as air and water pollution, the deterioration of Latin American fauna and vegetation, erosion of desert regions and the effect of urbanization and industrialization on the ecological balance in Latin America.

During November, a working group of 25 Latin American experts and representatives of national and international agencies concerned with the statistical measurement of income distribution met in Santiago, Chile.

Regional co-operation

During 1971, ECLA continued to co-operate and co-ordinate its activities with the governmental and regional agencies responsible for Latin American integration programmes and development plans.

Through its offices in Bogotá (Colombia), Mexico City (Mexico), Montevideo (Uruguay) and Port-of-Spain (Trinidad), ECLA continued to provide advisory services to regional and sub-regional economic integration movements; through its Rio de Janeiro (Brazil) office, it co-operated with Brazilian authorities in training and development programmes. The Commission also maintained permanent contact with the agencies of the United Nations system and with regional and inter-American organizations, through its Washington, D.C. (United States) office.

Documentation and publications

During 1971, the Latin American Centre for Economic and Social Documentation (CLADES) was set up in the ECLA secretariat. The Centre, made possible by a donation from the Netherlands Government, was intended to support development activities through the systematic organization of basic economic and social data.

As a substantive part of its research and analytical work, ECLA produced some 100 reports and studies in 1971. In addition to the *Economic Survey of Latin America, 1970*, and the semi-annual *Economic Bulletin for Latin America* and *Statistical Bulletin for Latin America*, the Commission prepared studies dealing with such topics as the distribution of income in selected major Latin American cities; the demographic situation and its policy implications; trade and financial relations between Latin America and Japan; international railways in Latin America; the metal-transforming industry in Latin America; and the institutional structure of Latin American integration and the export of manufactures.

Decisions by Economic and Social Council

At its July 1971 session, the Economic and Social Council considered the annual report of the Economic Commission for Latin America, covering the period from 8 May 1970 to 8 May 1971.

By a decision of 20 July 1971, the Council took note of the report and endorsed the programme of work and priorities of the Commission. These decisions by the Council were embodied in resolution 1607(LI), which was adopted, without objection, on the recommendation of the Economic Committee. The text, based on a draft submitted by ECLA, was approved without vote by the Economic Committee on 14 July 1971.

DOCUMENTARY REFERENCES

Economic and Social Council—51st session
Economic Committee, meetings 523-526, 530.
Plenary meetings 1773, 1777, 1785.

E/4935 and Add.1, Add.1/Corr.1, Add.2. Reports of Joint Inspection Unit (JIU). Report on activities of ECLA. Report by 3 members of JIU (June 1970), note by Secretary-General, and observations of Advisory Committee on Administrative and Budgetary Questions.
E/5027. Annual report of Economic Commission for Latin America (ECLA), 8 May 1970–8 May 1971, Vol. I.
E/5027/Add.1. Annual report of ECLA, 8 May 1970–8 May 1971, Vol. II (Part V: Draft programme of work and priorities, May 1971–April 1973).
E/5027/Summary. Summary of annual report of ECLA.
E/5027, Vol. I, Part IV. Draft resolution submitted by ECLA for action by Economic and Social Council, approved without vote by Economic Committee on 14 July 1971, meeting 526.
E/5039. Report of meetings of executive secretaries of regional economic commissions held in 1971 (New York, 27-29 January 1971; Geneva, Switzerland, 28-30 June and 3 July 1971).
E/AC.6/L.424. Regional co-operation. Note by Secretary-General (on participation of Intergovernmental Council of Copper Exporting Countries as observer in work of ECLA and Economic Commission for Africa).
E/5054 and Corr.1. Report of Economic Committee, draft resolution VIII.

RESOLUTION 1607(LI), as recommended by Economic Committee, E/5054, adopted without objection by Council on 20 July 1971, meeting 1785.

The Economic and Social Council
1. *Takes note* of the annual report of the Economic Commission for Latin America covering the period 8 May 1970 to 8 May 1971 and of the resolutions and recommendations contained in parts II and III of that report;
2. *Endorses* the programme of work and priorities contained in part V of that report.

Other documents
A/8401. Report of Secretary-General on work of the Organization, 16 June 1970–15 June 1971, Part Three, Chapter III C.
A/8403. Report of Economic and Social Council on work of its 50th and 51st sessions, Chapter XIII A.
Income Distribution in Latin America. U.N.P. Sales No.: E.71.II.G.2.
Statistical Bulletin for Latin America, Vol. VIII, No. 1, March 1971. U.N.P. Sales No.: E/S.71.II.G.4; *No. 2, October 1971.* U.N.P. Sales No.: E/S.72.II.G.3.
Economic Bulletin for Latin America, Vol. XVI, No. 1 (first half of 1971). U.N.P. Sales No.: E.71.II.G.5; *No. 2 (second half of 1971).* U.N.P. Sales No.: E.71.II.G.6.
Economic Survey of Latin America, 1970. U.N.P. Sales No.: E.72.II.G.1.

The Economic Commission for Africa (ECA)

The tenth biennial session of the Economic Commission for Africa (ECA) was held in Tunis, Tunisia, from 8 to 13 February 1971. In accordance with an ECA recommendation of 10 February 1969, the session was held at the ministerial level and was known as the Conference of Ministers.[3]

The Conference adopted a number of resolutions concerning the work of the Commission, including one setting forth an African strategy for development in the 1970s. These decisions served as the basis for the Commission's activities during the year.

Activities in 1971

Development strategy

At its 1971 session, the ECA Conference of Ministers adopted a strategy for Africa's economic and social development in the 1970s, within the framework of the International Development Strategy for the Second United Nations Development Decade.[4]

In so doing, the Conference recommended that the development programmes of individual member States of ECA be concentrated on a limited number of key areas and activities. Among the issues singled out by the Conference as requiring special attention were the following: agriculture; rural transformation; trade; external financial and technical co-operation; mobilization of domestic resources; industry; and the special problems of the least-developed, the land-locked and the island countries.

The Conference recommended that special programmes be initiated by ECA in pursuance of the aims of the African development strategy.

Population programme

An African Population Conference was held in Accra, Ghana, from 9 to 18 December 1971, followed by the first session of the Conference of African Demographers, held from 19 to 22 December.

The Population Programme Centre of ECA sent missions to Cameroon, Chad and Ghana to advise on the establishment of demographic training centres and the preparation of population projections, and assisted Ethiopia and Somalia in

[3]See Y.U.N., 1969, p. 409.
[4]See Y.U.N., 1970, pp. 319-29, text of resolution 2626(XXV) of 24 October 1970, containing the text of the International Development Strategy.

connexion with their forthcoming census projects.

A revised edition of the *Demographic Handbook of Africa* was published during the year, as were several issues of the *African Population Newsletter* and the *African Census Population Newsletter*.

Trade

In view of the vulnerable trade position of the African countries, the activities of the ECA secretariat placed emphasis on promoting and expanding intra-African trade and identifying new trade opportunities in non-traditional markets, while at the same time consolidating existing markets.

Among meetings and seminars held during 1971 were two training courses in export promotion (for English- and French-speaking countries, respectively), held in co-operation with the International Trade Centre.

The sixth Joint Meeting on Trade and Development of ECA and the Organization of African Unity (OAU) was held in Geneva, Switzerland, from 12 to 20 August. An African ministerial meeting to prepare for the third (1972) session of the United Nations Conference on Trade and Development (UNCTAD) was held in Addis Ababa, Ethiopia, from 8 to 14 October.

Two symposia were held in conjunction with the Second Ghana International Trade Fair: one on business development in West Africa, and another on trade expansion as a basis for industrial development.

Preparations were also begun for the All Africa Trade Fair, scheduled to be held in Nairobi, Kenya, early in 1972.

Natural resources

A conference on hydrology and hydrometeorology in the economic development of Africa was held in Addis Ababa from 19 September to 2 October 1971.

A mission was sent to the United Republic of Tanzania to discuss the establishment of a water resources development institute, and an expert on water resources visited Upper Volta to advise on the construction of a dam for irrigation and power purposes.

An adviser in mining and geology visited Ghana, the Ivory Coast, Nigeria, Senegal and Sierra Leone in August in connexion with a programme for training mining engineers and mining economists.

Transport and tourism

The first and second meetings of the Trans-African Highway Committee were held in Addis Ababa from 14 to 18 June and from 29 September to 1 October, respectively.

Advisory services were rendered in the fields of transport and tourism in Burundi, Ethiopia,

Rwanda and in the countries of the East African Community and North Africa.

Industry

A Conference of Ministers of Industry, sponsored jointly by ECA and OAU, was held in Addis Ababa from 3 to 7 May 1971, attended by representatives of 28 States. The Conference drew up a "Declaration on Industrial Development in Africa in the 1970s," dealing with the challenge of the mobilization of domestic resources for industrial development; problems of high installation and operating costs; private foreign investment; the relationship between industry and employment; and self-reliance in industrial development.

Several industrial project descriptions were formulated by ECA and submitted to Governments for examination and implementation; the projects prepared dealt with, among other things, wire drawing, soap, welded tubes, electromotors, transformers, agricultural hand tools, fertilizers, ceramics and cement. The Commission was also working to bring the projects to the attention of potential investors.

The third African Meeting to Promote Industrial Projects, jointly sponsored by the United Nations Industrial Development Organization (UNIDO), ECA and the African Development Bank, was held at Abidjan, Ivory Coast, from 24 November to 1 December 1971. Participants from 24 African countries considered more than 160 proposals submitted by potential foreign investors.

Members of the forest industries advisory group visited various member States.

Statistics

The seventh session of the Conference of African Statisticians was convened at Dakar, Senegal, from 13 to 22 October 1971.

An expert visited Dahomey, the Ivory Coast, Liberia and Togo to advise on accounting and statistical practices.

A course in demographic statistics was given at the Institute of Statistics and Applied Economics, Makerere University, Kampala, Uganda. An adviser in demographic statistics was sent to Cameroon, Dahomey, Ethiopia, the Ivory Coast, Mauritius, Nigeria and Somalia, mainly in connexion with formulating proposals for censuses.

Human resources

A number of activities were carried out during the year in the areas of rural life and institutions, and social welfare policy and training.

A symposium on rural development in Africa, attended by representatives of 27 international voluntary and United Nations agencies, was held in Addis Ababa from 9 to 13 August 1971. The participants discussed ways of fostering co-operation between ECA and international voluntary agencies operating rural development programmes in Africa.

A regional adviser in rural life and institutions was sent to Burundi, Rwanda and Zaire to assist in the review of the rural development policies of those Governments, including the questions of land tenure, agricultural development, farmers' co-operatives for credit, and marketing and job opportunities.

A regional adviser on social welfare policy and training carried out assignments in Gambia, Ghana, Liberia, Sierra Leone, Somalia, Sudan and the United Republic of Tanzania. In Dahomey, Gabon, Mali, Niger, Togo and Upper Volta, ECA assisted in the development of programmes aimed at securing greater participation of broad social groups in national development, and at the training and employment of youth.

In the field of manpower development, ECA had, in response to requests by member States, received more than 150 offers of scholarships and fellowships for training Africans in fields of development priority; as at the end of 1971, some 70 Africans had received awards under the programme.

Among the meetings and seminars conducted during the year were an expert group meeting on social welfare training and administration; a regional conference on vocational training and work opportunities for girls and women in Africa; and a training course in the techniques and methodology of manpower planning and training. Mobile workshops on modern training methods and teaching aids were held in eight African countries.

A country-by-country survey of pre-vocational, vocational and technical training for women was completed.

Agriculture

Missions to central, west, north and east Africa were undertaken by a joint ECA and Food and Agriculture Organization (FAO) team during the year; the missions discussed intra-regional co-operation and trade in agriculture.

A consultant visited seven countries of East Africa to appraise prospects for increased production and trade in livestock and livestock products; another consultant visited seven West African countries to gather data on the organization and administration of agricultural extension services.

A working group on the extension of the activities of the African Ground-nut Council to other African oil-seeds was held in Addis Ababa from 20 to 23 April. The Commission also participated in an FAO regional conference on the establishment of co-operative agricultural research programmes between countries with similar eco-

logical conditions in the Guinean ecological zone; the conference was held in Ibadan, Nigeria, from 23 to 28 August.

Economic co-operation

The work of the ECA Centre for Economic Co-operation involved joint sponsorship of projects, technical and economic evaluation of development projects and the provision of advisory services.

A working group of experts met from 29 November to 3 December in Addis Ababa to establish the procedures for the harmonization of development plans at the level of two or more countries.

A symposium on economic co-operation in Central Africa was held in Zaire in June.

In conjunction with the Centre for Development Planning, Projections and Policies, the Commission convened an East African expert meeting on economic co-operation from 1 to 10 November 1971. The meeting identified areas for strengthening economic co-operation in the various economic sectors within the sub-region and prepared action-oriented proposals on economic co-operation for submission to Governments.

Consideration by Economic and Social Council and General Assembly

The annual report of the Economic Commission for Africa, covering the period 15 February 1970 to 13 February 1971, was considered by the Economic and Social Council during its July 1971 session.

On 20 July 1971, the Council, in noting the report, endorsed the Commission's programme of work and priorities, 1971-1973, with projections to 1976. It took note of the recommendations made by the Commission on regional structures within the United Nations system. The Council also commended the Commission for the measures it had taken to chart a meaningful strategy for Africa's economic and social development in the 1970s, within the framework of the International Development Strategy for the Second United Nations Development Decade.

These decisions by the Council were set forth in resolution 1608(LI), which was adopted without objection on the recommendation of the Economic Committee. The text, based on a draft submitted by the Economic Commission for Africa, was approved without vote by the Economic Committee on 14 July 1971. (For text of resolution, see DOCUMENTARY REFERENCES below.)

Two other decisions regarding ECA were taken by the Economic and Social Council and the General Assembly during 1971.

At its mid-1971 session, the Council had before it a note by the Secretary-General transmitting to the Council the names of representatives of Angola, Guinea (Bissau) and Mozambique to ECA proposed by the Organization of African Unity in accordance with a 1969 resolution of ECA concerning the proposed associate membership in ECA of Angola, Guinea (Bissau) and Mozambique.

On 20 July 1971, the Council, without adopting a resolution, decided to transmit the note by the Secretary-General to the General Assembly for appropriate action at its 1971 session. The Council took this decision on the recommendation of its Economic Committee, which, on 16 July 1971, approved the draft decision, submitted by Ghana, by a roll-call vote of 18 to 0, with 6 abstentions.

On 10 December 1971, the General Assembly approved the arrangements relating to the representation of Angola, Mozambique and Guinea (Bissau) as associate members of the Economic Commission for Africa, as well as the list of the

representatives of those territories proposed by the Organization of African Unity.

This decision by the Assembly was set forth in resolution 2795(XXVI), paragraph 12. The Assembly adopted the resolution on the recommendation of its Fourth Committee. (For text of resolution 2795(XXVI), see pp. 574-76.)

Also, on 20 July 1971, the Economic and Social Council decided, without adopting a resolution, to take no action on the recommendation of ECA that the Intergovernmental Council of Copper Exporting Countries be allowed to participate in an observer capacity in Commission sessions and meetings of its subsidiary bodies concerned with issues of interest to the Intergovernmental Council, since the Commission was competent, under its terms of reference, to enter into the proposed arrangements with the Intergovernmental Council.

DOCUMENTARY REFERENCES

Economic and Social Council—51st session
Economic Committee, meetings 523-526, 528, 530.
Plenary meetings 1777, 1785.

E/4997, Vol. I. Annual report of Economic Commission for Africa (ECA), 15 February 1970–13 February 1971, Parts I-IV and Annexes.
E/4997, Vol. II. Annual report of ECA, 15 February 1970–13 February 1971, Part V: Programme of work and priorities, 1971-1973, with projections to 1976.
E/4997/Summary. Summary of annual report of ECA.
E/4997, Vol. I, Part IV. Draft resolution submitted by ECA for action by Economic and Social Council, approved without vote by Economic Committee on 14 July 1971, meeting 526.
E/5039. Report of meetings of executive secretaries of regional economic commissions held in 1971 (New York, 27-29 January 1971; Geneva, Switzerland, 28-30 June and 3 July 1971).
E/L.1376. Letter of 5 March 1971 from Portugal.
E/5054 and Corr.1. Report of Economic Committee, draft resolution IX.

RESOLUTION 1608(LI), as recommended by Economic Committee, E/5054, adopted without objection by Council on 20 July 1971, meeting 1785.

The Economic and Social Council
1. *Takes note* of the report of the Economic Commission for Africa covering the period from 15 February 1970 to 13 February 1971 and the recommendations and resolutions contained in parts II and III of that report;
2. *Endorses* the programme of work and priorities, 1971-1973, with projections to 1976, contained in part V of the report;
3. *Takes note* of the recommendations made in the Commission's resolution 217(X) on regional structures within the United Nations system with respect to the implementation of Council resolution 1553(XLIX) of 30 July 1970;
4. *Commends* the Commission for the measures it has taken to chart a meaningful strategy for Africa's economic and social development in the 1970s, within the framework of the global International Development Strategy for the Second United Nations Development Decade adopted by the General Assembly in resolution 2626(XXV) of 24 October 1970.

E/4779, Vol. I. Annual report of ECA (15 February 1970–13 February 1971), Part III (resolution 233(X)) and Annex II.
E/5051. Question of representation of Angola, Guinea (Bissau) and Mozambique in ECA. Note by Secretary-General.

E/AC.6/L.425. Ghana: draft decision, approved by Economic Committee on 16 July 1971, meeting 530, by roll-call vote of 18 to 0, with 6 abstentions, as follows:

In favour: Ceylon, Ghana, Greece, Haiti, Hungary, Indonesia, Jamaica, Kenya, Madagascar, Malaysia, New Zealand, Niger, Norway, Pakistan, Sudan, Tunisia, USSR, Yugoslavia.
Against: None.
Abstaining: Brazil, France, Italy, United Kingdom, United States, Uruguay.

E/5054 and Corr.1. Report of Economic Committee, draft decision XII.
E/5073. Resolutions adopted by Economic and Social Council during its 51st session, 5-30 July 1971. Other decisions, p. 10.

E/4997, Vol. I. Annual report of ECA (15 February 1970–13 February 1971), paras. 484-485.
E/AC.6/L.424. Note by Secretary-General (on participation of Intergovernmental Council of Copper Exporting Countries as observer in work of ECLA and ECA).
E/5054 and Corr.1. Report of Economic Committee, draft decision XIII.
E/5073. Resolutions adopted by Economic and Social Council during its 51st session, 5-30 July 1971. Other decisions, p. 10.

Other documents
A/8401. Report of Secretary-General on work of the Organization, 16 June 1970–15 June 1971, Part Three, Chapter III D.
A/8403. Report of Economic and Social Council on work of its 50th and 51st sessions, Chapter XIII A.
Economic Bulletin for Africa, Vol. VIII, Nos. 1 and 2. U.N.P. Sales No.: E.68.II.K.1.
Integrated Approach to Rural Development in Africa. U.N.P. Sales No: E.71.II.K.2.
Administration for Development. U.N.P. Sales No.: E.71.II.K.13.
A Survey of Economic Conditions in Africa, 1969 (Part I). U.N.P. Sales No.: E.71.II.K.5 and corrigendum; *(Part II).* U.N.P. Sales No.: E.71.II.K.6.
A Survey of Economic Conditions in Africa, 1970 (Part I). U.N.P. Sales No.: E.71.II.K.9; *(Part II).* U.N.P. Sales No.: E.72.II.K.5.
Foreign Trade Statistics for Africa, Series A, Direction of Trade, No. 17. U.N.P. Sales No.: E/F.71.II.K.15; *No. 18.* U.N.P. Sales No.: E/F.72.II.K.4.
Agricultural Economics Bulletin for Africa, No. 13, June 1971. U.N.P. Sales No.: E.72.II.K.2.

The United Nations Economic and Social Office at Beirut

At its mid-1971 session, the Economic and Social Council considered a report submitted by the Secretary-General on the activities of the United Nations Economic and Social Office at Beirut (UNESOB) during the period 15 April 1970 to 15 April 1971. The report noted, among other things, the efforts of UNESOB to contribute to the International Development Strategy of the Second United Nations Development Decade,[5] including the preparation of a statistical framework for evaluating economic and social progress in the region during that period.

It was also noted that an intensification of activities of UNESOB was envisaged over the five-year period 1972-1976, assuming that resources could be made available to meet the increasing demands for UNESOB services by Governments and United Nation bodies.

On 20 July 1971, the Economic and Social Council took note of the report of the Secretary-General by adopting, without objection, resolution 1609(LI), as recommended by its Economic Committee. The text, suggested by the Chairman of the Economic Committee, was approved without vote by that Committee on 14 July 1971.

[5]See Y.U.N., 1970, pp. 319-29, resolution 2626(XXV) of 24 October 1970, containing the text of the International Development Strategy.

DOCUMENTARY REFERENCES

Economic and Social Council—51st session
Economic Committee, meetings 523-526.
Plenary meetings 1773, 1777, 1785.

E/5006. Regional co-operation. Activities of United Nations Economic and Social Office at Beirut (UNESOB), 15 April 1970–15 April 1971. Report of Secretary-General.
E/5039. Report of meetings of executive secretaries of regional economic commissions held in 1971 (New York, 27-29 January 1971; Geneva, Switzerland, 28-30 June and 3 July 1971).
E/5054 and Corr.1. Report of Economic Committee, draft resolution X, as suggested by Committee Chairman, approved without vote by Economic Committee on 14 July 1971, meeting 526.

RESOLUTION 1609(LI), as recommended by Economic Committee, E/5054, adopted without objection by Council on 20 July 1971, meeting 1785, taking note of annual report of Secretary-General on activities of UNESOB, 15 April 1970–15 April 1971.

Other documents
A/8401. Report of Secretary-General on work of the Organization, 16 June 1970–15 June 1971, Part Three, Chapter III E.
A/8403. Report of Economic and Social Council on work of its 50th and 51st sessions, Chapter XIII A.
Studies on Selected Development Problems in Various Countries in the Middle East, 1971. U.N.P. Sales No.: E.71.II.C.2.
E/5010. Studies on selected development problems in various countries in Middle East, 1971. Summary.

Role of the regional commissions in the Second Development Decade

The Economic and Social Council and the General Assembly took several decisions in 1971 concerning the role of the regional economic commissions and the United Nations Economic and Social Office at Beirut (UNESOB) in the Second United Nations Development Decade. The contribution the commissions and UNESOB could make to the attainment of the goals and objectives of the Second Development Decade, and to the appraisal at the regional level of progress in the implementation of the International Development Strategy,[6] had been recognized by the General Assembly by its decisions of 11 December 1970[7] and 19 November 1970.[8]

Regional and sub-regional advisory services

At its mid-1971 session, on 20 July 1971, the Economic and Social Council took note of the fact that new responsibilities would be assumed by the regional economic commissions and UNESOB in the implementation of the International Development Strategy, in addition to various other responsibilities that had earlier been assumed by them in accordance with General Assembly requests. The Council recognized that the accretion of such responsibilities meant a considerable strain on the organizational and administrative resources of the commissions and UNESOB.

The Council recommended that, as a first step in relieving this burden, the General Assembly decide to establish a separate section in the United Nations regular budget to make provision for a unified system of regional and sub-regional advisory services, earmarked for the operations of the commissions and UNESOB, and to transfer the existing regional advisory services to this section. It further recommended that section 13 of the United Nations budget for the regular programme of technical assistance (dealing with various programmes of economic and social development) be maintained in 1972 at its current level; it recommended that these operations be concentrated in support of country programmes of the least developed among the developing

[6]See Y.U.N., 1970, pp. 319-29, text of resolution 2626(XXV) of 24 October 1970, setting forth the International Development Strategy.
[7]*Ibid.*, pp. 435-36, text of resolution 2687(XXV).
[8]*Ibid.*, pp. 329-30, text of resolution 2641(XXV).

countries, as well as of regional and sub-regional programmes of special interest to those countries.

These decisions by the Council were set forth in resolution 1601(LI), adopted on the recommendation of the Council's Economic Committee, by a roll-call vote of 20 to 5, with 1 abstention. The Committee approved the text, which was based on a proposal by Sudan, on 15 July 1971, by a roll-call vote of 21 to 5, with 1 abstention. (For text of resolution, see DOCUMENTARY REFERENCES below.)

On 14 December 1971, the General Assembly, recalling among other things the above Economic and Social Council resolution of 20 July 1971: (1) decided to establish a separate section in the United Nations regular budget to provide for a unified system of regional and sub-regional advisory services earmarked for the operations of the regional economic commissions and the United Nations Economic and Social Office in Beirut (UNESOB), and to transfer to that section the existing regional advisory services; (2) requested the Secretary-General to provide, as appropriate, directly to the commissions and UNESOB the respective amounts earmarked for regional and sub-regional advisory services and to authorize the executive secretaries of the commissions and the Director of UNESOB to administer those funds; and (3) decided that section 13 of the United Nations budget for the regular programme of technical assistance (dealing with various programmes of economic and social development) should be maintained for 1972 at its current level and its operations concentrated in support of country programmes of the least developed among the developing countries, as well as other programmes of special interest to those countries.

These decisions by the Assembly were set forth in resolution 2803(XXVI), which was adopted, by a vote of 92 to 10, with 7 abstentions, on the recommendation of the Second (Economic and Financial) Committee.

The text, approved by the Second Committee on 11 November 1971, by a vote of 88 to 13, with 5 abstentions, was based on a proposal by the following 35 powers: Brazil, Burundi, Cameroon, Chile, Colombia, Ethiopia, Guinea, Guyana, India, Indonesia, Iraq, Ireland, Kuwait, Lebanon, Lesotho, Libyan Arab Republic, Madagascar, Malaysia,

Mali, Mexico, Morocco, the People's Democratic Republic of Yemen, Peru, the Philippines, Rwanda, Sudan, Swaziland, Sweden, Thailand, Togo, Trinidad and Tobago, Tunisia, the United Republic of Tanzania, Upper Volta and Zaire.

(For text of resolution, see DOCUMENTARY REFERENCES below.)

(For further information on technical assistance appropriations, see pp. 644-45, text of resolution 2899 A (XXVI).)

Other decisions

The Economic and Social Council and the General Assembly took several other decisions concerning the role to be played by the regional economic commissions and UNESOB in the Second United Nations Development Decade.

On 30 July 1971, the Economic and Social Council, reaffirming the importance of identifying the least developed among the developing countries, included the regional economic commissions and UNESOB among the bodies which were to examine the economic and social advancement of those countries, keeping in view the possibility of modifications in the list of those countries at the time of the comprehensive appraisal which was scheduled for 1975, the middle of the Second Development Decade.

This decision was set forth in resolution 1628(LI). (For text of resolution, see page 235.)

On 14 December 1971, the General Assembly took a number of decisions concerning the review and appraisal of the objectives and policies of the International Development Strategy for the Second United Nations Development Decade.

Among other things, the Assembly requested competent secretariats at the sectoral and regional levels to co-operate with the Committee for Development Planning by collecting, processing and making available required data and information. It also invited the regional economic commissions and UNESOB, among other organizations, to integrate their activities with the preparatory work for the over-all review and appraisal so as to avoid unnecessary duplication in this field.

These decisions were set forth in resolution 2801(XXVI). (For text of resolution, see page 231.)

DOCUMENTARY REFERENCES

Economic and Social Council—51st session
Economic Committee, meetings 523-528.
Plenary meetings 1773, 1777, 1785.

E/4997, Vols. I and II. Annual report of Economic Commission for Africa, 15 February 1970–13 February 1971.
E/5001. Annual report of Economic Commission for Europe, 25 April 1970–30 April 1971.
E/5006. Regional co-operation. Activities of United Nations

Economic and Social Office in Beirut, 15 April 1970–15 April 1971. Report of Secretary-General.
E/5020. Annual report of Economic Commission for Asia and Far East, 28 April 1970–30 April 1971.
E/5027 (Vol. I) and Add.1 (Vol. II). Annual report of Economic Commission for Latin America, 8 May 1970–8 May 1971.
E/5039. Report of meetings of executive secretaries of regional economic commissions held in 1971 (New York, 27-29 January 1971; Geneva, Switzerland, 28-30 June and 3 July 1971).
E/AC.6/L.421 and Corr.1. Sudan: draft resolution, as orally

revised by sponsor, approved by Economic Committee on 15 July 1971, meeting 528, by roll-call vote of 21 to 5, with 1 abstention, as follows:

In favour: Brazil, Ceylon, Ghana, Greece, Haiti, Indonesia, Italy, Jamaica, Kenya, Lebanon, Madagascar, Malaysia, Niger, Norway, Pakistan, Peru, Sudan, Tunisia, Uruguay, Yugoslavia, Zaire.

Against: France, Hungary, USSR, United Kingdom, United States.

Abstaining: New Zealand.

E/AC.6/L.421/Add.1 and Corr.1. Administrative and financial implications of Sudanese draft resolution, E/AC.6/L.421. Statement by Secretary-General.

E/5054 and Corr.1. Report of Economic Committee, draft resolution II.

RESOLUTION 1601(LI), as recommended by Economic Committee, E/5054 and Corr.1, adopted by Council on 20 July 1971, meeting 1785, by roll-call vote of 20 to 5, with 1 abstention:

In favour: Brazil, Ceylon, Ghana, Greece, Haiti, Indonesia, Italy, Jamaica, Kenya, Lebanon, Madagascar, Niger, Norway, Pakistan, Peru, Sudan, Tunisia, Uruguay, Yugoslavia, Zaire.

Against: France, Hungary, USSR, United Kingdom, United States.

Abstaining: New Zealand.

The Economic and Social Council,

Recalling its resolution 793(XXX) of 3 August 1960 on decentralization of activities and operations, and General Assembly resolutions 1709(XVI) of 19 December 1961 and 1823(XVII) of 18 December 1962 on the decentralization of the economic and social activities of the United Nations and strengthening of the regional economic commissions,

Noting the Council's recommendation in its resolution 1442(XLVII) of 31 July 1969 that the regional economic commissions and the United Nations Economic and Social Office at Beirut play a more active role in the implementation of operational programmes for economic and social action,

Taking into account that the expansion of the membership of the regional economic commissions has required both an extension of the existing services of the commissions over a wider area and a reflection in their activities of new aspirations and new urges,

Recognizing that the regional economic commissions have been called upon to reorient their activities in response to the wide acceptance of new approaches to development, particularly the consideration and implementation, under the aegis of the commissions, of an increasing number and variety of schemes for regional and sub-regional economic co-operation and integration, multi-disciplinary approaches to development, the need to integrate economic and social aspects of development, and vast possibilities opened up recently in the field of the application of science and technology to development,

Taking note of the provisions on the new country programming approach, approved by the General Assembly in its resolution 2688(XXV) of 11 December 1970,

Considering that the adoption of a new country programming approach has called for a new orientation and a re-definition of the operational functions of the regional economic commissions,

Noting the conclusion of the Joint Inspection Unit that the regional economic commissions, while continuing their functions of economic studies and research and advisory services to member countries, have increasingly become operational bodies in the field of economic co-operation and will be called upon to undertake in the future even greater responsibilities in these directions,

Recalling that the General Assembly in its resolution 2563(XXIV) of 13 December 1969 and the Council in its resolution 1552(XLIX) of 30 July 1970 requested the Secretary-General together with the executive secretaries of the regional economic commissions and the Director of the United Nations Economic and Social Office at Beirut to initiate multinational interdisciplinary United Nations Development Advisory Teams,

Noting that a number of those Teams have been launched on a sub-regional basis, as indicated in the report of the meetings of the executive secretaries of the regional economic commissions held in 1971,

Recalling further that the General Assembly, in its resolution 2687(XXV) of 11 December 1970, requested the regional economic commissions and the United Nations Economic and Social Office at Beirut to continue and further intensify their efforts in helping to promote, on a regional, sub-regional or inter-regional basis, trade expansion, economic co-operation and integration among their member countries, as a concrete step towards the attainment of the goals and objectives of the Second United Nations Development Decade,

Considering that the regional economic commissions and the United Nations Economic and Social Office at Beirut will be called upon to assume major responsibilities for review and appraisal at the regional level of the progress in the implementation of the International Development Strategy,

Recognizing that the accretion of such responsibilities to the regional economic commissions has meant a considerable strain on their organizational and administrative resources,

Recalling that the General Assembly, in its resolution 2687(XXV), urged that the regional economic commissions and the United Nations Economic and Social Office at Beirut be provided with the means and resources necessary to fulfil their role for the benefit of their member countries,

Stressing that the increasing responsibilities being discharged by the regional economic commissions in the operational field are an integral part of their mandatory and policy functions and any distinction between these two categories of functions is arbitrary,

Taking note that the regional advisory services under the United Nations regular programme have in recent years been utilized by the regional economic commissions for the discharge of these responsibilities,

Welcoming the new orientation being imparted to the regular programme, in both its country and regional components, particularly through its concentration in the least developed among the developing countries and in areas which are of crucial importance to the development process of these countries,

1. *Recommends* that, as a first step and at least partially to relieve the financial and administrative burden on the regional economic commissions and the United Nations Economic and Social Office at Beirut imposed by the expanded scope of these responsibilities, the General Assembly should decide to establish at its twenty-sixth session a separate section in the United Nations regular budget to make provision for a unified system of regional and sub-regional advisory services, earmarked for the operations of the regional economic commissions and the United Nations Economic and Social Office at Beirut, and to transfer to this section the existing regional advisory services at present under part V;

2. *Further recommends* that the existing section 13 of part V of the United Nations budget for the regular programme of technical assistance be maintained for 1972 at its current level of $5,408,000 and concentrate its operations substantially to support country programmes of the least developed among the developing countries, as well as regional and sub-regional programmes of special interest to those countries.

General Assembly—26th session

Second Committee, meetings 1369-1382, 1394, 1395, 1397, 1400, 1404.

Fifth Committee, meetings 1478, 1479.

Plenary meeting 2017.

A/8401/Add.1. Introduction to report of Secretary-General on work of the Organization, September 1971, paras. 249-250.

A/8403. Report of Economic and Social Council on work of its 50th and 51st sessions, Chapter XIII.

A/C.2/265. Note by Secretary-General.

A/C.2/L.1148. Brazil, Burundi, Cameroon, Chile, Colombia, Ethiopia, Guinea, Guyana, India, Indonesia, Iraq, Kuwait, Lebanon, Lesotho, Libyan Arab Republic, Madagascar, Malaysia, Mali, Mexico, Morocco, People's Democratic Republic of

Yemen, Peru, Philippines, Rwanda, Sudan, Swaziland, Sweden, Thailand, Togo, Trinidad and Tobago, Tunisia, United Republic of Tanzania, Upper Volta, Zaire: draft resolution.

A/C.2/L.1148/Rev.1. Revised draft resolution, sponsored by above 34 powers and Ireland, approved by Second Committee on 11 November 1971, meeting 1404, by 88 votes to 13, with 5 abstentions.

A/C.2/L.1148/Add.1, A/C.5/1399 and Corr.1, A/8408/Add.19, A/8579. Administrative and financial implications of draft resolution II recommended by Second Committee in A/8578. Statements by Secretary-General and reports of Advisory Committee on Administrative and Budgetary Questions and Fifth Committee.

A/8578. Report of Second Committee (part I) (on report of Economic and Social Council), draft resolution II.

RESOLUTION 2803(XXVI), as recommended by Second Committee, A/8578, adopted by Assembly on 14 December 1971, meeting 2017, by 92 votes to 10, with 7 abstentions.

The General Assembly,

Recalling its resolutions 2563(XXIV) of 13 December 1969 and 2687(XXV) of 11 December 1970 on the role of the regional economic commissions in the Second United Nations Development Decade,

Recalling Economic and Social Council resolution 793(XXX) of 3 August 1960 and General Assembly resolution 1823(XVII) of 18 December 1962 on the decentralization of the economic and social activities of the United Nations and the strengthening of the regional economic commissions,

Recalling further Economic and Social Council resolution 1442(XLVII) of 31 July 1969 in which the Council called upon the regional economic commissions and the United Nations Economic and Social Office at Beirut to play a more active role in the implementation of operational programmes for economic and social action,

Recalling Economic and Social Council resolution 1601(LI) of 20 July 1971 on regional and sub-regional advisory services,

Considering that the regional economic commissions and the United Nations Economic and Social Office at Beirut will be called upon to assume major responsibilities for review and appraisal at the regional level of the progress in implementing the International

Development Strategy for the Second United Nations Development Decade, contained in General Assembly resolution 2626(XXV) of 24 October,

Stressing that the increasing responsibilities being discharged by the regional economic commissions in the operational fields have a distinctive identity of their own without duplicating United Nations Development Programme activities, that these functions are an integral part of their mandatory and policy functions and that any distinction between these two categories of functions is arbitrary,

Taking note that the regional advisory services under the United Nations regular programme have in recent years been utilized by the regional economic commissions for the discharge of those responsibilities,

I

1. *Decides,* as a practical step in strengthening the regional economic commissions and the United Nations Economic and Social Office at Beirut enabling them to carry out with increasing effectiveness their duties towards the States members of their respective regions, to establish a separate section in the United Nations regular budget to provide for a unified system of regional and sub-regional advisory services earmarked for the operations of the regional economic commissions and the United Nations Economic and Social Office at Beirut, and to transfer to that section the existing regional advisory services at present under section 13 of the budget;

2. *Requests* the Secretary-General to provide, as appropriate, directly to the regional economic commissions and the United Nations Economic and Social Office at Beirut, the respective amounts earmarked for regional and sub-regional advisory services and to authorize the executive secretaries of the regional economic commissions and the Director of the United Nations Economic and Social Office at Beirut to administer these funds;

II

Decides that the existing section 13 of the United Nations budget shall be maintained for 1972 at its current level of $5,408,000 and its operations shall be concentrated substantially to support country programmes of the least developed among the developing countries as well as regional and sub-regional programmes of special interest to those countries.

Other matters concerning regional economic activities

During 1971, the Economic and Social Council took a number of other decisions concerning the regional economic commissions and the United Nations Economic and Social Office at Beirut (UNESOB).

On 11 December 1970,[9] the General Assembly had recommended that the Council consider changing the names of the four regional economic commissions to "economic and social commissions." On 20 July 1971, the Council—after taking note of the views expressed by the regional economic commissions regarding the proposed renaming and of the views of the Secretary-General as reflected in the report of the 1971 meetings of the executive secretaries of the regional economic commissions—decided to retain the current names of the regional economic commissions.

This decision was set forth in resolution 1610(LI), which was adopted, without objection, on the recommendation of the Council's Economic Committee. The text had been proposed by the

Chairman of the Economic Committee and approved without vote by the Committee on 16 July 1971. (For text of resolution, see DOCUMENTARY REFERENCES below.)

Also at its mid-1971 session, the Council had before it a preliminary report by the Secretary-General on various aspects of the regional structures of the United Nations, prepared in accordance with a Council request of 30 July 1970.[10] The report took into account the responses to a questionnaire on the strengthening and co-ordination of the regional structures, which had been sent to Governments by the Secretary-General.

On 20 July 1971, the Council, on the recommendation of its Co-ordination Committee and without taking a vote, took note of the preliminary report of the Secretary-General, and of the

[9]See Y.U.N., pp. 437-38, text of resolution 2686(XXV).
[10]*Ibid.*, p. 439, text of resolution 1553(XLIX).

comments thereon of the Committee for Programme and Co-ordination, and endorsed the Secretary-General's suggestion that his final report on the subject be submitted to the Council at its mid-1972 session.

Also on 20 July 1971, the Council, without vote, took note with appreciation of the report on the two meetings of the executive secretaries of the regional economic commissions held in 1971 (in New York from 27 to 29 January, and in Geneva, Switzerland, from 28 to 30 June and on 3 July).

A series of other decisions by the Council in a variety of fields also concerned regional economic activities.

In calling for co-ordination of United Nations activities in the field of statistics, the Council requested the regional economic commissions and UNESOB, among other agencies, to co-operate fully with the Statistical Commission in achieving an integrated system in the collection, data processing and dissemination of international statistics by the organs and agencies of the United Nations system. This decision was set forth in resolution 1566(L), adopted on 3 May 1971. (For text of resolution, see pp. 331-32.)

In recognizing that the regional development approach could be an important instrument for achieving the goals and objectives of the International Development Strategy for the Second United Nations Development Decade, the Council: (*a*) endorsed the recommendation of the *Ad Hoc* Advisory Committee for the Research and Training Programme in Regional Development that vigorous efforts should be made to increase multinational as well as national research and training centres, within the context of existing

regional development projects; and (*b*) requested the Secretary-General, in co-operation with the specialized agencies, the United Nations Development Programme and other multilateral and regional institutions, to work out arrangements by which resources could be mobilized and utilized for research and training within regional development projects supported by them. These decisions were included in resolution 1582(L), which was adopted on 21 May 1971. (For text of resolution, see p. 369.)

In reaffirming the need for effective international assistance for the trade promotion efforts of the developing countries, as called for in the International Development Strategy for the Second Development Decade, the Council urged developed countries to give their full support to the regional export promotion centres, as well as to other agencies and organizations participating in the United Nations export promotion programme. This decision was set forth in resolution 1620(LI), adopted on 27 July 1971. (For text of resolution, see p. 287.)

Finally, in noting the need to increase private and public national savings in the developing countries, the Council requested the Secretary-General, the regional economic commissions and UNESOB to continue their technical assistance activities relating to the mobilization of financial resources, in co-operation with the International Bank for Reconstruction and Development, the International Monetary Fund, and other specialized agencies and Governments concerned. This decision was set forth in resolution 1631(LI), adopted on 30 July 1971. (For text of resolution, see p. 305.)

DOCUMENTARY REFERENCES

RENAMING OF COMMISSIONS

Economic and Social Council—51st session
Economic Committee, meetings 528, 530.
Plenary meetings 1773, 1785.

E/4997, Vols. I and II. Annual report of ECA, 15 February 1970–13 February 1971. (Vol. I, paras. 479, 480.)
E/5001. Annual report of ECE, 25 April 1970–30 April 1971, paras. 195, 196.
E/5020. Annual report of ECAFE, 28 April 1970–30 April 1971, paras. 484, 485, and Part III (resolution 113(XXVII)).
E/5027 (Vol.I) and Add.1 (Vol. II). Annual report of ECLA, 8 May 1970–8 May 1971 (Vol. I, paras. 517, 518 and 538).
E/5039. Report of meetings of executive secretaries of regional economic commissions held in 1971 (New York, 27-29 January 1971; Geneva, Switzerland, 28-30 June and 3 July 1971), Chapter X.
E/AC.6/L.423 and Rev.1. Proposal by Chairman of Economic Committee, and revision, approved without vote by Economic Committee on 16 July 1971, meeting 530.
E/5054 and Corr.1. Report of Economic Committee, draft resolution XI.

RESOLUTION 1610(LI), as recommended by Economic Commit-

tee, E/5054, adopted without objection by Council on 20 July 1971, meeting 1785.

The Economic and Social Council,
Having considered, as recommended in General Assembly resolution 2686(XXV) of 11 December 1970, the question of renaming the regional economic commissions,
Taking note of the views expressed by the regional economic commissions regarding the proposed renaming of the commissions,
Noting further the views of the Secretary-General as reflected in paragraph 54 of the report of the meetings of the executive secretaries of the regional economic commissions held in 1971,
Decides to retain the present names of the regional economic commissions.

STUDY ON REGIONAL STRUCTURES

Economic and Social Council—51st session
Co-ordination Committee, meeting 423.
Plenary meetings 1773, 1785.

E/5030 and Add.1,2. Preliminary report of Secretary-General.
E/5038. Report of Committee for Programme and Co-ordination on its 9th session, 24 May–14 June 1971, Chapter VII.

E/5039. Report of meetings of executive secretaries of regional economic commissions held in 1971 (New York, 27-29 January 1971; Geneva, Switzerland, 28-30 June and 3 July 1971), Chapter IV.

E/5053. Report of Co-ordination Committee.

E/5073. Resolutions adopted by Economic and Social Council during its 51st session, 5-30 July 1971. Other decisions, p. 10.

A/8403. Report of Economic and Social Council on work of its 50th and 51st sessions, Chapter XIII D.

REPORT ON MEETINGS OF EXECUTIVE SECRETARIES

Economic and Social Council—51st session
Co-ordination Committee, meeting 423.
Plenary meeting 1773, 1785.

E/5039. Report of meetings of executive secretaries of regional

economic commissions held in 1971 (New York, 27-29 January 1971; Geneva, Switzerland, 28-30 June and 3 July 1971).

E/5053. Report of Co-ordination Committee.

E/5073. Resolutions adopted by Economic and Social Council during its 51st session, 5-30 July 1971. Other decisions, p. 10.

A/8403. Report of Economic and Social Council on work of its 50th and 51st sessions, Chapter XIII B.

Other documents

A/C.2/272. Report of Economic and Social Council. Letter of 17 November 1971 from Bulgaria, Byelorussian SSR, Czechoslovakia, Hungary, Mongolia, Poland, Romania, Ukrainian SSR and USSR (transmitting "Comprehensive Programme for Further Extension and Improvement of Co-operation and Development of Socialist Economic Integration of CMEA Member Countries").

Chapter XIII

Matters pertaining to food problems

Protein resources

During 1971, both the Economic and Social Council and the General Assembly took up the question of protein resources and considered a report submitted by the Secretary-General entitled "Strategy Statement on Action to Avert the Protein Crisis in the Developing Countries."

In the report, which was prepared by a high-level panel of experts convened by the Secretary-General, it was proposed that the Protein Advisory Group, a co-operative venture of the Food and Agriculture Organization of the United Nations (FAO), the World Health Organization (WHO) and the United Nations Children's Fund (UNICEF), be expanded and strengthened to serve as the principal technical body to deal with protein questions in the United Nations system.

The report suggested also that a new inter-governmental committee, capable of mobilizing international opinion and action, and a special protein fund to assist in resolving the edible protein crisis be established.

On 30 July 1971, concerned at the critical edible protein situation in the developing countries and convinced that urgent and concerted effort was needed to avert a crisis, the Economic and Social Council asked the Administrator of the United Nations Development Programme (UNDP) to circulate the substantive portions of the Secretary-General's report to the resident representatives of UNDP, with a view to maximizing their efforts and collaboration with various Governments.

The Council urged that greater emphasis in meeting the problem be placed on national development planning. Governments of devel-

oped countries Members of the United Nations were urged to reinforce their support of programmes and projects dealing with the problem on bilateral and multilateral levels.

The Council recommended that appropriate United Nations organs and the specialized agencies participate in the FAO/WHO/UNICEF Protein Advisory Group so as to broaden the Group's activities and include in it all organizations concerned. The legislative bodies of UNICEF, FAO, WHO and the United Nations Educational, Scientific and Cultural Organization (UNESCO) and other appropriate bodies of the United Nations family were requested to discuss the strategy statement for solving the protein gap as proposed in the report. Experts of the Protein Advisory Group were asked to participate in those discussions. Finally, the Protein Advisory Group was requested to submit an annual progress report on its efforts in finding a solution to the problem of the protein gap, with suggestions and options for possible courses of action by the inter-governmental bodies concerned.

These decisions were embodied in resolution 1640(LI), which the Council adopted unanimously on the recommendation of its Co-ordination Committee, in which the text had been unanimously approved on 23 July 1971 on the basis of a proposal by Ghana, Kenya, the USSR and the United States, as orally amended by France. (For text of resolution, see DOCUMENTARY REFERENCES below.) The text approved in the Committee had combined the views presented in earlier texts proposed by Kenya and by the United States.

Later in the year, at its twenty-sixth session,

which opened on 21 September 1971, the General Assembly took decisions on the question of protein resources by adopting resolution 2848(XXVI), on 20 December 1971. Annexed to the resolution was a list of essential elements of the Strategy Statement on Action to Avert the Protein Crisis in the Developing Countries.

By preambular paragraphs of the resolution, the Assembly recognized that the protein problem was part of the general problem of food production and supply and that protein-calorie malnutrition was the primary cause of high infant and child mortality. It also considered that it was in the interests of developing countries to make increased use of assistance available for dealing with problems of food supply and nutrition.

The ultimate solution to the protein problem, the Assembly recognized, could only be found over the long term, but immediate action with respect to vulnerable groups was required.

By operative paragraphs, the developing countries were urged to establish or emphasize short-term priorities and undertake special action and information programmes with regard to protein malnutrition. They were also urged to draw up a comprehensive statement of national nutrition policy, to encourage studies of their food and nutrition situations and the training of professional personnel in this field.

The developed countries were urged to reinforce their support for both bilateral and multilateral projects and programmes dealing with the protein problem.

The Assembly recommended to the sponsoring agencies that the terms of reference of the Protein Advisory Group be modified to enable it to broaden its activities and play a more active and stimulative role. It urged all United Nations bodies concerned, in particular the World Food Programme, the International Labour Organisation, UNESCO and the International Atomic Energy Agency, to become full sponsors of the Protein Advisory Group so that the Group could effectively carry out its terms of reference in support of the United Nations system.

The Secretary-General was requested, in consultation with the Administrator of UNDP, the Secretary-General of the United Nations Conference on Trade and Development and the Executive Director of the United Nations Industrial Development Organization, to study and report to the Council in 1972 on the possible modalities of United Nations sponsorship of the Protein Advisory Group.

The Secretary-General was also requested, among other things, to seek the views of Governments on the recommendation for the establishment of a special protein fund under UNDP, and to report to the General Assembly in 1972 through

the Economic and Social Council on its feasibility.

Resolution 2848(XXVI) in which these decisions were embodied was adopted, by 109 votes to 0, with 10 abstentions, on the recommendation of the Assembly's Second (Economic and Financial) Committee. The Committee had approved the text on 15 December 1971, by 68 votes to 0, with 9 abstentions, on a revised proposal of Canada, Costa Rica, Denmark, Indonesia, Kenya, New Zealand, Nicaragua and the Philippines. (For text, see DOCUMENTARY REFERENCES below.)

Amendments proposed by Chile in the course of the Second Committee's discussion were withdrawn after the suggestions had been incorporated into the final revision approved by the Committee.

Annexed to resolution 2848(XXVI) were 16 elements considered essential to the Strategy Statement on Action to Avert the Protein Crisis in the Developing Countries. (For text, see DOCUMENTARY REFERENCES below.)

The green revolution

Before the Economic and Social Council at its July 1971 session was a report prepared by the Administrative Committee on Co-ordination on the implications of the so-called green revolution—the technology involving the introduction and increasing application of new varieties of high-yielding food crops and the complex variety of measures required to support it.

On 30 July 1971, the Council took note with appreciation of the report and endorsed the broad lines for inter-agency planning and concerted action-oriented programming indicated in it.

In this connexion, the Council recognized that the impact of the green revolution extended far beyond the field of agricultural technology, covered a wide social and economic field and therefore called for concerted multidisciplinary action by the United Nations system as a whole.

It was recommended that Governments of United Nations Members, bodies within the United Nations system and other international organizations concerned give close attention in their plans to the promotion of action-oriented projects in respect of the green revolution.

The Council recommended that attention be given to spreading the benefits of the green revolution to a wider range of agricultural conditions and income groups and that close attention be given to the impact of the new technology on socio-economic development.

The initiative of the Food and Agriculture Organization in intensifying contacts with potential sources of aid in order to further the objective of spreading the new technology was welcomed by the Council.

Finally, the Council decided that a review and

appraisal of progress in the application of the new technology be made in 1975, at the mid-term of the Second United Nations Development Decade.

These decisions were embodied in resolution 1645(LI) which was adopted, by 25 votes to 0, with 2 abstentions, on the recommendation of the Council's Co-ordination Committee. The Commit-

tee had approved the text without vote on 26 July 1971, on the basis of a proposal by Indonesia and the United States, as amended by Norway. (For text of resolution, see DOCUMENTARY REFERENCES below.)

(See also p. 461.)

DOCUMENTARY REFERENCES

Protein resources

Economic and Social Council—51st session
Co-ordination Committee, meetings 426-429, 433.
Plenary meeting 1799.

Strategy Statement on Action to Avert the Protein Crisis in the Developing Countries. Report of the Panel of Experts on the Protein Problem Confronting Developing Countries, 3–7 May 1971 (E/5018/Rev.1). U.N.P. Sales No.: E.71.II.A.17.
E/5012 (part I). Development and co-ordination of activities of organizations within United Nations system. Report of Administrative Committee on Co-ordination (ACC), Chapter I B, paras. 18, 19.
E/5047. Comments by ACC on report of meeting of Panel of Experts on protein problem.
E/AC.24/L.404. Kenya: draft resolution.
E/AC.24/L.405. United States: draft resolution.
E/AC.24/L.408. Ghana, Kenya, USSR, United States: draft resolution, as orally amended by France and as orally revised by sponsors, approved unanimously by Co-ordination Committee on 23 July 1971, meeting 429.
E/5068. Report of Co-ordination Committee, draft resolution IV.

RESOLUTION 1640(LI), as recommended by Co-ordination Committee, E/5068, adopted unanimously by Council on 30 July 1971, meeting 1799.

The Economic and Social Council,
Feeling that the Secretary-General's report on edible protein, distributed too late to be the subject of detailed examination by the Council, deserves further and more comprehensive study by national Governments and all appropriate intergovernmental bodies of the United Nations system,
Concerned at the critical edible protein situation in the developing countries,
Convinced that urgent and concerted effort is needed to avert a crisis,
Recognizing that in the United Nations system technical expertise at present exists in the FAO/WHO/UNICEF Protein Advisory Group,
Further convinced that the developing countries themselves must play a major role if a crisis is to be averted,
Recognizing that a basic problem is the question of spreading awareness of the acuteness of the problem, and of the means of dealing with it, at the appropriate governmental levels in both the developed and developing countries,
Recognizing further that the appropriate national policy-level representatives convene at present on a regular basis in the meetings of the legislative bodies of the United Nations Children's Fund, the Food and Agriculture Organization of the United Nations, the United Nations Educational, Scientific and Cultural Organization, the World Health Organization and other appropriate United Nations organizations,
1. *Commends* the Secretary-General for his report and the strategy statement of the high-level panel of independent experts, prepared in response to General Assembly resolution 2684(XXV) of 11 December 1970;
2. *Requests* the Administrator of the United Nations Development Programme to circulate the substantive portions of the report (chapters I, II, III and the annex) to the resident representatives of the Programme, with a view to maximizing their efforts and

collaboration with the various Governments, so that this very important problem can be brought more forcibly to the attention of the national development planning officials at the highest possible level;
3. *Urges* that greater emphasis in meeting this problem be placed on national development planning;
4. *Urges also* the Governments of developed countries Members of the United Nations to reinforce their support for programmes and projects dealing with the problem on bilateral and multilateral levels;
5. *Recommends* the appropriate United Nations organs and the specialized agencies to participate in the FAO/WHO/UNICEF Protein Advisory Group, in order to broaden its activities, and continues to urge the expansion of that Group to include all the organizations concerned;
6. *Requests* the legislative bodies of the United Nations Children's Fund, the Food and Agriculture Organization of the United Nations, the United Nations Educational, Scientific and Cultural Organization, the World Health Organization and other appropriate bodies of the United Nations family of organizations, including the Advisory Committee on the Application of Science and Technology to Development, to incorporate in their agendas as a major topic for consideration, at the earliest possible date, the discussion of the strategy statement for solving the protein gap as contained in chapters I, II and III and the annex of the report of the Secretary-General, and requests that appropriate experts of the Protein Advisory Group be invited to participate in the consideration of the strategy by these bodies;
7. *Requests* the Protein Advisory Group to submit to the appropriate intergovernmental bodies of the United Nations system an annual report giving an analysis of the progress and problems encountered in the solution of the problem of the protein gap, with suggestions and options for possible courses of action by these intergovernmental bodies.

General Assembly—26th session
Second Committee, meetings 1370-1382, 1436, 1445, 1446.
Plenary meeting 2026.

A/8403. Report of Economic and Social Council on work of its 50th and 51st sessions, Chapter XII E.
A/C.2/262. Questions relating to science and technology. Note by Secretary-General (Section C. The protein problem).
A/C.2/L.1211 and Rev.1. Canada, Denmark, Indonesia, Kenya, New Zealand: draft resolution and revision.
A/C.2/L.1211/Rev.2,3. Canada, Costa Rica, Denmark, Indonesia, Kenya, New Zealand, Nicaragua, Philippines: revised draft resolution, as further orally revised by sponsors, approved by Second Committee on 15 December 1971, meeting 1446, by 68 votes to 0, with 9 abstentions.
A/C.2/L.1217. Note by Secretary-General (transmitting extract from report of 16th session of Conference of FAO relating to question of production and use of edible protein).
A/C.2/L.1220. Chile: amendments to 8-power revised draft resolution, A/C.2/L.1211/Rev.2.
A/8578/Add.1. Report of Second Committee (part II) (on report of Economic and Social Council), Section XI and draft resolution XI.

RESOLUTION 2848(XXVI), as recommended by Second Committee, A/8578/Add.1, adopted by Assembly on 20 December 1971, meeting 2026, by 109 votes to 0, with 10 abstentions.

The General Assembly,

Recalling its resolutions 2416(XXIII) of 17 December 1968 and 2684(XXV) of 11 December 1970, Economic and Social Council resolution 1640(LI) of 30 July 1971, World Health Assembly resolution WHA22.56 of 25 July 1969 and resolutions 2/69 and 7/71 adopted by the Conference of the Food and Agriculture Organization of the United Nations on 26 November 1969 and 22 November 1971,

Recalling also paragraphs 18 and 69 of the International Development Strategy for the Second United Nations Development Decade,

Bearing in mind the Declaration on the world food problem adopted on 22 March 1968 by the United Nations Conference on Trade and Development at its second session,

Recognizing that the protein problem is part of the general problem of food production and supply, which depends on a great many economic, social, cultural and political factors, including social and economic under-development, which is manifested in unemployment and under-employment, extremely low incomes, poor nutritional habits, poor health and sanitary conditions, low agricultural productivity and serious defects in marketing,

Recognizing also that protein-calorie malnutrition is the primary cause of high infant and child mortality, reaching from 25 to 30 per cent in many developing countries, that it increases susceptibility to infection and can permanently impair growth and development in the survivors, to the detriment of later physical and intellectual performance,

Considering that it is in the interests of developing countries to make increased use of the external—and particularly multilateral—financial and technical assistance available for dealing with problems of food supply and nutrition since the direct and indirect costs of malnutrition to national development are often far more than the amount that would be required for its prevention,

Recognizing that, since the ultimate solution of the protein problem can only be found over the long term while immediate action with respect to vulnerable groups is required if irreversible damage is to be prevented, clear national and international priorities must be set now in taking remedial action, and that consequently external short-term assistance such as emergency food support must be combined with assistance for vital long-range projects,

Acknowledging the programme and assistance activities relating to the protein problem being undertaken by various organizations of the United Nations system and particularly by the Protein Advisory Group and its four sponsoring organizations—the United Nations Children's Fund, the Food and Agriculture Organization of the United Nations, the World Health Organization and the International Bank for Reconstruction and Development—and emphasizing that their efforts must be further integrated to achieve the maximum effectiveness,

Concerned that increasing awareness of the extent and implications of the problem of protein-calorie malnutrition has not led to the type and scope of national or international response required for an effective approach to the solution,

1. *Urges* developing countries to establish or emphasize short-term priorities and undertake special action and information programmes with regard to protein malnutrition in accordance with their respective national plans, since the alleviation of the situation in the short-term must be based upon the improved utilization of existing national and international resources;

2. *Urges* the developed countries to reinforce their support for both bilateral and multilateral projects and programmes dealing with the protein problem in a manner compatible with the requests of the developing countries;

3. *Urges* developing countries:

(a) To draw up comprehensive statements of national nutrition policy and related food and agricultural policy to be incorporated, under the most appropriate administrative arrangements, in their development plans;

(b) To encourage and make the maximum use of surveys and studies of their food and nutrition situations and to encourage the training of the necessary professional personnel in science and technology related to food, agriculture, nutrition and other relevant fields;

4. *Urges* Governments to implement as appropriate, but as soon as possible, the essential elements of the Strategy Statement on Action to Avert the Protein Crisis in the Developing Countries—prepared by the Panel to Assist the Secretary-General in the Formulation of a Strategy Statement on the Protein Problem Confronting the Developing Countries, convened in pursuance of General Assembly resolution 2684(XXV)—as set forth in the annex to the present resolution;

5. *Requests* appropriate United Nations organs, particularly the United Nations Development Programme, the specialized agencies and the International Atomic Energy Agency, to assist the developing countries, at their request, in all possible ways to implement the undertakings set out in paragraphs 1, 3 and 4 above;

6. *Recommends* to the sponsoring agencies that the terms of reference of the Protein Advisory Group should be modified as follows so as to enable the Group to broaden its activities and to play a more active and stimulative role:

(a) To advise on the technical, economic, educational, social and other related aspects of all the programmes within the United Nations system related to improving protein nutrition;

(b) To advise on current programmes and on new areas of activity;

(c) To provide guidelines for the formulation of the broad programmes of the United Nations system of organizations involved in the various aspects of the protein problem;

(d) To seek, evaluate and disseminate new information on all aspects of the protein problem;

(e) To advise on the improvement of procedures for project evaluation and feasibility studies;

(f) To identify, evaluate and advise on problems in protein resource development and protein-calorie malnutrition requiring scientific and technological research;

(g) To advise on such other matters as the various United Nations bodies refer to it;

7. *Urges* the United Nations bodies concerned, in particular the World Food Programme, the International Labour Organisation, the United Nations Educational, Scientific and Cultural Organization and the International Atomic Energy Agency, to become full sponsors of the Protein Advisory Group so that it can effectively carry out its terms of reference in support of the United Nations system;

8. *Requests*, to this same end, the Secretary-General, in consultation with the Administrator of the United Nations Development Programme, the Secretary-General of the United Nations Conference on Trade and Development and the Executive Director of the United Nations Industrial Development Organization, to study and report to the Economic and Social Council at its fifty-second session on the possible modalities of United Nations sponsorship of the Protein Advisory Group;

9. *Commends* paragraphs 6 and 7 of Economic and Social Council resolution 1640(LI) of 30 July 1971 relating to further discussion of the protein strategy in other forums and the submission of annual reports by the Protein Advisory Group;

10. *Welcomes* the recent establishment by the Council of the Food and Agriculture Organization of the United Nations, pursuant to resolution 7/71 adopted on 22 November 1971 by the Conference of that organization, of a special seven-member committee to review the work of the organization in the protein field;

11. *Requests* the Economic and Social Council, during its discussion of the terms of reference of its Committee on Science and Technology, to give sympathetic consideration to inviting appropriate representation of the Protein Advisory Group to sessions of the Committee held to review and focus attention on the protein problem and to urging Governments, the United Nations and the specialized agencies concerned to assign representatives at a high level to attend such meetings;

12. *Requests* the Secretary-General, in co-operation with the Administrator of the United Nations Development Programme and in consultation with the executive heads of the organizations sponsoring the Protein Advisory Group, to arrange, at the request of Governments, for persons who took part in the Panel convened by the Secretary-General in pursuance of General Assembly

resolution 2684(XXV) to visit the Governments in order to enhance the establishment of national policies and arrangements to deal with the protein problem, and to report as appropriate to the Committee on Science and Technology;

13. *Further requests* the Secretary-General to seek the views of Governments on the recommendation of the Panel and of the Advisory Committee on the Application of Science and Technology to Development for the establishment of a special protein fund under the United Nations Development Programme in order to ascertain the views of Governments on its feasibility and to ascertain whether significant resources would be made available to it without prejudice to the increased resources envisaged for the Programme, and to report to the General Assembly at its twenty-seventh session through the Economic and Social Council.

ANNEX

Essential elements of the Strategy Statement on Action to Avert the Protein Crisis in the Developing Countries

1. Make every effort to increase the production of food crops, particularly through the exploitation of new high-yield varieties, bearing in mind the special need for an expanded production of protein-rich pulses and oilseeds;

2. Encourage accelerated and expanded research designed to improve the nutritive value of cereal proteins through genetic engineering;

3. Encourage accelerated and expanded research designed to develop high-yielding pulses, legumes and oilseed crops;

4. Encourage the increased production of animal proteins, particularly through research on increasing forage yields and production;

5. Make every effort to prevent an unnecessary loss of protein-containing foods in field, storage, transport and home;

6. Encourage increased production from marine and fresh-water fishery resources;

7. Encourage the development, distribution and promotion of formulated protein foods;

8. Facilitate the application of science and technology to the development of new protein sources in order to supplement conventional food resources;

9. Develop and support regional and national centres for research and training in agricultural technology, food science, food technology and nutrition;

10. Conduct informational and educational campaigns related to protein production and consumption;

11. Improve protein utilization through the control and prevention of infectious diseases;

12. Review and improve policies, legislation and regulations regarding all aspects of food and protein production, processing and marketing so as to remove unnecessary obstacles and encourage appropriate activities;

13. Give special attention to the protein needs of vulnerable groups;

14. Initiate intervention programmes aimed at ensuring that vulnerable groups will receive the most appropriate type and a sufficient quantity of food by the most effective means;

15. Recognize the important relationships between family size, population growth and the protein problem;

16. Recognize the role of economic development and social modernization in solving the protein problem.

The green revolution

Economic and Social Council—51st session
Co-ordination Committee, meetings 413, 416-419, 431.
Plenary meeting 1799.

E/5012 (part II). Development and co-ordination of activities of organizations within United Nations system. Special report prepared by Administrative Committee on Co-ordination on implications of "green revolution."

E/5038. Report of Committee for Programme and Co-ordination on its 9th session, 24 May–14 June 1971, Chapter IV, para. 29.

E/AC.24/L.406. Indonesia and United States: draft resolution, as amended by Norway (E/AC.24/L.410, as orally sub-amended by Brazil and by Pakistan), approved without vote by Co-ordination Committee on 26 July 1971, meeting 431.

E/AC.24/L.410. Norway: amendments to 2-power draft resolution, E/AC.24/L.406.

E/5069. Report of Co-ordination Committee, draft resolution IV.

RESOLUTION 1645(LI), as recommended by Co-ordination Committee, E/5069, adopted by Council on 30 July 1971, meeting 1799, by 25 votes to 0, with 2 abstentions.

The Economic and Social Council,

Aware of the significant contribution which the wider application and spread of high-yielding varieties of food crops can make towards achieving the agricultural production goals of the Second United Nations Development Decade,

Realizing that attention should be given to the economic, social and human problems which inevitably accompany such a revolutionary process, such attention being a determining factor in ensuring the successful promotion of the new technology,

Noting the new initiative taken jointly by the United Nations Development Programme, the Food and Agriculture Organization of the United Nations and the International Bank for Reconstruction and Development to improve and strengthen international co-operation in the fields of agricultural and allied research,

Taking note with interest of the United Nations/UNDP research project at present being carried out by the United Nations Research Institute for Social Development, in consultation with the International Labour Organisation and the Food and Agriculture Organization of the United Nations, on the social implications of the large-scale introduction of high-yielding varieties of food grains,

Considering that the successful application of new high-yielding varieties of grains requires a more accessible and greatly increased availability of material inputs,

Recognizing that the impact of the green revolution extends far beyond the field of agricultural technology, covers also a wide field of social and economic aspects, and therefore calls for concerted multidisciplinary action by the United Nations system as a whole,

1. *Takes note with appreciation* of the special report prepared by the Administrative Committee on Co-ordination on the implications of the green revolution and the initiative of that Committee in thus bringing to the notice of the Council the opportunities offered by the spread of the new technology for a truly co-ordinated effort throughout the whole of the United Nations system;

2. *Endorses* the broad lines for inter-agency planning and concerted action-oriented programming in this particular area of economic and social development, indicated in the special report mentioned in paragraph 1 above;

3. *Recommends* the Governments of Member States, the regional economic commissions, the specialized agencies, the International Atomic Energy Agency and the other international organizations concerned to give close attention, in their short-term and medium-term plans, to the promotion of concerted and meaningful action-oriented projects in respect of the green revolution;

4. *Recommends* that attention also be given to spreading the benefits of the green revolution to a wider range of agricultural conditions and income groups, through continued research to develop high-yielding varieties of food crops not already covered by existing programmes;

5. *Further recommends* that close attention be given to the impact of the new technology on socio-economic development, including environmental aspects, taking into account, *inter alia,* the findings of the study on the social implications of the new agricultural technology now being undertaken by the United Nations Research Institute for Social Development;

6. *Welcomes* the initiative of the Food and Agriculture Organization of the United Nations in intensifying contacts with potential sources of both international and bilateral aid, especially in respect of research and food production resources, in order to further the objective of spreading the new technology;

7. *Urges* the United Nations Development Programme and other financial institutions to give careful consideration to the special report of the Administrative Committee on Co-ordination and to take it into account in assisting Governments in their country programming;

8. *Decides* that a review and appraisal of progress in the application of this new technology be made at the mid-term of the Second United Nations Development Decade, within the framework of the arrangements that may be established for that purpose and in co-operation with the Administrative Committee on Co-ordination.

A/8403. Report of Economic and Social Council on work of its 50th and 51st sessions, Chapter XXI C.

Chapter XIV

Population questions

During 1971, population questions were taken up by a number of bodies in the United Nations system, and the General Assembly took decisions concerning the United Nations Fund for Population Activities.

Preparations continued for the World Population Conference, scheduled to be held in 1974, and for World Population Year, 1974.

Technical assistance activities in the population field expanded, and meetings were held on various aspects of the subject.

Activities in 1971

The United Nations continued to provide advice and technical evaluation with respect to programme development in the population field, and to provide substantive support to projects financed under the United Nations Fund for Population Activities (UNFPA), the United Nations Development Programme (UNDP) and the regular programme of technical co-operation.

Approximately 140 projects of various types were taken up in 1971 with UNFPA financing. These included the services of experts, as well as fellowships and missions.

Twelve experts carried out assignments in Africa, Asia, the Caribbean, Latin America and the Middle East, to assist developing countries in identifying population problems and in preparing projects in the population field. They visited 62 countries in 1971—28 in Africa, 9 in Asia, 16 in Latin America and the Caribbean, and 9 in the Middle East; and were actively involved in the development of about 160 country projects in 85 countries.

In addition, the services of another 21 experts—5 in Africa, 6 in Asia, 8 in Latin America and 2 in the Middle East—were provided by the United Nations to 14 countries in 1971: Ceylon, China, Dominican Republic, Guatemala, Haiti, Honduras, Iran, Jordan, Nicaragua, Nigeria, the Philippines, Sierra Leone, the Syrian Arab Republic and Western Samoa.

Experts were also provided to the three regional demographic training and research centres supported by the United Nations in Chile, India and Egypt, which continued to provide basic training facilities for students. Two additional regional demographic centres were established in 1971 in Africa, one in Cameroon and the other in Ghana.

An expanded United Nations fellowship training programme was established during the year. About 175 fellowships were granted in 1971, one half for attendance at the regional demographic centres and one half for study at other institutes.

At the request of Iran and Ceylon, inter-agency missions visited those countries to review and advise on their family planning programmes.

An expert group on social welfare aspects of family planning met in New York in March 1971 to advise on policy and programme formulation, training of social welfare personnel, and co-operation at the international and regional levels.

Two expert groups were convened by the United Nations in June 1971: one on population research in national institutions, which met in Lyon, France; the other on methods of analysing fertility data for developing countries, which met in Budapest, Hungary.

An *ad hoc* consultative group of experts on population policy was convened in New York from 15 to 17 December 1971, to advise the Secretary-General on the nature and future development of United Nations activities in the field of population policy.

A variety of other meetings and seminars were convened under the auspices of the United Nations regional economic bodies in Africa, Asia and the Far East, the Middle East, and Latin America.

United Nations Fund for Population Activities

In 1971, funding targets for the United Nations Fund for Population Activities were surpassed (a $25 million goal for the year was oversubscribed by almost \$4 million) and the list of donors increased from 24 in 1970 to 46 in 1971.

Resources of the Fund were used in 1971 to assist 206 regional and inter-regional projects and 114 new national projects in 60 countries. New agreements were negotiated during the year for major country programmes in Iran, the Philippines and Thailand. A programme was launched in Indonesia with the collaboration for the first time of the International Bank for Reconstruction and Development.

Other executing agencies included the United Nations, the World Health Organization, the United Nations Children's Fund, the International Labour Organisation, the Food and Agriculture Organization and the United Nations Educational, Scientific and Cultural Organization.

Projects financed through the Fund covered a wide range of activities: the collection and analysis of demographic data; the provision of demographic research and training facilities; demonstration programmes in family planning; extension courses relating to population problems; the provision of fellowships in the field; the provision of contraceptive supplies and manufacturing materials; and the formulation of population policies and measures to be taken in accordance with national development objectives.

On 14 December 1971, the General Assembly invited Governments to make voluntary contributions to the Fund, noting that it had become a viable entity in the United Nations system and convinced that it should play a leading role in promoting programmes on the problem of fast population growth as well as on the problem of under-population, which, among other things, could hamper rapid economic development.

The Assembly requested the Secretary-General, in consultation with the Administrator of UNDP and the Executive Director of the Fund, to take action to improve the administrative machinery of the Fund aimed at the efficient and expeditious provision of population programmes, including measures to speed up recruitment and consideration of training experts and personnel in the developing countries.

At the same time, the Assembly recognized the need for the executing agencies of the Fund to implement with dispatch, in close co-operation with the Fund, population programmes requested by developing countries in order that such programmes might have the desired impact.

These decisions were embodied in resolution 2815(XXVI), adopted, by 94 votes to 0, with 20 abstentions, on the recommendation of the Assembly's Second (Economic and Financial) Committee, which approved the text on 1 December 1971, by 59 votes to 0, with 17 abstentions. The Committee acted on the basis of a text proposed by Denmark, Indonesia, Iran, Japan, Jordan, Kenya, the Netherlands, Norway, Pakistan, the Philippines, Singapore, Sweden and Thailand, as amended by Ethiopia. (For text of resolution, see DOCUMENTARY REFERENCES below.)

World Population Conference and Year

The Preparatory Committee for the 1974 World Population Conference, an inter-agency body established by the Secretary-General,[1] met twice in 1971. It recommended, *inter alia*, agenda items for the World Population Conference, the third of its kind, scheduled to be held from 19 to 30 August 1974 at United Nations Headquarters, New York.

The Preparatory Committee also made some general recommendations about a proposed world programme for observing the World Population Year.[2]

Taking into account the suggestions of the Preparatory Committee and recommendations of various other bodies within the United Nations system, the Secretary-General proposed a programme of measures and activities for World Population Year and submitted it for consideration by the Economic and Social Council Population Commission, which met in Geneva, Switzerland, from 1 to 12 November 1971.

Population Commission

The Population Commission reviewed progress during 1970–1971 in carrying out the programme of work it had recommended at its 1969 session, and drew up five-year and two-year programmes of work and priorities for the period 1972–76.

The Commission approved a four-part draft resolution on population and development, for final adoption by the Economic and Social Council in 1972. The four parts of the resolution dealt with: (*a*) population problems and the Second United Nations Development Decade; (*b*) the World Population Conference, 1974; (*c*) the World Population Year, 1974; and (*d*) work programmes and priorities.

By part A, the Council among other things would urge all Member States of the United Nations to: (*a*) give full attention to their demographic objectives and measures during the biennial review and appraisal of progress in achieving the objectives of the Second United Nations Development Decade, and take the necessary steps to improve demographic statistics, research, and the planning machinery needed for developing population policies and programmes; (*b*) co-operate in achieving a substantial reduction of the rate of population growth in those countries

---

[1]See Y.U.N., 1970, pp. 470-71, text of resolution 1484(XLVIII), authorizing the Secretary-General to establish the Preparatory Committee.
[2]*Ibid.*, pp. 468-469, text of resolution 1485(XLVIII), designating 1974 as World Population Year.

that considered their present rate too high; (c) ensure—in accordance with their national population policies and needs—that information and education on family planning, and the means to practise effectively such planning, were made available to all individuals by the end of the Second Development Decade.

By part B of the draft resolution, on the World Population Conference to be held in 1974, the Council would call upon all Member States to participate in the Conference and to report on the actions they had taken in developing their population policies, programmes and activities. The Council would also request the Secretary-General to elaborate further the programme and arrangements for the Conference.

By part C of the draft resolution, on the World Population Year, 1974, the Council, among other things, would invite all United Nations Member States to take part in World Population Year, especially to promote activities that would improve knowledge and awareness, as well as policies and measures relative to population and development, and would request the Secretary-General to render all possible assistance to Member States to enable them to participate fully in the activities of the Year.

By part D, on work programmes and priorities, the Council would invite the regional economic commissions to further develop their two-year and five-year programmes of work in the population field in conformity with their regional needs. It would also invite the United Nations agencies concerned to co-operate to support population activities and the implementation of population programmes requested by Governments. The Council would also request the Secretary-General to undertake a number of activities relating to population questions.

The Population Commission believed that it, and the World Population Conference, should give the highest priority to the consideration of social, economic and other conditions conducive to the attainment of national demographic objectives. It was of the opinion that it should keep under continuous review the progress achieved in carrying out the programmes and activities relevant to population and the Second United Nations Development Decade, the 1974 World Population Conference and World Population Year. It recommended therefore that a special short session of the Commission be held in mid-1972, preferably in New York.

Publications

A study on *Methods of Projecting the Economically Active Population*, produced by the United Nations and the International Labour Organisation, was published in 1971. It described methods of projecting the economically active population with regard to both the labour supply and the labour demand.

A Concise Summary of the World Population Situation in 1970 was published, as was a more extensive report on the same subject, entitled *The World Population Situation in 1970*.

The *Demographic Yearbook, 1970*, published in 1971, included historical trends of population for the period 1950-70, continuing those for 1920–60 that appeared in the 1960 issue, and the statistics on enumerated population by sex during 1900–70.

The *Monthly Bulletin of Statistics* expanded its coverage of demographic data in 1971, in response to a Population Commission recommendation that this be done by augmenting the demographic tables regularly published therein and by including in the special tables information of a demographic nature at least twice a year.

DOCUMENTARY REFERENCES

United Nations Fund for Population Activities

General Assembly—26th session
Second Committee, meetings 1385, 1425.
Plenary meeting 2017.

A/8401. Report of Secretary-General on work of the Organization, 16 June 1970–15 June 1971, Part Three, Chapters II A 3 and VI B 1.
A/8401/Add.1. Introduction to report of Secretary-General, September 1971, para. 244.
A/C.2/L.1187. Denmark, Indonesia, Japan, Jordan, Kenya, Netherlands, Norway, Philippines, Singapore, Sweden: draft resolution.
A/C.2/L.1187/Rev.1,2. Denmark, Indonesia, Iran, Japan, Jordan, Kenya, Netherlands, Norway, Pakistan, Philippines, Singapore, Sweden, Thailand: revised draft resolution, as orally amended by sponsors and by Ethiopia, approved by Second Committee on 1 December 1971, meeting 1425, by 59 votes to 0, with 17 abstentions.
A/8563. Report of Second Committee (on operational activities for development), draft resolution VII.

RESOLUTION 2815(XXVI), as recommended by Second Committee, A/8563, adopted by Assembly on 14 December 1971, meeting 2017, by 94 votes to 0, with 20 abstentions.

The General Assembly,
Recalling Economic and Social Council resolution 1084(XXXIX) of 30 July 1965 on the work programmes and priorities in the population fields,
Recalling further its resolution 2211(XXI) of 17 December 1966, in response to which a trust fund, subsequently named the United Nations Fund for Population Activities, was established in 1967 by the Secretary-General,
Bearing in mind the International Development Strategy for the Second United Nations Development Decade, contained in General Assembly resolution 2626(XXV) of 24 October 1970, with particular reference to the demographic objectives and policy measures set forth in paragraphs 13 and 65 of the Strategy,
Recognizing the responsibility of the Population Commission to assist the Economic and Social Council in accordance with its terms of reference, as defined in Council resolution 150(VII) of 10 August 1948,

Noting that the Secretary-General has requested the Administrator of the United Nations Development Programme to administer the United Nations Fund for Population Activities and that an Executive Director of the Fund has been appointed,

Further noting with satisfaction the progress made to date by the Fund to which, so far, thirty-two countries have contributed,

Aware that the Fund has now become a viable entity in the United Nations system,

Convinced that the Fund should play a leading role in the United Nations system in promoting population programmes—consistent with the decisions of the General Assembly and the Economic and Social Council—on the problem of fast population growth as well as on the problem of under-population, which could, among other things, hamper rapid economic development,

Recognizing the need for the executing agencies of the Fund to implement with dispatch, in close co-operation with the Fund, population programmes requested by developing countries in order that such programmes may have the desired impact,

Expressing its appreciation of the efforts of the Secretary-General, which have resulted in the unprecedented growth and expansion of the Fund, and of the support extended by the Administrator of the United Nations Development Programme,

1. *Invites* Governments which are in a position to do so and whose policies would allow it to make voluntary contributions to the United Nations Fund for Population Activities;

2. *Requests* the Secretary-General, in consultation with the Administrator of the United Nations Development Programme and the Executive Director of the United Nations Fund for Population Activities, to take the necessary steps to achieve the desired improvements in the administrative machinery of the Fund aimed at the efficient and expeditious delivery of population programmes, including measures to quicken the pace of recruiting the experts and personnel required to cope with the increasing volume of requests, as well as to consider the training of experts and personnel in the developing countries;

3. *Further requests* the Secretary-General to inform the Economic and Social Council at its fifty-third session and the General Assembly at its twenty-seventh session of the steps he has taken in the implementation of the present resolution and of any recommendations he may wish to make in this regard.

World Population Conference and Year

E/CONF.60/PC/1. Report of Preparatory Committee for World Population Conference, 1974, on its first session, Geneva, Switzerland, 22–26 February 1971.

E/CONF.60/PC/2. Report of Preparatory Committee for World Population Conference, 1974, on its 2nd session, Paris, France, 16–22 June 1971.

Population Commission

E/5090. Report of Population Commission on its 16th session, Geneva, Switzerland, 1–12 November 1971. (Annex III. List of documents before Commission.)

E/5090. Chapter IX. Recommendations requiring action by Economic and Social Council.

Publications and reports

Methods of Projecting the Economically Active Population (Manual V of Manuals on Methods of Estimating Population). Population Studies, No. 46. U.N.P. Sales No.: E.70.XIII.2.

A Concise Summary of the World Population Situation in 1970. Population Studies, No. 48. U.N.P. Sales No.:E.71.XIII.2.

The World Population Situation in 1970. Population Studies, No. 49. U.N.P. Sales No.: E.71.XIII.4.

Measures, Policies and Programmes Affecting Fertility, with Particular Reference to National Family Planning Programmes. Population Studies, No. 51. U.N.P. Sales No.: E.72.XIII.2.

Interim Report on Conditions and Trends of Fertility in the World, 1960–1965. Population Studies, No. 52. U.N.P. Sales No.: E.72.XIII.3 and corrigendum.

ST/SOA/SER.R/13. Population and family planning in Iran. Note by Secretary-General (attaching report).

ST/SOA/SER.R/14. Family planning evaluation mission to Ceylon. Note by Secretary-General (attaching report).

Demographic Yearbook, 1970. U.N.P. Sales No.: E/F.71.XIII.1; 1971. U.N.P. Sales No.: E/F.72.XIII.1.

Monthly Bulletin of Statistics, Vol. XXV, Nos. 1-12 (January-December 1971).

Population and Vital Statistics Report. Statistical Papers, Series A (ST/STAT/SER.A/95-98), Vol. XXIII, Nos. 1, 2, 3, 4 (data available as of 1 January, 1 April, 1 July, 1 October 1971).

Chapter XV

Social questions

Social development and policy

World social situation

During 1971, both the Economic and Social Council and the General Assembly took a number of decisions concerning the world social situation. Their deliberations on the subject were based primarily on the *1970 Report on the World Social Situation,* which discussed social development during the latter half of the First United Nations Development Decade, and considered social trends in both the developed and the developing countries by sector and region. Part One of the *Report* consisted of regional surveys of trends and programmes in all regions of the world. Part Two reviewed by sector (such as health, education, nutrition) the changes of levels of living and the policies and measures adopted to improve social conditions throughout the world.

The decisions of the Economic and Social Council on the world social situation were embodied in a three-part resolution (resolution 1581(L)), put to the vote on 21 May 1971.

By the first part of resolution 1581(L), the Economic and Social Council, considering that a number of countries had acquired considerable experience in the application of measures leading to social progress, asked the Secretary-General to forward to Members of the United Nations or members of the specialized agencies a questionnaire on their experience in achieving far-reaching social and economic changes for the purposes of social progress. It decided to consider the question again in 1972 or 1973.

The Council noted that the achievement of genuine social progress, including in particular the solution of the problem of employment and the establishment of an adequate standard of living for everyone, and cultural, scientific and educational development required efforts for the attainment of profound economic and social changes in countries which set these objectives.

These decisions were among those set forth in resolution 1581A(L), adopted by a vote of 15 to 0, with 1 abstention, on the recommendation of the Council's Social Committee, which approved the text, as amended by the United States on 10 May 1971, by 21 votes to 0, with 2 abstentions. The text was suggested by the Commission for Social Development. (For text of resolution, see DOCUMENTARY REFERENCES below.)

A United States amendment—to ask the Secretary-General to forward the questionnaire to States Members of the United Nations or members of the specialized agencies (rather than "to all States")—was adopted in the Social Committee by 13 votes to 5, with 4 abstentions.

By the second part of resolution 1581(L), the Council regretted that, despite limited improvement in some sectors, there had been continued deterioration of the world social situation, particularly that arising from growing disparities among the developed and developing countries. It reaffirmed that progress towards general and complete disarmament should release substantial additional resources which could be used for economic and social development.

The primary responsibility for the development of developing countries rested upon themselves, the Council emphasized, but the assistance of developed countries was necessary if developing countries were to achieve the desired goals. The Council called attention to the interdependence of economic and social development and to the consequent need for an integrated approach to planning and development. It also recognized the desirability for countries which considered that their rate of population growth hampered their development to adopt measures they deemed necessary in accordance with their concept of development.

The Council endorsed the conclusion of the *1970 Report on the World Social Situation* that reduction of disparities and inequality existing between developed and developing countries presupposed, among other things, a substantial rise in the income of the developing countries, which necessitated an enlightened, equitable and progressive approach by the developed countries

to the questions of trade, aid and the transfer of technology.

Governments were urged to accelerate development by such measures as increasing popular participation in all aspects of national life, promoting purposeful social change and giving appropriate emphasis to social objectives in planning and development.

It was recommended that the system ultimately adopted for review and appraisal of the objectives and policies of the International Development Strategy for the Second United Nations Development Decade provide for adequate consultation with international and regional trade-union and employers' federations and other major organizations of the people.

The Council reminded Governments of their obligations to implement the International Development Strategy, and developed countries were urged to accelerate the achievement of the targets for trade and financial transfer to developing countries established in the Strategy.

The Council recommended that the *1970 Report on the World Social Situation* should serve as a background document during the Second Development Decade and that in the preparation of future issues of the *Report,* due account should be taken of: evaluation and analysis at the national, sub-regional and regional levels; increased emphasis on an integrated, cross-sectoral analysis of trends and developments; drawing conclusions and making suggestions that would be useful for practical policy-making; and the social situation in colonial and dependent territories, whose progress was hampered by occupation and denial of self-determination.

These decisions were set forth in resolution 1581B(L), adopted, by 18 votes to 0, with 2 abstentions, on the recommendation of the Council's Social Committee, which had approved the text, as amended by Brazil and Pakistan and by Norway, on 10 May 1971, by 21 votes to 0, with 2 abstentions. The text had been suggested by the Commission for Social Development. (For text of resolution, see DOCUMENTARY REFERENCES below.)

A number of amendments to the text were proposed and voted upon in the Social Committee.

The Committee rejected by 14 votes to 5, with 3 abstentions, a United States proposal to delete the reference in the preamble to the deterioration of the world social situation particularly arising from growing disparities among the developed and developing countries and within countries.

Another United States proposal that was rejected, by 13 votes to 6, with 4 abstentions, was intended to replace the operative paragraphs by which the Council would endorse the conclusion of the *1970 Report on the World Social Situation* concerning disparities and inequality between developed and developing countries and by which Governments were reminded of their obligations to implement the International Development Strategy. Instead, the Council would, by the United States proposal, stress the importance of a substantial rise in the income of the developing countries and urge Governments of developed countries to make their greatest efforts to achieve the targets for trade and financial transfer to developing countries established in the Strategy, in order to bring about an early achievement of its goals and objectives.

Norwegian amendments urging consultation with employers' federations, among other social organizations, in the pursuit of social development, were adopted by the Committee.

By the third part of its resolution on the world social situation, the Council offered a number of recommendations to Member States on enhancing social progress and also made a number of decisions concerning the *Report on the World Social Situation.*

The Council recommended that United Nations Members intensify their efforts to enhance social progress and development by: mobilizing domestic resources and effecting necessary structural, administrative and institutional reforms; increasing popular participation in national development; and co-operating with other Members through bilateral assistance and international programmes.

It was recommended that Members pursue a unified approach to development, thus manifesting their belief that social and economic objectives were inseparable, and that they seek to improve the collection of data, analysis and reporting in the social field and undertake a continuing examination of development policies and programmes.

The Council decided that the *Report on the World Social Situation* should serve as a guide for the Second Development Decade and be updated periodically as part of the review and appraisal of social progress during the Decade and that the *1974 Report* should serve as a major assessment at mid-Decade.

It was also suggested, *inter alia,* that future issues of the *Report* contain suggestions for possible action by Governments and by agencies of the United Nations.

These were among decisions set forth in resolution 1581 C (L), adopted, by 11 votes to 4, with 5 abstentions, on the recommendation of the Social Committee, which on 10 May 1971 approved the text, as amended by the United States, by 12 votes to 3, with 7 abstentions. The text had been suggested by the Commission for Social Development. (For text of resolution, see DOCU-MENTARY REFERENCES below.)

On 22 November 1971, the General Assembly also took a number of decisions on the world social situation which, it said, had continued to deteriorate. The Assembly expressed concern that the persistence of poverty, unemployment, hunger, disease, illiteracy, inadequate housing and uncontrolled growth of population in certain parts of the world had acquired new dimensions and that many causes of the growing disparities between the developed and developing countries hindered the advancement of the developing countries.

The Assembly among other things reaffirmed the urgency of taking effective measures aimed at halting the deterioration of the world social situation and promoting social progress and development, and it endorsed the provisions of the second part of the Economic and Social Council's resolution of 21 May 1971 (1581 B (L)) summarized above.

The primary responsibility for the development of developing countries, the Assembly stressed, rested with these countries themselves, but, it also noted, their own efforts would not be sufficient to enable them to achieve the desired goals unless they were assisted by developed countries. The latter were urged to fulfil their obligation to implement the International Development Strategy.

The Assembly emphasized that it was necessary to raise levels of living in the developing countries and that colonialism, racial discrimination, *apartheid,* alien domination, foreign occupation, aggressive wars and other policies of oppression and exploitation were principal obstacles to social progress and development. At the same time, the Assembly reaffirmed the inherent rights of all peoples and the permanent sovereignty of all countries, particularly the developing countries, over their natural resources.

The Assembly, in addition, drew the attention of all States and the United Nations bodies and specialized agencies concerned to a listed number of conclusions and recommendations, based on the *1970 Report on the World Social Situation.* These had to do with such matters as: the improvement in social conditions being dependent on the improvement in international political and economic relations, the social situation of peoples under colonial and alien domination being mentioned as a source of great concern; the resources required for achieving a substantial rise in the incomes of developing countries; promoting economic growth with social justice; disparity in income levels; the growth of unemployment; science and technology; terms of trade; the outflow of qualified personnel from developing countries; the need for broad popular participation in planning and implementing development policies; the needs and aspirations of youth; discriminatory practices against women; and family and child welfare.

The Assembly further called upon Governments and United Nations bodies and agencies to co-operate with the Secretary-General in his preparation of the next report on the world social situation, which he was requested to submit in 1975 for consideration in conjunction with the mid-term over-all review and appraisal of the Second Development Decade.

These were among the decisions embodied in resolution 2771 (XXVI), adopted, by a recorded vote of 95 to 0, with 3 abstentions, on the recommendation of the Assembly's Third (Social, Humanitarian and Cultural) Committee, which approved the text on 20 October 1971, by 104 votes to 0, with 5 abstentions. The Committee acted on the basis of a proposal by Afghanistan, Algeria, Chile, Egypt, Ethiopia, Guyana, India, Indonesia, Iran, Jordan, Kenya, Kuwait, the Libyan Arab Republic, Malaysia, Morocco, Nigeria, Pakistan, Peru, Sierra Leone, Somalia, the United Republic of Tanzania, Yemen, Yugoslavia and Zambia, as amended.

(For text of resolution, see DOCUMENTARY REFERENCES below.)

In the course of discussion in the Third Committee, both oral and written amendments to the draft text were proposed. Several were withdrawn after the ideas contained in them had been incorporated into a revised version of the draft. Others were put to the vote on 20 October 1971.

Among the proposed amendments voted upon was a Hungarian suggestion, approved by 37 votes to 29, with 41 abstentions, that the Assembly state that the resources necessary for a substantial rise in incomes of the developing countries could be achieved, among other means, through a drastic reduction in military expenditures, leading finally to general and complete disarmament under effective international control. (The last phrase, "under effective international control," was suggested by the United Kingdom, and was approved by 31 votes to 17, with 49 abstentions.) The Hungarian amendment replaced wording by which the Assembly would have stated that the resources necessary could be achieved through a drastic reduction of military expenditures, which in some developed countries had reached unbearable proportions.

Rejected, by a roll-call vote of 82 to 11, with 20 abstentions, was an amendment proposed by the United States by which the Assembly would have described the implementation of the International Development Strategy as a responsibility rather than as an obligation.

Social policy and development planning

At its March 1971 session, the Commission for Social Development took up the question of the implementation of the International Development Strategy for the Second United Nations Development Decade. In this connexion, the Commission had before it a note by the Secretary-General and a report of the Working Group of the Committee for Development Planning on evaluating progress during the Second Development Decade.

On 19 March 1971, the Commission decided to recommend a draft resolution for adoption by the Economic and Social Council. By it, the Council would request the Commission to submit a report indicating the progress made towards the attainment of the objectives of the Second Development Decade in the context of an integrated approach and containing appropriate recommendations with a view to improving the implementation of the Strategy and defining more precisely its social objectives.

Also by the draft resolution, the Council would invite the Secretary-General to take steps to prepare an additional report on the methodology of appraisal, based on the integrated approach, so that this report might be submitted to the Commission.

On 21 May 1971, the Economic and Social Council decided to defer consideration of the matter to a later session in the year. It did so, without adopting a resolution, on the recommendation of its Social Committee, which had approved without objection the text of a decision proposed by the Chairman of the Committee.

By the decision, the Council deferred consideration of the text suggested by the Commission for Social Development as well as various proposals for postponement that had been presented to the Committee.

At the Council's mid-year session, the proposals were discussed in the Economic Committee which was considering the implementation of the International Development Strategy. On 30 July 1971, the Council decided to defer until 1972 its consideration of these proposals. It did this without adopting a resolution and without voting. The wording of the decision to defer was suggested by the United States.

(See also pp. 226-28.)

Other aspects of social development and policy

Declaration on Rights of Mentally Retarded

On 20 December 1971, the General Assembly proclaimed the Declaration on the Rights of Mentally Retarded Persons and called for national and international action to ensure that it would be used as a common basis and frame of reference for the protection of these rights.

In the Declaration, it was stated that the mentally retarded person had, to the maximum degree of feasibility, the same rights as other human beings, and that such a person had a right to proper medical care, to education, to economic security, to a qualified guardian if required, to protection from exploitation, and to legal procedures. Whenever possible, the mentally retarded person should live with his own family or with foster parents and participate in different forms of community life.

The necessity of assisting mentally retarded persons to develop their abilities in various fields of activities was noted, and the Assembly expressed its awareness that certain countries, at their present stage of development, could devote only limited efforts to this end.

The Declaration was embodied in resolution 2856(XXVI), adopted, by 110 votes to 0, with 9 abstentions, on the recommendation of the Assembly's Third Committee, which approved the text on 10 December 1971 by a recorded vote of 83 to 0, with 9 abstentions. (For text, see DOCUMENTARY REFERENCES below.)

The text of the Declaration—which had been drafted by the Commission for Social Development—was transmitted to the General Assembly on 21 May 1971 by the Economic and Social Council. The Council's decision to transmit the text was set forth in resolution 1585(L), adopted, by 21 votes to 0, with 2 abstentions, on the recommendation of the Council's Social Committee. The Committee approved the text on 10 May 1971, by 19 votes to 0, with 2 abstentions, on a proposal of France and the United Kingdom, as amended by Greece. (For text, see DOCUMENTARY REFERENCES below.)

The Greek amendment to the text, adopted on 10 May 1971 by 15 votes to 0, with 6 abstentions, referred to the paragraph in the draft declaration in which it was stated that the mentally retarded person had the same rights as other citizens. The amendment had the effect of modifying this to read that the mentally retarded person had, to the maximum degree of feasibility, the same rights as other human beings.

Research and training programme
in regional development

During 1971, both the Economic and Social Council and the Commission for Social Development considered the question of research and training in regional development. Before these bodies was a report by the *Ad Hoc* Advisory Committee for the Research and Training Programme in Regional Development and a related note by the Secretary-General.

On 21 May 1971, the Council endorsed the conclusions of the *Ad Hoc* Advisory Committee that regional development was a potential instrument for the integration and promotion of social and economic development efforts, and that more

vigorous efforts should be made to increase multinational and national research and training projects.

The Secretary-General was asked, in co-operation with various United Nations bodies, to work out arrangements by which resources could be mobilized and used for research and training within regional development projects.

Member States with experience in this field were called upon to make research and training facilities available, provide fellowships, and make other contributions.

These were among decisions set forth in resolution 1582(L), adopted by 18 votes to 1, with 1 abstention, on the recommendation of the Council's Social Committee, which had approved the draft on 10 May 1971, by 20 votes to 2, on the basis of a text proposed by the Commission for Social Development. (For text of resolution, see DOCUMENTARY REFERENCES below.)

Work programme of Commission

When, on 21 May 1971, the Economic and Social Council considered the work programme of the Commission for Social Development for the period 1971–1975, it noted the need for the Commission to orient its activities increasingly towards the essential aspects of over-all development.

The Council approved the priority given in the work programme to major questions relating to social policy, development planning, social reform and the use of human resources, and decided that the Commission should concentrate more on the major problems of social policy. The Council stressed the importance of an appropriate distribution of emphasis at the national, regional and global levels in the implementation of the work programme, and especially of an increased role for regional bodies.

Approving the work programme for 1971–73, the Council asked the Secretary-General to continue to place emphasis on practical action, particularly on technical co-operation and other operational activities. He was also requested to provide in 1972 a detailed programme for the Commission for Social Development for the period 1973–75, and to study the results of the United Nations Conference on the Human Environment, scheduled to be held in 1972, which might have implications for the social aspects of development.

The need for close and continuing co-operation between the United Nations and the specialized agencies was also stressed by the Council.

These decisions were embodied in resolution 1583(L), adopted by 20 votes to 0, with 2 abstentions, on the recommendation of the Social Committee, which had approved the text on 10 May 1971, by 21 votes to 0, with 2 abstentions, on the basis of a draft suggested by the Commission for Social Development. (For text of resolution, see DOCUMENTARY REFERENCES below.)

Report of United Nations Research Institute for Social Development

In 1971, the Commission for Social Development and the Economic and Social Council discussed the United Nations Research Institute for Social Development.

On 21 May 1971, the Council decided that the three-year term of office of nominated members of the Board of the Institute should be extended to four years to coincide with the biennial sessions of the Commission.

The Council took this decision without objection and without adopting a resolution, on the recommendation of its Social Committee, which had approved the decision without objection on 10 May 1971 on the basis of a proposal by the Commission for Social Development.

DOCUMENTARY REFERENCES

World social situation

Economic and Social Council—50th session
Social Committee, meetings 660-665, 667, 668.
Plenary meetings 1770, 1771.

1970 Report on the World Social Situation (ST/SOA/110). U.N.P. Sales No.: E.71.IV.13.
E/4984. Report of Commission for Social Development on its 22nd session, 1-22 March 1971, Chapter III (resolution 1(XXII)).
E/4984, Chapter X. Draft resolution I, as amended by United States, E/AC.7/L.587, approved by Social Committee on 10 May 1971, meeting 667, by 21 votes to 0, with 2 abstentions.
E/4989. Report of Committee for Programme and Co-ordination on its 8th session, 22 March–8 April 1971, Chapter VI D.
E/5005. Note by Secretary-General (transmitting summary (preface and introduction) of 1970 Report on the World Social Situation).
E/AC.7/L.587. United States: amendment to draft resolution I recommended by Commission for Social Development in E/4984.
E/5029. Report of Social Committee, draft resolution I.

RESOLUTION 1581 A(L), as recommended by Social Committee, E/5029, adopted by Council on 21 May 1971, meeting 1771, by 15 votes to 0, with 1 abstention.

The Economic and Social Council,
Taking note of the 1970 Report on the World Social Situation,
Recalling that under the terms of the Charter of the United Nations, it is essential to promote social progress and better standards of life,
Recalling also the Declaration on Social Progress and Development, particularly article 18(b), which recommends the promotion of democratically based social and institutional reforms and motivation for change basic to the elimination of all forms of discrimination and exploitation,
Considering that the International Development Strategy for the Second United Nations Development Decade calls for qualitative and structural changes in society,
Noting its resolution 1139(XLI) of 29 July 1966, which emphasized, *inter alia,* the significance of adequate structural social and economic changes for the achievement of social progress,
Bearing in mind that the achievement of genuine social progress, including in particular the solution of the problem of employment and the establishment of an adequate standard of living for everyone, and cultural, scientific and educational development require efforts for the attainment of profound economic and social changes in the countries which set these objectives,
Considering also that a number of countries have already acquired considerable experience in the application of measures of this kind,
1. *Considers it appropriate* to study the experience of the various countries of the world in this field;

2. *Requests* the Secretary-General, with this end in view and drawing on relevant work done in this field, to forward to States Members of the United Nations or members of the specialized agencies a questionnaire on their experience in achieving far-reaching social and economic changes for purposes of social progress;
3. *Decides* to consider this question, if possible at its fifty-second session, but not later than at its fifty-third session.

E/4984. Report of Commission for Social Development on its 22nd session, Chapter III (resolution 2(XXII)).
E/4984, Chapter X. Draft resolution II, as amended by 2 powers (E/AC.7/L.591) and by Norway (E/AC.7/L.593), approved by Social Committee on 10 May 1971, meeting 667, by 21 votes to 0, with 2 abstentions.
E/AC.7/L.588 and Rev.1. United States: amendments and revised amendments to draft resolution II recommended by Commission for Social Development in E/4984.
E/AC.7/L.591. Brazil and Pakistan: amendments to draft resolution II recommended by Commission for Social Development in E/4984.
E/AC.7/L.593. Norway: amendments to draft resolution II recommended by Commission for Social Development in E/4984.
E/5029. Report of Social Committee, draft resolution II.

RESOLUTION 1581 B(L), as recommended by Social Committee, E/5029, adopted by Council on 21 May 1971, meeting 1771, by 18 votes to 0, with 2 abstentions.

The Economic and Social Council,
Taking note of the 1970 Report on the World Social Situation,
Recalling that under the terms of the Charter of the United Nations all Member States are pledged to promote social progress and better standards of life,
Recalling further General Assembly resolutions 2542(XXIV) of 11 December 1969 on the Declaration on Social Progress and Development, 2436(XXIII) of 19 December 1968 on the world social situation and 2681(XXV) of 11 December 1970 on a unified approach to economic and social planning in national development, and Economic and Social Council resolution 1494(XLVIII) of 26 May 1970 on social policy and planning in national development,
Bearing in mind the goals and objectives embodied in the International Development Strategy for the Second United Nations Development Decade,
Regretting that, despite limited improvement in some sectors, there has been continued deterioration of the world social situation, particularly that arising from growing disparities among the developed and developing countries and within countries,
Reaffirming that progress towards general and complete disarmament should release substantial additional resources which could be utilized for the purpose of economic and social development, in particular that of the developing countries,
Emphasizing the need for the opportunities offered by science and technology to be equitably shared by developed and developing countries,

Re-emphasizing that the primary responsibility for the development of developing countries rests upon themselves, but that, however great their own efforts, these will not be sufficient to enable them to achieve the desired development goals as expeditiously as they must unless they are assisted through increased financial resources and more favourable economic and commercial policies on the part of the developed countries,

Calling renewed attention to the interdependence of economic and social development, and to the consequent need for an integrated approach to planning and development,

Recognizing the desirability for countries which consider that their rate of population growth hampers their development to adopt measures they deem necessary in accordance with their concept of development,

Stressing the necessity of intensified international co-operation among nations, regardless of their economic and social systems, on the basis of mutual respect and equality, in accordance with the Charter and the relevant resolutions of the United Nations,

Re-emphasizing the pressing need to raise levels of living in the developing countries so that disparities between developed and developing countries are reduced, and the need for all countries to pursue policies for the promotion of economic and social development throughout the world,

1. *Endorses* the conclusion of the *1970 Report on the World Social Situation,* that reduction of disparities and inequality existing between developed and developing countries presupposes, among other things, a substantial rise in the income of the developing countries, which necessitates an enlightened, equitable and progressive approach by the developed countries to the questions of trade, aid and transfer of technology;

2. *Urges* Governments to accelerate development by:

(a) Giving appropriate emphasis to social objectives in planning and development;

(b) Taking measures to greatly increase popular participation in all aspects of national life, including development, and to consult regularly with trade unions and employers' federations and other broad social organizations representing all sections of workers, peasants and other working people;

(c) Working towards the reduction and eventual elimination of dualism in all its manifestations;

(d) Giving high priority to the attainment of adequate levels of living for all, especially through measures to bring about more equitable distribution of income and to improve the effectiveness of social services;

(e) Promoting purposeful social change and necessary structural, institutional and administrative reforms;

(f) Ensuring that economic and physical development are planned with a view to serving a larger human and social purpose and are effectively co-ordinated with social development measures;

3. *Recommends* that the system ultimately adopted for review and appraisal of the objectives and policies of the International Development Strategy for the Second United Nations Development Decade provide for adequate consultation with international and regional trade-union and employers' federations and other major organizations of the people which can contribute to the comprehensive and realistic consideration of the social aspects and problems of development;

4. *Reminds* Governments of their obligations to implement the International Development Strategy, and urges the Governments of developed countries to accelerate the achievement of the targets for trade and financial transfer to developing countries established in the Strategy, in order to bring about an early achievement of its goals and objectives, which is so essential to the amelioration of the world situation;

5. *Requests* the Secretary-General to take the necessary steps to make resources available, to the extent possible, to meet requests by Governments for assistance in the review and reappraisal of objectives and policies in the context of the International Development Strategy;

6. *Recommends* that the *1970 Report on the World Social Situation* should serve as one of the background documents during the Second United Nations Development Decade, and that in the preparation of future issues of the *Report* due account be taken of the following:

(a) Evaluation and analysis at the national, subregional and regional levels as recommended in the International Development Strategy;

(b) Increased emphasis on an integrated, cross-sectoral analysis of trends and developments, with particular attention being given to appraisal of the real social and human aspects of development;

(c) Drawing conclusions and making suggestions that will be useful for purposes of practical policy-making and planning and for national and international action;

(d) The social situation in colonial and dependent territories whose progress in this field is hampered by occupation and denial of self-determination.

E/4984. Report of Commission for Social Development on its 22nd session, Chapter III (resolution 3(XXII)).

E/4984, Chapter X. Draft resolution III, as amended by United States (E/AC.7/L.586, as orally revised by France), approved by Social Committee on 10 May 1971, meeting 667, by 12 votes to 3, with 7 abstentions.

E/AC.7/L.586. United States: amendment to draft resolution III recommended by Commission for Social Development in E/4984.

E/5029. Report of Social Committee, draft resolution III.

RESOLUTION 1581 C (L), as recommended by Social Committee, E/5029, adopted by Council on 21 May 1971, meeting 1771, by 11 votes to 4, with 5 abstentions.

The Economic and Social Council,

Taking note of the *1970 Report on the World Social Situation,*

Expressing concern that, despite examples of improved conditions, there has been a regrettable deterioration in social conditions, especially in the developing countries,

Deploring the persistence of poverty, illiteracy, disease, poor housing and social inequities despite national and international efforts to overcome these evils,

Recognizing that in some countries excessive population growth and unplanned urbanization are among the factors retarding economic and social development and adversely affecting the human environment,

Affirming that primary responsibility for improvement in social conditions rests with Governments,

Recalling Article 56 of the Charter of the United Nations under which all Members pledge themselves to take joint and separate action in co-operation with the Organization for the achievement of higher standards of living, full employment and conditions of economic and social progress and development, and solutions of international economic, social, health and related problems,

Recalling further the Declaration on Social Progress and Development,

Bearing in mind the goals and objectives embodied in the International Development Strategy for the Second United Nations Development Decade,

1. *Recommends* that Member States intensify their efforts to enhance social progress and development by:

(a) Mobilizing domestic resources and effecting necessary structural, administrative and institutional reforms;

(b) Increasing popular participation in national development;

(c) Co-operating with other Members in the framework of bilateral assistance and with international agencies in multilateral programmes and other activities;

2. *Recommends* that Member States pursue a unified approach to development and improvement in the quality of life, thus manifesting their belief that social and economic objectives are inseparable;

3. *Recommends further* that Member States seek to improve the collection of data, analysis and reporting in the social field and to undertake a continuing examination of development policies and programmes with a view to enhancing social progress;

4. *Decides* that the *Report on the World Social Situation* should be utilized during the Second United Nations Development Decade in the following manner:

(a) The 1970 *Report* should serve as a guide for the Decade and be updated periodically as part of the continuing work programme of the Secretariat for purposes of review and appraisal of social progress during the Decade;

(*b*) The 1974 *Report* should serve as a major assessment at mid-Decade and provide an opportunity for modifying objectives in view of changing circumstances;

5. *Suggests* to the Secretary-General that future issues of the *Report on the World Social Situation* might take account of the following:

(*a*) They should be more analytical in nature;

(*b*) They should highlight issues deemed to require national and international action;

(*c*) They should contain suggestions for possible action by Governments and agencies of the United Nations.

General Assembly—26th session
Third Committee, meetings 1824–1844.
Plenary meeting 1991.

A/8380. Note by Secretary-General (transmitting *1970 Report on the World Social Situation*).

1970 Report on the World Social Situation (ST/SOA/110). U.N.P. Sales No.: E.71.IV.13.

A/8401. Report of Secretary-General on work of the Organization, 16 June 1970–15 June 1971, Part Three, Chapter II A 2.

A/8403. Report of Economic and Social Council on work of its 50th and 51st sessions, Chapter XV A.

A/C.3/L.1853. Afghanistan, Algeria, Chile, Egypt, Guyana, India, Indonesia, Jordan, Kenya, Kuwait, Libyan Arab Republic, Malaysia, Morocco, Nigeria, Pakistan, Peru, Sierra Leone, Somalia, United Republic of Tanzania, Yemen, Yugoslavia, Zambia: draft resolution.

A/C.3/L.1853/Rev.1. Afghanistan, Algeria, Chile, Egypt, Ethiopia, Guyana, India, Indonesia, Iran, Jordan, Kenya, Kuwait, Libyan Arab Republic, Malaysia, Morocco, Nigeria, Pakistan, Peru, Sierra Leone, Somalia, United Republic of Tanzania, Yemen, Yugoslavia, Zambia: revised draft resolution, as orally amended by sponsors and as amended by Brazil (A/C.3/L.1863/Rev.1), by Hungary (A/C.3/L.1862/Rev.1, para. 1, and para. 2 as sub-amended by United Kingdom, A/C.3/L.1868), by Iraq (A/C.3/L.1861) and by USSR (A/C.3/L.1859, as orally amended), approved by Third Committee on 20 October 1971, meeting 1843, by 104 votes to 0, with 5 abstentions.

A/C.3/L.1855. Algeria and Ukrainian SSR: amendments to 22-power draft resolution, A/C.3/L.1853.

A/C.3/L.1858. Guinea: amendment to 24-power revised draft resolution, A/C.3/L.1853/Rev.1.

A/C.3/L.1859. USSR: amendment to 24-power revised draft resolution, A/C.3/L.1853/Rev.1.

A/C.3/L.1860. Argentina: amendments to 24-power revised draft resolution, A/C.3/L.1853/Rev.1.

A/C.3/L.1861. Iraq: amendments to 24-power revised draft resolution, A/C.3/L.1853/Rev.1.

A/C.3/L.1862 and Rev.1. Hungary: amendments and revised amendments to 24-power revised draft resolution, A/C.3/L.1853/Rev.1.

A/C.3/L.1863 and Rev.1. Brazil: amendments and revised amendments to 24-power revised draft resolution, A/C.3/L.1853/Rev.1.

A/C.3/L.1864. Liberia: amendment to 24-power revised draft resolution, A/C.3/L.1853/Rev.1.

A/C.3/L.1865. Italy: amendment to 24-power revised draft resolution, A/C.3/L.1853/Rev.1.

A/C.3/L.1866. United States: amendments to 24-power revised draft resolution, A/C.3/L.1853/Rev.1.

A/C.3/L.1867. Mongolia: amendment to 24-power revised draft resolution, A/C.3/L.1853/Rev.1.

A/C.3/L.1868. United Kingdom: sub-amendment to Hungarian amendment, A/C.3/L.1862.

A/C.3/L.1869. Bolivia: amendment to 24-power revised draft resolution, A/C.3/L.1853/Rev.1.

A/8507. Report of Third Committee, draft resolution II.

RESOLUTION 2771 (XXVI), as recommended by Third Committee, A/8507, adopted by Assembly on 22 November 1971, meeting 1991, by recorded vote of 95 to 0, with 3 abstentions:

In favour: Algeria, Argentina, Australia, Austria, Bahrain, Barbados, Belgium, Bhutan, Bolivia, Brazil, Bulgaria, Burma, Burundi, Byelorussian SSR, Cameroon, Central African Republic, Ceylon, Chile, Colombia, Congo, Costa Rica, Cuba, Czechoslovakia, Dahomey, Denmark, Dominican Republic, Ecuador, Egypt, Equatorial Guinea, Finland, France, Gabon, Ghana, Greece, Guatemala, Guinea, Guyana, Honduras, Hungary, Iceland, India, Indonesia, Iran, Iraq, Ireland, Italy, Ivory Coast, Jamaica, Jordan, Khmer Republic, Kuwait, Laos, Lebanon, Lesotho, Liberia, Libyan Arab Republic, Luxembourg, Madagascar, Malawi, Mauritania, Mexico, Mongolia, Nepal, Netherlands, New Zealand, Nicaragua, Niger, Nigeria, Norway, Pakistan, Panama, People's Democratic Republic of Yemen, Peru, Philippines, Poland, Qatar, Romania, Saudi Arabia, Sierra Leone, Singapore, Spain, Sudan, Swaziland, Sweden, Syrian Arab Republic, Thailand, Togo, Tunisia, Turkey, Ukrainian SSR, USSR, Uruguay, Venezuela, Yugoslavia, Zambia.

Against: None.

Abstaining: Japan, Portugal, United States.

The General Assembly,

Recalling its resolutions 2436(XXIII) of 19 December 1968 on the world social situation and 2542(XXIV) of 11 December 1969 containing the Declaration on Social Progress and Development,

Bearing in mind the goals and objectives embodied in the International Development Strategy for the Second United Nations Development Decade, contained in its resolution 2626(XXV) of 24 October 1970,

Noting with appreciation the *1970 Report on the World Social Situation,*

Deeply concerned that the world social situation has continued to deteriorate, that the persistence of poverty, unemployment, hunger, disease, illiteracy, inadequate housing and uncontrolled growth of population in certain parts of the world has acquired new dimensions and that many causes of the growing disparities between the developed and developing countries hinder the advancement of the developing countries,

1. *Endorses* the provisions of Economic and Social Council resolution 1581 B(L) of 21 May 1971;

2. *Reaffirms* the urgency of taking effective measures aimed at halting the deterioration of the world social situation and promoting social progress and development;

3. *Emphasizes* the pressing need to raise levels of living in the developing countries, to reduce disparities between developed and developing countries and within countries, to accelerate economic and social reforms, and for all countries to pursue progressive and well co-ordinated policies for the promotion of economic and social progress and development throughout the world;

4. *Emphasizes further* that colonialism, racial discrimination, *apartheid,* alien domination, foreign occupation, aggressive wars and other policies of oppression and exploitation, and the violation of human rights and fundamental freedoms and economic exploitation by foreign monopolies constitute principal obstacles to social progress and development in many parts of the world and that urgent attention is required, particularly for the amelioration of the social situation of the peoples living in those parts of the world;

5. *Stresses* that the primary responsibility for the development of developing countries rests upon themselves, but that their own efforts, however great, will not be sufficient to enable them to achieve the desired development goals as expeditiously as they must, unless they are assisted through increased financial resources and more favourable economic and commercial policies on the part of the developed countries;

6. *Urges* Governments of developed countries to fulfil their obligation to implement the International Development Strategy for the Second United Nations Development Decade, and in particular to attain the targets for trade, financial resources and the provisions for the transfer of science and technology for the

development of developing countries embodied in the Strategy—and where possible to exceed those targets—which is essential to the amelioration of the world social situation;

7. *Reaffirms* the inherent rights of all peoples and the permanent sovereignty of all countries, particularly of developing countries, over their natural resources, calls upon Governments and international organizations concerned to refrain from any action which may detract from the exercise by other States of permanent sovereignty over their natural resources and emphasizes the importance for the developing countries of co-ordinating their actions within economic subregional, regional and continental organizations so as to derive the maximum benefits from their natural resources;

8. *Draws the attention* of all States and the United Nations bodies and specialized agencies concerned to the following conclusions and recommendations based upon the consideration of the *1970 Report on the World Social Situation*:

(*a*) The improvement of social conditions in many parts of the world has become, as never before, dependent upon the improvement of international political and economic relations. The social situation of the peoples under colonial and alien domination, or under foreign occupation, is a source of great concern. Their liberation is a prerequisite for the improvement of their social conditions.

(*b*) A substantial rise in the incomes of the developing countries, required for the reduction of inequality between developed and developing countries, presupposes, among other things, a positive approach by the developed countries to the questions of trade and aid; the resources necessary for the attainment of this objective could be achieved, among other means, through a drastic reduction in military expenditures, leading finally to general and complete disarmament under effective international control as well as through the exploitation of the resources of the sea-bed and the ocean floor beyond national jurisdiction for the benefit of all mankind, taking into account the special needs and interests of the developing countries, as referred to in General Assembly resolution 2749(XXV) of 17 December 1970.

(*c*) Economic growth has generally been accompanied by a considerable widening of disparities in the distribution of income, wealth and services. Effective measures for promoting economic growth with social justice should receive the highest priority. Social progress will depend, to a very large extent, upon the early and vigorous implementation of a wide range of structural and institutional reforms, such as agrarian reforms, reforms aimed at securing just distribution of national wealth and income, and such programmes as measures for family planning aimed at controlling the rate of population growth in countries which consider that that rate hampers their development.

(*d*) The growth of unemployment and underemployment, particularly in the developing countries, is acquiring serious proportions. Rapid expansion of employment opportunities should be regarded as an important objective of development planning. Far greater attention should be given to the application of labour intensive techniques for the purpose of drawing under-utilized labour in rural and urban areas into extensive programmes of development.

(*e*) The implementation of the International Development Strategy in all its interrelated aspects is an obligation of both developed and developing countries. A substantial improvement in the level of living of the masses in developing countries should be a central objective of the Second United Nations Development Decade. Improvement in the quality and distribution of social services, particularly in the fields of education, health, agriculture, housing, social welfare and social defence, should be recognized as an integral part of the over-all development effort.

(*f*) Increased utilization of science and technology will greatly help social progress and development. Equally important is its equitable sharing by the developed and developing countries. The Advisory Committee on the Application of Science and Technology to Development should study the implementation of the provisions of the present resolution and of the Declaration on Social Progress and Development on the question of science and technology in relation to social development.

(*g*) The unfavourable terms of trade, including the instability of prices of primary commodities which constitute the bulk of exports of many developing countries, are undermining the efforts of these countries to improve their social situation. These terms have been further aggravated by the recent disquieting developments in international economic relations and, in particular, by the instability of the international monetary system. The Economic and Social Council, in its consideration of the monetary and financial situation, should pay special attention to the influence of the current crisis on social progress in different countries, particularly in developing countries, and mention it in its report to the General Assembly.

(*h*) The outflow of qualified personnel from developing countries to developed countries seriously hampers economic and social development in developing countries.

(*i*) Broad popular participation, not only in the implementation of development programmes but also in the formulation of policies and plans and other forms of decision-making, should be regarded as both an objective and a means of development.

(*j*) Due attention should be paid to the needs and aspirations of the younger generation. Effective policy measures designed to involve fully the younger generation in the promotion of social progress and development should be undertaken.

(*k*) Adequate measures should be taken to remove discriminatory practices against women in all spheres. Greater attention should be paid to women's education, vocational training and guidance so as to ensure their full integration and participation in all aspects of economic and social life.

(*l*) Adequate attention should be given to multidisciplinary community services in the field of family and child welfare, particularly in situations of rapid urbanization and social change affecting family levels of living and especially the welfare of pre-school children.

9. *Calls upon* Governments and the United Nations bodies and specialized agencies concerned to co-operate with the Secretary-General in the preparation of the next report on the world social situation;

10. *Requests* the Secretary-General to submit the next report on the world social situation to the General Assembly at its thirtieth session, through the Economic and Social Council, for consideration in conjunction with the mid-term over-all review and appraisal of the Second United Nations Development Decade, and to evaluate and analyse trends relating to social development—their causes and manifestations and the experiences thereon —throughout the world, including the situation in colonial, dependent and occupied Territories, within the framework of the unified approach to development, bearing in mind the provisions of the present resolution, the deliberations on this item at the current session of the General Assembly, the fiftieth session of the Economic and Social Council and the twenty-second session of the Commission for Social Development, and the provisions of the Declaration on Social Progress and Development.

Social policy and development planning

Economic and Social Council—50th session
Social Committee, meetings 660-665, 667, 668.
Plenary meeting 1771.

E/4984 and Add.1. Report of Commission for Social Development on its 22nd session, 1-22 March 1971, Chapter VII (resolution 7(XXII)) and Chapter X (draft resolution VII).
E/AC.7/L.592. Pakistan: draft resolution.
E/AC.7/L.594. France, Italy, United Kingdom: draft decision.
E/AC.7/L.595. Proposal by Chairman of Social Committee.
E/5029. Report of Social Committee (on social development), paras. 11-13 and 19, draft decision I, and appendix (annex).
E/5044. Resolutions adopted by Economic and Social Council during its 50th session, 11-13 January and 26 April–21 May 1971. Decisions (item 2), pp. 14-15.

Economic and Social Council—51st session
Economic Committee, meetings 529, 530, 532, 533, 539.
Plenary meetings 1773-1782, 1794-1799.

E/5029. Report of Social Committee, appendix (annex).
E/L.1456. United States: draft decision.
E/5073. Resolutions adopted by Economic and Social Council
during its 51st session, 5-30 July 1971. Other decisions, p. 10.

Other aspects of social development and policy

Economic and Social Council—50th session
Social Committee, meetings 660-665, 667, 668.
Plenary meetings 1770, 1771.

DECLARATION ON RIGHTS OF MENTALLY RETARDED
E/4984. Report of Commission for Social Development on its 22nd
session, 1-22 March 1971, Chapter VI (resolution 8(XXII)) and
Chapter XI (draft declaration recommended for adoption by
General Assembly).
E/AC.7/L.589. Greece: amendments to draft declaration recom-
mended by Commission for Social Development in E/4984,
Chapter XI (and to 2-power draft resolution, E/AC.7/L.590).
E/AC.7/L.590. France and United Kingdom: draft resolution, as
amended by Greece, E/AC.7/L.589, approved by Social
Committee on 10 May 1971, meeting 667, by 19 votes to 0, with
2 abstentions.
E/5029. Report of Social Committee, draft resolution VII.

RESOLUTION 1585(L), as recommended by Social Committee,
E/5029, adopted by Council on 21 May 1971, meeting 1771, by
21 votes to 0, with 2 abstentions.

The Economic and Social Council,
Noting resolution 8(XXII) of the Commission for Social
Development in which it requested the Economic and Social
Council to recommend in its report to the General Assembly the
adoption of the Declaration concerning the rights of mentally
retarded persons,
Decides to transmit the text of the following draft Declaration to
the General Assembly for adoption at its twenty-sixth session.

[For text of Declaration, see General Assembly resolution
2856(XXVI) below.]

General Assembly—26th session
Third Committee, meeting 1905.
Plenary meeting 2027.

A/8403. Report of Economic and Social Council on work of its 50th
and 51st sessions, Chapter XV E.
A/C.3/L.1870. Note by Secretary-General, transmitting text of
Economic and Social Council resolution 1585(L) containing text
of draft Declaration on Rights of Mentally Retarded Persons,
approved by Third Committee on 10 December 1971, meeting
1905, by recorded vote of 83 to 0, with 9 abstentions, as follows:

In favour: Afghanistan, Algeria, Argentina, Australia, Austria,
Belgium, Brazil, Burma, Burundi, Cameroon, Canada, Central
African Republic, Chile, Colombia, Congo, Costa Rica, Cuba,
Denmark, Equatorial Guinea, Finland, France, Ghana, Greece,
Guatemala, Guinea, Guyana, Honduras, Iceland, India, In-
donesia, Iran, Iraq, Ireland, Israel, Italy, Ivory Coast, Jamaica,
Japan, Kenya, Khmer Republic, Kuwait, Laos, Lebanon, Liberia,
Libyan Arab Republic, Madagascar, Malaysia, Mali, Mauritania,
Mexico, Morocco, Nepal, Netherlands, New Zealand, Nigeria,
Norway, Pakistan, Panama, People's Democratic Republic of
Yemen, Peru, Philippines, Portugal, Rwanda, Saudi Arabia,
Senegal, Singapore, Somalia, Spain, Sudan, Swaziland, Swe-
den, Syrian Arab Republic, Thailand, Tunisia, Turkey, Uganda,
United Kingdom, United States, Uruguay, Venezuela, Yemen,
Yugoslavia, Zaire.
Against: None.

Abstaining: Bulgaria, Byelorussian SSR, Czechoslovakia,
Hungary, Mongolia, Poland, Ukrainian SSR, USSR, United
Republic of Tanzania.

A/8588. Report of Third Committee, draft resolution II.

RESOLUTION 2856 (XXVI), as recommended by Third Committee, A/8588, adopted by Assembly on 20 December 1971,
meeting 2027, by 110 votes to 0, with 9 abstentions.

The General Assembly,
Mindful of the pledge of the States Members of the United
Nations under the Charter to take joint and separate action in
co-operation with the Organization to promote higher standards of
living, full employment and conditions of economic and social
progress and development,
Reaffirming faith in human rights and fundamental freedoms and
in the principles of peace, of the dignity and worth of the human
person and of social justice proclaimed in the Charter,
Recalling the principles of the Universal Declaration of Human
Rights, the International Covenants on Human Rights, the
Declaration of the Rights of the Child and the standards already set
for social progress in the constitutions, conventions, recommendations and resolutions of the International Labour Organisation, the
United Nations Educational, Scientific and Cultural Organization,
the World Health Organization, the United Nations Children's Fund
and other organizations concerned,
Emphasizing that the Declaration on Social Progress and
Development has proclaimed the necessity of protecting the rights
and assuring the welfare and rehabilitation of the physically and
mentally disadvantaged,
Bearing in mind the necessity of assisting mentally retarded
persons to develop their abilities in various fields of activities and of
promoting their integration as far as possible in normal life,
Aware that certain countries, at their present stage of
development, can devote only limited efforts to this end,
Proclaims this Declaration on the Rights of Mentally Retarded
Persons and calls for national and international action to ensure
that it will be used as a common basis and frame of reference for
the protection of these rights:

1. The mentally retarded person has, to the maximum
degree of feasibility, the same rights as other human beings.
2. The mentally retarded person has a right to proper
medical care and physical therapy and to such education,
training, rehabilitation and guidance as will enable him to
develop his ability and maximum potential.
3. The mentally retarded person has a right to economic
security and to a decent standard of living. He has a right to
perform productive work or to engage in any other meaningful
occupation to the fullest possible extent of his capabilities.
4. Whenever possible, the mentally retarded person should
live with his own family or with foster parents and participate in
different forms of community life. The family with which he lives
should receive assistance. If care in an institution becomes
necessary, it should be provided in surroundings and other
circumstances as close as possible to those of normal life.
5. The mentally retarded person has a right to a qualified
guardian when this is required to protect his personal well-being
and interests.
6. The mentally retarded person has a right to protection
from exploitation, abuse and degrading treatment. If prosecuted
for any offence, he shall have a right to due process of law with
full recognition being given to his degree of mental responsibility.
7. Whenever mentally retarded persons are unable, because of the severity of their handicap, to exercise all their rights
in a meaningful way or it should become necessary to restrict or
deny some or all of these rights, the procedure used for that
restriction or denial of rights must contain proper legal
safeguards against every form of abuse. This procedure must be
based on an evaluation of the social capability of the mentally
retarded person by qualified experts and must be subject to
periodic review and to the right of appeal to higher authorities.

RESEARCH AND TRAINING PROGRAMME
IN REGIONAL DEVELOPMENT

E/4984. Report of Commission for Social Development on its 22nd session, 1-22 March 1971, Chapter IV B (resolution 4(XXII)).

E/4984, Chapter X. Draft resolution IV, approved by Social Committee on 10 May 1971, meeting 667, by 20 votes to 2.

E/5029. Report of Social Committee, draft resolution IV.

RESOLUTION 1582 (L), as recommended by Social Committee, E/5029, adopted by Council on 21 May 1971, meeting 1771, by 18 votes to 1, with 1 abstention.

The Economic and Social Council,

Recalling its resolutions 1086 C (XXXIX) of 30 July 1965 and 1141(XLI) of 29 July 1966 concerning the research and training programme in regional development,

Having considered the conclusions and recommendations of the *Ad Hoc* Advisory Committee for the Research and Training Programme in Regional Development and the note by the Secretary-General thereon,

Convinced that the regional development approach can be an important instrument for achieving the goals and objectives of the International Development Strategy for the Second United Nations Development Decade,

Recognizing that the regional development approach is being used more widely by Member States to achieve a more effective integration of social, economic and spatial aspects of development and also to spread more evenly the economic and social benefits of development efforts,

1. *Endorses* the conclusions of the *Ad Hoc* Advisory Committee for the Research and Training Programme in Regional Development that regional development is a potential instrument for the integration and promotion of social and economic development efforts within a country in order, particularly, to:

(a) Induce rapid structural change and social reform, especially to achieve a broader distribution of returns from development among less privileged groups in society;

(b) Increase popular participation in setting development goals and in developmental decision-making and organizational processes;

(c) Create more effective institutional and administrative arrangements and operational approaches to carry out development plans;

(d) Achieve a better distribution of population and human activities and settlement through a more effective integration of urban and rural development;

(e) Include more effectively environmental considerations in development programmes;

2. *Further endorses* the recommendations of the *Ad Hoc* Advisory Committee, particularly the recommendation that more vigorous efforts should be made to increase multinational as well as national research and training centres, including experimental pilot projects, within the context of selected existing regional development projects, while continuing to support and strengthen the centres already established by Member States;

3. *Requests* the Secretary-General, in co-operation with the specialized agencies, the United Nations Development Programme and other multilateral and regional institutions, to work out arrangements by which resources can be mobilized and utilized for research and training within regional development projects supported by them;

4. *Calls upon* those Member States which have acquired experience and have resources to offer in regional development to co-operate with the Secretary-General in increasing the resources and facilities for the research and training programme in this field by:

(a) Making research and training facilities available for training of persons from other countries;

(b) Providing fellowships for such training;

(c) Making other contributions in kind to advance the objectives of the research and training programme in regional development;

5. *Recommends* that the Secretary-General should avail himself, as needed, of the services of senior experts knowledge-able and experienced in regional development to advise him on further development of the programme.

WORK PROGRAMME OF COMMISSION

E/4984. Report of Commission for Social Development on its 22nd session, 1-22 March 1971, Chapters IV C (resolution 5(XXIV)) and XII.

E/4984, Chapter X. Draft resolution V, as orally corrected by Committee Chairman, approved by Social Committee on 10 May 1971, meeting 667, by 21 votes to 0, with 2 abstentions.

E/4989. Report of Committee for Programme and Co-ordination on its 8th session, 22 March–8 April 1971, Chapter VI D.

E/5029. Report of Social Committee, draft resolution V.

RESOLUTION 1583 (L), as recommended by Social Committee, E/5029, adopted by Council on 21 May 1971, meeting 1771, by 20 votes to 0, with 2 abstentions.

The Economic and Social Council,

Having taken note of the work programme of the Commission for Social Development proposed by the Secretary-General for the period 1971–1975,

Considering the need for the Commission to orient its activities increasingly towards the essential aspects of over-all development, with special reference to the Declaration on Social Progress and Development and the International Development Strategy for the Second United Nations Development Decade,

Taking into account that several of these questions are of equal interest to the United Nations, the specialized agencies and the regional economic commissions,

Bearing in mind General Assembly resolution 2188(XXI) of 13 December 1966, which was designed to increase the effectiveness of the work undertaken in the economic and social sectors of the United Nations and to avoid duplication,

1. *Expresses its appreciation* of the manner in which the work programme of the Commission for Social Development has been presented, particularly as concerns the formulation of a precise two-year programme within the framework of a five-year programme of activities;

2. *Approves* the priority given in the work programme to major questions relating to social policy, the concept and problems of development planning, social reform and institutional change, and the utilization of human resources;

3. *Requests* the Secretary-General to continue his effort to place emphasis on practical action, particularly on technical co-operation and other operational activities, and to strengthen co-operation with the United Nations Development Programme and ensure the availability of the expertise of the Social Development Division to the United Nations Development Programme;

4. *Stresses* the importance of an appropriate distribution of emphasis at the national, regional and global levels in the implementation of the work programme, and especially of an increased role for regional bodies in matters within the field of their competence;

5. *Stresses* the need for close and continuing co-operation between the United Nations and the specialized agencies;

6. *Decides* that the Commission for Social Development should concentrate more on the major problems of social policy;

7. *Approves* the work programme of the Commission for the period 1971–1973 and invites the Secretary-General, in implementing that programme, to take the fullest account of the foregoing considerations;

8. *Requests* the Secretary-General to submit to the Commission for Social Development at its twenty-third session a detailed programme for the period 1973-1975, incorporating such adjustments as may be deemed necessary on the basis of the views expressed by the Commission, the Committee for Programme and Co-ordination, the Economic and Social Council and the General Assembly;

9. *Further requests* the Secretary-General to study the results of the United Nations Conference on the Human Environment in 1972 which may have implications for the social aspects of development that should be reflected in future issues of the *Report*

on the *World Social Situation* and in the work programme of the Commission;

10. *Requests* the Centre for Development Planning, Projections and Policies to render advisory and methodological assistance to the relevant organs and organizations of the United Nations system in matters relating to the formulation of a general approach to planning, bearing in mind the needs of social development.

REPORT OF UNITED NATIONS RESEARCH
INSTITUTE FOR SOCIAL DEVELOPMENT
E/4984. Report of Commission for Social Development on its 22nd session, Chapter VIII (recommendation, para. 223).
E/5029. Report of Social Committee, paras. 17 and 19, draft decision III.
E/5044. Resolutions adopted by Economic and Social Council during its 50th session, 11-13 January and 26 April–21 May 1971. Other decisions, p. 27.

REPORT OF COMMISSION FOR SOCIAL DEVELOPMENT
E/4984. Report of Commission for Social Development on its 22nd session, 1-22 March 1971. (Annex III: List of documents before Commission at its 22nd session.)

E/4984/Summary. Summary of report of Commission for Social Development.
E/4984/Add.1. Administrative and financial implications of resolutions adopted by Commission at its 22nd session. Note by Secretary-General.
E/5029. Report of Social Committee, draft resolution VIII, as suggested by Committee Chairman, approved without vote by Social Committee on 11 May 1971, meeting 668.

RESOLUTION 1586(L), as recommended by Social Committee, E/5029, taking note of report of Commission for Social Development on its 22nd session, adopted without objection by Council on 21 May 1971, meeting 1771.

Other documents
International Social Development Review, No. 3: Unified Socio-Economic Development and Planning: Some New Horizons.
U.N.P. Sales No.: E.71.IV.9.
A/8401. Report of Secretary-General on work of the Organization, 16 June 1970–15 June 1971, Part Three, Chapter II D.
A/8403. Report of Economic and Social Council on work of its 50th and 51st sessions, Chapter XV.

Housing, building and planning

Technical aid activities and studies in 1971

During 1971, the services of 198 experts and 31 associate experts were provided to the following 64 countries and territories to advise on various aspects of housing, building and planning: Afghanistan, Antigua, Argentina, the Bahamas, Botswana, the British Virgin Islands, Burundi, the Cayman Islands, Ceylon, Chad, Chile, China, Colombia, the Congo, Dominica, Egypt, El Salvador, Ethiopia, Gambia, Grenada, Haiti, India, Indonesia, Iran, Iraq, the Ivory Coast, Jamaica, Jordan, Kenya, the Khmer Republic, Korea, Kuwait, Lebanon, Lesotho, Liberia, Madagascar, Malawi, Montserrat, Morocco, Nepal, Niger, Nigeria, Pakistan, Panama, Peru, the Philippines, St. Kitts-Nevis-Anguilla, St. Lucia, St. Vincent, Sierra Leone, Singapore, Somalia, Sudan, Swaziland, the Syrian Arab Republic, Togo, the Turks and Caicos Islands, Uganda, the United Republic of Tanzania, Upper Volta, Venezuela, Western Samoa, Yemen and Yugoslavia.

Missions were undertaken by four inter-regional advisers of the Centre for Housing, Building and Planning to the following countries and territory: El Salvador, Ethiopia, Haiti, Iran, Iraq, Lebanon, Panama, the Philippines, Saudi Arabia, the Seychelles, Sierra Leone and Togo.

One hundred and twenty-five fellowships were awarded for study abroad to nationals of the following 31 countries and territory: Afghanistan, Brazil, Burma, Czechoslovakia, Egypt, Gambia, India, Iran, Iraq, Jordan, the Khmer Republic, Korea, Lebanon, Liberia, Madagascar, Malawi, Mauritius, Mexico, Nepal, Niger, Pakistan, Panama, Peru, Poland, St. Lucia, Singapore, Sudan,

Thailand, Turkey, the United Republic of Tanzania and Yemen.

Sixty-four fellowships were awarded for participation in: the United Nations Inter-regional Seminar on Urban Land Policies and Land-Use Control Measures, held in Madrid, Spain, in November 1971; the Inter-regional Seminar on Low-Cost Construction Resistant to Earthquakes and Hurricanes, convened in Skopje, Yugoslavia, in November 1971; and the inter-regional Seminar on the Use of Wood in Housing (with emphasis on the needs of developing countries), held in Vancouver, British Columbia, Canada, in July 1971.

An Inter-regional Symposium on Training of Planners for Comprehensive Regional Development was held from 14 to 28 June 1971, in Warsaw, Poland, and an Expert Group Meeting on Social Indicators for Housing and Urban Development met in Dublin, Ireland, from 4 to 8 October.

A United Nations Advisory Group Meeting on Housing Policies and Programmes met in Puerto Rico from 30 August to 3 September 1971.

The number of projects in the field of housing, building and planning financed under the Special Fund component of the United Nations Development Programme increased by three during 1971, bringing the total of approved projects in the substantive field to 26.

Among publications issued in 1971 were: *Design of Low-Cost Housing and Community Facilities*, Vol. 1: "Climate and House Design"; *Improvement of Slums and Uncontrolled Settlements*, report of the Inter-regional Seminar held in Medellín, Colombia, 15 February–1 March 1970; and *Social Programming of Housing in Urban Areas.*

Decisions of Committee on
Housing, Building and Planning

The Committee on Housing, Building and Planning, at its seventh session, held in Geneva, Switzerland, from 18 to 29 October 1971, discussed: housing, building and planning in the Second United Nations Development Decade; problems of the human environment; social aspects of urban development and housing; rehabilitation of slums, squatter and other forms of uncontrolled settlements, and improvement of rural settlements; urban land policies and land-use control measures; finance for housing and community facilities; the industrialization of building; the economics of urban development; the campaign to focus world-wide attention on housing; a world housing survey; training of skilled manpower; funds expended in international programmes; and the work programme of the Committee.

The Committee, which had before it a report of the Secretary-General on housing, building and planning in the Second United Nations Development Decade and the problems and priorities in human settlements, noted: that plans for physical development should be based on social and economic considerations; that legislative frameworks were necessary to provide land tenure to permit the urban poor to build shelters on their own land; that essential urban infrastructure needed to be provided in portions of cities occupied by immigrants and other very low-income families; and that indigenous institutions and local skills needed to be developed.

The establishment of interdisciplinary teams in development planning was welcomed; it was requested that such teams include appropriate experts in urban and regional planning.

The Committee agreed with the Preparatory Committee for the United Nations Conference on the Human Environment that a proposal for an international housing programme be carefully studied by the United Nations system. (See pp. 307-13.)

On the problems of slums and squatter settlements, the Committee recommended to the Economic and Social Council that United Nations Members adopt measures for the improvement of slums and uncontrolled settlement areas and that they and the Secretary-General formulate a strategy for co-ordinated action and maximum utilization of United Nations resources to broaden the exchange of knowledge through monitoring and research and establish training programmes at all levels to encourage popular participation in solving the problems of slums and squatter settlements.

The Committee also recommended that the Secretary-General propose to the Secretariat of the United Nations Conference on the Human Environment that it accord high priority to the problem of slums and squatter settlements.

Taking note of the Secretary-General's recommendation on the Campaign to Focus World Attention on Housing, the Committee agreed to postpone this campaign to avoid duplicating efforts connected with the Second United Nations Development Decade and the Conference on the Human Environment.

The Committee, noting the inability of the International Labour Organisation (ILO) to continue its series of studies on the training of skilled manpower in housing, building and planning for developing countries, recommended that the Economic and Social Council urge ILO to restore this item to its work programme and requested the Secretary-General to search for the necessary resources for completion of this project.

In approving the six-year and two-year work programmes of the Centre for Housing, Building and Planning, the Committee emphasized that available resources should be concentrated on projects that would yield early and practical results and also recommended greater emphasis on specific problems of squatter settlements and a project on measures for the improvement of the building industry as a tool for human settlements development. The approved work programmes included continuing technical co-operation, servicing and periodic reporting of relevant United Nations meetings, collection and analysis of data, and study projects and seminars.

DOCUMENTARY REFERENCES

Decisions of Committee on
Housing, Building and Planning
E/5086. Report of Committee on Housing, Building and Planning on its 7th session, 18-29 October 1971, Geneva, Switzerland. (Chapter XII: Draft resolutions recommended for adoption by Economic and Social Council; Chapter XIII: Resolution to be drawn to attention of Council; Annex II: List of documents.)

Elections

Economic and Social Council—50th session
Plenary meeting 1770.

E/4968 and Add.1. Election of 9 members of Committee on Housing, Building and Planning. Note by Secretary-General.
E/5044. Resolutions adopted by Economic and Social Council during its 50th session, 11-13 January and 26 April–21 May 1971. Other decisions, pp. 30-31 (item 17).

Other documents
A/8401. Report of Secretary-General on work of the Organization, 16 June 1970–15 June 1971, Part Three, Chapter II F.
ST/TAO/SER.C/127. Report of United Nations Seminar on Physical Planning Techniques for Construction of New Towns, Moscow, USSR, 2-22 September 1968.

ST/TAO/SER.C/130. Symposium on Impact of Urbanization on Man's Environment, sponsored by United Nations in co-operation with International Trade Union of United Automotive, Aerospace and Agricultural Implement Workers of America, United Nations Headquarters, N.Y., and UAW Family Education Center, Onaway, Michigan, 13-20 June 1970.

ST/TAO/SER.C/131. Report of Inter-regional Seminar on Physical Planning for Tourism Development, Dubrovnik, Yugoslavia, 19 October-3 November 1970.

ST/TAO/SER.C/132. Report of Inter-regional Seminar on Physical Planning for Urban, Regional and National Development, held at Bucharest, Romania, 22 September-7 October 1969.

ST/TAO/SER.C/134. Report of the Inter-regional Seminar on the Financing of Housing and Urban Development, Copenhagen, Denmark, 25 May-10 June 1970.

ST/TAO/SER.C/137. Report of the Seminar on the Use of Wood in Housing (with emphasis on the needs of developing countries), Vancouver, British Columbia, Canada, 2-16 July 1971.

ST/TAO/SER.C./141. Report of Seminar on Prefabrication of Houses for Latin America, Copenhagen, Denmark, 13 August-1 September 1967.

Social services

Technical aid and studies in 1971

In 1971, United Nations activities in social welfare focused on the development of regional centres for training and research in social welfare and social development and on the expansion of programmes concerning social welfare aspects of family planning. Studies on the role of women in development and on the problems of the aged in society were also initiated.

During 1971, the services of 22 social welfare experts were made available to 17 countries under the United Nations technical co-operation programme. In addition, the services of three regional and two inter-regional advisers were provided. Nineteen fellowships were awarded to nationals of 11 Member States.

A study on rehabilitation of the war disabled, based on replies to a General Assembly questionnaire received from 23 countries, was published in 1971. The report of the United Nations interregional training course for instructors in prosthetics, held in 1969, was published, and the report of the 1971 course was issued in mimeographed form. A report entitled "Establishment of Technical Orthopaedic Services in Iran and Progression to International-scale Training Activities" was published in 1971.

Organization and administration
of social welfare services

Technical assistance advisory services in the planning, organization and administration of social welfare services were made available in 1971 to the following countries: Cyprus, Haiti, Iran, Jamaica, Korea, Liberia, Togo and Zambia.

A conference of Arab ministers of social affairs was convened in Cairo, Egypt, from 23 to 25 March 1971, as a follow-up to a 1968 international conference of social welfare ministers.

Two sub-regional training workshops on social welfare planning and plan implementation were convened by the Economic Commission for Asia and the Far East (ECAFE) from 19 to 28 August 1971 in Singapore, and from 1 to 9 September 1971 in Islamabad, Pakistan.

An inter-regional seminar on industrial social welfare was held in Moscow, the USSR, from 16 October to 5 November 1971.

A seminar on local participation in programmes for the elderly was convened under the European Programme in Gummersbach, near Cologne, the Federal Republic of Germany, during November 1971.

Family and child welfare

In 1971, advisory services in family and child welfare were provided to Colombia, the Republic of Viet-Nam and the Syrian Arab Republic.

The United Nations Children's Fund (UNICEF) continued its assistance to Governments in the field of family and child welfare. It also assisted in convening regional seminars on children and youth in Panama, Thailand and Togo.

An inter-regional meeting of experts on the social welfare aspects of family planning was convened at United Nations Headquarters in March 1971.

A seminar on family planning and social policy in Europe took place at Kiljava, Finland, in May 1971.

A regional conference on education, vocational training and work opportunities for girls and women was convened by the Economic Commission for Africa (ECA) in Rabat, Morocco, in May 1971.

Training of social welfare personnel

In 1971, advisory services in social welfare training were made available to China, Guyana, Korea, Iraq, Mali, the Philippines, the Republic of Viet-Nam, Thailand and Uganda.

Rehabilitation of the disabled

An inter-regional training course for instructors in prosthetics, organized by the United Nations and the Government of Denmark in co-operation with the International Society for Prosthetics and Orthotics, was held from 30 August to 25 September 1971 in Rungsted Kyst, Denmark. Nineteen participants, from Burma, the Dominican Republic, Egypt, Ethiopia, Ghana, Iran, Iraq, Jordan, Kenya, Liberia, the Republic of Korea, Sudan, Turkey and Uganda, attended the course. All 19 were awarded fellowships.

Technical assistance projects were completed in Iran, Israel and Nigeria while such projects were continued in the Dominican Republic, Laos and Spain. Short-term survey and advisory missions were sent to Afghanistan, Burma, Cyprus, Jordan, the Khmer Republic, Pakistan, Thailand and Yemen.

Conference of European social welfare ministers

Before the Commission for Social Development at its twenty-second session, held from 1 to 22 March 1971, was a note by the Secretary-General on the possibility of convening in 1972 a conference of European ministers responsible for social welfare. The Government of the Netherlands was prepared to provide host facilities.

On 18 March 1971, the Commission decided to recommend to the Economic and Social Council that, subject to a positive outcome of the Secretary-General's consultations with Governments of European Members of the United Nations or members of the specialized agencies on the merits of the proposal and provided that there would be no financial implications to the United Nations that could not be absorbed within the resources available to the Secretariat, the proposed Conference should be convened under United Nations auspices with the co-operation of the Netherlands.

On 21 May 1971, the Economic and Social Council, after being informed of the positive outcome of consultations between the Secretary-General and the Governments concerned and having noted that there would be no financial implications to the United Nations that could not be absorbed within the resources available to the Secretariat, decided (without adopting a resolution) to approve the convening of the Conference.

The Council acted on the recommendation of its Social Committee, which on 11 May 1971 had approved the text of the decision, which had been proposed by the Commission for Social Development.

Social security in context of national development

The Commission for Social Development at its session in March 1971 had before it a report entitled "Social Security in the Context of National Development," prepared by the International Labour Organisation (ILO) with the co-operation of the United Nations Secretariat.

On 22 March 1971, the Commission decided to include in its report to the Economic and Social Council a summary of its main conclusions on this question, as follows:

(1) Social security schemes were seen as an important instrument to achieve goals as outlined in the International Development Strategy for the Second United Nations Development Decade, such as those aiming to bring about a more equitable distribution of income and wealth to achieve a greater degree of income security and to expand and improve health facilities. A co-ordinated system of alternative social policies and programmes, nevertheless, would have to be evolved.

(2) Greater attention should be given by development planners to the role of social security and its possible contribution to over-all development objectives. However, it was recognized that for developing countries to undertake any comprehensive social security scheme was most difficult. Particular concern was expressed about the situation in developing countries in which the bulk of the population was not generally covered by social security schemes.

(3) In some industrialized countries, social security schemes were undergoing a thorough reassessment in order to ensure better protection particularly to the segments of the population with the most urgent and acute social needs.

(4) The disparity between the situations of developed and developing countries precluded any global standardization of social security schemes.

The ILO was urged to pursue the analysis initiated in the report and to undertake more experimentation and research, especially in developing countries.

DOCUMENTARY REFERENCES

Economic and Social Council—50th session
Social Committee, meetings 660-665, 667, 668.
Plenary meetings 1770, 1771.

Conference of European social welfare ministers
E/4984. Report of Commission for Social Development on its 22nd session, 1-22 March 1971, Chapter IV C (recommendation, para. 128).
E/5029. Report of Social Committee, paras. 17 and 19, draft decision II.
E/5044. Resolutions adopted by Economic and Social Council during its 50th session, 11-13 January and 26 April-21 May 1971. Decisions, p. 15.

Social security in context of national development
E/4984. Report of Commission for Social Development on its 22nd session, 1-22 March 1971, Chapter II.

Other documents
Report of the Inter-regional Meeting of Experts on the Social Welfare Aspects of Family Planning, United Nations Headquarters, 22-30 March 1971. U.N.P. Sales No.: E.71.IV.11.
Planning, Organization and Administration of National Rehabilita-

tion Programmes for the Disabled in Developing Countries, Geneva, Switzerland, 27 September–6 October 1971. U.N.P. Sales No.: E.72.IV.1.

ST/TAO/SER.C/140. Report of United Nations Inter-regional Seminar on Industrial Social Welfare, Moscow, USSR, 16 October–5 November 1971.

Social defence

Technical aid and publications in 1971

The activities of the United Nations in social defence during 1971 were directed towards the development of more effective international co-operation in the prevention and control of crime and the treatment of offenders. Major attention was given to the intensification of international efforts to advance knowledge, exchange theoretical and practical experience and develop policies in crime prevention consistent with comprehensive economic and social development.

The fifth session of the Advisory Committee of Experts on the Prevention of Crime and the Treatment of Offenders was held at United Nations Headquarters from 19 to 26 July 1971. Three closely linked subjects, social defence policies in relation to development planning, participation of the public in crime prevention, and the organization of research as a basis for policy development in social defence, were primary subjects of discussion.

During 1971, the United Nations Asia and Far East Institute for the Prevention of Crime and Treatment of Offenders in Fuchu, Japan, conducted three international training courses. A total of 66 trainees from 15 countries of the region participated in the courses.

The United Nations continued to extend technical support to the National Centre for Social and Criminological Research in Cairo, Egypt, during 1971. One training course was attended by 19 trainees from eight Middle Eastern and African countries; a seminar was attended by 25 participants from 11 Middle Eastern countries. The services of four short-term experts were provided by the United Nations during 1971 to assist in the further development of the Centre.

Ten fellowships and the services of experts were provided to the following countries, among others, during 1971: Burma, Ceylon, Costa Rica, Egypt, Guyana, Iran, Tunisia, Venezuela and Yugoslavia.

Two inter-regional advisers on social defence matters visited 35 countries during 1971 to advise on various aspects of social defence planning.

A special issue (No. 29) of the *International Review of Criminal Policy* was prepared in 1971. This issue dealt exclusively with social defence developments in the Eastern European countries.

Criminality and social change

Both the General Assembly and the Economic and Social Council took up questions concerning criminality and social change in 1971.

Their decisions were based on proposals of the Fourth United Nations Congress on the Prevention of Crime and the Treatment of Offenders and the Commission for Social Development.

The Commission for Social Development, at its twenty-second session (1-22 March 1971), had before it a note by the Secretary-General on the question of criminality and social change highlighting main issues and problems and containing a proposed work programme in social defence for the period 1971–1975, a summary of the conclusions and recommendations of the Fourth United Nations Congress on the Prevention of Crime and the Treatment of Offenders, and the report of the Advisory Committee of Experts on the Prevention of Crime and the Treatment of Offenders. (Both the Congress and the Committee of Experts met in Kyoto, Japan, in August 1970.)

The Commission incorporated the suggested work programme in social defence into its work programme in the whole field of social development for 1971–1975, and recommended a draft resolution for adoption by the Economic and Social Council.

On 21 May 1971, the Council adopted the proposal of the Commission. It endorsed the Declaration and the conclusions and recommendations of the Fourth United Nations Congress on the Prevention of Crime and the Treatment of Offenders.

The Secretary-General was requested to implement to the fullest extent the resolutions of the Congress applicable to the United Nations by intensifying international efforts to advance knowledge, exchange experiences and develop policy and practical and popular participation in crime prevention as proposed by the Secretary-General, especially through:

(a) direct aid to Governments requesting it;

(b) the development and extension of research institutes for training and research in the prevention of crime and the treatment of offenders;

(c) the promotion of action-oriented research into all aspects of crime prevention and control, especially through the United Nations Social Defence Research Institute;

(d) the organization of seminars, training courses, workshops and meetings of experts at the national, regional and inter-regional levels and the full involvement of Governments, universities and non-governmental organizations in this exchange of information and experience; and

(e) wider dissemination of information on the

prevention of crime and treatment of offenders.

The Council decided to enlarge the membership of the Advisory Committee on the Prevention of Crime and the Treatment of Offenders from 10 to 15 in order to provide the variety of professional expertise needed on social defence questions spread over a wide geographical area.

It recommended that the General Assembly consider fully the situation arising from increasing criminality and such measures as might be necessary to deal with it.

These decisions were among those embodied in resolution 1584(L), which the Council adopted, by 21 votes to 0, with 2 abstentions, on the recommendation of its Social Committee.

The Social Committee had approved the text submitted by the Commission, by 21 votes to 0, with 2 abstentions, on 10 May 1971.

(For text of resolution, see DOCUMENTARY REFERENCES below.)

Annexed to Council resolution 1584(L) was the text of the Declaration of the Fourth United Nations Congress on the Prevention of Crime and the Treatment of Offenders.

Later in the year, at its twenty-sixth session, which opened on 21 September 1971, the General Assembly took up the question of criminality and social change.

On 18 December 1971, the Assembly welcomed the Economic and Social Council's decisions on criminality and social change and decided, because of the limited time available to it at its 1971 session, to consider in depth the question of crime prevention and control at its 1972 session.

In this connexion, the Assembly recognized the importance of the Declaration adopted by the Fourth United Nations Congress on the Prevention of Crime and the Treatment of Offenders and noted that it was conscious of the serious threat that criminality presented to economic and social development and the quality of life.

These decisions were embodied in resolution 2843(XXVI), adopted, by 113 votes to 0, on the recommendation of the Assembly's Third (Social, Humanitarian and Cultural) Committee, which approved the text on 10 December 1971 by 73 votes to 0, on the basis of a proposal by Brazil, Canada, Costa Rica, Cyprus, Finland, France, Ghana, India, Japan, the Philippines, Romania, Sweden, the United Kingdom, the United States and Venezuela. (For text, see DOCUMENTARY REFERENCES below.)

DOCUMENTARY REFERENCES

Economic and Social Council—50th session
Social Committee, meetings 660-665, 667.
Plenary meetings 1770, 1771.

Fourth United Nations Congress on the Prevention of Crime and the Treatment of Offenders, Kyoto, Japan, 17–26 August 1970. Report prepared by Secretariat. U.N.P. Sales No.: E.71.IV.8.
International Review of Criminal Policy, No. 29, 1971. U.N.P. Sales No.: E.72.IV.2.
E/4984. Report of Commission for Social Development on its 22nd session, 1-22 March 1971, Chapter V (resolution 6(XXII)).
E/4984, Chapter X. Draft resolution VI, as corrected by Committee Chairman, approved by Social Committee on 10 May 1971, meeting 667, by 21 votes to 0, with 2 abstentions.
E/5029. Report of Social Committee, draft resolution VI.

RESOLUTION 1584 (L), as recommended by Social Committee, E/5029, adopted by Council on 21 May 1971, meeting 1771, by 21 votes to 0, with 2 abstentions.

The Economic and Social Council,

Having considered the note by the Secretary-General on criminality and social change, the conclusions and recommendations of the Fourth United Nations Congress on the Prevention of Crime and the Treatment of Offenders, held at Kyoto, Japan, from 17 to 26 August 1970, and the recommendations of the Advisory Committee of Experts on the Prevention of Crime and the Treatment of Offenders, which met after the Congress,

Recognizing the historic importance of the Declaration unanimously adopted by the Congress, calling attention to the urgent need for the United Nations and other international organizations to give high priority to the strengthening of international co-operation in crime prevention,

Being conscious of the serious threat that criminality presents to the quality of economic and social development and to the wholesomeness of economic and social progress and social change,

Recalling the responsibility assumed by the United Nations in the field of crime prevention as a consequence of General Assembly resolution 415(V) of 1 December 1950 and the affirmation of United Nations leadership in crime prevention reflected in Economic and Social Council resolutions 731 F (XXVIII) of 30 July 1959, 830 D (XXXII) of 2 August 1961 and 1086 B (XXXIX) of 30 July 1965,

Mindful of the need for closer working relationships in crime prevention among all United Nations bodies and especially the Commission for Social Development, the Commission on Narcotic Drugs and the Commission on Human Rights,

1. *Endorses* the Declaration of the Fourth United Nations Congress on the Prevention of Crime and the Treatment of Offenders, the text of which is annexed to the present resolution, commends it to the attention of Governments and urges the Secretary-General to give it the widest possible circulation;

2. *Further endorses* the conclusions and recommendations of the Congress;

3. *Requests* the Secretary-General to implement to the fullest extent those conclusions and recommendations of the Congress applicable to the United Nations, by intensifying international efforts to advance knowledge, exchange experience and develop policy, practice and public participation in crime prevention, as set out in his note, and especially by:

(a) Direct aid to Governments requesting it, including technical assistance to improve local services, the use of advisers at the country, regional and interregional levels, and the circulation of data as required by countries needing information to improve the quality of their crime preventive work;

(b) The development and extension of regional institutes for training and research in the prevention of crime and the treatment of offenders;

(c) The encouragement and promotion of research of an action-oriented character into all aspects of crime prevention and control, especially through the United Nations Social Defence Research Institute at Rome;

(d) The organization of seminars, training courses, workshops and meetings of experts at the national, regional and interregional levels, and the full involvement of Governments, universities and non-governmental organizations in this exchange of information and experience;

(e) Wider dissemination of information on the prevention of crime and the treatment of offenders through the publication in various languages, proposed by the Secretary-General, of the *International Review of Criminal Policy* and other means;

4. *Invites* Member States to give more immediate consideration to ways of strengthening national and international action for crime prevention, especially through the sharing of costs of international meetings and by acting as host to regional or international research centres or by any other measures deemed appropriate, and to give more consideration to the social and economic factors which are related to criminality;

5. *Decides* to enlarge from ten to fifteen the membership of the Advisory Committee of Experts on the Prevention of Crime and the Treatment of Offenders, established under General Assembly resolution 415(V), in order to provide the variety of professional expertise needed on social defence questions spread over a wider geographical area, and to consider terminating the former Consultative Group on the Prevention of Crime and the Treatment of Offenders in the light of this enlargement;

6. *Further decides* that the members of the Committee shall be appointed by the Economic and Social Council on the recommendation of the Secretary-General, that the Committee be renamed the Committee on Crime Prevention and Control and that it should report to the Commission for Social Development and, as appropriate on particular aspects, to the Commission on Human Rights and the Commission on Narcotic Drugs;

7. *Requests* the Secretary-General to consult with the heads of the regional economic commissions and the United Nations Economic and Social Office at Beirut, with a view to involving them more closely in international action in the field of the prevention of crime and the treatment of offenders;

8. *Further requests* the Secretary-General to include in the provisional agenda of the twenty-sixth session of the General Assembly an item entitled "Criminality and social change" to enable the General Assembly to consider fully the situation arising from increasing criminality and such measures as might be necessary to deal with it.

ANNEX

Declaration of the Fourth United Nations Congress on the Prevention of Crime and the Treatment of Offenders

The Fourth United Nations Congress on the Prevention of Crime and the Treatment of Offenders, meeting at Kyoto, Japan, from 17 to 26 August 1970, attended by participants from eighty-five countries representing all regions of the world,

Being deeply concerned with the increasing urgency of the need for the world community of nations to improve its planning for economic and social development by taking fuller account of the effects of urbanization, industrialization and the technological revolution upon the quality of life and the human environment,

Affirming that inadequacies in the attention paid to the quality of life in the process of development are manifest in the increasing seriousness and proportions of the problem of crime in many countries,

Observing that the world-wide crime problem has many ramifications, covering the range of conventional crime as well as the more subtle and sophisticated types of organized crime and corruption, and subsuming the violence of protest and the danger of increasing escapism through the abuse of drugs and narcotics, and observing that crime in all its forms saps the energies of a nation and undermines its efforts to achieve a more wholesome environment and a better life for its people,

Believing that the problem of crime in the world, in its new dimensions, is far more serious now than at any other time in the long history of these congresses,

Feeling an inescapable obligation to alert the world to the serious consequences for society of the insufficient attention which is now being given to measures of crime prevention, which by definition include the treatment of offenders,

1. *Calls upon* all Governments to take effective steps to co-ordinate and intensify their crime preventive efforts within the context of the economic and social development which each country envisages for itself;

2. *Urges* the United Nations and other international organizations to give high priority to the strengthening of international co-operation in crime prevention and, in particular, to ensure the availability of effective technical aid to countries desiring such assistance for the development of action programmes for the prevention and control of crime and delinquency;

3. *Recommends* that special attention be given to the administrative, professional and technical structure necessary for more effective action to be taken to move more directly and purposefully into the area of crime prevention.

General Assembly—26th session
Third Committee, meeting 1905.
Plenary meeting 2025.

A/8372. Note by Secretary-General.
A/8403. Report of Economic and Social Council on work of its 50th and 51st sessions, Chapter XV D.
A/C.3/L.1922. Brazil, Canada, Costa Rica, Cyprus, Finland, France, Ghana, India, Japan, Philippines, Romania, Sweden, United Kingdom, United States, Venezuela: draft resolution, approved by Third Committee on 10 December 1971, meeting 1905, by 73 votes to 0.
A/8595. Report of Third Committee.

RESOLUTION 2843 (XXVI), as recommended by Third Committee, A/8595, adopted by Assembly on 18 December 1971, meeting 2025, by 113 votes to 0.

The General Assembly,

Recalling the responsibility assumed by the United Nations in the field of crime prevention and control under General Assembly resolution 415(V) of 1 December 1950 and the leading role in this area assigned to it by the Economic and Social Council in resolution 155 C (VII) of 13 August 1948, which the Council reaffirmed in its resolutions 731 F (XXVIII) of 30 July 1959, 830 D (XXXII) of 2 August 1961 and 1086 B (XXXIX) of 30 July 1965,

Taking account of the note by the Secretary-General on criminality and social change,

Recognizing the importance of the Declaration unanimously adopted by the Fourth United Nations Congress on the Prevention of Crime and the Treatment of Offenders, held at Kyoto, Japan, from 17 to 26 August 1970, which underscored the seriousness of the crime problem in many countries and called attention to the urgent need to give priority to the strengthening of international co-operation for crime prevention,

Conscious of the serious threat that criminality in its diverse forms and new dimensions presents to economic and social development and the quality of life,

Aware of the limited time available at its twenty-sixth session for the General Assembly to consider the matter adequately,

1. *Welcomes* Economic and Social Council resolution 1584(L) of 21 May 1971 on criminality and social change and the action taken to implement the conclusions of the Fourth United Nations Congress on the Prevention of Crime and the Treatment of Offenders;

2. *Decides* to consider the question of crime prevention and control in depth at its twenty-seventh session.

Other documents
A Policy Approach to Planning in Social Defence. U.N.P. Sales No.: E.72.IV.9.

Regional and community development

In 1971, 44 advisers in various aspects of community and regional development (including short-term consultants) were sent to Botswana, the Central African Republic, China, Ecuador, Egypt, El Salvador, the Ivory Coast, Japan, Kenya, Laos, Mali, Mexico, Nepal, Niger, Nigeria, the Philippines, Saudi Arabia, Swaziland, Togo, Tunisia, the United Republic of Tanzania, Upper Volta, Venezuela, Yemen and Zambia. In addition, 73 fellowships were provided to trainees from 11 countries.

Work continued on projects financed by the United Nations Development Programme in Egypt, Saudi Arabia and Venezuela.

A regional adviser in community development was provided to the United Nations Economic and Social Office at Beirut, Lebanon, and an adviser in rural life and institutions was placed in the Office of the Economic Commission for Latin America.

A number of short-term consultants were also engaged to assist Member States in organizing research and training in regional development and to help in the preparation of teaching materials.

As in the past, a rural development training course for officers from English-speaking African countries was conducted at Holte, Denmark.

A course of training in regional development was conducted at the United Nations Centre for Regional Development in Nagoya, Japan. Another course was conducted at the Settlement Study Centre, Rehovot, Israel, for which the United Nations provided fellowships. A training course in regional and local development planning for participants from Latin American countries was also held.

The Inter-regional Symposium on Training Planners for Comprehensive Regional Development met in Warsaw, Poland, from 14 to 28 June 1971. Participants from more than 20 developing and developed countries exchanged views and experiences on regional planning as an instrument for comprehensive national development.

As a follow-up to the Warsaw meeting, the Symposium on European Co-operation in Training Regional Planners from Developing Countries was held in Stockholm, Sweden, from 5 to 11 September 1971. Participants, including both European and non-European specialists, discussed training implications of the social science approach to regional planning and European inputs to training processes.

A study entitled *Popular Participation in Development: Emerging Trends in Community Development* was published in 1971.

Chapter XVI

Questions relating to youth

During 1971, both the General Assembly and the Commission on Human Rights took decisions on questions relating to youth. Among other things, the Assembly called attention to the important role that young people have in social and economic development.

The General Assembly decided that a mural should be painted at United Nations Headquarters to commemorate the World Youth Assembly, which had been held in 1970. (See p. 665.)

The Assembly also made a number of recommendations concerning youth and dependence-producing drugs. (See p. 382.)

Decisions of Human Rights Commission

At its February-March 1971 session, the Commission on Human Rights studied the question of the education of youth all over the world for the development of its personality and the strengthening of its respect for the rights of man and fundamental freedoms.

The Commission urged Governments, organizations of the United Nations system and other interested bodies to devote attention to the problems involved in the education of youth for devotion to social progress and respect for human rights.

Among the Commission's decisions was one requesting the Secretary-General to make available information on conscientious objection to military service, to seek from Members up-to-date information on the subject and to submit a report on the matter to the Commission as soon as possible.

Also, the Commission requested the United Nations Educational, Scientific and Cultural Organization (UNESCO) to ask its members for information on how human rights were taught in their universities. It further requested UNESCO to consider the desirability of envisaging the systematic study and the development of an independent scientific discipline of human rights and to report on the matter to the Commission.

(See also p. 437.)

Decisions of General Assembly

On 22 November 1971, the General Assembly took decisions on the subject of youth, its problems and needs and its participation in national development.

After noting the serious problems still facing many of the world's youth with regard to health, education, training, employment, housing and social services and their opportunities to participate in national development as described in the *1970 Report on the World Social Situation,* the Assembly emphasized the need of the United Nations and the specialized agencies to increase their contribution to the education of youth and to enlarge their programmes and projects related to youth.

The Assembly asked the Secretary-General to invite comments from Governments on the implementation of the Declaration on the Promotion among Youth of the Ideals of Peace, Mutual Respect and Understanding between Peoples, which was adopted by the Assembly on 7 December 1965.[1]

It also decided to consider no later than at its 1973 session the question of youth, its education in the respect for human rights and fundamental freedoms, its problems and needs and its active participation in national development and international co-operation.

These decisions were embodied in resolution 2770(XXVI), adopted by a recorded vote of 91 to 0. The Assembly acted on the recommendation of its Third (Social, Humanitarian and Cultural) Committee, which approved the text unanimously

on 18 October 1971, on the basis of a proposal by Afghanistan, Austria, Bulgaria, Chile, Guinea, Honduras, Indonesia, Iran, Kenya, Malaysia, Mali, Mauritania, Mongolia, Morocco, Nigeria, Peru, Romania, Senegal, Somalia, Tunisia, the Ukrainian SSR, the United Republic of Tanzania and Yugoslavia. (For text, see DOCUMENTARY REFERENCES below.)

Assistance activities in 1971

At the regional level, a seminar on the role of youth in the dynamics of social development was held in Bucharest, Romania, from 16 to 26 May 1971 under the European Social Development Programme, and a seminar on national youth policies was held in Beirut, Lebanon, from 21 to 25 June 1971 under the sponsorship of the United Nations Economic and Social Office at Beirut.

These two seminars, together with similar meetings held in 1970 in Africa and in Asia and the Far East, preceded an international symposium on the participation of youth in the Second United Nations Development Decade, which was held by the United Nations in Geneva, Switzerland, from 27 September to 7 October 1971. Specialists from 24 developing and industrialized countries attended and adopted a report suggesting guidelines for United Nations action related to youth during the Second Development Decade.

Advisory missions were sent in 1971 to Barbados, British Honduras (Belize), Botswana, Burundi, Cameroon, Colombia, Costa Rica, Dominica, El Salvador, Gabon, Guatemala, Honduras, Iran, St. Lucia, St. Vincent, Swaziland, Togo, Trinidad and Tobago, Turkey, Uganda, Upper Volta and Venezuela.

During the year, long-term technical assistance advisers were requested by Hong Kong, Jamaica and Sudan.

A study of *New Trends in Service by Youth* was issued in 1971.

[1]See Y.U.N., 1965, pp. 480-81, text of resolution 2037(XX).

DOCUMENTARY REFERENCES

Decisions of Human Rights Commission

E/4949. Report of Commission on Human Rights on its 27th session, 22 February–26 March 1971, Geneva, Switzerland, Chapters VI and XIX (resolutions 11 A, B and C(XXVII)).

Decisions of General Assembly

General Assembly—26th session
Third Committee, meetings 1824-1839.
Plenary meeting 1991.

1970 Report on the World Social Situation (ST/SOA/110). U.N.P. Sales No.: E.71.IV.13.
A/8401. Report of Secretary-General on work of the Organization, 16 June 1970–15 June 1971, Part Three, Chapter I A 13.

A/C.3/L.1854. Austria, Bulgaria, Chile, Indonesia, Iran, Mali, Mauritania, Mongolia, Morocco, Nigeria, Romania, Senegal, Tunisia, Ukrainian SSR: draft resolution.
A/C.3/L.1854/Rev.1. Afghanistan, Austria, Bulgaria, Chile, Guinea, Honduras, Indonesia, Iran, Kenya, Malaysia, Mali, Mauritania, Mongolia, Morocco, Nigeria, Peru, Romania, Senegal, Somalia, Tunisia, Ukrainian SSR, United Republic of Tanzania, Yugoslavia: revised draft resolution, as orally amended by Chairman, approved unanimously by Third Committee on 18 October 1971, meeting 1839.
A/8507. Report of Third Committee (on world social situation), draft resolution I.

RESOLUTION 2770(XXVI), as recommended by Third Committee, A/8507, adopted by Assembly on 22 November 1971, meeting 1991, by recorded vote of 91 to 0, as follows:

In favour: Algeria, Argentina, Australia, Austria, Bahrain, Barbados, Belgium, Bhutan, Brazil, Bulgaria, Burma, Byelorussian SSR, Cameroon, Central African Republic, Ceylon, Chad, Chile, Colombia, Costa Rica, Cuba, Czechoslovakia, Dahomey, Denmark, Dominican Republic, Ecuador, Egypt, Equatorial Guinea, Finland, France, Gabon, Ghana, Greece, Guatemala, Guyana, Hungary, India, Indonesia, Iran, Iraq, Ireland, Italy, Ivory Coast, Jamaica, Japan, Jordan, Khmer Republic, Kuwait, Laos, Lebanon, Lesotho, Liberia, Libyan Arab Republic, Luxembourg, Madagascar, Mauritania, Mexico, Mongolia, Nepal, Netherlands, New Zealand, Nicaragua, Niger, Nigeria, Norway, Pakistan, People's Democratic Republic of Yemen, Peru, Philippines, Poland, Portugal, Qatar, Romania, Saudi Arabia, Sierra Leone, Singapore, Spain, Sudan, Swaziland, Sweden, Syrian Arab Republic, Thailand, Togo, Tunisia, Turkey, Ukrainian SSR, USSR, United States, Uruguay, Venezuela, Yugoslavia, Zambia.

Against: None.

The General Assembly,

Recognizing the important role of youth in the realization of the purposes of the Charter of the United Nations, in particular those concerning the promotion of higher standards of living and conditions of economic and social progress and development,

Emphasizing the tasks and responsibilities young people have been increasingly assuming in social and economic development, the promotion of human rights and the achievement of world peace, justice and progress,

Noting that serious problems still exist for the individual and social needs of many of the world's youth, in particular with regard to health, education, training, employment, housing and social services, and their opportunities to participate in national development as indicated in the *1970 Report on the World Social Situation,*

Aware of the need to increase the contribution of the United Nations and the specialized agencies concerned with the education of youth, in the spirit of peace, mutual understanding, friendly relations and co-operation among peoples, social justice, the dignity and value of the human person and respect for human rights and fundamental freedoms, as well as the need to enlarge their programmes and projects related to youth,

Noting that an analytical study in depth of the world social situation of youth, prepared in accordance with Economic and Social Council resolution 1407(XLVI) of 5 June 1969, will be completed in 1972,

Bearing in mind that a report of the Secretary-General on measures to be taken to establish channels of communication with youth and international youth organizations, requested by the General Assembly in resolution 2497(XXIV) of 28 October 1969, will be completed in 1972,

Desiring the realization of the aims of its resolution 2633(XXV) of 11 November 1970,

Recalling paragraph 16 of that resolution, in which the General Assembly decided to resume in the future the consideration of the item entitled "Youth, its education in the respect for human rights and fundamental freedoms, its problems and needs, and its participation in national development," taking into account in particular the advisability of considering the question of the implementation of the Declaration on the Promotion among Youth of the Ideals of Peace, Mutual Respect and Understanding between Peoples,

1.   *Requests* the Secretary-General to invite early comments from Governments on the question of the implementation of the Declaration on the Promotion among Youth of the Ideals of Peace, Mutual Respect and Understanding between Peoples;

2.   *Decides* to consider as soon as possible, but not later than at its twenty-eighth session, the item entitled "Youth, its education in the respect for human rights and fundamental freedoms, its problems and needs, and its active participation in national development and international co-operation."

Chapter XVII

Narcotic drugs

The aim of international control of narcotic drugs and psychotropic substances is to restrict the use of drugs to medical and scientific purposes through the co-operation of Governments. This co-operation takes place within the framework of the international narcotics treaties. By the end of 1971, the most recent of these treaties to come into force was the Single Convention on Narcotic Drugs, 1961, which, with some exceptions of detail, replaced the earlier treaties. The Convention on Psychotropic Substances, adopted February 1971, had not come into force by year's end.

The United Nations Economic and Social Council, with its Commission on Narcotic Drugs, formulates United Nations policies and co-ordinates the efforts of the international community in this field. The World Health Organization (WHO) recommends to the Commission the drugs that should be put under the different types of control, and generally advises on medical questions concerning drugs.

The International Narcotics Control Board ensures the supervising of the legal production and manufacture of, and trade in, narcotic drugs and also ensures that the aims of the international treaties are not endangered by the failure of Governments to carry out the provisions of these treaties.

The Commission on Narcotic Drugs, which had been put on a biennial cycle of sessions with effect from 1969, held its twenty-fourth regular session from 27 September to 21 October 1971 in Geneva, Switzerland.

The Government of Turkey informed the Commission of its decision to prohibit poppy cultivation and opium production in Turkey as at late 1972. The Commission was apprised of the text of a decree of 29 June 1971 by which the ban was enacted.

In view of the importance of the decision for the entire international community, the Commission unanimously expressed the hope that Turkey would be assisted in every possible way by all the agencies and organs of the United Nations system and all States interested in the problem in its efforts to compensate poppy cultivators for their loss of income resulting from the Government's decisions.

Convention on psychotropic substances

In response to an Economic and Social Council decision of 24 March 1970,[1] a United Nations Conference for the Adoption of a Protocol on Psychotropic Substances met in Vienna, Austria, from 11 January to 21 February 1971. Representatives from 71 States and observers from four attended the Conference. E. Nettel (Austria) was elected President.

Before the Conference was the text of the revised draft protocol on psychotropic substances, which had been prepared by the Commission on Narcotic Drugs at its first special session, in January 1970.[2]

The Conference decided to change the name of the instrument to be adopted from "Protocol" to "Convention," and on 21 February 1971 adopted and opened for signature the Convention on Psychotropic Substances. On that day, the Convention was signed on behalf of 23 States, all signatures being subject to ratification, with five of those States recording specific reservations.

The Convention was deposited with the Secretary-General and was to remain open for signature until 1 January 1972. It would come into force 90 days after 40 States had signed it without reservation or had deposited their instruments of ratification or accession. By 31 December 1971, 36 States had signed the Convention.

On 20 May 1971, the Economic and Social Council, expressing its satisfaction that the Convention on Psychotropic Substances had been adopted and opened for signature, and believing that the Convention constituted an essential contribution towards effective control of such substances and restriction of their use to medical and scientific purposes, invited States to give urgent consideration to becoming parties to the Convention.

The Council endorsed strongly the invitation of the Conference to States to apply provisionally the measures of control provided in the Convention, pending its entry into force for each of them, and it accepted the functions assigned by the Convention to the United Nations with regard to its execution.

These decisions were embodied in resolution 1576(L), which the Council adopted, by 23 votes to 0, with 3 abstentions, on the recommendation of its Social Committee. The Committee approved the text on 11 May 1971, by 20 votes to 0, with 4 abstentions, on the basis of a proposal by New Zealand, the United Kingdom and the United States, as orally amended by France.

(For text of resolution, see DOCUMENTARY REFERENCES below.)

Single Convention on Narcotic Drugs

On 20 May 1971, the Economic and Social Council, noting that amendments had been proposed to the 1961 Single Convention on Narcotic Drugs, decided to call a conference of plenipotentiaries to consider all amendments proposed to that Convention.

The Council requested the Secretary-General to convene such a conference as early as feasible in 1972, and to invite to the conference: parties to the Single Convention; other States Members of the United Nations or members of specialized agencies or the International Atomic Energy Agency or parties to the Statute of the International Court of Justice; the World Health Organization and other interested specialized agencies; the International Narcotics Control Board; and the International Criminal Police Organization.

The Commission on Narcotic Drugs was asked to study at its 1971 session proposals for amendments to the Single Convention, taking into consideration the need to ensure the effectiveness of control of both natural and synthetic drugs, with a view to submitting comments as appropriate to the conference.

These Council decisions were embodied in resolution 1577(L), which was adopted, by 24 votes to 2, on the recommendation of the Social Committee. The Committee approved the text on 11 May 1971, by 22 votes to 2, with 1 abstention, on the basis of a proposal by Greece, Indonesia, New Zealand, Norway, the United States, and Uruguay.

(For text of resolution, see DOCUMENTARY REFERENCES below.)

In letters dated 18 and 26 March 1971 to the Secretary-General, the United States had transmitted amendments to the Single Convention on Narcotic Drugs and requested that they be communicated to the parties to the Convention and to the Economic and Social Council. The United States Government had also proposed that the plenipotentiary conference be convened to consider any proposed amendments to the Single Convention.

On 17 December 1971, the Secretary-General communicated to all those invited to the conference the documents relating to the amendments to the Single Convention that had been considered by the Commission on Narcotic Drugs at its September-October 1971 session.

---

[1]See Y.U.N., 1970, pp. 493-94, text of resolution 1474(XLVIII).
[2]*Ibid.*, p. 490.

Implementation of treaties

Ratifications, accessions to and acceptance of treaties

During 1971, the following States became parties to the Single Convention on Narcotic Drugs, 1961: Fiji, Portugal, South Africa. As at 31 December 1971, the number of accessions to and ratifications of the 1961 Convention was 82.

Between 21 February and 31 December 1971, the following 36 States had signed the Convention on Psychotropic Substances: Argentina, Australia, Brazil, the Byelorussian SSR, Chile, China,[3] Costa Rica, Denmark, Egypt, the Federal Republic of Germany, Finland, France, Ghana, Greece, Guyana, the Holy See, Hungary, Iran, Japan, Lebanon, Liberia, Monaco, New Zealand, Paraguay, Poland, Rwanda, Sweden, Togo, Trinidad and Tobago, Turkey, the Ukrainian SSR, the United Kingdom, the United States, the USSR, Venezuela and Yugoslavia. (See section above on its adoption.)

The Government of Fiji, on 1 November 1971, deposited with the Secretary-General a notification of accession to the Protocol bringing under International Control Drugs Outside the Scope of the Convention of 13 July 1931 for Limiting the Manufacture and Regulating the Distribution of Narcotic Drugs, as amended by the Protocol signed at Lake Success, New York, on 11 December 1946, signed at Paris, on 19 November 1948.

Reports of Governments

Governments submit annual reports to the Secretary-General on the implementation of their obligations under the international narcotics treaties. In 1971, 122 countries and territories submitted annual reports for 1970.

During 1971, 21 Governments communicated to the Secretary-General the texts of 56 national laws and regulations on narcotics.

Illicit traffic

During 1971, the Secretary-General received 1,911 seizure reports covering a total of 2,208 individual seizures in respect of 39 countries. Information on illicit traffic in drugs was submitted by 124 Governments in their 1970 reports.

The main drugs involved continued to be opium and the opiates (morphine and heroin), cocaine, coca leaf and cannabis.

There were substantial increases in seizures of cocaine, heroin and cannabis, but illicit trafficking as a whole increased, and numerous reports of seizures of psychotropic substances were received.

Committee on illicit traffic

Following the resumption of opium production by Iran, the Commission at its 1971 session considered a report it had requested of the Secretary-General on contacts he was to make with Governments concerned with the problem of opium production and its illicit traffic. The report was prepared following a mission on behalf of the Secretary-General to Afghanistan, Iran, Pakistan and Turkey in 1969.

The Government of Iran's resumption of opium production, while under stringent control, was recognized to be a provisional measure which would be reviewed in the light of developments in other parts of the region from which illicit opium traffic into Iran originated. It was felt that the Government of Afghanistan should be encouraged to discuss and accept international assistance to contain and eliminate the illicit opium production in its territory.

The Commission decided to establish an *Ad Hoc* Committee on Illicit Traffic in the Near and Middle East to promote greater co-operation and mutual assistance among the States of the area.

The Commission decided that Iran, Pakistan and Turkey should be members of the *Ad Hoc* Committee and that Afghanistan should be invited to participate. The Committee was authorized to meet between the twenty-fourth (1971) and the twenty-fifth (1973) sessions of the Commission.

Action concerning drug abuses

At its 1971 session, the Commission on Narcotic Drugs noted that 74 replies had been received to a questionnaire on the abuse of psychotropic substances sent to 140 countries and territories by the Secretary-General. The Commission concluded that it was difficult to obtain an over-all view of the problem, since few statistics on addiction to psychotropic substances were available and since the phenomenon of multiple drug abuse made it extremely difficult to distinguish abusers.

The attention of the Commission was drawn repeatedly to the serious problem of khat-chewing in certain countries in the Middle East and Eastern Africa. The Commission recommended that the Economic and Social Council request WHO to move ahead on studies undertaken on khat.

The Commission also recommended to the Economic and Social Council that it recommend to Governments the application of the most severe control measures to prevent the abuse of and illicit traffic in cannabis.

[3]China is an original Member of the United Nations, the Charter having been signed and ratified on its behalf, on 26 June and 11 September 1945, respectively, by the Government of the Republic of China, which continued to represent China in the United Nations until 25 October 1971. On that date, the General Assembly adopted its resolution 2758(XXVI), by which it decided "to restore all its rights to the People's Republic of China and to recognize the representatives of its Government as the only legitimate representatives of China to the United Nations."

The above entry in respect of China refers to an action taken by the authorities representing China in the United Nations at the time of that action.

Fund for Drug Abuse Control

On 1 April 1971, the United Nations Fund for Drug Abuse Control was established. In this connexion, the Secretary-General proposed a plan for action against drug abuse, which the Commission on Narcotic Drugs considered at its 1971 session. The plan envisaged the expenditure of $95 million for the first five years: total contributions and firm pledges to the Fund amounted to $2,822,034 at the end of 1971.

Youth and dependence-producing drugs

At its twenty-sixth session, which opened on 21 September 1971, the General Assembly took a number of decisions on drug abuse. Considering that the abuse of narcotics and psychotropic drugs had become an extremely serious problem in many countries, the Assembly acknowledged that measures hitherto adopted in the fight against the abuse of drugs had not been sufficiently effective.

The Assembly acknowledged further that developing countries determined to prevent illicit production of and illicit traffic in narcotic drugs did not succeed in achieving their goal owing to economic and technical difficulties. It emphasized that the abuse of dependence-producing drugs presented an especially serious threat to the youth of the world.

The activities of the International Narcotics Control Board, the World Health Organization and other agencies were strongly endorsed by the Assembly, as it noted that only through the consistent implementation by States of their relevant measures coupled with international co-operation could the dangers of drug abuse be reduced. The Assembly warned in particular against attempts directed towards the weakening of existing controls over cannabis.

All States were urged to give wide support to the United Nations Fund for Drug Abuse Control and, in particular, to involve youth in activities aimed at controlling drug abuse. All competent bodies of the United Nations dealing with the question of narcotic drugs were requested to provide appropriate and effective assistance to developing countries to enable them to combat more effectively illicit production of and illicit traffic in narcotic drugs.

The Assembly appealed to all States to enact effective legislation against drug abuse, providing severe penalties for those engaged in illicit drug-trafficking, and it urged that steps be taken by Governments to inform in particular youth about the dangers of drug abuse, and to promote the establishment of comprehensive community-based drug treatment and rehabilitation facilities, especially for young drug users.

Finally, the Assembly requested the Secretary-General, in consultation with the specialized agencies concerned, to submit a report to the Economic and Social Council in 1972 on how the United Nations system could increase its effectiveness in the fight against drug abuse with special reference to the problems of youth in this respect.

These decisions were embodied in resolution 2859(XXVI), adopted on 20 December 1971, by 122 votes to 0, with 1 abstention, as recommended by the Third (Social, Humanitarian and Cultural) Committee. The Committee approved the text on 10 December 1971 by 94 votes to 0, on the basis of a proposal by Iceland, as amended by Afghanistan and Nigeria. (For text, see DOCUMENTARY REFERENCES below.)

A preambular amendment proposed by the Byelorussian SSR was adopted, by 103 votes to 0, with 8 abstentions, at the Assembly's plenary meeting on 20 December. This added a reference to the coupling of national action with international co-operation to reduce dangers of drug abuse.

Other activities

Technical assistance

A regional project was completed during the year: the Regional Training and Consultative Mission on Narcotics Control to Africa (Ghana, Liberia, Nigeria and Sierra Leone). A Regional and Consultative Mission on Narcotics Control to Europe visited Bulgaria, Greece, Romania and Yugoslavia in November and December 1971.

Fifty-five fellowships were awarded during the year to officials from Bolivia, Chile, China, Colombia, the Congo, Ecuador, Egypt, El Salvador, Greece, Honduras, Hong Kong, Indonesia, Iran, the Ivory Coast, Kenya, the Republic of Korea, Laos, Lebanon, Liberia, Malaysia, Mali, Niger, Pakistan, the Philippines, Senegal, Singapore, Somalia, the People's Democratic Republic of Yemen, the Syrian Arab Republic, Thailand, Togo, Yemen and Yugoslavia.

An officer of the Secretariat was posted to Bangkok, Thailand, to advise Governments in South-East Asia on narcotics questions and an expert was assigned to Iran as general narcotics adviser to the Government.

Publications

In 1971, four issues of the *Bulletin on Narcotics* were published, and the *Information Letter of the Division of Narcotic Drugs* series was published for the first time, under a grant from the United Nations Fund for Drug Abuse Control.

Scientific research

International collaboration was expanded in the United Nations research programmes on narcotic drugs. Scientists from many countries participated in the programmes; nominations of collaborating scientists were made by Belgium and Iceland. An institute was also designated for this purpose by Switzerland. Samples of cannabis and of opium and heroin were received, analysed and made available to collaborating scientists for research purposes.

Technical assistance, in the form of training in laboratory methods, was provided for fellowship holders from Colombia, El Salvador, Honduras, Iran, the Ivory Coast, Lebanon, Liberia, Niger, Pakistan, the Philippines, the Republic of Korea, Somalia, the People's Democratic Republic of Yemen and Yemen.

Drugs to be placed under international control

At its September–October 1971 session, the Commission on Narcotic Drugs decided to add the substance Algeril (the proposed international name of which is Propiram) to Schedule II of the Single Convention on Narcotic Drugs, 1961.

Report of International Narcotics Control Board

The report of the International Narcotics Control Board on its work in 1970 was published in 1971. The Board's annual report provided a digest of information on most aspects of the production, manufacture and utilization of narcotic drugs. It recorded the manner in which Governments had complied with the terms of the international treaties on narcotic drugs or failures of individual Governments to comply with their treaty obligations.

On 20 May 1971, the Economic and Social Council took note with appreciation of the Board's report by adopting, unanimously, resolution 1578(L), the text of which was recommended by the Social Committee. The Committee approved the text and amendments without a vote, on 10 and 11 May 1971, respectively, on the basis of a proposal by the Chairman. (For text, see DOCU-MENTARY REFERENCES below.)

DOCUMENTARY REFERENCES

REPORT OF COMMISSION ON NARCOTIC DRUGS
E/5082 and Corr.1. Report of Commission on Narcotic Drugs on its 24th session, 27 September–21 October 1971, Geneva, Switzerland. (Chapter XII: List of resolutions adopted by Commission; Chapter XIII: Draft resolutions recommended by Commission for action by Economic and Social Council; Annex IX: List of documents relevant to report of Commission.)
E/5073. Resolutions adopted by Economic and Social Council during its 51st session, 5–30 July 1971. Other decisions, p. 28 (Elections, para. (*b*)).

PROPOSAL FOR COMMISSION MEETING

Economic and Social Council—51st session
Plenary meeting 1799.

E/5073. Resolutions adopted by Economic and Social Council during its 51st session, 5–30 July 1971. Other decisions, p. 28 (Calendar of conferences and meetings for 1972, para. (*b*)).

PROHIBITION ON OPIUM PRODUCTION
E/L.1429 and Corr.1. Letter of 13 July 1971 from Turkey.
E/5082 and Corr.1. Report of 24th session of Commission on Narcotic Drugs, Chapter V.

Convention on Psychotropic Substances

Economic and Social Council—50th session
Social Committee, meetings 657, 659, 666, 668.
Plenary meetings 1769, 1770.

E/4966. Note by Secretary-General (transmitting Final Act of United Nations Conference for Adoption of Protocol on Psychotropic Substances and Text of Convention on Psychotropic Substances).
E/4966. Note by Secretary-General (resolution I).
E/AC.7/L.583 and Rev.1. New Zealand, United Kingdom, United States: draft resolution and revision, as orally amended by France, approved by Social Committee on 11 May 1971, meeting 668, by 20 votes to 0, with 4 abstentions.
E/5025. Report of Social Committee, draft resolution I.

RESOLUTION 1576(L), as recommended by Social Committee, E/5025, adopted by Council on 20 May 1971, meeting 1769, by 23 votes to 0, with 3 abstentions.

The Economic and Social Council,
Recalling its decision to convene a conference of plenipotentiaries for the adoption of a protocol on psychotropic substances,
Expressing its deep satisfaction that the United Nations Conference for the Adoption of a Protocol on Psychotropic Substances, held at Vienna from 11 January to 21 February 1971, adopted and opened for signature the Convention on Psychotropic Substances,
Believing that the Convention constitutes an essential contribution towards effective control of psychotropic substances and restriction of their use to medical and scientific purposes,
1. *Invites* States to give urgent consideration to becoming parties to the Convention on Psychotropic Substances;
2. *Endorses* strongly the invitation of the United Nations Conference for the Adoption of a Protocol on Psychotropic Substances to States, to the extent that they are able to do so, to apply provisionally the measures of control provided in the Convention pending its entry into force for each of them;
3. *Accepts* the functions assigned by the Convention to the United Nations in regard to its execution.

Single Convention on Narcotic Drugs

Economic and Social Council—50th session
Social Committee, meetings 657, 659, 666, 668.
Plenary meetings 1769, 1770.

E/4971 and Add.1. Letter of 18 March 1971 and memorandum from United States.
E/4985. Letter of 26 March 1971 from United States.
E/AC.7/L.584. France, Greece, Indonesia, New Zealand, Norway, United States, Uruguay: draft resolution.
E/AC.7/L.584/Rev.1. Greece, Indonesia, New Zealand, Norway, United States, Uruguay: revised draft resolution, approved by Social Committee on 11 May 1971, meeting 668, by 22 votes to 2, with 1 abstention.
E/AC.7/L.584/Add.1. Administrative and financial implications of

7-power draft resolution, E/AC.7/L.584. Note by Secretary-General.

E/5025. Report of Social Committee, draft resolution II.

RESOLUTION 1577(L), as recommended by Social Committee, E/5025, adopted by Council on 20 May 1971, meeting 1769, by 24 votes to 2.

The Economic and Social Council,
Noting that amendments have been proposed to the Single Convention on Narcotic Drugs, 1961,
Bearing in mind article 47 of that Convention,
Taking into consideration the Convention on Psychotropic Substances adopted at Vienna on 21 February 1971, and seeking to assure the effectiveness of control of both natural and synthetic drugs,
1. *Decides* to call, in accordance with Article 62, paragraph 4, of the Charter of the United Nations, a conference of plenipotentiaries to consider all amendments proposed to the Single Convention on Narcotic Drugs, 1961;
2. *Requests* the Secretary-General:
(a) To convene such a conference as early as feasible in 1972;
(b) To invite to the conference:
  (i) Parties to the Single Convention;
  (ii) Other States Members of the United Nations or members of specialized agencies or the International Atomic Energy Agency or parties to the Statute of the International Court of Justice;
  (iii) The World Health Organization and other interested specialized agencies, with the same rights as they have at sessions of the Economic and Social Council;
  (iv) The International Narcotics Control Board, with the same rights as it has at sessions of the Economic and Social Council;
  (v) The International Criminal Police Organization, with the same rights as it has at sessions of the Commission on Narcotic Drugs;
(c) To prepare provisional rules of procedure for the conference;
(d) To provide summary records for the conference and its committees;
3. *Requests* the Commission on Narcotic Drugs to study at its twenty-fourth session proposals for amendments to the Single Convention, taking into consideration the need to ensure the effectiveness of control of both natural and synthetic drugs, with a view to submitting comments as appropriate to the conference; these comments would be fully taken into account by the conference.

E/5082 and Corr.1. Report of Commission on Narcotic Drugs on its 24th session, Geneva, Switzerland, 27 September–21 October 1971, Chapter X and Annex VII.

Implementation of treaties

Estimated World Requirements of Narcotic Drugs and Estimates of World Production of Opium in 1971. U.N.P. Sales No.: E.71.XI.1; and *Supplements 1-4.* U.N.P. Sales Nos.: E/F/S.71.XI.4; E/F/S.71.XI.5; E/F/S.71.XI.7; E/F/S.71.XI.8.
Estimated World Requirements of Narcotic Drugs and Estimates of World Production of Opium in 1972. U.N.P. Sales No.: E.72.XI.1.
Comparative Statement of Estimates and Statistics on Narcotic Drugs for 1970 furnished by Governments in accordance with the International Treaties. U.N.P. Sales No.: E/F.72.XI.3 and corrigendum.
E/NA.1971/1 and Add.1. National authorities empowered to issue certificates and authorizations for import and export of narcotic drugs.
E/NF.1971/1. Manufacture of narcotic drugs.
E/NL.1965/Index/Add.4,5. National laws and regulations relating to control of narcotic drugs. Cumulative index 1947–1965, addenda Nos. 4 and 5.
E/5082 and Corr.1. Report of 24th session of Commission on Narcotic Drugs, Chapter II.

Illicit traffic

E/NS.1971/Summaries 1-4. Summaries of reports on illicit transactions and seizures of narcotic drugs and psychotropic substances received by Secretary-General from 1 January to 31 December 1971.
E/5082 and Corr.1. Report of 24th session of Commission on Narcotic Drugs, Chapter III and Annex V.

COMMITTEE ON ILLICIT TRAFFIC
E/5082 and Corr.1. Report of 24th session of Commission on Narcotic Drugs, Chapter VI.

Action concerning drug abuse

E/5082 and Corr.1. Report of 24th session of Commission on Narcotic Drugs, Chapters IV and IX.

FUND FOR DRUG ABUSE CONTROL
E/5082 and Corr.1. Report of 24th session of Commission on Narcotic Drugs, Chapters IV and IX.

YOUTH AND DEPENDENCE-PRODUCING DRUGS

General Assembly—26th session
Third Committee, meeting 1905.
Plenary meeting 2027.

A/8401. Report of Secretary-General on work of the Organization, 16 June 1970–15 June 1971, Part Three, Chapter VII B.
A/8403. Report of Economic and Social Council on work of its 50th and 51st sessions, Chapter XVI.
A/C.3/L.1917 and Rev.1. Iceland: draft resolution and revision, as orally amended by Nigeria and as amended by Afghanistan, A/C.3/L.1924/Rev.1, approved by Third Committee on 10 December 1971, meeting 1905, by 94 votes to 0.
A/C.3/L.1924 and Rev.1. Afghanistan: amendments and revised amendments to Icelandic draft resolution, A/C.3/L.1917.
A/L.668. Byelorussian SSR: amendment to draft resolution V recommended by Third Committee in A/8588.
A/8588. Report of Third Committee, draft resolution V.

RESOLUTION 2859(XXVI), as recommended by Third Committee, A/8588, and as amended by Byelorussian SSR, A/L.668, adopted by Assembly on 20 December 1971, meeting 2027, by 122 votes to 0, with 1 abstention.

The General Assembly,
Recalling its resolution 2719(XXV) of 15 December 1970, Economic and Social Council resolution 1578(L) of 20 May 1971 and World Health Assembly resolution WHA24.57 of 20 May 1971,
Considering that the abuse of narcotics and psychotropic drugs has become an extremely serious problem in many countries with disastrous results for the populations of these countries,
Acknowledging that measures hitherto adopted in the fight against the abuse of drugs have not been sufficiently effective, as some countries have taken positive steps while others have not yet taken adequate and effective measures for the suppression of illicit traffic in dependence-producing drugs,
Acknowledging further that developing countries determined to prevent illicit production of and illicit traffic in narcotic drugs do not succeed in achieving their goal owing to economic and technical difficulties,
Emphasizing that the abuse of dependence-producing drugs presents an especially serious threat to the youth of the world, among whom this disease has been growing at an alarming rate and now threatens the well-being of young people in a great number of countries,
Warning in particular against attempts directed towards the weakening of existing controls over the drug substance cannabis,
Noting that only through the consistent implementation by States of their relevant measures coupled with international co-operation can the dangers of drug abuse be reduced and this social malady effectively countered,
Strongly endorsing the activities of the International Narcotics Control Board, the World Health Organization and other agencies,

and their decision to redouble their efforts to control and combat drug abuse throughout the world,

1. *Urges* all States to give wide support to the United Nations Fund for Drug Abuse Control and, in particular, to involve youth in activities aimed at controlling drug abuse;

2. *Requests* all competent bodies of the United Nations dealing with the question of narcotic drugs to provide appropriate and effective assistance to developing countries with a view to enabling them to combat more effectively illicit production of and illicit traffic in narcotic drugs;

3. *Appeals* to all States to enact effective legislation against drug abuse, providing severe penalties for those engaged in illicit drug-trafficking;

4. *Urges* that steps be taken by Governments to inform in particular youth about the dangers of drug abuse, and to promote the establishment of comprehensive community-based drug treatment and rehabilitation facilities, especially for young drug users;

5. *Requests* the Secretary-General, in consultation with the specialized agencies concerned, to submit a report to the Economic and Social Council at its fifty-third session on how the United Nations system can increase its effectiveness in the fight against drug abuse with special reference to the problems of youth in this respect.

Report of International Narcotics Control Board

Economic and Social Council—50th session.
Social Committee, meetings 657, 659, 666, 668.
Plenary meetings 1769, 1770.

Report of the International Narcotics Control Board on its work in 1970 (E/INCB/9). U.N.P. Sales No.: E.71.XI.2.

E/4965. Report of INCB. Summary.

E/5025. Report of Social Committee, draft resolution III, as orally proposed by Chairman, approved without vote by Social Committee on 10 May 1971, meeting 666, as orally amended by New Zealand, Tunisia and Yugoslavia and by United States on 11 May 1971, meeting 668.

RESOLUTION 1578(L), as recommended by Social Committee, E/5025, adopted unanimously by Council on 20 May 1971, meeting 1769.

The Economic and Social Council

1. *Takes note with appreciation* of the report of the International Narcotics Control Board on its work in 1970;

2. *Expresses its appreciation* to the members of the Board for their valuable contribution during that year.

Report of the International Narcotics Control Board on its work in 1971 (E/INCB/13). U.N.P. Sales No.: E.72.XI.2.

Other documents

Bulletin on Narcotics (quarterly). *Vol. XXIII: No. 1, January–March 1971; No. 2, April–June 1971; No. 3, July–September 1971; No.4, October–December 1971.*

Information Letter of the Division of Narcotic Drugs (monthly) (NAR/INF.LETT./71), Nos: 1-10.

Chapter XVIII

Assistance to refugees

The Office of the United Nations High Commissioner for Refugees (UNHCR) continued during 1971 to provide international protection and assistance to refugees, in particular to new groups in Africa.

Activities in 1971

International protection

During 1971, the number of States parties to the 1951 Convention relating to the Status of Refugees rose to 61 with the accession of Malta and Uruguay, and the total number of States adhering to the 1967 Protocol was 48, with the accession of Burundi, Chile, Dahomey, Ethiopia, France, Luxembourg, Malta, Morocco and Uruguay. (This Protocol extended the scope of the 1951 Convention and made it applicable to new groups of refugees.)

The High Commissioner maintained close cooperation with Governments in determining refugee status under the 1951 Convention and the 1967 Protocol, and encouraged the establishment of procedures providing for the consideration of applications for refugee status.

The questions of asylum and *non-refoulement* continued to concern UNHCR in 1971. A *Colloquium* on the Law of Territorial Asylum, sponsored by the Carnegie Endowment for International Peace, New York, drew up a number of articles for inclusion in an inter-governmental instrument on asylum, a draft of which was to be considered by a further meeting of experts in 1972 prior to being considered by the General Assembly.

The Office continued its effort to further the improvement of the economic and social rights of refugees and to help refugees acquire the nationality of their country of residence. It continued to press for accessions to the 1961 Convention on the Reduction of Statelessness with a view to facilitating the acquisition of nationality by the children of refugees at birth.

In a number of countries, measures facilitating the travel of refugees were adopted, and the Office provided technical assistance to Governments in this connexion.

The Office continued to administer indemnification funds made available by the Government of the Federal Republic of Germany for the benefit of refugees who suffered persecution under the national socialist régime by reason of their nationality.

Material assistance programmes

The beneficiaries of UNHCR material assistance projects in 1971 totalled 250,000, most of whom were refugees settling on the land in Africa.

The total amount of funds committed and spent under UNHCR's 1971 Programme and its Emergency Fund amounted to $7,084,730. Trust funds were contributed in an amount of $1,216,353, most of which were earmarked by donors for complementary assistance projects, including educational assistance projects amounting to some $600,000, mainly in Africa.

In accordance with the principle whereby Governments of host countries have primary responsibility to assist refugees, many Governments again carried a considerable part of the burden of assistance.

Furthermore, supporting contributions were made from other sources, including, in particular, the World Food Programme, which supplied large quantities of food relief. Other United Nations bodies also lent support to the work of UNHCR, especially in respect of rural settlement and education.

In addition, other inter-governmental organizations, including the Intergovernmental Committee for European Migration and the Organization of African Unity, as well as non-governmental organizations, closely co-operated in the work of the Office.

Some 20,000 refugees, most of them African, opted for voluntary repatriation.

Local settlement again provided a solution for more than 95 per cent of all beneficiaries. Projects were focused on helping the refugees to become self-supporting so as to permit the phasing out of international assistance. Medical assistance and aid towards education and training constituted an essential element of the 1971 Programme.

Resettlement through migration remained in 1971 the most desired solution for new refugees in Europe, though the migratory flow was somewhat reduced because of less favourable conditions in traditional immigration countries. A number of countries continued to accept handicapped refugees for permanent settlement.

ASSISTANCE TO REFUGEES IN AFRICA

The number of refugees who were the concern of UNHCR in more than 25 African countries at the end of 1971 totalled some 1,000,000, the majority in Zaire (474,000) and Uganda (181,000). Over half the refugees in Africa were from territories under foreign administration, and so were the majority of the 18,500 new arrivals in 1971. The new influx during the year was offset by the number of refugees who opted for voluntary repatriation.

As further numbers of refugees were moved inland from reception areas near the border, the number of those established in UNHCR-assisted rural communities rose from about 200,000 at the end of 1970 to more than 235,000 at the end of 1971. The number of refugees requiring food rations increased to 83,000 from 77,000 in 1970.

Of the $4,080,657 committed under the 1971 Programme for assistance to refugees in Africa, $3,966,984 was used for their settlement on the land. Programme funds were supplemented by $131,820 from the Emergency Fund and $945,056 from trust funds.

The main repatriation movements in 1971 comprised some 9,000 Zambians of the Lumpa sect who had taken refuge in Zaire and 8,000 Zairians who chose to return to their homes following an amnesty promulgated by the Government. Financial aid was given by UNHCR in the repatriation of some 3,500 refugees.

Sustained efforts continued to be made in conjunction with the Bureau for the Placement and Education of African Refugees of the Organization of African Unity to promote migration for resettlement as a permanent solution for individual refugees.

As in previous years, the majority of beneficiaries under the UNHCR programmes in Africa were assisted to settle on the land. In the settlement areas, UNHCR assistance took a variety of forms designed in general to supplement the contribution of the Governments in arable land, roads, bridges, water supplies, electric power and community installations.

In a majority of the region's organized settlements, good progress was made with agriculture, the infrastructure was expanded with the assistance of UNHCR, more refugees were able to become self-supporting, and more young refugees benefited from educational assistance.

In order to deal with the growing problem of individual cases in some of the African capitals, UNHCR promoted the establishment of counselling services.

Of the funds committed for local settlement, about $900,000 was devoted to assisting agricultural development, an equal amount to facilities for primary education, some $575,000 for direct relief activities, and the remainder, amounting to about $1,340,000, for various other types of assistance.

ASSISTANCE TO REFUGEES
IN ASIA AND THE MIDDLE EAST

A major relief and repatriation operation was conducted for the benefit of East Bengali refugees in India, with UNHCR acting as focal point for the United Nations system. (See pp. 137-43.)

Problems of refugees other than East Bengalis in Asia continued to claim the attention of UNHCR, especially in the Far East, India, Nepal, and certain countries of the Middle East.

In addition, assistance was provided towards the rural settlement of over 3,000 refugee families in the Republic of Viet-Nam, and a contribution was made towards the improvement of facilities at a reception centre in the Khmer Republic.

About $850,000 was committed under the 1971 Programme and the Emergency Fund for assistance in Asia.

ASSISTANCE TO REFUGEES IN LATIN AMERICA

The number of refugees who were the concern of UNHCR in Latin America was estimated at about 105,000 as at the end of 1971. Of these, some 38,000 were residing in Brazil and 34,000 in Argentina. A growing proportion of the total —some 7,000 persons—were refugees from countries in Latin America.

Of the amount of $265,000 committed under the 1971 Programme and Emergency Fund, nearly half was allocated for assistance to refugees in Argentina, and smaller amounts for those in Brazil, Chile, Colombia, Guyana, Mexico, Paraguay, Peru and Venezuela. Most of the funds were used to assist refugees, including a high proportion of the handicapped, to settle permanently in their countries of residence.

ASSISTANCE TO REFUGEES IN EUROPE

There were some 615,000 refugees within the mandate of UNHCR in Europe as at the end of 1971. Their decrease through voluntary repatriation, migration and naturalization was offset by the number of newly recognized refugees and new arrivals, mainly from the Caribbean into Spain.

Of the amount of $667,000 committed under the 1971 Programme, a little more than half was applied towards local settlement projects. Most of the balance was used to facilitate resettlement and provide aid to individual refugees.

Decisions of Economic and Social Council

On 30 July 1971, the Economic and Social Council, without adopting a resolution, transmitted without debate the annual report of UNHCR, covering the period from 1 April 1970 to 31 March 1971, to the Assembly at its 1971 session.

Decisions of General Assembly

On 6 December 1971, the General Assembly requested the High Commissioner for Refugees to continue to provide international protection and assistance to refugees who were his concern and to promote permanent and speedy solutions to the problems of refugees through voluntary repatriation, integration in countries of asylum or resettlement in other countries.

In this connexion, the Assembly recognized the importance of voluntary repatriation as a permanent solution to the refugee problem and the useful role that United Nations bodies and non-governmental agencies could play in facilitating the rehabilitation of groups of refugees who had voluntarily returned to their countries of origin.

The Assembly noted its consideration of the increasing and fruitful co-operation between UNHCR and the other members of the United Nations system in the field of rural settlement, education and training of refugees in developing countries, particularly in Africa.

Noting with satisfaction the increasing number of Governments contributing to UNHCR's refugee assistance programme, the Assembly urged Governments to continue to lend their support both financially and in other ways.

These were among decisions embodied in resolution 2789(XXVI), adopted without a vote. The Assembly acted on the recommendation of its Third (Social, Humanitarian and Cultural) Committee, which unanimously approved the draft on 17 November 1971, on the basis of a proposal by Argentina, Australia, Austria, Belgium, Canada, Cyprus, Dahomey, Denmark, Egypt, Ethiopia, Finland, France, Greece, Iceland, Iran, Kenya, Lebanon, Lesotho, Liberia, the Libyan Arab Republic, Morocco, Nepal, the Netherlands, Niger, Nigeria, Norway, Pakistan, Senegal, Sierra Leone, Somalia, Sudan, Sweden, Togo, Tunisia, Turkey, Uganda, the United Kingdom, the United Republic of Tanzania, the United States, Yugoslavia, and Zaire, as amended by Saudi Arabia. (For text, see DOCUMENTARY REFERENCES below.)

Contribution pledges

Pledges towards the 1972 Programme of UNHCR were announced at a meeting of the *Ad Hoc* Committee of the General Assembly for the Announcement of Voluntary Contributions to the Programme of the United Nations High Commissioner for Refugees, held on 23 November 1971.

These pledges, as well as pledges made subsequent to the meeting of the *Ad Hoc* Committee, are shown in the table below.

Government contributions paid, pledged or conditionally pledged towards the financing of the UNHCR assistance programme for 1972

(As at 31 March 1972, in U.S. dollars)

Government	Contribution	Government	Contribution	Government	Contribution
Argentina	20,000	Greece	14,000	Morocco	10,730
Australia	208,432	Holy See	2,500	Netherlands	234,375
Austria	31,645	Iceland	6,318	Norway	403,437
Bahamas	3,075	India	13,738	Pakistan	2,499
Barbados	519	Indonesia	1,000	Peru	1,284
Belgium	227,272	Ireland	17,500	Philippines	1,250
Botswana	1,000	Israel	7,500	Saudi Arabia	8,000
Burundi	1,714	Italy	50,000	Senegal	3,968
Canada	400,000	Ivory Coast	2,976	Sweden	700,000
Chile	10,000	Jamaica	648	Switzerland	260,417
Congo	1,000	Japan	30,000	Tunisia	2,500
Cyprus	648	Kuwait	3,000	Turkey	5,357
Denmark	400,000	Liberia	5,000	United Kingdom	466,321
Dubai	3,000	Luxembourg	4,545	Uruguay	2,000
Egypt	6,900	Madagascar	992	Yugoslavia	10,000
Fed. Rep. of Germany	623,053	Malaysia	1,500	Zaire	4,000
Finland	100,000	Malta	1,000		
France	486,770	Mauritius	1,047	Total	4,809,240
Ghana	4,615	Monaco	195		

DOCUMENTARY REFERENCES

Decisions of Economic and Social Council

Economic and Social Council—51st session
Plenary meetings 1773, 1783, 1799.

E/5037 and Corr.1. Report of United Nations High Commissioner for Refugees (UNHCR) (A/8412).
E/5073. Resolutions adopted by Economic and Social Council during its 51st session, 5-30 July 1971. Other decisions, p. 27.

Decisions of General Assembly

General Assembly—26th session
Third Committee, meetings 1874-1880.
Plenary meeting 2001.

A/8401. Report of Secretary-General on work of the Organization, 16 June 1970–15 June 1971, Part Three, Chapter VII A.
A/8403. Report of Economic and Social Council on work of its 50th and 51st sessions, Chapter XVIII B.
A/8412 and Add.1. Report of UNHCR and addendum (containing report of 22nd session of Executive Committee of High Commissioner's Programme, Geneva, Switzerland, 4-12 October 1971).
A/C.3/L.1883. Argentina, Australia, Austria, Belgium, Canada, Cyprus, Dahomey, Denmark, Egypt, Ethiopia, Finland, France, Greece, Iceland, Iran, Kenya, Lebanon, Lesotho, Liberia, Libyan Arab Republic, Morocco, Nepal, Netherlands, Niger, Nigeria, Norway, Pakistan, Senegal, Sierra Leone, Somalia, Sudan, Sweden, Togo, Tunisia, Turkey, Uganda, United Kingdom, United Republic of Tanzania, United States, Yugoslavia, Zaire: draft resolution as amended by Saudi Arabia, A/C.3/L.1884, as orally sub-amended by sponsors, approved unanimously by Third Committee on 17 November 1971, meeting 1875.
A/C.3/L.1884. Saudi Arabia: amendment to 41-power draft resolution, A/C.3/L.1883.
A/8544. Report of Third Committee, draft resolution I.

RESOLUTION 2789(XXVI), as recommended by Third Committee, A/8544, adopted without vote by Assembly on 6 December 1971, meeting 2001.

The General Assembly,
Having considered the report of the United Nations High Commissioner for Refugees concerning his current activities and having heard his statement,

Noting with appreciation the results obtained by the High Commissioner in the accomplishment of his humanitarian task of providing international protection to refugees within his mandate and promoting permanent solutions to their problems,
Considering the increasing and fruitful co-operation between the High Commissioner and the other members of the United Nations system in the field of rural settlement, education and training of refugees in developing countries, particularly in Africa, which results in a better co-ordination of action and a greater efficiency of the United Nations system as a whole,
Noting with satisfaction the recent decision of the Executive Committee of the High Commissioner's Programme to approve the participation of the High Commissioner in the new country programming system adopted by the United Nations Development Programme and his association, where necessary, with any efforts made by Governments, with the assistance of the Programme, to develop regions where large groups of refugees are being settled with the assistance of the High Commissioner,
Recognizing the importance of voluntary repatriation as a permanent solution to the refugee problem and the useful role that United Nations bodies and non-governmental agencies can play in facilitating the rehabilitation of groups of refugees who have voluntarily returned to their countries of origin,
Noting with satisfaction the increasing number of Governments contributing to the High Commissioner's assistance programme and the substantial increase in some of these contributions,
Commending the growing number of accessions to the Convention relating to the Status of Refugees of 1951 and the Protocol relating to the Status of Refugees of 1967,
1. *Expresses its deep satisfaction* at the efficient manner in which the United Nations High Commissioner for Refugees and his staff continue to accomplish their humanitarian tasks;
2. *Requests* the High Commissioner to continue to provide international protection and assistance to refugees who are his concern, in accordance with the relevant resolutions of the General Assembly and the directives of the Executive Committee of the High Commissioner's Programme;
3. *Requests* the High Commissioner to continue his efforts, in co-operation with Governments, United Nations bodies and voluntary agencies, to promote permanent and speedy solutions to the problems of refugees who are his concern through voluntary repatriation, integration in countries of asylum or resettlement in other countries;
4. *Urges* Governments to continue to lend their support to the High Commissioner's humanitarian action by:
(a) Facilitating the accomplishment of his task in the field of international protection;

(b) Co-operating in the promotion of permanent solutions to refugee problems;

(c) Providing the necessary means to attain the financial targets established with the approval of the Executive Committee.

Contribution pledges

General Assembly—26th session

Ad Hoc Committee of General Assembly for Announcement of Voluntary Contributions to Programme of UNHCR, meeting of 23 November 1971 (A/AC.152/SR.1).

Other documents

As They Came in Africa. A photo documentary by the United Nations High Commissioner for Refugees. U.N.P. Sales No.: E.71,II.K.4.

HCR Bulletin. Quarterly record of activities. Published by UNHCR, Palais des Nations, Geneva, Switzerland. Nos. 13-16 (1st-4th quarters 1971).

UNHCR. What it is. What it does. How it helps refugees. Published by UNHCR, Palais des Nations, Geneva, Switzerland.

A/AC.96/465. List of documents issued at 22nd session of Executive Committee of High Commissioner's Programme.

A/AC.96/467. Report on UNHCR current operations in 1971.

Chapter XIX

The United Nations Children's Fund

The United Nations Children's Fund (UNICEF) celebrated its twenty-fifth anniversary in 1971. At its annual session, held from 13 to 29 April 1971 in Geneva, Switzerland, the Executive Board reviewed three main phases in the evolution of UNICEF during that period: the European phase, during which the Fund's resources were mainly devoted to meeting post-war emergency needs of children for food and clothing; the shift to the developing countries in the 1950s, with emphasis on programmes of long-range benefit to children; and the movement during the 1960s to aid children as an integral part of over-all development efforts.

At its 1971 session, the Executive Board also reviewed the role of UNICEF in the Second United Nations Development Decade and discussed, among other topics, the situation of children living in slums and shanty-towns.

During the year, UNICEF was aiding projects in 112 countries and territories: 38 in Africa; 33 in the Americas; 27 in Asia; 13 in the Eastern Mediterranean; and 1 in Europe.

Executive Board session

Role of UNICEF in Second Development Decade

At its 1971 session, the Executive Board discussed the growing difficulties encountered by developing countries in providing for the needs of their children and adolescents, in the light of the competing claims on resources and the fact that the number of children aged 15 and under—who currently constituted over 45 per cent of the population in UNICEF-assisted countries—was expected to increase by 250 million, or by 30 per cent, by 1980.

Board members viewed the International Development Strategy for the Second Development Decade as having great importance for systematic long-term efforts to improve the condition of children. It was felt that the Strategy provided a framework for two crucial elements in the welfare of children and adolescents: the adoption of a unified approach to economic and social development, viewed as interdependent goals; and a concern that children and youth receive their due share of attention and investment in the development process in each country.

The Board felt that programmes had to be designed to meet the specific needs of children in different situations—in various age groups, in rural and urban areas, and so forth—and that the principal task was to evolve, at both the national and international levels, effective methods of translating such an approach within each country into programmes of action. In this respect, mention was made of the need for innovations in programmes, new ways of training staff, greater attention to eliciting local support and a closer relationship between planning and programming both at headquarters and in the field.

Children in slums and shanty-towns

The Executive Board had before it, at its 1971 session, a study on the situation of children and adolescents in slums and uncontrolled settlements, or shanty-towns, in developing countries. It brought out the fact that, in terms of numbers involved, the problem was growing rapidly and was bound to become more serious in the future. One of the main conclusions of the study was that dwellers in slums and shanty-towns could do a great deal to help themselves if given the necessary framework of policy, institutions and technical support.

In approving guidelines for UNICEF aid, the Board agreed that, in addition to expanding its help for children in slums and shanty-towns in all fields in which UNICEF normally operated, certain special forms of assistance would be necessary. Although UNICEF would focus on the needs of children, the wider economic and social setting would have to be taken into account and would require the attention of various members of the United Nations development system.

Education and training of health personnel

The question of education and training programmes for health personnel was another main topic of discussion by the Board in 1971. The Board noted that despite the important advances that developing countries had made over the years in the extension of health services, with the aid of UNICEF and the World Health Organization, only a small proportion of families in most developing countries had access to even rudimentary health services; a radical reorientation of health training was needed, and more attention given to training for rural areas and the social and preventive aspects of medicine.

The Board recommended that greater use be made of auxiliaries and greater collaboration be carried out with non-medical personnel, including school-teachers, social workers, home economists and agricultural extension workers.

Activities in 1971

At its April 1971 session, the Executive Board approved commitments of UNICEF resources totalling $79.9 million. Health and education continued to receive the majority of resources, 47.8 and 28.3 per cent, respectively. (For a breakdown of 1971 commitments by sector, see Table I.)

There were several new characteristics of projects aided by UNICEF in 1971. An increasing number of projects were of a multidisciplinary character, linked to major segments of national development plans; greater attention was being paid to projects designed to help strengthen the ability of countries to assume full responsibility for the supported activities within the foreseeable future; increased efforts were being made at the time of project preparation to mobilize additional sources of financial support from multilateral and bilateral sources, wherever possible; and more emphasis was being placed on ensuring community participation in projects.

The guidelines for the equitable allocation of assistance among countries at various stages of development, discussed by the Board at its 1970 session, were being gradually put into effect. Under those guidelines, more aid would go to the economically poorer countries with large populations.

Health services

Aid for health services continued to be UNICEF's major investment. Commitments for these services in 1971 amounted to $32.1 million, or 49 per cent

of the total programme aid approved. About 90 per cent of this was for the building up of basic health services, with emphasis on maternal and child health care, including immunization, environmental sanitation, health and nutrition education, and family planning. The remaining 10 per cent was for malaria eradication.

Nutrition

Commitments totalling nearly $5 million were made for child nutrition in 1971, or 7.6 per cent of UNICEF programme commitments.

At its 1971 session, the Board expressed concern at the relatively low level of commitments for child nutrition in view of the adverse effects of malnutrition—many of them irreversible—on the future physical and mental development of the young child. It was felt that in part this reflected the slow recognition by some Governments that child malnutrition could be a serious deterrent to national development. The Board discussed the need for the establishment of national food and nutrition policies, of which UNICEF-assisted programmes could be an integral part.

Education

In 1971, UNICEF committed $18.9 million for education and pre-vocational training programmes, or 28.7 per cent of total programme aid.

The main emphasis in the Board's discussion of aid for schooling and pre-vocational training was on ways in which UNICEF might contribute, in co-operation with other members of the United Nations family, to an education more relevant to students' futures.

Some misgivings were expressed during the discussion that too large a proportion of UNICEF funds was being spent on education. On the other hand, it was held that project recommendations had followed the guidelines for UNICEF aid in that field approved by the Executive Board in 1968, as well as the general UNICEF policy of adapting its aid to government priorities. The Board decided to review UNICEF policy on aid to education at its 1972 session.

Training

The training of national auxiliary and para-professional personnel continued to be a major element in UNICEF aid. In 1971, over 170,000 persons received training with UNICEF stipends. In addition, a large number of trainees benefited from the material aid that UNICEF provided to various training institutions and centres.

Income and expenditures

Income in 1971

Total income of UNICEF in 1971 amounted to $63.7 million, including more than $2.9 million in funds-in-trust available for commitment by the Executive Board. This was an increase of $4.3 million over 1970. More than 68 per cent came from Governments; about 32 per cent from private sources (campaign collections, individual donations and greeting card profits) and the rest from miscellaneous sources.

In addition, UNICEF handled a large volume of funds from the United Nations system in connexion with emergencies on the Indian sub-continent. These were used partly for UNICEF-type aid and partly for other supplies for which UNICEF had a special purchasing capacity. That brought the total funds handled by UNICEF in 1971 (income, funds-in-trust available for commitment by the Board and other funds-in-trust) to $90.1 million, the largest annual volume of funds handled by UNICEF since its inception.

Contributions in kind valued at some $14 million were also received, mainly in the form of children's food and air freight services.

GOVERNMENTAL CONTRIBUTIONS

The over-all increase in 1971 income was largely due to a rise in the regular annual governmental contributions to UNICEF; a record number of 138 Governments made contributions totalling $42.8 million in 1971. Of this amount, $38.1 million was in regular contributions, $4 million (from 11 Governments) for relief and rehabilitation, and $700,000 (from two Governments) for specific long-term projects.

In addition, Governments provided $600,000 in funds-in-trust available for commitment by the Executive Board.

NON-GOVERNMENTAL CONTRIBUTIONS

Income from private fund-raising campaigns in 1971 (other than the greeting card operation) and unsolicited contributions rose to a record level of $10.4 million. Roughly one half originated from the Hallowe'en collections in the United States and Canada. Proceeds from television appeals in Europe rose to $1 million from $700,000 in 1970. In addition, UNICEF received $900,000 from non-governmental sources as funds-in-trust for use in relief and rehabilitation.

GREETING CARDS AND CALENDARS

More than 72.4 million greeting cards and 570,000 calendars were sold in the 1970/71 campaign, bringing to UNICEF net earnings of $4.7 million, an increase of $400,000 over 1970.

Expenditures in 1971

Expenditure from income in 1971 was $56.9 million and from trust funds $27.9 million, making a total expenditure of $84.8 million, the largest since the inception of UNICEF.

Decisions of Economic and Social Council

The report of the Executive Board of UNICEF was reviewed by the Economic and Social Council at its mid-1971 session.

On 27 July 1971, the Council: (1) endorsed the policies of UNICEF and commended its work as an important element in furthering economic and social development as well as in assisting countries whose children suffered from natural and other disasters; (2) requested the Fund to continue and expand the assistance it was providing to aid countries in the preparation of the younger generation for their future responsibilities; and (3) appealed to the Governments of Member States and other donors to make every effort to increase their contributions to the Fund, so as to enable it to reach its target figure of $100 million by 1975.

The decisions to this effect were embodied in resolution 1619(LI), which was adopted, unanimously, on the recommendation of the Economic Committee. On 19 July, the Committee had approved without a vote the text proposed by Indonesia, Norway, Peru and Yugoslavia.

(For text of resolution, see DOCUMENTARY REFERENCES below.)

Decisions of General Assembly

On 20 December 1971, the General Assembly, after considering the section of the report of the Economic and Social Council dealing with UNICEF, took the following action. It: (1) commended UNICEF for very substantial and significant achievements during its 25 years of operation; (2) endorsed the policies of the Fund; (3) requested the Fund to continue and expand its co-operation with countries for the protection of the younger generation and their preparation for future responsibilities; and (4) appealed to Governments and other donors to make every effort to increase their contributions to the Fund, so as to enable it to reach its target figure of $100 million by 1975.

The Assembly took this action in adopting, unanimously, resolution 2855 (XXVI), on the recommendation of the Third (Social, Humanitarian and Cultural) Committee.

The text was based on a proposal by the following States: Afghanistan, Algeria, Austria, Belgium, Bhutan, Brazil, Canada, Chile, Costa Rica, Denmark, Egypt, Ethiopia, Finland, Greece, Iceland, India, Indonesia, Iran, the Libyan Arab Republic, Mauritania, Morocco, Nigeria, Norway Pakistan, the Philippines, Poland, Sierra Leone, Sudan, Sweden, the Syrian Arab Republic, Tunisia, Uruguay and Yugoslavia. It was approved unanimously by the Third Committee on 10 December 1971.

(For text of resolution, see DOCUMENTARY REFERENCES below.)

Table I. Types of aid rendered by UNICEF in 1971

(By region and type of aid)

Type of aid	Number of countries and territories assisted					Total No. of countries (all regions)	Total commitments approved in 1971* (in thousands of U.S. dollars)
	Africa	Asia	Eastern Mediter- ranean	Europe	The Americas		
Child health	38	22	12	—	23	95	32,147
Child nutrition	22	16	8	—	13	59	4,966
Family and child welfare	29	11	8	—	3	51	4,613
Education	36	18	10	—	16	80	17,871
Pre-vocational training	5	6	4	—	1	16	1,001
Integrated services for children	2	1	1	1	9	14	2,211
Country planning and project preparation	—	—	—	—	—	—	1,070
Block commitment for Pacific Islands	—	—	—	—	—	—	145
Emergency aid	—	3	1	—	—	4	1,607
Total programme aid							65,631
Programme support services							9,045
Total assistance							74,676
Administrative costs							5,267
Total commitments							79,943

*Including funds-in-trust available for commitment by the Executive Board; excluding special funds-in-trust from United Nations system for relief and rehabilitation, reimbursable procurement and local budget costs ($26,904,100).

Table II. Countries and territories for which UNICEF aid was approved in 1971

Country or territory	Commitments (in thousands of U.S. dollars)	Country or territory	Commitments (in thousands of U.S. dollars)	Country or territory	Commitments (in thousands of U.S. dollars)
Afghanistan	1,050	Haiti	873	Papua New Guinea	98
Bolivia	129	Honduras	535	Paraguay	278
Brazil	1,373	Hong Kong	23	People's Democratic Republic	
British Honduras	18	India	10,127	of Yemen	1,100
Burma	47	Indonesia	2,444	Peru	1,384
Central African Republic	221	Iran	290	Philippines	2,023
Chad	419	Iraq	140	Republic of Korea	1,209
China*	543	Jamaica	236	Republic of Viet-Nam	49
Columbia	527	Jordan	453	Rwanda	104
Costa Rica	207	Kenya	573	Saudi Arabia	500
Cuba	863	Laos	90	Sierra Leone	46
Dahomey	119	Lebanon	626	Singapore	27
Dominican Republic	38	Liberia	300	Sudan	1,100
Ecuador	340	Madagascar	428	Thailand	385
Egypt	833	Malaysia	164	Tunisia	752
El Salvador	120	Mauritius	527	Uganda	92
Equatorial Guinea	73	Mexico	250	United Arab Republic	1,860
Ethiopia	1,369	Morocco	1,440	United Republic of	
Gambia	80	Nicaragua	415	Tanzania	1,880
Ghana	100	Niger	131	Western Samoa	78
Guatemala	471	Nigeria	5,125	Yugoslavia	200
Guinea	540	Pakistan	13,598	Regional and inter-	
Guyana	80	Panama	267	regional projects	3,851

*China is an original Member of the United Nations, the Charter having been signed and ratified on its behalf, on 26 June and 11 September 1945 respectively, by the Government of the Republic of China, which continued to represent China in the United Nations until 25 October 1971. On that date, the General Assembly adopted resolution 2758(XXVI), by which it decided "to restore all its rights to the People's Republic of China and to recognize the representatives of its Government as the only legitimate representatives of China to the United Nations. . . ."

The above entry in respect of China refers to an action taken by the authorities representing China in the United Nations at the time of that action.

Table III. Governmental contributions to UNICEF for 1971

Country or territory	Amount (in thousands of U.S. dollars)	Country or territory	Amount (in thousands of U.S. dollars)	Country or territory	Amount (in thousands of U.S. dollars)
Afghanistan	20.0	Bahrain	5.0	British Honduras	0.6
Algeria	87.3	Barbados	2.0	Brunei	4.9
Argentina	52.9	Belgium	347.1	Bulgaria	42.7
Australia	627.0	Bolivia	8.1	Burma	105.3
Austria	119.1	Botswana	2.0	Burundi	5.0
Bahamas	2.9	Brazil	142.9	Byelorussian SSR	62.5

Country or territory	Amount (in thousands of U.S. dollars)	Country or territory	Amount (in thousands of U.S. dollars)	Country or territory	Amount (in thousands of U.S. dollars)
Cameroon	25.2	Italy	480.8	Qatar	200.0
Canada	1,599.0	Ivory Coast	37.8	Republic of Korea	56.0
Central African Republic	10.8	Jamaica	12.2	Republic of Viet-Nam	26.0
Ceylon	26.2	Japan	786.0	Romania	25.0
Chad	5.4	Jordan	8.4	Rwanda	2.0
Chile	124.6	Kenya	8.4	St. Kitts-Nevis-Anguilla	0.8
China*	10.2	Khmer Republic	10.0	St. Lucia	3.0
Colombia	302.5	Kuwait	40.0	St. Vincent	0.8
Congo	14.4	Laos	3.0	San Marino	1.6
Costa Rica	30.0	Lebanon	18.4	Saudi Arabia	24.2
Cuba	70.6	Lesotho	2.8	Senegal	28.2
Cyprus	3.5	Liberia	20.0	Sierra Leone	19.2
Czechoslovakia	104.2	Libyan Arab Republic	21.8	Singapore	10.0
Dahomey	7.2	Liechtenstein	2.0	Somalia	10.0
Denmark	1,748.8	Luxembourg	14.0	South Africa	50.0
Dominica	1.0	Madagascar	18.0	Spain	100.0
Ecuador	18.0	Malawi	1.2	Sudan	25.2
Egypt	9.7	Malaysia	77.6	Swaziland	1.9
Ethiopia	53.1	Maldives	0.9	Sweden	6,007.8
Federal Republic of Germany	4,134.4	Mali	21.6	Switzerland	1,221.2
Fiji	2.0	Mauritania	10.8	Syrian Arab Republic	16.3
Finland	639.7	Mauritius	4.0	Thailand	243.1
France	1,780.9	Mexico	62.4	Togo	10.8
Gabon	26.9	Monaco	1.8	Tonga	1.0
Gambia	4.5	Mongolia	2.5	Trinidad and Tobago	10.0
Ghana	21.0	Montserrat	0.2	Tunisia	39.9
Greece	69.0	Morocco	82.1	Turkey	156.1
Grenada	0.8	Nepal	2.5	Uganda	67.7
Guatemala	15.0	Netherlands	386.2	Ukrainian SSR	125.0
Guinea	40.8	New Zealand	149.6	USSR	675.0
Guyana	6.0	Niger	10.8	United Arab Emirates	75.0
Holy See	1.0	Nigeria	.70.0	United Kingdom	1,695.0
Honduras	30.0	Norway	1,595.0	United Republic of Tanzania	31.0
Hong Kong	12.9	Oman	20.0	United States	13,827.9
Hungary	6.7	Pakistan	217.0	Upper Volta	10.0
Iceland	11.7	Panama	20.0	Western Samoa	1.4
India	1,160.0	Paraguay	20.0	Yugoslavia	220.0
Indonesia	202.2	People's Democratic Republic of Yemen	0.8	Zaire	23.6
Iran	336.9	Peru	100.0	Zambia	42.5
Iraq	84.2	Philippines	238.9	**Total**	**44,462.5**
Ireland	147.8	Poland	220.0		
Israel	42.5				

*See footnote to Table II.

DOCUMENTARY REFERENCES

Economic and Social Council—51st session
Economic Committee, meeting 531.
Plenary meeting 1793.

E/5035. United Nations Children's Fund (UNICEF). Report of Executive Board, 13–29 April 1971, Geneva, Switzerland.
E/AC.6/L.426. Indonesia, Norway, Peru, Yugoslavia: draft resolution, approved without vote by Economic Committee on 19 July 1971, meeting 531.
E/5056. Report of Economic Committee.

RESOLUTION 1619(LI), as recommended by Economic Committee, E/5056, adopted unanimously by Council on 27 July 1971, meeting 1793.

The Economic and Social Council,
Having considered the report of the Executive Board of the United Nations Children's Fund on its session held at Geneva in April 1971,
Recognizing the important role that the Fund is playing, in co-operation with the relevant technical and other agencies of the United Nations system, in helping developing countries to initiate and carry on programmes for the benefit of their children and adolescents,
Welcoming the Fund's current and prospective contribution to the furtherance of the objectives of the Second United Nations Development Decade, and the confirmation by the Executive Board of the Fund, in keeping with its established "country approach," that it will co-operate fully in the system of country programming under the leadership of the United Nations Development Programme,
Commending the prompt and considerable assistance being provided to meet the urgent needs of mothers, children and adolescents in emergency situations in many parts of the world, and the close co-operation in this work between the Fund, other members of the United Nations system, Governments and non-governmental organizations,
Welcoming also the increasing emphasis which the Fund is placing on the training within the developing countries of nationals for service in programmes benefiting children and the improvements proposed for such training as the result of joint studies with the World Health Organization and other organizations,
1. *Endorses* the policies of the United Nations Children's Fund and commends its work as an important element in furthering economic and social development, as well as in assisting countries whose children suffer from natural and other disasters;
2. *Requests* the Fund to continue and expand the assistance it is providing to aid countries in the preparation of the younger generation for their future responsibilities;
3. *Appeals* to the Governments of Member States and other donors to make every effort to increase their contributions to the Fund, so as to enable it to reach its target figure of $100 million by 1975.

General Assembly—26th session
Third Committee, meetings 1904, 1905.
Plenary meeting 2027.

A/8401. Report of Secretary-General on work of the Organization, 16 June 1970–15 June 1971, Part Three, Chapter VI E.

A/8403. Report of Economic and Social Council on work of its 50th and 51st sessions, Chapter VIII F.

A/C.3/L.1900. Afghanistan, Algeria, Austria, Belgium, Bhutan, Brazil, Canada, Chile, Costa Rica, Denmark, Egypt, Ethiopia, Finland, Greece, Iceland, India, Indonesia, Iran, Libyan Arab Republic, Mauritania, Morocco, Nigeria, Norway, Pakistan, Philippines, Poland, Sierra Leone, Sudan, Sweden, Syrian Arab Republic, Tunisia, Uruguay, Yugoslavia: draft resolution as orally amended by sponsors, approved unanimously by Third Committee on 10 December 1971, meeting 1905.

A/8588. Report of Third Committee (on report of Economic and Social Council), draft resolution I.

RESOLUTION 2855(XXVI), as recommended by Third Committee, A/8588, adopted unanimously by Assembly on 20 December 1971, meeting 2027.

The General Assembly,

Having considered the section of the report of the Economic and Social Council dealing with the United Nations Children's Fund,

Recognizing that, in countries assisted by the Fund, children and adolescents represent about half of the total population, and that their number will increase by nearly a third in the decade of the 1970s,

Convinced of the importance of ensuring that children and adolescents receive their due share of attention and investment in the developing process of developing countries,

Recognizing the valuable role the Fund is playing, in co-operation with Governments, the relevant technical and other agencies of the United Nations system and non-governmental organizations, in furthering the objectives of the Second United Nations Development Decade,

Welcoming the efforts of the Fund to bring the needs of children and adolescents in developing countries to world-wide attention and the practical aid the Fund gives to developing countries to enable them to provide services for children and adolescents within a unified approach to economic and social development,

Noting with approval the prompt and effective assistance that the Fund has provided in natural and other disasters to meet the urgent needs of mothers and children, who are particularly vulnerable and constitute the large majority of those affected by disasters,

1. *Commends* the United Nations Children's Fund for its very substantial and significant achievements during its twenty-five years of operation, and expresses its appreciation to all who helped contribute to those achievements;

2. *Endorses* the policies of the Fund;

3. *Requests* the Fund to continue and expand its co-operation with countries for the protection of the younger generation and their preparation for future responsibilities;

4. *Appeals* to Governments and other donors to make every effort to increase their contributions to the Fund, so as to enable it to reach its target figure of $100 million by 1975.

ELECTIONS TO EXECUTIVE BOARD

Economic and Social Council—50th session
Plenary meeting 1770.

E/L.1373. Election of 10 members of Executive Board of UNICEF. Note by Secretary-General.

E/5044. Resolutions adopted by Economic and Social Council during its 50th session, 11-13 January and 26 April–21 May 1971. Other decisions, p. 31.

Other documents

E/ICEF/608 and Corr.1 and Add.1-9. General progress report of Executive Director. Add.1: Programme developments in West and Central Africa; Add.2: Programme developments in Ghana and Nigeria; Add.3: Programme developments in East Africa; Add.4: Programme developments in Americas; Add.5: Programme developments in East Asia and Pakistan; Add.6: Programme developments in South Central Asia; Add.7: Programme developments in Eastern Mediterranean; Add.8: Programme developments in Europe, Turkey and North Africa; Add.9: First 25 years of UNICEF: a summary of policy evolution.

E/ICEF/609. Report of UNICEF/WHO Joint Committee on Health Policy, 18th session, 1-2 February 1971, Geneva, Switzerland.

E/ICEF/614. Report on organizational meeting of Executive Board for election of officers and committees for period 1 August 1971–31 July 1972.

E/ICEF/INF/33. Checklist of UNICEF documents, issued in connexion with session of Executive Board, 13-29 April 1971, Geneva, Switzerland.

UNICEF News. Issues 68-70 (Summer: *UNICEF at Twenty-five;* October: *India;* December: *Africa*).

Chapter XX

Human rights questions

Action against racism, racial discrimination, *apartheid*, nazism and racial intolerance

During 1971, which had been designated by the General Assembly as the International Year for Action to Combat Racism and Racial Discrimination, United Nations bodies intensified their efforts to take effective and practical measures against all forms of racism and racial discrimination.

Among the matters dealt with were: implementation of the Declaration and Convention on the Elimination of All Forms of Racial Discrimination; *apartheid* and racial discrimination in southern Africa; measures against incitement to racial discrimination; and other matters concerning the prevention of discrimination and protection of minorities.

Decisions on these and other related matters, such as violations of human rights and fundamental freedoms, taken by United Nations bodies during 1971 are described in the sections that follow.

In a message concerning the United Nations campaign against racial discrimination, which the President of the twenty-sixth (1971) session of the General Assembly forwarded to the heads of State or Government, the General Assembly stated that it was as convinced as ever that the continuation of national and international action against racial discrimination in all its forms, old and contemporary alike, was a matter of cardinal importance if the world was to live in peace and justice—the two interdependent and indispensable components of a better future for all mankind.

The Assembly declared that the primary aim of the United Nations and, therefore, of all its Member States in the sphere of human rights was the achievement by each individual of the maximum freedom and dignity and that, for the realization of this objective, the laws of every country should grant each individual—irrespective of race, sex, language, religion or political belief—all the rights inherent in all human beings on the basis of equality, and that the people of every country must be made fully aware of the evils of the policies of racial discrimination and of the ideologies based on racial supremacy and must join in condemning, resisting and combating them. The continuation of racism and colonialism could not but seriously hamper the efforts of the international community to achieve peace, justice and progress.

International Year for Action to Combat Racism and Racial Discrimination

The year 1971 was observed as International Year for Action to Combat Racism and Racial Discrimination, in accordance with a General Assembly decision of 11 December 1969.[1]

The General Assembly's Special Committee on *Apartheid* held a special session in New York from 22 to 24 March 1971 in connexion with observance of the International Year (see page 65). The Commission on Human Rights, the Economic and Social Council and the General Assembly also considered measures to combat racism and racial discrimination during and after 1971.

Decisions by Human Rights Commission and Economic and Social Council

At its twenty-seventh session, held from 22 February to 26 March 1971, the Commission on Human Rights generally agreed that although the programme for the observance of the International Year for Action to Combat Racism and Racial Discrimination consisted of commendable measures aimed at combating racism and racial discrimination, further measures were necessary to make the programme more successful. In particular, the Commission felt that effective action should be taken to combat racial discrimination in southern Africa.

On 1 March 1971, the Commission adopted a resolution by which, recalling that 1971 had been designated International Year for Action to Combat Racism and Racial Discrimination, it appealed to international public opinion to protest any attempt to violate the relevant provisions of the Security Council resolutions imposing an embargo on the sale of arms to South Africa. The Sub-Commission on Prevention of Discrimination and Protection of Minorities approved similar conclusions on 18 August 1972, at its twenty-fourth session.

The Economic and Social Council, at its April–May 1971 session, adopted a resolution (1588(L) of 21 May 1971) dealing among other things with observance of the International Year.

The Council recommended that the General Assembly: (*a*) request every competent United Nations organ, specialized agency, regional intergovernmental organization and non-governmental organization in consultative status to consider at their 1971 sessions as a matter of the highest priority the International Year for Action to Combat Racism and Racial Discrimination; (*b*) urge all States not parties to the International Convention on the Elimination of All Forms of Racial Discrimination to accelerate the process of ratifying that Convention, especially during the International Year; and (*c*) pursue, after 1971 and in co-operation with United Nations and other international organizations, a world-wide programme intended to build up public opinion—especially through radio and television broadcasts and the distribution of appropriate literature—to eradicate false racial beliefs.

(For text of resolution 1588(L), see pp. 413-14.)

Decisions by General Assembly

At its 1971 session, the General Assembly considered a report by the Secretary-General concerning measures and activities undertaken by Governments, by United Nations bodies and by other international organizations in observance of the International Year for Action to Combat Racism and Racial Discrimination.

On 6 December 1971, the Assembly among other things expressed its appreciation to the Governments, United Nations bodies and other inter-governmental and non-governmental organizations which had acted in good faith without political motivation and in accordance with the

---

[1]See Y.U.N., 1969, pp. 486-87, text of resolution 2544(XXIV).

United Nations Charter and contributed positively to the observance of the International Year. It recommended that the measures and activities which they had undertaken be continued, developed and enlarged, and that the initiatives which had emerged from the observance of the International Year should serve as guidelines for action-oriented programmes designed to ensure that the work accomplished in 1971 would be pursued.

The Assembly urged all States concerned to implement a programme of political, social, cultural and economic redress to improve the conditions of those suffering from the effects of past and present policies of racial discrimination; in particular, it appealed to Governments and all organizations in the United Nations system to devote urgent attention to the problems involved in the education of youth, in order to combat racial policies and to promote equal rights and economic, social and cultural progress for all.

It requested all competent United Nations bodies and regional inter-governmental and non-governmental organizations in consultative status, acting in good faith without political motivation and in accordance with the Charter, to consider as a matter of highest priority further actions they might take with a view to the speedy elimination of racial discrimination throughout the world.

Also, the Assembly endorsed the Economic and Social Council's invitation to the International Labour Organisation and the United Nations Educational, Scientific and Cultural Organization to report annually to the Human Rights Commission on the nature and effect of any racial discrimination of which they had knowledge; it also endorsed the Council's invitation to non-governmental organizations in consultative status with a special interest in the elimination of racism to advise on their endeavours in this regard biennially.

The Assembly also, among other things, requested the Secretary-General to study information programmes on all questions relating to racial discrimination and to pursue, as a major feature of action to combat racism and racial discrimination after the International Year, a world-wide programme intended to build up public opinion—especially through radio and television broadcasts and the distribution of appropriate literature—with a view to eradicating once and for all false racial beliefs based upon distortion or lack of scientific knowledge. The Secretary-General was also asked to submit to the Assembly in 1972 a report on measures taken by United Nations organs which would make possible a formulation of new methods and measures to combat racism, racial discrimination and *apartheid*.

These Assembly decisions were set forth in resolution 2785(XXVI), which was adopted by a recorded vote of 87 to 2, with 23 abstentions, on the recommendation of the Third (Social, Humanitarian and Cultural) Committee. The text was based on a proposal by Argentina, Costa Rica, Cyprus, Dahomey, the Dominican Republic, Ghana, Greece, Japan, Morocco, New Zealand and Uruguay; it was approved by the Third Committee on 11 November 1971 by a recorded vote of 76 to 6, with 31 abstentions.

(For text of resolution, see DOCUMENTARY REFERENCES below.)

Also on 6 December 1971, the Assembly adopted a resolution by which it expressed the conviction that the International Year for Action to Combat Racism and Racial Discrimination should be observed as the opening year of an ever-growing struggle against racial discrimination in all its forms and manifestations and for the purpose of promoting international solidarity with all those struggling against racism. The Assembly further considered that by arousing world public opinion and promoting action against racism, the International Year would contribute to the expansion of national and international efforts towards ensuring the rapid and total eradication of racial discrimination in all its forms.

The Assembly then, among other things, invited the Economic and Social Council to request the Commission on Human Rights to submit suggestions with a view to launching a decade for continued mobilization against racism and racial discrimination in all its forms.

Annexed to the resolution was a message from the President of the General Assembly to the heads of State or Government concerning the United Nations campaign against racial discrimination, including the observance of the International Year for Action to Combat Racism and Racial Discrimination.

(For text of resolution 2784(XXVI), see pp. 402-4.)

(See also page 80 and page 81, for texts of resolutions 2775 B(XXVI) and 2775 D(XXVI), respectively.)

DOCUMENTARY REFERENCES

Decisions of Human Rights Commission
E/4949. Report of Commission on Human Rights on its 27th session, 22 February–26 March 1971, Chapters II A and XIX (resolution 1(XXVII)).

E/CN.4/1070 and Corr.1. Report of Sub-Commission on Prevention of Discrimination and Protection on Minorities on its 24th session, 2–20 August 1971, Chapters III and XII (resolution 5(XXIV)).

Decisions of General Assembly

General Assembly—26th session
Third Committee, meetings 1844-1868.
Plenary meeting 2001.

A/8367 and Corr.1,2 and Add.1,2. Report of Secretary-General.
A/8401. Report of Secretary-General on work of the Organization, 16 June 1970–15 June 1971, Part Three, Chapter I A 1.
A/C.3/L.1872 and Rev.1. Argentina, Costa Rica, Cyprus, Dahomey, Dominican Republic, Ghana, Greece, Japan, Morocco, New Zealand, Senegal, Uruguay: draft resolution and revision.
A/C.3/L.1872/Rev.2. Argentina, Costa Rica, Cyprus, Dahomey, Dominican Republic, Ghana, Greece, Japan, Morocco, New Zealand, Uruguay: revised draft resolution, as orally revised by sponsors, approved by Third Committee on 11 November 1971, meeting 1867, by recorded vote of 76 to 6, with 31 abstentions:

In favour: Argentina, Australia, Austria, Barbados, Belgium, Bhutan, Brazil, Burma, Canada, Chad, Chile, Colombia, Costa Rica, Cyprus, Dahomey, Denmark, Dominican Republic, Ecuador, Egypt, El Salvador, Ethiopia, Fiji, Finland, France, Gabon, Gambia, Ghana, Greece, Guatemala, Guyana, Honduras, Iceland, India, Indonesia, Iran, Ireland, Israel, Italy, Ivory Coast, Jamaica, Japan, Lebanon, Lesotho, Liberia, Luxembourg, Madagascar, Malaysia, Mexico, Morocco, Nepal, Netherlands, New Zealand, Nicaragua, Nigeria, Norway, Panama, Peru, Philippines, Portugal, Senegal, Sierra Leone, Singapore, Somalia, Spain, Swaziland, Sweden, Thailand, Togo, Trinidad and Tobago, Tunisia, Turkey, United Kingdom, United States, Uruguay, Venezuela, Zaire.
Against: Byelorussian SSR, Iraq, Jordan, Syrian Arab Republic, Ukrainian SSR, USSR.
Abstaining: Afghanistan, Algeria, Bulgaria, Burundi, Cameroon, Central African Republic, Ceylon, Cuba, Czechoslovakia, Equatorial Guinea, Guinea, Hungary, Kenya, Kuwait, Libyan Arab Republic, Mali, Mauritania, Mongolia, Niger, People's Democratic Republic of Yemen, Poland, Romania, Rwanda, Saudi Arabia, Sudan, Uganda, United Republic of Tanzania, Upper Volta, Yemen, Yugoslavia, Zambia.

A/8542 and Corr.1. Report of Third Committee, draft resolution III.

RESOLUTION 2785(XXVI), as recommended by Third Committee, A/8542, adopted by Assembly on 6 December 1971, meeting 2001, by recorded vote of 87 to 2, with 23 abstentions, as follows:

In favour: Afghanistan, Argentina, Australia, Austria, Barbados, Botswana, Brazil, Burma, Burundi, Cameroon, Canada, Chad, Chile, Congo, Costa Rica, Cyprus, Dahomey, Denmark, Dominican Republic, Ecuador, Egypt, Equatorial Guinea, Ethiopia, Finland, France, Gabon, Gambia, Ghana, Greece, Guatemala, Guinea, Guyana, Honduras, Iceland, India, Indonesia, Iran, Ireland, Israel, Italy, Ivory Coast, Jamaica, Japan, Kenya, Lebanon, Liberia, Luxembourg, Madagascar, Malaysia, Mali, Malta, Mauritania, Mexico, Morocco, Nepal, Netherlands, New Zealand, Nicaragua, Niger, Nigeria, Norway, Pakistan, Panama, Paraguay, Peru, Philippines, Portugal, Qatar, Rwanda, Saudi Arabia, Senegal, Singapore, Somalia, Spain, Sudan, Sweden, Thailand, Togo, Tunisia, Turkey, Uganda, United Kingdom, United States, Uruguay, Venezuela, Zaire, Zambia.
Against: Belgium, People's Democratic Republic of Yemen.*
Abstaining: Algeria, Bahrain, Bulgaria, Byelorussian SSR, Central African Republic, Colombia, Cuba, Czechoslovakia, Hungary, Iraq, Jordan, Kuwait, Libyan Arab Republic, Mongolia, Oman, Poland, Romania, Syrian Arab Republic, Ukrainian SSR, USSR, United Republic of Tanzania, Yemen, Yugoslavia.

*Subsequently the People's Democratic Republic of Yemen advised the Secretariat that it had intended to vote in favour.

The General Assembly,
Firmly convinced that all forms of racial discrimination are a total negation of the purposes and principles of the Charter of the United Nations and that they militate against human progress, peace and justice,
Recalling its resolutions 2446(XXIII) of 19 December 1968, 2544(XXIV) of 11 December 1969, in which it designated the year 1971 as International Year for Action to Combat Racism and Racial Discrimination, and 2646(XXV) of 30 November 1970, in which it welcomed the observance of 1971 as the International Year for Action to Combat Racism and Racial Discrimination and urged all Governments, the specialized agencies and all other organizations concerned to make renewed efforts to take effective and practical measures to this end and, in particular, Economic and Social Council resolution 1588(L) of 21 May 1971, which provided for further action that should be taken to eliminate specifically racial discrimination in the political, economic, social and cultural spheres,
Noting the Secretary-General's second progress report, based on information received from Governments, the specialized agencies and other international organizations, on the observance of the International Year for Action to Combat Racism and Racial Discrimination and on the activities of United Nations organs to eliminate all forms of racial discrimination and *apartheid,*
Noting the Secretary-General's report on the review and reappraisal of United Nations information policies and activities, analysing the relationship of United Nations public information activities to the achievement of the substantive goals of the United Nations, including the elimination of *apartheid,* racial discrimination and colonialism, and stressing the need, within the principles of universality and objectivity, of a United Nations information programme more directly geared to the support of these goals,
Noting the measures that have been taken and the progress that has been achieved to date in the implementation of the programme for the observance of the International Year for Action to Combat Racism and Racial Discrimination by Governments, United Nations organs, specialized agencies, regional intergovernmental organizations and the national and international non-governmental organizations concerned,
1. *Expresses its appreciation* to the Governments, United Nations organs, specialized agencies, regional intergovernmental organizations and non-governmental organizations, which have acted in good faith without political motivation and in accordance with the Charter of the United Nations and contributed positively to the observance of the International Year for Action to Combat Racism and Racial Discrimination;
2. *Further expresses its appreciation* to the Secretary-General for the effective co-ordination of the measures and activities undertaken to date in connexion with the International Year for Action to Combat Racism and Racial Discrimination and for the informative progress reports he has submitted thereon to the General Assembly;
3. *Recommends* that the measures and activities undertaken on the occasion of the International Year for Action to Combat Racism and Racial Discrimination by Governments, United Nations organs, specialized agencies, regional intergovernmental organizations and non-governmental organizations genuinely concerned with the elimination of racism and racial discrimination be continued, developed and enlarged, and that the initiatives which have emerged from the observance of the International Year should serve as guidelines for action-oriented programmes designed to ensure that the work accomplished in 1971 will be pursued;
4. *Urges* all States concerned to implement a programme of political, social, cultural and economic redress to improve the conditions of those suffering from the effects of past and present policies of racial discrimination and, in particular, appeals to Governments and all organizations in the United Nations system to devote their urgent attention to the problems involved in the education of youth, in a spirit of world peace, justice, mutual respect and understanding, as well as respect for the value and dignity of the human person and generally recognized principles of morality and international law concerning friendly relations and co-operation among States, in order to combat racial policies and to promote equal rights and economic, social and cultural progress for all;

5. *Requests* every competent United Nations organ, specialized agency, regional intergovernmental organization and non-governmental organization in consultative status, acting in good faith without political motivation and in accordance with the Charter of the United Nations, to consider, as a matter of highest priority:

(a) The further action that it might itself take with a view to the speedy elimination of racial discrimination throughout the world;

(b) The action that it might suggest to its subsidiary organs, to States and to international and national bodies for this purpose;

(c) The follow-up measures required to ensure full and effective implementation of its decisions in this matter;

6. *Endorses* the invitation addressed by the Economic and Social Council to the International Labour Organisation and the United Nations Educational, Scientific and Cultural Organization to provide the Commission on Human Rights with reports on the nature and effect of any racial discrimination of whose existence they have knowledge in their sphere of competence and requests that such reports should be submitted annually, and also endorses the invitation addressed by the Council to the non-governmental organizations in consultative status referred to in paragraph 5 above which have a special interest in the elimination of racism and racial discrimination to communicate biennially to the Council, and for the information of any interested organ of the United Nations, their endeavours and progress in the struggle against racism, *apartheid* and racial discrimination in all its forms;

7. *Requests* the Secretary-General:

(a) In conformity with the conclusions stated in paragraphs 52 and 57 of his report on the review and reappraisal of United Nations information policies and activities, to study information programmes on all questions relating to racial discrimination, taking into account the views of the Economic and Social Council and its competent subsidiary bodies with a view to intensifying the realization of such programmes;

(b) To pursue, as a major feature of action to combat racism and racial discrimination after the International Year, a world-wide programme intended to build up public opinion, especially through radio and television broadcasts, and the distribution of appropriate literature such as the Statement on Race and Racial Prejudice, adopted by a committee of experts on the subject convened by the United Nations Educational, Scientific and Cultural Organization in Paris in September 1967, and the special study on racial discrimination in the political, economic, social and cultural spheres, prepared by the Special Rapporteur of the Sub-Commission on Prevention of Discrimination and Protection of Minorities, with a view to eradicating once and for all false racial beliefs based upon distortion or lack of scientific knowledge and showing how the different races complement one another;

8. *Requests* the Secretary-General to submit to the General Assembly at its twenty-seventh session a report on the measures taken by United Nations organs, which would make possible a detailed assessment and formulation of further new methods and measures to combat racism, racial discrimination and *apartheid*.

Implementation of Declaration and Convention on Elimination of All Forms of Racial Discrimination

Elimination of all forms of racial discrimination

On 6 December 1971, at its twenty-sixth session, the General Assembly adopted a resolution (2784(XXVI)) calling for continued international action to combat racism and racial discrimination. Annexed to the resolution was a special message—concerning the United Nations campaign against racial discrimination—which the Assembly asked its President to forward directly to the heads of State or Government of each State (see below).

The Secretary-General was asked to submit a report, based on information and comments received in accordance with that message, to the Commission on Human Rights at its 1972 session. The Economic and Social Council was invited to ask the Commission to submit suggestions with a view to launching continued international action to combat racism on the basis of a "Decade for vigorous and continued mobilization against racism and racial discrimination in all its forms."

The Assembly then reaffirmed that *apartheid* was a crime against humanity and declared that racial discrimination in all its forms was a criminal affront to the conscience and dignity of mankind. It reaffirmed emphatically its recognition and vigorous support of the struggles of all oppressed peoples everywhere—and in particular in southern Africa—against colonial, racial and alien domination or foreign occupation towards the achievement of their inalienable rights to equality and freedom, in accordance with the purposes and principles of the United Nations Charter. The Assembly called for increased and continued moral and material support to all peoples strug-

gling for their liberation, self-determination and the elimination of all forms of racial discrimination.

The Assembly took note with appreciation of the report of the Committee on the Elimination of Racial Discrimination established under the International Convention on the Elimination of All Forms of Racial Discrimination[2] and endorsed opinions and recommendations of that Committee.

The Assembly then called upon the trading partners of South Africa to abstain from any action that constituted an encouragement to the continued violation of the principles and objectives of the International Convention by South Africa and the illegal régime in Southern Rhodesia, and to use their influence towards ensuring the eradication of the policies of *apartheid* and racial discrimination in the international territory of Namibia and Southern Rhodesia.

The United Kingdom—the administering power for Southern Rhodesia—was called on by the Assembly to adopt all the necessary measures, including the use of force, with a view to ending the racist and illegal régime of Ian Smith. Portugal was condemned for persisting in its colonialist policies in Africa and for continuing its war against the peoples of the territories under its domination.

The Economic and Social Council was invited to request the Human Rights Commission to continue its comprehensive studies of policies and

[2]See Y.U.N., 1965, pp. 440-46, resolution 2106 A(XX) of 21 December 1965, containing text of International Convention.

practices of racial discrimination, taking into account in particular discrimination against peoples of African origin in all countries, and to report to the Assembly not later than at its 1973 session, together with recommendations for action to combat such policies and practices.

Finally, by this resolution the Assembly decided to consider the matter again at its twenty-seventh session in 1972.

The message to the heads of State or Government from the President of the General Assembly, annexed to the resolution, made the following points about the United Nations campaign against racial discrimination:

(*a*) The racist Government of South Africa and the illegal régime in Southern Rhodesia had blatantly continued to pursue policies of racial discrimination and *apartheid* in flagrant violation of the purposes and principles of the Charter and of those enshrined in the Universal Declaration of Human Rights.

(*b*) South Africa continued to effect an extensive arms build-up, thus posing a serious threat to the security and sovereignty of independent African States opposed to its racist policies, as well as to all those peoples struggling against the racial and inhuman policies in southern Africa.

(*c*) The racist policies in southern Africa had been permitted, even encouraged, to expand through: (i) the continued existence and operation of the white racist minority régime in Southern Rhodesia through the deliberate ineffectiveness of measures so far taken by the Government of the United Kingdom; and (ii) the illegal occupation of the territory of Namibia by the racist Government of South Africa.

(*d*) The racist Governments in southern Africa had been further strengthened through: (i) the maintenance by many States of political, commercial, military, economic, social and other relations with the racist Governments in southern Africa in utter disregard of United Nations resolutions and of Charter purposes and principles; and (ii) an unholy alliance between South Africa, Portugal and Southern Rhodesia, established to suppress the struggle of the peoples of that region and to silence the cry of Africa against racism, *apartheid*, economic exploitation and colonial domination.

(*e*) The United Nations had vigorously opposed all policies based on racial discrimination and consequently had: (i) declared that any States whose official policy or practice was based on racial discrimination contravened the purposes and principles of the Charter, and called on those Governments to desist forthwith from such policies; (ii) condemned the policies of States which, by political, economic or military collaboration with the racist régimes in southern Africa, enabled and encouraged those régimes to enforce and perpetu-

ate their racist policies, and called upon those States to desist forthwith from extending such collaboration; and (iii) reaffirmed time and again the legitimacy of the struggle of all oppressed peoples, in particular in the territories under racial, alien domination or foreign occupation, to obtain liberation and racial equality, and called for increased and continued moral and material support to those struggling peoples.

(*f*) However, the numerous resolutions that had been adopted by various United Nations organs still had little or no effect, owing to the arrogant, flagrant and stubborn disregard on the part of South Africa and its racist allies, transplanted to the soil of Africa, and to the continued political, economic and military aid coming from some States.

The President's message went on to state that the General Assembly was, therefore, as convinced as ever that the continuation of national and international action against racial discrimination in all its forms, old and contemporary alike, was a matter of cardinal importance if the world was to live in peace and justice—the two interdependent and indispensable components of a better future for all mankind.

The Assembly was also convinced, the message said, that the primary aim of the United Nations and therefore all its Member States in the sphere of human rights was the achievement by each individual of the maximum freedom and dignity and that, for the realization of this objective, the laws of every country should grant each individual—irrespective of race, sex, language, religion or political belief—all the rights inherent in all human beings on the basis of equality, and that the people of every country must be made fully aware of the evils of the policies of racial discrimination and of the ideologies based on racial supremacy and must join in condemning, resisting and combating them.

The General Assembly, the message added, was further convinced that the continuation of racism and colonialism could not but seriously hamper the efforts of the international community to achieve peace, justice and progress.

In the message, the President went on to say that the Assembly had authorized him to request the heads of State and Government to transmit the present text to the legislative, administrative, judicial, educational and trade union bodies of their countries, as well as to the mass media of information, in order to ensure the continuation of the world campaign against racial discrimination, bearing in mind that the International Year for Action to Combat Racism and Racial Discrimination should be considered as the opening year for a full decade of vigorous struggle against this evil, until the achievement of its total elimination.

To that end, the President said, the General Assembly recommended, among other things:

(a) discussion of the problem in all national and international conferences, especially in the fields of education, information, trade unions, etc.;

(b) inculcation through education of children and youth in the spirit of human rights by including in the curricula special and yearly programmes on the evils of racism and racial discrimination;

(c) continuation of the programmes designated to be carried out during 1971—the International Year for Action to Combat Racism and Racial Discrimination—and their development and updating, in order to intensify the efforts to combat racial discrimination;

(d) continuation of open moral support and increasing material aid to peoples struggling against racial discrimination and *apartheid;*

(e) termination of all relations with the Government of South Africa and all other racist régimes;

(f) exerting every effort to bring about the full implementation of all Security Council and General Assembly resolutions that reflected the world's resolve to end each and every case of discrimination and foreign exploitation; and

(g) repeal of all laws and regulations contributing to the maintenance and propagation of racial discrimination.

Finally, the message said, the Assembly had asked the Secretary-General to submit a report on the question to the Assembly's twenty-seventh (1972) session, in which would be included reports of Governments on the message.

The resolution, and its annex, was adopted by the Assembly on 6 December by a recorded vote of 93 to 5, with 15 abstentions, as recommended by the Assembly's Third (Social, Humanitarian and Cultural) Committee, which approved it—as revised by its sponsors—by a recorded vote of 93 to 6, with 11 abstentions, on 10 November. The text was sponsored by Afghanistan, Algeria, Burundi, Cameroon, the Congo, Cyprus, Dahomey, Egypt, Ethiopia, Ghana, Guinea, India, Kenya, Liberia, the Libyan Arab Republic, Mali, Mauritania, Morocco, Niger, Nigeria, Pakistan, the People's Democratic Republic of Yemen, Rwanda, Senegal, Sierra Leone, Somalia, Sudan, the Syrian Arab Republic, Togo, Uganda, the United Republic of Tanzania, Upper Volta, Yemen, Yugoslavia and Zambia. (For text of resolution 2784(XXVI), see DOCUMENTARY REFERENCES below.)

Report of Committee on Elimination of Racial Discrimination

The Committee on the Elimination of Racial Discrimination, set up under the terms of the International Convention on the Elimination of All Forms of Racial Discrimination, held its third and fourth sessions during 1971 and submitted its second annual report to the General Assembly in September.

At its third session, held from 12 to 23 April, the Committee continued its consideration of reports submitted under article 9 of the International Convention, by which States parties undertake to submit reports and information on the legislative, judicial, administrative or other measures adopted by them giving effect to the provisions of the Convention. With regard to the reports from 32 States parties it examined at its second and third sessions, the Committee decided that 17 contained incomplete information and it requested those States to supply further information. A similar request was addressed to eight other States parties at the Committee's fourth session—held from 23 August to 10 September.

The Committee's report drew the Assembly's attention to reports submitted by Panama and the Syrian Arab Republic relating to situations in the Panama Canal Zone and the Golan Heights, respectively. Since the information concerned States which were not parties to the Convention, the Committee, recognizing it had no competence to request information from such States, decided to draw the Assembly's attention to those situations.

At its fourth session, the Committee completed its examination of material concerning Trust and Non-Self-Governing Territories received from the Trusteeship Council and the Special Committee on the Situation with regard to the Implementation of the Declaration on the Granting of Independence to Colonial Countries and Peoples, and submitted its opinions and recommendations thereon to the General Assembly.

On 6 December 1971, the General Assembly adopted a resolution by which, among other things, it:

(1) urged all States not yet parties to the International Convention on the Elimination of All Forms of Racial Discrimination to ratify or accede to the Convention as soon as possible and asked them to report to the Assembly on measures taken to that effect, on any obstacles encountered and on any interim measures taken to comply strictly with the principles set out in the United Nations Declaration on the Elimination of All Forms of Racial Discrimination[3] and in the Convention;

(2) took note with appreciation of the report of the Committee on the Elimination of Racial Discrimination on the second year of its activities;

---

[3]See Y.U.N., 1963, pp. 344-46, resolution 1904(XVIII), containing text of Declaration.

(3) drew the attention of all States to the contents of that report;

(4) commended the Committee for its efforts to obtain extensive reports from States parties, as well as information concerning Trust and Non-Self-Governing Territories;

(5) expressed the view that the Committee's work would be facilitated if the reports submitted by States parties conformed with the guidelines laid down by the Committee for that purpose and if the Committee invited States to be present at its meetings when their reports were examined;

(6) recognized that the Assembly's consideration of the Committee's reports would be facilitated by the inclusion of the criteria used by the Committee when it examined in greater depth the substance of the reports submitted from States parties;

(7) drew the attention of the Trusteeship Council and the Special Committee on the Situation with regard to the Implementation of the Declaration on the Granting of Independence to Colonial Countries and Peoples to the Committee's report, and asked them to take appropriate action within their terms of reference in their respective spheres of activity, as expressed in the relevant parts of the report; and

(8) requested the Secretary-General to transmit to the Committee the records of the discussion on its report at the twenty-sixth (1971) session of the General Assembly.

The Assembly took these decisions when it adopted resolution 2783(XXVI), by a vote of 101 to 0, with 5 abstentions, on the recommendation of its Third Committee, where it was approved on 10 November by a recorded vote of 108 to 1, with 4 abstentions. The text was proposed and revised by Finland, and amended by the USSR.

By another resolution adopted on 6 December (2784(XXVI)), the General Assembly among other things took note with appreciation of the Committee's report and endorsed various opinions and recommendations submitted by the Committee (see above).

(For texts of resolutions 2783(XXVI) and 2784(XXVI), see DOCUMENTARY REFERENCES below.)

Status of International Convention on elimination of racial discrimination

The International Convention on the Elimination of All Forms of Racial Discrimination entered into force on 4 January 1969. By its terms, States parties among other things condemn "racial discrimination and undertake to pursue by all appropriate means and without delay a policy of eliminating racial discrimination in all its forms and promoting understanding among all races."

As at 31 December 1971, the following 58 States had ratified or acceded to the International Convention on the Elimination of All Forms of Racial Discrimination:

Argentina, Bolivia, Brazil, Bulgaria, the Byelorussian SSR, Cameroon, Canada, the Central African Republic, Chile, Costa Rica, Cyprus, Czechoslovakia, Denmark, Ecuador, Egypt, the Federal Republic of Germany, Finland, France, Ghana, Greece, the Holy See, Hungary, Iceland, India, Iran, Iraq, Jamaica, Kuwait, Lebanon, Lesotho, the Libyan Arab Republic, Madagascar, Malta, Mongolia, Morocco, Nepal, the Netherlands, Niger, Nigeria, Norway, Pakistan, Panama, Peru, the Philippines, Poland, Romania, Sierra Leone, Spain, Swaziland, Sweden, the Syrian Arab Republic, Tunisia, the Ukrainian SSR, the USSR, the United Kingdom, Uruguay, Venezuela and Yugoslavia.

At its twenty-sixth (1971) session, the General Assembly had before it a report by the Secretary-General on the status of the Convention containing, among other things, the texts of declarations and/or reservations made by some States.

By its resolution 2783(XXVI) adopted on 6 December 1971, the General Assembly among other things urged all States which were not yet parties to the Convention to ratify or accede to it as soon as possible and asked them to report to the Assembly on measures taken to that effect, on any obstacles encountered and on any interim measures taken to comply strictly with the principles set out in the United Nations Declaration on the Elimination of All Forms of Racial Discrimination and in the Convention.

(For text of resolution 2783(XXVI) and voting details, see DOCUMENTARY REFERENCES below.)

International Day for Elimination of Racial Discrimination

On 22 March 1971, the International Day for the Elimination of Racial Discrimination—proclaimed by the General Assembly in 1966—was commemorated for the fifth time. The Assembly in 1969 had invited all States and organizations to observe the International Day on the anniversary of the Sharpeville massacre in solidarity with the oppressed people of South Africa, and to make special contributions on that day in support of the struggle against *apartheid*.

At United Nations Headquarters in New York, representatives of Member States participated in a special meeting of the Special Committee on *Apartheid* on 22 March which was addressed by the Secretary-General, the President of the twenty-fifth (1970) session of the General Assembly, the President of the Security Council, the Acting Chairman of the Committee of Trustees of the United Nations Trust Fund for South Africa and the Chairman of the Special Committee on *Apartheid*.

The Commission on Human Rights also held a special meeting on 22 March in Geneva, Switzerland, attended by Commission members as well as by representatives of specialized agencies and non-governmental organizations.

As part of the International Day observance, a register for contributions for the victims of *apartheid* was opened at Headquarters on 19 and 22 March 1971. Contributions were accepted on those days for the United Nations Trust Fund for South Africa and for the United Nations Educational and Training Programme for Southern Africa, covering South Africa, Namibia, Southern Rhodesia and the territories under Portuguese administration.

DOCUMENTARY REFERENCES

Elimination of all forms of racial discrimination

General Assembly—26th session
Third Committee, meetings 1844-1868.
Plenary meeting 2001.

A/8403. Report of Economic and Social Council, Chapter XVIIB.
A/8418. Report of Committee on Elimination of Racial Discrimination.
A/C.3/L.1874. Afghanistan, Algeria, Cameroon, Congo, Dahomey, Egypt, Ethiopia, Ghana, Guinea, India, Kenya, Liberia, Libyan Arab Republic, Mali, Mauritania, Morocco, Niger, Nigeria, Pakistan, People's Democratic Republic of Yemen, Senegal, Sierra Leone, Somalia, Sudan, Syrian Arab Republic, Uganda, United Republic of Tanzania, Upper Volta, Yugoslavia, Zambia: draft resolution.
A/C.3/L.1874/Rev.1. Revised draft resolution, sponsored by above 30 powers and by Burundi, Cyprus, Rwanda, Togo and Yemen, as further orally revised by sponsors, approved by Third Committee on 10 November 1971, meeting 1866, by recorded vote of 93 to 6, with 11 abstentions, as follows:

In favour: Afghanistan, Algeria, Barbados, Bhutan, Brazil, Bulgaria, Burma, Burundi, Byelorussian SSR, Cameroon, Central African Republic, Ceylon, Chad, Chile, Colombia, Congo, Costa Rica, Cuba, Cyprus, Czechoslovakia, Dahomey, Denmark, Dominican Republic, Ecuador, Egypt, Equatorial Guinea, Ethiopia, Fiji, Finland, Gabon, Gambia, Ghana, Greece, Guatemala, Guinea, Guyana, Honduras, Hungary, Iceland, India, Indonesia, Iran, Iraq, Israel, Ivory Coast, Jamaica, Jordan, Kenya, Kuwait, Lebanon, Liberia, Libyan Arab Republic, Madagascar, Malaysia, Mali, Mauritania, Mexico, Mongolia, Morocco, Nepal, Nicaragua, Nigeria, Norway, Pakistan, People's Democratic Republic of Yemen, Peru, Philippines, Poland, Romania, Rwanda, Saudi Arabia, Senegal, Sierra Leone, Singapore, Somalia, Sudan, Sweden, Syrian Arab Republic, Thailand, Togo, Trinidad and Tobago, Tunisia, Turkey, Uganda, Ukrainian SSR, USSR, United Republic of Tanzania, Upper Volta, Venezuela, Yemen, Yugoslavia, Zaire, Zambia.
Against: Australia, Canada, France, Portugal, United Kingdom, United States.
Abstaining: Argentina, Austria, Belgium, Ireland, Italy, Japan, Luxembourg, Netherlands, New Zealand, Spain, Uruguay.

A/8542. Report of Third Committee, draft resolution II.

RESOLUTION 2784(XXVI), as recommended by Third Committee, A/8542, adopted by Assembly on 6 December 1971, meeting 2001, by recorded vote of 93 to 5, with 15 abstentions:

In favour: Afghanistan, Algeria, Bahrain, Barbados, Botswana, Brazil, Bulgaria, Burma, Burundi, Byelorussian SSR, Cameroon, Central African Republic, Ceylon, Chad, Chile, Congo, Costa Rica, Cuba, Cyprus, Czechoslovakia, Dahomey, Denmark, Dominican Republic, Ecuador, Equatorial Guinea, Ethiopia, Finland, Gabon, Gambia, Ghana, Greece, Guatemala, Guinea, Guyana, Honduras, Hungary, Iceland, India, Indonesia, Iran, Iraq, Israel, Ivory Coast, Jamaica, Jordan, Kenya, Kuwait, Lebanon, Liberia, Libyan Arab Republic, Madagascar, Malaysia, Mali, Malta, Mauritania, Mexico, Mongolia, Morocco, Nepal, Nicaragua, Niger, Nigeria, Norway, Oman, Pakistan, Panama, Paraguay, People's Democratic Republic of Yemen, Peru, Philippines, Poland, Qatar, Romania, Rwanda, Saudi Arabia, Senegal, Singapore, Somalia, Sudan, Sweden, Syrian Arab Republic, Thailand, Tunisia, Turkey, Uganda, Ukrainian SSR, USSR, United Republic of Tanzania, Venezuela, Yemen, Yugoslavia, Zaire, Zambia.
Against: Australia, France, Portugal, United Kingdom, United States.
Abstaining: Argentina, Austria, Belgium, Canada, Colombia, Ireland, Italy, Japan, Luxembourg, Netherlands, New Zealand, Spain, Swaziland, Togo, Uruguay.

The General Assembly,

Firmly convinced that all forms of racial discrimination are a total negation of the purposes and principles of the Charter of the United Nations and that they militate against human progress, peace and justice,

Fully aware that *apartheid* and all other forms of racial discrimination are instruments of colonialism and imperialism as well as of economic exploitation,

Reiterating its conviction that any doctrine of exclusiveness based on racial differentiation or ethnic or religious superiority is scientifically false, morally condemnable and socially unjust,

Reiterating also its firm determination to bring about the total and unconditional elimination of racial discrimination in all its forms,

Having designated the year 1971 as the International Year for Action to Combat Racism and Racial Discrimination,

Convinced that the International Year for Action to Combat Racism and Racial Discrimination should be observed as the opening year of an ever-growing struggle against racial discrimination in all its forms and manifestations and for the purpose of promoting international solidarity with all those struggling against racism,

Considering that by arousing world public opinion and promoting action against racism the International Year for Action to Combat Racism and Racial Discrimination would contribute to the expansion of national and international efforts towards ensuring the rapid and total eradication of racial discrimination in all its forms,

Believing in the urgent need for eliminating racial discrimination through continuous and vigorous national action and collective international measures in order to alleviate the suffering of millions of people the world over and to ensure them the dignity and equality inherent in all human beings,

I

1. *Requests* the President of the General Assembly to forward the message annexed to the present resolution directly to the heads of State or Government of each State;

2. *Requests* the Secretary-General to submit a report based on the information and comments received from Governments, in accordance with the message sent to heads of State or Government, to the Commission on Human Rights at its twenty-eighth session;

3. *Invites* the Economic and Social Council to request the Commission on Human Rights, bearing in mind the provisions of

paragraph 2 above, to submit suggestions with a view to launching continued international action to combat racism on the basis of a "Decade for vigorous and continued mobilization against racism and racial discrimination in all its forms;"

1. *Reaffirms* that *apartheid* is a crime against humanity;
2. *Declares* that racial discrimination in all its forms is a criminal affront to the conscience and dignity of mankind;
3. *Emphatically reaffirms* its recognition and vigorous support of the legitimacy of the struggles of all oppressed peoples everywhere, and in particular in southern Africa, against colonial, racial and alien domination or foreign occupation towards the achievement of their inalienable rights to equality and freedom, in accordance with the purposes and principles of the Charter of the United Nations, and calls for increased and continued moral and material support to all peoples struggling for their liberation, self-determination and the elimination of all forms of racial discrimination;
4. *Invites* the Economic and Social Council to request the Commission on Human Rights to study and make recommendations for the further elaboration of international instruments to deal with crimes against humanity, particularly those arising from the policies of *apartheid*;
5. *Condemns* those countries which, by their political, economic and military collaboration with the Government of South Africa, encourage and incite that Government to persist in its racist policy;
6. *Strongly condemns* all Governments that continue to supply arms to the Pretoria régime in violation of the relevant resolutions of the General Assembly and the Security Council;

III

1. *Takes note with appreciation* of the report of the Committee on the Elimination of Racial Discrimination, established under article 8 of the International Convention on the Elimination of All Forms of Racial Discrimination;
2. *Endorses* the opinions and recommendations submitted by the Committee on the Elimination of Racial Discrimination in its decisions 3(IV), 4(IV) and 5(IV);
3. *Calls upon* all the trading partners of South Africa to abstain from any action that constitutes an encouragement to the continued violation of the principles and objectives of the International Convention on the Elimination of All Forms of Racial Discrimination by South Africa and the illegal régime in Southern Rhodesia, and to use their influence with a view to ensuring the eradication of the policies of *apartheid* and racial discrimination in the international territory of Namibia and Southern Rhodesia;
4. *Also calls upon* the United Kingdom of Great Britain and Northern Ireland, the administering Power for Southern Rhodesia, to adopt all the necessary measures, including the use of force, with a view to ending the racist and illegal régime of Ian Smith;
5. *Condemns* the Government of Portugal for persisting in its colonialist policies in Africa and for continuing its war against the peoples of the Territories under its domination;
6. *Invites* the Economic and Social Council to request the Commission on Human Rights to continue its comprehensive studies of policies and practices of racial discrimination, taking into account in particular discrimination against peoples of African origin in all countries, and to submit a report to the General Assembly as soon as possible, but not later than at its twenty-eighth session, together with recommendations for action to combat such policies and practices;

IV

Decides to consider this item again at its twenty-seventh session.

ANNEX

Message from the President of the General Assembly to the heads of State or Government

I

1. The General Assembly at its twenty-sixth session on the occasion of celebrating the International Year for Action to Combat Racism and Racial Discrimination has requested me, as a matter of urgency, to put before you the following facts concerning the United Nations campaign against racial discrimination:

(a) The racist Government of South Africa and the illegal régime in Southern Rhodesia have blatantly continued to pursue policies of racial discrimination and *apartheid* in flagrant violation of the purposes and principles of the Charter of the United Nations and of those enshrined in the Universal Declaration of Human Rights.

(b) The racist Government of South Africa continues to effect an extensive arms build-up, thus posing a serious threat to the security and sovereignty of independent African States opposed to its racist policies, as well as to all those peoples struggling against the racial and inhuman policies in southern Africa.

(c) The racist policies in southern Africa have been permitted, even encouraged, to expand through:

(i) The continued existence and operation of the white racist minority régime in Southern Rhodesia through the deliberate ineffectiveness of measures so far taken by the Government of the United Kingdom of Great Britain and Northern Ireland, the administering Power;

(ii) The illegal occupation of the Territory of Namibia by the racist Government of South Africa.

(d) The racist Governments in southern Africa have been further strengthened through:

(i) The maintenance by many States of political, commercial, military, economic, social and other relations with the racist Governments in southern Africa in utter disregard of United Nations resolutions and of the purposes and principles of the Charter;

(ii) An unholy alliance between South Africa, Portugal and Southern Rhodesia, established in order to suppress the struggle of the peoples of that region and to silence the cry of Africa against racism, *apartheid*, economic exploitation and colonial domination.

(e) The United Nations has vigorously opposed all policies based on racial discrimination and, consequently, has:

(i) Declared that any State whose official policy or practice is based on racial discrimination contravenes the purposes and principles of the Charter, and called upon those Governments to desist forthwith from pursuing such policies;

(ii) Condemned the policies of States which, by political, economic or military collaboration with the racist régimes in southern Africa, enable and encourage those régimes to enforce and perpetuate their racist policies, and called upon those States to desist forthwith from extending such collaboration;

(iii) Reaffirmed time and again the legitimacy of the struggle of all oppressed peoples, in particular in the territories under racial, alien domination or foreign occupation, to obtain liberation and racial equality, and called for increased and continued moral and material support to these struggling peoples.

(f) However, the numerous resolutions that have been adopted by the various organs of the United Nations still have little or no effect, owing to the arrogant, flagrant and stubborn disregard on the part of South Africa and its racist allies, transplanted to the soil of Africa, and to the continued political, economic and military aid coming from some States.

II

2. The General Assembly, therefore, is as convinced as ever that the continuation of national and international action against racial discrimination in all its forms, old and contemporary alike, is a matter of cardinal importance if the world is to live in peace and justice, the two interdependent and indispensable components of a better future for all mankind.

3. The General Assembly is also convinced that the primary aim of the United Nations, and, therefore, of all its Member States in the sphere of human rights is the achievement by each individual of the maximum freedom and dignity and that, for the realization of this objective, the laws of every country should grant each individual, irrespective of race, sex, language, religion or

political belief, all the rights inherent in all human beings on the basis of equality, and that the people of every country must be made fully aware of the evils of the policies of racial discrimination and of the ideologies based on racial supremacy and must join in condemning, resisting and combating them.

4. The General Assembly is further convinced that the continuation of racism and colonialism cannot but seriously hamper the efforts of the international community to achieve peace, justice and progress.

III

5. The General Assembly, in view of the aforementioned facts and convictions, has authorized me to request you to transmit the present text to the legislative, administrative, judicial, educational and trade union bodies of your country, as well as to the mass media of information, in order to ensure the continuation of the world campaign against racial discrimination, bearing in mind that the International Year for Action to Combat Racism and Racial Discrimination should be considered as the opening year for a full decade of vigorous struggle against this evil, until the achievement of its total elimination. To that end, the General Assembly recommends, *inter alia*:

(*a*) The discussion of this problem in all national and international conferences, especially in the fields of education, information, trade unions, etc.;

(*b*) The inculcation through education of children and youth in the spirit of human rights by the inclusion in the curricula of special and yearly programmes on the evils of racism and racial discrimination;

(*c*) The continuation of the programmes designated to be carried out during 1971, the International Year for Action to Combat Racism and Racial Discrimination, and their development and updating, in order to intensify the efforts to combat racial discrimination;

(*d*) The continuation of open moral support and the increasing of material aid to the peoples struggling against racial discrimination and *apartheid*;

(*e*) The termination of all relations with the Government of South Africa and all other racist régimes;

(*f*) Exerting every effort to bring about the full implementation of all Security Council and General Assembly resolutions that reflect the world's resolve to end each and every case of discrimination and foreign exploitation;

(*g*) The repeal of all laws and regulations which contribute to the maintenance and propagation of racial discrimination.

IV

6. The General Assembly has requested the Secretary-General to submit a report on this subject to the Assembly at its twenty-seventh session, in which would be included reports of Governments on the above message.

Report of Committee on Elimination of Racial Discrimination

General Assembly—26th session
Third Committee, meetings 1844-1868.
Plenary meeting 2001.

A/8418. Report of Committee on Elimination of Racial Discrimination on its 3rd (12-23 April 1971) and 4th (23 August-10 September 1971) sessions. (Chapter VII: Decisions adopted by Committee at its 3rd (decisions 1(III) and 2(III)) and 4th (decisions 1(IV)-5(IV)) sessions.)

A/C.3/L.1873 and Rev.1. Finland: draft resolution and revision, as further orally amended by sponsor, and as amended by USSR (A/C.3/L.1876, as orally revised), approved by Third Committee on 10 November 1971, meeting 1866, by recorded vote of 108 to 1, with 4 abstentions, as follows:

In favour: Afghanistan, Algeria, Argentina, Australia, Austria, Barbados, Belgium, Bhutan, Brazil, Bulgaria, Burundi, Byelorus-

sian SSR, Cameroon, Canada, Ceylon, Chad, Chile, Colombia, Congo, Costa Rica, Cuba, Cyprus, Czechoslovakia, Dahomey, Denmark, Dominican Republic, Ecuador, Egypt, Equatorial Guinea, Ethiopia, Fiji, Finland, France, Gabon, Gambia, Ghana, Greece, Guatemala, Guinea, Guyana, Honduras, Hungary, Iceland, India, Indonesia, Iran, Iraq, Ireland, Italy, Ivory Coast, Jamaica, Japan, Jordan, Kenya, Kuwait, Laos, Lebanon, Lesotho, Liberia, Libyan Arab Republic, Luxembourg, Madagascar, Malawi, Malaysia, Mali, Mauritania, Mexico, Mongolia, Morocco, Nepal, Netherlands, New Zealand, Nicaragua, Nigeria, Norway, Pakistan, People's Democratic Republic of Yemen, Peru, Philippines, Poland, Romania, Rwanda, Saudi Arabia, Senegal, Sierra Leone, Singapore, Somalia, Spain, Sudan, Sweden, Syrian Arab Republic, Thailand, Togo, Trinidad and Tobago, Tunisia, Turkey, Uganda, Ukrainian SSR, USSR, United Kingdom, United Republic of Tanzania, Upper Volta, Uruguay, Venezuela, Yemen, Yugoslavia, Zaire, Zambia.

Against: Central African Republic.

Abstaining: Burma, Israel, Portugal, United States.

A/C.3/L.1876. USSR: amendment to Finnish draft resolution, A/C.3/L.1873.

A/8542. Report of Third Committee, draft resolution I.

RESOLUTION 2783(XXVI), as recommended by Third Committee, A/8542, adopted by Assembly on 6 December 1971, meeting 2001, by 101 votes to 0, with 5 abstentions.

The General Assembly,

Recalling its resolution 2106(XX) of 21 December 1965 in which it adopted and opened for signature and ratification the International Convention on the Elimination of All Forms of Racial Discrimination and invited eligible States under article 17 of that Convention to sign and ratify it without delay,

Stressing the significance of the coming into force of the International Convention on the Elimination of All Forms of Racial Discrimination and of the bringing into being of the Committee on the Elimination of Racial Discrimination, and requesting all States parties to the Convention to give full co-operation to that Committee in order that it may fulfil its mandate under the Convention,

Noting the recommendations contained in Economic and Social Council resolution 1588(L) of 21 May 1971,

Having received the report of the Committee on the Elimination of Racial Discrimination, established under the International Convention on the Elimination of All Forms of Racial Discrimination, on the second year of its activities,

Expressing its satisfaction at the ratification of or accession to the Convention by 55 States and at the intention expressed by various other States to ratify or accede to the Convention in the near future,

1. *Urges* all States which are not yet parties to the International Convention on the Elimination of All Forms of Racial Discrimination to ratify or accede to the Convention as soon as possible and requests them to report to the General Assembly on the measures taken by them to this effect, on any obstacles that may have been encountered and on any interim measures that have been taken to comply strictly with the principles set out in the United Nations Declaration on the Elimination of All Forms of Racial Discrimination and in the Convention;

2. *Takes note with appreciation* of the report of the Committee on the Elimination of Racial Discrimination on the second year of its activities, submitted under article 9 of the Convention;

3. *Draws the attention* of all States to the contents of that report;

4. *Commends* the Committee on the Elimination of Racial Discrimination for its efforts to obtain extensive reports from States parties, as provided in article 9, paragraph 1, of the Convention, as well as information concerning Trust and Non-Self-Governing Territories relating to matters referred to in article 15;

5. *Expresses the view* that the work of the Committee on the Elimination of Racial Discrimination would be facilitated if the reports submitted by States parties conformed with the guidelines

laid down by the Committee for that purpose and if the Committee invited States parties to be present at its meetings when their reports are examined;

6. *Recognizes* that the General Assembly's consideration of the reports of the Committee on the Elimination of Racial Discrimination would be facilitated by the inclusion of the criteria used by the Committee when it examines in greater depth the substance of the reports from States parties submitted under article 9 of the Convention;

7. *Draws the attention* of the Trusteeship Council and of the Special Committee on the Situation with regard to the Implementation of the Declaration on the Granting of Independence to Colonial Countries and Peoples to the report of the Committee on the Elimination of Racial Discrimination and requests them to take appropriate action within their terms of reference in their respective spheres of activity, as expressed in the relevant parts of the report;

8. *Requests* the Secretary-General to transmit to the Committee on the Elimination of Racial Discrimination the records of the discussion on its report at the twenty-sixth session of the General Assembly.

Status of International Convention on elimination of racial discrimination

A/8401. Report of Secretary-General on work of the Organization, 16 June 1970–15 June 1971, Part Three, Chapter I A 2.

A/8418. Report of Committee on Elimination of Racial Discrimination. Annex I: States Parties to International Convention on Elimination of All Forms of Racial Discrimination as of 10 September 1971.

A/8439. Report of Secretary-General.

Apartheid and racial discrimination in southern Africa

Policies of *apartheid* and racial discrimination

At its 1971 session, the Commission on Human Rights considered the report of the *Ad Hoc* Working Group of Experts which, in 1971, had conducted an investigation of the following matters: the question of capital punishment in southern Africa; the treatment of political prisoners and captured freedom fighters in southern Africa; the condition of Africans in the so-called native reserves and transit camps in South Africa, Namibia and Southern Rhodesia; grave manifestations of *apartheid* in South Africa; and grave manifestations of colonialism and racial discrimination in Namibia, Southern Rhodesia and the African territories under Portuguese administration.

After considering the *Ad Hoc* Working Group's report, the Commission adopted a resolution on 8 March stating, among other things, that it: looked forward to receiving the text of a study on the question of *apartheid* (which had been declared a crime against humanity) from the point of view of international penal law; endorsed the observations, conclusions and recommendations of the Working Group; and decided that the Working Group should continue to survey developments in South Africa, Namibia, Southern Rhodesia and the territories under Portuguese administration, with particular reference to grave manifestations of colonialism and racial discrimination present in the situation prevailing in those areas resulting from the actions of the illegal South African régime in Namibia, the illegal minority régime in Southern Rhodesia and the Portuguese régime in Angola, Mozambique and Guinea (Bissau).

The Commission also asked the Working Group to remain active and vigilant in its observation of colonial and racially discriminatory practices in Africa, to bring to the Commission's attention at its 1972 session new developments in the area, and to submit a report, including conclusions and recommendations, to the Commission at its 1973 session.

Also at its 1971 session, the Commission on Human Rights—after considering the 1970 report of the Sub-Commission on Prevention of Discrimination and Protection of Minorities relating to the special study on racial discrimination in the political, economic, social and cultural spheres prepared by its Special Rapporteur, Hernán Santa Cruz—recommended to the Economic and Social Council the adoption of a resolution on policies of *apartheid* and racial discrimination.

On 21 May 1971, at its fiftieth session, the Economic and Social Council adopted this text as its resolution 1591(L), by which, among other things, it:

(1) requested the Security Council to find means of rigidly enforcing its own resolutions, by which all Member States were called upon not to supply arms to South Africa, and of effectively implementing the relevant resolutions of the General Assembly;

(2) urged States and, in particular, the major trading partners of South Africa to apply fully the resolutions concerning *apartheid* adopted by the Assembly, the Security Council, and other organs of the United Nations;

(3) invited the specialized agencies and especially the financial institutions to follow, towards South Africa, a policy in conformity with those resolutions;

(4) invited all States to strengthen and expand their programmes of assistance to the victims of *apartheid* and to respond as promptly as possible to the General Assembly's appeal for substantial contributions to the United Nations Trust Fund for South Africa;

(5) invited all States to undertake—with the assistance of non-governmental organizations, including workers, religious, social and professional organizations, universities, youth and civic groups and national women's organizations, where appropriate—an educational programme designed to acquaint the public of each country and territory with the evil consequences of the policy of *apartheid*;

(6) also invited non-governmental organizations in consultative status with special interest in the elimination of racism and racial discrimination, independent of any action being undertaken by States, to mount a regular and constant campaign against *apartheid* both at the national and international levels and to report their endeavours and progress biennially to the Economic and Social Council;

(7) appealed to all humanitarian organizations and to the International Committee of the Red Cross, in particular, to take an active role in assisting the victims of *apartheid,* especially those who were detained or imprisoned;

(8) urged the General Assembly to provide funds on the scale required to combat effectively the propaganda undertaken by the Government of South Africa by which that Government sought to defend and justify the policy of *apartheid*;

(9) invited the Secretary-General to make special efforts, utilizing the existing information services available to the United Nations, to alert world public opinion, particularly that of the countries trading with South Africa, to the recommendations made by various United Nations bodies on the subject of *apartheid,* in order to facilitate compliance by Governments with those recommendations.

The Council adopted this text by a vote of 17 to 0, with 8 abstentions, on the recommendation of its Social Committee, which approved it on 19 May by a vote of 20 to 0, with 6 abstentions.

By its resolution 2784(XXVI), adopted on 6 December, the General Assembly among other things invited the Economic and Social Council to ask the Human Rights Commission to study and make recommendations for the further elaboration of international instruments to deal with crimes against humanity, particularly those arising from the policies of *apartheid.*

The Assembly, after reaffirming that *apartheid* was a crime against humanity and declaring that racial discrimination in all its forms was a criminal affront to the conscience and dignity of mankind, reaffirmed its recognition and vigorous support of the legitimacy of the struggles of all oppressed peoples everywhere, and particularly in southern Africa, against colonial, racial and alien domination or foreign occupation towards the achievement of their inalienable rights to equality and freedom, in accordance with the purposes and principles of the United Nations Charter; it called for increased and continued moral and material support to all peoples struggling for their liberation, self-determination and the elimination of all forms of racial discrimination.

Also by this resolution, the Assembly condemned those countries which, by their political, economic and military collaboration with the South African Government, encouraged and incited that Government to persist in its racist policy. It strongly condemned all Governments that continued to supply arms to the Pretoria régime in violation of the relevant resolutions of the General Assembly and the Security Council.

By other parts of this resolution, the General Assembly called upon all trading partners of South Africa to abstain from any action that constituted an encouragement to the continued violation of the principles and objectives of the International Convention on the Elimination of All Forms of Racial Discrimination by South Africa and the illegal régime in Southern Rhodesia, and to use their influence towards the eradication of the policies of *apartheid* and racial discrimination in the international territory of Namibia and Southern Rhodesia.

The Assembly called upon the United Kingdom—the administering power for Southern Rhodesia—to adopt all the necessary measures, including the use of force, with a view to ending the racist and illegal régime of Ian Smith. The Government of Portugal was condemned for persisting in its colonialist policies in Africa and for continuing its war against the peoples of the territories under its domination.

The Assembly then invited the Economic and Social Council to request the Human Rights Commission to continue its comprehensive studies of policies and practices of racial discrimination, taking into account in particular discrimination against peoples of African origin in all countries, and to submit a report to the General Assembly as soon as possible, but not later than at its twenty-eighth (1973) session, together with recommendations for action to combat such policies and practices.

(For details, see above, pp. 398-400.)

Draft convention on suppression and punishment of the crime of *apartheid*

On 6 December 1971, the General Assembly decided to defer consideration of a draft convention on the suppression and punishment of the crime of *apartheid* submitted by Guinea and the USSR on 5 November to the Assembly's Third (Social, Humanitarian and Cultural) Committee.

The Assembly invited the Secretary-General to transmit the draft convention, together with the relevant documentation, to the Commission on Human Rights; the Assembly recommended that the Commission and the Economic and Social Council should consider the item, in co-operation with the Special Committee on *Apartheid,* as a matter of priority at their sessions in 1972 and should submit the text of a draft convention on the suppression and punishment of the crime of *apartheid* to the Assembly at its twenty-seventh session, scheduled to convene in September 1972.

The Assembly took this decision when it adopted resolution 2786(XXVI)—by a recorded vote of 86 to 5, with 23 abstentions—on the recommendation of its Third Committee, which

approved it on 11 November by 79 votes to 5, with 27 abstentions, on a proposal by Bulgaria, the Syrian Arab Republic and the Ukrainian SSR.

(For text of resolution, see DOCUMENTARY REFERENCES below.)

DOCUMENTARY REFERENCES

Policies of apartheid *and racial discrimination*

Economic and Social Council—50th session
Social Committee, meetings 669-680.
Plenary meeting 1771.

E/4949. Report of Commission on Human Rights on its 27th session, 22 February–26 March 1971, Chapters II C (c) and E, VII and XIX (resolutions 6(XXVII) and 7(XXVII)).
E/4949, Chapter XX. Draft resolution V, as submitted by Commission on Human Rights, approved by Social Committee on 19 May 1971, meeting 680, by 20 votes to 0, with 6 abstentions.
E/4949/Add.1. Financial implications of resolutions adopted by Commission on Human Rights at its 27th session.
E/5032. Report of Social Committee, draft resolution V.

RESOLUTION 1591(L), as recommended by Social Committee, E/5032, adopted by Council on 21 May 1971, meeting 1771, by 17 votes to 0, with 8 abstentions.

The Economic and Social Council,
Strongly condemning the policies of racial discrimination pursued in South Africa, Namibia, Southern Rhodesia and the Territories under Portuguese domination, more particularly the doctrine of *apartheid,* which is scientifically false and whose application constitutes a crime against humanity and a threat to international peace and security,
Welcoming the recommendations concerning the policies of *apartheid* made in General Assembly resolutions of recent years, particularly resolutions 2396(XXIII) and 2397(XXIII) of 2 December 1968, 2544(XXIV) of 11 December 1969, 2547(XXIV) of 11 and 15 December 1969 and 2646(XXV) of 30 November 1970,
Convinced that, in order to ensure the complete effectiveness of the struggle being carried on against *apartheid,* it is essential for Member States, in particular the trading partners of South Africa, to apply as a matter of the utmost urgency and without reservation the resolutions concerning *apartheid* adopted by the General Assembly, the Security Council and other organs of the United Nations,
1. *Requests* the Security Council to find means of rigidly enforcing its own resolutions, in which all Member States are called upon not to supply arms to South Africa, and of effectively implementing the above-mentioned resolutions of the General Assembly;
2. *Urges* States and, in particular, the major trading partners of South Africa to apply fully the resolutions concerning *apartheid* adopted by the General Assembly, the Security Council, and other organs of the United Nations;
3. *Invites* the specialized agencies and, especially, the financial institutions to follow, towards South Africa, a policy in conformity with these resolutions;
4. *Invites* all States to strengthen and expand their programmes of assistance to the victims of *apartheid* and to respond as promptly as possible to the General Assembly's appeal for substantial contributions to the United Nations Trust Fund for South Africa;
5. *Invites* all States to undertake, with the assistance of non-governmental organizations, including workers, religious, social and professional organizations, universities, youth and civic groups and national women's organizations, where appropriate, an educational programme designed to acquaint the public of each country and Territory with the evil consequences of the policy of *apartheid;*

6. *Also invites* non-governmental organizations in consultative status with special interest in the elimination of racism and racial discrimination, independent of any action being undertaken by States, to mount a regular and constant campaign against *apartheid* both at the national and international levels and to report their endeavours and progress biennially to the Economic and Social Council;
7. *Appeals* to all humanitarian organizations and to the International Committee of the Red Cross, in particular, to take an active role in assisting the victims of *apartheid,* especially those who are detained or imprisoned;
8. *Urges* the General Assembly to provide funds on the scale required to combat effectively the propaganda undertaken by the Government of South Africa by which that Government seeks to defend and justify the policy of *apartheid;*
9. *Invites* the Secretary-General to make special efforts, utilizing the existing information services available to the United Nations, to alert world public opinion, particularly that of the countries trading with South Africa, to the recommendations made by various United Nations bodies on the subject of *apartheid,* in order to facilitate compliance by Governments with those recommendations.

OTHER DOCUMENTS
A/8342 and Add.1. Question of violation of human rights and fundamental freedoms, including policies of racial discrimination and segregation and of *apartheid,* in all countries, with particular reference to colonial and other dependent countries and territories. Report of Secretary-General.
A/8401. Report of Secretary-General on work of the Organization, 16 June 1970–15 June 1971, Part Three, Chapter I A 3.
A/8403. Report of Economic and Social Council on work of its 50th and 51st sessions, Chapter XVII C.

Draft convention on suppression and punishment of the crime of apartheid

General Assembly—26th session
Third Committee, meetings 1859-1868.
Plenary meeting 2001.

A/C.3/L.1871. Guinea and USSR: draft convention on suppression and punishment of crime of *apartheid.*
A/C.3/L.1875. Bulgaria, Syrian Arab Republic, Ukrainian SSR: draft resolution, as orally amended by sponsors, approved by Third Committee on 11 November 1971, meeting 1867, by recorded vote of 79 to 5, with 27 abstentions, as follows:

In favour: Afghanistan, Algeria, Barbados, Bhutan, Brazil, Bulgaria, Burma, Burundi, Byelorussian SSR, Cameroon, Ceylon, Chad, Chile, Colombia, Cuba, Cyprus, Czechoslovakia, Dahomey, Ecuador, Egypt, Equatorial Guinea, Ethiopia, Gabon, Gambia, Ghana, Guinea, Guyana, Hungary, Iceland, India, Indonesia, Iran, Iraq, Israel, Ivory Coast, Jamaica, Jordan, Kenya, Kuwait, Lebanon, Lesotho, Liberia, Libyan Arab Republic, Mali, Mauritania, Mexico, Mongolia, Nepal, Niger, Nigeria, Panama, People's Democratic Republic of Yemen, Peru, Philippines, Poland, Romania, Rwanda, Saudi Arabia, Senegal, Sierra Leone, Singapore, Somalia, Sudan, Syrian Arab Republic, Thailand, Togo, Trinidad and Tobago, Tunisia, Turkey, Uganda, Ukrainian SSR, USSR, United Republic of Tanzania, Upper Volta, Uruguay, Venezuela, Yemen, Yugoslavia, Zambia.
Against: Canada, Netherlands, Portugal, United Kingdom, United States.

Abstaining: Argentina, Australia, Austria, Belgium, Central African Republic, Costa Rica, Denmark, Dominican Republic, El Salvador, Fiji, Finland, France, Greece, Guatemala, Honduras, Ireland, Italy, Japan, Luxembourg, Madagascar, New Zealand, Nicaragua, Norway, Spain, Swaziland, Sweden, Zaire.

A/8542. Report of Third Committee, draft resolution IV.

RESOLUTION 2786(XXVI), as recommended by Third Committee, A/8542, adopted by Assembly on 6 December 1971, meeting 2001, by recorded vote of 86 to 5, with 23 abstentions, as follows:

In favour: Afghanistan, Albania, Algeria, Bahrain, Barbados, Brazil, Bulgaria, Burma, Burundi, Byelorussian SSR, Cameroon, Ceylon, Chad, Chile, China, Congo, Cuba, Cyprus, Czechoslovakia, Dahomey, Ecuador, Egypt, Equatorial Guinea, Ethiopia, Gabon, Gambia, Ghana, Guinea, Guyana, Honduras, Hungary, Iceland, India, Indonesia, Iran, Iraq, Israel, Ivory Coast, Jamaica, Jordan, Kenya, Kuwait, Lebanon, Liberia, Libyan Arab Republic, Malaysia, Mali, Malta, Mauritania, Mexico, Mongolia, Morocco, Nepal, Niger, Nigeria, Oman, Pakistan, Panama, People's Democratic Republic of Yemen, Peru, Philippines, Poland, Qatar, Romania, Rwanda, Saudi Arabia, Senegal, Sierra Leone, Singapore, Somalia, Sudan, Syrian Arab Republic, Thailand, Togo, Tunisia, Turkey, Uganda, Ukrainian SSR, USSR, United Republic of Tanzania, Uruguay, Venezuela, Yemen, Yugoslavia, Zaire, Zambia.
Against: Canada, Netherlands, Portugal, United Kingdom, United States.
Abstaining: Argentina, Australia, Austria, Belgium, Central

African Republic, Colombia, Costa Rica, Denmark, Dominican Republic, Finland, France, Greece, Guatemala, Ireland, Italy, Japan, Luxembourg, Madagascar, New Zealand, Nicaragua, Norway, Spain, Sweden.

The General Assembly,
Firmly convinced that *apartheid* constitutes a total negation of the purposes and principles of the Charter of the United Nations and is a crime against humanity,
Recognizing the need to take further effective measures with a view to the suppression and punishment of the crime of *apartheid*,
Recognizing that the conclusion of a convention on the suppression and punishment of the crime of *apartheid* under the auspices of the United Nations would be an important contribution to the struggle against *apartheid*, racism, economic exploitation, colonial domination and foreign occupation,
Considering that there has been no opportunity at the current session of the General Assembly to consider fully the draft convention submitted to the Third Committee,
1. *Invites* the Secretary-General to transmit to the Commission on Human Rights the draft convention on the suppression and punishment of the crime of *apartheid*, together with the relevant records of the discussion;
2. *Recommends* that the Commission on Human Rights at its twenty-eighth session and the Economic and Social Council at its fifty-second session should consider this item, in co-operation with the Special Committee on *Apartheid*, as a matter of priority, and should submit the text of the draft convention on the suppression and punishment of the crime of *apartheid* to the General Assembly at its twenty-seventh session.

Measures against incitement to racial discrimination

On 18 December 1971, the General Assembly took several decisions concerning measures to be taken against nazism and other totalitarian ideologies and practices based on incitement to hatred and racial intolerance.

In so doing, the Assembly observed that contemporary manifestations of resurgent nazism, like the earlier ones, combined racial prejudice and discrimination with terrorism, and that in some cases racism had been raised to the level of State policy as in the case of South Africa.

After condemning all manifestations of the ideology and practice of nazism and racial intolerance, wherever they might occur, the Assembly: (*a*) called upon States to take steps to bring to light any evidence of the manifestation and dissemination of the ideology and practice of nazism and racial intolerance and to ensure that they were rigorously suppressed and prohibited; (*b*) invited all eligible States which had not yet done so to ratify and to accede to the Convention on the Prevention and Punishment of the Crime of Genocide[4] and the Convention on the Non-Applicability of Statutory Limitations to War Crimes and Crimes against Humanity[5] as soon as possible; (*c*) invited all Member States of the United Nations or members of the specialized agencies to review their legislation, in the light of the above-mentioned Conventions, with a view to determining whether, in the light of their circum-

stances, further legal measures were required to eradicate for all time the danger of a revival of nazism, racial intolerance or other ideologies based on terror; (*d*) urgently called upon those States concerned to take immediate and effective measures, including legislative measures, to prevent the activities of nazi and racist organizations and groups; and (*e*) appealed to all States to prohibit activity by organizations propagating concepts of nazism and racial superiority.

The Assembly urged those States which were unable, for serious constitutional or other reasons, to implement fully the provisions of article 9 of the United Nations Declaration on the Elimination of All Forms of Racial Discrimination and article 4 of the International Convention on the Elimination of All Forms of Racial Discrimination—both of which condemned and outlawed all propaganda and organizations based on ideas or theories of the superiority of one race or group of persons of one colour or ethnic origin, or which attempted to justify or promote racial hatred and discrimination in any form—to take measures designed to ensure the speedy disbandment and disappearance of such organizations. The measures should provide, *inter alia*, that: (*a*) those organizations

[4]See Y.U.N., 1948-49, pp. 959-60, text of Convention.
[5]See Y.U.N., 1968, pp. 608-10, resolution 2391(XXIII), containing text of Convention.

should not be allowed to receive financial subsidies from organs of the State, private companies or individuals; they should be denied the use of public premises in which to establish headquarters or conduct meetings, the use of streets and squares in populated areas for holding demonstrations, and the use of public information media for disseminating propaganda; and they should be prohibited from forming militarized detachments on any pretext; and (b) persons employed by the State, particularly in the armed forces, should not be permitted to belong to such organizations. The above measures were to be taken only in so far as they were compatible with the principles of the Universal Declaration of Human Rights.

The Assembly requested the International Labour Organisation, the United Nations Educational, Scientific and Cultural Organization and other specialized agencies to consider, within their respective spheres of competence, the question of the danger of a revival of the concepts of nazism and racial intolerance; it also appealed to regional inter-governmental organizations to consider the question at the regional level.

The Assembly also called upon Governments, the United Nations and its various bodies, specialized agencies and international and national organizations to increase public awareness of the danger of a revival of nazism and racial intolerance, especially among young people, by education, by the preparation and dissemination of information on the subject and by recalling the history of nazism and of racial intolerance; and called upon all States to take legislative and administrative measures to prevent activities of any kind in favour of nazism and the concept of racial superiority. It confirmed the principles of international law with regard to the eradication of nazism, and appealed to all States to act in conformity with those principles.

Finally, the Assembly decided to keep under continuing review the question of measures to be taken against ideologies and practices based on terror or incitement to racial discrimination.

(For text of resolution, see DOCUMENTARY REFERENCES below.)

These decisions by the Assembly were set forth in resolution 2839(XXVI), adopted by a vote of 89 to 2, with 21 abstentions, on the recommendation of the Third (Social, Humanitarian and Cultural) Committee.

In the Third Committee, at the request of Italy, separate votes were taken on the provisions (a) inviting eligible States which had not yet done so to ratify or to accede as soon as possible to the Convention on the Prevention and Punishment of the Crime of Genocide and the Convention on the Non-Applicability of Statutory Limitations to War Crimes and Crimes against Humanity (approved by a vote of 33 to 2, with 45 abstentions); and (b) inviting all States Members of the United Nations or the specialized agencies to review their legislation in the light of the above Conventions with a view to determining whether further legal measures were required to eradicate for all time the danger of a revival of nazism, racial intolerance or other ideologies based on terror (approved by a vote of 36 to 2, with 45 abstentions).

At the request of Finland, the Committee also approved by separate votes the two references to the Convention on the Non-Applicability of Statutory Limitations to War Crimes and Crimes against Humanity.

The draft resolution as a whole was approved by the Third Committee by a vote of 58 to 2, with 23 abstentions.

The text was recommended to the Assembly by the Economic and Social Council by its resolution 1590(L) of 21 May 1971.

In recommending that the Assembly adopt the text, the Economic and Social Council also invited the Assembly to resume, as soon as possible, the study of the question of international criminal jurisdiction and the question of the draft code of offences against the peace and security of mankind, with a view to the preparation of effective measures to eliminate any possibility of a revival of nazism.

(For text of resolution, see DOCUMENTARY REFERENCES below.)

Resolution 1590(L) was adopted by a vote of 16 to 2, with 6 abstentions, on the recommendation of the Council's Social Committee. On 18 May 1971, by a vote of 15 to 2, with 5 abstentions, the Social Committee approved the text submitted by the Commission on Human Rights. That text was adopted by the Commission at its 1971 session (22 February–26 March 1971).

DOCUMENTARY REFERENCES

Economic and Social Council—50th session
Social Committee, meetings 669-678.
Plenary meeting 1771.

Racial Discrimination. Special Study on Racial Discrimination in the Political, Economic, Social and Cultural Spheres. U.N.P. Sales No.: E.71.XIV.2.
E/4949. Report of Commission on Human Rights on its 27th session, Chapters II B and D and XIX (resolution 5(XXVII)).

E/4949, Chapter XX. Draft resolution IV, as submitted by Commission on Human Rights, approved by Social Committee on 18 May 1971, meeting 678, by 15 votes to 2, with 5 abstentions.
E/5032. Report of Social Committee, draft resolution IV.

RESOLUTION 1590(L), as recommended by Social Committee, E/5032, adopted by Council on 21 May 1971, meeting 1771, by 16 votes to 2, with 6 abstentions.

The Economic and Social Council,

Noting resolution 4(XXIII) of the Sub-Commission on Prevention of Discrimination and Protection of Minorities, and resolution 5(XXVII) of the Commission on Human Rights on the danger of a revival of nazism and racial discrimination,

Having considered the special study of racial discrimination in the political, economic, social and cultural spheres, prepared by the Special Rapporteur of the Sub-Commission and, in particular, chapter XII of that study on the danger of the revival of nazism and racial discrimination,

1. *Invites* the General Assembly to resume, as soon as possible, the study of the question of international criminal jurisdiction and the question of the draft code of offences against the peace and security of mankind, with a view to the preparation of effective measures to eliminate any possibility of a revival of nazism;

2. *Recommends* to the General Assembly the adoption of the following draft resolution:

[For text of resolution, see General Assembly resolution 2839(XXVI) below.]

General Assembly—26th session
Third Committee, meeting 1902.
Plenary meeting 2025.

A/8332. Measures to be taken against nazism and other totalitarian ideologies and practices based on incitement to hatred and racial intolerance. Note by Secretary-General, transmitting Economic and Social Council resolution 1590(L), approved by Third Committee on 9 December 1971, meeting 1902, by 58 votes to 2, with 23 abstentions.
A/8401. Report of Secretary-General on work of the Organization, 16 June 1970–15 June 1971, Part Three, Chapter I A 4.
A/8403. Report of Economic and Social Council on work of its 50th and 51st sessions, Chapter XVII E.
A/8593. Report of Third Committee.

RESOLUTION 2839(XXVI), as recommended by Third Committee, A/8593, adopted by Assembly on 18 December 1971, meeting 2025, by 89 votes to 2, with 21 abstentions.

The General Assembly,

Recognizing that there still exist in the world convinced adherents of nazism and racial intolerance whose activities, if they are not opposed in sufficient time, could bring about a resurgence of those ideologies, which are clearly incompatible with the purposes and principles of the Charter of the United Nations, the United Nations Declaration on the Elimination of All Forms of Racial Discrimination and the International Convention on the Elimination of All Forms of Racial Discrimination, and that, accordingly, the danger of a revival or a development of new forms of nazism and racial discrimination combined with terrorism cannot be disregarded,

Considering that contemporary manifestations of resurgent nazism, like the earlier ones, combine racial prejudice and discrimination with terrorism, and that in some cases racism has been raised to the level of State policy, as in the case of South Africa,

Believing it essential, in order to remove this threat to the peace and security of peoples and to the realization of basic human rights and fundamental freedoms, to elaborate a series of urgent and effective measures which might be adopted by States with a view to suppressing the revival of nazism and preventing its revival, in any form or manifestation, in the future,

Firmly convinced that the best bulwark against nazism and racial discrimination is the establishment and maintenance of democratic institutions, that the existence of genuine political, social and economic democracy is an effective vaccine and an equally effective antidote against the formation or development of Nazi movements and that a political system which is based on freedom and effective participation by the people in the conduct of public affairs, and under which economic and social conditions are such as to ensure a decent standard of living for the population, makes it impossible for fascism, nazism or other ideologies based on terror to succeed,

Confirming that nazism and other forms of racial intolerance constitute a serious threat to the realization everywhere of human rights and freedoms and the maintenance of international peace and security,

Deeming it essential that the question of measures to be taken to combat nazism and racial intolerance should be kept under constant review by the appropriate United Nations bodies with a view to the timely and immediate adoption of the necessary measures for the complete eradication of nazism from the life of society,

1. *Condemns* all manifestations of the ideology and practice of nazism and racial intolerance, wherever they may occur;

2. *Calls upon* States to take steps to bring to light any evidence of the manifestation and dissemination of the ideology and practice of nazism and racial intolerance and to ensure that they are rigorously suppressed and prohibited;

3. *Invites* all eligible States which have not yet done so to ratify and to accede to the Convention on the Prevention and Punishment of the Crime of Genocide and the Convention on the Non-Applicability of Statutory Limitations to War Crimes and Crimes against Humanity as soon as possible, and requests them to report to the General Assembly at its twenty-seventh session on the measures taken by them to comply strictly with the provisions of those Conventions;

4. *Invites* all States Members of the United Nations or members of specialized agencies to review their legislation, in the light of the provisions of the Convention on the Prevention and Punishment of the Crime of Genocide and the Convention on the Non-Applicability of Statutory Limitations to War Crimes and Crimes against Humanity, with a view to determining whether, in the light of their circumstances, further legal measures are required to eradicate for all time the danger of a revival of nazism, racial intolerance or other ideologies based on terror;

5. *Urgently calls upon* those States concerned which have not yet done so to take immediate and effective measures, including legislative measures, with due regard to the principles contained in the Universal Declaration of Human Rights, to prevent the activities of Nazi and racist organizations and groups;

6. *Appeals* to all States to prohibit activity by organizations propagating concepts of nazism and racial superiority;

7. *Urges* those States which are unable, for serious constitutional or other reasons, to implement immediately and fully the provisions of article 9 of the United Nations Declaration on the Elimination of All Forms of Racial Discrimination and article 4 of the International Convention on the Elimination of All Forms of Racial Discrimination—both of which condemn and outlaw all propaganda and all organizations based on ideas or theories of the superiority of one race or group of persons of one colour or ethnic origin, or which attempt to justify or promote racial hatred and discrimination in any form—to take measures designed to ensure the speedy disbandment and disappearance of such organizations, these measures to provide, *inter alia,* that:

(*a*) Such organizations should not be allowed to receive financial subsidies from organs of the State, private companies or individuals;

(*b*) Such organizations should not be allowed the use of public premises in which to establish their headquarters or conduct meetings of their members, the use of streets and squares in populated areas for holding demonstrations, or the use of public information media for disseminating propaganda;

(*c*) Such organizations should not be allowed to form militarized detachments on any pretext, and offenders should be subject to prosecution in the courts;

(*d*) Persons employed by the State, particularly in the armed forces, should not be permitted to belong to such organizations; and all these measures to be taken only in so far as they are compatible with the principles of the Universal Declaration of Human Rights;

8. *Requests* the United Nations Educational, Scientific and Cultural Organization, the International Labour Organisation and other specialized agencies to consider, within their respective

spheres of competence, the question of the danger of a revival of the concepts of nazism and racial intolerance;

9. *Appeals* to regional intergovernmental organizations to consider this question at the regional level;

10. *Calls upon* Governments, particularly those which control mass information media of world or continental scope, the United Nations and its various bodies, specialized agencies and international and national organizations to increase public awareness of the danger of a revival of nazism and racial intolerance, especially among young people, by education, by the preparation and dissemination of information on this subject and by recalling the history of nazism and its crimes and of racial intolerance;

11. *Calls upon* all States to take legislative and administrative measures to prevent activities of any kind in favour of nazism and the concept of racial superiority;

12. *Decides* to place the question of measures to be taken against ideologies and practices based on terror or on incitement to racial discrimination or any other form of group hatred on its agenda and under continuing review, and urges other competent organs of the United Nations to do likewise, so that appropriate measures can be taken promptly as required;

13. *Confirms* the principles of international law with regard to the eradication of nazism, and appeals to all States to act in conformity with those principles.

Other matters concerning prevention of discrimination and protection of minorities

Studies on discrimination

Special study on racial discrimination in the political, economic, social and cultural spheres

During 1971, the Commission on Human Rights and the Economic and Social Council examined the final report on the special study on racial discrimination in the political, economic, social and cultural spheres, prepared by the Special Rapporteur of the Commission's Sub-Commission on Prevention of Discrimination and Protection of Minorities.

The special study included information on the historical background, meaning and causes of racial discrimination; international and national action to eliminate racial discrimination; racial discrimination in the political, economic, social and cultural spheres; measures taken in connexion with the protection of indigenous peoples; the racial policy of South Africa; characteristics and manifestations of the policy of segregation elsewhere in southern Africa; and the danger of the revival of nazism and racial intolerance.

On 21 May 1971, the Economic and Social Council adopted three resolutions concerning racial discrimination in the political, economic, social and cultural spheres.

By one of these, the Council, endorsing in general the conclusions of the special study on racial discrimination and bearing in mind that racial discrimination existed in many countries, and that in southern Africa especially it was being perpetuated as a device for maintaining a steady supply of cheap labour and minority rule by racist régimes, took the following action.

It recommended that the General Assembly should: (*a*) request every competent United Nations organ, specialized agency, regional intergovernmental organization and non-governmental organization in consultative status to consider as a matter of highest priority at sessions to be held in 1971—the International Year for Action to Combat Racism and Racial Discrimination—and in succeeding years: (i) further action it might take with a view to speedily eliminating racial discrimination throughout the world; (ii) action it might recommend to its subsidiary organs, to States and to international and national bodies for this purpose; and (iii) follow-up measures required to ensure the full and effective implementation of its decisions in this matter; (*b*) urge all States not parties to the International Convention on the Elimination of All Forms of Racial Discrimination to accelerate the process of ratifying that Convention, and request them to report to the General Assembly on the measures taken to this end, on any obstacles that might have been encountered and on any interim measures taken to comply strictly with the principles set out in the United Nations Declaration and International Convention on the Elimination of All Forms of Racial Discrimination; (*c*) pursue, as a major feature of action to combat racism and racial discrimination after the International Year, with the co-operation and assistance of every competent United Nations organ, specialized agency and affiliated national and international organization, a world-wide programme intended to build up public opinion—especially through radio and television broadcasts as well as through the distribution of appropriate literature—with a view to eradicating once and for all false racial beliefs based upon a lack of scientific knowledge; and (*d*) urge all States concerned to accelerate economic and social development of their minority groups with a view to eliminating *de facto* discrimination occasioned by their low standard of living, and also urge competent organs of the United Nations and specialized agencies to extend their full co-operation, including technical and financial assistance where appropriate, to enable the States concerned to achieve the foregoing objective.

The Council also invited non-governmental organizations in consultative status with special interest in the elimination of racism and racial discrimination to communicate biennially to the Economic and Social Council, and for the information of any interested organ of the United Nations, their endeavours and progress in the struggle against racism, *apartheid* and racial discrimination, especially in southern Africa. It invited the International Labour Organisation and the United Nations Educational, Scientific and Cultural Organization to provide the Commission on Human Rights with reports, at three-year intervals, on the nature and effect of any racial discrimination, especially in southern Africa, of whose existence they had knowledge in their sphere of competence.

The Council also stressed the significance of social and economic reforms that would lead to the acceleration of the social and economic development of countries and to the full participation of people in the process of such development and in its benefits as the basis for the actual realization of human rights and freedoms and the elimination of all forms of racial discrimination.

These Council decisions were set forth in resolution 1588(L), adopted, unanimously, as recommended by the Social Committee. The Social Committee unanimously approved the text recommended by the Commission on Human Rights on 18 May 1971.

(For text of resolution, see DOCUMENTARY REFERENCES below.)

In another series of decisions, the Council made the point that the international community should devote particular attention to the problems of indigenous populations, which often encountered racial prejudice and discrimination, sometimes as the result of special measures taken by the authorities to protect their unique culture and identity.

The Council: (*a*) recommended that the Governments of all States having indigenous populations take into account, in their policies of economic and social development, the special problems of indigenous populations with a view to eliminating prejudice and discrimination against such populations; (*b*) appealed to the States concerned to take appropriate legislative, administrative and other measures to protect the indigenous population and prevent any discrimination against it; and (*c*) recommended to all States having legislation for the protection of indigenous populations that they review that legislation with a view to determining whether in practice it had resulted, or might result, in discrimination, or whether its effect had been to place unjust and unnecessary restrictions on certain civil and political rights.

The Council invited all competent organs of the United Nations and, especially, the regional economic commissions and specialized agencies concerned, to co-operate with Governments in any actions they might undertake in compliance with the resolution.

The Council also noted with interest the efforts that had been made within the inter-American system in reviewing legislation for the protection of indigenous populations, and invited the Organization of American States, other regional bodies, and the specialized organs and bodies of the United Nations to assist in the eradication of any kind of discrimination against indigenous populations.

Finally, the Council authorized the Sub-Commission on Prevention of Discrimination and Protection of Minorities to make a complete and comprehensive study of the problem of discrimination against indigenous populations and to suggest the necessary national and international measures for eliminating such discrimination, in co-operation with the other organs and bodies of the United Nations and with the competent international organizations.

The Council took this action on 21 May 1971 in unanimously adopting resolution 1589(L), as recommended by its Social Committee, which on 19 May had approved, unanimously, a draft submitted by the Commission on Human Rights, as amended by Brazil.

Also on 21 May 1971, the Economic and Social Council, noting the unique contribution made by the special study on racial discrimination in the political, economic, social and cultural spheres prepared by the Special Rapporteur of the Sub-Commission on Prevention of Discrimination and Protection of Minorities, expressed its gratitude to the Special Rapporteur, Hernán Santa Cruz.

The Council took this action in unanimously adopting resolution 1587(L), as recommended by its Social Committee. The draft text, proposed by the Commission on Human Rights, had been approved unanimously by the Social Committee on 18 May 1971.

(For text of resolution, see DOCUMENTARY REFERENCES below.)

Study of equality in the administration of justice

During 1971, the Commission on Human Rights, the Economic and Social Council and the General Assembly took several decisions concerning human rights in the administration of justice.

At its 1971 session, the Commission on Human Rights considered the final report on the study of equality in the administration of justice submitted by its Special Rapporteur, Mohammed Ahmed Abu Rannat. It was unable, however, to examine the draft principles relating to equality in the administration of justice which had been adopted by the Sub-Commission on Prevention of Discrimination and Protection of Minorities in 1970.

On 21 May 1971, the Economic and Social

Council requested the Secretary-General to circulate the study and the draft principles adopted by the Sub-Commission, and recommended that the Commission on Human Rights should, at its 1972 session, examine the draft principles and take a decision on further action.

The Council took these decisions in unanimously adopting resolution 1594(L), as recommended by its Social Committee. The text was based on a draft submitted by the Commission on Human Rights and approved unanimously by the Social Committee on 18 May 1971.

(For text of resolution, see DOCUMENTARY REFERENCES below.)

Later in 1971, at its twenty-sixth session, the General Assembly reaffirmed the principles concerning human rights in the administration of justice as embodied in the Universal Declaration of Human Rights, namely, those referring to: the right not to be subjected to inhuman treatment or punishment; the right to a fair and public hearing by an independent and impartial tribunal in any civil or criminal proceedings; the right, if charged with a penal offence, to be presumed innocent until proved guilty; and the right not to be subjected to retrospective criminal sanctions.

Among other things, the Assembly also invited the attention of Member States to the Standard Minimum Rules for the Treatment of Prisoners, and recommended that they be effectively implemented in the administration of penal and correctional institutions and that favourable consideration be given to their incorporation in national legislation. The Assembly also expressed the hope that the Economic and Social Council would be able at its early-1972 session to consider final proposals of the Commission on Human Rights concerning the principles relating to equality in the administration of justice.

These Assembly decisions were set forth in resolution 2858(XXVI), which was adopted by a vote of 111 to 7, with 3 abstentions, on the recommendation of the Third (Social, Humanitarian and Cultural) Committee. On 10 December 1971, by a vote of 72 to 7, with 9 abstentions, the Third Committee approved the draft sponsored by Austria, Belgium, Brazil, Canada, Costa Rica, France, Italy, the Netherlands, New Zealand, Sweden, the United Kingdom and Uruguay.

(For text of resolution, see DOCUMENTARY REFERENCES below.)

Elimination of religious intolerance

On 18 December 1971, the General Assembly decided to consider the question of the elimination of all forms of religious intolerance at its 1972 session.

The Assembly took this action, among others, in adopting resolution 2844(XXVI), on the recommendation of its Third (Social, Humanitarian and Cultural) Committee, which on 10 December 1971 approved, by a vote of 96 to 0, a text proposed by Nigeria and Sudan.

(For text of resolution, see DOCUMENTARY REFERENCES below.)

DOCUMENTARY REFERENCES

Studies on discrimination

SPECIAL STUDY ON RACIAL DISCRIMINATION IN THE
POLITICAL, ECONOMIC, SOCIAL AND CULTURAL SPHERES
Racial Discrimination. Special Study on Racial Discrimination in the Political, Economic, Social and Cultural Spheres. U.N.P. Sales No.: E.71.XIV.2.

Economic and Social Council—50th session
Social Committee, meetings 669-680.
Plenary meeting 1771.

E/4949. Report of Commission on Human Rights on its 27th session, 22 February–26 March 1971, Chapters II C (a) and XIX (resolution 3(XXVII)).
E/4949, Chapter XX. Draft resolution II, as submitted by Commission on Human Rights, approved unanimously by Social Committee on 18 May 1971, meeting 678.
E/5032. Report of Social Committee, draft resolution II.

RESOLUTION 1588(L), as recommended by Social Committee, E/5032, adopted unanimously by Council on 21 May 1971, meeting 1771.

The Economic and Social Council,
Considering it necessary that immediate, effective and decisive steps should be taken to eradicate racial discrimination in the political, economic, social and cultural spheres,
Endorsing in general the conclusions concerning such discrimination set out in the special study of racial discrimination in the political, economic, social and cultural spheres,
Bearing in mind that racial discrimination exists in many countries and that in southern Africa especially it is being perpetuated as a device for maintaining a steady supply of cheap labour and the minority rule by the racist régimes,
1. *Recommends* that the General Assembly request every competent United Nations organ, specialized agency, regional intergovernmental organization and non-governmental organization in consultative status to consider, as a matter of the highest priority, at sessions to be held in 1971, the International Year for Action to Combat Racism and Racial Discrimination, and in succeeding years:
(a) The further action which it might itself take with a view to speedily eliminating racial discrimination throughout the world;
(b) The action which it might recommend to its subsidiary organs, to States and to international and national bodies for this purpose;
(c) The follow-up measures required to ensure the full and effective implementation of its decisions in this matter;
2. *Invites* non-governmental organizations in consultative status with special interest in the elimination of racism and racial discrimination to communicate biennially to the Economic and Social Council, and for the information of any interested organ of the United Nations, their endeavours and progress in the struggle against racism, *apartheid* and racial discrimination, especially in southern Africa;
3. *Recommends further* that the General Assembly urge all States which are not parties to the International Convention on the

Elimination of All Forms of Racial Discrimination to accelerate the process of ratifying that Convention, to ratify or accede to it as soon as possible, especially during the International Year for Action to Combat Racism and Racial Discrimination, and request them to report to the General Assembly on the measures taken by them to this effect, on any obstacles that may have been encountered and on any interim measures taken to comply strictly with the principles set out in the United Nations Declaration on the Elimination of All Forms of Racial Discrimination and the International Convention on the Elimination of All Forms of Racial Discrimination;

4. *Recommends further* that the General Assembly should pursue, as a major feature of action to combat racism and racial discrimination after the International Year, with the co-operation and assistance of every competent United Nations organ, specialized agency and affiliated national and international organization, a world-wide programme intended to build up public opinion, especially through radio and television broadcasts, as well as through the distribution of appropriate literature such as the Statement on Race and Racial Discrimination adopted by a conference of experts on the subject convened by the United Nations Educational, Scientific and Cultural Organization in Paris in 1967, with a view to eradicating once and for all false racial beliefs based upon a lack of scientific knowledge;

5. *Recommends further* that the General Assembly urge all States concerned to accelerate economic and social development of their minority groups with a view to eliminating *de facto* discrimination occasioned by their low standard of living, and urge also competent organs of the United Nations and specialized agencies to extend their full co-operation, including technical and financial assistance where appropriate, to enable the States concerned to achieve the foregoing objective;

6. *Stresses* the significance of social and economic reforms that lead to the acceleration of the social and economic development of countries and also to the full participation of people in the process of such development and in its benefits as the basis for the actual realization of human rights and freedoms and the elimination of all forms of racial discrimination;

7. *Invites* the International Labour Organisation and the United Nations Educational, Scientific and Cultural Organization to provide the Commission on Human Rights with reports, at three-year intervals, on the nature and effect of any racial discrimination, especially in southern Africa, of whose existence they have knowledge in their sphere of competence.

E/4949. Report of Commission on Human Rights on its 27th session, 22 February–26 March 1971, Chapters II C (*b*) and XIX (resolution 4(XXVII)).

E/4949, Chapter XX. Draft resolution III, as submitted by Commission on Human Rights, and as amended by Brazil (E/AC.7/L.600, paras. 1 and 2), approved unanimously by Social Committee on 19 May 1971, meeting 680.

E/AC.7/L.600. Brazil: amendments to draft resolution III submitted by Commission on Human Rights in E/4949.

E/5032. Report of Social Committee, draft resolution III.

RESOLUTION 1589(L), as recommended by Social Committee, E/5032, adopted unanimously by Council on 21 May 1971, meeting 1771.

The Economic and Social Council,
Noting that indigenous populations often encounter racial prejudice and discrimination and that sometimes the special measures taken by the authorities to protect their unique culture and identity— which they themselves earnestly wish to maintain —may, with the passage of time, become unnecessary or excessive and therefore may also be discriminatory in character,

Considering that the international community must therefore devote particular attention to the problems of indigenous populations if it is to succeed in its endeavour to eliminate all forms of discrimination,

Convinced that the policy of integration of indigenous populations in the national community, and not segregation or assimilation, is the most appropriate means of eliminating discrimination against those populations,

Convinced also that no integration policy for indigenous populations, whether they represent minority groups or a majority of a country's population, can proceed unless it is accompanied by a policy of economic, social and educational development aimed at achieving a rapid and substantial rise in the living standards of those populations,

Convinced further that every precaution must be taken to ensure that the process of integration is not carried out to the detriment of the institutions and traditions of the indigenous population and that its cultural and historical values are respected,

1. *Recommends* that the Governments of all States having indigenous populations take into account, in their policies of economic and social development, the special problems of indigenous populations with a view to eliminating prejudice and discrimination against such populations;

2. *Appeals* to the States concerned, if they have not yet done so, to take the appropriate legislative, administrative and other measures to protect the indigenous population and to prevent any discrimination against it;

3. *Invites* all competent organs of the United Nations and, especially, the regional economic commissions and specialized agencies concerned to co-operate with Governments in any actions which they may undertake in compliance with the present resolution;

4. *Recommends* to all States having legislation for the protection of indigenous populations that they review that legislation with a view to determining whether in practice it has not already resulted, or might not result, in discrimination, or whether its effect has been to place unjust and unnecessary restrictions on certain civil and political rights;

5. *Notes with interest* the efforts that have been made in this connexion within the inter-American system and invites the Organization of American States, and particularly its specialized organs and bodies, such as the Inter-American Commission on Human Rights and the Inter-American Indian Institute, to assist in the eradication of any kind of discrimination against indigenous populations;

6. *Invites similarly* the specialized organs and bodies of the United Nations and the other regional bodies to take the necessary steps for the same purpose of assisting in the eradication of any discrimination against indigenous populations;

7. *Authorizes* the Sub-Commission on Prevention of Discrimination and Protection of Minorities to make a complete and comprehensive study of the problem of discrimination against indigenous populations and to suggest the necessary national and international measures for eliminating such discrimination, in co-operation with the other organs and bodies of the United Nations and with the competent international organizations.

E/4949. Report of Commission on Human Rights on its 27th session, 22 February–26 March 1971, Chapters II C (*d*) and XIX (resolution 2(XXVII)).

E/4949, Chapter XX. Draft resolution I, as submitted by Commission on Human Rights, approved unanimously by Social Committee on 18 May 1971, meeting 678.

E/5032. Report of Social Committee, draft resolution I.

RESOLUTION 1587(L), as recommended by Social Committee, E/5032, adopted unanimously by Council on 21 May 1971, meeting 1771.

The Economic and Social Council,
Taking into account the unique contribution made by the special study of racial discrimination in the political, economic, social and cultural spheres, submitted to the Sub-Commission on Prevention of Discrimination and Protection of Minorities at its twenty-third session and to the Commission on Human Rights at its twenty-seventh session by the Special Rapporteur of the Sub-Commission, Mr. Hernán Santa Cruz,

Expresses its appreciation to Mr. Santa Cruz for his valuable study.

E/CN.4/1070 and Corr.1. Report of Sub-Commission on Prevention of Discrimination and Protection of Minorities on its 24th session, 2–20 August 1971, Chapters IX and XII (resolution 8(XXIV)).

Other documents

A/8401. Report of Secretary-General on work of the Organization, 16 June 1970–15 June 1971, Part Three, Chapter I A 3.

A/8403. Report of Economic and Social Council on work of its 50th and 51st sessions, Chapter XVII B and F.

E/CN.4/1070 and Corr.1. Report on 24th session of Sub-Commission on Prevention of Discrimination and Protection of Minorities, 2–20 August 1971, Chapters VII and XII (resolution 6(XXIV)).

STUDY OF EQUALITY IN THE
ADMINISTRATION OF JUSTICE

Economic and Social Council—50th session
Social Committee, meetings 669-678.
Plenary meeting 1771.

Study of Equality in the Administration of Justice. U.N.P. Sales No.: E.71.XIV.3.

E/4949. Report of Commission on Human Rights on its 27th session, 22 February–26 March 1971, Chapters VIII and XIX (resolution 13(XXVII)).

E/4949, Chapter XX. Draft resolution VIII, as submitted by Commission on Human Rights, approved unanimously by Social Committee on 18 May 1971, meeting 678.

E/4949/Add.1. Financial implications of resolutions adopted by Commission on Human Rights at its 27th session.

E/5032. Report of Social Committee, draft resolution VIII.

RESOLUTION 1594(L), as recommended by Social Committee, E/5032, adopted unanimously by Council on 21 May 1971, meeting 1771.

The Economic and Social Council,
Recalling its resolution 1499(XLVIII) of 27 May 1970 on the study of equality in the administration of justice,
Noting resolution 3(XXIII) of the Sub-Commission on Prevention of Discrimination and Protection of Minorities,
Noting also that the Sub-Commission has completed its consideration of the draft principles contained in the study prepared by the Special Rapporteur, Mr. Abu Rannat, and has adopted certain principles relating to equality in the administration of justice,
Considering however that, owing to lack of time, the Commission on Human Rights was unable to examine the above draft principles in detail,
1. *Expresses its appreciation* to Mr. Abu Rannat for his valuable study;
2. *Requests* the Secretary-General to print the Special Rapporteur's study, together with the general principles adopted by the Sub-Commission on Prevention of Discrimination and Protection of Minorities in its resolution 3(XXIII), and to circulate them as widely as possible;
3. *Recommends* that the Commission on Human Rights should, at its twenty-eighth session, examine the draft principles relating to equality in the administration of justice and take a decision on further action.

General Assembly—26th session
Third Committee, meeting 1905.
Plenary meeting 2027.

A/8401. Report of Secretary-General on work of the Organization, 16 June 1970–15 June 1971, Part Three, Chapter I A 3.

A/8403. Report of Economic and Social Council on work of its 50th and 51st sessions, Chapter XVII H.

A/C.3/L.1909. Austria, Belgium, Brazil, Canada, Costa Rica, France, Italy, Netherlands, New Zealand, Sweden, United Kingdom, Uruguay: draft resolution, approved by Third Committee on 10 December 1971, meeting 1905, by 72 votes to 7, with 9 abstentions.

A/8588. Report of Third Committee (on report of Economic and Social Council), draft resolution IV.

RESOLUTION 2858(XXVI), as recommended by Third Committee, A/8588, adopted by Assembly on 20 December 1971, meeting 2027, by 111 votes to 7, with 3 abstentions.

The General Assembly,
Recalling articles 5, 10 and 11 of the Universal Declaration of Human Rights,
Recalling Economic and Social Council resolution 663 C (XXIV), section I, of 31 July 1957, by which the Council approved the Standard Minimum Rules for the Treatment of Prisoners,
Convinced of the need for further concerted action in promoting respect for and implementation of the principles embodied in the aforementioned articles of the Universal Declaration of Human Rights,
1. *Solemnly reaffirms* the principles concerning human rights in the administration of justice as embodied in articles 5, 10 and 11 of the Universal Declaration of Human Rights, namely, those referring to the right not to be subjected to inhuman treatment or punishment, the right to a fair and public hearing by an independent and impartial tribunal in any civil or criminal proceedings, the right, if charged with a penal offence, to be presumed innocent until proved guilty and the right not to be subjected to retrospective criminal sanctions;
2. *Invites* the attention of Member States to the Standard Minimum Rules for the Treatment of Prisoners and recommends that they shall be effectively implemented in the administration of penal and correctional institutions and that favourable consideration shall be given to their incorporation in national legislation;
3. *Takes note with satisfaction* of the establishment within the work programme of the Commission for Social Development of the Working Group on Standard Minimum Rules for the Treatment of Prisoners to advise on methods of strengthening the implementation of the Rules and of improving the reporting procedures thereon;
4. *Endorses* the recommendation contained in Economic and Social Council resolution 1594(L) of 21 May 1971 that the Commission on Human Rights should, at its twenty-eighth session, examine the draft principles relating to equality in the administration of justice adopted by the Sub-Commission on Prevention of Discrimination and Protection of Minorities and take a decision on further action;
5. *Expresses the hope* that the Economic and Social Council at its fifty-second session will be able to consider final proposals of the Commission on Human Rights on these principles.

Elimination of religious intolerance

General Assembly—26th session
Third Committee, meeting 1905.
Plenary meeting 2025.

A/8330. Note by Secretary-General.

A/C.3/L.1925. Nigeria and Sudan: draft resolution, approved by Third Committee on 10 December 1971, meeting 1905, by 96 votes to 0.

A/8590. Report of Third Committee.

RESOLUTION 2844(XXVI), as recommended by Third Committee, A/8590, adopted by Assembly on 18 December 1971, meeting 2025, by 114 votes to 0.

The General Assembly,
Considering that there is not enough time for the consideration of all the items on the agenda of the Third Committee,
Bearing in mind the need for a full discussion of all the items,
Decides to consider at its twenty-seventh session the items entitled "Freedom of information," "Human rights and scientific

and technological developments" and "Elimination of all forms of religious intolerance."

Consideration of future work of Sub-Commission
E/CN.4/1070 and Corr.1. Report of Sub-Commission on Prevention of Discrimination and Protection of Minorities on its 24th session, 2-20 August 1971, Chapters X and XII (resolutions 4(XXIV) and 9(XXIV)).

Report of Sub-Commission
E/4949. Report of Commission on Human Rights on its 27th session, 22 February–26 March 1971, Chapters VI, VIII, XIV, XV and XIX B (other decisions, pp. 95 and 96).
E/CN.4/1070 and Corr.1. Report of Sub-Commission on Prevention of Discrimination and Protection of Minorities on its 24th session, 2–20 August 1971, Headquarters, New York. (Annex III: List of documents before Sub-Commission at its 24th session.)

Violations of human rights and fundamental freedoms

During 1971, various questions concerning violations of human rights and fundamental freedoms were again considered by the General Assembly, the Economic and Social Council, the Commission on Human Rights and certain subsidiary bodies.

Among the matters considered were: the violation of human rights in the territories occupied as a result of hostilities in the Middle East; the study of situations revealing a consistent pattern of human rights violations; and rules of procedure for bodies dealing with violations.

Decisions on these and related matters by the various bodies concerned are described in the sections that follow.

Study of violations

Questions of human rights in occupied territories

During 1971, the Commission on Human Rights considered the first report of the Special Committee to Investigate Israeli Practices Affecting the Human Rights of the Population of the Occupied Territories, established by the General Assembly on 19 December 1968.[6] The second report of the Special Committee was considered in 1971 by the General Assembly at its twenty-sixth (1971) session.

Also during 1971, the Security Council received a number of communications from Arab countries concerning the treatment of the civilian population in territories occupied by Israel, and Israel's replies to these (see pp. 188-90).

Decisions of Human Rights Commission

The 1970 report of the Special Committee to Investigate Israeli Practices Affecting the Human Rights of the Population of the Occupied Territories, which had been considered by the General Assembly at its twenty-fifth (1970) session, was also studied by the Commission on Human Rights at its twenty-seventh (1971) session. On 15 March, the Commission adopted a resolution based on the recommendations and conclusions contained in the 1970 report.

Among other things, the Commission condemned Israel's continued violations of human rights in the occupied territories, including policies aimed at changing the status of the territories, and condemned specifically the following policies and practices of Israel: (a) denial of the right of the refugees and displaced persons to return to their homes; (b) resort to collective punishment; (c) the deportation and expulsion of the citizens of the occupied territories; (d) arbitrary arrest and detention of the citizens of the occupied territories; (e) ill-treatment and torture of prisoners; (f) destruction and demolition of villages, town quarters, houses, and confiscation and expropriation of property; (g) evacuation and transfer of sections of the population of the occupied territories; and (h) transfer of parts of its own civilian population into the occupied territories.

The Commission strongly deplored Israel's policies in the occupied territories aimed at placing the population in a general state of repression, fear and deprivation, and particularly deplored: (a) requisition of hospitals and their transformation into police stations; (b) abrogation of the national laws and interference with the judicial system; and (c) refusal to allow use of the textbooks approved by the United Nations Educational, Scientific and Cultural Organization for schools in the occupied territories, and the insistence on forcing upon school children an alien system of education.

The Commission again called upon Israel: to comply fully with its obligations under the fourth Geneva Convention of 12 August 1949 (having to do with the protection of civilian persons in time of war); to enable forthwith the refugees and displaced persons to return to their homes; and to heed and implement the many resolutions adopted by United Nations organs and the specialized agencies for the safeguarding of human rights in the occupied territories.

The Commission reaffirmed that all measures taken by Israel to colonize the occupied territories, including occupied Jerusalem, were completely null and void and declared that Israel's continued

[6]See Y.U.N., 1968, pp. 555-56, text of resolution 2443(XXIII).

and increasing violations of the human rights of the population of the occupied territories—and its deliberate and persistent refusal to abide by its legal obligations under the United Nations Charter, international law, and the fourth Geneva Convention of 1949—indicated the necessity of collective action on the part of the international community to ensure respect for the human rights of the population of the occupied territories.

The International Committee of the Red Cross was urged by the Commission to co-operate with United Nations organs, and particularly with the Special Committee to Investigate Israeli Practices Affecting the Human Rights of the Population of the Occupied Territories in the fulfilment of its task to ensure the safeguarding of the human rights of the population of the occupied territories, and to inform the Human Rights Commission at its 1972 session of the steps taken. The Secretary-General was asked to give wide publicity to United Nations documents dealing with violations of human rights in the occupied territories, and in particular to the report of the Special Committee, and to use United Nations information media in disseminating information on the conditions of the population of the occupied territories, the refugees and displaced persons.

Reports of the Special Committee in 1971

The Special Committee to Investigate Israeli Practices Affecting the Human Rights of the Population of the Occupied Territories carried out further investigations from 7 to 16 July 1971. It held meetings in Amman (Jordan), Beirut (Lebanon), Geneva (Switzerland) and New York; 49 witnesses were heard, and written evidence was also received. Its second report was issued on 5 October, and a supplementary report on 10 December.

The Special Committee noted that since the presentation of its first report in 1970 certain policies and practices found to exist in the occupied territories had been continued, in some instances on an even wider scale than before, especially with regard to the policy of encouraging the movement of Israeli settlers into settlements in the occupied territories.

The practice of deporting civilians from the occupied territories had continued unabated, the Special Committee reported, and it recorded its grave concern that this practice, together with the policy of establishing settlements in the occupied territories, seemed calculated to eliminate an identifiable Palestinian community altogether from those territories.

For these reasons, the Special Committee reiterated the recommendations it had made in 1970: that the States whose territory was occupied by Israel appoint immediately either a neutral State or States, or an international organization offering all guarantees of impartiality and effectiveness, to safeguard the human rights of the population of the occupied territories; that suitable arrangements be made for the proper representation of the interests of the large population in the occupied territories which had not been given the opportunity of exercising the right of self-determination; and that a neutral State or international organization be nominated by Israel and be associated in this arrangement.

The Special Committee further recommended that the State or States or international organization duly nominated under this arrangement might be authorized to undertake the following activities: (*a*) to secure the scrupulous implementation of the provisions relating to human rights contained in the third and fourth Geneva Conventions of 12 August 1949 (the third Convention having to do with the treatment of prisoners of war, the fourth Convention with the treatment of civilian persons in time of war), and particularly to investigate allegations of violations of the human rights provisions of these Conventions or of other applicable international instruments; (*b*) to ensure that the population of the occupied territories was treated in accordance with the applicable law; and (*c*) to report on its work to the States concerned and to the General Assembly.

In its supplementary report issued on 10 December, the Special Committee took note of a statement that had been made by the International Committee of the Red Cross (ICRC) to the effect that it was willing under certain conditions to assume the role of a protecting power under the Geneva Conventions. The Special Committee noted that ICRC had expressed its readiness to assume these functions after giving careful consideration to the question of the reinforcement of the implementation of the existing Geneva Conventions and arriving at the conclusion that all tasks falling to a protecting power under the Conventions could be considered humanitarian functions.

The Special Committee therefore modified its original recommendations and recommended that the General Assembly might: (*a*) request the Secretary-General to inform the parties concerned of ICRC's readiness to take upon itself all the functions envisaged for protecting powers in the Geneva Conventions and to invite them to avail themselves of the services of ICRC in dealing with the application of the provisions of the Geneva Conventions in the occupied territories in the Middle East; (*b*) request ICRC to consider the need for keeping the United Nations fully informed, through the Secretary-General, of its activities as a protecting power, in addition to reporting to the parties concerned; and (*c*) reconsider the mandate of the Special Committee as to whether or not there was need for the continuation of its activities once ICRC began in fact to function as a protecting power.

Consideration by General Assembly

On 20 December 1971, at its twenty-sixth session, the General Assembly adopted a resolution (2851(XXVI)) on the 1971 reports of the Special Committee to Investigate Israeli Practices Affecting the Human Rights of the Population of the Occupied Territories.

By the preambular parts of this text, the Assembly among other things expressed its grave concern about the violations of the human rights of the inhabitants of the occupied territories. The Assembly considered that the system of investigation and protection was essential for ensuring effective implementation of international instruments, such as the 1949 (fourth) Geneva Convention relative to the Protection of Civilian Persons in Time of War, and regretted that the relevant provisions of that Convention had not been implemented by the Israeli authorities. The Assembly also recalled that States parties to that Convention had undertaken not only to respect but also to ensure respect for the Convention in all circumstances.

The Assembly then noted with satisfaction that the International Committee of the Red Cross (ICRC) had concluded that all tasks falling to a protecting power under the 1949 Geneva Conventions could be considered humanitarian functions and ICRC had declared itself ready to assume all the functions envisaged for protecting powers in the Conventions.

By the operative part of the text, the Assembly among other things strongly called upon Israel to rescind forthwith all measures and to desist from all policies and practices such as: (a) the annexation of any part of the occupied Arab territories; (b) the establishment of Israeli settlements on those territories and the transfer of parts of Israel's civilian population into the occupied territory; (c) the destruction and demolition of villages, quar-

ters and houses and the confiscation and expropriation of property; (d) the evacuation, transfer, deportation and expulsion of the inhabitants of the occupied Arab territories; (e) the denial of the right of the refugees and displaced persons to return to their homes; (f) the ill-treatment and torture of prisoners and detainees; and (g) collective punishment.

The Assembly then called upon Israel to permit all persons who had fled from the occupied territories or had been deported or expelled therefrom to return to their homes. It reaffirmed that all measures taken by Israel to settle the occupied territories, including occupied Jerusalem, were completely null and void.

Israel was called on by the Assembly to comply fully with its obligations under the fourth Geneva Convention of 1949, and States parties to the Convention were asked to do their utmost to ensure that Israel respected and fulfilled such obligations.

The Assembly asked the Special Committee—pending the early termination of Israeli occupation of Arab territories—to continue its work and to consult as appropriate with ICRC to ensure the safeguarding of the welfare and human rights of the population of the occupied territories. It urged Israel to co-operate with the Special Committee and to facilitate its entry into the occupied territories so that it could perform its functions.

The resolution was adopted on the recommendation of the Assembly's Special Political Committee, which approved it on 16 December by a roll-call vote of 48 to 16, with 42 abstentions, on the basis of a proposal by Mali and Mauritania. Amendments proposed by Indonesia and Nigeria were accepted by the sponsors. The resolution was adopted by the Assembly on 20 December by a recorded vote of 53 to 20, with 46 abstentions, as resolution 2851(XXVI).

(For text of resolution and voting details, see pp. 194-95; for debate in Special Political Committee, see pp. 192-94.)

DOCUMENTARY REFERENCES

Question of human rights in occupied territories

DECISIONS OF HUMAN RIGHTS COMMISSION

E/4949. Report of Commission on Human Rights on its 27th session, 22 February–26 March 1971, Chapters IV and XIX (resolution 9(XXVII)).
E/L.1395. Note of 5 May 1971 by Secretary-General (transmitting communication from International Committee of Red Cross).

DECISIONS OF GENERAL ASSEMBLY

RESOLUTION 2851(XXVI), as recommended by Special Political Committee, A/8630, adopted by Assembly on 20 December 1971, meeting 2027, by recorded vote of 53 to 20, with 46 abstentions.

[For text of resolution, recorded vote, relevant meetings and supporting documentation, see p. 195.]

Other matters relating to violations of human rights and fundamental freedoms

Questions concerning procedures

Procedures for dealing with communications
relating to violations of human rights

At its 1971 session (22 February–26 March), the Commission on Human Rights had before it a number of proposals on provisional procedures concerning the admissibility of communications relating to violations of human rights received by the Secretary-General under an Economic and Social Council resolution of 30 July 1959.[7] The proposals had been transmitted to the Commission following their consideration by the Sub-Commission on Prevention of Discrimination and Protection of Minorities in 1970, in accordance with an Economic and Social Council request of 27 May 1970.[8]

Because of lack of time, the Commission was unable to examine the draft proposals.

At its twenty-fourth session held in August 1971, the Sub-Commission approved a set of provisional procedures, under which, among other things, a communication was to be considered admissible only if: (i) there were reasonable grounds to believe it revealed a consistent pattern of gross and reliably attested violations of human rights and fundamental freedoms; (ii) the object of the communication was consistent with the relevant principles of the United Nations Charter, the Universal Declaration of Human Rights and other applicable instruments in the field; and (iii) the communication originated from a person or group of persons who could reasonably be presumed to be victims of the violations, a person or persons who had direct and reliable knowledge of the violations, or non-governmental organizations having direct and reliable knowledge of such violations. Each communication was to contain a description of the facts and indicate the purpose of the petition and the rights that had been violated.

A communication would be held inadmissible if: it were anonymous, written in abusive language or manifestly politically motivated; it appeared to be based exclusively on reports disseminated by the mass media; it would prejudice by its admission the functions of the specialized agencies; domestic remedies had not been exhausted; the case had been settled by the State concerned in accordance with the principles set forth in the Universal Declaration of Human Rights and other relevant instruments; or it was not submitted to the United Nations within a reasonable time after the exhaustion of domestic remedies.

Also during 1971, the Sub-Commission on Prevention of Discrimination and Protection of Minorities appointed a five-member working group to consider all communications received by the Secretary-General under the Council's resolution of 30 July 1959, with a view to bringing to the attention of the Sub-Commission those communications, together with the replies of Governments, which appeared to reveal a consistent pattern of gross and reliably attested violations of human rights and fundamental freedoms. The Sub-Commission took this action at the request of the Economic and Social Council.[9]

Rules of procedure for bodies dealing
with violations of human rights

At its 1971 session, the Commission on Human Rights adopted a resolution by which it decided to establish a five-member working group to examine draft model rules of procedure for United Nations bodies dealing with violations of human rights; the model rules had been submitted to the Commission by the Secretary-General in 1970.

The Commission asked the Secretary-General to transmit the model rules to Member States for their comments, and to submit the comments received to the working group and the Commission. It requested the working group to report to it on this question in 1972.

[7]See Y.U.N., 1959, p. 221, text of resolution 728 F (XXVIII).
[8]See Y.U.N., 1970, pp. 530-31, text of resolution 1503(XLVIII).
[9]*Ibid.*

DOCUMENTARY REFERENCES

Questions concerning procedures

PROCEDURES FOR DEALING WITH COMMUNICATIONS
RELATING TO VIOLATIONS OF HUMAN RIGHTS
E/4949. Report of Commission on Human Rights on its 27th session, 22 February–26 March 1971, Chapter VII A.
A/8401. Report of Secretary-General on work of the Organization, 16 June 1970–15 June 1971, Part Three, Chapter I A 17.
E/CN.4/1070 and Corr.1. Report of Sub-Commission on Prevention of Discrimination and Protection of Minorities on its 24th session, 2–20 August 1971, Chapters II and XII (resolutions 1(XXIV) and 2(XXIV)).

RULES OF PROCEDURE FOR BODIES DEALING
WITH VIOLATIONS OF HUMAN RIGHTS
E/4949. Report of Commission on Human Rights on its 27th session, 22 February–26 March 1971, Chapters VII B and XIX (resolution 14(XXVII)).
E/4949/Add.1. Financial implications of resolutions adopted by Commission on Human Rights at its 27th session.

The importance of the right to self-determination

During 1971, various aspects of the question of the importance of the right to self-determination were considered by the General Assembly, the Economic and Social Council and the Commission on Human Rights.

At its 1971 session (22 February–26 March), the Commission on Human Rights adopted two resolutions concerning the implementation of United Nations resolutions relating to the right to self-determination of peoples under colonial and alien domination.

By the first text, the Commission requested the Secretary-General to prepare an annotated collection of all such resolutions which had been adopted by the various organs of the United Nations, the specialized agencies and the regional organizations.

By its second text, the Commission recommended to the Economic and Social Council, for eventual adoption by the General Assembly, a draft resolution on the right to self-determination.

On 21 May 1971, the Council adopted resolution 1592(L), by which it transmitted the Commission's text, as requested, to the General Assembly, with the recommendation that the Assembly adopt it.

By the preambular paragraphs of this draft, the Assembly would:

(*a*) solemnly reaffirm that the subjection of peoples to alien subjugation, domination and exploitation was a violation of the principle of self-determination as well as a denial of basic human rights and was contrary to the United Nations Charter;

(*b*) express concern at the fact that many peoples continued to be denied the right to self-determination and were living under conditions of colonial and foreign domination;

(*c*) express concern at the fact that some countries, notably Portugal, with the support of its North Atlantic Treaty Organization allies, were waging war against the national liberation movement in colonial and developing countries;

(*d*) confirm that colonialism in all its forms and manifestations, including the methods of neo-colonialism, constituted a gross encroachment on the rights of peoples and the basic human rights and freedoms;

(*e*) express the conviction that effective application of the principles of self-determination of peoples was of paramount importance for promoting the development of friendly relations between countries and peoples and for ensuring human rights.

By the operative paragraphs of the draft, the Assembly would:

(1) confirm the legality of the peoples' struggle for self-determination and liberation from colonial and foreign domination by all available means;

(2) affirm man's basic human right to fight for the self-determination of his people under colonial and foreign domination;

(3) express belief that the main objectives and principles of international protection of human rights could not be effectively implemented while some States pursued the imperialist policy of colonialism, used force against developing countries and peoples fighting for self-determination and supported régimes that applied the criminal policy of racism and *apartheid;*

(4) condemn the colonial powers that were suppressing the right of peoples to self-determination and hampering the liquidation of the last hotbeds of colonialism and racism in the African continent and other parts of the world;

(5) condemn States that contributed to the creation in southern Africa of a military-industrial complex whose aim was to suppress the movement of peoples struggling for their self-determination and to interfere in the affairs of independent African States;

(6) recall that it was the duty of every State to contribute through joint and independent action to the implementation of the principle of self-determination, in accordance with the provisions of the Charter, and to assist the United Nations in discharging the responsibilities vested in it by the Charter for the implementation of this principle;

(7) urge States to discharge their duty and to co-operate in bringing about universal respect for and observance of human rights and fundamental freedoms and in eliminating all forms of racial discrimination; and

(8) resolve to devote constant attention to the question of flagrant large-scale violations of human rights and fundamental freedoms resulting from the denial to peoples under colonial and foreign domination of their right to self-determination.

Council resolution 1592(L) was adopted by a vote of 16 to 5, with 3 abstentions, as recommended by the Social Committee. The Social Committee approved the text submitted by the Commission on Human Rights on 18 May 1971, by a vote of 15 to 5, with 3 abstentions.

(For text of resolution, see DOCUMENTARY REFERENCES below.)

In explanation of vote, the United States said that it had voted against the draft because it contained tendentious and unrealistic statements. France said that it had opposed the text because it believed that the question of the right to self-determination was political in nature and beyond the competence of the Commission on Human Rights;

moreover, the wording of the text was in conflict with that of the United Nations Charter.

When the Council's text was discussed in the General Assembly's Third (Social, Humanitarian and Cultural) Committee, a number of amendments were put forward by Committee members.

The text that was approved by the Third Committee incorporated amendments sponsored by: the Syrian Arab Republic; six powers—Algeria, Guinea, the Libyan Arab Republic, Mali, Mauritania and Tunisia; 12 powers—Barbados, the Congo, Guyana, Jamaica, Kenya, Mauritania, Nigeria, Sierra Leone, Somalia, Uganda, the United Republic of Tanzania, and Zambia; Pakistan; Afghanistan; Iraq; and the United States. A number of other amendments put forward by the United States were rejected by the Committee.

On 6 December 1971, the Assembly adopted, as its resolution 2787(XXVI), the text that was recommended by the Third Committee.

By the preambular paragraphs of the resolution, the Assembly:

(a) solemnly reaffirmed that the subjection of peoples to alien subjugation, domination and colonial exploitation was a violation of the principle of self-determination as well as a denial of basic human rights and was contrary to the Charter of the United Nations;

(b) expressed concern that many peoples continued to be denied the right to self-determination and were living under conditions of colonial and foreign domination;

(c) expressed concern that some countries, notably Portugal, with the support of their North Atlantic Treaty Organization (NATO) allies, were waging war against the national liberation movement of the colonies and against certain independent States of Africa and Asia and the developing countries;

(d) confirmed that colonialism in all its forms and manifestations, including the methods of neo-colonialism, constituted a gross encroachment on the rights of peoples and on the basic human rights and freedoms;

(e) expressed the conviction that the effective application of the principle of self-determination of peoples was of paramount importance for the promotion of friendly relations between countries and peoples, the guarantee of human rights and the maintenance of peace in the world;

(f) affirmed that the future of Zimbabwe [Southern Rhodesia] could not be negotiated with an illegal régime and that any settlement must be made on the basis of "no independence before majority rule";

(g) reaffirmed the inalienable rights of all peoples, and in particular those of Zimbabwe, Namibia, Angola, Mozambique and Guinea (Bissau) and the Palestinian people, to freedom, equality and self-determination, and the legitimacy of their struggles to restore those rights;

(h) reaffirmed the Declaration on Principles of International Law concerning Friendly Relations and Co-operation among States in accordance with the Charter of the United Nations,[10] which elaborated the principle of self-determination of peoples;

(i) considered that the establishment of a sovereign and independent State freely determined by all the people belonging to the territory constituted a mode of implementing the right of self-determination;

(j) further considered that any attempt aimed at the partial or total disruption of the national unity and territorial integrity of a State established in accordance with the right of self-determination of its people was incompatible with the purposes and principles of the Charter;

(k) had in mind that interference in the internal affairs of States was a violation of the Charter and could pose a serious threat to the maintenance of peace.

By the operative paragraphs of the resolution, the Assembly:

(1) confirmed the legality of the people's struggle for self-determination and liberation from colonial and foreign domination and alien subjugation, notably in southern Africa and in particular that of the peoples of Zimbabwe, Namibia, Angola, Mozambique and Guinea (Bissau), as well as of the Palestinian people, by all available means consistent with the United Nations Charter;

(2) affirmed man's basic human right to fight for the self-determination of his people under colonial and foreign domination;

(3) called upon all States dedicated to the ideals of freedom and peace to give all their political, moral and material assistance to peoples struggling for liberation, self-determination and independence against colonial and alien domination;

(4) expressed the belief that the main objectives and principles of international protection of human rights could not be effectively implemented while some States, particularly Portugal and South Africa, pursued the imperialist policy of colonialism, used force against independent African States and developing countries and peoples fighting for self-determination and supported régimes that were applying the criminal policy of racism and *apartheid;*

(5) condemned the colonial and usurping powers that were suppressing the right of peoples to self-determination and hampering the liquida-

---

[10]See Y.U.N., 1970, pp. 788-92, resolution 2625(XXV) of 24 October 1970, containing text of Declaration.

tion of the last hotbeds of colonialism and racism in the African and Asian continents and in other parts of the world;

(6) condemned the policy of certain States members of NATO that contributed to the creation in southern Africa of a military-industrial complex whose aim was to suppress the movement of peoples struggling for self-determination and to interfere in the affairs of independent African States;

(7) recalled that it was the duty of every State to contribute through joint and independent action to the implementation of the principle of self-determination in accordance with the provisions of the Charter, and to assist the United Nations in discharging the responsibilities vested in it by the Charter for the implementation of this principle;

(8) urged the Security Council as well as States Members of the United Nations or members of specialized agencies to take effective steps to ensure the implementation of the relevant United Nations resolutions on the elimination of colonialism and racism and to report to the General Assembly at its 1972 session;

(9) resolved to devote constant attention to the

question of flagrant large-scale violations of human rights and fundamental freedoms resulting from the denial to peoples under colonial and foreign domination of their right to self-determination;

(10) called upon all States to observe the principles of the sovereign equality of States, non-interference in the internal affairs of other States and respect for their sovereign rights and territorial integrity.

Resolution 2787(XXVI) was adopted by a recorded vote of 76 to 10, with 33 abstentions.

Separate votes were taken on the references to the Palestinian people which appeared in the text: by a recorded vote of 50 to 23, with 43 abstentions, the Assembly decided to retain the reference which appeared in the preamble; by a recorded vote of 50 to 24, with 44 abstentions, it decided to retain the reference in the first operative paragraph.

The Third Committee approved the draft on 25 November 1971, by a recorded vote of 74 to 12, with 27 abstentions.

(For text of resolution, see DOCUMENTARY REFERENCES below.)

DOCUMENTARY REFERENCES

Economic and Social Council—50th session
Social Committee, meetings 669-678.
Plenary meeting 1771.

E/4949. Report of Commission on Human Rights on its 27th session, 22 February–26 March 1971, Chapters III and XIX (resolution 8 A and B (XXVII)).
E/4949, Chapter XX. Draft resolution VI, as submitted by Commission on Human Rights, approved by Social Committee on 18 May 1971, meeting 678, by 15 votes to 5, with 3 abstentions.
E/5032. Report of Social Committee, draft resolution VI.

RESOLUTION 1592(L), as recommended by Social Committee, E/5032, adopted by Council on 21 May 1971, meeting 1771, by 16 votes to 5, with 3 abstentions.

The Economic and Social Council,
Recalling General Assembly resolution 1514(XV) of 14 October 1960 containing the Declaration on the Granting of Independence to Colonial Countries and Peoples, and General Assembly resolution 2621(XXV) of 12 October 1970 concerning a programme of action for the full implementation of the said Declaration,
Guided by the Declaration on Principles of International Law concerning Friendly Relations and Co-operation among States in accordance with the Charter of the United Nations,
Recommends that the General Assembly adopt the following draft resolution:
"The General Assembly,
"Solemnly reaffirming that the subjection of peoples to alien subjugation, domination and exploitation is a violation of the principle of self-determination as well as a denial of basic human rights and is contrary to the Charter of the United Nations,
"Concerned at the fact that many peoples continue to be denied the right to self-determination and are living under conditions of colonial and foreign domination,
"Expressing concern at the fact that some countries, notably

Portugal, with the support of its North Atlantic Treaty Organization allies, are waging war against the national liberation movement in colonial and developing countries,
"Confirming that colonialism in all its forms and manifestations, including the methods of neo-colonialism, constitutes a gross encroachment on the rights of peoples and the basic human rights and freedoms,
"Convinced that effective application of the principles of self-determination of peoples is of paramount importance for promoting the development of friendly relations between countries and peoples and for ensuring human rights,
"1. *Confirms* the legality of the peoples' struggle for self-determination and liberation from colonial and foreign domination by all available means;
"2. *Affirms* man's basic human right to fight for the self-determination of his people under colonial and foreign domination;
"3. *Believes* that the main objectives and principles of international protection of human rights cannot be effectively implemented while some States pursue the imperialist policy of colonialism, use force against developing countries and peoples fighting for self-determination and support regimes that are applying the criminal policy of racism and *apartheid;*
"4. *Condemns* the colonial Powers that are suppressing the right of peoples to self-determination and hampering the liquidation of the last hotbeds of colonialism and racism in the African continent and in other parts of the world;
"5. *Condemns* States that contribute to the creation in southern Africa of a military-industrial complex whose aim is the suppression of the movement of peoples struggling for their self-determination and interference in the affairs of independent African States;
"6. *Recalls* that it is the duty of every State to contribute through joint and independent action to the implementation of the principle of self-determination, in accordance with the provisions of the Charter, and to assist the United Nations in discharging the responsibilities vested in it by the Charter for the implementation of this principle;
"7. *Urges* States to discharge their duty and to co-operate in

bringing about universal respect for and observance of human rights and fundamental freedoms and eliminating all forms of racial discrimination;

"8. *Resolves* to devote constant attention to the question of flagrant large-scale violations of human rights and fundamental freedoms resulting from the denial to peoples under colonial and foreign domination of their right to self-determination."

General Assembly—26th session
Third Committee, meetings 1868-1873, 1880-1884.
Plenary meeting 2001.

A/8331. Importance of universal realization of right of peoples to self-determination and of speedy granting of independence to colonial countries and peoples for effective guarantee and observance of human rights. Note by Secretary-General, transmitting Economic and Social Council resolution 1592(L), as amended by Afghanistan (A/C.3/L.1879), by Iraq (A/C.3/L.1877/Rev.1, as orally sub-amended by Morocco), by Pakistan (A/C.3/L.1886/Rev.1, as amended by India (A/C.3/L.1893, para. 1, as orally revised)), by Syrian Arab Republic (A/C.3/L.1878, as orally sub-amended), by United States (A/C.3/L.1881/Rev.1, para. 3), by 6 powers (A/C.3/L.1882, as sub-amended by Barbados (A/C.3/L.1888, as orally sub-amended by Morocco) and as orally sub-amended by Jamaica and by sponsors), and by 12 powers (A/C.3/L.1880), approved by Third Committee on 25 November 1971, meeting 1883, by recorded vote of 74 to 12, with 27 abstentions, as follows:

In favour: Afghanistan, Albania, Algeria, Bahrain, Bolivia, Botswana, Bulgaria, Burma, Burundi, Byelorussian SSR, Cameroon, Central African Republic, Ceylon, Chad, Chile, China, Congo, Cuba, Cyprus, Czechoslovakia, Dominican Republic, Ecuador, Egypt, El Salvador, Ghana, Greece, Guatemala, Guinea, Guyana, Hungary, India, Indonesia, Iran, Iraq, Ivory Coast, Jordan, Kenya, Kuwait, Lebanon, Libyan Arab Republic, Malaysia, Mali, Mauritania, Mexico, Mongolia, Morocco, Nepal, Niger, Nigeria, Pakistan, People's Democratic Republic of Yemen, Peru, Poland, Qatar, Romania, Rwanda, Saudi Arabia, Senegal, Sierra Leone, Singapore, Somalia, Sudan, Syrian Arab Republic, Togo, Trinidad and Tobago, Tunisia, Turkey, Uganda, Ukrainian SSR, USSR, United Republic of Tanzania, Yemen, Yugoslavia, Zambia.

Against: Australia, Belgium, France, Israel, Italy, Luxembourg, Netherlands, New Zealand, Nicaragua, Portugal, United Kingdom, United States.

Abstaining: Argentina, Austria, Barbados, Brazil, Canada, Colombia, Costa Rica, Dahomey, Denmark, Ethiopia, Finland, Gambia, Ireland, Jamaica, Japan, Laos, Lesotho, Liberia, Madagascar, Malawi, Norway, Panama, Philippines, Spain, Sweden, Uruguay, Venezuela.

A/8401. Report of Secretary-General on work of the Organization, 16 June 1970–15 June 1971, Part Three, Chapter I A 8.
A/8403. Report of Economic and Social Council on work of its 50th and 51st sessions, Chapter XVII D.
A/C.3/L.1877 and Rev.1. Iraq: amendments and revised amendments to draft resolution recommended by Economic and Social Council in A/8331.
A/C.3/L.1878. Syrian Arab Republic: amendment to draft resolution recommended by Economic and Social Council in A/8331.
A/C.3/L.1879. Afghanistan: amendment to draft resolution recommended by Economic and Social Council in A/8331.
A/C.3/L.1880. Barbados, Congo, Guyana, Jamaica, Kenya, Mauritania, Nigeria, Sierra Leone, Somalia, Uganda, United Republic of Tanzania, Zambia: amendment to draft resolution recommended by Economic and Social Council in A/8331.
A/C.3/L.1881 and Rev.1. United States: amendments and revised amendments to draft resolution recommended by Economic and Social Council in A/8331.
A/C.3/L.1882. Algeria, Guinea, Libyan Arab Republic, Mali, Mauritania, Tunisia: amendments to draft resolution recommended by Economic and Social Council in A/8331.

A/C.3/L.1886 and Rev.1. Pakistan: amendments and revised amendments to draft resolution recommended by Economic and Social Council in A/8331.
A/C.3/L.1888. Barbados and Uganda: sub-amendments to 6-power amendments, A/C.3/L.1882.
A/C.3/L.1889. Barbados and Uganda: sub-amendment to Iraqi revised amendment, A/C.3/L.1877/Rev.1.
A/C.3/L1893. India: sub-amendments to Pakistani revised amendments, A/C.3/L.1886/Rev.1.
A/C.3/L.1901. Text of draft resolution adopted by Third Committee on 25 November 1971, meeting 1883.
A/8543. Report of Third Committee.

RESOLUTION 2787(XXVI), as recommended by Third Committee, A/8543, adopted by Assembly on 6 December 1971, meeting 2001, by recorded vote of 76 to 10, with 33 abstentions, as follows:

In favour: Afghanistan, Albania, Algeria, Bahrain, Botswana, Bulgaria, Burma, Burundi, Byelorussian SSR, Cameroon, Central African Republic, Ceylon, Chad, Chile, China, Congo, Cuba, Cyprus, Czechoslovakia, Ecuador, Egypt, Equatorial Guinea, Ethiopia, Gabon, Ghana, Greece, Guatemala, Guinea, Guyana, Honduras, Hungary, India, Indonesia, Iran, Iraq, Ivory Coast, Jordan, Kenya, Kuwait, Lebanon, Libyan Arab Republic, Malaysia, Mali, Malta, Mauritania, Mexico, Mongolia, Morocco, Nepal, Niger, Nigeria, Oman, Pakistan, People's Democratic Republic of Yemen, Peru, Poland, Qatar, Romania, Rwanda, Saudi Arabia, Senegal, Sierra Leone, Singapore, Somalia, Sudan, Syrian Arab Republic, Togo, Tunisia, Turkey, Uganda, Ukrainian SSR, USSR, United Republic of Tanzania, Yemen, Yugoslavia, Zambia.

Against: Australia, Belgium, France, Israel, Luxembourg, Netherlands, New Zealand, Portugal, United Kingdom, United States.

Abstaining: Argentina, Austria, Barbados, Brazil, Canada, Colombia, Costa Rica, Dahomey, Denmark, Dominican Republic, Finland, Gambia, Iceland, Ireland, Italy, Jamaica, Japan, Laos, Lesotho, Liberia, Madagascar, Malawi, Nicaragua, Norway, Panama, Paraguay, Philippines, Spain, Swaziland, Sweden, Thailand, Uruguay, Venezuela.

The General Assembly,
Reaffirming its resolutions 1514(XV) of 14 December 1960, 1803(XVII) of 14 December 1962, 1904(XVIII) of 20 November 1963, 2200(XXI) of 16 December 1966, 2535 B(XXIV) of 10 December 1969, 2625(XXV) of 24 October 1970, 2649(XXV) of 30 November 1970 and 2672 C(XXV) of 8 December 1970 and resolution VIII adopted by the International Conference on Human Rights held at Teheran in 1968,
Solemnly reaffirming that the subjection of peoples to alien subjugation, domination and colonial exploitation is a violation of the principle of self-determination as well as a denial of basic human rights and is contrary to the Charter of the United Nations,
Concerned that many peoples continue to be denied the right to self-determination and are living under conditions of colonial and foreign domination,
Expressing concern that some countries, notably Portugal, with the support of their North Atlantic Treaty Organization allies, are waging war against the national liberation movement of the colonies and against certain independent States of Africa and Asia and the developing countries,
Confirming that colonialism in all its forms and manifestations, including the methods of neo-colonialism, constitutes a gross encroachment on the rights of peoples and on the basic human rights and freedoms,
Convinced that effective application of the principle of self-determination of peoples is of paramount importance for the promotion of friendly relations between countries and peoples, the guarantee of human rights and the maintenance of peace in the world,
Affirming that the future of Zimbabwe cannot be negotiated with an illegal régime and that any settlement must be made on the basis of "no independence before majority rule,"
Reaffirming the inalienable rights of all peoples, and in particular

those of Zimbabwe, Namibia, Angola, Mozambique and Guinea (Bissau) and the Palestinian people, to freedom, equality and self-determination, and the legitimacy of their struggles to restore those rights,

Reaffirming the Declaration on Principles of International Law concerning Friendly Relations and Co-operation among States in accordance with the Charter of the United Nations, which elaborated the principle of self-determination of peoples,

Considering that the establishment of a sovereign and independent State freely determined by all the people belonging to the territory constitutes a mode of implementing the right of self-determination,

Further considering that any attempt aimed at the partial or total disruption of the national unity and territorial integrity of a State established in accordance with the right of self-determination of its people is incompatible with the purposes and principles of the Charter,

Mindful that interference in the internal affairs of States is a violation of the Charter and can pose a serious threat to the maintenance of peace,

1. *Confirms* the legality of the peoples' struggle for self-determination and liberation from colonial and foreign domination and alien subjugation, notably in southern Africa and in particular that of the peoples of Zimbabwe, Namibia, Angola, Mozambique and Guinea (Bissau), as well as of the Palestinian people, by all available means consistent with the Charter of the United Nations;

2. *Affirms* man's basic human right to fight for the self-determination of his people under colonial and foreign domination;

3. *Calls upon* all States dedicated to the ideals of freedom and peace to give all their political, moral and material assistance to peoples struggling for liberation, self-determination and independence against colonial and alien domination;

4. *Believes* that the main objectives and principles of international protection of human rights cannot be effectively implemented while some States, particularly Portugal and South Africa, pursue the imperialist policy of colonialism, use force against independent African States and developing countries and peoples fighting for self-determination and support régimes that are applying the criminal policy of racism and *apartheid*;

5. *Condemns* the colonial and usurping Powers that are suppressing the right of peoples to self-determination and hampering the liquidation of the last hotbeds of colonialism and racism in the African and Asian continents and in other parts of the world;

6. *Condemns* the policy of certain States members of the North Atlantic Treaty Organization that contribute to the creation in southern Africa of a military-industrial complex whose aim is to suppress the movement of peoples struggling for self-determination, and to interfere in the affairs of independent African States;

7. *Recalls* that it is the duty of every State to contribute through joint and independent action to the implementation of the principle of self-determination, in accordance with the provisions of the Charter, and to assist the United Nations in discharging the responsibilities vested in it by the Charter for the implementation of this principle;

8. *Urges* the Security Council as well as States Members of the United Nations or members of specialized agencies to take effective steps to ensure the implementation of the relevant United Nations resolutions on the elimination of colonialism and racism, and to report to the General Assembly at its twenty-seventh session;

9. *Resolves* to devote constant attention to the question of flagrant large-scale violations of human rights and fundamental freedoms resulting from the denial to peoples under colonial and foreign domination of their right to self-determination;

10. *Calls upon* all States to observe the principles of the sovereign equality of States, non-interference in the internal affairs of other States and respect for their sovereign rights and territorial integrity.

Human rights in armed conflicts

Respect for human rights in armed conflicts

In response to a General Assembly request of 9 December 1970,[11] the Secretary-General submitted to the Assembly in 1971 a report on respect for human rights in armed conflicts.

The report included: a brief survey of the origin and nature of United Nations concern with the question of human rights in armed conflicts; a summary of the work of the Conference of Government Experts on the Reaffirmation and Development of International Humanitarian Law Applicable in Armed Conflicts, convened in May–June 1971 by the International Committee of the Red Cross (ICRC); and information on other relevant developments relating to the protection of human rights in armed conflicts.

Among the questions discussed at the Conference of Government Experts were the following: protection of civilians; protection of combatants in international armed conflicts; prohibition and limitation of certain methods and means of warfare; non-international armed conflicts; guerrilla warfare; protection of civilians and combatants in conflicts arising from the struggles of peoples under colonial and foreign rule for liberation and self-determination; protection of the wounded and sick; protection of journalists engaged in dangerous missions; international assistance in, and supervision of, humanitarian rules relating to armed conflicts; and better application and reaffirmation of humanitarian international conventions and rules.

The Assembly also had before it comments by Governments on the 1969 and 1970 reports of the Secretary-General on respect for human rights in armed conflicts.

On 20 December 1971, the General Assembly adopted two resolutions concerning respect for human rights in armed conflicts.

By the preamble to the first resolution (2852(XXVI)), the Assembly among other things: reaffirmed its determination to continue all efforts to eliminate the threat or use of force in international relations, in conformity with the United Nations Charter, and to bring about general and complete disarmament under effective international control; reaffirmed its desire to secure full observance of human rights applicable in all armed conflicts pending the earliest possible termination of such conflicts; and reaffirmed that, in order effectively to guarantee human rights, all States should devote their efforts to averting the

[11]See Y.U.N., 1970, pp. 540-41, text of resolution 2677(XXV).

unleashing of aggressive wars and armed conflicts that violated the Charter and the provisions of the Declaration on Principles of International Law concerning Friendly Relations and Co-operation among States in accordance with the Charter of the United Nations.[12]

The Assembly also: expressed its deep concern over the terrible suffering that armed conflicts continued to inflict on combatants and civilians, particularly through the use of cruel means and methods of warfare and through inadequate restraints in defining military objectives; and noted that current disarmament negotiations did not deal with the question of prohibiting or restricting certain cruel methods of warfare, such as napalm, or methods that indiscriminately affected civilians and combatants.

The Assembly welcomed the decision of ICRC to convene in 1972 a second session of the Conference of Government Experts on the Reaffirmation and Development of International Humanitarian Law Applicable in Armed Conflicts, and stressed the importance of further close co-operation between the United Nations and ICRC.

By the operative paragraphs of the resolution, the Assembly among other things called again upon all parties to any armed conflict to observe the rules laid down in the Hague Conventions of 1899 and 1907, the Geneva Protocol of 1925, the Geneva Conventions of 1949 and other humanitarian rules applicable in armed conflicts, and invited those States which had not yet done so to adhere to those instruments.

It reaffirmed that persons participating in resistance movements and freedom fighters in southern Africa and in territories under colonial and alien domination and foreign occupation who were struggling for their liberation and self-determination should, in case of arrest, be treated as prisoners of war in accordance with the principles of the Hague Convention of 1907 and the Geneva Conventions of 1949.

The International Committee of the Red Cross (ICRC) was invited to continue the work that was begun with the assistance of government experts in 1971, and, taking into account all relevant United Nations resolutions on human rights in armed conflicts, to devote special attention to: the need to ensure better application of existing rules relating to armed conflicts; the need for a reaffirmation and development of relevant rules, as well as other measures to improve the protection of the civilian population during armed conflicts, including legal restraints and restrictions on certain methods of warfare and weapons that had proved particularly perilous to civilians; the need to evolve norms designed to increase the protection of persons struggling against colonial and alien domination, foreign occupation and

racist régimes; the need for development of the rules concerning the status, protection and humane treatment of combatants in international and non-international armed conflicts and the question of guerrilla warfare; and the need for additional rules regarding the protection of the wounded and sick.

The Assembly called upon all States to disseminate widely information on, and to provide instruction concerning, human rights in armed conflicts and to take all necessary measures to ensure full observance by their own armed forces of humanitarian rules applicable in armed conflicts.

The Secretary-General was requested to prepare as soon as possible, with the help of qualified governmental consultant experts, a report on napalm and other incendiary weapons and all aspects of their possible use.

The Assembly also asked the Secretary-General to encourage the study and teaching of principles of respect for human rights applicable to armed conflicts by the means at his disposal, and to report to the General Assembly at its 1972 session on the results of the second session of the Conference of Government Experts and any other relevant developments.

The Assembly decided to consider the question of human rights in armed conflict in all its aspects again at its 1972 session.

(For text of resolution, see DOCUMENTARY REFERENCES below.)

Resolution 2852(XXVI) was adopted by a vote of 110 to 1, with 5 abstentions, on the recommendation of the Assembly's Third (Social, Humanitarian and Cultural) Committee, which approved the text on 7 December 1971 by a vote of 88 to 1, with 5 abstentions.

The draft approved by the Third Committee was based on a proposal sponsored by 12 States—Austria, Chile, Ecuador, Egypt, Ireland, Kenya, Mexico, Morocco, Norway, Peru, Sweden and Yugoslavia—as amended by the Byelorussian SSR and jointly by nine powers: Algeria, Ghana, Guinea, Mali, Mauritania, Sierra Leone, Tunisia, the United Republic of Tanzania, and Zambia.

Among the amendments approved by the Committee were: amendments by the Byelorussian SSR adding the preambular paragraph referring to the need to avert aggressive wars, and adding an operative provision asking the ICRC to devote special attention to the need to evolve norms to increase the protection of persons struggling against colonial, foreign and racist régimes; and an amendment by the nine powers adding the operative paragraph concerning the

---

[12]See Y.U.N., 1970, pp. 788-92, resolution 2625(XXV) of 24 October 1970, containing text of Declaration.

treatment of freedom fighters in southern Africa.

The Committee rejected an amendment by the Byelorussian SSR to delete the provision calling on the Secretary-General to use qualified governmental experts in preparing the napalm report.

Also on 20 December 1971, the Assembly adopted resolution 2853(XXVI) concerning human rights in cases of armed conflict.

By the preambular paragraphs, the Assembly among other things: emphasized that effective protection for human rights in situations of armed conflict depended primarily on universal respect for humanitarian rules; recognized that the humanitarian rules which existed did not in all respects meet the need of contemporary situations and that it was necessary to strengthen and develop them; and affirmed that the successful development of humanitarian rules applicable in armed conflicts required the negotiation of instruments which could be effectively implemented and could command the widest possible support.

By the operative paragraphs of the resolution, the Assembly among other things reiterated its calls upon all parties to any armed conflict to observe the rules laid down in the Hague Conventions of 1899 and 1907, the Geneva Protocol of 1925, the Geneva Conventions of 1949 and other humanitarian rules applicable in armed conflicts, and invited those States which had not yet done so to adhere to those instruments.

The Assembly welcomed the progress made by the 1971 Conference of Government Experts convened by ICRC with regard to the following questions: protection of the wounded and sick; protection of victims of non-international armed conflicts; rules applicable in guerrilla warfare; protection of the civilian population against dangers of hostilities; strengthening of the guarantees afforded by international humanitarian law for non-military civil defence organizations; rules relative to the behaviour of combatants; and measures intended to reinforce the implementation in armed conflicts of existing international humanitarian law.

The Assembly expressed the hope that the second session of the Conference of Government Experts would make recommendations for the further development of international humanitarian law in this field—including, as appropriate, draft protocols to the 1949 Geneva Conventions—for subsequent consideration at one or more plenipotentiary diplomatic conferences.

The Assembly called upon States parties to the existing international agreements to review as a matter of priority any reservations they might have made to those instruments.

(For text of resolution, see DOCUMENTARY REFERENCES below.)

Resolution 2853(XXVI) was adopted by a vote

of 83 to 15, with 14 abstentions, as recommended by the Third Committee. The Third Committee approved, on 7 December 1971, a text proposed by Japan, New Zealand and the United Kingdom, by a roll-call vote of 54 to 18, with 26 abstentions.

The Committee rejected several amendments to the draft which were sponsored by Bulgaria and the Ukrainian SSR.

Preliminary draft convention on protection of journalists

By a decision of 9 December 1970, the General Assembly invited the Economic and Social Council to request the Commission on Human Rights to study the possibility of preparing a draft international agreement ensuring the protection of journalists engaged in dangerous missions and providing, among other things, for the creation of a universally recognized and guaranteed identification document. In so doing, the Assembly recognized that, although certain types of protection were granted to journalists under the Geneva Conventions of 1949, the provisions did not cover some categories of journalists engaged in dangerous missions and did not correspond to their current needs.[13]

The Commission on Human Rights considered the question at its 1971 session (22 February–26 March), at which it had before it a preliminary draft international convention on the protection of journalists engaged in dangerous missions, submitted by Austria, Finland, France, Iran, Turkey and Uruguay.

The Commission adopted a resolution by which, among other things, it: (a) expressed its conviction of the urgent need to examine the question, both on humanitarian grounds and in order to enable journalists to seek, receive and impart information fully, objectively and faithfully; (b) noted that it had not had sufficient time to examine in detail the preliminary draft international convention on protection of journalists engaged in dangerous missions; (c) recommended that the Economic and Social Council consider and transmit the preliminary draft convention to the General Assembly at its 1971 session; and (d) requested the Secretary-General to solicit the observations of Governments on the draft convention and to establish a working group of experts to consider various aspects of the question.

On 21 May 1971, the Economic and Social Council, taking note of that resolution of the Commission on Human Rights, decided to transmit the preliminary draft international convention to the General Assembly.

The Council took this decision in adopting, by a vote of 21 to 0, with 3 abstentions, resolution

[13]See Y.U.N., 1970, pp. 541-42, text of resolution 2673(XXV).

1597(L), to which the preliminary draft convention was annexed. The text of the resolution, based on a proposal of France, Madagascar, Tunisia and Uruguay, had been recommended and approved by the Social Committee on 18 May 1971 by a vote of 22 to 0, with 3 abstentions.

(For text of resolution, see DOCUMENTARY REFERENCES below.)

At its 1971 session, the General Assembly had before it a report by the Secretary-General containing, among other things, Government comments on the draft text of the convention on the protection of journalists engaged in dangerous missions in areas of armed conflict.

Also before the Assembly was the report of the Working Group of Experts established by the Secretary-General in accordance with the request of the Human Rights Commission; the report contained a draft protocol concerning the International Professional Committee to be established pursuant to the provisions of the draft international convention for the protection of journalists engaged in dangerous missions.

Also, the Assembly had before it another draft convention and a working paper on the draft convention on protection of journalists, submitted by Australia and the United States, respectively.

On 20 December 1971, the General Assembly expressed its belief that it was necessary to adopt a convention providing for the protection of journalists engaged in dangerous missions in areas of armed conflict. It invited the Economic and Social Council to ask the Human Rights Commission to consider, as a matter of priority at its 1972 session, the draft conventions and all other related documents which had been submitted.

The Assembly further asked the Commission to send its report to the 1972 session of the Conference of Government Experts on the Reaffirmation and Development of International Humanitarian Law Applicable in Armed Conflicts, so that the International Committee of the Red Cross might submit observations to the General Assembly.

Finally, the Assembly invited Governments to transmit their observations on that part of the Commission's report dealing with the question, and requested the Secretary-General to submit to the General Assembly the replies received and an analytic report on them. It decided to examine the question as a matter of the highest priority at its 1972 session.

(For text of resolution, see DOCUMENTARY REFERENCES below.)

These decisions of the Assembly were set forth in resolution 2854(XXVI), which was adopted by a vote of 96 to 2, with 20 abstentions, as recommended by the Third Committee.

The Committee approved the text on 7 December 1971 by a vote of 79 to 1, with 19 abstentions. The text was based on a proposal sponsored by Austria, Finland, France, Iran, Madagascar, Senegal, Tunisia, Turkey and Uruguay; it incorporated certain amendments sponsored jointly by Argentina, Brazil, Canada, Costa Rica, Ecuador, Guatemala, Nicaragua, Nigeria, Panama, Venezuela, and Zambia.

Separate votes were taken on several provisions, including a roll-call vote on the provision which called for the Assembly to consider the question of the protection of journalists engaged in dangerous missions "as a matter of the highest priority" in 1972. The words were retained by a vote of 37 to 6, with 59 abstentions.

DOCUMENTARY REFERENCES

Respect for human rights
in armed conflicts

General Assembly—26th session
Third Committee, meetings 1885-1887, 1889-1898.
Fifth Committee, meeting 1486.
Plenary meeting 2027.

A/8313 and Add.1-3. Comments by Governments on reports of Secretary-General. Note by Secretary-General.
A/8370 and Add.1. Report of Secretary-General.
A/8401. Report of Secretary-General on work of the Organization, 16 June 1970–15 June 1971, Part Three, Chapter I A 10.
A/C.3/L.1896. Chile, Egypt, Kenya, Mexico, Sweden, Yugoslavia: draft resolution.
A/C.3/L.1896/Rev.1. Chile, Ecuador, Egypt, Ireland, Kenya, Mexico, Morocco, Peru, Sweden, Yugoslavia: revised draft resolution.
A/C.3/L.1896/Rev.2. Revised draft resolution, sponsored by above 10 powers and by Austria and Norway, as amended by Byelorussian SSR (A/C.3/L.1914/Rev.1, paras. 1 and 2) and by 9 powers (A/C.3/L.1911, as orally sub-amended), approved by Third Committee on 7 December 1971, meeting 1898, by 88 votes to 1, with 5 abstentions.

A/C.3/L.1910. Syrian Arab Republic: amendment to 10-power revised draft resolution, A/C.3/L.1896/Rev.1.
A/C.3/L.1911. Algeria, Ghana, Guinea, Mali, Mauritania, Sierra Leone, Tunisia, United Republic of Tanzania, Zambia: amendment to 10-power revised draft resolution, A/C.3/L.1896/Rev.1.
A/C.3/L.1912. Greece: amendment to 10-power revised draft resolution, A/C.3/L.1896/Rev.1.
A/C.3/L.1913. Austria: amendment to 10-power revised draft resolution, A/C.3/L.1896/Rev.1.
A/C.3/L.1914. Byelorussian SSR: amendment to 10-power revised draft resolution, A/C.3/L.1896/Rev.1.
A/C.3/L.1914/Rev.1. Byelorussian SSR: revised amendment to 12-power revised draft resolution, A/C.3/L.1896/Rev.2.
A/C.3/L.1916. Administrative and financial implications of 10-power revised draft resolution, A/C.3/L.1896/Rev.1. Statement by Secretary-General.
A/C.5/1420, A/8612. Administrative and financial implications of draft resolution I recommended by Third Committee in A/8589. Reports of Secretary-General and Fifth Committee.
A/8589. Report of Third Committee, draft resolution I.

RESOLUTION 2852(XXVI), as recommended by Third Committee, A/8589, adopted by Assembly on 20 December 1971, meeting 2027, by 110 votes to 1, with 5 abstentions.

The General Assembly,

Reaffirming its determination to continue all efforts to eliminate the threat or use of force in international relations, in conformity with the Charter of the United Nations, and to bring about general and complete disarmament under effective international control, and reaffirming its desire to secure full observance of human rights applicable in all armed conflicts pending the earliest possible termination of such conflicts,

Reaffirming that, in order effectively to guarantee human rights, all States should devote their efforts to averting the unleashing of aggressive wars and armed conflicts that violate the Charter and the provisions of the Declaration on Principles of International Law concerning Friendly Relations and Co-operation among States in accordance with the Charter of the United Nations,

Recalling the successive resolutions that have been adopted by the United Nations relating to human rights in armed conflicts, in particular General Assembly resolutions 2652(XXV) of 3 December 1970, 2674(XXV) and 2678(XXV) of 9 December 1970 and 2707(XXV) of 14 December 1970, and taking into account relevant resolutions of international conferences of the Red Cross,

Deeply concerned over the terrible suffering that armed conflicts continue to inflict upon combatants and civilians, particularly through the use of cruel means and methods of warfare and through inadequate restraints in defining military objectives,

Desiring to ensure the effective application of all existing rules relating to human rights in armed conflicts, as well as the development of these rules, and aware that progress in this regard will depend upon the political readiness and willingness of Member States,

Conscious that, although negotiations are going on in the field of disarmament concerning general and complete disarmament and the limitation and elimination of nuclear, biological and chemical weapons, those deliberations do not deal with the question of prohibiting or restricting the use of other methods of warfare that are cruel, such as napalm, or that indiscriminately affect civilians and combatants,

Noting the comments by Governments on the reports of the Secretary-General on respect for human rights in armed conflicts,

Noting with appreciation the report of the Secretary-General on the comprehensive discussions undertaken at the first session of the Conference of Government Experts on the Reaffirmation and Development of International Humanitarian Law Applicable in Armed Conflicts, which was held at Geneva from 24 May to 12 June 1971 at the invitation of the International Committee of the Red Cross,

Having taken cognizance of the report prepared by the International Committee of the Red Cross on the work of the Conference of Government Experts,

Welcoming the decision of the International Committee of the Red Cross to convene in 1972 a second session of the Conference of Government Experts with broader participation to include all the States parties to the Geneva Conventions of 1949 and to circulate in advance of that session a series of draft protocols,

Stressing the importance of further close co-operation between the United Nations and the International Committee of the Red Cross,

Determined to continue its efforts to achieve better application of existing rules relating to armed conflicts, as well as the reaffirmation and development of these rules,

1. *Calls again upon* all parties to any armed conflict to observe the rules laid down in the Hague Conventions of 1899 and 1907, the Geneva Protocol of 1925, the Geneva Conventions of 1949 and other humanitarian rules applicable in armed conflicts, and invites those States which have not yet done so to adhere to those instruments;

2. *Reaffirms* that persons participating in resistance movements and freedom fighters in southern Africa and in territories under colonial and alien domination and foreign occupation who are struggling for their liberation and self-determination should, in case of arrest, be treated as prisoners of war in accordance with the principles of the Hague Convention of 1907 and the Geneva Conventions of 1949;

3. *Invites* the International Committee of the Red Cross to continue the work that was begun with the assistance of government experts in 1971 and, taking into account all relevant United Nations resolutions on human rights in armed conflicts, to devote special attention, among the questions to be taken up, to the following:

(a) The need to ensure better application of existing rules relating to armed conflicts, particularly the Hague Conventions of 1899 and 1907, the Geneva Protocol of 1925 and the Geneva Conventions of 1949, including the need for strengthening the system of protecting Powers contained in such instruments;

(b) The need for a reaffirmation and development of relevant rules, as well as other measures to improve the protection of the civilian population during armed conflicts, including legal restraints and restrictions on certain methods of warfare and weapons that have proved particularly perilous to civilians, and also arrangements for humanitarian relief;

(c) The need to evolve norms designed to increase the protection of persons struggling against colonial and alien domination, foreign occupation and racist régimes;

(d) The need for development of the rules concerning the status, protection and humane treatment of combatants in international and non-international armed conflicts and the question of guerrilla warfare;

(e) The need for additional rules regarding the protection of the wounded and the sick;

4. *Expresses the hope* that the second session of the Conference of Government Experts on the Reaffirmation and Development of International Humanitarian Law Applicable in Armed Conflicts will result in specific conclusions and recommendations for action at the government level;

5. *Requests* the Secretary-General, in line with paragraph 126 of his report on respect for human rights in armed conflicts submitted to the General Assembly at its twenty-fifth session, to prepare as soon as possible, with the help of qualified governmental consultant experts, a report on napalm and other incendiary weapons and all aspects of their possible use;

6. *Further calls upon* all States to disseminate widely information and to provide instruction concerning human rights in armed conflicts and to take all the necessary measures to ensure full observance by their own armed forces of humanitarian rules applicable in armed conflicts;

7. *Requests* the Secretary-General to encourage the study and teaching of principles of respect for human rights applicable in armed conflicts by the means at his disposal;

8. *Requests* the Secretary-General to report to the General Assembly at its twenty-seventh session on the results of the second session of the Conference of Government Experts and any other relevant developments;

9. *Decides* to include in the provisional agenda of its twenty-seventh session an item entitled "Human rights in armed conflicts" and to consider it in all its aspects.

A/C.3/L.1895 and Rev.1. Japan, New Zealand, United Kingdom: draft resolution and revision, as further orally amended by sponsors, approved by Third Committee on 7 December 1971, meeting 1898, by roll-call vote of 54 to 18, with 26 abstentions, as follows:

In favour: Argentina, Australia, Austria, Barbados, Belgium, Brazil, Canada, Colombia, Costa Rica, Cyprus, Denmark, Dominican Republic, Ethiopia, Finland, France, Ghana, Greece, Guatemala, Guyana, India, Indonesia, Iran, Ireland, Israel, Italy, Ivory Coast Jamaica, Japan, Kenya, Khmer Republic, Liberia, Madagascar, Malaysia, Netherlands, New Zealand, Nicaragua, Niger, Nigeria, Norway, Panama, Philippines, Portugal, Rwanda, Singapore, Spain, Swaziland, Thailand, Turkey, United Kingdom, United States, Uruguay, Venezuela, Zaire, Zambia.

Against: Algeria, Bulgaria, Byelorussian SSR, Chile, Cuba, Czechoslovakia, Ecuador, Guinea, Hungary, Iraq, Mexico, Mongolia, Morocco, Poland, Romania, Syrian Arab Republic, Ukrainian SSR, USSR.

Abstaining: Afghanistan, Burma, Burundi, Cameroon, Central African Republic, Congo, Dahomey, Egypt, Iceland, Kuwait,

Libyan Arab Republic, Mali, Mauritania, People's Democratic Republic of Yemen, Peru, Saudi Arabia, Sierra Leone, Somalia, Sudan, Sweden, Togo, Tunisia, Uganda, United Republic of Tanzania, Yemen, Yugoslavia.

A/C.3/L.1915. Bulgaria and Ukrainian SSR: amendments to 3-power revised draft resolution, A/C.3/L.1895/Rev.1.
A/8589. Report of Third Committee, draft resolution II.

RESOLUTION 2853(XXVI), as recommended by Third Committee, A/8589, adopted by Assembly on 20 December 1971, meeting 2027, by 83 votes to 15, with 14 abstentions.

The General Assembly,
Recalling its resolutions 2674(XXV), 2675(XXV), 2676(XXV) and 2677(XXV) of 9 December 1970,
Noting also that the twenty-first International Conference of the Red Cross, held at Istanbul in 1969, adopted resolution XIII concerning the reaffirmation and development of the laws and customs applicable in armed conflicts,
Noting with appreciation the report of the Secretary-General on respect for human rights in armed conflicts, concerning in particular the results of the first session of the Conference of Government Experts on the Reaffirmation and Development of International Humanitarian Law Applicable in Armed Conflicts, which was held at Geneva from 24 May to 12 June 1971 at the invitation of the International Committee of the Red Cross, as well as the report of the International Committee on the work of the Conference,
Emphasizing that effective protection for human rights in situations of armed conflict depends primarily on universal respect for humanitarian rules,
Recognizing that existing humanitarian rules relating to armed conflicts do not in all respects meet the need of contemporary situations and that it is therefore necessary to strengthen the procedure for implementing these rules and to develop their substance,
Welcoming the decision of the International Committee of the Red Cross to convene a second session of the Conference of Government Experts with the task of reaching agreement on the wording of various texts to facilitate discussion at a future diplomatic conference, and noting that all States parties to the Geneva Conventions of 1949 have been invited to participate,
Affirming that the successful development of humanitarian rules applicable in armed conflicts requires the negotiation of instruments which can be effectively implemented and which command the widest possible support,
Emphasizing the importance of continued close collaboration between the United Nations and the International Committee of the Red Cross,
1. *Reiterates* its call upon all parties to any armed conflict to observe the rules laid down in the Hague Conventions of 1899 and 1907, the Geneva Protocol of 1925, the Geneva Conventions of 1949 and other humanitarian rules applicable in armed conflicts, and invites those States which have not yet done so to adhere to those instruments;
2. *Welcomes* the progress made by the Conference of Government Experts on the Reaffirmation and Development of International Humanitarian Law Applicable in Armed Conflicts, as shown in its report, with regard to the following questions:
   (a) Protection of the wounded and the sick;
   (b) Protection of victims of non-international armed conflicts;
   (c) Rules applicable in guerrilla warfare;
   (d) Protection of civilian population against dangers of hostilities;
   (e) Strengthening of the guarantees afforded by international humanitarian law for non-military civil defence organizations;
   (f) Rules relative to the behaviour of combatants;
   (g) Measures intended to reinforce the implementation, in armed conflicts, of existing international humanitarian law;
3. *Expresses the hope* that the second session of the Conference of Government Experts will make recommendations for the further development of international humanitarian law in this field including, as appropriate, draft protocols to the Geneva Conventions of 1949, for subsequent consideration at one or more plenipotentiary diplomatic conferences;
4. *Calls upon* States parties to the existing international instruments to review, as a matter of priority, any reservations they may have made to those instruments;
5. *Requests* the Secretary-General:
   (a) To transmit his latest report, together with any further observations received from Governments as well as the records of relevant discussions and resolutions of the General Assembly, to the International Committee of the Red Cross for consideration, as appropriate, by the Conference of Government Experts at its second session;
   (b) To report to the General Assembly at its twenty-seventh session on the progress made in the implementation of the present resolution;
6. *Decides* to consider this question again, in all its aspects, at its twenty-seventh session.

Preliminary draft convention on protection of journalists

Economic and Social Council—50th session
Social Committee, meetings 669-678.
Plenary meeting 1771.

E/4949. Report of Commission on Human Rights on its 27th session, 22 February–26 March 1971, Chapters IX and XIX (resolution 15(XXVII)).
E/4949/Add.1. Financial implications of resolutions adopted by Commission on Human Rights at its 27th session.
E/AC.7/L.597. France, Madagascar, Tunisia, Uruguay: draft resolution, approved by Social Committee on 18 May 1971, meeting 678, by 22 votes to 0, with 3 abstentions.
E/5032. Report of Social Committee, draft resolution XI.

RESOLUTION 1597(L), as recommended by Social Committee, E/5032, adopted by Council on 21 May 1971, meeting 1771, by 21 votes to 0, with 3 abstentions.

The Economic and Social Council,
Recalling General Assembly resolution 2673(XXV) of 9 December 1970 in which it invited the Economic and Social Council to request the Commission on Human Rights to study the possibility of preparing a draft international agreement ensuring the protection of journalists engaged in dangerous missions and providing, *inter alia,* for the creation of a universally recognized and guaranteed identification document,
Having taken cognizance with interest of the preliminary draft international convention on the protection of journalists engaged in dangerous missions which was transmitted to it by the Commission on Human Rights,
Noting that the Commission on Human Rights, in its resolution 15(XXVII), recommended to the Economic and Social Council that it consider and transmit to the General Assembly the preliminary draft international convention on the protection of journalists engaged in dangerous missions, together with the relevant records of the discussions held in the Commission and in the Council, as a valid basis for discussion on this subject by the General Assembly at its twenty-sixth session,
Noting also that, in the same resolution, the Commission requested the Secretary-General to communicate the preliminary draft convention together with the same documentation to the Governments of the States mentioned in the resolution as well as to the Intergovernmental Conference of Experts of the International Committee of the Red Cross to be held in May 1971 so that the General Assembly may have their observations before it at its twenty-sixth session,
Noting further that the Commission requested the Secretary-General to establish a group of experts for the purpose of preparing a draft protocol, annexed to the draft convention, prescribing the composition, duties and methods of the Internation-

al Professional Committee provided for in article 3 of the preliminary draft convention,

Recalling further that the General Assembly decided to give the highest priority to the consideration of this question at its twenty-sixth session,

Decides to transmit to the General Assembly the preliminary draft international convention on the protection of journalists engaged in dangerous missions contained in the annex to the present resolution, as well as the relevant records of the Commission on Human Rights and of the Economic and Social Council, as a valid basis for the discussions of the General Assembly at its twenty-sixth session.

ANNEX

Preliminary Draft International Convention on the Protection of Journalists Engaged in Dangerous Missions

The High Contracting Parties,

Considering that the Universal Declaration of Human Rights has proclaimed in its article 19 the right of everyone to freedom of opinion and expression, including freedom to seek, receive and impart information through any media and regardless of frontiers,

Considering that it is important to promote the right to complete, objective and truthful information,

Considering that the press plays a vital role in that connexion,

Considering that the quest for information may expose journalists to dangerous situations when their mission leads them to carry on their activity in areas where there is armed conflict,

Considering that those whose recognized function is to gather information for dissemination through an information organ should be afforded adequate protection in time of armed conflict,

Considering that without prejudice to the application of the Geneva Conventions of 12 August 1949 it is desirable to guarantee for all categories of journalists, in view of the present-day requirements of their profession, effective protection when they carry out dangerous missions,

Have agreed on the following provisions:

Article 1

This Convention shall apply to journalists who engage in dangerous missions and who hold the safe-conduct card provided for in article 3 below.

It shall not apply to war correspondents covered by the provisions of the Geneva Conventions of 12 August 1949.

Article 2

For the purposes of the application of this Convention, the word "journalist" shall mean any correspondent, reporter, photographer, film cameraman or press technician who has that status by virtue of his country's law or practice, in the case of a State Member of the United Nations or member of a specialized agency or of the International Atomic Energy Agency or any other State party to the Statute of the International Court of Justice or Party to this Convention.

The words "dangerous mission" shall mean any mission carried out in an area where there is an armed conflict, whether or not of an international character, for the purpose of gathering information for dissemination through a medium of public information.

Article 3

A journalist who is to carry out a dangerous mission may hold a safe-conduct card.

The said card shall be issued by the International Professional Committee for the Protection of Journalists Engaged in Dangerous Missions, whose composition and functions are defined in a Protocol annexed to this Convention.

Article 4

The validity of the safe-conduct card shall be limited to a specified geographical area and to the expected duration of the mission.

It shall certify the status of the journalist and the references which entitle him to that status within the meaning of article 2

above; it shall, in particular, bear his photograph and state his name, date and place of birth, habitual residence and nationality.

Article 5

Every party to an armed conflict shall recognize the validity of the safe-conduct cards issued by the International Committee.

The Committee shall give wide circulation to the model of the card and to the distinguishing mark provided for in the following article.

Article 6

When engaged in a dangerous mission, a journalist who holds a safe-conduct card must be able to produce it on any occasion and, in particular, at the request of any competent authority.

A journalist who holds a safe-conduct card may also, at his discretion, wear a readily recognizable distinguishing mark, an exact description of which shall be drawn up by the International Committee.

Article 7

The States Parties to this Convention and all parties to the conflict shall:

(1)   Recognize persons holding a safe-conduct card as journalists within the meaning of the provisions of articles 2, 3 and 4 above;

(2)   Enable such persons to identify themselves;

(3)   Extend to them the same protection of their persons as to their own journalists;

(4)   Recognize, in case of internment, that the regulations for the treatment of internees laid down in the Geneva Convention relative to the Protection of Civilian Persons in Time of War, of 12 August 1949, shall apply;

(5)   Make public the internment order;

(6)   Also make public any information on journalists who have been wounded or who have died.

Such facts may be made public through all appropriate media, in the quickest and most effective manner and, preferably, through the International Committee of the Red Cross or any organ of the United Nations family in order that the International Professional Committee for the Protection of Journalists Engaged in Dangerous Missions may be informed without delay.

Article 8

The application of this Convention shall have no legal effect on the situation of the parties to a conflict.

Article 9

This Convention shall not affect national regulations concerning the crossing of frontiers or the movement or residence of aliens.

Article 10

None of the provisions of this Convention may be interpreted as affecting the provisions of the Geneva Conventions of 12 August 1949.

General Assembly—26th session
Third Committee, meetings 1885-1887, 1889-1898.
Plenary meeting 2027.

A/8370 and Add.1. Respect for human rights in armed conflicts. Report of Secretary-General, Chapter H.

A/8371 and Add.1,2. Protection of journalists engaged in dangerous missions in areas of armed conflict. Report of Secretary-General. (Annex I: Preliminary draft international convention on protection of journalists engaged in dangerous missions.)

A/8403. Report of Economic and Social Council on work of its 50th and 51st sessions, Chapter XVII A.

A/8438. Note by Secretary-General (transmitting report of Working Group established under resolution 15(XXVII) of Commission on Human Rights. Annex: Draft protocol relating to composition and functions of International Professional Committee for protection of journalists engaged in dangerous missions pursuant to article 3 of draft international convention).

A/8438/Add.1. Administrative and financial implications of recommendations of Working Group of Commission on Human Rights in A/8438. Statement by Secretary-General.

A/C.3/L.1902. Australia: draft convention on protection of journalists engaged in dangerous missions in areas of armed conflict.

A/C.3/L.1903. United States: working paper on draft international convention on protection of journalists engaged in dangerous missions.

A/C.3/L.1904 and Rev.1,2. Austria, Finland, France, Iran, Madagascar, Senegal, Tunisia, Turkey, Uruguay: draft resolution and revisions, as further orally revised by sponsors, approved by Third Committee on 7 December 1971, meeting 1898, by 79 votes to 1, with 19 abstentions.

A/C.3/L.1905. Austria, Iran, France, Uruguay: draft of final clauses of preliminary draft international convention on protection of journalists engaged in dangerous missions.

A/C.3/L.1919 and Rev.1. Argentina, Brazil, Canada, Costa Rica, Ecuador, Guatemala, Nicaragua, Nigeria, Panama, Venezuela, Zambia: amendments to 9-power draft resolution, A/C.3/L.1904, and revised amendments to 9-power revised draft resolution, A/C.3/L.1904/Rev.2.

A/8589. Report of Third Committee, draft resolution III.

RESOLUTION 2854(XXVI), as recommended by Third Committee, A/8589, adopted by Assembly on 20 December 1971, meeting 2027, by 96 votes to 2, with 20 abstentions.

The General Assembly,

Recalling its resolution 2444(XXIII) of 19 December 1968 concerning, in particular, the studies to be undertaken by the Secretary-General in consultation with the International Committee of the Red Cross and other appropriate international organizations with regard, *inter alia,* to the need for additional humanitarian international conventions or for other appropriate legal instruments to ensure the better protection of civilians, prisoners and combatants in all armed conflicts,

Recalling also its resolution 2673(XXV) of 9 December 1970, in which it expressed its conviction that there was a need for an additional humanitarian international instrument to ensure the better protection of journalists engaged in dangerous missions, particularly in areas where an armed conflict was taking place,

Being aware that the provisions of the humanitarian conventions at present in force do not cover some categories of journalists engaged in dangerous missions and do not correspond to their present needs,

Noting Commission on Human Rights resolution 15(XXVII) of 24 March 1971, in which the Commission expressed its conviction that there was an urgent need to examine the question of the protection of journalists engaged in dangerous missions, both on humanitarian grounds and in order to enable journalists with due respect for the law to seek, receive and impart information fully, objectively and faithfully in the spirit of the purposes and principles of the Charter of the United Nations and the Universal Declaration of Human Rights concerning freedom of information,

Noting Economic and Social Council resolution 1597(L) of 21 May 1971, in which the Council decided to transmit to the General Assembly the preliminary draft international convention on the

protection of journalists engaged in dangerous missions, submitted to it by the Commission on Human Rights, as well as the relevant records of the Commission and of the Council, as a valid basis for the discussions of the Assembly at its twenty-sixth session,

Noting the report of the Secretary-General containing the preliminary draft international convention on the protection of journalists engaged in dangerous missions, the observations received from Governments concerning the preliminary draft and the observations of the Conference of Government Experts on the Reaffirmation and Development of International Humanitarian Law Applicable in Armed Conflicts, which was held at Geneva from 24 May to 12 June 1971 at the invitation of the International Committee of the Red Cross,

Noting with appreciation the report of the Working Group established by the Secretary-General in accordance with Commission on Human Rights resolution 15(XXVII), and the annexed draft protocol relating to the composition and functions of the International Professional Committee for the Protection of Journalists Engaged in Dangerous Missions referred to in article 3 of the aforementioned preliminary draft convention,

Having considered the observations submitted by some Member States in accordance with Commission on Human Rights resolution 15(XXVII) and the observations of the Conference of Government Experts as well as the discussions on the item and the alternate draft convention submitted during the debate at the twenty-sixth session of the General Assembly,

1. *Believes* that it is necessary to adopt a convention providing for the protection of journalists engaged in dangerous missions in areas of armed conflict;

2. *Invites* the Economic and Social Council to request the Commission on Human Rights to consider as a matter of priority at its twenty-eighth session the preliminary draft convention contained in Council resolution 1597(L), taking into consideration the draft conventions submitted by Australia and by the United States of America, and the observations of Governments, as well as all subsequent documents including the draft protocol prepared by the Working Group in accordance with resolution 15(XXVII) of the Commission;

3. *Further requests* the Commission on Human Rights to transmit its report on its twenty-eighth session to the Conference of Government Experts on the Reaffirmation and Development of International Humanitarian Law Applicable in Armed Conflicts at its second session to be convened in 1972 by the International Committee of the Red Cross, in order that the International Committee may submit its observations to the General Assembly at its twenty-seventh session;

4. *Invites* Governments to transmit their observations on that part of the report of the Commission on Human Rights on its twenty-eighth session relating to this question;

5. *Requests* the Secretary-General to submit the replies received and an analytic report on those replies to the General Assembly at its twenty-seventh session;

6. *Decides* to examine this question as a matter of the highest priority at its twenty-seventh session, taking into consideration the recommendations transmitted to the General Assembly by the Economic and Social Council.

The status of women

The Commission on the Status of Women did not meet during 1971, following a decision of the Economic and Social Council in 1970 that the Commission should meet biennially.[14] The twenty-fourth session of the Commission was to be held in 1972.

The Secretary-General submitted a report on the political rights of women to the General Assembly at its 1971 session. The report contained

a summary of information on relevant constitutional provisions, electoral laws and other legal instruments relating to the political rights of women which had become available since the previous report was issued in 1970, as well as a summary of additonal replies received from Member States on the implementation of the 1952

[14]See Y.U.N., 1970, p. 549.

Convention on the Political Rights of Women.[15]

Several studies relating to the role of women in community, national and international life were prepared by the Secretary-General during the year. These included reports on the following subjects: the participation of women in community development; the condition of women and children during emergency and armed conflicts in the struggle for peace, self-determination, national liberation and independence; the status of women in Trust and Non-Self-Governing Territories; and the status of the unmarried mother—law and practice. A preliminary report on the status of women in private law was also issued during 1971.

Activities carried out during the year in connexion with the programme of concerted international action for the advancement of women, proclaimed by the General Assembly in 1970,[16] included a regional seminar on the participation of women in economic life, held at Libreville, Gabon. (See also section below on ADVISORY SERVICES IN HUMAN RIGHTS.)

[15]See Y.U.N., 1952, pp. 484-85, text of Convention.
[16]See Y.U.N., 1970, pp. 553-55 text of resolution 2716(XXV) of 15 December 1970.

DOCUMENTARY REFERENCES

A/8481 and Corr.1. Political rights of women. Report of Secretary-General.
A/8401. Report of Secretary-General on work of the Organization, 16 June 1970–15 June 1971, Part Three, Chapter I B.
The Status of the Unmarried Mother: Law and Practice. Report of the Secretary-General. U.N.P. Sales No.: E.71.IV.4.
Participation of Women in Community Development. Report of the

United Nations Secretary-General. U.N.P. Sales No.: E.72.IV.8. ST/TAO/HR/43. Seminar on Participation of Women in Economic Life (with reference to implementation of article 10 of Declaration on Elimination of Discrimination against Women and of General Assembly resolution 2716(XXV)), Libreville, Gabon, 17 July–9 August 1971.

Advisory services in human rights

Under the programme of advisory services in the field of human rights, established by the General Assembly in 1955,[17] the United Nations provides, at the request of Governments, fellowships and expert advisory services and organizes seminars on human rights problems.

Activities in 1971

The following seminars were held in 1971: (*a*) an international seminar on measures to be taken on the national level for the implementation of United Nations instruments aimed at combating and eliminating racial discrimination and for the promotion of harmonious race relations—a symposium on the evils of racial discrimination, held from 16 to 29 June, at Yaoundé, Cameroon (organized as part of the programme for the observance of the International Year for Action to Combat Racism and Racial Discrimination); (*b*) a regional seminar on the participation of women in economic life, held from 27 July to 9 August, at Libreville, Gabon; and (*c*) an international seminar on the dangers of a recrudescence of intolerance in all its forms and the search for ways of preventing and combating it, which took place at Nice, France, from 24 August to 6 September.

At the request of the Government of Cameroon, an expert continued in 1971 to advise on the promotion of the participation of women in national affairs and national development in Cameroon, with particular emphasis on community development, concluding his work in October.

During 1971, 63 fellowships in the field of human rights were awarded to nationals of 41

countries, namely: Afghanistan, Argentina, Austria, Barbados, Bolivia, Ceylon, Colombia, Costa Rica, El Salvador, Fiji, Guyana, India, Indonesia, Iran, Iraq, the Khmer Republic, Lesotho, Madagascar, Nepal, New Zealand, Nigeria, Pakistan, Paraguay, the Philippines, Poland, Saudi Arabia, Senegal, Sierra Leone, Singapore, Somalia, Spain, Sudan, Sweden, the Syrian Arab Republic, Thailand, Togo, Trinidad and Tobago, Turkey, the United Republic of Tanzania, Yemen and Yugoslavia.

Decisions by Human Rights Commission

At its February-March 1971 session, the Commission on Human Rights adopted a resolution by which, among other things, it expressed the hope that further seminars on the role of youth in the promotion and protection of human rights would be organized under the programme of advisory services, if possible, in all regions of the world. The Commission invited the Secretary-General to explore, through such seminars and other techniques, ways and means by which youth might be encouraged to participate constructively and to assist in the effective implementation of United Nations principles concerning human rights at the national and international levels.

Decision by General Assembly

On 22 December 1971, in adopting resolution 2899 A (XXVI) on budget appropriations for

[17]See Y.U.N., 1955, pp. 164-65, text of resolution 926(X) of 14 December 1955.

1972, the General Assembly appropriated funds for United Nations programmes of technical co-operation, including funds for the programme of advisory services in the field of human rights.

(For text of resolution 2899 A (XXVI) see pp. 644-45.)

DOCUMENTARY REFERENCES

E/4949. Report of Commission on Human Rights on its 27th session, 22 February–26 March 1971, Chapters XVI and XIX A (resolution 11 A (XXVII)) and B (other decisions, p. 95).

A/8401. Report of Secretary-General on work of the Organization, 16 June 1970–15 June 1971, Part Three, Chapter I A 19.

ST/TAO/HR/42. Seminar on Measures to be Taken on National Level for Implementation of United Nations Instruments Aimed at Combating and Eliminating Racial Discrimination and for Promotion of Harmonious Race Relations: Symposium on Evils

of Racial Discrimination, Yaoundé, Cameroon, 16-29 June 1971.

ST/TAO/HR/43. Seminar on Participation of Women in Economic Life (with reference to implementation of article 10 of Declaration on Elimination of Discrimination against Women and of General Assembly resolution 2716(XXV)), Libreville, Gabon, 27 July–9 August 1971.

ST/TAO/HR/44. Seminar on Dangers of Recrudescence of Intolerance in All its Forms and Search for Ways of Preventing and Combating It, held at Nice, France, 24 August–6 September 1971.

Other human rights questions

Punishment of war criminals and persons committing crimes against humanity

The question of the punishment of war criminals and of persons who had committed crimes against humanity was considered again during 1971 by various United Nations organs.

At its February-March 1971 session, the Commission on Human Rights adopted a resolution asking the Secretary-General to continue reporting on the question in 1972, in the light of information received from Governments pursuant to General Assembly requests of 15 December 1969 and 15 December 1970.[18]

A report of the Secretary-General on the subject, prepared in accordance with the above requests, was before the Assembly at its 1971 session. The report contained information and views of Governments concerning, among other things: the legal basis for the prosecution and punishment of war criminals and of persons guilty of crimes against humanity; the non-applicability of statutory limitations of such offences; the competent organs and authorities and applicable procedures for the prosecution and trial of war criminals and persons committing crimes against humanity; international co-operation in finding and collecting evidence of war crimes; the extradition of persons responsible for war crimes and crimes against humanity; and the criteria for determining compensation to the victims of such crimes.

On 18 December 1971, the Assembly, noting with regret that the numerous decisions of the United Nations on the punishment of war criminals and of persons who had committed crimes against humanity were still not being fully complied with, affirmed that refusal by States to co-operate in the arrest, extradition, trial and punishment of persons guilty of war crimes and

crimes against humanity was contrary to the purposes and principles of the United Nations Charter and to generally recognized norms of international law.

The Assembly urged all States (a) to implement the relevant resolutions of the General Assembly and to take measures in accordance with international law to put an end to and prevent war crimes and crimes against humanity and to ensure the punishment of all persons guilty of such crimes, including their extradition to those countries where they had committed such crimes; and (b) to co-operate in particular in the collection and exchange of information which would lead to the punishment of such persons. The Assembly further called upon all States which had not done so to become parties to the Convention on the Non-Applicability of Statutory Limitations to War Crimes and Crimes against Humanity.[19]

The Commission on Human Rights was requested to submit to the Assembly at its 1972 session a report on the principles of international co-operation in the detection, arrest, extradition and punishment of persons guilty of war crimes and of crimes against humanity.

The Assembly took this action in adopting resolution 2840(XXVI), by a vote of 71 to 0, with 42 abstentions, as recommended by its Third (Social, Humanitarian and Cultural) Committee. On 9 December 1971, the Third Committee, by a vote of 42 to 0, with 38 abstentions, had approved the text, proposed by Bulgaria, the Byelorussian SSR, Czechoslovakia and Mongolia, as orally amended by the United Kingdom.

---

[18]See Y.U.N., 1969, pp. 549-50, text of resolution 2583(XXIV); and Y.U.N., 1970, pp. 572-73, text of resolution 2712(XXV).

[19]See Y.U.N., 1968, pp. 608-10, resolution 2391(XXIII) of 26 November 1968, containing text of Convention.

Slavery and practices of
apartheid and colonialism

Two reports on the question of slavery and the slave trade in all their practices and manifestations, including *apartheid* and colonialism, were considered by the Commission on Human Rights and the Economic and Social Council in 1971. The first was a progress report submitted in 1970 by the Special Rapporteur of the Sub-Commission on Prevention of Discrimination and Protection of Minorities, Mohamed Awad, and the second was a report by the Secretary-General, submitted in accordance with Economic and Social Council decisions of 31 May 1968.[20]

The Human Rights Commission recommended to the Council adoption of a draft resolution on the subject which had originated with the Sub-Commission. This text as amended was adopted by the Council on 21 May 1971.

The Council thereby, among other things, expressed its appreciation to the Special Rapporteur for its valuable report and invited him to submit a final report containing his conclusions and recommendations to the Sub-Commission on Prevention of Discrimination and Protection of Minorities at its 1971 session, scheduled for August.

The Council invited the Special Rapporteur to elaborate in his final report on ways in which national and international work in the fields of narcotics control and the protection of refugees might be applied in order to secure the better implementation of existing international instruments relating to the suppression of slavery and slavery-like practices.

The Council requested the Secretary-General: (a) to urge those States which had not yet ratified the 1956 Supplementary Convention on the Abolition of Slavery, the Slave Trade, and Institutions and Practices Similar to Slavery to expedite their ratification procedures; (b) to extend his assistance to the States parties for the purpose of arranging for the exchange of information called for by the Supplementary Convention; and (c) to supplement such information by information from other official sources, and to present it to the Sub-Commission on Prevention of Discrimination and Protection of Minorities.

The Secretary-General was also requested to seek the co-operation of those organizations, both inter-governmental and non-governmental, which could provide assistance in particular in the eradication of slavery, the slave trade and other forms of servitude.

The Council took these actions in adopting, unanimously, resolution 1593(L), on the recommendation of its Social Committee.

(For text of resolution, see DOCUMENTARY REFERENCES below.)

The text, unanimously approved by the Social Committee on 19 May 1971, was based on the draft resolution recommended by the Commission on Human Rights, as amended by Greece and the United Kingdom.

The amendment added a new provision by which the Council invited the Special Rapporteur to elaborate on ways in which work in the fields of narcotics control and the protection of refugees might be applied to secure better implementation of international instruments relating to the suppression of slavery and slavery-like practices.

At its 1971 session, held from 2 to 20 August, the Sub-Commission on Prevention of Discrimination and Protection of Minorities considered the final report on the question of slavery and the slave trade submitted by its Special Rapporteur.

The Sub-Commission transmitted the report to the Commission on Human Rights for consideration at its 1972 session, with the request that the Commission transmit it to the Economic and Social Council and recommend to the Council the adoption of a draft resolution whereby the Council would, among other things, call upon States to enact legislation to prohibit slavery and the slave trade in all their practices and manifestations.

Trade union rights

During 1971, the *Ad Hoc* Working Group of Experts established by the Commission on Human Rights continued its investigation of infringements of trade union rights in South Africa, Namibia and Southern Rhodesia and considered certain labour matters relating to Angola and Mozambique. In its report to the Economic and Social Council, the Working Group reiterated the conclusions and recommendations of its 1969 and 1970 reports[21] and added the following new conclusions and recommendations.

With regard to South Africa, the Working Group expressed its concern that the measures against African labour contained in the Bantu Laws Amendment Act of 1970 were more restrictive than those of earlier legislation. It concluded that discrimination in the matter of wages existed between white and black workers, and that trade union leaders continued to be persecuted. It recommended that the International Labour Organisation (ILO) be invited to continue its efforts towards removing discrimination against African workers in South Africa.

The Working Group described as similar to slavery the method of recruitment of African workers in Namibia by the South West Africa

[20]See Y.U.N., 1968, pp. 602-3 and 578-79, texts of resolutions 1330(XLIV) and 1331(XLIV), respectively.
[21]See Y.U.N., 1969, pp. 534-35, and Y.U.N., 1970, p. 564.

Native Labour Association (SWANLA) under a system of labour contracts. It recommended that this recruitment system be thoroughly investigated and brought to the knowledge of world public opinion. It also recommended that in all collective labour negotiations in Namibia, African workers be represented by an African non-official and not by a South African official.

With regard to Southern Rhodesia, the Working Group concluded that a number of trade unionists continued to be detained, without trial, solely on account of their trade union activities. It considered that the Land Tenure Act of 1969 contained provisions which greatly hampered the activities of African trade unions in white areas. It also expressed the view that a system of job reservation discriminating against Africans had developed. The Working Group recommended that its report be brought to the attention of ILO and the Government of the United Kingdom—the administering power—and that, since the authorities of Southern Rhodesia appeared to have violated the International Convention on the Elimination of All Forms of Racial Discrimination,[22] ways should be studied of bringing the relevant facts to the attention of the Committee on the Elimination of Racial Discrimination.

Regarding the African territories administered by Portugal, the Working Group concluded that, among other things: African producers of primary products were often dispossessed by Portuguese colonists, subjected to discriminatory taxes and obliged by the State to sell their products at very low prices; unorganized labour governed by Portuguese law was reported to amount to forced labour; and the labour conditions imposed upon African workers from Angola and Mozambique who were employed in South Africa, Namibia and Southern Rhodesia were a matter of great concern.

The Working Group recommended that its report be transmitted to ILO, and that the Government of Portugal be called upon to discontinue the confiscation of African lands and the use of African workers as cheap manpower. It further recommended that the labour conditions of African workers from the Portuguese territories employed in South Africa and Southern Rhodesia be investigated with a view to determining the possible existence of forced labour.

On 21 May 1971, the Economic and Social Council endorsed the conclusions and recommendations of the Ad Hoc Working Group of Experts.

It condemned the repression and detention of trade union leaders in southern Africa and called for their immediate and unconditional release. It condemned also the treatment of African producers of primary products in the territories under Portuguese domination.

The Council called upon Portugal to stop immediately the confiscation of African lands, and called upon the United Kingdom to fulfil its responsibility to put an immediate end to discrimination and repression against African workers and trade unionists in Southern Rhodesia.

The International Labour Organisation was asked to continue its efforts to eliminate discrimination against African workers in southern Africa and to report on this question to the Council as soon as possible but no later than at its fifty-fourth (early 1973) session.

The Ad Hoc Working Group of Experts was also requested to report to the Council by early 1973 on its investigations of the recruitment system of African workers in Namibia, Southern Rhodesia and the territories under Portuguese domination.

The Secretary-General was asked to transmit this resolution and the Working Group's report to the General Assembly at its 1972 session, and to the Committee on the Elimination of Racial Discrimination.

These decisions by the Council were set forth in resolution 1599(L), which was adopted by a vote of 20 to 0, with 7 abstentions, as recommended by the Social Committee. On 19 May 1971, the Social Committee approved, by a vote of 19 to 0, with 8 abstentions, the text proposed by Ghana, Indonesia, Jamaica, Kenya, Malaysia, Sudan and Yugoslavia.

(For text of resolution, see DOCUMENTARY REFERENCES below.)

Also before the Economic and Social Council at its April-May 1971 session were two communications concerning the report of the Ad Hoc Working Group of Experts.

The first was a letter dated 30 April 1971 from the Chargé d'affaires of Portugal to the United Nations, addressed to the Secretary-General, denying certain assertions contained in the report and stating that the validity of the conclusions and recommendations concerning Angola and Mozambique was questionable and unacceptable, since the Working Group had a predetermined political aim which was implied in its mandate.

A second letter, dated 5 May 1971, from the Chairman/Rapporteur of the Ad Hoc Working Group of Experts and replying to the above letter, noted that Portugal had denied the Working Group entry into Mozambique and Angola, and that the Group's conclusions and recommendations were thus based on evidence received from witnesses who crossed borders in order to testify before the Group.

Subsequently, there was circulated as an official document of the Economic and Social Council a

---

[22]See Y.U.N., 1965, pp. 440-46, resolution 2106 A (XX) of 21 December 1965, containing text of International Convention.

letter of 28 May 1971 from the Chargé d'affaires of Portugal to the United Nations, addressed to the Secretary-General, with two annexes containing sections of the report of the Committee of Experts on the Application of Conventions and Recommendations, issued in 1971 by ILO. It was the conclusion of that Committee that in the light of the information on the situation in Angola and Mozambique which had become available as a result of direct contacts, there was no evidence from which it could be inferred that at the present time the legislative provisions which prohibited recourse to forced or compulsory labour and any form of coercion or improper pressure in connexion with the recruiting of workers were not being observed.

Creation of post of United Nations High Commissioner for Human Rights

A proposal to create the post of United Nations High Commissioner for Human Rights, originally made in 1965, was again before the Assembly in 1971.

On 18 December 1971, in view of the fact that there had not been sufficient time to conclude the study of the item at its 1971 session, the Assembly decided to consider the question again in 1973.

The Assembly took this action in plenary meeting by adopting resolution 2841(XXVI), by a recorded vote of 78 to 11, with 25 abstentions, on the recommendation of its Third (Social, Humanitarian and Cultural) Committee.

Prior to the plenary vote, the Assembly adopted a Sudanese amendment deferring consideration to 1973, rather than 1972, as called for in the text recommended by the Third Committee.

(For text of resolution, see DOCUMENTARY REFERENCES below.)

The text, approved by the Third Committee on 9 December 1971 by a recorded vote of 54 to 12, with 39 abstentions, was sponsored by 10 powers: Afghanistan, Canada, Costa Rica, Iran, Lesotho, Madagascar, the Netherlands, the Philippines, Sweden and Uruguay, as orally revised and amended.

An earlier draft resolution submitted in the Third Committee by the same 10 powers would have had the Assembly establish a United Nations High Commissioner's Office for Human Rights. Two draft resolutions submitted by Saudi Arabia would have called for a postponement of consideration of the question pending further studies regarding the advisability of creating the post and its long-term financial implications. No action was taken on these drafts.

Capital punishment

As requested by the General Assembly on 26 November 1968,[23] the Secretary-General submit-

ted to the Economic and Social Council at its April-May 1971 session a note summarizing data received from Member States with regard to capital punishment. The note augmented information provided in two earlier reports on capital punishment which covered developments to 1960, and from 1961 to 1965.

The note reviewed the legal safeguards provided in the reporting countries for persons liable to capital punishment for ordinary crimes, as well as for persons accused of offences against the State and certain other military and exceptional crimes. The note also listed changes that had taken place in the reporting States since 1965 in respect of the restriction of the use of, or the abolition of, the death penalty.

On 20 May 1971, the Council took the following decision, among others, concerning the question of capital punishment. It noted with satisfaction the measures already taken by a number of States to ensure the most careful legal procedures and the greatest possible safeguards for the accused in capital cases in countries where the death penalty still obtained; it considered that further efforts should be made by Member States to ensure the full and strict observance of the relevant principles contained in the Universal Declaration of Human Rights[24] and the International Covenant on Civil and Political Rights;[25] it affirmed the objective of progressively restricting the number of offences for which capital punishment might be imposed, with a view to the desirability of abolishing this punishment in all countries; and it invited Member States which had not yet done so to inform the Secretary-General of their attitude to possible further restriction of the use of the death penalty or to its total abolition.

These decisions were set forth in resolution 1574(L), which was adopted by a vote of 14 to 0, with 6 abstentions. The Council acted on the recommendation of its Social Committee, which approved the text on 28 April 1971 by a vote of 21 to 0, with 5 abstentions. The text was based on a draft submitted by Italy, Norway, the United Kingdom and Uruguay. Amendments put forth by the USSR were not pressed to a vote.

(For text of resolution, see DOCUMENTARY REFERENCES below.)

On 20 December 1971, the General Assembly reiterated the provisions contained in the Economic and Social Council resolution of 20 May 1971.

It also requested the Secretary-General, on the basis of material furnished by Governments of

[23]See Y.U.N., 1968, pp. 605-6, text of resolution 2393(XXIII).
[24]See Y.U.N., 1948-49, pp. 535-37, text of Universal Declaration of Human Rights.
[25]See Y.U.N., 1966, pp. 418-32, resolution 2200 A (XXI) of 16 December 1966, containing text of International Covenant on Economic, Social and Cultural Rights, International Covenant on Civil and Political Rights, and Optional Protocol to International Covenant on Civil and Political Rights.

Member States where capital punishment still existed, to report to the General Assembly on practices and statutory rules which might govern the right of a person sentenced to capital punishment to petition for pardon, commutation or reprieve.

These decisions were embodied in resolution 2857(XXVI), which was adopted by a recorded vote of 59 to 1, with 54 abstentions, on the recommendation of the Third (Social, Humanitarian and Cultural) Committee. The Committee approved, on 10 December 1971 by a recorded vote of 45 to 0, with 51 abstentions, the text sponsored by Austria, Costa Rica, Italy, the Netherlands, New Zealand, Norway, Sweden, the United Kingdom, Uruguay and Venezuela.

(For text of resolution, see DOCUMENTARY REFERENCES below.)

Education of youth in respect for human rights

The question of the education of youth in the respect for human rights and fundamental freedoms was discussed by the Human Rights Commission and by the General Assembly during 1971.

The Commission, among other things: urged Governments, organizations of the United Nations system and other interested bodies to devote attention to· the problems involved in educating youth in the respect for human rights; requested the Secretary-General to report to it regarding conscientious objection to military service; and requested the United Nations Educational, Scientific and Cultural Organization to seek information on the teaching of human rights in universities.

The General Assembly, in adopting resolution 2770(XXVI) on 22 November 1971, decided to consider no later than at its 1973 session the question of youth, its education in the respect for human rights and fundamental freedoms, its problems and needs, and its active participation in national development and international co-operation.

(For text of resolution 2770(XXVI), see pp. 378-79.)

International Covenants on Human Rights

The International Covenant on Economic, Social and Cultural Rights and the International Covenant on Civil and Political Rights (with Optional Protocol) were adopted by the General Assembly on 16 December 1966 and opened for signature, ratification and accession.[26]

Each Covenant was to enter into force three months after the date of deposit with the Secretary-General of the United Nations of the thirty-fifth instrument of ratification or accession. The Optional Protocol to the International Covenant on Civil and Political Rights was to enter into

force three months after the date of deposit with the Secretary-General of the tenth instrument of ratification or accession (subject to the entry into force of the Covenant).

As at 31 December 1971, 45 States had signed the International Covenant on Economic, Social and Cultural Rights and 44 had signed the International Covenant on Civil and Political Rights. Each Covenant had been ratified or acceded to by 12 States. The Optional Protocol had been signed by 16 States and ratified by 5.

On 6 December 1971, the General Assembly, in adopting, without vote, resolution 2788(XXVI), recommended that Member States give special attention to the possibilities of accelerating the process of ratification of the Covenants and the Optional Protocol. The Assembly requested the Secretary-General to report to it on the progress made in the matter.

The Assembly took this action on the recommendation of its Third (Social, Humanitarian and Cultural) Committee, which approved the text by acclamation on 26 November 1971, on a proposal by Bulgaria, Cyprus, the Libyan Arab Republic, Madagascar, the Syrian Arab Republic and Tunisia, as amended by Costa Rica, the Netherlands, Sweden and Uruguay.

(For text of resolution, see DOCUMENTARY REFERENCES below).

Human rights and scientific and technological developments

At its 1971 session, the Commission on Human Rights considered a preliminary report on human rights and scientific and technological developments, prepared by the Secretary-General at the request of the General Assembly.[27]

The Commission adopted a resolution by which, among other things, it: considered that each State should make use of scientific and technological developments to promote the exercise of human rights and fundamental freedoms; considered that problems of protecting human rights and fundamental freedoms in the context of scientific and technological progress should be tackled at the national and international levels; and recognized the need to concentrate attention on these problems during the Second United Nations Development Decade.

The Commission also: requested the Secretary-General to continue his study of the consequences, for the observance of human rights, of current developments in science and technology; requested Governments, the specialized agencies and the International Atomic Energy Agency, and other

---

[26]*Ibid.*
[27]See Y.U.N., 1968, pp. 615-16, text of resolution 2450(XXIII) of 19 December 1968.

inter-governmental and non-governmental organizations to provide the Secretary-General with reports, comments and observations on problems arising in connexion with the protection of human rights within the context of scientific and technological progress; requested the Secretary-General to submit to the Commission one or more reports which could be used as a basis for preparing international instruments designed to strengthen the protection of the human rights proclaimed in the Universal Declaration of Human Rights; and requested the Secretary-General to bring the resolution and the relevant documentation to the attention of the Preparatory Committee for the United Nations Conference on the Human Environment and of the Economic and Social Council, in connexion with efforts to ensure the success of the Second Development Decade.

The Commission decided to retain the question of human rights and technological developments as a standing item on its agenda.

The General Assembly, on 18 December 1971, decided to consider the question of human rights and technological developments at its 1972 session. This decision was one of several set forth in resolution 2844(XXVI), which was adopted by a vote of 114 to 0, as recommended by the Third (Social, Humanitarian and Cultural) Committee. The Committee approved the text to this effect, proposed by Nigeria and Sudan, on 10 December 1971, by a vote of 96 to 0.

(For text of resolution, see DOCUMENTARY REFERENCES below.)

Twenty-fifth anniversary of the Universal Declaration of Human Rights

At its 1971 session the General Assembly took note of the fact that Human Rights Day in 1973 would mark the twenty-fifth anniversary of the proclamation of the Universal Declaration of Human Rights, adopted by the Assembly on 10 December 1948.[28] The Assembly recalled that the United Nations had provided for special observances of previous anniversaries of the Universal Declaration, including the observance of the twentieth anniversary, in 1968, as the International Year for Human Rights, and expressed its desire to mark the twenty-fifth anniversary in a manner which would fit the occasion and serve the cause of human rights.

The Assembly decided to consider at its 1972 session the question of the preparation of an appropriate programme to observe the twenty-fifth anniversary of the Universal Declaration, and requested the Secretary-General to present to it at that time suggestions for suitable activities.

The Assembly took this action on 20 December

1971 in unanimously adopting resolution 2860(XXVI), as recommended by its Third (Social, Humanitarian and Cultural) Committee. The text was based on a proposal by Cyprus, Ghana, Nigeria, Norway, Senegal, Sierra . Leone and Zambia; it was approved unanimously by the Third Committee on 10 December 1971.

(For text of resolution, see DOCUMENTARY REFERENCES below.)

Realization of economic, social and cultural rights

By a decision of 6 June 1969,[29] the Economic and Social Council had confirmed the appointment by the Commission on Human Rights of a Special Rapporteur to prepare a comprehensive report on the realization of economic, social and cultural rights set forth in the Universal Declaration of Human Rights[30] and the International Covenant on Economic, Social and Cultural Rights,[31] taking particular account of the special problems of developing countries. The report was to be submitted to the Commission at its 1971 session.

Because the report was not completed, the Commission decided at its 1971 session to place this question, as a high-priority matter, on the agenda of its 1972 session.

On 21 May 1971, on the Commission's recommendation, the Economic and Social Council requested the Special Rapporteur, in preparing his study, to take into account the provisions of the 1969 Declaration on Social Progress and Development as well as the Assembly's resolution concerning implementation of that Declaration,[32] and to submit his final report to the Commission on Human Rights not later than at its twenty-eighth (1972) session.

These decisions by the Council were set forth in resolution 1595(L), which was adopted, unanimously, as recommended by the Social Committee. On 18 May 1971, the Social Committee unanimously approved a draft submitted by the Commission on Human Rights.

(For text of resolution, see DOCUMENTARY REFERENCES below.)

Periodic reports on human rights

At its 1971 session, the Commission on Human Rights continued consideration of periodic reports on human rights submitted by Governments and specialized agencies. The reports before the Commission dealt with economic, social and

[28]See footnote 24.
[29]See Y.U.N., 1969, pp. 553-54, text of resolution 1421(XLVI).
[30]See footnote 24.
[31]See footnote 25.
[32]See Y.U.N., 1969, pp. 433-38, resolution 2542(XXIV) of 11 December 1969, containing text of Declaration, and p. 438, text of resolution 2543(XXIV) of 11 December 1969.

cultural rights for the period 1 July 1966 to 30 June 1969 received subsequent to the 1970 session of the Commission's *Ad Hoc* Committee on Periodic Reports on Human Rights.

The Commission adopted a resolution by which, among other things, it: drew the attention of the Special Rapporteur on the question to these periodic reports; deplored the absence of information on the exercise of economic, social and cultural rights in some territories still under colonial rule; and emphasized that it was only through the timely submission of concise reports by Member States and specialized agencies, and objective information by non-governmental organizations, that the international community could appreciate the progress achieved and the problems to be overcome.

On 21 May 1971, the Economic and Social Council took note of the Commission's decisions. Recognizing that the number of reporting obligations imposed upon Member States made it difficult to prepare comprehensive periodic reports on human rights each year, the Council decided that Member States should be asked to submit periodic reports every two years in a continuing cycle: the first, on civil and political rights, to be submitted in 1972; the second, on economic, social and cultural rights, in 1974; and the third, on freedom of information, in 1976. Previously, in accordance with a schedule established by the Economic and Social Council in 1965,[33] the reports had been submitted annually in a continuing three-year cycle.

The Council also expressed the hope that an increasing number of Member States would report in the future, and observed that the reports could be of value only to the extent that they included detailed information on specific difficulties encountered and on practical measures applied, or assistance needed, to overcome them.

The Council took these decisions in adopting, unanimously, resolution 1596(L), as recommended by its Social Committee. On 18 May 1971, the Committee had approved unanimously a text proposed by Italy, Pakistan, the United Kingdom and Uruguay.

(For text of resolution, see DOCUMENTARY REFERENCES below.)

Freedom of information

On 18 December 1971, the General Assembly, bearing in mind the need for a full discussion of the question of freedom of information, decided to consider the item at its 1972 session. The Assembly took this decision, among others, in adopting resolution 2844(XXVI).

(For text of resolution, see DOCUMENTARY REFERENCES below, p. 444.)

Earlier, in adopting resolution 1596(L) on 21

May 1971, the Economic and Social Council had decided that Governments and specialized agencies should submit their periodic reports on freedom of information in 1971 and again in 1976.

(For text of resolution, see DOCUMENTARY REFERENCES below, p. 445.)

Communications on human rights

In accordance with procedures established by the Economic and Social Council, communications dealing with the principles involved in promoting respect for human rights are summarized in a non-confidential list submitted every year to the Commission on Human Rights.

Other communications concerning human rights are summarized in confidential lists, which are transmitted monthly to members of the Sub-Commission on Prevention of Discrimination and Protection of Minorities and annually to members of the Commission. Copies of the communications are sent to the Member States concerned, and replies from Governments are submitted to members of the Commission and the Sub-Commission. Allegations concerning infringements of trade union rights are forwarded to the International Labour Organisation. Information received concerning the plight of survivors of concentration camps who had been the victims of so-called scientific experiments during the nazi régime is sent to the Government of the Federal Republic of Germany.

The Secretary-General submitted non-confidential and confidential lists of communications to the Commission on Human Rights at its 1972 session, together with Government replies and a statistical summary of the confidential lists. The Commission did not consider the item.

(See also p. 419.)

Work programme of Human Rights Commission

At its April-May 1971 session, the Economic and Social Council considered the question of the rationalization of the work of the Commission on Human Rights.

A draft resolution on this subject was submitted in the Social Committee by France and the United Kingdom. By the draft, the Council would note that the Commission was expected to deal with numerous and complicated questions in an increasingly important field, that it was experiencing difficulty in giving proper consideration to all the items on its agenda and that this created a backlog detrimental to the effectiveness of its work.

The Council would then recommend that the Commission (1) take effective measures at its 1972

[33]See Y.U.N., 1965, pp. 487-88, text of resolution 1074C(XXXIX) of 28 July 1965.

session to prepare a work programme which would enable it at future sessions gradually to consider and dispose of the items which had accumulated on its agenda, and (2) endeavour in future to maintain a proper balance among the matters referred to it. The Secretary-General would be requested, when preparing the provisional agenda of the Commission, to combine items which could be considered simultaneously, except when a member of the Commission had expressly requested that an item be considered separately.

On 21 May 1971, the Council, on the recommendation of the Social Committee but without adopting a resolution, decided to transmit to the Commission on Human Rights the summary records of the discussions concerning the work programme of the Commission which took place in the Social Committee during discussion of the draft resolution.

DOCUMENTARY REFERENCES

Punishment of war criminals and persons committing crimes against humanity

E/4949. Report of Commission on Human Rights on its 27th session, 22 February–26 March 1971, Chapters X and XIX (resolution 16(XXVII)).

General Assembly—26th session
Third Committee, meeting 1902.
Plenary meeting 2025.

A/8345. Report of Secretary-General.
A/8401. Report of Secretary-General on work of the Organization, 16 June 1970–15 June 1971, Part Three, Chapter I A 7.
A/C.3/627. Communication of 30 June 1971 from Saudi Arabia.
A/C.3/L.1918: Bulgaria, Byelorussian SSR, Czechoslovakia, Mongolia: draft resolution, as orally amended by United Kingdom, approved by Third Committee on 9 December 1971, meeting 1902, by 42 votes to 0, with 38 abstentions.
A/8592. Report of Third Committee.

RESOLUTION 2840(XXVI), as recommended by Third Committee, A/8592, adopted by Assembly on 18 December 1971, meeting 2025, by 71 votes to 0, with 42 abstentions.

The General Assembly,
Recalling its resolutions 3(I) of 13 February 1946 and 170(II) of 31 October 1947 on the extradition and punishment of war criminals and its resolution 95(I) of 11 December 1946 affirming the principles of international law recognized by the Charter of the International Military Tribunal, Nuremberg, and the judgement of that Tribunal,
Recalling further its resolution 2712(XXV) of 15 December 1970 in which it condemned the war crimes and crimes against humanity at present being committed as a result of aggressive wars and the policies of racism, *apartheid* and colonialism,
Again noting with regret that the numerous decisions adopted by the United Nations on the question of the punishment of war criminals and of persons who have committed crimes against humanity are still not being fully complied with,
Recalling the Convention on the Non-Applicability of Statutory Limitations to War Crimes and Crimes against Humanity,
Convinced that the effective punishment of war crimes and crimes against humanity is an important element in putting an end to and preventing such crimes, in the protection of human rights and fundamental freedoms, in the strengthening of confidence and in promoting co-operation between peoples as well as peace and international security,
Expressing its deep concern at the fact that many war criminals and persons who have committed crimes against humanity are continuing to take refuge in the territories of certain States and are enjoying their protection,
Affirming that war crimes and crimes against humanity are among the most dangerous crimes under international law,
Firmly convinced of the need for international co-operation in the thorough investigation of war crimes and crimes against humanity, as defined in article I of the Convention on the Non-Applicability of Statutory Limitations to War Crimes and Crimes against Humanity, and in bringing about the detection,

arrest, extradition and punishment of all war criminals and persons guilty of crimes against humanity who have not yet been brought to trial or punished,
1. *Urges* all States to implement the relevant resolutions of the General Assembly and to take measures in accordance with international law to put an end to and prevent war crimes and crimes against humanity and to ensure the punishment of all persons guilty of such crimes, including their extradition to those countries where they have committed such crimes;
2. *Further urges* all States to co-operate in particular in the collection and exchange of information which will contribute to the detection, arrest, extradition, trial and punishment of persons guilty of war crimes and crimes against humanity;
3. *Again calls upon* all States which have not yet done so to become as soon as possible parties to the Convention on the Non-Applicability of Statutory Limitations to War Crimes and Crimes against Humanity;
4. *Affirms* that refusal by States to co-operate in the arrest, extradition, trial and punishment of persons guilty of war crimes and crimes against humanity is contrary to the purposes and principles of the Charter of the United Nations and to generally recognized norms of international law;
5. *Requests* the Commission on Human Rights to consider the principles of international co-operation in the detection, arrest, extradition and punishment of persons guilty of war crimes and crimes against humanity and to submit a report on this question to the General Assembly at its twenty-seventh session.

Slavery and practices of apartheid and colonialism

Economic and Social Council—50th session
Social Committee, meetings 669-680.
Plenary meeting 1771.

E/4949. Report of Commission on Human Rights on its 27th session, 22 February–26 March 1971, Chapters VIII and XIX (resolution 12(XXVII)).
E/4949, Chapter XX. Draft resolution VII, as submitted by Commission on Human Rights, and as amended by Greece and United Kingdom, E/AC.7/L.599, approved unanimously by Social Committee on 19 May 1971, meeting 680.
E/AC.7/L.599. Greece and United Kingdom: amendment to draft resolution VII recommended by Commission on Human Rights in E/4949.
E/5032. Report of Social Committee, draft resolution VII.

RESOLUTION 1593(L), as recommended by Social Committee, E/5032, adopted unanimously by Council on 21 May 1971, meeting 1771.

The Economic and Social Council,
Having considered the progress report on the question of slavery and the slave trade in all their practices and manifestations, including the slavery-like practices of *apartheid* and colonialism, submitted by the Special Rapporteur, Mr. Mohamed Awad,
Having noted the information on the same question presented by the Secretary-General in accordance with resolution 4(XXII) of

the Sub-Commission on Prevention of Discrimination and Protection of Minorities and resolution 1331(XLIV) of the Economic and Social Council of 31 May 1968,

1. *Expresses its appreciation* to Mr. Mohamed Awad for his valuable report;

2. *Invites* the Special Rapporteur to continue his important task, taking into account the exchange of views on his progress report during the twenty-third session of the Sub-Commission on Prevention of Discrimination and Protection of Minorities and the twenty-seventh session of the Commission on Human Rights, and to submit in his final report to the Sub-Commission at its twenty-fourth session his conclusions and recommendations, having regard to the urgent need for the proper implementation of the Supplementary Convention on the Abolition of Slavery, the Slave Trade, and Institutions and Practices Similar to Slavery, of 30 April 1956;

3. *Further invites* the Special Rapporteur to elaborate, in his final report, on his previous studies of ways in which national and international work in the fields of narcotics control and the protection of refugees may be applied in order to secure the better implementation of existing international instruments relating to the suppression of slavery and slavery-like practices;

4. *Requests* the Secretary-General once again to urge those States which have not yet ratified the Supplementary Convention of 1956 to expedite their ratification procedures;

5. *Requests* the Secretary-General to extend his assistance to the States parties for the purpose of arranging for the exchange of information called for by article 3, paragraph 3, of the Supplementary Convention of 1956;

6. *Authorizes* the Secretary-General to supplement the information received from States parties to that Convention by information which may be available from other official sources, including States that have not yet adhered to the Convention and the appropriate international organizations, and to present such information to the Sub-Commission on Prevention of Discrimination and Protection of Minorities;

7. *Requests* the Secretary-General to seek the co-operation of those organizations, both intergovernmental and non-governmental, which can provide assistance in particular in the eradication of slavery, the slave trade and other forms of servitude.

A/8401. Report of Secretary-General on work of the Organization, 16 June 1970–15 June 1971, Part Three, Chapter I A 5.

A/8403. Report of Economic and Social Council on work of its 50th and 51st sessions, Chapter XVII G.

E/CN.4/1070 and Corr.1. Report of 24th session of Sub-Commission on Prevention of Discrimination and Protection of Minorities, 2-20 August 1971, Chapters IV and XII (resolution 3(XXIV)).

Trade union rights

Economic and Social Council—50th session
Social Committee, meetings 669, 671-680.
Plenary meeting 1771.

E/4953. Report on trade union rights in southern Africa, submitted in accordance with Economic and Social Council resolution 1412(XLVI), by *Ad Hoc* Working Group of Experts established under resolution 2(XXIII) of Commission on Human Rights.

E/4956. Report of Secretary-General on publicity given to report of *Ad Hoc* Working Group of Experts (paragraph 9 of Council resolution 1509(XLVIII)).

E/L.1390. Letter of 30 April 1971 from Portugal to Secretary-General.

E/L.1396. Letter of 5 May 1971 from Chairman/Rapporteur of *Ad Hoc* Working Group of Experts to President of Economic and Social Council.

E/AC.7/L.598. Ghana, Indonesia, Jamaica, Kenya, Malaysia, Sudan, Yugoslavia: draft resolution, as orally revised by sponsors, approved by Social Committee on 19 May 1971, meeting 680, by 19 votes to 0, with 8 abstentions.

E/AC.7/L.602. New Zealand: amendment to 7-power draft resolution, E/AC.7/L.598.

E/5032. Report of Social Committee, draft resolution XIII.

RESOLUTION 1599(L), as recommended by Social Committee, E/5032, adopted by Council on 21 May 1971, meeting 1771, by 20 votes to 0, with 7 abstentions.

The Economic and Social Council,

Recalling its resolutions 1216(XLII) of 1 June 1967, 1302(XLIV) of 28 May 1968, 1412(XLVI) of 6 June 1969 and 1509(XLVIII) of 28 May 1970,

Having examined the report on trade union rights in southern Africa, submitted in accordance with Economic and Social Council resolution 1412(XLVI), by the *Ad Hoc* Working Group of Experts established under resolution 2(XXIII) of the Commission on Human Rights,

Gravely concerned at the continued suppression of trade union rights in South Africa, Namibia, Angola, Mozambique and Southern Rhodesia,

1. *Endorses* the conclusions and recommendations of the *Ad Hoc* Working Group of Experts,

2. *Strongly condemns* the repression and detention of trade union leaders in southern Africa and calls for their immediate and unconditional release;

3. *Condemns also* the treatment of African producers of primary products in the Territories under Portuguese domination;

4. *Calls upon* Portugal to stop immediately the confiscation of African lands;

5. *Calls upon* the Government of the United Kingdom of Great Britain and Northern Ireland to fulfil its responsibility to put an immediate end to discrimination and repression against African workers and trade unionists in Southern Rhodesia;

6. *Requests* the Secretary-General to bring the report of the *Ad Hoc* Working Group of Experts to the attention of the International Labour Organisation;

7. *Welcomes* the activities of the International Labour Organisation in this field and requests it to continue its efforts to bring to an end the discrimination against African workers in southern Africa and to submit the results of its endeavours to the Economic and Social Council as soon as possible but not later than at its fifty-fourth session;

8. *Requests* the *Ad Hoc* Working Group of Experts to investigate thoroughly the system of recruitment of African workers in Namibia, Southern Rhodesia and the Territories under Portuguese domination and to report to the Economic and Social Council as soon as possible but not later than at its fifty-fourth session;

9. *Requests* the Secretary-General to bring the present resolution and the report of the *Ad Hoc* Working Group of Experts to the attention of the Committee on the Elimination of Racial Discrimination;

10. *Requests* the Secretary-General to transmit the present resolution and the report of the *Ad Hoc* Working Group of Experts to the General Assembly at its twenty-sixth session.

A/8403. Report of Economic and Social Council on work of its 50th and 51st sessions, Chapter XVII M.

E/L.1403. Letter of 28 May 1971 from Portugal to Secretary-General.

Creation of post of United Nations High Commissioner for Human Rights

General Assembly—26th session
Third Committee, meetings 1899-1902.
Plenary meeting 2025.

A/8333. Report of Secretary-General. (Annex I: Economic and Social Council resolution 1237(XLII); Annex II: United Republic of Tanzania: amendments to Council resolution 1237(XLII).)

A/8401. Report of Secretary-General on work of the Organization, 16 June 1970–15 June 1971, Part Three, Chapter I A 15.

A/C.3/L.1851. Afghanistan, Canada, Costa Rica, Iran, Lesotho, Madagascar, Netherlands, Philippines, Sweden, Uruguay: draft resolution.

A/C.3/L.1852. Administrative and financial implications of Council resolution 1237(XLII) and amendments submitted thereto by United Republic of Tanzania in A/8333, annexes I and II. Report of Secretary-General.

A/C.3/L.1856. Saudi Arabia: draft resolution.

A/C.3/L.1857. Saudi Arabia: draft resolution.

A/C.3/L.1921. Afghanistan, Canada, Costa Rica, Iran, Lesotho, Madagascar, Netherlands, Philippines, Sweden, Uruguay: draft resolution, as orally revised by Committee, on proposal of Somalia, by roll-call vote of 43 to 37, with 26 abstentions), and as amended by Ghana and Nigeria (A/C.3/L.1923), approved by Third Committee on 9 December 1971, meeting 1901, by recorded vote of 54 to 12, with 39 abstentions, as follows:

In favour: Afghanistan, Argentina, Australia, Austria, Barbados, Belgium, Cameroon, Canada, Central African Republic, Chad, Colombia, Costa Rica, Cyprus, Denmark, Fiji, Finland, France, Greece, Guatemala, Guyana, Honduras, Iceland, Iran, Ireland, Israel, Italy, Ivory Coast, Japan, Khmer Republic, Laos, Lesotho, Liberia, Madagascar, Malta, Morocco, Netherlands, New Zealand, Nicaragua, Norway, Pakistan, Panama, Philippines, Singapore, Spain, Swaziland, Sweden, Uganda, United Kingdom, United States, Upper Volta, Uruguay, Venezuela, Zaire, Zambia.

Against: Bulgaria, Byelorussian SSR, Cuba, Czechoslovakia, Ethiopia, Hungary, Mongolia, Poland, Romania, Saudi Arabia, Ukrainian SSR, USSR.

Abstaining: Algeria, Brazil, Burma, Burundi, Chile, Congo, Dahomey, Ecuador, Egypt, Ghana, India, Indonesia, Iraq, Jamaica, Jordan, Kenya, Kuwait, Lebanon, Libyan Arab Republic, Malaysia, Mauritania, Mexico, Nepal, Nigeria, People's Democratic Republic of Yemen, Peru, Portugal, Rwanda, Senegal, Sierra Leone, Somalia, Sudan, Syrian Arab Republic, Togo, Tunisia, Turkey, United Republic of Tanzania, Yemen, Yugoslavia.

A/C.3/L.1923. Ghana and Nigeria: amendment to 10-power draft resolution, A/C.3/L.1921.

A/L.667. Sudan: amendment to draft resolution recommended by Third Committee in A/8594.

A/8594. Report of Third Committee.

RESOLUTION 2841(XXVI), as recommended by Third Committee, A/8594, as amended by Sudan, A/L.667, adopted by Assembly on 18 December 1971, meeting 2025, by recorded vote of 78 to 11, with 25 abstentions, as follows:

In favour: Afghanistan, Algeria, Argentina, Australia, Austria, Belgium, Burundi, Canada, Central African Republic, Congo, Costa Rica, Cyprus, Denmark, Dominican Republic, Ecuador, Equatorial Guinea, Ethiopia, Fiji, Finland, France, Gambia, Greece, Guatemala, Guinea, Honduras, India, Indonesia, Iran, Ireland, Israel, Italy, Ivory Coast, Japan, Jordan, Kenya, Khmer Republic, Laos, Lebanon, Liberia, Libyan Arab Republic, Luxembourg, Madagascar, Malawi, Mali, Malta, Mauritania, Mexico, Morocco, Netherlands, New Zealand, Nicaragua, Niger, Nigeria, Norway, Pakistan, Panama, People's Democratic Republic of Yemen, Philippines, Qatar, Sierra Leone, Singapore, Spain, Sudan, Swaziland, Sweden, Syrian Arab Republic, Trinidad and Tobago, Uganda, United Arab Emirates, United Kingdom, United Republic of Tanzania, United States, Upper Volta, Uruguay, Venezuela, Yemen, Zaire, Zambia.

Against: Bulgaria, Byelorussian SSR, Cuba, Czechoslovakia, Hungary, Mongolia, Poland, Romania, Saudi Arabia, Ukrainian SSR, USSR.

Abstaining: Bahrain, Botswana, Brazil, Burma, Cameroon, Chile, Colombia, Egypt, El Salvador, Gabon, Haiti, Jamaica, Kuwait, Malaysia, Nepal, Peru, Portugal, Rwanda, Senegal, Somalia, Thailand, Togo, Tunisia, Turkey, Yugoslavia.

The General Assembly,

Recalling its resolutions 2062(XX) of 16 December 1965, 2333(XXII) of 18 December 1967, 2437(XXIII) of 19 December 1968 and 2595(XXIV) of 16 December 1969 concerning the creation of the post of United Nations High Commissioner for Human Rights,

Taking note of Economic and Social Council resolution 1237(XLII) of 6 June 1967 on the creation of an Office of the United Nations High Commissioner for Human Rights, and of Council resolution 1238(XLII) of 6 June 1967 concerning the implementation of human rights through a United Nations High Commissioner for Human Rights or some other appropriate international machinery,

Taking further note of the views expressed in the general debate on this question and of the draft resolution submitted to the Third Committee for consideration during the current session,

Considering that there was not sufficient time during its twenty-sixth session to conclude the study of this item,

1. *Decides* to give consideration to this item at its twenty-eighth session;

2. *Requests* the Secretary-General to transmit to the General Assembly at its twenty-eighth session the documentation pertaining to the study of this question.

Capital punishment

Economic and Social Council—50th session
Social Committee, meetings 648-651.
Plenary meeting 1769.

E/4947 and Corr.1 and Add.1. Note by Secretary-General.

E/L.1378. Letter of 31 March 1971 from Austria.

E/AC.7/L.578. Italy, Norway, United Kingdom, Uruguay: draft resolution, as orally revised by sponsors, approved by Social Committee on 28 April 1971, meeting 651, by 21 votes to 0, with 5 abstentions.

E/AC.7/L.579. USSR: amendment to 4-power draft resolution, E/AC.7/L.578.

E/4993 and Corr.1. Report of Social Committee.

RESOLUTION 1574(L), as recommended by Social Committee, E/4993, adopted by Council on 20 May 1971, meeting 1769, by 14 votes to 0, with 6 abstentions.

The Economic and Social Council,

Having examined the report submitted by the Secretary-General in accordance with paragraph 3 of General Assembly resolution 2393(XXIII) of 26 November 1968,

1. *Takes note with satisfaction* of the measures already taken by a number of States in order to ensure the most careful legal procedures and the greatest possible safeguards for the accused in capital cases in countries where the death penalty still obtains;

2. *Considers* that further efforts should be made by Member States to ensure the full and strict observance anywhere of the principles contained in articles 5, 10 and 11 of the Universal Declaration of Human Rights, reaffirmed by articles 7, 14 and 15 of the International Covenant on Civil and Political Rights, and in particular of the principles that no one shall be subjected to torture or to cruel, inhuman or degrading treatment or punishment, that everyone is entitled to a fair and public hearing by an independent and impartial tribunal, that everyone charged with a penal offence has the right to be presumed innocent until proved guilty by a final sentence, and that every accused has the right to enjoy all the guarantees necessary for his defence;

3. *Affirms* that the main objective to be pursued is that of progressively restricting the number of offences for which capital punishment might be imposed with a view to the desirability of abolishing this punishment in all countries so that the right to life, provided for in article 3 of the Universal Declaration of Human Rights, may be fully guaranteed;

4. *Invites* Member States which have not yet done so to inform the Secretary-General of their attitude to possible further restriction of the use of the death penalty or to its total abolition, by providing the information requested in paragraph 2 of General Assembly resolution 2393(XXIII);

5. *Requests* the Secretary-General to circulate as soon as

possible to Member States all the replies to the queries contained in paragraphs 1 and 2 of General Assembly resolution 2393(XXIII) submitted by Member States either before or after the adoption of the present resolution.

General Assembly—26th session
Third Committee, meeting 1905.
Plenary meeting 2027.

A/8403. Report of Economic and Social Council on work of its 50th and 51st sessions, Chapter XVIII C.
A/C.3/L.1908. Austria, Costa Rica, Italy, Netherlands, New Zealand, Norway, Sweden, United Kingdom, Uruguay, Venezuela: draft resolution, as orally revised by sponsors, approved by Third Committee on 10 December 1971, meeting 1905, by recorded vote of 45 to 0, with 51 abstentions, as follows:

In favour: Australia, Austria, Belgium, Bulgaria, Byelorussian SSR, Canada, Colombia, Costa Rica, Cyprus, Czechoslovakia, Denmark, Ecuador, Ethiopia, Finland, France, Ghana, Greece, Guatemala, Honduras, Hungary, Iceland, India, Ireland, Israel, Italy, Ivory Coast, Laos, Luxembourg, Madagascar, Mongolia, Netherlands, New Zealand, Nicaragua, Norway, Philippines, Poland, Portugal, Spain, Sweden, Ukrainian SSR, USSR, United Kingdom, Uruguay, Venezuela, Yugoslavia.
Against: None.
Abstaining: Afghanistan, Algeria, Argentina, Bahrain, Barbados, Brazil, Burma, Burundi, Cameroon, Central African Republic, Chile, Dahomey, Egypt, Equatorial Guinea, Guinea, Guyana, Indonesia, Iran, Iraq, Jamaica, Japan, Kenya, Kuwait, Lebanon, Liberia, Libyan Arab Republic, Malaysia, Mali, Mauritania, Mexico, Morocco, Nepal, Nigeria, People's Democratic Republic of Yemen, Peru, Rwanda, Saudi Arabia, Senegal, Sierra Leone, Singapore, Somalia, Sudan, Swaziland, Syrian Arab Republic, Togo, Tunisia, Turkey, Uganda, United Republic of Tanzania, United States, Yemen.

A/8588. Report of Third Committee (on report of Economic and Social Council), draft resolution III.

RESOLUTION 2857(XXVI), as recommended by Third Committee, A/8588, adopted by Assembly on 20 December 1971, meeting 2027, by recorded vote of 59 to 1, with 54 abstentions, as follows:

In favour: Austria, Belgium, Bulgaria, Byelorussian SSR, Canada, Central African Republic, Chad, Colombia, Costa Rica, Cyprus, Czechoslovakia, Denmark, Ecuador, Ethiopia, Finland, France, Ghana, Greece, Guatemala, Honduras, Hungary, Iceland, India, Ireland, Israel, Italy, Ivory Coast, Laos, Luxembourg, Madagascar, Malta, Nepal, Netherlands, New Zealand, Nicaragua, Niger, Nigeria, Norway, Pakistan, Panama, Paraguay, Philippines, Poland, Portugal, Romania, Senegal, Singapore, Somalia, Spain, Sweden, Togo, Ukrainian SSR, USSR, United Arab Emirates, United Kingdom, Upper Volta, Uruguay, Venezuela, Yugoslavia.
Against: Saudi Arabia.
Abstaining: Afghanistan, Algeria, Argentina, Australia, Bahrain, Barbados, Bolivia, Botswana, Brazil, Burma, Burundi, Cameroon, Ceylon, Chile, Congo, Dahomey, Dominican Republic, El Salvador, Equatorial Guinea, Guinea, Guyana, Haiti, Indonesia, Iran, Jamaica, Japan, Kenya, Kuwait, Lesotho, Liberia, Libyan Arab Republic, Malaysia, Mali, Mauritania, Mexico, Morocco, People's Democratic Republic of Yemen, Peru, Qatar, Rwanda, Sierra Leone, Sudan, Swaziland, Syrian Arab Republic, Thailand, Trinidad and Tobago, Tunisia, Turkey, Uganda, United Republic of Tanzania, United States, Yemen, Zaire, Zambia.

The General Assembly,
Recalling its resolution 2393(XXIII) of 26 November 1968 concerning the application of the most careful legal procedures and the greatest possible safeguards for the accused in capital

cases as well as the attitude of Member States to possible further restriction of the use of capital punishment or to its total abolition,
Taking note of the section of the report of the Economic and Social Council concerning the consideration by the Council of the report on capital punishment submitted by the Secretary-General in implementation of the aforementioned resolution,
Expressing the desirability of continuing and extending the consideration of the question of capital punishment by the United Nations,
1. *Notes with satisfaction* the measures already taken by a number of States in order to ensure careful legal procedures and safeguards for the accused in capital cases in countries where the death penalty still exists;
2. *Considers* that further efforts should be made to ensure such procedures and safeguards in capital cases everywhere;
3. *Affirms* that, in order fully to guarantee the right to life, provided for in article 3 of the Universal Declaration of Human Rights, the main objective to be pursued is that of progressively restricting the number of offences for which capital punishment may be imposed, with a view to the desirability of abolishing this punishment in all countries;
4. *Invites* Member States which have not yet done so to inform the Secretary-General of their legal procedures and safeguards as well as of their attitude to possible further restriction of the use of the death penalty or its total abolition, by providing the information requested in paragraphs 1 (c) and 2 of General Assembly resolution 2393(XXIII);
5. *Requests* the Secretary-General to circulate as soon as possible to Member States all the replies already received from Member States to the queries contained in paragraphs 1 (c) and 2 of resolution 2393(XXIII) and those to be received after the adoption of the present resolution, and to submit a supplementary report to the Economic and Social Council at its fifty-second session;
6. *Further requests* the Secretary-General, on the basis of material furnished in accordance with paragraph 4 above by Governments of Member States where capital punishment still exists, to prepare a separate report regarding practices and statutory rules which may govern the right of a person sentenced to capital punishment to petition for pardon, commutation or reprieve, and to submit that report to the General Assembly.

Education of youth in respect for human rights
E/4949. Report of Commission on Human Rights on its 27th session, 22 February–26 March 1971, Chapters VI and XIX (resolutions 11 A-C (XXVII)).

RESOLUTION 2770(XXVI), as recommended by Third Committee (A/8507, draft resolution I), adopted by Assembly on 22 November 1971, meeting 1991, by recorded vote of 91 to 0.

[For text of resolution, relevant meetings, recorded vote and supporting documentation, see pp. 378-79.]

International Covenants on Human Rights

General Assembly—26th session
Third Committee, meetings 1869, 1884, 1885.
Plenary meeting 2001.

A/8390. Status of International Covenant on Economic, Social and Cultural Rights, International Covenant on Civil and Political Rights and Optional Protocol to International Covenant on Civil and Political Rights. Report of Secretary-General.
A/8401. Report of Secretary-General on work of the Organization, 16 June 1970–15 June 1971, Part Three, Chapter I A 9.
A/C.3/L.1894. Bulgaria, Cyprus, Libyan Arab Republic, Madagascar, Syrian Arab Republic, Tunisia: draft resolution, as amended by 4 powers, A/C.3/L.1898, approved by acclamation by Third Committee on 26 November 1971, meeting 1885.
A/C.3/L.1898. Costa Rica, Netherlands, Sweden, Uruguay: amendments to 6-power draft resolution, A/C.3/L.1894.
A/8546. Report of Third Committee.

RESOLUTION 2788(XXVI), as recommended by Third Committee, A/8546, adopted without vote by Assembly on 6 December 1971, meeting 2001.

The General Assembly,

Having noted the report of the Secretary-General on the status of the International Covenant on Economic, Social and Cultural Rights, the International Covenant on Civil and Political Rights and the Optional Protocol to the International Covenant on Civil and Political Rights,

Firmly believing that the entry into force of the International Covenants on Human Rights and the Optional Protocol will greatly enhance the ability of the United Nations to promote and encourage respect for human rights and fundamental freedoms for all, without distinction as to race, sex, language or religion, and will contribute to the attainment of the purposes and principles of the Charter of the United Nations,

Desirous of making all possible efforts that may be appropriate to assist in hastening the process of ratification and, if possible, in bringing into force those instruments by the twenty-fifth anniversary of the proclamation of the Universal Declaration of Human Rights, in 1973,

1. *Recommends* that Member States should give special attention to possibilities of accelerating as far as possible the internal procedures that would lead to the ratification of the International Covenant on Economic, Social and Cultural Rights, the International Covenant on Civil and Political Rights and the Optional Protocol to the International Covenant on Civil and Political Rights;

2. *Requests* the Secretary-General on the basis of communications from Governments, to report to the General Assembly at its twenty-seventh session and at such other times as he may consider appropriate on the progress of the ratification of the Covenants and the Optional Protocol.

Human rights and scientific and technological developments

E/4949. Report of Commission on Human Rights on its 27th session, 22 February–26 March 1971, Chapters V and XIX (resolution 10(XXVII)).

General Assembly—26th session
Third Committee, meeting 1905.
Plenary meeting 2025.

A/8339. Report of Secretary-General.
A/8401. Report of Secretary-General on work of the Organization, 16 June 1970–15 June 1971, Part Three, Chapter I A 14.
A/C.3/L.1925. Nigeria and Sudan: draft resolution, approved by Third Committee on 10 December 1971, meeting 1905, by 96 votes to 0.
A/8590. Report of Third Committee.

RESOLUTION 2844(XXVI), as recommended by Third Committee, A/8590, adopted by Assembly on 18 December 1971, meeting 2025, by 114 votes to 0.

The General Assembly,

Considering that there is not enough time for the consideration of all the items on the agenda of the Third Committee,

Bearing in mind the need for a full discussion of all the items,

Decides to consider at its twenty-seventh session the items entitled "Freedom of information," "Human rights and scientific and technological developments" and "Elimination of all forms of religious intolerance."

Twenty-fifth anniversary of the Universal Declaration of Human Rights

General Assembly—26th session
Third Committee, meeting 1905.
Plenary meeting 2027.

A/C.3/L.1926. Cyprus, Ghana, Nigeria, Norway, Senegal, Sierra Leone, Zambia: draft resolution, as orally amended by sponsors, approved unanimously by Third Committee on 10 December 1971, meeting 1905.
A/8588. Report of Third Committee (on report of Economic and Social Council), draft resolution VI.

RESOLUTION 2860(XXVI), as recommended by Third Committee, A/8588, adopted unanimously by Assembly on 20 December 1971, meeting 2027.

The General Assembly,

Noting that Human Rights Day in 1973 will mark the twenty-fifth anniversary of the adoption and proclamation by the General Assembly of the Universal Declaration of Human Rights,

Convinced of the historic significance and enduring value of the Universal Declaration as a common standard of achievement for all peoples and all nations,

Recalling that the United Nations provided for special observances of the tenth, fifteenth and twentieth anniversaries of the Universal Declaration, including the observance of the twentieth anniversary, in 1968, as the International Year for Human Rights,

Desiring to mark, in 1973, the twenty-fifth anniversary of the Universal Declaration in a manner which would fit the occasion and serve the cause of human rights,

1. *Decides* to consider at its twenty-seventh session the question of the preparation of an appropriate programme to observe the twenty-fifth anniversary of the Universal Declaration of Human Rights;

2. *Requests* the Secretary-General to present, for consideration by the General Assembly at its twenty-seventh session, such suggestions as he may consider appropriate concerning suitable activities which could be undertaken in celebration of the twenty-fifth anniversary of the Universal Declaration.

Realization of economic, social and cultural rights

Economic and Social Council—50th session
Social Committee, meetings 669-678.
Plenary meeting 1771.

E/4949. Report of Commission on Human Rights on its 27th session, 22 February–26 March 1971, Chapters XI and XIX (resolution 17(XXVII)).
E/4949, Chapter XX. Draft resolution IX, as submitted by Commission on Human Rights, approved unanimously by Social Committee on 18 May 1971, meeting 678.
E/5032. Report of Social Committee, draft resolution IX.

RESOLUTION 1595(L), as recommended by Social Committee, E/5032, adopted unanimously by Council on 21 May 1971, meeting 1771.

The Economic and Social Council,

Recalling its resolutions 1421(XLVI) of 6 June 1969 and 1502(XLVIII) of 27 May 1970,

1. *Draws attention* to the fact that, since the adoption of resolution 1421(XLVI) by the Council, the, General Assembly has adopted on 11 December 1969 resolution 2542(XXIV) containing the Declaration on Social Progress and Development and resolution 2543(XXIV) on the implementation of that Declaration;

2. *Requests* the Special Rapporteur while preparing his study to take into account the provisions of the above-mentioned resolutions and to submit his final report to the Commission on Human Rights not later than at its twenty-eighth session, in 1972.

A/8401. Report of Secretary-General on work of the Organization, 16 June 1970–15 June 1971, Part Three, Chapter I A 12.
A/8403. Report of Economic and Social Council on work of its 50th and 51st sessions, Chapter XVII I.

Periodic reports on human rights

Economic and Social Council—50th session
Social Committee, meetings 669-678.
Plenary meeting 1771.

E/4949. Report of Commission on Human Rights on its 27th session, 22 February–26 March 1971, Chapters XII and XIX (resolution 18(XXVII)).
E/AC.7/L.596 and Rev.1. Italy, Pakistan, United Kingdom, Uruguay: draft resolution and revision, approved unanimously by Social Committee on 18 May 1971, meeting 678.
E/5032. Report of Social Committee, draft resolution X.

RESOLUTION 1596(L), as recommended by Social Committee, E/5032, adopted unanimously by Council on 21 May 1971, meeting 1771.

The Economic and Social Council,
Bearing in mind section III of its resolution 1458(XLVII) of 8 August 1969 concerning requests for information from Member States regarding the United Nations programme in the field of human rights,
Recalling its resolution 1074 C (XXXIX) of 28 July 1965 concerning periodic reports on human rights and reports on freedom of information,
Noting resolution 18(XXVII) of the Commission on Human Rights,
Believing that it is only through the timely submission of concise reports by Member States and specialized agencies and objective information by non-governmental organizations in consultative status that the international community can appreciate both the progress achieved and problems still to be overcome,
Believing also that the value of these reports rests on their being submitted by as many Member States as possible,
Recognizing that the number of reporting obligations imposed upon Member States may make more difficult the preparation of comprehensive periodic reports on human rights each year,
1. *Decides* that, without prejudice to the submission of reports on freedom of information in 1971 and with effect from the date of the present resolution, Member States shall be asked to submit periodic reports once every two years in a continuing cycle: the first, on civil and political rights, to be submitted in 1972; the second, on economic, social and cultural rights, in 1974; the third, on freedom of information, in 1976;
2. *Expresses the hope* that an increasing number of Member States will report in the future;
3. *Invites* Member States, in submitting their periodic reports, to follow closely the outline of headings for the reports sent to them by the Secretary-General and to pay greater attention to the guidelines contained in paragraph 1 of resolution 16 B (XXIII) of the Commission on Human Rights, which was adopted unanimously on 22 March 1967;
4. *Considers* in particular that the assessment of progress and problems in the promotion and protection of human rights by the Commission on Human Rights and its *Ad Hoc* Committee on Periodic Reports on Human Rights can be of practical value only to the extent that Governments include in their reports detailed information concerning specific difficulties encountered, practical measures or methods applied or assistance needed to overcome them.

A/8401. Report of Secretary-General on work of the Organization, 16 June 1970–15 June 1971, Part Three, Chapter I A 11.
A/8403. Report of Economic and Social Council on work of its 50th and 51st sessions, Chapter XVII J.

Freedom of information

Economic and Social Council—50th session
Social Committee, meetings 669-678.
Plenary meeting 1771.

RESOLUTION 1596(L), as recommended by Social Committee (E/5032, draft resolution X), adopted unanimously by Council on 21 May 1971, meeting 1771.

[For text of resolution and supporting documentation, see section above on PERIODIC REPORTS ON HUMAN RIGHTS.]

General Assembly—26th session
Third Committee, meeting 1905.
Plenary meeting 2025.

A/8340. Note by Secretary-General.
A/8401. Report of Secretary-General on work of the Organization, 16 June 1970–15 June 1971, Part Three, Chapter I A 16.
A/8403. Report of Economic and Social Council on work of its 50th and 51st sessions, Chapter XVII J.
A/C.3/L.1925. Nigeria and Sudan: draft resolution, approved by Third Committee on 10 December 1971, meeting 1905, by 96 votes to 0.
A/8590. Report of Third Committee.

RESOLUTION 2844(XXVI), as recommended by Third Committee, A/8590, adopted by Assembly on 18 December 1971, meeting 2025, by 114 votes to 0.

[For text of resolution, see section above on HUMAN RIGHTS AND SCIENTIFIC AND TECHNOLOGICAL DEVELOPMENTS.]

Communications on human rights

A/8401. Report of Secretary-General on work of the Organization, 16 June 1970–15 June 1971, Part Three, Chapter I A 17.
E/4949. Report of Commission on Human Rights on its 27th session, 22 February–26 March 1971, Chapter XVII.
E/CN.4/1070 and Corr.1. Report of Sub-Commission on Prevention of Discrimination and Protection of Minorities on its 24th session, 2–20 August 1971, Chapter V.

Studies of specific rights or groups of rights

E/4949. Report of Commission on Human Rights on its 27th session, 22 February–26 March 1971, Chapters XIII and XIX B (Other decisions, p. 96, sub-paras. (a), (c) and (d)).
E/4949/Add.1. Financial implications of resolutions adopted by Commission on Human Rights at its 27th session (decisions taken at 1136th meeting of Commission).

Genocide

E/CN.4/1070 and Corr.1. Report of Sub-Commission on Prevention of Discrimination and Protection of Minorities on its 24th session, 2–20 August 1971, Chapters VIII and XII (resolution 7(XXIV)).

Work programme of Human Rights Commission

Economic and Social Council—50th session
Social Committee, meetings 679, 680.
Plenary meeting 1771.

E/4949. Report of Commission on Human Rights on its 27th session, Chapter XIX B (Other decisions, p. 96, sub-paragraph (b)).
E/AC.7/L.601. France and United Kingdom: draft resolution.
E/5032. Report of Social Committee, paras. 34-36.
E/5044. Resolutions adopted by Economic and Social Council during its 50th session, 11-13 January and 26 April–21 May 1971. Decision, p. 22.
A/8403. Report of Economic and Social Council on work of its 50th and 51st sessions, Chapter XVII K.

Report of Human Rights Commission

Economic and Social Council—50th session
Social Committee, meetings 669-680.
Plenary meeting 1771.

E/4949. Report of Commission on Human Rights on its 27th session, Geneva, Switzerland, 22 February–26 March 1971. (Annex III: List of documents before Commission at its 27th session.)

E/4949, Chapter XX. Draft resolution X, submitted by Commission on Human Rights, approved unanimously by Social Committee on 19 May 1971, meeting 680.

E/4949/Summary. Summary of report of Commission on Human Rights on its 27th session.

E/4949/Add.1. Financial implications of resolutions adopted by Commission on Human Rights at its 27th session.

E/5032. Report of Social Committee, draft resolution XII.

RESOLUTION 1598(L), as recommended by Social Committee, E/5032, taking note of report of Commission on Human Rights

on its 27th session. adopted unanimously by Council on 21 May 1971, meeting 1771.

Other documents

Yearbook on Human Rights for 1969. U.N.P. Sales No: E.72.XIV.1.

A/8401. Report of Secretary-General on work of the Organization, 16 June 1970–15 June 1971, Part Three, Chapter I.

A/8401/Add.1. Introduction to report of Secretary-General, September 1971, Part Two, Chapter VI.

A/8403. Report of Economic and Social Council on work of its 50th and 51st sessions, Chapter XVII.

A/INF/147. Human Rights Day: observance of 22nd anniversary of adoption of Universal Declaration of Human Rights. Report of Secretary-General.

Chapter XXI

Consultative arrangements with non-governmental organizations

During 1971, the Committee on Non-Governmental Organizations of the Economic and Social Council undertook its annual consideration of applications and re-applications for consultative status as well as requests for reclassification received from non-governmental organizations (NGOs).

In October 1971, the Economic and Social Council instructed its Committee on Non-Governmental Organizations to study how NGOs could help in the achievement of the objectives of the Declaration on the Granting of Independence to Colonial Countries and Peoples. The General Assembly, in December 1971, asked its Special Committee on the implementation of the Declaration to assist in the study. (See pp. 519-20 and 525-26.) The Assembly also asked its Special Committee to study, in particular, the efforts being made by NGOs to acquaint world public opinion with the role of foreign economic and other interests in impeding the implementation of the Declaration. (See pp. 532-33.)

By a decision taken in May 1971, the Council recommended that the Assembly request NGOs, among other bodies, to consider measures that might be taken with a view to speedily eliminating racial discrimination throughout the world. (See pp. 411-12.)

The Council, at its fiftieth session, held from 26 April to 21 May 1971, considered the report of its Committee on Non-Governmental Organizations, which contained recommendations on the categorization of various organizations.

At the end of 1971, there were 469 NGOs that the Economic and Social Council could consult on questions relative to those organizations.

In accordance with the criteria set forth in a Council decision of 23 May 1968,[1] those NGOs were divided into three groups.

In Category I were organizations that were concerned with most of the activities of the Council and could demonstrate to the satisfaction of the Council: that they had marked and sustained contributions to make to the achievements of the United Nations in the social, cultural, educational, health, scientific, technological and human rights fields; that they were closely involved with the economic and social life of the peoples of the areas they represented; and that their membership was broadly representative of major segments of population in a large number of countries.

In Category II were organizations that had a special competence in, and were concerned specifically with, only a few of the fields of activity covered by the Council and that were known internationally within the fields for which they had consultative status.

On the Roster were organizations that the Council, or the Secretary-General, in consultation with the Council or its Committee on Non-Governmental Organizations, considered could make occasional and useful contributions to the work of the Council or other United Nations bodies, within their competence.

At the end of 1971, there were 16 NGOs with Category I status, 157 with Category II status and 296 on the Roster.

Organizations in Categories I and II may send

---

[1]See Y.U.N., 1968, pp. 647-52, text of resolution 1296(XLIV).

observers to public meetings of the Council and its subsidiary bodies. Those on the Roster may have representatives present at those of the public meetings which are concerned with matters within their fields of competence.

Organizations in Categories I and II may submit for circulation written statements relevant to the work of the Council on subjects in which these organizations have a special competence. The Secretary-General, in consultation with the President of the Council, or the Council or its Committee on Non-Governmental Organizations, may invite organizations on the Roster to submit written statements.

Category I organizations may present their views orally and also propose items for possible inclusion in the Council's provisional agenda. Such proposals must first be submitted to the Council's Committee on Non-Governmental Organizations for subsequent action by the Secretary-General. Category I organizations, however, may propose items directly for the provisional agendas of the Council's commissions.

In addition, all three groups of NGOs may consult with the United Nations Secretariat on matters of mutual concern.

At its April-May 1971 session, the Council also considered the question of a special arrangement for co-operation between the United Nations and the International Criminal Police Organization (INTERPOL).

The Council at the same session also took up the question of the contribution of NGOs to the International Development Strategy for the Second United Nations Development Decade.

Details of these and related matters are discussed in the sections that follow.

Contribution of NGOs to International Development Strategy

On 20 May 1971, the Economic and Social Council emphasized the need for NGOs in consultative status with the Council and active primarily in the field of economic and social development to endeavour to develop more meaningful and productive relationships with the Council, enabling them to contribute effectively towards the implementation of the International Development Strategy for the Second Development Decade.[2]

The Council requested its Committee on Non-Governmental Organizations to examine the contributions to development already made or being planned by NGOs active in the field of economic and social development; and asked the Committee to submit recommendations on improving the contributions of those NGOs towards the implementation of the Strategy.

These decisions were embodied in resolution 1580(L), which the Council adopted, unanimously,

on the recommendation of its Social Committee. The Committee approved the text unanimously on 29 April 1971, on the basis of a proposal by Brazil, Ghana, Pakistan and Sudan. (For text, see DOCUMENTARY REFERENCES below.)

Review of NGOs granted consultative status

On 20 May 1971, the Council approved the report of its Committee on Non-Governmental Organizations containing recommendations on the granting of consultative status to NGOs. It took a series of decisions on the recommendations and on proposals by Council members, without adopting resolutions.

Granting of consultative status

On 20 May 1971, the Council decided to place the World Council for the Welfare of the Blind in Category II. (This organization claimed to have had a valid or technical reason for not having replied to the questionnaire of the Committee on Non-Governmental Organizations during the Committee's review.)

It decided to place in Category II or on the Roster the following NGOs that had been put on the Roster by the Secretary-General as an interim measure: the Union of International Associations and St. Joan's International Alliance, placed in Category II; the International Association of Gerontology and the International Real Estate Federation, placed on the Roster.

The Council decided to place the following organizations, which had newly applied for consultative status, in Category II:

Arab Lawyers Union
European League for Economic Co-operation
International Association of Lawyers
International Association for Water Law
International Defence and Aid Fund for Southern Africa
Pan American Federation of Engineering Societies (UPADI)
Société internationale de prophylaxie criminelle
World Federation for the Protection of Animals.

The Council decided to place the following organizations, which had newly applied, on the Roster:

Asian Development Center
International Federation of Operational Research Societies
International Organization of Experts (ORDINEX)
International Union of Police Federations
International Union of Social Democratic Teachers
International Working Group for the Construction of Sports Premises (IAKS)
Young Lawyers International Association (AIJA).

[2]See Y.U.N., 1970, pp. 319-29, resolution 2626(XXV), containing text of Strategy.

The following organizations were reclassified from the Roster to Category II:

Boy Scouts World Bureau
International Chamber of Shipping
International Council of Scientific Unions
International Council of Social Democratic Women
International Hotel Association
International Prisoners Aid Association
International Savings Banks Institute
International Touring Alliance
World University Service.

During the Council's discussions of these organizations, a proposal by the United States to place the Asian Development Center in Category II was rejected by 8 votes to 8, with 9 abstentions. Its inclusion on the Roster was approved by 18 votes to 0, with 4 abstentions.

A proposal by the USSR that the European League for Economic Co-operation be placed on the Roster was rejected by 7 votes to 2, with 16 abstentions. Its inclusion in Category II was approved by 18 votes to 2, with 3 abstentions.

The inclusion of the International Association for Water Law in Category II was approved by 21 votes to 0, with 4 abstentions.

A proposal by the USSR to place the International Working Group for the Construction of Sports Premises (IAKS) in Category II was rejected by 2 votes to 2, with 22 abstentions; its inclusion on the Roster was approved unanimously.

A proposal by the USSR to place the International Council of Social Democratic Women on the Roster was rejected by 7 votes to 2, with 14 abstentions; the Committee's recommendation to reclassify it to Category II was adopted by 20 votes to 0, with 3 abstentions.

At its May session, the Council received a note by the Secretary-General informing it of his intention to place the Lutheran World Federation on the Roster.

The Council also took the view that an item concerning the teaching of the purposes and principles, the structure and activities of the United Nations and the specialized agencies, in schools and other educational institutions of Member States, requested by the World Federation of United Nations Associations to be placed by the Council on the agenda of one of its 1971 sessions, might more appropriately be considered by the United Nations Educational, Scientific and Cultural Organization.

Special arrangement with INTERPOL

On 20 May 1971, the Council approved an arrangement for co-operation between the United Nations and the International Criminal Police Organization (INTERPOL), which had been recommended by its Committee on Non-Governmental

Organizations following consideration in 1970.[3]

This decision was embodied in resolution 1579(L), adopted by 24 votes to 0, with 2 abstentions, on the recommendation of the Council's Social Committee, which unanimously approved the text on 28 April 1971, on the basis of a text submitted by the Committee on Non-Governmental Organizations.

Annexed to resolution 1579(L) was the text of the arrangement for co-operation between the United Nations and INTERPOL. It covered matters of concern to INTERPOL, the question of exchange of information and documentation, consultations and technical co-operation, representation by observers at meetings, exchange of written statements and the mutual proposing of agenda items. (For text of resolution and Annex, see DOCUMENTARY REFERENCES below.)

Operating consultative arrangements

Written statements

Twenty statements by 16 individual NGOs were submitted to the Council in 1971 under the arrangements for consultation. In addition, one joint statement by 12 organizations was submitted to the Council.

Written statements were submitted not only to the Council but to the following: the United Nations Children's Fund; the Commission on Human Rights; the Sub-Commission on Prevention of Discrimination and Protection of Minorities; the Commission for Social Development; the Commission on the Status of Women; and the United Nations Conference on Trade and Development.

Hearings of NGOs

During the Council's April-May 1971 session, two NGOs in Category I consultative status made statements on agenda items as follows: the International Confederation of Free Trade Unions, on social development and on human rights; the World Federation of Trade Unions, on social development and on human rights.

During the Council's July 1971 session, six NGOs in Category I consultative status made statements on agenda items, as follows: the International Chamber of Commerce, on the Second United Nations Development Decade; the International Confederation of Free Trade Unions, on general discussion of international economic and social policy and on the Second Development Decade; the Inter-Parliamentary Union, on the Second Development Decade; the League of Red Cross Societies, on the United Nations Conference on the Human Environment and on assistance in

[3]See Y.U.N., 1970, p. 625, for background.

cases of natural disaster; the Women's International Democratic Federation and the World Federation of Trade Unions, on general discussion of economic and social policy and on the Second Development Decade.

During the Council's July 1971 session, three NGOs in Category II were heard by the Council Committee on Non-Governmental Organizations, as follows: the International Student Movement for the United Nations, on the United Nations

Volunteers programme, on the Report of the United Nations High Commissioner for Refugees and on assistance in cases of natural disaster; the St. Joan's International Alliance, on the United Nations Conference on the Human Environment; the World Jewish Congress, on the role of the United Nations in training national technical personnel for the accelerated industrialization of developing countries.

Non-governmental organizations in consultative status
(As at 31 December 1971)

Category I
International Chamber of Commerce
International Confederation of Free Trade Unions
International Co-operative Alliance
International Council of Women
International Federation of Agricultural Producers
International Organization of Employers
International Union of Local Authorities
International Union of Official Travel Organizations
Inter-Parliamentary Union
League of Red Cross Societies
United Towns Organization
Women's International Democratic Federation
World Confederation of Labour
World Federation of Trade Unions
World Federation of United Nations Associations
World Veterans Federation

Category II
Afro-Asian Organization for Economic Co-operation
Agudas Israel World Organization
All-African Women's Conference
All-India Women's Conference
All-Pakistan Women's Association
Amnesty International
Anti-*apartheid* Movement, The
Anti-Slavery Society, The
Arab Lawyers Union
Associated Country Women of the World
Bahá'i International Community
Boy Scouts World Bureau
CARE (Cooperative for American Relief Everywhere, Inc.)
Carnegie Endowment for International Peace
Catholic International Union for Social Service
Centre for Latin American Monetary Studies
Centro de Investigación para el Desarrollo Económico Social
Chamber of Commerce of the United States of America
Christian Democratic World Union
Commission of the Churches on International Affairs, The
Community Development Foundation, Inc.
Consultative Council of Jewish Organizations
Co-ordinating Board of Jewish Organizations (CBJO)
Co-ordinating Committee for International Voluntary Service
Eastern Regional Organization for Public Administration

European Insurance Committee
European League for Economic Co-operation
Friends World Committee for Consultation
Howard League for Penal Reform
Inter-American Council of Commerce and Production
Inter-American Federation of Public Relations Associations
Inter-American Planning Society
Inter-American Press Association
Inter-American Statistical Institute
International Abolitionist Federation
International Air Transport Association
International Alliance of Women—Equal Rights, Equal Responsibilities
International Association for Social Progress
International Association for the Promotion and Protection of Private Foreign Investments
International Association for the Protection of Industrial Property
International Association for Water Law (IAWL)
International Association of Democratic Lawyers
International Association of Lawyers
International Association of Penal Law
International Association of Ports and Harbours (IAPH)
International Association of Schools of Social Work
International Association of Youth Magistrates
International Astronautical Federation
International Bar Association
International Cargo Handling Co-ordination Association
International Catholic Child Bureau
International Catholic Migration Commission
International Catholic Union of the Press
International Chamber of Shipping
International Christian Union of Business Executives (UNIAPAC)
International College of Surgeons
International Commission of Jurists
International Commission on Irrigation and Drainage
International Committee of the Red Cross
International Conference of Catholic Charities
International Council for Building Research, Studies and Documentation
International Council for Scientific Management
International Council of Jewish Women
International Council of Scientific Unions
International Council of Social Democratic Women
International Council on Jewish Social and Welfare Services
International Council on Social Welfare

International Criminal Police Organization (INTERPOL)*
International Defence and Aid Fund for Southern Africa
International Federation for Housing and Planning
International Federation for the Rights of Man
International Federation of Business and Professional Women
International Federation of Journalists
International Federation of Senior Police Officers
International Federation of Settlements and Neighbourhood Centres
International Federation of Social Workers
International Federation of University Women
International Federation of Women in Legal Careers
International Federation of Women Lawyers
International Hotel Association
International Information Centre for Local Credit
International Institute of Administrative Sciences
International Institute of Public Finance
International Law Association
International League for the Rights of Man
International Movement for Fraternal Union Among Races and Peoples
International Organization for Standardization
International Organization—Justice and Development
International Organization of Consumer's Unions
International Organization of Journalists (IOJ)
International Organization of Supreme Audit Institutions (INTOSAI)
International Planned Parenthood Federation
International Prisoners Aid Association
International Recreation Association
International Road Federation
International Road Transport Union
International Savings Banks Institute
International Social Service
International Society for Criminology
International Society for Rehabilitation of the Disabled
International Society of Social Defence
International Statistical Institute
International Student Movement for the United Nations
International Touring Alliance
International Union for Child Welfare
International Union for Conservation of Nature and Natural Resources
International Union for Inland Navigation
International Union for the Scientific Study of Population
International Union of Architects
International Union of Building Societies and Savings Associations
International Union of Family Organizations
International Union of Producers and Distributors of Electrical Energy
International Union of Public Transport
International Union of Railways
International Young Christian Workers
Junior Chamber International
Latin American Iron and Steel Institute
Lions International—The International Association of Lions Clubs
Movement for Colonial Freedom
Pan American Federation of Engineering Societies (UPADI)
Pan-Pacific and South-East Asia Women's Association

Pax Romana
    International Catholic Movement for Intellectual and Cultural Affairs
    International Movement of Catholic Students
Permanent International Association of Road Congresses (PIARC)
Rotary International
Salvation Army, The
Society for Comparative Legislation
Société internationale de prophylaxie criminelle
Soroptimist International Association
St. Joan's International Alliance
Studies and Expansion Society—International Scientific Association (SEC)
Union of International Fairs
Union of International Associations
Universal Federation of Travel Agents Associations
Women's International League for Peace and Freedom
Women's International Zionist Organization
World Alliance of Young Men's Christian Associations
World Assembly of Youth
World Association of World Federalists
World Confederation of Organizations of the Teaching Profession
World Council for the Welfare of the Blind
World Energy Conference
World Federation for Mental Health
World Federation for the Protection of Animals
World Federation of Catholic Youth
World Federation of the Deaf
World Federation of Democratic Youth
World Jewish Congress
World Movements of Mothers
World Muslim Congress
World Peace Through Law Centre
World Student Christian Federation
World Union of Catholic Women's Organizations
World Union of Organizations for the Safeguard of Youth
World Young Women's Christian Association
World Woman's Christian Temperance Union
World University Service
Zonta International

*INTERPOL retained its status as an NGO until the text of the Special Arrangement between it and the Economic and Social Council, adopted by the Council on 20 May 1971, was approved by the General Assembly of INTERPOL in September 1971.

Roster

Organizations included by action of Economic and Social Council
American Foreign Insurance Association
Asian Development Center
Battelle Memorial Institute
Boy Scouts World Bureau
Comité d'études économiques de l'industrie du gaz
Committee for Economic Development
Confederation of Asian Chambers of Commerce
Engineers Joint Council
European Alliance of Press Agencies
European Confederation of Woodworking Industries
Federation of International Furniture Removers

Inter-American Federation of Touring and Automobile Clubs

International Association for the Exchange of Students for Technical Experience

International Association of Gerontology

International Automobile Federation

International Bureau of Motor-Cycle Manufacturers

International Bureau for the Suppression of Traffic in Persons

International Committee of Outer Space Onomastics (ICOSO)

International Confederation of Associations of Experts and Consultants

International Container Bureau

International Council of Commerce Employers

International Council of Voluntary Agencies (ICVA)

International Council on Alcohol and Addictions

International Federation for Documentation

International Federation of Cotton and Allied Textile Industries

International Federation of Forwarding Agents Associations

International Federation of Free Journalists

International Federation of Operational Research Societies

International Federation of Surveyors

International Fiscal Association

International League of Surveillance Societies, The

International Olive Growers Federation

International Organization of Experts (ORDINEX)

International Permanent Bureau of Automobile Manufacturers

International Police Association

International Real Estate Federation

International Schools Association

International Senior Citizens Association, Inc., The

International Shipping Federation

International Society for the Protection of Animals

International Union of Marine Insurance

International Union of Police Federations

International Union of Social Democratic Teachers

International Voluntary Service

International Working Group for the Construction of Sports Premises (IAKS)

Mutual Assistance of the Latin American Government Oil Companies

Open Door International (for the Economic Emancipation of the Woman Worker)

Permanent International Association of Navigation Congresses

Prévention routière internationale, La (International Road Safety Association)

Society for International Development

Vienna Institute for Development

World Association of Girl Guides and Girl Scouts

World Confederation for Physical Therapy

World Union for Progressive Judaism

Young Lawyers International Association (AIJA)

Organizations included by action of Secretary-General

Association for the Advancement of Agricultural Sciences in Africa

Lutheran World Federation

Organisation internationale pour le développement rural

World Society of Ekistics

Organizations included because of consultative status with specialized agencies or United Nations bodies

The organizations listed below had consultative status with the following specialized agencies and other bodies of the United Nations system: the International Labour Organisation (ILO); the Food and Agriculture Organization of the United Nations (FAO); the United Nations Educational, Scientific and Cultural Organization (UNESCO); the World Health Organization (WHO); the International Civil Aviation Organization (ICAO); the Inter-Governmental Maritime Consultative Organization (IMCO); the United Nations Conference on Trade and Development (UNCTAD); the United Nations Industrial Development Organization (UNIDO).

Organization	In consultative status with
Aerospace Medical Association	ICAO
African Trade Union Confederation	UNCTAD
Asian Broadcasting Union	UNESCO, FAO
Association des universités partiellement ou entièrement de langue française	UNESCO
Association for the Promotion of the International Circulation of the Press	UNESCO
Association of Commonwealth Universities	UNESCO
Association of Official Analytical Chemists	FAO
Baltic and International Maritime Conference, The	IMCO
Biometric Society, The	WHO
B'nai B'rith International Council	UNESCO
Catholic International Education Office	UNESCO
Central Council for Health Education	WHO
Christian Medical Commission	WHO
Confederation of Latin American Teachers	UNESCO
Council for International Organizations of Medical Sciences (CIOMS)	WHO, UNESCO
European Alliance of Press Agencies	UNESCO
European Association for Animal Production	FAO
European Association for Personnel Management	ILO
European Bureau for Youth and Childhood	ILO
European Centre for Overseas Industrial Development	UNIDO
European Confederation of Agriculture	FAO
European Federation of Associations of Engineers and Heads of Industrial Safety Services and Industrial Physicians	ILO
European Federation of National Associations of Engineers	UNESCO
European Mechanical Handling Confederation	ILO

Organization	In consultative status with	Organization	In consultative status with
European Nitrogen Produce Association	IMCO	International Association of Students in Economic and Commercial Sciences	UNESCO, ILO
European Society of Culture	UNESCO	International Association of Universities	UNESCO
European Union of Coachbuilders	UNIDO	International Association of University Professors and Lecturers	UNESCO
European Writers' Community	UNESCO		
Experiment in International Living	UNESCO	International Association of Workers for Maladjusted Children	UNESCO
Institute of International Law	ICAO		
Institute of Man and Science	UNESCO	International Board on Books for Young People	UNESCO
Inter-American Association of Broadcasters	UNESCO	International Brain Research Organization	UNESCO, WHO
Inter-American Association of Sanitary Engineering	WHO	International Bureau of Social Tourism	ILO
International Academy of Legal Medicine and of Social Medicine	WHO	International Catholic Association for Radio and Television (UNDA)	UNESCO
International Aeronautical Federation	ICAO	International Catholic Secretariat for Technologists, Agriculturists and Economists	ILO
International Airline Navigators Council	ICAO		
International Association for Accident and Traffic Medicine	WHO	International Cell Research Organization	UNESCO
International Association for Child Psychiatry and Allied Professions	WHO	International Centre of Research and Information on Collective Economy	ILO
International Association for Earthquake Engineering	UNESCO	International Cocoa Trade Federation	UNCTAD
International Association for Educational and Vocational Guidance	UNESCO, ILO	International Commission Against Concentration Camp Practices	ILO
International Association for Educational and Vocational Information	UNESCO, ILO	International Commission of Agricultural Engineering	FAO
International Association for Mass Communication Research	UNESCO	International Commission on Illumination	IMCO, ICAO, ILO
International Association for Prevention of Blindness	WHO	International Commission on Radiation Units and Measurements	WHO
International Association for Religious Freedom	UNESCO	International Commission on Radiological Protection	WHO
International Association for the Advancement of Educational Research	UNESCO	International Committee for Social Sciences Documentation	UNESCO
International Association for the Physical Sciences of the Ocean	ICAO	International Committee of Catholic Nurses and Medico-Social Workers	WHO, ILO
International Association of Agricultural Librarians and Documentalists	FAO	International Community of Booksellers Associations	UNESCO
International Association of Agricultural Medicine	WHO, ILO	International Confederation of Midwives	WHO, ILO
International Association of Art—Painting, Sculpture, Graphic Art	UNESCO	International Confederation of Societies of Authors and Composers	UNESCO
International Association of Art Critics	UNESCO	International Congress of University Adult Education	UNESCO
International Association of Classification Societies	IMCO	International Coordinating Committee for the Presentation of Science and Development of Out-of-School Scientific Activities	UNESCO
International Association of Crafts and Small and Medium-Sized Enterprises	UNIDO		
International Association of Fish Meal Manufacturers	FAO	International Council for Philosophy and Humanistic Studies	UNESCO
International Association of Horticultural Producers	FAO	International Council for Educational Films	ILO
International Association of Legal Science	UNESCO	International Council of Monuments and Sites	UNESCO
International Association of Lighthouse Authorities	IMCO	International Council of Museums	UNESCO
		International Council of Nurses	WHO, ILO
International Association of Literary Critics	UNESCO	International Council of Societies of Industrial Design	UNESCO
International Association of Logopedics and Phoniatrics	UNESCO, WHO	International Council of Societies of Pathology	WHO
International Association of Medical Laboratory Technologists	WHO	International Council of Sport and Physical Education	UNESCO
International Association of Microbiological Societies	WHO	International Council on Archives	UNESCO

Organization	In consultative status with	Organization	In consultative status with
International Council on Correspondence Education	UNESCO	International Federation of the Periodical Press	UNESCO
International Dairy Federation	FAO	International Federation of the Phonographic Industry	UNESCO
International Dental Federation	WHO	International Federation of Translators	UNESCO
International Diabetes Federation	WHO	International Federation of Workers' Educational Associations	UNESCO
International Economic Association	UNESCO	International Fertility Associations	WHO
International Electrotechnical Commission	IMCO	International Film and Television Council	UNESCO
International Epidemiological Association	IMCO	International Geographical Union	ICAO
International Ergonomics Association	ILO	International Hospital Federation	WHO
International Falcon Movement	UNESCO	International Humanistic and Ethical Union	UNESCO
International Federation for Information Processing	UNESCO	International Hydatidological Association	WHO
International Federation for Medical and Biological Engineering	WHO	International League Against Epilepsy	WHO
International Federation for Parent Education	UNESCO	International League against Rheumatism	WHO
International Federation of Air Line Pilots Associations	ICAO	International League for Child and Adult Education	UNESCO
International Federation of Automatic Control	UNIDO	International League of Dermatological Societies	WHO
International Federation of Beekeepers' Associations	FAO	International League of Societies for the Mentally Handicapped	ILO
International Federation of Catholic Universities	UNESCO	International Leprosy Association	WHO
International Federation of Children's Communities	UNESCO	International Literary and Artistic Association	UNESCO
International Federation of Free Teachers' Unions	UNESCO	International Marine Radio Association	IMCO
International Federation of Gynecology and Obstetrics	WHO	International Maritime Committee	IMCO
International Federation of Home Economics	FAO	International Medical Association for the Study of Living Conditions and Health	FAO
International Federation of Independent Air Transport	ICAO	International Movement of Catholic Agricultural and Rural Youth	FAO, ILO, UNESCO
International Federation of Landscape Architects	UNESCO	International Music Council	UNESCO
International Federation of Library Associations	UNESCO	International Organization Against Trachoma	WHO
International Federation of Margarine Associations	FAO	International Paediatric Association	WHO
International Federation of Modern Language Teachers	UNESCO	International Peace Research Association	UNESCO
International Federation of Multiple Sclerosis Societies	WHO	International PEN	UNESCO
International Federation of Newspaper Publishers	UNESCO	International Pharmaceutical Federation	WHO
International Federation of Organizations for School Correspondence and Exchange	UNESCO	International Political Science Association	UNESCO
International Federation of Pharmaceutical Manufacturers Associations	WHO	International Publishers Association	UNESCO
International Federation of Physical Medicine	WHO	International Radio and Television Organization	UNESCO
International Federation of Plantation, Agricultural and Allied Workers	FAO	International Rayon and Synthetic Fibres Committee	UNCTAD
International Federation of Popular Travel Organizations	UNESCO	International Scientific Film Association	UNESCO
International Federation of Purchasing	UNCTAD	International Shrimp Council	FAO
International Federation of Sportive Medicine	WHO	International Social Science Council	UNESCO, ILO
International Federation of Surgical Colleges	WHO	International Society for Education through Art	UNESCO
		International Society for Labour Law and Social Legislation	ILO
		International Society for Research on Moors	FAO
		International Society for Biometeorology	WHO
		International Society of Blood Transfusion	WHO

Organization	In consultative status with	Organization	In consultative status with
International Society of Cardiology	WHO	Pan-American Union of Associations of Engineering	UNESCO
International Society of Orthopaedic Surgery and Traumatology	WHO	Permanent Commission and International Association on Occupational Health	WHO, ILO
International Society of Radiographers and Radiological Technicians	WHO	Permanent International Committee on Canned Foods	FAO
International Society of Soil Science	FAO, UNESCO	Society of African Culture	UNESCO
International Sociological Association	UNESCO	Sri Aurobindo Society	UNESCO
International Solid Waste and Public Cleansing Associations	WHO	Standing Conference of Chambers of Commerce and Industry of the European Economic Community	UNCTAD
International Superphosphate Manufacturers' Association	IMCO	Standing Conference of Rectors and Vice-Chancellors of the European Universities	UNESCO
International Theatre Institute	UNESCO	Transplantation Society	WHO
International Travel Journalists and Writers Federation	UNESCO	UNDA—Catholic International Association for Radio and Television	UNESCO
International Union Against Cancer	WHO	Union of Industries of the European Community	UNIDO, UNCTAD
International Union Against the Venereal Diseases and the Treponematoses	WHO	Union of International Engineering Organizations	UNESCO
International Union Against Tuberculosis	WHO, ILO	Union of Latin American Universities	UNESCO
International Union for Health Education	WHO, UNESCO	Union of National Radio and Television Organizations of Africa	UNESCO, ILO
International Union for Liberty of Education	UNESCO	United Seamen's Service	ILO
International Union of Aviation Insurers	ICAO	Universal Esperanto Association	UNESCO
International Union of Food and Allied Workers Associations	FAO	World Association for Christian Broadcasting	UNESCO
International Union of Forestry Research Organizations	FAO	World Association for Public Opinion Research	UNESCO
International Union of Geodesy and Geophysics	ICAO	World Council of Peace	UNESCO
International Union of Independent Laboratories	UNIDO	World Crafts Council	UNESCO
International Union of Judges	ILO	World Education Fellowship	UNESCO
International Union of Nutritional Sciences	FAO	World Federation of Engineering Organizations	UNESCO, UNIDO
International Union of Pharmacology	WHO	World Federation of Neurology	WHO
International Union of Psychological Science	UNESCO	World Federation of Occupational Therapists	WHO
International Union of Pure and Applied Chemistry	WHO	World Federation of Public Health Associations	WHO
International Union of School and University Health and Medicine	WHO, UNESCO	World Federation of Scientific Workers	UNESCO
International Union of Socialist Youth	UNESCO, ILO	World Federation of Societies of Anaesthesiologists	WHO
International Union of Students	UNESCO	World Federation of Teachers' Unions	UNESCO
International Water Supply Association	WHO	World Fellowship of Buddhists	UNESCO
International Wholesale and Foreign Trade Centre	UNCTAD	World Medical Association	WHO, ILO
International Writers Guild	UNESCO	World Movement of Christian Workers	ILO
International Young Catholic Students	UNESCO	World Organization for Early Childhood Education	UNESCO
International Youth Hostel Federation	UNESCO	World OSE Union (Worldwide organization for child care, health and hygiene among Jews)	WHO
Latin American Shipowners Association	UNCTAD	World Psychiatric Association	WHO
Medical Women's International Association	WHO	World's Poultry Science Association	FAO
Pacific Science Association	UNESCO	World Union of Catholic Teachers	UNESCO
		World Veterinary Association	WHO, FAO

DOCUMENTARY REFERENCES

Contribution of NGOs to International Development Strategy

Economic and Social Council—50th session

Council Committee on Non-Governmental Organizations, meetings 307-318.
Social Committee, meetings 652, 653.
Plenary meeting 1769.

E/4945. Report of Council Committee on NGOs.

E/AC.7/L.580. Brazil, Pakistan, Sudan: draft resolution.

E/AC.7/L.580/Rev.1. Brazil, Ghana, Pakistan, Sudan: revised draft resolution, as orally amended by sponsors and by Italy, approved unanimously by Social Committee on 29 April 1971, meeting 653.

E/5021. Report of Social Committee, draft resolution II.

RESOLUTION 1580(L), as recommended by Social Committee, E/5021, adopted unanimously by Council on 20 May 1971, meeting 1769.

The Economic and Social Council,

Recalling its resolution 1296(XLIV) of 23 May 1968 on arrangements for consultation with non-governmental organizations,

Having considered the report of the Council Committee on Non-Governmental Organizations,

Believing that non-governmental organizations in consultative status with the Council active primarily in the field of economic and social development can contribute significantly to the achievement of the goals and objectives of the International Development Strategy for the Second United Nations Development Decade,

1. *Emphasizes* the need for non-governmental organizations in consultative status active primarily in the field of economic and social development to endeavour to develop more meaningful and productive relationships with the Economic and Social Council, to enable them to contribute effectively towards the implementation of the International Development Strategy for the Second United Nations Development Decade;

2. *Requests* its Committee on Non-Governmental Organizations to examine, bearing in mind the goals and objectives of the International Development Strategy, the contributions to development already made or being planned by non-governmental organizations in consultative status active primarily in the field of economic and social development;

3. *Further requests* its Committee on Non-Governmental Organizations, subsequent to the examination provided for in paragraph 2 above, to submit to the Council at its fifty-fourth session recommendations on improving their contribution towards the implementation of the International Development Strategy.

Review of NGOs granted consultative status

Economic and Social Council—50th session

Council Committee on Non-Governmental Organizations, meetings 307-318.

Social Committee, meeting 652.

Plenary meeting 1769.

E/4945. Report of Council Committee on NGOs, Chapter III A, B and D, and Chapter V.

E/5026. Action by Secretary-General to place non-governmental organization on Roster. Note by Secretary-General.

E/5044. Resolutions adopted by Economic and Social Council during its 50th session, 11-13 January and 26 April–21 May 1971. Decisions, pp. 24-25.

E/4945. Report of Council Committee on NGOs, Chapter II.

E/4945, Annex III. Draft resolution, approved unanimously by Social Committee on 28 April 1971, meeting 652.

E/5021. Report of Social Committee, draft resolution I.

RESOLUTION 1579(L), as recommended by Social Committee, E/5021, adopted by Council on 20 May 1971, meeting 1769, by 24 votes to 0, with 2 abstentions.

The Economic and Social Council,

Noting the relevant recommendations of the Council Committee on Non-Governmental Organizations,

Approves the arrangement for co-operation between the United Nations and the International Criminal Police Organization (INTERPOL) set out in the annex to the present resolution.

ANNEX

Arrangement for co-operation between the United Nations and the International Criminal Police Organization

1. *Matters of concern to the International Criminal Police Organization*

Note is taken that the aims of the International Criminal Police Organization, as stated in article 2 of its Constitution, are:

(a) To ensure and promote the widest possible mutual assistance between all criminal police authorities within the limits of the laws existing in the different countries in the spirit of the Universal Declaration of Human Rights;

(b) To establish and develop all institutions likely to contribute effectively to the prevention and suppression of ordinary law crimes; and that, according to article 3 of its Constitution, it is strictly forbidden to undertake any intervention or activities of a political, military, religious or racial character.

In the execution of these aims, the International Criminal Police Organization is concerned in all criminal police matters, including the police aspects of drug abuse, prevention of crime and treatment of offenders, traffic in persons, certain human rights questions specified by its Constitution, counterfeiting and new forms of crime that may arise.

2. *Exchange of information and documentation*

The United Nations Secretariat and the International Criminal Police Organization shall exchange, as may be appropriate, information and documentation relevant to matters of mutual interest.

3. *Consultations and technical co-operation*

The United Nations Secretariat and the International Criminal Police Organization, at the request of either, shall consult together on matters of common interest. They may collaborate in the study of such matters and may undertake technical co-operation in substantive projects.

4. *Representation by observers*

Representatives of the United Nations Secretariat shall be invited to attend in an observer capacity meetings of bodies of the International Criminal Police Organization and other meetings organized by it which deal with matters of common interest. Representatives of that organization shall be invited to attend in an observer capacity meetings of the Economic and Social Council, of its subsidiary organs, conferences convened by it and meetings of other United Nations bodies which deal with matters of common interest. Observers invited pursuant to the present paragraph may participate, with the approval of the body concerned and without the right to vote, in debates on questions of concern to their organizations.

5. *Written statements*

The United Nations Secretariat may submit written statements to meetings of bodies of the International Criminal Police Organization and other meetings organized by it on matters of common interest which are relevant to the work of those bodies. The International Criminal Police Organization may submit written statements to the Economic and Social Council, to its subsidiary organs and to conferences convened by it, on matters of common interest which are relevant to the work of those bodies, subject to the same conditions and procedures as are applicable to written statements by organizations having consultative status in category I with the Council.

6. *Proposal of agenda items*

The United Nations may propose items for the provisional agenda of bodies of the International Criminal Police Organization and other meetings organized by it. The International Criminal Police Organization may propose items for the provisional agenda of the Economic and Social Council and its subsidiary bodies, subject to the same conditions and procedures as are applicable to such proposals by organizations having consultative status in category I with the Council.

E/INF/117. NGOs in consultative status with Economic and Social
   Council in 1971.
A/8401. Report of Secretary-General on work of the Organization,
   16 June 1970–15 June 1971, Part Three, Chapter II H.
A/8403. Report of Economic and Social Council on work of its 50th
   and 51st sessions, Chapter XXIII.

Operating consultative arrangements

WRITTEN STATEMENTS

E/C.2/722-727, 728 and Corr.1, 729-732, 734-743. Statements
   submitted to Economic and Social Council.

[For written statements submitted by non-governmental organizations to subsidiary bodies of Council, see report of those bodies
to Council.]

HEARINGS OF NGOs

Economic and Social Council—50th session
Council Committee on NGOs, meeting 316.
Social Committee, meetings 661, 671, 672.
Plenary meeting 1750.

E/5008. Applications for hearings. Report of Council Committee
   on NGOs.

Economic and Social Council—51st session
Council Committee on NGOs, meetings 317, 318.
Economic Committee, meetings 529, 532.
Plenary meetings 1776, 1779, 1781, 1787.

E/5055. Applications for hearings. Report of Council Committee
   on NGOs.

Chapter XXII

Co-ordination and organizational questions

Development and co-ordination of activities of the United Nations family of organizations

In accordance with past practice, the Economic
and Social Council reviewed questions of inter-
agency co-ordination and co-operation at its
mid-1971 session. The review was based, as in
previous years, on reports of the Council's
Committee for Programme and Co-ordination
(CPC), the annual reports of the Administrative
Committee on Co-ordination (ACC), those of the
specialized agencies and the International Atomic
Energy Agency (IAEA), and the report of the
annual Joint Meetings of CPC and ACC.

The report of ACC, which is composed of the
executive heads of the specialized agencies, IAEA,
the General Agreement on Tariffs and Trade
(GATT), the World Food Programme (WFP), the
United Nations Children's Fund (UNICEF), the
Office of the United Nations High Commissioner
for Refugees (UNHCR), the United Nations Relief
and Works Agency for Palestine Refugees in the
Near East (UNRWA), the United Nations Institute
for Training and Research (UNITAR), the United
Nations Conference on Trade and Development
(UNCTAD), the United Nations Industrial Development Organization (UNIDO) and the United Nations Development Programme (UNDP), under the
chairmanship of the Secretary-General, outlined
developments of inter-agency concern in several
programme and administrative areas.

In the administrative and financial sector,
attention was devoted to questions of budgeting
and programming and to co-ordination in the use

of computers. Programme matters dealt with in
the report included the Second United Nations
Development Decade, population, outer space,
action against drug abuse, the human environment and science and technology.

The report of the Joint Meetings of CPC and
ACC, held on 1 and 2 July 1971 immediately prior
to the Economic and Social Council's session, also
dealt with future institutional arrangements for
science and technology. However, it was principally concerned with the review of the sphere of
activities and competence of ACC. The role of ACC
and the ways in which ACC could better assist the
Council and other inter-governmental organs in
carrying out their co-ordination responsibilities,
had been dealt with at some length by CPC during
two sessions, held in April and May-June.

The Council, at its July 1971 session, considered
the role of ACC in the context of the over-all
functioning and effectiveness of the central machinery for co-ordination. In addition to adopting a
resolution on ACC's sphere of activities, the
Economic and Social Council took a number of
decisions aimed at improving its own methods of
work. These decisions reflected a continuing
concern on the part of the Council with the
strengthening of its co-ordinating functions.

By one decision, for example, the Council
referred to the need for greater precision and
efficiency in the exercise of its co-ordinating
responsibilities under the United Nations Charter,

and recommended that the Assembly instruct it to propose effective methods to remedy current shortcomings.

By another decision, the Council decided to review in 1972 its co-ordinating machinery, including the possibility of holding inter-sessional meetings of its Co-ordination Committee (one of the Council's sessional committees) to deal with tasks currently entrusted to the Committee for Programme and Co-ordination (a standing committee with different membership from that of the Council).

(For further details on these decisions, see immediately below.)

Developments regarding co-ordination machinery

Role of ACC

By a decision of 30 July 1970,[1] the Council had instructed the Committee for Programme and Co-ordination (CPC) to review the sphere of activities and competence of the Administrative Committee on Co-ordination (ACC) so that the Council might achieve more effective co-ordination of the social, economic and technical activities of the United Nations system.

The relevant discussions in CPC and in the Joint Meetings of CPC and ACC centred on two main issues: co-operation between ACC and the Council, in the light of the respective competences of inter-governmental organs and secretariats; and ACC's reporting procedures and methods of work.

Some members of CPC, while recognizing the importance of the role of ACC as the main co-ordinating body at the secretariat level, emphasized that ACC should not infringe upon the prerogatives of inter-governmental organs, particularly in policy formulation and decision making. Those were functions that properly belonged to inter-governmental bodies in the same way as the implementation of programmes and decisions were mainly the responsibility of secretariats. In that connexion, those members called for a stricter implementation of the Economic and Social Council's 1947 decision which had given ACC the mandate of ensuring the effective implementation of the agreements entered into between the United Nations and the specialized agencies.[2]

Other CPC members noted that the expansion of ACC's activities since 1947 had been the result of a general acceleration of the pace of the activities of international organizations, and had taken place in response to demands made upon ACC by the Council and the General Assembly. They pointed out that the term "policy formulation" defined a complex set of inter-related functions, comprising the preparation and evaluation of alternative courses of action and choices among these alternatives, and that it was seldom possible or desirable to draw a distinct line between such functions. They felt that ACC should be given the necessary flexibility to do its work effectively, and that the submission of recommendations by ACC would facilitate the performance by the Council of its co-ordination functions.

For their part, members of the Administrative Committee on Co-ordination noted, at the Joint Meetings with CPC, that the main contribution of ACC was to provide the machinery through which the preoccupations and decisions of the governing bodies of all the organizations of the system could be taken into proper account. The recent evolution in inter-agency relations from "negative co-ordination"—aimed merely at the avoidance of duplication—to a search for common approaches needed to be strengthened, and ACC was in a unique position to contribute to the furthering of this process, with the clear understanding, of course, that the taking of the necessary decisions was the exclusive prerogative of Governments. To facilitate this, fuller co-operation was needed between the Council and CPC, on the one hand, and ACC, on the other, rather than any rigid allocation of functions.

With regard to the methods of work of ACC, members of CPC considered that there was a need for improved communication between ACC and the competent inter-governmental organs, and that the annual reports of ACC had not, so far, met the requirements of those organs. In particular, they seldom provided information on problems and difficulties encountered, which would enable the Economic and Social Council to take informed decisions on them.

By the terms of a resolution adopted unanimously on 30 July 1971, the Council requested ACC to give priority to the study of methods that would enable the system to achieve greater productivity and efficiency, and invited it to maintain under review measures aimed at ensuring the fullest implementation of the agreements between the United Nations, the specialized agencies, and the International Atomic Energy Agency (IAEA). It further called upon ACC to state options and alternative courses of action in its reports, in order to facilitate the decision-making role of the legislative organs concerned.

With regard to the format and contents of ACC's annual reports, the Council called for concise descriptions of the way in which the system

---

[1]See Y.U.N., 1970, pp. 605-6, text of resolution 1547(XLIX).
[2]See Y.U.N., 1946-47, p. 546, text of resolution 13(III).

operated in the various fields, highlighting un-resolved problems for action at the inter-govern-mental level, and putting forward suggestions to facilitate the implementation of the Council's decisions within the system. Fuller information on the results of the work of ACC's subsidiary bodies were also requested. In addition, the Council provided for the preparation by ACC of separate reports on topics of system-wide interest, to be selected by the Council for in-depth study at the suggestion of the Administrative Committee on Co-ordination.

As far as ACC's working procedures were concerned, the Council requested the Secretary-General to pursue his consideration of the possibility of associating the executive secretaries of the regional economic commissions and the Director of the United Nations Economic and Social Office at Beirut with the work of ACC. The Council also called on ACC to ensure close control over all inter-agency meetings and to notify the members of the Council and CPC of the holding of these meetings. Finally, ACC was requested to continue to make arrangements for prior consulta-tions among interested secretariats, before pro-posed work programmes were presented to the legislative bodies concerned for approval.

The Council's decisions were embodied in resolution 1643(LI), adopted on the recommenda-tion of the Co-ordination Committee. The text was based on a draft resolution proposed by CPC, which the Co-ordination Committee revised dur-ing discussions and approved by consensus on 19 July 1971.

Amendments proposed by Ghana, by Sudan and jointly by Brazil, France, Uruguay and the USSR were not pressed to the vote following Committee consensus on amending CPC's text. Similarly, a proposal by Ghana to defer considera-tion of CPC's text was not pursued.

(For text of resolution, see DOCUMENTARY REFERENCES below.)

Reports of specialized agencies and IAEA

On 30 July 1971, the Economic and Social Council, noting with appreciation the analytical reports submitted by the specialized agencies and IAEA, requested these organizations to continue to provide such reports, bearing in mind the guide-lines laid down for this purpose, and agreed on some changes in the procedures followed for their consideration.

Expressing the view that there could be an improvement in its consideration of these reports, the Council referred to a suggestion by the Director-General of WHO for an annual in-depth review of selected organizations.

Thus, a procedure by which the Council would give detailed consideration each year to the reports of two or three agencies was agreed on, with the proviso that the reports of all the agencies should be examined in depth over a five-year period. In addition, CPC was instructed to assist the Council by recommending the arrangements and the choice of the reports.

The Council also decided that, after the discussion in depth of the reports selected, sufficient time should be allowed at each mid-year session for consideration of any of the other reports.

These Council decisions were set forth in resolution 1642(LI) which was adopted, unani-mously, on the recommendation of the Co-ordina-tion Committee. The text was sponsored in the Committee by Brazil, Peru, the USSR, the United Kingdom, the United States, Uruguay and Yugo-slavia, and was approved by the Committee without objection, on 26 July 1971.

(For text of resolution, see DOCUMENTARY REFERENCES below.)

DOCUMENTARY REFERENCES

Role of ACC

Economic and Social Council—51st session
Co-ordination Committee, meetings 413, 416-419, 422, 424, 425.
Plenary meeting 1799.

E/4989. Report of Committee for Programme and Co-ordination (CPC) on its 8th session, 22 March-8 April 1971, Chapters II-IV and Annexes III and IV.
E/5038. Report of CPC on its 9th session, 24 May-14 June 1971, Chapters III, IV and IX.
E/5038, para. 25. Draft resolution, recommended by CPC for adoption by Economic and Social Council, as orally amended by Co-ordination Committee by consensus, approved by Co-ordi-nation Committee by consensus on 19 July 1971, meeting 425.
E/5045. Report of Chairman of CPC and Acting Chairman of Administrative Committee on Co-ordination (ACC) on Joint Meetings of CPC and ACC, Geneva, Switzerland, 1 and 2 July 1971.
E/5045/Add.1. Annex II: Letter of 7 May 1971 from Secretary-General to Chairman of CPC.

E/AC.24/L.400. Ghana: draft resolution.
E/AC.24/L.401. Ghana: amendments to draft resolution proposed by CPC in E/5038.
E/AC.24/L.402. Brazil, France, Uruguay, USSR: amendments to draft resolution proposed by CPC in E/5038.
E/AC.24/L.403. Sudan: amendments to draft resolution proposed by CPC in E/5038.
E/5069. Report of Co-ordination Committee, draft resolution II.

RESOLUTION 1643(LI), as recommended by Co-ordination Committee, E/5069, and as orally corrected by Council President, adopted unanimously by Council on 30 July 1971, meeting 1799.

The Economic and Social Council,
Recalling the provisions of Chapter IX of the Charter of the United Nations concerning international economic and social co-operation and, in particular, Article 58 concerning recommen-dations to be made by the Organization for the co-ordination of the policies and activities of the specialized agencies, and the provisions of Chapter X of the Charter, in particular Article 63,

paragraph 2, which provides that the Council may co-ordinate the activities of the specialized agencies through consultation with and recommendations to such agencies and through recommendations to the General Assembly and to the Members of the United Nations,

Recalling the establishment of the Administrative Committee on Co-ordination in pursuance of Council resolution 13(III) of 21 September 1946 and the concurring decisions of the competent organs of the specialized agencies and the International Atomic Energy Agency and, in some cases, the relationship agreements concluded between the Council and the agencies,

Recalling further its resolutions 1367(XLV) of 2 August 1968 and 1547(XLIX) of 30 July 1970,

Considering the need to increase the efficiency of the activities of the United Nations system in the economic, social and related fields, *inter alia*, through a move by the United Nations family of organizations towards a more co-ordinated and rational approach in terms of the formulation and implementation of programmes on a system-wide basis,

Noting that the implementation of the goals and objectives set forth in the International Development Strategy for the Second United Nations Development Decade will require, on the part of the United Nations system, dynamic action for the fulfilment of the needs of the developing countries, the maximum productivity and impact through adequate planning and programming and the rational utilization of all available resources,

Recalling that the policy-making role in the United Nations system is the prerogative of Member States represented in the competent organs of the system and that the different secretariats perform the functions assigned to them by those organs, in accordance with the constitutional provisions of each organization and agency,

Noting further that suggestions by various secretariats and secretariat bodies on possible courses of action would assist the competent intergovernmental bodies in exercising their decision-making role,

Noting also that, in accordance with the constitutional provisions and responsibilities of each of its components, the Administrative Committee on Co-ordination, in carrying out its functions as the main co-ordinating body at the secretariat level, can, *inter alia*, effectively assist the Council in fulfilling its task of co-ordinating the activities of the system in the economic, social and related fields by providing the necessary information and basic data, by serving as a clearing-house for matters that can more effectively be dealt with on a system-wide basis, by providing a suitable forum for consultations at the secretariat level on work programmes and by performing such other tasks as may be specifically entrusted to it by the Council,

Stressing the importance of securing the effective implementation of the agreements entered into between the United Nations, the specialized agencies and the International Atomic Energy Agency,

Stressing further the need for a more effective participation of the regional economic commissions in the co-ordination arrangements at the secretariat level,

1. *Invites* the Administrative Committee on Co-ordination to maintain under constant review measures to be suggested to the Economic and Social Council, in order to ensure the fullest and most effective implementation of the agreements entered into between the United Nations, the specialized agencies, and the International Atomic Energy Agency;

2. *Requests* the Committee to give priority to the study of uniform and co-ordinated methods which would enable the United Nations system to achieve greater productivity and efficiency through economies of scale and related advantages;

3. *Further requests* the Committee to present annually to the Council and, as appropriate, to the competent legislative bodies of the specialized agencies and the International Atomic Energy Agency a concise report on the way in which the system operates, bringing out the problems solved and in addition highlighting those which are unresolved, for action at the intergovernmental level, and making suggestions and proposals designed to facilitate the implementation by the organizations concerned of decisions taken by the Council in the field of co-ordination, in order to ensure that actions taken are mutually supporting and complementary;

4. *Calls upon* the Committee to present annually to the Council a list of possible topics for in-depth consideration, with a system-wide coverage, and, once the list has been approved in principle by the Council, to present to the Council and, as appropriate, the competent legislative bodies of the specialized agencies and the International Atomic Energy Agency separate reports on each topic containing a concise and factual picture of the way in which the system as a whole operates, pointing out in particular any shortfalls or duplication and also the practical difficulties arising from the implementation of policies and programmes of work related to the topic in question;

5. *Invites* the Committee to make available to the Council and the competent legislative bodies of the specialized agencies and the International Atomic Energy Agency the results of the work of its subsidiary bodies, including *ad hoc* groups or panels, or, where appropriate, brief summaries including the main topics and trends of discussions;

6. *Urges* the Committee, in order to ensure greater efficiency and avoid duplication, to continue to make the necessary arrangements for prior consultations among interested secretariats of the United Nations system before proposals on draft programmes are presented to the legislative bodies and also before changes are made in the execution of approved programmes, keeping the Council informed on developments by means of periodic reports;

7. *Calls upon* the Committee, when it submits suggestions and studies, to state options and alternative courses of action in order to facilitate the decision-making role of the appropriate legislative organs;

8. *Further calls upon* the Committee to ensure, where appropriate, close control over all inter-agency meetings held for purposes of consultation and co-ordination;

9. *Decides* that all members of the Council and of the Committee for Programme and Co-ordination should receive notification of the meetings of the Administrative Committee on Co-ordination, its Preparatory Committee and other subsidiary bodies, together with an indication of the agendas of those meetings;

10. *Requests* the Secretary-General to pursue his consideration of the possibility of associating, where and when necessary, the executive secretaries of the regional economic commissions and the Director of the United Nations Economic and Social Office at Beirut with the meetings of the Administrative Committee on Co-ordination and its Preparatory Committee.

Reports of specialized agencies and IAEA

Economic and Social Council—51st session
Co-ordination Committee, meetings 413-416, 431.
Plenary meetings 1780, 1799.

E/4974 and Add.1. Report of IAEA.
E/4975. Report of UNESCO.
E/4976. Report of UPU. Analytical report on work of UPU in 1970.
E/4977. Report of ILO(Summary).
E/4978. Report of WHO (Summary).
E/4979. Report of ITU.
E/4980. Report of ICAO (Summary).
E/4981. Report of IMCO (Summary).
E/4982. Report of WMO (Summary).
E/4983. Report of FAO.
E/5038. Report of CPC on its 9th session, 24 May–14 June 1971, Chapter IV.
E/L.1424. Letter of 30 April 1971 from Director-General of IAEA.
E/AC.24/L.409. Brazil, Peru, USSR, United Kingdom, United States, Uruguay, Yugoslavia: draft resolution, as orally amended by sponsors, approved without objection by Co-ordination Committee on 26 July 1971, meeting 431.
E/5069. Report of Co-ordination Committee, draft resolution I.

RESOLUTION 1642(LI), as recommended by Co-ordination Committee, E/5069, adopted unanimously by Council on 30 July 1971, meeting 1799.

The Economic and Social Council,

Having examined the analytical summaries of the reports of the specialized agencies and the International Atomic Energy Agency and the comments of the Committee for Programme and Co-ordination in its report on its ninth session,

Believing that there should be an improvement in the Council's consideration of these reports,

Having heard the suggestion of the Director-General of the World Health Organization for an annual in-depth review of two or three agencies, as well as other suggestions made during the course of the fifty-first session of the Council,

1. *Takes note with appreciation* of the analytical summaries provided by the specialized agencies and the International Atomic Energy Agency and in particular the improvements introduced in the summaries;

2. *Requests* the specialized agencies and the International Atomic Energy Agency to continue to furnish such analytical summaries, bearing in mind the guidelines laid down by the Council, in particular in its resolution 1548(XLIX) of 30 July 1970;

3. *Instructs* the Committee for Programme and Co-ordination to recommend that the Council approve at its spring session the choice of the reports of two or three agencies which the Council might appropriately examine in depth, and to recommend procedures to be followed, having regard to the desirability of ensuring that the reports of all the agencies should receive detailed consideration over a five-year period;

4. *Decides* that, at the Council's summer session, after finishing the in-depth discussion of the reports selected on the recommendation of the Committee, sufficient time should be allowed for the discussion of any of the other reports.

Co-ordination of programme activities

Second United Nations Development Decade

In its 1971 annual report to the Economic and Social Council, the Administrative Committee on Co-ordination (ACC) stressed the importance it attached to the International Development Strategy for the Second United Nations Development Decade, not only as an expression of political will—because the primary responsibility for the implementation of the policy measures embodied therein rested with the Governments themselves —but also as a frame of reference for further co-operation and co-ordination in the activities of the United Nations family during the Decade.

The report referred to current deliberations in the Economic and Social Council and the General Assembly regarding the mechanisms and procedures for review and appraisal of progress in the implementation of the Strategy. Pending action by these organs, ACC stated, preliminary consultations were being undertaken at the secretariat level on technical issues of an inter-disciplinary character.

One such issue was the attainment of a proper degree of harmonization of the sectoral reviews conducted by the various organizations in their respective areas of activity. Consideration was also being given to ways of ensuring that appraisals carried out at different levels and in various forums drew on each other, as well as on relevant information gathered outside the United Nations system. In particular, reviews by Governments at the national level were basic to the whole process, and the United Nations family of organizations was already active in assisting Governments in this field. Moreover, arrangements were being made for the preparation of an agreed list of indicators in the economic and social field, so as to ensure that the information and data used were common to all appraisals.

It was pointed out by ACC that, inasmuch as responsibility for over-all review and appraisal would be entrusted to the General Assembly and the Economic and Social Council, the United Nations Secretariat would act as the focal point for, and take the lead in, the consideration of issues relating to the collection, analysis and correlation of sectoral data.

Members of the Council's Committee for Programme and Co-ordination (CPC) expressed satisfaction at the inter-secretariat arrangements reported by ACC. Some reservations were expressed, however, regarding the extent of the involvement of inter-secretariat bodies, such as ACC and its Sub-Committee on the Second Development Decade, in the appraisal of the Decade's results.

Science and technology

The question of future institutional arrangements for science and technology was considered by CPC at its March-April 1971 session. It was unable to reach any agreement on a recommendation to the Economic and Social Council regarding changes in the current machinery, and limited its report to a list of suggestions formulated during the meeting.

The framework of the discussions was provided by the conclusion of the Advisory Committee on the Application of Science and Technology to Development that its recommendations would receive fuller attention if they were considered by an inter-governmental body in which those concerned with policy decisions on scientific matters at the national level would participate.

Commenting on this question in its annual report, ACC reconfirmed its preference for a centralized advisory body concerned with global policy issues in the field of science and technology, and so constituted as to include a balanced representation to cover areas of activity involving more than one organization in the United Nations system.

At the Joint Meetings of CPC and ACC, held on 1 and 2 July 1971, it was agreed not to comment on the specific proposals for future institutional arrangements before the Economic and Social Council, and to concentrate on a general discussion of the over-all requirements of the United

Nations system of organizations regarding this area.

Also, the belief was expressed that there was a continuing need for a centralized advisory body capable of responding to new developments in science and technology and to the changing requirements of United Nations organizations. During the discussions, it was stated that while the United Nations system had traditionally used a sectoral approach to problems of this type, it was particularly important that an inter-disciplinary approach to questions of science and technology be encouraged, in terms of removing economic and financial constraints, tackling general problems of planning, and enlarging the areas of political agreement.

(For further information, see pp. 315-16.)

In the context of science and technology, both CPC and ACC reviewed during 1971 the inter-agency implications of the establishment by the United Nations Conference on Trade and Development (UNCTAD) of a new inter-governmental group to consider problems relating to the transfer of operative technology.

The "green revolution"

In 1971, ACC submitted to the Economic and Social Council its first study of a key issue which provided an opportunity for concerted inter-agency action in economic and social development. The study related to the "green revolution"—the technology involving the introduction and increasing application of new varieties of high-yielding food crops.

The aim of the study, ACC indicated, was to assist the governing organs of United Nations organizations in the development of relevant programme initiatives. However, ACC hoped that an agreed analysis of the opportunities offered by the green revolution, together with its economic and social implications, could also provide valuable assistance to member States in deciding on policies to be formulated, and in stimulating closer co-operation among national departments concerned.

On 30 July 1971, the Economic and Social Council, by the adoption of resolution 1645(LI), endorsed the broad lines for inter-agency action outlined in the ACC report. Governments and international organizations were invited to give close attention, in their short- and medium-term plans, to the promotion of projects related to the green revolution, taking due account of the impact of the new technology on socio-economic development.

Among other things, the Council also decided to review, in co-operation with ACC, progress made in the application of this technology at the mid-term of the Second Development Decade.

(For further details and text of resolution 1645(LI), see pp. 352-53 and 355-56, respectively.)

The human environment

A second functional group to deal with the questions concerning the human environment was established by ACC in 1971. This group was to concentrate on the preparation of a consolidated report on current and planned activities of the United Nations system, for submission to the United Nations Conference on the Human Environment (scheduled for June 1972) in connexion with its consideration of the organizational implications of action proposals.

This and related developments were reviewed by CPC at its May-June 1971 session.

The question of reviewing the co-ordination of activities relating to the uses of the seas was postponed by CPC.

Other programme matters

Among the other programme matters reviewed by ACC in 1971 were the long-term plans for action against drug abuse, drawn up by the Secretary-General following the establishment of the United Nations Fund for Drug Abuse Control. The maximum contribution of the specialized agencies in the implementation of these plans was urged.

Also, ACC reported to the Economic and Social Council that it had agreed to the suggestion of the sponsoring agencies of the Protein Advisory Group (the Food and Agriculture Organization of the United Nations (FAO), the World Health Organization (WHO) and the United Nations Children's Fund (UNICEF)) that the Group should be broadened to become the principal technical advisory body on protein nutrition for the entire system. All United Nations organizations had been invited to become sponsors and to contribute financially towards the budget of the Group. (See also pp. 351-52.)

The preparations for the World Population Conference and the World Population Year were examined by ACC, which called for active support thereto of all organizations concerned.

With regard to the programmes of the United Nations system dealing with the peaceful uses of outer space, ACC informed the Economic and Social Council of the results of recent inter-agency consultations in this area, and of the arrangements made to co-ordinate the activities of the United Nations, the United Nations Educational, Scientific and Cultural Organization (UNESCO) and the International Telecommunication Union (ITU) relating to direct broadcasting satellites.

General support for the organizational and other proposals contained in the comprehensive report prepared by the Secretary-General on assistance in disaster relief was recorded in the ACC report to the Council. (See also pp. 473-79.)

Also included in ACC's report was information on the activities undertaken by United Nations organizations in the implementation of the Declaration on the Granting of Independence to Colonial Countries and Peoples, and other relevant General Assembly resolutions. (See pp. 524-29.)

Programme co-ordination was reviewed by CPC on the basis of the ACC report. In addition, CPC considered co-ordination arrangements in the field of tourism and held a preliminary discussion on the activities of the United Nations system at the regional level, with particular reference to an Economic and Social Council request of 30 July 1970[3] calling for a study on the regional structures of the system.

[3]See Y.U.N., 1970, p. 439, text of resolution 1553(XLIX).

DOCUMENTARY REFERENCES

Second United Nations Development Decade
E/5012 (Part I). Thirty-seventh report of ACC, Chapter I A.
E/5038. Report of CPC on its 9th session, 24 May–14 June 1971, Chapter IV, para. 30.

Science and technology
E/4989. Report of CPC on its 8th session, 22 March–8 April 1971, Chapter VII.
E/5012 (Part I). Thirty-seventh report of ACC, Chapter I B.

The "green revolution"

Economic and Social Council—51st session
Co-ordination Committee, meetings 413, 416-419, 531.
Plenary meeting 1799.

RESOLUTION 1645(LI), as recommended by Co-ordination Committee (E/5069, draft resolution IV), adopted by Council on 30 July 1971, meeting 1799, by 25 votes to 0, with 2 abstentions.

[For text and supporting documentation, see pp. 355-56.]

The human environment
E/5012 (Part I). Thirty-seventh report of ACC, Chapter I C.
E/5038. Report of CPC on its 9th session, 24 May–14 June 1971, Chapter VIII A.

Other programme matters
E/4989. Report of CPC on its 8th session, 22 March–8 April 1971, Chapter IX: Development of tourism.
E/5012 (Part I). Thirty-seventh report of ACC. Chapter I: Section D, Outer space; Section E, Statistical activities; Section F, Population questions; Section G, Action against drug abuse; Section H, Assistance in cases of natural disaster. Chapter II: Questions relating to implementation of Declaration on Granting of Independence to Colonial Countries and Peoples by members of United Nations system.
E/5038. Report of CPC on its 9th session, 24 May–14 June 1971, Chapter VII: Study of regional structures.
E/5072/Rev.1. Report of CPC on its 10th session, 13–17 September and 5, 8, 10, 12 and 17 November 1971, Chapter II.

Co-ordination of administrative and financial activities

Joint Inspection Unit

A number of reports of the Joint Inspection Unit dealing with the activities of the Economic Commission for Latin America, the work of the United Nations family of organizations in some Central American countries and the operations of the United Nations in Madagascar and Nepal were reviewed by the Committee for Programme and Co-ordination (CPC) during 1971.

By a decision taken on 30 July 1971, without adoption of a formal resolution, the Economic and Social Council noted these reports with appreciation and drew the attention of all concerned to the comments of CPC.

In this connexion, CPC had: expressed satisfaction with the positive response of the executive heads of the organizations to the reports of the Joint Inspection Unit; suggested that, in commenting on these reports, the Secretary-General and the Administrator of the United Nations Development Programme (UNDP) should give particular attention to recommendations with which they could not concur, and explain the reasons for their objections; and recommended that steps be taken within the United Nations to expedite the circulation and consideration of these reports.

The Council's decision, unanimously recommended by the Co-ordination Committee on the proposal of the United Kingdom, was approved by 24 votes to 1, with 2 abstentions.

Computers

Recent developments in the United Nations system with regard to the use of computers were described in the annual report of the Administrative Committee on Co-ordination (ACC) to the Economic and Social Council.

During 1971, ACC had agreed on the terms of reference of the newly established Inter-Organization Board for Information Systems and Related Activities, as follows:

(a) under the over-all direction of ACC, to develop inter-organization management information systems, particularly in support of social and economic development activities;

(b) to approve the necessary work programme, including cost estimates, for the development of such systems and to monitor progress in its implementation;

(c) to establish and maintain close co-operation with organizations outside the United Nations system, whose activities were relevant to the Board's work programme; and

(d) to establish the necessary policy guidelines for the planning and development of the International Computing Centre.

The Computing Centre became operational on 1 March 1971.

The terms of reference of the Board were noted with approval by CPC, which expressed the hope that, bearing in mind their specific requirements, other organizations of the United Nations system represented on the Board would join the International Computing Centre.

These developments were briefly reviewed by the Council at its mid-1971 session.

Later in the year, on 22 December 1971, the General Assembly, on the recommendation of its Fifth (Administrative and Budgetary) Committee, urged all organizations concerned to review their policies in the field of electronic data processing so that the International Computing Centre could, at a very early date, become a truly common facility for the United Nations family of organizations. (See also pp. 674-75.)

Other administrative and financial questions

The 1971 report of ACC to the Economic and Social Council described at some length the efforts being made at the inter-agency level to standardize as far as possible the presentation of the programmes and budgets of the various organizations, and to synchronize their budget cycles.

For example, ACC reported that inter-agency agreements had been reached during the past year on a standard classification for objects of expenditure, to be used by all organizations for budget and accounting purposes, and on some standard annexes to the programme and budget documents of the various organizations.

With regard to synchronization of budget periods, ACC recommended that those organizations that faced no constitutional obstacles to changing to a two-year period should aim to do so on a synchronized basis, as soon as possible. In this respect, ACC also drew attention to the advantages that the system would derive from the adoption by the United Nations of biennial programme budgeting.

Finally, ACC drew the Council's attention to the new classification of activities it had used in the preparation of its annual report on the expenditures of the system in relation to programmes, and expressed the hope that its new format would provide the Council with a more adequate tool for the comparison of the magnitude and balance of programmes.

On 30 July 1971, the Council welcomed the new format of the annual report of ACC on expenditures of the United Nations system in relation to programmes, which presented those expenditures broken down by programme sectors and sub-sectors. The Council felt that the new format provided an over-all view of the activities of the system that would be helpful to it in carrying out its policy-making and co-ordination roles.

The Council requested UNDP, the Inter-Organization Board and other organs concerned to utilize the new framework as far as possible in their information system and reporting activities. Some refinements in the framework, aimed at better relating the figures to the programmes they paid for, were also recommended.

This Council decision was embodied in resolution 1646(LI), adopted, by 19 votes to 0, with 7 abstentions, on the recommendation of the Co-ordination Committee. The draft resolution was sponsored by the United States, and approved by the Co-ordination Committee, on 26 July 1971, by 14 votes to 0, with 9 abstentions. (For text of resolution, see DOCUMENTARY REFERENCES below.)

A proposal by the USSR that consideration of the draft resolution be postponed until the views of the Advisory Committee on Administrative and Budgetary Questions (ACABQ) were available was rejected by 9 votes to 3, with 10 abstentions. (See pp. 673-74 for information on ACABQ reports and General Assembly action.)

DOCUMENTARY REFERENCES

Joint Inspection Unit

Economic and Social Council—51st session
Co-ordination Committee, meetings 431, 432.
Plenary meeting 1799.

E/4932. Observations on work of United Nations Office for Technical Co-operation in Madagascar. Note by Advisory Committee on Administrative and Budgetary Questions (ACABQ) (transmitting report of Joint Inspection Unit (JIU)).
E/4935 and Add.1 and Add.1/Corr.1 and Add.2. Report on activities of Economic Commission for Latin America (ECLA).
E/4941 and Add.1,2. Report on activities of United Nations family of organizations in some Central American countries. Report of JIU; report of Secretary-General to ACABQ; comments of ACABQ.
E/4941/Add.3. Report on activities of United Nations family of organizations in some Central American countries; report on activities of United Nations in some Central American countries. Report of Secretary-General to ACABQ.
E/4941/Rev.1. Report on activities of United Nations family of organizations in some Central American countries; report on activities of United Nations in some Central American countries. Reports of JIU.
E/4941/Rev.1/Add.4-7. Report on activities of United Nations family of organizations in some Central American countries. Comments of specialized agencies; comments of Secretary-General of ICAO and action taken by ICAO Council; comments of Director-General of UPU and action taken by UPU Council; comments of Director-General of UNESCO and action taken by Executive Board of UNESCO.
E/4951 and Add.1-5. United Nations activities and operations in Nepal.
E/4952. Work programme of Joint Inspection Unit for 1971. Note by Secretary-General.
E/4957. Overhead costs of extra-budgetary programmes and on

methods of measuring performances and costs; some aspects of technical assistance activities of United Nations; programming and budgets in United Nations family of organizations; visit to Malaysia and Singapore; selected ideas for improving field operations; visit of inspection to Malawi; United Nations activities and operations in Nepal; report on activities of United Nations family of organizations in some Central American countries. Action taken by Executive Committee of WMO.

E/4989. Report of Committee for Programme and Co-ordination (CPC) on its 8th session, 22 March–8 April 1971, Chapter V.

E/5038. Report of CPC on its 9th session, 24 May–14 June 1971, Chapter VIII C.

E/5048 and Add.1-5. United Nations activities in Indonesia.

E/5049 and Add.1. Observations on work of Office for Technical Co-operation of United Nations in Burma.

E/L.1428. Note by Secretariat.

E/AC.24/L.414. United Kingdom: draft decision.

E/5067. Report of Co-ordination Committee.

E/5073. Resolutions adopted by Economic and Social Council during its 51st session, 5-30 July 1971. Other decision, p. 20.

A/8403. Report of Economic and Social Council on work of its 50th and 51st sessions, Chapter XXII.

Computers

E/5013 and Corr.1,2 and Add.1. Report of ACC on recent developments in use of computers and common information needs in United Nations system.

E/5038. Report of CPC on its 9th session, Chapter IV, para. 40.

Other administrative and financial questions

EXPENDITURES IN RELATION TO PROGRAMMES

Economic and Social Council—51st session
Co-ordination Committee, meetings 413, 416, 418, 431.
Plenary meeting 1799.

E/5014. Report of ACC.

E/AC.24/L.407. United States: draft resolution, approved by Co-ordination Committee on 26 July 1971, meeting 431, by 14 votes to 0, with 9 abstentions.

E/5069. Report of Co-ordination Committee, draft resolution V.

RESOLUTION 1646(LI), as recommended by Co-ordination Committee, E/5069, adopted by Council on 30 July 1971, meeting 1799, by 19 votes to 0, with 7 abstentions.

The Economic and Social Council,

Recalling its resolution 984(XXXVI) of 2 August 1963 concerning the preparation of a framework of functional classification for the activities of the United Nations system of organizations in connexion with the first United Nations Development Decade, and section I of its resolution 1090 D (XXXIX) of 31 July 1965, concerning the submission to the Council of a separate report containing a list of activities of the organizations in the United Nations system in the fields of interest to the Council, with an indication of the expenditures involved under both the regular budget and the extra-budgetary programmes of these organizations,

Recalling further that the Council at its forty-fifth session concluded that the headings used in the report of the Administrative Committee on Co-ordination on expenditures in relation to programmes, and the allocation of expenditures under each heading, needed to be reviewed in the light of the requirements of those bodies with responsibilities for co-ordinating the activities of the United Nations system in the economic, social and human rights fields,

Bearing in mind recommendation G in the final report of the Enlarged Committee for Programme and Co-ordination, in which that Committee considered the improvements that could be made in the existing framework of headings, particularly from the standpoint of the requirements of coherent programme review and co-ordination, and stressed the need for the establishment of mutually exclusive categories by excluding as far as possible cross-sectoral headings,

1. *Takes note* of the new format of the annual report of the Administrative Committee on Co-ordination on expenditures of the United Nations system in relation to programmes, which presents these expenditures broken down by programme sectors and sub-sectors;

2. *Welcomes* this new format as providing an over-all view of the activities of the system that will be helpful to the Council in carrying out its policy-making and co-ordinating roles;

3. *Requests* the United Nations Development Programme, the Inter-Organization Board and other organs of the United Nations system concerned to utilize this framework as far as possible in their information system and reporting activities;

4. *Requests* the Administrative Committee on Co-ordination to consider the possibility of including cross-references, in the notes to table 4, to the corresponding parts of the budget documents of those organizations whose budgets are presented on a "programme" basis, so that it would be possible to relate the figures to the programmes they pay for.

United Nations work programme in the economic, social and human rights fields

Reports to Economic and Social Council

At its mid-1971 session, the Economic and Social Council considered the work programme performance of the United Nations in the economic, social and human rights fields. The Council had before it a report of the Secretary-General on the work programme performance in the economic, social and human rights fields for the financial year 1970 and the related reports of the Committee for Programme and Co-ordination (CPC).

The Secretary-General's report evaluated the programme performance during 1970 for the following units: (*a*) Division of Human Rights; (*b*) Department of Economic and Social Affairs, including the regional economic commissions; (*c*)

United Nations economic and social activities in Geneva, Switzerland; (*d*) the United Nations Conference on Trade and Development (UNCTAD); and (*e*) the United Nations Industrial Development Organization (UNIDO).

The Committee for Programme and Co-ordination reported to the mid-1971 session of the Economic and Social Council that it had examined the performance report at its May-June 1971 session and had agreed that it represented a significant improvement over previous reports of a similar nature. Nevertheless, both the format and the content could be further improved to enhance its usefulness.

Members of CPC had also stressed the importance of the earlier development of an integrated system of programme planning and budgeting, which would yield the kind of information the Committee needed to determine priorities and allocation of resources. The Committee gave considerable attention to the impact of recruiting difficulties on the implementation of the work programme.

Later in 1971, at meetings held in November, CPC considered the report of the Secretary-General on the new form of presentation of the United Nations budget. The majority of CPC members agreed that the introduction of programme budgeting would strengthen legislative control over programme objectives and content, as well as over the level of resources required for their implementation.

Decisions of Economic and Social Council

At its mid-1971 session the Economic and Social Council took up the recommendation of CPC dealing with programme implementation in 1970 and related matters.

On 30 July 1971, the Council, while recognizing the significant improvement of the Secretary-General's report on work programme performance in the economic, social and human rights fields for the financial year 1970 over reports of previous years, noted CPC's opinion that the report could still be further improved both in format and in content to enhance its usefulness.

The Council asked the Secretary-General in future reports to ensure that: (a) the format of the budget performance document should have a direct correlation with the work programme for the same year to enable meaningful comparisons to be made; (b) the document should be more detailed and give more output-oriented information, since it continued to emphasize input factors, such as man-months spent in preparation of projects, to the detriment of information on allocation of resources and even on non-administrative impediments to the implementation of the approved programmes; (c) the United Nations Secretariat should exercise greater central supervision over the preparation of the document to ensure the consistency of its parts, and, pending the study on a system of programme budgeting, should provide specified over-all information; (d) the period covered by the data presented should be extended to five years to enable easy comparisons; and (e) the reports should be circulated early in the year and considered by each organization, and the results, in turn, should be examined by CPC.

These Council decisions were set forth in resolution 1644(LI), adopted by 25 votes to 0, with 2 abstentions. The text of the resolution was recommended to the Council by the Co-ordination Committee which approved it without objection on 26 July, on a proposal by Norway and the United States.

(For text of resolution, see DOCUMENTARY REFERENCES below.)

In connexion with CPC's comments on the new form of presentation of the United Nations budget, the Council, on 30 November 1971, transmitted CPC's report to the Advisory Committee on Administrative and Budgetary Questions for consideration, and to the General Assembly, together with the report of the Secretary-General on the subject.

(See page 641 for General Assembly consideration.)

DOCUMENTARY REFERENCES

Economic and Social Council—50th session
Plenary meeting 1767.

E/4989. Report of CPC on its 8th session, 22 March–8 April 1971.
E/4998. Financial implications of recommendations of commissions and committees of Council. Note by Secretary-General.
E/5044. Resolutions adopted by Economic and Social Council during its 50th session, 11-13 January and 26 April–21 May 1971. Decisions, p. 26.

Economic and Social Council—51st session
Co-ordination Committee, meetings 413, 417-419, 422, 425, 431.
Plenary meetings 1799, 1806, 1807.

E/5038. Report of CPC on its 9th session, 24 May–14 June 1971, Chapter II.
E/5072/Rev.1. Report of CPC on its 10th session, 13-17 September and 5, 8, 10, 12 and 17 November 1971, Chapter III and Annex III.
E/AC.51/52 and Corr.1 and Add.1. Report of Secretary-General.
E/AC.51/53. Implementation of 1971 work programme in economic, social and human rights fields. Note by Secretary-General.
E/AC.24/L.399. Norway and United States: draft resolution.

approved without objection by Co-ordination Committee on 26 July 1971, meeting 431.
E/5069. Report of Co-ordination Committee, draft resolution III.

RESOLUTION 1644(LI), as recommended by Co-ordination Committee, E/5069, adopted by Council on 30 July 1971, meeting 1799, by 25 votes to 0, with 2 abstentions.

The Economic and Social Council,
Recognizing the significant improvement of the Secretary-General's report on work programme performance in the economic, social and human rights fields for the financial year 1970 over reports of previous years,
Noting that the Committee for Programme and Co-ordination felt that the report could still be further improved, in terms of both format and content, to enhance its usefulness,
Noting further that future reports should be more output-oriented and should provide an over-all analysis of performance,
Requests that the Secretary-General in future reports should ensure that:
(a) The format of the budget performance document for any given year should have a direct correlation with the work programme document for that year, in order to enable meaningful comparisons to be made;

(b) The document should be amplified by more detailed and more output-oriented information, since it continues to emphasize input factors, such as man-months spent in preparation of projects in progress, to the detriment of information on allocation of resources and even on non-administrative impediments to the implementation of the approved programmes;

(c) The Secretariat should exercise greater central supervision over the preparation of the document, to ensure the consistency of its various parts, and, pending the study on a system of programme budgeting, the Secretariat should prepare an overview section in which the various parts are synthesized, in which the over-all problems of the work programme performance are analysed, and in which, where possible, and provided this is based on the decisions taken and the priorities set by the intergovernmental organs concerned, the allocations of resources between the various sections of the work programme are explained;

(d) The period covered by the data presented in the tables should be extended to five years, i.e. the authorization with reference to the specific decisions taken by the competent intergovernmental bodies and performance data for the four previous years together with the authorization data for the current year should be presented for each programme, so as to permit an easy comparison of the shifting of emphasis within and between sections, explanations of the causes of which should be incorporated in the explanatory texts, due regard also being paid to the fact that the inclusion of the current year's authorizations would be most useful in ascertaining the future direction programmes may take and would be of assistance to the various intergovernmental bodies in their decision making;

(e) The reports should be circulated early in the year to the intergovernmental organs concerned and, as far as practicable, incorporated in the agendas and documentation for consideration by each organization or commission, and the results of such consideration, in turn, should be examined by the Committee for Programme and Co-ordination in its review of the topic.

E/5073/Add.1. Resolutions adopted by Economic and Social Council during its resumed 51st session, 27-29 October, 23 and 30 November and 20 December 1971. Other decisions, p. 4.

A/8403/Add.1. Addendum to report of Economic and Social Council, resumed 51st session, Chapter VI.

Developments regarding organizational questions

Organization of work of Council

Enlargement of Council

The question of enlarging the membership of the Economic and Social Council was discussed in 1971 in conjunction with consideration of measures to improve the organization of its work.

The Council began its discussion at meetings held in January. At its April-May session a number of draft resolutions were submitted. However, debate was adjourned to the July session.

On 30 July 1971, with the adoption of resolution 1621 A (LI), the Council took a decision on the enlargement of its membership. Reaffirming that its role as a principal organ of the United Nations should be enhanced and its methods of work improved to enable it to discharge more effectively the functions conferred upon it by the United Nations Charter, the Council observed that the participation of a larger number of States Members of the United Nations would strengthen the representative character, the authority and the dynamism of the Council.

It thus recommended that the General Assembly take, at its 1971 session, all necessary steps to amend the Charter to ensure an early enlargement of the Council to 54 members, the additional 27 seats to be allocated in accordance with the present geographical distribution in the Council.

The Council also decided to enlarge, in the interim period, the membership of its sessional committees and the Committee on Natural Resources to 54 members as from 1 January 1972. It asked the General Assembly to elect, at its 1971 session, 27 States Members of the United Nations to serve on the sessional committees of the Council in accordance with the current geographical distribution of seats in the Council.

At the same time, the Council decided: that in the interim period, all substantive agenda items would be submitted to sessional committees, with a view to submitting concrete recommendations to the Council; and that in mid-1972 it would review its co-ordinating machinery, including the possibility of inter-sessional meetings of the Co-ordination Committee to deal with the work currently entrusted to the Committee for Programme and Co-ordination.

(For text of resolution 1621 A (LI), see DOCUMENTARY REFERENCES below. Parts B and C of the Council's resolution dealt with future institutional arrangements for science and technology and with the machinery for appraisal of progress during the Second United Nations Development Decade, respectively. See pp. 315-16 and 226.)

Part A of the resolution was adopted by a roll-call vote of 17 to 10; the resolution as a whole was adopted by a roll-call vote of 17 to 7, with 3 abstentions.

The text was sponsored by Ghana, Haiti, Indonesia, Italy, Jamaica, Kenya, Lebanon, Madagascar, Malaysia, New Zealand, Niger, Norway, Sudan, Tunisia, the United States and Zaire.

A proposal by Greece to defer to a later date in 1971 the adoption of decisions on questions relating to structural reform was rejected in the Council.

On 20 December 1971, the General Assembly acted on the recommendation of the Economic and Social Council. It decided to adopt an amendment to the United Nations Charter providing for enlargement of the Council and to submit it for ratification to Member States.

The amendment provided for enlarging the Council from 27 to 54 members. Members of the Council were to be elected by the General

Assembly in accordance with the following pattern:

(*a*) 14 members from African States;

(*b*) 11 members from Asian States;

(*c*) 10 members from Latin American States;

(*d*) 13 members from Western European and other States; and

(*e*) 6 members from socialist States of Eastern Europe.

The Assembly also welcomed the Council's decision to enlarge its sessional committees to 54 members and invited it to elect the new members to serve on those committees at its first meetings in 1972.

The Assembly's decisions on the matter were set forth in resolution 2847(XXVI), which was adopted, by a roll-call vote of 105 to 2, with 15 abstentions, on the recommendation of the Second (Economic and Financial) Committee.

When the Second Committee considered the question, it had before it a 41-power draft resolution giving effect to the Economic and Social Council's recommendations.

During the discussion, amendments to the 41-power draft text were proposed. These dealt with the geographical distribution of Council seats. Proposals by the Congo and Rwanda to the effect that the seats in the enlarged Council should be apportioned in such a manner that the principle of equitable geographical distribution was the main criterion were rejected by roll-call vote.

The other amendments before the Second Committee, with the exception of those proposed by Australia, were withdrawn. A motion to defer the question to the 1972 session of the General Assembly, proposed by Upper Volta, was defeated. The Australian amendments to the draft resolution—setting forth the geographical pattern of seats on the Council and the sessional committees—were then adopted by roll-call vote. A Lebanese sub-amendment, which would have had the Assembly review the distribution of seats in 1972, was rejected.

Finally, the Committee, after approving separately by a roll-call vote of 93 to 4, with 16 abstentions, the provision to amend the Charter so as to enlarge the Council to 54 members, approved the text as a whole by another roll-call vote; this last vote was 93 in favour to 4 against, with 17 abstentions.

The 41 sponsors of the draft resolution in the Second Committee were: Algeria, Argentina, Austria, Cameroon, Canada, Central African Republic, Chad, Colombia, Denmark, the Dominican Republic, Egypt, Finland, Ghana, Guinea, Indonesia, Italy, the Ivory Coast, Jamaica, Japan, Kenya, Lebanon, Lesotho, Liberia, the Libyan Arab Republic, Madagascar, Malaysia, Mali, Mauritania, Mexico, Morocco, the Netherlands, Niger, Nigeria, Norway, the People's Democratic Repub-

lic of Yemen, Spain, Sudan, Sweden, Tunisia, the United States and Zaire.

(For text of resolution 2847(XXVI), see DOCU-MENTARY REFERENCES below.)

Organization of Council's work

During 1971, the Economic and Social Council took a number of decisions concerning the organization of its work.

On 30 July, it recommended that the General Assembly adopt a resolution by which that body would: (1) deem it advisable for any new economic, social, scientific or technical questions appearing on the Assembly agenda to be considered, as a rule, first by the Economic and Social Council, which would make specific recommendations concerning possible Assembly decisions thereon; (2) instruct the Council to submit a list of questions concerning the economic, social, scientific and technical activities of the United Nations, accompanied by recommendations for consideration at Assembly sessions; (3) ask the Council to indicate the range of problems on which the Council itself, in accordance with the Charter, considered it advisable to take final decisions, and to submit proposals on that question to the General Assembly in 1972; (4) invite the Council to regulate and improve co-ordination of economic, social, scientific and technical activities within the United nations system; and (5) instruct the Council to submit to the 1972 Assembly session proposals concerning effective measures to remedy current shortcomings in the co-ordination of economic and social development programmes and thereby to eliminate overlapping, duplication, overstaffing, and over-expenditure of budgetary funds.

This Council decision was embodied in resolution 1622(LI), adopted by 8 votes in favour to 4 against, with 15 abstentions, on a proposal of the USSR. (For text of resolution, see DOCUMENTARY REFERENCES below.)

The second Council decision on the organization of its work was embodied in resolution 1623(LI), also adopted on 30 July 1971.

Observing that its role as a principal organ of the United Nations should be reaffirmed, its authority enhanced and its methods of work improved, the Council reaffirmed that because of the expansion of the activities of the United Nations system, greatly increased importance had been assumed by its functions as: (*a*) the governing body for the United Nations work programme in the economic, social, human rights and related fields; (*b*) the co-ordinator of the activities of the United Nations system of organizations in these fields; and (*c*) a forum for the discussion of issues of international economic and social policy, and for formulating recommendations for the United

Nations system of organizations on these issues.

The Council also noted that the appraisal it was to make of the progress of the International Development Strategy for the Second United Nations Development Decade would bring its functions into sharper focus and require increased emphasis on the definition of priorities and the resolution of conflicts of interests within the United Nations system.

The Council decided that in its review of the over-all economic and social situation it should formulate new policy recommendations to meet the challenges of development, define major development lags and constraints and recommend means for their removal.

It also set forth the annual arrangements for its work programme, for documentation, and for related matters.

The Council welcomed the participation in its deliberations of United Nations Member States that were not members of the Council, in the conviction that such participation would ensure a politically more solid and wider basis for decisions.

(For text of resolution, see DOCUMENTARY REFERENCES below.)

The text of this resolution was proposed jointly by Greece and New Zealand; certain Brazilian amendments were accepted by the sponsors, others were not pressed to the vote. Also, eight-power amendments (Brazil, Ghana, Jamaica, Lebanon, Pakistan, Peru, Tunisia, Yugoslavia) were not pressed to a vote.

The Council adopted resolution 1623(LI) by 26 votes to 0, with 1 abstention.

At its 1971 session, which opened on 21 September, the General Assembly referred to its Second Committee the draft resolution on the organization of the Council's work, proposed by the Council on 30 July (resolution 1622(LI)).

Five Members of the Second Committee— Brazil, the Netherlands, the Philippines, Sudan and Tunisia—proposed extensive amendments to the operative part of the draft text, without, however, altering the basic thrust of the draft.

After some discussion, the Second Committee—on 16 December 1971—recommended to the Assembly that it defer further consideration of these proposals to its 1972 session. The Assembly accepted the recommendation on 20 December.

Documentation

The Economic and Social Council examined various measures to improve its documentation and took several decisions thereon at its mid-1971 session.

By resolution 1623(LI), which dealt mainly with the organization of its work, the Council set out certain guidelines relating to the form, content and submission of reports.

Another resolution—1624(LI)—was mainly concerned with the circulation of Council documentation in sufficient time and simultaneously in the working languages. The Council among other things asked its Committee for Programme and Co-ordination to make practical suggestions in this regard. The resolution was adopted, unanimously, on 30 July 1971, on the proposal of Brazil, France, Tunisia and Uruguay. (For text of resolution, see DOCUMENTARY REFERENCES below.)

(See also pp. 660-64.)

DOCUMENTARY REFERENCES

ENLARGEMENT OF COUNCIL

Economic and Social Council—50th session
Plenary meetings 1734-1739, 1743, 1745, 1761, 1765, 1768, 1772.

E/4986 and Add.1-9. Measures to improve organization of work of Council. Views and proposals of Governments. Note by Secretary-General.
E/L.1369. Note of 31 December 1970 by Council President.
E/5044. Resolutions adopted by Economic and Social Council during its 50th session, 11-13 January and 26 April–21 May 1971. Decisions, p. 26.

Economic and Social Council—51st session
Plenary meetings 1784, 1789, 1794-1799, 1808.

E/L.1451. Ghana, Haiti, Indonesia, Italy, Jamaica, Kenya, Lebanon, Madagascar, Malaysia, New Zealand, Niger, Norway, Sudan, Tunisia, United States, Zaire: draft resolution, part A.
E/L.1451/Add.1. Administrative and financial implications of 16-power draft resolution, E/L.1451. Statement by Secretary-General.
E/L.1458. Greece: draft resolution.

RESOLUTION 1621 A(LI), as proposed by 16 powers, E/L.1451,

part A, adopted by Council on 30 July 1971, meeting 1798, by roll-call vote of 17 to 10, as follows:

In favour: Ghana, Haiti, Indonesia, Italy, Jamaica, Kenya, Lebanon, Madagascar, Malaysia, New Zealand, Niger, Norway, Pakistan, Sudan, Tunisia, United States, Zaire.
Against: Brazil, Ceylon, France, Greece, Hungary, Peru, United Kingdom, USSR, Uruguay, Yugoslavia.

Draft resolution, as a whole (including parts B and C),* adopted by Council on 30 July 1971, meeting 1798, by roll-call vote of 17 to 7, with 3 abstentions, as follows:

In favour: Ghana, Haiti, Indonesia, Italy, Jamaica, Kenya, Lebanon, Madagascar, Malaysia, New Zealand, Niger, Norway, Pakistan, Sudan, Tunisia, United States, Zaire.
Against: Brazil, Ceylon, Hungary, Peru, USSR, Uruguay, Yugoslavia.
Abstaining: France, Greece, United Kingdom.

A

The Economic and Social Council,
Reaffirming that its role as a principal organ of the United Nations should be enhanced and its methods of work improved to enable it to discharge more effectively the functions conferred upon it by the Charter of the United Nations in the formulation of

general economic and social policies to meet the challenges of the modern world,

Considering that the participation of a larger number of States Members of the United Nations would strengthen the representative character, the authority and the dynamism of the Council,

1. *Recommends* the General Assembly to take, at its twenty-sixth session, all necessary steps to amend the Charter to ensure an early enlargement of the Council to 54 members, the additional 27 seats to be allocated in accordance with the present geographical distribution in the Council;

2. *Decides* to enlarge, in the interim period, the membership of its sessional committees and the Committee on Natural Resources to 54 members as from 1 January 1972;

3. *Requests* the General Assembly to elect, at its twenty-sixth session, in addition to the 9 new members of the Council, 27 States Members of the United Nations to serve on the sessional committees of the Council in accordance with the present geographical distribution of seats in the Council;

4. *Decides also* that, in the interim period, all substantive items on the agenda of a session of the Council, apart from the general debate, shall be allocated to the sessional committees for their in-depth consideration, with a view to submitting concrete recommendations to the Council;

5. *Decides further* to review at its fifty-third session its co-ordinating machinery, including the possibility of inter-sessional meetings of the Co-ordination Committee to deal with the task currently entrusted to the Committee for Programme and Co-ordination, with a view to strengthening the co-ordination role of the Council.

*For texts, roll-call votes and supporting documentation for parts B and C of resolution 1621(LI), which dealt with future institutional arrangements for science and technology and with the system of over-all appraisal of progress in implementing the International Development Strategy for the Second United Nations Development Decade, respectively, see pp. 319-20 and 229-30.

General Assembly—26th session
Second Committee, meetings 1370-1382, 1426, 1442-1446.
Plenary meeting 2026.

A/8403. Report of Economic and Social Council on work of its 50th and 51st sessions, Chapter IV.
A/C.2/264. Measures to improve organization of work of Council. Note by Secretary-General.
A/C.2/L.1184/Rev.1. Algeria, Argentina, Austria, Cameroon, Canada, Central African Republic, Chad, Colombia, Denmark, Dominican Republic, Egypt, Finland, Ghana, Guinea, Indonesia, Italy, Ivory Coast, Jamaica, Japan, Kenya, Lebanon, Lesotho, Liberia, Libyan Arab Republic, Madagascar, Malaysia, Mali, Mauritania, Mexico, Morocco, Netherlands, Niger, Nigeria, Norway, People's Democratic Republic of Yemen, Spain, Sudan, Sweden, Tunisia, United States, Zaire: revised draft resolution, as amended by Australia, A/C.2/L.1221, approved by Second Committee on 15 December 1971; meeting 1446, by roll-call vote of 93 to 4, with 17 abstentions, as follows:

In favour: Afghanistan, Albania, Algeria, Argentina, Australia, Austria, Bahrain, Barbados, Bhutan, Bolivia, Brazil, Burma, Cameroon, Canada, Ceylon, Chile, Colombia, Costa Rica, Cuba, Cyprus, Dahomey, Denmark, Dominican Republic, Ecuador, Egypt, El Salvador, Fiji, Finland, Ghana, Guatemala, Guyana, Haiti, Honduras, Iceland, India, Indonesia, Iran, Iraq, Ireland, Israel, Italy, Ivory Coast, Jamaica, Japan, Jordan, Kenya, Khmer Republic, Kuwait, Lebanon, Liberia, Libyan Arab Republic, Madagascar, Malawi, Malaysia, Mali, Malta, Mauritania, Mexico, Morocco, Nepal, Netherlands, New Zealand, Nicaragua, Nigeria, Norway, Panama, People's Democratic Republic of Yemen, Peru, Philippines, Qatar, Romania, Saudi Arabia, Senegal, Singapore, Spain, Sudan, Swaziland, Sweden, Syrian Arab Republic, Thailand, Togo, Trinidad and Tobago, Tunisia, Turkey, Uganda, United Republic of Tanzania, United States, Uruguay, Venezuela, Yemen, Yugoslavia, Zaire, Zambia.

Against: Ethiopia, France, Greece, United Kingdom.
Abstaining: Belgium, Bulgaria, Byelorussian SSR, Congo, Czechoslovakia, Hungary, Laos, Luxembourg, Mongolia, Oman, Poland, Portugal, Rwanda, South Africa, Ukrainian SSR, USSR, Upper Volta.

A/C.2/L.1190. Upper Volta: amendments to 41-power revised draft resolution, A/C.2/L.1184/Rev.1.
A/C.2/L.1208 and Rev.1. Congo: amendments and revised amendments to 41-power revised draft resolution, A/C.2/L.1184/Rev.1.
A/C.2/L.1208/Rev.2,3. Congo and Rwanda: revised amendments to 41-power revised draft resolution, A/C.2/L.1184/Rev.1.
A/C.2/L.1210. Bahrain, Burma, Ceylon, Fiji, Iraq, Khmer Republic, Kuwait, Laos, Nepal, Oman, Pakistan, Philippines, Qatar, Saudi Arabia, Singapore, Thailand, Yemen: amendments to 41-power revised draft resolution, A/C.2/L.1184/Rev.1.
A/C.2/L.1221. Australia: amendments to 41-power revised draft resolution, A/C.2/L.1184/Rev.1.
A/8578/Add.1 and Corr.1. Report of Second Committee (part II) (on report of Economic and Social Council), draft resolution X.

RESOLUTION 2847(XXVI), as recommended by Second Committee, A/8578/Add.1, adopted by Assembly on 20 December 1971, meeting 2026, by roll-call vote of 105 to 2, with 15 abstentions, as follows:

In favour: Afghanistan, Albania, Algeria, Argentina, Australia, Austria, Bahrain, Belgium, Bolivia, Brazil, Burma, Burundi, Cameroon, Canada, Central African Republic, Ceylon, Chad, Chile, Colombia, Congo, Costa Rica, Cuba, Cyprus, Dahomey, Denmark, Dominican Republic, Ecuador, Egypt, El Salvador, Equatorial Guinea, Finland, Gabon, Gambia, Ghana, Guatemala, Guinea, Guyana, Haiti, Honduras, Iceland, India, Indonesia, Iran, Iraq, Ireland, Israel, Italy, Ivory Coast, Jamaica, Japan, Jordan, Kenya, Kuwait, Laos, Lebanon, Lesotho, Liberia, Libyan Arab Republic, Luxembourg, Madagascar, Malawi, Malaysia, Mali, Malta, Mauritania, Mexico, Morocco, Nepal, Netherlands, New Zealand, Nicaragua, Nigeria, Norway, Pakistan, Panama, Paraguay, People's Democratic Republic of Yemen, Peru, Philippines, Qatar, Romania, Saudi Arabia, Senegal, Singapore, Somalia, Spain, Sudan, Swaziland, Sweden, Syrian Arab Republic, Thailand, Togo, Trinidad and Tobago, Tunisia, Turkey, Uganda, United Arab Emirates, United Republic of Tanzania, United States, Uruguay, Venezuela, Yemen, Yugoslavia, Zaire, Zambia.

Against: France, United Kingdom.
Abstaining: Bulgaria, Byelorussian SSR, Czechoslovakia, Ethiopia, Greece, Hungary, Mongolia, Oman, Poland, Portugal, Rwanda, South Africa, Ukrainian SSR, USSR, Upper Volta.

The General Assembly,
Recognizing that an enlargement of the Economic and Social Council will provide broad representation of the United Nations membership as a whole and make the Council a more effective organ for carrying out its functions under Chapters IX and X of the Charter of the United Nations,

Having considered the report of the Economic and Social Council,

1. *Takes note* of Economic and Social Council resolution 1621(LI) of 30 July 1971;

2. *Decides* to adopt, in accordance with Article 108 of the Charter of the United Nations, the following amendment to the Charter and to submit it for ratification by the States Members of the United Nations:

"Article 61
"1. The Economic and Social Council shall consist of fifty-four Members of the United Nations elected by the General Assembly.

"2. Subject to the provisions of paragraph 3, eighteen members of the Economic and Social Council shall be elected each year for a term of three years. A retiring member shall be eligible for immediate re-election.

"3. At the first election after the increase in the membership of the Economic and Social Council from twenty-seven to fifty-four members, in addition to the members elected in place of the nine members whose term of office expires at the end of that year, twenty-seven additional members shall be elected. Of these twenty-seven additional members, the term of office of nine members so elected shall expire at the end of one year, and of nine other members at the end of two years, in accordance with arrangements made by the General Assembly.

"4. Each member of the Economic and Social Council shall have one representative.";

3. *Urges* all Member States to ratify the above amendment in accordance with their respective constitutional processes as soon as possible and to deposit their instruments of ratification with the Secretary-General;

4. *Further decides* that the members of the Economic and Social Council shall be elected according to the following pattern:

(a) Fourteen members from African States;
(b) Eleven members from Asian States;
(c) Ten members from Latin American States;
(d) Thirteen members from Western European and other States;
(e) Six members from socialist States of Eastern Europe;

5. *Welcomes* the decision of the Economic and Social Council, pending the receipt of the necessary ratifications, to enlarge its sessional committees to fifty-four members;

6. *Invites* the Economic and Social Council, as soon as possible and not later than the organizational meetings of its fifty-second session, to elect the twenty-seven additional members from States Members of the United Nations to serve on the enlarged sessional committees; such elections should be in accordance with paragraph 4 above and should be held each year pending the coming into force of the enlargement of the Council;

7. *Decides* that, as of the date of the entry into force of the above amendments, rule 147 of the rules of procedure of the General Assembly shall be amended to read:

"Rule 147*

"The General Assembly shall each year, in the course of its regular session, elect eighteen members of the Economic and Social Council for a term of three years."

*Formerly rule 146 (see page 611, text of resolution 2837(XXVI), annex I, para. 9).

ORGANIZATION OF COUNCIL'S WORK

Economic and Social Council—50th session
Plenary meetings 1734-1739, 1743, 1745, 1761, 1765, 1768, 1772.

E/4986 and Add.1-9. Measures to improve organization of work of Council. Views and proposals of Governments. Note by Secretary-General.
E/L.1369. Note of 31 December 1970 by Council President.
Ξ/L.1382. USSR: draft resolution.
E/L.1408 and Rev.1. Greece and New Zeland: draft resolution and revision.
E/L.1421. Ghana, Indonesia, Italy, Kenya, Lebanon, Madagascar, Pakistan, Sudan, Tunisia, Zaire: amendments to 2-power draft resolution, E/L.1408.
E/L.1421/Rev.1. Ghana, Indonesia, Italy, Kenya, Lebanon, Madagascar, Niger, Norway, Pakistan, Sudan, Tunisia, Zaire: revised amendments to 2-power revised draft resolution, E/L.1408/Rev.1.
E/L.1422. Brazil: amendments to 2-power draft resolution, E/L.1408.
E/L.1423. United States: amendment to 2-power draft resolution, E/L.1408.
E/5044. Resolutions adopted by Economic and Social Council during its 50th session, 11-13 January and 26 April–21 May 1971. Decisions, p. 26 (items 5 and 16).

Economic and Social Council—51st session
Plenary meetings 1784, 1789, 1794, 1796-1799.

E/L.1382. USSR: draft resolution.

RESOLUTION 1622(LI), as proposed by USSR, E/L.1382, adopted by Council on 30 July 1971, meeting 1798, by 8 votes to 4, with 15 abstentions.

The Economic and Social Council
Recommends to the General Assembly the adoption of the following draft resolution:

"The General Assembly,

"Taking into account the considerable increase over the past twenty-five years in the volume of activities undertaken by organs and organizations of the United Nations system in the economic, social, scientific and technical fields, and the resulting need for the closer and more effective co-ordination of those activities,

"Recalling its resolution 2188(XXI) of 13 December 1966, 2360(XXII) of 19 December 1967 and, in particular, 2579(XXIV) of 15 December 1969, in which, *inter alia*, the Economic and Social Council was requested to introduce as soon as possible such improvements or modifications with regard to co-ordination and programme review as might appear necessary, in the light of the experience gained and of relevant developments within the United Nations system of organizations,

"Supporting, in that connexion, the recommendations contained in Economic and Social Council resolution 1547(XLIX) of 30 July 1970,

"Recalling that, under Chapter IX of the Charter of the United Nations, responsibility for the development of international, economic and social co-operation is vested in the General Assembly and, under its authority, in the Economic and Social Council,

"Emphasizing that, under Chapter X of the Charter, the Economic and Social Council is required to play a key role within the United Nations system in the economic and social fields and in the field of human rights,

"Noting the need for the establishment of a more rational procedure for the consideration of economic, social, scientific and technical questions at the sessions of the General Assembly and of the Economic and Social Council,

"1. *Deems it advisable* for any new economic, social, scientific or technical questions appearing on the agenda of the General Assembly to be considered, as a rule, first by the Economic and Social Council, which would make specific recommendations concerning the nature of possible future decisions to be adopted by the General Assembly on such questions;

"2. *Instructs* the Economic and Social Council to submit, in due time, a list of questions concerning the economic, social, scientific and technical activities of the United Nations, accompanied by appropriate recommendations for consideration at sessions of the General Assembly;

"3. *Requests* the Economic and Social Council, at one of its forthcoming sessions, to indicate the range of problems on which the Council itself, in accordance with the Charter, considers it advisable to take final decisions and to submit its proposals on that question for the approval of the General Assembly at its twenty-seventh session;

"4. *Invites* the Economic and Social Council to take appropriate measures with a view to the regulation and improved co-ordination of economic, social, scientific and technical activities within the United Nations system and, in that connexion, calls the attention of the Council to the need for greater precision and efficiency in the exercise of its functions and powers, as defined in the Charter, in particular in Article 63;

"5. *Instructs* the Economic and Social Council, having regard to paragraph 4 above, to prepare and submit to the General Assembly, for consideration at its twenty-seventh session, proposals concerning effective measures to remedy present shortcomings in the co-ordination of economic and social development programmes and thereby to eliminate overlapping, duplication, over-staffing and over-expenditure of budgetary funds."

E/L.1408/Rev.2. Greece and New Zealand: revised draft resolution.
E/L.1422. Brazil: amendments to 2-power draft resolution, E/L.1408.
E/L.1431. Brazil, Ghana, Jamaica, Lebanon, Pakistan, Peru, Tunisia, Yugoslavia: amendment to 2-power revised draft resolution, E/L.1408/Rev.2.

RESOLUTION 1623(LI), as proposed by 2 powers, E/L.1408/Rev.2, and as amended by Brazil (E/L.1422, first part of para. 3), adopted by Council on 30 July 1971, meeting 1798, by 26 votes to 0, with 1 abstention.

The Economic and Social Council,
Considering that its role as a principal organ of the United Nations should be reaffirmed and that its authority should be enhanced and its methods of work improved to enable it to discharge more effectively the functions conferred upon it by the Charter of the United Nations in the formulation of general economic and social policies to meet the challenges of development,

Reaffirming that, because of the expansion of the activities of the United Nations system during recent years, greatly increased importance has been assumed by the functions of the Council as set out in its resolution 1156(XLI) of 5 August 1966, namely its functions as:

(a) The governing body for the United Nations work programme in the economic, social, human rights and related fields,

(b) The co-ordinator of the activities of the United Nations system of organizations in these fields,

(c) A forum for the discussion of issues of international economic and social policy, and for formulating recommendations for the United Nations system of organizations,

Noting that paragraph 83 of the International Development Strategy for the Second United Nations Development Decade, approved by the General Assembly in its resolution 2626(XXV) of 24 October 1970 and providing for an over-all appraisal by the General Assembly, through the Economic and Social Council, of the progress in implementing the Strategy, will bring these functions into sharper focus and require increased emphasis on the definition of priorities and the resolution of conflicts of interests within the United Nations system,

I

1. *Decides* that in its review of the over-all economic and social situation the Council should formulate new policy recommendations to meet the challenges of development, define major lags and constraints in the field of development and recommend ways and means for their removal;

2. *Decides* to arrange its programme of work, taking into account the rules of procedure of the Council, to provide for:

(a) A short organizational session in January;

(b) A session in the second quarter of the calendar year devoted mainly to social questions, the reports of subsidiary bodies and elections;

(c) A session in the third quarter of the calendar year at Geneva devoted to major questions arising from the world economic situation and in alternate years a debate on the implementation of the International Development Strategy for the Second United Nations Development Decade, with a view to assisting the General Assembly in the over-all appraisal, and to the co-ordination of the activities of the United Nations system in the economic and social fields;

(d) A brief resumed session during the session of the General Assembly to deal with items that cannot normally be considered at the regular sessions of the Council;

II

3. *Requests* the Secretary-General, in consultation with the members of the Council, to develop a more rational agenda

designed to avoid duplication of discussion and to enable the Council to concentrate on policy issues, grouping items on related issues and providing for the consideration of important substantive issues on a longer-term planning cycle, where this is appropriate;

4. *Reaffirms* its decision that the report of the United Nations High Commissioner for Refugees should be transmitted to the General Assembly without debate, unless the Council decides otherwise, at the specific request of one or more of its members or of the High Commissioner, at the time of the adoption of its agenda;

5. *Decides* that, as a general rule and in order to avoid repetitious debates, consideration of the reports of all its functional commissions and subsidiary bodies should be confined, as far as possible, to matters which require decisions or guidance from the Council;

6. *Invites* the Secretary-General, in consultation with delegations, to circulate a more detailed schedule of work for each session and to ensure that the annotated provisional agenda for each session is more informative;

7. *Requests* the Secretary-General to prepare for each substantive agenda item a short document summarizing the previous consideration of the question and the various options for decision by the Council, as well as the consequences likely to arise from such decisions;

III

8. *Requests* the Secretary-General to take urgent steps to reform the nature, scope and form of documentation submitted to the Council to ensure that Governments can review reports adequately and also that the Council is able to concentrate on issues requiring intergovernmental consideration, that reports submitted to the Council are action-oriented and concise (normally not more than thirty-two pages), and present clear and precise recommendations drawing attention to issues that should be taken into account by the Council and possible alternative courses of action proposed for the Council and their implications, and to ensure also that, in the case of meetings of experts convened by the Secretary-General, only a concise report by the Secretary-General setting out the relevant recommendations for action by the Council is submitted;

9. *Requests* the Secretary-General to ensure that these guidelines are observed in reports submitted to the Council and its functional commissions and subsidiary bodies, beginning in 1972;

10. *Decides* that the reports of its functional commissions and subsidiary bodies should contain, in addition to a résumé of the discussions, a concise summary of recommendations and a statement of issues requiring action by the Council, and that all resolutions adopted by its functional commissions and subsidiary bodies should normally be in the form of drafts for approval by the Council;

11. *Decides* that the Council's report to the General Assembly should be reorganized to provide the Assembly with an effective basis for discussion, and that it should consist of a clear statement of the issues on which Assembly action is required and a summary of the Council's discussions and a record of its decisions, including details of votes;

12. *Reaffirms* the importance of the strict observance of rule 14, paragraph 4, of the rules of procedure of the Council and decides that the calendar of conferences should be drawn up in such a way as to permit the observance of this rule;

13. *Invites* the specialized agencies and the International Atomic Energy Agency to continue to provide analytical reports, bearing in mind the recommendations in Council resolution 1548(XLIX) of 30 July 1970;

IV

14. *Welcomes* the participation in its deliberations, in accordance with rule 75 of the rules of procedure of the Council, of Member States which are not members of the Council, in the conviction that such participation will ensure a politically more solid and wider basis for decisions.

General Assembly—26th session
Second Committee, meeting 1370-1382, 1410, 1446.
Plenary meeting 2026.

A/8403. Report of Economic and Social Council on work of its 50th and 51st sessions, Chapter IV.

A/C.2/264. Measures to improve organization of work of Council. Note by Secretary-General.

A/C.2/266. Review of machinery for co-ordination and programme review. Note by Secretariat.

A/C.2/L.1181 and Rev.1. Brazil, Netherlands, Philippines, Sudan, Tunisia: amendments and revised amendments to draft resolution recommended for adoption by Assembly in Council resolution 1622(LI).

A/8578/Add.1. Report of Second Committee (part II) (on report of Economic and Social Council), paras. 43-47 and 49.

A/8429. Resolutions adopted by Assembly during its 26th session, 21 September–22 December 1971. Other decisions, p. 73.

DOCUMENTATION

Economic and Social Council—51st session
Plenary meetings 1784, 1789, 1794, 1796, 1798.

E/L.1435. Brazil, France, Tunisia, Uruguay: draft resolution.

RESOLUTION 1624(LI), as proposed by 4 powers, E/L.1435, as orally amended by sponsors, adopted unanimously by Council on 30 July 1971, meeting 1798.

The Economic and Social Council,

Noting the difficulties encountered by delegations as a result of the late date on which they sometimes receive working papers for the session in the language of their choice,

Recalling rule 14, paragraph 4, of its rules of procedure,

Recalling further its resolution 1090 E (XXXIX) of 31 July 1965,

Noting that General Assembly resolution 2247(XXI) of 20 December 1966 asked the Secretary-General to ensure that documents should be available to the Member States in sufficient time and simultaneously in the working languages envisaged,

Noting further that General Assembly resolution 2292(XXII) of 8 December 1967 requested the Secretary-General to take all measures to ensure a more effective presentation and communication of the documents in due time and simultaneously in the working languages,

1. *Again calls upon* the Secretary-General to take such action as will ensure that the documents submitted to the Council and to its subsidiary organs are available to Member States in sufficient time (at least six weeks before the beginning of the session) and simultaneously in the working languages of the Council and of its organs, without prejudice to the other languages;

2. *Decides* that, for the future, the calendar of conferences shall be so established that paragraph 1 above can be complied with and requests the Committee for Programme and Co-ordination to submit to it, at its fifty-third session, practical suggestions for attaining that objective;

3. *Requests* the Secretary-General, after consultations with the Advisory Committee on Administrative and Budgetary Questions and after obtaining any outside advice which he may think helpful, to review the measures currently in force with respect to the preparation, translation and distribution of documents submitted to the Council or to its subsidiary organs;

4. *Further requests* the Secretary-General to submit to it, at its fifty-third session, through the Committee for Programme and Co-ordination, a report giving the results of the study defined in paragraph 3 above and indicating what new measures have been taken or envisaged to improve the present situation.

RESOLUTION 1623(LI) (part III), as proposed by 2 powers, E/L.1408/Rev.2, adopted by Council on 30 July 1971, meeting 1798, by 26 votes to 0, with 1 abstention.

The Economic and Social Council,
    . . .

III

8. *Requests* the Secretary-General to take urgent steps to reform the nature, scope and form of documentation submitted to the Council to ensure that Governments can review reports adequately and also that the Council is able to concentrate on issues requiring intergovernmental consideration, that reports submitted to the Council are action-oriented and concise (normally not more than thirty-two pages), and present clear and precise recommendations drawing attention to issues that should be taken into account by the Council and possible alternative courses of action proposed for the Council and their implications, and to ensure also that, in the case of meetings of experts convened by the Secretary-General, only a concise report by the Secretary-General setting out the relevant recommendations for action by the Council is submitted;

9. *Requests* the Secretary-General to ensure that these guidelines are observed in reports submitted to the Council and its functional commissions and subsidiary bodies, beginning in 1972;

10. *Decides* that the reports of its functional commissions and subsidiary bodies should contain, in addition to a résumé of the discussions, a concise summary of recommendations and a statement of issues requiring action by the Council, and that all resolutions adopted by its functional commissions and subsidiary bodies should normally be in the form of drafts for approval by the Council;

11. *Decides* that the Council's report to the General Assembly should be reorganized to provide the Assembly with an effective basis for discussion, and that it should consist of a clear statement of the issues on which Assembly action is required and a summary of the Council's discussions and a record of its decisions, including details of votes;

12. *Reaffirms* the importance of the strict observance of rule 14, paragraph 4, of the rules of procedure of the Council and decides that the calendar of conferences should be drawn up in such a way as to permit the observance of this rule;

13. *Invites* the specialized agencies and the International Atomic Energy Agency to continue to provide analytical reports, bearing in mind the recommendations in Council resolution 1548(XLIX) of 30 July 1970;

    . . . .

[For full text of resolution 1623(LI), supporting documentation and relevant meetings, see section above on ORGANIZATION OF COUNCIL'S WORK.]

Chapter XXIII

Other economic and social questions

Assistance in cases of natural disaster

Assistance in 1971

During 1971, the Secretary-General, under authority granted to him by the General Assembly, made a number of allocations from the Working Capital Fund for natural disaster emergency aid.

These allocations were for assistance to Nicaragua during February, for the purchase of tools and related materials for reconstruction, following a volcanic eruption; to Malaysia during April, for the purchase of school textbooks to replace those damaged following floods; to Jordan during April, for the purchase of tents and blankets following floods; to Turkey during June, for the purchase of medical supplies following earthquakes; to Afghanistan during October for the purchase of trucks following a prolonged drought; and to Somalia during December, for the purchase of building materials following a cyclone.

The Secretary-General also approved a grant to the Syrian Arab Republic for two fellowships in pre-disaster planning.

Assistance to Chile and Colombia

During July 1971, the Economic and Social Council considered the situation resulting from natural disasters in Chile and Colombia.

On 21 July, the Council asked the executive heads of the specialized agencies and United Nations programmes concerned to devote the largest possible volume of resources to meet assistance requests from the Governments of Colombia and Chile for reconstruction work.

The Council also expressed the desire that the United Nations Development Programme should consider favourably such requests for assistance as might be submitted by these Governments, in line with their special rehabilitation programmes.

These decisions were set forth in resolution 1611(LI), adopted unanimously by the Council on the basis of a proposal by Brazil, Haiti, Jamaica, Peru and Uruguay. (For text, see DOCUMENTARY REFERENCES below.)

Various amendments, proposed both formally and orally, were taken into account.

Assistance to Afghanistan

On 11 October 1971, the General Assembly took note with concern of the grave results in Afghanistan of two successive years of drought, the resulting shortage of foodstuffs, and in particular the serious damage caused by the drought to the country's livestock industry, which was basic to its export-earning capacity.

The Assembly invited States Members of the United Nations or specialized agencies, and governmental and non-governmental organizations, to make generous contributions towards alleviating the severe conditions prevailing in the disaster areas of Afghanistan.

It also invited the Secretary-General to study ways and means of providing additional assistance from the United Nations to the Afghan Government, and asked that the specialized agencies and United Nations programmes concerned take into consideration the pressing needs of the Government in this respect when determining assistance allocations to Member States.

The Assembly took these decisions by adopting, unanimously, resolution 2757(XXVI), as recommended by the Third (Social, Humanitarian and Cultural) Committee, which approved the text by acclamation on 5 October 1971, on a proposal by Algeria, Australia, Bhutan, Canada, Chile, Costa Rica, Cyprus, Denmark, Egypt, Ethiopia, Ghana, Greece, Honduras, India, Indonesia, Iran, Iraq, Japan, Kuwait, Lebanon, the Libyan Arab Republic, Madagascar, Malaysia, Morocco, Nepal, Nigeria, Pakistan, Peru, the Philippines, Sudan, the Syrian Arab Republic, Tunisia, Turkey, the United Kingdom, Uruguay, Yemen and Yugoslavia. (For text of resolution, see DOCUMENTARY REFERENCES below.)

Procedures for assistance

The Economic and Social Council considered the general question of assistance in cases of natural disaster at its July 1971 session. It had before it a comprehensive report submitted by the Secretary-General which stressed that, while the primary responsibility in disaster situations inevitably rested with the Government of the stricken country, other Governments and international organizations, as well as voluntary agencies, had an important contribution to make in many areas.

The report listed four main areas in which international assistance might be strengthened:

prevention, control and prediction; planning and preparedness; organization of relief action when a disaster strikes; and rehabilitation and reconstruction. It also set out a number of recommendations addressed to disaster-prone countries, to countries which expected to give aid, to the League of Red Cross Societies and other international voluntary agencies and to the United Nations itself. The report emphasized the urgent need for improved organizational arrangements in the provision of assistance by and through the United Nations system and outlined the nature and extent of the functions of the permanent office within the United Nations Secretariat (envisaged in a General Assembly decision of 15 December 1970)[1] for the co-ordination of action relating to natural disasters.

The Council also considered a recommendation of the World Administrative Radio Conference for Space Telecommunications which noted that the use of space radio-communications systems was one of the means by which rapid and reliable telecommunications could be provided for relief operations. It accordingly recommended that administrations individually or in collaboration should provide for the needs of eventual relief operations in planning their space radio-communications systems and should identify, for this purpose, preferred radio-frequency channels and facilities which could quickly be made available for relief operations.

On 23 July 1971, the Council called on the Secretary-General to appoint a disaster relief co-ordinator who would be authorized, on behalf of the Secretary-General, to carry on activities, listed by the Council, having to do with the mobilization, direction and co-ordination of disaster relief activities.

The Council also recommended that the Disaster Relief Co-ordinator be appointed by the Secretary-General normally for a term of five years, and that he head a small permanent office in the United Nations which should be the focal point in the United Nations system for disaster relief matters.

The Secretary-General was requested to prepare a study for one of the Council's 1972 sessions, taking into account any relevant suggestions and the experience gained by the Disaster Relief Co-ordinator, on ways and means of enabling the Disaster Relief Co-ordinator adequately to perform the functions entrusted to him.

It endorsed the plan for a roster of volunteers to be drawn from experienced staff members of the United Nations system and interested non-governmental organizations who could be made available at very short notice.

It recommended that the Disaster Relief Co-ordinator should maintain contact with the Gov-

ernments of Members of the United Nations and members of the specialized agencies and the International Atomic Energy Agency (IAEA) concerning available aid in emergency situations, such as food supplies, medicines, personnel, transportation and communications, as well as advice to countries in pre-disaster planning and preparedness.

Potential recipient Governments were invited to take certain measures to facilitate the receipt of international aid in times of emergency. Potential donor Governments were invited to respond promptly to any call by the Secretary-General or by the Disaster Relief Co-ordinator on his behalf; to offer on a wider basis emergency assistance in disaster situations; and to inform the Disaster Relief Co-ordinator in advance about the facilities and services they might be in a position to provide immediately, including relief units, logistical support and means of effective communications.

The Council further invited all organizations of the United Nations system and all other organizations involved to co-operate with the Disaster Relief Co-ordinator.

Finally, the Council recommended that the General Assembly at its 1971 session endorse these proposals.

The Council's recommendations were set forth in resolution 1612(LI), adopted by 24 votes to 0, with 2 abstentions, on a proposal of Greece, Indonesia, Jamaica, Kenya, Lebanon, Malaysia, New Zealand, Norway, Pakistan, Peru, Turkey, the United Kingdom and the United States, as amended by France. (For text, see DOCUMENTARY REFERENCES below.)

A number of amendments were proposed during the Council's discussion, several of which were either taken into account in the revision of the draft text or withdrawn. Others were voted upon on 23 July 1971.

A French proposal to delete the idea that the Disaster Relief Co-ordinator should be appointed at a level equivalent to that of an Under-Secretary-General of the United Nations was adopted by 10 votes to 9, with 5 abstentions.

A Hungarian proposal which referred to the operative paragraph by which it was recommended that the Disaster Relief Co-ordinator should maintain contact with Governments of States Members of the United Nations and of the specialized agencies and IAEA was rejected by 14 votes to 6, with 5 abstentions. It would have had the effect of deleting reference to "States Members of the United Nations and of the specialized agencies and the IAEA."

Rejected, by 16 votes to 5, with 4 abstentions, was a USSR proposal which would have called for

[1]See Y.U.N., 1970, pp. 643-44, text of resolution 2717(XXV).

the functions of a disaster relief co-ordinator to be taken over by one of the existing Under-Secretaries-General or Assistant Secretaries-General and for the office of the Disaster Relief Co-ordinator to be staffed within the limits of the current staff of the Secretariat.

Later in 1971, on 14 December, the General Assembly discussed the general question of assistance in cases of natural disaster and other disaster situations.

The Assembly, as the Council had recommended, called upon the Secretary-General to appoint a disaster relief co-ordinator to carry out a number of measures listed by the Assembly.

The Assembly called for the same action the Council had asked for on 23 July 1971 (see above) and was specific on a number of points. It recommended that the Disaster Relief Co-ordinator be appointed at a level comparable to that of an Under-Secretary-General of the United Nations and that the office he would head be located in Geneva, Switzerland.

It also authorized the Secretary-General to draw on the Working Capital Fund in the amount of $200,000 for emergency assistance in any one year, with a normal ceiling of $20,000 per country in the case of any one disaster.

The Assembly's recommendations were embodied in resolution 2816(XXVI), adopted by 86 votes to 0, with 10 abstentions, on the recommendation of the Third Committee. The Committee had

approved the text on 1 December 1971, by 85 votes to 0, with 8 abstentions, on the basis of a proposal of the following 60 powers: Afghanistan, Algeria, Australia, Austria, Belgium, Burundi, Canada, the Congo, Costa Rica, Cyprus, Denmark, Ecuador, Egypt, Finland, Greece, Guinea, Indonesia, Iran, Iraq, Italy, Jamaica, Japan, Jordan, Kenya, Kuwait, Lebanon, Lesotho, Liberia, the Libyan Arab Republic, Madagascar, Malaysia, Mali, Mauritania, Morocco, the Netherlands, New Zealand, Nicaragua, Niger, Nigeria, Norway, Pakistan, Panama, the People's Democratic Republic of Yemen, Peru, the Philippines, Senegal, Sierra Leone, Somalia, Swaziland, Sweden, the Syrian Arab Republic, Trinidad and Tobago, Tunisia, Turkey, Uganda, the United Kingdom, the United Republic of Tanzania, the United States, Uruguay and Yemen.

(For text of resolution, see DOCUMENTARY REFERENCES below.)

In the course of the Third Committee's discussion, amendments were proposed jointly by Dahomey and France. A proposal to locate the Disaster Relief Co-ordinator's office in Geneva was adopted by 72 votes to 5, with 12 abstentions. Rejected, by 51 votes to 10, with 29 abstentions, was a proposal that the Disaster Relief Co-ordinator be appointed at a level comparable to that of an Assistant Secretary-General (rather than at a level of an Under-Secretary-General, as the final text read).

DOCUMENTARY REFERENCES

Assistance in 1971

Economic and Social Council—51st session
Plenary meetings 1778, 1785-1787.

E/4994. Comprehensive report of Secretary-General.
E/5012 (Part I). Development and co-ordination of activities of organizations within United Nations system. Thirty-seventh report of Administrative Committee on Co-ordination, Chapter I H.
E/5038. Report of Committee for Programme and Co-ordination on its 9th session, 24 May–14 June 1971, Chapter VI.
E/L.1434. Brazil, Haiti, Jamaica, Peru, Uruguay: draft resolution.
E/L.1436. Communication of 16 July 1971 from Chile.
E/L.1437. USSR: amendment to 5-power draft resolution, E/L.1434.

RESOLUTION 1611(LI), as proposed by 5 powers, E/L.1434, as orally revised by sponsors, adopted unanimously by Council on 21 July 1971, meeting 1787.

The Economic and Social Council,
Considering that areas of Colombia and Chile have recently suffered the effects of natural disasters which have caused considerable loss of human life and property and serious damage to the economies of both countries,
Bearing in mind that assistance to Members of the United Nations which have suffered major natural disasters is in keeping with the concept of international solidarity embodied in the Charter of the United Nations,
1. *Expresses* to the people and Governments of Colombia and

Chile its heartfelt condolences for the loss of life and devastation sustained as a result of the recent natural disasters;
2. *Requests* the Secretary-General to ask the Governing Council of the United Nations Development Programme and the Administrator of that Programme, the specialized agencies, more especially the International Bank for Reconstruction and Development, and also the Food and Agriculture Organization of the United Nations and the United Nations Educational, Scientific and Cultural Organization, and the International Atomic Energy Agency, the United Nations Conference on Trade and Development, the United Nations Industrial Development Organization, the United Nations Children's Fund, and United Nations Institute for Training and Research and the World Food Programme, to devote the largest possible volume of resources, within their respective programmes, to meeting assistance requests from the Governments of Colombia and Chile relating to reconstruction work contemplated in their initial emergency programmes;
3. *Conveys its desire* to the Governing Council and the Administrator of the United Nations Development Programme that they should consider favourably such requests for assistance within the purview of that Programme as may be submitted by the Governments of Colombia and Chile in connexion with their special medium-term and long-term programmes of rehabilitation.

General Assembly—26th session
Third Committee, meeting 1827.
Plenary meeting 1971.

A/8401. Report of Secretary-General on work of the Organization, 16 June 1970–15 June 1971, Part Three, Chapter VII C.

A/8403. Report of Economic and Social Council on work of its 50th and 51st sessions, Chapter XIX.

A/C.3/L.1850. Algeria, Australia, Bhutan, Canada, Chile, Costa Rica, Cyprus, Denmark, Egypt, Ethiopia, Ghana, Greece, Honduras, India, Indonesia, Iran, Iraq, Japan, Kuwait, Lebanon, Libyan Arab Republic, Madagascar, Malaysia, Morocco, Nepal, Nigeria, Pakistan, Peru, Philippines, Sudan, Syrian Arab Republic, Tunisia, Turkey, United Kingdom, Uruguay, Yemen, Yugoslavia: draft resolution, as orally amended by sponsors, approved by acclamation by Third Committee on 5 October 1971, meeting 1827.

A/8430. Report of Third Committee (part I).

RESOLUTION 2757(XXVI), as recommended by Third Committee, A/8430 (part I), adopted unanimously by Assembly on 11 October 1971, meeting 1961.

The General Assembly,

Taking note with concern of the grave results in Afghanistan of two successive years of drought, the resulting shortage of food-stuffs, and in particular the serious damage caused by the drought to the country's livestock industry, which is basic to its export-earning capacity,

Recalling its resolutions 2034(XX) of 7 December 1965, 2435(XXIII) of 19 December 1968, 2608(XXIV) of 16 December 1969 and 2717(XXV) of 15 December 1970,

Aware of the adverse effects of this natural disaster on the economic and social development of Afghanistan,

Aware also of the urgent efforts of the Government of Afghanistan to obtain food-stuffs, fodder and equipment to combat the water shortage and to restore satisfactory living conditions in the devastated areas,

Recognizing the very high cost involved and the great problems of distribution to the remote areas of the country,

Recalling the statement of the President of the Trade and Development Board, made at the eleventh session in the name of the entire membership of the Board, in which Member States and international organizations were requested to consider practical measures that might be taken to bring prompt relief and assistance to Afghanistan,

Noting with satisfaction the assistance already offered by some countries and organizations and by the United Nations,

1. *Assures* the people and the Government of Afghanistan of its deep sympathy in the face of this catastrophe;

2. *Invites* States Members of the United Nations or members of specialized agencies and governmental and non-governmental organizations to study all possible ways in which they could provide assistance to Afghanistan and to make generous contributions towards alleviating the severe conditions prevailing in the disaster areas;

3. *Invites* the Secretary-General to study ways and means of providing, on an emergency basis, additional assistance from the United Nations to the Government of Afghanistan and to make this assistance available as soon as possible;

4. *Requests* the Secretary-General of the United Nations, the Administrator of the United Nations Development Programme, the executive heads of specialized agencies, the Executive Director of the World Food Programme and the Director-General of the United Nations Children's Fund, bearing in mind their available resources, to take into consideration the pressing needs of the Government of Afghanistan in this respect when determining the allocation of their assistance to Member States.

Procedures for assistance

Economic and Social Council—51st session
Plenary meetings 1773, 1778, 1785-1787, 1790.

E/4970. Eighth report of Advisory Committee on Application of Science and Technology to Development, March 1971, para. 31.

E/4994. Comprehensive report of Secretary-General.

E/5012 (Part I). Development and co-ordination of activities of organizations within United Nations system. Thirty-seventh report of Administrative Committee on Co-ordination, Chapter I H.

E/5038. Report of Committee for Programme and Co-ordination on its 9th session, 24 May–14 June 1971, Chapter VI.

E/5131. Ninth report of Advisory Committee on Application of Science and Technology to Development, May 1972, para. 52.

E/L.1404. Memorandum of 4 March 1971 from United Kingdom.

E/L.1425. Memorandum of 4 June 1971 from Turkey.

E/L.1430. Note by Secretary-General (transmitting recommendation adopted by World Administrative Radio Conference for Space Telecommunications, Geneva, Switzerland, 1971).

E/L.1438. Greece, Indonesia, Jamaica, Kenya, Lebanon, Malaysia, New Zealand, Norway, Pakistan, Peru, United Kingdom, United States: draft resolution.

E/L.1438/Rev.1. Greece, Indonesia, Jamaica, Kenya, Lebanon, Malaysia, New Zealand, Norway, Pakistan, Peru, Turkey, United Kingdom, United States: revised draft resolution.

E/L.1438/Add.1. Administrative and financial implications of 12-power draft resolution, E/L.1438. Statement by Secretary-General.

E/L.1440 and Corr.1. USSR: amendments to 12-power draft resolution, E/L.1438.

E/L.1442. France: amendments to 12-power draft resolution, E/L.1438.

E/L.1443. Hungary: amendment to 12-power draft resolution, E/L.1438.

RESOLUTION 1612(LI), as proposed by 13 powers, E/L.1438/Rev.1, as amended by France (E/L.1442, para. 2) and as orally revised by sponsors, adopted by Council on 23 July 1971, meeting 1790, by 24 votes to 0, with 2 abstentions.

The Economic and Social Council,

Bearing in mind that throughout history natural disasters and emergency situations have inflicted heavy loss of life and property, affecting every people and every country,

Aware of the varying needs of nations experiencing such disorders, which present new challenges for international co-operation,

Concerned over the ability of the international community to come to the aid of countries in a disaster situation,

Recalling General Assembly resolutions 2435(XXIII) of 19 December 1968 and 2717(XXV) of 15 December 1970 on assistance in cases of natural disaster,

Expressing appreciation for the Secretary-General's comprehensive report, and for its perceptive examination of all aspects of the question and taking note of the relevant passage in his statement to the Council on 5 July 1971,

Noting the study, annexed to the Secretary-General's report, on the legal status of disaster relief units made available through the United Nations,

Mindful of recent steps taken to improve evolving procedures in the United Nations system, voluntary agencies and individual Governments in the field of international disaster assistance,

Bearing in mind that assistance to meet the requests of the stricken countries without prejudice to their individual country programmes under the United Nations Development Programme can be an effective contribution to the rehabilitation and development of the stricken areas,

Bearing in mind also that the possible response of the International Bank for Reconstruction and Development and other credit organizations and development agencies to a request from the Governments concerned for complementary assistance for the stricken areas, without prejudice to the assistance provided by these organizations for the normal development programmes of the stricken countries, can be an important element in the reconstruction and development of the stricken areas,

Noting the competence of the United Nations and its agencies, the United Nations Children's Fund, the United Nations High Commissioner for Refugees and the World Food Programme, to render assistance in disasters and other emergency situations,

Noting further the key role which the resident representative of the United Nations Development Programme should play at the country level,

Recognizing the vital roles in international relief of the International Red Cross and other voluntary societies,

Recognizing further the necessity to ensure prompt, effective and efficient response to a Government's need for assistance at the time of a natural disaster or other emergency situation, that will bring to bear the resources of the United Nations, prospective donor countries, and voluntary agencies,

1. *Calls on* the Secretary-General to appoint a disaster relief co-ordinator, who would report directly to him, and who would be authorized, on behalf of the Secretary-General:

   (a) To mobilize, direct and co-ordinate the relief activities of the various organizations of the United Nations system in response to a request for disaster assistance from a stricken State;

   (b) To receive on behalf of the Secretary-General contributions offered to him for disaster relief assistance to be carried out by the United Nations, its agencies, and programmes, for particular emergency situations;

   (c) To co-ordinate United Nations assistance with assistance given by intergovernmental and non-governmental organizations;

   (d) To assist the Government of the stricken country to assess relief and other needs and to evaluate the priority of these needs, to disseminate this information to prospective donors and others concerned and to serve as a clearing-house for assistance extended or planned by all sources of external aid;

   (e) To promote the study, prevention, control and prediction of natural disasters, including the collection and dissemination of information concerning technological developments;

   (f) To assist in providing advice to Governments on pre-disaster planning in association with relevant voluntary organizations, particularly with the League of Red Cross Societies, and draw upon United Nations resources available for such purposes;

   (g) To acquire and disseminate information relevant to planning and co-ordinating relief for disasters, including the improvement and establishment of stockpiles in disaster-prone areas, and to prepare suggestions to ensure the most effective use of available resources;

   (h) To phase out relief operations under his aegis as the stricken country moves into the stage of rehabilitation and reconstruction but to continue to interest himself, within the framework of his responsibilities for relief, in the activities of the United Nations agencies concerned with rehabilitation and reconstruction;

   (i) To prepare an annual report for the Secretary-General, to be submitted to the Economic and Social Council and the General Assembly;

2. *Recommends* that the Disaster Relief Co-ordinator be appointed by the Secretary-General normally for a term of five years;

3. *Endorses* the Secretary-General's proposals for a small permanent office in the United Nations which shall be the focal point in the United Nations system for disaster relief matters;

4. *Recommends* that this office be headed by the Disaster Relief Co-ordinator, be a distinct element within the United Nations Secretariat, and be augmented as necessary by short-term secondment of personnel for individual emergencies;

5. *Requests* the Secretary-General to prepare a study for its fifty-third session, taking into account any relevant suggestions and the experience gained by the Disaster Relief Co-ordinator, on ways and means to enable the Disaster Relief Co-ordinator adequately to perform the functions entrusted to him under the present resolution;

6. *Further endorses* the plan for a roster of volunteers to be drawn from experienced staff members of the United Nations system and interested non-governmental organizations, who could be made available at very short notice;

7. *Recommends* that the Disaster Relief Co-ordinator should maintain contact with the Governments of States Members of the United Nations and members of the specialized agencies and the International Atomic Energy Agency concerning available aid in emergency situations, such as food supplies, medicines, personnel, transportation and communications, as well as advice to countries in pre-disaster planning and preparedness;

8. *Invites* potential recipient Governments:

   (a) To establish disaster contingency plans with appropriate assistance from the Disaster Relief Co-ordinator;

   (b) To appoint a single national disaster relief co-ordinator to facilitate the receipt of international aid in times of an emergency;

   (c) To establish stockpiles of emergency supplies such as tents, blankets, medicine and non-perishable food-stuffs;

   (d) To consider appropriate legislative or other measures to facilitate the receipt of aid, including overflight and landing rights and necessary privileges and immunities for relief units;

   (e) To improve national disaster warning systems;

9. *Invites* potential donor Governments:

   (a) To respond promptly to any call by the Secretary-General or by the Disaster Relief Co-ordinator on his behalf;

   (b) To consider and to continue offering on a wider basis emergency assistance in disaster situations;

   (c) To inform the Disaster Relief Co-ordinator in advance about the facilities and services they might be in a position to provide immediately, including where possible relief units, logistical support and means of effective communications;

10. *Further invites* all organizations of the United Nations system and all other organizations involved to co-operate with the Disaster Relief Co-ordinator;

11. *Recommends* that the General Assembly at its twenty-sixth session endorse the foregoing proposals and recommendations.

General Assembly—26th session
Third Committee, meetings 1888, 1890, 1891.
Fifth Committee, meetings 1475-1478.
Plenary meeting 2018.

A/8401. Report of Secretary-General on work of the Organization, 16 June 1970–15 June 1971, Part Three, Chapter VII C.
A/8401/Add.1. Introduction to report of Secretary-General, September 1971, Part Two, Chapter IX, paras. 320-323.
A/8403. Report of Economic and Social Council on work of its 50th and 51st sessions, Chapter XIX.
A/8436. Note by Secretary-General.
A/C.3/L.1897. Afghanistan, Algeria, Australia, Austria, Belgium, Burundi, Canada, Congo, Costa Rica, Cyprus, Denmark, Ecuador, Egypt, Finland, Greece, Guinea, Indonesia, Iran, Iraq, Italy, Jamaica, Japan, Jordan, Kenya, Kuwait, Lebanon, Lesotho, Liberia, Libyan Arab Republic, Madagascar, Malaysia, Mali, Mauritania, Morocco, Netherlands, New Zealand, Nicaragua, Niger, Nigeria, Norway, Pakistan, Panama, People's Democratic Republic of Yemen, Peru, Philippines, Senegal, Sierra Leone, Somalia, Swaziland, Sweden, Syrian Arab Republic, Trinidad and Tobago, Tunisia, Turkey, Uganda, United Kingdom, United Republic of Tanzania, United States, Uruguay, Yemen: draft resolution, as orally revised by sponsors and as amended by 2 powers (A/C.3/L.1906, para. 3), approved by Third Committee on 1 December 1971, meeting 1890, by 85 votes to 0, with 8 abstentions.
A/C.3/L.1899, A/C.5/1409 and Corr.1, A/8408/Add.18, A/8499. Administrative and financial implications of draft resolution recommended by Third Committee in A/8430/Add.1. Statements by Secretary-General and reports of Advisory Committee on Administrative and Budgetary Questions and Fifth Committee.
A/C.3/L.1906. Dahomey and France: amendment to 60-power draft resolution, A/C.3/L.1897.
A/8430/Add.1. Report of Third Committee (part II).

RESOLUTION 2816(XXVI), as recommended by Third Committee, A/8430/Add.1, adopted by Assembly on 14 December 1971, meeting 2018, by 86 votes to 0, with 10 abstentions.

The General Assembly,
Bearing in mind that throughout history natural disasters and emergency situations have inflicted heavy loss of life and property, affecting every people and every country,
Aware of and concerned about the suffering caused by natural

disasters and the serious economic and social consequences for all, especially the developing countries,

Also aware of the varying needs of nations experiencing such disorders, which present new challenges for international co-operation,

Concerned about the ability of the international community to come to the aid of countries in a disaster situation,

Recalling its resolutions 2034(XX) of 7 December 1965, 2435(XXIII) of 19 December 1968, 2608(XXIV) of 16 December 1969 and 2717(XXV) of 15 December 1970, and Economic and Social Council resolutions 1533(XLIX) of 23 July 1970 and 1546(XLIX) of 30 July 1970 on assistance in cases of natural disaster,

Expressing appreciation of the Secretary-General's comprehensive report and of its perceptive examination of all aspects of the question, and taking note of the relevant passage in his statement to the Economic and Social Council on 5 July 1971,

Taking note of Economic and Social Council resolution 1612(LI) of 23 July 1971 on assistance in cases of natural disaster and other emergency situations,

Noting the study, annexed to the Secretary-General's report, on the legal status of disaster relief units made available through the United Nations,

Mindful of the need to strengthen and make more effective the collective efforts of the international community, and particularly the United Nations system, in the field of international disaster assistance,

Bearing in mind that assistance provided at the request of the stricken countries, without prejudice to their individual country programmes under the United Nations Development Programme, can be an effective contribution to the rehabilitation and development of the stricken areas,

Bearing in mind also that the possible response of the International Bank for Reconstruction and Development and other credit organizations and development agencies to a request from the Governments concerned for complementary assistance to the stricken areas, without prejudice to the assistance provided by those organizations for the normal development programmes of the stricken countries, can be an important element in the reconstruction and development of those areas,

Noting the competence of the United Nations and its related agencies, the United Nations Children's Fund, the United Nations High Commissioner for Refugees and the World Food Programme to render assistance in cases of natural disaster and other disaster situations,

Noting further the key role which the resident representatives of the United Nations Development Programme could play at the country level,

Recognizing the vital role in international relief played by the International Red Cross and other voluntary societies,

Recognizing further the necessity to ensure prompt, effective and efficient response to a Government's need for assistance, at the time of a natural disaster or other disaster situation, that will bring to bear the resources of the United Nations system, prospective donor countries and voluntary agencies,

1. *Calls upon* the Secretary-General to appoint a Disaster Relief Co-ordinator, who will report directly to him and who will be authorized, on his behalf:

(a) To establish and maintain the closest co-operation with all organizations concerned and to make all feasible advance arrangements with them for the purpose of ensuring the most effective assistance;

(b) To mobilize, direct and co-ordinate the relief activities of the various organizations of the United Nations system in response to a request for disaster assistance from a stricken State;

(c) To co-ordinate United Nations assistance with assistance given by intergovernmental and non-governmental organizations, in particular by the International Red Cross;

(d) To receive, on behalf of the Secretary-General, contributions offered to him for disaster relief assistance to be carried out by the United Nations, its agencies and programmes for particular emergency situations;

(e) To assist the Government of the stricken country to assess its relief and other needs and to evaluate the priority of those needs, to disseminate that information to prospective donors and others concerned, and to serve as a clearing-house for assistance extended or planned by all sources of external aid;

(f) To promote the study, prevention, control and prediction of natural disasters, including the collection and dissemination of information concerning technological developments;

(g) To assist in providing advice to Governments on pre-disaster planning in association with revelant voluntary organizations, particularly with the League of Red Cross Societies, and to draw upon United Nations resources available for such purposes;

(h) To acquire and disseminate information relevant to planning and co-ordinating disaster relief, including the improvement and establishment of stockpiles in disaster-prone areas, and to prepare suggestions to ensure the most effective use of available resources;

(i) To phase out relief operations under his aegis as the stricken country moves into the stage of rehabilitation and reconstruction, but to continue to interest himself, within the framework of his responsibilities for relief, in the activities of the United Nations agencies concerned with rehabilitation and reconstruction;

(j) To prepare an annual report for the Secretary-General, to be submitted to the Economic and Social Council and to the General Assembly;

2. *Recommends* that the Disaster Relief Co-ordinator should be appointed by the Secretary-General normally for a term of five years and at a level comparable to that of an Under-Secretary-General of the United Nations;

3. *Endorses* the Secretary-General's proposals for an adequate permanent office in the United Nations which shall be the focal point in the United Nations system for disaster relief matters;

4. *Recommends* that that office should be headed by the Disaster Relief Co-ordinator and located in Geneva, be a distinct element within the United Nations Secretariat and be augmented as necessary by short-term secondment of personnel for individual emergencies;

5. *Requests* the Secretary-General to prepare for the Economic and Social Council at its fifty-third session, taking into account any relevant suggestions and the experience gained by the Disaster Relief Co-ordinator, a report on any further steps which may be required to enable the Disaster Relief Co-ordinator adequately to perform the functions entrusted to him under the present resolution;

6. *Further endorses* the plan for a roster of volunteers, to be drawn from experienced staff members of the United Nations system and interested non-governmental organizations, who could be made available at very short notice;

7. *Recommends* that the Disaster Relief Co-ordinator should maintain contact with the Governments of States Members of the United Nations or members of specialized agencies or of the International Atomic Energy Agency concerning available aid in emergency situations, such as food supplies, medicines, personnel, transportation and communications, as well as advice to countries in pre-disaster planning and preparedness;

8. *Invites* potential recipient Governments:

(a) To establish disaster contingency plans with appropriate assistance from the Disaster Relief Co-ordinator;

(b) To appoint a single national disaster relief co-ordinator to facilitate the receipt of international aid in times of emergency;

(c) To establish stockpiles of emergency supplies, such as tents, blankets, medicines and non-perishable food-stuffs;

(d) To make necessary arrangements for the training of administrative and relief personnel;

(e) To consider appropriate legislative or other measures to facilitate the receipt of aid, including overflight and landing rights and necessary privileges and immunities for relief units;

(f) To improve national disaster warning systems;

9. *Invites* potential donor Governments:

(a) To respond promptly to any call by the Secretary-General or, on his behalf, by the Disaster Relief Co-ordinator;

(b) To consider and to continue offering on a wider basis emergency assistance in disaster situations;

(c) To inform the Disaster Relief Co-ordinator in advance about the facilities and services they might be in a position to provide immediately, including where possible relief units, logistical support and means of effective communication;

10. *Decides* to authorize the Secretary-General to draw on the Working Capital Fund in the amount of $200,000 for emergency assistance in any one year, with a normal ceiling of $20,000 per country in the case of any one disaster;

11. *Further invites* all organizations of the United Nations system and all other organizations involved to co-operate with the Disaster Relief Co-ordinator.

Other documents

The Role of Science and Technology in Reducing the Impact of Natural Disasters on Mankind. Report of the Advisory Committee on the Application of Science and Technology to Development. U.N.P. Sales No.: E.72.II.A.8 and corrigendum.

The United Nations Institute for Training and Research

Activities in 1971

In an effort to take a forward look at the training programmes in diplomacy and international organization and in technical and economic co-operation, the Executive Director of the United Nations Institute for Training and Research (UNITAR) was assisted in 1971 by two panels of consultants. The year was marked by UNITAR's effort to break away from traditional patterns of training.

Several training courses were offered during the year to civil servants at both the national and the international levels. A three-month basic course in diplomacy was organized in Dakar, Senegal, for young civil servants from Africa and Asia.

Seminars on the organization and functioning of the United Nations in New York were held for diplomatic personnel newly appointed to permanent missions and new staff members of the United Nations in New York. A three-day briefing for new delegates was held prior to the twenty-sixth session of the General Assembly, which opened on 21 September 1971.

Orientation seminars for permanent missions in Geneva, Switzerland, on documentation of international organizations, were held both in English and in French in March 1971. Senior officials in the United Nations system attended a *colloquium* on the inter-cultural factor in international administration, held from 10 to 12 June in Austria.

During 1971, 20 persons participated in the international-law training programme, and a regional symposium on international law was held in Accra, Ghana.

In May 1971, a symposium on environment and development was held. Also during the year, UNITAR sponsored a seminar on the major problems of technical and financial co-operation.

The Institute's research activities continued to concentrate on six main areas—namely, the functioning and procedures of United Nations organs and agencies; the peaceful settlement of disputes; economic and social development; information and communication; the implications of science and technology for international organizations; and international law and human rights.

Specifically, research projects were carried out on the following subjects: relations between the United Nations and regional inter-governmental organizations; General Assembly procedures; functioning of the Economic and Social Council; international youth organizations and the United Nations system; the peaceful settlement of disputes; the international migration of professionals from developing to developed countries; the transfer of operative technology from enterprise to enterprise; the financing of international waterway systems; new methods and techniques of managerial training; communications, computers and automation for development; new research on technical co-operation; the United Nations and the news media; access to United Nations data for research purposes; use of United Nations documents; environmental problems; verification of atomic safeguards system; international law studies; and racial discrimination.

Twenty-five research papers and books on these subjects were published during the year.

The research carried out by UNITAR was generally action-oriented. For example, the activities on the environment were aimed at contributing to the preparations for the United Nations Conference on the Human Environment; studies of the functioning of the General Assembly and the Economic and Social Council were aimed at helping officials and committees examine the roles of these bodies.

In addition to its regular contacts with academic institutions, UNITAR was host to 20 interns and visiting scholars from ten countries in the course of 1971.

During the year, the Institute contributed to the preparation of proposals relating to the establishment of an international university. (See pp. 488-90.)

Also in 1971, a UNITAR study recommended that steps be taken to establish a staff college to serve the United Nations system. The college was to provide courses both in development and in management techniques and was to have a small core-staff supplemented by visiting lecturers. Initially, its operations were to consist of holding short courses for officials with important supervisory functions. The establishment of the staff college was to be accomplished in two stages, as follows: during the first stage, courses would be organized on a decentralized basis, serving only staff members of the United Nations system; in the second stage, the college would acquire its own premises and might also cater to national officials and officials of non-governmental organizations.

Following approval of these recommendations, the UNITAR Board submitted to the Administrative Committee on Co-ordination (ACC) the following proposals for action, with which ACC concurred on 27 April 1971: a small staff college advisory committee, whose priority task would be to plan the programme of studies, should be appointed at once; steps should be taken to appoint the first principal (head of the college) early, so that he could be associated with the planning of the college. The aim should be to bring the first stage of the college into operation in 1972; *ad hoc* courses might be introduced in late 1971.

The staff college was to be financed by contributions from the members of the United Nations system, and discussions on an agreed scheme for this purpose were in progress.

On 21 December 1971, the General Assembly, without adopting a resolution, approved in principle the idea of establishing a staff college.

(See also pp. 636-37.)

Decision of General Assembly

On 18 November 1971, the General Assembly noted with satisfaction the increasing effectiveness of UNITAR and expressed the hope that it would have greater and wider financial support. It did this while taking note of the report of the Executive Director of UNITAR.

The Assembly acted by adopting, without objection, resolution 2767(XXVI), on the recommendation of its Second (Economic and Financial) Committee, which approved the text without objection on 13 October 1971, on a proposal of Brazil, Canada, Chile, Denmark, El Salvador, Ghana, India, Iran, Jamaica, Kenya, Kuwait, Laos, Lebanon, Lesotho, the Libyan Arab Republic, Nigeria, Singapore, Uganda, Upper Volta, Uruguay and Venezuela. (For text of resolution, see DOCUMENTARY REFERENCES below.)

Pledges and contributions

The following table shows governmental contributions to UNITAR in 1971.

In addition to the contributions listed below, grants were given to UNITAR for special purposes. Twelve non-governmental sources donated a total of $854,656, and a total of $382,200 was donated by Argentina, France, Sweden and the United States.

The Governments of Hungary and the USSR donated 100,000 forints and 300,000 roubles, respectively, for UNITAR projects to be carried out in those countries.

Contributions to UNITAR during 1971

(In U.S. dollars)

Country	Amount	Country	Amount	Country	Amount
Algeria	5,000	Iran	22,000	Philippines	29,830
Argentina	60,000	Iraq	34,000	Republic of Korea	6,000
Barbados	500	Ireland	15,000	Rwanda	6,000
Belgium	300,375	Israel	12,000	Saudi Arabia	40,000
Brazil	5,000	Italy	59,840	Senegal	8,138
Brunei	19,601	Ivory Coast	117,986	Singapore	1,500
Cameroon	2,899	Jamaica	2,500	Sudan	5,000
Canada	335,749	Japan	282,000	Sweden	177,139
Central African		Jordan	8,000	Switzerland	210,463
Republic	40	Kenya	14,002	Syrian Arab	
Ceylon	3,000	Kuwait	110,000	Republic	10,471
Chile	3,000	Laos	1,000	Thailand	28,200
China	5,000	Lebanon	10,000	Togo	5,179
Cyprus	550	Liberia	7,500	Trinidad and	
Czechoslovakia	2,000	Libyan Arab		Tobago	5,000
Denmark	150,000	Republic	15,000	Tunisia	10,000
Dubai	1,000	Liechtenstein	4,630	Turkey	5,000
Ecuador	7,025	Luxembourg	12,000	USSR	120,000
Egypt	4,600	Malaysia	3,288	United Kingdom	701,584
Ethiopia	5,000	Mali	2,000	United Republic	
Federal Republic		Malta	600	of Tanzania	25,602
of Germany	375,000	Morocco	20,000	United States	1,900,000
Finland	60,205	Netherlands	100,663	Upper Volta	3,000
Ghana	42,000	Niger	3,054	Venezuela	60,000
Greece	45,000	Nigeria	30,800	Yugoslavia	28,000
Guinea	5,000	Norway	109,200	Zaire	60,000
Guyana	2,000	Pakistan	20,000	Zambia	2,000
Holy See	2,000	People's Democratic		Total	5,956,953
India	50,000	Republic of Yemen	240		

DOCUMENTARY REFERENCES

General Assembly—26th session
Second Committee, meetings 1383, 1384.
Plenary meeting 1988.

A/8401. Report of Secretary-General on work of the Organization, 16 June 1970–15 June 1971, Part Five, Chapter II.
A/8414. Report of Executive Director of United Nations Institute for

Training and Research (UNITAR) (covering period 1 July 1970–30 June 1971). (Annex V: List of UNITAR publications available or in preparation.)

A/C.2/L.1144. Brazil, Canada, Chile, Denmark, El Salvador, Ghana, India, Iran, Jamaica, Kenya, Kuwait, Laos, Lebanon, Lesotho, Libyan Arab Republic, Nigeria, Singapore, Uganda, Upper Volta, Uruguay, Venezuela: draft resolution, approved without objection by Second Committee on 13 October 1971, meeting 1384.

A/8517. Report of Second Committee (on United Nations Institute for Training and Research), draft resolution.

RESOLUTION 2767(XXVI), as recommended by Second Committee, A/8517, adopted without objection by Assembly on 18 November 1971, meeting 1988.

The General Assembly,

Recalling its past resolutions relating to the United Nations Institute for Training and Research, particularly resolution 2640(XXV) of 19 November 1970, and the resolutions of the Economic and Social Council on the same subject,

1. *Takes note* of the report of the Executive Director of the United Nations Institute for Training and Research;

2. *Notes with satisfaction* the increasing effectiveness of the Institute in the discharge of its responsibilities;

3. *Expresses the hope* that the Institute will have greater and wider financial support.

Outflow of trained personnel

At its April-May 1971 session, the Economic and Social Council had before it a report by the Secretary-General on the outflow of trained personnel from developing to developed countries and two progress reports on the subject by the United Nations Institute for Training and Research (UNITAR).

The Secretary-General's report supported the view that there were serious shortages at various levels of trained personnel in some of the developing countries and that the migration of those cadres had contributed to retarding development.

On 19 May 1971, the Council expressed its concern that developing countries were suffering material loss from the "brain drain" to some advanced countries. The Council considered it necessary to pursue the study of this problem with a view to submitting measures for its solution.

The Council asked the Secretary-General to continue to study, in close co-operation with UNITAR, the problem of the "brain drain." In particular, he was asked: to prepare a study on the effect of the influx of foreign specialists on the economies of countries that admitted them to their enterprises; to devise methods of assessing the impact of the "brain drain" on the economies of developing countries; and to prepare a preliminary study of ways of strengthening co-operation among developing countries for the purpose of overcoming the problem by greater common utilization of their experts and trained personnel.

The attention of Governments of the developing countries was drawn to the need, as part of their development plans and with respect for the Universal Declaration of Human Rights, to take certain measures to deal with the "brain drain": to adapt educational programmes to national requirements, to provide correct vocational guidance, to encourage the return of scientists and other skilled personnel and to promote the training of technicians, to exchange information with other countries on measures taken, and to seek the necessary technical assistance from the developed countries, the United Nations Development Programme (UNDP) and other international agencies.

Developed countries and various bodies connected with the United Nations system were called upon to assist developing countries to establish and strengthen scientific and technological research centres, at both the national and regional levels. Governments of developed countries were invited to refrain from taking any special measures to induce scholarship students and trainees from the developing countries to settle permanently in their countries.

Developed countries were asked to encourage their private investors in developing countries to absorb local trained personnel within existing and planned projects, as a means of reducing the outflow. The organizations of the United Nations system, and especially UNDP, were asked to increase employment of local qualified experts and to use indigenous technology and services in the planning and implementation of projects in the field.

The Council also urged the International Labour Organisation to assist in the implementation of appropriate training and employment measures that would help developing countries combat the outflow.

These decisions were embodied in resolution 1573(L), which was adopted by consensus. The text was proposed by a working group composed of the sponsors of two draft resolutions that had been put before the Council and of other members who had made suggestions. The text that was finally adopted was essentially a combination of the ideas presented in those draft resolutions, one of which was sponsored by France, Hungary, Madagascar, Tunisia, the USSR and Yugoslavia, and the other by Uruguay. (For text, see DOCUMENTARY REFERENCES below.)

Amendments proposed to the working group's first draft text—by Brazil, Haiti, Jamaica and Kenya, by Sudan, and by the USSR—were taken into account in the revised version.

DOCUMENTARY REFERENCES

Economic and Social Council—50th session
Plenary meetings 1756, 1759, 1760, 1763, 1765, 1767, 1768.

E/4798. Outflow of trained personnel from developing to developed countries. Report of Executive Director of United Nations Institute for Training and Research (UNITAR).
E/4820 and Corr.1 and Add.1 and Add.1/Corr.1. Report of Secretary-General.
E/4820 (Summary). Summary of report of Secretary-General, prepared by Secretariat.
E/4948 and Corr.1. Progress report by Executive Director of UNITAR.
E/L.1379. USSR: draft resolution.
E/L.1379/Rev.1. France, Hungary, Madagascar, Tunisia, USSR, Yugoslavia: revised draft resolution.
E/L.1379/Rev.1/Add.1. Administrative and financial implications of 6-power revised draft resolution, E/L.1379/Rev.1. Statement by Secretary-General.
E/L.1409. Uruguay: draft resolution.
E/L.1412 and Rev.1. Draft resolution and revision prepared by Working Group.
E/L.1416. Sudan: amendments to draft resolution prepared by Working Group, E/L.1412.
E/L.1417. USSR: amendment to draft resolution prepared by Working Group, E/L.1412.
E/L.1418. Brazil, Haiti, Jamaica, Kenya: amendments to draft resolution prepared by Working Group, E/L.1412.

RESOLUTION 1573(L), as proposed by Working Group, E/L.1412/Rev.1, adopted by consensus by Council on 19 May 1971, meeting 1768.

The Economic and Social Council,
Taking into account the valuable report of the Secretary-General and the work of the United Nations and the United Nations Institute for Training and Research,
Recalling General Assembly resolutions 2320(XXII) of 15 December 1967 and 2417(XXIII) of 17 December 1968 on the outflow of trained personnel from the developing countries,
Concerned by the fact that developing countries are suffering material loss from the "brain drain" to some advanced countries,
Believing that this state of affairs calls for action by both developing and developed countries,
Noting that the most serious type of personnel outflow from developing countries consists of scientists and technically trained people migrating from their countries to permanently settle and work in the developed countries,
Considering it necessary to pursue the study of this problem with a view to subsequently submitting effective measures for its solution,
1. *Takes note* of the Secretary-General's report on the outflow of trained personnel from developing to developed countries, prepared in pursuance of General Assembly resolution 2417(XXIII);
2. *Requests* the Secretary-General to continue to study, in close co-operation with the United Nations Institute for Training and Research, the problem of the "brain drain" with a view to assessing its consequences for the economic development of the developing countries and, in particular:
(*a*) To prepare a study on the effect of the influx of foreign specialists on the economies of countries which admit foreign specialists to their enterprises and institutions;
(*b*) To devise methods of assessing the impact of the "brain drain" on the economies of developing countries;
(*c*) To prepare, in conjunction with the specialized agencies concerned, a preliminary study of the means and methods of strengthening co-operation among developing countries for the purpose of overcoming the problem of the "brain drain" by greater common utilization of their experts and trained personnel;
3. *Draws the attention* of the Governments of the developing countries to the need, as part of their development plans and with respect for the Universal Declaration of Human Rights:
(*a*) To adapt educational programmes to national requirements, in order to achieve so far as possible a suitable correlation between the training of skilled personnel and employment opportunities;
(*b*) To provide correct vocational guidance for the personnel to be trained, by first studying their aptitudes;
(*c*) To encourage the return of scientists and skilled personnel and to promote the training of technicians, by providing special allowances and benefits, by creating and exchanging fellowships with other countries and by measures such as the provision of favourable working and housing conditions;
(*d*) To exchange information with other countries about the measures taken and the results achieved in halting the outflow of technicians and skilled personnel;
(*e*) To seek the necessary technical assistance from developed countries, the United Nations Development Programme and other international agencies, in accordance with the International Development Strategy for the Second United Nations Development Decade;
4. *Calls upon* developed countries, the United Nations Industrial Development Organization, the United Nations Development Programme, the International Atomic Energy Agency and the various organs, commissions and agencies in the United Nations system to assist developing countries, upon their request, to establish and strengthen the existing scientific and technological research centres, at both the national and regional levels, in accordance with the International Development Strategy for the Second United Nations Development Decade;
5. *Invites* the Governments of the developed countries, without prejudice to the international agreements in force and with respect for the Universal Declaration of Human Rights, to refrain from taking any special measures to induce scholarship students and trainees from the developing countries to settle permanently in their countries;
6. *Requests* developed countries to encourage, as appropriate, their private investors in developing countries to absorb local, trained personnel, scientists and technicians within existing and planned projects, as a means of helping the developing countries to reduce the outflow;
7. *Urges* the International Labour Organisation, as a part of its jobs and skills programme for developing countries—in connexion with the World Employment Programme—to assist, upon request and in co-operation with the United Nations Development Programme and other international organizations, in the implementation of appropriate training and employment measures which would help developing countries to combat the outflow;
8. *Further urges* the organizations of the United Nations system and especially the United Nations Development Programme, with due regard to their recruitment, contracting and sub-contracting procedures and taking into full consideration the provisions of General Assembly resolution 2688(XXV) of 11 December 1970, to further increase employment of local, qualified experts and to use, as far as possible, indigenous technology and services in the planning and implementation of projects they carry out in the field.

Other documents
A/8401. Report of Secretary-General on work of the Organization, 16 June 1970–15 June 1971, Part Three, Chapter II D 3.
A/8403. Report of Economic and Social Council on work of its 50th and 51st sessions, Chapters II (p.3) and X C.
A/C.2/261. Note by Secretary-General.

Transport

Technical aid in 1971

Technical co-operation and assistance for the development of transport, including public works connected with transport in developing countries, continued during 1971. Large-scale country projects were in operation in Afghanistan, the Ivory Coast, Madagascar, Nepal, Paraguay and the People's Democratic Republic of Yemen.

In addition, two regional projects for the feasibility and pre-investment study of the Trans-Saharan Road and the navigability and port development of the Senegal River covered Algeria, Mali, Niger, Tunisia and Guinea, and Mali, Mauritania and Senegal, respectively. Two projects for the improvement of road and water transport were in operation in West Irian, Indonesia, under the programme of the United Nations Fund for the Development of West Irian.

The following countries were assisted through the provision of about 70 individual experts or teams: Afghanistan, Bolivia, the Central African Republic, China, Colombia, the Congo, Costa Rica, Egypt, Gabon, Guatemala, Haiti, India, Indonesia, Kenya, Lesotho, Madagascar, Nepal, Niger, Pakistan, Saudi Arabia, Sierra Leone, Swaziland, the Syrian Arab Republic, Togo, the United Republic of Tanzania, Upper Volta, Venezuela, Western Samoa, Zaire and Zambia. Assistance was offered in transport administration, planning, programming and co-ordination, port management and administration, railway accounting and auditing, highway building, design and construction and material testing, inland water transport and coastal shipping.

Conference on container traffic

On 10 May 1971, the Economic and Social Council agreed that a Conference on International Container Traffic, to be convened jointly by the United Nations and the Inter-Governmental Maritime Consultative Organization (IMCO), should begin at Geneva, Switzerland, on 13 November 1972, not to extend beyond five weeks.

It noted that the Conference was supposed to deal, among other questions, with the legal problems concerning the liability of combined transport operators and related questions.

The Council stressed that the Conference should have its scope limited to the international aspects of containerization, and should have as its guiding principle the development and facilitation of container traffic on a global basis while safeguarding the interests of the developing countries.

The Secretary-General was asked to ascertain the views of Governments of Member States on their priorities for the Conference. The Council also asked that a small inter-governmental preparatory group be convened to review the responses of Governments and propose a specific provisional agenda to the Council.

The Secretary-General was also requested to prepare a study on the economic implications, in particular for the developing countries, of the proposed Convention on the International Combined Transport of Goods and to distribute the study to Governments. He was to prepare the study in co-operation with the United Nations Conference on Trade and Development (UNCTAD), the United Nations regional commissions and IMCO. The views of Governments were to be ascertained.

The UNCTAD Committee on Shipping, the United Nations regional commissions and IMCO were to consider, in the light of the results of the study, whether the draft Convention or alternative proposals were ready for international consideration.

These Council decisions were embodied in resolution 1568(L), adopted by 19 votes to 2, on the basis of a proposal by three Council members (Brazil, New Zealand and the United States) and by two observers, Chile and India. (For text of resolution, see DOCUMENTARY REFERENCES below.)

Two days later, on 12 May, the Economic and Social Council decided that the following bodies should be invited to the United Nations/IMCO Conference on International Container Traffic: all States Members of the United Nations or members of specialized agencies or of the International Atomic Energy Agency (IAEA) and, in an advisory capacity, the specialized agencies and IAEA and also, as observers, interested inter-governmental organizations and non-governmental organizations having consultative status with the Council or with IMCO.

This decision was embodied in resolution 1569(L), adopted by 19 votes to 3, with 4 abstentions, on the basis of a proposal by France, the United Kingdom and the United States. (For text of resolution, see DOCUMENTARY REFERENCES below.)

An amendment proposed by Ceylon to the effect that all States should be invited to the Conference was rejected on 12 May 1971 by 13 votes to 6, with 7 abstentions.

Withdrawn was a draft decision, proposed by Hungary, Sudan, the USSR and Yugoslavia, which was also intended to have all States invited to the Conference.

Transport documentation centre

Before the Council at its May 1971 session was a report by the Secretary-General on the establishment of a United Nations transport economics and technology documentation centre. The report outlined the role and basic functions of such a centre, its terms of reference, its organization and its co-operation responsibilities with other organizations. The centre's role as a clearing-house for information on new transport technologies and their economics was stressed.

Two draft resolutions were presented to the Council during its discussion of the transport documentation centre. On 12 May 1971, however, the Council decided not to take any decision on the substance of these proposals. On 21 May, it decided to take up the question at its first session in 1972. These decisions were taken without adopting a formal resolution.

One draft resolution before the Council was sponsored by the United States and the other by Brazil, Kenya, Sudan, Tunisia, Yugoslavia and Zaire. The sponsors of both drafts recognized that more systematic evaluation and dissemination of the results of research on transport planning was of importance.

The difference between the draft texts was mainly in the institutional approach to achieving that purpose.

By the United States text, the Council would have expressed the belief that the purpose could be achieved without establishing a separate centre, at least initially, and it would have suggested that the Secretary-General develop the activities outlined in his report within the Department of Economic and Social Affairs gradually over the next few years as budgetary or extra-budgetary resources became available for the purpose.

The six-power text would have had the Council decide to set up a centre within the Department of Economic and Social Affairs, the establishment to be phased over a period of not more than three years.

Accession of Republic of Korea to Convention on Road Traffic

In a communication dated 16 February 1971 addressed to the Secretary-General, the Government of the Republic of Korea expressed the wish to accede to the Convention on Road Traffic of 19 September 1949. The Secretary-General brought this matter to the attention of the Economic and Social Council at meetings held in April 1971.

On 28 April 1971, the Council took note of the Korean communication and declared that the Republic of Korea was eligible to accede to the Convention on Road Traffic. The Council took this action in adopting resolution 1563(L), by 16 votes to 5, with 4 abstentions, on a proposal by New Zealand. (For text, see DOCUMENTARY REFERENCES below.)

International transport of dangerous goods

During 1971, a number of meetings were held under the auspices of the Inland Transport Committee of the Economic Commission for Europe (ECE). In February 1971, *ad hoc* groups on the marking of vehicles carrying dangerous goods and on the listing of particularly dangerous goods met. In March, a group of experts on the transport of dangerous goods (radioactive materials) met, and in April, experts on the transport of dangerous goods met to study provisions concerning the design and testing of tanks.

The revision of the European Agreement regulating the international carriage of dangerous goods by road, in harmony with the revision of the corresponding railway regulations, continued, and steps were taken towards the preparation of a similar agreement on inland waterway transport.

In August 1971, the group of experts on explosives met and discussed, among other things, the classification of explosives, tests to determine and classify the risks inherent in explosives, the labelling of explosives, the determination of maximum weights of packages of explosives and the work of IMCO on the carriage of explosives.

DOCUMENTARY REFERENCES

Preparations for conference on container traffic

Economic and Social Council—50th session
Plenary meetings 1747-1751, 1755, 1757, 1760, 1762.

E/4963. Note by Secretary-General.
E/L.1380. Note by Secretariat (transmitting extracts from report of UNCTAD Committee on Shipping on its 5th session, Geneva, Switzerland, 22 March–3 April 1971).
E/L.1388. Note by Secretariat (transmitting cable from IMCO).
E/L.1391. Brazil and India: draft resolution.
E/L.1391/Rev.1. Brazil, Chile, India: revised draft resolution.
E/L.1391/Rev.1/Add.1. Administrative and financial implications of E/L.1391/Rev.1. Statement by Secretary-General.
E/L.1391/Rev.2. Brazil, Chile, India, New Zealand, United States: revised draft resolution.

E/L.1393. United Kingdom: amendments to 2-power draft resolution, E/L.1391.
E/L.1393/Rev.1. United Kingdom: amendments to 5-power revised draft resolution, E/L.1391/Rev.2.
E/L.1394. Brazil, Ghana, Yugoslavia: draft decision.
E/L.1398. USSR: amendment to 5-power revised draft resolution, E/L.1391/Rev.2.

RESOLUTION 1568(L), as proposed by 5 powers, E/L.1391/Rev.2, adopted by Council on 10 May 1971, meeting 1757, by 19 votes to 2.

The Economic and Social Council,
Recalling its decision taken at the forty-eighth session that a Conference on International Container Traffic should be convened

jointly by the United Nations and the Inter-Governmental Maritime Consultative Organization,

Having received the Secretary-General's note on the preparation for the Conference,

Aware that technological advancements in international container transport have important economic implications for conditions of development in developing countries,

Recognizing the desirability of more extensive discussion among Governments with respect to elaborating more precisely the scope and objectives of the Conference,

Noting that the Conference is supposed to deal, among other questions, with the legal problems concerning in particular the liability of combined transport operators and related questions,

Noting that a preliminary draft of a Convention on the International Combined Transport of Goods (TCM) has been considered by the Inter-Governmental Maritime Consultative Organization and the Economic Commission for Europe,

Noting further that the Committee on Shipping of the United Nations Conference on Trade and Development, in its resolution 17(V) of 3 April 1971, recommended that the Economic and Social Council be invited to consider undertaking a study on the economic implications, in particular for developing countries, of the proposed Convention on the International Combined Transport of Goods so that such implications may be fully taken into account,

1. *Agrees* that the Conference on International Container Traffic should begin at Geneva on 13 November 1972 and that it should not extend beyond five weeks;

2. *Stresses* that the Conference should have its scope limited to the international aspects of containerization, including in particular those international aspects related to combined transport and its requirements, and that this scope should not comprehend over-all transport control;

3. *Stresses further* that the Conference should have as its guiding principle the development and facilitation of container traffic on a global basis while safeguarding the interests of the developing countries;

4. *Requests* the Secretary-General to ascertain the views of Governments of Member States as to their priorities for the Conference from among the topics and areas of action referred to in the decision taken by the Council at its forty-eighth session;

5. *Requests further* that a small intergovernmental preparatory group, half of its members to be designated by the President of the Economic and Social Council and the other half by the Chairman of the Council of the Inter-Governmental Maritime Consultative Organization, with due regard to geographical representation, be convened as early as practicable to review the responses of Governments and propose a specific provisional agenda to the Economic and Social Council;

6. *Requests* also that the Secretary-General, in close co-operation with the United Nations Conference on Trade and Development, the regional economic commissions and the United Nations Economic and Social Office at Beirut, and in consultation with the Inter-Governmental Maritime Consultative Organization, prepare a study on the economic implications, in particular for developing countries, of the proposed Convention on the International Combined Transport of Goods, such study to be conducted with the assistance of experts, after ascertaining the views of Governments of Member States on those aspects and questions which in their view require clarification;

7. *Requests* also that the Secretary-General distribute the study to the Governments of Member States as soon as it is available;

8. *Invites* the Committee on Shipping of the United Nations Conference on Trade and Development, the regional economic commissions, the United Nations Economic and Social Office at Beirut and the Inter-Governmental Maritime Consultative Organization to review the matter in the light of the results of the study in order to consider whether the draft Convention on the International Combined Transport of Goods or alternative proposals are ready for international consideration.

E/L.1402. France, United Kingdom, United States: draft resolution.
E/L.1405. Hungary, Sudan, USSR, Yugoslavia: draft decision.

RESOLUTION 1569(L), as proposed by 3 powers, E/L.1402, and as orally revised by sponsors, adopted by Council on 12 May 1971, meeting 1760, by 19 votes to 3, with 4 abstentions.

The Economic and Social Council,

Recalling its decision taken at the forty-eighth session that a Conference on International Container Traffic should be convened jointly by the United Nations and the Inter-Governmental Maritime Consultative Organization,

Having considered the arrangements proposed by the Secretary-General in his note on the preparation for the Conference,

Decides that all States Members of the United Nations or members of specialized agencies or of the International Atomic Energy Agency and, in an advisory capacity, the specialized agencies and the International Atomic Energy Agency and also, as observers, interested intergovernmental organizations and interested non-governmental organizations having consultative status with the Council or having such status or special working arrangements with the Inter-Governmental Maritime Consultative Organization shall be invited to the Conference.

OTHER DOCUMENTS

E/5046. Establishment of inter-governmental preparatory groups. Note by Secretary-General.
A/8401. Report of Secretary-General on work of the Organization, 16 June 1970–15 June 1971, Part Three, Chapter II G.
A/8403. Report of Economic and Social Council on work of its 50th and 51st sessions, Chapter VII D.
ST/ECA/160. Economic implications, in particular for developing countries, of proposed Convention on International Combined Transport of Goods. Study by Secretary-General.

Transport documentation centre

Economic and Social Council—50th session
Plenary meetings 1741, 1751, 1752, 1757, 1759, 1760, 1772.

E/4964. Transport development. Establishment of United Nations transport economics and technology documentation centre. Report of Secretary-General.
E/4964/Add.1. Comments of International Civil Aviation Organization.
E/2964/Add.2. Administrative and financial implications of report of Secretary-General, E/4964. Statement by Secretary-General.
E/4964/Add.3. Note by Secretary-General.
E/4964/Add.4. Extract from report of Economic Commission for Europe.
E/4989. Report of Committee for Programme and Co-ordination on its 8th session, 22 March–8 April 1971, Chapter VIII.
E/L.1381. Note by Secretariat (transmitting decision of UNCTAD Committee on Shipping at its 5th session).
E/L.1397. United States: draft resolution.
E/L.1401. Brazil, Kenya, Sudan, Tunisia, Yugoslavia, Zaire: draft resolution.
E/5044. Resolutions adopted by Economic and Social Council during its 50th session, 11-13 January and 26 April–21 May 1971. Decisions, p. 14.
A/8403. Report of Economic and Social Council on work of its 50th and 51st sessions, Chapter VII C.

Accession of Republic of Korea to Convention on Road Traffic

Economic and Social Council—50th session
Plenary meeting 1742.

E/4972. Note by Secretary-General (transmitting communication of 16 February 1971 from Acting Permanent Observer of Republic of Korea).
E/L.1383. New Zealand: draft resolution.

RESOLUTION 1563(L), as proposed by New Zealand, E/L.1383, adopted by Council on 28 April 1971, meeting 1742, by 16 votes to 5, with 4 abstentions.

The Economic and Social Council,
Taking note of the communication dated 16 February 1971 from the Republic of Korea concerning the desire of that State to become a party to the Convention on Road Traffic, signed at Geneva on 19 September 1949,

Declares that the Republic of Korea is eligible to accede to the aforementioned Convention on Road Traffic.

A/8403. Report of Economic and Social Council on work of its 50th and 51st sessions, Chapter VII E.

International transport of dangerous goods
E/CN.2/CONF.5/43. Report of Group of Experts on Explosives on its 11th session, Geneva, Switzerland, 4-5 August 1971.

International tourism

Technical aid

During 1971, 14 individual experts were provided for technical assistance in tourism to Afghanistan, India, Iran, Kenya, Lesotho and Senegal. Assistance was provided in such fields as passenger transportation, tourism surveys and statistics, tourism promotion, development and planning, operation of travel agencies and hotel management.

Relations with World Tourism Organization

During 1971, the question of co-operation and relations between the United Nations and the World Tourism Organization was considered by the Economic and Social Council's Committee for Programme and Co-ordination, the Council itself and the General Assembly.

Before the Assembly was a note by the Secretary-General on co-operation and relations between the United Nations and the World Tourism Organization which dealt, among other things, with arrangements for a meeting to be held in 1972 between the United Nations and the International Union of Official Travel Organizations (IUOTO).

(The General Assembly of IUOTO had met in September 1970 to revise the statutes of IUOTO to enable it to acquire an inter-governmental character. The United Nations was to establish an operational link with the transformed Union, which was to be known as the World Tourism Organization, after the statutes entered into force.)[2]

By a decision of 20 May 1971, the Economic and Social Council expressed the hope that consultations between the United Nations and the International Union of Official Travel Organizations (IUOTO) would continue.

The Council recommended that the following considerations be kept in mind during such negotiations: the World Tourism Organization should have the decisive and central role in the field of world tourism, and the fundamental aim of that organization should be the promotion and development of tourism, with particular attention being paid to the interests of the developing countries.

Steps should be taken, the Council recommend-

ed, to enable the World Tourism Organization to be designated as a participating and executing agency of the United Nations Development Programme (UNDP). Finally, the Council recommended that the Secretary-General should submit proposals to the Council on measures to improve the planning and co-ordination of activities by the United Nations system in tourism.

Without adopting a resolution, the Council took these actions on the recommendation of its Social Committee, which had approved the text of this decision without objection on 4 May 1971.

Later in the year, at its twenty-sixth session, which opened on 21 September 1971, the General Assembly endorsed the recommendations of the Economic and Social Council with regard to co-operation between the United Nations and the World Tourism Organization. In particular, the Assembly recommended that steps should be taken to enable the World Tourism Organization to be designated as a participating and executing agency of UNDP.

The Assembly invited States whose national tourism organizations were members of IUOTO to approve the statutes of the World Tourism Organization and emphasized that an agreement between the United Nations and the World Tourism Organization should be concluded soon after the establishment of that organization.

It was further recommended that the report of the Secretary-General on co-operation and relationships between the United Nations and IUOTO should be revised in the light of discussions held in 1971 by the Committee for Programme and Co-ordination, the Economic and Social Council and the General Assembly and be submitted to the Council in 1972.

The Assembly acted by adopting resolution 2802(XXVI), on 14 December 1971, by 106 votes to 0, with 5 abstentions, on the recommendation of its Second (Economic and Financial) Committee, which approved the text on 20 October 1971 by 91 votes to 0, with 5 abstentions. The text was proposed by Burundi, Cameroon, Chile, Colombia, the Dominican Republic, Ethiopia, Guatemala, Guinea, Honduras, India, Indonesia, Kenya,

[2]See Y.U.N., 1970, pp. 661-63.

Kuwait, Lebanon, Madagascar, Malaysia, Mexico, Morocco, Nigeria, Pakistan, Peru, the Philippines, Sudan, Thailand, Trinidad and Tobago, Tunisia, Turkey, the United Republic of Tanzania and Yugoslavia. (For text of resolution, see DOCUMENTARY REFERENCES below.)

DOCUMENTARY REFERENCES

Economic and Social Council—50th session
Social Committee, meetings 656, 658, 659.
Plenary meeting 1769.

E/4861 and Corr.1. Co-operation and relationships between United Nations and International Union of Official Travel Organizations. Report of Secretary-General.
E/4955. Co-operation and relations between United Nations and World Tourism Organization. Note by Secretary-General.
E/4961. Relations with non-United Nations inter-governmental organizations in economic and social field. Report of Secretary-General.
E/4989. Report of Committee for Programme and Co-ordination on its 8th session, 22 March–8 April 1971, Chapter IX.
E/AC.7/L.585 and Rev.1. Indonesia, Sudan, Yugoslavia and observer for India: proposal and revised proposal for decision by Council, approved without objection by Social Committee on 4 May 1971, meeting 659.
E/5023. Report of Social Committee (on relations with inter-governmental organizations).
E/5044. Resolutions adopted by Economic and Social Council during its 50th session, 11-13 January and 26 April–21 May 1971. Decisions, pp. 25-26 (item 12 (*b*)).

Economic and Social Council—51st session
Plenary meeting 1799.

General Assembly—26th session
Second Committee, meetings 1370-1382, 1394.
Plenary meeting 2017.

A/8401. Report of Secretary-General on work of the Organization, 16 June 1970–15 June 1971, Part Three, Chapter II G.
A/8403. Report of Economic and Social Council on work of its 50th and 51st sessions, Chapter XXI D, paras. 751-761.
A/C.2/L.1147. Burundi, Cameroon, Chile, Colombia, Dominican Republic, Ethiopia, Guatemala, Guinea, Honduras, India, Indonesia, Kenya, Kuwait, Lebanon, Madagascar, Malaysia, Mexico, Morocco, Nigeria, Pakistan, Peru, Philippines, Sudan, Thailand, Trinidad and Tobago, Tunisia, Turkey, United Republic of Tanzania, Yugoslavia: draft resolution, as orally amended by Japan and by sponsors, approved by Second Committee on 20 October 1971, meeting 1394, by 91 votes to 0, with 5 abstentions.
A/8578. Report of Second Committee (part I) (on report of Economic and Social Council), draft resolution I.

RESOLUTION 2802(XXVI), as recommended by Second Committee, A/8578, adopted by Assembly on 14 December 1971, meeting 2017, by 106 votes to 0, with 5 abstentions.

The General Assembly,
Recalling its resolution 2529(XXIV) of 5 December 1969 on the establishment of an intergovernmental tourism organization,

Noting that the International Union of Official Travel Organizations at its Extraordinary General Assembly held at Mexico City adopted, on 28 September 1970, the statutes of the World Tourism Organization,
Believing that the World Tourism Organization should be established as early as possible,
Taking note of the decision taken by the Economic and Social Council on 20 May 1971,
1. *Invites* States whose national tourism organizations are members of the International Union of Official Travel Organizations to approve, as soon as possible, the statutes of the World Tourism Organization;
2. *Emphasizes* that an agreement between the United Nations and the World Tourism Organization, defining the role and sphere of competence of the latter, should be concluded soon after the establishment of the organization;
3. *Recommends* that intensified negotiations to that end be held between the United Nations and the International Union of Official Travel Organizations with a view to finalizing a draft agreement;
4. *Endorses* the recommendation of the Economic and Social Council that the following guidelines be kept in mind during those negotiations:
(*a*) The World Tourism Organization shall have the decisive and central role in the field of world tourism in co-operation with the existing machinery within the United Nations;
(*b*) The fundamental aim of the World Tourism Organization shall be the promotion and development of tourism and particular attention shall be paid to the interests of the developing countries in this regard;
5. *Recommends* that the report of the Secretary-General on co-operation and relationships between the United Nations and the International Union of Official Travel Organizations should be revised in the light of the discussions at the eighth session of the Committee for Programme and Co-ordination, the fiftieth session of the Economic and Social Council and the twenty-sixth session of the General Assembly, and submitted to the Council at its fifty-third session in order to enable the Council to give concrete directions to determine the course of the negotiations;
6. *Requests* the Secretary-General to submit to the Economic and Social Council at its fifty-third session, through the Committee for Programme and Co-ordination, a report on the activities of the United Nations family in the field of development of tourism;
7. *Recommends* that steps should be taken, as appropriate and with due regard to procedures of the United Nations Development Programme, to enable the designation of the World Tourism Organization as a participating and executing agency of the Programme in order to assist that organization in carrying out its functions related to the development of tourism.

Other documents
ST/TAO/SER.C/131. Report of Inter-regional Seminar on Physical Planning for Tourism Development, Dubrovnik, Yugoslavia, 19 October–3 November 1970.

International co-operation in cartography

During 1971, ten experts under the programme of technical assistance were provided in such fields as geodetic, land and topographic surveying, hydrography, and administration of survey departments to Afghanistan, Burundi, Guyana, Laos, Madagascar, Nepal and Somalia.

Six major projects under the Special Fund component of the United Nations Development Programme were in operation during the year. In Ceylon, work continued in the Institute of Surveying and Mapping at Diyatalawa, and advanced training courses in cadastral mapping and land registration were established. In Colombia, progress was made on the surveying and mapping aspects of the Chaco Valley Project. The assistance to the Survey of India for pre-investment surveying, mapping and training was extended by two years. Assistance to the Geographic Institute in the Ivory Coast, strengthening of the topographical survey division in Sudan and assistance to the Survey Department of Jamaica continued.

Twenty-seven fellowships were awarded during the year for the study of surveying and mapping.

The Inter-regional Seminar on Photogrammetric Techniques, held in Zurich, Switzerland, from 15 March to 3 April 1971, discussed the latest photogrammetric techniques and their application to the economic development of developing countries.

The third session of the *Ad Hoc* Group of Experts on Geographical Names was convened in New York from 2 to 12 February 1971 to prepare and discuss the agenda of the second United Nations Conference on the Standardization of Geographical Names, to be convened in 1972.

An *Ad Hoc* Group of Experts on Projections and

Planning of United Nations activities in Cartography for the Second United Nations Development Decade was convened in New York from 8 to 19 November 1971.

The report of the Sixth United Nations Regional Cartographic Conference for Asia and the Far East (convened at Teheran, Iran, from 24 October to 7 November 1970) was before the Economic and Social Council at its May 1971 session.

On 13 May 1971, the Council approved the holding of a Seventh United Nations Regional Conference for Asia and the Far East in the second half of 1973 in Japan and requested the Secretary-General to make the necessary arrangements.

The Secretary-General was also asked to take practical measures for the implementation, as appropriate, of the recommendations of the Sixth United Nations Regional Conference for Asia and the Far East.

These decisions were embodied in resolution 1570(L), adopted by 22 votes to 2, on the basis of a proposal by Indonesia, Malaysia and New Zealand. (For text of resolution, see DOCUMENTARY REFERENCES below.)

DOCUMENTARY REFERENCES

Economic and Social Council—50th session
Plenary meetings 1758, 1762.

E/4943. Sixth United Nations Regional Cartographic Conference for Asia and Far East. Report of Secretary-General.
E/4943/Add.1. Administrative and financial implications of proposals contained in report of Secretary-General, E/4943. Statement by Secretary-General.
E/4969. Report of Committee on Natural Resources on its first session, 22 February–10 March 1971, Chapter VI C.
E/L.1406. Indonesia, Malaysia, New Zealand: draft resolution.

RESOLUTION 1570(L), as proposed by 3 powers, E/L.1406, and as orally revised by sponsors, adopted by Council on 13 May 1971, meeting 1762, by 22 votes to 2.

The Economic and Social Council,
Having considered the report of the Secretary-General on the Sixth United Nations Regional Cartographic Conference for Asia and the Far East, which was held at Teheran from 24 October to 7 November 1970,
Appreciating the valuable contributions of the Conference to economic and social development in furthering cartographic work in the countries of the region,
Noting the recommendation of the Conference that a Seventh

United Nations Regional Cartographic Conference for Asia and the Far East be convened during October/November 1973,
Noting also with appreciation that the Government of Japan has offered to act as host to the conference and to extend full co-operation in this regard,
1. *Requests* the Secretary-General to make the necessary arrangements, in accordance with General Assembly resolution 2609(XXIV) of 16 December 1969, and to convene in Japan in the second half of 1973 the Seventh United Nations Regional Cartographic Conference for Asia and the Far East, including the sending of invitations to Governments of States Members of the United Nations or members of specialized agencies and to the specialized agencies concerned and other interested international organizations;
2. *Further requests* the Secretary-General to take practical measures for the implementation, as appropriate, of the recommendations of the Sixth United Nations Regional Cartographic Conference for Asia and the Far East.

Other documents
A/8403. Report of Economic and Social Council on work of its 50th and 51st sessions, Chapter VII F.
Supplement No. 1 to *International Map of the World on the Millionth Scale (IMW)* (ST/ECA/SER.D/15, U.N.P. Sales No.: E/F.70.I.19). Status of publication of IMW sheets as at 31 January 1971 (ST/ECA/SER.D/Supp.1).

The establishment of an international university

In 1971, both the Economic and Social Council and the General Assembly took up the question of the establishment of an international university. Before those bodies was a report of the Secretary-General containing a report and comments of the Director-General of the United Nations Educa-

tional, Scientific and Cultural Organization (UNESCO) on the results of a feasibility study concerning the university, as well as recommendations of the United Nations Institute for Training and Research and a report of the Panel of Experts on the Establishment of an International University, a body set up by the General Assembly in 1970.[3]

On 23 November 1971, the Economic and Social Council, having taken note of the report of the Secretary-General, transmitted it to the General Assembly. The Council drew the attention of the Assembly to the fact that it had not had an opportunity to discuss the report and accordingly recommended that the Assembly defer consideration of the item to its 1972 session so that the Council might have an opportunity to submit recommendations of a concrete nature.

The Council acted by adopting, without a vote, resolution 1653(LI), the text of which had been suggested by the Council President and amended by the USSR. (For text, see DOCUMENTARY REFERENCES below.)

The amendment proposed by the USSR and sub-amended by the United Kingdom was the recommendation that the Assembly defer consideration of the item to 1972.

Later in 1971, at its twenty-sixth session, which opened on 21 September, the General Assembly did take up the question of the establishment of an international university and decided to consider the matter fully in 1972.

The Assembly noted with appreciation the report of the Secretary-General and requested him to continue his studies, in consultation with UNESCO and other interested bodies.

The Secretary-General was authorized to call on the assistance of the Panel of Experts on the Establishment of an International University, the membership of which, the Assembly stated, should be increased (from 10) to not more than 20 to allow for the designation of additional experts by the Director-General of UNESCO, in consultation with the Secretary-General and interested agencies.

The General Conference and the Executive Board of UNESCO were invited to submit further observations and recommendations on the subject. The Economic and Social Council was requested to consider the matter further and to submit a report to the Assembly in 1972, together with any recommendations on the question.

These decisions were among those embodied in resolution 2822(XXVI), adopted on 16 December 1971, by 100 votes to 0, with 10 abstentions, on the recommendation of the Assembly's Second (Economic and Financial) Committee, which approved a revised text on 13 December 1971, by 86 votes to 0, with 9 abstentions. The text was proposed in the Second Committee by Austria, Cyprus, Egypt, Greece, Honduras, India, Indonesia, Japan, Lebanon, New Zealand, the Philippines, Sierra Leone and Yugoslavia. (For text of resolution, see DOCUMENTARY REFERENCES below.)

During the discussion in the Second Committee, amendments to an earlier text proposed by Colombia and Japan and by Egypt were incorporated into the revised text.

---

[3]See Y.U.N., 1970, pp. 651-52, text of resolution 2691(XXV) of 11 December 1970.

DOCUMENTARY REFERENCES

Economic and Social Council—51st session
Plenary meeting 1806.

E/5083. Report of Secretary-General (covering note transmitting A/8510).
E/5077. Organization and financing of an international university: recommendations of United Nations Institute for Training and Research (UNITAR). Note by Executive Director of UNITAR.
E/L.1461. Note by Secretary-General (transmitting progress report of Panel of Experts on Establishment of an International University).

RESOLUTION 1653(LI), as suggested by Council President and as orally amended by USSR, as orally sub-amended by United Kingdom, adopted without vote by Council on 23 November 1971, meeting 1806.

The Economic and Social Council,
Having taken note of the report of the Secretary-General, with its annexes, on the studies undertaken in pursuance of General Assembly resolution 2691(XXV) of 11 December 1970,
1. *Transmits* this report to the General Assembly at its twenty-sixth session;
2. *Draws the attention* of the General Assembly to the comments and observations on the subject made in the Economic and Social Council;
3. *Also draws the attention* of the General Assembly to the fact that the Council did not have an opportunity to discuss the report of the Secretary-General submitted to it on the question of the establishment of an international university, and accordingly

recommends that the General Assembly defer consideration of this item to its twenty-seventh session in order that the Council may have an opportunity to submit to the Assembly recommendations of a concrete nature.

General Assembly—26th session
Second Committee, meetings 1440, 1441, 1443.
Fifth Committee, meeting 1486.
Plenary meeting 2021.

A/8401/Add.1. Introduction to report of Secretary-General on work of the Organization, September 1971, Part Two, Chapter IX, paras. 324-330.
A/8403/Add.1. Addendum to report of Economic and Social Council, resumed 51st session, Chapter V.
A/8510 and Add.1 and Add.1/Rev.1. Report of Secretary-General, and addendum.
A/C.2/L.1200 and Rev.1. Austria, Egypt, Greece, Honduras, Indonesia, Japan, Lebanon, New Zealand, Philippines, Sierra Leone, Yugoslavia: draft resolution and revision.
A/C.2/L.1200/Rev.2. Austria, Cyprus, Egypt, Greece, Honduras, India, Indonesia, Japan, Lebanon, New Zealand, Philippines, Sierra Leone, Yugoslavia: revised draft resolution, approved by Second Committee on 13 December 1971, meeting 1443, by 86 votes to 0, with 9 abstentions.
A/C.2/L.1203. Egypt: amendments to 6-power draft resolution, A/C.2/L.1200.
A/C.2/L.1204. Colombia and Japan: amendments to 6-power draft resolution, A/C.2/L.1200.
A/C.2/L.1219, A/C.5/1421. Administrative and financial implica-

tions of draft resolution recommended by Second Committee in A/8596. Statements by Secretary-General.
A/8596. Report of Second Committee.

RESOLUTION 2822(XXVI), as recommended by Second Committee, A/8596, adopted by Assembly on 16 December 1971, meeting 2021, by 100 votes to 0, with 10 abstentions.

The General Assembly,

Recalling its resolution 2691(XXV) of 11 December 1970,

Recalling also Economic and Social Council resolution 1653(LI) of 23 November 1971,

Emphasizing the importance of adequate consideration by appropriate intergovernmental bodies of the United Nations system of all factors relating to the question of the establishment of an international university,

1. *Takes note with appreciation* of the report of the Secretary-General, containing the report and comments of the Director-General of the United Nations Educational, Scientific and Cultural Organization on the results of the feasibility study concerning the international university, the decision adopted by the Executive Board of that organization on 18 October 1971, the recommendations of the United Nations Institute for Training and Research and the report of the Panel of Experts on the Establishment of an International University;

2. *Requests* the Secretary-General to continue his studies, in consultation with the United Nations Educational, Scientific and Cultural Organization and other interested bodies, taking into account the views expressed in the General Assembly at its twenty-sixth session, and to submit any additional information to the Economic and Social Council at its fifty-third session;

3. *Authorizes* the Secretary-General to call on the assistance of the Panel of Experts on the Establishment of an International University, set up in accordance with General Assembly resolution 2691(XXV), the membership of which should be increased to not more than twenty to allow for the designation of five additional experts by the Director-General of the United Nations Educational, Scientific and Cultural Organization, in consultation with the Secretary-General and interested agencies and programmes;

4. *Invites* the Executive Board of the United Nations Educational, Scientific and Cultural Organization to submit to the Economic and Social Council at its fifty-third session such further observations and recommendations on the subject as it may consider appropriate;

5. *Requests* the Economic and Social Council to give detailed consideration, in conformity with its resolution 1653(LI), to reports and recommendations contained in the report of the Secretary-General, the further report of the Secretary-General and the views of the Executive Board of the United Nations Educational, Scientific and Cultural Organization and to submit to the General Assembly at its twenty-seventh session a report, together with any recommendations it may make on the question of the establishment of an international university;

6. *Requests* the Economic and Social Council to take into account also the views expressed in the General Assembly at its twenty-sixth session;

7. *Invites* the General Conference of the United Nations Educational, Scientific and Cultural Organization at its seventeenth session to submit to the General Assembly at its twenty-seventh session such comments and observations on the subject as it may consider appropriate;

8. *Decides* to consider the matter fully at its twenty-seventh session.

International Book Year

On 20 May 1971, having examined a report of the United Nations Educational, Scientific and Cultural Organization (UNESCO) on book development in the service of education, the Economic and Social Council made a number of decisions in support of the UNESCO proclamation of 1972 as International Book Year.

The Council noted that, pending the wider and more enlightened use of other media, the book remained the indispensable instrument for education, that books contributed to knowledge and mutual understanding of cultures and thus strengthened international understanding, but that there existed a gap between developed and developing countries, the latter suffering from serious shortages of printing and distribution facilities and of authors' manuscripts.

It was urgent, the Council considered, that these shortages be overcome without delay and that an adequate infrastructure to develop national book production be developed.

Countries were invited to respond to the requirements of the developing countries in revising the Berne Convention for the Protection of Literary and Artistic Works and the Universal Copyright Convention, and developed countries were invited to grant the greatest possible copyright facilities to developing countries.

It was recommended that international assistance be provided for low-cost local production of books produced in developed countries for higher education. Further, it was recommended that financial and technical assistance be provided to create an adequate infrastructure in the developing countries for the promotion of domestic book production.

The Food and Agriculture Organization of the United Nations was asked to continue its work for the promotion of paper industries, in particular in the developing countries.

Finally, Member States and inter-governmental organizations were invited to take appropriate steps to attain the objectives of International Book Year, and UNESCO was invited to submit a report to the Council in 1974 on the results achieved.

These decisions were embodied in resolution 1575(L), adopted by the Council, unanimously, on the recommendation of its Social Committee, which approved the text unanimously on 4 May 1971, on a proposal of Lebanon, Madagascar, Pakistan, Sudan and Tunisia. (For text of resolution, see DOCUMENTARY REFERENCES below.)

During the discussion of the text in the Social Committee, an amendment sponsored by Kenya was adopted, by a vote of 25 to 0, with 1 abstention, by which the Council recommended that financial and technical assistance be provided to create an adequate infrastructure in developing countries for the promotion of domestic book production.

DOCUMENTARY REFERENCES

Economic and Social Council—50th session
Social Committee, meetings 653-656, 658.
Plenary meeting 1769.

E/4958. Development of information media. Book development in service of education. Report by UNESCO secretariat.
E/AC.7/L.581. Lebanon, Madagascar, Pakistan, Sudan, Tunisia: draft resolution, as orally amended by sponsors, by France and by Greece, and as amended by Kenya (E/AC.7/L.582, as orally amended), approved unanimously by Social Committee on 4 May 1971, meeting 658.
E/AC.7/L.582. India (sponsorship assumed by Kenya): amendment to 5-power draft resolution, E/AC.7/L.581.
E/4987. Report of Social Committee.

RESOLUTION 1575(L), as recommended by Social Committee, E/4987, adopted unanimously by Council on 20 May 1971, meeting 1769.

The Economic and Social Council,
Recalling its resolution 1278(XLIII) of 4 August 1967 on the development of information media, in which it requested the United Nations Educational, Scientific and Cultural Organization to submit a report on the application of new techniques of communication for the achievement of rapid progress in education, notably in the field of book development,
Having examined the report of the secretariat of the United Nations Educational, Scientific and Cultural Organization on book development in the service of education,
Noting that:
(a) Pending the wider and more enlightened use of other media, in particular radio and television, the book remains the indispensable instrument for education, now recognized as an essential factor in development,
(b) Books in the service of education, and particularly of life-long education, contribute to knowledge and mutual understanding of cultures and thus strengthen international understanding and peaceful co-operation,
(c) There exists, nevertheless, a profound gap between developed and developing countries and that the latter suffer from serious shortages, not only of printing and distribution facilities, but also of authors' manuscripts,
Considering that:
(a) It is urgent that these shortages be overcome without delay, especially since the book requirements of developing countries are increasing steadily, particularly as a result of progress in the spread of education and adult literacy training,

(b) It is essential, in the first instance, to develop national book production by creating an adequate infrastructure,
(c) The attainment of these objectives requires concerted international action on a global scale,
Considering moreover that the decision taken by the General Conference of the United Nations Educational, Scientific and Cultural Organization at its sixteenth session, in its resolution 4.121, to proclaim 1972 International Book Year provides the opportunity for such action,
1. *Supports* this initiative taken by the United Nations Educational, Scientific and Cultural Organization within the framework of its long-term programme for book development;
2. *Invites* the countries participating in the conferences being organized by the United Nations Educational, Scientific and Cultural Organization in July 1971 to respond to the requirements of the developing countries in revising, respectively, the Berne Convention for the Protection of Literary and Artistic Works and the Universal Copyright Convention, including their requirements in the field of school and university education;
3. *Invites further* the developed countries to grant the greatest possible copyright facilities to developing countries within the framework of the International Copyright Information Centre of the United Nations Educational, Scientific and Cultural Organization;
4. *Recommends* the provision of international assistance for low-cost local reprint and translation or adaptation into national languages of developing countries of books written and produced in developed countries for higher education;
5. *Recommends further* that financial and technical assistance be provided to create an adequate infrastructure in the developing countries for the promotion of domestic book production;
6. *Requests* the Food and Agriculture Organization of the United Nations to continue its work for the promotion of paper industries, in particular in the developing countries;
7. *Invites* Member States and, within their respective fields of competence, the institutions and organs of the United Nations system, as well as other interested intergovernmental organizations, to take appropriate steps to attain the objectives of International Book Year;
8. *Invites* the United Nations Educational, Scientific and Cultural Organization to submit to the Economic and Social Council, at its fifty-sixth session, a report on the results achieved as a result of International Book Year and particularly on the ways in which these results can contribute to the goals of the International Development Strategy for the Second United Nations Development Decade.

A/8403. Report of Economic and Social Council on work of its 50th and 51st sessions, Chapter XVIII A.

Question of the elderly and the aged

Before the General Assembly at its twenty-sixth session, which opened on 21 September 1971, was a note by the Secretary-General giving a review of recent trends in the situation of the aged and another note by him transmitting a World Health Organization (WHO) communication on the activities of WHO in gerontology and geriatrics.

The Secretary-General's note contained a description of the aging process, a brief demographic discussion of trends in the aging population, the status and role of the aged in developing and developed countries, a listing of the major needs of the aged, and recommendations for international action related to the aged.

On 18 December 1971, the Assembly asked the

Secretary-General to continue the study of the changing socio-economic and cultural role and status of the aged in countries of different levels of development and to prepare, in co-operation with interested specialized agencies, a report suggesting guidelines for national policies and international action related to the needs of the elderly and the aged in society.

In this connexion, the Assembly noted that demographic projections and anticipated social change indicated that the position of the elderly and the aged in society was expected to deteriorate in many countries unless appropriate policies were initiated to deal with their needs.

The Assembly also noted the importance for the

elderly and the aged to be informed of the interest and concern of the United Nations about their welfare and needs.

Governments were requested to disseminate information contained in these Assembly decisions for the benefit of the elderly and the aged, and the Secretary-General was asked to submit a report on the subject to the Economic and Social Council and the General Assembly in 1973.

The Assembly took these decisions by unanimously adopting resolution 2842(XXVI), the text of which had been recommended by its Third (Social, Humanitarian and Cultural) Committee.

The Committee approved the text by acclamation on 9 December 1971, on a proposal by Canada, Chile, Costa Rica, Cyprus, Denmark, Ecuador, France, Greece, Guyana, Hungary, Iceland, India, Italy, Jamaica, Kenya, Lebanon, the Libyan Arab Republic, Malta, Mongolia, the Philippines, Romania, the Syrian Arab Republic and the United States. (For text, see DOCUMENTARY REFERENCES below.)

In the course of the Third Committee discussion, Cyprus proposed amendments which were accepted by the sponsors of the draft text.

DOCUMENTARY REFERENCES

General Assembly—26th session
Third Committee, meetings 1894, 1903.
Plenary meeting 2025.

A/8364. Note by Secretary-General.
A/C.3/616. Note by Secretary-General (transmitting World Health Organization (WHO) communication, "Activities of WHO in Gerontology and Geriatrics").
A/C.3/L.1907. Canada, Chile, Costa Rica, Cyprus, Denmark, Ecuador, France, Greece, Guyana, Hungary, Iceland, India, Italy, Jamaica, Kenya, Lebanon, Libyan Arab Republic, Malta, Mongolia, Philippines, Romania, Syrian Arab Republic, United States: draft resolution, as amended by Cyprus, A/C.3/L.1920, orally revised by sponsors, approved by acclamation by Third Committee on 9 December 1971, meeting 1903.
A/C.3/L.1920. Cyprus: amendment to 23-power draft resolution, A/C.3/L.1907.
A/8591. Report of Third Committee.

RESOLUTION 2842(XXVI), as recommended by Third Committee, A/8591, adopted unanimously by Assembly on 18 December 1971, meeting 2025.

The General Assembly,
Recalling its resolution 2599(XXIV) of 16 December 1969 and its decision of 15 December 1970 recommending that a high priority be given to the question of the elderly and the aged,
Taking note with appreciation of the preliminary report of the Secretary-General, which reviews the major socio-economic problems of the elderly and the aged and the impact of technological and scientific advances on their well-being,
Bearing in mind the principles embodied in the Charter of the United Nations and in the Universal Declaration of Human Rights, with reference to respect for the dignity and worth of the human person,
Recalling the Declaration on Social Progress and Development

which emphasizes the protection of the rights and the assuring of the welfare of the aged,
Bearing in mind that demographic projections and anticipated social change indicate that the position of the elderly and the aged in society is expected to deteriorate in many industrialized as well as in many developing countries unless appropriate policies are initiated to deal with their needs and to ensure opportunities for their participation in national life and their contribution to the development of their communities,
Considering that the interaction of social, cultural, economic and technological factors affecting the elderly and the aged calls for integrated policies and appropriate programmes at the country level,
Noting that an exploratory cross-national survey is being conducted by the Secretary-General, in co-operation with several countries, to analyse the changing socio-economic role and status of old people,
Bearing in mind the importance for the elderly and the aged to be informed of the interest and concern of the United Nations about their welfare and needs,
1.   *Requests* the Secretary-General to continue the study of the changing socio-economic and cultural role and status of the aged in countries of different levels of development and to prepare, within existing resources and in co-operation with the International Labour Organisation, the World Health Organization and other interested specialized agencies, a report suggesting guidelines for national policies and international action related to the needs and the role of the elderly and the aged in society in the context of over-all development, particularly in countries where the socio-economic problems of the aged are marked;
2.   *Requests* Governments to disseminate, in the best way they deem appropriate, the information contained in the present resolution for the benefit of the elderly and the aged;
3.   *Further requests* the Secretary-General to submit a report on this subject to the Economic and Social Council in 1973, through the Commission for Social Development, and to report to the General Assembly at its twenty-eighth session on the action taken on the present resolution.

Town twinning

The General Assembly, at its twenty-sixth session, which opened on 21 September 1971, took up the question of town twinning as a means of international co-operation.

Considering that world co-operation between municipalities was a natural complement to co-operation between States and inter-governmental organizations, the Assembly, on 20 December 1971, invited the Secretary-General: to study, in

liaison with the United Towns Organization and other non-governmental organizations whose orientation was essentially communal and municipal, the means by which the United Nations and its specialized agencies could contribute effectively to the development of international co-operation between municipalities; and to study any suggestions for world co-operation between municipalities.

The Secretary-General was asked to report to the Economic and Social Council in 1973 on measures taken by him to revitalize methods of co-operation and to facilitate the participation of local and regional bodies in development.

In this connexion, the Assembly noted its conviction that town twinning was an exceptionally valuable means of co-operation and that, if carried out between towns in industrialized countries and in developing countries, twinning afforded intellectual and spiritual enrichment to those parties to it, as well as technical and material support for growing towns.

Earlier Assembly and Council resolutions were recalled, in which non-governmental organizations had been asked to prepare a programme of measures to encourage town twinning.[4]

Among other things, the Assembly noted that United Nations Member States supported the principle of international co-operation between local bodies and that the twinning already undertaken had had positive results. It also noted that the United Towns Organization had acquired unquestionable competence in the field of twinning co-operation, and had been recognized by a number of States as serving the public interest. The resources available to the United Towns Organization for implementing twinning, the Assembly noted, were not commensurate with the needs.

These decisions were embodied in resolution 2861(XXVI) adopted, by 85 votes to 4, with 27 abstentions, on the recommendation of the Assembly's Third (Social, Humanitarian and Cultural) Committee, which approved the text on 10 December 1971, by 53 votes to 5, with 22 abstentions, on a proposal of Cameroon, Colombia, France, Greece, Iran, Kuwait, Laos, the Libyan Arab Republic, Madagascar, Malawi, Mali, Morocco, Niger, Rwanda, Senegal, Togo, Tunisia, Upper Volta and Uruguay, as amended. (For text of resolution, see DOCUMENTARY REFERENCES below.)

In the course of the Third Committee discussion, five amendments were proposed by Egypt and Nigeria and six by the Netherlands, New Zealand, Nicaragua and the United Kingdom. All were voted upon on 10 December 1971.

Two of the two-power amendments were incorporated by the sponsors of the resolution into a revised version of the text; two were withdrawn. The other two-power amendment, adopted by 35 votes to 30, with 14 abstentions, had the effect of deleting an operative paragraph by which the Assembly would have recognized the United Towns Organization as an agency for the implementation of this form of co-operation and invited the United Nations Development Programme to adopt the principle of participating in such programmes as that organization might undertake in the field.

Six amendments were proposed by the four powers. Adopted, by 29 to 24, with 25 abstentions, was a proposal to delete a sub-paragraph by which the Assembly would have considered it desirable that practical co-operation between the United Nations and basic municipal and communal bodies should take the form of moral and material support provided by the former to the latter.

A second four-power amendment was rejected by 37 to 32, with 9 abstentions. It would have had the effect of deleting the preambular paragraph by which the Assembly noted that the United Towns Organization had acquired unquestionable competence in the field and that resources available to that organization were not commensurate with the needs. Instead, the Assembly would have noted that non-governmental organizations competent in the field had made a valuable contribution towards co-operation between local government bodies throughout the world.

A third amendment proposed by the four powers was adopted by 44 to 22, with 10 abstentions. By this amendment, the Assembly invited the Secretary-General to study the means by which the United Nations and its specialized agencies could contribute (rather than "could contribute morally and materially") to the development of international co-operation between municipalities.

Adopted, by 45 votes to 18, with 14 abstentions, was a fourth proposal by the four powers, which had the effect of inserting the operative paragraph inviting the Secretary-General to study any suggestions for world co-operation between municipalities. That paragraph replaced one that would have invited the Secretary-General to study, with a view to implementation, the projects included in the programmes for world co-operation between communities which had been suggested to the United Nations by the United Towns Organization.

A recommendation in the original draft text that the specialized agencies adopt similar measures relating to the programmes of the United Towns Organization was deleted by the adoption of another four-power amendment, by 36 to 33, with 12 abstentions.

The final amendment proposed by the four powers was adopted by 37 to 25, with 15 abstentions. This amendment had the effect, in the operative paragraph asking the Secretary-General to report to the Council in 1973, of deleting a phrase asking him to report on measures to "achieve a better division of efforts and funds."

---

[4] See Y.U.N., 1965, p. 529, text of Assembly resolution 2058(XX) and Y.U.N., 1967, p. 588, text of Council resolution 1217(XLII).

DOCUMENTARY REFERENCES

General Assembly—26th session
Third Committee, meeting 1905.
Plenary meeting 2027.

A/8434. Note by Secretary-General.
A/C.3/L.1892. Cameroon, Colombia, France, Iran, Kuwait, Laos, Libyan Arab Republic, Madagascar, Malawi, Mali, Morocco, Niger, Senegal, Togo, Tunisia, Uruguay: draft resolution.
A/C.3/L.1892/Rev.1. Revised draft resolution sponsored by above 16 powers and by Greece, Rwanda and Upper Volta, as orally revised by sponsors and as amended by 2 powers (A/C.3/L.1927, paras. 1, 3 and 5) and by 4 powers (A/C.3/L.1928, paras. 1, 3 and 4 as orally amended, and paras. 5 and 6), approved by Third Committee on 10 December 1971, meeting 1905, by 53 votes to 5, with 22 abstentions.
A/C.3/L.1927. Egypt and Nigeria: amendments to 19-power revised draft resolution, A/C.3/L.1892/Rev.1.
A/C.3/L.1928. Netherlands, New Zealand, Nicaragua, United Kingdom: amendments to 19-power revised draft resolution, A/C.3/L.1892/Rev.1.
A/C.3/L.1929. Text of draft resolution as approved by Third Committee on 10 December 1971, meeting 1905.
A/8600. Report of Third Committee.

RESOLUTION 2861(XXVI), as recommended by Third Committee, A/8600, adopted by Assembly on 20 December 1971, meeting 2027, by 85 votes to 4, with 27 abstentions.

The General Assembly,
Considering that:
(a) It is a function of the United Nations to serve as the nodal point of the efforts of all peoples to achieve peace and international co-operation,
(b) It is necessary therefore to establish active co-operation between the Secretariat and collaborating local and regional bodies whose objectives are the same as those of the Organization,
Convinced that:
(a) Town twinning is an exceptionally valuable means of co-operation in that, between countries, it brings into contact not only local leaders but also whole populations,
(b) If carried out between towns in industrialized countries and those in developing countries, twinning affords, in addition to the intellectual and spiritual enrichment of those parties to it, technical and material support for growing towns which is sometimes considerable and can be brought to bear directly without administrative expenditure and without detriment to the sense of equality existing between the partners,
(c) The international co-operation of local bodies can play an important role in bringing peoples together,
Recalling:
(a) Economic and Social Council resolution 1028(XXXVII) of 13 August 1964, in which the Council considered town twinning as

one of the means of co-operation that should be encouraged by the international Organization,
(b) General Assembly resolution 2058(XX) of 16 December 1965, in which the Assembly requested the Economic and Social Council, in collaboration with the appropriate non-governmental organizations in consultative status, to prepare a programme of measures through which the United Nations and the United Nations Educational, Scientific and Cultural Organization might take concrete steps to encourage further the achievement of the largest possible number of twinned towns,
(c) Economic and Social Council resolution 1217(XLII) of 1 June 1967, in which the Council considered that there are non-governmental organizations in consultative status which can assist in promoting town twinning as a means of co-operation and recommended that the United Nations Development Programme bear in mind the experience of those non-governmental organizations when arranging for the implementation of such projects,
Noting that:
(a) Member States support the principle of international co-operation between local bodies, and that the twinning already undertaken throughout the world has had positive results,
(b) The United Towns Organization, a non-governmental organization in consultative status, in category I, with the Economic and Social Council and in consultative status, in category A, with the United Nations Educational, Scientific and Cultural Organization, has acquired unquestionable competence in the field of twinning co-operation, was expressly described by the Fifteenth General Conference of the United Nations Educational, Scientific and Cultural Organization, in its resolution 9.11 of 15 November 1968 on peace, as an instrumentality which mobilizes public support in communes for understanding and international co-operation, and has been recognized by a number of States as serving the public interest,
(c) The resources available to the United Towns Organization for the implementation of such twinning are not commensurate with the corresponding needs,
1. *Considers* that world co-operation between municipalities is a natural complement to co-operation between States and intergovernmental organizations;
2. *Invites* the Secretary-General:
(a) To study, in liaison with the United Towns Organization and those non-governmental organizations whose orientation is essentially communal and municipal with the same universalist character and having the same objectives, the means by which the United Nations and its specialized agencies can contribute effectively to the development of international co-operation between municipalities;
(b) To study any suggestions for world co-operation between municipalities;
3. *Requests* the Secretary-General to report to the Economic and Social Council at its fifty-fourth session on the results of the measures taken by him, pursuant to the present resolution, to revitalize methods of co-operation and to facilitate the participation of local and regional bodies in development.

Relations with non-United Nations inter-governmental organizations in the economic and social field

At its April-May 1971 session, the Economic and Social Council had before it a report by the Secretary-General on the functioning of arrangements for relations between the Council and non-United Nations inter-governmental organizations in the economic and social field.

The Secretary-General's report covered the participation of those organizations in the work of

the Council and its subsidiary bodies, as well as relations between the United Nations and such organizations at the secretariat level. It also contained recommendations for action by the Council.

On 20 May 1971, the Council took note of the Secretary-General's report and approved the recommendations contained therein. It decided to extend a standing invitation to the Council of Europe, the Council for Mutual Economic Assistance, the European Economic Community and the Organisation for Economic Co-operation and Development to be represented by observers at its sessions, and requested the Secretary-General to invite the League of Arab States, the Organization of African Unity, the Organization of American States, the Organization of Petroleum Exporting Countries, the Regional Co-operation for Development organization and the World Intellectual Property Organization as observers to all future sessions.

The Council, further, authorized the Secretary-General to propose from time to time that certain other inter-governmental organizations might be represented by observers at specific sessions when questions of concern to them were to be discussed.

Finally, it decided that the functional commissions and standing committees should continue to invite to their meetings inter-governmental organs in fields of concern to them. All the inter-governmental organizations invited to sessions of the Council and its subsidiary organs would be entitled to participate with the approval of the Council or the subsidiary organ concerned and without the right to vote in debates on questions of concern to them.

These decisions, made without the adoption of a resolution, were taken on the recommendation of the Council's Social Committee, which had recommended the decision on 30 April 1971, on the basis of a proposal by three Council members (Indonesia, Sudan and Yugoslavia) and the observer of India.

DOCUMENTARY REFERENCES

Economic and Social Council—50th session
Social Committee, meeting 655.
Plenary meeting 1769.

E/4961. Report of Secretary-General.
E/5023. Report of Social Committee, para. 8.

E/5044. Resolutions adopted by Economic and Social Council during its 50th session, 11-13 January and 26 April–21 May 1971. Decisions, p. 25 (item 12 (a)).
A/8403. Report of Economic and Social Council on work of its 50th and 51st sessions, Chapter XXI D.

Questions relating to Trust and Non-Self-Governing Territories and the Declaration on granting independence

Chapter I

The International Trusteeship System

General aspects

Territories under the System

Under the International Trusteeship System established by the Charter of the United Nations, Member States administering Trust Territories are accountable to the United Nations for the discharge of their responsibilities and obligations in the administration of the Territories.

At the end of 1971, there remained two of the 11 Trust Territories originally placed under the International Trusteeship System. The Territories, situated in the Pacific, were: New Guinea, administered by Australia; and the Trust Territory of the Pacific Islands (a strategic area in accordance with Article 83 of the United Nations Charter),[1] administered by the United States.

Examination of annual reports

The Trusteeship Council, in supervising the administration of the Trust Territories on behalf of the General Assembly or, in the case of the strategic area, on behalf of the Security Council, examines the annual reports submitted by the Administering Authorities. At the same time, it also examines, among other things, petitions affecting the Trust Territories, reports of United Nations visiting missions, and observations on conditions in the Territories which may have been submitted by specialized agencies, and which are within their sphere of competence.

Under the procedures followed, the Special Representative of the Administering Authority makes an opening statement in which he brings the Trusteeship Council up to date on events in the Territory concerned. This statement is supplemented by the comments of indigenous representatives attached to the delegation of the Administering Authority. The Administering Authority's representative on the Council and its Special Representative then reply to questions put to them by members of the Council. After a general debate in which each Council member gives his opinion on conditions in the particular Territory, a draft report (drawn up by a drafting committee) is submitted to the Council, which votes on various conclusions and recommendations. A summary of observations made by individual members representing their individual opinions only is also contained in the report.

The report on conditions in the Trust Territories forms part of the Council's annual report to the General Assembly, or to the Security Council in the case of the Trust Territory of the Pacific Islands.

The Trusteeship Council held its thirty-eighth regular session at United Nations Headquarters, New York, from 25 May to 18 June 1971, during which it examined the annual reports submitted by the Administering Authorities of the two Trust Territories and adopted conclusions and recommendations on each of them.

In accordance with its normal practice, the Council adopted two reports: one to the General Assembly which included a chapter on conditions in the Trust Territory of New Guinea; and one to the Security Council, which contained a chapter on conditions in the Trust Territory of the Pacific Islands.

(For further details, see sections below, pp. 502-10 and 510-14.)

Composition of Trusteeship Council

In 1971, the Trusteeship Council was composed of two Administering Authorities—Australia (New Guinea) and the United States (Trust Territory of the Pacific Islands)—and four non-administering members, by virtue of their being permanent

[1]For text of Article 83 of the Charter, see APPENDIX II.

members of the Security Council—China, France, the USSR and the United Kingdom.

Petitions and oral hearings

The examination of petitions concerning Trust Territories derives from Article 87 of the United Nations Charter, which provides that the General Assembly and, under its authority, the Trusteeship Council, may accept petitions and examine them in consultation with the Administering Authority.[2] Petitions relating to a strategic area are governed by Article 83 of the United Nations Charter and the terms of the relevant Trusteeship Agreement.

Under its rules of procedure, the Council considers petitions concerning specific complaints and petitions and communications which relate to general questions pertaining to a Trust Territory or to the operation of the International Trusteeship System. The Council considers the petitions and communications in the course of its examination of the annual report on the particular Trust Territory concerned. Hearings are granted to petitioners by both the Trusteeship Council and the General Assembly.

In 1971, the Trusteeship Council considered 29 written petitions and communications: four concerning New Guinea and 25 concerning the Trust Territory of the Pacific Islands. The Council also heard four petitioners on the Trust Territory of the Pacific Islands.[3]

Visiting missions

Trust Territory of New Guinea

In 1971, the Trusteeship Council examined the report of its periodic Visiting Mission to the Trust Territory of New Guinea.

Consisting of members nominated by France, Iraq, Sierra Leone and the United Kingdom, the Mission visited the Territory from 24 January to 6 March 1971. Subsequently, it held discussions in Canberra, Australia, with the Minister for External Territories and officials of the Department of Foreign Affairs, as well as with members of the Foreign Affairs Committee of the Parliament.

On 18 June 1971, the Council adopted a resolution drawing attention to the fact that, in formulating its conclusions and recommendations on conditions in the Trust Territory, it had taken into account the recommendations and observations of the Visiting Mission and the observations of the Administering Authority thereon. The Council also invited the Administering Authority to take into account the recommendations and conclusions of the Visiting Mission, as well as the comments of Council members thereon.

The decisions to this effect were embodied in the Council's resolution 2155(XXXVIII), adopted by a

vote of 5 to 0, with 1 abstention. (For text of resolution, see DOCUMENTARY REFERENCES below.)

Prior to the vote, the USSR stated that, although it approved some of the conclusions and recommendations contained in the report of the Visiting Mission, it could not support the report as a whole or a series of recommendations which it believed were inadequate and not in keeping with the requirements contained in the Declaration on the Granting of Independence to Colonial Countries and Peoples. For example, the Visiting Mission did not say that the Administering Authority was not carrying out the decisions of that Declaration concerning the setting of a time-limit for self-determination and independence. Nor did it make specific recommendations on such important questions as the cessation of military activity in the Territory, the restriction of the exploitative activity of Australian and other foreign monopolies or the removal of the Administrator's right of veto.

In a letter dated 11 June 1971, the Permanent Representative of Australia invited the Trusteeship Council to send a visiting mission to observe the elections to the Papua New Guinea House of Assembly in 1972. Australia suggested that the composition of the mission be determined in the manner requested by the Assembly on 16 December 1969,[4] and that the mission comprise four members, two to be chosen from the Trusteeship Council and two on the basis of consultation with the Special Committee on the Situation with regard to the Implementation of the Declaration on the Granting of Independence to Colonial Countries and Peoples.

On 18 June 1971, following conversations with the Chairman of the Special Committee, the President of the Trusteeship Council informed the Council of the views of the Committee. The Special Committee: (1) would agree to participate in the proposed visiting mission to Papua New Guinea in 1972, should the Council decide to accept the invitation of Australia; (2) would agree to accept the composition proposed by Australia, although in the Special Committee's view, for the purpose of ensuring equitable geographic distribution and the necessary political balance, the mission should consist of at least five members, two to be drawn from the Trusteeship Council and three from the Special Committee; and (3) would authorize its Chairman to continue consultations concerning the two members of the proposed

---

[2]For text of Article 87 of the Charter, see APPENDIX II.

[3]For details on the petitions concerning the Trust Territory of the Pacific Islands, see "Report of the Trusteeship Council to the Security Council" (S/10237), Part I, paras. 9-14. For details on the petitions concerning New Guinea, see "Report of the Trusteeship Council to the General Assembly" (A/8404), Part I, Chapter III, paras. 18-21.

[4]See Y.U.N., 1969, p. 620, text of resolution 2590(XXIV), operative para. 5.

mission to be chosen from the Special Committee.

On the same day, the Council decided to send a visiting mission to observe the elections to the Papua New Guinea House of Assembly in 1972. The Council decided that the Mission should be composed of two members nominated by the United Kingdom and the United States, and two members from States to be designated by the President of the Council on the basis of consultations with members of the Council, the Special Committee and the Administering Authority.

The Council directed the Visiting Mission to observe the elections to the House of Assembly in Papua New Guinea in 1972, including electoral arrangements, the activities of candidates and political parties, the casting of votes, the closure of voting, the counting of ballots and the declaration of results.

The Visiting Mission was requested to submit to the Council, as soon as practicable, a report on its findings, with such observations, conclusions and recommendations as it might wish to make.

These decisions by the Council were set forth in resolution 2156(XXXVIII), adopted by a vote of 5 to 0, with 1 abstention. (For text of resolution, see DOCUMENTARY REFERENCES below.)

Prior to taking this decision, the Trusteeship Council rejected, by a vote of 3 to 1, with 2 abstentions, a USSR proposal whereby the Mission would be asked to submit its report both to the Council and to the Assembly's Special Committee on the Situation with regard to the Implementation of the Declaration on the Granting of Independence to Colonial Countries and Peoples.

The United Kingdom, in explanation of vote, said that it supported the resolution on the understanding that the scope of the Mission was limited to the purpose of observing the elections in Papua New Guinea and that it was not intended that the Mission would conduct a general investigation into conditions in Papua.

France said that Australia was entitled to accept, taking into account specific problems of Papua New Guinea, practices different from those provided for in the Charter, such as calling upon the Special Committee to nominate members of the Mission, in the case of the Trust Territory of New Guinea, and sending a Mission to the Non-Self-Governing Territory of Papua. But in France's view, this should not be considered a precedent to be used in regard to States which, by abstaining in the vote, had shown their desire not to ratify such practices.

Subsequently, Mohammad Hakim Aryubi (Afghanistan), Sir Derek Jakeway (United Kingdom), W. Tapley Bennett, Jr. (United States) and Aleksandar Psoncak (Yugoslavia) were nominated as members of the Mission. Mr. Bennett was elected Chairman.

Attainment of self-government or independence

In 1971, during its examination of conditions in the Trust Territories, the Trusteeship Council considered the question of the attainment by the Trust Territories of self-government or independence. Special attention was paid to the measures being taken to transfer all powers to the peoples of those Territories in accordance with their freely expressed will and desire in order to enable them to enjoy self-government or complete independence within the shortest time practicable.

The Council's conclusions and recommendations on the subject, as well as a brief summary of the observations made by members, are set out below in the sections dealing with each of the Territories. (See pp. 502-10 and 510-14.)

In 1961, when the General Assembly established its Special Committee on the Situation with regard to the Implementation of the Declaration on the Granting of Independence to Colonial Countries and Peoples, it requested the Trusteeship Council to assist that Committee in its work.

In accordance with this request and following a decision taken by the Trusteeship Council, the President of the Council informed the Chairman of the Special Committee that the Council had in 1971 examined conditions in the Trust Territories of the Pacific Islands and New Guinea, and that the conclusions and recommendations of the Council, as well as the observations of the Council members representing their individual opinions only, were contained in the report to the Security Council relating to the Trust Territory of the Pacific Islands and in the report to the General Assembly with regard to New Guinea.

The President expressed willingness to discuss with the Chairman of the Special Committee any further assistance that the Special Committee might require from the Council. The Council also decided to draw the attention of the General Assembly to the fruitful co-operation that had again taken place during the year between the Special Committee and the Trusteeship Council, which had again led to the inclusion of non-members of the Council in a visiting mission.

Offers of study and training facilities

In 1971, the Secretary-General submitted his annual report to the Trusteeship Council on the programme of scholarships and fellowships for inhabitants of Trust Territories, initiated by the General Assembly in 1952.

During the period covered by the report—1 June 1970 to 31 May 1971—scholarships and training facilities had been offered by 11 Member States: Czechoslovakia, Hungary, Indonesia, Italy, Mexico, Pakistan, the Philippines, Poland, Tunisia, the USSR and Yugoslavia. According to information made available to the Secretary-General, no applications for scholarships offered by those Member States were received from either of the two remaining Trust Territories during the period under review.

On 17 June 1971, the Trusteeship Council, without adopting a formal resolution, took note of the report of the Secretary-General.

Dissemination of Information on the United Nations and the Trusteeship System

In accordance with decisions by the Trusteeship Council and the General Assembly, the Secretary-General reports annually to the Trusteeship Council on arrangements undertaken in co-operation with the Administering Authorities for distributing official records of the United Nations and for disseminating information concerning the aims and activities of the United Nations and the International Trusteeship System in the Trust Territories.

The report submitted by the Secretary-General to the Council's 1971 session, covering the period from 1 June 1970 to 31 May 1971, contained information on United Nations publications, films and radio programmes. It indicated that there had been wide distribution of a number of publications prepared by the Office of Public Information, including pamphlets, brochures and press releases.

During discussion in the Council, Australia said that the Administration in New Guinea considered the spread of information about the United Nations to be an important part of its political education programme. The 1971 Visiting Mission itself had been the most effective means of disseminating information about, and consciousness of, the United Nations in the Territory. The Mission had referred to the need for increasing the capability of the United Nations Information Centre in Port Moresby, New Guinea, including more extensive travel by its Director and staff. The representative of Australia stated that it should be possible for the Administration to arrange air transport for the Director at little or no cost.

The United States said it had continued widespread dissemination of United Nations information throughout the Trust Territory of the Pacific Islands. The Administering Authority welcomed the availability of United Nations information and was prepared to consider means of enhancing the United Nations image there.

The United Kingdom, noting that the dissemination of information to the Trust Territory of the Pacific Islands was carried out through the United Nations Information Centre in Washington, D.C., asked whether consideration had been given to the possibility of making use of the expertise of geographically closer Centres, such as the ones in Port Moresby and Manila, the Philippines.

France noted the impression of the Visiting Mission that the Port Moresby Information Centre had not lacked material but that it had not always suited the needs of the Territory; the small staff did all it could to fulfil its obligations with the material available to it.

The United Nations Assistant Secretary-General for Public Information referred to the recommendation by the 1971 Visiting Mission that the budget and staff of the Information Centre at Port Moresby be increased; if implemented, the recommendation would make it possible for the Centre to increase its production capability in a form that would make information more accessible to the population of the Territory. The Centre at Port Moresby had been set up at the specific request of the General Assembly, and it was to be presumed that the Assembly would give special attention to any recommendation by the Trusteeship Council in this respect.

The Assistant Secretary-General said that the suggestion by the representative of the United Kingdom regarding the Trust Territory of the Pacific Islands would be examined, and if it was found that any other Information Centre could help the spread of information in the Trust Territory, that would certainly be done.

Australia said it would be difficult for the Council to ask for any significant increase in the budget for the Port Moresby Centre, but it would be worth examining whether a small increase might not make it possible for the Centre to increase its production in pidgin.

The USSR representative could not agree to the suggestion that the budget of the Port Moresby Centre be increased because that might lead to increases in the budgets of other Information Centres, to which he was opposed. He thought that funds for the Centre could be found by the Administering Authority.

The representative of Australia said the Administering Authority had already assisted the Centre considerably but would be ready to examine the suggestion of the USSR.

On 15 June 1971, the Trusteeship Council, without adopting a formal resolution, took note of the report of the Secretary-General and of the comments made during consideration of the item.

Co-operation with Committee on Elimination of Racial Discrimination

By the terms of article 15 of the International Convention on the Elimination of All Forms of Racial Discrimination,[5] and of a General Assembly resolution of 21 December 1965,[6] the Trusteeship

---

[5]See Y.U.N., 1965, pp. 440-46, resolution 2106 A (XX), containing text of International Convention.
[6]*Ibid.*, pp. 446-47, text of resolution 2106 B (XX).

Council transmits to the Committee on the Elimination of Racial Discrimination copies of the reports of the Administering Authorities as well as of petitions it receives relating to racial discrimination.

In 1971, the Council had before it a communication from the Committee on the Elimination of Racial Discrimination requesting it to obtain from the Administering Authorities information on a number of matters relating to the principles and the objectives of the International Convention.

On 8 June 1971, the Council decided to invite the Administering Authorities to include in their annual reports information on the matters noted in the communication of the Committee. On 17 June 1971, the Council decided to transmit to the Committee two petitions concerning New Guinea, together with relevant documentation. Both these decisions were taken without the adoption of a formal resolution.

DOCUMENTARY REFERENCES

Examination of annual reports

Trusteeship Council—38th session
Plenary meetings 1372-1382, 1384, 1386, 1387.

T/L.1160 and Add.1. Outline of conditions in Trust Territory of Pacific Islands. Working paper prepared by Secretariat and draft amendments thereto.

T/L.1162. Draft report of Trusteeship Council to Security Council on Trust Territory of Pacific Islands covering period 20 June 1970–18 June 1971. Working paper prepared by Secretariat, adopted by Council on 18 June 1971, meeting 1387, by 5 votes to 0, with 1 abstention.

T/L.1163. Conditions in Trust Territory of Pacific Islands. Report of Drafting Committee. (Annex: Draft recommendations and conclusions.)

S/10237. Report of Trusteeship Council to Security Council on Trust Territory of Pacific Islands, 20 June 1970–18 June 1971 *(Security Council Official Records, 26th Year, Special Supplement No. 1):* Part I A; Part II.

T/L.1165. Draft report of Trusteeship Council to General Assembly for period covering 20 June 1970–18 June 1971. Working paper prepared by Secretariat, adopted by Council on 18 June 1971, meeting 1387, by 5 votes to 0, with 1 abstention.

A/8404. Report of Trusteeship Council to General Assembly, 20 June 1970–18 June 1971: Part I, Chapter II; Part II.

T/1727. Resolutions adopted by Trusteeship Council at its 38th session, 25 May-18 June 1971. Other decisions, p. 3.

[See also DOCUMENTARY REFERENCES for sections on New Guinea and Trust Territory of the Pacific Islands, below.]

Petitions and oral hearings

Trusteeship Council—38th session
Plenary meetings 1373, 1374, 1381, 1382.

T/1714/Add.1. Provisional agenda of 38th session of Trusteeship Council, Annex: List of petitions and communications received by Secretary-General and circulated to members of Trusteeship Council.

A/8404. Report of Trusteeship Council to General Assembly, Part I, Chapter III.

S/10237. Report of Trusteeship Council to Security Council on Trust Territory of Pacific Islands, Part I B.

T/1727. Resolutions adopted by Trusteeship Council at its 38th session. Other decisions, pp. 3-4.

Visiting missions

TRUST TERRITORY OF NEW GUINEA, 1971

Trusteeship Council—38th session
Plenary meetings 1381, 1382, 1384, 1386, 1387.

A/8404. Report of Trusteeship Council to General Assembly, Part I, Chapter IV A.

T/1728 (T/1717). Report of United Nations Visiting Mission to Trust Territory of New Guinea, 1971, together with relevant resolution of Trusteeship Council, Annex III.

T/L.1166. United States: draft resolution.

RESOLUTION 2155(XXXVIII), as proposed by United States, T/L.1166, adopted by Council on 18 June 1971, meeting 1387, by 5 votes to 0, with 1 abstention.

The Trusteeship Council,
Having examined at its thirty-eighth session the report of the United Nations Visiting Mission to the Trust Territory of New Guinea, 1971,
Having heard the oral observations made by the representative of Australia concerning the report,

1. *Takes note* of the report of the Visiting Mission and of the observations of the Administering Authority thereon;

2. *Expresses* its appreciation of the work accomplished by the Visiting Mission on its behalf;

3. *Draws attention* to the fact that, at its thirty-eighth session, in formulating its own conclusions and recommendations on conditions in the Trust Territory, the Trusteeship Council took into account the recommendations and observations of the Visiting Mission and the observations of the Administering Authority thereon;

4. *Decides* that it will continue to take these recommendations, conclusions and observations into account in future examination of matters relating to the Trust Territory concerned;

5. *Invites* the Administering Authority to take into account the recommendations and conclusions of the Visiting Mission as well as the comments made thereon by the members of the Trusteeship Council;

6. *Decides,* in accordance with rule 98 of its rules of procedure, that the report of the Visiting Mission and the text of the present resolution shall be distributed in an appropriate form.

TRUST TERRITORY OF NEW GUINEA, 1972

Trusteeship Council—38th session
Plenary meetings 1385-1387.

A/8404. Report of Trusteeship Council to General Assembly, Part I, Chapter IV B.

T/1725. Letter of 11 June 1971 from Australia.

T/L.1167. Draft resolution.

T/L.1168. Draft resolution.

T/L.1169. Administrative and financial implications of draft resolutions T/L.1167 and T/L.1168. Statement by Secretary-General.

RESOLUTION 2156(XXXVIII), as proposed by Council members, T/L.1168, as orally amended by President, adopted by Council on 18 June 1971, meeting 1387, by 5 votes to 0, with 1 abstention.

The Trusteeship Council,
Being aware of the elections to the Papua New Guinea House of Assembly due to be held in the period March/April 1972,

Having been invited by the Administering Authority to dispatch a mission to observe these elections,

Recalling the request made to the Trusteeship Council by the General Assembly, in paragraph 5 of its resolution 2590(XXIV) of 16 December 1969, to include non-members of the Trusteeship Council in its periodic visiting missions to the Trust Territory of New Guinea, in consultation with the Special Committee on the Situation with regard to the Implementation of the Declaration on the Granting of Independence to Colonial Countries and Peoples and with the Administering Authority, in accordance with the Charter of the United Nations,

Noting that the consultations requested by the General Assembly cannot be completed until after the conclusion of its present session,

1. *Decides* to send a visiting mission to observe the elections to the Papua New Guinea House of Assembly in 1972;

2. *Decides* that the Mission should be composed of .... (United Kingdom of Great Britain and Northern Ireland), ... (United States of America), ... ( ), ... ( ),* the two latter to be designated by the President of the Council on the basis of consultations with the members of the Council, the Special Committee on the Situation with regard to the Implementation of the Declaration on the Granting of Independence to Colonial Countries and Peoples and the Administering Authority;

3. *Directs* the Visiting Mission to observe the elections to the House of Assembly in Papua New Guinea in 1972, including electoral arrangements, the activities of candidates and political parties, the casting of votes, the closure of voting, the counting of ballots and the declaration of results;

4. *Requests* the Visiting Mission to submit to the Council, as soon as practicable, a report on its observations of the elections containing its findings, with such observations, conclusions and recommendations as it may wish to make.

*On 18 June 1971, the Council decided that the nominations to be submitted would automatically be approved when received. Subsequently, and on the basis of consultations, the President designated Afghanistan and Yugoslavia as the two States to nominate the other members of the Visiting Mission.

T/1729. Arrangements for dispatch of visiting mission to observe elections to Papua New Guinea House of Assembly in 1972. Report of 31 August 1971 by President of Trusteeship Council.

Attainment of self-government or independence

Trusteeship Council—38th session
Plenary meeting 1385.

A/8404. Report of Trusteeship Council to General Assembly: Part I, Chapter V; Part II, Section F.

S/10237. Report of Trusteeship Council to Security Council on Trust Territory of Pacific Islands, Part II, Section F.

T/1727. Resolutions adopted by Trusteeship Council at its 38th session. Other decisions, p. 4.

Offers of study and training facilities

Trusteeship Council—38th session
Plenary meeting 1386.

A/8404. Report of Trusteeship Council to General Assembly, Part I, Chapter VI A.

T/1726. Offers by Member States of study and training facilities for inhabitants of Trust Territories. Report of Secretary-General.

T/1727. Resolutions adopted by Trusteeship Council at its 38th session. Other decisions, p. 5.

Dissemination of information on the United Nations and the Trusteeship System

Trusteeship Council—38th session
Plenary meetings 1383, 1385.

A/8404. Report of Trusteeship Council to General Assembly, Part I, Chapter VI B.

T/1718 and Corr.1. Dissemination of information on United Nations and International Trusteeship System in Trust Territories. Report of Secretary-General.

T/1727. Resolutions adopted by Trusteeship Council at its 38th session. Other decisions, p. 5.

Co-operation with Committee on Elimination of Racial Discrimination

Trusteeship Council—38th session
Plenary meetings 1381, 1383, 1386.

A/8404. Report of Trusteeship Council to General Assembly, Part I, Chapter VI C.

T/1722. Communication of 4 June 1971 from Committee on Elimination of Racial Discrimination.

T/1727. Resolutions adopted by Trusteeship Council at its 38th session. Other decisions, p. 5.

Other documents

T/1724. Report of 14 June 1971 by Secretary-General on credentials.

T/1730. Letter of 26 October 1971 from Secretary-General to President of Trusteeship Council.

Conditions in individual Trust Territories

Trust Territory of New Guinea

The Trust Territory of New Guinea comprises part of the island of New Guinea north of the Papuan border and east of the 141st meridian of longitude, the islands of the Bismarck Archipelago, and the two northernmost islands of the Solomon Group, namely Buka and Bougainville. The total land area covers 92,160 square miles.

As at 30 June 1970, the indigenous population of the Trust Territory totalled 1,763,429. The non-indigenous population numbered 20,265 at the census of June 1966.

The Trust Territory and the neighbouring territory of Papua are administered jointly by Australia under the Papua and New Guinea Act, 1949-1968.[7]

During 1971, conditions in the Trust Territory were considered by the Trusteeship Council, by the General Assembly's Special Committee on the Situation with regard to the Implementation of the Declaration on the Granting of Independence to

[7]The territory of Papua has a total area of 86,100 square miles. As at 30 June 1970, the indigenous population totalled 668,964. At the 1966 census, the non-indigenous population was 14,377.

Colonial Countries and Peoples, and by the General Assembly.

Consideration by Trusteeship Council

At its thirty-eighth session, held at United Nations Headquarters, New York, from 25 May to 18 June 1971, the Trusteeship Council considered the report of its 1971 Visiting Mission to the Trust Territory of New Guinea, as well as the annual report of the Administering Authority (Australia).

Political advancement

The Trusteeship Council shared the impression of the 1971 Visiting Mission to the Trust Territory of New Guinea that recent arrangements involving a substantial transfer of authority to ministerial and assistant ministerial members were working well and had given ministerial members a wide measure of authority over their own departments, including control of expenditures.

The Council was pleased to note the statement by the Prime Minister of Australia that the Australian Parliament would not exercise its veto power in relation to ordinances passed by the House of Assembly of the Trust Territory, if those ordinances affected the actual responsibilities handed over to ministerial members. The Council also noted that the Administering Authority would devote itself to the formulation of flexible plans for the smooth handing over of powers.

The Council was pleased to note the Visiting Mission's finding that local government bodies were playing an important role in introducing people to the responsibilities of self-government, in overcoming local animosities and in contributing to the general welfare. The Council noted at the conclusion of the Visiting Mission that localization needed a new impetus, particularly as the Territory advanced towards self-government and independence. It shared the belief of the Administering Authority that the formation of an Australian service for overseas co-operation and other measures to guarantee employment security for overseas officers should help to speed the localization of the public service.

The representative of the United Kingdom noted with approval the recent widening of the portfolios of ministerial members, and the fact that a departmental committee had been set up to study the further handing over of responsibilities.

The representative of the United States agreed with the Visiting Mission that the process of transferring authority should be continued in the vital areas of internal administration and economic development, and that an early start should be made towards bringing them within the ambit of the ministerial system.

The representative of France said that there were still too many political groups. It was important that members of the local executive would be able to be considered as representatives of a definite trend and that in 1972, unlike 1968, voters could vote for representatives of a certain orientation rather than for individuals. He also suggested that voters be required to be able to read and write.

The representative of the USSR stated that in implementing partial reforms in the constitutional field, as well as in certain other fields, the Administering Authority firmly maintained the reins of power in its own hands. The House of Assembly did not have legislative rights, and the right of veto of the Administrator of the Territory had not been eliminated. The Select Committee on Constitutional Development of the House of Assembly, which had made recommendations on the date for self-government, had not dared to express its opinion on questions of decisive importance for the development of the Territory towards self-government and independence.

The Special Representative of the Administering Authority said that as responsibility and authority were transferred, the areas in which the veto power formally existed diminished. It was the stated intention of the Administering Authority to transfer power as rapidly as the government in the Territory was ready to accept it. In February 1971, there had been a new extension of powers; in June, over-all responsibility for development planning had been brought within the scope of a committee of the Administrator's Executive Council, and a department had been established for programming and co-ordination, under the control of a ministerial member.

Economic advancement

Primary production, mainly agriculture, formed the basis of the Territory's economy, with agricultural products making up approximately 85 per cent of the total value of exports in 1971. Although the economy was still largely dependent on copra and copra products, it was becoming more diversified. More cocoa and coffee were being exported; tea and oil-palm industries were being established; and manufacturing and service industries were developing rapidly. Intensive mineral exploration had established the presence of large low-grade deposits of copper and gold-bearing areas.

The Trusteeship Council noted that the five-year economic development programme (1968-1973) had been revised, and that the Administration had sought the help of the International Bank for Reconstruction and Development in the formulation of a second programme, for the period 1973-1978. In this connexion, the Council invited the Administering Authority to see to it that any imbalance in economic development which might be caused by a project such as the Bougainville copper project was adjusted to the advantage of the population of the Territory.

The Council noted that an agreement had recently been reached with the International Bank for Reconstruction and Development for a loan of A$20.7 million to enable work to begin on the Upper Ramu hydroelectric scheme.

The Council reiterated its belief that no effort should be spared to increase the participation of the indigenous population in the economic advancement of the Territory. It welcomed the fact that the loans granted by the Papua and New Guinea Development Bank to Papuans and New Guineans for the period 1 July 1970–14 February 1971 amounted to A$1.2 million, exceeding the A$866,000 in loans contracted by expatriates. The Council noted with satisfaction that the House of Assembly had adopted an ordinance to set up an investment corporation.

The Council noted the increase in the budgetary grant from the Administering Authority, which reached A$92,270,921 in 1969-1970. It welcomed the fact that for 1971-1972, the Administrator's Executive Council would prepare the budget and negotiate with the Administering Authority, and that a ministerial member had been placed in charge of economic development and planning. It recommended that the Administering Authority continue the progressive transfer of financial responsibility to elected representatives.

The Council noted the possibilities for increasing indigenous ownership through companies, partnerships and individual entrepreneurs as well as through co-operatives and joint ventures between indigenes and expatriates. It expressed the hope that the Administering Authority would expand its efforts to increase the extent of indigenous ownership by such means as the proposed investment corporation and the recently established Department of Business Development.

The representative of the United Kingdom expressed satisfaction that the Administration, in accordance with the Council's recommendations, had revised the five-year development programme to take account of the impact of the Bougainville copper project and to take advantage of new market opportunities which had emerged.

The United States was happy to note the Visiting Mission's opinion that the fast rate of development was due to both overseas investment and the efforts of the Administration to encourage local enterprise. It hoped that as new cash crops realized their potential and as the benefits of the Bougainville copper scheme were realized, the Territory's unfavourable balance of trade would be corrected and its revenues substantially increased.

The representative of the USSR said that the entire policy of the Administering Authority in the Territory amounted to transforming the Territory into a source of raw material for Australia. He stated that there had been a catastrophic deterioration of the trade balance in the Territory in the last year, and that indirect taxes had increased from A$17.4 million in 1969 to A$23.9 million in 1970. All this had affected the standard of living of the population, which had to carry the heavy burden of the activities of the foreign monopolies in the Territory. A study of the Visiting Mission's report confirmed that those monopolies were mercilessly exploiting the country's natural and human resources.

France stated that foreign investments could advance the Territory's development, on the condition that the public authorities controlled their flow and utilization. If it had closed the door of New Guinea to capital, the Administering Authority would have failed in its responsibilities to the indigenous population.

Charles Wyse (Sierra Leone), member of the 1971 Visiting Mission, stated that the private sector in New Guinea should follow the example of the Bougainville copper project. While the primary aim of businessmen was profit-making, they should realize that it was only in a stable political climate that they could operate without fear of expropriation, and should regard the indigenous population as partners.

Adnan Raouf (Iraq), member of the Visiting Mission, noted that other countries which had gained independence in similar circumstances had had their political and economic convulsions later, and that it would be wise to anticipate such a disruptive stage in the future independent Papua New Guinea. He felt that the Administration should make a serious effort to bring the expatriate private sector in line with the established policy, to enlarge the role of the public sector, and to create joint enterprises, in order to identify the interests of the individual investors with the larger interests of the community.

Referring to remarks by the representatives of France and the United Kingdom on the implications for Papua New Guinea of the United Kingdom's entry into the European Economic Community (EEC), the Special Representative of the Administering Authority said he hoped that the confidence they had expressed concerning the safeguarding of the Territory's agricultural exports would be justified. But he reminded the Council that traditionally almost 30 per cent of the Territory's exports had gone to the United Kingdom, and that the Territory would be placed at a disadvantage compared to many of its Pacific Ocean neighbours which had or might obtain associate status in EEC.

Social and educational advancement

The Administering Authority reported that all elements of the population were secure in the enjoyment of human rights and fundamental freedoms without discrimination on grounds of race, sex, language or religion. However, it was still considered necessary to retain certain legislative provisions in order to protect the interests of the indigenous people in such matters as land acquisition and employment.

The Trusteeship Council noted with satisfaction that the 1971 Visiting Mission had found no real evidence of overt discrimination on racial grounds and that relations between the communities were relaxed and easy. It hoped, however, that efforts would continue to be made jointly by indigenous people and expatriates to eliminate social separateness.

Expenditure on health services amounted to A$10,072,211 during 1969-1970. Capital expenditure on hospital buildings and facilities, including water supplies and sewerage, amounted to A$2,665,184, while grants-in-aid to missions for health services totalled A$508,491.

The Trusteeship Council welcomed the legislation recently adopted by the House of Assembly which provided, among other things, for the establishment of a Minimum Wage Board to determine minimum wage rates and for the introduction into the rural sector of the concept of all-cash wages.

The number of Administration schools increased from 385 to 392 during 1969-1970 and the number of pupils enrolled from 60,325 to 63,173. The number of recognized mission schools decreased from 892 to 836, while enrolment increased from 103,473 to 104,483. Expenditure on educational services for 1969-1970 was A$13,829,016; grants-in-aid to mission schools totalled A$2,102,000.

The Trusteeship Council was pleased to note that the House of Assembly had passed legislation to establish a Territory Board of Education, which had been given major functions in the planning and administration of education at the national level.

The Council also took note that the Teaching Service Commission, an employing authority for all teachers in the national system, was headed by an indigenous Commissioner. The Council further noted the statement by the Special Representative that the dismissal of unqualified teachers and the consolidation of schools had resulted in an improvement in the quality of education in the Territory.

The Council expressed the view that education played a crucial role in developing a sense of national unity and that it should be geared to present and future opportunities for employment.

The Council hoped that the impressive record of achievement of the Administration in recent years would continue as the Territory advanced towards self-government and independence.

Attainment of self-government or independence

The Trusteeship Council noted with satisfaction that the Administering Authority had accepted the report of the Select Committee on Constitutional Development, adopted by the House of Assembly in 1971, and that legislation had been passed which would give full effect to those parts of the report dealing with the 1972 House of Assembly elections. The Council also noted the intention of the Administering Authority to pass additional legislation to give further effect to the Committee's report.

The Council sought to ensure that the people of the Territory were brought to self-determination as swiftly as possible, in accordance with the Council's mandate under the United Nations Charter and the provisions of the Trusteeship Agreement, and bearing in mind the provisions of the relevant General Assembly resolutions—including those of 14 December 1960 (containing the text of the Declaration on the Granting of Independence to Colonial Countries and Peoples)[8] and 15 December 1960.[9] The Council welcomed the declaration by the Administering Authority that the approximate time-table for self-government set by the House of Assembly had been accepted, and that further movement towards internal self-government would require consultations with the Territory's leadership after the 1972 elections. The Council noted with interest the statement of the Minister for External Territories that, should a cohesive group of ministers emerge from the 1972 elections with a majority backing in the House, Australia would regard the group as constituting a government and would negotiate with its leader for the handing over of further authority; when this process was completed, the Administering Authority would give formal recognition to the attainment of full internal self-government.

The Council took note of the conclusion of the 1971 Visiting Mission that although the chief responsibility for setting a date for independence should rest with the government of a self-governing Papua New Guinea, it was realistic to assume for planning purposes that independence would be achieved during the life of the fourth House of Assembly (1976-1980). The Council nevertheless agreed with the stated policy of the Administering Authority that it was for the elected leaders of a self-governing Papua New Guinea to determine

---

[8]See Y.U.N., 1960, pp. 49-50, text of resolution 1514(XV).
[9]*Ibid.*, pp. 509-10, text of resolution 1541(XV).

when independence was to be achieved. In this regard, the Council noted the statement of Tore Lokoloko, Special Adviser to the Special Representative of the Administering Authority, that the Mission's recommendations on achieving independence did not reflect the wishes of the people and that neither the Administering Authority nor the people of the Territory should set a target date until the people themselves were confident that they could stand on their own feet.

The United Kingdom representative noted that in accepting the recommendations of the Select Committee, the Administering Authority, in conjunction with the elected representatives of the Territory, had set a tentative time-table for full internal self-government within the period 1972-1976. In deferring the final decision until the wishes of the House of Assembly to be elected in 1972 were known, the Administering Authority was fulfilling its responsibilities under the Trusteeship Agreement and the relevant provisions of the United Nations Charter.

The United States agreed with the Administering Authority that the freely expressed views of a fully self-governing Territory, and not the setting of approximate time-tables or target dates by outsiders, should determine when independence was to be achieved. However, the United States felt that the approximate time-table recommended by the Select Committee would give a sense of direction to the Territory and encourage greater political awareness.

The representative of the USSR said that in line with its consistent policy of supporting peoples who were struggling for their freedom and independence, the USSR strongly favoured granting to the people of Papua New Guinea their inalienable right to freedom and independence, in accordance with the Declaration on the Granting of Independence to Colonial Countries and Peoples. The USSR continued to oppose the policy of Australia, which was preventing the political, social, cultural and economic development of the Trust Territory; that policy was rather directed at the annexation of the Territory and its utilization as a source of raw material and as a military and strategic base for the metropolitan country. The Administering Authority should implement its obligations under the Charter and the various United Nations resolutions which called for the rapid granting of independence to the peoples of Papua New Guinea.

Charles Wyse, member of the Visiting Mission, stated that the Mission had been guided in its suggestions concerning the timing of self-government by the recommendations of the Select Committee on Constitutional Development. His visit to the Territory had convinced him that the Territory was gradually preparing itself to take its place among the community of independent nations, and that it was the intention of the Administering Authority to bring the Territory to self-government and independence.

Adnan Raouf, member of the Visiting Mission, stated that in view of the sentiments expressed by people in certain areas of the Territory, the time-table set up by the Select Committee might seem overly optimistic. However, although the tendency to avoid assuming full responsibility was noticeable, it was to a great extent balanced by the responsible attitudes of members of the House of Assembly.

The representative of the Administering Authority, referring to the comments of the USSR representative concerning self-government and independence, regretted that the USSR had not properly understood the situation. His Government agreed with the House of Assembly that planning should be directed towards the likelihood of full self-government in the period 1972-1976. Australia was firmly committed to extending full self-government to Papua New Guinea in that period if the government of Papua New Guinea asked for it; it was firmly committed to granting independence as soon thereafter as a fully self-governing government of Papua New Guinea requested.

Mr. Lokoloko, Special Adviser to the Special Representative, stated that the people of Papua New Guinea did not want to be forced into full self-government until they had made progress in the political, economic and social fields. Yakob Talis, Special Adviser to the Special Representative, held that the people of Papua New Guinea wanted development in the Territory to be steady and without discrimination, racial struggle or bloodshed.

Consideration by Special Committee

The situation in Papua and the Trust Territory of New Guinea was considered by the General Assembly's Special Committee on the Situation with regard to the Implementation of the Declaration on the Granting of Independence to Colonial Countries and Peoples at meetings held between 7 September and 21 October 1971.

In its conclusions and recommendations adopted on 21 October 1971, the Special Committee noted the statement of the representative of the administering power concerning separatist tendencies in several regions of Papua New Guinea. Mindful that the period immediately preceding independence was of crucial importance and that the administering power was responsible for leaving the country united and intact, the Special Committee strongly urged the administering power to discourage separatist movements.

The Special Committee welcomed the fact that a

proposal for a single citizenship for all inhabitants of the Territory was before the House of Assembly, and expressed the hope that a common citizenship would be introduced as soon as possible. The Special Committee also urged the intensification of the campaign to promote national unity and the programme of mass political education.

Noting that the administering power had affirmed that the interval between the attainment of full self-government and independence would be a matter to be determined by the then government of Papua New Guinea, and the fact that the recommendation of the Select Committee on Constitutional Development regarding progress towards self-government had been agreed to by the House of Assembly and the administering power, the Special Committee considered that the administering power should be in a position to set the time-table for independence which had been requested by the General Assembly on 14 December 1970.[10]

The Special Committee recognized the importance of increased participation by the people of Papua New Guinea in the management of their own affairs. It urged the administering power to expedite the implementation of the programme for accelerated localization of the Papua New Guinea public service, and recommended the discontinuation of recruitment of expatriate officers for any posts except those for which no Papuan or New Guinean was qualified.

The Committee expressed regret that indigenous participation in the ownership and management of private economic enterprises, particularly in the industrial sector, was still on a very small scale and that the majority of private enterprises continued to be dominated by expatriates, most of whom made little effort to identify themselves with the country in which they were living.

The Special Committee endorsed the view of the 1971 Visiting Mission to the effect that economic development would have to take account of political and social changes. Noting that in its revised five-year development programme, the Administration had called for maximum participation in the economy by Papuans and New Guineans at all levels, the Special Committee urged the administering power to accelerate the rate at which this objective would be achieved and to intensify efforts to facilitate the entry of the people of the Territory into modern economic life. It noted that some progress had been achieved in the field of education, and expressed the hope that the administering power would give greater attention to the problem of drop-outs.

The Special Committee urged the administering power to do all that it could to preserve the cultural heritage of the people of Papua New Guinea, as well as their national unity. It welcomed the spirit of co-operation shown by the administering power in adopting some of the measures suggested by the 1971 Visiting Mission. It also welcomed the administering power's invitation to the Trusteeship Council to dispatch a special mission to observe the elections to the House of Assembly in 1972, and the fact that this mission would be composed in the manner set out by the General Assembly on 16 December 1969.[11] (See also pp. 498-99.) It considered that the reports of future missions of the Trusteeship Council should be submitted simultaneously to the Trusteeship Council and the Special Committee.

The representative of the Administering Authority informed the Special Committee that since the report of the Select Committee on Constitutional Development had been adopted by the Papua New Guinea House of Assembly and agreed to by the Administering Authority, it was the view of his Government and of the government of Papua New Guinea that in effect the time-table for the attainment of full internal self-government, and subsequently independence, had been set. However, until the elections early in 1972, which would result in the formation of a new government in Papua New Guinea, it would not be possible to be more specific about the date for self-government.

Consideration by General Assembly

Later in 1971, at its twenty-sixth session, the General Assembly considered the 1970-1971 report of the Trusteeship Council and the report of the Special Committee concerning Papua and the Trust Territory of New Guinea.

During discussion in the Assembly's Fourth Committee—to which the question was referred—the representative of Australia stated that there was already a large measure of self-government in Papua New Guinea, which would be extended considerably by constitutional process after the elections of 1972; it would be left to the new House of Assembly, which would meet in April 1972, to decide when it should assume responsibility for those few matters affecting internal self-government which were still the responsibility of the Administering Authority. His Government had made it clear that the period of time which would elapse between the assumption of full internal self-government and independence would be a matter for the then government of Papua New Guinea to determine. The Australian Government believed that it had done what the United Nations had called on it to do.

---

[10]See Y.U.N., 1970, pp. 680-81, text of resolution 2700(XXV).
[11]See Y.U.N., 1969, p. 620, text of resolution 2590(XXIV), operative para. 5.

Kenya said that Australia should be commended for the spirit of co-operation it had shown the Special Committee on the Situation with regard to the Implementation of the Declaration on the Granting of Independence to Colonial Countries and Peoples, and for inviting a mission to Papua New Guinea in 1972. The Australian attitude was very different from that of other administering powers in Africa and elsewhere, Kenya felt.

The representative of Iraq stated that Australia had to some extent fulfilled the request of the General Assembly of 14 December 1970 calling upon it to prescribe a specific time-table for the free exercise by the people of Papua and New Guinea of their right to self-determination and independence.[12]

France held that New Guineans did not desire too speedy a political change because they feared a consequent loss of external assistance. It noted that the Administering Authority was taking steps to encourage local enterprise and develop national feeling.

Ghana endorsed the appeal by the Special Committee for an intensification of the campaign to promote national unity.

On 14 December 1971, the Fourth Committee approved without objection the text of a draft resolution, which was adopted by the General Assembly on 20 December.

The Assembly thereby reaffirmed the inalienable right of the people of Papua and the Trust Territory of New Guinea to self-determination and independence in accordance with the 1960 Declaration on the Granting of Independence to Colonial Countries and Peoples and the Trusteeship Agreement of 13 December 1946.

The Assembly decided that, in accordance with the express desire of the peoples of the territories, the name to be applied for United Nations purposes to the territory of Papua and the Trust Territory of New Guinea would henceforth be "Papua New Guinea."

The administering power was called upon to take all necessary steps to ensure the speedy attainment by Papua New Guinea of self-government and independence as a single political and territorial entity and, in that regard, to establish, in consultation with the freely elected representatives of the people, a specific time-table for the free exercise by the people of Papua New Guinea of their right to self-determination and independence. The administering power was urged to discourage separatist movements and to ensure that the unity of Papua New Guinea was preserved throughout the period leading to independence.

The Assembly requested the Trusteeship Council, while continuing to exercise its specific responsibilities towards the Trust Territory of New Guinea, and the Special Committee on the

Situation with regard to the Implementation of the Declaration on the Granting of Independence to Colonial Countries and Peoples, to bear in mind the need to consider Papua New Guinea as a single political and territorial entity and to take account of this when determining the itineraries of future visiting missions in consultation with the administering power. The Council was also asked to continue to include non-members of the Council in its periodic visiting missions on the basis recommended by the General Assembly on 16 December 1969.[13]

The Assembly welcomed the invitation extended by the administering power to the Trusteeship Council to dispatch a special mission to observe the elections to the Papua New Guinea House of Assembly in 1972, and the fact that the mission would be composed as recommended by the General Assembly on 16 December 1969.[14] It recommended that the reports of this special mission and those of future missions should be submitted both to the Trusteeship Council and to the Special Committee.

Also, the Assembly urged the administering power to intensify its programme of political education in Papua New Guinea and to expedite the implementation of the programme for accelerated localization of the Papua New Guinea public service. It requested the administering power: to intensify and extend the educational services, including technical and administrative training, provided for the people of Papua New Guinea; to continue to expand the measures being taken to promote ownership, management and participation by the inhabitants of Papua New Guinea in enterprises in all sectors of the economy; and to report to the Trusteeship Council and the Special Committee on the implementation of this resolution.

Finally, the Assembly requested the Trusteeship Council and the Special Committee to continue to examine the question and to report thereon to the General Assembly in 1972.

These decisions by the Assembly were set forth in resolution 2865(XXVI), which was adopted by a recorded vote of 119 to 0, with 1 abstention. (For text of resolution, see DOCUMENTARY REFERENCES below.)

The text was based on a proposal sponsored in the Fourth Committee by: Afghanistan, Cameroon, Egypt, Ethiopia, Ghana, India, Indonesia, Iran, Iraq, Ireland, Mali, Mauritania, Nigeria, the Philippines, Sierra Leone, Sudan, Trinidad and Tobago, Tunisia, the United Republic of Tanzania, Yugoslavia and Zambia.

---

[12]See footnote 10.
[13]See footnote 11.
[14]*Ibid.*

DOCUMENTARY REFERENCES

Trusteeship Council—38th session
Plenary meetings 1377-1379, 1381, 1382, 1384, 1387.

Commonwealth of Australia: Administration of the Territory of New Guinea, 1 July 1969–30 June 1970. Report to the General Assembly of the United Nations. Government Printing Office, Canberra, Australia.

T/1715 and Add.1. Notes by Secretary-General (transmitting report of Australia on administration of Trust Territory of New Guinea for period 1 July 1969–30 June 1970 and supplementary report for 1 July 1970–31 March 1971).

T/1720. Observations of World Health Organization.

T/1723. Observations of United Nations Educational, Scientific and Cultural Organization.

T/1728 (T/1717). Report of United Nations Visiting Mission to Trust Territory of New Guinea, 1971, together with relevant resolution of Trusteeship Council.

T/L.1161 and Add.1. Conditions in Trust Territory of New Guinea. Working paper prepared by Secretariat and draft amendments to working paper.

T/L.1164. Conditions in Trust Territory of New Guinea. Report of Drafting Committee, annexing draft conclusions and recommendations, adopted by Trusteeship Council on 18 June 1971, meeting 1387, by 4 votes to 0, with 2 abstentions.

T/1727. Resolutions adopted by Trusteeship Council during its 38th session, 25 May–18 June 1971. Other decisions, p. 4.

Special Committee on Situation with regard to Implementation of Declaration on Granting of Independence to Colonial Countries and Peoples, meetings 799-801, 819-822, 825, 830.

General Assembly—26th session
Fourth Committee, meetings 1953, 1956, 1957, 1962-1965, 1967, 1968.
Plenary meeting 2028.

A/8360. Note by Secretary-General (transmitting report of Commonwealth of Australia on administration of Trust Territory of New Guinea for period 1 July 1969–30 June 1970).

A/8401. Report of Secretary-General on work of the Organization, 16 June 1970–15 June 1971, Part Two, Chapter II B 1.

A/8404. Report of Trusteeship Council to General Assembly, 20 June 1970–18 June 1971: Part I, Chapters II-VI; Part II.

A/8423/Rev.1. Report of Special Committee on Situation with regard to Implementation of Declaration on Granting of Independence to Colonial Countries and Peoples (covering its work during 1971), Chapters IV and XIX.

A/C.4/L.1004. Afghanistan, Cameroon, Egypt, Ethiopia, Ghana, India, Indonesia, Iran, Iraq, Ireland, Mali, Mauritania, Nigeria, Philippines, Sierra Leone, Sudan, Trinidad and Tobago, Tunisia, United Republic of Tanzania, Yugoslavia, Zambia: draft resolution, as orally revised by sponsors, approved without objection by Fourth Committee on 14 December 1971, meeting 1968.

A/8615. Report of Fourth Committee.

RESOLUTION 2865(XXVI), as recommended by Fourth Committee, A/8615, adopted by Assembly on 20 December 1971, meeting 2028, by recorded vote of 119 to 0, with 1 abstention, as follows:

In favour: Afghanistan, Algeria, Argentina, Australia, Austria, Bahrain, Barbados, Belgium, Botswana, Brazil, Bulgaria, Burma, Burundi, Byelorussian SSR, Cameroon, Canada, Central African Republic, Ceylon, Chile, Colombia, Costa Rica, Cuba, Cyprus, Czechoslovakia, Dahomey, Denmark, Dominican Republic, Ecuador, Egypt, El Salvador, Equatorial Guinea, Ethiopia, Fiji, Finland, Gambia, Ghana, Greece, Guatemala, Guinea, Guyana, Haiti, Honduras, Hungary, Iceland, India, Indonesia, Iran, Iraq, Ireland, Israel, Italy, Ivory Coast, Jamaica, Japan, Jordan, Kenya, Khmer Republic, Kuwait, Laos, Lebanon,

Lesotho, Liberia, Libyan Arab Republic, Luxembourg, Madagascar, Malawi, Malaysia, Mali, Malta, Mauritania, Mexico, Mongolia, Morocco, Nepal, Netherlands, New Zealand, Nicaragua, Nigeria, Norway, Oman, Pakistan, Panama, Paraguay, People's Democratic Republic of Yemen, Peru, Philippines, Poland, Portugal, Romania, Rwanda, Saudi Arabia, Senegal, Sierra Leone, Singapore, Somalia, Spain, Sudan, Swaziland, Sweden, Syrian Arab Republic, Thailand, Togo, Trinidad and Tobago, Tunisia, Turkey, Uganda, Ukrainian SSR, USSR, United Arab Emirates, United Kingdom, United Republic of Tanzania, United States, Upper Volta, Uruguay, Venezuela, Yemen, Yugoslavia, Zaire, Zambia.
Against: None.
Abstaining: France.

The General Assembly,

Recalling the provisions of the Charter of the United Nations and General Assembly resolution 1514(XV) of 14 December 1960, containing the Declaration on the Granting of Independence to Colonial Countries and Peoples,

Recalling its previous resolutions concerning Papua and the Trust Territory of New Guinea, in particular resolutions 2590(XXIV) of 16 December 1969 and 2700(XXV) of 14 December 1970,

Having considered the report of the Trusteeship Council covering the period from 20 June 1970 to 18 June 1971 and the relevant chapters of the report of the Special Committee on the Situation with regard to the Implementation of the Declaration on the Granting of Independence to Colonial Countries and Peoples,

Having heard the statement of the representative of the administering Power,

Taking into account the conclusions and recommendations of the Special Committee and the Trusteeship Council regarding developments in Papua and the Trust Territory of New Guinea,

Noting in particular the express desire of the people of Papua and the Trust Territory of New Guinea for national unity and independence as a single political and territorial entity,

Taking note of the decision of the House of Assembly of Papua and the Trust Territory of New Guinea that the Territory formed from the administrative union of those two Territories should be named Papua New Guinea,

Bearing in mind the decisions taken during 1971 by the House of Assembly of Papua and the Trust Territory of New Guinea and the administering Power with regard to the attainment of full internal self-government during the period 1972-1976, and the affirmation by the Government of Australia, as the administering Power, that the interval between the attainment of full self-government and independence will be a matter to be determined by the then Government of Papua and the Trust Territory of New Guinea,

Noting further the decision of the Government of Australia to invite a special mission of the Trusteeship Council, including two members of the Special Committee, to observe the elections to the Third House of Assembly of Papua and the Trust Territory of New Guinea in 1972,

Mindful of the responsibility of the United Nations to render all help to the people of Papua and the Trust Territory of New Guinea in their efforts freely to decide their own future,

1. *Reaffirms* the inalienable right of the people of Papua and the Trust Territory of New Guinea to self-determination and independence in accordance with General Assembly resolution 1514(XV) and the Trusteeship Agreement of 13 December 1946;

2. *Decides* that, in accordance with the express desire of the people of the Territories, the name to be applied for United Nations purposes to the Territory of Papua and the Trust Territory of New Guinea shall henceforth be "Papua New Guinea";

3. *Calls upon* the administering Power to take all necessary steps to ensure the speedy attainment by Papua New Guinea of self-government and independence as a single political and territorial entity and, in that regard, to establish, in consultation with the freely elected representatives of the people, a specific time-table for the free exercise by the people of Papua New Guinea of their right to self-determination and independence;

4. *Urges* the administering Power to discourage separatist movements and to ensure that the unity of Papua New Guinea is preserved throughout the period leading up to independence;

5. *Requests* the Trusteeship Council, while continuing to exercise its specific responsibilities towards the Trust Territory of New Guinea, and the Special Committee on the Situation with regard to the Implementation of the Declaration on the Granting of Independence to Colonial Countries and Peoples to bear in mind the need to consider Papua New Guinea as a single political and territorial entity and to take account of this when determining the itineraries of future visiting missions in consultation with the administering Power;

6. *Further requests* the Trusteeship Council to continue to include non-members of the Trusteeship Council in its periodic visiting missions on the basis recommended in General Assembly resolution 2590(XXIV);

7. *Welcomes* the invitation extended by the administering Power to the Trusteeship Council to dispatch a special mission to observe the elections to the Papua New Guinea House of Assembly in 1972 and the fact that the mission will be composed as recommended in General Assembly resolution 2590(XXIV);

8. *Recommends* that the report of this special mission and those of future missions should be submitted both to the Trusteeship Council and to the Special Committee;

9. *Urges* the administering Power to intensify its programme of political education in Papua New Guinea and to expedite the implementation of the programme for accelerated localization of the Papua New Guinea public service;

10. *Requests* the administering Power further to intensify and extend the educational services, including technical and administrative training, provided for the people of Papua New Guinea;

11. *Further requests* the administering Power to continue to expand the measures being taken to promote ownership, management and participation by the inhabitants of Papua New Guinea in enterprises throughout all sectors of the economy;

12. *Requests* the administering Power to report to the Trusteeship Council and the Special Committee on the implementation of the present resolution;

13. *Requests* the Trusteeship Council and the Special Committee to continue to examine this question and to report thereon to the General Assembly at its twenty-seventh session.

Trust Territory of the Pacific Islands

The Trust Territory of the Pacific Islands, administered by the United States, covers some 3 million square miles of the western Pacific Ocean north of the Equator. It embraces more than 2,000 islands and atolls with a combined land area of 700 square miles. Collectively known as Micronesia, these islands form three major archipelagos: the Marianas, the Carolines and the Marshalls. (Guam, the largest island in the Marianas, is not part of the Trust Territory.)

As at June 1970, the population of the Trust Territory totalled 102,250. Saipan, in the Mariana Islands, is the provisional headquarters of the Administration.

In 1971, conditions in the Trust Territory were considered by the Trusteeship Council and by the Special Committee on the Situation with regard to the Implementation of the Declaration on the Granting of Independence to Colonial Countries and Peoples.

Consideration by Trusteeship Council

The Trusteeship Council considered the Trust Territory of the Pacific Islands at its thirty-eighth session, held at United Nations Headquarters, New York, from 25 May to 18 June 1971. The Council reported to the Security Council on this Territory, a strategic area in accordance with Article 83 of the United Nations Charter.[15]

Population movements

The Trusteeship Council noted with satisfaction the statement by the Special Representative of the Administering Authority that the rehabilitation of Bikini Atoll was continuing on schedule. The Council reiterated the hope that, as soon as feasible, similar measures would be taken in respect of other displaced communities.

War damage claims

With regard to the question of the settlement of Micronesian claims for compensation for war and other damages, the Trusteeship Council noted that legislation aimed at the settlement of both categories of claims was still before the United States Congress.

In view of the impression reported by the 1970 Visiting Mission to the Trust Territory that the settlement of the claims was a matter of major importance to many Micronesians, in some cases to the exclusion of any other aspect of the Territory's affairs, the Council regretted the continuing delay in resolving the problem and once again expressed the hope that a definite solution would soon be arrived at so that payments would be made at the earliest possible date.

Political advancement

The Trusteeship Council was glad to note that the Congress of Micronesia had taken on greater responsibilities in 1970-1971 and had enacted several important legislative measures. The Council also welcomed the greater participation by the Micronesian Congress and by the district legislatures in the preparation of the Territory's budget. The Council recalled the hope expressed at its 1970 session that steps would be taken to enlarge the financial responsibility of the Micronesian Congress by progressively extending its powers to include appropriation of United States financial subsidies.

The Council commended the Administering Authority for further appointments of Micronesians to senior positions in the Executive. It noted that the Executive was in accord with legislation

[15]For text of Article 83 of the Charter, see APPENDIX II.

passed by the Micronesian Congress providing for submission to the latter, for its advice and consent, appointments to certain positions, including department heads of cabinet rank within the government of the Trust Territory. The Council nevertheless recalled its endorsement of the comments of the 1970 Visiting Mission regarding the desirability of including popularly elected Micronesians as soon as possible in the senior councils of the Executive.

The Council welcomed the further appointments of Micronesians to positions of responsibility; it noted the statement of the Special Representative that out of a civil service totalling approximately 5,700 persons, 5,200 were Micronesian citizens.

The Council noted the statement of the Special Representative that, under the Administration's decentralization programme, the district administrators occupied the most important positions in the Territory's government and welcomed the comments by the Special Representative commending the work of Micronesians occupying those positions.

The representative of the USSR stated that the Congress of Micronesia could not act as a sovereign organ. He had attempted in vain to ascertain from the High Commissioner what constitutional changes had been made to expand the rights of the Congress and restrict those of the High Commissioner, so as to prepare the way to self-determination and independence.

The representative of France said it appeared that members of the Congress were helping to develop a sense of territorial unity among their people. Nevertheless, he wondered whether the term of office of representatives was not too short; in a country at the beginning of democracy, the electors should not be called to the polls too often and those elected should have sufficient time to become aware of public affairs.

The United Kingdom had hoped that there might have been a movement towards establishing a territorial executive that would include elected members, as was the case in the Trust Territory of New Guinea and in the Gilbert and Ellice Islands.

Economic development

The Trusteeship Council noted that the gross national product of the Territory amounted to approximately $1,000 per capita, a figure comparable to that of a developed country. It pointed out, however, that this figure concealed considerable inequalities, particularly between urban and rural dwellers and between civil servants and farmers or fishermen, and that large outside financial contributions had been included in the calculations. The Council recommended that an effort be made to harmonize and co-ordinate action by the Adminis-

tration in various fields and to reduce inequalities in the standard of living. The Council also recommended that special attention continue to be paid to anti-inflationary measures.

The Council noted with satisfaction that the grants made available to the Administration had increased, exceeding the sum of $50 million in the last fiscal year. Nevertheless, as excessive dependence on external assistance prevented the establishment of a solid financial base within the Territory, the Council welcomed the fact that the Congress of Micronesia had passed legislation introducing an income tax, which would increase the Territory's revenue and develop a sense of financial autonomy among the inhabitants.

The Trusteeship Council noted that under the Land Commission Act of 1966, five of the six proposed land commissions had been established, and that over 1,000 parcels had been surveyed and 500 land titles had been issued; nevertheless, that was only a fraction of the 348,000 parcels of land in the Territory. The Council expressed the hope that the sixth land commission would soon be set up and again recommended a reduction in the amount of public land in the Territory so that it might be made available to the population.

The Council was pleased to note that agricultural production was growing; for example, over a two-year period, copra production had risen by 2,000 tons and vegetable production had increased tenfold. It regretted that in a' predominantly agricultural area, food imports had amounted to $7 million in 1970, an increase over 1969, and expressed the hope that the increase in locally produced foodstuffs would lessen dependence on imports.

Noting that the sale of fish ranked second in Micronesia's foreign trade—a position in keeping with the maritime character of the Territory—the Council regretted that the value of fish exports still barely exceeded that of tinned fish imports.

The Council noted with satisfaction that tourism was expanding at a considerably faster rate than had been foreseen, that it currently ranked third among the Territory's external sources of revenue and that there was a senior official responsible for promoting tourism. It recommended that efforts be made to ensure that all the archipelagos benefit from the increase in tourism and that Micronesians play a more active role in tourist activities at all levels.

The Council was pleased that approximately one quarter of the working population belonged to co-operatives, whose annual volume of business had increased by more than $1 million.

The representative of the USSR stated that the policy of the administering power in the economic field was designed to convert the Territory into an economic appendage of the metropolitan country:

a source of raw material for the United States, a market for American goods and a destination for American capital. If anything, the Territory had undergone a state of economic stagnation, he said.

The United Kingdom representative said it was important that the maximum possible use be made of the Territory's own resources, both for internal consumption and for export. As the Visiting Mission had observed in 1970, the excessive financial dependence of the Territory upon the Administration was one of its most serious problems; the United Kingdom therefore noted with approval the introduction of an income tax system in the Territory.

Australia said there appeared to be no reason why a system of progressive taxation could not be made simple enough to conform with the economy of the Territory; it hoped that in future the Congress might consider raising the tax rate on higher personal and business incomes.

Social advancement

The Trusteeship Council noted with pleasure the fact that 70 per cent of the population of the Territory had direct access to a district or sub-district hospital and that recurrent expenditure on public health had increased by almost $1 million over the period 1968-1970. It regretted that the number and capacity of hospitals had not substantially changed since consideration of the 1966-1967 report, and hoped that the construction planned for the future would be completed as soon as possible. It endorsed the view of the representative of the World Health Organization that in the islands out of reach of hospitals, the most critical need was at the dispensary and health aid level, and noted with approval that the Administering Authority was giving priority to these areas.

The representative of the USSR observed that the situation with regard to medical services in the Territory was still unsatisfactory; there was a severe shortage of doctors, other medical personnel and medical facilities.

Educational advancement

The Trusteeship Council reiterated its view that the main requirements in education were: to improve teaching standards; to improve and expand vocational and technical education, especially at the high school level; to operate one or two selective high schools as a preparation for students proceeding to higher education; and to reform the curricula in elementary and secondary schools. In this regard, the Council noted with approval the Administering Authority's efforts to establish a comprehensive vocational training programme in each district to supplement the work of the Micronesian Occupational Center in Koror, as well

as the establishment of a Curriculum Council and the intention to make the curriculum more responsive to the needs of the people of Micronesia.

The Council noted that the percentage of non-indigenous teachers was still high but appreciated the difficulties facing the Administering Authority in recruiting local staff. It hoped that every effort would be made to localize the teaching service, with particular emphasis on the elementary level.

The representative of the USSR stated that after 24 years of administration by the United States, education was still not universal. The education policy of the Administering Authority was part of a well thought out programme of Americanization of Micronesian culture and society.

The representative of France stated that the Territory enjoyed a relatively high literacy rate for a developing country. The number of non-indigenous teachers remained very high, however; it would be desirable if the entire teaching staff at the elementary level could be Micronesian as soon as possible.

Attainment of self-government or independence

The Trusteeship Council noted the appointment of a Joint Political Status Committee of the Congress of Micronesia and the appointment of a personal representative of the President of the United States to discuss the future political status of the Territory. It noted with approval that further discussions were due to take place during 1971.

The Council noted that the Administering Authority had proposed commonwealth status for the Territory and that the Congress of Micronesia had declared the offer unacceptable. It also noted the statement by the representative of the Administering Authority that the Administering Authority was not attempting to impose any particular solution on the Micronesian people but was working with the Joint Political Status Committee to achieve a mutually agreed status of self-government in association with the United States. The Council further noted that the Administering Authority had studied the principles which the Micronesian Congress considered essential to the status of free association, and that it was optimistic that a mutually agreed status could be achieved. The Council believed that the statements of the Administering Authority, while not committing it to any particular status for the Trust Territory, were indicative of an open-minded, flexible approach and augured well for the success of the forthcoming talks.

The Council reaffirmed its conviction that in view of the particular situation of the Trust Territory, it would be desirable for the people of

Micronesia to determine their future status sooner rather than later.

The representative of the USSR said that despite its obligations under the Charter and the Trusteeship Agreement, the United States was virtually turning the Territory into an appendage of the metropolitan country and depriving the people of any development towards independence or the possibility of achieving independence, even in the remote future. The United States had in fact embarked on a policy of converting the Territory into its military and strategic bulwark in the western Pacific. The USSR fully shared the view of the Micronesian delegation that Micronesia considered the right to independence a fundamental and inalienable right of its people and that independence was the future political status most in keeping with the purpose of the Trusteeship Agreement.

The representative of the Administering Authority rejected the statement of the USSR that the United States was seeking to make Micronesia its military and strategic appendage. Rather, it was working with the Joint Political Status Committee to achieve a mutually agreed status of self-government in association with the United States—the stated preference of Micronesia.

Australia felt that the views of both sides regarding the future status of the Territory seemed to be very close and was optimistic that this would prove to be the case when the Council met in 1972.

The United Kingdom felt encouraged by what it had heard at the current session, and had every hope that an agreement on the future status of Micronesia might soon be reached between the Administering Authority and the Joint Political Status Committee.

France said that the creation of organs such as co-operatives and credit unions, through which the Micronesians could manage their own affairs, could be speeded up by organizing political education campaigns. France was gratified that such campaigns had been undertaken and were to be expanded in future.

Consideration by Special Committee

The situation in the Trust Territory of the Pacific Islands was discussed in 1971 by the General Assembly's Special Committee on the Situation with regard to the Implementation of the Declaration on the Granting of Independence to Colonial Countries and Peoples.

On 4 June 1971, Lazarus Salii and Erpap Silk,

Co-Chairmen of the Joint Political Status Committee of Micronesia, addressed the Special Committee.

In its conclusions and recommendations, adopted on 5 November 1971, the Special Committee among other things reaffirmed the inalienable right of the people of the Trust Territory of the Pacific Islands to self-determination, in conformity with the Declaration on the Granting of Independence to Colonial Countries and Peoples,[16] and reiterated its view that the size, isolation and limited resources of the Trust Territory should in no way delay the speedy implementation of the Declaration.

The Special Committee expressed its serious concern that a representative of the Administering Authority was not present during discussions concerning the Trust Territory. It urged the United States to reconsider its position and to co-operate with the Committee by supplying the information necessary to assist the Committee in formulating its conclusions and recommendations.

The Special Committee urged the Administering Authority to cease pursuing a policy which tended to maintain the Trust Territory permanently dependent upon the United States. It reiterated its previous recommendations that the Administering Authority should in no way prejudge the future of the Trust Territory, which was a matter for the inhabitants to decide.

The Special Committee drew the attention of the Administering Authority to the danger that increasing the volume of grants without a definite programme to develop and diversify the economy of the Trust Territory might make Micronesia totally dependent on such grants.

The Committee took note of the invitation that had been extended to the Special Committee by the Congress of Micronesia to visit the Trust Territory, and expressed regret that the Administering Authority was not agreeable to such a visit. The Committee recalled that it would be participating in other missions to the Pacific area in 1972, and stressed the importance it attached to such missions. It considered that the consultations between the Chairman of the Special Committee, the President of the Trusteeship Council and representatives of the Administering Authority on the question of a visiting mission should be continued and once again urged the Administering Authority to reconsider its position.

[16]See Y.U.N., 1960, pp. 49-50, resolution 1514(XV), containing text of Declaration.

DOCUMENTARY REFERENCES

Trusteeship Council—38th session
Plenary meetings 1372-1376, 1380, 1386, 1387.

Twenty-third Annual Report to the United Nations on the Administration of the Trust Territory of the Pacific Islands, 1 July

1969 to 30 June 1970. Transmitted by the United States of America to the United Nations pursuant to Article 88 of the Charter of the United Nations. Department of State Publication 8520, International Organization and Conference Series 91. Government Printing Office, Washington D. C., 1971.

T/1716 (S/10196). Note by Secretary-General (transmitting report of United States on administration of Trust Territory of Pacific Islands for period 1 July 1969–30 June 1970).

T/1719. Observations of World Health Organization on annual report on Trust Territory of Pacific Islands for year ended 30 June 1970.

T/L.1160 and Add.1. Outline of conditions in Trust Territory of Pacific Islands. Working paper prepared by Secretariat and draft amendments thereto.

T/L.1162. Draft report of Trusteeship Council to Security Council on Trust Territory of Pacific Islands covering period 20 June 1970–18 June 1971. Working paper, prepared by Secretariat, adopted by Council on 18 June 1971, meeting 1387, by 5 votes to 0, with 1 abstention.

T/L.1163. Conditions in Trust Territory of Pacific Islands. Report of Drafting Committee, annexing draft recommendations and conclusions, adopted by Council on 17 June 1971, meeting 1386, by 5 votes to 0, with 1 abstention.

S/10237. Report of Trusteeship Council to Security Council on

Trust Territory of Pacific Islands, 20 June 1970–18 June 1971 (*Security Council Official Records, 26th Year, Special Supplement No. 1*).

T/1727. Resolutions adopted by Trusteeship Council during its 38th session, 25 May–18 June 1971. Other decisions, p. 4.

Special Committee on Situation with regard to Implementation of Declaration on Granting of Independence to Colonial Countries and Peoples, meetings 796, 798, 819-822, 830, 831.

Consideration by General Assembly

A/8401. Report of Secretary-General on work of the Organization, 16 June 1970–15 June 1971, Part Two, Chapter II B 2.

A/8404. Report of Trusteeship Council to General Assembly, 20 June 1970–18 June 1971, Chapter II.

A/8423/Rev.1. Report of Special Committee on Situation with regard to Implementation of Declaration on Granting of Independence to Colonial Countries and Peoples (covering its work during 1971), Chapter XVIII.

Other documents

A/8402. Report of Security Council, 16 June 1970–15 June 1971, Chapter 19.

Chapter II

The Situation with regard to the Implementation of the Declaration on the Granting of Independence to Colonial Countries and Peoples

During 1971, the General Assembly's Special Committee on the Situation with regard to the Implementation of the Declaration on the Granting of Independence to Colonial Countries and Peoples[1] continued to discharge its mandate as set forth by the General Assembly, and to seek suitable means for the immediate and full implementation of the Declaration in territories which had not yet attained independence.

In this chapter an account is given of the Special Committee's work in general during 1971, the consideration of its report by the General Assembly, and related action by other United Nations

bodies. Details are given of the Special Committee's and the General Assembly's consideration of and recommendations on individual territories.

Information on the action taken in 1971 by the General Assembly, the Special Committee and other bodies on matters concerning Southern Rhodesia, Namibia, the territories under Portuguese administration and Oman will be found in other chapters (see pp. 88-112, 546-64, 564-76, 211-12).

[1]See Y.U.N., 1960, pp. 49-50, resolution 1514(XV) of 14 December 1960 containing text of Declaration.

General questions

System of examination

During 1971, the General Assembly's Special Committee on the Situation with regard to the Implementation of the Declaration on the Granting of Independence to Colonial Countries and Peoples[2] continued to use the methods of work developed in preceding years and endorsed by the General Assembly.

Under this procedure, it examined special

questions relating to the implementation of the Declaration as well as its implementation in individual territories, the order of priority being decided on the basis of recommendations made by its working group.

[2]See Y.U.N., 1960, pp. 49-50, resolution 1514(XV) of 14 December 1960, containing text of Declaration.

To assist in its examination of conditions in each territory, the Special Committee normally has before it an information paper prepared by the United Nations Secretariat describing recent political and constitutional developments as well as current economic, social and educational conditions. This information is derived from published sources and, in relevant cases, from the information transmitted by administering powers under Article 73e of the United Nations Charter.[3]

In addition, the Special Committee requests the administering powers to submit information on political and constitutional developments in the territories they administer. The Committee hears statements from the administering powers, inviting those which are not members of the Committee to participate in its examination of the territories concerned. Petitions are circulated and the Committee may decide to hear petitioners at its meetings.

The Special Committee adopts its recommendations in the form of a consensus formulated by its Chairman or a resolution adopted by vote. The Special Committee is empowered by the General Assembly to send out visiting missions to territories in co-operation with administering powers. It also establishes sub-committees whenever it considers them necessary.

Each year, the Special Committee adopts a report to the General Assembly which includes separate chapters on the situation in each territory or group of territories which it has considered, as well as on special questions which it has decided to take up separately. It is on the basis of this report that the Assembly considers the implementation of the Declaration in general and with respect to individual territories.

The Special Committee held 52 plenary meetings from 11 February to 26 November 1971. The Committee considered general aspects of the implementation of the Declaration and also its implementation with respect to the following territories: Southern Rhodesia, Namibia, the territories under Portuguese administration, Spanish Sahara, the French Territory of the Afars and the Issas (former French Somaliland), British Honduras, Hong Kong, Gibraltar, the Falkland Islands (Malvinas), Oman, Seychelles, St. Helena, the Gilbert and Ellice Islands, Pitcairn, the Solomon Islands, American Samoa, Guam, Niue, the Tokelau Islands, the New Hebrides, the Trust Territory of the Pacific Islands, Papua and the Trust Territory of New Guinea, Cocos (Keeling) Islands, Brunei, Bermuda, Montserrat, the Bahamas, the British Virgin Islands, the United States Virgin Islands, Cayman Islands, Turks and Caicos Islands, Antigua, Dominica, Grenada, St. Kitts-Nevis-Anguilla, St. Lucia and St. Vincent.

During 1971, the Sub-Committee on Petitions considered 62 communications, 52 of which it decided to circulate as petitions. It also submitted recommendations concerning petitions relating to Namibia and the International Convention on the Elimination of all Forms of Racial Discrimination.

[3]For text of article 73e of the Charter, see APPENDIX II.

DOCUMENTARY REFERENCES

Special Committee on Situation with regard to Implementation of Declaration on Granting of Independence to Colonial Countries and Peoples, meetings 781-832.
Sub-Committee on Petitions, meetings 162-169.

A/AC.109/L.691, 693 and Corr.1, 705, 707, 710, 720, 743, 757. Reports (155th-162nd) of Special Committee's Sub-Committee on Petitions.

General aspects of implementation of Declaration

Consideration by Special Committee

The withdrawal from membership in the General Assembly's Special Committee on the Situation with regard to the Implementation of the Declaration on the Granting of Independence to Colonial Countries and Peoples of the United Kingdom and the United States was noted with regret by a number of members when the Committee convened in 1971. Both States, it was observed, had served on the Committee since its inception and together were responsible for the administration of the majority of the remaining dependent territories. In the view of some Committee members, the withdrawal of the administering powers impeded the full and speedy implementation of the General Assembly's resolution of 14 December 1960 concerning the granting of independence.[4]

During the year, the Special Committee carried out specific tasks entrusted to it by the General Assembly or arising from its own previous decisions. Thus, among general questions, it continued its study of the activities of foreign economic and other interests and its study of military activities and arrangements by colonial powers in territories under their administration which might be impeding the implementation of the Declaration. It also considered the compliance of Member States with the Declaration and other relevant resolutions on the question of decolonization, the implementation of the Declaration by the

[4]See Y.U.N., 1960, pp. 49-50, text of resolution 1514(XV).

specialized agencies and the international institutions associated with the United Nations and the question of sending visiting missions to the territories.

Within the context of the General Assembly resolutions by which the Special Committee was directed to continue to send visiting missions to colonial territories and to hold meetings at places where it could best obtain first-hand information on the situation in those territories, the Committee at the outset of the year decided to send an *Ad Hoc* Group to Africa for the purpose of maintaining contact with representatives of national liberation movements of colonial territories on that continent and obtaining first-hand information on the situation in those territories. The group visited Lusaka (Zambia), Dar es Salaam (United Republic of Tanzania) and Addis Ababa (Ethiopia), and met with representatives of 10 groups of national liberation movements of the territories concerned and with officials of the Organization of African Unity (OAU).

The Special Committee once again examined the question of publicity to be given to the work of the United Nations in the field of decolonization. The Committee considered that a sustained effort must be made to keep world public opinion adequately acquainted with the situation in the colonial territories and with the continuing struggle for liberation being waged by the colonial peoples, so as to mobilize the international community more effectively in favour of the implementation of the Declaration.

On the question of military activities and arrangements, the Special Committee, on 5 November 1971, adopted conclusions and recommendations proposed by its Sub-Committee I. Reservations to these were expressed by the representative of Sweden.

By these conclusions, the Special Committee noted with grave concern that there had been no compliance with the provisions of General Assembly resolutions on this question, in particular with the resolution of 14 December 1970, by which the General Assembly had requested the colonial powers to withdraw immediately and unconditionally their military bases and installations from colonial territories and to refrain from establishing new ones.[5] Also, little had been done to comply in this respect with the Programme of Action for the full implementation of the Declaration on the Granting of Independence to Colonial Countries and Peoples, embodied in the General Assembly's resolution of 12 October 1970.[6] Despite these resolutions, the colonial powers continued to engage in ever-increasing military activities aimed at subjugating the colonial peoples, providing protection for foreign monopolies and perpetuating colonialist and racist régimes.

The Special Committee viewed with great concern the situation in the territories of southern Africa and declared that its study proved there had been increasing collaboration during the year under review between the Governments of South Africa and Portugal and the illegal régime of Southern Rhodesia, which had formed a military *entente*. Their representatives continued to meet regularly to exchange information and to draw up joint plans for military operations against the liberation movements in Africa.

Representatives of the liberation movements had reported to the *Ad Hoc* Group of the Special Committee that there had been an over-all intensification of repressive acts against their movements. These representatives held that States members of the North Atlantic Treaty Organization (NATO) were responsible for the continuing provision of arms and other military and logistic equipment and supplies to the colonial powers.

The Special Committee concluded that the continuing escalation of armed repression in the territories of southern Africa, the intensification of military preparations, and of collaboration between South Africa, Portugal and the illegal régime in Southern Rhodesia had created a grave and ever-increasing threat to the security of independent African States and to international peace and security.

In regard to the smaller territories, such as Guam, the Trust Territory of the Pacific Islands, Bermuda and the Bahamas among others, the Special Committee noted that the colonial powers and their allies had continued to maintain a great number of military bases and installations in a manner detrimental to the interests of the indigenous peoples. The Committee reiterated its previous finding that such military activities, which were determined by the strategic military interests of the colonial powers, inevitably impeded the process of decolonization.

The Special Committee concluded that its study revealed once again conclusive evidence that the military activities and arrangements by colonial powers in the territories under their administration constituted one of the most serious impediments to the implementation of the Declaration on the granting of independence and posed a grave threat to international peace and security.

On the basis of the above conclusions, the Special Committee condemned once again the use of military force by colonial powers to suppress the legitimate aspirations of colonial peoples to self-determination and independence. It condemned once more the military *entente* between the Governments of South Africa and Portugal and

[5]See Y.U.N., 1970, pp. 709-10, text of resolution 2708(XXV).
[6]*Ibid.*, pp. 706-8, text of resolution 2621(XXV).

the illegal racist minority régime of Southern Rhodesia aimed at suppressing by armed force the inalienable right of the oppressed peoples of the colonial territories of southern Africa to self-determination and independence. The Committee called upon all States to withhold all support and assistance to those countries.

The Special Committee requested all States responsible for the administration of colonial and Trust Territories to discontinue all military activities which impeded the implementation of the Declaration. The Committee deplored once again, and called for an end to, the alienation of land for military installations and asked for return of the land already alienated to its rightful owners.

The Special Committee also called upon the colonial powers to desist from utilizing the economic and manpower resources of the territories for military activities and arrangements and to terminate the practice of conscripting men from the indigenous population for service in the armed forces of the administering power concerned.

The Committee, finally, asked the Secretary-General to give publicity to the information on military activities and arrangements by colonial powers in territories under their administration which might be impeding the implementation of the Declaration.

During its consideration of the question of sending visiting missions to the territories, the Special Committee had before it a report by its Chairman on his consultations on the subject with representatives of the administering powers.

The Chairman advised that the Government of Australia had decided to invite the Trusteeship Council to send a visiting mission to observe the elections to the Papua New Guinea House of Assembly in 1972. Australia had suggested following the precedent established for the periodic visiting mission to the Trust Territory of New Guinea of two members chosen from the Trusteeship Council and two chosen on the basis of consultation with the Special Committee and the Administering Authority.

New Zealand had decided that, in the light of the political developments in Niue and the Tokelau Islands, it might be appropriate for the Special Committee to send a small visiting mission, at a suitable time in 1972, in order that the United Nations might obtain first-hand information on the wishes of the people, the situation prevailing in, and the problems being faced by, those territories.

The United Kingdom had stated, the Chairman also reported, that, while it did not deny the useful role played by some visiting groups dispatched in the past by the United Nations, its basic position on the question remained unchanged. The position was that although there was no question of the

United Kingdom Government categorically excluding for all time the possibility of any visiting mission, little encouragement could be given to the Committee to believe that the United Kingdom could agree to such a proposal. The United Kingdom representative considered that the material already at the disposal of the Committee was not in any way insufficient.

The United States had stated it remained of the view that visiting missions to the non-self-governing territories under its administration—namely, American Samoa, Guam and the United States Virgin Islands—were not warranted at the present time. Accordingly, it could not at the present stage respond favourably to any request to permit a visiting mission to those territories, although it did not exclude the possibility in the future of making appropriate arrangements for a United Nations presence in the territories under its administration.

During the Special Committee's discussion of visiting missions, many members, including Sweden and Yugoslavia, noted with satisfaction the invitations of Australia and New Zealand.

A number of speakers, including those representing Iraq, the USSR and Yugoslavia, regretted that the unco-operative attitude of certain administering powers towards the sending of visiting missions by the Committee had continued to impede the full, speedy and effective implementation of the Declaration on the granting of independence.

On 1 September 1971, the Special Committee unanimously adopted a resolution by which it noted with satisfaction that New Zealand had responded positively to the requests contained in the relevant General Assembly resolutions by extending an invitation to the Special Committee to send a visiting mission to Niue and the Tokelau Islands in 1972. It also noted that the Trusteeship Council had decided, on the invitation of Australia and in consultation with the Special Committee, to dispatch a visiting mission to observe the elections to the Papua New Guinea House of Assembly in 1972 and that the membership of the mission would include two members of the Special Committee.

The Special Committee deeply regretted the negative attitude of certain administering powers which continued to ignore the repeated appeals made in that regard by the General Assembly and the Special Committee, thereby impeding the full implementation of the Declaration with respect to the territories under their administration. It called upon those administering powers to co-operate fully with the Committee by permitting the access of visiting groups to the territories under their administration.

The Committee asked its Chairman to continue

his consultations with the administering powers concerned.

Consideration by General Assembly

General aspects of the question of the implementation of the Declaration on the Granting of Independence to Colonial Countries and Peoples were considered by the General Assembly at plenary meetings held between 13 and 20 December 1971.

The Assembly had before it the report of the Special Committee covering its work in 1971. Chapters of the Special Committee's report dealing with the situation in specific territories were referred to the Assembly's Fourth Committee.

Also before the Assembly was a report of the Secretary-General on a Joint Meeting of the Special Committee on *Apartheid*, the Special Committee on the implementation of the Declaration on granting independence and the United Nations Council for Namibia. A consensus adopted by the Joint Meeting on 13 September 1971 was attached. The consensus referred to the agreement by the three bodies on the importance of periodic consultations with a view to achieving greater co-ordination and more effective action. The consensus also set forth a number of recommendations of the Joint Meeting, including one for an intensified information programme.

During the General Assembly debate, Members expressed the view that the process of decolonization was painfully slow.

The representative of Syria, who was Chairman of the Special Committee on the Implementation of the Declaration, said that the task of the Committee had been all the more difficult during the current year as the obstacles being placed in the path of decolonization were of the most arduous kind. In southern Africa, the adherents to colonialism and *apartheid* had continued to strengthen their position. The representatives of liberation movements and the Organization of African Unity (OAU) had confirmed to the members of the Special Committee's *Ad Hoc* Group which visited Africa in 1971 that the situation in the African colonial territories had further deteriorated. The only choice remaining to the Committee was to ask the United Nations, the States, and the specialized agencies to increase their material, financial, political and moral assistance to the colonial peoples.

The representative of Yugoslavia felt that on the part of some administering powers—namely, Australia and New Zealand—there was a more positive approach and readiness to co-operate in a meaningful way with the United Nations regarding the territories under their administration. He believed that the ending of the non-self-governing status of the territories under their administration

was already perceivable and that it was only a matter of time. In contrast, a total stagnation had occurred once again in the decolonization process in southern Africa. As a result, there was further deterioration of the situation in the area, which was increasingly becoming a potential hotbed of wider and dangerous conflicts.

The USSR pointed out that in the year that had just passed the world had witnessed the strengthening of resistance to the process of decolonization on the part of the imperialist powers, which were striving to keep colonial territories under their domination for the purpose of exploiting them economically and using them as military and strategic spring-boards. As the result of the liberation struggle, the majority of the countries of Africa had wrested their freedom from the colonial shackles, but world imperialism was making a desperate effort to maintain racist and colonial régimes on the continent.

Referring to the smaller territories, the USSR said that, using the pretext of association or integration, the colonial powers were attempting to keep them in their hands in order to use them for their economic, military and strategic purposes. The Special Committee should further intensify its efforts to implement the Declaration; it should concentrate its attention on trying to achieve the full and immediate implementation of decisions already taken by the United Nations on questions relating to the struggle against colonialism and racism.

The United Republic of Tanzania said the United Nations was faced, on the one hand, with new levels of determination by the colonial régimes to consolidate and perfect their machinery for holding people in bondage and, on the other, with negative and outright obstructionist attitudes of some major Western powers on decolonization. Thus, the struggle for freedom and independence by colonial peoples had become more difficult than it was in 1960, when the Declaration was adopted. In the year under review, the Special Committee had operated under very difficult circumstances. In the years ahead, the Special Committee would be faced with more and stronger opponents. It would be necessary for the Committee to expand the area of co-operation with the specialized agencies and other international organizations associated with the United Nations, and with non-governmental organizations. Also, it would be necessary to establish better channels of communication and co-operation with OAU and its subsidiary organ, the Liberation Committee, as well as with the liberation movements themselves.

Zambia observed that the urgent yet vexing question of the full implementation of the Declaration on the granting of independence was becoming academic in practice. The African peoples of Angola, Mozambique and Guinea (Bissau), of Zimbabwe, Namibia and South Africa, and, indeed, of certain other parts of the world, still languished under the yoke of colonial and racist oppression.

The situation in Angola, Mozambique, Guinea (Bissau), Namibia and Southern Rhodesia represented a great challenge to the international community, in the view of Chile. Committees and sub-committees had been set up and special assistance funds had been established for those peoples. However, positive results had not yet been produced and they could not be so long as the major Western powers continued to trade with, to give military assistance to, and indirectly to support, the white racist minorities and allow them to have complete control over entire populations.

Chile felt that large sections of world public opinion had not been adequately informed on that situation. There was a need for a massive world-wide campaign by the United Nations in order to do away with that state of affairs.

For the representative of Afghanistan, it was a matter of deep concern and disappointment to note that since the adoption of the Declaration in 1960, the process of decolonization, owing to the negative attitude of colonial powers, had been very slow. Some colonial powers, in open defiance of the relevant resolutions of the various organs of the United Nations, continued to perpetuate their illegal rule over colonial countries and peoples in different parts of the world.

Egypt observed that, 11 years after the adoption of the Declaration, the world was not yet rid of the old colonialism and the colonial battle line in Africa still held. This situation was a challenge to the United Nations Charter. A new resolution was the answer suggested to this challenge. Egypt was of the opinion that the defence of the Charter needed more than resolutions, strong as they might be. It was time for the Members to reflect on how the Charter could meet the challenge. Had the Charter been used sufficiently? Members should come with an answer.

On 20 December 1971, the General Assembly took a series of decisions on the implementation of the Declaration, with the adoption of resolution 2878(XXVI).

By the preamble of this resolution, the Assembly among other things expressed deep concern that, 11 years after the adoption of the Declaration on granting independence, millions of people lived under colonialist and racial repression, and it deplored the continued refusal of colonial powers to implement the Declaration. The Assembly also reiterated its view that racial discrimination in dependent territories could be eradicated fully by implementation of the Declaration.

By the operative part of the resolution, the Assembly among other things:

(1) reaffirmed its resolution 1514(XV) of 14 December 1960[7] and all other resolutions on decolonization, and called upon the administering powers to take all the necessary steps to enable the dependent peoples of the territories concerned to exercise fully and without further delay their inalienable right to self-determination and independence;

(2) approved the report of the Special Committee and its programme of work envisaged for 1972;

(3) urged all States, in particular the administering powers, and the specialized agencies and other organizations within the United Nations system to give effect to the recommendations contained in the report of the Special Committee;

(4) reaffirmed that the continuation of colonialism in all its forms and manifestations—including racism, *apartheid,* foreign economic exploitation and the waging of colonial wars—was incompatible with the Charter of the United Nations, the Universal Declaration of Human Rights and the Declaration on the Granting of Independence to Colonial Countries and Peoples and posed a threat to international peace and security;

(5) reaffirmed its recognition of the legitimacy of the struggle of the colonial peoples and peoples under alien domination to exercise their right to self-determination and independence by all the necessary means at their disposal;

(6) condemned the policies, pursued by certain colonial powers in the territories under their domination, of imposing non-representative régimes and constitutions, strengthening the position of foreign economic and other interests, misleading world opinion and encouraging foreign immigrants while evicting indigenous inhabitants;

(7) urged all States and the specialized agencies and other organizations within the United Nations system to provide, in consultation, as appropriate, with OAU, moral and material assistance to all peoples struggling for their freedom and independence in the colonial territories, and, in particular, to the national liberation movements of the territories in southern Africa and called attention in that connexion to OAU's Assistance Fund;

(8) requested all States to withhold assistance of any kind from the Governments of Portugal and South Africa and from the illegal racist minority régime in Southern Rhodesia until they renounced their policy of colonial domination and racial discrimination;

(9) requested the colonial powers to withdraw

---

[7]See footnote 4.

immediately and unconditionally their military bases and installations from colonial territories and to refrain from establishing new ones;

(10) requested the Special Committee to continue to seek suitable means for the immediate and full implementation of the Declaration on granting independence;

(11) requested the Special Committee to make concrete suggestions which could assist the Security Council in considering appropriate measures under the United Nations Charter with regard to developments in colonial territories which were likely to threaten international peace and security;

(12) requested the Special Committee to undertake a special study on the compliance of Member States with the Declaration and with other relevant resolutions on decolonization;

(13) requested the Special Committee to intensify its consideration of the small territories and to recommend to the General Assembly the most appropriate methods to enable the populations of those territories to exercise fully and without further delay their right to self-determination and independence;

(14) endorsed the proposal of the Special Committee to take steps, in consultation with OAU, to enable representatives of national liberation movements in the colonial territories in southern Africa to participate, whenever necessary and in an appropriate capacity, in its deliberations relating to those territories;

(15) requested the administering powers to co-operate with the Special Committee in the discharge of its mandate and, in particular, to participate in the work of the Committee relating to the territories under their administration;

(16) called upon the administering powers to co-operate fully with the Special Committee by permitting the access of visiting groups to colonial territories in order to secure first-hand information concerning the territories and to ascertain the wishes and aspirations of the inhabitants of those territories under their administration; and

(17) requested the Special Committee to assist the Economic and Social Council in the study to be made by the Council's Committee on Non-Governmental Organizations on how those organizations might assist in achieving the objectives of the Declaration on granting independence, bearing in mind the need to enlist the support of the non-governmental organizations.

General Assembly resolution 2878(XXVI) was adopted, by a recorded vote of 96 to 5, with 18 abstentions, on the proposal of Afghanistan, Algeria, Burundi, Cameroon, the Congo, Egypt, Equatorial Guinea, Ethiopia, Ghana, Guinea, India, Indonesia, Iraq, Kenya, the Libyan Arab Republic, Mali, Mongolia, Morocco, Nigeria, the People's Democratic Republic of Yemen, Rwanda,

Sierra Leone, Somalia, Sudan, the Syrian Arab Republic, Tunisia, Uganda, the United Republic of Tanzania, Yemen, Yugoslavia, Zaire and Zambia.

(For text of resolution and voting details, see DOCUMENTARY REFERENCES below.)

Turkey said that, while supporting the resolution, it had reservations with regard to the operative paragraphs calling for aid to liberation movements and for removal of military bases from territories. Turkey hoped that in the years ahead the Special Committee, together with the Committee on *Apartheid* and the Council for Namibia, would continue to seek appropriate and practical means for the full implementation of the Declaration.

On 20 December 1971, the General Assembly also took decisions on the question of dissemination of information on decolonization. Among other things, the Assembly approved the Special Committee's report on publicity for the work of the United Nations in the field of decolonization and affirmed the vital importance of urgently effecting the widest possible dissemination of information on the evils and dangers of colonialism, the continuing struggle for liberation being waged by the colonial peoples, particularly in southern Africa, and the efforts being made by the international community to eliminate the remaining vestiges of colonialism in all its forms and manifestations.

The Assembly asked the Secretary-General to continue to take concrete measures through all the media at his disposal, including publications, radio and television, to give widespread and continuous publicity to the work of the United Nations in the field of decolonization, to the situation in the colonial territories and to the continuing struggle for liberation being waged by the colonial peoples. Also, it asked him to intensify the activities of information centres in southern Africa, to maintain a close working relationship with OAU, to enlist help from non-governmental organizations in the dissemination of relevant information and to continue certain specified publications in other languages besides English and French.

The Assembly asked Member States, in particular the administering powers, to co-operate fully with the Secretary-General in disseminating information on decolonization.

Also, it invited all States, the specialized agencies and other governmental and non-governmental organizations to undertake, in co-operation with the Secretary-General and within their respective spheres of competence, the large-scale dissemination of the information referred to above.

These decisions were taken in adopting resolution 2879(XXVI), on the proposal of Algeria, Cameroon, Equatorial Guinea, Ethiopia, Ghana,

Guinea, India, Iran, Kenya, Malaysia, Morocco, Nigeria, the People's Democratic Republic of Yemen, Rwanda, Uganda, the United Republic of Tanzania, Yemen, Yugoslavia, Zaire and Zambia.

The resolution was adopted by a recorded vote of 110 to 2, with 8 abstentions. (For text of resolution and voting details, see DOCUMENTARY REFERENCES below.)

At its 1971 session, the General Assembly also adopted a resolution—2784(XXVI)—on the elimination of all forms of racial discrimination and a resolution—2787(XXVI)—on the importance of the universal realization of the right of peoples to self-determination and of the speedy granting of independence to colonial countries and peoples for the effective guarantee and observance of human rights. These two resolutions were adopted on 6 December 1971 on the recommendation of the Assembly's Third (Social, Humanitarian and Cultural) Committee.

By resolution 2784(XXVI), the General Assembly among other things: reaffirmed that *apartheid* was a crime against humanity; declared that racial discrimination in all its forms was a criminal affront to the conscience and dignity of mankind and emphatically reaffirmed its recognition and vigorous support of the legitimacy of the struggle of oppressed peoples everywhere, in particular in southern Africa, against colonial, racial and alien domination. (For text of resolution 2784(XXVI), see pp. 402-4.)

By resolution 2787(XXVI), the General Assembly among other things: confirmed the legality of the peoples' struggle for self-determination and liberation from colonial and foreign domination and alien subjugation by all available means consistent with the United Nations Charter; called upon all States dedicated to the ideals of freedom and peace to give all their political, moral and material assistance to peoples struggling for liberation, self-determination and independence against colonial and alien domination; recalled that it was the duty of every State to contribute through joint and independent action to the implementation of the principle of self-determination, in accordance with the provisions of the Charter; and urged the Security Council as well as States Members of the United Nations or members of the specialized agencies to take effective steps to ensure the implementation of the relevant United Nations resolutions on the elimination of colonialism and racism.

(For text of resolution 2787(XXVI), see pp. 423-24.)

DOCUMENTARY REFERENCES

Consideration by Special Committee

Special Committee on Situation with regard to Implementation of Declaration on Granting of Independence to Colonial Countries and Peoples, meetings 781-832.

Consideration by General Assembly

General Assembly—26th session
Fifth Committee, meeting 1488.
Plenary meetings 2016, 2020, 2023, 2024, 2028.

A/8388. Implementation of Declaration on Granting of Independence to Colonial Countries and Peoples; policies of *apartheid* of Government of South Africa; question of Namibia. Report of Secretary-General (attaching letter of 15 September 1971 from Chairman of 9th Meeting of Joint Meeting of Special Committee on *Apartheid*, Special Committee on Situation with regard to Implementation of Declaration on Granting of Independence to Colonial Countries and Peoples, and United Nations Council for Namibia, transmitting consensus of 13 September 1971).
A/8401. Report of Secretary-General on work of the Organization, 16 June 1970–15 June 1971, Part Two, Chapter I.
A/8401/Add.1. Introduction to report of Secretary-General, September 1971: Part One, Chapter V; Part II, Chapter VIII.
A/8423/Rev.1. Report of Special Committee on Situation with regard to Implementation of Declaration on Granting of Independence to Colonial Countries and Peoples (covering its work during 1971). Chapter I: Establishment, organization and activities of Special Committee; Chapter II: Military activities and arrangements by colonial powers in territories under their administration which might be impeding implementation of Declaration on Granting Independence to Colonial Countries and Peoples; Chapter IV: Question of sending visiting missions to territories.
A/8486. Letters of 26 October 1971 from Mongolia (transmitting letter of 24 September from German Democratic Republic).
A/L.662 And Add.1. Afghanistan, Algeria, Burundi, Cameroon, Congo, Egypt, Equatorial Guinea, Ethiopia, Ghana, Guinea, India, Indonesia, Iraq, Kenya, Libyan Arab Republic, Mali, Mongolia, Morocco, Nigeria, People's Democratic Republic of Yemen, Rwanda, Sierra Leone, Somalia, Sudan, Syrian Arab Republic, Tunisia, Uganda, United Republic of Tanzania, Yemen, Yugoslavia, Zaire, Zambia: draft resolution.
A/C.5/1428, A/8632. Administrative and financial implications of, *inter alia*, 32-power draft resolution, A/L.662. Statement by Secretary-General and report of Fifth Committee.

RESOLUTION 2878(XXVI), as proposed by 32 powers, A/L.662, adopted by Assembly on 20 December 1971, meeting 2028, by recorded vote of 96 to 5, with 18 abstentions, as follows:

In favour: Afghanistan, Albania, Algeria, Argentina, Bahrain, Botswana, Bulgaria, Burma, Burundi, Byelorussian SSR, Cameroon, Central African Republic, Ceylon, Chad, Chile, Colombia, Congo, Cuba, Cyprus, Czechoslovakia, Dahomey, Dominican Republic, Ecuador, Egypt, El Salvador, Equatorial Guinea, Ethiopia, Ghana, Greece, Guatemala, Guinea, Guyana, Haiti, Honduras, Hungary, India, Indonesia, Iran, Iraq, Israel, Ivory Coast, Jamaica, Jordan, Kenya, Khmer Republic, Kuwait, Laos, Lebanon, Lesotho, Liberia, Libyan Arab Republic, Madagascar, Malaysia, Malta, Mauritania, Mexico, Mongolia, Morocco, Nepal, Nicaragua, Niger, Nigeria, Oman, Pakistan, Panama, People's Democratic Republic of Yemen, Peru, Philippines, Poland, Romania, Rwanda, Saudi Arabia, Senegal, Sierra Leone, Singapore, Somalia, Sudan, Swaziland, Syrian Arab Republic, Thailand, Togo, Trinidad and Tobago, Tunisia, Turkey, Uganda, Ukrainian SSR, USSR, United Arab Emirates, United Republic of Tanzania, Upper Volta, Uruguay, Venezuela, Yemen, Yugoslavia, Zaire, Zambia.
Against: France, Portugal, South Africa, United Kingdom, United States.

Abstaining: Australia, Austria, Belgium, Brazil, Canada, Denmark, Fiji, Finland, Iceland, Ireland, Italy, Japan, Luxembourg, Netherlands, New Zealand, Norway, Spain, Sweden.

The General Assembly,

Recalling the Declaration on the Granting of Independence to Colonial Countries and Peoples, contained in its resolution 1514(XV) of 14 December 1960, and the programme of action for the full implementation of the Declaration, contained in its resolution 2621(XXV) of 12 October 1970,

Recalling all its previous resolutions concerning the implementation of the Declaration, in particular resolution 2708(XXV) of 14 December 1970,

Deeply concerned that eleven years after the adoption of the Declaration many Territories are still under colonial domination and that millions of dependent peoples live under conditions of ruthless and undisguised colonialist and racialist repression,

Deeply deploring the continued refusal of the colonial Powers, especially Portugal and South Africa, to implement the Declaration and other relevant resolutions on decolonization, particularly those relating to the Territories under Portuguese domination, Namibia and Southern Rhodesia,

Strongly deploring the policies of those States which, in defiance of the relevant resolutions of the Security Council, the General Assembly and the Special Committee on the Situation with regard to the Implementation of the Declaration on the Granting of Independence to Colonial Countries and Peoples, continue to co-operate with the Governments of Portugal and South Africa and with the illegal racist minority régime in Southern Rhodesia,

Deeply disturbed at the intransigent attitude of certain administering Powers which, despite the repeated appeals addressed to them by the General Assembly and the Special Committee, refuse to co-operate with the Special Committee in the discharge of the mandate entrusted to it by the General Assembly,

Reiterating its view that racial discrimination in dependent Territories can be eradicated fully and with the greatest speed by the faithful and complete implementation of the Declaration,

Noting with satisfaction that the Organization of African Unity has decided to convene an international conference against colonialism and *apartheid,* to be held at Oslo in May and June 1972,

1. *Reaffirms* its resolutions 1514(XV) and 2621(XXV) and all other resolutions on decolonization, and calls upon the administering Powers, in accordance with those resolutions, to take all the necessary steps to enable the dependent peoples of the Territories concerned to exercise fully and without further delay their inalienable right to self-determination and independence;

2. *Approves* the report of the Special Committee on the Situation with regard to the Implementation of the Declaration on the Granting of Independence to Colonial Countries and Peoples covering its work during 1971, including the programme of work envisaged for 1972;

3. *Urges* all States, in particular the administering Powers, and the specialized agencies and other organizations within the United Nations system to give effect to the relevant provisions of the programme of action contained in General Assembly resolution 2621(XXV) and to the recommendations contained in the report of the Special Committee for the speedy implementation of the Declaration and the relevant United Nations resolutions;

4. *Reaffirms* that the continuation of colonialism in all its forms and manifestations—including racism, *apartheid* and activities of foreign economic and other interests which exploit colonial peoples, as well as the waging of colonial wars to suppress national liberation movements in southern Africa—is incompatible with the Charter of the United Nations, the Universal Declaration of Human Rights and the Declaration on the Granting of Independence to Colonial Countries and Peoples and poses a threat to international peace and security;

5. *Reaffirms* its recognition of the legitimacy of the struggle of the colonial peoples and peoples under alien domination to exercise their right to self-determination and independence by all

the necessary means at their disposal, and notes with satisfaction the progress made in the colonial Territories by the national liberation movements, both through their struggle and through reconstruction programmes;

6. *Condemns* the policies, pursued by certain colonial Powers in the Territories under their domination, of imposing non-representative régimes and constitutions, strengthening the position of foreign economic and other interests, misleading world public opinion and encouraging the systematic influx of foreign immigrants while evicting, displacing and transferring the indigenous inhabitants to other areas, and calls upon those Powers to desist forthwith from such policies;

7. *Urges* all States and the specialized agencies and other organizations within the United Nations system to provide, in consultation, as appropriate, with the Organization of African Unity, moral and material assistance to all peoples struggling for their freedom and independence in the colonial Territories and, in particular, to the national liberation movements of the Territories in southern Africa, and in that connexion draws the attention of all States to the Assistance Fund for the Struggle against Colonialism and *Apartheid* of the Organization of African Unity;

8. *Requests* all States, directly and through their action in the specialized agencies and other organizations within the United Nations system, to withhold or continue to withhold assistance of any kind from the Governments of Portugal and South Africa and from the illegal racist minority régime in Southern Rhodesia until they renounce their policy of colonial domination and racial discrimination;

9. *Requests* the colonial Powers to withdraw immediately and unconditionally their military bases and installations from colonial Territories and to refrain from establishing new ones;

10. *Requests* the Special Committee to continue to seek suitable means for the immediate and full implementation of General Assembly resolutions 1514(XV) and 2621(XXV) in all Territories which have not yet attained independence and, in particular, to formulate specific proposals for the elimination of the remaining manifestations of colonialism and report thereon to the General Assembly at its twenty-seventh session;

11. *Requests* the Special Committee to make concrete suggestions which could assist the Security Council in considering appropriate measures under the Charter with regard to developments in colonial Territories which are likely to threaten international peace and security, and recommends that the Council take such suggestions fully into consideration;

12. *Requests* the Special Committee to undertake a special study on the compliance of Member States with the Declaration and with other relevant resolutions on decolonization, particularly those relating to the Territories under Portuguese domination, Namibia and Southern Rhodesia, and to report thereon to the General Assembly at its twenty-seventh session;

13. *Requests* the Special Committee to intensify its consideration of the small Territories and to recommend to the General Assembly the most appropriate methods and also the steps to be taken to enable the populations of those Territories to exercise fully and without further delay their right to self-determination and independence;

14. *Endorses* the proposal of the Special Committee to take steps, in consultation with the Organization of African Unity, to enable representatives of national liberation movements in the colonial Territories in southern Africa to participate, whenever necessary and in an appropriate capacity, in its deliberations relating to those Territories;

15. *Requests* the administering Powers to co-operate with the Special Committee in the discharge of its mandate and, in particular, to participate in the work of the Committee relating to the Territories under their administration;

16. *Calls upon* the administering Powers to co-operate fully with the Special Committee by permitting the access of visiting groups to the colonial Territories in order to secure first-hand information concerning the Territories and to ascertain the wishes and aspirations of the inhabitants of those Territories under their administration;

17. *Requests* the Special Committee to assist the Economic

and Social Council in the study envisaged in Council resolution 1651(LI) of 29 October 1971, bearing in mind the need to enlist the support of non-governmental organizations in consultative status with the Council in the achievement of the objectives of the Declaration and in the implementation of the relevant resolutions of the United Nations;

18. *Requests* the Secretary-General to provide the Special Committee with the facilities and personnel necessary for the implementation of the present resolution as well as the various resolutions on decolonization adopted by the General Assembly and the Special Committee.

A/L.663 and Corr.1 and Add.1. Algeria, Cameroon, Equatorial Guinea, Ethiopia, Ghana, Guinea, India, Iran, Kenya, Malaysia, Morocco, Nigeria, People's Democratic Republic of Yemen, Rwanda, Uganda, United Republic of Tanzania, Yemen, Yugoslavia, Zaire, Zambia: draft resolution.
A/C.5/1428, A/8632. Administrative and financial implications of, *inter alia*, 20-power draft resolution, A/L.663. Statement by Secretary-General and report of Fifth Committee.

RESOLUTION 2879(XXVI), as proposed by 20 powers, A/L.663, adopted by Assembly on 20 December 1971, meeting 2028, by recorded vote of 110 to 2, with 8 abstentions, as follows:

In favour: Afghanistan, Algeria, Argentina, Australia, Austria, Bahrain, Botswana, Bulgaria, Burma, Burundi, Byelorussian SSR, Cameroon, Canada, Central African Republic, Ceylon, Chad, Chile, Colombia, Congo, Cuba, Cyprus, Czechoslovakia, Dahomey, Denmark, Dominican Republic, Ecuador, Egypt, El Salvador, Equatorial Guinea, Ethiopia, Fiji, Finland, Ghana, Greece, Guatemala, Guinea, Guyana, Haiti, Honduras, Hungary, Iceland, India, Indonesia, Iran, Iraq, Ireland, Israel, Ivory Coast, Jamaica, Japan, Jordan, Kenya, Khmer Republic, Kuwait, Laos, Lebanon, Lesotho, Liberia, Libyan Arab Republic, Madagascar, Malawi, Malaysia, Mali, Malta, Mauritania, Mexico, Mongolia, Morocco, Nepal, New Zealand, Nicaragua, Niger, Nigeria, Norway, Oman, Pakistan, Panama, People's Democratic Republic of Yemen, Peru, Philippines, Poland, Romania, Rwanda, Saudi Arabia, Senegal, Sierra Leone, Singapore, Somalia, Spain, Sudan, Swaziland, Sweden, Syrian Arab Republic, Thailand, Togo, Trinidad and Tobago, Tunisia, Turkey, Uganda, Ukrainian SSR, USSR, United Arab Emirates, United Republic of Tanzania, Upper Volta, Uruguay, Venezuela, Yemen, Yugoslavia, Zaire, Zambia.
Against: Portugal, South Africa.
Abstaining: Belgium, Brazil, France, Italy, Luxembourg, Netherlands, United Kingdom, United States.

The General Assembly,

Having examined the chapters of the report of the Special Committee on the Situation with regard to the Implementation of the Declaration on the Granting of Independence to Colonial Countries and Peoples relating to the question of publicity for the work of the United Nations in the field of decolonization,

Recalling its resolution 1514(XV) of 14 December 1960, containing the Declaration on the Granting of Independence to Colonial Countries and Peoples, and its resolution 2621(XXV) of 12 October 1970, containing the programme of action for the full implementation of the Declaration,

Conscious of the urgent need to intensify widespread and continuous dissemination of information on the work of the United Nations in the field of decolonization, on the situation in the colonial Territories and on the continuing struggle for liberation being waged by the colonial peoples and the activities of their national liberation movements,

Taking into account the suggestions of the Special Committee as well as the views of the Office of Public Information on the implementation of these suggestions, as reflected in the relevant chapters of the report of the Special Committee,

Taking into account the recommendations of the Fifth Committee relating to the report of the Secretary-General on the review and reappraisal of United Nations information policies and activities, and noting the report of the Secretary-General on the joint meeting of the Special Committee on the Situation with regard to the Implementation of the Declaration on the Granting of Independence to Colonial Countries and Peoples, the Special Committee on *Apartheid* and the United Nations Council for Namibia,

Recognizing the importance of publicity as an instrument for furthering the aims and purposes of the Declaration and the need for the Office of Public Information to intensify its efforts to acquaint world public opinion with all aspects of the problems of decolonization,

1. *Approves* the chapters of the report of the Special Committee on the Situation with regard to the Implementation of the Declaration on the Granting of Independence to Colonial Countries and Peoples relating to the question of publicity for the work of the United Nations in the field of decolonization;

2. *Affirms* the vital importance of urgently effecting the widest possible dissemination of information on the evils and dangers of colonialism, the continuing struggle for liberation being waged by the colonial peoples, particularly in southern Africa, and the efforts being made by the international community to eliminate the remaining vestiges of colonialism in all its forms and manifestations;

3. *Requests* the Secretary-General, having regard to the suggestions of the Special Committee, to continue to take concrete measures through all the media at his disposal, including publications, radio and television, to give widespread and continuous publicity to the work of the United Nations in the field of decolonization, to the situation in the colonial Territories and to the continuing struggle for liberation being waged by the colonial peoples and, *inter alia:*

(*a*) To intensify the activities of the information centres located in southern Africa, including the establishment of an additional information centre where appropriate;

(*b*) To maintain a close working relationship with the Organization of African Unity by holding periodic consultations and a systematic exchange of the relevant information with that organization;

(*c*) To enlist, from the non-governmental organizations in consultative status with the Economic and Social Council and from those non-governmental organizations having a special interest in the field of decolonization, support in the dissemination of the relevant information;

(*d*) To continue to publish, in consultation with the Special Committee, selected issues of the periodical *Objective: Justice* and the bulletin "United Nations and Southern Africa" in other languages besides English and French;

4. *Requests* Member States, in particular the administering Powers, to co-operate fully with the Secretary-General in the discharge of the tasks entrusted to him under paragraph 3 above;

5. *Invites* all States, the specialized agencies and other organizations within the United Nations system and non-governmental organizations in consultative status with the Economic and Social Council, as well as other non-governmental organizations having a special interest in the field of decolonization, to undertake, in co-operation with the Secretary-General and within their respective spheres of competence, the large-scale dissemination of the information referred to in paragraph 2 above;

6. *Requests* the Secretary-General, in consultation with the Special Committee, to collect and prepare on a continuous basis for redissemination by the Office of Public Information, basic material, studies and articles relating to various aspects of the problems of decolonization;

7. *Requests* the Secretary-General to report to the Special Committee on the implementation of the present resolution;

8. *Requests* the Special Committee to continue to examine the question at its next session and to report thereon to the General Assembly at its twenty-seventh session.

Membership of Special Committee
A/8276. Letter of 11 January 1971 from United Kingdom.
A/8277. Letter of 11 January 1971 from United States.

A/8611. Letter of 13 December 1971 from Poland.
A/8429. Resolutions adopted by General Assembly during its 26th

session, 21 September–22 December 1971. Other decisions, p. 23.

Implementation of Declaration by specialized agencies and other international institutions

Consideration by Special Committee

In 1971, the General Assembly's Special Committee on the Situation with regard to the Implementation of the Declaration on the Granting of Independence to Colonial Countries and Peoples[8] again examined the question of the implementation of the Declaration by the specialized agencies and the international institutions associated with the United Nations. The Committee considered this question at plenary meetings held between 16 July and 21 October.

The Special Committee had before it a report submitted by the Secretary-General in accordance with a General Assembly resolution of 14 December 1970[9] containing information on the implementation of the Declaration and other relevant Assembly resolutions by the following specialized agencies and international institutions: the International Labour Organisation (ILO); the Food and Agriculture Organization of the United Nations (FAO); the United Nations Educational, Scientific and Cultural Organization (UNESCO); the World Health Organization (WHO); the International Bank for Reconstruction and Development; the International Monetary Fund; the International Civil Aviation Organization (ICAO); the Universal Postal Union (UPU); the International Telecommunication Union (ITU); the World Meteorological Organization (WMO); the Inter-Governmental Maritime Consultative Organization (IMCO); the International Atomic Energy Agency (IAEA); the United Nations Conference on Trade and Development (UNCTAD); the United Nations Industrial Development Organization (UNIDO); the United Nations Development Programme (UNDP); the United Nations Children's Fund (UNICEF); the Office of the United Nations High Commissioner for Refugees (UNHCR); the United Nations Institute for Training and Research (UNITAR); the United Nations/FAO World Food Programme (WFP); the League of Arab States; the Organization of African Unity (OAU); and the Organization of American States (OAS).

The Special Committee also had before it a draft resolution on the question sponsored by Afghanistan, Bulgaria, Ecuador, Ethiopia, India, Iraq, Mali, Sierra Leone, the Syrian Arab Republic and the United Republic of Tanzania.

In the course of the discussion, India said the specialized agencies had played an important role in assisting the liberation movements in their struggle to put an end to colonialism. India had noted with satisfaction the specific steps taken by

agencies—such as UNESCO, WHO, ILO, FAO, the High Commissioner for Refugees and ICAO—in implementing the Declaration. It had, however, read with regret the replies of the International Bank and of the International Monetary Fund contained in the report of the Secretary-General. These two agencies were in positions of considerable means and possibilities, and it was in that context that India regretted the lack of assistance from them.

Ethiopia said it was grateful to the many organizations of the United Nations family which had, in close co-operation with the United Nations High Commissioner for Refugees and in consultation with OAU, increased their assistance to refugees from the colonial territories in southern Africa. At the same time, there still remained the urgent need for larger participation, by such organizations as UNDP and the International Bank in this field of endeavour, in particular in the formulation and execution of projects beneficial to refugees, including the extension of advice and assistance to Governments of countries of asylum in the preparation of the necessary requests.

The representative of the USSR said only a few specialized agencies and international organizations like UNESCO, WHO, UNICEF and ILO had endeavoured to implement the Declaration on granting independence. He observed that while certain measures had been adopted by the above-mentioned organizations in the field of assistance to refugees, other specialized agencies like the International Bank and the International Monetary Fund had done little or nothing from the point of view of granting assistance to colonial peoples. The USSR representative did not agree with the claims that the basic charters of various specialized agencies prevented them from any possibility of implementing the measures that had been recommended by the General Assembly. In the view of the USSR, a specific course of action based upon the principles and objectives of the United Nations Charter and instituted by the General Assembly and the Security Council must be followed by all organizations within the United Nations family.

Sweden welcomed the fact that several agencies had begun to plan or had embarked on concrete programmes of assistance to the colonized peo-

[8]See Y.U.N., 1960, pp. 49-50, resolution 1514(XV) of 14 December 1960, containing text of Declaration.
[9]See Y.U.N., 1970 pp. 711-13, text of resolution 2704(XXV).

ples. The difficulties with which the agencies were faced must be recognized and respected, however. Sweden held that the agencies could not act outside their own statutes and should not be pressed to do so. Concerning the draft resolution before the Special Committee, the representative of Sweden said some provisions did not take sufficiently into account the constitutional position of the various agencies. Sweden was not, therefore, able to support the draft resolution as a whole.

Several Special Committee members, including Fiji, Trinidad and Tobago, Venezuela and the Ivory Coast, while being in favour of the draft resolution, had reservations with regard to those paragraphs which, in their view, did not take into account the constitutional position of the various agencies.

The Special Committee adopted the draft resolution on 21 October 1971. It thereby, among other things:

(*a*) reaffirmed that the recognition by the General Assembly, the Security Council and other United Nations bodies of the legitimacy of the struggle of colonial peoples to achieve freedom and independence entailed the extension by the United Nations system of organizations of all the necessary moral and material assistance to the national liberation movements in colonial territories, including especially the populations in the liberated areas of those territories;

(*b*) expressed its appreciation to the Office of the United Nations High Commissioner for Refugees, to UNESCO and to those specialized agencies and other organizations which had co-operated in varying degrees with the United Nations in the implementation of the relevant General Assembly resolutions;

(*c*) reiterated its request that the specialized agencies and other organizations within the United Nations system, including in particular UNDP and the International Bank, should take measures, within their respective spheres of competence, to increase the scope of their assistance to refugees from colonial territories, including assistance to the Governments concerned in the preparation and execution of projects beneficial to those refugees, and to introduce the greatest possible measure of flexibility in the relevant procedures;

(*d*) reiterated its urgent appeal to the specialized agencies and other organizations within the United Nations system to render all possible moral and material assistance to the peoples struggling for their liberation from colonial rule and, in particular, to work out, with the active co-operation of OAU and, through it, of the national liberation movements, concrete programmes for assisting the peoples of Southern Rhodesia, Namibia and the territories under Portuguese administration, including in particular the populations in the liberated areas of those territories;

(*e*) recommended that the General Assembly should once again urge the specialized agencies and other organizations within the United Nations system to discontinue all collaboration with the Governments of Portugal and South Africa, as well as with the illegal régime of Southern Rhodesia, in accordance with the relevant resolutions of the General Assembly and those of the Security Council relating to the colonial territories in southern Africa; and

(*f*) urged once again that the specialized agencies and other organizations within the United Nations system, and in particular the International Bank and the International Monetary Fund, take all the necessary measures to withhold financial, economic, technical and other assistance from the Governments of Portugal and South Africa until they renounced their policies of racial discrimination and colonial domination.

Consideration by Economic and Social Council

Implementation by the specialized agencies and international institutions associated with the United Nations of the Declaration on granting independence to colonial countries and peoples was also considered in 1971 by the Economic and Social Council. Among other things, the Council discussed the report of its President on this subject.

In his report, the Council President stated he had held consultations with the Chairman of the General Assembly's Special Committee on the implementation of the Declaration. Among other things, they had agreed that considerable progress had been made under the aegis of the High Commissioner for Refugees in enlarging participation in refugee assistance programmes benefiting colonial peoples in Africa. However, the High Commissioner's capacity to help the refugees would be enhanced if host Governments were to give high priority to development projects carried out in co-operation with the agencies which would benefit the refugees, and if the Governments would grant the refugees adequate legal status, including, among other things, work permits.

With reference to the Special Committee's wish that UNDP and the International Bank participate more actively in refugee assistance programmes, the President stated he had been informed of UNDP's readiness, subject to submission of requests by Governments and authorization by the UNDP Governing Council, to consider educational and training projects beneficial to refugees from within the resources available for inter-regional projects. UNDP was also considering certain proposals for co-operation with OAU. The President and the Chairman had agreed on the need to bring into proper relationship the education and training activities of the various United Nations organizations and to maintain close contact with OAU's Bureau for the Placement and Education of African Refugees.

The President noted that a number of agencies had sent special missions to consult with OAU on the extension of moral and material assistance, through OAU, to national liberation movements in colonial territories.

The Council President also reported that he and the Special Committee Chairman had agreed that it was for the executive heads of the agencies to bring to the attention of their respective legislative bodies, for necessary decisions, any constitutional, legal or other difficulties in connexion with the Assembly's call for discontinuance of aid to régimes pursuing colonialist and racialist policies in southern Africa. Action in this respect by the UNESCO General Conference was commended.

The President and the Chairman, in addition, felt that difficulties faced by some agencies in providing for participation of representatives of liberation movements of the territories in agency conferences and other meetings were not incapable of solution.

On 29 October 1971, the Economic and Social Council took several decisions on the subject. Endorsing the conclusions and suggestions contained in the Council President's report, it recommended them for action by the specialized agencies and organizations within the United Nations system.

The Council instructed its Committee on Non-Governmental Organizations to study how non-governmental organizations in consultative status with the Council assisted in the achievement of the objectives of the Declaration and other relevant resolutions of the General Assembly.

It also decided to transmit to the General Assembly the reports of the President of the Council and the Committee for Programme and Co-ordination in order to facilitate the Assembly's consideration of the matter.

These decisions were set forth in Council resolution 1651(LI), which was adopted, by 16 votes to 0, with 7 abstentions, on a proposal by Pakistan, Tunisia and Yugoslavia. (For text of resolution, see DOCUMENTARY REFERENCES below.)

Consideration by General Assembly

General Assembly discussion on the implementation of the Declaration on the Granting of Independence to Colonial Countries and Peoples by the specialized agencies and the international institutions associated with the United Nations took place mainly in the Assembly's Fourth Committee.

On 20 December 1971, the Assembly adopted a resolution setting forth its decisions on the question.

By the preamble, the Assembly among other things expressed its awareness of the urgent need of the peoples and the national liberation movements of several colonial territories, particularly in the liberated areas of some of those territories, for assistance from the specialized agencies and other organizations in the United Nations system, especially in the fields of education, training, health and nutrition.

By the operative provisions of the resolution, the Assembly approved the Special Committee's report on the question and reaffirmed that the recognition by the General Assembly, the Security Council and other United Nations bodies of the legitimacy of the struggle of colonial peoples to achieve freedom and independence entailed the extension by the United Nations system of organizations of all necessary moral and material assistance to the national liberation movements, including especially the liberated areas of the colonial territories.

The Assembly expressed its appreciation to the Office of the United Nations High Commissioner for Refugees, to UNESCO and to those other specialized agencies and organizations which had co-operated in varying degrees with the United Nations in the implementation of the relevant resolutions of the General Assembly. It reiterated its urgent appeal to the specialized agencies and other organizations within the United Nations system to render all possible moral and material assistance to the peoples in Africa struggling for their liberation from colonial rule and, in particular, to work out, with the active co-operation of OAU and, through it, of the national liberation movements, concrete programmes for assisting the peoples of Southern Rhodesia, Namibia and the territories under Portuguese administration, including in particular the populations in the liberated areas of those territories.

Also, the Assembly reiterated its request that the specialized agencies and other organizations within the United Nations system, including in particular UNDP and the International Bank, should take measures, within their respective spheres of competence, to increase the scope of their assistance to refugees from colonial territories, including assistance to the Governments concerned in the preparation and execution of projects beneficial to these refugees.

It then requested the specialized agencies and other organizations within the United Nations system to discontinue all collaboration with the Governments of Portugal and South Africa, as well as with the illegal régime in Southern Rhodesia.

The Assembly urged once again that the

specialized agencies and other organizations within the United Nations system, in particular the International Bank and the International Monetary Fund, take all necessary measures to withhold financial, economic, technical and other assistance from the Governments of Portugal and South Africa until they renounced their policies of racial discrimination and colonial domination.

Also, it urged all the specialized agencies and other international institutions concerned, in particular the Bank, the Monetary Fund, ICAO, UPU, ITU and IMCO, to intensify their efforts aimed at facilitating the effective implementation, without further delay, of the relevant provisions of the various Security Council resolutions on colonial territories in southern Africa.

The Assembly invited the specialized agencies to continue to examine, in consultation with OAU, procedures for the participation, where necessary and appropriate, in conferences, seminars and other regional meetings convened by the specialized agencies, of representatives of the national liberation movements in the colonial territories in Africa in an appropriate capacity and, to facilitate this, asked the Economic and Social Council to submit appropriate recommendations in consultation with the Special Committee.

It recommended that all Governments intensify their efforts in the specialized agencies and other organizations within the United Nations system of which they were members in order to ensure the full and effective implementation of the Declaration and other relevant resolutions of the United Nations; and it recommended that, in order to facilitate such action, the specialized agencies and other organizations within the United Nations system should request their executive heads to present to their respective governing and legislative organs, in a specific and systematic manner, recommendations on decolonization adopted by competent United Nations bodies, together with a full analysis of the issues and problems involved, if any, and concrete suggestions for the implementation of these recommendations.

Also, the Assembly asked the Economic and Social Council to continue to consider, in consultation with the Special Committee, appropriate measures for co-ordination of the policies and activities of the specialized agencies and other organizations within the United Nations system in implementing the relevant resolutions of the General Assembly.

The General Assembly adopted this resolution—2874(XXVI)—by a recorded vote of 93 to 4, with 27 abstentions. It acted on the recommendation of its Fourth Committee, which approved the text by a recorded vote of 73 to 4, with 23 abstentions. The text was sponsored in the Fourth Committee by Afghanistan, Bulgaria, Chile, Ecuador, Egypt, Ethiopia, Ghana, Guinea, Guyana, India, Indonesia, Iraq, Kenya, Mali, Mauritania, Mongolia, Nigeria, the People's Democratic Republic of Yemen, Rwanda, Sierra Leone, Sudan, the Syrian Arab Republic, the United Republic of Tanzania, Yugoslavia and Zambia. (For text of resolution and voting details, see DOCUMENTARY REFERENCES below.)

At the time of the vote in the Fourth Committee, a number of Members, including Colombia, Costa Rica, Honduras, the Ivory Coast, Madagascar, Trinidad and Tobago, Turkey and Venezuela, expressed reservations regarding certain paragraphs of the resolution, in particular those that could give the impression that the constitutional limitations of the United Nations institutions had not been taken fully into account.

The United States said it was concerned at the trend among the specialized agencies to deal with political matters and it felt the resolution encouraged that trend. The politicization of the specialized agencies would prevent them from carrying out the task entrusted to them, in the view of the United States.

At the plenary meeting of the General Assembly on 20 December 1971, the United Kingdom declared that it was increasingly concerned by the tendency of the specialized agencies to become involved in political matters at the expense and to the detriment of their legitimate activities. The United Kingdom was convinced that it was improper for the General Assembly to seek to exert pressure on the agencies in respect of issues both of principle and of policy which should be decided in the light of their respective constitutions.

Norway said that it could not support the request that all collaboration between the agencies and certain Governments and régimes should be discontinued. Denmark and Honduras also expressed reservations on the text.

DOCUMENTARY REFERENCES

Special Committee, meetings 798, 809, 823, 829, 830.

Economic and Social Council—51st session
Plenary meetings 1792, 1805.

E/5012 (Part I). Development and co-ordination of activities of organizations within United Nations system. Report of Administrative Committee on Co-ordination, Chapter II.

E/5033 and Add.1-4. Report of Secretary-General (transmitting documents A/8314 and Add.1-4).
E/5038. Report of Committee for Programme and Co-ordination (CPC) on its 9th session, 24 May–14 June 1971, Chapter V.
E/5073. Resolutions adopted by Economic and Social Council during its 51st session, 5-31 July 1971. Other decisions, p. 27.
E/5072/Rev.1. Report of CPC on its 10th session, 13-17 September and 5, 8, 10, 12 and 17 November 1971, Chapter II.

E/5079. Report of President of Economic and Social Council.

E/L.1467. Pakistan, Tunisia, Yugoslavia: draft resolution.

RESOLUTION 1651(LI), as proposed by 3 powers, E/L.1467, as orally revised by sponsors, adopted by Council on 29 October 1971, meeting 1805, by 16 votes to 0, with 7 abstentions.

The Economic and Social Council,

Having considered the item entitled "Implementation of the Declaration on the Granting of Independence to Colonial Countries and Peoples by the specialized agencies and the international institutions associated with the United Nations,"

Having examined the comprehensive report of the Secretary-General on the item,

Having also examined the report of the President of the Council, the report of the Committee for Programme and Co-ordination on its tenth session, as well as the relevant chapter of the thirty-seventh report of the Administrative Committee on Co-ordination,

1. *Takes note* of the report of the President of the Council and endorses the conclusions and suggestions contained therein;

2. *Recommends* these conclusions and suggestions for action by the specialized agencies and organizations within the United Nations system;

3. *Instructs* its Committee on Non-Governmental Organizations to study how non-governmental organizations in consultative status with the Council assist in the achievement of the objectives of the Declaration and other relevant resolutions of the General Assembly, and to report to the Council at its fifty-fourth session, taking into due account the deliberations on this item at the resumed fifty-first session of the Council;

4. *Decides* to transmit to the General Assembly the reports of the President of the Council and the Committee for Programme and Co-ordination in order to facilitate the consideration of the item by the Fourth Committee.

General Assembly—26th session
Fourth Committee, meetings 1953, 1956-1958, 1960, 1962-1965, 1968-1971.
Plenary meeting 2028.

A/8314 and Add.1-5 and Add.6 (Parts I and II). Report of Secretary-General.

A/8401. Report of Secretary-General on work of the Organization, 16 June 1970–15 June 1971, Part Two, Chapter I C 5.

A/8403. Report of Economic and Social Council on work of its 50th and 51st sessions, Chapter XX.

A/8403/Add.1. Addendum to report of Economic and Social Council on its resumed 51st session, Chapter VII.

A/8423/Rev.1. Report of Special Committee, Chapter III.

A/8480. Report of Secretary-General (on report of Economic and Social Council, Chapter XX).

A/C.4/L.1007. Afghanistan, Bulgaria, Chile, Ecuador, Egypt, Ethiopia, Ghana, Guinea, Guyana, India, Indonesia, Iraq, Kenya, Mali, Mauritania, Mongolia, Nigeria, People's Democratic Republic of Yemen, Rwanda, Sierra Leone, Sudan, Syrian Arab Republic, United Republic of Tanzania, Yugoslavia, Zambia: draft resolution, approved by Fourth Committee on 15 December 1971, meeting 1970, by recorded vote of 73 to 4, with 23 abstentions, as follows:

In favour: Afghanistan, Algeria, Barbados, Botswana, Bulgaria, Burma, Burundi, Byelorussian SSR, Cameroon, Central African Republic, Ceylon, Chile, Colombia, Cuba, Czechoslovakia, Ecuador, Egypt, Equatorial Guinea, Ethiopia, Gambia, Ghana, Guyana, Hungary, India, Indonesia, Iran, Iraq, Israel, Ivory Coast, Jamaica, Jordan, Kenya, Khmer Republic, Kuwait, Lebanon, Liberia, Libyan Arab Republic, Madagascar, Malaysia, Mali, Mexico, Mongolia, Morocco, Nepal, Niger, Nigeria, People's Democratic Republic of Yemen, Peru, Philippines,

Poland, Qatar, Romania, Rwanda, Saudi Arabia, Senegal, Singapore, Sudan, Swaziland, Syrian Arab Republic, Togo, Trinidad and Tobago, Tunisia, Turkey, Uganda, Ukrainian SSR, USSR, United Republic of Tanzania, Upper Volta, Venezuela, Yemen, Yugoslavia, Zaire, Zambia.

Against: Portugal, South Africa, United Kingdom, United States.

Abstaining: Argentina, Australia, Austria, Belgium, Brazil, Canada, Costa Rica, Denmark, Fiji, Finland, France, Greece, Iceland, Ireland, Italy, Japan, Luxembourg, Netherlands, New Zealand, Norway, Spain, Sweden, Uruguay.

A/8620. Report of Fourth Committee.

RESOLUTION 2874(XXVI), as recommended by Fourth Committee, A/8620, adopted by Assembly on 20 December 1971, meeting 2028, by recorded vote of 93 to 4, with 27 abstentions, as follows:

In favour: Afghanistan, Algeria, Bahrain, Barbados, Botswana, Bulgaria, Burma, Burundi, Byelorussian SSR, Cameroon, Central African Republic, Ceylon, Chad, Chile, Colombia, Congo, Cuba, Cyprus, Czechoslovakia, Dahomey, Dominican Republic, Ecuador, Egypt, El Salvador, Equatorial Guinea, Ethiopia, Gambia, Ghana, Guatemala, Guinea, Guyana, Haiti, Honduras, Hungary, India, Indonesia, Iran, Iraq, Israel, Ivory Coast, Jamaica, Jordan, Kenya, Khmer Republic, Kuwait, Laos, Lebanon, Liberia, Libyan Arab Republic, Madagascar, Malaysia, Mali, Malta, Mauritania, Mexico, Mongolia, Morocco, Nepal, Niger, Nigeria, Oman, Pakistan, Panama, People's Democratic Republic of Yemen, Peru, Philippines, Poland, Romania, Rwanda, Saudi Arabia, Senegal, Sierra Leone, Singapore, Somalia, Sudan, Swaziland, Syrian Arab Republic, Thailand, Togo, Trinidad and Tobago, Tunisia, Turkey, Uganda, Ukrainian SSR, USSR, United Arab Emirates, United Republic of Tanzania, Upper Volta, Venezuela, Yemen, Yugoslavia, Zaire, Zambia.

Against: Portugal, South Africa, United Kingdom, United States.

Abstaining: Argentina, Australia, Austria, Belgium, Brazil, Canada, Costa Rica, Denmark, Fiji, Finland, France, Greece, Iceland, Ireland, Italy, Japan, Lesotho, Luxembourg, Malawi, Netherlands, New Zealand, Nicaragua, Norway, Paraguay, Spain, Sweden, Uruguay.

The General Assembly,

Having considered the item entitled "Implementation of the Declaration on the Granting of Independence to Colonial Countries and Peoples by the specialized agencies and the international institutions associated with the United Nations,"

Recalling the Declaration on the Granting of Independence to Colonial Countries and Peoples, contained in its resolution 1514(XV) of 14 December 1960, and the programme of action for the full implementation of the Declaration, contained in its resolution 2621(XXV) of 12 October 1970,

Recalling further its resolutions 2311(XXII) of 14 December 1967, 2426(XXIII) of 18 December 1968, 2555(XXIV) of 12 December 1969 and 2704(XXV) of 14 December 1970, as well as other relevant resolutions,

Taking into account the relevant resolutions of the Security Council on southern Africa, in particular resolution 277(1970) of 18 March 1970 on the question of Southern Rhodesia and resolution 283(1970) of 29 July 1970 on the question of Namibia,

Taking into account with appreciation the reports submitted on the item by the Secretary-General, the Economic and Social Council and the Special Committee on the Situation with regard to the Implementation of the Declaration on the Granting of Independence to Colonial Countries and Peoples,

Conscious of the urgent need of the peoples and the national liberation movements of several colonial Territories, particularly in the liberated areas of some of those Territories, for assistance from the specialized agencies and other organizations within the United Nations system, especially in the fields of education, training, health and nutrition,

Recognizing the need for further and more effective measures to be taken for the speedy implementation of the Declaration and other relevant resolutions of the General Assembly, the Security Council and the Special Committee by all the organizations of the United Nations system within their respective spheres of competence,

Noting with deep concern that, while several of the specialized agencies and organizations within the United Nations system have provided considerable assistance to refugees from the colonial Territories in Africa, many of them have not extended their full co-operation to the United Nations in the implementation of the provisions of the relevant resolutions relating to providing assistance to the national liberation movements and to discontinuing all collaboration with the Governments of Portugal and South Africa, as well as with the illegal régime in Southern Rhodesia,

Noting with appreciation that some of the organizations have embarked on or are taking steps to formulate, in consultation with the Organization of African Unity, concrete programmes for providing assistance, within their spheres of competence, to the peoples of the colonial Territories striving to liberate themselves from colonial domination,

Mindful of the necessity to keep under continuous review the activities of the specialized agencies and other organizations within the United Nations system in the implementation of the various United Nations decisions relating to decolonization,

1. *Approves* the chapter of the report of the Special Committee on the Situation with regard to the Implementation of the Declaration on the Granting of Independence to Colonial Countries and Peoples relating to the item;

2. *Reaffirms* that the recognition by the General Assembly, the Security Council and other United Nations bodies of the legitimacy of the struggle of colonial peoples to achieve freedom and independence entails, as a corollary, the extension by the United Nations system of organizations of all necessary moral and material assistance to the national liberation movements in those Territories, including especially the liberated areas of the colonial Territories;

3. *Expresses its appreciation* to the Office of the United Nations High Commissioner for Refugees, to the United Nations Educational, Scientific and Cultural Organization and to those other specialized agencies and organizations within the United Nations system which have co-operated in varying degrees with the United Nations in the implementation of the relevant resolutions of the General Assembly;

4. *Reiterates* its urgent appeal to the specialized agencies and other organizations within the United Nations system to render all possible moral and material assistance to the peoples in Africa struggling for their liberation from colonial rule and, in particular, to work out, with the active co-operation of the Organization of African Unity and, through it, of the national liberation movements, concrete programmes for assisting the peoples of Southern Rhodesia, Namibia and the Territories under Portuguese administration, including in particular the populations in the liberated areas of those Territories;

5. *Reiterates* its request that the specialized agencies and other organizations within the United Nations system, including in particular the United Nations Development Programme and the International Bank for Reconstruction and Development, should take measures, within their respective spheres of competence, to increase the scope of their assistance to refugees from colonial Territories, including assistance to the Governments concerned in the preparation and execution of projects beneficial to these refugees, and to introduce the greatest possible measure of flexibility in the relevant procedures:

6. *Requests* the specialized agencies and other organizations within the United Nations system to discontinue all collaboration with the Governments of Portugal and South Africa as well as with the illegal régime in Southern Rhodesia, in accordance with the relevant resolutions of the General Assembly and those of the Security Council relating to colonial Territories in southern Africa;

7. *Urges once again* the specialized agencies and other organizations within the United Nations system, in particular the International Bank for Reconstruction and Development and the International Monetary Fund, to take all necessary measures to withhold financial, economic, technical and other assistance from the Governments of Portugal and South Africa until they renounce their policies of racial discrimination and colonial domination;

8. *Urges* all the specialized agencies and other international institutions concerned, in particular the International Bank for Reconstruction and Development, the International Monetary Fund, the International Civil Aviation Organization, the Universal Postal Union, the International Telecommunication Union and the Inter-Governmental Maritime Consultative Organization, to intensify their efforts aimed at facilitating the effective implementation, without further delay, of the relevant provisions of the various Security Council resolutions on colonial Territories in southern Africa, especially paragraphs 9 (*b*), 11 and 23 of resolution 277(1970) and paragraph 14 of resolution 283(1970);

9. *Invites* the specialized agencies to continue to examine, in consultation with the Organization of African Unity, procedures for the participation, where necessary and appropriate, in conferences, seminars and other regional meetings convened by the specialized agencies, of representatives of the national liberation movements in the colonial Territories in Africa in an appropriate capacity and, in order to facilitate examination of this matter by the specialized agencies, requests the Economic and Social Council, in consultation with the Special Committee and taking into account the views of the Organization of African Unity, to submit appropriate recommendations;

10. *Recommends* that all Governments intensify their efforts in the specialized agencies and other organizations within the United Nations system of which they are members in order to ensure the full and effective implementation of the Declaration and other relevant resolutions of the United Nations;

11. *Recommends* that, in order to facilitate implementation of paragraph 10 above, the specialized agencies and other organizations within the United Nations system should request their executive heads to present to their respective governing and legislative organs, in a specific and systematic manner, recommendations on decolonization adopted by competent United Nations bodies, together with a full analysis of the issues and problems involved, if any, and concrete suggestions for the implementation of these recommendations;

12. *Requests* the Economic and Social Council to continue to consider, in consultation with the Special Committee, appropriate measures for co-ordination of the policies and activities of the specialized agencies and other organizations within the United Nations system in implementing the relevant resolutions of the General Assembly;

13. *Requests* the Secretary-General:

(*a*) To prepare for submission to the relevant bodies concerned with related aspects of the present item, with the assistance of the specialized agencies and other organizations within the United Nations system, a report on the action taken since the circulation of his comprehensive report, or envisaged by those organizations in implementation of the relevant United Nations resolutions, including the present resolution;

(*b*) To continue to assist the specialized agencies and other organizations within the United Nations system in working out appropriate measures for implementing the present resolution and to report thereon to the General Assembly at its twenty-seventh session;

14. *Requests* the Special Committee to continue to examine the question and to report thereon to the General Assembly at its twenty-seventh session.

Activities of foreign economic and other interests

Consideration by Special Committee

In October 1971, the General Assembly's Special Committee on the Situation with regard to the Implementation of the Declaration on the Granting of Independence to Colonial Countries and Peoples[10] adopted conclusions and recommendations on the activities of foreign economic and other interests impeding the implementation of the Declaration on granting independence in Southern Rhodesia, in Namibia, in the territories under Portuguese domination and in all other territories under colonial domination. The Special Committee's decisions were based on a report of its Sub-Committee I, which the Committee adopted without objection.

The Special Committee drew the following conclusions, among others.

The colonial powers and the States whose nationals were engaged in economic activities in colonial territories had continued to disregard United Nations decisions on the question of those activities. The monopolies and other foreign concerns operating in those territories were guided solely by their own interests, and the support which they gave to the colonialist and minority racist régimes had increased. Foreign monopolies continued to follow economic and financial policies without regard to the legitimate interests of the inhabitants of the territories. The monopolies supplied the colonial régimes with funds and other forms of assistance, including military aid, with the aim of liquidating the national liberation movements.

In colonial territories, the major feature in the process of expansion of foreign economic interests was the creation, with the assistance of big monopolies controlled from the United Kingdom, the United States, France, the Federal Republic of Germany and Japan, of a new military and paramilitary industrial complex under the aegis of South Africa, which was penetrating deeply into neighbouring territories of southern Africa.

There were further developments connected with the Cabora Bassa dam project on the Zambezi River, in particular the awarding of a contract for the construction of the project to the Zamco-Zambeze Consórcio Hidroeléctrico, a consortium headed by South African interests and comprising 17 companies, mostly from the Federal Republic of Germany, France and South Africa. Several new firms were involved directly or indirectly, including interests from South Africa, the United Kingdom and the United States, and some firms already involved in the project had been awarded additional contracts in connexion with the scheme. For example, five British concerns were participating in the projects, including Barclay's Bank D.C.O. and Imperial Chemical Industries, which were closely connected with South African financial interests. As a result of the new development, South African firms were responsible for about two thirds, in terms of value, of the contracts connected with the scheme.

New developments had taken place concerning the Cunene River Basin scheme in Angola, which had the purpose of consolidating and further strengthening the control of colonialist and racist minority régimes over the colonial territories of southern Africa. The project included the building of dams and hydroelectric stations and was to involve bringing between 500,000 and 1 million European settlers into Namibia and Angola.

The Special Committee noted with appreciation that the representatives of the national liberation movements had provided the *Ad Hoc* Group of the Special Committee (which had visited Africa in 1971) with some information concerning the operation of the huge economic and financial interests from the United States, the United Kingdom, France, Canada, the Federal Republic of Germany, South Africa and Japan in Angola, Mozambique, Namibia and Southern Rhodesia. They had pointed out that in Namibia foreign companies had been granted thousands of square miles of concession rights to explore for oil and base minerals. In the territories under Portuguese domination, Portugal had continued to make it easy for powerful imperialist economic interests to establish themselves.

In Southern Rhodesia, the private sector of the economy was still almost wholly dominated by foreign economic and other interests, with the co-operation and support of the illegal régime. Six of the 10 major companies in the territory were entirely South African-owned. The total impact of certain set-backs in the economy caused by economic sanctions had been offset by the expansion of the mining industry by Japanese and South African financial interests. The representatives of liberation movements had been unanimous in the belief that both the Cabora Bassa and Cunene River Basin projects, in which South Africa was taking a leading part, were military-economic projects that formed part of South Africa's aggressive policy against the liberation movements in southern Africa and against neighbouring independent States. These projects had been condemned as a further commitment and involvement of the imperialist powers in defence of the

---

[10]See Y.U.N., 1960, pp. 49-50, resolution 1514(XV) of 14 December 1960, containing text of Declaration.

racist and colonialist régime of southern Africa. Once these schemes were completed, the colonialist hold over the region would be further consolidated and strengthened, and a military and political presence would be established to protect them.

Protest campaigns against the involvement of foreign economic interests in the exploitation of the colonial territories took place all over the world in the previous year, the Special Committee noted. Prominent among those protesting had been the United Church of Christ, the Presbyterian Church, the Southern Africa Committee and the American Committee on Africa, which had protested against the involvement of the Gulf Oil Company in the exploitation of Angolan oil. During April 1971, several members of the United States Congress announced their support for these protest campaigns. Other campaigns had been directed against the participation of the General Electric Company and Barclay's Bank, which were participating in the Cabora Bassa project, and two Canadian companies which were reported to be similarly involved.

The Special Committee concluded that information on the situation in the territories in the Caribbean and Pacific Ocean areas showed that big multinational corporations were depriving the indigenous people of their rights to the wealth of their countries. In spite of the appeal by the General Assembly, the administering powers had failed to put restrictions on the sale of land to foreigners, and the loss of ownership of land by the inhabitants of the territories had continued to be the most obvious consequence of this practice in the region.

The Special Committee approved the following as its recommendations.

(a) It reaffirmed once again that foreign economic, financial and other interests, as they were continuing to operate in the colonial territories, constituted a major obstacle in the way of political independence as well as social and economic justice for the indigenous people.

(b) It strongly condemned the activities and operating methods of those foreign economic and other interests in the territories under colonialist domination which were designed to keep the colonial peoples subjugated and to thwart their efforts and initiatives towards independence.

(c) It reaffirmed the inalienable right of the indigenous population of the territories over their natural resources and their right to enjoy the benefits thereof.

(d) It condemned the colonialist powers and States which gave their active support to foreign economic and other interests engaged in exploiting the natural and human resources of the territories without regard to the welfare of the indigenous people, and depriving them of the means of stabilizing their economies and achieving independence.

(e) It strongly condemned the construction of the Cabora Bassa project in Mozambique and the Cunene River Basin project in Angola as being designed to strengthen and perpetuate colonialist and racist domination over the territories of southern Africa and fraught with serious implications for international peace and security in Africa.

(f) It condemned the positions of the Governments of Portugal, South Africa, the United Kingdom, the United States, the Federal Republic of Germany, France, Canada and other States which had failed to prevent their nationals and companies from participating in the Cabora Bassa and the Cunene River Basin projects, and urged those Governments to withdraw their support from the projects and put an end to participation by companies or individuals of their nationality in those projects.

(g) It reiterated its urgent request that the colonial powers and States concerned should take legislative, administrative and other measures in respect of their companies and nationals who owned and operated enterprises in the colonial territories.

(h) It requested the Secretary-General to give the widest publicity possible to the information on the pernicious activities of foreign economic and other interests in all colonial territories.

(i) It once again requested the colonial powers and States concerned to comply fully with the provisions of relevant General Assembly resolutions and asked them to adopt effective measures to prevent new investments, particularly in southern Africa, which were contrary to those resolutions.

During the discussion of the Sub-Committee's report, the USSR said that representatives of numerous Governments had, over the past years, referred to the plundering activities of foreign monopolies and had stated that those activities formed one of the main obstacles to decolonization. That view was shared by the overwhelming majority of the United Nations Member States and had been reflected in General Assembly resolutions. In spite of this general condemnation, the scope of colonial operations, and the scope of the support given by those foreign monopolies to the reactionary and racist colonial régimes, had increased each year.

The USSR said the main purpose of projects like the Cabora Bassa Dam was to reinforce the forces of reaction in southern Africa and to change the area into a paradise for colonialism where European immigrants who would support colonialism could settle. At the same time, there would be cheap electric energy from the new power stations to expand the scope of activities of the international monopolies. The activities of foreign monopolies in the smaller territories, though on a smaller scale, were no less predatory. Particular criticism had been levelled at the practice of the alienation of land. All available information, the USSR observed, indicated that monopolies and colonialist, racist régimes were forming a united front in their action against the national liberation struggle in the colonial territories.

The representative of the Ivory Coast said that, since the Special Committee began discussing the question of foreign economic interests, it had been his delegation's view that in its conclusions on the specific problem of economic interests in the territories yet to be decolonized, the Committee should try to avoid generalities. The report before the Committee showed that that principle had not been respected. He went on to say that he would like the record to show that the views expressed in the report of the Sub-Committee did not meet with the agreement of the Ivory Coast.

The representative of Mali emphasized that southern Africa, with its great resources, could achieve independence only if the major powers, such as the United Kingdom, the United States, Japan and the Federal Republic of Germany, refrained from giving direct political and economic assistance to the colonialists. That assistance increased as new mineral resources were discovered. The Portuguese régime received assistance from its allies in the North Atlantic Treaty Organization on the basis of a kind of mortgage on the resources of that part of Africa. It was strange that during the general debate in the Assembly the same powers were the first to state how sympathetic they were towards the peoples who should be gaining independence. But it was a different situation when it came to assisting the economic interests which were making it impossible for those peoples to achieve their independence.

Venezuela repeated the reservations it had expressed on other occasions concerning the Special Committee's criteria on the Cabora Bassa project in Mozambique and the Cunene River Basin project in Angola. Venezuela wished to put on record that it did not agree with certain provisions in the conclusions and the recommendations of the Committee's report.

Madagascar said it had always taken a highly qualified stand on the question of foreign economic interests, since it believed that no one could live in a state of autarchy from the economic standpoint; perhaps in those terms it might be said that where there was dependence, there was interdependence. Madagascar did not wish to see texts on foreign economic interests couched in such

general terms without qualifications. Madagascar would not take part in the vote on the report.

Sweden had no difficulty in condemning foreign economic interests shown to be harmful to the territories where they were active, but it felt that the present report made the same mistakes of generalizing as did earlier reports; Sweden could not subscribe to that. There had not been any study in depth of the question, and the conclusions and the recommendations in the report contained a blanket condemnation of all foreign economic activities.

Consideration by General Assembly

The question of the activities of foreign economic interests in colonial territories was taken up in the General Assembly's Fourth Committee on the basis of the report of the Special Committee.

On the recommendation of the Fourth Committee, the Assembly, on 20 December 1971, adopted a resolution by which it took the following decisions on the question, among others.

Noting with deep concern the intensified activities of foreign economic, financial and other interests in the territories, the Assembly reaffirmed the inalienable right of the peoples of dependent territories to self-determination and independence and to the enjoyment of the natural resources of their territories, as well as their right to dispose of those resources in their best interests.

The Assembly also affirmed that the activities of foreign economic, financial and other interests operating in the territories of Southern Rhodesia, Namibia and those under Portuguese domination, constituted a major obstacle to political independence and to the enjoyment of their natural resources by the indigenous inhabitants.

Approving the Special Committee's report on the question, the Assembly reiterated its declaration that any administering power, by depriving the colonial peoples of the exercise of their rights or by subordinating them to foreign economic and financial interests, violated the obligations it had assumed under Chapters XI and XII of the United Nations Charter.[11]

The Assembly condemned the current activities and operating methods of those foreign economic and other interests in the territories under colonial domination which were designed to perpetuate the subjugation of dependent peoples.

It deplored the support given by the colonial powers and other States to those foreign economic and other interests engaged in exploiting the natural and human resources of the territories without regard to the welfare of the indigenous peoples, thus violating the political, economic and social rights and interests of the indigenous

[11]For text of Chapters XI and XII of the Charter, see APPENDIX II.

peoples and obstructing the full and speedy implementation of the Declaration on the granting of independence in respect of those territories.

It also condemned the construction of the Cabora Bassa project in Mozambique and the Cunene River Basin project in Angola, which were designed to further entrench colonialist and racialist domination over the territories of southern Africa and which were a source of international tension.

The Assembly, further, deplored the policies of those Governments which had not yet prevented their nationals and bodies corporate under their jurisdiction from participating in the Cabora Bassa and Cunene River Basin projects, and urgently requested the Governments concerned to take all the necessary measures to terminate that participation and to have them withdraw immediately from all activities related to those projects.

It called upon the administering powers to abolish every discriminatory and unjust wage system which prevailed in the territories under their administration and to apply in each territory a uniform system of wages to all the inhabitants without any discrimination.

In addition, the Assembly called upon the colonial powers and States concerned to take legislative, administrative and other measures in respect of their nationals who owned and operated enterprises in colonial territories, particularly in southern Africa, which were detrimental to the interests of the inhabitants of those territories, in order to put an end to such enterprises and to prevent new investments which ran counter to the interests of the inhabitants.

The Assembly asked all States to take effective measures to end the supply of funds and other forms of assistance, including military equipment, to those régimes which used such assistance to repress the national liberation movements.

Finally, it asked the Special Committee to continue to study this question, including in particular the efforts being made by non-governmental organizations to acquaint world public opinion with the role of foreign economic and other interests in impeding the implementation of the Declaration; and it asked the Secretary-General to assist in preparing the study and to publicize it when completed.

These decisions were taken with the adoption of resolution 2873(XXVI), by a roll-call vote of 103 to 8, with 13 abstentions.

The Fourth Committee approved the text on 14 December 1971 by a recorded vote of 86 to 7, with 13 abstentions.

(For text of resolution and voting details, see DOCUMENTARY REFERENCES below.)

The sponsors of the text in the Fourth Committee were: Algeria, Cameroon, the Congo, Egypt, Equatorial Guinea, Ghana, Guinea, the Libyan Arab Republic, Mali, Mongolia, Nigeria, the Sudan, the Syrian Arab Republic, the United Republic of Tanzania, Yugoslavia, Zaire and Zambia.

The majority of the Members that took part in the debate, including the Byelorussian SSR, Bulgaria, Cuba, Czechoslovakia, Ecuador, Egypt, Guinea, Pakistan, Romania, Somalia, the Syrian Arab Republic, the USSR, Yugoslavia and Zaire, were of the opinion that foreign economic interests were the major obstacles to the attainment of independence by colonial peoples.

The representative of the Ukrainian SSR maintained that the international monopolies were the parties most interested in maintaining colonial rule. High profits and low salaries were attracting an increasing flow of Western capital to the colonial territories, which were a source of vitally important strategic and industrial materials.

The Ukrainian representative went on to say that Portugal and South Africa, with the support of the international monopolies, had been responsible for the breakdown of the sanctions imposed on the régime in Southern Rhodesia and had ensured its survival. The recent agreement between that régime and the United Kingdom Government was due to the pressure of economic interests eager to exploit the Zimbabwe people. Also, he pointed out that, according to press reports, the decision of the United States Congress to permit the import of chrome from Southern Rhodesia resulted from the pressure brought to bear by large metallurgical firms with investments in the mining industry of the territory. The Ukrainian SSR considered that the Cabora Bassa and Cunene River Basin projects would strengthen the alliance between the colonialists and the international monopolies and would impede the Africans' struggle for independence. It therefore supported the determined opposition of the national liberation movements to those projects.

The representative of the United Republic of Tanzania said that the monopolies served as a means of generating extra force for the purpose of perpetuating oppression. That was the sole purpose of the Cabora Bassa project. All progressive forces had condemned it, and the indigenous people of Mozambique continued to oppose the construction of the dam; they were fighting and dying to prevent its completion, for good reason. He said the project was designed to bring outcasts from Western European societies to Mozambique, provide them with free land taken from the Africans and establish for such European social misfits a special régime of privilege based on the South African *apartheid* model. The Tanzanian representative could not accept the contention that the activities of any foreign economic interests were beneficial to the indigenous peoples of the territories of southern Africa.

Australia observed that a most important aspect of political control was control over foreign investment. The question was how to obtain real benefits from foreign investment without being dominated by it. There could be no doubt that Papua New Guinea (administered by Australia) needed foreign investment if development was to be maintained.

Speaking in the Fourth Committee before the vote, South Africa said it would oppose the resolution, which expressed mischievous views, was ideologically motivated and contained unsubstantiated allegations against particular States. The condemnation of the Cabora Bassa and Cunene River Basin projects was an attempt to deprive the populations concerned of an element basic to their welfare—namely, water. The Governments of the region in question had a duty to develop water and energy resources in the interests of its inhabitants. The view that the projects mentioned in the paragraph were a source of international tension was unacceptable to South Africa.

The representative of Japan said that Japan would support the resolution, but that it reserved its position with regard to the Assembly's approval of the report of the Special Committee since that report contained a set of recommendations based on the idea that all the activities considered were inherently detrimental to the peoples concerned.

The fact was that foreign economic interests could play a beneficial role in developing the human and natural resources of those peoples, even before independence. The Special Committee report also contained false allegations with regard to Japanese interests in southern Africa. Japan's categorical rejection of the allegations and its position of strict compliance with relevant Security Council decisions had been stated in detail in a letter of 11 November 1971 addressed to the Secretary-General.

Reservations to various provisions of the resolution, principally to those pertaining to the Cabora Bassa and Cunene River Basin projects, were also expressed by Turkey, Uruguay and Venezuela, among others. The Netherlands stated that it abstained in the vote because it could not endorse the principle that foreign investment impeded the implementation of the General Assembly's resolution on the granting of independence. The point that not all ventures involving foreign interests were necessarily harmful was also made by Ireland, among others.

DOCUMENTARY REFERENCES

Special Committee, meeting 829.

General Assembly—26th session
Fourth Committee, meetings 1953, 1956-1958, 1960, 1962-1965, 1967, 1968.
Plenary meeting 2028.

A/8401. Report of Secretary-General on work of the Organization, 16 June 1970–15 June 1971, Part Two, Chapter I C 2.
A/8423/Rev.1/Add.1 (A/8398 and Add.1). Activities of foreign economic and other interests impeding implementation of Declaration on Granting of Independence to Colonial Countries and Peoples in Southern Rhodesia, Namibia and territories under Portuguese domination and in all other territories under colonial domination and efforts to eliminate colonialism, *apartheid* and racial discrimination in southern Africa. Report of Special Committee.
A/8513. Letter of 11 November 1971 from Japan.
A/C.4/L.1005. Algeria, Cameroon, Congo, Egypt, Equatorial Guinea, Ghana, Guinea, Libyan Arab Republic, Mali, Mongolia, Nigeria, Sudan, Syrian Arab Republic, United Republic of Tanzania, Yugoslavia, Zaire, Zambia: draft resolution, approved by Fourth Committee on 14 December 1971, meeting 1968, by recorded vote of 86 to 7, with 13 abstentions, as follows:

In favour: Afghanistan, Albania, Algeria, Argentina, Barbados, Botswana, Bulgaria, Burma, Burundi, Byelorussian SSR, Cameroon, Central African Republic, Ceylon, Chad, Chile, Colombia, Congo, Cuba, Czechoslovakia, Dominican Republic, Ecuador, Egypt, Equatorial Guinea, Ethiopia, Fiji, Ghana, Greece, Guinea, Guyana, Hungary, Iceland, India, Indonesia, Iran, Iraq, Ireland, Israel, Ivory Coast, Jamaica, Japan, Jordan, Kenya, Khmer Republic, Kuwait, Lebanon, Lesotho, Liberia, Libyan Arab Republic, Madagascar, Malaysia, Mali, Mauritania, Mexico, Mongolia, Morocco, Nepal, Nicaragua, Niger, Nigeria, People's Democratic Republic of Yemen, Peru, Philippines, Poland, Romania, Senegal, Singapore, Somalia, Sudan, Swaziland, Syrian Arab Republic, Thailand, Togo, Trinidad and Tobago, Tunisia, Turkey, Uganda, Ukrainian SSR, USSR, United Republic of Tanzania, Upper Volta, Uruguay, Venezuela, Yemen, Yugoslavia, Zaire, Zambia.
Against: Belgium, Canada, France, Portugal, South Africa, United Kingdom, United States.
Abstaining: Australia, Austria, Brazil, Costa Rica, Denmark, Finland, Italy, Malawi, Netherlands, New Zealand, Norway, Spain, Sweden.

A/8619. Report of Fourth Committee.

RESOLUTION 2873(XXVI), as recommended by Fourth Committee, A/8619, adopted by Assembly on 20 December 1971, meeting 2028, by roll-call vote of 103 to 8, with 13 abstentions:

In favour: Afghanistan, Albania, Algeria, Argentina, Bahrain, Barbados, Botswana, Bulgaria, Burma, Burundi, Byelorussian SSR, Cameroon, Central African Republic, Ceylon, Chad, Chile, Colombia, Costa Rica, Cuba, Cyprus, Czechoslovakia, Dahomey, Dominican Republic, Ecuador, Egypt, El Salvador, Equatorial Guinea, Ethiopia, Fiji, Gambia, Ghana, Greece, Guatemala, Guinea, Guyana, Haiti, Honduras, Hungary, Iceland, India, Indonesia, Iran, Iraq, Ireland, Israel, Ivory Coast, Jamaica, Japan, Jordan, Kenya, Khmer Republic, Kuwait, Laos, Lebanon, Lesotho, Liberia, Libyan Arab Republic, Madagascar, Malaysia, Mali, Malta, Mauritania, Mexico, Mongolia, Morocco, Nepal, Nicaragua, Niger, Nigeria, Oman, Pakistan, Panama, Paraguay, People's Democratic Republic of Yemen, Peru, Philippines, Poland, Romania, Rwanda, Saudi Arabia, Senegal, Sierra Leone, Singapore, Somalia, Sudan, Syrian Arab Republic, Thailand, Togo, Trinidad and Tobago, Tunisia, Turkey, Uganda, Ukrainian SSR, USSR, United Arab Emirates, United Republic of Tanzania, Upper Volta, Uruguay, Venezuela, Yemen, Yugoslavia, Zaire, Zambia.

Against: Belgium, Canada, France, Luxembourg, Portugal, South Africa, United Kingdom, United States.

Abstaining: Australia, Austria, Brazil, Denmark, Finland, Italy, Malawi, Netherlands, New Zealand, Norway, Spain, Swaziland,* Sweden.

*Subsequently, Swaziland advised the Secretariat that it had intended to vote in favour.

The General Assembly,

Having considered the item entitled "Activities of foreign economic and other interests which are impeding the implementation of the Declaration on the Granting of Independence to Colonial Countries and Peoples in Southern Rhodesia, Namibia and Territories under Portuguese domination and in all other Territories under colonial domination and efforts to eliminate colonialism, *apartheid* and racial discrimination in southern Africa,"

Having examined the report of the Special Committee on the Situation with regard to the Implementation of the Declaration on the Granting of Independence to Colonial Countries and Peoples relating to this question,

Recalling its resolution 1514(XV) of 14 December 1960, containing the Declaration on the Granting of Independence to Colonial Countries and Peoples, and its resolution 2621(XXV) of 12 October 1970, containing the programme of action for the full implementation of the Declaration,

Recalling further its previous resolutions on the item, in particular resolution 2703(XXV) of 14 December 1970,

Reaffirming that the administering Powers, in accordance with Chapters XI and XII of the Charter of the United Nations, have the obligation to ensure the political, economic, social and educational advancement of the inhabitants of the Territories under their administration and to protect the human and natural resources of those Territories against abuses,

Reiterating its conviction that any economic or other activity which impedes the implementation of the Declaration and obstructs efforts aimed at the elimination of colonialism, *apartheid* and racial discrimination in southern Africa and other colonial Territories violates the political, economic and social rights and interests of the people in those Territories and is therefore incompatible with the purposes and principles of the Charter,

Noting with deep concern the intensified activities of those foreign economic, financial and other interests in those Territories which, contrary to the relevant resolutions of the General Assembly, are directly and indirectly assisting the Governments of South Africa and Portugal, as well as the illegal racist minority régime in Southern Rhodesia, and impeding the realization by the peoples of the Territories of their legitimate aspirations for self-determination and independence,

1. *Reaffirms* the inalienable right of the peoples of dependent Territories to self-determination and independence and to the enjoyment of the natural resources of their Territories, as well as their right to dispose of those resources in their best interests;

2. *Affirms* that the activities of foreign economic, financial and other interests operating at present in the colonial Territories of Southern Rhodesia and Namibia, as well as in those under Portuguese domination, constitute a major obstacle to political independence and to the enjoyment of the natural resources of those Territories by the indigenous inhabitants;

3. *Approves* the report of the Special Committee on the Situation with regard to the Implementation of the Declaration on the Granting of Independence to Colonial Countries and Peoples relating to this question;

4. *Reiterates* its declaration that any administering Power, by depriving the colonial peoples of the exercise of their rights or by subordinating them to foreign economic and financial interests, violates the obligations it has assumed under Chapters XI and XII of the Charter of the United Nations;

5. *Condemns* the present activities and operating methods of those foreign economic and other interests in the Territories under colonial domination which are designed to perpetuate the subjugation of dependent peoples;

6. *Deplores* the support given by the colonial Powers and other States to those foreign economic and other interests engaged in exploiting the natural and human resources of the Territories without regard to the welfare of the indigenous peoples, thus violating the political, economic and social rights and interests of the indigenous peoples and obstructing the full and speedy implementation of the Declaration in respect of those Territories;

7. *Condemns* the construction of the Cabora Bassa project in Mozambique and the Cunene River Basin project in Angola, which are designed to entrench further colonialist and racialist domination over the Territories of southern Africa and which are a source of international tension;

8. *Deplores* the policies of those Governments which have not yet prevented their nationals and bodies corporate under their jurisdiction from participating in the Cabora Bassa and the Cunene River Basin projects, and urgently requests the Governments concerned to take all the necessary measures to terminate this participation and to have them withdraw immediately from all activities related to those projects;

9. *Calls upon* the administering Powers to abolish every discriminatory and unjust wage system which prevails in the Territories under their administration and to apply in each Territory a uniform system of wages to all the inhabitants without any discrimination;

10. *Calls upon* the colonial Powers and States concerned to take legislative, administrative and other measures in respect of their nationals who own and operate enterprises in colonial Territories, particularly in southern Africa, which are detrimental to the interests of the inhabitants of those Territories, in order to put an end to such enterprises and to prevent new investments which run counter to the interests of the inhabitants;

11. *Requests* all States to take effective measures to end the supply of funds and other forms of assistance, including military equipment, to those régimes which use such assistance to repress the national liberation movements;

12. *Requests* the Special Committee to continue to study this question, including in particular the efforts being made by non-governmental organizations to acquaint world public opinion with the role of foreign economic and other interests in impeding the implementation of the Declaration, and to report thereon to the General Assembly at its twenty-seventh session;

13. *Requests* the Secretary-General to render all possible assistance to the Special Committee in the preparation of the study and to give the widest possible publicity to that study when it is completed, as well as to previous studies and any other related aspects of the question.

United Nations Educational and Training Programme for Southern Africa

The United Nations Educational and Training Programme for Southern Africa continued during 1970-1971 to grant scholarships for education and training to persons from Namibia, South Africa, Southern Rhodesia and the territories under Portuguese administration. During the period from 1 November to 8 December 1971, 25 States had pledged an amount equivalent to $689,036.

On 20 December 1971, the General Assembly, noting that the voluntary contributions received in the period from 1968 to 1971 had fallen far short of the original three-year target, urgently appealed to all States, organizations and individuals to make generous contributions to the trust fund for the Programme. The Assembly also decided that, as a transitional measure, provision should be made under the regular budget of the United Nations for the financial year 1972 for $100,000 to ensure continuity of the Programme pending the receipt of adequate voluntary contributions.

These decisions were set forth in resolution 2875(XXVI). (For further details and for text of resolution, see pp. 123-25.)

Questions concerning individual territories

The following pages give brief accounts of decisions taken on various individual territories in 1971 by the General Assembly and by its Special Committee on the Situation with regard to the Implementation of the Declaration on the Granting of Independence to Colonial Countries and Peoples.[12] (See also pp. 88-112, 546-64, 564-76 and 502-14 for details on questions concerning Southern Rhodesia, Namibia, territories under Portuguese administration, Papua and the Trust Territory of New Guinea and the Trust Territory of the Pacific Islands.)

Falkland Islands (Malvinas)

The Special Committee considered the question of the Falkland Islands (Malvinas) at a meeting held on 25 March 1971.

The Special Committee had before it a working paper prepared by the Secretariat containing information on action previously taken by the Special Committee and the General Assembly, and on the latest developments concerning the territory.

The Committee also had before it identical letters, dated 12 August 1971, from the Permanent Representatives of Argentina and the United Kingdom, addressed to the Secretary-General and stating that the Argentine and United Kingdom delegations—the latter including participants from the Falkland Islands (Malvinas)—had held special talks in Buenos Aires, Argentina, in June 1971. The talks had resulted in the adoption of measures aimed at facilitating the movement of persons and goods between the Argentine mainland and the islands and at promoting the establishment of cultural, social and economic links. Both Governments declared they would continue to exchange views on these matters.

Annexed to the letters were copies of notes exchanged between the two Governments by which both parties agreed that nothing contained in the joint statement issued at the conclusion of the talks should be interpreted as a renunciation by either Government of any right to territorial sovereignty over the islands or as a recognition of, or support for, the other Government's position with regard to such territorial sovereignty; and that no acts or activities undertaken pursuant to the joint statement should constitute a basis for asserting, supporting or denying the position of either Government with regard to territorial sovereignty over the islands.

On 21 October 1971, the Special Committee decided to transmit the Secretariat working paper to the General Assembly and, subject to any directives which the General Assembly might give, to consider the item at its 1972 session.

On 20 December 1971, on the recommendation of its Fourth Committee, the General Assembly adopted a consensus relating to the question of the Falkland Islands (Malvinas). By the consensus, the Assembly noted with satisfaction the progress achieved in the special talks on communications which had taken place within the general framework of the negotiations reported in the letters of 12 August 1971 from the Permanent Representatives of Argentina and the United Kingdom addressed to the Secretary-General. The Assembly urged the parties to continue their efforts to reach a definitive solution to the dispute as soon as possible and to keep the Special Committee and the General Assembly informed during 1972 of the development of the negotiations on this colonial situation, the elimination of which was of interest to the United Nations within the context of the Declaration on the Granting of Independence to Colonial Countries and Peoples.[13]

The Fourth Committee approved the draft consensus without objection on 13 December 1971; the text had been suggested by Uruguay and Argentina. (For text of consensus, see DOCUMENTARY REFERENCES below.)

French Territory of the Afars and the Issas

On 6 October 1971, the Special Committee decided without objection to transmit to the General Assembly the working paper prepared by the Secretariat on the French Territory of the Afars and the Issas, in order to facilitate consideration of the item by the Assembly, and, subject to any Assembly directives, to consider the question in 1972.

On 20 December 1971, the General Assembly endorsed a recommendation of its Fourth Committee that consideration of the question be postponed to its twenty-seventh session, to be held in 1972.

[12]See Y.U.N., 1960, pp. 49-50, resolution 1514(XV), containing text of Declaration.
[13]*Ibid.*

Gibraltar

On 6 October 1971, the Special Committee decided without objection to transmit to the General Assembly the working paper on Gibraltar prepared by the Secretariat, in order to facilitate consideration of the item by the Fourth Committee of the Assembly, and, subject to any Assembly directives, to consider the question in 1972.

On 20 December 1971, the General Assembly endorsed a recommendation of its Fourth Committee that consideration of the question of Gibraltar be postponed to 1972.

Spanish Sahara

On 6 October 1971, the Special Committee decided without objection to transmit to the General Assembly the working paper on Spanish Sahara prepared by the Secretariat, in order to facilitate consideration of the item by the Fourth Committee of the Assembly, and, subject to any Assembly directives, to consider the question in 1972.

On 20 December 1971, the General Assembly endorsed a recommendation of its Fourth Committee that consideration of the question of Spanish Sahara be postponed to 1972.

Other territories

In 1971, the General Assembly and its Special Committee on the Situation with regard to the Implementation of the Declaration on the Granting of Independence to Colonial Countries and Peoples[14] considered the situation in the following territories (in addition to the territories covered in the preceding sections): American Samoa, Antigua, the Bahamas, Bermuda, British Honduras, the British Virgin Islands, Brunei, the Cayman Islands, the Cocos (Keeling) Islands, Dominica, the Gilbert and Ellice Islands, Grenada, Guam, Hong Kong, Montserrat, the New Hebrides, Niue, Pitcairn, St. Helena, St. Kitts-Nevis-Anguilla, St. Lucia, St. Vincent, the Seychelles, the Solomon Islands, the Tokelau Islands, the Turks and Caicos Islands and the United States Virgin Islands.

The Special Committee referred 19 of these territories to its Sub-Committees I, II and III for consideration and report. Seven territories—Antigua, British Honduras, Dominica, Grenada, St. Kitts-Nevis-Anguilla, St. Lucia and St. Vincent —were considered by the full Committee.

The Special Committee adopted the Sub-Committees' reports on 18 territories and endorsed their conclusions and recommendations, on the understanding that any reservations made by Committee members would be included in the records. Owing to lack of time, Sub-Committee II was unable to complete its consideration of Brunei, and the Special Committee therefore took no action on this territory.

With regard to Antigua, Dominica, Grenada, St. Kitts-Nevis-Anguilla, St. Lucia and St. Vincent, the Special Committee decided to transmit to the General Assembly the working paper on these territories prepared by the Secretariat and, subject to any Assembly directives, to consider the item in 1972.

The Special Committee also decided to defer consideration of British Honduras until 1972, subject to any directives it might receive from the General Assembly at its 1971 session.

The Special Committee decided to take up Hong Kong as a separate item and to consider it during plenary meetings. The Committee took no action on the territory, but decided to consider it again in 1972, subject to any Assembly directives.

Consideration by the Special Committee

SEYCHELLES AND ST. HELENA

On 13 August 1971, the Special Committee adopted the conclusions and recommendations contained in the report of Sub-Committee I concerning the Seychelles and St. Helena.

The Special Committee noted with deep regret that the administering power (the United Kingdom) had failed to implement its previous recommendations in respect of the Seychelles.

Noting that a new constitution had been introduced in the territory and that the first elections under the new constitutional arrangements had taken place in November 1970, the Special Committee reiterated its opinion that, although this step represented some progress in the process of self-determination, it was nevertheless inadequate to promote the process of complete decolonization in accordance with the Declaration on the Granting of Independence to Colonial Countries and Peoples.[15]

The Special Committee noted that the policies of the administering power threatened to cause dissension and conflict among the inhabitants of the territory concerning its future, and that there was an urgent need to create conditions under which the people of the Seychelles could exercise their right to self-determination. It noted with regret that the administering power refused to restore the territorial integrity of the Seychelles by returning to it the islands detached from the territory in 1965.

It noted with serious concern the report that the United Kingdom and the United States intended to begin in March 1971 construction of military facilities in the so-called British Indian Ocean Territory, in violation of various General Assem-

---

[14]See Y.U.N., 1960, pp. 49-50, resolution 1514(XV), containing text of Declaration.
[15]*Ibid.*

bly decisions, and that this constituted a threat to international peace and security. The Committee condemned the direct intervention of South Africa in the economy of the Seychelles and St. Helena, which had been reported by the Secretary-General of the Seychelles People's United Party; it called upon the administering power to take immediate and effective measures to stop the sale of land to foreign firms and to prevent the economic intervention of South Africa, with a view to safeguarding the interests of the local population.

BAHAMAS, BERMUDA, BRITISH VIRGIN ISLANDS, CAYMAN ISLANDS, MONTSERRAT, TURKS AND CAICOS ISLANDS

On 6 October 1972, the Special Committee adopted conclusions and recommendations concerning six Caribbean territories, on the basis of a report by its Sub-Committee III.

In its general conclusions and recommendations, the Special Committee reaffirmed the inalienable right to self-determination and independence of the peoples of the Bahamas, Bermuda, the British Virgin Islands, the Cayman Islands, Montserrat and the Turks and Caicos Islands. It reiterated its view that the question of size, limited population and restricted resources should in no way delay a speedy implementation of the Declaration on granting independence with respect to those territories. It also reiterated its request to the administering power (the United Kingdom) to take immediately the necessary measures to transfer all powers to the people of the territories, without any conditions and reservations, and to encourage them to discuss openly and freely the various alternatives available for the realization of their aspirations, in accordance with their freely expressed will and desire. The Special Committee reiterated its belief that a United Nations presence and participation before and/or during the procedures for the exercise of the right of self-determination was essential.

The Special Committee once again urged the administering power to enable the United Nations to send visiting missions to the territories. It also considered that it would be desirable to invite representatives of groups representing various shades of opinion in each territory to participate in meetings of the Special Committee and its Sub-Committees.

The Committee reiterated its concern over the continued existence of separate economic and financial entities in some territories which, it felt, were not subject to the proper control of government authority; and it requested the administering power to take effective measures, without further delay, which would guarantee and safeguard the rights of the people of the territories to dispose of their resources and to establish and

maintain control over their future development. Finally, in taking note of the number of projects which continued to be carried out in some territories under the auspices of the United Nations and its specialized agencies, the Committee maintained that such assistance was useful and expressed the hope that it would be further increased.

In its specific conclusions and recommendations, the Special Committee expressed the hope that the Bahamas would be granted full self-determination and independence at an early stage.

The Committee expressed concern over continuing racial inequalities and tension prevailing in Bermuda and called upon the administering power to take, without further delay, effective measures which would ensure that the people of the territory enjoyed equal opportunities, without any distinction. It further urged the administering power to take immediate steps for the full implementation of the Declaration on granting independence with respect to the territory.

The Special Committee expressed regret that recent constitutional changes in the British Virgin Islands represented no substantial advancement towards a speedy implementation of the Declaration with respect to the territory.

The Committee expressed the hope that the consultations which were taking place concerning the Cayman Islands would result in further constitutional advances leading to the implementation of the provisions of the Declaration with respect to the territory.

The Special Committee reiterated the hope that discussions which had taken place in 1970 concerning the possibility of sending a visiting mission to Montserrat would be followed by practical steps on the part of the administering power leading to the dispatch of a visiting mission to the territory.

Finally, the Special Committee expressed its concern at the difficult economic and social situation prevailing in the Turks and Caicos Islands and appealed to the administering power to take positive and effective steps that would lead towards the full implementation of the objectives of the Declaration.

GILBERT AND ELLICE ISLANDS, PITCAIRN, SOLOMON ISLANDS

The Special Committee adopted its conclusions and recommendations concerning the Gilbert and Ellice Islands, Pitcairn and the Solomon Islands on 1 September 1971, on the basis of a report by its Sub-Committee II.

Expressing serious concern that a representative of the administering power (the United Kingdom) had not been present during discussions concerning those territories, the Special Committee urged the administering power to reconsider its position and to co-operate with the Committee.

Because of lack of information, the Special Committee was not in a position to evaluate fully the progress made in constitutional developments. It would welcome more information on the results of the 1971 elections in the Gilbert and Ellice Islands and on the time-table for complete localization of the public service.

Noting that the economy of the Gilbert and Ellice Islands was still based mainly on phosphate mining, the Special Committee said it would also welcome information concerning the economic situation that would obtain in the territory when the phosphates were depleted. The Special Committee also invited the administering power to furnish more specific information as to the composition and operations of the Wholesale Society, which appeared to have a monopoly of imports and internal trade in the territory.

With regard to the Solomon Islands, the Special Committee noted that one third of the members of its legislature remained *ex officio* and that the High Commissioner retained extensive control. The Committee reiterated its previous recommendations that the administering power transfer full responsibility of government to the representatives of the people, in accordance with the Declaration on granting independence. It endorsed the motion adopted by the Governing Council of the Solomon Islands calling for the drawing up of a time-table leading to independence.

The Special Committee felt that the need for a substantial upgrading of education was obvious and urged the administering power to accord greater importance and support to secular education in the territories.

Finally, it urged the administering power to reconsider its position and to allow a mission to visit the territories.

NIUE AND THE TOKELAU ISLANDS

On 16 August 1971, the Special Committee adopted its conclusions and recommendations concerning Niue and the Tokelau Islands on the basis of a report by its Sub-Committee II.

It considered that the problems of area, remoteness, lack of resources and size of population should not prevent the ultimate implementation in the territories of the Declaration on granting independence. The Special Committee noted that the Niue Assembly had approved the recommendations of the Constitutional Adviser concerning Niue's future constitutional development, which it viewed as an encouraging sign. It would welcome information on the future role of the Resident Commissioner in the Niue Assembly, and noted with satisfaction that the Assembly had power to control all public expenditure in the territory.

The Special Committee noted that although there had been a marked increase in the value of exports—owing to a higher level of passion-fruit exports—the territory continued to rely on material aid from the administering power (New Zealand). It noted further that the construction of an airport in Niue would increase the territory's communication with the outside world.

The Special Committee noted the serious economic difficulties faced by the people of the Tokelau Islands and their widely felt need for continued assistance from New Zealand. It considered that further efforts should be made by the administering power to develop the islands' resources.

Finally, the Special Committee welcomed New Zealand's invitation to send a small mission to the territories and requested the Committee Chairman to take the necessary steps to dispatch such a mission during 1972.

Statements concerning the report of Sub-Committee II were made by the representative of New Zealand and by the Chairman of the Special Committee.

NEW HEBRIDES

On 11 August 1971, the Special Committee adopted conclusions and recommendations concerning the New Hebrides, on the basis of a report by its Sub-Committee II.

The Special Committee noted with regret the absence of the representatives of the two administering powers (France and the United Kingdom) from the discussions, and expressed its deep concern that France continued to find it impossible to co-operate with the Committee concerning the territory. It appealed to the two Governments to reconsider their positions and provide more information on the territory.

The Committee noted that the general impression was that of very little political progress in the territory. Although the Advisory Council had been enlarged, its functions were restricted and New Hebridean members remained in a minority.

The Special Committee reiterated its hope that constitutional development would take place so as to transfer full government authority to an elected body. It would also welcome information concerning training programmes aimed at localizing the public service.

It regretted that no information had been forthcoming on the system of land tenure in the territory. The Committee urged the restoration of land to indigenous ownership and asked to be kept informed of developments. It also expressed the hope that immediate steps would be taken to halt investments that were detrimental to the people of the territory and that would have inevitable political repercussions.

The Special Committee shared the concern of the territory's Advisory Council over the exodus of labour from the territory and suggested that a study be made of the subject. Finally, the Committee again stressed the importance it attached to the dispatch of a visiting mission to the territory and urged the administering powers to reconsider their position concerning missions and allow one to visit the New Hebrides.

AMERICAN SAMOA AND GUAM

On 21 October 1971, the Special Committee approved the report of Sub-Committee II concerning American Samoa and Guam, and endorsed the conclusions and recommendations contained therein. The two territories are administered by the United States.

The Committee remained of the opinion that the economic development of Guam revolved around the existence of military bases and reiterated its view that the dependence of the territory on military installations, and particularly the presence of military bases, should be brought to an end as soon as possible. Noting with regret that the residency requirement for voters in Guam was only one year, and that it was difficult to determine what percentage of voters were from the United States, it considered that measures should be adopted to ensure that United States voters did not influence the elections to the detriment of the indigenous inhabitants and the exercise of their political rights.

The Special Committee reiterated its view that all options, including independence, should be left open to the people of the territory and urged the administering power to take steps aimed at reducing the dependence of the territory on the United States and to allow the indigenous inhabitants to participate fully and freely in an act of self-determination in conformity with the Declaration on granting independence.

The Committee said it would welcome information concerning the number of indigenous inhabitants holding key posts in the public service, the number of workers imported from abroad and the number of indigenous inhabitants seeking employment overseas.

Regarding American Samoa, the Special Committee reiterated a view similar to the one it held on the future of Guam; in this connexion, it looked forward to receiving the conclusions of the study made by the Political Status Commission concerning the future of the territory. It also looked forward to the establishment of a community college in American Samoa and expressed the hope that more attention would be paid to education in the territory, in particular to higher education and the training of cadres.

Finally, the Special Committee again stressed the importance it attached to the dispatch of visiting missions to the territories and expressed the hope that the administering power would agree that the time had come for it to reconsider its negative position and allow a mission to visit these territories.

The representative of the United States participated in the work of the Special Committee during its consideration of the item and made a statement concerning the conclusions and recommendations of the Sub-Committee's report.

UNITED STATES VIRGIN ISLANDS

The Special Committee adopted its conclusions and recommendations on the United States Virgin Islands on 13 August 1971, on the basis of a report by its Sub-Committee III.

The Special Committee noted with regret that no significant constitutional progress towards the full implementation of the Declaration on granting independence had taken place in the territory. It noted, however, that in November 1970, for the first time in the territory's history, the Governor had been elected in general elections, and expressed the hope that the Constitutional Convention to be held in September 1971 would bring the necessary political and constitutional advancement.

Recognizing the importance of the alien population in the United States Virgin Islands to its sustained economic development, the Committee viewed with concern the recent disturbances caused by the unsatisfactory and even critical conditions of life of the alien population, and took note of the action taken by the administering power (the United States) in dealing with the situation; the Committee once again urged the administering power to take appropriate measures with a view to the immediate solution of the most pressing problems in the fields of housing, welfare, economics and education. Finally, the Committee once again urged the administering power to enable the United Nations to send a visiting mission to the territory, extending to it full co-operation and assistance.

The representative of the United States participated in the work of the Special Committee during its consideration of the item and made a statement concerning the report of Sub-Committee III.

COCOS (KEELING) ISLANDS

On 21 October 1971, the Special Committee adopted conclusions and recommendations concerning the Cocos (Keeling) Islands (administered by Australia) on the basis of a report by Sub-Committee II.

The Special Committee reaffirmed the inalienable right of the people of the territory to self-determination and independence in conformity with the Declaration on granting independence. It reiterated its view that the question of size, location and limited resources should in no way delay the speedy implementation of the Declaration in the territory.

Consideration by General Assembly

Later in 1971, at its twenty-sixth session, the General Assembly took up the Special Committee's report on the territories.

On 20 December, the Assembly adopted a number of resolutions regarding the various territories.

With regard to the Seychelles, the Assembly, noting the statement of the Chief Minister of the Seychelles that he would welcome the dispatch of a United Nations mission to the territory, and would agree to the holding of a referendum on the future status of the territory under the auspices of the United Nations: (1) reaffirmed the inalienable right of the people of the Seychelles to self-determination and independence, in conformity with the 1960 Declaration on the Granting of Independence to Colonial Countries and Peoples, and called upon the United Kingdom, as the administering power, to take all necessary measures to enable the people to exercise that right without further delay; (2) requested the administering power to receive the special mission of the United Nations envisaged under the provisions of the relevant Assembly resolutions and to make the necessary arrangements, in consultation with the special mission, for the holding of a referendum on the future status of the territory; (3) requested the Special Committee on the Situation with regard to the Implementation of the Declaration on the Granting of Independence to Colonial Countries and Peoples, in consultation with the administering power and with the assistance of the Secretary-General, to appoint immediately a special mission to visit the Seychelles for the purpose of recommending practical steps to be taken for the full implementation of the relevant Assembly resolutions—in particular concerning the extent of United Nations participation in the holding of a referendum on the future status of the territory; and (4) requested the Special Committee to continue to examine the question and to report thereon to the Assembly in 1972.

These decisions were set forth in resolution 2866(XXVI), adopted by a vote of 101 to 3, with 16 abstentions. The Assembly acted on the recommendation of its Fourth Committee which approved the text on 13 December 1971, by a vote of 78 to 4, with 15 abstentions. The text was based on a proposal by Burundi, Cameroon, Egypt, Ethiopia, Ghana, India, Iraq, Kenya, Nigeria, Rwanda, Sudan, the Syrian Arab Republic, Ugan-

da, the United Republic of Tanzania, Yugoslavia and Zambia. (For text of resolution, see DOCUMENTARY REFERENCES below.)

With regard to the Caribbean territories of Antigua, Dominica, Grenada, St. Kitts-Nevis-Anguilla, St. Lucia and St. Vincent, the General Assembly: (1) took note of the chapter of the report of the Special Committee relating to these territories; and (2) requested the Special Committee to give full consideration to the question in accordance with the provisions of the relevant General Assembly resolutions, in particular its resolution of 16 December 1969,[16] and to report thereon to the Assembly in 1972.

The Assembly took these decisions in adopting resolution 2867(XXVI), by a recorded vote of 110 to 0, with 7 abstentions. It acted on the recommendation of the Fourth Committee, which approved the text by a vote of 66 to 0, with 3 abstentions, on 14 December 1971. The text had been proposed by Cameroon, Egypt, Ghana, Guyana, Jamaica, Nigeria, Trinidad and Tobago, the United Republic of Tanzania and Zambia. (For text of resolution, see DOCUMENTARY REFERENCES below.)

In another action, the Assembly: (1) reaffirmed the inalienable right of the people of Niue and the Tokelau Islands to self-determination, in accordance with the Declaration on the Granting of Independence to Colonial Countries and Peoples; (2) called upon the administering power to take further measures to enable the people of the territory to exercise their right to self-determination as soon as possible; (3) took note of the arrangements made by the Special Committee for the dispatch of a visiting mission to Niue in 1972 and requested the Special Committee to instruct the mission to obtain first-hand information on conditions in the territory, and on the wishes and aspirations of its people, and to recommend practical steps for their advancement towards self-government and self-determination.

Among other things, the Assembly also requested the Special Committee to report to it on this question in 1972.

These decisions were set forth in resolution 2868(XXVI), adopted by a recorded vote of 117 to 0, with 1 abstention, on the recommendation of the Fourth Committee. On 15 December 1971, by a recorded vote of 79 to 0, with 1 abstention, the Fourth Committee approved the text sponsored by Afghanistan, Ecuador, Ethiopia, Fiji, Ghana, India, Indonesia, Iran, Iraq, Kenya, Nigeria, the Philippines, Sierra Leone, Sweden, Trinidad and Tobago, Yugoslavia and Zambia. (For text of resolution, see DOCUMENTARY REFERENCES below.)

By another resolution, the Assembly took decisions concerning 17 territories: American

[16]See Y.U.N., 1969, p. 675, text of resolution 2593(XXIV).

Samoa, the Bahamas, Bermuda, the British Virgin Islands, Brunei, the Cayman Islands, the Cocos (Keeling) Islands, the Gilbert and Ellice Islands, Guam, Montserrat, the New Hebrides, Pitcairn, St. Helena, the Seychelles, the Solomon Islands, the Turks and Caicos Islands and the United States Virgin Islands.

By the preambular paragraphs, the Assembly: (*a*) deplored the policy of some administering powers in establishing and maintaining military bases in some of the territories under their administration; (*b*) deeply deplored the attitude of those administering powers which continued to refuse to allow United Nations missions to visit the territories under their administration; (*c*) expressed its conviction of the vital importance of such missions as a means of securing first-hand information in regard to political, economic and social conditions in the territories and to the views and aspirations of the people in those territories; (*d*) declared that the territories required the continued attention and assistance of the United Nations in the achievement by their peoples of the objectives embodied in the United Nations Charter and in the Declaration on the Granting of Independence to Colonial Countries and Peoples; and (*e*) noted the special circumstances of the geographical location and economic conditions of those territories.

By the operative paragraphs of the resolution, the Assembly: (1) approved the report of the Special Committee on the above territories; (2) reaffirmed the inalienable right of the people of the territories to self-determination and independence in accordance with the Declaration on granting independence; (3) called upon the administering powers to take all necessary steps, without delay, to ensure the full and speedy attainment of the goals set forth in the Declaration with respect to those territories; (4) reaffirmed its conviction that the questions of size, geographical isolation and limited resources should in no way delay implementation of the Declaration with respect to those territories; (5) deprecated any attempt aimed at the partial or total disruption of the national unity and territorial integrity of colonial territories and the establishment of military bases and installations in those territories as being incompatible with the purposes and principles of the United Nations Charter and the Declaration on granting independence; (6) called upon the administering powers to reconsider their attitude towards the receiving of visiting missions to the above-mentioned territories and to permit access by such missions to territories under their administration; (7) decided that the United Nations should render all help to the peoples of those territories in their efforts freely to decide their future status; and (8) requested the Special Committee to continue to give full consideration to the question, in particular the dispatch of missions to those territories, and to report to the Assembly in 1972.

These decisions were embodied in resolution 2869(XXVI), adopted by a recorded vote of 98 to 1, with 19 abstentions. The Assembly acted on the recommendation of its Fourth Committee, which approved the text on 16 December 1971, by a recorded vote of 73 to 0, with 18 abstentions; the sponsors of the draft were Cameroon, the Congo, Ethiopia, Ghana, Guinea, India, Kenya, Mongolia, the People's Democratic Republic of Yemen, Rwanda, Sierra Leone, the Syrian Arab Republic, Uganda, the United Republic of Tanzania, Yugoslavia and Zambia. (For text of resolution, see DOCUMENTARY REFERENCES below.)

Also on 20 December 1971, the General Assembly, on the recommendation of the Fourth Committee, decided without objection to defer consideration of the question of British Honduras until its 1972 session.

DOCUMENTARY REFERENCES

Falkland Islands (Malvinas)

Special Committee on Situation with regard to Implementation of Declaration on Granting of Independence to Colonial Countries and Peoples, meeting 830.

General Assembly—26th session
Fourth Committee, meetings 1953, 1964-1967.
Plenary meetings 1948, 2028.

A/8368. Letter of 12 August 1971 from Argentina (circulating notes of 5 August 1971 exchanged between Argentina and United Kingdom, and Joint Statement of 1 July 1971).
A/8369. Letter of 12 August 1971 from United Kingdom (circulating notes of 5 August 1971 exchanged between Argentina and United Kingdom, and Joint Statement of 1 July 1971).
A/8423/Rev.1. Report of Special Committee (covering its work during 1971), Chapter XXV.

A/8527. Letter of 17 November 1971 from United Kingdom.
A/C.4/L.1000. Uruguay and Venezuela: draft consensus, approved without objection by Fourth Committee on 13 December 1971, meeting 1967.
A/8616. Report of Fourth Committee (on territories not considered separately), Section I and paras. 5 and 24: draft consensus.
A/8429, pp. 111-112. Consensus, as recommended by Fourth Committee, A/8616, adopted by Assembly on 20 December 1971, meeting 2028.

The General Assembly, having regard to its resolution 2065(XX) of 16 December 1965 and to the consensuses which it approved on 20 December 1966, 19 December 1967 and 16 December 1969, concerning the question of the Falkland Islands (Malvinas), takes note of the communications dated 12 August 1971 from the Permanent Representatives of Argentina and the United Kingdom of Great Britain and Northern Ireland addressed to the Secretary-General.

In this connexion, the General Assembly notes with satisfaction the progress achieved in the special talks on communications which took place within the general framework of the negotiations that were reported in the notes of 12 August 1971, and urges the parties, bearing particularly in mind resolution 2065(XX) and the consensuses mentioned above, to continue their efforts to reach, as soon as possible, a definitive solution to the dispute as envisaged in the notes referred to, and to keep the Special Committee on the Situation with regard to the Implementation of the Declaration on the Granting of Independence to Colonial Countries and Peoples and the General Assembly informed during the coming year of the development of the negotiations on this colonial situation, the elimination of which is of interest to the United Nations within the context of General Assembly resolution 1514(XV) of 14 December 1960.

French Territory of the Afars and the Issas

Special Committee on Situation with regard to Implementation of Declaration on Granting of Independence to Colonial Countries and Peoples, meeting 828.

General Assembly—26th session
Fourth Committee, meetings 1953, 1957, 1964, 1965, 1967.
Plenary meeting 2028.

A/8401. Report of the Secretary-General on work of the Organization, 16 June 1970–15 June 1971, Part Two, Chapter I B 6.
A/8423/Rev.1. Report of Special Committee (covering its work during 1971), Chapter XII.
A/8616. Report of Fourth Committee (on territories not considered separately), paras. 9 and 26.
A/8429. Resolutions adopted by General Assembly during its 26th session, 21 September–22 December 1971. Other decisions, pp. 111-12.

Gibraltar

Special Committee on Situation with regard to Implementation of Declaration on Granting of Independence to Colonial Countries and Peoples, meeting 828.

General Assembly—26th session
Fourth Committee, meetings 1953, 1957, 1960, 1964, 1965, 1967.
Plenary meeting 2028.

A/8401. Report of Secretary-General on work of the Organization, 16 June 1970–15 June 1971, Part Two, Chapter I B 5.
A/8423/Rev.1. Report of Special Committee (covering its work during 1971), Chapter XI.
A/8616. Report of Fourth Committee (on territories not considered separately), paras. 9 and 26.
A/8429. Resolutions adopted by General Assembly during its 26th session, 21 September–22 December 1971. Other decisions, pp. 111-12.

Spanish Sahara

Special Committee on Situation with regard to Implementation of Declaration on Granting of Independence to Colonial Countries and Peoples, meetings 828, 832.

General Assembly—26th session
Fourth Committee, meetings 1953, 1957, 1964-66.
Plenary meeting 2028.

A/8401. Report of Secretary-General on work of the Organization, 16 June 1970–15 June 1971, Part Two, Chapter I B 4.
A/8423/Rev.1. Report of Special Committee, Chapter X.
A/8616. Report of Fourth Committee (on territories not considered separately), paras. 9 and 26.
A/8429. Resolutions adopted by General Assembly during its 26th

session, 21 September–22 December 1971. Other decisions, pp. 111-12.

Other territories

Special Committee on Situation with regard to Implementation of Declaration on Granting of Independence to Colonial Countries and Peoples, meetings 811, 813-816, 819-822, 824, 828, 830, 832.

DECISIONS OF GENERAL ASSEMBLY

General Assembly—26th session
Fourth Committee, meetings 1926-1928, 1953, 1956-1958, 1960, 1962-1968, 1970, 1971.
Fifth Committee, meeting 1488.
Plenary meetings 1947, 2028.

A/8401. Report of Secretary-General on work of the Organization, 16 June 1970–15 June 1971, Part Two, Chapter I B 9.
A/8401/Add.1. Introduction to report of Secretary-General, September 1971, Part Two, Chapter VIII, paras. 304, 305.
A/8423/Rev.1. Report of Special Committee (covering its work during 1971). Chapter I, Sections E-G and N, and Annex I; Chapter IX: Seychelles and St. Helena; Chapter X: Spanish Sahara; Chapter XI: Gibraltar; Chapter XII: French Somaliland; Chapter XIV: New Hebrides; Chapter XV: Niue and Tokelau Islands; Chapter XVI: Gilbert and Ellice Islands, Pitcairn and Solomon Islands; Chapter XVII: American Samoa and Guam; Chapter XVIII: Trust Territory of Pacific Islands; Chapter XIX: Cocos (Keeling) Islands, Papua and Trust Territory of New Guinea; Chapter XX: Brunei; Chapter XXI: Hong Kong; Chapter XXII: Antigua, Dominica, Grenada, St. Kitts-Nevis-Anguilla, St. Lucia and St. Vincent; Chapter XXIII: United States Virgin Islands; Chapter XXIV: Bahamas, Bermuda, British Virgin Islands, Cayman Islands, Montserrat and Turks and Caicos Islands; Chapter XXVI: British Honduras.
A/C.4/L.996. Burundi, Cameroon, Egypt, Ethiopia, Ghana, India, Iraq, Kenya, Nigeria, Rwanda, Sudan, Syrian Arab Republic, Uganda, United Republic of Tanzania, Yugoslavia, Zambia: draft resolution, as orally revised by sponsors, approved by Fourth Committee on 13 December 1971, meeting 1967, by 78 votes to 4, with 15 abstentions.
A/C.4/L.999. Administrative and financial implications of 16-power draft resolution, A/C.4/L.996. Statement by Secretary-General.
A/C.5/1428, A/8632. Administrative and financial implications of, *inter alia*, draft resolution I recommended by Fourth Committee in A/8616. Statement by Secretary-General and report of Fifth Committee.
A/8616. Report of Fourth Committee, draft resolution I.

RESOLUTION 2866(XXVI), as recommended by Fourth Committee, A/8616, adopted by Assembly on 20 December 1971, meeting 2028, by 101 votes to 3, with 16 abstentions.

The General Assembly,
Having considered the question of the Seychelles,
Having considered the relevant chapter of the report of the Special Committee on the Situation with regard to the Implementation of the Declaration on the Granting of Independence to Colonial Countries and Peoples,
Recalling its resolution 1514(XV) of 14 December 1960, containing the Declaration on the Granting of Independence to Colonial Countries and Peoples, and its resolution 2621(XXV) of 12 October 1970, containing the programme of action for the full implementation of the Declaration,
Recalling further its previous resolutions relating to the question, in particular resolution 2709(XXV) of 14 December 1970,
Affirming that the Seychelles should accede to independence without any prejudice to their territorial integrity,
Mindful of the views expressed to the Special Committee by the leader of the Seychelles People's United Party,
Noting the statement of the Chief Minister of the Seychelles that

he would welcome the dispatch of a United Nations mission to the Territory and would agree to the holding of a referendum on the future status of the Territory under the auspices of the United Nations,

1. *Reaffirms* the inalienable right of the people of the Seychelles to self-determination and independence in conformity with General Assembly resolution 1514(XV), and calls upon the Government of the United Kingdom of Great Britain and Northern Ireland, as the administering Power, to take all necessary measures to enable the people to exercise that right without further delay;

2. *Requests* the administering Power, in accordance with the provisions of the relevant resolutions of the General Assembly, to receive the special mission of the United Nations envisaged hereunder and to make the necessary arrangements, in consultation with the special mission, for the holding of a referendum on the future status of the Territory;

3. *Requests* the Special Committee on the Situation with regard to the Implementation of the Declaration on the Granting of Independence to Colonial Countries and Peoples, in consultation with the administering Power and with the assistance of the Secretary-General, to appoint immediately a special mission to visit the Seychelles for the purpose of recommending practical steps to be taken for the full implementation of the relevant resolutions of the General Assembly—in particular for the purpose of determining the extent of United Nations participation in the preparation and supervision of the referendum on the future status of the Territory—and to submit a report thereon to the Special Committee;

4. *Requests* the Special Committee to continue its examination of the question and to report thereon to the General Assembly at its twenty-seventh session.

A/C.4/L.1002. Cameroon, Egypt, Ghana, Guyana, Jamaica, Nigeria, Trinidad and Tobago, United Republic of Tanzania, Zambia: draft resolution, approved by Fourth Committee on 14 December 1971, meeting 1968, by 66 votes to 0, with 3 abstentions.

A/8616. Report of Fourth Committee, draft resolution II.

RESOLUTION 2867(XXVI), as recommended by Fourth Committee, A/8616, adopted by Assembly on 20 December 1971, meeting 2028, by recorded vote of 110 to 0, with 7 abstentions, as follows:

In favour: Afghanistan, Algeria, Australia, Austria, Bahrain, Botswana, Brazil, Bulgaria, Burma, Burundi, Byelorussian SSR, Cameroon, Canada, Central African Republic, Ceylon, Chile, Colombia, Costa Rica, Cuba, Cyprus, Czechoslovakia, Dahomey, Denmark, Dominican Republic, Ecuador, Egypt, El Salvador, Equatorial Guinea, Ethiopia, Fiji, Finland, Gambia, Ghana, Greece, Guatemala, Guinea, Guyana, Haiti, Hungary, Iceland, India, Indonesia, Iran, Iraq, Ireland, Israel, Italy, Ivory Coast, Jamaica, Japan, Jordan, Kenya, Khmer Republic, Kuwait, Laos, Lebanon, Lesotho, Liberia, Libyan Arab Republic, Madagascar, Malaysia, Mali, Malta, Mauritania, Mexico, Mongolia, Morocco, Nepal, Netherlands, New Zealand, Nicaragua, Nigeria, Norway, Oman, Pakistan, Panama, Paraguay, People's Democratic Republic of Yemen, Peru, Philippines, Poland, Romania, Rwanda, Saudi Arabia, Senegal, Sierra Leone, Singapore, Somalia, Spain, Sudan, Swaziland, Sweden, Syrian Arab Republic, Thailand, Togo, Trinidad and Tobago, Tunisia, Turkey, Uganda, Ukrainian SSR, USSR, United Arab Emirates, United Republic of Tanzania, Upper Volta, Uruguay, Venezuela, Yemen, Yugoslavia, Zaire, Zambia.

Against: None.

Abstaining: Argentina, Barbados, Belgium, France, Luxembourg, Malawi, United States.

The General Assembly,

Having considered the question of Antigua, Dominica, Grenada, St. Kitts-Nevis-Anguilla, St. Lucia and St. Vincent,

Recalling its resolution 1514(XV) of 14 December 1960,

containing the Declaration on the Granting of Independence to Colonial Countries and Peoples, and its resolution 2621(XXV) of 12 October 1970, containing the programme of action for the full implementation of the Declaration,

Recalling further its previous resolutions relating to the question, in particular resolution 2710(XXV) of 14 December 1970,

Having examined the relevant chapter of the report of the Special Committee on the Situation with regard to the Implementation of the Declaration on the Granting of Independence to Colonial Countries and Peoples,

1. *Takes note* of the chapter of the report of the Special Committee on the Situation with regard to the Implementation of the Declaration on the Granting of Independence to Colonial Countries and Peoples relating to Antigua, Dominica, Grenada, St. Kitts-Nevis-Anguilla, St. Lucia and St. Vincent;

2. *Requests* the Special Committee to give full consideration to this question in accordance with the provisions of the relevant resolutions of the General Assembly, in particular resolution 2593(XXIV) of 16 December 1969, and to report thereon to the Assembly at its twenty-seventh session.

A/C.4/L.1006. Afghanistan, Ecuador, Ethiopia, Fiji, Ghana, India, Indonesia, Iran, Iraq, Kenya, Nigeria, Philippines, Sierra Leone, Sweden, Trinidad and Tobago, Yugoslavia, Zambia: draft resolution, approved by Fourth Committee on 15 December 1971, meeting 1970, by recorded vote of 79 to 0, with 1 abstention, as follows:

In favour: Afghanistan, Algeria, Argentina, Australia, Austria, Barbados, Belgium, Botswana, Brazil, Bulgaria, Burundi, Byelorussian SSR, Cameroon, Canada, Ceylon, Chile, Costa Rica, Denmark, Ethiopia, Finland, Ghana, Greece, Guyana, Hungary, Iceland, India, Indonesia, Iran, Ireland, Italy, Ivory Coast, Jamaica, Japan, Jordan, Kenya, Khmer Republic, Laos, Lebanon, Libyan Arab Republic, Luxembourg, Madagascar, Malaysia, Mali, Mexico, Mongolia, Morocco, Netherlands, New Zealand, Nicaragua, Niger, Nigeria, Norway, People's Democratic Republic of Yemen, Peru, Philippines, Poland, Romania, Rwanda, Saudi Arabia, Senegal, Singapore, Spain, Sweden, Syrian Arab Republic, Togo, Trinidad and Tobago, Tunisia, Turkey, Uganda, Ukrainian SSR, USSR, United Kingdom, United Republic of Tanzania, United States, Upper Volta, Venezuela, Yugoslavia, Zaire, Zambia.

Against: None.

Abstaining: France.

A/C.4/L.1010. Administrative and financial implications of 17-power draft resolution, A/C.4/L.1006. Statement by Secretary-General.

A/C.5/1428, A/8632. Administrative and financial implications of, *inter alia,* draft resolution III recommended by Fourth Committee in A/8616. Statement by Secretary-General and report of Fifth Committee.

A/8616. Report of Fourth Committee, draft resolution III.

RESOLUTION 2868(XXVI), as recommended by Fourth Committee, A/8616, adopted by Assembly on 20 December 1971, meeting 2028, by recorded vote of 117 to 0, with 1 abstention, as follows:

In favour: Afghanistan, Algeria, Argentina, Australia, Austria, Bahrain, Barbados, Belgium, Botswana, Brazil, Bulgaria, Burma, Burundi, Byelorussian SSR, Cameroon, Canada, Central African Republic, Ceylon, Chile, Colombia, Costa Rica, Cuba, Cyprus, Czechoslovakia, Dahomey, Denmark, Dominican Republic, Ecuador, Egypt, El Salvador, Equatorial Guinea, Ethiopia, Fiji, Finland, Gambia, Ghana, Greece, Guatemala, Guinea, Guyana, Haiti, Honduras, Hungary, Iceland, India, Indonesia, Iran, Iraq, Ireland, Israel, Italy, Ivory Coast, Jamaica, Japan, Jordan, Kenya, Khmer Republic, Kuwait, Laos, Lebanon, Lesotho, Liberia, Libyan Arab Republic, Luxembourg, Madagascar, Malawi, Malaysia, Mali, Malta, Mauritania, Mexico, Mongolia, Morocco, Nepal, Netherlands, New Zealand, Nicaragua,

Nigeria, Norway, Oman, Pakistan, Panama, Paraguay, People's Democratic Republic of Yemen, Peru, Philippines, Poland, Romania, Rwanda, Saudi Arabia, Senegal, Sierra Leone, Singapore, Somalia, Spain, Sudan, Swaziland, Sweden, Syrian Arab Republic, Thailand, Togo, Trinidad and Tobago, Tunisia, Turkey, Uganda, Ukrainian SSR, USSR, United Arab Emirates, United Kingdom, United Republic of Tanzania, United States, Upper Volta, Uruguay, Venezuela, Yemen, Zaire, Zambia.

Against: None.

Abstaining: France.

The General Assembly,

Having considered the question of Niue and the Tokelau Islands,

Having examined the relevant chapters of the report of the Special Committee on the Situation with regard to the Implementation of the Declaration on the Granting of Independence to Colonial Countries and Peoples,

Recalling its resolution 1514(XV) of 14 December 1960, containing the Declaration on the Granting of Independence to Colonial Countries and Peoples,

Having heard the statement of the representative of the administering Power,

Taking into account the conclusions and recommendations of the Special Committee regarding developments in Niue and the Tokelau Islands,

Noting the recent constitutional developments in Niue which have been embodied in the Niue Amendment Act, enacted in 1971 by the Government of New Zealand as the administering Power,

Noting with appreciation that the administering Power has responded positively to the requests contained in the relevant resolutions of the General Assembly by extending an invitation to the Special Committee to send a visiting mission to Niue and the Tokelau Islands in 1972,

1. *Reaffirms* the inalienable right of the people of Niue and the Tokelau Islands to self-determination in conformity with General Assembly resolution 1514(XV);

2. *Calls upon* the administering Power to take further measures, in accordance with the wishes of the people, to enable the people of the Territory to exercise their right to self-determination as soon as possible;

3. *Takes note* of the arrangements made by the Special Committee on the Situation with regard to the Implementation of the Declaration on the Granting of Independence to Colonial Countries and Peoples for the dispatch of a visiting mission to Niue in 1972 and requests the Special Committee to instruct the visiting mission to obtain first-hand information on conditions in the Territory and on the wishes and aspirations of its people and to recommend practical steps for their advancement as soon as possible towards self-government and self-determination;

4. *Requests* the administering Power to provide all the necessary assistance and facilities to the visiting mission in the discharge of its tasks ;

5. *Requests* the Special Committee to continue to examine this question and to report thereon to the General Assembly at its twenty-seventh session.

A/C.4/L.1011. Cameroon, Congo, Ethiopia, Ghana, Guinea, India, Kenya, Mongolia, People's Democratic Republic of Yemen, Rwanda, Sierra Leone, Syrian Arab Republic, Uganda, United Republic of Tanzania, Yugoslavia, Zambia: draft resolution, approved by Fourth Committee on 16 December 1971, meeting 1971, by recorded vote of 73 to 0, with 18 abstentions, as follows:

In favour: Afghanistan, Algeria, Argentina, Barbados, Botswana, Brazil, Bulgaria, Burma, Burundi, Byelorussian SSR, Cameroon, Ceylon, Chad, Chile, Colombia, Cuba, Czechoslovakia, Ecuador, Equatorial Guinea, Ethiopia, Gambia, Ghana, Greece, Guatemala, Guinea, Guyana, Hungary, India, Indonesia, Iran, Iraq, Ireland, Ivory Coast, Jamaica, Jordan, Lebanon, Liberia, Libyan Arab Republic, Madagascar, Malaysia, Mali, Mexico, Mongolia, Morocco, Nepal, Nigeria, Peru, Philip-

pines, Poland, Romania, Rwanda, Saudi Arabia, Senegal, Singapore, Somalia, Spain, Sudan, Swaziland, Syrian Arab Republic, Thailand, Togo, Trinidad and Tobago, Tunisia, Turkey, Ukrainian SSR, USSR, United Republic of Tanzania, Upper Volta, Venezuela, Yemen, Yugoslavia, Zaire, Zambia.

Against: None.

Abstaining: Australia, Austria, Belgium, Canada, Denmark, Finland, France, Iceland, Italy, Japan, Luxembourg, Netherlands, New Zealand, Norway, Portugal, Sweden, United Kingdom, United States.

A/8616. Report of Fourth Committee, draft resolution IV.

RESOLUTION 2869(XXVI), as recommended by Fourth Committee, A/8616, adopted by Assembly on 20 December 1971, meeting 2028, by recorded vote of 98 to 1, with 19 abstentions, as follows:

In favour: Afghanistan, Algeria, Argentina, Bahrain, Barbados, Botswana, Brazil, Bulgaria, Burma, Burundi, Byelorussian SSR, Cameroon, Central African Republic, Ceylon, Chile, Colombia, Cuba, Cyprus, Czechoslovakia, Dahomey, Dominican Republic, Ecuador, Egypt, El Salvador, Equatorial Guinea, Ethiopia, Gambia, Ghana, Greece, Guatemala, Guinea, Guyana, Haiti, Honduras, Hungary, India, Indonesia, Iran, Iraq, Ireland, Israel, Ivory Coast, Jamaica, Jordan, Kenya, Khmer Republic, Kuwait, Laos, Lebanon, Lesotho, Liberia, Libyan Arab Republic, Madagascar, Malaysia, Mali, Malta, Mauritania, Mexico, Mongolia, Morocco, Nepal, Nicaragua, Nigeria, Oman, Pakistan, Panama, Paraguay, People's Democratic Republic of Yemen, Peru, Philippines, Poland, Romania, Rwanda, Saudi Arabia, Senegal, Sierra Leone, Singapore, Somalia, Spain, Sudan, Swaziland, Syrian Arab Republic, Thailand, Togo, Trinidad and Tobago, Tunisia, Turkey, Uganda, Ukrainian SSR, USSR, United Arab Emirates, United Republic of Tanzania, Upper Volta, Uruguay, Venezuela, Yemen, Zaire, Zambia.

Against: Costa Rica.*

Abstaining: Australia, Austria, Belgium, Canada, Denmark, Finland, France, Iceland, Italy, Japan, Luxembourg, Malawi, Netherlands, New Zealand, Norway, Portugal, Sweden, United Kingdom, United States.

*Subsequently, Costa Rica advised the Secretariat that it had intended to abstain.

The General Assembly,

Having considered the question of American Samoa, Bahamas, Bermuda, British Virgin Islands, Brunei, Cayman Islands, Cocos (Keeling) Islands, Gilbert and Ellice Islands, Guam, Montserrat, New Hebrides, Pitcairn, St. Helena, Seychelles, Solomon Islands, Turks and Caicos Islands and the United States Virgin Islands,

Having examined the relevant chapters of the report of the Special Committee on the Situation with regard to the Implementation of the Declaration on the Granting of Independence to Colonial Countries and Peoples,

Recalling its resolution 1514(XV) of 14 December 1960, containing the Declaration on the Granting of Independence to Colonial Countries and Peoples, and its resolution 2621(XXV) of 12 October 1970, containing the programme of action for the full implementation of the Declaration,

Recalling its previous resolutions relating to those Territories, in particular resolution 2709(XXV) of 14 December 1970,

Deploring the policy of some administering Powers in establishing and maintaining military bases in some of the Territories under their administration, in contravention of the relevant resolutions of the General Assembly,

Deeply deploring the attitude of those administering Powers which continue to refuse to allow United Nations missions to visit the Territories under their administration,

Convinced of the vital importance of visiting missions as a means of securing adequate and first-hand information in regard to political, economic and social conditions in the Territories and to the views, wishes and aspirations of the people in those Territories,

Conscious that those Territories require the continued attention and assistance of the United Nations in the achievement by their peoples of the objectives embodied in the Charter of the United Nations and in the Declaration on the Granting of Independence to Colonial Countries and Peoples,

Aware of the special circumstances of the geographical location and the economic conditions of those Territories,

1. *Approves* the chapters of the report of the Special Committee on the Situation with regard to the Implementation of the Declaration on the Granting of Independence to Colonial Countries and Peoples relating to those Territories;

2. *Reaffirms* the inalienable right of the peoples of those Territories to self-determination and independence in accordance with the Declaration on the Granting of Independence to Colonial Countries and Peoples;

3. *Calls upon* the administering Powers to take all necessary steps, without further delay, to ensure the full and speedy attainment of the goals set forth in the Declaration with respect to those Territories;

4. *Reaffirms its conviction* that the questions of territorial size, geographical isolation and limited resources should in no way delay the implementation of the Declaration with respect to those Territories;

5. *Deprecates* any attempt aimed at the partial or total disruption of the national unity and territorial integrity of colonial Territories and the establishment of military bases and installations in those Territories, as being incompatible with the purposes and principles of the Charter of the United Nations and General Assembly resolution 1514(XV);

6. *Calls upon* the administering Powers concerned to reconsider their attitude towards the receiving of visiting missions to the above-mentioned Territories and to permit access by such missions to Territories under their administration;

7. *Decides* that the United Nations should render all help to the peoples of those Territories in their efforts freely to decide their future status;

8. *Requests* the Special Committee to continue to give full consideration to this question, including in particular the dispatch of visiting missions to those Territories, and to report to the General Assembly at its twenty-seventh session on the implementation of the present resolution.

British Honduras

A/8453. Letter of 4 October 1971 from United Kingdom.

A/8616. Report of Fourth Committee, paras. 9 and 26.

A/8429. Resolutions adopted by General Assembly during its 26th session, 21 September–22 December 1971. Other decisions, pp. 111-112.

Chapter III

The question of Namibia

During 1971, decisions concerning Namibia were taken by various United Nations bodies, including the Security Council, the General Assembly and the Assembly's Special Committee on the Situation with regard to the Implementation of the Declaration on the Granting of Independence to Colonial Countries and Peoples.

On 21 June 1971, the International Court of Justice delivered an advisory opinion—in response to a 1970 Security Council request for an opinion as to the legal consequences for States of South Africa's continued presence in Namibia—by which it held, among other things, that the continued presence of South Africa in Namibia being illegal, South Africa was under an obligation to withdraw its administration from the territory immediately, and that United Nations Member States were under an obligation to recognize the illegality of South Africa's presence in Namibia and the illegality of its acts concerning the territory.

On 22 June, the Chairman of the Special Committee issued a statement declaring that the Court's opinion underlined the urgent need for the Security Council to consider taking effective measures envisaged under the Charter to eliminate the illegal colonial oppression of the Namibians. Subsequently, on 2 September 1971, the Special Committee approved a consensus by which

it expressed the hope that the Security Council would, in the light of the advisory opinion, consider taking all effective measures envisaged under the Charter so as to ensure attainment, with respect to Namibia, of the goals set out in the 1960 Declaration on the Granting of Independence to Colonial Countries and Peoples.[1]

The Security Council, meeting in September-October 1971 to consider the question of Namibia, adopted a resolution on 20 October by which, among other things, it declared that South Africa's continued illegal presence in Namibia constituted an internationally wrongful act and a breach of international obligations; agreed with the Court's advisory opinion of 21 June 1971; called once again upon South Africa to withdraw from Namibia; declared that any further refusal of South Africa to withdraw could create conditions detrimental to the maintenance of peace and security in the region; and called upon all States to take various specific measures in discharge of their responsibilities towards the people of Namibia.

The General Assembly, considering the question later in 1971, had before it the report of the United Nations Council for Namibia. The Council

[1]See Y.U.N., 1960, pp. 49-50, resolution 1514(XV) of 14 December 1960, containing text of Declaration.

reported that South Africa not only had continued its illegal occupation of the territory but had persisted in applying the policies of *apartheid* and other repressive measures designed to destroy the unity and territorial integrity of Namibia and to consolidate its hold over the territory. In view of the advisory opinion of the International Court of Justice that the South African presence in Namibia was illegal, the Council concluded that the United Nations was the only entity which could lawfully administer the territory and that the Council was the (interim) *de jure* Government of Namibia.

On 20 December 1971, the Assembly adopted two resolutions concerning Namibia. By the first, among other things it: reaffirmed the inalienable right of the people of Namibia to self-determination and independence; welcomed the advisory opinion of the Court; invited the Security Council to take effective measures, in conformity with relevant provisions of the United Nations Charter, to secure the withdrawal by South Africa of its illegal administration from Namibia; called upon all States to take effective economic and other measures designed to ensure the withdrawal of South Africa; reaffirmed the direct responsibility

of the United Nations in regard to the territory of Namibia; and asked the Council for Namibia to continue to discharge the functions entrusted to it.

By the second resolution, the Assembly among other things reaffirmed its previous decision to establish a United Nations Fund for Namibia and decided, as a transitional measure, to allocate to the Fund the sum of $50,000 from the regular United Nations budget.

Other resolutions affecting Namibia adopted by the General Assembly in 1971 dealt with, among other things, the implementation of the Declaration on the Granting of Independence to Colonial Countries and Peoples;[2] the activities of foreign economic interests which impeded the implementation of the Declaration; and measures to combat racial discrimination and *apartheid* in southern Africa.

Decisions relating to Namibia were also taken by the Economic and Social Council and the Commission on Human Rights.

These decisions and related matters are described below.

[2] *Ibid.*

Political and related developments

Communications to Security Council

By a letter dated 13 July 1971, addressed to the President of the Security Council, the Executive Secretary of the Organization of African Unity (OAU) transmitted the text of a resolution concerning Namibia, adopted by the eighth Assembly of Heads of State and Government of OAU on 23 June 1971. Among other things, the resolution noted with approval the advisory opinion of the International Court of Justice of 21 June 1971 and called for a special meeting of the Security Council to discuss ways and means of enforcing the past decisions of the United Nations with regard to Namibia, in the light of the advisory opinion.

On 30 July 1971, the Secretary-General informed the President of the Security Council that by a letter of 12 July, the Minister for Foreign Affairs of Sudan, in his capacity as Chairman of the Council of Ministers of OAU, had requested that a meeting of the Council be convened on 27 September 1971 to consider the question of Namibia, in the light of the Court's advisory opinion of 21 June.

Opinion of International Court of Justice

On 16 July 1971, the Secretary-General transmitted to members of the Security Council the text of the advisory opinion given by the International Court of Justice on 21 June 1971 concerning the legal consequences for States of the continued

presence of South Africa in Namibia (South West Africa), notwithstanding Security Council resolution 276(1970).[3] The question had been put to the International Court by the Security Council on 29 July 1970.[4]

The Court was of the opinion: (1) that, the continued presence of South Africa in Namibia being illegal, South Africa was under obligation to withdraw its administration from Namibia immediately and thus put an end to its occupation of the territory; (2) that States Members of the United Nations were under obligation to recognize the illegality of South Africa's presence in Namibia and the invalidity of its acts on behalf of or concerning Namibia, and to refrain from any acts and in particular any dealings with the Government of South Africa implying recognition of the legality of, or lending support or assistance to, such presence and administration; and (3) that it was incumbent upon States which were not Members of the United Nations to give assistance, within the scope of sub-paragraph (2) above, in the action which had been taken by the United Nations with regard to Namibia.

(For further information on the Court's advisory opinion, see pp. 581-86.)

[3] See Y.U.N., 1970, pp. 752-53, text of resolution 276(1970) of 30 January 1970.
[4] *Ibid.*, p. 754, text of resolution 284 (1970).

Consideration by Security Council

By a letter of 17 September 1971, addressed to the President of the Security Council, representatives of 37 African Member States noted that on 23 June 1971, the eighth Assembly of Heads of State and Government of OAU had adopted a resolution urging that the Council be convened immediately to discuss ways and means of enforcing the past decisions of the United Nations with respect to Namibia, in the light of the legal obligation imposed on the world community by the decision of the International Court of Justice of 21 June 1971. The letter asked that the Council be convened on 27 September in order to enable Moktar Ould Daddah, President of Mauritania and current President of OAU, to participate in the debate, at the head of a delegation of ministers from African countries.

The security Council considered the situation in Namibia at meetings held between 27 September and 20 October 1971. The President of OAU and the President of the United Nations Council for Namibia addressed the Council; representatives of Chad, Ethiopia, Guyana, India, Liberia, Mauritius, Nigeria, Saudi Arabia, South Africa, Sudan and Uganda also participated in the discussion, without the right to vote.

The Council had before it a report of its *Ad Hoc* Sub-Committee on Namibia, established in 1970 to study ways and means by which the relevant resolutions of the Council could be effectively implemented, in the light of the flagrant refusal of South Africa to withdraw from Namibia.[5] The report, the third submitted by the Sub-Committee, covered 17 meetings held between 21 August 1970 and 23 September 1971 and took into account the Court's advisory opinion of 21 June 1971.

The report included: (*a*) proposals relating to political, economic, legal, military and other aspects of the question of Namibia which were generally acceptable to the *Ad Hoc* Sub-Committee; (*b*) proposals submitted by Burundi, Sierra Leone, Somalia and the Syrian Arab Republic, on which agreement could not be reached; and (*c*) a proposal by Italy and the United States on which agreement also could not be reached.

Opening the general debate in the Security Council, the President of OAU said his organization had welcomed the conclusions of the International Court of Justice as set forth in its advisory opinion of 21 June 1971. Consequently, OAU had asked that the Security Council apply the pertinent provisions of Chapter VII of the United Nations Charter (concerning action to be taken with respect to threats to the peace and acts of aggression)[6] to achieve the immediate and unconditional withdrawal of South Africa's illegal administration from the international territory of Namibia. Once this had been accomplished, the

United Nations should create the necessary conditions for the independence of Namibia, in consultation with the Namibian people and OAU. The international community should also be called upon to apply appropriate political, military and economic sanctions against South Africa. It was the duty of the Council to assume its responsibilities and ensure that the objectives and decisions of the United Nations were respected, the President of OAU held.

The representative of Burundi, speaking as Chairman of the *Ad Hoc* Sub-Committee on Namibia, stated that despite the divergent viewpoints expressed on various parts of the Sub-Committee's report, all members of the Security Council were aware of the need to approve and to implement the opinion handed down by the International Court of Justice. To fail to discharge an obligation to protect the integrity of the Court would be tantamount to a serious infringement of the very prestige of the organs of the United Nations.

The President of the United Nations Council for Namibia said that by confirming once again that South Africa's continued occupation of Namibia was illegal, the International Court of Justice had recognized the United Nations Council for Namibia as the *de jure* Government of Namibia. But although within its current terms of reference the Council had the legal powers of a sovereign entity vis-à-vis Namibia, it was unable to exercise those powers, particularly inside the territory. The scope of activities of the Council must be broadened in conformity with its proper status, the President of the Council said. Once South Africa's occupation of Namibia was terminated, the Council should be provided with adequate funds and resources from the United Nations regular budget. The appointment of a full-time Commissioner for Namibia would also strengthen the Council.

The Minister for Foreign Affairs of South Africa declared that the advisory opinion of the International Court of Justice concerning Namibia was completely unacceptable to his Government. The Court had evaded the fundamental issue—namely, whether there was any provision of the Charter under which the General Assembly had the power to terminate South Africa's Mandate. The Court had said only that it would not be correct to assume that, because the General Assembly was in principle vested with recommendatory powers, it was debarred from adopting, in specific cases within the framework of its competence, resolutions that made determinations or had operative design. It followed from the Court's opinion that merely by invoking Article 10 of the Charter,[7] the

---

[5]See footnote 3.
[6]For text of Chapter VII, see APPENDIX II.
[7]For text of Article 10, see APPENDIX II.

General Assembly could oblige States to submit reports and to accept its supervision in regard to any matter the Assembly might choose to discuss. Moreover, within the framework of its competence, the Assembly would even be able to abrogate or alter territorial rights.

The Court's findings in regard to the powers of the Security Council were even more unreasoning and unconvincing, the Foreign Minister continued. The Court had stated that Article 24 of the Charter conferred upon the Council general powers which might be exercised whenever a situation might lead to a breach of the peace, and that such powers were additional to those specifically granted to the Council under the Charter (Chapters VI, VII, VIII and XII); moreover, the Court had stated that, should the Council so intend, any decision it might take would be binding in terms of Article 25.[8] According to the Court, the Council would no longer be restricted to acting in situations that constituted a threat to the peace or were likely to endanger the peace. It would be sufficient that in the Council's view a situation might lead to a breach of the peace.

The South African Foreign Minister said that the Court, in arriving at its opinion, had ignored or brushed aside its earlier judgements which had substantiated South Africa's contention. Moreover, the Court had gone out of its way to censure South Africa's policies in the territory; the purpose of this censure was clearly political rather than legal and emphasized the basically political nature of the opinion.

The Foreign Minister of South Africa asserted that South West Africa enjoyed peace, prosperity and progress and posed no threat to international peace and security. South Africa was making determined efforts to bring the peoples of South West Africa towards self-government; the process would continue until the stage of full self-determination was reached. The tangible benefits of South Africa's administration of the territory, in both human and material terms, were there to be seen; the Foreign Minister again invited the Secretary-General or his representative to visit the territory.

Later in the debate, South Africa explained that, in its view, the principle of self-determination entailed that a nation might choose independence or, if it preferred, political union or federation with another consenting nation or nations. This conception was in accordance with the United Nations Charter, which spoke of the self-determination of peoples and not of territories, South Africa said.

Most African and Asian representatives participating in the Council's discussion welcomed the Court's advisory opinion. They held that the Security Council, and especially its permanent members, now had the duty to act effectively to end South Africa's illegal occupation of Namibia.

Somalia and Nigeria said the Security Council should call on South Africa to enter into discussions with the Secretary-General to arrange for its withdrawal from the territory. Ethiopia held that if South Africa genuinely desired to recognize change in Namibia, it should voluntarily end its illegal occupation; failing that, the Security Council was duty-bound to invoke the appropriate enforcement measures. A number of African States said the Council should declare that South Africa's failure to withdraw from Namibia would constitute an act of aggression and a threat to international peace and security within the context of Article VII of the Charter.

Poland and the USSR declared that the advisory opinion of the Court had confirmed all previous United Nations decisions concerning Namibia. The Security Council could not now limit itself to adopting resolutions but had to take practical measures to ensure South Africa's withdrawal from the territory.

The USSR and many African and Asian representatives also charged that the Western powers were encouraging South Africa's defiance of the United Nations by providing economic and military assistance to that régime. They called for an immediate end to all economic support of South Africa and a strict embargo on the supply of arms and military equipment to that country.

A number of members held that the Council should recognize the legitimacy of the struggle being waged by the national liberation movement in Namibia.

The President of the South West Africa People's Organization (SWAPO), Sam Nujoma, who was invited to speak under rule 39 of the provisional rules of procedure, said that the people of Namibia enthusiastically welcomed the Court's advisory opinion. It was now up to the Security Council to take concrete and immediate action under Chapter VII of the Charter. Contrary to the claim of the South African Foreign Minister, the African majority did not benefit financially or materially from the economic development of Namibia; in Namibia, as in South Africa, everything was geared towards benefiting the white section of the population. The people of Namibia wanted an immediate end to South African rule; unless the Security Council acted decisively to secure South Africa's withdrawal, they would have no alternative but to continue their armed struggle, the President of SWAPO said.

Several Council members took issue with the arguments advanced by South Africa challenging the legality of the Court's opinion. The representative of Liberia stated that the General Assembly

---

[8]For text of articles and chapters mentioned herein, see APPENDIX II.

had the power to terminate the Mandate of South West Africa, even though such power was not specifically expressed in the Covenant of the League of Nations. Moreover, the representative said, it was a fundamental principle of law that the continuation of a right depended on the performance of the corresponding duty; although South Africa claimed that the General Assembly did not have the power to terminate the Mandate, it ascribed to itself the right unilaterally to terminate its obligation under the same Mandate.

The representative of Sierra Leone said that contrary to the statement by the Foreign Minister of South Africa, the Court had not evaded the issue of whether the United Nations had the power to terminate South Africa's Mandate. It was the Court's opinion that resolutions of the General Assembly were not, in respect of Mandates, limited only to the form of recommendations and that in adopting its resolutions concerning Namibia the Security Council was acting in exercise of what it considered its prime responsibility: the maintenance of peace and security. South Africa could not now renounce Article 93 of the United Nations Charter, under which all Member States were declared *ipso facto* parties to the Statute of the International Court of Justice, the representative said.[9]

India maintained that it was irrelevant whether or not the League of Nations had the power to terminate the Mandate unilaterally; since it had been clearly recognized that no advantage should accrue to a mandatory power as a consequence of the Mandate, it would be illegal to allow South Africa to annex Namibia.

Reservations concerning the advisory opinion were expressed by several members. France and the United Kingdom rejected the Court's conclusions that the General Assembly could take binding decisions for States within the framework of its competence, and that the Security Council could take binding decisions outside the framework of Chapter VII of the Charter.

The United Kingdom held that the notion of the revocability of the Mandate was not incorporated in the Covenant of the League of Nations or in the individual Mandates; even if the possibility of revocation existed, that power could not have been exercised without the consent of the Mandatary. The United Kingdom stated further that the advisory opinion of the Court was not binding on the international community.

Both France and the United Kingdom held that the solution to the problem lay in negotiations with South Africa.

The representatives of Argentina, Belgium, Italy and Japan agreed with the Court's conclusions, although they had reservations about some of its reasoning.

On 20 October 1971, a draft resolution sponsored by Burundi, Sierra Leone, Somalia and the Syrian Arab Republic was adopted by the Security Council as its resolution 301(1971).

The Council thereby:

(1) reaffirmed that the territory of Namibia was the direct responsibility of the United Nations and that this responsibility included the obligation to support and promote the rights of the people of Namibia in accordance with the Declaration on the Granting of Independence to Colonial Countries and Peoples;[10]

(2) reaffirmed the national unity and territorial integrity of Namibia;

(3) condemned all moves by South Africa designed to destroy that unity and territorial integrity, such as the establishment of Bantustans;

(4) declared that South Africa's continued illegal presence in Namibia constituted an internationally wrongful act and breach of international obligations, and that South Africa remained accountable to the international community for any violations of its international obligations or the rights of the people of the territory of Namibia;

(5) took note with appreciation of the advisory opinion of the International Court of Justice of 21 June 1971;

(6) agreed with the above opinion;

(7) declared that all matters affecting the rights of the people of Namibia were of immediate concern to all States Members of the United Nations, and that States should take this into account in their dealings with South Africa, in particular in any dealings implying recognition of the legality of, or lending support or assistance to, such illegal presence and administration;

(8) called once again on South Africa to withdraw from the territory of Namibia;

(9) declared that any further refusal of South Africa to withdraw from Namibia could create conditions detrimental to the maintenance of peace and security in the region;

(10) reaffirmed the provisions of its resolution 283(1970) of 29 July 1970, concerning Namibia;[11]

(11) called upon all States in discharge of their responsibilities towards the people of Namibia and, subject to the exceptions set forth in the advisory opinion of the International Court of Justice of 21 June 1971: (*a*) to abstain from entering into treaty relations with South Africa in all cases in which South Africa purported to act on behalf of or concerning Namibia; (*b*) to abstain from invoking or applying those treaties or provisions of treaties concluded by South Africa on behalf of or concerning Namibia which

---

[9]For text of Article 93, see APPENDIX II.
[10]See Y.U.N., 1960, pp. 49-50, resolution 1514(XV) of 14 December 1960, containing text of Declaration.
[11]See Y.U.N., 1970, pp. 753-54.

involved active inter-governmental co-operation; (c) to review their bilateral treaties with South Africa in order to ensure that they were not inconsistent with the advisory opinion of the Court of 21 June 1971; (d) to abstain from sending diplomatic or special missions to South Africa that included the territory of Namibia in their jurisdiction; (e) to abstain from sending consular agents to Namibia and to withdraw any such agents already there; (f) to abstain from entering into economic and other forms of relationship or dealings with South Africa on behalf of or concerning Namibia which might entrench its authority over the territory;

(12) declared that franchises, rights, titles or contracts relating to Namibia granted to individuals or companies by South Africa after the adoption of the General Assembly resolution of 27 October 1966 (which terminated South Africa's Mandate over Namibia)[12] were not subject to protection or espousal by their States against claims of a future lawful Government of Namibia;

(13) requested the *Ad Hoc* Sub-Committee on Namibia to continue to carry out the tasks entrusted to it by the Security Council on 29 July 1970[13] and, in particular, to study appropriate measures for the fulfilment of the responsibility of the United Nations towards Namibia;

(14) requested the *Ad Hoc* Sub-Committee on Namibia to review and report periodically on all treaties and agreements which were contrary to the provisions of the present resolution in order to ascertain whether States had entered into agreements which recognized South Africa's authority over Namibia;

(15) called upon all States to support and promote the rights of the people of Namibia and to this end to implement fully the provisions of the present resolution;

(16) requested the Secretary-General to report periodically on the implementation of the provisions of the present resolution.

The above resolution was adopted by a vote of 13 to 0, with 2 abstentions. (For text, see DOCUMENTARY REFERENCES below.)

Before the vote, France and the United Kingdom explained that they would abstain. France said it could not support a resolution which implicitly accepted the advisory opinion of the International Court of Justice; the United Kingdom could not accept the premises on which most of the provisions of the text were based.

The United States said that it supported the text, but that this should not be construed as reflecting any change in its position with regard to earlier resolutions mentioned in the text on which the United States had abstained; the United States noted that it had supported the Assembly resolution of 27 October 1966 terminating South

Africa's Mandate over the territory of Namibia.

Belgium stated that it would carry out with regard to the future only the provision by which the Assembly declared that franchises, rights, titles or contracts relating to Namibia which South Africa granted to individuals or companies after the General Assembly's termination of the Mandate on 27 October 1966 were not subject to protection or espousal by their States against claims of a future lawful Government of Namibia. Belgium did not believe that a retroactive effect should have been given to the provision.

Following the adoption of resolution 301(1971) on 20 October, a draft resolution was introduced in the Security Council by Argentina. As subsequently amended, it would have the Council: (1) invite the Secretary-General, acting on behalf of the United Nations, to initiate as soon as possible contacts with all parties concerned, with a view to establishing the necessary conditions so as to enable the people of Namibia, freely and with strict regard to the principles of human equality, to exercise their right to self-determination and independence, in accordance with the United Nations Charter; (2) call on South Africa to co-operate fully with the Secretary-General in the implementation of the present resolution; and (3) request the Secretary-General to report to the Security Council on the implementation of the resolution not later than 30 April 1972.

The representative of Argentina stated that the draft was not incompatible with the course of action laid down in resolution 301(1971), and that every possible alternative to ensure the future of Namibia should be explored.

The Council decided to defer consideration of the Argentine draft resolution.

On 16 November 1971, the President of the Security Council circulated a telegram dated 12 November from the Minister of Foreign Affairs of the German Democratic Republic expressing the support of his Government for the Security Council's decisions of 20 October embodied in resolution 301(1971).

Decisions of Human Rights Commission and of Economic and Social Council

On 21 May 1971, during its fiftieth session, the Economic and Social Council adopted several resolutions concerning the situation in the territories of southern Africa, including Namibia.

By resolution 1592(L), the Council recommended for adoption by the General Assembly a text concerning the implementation of United Nations resolutions relating to the right to self-determination of peoples under colonial and

---

[12]See Y.U.N., 1966, pp. 605-6, text of resolution 2145(XXI).
[13]See footnote 11.

alien domination. This text, in a revised form, was subsequently adopted by the Assembly as its resolution 2787(XXVI) (see below, page 559). (For text of resolution 1592(L), see pp. 422-23.)

By resolution 1599(L), the Council, after considering the report of its *Ad Hoc* Working Group of Experts on infringements of trade union rights in southern Africa: (1) strongly condemned the repression and detention of trade union leaders in southern Africa and called for their immediate release; and (2) requested the *Ad Hoc* Working Group to investigate and report to the Council on the system of recruitment of African workers in Namibia, Southern Rhodesia and the territories under Portuguese domination. (For text of resolution 1599(L), see page 441.)

Resolution 1591(L) concerned measures to be taken by the Assembly, the Security Council and other organs of the United Nations to combat policies of *apartheid* and racial discrimination in southern Africa. (For text of resolution 1591(L), see page 407.)

The Commission on Human Rights, at its twenty-seventh session (February-March 1971), adopted a resolution by which, among other things, it decided that its *Ad Hoc* Working Group of Experts should continue to survey developments in South Africa, Namibia, Southern Rhodesia and the territories under Portuguese administration, with particular reference to grave manifestations of colonialism and racial discrimination present in the situation prevailing in those areas resulting from the actions of the illegal South African régime in Namibia, the illegal minority régime in Southern Rhodesia and the Portuguese régime in Angola, Mozambique and Guinea (Bissau). The Commission asked the Group to remain active and vigilant in its observations of colonial and racially discriminatory practices in Africa and to bring to the Commission's attention at its 1972 session new developments in the area. (See also page 405.)

Consideration by Special Committee

The Special Committee on the Situation with regard to the Implementation of the Declaration on the Granting of Independence to Colonial Countries and Peoples[14] considered the question of Namibia at meetings held between 4 March and 9 September 1971.

In addition, the *Ad Hoc* Group established by the Special Committee held meetings in Africa during May. With respect to Namibia, the *Ad Hoc* Group heard statements, in public meetings, by the following petitioners: Duma Nokwe, African National Congress of South Africa (ANC); Moses Garoeb, Andreas Chipanga and Jesaya Nyamu, South West Africa People's Organization (SWAPO); A. Fataar and Miss Jane Gool, Unity Movement of

South Africa; Mrs. Ray E. Simons, South African Congress of Trade Unions (SACTU); Ahmed E. Ebrahim, Pan Africanist Congress (PAC); and a representative of the Movimento Popular de Libertação de Angola (MPLA).

The petitioners told the *Ad Hoc* Group that they opposed the policy of dialogue with South Africa; condemned the decision of the United Kingdom to resume arms sales to South Africa, which, they said, would constitute a further threat to international peace and security in the region; and rejected any plebiscite conducted in Namibia under the auspices of South Africa. They reported an intensification of repressive acts against their movements and collaboration between South Africa, Portugal and the illegal régime in Southern Rhodesia, and stated that armed struggle was the only means available to them to achieve self-determination and independence.

The Special Committee took a number of decisions concerning Namibia during 1971.

On 4 March, it approved a consensus deploring a decision by the United Kingdom to grant export licences for helicopters and spare parts to South Africa, which, it said, would have serious repercussions throughout the whole of southern Africa.

On 22 June 1971, the Chairman of the Special Committee made a statement regarding the International Court of Justice's advisory opinion of 21 June. The Chairman said that while the Special Committee had never had any doubt about the consequences of the continued illegal occupation of Namibia by South Africa, the opinion delivered by the Court once again underlined the anomaly existing in that part of Africa and the urgent need for the Security Council to consider taking effective measures envisaged under the Charter to eliminate the illegal colonial oppression of the Namibians.

On 2 September 1971, the Special Committee approved a consensus by which, *inter alia,* it noted that despite the repeated demands of the General Assembly and the Security Council to withdraw immediately from the territory, South Africa had not only continued its illegal occupation of Namibia but had persisted in the application of the criminal policies of *apartheid* and other repressive measures designed to destroy the unity and territorial integrity of Namibia and to consolidate its illegal presence in the territory. In so doing, South Africa had intensified its collaboration with Portugal and the illegal régime in Southern Rhodesia by extending further military assistance to these régimes; Portugal, South Africa and the illegal régime in Southern Rhodesia had stepped up their military operations against the peoples under their domination who were struggling to

[14]See footnote 10.

assert their legitimate right to freedom and independence, and the resultant situation continued to threaten the peace and security of neighbouring independent African States.

The Special Committee condemned the support South Africa received in pursuit of its policies of economic exploitation of the Namibians, in particular from its major trading partners and financial, economic and other interests operating in Namibia. The Special Committee called upon the Governments concerned to withdraw forthwith the support they accorded South Africa.

The Committee expressed the hope that in the light of the advisory opinion of the International Court of Justice of 21 June 1971, the Security Council would consider, without further delay, taking all effective measures envisaged under the Charter so as to ensure attainment, with respect to Namibia, of the goals set out in the Declaration on the Granting of Independence to Colonial Countries and Peoples. It endorsed the call for a special meeting of the Security Council contained in a resolution adopted by the Assembly of Heads of State and Government of the Organization of African Unity (OAU) on 23 June 1971.

Also, the Special Committee called upon all States, specialized agencies and other organizations within the United Nations system, in consultation with OAU, to provide increased moral and material assistance to the people of Namibia in their struggle against foreign occupation and oppression. In view of the armed conflict in the territory and the inhuman treatment of prisoners, the Special Committee invited the International Committee of the Red Cross to exercise its good offices with a view to securing application to that situation of the 1949 Geneva Conventions relative to the Treatment of Prisoners of War and to the Protection of Civilian Persons in Time of War.

On 9 September 1971, the Special Committee adopted a resolution concerning all territories in southern Africa. The Committee thereby, among other things, reaffirmed the legitimate right of the peoples in Southern Rhodesia, Namibia and the territories under Portuguese domination to struggle by all necessary means at their disposal against the colonialist authorities which denied them their freedom and independence, as well as the obligation of Member States to render all necessary moral and material assistance to those peoples. The Committee condemned the increasing collaboration between Portugal, South Africa and the illegal racist minority régime in Southern Rhodesia, which was designed to perpetuate colonialism and oppression in southern Africa. It urged all States to increase their financial and material assistance to the peoples of those territories in their struggle for the restoration of their inalienable rights and requested all States, directly

and through the organizations of the United Nations system, to discontinue all collaboration with the Governments of Portugal and South Africa, and with the illegal régime in Southern Rhodesia.

Report of United Nations Council for Namibia

In its report to the General Assembly's 1971 session, the United Nations Council for Namibia gave an account of its activities during the period 13 October 1970 to 28 October 1971, including the progress it had made towards discharging the tasks entrusted to it by the General Assembly. These related, among other things, to the issuance of travel documents for Namibians; the establishment of a co-ordinated emergency programme of technical and financial assistance to Namibia; the organization of an educational and training programme for Namibians; a review of laws and practices established in the territory by South Africa which were contrary to the purposes and principles of the United Nations Charter; and consultation with representatives of the Namibian people and with the Organization of African Unity (OAU).

During a visit to various countries of Africa and Europe during June 1971, the Council reached agreement with the Governments of Kenya and Nigeria concerning recognition of the Council's travel documents for Namibians, and held substantive discussions with the Governments of Kenya, Nigeria and Zambia regarding the possibility of issuing the Council's identity document to Namibians within the borders of those countries.

Delegations from the Council attended the formal opening of the regional office of the United Nations Council for Namibia in Lusaka, Zambia, and the seventeenth session of the Council of Ministers of OAU, held in Addis Ababa, Ethiopia.

In its report to the Assembly, the Council for Namibia noted that there had been no apparent change in South Africa's policy regarding Namibia during the last year. Despite the repeated demands of the General Assembly and the Security Council to withdraw immediately from the territory, South Africa had not only continued its illegal occupation but had persisted in applying the condemned policies of *apartheid* and other repressive measures designed to destroy the unity and territorial integrity of Namibia and to consolidate its hold over the territory.

The Council noted further that in view of the advisory opinion of the International Court of Justice holding that the South African presence in Namibia was illegal, the United Nations was the only entity that could lawfully administer the territory and that the Council for Namibia was the (interim) *de jure* Government of Namibia.

The Council recommended that, particularly in view of the Court's decision, the Assembly take a number of steps, including appointing a full-time United Nations Commissioner for Namibia; enlarging the membership of the Council to ensure broader representation; and making adequate budgetary provisions for the Council to continue its existing responsibilities and undertake future activities, including the development of an educational programme and institutions for Namibians.

Consideration by General Assembly

General aspects

At its twenty-sixth session in 1971, the General Assembly referred the question of Namibia to its Fourth Committee, which considered it at meetings held between 14 October and 10 November 1971. The Fourth Committee had before it the report of the Special Committee on the Situation with regard to the Implementation of the Declaration on the Granting of Independence to Colonial Countries and Peoples, as well as the report of the United Nations Council for Namibia.

The Fourth Committee heard statements by the following petitioners: the Reverend Michael Scott, International League for the Rights of Man; Miss Barbara J. Rogers, Friends of Namibia Committee; Joel Carlson, Romesh Chandra, Lucio Luzzatto, Emilson Randriamihasinoro and Nikolai Voshinin, World Peace Council; Jariretundu Kozonguizi; Gidon Gottlieb; and I. B. Tabata, Unity Movement of South Africa.

All speakers in the debate expressed concern at South Africa's refusal to withdraw its administration from Namibia, in defiance of numerous resolutions of the General Assembly and the Security Council, as well as of the International Court of Justice's advisory opinion of 21 June 1971. Some speakers said the situation in Namibia was deteriorating because of South Africa's extension of its *apartheid* policies to the territory.

Turkey said that South Africa's persistent defiance of United Nations resolutions was the main proof of its insincerity in speaking of self-determination for Namibians; the Bantustan policy South Africa was applying clearly indicated its desire to divide and rule in the territory. Sweden also held that although South Africa was trying to convince the world it was guiding Namibians towards self-determination and independence, in fact it was pursuing in the territory a policy of *apartheid* pushed to an extreme.

A number of speakers expressed concern at the military and economic assistance being given to South Africa by some Member States. The USSR maintained that the support given by the Western powers to the régimes of South Africa, Southern Rhodesia and the Portuguese colonialists was dictated by monopoly groups which had enormous investments in southern

Africa and derived vast profits from the exploitation of its natural and human resources; South Africa was being maintained as a stronghold of imperialism by the Western powers. The USSR called for implementation of all United Nations resolutions on the elimination of colonial régimes in southern Africa.

Peru held that it was common knowledge that foreign monopolies in Namibia were pursuing policies aimed solely at obtaining profits and were developing only those economic sectors of use to them; they therefore ignored United Nations resolutions on Namibia, as well as the legitimate interests of Namibians.

Nigeria said it fully shared the concern of the Special Committee on the Situation with regard to the Implementation of the Declaration on the Granting of Independence to Colonial Countries and Peoples concerning the supply of arms to South Africa by certain Western powers.

A number of suggestions were made with regard to action that could be taken by the United Nations, especially in the light of the International Court of Justice's advisory opinion of 21 June 1971.

Pakistan suggested that the General Assembly make a formal declaration accepting the advisory opinion, and call upon all States to comply with its conclusions. Zambia held that since the status of Namibia had been clearly determined, the Security Council should put an immediate end to South Africa's illegal occupation and exploitation of the territory, through the full application of Chapter VII of the Charter.[15] Indonesia held that the United Nations should make it clear to South Africa that it took seriously the "sacred trust" that all Member States exercised jointly on behalf of the Namibian people; it called for the establishment of an interim international body to administer the territory.

Other Members held that the powers of the United Nations Council for Namibia should be strengthened. Zambia noted that the Council should be given all powers necessary to administer the territory on the spot; it should be empowered to recognize foreign economic and other interests operating in the territory and to ensure that all royalties and other dues collected from them were used for the education and training of Namibians. Guyana held that the composition of the Council should be modified to enable any of the permanent members of the Security Council willing to serve to participate in its deliberations and decisions.

A number of speakers—including Algeria, Bulgaria, Ethiopia, Iceland, India, Morocco, Nigeria, the Syrian Arab Republic, the USSR, Yugo-

---

[15]For text of Chapter VII, see APPENDIX II.

slavia, Zaire and Zambia—urged the United Nations to give greater moral and material assistance to the liberation movements in Namibia, as well as elsewhere in southern Africa. Zambia said that the General Assembly should examine the possibility of a special fund to provide assistance to the Namibian liberation movements. Albania held that the only path of liberation in southern Africa was that of armed struggle; Cameroon also said that all available means, including the use of force, must be considered to enable the people of Namibia to exercise their right to self-determination and independence as soon as possible.

Canada said it did not believe that violence could provide a realistic and lasting solution to the problem; it supported the proposal that the Security Council take the necessary steps to create the conditions that would enable the people of Namibia to exercise their right to self-determination. Austria felt that, despite the lack of progress, consideration should be given to all methods that might contribute to a peaceful attainment of independence for the peoples of southern Africa. Lesotho favoured a visit to Namibia by the Secretary-General to obtain first-hand information on the situation

The representative of Saudi Arabia believed that it had been a mistake to terminate the South African Mandate over Namibia at a time when the United Nations was not in a position to enforce its decision. That error should be rectified through private negotiations with South Africa aimed at making Namibia a Trust Territory. The representative of the Ivory Coast also favoured negotiations with South Africa as the only realistic course.

On 14 December 1971, the Fourth Committee approved a draft resolution concerning Namibia, which was subsequently adopted by the General Assembly—on 20 December—as its resolution 2871(XXVI).

By the preambular paragraphs of the resolution, the Assembly among other things expressed its deep concern at South Africa's continued occupation of Namibia, in defiance of the General Assembly's resolution of 27 October 1966[16] and in flagrant violation of its obligations under the United Nations Charter; expressed its further concern at the use of the territory of Namibia by South Africa as a base for taking actions that violated the sovereignty and territorial integrity of independent African States; and noted that the direct responsibility of the United Nations for Namibia included the solemn obligation to protect and safeguard the rights and interests of the people of the territory pending their exercise of self-determination and attainment of independence.

By the operative paragraphs of the resolution,

the Assembly reaffirmed the inalienable right of the people of Namibia to self-determination and independence, as recognized in the General Assembly resolution of 14 December 1960 (containing the text of the Declaration on the Granting of Independence to Colonial Countries and Peoples)[17] and subsequent resolutions, and the legitimacy of their struggle by all means against the illegal occupation of their territory by South Africa.

It welcomed the advisory opinion of the International Court of Justice of 21 June 1971 concerning Namibia.

The Assembly condemned South Africa for its continued refusal to put an end to its illegal occupation and administration of Namibia, as well as for its continued extension to Namibia of the policies of *apartheid* and for its policies aimed at destroying the territorial integrity of Namibia and the unity of its people through establishment of separate "homelands."

The Assembly called for the termination of all support given by any State to South Africa and by any financial, economic and other interests operating in Namibia. It called upon all States: (*a*) to respect strictly the resolutions of the General Assembly and the Security Council concerning Namibia, and the advisory opinion of the International Court of Justice of 21 June 1971; (*b*) to refrain from any direct or indirect relations, economic or otherwise, with South Africa, where those relations concerned Namibia; (*c*) not to recognize as legally valid any rights or interests in Namibian property or resources purportedly acquired from the South African Government after 27 October 1966; and (*d*) to take effective economic and other measures designed to ensure the immediate withdrawal of the South African administration from Namibia.

The Security Council was invited to take effective measures, in conformity with the relevant provisions of the Charter, to secure the withdrawal by South Africa of its illegal administration from Namibia, and the implementation of the resolutions of the General Assembly and the Security Council designed to enable the people of Namibia to exercise their right to self-determination.

South Africa was called upon once again to treat Namibians captured during their struggle for freedom as prisoners of war in accordance with the 1949 Geneva Convention relative to the Treatment of Prisoners of War, and to comply with the 1949 Geneva Convention relative to the Protection of Civilian Persons in Time of War; the International Committee of the Red Cross was invited to exercise its good offices to secure South

[16]See Y.U.N., 1966, pp. 605-6, text of resolution 2145(XXI).
[17]See Y.U.N., 1960, pp. 49-50, text of resolution 1514(XV).

Africa's compliance with those 1949 Conventions.

The Assembly requested all States, the specialized agencies and other United Nations organizations, in co-operation with the Organization of African Unity (OAU), to render to the Namibian people all moral and material assistance necessary to continue their struggle for the restoration of their inalienable right to self-determination and independence, and to work out, in active co-operation with the United Nations Council for Namibia and OAU, concrete programmes of assistance to Namibia.

The Assembly reaffirmed the direct responsibility of the United Nations in regard to the territory of Namibia and its obligation to lead the Namibian people to self-determination and independence.

The United Nations Council for Namibia was requested to continue to discharge its functions and responsibilities, and in particular (*a*) to represent Namibia whenever it was required; (*b*) to continue its consultations, at United Nations Headquarters, in Africa or elsewhere, with the representatives of the Namibian people and OAU; and (*c*) to assume responsibility for the urgent establishment of a short-term and long-term co-ordinated programme of technical and financial assistance to Namibia.

The Assembly also asked the Secretary-General to take several steps, including the following: (*a*) to hold consultations among the permanent members of the Security Council and other regional groups not represented on the United Nations Council for Namibia concerning the enlargement of the membership of the Council for Namibia; (*b*) to undertake the necessary consultations to nominate as soon as possible a full-time United Nations Commissioner for Namibia; (*c*) to continue to provide the necessary assistance and facilities to the Council for Namibia and to the United Nations Commissioner for Namibia; and (*d*) to intensify publicity relating to Namibia, including issues of a series of commemorative United Nations postage stamps.

Resolution 2871(XXVI) was adopted by a roll-call vote of 111 to 2, with 10 abstentions.

The Fourth Committee approved the text by a recorded vote of 88 to 2, with 8 abstentions. The following Members sponsored the draft: Afghanistan, Burundi, Cameroon, Chad, Ethiopia, Ghana, Guinea, Guyana, India, Indonesia, Iraq, Jamaica, Kenya, Kuwait, Liberia, the Libyan Arab Republic, Mali, Mauritania, Niger, Nigeria, Pakistan, the People's Democratic Republic of Yemen, the Philippines, Rwanda, Senegal, Singapore, Somalia, Sudan, the Syrian Arab Republic, Tunisia, Uganda, the United Republic of Tanzania, Yugoslavia and Zambia. (For text of resolution, see DOCUMENTARY REFERENCES below.)

United Nations Fund for Namibia

By a decision of 9 December 1970, the General Assembly decided to establish a comprehensive United Nations Fund for Nambia and asked the Secretary-General to report to it on the details involved in the creation of such a programme.[18]

In his report, which was before the Assembly at its 1971 session, the Secretary-General proposed a number of short- and intermediate-term measures to aid Namibia.

The short-term measures related to (1) refugee relief; (2) legal aid and relief for Namibian victims of persecution, detainees and their families; and (3) a variety of measures to assist in the education and training of Namibians, including assistance to secondary and higher education; remedial (upgrading) education for students over the normal school age to bring them up to the standards required for entry to technical and vocational training institutions; apprenticeships; advanced training in public administration; and creation of employment opportunities for trained Namibians.

The intermediate-term measures involved a study of the question of remedial education of over-school-age students, including the possibility of providing such education either through contractual arrangements with existing institutions or through the establishment of a separate college for further education of Namibians.

On 20 December 1971, the Assembly reaffirmed its decision of 9 December 1970[19] to establish a United Nations Fund for Namibia for the purpose of putting into effect the comprehensive programme of assistance to Namibians outlined in the report of the Secretary-General.

The Assembly decided, as a transitional measure, to allocate to the Fund the sum of $50,000 from the 1972 regular budget of the United Nations. It authorized the Secretary-General to appeal to Governments for voluntary contributions to the Fund, and invited Governments to appeal to their national organizations and institutions for voluntary financial contributions also.

The Secretary-General was authorized to implement the short-term and intermediate-term measures contained in his report as soon as the necessary funds were available, and to make the necessary arrangements for the administration of the Fund. Pending the entry into full operation of the comprehensive programme, Namibians would continue to be eligible for assistance under the United Nations Educational and Training Programme for Southern Africa and the United Nations Trust Fund for South Africa.

The Secretary-General was further requested to

[18]See Y.U.N., 1970, pp. 757-58, text of resolution 2679(XXV).
[19]*Ibid.*

undertake a study of the economic, social and cultural needs of Namibia, with a view to formulating a contingency plan of co-ordinated international and technical assistance, to be implemented in Namibia following the withdrawal of South Africa from the territory.

The Assembly took these decisions in adopting resolution 2872(XXVI), by a recorded vote of 113 to 2, with 7 abstentions. The Assembly acted on the recommendation of its Fourth Committee, which approved the text on 14 December 1971, by a recorded vote of 90 to 2, with 7 abstentions, as sponsored by: Burundi, Cameroon, Finland, Guinea, Iran, Japan, Mexico, Nepal, Nigeria, Sierra Leone, Yugoslavia and Zambia.

(For text of resolution, see DOCUMENTARY REFERENCES below.)

Following the adoption of resolution 2872(XXVI), the President of the General Assembly drew attention to a proposal by the Secretary-General that Lord Caradon (United Kingdom) be appointed as United Nations Commissioner for Namibia, for an initial period of one year.

Commenting on the proposal, the representative of Nigeria stressed the need for a full-time Commissioner and said that the candidate proposed was acceptable to representatives of the Namibian people.

The USSR said it categorically opposed the appointment of Lord Caradon, who was the representative of a colonial power which maintained a number of territories under colonial rule and extended various forms of assistance, including military assistance, to the racist and colonial régimes of southern Africa; such a representative could not further the liberation of the peoples of Namibia from the tyrannical rule of South Africa. The USSR said the question of appointing a Commissioner for Namibia should be postponed until after the current session of the General Assembly. If the proposal to approve the candidacy of Lord Caradon were put to a vote, the USSR would vote against it.

On 23 December 1971, the President of the Assembly called attention to a note by the Secretary-General withdrawing the nomination of Lord Caradon as United Nations Commissioner for Namibia. The President announced that the Secretary-General had no further communications on the matter.

Other Assembly decisions

DECLARATION ON GRANTING INDEPENDENCE

On 20 December 1971, in adopting resolution 2878(XXVI) on the implementation of the Declaration on the Granting of Independence to Colonial Countries and Peoples, the General Assembly took several decisions directly concerning Namibia.

The Assembly deeply deplored the continued refusal of the colonial powers, especially Portugal and South Africa, to implement the Declaration and other relevant resolutions on decolonization, particularly those relating to the territories under Portuguese domination, Namibia and Southern Rhodesia.

The Assembly reaffirmed that the continuation of colonialism in all its forms and manifestations —including racism, *apartheid,* activities of foreign economic and other interests which exploited colonial peoples and the waging of colonial wars to suppress national liberation movements in southern Africa—was incompatible with the United Nations Charter, the Universal Declaration of Human Rights and the Declaration on the Granting of Independence to Colonial Countries and Peoples, and posed a threat to international peace and security. In particular, the Assembly condemned the following policies pursued by certain colonial powers in the territories under their domination: imposing non-representative régimes and constitutions, strengthening the position of foreign economic and other interests, misleading world public opinion and encouraging the systematic influx of foreign immigrants while evicting, displacing and transferring the indigenous inhabitants to other areas; it called upon those powers to desist forthwith from such policies.

The Assembly reaffirmed the legitimacy of the struggle of the colonial peoples and peoples under alien domination to exercise their right to self-determination and independence by all necessary means at their disposal. It urged all States and organizations within the United Nations system to provide moral and material support to all peoples struggling for their independence in the colonial territories, in particular to the national liberation movements of the territories of southern Africa.

The Special Committee on the Implementation of the Declaration on the Granting of Independence to Colonial Countries and Peoples was requested to undertake a special study on the compliance of Member States with the Declaration and with other relevant resolutions on decolonization, particularly those relating to the territories under Portuguese domination, Namibia and Southern Rhodesia, and to report thereon to the Assembly in 1972.

(For text of resolution 2878(XXVI), see pp. 521-23.)

In adopting another resolution (2874(XXVI) of 20 December 1971) on the implementation of the Declaration on granting independence, the Assembly—taking into account the relevant resolutions of the Security Council on southern Africa, including resolution 283(1970) of 29 July 1970[20] on the question of Namibia—took the following action, among others: (1) reiterated its urgent appeal to the specialized agencies and other organizations within the United Nations system to render all possible moral and material assistance to the peoples in Africa struggling for their liberation from colonial rule and, in particular, to work out, with the active co-operation of the Organization of African Unity, and through it, of the national liberation movements, concrete programmes for assisting the peoples of Southern Rhodesia, Namibia and the territories under Portuguese administration, including, in particular, the populations in the liberated areas of those territories.

(For text of resolution 2874(XXVI), see pp. 528-29.)

ESTABLISHMENT OF BANTUSTANS

On 29 November 1971, the General Assembly adopted a resolution (2775 E (XXVI)) concerning the Bantustans (Bantu homelands). In so doing, the Assembly considered that the establishment of Bantustans and other measures adopted by South Africa in pursuance of *apartheid* were designed to consolidate and perpetuate domination by a white minority and the dispossession and exploitation of the African and other non-white people of South Africa and of Namibia.

The Assembly then: (1) again condemned the establishment by South Africa of Bantustans and the forcible removal of the African people of South Africa and Namibia to those areas as a violation of their inalienable rights, contrary to the principle of self-determination and prejudicial to the territorial integrity of the countries and the unity of their peoples; (2) declared that the United Nations would continue to encourage and promote a solution to the situation in South Africa through the full application of human rights and fundamental freedoms, including political rights, to all inhabitants of the territory of South Africa as a whole, regardless of race, colour or creed; and (3) decided to keep the situation in South Africa constantly under review. (For text of resolution 2775 E (XXVI), see p. 82.)

FOREIGN ECONOMIC INTERESTS

On 20 December 1971, the General Assembly adopted resolution 2873(XXVI) on the activities of foreign and other economic interests which were impeding (*a*) the implementation of the Declaration on the Granting of Independence to Colonial Countries and Peoples in territories under colonial domination and (*b*) efforts to eliminate colonialism, *apartheid* and racial discrimination in southern Africa.

Among other things, by this resolution, the Assembly: (1) reaffirmed the inalienable right of the peoples of the dependent territories to self-determination and independence and to the natural resources of their territories, as well as their right to dispose of those resources in their best interest; (2) affirmed that activities of foreign economic and other interests operating in Southern Rhodesia, Namibia and the territories under Portuguese domination constituted a major obstacle to political independence and to the enjoyment of the natural resources of the territories by the indigenous inhabitants; (3) condemned the present activities and operating methods of foreign economic and other interests in the territories under colonial domination which were designed to perpetuate the subjugation of dependent peoples; (4) called upon the administering powers to abolish every discriminatory and unjust wage system which prevailed in the territories under their administration, and, in each territory, to apply a uniform system of wages to all the inhabitants without any discrimination; (5) called upon the colonial powers and States concerned to take legislative, administrative and other measures of respect of their nationals who owned and operated enterprises in colonial territories, particularly in southern Africa, which were detrimental to the interests of the inhabitants of those territories, in order to put an end to such enterprises and to prevent new investments which ran counter to the interests of the inhabitants; and (6) requested all States to take effective measures to end the supply of funds and other forms of assistance, including military equipment, to those régimes which used such assistance to repress the national liberation movements.

(For text of resolution 2873(XXVI), see pp. 534-35.)

ELIMINATION OF DISCRIMINATION

On 6 December 1971, the Assembly, in adopting resolution 2784(XXVI), took a number of decisions concerning the elimination of all forms of racial discrimination. Thus, among other things, the Assembly emphatically reaffirmed its recognition and vigorous support of the legitimacy of the struggles of all oppressed peoples everywhere, and in particular in southern Africa, against colonial, racial and alien domination or foreign occupation, and towards the achievement of their inalienable right to equality and freedom, in accordance with the Charter of the United Nations.

The Assembly also called upon all trading partners of South Africa to abstain from any action that constituted an encouragement to the

[20]See Y.U.N., 1970, pp. 753-54.

continued violation of the principles and objectives of the International Convention on the Elimination of All Forms of Racial Discrimination by South Africa and the illegal régime in Southern Rhodesia, and to use their influence with a view to ensuring the eradication of the policies of *apartheid* and racial discrimination in the international territory of Namibia and Southern Rhodesia.

Annexed to resolution 2784(XXVI) was the text of a message from the President of the General Assembly to heads of State or Government concerning the United Nations campaign against racial discrimination.

The President noted, among other things, that the racist policies in southern Africa had been permitted and even encouraged to expand through the illegal occupation of the territory of Namibia by the racist Government of South Africa; and that the numerous resolutions opposing racial discrimination adopted by the various organs of the United Nations had had little or no effect, owing to the arrogant, flagrant and stubborn disregard of them by South Africa and its racist allies, and to the continued political, economic and military aid coming from some States.

The President requested the heads of State or Government to transmit the text of the message to legislative, administrative, judicial, educational and trade union bodies in their countries, in order to ensure the continuation of the world campaign against racial discrimination.

(For text of resolution 2784(XXVI), see pp. 402-4.)

THE RIGHT TO SELF-DETERMINATION

On 6 December 1971, the General Assembly took several decisions concerning the importance of the universal realization of the right of peoples to self-determination and of the speedy granting of independence to colonial countries and peoples for the effective guarantee and observance of human rights.

In adopting resolution 2787(XXVI), the Assembly, among other things: (1) confirmed the legality of the peoples' struggle for self-determination and liberation from colonial and foreign subjugation, notably in southern Africa and in particular that of the peoples of Zimbabwe, Namibia, Angola, Mozambique and Guinea (Bissau), as well as of the Palestinian people, by all available means consistent with the United Nations Charter; and (2) expressed its belief that the main objectives and principles of international protection of human rights could not be effectively implemented while some States, particularly Portugal and South Africa, pursued the imperialist policy of colonialism, used force against independent African States and developing countries and peoples fighting for self-determination, and supported régimes that were applying the criminal policy of racism and *apartheid.*

(For text of resolution 2787(XXVI), see pp. 423-24.)

United Nations Educational and Training Programme for Southern Africa

Under the United Nations Educational and Training Programme for Southern Africa, scholarships were provided to persons from Namibia, South Africa, Southern Rhodesia and the territories under Portuguese administration.

On 20 December 1971, the General Assembly took several decisions concerning the Programme. After expressing its conviction that the provision of assistance for the education and training of persons from territories in southern Africa was as essential as ever and should be expanded, the Assembly, among other things: (*a*) appealed urgently to all States, organizations and individuals to make generous contributions to the trust fund for the Programme; and (*b*) decided that, as a transitional measure, provision should be made under the 1972 regular budget of the United Nations for an amount of $100,000 to ensure continuity of the Programme, pending the receipt of adequate voluntary contributions. (For details, see pp. 123-25.)

DOCUMENTARY REFERENCES

Communications to Security Council (January-September 1971)

S/10086. Letter of 19 January 1971 from Secretary-General (transmitting text from Assembly resolution 2678(XXV)).

S/10108. Letter of 8 February 1971 from President of United Nations Council for Namibia (transmitting letter of 11 January 1971 from Acting Commissioner for Namibia).

S/10178. Letter of 16 April 1971 from Chile.

S/10240. Letter of 22 June 1971 from Finland.

S/10267. Legal consequences for States of continued presence of South Africa in Namibia (South West Africa) notwithstanding Security Council resolution 276(1970): advisory opinion of International Court of Justice (ICJ). Note by Secretary-General (transmitting ICJ advisory opinion of 21 June 1971).

S/10272. Letter of 13 July 1971 from Executive Secretary of Organization of African Unity (OAU) (transmitting resolutions adopted by 8th Assembly of Heads of State and Government of OAU).

S/10277. Letter of 30 July 1971 from Secretary-General to President of Security Council.

S/10288. Review of multilateral treaties to which South Africa became a party, and which either by direct reference or on basis of relevant provisions of international law might be considered to apply to Namibia. Report of 12 August 1971 of Secretary-General.

S/10303. Letter of 2 September 1971 from Acting Chairman of Special Committee on Situation with regard to Implementation of Declaration on Granting of Independence to Colonial Countries and Peoples (transmitting consensus adopted by Special Committee on 2 September 1971).

S/10312. Letter of 10 September 1971 from Acting Chairman of Special Committee on Situation with regard to Implementation of Declaration on Granting of Independence to Colonial Countries and Peoples (transmitting relevant text of resolution adopted by Special Committee on 9 September 1971).

Consideration by Security Council
(September-October)

Security Council, meetings 1583-1585, 1587-1589, 1593-1595, 1597, 1598.

S/10326. Letter of 17 September 1971 from Algeria, Botswana, Burundi, Cameroon, Central African Republic, Chad, Congo, Dahomey, Egypt, Equatorial Guinea, Ethiopia, Gabon, Ghana, Guinea, Kenya, Liberia, Libyan Arab Republic, Madagascar, Mali, Mauritania, Mauritius, Morocco, Niger, Nigeria, Rwanda, Senegal, Sierra Leone, Somalia, Sudan, Swaziland, Togo, Tunisia, Uganda, United Republic of Tanzania, Upper Volta, Zaire, Zambia (request to convene Council).

S/10330 and Corr.1 and Add.1. Report of *Ad Hoc* Sub-Committee on Namibia (*Security Council Official Records, 26th Year, Special Supplement No. 5*).

S/10331. Letter of 23 September 1971 from Chairman of 9th Meeting of Joint Meeting of Special Committee on *Apartheid*, Special Committee on Situation with regard to Implementation of Declaration on Granting of Independence to Colonial Countries and Peoples and United Nations Council for Namibia (transmitting consensus adopted at 9th meeting, on 13 September 1971 (A/8388)).

S/10332. Letter of 23 September 1971 from President of United Nations Council for Namibia (request to participate in Security Council's discussion).

S/10333, S/10334, S/10336, S/10339, S/10340. Letters of 23, 24 and 27 September 1971 from Ethiopia, South Africa, Sudan, Liberia and Guyana (requests to participate in Council's discussion).

S/10346. Letter of 30 September 1971 from Burundi, Sierra Leone and Somalia (request for President of South West Africa People's Organization to participate in Council's discussion).

S/10347, S/10353. Letters of 29 September and 6 October 1971 from Mauritius and Saudi Arabia (requests to participate in Council's discussion).

S/10356. Letter of 6 October 1971 from President of United Nations Council for Namibia (transmitting letter of 3 September 1971 from Chief of Herero Peoples, Namibia, to his solicitor in London, United Kingdom).

S/10372 and Rev.1. Burundi, Sierra Leone, Somalia, Syrian Arab Republic: draft resolution and revision.

S/10373, S/10374. Letters of 15 October 1971 from India and Uganda (requests to participate in Council's discussion).

S/10376 and Rev.1. Argentina: draft resolution and revision.

RESOLUTION 301(1971), as proposed by 4 powers, S/10372/Rev.1, as orally amended by sponsors, adopted by Council on 20 October 1971, meeting 1598, by 13 votes to 0, with 2 abstentions (France and United Kingdom).

The Security Council,

Reaffirming the inalienable right of the people of Namibia to freedom and independence, as recognized in General Assembly resolution 1514(XV) of 14 December 1960,

Recognizing that the United Nations has direct responsibility for Namibia, following the adoption of General Assembly resolution 2145(XXI) of 27 October 1966, and that States should conduct any relations with or involving Namibia in a manner consistent with that responsibility,

Reaffirming its resolutions 264(1969) of 20 March 1969, 276(1970) of 30 January 1970 and 283(1970) of 29 July 1970,

Recalling its resolution 284(1970) of 29 July 1970, in which it requested the International Court of Justice for an advisory opinion on the question:

"What are the legal consequences for States of the continued presence of South Africa in Namibia, notwithstanding Security Council resolution 276(1970)?,"

Gravely concerned at the refusal of the Government of South Africa to comply with the resolutions of the Security Council pertaining to Namibia,

Recalling its resolution 282(1970) of 23 July 1970 on the arms embargo against the Government of South Africa and stressing the significance of that resolution with regard to the Territory of Namibia,

Recognizing the legitimacy of the movement of the people of Namibia against the illegal occupation of their Territory by the South African authorities and their right to self-determination and independence,

Taking note of the statements of the delegation of the Organization of African Unity, led by the President of Mauritania in his capacity as current Chairman of the Assembly of Heads of State and Government of that organization,

Noting further the statement of the President of the United Nations Council for Namibia,

Having heard the statements of the delegation of the Government of South Africa,

Having considered the report of the *Ad Hoc* Sub-Committee on Namibia,

1. *Reaffirms* that the Territory of Namibia is the direct responsibility of the United Nations and that this responsibility includes the obligation to support and promote the rights of the people of Namibia in accordance with General Assembly resolution 1514(XV);

2. *Reaffirms* the national unity and territorial integrity of Namibia;

3. *Condemns* all moves by the Government of South Africa designed to destroy that unity and territorial integrity, such as the establishment of Bantustans;

4. *Declares* that South Africa's continued illegal presence in Namibia constitutes an internationally wrongful act and a breach of international obligations and that South Africa remains accountable to the international community for any violations of its international obligations or the rights of the people of the Territory of Namibia;

5. *Takes note with appreciation* of the advisory opinion of the International Court of Justice of 21 June 1971;

6. *Agrees* with the Court's opinion, as expressed in paragraph 133 of its advisory opinion:

"(1) that, the continued presence of South Africa in Namibia being illegal, South Africa is under obligation to withdraw its administration from Namibia immediately and thus put an end to its occupation of the Territory;

"(2) that States Members of the United Nations are under obligation to recognize the illegality of South Africa's presence in Namibia and the invalidity of its acts on behalf of or concerning Namibia, and to refrain from any acts and in particular any dealings with the Government of South Africa implying recognition of the legality of, or lending support or assistance to, such presence and administration;

"(3) that it is incumbent upon States which are not Members of the United Nations to give assistance, within the scope of subparagraph (2) above, in the action which has been taken by the United Nations with regard to Namibia.";

7. *Declares* that all matters affecting the rights of the people of Namibia are of immediate concern to all Members of the United Nations and, as a result, the latter should take this into account in their dealings with the Government of South Africa, in particular in any dealings implying recognition of the legality of, or lending support or assistance to, such illegal presence and administration;

8. *Calls once again* upon South Africa to withdraw from the Territory of Namibia;

9. *Declares* that any further refusal of the South African Government to withdraw from Namibia could create conditions detrimental to the maintenance of peace and security in the region;

10. *Reaffirms* the provisions of resolution 283(1970), in particular paragraphs 1 to 8 and 11;

11. *Calls upon* all States, in the discharge of their responsibilities towards the people of Namibia and subject to the exceptions set forth in paragraphs 122 and 125 of the advisory opinion of 21 June 1971:

(a) To abstain from entering into treaty relations with South Africa in all cases in which the Government of South Africa purports to act on behalf of or concerning Namibia;

(b) To abstain from invoking or applying those treaties or provisions of treaties concluded by South Africa on behalf of or concerning Namibia which involve active intergovernmental co-operation;

(c) To review their bilateral treaties with South Africa in order to ensure that they are not inconsistent with paragraphs 5 and 6 above;

(d) To abstain from sending diplomatic or special missions to South Africa that include the Territory of Namibia in their jurisdiction;

(e) To abstain from sending consular agents to Namibia and to withdraw any such agents already there;

(f) To abstain from entering into economic and other forms of relationship or dealings with South Africa on behalf of or concerning Namibia which may entrench its authority over the Territory;

12. *Declares* that franchises, rights, titles or contracts relating to Namibia granted to individuals or companies by South Africa after the adoption of General Assembly resolution 2145(XXI) are not subject to protection or espousal by their States against claims of a future lawful Government of Namibia;

13. *Requests* the *Ad Hoc* Sub-Committee on Namibia to continue to carry out the tasks entrusted to it under paragraphs 14 and 15 of Security Council resolution 283(1970) and, in particular, taking into account the need to provide for the effective protection of Namibian interests at the international level, to study appropriate measures for the fulfilment of the responsibility of the United Nations towards Namibia;

14. *Requests* the *Ad Hoc* Sub-Committee on Namibia to review all treaties and agreements which are contrary to the provisions of the present resolution in order to ascertain whether States have entered into agreements which recognize South Africa's authority over Namibia, and to report periodically thereon;

15. *Calls upon* all States to support and promote the rights of the people of Namibia and to this end to implement fully the provisions of the present resolution;

16. *Requests* the Secretary-General to report periodically on the implementation of the provisions of the present resolution.

S/10389. Telegram of 12 November 1971 from Minister of Foreign Affairs of German Democratic Republic.

Communication to Security Council

S/10379. Letter of 27 October 1971 from Acting Chairman of Special Committee on Situation with regard to Implementation of Declaration on Granting of Independence to Colonial Countries and Peoples (transmitting petition on Namibia).

Consideration by Special Committee

Special Committee on Situation with regard to Implementation of Declaration on Granting of Independence to Colonial Countries and Peoples, meetings 782, 785, 789, 792-796, 802-805, 807, 809, 811, 813, 814, 821-825.

A/8423/Rev.1. Report of Special Committee to General Assembly (covering its work during 1971). Chapter V B (Resolution adopted by Special Committee on 9 September 1971); Chapter VI B, para. 31 (Consensus adopted by Special Committee on 4 March 1971); Chapter VII B (Consensus adopted by Special Committee on 2 September 1971) and D (Decision of Special Committee relating to petitions).

Report of United Nations Council for Namibia

A/8424. Report of United Nations Council for Namibia.

Consideration by General Assembly

General Assembly—26th session
Fourth Committee, meetings 1919, 1921-1926, 1928-1936, 1938-1950, 1952-1954, 1960, 1965-1969.
Fifth Committee, meeting 1487.
Plenary meetings 2028, 2030, 2031.

GENERAL ASPECTS

A/8388. Implementation of Declaration on Granting of Independence to Colonial Countries and Peoples; policies of *apartheid* of Government of South Africa; question of Namibia. Report of Secretary-General (attaching letter of 15 September 1971 from Chairman of 9th Meeting of Joint Meeting of Special Committee on *Apartheid*, Special Committee on Situation with regard to Implementation of Declaration on Granting of Independence to Colonial Countries and Peoples, and United Nations Council for Namibia, transmitting consensus of 13 September 1971).

A/8401. Report of Secretary-General on work of the Organization, 16 June 1970–15 June 1971, Part Two, Chapter I B 2.

A/8401/Add.1. Introduction to report of Secretary-General, September 1971: Part One, Chapter V, paras. 56-58; Part Two, Chapter VIII, paras. 295-299.

A/8402. Report of Security Council, 16 June 1970–15 June 1971, Chapter 3.

A/8423/Rev.1. Report of Special Committee (covering its work during 1971), Chapters V and VII.

A/8424. Report of United Nations Council for Namibia.

A/C.4/735 and Add.1-6. Requests for hearings.

A/C.4/736 and Add.1. Question of Namibia; question of territories under Portuguese administration; question of Southern Rhodesia. Requests for hearings.

A/C.4/738 and Add.1. Statement by member of Friends of Namibia Committee, London, United Kingdom, in Fourth Committee on 8 October 1971, meeting 1922.

A/C.4/740. Statement by member of International League for Rights of Man in Fourth Committee on 7 October 1971, meeting 1921.

A/C.4/L.994. Afghanistan, Burundi, Cameroon, Chad, Ethiopia, Ghana, Guinea, Guyana, India, Indonesia, Iraq, Jamaica, Kenya, Kuwait, Liberia, Libyan Arab Republic, Mali, Mauritania, Niger, Nigeria, Pakistan, People's Democratic Republic of Yemen, Philippines, Rwanda, Senegal, Sinagapore, Somalia, Sudan, Syrian Arab Republic, Tunisia, Uganda, United Republic of Tanzania, Yugoslavia, Zambia: draft resolution, as orally amended by sponsors, approved by Fourth Committee on 14 December 1971, meeting 1968, by recorded vote of 88 to 2, with 8 abstentions, as follows:

In favour: Afghanistan, Albania, Algeria, Argentina, Austria, Barbados, Brazil, Bulgaria, Burma, Burundi, Byelorussian SSR, Cameroon, Central African Republic, Ceylon, Chad, Chile, Colombia, Congo, Costa Rica, Cuba, Czechoslovakia, Denmark, Dominican Republic, Ecuador, Egypt, Equatorial Guinea, Ethiopia, Finland, Ghana, Greece, Guinea, Guyana, Honduras, Hungary, India, Indonesia, Iran, Iraq, Ireland, Israel, Ivory Coast, Jamaica, Japan, Kenya, Khmer Republic, Kuwait, Liberia, Libyan Arab Republic, Madagascar, Malaysia, Mali, Mauritania, Mexico, Mongolia, Morocco, Nepal, Netherlands, Nicaragua, Niger, Nigeria, Norway, People's Democratic Republic of Yemen, Peru, Philippines, Poland, Romania, Senegal, Singapore, Somalia, Spain, Sudan, Sweden, Syrian Arab Republic, Thailand, Togo, Trinidad and Tobago, Tunisia, Turkey, Uganda, Ukrainian SSR, USSR, United Republic of Tanzania, Upper Volta, Uruguay, Venezuela, Yugoslavia, Zaire, Zambia.

Against: Portugal, South Africa.

Abstaining: Australia, Belgium, Canada, France, Italy, New Zealand, United Kingdom, United States.

A/C.5/L.1422, A/C.4/L.1008. Administrative and financial implications of 34-power draft resolution, A/C.4/L.994. Statements by Secretary-General.

A/8633. Administrative and financial implications of draft resolutions I and II recommended by Fourth Committee in A/8618. Report of Fifth Committee.

A/8618. Report of Fourth Committee, draft resolution I.

RESOLUTION 2871(XXVI), as recommended by Fourth Committee, A/8618, adopted by Assembly on 20 December 1971, meeting 2028, by roll-call vote of 111 to 2, with 10 abstentions:

In favour: Afghanistan, Albania, Algeria, Argentina, Austria, Bahrain, Barbados, Botswana, Brazil, Bulgaria, Burma, Burundi, Byelorussian SSR, Cameroon, Central African Republic, Ceylon, Chad, Chile, Colombia, Costa Rica, Cuba, Cyprus, Czechoslovakia, Dahomey, Denmark, Dominican Republic, Ecuador, El Salvador, Equatorial Guinea, Ethiopia, Fiji, Finland, Gambia, Ghana, Greece, Guatemala, Guinea, Guyana, Haiti, Honduras, Hungary, Iceland, India, Indonesia, Iran, Iraq, Ireland, Israel, Ivory Coast, Jamaica, Japan, Jordan, Kenya, Khmer Republic, Kuwait, Laos, Lebanon, Lesotho, Liberia, Libyan Arab Republic, Madagascar, Malaysia, Mali, Malta, Mauritania, Mexico, Mongolia, Morocco, Nepal, Netherlands, Nicaragua, Niger, Nigeria, Norway, Oman, Pakistan, Panama, Paraguay, People's Democratic Republic of Yemen, Peru, Philippines, Poland, Romania, Rwanda, Saudi Arabia, Senegal, Sierra Leone, Singapore, Somalia, Spain, Sudan, Swaziland, Sweden, Syrian Arab Republic, Thailand, Togo, Trinidad and Tobago, Tunisia, Turkey, Uganda, Ukrainian SSR, USSR, United Arab Emirates, United Republic of Tanzania, Upper Volta, Uruguay, Venezuela, Yemen, Yugoslavia, Zaire, Zambia.

Against: Portugal, South Africa.

Abstaining: Australia, Belgium, Canada, France, Italy, Luxembourg, Malawi, New Zealand, United Kingdom, United States.

The General Assembly,

Having considered the question of Namibia,

Having examined the report of the United Nations Council for Namibia,

Having examined the relevant chapters of the report of the Special Committee on the Situation with regard to the Implementation of the Declaration on the Granting of Independence to Colonial Countries and Peoples,

Having heard the statements of the petitioners and bearing in mind the views expressed by the representatives of national liberation movements,

Recalling its resolutions 1514(XV) of 14 December 1960, 2145(XXI) of 27 October 1966, 2248(S-V) of 19 May 1967 and subsequent resolutions on the question of Namibia, as well as Security Council resolutions 264(1969) of 20 March 1969, 269(1969) of 12 August 1969, 276(1970) of 30 January 1970 and 283(1970) of 29 July 1970,

Recalling further the relevant provisions of its resolution 2621(XXV) of 12 October 1970, containing the programme of action for the full implementation of the Declaration on the Granting of Independence to Colonial Countries and Peoples,

Bearing in mind the direct responsibility of the United Nations with regard to the Territory of Namibia and its people,

Noting with satisfaction the advisory opinion of the International Court of Justice of 21 June 1971 delivered in response to the request addressed to it by the Security Council in its resolution 284(1970) of 29 July 1970,

Noting also the provisions of Security Council resolution 301(1971) of 20 October 1971,

Deeply concerned at South Africa's continued occupation of Namibia in defiance of General Assembly resolution 2145(XXI) and in flagrant violation of its obligations under the Charter of the United Nations,

Deeply concerned also at the use of the Territory of Namibia by

South Africa as a base for taking actions which violate the sovereignty and territorial integrity of independent African States,

Considering that the basic condition for the fulfilment of the responsibility of the United Nations towards Namibia is the removal of South Africa's presence from the Territory,

Mindful of the obligations of all Member States under Article 25 of the Charter,

Mindful also that the direct responsibility of the United Nations for Namibia includes the solemn obligation to protect and safeguard the rights and interests of the people of the Territory pending their exercise of self-determination and attainment of independence,

1. *Reaffirms* the inalienable right of the people of Namibia to self-determination and independence, as recognized in General Assembly resolution 1514(XV) and subsequent resolutions, and the legitimacy of their struggle by all means against the illegal occupation of their territory by South Africa;

2. *Welcomes* the advisory opinion of the International Court of Justice of 21 June 1971, as expressed in paragraph 133 thereof;

3. *Condemns* the Government of South Africa for its continued refusal to put an end to its illegal occupation and administration of the Territory of Namibia and to comply with the pertinent resolutions of the Security Council and the General Assembly;

4. *Further condemns* the Government of South Africa for its continued extension to the Territory of Namibia of the policies of *apartheid,* and for its policies aimed at destroying the unity of the people and the territorial integrity of Namibia through the establishment of separate "homelands" based on racial and tribal distinctions;

5. *Deplores* any support given by any State to South Africa, and by any financial, economic and other interests operating in Namibia, which enables South Africa to pursue its repressive policies in the Territory, and calls for the termination of all such support;

6. *Calls upon* all States:

(*a*) To respect strictly the resolutions of the General Assembly and the Security Council concerning Namibia, and the advisory opinion of the International Court of Justice of 21 June 1971;

(*b*) To refrain from all direct or indirect relations, economic or otherwise, with South Africa, where those relations concern Namibia;

(*c*) Not to recognize as legally valid any rights or interests in Namibian property or resources purportedly acquired from the South African Government after 27 October 1966;

(*d*) To take effective economic and other measures designed to ensure the immediate withdrawal of the South African administration from Namibia, thereby making possible the implementation of General Assembly resolutions 2145(XXI) and 2248(S-V);

7. *Invites* the Security Council to take effective measures, in conformity with the relevant provisions of the Charter, to secure the withdrawal by South Africa of its illegal administration from Namibia, and the implementation of the resolutions of the General Assembly and the Security Council designed to enable the people of Namibia to exercise their right to self-determination;

8. *Calls once again* upon South Africa to treat Namibians captured during their struggle for freedom as prisoners of war in accordance with the Geneva Convention relative to the Treatment of Prisoners of War, of 12 August 1949, and to comply with the Geneva Convention relative to the Protection of Civilian Persons in Time of War, of 12 August 1949, and, in this regard, invites the International Committee of the Red Cross to exercise its good offices to secure South Africa's compliance with those Conventions;

9. *Requests* all States and the specialized agencies and other organizations within the United Nations system, in co-operation with the Organization of African Unity, to render to the Namibian people all moral and material assistance necessary to continue their struggle for the restoration of their inalienable right to self-determination and independence, and to work out, in active co-operation with the United Nations Council for Namibia and the Organization of African Unity, concrete programmes of assistance to Namibia;

10. *Invites* the specialized agencies to give full publicity,

through all media, to the question of Namibia and to the conditions prevailing in the Territory to which their respective spheres of competence are related;

11. *Recommends* the report of the United Nations Council for Namibia to all States and to the subsidiary organs of the General Assembly and other competent organs of the United Nations, as well as the specialized agencies and other organizations within the United Nations system, for appropriate action, in conformity with the relevant resolutions of the General Assembly and the Security Council;

12. *Reaffirms* the direct responsibility of the United Nations in regard to the Territory of Namibia and its obligation to lead the Namibian people to self-determination and independence;

13. *Requests* the United Nations Council for Namibia, in accordance with the provisions of the relevant resolutions of the General Assembly, to continue to discharge its functions and responsibilities, and in particular:

(a) To represent Namibia whenever it is required;

(b) To continue its consultations, at United Nations Headquarters, in Africa or elsewhere, with the representatives of the Namibian people and the Organization of African Unity;

(c) To assume responsibility for the urgent establishment of a short-term and long-term co-ordinated programme of technical and financial assistance to Namibia, as explained in the report of the Secretary-General, in line with the relevant provisions of General Assembly resolution 2248(S-V);

14. *Notes with appreciation* the recognition by a large number of States of the identity certificates and travel documents issued to Namibians by the United Nations Council for Namibia and once again calls upon all other States which have not yet done so to recognize those documents;

15. *Calls upon* all States to co-operate fully with the United Nations Council for Namibia in its efforts to discharge its responsibilities;

16. *Requests* the Secretary-General, bearing in mind the recommendation of the United Nations Council for Namibia concerning the enlargement of its membership with a view to ensuring broader representation on the Council, to hold consultations among the permanent members of the Security Council and other regional groups not represented on the United Nations Council for Namibia and to report thereon to the General Assembly;

17. *Urges* the Secretary-General, in view of the recommendation of the United Nations Council for Namibia, to undertake the necessary consultations to nominate as soon as possible a full-time United Nations Commissioner for Namibia;

18. *Requests* the Secretary-General to continue to provide the necessary assistance and facilities to the United Nations Council for Namibia and to the United Nations Commissioner for Namibia for the discharge of their respective duties and functions;

19. *Requests* the Secretary-General to take the necessary steps to intensify publicity relating to Namibia, and to issue a series of United Nations commemorative postage stamps to publicize the direct responsibility of the United Nations for Namibia;

20. *Requests* the Secretary-General to transmit the present resolution to the competent subsidiary organs of the General Assembly, other organs of the United Nations, the specialized agencies and other organizations within the United Nations system;

21. *Further requests* the Secretary-General to report to the General Assembly at its twenty-seventh session on the implementation of the present resolution.

UNITED NATIONS FUND FOR NAMIBIA

A/8473. Report of Secretary-General.

A/C.4/L.997. Burundi, Cameroon, Finland, Guinea, Iran, Japan, Mexico, Nepal, Nigeria, Sierra Leone, Yugoslavia, Zambia: draft resolution, approved by Fourth Committee on 14 December 1971, meeting 1969, by recorded vote of 90 to 2, with 7 abstentions, as follows:

In favour: Afghanistan, Algeria, Argentina, Australia, Austria, Barbados, Belgium, Botswana, Brazil, Burma, Burundi, Came-

roon, Canada, Ceylon, Chad, Chile, Colombia, Congo, Costa Rica, Cyprus, Denmark, Dominican Republic, Ecuador, Egypt, Equatorial Guinea, Ethiopia, Finland, France, Gambia, Ghana, Greece, Guyana, Iceland, India, Indonesia, Iran, Iraq, Ireland, Italy, Ivory Coast, Jamaica, Japan, Jordan, Kenya, Khmer Republic, Lebanon, Liberia, Libyan Arab Republic, Madagascar, Malaysia, Mali, Mauritania, Mexico, Mongolia, Morocco, Nepal, Netherlands, New Zealand, Nicaragua, Nigeria, Norway, Pakistan, People's Democratic Republic of Yemen, Peru, Philippines, Poland, Romania, Rwanda, Senegal, Singapore, Spain, Sudan, Swaziland, Sweden, Syrian Arab Republic, Thailand, Togo, Trinidad and Tobago, Tunisia, Turkey, Uganda, United Kingdom, United Republic of Tanzania, United States, Upper Volta, Uruguay, Venezuela, Yugoslavia, Zaire, Zambia.

Against: Portugal, South Africa.

Abstaining: Bulgaria, Byelorussian SSR, Cuba, Czechoslovakia, Hungary, Ukrainian SSR, USSR.

A/C.4/L.1009, A/C.5/L.1423. Administrative and financial implications of 12-power draft resolution A/C.4/L.997. Statements by Secretary-General.

A/8633. Administrative and financial implications of draft resolutions I and II recommended by Fourth Committee in A/8618. Report of Fifth Committee.

A/8618. Report of Fourth Committee, draft resolution II.

RESOLUTION 2872(XXVI), as recommended by Fourth Committee, A/8618, adopted by Assembly on 20 December 1971, meeting 2028, by recorded vote of 113 to 2, with 7 abstentions, as follows:

In favour: Afghanistan, Algeria, Argentina, Australia, Austria, Bahrain, Barbados, Belgium, Botswana, Brazil, Burma, Burundi, Cameroon, Canada, Central African Republic, Ceylon, Chad, Chile, Colombia, Costa Rica, Cyprus, Dahomey, Denmark, Dominican Republic, Ecuador, El Salvador, Equatorial Guinea, Ethiopia, Fiji, Finland, France, Gambia, Ghana, Greece, Guatemala, Guinea, Guyana, Haiti, Honduras, Iceland, India, Indonesia, Iran, Iraq, Ireland, Israel, Italy, Ivory Coast, Jamaica, Japan, Jordan, Kenya, Khmer Republic, Kuwait, Laos, Lebanon, Lesotho, Liberia, Libyan Arab Republic, Luxembourg, Madagascar, Malawi, Malaysia, Mali, Malta, Mauritania, Mexico, Mongolia, Morocco, Nepal, Netherlands, New Zealand, Nicaragua, Niger, Nigeria, Norway, Oman, Pakistan, Panama, Paraguay, People's Democratic Republic of Yemen, Peru, Philippines, Poland, Romania, Rwanda, Saudi Arabia, Senegal, Sierra Leone, Singapore, Somalia, Spain, Sudan, Swaziland, Sweden, Syrian Arab Republic, Thailand, Togo, Trinidad and Tobago, Tunisia, Turkey, Uganda, United Arab Emirates, United Kingdom, United Republic of Tanzania, United States, Upper Volta, Uruguay, Venezuela, Yemen, Yugoslavia, Zaire, Zambia.

Against: Portugal, South Africa.

Abstaining: Bulgaria, Byelorussian SSR, Cuba, Czechoslovakia, Hungary, Ukrainian SSR, USSR.

The General Assembly,

Recalling its resolution 2145(XXI) of 27 October 1968, by which the United Nations decided to terminate the Mandate of South Africa over Namibia and assume direct responsibility for the Territory until its independence,

Reaffirming its resolve to discharge that responsibility in regard to the Territory,

Mindful that, by assuming direct responsibility for Namibia, the United Nations incurred a solemn obligation to assist and prepare the people of the Territory for self-determination and independence,

Recalling further its resolution 2679(XXV) of 9 December 1970, whereby it decided to establish a United Nations Fund for Namibia to provide comprehensive assistance to the people of the Territory,

Recognizing that South Africa's continued illegal occupation of Namibia at present prevents the United Nations from furnishing needed large-scale assistance within the Territory,

Having examined the report of the Secretary-General on the development, planning, execution and administration of a comprehensive programme of assistance to Namibians in various fields,

Having considered the recommendations set out in that report and having noted that the assistance envisaged consists of:

(a) Short-term and intermediate-term assistance to those Namibians who are at present accessible to international aid,

(b) The drawing up of a plan of co-ordinated international assistance to be implemented within Namibia following the withdrawal of South Africa from the Territory,

Bearing in mind that the scope of the programme, as well as its financing and administrative machinery, will be subject to review by the General Assembly when South Africa's illegal occupation of Namibia is terminated,

1. *Expresses its appreciation* of the report of the Secretary-General and the conclusions and recommendations contained therein;

2. *Reaffirms* its previous decision, contained in resolution 2679(XXV), to establish a United Nations Fund for Namibia for the purpose of putting into effect the comprehensive programme of assistance to Namibians outlined in the report of the Secretary-General;

3. *Decides*, as a transitional measure, to allocate to the Fund the sum of $50,000 from the regular budget of the United Nations for 1972;

4. *Authorizes* the Secretary-General to appeal to Governments for voluntary contributions to the Fund;

5. *Invites* Governments to appeal to their national organizations and institutions for voluntary financial contributions to the Fund;

6. *Authorizes* the Secretary-General to implement the short-term and intermediate-term measures contained in his report as soon as the necessary funds are available;

7. *Requests* the Secretary-General to make the necessary arrangements for the administration of the Fund and for the comprehensive programme, in conformity with the proposals and suggestions set out in paragraphs 77 to 85 of the report;

8. *Requests* the United Nations High Commissioner for Refugees, the specialized agencies and other organizations within the United Nations system to render all necessary assistance to the Secretary-General in carrying out the tasks assigned to him under the present resolution;

9. *Decides*, pending the entry into full operation of the comprehensive programme, that Namibians shall continue to be eligible for assistance through the United Nations Educational and Training Programme for Southern Africa and the United Nations Trust Fund for South Africa;

10. *Requests* the Secretary-General to undertake a study of the economic, social and cultural needs of Namibia, with a view to the formulation of a contingency plan of co-ordinated international and technical assistance, to be implemented in Namibia following the withdrawal of South Africa from the Territory;

11. *Requests* the Secretary-General to report to the General Assembly at its twenty-seventh session on the implementation of the present resolution.

Appointment of United Nations Commissioner for Namibia

A/8638 and Add.1. Notes by Secretary-General.

A/8429. Resolutions adopted by General Assembly during its 26th session, 21 September–22 December 1971. Decisions, p. 21.

Chapter IV

Territories under Portuguese administration

During 1971, various aspects of the situation in the Portuguese-administered territories of Angola, Mozambique, Guinea, called Portuguese Guinea, the Cape Verde Archipelago, São Tomé e Príncipe, Macau and dependencies, and Timor and dependencies were discussed in the Security Council (see pp. 116-23), the General Assembly, and the Assembly's Special Committee on the Situation with regard to the Implementation of the Declaration on the Granting of Independence to Colonial Countries and Peoples,[1] as well as by the Commission on Human Rights and the Economic and Social Council.

Consideration by Special Committee

The Special Committee on the Situation with regard to the Implementation of the Declaration on the Granting of Independence to Colonial Countries and Peoples discussed the territories under Portuguese administration at meetings held between 4 March and 14 September 1971.

The Committee had before it a number of written petitions and heard the following petitioners: Boubaker Adjali; Jack Seaton, Project Mo-

zambique, Canada; Abdul S. Minty, Anti-*Apartheid* Movement, the United Kingdom; and a delegation from the World Peace Council.

It also took into account the report of its *Ad Hoc* Group which visited Africa from 8 to 25 May 1971. The Group heard the following petitioners from the Portuguese-administered territories: Agostinho Neto and Pascal Luvualu, *Movimento Popular de Libertação de Angola* (MPLA); Grielme Chippia, *União Nacional para a Independência Total de Angola* (UNITA), Paulo J. Gumane and Miniban J. Ntundumula, *Comité Revolucionário de Moçambique* (COREMO); and Joaquim Chissano and Sérgio Vieira, *Frente de Libertação de Moçambique* (FRELIMO).

In connexion with its consideration of the Portuguese-administered territories, the Special Committee sent delegations of observers to the Assembly of the World Peace Council (held in Budapest, Hungary, 13-16 May 1971) and to the special meeting of the Executive Committee of the

---

[1]See Y.U.N., 1960, pp. 49–50, text of resolution 1514(XV), containing text of Declaration.

Afro-Asian Peoples' Solidarity Organization (held in Damascus, Syrian Arab Republic, on 23 and 24 June 1971). The reports of the two delegations were annexed to the Special Committee's report.

On 7 April 1971, the Special Committee decided to give consideration, as a matter of urgency, to a communication from Agostinho Neto, president of MPLA, concerning the use by Portugal of chemical substances, including herbicides and defoliants, in the liberated areas of Angola which had destroyed crops and killed a number of people.

Most of the members who took part in the debate considered that it was incumbent upon the Special Committee to condemn such chemical warfare. The representatives of Bulgaria, Ethiopia, India, Poland, the USSR and the United Republic of Tanzania supported the suggestion that the Committee adopt a resolution condemning the use of such methods of warfare by Portugal and expressing solidarity with the freedom fighters.

Bulgaria and the USSR linked the intensification of Portugal's war activities against the liberation movements in the territories to the assistance it received from North Atlantic Treaty Organization (NATO) members. India said that the latest information should dispel any further doubts some members had on the barbarous acts of the Portuguese Government. The United Republic of Tanzania expressed the hope that large-scale and effective measures of assistance would be taken as a matter of urgency by the Special Committee, as well as by the Food and Agriculture Organization (FAO), the World Health Organization (WHO) and other specialized agencies.

On 13 April 1971, the Special Committee adopted a resolution by which it condemned the use by Portugal of chemical substances, such as herbicides and defoliants, in Angola or in other territories. It called upon Portugal to cease forthwith from using chemical and biological methods of warfare against the peoples of the territories under its domination, in accordance with the relevant provisions of a General Assembly resolution of 14 December 1970[2] and of the Geneva Protocol of 17 June 1925 on the Prohibition of the Use in War of Asphyxiating, Poisonous or Other Gases, and of Bacteriological Methods of Warfare.

The Committee drew the attention of the Security Council to the urgent need to take measures to ensure the immediate cessation by Portugal of its colonial wars in Africa and its use of herbicides and defoliants, and requested the Chairman of the Special Committee to bring the communication from Agostinho Neto to the attention of the Organization of African Unity (OAU), with an appeal that urgent action be taken

thereon. It also appealed to FAO, WHO and other concerned organizations within the United Nations system, in consultation with OAU, to give urgent and favourable consideration to Mr. Neto's request for assistance.

The Special Committee's resolution to this effect was based on a proposal by Afghanistan, Bulgaria, Ethiopia, India, Mali, Poland, Sierra Leone, the Syrian Arab Republic, Trinidad and Tobago, Tunisia, the United Republic of Tanzania and Yugoslavia. It was adopted by a vote of 19 to 0, with 1 abstention.

Sweden, which abstained, commented before the vote that, although it agreed with the general purpose of a resolution that rejected inhuman methods of warfare, the facts available did not establish an adequate case against Portugal.

On 2 June 1971, again as a matter of urgency, the Special Committee considered a communication from Amílcar Cabral, Secretary-General of the *Partido Africano da Independência da Guiné e Cabo Verde* (PAIGC), concerning the forthcoming meeting in Lisbon, Portugal, of the Council of Ministers of NATO.

Several members of the Committee, including Bulgaria, Ecuador, Iraq, Mali, Poland, the Syrian Arab Republic, Trinidad and Tobago, the USSR and the United Republic of Tanzania, considered the meeting an expression of NATO support for Portugal's colonial policy and felt it should be condemned by the Committee.

The representatives of Fiji and Madagascar held that the Special Committee had no competence to interfere in the internal procedures of NATO. The Ivory Coast spokesman said that the adoption of a resolution by the Committee would not have any effect since the meeting was to be held the following day; in any case, it was doubtful whether the Committee could prevent NATO from holding a meeting wherever it wanted. Had the Committee taken up the matter earlier, it might have induced members of NATO to reconsider, if they understood that the meeting would be interpreted as a manifestation of political support for Portugal's colonial policy.

On the same day (2 June 1971), the Committee adopted a resolution by which it considered that the meeting of the NATO Council of Ministers in Lisbon could not but afford political and moral encouragement to Portugal in the pursuit of its colonialist policies; deplored this manifestation of collaboration with Portugal by States members of NATO; and urged those States to desist from any acts that might encourage Portugal to continue its oppression of the peoples of the territories under its domination.

The Committee's resolution to this effect was

[2]See Y.U.N., 1970, pp. 770–72, text of resolution 2707(XXV).

adopted by a roll-call vote of 16 to 0, with 3 abstentions.

In explanation of vote, Sweden said that, although it understood the reasons for the votes of some delegations, it would have preferred a consensus expressing the unanimous position of the Committee.

On 3 June 1971, the Chairman of the Special Committee transmitted the text of the resolution to States members of NATO for the attention of their Governments, and to OAU.

The Special Committee's general discussion on the territories under Portuguese administration was opened by Sweden, which deplored Portugal's colonial policies and its endeavour to conquer the spirit of the peoples of the African territories by force of arms. Sweden attached great importance to the arms embargo called for by the Security Council. The Swedish representative noted that Portugal had not responded to United Nations resolutions; instead, its concept of decolonization involved transforming Africans into Portuguese. The facts did not support Portugal's own version of decolonization and self-determination, however, since so few Africans had the right to vote. The proposed constitutional changes, which Portugal said were intended to give a degree of autonomy to the territories, would in no way change the status of the Africans, Sweden stated.

As in previous years, many members of the Special Committee, including Bulgaria, India, the USSR and the United Republic of Tanzania, expressed concern over the assistance provided to Portugal by States members of NATO and the further strengthening of the collaboration between Portugal, South Africa and Southern Rhodesia, which enabled Portugal to carry on its colonial war. The USSR charged that the overwhelming majority of the war material used by the Portuguese armed forces was supplied by NATO countries.

Bulgaria, India and the USSR also criticized foreign economic interests in Angola and Mozambique which supported Portugal's colonial policies. Together with the United Republic of Tanzania, they called for greater assistance to the liberation movements by the specialized agencies and international institutions. The United Republic of Tanzania suggested, among other things, that the Special Committee hold meetings in Africa, and that it co-operate more closely with OAU.

On 9 September 1971, the Special Committee adopted a resolution whereby, among other things, it reaffirmed the legitimate right of the peoples in Southern Rhodesia, Namibia and the territories under Portuguese domination to struggle by all necessary means at their disposal against the colonialist authorities which denied them their freedom and independence, and reaffirmed the obligation of Member States to render all necessary moral and material assistance to those peoples. The Special Committee condemned the increasing collaboration between Portugal, South Africa and the illegal racist minority régime in Southern Rhodesia, designed to perpetuate colonialism and oppression in southern Africa. It urged all States to increase their financial and material assistance to the peoples of those territories in their struggle for the restoration of their inalienable rights, and requested all States, directly and through their action in the organizations of the United Nations system, to discontinue all collaboration with the Governments of Portugal and South Africa, and with the illegal régime in Southern Rhodesia.

The Special Committee drew the attention of the Security Council to the urgent need to take effective measures to put an end to the grave situation—which threatened international peace and security—created by the continued defiance by the authorities concerned of their obligations under the United Nations Charter, in respect of Southern Rhodesia, Namibia and the territories under Portuguese administration.

It also decided to request its Working Group to study the possibility of associating more closely with the Committee's work the representatives of the national liberation movements of the territories concerned, and to report to the Committee thereon in 1972.

The Special Committee's resolution to this effect was adopted by a vote of 17 to 0, with 1 abstention. The text was based on a proposal sponsored by Afghanistan, Ethiopia, India, Iraq, Mali, Sierra Leone, the Syrian Arab Republic, Trinidad and Tobago, the United Republic of Tanzania, and Yugoslavia.

On 14 September 1971, the Special Committee adopted another resolution whereby it: condemned the persistent refusal of the Government of Portugal to implement the General Assembly's resolution of 14 December 1960 (containing the text of the Declaration on the Granting of Independence to Colonial Countries and Peoples)[3] and other relevant resolutions of the General Assembly and the Security Council; also condemned the colonial war Portugal waged against the African peoples in Angola, Mozambique and Guinea (Bissau) which threatened the security and violated the territorial integrity and sovereignty of neighbouring independent African States; further condemned violations by Portugal of the territorial integrity and sovereignty of independent African States, in particular those bordering the Portuguese-administered territories.

The Special Committee called upon Portugal: to

[3]See footnote 1.

cease all repressive activities and military operations against the people of the territories; to withdraw all military and other forces; to give full implementation to the Assembly's resolution of 14 December 1960 and all other relevant resolutions of the Assembly and the Security Council; and to ensure, in connexion with the conflict, the application in the territories of the 1949 Geneva Conventions relative to the Treatment of Prisoners of War and to the Protection of Civilian Persons in Time of War.

The Committee again appealed to all States, particularly Portugal's military allies within NATO, to discontinue all military assistance to Portugal and to prevent the sale or supply of weapons, military equipment and material to Portugal for use in its colonial wars in Africa.

The Committee further called upon all States to put an end to all practices that exploited the territories and their peoples, and to discourage their nationals and companies from economic activities that strengthened Portugal's domination. In particular, the Committee condemned the continuing foreign participation in the Cabora Bassa dam project in Mozambique and the Cunene River Basin project in Angola; it appealed to those Governments which had not yet done so to withdraw immediately from all activities relating to the projects and to prevent any further participation therein by companies or individuals under their jurisdiction.

The Special Committee urged all States and specialized agencies and other organizations within the United Nations system, in co-operation with OAU, to render to the peoples of the territories the moral and material assistance necessary to continue their struggle for the restoration of their inalienable rights. It reiterated its appeals to the specialized agencies and the international institutions associated with the United Nations, in particular the International Bank for Reconstruction and Development and the International Monetary Fund, to refrain from granting Portugal any financial, economic or technical assistance as long as Portugal refused to implement the Assembly resolution of 14 December 1960. The Special Committee also drew the attention of the Security Council to the urgent need to take all effective measures, in accordance with the relevant provisions of the United Nations Charter, to secure the implementation by Portugal of that resolution and of the Security Council decisions on the territories under Portuguese domination.

In view of the Special Committee's acceptance of the invitations extended by the *Movimento Popular de Libertação de Angola* (MPLA) and the *Frente de Libertação de Moçambique* (FRELIMO) to visit the liberated areas of Angola and Mozambique, the Special Committee requested its Chairman to work out the necessary modalities in consultation with OAU and those liberation movements.

The Special Committee's decisions to this effect were based on a proposal by Afghanistan, Ethiopia, India, Iraq, Mali, Sierra Leone, the Syrian Arab Republic, Trinidad and Tobago, the United Republic of Tanzania, and Yugoslavia, and were set forth in a resolution adopted by a roll-call vote of 17 to 0.

Venezuela explained that it had not participated in the vote because the Special Committee had rejected its proposals for separate votes on several paragraphs of the resolution. In Venezuela's view, the Committee was not competent to raise the question of Portuguese violations of the territory of other States, as this was strictly within the competence of the Security Council.

Decisions of Human Rights Commission and of Economic and Social Council

During 1971, the Commission on Human Rights and the Economic and Social Council took several decisions concerning the violation of human rights and fundamental freedoms, including policies of racial discrimination and *apartheid*, with particular reference to colonial and other dependent countries and territories, including the Portuguese-administered territories.

By a resolution adopted on 8 March 1971, the Commission among other things decided that its *Ad Hoc* Working Group of Experts should continue to survey developments in southern Africa, particularly in reference to grave manifestations of colonialism and racial discrimination in Namibia, Southern Rhodesia, Angola, Mozambique and Guinea (Bissau).

The Commission requested the Group to bring any new developments of such manifestations to its attention at its 1972 session, and to submit a report to its 1973 session. (See also p. 405.)

On 11 March 1971, the Commission on Human Rights recommended to the Economic and Social Council a draft resolution whereby the Council would recommend that, among other things, the General Assembly: express its concern that some countries, notably Portugal, with the support of its NATO allies, were waging war against the national liberation movement in colonial and developing countries; confirm the legality of the people's struggle for self-determination and liberation from colonial and foreign domination by all available means; and condemn States that contributed to the creation in southern Africa of a military-industrial complex whose aim was the suppression of the movement of peoples struggling for their self-determination, and interference in the affairs of independent African States.

On 21 May 1971, the Economic and Social Council adopted the text as its resolution 1592(L).

(For text of Economic and Social Council resolution 1592(L), see pp. 422-23.)

Also on 21 May 1971, the Economic and Social Council adopted a resolution (1599(L)) by which it expressed its grave concern at the continued suppression of trade union rights in South Africa, Namibia, Angola, Mozambique and Southern Rhodesia. It condemned the repression and detention of trade union leaders in southern Africa and called for their immediate and unconditional release. It also condemned the treatment of African producers of primary products in the territories under Portuguese domination.

The Council called upon Portugal to stop immediately the confiscation of African lands. It requested the *Ad Hoc* Working Group of Experts of the Commission on Human Rights to investigate thoroughly the system of recruitment of African workers in Namibia, Southern Rhodesia and the territories under Portuguese domination and to report to the Council on this question by early 1973.

(For text of resolution 1599(L), see p. 441.)

Consideration by General Assembly

General questions

At its 1971 session, the General Assembly referred the question of the territories under Portuguese administration to its Fourth Committee.

In addition to the report of the Special Committee on the Situation with regard to the Implementation of the Declaration on the Granting of Independence to Colonial Countries and Peoples, the Fourth Committee had before it the following: a report by the Secretary-General containing replies of Governments on the implementation of the Assembly resolution of 14 December 1970, which, among other things, called for States to withhold from Portugal assistance that enabled it to prosecute its colonial war in Africa;[4] a note by the Secretary-General concerning the question of the representation of Angola, Guinea (Bissau) and Mozambique in the Economic Commission for Africa (ECA); and a letter dated 2 December 1971 from the Permanent Representative of Zambia to the United Nations, addressed to the Secretary-General, transmitting the text of a cable from Amílcar Cabral, Secretary-General of the *Partido Africano da Independência da Guiné e Cabo Verde* (PAIGC), concerning Portuguese actions against Guinea (Bissau).

The Fourth Committee heard the following petitioners on the territories under Portuguese administration: Raymond F. Mbala, *Gouvernement révolutionnaire de l'Angola en exil* (GRAE); Sharfudine M. Khan, *Frente de Libertação de Moçambique* (FRELIMO); Romesh Chandra, Lucio Luzzatto,

Emilson Randriamihasinoro and Nicolai Voshinin, World Peace Council; I. B. Tabata, Unity Movement of South Africa; and Gil Fernandes, *Partido Africano da Independência da Guiné e Cabo Verde* (PAIGC).

Discussion in the Fourth Committee on the territories under Portuguese administration was concerned in particular with action that could be taken by the international community to find a solution to what was felt by many Members to be a growing threat to international peace and security posed by Portugal.

Many Members, including Albania, Algeria, Guinea, Hungary, Mali, Romania, Senegal, Togo, Yemen and Yugoslavia, stated that Portugal had become increasingly aggressive, as evidenced by its use of chemical substances and defoliants and attacks on sovereign States sharing common borders with its territories.

The Central African Republic, Czechoslovakia, Egypt, Haiti, Somalia, the Syrian Arab Republic, Trinidad and Tobago and the United Republic of Tanzania, among others, held that there was increased collaboration between Portugal, South Africa and Southern Rhodesia, which aimed at consolidating control of their white minority régimes.

Some speakers, including Argentina, Indonesia, Mongolia, Pakistan and Sweden, expressed disappointment that the constitutional reforms enacted by Portugal in 1971 had not introduced any real changes in the political status of the territories. Sweden stated that the reforms did not open the way to self-determination and political freedom for the peoples concerned.

Many Members considered that there could be no peaceful solution to the problem so long as Portugal refused to recognize the right of the peoples of the territories to self-determination. Cameroon and Norway, among others, expressed regret that Portugal had not found it possible to accept the offer contained in the Manifesto on Southern Africa (Lusaka Manifesto)—adopted by the Heads of State and Government of the Organization of African Unity (OAU) in 1969—that, if Portugal changed its policy and accepted the principle of self-determination, the African States would urge the liberation movements to desist from armed struggle and co-operate in a peaceful transfer of power.[5] Several Members, including Canada, Japan, Nepal and Tunisia, expressed the hope that Portugal would recognize the irreversible tide of history and realize the need to change its colonial policy.

A number of Members shared the view that the major powers were responsible for Portugal's

---

[4]See footnote 2.
[5]See Y.U.N., 1969, pp. 147-52, for information on Manifesto.

intransigence through the support and assistance they provided to it. Algeria, the Byelorussian SSR, Cuba, Guyana, Hungary, Jamaica, Mali, Mauritania, Nepal, Nigeria, Poland and the Syrian Arab Republic were among those holding that the assistance Portugal received from Western countries, particularly its allies in the NATO alliance, enabled it to carry on its wars against the independence movements and constituted one of the major obstacles to the victory of the liberation movements. Kenya said that at the General Assembly's 1970 session, three permanent members of the Security Council had sided with Portugal in the voting on the resolution on territories under Portuguese administration.[6]

The activities of foreign economic interests in the territories, in particular their participation in the Cabora Bassa and Cunene River Basin projects, were criticized by a number of Members as designed to further entrench colonialism in the territories and to create a centre of white power in southern Africa. Members who shared this view included the Central African Republic, Egypt, Jamaica, Mongolia, Nepal, Nigeria, Pakistan, Trinidad and Tobago and Uganda.

Some Members felt that the major powers must take steps to persuade Portugal to change its policy; others advocated stronger action by the United Nations. Peru, Uruguay and Yugoslavia were among those who urged that the Security Council take measures to ensure the implementation by Portugal of the relevant United Nations resolutions; in this connexion, several Members referred to the programme of action, adopted by the General Assembly in 1970,[7] for the full implementation of the Declaration on the Granting of Independence to Colonial Countries and Peoples.

The suggestion was made by the USSR that sanctions be extended to Portugal and South Africa, and by the United Republic of Tanzania that a united front be established to find ways of isolating Portugal and other minority régimes and to expel them from all specialized agencies associated with the United Nations. Sweden considered that the greater the support a United Nations decision received from Member States that could exert direct influence on the responsible régimes in southern Africa, the greater would be the hope of achieving a real solution.

It was suggested by a number of Members that action by the various United Nations bodies concerned with the territories in question should be more carefully co-ordinated and planned. Other members urged more United Nations activities to mobilize public opinion and moral pressure. Some Members—including the Congo, Guinea, India, Mexico, Morocco, Romania, Yugoslavia and Zambia—called for increased material

assistance to the liberation movements by the United Nations.

The representative of Portugal stated that Portuguese policy had always been aimed at establishing a multiracial society based on the principles of equal rights and non-discrimination. Portugal had never sought to impose its culture on other peoples.

The 1971 constitutional reforms promulgated by the Portuguese Government aimed at granting increased administrative, political and economic autonomy to the territories, the representative said. In order for the population to be able to exercise such rights, they needed certain qualifications and a certain level of education; the progress made in school enrolment testified to Portugal's policy of encouraging fuller participation by the inhabitants in the political life of the nation.

The Portuguese representative denied that Portugal's presence in the territories was dependent upon the assistance it received from its allies in NATO, a view that was based on the false premise that the territories were in a state of rebellion. The economic activities that Members had criticized were aimed solely at the development of the territories themselves.

Portugal had rejected the proposals in the Lusaka Manifesto because of the insulting accusations the Manifesto contained, but it had repeatedly offered to co-operate with Member States sharing common borders with the territories under Portuguese administration; in particular, it had put forward proposals in 1963, 1965 and 1971 for the establishment of an impartial commission to supervise those frontiers. Noting that some constructive suggestions had been put forward during the Fourth Committee's discussion, the Portuguese representative declared that Portugal was ready to hold a dialogue, which could be a prelude to an agreement.

On 3 December 1971, the Fourth Committee approved a draft resolution which was adopted by the General Assembly on 10 December 1971.

The Assembly thereby, among other things, expressed its grave concern at the critical and explosive situation created by Portugal's further intensification of its military operations and other oppressive measures against the peoples of Angola, Mozambique and Guinea (Bissau) who were struggling to attain their freedom and independence and about any use of chemical substances by Portugal in its colonial wars against the peoples of the territories under its domination.

The Assembly noted with concern that the constitutional changes introduced by the Por-

[6]See footnote 2.
[7]See Y.U.N., 1970, pp. 706-8, text of resolution 2621(XXV) of 12 October 1970.

tuguese Government in 1971 were not intended to lead to the exercise of self-determination and attainment of independence by the African people of the territories but were designed to perpetuate Portuguese domination. It noted with satisfaction the progress made towards national independence and freedom by the national liberation movements in those territories, both through their struggle and through reconstruction programmes and the arrangements relating to the representation of Angola, Mozambique and Guinea (Bissau) as associate members in the Economic Commission for Africa.

By the operative part of the resolution, the General Assembly reaffirmed the inalienable right of the peoples of the territories under Portuguese administration to self-determination and independence, as recognized by the General Assembly in its resolution of 14 December 1960,[8] and the legitimacy of their struggle to achieve that right. It strongly condemned Portugal's persistent refusal to implement that resolution and other relevant resolutions, including those of the Security Council.

It also condemned: (a) Portugal's colonial wars against the peoples of Angola, Mozambique and Guinea (Bissau) and its violation of the territorial integrity and sovereignty of neighbouring independent African States, which seriously disturbed international peace and security; (b) the indiscriminate bombing of civilians and the ruthless and wholesale destruction of villages and properties by the Portuguese military forces in Angola, Mozambique and Guinea (Bissau); and (c) the collaboration between Portugal, South Africa and the illegal régime of Southern Rhodesia, designed to perpetuate colonialism and oppression in southern Africa, as well as the continued intervention of South African forces against the peoples of Angola and Mozambique.

The Assembly called upon the Government of Portugal to refrain from the use of chemical substances in its colonial wars; to treat captured freedom fighters of Angola, Mozambique and Guinea (Bissau) as prisoners of war in accordance with the principles of the 1949 Geneva Convention relative to the Treatment of Prisoners of War; and to comply with the 1949 Geneva Convention relative to the Protection of Civilian Persons in Time of War.

It also urgently called upon the Government of Portugal: (a) to recognize immediately the right of the peoples under its administration to self-determination and independence in accordance with relevant United Nations resolutions; (b) to cease immediately its colonial wars and acts of repression against the peoples of Angola, Mozambique and Guinea (Bissau), to withdraw military and other forces employed for that purpose and to

eliminate all practices that violated the inalienable rights of the African populations, including arbitrary eviction and regrouping of African populations and settlement of immigrants in the territories; (c) to proclaim an unconditional political amnesty, to restore democratic political rights and to transfer powers to freely elected institutions representative of the population; (d) to cease all attacks on, and violations of, the security and territorial integrity of neighbouring sovereign countries; and (e) to release the men and property it was holding as a result of those attacks and violations.

It appealed once again to all States, particularly to those members of NATO which continued to render assistance to Portugal, to withdraw any assistance and to prevent the sale or supply of weapons, military equipment and material to Portugal, used to perpetuate its colonial domination in Africa. It called upon all States to put an end to all activities that helped to exploit the territories and to discourage activities by their nationals and companies which impeded the implementation of the Declaration; and requested Governments that had not yet done so to prevent their nationals and companies under their jurisdiction from participating in the Cabora Bassa project in Mozambique and the Cunene River Basin project in Angola, and to withdraw immediately from all activities related to those projects. It also requested all States, and the specialized agencies and other organizations within the United Nations system, in consultation with the Organization of African Unity, to render to the peoples of the territories all the moral and material assistance necessary to continue their struggle for the restoration of their inalienable rights.

The Assembly drew the attention of the Security Council, in view of the further deterioration of the situation in the territories which seriously disturbed international peace and security, to the urgent need to consider taking steps, in accordance with the provisions of the Charter of the United Nations, to secure the implementation by Portugal of the General Assembly's resolution of 14 December 1960 and decisions of the Security Council concerning the territories under Portuguese domination.

The Assembly approved the arrangements relating to the representation of Angola, Mozambique and Guinea (Bissau) as associate members of the Economic Commission for Africa (ECA), as well as the list of representatives of those territories proposed by the Organization of African Unity, and noted with satisfaction the intention of the Special Committee to send a group to visit the

[8]See footnote 1.

liberated areas of Angola, Mozambique and Guinea (Bissau). It invited the Secretary-General to further intensify educational and training programmes for the peoples of the territories in accordance with their needs and within the framework of the United Nations Educational and Training Programme for Southern Africa, and to report thereon to the General Assembly at its 1972 session. It also requested the Secretary-General to transmit the resolution to all States and to report to the Assembly in 1972 on the implementation of its provisions.

The above decisions were set forth in resolution 2795(XXVI), which the Assembly adopted by a roll-call vote of 105 to 8, with 5 abstentions. (For text of resolution, see DOCUMENTARY REFERENCES below.)

The draft text to this effect was based on a proposal in the Fourth Committee by the following 38 Members: Afghanistan, Algeria, Cameroon, Ceylon, Chad, the Congo, Dahomey, Equatorial Guinea, Ethiopia, Ghana, Guinea, India, Indonesia, Iraq, Kenya, Liberia, Malaysia, Mali, Mauritania, Mongolia, Morocco, Niger, Nigeria, Pakistan, Rwanda, Senegal, Sierra Leone, Singapore, Somalia, Sudan, Togo, Tunisia, Uganda, the United Republic of Tanzania, Upper Volta, Yugoslavia, Zaire and Zambia. The text was approved by the Fourth Committee by a roll-call vote of 99 to 6, with 6 abstentions.

Speaking before the vote, the representative of Portugal stated that the text contained the same accusations, condemnations and exhortations as in previous years. He took issue especially with the paragraph approving the arrangements relating to the representation of Angola, Mozambique and Guinea (Bissau) as associate members of ECA. In his view, the procedures recommended by ECA were contrary to the principles of international law and to the provisions of the Charter of the United Nations; there was no legal basis for attributing to the Organization of African Unity competence to appoint representatives of the territories, nor could ECA give it such competence. Portugal had exclusive competence in the matter; even if the territories were considered non-self-governing under Portuguese administration, it still would be for Portugal, as the administering power, to appoint representatives from those territories or to authorize the governments of those territories to do so, the Portuguese representative held.

Australia, Austria, Canada, Ecuador, Finland, Greece, Guatemala, Honduras, Ireland, Japan, Mexico, the Netherlands, New Zealand, Nicaragua, Norway, the Philippines, Sweden, Uruguay and Venezuela supported the resolution as a whole but expressed reservations regarding, among other things, the operative paragraph approving arrangements for ECA representation of

Angola, Mozambique and Guinea (Bissau); in the view of many of these Members, the provision raised questions of a legal and procedural nature. France, the United Kingdom and South Africa also expressed reservations on the paragraph.

Other Assembly decisions

DECLARATION ON GRANTING INDEPENDENCE

In another decision bearing on the question of the territories under Portuguese administration, the General Assembly on 20 December 1971 adopted a resolution (2878(XXVI)) on the implementation of the Declaration on the Granting of Independence to Colonial Countries and Peoples.

Among other things, the Assembly thereby deplored the continued refusal of the colonial powers, especially Portugal and South Africa, to implement the Declaration and other relevant resolutions on decolonization, particularly those relating to the territories under Portuguese domination and to Namibia and Southern Rhodesia. It also strongly deplored the policies of those States that continued to co-operate with the Governments of Portugal and South Africa and the illegal régime in Southern Rhodesia, in defiance of resolutions of the General Assembly, the Security Council and the Special Committee.

The Assembly condemned the policies, pursued by certain colonial powers in the territories under their domination, of imposing non-representative régimes and constitutions, strengthening the position of foreign economic and other interests, misleading public opinion and encouraging the systematic influx of foreign immigrants while evicting, displacing and transferring the indigenous inhabitants to other areas, and called upon those powers to desist forthwith from such policies.

The Assembly urged all States and the specialized agencies and other organizations within the United Nations system to provide, in consultation, as appropriate, with the Organization of African Unity (OAU) moral and material assistance to all peoples struggling for their freedom and independence in the colonial territories, in particular to the national liberation movements of the territories in southern Africa, and in that connexion drew the attention of all States to the OAU Assistance Fund for the Struggle against Colonialism and *Apartheid.*

All States were asked to withhold or continue to withhold any assistance from the Governments of Portugal and South Africa and from the illegal régime in Southern Rhodesia until they renounced their policy of colonial domination and racial discrimination.

Also, the Assembly requested the colonial

powers to withdraw immediately and unconditionally their military bases and installations from colonial territories and to refrain from establishing new ones. The Assembly asked the Special Committee to make concrete suggestions which might assist the Security Council in considering appropriate measures under the Charter regarding developments in colonial territories which were likely to threaten international peace and security, and recommended that the Council take such suggestions fully into consideration.

The Assembly endorsed the proposal of the Special Committee to take steps, in consultation with OAU, to enable representatives of national liberation movements in the colonial territories in southern Africa to participate, whenever necessary and in an appropriate capacity, in its deliberations relating to those territories.

(For text of resolution 2878(XXVI), see pp. 521-23.)

Also on 20 December 1971, the General Assembly took another series of decisions concerning the implementation of the Declaration.

By resolution 2874(XXVI), the Assembly among other things reaffirmed that recognition by the Assembly, the Security Council and other United Nations bodies of the legitimacy of the struggle of colonial peoples to achieve freedom and independence entailed, as a corollary, the extension by the United Nations system of organizations of all necessary moral and material assistance to national liberation movements in those territories, including especially the liberated areas of the colonial territories.

The Assembly reiterated its urgent appeal to specialized agencies and other organizations within the United Nations system to render all possible moral and material assistance to the peoples struggling to liberate themselves from colonial rule and in particular to work out, in co-operation with OAU and through it, with the national liberation movements, concrete programmes for assisting the peoples of Southern Rhodesia, Namibia and the territories under Portuguese administration, including in particular the populations in the liberated areas of those territories.

The Assembly also requested the specialized agencies and other organizations within the United Nations system to discontinue all collaboration with the Governments of Portugal and South Africa and with the illegal régime in Southern Rhodesia, in accordance with relevant resolutions of the General Assembly and of the Security Council relating to colonial territories in southern Africa. In particular, it urged the International Bank for Reconstruction and Development and the International Monetary Fund to take all necessary measures to withhold financial, economic, technical and other assistance from the Govern-

ments of Portugal and South Africa until they renounced their policies of racial discrimination and colonial domination.

(For text of resolution 2874(XXVI), see pp. 528-29.)

RIGHT TO SELF-DETERMINATION

On 6 December 1971, the General Assembly adopted a resolution (2787(XXVI)) on the importance of the universal realization of the rights of peoples to self-determination and of the speedy granting of independence to colonial countries and peoples for the effective guarantee and observance of human rights.

In so doing, the Assembly among other things expressed concern that some countries—notably Portugal, with the support of its NATO allies—were waging wars against the national liberation movements of the colonies and against certain independent States of Africa and Asia and the developing countries; it confirmed that colonialism in all its forms and manifestations, including methods of neo-colonialism, constituted a gross encroachment on the rights of peoples and on the basic human rights and freedoms.

The Assembly confirmed the legality of the peoples' struggle for self-determination and liberation from colonial and foreign domination and alien subjugation, notably the peoples in southern Africa—particularly those of Zimbabwe [Southern Rhodesia], Namibia, Angola, Mozambique and Guinea (Bissau)—as well as the Palestinian people, by all available means consistent with the Charter of the United Nations. It affirmed man's basic human right to fight for the self-determination of his people under colonial and foreign domination; and called upon all States dedicated to the ideals of freedom and peace to give all political, moral and material assistance to peoples struggling for liberation, self-determination and independence.

The Assembly further expressed its belief that the main objectives and principles of international protection of human rights could not be effectively implemented while some States, particularly Portugal and South Africa, pursued the imperialist policy of colonialism, used force against independent African States and developing countries and peoples fighting for self-determination and supported régimes that were applying the criminal policy of racism and *apartheid*.

The Assembly condemned: (*a*) the colonial and usurping powers that were suppressing the right of peoples to self-determination and hampering the liquidation of the last hotbeds of colonialism and racism in the African and Asian continents and in other parts of the world; and (*b*) the policy of certain NATO members which contributed to the creation of a military-industrial complex in southern Africa which aimed at suppressing the movements of peoples struggling for self-determination and at interfering in the affairs of independent African States.

(For text of resolution 2787(XXVI), see pp. 423-24.)

FOREIGN ECONOMIC INTERESTS

On 20 December 1971, the General Assembly adopted resolution 2873(XXVI) on the activities of foreign economic and other interests impeding the implementation of the Declaration on the Granting of Independence to Colonial Countries and Peoples in Southern Rhodesia, Namibia and territories under Portuguese domination and in other territories under colonial domination, and impeding efforts to eliminate colonialism, *apartheid* and racial discrimination in southern Africa.

By this resolution, the Assembly among other things reaffirmed the inalienable right of the peoples of the territories to self-determination and independence and to the enjoyment of the natural resources of the territories by the indigenous inhabitants.

The Assembly again condemned the activities and operating methods of those foreign economic and other interests in the territories under colonial domination which were designed to perpetuate the subjugation of dependent peoples; and it deplored the support given by the colonial powers and other States to those foreign and other interests engaged in exploiting the natural and human resources of the territories without regard to the welfare of the indigenous peoples, thus violating the rights of the indigenous peoples and obstructing the full and speedy implementation of the Declaration.

The Assembly also condemned the construction of the Cabora Bassa and Cunene River Basin projects, which were designed to further entrench colonialist and racialist domination over the territories of southern Africa and which were a source of international tension, and deplored the policies of those Governments that had not yet prevented their nationals and companies from participating in the two projects, urgently requesting the Governments concerned to take all necessary measures to terminate this participation and withdraw immediately from all activities related to them.

(For text of resolution 2873(XXVI), see pp. 534-35.)

HUMAN RIGHTS IN ARMED CONFLICTS

On 20 December 1971, the General Assembly, in adopting resolution 2852(XXVI) concerning respect for human rights in armed conflicts, reaffirmed that persons participating in resistance movements and freedom fighters in southern Africa and in territories under colonial and alien domination who were struggling for their liberation and self-determination should, in case of arrest, be treated as prisoners of war in accordance with the principles of the Hague Convention of 1907 and the Geneva Conventions of 1949.

It invited the International Committee of the Red Cross to devote special attention to, among other things, the need to evolve norms designed to increase the protection of persons struggling against colonial and alien domination, foreign occupation and racist régimes; and the need for development of rules concerning the status, protection and humane treatment of combatants in international and non-international armed conflicts and the question of guerrilla warfare.

(For text of resolution 2852(XXVI), see pp. 427-28.)

ELIMINATION OF RACIAL DISCRIMINATION

On 6 December 1971, in adopting resolution 2784(XXVI) on the elimination of all forms of racial discrimination, the Assembly emphatically reaffirmed its recognition and vigorous support of the legitimacy of the struggles of oppressed peoples everywhere, in particular in southern Africa, against colonial, racial and alien domination towards the achievement of their inalienable rights to equality and freedom. It particularly condemned Portugal for persisting in its colonialist policies in Africa and for continuing its war against the peoples of the territories under its domination.

The Assembly requested the President of the General Assembly to forward directly to the Heads of State or Government of each State a message annexed to the resolution putting before them, among other things, the fact that the racist Governments in southern Africa had been further strengthened through an unholy alliance between South Africa, Portugal and the minority régime in Southern Rhodesia.

(For text of resolution 2784(XXVI), see pp. 402-4.)

United Nations Educational and Training Programme for Southern Africa

Under the United Nations Educational and Training Programme for Southern Africa, 205 applications from territories under Portuguese administration were received during the period 1 November 1970 to 8 October 1971. Fifty-eight new awards were made and another 129 were extended. By 8 October 1971, there were 187 fellowship holders from Portuguese territories studying abroad in 23 countries.

By a resolution (2875(XXVI)) adopted on 20 December 1971, the General Assembly noted that voluntary contributions to the Programme received from 1968 to 1971 had fallen far short of the target set by the Assembly in 1967.[9] The Assembly appealed urgently to all States, organizations and individuals to make generous contributions and decided that, as a further transitional measure, provision should be made, under the regular budget for the financial year 1972, for an amount of $100,000 to ensure continuity of the Programme.

(For text of resolution 2875(XXVI), see pp. 124-25.)

By the resolution dealing with the situation in the Portuguese territories (2795(XXVI)), which it adopted on 10 December 1971, the Assembly invited the Secretary-General, within the frame-work of the United Nations Educational and Training Programme for Southern Africa, to intensify educational and training programmes for the people of the territories under Portuguese domination, taking into account their needs for qualified administrative, technical and professional personnel to assume responsibility for the public administration and the economic and social development of their countries, and to report on the question to the General Assembly in 1972.

(For text of resolution 2795(XXVI), operative para. 15, see p. 576.)

[9]See Y.U.N., 1967, pp. 649-50, text of resolution 2349(XXII).

DOCUMENTARY REFERENCES

Consideration by Special Committee

Special Committee on Situation with regard to Implementation of Declaration on Granting of Independence to Colonial Countries and Peoples, meetings 782, 784, 785, 787, 789-791, 795-797, 802, 806, 811-814, 824-826, 830.

A/8423/Rev.1. Report of Special Committee (covering its work during 1971), Chapter V (Section B: Decisions of Special Committee, including resolution adopted on 9 September 1971) and Chapter VIII (Section B: Resolutions adopted by Special Committee on 13 April, 2 June and 14 September 1971).

Consideration by General Assembly

General Assembly—26th session
Fourth Committee, meetings 1922-1926, 1928-1946, 1949, 1954, 1958-1961.
Plenary meeting 2012.

A/8348 and Add.1. Report of Secretary-General.
A/8401. Report of Secretary-General on work of the Organization, 16 June 1970–15 June 1971, Part Two, Chapter I B 3.
A/8401/Add.1. Introduction to report of Secretary-General on work of the Organization, September 1971: Part One, Chapter V; Part Two, Chapter VIII.
A/8402. Report of Security Council, 16 June 1970–15 June 1971, Chapter 11.
A/C.4/736 and Add.1. Question of Namibia; question of territories under Portuguese administration; question of Southern Rhodesia. Requests for hearings.
A/C.4/739 and Add.1. Requests for hearings.
A/C.4/742. Letter of 2 December 1971 from Zambia.
A/C.4/L.922. Afghanistan, Algeria, Cameroon, Ceylon, Chad, Congo, Dahomey, Equatorial Guinea, Ethiopia, Ghana, Guinea, India, Indonesia, Iraq, Kenya, Liberia, Malaysia, Mali, Mauritania, Mongolia, Morocco, Niger, Nigeria, Pakistan, Rwanda, Senegal, Sierra Leone, Singapore, Somalia, Sudan, Togo, Tunisia, Uganda, United Republic of Tanzania, Upper Volta, Yugoslavia, Zaire, Zambia: draft resolution, approved by Fourth Committee on 3 December 1971, meeting 1961, by roll-call vote of 99 to 6, with 6 abstentions, as follows:

In favour: Afghanistan, Albania, Algeria, Australia, Austria, Bahrain, Barbados, Botswana, Bulgaria, Burma, Byelorussian SSR, Cameroon, Canada, Central African Republic, Ceylon, Chad, Chile, Colombia, Congo, Cuba, Czechoslovakia, Dahomey, Denmark, Dominican Republic, Ecuador, Egypt, Ethiopia, Fiji, Finland, Gabon, Gambia, Ghana, Greece, Guatemala, Guinea, Guyana, Honduras, Hungary, India, Indonesia, Iran, Iraq, Ireland, Israel, Ivory Coast, Jamaica, Japan, Jordan, Kenya, Khmer Republic, Kuwait, Lebanon, Lesotho, Liberia, Libyan Arab Republic, Madagascar, Malaysia, Mali, Mauritania, Mexico, Mongolia, Morocco, Nepal, Netherlands, New Zealand, Nicaragua, Nigeria, Norway, Pakistan, People's Democratic Republic of Yemen, Peru, Philippines, Poland, Romania, Rwanda, Saudi Arabia, Senegal, Sierra Leone, Singapore, Somalia, Sudan, Sweden, Syrian Arab Republic, Thailand, Togo, Trinidad and Tobago, Tunisia, Turkey, Uganda, Ukrainian SSR, USSR, United Republic of Tanzania, Upper Volta, Uruguay, Venezuela, Yemen, Yugoslavia, Zaire, Zambia.

Against: Brazil, Portugal, South Africa, Spain, United Kingdom, United States.

Abstaining: Argentina, Belgium, Costa Rica, France, Italy, Malawi.

A/C.4/L.993. Statement made by member of *Frente de Libertação de Moçambique* in Fourth Committee on 1 November 1971, meeting 1937.
A/8549. Report of Fourth Committee.

RESOLUTION 2795(XXVI), as recommended by Fourth Committee, A/8549, adopted by Assembly on 10 December 1971, meeting 2012, by roll-call vote of 105 to 8, with 5 abstentions, as follows:

In favour: Afghanistan, Albania, Algeria, Australia, Austria, Bahrain, Barbados, Botswana, Bulgaria, Burma, Burundi, Byelorussian SSR, Cameroon, Canada, Central African Republic, Ceylon, Chad, Chile, Colombia, Congo, Cuba, Cyprus, Czechoslovakia, Dahomey, Denmark, Dominican Republic, Ecuador, Egypt, Equatorial Guinea, Ethiopia, Fiji, Finland, Gabon, Gambia, Ghana, Greece, Guatemala, Guyana, Haiti, Honduras, Hungary, Iceland, India, Indonesia, Iran, Iraq, Ireland, Israel, Ivory Coast, Jamaica, Japan, Jordan, Kenya, Khmer Republic, Kuwait, Laos, Lesotho, Liberia, Libyan Arab Republic, Madagascar, Malaysia, Mali, Mauritania, Mexico, Mongolia, Morocco, Nepal, Netherlands, New Zealand, Nicaragua, Niger, Nigeria, Norway, Oman, Pakistan, Panama, People's Democratic Republic of Yemen, Peru, Philippines, Poland, Qatar, Romania, Rwanda, Saudi Arabia, Senegal, Singapore, Somalia, Sudan, Sweden, Syrian Arab Republic, Togo, Trinidad and Tobago, Tunisia, Turkey, Uganda, Ukrainian SSR, USSR, United Republic of Tanzania, Upper Volta, Uruguay, Venezuela, Yemen, Yugoslavia, Zaire, Zambia.

Against: Brazil, Costa Rica, France, Portugal, South Africa, Spain, United Kingdom, United States.

Abstaining: Argentina, Belgium, El Salvador, Italy, Malawi.

The General Assembly,
Having considered the question of Territories under Portuguese domination,
Having examined the relevant chapters of the report of the Special Committee on the Situation with regard to the Implementa-

tion of the Declaration on the Granting of Independence to Colonial Countries and Peoples,

Having examined the report of the Secretary-General concerning the item,

Having heard the statements of the petitioners and bearing in mind the views expressed by representatives of national liberation movements,

Reaffirming its resolution 1514(XV) of 14 December 1960, containing the Declaration on the Granting of Independence to Colonial Countries and Peoples, and its resolution 2621(XXV) of 12 October 1970, containing the programme of action for the full implementation of the Declaration,

Recalling all previous resolutions concerning the question of Territories under Portuguese administration adopted by the General Assembly, the Security Council and the Special Committee,

Deploring the persistent refusal of the Government of Portugal to recognize the inalienable right of the peoples in the Territories under its domination to self-determination and independence in accordance with the Declaration on the Granting of Independence to Colonial Countries and Peoples,

Gravely concerned at the critical and explosive situation created by that Government's further intensification of its military operations and other oppressive measures against the peoples in Angola, Mozambique and Guinea (Bissau) who are struggling to attain their freedom and independence,

Deeply disturbed by the repeated occurrence of aggressive acts committed by Portugal against independent African States that border the Territories under its domination,

Deeply concerned at the continued and intensified activities of those foreign economic, financial and other interests which, contrary to the relevant resolutions of the General Assembly, are directly and indirectly assisting the Government of Portugal in its colonial wars and impeding the realization by the peoples of the Territories under Portuguese domination of their legitimate aspirations for self-determination and independence,

Deploring the policies of those States which, in disregard of the repeated appeals addressed to them by the United Nations, continue to provide Portugal with military and other assistance, which it uses to pursue its policies of colonial domination and oppression of the peoples of Angola, Mozambique and Guinea (Bissau),

Deeply concerned about any use of chemical substances by Portugal in its colonial wars against the peoples in the Territories under its domination,

Noting with concern that the constitutional changes introduced by the Portuguese Government in 1971 are not intended to lead to the exercise of self-determination and the attainment of independence by the African people of the Territories, but are designed to perpetuate Portuguese domination,

Noting with satisfaction the progress towards national independence and freedom made by the national liberation movements in those Territories, both through their struggle and through reconstruction programmes and the arrangements relating to the representation of Angola, Mozambique and Guinea (Bissau) as associate members in the Economic Commission for Africa,

1. *Reaffirms* the inalienable right of the peoples of Angola, Mozambique, Guinea (Bissau) and other Territories under Portuguese domination to self-determination and independence, as recognized by the General Assembly in its resolution 1514(XV), and the legitimacy of their struggle to achieve that right;

2. *Strongly condemns* the persistent refusal of the Government of Portugal to implement resolution 1514(XV) and all other relevant resolutions of the General Assembly and the Security Council;

3. *Condemns* the colonial war being waged by the Government of Portugal against the peoples of Angola, Mozambique and Guinea (Bissau) and the violations by that Government of the territorial integrity and sovereignty of neighbouring independent African States, which seriously disturb international peace and security;

4. *Condemns* the indiscriminate bombing of civilians and the ruthless and wholesale destruction of villages and property being carried out by the Portuguese military forces in Angola, Mozambique and Guinea (Bissau);

5. *Condemns* the collaboration among Portugal, South Africa and the illegal racist minority régime in Southern Rhodesia, designed to perpetuate colonialism and oppression in southern Africa, and the continued intervention of South African forces against the peoples of Angola and Mozambique;

6. *Calls upon* the Government of Portugal to refrain from the use of chemical substances in its colonial wars against the peoples of Angola, Mozambique and Guinea (Bissau), as such practice is contrary to the generally recognized rules of international law embodied in the Protocol for the Prohibition of the Use in War of Asphyxiating, Poisonous or Other Gases, and of Bacteriological Methods of Warfare, signed at Geneva on 17 June 1925, and to General Assembly resolution 2707(XXV) of 14 December 1970;

7. *Calls upon* the Government of Portugal to treat the freedom fighters of Angola, Mozambique and Guinea (Bissau) captured during the struggle for freedom as prisoners of war in accordance with the principles of the Geneva Convention relative to the Treatment of Prisoners of War, of 12 August 1949, and to comply with the Geneva Convention relative to the Protection of Civilian Persons in Time of War, of 12 August 1949;

8. *Appeals once again* to all States, particularly to those members of the North Atlantic Treaty Organization which continue to render assistance to Portugal, to withdraw any assistance that enables Portugal to prosecute the colonial war in Angola, Mozambique and Guinea (Bissau) and to prevent the sale or supply of weapons, military equipment and material to the Government of Portugal, as well as all supplies, equipment and material for the manufacture or maintenance of weapons and ammunition that it uses to perpetuate its colonial domination in Africa;

9. *Urgently calls upon* the Government of Portugal to take the following steps:

(a) The immediate recognition of the right of the peoples under its administration to self-determination and independence in accordance with General Assembly resolution 1514(XV) and other relevant resolutions of the Assembly and the Security Council;

(b) The immediate cessation of colonial wars and all acts of repression against the peoples of Angola, Mozambique and Guinea (Bissau), the withdrawal of military and other forces employed for that purpose and the elimination of all practices that violate the inalienable rights of the African populations, including arbitrary eviction and regrouping of the African populations and the settlement of immigrants in the Territory;

(c) The proclamation of an unconditional political amnesty, the restoration of democratic political rights and the transfer of all powers to freely elected institutions representative of the population, in accordance with resolution 1514(XV);

(d) The cessation of all attacks on, and violations of, the security and territorial integrity of neighbouring sovereign countries;

(e) The release of the men and property being held at present by Portugal following the attacks and violations committed against those sovereign States;

10. *Calls upon* all States to take immediate measures to put an end to all activities that help to exploit the Territories under Portuguese domination and the peoples therein and to discourage their nationals and bodies corporate under their jurisdiction from entering into any transactions or arrangements that strengthen Portugal's domination over, and impede the implementation of the Declaration with respect to, those Territories;

11. *Requests* those Governments that have failed to prevent their nationals and the companies under their jurisdiction from participating in the Cabora Bassa project in Mozambique and the Cunene River Basin project in Angola to take all the necessary measures to terminate their participation and to withdraw immediately from all activities related to those projects;

12. *Approves* the arrangements relating to the representation of Angola, Mozambique and Guinea (Bissau) as associate members of the Economic Commission for Africa, as well as the list of the representatives of those Territories proposed by the Organization of African Unity;

13. *Requests* all States and the specialized agencies and

other organizations within the United Nations system, in consultation with the Organization of African Unity, to render to the peoples of the Territories under Portuguese domination, in particular the population in the liberated areas of those Territories, all the moral and material assistance necessary to continue their struggle for the restoration of their inalienable right to self-determination and independence;

14. *Draws the attention* of the Security Council, in view of the further deterioration of the situation in the Territories of Angola, Mozambique and Guinea (Bissau) which seriously disturbs international peace and security, to the urgent need to consider taking all effective steps, in accordance with the relevant provisions of the Charter of the United Nations, to secure the full and speedy implementation by Portugal of General Assembly resolution 1514(XV) and of the decisions of the Security Council concerning the Territories under Portuguese domination;

15. *Invites* the Secretary-General, within the framework of the United Nations Educational and Training Programme for Southern Africa and in consultation with the specialized agencies, the United Nations High Commissioner for Refugees, the Governments of the host countries and the Organization of African Unity, to further intensify educational and training programmes for the people of the Territories under Portuguese domination, taking into account their needs for qualified administrative, technical and professional personnel to assume responsibility for the public administration and the economic and social development of their own countries, and to include information on the progress achieved in that regard

in the report concerning that Programme to be submitted by the Secretary-General to the General Assembly at its twenty-seventh session;

16. *Notes with satisfaction* the intention of the Special Committee on the Situation with regard to the Implementation of the Declaration on the Granting of Independence to Colonial Countries and Peoples to send a group to visit the liberated areas of Angola, Mozambique and Guinea (Bissau);

17. *Requests* the Secretary-General to transmit the present resolution to all States and to report to the General Assembly at its twenty-seventh session on the steps taken or envisaged by States in the implementation of the various provisions contained therein;

18. *Requests* the Special Committee to keep the situation in the Territories under review.

Other documents

S/10176. Letter of 13 April 1971 from Chairman of Special Committee on Situation with regard to Implementation of Declaration on Granting of Independence to Colonial Countries and Peoples to President of Security Council (transmitting operative text of resolution adopted on 13 April 1971).

S/10312. Letter of 10 September 1971 from Acting Chairman of Special Committee to President of Security Council (transmitting operative text of resolution adopted on 9 September 1971).

S/10320. Letter of 14 September 1971 from Acting Chairman of Special Committee to President of Security Council (transmitting operative text of resolution adopted on 14 September 1971).

Chapter V

The situation in Southern Rhodesia

The situation in Southern Rhodesia continued in 1971 to receive consideration by the Security Council, the General Assembly and the Assembly's Special Committee on the Situation with regard to the Implementation of the [1960] Declaration on the Granting of Independence to Colonial Countries and Peoples, as well as by the Commission on Human Rights and the Economic and Social Council.

These bodies were concerned with bringing to an end the situation in Southern Rhodesia created by the white minority régime of Ian Smith—which had unilaterally declared its independence from the United Kingdom in 1965—and with enabling the African people of the territory to exercise their basic human rights, particularly their inalienable right to freedom and independence in accordance with the 1960 Declaration on granting independence.

The Security Council met in November and December 1971 to consider the question of Southern Rhodesia in the light of the proposals for a settlement agreed upon between the illegal régime and the United Kingdom Government; a draft resolution sponsored by four African and Asian States failed to be adopted owing to the negative vote of the United Kingdom, a perma-

nent member of the Security Council of the United Nations.

The Special Committee adopted three resolutions on the question: one on 30 April relating to Southern Rhodesia's participation in the XXth Olympic Games; another on 2 July relating to the continuation of talks between the United Kingdom Government and the illegal régime; and a third on 24 August on the question of Southern Rhodesia as a whole.

At its twenty-sixth session, later in 1971, the General Assembly adopted four resolutions on the question. By the first, adopted on 16 November, it called on the United States to prevent the importation of chrome into the United States from Southern Rhodesia. By the second, adopted on 22 November, it reaffirmed the principle that there should be no independence before majority rule in Southern Rhodesia and affirmed that any settlement must be worked out with the participation of the nationalist leaders of Zimbabwe [Southern Rhodesia] and endorsed freely by the people.

A third resolution, adopted by the Assembly on 10 December, laid down a number of provisions on the general aspects of the situation in Southern Rhodesia. On 20 December, the Assembly adopted a fourth resolution by which, among other things, it rejected the proposals for a settlement agreed upon by the United Kingdom and the racist minority régime as constituting a flagrant violation of the inalienable right of the Zimbabwe people to self-determination and independence.

(For details of these and other related decisions on Southern Rhodesia, see pp. 88-112.)

Chapter VI

Other questions relating to Non-Self-Governing Territories

Transmission of information

Territories on which information was submitted in 1971

In accordance with Chapter XI, Article 73e of the United Nations Charter, Members responsible for the administration of territories whose peoples have not yet attained a full measure of self-government have the obligation to send each year to the Secretary-General information on economic, social and educational conditions in the territories for which they have responsibilities, subject to such limitations as security and constitutional considerations may require.[1]

Australia, France, New Zealand, Spain, the United Kingdom and the United States regularly include information on political and constitutional developments in the territories on which they transmit information. Additional information on political and constitutional developments in the territories under their administration is also given by Australia, New Zealand and the United States when the territories for which they have responsibility are discussed in the General Assembly's Special Committee on the Situation with regard to the Implementation of the Declaration on the Granting of Independence to Colonial Countries and Peoples. Supplementary information is also made available by the United Kingdom concerning territories under its administration.

During 1971, information relating to 1970 was transmitted to the Secretary-General with respect to the following territories:

Australia: Cocos (Keeling) Islands; Papua
France: New Hebrides (condominium with the United Kingdom)
New Zealand: Niue Island; Tokelau Islands
Spain: Spanish Sahara
United Kingdom: Bahamas; Bermuda; British Honduras; British Virgin Islands; Brunei; Cayman Islands; Falkland Islands (Malvinas); Gibraltar; Gilbert and Ellice Islands; Hong Kong; Montserrat; New Hebrides (condominium with France); Pitcairn Island; St. Helena; Seychelles; Solomon Islands; Southern Rhodesia; Turks and Caicos Islands

United States: American Samoa; Guam; United States Virgin Islands.

The Secretary-General reported to the General Assembly at its 1971 session, which opened on 21 September, that he had received no information concerning territories under Portuguese administration, which the General Assembly by a decision of 15 December 1960[2] considered to be non-self-governing territories within the meaning of Chapter XI of the Charter.

Nor had the Secretary-General received any information on Antigua, Dominica, Grenada, St. Kitts-Nevis-Anguilla and St. Lucia. The representative of the United Kingdom had stated in the Fourth Committee, on 15 December 1967, that these territories, having achieved the status of Associated States, had achieved a full measure of self-government and that information on them would not be transmitted in future. A similar statement with respect to St. Vincent was made by the representative of the United Kingdom in the Fourth Committee on 10 December 1969.

Study of information from administering Members

Up to 1963, information transmitted by administering Members on non-self-governing territories was examined by the General Assembly's Committee on Information from Non-Self-Governing Territories. When the General Assembly decided, on 16 December 1963, to discontinue this Committee,[3] it requested the Special Committee on the Situation with regard to the Implementation of the Declaration on the Granting of Independence to Colonial Countries and Peoples to study this information and take it fully into account in examining the situation in each of the non-self-governing territories.

On 20 December 1971, the General Assembly approved the chapter of the report of the Special Committee relating to the information from

[1]For text of Chapter XI of the Charter, see APPENDIX II.
[2]See Y.U.N., 1960, p. 513, text of resolution 1542(XV).
[3]See Y.U.N., 1963, pp. 441-42, text of resolution 1970(XVIII).

non-self-governing territories transmitted under Article 73e of the Charter of the United Nations. It deeply deplored that, despite the repeated recommendations of the General Assembly and the Special Committee, some Member States having responsibilities for the administration of non-self-governing territories had ceased to transmit information under Article 73e of the Charter, had transmitted insufficient information or had transmitted information too late.

The Assembly strongly condemned the Government of Portugal for its continued refusal to recognize the colonial status of the territories under its domination and to transmit information on them under Article 73e of the Charter.

The Assembly then reaffirmed that, in the absence of a decision by the General Assembly itself that a non-self-governing territory had attained a full measure of self-government in terms of Chapter XI of the Charter, the administering power concerned should continue to transmit information under Article 73e of the Charter with respect to that territory. It asked the administering powers concerned to transmit, or continue to transmit, to the Secretary-General such information, as well as the fullest possible information on political and constitutional developments in the territories concerned as early as possible and, at the latest, within a maximum period of six months following the expiration of the administrative year in the non-self-governing territories concerned.

Finally, the Assembly requested the Special Committee to continue to discharge its functions in this connexion.

These decisions were embodied in resolution 2870(XXVI), which the Assembly adopted by 111 votes to 2, with 10 abstentions. The Assembly acted on the recommendation of its Fourth Committee, which approved the text on 13 December 1971 by 86 votes to 2, with 8 abstentions. The sponsors of the text in the Fourth Committee were: Algeria, Cameroon, the Congo, Egypt, Equatorial Guinea, Ethiopia, Ghana, Guinea, India, Iran, Kenya, Mali, Mauritania, Mongolia, Nigeria, Pakistan, Rwanda, Sudan, the Syrian Arab Republic, the United Republic of Tanzania, Yugoslavia and Zambia. (For text of resolution, see DOCUMENTARY REFERENCES below.)

The text was based on a resolution approved on 6 October 1971 by the Special Committee on the Situation with regard to the Implementation of the Declaration on the Granting of Independence to Colonial Countries and Peoples. One provision of the Special Committee's resolution—deploring the refusal of the Government of the United Kingdom to transmit information on the territories of Antigua, Dominica, Grenada, St. Kitts-Nevis-Anguilla, St. Lucia and St. Vincent—was omitted from the text approved by the Fourth Committee and adopted by the Assembly.

Offers of study and training facilities

In 1971, the Secretary-General reported to the General Assembly that, up to 31 October 1971, the following 25 Member States had made scholarships available to persons from non-self-governing territories for secondary, vocational, university and post-graduate studies: Austria, Brazil, Bulgaria, Ceylon, Cyprus, Czechoslovakia, Egypt, Ghana, Greece, Hungary, India, Iran, Israel, Italy, Mexico, Pakistan, the Philippines, Poland, Romania, Tunisia, Turkey, Uganda, the USSR, the United States and Yugoslavia.

The General Assembly, on 20 December 1971, expressed its appreciation to the Member States that had made scholarships available, and it invited all States to make generous offers of such study and training facilities. It also requested the States offering scholarships to inform the Secretary-General of the details of the offers made under this programme and, whenever possible, to provide travel funds to prospective students.

The Assembly also requested the administering powers concerned to give widespread publicity in territories under their administration to offers of study and training facilities made by States and to provide all the necessary facilities to enable students to avail themselves of such offers. It asked the Secretary-General to report to the Assembly in 1972 on the implementation of these decisions.

These Assembly decisions were set forth in resolution 2876(XXVI), adopted without objection, on the recommendation of the Fourth Committee, which approved the text without objection on 10 December 1971.

The draft had been proposed in the Committee by Afghanistan, Ethiopia, Ghana, Guinea, India, Indonesia, Iran, Kenya, Liberia, the Libyan Arab Republic, Mongolia, Pakistan, Senegal, Sierra Leone, Somalia, Sudan, the Syrian Arab Republic, the United Republic of Tanzania, Yugoslavia and Zambia. (For text of resolution, see DOCUMENTARY REFERENCES below.)

DOCUMENTARY REFERENCES

Transmission of information

Special Committee on Situation with regard to Implementation of Declaration on Granting of Independence to Colonial Countries and Peoples, meeting 828.

General Assembly—26th session
Fourth Committee, meetings 1953, 1956-1958, 1960, 1962-1967. Plenary meeting 2028.

A/8401. Report of Secretary-General on work of the Organization

16 June 1970–15 June 1971, Part Two, Chapter III, Section A.

A/8423/Rev.1. Report of Special Committee (covering its work during 1971), Chapter XXVII. (Section B: Resolution adopted by Special Committee on 6 October 1971.)

A/8520 and Add.1. Information from non-self-governing territories transmitted under Article 73e of Charter of United Nations. Report of Secretary-General.

A/C.4/L.998. Algeria, Cameroon, Congo, Egypt, Equatorial Guinea, Ethiopia, Ghana, Guinea, India, Iran, Kenya, Mali, Mauritania, Mongolia, Nigeria, Pakistan, Rwanda, Sudan, Syrian Arab Republic, United Republic of Tanzania, Yugoslavia, Zambia: draft resolution, approved by Fourth Committee on 13 December 1971, meeting 1967, by 86 votes to 2, with 8 abstentions.

A/8617. Report of Fourth Committee.

RESOLUTION 2870(XXVI), as recommended by Fourth Committee, A/8617, adopted by Assembly on 20 December 1971, meeting 2028, by 111 votes to 2, with 10 abstentions.

The General Assembly,
Recalling its resolution 1970(XVIII) of 16 December 1963, in which it requested the Special Committee on the Situation with regard to the Implementation of the Declaration on the Granting of Independence to Colonial Countries and Peoples to study the information transmitted to the Secretary-General in accordance with Article 73e of the Charter of the United Nations and to take such information fully into account in examining the situation with regard to the implementation of the Declaration,

Recalling also its resolution 2701(XXV) of 14 December 1970 by which it, *inter alia*, requested the Special Committee to continue to discharge the functions entrusted to it under resolution 1970(XVIII), in accordance with the procedures approved by the General Assembly in its resolution 2109(XX) of 21 December 1965,

Recalling further the provisions of paragraph 5 of its resolution 2701(XXV), in which it urged the administering Powers concerned to transmit, or continue to transmit, to the Secretary-General the information prescribed in Article 73e of the Charter, as well as the fullest possible information on political and constitutional developments in the Territories concerned,

Having examined the chapter of the report of the Special Committee dealing with the transmittal of information under Article 73e of the Charter and the action taken by it in respect of that information,

Having also examined the report of the Secretary-General on this item,

1. *Approves* the chapter of the report of the Special Committee on the Situation with regard to the Implementation of the Declaration on the Granting of Independence to Colonial Countries and Peoples relating to the information from Non-Self-Governing Territories transmitted under Article 73e of the Charter of the United Nations;

2. *Deeply deplores* that, despite the repeated recommendations of the General Assembly and the Special Committee, some Member States having responsibilities for the administration of Non-Self-Governing Territories have ceased to transmit information under Article 73e of the Charter, have transmitted insufficient information or have transmitted information too late;

3. *Strongly condemns* the Government of Portugal for its continued refusal to recognize the colonial status of the Territories under its domination and to transmit information under Article 73e of the Charter on those Territories, in complete disregard of the provisions of the relevant resolutions of the General Assembly and the Special Committee;

4. *Reaffirms* that, in the absence of a decision by the General Assembly itself that a Non-Self-Governing Territory has attained a full measure of self-government in terms of Chapter XI of the Charter, the administering Power concerned should continue to transmit information under Article 73e of the Charter with respect to that Territory;

5. *Requests* the administering Powers concerned to transmit, or continue to transmit, to the Secretary-General the information prescribed in Article 73e of the Charter, as well as the fullest possible information on political and constitutional developments in the Territories concerned;

6. *Reiterates* its request that the administering Powers concerned transmit such information as early as possible and, at the latest, within a maximum period of six months following the expiration of the administrative year in the Non-Self-Governing Territories concerned;

7. *Requests* the Special Committee to continue to discharge the functions entrusted to it under General Assembly resolution 1970(XVIII), in accordance with established procedures.

Offers of study and training facilities

General Assembly—26th session
Fourth Committee, meetings 1953, 1956-1958, 1960, 1962-1966.
Plenary meeting 2028.

A/8401. Report of Secretary-General on work of the Organization, 16 June 1970–15 June 1971, Part Two, Chapter III B.

A/8530. Offers by Member States of study and training facilities for inhabitants of non-self-governing territories. Report of Secretary-General.

A/C.4/L.995. Afghanistan, Ethiopia, Ghana, Guinea, India, Indonesia, Iran, Kenya, Liberia, Libyan Arab Republic, Mongolia, Pakistan, Senegal, Sierra Leone, Somalia, Sudan, Syrian Arab Republic, United Republic of Tanzania, Yugoslavia, Zambia: draft resolution, approved without objection by Fourth Committee on 10 December 1971, meeting 1966.

A/8622. Report of Fourth Committee.

RESOLUTION 2876(XXVI), as recommended by Fourth Committee, A/8622, adopted without objection by Assembly on 20 December 1971, meeting 2028.

The General Assembly,
Recalling its resolution 2705(XXV) of 14 December 1970,

Having examined the report of the Secretary-General on offers by Member States of study and training facilities for inhabitants of Non-Self-Governing Territories, prepared under the terms of General Assembly resolution 845(IX) of 22 November 1954,

Bearing in mind the need to provide increased educational and training facilities, at all levels, for the inhabitants of Non-Self-Governing Territories,

1. *Takes note* of the report of the Secretary-General;

2. *Expresses its appreciation* to those Member States which have made scholarships available to the inhabitants of Non-Self-Governing Territories;

3. *Invites* all States to make generous offers of study and training facilities to inhabitants of Non-Self-Governing Territories;

4. *Requests* those States offering scholarships and those which might subsequently do so to inform the Secretary-General of the details of the offers made under this programme and, whenever possible, to provide travel funds to prospective students;

5. *Requests* the administering Powers concerned to give widespread publicity in Territories under their administration to offers of study and training facilities made by States and to provide all the necessary facilities to enable students to avail themselves of such offers;

6. *Requests* the Secretary-General to report to the General Assembly at its twenty-seventh session on the implementation of the present resolution;

7. *Draws the attention* of the Special Committee on the Situation with regard to the Implementatio. of the Declaration on the Granting of Independence to Colonial Countries and Peoples to the present resolution.

Legal questions

The International Court of Justice

Legal consequences for States of the continued presence of South Africa in Namibia (South West Africa) notwithstanding Security Council resolution 276(1970) (Request for advisory opinion)

In June 1971, the International Court of Justice delivered an advisory opinion on the following question: "What are the legal consequences for States of the continued presence of South Africa in Namibia, notwithstanding Security Council resolution 276(1970)?"[1]

The question had been put to the Court by the Security Council on 29 July 1970,[2] and written statements thereon had been received from the Secretary-General of the United Nations and the Governments of Czechoslovakia, Finland, France, India, the Netherlands, Nigeria, Pakistan, Poland, South Africa, the United States and Yugoslavia.[3]

On 26 January 1971, the Court made three Orders whereby it decided not to accede to objections raised in the written statement of the Government of South Africa against the participation of President Sir Muhammad Zafrulla Khan and Judges Padilla Nervo and Morozov in the proceedings. These objections were based on statements made or other participation by the Judges concerned in their former capacity as representatives of their Governments in United Nations organs dealing with matters concerning Namibia. The Court came to the conclusion, unanimously with regard to President Sir Muhammad Zafrulla Khan and Judge Padilla Nervo, and by 10 votes to 4 with regard to Judge Morozov, that there was no reason to apply Article 17, paragraph 2, of its Statute.[4]

At a closed sitting held on 27 January 1971, the Court heard the contentions submitted by J. D. Viall and D. P. de Villiers on behalf of the Government of South Africa on the question of an application made by that Government in a letter of 13 November 1970 for leave, under Article 31, paragraph 2, of the Statute of the Court, to choose a judge *ad hoc* to sit in the proceedings.[5] By an Order made on 29 January 1971, the Court

decided, by 10 votes to 5, to reject that application. Judges Sir Gerald Fitzmaurice, Gros and Petrén on the one hand, and Judges Onyeama and Dillard on the other, appended joint declarations.

The Court was consequently composed for the proceedings as follows: President Sir Muhammad Zafrulla Khan; Vice-President Ammoun; Judges Sir Gerald Fitzmaurice, Padilla Nervo, Forster, Gros, Bengzon, Petrén, Lachs, Onyeama, Dillard, Ignacio-Pinto, de Castro, Morozov and Jiménez de Aréchaga.

From 8 February to 17 March 1971, the Court held 23 public sittings, at which oral statements were presented by C. A. Stavropoulos and D. B. H. Vickers on behalf of the Secretary-General of the United Nations; T. O. Elias on behalf of the Organization of African Unity; E. J. S. Castrén on behalf of Finland; M. C. Chagla on behalf of India; W. Riphagen on behalf of the Netherlands; Mr. Elias on behalf of Nigeria; S. S. Pirzada on behalf of Pakistan; Le Tai Trien on behalf of the Republic of Viet-Nam; Mr. Viall, Mr. de Villiers, E. M. Grosskopf, H. J. O. van Heerden, R. F. Botha and M. Wiechers on behalf of South Africa; and J. R. Stevenson on behalf of the United States.

On 8 February, at the opening of these sittings, the President made the following statement:

---

[1] See Y.U.N., 1970, pp. 752–53, for text of resolution 276(1970), of 30 January 1970.

[2] See Y.U.N., 1970, p. 754, text of resolution 284(1970).

[3] See also Y.U.N., 1950, pp. 807-14; Y.U.N., 1955, p. 265; Y.U.N., 1956, pp. 378-79; Y.U.N., 1962, pp. 469-72; Y.U.N., 1966, pp. 623-892; and Y.U.N., 1970, p. 779.

[4] Article 17, paragraph 2, of the Statute of the International Court of Justice states that "no member [of the Court] may participate in the decision of any case in which he has previously taken part as agent, counsel, or advocate for one of the parties, or as a member of a national or international court, or of a commission of enquiry, or in any other capacity."

[5] Article 31, paragraph 2, of the Statute of the Court states, in part, that "if the Court includes upon the Bench a judge of the nationality of one of the parties, any other party may choose a person to sit as judge." For full text, see APPENDIX II.

The Court has decided to examine first of all the observations which the Government of the Republic of South Africa has made in its written statement and in its letter of 14 January 1971 concerning the supposed disability of the Court to give the advisory opinion requested by the Security Council, because of political pressure to which the Court, according to the Government of the Republic of South Africa, had been or might be subjected.

After having deliberated upon the matter, the Court has unanimously decided that it was not proper for it to entertain these observations, bearing as they do on the very nature of the Court as the principal judicial organ of the United Nations, an organ which, in that capacity, acts only on the basis of the law, independently of all outside influence or interventions whatsoever, in the exercise of the judicial function entrusted to it alone by the Charter and its Statute. A court functioning as a court of law can act in no other way.

On 17 March 1971, at the close of the hearings, the President announced that the Court considered it appropriate to defer its decision regarding requests by the Government of South Africa concerning the holding of a plebiscite and the supply of further factual information (proposals put forward in letters of 27 January and 6 February 1971 and in the course of the hearings). In a letter of 14 May 1971, the President informed the representatives of the States and organizations that had participated in the oral proceedings that the Court, having examined the matter, did not find itself in need of further arguments or information, and had decided to refuse both these requests.

At a public sitting on 21 June 1971, the Court delivered its advisory opinion, the text of which was transmitted immediately to the Secretary-General of the United Nations.

A summary of the reasoning of the Court is given below.

Objections against Court's dealing with the question

The Government of South Africa contended that the Court was not competent to deliver the opinion because Security Council resolution 284(1970) of 29 July 1970[6] was invalid, for the following reasons: (*a*) two permanent members of the Security Council had abstained during the voting on the resolution, which consequently was not adopted by an affirmative vote of nine members, including the concurring votes of the permanent members, as required by Article 27, paragraph 3, of the Charter of the United Nations;[7] (*b*) as the question related to a dispute between South Africa and other Members of the United Nations, South Africa should have been invited under Article 32 of the Charter to participate in the discussion in the Security Council,[8] and the proviso of Article 27, paragraph

3, of the Charter, requiring members of the Security Council which were parties to a dispute to abstain from voting, should have been complied with.[9]

The Court pointed out that (*a*) for a long period the voluntary abstention of a permanent member had consistently been interpreted as not constituting a bar to the adoption of resolutions by the Security Council; (*b*) the question of Namibia had been placed on the agenda of the Council as a "situation" and not as a "dispute"; since the South African Government had failed to draw the Council's attention to the necessity, in its view, of treating the matter as a "dispute" it was not open to it to raise the issue before the International Court at this time.

In the alternative, the Government of South Africa maintained that even if the Court had competence it should nevertheless, as a matter of judicial propriety, have refused to give the opinion requested on account of political pressure to which, it was contended, the Court had been or might be subjected. At the opening of the public sittings, the President of the Court made, on this contention, the statement reproduced above.

The Government of South Africa also advanced another reason for the Court's not giving the advisory opinion requested, namely, that the question was in reality contentious, because it related to an existing dispute between South Africa and other States.

The Court considered that it was asked to deal with a request put forward by a United Nations organ with a view to seeking legal advice on the consequences of its own decisions. The fact that, in order to give its answer, the Court might have to pronounce on legal questions upon which divergent views existed between South Africa and the United Nations did not convert the case into a dispute between States. That was also the reason why the Court considered (in its Order of 29 January 1971) that there was no occasion for the application of Article 83 of its Rules, according to which, if an advisory opinion was requested upon a legal question "actually pending between two or more States," Article 31 of the Statute, dealing with judges *ad hoc*, was applicable (see above).

In sum, the Court saw no reason to decline to answer the request for an advisory opinion.

History of the Mandate

The Court recalled that in its 1950 advisory opinion on the *International Status of South West Africa*,[10] it had found that the Mandates System

---

[6]See footnote 2.
[7]For text of Article 27, paragraph 3, of the Charter, see APPENDIX II.
[8]For text of Article 32, see APPENDIX II.
[9]See footnote 7.
[10]See Y.U.N., 1950, pp. 807-14.

established by Article 22 of the Covenant of the League of Nations was based upon two principles of paramount importance: the principle of non-annexation and the principle that the well-being and development of the peoples concerned formed a sacred trust of civilization.

Taking the developments of the past half century into account, the Court in its 1971 opinion said, there could be little doubt that the ultimate objective of the sacred trust was self-determination and independence. The Mandatory was to observe a number of obligations, and the Council of the League was to see that they were fulfilled. The rights of the Mandatory as such had their foundation in those obligations. When the League of Nations was dissolved, the *raison d'être* and original objective of these obligations remained. Since the fulfilment of these obligations did not depend on the existence of the League, the Court added, they could not be brought to an end merely because the supervisory organ had ceased to exist. The Members of the League had not declared, or accepted even by implication, that the Mandates would be cancelled or lapse with the dissolution of the League. The last resolution of the League Assembly and Article 80, paragraph 1, of the United Nations Charter[11] maintained the obligations of Mandatories. The Court had consistently recognized that the Mandate survived the demise of the League, and South Africa also admitted as much for a number of years. Thus the supervisory element, which was an essential part of the Mandate, was bound to survive, the Court maintained.

The United Nations, it noted, had suggested a system of supervision which would not exceed that which applied under the Mandates System, but this proposal had been rejected by South Africa.

Resolutions by General Assembly and Security Council

Eventually, the Court recalled, the General Assembly of the United Nations had decided, on 27 October 1966,[12] that the Mandate was terminated and that South Africa had no other right to administer the Territory.

Subsequently the Security Council adopted various resolutions, including its resolution of 30 January 1970,[13] declaring the continued presence of South Africa in Namibia illegal.

Objections challenging the validity of these resolutions having been raised, the Court pointed out that it did not possess powers of judicial review or appeal in relation to the United Nations organs in question. Nor did the validity of the resolutions form the subject of the request for an advisory opinion. The Court nevertheless, in the exercise of its judicial function, and since these objections had been advanced, considered them in the course of

its reasoning before determining the legal consequences arising from those resolutions.

In its 1971 opinion, the Court recalled in the first place that the entry into force of the United Nations Charter had established a relationship between all Members of the United Nations on the one side, and each mandatory power on the other, and that one of the fundamental principles governing that relationship was that the party which disowned or did not fulfil its obligations could not be recognized as retaining the rights which it claimed to derive from the relationship. On 27 October 1966, the Assembly determined that there had been a material breach of the Mandate, which South Africa had in fact disavowed.

It had been contended, the Court noted: (a) that the Covenant of the League of Nations did not confer on the Council of the League power to terminate a Mandate for misconduct of the Mandatory and that the United Nations could not derive from the League greater powers than the latter itself had; (b) that, even if the Council of the League had possessed the power of revocation of the Mandate, it could not have been exercised unilaterally but only in co-operation with the Mandatory; (c) that in its resolution of 27 October 1966 on the matter, the General Assembly had made pronouncements which, not being a judicial organ, it was not competent to make; (d) that a detailed factual investigation was called for; (e) that one part of the Assembly's resolution of 27 October 1966 had decided in effect a transfer of territory.

With regard to these contentions, the Court observed: (a) that, according to a general principle of international law (incorporated in the Vienna Convention on the Law of Treaties), the right to terminate a treaty on account of breach must be presumed to exist in respect of all treaties, even if unexpressed; (b) that the consent of the wrongdoer to such a form of termination could not be required; (c) that the United Nations, as a successor to the League, acting through its competent organs, must be seen above all as the supervisory institution competent to pronounce on the conduct of the Mandatory; (d) that the failure of South Africa to comply with the obligation to submit to supervision could not be disputed; (e) that the General Assembly was not making a finding on facts, but formulating a legal

---

[11]Article 80, paragraph 1, of the Charter states that "except as may be agreed upon in individual trusteeship agreements, made under articles 77, 79 and 81, placing each territory under the trusteeship system, and until such agreements have been concluded, nothing in this Chapter shall be construed in or of itself to alter in any manner the rights whatsoever of any states or any peoples or the terms of existing international instruments to which Members of the United Nations may respectively be parties."

[12]See Y.U.N., 1966, pp. 605-6, text of resolution 2145(XXI).

[13]See footnote 1.

situation; it would not be correct to assume that, because it is in principle vested with recommendatory powers, it was debarred from adopting, in special cases within the framework of its competence, resolutions which made determinations or had operative design.

The Court recalled further that the General Assembly lacked the necessary powers to ensure the withdrawal of South Africa from the Territory and therefore, acting in accordance with Article 11, paragraph 2, of the Charter, enlisted the co-operation of the Security Council.[14]

The Council for its part, when it adopted the resolutions concerned, was acting in the exercise of what it deemed to be its primary responsibility for the maintenance of peace and security. Article 24 of the Charter vested in the Security Council the necessary authority.[15] Its decisions were taken in conformity with the purposes and principles of the Charter, under Article 25 of which it was for Member States to comply with those decisions, even those members of the Security Council which voted against them and those Members of the United Nations which were not members of the Council.[16]

Legal consequences of presence of South Africa in Namibia

The Court stressed that a binding determination made by a competent organ of the United Nations to the effect that a situation was illegal could not remain without consequence.

South Africa, being responsible for having created and maintained that situation, had the obligation to put an end to it and withdraw its administration from the Territory, the Court considered. By occupying the Territory without title, South Africa had incurred international responsibilities arising from a continuing violation of an international obligation. It also remained accountable for any violations of the rights of the people of Namibia, or of its obligations under international law towards other States in respect of the exercise of its powers in relation to the Territory.

The Court held that United Nations Member States were under the obligation to recognize the illegality and invalidity of South Africa's continued presence in Namibia and to refrain from lending any support or any form of assistance to South Africa with reference to its occupation of Namibia.

The precise determination of the acts permitted—what measures should be selected, what scope they should be given and by whom they should be applied—was a matter which lay within the competence of the appropriate political organs of the United Nations acting within their authority under the Charter, the Court said. Thus, it was for the Security Council to determine any further

measures consequent upon the decisions already taken by it.

The Court in consequence confined itself to giving advice on those dealings with the Government of South Africa which, under the Charter of the United Nations and general international law, should be considered as inconsistent with the Security Council resolution of 30 January 1970 because they might imply recognizing South Africa's presence in Namibia as legal:

(a) Member States were under obligation (subject to the provisions set forth in (d) below) to abstain from entering into treaty relations with South Africa in all cases in which the Government of South Africa purported to act on behalf of or concerning Namibia. With respect to existing bilateral treaties, Member States must abstain from invoking or applying those treaties or provisions of treaties concluded by South Africa on behalf of or concerning Namibia which involved active intergovernmental co-operation. With respect to multilateral treaties, the same rule could not be applied to certain general conventions such as those with a humanitarian character, the non-performance of which might adversely affect the people of Namibia: it would be for the competent international organs to take specific measures in this respect.

(b) Member States were under an obligation to abstain from sending diplomatic or special missions to South Africa including in their jurisdiction the Territory of Namibia, to abstain from sending consular agents to Namibia, and to withdraw any such agents already there; and to make it clear to South Africa that the maintenance of diplomatic or consular relations did not imply any recognition of its authority with regard to Namibia.

(c) Member States were under an obligation to abstain from entering into economic and other forms of relations with South Africa on behalf of or concerning Namibia which might entrench its authority over the Territory.

(d) However, non-recognition should not result in depriving the people of Namibia of any advantages derived from international co-operation. In particular, the illegality or invalidity of acts performed by the Government of South Africa on behalf of or concerning Namibia after the termination of the Mandate could not be extended to such acts as the registration of births, deaths and marriages.

As to States not members of the United Nations, the Court held that although they were not bound by Articles 24 and 25 of the Charter, they had been called upon by the Security Council by its

[14]For text of Article 11, paragraph 2, see APPENDIX II.
[15]For text of Article 24, see APPENDIX II.
[16]For text of Article 25, see APPENDIX II.

resolution of 30 January 1970[17] to give assistance in the action which had been taken by the United Nations with regard to Namibia.

In the view of the Court, the termination of the Mandate and the declaration of the illegality of South Africa's presence in Namibia were opposable to all States in the sense of barring *erga omnes* the legality of the situation which was maintained in violation of international law. In particular, no State which had entered into relations with South Africa concerning Namibia might expect the United Nations or its Members to recognize the validity or effects of any such relationship. The Mandate having been terminated by a decision of the international organization in which the supervisory authority was vested, it was for non-member States to act accordingly. All States should bear in mind that the entity injured by the illegal presence of South Africa in Namibia was a people which must look to the international community for assistance in its progress towards the goals for which the sacred trust was instituted.

Requests by South Africa

The Court gave finally the reasons for the decision which the President of the Court announced in his letter of 14 May 1971 (see above) concerning two requests put forward by the Government of South Africa.

That Government had expressed the desire to supply the Court with further factual information concerning the purposes and objectives of its policy of separate development in Namibia, contending that to establish a breach of its substantive international obligations under the Mandate it would be necessary to prove that South Africa had failed to exercise its powers with a view to promoting the well-being and progress of the inhabitants.

The Court found that no factual evidence was needed for the purpose of determining whether the policy of *apartheid* applied in Namibia was in conformity with the international obligations assumed by South Africa. It was undisputed that the official governmental policy pursued by South Africa in Namibia was to achieve a complete physical separation of races and ethnic groups. This meant the enforcement of distinctions, exclusions, restrictions and limitations exclusively based on grounds of race, colour, descent or national or ethnic origin which constituted a denial of fundamental human rights. This the Court viewed as a flagrant violation of the purposes and principles of the Charter of the United Nations.

The Government of South Africa had also submitted a request that a plebiscite be held in the Territory of Namibia under the joint supervision of the Court and the Government of South Africa. The Court having concluded that no further evidence was required, that the Mandate had been validly terminated and that in consequence South Africa's presence in Namibia was illegal and its acts on behalf of or concerning Namibia illegal and invalid, it was not able to entertain this proposal.

Opinion of Court

The Court was of the opinion:

(1) That, the continued presence of South Africa in Namibia being illegal, South Africa was under obligation to withdraw its administration from Namibia immediately and thus put an end to its occupation of the Territory (the vote in the Court on this sub-paragraph was 13 to 2);

(2) That States Members of the United Nations were under obligation to recognize the illegality of South Africa's presence in Namibia and the invalidity of its acts on behalf of or concerning Namibia, and to refrain from any acts and in particular any dealings with the Government of South Africa implying recognition of the legality of, or lending support or assistance to, such presence and administration (the vote in the Court on this sub-paragraph was 11 to 4);

(3) That it was incumbent upon States which were not Members of the United Nations to give assistance, within the scope of sub-paragraph 2 above, in the action which had been taken by the United Nations with regard to Namibia (the vote in the Court on this sub-paragraph was 11 to 4).

The President of the Court, Sir Muhammad Zafrulla Khan, appended a declaration to the Advisory Opinion. Vice-President Ammoun and Judges Padilla Nervo, Petrén, Onyeama, Dillard and de Castro appended separate opinions. Judge Sir Gerald Fitzmaurice and Judge Gros appended dissenting opinions.

Judge Sir Gerald Fitzmaurice considered that the Mandate had not been validly revoked, that the Mandatory was still subject to the obligations of the Mandate whatever those might be, and that States Members of the United Nations were bound to respect the position unless and until it was changed by lawful means.

Judge Gros disagreed with the Court's conclusions as to the legal validity and effects of the General Assembly resolution of 27 October 1966[18] but considered that South Africa ought to agree to negotiate on the conversion of the Mandate into a United Nations trusteeship.

Judges Petrén and Onyeama stated that they had voted for sub-paragraph 1 but against sub-paragraphs 2 and 3, which in their view ascribed too broad a scope to the effects of non-recognition.

Judge Dillard, concurring in the operative

[17] See footnote 1.
[18] See footnote 12.

clause, added certain mainly cautionary comments on sub-paragraph 2.

Furthermore, Judges Sir Gerald Fitzmaurice, Gros, Petrén, Onyeama and Dillard disagreed with some of the decisions taken by the Court concerning the Court's composition in the proceedings.

The President and Judges Padilla Nervo and de Castro accepted the operative clause of the Advisory Opinion in full.

The Vice-President, while sharing the views expressed in the Advisory Opinion, considered that the operative clause was not sufficiently explicit or decisive.

DOCUMENTARY REFERENCES

Legal Consequences for States of the Continued Presence of South Africa in Namibia (South West Africa) notwithstanding Security Council Resolution 276(1970). Orders Nos. 1, 2 and 3 of 26 January 1971, I.C.J. Reports 1971, pp. 3, 6 and 9. I.C.J. Sales Nos.: 348, 349, 350; Order of 29 January 1971, I.C.J. Reports 1971, p. 12. I.C.J. Sales No.: 351.

Legal Consequences for States of the Continued Presence of South Africa in Namibia (South West Africa) notwithstanding Security Council Resolution 276(1970), Advisory Opinion, I.C.J. Reports 1971, p. 16. I.C.J. Sales No.: 352.

Pleadings, Oral Arguments, Documents. Legal Consequences for States of the Continued Presence of South Africa in Namibia (South West Africa) notwithstanding Security Council Resolution 276(1970). Vol. I: Request for Advisory Opinion, Documents, Written Statements. I.C.J. Sales No.: 356; Vol. II: Oral Statements and Correspondence. I.C.J. Sales No.: 360.

A/8401. Report of Secretary-General on work of the Organization, 16 June 1970–15 June 1971, Part Four, Chapter I.

A/8405. Report of International Court of Justice, 1 August 1970–31 July 1971, Chapter III A.

Appeal relating to the jurisdiction of the Council of the International Civil Aviation Organization (India v. Pakistan)

On 30 August 1971, the Government of India filed in the Registry of the International Court of Justice an Application instituting proceedings against Pakistan.

The Application stated that India and Pakistan were parties to two instruments concluded at Chicago, United States, in 1944: the Convention on International Civil Aviation and the International Air Services Transit Agreement. Under these two instruments, aircraft of each of the two countries had the right to overfly the territory of the other.

According to the Application, this régime was suspended between the two States in August-September 1965. In February 1966, the two Governments concluded a special agreement under which a new concession to overfly each other's territory was granted, subject to the permission of the Government concerned.

In February 1971, the Government of India suspended overflights of its own aircraft over Pakistan territory and withdrew permission for Pakistan aircraft to overfly the territory of India. On 3 March 1971, the Government of Pakistan, by means of an Application and a Complaint, submitted the matter to the Council of the International Civil Aviation Organization (ICAO), which was empowered to deal with disputes concerning the interpretation or application of the 1944 Convention and Transit Agreement.

India argued that the Council had no jurisdiction in the current dispute, which related on the contrary to the termination or suspension of those two instruments in so far as they concerned overflights between two States.

On 29 July 1971, the ICAO Council decided that

it had jurisdiction. In its Application, the Government of India appealed from that decision to the Court, on the basis of article 84 of the Convention on International Civil Aviation, article II of the Air Services Transit Agreement, and Articles 36 and 37 of the Statute of the Court.[19]

By Order of 16 September 1971, Vice-President Fouad Ammoun, Acting President in this case by virtue of Article 13, paragraph 1, of the Rules of Court (President Sir Muhammad Zafrulla Khan being a national of Pakistan), fixed 16 December 1971 as the time-limit for the filing of the Memorial of the Government of India. At the request of the Government of India, the time-limit was extended to 22 December by an Order made by the Vice-President on 3 December.

On 22 December 1971, the Government of India filed its Memorial, in which it enlarged upon its grounds for denying the jurisdiction of the ICAO Council to handle the matters presented by Pakistan or to consider Pakistan's complaint.

The next step in the proceedings was to be the filing of a Counter-Memorial by Pakistan.

In accordance with Article 31 of the Court's Statute,[20] the Government of India chose, to sit as judge *ad hoc* in this case, Nagendra Singh, Secretary to the President of India and a Member of the Permanent Court of Arbitration and of the International Law Commission. The Government of Pakistan indicated that it had no objection to this appointment.

---

[19]For text of Articles 36 and 37 of the Statute of the Court, see APPENDIX II.

[20]Article 31 of the Statute states, in part, that "if the Court includes upon the Bench a judge of the nationality of one of the parties, any other party may choose a person to sit as judge." For text of Article, see APPENDIX II.

DOCUMENTARY REFERENCES

Appeal Relating to the Jurisdiction of the ICAO Council. Order of 16 September 1971, I.C.J. Reports 1971, p. 347. I.C.J. Sales No.: 357.
Appeal Relating to the Jurisdiction of the ICAO Council. Order of 3 December 1971, I.C.J. Reports 1971, p. 350. I.C.J. Sales No.: 358.

Other documents

Yearbook of the International Court of Justice, 1970–1971, No. 25 (covering period 1 August 1970–31 July 1971). I.C.J. Sales No.: 355.

Review of the role of the Court

An item concerning a review of the role of the International Court of Justice, which the General Assembly had considered at its 1970 session,[21] was included in the agenda of its 1971 session and allocated to the Sixth (Legal) Committee.

The Sixth Committee had before it a report by the Secretary-General reproducing the views and suggestions concerning the role of the Court expressed by Member States and States parties to the Statute of the International Court of Justice; the report had been prepared in response to a General Assembly request of 15 December 1970.[22]

Also before the Sixth Committee was a request by Switzerland for permission to participate in the discussion. In that connexion, the Chairman observed that, pursuant to the Assembly resolution of 15 December 1970,[23] Switzerland had been invited, like all other States parties to the Statute of the Court, to submit in writing its views and suggestions concerning the role of the Court, and that it therefore seemed logical to allow it to express its views in the course of the debate on the subject. The Committee accordingly decided that Switzerland would be invited to present its views and suggestions on the item.

The representative of the USSR, noting that Switzerland was being allowed to submit its observations as a matter of courtesy, expressed the hope that the same attitude would be adopted in future in regard to other States non-members of the United Nations.

Consideration by General Assembly

Discussion in Sixth Committee

All the representatives who spoke during the discussion in the Sixth Committee stressed the importance of the role of the International Court of Justice as the principal judicial organ of the United Nations. However, while some Members, including Brazil, the Netherlands, and Pakistan, expressed the view that judicial settlement was a foremost means of peaceful settlement of disputes provided for by Article 33 of the Charter, other Members, among them Bulgaria and Poland, felt that recourse to the Court was only one of several means of peaceful settlement and was given no priority under the Charter.[24]

Many representatives emphasized the positive influence that the Court's judgements and opinions had had on relations between States and on the progressive development and codification of international law. Although several Members—among them Ethiopia and the Ukrainian SSR—felt that the Court had handed down some decisions which they considered questionable, others, in particular Finland, believed that a renewed confidence in the Court was emerging. Most Members were agreed, however, that the Court had not discharged in full the role originally envisaged, as evidenced by its relative inactivity.

The current situation of the Court was attributed to various general factors, including the lack of homogeneity of international society, the current state of political relations between States and the excessive attachment of States to the concept of national sovereignty.

A number of Members, including Burma and Iraq, expressed the opinion that the law the Court was required to apply under Article 38 of its Statute did not correspond to the current realities or the legitimate aspirations of many States.[25] Other delegations, however—for example those of Italy and Uruguay—considered that existing international law showed universality in many areas, particularly as a result of the work of the International Law Commission and the United Nations system generally.

Among the specific factors mentioned as relevant to the situation of the Court were its organization, jurisdiction and procedures and methods of work.

[21]See Y.U.N., 1970, pp. 779-83.
[22]*Ibid.*, p. 783, text of resolution 2723(XXV).
[23]*Ibid.*
[24]Article 33 of the Charter states, in part: "The parties to any dispute, the continuance of which is likely to endanger the maintenance of international peace and security, shall, first of all, seek a solution by negotiation, enquiry, mediation, conciliation, arbitration, judicial settlement, resort to regional agencies or arrangements, or other peaceful means of their own choice."
[25]Article 38, paragraph 1, of the Statute of the Court states as follows: "The Court, whose function is to decide in accordance with international law such disputes as are submitted to it, shall apply: (a) international conventions, whether general or particular, establishing rules expressly recognized by the contesting states; (b) international custom, as evidence of a general practice accepted as law; (c) the general principles of law recognized by civilized nations; (d) subject to the provisions of Article 59, judicial decisions and the teachings of the most highly qualified publicists of the various nations, as subsidiary means for the determination of rules of law."

Cuba and Ecuador, among others, felt that the composition of the Court was not representative of the various legal systems in the world. This was disputed by other Members, including Australia, which held that the main forms of civilization and principal legal systems of the world could be said to be properly represented on it.

A number of representatives, including those of Iran, Japan and New Zealand, considered that the recourse to the chamber of summary procedure (provided for by Article 29 of the Statute of the Court) and the formation of chambers for dealing with particular categories of cases (Article 26) might encourage States to resort to the Court more frequently.[26] The representative of Austria, however, felt that the manifest disinclination of States to call upon chambers should dictate caution and that the benefits and drawbacks should be carefully studied before any course of action was recommended.

Most of the representatives who commented on the subject of regional chambers were not in favour of the idea.

With regard to the jurisdiction of the Court, it was held by several Members that under Article 36, paragraph 3, of the United Nations Charter, judicial settlement by the Court was limited to legal disputes.[27]

The question of the compulsory jurisdiction of the Court was raised by a number of Members. Many representatives considered that, for a long time to come, the system established by Article 36, paragraph 2, of the Court's Statute would probably remain the only realistic means of reconciling the principle of sovereignty with the compulsory jurisdiction of the Court.[28] Some Members, among them Uruguay, expressed regret that only 47 States had accepted the optional clause on compulsory jurisdiction and that some of these had done so with reservations that greatly reduced the scope of their acceptance. Others, including the USSR, disagreed with the view that the Court's difficulties would be overcome if all States recognized its compulsory jurisdiction. In its opinion, it was for States to decide whether to refer a matter to the Court.

Most of the representatives who commented on the question considered that international organizations, in view of their increasingly important role, should be allowed to appear before the Court. The representative of the USSR, on the other hand, felt that to allow international organizations access to the Court would be a violation of the Charter.

With respect to the question of disputes relating to the interpretation and application of treaties, some representatives, in particular those of El Salvador and Madagascar, considered it desirable to encourage the inclusion in treaties of a stipulation that disputes concerning their interpretation and application be submitted to the jurisdiction of the Court.

A number of Members expressed regret that little use had been made of the possibilities offered under Article 96 of the Charter for requesting advisory opinions from the Court.[29]

Ethiopia and the United States, among others, considered that inter-governmental organizations other than specialized agencies, in particular the regional organizations, should be given access to the Court. Some Members, including Austria, supported proposals to permit States to request advisory opinions from the Court. Other Members, including Brazil, were opposed to the idea of extending the advisory jurisdiction of the Court to regional organizations and States: they argued that such an extension of the advisory role of the Court could be prejudicial to the Court's judicial jurisdiction proper which, under its Statute, was its primary responsibility.

A number of representatives considered that it was necessary to simplify and expedite the Court's procedures and methods of work.

The question of the revision of the Court's Statute and of other measures to improve the Court's functioning were also raised.

Some representatives, among them those of Colombia and Finland, said they would favour a revision of the Statute of the Court. Many representatives, however, including those of Australia and Pakistan, felt it would be premature to approach the review of the role of the Court from the standpoint of a possible revision of the Statute and the Charter. A third group, which included the representatives of Bulgaria and the Ukrainian SSR, expressed strong opposition to any attempt to revise the Statute and the Charter.

Many representatives expressed the view that certain improvements could be made in the Court's procedure; in this connexion, they noted with satisfaction that in 1967 the Court had undertaken a revision of its Rules. While some Members pointed out that under Article 30 of the Statute, the Court had exclusive competence with regard to its procedure,[30] others expressed the opinion that the Court would no doubt wish to take into account the views of Governments and of the General Assembly, and that the General

---

[26]For texts of Articles 29 and 26 of the Statute, see APPENDIX II.

[27]For text of Article 36, paragraph 3, of the Charter, see APPENDIX II.

[28]Article 36, paragraph 2, of the Statute provides that "The states parties to the present Statute may at any time declare that they recognize as compulsory *ipso facto* and without special agreement, in relation to any other state accepting the same obligation, the jurisdiction of the Court in all legal disputes concerning: (*a*) the interpretation of a treaty; (*b*) any question of international law; (*c*) the existence of any fact which, if established, would constitute a breach of an international obligation; (*d*) the nature or extent of the reparation to be made for the breach of an international obligation."

[29]For text of Article 96 of the Charter, see APPENDIX II.

[30]For text of Article 30 of the Statute, see APPENDIX II.

Assembly could appropriately make recommendations on the subject.

A number of Members, among them Canada and the United States, observed that the Secretary-General's report contained many suggestions that went beyond the scope of the Court's review of its Rules yet would not require amendment of the Statute.

Decisions of General Assembly

Three approaches emerged with regard to the general question of the review of the role of the Court.

The first of these, held by such Members as Greece, Japan, Nigeria, the Philippines and Uruguay, was that the report of the Secretary-General indicated that Governments considered the question important and urgent. These Members felt the time had come to establish a specialized body to study the various suggestions made by Governments with regard to the role of the Court.

A second group, including among others the Byelorussian SSR, Czechoslovakia and the USSR, argued that the review of the role of the Court was not an urgent issue and that the review had already achieved such objectives as were feasible. These Members declared themselves strongly opposed to the establishment of a committee to study the matter further, the real purpose of which, they maintained, would be to set in motion the process of revising the Statute.

A third group of representatives, which included those of France, Iraq and Mexico, held that the fact that not all States had replied to the Secretary-General's request for opinions proved the need for reflecting at greater length on the question. They noted the uncertainty on the appropriate direction for efforts to solve the problem, and expressed the fear that to establish a committee whose terms of reference would of necessity be vague would be both dangerous and useless. It would be advisable, they felt, to defer any decision concerning the establishment of such a committee until additional replies had been received from Governments.

These three approaches found expression in three draft resolutions introduced into the Sixth Committee.

The first draft was sponsored by the following 32 States: Argentina, Austria, Barbados, Belgium, Canada, Cyprus, Denmark, Ethiopia, Finland, Ghana, Greece, Guatemala, Guyana, Haiti, Italy, the Ivory Coast, Japan, the Khmer Republic, Liberia, the Netherlands, New Zealand, Nicaragua, Nigeria, Norway, Pakistan, the Philippines, Sierra Leone, Sweden, Turkey, the United Kingdom, the United States and Uruguay. It would have had the General Assembly establish an *ad hoc* committee on the role of the International Court of Justice, composed of 25 States parties to the Statute of the Court, to be appointed by the President of the General Assembly.

Three series of amendments were submitted to the 32-power draft by the USSR, by Kuwait and Lebanon, and by Uganda, respectively. The amendments submitted by the USSR would, among other things, have deleted the provision that called for the establishment of an *ad hoc* committee and would have postponed further consideration of the question of the review of the Court until the Court had completed revision of its Rules. The amendments by Kuwait and Lebanon, some of which were accepted by the sponsors of the draft resolution, involved certain procedural and wording changes, as did the amendments of Uganda.

A second draft was sponsored by eight Members: Bulgaria, the Byelorussian SSR, Czechoslovakia, Hungary, Mongolia, Poland, the Ukrainian SSR and the USSR. By it, the General Assembly, among other things, would have noted that the possibilities afforded by the Statute of the Court were not being fully realized and that the Court was taking measures to enhance the effectiveness of its procedures, in particular through revision of its Rules. The Assembly would have requested the Court to accelerate the revision of its Rules and decided to postpone further consideration of the question of the review of the role of the Court until the revision had been completed.

A third draft was sponsored by the following nine Members: Dahomey, Ecuador, El Salvador, France, Kenya, Madagascar, Morocco, Spain and Sudan. It would have the Assembly invite Member States and States parties to the Statute of the Court which had not yet done so to transmit to the Secretary-General, by 1 July 1972, their comments on the questionnaire prepared in accordance with the General Assembly request of 15 December 1970;[31] would request the Secretary-General to submit the comments to the Assembly at its 1972 session; and would decide to include the item in the provisional agenda of its 1972 session.

On 30 November 1971, at the request of Ecuador, a recorded vote was taken on an Egyptian proposal that priority in the voting be given to the nine-power draft; the proposal was adopted by 54 votes to 42, with 13 abstentions. The sponsors of the eight-power draft proposal then withdrew their draft in favour of the nine-power draft.

At the request of Madagascar, a recorded vote was taken on the nine-power proposal. It was approved by 57 votes to 40, with 12 abstentions.

[31]See footnote 22.

The Sixth Committee then decided, by a vote of 55 to 29, with 17 abstentions, not to vote on the remaining proposals before it.

The text as recommended by the Sixth Committee was adopted without objection by the General Assembly on 15 December 1971, as its resolution 2818(XXVI).

The Assembly thereby: requested Member States and States parties to the Statute of the Court which had not yet been able to do so to transmit to the Secretary-General, by 1 July 1972, their comments on the review of the role of the Court; requested the Secretary-General to submit those comments to the Assembly at its 1972 session and also to transmit the relevant documentation to the Court; invited the Court to state its views, should it so desire; expressed the hope that the Court would complete the revision of its rules as soon as possible; and decided to include the item in the provisional agenda of its 1972 session.

(For text of resolution, see DOCUMENTARY REFERENCES below.)

DOCUMENTARY REFERENCES

General Assembly—26th session
Sixth Committee, meetings 1277-1284, 1288, 1291, 1293-1296.
Fifth Committee, meeting 1472.
Plenary meeting 2019, 2024.

A/8382 and Add.1-4. Report of Secretary-General.
A/8401. Report of Secretary-General on work of the Organization, 16 June 1970–15 June 1971, Part Four, Chapter I.
A/8401/Add.1. Introduction to report of Secretary-General, September 1971, Part Two: Chapter IX, paras. 306–308.
A/8405. Report of International Court of Justice, 1 August 1970–31 July 1971.
A/8405. Report of International Court of Justice, 1 August 1970–31 July 1971, Chapter IV A.
A/C.6/407. Letter of 6 October 1971 from Secretary-General to Chairman of Sixth Committee (containing request by Switzerland).
A/C.6/L.829. Argentina, Austria, Barbados, Belgium, Canada, Cyprus, Denmark, Ethiopia, Finland, Ghana, Greece, Guatemala, Guyana, Haiti, Italy, Ivory Coast, Japan, Khmer Republic, Liberia, Netherlands, New Zealand, Nicaragua, Nigeria, Norway, Pakistan, Philippines, Sierra Leone, Sweden, Turkey, United Kingdom, United States, Uruguay: draft resolution.
A/C.6/L.830. Bulgaria, Byelorussian SSR, Czechoslovakia, Hungary, Mongolia, Poland, Ukrainian SSR, USSR: draft resolution.
A/C.6/L.831. Dahomey, Ecuador, El Salvador, France, Kenya, Madagascar, Morocco, Spain, Sudan: draft resolution, approved by Sixth Committee on 30 November 1971, meeting 1295, by recorded vote of 57 to 40, with 12 abstentions:

In favour: Algeria, Australia, Bahrain, Brazil, Bulgaria, Byelorussian SSR, Central African Republic, Ceylon, Chile, Colombia, Cuba, Czechoslovakia, Dahomey, Ecuador, Egypt, El Salvador, Equatorial Guinea, France, Guinea, Hungary, India, Iran, Iraq, Jamaica, Jordan, Kenya, Kuwait, Lebanon, Libyan Arab Republic, Madagascar, Malaysia, Mauritania, Mexico, Mongolia, Morocco, People's Democratic Republic of Yemen, Peru, Poland, Portugal, Qatar, Romania, Rwanda, Saudi Arabia, Senegal, Spain, Sudan, Syrian Arab Republic, Togo, Tunisia, Uganda, Ukrainian SSR, USSR, Upper Volta, Venezuela, Yemen, Yugoslavia, Zambia.

Against: Austria, Belgium, Burma, Cameroon, Canada, Costa Rica, Cyprus, Denmark, Dominican Republic, Ethiopia, Finland, Ghana, Greece, Guatemala, Guyana, Haiti, Honduras, Iceland, Ireland, Italy, Ivory Coast, Japan, Khmer Republic, Lesotho, Liberia, Netherlands, New Zealand, Nicaragua, Nigeria, Norway, Pakistan, Panama, Paraguay, Philippines, Sierra Leone, Sweden, Trinidad and Tobago, Turkey, United Kingdom, United States.

Abstaining: Afghanistan, Argentina, Indonesia, Israel, Laos, Mali, Nepal, Niger, Singapore, South Africa, United Republic of Tanzania, Uruguay.

A/C.6/L.833. Administrative and financial implications of 32-power draft resolution, A/C.6/L.829. Statement by Secretary-General.

A/C.6/L.834. USSR: amendments to 32-power draft resolution, A/C.6/L.829.
A/C.6/L.836. Kuwait and Lebanon: amendments to 32-power draft resolution, A/C.6/L.829.
A/C.6/L.837. Uganda: amendments to 32-power draft resolution A/C.6/L.829.
A/C.5/1410, A/8408/Add.15, A/8569. Administrative and financial implications of draft resolution recommended by Sixth Committee in A/8568. Statement by Secretary-General and reports of Advisory Committee on Administrative and Budgetary Questions and Fifth Committee.
A/8568. Report of Sixth Committee.

RESOLUTION 2818(XXVI), as recommended by Sixth Committee, A/8568, adopted without objection by Assembly on 15 December 1971, meeting 2019.

The General Assembly,

Recalling that the International Court of Justice is the principal judicial organ of the United Nations,

Recalling further that, in accordance with Article 2, paragraph 3, of the Charter of the United Nations, all Members shall settle their international disputes by peaceful means in such a manner that international peace and security, and justice, are not endangered,

Emphasizing that, in conformity with that principle, as solemnly proclaimed in the Declaration on Principles of International Law concerning Friendly Relations and Co-operation among States in accordance with the Charter of the United Nations, judicial settlement is one of the means to which States can have recourse in seeking a just settlement of their disputes,

Considering the desirability of finding ways and means of enhancing the effectiveness of the Court,

Noting that the Court has undertaken a revision of its Rules,

Having noted the report of the Secretary-General containing the replies received from certain Member States and from Switzerland to the questionnaire prepared in accordance with General Assembly resolution 2723(XXV) of 15 December 1970 and the text of the letter addressed to the Secretary-General by the President of the Court,

1. *Invites* Member States and States parties to the Statute of the International Court of Justice which have not yet been able to do so to transmit to the Secretary-General, by 1 July 1972, their comments on the questionnaire prepared in accordance with General Assembly resolution 2723(XXV);

2. *Requests* the Secretary-General to submit those comments to the General Assembly at its twenty-seventh session;

3. *Also requests* the Secretary-General to transmit to the Court the above-mentioned report, together with the summary records of the discussions held in the Sixth Committee on this subject at the twenty-sixth session;

4. *Invites* the Court to submit its views on the matter if it so desires;

5. *Expresses the hope* that the Court will complete the revision of its Rules as soon as possible;

6. *Decides* to include in the provisional agenda of its twenty-seventh session an item entitled "Review of the role of the International Court of Justice."

A/8429. Resolutions adopted by General Assembly during its 26th session, 21 September–22 December 1971. Other decisions, page 20.

Proposal to amend Statute of the International Court of Justice

An item concerning the amendment of Articles 22, 23 and 28 of the Statute of the International Court of Justice (regarding the seat of the Court) was included in the provisional agenda of the 1971 session of the General Assembly. Consideration of the item, which, at the request of the Court, had first been included in the agenda of the 1969 session of the Assembly, had been postponed both at that session and at the Assembly's 1970 session.[32]

On 24 September 1971, the General Assembly, on the recommendation of its General Committee, decided to include the item in the provisional agenda of its 1972 session.

[32]See Y.U.N., 1969, pp. 720–23 and Y.U.N., 1970, pp. 783-84.

DOCUMENTARY REFERENCES

General Assembly—26th session
General Committee, meeting 191.
Plenary meeting 1937.

A/8378. Amendment to Article 22 of Statute of International Court of Justice (Seat of Court) and consequential amendments to Articles 23 and 28. Note by Secretary-General.
A/8401. Report of Secretary-General on work of the Organization, 16 June 1970–15 June 1971, Part Four, Chapter I.

A/8405. Report of International Court of Justice, 1 August 1970–31 July 1971, Chapter IV B.
A/8500. Organization of 26th regular session of General Assembly, adoption of agenda and allocation of items. First report of General Committee, para. 15 (i).
A/8429. Resolutions adopted by General Assembly during its 26th session, 21 September–22 December 1971. Other decisions, p. 19.

Chapter II

Questions concerning the International Law Commission

The International Law Commission held its twenty-third session in Geneva, Switzerland, from 26 April to 30 July 1971. The major part of the session was devoted to concluding consideration of the topic "relations between States and international organizations." The General Assembly considered and took a number of decisions concerning the report of the work of the Commission at its 1971 session. (For details see below.)

Report of International Law Commission

Relations between States and international organizations

At its 1968, 1969 and 1970 sessions, the International Law Commission adopted Parts I, II, III and IV of its provisional draft on representatives of States to international organizations.[1]

At the 1971 session of the Commission, the Special Rapporteur, Abdullah El-Erian, submitted a sixth report which summarized the written comments on the provisional draft submitted by Governments and by the secretariats of the United Nations, the specialized agencies and the International Atomic Energy Agency (IAEA), as well as the oral comments made by Members during discussion in the General Assembly; the report also contained proposals for the revision of the articles.

The Special Rapporteur also submitted to the Commission three working papers in which he examined: the possible effects of exceptional situations—such as absence of recognition, severance of diplomatic and consular relations and the effects of armed conflict—on the representation of States in international organizations; the inclusion in the draft articles of a provision on the settlement of disputes; and proposed draft articles on observer delegations of States to organs and to conferences.

After considering the sixth report of the Special Rapporteur and the working papers, the Commission established a Working Group to assist in revising, co-ordinating and consolidating the different parts of the draft articles. The Working Group proposed a new organization of the draft articles and a substantial reduction in their

[1]For further information, see Y.U.N., 1968, pp. 813–14; Y.U.N., 1969, pp. 723–25; and Y.U.N., 1970, pp. 798–800.

number. The proposals of the Working Group were considered by the Commission, which adopted some new articles, revised the title of the draft and of various articles, and decided upon the order and structure of all the articles.

The final draft approved by the Commission consisted of 82 articles on the representation of States in their relations with international organizations, together with an Annex. The Commission submitted the draft articles to the General Assembly and recommended that the Assembly convene an international conference of plenipotentiaries to conclude a convention on the subject, on the basis of the Commission's draft articles. The Commission expressed the hope that appropriate arrangements would be made by the General Assembly for involving the United Nations, the specialized agencies and the International Atomic Energy Agency (IAEA) in the adoption of the convention.

The draft articles approved by the Commission were divided into four parts. Part I, entitled *Introduction* (articles 1-4), consisted of provisions which were intended to apply to the draft articles as a whole; Part II, entitled *Missions to international organizations* (articles 5-41), contained provisions dealing, under the generic term "missions," with both permanent missions and permanent observer missions; Part III, entitled *Delegations to organs and to conferences* (articles 42–71), contained provisions dealing specifically with delegations to organs and to conferences; Part IV, entitled *General provisions* (articles 72-82), consisted of further provisions which were generally applicable to missions to international organizations and to delegations to organs and conferences.

Twenty-four draft articles on observer delegations to organs and conferences were included as an Annex to the draft; these provisions had not been included in the provisional draft and therefore Governments and international organizations had not had an opportunity to comment on them.

The draft articles approved by the Commission dealt only with the representation of States in their relations with international organizations. They did not extend to the representation of organizations to States nor contain provisions concerning representatives of entities other than States which might participate in the work of organs of international organizations or conferences convened by or under the auspices of international organizations. As in the case of previous topics, the Commission did not think it advisable to deal with the possible effects of armed conflict on the representation of States in their relations with international organizations.

Other topics

Also at its 1971 session, the Commission had before it further reports submitted by the following Special Rapporteurs: Sir Humphrey Waldock, on "succession of States and Governments in respect of treaties"; Mohammed Bedjaoui, on "succession of States in respect of matters other than treaties"; and Roberto Ago, on "State responsibility." Owing to lack of time, the Commission did not consider these topics, or the topic "the most-favoured-nation clause." However, it included in its report an account of the progress made to date in its work.

Other aspects of work of International Law Commission

On the basis of a report from a sub-committee especially set up to consider preliminary problems involved in the study of the question of treaties concluded between States and international organizations, or between two or more international organizations, the Commission, in 1971, decided to appoint Paul Reuter as Special Rapporteur on the topic and reconfirmed its 1970 request to the Secretary-General to prepare relevant documentation.[2]

In accordance with a General Assembly recommendation of 8 December 1970,[3] the Commission decided to include the question of "non-navigational uses of international watercourses" in its general programme of work, without prejudging the priority to be given to the topic. The Commission requested the Secretariat to compile relevant material on State practice with regard to this matter.

At its 1970 session, the Commission had requested the Secretary-General to prepare a working paper listing topics that might be included in its long-term programme of work. The working paper, "Survey of International Law," was before the Commission at its 1971 session. The Commission decided to place the question on the provisional agenda of its 1972 session and to invite members of the Commission to submit written statements on the review of its long-term programme of work.

The suggestion was made at its 1971 session that the Commission consider the possibility of preparing draft articles regarding such crimes as murder, kidnapping and assaults upon diplomats and other persons entitled to special protection under international law. The Commission recognized the importance and urgency of the matter, but deferred its decision in view of the priority that

[2]See Y.U.N., 1970, p. 801.
[3]*Ibid.*, pp. 818–19, text of resolution 2669(XXV).

had been given to completion of the draft articles on relations between States and international organizations. However, the Commission agreed that, if the General Assembly requested it to do so, it would prepare at its 1972 session draft articles on this subject, with a view towards submitting them to the 1972 session of the General Assembly.

Decisions by General Assembly

Later in 1971, the report of the International Law Commission was considered by the General Assembly, mainly in its Sixth (Legal) Committee.

On 3 December 1971, on the recommendation of the Sixth Committee, the General Assembly took the following decisions, among others, with regard to the work of the Commission.

It approved the programme and organization of work for the 1972 session of the Commission, including the decision to place on the provisional agenda of that session an item concerning a review of the Commission's long-term programme of work.

The Assembly also recommended that the Commission continue its work on the following topics: (*a*) succession of States, with a view to completing in 1972 the first reading of draft articles on succession of States in respect of treaties and making progress in the consideration of succession of States in respect of matters other than treaties; (*b*) State responsibility, with a view to making in 1972 substantial progress in the preparation of draft articles on the topic; (*c*) the most-favoured-nation clause; and (*d*) the question of treaties concluded between States and international organizations or between two or more international organizations. The Assembly recommended further that the Commission, in the light of its scheduled programme of work, decide upon the priority to be given to the topic of the law of the non-navigational uses of international watercourses.

The Assembly expressed its desire that an international convention on the representation of States in their relations with international organizations be elaborated and concluded expeditiously, on the basis of the draft articles adopted by the Commission in 1971 and in the light of the comments and observations on them submitted by Member States, and by Switzerland as a host State, and by the Secretary-General and the executive heads of the specialized agencies and IAEA. The Assembly also decided to include the item in the provisional agenda of its 1972 session.

Finally, the Assembly requested the Secretary-General to invite comments from Member States on the question of the protection of diplomats and to transmit them to the Commission at its 1972 session. It then requested the Commission to study, in the light of the comments, the question of the protection and inviolability of diplomatic agents and other persons entitled to special protection under international law, with a view to preparing a set of draft articles on the subject for submission to the General Assembly at the earliest date the Commission considered appropriate.

These decisions by the General Assembly were set forth in resolution 2780 (XXVI), which was adopted by a vote of 107 to 0. (For text, see DOCUMENTARY REFERENCES below.)

At the request of Jamaica, a separate vote was taken on the provision of the resolution by which the General Assembly recommended that the International Law Commission should continue its study of the most-favoured-nation clause; the provision was adopted by a vote of 94 to 0, with 8 abstentions.

At the request of Cuba, a separate vote was taken on the section of the resolution dealing with the work of the Commission on the question of the protection of diplomats; the section was adopted by a vote of 88 to 2, with 11 abstentions.

The text was based on a proposal put forward in the Sixth Committee by Canada, the Central African Republic, Cyprus, Egypt, Finland, Greece, India, Iran, Japan, Poland, Thailand, Tunisia, Turkey, the United States, Upper Volta and Uruguay, as orally amended by Cameroon. It was approved by the Sixth Committee on 12 November 1971, by a vote of 82 to 0.

On 22 September 1971, the General Assembly, acting on the recommendation of its General Committee, decided not to place on its agenda the item entitled "Declaration on Universal Participation in the Vienna Convention on the Law of Treaties," but to place it on the provisional agenda of its 1972 session. The item had been deferred from the Assembly's 1969 and 1970 sessions.

The item concerned the request of the Conference on the Law of Treaties (held at Vienna, Austria, in 1968 and 1969) to the General Assembly to issue special invitations to become parties to the Vienna Convention to States not Members of the United Nations, of the specialized agencies or of the International Atomic Energy Agency, or parties to the Statute of the International Court of Justice.

On the same date, the Assembly also decided not to place on its agenda an item concerning the issuance of invitations in order to ensure the widest possible participation in the Convention on Special Missions. In this case as well, the Assembly placed the item on the provisional agenda of its 1972 session.

DOCUMENTARY REFERENCES

General Assembly—26th session
General Committee, meeting 191.
Sixth Committee, meetings 1255–1265, 1279, 1280.
Plenary meeting 1999.

REPORT OF INTERNATIONAL LAW COMMISSION

*Yearbook of the International Law Commission, 1971, Vol. I:
Summary records of 23rd session, 26 April–30 July 1971.*
U.N.P. Sales No.: E.72.V.5.
A/8401. Report of Secretary-General on work of the Organization,
16 June 1970–15 June 1971, Part Four, Chapter II.
A/8401/Add.1. Introduction to report of Secretary-General, Sep-
tember 1971, para. 309.
A/8410/Rev.1. Report of International Law Commission on work
of its 23rd session, 26 April–30 July 1971.
A/C.6/L.821. Note by Secretariat.
A/C.6/L.822. Uruguay: working paper concerning problem of
protection and inviolability of diplomatic agents and other
persons entitled to special protection under international law,
referred to in A/8410/Rev.1, Chapter V D.
A/C.6/L.825. Uruguay: draft resolution concerning problem of
protection and inviolability of diplomatic agents and other
persons entitled to special protection under international law,
referred to in A/8410/Rev.1, Chapter V D.
A/C.6/L.826. Canada, Central African Republic, Cyprus, Egypt,
Finland, Greece, India, Iran, Japan, Poland, Thailand, Tunisia,
Turkey, United States, Upper Volta, Uruguay: draft resolution, as
orally amended by Cameroon, approved by Sixth Committee on
12 November 1971, meeting 1280, by 82 votes to 0.
A/8537. Report of Sixth Committee.

RESOLUTION 2780 (XXVI), as recommended by Sixth Committee, A/8537, adopted by Assembly on 3 December 1971,
meeting 1999, by 107 votes to 0.

The General Assembly,
Having considered the report of the International Law Commission on the work of its twenty-third session,
Emphasizing the need for the further codification and progressive development of international law in order to make it a more
effective means of implementing the purposes and principles set
forth in Articles 1 and 2 of the Charter of the United Nations and to
give increased importance to its role in relations among nations,
Recalling the recommendations it made in resolution 2634(XXV)
of 12 November 1970 concerning the codification and progressive
development of the rules of international law governing the
representation of States in their relations with international
organizations, succession of States, State responsibility, the
most-favoured-nation clause and the question of treaties concluded between States and international organizations or between two
or more international organizations,
Noting with satisfaction that at its twenty-third session, in 1971,
the International Law Commission, in the light of the observations
and comments of Member States, Switzerland and the secretariats
of various international organizations and taking into account the
relevant resolutions and debates of the General Assembly, revised
the provisional draft articles on the representation of States in their
relations with international organizations, prepared at its twentieth,
twenty-first and twenty-second sessions, and finally adopted the
draft articles as the basis of a convention,
Believing that the Vienna Convention on Diplomatic Relations,
the Vienna Convention on Consular Relations and the Convention
on Special Missions constitute instruments the purpose of which is
to contribute to the fostering of friendly relations among nations,
irrespective of their constitutional and social systems, and that it is
desirable to conclude a convention on the representation of States
in their relations with international organizations,
Recognizing the views expressed by the International Law
Commission in paragraphs 133 and 134 of its report, in particular
those on the importance and urgency of dealing with the problem

of the protection and inviolability of diplomatic agents and other
persons entitled to special protection under international law,
Noting with appreciation that the United Nations Office at
Geneva organized, during the twenty-third session of the
International Law Commission, a seventh session of the Seminar
on International Law,

I

1. *Takes note* of the report of the International Law Commission on the work of its twenty-third session;
2. *Expresses its appreciation* to the International Law Commission for the work it accomplished at its twenty-third session;
3. *Approves* the programme and organization of work of the
twenty-fourth session of the International Law Commission to be
held in 1972, including the decision to place on the provisional
agenda of that session an item entitled "Review of the
Commission's long-term programme of work: 'Survey of International Law' prepared by the Secretary-General";
4. *Recommends* that the International Law Commission
should:
  (*a*) Continue its work on succession of States, taking into
account the views and considerations referred to in General
Assembly resolutions 1765(XVII) of 20 November 1962 and
1902(XVIII) of 18 November 1963, with a view to completing in
1972 the first reading of draft articles on succession of States in
respect of treaties and making progress in the consideration of
succession of States in respect of matters other than treaties;
  (*b*) Continue its work on State responsibility, taking into
account the views and considerations referred to in General
Assembly resolutions 1765(XVII) of 20 November 1962,
1902(XVIII) of 18 November 1963 and 2400(XXIII) of 11 December
1968, with a view to making in 1972 substantial progress in the
preparation of draft articles on the topic;
  (*c*) Continue its study of the most-favoured-nation clause;
  (*d*) Continue its consideration of the question of treaties
concluded between States and international organizations or
between two or more international organizations;
5. *Recommends further* that the International Law Commission, in the light of its scheduled programme of work, decide upon
the priority to be given to the topic of the law of the
non-navigational uses of international watercourses;
6. *Expresses the wish* that, in conjunction with future sessions
of the International Law Commission, other seminars might be
organized, which should continue to ensure the participation of an
increasing number of jurists of developing countries;
7. *Requests* the Secretary-General to forward to the International Law Commission the records of the discussion on the report
of the Commission at the twenty-sixth session of the General
Assembly;

II

1. *Expresses its appreciation* to the International Law Commission for its valuable work on the question of representation of
States in their relations with international organizations and to the
Special Rapporteur on the topic for his contribution to this work;
2. *Invites* Member States and Switzerland as a host State to
submit, not later than 1 June 1972, their written comments and
observations on the draft articles on representation of States in
their relations with international organizations, and on the
procedure to be adopted for the elaboration and conclusion of a
convention on the subject;
3. *Invites also* the Secretary-General and the executive heads
of the specialized agencies and the International Atomic Energy
Agency to submit within the same period their written comments
and observations on the said draft articles;
4. *Requests* the Secretary-General to circulate, before the
twenty-seventh session of the General Assembly, the comments
and observations submitted in accordance with paragraphs 2 and
3 above;
5. *Expresses its desire* that an international convention be
elaborated and concluded expeditiously on the basis of the draft

articles adopted by the International Law Commission and in the light of the comments and observations submitted in accordance with paragraphs 2 and 3 above;

6. *Decides* to include in the provisional agenda of its twenty-seventh session an item entitled "Representation of States in their relations with international organizations";

III

1. *Requests* the Secretary-General to invite comments from Member States before 1 April 1972 on the question of the protection of diplomats and to transmit them to the International Law Commission at its twenty-fourth session;

2. *Requests* the International Law Commission to study as soon as possible, in the light of the comments of Member States, the question of the protection and inviolability of diplomatic agents

and other persons entitled to special protection under international law, with a view to preparing a set of draft articles dealing with offences committed against diplomats and other persons entitled to special protection under international law for submission to the General Assembly at the earliest date which the Commission considers appropriate.

*Election of members of
International Law Commission*
A/8429. Resolutions adopted by General Assembly during its 26th session, 21 September–22 December 1971, p. xiv.

Other questions
A/8401. Report of Secretary-General on work of the Organization, 16 June 1970–15 June 1971, Part IV, Chapter IV H and N.

Chapter III

International trade law

Report of Commission on International Trade Law

The United Nations Commission on International Trade Law (UNCITRAL) held its fourth session in Geneva, Switzerland, from 29 March to 20 April 1971. The Commission continued consideration of four priority subjects: the international sale of goods, international payments, international commercial arbitration, and international legislation on shipping. The Commission's action with respect to these and other subjects is summarized below.

International sale of goods

At its 1971 session, the Commission considered the recommendations of its Working Group on Sales concerning the simplification and clarification of the Uniform Law on the International Sale of Goods, with a view towards making it more widely acceptable.

The Commission asked the Working Group to continue its work. It also asked the Secretary-General to continue an inquiry to ascertain whether certain general conditions of sale drawn up under the auspices of the United Nations Economic Commission for Europe (ECE) could be utilized in regions outside Europe, and to complete a study of the feasibility of developing general conditions that would embrace a wider scope of commodities than was included in existing formulations.

After considering a preliminary draft of a Uniform Law on Prescription (Limitation) in the international sale of goods, prepared by the Working Group on Time-limits and Limitations, the Commission asked the Working Group to prepare a final draft of the Uniform Law for submission to the Commission at its fifth (1972) session.

International payments

The Commission continued its consideration of measures for the harmonization and unification of the law relating to negotiable instruments used in international payments. At its 1971 session, the Commission analysed information supplied by Governments and banking and trade institutions on current international payment practices and on the problems encountered in settling international transactions. The Commission also considered an analysis prepared by the Secretary-General setting forth suggestions regarding the possible content of uniform rules relating to a special negotiable instrument for optional use in international payments. The Secretary-General was requested to prepare draft rules for consideration in 1972.

Other pending projects in the field of international payments considered by the Commission related to uniform customs for documentary credits (letters of credit), bank guarantees and security interests in goods.

International shipping legislation

At the invitation of the United Nations Conference on Trade and Development (UNCTAD) Working Group, and on the recommendation of the Commission's Working Group on International Legislation on Shipping, which met at Geneva in March 1971, the Commission decided that consideration should be given to the rules and practices concerning the responsibility of ocean carriers for cargo in the context of bills of lading. The Commission requested the Secretary-General to prepare a report making proposals directed towards the removal of uncertainties and ambiguities in existing international conventions and the establishment of a balanced allocation of risks between the cargo owner and the carrier.

Publications and training

The Commission recommended the publication of a second volume of the *Register of Texts of Conventions and Other Instruments concerning International Trade Law.* It also decided that its training and assistance programme should be expanded to include practical programmes of apprenticeship in the field of international trade law.

Consideration by General Assembly

The report of UNCITRAL to the General Assembly on the work of its fourth session was considered by the Assembly's Sixth (Legal) Committee at the Assembly's 1971 session.

On 17 November 1971, on the recommendation of the Sixth Committee, the Assembly among other things recommended that the Commission continue its work on the priority subjects, accelerate its work on training and assistance in the field of international trade law, and continue to collaborate with international organizations active in the field of international trade law. The Assembly also authorized the Secretary-General to publish a second volume of the *Register of Texts.*

These decisions were set forth in resolution 2766(XXVI), which was adopted unanimously. The text was sponsored in the Sixth Committee by Australia, Austria, Guyana, Hungary, India, Japan and Romania. It was approved without objection by the Committee on 25 October 1971. (For text of resolution, see DOCUMENTARY REFERENCES below.)

DOCUMENTARY REFERENCES

General Assembly—26th session
Sixth Committee, meetings 1247-1254, 1266, 1267.
Fifth Committee, meeting 1455.
Plenary meeting 1986.

A/8401. Report of Secretary-General on work of the Organization, 16 June 1970–15 June 1971, Part Four, Chapter III.
A/8401/Add.1. Introduction to report of Secretary-General, September 1971, para. 310.
A/8417. Report of United Nations Commission on International Trade Law (UNCITRAL) on work of its 4th session, Geneva, Switzerland, 29 March–20 April 1971. (Annex IV: List of documents before Commission.)
A/C.6/L.820. Note by Secretary-General (transmitting extract from report of Trade and Development Board of United Nations Conference on Trade and Development on its 11th session).
A/C.6/L.823. Australia, Austria, Guyana, Hungary, India, Japan, Romania: draft resolution, approved without objection by Sixth Committee on 25 October 1971, meeting 1267.
A/C.6/L.824, A/C.5/1393, A/8408/Add.5, A/8519. Administrative and financial implications of draft resolution recommended by Sixth Committee in A/8506. Statements by Secretary-General and reports of Advisory Committee on Administrative and Budgetary Questions and Fifth Committee.
A/8506. Report of Sixth Committee.

RESOLUTION 2766(XXVI), as recommended by Sixth Committee, A/8506, adopted unanimously by Assembly on 17 November 1971, meeting 1986.

The General Assembly,
Having considered the report of the United Nations Commission on International Trade Law on the work of its fourth session,
Recalling its resolution 2205(XXI) of 17 December 1966 establishing the United Nations Commission on International Trade Law and defining the object and terms of reference of the Commission,
Further recalling its resolutions 2421(XXIII) of 18 December 1968, 2502(XXIV) of 12 November 1969 and 2635(XXV) of 12 November 1970 on the reports of the United Nations Commission on International Trade Law on the work of its first, second and third sessions,
Reaffirming its conviction that the progressive harmonization and unification of international trade law, in reducing or removing legal obstacles to the flow of international trade, especially those affecting the developing countries, would significantly contribute to universal economic co-operation among all peoples on a basis of equality and, thereby, to their well-being,
Noting that the Trade and Development Board, at its eleventh session, considered the report of the United Nations Commission on International Trade Law on its fourth session and expressed satisfaction with the co-ordination of the work programmes of the Commission and of the United Nations Conference on Trade and Development in the field of international legislation on shipping,
1. *Takes note with appreciation* of the report of the United Nations Commission on International Trade Law on the work of its fourth session and commends its members for their contribution to the progress made in the work of the Commission;
2. *Recommends* that the United Nations Commission on International Trade Law should:
(*a*) Continue, in its work, to pay special attention to the topics to which it has decided to give priority, that is, the international sale of goods, international payments, international commercial arbitration and international legislation on shipping;
(*b*) Accelerate its work on training and assistance in the field of international trade law, with special regard to developing countries;
(*c*) Continue to collaborate with international organizations active in the field of international trade law;
(*d*) Continue to give special consideration to the interests of developing countries and to bear in mind the special problems of land-locked countries;
(*e*) Continue, in its use of working groups and other working methods, to seek to enhance its efficiency and to ensure full consideration of the needs of all regions;
(*f*) Keep its programme of work under constant review;
3. *Notes with satisfaction* the publication of the first volume of the *Yearbook of the United Nations Commission on International Trade Law* and the first volume of the *Register of Texts of Conventions and Other Instruments concerning International Trade Law* and authorizes the Secretary-General to publish the second volume of the *Register of Texts* in accordance with the decision of the Commission contained in paragraph 131 of its report;
4. *Requests* the Secretary-General to forward to the United Nations Commission on International Trade Law the records of the discussions at the twenty-sixth session of the General Assembly on the Commission's report on the work of its fourth session.

Other documents
Yearbook of the United Nations Commission on International Trade Law, Vol. II: 1971. U.N.P. Sales No.: E.72.V.4.

Chapter IV

The question of defining aggression

Consideration by Special Committee

The Special Committee on the Question of Defining Aggression met at United Nations Headquarters, New York, from 1 February to 5 March 1971 to resume its work, as requested by the General Assembly on 25 November 1970.[1]

The Special Committee decided to consider the specific questions mentioned in the 1970 report of its Working Group, namely: a general definition of aggression; the principle of priority; political entities other than States; legitimate use of force; aggressive intent; acts proposed for inclusion in the definition; principle of proportionality; legal consequences of aggression; and the right of peoples to self-determination.

The Special Committee reconstituted its Working Group, instructing it to formulate an agreed or generally accepted definition of aggression and, in case it was unable to reach such a definition, to report its assessment of the progress made, indicating both the points of agreement and disagreement.

The Working Group held 23 meetings in 1971, and submitted two successive reports to the Special Committee. The first report reflected the outcome of its discussions on the general definition of aggression and the principle of priority; the second report reflected the results of its discussions on the questions of political entities other than States, legitimate use of force, aggressive intent, acts proposed for inclusion in the definition of aggression, proportionality, legal consequences of aggression and the right of peoples to self-determination.

The Special Committee considered the first report of the Working Group, but for lack of time was unable to examine the second report. Both reports were annexed to the 1971 report of the Special Committee to the General Assembly.

On 5 March 1971, the Special Committee unanimously adopted a resolution, submitted by Czechoslovakia and Mexico, by which, *inter alia*, it noted the common desire of its members to continue their work on the basis of the results attained and arrive at a draft definition, and it recommended to the General Assembly that the Committee be invited to resume its work in 1972.

General Assembly discussion

The report of the Special Committee on its 1971 session was taken up by the General Assembly at its twenty-sixth (1971) session. The report was referred to the Assembly's Sixth (Legal) Committee,

which discussed it at 11 meetings held between 26 October and 18 November 1971. Some of the main points raised are summarized below.

Views on general aspects of question of defining aggression

Many Members expressed the view that there was an urgent need for a definition of aggression. The representatives of Bulgaria, Poland, the Syrian Arab Republic, the USSR and Yugoslavia, among others, felt that the adoption of a definition of aggression would not only contribute to the codification of international law but also strengthen the system of collective security established by the United Nations Charter and promote the rule of law. It was further held, by those States among others, that a definition of aggression could contribute towards the formation of an enlightened public opinion; could be a yardstick against which to measure the conduct of States in the light of their obligations under the Charter; could serve as a warning to any potential aggressor; would be useful for protecting small countries; and would supply a legal basis, within the framework of the United Nations, for eliminating the lack of precision and the subjective nature of political judgements.

Other Members, including Cameroon, Israel and the United States, expressed doubt regarding the usefulness of a definition of aggression. The representative of the United States felt that although the clarification of legal norms was a useful step in promoting the rule of law, an agreed definition of aggression was not vital to the attainment of the purposes and principles of the Charter; a determination to make the United Nations collective security system as effective as possible was far more important.

The representative of Israel argued that even if such a definition could be established, it could neither have any impact on the development of international penal law nor remove provocation and aggression.

The representative of Cameroon held that international peace in fact depended on the political will of States; it would be wrong to believe that the cause of peace could be furthered by working out new rules of law, since the various juridical instruments of general application at the disposal of the international community were quite adequate for its needs.

[1]See Y.U.N., 1970, pp. 797–98, text of resolution 2644(XXV).

The Cameroonian representative said he was unable to share the optimism of those who believed that the Special Committee was on the verge of completing its work and could not support the proposal that the mandate of the Special Committee be renewed in 1972, a position that was also taken by the representative of Israel.

Most of the representatives who spoke, however, felt that the Special Committee had made encouraging progress which gave grounds for hope that a generally acceptable definition of aggression could be formulated in the near future.

With regard to the procedure to be followed for the formulation and adoption of a definition of aggression, the representatives of Ceylon, Finland, Greece and Hungary were among those who considered that the only way of arriving at an acceptable and lasting definition of aggression was by consensus.

Other representatives, including those of Iraq, the Ukrainian SSR and the United Republic of Tanzania, felt that if it was not possible to reach a consensus the definition should be adopted by a simple majority. (The representative of the United Republic of Tanzania held that the method of seeking the consent of all the permanent members of the Security Council was obstructive and undemocratic and should be abandoned.)

Mexico and the USSR felt that a definition of aggression would gain in importance if it were adopted in a General Assembly resolution similar to that by which the Assembly had adopted the Declaration on Principles of International Law concerning Friendly Relations and Co-operation among States in accordance with the Charter of the United Nations.[2]

Views on content of definition

THE DEFINITION AND THE POWER OF THE SECURITY COUNCIL

It was generally accepted in principle that the definition of aggression should safeguard the discretionary power of the Security Council as the United Nations organ with primary responsibility for the maintenance of international peace and security. Italy held that no definition of aggression could bind the Security Council in determining a particular case of aggression; the Security Council was and remained an organ of security. Mexico inquired whether the incorporation of a definition of aggression in international law would not have the effect of curtailing the powers of the Security Council.

POLITICAL ENTITIES TO WHICH DEFINITIONS SHOULD APPLY

A number of representatives, including those of Afghanistan, Bulgaria, Costa Rica, Cuba, Ghana,

Greece, Iraq and Peru, opposed the inclusion in the definition of aggression of a reference to "political entities other than States."

The representative of Ghana held that the definition should apply to all sovereign and independent States, whether they were Members of the United Nations or not; the notion of "political entity" was not embodied in the Charter, which had no provision for making the existence of a sovereign State dependent on its recognition by other States.

The Peruvian representative maintained that only States should be taken into consideration, regardless of the question of their recognition; States should be regarded in the definition as the only subjects of international law capable of committing or being the victim of an act of aggression.

To ensure that the definition was given the widest possible application, some representatives, including those of Italy and Zambia, suggested resorting to the compromise solution envisaged in the Working Group's 1971 report, namely, to annex to the definition an explanatory note to the effect that the term "State" included States whose statehood was disputed.

The representative of the United States, among others, felt that the definition of aggression, if it was to be complete, should include the concept of political entities; agreement on certain aspects of that problem had already been achieved in the Declaration on Principles of International Law concerning Friendly Relations and Co-operation among States in accordance with the Charter of the United Nations, he noted.

ACTS PROPOSED FOR INCLUSION IN DEFINITION

Many Members expressed the view that the definition should be limited, at least at the current stage, to the use of armed force. Different opinions were expressed, however, with regard to whether the definition should cover the so-called indirect use of armed force for the purposes of the exercise of the right of self-defence. Several representatives, including those of France, Ghana and Iraq, maintained that at the current stage of its work the Special Committee should not concern itself with defining "indirect aggression" because of the difficulty of finding a precise definition and the time-consuming process of determining a consensus.

The representative of Ghana noted that care should be taken not to confuse the concept of "breach of the peace" with that of "armed attack" or "aggression"; the Special Committee's report had cited as examples of acts constituting aggression acts which, in fact, would only result in a

[2]See Y.U.N., 1970, pp. 784–92.

breach of the peace if they were of such intensity as to necessitate recourse to self-defence, in which case they would pose an imminent danger to life and property as well as to the existence of a State. The French representative proposed that the definition contain a list of the most serious kinds of aggression, i.e. those contemplated in Articles 39 and 51 of the Charter.[3] He felt that the sending of armed bands by one State into the territory of another might be included in the list, but that unduly vague concepts, such as support for acts of subversion, should be excluded, since a State might use them as a pretext for aggression under the guise of self-defence.

Other representatives, including those of Canada, Israel and the United States, maintained that the definition of aggression should cover any illegal use of armed force, whether direct or indirect.

The United States representative held that a definition of aggression must be exhaustive and not partial and that attempts to draw a distinction between "direct" and "indirect" aggression sometimes served as an excuse for accepting a partial definition; such a distinction had no basis in the Charter, where the various kinds of illegal force or aggression were not differentiated.

The representative of Israel contended that indirect aggression was probably the most serious contemporary manifestation of aggression and that any enumeration of acts of aggression which overlooked that particular form would have no great practical value. It was common knowledge that current violations of the provisions of the Charter were due as much to indirect as to direct aggression and that certain States had used force through the agency of terrorists or armed bands or had permitted such groups to operate from their territories against the territorial integrity and political independence of other States, the Israeli representative added.

Chile, Cuba and India were among those holding that the definition should not be limited to armed aggression; for example, it was noted by Cuba, France and Zambia that the Special Committee should consider including in the definition a reference to economic aggression as one of the most serious forms of attack or challenge.

The notions of declaration of war, occupation and annexation were among the specific acts mentioned for enumeration in the definition as examples of aggression. The Canadian representative noted that a view seemed to be emerging that a declaration of war did not necessarily constitute aggression but was an important element in determining an act of aggression, because of its inherent seriousness and the formal juridical consequences that followed from it.

Egypt felt that the most serious act of aggression

was occupation or annexation of the territory of a State by force.

Romania held that the definition should include cases in which a State made its territory available to another State so that it could commit aggression against a third State.

PRINCIPLE OF PRIORITY

No basic objection to the inclusion of the principle of priority in the definition of aggression was expressed. Several Members, including Bulgaria, Hungary and Iraq, felt that the principle must be retained as being a basic and determinative criterion. Hungary noted that the principle of priority made it impossible for an aggressor State to plead innocence on the grounds that it was conducting a preventive war: the burden of proof was placed on the State that first resorted to force.

Others, including Canada, Italy and the United States, were of the opinion that the principle of priority could not in itself constitute a determining factor and should figure in the definition as only one element among others. The Canadian representative suggested that the question of priority might be solved by postulating that the Security Council should determine, in each case, which party first used force and treat its finding as a fact of considerable significance but without prejudice to the ultimate consequences of the finding.

AGGRESSIVE INTENT

In the view of some Members, including Burma, El Salvador, the USSR, the United Kingdom and the United States, the element of intent should be a fundamental ingredient of any definition of aggression.

The USSR said that if the definition did not include the element of intent, its sphere of application would be limited; in particular, it would not apply to cases where exercise of the right of self-defence developed into actual aggression.

The United States considered that *animus aggressionis* was an essential element of a definition of aggression.

Others—France, Ghana, Iraq and Israel, for instance—were opposed to including the element of intent in the definition. Since aggressive intent was necessarily implied in any act of aggression, Ghana said, it was not necessary to include the principle in the definition; the inclusion of the element of intent in a definition would in fact permit an aggressor State to seek to justify its action, but the burden of proof should always be on the aggressor and not on the victim State.

The representative of Israel felt that the question of aggressive intent should be left to the

---

[3]For text of Articles 39 and 51 of the Charter, see APPENDIX II.

discretionary power of the Security Council, which should take motive and purpose into consideration in determining the existence or non-existence of aggression; inclusion of the notion of intent in the definition could only add to the complexity of the problem.

LEGITIMATE USE OF FORCE

Egypt and the USSR were among those maintaining that the definition of aggression should distinguish clearly between aggression and the legitimate use of force. Article 51 of the Charter expressly provided that the right of self-defence could be exercised in the event of armed attack, the USSR noted. Egypt said that a definition not totally based on Article 51 would run the risk of encouraging the use of force in violation of the provisions of the Charter.

On the other hand, the United Kingdom felt that any attempt to incorporate in the definition of aggression a definition of the right of self-defence was misconceived and dangerous; the Special Committee's terms of reference did not entitle it to embark on a definition of the right of self-defence. All that was required, the United Kingdom said, was that the definition should contain a suitable saving provision to the effect that the definition did not apply to what was done in the exercise of the right of self-defence.

The representatives of the Byelorussian SSR, France, Ghana, Hungary, Israel and Mongolia were opposed to including the principle of proportionality in the definition of aggression. They made the following points: no such principle appeared in the Charter and it was by no means universally recognized in international law; its inclusion in the definition would favour the aggressor by throwing the burden of proof on the victim of aggression; such a principle might be applied in the case of indirect armed attack or breaches of the peace, which were less urgent; and, in any case, Article 51 of the Charter recognized the right of self-defence as an inherent right without any restrictions whatsoever.

Other representatives, including those of Burma, Costa Rica, Greece and the United States, considered that it would be useful to include the principle of proportionality in the definition. The United States representative felt that the fear that incorporating the principle of proportionality in the definition of aggression would only encourage aggression was not supported by the facts; proportionality should be based on the danger rationally perceived by the victim. He noted that the principle was not a new concept in municipal law and that it would be relatively easy to transfer it to international law.

It was observed by the representative of Greece that the principle of proportionality was an excellent criterion for determining whether an action was defensive or aggressive.

With regard to the organs empowered to use force, some Members, including Cuba and the Ukrainian SSR, maintained that the Security Council alone could decide on the use of force. Article 11 of the Charter, the Ukrainian representative said, left no room for doubt on that question; any attempt to grant such powers to other organs would be tantamount to a revision of the Charter. Cuba was unable to accept any definition which recognized that force could be used legitimately under regional arrangements or by regional agencies without the authorization of the Security Council, as required by Article 53 of the Charter.[4]

THE RIGHT OF SELF-DETERMINATION

Several Members, including Ghana and Romania, said that logically it was the duty of the Special Committee, as the body responsible for defining aggression—namely, the illegal use of force—to consider situations in which the use of force was legitimate, in particular the inalienable right of colonial peoples to oppose any attempt to deprive them by force of their right to self-determination.

Other Members, including Italy and the United Kingdom, said the right of self-determination should not be mentioned in the definition of aggression. It was argued that this right had been dealt with in other instruments, and therefore was not relevant to the definition of aggression; it could not be made part of the definition without an unacceptable distortion of the definition's scope and function.

LEGAL CONSEQUENCES OF AGGRESSION

Several representatives, including those of Egypt and Iraq, said the definition of aggression should include a provision concerning the legal consequences of aggression. In the view of the representative of Iraq, it must be stated that aggression, once established, entailed responsibility; it was also important to mention the principle of non-recognition and to declare that no territorial gain from aggression should be recognized.

The representatives of Italy and the United States, among others, maintained that the definition of aggression should not mention the legal consequences of aggression; the question went beyond the Special Committee's terms of reference and, in any case, had been adequately dealt with in the Declaration on Principles of International Law concerning Friendly Relations and Co-operation among States.[5]

---

[4]For text of Articles 11 and 53 of the Charter, see APPENDIX II.
[5]See footnote 2.

Decisions by General Assembly

On 3 December 1971, the General Assembly: (1) decided that the Special Committee on the Question of Defining Aggression should resume its work as early as possible in 1972; (2) requested the Secretary-General to provide the Special Committee with the necessary facilities and services; and (3) decided to include the question in the provisional agenda of its 1972 session.

These decisions by the Assembly were set forth in resolution 2781(XXVI), which was adopted, by a vote of 110 to 0, with 3 abstentions, on the recommendation of the Sixth Committee.

The resolution was based on a proposal put forward in the Sixth Committee by the following 33 Members: Bulgaria, the Byelorussian SSR, Colombia, Cyprus, Czechoslovakia, Ecuador, Egypt, Ethiopia, Ghana, Guinea, Guyana, Haiti, Hungary, India, Iran, Jordan, Kenya, the Libyan Arab Republic, Madagascar, Mali, Mexico, Mongolia, Pakistan, Poland, Romania, Sierra Leone, the Syrian Arab Republic, Uganda, the Ukrainian SSR, the USSR, the United Republic of Tanzania, Yugoslavia and Zambia.

The text was approved by the Sixth Committee on 15 November 1971 by a vote of 85 to 0, with 3 abstentions. (For text of resolution, see DOCU-MENTARY REFERENCES below.)

On 21 December 1971, the Assembly, in taking decisions concerning the implementation of the Declaration on the Strengthening of International Security, called for an early agreement on the definition of aggression. (For text of resolution 2880 (XXVI), see pp. 40-41.)

DOCUMENTARY REFERENCES

General Assembly—26th session
Sixth Committee, meetings 1268-1276, 1281, 1285.
Fifth Committee, meeting 1460.
Plenary meeting 1999.

A/8401. Report of Secretary-General on work of the Organization, 16 June 1970–15 June 1971, Part Four, Chapter IV B.
A/8419. Report of Special Committee on Question of Defining Aggression, 1 February–5 March 1971. (Chapter IV: Recommendation of Special Committee.)
A/C.6/L.827. Bulgaria, Byelorussian SSR, Colombia, Cyprus, Czechoslovakia, Ecuador, Egypt, Ethiopia, Ghana, Guinea, Guyana, Haiti, Hungary, India, Iran, Jordan, Kenya, Libyan Arab Republic, Madagascar, Mali, Mexico, Mongolia, Pakistan, Poland, Romania, Sierra Leone, Syrian Arab Republic, Uganda, Ukrainian SSR, USSR, United Republic of Tanzania, Yugoslavia, Zambia: draft resolution, approved by Sixth Committee on 15 November 1971, meeting 1281, by 85 votes to 0, with 3 abstentions.
A/C.6/L.828, A/C.5/1401, A/8533. Administrative and financial implications of draft resolution recommended by Sixth Committee in A/8525. Statements by Secretary-General and report of Fifth Committee.
A/8525. Report of Sixth Committee.

RESOLUTION 2781(XXVI), as recommended by Sixth Committee, A/8525, adopted by Assembly on 3 December 1971, meeting 1999, by 110 votes to 0, with 3 abstentions.

The General Assembly,
Having considered the report of the Special Committee on the Question of Defining Aggression on the work of its session held in New York from 1 February to 5 March 1971,
Taking note of the progress made by the Special Committee in its consideration of the question of defining aggression and on the draft definition, as reflected in the report of the Special Committee,
Considering that it was not possible for the Special Committee to complete its task at its session held in 1971,
Considering that in its resolutions 2330(XXII) of 18 December 1967, 2420(XXIII) of 18 December 1968, 2549(XXIV) of 12 December 1969 and 2644(XXV) of 25 November 1970 the General Assembly recognized the widespread conviction of the need to expedite the definition of aggression,
Considering the urgency of bringing the work of the Special Committee to a successful conclusion and the desirability of achieving the definition of aggression as soon as possible,
Noting also the common desire of the members of the Special Committee to continue their work on the basis of the results achieved and to arrive at a draft definition,
1. *Decides* that the Special Committee on the Question of Defining Aggression shall resume its work, in accordance with General Assembly resolution 2330(XXII), as early as possible in 1972;
2. *Requests* the Secretary-General to provide the Special Committee with the necessary facilities and services;
3. *Decides* to include in the provisional agenda of its twenty-seventh session an item entitled "Report of the Special Committee on the Question of Defining Aggression."

Chapter V

United Nations programme of assistance to promote teaching and knowledge of international law

Activities in 1971

Activities were continued in 1971 under the United Nations Programme of Assistance in the Teaching, Study, Dissemination and Wider Appreciation of International Law.

Under a fellowship scheme jointly administered by the United Nations and the United Nations Institute for Training and Research (UNITAR), 15 fellowships to persons from developing countries were awarded by the United Nations and five fellowships were awarded by UNITAR. The fellowship holders were government officials and university teachers from the following countries: Barbados, Ecuador, Ethiopia, Guatemala, Haiti, India, Lesotho, Malawi, Mexico, Nigeria, the People's Democratic Republic of Yemen, Romania, Singapore, Somalia, Sudan, the Syrian Arab Republic, Thailand, the United Kingdom, Uruguay and Western Samoa.

Fellowship holders attended a seminar on international law, organized by the United Nations and The Hague Academy of International Law, Netherlands, and, in some instances, received practical training in the legal offices of the United Nations and in those of its associated agencies.

A regional symposium on international law for participants from African States, organized by UNITAR, was held in Accra, Ghana, from 14 to 28 January 1971. The meeting was attended by officials and scholars from 23 African countries, who discussed the following topics: State succession in matters other than treaties; economic development agreements; and the pre-colonial and current contribution of Africa to international law.

In accordance with a decision of the United Nations Commission on International Trade Law (UNCITRAL), the Secretary-General continued his consultations with interested organizations with a view to developing programmes of training and assistance in international trade law, in particular arrangements whereby practical experience could be made available to persons, especially those from developing countries.

The participation of the United Nations Educational, Scientific and Cultural Organization (UNESCO) in the Programme included the provision of fellowships for post-graduate study in international law and related topics, and various forms of assistance for the teaching of international law, especially in Africa.

Consideration by General Assembly

Report by Secretary-General

In his 1971 report on the United Nations Programme of Assistance in the Teaching, Study, Dissemination and Wider Appreciation of International Law, the Secretary-General proposed that the Programme in 1972 and 1973 be conducted along broadly the same lines as in previous years, with the continued participation of the United Nations, UNITAR and UNESCO. It was noted that in addition to supplying fellowships, UNITAR planned to hold a regional training and refresher course in Latin America in 1972 and a regional symposium in Asia in 1973.

The Secretary-General reported that the Programme had been in operation for six years and that it was unlikely that major modifications in its activities would be called for in the immediate future. He therefore proposed that the General Assembly be invited to approve the recommendations for the two-year period 1972–1973, and that he submit his next report on the Programme to the 1973 session of the General Assembly.

This proposal was endorsed by the Advisory Committee on the Programme of Assistance in the Teaching, Study, Dissemination and Wider Appreciation of International Law at its sixth session, held from 12 October to 8 November 1971.

Decisions of General Assembly

The Secretary-General's report, together with the views expressed by the Advisory Committee, was considered by the General Assembly's Sixth (Legal) Committee at the Assembly's 1971 session.

On 18 December 1971, the Assembly authorized the Secretary-General to carry out in 1972 and 1973 the activities specified in his report, to be financed from budgetary provisions in the regular budget. These activities were to include the provision of a minimum of 15 fellowships in 1972 and 1973 at the request of Governments of developing countries, and assistance, in the form of travel grants, for participants from developing countries invited to the regional meetings to be organized by UNITAR in Latin America in 1972 and in Asia in 1973.

The Assembly also, among other things, expressed its appreciation to UNESCO and UNITAR for their participation in the Programme; requested the Secretary-General to continue to publicize the Programme by periodically inviting Member States, universities, foundations and other bodies, and individuals, to make voluntary contributions towards the financing and implementation of the Programme; and reiterated its request to Member States and interested organizations and individuals to make voluntary financial contributions to the Programme.

The Secretary-General was requested to report to the General Assembly at its 1973 session on the implementation of the Programme and, following consultations with the Advisory Committee, to submit recommendations for the future.

These decisions were set forth in resolution 2838(XXVI), which was adopted, without objection, on the recommendation of the Sixth Committee. (For text of resolution, see DOCUMENTARY REFERENCES below.)

The text, which was approved without objection by the Sixth Committee on 10 December 1971, was based on a proposal put forward by 17 Members: Afghanistan, Algeria, Cameroon, the Congo,

Costa Rica, Cyprus, the Dominican Republic, Ecuador, El Salvador, Ethiopia, Ghana, Guatemala, Kenya, the Philippines, Rwanda, the United Republic of Tanzania and Zambia. The 17-power draft was a revised version of a 7-power proposal and incorporated certain amendments to the latter put foward by, respectively, the Ukrainian SSR; Greece; and the Congo, Kenya and the United Republic of Tanzania.

Two amendments, submitted jointly by Canada, France, the United Kingdom and the United States, were rejected. The first amendment would have replaced the words "a minimum of" with the words "in principle" in the authorization to provide a minimum of 15 fellowships in 1972 and 1973. The second amendment concerned the authorization to provide travel grants to participants in the regional meetings; it would have added the words "providing that a contribution to the cost of such travel, amounting to at least half of that cost, is forthcoming from the Government of that country."

At the request of the United Kingdom, a separate vote was taken on the operative paragraph authorizing the Secretary-General to carry out the activities specified in his report. The paragraph was approved by the Sixth Committee.

DOCUMENTARY REFERENCES

General Assembly—26th session
Sixth Committee, meetings 1300, 1301, 1304–1307.
Fifth Committee, meeting 1486.
Plenary meeting 2025.

A/8379. Addendum to register of experts and scholars in international law.
A/8401. Report of Secretary-General on work of the Organization, 16 June 1970–15 June 1971, Part Four, Chapter IV C.
A/8508 and Corr.1. Report of Secretary-General.
A/C.6/412. Appointment of members of Advisory Committee on United Nations Programme of Assistance in Teaching, Study, Dissemination and Wider Appreciation of International Law. Note by Secretary-General.
A/C.6/L.843. Costa Rica, Cyprus, Ecuador, El Salvador, Ghana, Guatemala, Philippines: draft resolution.
A/C.6/L.843/Rev.1. Afghanistan, Algeria, Cameroon, Congo, Costa Rica, Cyprus, Dominican Republic, Ecuador, El Salvador, Ethiopia, Ghana, Guatemala, Kenya, Philippines, Rwanda, United Republic of Tanzania, Zambia: revised draft resolution, approved without objection by Sixth Committee on 10 December 1971, meeting 1307.
A/C.6/L.844. Ukrainian SSR: amendment to 7-power draft resolution, A/C.6/L.843.
A/C.6/L.845. Greece: amendment to 7-power draft resolution, A/C.6/L.843.
A/C.6/L.846. Administrative and financial implications of 7-power draft resolution, A/C.6/L.843. Note by Secretary-General.
A/C.6/L.847. Canada, France, United Kingdom, United States: amendments to 7-power draft resolution, A/C.6/L.843.
A/C.6/L.848. Congo, Kenya, United Republic of Tanzania: amendments to 7-power draft resolution, A/C.6/L.843.
A/C.5/1418, A/8609. Administrative and financial implications of draft resolution recommended by Sixth Committee in A/8570. Statement by Secretary-General and report of Fifth Committee.
A/8570. Report of Sixth Committee.

RESOLUTION 2838(XXVI), as recommended by Sixth Committee, A/8570, adopted by Assembly without objection on 18 December 1971, meeting 2025.

The General Assembly,
Noting with appreciation the report of the Secretary-General on the implementation of the United Nations Programme of Assistance in the Teaching, Study, Dissemination and Wider Appreciation of International Law and the recommendations made to the Secretary-General by the Advisory Committee on the United Nations Programme of Assistance in the Teaching, Study, Dissemination and Wider Appreciation of International Law, which are contained in that report,

Considering that international law should occupy an appropriate place in the teaching of legal disciplines at all universities,
Noting with appreciation the efforts made by States at the bilateral level to provide assistance in the teaching and study of international law,
Convinced nevertheless that States, international organizations and institutions should be encouraged to give further support to the Programme and to increase their activities to promote the teaching, study, dissemination and wider appreciation of international law, in particular those activities which are of special benefit to persons from developing countries,
Recalling that, in the conduct of the Programme, it is desirable to use as far as possible the resources and facilities made available by Member States, international organizations and others,
1. *Authorizes* the Secretary-General to carry out in 1972 and 1973 the activities specified in his report to be financed from budgetary provisions in the regular budget, including the provision of:
(a) A minimum of fifteen fellowships in 1972 and 1973 at the request of Governments of developing countries;
(b) Assistance in the form of a travel grant for one participant from each developing country who will be invited to the regional training and refresher course to be held in Latin America in 1972 and to the regional symposium to be held in Asia in 1973;
2. *Expresses its appreciation* to the Secretary-General for his constructive efforts to promote training and assistance in international law within the framework of the United Nations Programme of Assistance in the Teaching, Study, Dissemination and Wider Appreciation of International Law in 1971;
3. *Expresses its appreciation* to the United Nations Educational, Scientific and Cultural Organization for its participation in the Programme, in particular for the efforts made to support the teaching of international law;
4. *Expresses its appreciation* to the United Nations Institute for Training and Research for its participation in the Programme, particularly in the organization of regional meetings and in the conduct of the fellowship programme in international law sponsored jointly by the United Nations and the Institute;
5. *Expresses its appreciation* for the offer of the Government of Venezuela to provide host facilities for the regional training and refresher course to be held in 1972;
6. *Urges* all Governments to encourage the inclusion of courses on international law in the programmes of legal studies offered at institutions of higher learning;
7. *Requests* the Secretary-General to continue to publicize the Programme by periodically inviting Member States, universities, philanthropic foundations and other interested national and international institutions and organizations, and individuals to make voluntary contributions towards the financing of the Programme or otherwise towards assisting in its implementation and possible expansion;

8. *Reiterates* its request to Member States and to interested organizations and individuals to make voluntary contributions towards the financing of the Programme and expresses its appreciation to those Member States which have made voluntary contributions for this purpose;

9. *Decides* to appoint the following thirteen Member States as members of the Advisory Committee on the United Nations Programme of Assistance in the Teaching, Study, Dissemination and Wider Appreciation of International Law, for a period of four years beginning on 1 January 1972: Barbados, Belgium, Cyprus, El Salvador, France, Ghana, Hungary, Iraq, Mali, Union of Soviet Socialist Republics, United Kingdom of Great Britain and Northern Ireland, United Republic of Tanzania and United States of America;

10. *Requests* the Secretary-General to report to the General Assembly at its twenty-eighth session on the implementation of the Programme during 1972 and 1973 and, following consultations with the Advisory Committee, to submit recommendations regarding the execution of the Programme in subsequent years;

11. *Decides* to include in the provisional agenda of its twenty-eighth session an item entitled "United Nations Programme of Assistance in the Teaching, Study, Dissemination and Wider Appreciation of International Law."

Chapter VI

Treaties and multilateral conventions

Privileges and immunities

Convention on the Privileges and Immunities of the United Nations

During 1971, Burundi acceded and Fiji succeeded to the Convention on the Privileges and Immunities of the United Nations.

At the end of 1971, the following 104 States were parties to the Convention:

Afghanistan, Albania, Algeria, Argentina, Australia, Austria, Belgium, Bolivia, Brazil, Bulgaria, Burma, Burundi, the Byelorussian SSR, Cameroon, Canada, the Central African Republic, Chile, the Congo, Costa Rica, Cuba, Cyprus, Czechoslovakia, Denmark, the Dominican Republic, Ecuador, Egypt, El Salvador, Ethiopia, Fiji, Finland, France, Gabon, Gambia, Ghana, Greece, Guatemala, Guinea, Haiti, Honduras, Hungary, Iceland, India, Iran, Iraq, Ireland, Israel, Italy, the Ivory Coast, Jamaica, Japan, Jordan, Kenya, the Khmer Republic, Kuwait, Laos, Lebanon, Lesotho, Liberia, the Libyan Arab Republic, Luxembourg, Madagascar, Malawi, Malaysia, Mali, Malta, Mauritius, Mexico, Mongolia, Morocco, Nepal, the Netherlands, New Zealand, Nicaragua, Niger, Nigeria, Norway, Pakistan, Panama, Paraguay, Peru, the Philippines, Poland, Romania, Rwanda, Senegal, Sierra Leone, Singapore, Somalia, Sweden, the Syrian Arab Republic, Thailand, Togo, Trinidad and Tobago, Tunisia, Turkey, the Ukrainian SSR, the USSR, the United Kingdom, the United Republic of Tanzania, the United States, Upper Volta, Yemen, Yugoslavia and Zaire.

Convention on the Privileges and Immunities of Specialized Agencies

In the course of 1971, one more State—Barbados—acceded to the Convention on the Privileges and Immunities of the Specialized Agencies. At the end of 1971, there were 74 States parties to the Convention. (For further details, see table below.)

Barbados undertook to apply the Convention to the World Health Organization (WHO), the International Civil Aviation Organization (ICAO), the International Labour Organisation (ILO), the Food and Agriculture Organization (FAO), the United Nations Educational, Scientific and Cultural Organization (UNESCO), the International Monetary Fund, the Universal Postal Union (UPU), the International Telecommunication Union (ITU), the World Meteorological Organization (WMO) and the Inter-Governmental Maritime Consultative Organization (IMCO).

The following table shows, as at the end of 1971, the States parties to the Convention, as well as the specialized agencies in respect of which each of these States has undertaken to apply the Convention.

Parties to Convention on the Privileges and Immunities of the Specialized Agencies

(As at 31 December 1971)

States Parties	Agencies in respect of which Convention is applicable*												
	ILO	FAO	UNESCO	WHO	IBRD	IFC	IDA	IMF	ICAO	UPU	ITU	WMO	IMCO
Algeria	x	x	x	x	x			x	x	x	x	x	x
Argentina	x	x	x	x	x	x		x	x	x	x	x	x
Austria	x	x	x	x	x	x	x	x	x	x	x	x	
Barbados	x	x	x	x				x	x	x	x	x	x
Belgium	x	x	x	x	x	x	x	x	x	x	x	x	x

Agencies in respect of which Convention is applicable*

States Parties	ILO	FAO	UNESCO	WHO	IBRD	IFC	IDA	IMF	ICAO	UPU	ITU	WMO	IMCO
Brazil	x	x	x	x	x	x	x	x	x	x	x	x	x
Bulgaria	x	x	x	x						x	x	x	x
Byelorussian SSR	x		x								x	v	
Central African Republic	x	x	x	x					x			v	
Chile	x	x	x	x	x			x	x	x	x		
Cyprus	x	x	x	x					x	x	x	x	x
Czechoslovakia	x		x	x					x	x	x	x	x
Denmark	x	x	x	x	x	x	x	x	x	x	x	x	x
Ecuador	x	x	x	x	x			x	x	x	x	x	
Egypt	x	x	x	x	x			x	x	x		x	
Federal Republic of Germany	x	x	x	x	x	x		x	x	x	x	x	x
Finland	x	x	x	x	x	x	x	x	x	x	x	x	x
Gabon											x		
Gambia	x	x	x	x	x	x	x	x	x	x	x	x	x
Ghana	x	x	x	x	x			x	x	x	x	x	
Guatemala	x	x	x	x	x		x	x	x	x	x	x	
Guinea	x	x	x	x	x	x	x	x	x	x	x	x	x
Haiti	x	x	x	x	x			x	x	x	x	x	x
Hungary	x		x	x						x	x	x	x
India	x	x	x	x	x	x		x	x	x	x	x	
Iraq	x	x	x	x	x			x	x	x	x	x	
Ireland	x	x	x	x	x	x	x	x	x	x	x	x	x
Ivory Coast	x	x	x	x	x	x	x	x	x	x	x	x	
Jamaica	x	x	x	x					x	x	x	x	
Japan	x	x	x	x	x	x	x	x	x	x	x	x	x
Jordan		x	x	x					x	x	x	x	
Kenya	x	x	x	x	x	x	x	x	x	x	x	x	x
Khmer Republic		x	x	x					x	x	x	x	
Kuwait	x	x	x	x	x	x	x	x	x	x	x	x	x
Laos	x	x	x	x	x	x		x	x	x	x	x	x
Lesotho	x	x	x	x	x	x	x	x	x	x	x	x	
Libyan Arab Republic	x	x	x	x	x			x	x		x	x	
Luxembourg	x	x	x	x	x			x	x	x	x	x	
Madagascar	x	x	x	x	x	x		x	x	x	x	x	x
Malawi	x	x	x	x	x	x	x	x	x	x	x	x	x
Malaysia	x	x	x	x					x	x	x	x	
Maldives				x						x	x		x
Mali	x	x	x	x	x			x	x	x	x	x	
Malta	x	x	x	x	x	x	x	x	x	x	x	x	x
Mauritius	x	x	x	x					x	x	x	x	x
Mongolia	x		x	x						x	x	x	
Morocco	x	x	x	x					x	x	x	x	
Nepal		x	x	x	x			x	x	x	x		
Netherlands	x	x	x	x	x	x	x	x	x	x	x	x	x
New Zealand	x	x	x	x					x	x	x	x	x
Nicaragua	x	x	x	x	x			x	x	x	x	x	
Niger	x	x	x	x	x		x	x	x	x	x	x	
Nigeria	x	x	x	x					x	x	x	x	x
Norway	x	x	x	x	x	x		x	x	x	x	x	x
Pakistan	x	x	x	x	x	x	x	x	x	x	x	x	x
Philippines	x	x	x	x	x	x		x	x			x	
Poland	x	x	x	x					x	x	x	x	x
Romania	x	x	x	x					x	x	x	x	
Rwanda	x	x	x	x	x		x	x	x	x	x	x	
Senegal	x	x	x	x	x	x	x	x	x	x	x	x	x
Sierra Leone	x	x	x	x					x	x	x	x	x
Singapore	x	x	x	x					x	x	x	x	
Sweden	x	x	x	x	x	x	x	x	x	x	x	x	x
Thailand	x	x	x	x	x	x		x	x	x	x	x	
Togo				x									
Trinidad and Tobago	x	x	x	x	x			x	x	x	x	x	x
Tunisia	x	x	x	x	x			x	x	x	x	x	
Ukrainian SSR	x		x							x	x	x	
USSR	x		x	x						x	x	x	x
United Kingdom	x	x	x	x					x	x	x	x	x
United Republic of Tanzania	x	x	x	x	x	x		x	x		x	x	
Upper Volta	x	x	x	x	x	x		x	x	x	x	x	x
Yugoslavia	x	x	x	x	x	x	x	x	x	x	x	x	x
Zaire	x	x	x	x	x	x	x	x	x	x	x	x	

*Abbreviations used in table above.

ILO	International Labour Organisation	IMF	International Monetary Fund
FAO	Food and Agriculture Organization of the United Nations	ICAO	International Civil Aviation Organization
UNESCO	United Nations Educational, Scientific and Cultural Organization	UPU	Universal Postal Union
WHO	World Health Organization	ITU	International Telecommunication Union
IBRD	International Bank for Reconstruction and Development	WMO	World Meteorological Organization
IFC	International Finance Corporation	IMCO	Inter-Governmental Maritime Consultative Organization
IDA	International Development Association		

Registration and publication of treaties and agreements

During 1971, a total of 728 treaties and agreements was registered with the United Nations Secretariat: 49 *ex officio*, 517 by 32 Governments and 162 by 10 specialized agencies and eight international organizations. In addition, three treaties were filed and recorded, two by the Secretariat and one by a specialized agency.

This brought the total number of treaties and agreements registered and filed and recorded as at 31 December 1971 to 16,986. In addition, 431 certified statements relating to these treaties and agreements were registered during 1971, bringing the total of certified statements registered or filed and recorded by the end of 1971 to 7,817.

The texts of treaties registered or filed and recorded are published by the Secretariat in the United Nations *Treaty Series* in the original languages, followed by translations in English and French.

New conventions concluded under United Nations auspices

The following conventions, of which the Secretary-General is the depositary, were drawn up under United Nations auspices and deposited with the Secretary-General during 1971:

Convention on Psychotropic Substances. Done at Vienna, Austria, on 21 February 1971;

European Agreement concerning the Work of Crews of Vehicles Engaged in International Road Transport (AETR), with annex and Protocol of Signature. Done at Geneva, Switzerland, on 1 July 1970 (deposited with the Secretary-General in 1971);

Agreement on the International Carriage of Perishable Foodstuffs and on the Special Equipment to be used for such Carriage (ATP), with annexes. Done at Geneva on 1 September 1970 (deposited with the Secretary-General in 1971);

Agreement establishing the Pepper Community. Opened for signature at Bangkok, Thailand, on 16 April 1971;

Convention for the Protection of Producers of Phonograms against Unauthorized Duplication of their Phonograms. Done at Geneva on 29 October 1971.

Status of multilateral conventions in 1971

The number of conventions for which the Secretary-General exercises depositary functions rose to 195 by the end of 1971.

During the year, 83 signatures, including one definitive signature, were affixed to conventions for which the Secretary-General exercises depositary functions, and 158 instruments of ratification, accession and acceptance or notifications were transmitted to the Secretary-General. In addition, the Secretary-General received 64 communications from States expressing observations on declarations and reservations made by certain States at the time of signature, ratification or accession.

No convention in respect of which the Secretary-General acts as depositary came into force during 1971.

DOCUMENTARY REFERENCES

Registration and publication of treaties and agreements

United Nations *Treaty Series*, Vols. 609, 631, 632, 637, 640, 643–655, 657–660, 662–666, 668, 669, 674, 761, 762. Issued in 1971, covering treaties registered or filed and recorded in 1967, 1968 and 1969.
Statement of Treaties and International Agreements Registered or Filed and Recorded with the Secretariat during 1971 (ST/LEG/SER.A/287-298). Issued monthly.

New conventions concluded under United Nations auspices

E/CONF.58/6. *Convention on Psychotropic Substances.* Done at Vienna, Austria, on 21 February 1971. (Circulated by Secretary-General in E/4966.)
E/ECE/810 (E/ECE/TRANS/563). *Agreement on the International Carriage of Perishable Foodstuffs and on the Special Equipment to be used for such Carriage (ATP), with annexes,* Done at Geneva, Switzerland, on 1 September 1970.

E/ECE/811 (E/ECE/TRANS/564). *European Agreement concerning the Work of Crews of Vehicles Engaged in International Road Transport (AETR), with annex and Protocol of Signature.* Done at Geneva, Switzerland, on 1 July 1970.

Status of multilateral conventions in 1971

Multilateral treaties in respect of which the Secretary-General Performs Depositary Functions. List of Signatures, Ratifications, Accessions, etc., as at 31 December 1971 (ST/LEG/SER.D/5). U.N.P. Sales No.: E.72.V.7.
Multilateral Treaties in respect of which the Secretary-General Performs Depositary Functions. Supplement No. 3. Annex: Final Clauses (ST/LEG/SER.D/1. Annex). U.N.P. Sales No.: E.72.V.8.

Other documents

A/8401. Report of Secretary-General on work of the Organization, 16 June 1970–15 June 1971, Part Four, Chapter IV I and J.

United Nations Juridical Yearbook, 1970. U.N.P. Sales No.: E.72.V.1.
National Legislation and Treaties relating to the Territorial Sea, the *Contiguous Zone, the Continental Shelf, the High Seas and to Fishing and Conservation of the Living Resources of the Sea (ST/LEG/SER.B/15).* U.N.P. Sales No.: E/F.70.V.9.

Chapter VII

Other legal questions

Procedures and organization of General Assembly

Work of Special Committee

At its 1970 session, the General Assembly established the Special Committee on the Rationalization of the Procedures and Organization of the General Assembly and instructed it to study ways and means of improving the procedures and organization of the Assembly, including the allocation of agenda items, the organization of work, documentation, rules of procedure, and related questions, methods and practices.[1]

The Special Committee held a total of 45 meetings during the periods 2 February to 9 July and 8 to 17 September 1971. It decided to hold closed meetings but to allow representatives of Member States not members of the Special Committee to attend the meetings and to elaborate on the written observations submitted by their Governments.

The Special Committee also decided to invite all former Presidents of the General Assembly and the Chairmen of the Main Committees for the twentieth to the twenty-fifth (1965–1970) sessions of the Assembly to submit in writing to the Committee, if they so desired, any views and suggestions they might wish to put forward with regard to the rationalization of the procedures and organization of the Assembly.

After a general debate, the Special Committee considered in detail the various suggestions that had been submitted to it. All decisions of the Committee were approved by consensus.

The Special Committee established two working groups to consider the following subjects: (*a*) General Committee and agenda; and (*b*) documentation. It also created three drafting groups entrusted with consideration of the following matters: (*a*) opening of meetings at the scheduled time and quorum; (*b*) limiting the length of speeches or number of speakers, explanations of vote, right of reply and points of order; and (*c*) congratulations and condolences.

The members of the Special Committee agreed that the existing rules of procedure were generally satisfactory and that most improvements would be achieved not through changes in the rules of procedure but through better application of those rules, due account being taken of the conclusions of the Special Committee and of the various committees responsible for reviewing the procedures and organization of the General Assembly. Therefore, although the Special Committee submitted to the General Assembly for its approval a number of amendments to the rules, most of its conclusions were presented in the form of recommendations.

The report of the Special Committee was submitted to the General Assembly at its 1971 session. The report gave an account of all the proposals presented to the Committee, stating in each case the arguments in favour, those against and the conclusions reached by the Committee. Two documents, "Statistical data on the General Assembly and the Main Committees" and "Analytical summary of views and suggestions submitted to the Special Committee," were appended to the report.

Also included in the Special Committee's report was a draft resolution for the General Assembly's approval, by which the Assembly would, among other things, adopt a number of amendments to its rules of procedure and approve the conclusions of

---

[1]See Y.U.N., 1970, p. 822, text of resolution 2632(XXV) of 9 November 1970.

the Special Committee which were not the subject of amendments to the rules.

The proposed amendments to the rules of procedure of the General Assembly were included as Annex I to the draft resolution; the conclusions reached by the Committee which were not the subject of amendments to the rules were included in Annex II.

Decisions of General Assembly

When the General Assembly took up the Committee's report at its 1971 session, it decided that the item as a whole would be discussed in plenary meetings, and it referred the section of the report dealing with documentation to its Fifth (Administrative and Budgetary) Committee (see page 661) and the section relating to amendments to the rules of procedure to its Sixth (Legal) Committee.

On 3 December 1971, the Sixth Committee considered the text of the proposed amendments contained in Annex I, as drafted by the Special Committee. After modifying, at the proposal of Colombia, the suggested amendments to rules 69 and 110 (dealing with quorums), the Committee approved without a vote the amendments and recommended to the General Assembly that it adopt them, as amended.

The General Assembly considered the report of the Special Committee and of the Sixth Committee at a plenary meeting of its twenty-sixth session held on 17 December 1971.

The Assembly approved, by 83 votes to 2, the modifications recommended by the Sixth Committee in the proposed amendments to rules 69 and 110, and, by 81 votes to 0, with 1 abstention, a drafting change subsequently proposed by Cameroon, Ecuador, Guyana, Jamaica, Kenya and Lebanon in the proposed new rule 112 (on congratulations); the drafting change applied only to the English and Russian texts.

The General Assembly then adopted without a vote, as resolution 2837(XXVI), the draft resolution which had been recommended by the Special Committee.

The Assembly thereby endorsed the view expressed by the Special Committee on the Rationalization of the Procedures and Organization of the General Assembly that the existing rules of procedure were generally satisfactory and that most improvements would be achieved not through changes in the rules of procedure but through their better application. It also expressed its consciousness of the need to discharge in the most efficient manner the functions incumbent upon it under the provisions of the United Nations Charter.

The Assembly then: (1) decided to amend its rules of procedure by incorporating therein the amendments set forth in Annex I to the resolution; (2) approved the conclusions of the Special Committee as they appeared in Annex II to the resolution; declared these conclusions useful and worthy of consideration by the Assembly, its committees and other relevant organs; and decided that they be reproduced as an annex to its rules of procedure; and (3) decided to review from time to time the progress achieved in rationalizing its work and requested the Secretary-General, as appropriate, to report on the extent to which the conclusions of the Special Committee had been reflected in the practice of the Assembly.

The major changes approved by the Assembly in its rules of procedure are summarized in the paragraphs below.

(1) Rule 60, entitled "Verbatim records," which no longer reflected the actual practice followed by the General Assembly and its committees, was thoroughly revised and given a new title, "Records and sound recordings of meetings."

(2) Rules 69 and 110, according to which a majority of the Members of the General Assembly and one third of the members of a committee constituted a quorum, were amended so as to allow the presiding officer to declare a meeting open and permit the debate to proceed when at least one third of the Members of the General Assembly or one quarter of the members of a committee were present. The presence of a majority of the members was still required for any decision to be taken either by the General Assembly or in the committees.

(3) Under rules 74 and 115, the General Assembly or a committee could limit the time to be allowed to each speaker and the number of times each representative could speak on any question. The amended text of these rules contained an additional provision whereby two representatives might speak in favour of, and two against, a proposal to set such limits. (Rule 115 became rule 116 with the renumbering of old rules 112 to 164; see below.)

(4) Rule 100, referring to priorities in the Main Committees, was renumbered as 101 and broadened in scope to deal with the general organization of work of the Main Committees, including such matters as the holding of elections, the adoption of a programme of work and the setting of target dates. (Rule 101 consequentially became rule 100.)

(5) Rule 105, which provided that each committee was to elect its own Chairman, Vice-Chairman and Rapporteur, was amended to stipulate that each Main Committee elect a Chairman, two Vice-Chairmen and a Rapporteur and that, in the case of other committees, each elect a Chairman, one or more Vice-Chairmen and a Rapporteur. Consequential amendments were made to rules 39 and 107.

(6) A new rule 112 was inserted and former rules 112 to 164 were renumbered accordingly (113 to 165). Under the new rule 112, congratulations to the officers of a Main Committee were not to be expressed except by the Chairman of the previous session—or, in his absence, by a member of his delegation—after all the officers of that Committee had been elected.

Among the recommendations submitted by the Special Committee and approved by the General Assembly—as contained in Annex II to resolution 2837 (XXVI)—several reaffirmed previous decisions of the Assembly or confirmed established practice; others reflected new ideas aimed at improving the procedures and organization of the Assembly.

Some of the innovations introduced by the General Assembly and incorporated into the resolution were as follows:

(1) The Secretary-General should communicate to Member States, by not later than 15 February, the unofficial list of items proposed for inclusion in the provisional agenda of the Assembly. (Under rule 12 of the rules of procedure, the provisional agenda was to be circulated at least 60 days before the opening of the session, i.e. approximately by mid-July.)

(2) The Secretary-General should also communicate to Member States, by not later than 15 June, an annotated list of the items proposed for inclusion in the provisional agenda, briefly indicating the history of each item, the available documentation, the substance of the matter to be discussed and earlier decisions by United Nations organs. An addendum to the annotated list should be circulated to Member States before the opening of the session.

(3) Member States requesting the inclusion of an agenda item should, if they deemed it advisable, make a suggestion concerning its referral to a Main Committee or to the plenary Assembly.

(4) The general debate in the plenary Assembly should take place intensively and without interruption; its length should not normally exceed two and a half weeks.

(5) The President of the General Assembly or the Chairman of a Main Committee should, soon after the beginning of the debate on an item, indicate a date for the closing of the list of speakers; he should endeavour to have the list closed at the latest after one third of the meetings allocated to the item had been held. In the case of the general debate in the plenary Assembly, the list of speakers should be closed at the end of the third day after the opening of the debate.

(6) The nomination of officers to the Main Committees should be limited to one statement for each candidate, after which the Committee would proceed to the election immediately.

(7) All the Main Committees, with the possible exception of the First Committee, should begin their work on the working day following the receipt of the list of items referred to them by the General Assembly.

(8) A comprehensive description of the concept of a point of order was adopted.

(9) In subsidiary organs of the General Assembly, congratulations to the Chairman should be expressed only by the temporary Chairman and congratulations to other officers should be expressed only by the Chairman.

(10) Condolences addressed to a delegation on the death of a prominent person or in the event of a disaster should be expressed solely by the President of the General Assembly, by the Chairman of a Main Committee or by the Chairman of a subsidiary organ on behalf of all members.

(11) All the subsidiary organs of the General Assembly should be required to complete their work and submit their reports before the opening of each regular session of the Assembly.

(12) The composition of subsidiary organs should be subject to periodic change.

(For the full text of resolution 2837(XXVI), including Annexes I and II, see DOCUMENTARY REFERENCES below.)

DOCUMENTARY REFERENCES

General Assembly—26th session
Sixth Committee, meeting 1299.
Fifth Committee, meetings 1469–1473, 1486.
Plenary meeting 2024.

Rules of Procedure of the General Assembly (embodying amendments and additions adopted by the General Assembly up to 31 December 1971) (A/520/Rev.11). U.N.P. Sales No.: E.72.I.13.
A/8319 and Corr.1. Pattern of conferences. Report of Joint Inspection Unit (JIU) on United Nations documentation and on organization of proceedings of General Assembly and its main bodies. Note by Secretary-General (transmitting JIU report).
A/8401. Report of Secretary-General on work of the Organization, 16 June 1970–15 June 1971, Part Four, Chapter IV G.

A/8401/Add.1. Introduction to report of Secretary-General, September 1971. Part One: para. 100; Part Two: paras. 313, 314.
A/8426. Report of Special Committee on Rationalization of Procedures and Organization of General Assembly. (Annex II: List of documents.)
A/8426. Report of Special Committee, Section IX (Documentation).
A/8426, Section XII, Annex I: Annex I of draft resolution recommended by Special Committee for adoption by General Assembly, as orally amended by Colombia (rules 69 and 110), approved without vote by Sixth Committee on 3 December 1971, meeting 1299.
A/8488. Pattern of conferences. Report of JIU on United Nations documentation and on organization of proceedings of General Assembly and its main bodies. Note by Advisory Committee on

Administrative and Budgetary Questions (ACABQ) (transmitting comments by Secretary-General on JIU report).

A/8532 and Corr.1,2. Publications and documentation of United Nations; pattern of conferences; rationalization of procedures and organization of General Assembly. Report of JIU on United Nations documentation and on organization of proceedings of General Assembly and its main bodies. Report of ACABQ.

A/8572. Report of Sixth Committee, para. 6.

A/8608. Report of Fifth Committee (part I), para. 6.

A/L.660. Cameroon, Ecuador, Guyana, Jamaica, Kenya, Lebanon: amendment to proposed new rule 112 recommended by Special Committee (A/8426, Section XII, Annex I, para. 9).

RESOLUTION 2837(XXVI), as recommended by Special Committee (A/8426, Section XII), adopted by Assembly on 17 December 1971, meeting 2024, as follows: Annex I, as amended by Sixth Committee (A/8572, para. 6, adopted by 83 votes to 2) and as further amended by 6 powers (A/L.660, adopted by 81 votes to 0, with 1 abstention); draft resolution as a whole, with Annexes, as amended, adopted without vote.

The General Assembly,

Recalling its resolution 2632(XXV) of 9 November 1970 on the rationalization of the procedures and organization of the General Assembly,

Having considered the report of the Special Committee on the Rationalization of the Procedures and Organization of the General Assembly,

Endorsing the view expressed by the Special Committee that the existing rules of procedure were generally satisfactory and that most improvements would be achieved not through changes in the rules of procedure but through their better application,

Conscious of the need to discharge in the most efficient manner the functions incumbent upon it under the Charter of the United Nations,

1. *Decides* to amend its rules of procedure by incorporating therein the modifications set forth in annex I to the present resolution;

2. *Approves* the conclusions of the Special Committee on the Rationalization of the Procedures and Organization of the General Assembly as they appear in annex II to the present resolution;

3. *Declares* the conclusions of the Special Committee to be useful and worthy of consideration by the General Assembly, its committees and other relevant organs;

4. *Decides* that the conclusions referred to in paragraph 2 above shall be reproduced as an annex to its rules of procedure;

5. *Further decides* to review from time to time the progress achieved in rationalizing its work and requests the Secretary-General, as appropriate, to report on the extent to which the conclusions of the Special Committee have been reflected in the practice of the General Assembly.

ANNEX I

Amendments to the rules of procedure of the General Assembly

1. Replace the present rule 39 by the following text [*para. 130 of the report of the Special Committee*]:

"If a Vice-President of the General Assembly finds it necessary to be absent during a meeting of the General Committee, he may designate a member of his delegation as his substitute. The Chairman of a Main Committee shall, in case of absence, designate one of the Vice-Chairmen of the Committee as his substitute. A Vice-Chairman shall not have the right to vote if he is of the same delegation as another member of the General Committee."

2. Replace the present rule 60 by the following text [*para. 308*]:

"*Records of meetings and sound recordings*

"(a) Verbatim records of the meetings of the General Assembly and of the Political and Security Committee (First Committee) shall be drawn up by the Secretariat and submitted to those organs after approval by the presiding officer. The General Assembly shall decide upon the form of the records of the meetings of the other Main Committees and, if any, of the subsidiary organs and of special meetings and conferences. No organ of the General Assembly shall have both verbatim and summary records.

"(b) Sound recordings of the meetings of the General Assembly and of the Main Committees shall be made by the Secretariat. Such recordings shall also be made of the proceedings of subsidiary organs and special meetings and conferences when they so decide."

3. Replace the present rule 69 by the following text [*para. 198*]:

"The President may declare a meeting open and permit the debate to proceed when at least one third of the members of the General Assembly are present. The presence of a majority of the members shall be required for any decision to be taken."

4. Replace the present rule 74 by the following text [*para. 210*]:

"The General Assembly may limit the time to be allowed to each speaker and the number of times each representative may speak on any question. Before a decision is taken, two representatives may speak in favour of, and two against, a proposal to set such limits. When the debate is limited and a representative has spoken his allotted time, the President shall call him to order without delay."

5. Replace the present rule 100 by the following text, to be inserted after the present rule 101 [*para. 175*]:

"*Organization of work*

"(a) All the Main Committees shall, during the first week of the session, hold the elections provided for in rule 105.

"(b) Each Main Committee, taking into account the closing date for the session fixed by the General Assembly on the recommendation of the General Committee, shall adopt its own priorities and meet as may be necessary to complete the consideration of the items referred to it. It shall at the beginning of the session adopt a programme of work indicating, if possible, a target date for the conclusion of its work, the approximate dates of consideration of items and the number of meetings to be allocated to each item."

The present rule 101 will become rule 100.

6. Replace the present rule 105 by the following text [*paras. 130 and 165*]:

"Each Main Committee shall elect a Chairman, two Vice-Chairmen and a Rapporteur. In the case of other committees, each shall elect a Chairman, one or more Vice-Chairmen and a Rapporteur. These officers shall be elected on the basis of equitable geographical distribution, experience and personal competence. The elections shall be held by secret ballot unless the committee decides otherwise in an election where only one candidate is standing. The nomination of each candidate shall be limited to one speaker, after which the committee shall proceed to the election immediately."

7. Replace the present rule 107 by the following text [*para. 130*]:

"If the Chairman finds it necessary to be absent during a meeting or any part thereof, he shall designate one of the Vice-Chairmen to take his place. A Vice-Chairman acting as Chairman shall have the same powers and duties as the Chairman. If any officer of the committee is unable to perform his functions, a new officer shall be elected for the unexpired term."

8. Replace the present rule 110 by the following text [*para. 198*]:

"The Chairman may declare a meeting open and permit the debate to proceed when at least one quarter of the members of the committee are present. The presence of a majority of the members shall be required for any decision to be taken."

9. Insert the following rule after the present rule 111 and renumber the present rules 112 to 164 accordingly [*para. 236*]:

"Congratulations to the officers of a Main Committee shall not be expressed except by the Chairman of the previous session—or, in his absence, by a member of his delegation—after all the officers of that committee have been elected."

10. Replace the present rule 115 by the following text [*para. 210*]:

"The committee may limit the time to be allowed to each speaker and the number of times each representative may speak on any question. Before a decision is taken, two representatives may speak in favour of, and two against, a proposal to set such limits. When the debate is limited and a representative has spoken his allotted time, the Chairman shall call him to order without delay."

As a result of the amendment in paragraph 9 above, rule 115 will become rule 116.

ANNEX II

Conclusions of the Special Committee on the Rationalization of the Procedures and Organization of the General Assembly

CONTENTS

I. MANDATE OF THE SPECIAL COMMITTEE

1. The members of the Special Committee agreed that the existing rules of procedure were generally satisfactory and that most improvements would be achieved not through changes in the rules of procedure but through better application of the existing rules, due account being taken of the conclusions of the Special Committee and of the various committees responsible for reviewing the procedures and organization of the General Assembly [para. 12 of the report of the Special Committee].

2. The Special Committee considered, moreover, that it would be desirable to review from time to time the procedures and organization of the General Assembly [para. 13].

II. GENERAL ORGANIZATION OF SESSIONS

A. Opening date

3. The Special Committee is of the opinion that it would not be desirable to change the date fixed for the opening of sessions [para. 18].

B. Duration of sessions

4. The Special Committee, noting that, despite the appreciable increase in the number of Member States, it has been possible to maintain an average duration of 13 weeks for regular sessions, is of the view that this period should not be changed and that, in any case, the session should end before Christmas [para. 22].

5. The Special Committee did not endorse the suggestion that the session should be divided into two parts. The Committee likewise did not endorse the suggestion that the session should theoretically last a whole year and should merely be adjourned after a two-month main session [para. 23].

C. Residuary sessions

6. The Special Committee did not endorse the suggestion that a brief meeting of the General Assembly, to be called a "residuary session," might be held at head-of-mission level about the end of April for the discussion of certain administrative and routine questions [para. 24].

III. GENERAL COMMITTEE

A. Composition of the General Committee

1. *Increase in membership*

7. The Special Committee decided not to take any action on the question of either maintaining or increasing the present membership of the General Committee [para. 31].

8. Furthermore, the Special Committee did not retain the suggestion that the Chairman of the Credentials Committee should be authorized to participate in the work of the General Committee [para. 32].

2. *Absence of members of the General Committee elected in their personal capacity*

9. The Special Committee considers that the problems which arise when the Chairman or Vice-Chairman of a Main Committee cannot attend a meeting of the General Committee would be settled for the most part if the General Assembly decided to increase the number of Vice-Chairmen of the Main Committees [para. 36].

10. The Special Committee also considers that, if the General Assembly took such a decision, the Chairman of a Main Committee, in designating a Vice-Chairman as his substitute, should take into account the representative character of the General Committee [para. 37].

B. Functions of the General Committee

1. *Importance of the role of the General Committee*

11. The Special Committee considers that the General Committee, in view of the functions conferred on it by the rules of procedure, should play a major role in advancing the rational organization and general conduct of the proceedings of the General Assembly. The Committee is of the opinion that the General Committee should discharge completely and effectively the functions assigned to it under rules 40, 41 and 42 of the rules of procedure the purpose of which is to assist the Assembly in the general conduct of its work [para. 41].

2. *Adoption of the agenda and allocation of items*

12. The Special Committee recommends that, within the framework of the functions conferred on it by the rules of procedure, and subject to the limitation prescribed in rule 40 as regards the discussion of the substance of an item, the General Committee should examine the provisional agenda, together with the supplementary list and requests for the inclusion of additional items, more attentively and carry out more fully and consistently its functions of recommending with regard to each item its inclusion in the agenda, the rejection of the request for inclusion or its inclusion in the provisional agenda of a future session, as well as of allocating items to the Main Committees regard being had to rules 99 and 101 of the rules of procedure, with a view to ensuring that all items inscribed on the agenda can be taken up by the end of the session [para. 45].

3. *Organization of the work of the General Assembly*

13. The Special Committee recalls the recommendation, in subparagraph *(f)* of General Assembly resolution 1898(XVIII), that the General Committee should meet at least once every three weeks. The Special Committee notes that the recommendation has not been complied with and expresses the hope that the General Committee will be able to hold more frequent meetings, in conformity with rule 42 of the rules of procedure, without thereby interfering with the normal meeting schedule of the plenary and the Main Committees [para. 49].

14. The Special Committee also considers that, in the discharge of the functions conferred by rules 41 and 42 of the rules of procedure and subject to the limitation prescribed in rule 41 regarding the decision of any political question, the General Committee should review the progress of the General Assembly and the Main Committees and should, as required, assist and make recommendations to the President and the Assembly for the co-ordination of the proceedings of the Main Committees and for expediting the general conduct of business [para. 50].

C. Ways of facilitating the work of the
General Committee

1. *Preparatory meetings*

15. The Special Committee does not consider that it is in a position to make any recommendation with regard to the holding of preparatory meetings of the General Committee [para. 54].

2. *Subsidiary organs*

16. The Special Committee does not consider that it is in a position to make any recommendation with regard to the establishment of subsidiary organs of the General Committee [para. 58].

IV. AGENDA

A. Presentation and preliminary consideration of the provisional agenda

17. The Special Committee, aware of the need to assist delegations, to the greatest extent possible, to prepare for the work of the General Assembly, recommends to the Assembly that the Secretary-General should be requested:

(a) To communicate to Member States, not later than 15 February, the unofficial list of items proposed for inclusion in the provisional agenda of the Assembly;

(b) To communicate to Member States, not later than 15 June, an annotated list of items which would indicate briefly the history of each item, the available documentation, the substance of the matter to be discussed and earlier decisions by United Nations organs;

(c) To communicate to Member States before the opening of the session an addendum to the annotated list [para. 64].

18. Furthermore, the Special Committee recommends that Member States requesting the inclusion of an item should, if they deem it advisable, make a suggestion concerning its referral to a Main Committee or to the plenary Assembly [para. 65].

B. Reduction in the number of agenda items

1. *Non-inclusion of certain items*

19. The Special Committee, considering that the General Assembly should take into account the relative importance of agenda items in the light of the purposes and principles of the Charter of the United Nations, recommends to the Assembly that, in the context of rules 22 and 40 of the rules of procedure, Member States should take special interest in the contents of the Assembly's agenda and, in particular, in deciding on the appropriate solution of questions or on the elimination of items which have lost their urgency or relevance, are not ripe for consideration or could be dealt with and even disposed of equally well by subsidiary organs of the General Assembly [para. 70].

2. *Staggering of items over two or more years and grouping of related items*

20. The Special Committee considers that the staggering of items over two or more years constitutes one means of rationalizing the procedures of the General Assembly [para. 74].

21. Moreover, the Special Committee recommends to the General Assembly that, as far as possible and appropriate, related items should be grouped under the same title [para. 75].

3. *Referral to other organs*

22. The Special Committee recommends that the General Assembly should, where relevant, refer specific items to other United Nations organs or to specialized agencies, taking into account the nature of the question [para. 79].

23. The Special Committee also recommends that the General Assembly should give due weight to the debates that have taken place in other organs [para. 80].

4. *Non-receivability of certain additional items*

24. The Special Committee recommends to the General Assembly that additional items, which are proposed for inclusion in the agenda less than 30 days before the opening of a session, should be included only if the conditions prescribed by rule 15 of the rules of procedure are fully satisfied [para. 84].

C. Allocation of agenda items

1. *Division of work among the Main Committees*

25. The Special Committee wishes to draw attention to the importance of a rational distribution of agenda items among the Main Committees. In this connexion, the Committee, recognizing that the structure of the Main Committees gives them specialization and experience, recommends that the allocation of agenda items should be based not only on the workload of the Committees but also on the nature of the item, regard being had to rules 99 and 101 of the rules of procedure [para. 89].

26. The Special Committee also considers that it would be helpful if suggestions concerning the allocation of items were made much earlier so that Member States might have more time to study them [para. 90].

27. Lastly, the Special Committee recommends that the General Committee and the General Assembly should consider, in some cases, the possibility of referring more items directly to the plenary [para. 91].

2. *Non-referral of certain items to two or more Committees*

28. The Special Committee recommends to the General Assembly that agenda items should be so allocated as to ensure, as far as possible, that the same questions or the same aspects of a question are not considered by more than one Committee [para. 95].

V. ORGANIZATION OF THE WORK OF THE MAIN COMMITTEES

A. Functions of the individual Committees

29. There was general agreement among the members of the Special Committee that a flexible approach should be adopted towards the whole question of the division of work among the Main Committees and that the Committee should not make any recommendation concerning the referral of specific items, in order not to go beyond its field of competence [para. 97].

30. The Special Committee, considering that the potential of the seven Main Committees should be utilized to the full, recommends that the General Assembly should ensure a more balanced division of work among the Committees, giving due account to the nature of items. The Committee does not, however, feel that it should specify which items might be transferred from one Committee to another [para. 98].

31. The Special Committee, recognizing that the workload of a number of Committees is extremely heavy, is of the opinion that the General Assembly should advise those Committees so to organize their work as to enable them to consider their agenda in the most effective way [para. 99].

1. *First Committee*

32. The Special Committee, recognizing that the role of the First Committee is essentially political, recommends that this Committee devote itself primarily to problems of peace, security and disarmament [para. 103].

33. The Special Committee, not wishing to make any specific recommendation concerning the allocation of agenda items, did not feel that it should take any decision on the proposal that the reports of the International Atomic Energy Agency and the United Nations Scientific Committee on the Effects of Atomic Radiation should be submitted to the First Committee [para. 104].

2. *Special Political Committee*

34. The Special Committee, reaffirming the major role which must be played by the Special Political Committee and recognizing further that the agenda of that Committee is relatively light, recommends that the General Assembly should consider transferring to the Special Political Committee one or two items usually

considered by other Committees with a view to ensuring a better division of work among the Main Committees [para. 108].

35.   The Special Committee did not endorse the suggestions concerning the renaming of the Special Political Committee [para. 109].

3. *Second Committee*

36.   The Special Committee did not feel that it should take any decision on the proposals that all the social aspects of development should be dealt with by the Second Committee. Accordingly, it did not endorse the suggestion to change the name of that Committee [para. 113].

4. *Third Committee*

37.   The Special Committee did not feel it should take a decision on the proposal that some of the items on the agenda of the Third Committee should be transferred to other Main Committees [para. 117].

5. *Conflicts of competence among Committees*

38.   The Special Committee considers that conflicts of competence among the Main Committees should be avoided whenever possible. Without prejudging the decision to be taken in each individual case, the Committee wishes to draw attention to the existence of this problem and to the advisability for the General Committee and the General Assembly to consider the most effective ways of remedying it [para. 119].

B. Role of the presiding officers

39.   The Special Committee recommends to the General Assembly that the Chairmen of the Main Committees should fully exercise the functions assigned to them in the rules of procedure and, in particular, make use of the prerogatives given them in rule 108 [para. 123].

40.   The Special Committee also reaffirms that the Chairmen of the Main Committees should be elected on the basis of equitable geographical distribution as well as on that of experience and competence, as provided for in rule 105 of the rules of procedure [para. 124].

41.   The Special Committee did not endorse the suggestion that candidates should have had at least one year's experience in one of the Main Committees or the suggestion that Chairmen should be elected at the end of the previous session [para. 125].

C. Number of Vice-Chairmen[a]

42.   From its own experience, the Special Committee recommends to the General Assembly that its subsidiary organs should consider, as far as possible, the designation of three Vice-Chairmen in order to ensure the representative character of their officers [para. 131].

D. Reports of the Committees

43.   The Special Committee, recalling General Assembly resolution 2292(XXII), recommends to the Assembly that the reports of the Main Committees should be as concise as possible and, save in exceptional cases, should not contain a summary of the debates [para. 133].[b]

VI. MAXIMUM UTILIZATION OF AVAILABLE TIME

A. Plenary Assembly

1. *General debate*

(a) *Frequency*

44.   The Special Committee, recognizing the unquestionable value of the general debate, considers that it should continue to be held every year and that the time devoted to it should be utilized to the maximum. It wishes to stress also the importance of participation by heads of State or Government, Ministers for Foreign Affairs and other high officials as a means of enhancing the significance of the general debate [para. 137].

(b) *Organization of meetings*
(i) *Length of the general debate*
45.   The Special Committee feels that the general debate

would be more meaningful, as far as organization was concerned, if it took place intensively and without interruption. Its length should not normally exceed two and a half weeks if the time available were utilized to the maximum [para. 142].

(ii) *Closure of the list of speakers*
46.   Considering that the organization of the general debate would be improved if delegations were required to decide more quickly when to speak, the Special Committee recommends to the General Assembly that the list of speakers wishing to take part in the general debate should be closed at the end of the third day after the opening of the debate [para. 144].

(c) *Length of statements*
47.   The Special Committee, noting that during the session commemorating the twenty-fifth anniversary of the United Nations it had been possible to hear a large number of speakers during a relatively short period without limiting the duration of statements, considers that this result was due to a better utilization of the time available and not to the imposition of a limitation on the length of speeches [para. 147].

48.   The Committee notes that during recent sessions of the General Assembly the average length of speeches has been 35 minutes and expresses the hope that delegations will ensure that their statements will not be excessively long [para. 148].

(d) *Submission of written statements*
49.   The Special Committee considers that the submission of written statements should not be formally instituted with regard to the general debate [para. 152].

2. *Debate on items already considered in Committee*
50.   The Special Committee is of the opinion that rule 68 of the rules of procedure has been applied judiciously and with satisfactory results [para. 155].

3. *Non-utilization of the rostrum*
51.   The Special Committee thinks that it would be useful to draw the attention of representatives to the possibility of speaking without going to the rostrum. It considers, however, that in all cases it is for representatives to decide whether they prefer to speak from their seats or from the rostrum, whether on a point of order, for an explanation of vote or in exercise of their right of reply [para. 157].

4. *Presentation of the reports of the Main Committees*
52.   The Special Committee wishes to recall the recommendation made in 1947 by the Committee on Procedures and Organization of the General Assembly that Rapporteurs should not read out their reports in plenary meetings. It wishes to stress that the presentation of reports in plenary meetings should be limited to brief introductory statements [para. 158].

53.   The Special Committee recommends also that the General Assembly should confirm the practice whereby certain related reports of a non-controversial nature may be introduced simultaneously to the plenary Assembly by the Rapporteur [para. 159].

B. Main Committees

1. *Nomination of officers*
54.   The members of the Special Committee agreed that the nomination of candidates involved a significant loss of time. They also recognized that the terms of rule 105 of the rules of procedure, which provided that elections should be held by secret ballot, no longer corresponded to the present practice, since in most cases, as a result of prior consultations, there was only one candidate for each post and voting by secret ballot was therefore superfluous [para. 161].

---

[a]For the number of Vice-Chairmen of the Main Committees, see annex I, para. 6, above.

[b]For the recommendations concerning the reports of subsidiary organs, see para. 107 below.

55. The Special Committee, bearing in mind particularly the financial implications of such a procedure, did not retain the suggestion that nominations should be made in writing [para. 162].

56. Furthermore, in view of the dictates of courtesy and the possibility that cases might arise in which nominees would not be known until the last moment, the Special Committee did not deem it advisable to dispense completely with the oral nomination of candidates [para. 163].

57. The Special Committee considers that the nomination of candidates should be limited to one statement for each candidate, after which the Committee would proceed to the election immediately. The Special Committee considers, however, that the general principle that elections are held by secret ballot should be retained [para. 164].c

2. *Commencement of work*d

58. The Special Committee recommends that all the Main Committees, with the possible exception of the First Committee, should begin their work on the working day following the receipt of the list of items referred to them by the General Assembly [para. 170].

59. The Special Committee also recommends that the First Committee should be ready to meet whenever no plenary meeting of the Assembly is being held [para. 171].

3. *Progress of work*e

60. The Special Committee recommends that the Main Committees should from time to time review the progress of their work [para. 176].

4. *General debate in Committee*

61. The Special Committee, while recognizing the unquestionable usefulness and importance of the general debate, considers that Chairmen should encourage the Main Committees:

(a) To recognize the advisability of shortening the general debate, whenever that is possible without detriment to the work of the Committees;

(b) To extend, whenever appropriate, the practice of holding a single debate on related and logically linked agenda items [para. 180].

62. The Special Committee recognizes that a general debate on questions previously considered by a United Nations organ and covered by a report of the organ concerned should be retained. The Committee, however, draws the attention of the Chairmen of the Main Committees to the possibility of consulting their Committees in every case when a general debate on a certain item does not seem to be needed. The Chairmen may resort to this practice to ascertain in particular whether the Committees desire to hold a general debate on every question referred to them by other organs [para. 181].

63. At the same time, the Special Committee wishes to reaffirm that the general debate serves a necessary and very useful purpose in the work of the Main Committees and that its organization should in no circumstances be changed without the consent of the Committees concerned, which therefore should decide on the applicability of the above-mentioned suggestions [para. 182].

64. The Special Committee did not deem it appropriate to make a recommendation concerning the suggestion that delegations sharing the same point of view could use a spokesman who would express those views in a single statement. Nor did the Committee retain the suggestion that the consideration of certain items already debated in previous sessions might be introduced by specially appointed rapporteurs who would summarize the main issues emerging from previous debates [para. 183].

5. *Concurrent consideration of several agenda items*

65. The Special Committee considers that in certain cases, when a Main Committee cannot proceed with its discussion of one item, it should be prepared to begin considering the next item on its agenda [para. 187].

6. *Establishment of sub- committees or working groups*

66. The Special Committee wishes to remind the General Assembly of the desirability of the Main Committees' making use of sub-committees or working groups [para. 188].

C. Measures applicable both to the plenary Assembly and to the Main Committees

1. *Opening of meetings at the scheduled time*

67. The members of the Special Committee agreed that the General Assembly would operate much more efficiently if the presiding officers made a special effort to open meetings at the scheduled time [para. 190].f

68. The Special Committee did not endorse the suggestion to have meetings begin at 9.30 a.m. and 2.30 p.m. in view of the practical difficulties that such a measure would entail [para. 192].

2. *List of speakers*

69. The Special Committee recommends to the General Assembly that the President of the Assembly or the Chairman of a Main Committee should, soon after the beginning of the debate on an item, indicate a date for the closing of the list of speakers. He should endeavour to have the list of speakers closed at the latest after one third of the meetings allocated to the item have been held [para. 202].

70. Moreover, the Special Committee considers that speakers should, as far as possible, avoid putting down their names to speak on a given item and at the same time indicating an alternative meeting if they are unable to keep to their original schedule [para. 203].

71. Finally, the Special Committee wishes to reaffirm the practice whereby presiding officers should invite representatives to speak in the order of their inscription on the list of speakers, on the understanding that those prevented from doing so should normally be moved to the end of the list, unless they have arranged to change places with other representatives [para. 204].

3. *Limiting the length of speeches or number of speakers*

72. The Committee wishes to stress that the amendment on this subject9 is of a purely technical nature, its only purpose being to limit the number of representatives who could speak on a proposal submitted under rules 74 and 115h of the rules of procedure [para. 210].

73. With regard to the general question of setting a time-limit on interventions, the Special Committee, while recognizing that, in so far as possible, statements should be kept brief so as to allow all delegations to present the views of their Governments, considers that no rigid rule on the question could be applied [para. 211].

4. *Explanations of vote*

74. The Special Committee considers that, in explaining their votes, delegations should limit their statements to an explanation, as brief as possible, of their own votes and should not use the occasion to reopen the debate [para. 216].

75. The Special Committee also considers that presiding officers should be encouraged to use, whenever they deem it appropriate, their powers under rules 90 and 129i of the rules of procedure [para. 217].

76. Finally, the Special Committee recommends to the General Assembly that a delegation should explain its vote only once on the same proposal, in either a Main Committee or a plenary meeting, unless the delegation considers it essential to explain it in both meetings. It recommends further that the sponsor of a draft resolution adopted by a Main Committee should refrain

---

cFor the relevant amendment to the rules of procedure, see annex I, para. 6, above.

dFor the election of officers of the Committees, see annex I, para. 5 (a), above.

eFor the programme of work, see annex I, para. 5 (b), above.

fFor the quorum, see annex I, paras. 3 and 8, above.

9For the relevant amendment to the rules of procedure, see annex I, paras. 4 and 10, above.

hNow rule 116 (see annex I, para. 9, above).

iNow rule 130.

from explaining its vote during the consideration of that draft resolution in the plenary unless it deems it essential to do so [para. 218].

5. *Right of reply*

77. The Special Committee recommends to the General Assembly that delegations should use restraint in the exercise of their right of reply, both in plenary meetings and in the Main Committees, and that their statements in exercise of that right should be as brief as possible [para. 223].

78. The Special Committee recommends, furthermore, that statements made in the exercise of the right of reply should be delivered, as a general rule, at the end of meetings [para. 224].

6. *Points of order*

79. The Special Committee recommends to the General Assembly the adoption of the following text as a description of the concept of a point of order [para. 229]:

"*(a)* A point of order is basically an intervention directed to the presiding officer, requesting him to make use of some power inherent in his office or specifically given him under the rules of procedure. It may, for example, relate to the manner in which the debate is conducted, to the maintenance of order, to the observance of the rules of procedure or to the way in which presiding officers exercise the powers conferred upon them by the rules. Under a point of order, a representative may request the presiding officer to apply a certain rule of procedure or he may question the way in which the officer applies the rule. Thus, within the scope of the rules of procedure, representatives are enabled to direct the attention of the presiding officer to violations or misapplications of the rules by other representatives or by the presiding officer himself. A point of order has precedence over any other matter, including procedural motions (rules 73 [114^j] and 79 [120^k]).

"*(b)* Points of order raised under rule 73 [114^j] involved questions necessitating a ruling by the presiding officer, subject to possible appeal. They are therefore distinct from the procedural motions provided for in rules 76 [117^l] to 79 [120^k], which can be decided only by a vote and on which more than one motion may be entertained at the same time, rule 79 [120^k] laying down the precedence of such motions. They are also distinct from requests for information or clarification, or from remarks relating to material arrangements (seating, interpretation system, temperature of the room), documents, translations etc., which—while they may have to be dealt with by the presiding officer—do not require rulings from him. However, in established United Nations practice, a representative intending to submit a procedural motion or to seek information or clarification often rises to 'a point of order' as a means of obtaining the floor. The latter usage, which is based on practical grounds, should not be confused with the raising of points of order under rule 73 [114^j].

"*(c)* Under rule 73 [114^j], a point of order must be immediately decided by the presiding officer in accordance with the rules of procedure; any appeal arising therefrom must also be put immediately to the vote. It follows that as a general rule:

"(i) A point of order and any appeal arising from a ruling thereon is not debatable;

"(ii) No point of order on the same or a different subject can be permitted until the initial point of order and any appeal arising therefrom have been disposed of.

"Nevertheless, both the presiding officer and delegations may request information or clarification regarding a point of order. In addition, the presiding officer may, if he considers it necessary, request an expression of views from delegations on a point of order before giving his ruling; in the exceptional cases in which this practice is resorted to, the presiding officer should terminate the exchange of views and give his ruling as soon as he is ready to announce that ruling.

"*(d)* Rule 73 [114^j] provides that a representative rising to a point of order may not speak on the substance of the matter under discussion. Consequently, the purely procedural nature of points of order calls for brevity. The presiding officer is responsible for ensuring that statements made on a point of order are in conformity with the present description."

7. *Congratulations*

80. The Special Committee is of the opinion that it would be better to retain the current practice of the plenary Assembly whereby congratulations to the President are confined to brief remarks included in the speeches made during the general debate [para. 235].

81. With regard to subsidiary organs of the General Assembly, the Special Committee recommends that, in the case of a newly established organ or of the rotation of officers on an existing one, congratulations to the Chairman should be expressed only by the temporary Chairman and congratulations to other officers should be expressed only by the Chairman [para. 237].^{m}

8. *Condolences*

82. The Special Committee recommends to the General Assembly that condolences addressed to a delegation on the death of a prominent person or in the event of a disaster should be expressed solely by the President of the General Assembly, by the Chairman of a Main Committee or by the Chairman of a subsidiary organ on behalf of all members. Where circumstances warrant it, the President of the General Assembly might call a special plenary meeting for that purpose [para. 242].

83. The Special Committee moreover takes note of the practice whereby the President of the General Assembly, on behalf of all members, dispatches a cable to the country concerned [para. 243].

9. *Roll-call votes*

84. The Special Committee, while believing that there is no need to change the rules of procedure relating to roll-call votes, recommends that delegations should endeavour not to request such a vote except when there are good and sound reasons for doing so [para. 247].

10. *Electronic devices*

85. The Special Committee did not believe that it should express any views on the possible use of an electronic voting system by all Committees, since the question of the installation of mechanical means of voting was included in the draft agenda of the twenty-sixth session of the General Assembly [para. 249].

86. The Special Committee did not retain the suggestion that a mechanical or electronic timing device might be installed in the General Assembly Hall and the Main Committee rooms [para. 250].

VII. RESOLUTIONS

A. Submission of draft resolutions

1. *Date of submission of draft resolutions*

87. The Special Committee recommends to the General Assembly that draft resolutions should be submitted as early as possible so as to give debates a more concrete character. It considers, however, that no rigid rule should be established in the matter, since it is for delegations to determine, in each case, the most appropriate moment for submitting draft resolutions [para. 254].

88. So as to ensure that debates take shape as quickly as possible without making it mandatory for delegations to submit a formal draft resolution, the Special Committee also considers that delegations might resort more often to the possibility of circulating draft resolutions as informal working papers which would provide a basis for the discussion but whose contents would be strictly provisional [para. 255].

---

^{j}Now rule 115.
^{k}Now rule 121.
^{l}Now rule 118.
^{m}For congratulations in the Main Committees, see annex I, para. 9, above.

2. *Submission of draft resolutions in writing*

89. Because of the appreciable loss of time that such a procedure could entail, the Special Committee decided not to endorse the suggestion that proposals and amendments should be submitted in writing only [para. 256].

3. *Consultations*

90. The Special Committee, recognizing the indisputable value of consultations, believes that delegations should explore every avenue for arriving at negotiated texts. It considers, however, that the initiative for such consultations must rest solely with the delegations concerned and can, under no circumstances, be dictated in mandatory provisions [para. 258].

91. The Special Committee also believes that the Chairmen of the Main Committees should be invited to bear in mind the possibility of establishing, where necessary, working groups for the purpose of facilitating the adoption of agreed texts. Such groups may be open, as appropriate, to interested delegations. It does not, however, consider it advisable to contemplate the establishment of such working groups whenever two or more draft resolutions have been introduced on the same matter [para. 259].

4. *Number of sponsors*

92. The Special Committee did not endorse the suggestion that the number of sponsors of a draft resolution should be limited [para. 260].

93. The Special Committee does, however, wish to draw attention to the practice whereby the sponsors of a proposal decide whether other delegations can become co-sponsors [para. 261].

5. *Time-lapse between the submission and the consideration of draft resolutions*

94. The Special Committee, while recognizing the difficulties experienced by some delegations in consulting their Governments within the time laid down by rules 80 and 121[n] of the rules of procedure, does not deem it advisable to propose an amendment to those rules [para. 265].

B. Content of resolutions

95. The Special Committee is of the opinion that the wording of resolutions, to be effective, must be as clear and succinct as possible. It recognizes, however, that only the delegations concerned can decide upon the content of the proposals which they are sponsoring [para. 267].

96. The Special Committee also wishes to emphasize that the text of a draft resolution should not go beyond the competence of the Committee in which it is submitted. Where, however, it is suggested that a draft resolution does so, the Special Committee feels that it is up to the Committee concerned to take a decision in the matter [para. 268].

C. Financial implications

1. *Financial controls*

97. The Special Committee feels that the provisions of rules 154[o] and 155[p] of the rules of procedure are satisfactory and should be strictly applied [para. 272].

98. The Special Committee is also of the opinion that the financial implications of draft resolutions should be viewed in terms of an over-all assessment of priorities and that the principal organs should give careful consideration to the draft resolutions adopted by their subsidiary organs where such drafts call for the appropriation of funds [para. 273].

2. *Work of the Advisory Committee on Administrative and Budgetary Questions*

99. The Special Committee recognizes that the Advisory Committee on Administrative and Budgetary Questions should meet more frequently, but does not consider itself qualified to make detailed recommendations on the matter [para. 275].

3. *Resolutions setting up new organs*

100. While acknowledging that new organs should be set up only after mature consideration, the Special Committee believes that it would be inadvisable to amend the rules of procedure and lay down hard and fast rules in the matter [para. 277].

D. Voting procedure

1. *Required majority*

101. The Special Committee considers that rules 88 and 127[q] of the rules of procedure should be left unchanged [para. 282].

102. The Special Committee also considers that the suggestion referred to in paragraph 279 of the report is unacceptable and, moreover, goes beyond its mandate [para. 283].

2. *Measures to accelerate procedures*

103. The Special Committee, recalling the recommendations which it has made elsewhere concerning debate on items already considered in Committee (see para. 50 above) and roll-call votes (see para. 84 above), feels that it is inadvisable to make any changes in the relevant provisions of the rules of procedure [para. 287].

3. *Consensus*

104. The Special Committee considers that the adoption of decisions and resolutions by consensus is desirable when it contributes to the effective and lasting settlement of differences, thus strengthening the authority of the United Nations. It wishes, however, to emphasize that the right of every Member State to set forth its views in full must not be prejudiced by this procedure [para. 289].

E. Reduction in the number of resolutions

105. The Special Committee did not endorse the suggestions aimed at reducing the number of resolutions adopted by the General Assembly [para. 293].

VIII. DOCUMENTATION

A. Reduction in the volume of documentation

106. The Special Committee recommends that the General Assembly should:

(a) Draw attention to the provisions of its resolutions 2292(XXII) and 2538(XXIV) summarized in document A/INF/136, and stress the need for strict adherence to them, not only in letter, but also in spirit, by Member States and also, in the light of its internal rules, by the Secretariat;

(b) Instruct its subsidiary organs to include in the agenda of each session an item on the control and limitation of the documentation of the organ itself in the spirit of paragraph 3 of General Assembly resolution 1272(XIII) [para. 300].

B. Preparation and distribution of documents

107. The Special Committee recommends to the General Assembly that:

(a) Timely distribution of documents in all working languages should be scrupulously observed;

(b) All the subsidiary organs of the General Assembly should be required to complete their work and submit their reports before the opening of each regular session of the Assembly;

(c) Reports to be considered by the General Assembly should be as brief as possible and contain precise information confined to a description of the work done by the organ concerned, to the conclusions it has reached, to its decisions and to the recommendations made to the Assembly; the reports should include, where appropriate, a summary of proposals, conclusions

[n]Now rule 122.
[o]Now rule 155.
[p]Now rule 156.
[q]Now rule 128.

and recommendations. As a rule, no previously issued material (working papers and other basic documents) should be incorporated in or appended to such reports, but, where necessary, referred to;

(d) Taking into account the needs of Member States, the number of copies of reports and other United Nations documents should, whenever appropriate, be limited, i.e., they should be issued in the /L. series [para. 304].[r]

C. Records of meetings and sound recordings

108. The Special Committee recommends that rule 60, as revised,[s] should be applied in accordance with the following observations:

(a) Summary records should continue to be provided for the General Committee and for all Main Committees other than the First Committee;

(b) The General Assembly, on the recommendation of the General Committee, should decide annually whether the option that has traditionally been approved for the Special Political Committee to have, on specific request, transcriptions of the debates of some of its meetings, or portions thereof, should be maintained;

(c) The provision of summary records to subsidiary organs should be reviewed periodically by the General Assembly in the light of the report of the Joint Inspection Unit on the use of minutes instead of summary records, and of the comments of the Secretary-General and the Advisory Committee on Administrative and Budgetary Questions thereon;

(d) Sound recordings should be kept by the Secretariat in accordance with its practice [para. 309].

IX. SUBSIDIARY ORGANS OF THE GENERAL ASSEMBLY

A. Reduction of the number of organs

109. The Special Committee recommends that the General Assembly should review, either periodically or when considering their reports, the usefulness of its various subsidiary organs [para. 313].

110. The Special Committee also recommends that the General Assembly should consider the possibility of merging some of these organs [para. 314].

B. Composition of organs

111. The Special Committee considers that membership of a body depends on the nature and function of that body and that it cannot, therefore, be subject to any general rule [para. 318].

112. The Special Committee is of the opinion that subsidiary organs of the General Assembly should, where appropriate, have the authority to invite a Member State which is not a member of the organ concerned to participate without vote in the discussion of a matter which the organ considers to be of particular interest to that Member State [para. 319].

113. The Special Committee is also of the opinion that the composition of subsidiary organs should be subject to periodic change [para. 320].

114. Finally, the Special Committee considers that visits of subsidiary organs away from their normal meeting places should be authorized by the General Assembly only when the nature of the work renders such visits essential [para. 321].

C. Calendar of meetings

115. The Special Committee recommends to the General Assembly that the Secretary-General should play a greater role in drawing up the calendar of meetings, it being understood that in every case the final decision rests with the organ concerned [para. 323].

X. OTHER QUESTIONS

A. Credentials of delegations

116. The Special Committee, while aware of the problems posed by the non-recognition by the General Assembly of a

delegation's credentials, feels that it is not in a position to make any proposal on the matter [para. 327].

B. Role of the Secretary-General

117. The Special Committee is of the opinion that the Secretary-General should play an active role in making suggestions with regard to the organization of sessions, it being understood that the final decision on the recommendations he makes lies with the General Assembly [para. 331].

C. Secretariat

118. The Special Committee considers that the question of the reorganization of the Secretariat, however valid it might be, does not come within its terms of reference. It is of the opinion, therefore, that it should not make any recommendation on the matter [para. 333].

D. Guidance regarding General Assembly procedure and assistance to presiding officers

1. Preparation of a manual on procedure

119. The Special Committee recommends that the General Assembly should consider requesting the Secretary-General to prepare a systematic and comprehensive compilation of the conclusions which the Assembly may adopt on the basis of the reports of the Special Committee and of the Joint Inspection Unit, this compilation to form an annex to the rules of procedure of the General Assembly [para. 339].

2. Repertory of Practice of United Nations Organs

120. The Special Committee, recognizing the usefulness of the *Repertory of Practice of United Nations Organs*, expresses the hope that it will be brought up to date as quickly as possible [para. 341].

3. Preparation of a repertory of practice on the rules of procedure of the General Assembly

121. The Special Committee did not consider that it should endorse the proposal to issue a repertory of practice on the rules of procedure of the General Assembly [para. 344].

4. Reminders of previous recommendations

122. It was suggested that at the beginning of the session the President of the General Assembly should remind the Assembly of, and particularly invite the attention of the Chairmen of Main Committees to, the recommendations for improving the methods of work which were specifically approved in General Assembly resolution 1898(XVIII). While there was general agreement on the principle underlying that suggestion, the Special Committee did not feel that it need make any specific recommendation in that regard [paras. 345 and 346].

123. The Special Committee did not retain the suggestion that the report of the *Ad Hoc* Committee on the Improvement of the Methods of Work of the General Assembly should be reissued on account of the financial implications that such a measure would entail [paras. 345 and 346].

5. Assistance in procedural matters

124. The Special Committee noted that it was not possible to assign a member of the Office of Legal Affairs continuously to each of the Main Committees but that legal advice was always furnished, either orally or in writing, when requested [para. 348].

125. The Special Committee did not consider that it should make any recommendation on the proposal that the President of the General Assembly and the Chairmen of Main Committees

---

[r]For the recommendations concerning the reports of the Main Committees, see para. 43 above.

[s]See annex I, para. 2, above.

should enlist several assistants under them, both from the Secretariat and, wherever possible, from the delegations themselves, to whom they would allocate items on the agenda for the purpose of closely following them up with the delegations directly concerned and expediting the progress of the General Assembly [paras. 347 and 348].

E. Studies of the rules of procedure

126. The Special Committee did not consider that it should retain the suggestions concerning the insertion in the rules of procedure of the General Assembly of provisions similar to those in the rules of procedure of the Economic and Social Council [para. 352].

127. The Special Committee took note of the proposal concerning a comparative study of the rules of procedure of the General Assembly and those of the governing bodies of the specialized agencies and suggests that the United Nations Institute for Training and Research should consider undertaking such a project [para. 353].

128. Lastly, the Special Committee recommends to the General Assembly that the Secretariat should be instructed to undertake a comparative study of the versions of the General Assembly's rules of procedure in the various official languages in order to ensure their concordance [para. 354].

F. Special training programme

129. The Special Committee, aware of the training problems facing delegations, particularly as regards newly arrived representatives, suggests that the United Nations Institute for Training and Research should consider ways of helping to solve these problems [para. 356].

G. Regional groups

130. The Special Committee endorses the suggestion that the names of chairmen of the regional groups for the month should be published in the *Journal of the United Nations* and recommends that it should be left to the Secretariat to decide how often it should be applied [paras. 357 and 358].

A/8429. Resolution adopted by General Assembly during its 26th session, 21 September—22 December 1971. Other decisions, p. 133.

Relations with the host country

On 17 December 1970,[2] the General Assembly requested the Secretary-General to convene the Informal Joint Committee on Host Country Relations in January 1971, and thereafter as frequently as appropriate, in order that the Committee might examine the matters specified in its terms of reference and seek solutions to problems falling within the broad context of relations with the host country. The General Assembly recommended that the Committee undertake a systematic consideration of the implementation of the Convention on the Privileges and Immunities of the United Nations and the Agreement between the United Nations and the United States regarding the Headquarters of the United Nations, as well as conditions of life and obligations of members of permanent missions to the United Nations.

The Informal Joint Committee, originally established in 1966, was composed of representatives of permanent missions to the United Nations in New York, of the host country and of the Secretariat. The Secretary-General served as chairman of the Committee.

Work of the Informal Joint Committee

The Informal Joint Committee held eight meetings during 1971, at which it discussed the following subjects: (*a*) protection of missions and diplomatic personnel; (*b*) studies comparing the privileges, immunities and facilities at major duty stations; (*c*) obligations of permanent missions and individuals protected by diplomatic immunity; (*d*) exemption from taxes levied by states other than New York; (*e*) the possibility of establishing a commissary at United Nations Headquarters for diplomatic personnel and Secretariat staff; (*f*) housing for diplomatic personnel and Secretariat staff; (*g*) transportation; (*h*) insurance; (*i*) the public relations of the United Nations community in the host city, New York.

The major part of the Committee's time was devoted to the question of protection of permanent missions and their staff. In this connexion, the Secretary-General received communications from a number of permanent missions to the United Nations. At their request, communications from the following permanent missions were issued as official documents of the Committee: the Byelorussian SSR, Iraq, Spain, the Syrian Arab Republic, the USSR and the United States.

The communications from permanent missions, other than that of the host country, contained inquiries, complaints or protests concerning various incidents that had taken place in New York City. A number of grievances were also presented and considered during meetings of the Committee.

The incidents complained of fell into several categories. Some complaints concerned thefts, burglaries or robberies to which diplomats or permanent missions had been subjected, including the theft of the official car of a permanent mission. One protest was directed against a serious assault committed against a permanent representative. There were many complaints about harassment in various forms against members of permanent missions and the Secretariat staff, or their families.

A further category consisted of threats, most of them anonymous, made against the premises of

[2]See Y.U.N., 1970, p. 826, text of resolution 2747(XXV).

diplomatic missions, their personnel or members of the families. Several threats were made to bomb or destroy the buildings of certain permanent missions or cars with diplomatic licence plates belonging to those missions. Several cars were fire-bombed, and explosives and incendiary devices were found on the premises of the residence of a permanent representative; in one case, a fire-bomb was thrown against the wall of a permanent mission.

In a number of cases considered by the Committee, reference was made to certain associations and groups (in particular, one radical Zionist group) which, it was stated, in spite of the generally hospitable attitude of the citizens of New York, appeared to have adopted policies deliberately designed to impede the work of various permanent missions. Individual members of those missions and their families had been persistently harassed when in the streets and, on occasion, threatened with violence, and demonstrations (sometimes prolonged over a number of days) had been organized near the missions concerned, which interfered with the safe and unimpeded conduct of official functions.

The representative of the host country informed the Committee of the measures taken or proposed by the host authorities to deal with the problems in question. The Committee was assured that the authorities of the host country would take all necessary and legally appropriate measures to protect mission premises and to enable mission staff to carry out their duties without interference. Information was also given concerning legislation that had been proposed to the United States Congress designed to provide increased protection for foreign officials. In essence, the proposed legislation would give United States federal authorities investigative and prosecutive jurisdiction concurrent with that already possessed by individual states within the United States.

The questions of transportation and housing were considered by a working group, which submitted two interim reports to the Committee. The Committee was informed that there were 432 parking spaces reserved for members of the diplomatic and consular corps in New York City. (There was a total of 1,572 cars with diplomatic or consular licence plates in the city.) In view of the traffic situation in Manhattan, especially in the midtown area, no general increase in the number of reserved parking spaces was obtained; however, because of the special conditions prevailing at the permanent mission of the USSR, an additional 10 parking spaces were designated in that area.

On the question of housing facilities for the personnel of permanent missions and Secretariat staff, the Committee studied a working paper, prepared by the mission of the host country, which surveyed the housing situation for the United Nations community in New York.

Other issues taken up by the Committee were not studied in detail.

Consideration by General Assembly

The report of the Secretary-General on the status of the work of the Informal Joint Committee on Host Country Relations was included as an item on the agenda of the 1972 session of the General Assembly.

A second item, "Security of missions accredited to the United Nations and safety of their personnel," was included on the agenda at the request of the representatives of Cuba, Iraq, Kuwait, Mauritius, the Syrian Arab Republic and the USSR.

The two agenda items were considered jointly by the Assembly's Sixth (Legal) Committee.

The Sixth Committee had before it the report of the Secretary-General on the work of the Informal Joint Committee, in which it was noted that that Committee had provided a useful forum for discussion of the different problems faced by the United Nations community in New York City. Although such problems were not easily solved, the Secretary-General noted, improvements might be achieved through a continued examination of those problems and of the other issues which the Informal Joint Committee had not yet studied in depth.

With regard to the second agenda item, the Sixth Committee had before it a letter dated 28 October 1971 from the Permanent Representative of the USSR addressed to the Secretary-General; attached to the letter were copies of a note dated 22 October 1971, from the Government of the USSR to the Government of the United States, and a note dated 21 October 1971, from the Permanent Mission of the USSR to the Permanent Mission of the United States in connexion with the shots fired at the Mission of the USSR on 20 October 1971.

Also before the Committee was a letter, dated 12 November 1971, from the Permanent Representative of the United States addressed to the Secretary-General, to which was attached a copy of a note, dated 12 November 1971, from the United States Mission to the United Nations addressed to the Mission of the USSR concerning the shooting incident.

In addition, the Committee had before it a document submitted by the Permanent Mission of the USSR, entitled "Violations of the immunity of the Permanent Mission of the USSR to the United Nations and safety of its personnel (November 1970 to November 1971)."

The debate in the Sixth Committee centred mostly on the protection and security of permanent missions accredited to the United Nations and of their personnel.

A number of representatives from Eastern European and Arab countries described incidents in the area of New York to which their missions or personnel had been subjected during 1971. Those representatives requested that the host country authorities take more effective measures to protect missions and their personnel, and that those responsible for the incidents be found, convicted and punished.

The representative of the host country explained the measures being taken to prevent such incidents from occurring, and reassured all representatives that his Government deplored and condemned criminal acts directed against permanent missions accredited to the United Nations and their personnel.

The Sixth Committee also considered the question whether the mandate of the Secretary-General to continue the Informal Joint Committee should be renewed or whether a regular sub-committee of the General Assembly should be established in its stead.

Three draft resolutions on this subject were introduced into the Sixth Committee.

The first draft as subsequently revised was sponsored by 12 Members: Bulgaria, the Byelorussian SSR, Czechoslovakia, Hungary, Iraq, Kuwait, Mongolia, the People's Democratic Republic of Yemen, the Syrian Arab Republic, the Ukrainian SSR, the USSR and Yemen.

By this 12-power text, the General Assembly would establish, in the place of the Informal Joint Committee, a Special Committee, chosen by the Chairman of the Sixth Committee, to deal with the question of security of missions and the safety of their personnel, as well as with all the categories of issues previously considered by the Informal Joint Committee. The Assembly would also have included an item on security of missions accredited to the United Nations and safety of their personnel on the provisional agenda of its 1972 session.

By the second draft, sponsored by Barbados, Malaysia, the Netherlands and the United Kingdom, the General Assembly would decide to retain the Informal Joint Committee on Host Country Relations and request that it be convened as frequently as possible and that it adopt a vigorous and constructive approach to the problems brought before it. In addition, the Assembly would ask the Secretary-General to report to the 1972 session of the Assembly on the status of the work of the Committee.

By the third proposal, sponsored by Belgium, the Assembly would establish an *Ad Hoc* Advisory Committee on Host Country Relations, composed of the Secretary-General or his representative, the host country and 25 members to be chosen by the

President of the General Assembly. This body would be instructed to consider in particular and systematically the problems related to the security of missions and of their personnel, as well as all the categories of issues previously considered by the Informal Joint Committee on Host Country Relations, and to report to the General Assembly in 1972 on the status of its work.

Belgium subsequently put forward a revised version of this draft, which it later withdrew, putting forward instead a number of amendments to the 12-power text.

Two Belgian amendments—incorporated in the 12-power text after being modified by the sponsors—dealt with the active participation by the Secretary-General in the work of the Committee so as to ensure representation of all interests concerned, and with the convening of the Committee.

Another Belgian amendment dealt with the question of recommendations by the Committee to the Assembly. Belgium subsequently withdrew its amendment; a similar proposal that the Committee make appropriate recommendations, if it deemed that necessary, was made orally by Lebanon and incorporated in the 12-power text.

On 7 December 1971, the Sixth Committee approved without objection the text of the draft resolution as amended. As a consequence, the four-power draft resolution was not put to a vote.

On 15 December 1971, the General Assembly unanimously adopted the text as recommended by the Sixth Committee as its resolution 2819(XXVI).

The Assembly thereby, among other things: (*a*) noted with extreme concern the illegal acts of individuals or groups against the inviolability of various missions accredited to the United Nations; (*b*) recalled the responsibilities of the host country under the Agreement between the United Nations and the United States regarding the Headquarters of the United Nations, the Convention on the Privileges and Immunities of the United Nations and general international law; (*c*) took into account the profound concern expressed by representatives of States at the 1971 session of the General Assembly over the perpetration and repetition of violent and increasingly dangerous attacks against the premises of certain missions, and over the repeated threats and hostile and intimidating acts against the personnel of these missions; and (*d*) noted that the problem was of mutual concern to Member States, including the host country, and to the Secretary-General.

The Assembly then strongly condemned the acts of violence and other criminal acts against the premises of certain missions accredited to the United Nations and against their personnel as being flagrantly incompatible with their status under international law.

It urged the Government of the United States,

the host country, to take all requisite measures to ensure the protection and security of the United Nations Headquarters, of the missions accredited to it and of their personnel so as to ensure normal conditions for the performance of their functions; and called upon it to take all possible measures, including the use of information and publicity, to ensure a favourable atmosphere for the normal functioning of the United Nations and the missions accredited to it.

The Assembly noted with appreciation the assurances given by the representative of the host country that it would intensify its efforts to strengthen the protection and safety of the missions and their personnel.

The Assembly decided to establish a Committee on Relations with the Host Country, to be composed of the host country and 14 Member States chosen by the President of the General Assembly in consultation with the regional groups.

The Committee was instructed to deal with the question of the security of missions and the safety of their personnel, as well as with all categories of issues previously considered by the Informal Joint Committee on Host Country Relations. In particular, the Committee was authorized to study the Convention on the Privileges and Immunities of the United Nations and to consider and advise the host country on issues arising in connexion with the implementation of the Agreement between the United Nations and the United States regarding the Headquarters of the United Nations.

The Committee was to convene on a periodic basis and whenever it was convoked by its Chairman at the request of any State Member of the United Nations or the Secretary-General.

The Secretary-General was requested to participate actively in the work of the Committee with a view to ensuring the representation of the interests concerned. He was also requested, among other things, to solicit the views of Member States with respect to the measures needed to ensure the future security of missions and the safety of their personnel, and to transmit such replies to the Committee, and to bring to the Committee's attention, if so requested by missions accredited to the United Nations, cases involving infringements in their status.

Finally, the Assembly requested the Committee to submit to the General Assembly at its 1972 session a report on the progress of its work and to make, if it deemed it necessary, appropriate recommendations.

(For text of resolution, see DOCUMENTARY REFERENCES below.)

DOCUMENTARY REFERENCES

General Assembly—26th session
General Committee, meeting 195.
Sixth Committee, meetings 1285–1292, 1296–1298, 1302, 1303.
Plenary meetings 1975, 1980, 2019, 2029.

A/8401. Report of Secretary-General on work of the Organization, 16 June 1970–15 June 1971, Part Four, Chapter IV O.
A/8474. Status of work of Informal Joint Committee on Host Country Relations. Report of Secretary-General.
A/8479. Statement made by USSR on 22 October 1971, plenary meeting 1975. Note by Secretary-General (transmitting photographs).
A/8493. Letter of 2 November 1971 from Cuba, Iraq, Kuwait, Mauritius, Syrian Arab Republic and USSR (request for inclusion in agenda of item entitled: "Security of missions accredited to the United Nations and safety of their personnel").
A/8500/Add.2. Third report of General Committee.
A/8505. Letter of 28 October 1971 from USSR (transmitting note of 22 October 1971 from USSR Government to United States Government and note of 21 October 1971 from Permanent Mission of USSR to Permanent Mission of United States).
A/8522. Letter of 12 November 1971 from United States (transmitting note of 12 November 1971 from Permanent Mission of United States to Permanent Mission of USSR).
A/C.6/408. Letter of 8 November 1971 from President of General Assembly to Chairman of Sixth Committee.
A/C.6/409. Violations of immunity of Permanent Mission of USSR to United Nations and safety of its personnel (November 1970–November 1971). Document submitted to Sixth Committee by USSR.
A/C.6/L.832. Hungary, Iraq, Kuwait, Mongolia, Syrian Arab Republic, USSR: draft resolution.
A/C.6/L.832/Rev.1, Rev.1/Corr.1 and Rev.2. Bulgaria, Byelorussian SSR, Czechoslovakia, Hungary, Iraq, Kuwait, Mongolia, People's Democratic Republic of Yemen, Syrian Arab Republic,

Ukrainian SSR, USSR, Yemen: revised draft resolution, as orally amended by sponsors, approved without objection by Sixth Committee on 7 December 1971, meeting 1303.
A/C.6/L.835. Barbados, Malaysia, Netherlands, United Kingdom: draft resolution.
A/C.6/L.838. Italy and New Zealand: amendments to 12-power revised draft resolution, A/C.6/L.832/Rev.1 and Corr.1.
A/C.6/L.839. Australia: amendments to 12-power revised draft resolution, A/C.6/L.832/Rev.1 and Corr.1.
A/C.6/L.840 and Rev.1. Belgium: draft resolution and revision.
A/C.6/L.841. Belgium: amendments to revised 12-power draft resolution, A/C.6/L.832/Rev.2.
A/C.6/L.842. Bulgaria, Byelorussian SSR, Czechoslovakia, Hungary, Iraq, Kuwait, Mongolia, People's Democratic Republic of Yemen, Syrian Arab Republic, Ukrainian SSR, USSR, Yemen: sub-amendments to Belgian amendments, A/C.6/L.841.
A/8585. Report of Sixth Committee.

RESOLUTION 2819(XXVI), as recommended by Sixth Committee, A/8585, adopted unanimously by Assembly on 15 December 1971, meeting 2019.

The General Assembly,

Having considered the item entitled "Security of missions accredited to the United Nations and safety of their personnel" and the report of the Secretary-General on the work of the Informal Joint Committee on Host Country Relations,

Drawing attention to its resolution 2747(XXV) of 17 December 1970, in which it urges the Government of the host country to make certain that the measures taken to ensure the protection and security of diplomatic missions and their diplomatic personnel are adequate to enable permanent missions to the United Nations to perform properly the functions entrusted to them by their Governments,

Expressing its gratitude to the Secretary-General for his

valuable contribution to the work of the Informal Joint Committee on Host Country Relations,

Noting with extreme concern the illegal acts of individuals or groups against the inviolability of various missions accredited to the United Nations involving the commission and the repetition of violent and other criminal acts, including in some cases the use of bombs or firearms, against their premises and the residences of their personnel and also the assaults, the uttering of threats and insults against such personnel, and picketing accompanied by violence,

Expressing its deep sympathy with the missions and their personnel that have become the victims of such acts,

Recalling the responsibilities of the Government of the host country with respect to the United Nations and missions accredited to it and their personnel under the Agreement between the United Nations and the United States of America regarding the Headquarters of the United Nations, the Convention on the Privileges and Immunities of the United Nations and general international law,

Taking into account the profound concern expressed by representatives of States at the twenty-sixth session of the General Assembly over the perpetration and repetition of violent and increasingly dangerous attacks against the premises of certain missions accredited to the United Nations, and also over the repeated threats and the hostile and intimidating acts against the personnel of these missions, which indicates a deterioration in the security of missions and the safety of their personnel,

Considering that the problems related to the privileges and immunities of the United Nations and to the status of the diplomatic missions accredited to it are of mutual concern to Member States, including the host country, as well as to the Secretary-General,

1. *Strongly condemns* the acts of violence and other criminal acts against the premises of certain missions accredited to the United Nations and against their personnel as being flagrantly incompatible with their status under international law;

2. *Urges* that the Government of the United States of America, the host country of the United Nations, should take all requisite measures to ensure, in conformity with its international obligations, the protection and security of the United Nations Headquarters, of the missions accredited to it and of their personnel, thereby ensuring normal conditions for the performance of their functions;

3. *Calls upon* the Government of the United States of America, in consultation with the Secretary-General, to take all possible measures, including the use of information and publicity, to ensure a favourable atmosphere for the normal functioning of the United Nations and the missions accredited to it;

4. *Notes with appreciation* the assurances given by the representative of the host country that it will intensify in a diligent and energetic manner its efforts to strengthen the protection and safety of the missions accredited to the United Nations and their personnel;

5. *Decides* to establish a Committee on Relations with the Host Country, composed of the host country and fourteen Member States to be chosen by the President of the General Assembly in consultation with regional groups and taking into consideration equitable geographic representation thereon;

6. *Requests* the Secretary-General to participate actively in the work of the Committee on Relations with the Host Country with a view to ensuring the representation of the interests concerned;

7. *Instructs* the Committee on Relations with the Host Country to deal with the question of the security of missions and the safety of their personnel, as well as all the categories of issues previously considered by the Informal Joint Committee on Host Country Relations; the Committee is authorized to study the Convention on the Privileges and Immunities of the United Nations and shall consider, and advise the host country on, issues arising in connexion with the implementation of the Agreement between the United Nations and the United States of America regarding the Headquarters of the United Nations;

8. *Authorizes* the Committee on Relations with the Host Country to have summary records of its meetings and to convene on a periodic basis and whenever it is convoked by its Chairman at the request of any State Member of the United Nations or the Secretary-General;

9. *Requests* the Secretary-General to solicit the views of Member States with respect to the measures needed to ensure the future security of missions and the safety of their personnel and to transmit such replies to the Committee on Relations with the Host Country;

10. *Requests* the Secretary-General to bring to the attention of the Committee on Relations with the Host Country, if so requested by missions accredited to the United Nations, cases involving infringements of their status;

11. *Requests* the Secretary-General to furnish all appropriate assistance to the Committee on Relations with the Host Country and to bring to its attention issues of mutual concern relating to the implementation of the Agreement between the United Nations and the United States of America regarding the Headquarters of the United Nations and the Convention on the Privileges and Immunities of the United Nations;

12. *Requests* the Committee on Relations with the Host Country to submit to the General Assembly at its twenty-seventh session a report on the progress of its work and to make, if it deems it necessary, appropriate recommendations;

13. *Decides* to include in the provisional agenda of its twenty-seventh session an item entitled "Report of the Committee on Relations with the Host Country."

Legal aspects of the peaceful uses of outer space

In 1971, after nearly eight years of consideration, the General Assembly's Committee on the Peaceful Uses of Outer Space and its Legal Sub-Committee completed work on a Convention on International Liability for Damage Caused by Space Objects. The General Assembly, on 29 November 1971, expressed the hope that as many States as possible would adhere to it, and requested the Depositary Governments to open the Convention for signature and ratification at the earliest possible date. It did this with the adoption of resolution 2777(XXVI), by 93 votes to 0, with 4 abstentions. (For further details, see pp. 49-55.)

The draft convention on liability was completed at the ninth session of the Legal Sub-Committee held at Geneva, Switzerland, from 7 June to 2 July. The draft was subsequently adopted by the Committee on Outer Space at its session held in New York from 1 to 10 September, and submitted to the General Assembly for final consideration and adoption.

At the request of the Sub-Committee, the Committee recommended that in its future work the Sub-Committee give priority to matters relating to the registration of space objects and to questions relating to the moon. The Committee noted that the USSR had submitted to the Assembly a draft treaty concerning the moon, on which some members made observations.

The Assembly, on 29 November 1971, took note of the draft treaty concerning the moon, and it requested the Committee on Outer Space and its Legal Sub-Committee to consider, as a matter of priority, the question of the elaboration of a draft international treaty concerning the moon and to report thereon to the Assembly in 1972. These decisions were set forth in resolution 2779(XXVI), adopted unanimously by the Assembly. (See page 50.)

Also on 29 November 1971, the Assembly took note of the programmes being undertaken by the United Nations Educational, Scientific and Cultur-al Organization and the International Telecommunication Union in satellite broadcasting, and it drew attention to the fact that questions relating to the legal implications of space communications were on the agenda of the Legal Sub-Committee of the Committee on Outer Space, with which the two agencies should co-ordinate their activities in this field. This decision was one of those embodied in resolution 2776(XXVI), adopted unanimously by the Assembly. (See page 50.)

Developments pertaining to Article 19 of the United Nations Charter

At the opening of its twenty-sixth (1971) session, the General Assembly had before it a letter dated 21 September 1971 from the Secretary-General, indicating that at that time one Member State, namely Yemen, was in arrears in the payment of its contributions to the regular budget of the United Nations within the terms of Article 19 of the Charter.[3] The same information was also before the Assembly in the form of the Report of the Committee on Contributions, and an addendum by its Chairman dated 21 September 1971.

The Secretary-General's letter had annexed to it a communication from the Permanent Representative of Yemen, in which the latter indicated that the prime factor hampering the remittance of the contributions of Yemen had been the rapid and successive political changes his country had been experiencing recently. The Prime Minister of Yemen had however assured him that the necessary remittance would be forthcoming immediately. Having in mind the communications delay between Sana'a', Yemen, and New York, the Permanent Representative requested that his delegation be permitted to vote pending the arrival of the necessary remittance.

Before the first vote of the twenty-sixth regular session (namely, the election of the President), the Temporary President of the Assembly drew the Assembly's attention to the Secretary-General's letter and to the explanation for delay in receipt of the contributions of Yemen which had been submitted by the Permanent Representative of Yemen. The Temporary President referred to the second sentence of Article 19, under which the Assembly could permit a Member State in arrears under that Article to vote if it was satisfied that the failure to pay was due to conditions beyond the control of the Member. He then suggested that the Assembly might wish to permit Yemen to vote under the second sentence of Article 19 for the brief period that would be required for the remittance to reach the Secretary-General, who should report as soon as the money was received and in any event not later than 27 September. The Assembly agreed to this suggestion without objection.

On 23 September 1971, the Secretary-General informed the President of the General Assembly by letter that a payment had been received from Yemen which reduced its arrears of contributions well below the amount specified in Article 19. On 27 September, the President drew the attention of the General Assembly to the letter and stated that, with the receipt of the payment from Yemen, the matter was closed.

---

[3]Article 19 of the Charter provides as follows: "A Member of the United Nations which is in arrears in the payment of its financial contributions to the Organization shall have no vote in the General Assembly if the amount of its arrears equals or exceeds the amount of the contributions due from it for the preceding two full years. The General Assembly may, nevertheless, permit such a Member to vote if it is satisfied that the failure to pay is due to conditions beyond the control of the Member."

For developments in previous years relating to the application of Article 19, see Y.U.N., 1964, pp. 3–60; Y.U.N., 1965, p. 16; Y.U.N., 1968, pp. 859–65; and Y.U.N., 1969, pp. 791–92.

DOCUMENTARY REFERENCES

General Assembly—26th session
Plenary meetings 1934, 1940.

A/8397. Letter of 21 September 1971 from Secretary-General to President of General Assembly.

A/8397/Add.1. Scale of assessments for apportionment of expenses of United Nations. Letter of 23 September 1971 from Secretary-General to President of General Assembly.
A/8411 and Add.1,2 and Add.2/Corr.1. Report of Committee on Contributions on its 31st session, 20-30 April 1971.

Declaration on Universal Participation in Vienna Convention on Law of Treaties

On 24 September 1971, the General Assembly, acting on the recommendation of its General Committee, decided not to place on its agenda the item entitled "Declaration on Universal Participation in the Vienna Convention on the Law of Treaties," but to place it instead on the provisional agenda of its 1972 session. The item had been deferred from the Assembly's 1969 and 1970 sessions.

The item concerned the request of the Conference on the Law of Treaties (held at Vienna, Austria, in 1968 and 1969) to the General Assembly to issue special invitations to become parties to the Vienna Convention to States not Members of the United Nations or members of any of the specialized agencies or of the International Atomic Energy Agency, or parties to the Statute of the International Court of Justice.

DOCUMENTARY REFERENCES

General Assembly—26th session
General Committee, meeting 191
Plenary meeting 1937

A/8376. Note by Secretary-General.
A/8401. Report of Secretary-General on work of the Organization, 16 June 1970–15 June 1971, Part Four, Chapter IV F.

A/8500. Organization of 26th regular session of General Assembly, adoption of agenda and allocation of items. First report of General Committee, para. 15(*g*).
A/8429. Resolutions adopted by General Assembly during its 26th session, 21 September–22 December 1971. Other decisions, p. 19.

Special missions

On 24 September 1971, the General Assembly decided not to place on its agenda an item postponed from its 1970 session concerning the issuance of invitations in order to ensure the widest possible participation in the Convention on Special Missions and the Optional Protocol concerning the Compulsory Settlement of Disputes. The Convention was adopted by the Assembly and opened for signature on 8 December 1969.[4]

The Assembly placed the item on the provisional agenda of its twenty-seventh session, scheduled to open in September 1972.

The action was taken, without vote, on the recommendation of the Assembly's General Committee.

[4]See Y.U.N., 1969, pp. 750–58, texts of resolution 2530(XXIV) and of Convention and Optional Protocol.

DOCUMENTARY REFERENCES

General Assembly—26th session
General Committee, meeting 191
Plenary meeting 1937

A/8377. Question of issuing special invitations to States not Members of United Nations or members of any of specialized agencies or of International Atomic Energy Agency or parties to Statute of International Court of Justice to become parties to Convention on Special Missions. Note by Secretary-General.

A/8401. Report of Secretary-General on work of the Organization, 16 June 1970–15 June 1971, Part Four, Chapter IV F.
A/8500. Organization of 26th regular session of General Assembly, adoption of agenda and allocation of items. First report of General Committee, para. 15 (*h*).
A/8429. Resolutions adopted by General Assembly during its 26th session, 21 September–22 December 1971. Other decisions, p. 19.

Administrative and budgetary questions

Administrative arrangements

The composition of the United Nations Secretariat

In 1971, the General Assembly examined the composition of the Secretariat on the basis of the annual report of the Secretary-General on the subject.

Report by Secretary-General

In his report, the Secretary-General reviewed the measures that had been taken in application of the recruitment guidelines laid down by the General Assembly in a resolution of 17 December 1970.[1] As part of his continuing effort to recruit staff from under-represented countries, the Secretary-General authorized two special recruitment missions, one to Japan and the other to the USSR. A similar mission attended the annual conference of a professional association in the United States which included among its members nationals of many countries. In addition, the regional economic commissions were invited to assist in the search for candidates from under-represented countries. The annual circular of vacancies and its quarterly supplements were revised to announce all vacancies anticipated during 1971.

In accordance with the Assembly guidelines, the Secretary-General added, special attention was paid to the improvement of geographical distribution at the senior (Director and Principal Officer) levels; an effort was made to seek out candidates willing to accept career or long-term appointments in the filling of posts entailing complex duties and responsibilities; and greater emphasis was placed on the recruitment of young candidates.

The 1971 report of the Secretary-General contained no recommendations on recruitment policy for the consideration of the General Assembly. The Secretary-General was of the view that before further recommendations were formulated it would be preferable to await the outcome of the review being undertaken by the General Assembly's Special Committee for the Review of the United Nations Salary System (see page 632) and the follow-up action proposed in the report on United Nations personnel problems

prepared by the Joint Inspection Unit (JIU) (see page 636).

The Secretary-General's report contained an analysis of the changes in the composition of the Secretariat that had taken place during the year ended on 31 August 1971.

The number of nationalities represented in the Secretariat increased from 118 to 122, including five from non-member States. Of the 10 Member States which were not represented in the Secretariat, six were countries in Africa. In terms of regional distribution, the largest net increase of staff was registered by North America and the Caribbean (6.7 per cent), followed by Latin America (5.6 per cent), Africa (4.4 per cent), Western Europe (3.0 per cent) and the Middle East (2.0 per cent). The two regions which shared a slight loss were Asia and the Far East (0.6 per cent) and Eastern Europe (0.4 per cent).

Among the factors entering into these regional shifts, the disparity in the rate of separations continued to be one of particular importance. The largest number of separations during the year were those of nationals of Western Europe (41), followed by Eastern Europe (40) and North America (37). These figures represented a rate of separation of 15.2 per cent for Eastern Europe, as compared to 8.1 for Western Europe and 7.1 for North America. Moreover, of the 188 staff who were separated during the year, 109 held fixed-term appointments, 38 of whom left before the expiration of their contracts. Thus the rate of resignations for fixed-term staff was 5.0 per cent as against 2.9 for career staff. As a result of the greater number of separations of fixed-term staff, the percentage of staff holding fixed-term appointments showed a decrease, for the first time in recent years, from 35.2 to 34.8.

The Secretary-General's report also included statistical data on the employment of women in the United Nations and its related agencies. The

[1]See Y.U.N., 1970, pp. 832-33, text of resolution 2736(XXV).

information was submitted in response to a resolution adopted by the General Assembly on 15 December 1970,[2] urging the United Nations and its related agencies "to take or continue to take appropriate measures to ensure opportunities for the employment of qualified women in senior and other professional positions."

Consideration by General Assembly

Discussion at the General Assembly's 1971 session on the composition of the Secretariat took place principally in the Assembly's Fifth (Administrative and Budgetary) Committee. The main emphasis was to ensure full implementation of the previous decisions adopted by the Assembly towards the objective of achieving a more equitable geographical distribution of the Secretariat staff, rather than to formulate or provide further guidelines.

On a proposal by Poland and the Ukrainian SSR, as amended by the United States, the Fifth Committee decided to include in its report to the Assembly a statement expressing its concern at the inadequate progress in achieving equitable geographical distribution within the Secretariat and requesting the Secretary-General to take effective measures to ensure the rapid implementation of General Assembly resolutions of 11 December 1969[3] and 17 December 1970[4] and other Assembly decisions relating to this question.

In this connexion, the Fifth Committee also stated that particular attention should be given to the application of the guidelines for the recruitment of staff set out in Article 101 of the United Nations Charter[5] and by the General Assembly in its resolution 2736(XXV) of 17 December 1970, and in particular to the principle that, in the recruitment of staff for posts at all levels which were subject to geographical distribution, especially posts at the senior level, preference should be given to qualified candidates from under-represented countries.

The Fifth Committee also requested the Secretary-General to include in his 1972 report on the composition of the Secretariat information on the situation with regard to the implementation of the aforementioned General Assembly decisions along with a long-term plan of recruitment, bearing in mind discussions in the Fifth Committee in recent years regarding the achievement of equitable geographical distribution of staff.

On a proposal by Norway, the Fifth Committee decided to include in its report a request that the Secretary-General include in his annual report on the subject a table showing each country's position in relation to the desirable ranges of posts over the previous 10 years so as to enable the Committee to acquire a clear picture of the long-term trend in changes in the Secretariat's composition.

The Fifth Committee also decided, on a proposal by Austria, that the deadlines applied to the reports of the Secretary-General concerning the staff of the United Nations Secretariat and its composition should be advanced from 31 August to 30 June each year, beginning in 1972, and requested the Secretary-General to circulate these reports to United Nations Member States each year not later than 1 September.

On 17 December 1971, the General Assembly took note of the decisions of the Fifth Committee without adopting a formal resolution.

In a related decision taken the same day, the Assembly, also without adopting a resolution, took note of a Fifth Committee decision to ask the Secretary-General, when implementing an Assembly decision of 21 December 1968[6] (designed to ensure linguistic balance within the Secretariat), to safeguard the interests of those staff members whose mother tongue was not one of the official languages of the United Nations and to report, through his annual reports on the composition of the Secretariat, on measures taken in this regard. This decision was based on a proposal in the Fifth Committee put forward by Ghana and Japan and approved on 24 November, as amended by India. (See also pp. 635-36 for further details on measures taken by the General Assembly in regard to linguistic balance within the Secretariat.)

During its discussions on the composition of the Secretariat, the Fifth Committee received a Colombian proposal concerning the interpretation of the principle of geographical representation. By this proposal, the Secretary-General would be asked to give citizens from Latin America, Asia and Africa greater participation in the administration by appointing them to permanent posts at a senior level. Also, an appeal would be made to the Secretary-General to give young persons from all regions permanent senior-level posts.

Members supporting the Colombian proposal felt that the principle of geographical distribution should not merely take into account the number of nationals of a State, but should place greater emphasis on the quality or level of posts, and that developing countries should be more equitably represented in policy-making senior administrative posts.

Members against the Colombian proposal felt that it appeared to go beyond the principle of equitable geographical distribution by selecting particular regions and age brackets for greater participation in the Secretariat at the senior level.

---

[2]*Ibid.*, p. 833, text of resolution 2715(XXV).
[3]See Y.U.N., 1969, pp. 803-4, text of resolution 2539(XXIV).
[4]See footnote 1.
[5]For text of Article 101 of the Charter, see APPENDIX II.
[6]See Y.U.N., 1968, pp. 875-76, text of resolution 2480 B (XXIII).

There was general agreement that youth should be favoured in recuitment policies.

In the absence of a consensus on the Colombian proposal, it was agreed that the proposal and the views expressed thereon would be reflected in the Fifth Committee's report to the Assembly.

DOCUMENTARY REFERENCES

General Assembly—26th session
Fifth Committee, meetings 1457, 1459-1461, 1464, 1480, 1481.
Plenary meeting 2023.

A/8401. Annual report of Secretary-General on work of the Organization, 16 June 1970–15 June 1971, Part Five, Chapter III A.
A/8401/Add.1. Introduction to report of Secretary-General, September 1971, Part One, Chapter IX.

A/8483. Personnel questions: composition of Secretariat. Report of Secretary-General.
A/C.5/L.1061 and Add.1. Staff of United Nations Secretariat. Report of Secretary-General (covering notes).
A/8604. Report of Fifth Committee (part I).
A/8429. Resolutions adopted by General Assembly during its 26th session, 21 September–22 December 1971. Other decisions, p. 133 (item 84, first para.).

The United Nations Joint Staff Pension Fund

Eleven organizations are members of the United Nations Joint Staff Pension Fund. They are: the United Nations (including the Registry of the International Court of Justice); the International Labour Organisation; the Food and Agriculture Organization of the United Nations; the United Nations Educational, Scientific and Cultural Organization; the World Health Organization; the International Civil Aviation Organization; the International Telecommunication Union; the World Meteorological Organization; the Inter-Governmental Maritime Consultative Organization; the Interim Commission for the International Trade Organization; and the International Atomic Energy Agency.

Operation of the Fund

During the 12 months ending 30 September 1971, the number of participants increased from 32,336 to 34,855 and the number of associate participants (death and disability coverage only) decreased from 404 to 5, owing to the discontinuance of the associate participant scheme for new entrants as of 1 January 1967 in accordance with a General Assembly decision of 15 December 1966.[7]

The principal of the Fund increased during this period from $505,555,040.77 to $592,381,574.83. The cash income on the average investments of the Fund was at the annual rate of 4.29 per cent, as against 4.35 per cent for the preceding year.

As at 30 September 1971, 1,966 retirement benefits, 982 withdrawal settlements in the form of life annuities, 742 widow's benefits, 145 disability benefits, 1,350 children's benefits and 18 secondary dependant's benefits were payable by the Fund.

Pension Board's annual report

The United Nations Joint Staff Pension Board held its sixteenth session at the headquarters of the World Health Organization in Geneva, Switzerland, from 19 to 30 July 1971.

Its subsequent report to the General Assembly of the United Nations contained: the audited accounts of the Fund for the fiscal year ended 30 September 1970; a summary of the investments of the Fund as at that date; various statistical tables reflecting the operation of the Fund during the year; and a summary of the Board's decisions relating to the general administrative control which it is required to exercise, within its own competence, over the affairs of the Fund, together with summaries of discussions of particular importance.

The matters dealt with in these discussions included: a review of the benefits system of the Fund and possible improvements to be made therein; a review of the Fund's organizational structure, including the composition and functioning of its organs; the conclusion of an agreement with the Board of Auditors setting out the scope and manner in which the external audit of the Fund should be carried out; a full examination of the investments policy of the Fund; and consideration of the problems posed for pensioners by the revaluation of currencies.

The report formulated three main recommendations for action by the General Assembly.

The first concerned a number of improvements in the benefits system:

(i) a change in the formula used for computing the final average remuneration so that instead of its being the average annual pensionable remuneration over the last five years of contributory service it would be the annual average over the best three years out of the last five of contributory service;
(ii) a reduction—from five to three years—in the period over which the movement of the post adjustment element in pensionable remuneration is averaged in order to produce the index by which cost-of-living supplements are applied by the Fund to benefits in payment;

[7]See Y.U.N., 1966, pp. 933-34.

(iii) a change in the formula for computing the early retirement benefit under which the existing reduction in the pension of about 6 per cent for each year short of age 60 would be diminished to 2 per cent per year where the retiring participant had at least 25 years of contributory service to his or her credit. This latter recommendation was linked to the qualified undertaking given by the executive heads of the participating organizations—in the inter-agency Administrative Committee on Co-ordination—that they would in the future, in all appropriate cases, extend the application of their discretion to retain staff on an individual basis beyond the statutory retirement age of 60;

(iv) an increase in the minimum benefit to $300 per annum whenever the annual amount of a disability, retirement, widow's or widower's benefit would, under the existing provisions, be less than that amount, subject to the benefit in question being the only benefit payable and to its not exceeding the final average remuneration of the participant; and

(v) a change whereby a married female participant entitled to a normal, early or deferred retirement benefit would be able to opt to receive an appropriately reduced benefit in consideration of payment by the Fund to her spouse, in the event of his surviving her, of a widower's benefit at the rate provided for under the Regulations.

The second main recommendation in the Pension Board's report concerned estimates of administrative expenses for 1972 and supplementary estimates for 1971.

The third contained a number of amendments to the Regulations of the Fund, in addition to those required to implement the benefit changes referred to above. These dealt with leave without pay and the payment of contributions after return from, rather than concurrently with, such leave.

The Board's report also contained, for the information of the General Assembly, amendments to two sections of the Administrative Rules of the Fund. The first one, dealing with leave without pay, became necessary as a consequence of the proposed amendment in the Regulations on that subject, while the second dealt with the computation and payment of benefits.

On 21 December 1971, the General Assembly, upon the recommendation of its Fifth (Administrative and Budgetary) Committee, adopted by 97 votes to 10 a resolution (2887(XXVI)) by which it decided that the Regulations should be amended as recommended, set forth the manner in which the amendments should be applied to participants and former participants in the Fund, approved the recommendation concerning the adjustment of benefits in respect of cost-of-living changes and approved the administrative expenses for 1972 and supplementary expenses for 1971.

(For text of resolution, see DOCUMENTARY REFERENCES below.)

DOCUMENTARY REFERENCES

General Assembly—26th session
Fifth Committee, meetings 1485, 1486.
Plenary meeting 2030.

A/8409. Report of United Nations Joint Staff Pension Board.
A/8409, annex IV. Draft resolution, proposed by Board for adoption by General Assembly, approved by Fifth Committee on 16 December 1971, meeting 1486, by 58 votes to 8, with 1 abstention.
A/8598. Report of Advisory Committee on Administrative and Budgetary Questions.
A/8628. Report of Fifth Committee.

RESOLUTION 2887(XXVI), as recommended by Fifth Committee, A/8628, adopted by Assembly on 21 December 1971, meeting 2030, by 97 votes to 10.

The General Assembly,
Having considered the report of the United Nations Joint Staff Pension Board to the General Assembly and to the member organizations of the United Nations Joint Staff Pension Fund for 1971 and the related report of the Advisory Committee on Administrative and Budgetary Questions,

I
Amendments to the Regulations of the United Nations Joint Staff Pension Fund

Decides that the Regulations of the United Nations Joint Staff Pension Fund shall be amended, with effect from 1 January 1972, as set forth in annex V of the report of the United Nations Joint Staff Pension Board;

II
Application of the Regulations, as Amended, to Participants and Former Participants in the United Nations Joint Staff Pension Fund

Decides that:
(a) Benefits payable to or on the account of participants whose last day of contributory service was after 31 December 1971 shall be calculated in accordance with the Regulations as amended in section I above;
(b) Benefits payable in periodic form to or on the account of participants whose last day of contributory service was prior to 1 January 1972, other than benefits derived from voluntary deposits under article 54 of the Regulations, shall be increased by 5 per cent with effect from that date; no increase shall be applied to benefits paid or payable in a lump sum to or on the account of participants whose last day of contributory service was prior to 1 January 1972;
(c) Benefits as in (b) above payable under article 30 of the Regulations shall, prior to the application of the increase, be recalculated in accordance with article 30 (b) (ii) of the Regulations as amended, if the contributory service of the participant on the date of his retirement was twenty-five years or more;

III
Adjustment of Benefits in Respect of Cost-of-Living Changes

Decides that the system of adjustment of benefits in payment contained in General Assembly resolution 2122(XX) of 21 December 1965 shall be varied, with effect from 1 January 1972, in such manner that the index provided for therein is calculated thenceforward according to the average values of the post adjustment element in the pensionable remuneration of Professional staff in each of the three years immediately preceding the 1 January upon which the adjustment is applied;

IV
Administrative Expenses

Approves expenses totalling $907,830 net for 1972 and

IV
Administrative Expenses

Approves expenses totalling $907,830 net for 1972 and supplementary expenses totalling $92,230 net for 1971 for the administration of the United Nations Joint Staff Pension Fund, as estimated in annex VI to the report of the United Nations Joint Staff Pension Board.

Pension scheme and emoluments of members of the International Court of Justice

Pension

On 22 December 1971, the General Assembly authorized adjustments to the annual pensions being paid to former members of the International Court of Justice and their eligible beneficiaries.

The annual value of all pensions in payment on 31 December 1971 to retired Judges and their survivors was increased with effect from 1 January 1972 by 17 per cent, with the exception of the maximum child's benefit payable to widows receiving a pension, which would remain at $600 a year.

Emoluments

The Assembly also authorized the following increases in the emoluments of the members of the Court (which had remained unchanged since 1968):

(i) the net salaries of members of the Court were increased from $30,000 to $35,000;

(ii) the duty allowance for the President of the Court was increased from $7,200 to $8,400, and so was the special duty allowance for the Vice-President increased for every day he acted as President; his allowance was raised from $45 a day (subject to a maximum of $4,500 a year) to $53 a day (subject to a maximum of $5,300 a year); and

(iii) the combined fee and subsistence payment to *ad hoc* judges was increased from $82 a day to $96.

The Assembly's decisions on pensions and emoluments were embodied in a two-part resolution (2890(XXVI)) adopted at a plenary meeting on 22 December 1971 by 107 votes to 9, with 1 abstention. The Assembly's action was taken on the recommendation of its Fifth (Administrative and Budgetary) Committee which approved the text on 25 October 1971 by 72 votes to 9, as proposed by the Assembly's Advisory Committee on Administrative and Budgetary Questions. (For text of resolution, see DOCUMENTARY REFERENCES below.)

DOCUMENTARY REFERENCES

General Assembly—26th session
Fifth Committee, meeting 1438.
Plenary meeting 2031.

A/C.5/1364. Arrangements concerning emoluments and pensions of members of International Court of Justice. Report of Secretary-General.
A/8408/Add.2. Report of Advisory Committee on Administrative and Budgetary Questions (ACABQ).
A/8531/Add.1. Report of Fifth Committee (part II) (on budget estimates for financial year 1972), paras. 51 and 52, and draft resolution II A, based on recommendations of ACABQ (A/8408/Add.2, paras. 7-10), approved by Fifth Committee on 25 October 1971, meeting 1438, by 72 votes to 9.

RESOLUTION 2890(XXVI), as recommended by Fifth Committee, A/8531/Add.1, adopted by Assembly on 22 December 1971, meeting 2031, by 107 votes to 9, with 1 abstention.

A. Pension Scheme

The General Assembly,

Recalling its resolutions 1562(XV) of 18 December 1960, 1925(XVIII) of 11 December 1963 and 2367(XXII) of 19 December 1967 on the pension scheme for members of the International Court of Justice,

Having considered the reports of the Secretary-General and of the Advisory Committee on Administrative and Budgetary Questions,

Desirous of protecting former members of the International Court of Justice and their eligible beneficiaries from the rise in the cost of living that has occurred since their pensions were last adjusted,

Decides that, with effect from 1 January 1972 and notwithstanding any provision to the contrary contained in the Pension Scheme Regulations for members of the International Court of Justice, the annual value of all pensions in course of payment as at 31 December 1971, including the pensions of any members of the Court who retire on or before that date, shall be increased by 17 per cent, except that the maximum child's benefit payable under article IV, paragraph 1 (a), of the Regulations shall remain $600 a year.

B. Emoluments

The General Assembly,

Having considered the reports of the Secretary-General and of the Advisory Committee on Administrative and Budgetary Questions,

Decides that, with effect from 1 January 1972, the emoluments of the members of the International Court of Justice shall be as follows:

	(U.S. dollars)
President:	
Annual salary	35,000
Special allowance	8,400
Vice-President:	
Annual salary	35,000
Allowance of $53 for every day on which he acts as President, up to an annual maximum of	5,300
Other members:	
Annual salary	35,000
Ad hoc judges referred to in Article 31 of the Statute of the Court; Fee of $67 for each day on which ad hoc judges exercise their functions, plus, as appropriate, a daily subsistence allowance of $29.	

Salaries and allowances

Salary and retirement allowance
of the Secretary-General

On 29 November 1971, acting on the recommendation of its Fifth (Administrative and Budgetary) Committee, the General Assembly revised the salary and retirement allowance of the Secretary-General.

Noting that the base salary of the Secretary-General had remained unchanged since 1 January 1968 at $50,000 gross ($31,600 net) per annum, while other United Nations salaries had been rising, the Assembly decided to increase, as from 1 December 1971, the Secretary-General's annual salary to $62,500 gross ($37,850 net) per annum. It also set his annual retirement allowance as one half of his gross salary after completion of a full term of office, with a schedule of smaller allowances for lesser periods.

At the same time, the Assembly established certain benefits for the widow and minor children of a Secretary-General who died in office or while receiving a retirement allowance. The widow's benefit was set at one half the retirement allowance of the Secretary-General. In addition, provision was made for benefits to the Secretary-General or his survivors, as the case might be, to be paid in the event of death, injury or illness of the Secretary-General attributable to the performance of official duties on behalf of the United Nations.

The Assembly took these decisions in adopting resolution 2772(XXVI) by 95 votes to 0, with 8 abstentions. The Fifth Committee had approved the text on 23 November 1971 by 68 votes to 0, with 7 abstentions, acting on a proposal by Afghanistan, Algeria, Barbados, Chile, Colombia, Costa Rica, Cyprus, Denmark, Ecuador, India, Indonesia, Iran, Ireland, Italy, the Ivory Coast, Kuwait, Lebanon, the Libyan Arab Republic, Mexico, Nicaragua, Niger, Nigeria, Pakistan, Peru, Poland, Somalia, Sudan, Tunisia and Yugoslavia.

(For text of resolution, see DOCUMENTARY REFERENCES below.)

(See also p. 218).

Special Committee for the Review
of the United Nations Salary System

By a resolution of 17 December 1970,[8] the General Assembly established a Special Committee for the Review of the United Nations Salary System to undertake a thorough review of the long-term principles and criteria governing the whole United Nations common system of salaries, allowances, grants, pensions and other benefits

and to report its conclusions and recommendations on the matter to the Assembly in 1971.

The Special Committee, composed of government experts from 11 Member States, held its first session from 1 June to 24 August 1971. In its interim report to the General Assembly covering its work during that period, the Special Committee did not enter into the substance of its task, but proposed a programme of work for 1972, subject to an extension of its mandate by the General Assembly.

On the basis of the proposed work programme of the Special Committee, the Secretary-General estimated that costs would amount to $524,485. In its report, the Assembly's Advisory Committee on Administrative and Budgetary Questions recommended that the costs be kept to $270,000 by certain economy measures, including the possibility of dispensing with detailed minutes, requesting documentation in all working languages to eliminate translation requirements and reconsidering the need for field visits. The Advisory Committee also recommended that the General Assembly request the Special Committee to review its work programme so as to enable it to complete its report at an earlier date than envisaged.

On 22 November 1971, the Assembly's Fifth (Administrative and Budgetary) Committee decided without objection that the mandate of the Special Committee be extended to 1972. By a roll-call vote of 74 to 3, with 1 abstention, the Fifth Committee approved the Advisory Committee's recommendation that $270,000 be provided for the Special Committee in the budget estimates for 1972. In addition, it approved a recommendation that the Secretary-General should be asked to submit the reports of the Special Committee and Advisory Committee to the executive heads of agencies in the common system of salaries and seek their co-operation. The Fifth Committee also adopted, by 75 votes to 2, the proposal to request the Special Committee to reorganize its work, taking into account the recommendations of the Advisory Committee.

The General Assembly approved the allocation of $270,000 for the Special Committee as part of the budget appropriations for 1972 adopted at a plenary meeting on 22 December 1971.

---

[8]See Y.U.N., 1970, pp. 841-42, text of resolution 2743 (XXV).

Accelerated salary increments

A change in the interval between periodic salary increments for staff in the professional and higher categories was approved by the General Assembly on 21 December 1971.

This change was designed to bring the Staff Regulations into line with a General Assembly resolution of 21 December 1968[9] which had envisaged, with effect from 1 January 1972, the award of salary increments at shorter intervals to staff subject to geographical distribution who had an adequate and confirmed knowledge of a second official language of the United Nations. The Assembly authorized the Secretary-General to reduce the intervals between salary increments from the normal period of one year to two years, depending on the case, to 10 months or 20 months, respectively, in favour of staff members who met the requisite language qualifications.

The text for incorporation into the Staff Regulations was included in resolution 2888 (XXVI), adopted by the Assembly at a plenary meeting on 21 December 1971, by 99 votes to 2, with 7 abstentions, after the Assembly amended a text put forward by the Fifth (Administrative and Budgetary) Committee. The amendment was proposed by Belgium, Canada, France and Tunisia and approved by 46 votes to 30, with 28 abstentions.

By the text as approved by the Assembly, the interval between salary increments within a particular grade in the case of staff members subject to geographical distribution who had an adequate and confirmed knowledge of a second official language would be reduced from 12 months to 10 in the case of staff members below step IV of the Principal Officer (D-1) level, and from 24 months to 20 in the case of those above step IV of the D-1 level. In each case the Secretary-General was to take account of the staff member's length of service prior to 1 January 1972 in the step of his grade. Thus, a qualified staff member whose normal salary increment was 12 months and who, at 1 January 1972, had already served 10 months at a particular step in his grade (below the top step) would move to the next higher step immediately on 1 January 1972 rather than on 1 March 1972.

By an alternative interpretation pointed out by the Assembly's Advisory Committee on Administrative and Budgetary Questions, a representative of the Secretary-General informed the Fifth Committee, no such staff member could benefit from an accelerated increment until November 1972 at the earliest and many would not benefit until 1973 or later. Under the Secretary-General's interpretation, on the other hand, all qualified staff members would benefit in 1972.

(For text of resolution 2888(XXVI), see DOCUMENTARY REFERENCES below.)

Salary of Administrator of United Nations Development Programme

On 21 December 1971, the General Assembly approved an increase in the annual salary for the Administrator of the United Nations Development Programme from $47,000 to $56,000 with effect from 1 January 1972.

The increase was proposed by the Secretary-General in order to bring the salary into line with that of the executive head of a major specialized agency.

The Assembly's action was taken in the form of an amendment to the United Nations Staff Regulations. This was embodied in resolution 2888(XXVI) which was adopted by 99 votes to 2, with 7 abstentions. (For text of resolution, see DOCUMENTARY REFERENCES below.)

The Fifth Committee had previously approved the proposal on 13 December, without vote.

---

[9]See Y.U.N., 1968, pp. 875-76, text of resolution 2480 B (XXIII).

DOCUMENTARY REFERENCES

*Salary and retirement allowance
of the Secretary-General*

General Assembly—26th session
Fifth Committee, meetings 1440, 1446, 1460.
Plenary meeting 1997.

A/8407/Add.9. Tenth report of Advisory Committee on Administrative and Budgetary Questions (ACABQ) on budget estimates for 1972. (Annex: Financial implications of 29-power draft resolution, A/C.5/L.1062/Rev.1. Report of Controller.)
A/C.5/L.1062. Afghanistan, Chile, Colombia, Costa Rica, India, Italy, Ivory Coast, Kuwait, Libyan Arab Republic, Mexico, Nicaragua, Niger, Pakistan, Peru, Poland, Somalia, Sudan: draft resolution.
A/C.5/L.1062/Rev.1. Afghanistan, Algeria, Barbados, Chile, Colombia, Costa Rica, Cyprus, Denmark, Ecuador, India, Indonesia, Iran, Ireland, Italy, Ivory Coast, Kuwait, Lebanon,

Libyan Arab Republic, Mexico, Nicaragua, Niger, Nigeria, Pakistan, Peru, Poland, Somalia, Sudan, Tunisia, Yugoslavia: revised draft resolution, as amended by ACABQ (A/8408/Add.9, para. 12), approved by Fifth Committee on 23 November 1971, meeting 1460, by 68 votes to 0, with 7 abstentions.
A/8531. Report of Fifth Committee (part I).

RESOLUTION 2772(XXVI), as recommended by Fifth Committee, A/8531, adopted by Assembly on 29 November 1971, meeting 1997, by 95 votes to 0, with 8 abstentions.

The General Assembly,
Noting that the net base salary of the Secretary-General has remained unchanged since 1 January 1968, when it was established at $31,600 net per annum ($50,000 gross per annum) and when provision was made for the appropriate post adjustments to be continued,

Noting also that the gross salaries of staff in the Professional and higher categories were revised by a 5 per cent increase and by the consolidation of one class of post adjustment into the base scales effective on 1 January 1969, and that subsequently the gross salaries were revised by the consolidation of two classes of post adjustment and by an 8 per cent increase effective on 1 July 1971,

Noting further the increases that have been made since 1 January 1968 in the salaries and allowances of the executive heads of the specialized agencies, and aware of the need to maintain an appropriate relationship between these salaries and the salary and allowances of the Secretary-General,

Recognizing that since it last considered, at its seventeenth session, the annual retirement allowance for the Secretary-General established in 1946 at one half of his net salary (excluding allowances), all retirement pensions payable by the United Nations Joint Staff Pension Fund, including those of the executive heads of the specialized agencies, have been based on gross annual salaries as a result of decisions taken by the General Assembly,

1. *Decides* that, with effect from 1 December 1971, the salary of the Secretary-General shall be $62,500 gross ($37,850 net) per annum;

2. *Decides further* that the provisions relating to the retirement allowance of the Secretary-General shall henceforth be as follows:

(a) On retirement on the completion of a full term of office, the annual retirement allowance of the Secretary-General shall be one half of the gross salary;

(b) In the event of the Secretary-General's retirement before the completion of the full term of his appointment, he shall be provided with a retirement allowance equal to one half of the full allowance if he has served at least one year, but less than two years; for longer periods, the retirement allowance shall increase by one eighth of the full allowance for each completed year of service beyond one year until reaching its full level on the completion of five years of service;

(c) (i) If the Secretary-General should die in office, his widow shall receive a pension equal to one half of the retirement allowance to which the Secretary-General would have been entitled had he retired on the date of his death; in no case shall the widow's pension be less than one half of the retirement allowance which would have been payable to the Secretary-General after one year of service;

(ii) If the Secretary-General should die while he is in receipt of a retirement allowance, his widow shall receive a pension equal to one half of that retirement allowance;

(iii) If the Secretary-General should die while in office or while he is in receipt of a retirement allowance, benefits equal to those provided for in the Regulations of the United Nations Joint Staff Pension Fund shall be paid to his surviving children or secondary dependants;

(iv) The conditions under which the benefits listed in (i), (ii) and (iii) above will be payable shall be consistent with those applicable to such benefits when they are paid by the United Nations Joint Staff Pension Fund;

(d) The provisions contained in appendix D of the Staff Rules of the United Nations shall be applicable *mutatis mutandis* in the event of death, injury or illness of the Secretary-General attributable to the performance of official duties on behalf of the United Nations.

Special Committee for the Review of the United Nations Salary System

General Assembly—26th session
Fifth Committee, meetings 1458, 1459, 1491.
Plenary meeting 2031.

A/8428 and Corr.1. Report of Special Committee for Review of United Nations Salary System, 1 June–24 August 1971. (Annex IV: List of documents.)
A/C.5/1388 and Corr.1, A/8408/Add.6. Special Committee for Review of United Nations Salary System established in

accordance with General Assembly resolution 2743(XXV) of 17 December 1970. Revised estimates under expenditure section 2 (Special meetings and conferences). Reports of Secretary-General and ACABQ.

Accelerated salary increments

General Assembly—26th session
Fifth Committee, meetings 1483, 1485, 1489.
Plenary meeting 2030.

A/C.5/1371. Amendments to Staff Rules. Note by Secretary-General.
A/C.5/1398. Amendment to Staff Regulations of United Nations. Note by Secretary-General, paragraph 4, approved without objection by Fifth Committee on 15 December 1971, meeting 1485.
A/C.5/1408, A/8408/Add.20. Implementation of General Assembly resolution 2480 B (XXIII). Revised estimates under expenditure section 3 (Salaries and wages), 4 (Common staff costs), 15 (UNCTAD) and 16 (UNIDO). Reports of Secretary-General and ACABQ.
A/8604/Add.1. Report of Fifth Committee (part II) (on personnel questions), containing draft resolution (para. 1 (b)), suggested by Committee Chairman based on proposals of Secretary-General (A/C.5/1398, paras. 3 and 4), approved without vote by Fifth Committee on 15 December 1971, meeting 1485.
A/L.669. Belgium, Canada, France, Tunisia: amendment to draft resolution recommended by Fifth Committee in A/8604/Add.1.

RESOLUTION 2888(XXVI), as recommended by Fifth Committee, A/8604/Add.1, as amended by 4 powers, A/L.669, adopted by Assembly on 21 December 1971, meeting 2030, by 99 votes to 2, with 7 abstentions.

The General Assembly,

Having considered the note by the Secretary-General on amendments to the Staff Regulations of the United Nations and the related report of the Advisory Committee on Administrative and Budgetary Questions,

1. *Decides* that the Staff Regulations of the United Nations shall be modified by the following amendments, with effect from 1 January 1972:

. . .

(b) Replace the present text of annex I, paragraph 4, by the following:

"Annex I, paragraph 4

"Subject to satisfactory service, salary increments within the levels set forth in paragraph 3 of the present annex shall be awarded annually except that any increment above step IV of the Principal Officer level shall be preceded by two years at the previous step. The Secretary-General is authorized to reduce the interval between salary increments to ten months and twenty months, respectively, in the case of staff subject to geographical distribution who have an adequate and confirmed knowledge of a second official language of the United Nations.";

2. *Decides* that, in the application of annex I, paragraph 4, of the Staff Regulations of the United Nations in its revised form, the Secretary-General shall take account in each case of the staff member's length of service prior to 1 January 1972 in the step of his grade;

3. *Takes note* of the changes made by the Secretary-General in the Staff Rules of the United Nations in the year ending on 31 August 1971, as set forth in his report.

[For text of paragraph 1 (a), see below under SALARY OF ADMINISTRATOR OF UNITED NATIONS DEVELOPMENT PROGRAMME.]

Salary of Administrator of United Nations Development Programme

General Assembly—26th session
Fifth Committee, meetings 1480, 1489.
Plenary meeting 2030.

A/8565. Amendments to Staff Regulations of United Nations. Report of ACABQ.

A/C.5/1371. Amendments to Staff Rules. Note by Secretary-General.

A/C.5/1398/Add.1. Amendment to Staff Regulations of United Nations. Note by Secretary-General, approved without vote by Fifth Committee on 13 December 1971, meeting 1480.

A/8604/Add.1. Report of Fifth Committee (part II) (on personnel questions), containing draft resolution (para. 1 (a)), suggested by Committee Chairman based on proposals of Secretary-General (A/C.5/1398/Add.1), approved without vote by Fifth Committee on 13 December 1971, meeting 1480.

RESOLUTION 2888 (XXVI), as recommended by Fifth Committee, A/8604/Add.1, adopted by Assembly on 21 December 1971, meeting 2030, by 99 votes to 2, with 7 abstentions.

The General Assembly,

Having considered the note by the Secretary-General on amendments to the Staff Regulations of the United Nations and the related report of the Advisory Committee on Administrative and Budgetary Questions,

1. *Decides* that the Staff Regulations of the United Nations shall be modified by the following amendments, with effect from 1 January 1972:

(a) Replace the present text of annex I, paragraph 1, by the following:

"Annex I, paragraph 1

"The Administrator of the United Nations Development Programme, having a status equivalent to that of the executive head of a major specialized agency, shall receive a salary of $US 56,000 per year, an Under-Secretary-General shall receive a salary of $US 43,750 per year and an Assistant Secretary-General shall receive a salary of $US 39,150 per year, subject to the staff assessment plan provided in staff regulation 3.3 and to post adjustments wherever applied. If otherwise eligible, they shall receive the allowances which are available to staff members generally.";

. . .

Other personnel questions

Measures on linguistic balance and proficiency in the Secretariat

In 1971, the General Assembly took a number of steps in anticipation of the coming into effect of the measures it had decided upon on 21 December 1968[10] with a view to promoting linguistic balance and language proficiency within the Secretariat.

To this end, the Assembly had then asked the Secretary-General to apply, with effect from 1 January 1972, two incentive measures designed to promote language proficiency of staff in the professional and higher categories.

The first one was that promotions of staff in the professional and higher categories subject to geographical distribution would normally be conditional upon adequate and confirmed knowledge of a second official language of the United Nations, i.e. Chinese, English, French, Russian or Spanish.

The second measure was that such knowledge would permit staff members to pass more rapidly through the steps within each grade. For the purpose of these incentive measures, the 1968 resolution prescribed that confirmation of the knowledge of a second language would be the obtaining of a language proficiency certificate award by the United Nations.

In 1971, the steps to be taken in 1972 were discussed both in the Assembly's Fifth (Administrative and Budgetary) Committee and in plenary meetings of the Assembly.

In connexion with its consideration of the question of the composition of the Secretariat, the Fifth Committee decided, on 24 November 1971 on the basis of a proposal by Ghana and Japan as amended by India, to include in its report to the

Assembly a statement requesting the Secretary-General, in the implementation of the Assembly's resolution of 21 December 1968, to safeguard the interests of those staff members whose mother tongue was not one of the official languages of the United Nations and to report, through his annual reports on the composition of the Secretariat, on measures taken in this regard. On 17 December 1971, without adopting a resolution, the General Assembly took note of this decision by the Fifth Committee.

A further action taken by the Fifth Committee was to endorse a recommendation by the Assembly's Advisory Committee on Administrative and Budgetary Questions to the effect that, for the purpose of implementing the incentive measures, the language proficiency certificate should be required in all cases, including those cases in which staff members whose mother tongue was an official language were required under the terms of their appointment to work in another official language. This was reflected in the report of the Fifth Committee on other personnel questions approved by the Assembly on 21 December 1971.

Accordingly, the Secretary-General issued administrative instructions which stipulated that in order to establish their eligibility for the incentive measures, staff members whose mother tongue was one of the official languages of the United Nations must obtain a language proficiency certificate in an official language other than their mother tongue, and those whose mother tongue was not an official language must obtain a certificate in one of the official languages that was not the language

[10]See Y.U.N., 1968, pp. 875-76, text of resolution 2480 B (XXIII).

in which they were required to work under the terms of their appointment.

In addition, on 21 December 1971, the Assembly in adopting resolution 2888(XXVI) approved accelerated salary increments for qualified staff members in conformity with the provisions of the Assembly's resolution of 21 December 1968 on incentive measures to promote language proficiency in the staff.

(For further details, see p. 633 above.)

Joint Inspection Unit report on United Nations personnel problems

Among the personnel questions considered by the General Assembly in 1971 was the matter of personnel problems of the United Nations.

Before the Assembly was a report on this subject prepared by Maurice Bertrand, a member of the Joint Inspection Unit. The report, transmitted to the Assembly by the Secretary-General, contained an analysis of the methods currently used in the United Nations in the recruitment, training, promotion and administration of its staff in the professional category and above, as well as an assessment of the reasons for the difficulties encountered.

It presented a series of recommendations that fell into five broad categories: (a) revision of basic concepts underlying the current personnel policy; (b) modernization of administrative practices; (c) reform of recruitment methods; (d) introduction of a career development system; and (e) modification of the structure and emoluments of the staff. Another recommendation dealt with the manner in which the work initiated by the report might be carried forward by the establishment of a task force.

The Secretary-General, setting forth his preliminary comments to the Assembly on the report of the Joint Inspection Unit, indicated that, since the report raised questions likely to be of interest to the Assembly's Special Committee for the Review of the United Nations Salary System and to the Administrative Management Service—which had not yet carried out a proposed survey of the Office of Personnel—he believed that comments on the substance of the report should be deferred until the 1972 session of the Assembly. In the meantime, he proposed to follow up on some of the recommendations contained in the report by undertaking supplementary studies.

In the course of the discussion of the report in the General Assembly's Fifth (Administrative and Budgetary) Committee, the representatives who spoke on the subject agreed that, in view of the importance and highly complex and technical

nature of the report, Assembly consideration of its substance should be deferred to 1972.

On a proposal by Canada, the Fifth Committee recommended to the Assembly that the Secretary-General be requested:

(a) to refer the Joint Inspection Unit report to the heads of the specialized agencies and the International Atomic Energy Agency;

(b) to initiate early discussions in the inter-agency Administrative Committee on Co-ordination (ACC) to determine areas where close co-operation in personnel questions arising from that report would be of mutual benefit to member organizations within the United Nations system;

(c) if possible, to transmit the views of ACC in this regard to the Special Committee for the Review of the United Nations Salary System.

At the suggestion of its Chairman, the Fifth Committee further decided to recommend to the General Assembly that the Secretary-General and the Assembly's Advisory Committee on Administrative and Budgetary Questions be requested to make a full submission to the Assembly in 1972 on the report of the Joint Inspection Unit, taking into account the views and recommendations of the Special Committee for the Review of the United Nations Salary System as well as the results of the forthcoming administrative management survey of the Office of Personnel.

On 21 December 1971, the General Assembly approved without objection the recommendations of the Fifth Committee. It did so without adopting a formal resolution.

Staff training

In 1971, the General Assembly had before it a report of the Secretary-General on staff training and the related report of the Assembly's Advisory Committee on Administrative and Budgetary Questions.

In his report, the Secretary-General proposed a significant increase in staff training programmes with the request for an additional appropriation of $436,450 to cover the costs in 1972. The major item of the proposal was the provision from the United Nations regular budget of a subvention of $200,000 as a contribution to the first-year budget of a United Nations staff college, the establishment of which had been proposed as an inter-agency project by the United Nations Institute for Training and Research with the concurrence of the Administrative Committee on Co-ordination (see pp. 479-80).

The Advisory Committee stated in its report that, while recognizing the importance of staff training, it favoured a cautious approach in view of the fact that several studies bearing on the subject were still to be considered. It recommended that the additional appropriation for staff training programmes be reduced to $88,350, the amount requested for the proposed staff college being specifically excluded. The Advisory Committee recommended instead that the General Assembly defer consideration of the proposal to set up a staff college until its session in 1972.

In the Assembly's Fifth (Administrative and Budgetary) Committee, on 15 December 1971, Ethiopia, France and Nigeria proposed approval of the Secretary-General's request for an appropriation of $200,000 as the United Nations contribution to the core budget of the staff college for 1972. The proposal was rejected by a vote of 33 to 31, with 11 abstentions.

On the same date, the Fifth Committee ap-proved by 52 votes to 2, with 20 abstentions, a proposal by Brazil, based on the Advisory Committee's recommendation, that the General Assembly should approve in principle the idea of establishing a United Nations staff college but defer consideration of the proposal to set up such a college until 1972.

The Fifth Committee also approved, by a vote of 74 to 0, with 1 abstention, the recommendations of the Advisory Committee for an additional appropriation of $88,350 for staff training programmes. Subsequently, the Fifth Committee rejected a proposal by Kenya and Liberia to reopen the debate on the question.

The General Assembly approved the Fifth Committee's decisions on 21 December 1971, without adopting a formal resolution.

DOCUMENTARY REFERENCES

*Measures on linguistic balance
and proficiency in the Secretariat*

General Assembly—26th session
Fifth Committee, meetings 1459-1461, 1464, 1480, 1481, 1483-1485, 1489.
Plenary meetings 2023, 2030.

A/8483. Personnel questions: composition of Secretariat. Report of Secretary-General.
A/C.5/1398. Amendment to Staff Regulations of United Nations. Note by Secretary-General, para. 4.
A/C.5/1398/Add.1. Amendment to Staff Regulations of United Nations. Note by Secretary-General.
A/C.5/1404. Other personnel questions: staff training. Report of Secretary-General, Chapter II.
A/C.5/1408, A/8408/Add.20. Implementation of General Assembly resolution 2480B(XXIII). Revised estimates under expenditure sections 3 (Salaries and wages), 4 (Common staff costs), 15 (UNCTAD) and 16 (UNIDO). Reports of Secretary-General and ACABQ.
A/8408/Add.21. Other personnel questions: staff training. Report of ACABQ, para. 6.
A/8604. Report of Fifth Committee (part I) (on personnel questions), para. 36.
A/8604/Add.1. Report of Fifth Committee (part II), section IV and para. 32.
A/8429. Resolutions adopted by Assembly during its 26th session, 21 September–22 December 1971. Other decisions, p. 133 (item 84).

[See also DOCUMENTARY REFERENCES, p. 634 above, on ACCELERATED SALARY INCREMENTS.]

*Joint Inspection Unit report on
United Nations personnel problems*

General Assembly—26th session
Fifth Committee, meetings 1480-1483, 1489
Plenary meeting 2030.

A/8454 (parts I and II). Report of Joint Inspection Unit (JIU) on personnel problems in United Nations. Note by Secretary-General (transmitting report).
A/8545. Note by Advisory Committee on Administrative and Budgetary Questions (ACABQ) (transmitting preliminary comments of Secretary-General on report of JIU (A/8454)).
A/8552. Report of ACABQ.
A/8604/Add.1. Report of Fifth Committee (part II), section I and para. 34 (a) and (b).
A/8429. Resolutions adopted by General Assembly during its 26th session, 21 September–22 December 1971. Other decisions, p. 133 (item 84, 2nd para.).

Staff training

General Assembly—26th session
Fifth Committee, meetings 1482, 1484, 1489, 1491.
Plenary meeting 2030.

A/C.5/1404. Staff training. Report of Secretary-General.
A/8408/Add.21. Budget estimates for financial year 1972. Staff training. Report of ACABQ.
A/8414. Report of Executive Director of United Nations Institute for Training and Research, Chapter III.
A/8604/Add.1. Report of Fifth Committee (part II), section II and para. 34 (c).
A/8429. Resolutions adopted by General Assembly during its 26th session, 21 September–22 December 1971. Other decisions, p. 133 (item 84, 2nd para.).

Chapter II

Budgetary arrangements

The United Nations budget for 1972

On 22 December 1971, at its twenty-sixth session, the General Assembly voted appropriations totalling $213,124,410 to meet the expenses of the United Nations in 1972. It also approved estimates of income in the amount of $35,921,650 (which included $25,313,650 to be derived from staff assessment on wages and salaries).

The gross amount to be contributed by Member States for 1972 was set by the Assembly at $203,203,426, after taking into account the surplus amount for the financial year 1970, contributions of new Member States for the financial years 1970 and 1971, and certain revisions to the income estimates for 1971. The gross assessment on United Nations Member States was to be offset by their respective shares in staff assessment income through the Tax Equalization Fund, in a total amount of $26,091,165.

These decisions were embodied in the three-part Assembly resolution 2899(XXVI). (For text and voting details, see DOCUMENTARY REFERENCES below.)

The Assembly's action was taken on the recommendation of its Fifth (Administrative and Budgetary) Committee, on the basis of reports of the Secretary-General and recommendations thereon by the Assembly's Advisory Committee on Administrative and Budgetary Questions.

The original expenditure estimates for 1972 submitted by the Secretary-General amounted to $207,721,500. Those recommended by the Advisory Committee amounted to $204,255,300, representing a reduction of $3,466,200 from the Secretary-General's estimates. Income estimates originally submitted by the Secretary-General amounted to $35,570,800. The Advisory Committee recommended a reduction of $365,000 in the income estimates submitted by the Secretary-General. The final figures approved by the Assembly, $213,124,410 and $35,921,650, were the consequence of revisions subsequent to the submission of the initial estimates and of inclusion of appropriations to meet the financial implications of decisions taken by the General Assembly during its 1971 session. (For details, see DOCUMENTARY REFERENCES below.)

As in previous years, certain Members, including Bulgaria, the Byelorussian SSR, Czechoslovakia, Hungary, Mongolia, Poland, the Ukrainian SSR and the USSR, reiterated their reserva-

tions regarding the inclusion in the regular budget of such items as the United Nations bond issue, the financing of the United Nations Commission for the Unification and Rehabilitation of Korea and the United Nations Memorial Cemetery in Korea. They also expressed reservations about various items relating to technical assistance programmes which they considered to be in contravention of the United Nations Charter; those activities, they believed, should be financed solely from voluntary contributions and not from the regular budget.

Argentina, Brazil, Ecuador, India, Nigeria and Sudan were among those who reserved their position of principle with regard to the United Nations bond issue; in their view, since funds raised thereby were used exclusively to cover expenditures resulting from peace-keeping operations, they should be financed on the principles approved by the Assembly for that purpose rather than on the same basis as the regular expenditures of the Organization.

Financial position of the Organization

In an oral statement before the Assembly's Fifth Committee on 6 October 1971, the Secretary-General described the financial position of the Organization as having reached a stage of near and hopeless insolvency. He felt he might have no alternative but to introduce a series of restrictive financial measures in order to arrest any further increase in the deficit, but would refrain from doing so while consultations were still in progress under the good offices of Ambassador Edvard Hambro, of Norway, the President of the twenty-fifth session of the General Assembly, in an effort to find a means of resolving the Organization's serious financial problem.

Ambassador Hambro explained to the Fifth Committee on 21 October that the basis of his approach in an appeal he had sent to all Member States on steps to be taken for an over-all solution of the problem was that positions of principle which had been taken in respect of the financing of controversial peace-keeping operations should be fully respected but that, at the same time, it needed to be realized that safeguarding the continued functioning of the United Nations was in the common interest of all Members.

During the Fifth Committee's general discussion on the budget estimates for 1972, an atmosphere of serious concern over the urgent financial difficulties of the Organization prevailed.

A number of Members expressed their appreciation of Ambassador Hambro's efforts and their hope that voluntary contributions might be forthcoming.

Among the various suggestions for achieving a solution to the long-term deficit problem and the immediate cash problem were the following: voluntary contributions; the establishment of a group to study the matter and make recommendations; the exclusion from the regular budget of expenditures which some considered to be in contravention of the Charter and to which they did not contribute; a régime of strict economy through administrative, financial and programme restraint; and the prompt payment of assessed contributions, with attendant deadlines and penalties.

In a letter to the Secretary-General dated 10 December, circulated to Assembly Members, Ambassador Hambro reported on his efforts to resolve the financial situation. Despite Member States' awareness of the seriousness of the situation and the need for drastic measures, he said, he had not been able to register any tendency to general agreement on how the problems could be solved or on what basis any voluntary contributions should be made within the framework of reasonable equitability. He suggested that, in order to use the time between sessions of the Assembly, and if possible to prepare the 1972 Assembly session fully for action, Members might consider establishing an inter-governmental working group or *ad hoc* committee to study the facts and propose suggestions for a solution.

On 18 December, the President of the General Assembly proposed the creation of a 15-member Special Committee on the Financial Situation of the United Nations. The Committee would be composed of the permanent members of the Security Council, three African States, two Asian States, one Eastern European State, two Latin American States and two Western European and other States. On 22 December, the Assembly approved the President's proposal without objection.

Subsequent to the general discussion of the 1972 budget in the Fifth Committee, the United Nations Controller informed the Committee that, in order to arrest any further increase in the deficit—estimated at $3.9 million for 1972—the Secretary-General had suggested he be authorized to credit to a special account for the purpose, or to the Working Capital Fund, the net surplus of $1.8 million which had accrued in 1970 and in prior years instead of making it available for credit to Member States against their assessed contributions for 1972, as would normally be the case. The Secretary-General would then endeavour to administer the appropriations in such a way as to aim at an unexpended balance of $2.1 million, or approximately 1 per cent under the budget as a whole.

The Assembly took no action on the Secretary-General's suggestion. The United States expressed the opinion that the Secretary-General's proposal would mean transferring to all Member States the burden resulting from the failure of a few to pay what they owe.

Manpower utilization and staffing requirements of the Secretariat

MANPOWER SURVEY

The progress made by the Administrative Management Service in conducting the survey of manpower utilization in the Secretariat, proposed in 1968,[1] was discussed in the Fifth Committee in conjunction with the budget estimates.

A progress report by the Secretary-General on the subject also included, *inter alia,* an outline of the future role and activities which the Secretary-General planned to assign to the Administrative Management Service and the estimated time schedule for completing the survey.

The Advisory Committee on Administrative and Budgetary Questions, in a related report, expressed the hope that the Administrative Management Service would be associated with any review of departmental requests for additional manpower, so that full account could be taken of any absorptive capacity which implementation of the recommendations of the Administrative Management Service had generated in the departments concerned. The Advisory Committee also called attention to a tendency for the Administrative Management Service and the Joint Inspection Unit to operate in the same fields and recommended that the two bodies keep each other fully informed of their respective work programmes to avoid overlapping. In addition, it expressed the hope that the Administrative Management Service would in future place more emphasis on work measurement and provide work statistics indicative of output.

After a brief discussion of the reports of the Secretary-General and the Advisory Committee, the Fifth Committee decided, on 18 December 1971, by a vote of 60 to 9, to take note of the reports and approved additional appropriations recommended by the Advisory Committee in connexion with the matters raised.

The General Assembly took note of this decision on 22 December 1971, without adopting a formal resolution.

[1]See Y.U.N., 1968, pp. 890-92.

HIRING OF EXPERTS AND CONSULTANTS
AND SECRETARIAT STAFFING NEEDS

During the Fifth Committee's discussion of the budget estimates for the financial year 1972, a number of representatives also commented on staffing requirements. Several objected to what they considered a constant increase in staff and emphasized the need for increased productivity through better management and redeployment of existing staff. A number of Members—including Colombia, France, Greece, Hungary, Japan, Mexico, Pakistan, Poland, Spain, Togo, the USSR, the United Republic of Tanzania, and the United States—were seriously concerned with what they considered to be an undue reliance by the Secretariat on the use of outside consultants and temporary assistance.

Finding it unreasonable to consider further increases in the Secretariat staff in the light of the Organization's serious financial situation, the USSR, on 5 November 1971, introduced a draft resolution proposing that the staff in 1972 be kept at the 1971 level. It also proposed that the financing of all provisional posts be discontinued as from 1 January 1972, and that the Secretary-General urgently undertake a study on how to reduce the number of external consultants and temporary staff and improve the efficiency of the permanent staff.

The USSR subsequently revised its proposal, adding provisions whereby appropriations for the retention of provisional Secretariat staff hired before 15 November 1971 would be included in the 1972 budget, and the appropriations requested by the Secretary-General in the 1972 budget estimates for temporary assistance, overtime and night differential would be reduced by 20 per cent. In lieu of the study previously requested, the revised proposal asked the Secretary-General to organize the work of the existing staff of the Secretariat and the secretariats of the regional economic commissions so that they could carry out in full the measures incumbent on them in connexion with the implementation of the Second United Nations Development Decade.

Saudi Arabia proposed several amendments to the original USSR text.

Among other things, these amendments would have given the Secretary-General discretionary powers, after consultation with the Controller, to increase staff resources in 1972 if he felt it was imperative to do so, provided that the increase did not exceed the amount of new posts he had proposed in the budget estimates for 1972. The Saudi Arabian amendments would also have modified the original USSR proposal that all provisional posts be eliminated effective 1 January 1972 by calling for an approximate annual 5 per cent elimination of most of the current provisional

staff, for a period of three years, to be achieved by the pooling of professional and secretarial work in Secretariat departments, where feasible.

On 11 November 1971, the United States formally proposed that the Fifth Committee should: approve only those new posts requested by the Secretary-General that had been specifically recommended or approved by the Administrative Management Service; consider requests for new established posts arising from decisions taken subsequent to the preparation of the Secretary-General's initial budget estimates on the basis of the special circumstances in each case; apply turnover deductions of 80 and 40 per cent, respectively, to new established professional and higher-level posts and to new established general service posts for 1972; appropriate the same amounts in 1972 as were expended in 1970 for temporary assistance and for overtime and night differential, at the same time trying to apply 65 per cent of the resulting reduction in the estimates to individual experts and consultants; and approve no new provisional posts for 1972, but approve the continuation into 1972 of such posts provided for in 1971 but not converted into established posts.

Several Members expressed reservations about the USSR and the United States proposals.

Ghana, Iran, Ireland, Nigeria, Thailand, Togo and Tunisia were among those who saw no link between the level of budget expenditure and the financial crisis.

Algeria, Argentina, Colombia, Ecuador, Pakistan, Uruguay and Yugoslavia, moreover, feared that any reductions beyond those already recommended by the Assembly's Advisory Committee on Administrative and Budgetary Questions would affect the Organization's work programme and hamper the attainment of the objectives of the Second United Nations Development Decade.

Belgium, Canada, France and Tunisia were concerned with the effect the United States proposals would have on the three new posts requested for the establishment of a French Language Unit in the Office of Public Information, in response to a request expressed by the Fifth Committee in 1970.[2] Although the Administrative Management Service had not recommended the posts in its survey of the department, the United States proposal would not affect the three posts, these Members were assured, since the Service had subsequently recognized the need for the posts.

The USSR and the United States subsequently decided not to press for a vote on their proposals.

However, on 17 November 1971, acting on a proposal by Poland, the Fifth Committee agreed,

---

[2]See Y.U.N., 1970, p. 849.

without objection, that the following text of its request to the Joint Inspection Unit on the hiring of experts and consultants be inserted in its report to the Assembly on the budget estimates for 1972:

The Fifth Committee requests the Joint Inspection Unit to include in its programme of work for 1972 an over-all review of the question of experts and consultants hired by different services of the United Nations and to submit its report, with any related recommendations, to the General Assembly at its twenty-seventh session.

The Assembly took note of the Fifth Committee's decision on 22 December, without adopting a formal resolution, when it took up the report of the Fifth Committee.

Planning estimates for 1973

The General Assembly, on 17 December 1971, approved without objection a recommendation of its Fifth (Administrative and Budgetary) Committee to defer for one further year[3] the implementation of the provision of the Assembly's resolution of 19 December 1967[4] that envisaged the consideration and approval of planning estimates for the United Nations budget estimates for the second succeeding (forecast) budgetary period—originally 1971, now set for 1973.

During the discussion of the question in the Fifth Committee, the view was expressed that a planning estimate and its possible application depended on whether a proposed new form of presentation of the United Nations budget by programme might be adopted. The United States said it would agree to a postponement for another year on the understanding that this action would in no way affect the principle that planning estimates should be approved by the Assembly every year for the forthcoming second budgetary period.

Form of presentation of United Nations budget

On 21 December 1971, the General Assembly endorsed a decision taken by its Fifth (Administrative and Budgetary) Committee to postpone until 1972 consideration of the form of presentation of the United Nations budget.

Pursuant to a decision taken by the Fifth Committee in 1970,[5] the Secretary-General submitted to the Assembly in 1971 a mock-up of the budget estimates for 1972 in a proposed new form of presentation on a programme basis.

In an oral statement before the Fifth Committee, the Chairman of the Advisory Committee on Administrative and Budgetary Questions explained that the Advisory Committee had not received the mock-up in time to give it adequate attention. Moreover, an alternative form of presentation of the budget had emerged from the

Economic and Social Council's Committee for Programme and Co-ordination (CPC), which had considered the matter at its session held during the period September–November 1971 (see pp. 464-66). The Advisory Committee was therefore called upon to consider both the mock-up and the alternative presentation, as well as the question of what changes would need to be made in the executive and deliberative machinery in the event the new form were to be adopted. Consequently, the Advisory Committee believed it would be wise to defer consideration of a new form of the budget until the following year.

After a brief discussion, a text to the following effect, proposed by India, was approved without objection, on 15 December 1971, for inclusion in the Fifth Committee's report to the General Assembly:

Owing to various practical considerations, it was not possible for the Fifth Committee to consider the question of the form of presentation of the United Nations budget. The Fifth Committee, therefore, decided to postpone consideration of this item until the twenty-seventh session of the General Assembly. In order to aid it in its consideration of this item, the Fifth Committee recommends that:

(a) The Advisory Committee on Administrative and Budgetary Questions should submit to it, at the beginning of the Assembly's 1972 session, detailed comments and recommendations on the form of presentation of the budget, including the submissions to the Committee for Programme and Co-ordination;

(b) The Secretary-General should present to it through the Advisory Committee on Administrative and Budgetary Questions: (i) a miniature mock-up covering a small segment of the 1973 estimates; and (ii) a report setting out the probable legal, institutional and organizational implications of switching to programme budgeting, bearing in mind the possibility of adoption of a biennial budget cycle;

(c) The Secretary-General's reports in (b) above should be transmitted to the Economic and Social Council and its Committee for Programme and Co-ordination for comments and suggestions, in order that the Advisory Committee on Administrative and Budgetary Questions can take them into account.

The Assembly took note of this decision, without objection, when it considered the Fifth Committee's report to the Assembly on the implementation of the recommendations of the *Ad Hoc* Committee of Experts to Examine the Finances of the United Nations and the Specialized Agencies.

Unforeseen and extraordinary expenses

On 21 December 1971, the Assembly's Fifth (Administrative and Budgetary) Committee ap-

---

[3]See Y.U.N., 1970, pp. 846-47.
[4]See Y.U.N., 1967, pp. 802-3, text of resolution 2370(XXII).
[5]See Y.U.N., 1970, p. 866.

proved, by 59 votes to 10, with 1 abstention, a draft resolution on unforeseen and extraordinary expenses for the financial year 1972. The resolution was adopted by the General Assembly on 22 December 1971 by a recorded vote of 112 to 10, with 2 abstentions, as resolution 2900(XXVI).

The Assembly thereby established the conditions under which the Secretary-General was authorized to enter into commitments to meet any unforeseen expenses which might arise in 1972 for which no provision had been made in the 1972 budget.

At the suggestion of the Assembly's Advisory Committee on Administrative and Budgetary Questions, in its report on the financial implications of a General Assembly resolution of 14 December 1971 on emergency aid in connexion with natural disasters (see p. 475), a provision was included whereby the Secretary-General was authorized, without prior concurrence of the Advisory Committee, to make commitments for such purposes not exceeding $200,000. A normal ceiling of $20,000 per country in the case of any one disaster was stipulated.

(For text of resolution, see DOCUMENTARY REFERENCES below.)

Working Capital Fund for 1972

On 22 December 1971, the General Assembly, acting on the recommendation of its Fifth (Administrative and Budgetary) Committee, established the level of the Working Capital Fund for 1972 at $40 million, the same level as for 1971.

As in previous years, the Assembly also set forth terms under which Member States would make advances to the Fund, credits and advances to be set off against those amounts, as well as conditions under which the Secretary-General was authorized to advance from the Working Capital Fund sums as might be necessary to finance certain budgetary appropriations and authorized commitments.

These decisions were embodied in Assembly resolution 2901(XXVI), adopted by a recorded vote of 111 to 0, with 12 abstentions. The Fifth Committee had approved the text on 21 December 1971, by 59 votes to 0, with 10 abstentions.

(For text of resolution, see DOCUMENTARY REFERENCES below.)

DOCUMENTARY REFERENCES

The United Nations budget for 1972

General Assembly—26th session
Fifth Committee, meetings 1427-1444, 1446-1470, 1472, 1474-1479, 1481-1491.
Plenary meetings 1997, 2021, 2031.

A/8322. Budget performance of United Nations for financial year 1970. Report of Secretary-General.
A/8401. Report of Secretary-General on work of the Organization, 16 June 1970–15 June 1971, Part Five, Chapter III C.
A/8403. Report of Economic and Social Council on work of its 50th and 51st sessions, Chapter XXIV C.
A/8406, Vol.I and Corr.1,3, Vol. II and Vol. III. Budget estimates for financial year 1972 and information annexes.
A/8406/Add.1. Budget for financial year 1972.
A/8408 and Corr.1,2. First report of Advisory Committee on Administrative and Budgetary Questions (ACABQ) on budget estimates for financial year 1972.
A/8408/Add.1-30. Second to thirty-first reports of ACABQ on budget estimates for financial year 1972.
A/8446 and Add.1. Report of Joint Inspection Unit (JIU) on United Nations Department of Economic and Social Affairs. Notes by ACABQ (transmitting report, preliminary observations of Secretary-General and comments of Administrator of UNDP on JIU report).
A/8455. Letter of 4 October 1971 from President of General Assembly to Chairmen of Main Committees (transmitting letter of 29 September 1971 from Chairman of Fifth Committee).
A/8497. Letter of 10 December 1971 from Norway.
A/8635. Note of 18 December 1971 by President of General Assembly.
A/C.5/1362. Joint UNCTAD/GATT International Trade Centre (ITC). Note by Secretary-General (transmitting budget estimates for financial year 1972 for ITC, submitted by Secretary-General of UNCTAD and Director-General of GATT (ITC/AG/17)).
A/C.5/1372. Distribution of Secretariat functions between different locations. Note by Secretary-General.
A/C.5/1376. Statement of Secretary-General at 1427th meeting of Fifth Committee, 6 October 1971.

A/C.5/1377. Statement by Chairman of ACABQ at 1427th meeting of Fifth Committee, 6 October 1971.
A/C.5/1380 and Corr.1, A/8408/Add.13. Restructuring Department of Economic and Social Affairs: response to 2nd United Nations Development Decade. Report of Secretary-General and report of Advisory Committee on Administrative and Budgetary Questions.
A/C.5/1381. Headquarters accommodation. Report of Secretary-General.
A/C.5/1383. Budget estimates for financial year 1972, Section 12, Chapter IV: Triangular fellowship programme. Note by Secretary-General.
A/C.5/1384. Letter of 20 October 1971 from France.
A/C.5,1385 and Corr.1,2, A/8408/Add.14. Progress made by Administrative Management Service in conducting survey of manpower utilization in Secretariat. Reports of Secretary-General and ACABQ.
A/C.5/1392, A/8408/Add.8. United Nations accommodation in Bangkok and Addis Ababa. Reports of Secretary-General and ACABQ.
A/C.5/1396, A/8408/Add.11. United Nations building in Santiago, Chile. Reports of Secretary-General and ACABQ.

Administrative and financial implications of Assembly decisions and recommendations of Main Committees

A/C.5/1393, A/8408/Add.5, A/8519. Report of United Nations Commission on International Trade Law on work of its 4th session (Sixth Committee). Statement by Secretary-General and reports of ACABQ and Fifth Committee.
A/C.5/1399 and Corr.1, A/8408/Add.19, A/8579. Report of Economic and Social Council (Regional and sub-regional advisory services under United Nations regular programme of technical co-operation) (Second Committee). Statement by Secretary-General and reports of ACABQ and Fifth Committee.
A/C.5/1401, A/8533. Report of Special Committee on Question of Defining Aggression (Sixth Committee). Statement by Secretary-General and report of Fifth Committee.
A/C.5/1402, A/8535. International co-operation in peaceful uses of outer space: report of Committee on Peaceful Uses of Outer

Space (First Committee). Statement by Secretary-General and report of Fifth Committee.

A/C.5/1403, A/8408/Add.12, A/8534. Policies of *apartheid* of Government of South Africa (Special Political Committee). Statement by Secretary-General and reports of ACABQ and Fifth Committee.

A/C.5/1409 and Corr.1, A/8408/Add.18, A/8499. Assistance in cases of natural disaster (Third Committee). Statement by Secretary-General and reports of ACABQ and Fifth Committee.

A/C.5/1410, A/8408/Add.15, A/8569. Review of role of International Court of Justice (Sixth Committee). Statement by Secretary-General and reports of ACABQ and Fifth Committee.

A/C.5/1411, A/8548. United Nations Relief and Works Agency for Palestine Refugees in Near East (Special Political Committee). Statement by Secretary-General and report of Fifth Committee.

A/C.5/1412, A/8408/Add.17, A/8554. Scientific work on peace research (Plenary). Statement by Secretary-General and reports of ACABQ and Fifth Committee.

A/C.5/1414 and Corr.1, A/8408/Add.23, A/8599. United Nations Conference on Trade and Development: report of Trade and Development Board (Second Committee). Statement by Secretary-General and reports of ACABQ and Fifth Committee.

A/C.5/1415, A/8408/Add.22, A/8602. United Nations Industrial Development Organization (UNIDO): report of special international conference of UNIDO (Second Committee). Statement by Secretary-General and reports of ACABQ and Fifth Committee.

A/C.5/1416 and Corr.1, A/8408/Add.26, A/8601. United Nations Conference on Human Environment (Second Committee). Statement by Secretary-General and reports of ACABQ and Fifth Committee.

A/C.5/1418, A/8609. United Nations Programme of Assistance in Teaching, Study, Dissemination and Wider Appreciation of International Law (Sixth Committee). Statement by Secretary-General and report of Fifth Committee.

A/C.5/1419, A/8603. Economic and social consequences of armaments race and its extremely harmful effects on world peace and security (First Committee). Statement by Secretary-General and report of Fifth Committee.

A/C.5/1420, A/8612. Respect for human rights in armed conflicts: report of Secretary-General (Third Committee). Statement by Secretary-General and report of Fifth Committee.

A/C.5/1421. Question of establishment of an international university (Second Committee). Statement by Secretary-General. (Oral report of Fifth Committee submitted to Assembly on 16 December 1971, meeting 2021.)

A/C.5/1422, A/8633. Question of Namibia (Fourth Committee). Statement by Secretary-General and report of Fifth Committee.

A/C.5/1423, A/8633. United Nations Fund for Namibia (Fourth Committee). Statement by Secretary-General and report of Fifth Committee.

A/C.5/1424, A/8634. United Nations Educational and Training Programme for Southern Africa (Fourth Committee). Statement by Secretary-General and report of Fifth Committee.

A/C.5/1425, A/8627. Reservation exclusively for peaceful purposes of sea-bed and ocean floor, and subsoil thereof, underlying high seas beyond limits of present national jurisdiction and use of their resources in interests of mankind, and convening of conference on law of sea (First Committee). Statement by Secretary-General and report of Fifth Committee.

A/C.5/1426, A/8636. Report of Special Committee to Investigate Israeli Practices Affecting Human Rights of Population of Occupied Territories (Special Political Committee). Statement by Secretary-General and report of Fifth Committee.

A/C.5/1427, A/8631. Co-operation between United Nations and Organization of African Unity (Plenary). Statement by Secretary-General and report of Fifth Committee.

A/C.5/1428, A/8632. Implementation of Declaration on Granting of Independence to Colonial Countries and Peoples (Plenary and Fourth Committee). Statement by Secretary-General and report of Fifth Committee.

A/C.5/L.1062/Rev.1, A/8408/Add.9, A/8531. Salary and retirement allowance of Secretary-General (Fifth Committee). Twenty-nine-power draft resolution and reports of ACABQ and Fifth Committee.

Revised estimates

A/8406/Add.2. Budget estimates for financial year 1972. Revised estimates.

A/8454 (Parts I and II), A/8545, A/8552. Personnel questions: report of JIU on personnel problems in United Nations. Note by Secretary-General (transmitting report), note by Advisory Committee on Administrative and Budgetary Questions (transmitting preliminary comments of Secretary-General on JIU report) and report of ACABQ.

A/C.5/1320 and Corr.1, A/C.5/1320/Rev.1 and Rev.1/Add.1, A/8508/Add.4. Review and reappraisal of United Nations information policies and activities. Reports of Secretary-General and ACABQ.

A/C.5/1364, A/8408/Add.2. Arrangements concerning emoluments and pensions of members of International Court of Justice. Reports of Secretary-General and ACABQ.

A/C.5/1365, A/8408/Add.3. Honorarium of Chairman of ACABQ. Reports of Secretary-General and ACABQ.

A/C.5/1366 and Add.1 and Add.1/Corr.1, A/8408/Add.1 and Add.1/Corr.1. Revised estimates resulting from decisions of Economic and Social Council at its 50th and 51st sessions. Reports of Secretary-General and ACABQ.

A/C.5/1366/Add.2, A/8408/Add.25. Revised estimates resulting from decisions of Economic and Social Council at its 50th and 51st sessions. Reports of Secretary-General and ACABQ.

A/C.5/1378 and Corr.1, A/8408/Add.16. Electronic data-processing in United Nations family of organizations. Reports of Secretary-General and ACABQ.

A/C.5/1388 and Corr.1, A/8408/Add.6. Special Committee for Review of United Nations Salary System established in accordance with General Assembly resolution 2743(XXV) of 17 December 1970. Revised estimates under expenditure section 2 (Special meetings and conferences). Reports of Secretary-General and ACABQ.

A/C.5/1389 and Corr.1,2, A/8408/Add.10. Extension of Palais des Nations [Geneva]. Reports of Secretary-General and ACABQ.

A/C.5/1390 and Corr.1, A/8408/Add.10. Programme of major maintenance of and improvements to Palais des Nations, Geneva. Reports of Secretary-General and ACABQ.

A/C.5/1391, A/8408/Add.7. Additional seating facilities in principal meeting areas. Reports of Secretary-General and ACABQ.

A/C.5/1400, A/8408/Add.24. Revised estimates under expenditure section 16 (UNIDO). Reports of Secretary-General and ACABQ.

A/C.5/1404, A/8408/Add.21. Other personnel questions: staff training. Reports of Secretary-General and ACABQ.

A/C.5/1405, A/8408/Add.28. Requirements for security staff at Headquarters. Reports of Secretary-General and ACABQ.

A/C.5/1406, A/8408/Add.27 and Add.27/Corr.1. Revised estimates under expenditure sections 3 (Salaries and wages), 4 (Common staff costs), 5 (Travel of staff), 8 (Permanent equipment), 9 (Maintenance, operation and rental of premises) and 10 (General expenses), and revised estimates of income under income sections 1 (Income from staff assessment) and 4 (Revenue-producing activities), arising from decisions of Secretary-General based on manpower utilization surveys by Administrative Management Service. Reports of Secretary-General and ACABQ.

A/C.5/1407, A/8408/Add.30. Problems concerning United Nations *Treaty Series*. Reports of Secretary-General and ACABQ.

A/C.5/1408, A/8408/Add.20. Implementation of General Assembly resolution 2480 B (XXIII). Revised estimates under expenditure sections 3, 4, 15 (UNCTAD) and 16. Reports of Secretary-General and ACABQ.

A/C.5/1417 and Corr.1, A/8408/Add.29. Revised estimates under expenditure sections 1 (Travel and other expenses of representatives and members of commissions, committees and other subsidiary bodies), 2, 3, 4, 5, 7 (Construction, alteration, improvement and major maintenance of premises), 8, 9, 10, 11 (Printing), 15, 16, 18 (UNHCR) and 19 (ICJ) and income sections 1 and 3 (General income). Reports of Secretary-General and ACABQ.

Other documents

A/8564. Installation of mechanical means of voting. Report of Secretary-General.

E/5070. Financial implications of actions taken by Economic and Social Council at its 51st session.

E/L.1460. Letter of 4 August 1971 from Chairman of ACABQ to President of Economic and Social Council.

DECISIONS ON BUDGET FOR 1972

A/8406, Vol. I. Draft resolution I A, relating to budget estimates, submitted by Secretary-General for adoption by General Assembly, approved by Fifth Committee on 21 December 1971, meeting 1491, by 55 votes to 8, with 7 abstentions.

A/8408 and Corr.1,2. First report of ACABQ on budget estimates for financial year 1972, Chapter II, para. 68: comparative table of appropriations as proposed by Secretary-General and recommended by ACABQ—Expenditure estimates.

A/8531/Add.2. Report of Fifth Committee (part III), draft resolution XI A.

RESOLUTION 2899 A (XXVI), as recommended by Fifth Committee, A/8531/Add.2, adopted by Assembly on 22 December 1971, meeting 2031, by recorded vote of 106 o 9, with 7 abstentions, as follows:

In favour: Afghanistan, Algeria, Argentina, Australia, Austria, Barbados, Belgium, Bhutan, Bolivia, Brazil, Burma, Burundi, Cameroon, Canada, Ceylon, Chad, Chile, Colombia, Congo, Ccsta Rica, Cyprus, Denmark, Dominican Republic, Ecuador, Egypt, El Salvador, Equatorial Guinea, Ethiopia, Finland, Gabon, Gambia, Ghana, Greece, Guatemala, Guinea, Guyana, Haiti, Honduras, Iceland, India, Indonesia, Iran, Ireland, Israel, Italy, Ivory Coast, Jamaica, Japan, Jordan, Kenya, Khmer Republic, Kuwait, Laos, Lebanon, Lesotho, Liberia, Libyan Arab Republic, Luxembourg, Madagascar, Malawi, Malaysia, Mali, Malta, Mauritania, Mexico, Morocco, Nepal, Netherlands, New Zealand, Nicaragua, Niger, Nigeria, Norway, Pakistan, Panama, Paraguay, People's Democratic Republic of Yemen, Peru, Philippines, Qatar, Rwanda, Saudi Arabia, Senegal, Sierra Leone, Singapore, Somalia, Spain, Sudan, Swaziland, Sweden, Syrian Arab Republic, Thailand, Togo, Trinidad and Tobago, Tunisia, Turkey, Uganda, United Arab Emirates, United Republic of Tanzania, Upper Volta, Uruguay, Venezuela, Yemen, Yugoslavia, Zaire, Zambia.

Against: Albania, Bulgaria, Byelorussian SSR, Czechoslovakia, Hungary, Mongolia, Poland, Ukrainian SSR, USSR.

Abstaining: Cuba, France, Portugal, Romania, South Africa, United Kingdom, United States.

A. Budget Appropriations for the Financial Year 1972

The General Assembly
Resolves that for the financial year 1972:

1. Appropriations totalling $US 213,124,410 are hereby voted for the following purposes:

Section	(U.S. dollars)	
PART I. *Sessions of the General Assembly, the councils, commissions and committees; special meetings and conferences*		
1. Travel and other expenses of representatives and members of commissions, committees and other subsidiary bodies	1,449,900	
2. Special meetings and conferences	2,903,600	
Total, Part I		4,353,500
PART II. *Staff costs and related expenses*		
3. Salaries and wages	96,189,160	
4. Common staff costs	21,951,100	
5. Travel of staff	2,656,100	
6. Payments under annex I, paragraphs 2 and 5, of the Staff Regulations; hospitality	159,000	
Total, Part II		120,955,360
PART III. *Construction, alteration, improvement and major maintenance of premises*		
7. Construction, alteration, improvement and major maintenance of premises	9,614,000	
Total, Part III		9,614,000
PART IV. *Equipment, supplies and services*		
8. Permanent equipment	1,413,300	
9. Maintenance, operation and rental of premises	6,897,900	
10. General expenses	6,037,000	
11. Printing	3,376,700	
Total, Part IV		17,724,900
PART V. *Technical programmes*		
12. Regional and subregional advisory services	1,825,000	
13. Economic development, social development and public administration; human rights advisory services; narcotic drugs control	5,408,000	
14. Industrial development	1,500,000	
Total, Part V		8,733,000
PART VI. *United Nations Conference on Trade and Development*		
15. United Nations Conference on Trade and Development	12,525,000	
Total, Part VI		12,525,000

Section		(U.S. dollars)
PART VII. *United Nations Industrial Development Organization*		
16. United Nations Industrial Development Organization	14,419,000	
Total, Part VII		14,419,000
PART VIII. *Special missions*		
17. Special missions	8,370,700	
Total, Part VIII		8,370,700
PART IX. *Office of the United Nations High Commissioner for Refugees*		
18. Office of the United Nations High Commissioner for Refugees	5,398,500	
Total, Part IX		5,398,500
PART X. *International Court of Justice*		
19. International Court of Justice	1,706,150	
Total, Part X		1,706,150
PART XI. *Special expenses*		
20. Special expenses	10,574,300	
Total, Part XI		10,574,300
		214,374,410
Global reduction to be achieved under various sections of the budget concerning United Nations documentation approved at the 1473rd meeting of the Fifth Committee		(1,250,000)
GRAND TOTAL		213,124,410

2. The Secretary-General shall be authorized to transfer credits between sections of the budget with the prior concurrence of the Advisory Committee on Administrative and Budgetary Questions;

3. The appropriations for technical assistance programmes under part V shall be administered in accordance with the Financial Regulations of the United Nations, except that the definition of obligations and the period of validity of obligations shall be in accordance with the procedures and practices established for the Technical Assistance component of the United Nations Development Programme;

4. The provisions under sections 1, 3, 5 and 11, in a total amount of $309,630 relating to the International Narcotics Control Board, shall be administered as a unit;

5. In addition to the appropriations voted under paragraph 1 above, an amount of $19,000 is appropriated from the accumulated income of the Library Endowment Fund for the purchase of books, periodicals, maps and library equipment and for such other expenses of the Library at the Palais des Nations as are in accordance with the objects and provisions of the endowment.

A/8406, Vol. I. Draft resolution I B, relating to budget estimates, submitted by Secretary-General for adoption by General Assembly, approved by Fifth Committee on 21 December 1971, meeting 1491, by 55 votes to 8, with 7 abstentions.

A/8408 and Corr.1,2. First report of ACABQ on budget estimates for financial year 1972, Chapter II, para. 68: Comparative table of appropriations as proposed by Secretary-General and recommended by ACABQ—Income estimates.

A/8531/Add.2. Report of Fifth Committee (part III), draft resolution XI B.

RESOLUTION 2899 B (XXVI), as recommended by Fifth Committee, A/8531/Add.2, adopted by Assembly on 22 December 1971, meeting 2031, by recorded vote of 122 to 0, as follows:

In favour: Afghanistan, Albania, Algeria, Argentina, Australia, Austria, Barbados, Belgium, Bhutan, Bolivia, Brazil, Bulgaria, Burma, Burundi, Byelorussian SSR, Cameroon, Canada, Ceylon, Chad, Chile, Colombia, Congo, Costa Rica, Cuba, Cyprus, Czechoslovakia, Dahomey, Denmark, Dominican Re- public, Ecuador, Egypt, El Salvador, Equatorial Guinea, Ethiopia, Finland, France, Gabon, Gambia, Ghana, Greece, Guatemala, Guinea, Guyana, Haiti, Honduras, Hungary, Iceland, India, Indonesia, Iran, Ireland, Israel, Italy, Ivory Coast, Jamaica, Japan, Jordan, Kenya, Khmer Republic, Kuwait, Laos, Lebanon, Lesotho, Liberia, Libyan Arab Republic, Luxembourg, Madagascar, Malawi, Malaysia, Mali, Malta, Mauritania, Mexico, Mongolia, Morocco, Nepal, Netherlands, New Zealand, Nicaragua, Niger, Nigeria, Norway, Pakistan, Panama, Paraguay, People's Democratic Republic of Yemen, Peru, Philippines, Poland, Portugal, Qatar, Romania, Rwanda, Senegal, Sierra Leone, Singapore, Somalia, South Africa, Spain, Sudan, Swaziland, Sweden, Syrian Arab Republic, Thailand, Togo, Trinidad and Tobago, Tunisia, Turkey, Uganda, Ukrainian SSR, USSR, United Arab Emirates, United Kingdom, United Republic of Tanzania, United States, Upper Volta, Uruguay, Venezuela, Yemen, Yugoslavia, Zaire, Zambia.

Against: None.
Abstaining: None.

B. Income Estimates for the Financial Year 1972

The General Assembly
Resolves that for the financial year 1972:

1. Estimates of income other than assessments on Member States totalling $US 35,921,650 are approved as follows:

Income section   *(U.S. dollars)*

PART I. Income from staff assessment
1. Income from staff assessment   25,313,650

                                  Total, Part I   25,313,650

PART II. Other income
2. Funds provided from extra-budgetary accounts   2,499,400
3. General income   4,910,000
4. Revenue-producing activities   3,198,600

                                  Total, Part II   10,608,000

                                  GRAND TOTAL   35,921,650

2. The income from staff assessment shall be credited to the Tax Equalization Fund in accordance with the provisions of General Assembly resolution 973(X) of 15 December 1955;

3. Direct expenses of the United Nations Postal Administration, services to visitors, catering and related services, and the sale of publications shall be charged against the income derived from those activities.

A/8406, Vol. I. Draft resolution I C, relating to budget estimates, submitted by Secretary-General for adoption by General Assembly, approved by Fifth Committee on 21 December 1971, meeting 1491, by 55 votes to 8, with 7 abstentions.

A/8531/Add.2. Report of Fifth Committee (part III), draft resolution XI C.

RESOLUTION 2899 C (XXVI), as recommended by Fifth Committee, A/8531/Add.2, adopted by Assembly on 22 December 1971, meeting 2031, by recorded vote of 110 to 0, with 13 abstentions, as follows:

In favour: Afghanistan, Algeria, Argentina, Australia, Austria, Barbados, Belgium, Bhutan, Bolivia, Brazil, Burma, Burundi, Cameroon, Canada, Central African Republic, Ceylon, Chad, Chile, Colombia, Congo, Costa Rica, Cyprus, Denmark, Dominican Republic, Ecuador, Egypt, El Salvador Equatorial Guinea, Ethiopia, Fiji, Finland, France, Gabon, Gambia, Ghana, Greece, Guatemala, Guinea, Guyana, Haiti, Honduras, Iceland, India, Indonesia, Iran, Ireland, Israel, Italy, Ivory Coast, Jamaica, Japan, Jordan, Kenya, Khmer Republic, Kuwait, Laos, Lebanon, Lesotho, Liberia, Libyan Arab Republic, Luxembourg, Madagascar, Malawi, Malaysia, Mali, Malta, Mauritania, Mexico, Morocco, Netherlands, New Zealand, Nicaragua, Niger, Nigeria, Norway, Pakistan, Panama, Paraguay, Peru, Philippines, Portugal, Qatar, Rwanda, Saudi Arabia, Senegal, Sierra Leone, Singapore, Somalia, South Africa, Spain, Sudan, Swaziland, Sweden, Syrian Arab Republic, Thailand, Togo, Trinidad and Tobago, Tunisia, Turkey, Uganda, United Arab Emirates, United Kingdom, United Republic of Tanzania, Upper Volta, Uruguay, Venezuela, Yemen, Yugoslavia, Zaire, Zambia.

Against: None.

Abstaining: Albania, Bulgaria, Byelorussian SSR, Cuba, Czechoslovakia, Hungary, Mongolia, People's Democratic Republic of Yemen, Poland, Romania, Ukrainian SSR, USSR, United States.

C. Financing of Appropriations for the Financial Year 1972

The General Assembly

Resolves that for the financial year 1972:

1. Budget appropriations totalling $US 213,124,410, together with supplementary appropriations for 1971 totalling $2,478,500, as well as the additional requirement to cover the decrease in estimated income other than staff assessment for 1971 of $158,500, shall be financed in accordance with regulations 5.1 and 5.2 of the Financial Regulations of the United Nations as follows:

    (a) As to $10,608,000, by income other than staff assessment approved under resolution B above;

    (b) As to $1,874,033, by the amount available in surplus account for the financial year 1970;

    (c) As to $75,951, by contribution of new Member States for the financial years 1970 and 1971;

    (d) As to $203,203,426, by assessment on Member States in accordance with General Assembly resolution 2654(XXV) of 4 December 1970 on the scale of assessments for the financial years 1971, 1972 and 1973;

2. There shall be set off against the assessment on Member States, in accordance with the provisions of General Assembly resolution 973(X) of 15 December 1955, their respective shares in the Tax Equalization Fund in a total amount of $26,091,165, comprising:

    (a) $25,313,650, being the estimated staff assessment income for 1972;

    (b) $140,515, being the excess of actual income over the approved estimates of income from staff assessment for 1970;

    (c) $637,000, being the increase in the revised income from staff assessment for 1971.

FINANCIAL POSITION OF THE ORGANIZATION

General Assembly—26th session
Fifth Committee, meetings 1427-1440, 1458, 1480, 1487, 1489, 1491.
Plenary meeting 2031.

A/8401/Add.1. Introduction to report of Secretary-General on work of the Organization, September 1971, Part One, Chapter XI.

A/8497. Letter of 10 December 1971 from Norway.

A/8635. Note of 18 December 1971 by President of General Assembly.

A/C.5/1376. Statement by Secretary-General at 1427th meeting of Fifth Committee, 6 October 1971.

A/C.5/1377. Statement by Chairman of ACABQ at 1427th meeting of Fifth Committee, 6 October 1971.

A/C.5/1384. Letter of 20 October 1971 from France.

A/8531/Add.1. Report of Fifth Committee (part II), paras. 6-13.

A/8531/Add.2. Report of Fifth Committee (part III), paras. 13-19.

A/8429. Resolutions adopted by General Assembly during its 26th session, 21 September–22 December 1971. Other decisions, pp. 132-33 (Item 76: Establishment of Special Committee on Financial Situation of United Nations).

MANPOWER UTILIZATION AND STAFFING
REQUIREMENTS OF THE SECRETARIAT

Manpower survey

General Assembly—26th session
Fifth Committee, meetings 1487, 1488.
Plenary meeting 2031.

A/8401/Add.1. Introduction to report of Secretary-General on work of the Organization, September 1971, Part II, Chapter IX, paras. 315-319.
A/C.5/1385 and Corr.1,2, A/8408/Add.14. Progress made by Administrative Management Service in conducting survey of manpower utilization in Secretariat. Reports of Secretary-General and ACABQ.
A/C.5/1406, A/8408/Add.27 and Corr.1. Revised estimates under expenditure sections 3-5 and 8-10, and revised estimates of income under income sections 1 and 4, arising from decisions of Secretary-General based on manpower utilization surveys by Administrative Management Service. Reports of the Secretary-General and ACABQ.
A/8531/Add.2. Report of Fifth Committee (Part III), paras. 5-12.
A/8429. Resolutions adopted by General Assembly during its 26th session, 21 September–22 December 1971. Other decisions, p. 132 (item 76, 2nd para.).

**Hiring of experts and consultants
and Secretariat staffing needs**

General Assembly—26th session
Fifth Committee, meetings 1446-1449, 1452-1455, 1457, 1458, 1489.
Plenary meeting 2031.

A/8408 and Corr.1,2. First report of ACABQ on budget estimates for financial year 1972, paras. 29-43 and 98-136.
A/8531/Add.1. Report of Fifth Committee (part II), paras, 20-23.
A/C.5/L.1065 and Rev.1. USSR: draft resolution and revision.
A/C.5/L.1067. Saudi Arabia: amendment to USSR draft resolution, A/C.5/L.1065.
A/8531/Add.1. Report of Fifth Committee (part II), paras. 24-32.
A/8429. Resolutions adopted by General Assembly during its 26th session. Other decisions, p. 132 (item 76).

PLANNING ESTIMATES FOR 1973

General Assembly—26th session
Fifth Committee, meetings 1475, 1476.
Plenary meeting 2023.

A/8605. Report of Fifth Committee.
A/8429. Resolutions adopted by General Assembly during its 26th session. Other decisions, p. 133

FORM OF PRESENTATION OF UNITED NATIONS BUDGET

Economic and Social Council—51st session
Plenary meetings 1806, 1807.

E/5072/Rev.1. Report of Committee for Programme and Co-ordination on its 10th session, 13-17 September and 5, 8, 10, 12 and 17 November 1971, Chapter III and Annex III.
E/5073/Add.1. Resolutions adopted by Economic and Social Council during its resumed 51st session. Other decisions, p. 4.

General Assembly—26th session
Fifth Committee, meetings 1475, 1476, 1480, 1484.
Plenary meeting 2030.

A/C.5/1363 and Add.1. Implementation of recommendations of *Ad Hoc* Committee of Experts to Examine Finances of United Nations and Specialized Agencies. Form of presentation of United Nations budget. Report of Secretary-General.

A/8629 and Corr.1. Report of Fifth Committee, Section IV.
A/8429. Resolutions adopted by General Assembly during its 26th session, 21 September–22 December 1971. Other decisions, p. 133 (item 82).

Unforeseen and extraordinary expenses

General Assembly—26th session
Fifth Committee, meetings 1477, 1491.
Plenary meeting 2031.

A/8406 and Corr.1,3, Vol. I. Budget estimates for financial year 1972 and information annexes. Draft resolution II, as submitted by Secretary-General and as amended on suggestion of ACABQ (A/8408/Add.18, para. 11) approved by Fifth Committee on 21 December 1971, meeting 1491, by 59 votes to 10, with 1 abstention.
A/8408 and Corr.1,2. First report of ACABQ on budget estimates for financial year 1972, para. 69.
A/8408/Add.18, A/8499. Assistance in cases of natural disaster and other disaster situations. Administrative and financial implications of draft resolution recommended by Third Committee in A/8430/Add.1. Reports of ACABQ (para. 11) and Fifth Committee (para. 12).
A/8531/Add.2. Report of Fifth Committee (part III), draft resolution XII.

RESOLUTION 2900(XXVI), as recommended by Fifth Committee, A/8531/Add.2, adopted by Assembly on 22 December 1971, meeting 2031, by recorded vote of 112 to 10, with 2 abstentions:

In favour: Afghanistan, Algeria, Argentina, Australia, Austria, Belgium, Bhutan, Bolivia, Brazil, Burma, Burundi, Cameroon, Canada, Central African Republic, Ceylon, Chad, Chile, Colombia, Congo, Costa Rica, Cyprus, Dahomey, Denmark, Dominican Republic, Ecuador, Egypt, El Salvador, Equatorial Guinea, Ethiopia, Fiji, Finland, France, Gabon, Gambia, Ghana, Greece, Guatemala, Guinea, Guyana, Haiti, Honduras, Iceland, India, Indonesia, Iran, Ireland, Israel, Italy, Ivory Coast, Jamaica, Japan, Jordan, Kenya, Khmer Republic, Kuwait, Laos, Lebanon, Lesotho, Liberia, Libyan Arab Republic, Luxembourg, Madagascar, Malawi, Malaysia, Mali, Malta, Mauritania, Mexico, Morocco, Nepal, Netherlands, New Zealand, Nicaragua, Niger, Nigeria, Norway, Pakistan, Panama, Paraguay, People's Democratic Republic of Yemen, Peru, Philippines, Qatar, Rwanda, Saudi Arabia, Senegal, Sierra Leone, Singapore, Somalia, South Africa, Spain, Sudan, Swaziland, Sweden, Syrian Arab Republic, Thailand, Togo, Trinidad and Tobago, Tunisia, Turkey, Uganda, United Arab Emirates, United Kingdom, United Republic of Tanzania, United States, Upper Volta, Uruguay, Venezuela, Yemen, Yugoslavia, Zaire, Zambia.
Against: Albania, Bulgaria, Byelorussian SSR, Cuba, Czechoslovakia, Hungary, Mongolia, Poland, Ukrainian SSR, USSR.
Abstaining: Portugal, Romania.

The General Assembly
1. *Authorizes* the Secretary-General, with the prior concurrence of the Advisory Committee on Administrative and Budgetary Questions and subject to the Financial Regulations of the United Nations and the provisions of paragraph 3 below, to enter into commitments to meet unforeseen and extraordinary expenses in the financial year 1972, provided that the concurrence of the Advisory Committee shall not be necessary for:
(a) Such commitments, not exceeding a total of $US 2 million, as the Secretary-General certifies relate to the maintenance of peace and security;
(b) Such commitments as the President of the International Court of Justice certifies relate to expenses occasioned by:
(i) The designation of *ad hoc* judges (Statute of the Court, Article 31), not exceeding a total of $37,500;
(ii) The appointment of assessors (Statute, Article 30), or the calling of witnesses and the appointment of experts (Statute, Article 50), not exceeding a total of $25,000;

(iii) The holding of sessions of the Court away from The Hague (Statute, Article 22), not exceeding a total of $75,000;

(c) Such commitments made in accordance with paragraph 10 of General Assembly resolution 2816(XXVI) of 14 December 1971, not exceeding a total of $200,000, as the Secretary-General certifies relate to emergency aid in connexion with natural disasters, with a normal ceiling of $20,000 per country in the case of any one disaster;

2. *Resolves* that the Secretary-General shall report to the Advisory Committee on Administrative and Budgetary Questions and to the General Assembly at its twenty-seventh session all commitments made under the provisions of the present resolution, together with the circumstances relating thereto, and shall submit supplementary estimates to the Assembly in respect of such commitments;

3. *Decides* that if, as a result of a decision of the Security Council, commitments relating to the maintenance of peace and security should arise in an estimated total exceeding $10 million before the twenty-seventh session of the General Assembly, a special session of the Assembly shall be convened by the Secretary-General to consider the matter.

Working Capital Fund for 1972

General Assembly—26th session
Fifth Committee, meetings 1427, 1487, 1491.
Plenary meeting 2031.

A/8406 and Corr.1,3, Vol. I. Budget estimates for financial year 1972 and information annexes.
A/8406, Vol. I. Draft resolution III, as submitted by Secretary-General for adoption by General Assembly, approved by Fifth Committee on 21 December 1971, meeting 1491, by 59 votes to 0, with 10 abstentions.
A/8408 and Corr.1,2. First report of ACABQ on budget estimates for financial year 1972, paras. 70 and 71.
A/8531/Add.2. Report of Fifth Committee (part III), draft resolution XIII.

RESOLUTION 2901(XXVI), as recommended by Fifth Committee, A/8531/Add.2, adopted by Assembly on 22 December 1971, meeting 2031, by recorded vote of 111 to 0, with 12 abstentions, as follows:

In favour: Afghanistan, Algeria, Argentina, Australia, Austria, Barbados, Belgium, Bhutan, Bolivia, Brazil, Burma, Burundi, Cameroon, Canada, Central African Republic, Ceylon, Chad, Chile, Colombia, Congo, Costa Rica, Cyprus, Denmark, Dominican Republic, Ecuador, Egypt, El Salvador, Equatorial Guinea, Ethiopia, Fiji, Finland, France, Gabon, Gambia, Ghana, Greece, Guatemala, Guinea, Guyana, Haiti, Honduras, India, Indonesia, Iran, Ireland, Israel, Italy, Ivory Coast, Jamaica, Japan, Jordan, Kenya, Khmer Republic, Kuwait, Laos, Lebanon, Lesotho, Liberia, Libyan Arab Republic, Luxembourg, Madagascar, Malawi, Malaysia, Mali, Malta, Mauritania, Mexico, Morocco, Nepal, Netherlands, New Zealand, Nicaragua, Niger, Nigeria, Norway, Pakistan, Panama, Paraguay, People's Democratic Republic of Yemen, Peru, Philippines, Qatar, Rwanda, Saudi Arabia, Senegal, Sierra Leone, Singapore, Somalia, South Africa, Spain, Sudan, Swaziland, Sweden, Syrian Arab Republic, Thailand, Togo, Trinidad and Tobago, Tunisia, Turkey, Uganda, United Arab Emirates, United Kingdom, United Republic of Tanzania, United States, Upper Volta, Uruguay, Venezuela, Yemen, Yugoslavia, Zaire, Zambia.

Against: None.
Abstaining: Albania, Bulgaria, Byelorussian SSR, Cuba, Czechoslovakia, Hungary, Mongolia, Poland, Portugal, Romania, Ukrainian SSR, USSR.

The General Assembly
Resolves that:

1. The Working Capital Fund shall be established for the year ending 31 December 1972 in the amount of $US 40 million;

2. Member States shall make advances to the Working Capital Fund in accordance with the scale adopted by the General Assembly for contributions of Members to the budget for the financial year 1972;

3. There shall be set off against this allocation of advances:

(a) Credits to Member States resulting from transfers made in 1959 and 1960 from surplus account to the Working Capital Fund in a total amount of $1,079,158;

(b) Cash advances paid by Member States to the Working Capital Fund for the financial year 1971 under General Assembly resolution 2740(XXV) of 17 December 1970;

4. Should the credits and advances paid by any Member State to the Working Capital Fund for 1971 exceed the amount of that Member State's advance under the provisions of paragraph 2 above, the excess shall be set off against the amount of the contribution payable by the Member State in respect of the financial year 1972;

5. The Secretary-General is authorized to advance from the Working Capital Fund:

(a) Such sums as may be necessary to finance budgetary appropriations pending the receipt of contributions; sums so advanced shall be reimbursed as soon as receipts from contributions are available for the purpose;

(b) Such sums as may be necessary to finance commitments which may be duly authorized under the provisions of the resolutions adopted by the General Assembly, in particular resolution 2900(XXVI) of 22 December 1971 relating to unforeseen and extraordinary expenses; the Secretary-General shall make provision in the budget estimates for reimbursing the Working Capital Fund;

(c) Such sums as, together with net sums outstanding for the same purpose, do not exceed $150,000, to continue the revolving fund to finance miscellaneous self-liquidating purchases and activities; advances in excess of the total of $150,000 may be made with the prior concurrence of the Advisory Committee on Administrative and Budgetary Questions;

(d) With the prior concurrence of the Advisory Committee on Administrative and Budgetary Questions, such sums as may be required to finance payments of advance insurance premiums where the period of insurance extends beyond the end of the financial year in which payment is made; the Secretary-General shall make provision in the budget estimates of each year, during the life of the related policies, to cover the charges applicable to each such year;

(e) Such sums as may be necessary to enable the Tax Equalization Fund to meet current commitments pending the accumulation of credits; such advances shall be repaid as soon as credits are available in the Tax Equalization Fund;

6. Should the provision in paragraph 1 above prove inadequate to meet the purposes normally related to the Working Capital Fund, the Secretary-General is authorized to utilize, in 1972, cash from special funds and accounts in his custody, under the conditions approved in General Assembly resolution 1341(XIII) of 13 December 1958, or the proceeds of loans authorized by the Assembly.

Supplementary estimates for the financial year 1971

In 1970, the General Assembly, in adopting the United Nations budget for 1971, approved: gross appropriations amounting to $192,149,300; an estimate of income from staff assessment of $21,663,000; and an estimate of $10,114,000 in income from other sources.[6] On 21 December

[6] See Y.U.N., 1970, pp. 852-54, text of resolution 2738 B (XXV).

1971, the Assembly approved revised appropriations for 1971 in the amount of $194,627,800, representing an increase of $2,478,500 over the original appropriations voted in 1970. Income from staff assessment was increased by $637,000 for a revised estimate of $22,300,000 and income from other sources was decreased by $158,500 for a revised estimate of $9,955,500.

The revised appropriations and income estimates were approved by the Assembly on the basis of a recommendation by its Fifth (Administrative and Budgetary) Committee, following consideration of reports by the Secretary-General and the Advisory Committee on Administrative and Budgetary Questions.

In his report, the Secretary-General requested an additional provision of $2,689,600 and proposed a net increase in estimated income of $478,500. In determining his request for additional credits, the Secretary-General took into account: additional costs, estimated at $1.1 million, resulting from the revaluation in May 1971 of the Swiss franc and the Austrian schilling; and additional requirements estimated at $1.2 million resulting from increased staff costs due to the movement of cost-of-living indexes, higher rates for utilities and certain other contractual services, and increases in the cost of air and sea travel fares.

The balance of the additional credits requested by the Secretary-General related to commitments that had been initially entered into under the terms of a General Assembly resolution of 17 December 1970 on unforeseen and extraordinary expenses for 1971,[7] or within the provisions of General Assembly resolutions relating to United Nations assistance in cases of natural disaster.

The Secretary-General, in his report, drew attention to the fact that an amount of $2 million appropriated for 1971 costs for new construction and major alterations at United Nations Headquarters, New York, authorized by the General Assembly on 17 December 1969,[8] would not be utilized in 1971 since it had not proved possible to achieve the total financing plan envisaged as a prior condition to the initiation of the project. If the $2 million were to be surrendered, the net additional requirements for 1971 would amount to $211,100 which, in view of their "manageable proportions," the Secretary-General would endeavour to absorb within resources available to him under the budget as a whole. If the Assembly agreed to such a procedure, there would be no increase in the assessed contributions of Member States for 1971.

The Assembly's Advisory Committee on Administrative and Budgetary Questions, in its related report, recommended that the Secretary-General's over-all request for additional appropriations be reduced by $211,100 and, on the assumption that the Assembly might decide to apply the $2 million which remained unspent to reduce the total level of appropriations for 1971, recommended that the gross expenditures for 1971 should be set at $192,627,800 and the estimate of income increased by $478,500 as recommended by the Secretary-General.

The discussion on this subject in the Fifth Committee centred mainly on the question of how to treat the unused appropriation of $2 million which had been intended for construction purposes at Headquarters in 1971. On 2 November 1971, the Fifth Committee, by a roll-call vote of 50 to 32, with 6 abstentions, rejected the proposal that the unspent $2 million appropriated in 1971 for construction purposes at Headquarters be surrendered. (See also pp. 664-65.)

The Committee then approved, by 65 votes to 6, with 14 abstentions, a total revised appropriation for 1971 in the amount of $194,627,800, and unanimously approved revised estimates of income for 1971 in a total amount of $32,255,500. Draft resolutions embodying these decisions were approved by the Fifth Committee on 16 December 1971. On 21 December, acting on the recommendation of the Fifth Committee, the Assembly approved the revised appropriations for 1971 in adopting resolution 2882 A (XXVI), by 92 votes to 10, with 4 abstentions. The income estimates for 1971 were unanimously approved by the Assembly with the adoption of resolution 2882 B (XXVI). (For texts, see DOCUMENTARY REFERENCES below.)

---

[7] See Y.U.N., 1970, p. 854, text of resolution 2739 (XXV).
[8] See Y.U.N., 1969, pp. 839-40, text of resolution 2618 (XXIV).

DOCUMENTARY REFERENCES

General Assembly—26th session
Fifth Committee, meetings 1431, 1434-1437, 1445, 1486.
Plenary meeting 2030.

A/8458. Report of Secretary-General.
A/8458, Annex I. Draft resolutions, proposed by Advisory Committee on Administrative and Budgetary Questions (ACABQ) for adoption by General Assembly, containing appropriations, as revised by Fifth Committee, approved by Fifth Committee on 2 November 1971, meeting 1445, as follows: appropriations in Part A, as revised, by 65 votes to 6, with 14 abstentions, income estimates, Part B, as revised, unanimously.

A/8471. Report of ACABQ.
A/C.5/1381. Budget estimates for financial year 1972. Headquarters accommodation. Report of Secretary-General.
A/8610. Report of Fifth Committee, draft resolutions, approved by Fifth Committee on 16 December 1971, meeting 1486, as follows: draft resolution A, by 57 votes to 8, with 3 abstentions; draft resolution B, by 60 votes to 0, with 7 abstentions.

RESOLUTIONS 2882 A and B (XXVI), as recommended by Fifth Committee, A/8610, adopted by Assembly on 21 December 1971, meeting 2030, as follows: Part A, by 92 votes to 10, with 4 abstentions; Part B, unanimously.

A. Budget Appropriations for the Financial Year 1971

The General Assembly
Resolves that for the financial year 1971:
1. The amount of $US 192,149,300 appropriated by its resolution 2738A(XXV) of 17 December 1970 shall be increased by $US 2,478,500 as follows:

Section	Amount appro-priated by resolution 2738A(XXV)	Increase or (decrease) (U.S. dollars)	Revised appro-priation
PART I. Sessions of the General Assembly, the councils, commissions and committees; special meetings and conferences			
1. Travel and other expenses of representatives and members of commissions, committees and other subsidiary bodies	1,387,100		1,387,100
2. Special meetings and conferences	3,317,800	227,300	3,545,100
Total, Part I	4,704,900	227,300	4,932,200
PART II. Staff costs and related expenses			
3. Salaries and wages	86,158,700	466,300	86,625,000
4. Common staff costs	19,585,300	237,600	19,822,900
5. Travel of staff	2,598,300	150,000	2,748,300
6. Payments under annex I, paragraphs 2 and 5, of the Staff Regulations; hospitality	159,000	—	159,000
Total, Part II	108,501,300	853,900	109,355,200
PART III. Premises, equipment, supplies and services			
7. Buildings and improvements to premises	9,040,900	(59,000)	8,981,900
8. Permanent equipment	962,700	(34,600)	928,100
9. Maintenance, operation and rental of premises	6,318,000	309,000	6,627,000
10. General expenses	5,349,900	635,000	5,984,900
11. Printing	3,112,300	—	3,112,300
Total, Part III	24,783,800	850,400	25,634,200
PART IV. Special expenses			
12. Special expenses	10,647,500	(101,400)	10,546,100
Total, Part IV	10,647,500	(101,400)	10,546,100
PART V. Technical programmes			
13. Economic development, social development and public administration; human rights advisory services; narcotic drugs control	5,408,000	—	5,408,000
14. Industrial development	1,500,000	—	1,500,000
Total, Part V	6,908,000	—	6.908,000
PART VI. United Nations Conference on Trade and Development			
15. United Nations Conference on Trade and Development	10,072,300	258,100	10,330,400
Total, Part VI	10,072,300	258,100	10,330,400
PART VII. United Nations Industrial Development Organization			
16. United Nations Industrial Development Organization	12,222,500	286,000	12,508,500
Total, Part VII	12,222,500	286,000	12.508,500
PART VIII. Special missions			
17. Special missions	8,133,100	—	8,133,100
Total, Part VIII	8,133,100	—	8,133,100

Section	Amount appropriated by resolution 2738 A (XXV)	Increase or (decrease) (U.S. dollars)	Revised appropriation
PART IX. Office of the United Nations High Commissioner for Refugees			
18. Office of the United Nations High Commissioner for Refugees	4,722,000	59,000	4,781,000
Total, Part IX	4,722,000	59,000	4,781,000
PART X. International Court of Justice			
19. International Court of Justice	1,453,900	45,200	1,499,100
Total, Part X	1,453,900	45,200	1,499,100
GRAND TOTAL	192,149,300	2,478,500	194,627,800

2. The Secretary-General shall be authorized to transfer credits between sections of the budget with the concurrence of the Advisory Committee on Administrative and Budgetary Questions;

3. The appropriations for technical assistance programmes under part V shall be administered in accordance with the Financial Regulations of the United Nations, except that the definition of obligations and the period of validity of obligations shall be in accordance with the procedures and practices established for the Technical Assistance component of the United Nations Development Programme;

4. The provisions under sections 1, 3, 5 and 11, in a total amount of $281,000 relating to the International Narcotics Control Board, shall be administered as a unit;

5. In addition to the appropriations voted under paragraph 1 above, an amount of $19,000 is appropriated from the accumulated income of the Library Endowment Fund for the purchase of books, periodicals, maps and library equipment and for such other expenses of the Library at the Palais des Nations as are in accordance with the objects and provisions of the endowment.

B. Income Estimates for the Financial Year 1971

The General Assembly

Resolves that for the financial year 1971:

1. The estimates of income approved by its resolution 2738 B (XXV) of 17 December 1970 shall be revised as follows:

Income section	Estimate approved by resolution 2738 B (XXV)	Increase or (decrease) (U.S. dollars)	Revised estimate
PART I. Income from staff assessment			
1. Income from staff assessment	21,663,000	637,000	22,300,000
Total, Part I	21,663,000	637,000	22,300,000
PART II Other income			
2. Funds provided from extra-budgetary accounts	2,436,400	139,000	2,575,400
3. General income	4,755,400	65,500	4,820,900
4. Revenue-producing activities	2,922,200	(363,000)	2,559,200
Total, Part II	10,114,000	(158,500)	9,955,500
GRAND TOTAL	31,777,000	478,500	32,255,500

2. The income from staff assessment shall be credited to the Tax Equalization Fund in accordance with the provisions of General Assembly resolution 973(X) of 15 December 1955;

3. Direct expenses of the United Nations Postal Administration, services to visitors, catering and related services, and the sale of publications shall be charged against the income derived from those activities.

Scale of assessments for the apportionment of United Nations expenses

On 8 November 1971, acting on the recommendation of its Fifth (Administrative and Budgetary) Committee, the General Assembly adopted, without a vote, a resolution (2762(XXVI)) establishing the rates of assessments for Bhutan and Fiji. These States had been admitted to membership in the United Nations subsequent to adoption, in 1970, of the scale of assessments for 1972.[9] The Fifth Committee approved the text on 13 October 1971,

[9]See Y.U.N., 1970, pp. 863-64, text of resolution 2654(XXV) of 4 December 1970.

by 69 votes to 0, on the recommendation of the Assembly's Committee on Contributions.

(For text of resolution, see DOCUMENTARY REFERENCES below.)

When the Chairman of the Committee on Contributions introduced that body's report to the Fifth Committee, he expressed the Committee's concern for the serious natural disasters that had occurred after the current scale of assessments had been drawn up, and referred to appeals submitted by Pakistan and Romania for changes in their assessments in the light of such disasters.

He said the Committee on Contributions had recognized the magnitude of the calamities suffered by the two States, but it felt that any adjustment in the scale could only offer them insignificant relief in relation to the size of the disasters. In the next review of the assessment scale in 1973, the Committee on Contributions would take such events into account and could also make special allowance, as in the past, for the serious economic effects of natural disasters which had occurred during the three-year interval.

The Chairman reported that the Committee on Contributions had also examined the possibility of further improving its methods for the establishment of the scale and had given particular attention to: (*a*) the implication of changes in price levels and exchange rates in determining the relative capacities to pay of Member States; (*b*) the possibility of taking into account in a more systematic way the ability of Members to secure foreign currency with which to pay their contributions; and (*c*) the effects on the scale of possible variations in the allowances for low per capita income.

During the ensuing discussion in the Fifth Committee, several Members, including Brazil and Ghana, expressed regret that the Committee on Contributions had not found it possible to make a positive response to the appeals of Pakistan and Romania for a decrease in their assessments. Brazil observed that while a downward adjustment would not have constituted any real relief, it would have served to acknowledge that capacity to pay had been affected and would thus have reaffirmed the principle that relative capacity to pay was the overriding factor in determining the scale of contributions.

Other Fifth Committee Members, however, had doubts about the advisability of making immediate reductions in the assessments of countries in such circumstances. Thus, Japan noted that the triennial review of the scale would take into account the special situation of the countries concerned.

The importance of ensuring that the methods used in determining assessments were realistically adjusted to the changing world economic situation was emphasized by Argentina, Brazil, Italy, Japan and Norway, among others. Proposals made in 1970 that the different elements of the allowance formula for low per capita income be revised so as to adjust to the changing world economic situation were recalled in this connexion and Members welcomed the announced study of the possible effects on the scale of the suggested changes in the allowance formula. The intention of the Committee on Contributions to give particular attention to the effect of noticeable differential changes in price levels which were not reflected in exchange rates in the case of certain countries was noted.

In connexion with the collection of contributions in currencies other than United States dollars, the United Nations Controller informed the Fifth Committee that, in arranging for the payment of contributions during 1971 in such currencies, the Secretary-General had taken into account a Fifth Committee recommendation made in 1970.[10] Thus, where the Organization's needs for currency in which several Member States wished to pay had been less than the assessed contribution of the State whose currency it was, the Secretary-General had given absolute priority for payments in non-United States currencies to the country whose currency it was.

Representatives noted there was a difference of view between the members of the Committee on Contributions regarding the interpretation of the Fifth Committee's directive. The representative of the USSR felt that the Secretary-General should not be deprived of a certain amount of flexibility in the matter and that, in accordance with the Assembly's resolution of 4 December 1970 establishing the scale, he should retain the right to determine the procedure for acceptance of currencies other than United States dollars, and to accept a portion of the contribution of any of the Member States in currencies other than United States dollars, as needed by the United Nations.

Brazil, India and Pakistan proposed and the Fifth Committee approved the inclusion in the Fifth Committee's report of the following statement so as to dispel any remaining doubts that the interpretation of the word "priority" in the Fifth Committee's directive meant absolute priority:

> The Fifth Committee took note of the fact that, in making arrangements for payments by Member States of 1971 contributions in currencies other than United States dollars, the Secretary-General had taken into account the recommendation of the Fifth Committee [in 1970]. . . . In that connexion, the Fifth Committee approved the interpretation given by the Secretary-General to the meaning of the word "priority" mentioned in that directive, which he had correctly taken to mean absolute priority, and recommended

---

[10]See Y.U.N., 1970, p. 860.

that the Secretary-General should continue to implement that directive in the same manner in the future.

India, Pakistan and the United Republic of Tanzania then proposed and the Fifth Committee approved the inclusion of the following paragraph in the report:

The Fifth Committee recommends that the Committee on Contributions should review the criteria of

selection of currencies other than the United States dollar for payment of contributions to the regular budget and report to the General Assembly at its twenty-seventh session [in 1973].

These decisions were taken without objection on 13 October 1971.

A table showing the percentage scale of assessments for 1972 and net contributions payable for 1972 appears below.

Percentage scale of assessments for the United Nations budget for 1972[a] and net contributions payable by member states for 1972

Member State	Percentage Scale of Assessments[b]	Net Contribution to United Nations Regular Budget[c] (in U.S. dollars)	Member State	Percentage Scale of Assessments[b]	Net Contribution to United Nations Regular Budget[c] (in U.S. dollars)	Member State	Percentage Scale of Assessments[b]	Net Contribution to United Nations Regular Budget[c] (in U.S. dollars)
Afghanistan	0.04	70,788	Greece	0.29	513,215	Pakistan	0.34	601,701
Albania	0.04	70,788	Guatemala	0.05	88,486	Panama	0.04	70,788
Algeria	0.09	159,274	Guinea	0.04	70,788	Paraguay	0.04	70,788
Argentina	0.85	1,504,251	Guyana	0.04	70,788	People's		
Australia	1.47	2,601,469	Haiti	0.04	70,788	Democratic		
Austria	0.55	973,339	Honduras	0.04	70,788	Republic of		
Barbados	0.04	70,788	Hungary	0.48	849,549	Yemen	0.04	70,788
Belgium	1.05	1,858,193	Iceland	0.04	70,788	Peru	0.10	176,971
Bhutan	0.04	70,788	India	1.55	2,743,046	Philippines	0.31	548,610
Bolivia	0.04	70,788	Indonesia	0.28	495,518	Poland	1.41	2,495,287
Botswana	0.04	70,788	Iran	0.22	389,336	Portugal	0.16	283,153
Brazil	0.80	1,415,765	Iraq	0.07	123,880	Romania	0.36	637,095
Bulgaria	0.18	318,547	Ireland	0.15	265,456	Rwanda	0.04	70,788
Burma	0.05	88,486	Israel	0.20	353,941	Saudi Arabia	0.07	123,880
Burundi	0.04	70,788	Italy	3.54	6,264,763	Senegal	0.04	70,788
Byelorussian			Ivory Coast	0.04	70,788	Sierra Leone	0.04	70,788
SSR	0.50	884,853	Jamaica	0.04	70,788	Singapore	0.05	88,486
Cameroon	0.04	70,788	Japan	5.40	9,556,417	Somalia	0.04	70,788
Canada	3.08	5,450,697	Jordan	0.04	70,788	South Africa	0.54	955,642
Central African			Kenya	0.04	70,788	Spain	1.04	1,840,496
Republic	0.04	70,788	Khmer Republic	0.04	70,788	Sudan	0.04	70,788
Ceylon	0.05	88,486	Kuwait	0.08	141,577	Swaziland	0.04	70,788
Chad	0.04	70,788	Laos	0.04	70,788	Sweden	1.25	2,212,134
Chile	0.20	353,941	Lebanon	0.05	88,486	Syrian Arab		
China	4.00	7,078,828	Lesotho	0.04	70,788	Republic	0.04	70,788
Colombia	0.19	336,244	Liberia	0.04	70,788	Thailand	0.13	230,062
Congo	0.04	70,788	Libyan Arab			Togo	0.04	70,788
Costa Rica	0.04	70,788	Republic	0.07	123,880	Trinidad and		
Cuba	0.16	283,153	Luxembourg	0.05	88,486	Tobago	0.04	70,788
Cyprus	0.04	70,788	Madagascar	0.04	71,167	Tunisia	0.04	70,788
Czechoslovakia	0.90	1,592,736	Malawi	0.04	70,788	Turkey	0.35	620,025
Dahomey	0.04	70,788	Malaysia	0.10	176,971	Uganda	0.04	70,810
Denmark	0.62	1,097,219	Maldives	0.04	70,788	Ukrainian SSR	1,87	3,309,352
Dominican			Mali	0.04	70,788	USSR	14.18	25,094,443
Republic	0.04	70,788	Malta	0.04	70,788	United Kingdom	5.90	10,441,271
Ecuador	0.04	70,788	Mauritania	0.04	70,788	United Republic		
Egypt	0.18	318,547	Mauritius	0.04	70,788	of Tanzania	0.04	71,484
El Salvador	0.04	70,788	Mexico	0.88	1,557,342	United States	31.52	63,998,521
Equatorial			Mongolia	0.04	70,788	Upper Volta	0.04	70,788
Guinea	0.04	70,788	Morocco	0.09	159,274	Uruguay	0.07	123,880
Ethiopia	0.04	70,788	Nepal	0.04	70,788	Venezuela	0.41	725,581
Fiji	0.04	70,788	Netherlands	1.18	2,088,254	Yemen	0.04	70,788
Finland	0.45	796,368	New Zealand	0.32	566,307	Yugoslavia	0.38	672,489
France	6.00	10,618,241	Nicaragua	0.04	70,788	Zaire	0.04	71,092
Gabon	0.04	70,788	Niger	0.04	70,788	Zambia	0.04	70,788
Gambia	0.04	70,788	Nigeria	0.12	212,365			
Ghana	0.07	123,880	Norway	0.43	760,974			

[a]Percentage scales of assessments for 1972 also apply to the United Nations regular budget for 1973.

[b]As approved by the General Assembly on 4 December 1970 (resolution 2654(XXV)), and as amended by the General Assembly on 8 November 1971 (resolution 2762(XXVI)).

[c] The amounts listed are the net contributions for 1972 after allowing for credits from the Tax Equalization Fund and other revenues and after an adjustment to take into account advances to the Working Capital Fund.

DOCUMENTARY REFERENCES

General Assembly—26th session
Fifth Committee, meetings 1427-1430, 1443.
Plenary meetings 1934, 1940, 1979.

A/8397 and Add.1. Letters of 21 and 23 September 1971 from
Secretary-General to President of General Assembly.
A/8411 and Add.1,2 and Add.2/Corr.1. Report of Committee on
Contributions.
A/8411, Chapter V. Draft resolution recommended by Committee
on Contributions for adoption by General Assembly, approved
by Fifth Committee on 13 October 1971, meeting 1430, by 69
votes to 0.
A/8489. Report of Fifth Committee.

RESOLUTION 2762(XXVI), as recommended by Fifth Committee,
A/8489, adopted without vote by Assembly on 8 November
1971, meeting 1979.

The General Assembly
Resolves that:
(a) The rates of assessment for the following States, which were
admitted to membership in the United Nations at the twenty-fifth
and twenty-sixth sessions of the General Assembly, shall be as
follows:

Member State	Per cent
Bhutan	0.04
Fiji	0.04

These rates shall be added to the scale of assessments for 1972
and 1973 contained in subparagraph (a) of General Assembly
resolution 2654(XXV) of 4 December 1970;
(b) For the financial year 1970, Fiji, which became a Member of
the United Nations on 13 October 1970, shall contribute an amount
equal to one ninth of 0.04 per cent applied to the same basis of
assessment for 1970 as for other Member States;
(c) For the financial year 1971, Fiji shall contribute at the rate of
0.04 per cent and Bhutan, which became a Member of the United
Nations on 21 September 1971, at the rate of one ninth of 0.04 per
cent, these rates to be applied to the same basis of assessment for
1971 as for other Member States;
(d) The contributions payable by Fiji for 1970 and 1971 and by
Bhutan for 1971 shall be used for the financing of the budget for
1972 under regulation 5.2 (c) of the Financial Regulations of the
United Nations;
(e) The advances to the Working Capital Fund by Bhutan and Fiji
under regulation 5.8 of the Financial Regulations of the United
Nations shall for each of these States be 0.04 per cent of the total
amount of the Fund, and these advances shall be carried as
additional to the authorized level of the Fund.

A/8429. Resolutions adopted by General Assembly during its 26th
session. Other decisions, p. 133 (item 80).

Chapter III

Other administrative and budgetary questions

Review and reappraisal of United Nations information policies and practices

Report of the Secretary-General

In 1971, during the twenty-sixth session of the
General Assembly, public information activities of
the United Nations were discussed on the basis of a
report of the Secretary-General on the review and
reappraisal of United Nations information policies
and activities.[1]

The report, examined in the course of the
debates in the Assembly's Fifth (Administrative
and Budgetary) Committee on the 1972 budget,
contained a detailed analysis of the operations
conducted by the Office of Public Information
since the creation of the Organization, as well as of
the criteria on which those operations were based.
The Secretary-General concluded that the basic
principles laid down in the resolution adopted by
the General Assembly on 13 February 1946[2] and
reaffirmed by an Assembly resolution of 4 February 1952[3] did not need to be revised, amended or
enlarged. By these two resolutions, the Assembly
determined that activities in the field of informa-

tion "should be so organized and directed as to
promote to the greatest possible extent an informed understanding of the work and purposes
of the United Nations among the peoples of the
world. To this end, the Department [of Public
Information—renamed the Office of Public Information in 1958] should primarily assist and rely
upon the co-operation of the established governmental and non-governmental agencies of information to provide the public with information
about the United Nations. The Department
. . . should not engage in 'propaganda'."

The report added that responsibility for more
efficient use of mass communication media rested
primarily with national Governments; the Office of
Public Information should, however, be prepared
to supply its expert knowledge and services, upon

[1]See also Y.U.N., 1970, pp. 848-50.
[2]See Y.U.N., 1946-47, pp. 83-85, text of resolution 13(I).
[3]See Y.U.N., 1951, p. 137, text of resolution 595(VI).

request. Moreover, it should try harder to enlist the support of national Governments and agencies in the production and distribution of its material.

In its own information operations, the report continued, the Office should concentrate on activities which depended for their execution or full effectiveness upon international rather than national management.

In the light of a quarter of a century of experience, and within the limits imposed upon it by the requirements of "universality" and "objectivity," the Office of Public Information, according to the report, should pursue a more active information programme in regard to such universally accepted causes as disarmament, decolonization, the elimination of *apartheid* and racial discrimination, as well as economic and social development. In this connexion, it should devote special efforts to serving the needs of selected groups and institutions throughout the world with high opinion-building potential, e.g. the specialist press, schools and universities, the professions, non-governmental organizations, etc.

The Office should equip itself with the necessary modern skills and technical facilities, such as those needed for utilizing communication satellites and colour television, and, where recruitment of personnel with the necessary talent was not possible, it should make greater use of hiring on a temporary contractual basis.

Finally, the Office should establish a mechanism for the central planning of policy for its activities and for keeping itself constantly informed of their effectiveness and utilization, both at Headquarters and in the field.

The Assembly's Advisory Committee on Administrative and Budgetary Questions, in its report on cost estimates of the Secretary-General's proposals, proceeded on the basis that questions of information policy raised by the Secretary-General were not within its competence but rather called for consideration by the General Assembly. It did, however, provide a general picture, for each of the years 1972 to 1976, of the financial implications of those proposals that could be costed, which involved expenditure of approximately $4 million over the five-year period.

Decisions of General Assembly

The Secretary-General's report gave rise to an extensive debate in the General Assembly's Fifth Committee on United Nations activities. Among the main issues discussed were: (1) the principles on which the Office of Public Information based its activities; (2) central policy control under the authority of the Secretary-General; (3) the reorganization of the Office of Public Information; (4) the staffing of United Nations information centres; and (5) the convening by the Secretary-General of the Consultative Panel on Public Information.

In regard to the first issue listed above, most speakers in the Fifth Committee expressed the view that the basic principles which had guided the Office had stood the test of time. This view was supported by France, Iraq, the USSR, the United Kingdom and the United Republic of Tanzania, among others. It was emphasized that care should be taken not to cross the boundary separating information *per se* from propaganda or promotion, for fear not only of encroaching on the principles on which the Office was grounded but also, in the long term, of damaging the Organization's interests. On the other hand, some delegations —among them Indonesia, the Netherlands and the Philippines—considered that, while the original principles remained valid in regard to politically contentious issues, the Office of Public Information should be entitled to a greater degree of freedom in promoting such universally recognized causes as that of economic and social development.

Closely linked to the nature of the Organization's information policies was the question of control to be exercised in the implementation of those policies.

A number of representatives, including those of Iran, Iraq, Pakistan, the USSR, the United Kingdom and the United Republic of Tanzania, emphasized the need for information activities to be fully co-ordinated and subject to central control. In their view, such central control was essential to ensure that policy directives were translated into action to produce well-formulated and closely integrated programmes in which waste and duplication would be minimal.

In this connexion, many Members felt that the Secretary-General's report failed to bring into focus the exact relationship between the Office of Public Information and units such as the Centre for Economic and Social Information (CESI).

Canada, Denmark, Indonesia, the Netherlands, Norway, the Philippines and Sweden were among those who supported the internal administrative arrangements made by the Secretary-General in the field of information. In their view, it could not be argued that shortcomings existed in the formulation and execution of information programmes and activities, particularly in so far as they related to economic and social affairs. There was therefore no need for CESI to be integrated into the Office of Public Information as some representatives had proposed.

In the course of the debate, a message was read on behalf of the Secretary-General in which it was indicated that the administrative arrangements in regard to this matter would be reviewed in the light of comments made in the Fifth Committee. He assured the Committee that he would spare no effort to improve the performance of the information machinery in general, and not least in the field of economic and social development.

In examining issues relating to the type of policy control to be exercised in the field of information, the Fifth Committee also discussed the arrangements—structural and otherwise—under which the Office of Public Information performed its mandate. In this connexion, the United Republic of Tanzania emphasized the need for the Office to be given importance commensurate with its difficult task. The Office itself should be thoroughly reorganized. Other delegations sharing this view felt that the present structure of the Office of Public Information could only lead to fragmentation and lack of clarity. Emphasized, too, in this regard were the dangers of overlapping and proliferation.

Also discussed by the Fifth Committee was the staffing of United Nations information centres. The matter was raised in the context of recommendations put forward by the Administrative Management Service which had been approved by the Secretary-General, tending towards the consolidation of United Nations Development Programme (UNDP) and Office of Public Information field resources. In line with these recommendations, UNDP Resident Representatives in certain countries would be entrusted with the functions of the United Nations Information Centre Director.

A number of representatives, including those of Colombia, Indonesia, Somalia and the United Republic of Tanzania, objected to this proposal on the grounds that Resident Representatives could not be expected to concern themselves with the dissemination of information on such matters as decolonization and the elimination of racism which formed an integral part of the Office's responsibilities. The proposed consolidation of resources could, in the eyes of many, only result in the reduction of professional knowledge and experience in the field of information necessary for the effective conduct of such activities in the field. Whatever budgetary savings might be achieved from such a consolidation would be more than offset by the self-defeating restraint placed on United Nations information activities.

During the early stages of the Fifth Committee's debates on public information, the representative of the USSR proposed that the Secretary-General's report on public information policies and activities should first be submitted to the Consultative Panel on Public Information, which had been established by an Assembly decision of 1 December 1959.[4] Consisting of 13 Member States selected by the Secretary-General to advise him on information matters, the Consultative Panel had not been convened since 1967, it was pointed out. Certain delegations shared the view of the USSR that the Consultative Panel should be reactivated and consulted prior to any decisions by the General Assembly on the Secretary-General's report.

Other delegations, while not opposed to reactivation of the Panel provided its membership was reviewed to ensure it was fully representative of the Organization, felt that prior consultation would entail an unacceptable delay in consideration of the report by the Assembly. A USSR proposal for prior study by the Consultative Panel was rejected by the Fifth Committee on 2 December 1971, by 35 votes against to 18 in favour, with 31 abstentions.

The Fifth Committee, also on 2 December 1971, by a roll-call vote of 59 to 1, with 33 abstentions, approved a resolution embodying the views of the Committee on the above points. The text was sponsored by Algeria, Ethiopia, Ghana, Iran, Iraq, Kenya, Nigeria, Pakistan, Sudan, the Syrian Arab Republic, Uganda, the United Republic of Tanzania, Upper Volta and Zambia.

Prior to this decision, the Fifth Committee had on the same day rejected, by 36 votes to 33, with 20 abstentions, an amendment put forward by the Netherlands to delete a provision for reorganizing the Office of Public Information with a view to ensuring central control and direction in the implementation of information policies and guidelines.

On 22 December 1971, the General Assembly approved the text submitted to it by the Fifth Committee by 96 votes in favour to 1 against, with 23 abstentions, as resolution 2897(XXVI).

By this resolution, the Assembly among other things reaffirmed its resolutions of 13 February 1946 and 4 February 1952 and its subsequent resolutions on public information, and decided that the basic principles laid down by the Assembly in those resolutions remained valid and did not require revision, amendment or enlargement. Those principles should remain applicable, subject to directives the Assembly had already given or might give in future.

It was recommended that the Secretary-General review the composition of the Consultative Panel on Public Information to ensure that it reflected the current situation in the United Nations, and he was asked to convene the Consultative Panel before the Assembly's 1972 session to advise him on the information policies and activities of the United Nations.

The Secretary-General was also requested: (a) to ascertain the publicity and promotional needs of various United Nations bodies which undertook approved universal causes so their financial requirements could be taken into account in preparing the budget; (b) to appoint to United Nations information centres highly qualified

---

[4]See Y.U.N., 1959, p. 439, text of resolution 1405(XIV).

professional staff to give their undivided attention to the dissemination of, and building support for, United Nations activities particularly in the economic, social and political fields; (c) to intensify his efforts to eliminate shortcomings in formulating and executing information programmes and activities, especially in the economic and social fields; (d) to ensure that the United Nations Conference on Trade and Development and the United Nations Industrial Development Organization were allocated sufficient resources to meet their increased informational activity needs during the Second United Nations Development Decade; (e) to review current administrative arrangements for the Centre for Economic and Social Information and to reorganize the Office of Public Information to ensure central control and direction and to carry out its mandate more effectively; and (f) to report on this matter to the Assembly in 1972.

It was also recommended that the Governing Council of UNDP should entrust as many of its information activities as possible to the United Nations and other executing agencies.

This resolution also covered other aspects of public information of a more specific character, such as approval in principle of the Secretary-General's proposal to set up a regional production bureau in Africa—in Addis Ababa, Ethiopia—and approval of a programme of acquisition and replacement of audio-visual equipment.

It also endorsed proposals for: maintenance of the Office of Public Information's output of publications (including the *UN Monthly Chronicle*, the *Yearbook of the United Nations*, pamphlets, etc.) at its current level, leaving open the possibility of an additional annual allocation to offset increased operating costs and increased output during the Disarmament and Development Decades; additional funds for a French edition of the publication entitled *Objective: Justice*; seeking payment for United Nations television services from users and encouraging co-production and cost-sharing with national television organizations; improvement of photographic processing equipment; provision of additional travel funds for seminars and conferences and funds for expansion of fellowship and seminar programmes; and, resuming in 1973, the practice of holding periodic meetings of information centre directors every five years.

(For full text of resolution, see DOCUMENTARY REFERENCES below.)

DOCUMENTARY REFERENCES

General Assembly—26th session
Fifth Committee, meetings 1425, 1447-1454, 1456, 1458, 1462, 1464, 1467-1469, 1489.
Plenary meeting 2031.

A/8401. Report of Secretary-General on work of the Organization, 16 June 1970–15 June 1971, Part V, Chapter I.
A/8408 and Corr.1,2. Report of Advisory Committee on Administrative and Budgetary Questions (ACABQ) on budget estimates for 1972, paras. 49-54.
A/8408/Add.4. Report of ACABQ.
A/C.5/1320/Rev.1 and Rev.1/Add.1. Report of Secretary-General.
A/C.5/L.1066. USSR: draft resolution.
A/C.5/L.1068 and Rev.1,2. Algeria, Ethiopia, Ghana, Iran, Iraq, Kenya, Nigeria, Pakistan, Sudan, Syrian Arab Republic, Uganda, United Republic of Tanzania, Upper Volta, Zambia: draft resolution and revisions, as amended by Colombia (A/C.5/L.1076, para. 1, as orally revised, and para. 2), by Indonesia (A/C.5/L.1074, para. 2) and by Somalia (A/C.5/L.1073, as orally revised), approved by Fifth Committee on 2 December 1971, meeting 1468, by roll-call vote of 59 to 1, with 33 abstentions, as follows:

In favour: Algeria, Argentina, Australia, Austria, Bahrain, Barbados, Brazil, Cameroon, Chile, Cyprus, Denmark, Ecuador, Egypt, Ethiopia, Gabon, Ghana, Greece, Guinea, Guyana, Iceland, Iran, Iraq, Ireland, Italy, Ivory Coast, Jamaica, Japan, Jordan, Kenya, Khmer Republic, Kuwait, Liberia, Libyan Arab Republic, Mali, Mexico, Morocco, New Zealand, Nigeria, Norway, Pakistan, People's Democratic Republic of Yemen, Qatar, Rwanda, Saudi Arabia, Senegal, Somalia, Sudan, Sweden, Syrian Arab Republic, Togo, Trinidad and Tobago, Turkey, Uganda, United Republic of Tanzania, Venezuela, Yemen, Yugoslavia, Zaire, Zambia.
Against: Portugal.
Abstaining: Afghanistan, Belgium, Bulgaria, Burma, Byelorussian SSR, Canada, Ceylon, Colombia, Cuba, Czechoslovakia, Dominican Republic, Finland, France, Guatemala, Hungary, India, Indonesia, Israel, Mongolia, Netherlands, Peru, Philippines, Poland, Romania, South Africa, Spain, Thailand, Tunisia, Ukrainian SSR, USSR, United Kingdom, United States, Uruguay.

A/C.5/L.1069. Canada, Denmark, India. Netherlands, Philippines, Sweden: amendments to 14-power revised draft resolution, A/C.5/L.1068/Rev.1.
A/C.5/L.1070. Czechoslovakia: amendments to 14-power revised draft resolution, A/C.5/L.1068/Rev.1.
A/C.5/L.1072. Byelorussian SSR: amendment to 14-power revised draft resolution, A/C.5/L.1068/Rev.1.
A/C.5/L.1073. Somalia: amendment to 14-power revised draft resolution, A/C.5/L.1068/Rev.2.
A/C.5/L.1074. Indonesia: amendments to 14-power revised draft resolution, A/C.5/L.1068/Rev.2.
A/C.5/L.1075. Netherlands: amendment to 14-power revised draft resolution, A/C.5/L.1068/Rev.2.
A/C.5/L.1076. Colombia: amendments to 14-power revised draft resolution, A/C.5/L.1068/Rev.2.
A/8531/Add.1. Report of Fifth Committee (part II) (on budget estimates for financial year 1972), draft resolution IX.

RESOLUTION 2897(XXVI), as recommended by Fifth Committee, A/8531/Add.1, adopted by Assembly on 22 December 1971, meeting 2031, by recorded vote of 96 to 1, with 23 abstentions, as follows:

In favour: Afghanistan, Algeria, Argentina, Australia, Austria, Bhutan, Bolivia, Brazil, Burma, Burundi, Cameroon, Canada, Ceylon, Chad, Chile, Colombia, Congo, Costa Rica, Cyprus, Dahomey, Denmark, Dominican Republic, Ecuador, Egypt, El Salvador, Equatorial Guinea, Ethiopia, Finland, Gambia, Ghana, Greece, Guatemala, Guyana, Haiti, Honduras, Iceland, Indonesia, Iran, Ireland, Israel, Italy, Ivory Coast, Jamaica, Japan, Jordan, Kenya, Khmer Republic, Kuwait, Laos, Lebanon, Lesotho, Liberia, Libyan Arab Republic, Madagascar, Malawi, Malaysia, Malta, Mauritania, Mexico, Morocco, Nepal, New Zealand, Nicaragua, Niger, Nigeria, Norway, Pakistan, Panama,

Paraguay, People's Democratic Republic of Yemen, Peru, Qatar, Rwanda, Senegal, Sierra Leone, Singapore, Somalia, Spain, Sudan, Swaziland, Sweden, Syrian Arab Republic, Thailand, Togo, Trinidad and Tobago, Turkey, Uganda, United Arab Emirates, United Republic of Tanzania, Upper Volta, Uruguay, Venezuela, Yemen, Yugoslavia, Zaire, Zambia.

Against: Portugal.

Abstaining: Belgium, Bulgaria, Byelorussian SSR, Cuba, Czechoslovakia, France, Gabon, Guinea, Hungary, India, Luxembourg, Mali, Mongolia, Netherlands, Philippines, Poland, Romania, South Africa, Tunisia, Ukrainian SSR, USSR, United Kingdom, United States.

The General Assembly,

Having considered the report of the Secretary-General on the review and reappraisal of United Nations information policies and activities, the related report of the Advisory Committee on Administrative and Budgetary Questions and the relevant statements made in the Fifth Committee by the representatives of the Secretary-General,

Reaffirming its resolutions 13(I) of 13 February 1946 and 595(VI) of 4 February 1952 and subsequent resolutions on public information in the United Nations,

Bearing in mind that various United Nations bodies make recommendations on policy guidelines related to information in their area of concern,

Reaffirming the importance of United Nations information centres as appropriate instruments for informing the peoples of the world about the Organization's objectives and activities,

Stressing the need for maintaining central control and direction in the implementation of information policies and guidelines,

1. *Takes note with appreciation* of the report of the Secretary-General on the review and reappraisal of United Nations information policies and activities;

2. *Decides* that the basic principles laid down in General Assembly resolution 13(I) and confirmed in resolution 595(VI) do not need to be revised, amended or enlarged and that they should continue to be applied, subject to such directives as the Assembly has already given or may give from time to time;

3. *Approves* the Secretary-General's proposals for the acquisition and replacement of equipment for 1972, as set out in annex I of the addendum to his report, and decides to consider at the twenty-seventh session the balance of the Secretary-General's programme of future acquisition and replacement;

4. *Endorses* the proposals contained in subparagraphs 261 (iii), (iv), (viii), (x), (xii) and (xiv) of the Secretary-General's report;

5. *Approves in principle* the Secretary-General's proposal on the establishment of a regional production bureau and decides to consider all aspects of its implementation at the twenty-seventh session;

6. *Recommends* that the Secretary-General, in accordance with the provisions of General Assembly resolution 1405(XIV) of 1 December 1959, should review the composition of the Consultative Panel on Public Information to ensure that it reflects the present situation in the United Nations, and requests the Secretary-General to convene the Panel before the twenty-seventh session to advise him on the information policies and activities of the United Nations;

7. *Requests* the Secretary-General to ascertain the publicity and promotional needs of the various bodies of the United Nations which undertake universal causes approved by the General Assembly, in order that those needs may be taken into account when considering the budgetary requirements for the Office of Public Information for 1973 and subsequent years;

8. *Requests* the Secretary-General to appoint to the United Nations information centres highly qualified Professional staff in the field of information, who should give their undivided attention to the dissemination of information and the building of public support for United Nations activities, particularly in the economic, social and political fields;

9. *Requests* the Secretary-General to intensify his efforts to eliminate any shortcomings that may persist in the formulation and execution of information programmes and activities, particularly in the economic and social fields;

10. *Further requests* the Secretary-General to ensure the allocation of adequate resources effectively to meet additional needs in the information activities of the United Nations Conference on Trade and Development and the United Nations Industrial Development Organization during the Second United Nations Development Decade;

11. *Takes note* of the Secretary-General's statement of 16 November 1971 and requests him, bearing in mind the relevant provisions of General Assembly resolutions 13(I) of 13 February 1946, 595(VI) of 4 February 1952 and 2567(XXIV) of 13 December 1969, to review the present administrative arrangements for the Centre for Economic and Social Information and to reorganize the Office of Public Information with a view to ensuring central control and direction in the implementation of information policies and guidelines and thereby enabling the Office to carry out its mandate more effectively;

12. *Recommends* to the Governing Council of the United Nations Development Programme, when it considers at its thirteenth session the Administrator's proposal on the Development Support Information Service, that it should entrust as many as possible of its information activities to the United Nations and other executing agencies;

13. *Requests* the Secretary-General to report to the General Assembly at its twenty-seventh session on the implementation of the present resolution.

Pattern of United Nations conferences

Discussion of the pattern of United Nations conferences and meetings took place during 1971 in both the Economic and Social Council and in the General Assembly.

On 30 July 1971, the Council decided, *inter alia,* to arrange its programme of work to provide for:

(*a*) a short organizational session in January;

(*b*) a session in the second quarter of the calendar year devoted mainly to social questions, the reports of subsidiary bodies and elections;

(*c*) a session in the third quarter of the calendar year at Geneva, Switzerland, devoted to major questions arising from the world economic situation and, in alternate years, a debate on the implementation of the International Development

Strategy for the Second United Nations Development Decade with a view to assisting the General Assembly in the over-all appraisal, and to the co-ordination of United Nations activities in the economic and social fields; and

(*d*) a brief resumed session during the session of the General Assembly to deal with items that could not normally be considered at the regular sessions of the Council.

These decisions were embodied in resolution 1623(LI), which was adopted by 26 votes to 0, with 1 abstention, on the basis of a proposal by Greece and New Zealand. (For text of relevant part of resolution, see DOCUMENTARY REFERENCES below, and for further information about other measures to improve the organization of the Council's work, see pp. 466-72.)

On the same date, the Council also approved, without a vote and without adopting a formal resolution, the calendar of conferences for 1972 as proposed by the Secretary-General and as approved by the Council's Co-ordination Committee, on the understanding that the Secretary-General, in administering the programme of meetings, would take into account the observations made by delegations in the course of the discussion of the draft calendar in the Council and its Co-ordination Committee.

The calendar of conferences for 1972 was approved without vote by the Co-ordination Committee on 23 July 1971 with the reservation that the Secretariat, when administering the programme of conferences and meetings, would also take into account the relative importance of different United Nations organs and in that respect would place the Economic and Social Council immediately after the General Assembly and before the other organs.

The General Assembly, on 17 December 1971, acting on the recommendation of its Fifth (Administrative and Budgetary) Committee, approved the calendar of conferences and meetings of the United Nations for 1972 as submitted by the Secretary-General.

The Assembly also asked the Secretary-General to submit in 1972 a study on conference location and servicing which it had called for on 16 December 1969,[5] and to include in that study consideration of locations other than Headquarters and the United Nations Office at Geneva, as well as an assessment of possible measures to ensure the most effective and efficient organization of the pattern of conferences. The Secretary-General was also asked to submit in 1972 a calendar of conferences for 1973 and a preliminary calendar for 1974.

These were among the decisions embodied in resolution 2834(XXVI), adopted at an Assembly plenary meeting on 17 December 1971 by 75 votes to 0, with 1 abstention.

Previously, on 4 December, the resolution had been agreed to in the Fifth Committee by 64 votes to 0, with 6 abstentions, on the basis of a proposal by the Committee's Chairman, as amended by Austria, Indonesia and the United Kingdom.

In taking these decisions, the Assembly, *inter alia*, stated its awareness that the increasing number of conferences and meetings was one of the causes of the growth in the United Nations budget and in United Nations documentation.

(For text of resolution, see DOCUMENTARY REFERENCES below.)

[5]See Y.U.N., 1969, pp. 834-35, text of resolution 2609(XXIV).

DOCUMENTARY REFERENCES

Decisions of Economic and Social Council

Economic and Social Council—51st session
Co-ordination Committee, meeting 433.
Plenary meeting 1799.

E/L.1441. Calendar of conferences for 1972. Note by Secretary-General.
E/L.1452. Letter of 21 July 1971 from Kenya.
E/5063. Report of Co-ordination Committee.
E/5073. Resolutions adopted by Economic and Social Council during its 51st session, 5-30 July 1971. Other decisions, p. 28.

Economic and Social Council—50th session
Plenary meetings 1734-1739, 1743, 1745, 1761, 1765, 1768, 1772.

E/4986 and Add.1-9. Measures to improve organization of work of Council. Views and proposals of Governments. Note by Secretary-General.
E/L.1369. Note of 31 December 1970 by Council President.
E/L.1408 and Rev.1. Greece and New Zealand: draft resolution and revision.
E/L.1421. Ghana, Indonesia, Italy, Kenya, Lebanon, Madagascar, Pakistan, Sudan, Tunisia, Zaire: amendments to 2-power draft resolution, E/L.1408.
E/L.1421/Rev.1. Ghana, Indonesia, Italy, Kenya, Lebanon, Madagascar, Niger, Norway, Pakistan, Sudan, Tunisia, Zaire: revised amendments to 2-power revised draft resolution, E/L.1408/Rev.1.
E/L.1422. Brazil: amendments to 2-power draft resolution, E/L.1408.

E/L.1423. United States: amendment to 2-power draft resolution, E/L.1408.
E/5044. Resolutions adopted by Economic and Social Council during its 50th session, 11-13 January and 26 April-21 May 1971. Decisions, p. 26 (items 5 and 16).

Economic and Social Council—51st session
Plenary Meetings 1773-1782, 1784, 1789, 1791, 1794-1796, 1798, 1799.

E/L.1408/Rev.2. Greece and New Zealand: revised draft resolution.
E/L.1431. Brazil, Ghana, Jamaica, Lebanon, Pakistan, Peru, Tunisia, Yugoslavia: amendment to 2-power revised draft resolution, E/L.1408/Rev.2.

RESOLUTION 1623(LI) (section I), as proposed by 2 powers, E/L.1408/Rev.2, adopted by Council on 30 July 1971, meeting 1798, by 26 votes to 0, with 1 abstention.

The Economic and Social Council,

. . .

I

1. *Decides* that in its review of the over-all economic and social situation the Council should formulate new policy recommendations to meet the challenges of development, define major lags and constraints in the field of development and recommend ways and means for their removal;
2. *Decides* to arrange its programme of work, taking into account the rules of procedure of the Council, to provide for:
   (a) A short organizational session in January;
   (b) A session in the second quarter of the calendar year

devoted mainly to social questions, the reports of subsidiary bodies and elections;

(c) A session in the third quarter of the calendar year at Geneva devoted to major questions arising from the world economic situation and in alternate years a debate on the implementation of the International Development Strategy for the Second United Nations Development Decade, with a view to assisting the General Assembly in the over-all appraisal, and to the co-ordination of the activities of the United Nations system in the economic and social fields;

(d) A brief resumed session during the session of the General Assembly to deal with items that cannot normally be considered at the regular sessions of the Council;

. . .

[For full text of resolution 1623(LI), see p. 471.]

Decisions of General Assembly

General Assembly—26th session
Fifth Committee, meetings 1469-1471, 1484.
Plenary meeting 2023.

A/8319 and Corr.1. Report of Joint Inspection Unit (JIU) on United Nations documentation and on organization of proceedings of General Assembly and its main bodies. Note by Secretary-General (transmitting JIU report).
A/8403. Report of Economic and Social Council on work of its 50th and 51st sessions, Chapters IV and XXIV B.
A/8848 and Add.1,2. Report of Secretary-General.
A/8488. Note by Advisory Committee on Administrative and Budgetary Questions (ACABQ) (transmitting observations of Secretary-General on JIU report).
A/8532 and Corr.1,2. Publications and documentation of United Nations; pattern of conferences; rationalization of procedures and organization of United Nations. Report of JIU on United Nations documentation and on organization of proceedings of General Assembly and its main bodies. Report of ACABQ.

A/C.5/1372. Budget estimates for financial year 1972. Distribution of Secretariat functions between different locations. Note by Secretary-General.
A/8606. Report of Fifth Committee, draft resolution, as proposed by Committee Chairman and as amended by Austria and by United Kingdom, sub-amended by Indonesia, approved by Fifth Committee on 4 December 1971, meeting 1471, by 64 votes to 0, with 6 abstentions.

RESOLUTION 2834(XXVI), as recommended by Fifth Committee, A/8606, adopted by Assembly on 17 December 1971, meeting 2023, by 75 votes to 0, with 1 abstention.

The General Assembly,
Aware that the increasing number of conferences and meetings is one of the causes of the growth in the budget and in documentation,

1. *Takes note* of the Secretary-General's report on the pattern of conferences;

2. *Requests* the Secretary-General to present to the General Assembly at its twenty-seventh session the study called for under the terms of paragraph 6 (b) of its resolution 2609(XXIV) of 16 December 1969 and to include in the study consideration of other locations;

3. *Decides* to continue in force for 1972 the provisions of paragraph 9 of resolution 2609(XXIV) relating to the pattern of conferences;

4. *Approves* the calendar of conferences and meetings of the United Nations for 1972, as submitted by the Secretary-General in his report;

5. *Requests* the Secretary-General to submit to the General Assembly at its twenty-seventh session a calendar of conferences for 1973 and a preliminary calendar for 1974;

6. *Further requests* the Secretary-General to include in the study to be undertaken in accordance with paragraph 6 (b) of resolution 2609(XXIV) an assessment of possible measures to ensure that the pattern of conferences is organized on the most effective and efficient basis.

Publications and documentation of the United Nations

During 1971, continuing efforts were made in various United Nations organs to reduce the volume of documentation and its concomitant expenditures in the Organization.

The Economic and Social Council took a number of decisions in this regard following consideration of measures to improve the organization of its work.

Thus, on 30 July 1971, the Council—on the basis of a proposal by Brazil, France, Tunisia and Uruguay—called on the Secretary-General to ensure that Council documents were available in all working languages at least six weeks before the beginning of each session. The Council requested its Committee for Programme and Co-ordination (CPC) to submit in 1972 practical suggestions for establishing its calendar of conferences in such a way as to comply with those provisions. It also asked the Secretary-General to review measures in force regarding the preparation, translation and distribution of Council documents and to report in 1972, through CPC, on new measures taken or envisaged to improve the situation.

The Council took these decisions in unanimous-

ly adopting resolution 1624(LI). (For text of resolution, see DOCUMENTARY REFERENCES below.)

By another resolution, the Council asked the Secretary-General, beginning in 1972, to reform the nature, scope and form of documentation submitted to the Council and its organs to ensure, among other things, that: Governments were able to review reports adequately and the Council could concentrate on issues requiring inter-governmental consideration; reports were action-oriented, concise, and contained precise recommendations drawing attention to issues to be taken into account by the Council as well as alternative courses of action and their implications.

The Council also set out guidelines relating to the content of reports and the form of resolutions of its functional commissions and subsidiary bodies, and of its own report to the General Assembly. It reaffirmed its procedural rule requiring documentation for agenda items six weeks before each session, and invited the specialized agencies and the International Atomic Energy Agency to continue to provide analytical reports in accordance with the format it had outlined on 30

July 1970 contained in its resolution 1548(XLIX).[6]

These decisions were embodied in section III of resolution 1623(LI), adopted on 30 July 1971 on the basis of a proposal by Greece and New Zealand by 26 votes to 0, with 1 abstention. (For text of section III of resolution 1623(LI), see DOCUMENTARY REFERENCES below.)

Two reports of the Joint Inspection Unit dealing with documentation came before the General Assembly at its 1971 session together with related comments and observations of the Secretary-General and the Assembly's Advisory Committee on Administrative and Budgetary Questions.

One report, requested by the Assembly on 11 December 1970 in connexion with its consideration of the pattern of conferences,[7] dealt with the matter of documentation as well as the organization of the proceedings of the General Assembly and its main bodies; the other, a report by Inspector Robert M. Macy, dealt specifically with the programme of recurrent publications of the United Nations.

The question of documentation was also reviewed in the Assembly's Special Committee on the Rationalization of the Procedures and Organization of the General Assembly. In this regard, considerable attention was paid to the rationalization of the work of the Assembly's Fifth (Administrative and Budgetary) Committee itself.

On 6 December 1971, the Fifth Committee approved the text of a paragraph for its report to the Assembly requesting the Secretary-General to prepare and distribute documents for the Fifth Committee earlier than had been the case in recent years, thereby making it possible for the Assembly's Advisory Committee on Administrative and Budgetary Questions to complete more of its work and submit more of its reports before the opening and during the early part of the regular session of the General Assembly.

The Assembly on 17 December took note of the Fifth Committee's decision without adopting a formal resolution.

Also, the Assembly, acting on the recommendation of its Fifth Committee, adopted resolution 2836(XXVI) by which, among other things it took note of the section of the Joint Inspection Unit's report pertaining to documentation as well as the related comments of the Secretary-General and the Advisory Commitee, and of the report of the Special Committee.

The Assembly then asked the Secretary-General to take the necessary administrative action—including establishment of departmental quotas—to reduce in 1972 the volume of documentation originating in the Secretariat by 15 per cent as compared to 1970, thus to reduce the budget expenditure for documentation in 1972 by $1.25 million. It set forth principles for drafting the reports of its subsidiary organs and their governing bodies, its Main Committees, and the subsidiary bodies of the Economic and Social Council.

The Assembly invited the Security Council to implement the Joint Inspection Unit's recommendation that requests by Member States for participation in Council proceedings should not be issued as Security Council documents. It invited the Security Council, the Economic and Social Council, the Trusteeship Council, the Trade and Development Board and the Industrial Development Board not to provide verbatim or summary records for a newly established body, special meeting or conference unless specifically authorized to do so in the enabling resolution, and asked its Main Committees to review the possibility of less frequent submission of annual reports of subsidiary bodies.

The Assembly drew the attention of the Economic and Social Council to the Joint Inspection Unit's recommendations that: periodic reports to the Commission on Human Rights should be reproduced in the original language only (analytical summaries in four languages); country and subject indexes should be dispensed with; and only the draft and final reports of the Sub-Commission on Prevention of Discrimination and Protection of Minorities should receive general distribution.

The General Assembly also asked the Secretary-General to implement, in the light of the observations of the Advisory Committee, those Joint Inspection Unit recommendations which could be implemented without specific Assembly authorization.

Finally, the Assembly asked the Secretary-General to ensure that documents for consideration by the Assembly were distributed, as far as possible, before the opening of the session.

The resolution, which originated in the Advisory Committee on Administrative and Budgetary Questions following that body's consideration of the recommendations of the Joint Inspection Unit, was amended in the Fifth Committee by Brazil, Denmark, Ecuador, the United States and Yugoslavia before the Fifth Committee approved it, on 6 December 1971, by 73 votes to 0, with 1 abstention. The Assembly adopted it on 17 December by 85 votes to 0. (For text of resolution, see DOCUMENTARY REFERENCES below.)

On 21 December 1971, the Assembly took note of the report of the Joint Inspection Unit on the programme of recurrent publications of the United Nations and the comments thereon by the Secretary-General and the Advisory Committee on Administrative and Budgetary Questions.

---

[6]See Y.U.N., 1970, p. 607, text of resolution 1548(XLIX).
[7]*Ibid.*, p. 879, text of resolution 2693(XXV).

The Assembly requested the inter-governmental bodies concerned, as well as the Secretary-General and the Advisory Committee, to consider the recommendations of the Joint Inspection Unit on this matter and to transmit their observations and recommendations to the Assembly, through the Economic and Social Council in 1972.

The Assembly took this action in adopting resolution 2886(XXVI), without objection, on the recommendation of its Fifth Committee, which had approved the text as suggested by its Chairman, without vote, on 17 December 1971. (For text of resolution, see DOCUMENTARY REFERENCES below.)

DOCUMENTARY REFERENCES

Decisions of Economic and Social Council

MEASURES TO SPEED UP COUNCIL DOCUMENTATION

Economic and Social Council—51st session
Plenary meetings 1784, 1796, 1798.

E/L.1435. Brazil, France, Tunisia, Uruguay: draft resolution.

RESOLUTION 1624(LI), as proposed by 4 powers, E/L.1435, as orally amended by sponsors, adopted unanimously by Council on 30 July 1971, meeting 1798.

The Economic and Social Council,
Noting the difficulties encountered by delegations as a result of the late date on which they sometimes receive working papers for the session in the language of their choice,
Recalling rule 14, paragraph 4, of its rules of procedure,
Recalling further its resolution 1090 E (XXXIX) of 31 July 1965,
Noting that General Assembly resolution 2247(XXI) of 20 December 1966 asked the Secretary-General to ensure that documents should be available to the Member States in sufficient time and simultaneously in the working languages envisaged,
Noting further that General Assembly resolution 2292(XXII) of 8 December 1967 requested the Secretary-General to take all measures to ensure a more effective presentation and communication of the documents in due time and simultaneously in the working languages,
1. *Again calls upon* the Secretary-General to take such action as will ensure that the documents submitted to the Council and to its subsidiary organs are available to Member States in sufficient time (at least six weeks before the beginning of the session) and simultaneously in the working languages of the Council and of its organs, without prejudice to the other languages;
2. *Decides* that, for the future, the calendar of conferences shall be so established that paragraph 1 above can be complied with and requests the Committee for Programme and Co-ordination to submit to it, at its fifty-third session, practical suggestions for attaining that objective;
3. *Requests* the Secretary-General, after consultations with the Advisory Committee on Administrative and Budgetary Questions and after obtaining any outside advice which he may think helpful, to review the measures currently in force with respect to the preparation, translation and distribution of documents submitted to the Council or to its subsidiary organs;
4. *Further requests* the Secretary-General to submit to it, at its fifty-third session, through the Committee for Programme and Co-ordination, a report giving the results of the study defined in paragraph 3 above and indicating what new measures have been taken or envisaged to improve the present situation.

Economic and Social Council—50th session
Plenary meetings 1734-1739, 1743, 1745, 1761, 1765, 1768, 1772.

E/4986 and Add.1-9. Measures to improve organization of work of Council. Views and proposals of Governments. Note by Secretary-General.
E/L.1369. Note of 31 December 1970 by Council President.
E/L.1408 and Rev.1 Greece and New Zealand: draft resolution and revision.

E/L.1421. Ghana, Indonesia, Italy, Kenya, Lebanon, Madagascar, Pakistan, Sudan, Tunisia, Zaire: amendments to 2-power draft resolution, E/L.1408.
E/L.1421/Rev.1. Ghana, Indonesia, Italy, Kenya, Lebanon, Madagascar, Niger. Norway, Pakistan, Sudan, Tunisia, Zaire: revised amendments to 2-power revised draft resolution, E/L.1408/Rev.1.
E/L.1422. Brazil: amendments to 2-power draft resolution, E/L.1408.
E/L.1423. United States: amendment to 2-power draft resolution, E/L.1408.
E/5044. Resolutions adopted by Economic and Social Council during its 50th session, 11-13 January and 26 April–21 May 1971. Decisions, p. 26 (items 5 and 16).

IMPROVEMENT OF COUNCIL'S DOCUMENTATION

Economic and Social Council—51st session
Plenary meetings 1773-1782, 1784, 1789, 1791, 1794-1799.

E/L.1408/Rev.2. Greece and New Zealand: revised draft resolution.
E/L.1431. Brazil, Ghana, Jamaica, Lebanon, Pakistan, Peru, Tunisia, Yugoslavia: amendment to 2-power revised draft resolution, E/L.1408/Rev.2.

RESOLUTION 1623(LI) (section III), as proposed by 2 powers, E/L.1408/Rev.2, adopted by Council on 30 July 1971, meeting 1798, by 26 votes to 0, with 1 abstention.

The Economic and Social Council,
. . .

III

8. *Requests* the Secretary-General to take urgent steps to reform the nature, scope and form of documentation submitted to the Council to ensure that Governments can review reports adequately and also that the Council is able to concentrate on issues requiring intergovernmental consideration, that reports submitted to the Council are action-oriented and concise (normally not more than thirty-two pages), and present clear and precise recommendations drawing attention to issues that should be taken into account by the Council and possible alternative courses of action proposed for the Council and their implications, and to ensure also that, in the case of meetings of experts convened by the Secretary-General, only a concise report by the Secretary-General setting out the relevant recommendations for action by the Council is submitted;
9. *Requests* the Secretary-General to ensure that these guidelines are observed in reports submitted to the Council and its functional commissions and subsidiary bodies, beginning in 1972;
10. *Decides* that the reports of its functional commissions and subsidiary bodies should contain, in addition to a résumé of the discussions, a concise summary of recommendations and a statement of issues requiring action by the Council, and that all resolutions adopted by its functional commissions and subsidiary bodies should normally be in the form of drafts for approval by the Council;
11. *Decides* that the Council's report to the General Assembly should be reorganized to provide the Assembly with an effective basis for discussion, and that it should consist of a clear statement

of the issues on which Assembly action is required and a summary of the Council's discussions and a record of its decisions, including details of votes;

12. *Reaffirms* the importance of the strict observance of rule 14, paragraph 4, of the rules of procedure of the Council and decides that the calendar of conferences should be drawn up in such a way as to permit the observance of this rule;

13. *Invites* the specialized agencies and the International Atomic Energy Agency to continue to provide analytical reports, bearing in mind the recommendations in Council resolution 1548(XLIX) of 30 July 1970;

. . .

[For full text of resolution 1623 (LI), see p. 471.]

Decisions of General Assembly

General Assembly—26th session
Fifth Committee, meetings 1469-1473, 1486, 1487.
Sixth Committee, meetings 1304, 1306, 1307.
Plenary meetings 2024, 2030.

UNITED NATIONS PUBLICATIONS AND DOCUMENTATION
A/8319 and Corr.1. Pattern of conferences. Report of Joint Inspection Unit (JIU) on United Nations documentation and on organization of proceedings of General Assembly and its main bodies. Note by Secretary-General (transmitting JIU report).
A/8401. Report of Secretary-General on work of the Organization, 16 June 1970–15 June 1971, Part Five, Chapter III B.
A/8408 and Corr.1,2. First report of Advisory Committee on Administrative and Budgetary Questions (ACABQ) on budget estimates for financial year 1972, paras. 47-48.
A/8426. Report of Special Committee on Rationalization of Procedures and Organization of General Assembly, Chapter IX.
A/8437. Report of Secretary-General.
A/8488. Pattern of conferences. Report of JIU on United Nations documentation and on organization of proceedings of General Assembly and its main bodies. Note by ACABQ (transmitting comments by Secretary-General on JIU report).
A/8532 and Corr.1,2. Publications and documentation of United Nations; pattern of conferences; rationalization of procedures and organization of General Assembly. Report of JIU on United Nations documentation and on organization of proceedings of General Assembly and its main bodies. Report of ACABQ.
A/8532, Annex III. Draft resolution, proposed by ACABQ for adoption by Assembly, as amended in Fifth Committee by Brazil, by Denmark, by Ecuador, by United States and by Yugoslavia, approved by Fifth Committee on 6 December 1971, meeting 1473, by 73 votes to 0, with 1 abstention.
A/8608. Report of Fifth Committee (part I).

RESOLUTION 2836(XXVI), as recommended by Fifth Committee, A/8608, adopted by Assembly on 17 December 1971, meeting 2024, by 85 votes to 0.

The General Assembly,

Recalling its resolutions 593(VI) of 4 February 1952, 789 (VIII) of 9 December 1953, 1202(XII) and 1203(XII) of 13 December 1957, 1272(XIII) of 14 November 1958, 1851(XVII) of 19 December 1962, 1987(XVIII) of 17 December 1963, 2116(XX) of 21 December 1965, 2150(XXI) of 4 November 1966, 2292(XXII) of 8 December 1967, 2361(XXII) of 19 December 1967, 2478(XXIII) of 21 December 1968, 2538(XXIV) of 11 December 1969 and 2732(XXV) of 16 December 1970,

Having considered part A of the report of the Joint Inspection Unit, section IX of the report of the Special Committee on the Rationalization of the Procedures and Organization of the General Assembly and the comments of the Secretary-General and of the Advisory Committee on Administrative and Budgetary Questions,

Welcoming the action taken by the Economic and Social Council, in section III of resolution 1623(LI) of 30 July 1971, to improve the effectiveness and reduce the volume of its documentation,

Expressing its appreciation to the Joint Inspection Unit and the Advisory Committee on Administrative and Budgetary Questions for their reports,

Convinced that the control and limitation of United Nations documentation is necessary for the effective and economical operation of the Organization,

1. *Takes note* of part A, relating to documentation, of the report of the Joint Inspection Unit, and the related comments of the Secretary-General and of the Advisory Committee on Administrative and Budgetary Questions, and section IX, relating to documentation, of the report of the Special Committee on the Rationalization of the Procedures and Organization of the General Assembly;

2. *Requests* the Secretary-General to reduce in 1972 the volume of documentation originating in the Secretariat, other than meetings records, by 15 per cent over-all, compared with the volume of such documentation in 1970 and, to that end, to take such administrative action as may be necessary, including the establishment of departmental quotas, to achieve that target;

3. *Decides* that the reports submitted to it by its subsidiary organs, by its Main Committees, by the Trade and Development Board and by the Industrial Development Board shall be drafted on the basis of the following principles:
   (a) The reports should be action-oriented and concise and should contain precise information confined to a description of the work done by the organ concerned, to the conclusions it has reached to its decisions and to the recommendations made to the General Assembly;
   (b) Introductions containing background information should, as far as possible, be confined to matters of substance rather than procedure and should contain only what it is essential to bring to the notice of the General Assembly;
   (c) The account of the deliberations should be concise and should be supplemented, as necessary, by cross-references to the summary records;
   (d) Texts available in easily accessible documents should not be incorporated in or annexed to the report;
   (e) Texts which are not easily accessible should not be annexed when their substance can reasonably be incorporated in the main body of the report;
   (f) Participants should not be listed by name, unless they are serving in their individual capacity;
   (g) Where appropriate, reports should include a summary of the proposals, conclusions and recommendations contained therein;

4. *Invites* the Economic and Social Council to request its subsidiary bodies to follow the principles set forth in paragraph 3 above when preparing their reports to the Council;

5. *Requests* the Trade and Development Board and the Industrial Development Board to adopt decisions for the control of their documentation, applying *mutatis mutandis* the guidelines set out in section III of Economic and Social Council resolution 1623(LI);

6. *Invites* the Security Council to implement recommendation 7 contained in part A, section IX, of the report of the Joint Inspection Unit;

7. *Invites* the Security Council, the Economic and Social Council, the Trusteeship Council, the Trade and Development Board and the Industrial Development Board to adopt decisions containing provisions similar to those in paragraph 10 (b) of General Assembly resolution 2538(XXIV);

8. *Decides* that for the purposes of paragraph 10 (b) of resolution 2538(XXIV) the term "summary records" shall mean any meetings records that are prepared by précis-writers and/or translators;

9. *Requests* all its Main Committees, when considering items on their agenda which involve the submission of annual reports of subsidiary organs or of the Secretary-General, to review whether such reports can be submitted at less frequent intervals;

10. *Draws the attention* of the Economic and Social Council to recommendation 10 contained in part A, section IX, of the report of the Joint Inspection Unit;

11. *Invites* the Secretary-General to take appropriate steps to implement recommendations 14 to 26 contained in part A, section IX, of the report of the Joint Inspection Unit, in the light of the

observations of the Advisory Committee on Administrative and Budgetary Questions;

12. *Decides* to make an over-all reduction of $1,250,000 in the provision for documentation in the budget of the United Nations for the financial year 1972;

13. *Requests* the Secretary-General to reflect in his budget estimates for 1973 and subsequent years the progressive savings which can be expected to flow from the implementation of the recommendations relating to the control and limitation of documentation;

14. *Requests* the Secretary-General to submit to the General Assembly at its twenty-eighth session a concise report on the implementation of the present resolution;

15. *Further requests* the Secretary-General to take such measures including the possible application of modern management techniques, as he deems appropriate to ensure that documents for consideration by the General Assembly are distributed, as far as possible, before the opening of the session.

RECURRENT PUBLICATIONS

A/8362. Reports of JIU on programme of recurrent publications of United Nations. Note by Secretary-General (transmitting JIU report).

A/8540. Report of JIU on programme of recurrent publications of United Nations. Note by ACABQ (transmitting observations of Secretary-General on JIU report).

A/8624. Report of JIU on programme of recurrent publications of United Nations. Report of ACABQ.

A/C.5/1407, A/8408/Add.30. Budget estimates for financial year 1972. Problems concerning United Nations *Treaty Series*. Reports of Secretary-General and ACABQ.

A/C.6/410 and Corr.1. Programme of recurrent publications of United Nations: report of JIU. Observations of Secretary-General regarding legal publications.

A/C.6/411. Letter of 1 December 1971 from President of General Assembly to Chairman of Sixth Committee (transmitting letter of 30 November 1971 from Chairman of Fifth Committee to Assembly President).

A/8608/Add.1. Report of Fifth Committee (part II), draft resolution, as suggested by Committee Chairman, approved without vote by Fifth Committee on 17 December 1971, meeting 1487.

RESOLUTION 2886(XXVI), as recommended by Fifth Committee, A/8608/Add.1, adopted without objection by Assembly on 21 December 1971, meeting 2030.

The General Assembly

1. *Takes note* of the report of the Joint Inspection Unit on the programme of recurrent publications of the United Nations, and of the preliminary observations thereon by the Secretary-General and the Advisory Committee on Administrative and Budgetary Questions;

2. *Requests* the intergovernmental bodies concerned to consider the specific recommendations contained in the report of the Joint Inspection Unit and to transmit their observations, through the Economic and Social Council where appropriate, to the General Assembly in time for consideration at its twenty-seventh session;

3. *Further requests* the Secretary-General and the Advisory Committee on Administrative and Budgetary Questions to submit their observations and recommendations to the General Assembly at its twenty-seventh session.

A/8429. Resolutions adopted by General Assembly during its 26th session, 21 September–22 December 1971. Other decisions, p. 133.

Extensions to United Nations conference and office facilities

United Nations Headquarters accommodation

In a report to the General Assembly on the subject of United Nations Headquarters accommodation, the Secretary-General informed the Assembly that it had not proved possible to complete the financial package envisaged to implement the Headquarters construction project authorized by the Assembly on 17 December 1969[8] and that it appeared unlikely that the plan which had been approved by the Assembly would be implemented.

Meanwhile, he added, the $2 million which had been appropriated under the regular budget for the purpose for 1971[9] would not be utilized nor would the $1 million estimated for 1972.

The Assembly's Fifth (Administrative and Budgetary) Committee, during discussion of the supplementary budget estimates for 1971, had rejected a proposal to surrender for other uses the unused $2 million appropriated for United Nations Headquarters construction purposes (see p. 649).

On 30 November 1971, the Fifth Committee decided, by 39 votes to 20, with 11 abstentions, to approve a draft resolution introduced by Brazil and co-sponsored by Argentina, Canada, India, Iraq, Kenya, New Zealand, Nigeria, Norway,

Pakistan and Uruguay, under the terms of which the Assembly would decide to defer the question of new construction and major alterations at Headquarters until 1972. It also asked the Secretary-General to undertake detailed studies of the situation created by the space shortage at Headquarters, and to complete studies previously requested on optimum distribution of Secretariat functions among various United Nations locations, including the possibility of relocating certain units of the United Nations, and report to the Assembly at its twenty-seventh (1972) session.

On the same date, the Fifth Committee also approved, by 42 votes to 5, with 19 abstentions, a proposal by the United States that the $1 million estimated for 1972 for the proposed Headquarters construction be eliminated from the budget estimates and the $2 million which remained unspent in 1971 be applied to the 1972 estimates for over-all construction purposes.

A second draft resolution before the Fifth Committee—submitted by Algeria, the Byelorussian SSR, Cuba, Czechoslovakia, Equatorial Guinea, Mongolia, Poland, the Syrian Arab Republic,

---

[8] See Y.U.N., 1969, pp. 839-40, text of resolution 2618(XXIV).
[9] See Y.U.N., 1970, p. 874.

the United Republic of Tanzania, and Upper Volta—would have the Assembly, among other things: rescind as inapplicable the provisions of the 1969 resolution authorizing new construction and expansion of premises at Headquarters, and delete those items from the budget; transfer the unused $2-million 1971 appropriation and use it for any work required at other United Nations offices outside New York City, and reduce the appropriations for new construction for 1972; and bring this decision to the attention of the United Nations Development Programme and the United Nations Children's Fund. The Committee rejected—by 36 votes to 27, with 9 abstentions—a proposal to put this resolution to a vote following the adoption of the 11-power text.

The General Assembly, on 22 December 1971, endorsed the Fifth Committee's text in adopting resolution 2895(XXVI) by a recorded vote of 93 to 16, with 10 abstentions. (For text of resolution, see DOCUMENTARY REFERENCES below.) It also approved, on the same date, without adopting a formal resolution, the Committee's recommendation to transfer the $2-million appropriation from the 1971 to the 1972 budget estimates.

Commemorative mural to World Youth Assembly

Acting on the recommendation of its Fifth (Administrative and Budgetary) Committee, the General Assembly, on 22 December 1971, adopted by a recorded vote of 75 to 17, with 26 abstentions, resolution 2896(XXVI), under the terms of which a mural would be painted at United Nations Headquarters to commemorate the World Youth Assembly held in 1970 within the framework of the twenty-fifth anniversary of the United Nations.[10]

The draft resolution, which the Fifth Committee approved on 30 November 1971 by 27 votes to 19, with 32 abstentions, was proposed by Saudi Arabia which accepted oral amendments by Indonesia. The text stipulated that the cost of the mural would be financed from the surplus voluntary funds of the World Youth Assembly, within a maximum of $10,000. (For text of resolution, see DOCUMENTARY REFERENCES below.)

Mechanical means of voting

By a decision of 4 December 1969,[11] the General Assembly approved a recommendation of the Secretary-General that the United Nations should design, construct and install its own mechanical voting system on the understanding that before any expenditures were incurred, a demonstration model would be tested to assure the technical feasibility of the project.

In January 1970 a model of the voting machine was tested and found to be satisfactory. Accordingly, a detailed design was developed, various

components fabricated, and the machine was installed in one of the conference rooms.

In his report on the voting machine, to the 1971 session of the General Assembly, the Secretary-General stated that, although he was satisfied that the equipment met the requirements of mechanical voting as provided in the rules of procedure, he still wished it to be considered as experimental. He intended to review the use of the machine after the Assembly's 1971 session to ascertain whether changes would be desirable in the light of experience.

In the meantime, the Secretary-General suggested that the Main Committees make full use, on a rotating basis, of the mechanical voting equipment.

On 22 September 1971, the Assembly's General Committee recommended that the item on mechanical means of voting be deferred to the 1972 session. The General Assembly approved this recommendation on 24 September 1971 without adopting a formal resolution.

Extension of Palais des Nations

The General Assembly on 22 December 1971 adopted, by a recorded vote of 110 to 0, with 10 abstentions, a resolution dealing with the construction of the extension to the Palais des Nations, headquarters of the United Nations Office at Geneva, Switzerland. The construction plan was originally authorized by the Assembly on 21 December 1968.[12]

The Assembly further authorized the Secretary-General to continue the construction project within a revised estimated cost of $31,186,000 and an appropriation of $2.5 million. Also revised was the amortization period of a loan of 61 million Swiss francs as well as the schedule of annual budget instalments established in the 1968 resolution. In addition, the Assembly authorized the establishment of an informal *ad hoc* committee at Geneva to review the progress of work and to advise the Secretary-General on any special problems, particularly those bearing on cost estimates.

(For text of resolution, see DOCUMENTARY REFERENCES below.)

The Assembly took these decisions on the recommendation of its Fifth (Administrative and Budgetary) Committee, embodying them in resolution 2891(XXVI).

The Committee's proposals were based on a progress report of the Secretary-General on the extension work at the Palais and on recommendations and a suggestion of the Assembly's Advisory Committee on Administrative and Budgetary

---

[10] See Y.U.N., 1970, pp. 113-14.
[11] See Y.U.N., 1969, p. 840, text of resolution 2519(XXIV).
[12] See Y.U.N., 1968, pp. 924-25, text of resolution 2488(XXIII).

Questions. An increase of $7.4 million over the original estimate of $22 million approved in 1968 was attributed to major modifications to the original plans, increases in labour and supply costs and in fees for architectural and engineering services and administrative expenses, unforeseen supplementary work, and underestimation of earlier cost estimates. The recommendations were approved by the Fifth Committee on 30 November 1971 by 61 votes to 0, with 7 abstentions.

Programme of major maintenance of and improvements to Palais des Nations

A resolution dealing with the programme of major maintenance of and improvements to the Palais des Nations at Geneva, Switzerland, was adopted by the Assembly on 22 December 1971, by a recorded vote of 112 to 0, with 9 abstentions.

Under the terms of this resolution (2892(XXVI))—recommended by the Assembly's Fifth (Administrative and Budgetary) Committee on 30 November 1971 on the basis of observations and suggestions of the Advisory Committee on Administrative and Budgetary Questions as approved by the Fifth Committee by 61 votes to 0, with 9 abstentions—the Secretary-General was authorized to continue with the programme of major maintenance and improvements at the Palais at an estimated cost of $6,773,847. This represented an increase of $240,000 over the amount approved in 1970, attributable mainly to the revaluation during 1971 of the Swiss franc in relation to the United States dollar.

By this resolution the Assembly also increased the annual budgetary appropriation for the programme in 1972 from $1,098,000 to $1,238,000, and authorized a like amount for 1973 and 1974 to finance the balance of the programme.

(For text of resolution, see DOCUMENTARY REFERENCES below.)

United Nations building in Santiago, Chile

On the basis of recommendations of the General Assembly's Advisory Committee on Administrative and Budgetary Questions—commenting on a progress report of the Secretary-General—the Assembly's Fifth (Administrative and Budgetary) Committee on 30 November 1971 approved by 72 votes to 1, with 1 abstention, a draft resolution dealing with the proposed new construction and the programme of modification and improvement to the existing United Nations premises in Santiago, Chile.

Under the terms of this resolution, which the Assembly adopted on 22 December 1971 as resolution 2893(XXVI) by a recorded vote of 120 to 0, with 2 abstentions, the Assembly concurred in the recommendations of its Advisory Committee.

The Advisory Committee had suggested that the Assembly seek the views of the Economic Commission for Latin America, the Economic and Social Council and the United Nations Development Programme on responsibility for accommodating the Latin American Institute for Economic and Social Planning before a final decision was taken to proceed with the proposed construction of a building to house the Institute. It also recommended that the Secretary-General proceed with construction of a Documents Research Centre with funds from a donation for that purpose by the Netherlands.

In addition, the Assembly authorized the Secretary-General to carry forward into 1972 an unencumbered balance of $71,150 from unspent funds provided in 1971 for the modification and improvement programme of the existing Santiago premises.

(For text of resolution, see DOCUMENTARY REFERENCES below.)

United Nations accommodation in Bangkok and Addis Ababa

On 22 December 1971, the General Assembly adopted, by a recorded vote of 112 to 0, with 9 abstentions, resolution 2894(XXVI) dealing with United Nations accommodation in Bangkok, Thailand, and Addis Ababa, Ethiopia.

Under the terms of this resolution, the Assembly expressed its gratitude to the host countries for their generosity and co-operation, and took note of the comments of its Advisory Committee on Administrative and Budgetary Questions.

The Advisory Committee, commenting on a progress report of the Secretary-General, noted that the work on both projects was behind schedule and that expenditures during 1971 therefore were likely to be about one sixth of the approved appropriations for that year. It expressed the belief that the Secretary-General would have to proceed vigorously in 1972 in order to meet the target date for completion—a matter of importance if cost estimates were not to be exceeded. The Assembly agreed to proposed modifications in the four-year (1971-1974) schedule of budgetary payments for the two projects endorsed by an Assembly decision of 17 December 1970[13]—which had authorized the Secretary-General to proceed with the construction of new premises for the Economic Commission for Africa in Addis Ababa and for the Economic Commission for Asia and the Far East in Bangkok—and approved a new financing schedule.

(For text of resolution 2894(XXVI), see DOCUMENTARY REFERENCES below.)

[13]See Y.U.N., 1970, p. 875, text of resolution 2745(XXV).

The Assembly took its decisions on the basis of recommendations by its Fifth (Administrative and Budgetary) Committee, which had approved, without vote, oral proposals of its Chairman to this effect on 30 November 1971.

Agreement on the use of the Peace Palace by the International Court of Justice

On 22 December 1971, following consideration of the budget estimates for 1972, the General Assembly adopted a resolution concerning the Agreement between the United Nations and the Carnegie Foundation on the use of the premises of the Peace Palace at The Hague, Netherlands, by the International Court of Justice.

The Court's occupancy of the Peace Palace is governed by a special agreement with the Carnegie Foundation in the Netherlands, which owns the building and is responsible for its maintenance and operation. In accordance with this Agreement, as approved by the General Assembly on 11 December 1946[14] the United Nations makes an annual contribution in respect of the use of the premises by the Court in an amount which has been increased from time to time[15] at the request of the Board of Directors of the Carnegie Foundation.

In response to such a request, the Secretary-General in his initial budget estimates for 1972, recommended that the General Assembly approved a Supplementary Agreement between the United Nations and the Carnegie Foundation whereby the annual contribution payable by the Court would be raised from the 1971 level of 150,000 Netherlands florins net to 225,000 florins net, with effect from 1 January 1972.

The Advisory Committee on Administrative and Budgetary Questions in its report noted that the proposed increase of 75,000 florins consisted of two different elements, one of which (amounting to 50,000 florins) constituted an increase in the amount of the annual contributions and the other (amounting to 25,000 florins) a supplementary payment towards the cost of the restoration of the Peace Palace, on which work was expected to be completed in 1974. The latter amount would therefore only be payable during the years 1972, 1973 and 1974. The Advisory Committee recommended that the Supplementary Agreement annexed to the draft resolution proposed by the Secretary-General be amended accordingly.

The Assembly's Fifth (Administrative and Budgetary) Committee, on 21 December 1971, approved, by 70 votes to 0, a draft resolution and the annex containing the Supplementary Agreement, as amended following the recommendations of the Advisory Committee. On the recommendation of the Fifth Committee, the Assembly adopted the text unanimously as resolution 2902(XXVI). (For text of resolution, see DOCUMENTARY REFERENCES below.)

---

[14] See Y.U.N., 1946-47, pp. 245-46, text of annex A to resolution 84(I).
[15] See Y.U.N., 1951, p. 151, text of annex to resolution 586(VI) of 21 December 1951, and Y.U.N., 1958, p. 410, text of resolution 1343(XIII) of 13 December 1958.

DOCUMENTARY REFERENCES

General Assembly—26th session
Fifth Committee, meetings 1443-1445, 1459, 1461, 1465-1467.
Plenary meeting 2031.

A/8406 and Corr.1,3, Vol. 1. Budget estimates for financial year 1972 and information annexes. (Part III, Section 7: Construction, alteration, improvement and major maintenance of premises.)
A/8408 and Corr.1,2. First report of Advisory Committee on Administrative and Budgetary Questions (ACABQ) on budget estimates for financial year 1972, paras. 55-59, and Part III, Section 7.

United Nations Headquarters accommodation
A/C.5/1372. Distribution of Secretariat functions between different locations. Note by Secretary-General.
A/C.5/1381. Report of Secretary-General.
A/C.5/1391, A/8408/Add.7. Additional seating facilities in principal meeting areas. Reports of Secretary-General and ACABQ.
A/C.5/L.1063. Argentina, Brazil, Canada, India, Iraq, Kenya, New Zealand, Nigeria, Norway, Pakistan, Uruguay: draft resolution, approved by Fifth Committee on 30 November 1971, meeting 1466, by 39 votes to 20, with 11 abstentions.
A/C.5/L.1064. Algeria, Byelorussian SSR, Cuba, Czechoslovakia, Poland, Syrian Arab Republic: draft resolution.
A/C.5/L.1064 Rev.1. Algeria, Byelorussian SSR, Cuba, Czechoslovakia, Equatorial Guinea, Mongolia, Poland, Syrian Arab Republic, United Republic of Tanzania, Upper Volta: revised draft resolution.
A/8531/Add.1. Report of Fifth Committee (part II) (on budget estimates for financial year 1972), paras. 74-88, and draft resolution VII.

RESOLUTION 2895(XXVI), as recommended by Fifth Committee, A/8531/Add.1, adopted by Assembly on 22 December 1971, meeting 2031, by recorded vote of 93 to 16, with 10 abstentions, as follows:

In favour: Afghanistan, Argentina, Australia, Austria, Belgium, Bhutan, Bolivia, Brazil, Burundi, Cameroon, Canada, Ceylon, Chad, Colombia, Congo, Costa Rica, Cyprus, Dahomey, Denmark, Dominican Republic, Ecuador, Egypt, El Salvador, Ethiopia, Fiji, Finland, Gabon, Gambia, Ghana, Greece, Guatemala, Guyana, Haiti, Honduras, Iceland, India, Indonesia, Iran, Ireland, Israel, Italy, Ivory Coast, Jamaica, Japan, Jordan, Kenya, Khmer Republic, Laos, Lebanon, Lesotho, Liberia, Luxembourg, Madagascar, Malawi, Malaysia, Mali, Malta, Mauritania, Mexico, Morocco, Nepal, Netherlands, New Zealand, Nicaragua, Nigeria, Norway, Pakistan, Panama, Paraguay, Philippines, Portugal, Rwanda, Saudi Arabia, Senegal, Sierra Leone, Singapore, Somalia, South Africa, Spain, Sweden, Thailand, Togo, Trinidad and Tobago, Tunisia, Turkey, Uganda, United Kingdom, United States, Uruguay, Venezuela, Yugoslavia, Zaire, Zambia.
Against: Bulgaria, Byelorussian SSR, Chile, Cuba, Czechoslovakia, Equatorial Guinea, Hungary, Kuwait, Mongolia, People's Democratic Republic of Yemen, Peru, Poland, Ukrainian SSR, USSR, Upper Volta, Yemen.
Abstaining: Algeria, Burma, France, Guinea, Libyan Arab

Republic, Qatar, Romania, Sudan, Syrian Arab Republic, United Republic of Tanzania.

The General Assembly,
Recalling its resolution 2618(XXIV) of 17 December 1969 on new construction and major alterations at United Nations Headquarters,
Noting the reports on this matter submitted by the Advisory Committee on Administrative and Budgetary Questions and by the Secretary-General to the General Assembly at its twenty-sixth session,
Noting with regret that there are no prospects at the present time for the execution of the projected new construction and major alterations to existing premises at United Nations headquarters, as authorized by resolution 2618(XXIV),
Recognizing that the shortage of space at Headquarters, as well as at many other major United Nations locations, grows continuously more acute,
1. *Decides* to defer until the twenty-seventh session the question of new construction and major alterations at United Nations Headquarters;
2. *Requests* the Secretary-General to undertake a detailed and comprehensive study of the situation created by the shortage of space at Headquarters, including the prospects of executing the project referred to in General Assembly resolution 2618(XXIV), and to submit a report to the Assembly at its twenty-seventh session, together with the concrete proposals and recommendations he might consider appropriate to meet that situation in the light of any new development;
3. *Further requests* the Secretary-General to present to the General Assembly at its twenty-seventh session, in a detailed and comprehensive manner, the studies mentioned in paragraphs 3, 4 and 5 of resolution 2618(XXIV), which were to have been submitted at the twenty-sixth session.

A/8429. Resolutions adopted by General Assembly during its 26th session, 21 September–22 December 1971. Other decisions, p. 132 (item 76, first para.).

COMMEMORATIVE MURAL TO WORLD YOUTH ASSEMBLY
A/C.5/L.1071. Saudi Arabia: draft resolution, as orally amended by Indonesia, approved by Fifth Committee on 30 November 1971, meeting 1466, by 27 votes to 19, with 32 abstentions.
A/8531/Add.1. Report of Fifth Committee (part II), paras. 89-93, and draft resolution VIII.

RESOLUTION 2896(XXVI), as recommended by Fifth Committee, A/8531/Add.1, adopted by Assembly on 22 December 1971, meeting 2031, by recorded vote of 75 to 17, with 26 abstentions, as follows:

In favour: Afghanistan, Algeria, Austria, Barbados, Bhutan, Bolivia, Burma, Burundi, Cameroon, Ceylon, Chile, Colombia, Congo, Costa Rica, Cyprus, Denmark, Dominican Republic, Egypt, Equatorial Guinea, Ethiopia, Fiji, Finland, Gambia, Greece, Guatemala, Guinea, Haiti, Iceland, India, Indonesia, Iran, Ivory Coast, Jamaica, Jordan, Khmer Republic, Kuwait, Laos, Lebanon, Lesotho, Liberia, Libyan Arab Republic, Madagascar, Malaysia, Mali, Malta, Mauritania, Mexico, Morocco, Nepal, Nicaragua, Nigeria, Norway, Pakistan, Panama, Paraguay, Peru, Philippines, Qatar, Romania, Rwanda, Saudi Arabia, Senegal, Sierra Leone, Sudan, Swaziland, Syrian Arab Republic, Togo, Trinidad and Tobago, Tunisia, Turkey, Uganda, Venezuela, Yemen, Yugoslavia, Zambia.
Against: Belgium, Brazil, Bulgaria, Canada, France, Ghana, Ireland, Israel, Italy, Netherlands, Portugal, South Africa, Sweden, United Kingdom, United Republic of Tanzania, United States, Upper Volta.
Abstaining: Australia, Byelorussian SSR, Chad, Cuba, Czechoslovakia, Dahomey, Ecuador, El Salvador, Gabon, Guyana, Honduras, Hungary, Japan, Kenya, Luxembourg, Malawi, Mongolia, New Zealand, People's Democratic Republic of Yemen, Poland, Somalia, Thailand, Ukrainian SSR, USSR, Uruguay, Zaire.

The General Assembly,
Considering that the World Youth Assembly, held within the framework of the twenty-fifth anniversary of the United Nations, recognized the important role that youth should play in the world,
Taking into account that youth constitutes more than half the population of the world,
Recognizing that the World Youth Assembly served a most useful purpose in bringing together the youth from nearly all the countries of the world, irrespective of the political or ideological systems to which those countries belonged,
Noting that the World Youth Assembly paved the way for a better understanding among youth designed to contribute to efforts for bringing about peace, justice and progress in the world,
1. *Decides* that a mural shall be painted at United Nations Headquarters to commemorate the World Youth Assembly;
2. *Decides* that the cost of such a mural shall be financed from the surplus voluntary funds of the World Youth Assembly, within the maximum amount of $10,000.

MECHANICAL MEANS OF VOTING

General Assembly—26th session
General Committee, meeting 191.
Plenary meeting 1937.

A/8374. Installation of mechanical means of voting. Report of Secretary-General.
A/8500. Organization of 26th regular session of General Assembly, adoption of agenda and allocation of items. First report of General Committee, para. 15 (*b*).

Extension of Palais des Nations
A/C.5/1389 and Corr.1,2. Report of Secretary-General.
A/8408/Add.10. Programme of major maintenance of and improvements to Palais des Nations, Geneva; extension of Palais des Nations. Report of ACABQ. Section II: recommendations and suggestion approved by Fifth Commitee on 30 November 1971, meeting 1466, as follows: recommendations in paras. 25 and 26, by 61 votes to 0, with 7 abstentions; suggestion in para. 23, without vote.
A/8531/Add.1. Report of Fifth Committee (part II), paras. 53-60, and draft resolution III, prepared on basis of recommendations and suggestion of ACABQ (A/8408/Add.10, paras. 23, 25 and 26) approved without vote by Fifth Committee on 30 November 1971, meeting 1466.

RESOLUTION 2891(XXVI), as recommended by Fifth Committee, A/8531/Add.1, adopted by Assembly on 22 December 1971, meeting 2031, by recorded vote of 110 to 0, with 10 abstentions, as follows:

In favour: Afghanistan, Algeria, Argentina, Australia, Austria, Belgium, Bhutan, Bolivia, Brazil, Burma, Burundi, Cameroon, Canada, Ceylon, Chad, Chile, Colombia, Congo, Costa Rica, Cuba, Cyprus, Dahomey, Denmark, Dominican Republic, Ecuador, Egypt, Equatorial Guinea, Ethiopia, Fiji, Finland, France, Gabon, Gambia, Ghana, Greece, Guatemala, Guinea, Guyana, Haiti, Honduras, Iceland, India, Indonesia, Iran, Ireland, Israel, Italy, Ivory Coast, Jamaica, Japan, Jordan, Kenya, Khmer Republic, Kuwait, Laos, Lebanon, Lesotho, Liberia, Libyan Arab Republic, Luxembourg, Madagascar, Malawi, Malaysia, Mali, Malta, Mauritania, Mexico, Morocco, Nepal, Netherlands, New Zealand, Nicaragua, Niger, Nigeria, Norway, Pakistan, Panama, Paraguay, People's Democratic Republic of Yemen, Peru, Philippines, Portugal, Qatar, Rwanda, Senegal, Sierra Leone, Singapore, Somalia, South Africa, Spain, Sudan, Swaziland, Sweden, Syrian Arab Republic, Thailand, Togo, Trinidad and Tobago, Tunisia, Uganda, United Arab Emirates, United Kingdom, United Republic of Tanzania, United States, Upper Volta, Uruguay, Venezuela, Yemen, Yugoslavia, Zaire, Zambia.
Against: None.
Abstaining: Bulgaria, Byelorussian SSR, Czechoslovakia, El Salvador, Hungary, Mongolia, Poland, Romania, Ukrainian SSR, USSR.

The General Assembly,

Recalling its resolution 2488(XXIII) of 21 December 1968 on plans for the extension of conference facilities at the Palais des Nations at Geneva,

Having considered the reports of the Secretary-General and of the Advisory Committee on Administrative and Budgetary Questions on the extension of the Palais des Nations,

1. *Authorizes* the Secretary-General to continue the construction project within the total new revised estimated cost of $US 31,186,000;

2. *Decides* to increase from $1.5 million to $2.5 million the budgetary appropriation for the project in 1972;

3. *Decides* that the repayment of the loan of 61 million Swiss francs shall be amortized over a ten-year period beginning in 1975;

4. *Decides* that the schedule of annual budget instalments contained in paragraph 3 of its resolution 2488 (XXIII) shall be amended as follows:

Year	(U.S. dollars)
1973	4,905,000
1974	4,108,000
1975	1,660,300
1976	1,960,300
1977	1,914,800
1978	1,868,800
1979	1,822,300
1980	1,775,800
1981	1,729,800
1982	1,683,300
1983	1,636,800
1984	1,590,800

5. *Approves* the establishment of an informal *ad hoc* committee at Geneva as recommended by the Advisory Committee on Administrative and Budgetary Questions in paragraph 23 of its report.

PROGRAMME OF MAJOR MAINTENANCE OF AND
IMPROVEMENTS TO PALAIS DES NATIONS

A/C.5/1390 and Corr.1. Report of Secretary-General.

A/8408/Add.10. Programme of major maintenance of and improvements to Palais des Nations, Geneva; extension of Palais des Nations. Report of ACABQ. Section I: observations and suggestion approved by Fifth Committee on 30 November 1971, meeting 1466, as follows: observations in paras. 4-6, without vote; suggestion in para. 7, by 61 votes to 0, with 9 abstentions.

A/8531/Add.1. Report of Fifth Committee (part II), paras. 53-60, and draft resolution IV, prepared, as suggested by Committee Chairman, on basis of observations and suggestion of ACABQ (A/8408/Add.10, paras. 4-7), approved without vote by Fifth Committee on 30 November 1971, meeting 1466.

RESOLUTION 2892(XXVI), as recommended by Fifth Committee, A/8531/Add.1, adopted by Assembly on 22 December 1971, meeting 2031, by recorded vote of 112 to 0, with 9 abstentions, as follows:

In favour: Afghanistan, Algeria, Argentina, Australia, Austria, Belgium, Bhutan, Bolivia, Brazil, Burma, Burundi, Cameroon, Canada, Ceylon, Chad, Chile, Colombia, Congo, Costa Rica, Cuba, Cyprus, Dahomey, Denmark, Dominican Republic, Ecuador, Egypt, Equatorial Guinea, Ethiopia, Fiji, Finland, France, Gabon, Gambia, Ghana, Greece, Guatemala, Guinea, Guyana, Haiti, Honduras, Iceland, India, Indonesia, Iran, Ireland, Israel, Italy, Ivory Coast, Jamaica, Japan, Jordan, Kenya, Khmer Republic, Kuwait, Laos, Lebanon, Lesotho, Liberia, Libyan Arab Republic, Luxembourg, Madagascar, Malawi, Malaysia, Mali, Malta, Mauritania, Mexico, Morocco, Nepal, Netherlands, New Zealand, Nicaragua, Niger, Nigeria, Norway, Pakistan, Panama, Paraguay, People's Democratic Republic of Yemen, Peru, Philippines, Portugal, Qatar, Romania, Rwanda, Senegal, Sierra Leone, Singapore, Somalia, South Africa,

Spain, Sudan, Swaziland, Sweden, Syrian Arab Republic, Thailand, Togo, Trinidad and Tobago, Tunisia, Turkey, Uganda, United Arab Emirates, United Kingdom, United Republic of Tanzania, United States, Upper Volta, Uruguay, Venezuela, Yemen, Yugoslavia, Zaire, Zambia.

Against : None.

Abstaining: Bulgaria, Byelorussian SSR, Czechoslovakia, El Salvador, Hungary, Mongolia, Poland, Ukrainian SSR, USSR.

The General Assembly,

Having considered the reports of the Secretary-General and of the Advisory Committee on Administrative and Budgetary Questions on the programme of major maintenance of and improvements to the Palais des Nations at Geneva,

1. *Takes note* of the observations of the Advisory Committee on Administrative and Budgetary Questions in paragraphs 4,5 and 6 of its report;

2. *Authorizes* the Secretary-General to continue with the programme of major maintenance and improvements, at an estimated cost of $US 6,773,847;

3. *Decides* that the budgetary appropriation for the programme in 1972 shall be increased from $1,098,000 to $1,238,000;

4. *Decides* that further annual appropriations of $1,238,000 shall be authorized for 1973 and 1974 to finance the balance of the programme.

United Nations Building in Santiago, Chile

A/C.5/1396. Report of Secretary-General.

A/8408/Add.11. Report of ACABQ, recommendations in paras. 10-12, approved by Fifth Committee on 30 November 1971, meeting 1466, by 72 votes to 1, with 1 abstention.

A/8531/Add.1. Report of Fifth Committee (part II), paras. 61-67, and draft resolution V, prepared, as suggested by Committee Chairman, on basis of recommendations of ACABQ (A/8408/Add.11, paras. 10-12), approved without vote by Fifth Committee on 30 November 1971, meeting 1466.

RESOLUTION 2893(XXVI), as recommended by Fifth Committee, A/8531/Add.1, adopted by Assembly on 22 December 1971, meeting 2031, by recorded vote of 120 to 0, with 2 abstentions, as follows:

In favour: Afghanistan, Algeria, Argentina, Australia, Austria, Belgium, Bhutan, Bolivia, Brazil, Bulgaria, Burma, Burundi, Byelorussian SSR, Cameroon, Canada, Ceylon, Chad, Chile, Colombia, Congo, Costa Rica, Cuba, Cyprus, Czechoslovakia, Dahomey, Denmark, Dominican Republic, Ecuador, Egypt, El Salvador, Equatorial Guinea, Ethiopia, Fiji, Finland, France, Gabon, Gambia, Ghana, Greece, Guatemala, Guinea, Guyana, Haiti, Honduras, Hungary, Iceland, India, Indonesia, Iran, Ireland, Israel, Italy, Ivory Coast, Jamaica, Japan, Jordan, Kenya, Khmer Republic, Kuwait, Laos, Lebanon, Lesotho, Liberia, Libyan Arab Republic, Luxembourg, Madagascar, Malaysia, Mali, Malta, Mauritania, Mexico, Mongolia, Morocco, Nepal, Netherlands, New Zealand, Nicaragua, Niger, Nigeria, Norway, Oman, Pakistan, Panama, Paraguay, People's Democratic Republic of Yemen, Peru, Philippines, Poland, Portugal, Qatar, Romania, Rwanda, Senegal, Sierra Leone, Singapore, Somalia, South Africa, Spain, Sudan, Swaziland, Sweden, Syrian Arab Republic, Thailand, Togo, Trinidad and Tobago, Tunisia, Turkey, Uganda, Ukrainian SSR, USSR, United Arab Emirates, United Kingdom, United Republic of Tanzania, Upper Volta, Uruguay, Venezuela, Yemen, Yugoslavia, Zaire, Zambia.

Against: None.

Abstaining: Malawi, United States.

The General Assembly

1. *Takes note* of the report of the Secretary-General on the proposed new construction and the programme of modification and improvement of existing premises in Santiago, Chile, as well as the related report of the Advisory Committee on Administrative and Budgetary Questions;

2. *Concurs* in the recommendations of the Advisory Commit-

tee on Administrative and Budgetary Questions as set forth in paragraphs 10 to 12 of its report;

3. *Authorizes* the Secretary-General to carry forward into 1972 the unencumbered balance of the funds provided in 1971 for the programme of modification and improvement of the existing United Nations building in Santiago.

United Nations accommodation in Bangkok and Addis Ababa

A/C.5/1392. Report of Secretary-General.
A/8408/Add.8. Report of ACABQ.
A/8531/Add.1. Report of Fifth Committee (part II), paras. 68-73, and draft resolution VI, as orally suggested by Committee Chairman, approved without vote by Fifth Committee on 30 November 1971, meeting 1466.

RESOLUTION 2894(XXVI), as recommended by Fifth Committee, A/8531/Add.1, adopted by Assembly on 22 December 1971, meeting 2031, by recorded vote of 112 to 0, with 9 abstentions:

In favour: Afghanistan, Algeria, Argentina, Australia, Austria, Belgium, Bhutan, Bolivia, Brazil, Burma, Burundi, Cameroon, Canada, Ceylon, Chad, Chile, Colombia, Congo, Costa Rica, Cuba, Cyprus, Dahomey, Denmark, Dominican Republic, Ecuador, Egypt, El Salvador, Equatorial Guinea, Ethiopia, Fiji, Finland, France, Gabon, Gambia, Ghana, Greece, Guatemala, Guinea, Guyana, Haiti, Honduras, India, Indonesia, Iran, Ireland, Israel, Italy, Ivory Coast, Jamaica, Japan, Jordan, Kenya, Khmer Republic, Kuwait, Laos, Lebanon, Lesotho, Liberia, Libyan Arab Republic, Luxembourg, Madagascar, Malawi, Malaysia, Mali, Malta, Mauritania, Mexico, Morocco, Nepal, Netherlands, New Zealand, Nicaragua, Niger, Nigeria, Norway, Pakistan, Panama, Paraguay, People's Democratic Republic of Yemen, Peru, Philippines, Portugal, Qatar, Romania, Rwanda, Saudi Arabia, Senegal, Sierra Leone, Singapore, Somalia, South Africa, Spain, Swaziland, Sweden, Syrian Arab Republic, Thailand, Togo, Trinidad and Tobago, Tunisia, Turkey, Uganda, United Arab Emirates, United Kingdom, United Republic of Tanzania, United States, Upper Volta, Uruguay, Venezuela, Yemen, Yugoslavia, Zaire, Zambia.
Against: None.
Abstaining: Bulgaria, Byelorussian SSR, Czechoslovakia, Hungary, Mongolia, Poland, Sudan,* Ukrainian SSR, USSR.

* Subsequently, Sudan advised the Secretariat that it had intended to vote in favour.

The General Assembly
1. *Takes note with appreciation* of the report of the Secretary-General on United Nations accommodation in Bangkok and Addis Ababa and of the related report of the Advisory Committee on Administrative and Budgetary Questions;
2. *Expresses its gratitude* to the Governments of the host countries for their generosity and co-operation;
3. *Takes note* of the observations of the Advisory Committee on Administrative and Budgetary Questions in paragraph 3 of its report;
4. *Agrees* to the modification of the schedule of budgetary payments for the two projects endorsed in its resolution 2745(XXV) of 17 December 1970;
5. *Approves* the new schedule for financing the two projects as set forth in paragraph 4 of the report of the Advisory Committee on Administrative and Budgetary Questions.

Agreement on the use of the Peace Palace by the International Court of Justice

General Assembly—26th session
Fifth Committee, meeting 1491.
Plenary meeting 2031.

A/8406 and Corr.1,3, Vol. I. Budget estimates for financial year 1972 and information annexes, draft resolution IV.
A/8408 and Corr.1,2. First report of ACABQ on budget estimates for financial year 1972, paras. 72 and 73.
A/8531/Add.2. Report of Fifth Committee (part III), draft resolution XIV, as proposed by Secretary-General (A/8406, Vol. I) and as amended by ACABQ (A/8408, para. 73), approved by Fifth Committee on 21 December 1971, meeting 1491, by 70 votes to 0.

RESOLUTION 2902(XXVI), as recommended by Fifth Committee, A/8531/Add.2, adopted unanimously by Assembly on 22 December 1971, meeting 2031.

The General Assembly,
Considering that the contribution payable by the International Court of Justice in respect of the use of the Peace Palace at The Hague under the terms of article II of the Agreement between the United Nations and the Carnegie Foundation concerning the use of the premises of the Peace Palace as contained in annex A to General Assembly resolution 84(I) of 11 December 1946, as amended by the supplementary agreements contained in the annexes to Assembly resolutions 586(VI) of 21 December 1951 and 1343(XIII) of 13 December 1958, is no longer sufficient to defray the costs which the Carnegie Foundation is required to pay under the terms of the said Agreement, as amended,
Approves the Supplementary Agreement between the United Nations and the Carnegie Foundation concerning the use of the Peace Palace as set forth in the annex to the present resolution.

ANNEX

Supplementary Agreement between the United Nations and the Carnegie Foundation concerning the Use of the Peace Palace

1. The United Nations and the Carnegie Foundation hereby agree that article II of the Agreement between the United Nations and the Carnegie Foundation concerning the use of the premises of the Peace Palace at The Hague as contained in annex A to General Assembly resolution 84(I) of 11 December 1946, as amended by the supplementary agreements contained in the annexes to Assembly resolutions 586(VI) of 21 December 1951 and 1343(XIII) of 13 December 1958, shall be amended to read as follows:

"Article II
"The annual contribution payable by the International Court of Justice in respect of the use of the Peace Palace is hereby fixed at 200,000 Netherlands florins net."

2. The two parties further agree that in 1972, 1973 and 1974 the International Court of Justice shall pay to the Carnegie Foundation a supplementary contribution of 25,000 Netherlands florins a year towards the cost of the restoration of the Peace Palace.
3. This Supplementary Agreement shall enter into force with effect from 1 January 1972.

The United Nations Postal Administration

In 1971, gross revenue of the United Nations Postal Administration from the sale of philatelic items at United Nations Headquarters, New York, and overseas offices exceeded $3.5 million. (Reve-

nue derived from the sale of stamps for philatelic purposes is retained by the United Nations; revenue from stamps used for postage purposes from United Nations Headquarters in New York is retained by the United States Postal Service, in accordance with an agreement between the United Nations and the United States Government. Similarly, revenue from stamps used for postage from the Palais des Nations, Geneva, Switzerland, is retained by the Swiss Postal, Telephone and Telegraph Enterprise (PTT) in accordance with an agreement between the United Nations and the Swiss Government.)

During 1971, United Nations commemorative stamps were issued for the first time both in United States and Swiss denominations. Six commemoratives and two definitives were issued during the year.

The theme of the first commemorative, issued on 25 January, was "Peaceful Uses of the Sea-Bed"; the denominations were 6c and 0.30 Swiss francs.

The second commemorative stamp, issued on 12 March, was to encourage "International Support for Refugees"; denominations were 6c, 13c and 0.50 Swiss francs.

The third commemorative stamp, issued on 13 April in denominations of 13c and 0.50 Swiss francs, paid tribute to the World Food Programme.

On 28 May, the fourth commemorative stamp,

depicting the Universal Postal Union Building, was issued in denominations of 20c and 0.75 Swiss francs.

"Eliminate Racial Discrimination" was the theme of the fifth commemorative issued on 21 September, in denominations of 8c and 13c and of 0.30 and 0.50 Swiss francs.

Two definitives, in United States denominations of 8c and 60c, were issued on 22 October, to meet revised postage rates.

The sixth and final commemorative stamp for 1971 was issued on 19 November, in denominations of 8c, 21c and 1.10 Swiss francs, for the United Nations International School.

By the end of 1971, United Nations stamps were available for purchase in local currency to collectors in 77 countries outside the United States.

The number of first day covers serviced for the various issues in 1971 was as follows:

Peaceful Uses of the Sea-Bed	558,144
International Support for Refugees	713,005
World Food Programme	560,984
Universal Postal Union Building	515,798
Eliminate Racial Discrimination	769,523
Definitives: 8c and 60c	336,013
United Nations International School	774,809

Financial regulations governing external audit procedures

On 21 December 1971, the General Assembly amended, with effect from 1 January 1972, the Financial Regulations of the United Nations dealing with external audit, as well as the annex to the Financial Regulations containing the principles to govern the audit procedures of the United Nations.

These changes were based on proposals put forward by the Secretary-General and on consequent comments by the Assembly's Advisory Committee on Administrative and Budgetary Questions.

Most of the changes recommended by the Secretary-General related to technical points of

detail with the exception of two amendments which introduced changes of substance: one of these related to the nature of certification by the External Auditors and affected all the organizations in the United Nations system; the other related to the scope of audit and was of concern only to the United Nations.

The changes in the Financial Regulations approved by the General Assembly were embodied in resolution 2885(XXVI), adopted by 105 votes to 0, with 1 abstention, on the basis of a text recommended by the Assembly's Fifth (Administrative and Budgetary) Committee. (For full text, see DOCUMENTARY REFERENCES below.)

DOCUMENTARY REFERENCES

General Assembly—26th session
Fifth Committee, meetings 1445, 1467.
Plenary meeting 2030.

A/C.5/1375. Implementation of recommendations of *Ad Hoc* Committee of Experts to Examine Finances of United Nations and Specialized Agencies. Standardization of financial regulations: financial regulations governing external audit. Report of Secretary-General.
A/C.5/1375, Annex. Proposed standard provisions for financial regulations relating to external audit and additional terms of

reference, as amended by Advisory Committee on Administrative and Budgetary Questions (ACABQ) (A/8482, para. 9), approved by Fifth Committee on 2 November 1971, meeting 1445, by 72 votes to 0, with 1 abstention.
A/8482. Report of ACABQ.
A/8629 and Corr.1. Report of Fifth Committee, draft resolution, prepared on oral suggestion of Committee Chairman.

RESOLUTION 2885(XXVI), as recommended by Fifth Committee, A/8629, adopted by Assembly on 21 December 1971, meeting 2030, by 105 votes to 0, with 1 abstention.

The General Assembly,

Having considered the report of the Secretary-General on the standardization of the financial regulations governing external audit and the recommendations of the Advisory Committee on Administrative and Budgetary Questions thereon,

Decides that, with effect from 1 January 1972, article XII of the Financial Regulations of the United Nations, dealing with external audit, as well as the annex to the Financial Regulations, containing the principles to govern the audit procedures of the United Nations, shall be amended as set forth in the annex to the present resolution.

ANNEX

Amendments to the Financial Regulations of the United Nations

1. Article XII of the Financial Regulations of the United Nations shall be amended to read as follows:

"ARTICLE XII. EXTERNAL AUDIT

"Appointment of a Board of Auditors
"Regulation 12.1: The General Assembly shall appoint a Board of Auditors to perform the audit of the accounts of the United Nations. This Board shall consist of three members, each of whom shall be the Auditor-General (or officer holding the equivalent title) of a Member State.

"Tenure of office of the members of the Board of Auditors
"Regulation 12.2: The members of the Board of Auditors shall be elected for a three-year term of office. The term of office shall commence on 1 July and expire on 30 June three years subsequent thereto. The term of office of one of the members shall expire each year. Consequently, the General Assembly shall elect each year a member to take office from 1 July of the following year.
"Regulation 12.3: If a member of the Board of Auditors ceases to hold office as Auditor-General (or equivalent title) in his own country, his tenure of office shall thereupon be terminated and he shall be succeeded as a member of the Board by his successor as Auditor-General. A Board member may not otherwise be removed during his tenure of office except by the General Assembly.

"Scope of audit
"Regulation 12.4: The audit shall be conducted in conformity with generally accepted common auditing standards and, subject to any special directions of the General Assembly, in accordance with the additional terms of reference set out in the annex to the present Regulations.
"Regulation 12.5: The Board of Auditors may make observations with respect to the efficiency of the financial procedures, the accounting system, the internal financial controls and, in general, the administration and management of the Organization.
"Regulation 12.6: The Board of Auditors shall be completely independent and solely responsible for the conduct of the audit.
"Regulation 12.7: The Advisory Committee on Administrative and Budgetary Questions may request the Board of Auditors to perform certain specific examinations and issue separate reports on the results.

"Facilities
"Regulation 12.8: The Secretary-General shall provide the Board of Auditors with the facilities it may require in the performance of the audit.
"Regulation 12.9: For the purpose of making a local or special examination or of effecting economies in the audit cost, the Board of Auditors may engage the services of any national Auditor-General (or equivalent title) or commercial public auditors of known repute, or any other person or firm who, in the opinion of the Board, is technically qualified.

"Reporting
"Regulation 12.10: The Board of Auditors shall issue a report on the audit of the financial statements and relevant schedules, which shall include such information as the Board deems necessary with regard to matters referred to in regulation 12.5 and in the additional terms of reference.
"Regulation 12.11: The reports of the Board of Auditors shall be transmitted to the General Assembly through the Advisory Committee on Administrative and Budgetary Questions, together with the audited financial statements, in accordance with any directions given by the Assembly. The Advisory Committee shall examine the financial statements and the audit reports and shall forward them to the Assembly with such comments as it deems appropriate.
"Audit assignment allocation
"Regulation 12.12: The Board of Auditors shall, subject to the concurrence of the Advisory Committee on Administrative and Budgetary Questions, allocate and rotate the audit work among the members of the Board."

2. The annex to the Financial Regulations of the United Nations shall be amended to read as follows:

"ANNEX TO THE FINANCIAL REGULATIONS

"Additional terms of reference governing the audit of the United Nations

"1. The Board of Auditors shall perform jointly and severally such audit of the accounts of the United Nations, including all trust funds and special accounts, as it deems necessary in order to satisfy itself:

"(a) That the financial statements are in accord with the books and records of the Organization;

"(b) That the financial transactions reflected in the statements have been in accordance with the Rules and Regulations, the budgetary provisions and other applicable directives;

"(c) That the securities and moneys on deposit and on hand have been verified by certificate received direct from the Organization's depositaries or by actual count;

"(d) That the internal controls, including the internal audit, are adequate in the light of the extent of reliance placed thereupon;

"(e) That procedures satisfactory to the Board of Auditors have been applied to the recording of all assets, liabilities, surpluses and deficits.

"2. The Board of Auditors shall be the sole judge as to the acceptance in whole or in part of certifications and representations by the Secretary-General and may proceed to such detailed examination and verification as it chooses of all financial records, including those relating to supplies and equipment.

"3. The Board of Auditors and its staff shall have free access at all convenient times to all books, records and other documentation which are, in the opinion of the Board of Auditors, necessary for the performance of the audit. Information which is classified as privileged and which the Secretary-General (or his designated senior official) agrees is required by the Board for the purposes of the audit and information classified as confidential shall be made available on application. The Board of Auditors and its staff shall respect the privileged and confidential nature of any information so classified which has been made available and shall not make use of it except in direct connexion with the performance of the audit. The Board may draw the attention of the General Assembly to any denial of information classified as privileged which, in its opinion, was required for the purpose of the audit.

"4. The Board of Auditors shall have no power to disallow items in the accounts but shall draw to the attention of the Secretary-General for appropriate action any transaction concerning which it entertains doubt as to legality or propriety. Audit objections, to these or any other transactions, arising during the examination of the accounts shall be communicated immediately to the Secretary-General.

"5. The Board of Auditors (or such of its officers as it may designate) shall express and sign an opinion in the following terms:

'We have examined the following appended financial statements, numbered _____ to _____, properly identified, and relevant schedules of _____ [*name of the body*] for the year ended 31 December 19 _____. Our examination included a general review of the accounting procedures and such tests of the accounting records and other supporting evidence as we considered necessary in the circumstances. As a result of our examination, we are of the opinion that the financial statements properly reflect the recorded financial transactions for the year, which transactions were in accordance with the Financial Regulations and legislative authority, and present fairly the financial position as at _____ 19 _____,'

adding, should it be necessary:

'subject to the observations in our foregoing report.'

"6. The report of the Board of Auditors on the financial statements should mention:

"(*a*) The type and scope of its examination;

"(*b*) Matters affecting the completeness or accuracy of the accounts, including where appropriate:

"(i) Information necessary to the correct interpretation of the accounts;

"(ii) Any amounts which ought to have been received but which have not been brought to account;

"(iii) Any amounts for which a legal or contingent obligation exists and which have not been recorded or reflected in the financial statements;

"(iv) Expenditures not properly substantiated;

"(v) Whether proper books of accounts have been kept—where in the presentation of statements there are deviations of a material nature from the generally accepted accounting principles applied on a consistent basis, these should be disclosed;

"(*c*) Other matters which should be brought to the notice of the General Assembly, such as:

"(i) Cases of fraud or presumptive fraud;

"(ii) Wasteful or improper expenditure of the Organization's money or other assets (notwithstanding that the accounting for the transaction may be correct);

"(iii) Expenditure likely to commit the Organization to further outlay on a large scale;

"(iv) Any defect in the general system or detailed regulations governing the control of receipts and disbursements or of supplies and equipment;

"(v) Expenditure not in accordance with the intention of the General Assembly after making allowance for duly authorized transfers within the budget;

"(vi) Expenditure in excess of appropriations as amended by duly authorized transfers within the budget;

"(vii) Expenditure not in conformity with the authority which governs it;

"(*d*) The accuracy or otherwise of the supplies and equipment records as determined by stock-taking and examination of the records;

"(*e*) If appropriate, transactions accounted for in a previous year concerning which further information has been obtained or transactions in a later year concerning which it seems desirable that the General Assembly should have early knowledge.

"7. The Board of Auditors may make such observations with respect to its findings resulting from the audit and such comments on the Secretary-General's financial report as it deems appropriate to the General Assembly or to the Secretary-General.

"8. Whenever the scope of audit of the Board of Auditors is restricted, or whenever the Board is unable to obtain sufficient evidence, it shall refer to the matter in its report, making clear the reasons for its comments, and the effect on the financial position and the financial transactions as recorded.

"9. In no case shall the Board of Auditors include criticism in its report without first affording the Secretary-General an adequate opportunity of explanation on the matter under observation."

Administrative and budgetary co-ordination

General co-ordination matters

On 21 December 1971, the General Assembly, on the recommendation of its Fifth (Administrative and Budgetary) Committee, adopted without objection a resolution (2884(XXVI)) on administrative and budgetary co-ordination of the United Nations with the specialized agencies and the International Atomic Energy Agency (IAEA). The Fifth Committee approved the resolution without objection on 10 December 1971, on the basis of a text orally presented by the Committee Chairman.

By this resolution, the Assembly took note of three reports of its Advisory Committee on Administrative and Budgetary Questions that the Fifth Committee had before it when discussing this subject: a report dealing with the review of administrative and management procedures concerning the programme and budget of IAEA; one dealing with general co-ordination matters; and a third on the administrative budgets of the specialized agencies.

The Assembly asked the Secretary-General to refer the report on general co-ordination matters to the executive heads of the specialized agencies and IAEA through the inter-agency Administrative Committee on Co-ordination, to the Economic and Social Council's Committee for Programme and Co-ordination for information and comment, and to the Board of Auditors and the Joint Inspection Unit for information. The Secretary-General was also asked to refer to the specialized agencies and IAEA the Advisory Committee's detailed comments on their 1972 budgets, and to transmit the report on the review of administrative and management procedures on IAEA's programme and budget to that Agency's Director-General to be brought to the attention of IAEA's Board of Governors.

(For text of resolution, see DOCUMENTARY REFERENCES below.)

On the same date, the Assembly took note of a decision taken by the Fifth Committee, by a vote of 47 to 8, with 15 abstentions, which arose from Advisory Committee comments on the means by which IAEA financed certain meetings held away from its headquarters by pooling amounts received from a system of standard charges applied to host countries for each such meeting —developed countries serving as host countries being charged more than developing countries. The Fifth Committee by its decision—the text of which was proposed by the United Republic of Tanzania—noted the system used by IAEA and recommended:

. . .that the Secretary-General, with the co-operation and assistance of the Director-General of the International Atomic Energy Agency, study the full operation of the methods of financing by IAEA of certain meetings and conferences of the Agency held away from headquarters and report as appropriate to the General Assembly at its twenty-seventh [1972] session on the possible application of those methods to similar conferences and meetings held by United Nations bodies away from United Nations Headquarters.

Harmonization of budgets and programmes

During 1971, the the Economic and Social Council and the General Assembly both considered the subject of the harmonization of budgets and programmes.

Before the Economic and Social Council at its fifty-first session, held from 5 to 30 July 1971, was a report of the Secretary-General submitted to the Council's Committee for Programme and Co-ordination (CPC) on work programme performance in the economic, social and human rights fields for the financial year 1970, as well as the report of CPC on its ninth session, held from 24 May to 14 June 1971.

The Secretary-General's report contained information submitted by, and evaluated the work programme performance in 1970 of, substantive units in the Division of Human Rights, the Department of Economic and Social Affairs (including the secretariats of the regional economic commissions), United Nations economic and social activities in Geneva, Switzerland, the United Nations Conference on Trade and Development and the United Nations Industrial Development Organization, in response to guidelines for the preparation of the 1972 budget estimates and the 1970 performance report. The report reiterated the urgent need for establishing an integrated system of planning, programming and budgeting for all activities in the economic and social fields, regardless of the sources of financing.

The Committee for Programme and Co-ordination agreed that the Secretary-General's report represented a significant improvement over previous reports of a similar nature. The Committee nevertheless felt that both the format and the content could be further improved to enhance its usefulness.

In order to ensure that future reports would be more output-oriented and provide an over-all analysis of performance, and would also provide a table comparing programmes executed to programmes approved, CPC recommended *inter alia*

that the format of the budget performance document for any given year should have a direct correlation with the work programme document for that year, in order to enable meaningful comparisons to be made.

On 30 July 1971, the Economic and Social Council requested that the Secretary-General should ensure that this recommendation, among others made by CPC, should be taken into account in future reports. The Council took this action in adopting resolution 1644(LI). (For text of resolution, see pp. 465-66.)

By a decision taken on 21 December 1971, but without adopting a formal resolution, the General Assembly—on the recommendation of its Fifth (Administrative and Budgetary) Committee which approved a text proposed by India—endorsed the Economic and Social Council's resolution relating to the format of the report on budget performance.

(See also p. 641.)

Electronic data-processing in United Nations family

The International Computing Centre at Geneva, Switzerland—the establishment of which was authorized by the General Assembly on 17 December 1970[16]—became operational on 1 March 1971 and was being used by the United Nations, the United Nations Development Programme and the World Health Organization.

All other agencies in the United Nations system had been invited to consider joining, as partners, the United Nations and the two agencies already participating in the Centre.

The Secretary-General, in a report on electronic data-processing in the United Nations family of organizations, proposed that the Centre should have primarily servicing and processing functions and that the bulk of systems analysis and programming be carried out by user staff. He also recommended an increase in staff at the New York Computing Centre and that machinery be established to provide centralized supervision of United Nations electronic data-processing needs.

In the course of the general debate on the budget estimates for 1972 in the Assembly's Fifth (Administrative and Budgetary) Committee, a number of delegations commenting on the Centre were concerned with the lack of participation of the other agencies in the work of the Centre.

A report before the Fifth Committee by the Assembly's Advisory Committee on Administrative and Budgetary Questions indicated that although the Advisory Committee appreciated the reluctance of agencies to commit themselves to full participation while the Centre was still in its

[16]See Y.U.N., 1970, pp. 872–73, text of resolution 2441(XXV).

formative stage, it felt nonetheless that such hesitation could jeopardize the Centre's success. The Advisory Committee, therefore, urged all concerned to review their policies so that the Centre might soon become the truly common facility envisaged when it was created.

Acting on a proposal by Brazil, the Fifth Committee on 15 December 1971 decided, without objection, to take note of the views of the Secretary-General and the Advisory Committee, endorsed the views expressed by the Advisory Committee concerning the need for agency participation, and recommended that the Assembly urge all organizations concerned within the United Nations system to review their policies in the field of electronic data-processing so that the International Computing Centre might at a very early date become a truly common facility for the United Nations system of organizations.

The General Assembly approved the Fifth Committee's recommendations on 22 December 1971, without adopting a formal resolution, when it considered the Fifth Committee's report on the budget estimates for 1972.

DOCUMENTARY REFERENCES

General co-ordination matters

General Assembly—26th session
Fifth Committee, meetings 1469, 1476, 1478, 1479.
Plenary meeting 2030.

A/8001. Report of Secretary-General on work of the Organization, 16 June 1970–15 June 1971, Part Five, Chapter IV.
A/8403. Report of Economic and Social Council on work of its 50th and 51st sessions, Chapters XXI and XXII.
A/8408 and Corr.1,2. First report of Advisory Committee on Administrative and Budgetary Questions (ACABQ) on budget estimates for 1972, paras. 60-62.
A/8447/Rev.1. Review of administrative and management procedures concerning programme and budget of International Atomic Energy Agency. Report of ACABQ.
A/8490. General co-ordination matters. Report of ACABQ.
A/8538. Administrative budgets of agencies. Report of ACABQ.
A/C.5/1394. Report of Economic and Social Council. Note by Secretary-General.
A/8607. Report of Fifth Committee, draft resolution, as orally presented by Committee Chairman, approved without objection by Fifth Committee on 10 December 1971, meeting 1479.

RESOLUTION 2884(XXVI), as recommended by Fifth Committee, A/8607, adopted without objection by Assembly on 21 December 1971, meeting 2030.

The General Assembly

1. *Takes note* of the reports of the Advisory Committee on Administrative and Budgetary Questions on general co-ordination matters, on the administrative budgets of the agencies for 1972 and on the review of the administrative and management procedures concerning the programme and budget of the International Atomic Energy Agency;

2. *Requests* the Secretary-General to refer the report on general co-ordination matters to the executive heads of the specialized agencies and the International Atomic Energy Agency through the consultative machinery of the Administrative Committee on Co-ordination, as well as to the members of the Committee for Programme and Co-ordination for their information and comment, and to the members of the Board of Auditors and of the Joint Inspection Unit for their information;

3. *Also requests* the Secretary-General to refer to the executive heads of the specialized agencies and the International Atomic Energy Agency the observations of the Advisory Committee on Administrative and Budgetary Questions contained in chapter III of its report on the administrative budgets of the agencies for 1972;

4. *Further requests* the Secretary-General to transmit the report on the review of the administrative and management procedures concerning the programme and budget of the International Atomic Energy Agency to the Director-General of that organization so that the report may be brought to the attention of the Board of Governors of the Agency.

A/8429. Resolutions adopted by General Assembly during its 26th session, 21 September–22 December 1971. Other decisions, p. 133.

Harmonization of budgets and programmes

Economic and Social Council—51st session
Co-ordination Committee, meetings 413, 417-419, 422, 425, 431.
Plenary meetings 1799, 1806, 1807.

RESOLUTION 1644(LI), as recommended by Co-ordination Committee (E/5069, draft resolution III), adopted by Council on 30 July 1971, meeting 1799, by 25 votes to 0, with 2 abstentions.

[For text of resolution and supporting documentation, see pp. 465-66.]

General Assembly—26th session
Fifth Committee, meetings 1469, 1476, 1479, 1480.
Plenary meeting 2030.

A/8403. Report of Economic and Social Council on work of its 50th and 51st sessions, Chapters XXI and XXII.
A/8490. General co-ordination matters. Report of ACABQ.
A/C.5/1394. Report of Economic and Social Council. Note by Secretary-General.
A/8613. Report of Fifth Committee (on report of Economic and Social Council).
A/8429. Resolutions adopted by General Assembly during its 26th session, 21 September–22 December 1971, p. 132 (item 12).

*Electronic data-processing
in United Nations family*

General Assembly—26th session
Fifth Committee, meetings 1481, 1483, 1485.
Plenary meeting 2031.

A/8408 and Corr.1,2. First report of ACABQ on budget estimates for financial year 1972, paras. 44-46 and 218.
A/8408/Add.16. Report of ACABQ.
A/8490. General co-ordination matters. Report of ACABQ, Chapter II B.
A/C.5/1378 and Corr.1. Report of Secretary-General.
A/8531/Add.1. Report of Fifth Committee (part II) (on budget estimates for financial year 1972), paras. 146-150.
A/8429. Resolutions adopted by General Assembly during its 26th session, 21 September–22 December 1971. Other decisions, p. 132 (item 76, first para.).
Report of Interregional Seminar on Electronic Data-Processing in Government, Bratislava, Czechoslovakia, 22-30 November 1971. Vol. I. Report and technical papers. U.N.P. Sales No.: E.72.II.H.3; Vol. II. Papers submitted by participants. U.N.P. Sales No.: E/F/S.72.II.H.4.

Financial reports and accounts and reports of the Board of Auditors for 1970

On 8 November 1971, the General Assembly approved the financial reports and accounts for the year ending 31 December 1970 and the relevant reports of the Board of Auditors for the United Nations, the United Nations Development Programme, the United Nations Children's Fund, the United Nations Relief and Works Agency for Palestine Refugees in the Near East, the United Nations Institute for Training and Research and the voluntary funds administered by the United Nations High Commissioner for Refugees.

The Assembly did so in adopting resolutions 2759 A-F (XXVI), on the basis of recommendations by its Fifth (Administrative and Budgetary) Committee, which also had before it the related report of the Advisory Committee on Administrative and Budgetary Questions and a note by the Secretary-General containing a consolidated statement of the accounts. (For texts of resolutions and voting details, see DOCUMENTARY REFERENCES below.)

During the discussion of the reports and accounts in the Fifth Committee, the necessity of having in future reports a clear indication of what action had been taken to correct irregularities

pointed out by the Board of Auditors was stressed by some delegations. India and Pakistan, among others, suggested that the customary resolution on the United Nations accounts which the Fifth Committee recommended to the Assembly for adoption was inadequate in this respect. The Committee decided to add a paragraph to the customary draft resolution requesting the Secretary-General, in the light of the discussion in the Fifth Committee, to take such remedial action as might be required by the comments of the Board of Auditors.

Poland and the USSR reiterated their objections to the inclusion in the regular budget of expenditures related to the financing of the repayment of amortization and interest charges on United Nations bonds, to the maintenance of the United Nations Commission for the Unification and Rehabilitation of Korea, to the United Nations Memorial Cemetery in Korea, and to the financing of technical assistance from the regular budget rather than solely from voluntary contributions. They considered the inclusion of such items of expenditure in the budget were in contravention of the United Nations Charter.

DOCUMENTARY REFERENCES

General Assembly—26th session
Fifth Committee, meetings 1426-1428, 1435.
Plenary meeting 1979.

A/8322. Budget performance of United Nations for financial year 1970. Report of Secretary-General.
A/8350. Report of Advisory Committee on Administrative and Budgetary Questions (ACABQ).
A/C.5/1395. Note by Secretary-General (annexing combined statement of assets and liabilities as at 31 December 1970, and of income, expenditure and surplus for 1970 covering all United Nations-financed or -sponsored activities and funds in custody of Secretary-General).
A/8477. Report of Fifth Committee, containing draft resolutions A-F.

UNITED NATIONS
A/8407. Financial report and accounts for year ended 31 December 1970 and report of Board of Auditors.
A/8350. Report of ACABQ, paras. 1-9.
A/8477. Report of Fifth Committee, draft resolution A, as suggested by Committee Chairman, and as amended by Pakistan, adopted without objection by Fifth Committee on 7 October 1971, meeting 1428.

RESOLUTION 2759 A (XXVI), as recommended by Fifth Committee, A/8477, adopted without objection by Assembly on 8 November 1971, meeting 1979.

The General Assembly
1. Accepts the financial report and accounts of the United Nations for the year ended 31 December 1970 and the certificates of the Board of Auditors;
2. Concurs in the observations of the Advisory Committee on

Administrative and Budgetary Questions as set forth in its report;
3. Requests the Secretary-General, in the light of the discussion in the Fifth Committee, to take such remedial action as may be required by the comments of the Board of Auditors.

UNITED NATIONS DEVELOPMENT PROGRAMME
A/8407/Add.1. Financial report and accounts for year ended 31 December 1970 and report of Board of Auditors.
A/8350. Report of ACABQ, paras. 10-12.
A/8477. Report of Fifth Committee, draft resolution B, as suggested by Committee Chairman, adopted without objection by Fifth Committee on 4 October 1971, meeting 1426.

RESOLUTION 2759 B (XXVI), as recommended by Fifth Committee, A/8477, adopted without objection by Assembly on 8 November 1971, meeting 1979.

The General Assembly
1. Accepts the financial report and accounts of the United Nations Development Programme for the year ended 31 December 1970 and the certificates of the Board of Auditors;
2. Takes note of the observations of the Advisory Committee on Administrative and Budgetary Questions as set forth in its report.

UNITED NATIONS CHILDREN'S FUND
A/8407/Add.2. Financial report and accounts for year 1970 and reports of Board of Auditors.
A/8350. Report of ACABQ, para. 13.
A/8477. Report of Fifth Committee, draft resolution C, as suggested by Committee Chairman, adopted without objection by Fifth Committee on 4 October 1971, meeting 1426.

RESOLUTION 2759 C (XXVI), as recommended by Fifth Committee, A/8477, adopted without objection by Assembly on 8 November 1971, meeting 1979.

The General Assembly
1. *Accepts* the financial report and accounts of the United Nations Children's Fund for the year ended 31 December 1970 and the certificates of the Board of Auditors;
2. *Takes note* of the report of the Advisory Committee on Administrative and Budgetary Questions.

UNITED NATIONS RELIEF AND WORKS AGENCY
FOR PALESTINE REFUGEES IN THE NEAR EAST
A/8407/Add.3. Accounts for year ended 31 December 1970 and report of Board of Auditors.
A/8350. Report of ACABQ, paras. 14-16.
A/8477. Report of Fifth Committee, draft resolution D, as suggested by Committee Chairman, adopted without objection by Fifth Committee on 4 October 1971, meeting 1426.

RESOLUTION 2759 D (XXVI), as recommended by Fifth Committee, A/8477, adopted without objection by Assembly on 8 November 1971, meeting 1979.

The General Assembly
1. *Accepts* the accounts of the United Nations Relief and Works Agency for Palestine Refugees in the Near East for the year ended 31 December 1970 and the certificates of the Board of Auditors;
2. *Takes note* of the observations of the Advisory Committee on Administrative and Budgetary Questions as set forth in its report.

UNITED NATIONS INSTITUTE
FOR TRAINING AND RESEARCH
A/8407/Add.4. Financial report and accounts for year ended 31 December 1970 and report of Board of Auditors.
A/8350. Report of ACABQ, para. 17.

A/8477. Report of Fifth Committee, draft resolution E, as suggested by Committee Chairman, adopted without objection by Fifth Committee on 4 October 1971, meeting 1426.

RESOLUTION 2759 E (XXVI), as recommended by Fifth Committee, A/8477, adopted without objection by Assembly on 8 November 1971, meeting 1979.

The General Assembly
1. *Accepts* the financial report and accounts of the United Nations Institute for Training and Research for the year ended 31 December 1970 and the certificates of the Board of Auditors;
2. *Takes note* of the report of the Advisory Committee on Administrative and Budgetary Questions.

VOLUNTARY FUNDS ADMINISTERED BY UNITED
NATIONS HIGH COMMISSIONER FOR REFUGEES
A/8407/Add.5. Accounts for year ended 31 December 1970 and report of Board of Auditors.
A/8350. Report of ACABQ, paras. 18, 19.
A/8477. Report of Fifth Committee, draft resolution F, as suggested by Committee Chairman, adopted without objection by Fifth Committee on 4 October 1971, meeting 1426.

RESOLUTION 2759 F (XXVI), as recommended by Fifth Committee, A/8477, adopted without objection by Assembly on 8 November 1971, meeting 1979.

The General Assembly
1. *Accepts* the accounts of the voluntary funds administered by the United Nations High Commissioner for Refugees for the year ended 31 December 1970 and the certificates of the Board of Auditors;
2. *Takes note* of the observations of the Advisory Committee on Administrative and Budgetary Questions as set forth in its report.

Other administrative and budgetary matters

Recommendations on the finances of the United Nations and specialized agencies

On 21 December 1971, the General Assembly without adopting a formal resolution took note of decisions taken by its Fifth (Administrative and Budgetary) Committee concerning reports of the Joint Inspection Unit.

When the subject was discussed in the Fifth Committee, the Committee had before it a report of the Secretary-General on the implementation of the recommendations of the Assembly's *Ad Hoc* Committee to Examine the Finances of the United Nations and the Specialized Agencies, by which report he transmitted, *inter alia,* a report of the Joint Inspection Unit on its activities from 1 July 1970 to 30 June 1971.

Also before the Fifth Committee were two reports of the Assembly's Advisory Committee on Administrative and Budgetary Questions: one contained the Advisory Committee's comments and observations on the Secretary-General's report; the other, among other things, indicated the Unit reports, and related comments thereon by United Nations organs, which the Advisory Committee had considered since mid-1970.

The Advisory Committee held an informal meeting with the Joint Inspection Unit in May 1971 during which the two bodies reviewed matters of common interest. Both agreed that brevity and clarity should be the goal in reporting to the Assembly on the implementation of the Unit's recommendations, and that the Secretary-General should precisely indicate those areas where further action was needed.

After discussing the matter of the reports, the Fifth Committee on 15 November 1971 decided, without objection:

(a) to accept the Secretary-General's suggestions, as set out in his report, that Joint Inspection Unit reports be discussed in the Fifth Committee during the current session under the pertinent agenda items;
(b) to inform the Economic and Social Council of the Fifth Committee's acceptance of the Advisory Committee's recommendations that, should the Council agree, circulation of the specialized agencies' comments on the Joint Inspection Unit reports should normally be limited to those issued in time for discussion in the Council's Committee for Programme and Co-ordination;
(c) to endorse the views expressed by the Advisory

Committee that, when the Assembly reviewed the question of the future of the Joint Inspection Unit, as it had decided to do on 17 December 1970,[17] the Advisory Committee trusted that the bodies whose views were requested—the Secretary-General as Chairman of the Administrative Committee on Co-ordination, the governing bodies of the specialized agencies concerned, the Economic and Social Council, the Committee for Programme and Co-ordination, the Advisory Committee and the Unit itself—would take the appropriate action to ensure that their views were available to the General Assembly at its 1972 session.

Restructuring of the Department of Economic and Social Affairs

Acting on the recommendation of its Fifth (Administrative and Budgetary) Committee, the General Assembly on 22 December 1971, when considering the Committee's report on budget estimates for 1972, adopted a resolution concerning a restructuring of the Secretariat's Department of Economic and Social Affairs as a response to the Second United Nations Development Decade.

The proposals of the Secretary-General contained in his report on the subject to the Assembly resulted from an initial manpower utilization study of the Department being conducted by the Administrative Management Service within the framework of the survey of the Secretariat as a whole, which, in turn, had taken account of a related report on the Department by Robert M. Macy, a member of the Joint Inspection Unit.

The Assembly's Advisory Committee on Administrative and Budgetary Questions, commenting on the report, felt it was difficult to judge the merits of the Secretary-General's proposals on reorganization and on the creation of five new high-level posts at a point when the study was not yet completed. The Advisory Committee was convinced that the Secretary-General had available to him sufficient management expertise and experience to continue with the study and that any advantages which might accrue from the immediate creation of the new posts would be more than offset by the loss of flexibility which would occur if the ultimate structure of the Department were to be determined before the survey was completed. The Advisory Committee suggested that the Secretary-General might wish to return to the question in 1972, at the conclusion of the survey, at which time he would be in a position to put forward firm recommendations on the organization of the Department.

After a brief discussion of the subject, the Fifth Committee, on 6 December, without a vote and on the basis of a proposal by its Chairman, decided to recommend that the Assembly take note of the relevant reports of the Secretary-General, the Advisory Committee and the Joint Inspection Unit

and endorse the Advisory Committee's suggestion that the Secretary-General return to the question in 1972. The Assembly adopted without objection resolution 2898(XXVI) embodying these recommendations of the Fifth Committee.

(For text of resolution, see DOCUMENTARY REFERENCES below.)

Honorarium of Chairman of Advisory Committee on Administrative and Budgetary Questions

On 22 December 1971, during consideration of the budget estimates for 1972, the General Assembly adopted a resolution dealing with the honorarium paid to the Chairman of the Assembly's Advisory Committee on Administrative and Budgetary Questions. It did so on the recommendation of its Fifth (Administrative and Budgetary) Committee, which had taken its decision on the basis of a proposal by the Secretary-General and a related report by the Advisory Committee.

After a brief discussion of the subject in the Fifth Committee, the Committee decided on 29 October 1971, by 47 votes to 14, with 17 abstentions, to approve the proposal of the Secretary-General that the honorarium of the Chairman of the Advisory Committee be increased from $5,000—an amount fixed by the Assembly on 21 December 1968[18]—to $25,000 net a year beginning in 1972, provided he was not actively engaged on behalf of his Government or any other body. Further, it decided that a daily subsistence allowance of $10, payable under the provisions of another Assembly resolution of 21 December 1968[19] to eligible members of United Nations organs and subsidiaries while attending meetings at the place of residence or duty station, should not be paid concurrently with the $25,000 honorarium.

The Fifth Committee also decided, without objection, to include in its recommendation to the Assembly its opinion that, in view of the special character of the functions of the Chairman of the Advisory Committee, the decision in respect of the Chairman's honorarium should not be considered as setting a precedent.

The Assembly adopted the Fifth Committee's recommendations as resolution 2889(XXVI) by a recorded vote of 107 to 11, with 2 abstentions. (For text of resolution, see DOCUMENTARY REFERENCES below.)

Without adopting a formal resolution, the Assembly also took note of the Fifth Committee's opinion regarding its action as not setting a precedent.

[17]See Y.U.N., 1970, pp. 866-67, text of resolution 2735 A (XXV).
[18]See Y.U.N., 1968, pp. 899-900, text of resolution 2489(XXIII).
[19]*Ibid.*, p. 901, text of resolution 2491(XXIII).

DOCUMENTARY REFERENCES

*Recommendations on the finances of the
United Nations and specialized agencies*

General Assembly—26th session
Fifth Committee, meetings 1454, 1455, 1467,
Plenary meeting 2030.

A/C.5/1368. Implementation of recommendations of *Ad Hoc*
Committee of Experts to Examine Finances of United Nations
and Specialized Agencies. Report of Secretary-General (trans-
mitting Joint Inspection Unit (JIU) report).
A/8408 and Corr.1,2. First report of Advisory Committee on
Administrative and Budgetary Questions (ACABQ) on budget
estimates for financial year 1972, paras. 63-65.
A/8503. Report of ACABQ.
A/8629 and Corr.1. Report of Fifth Committee, Section II.
A/8429. Resolutions adopted by General Assembly during its 26th
session, 21 September–22 December 1971. Other decisions,
p. 133 (item 82).

*Restructuring of the Department
of Economic and Social Affairs*

General Assembly—26th session
Fifth Committee, meetings 1472, 1489.
Plenary meeting 2031.

A/C.5/1380 and Corr.1. Budget estimates for financial year 1972.
Report of Secretary-General.
A/8408/Add.13. Budget estimates for financial year 1972.
Restructuring Department of Economic and Social Affairs:
response to 2nd United Nations Development Decade. Report of
ACABQ.
A/8446 and Add.1. Report of JIU on United Nations Department of
Economic and Social Affairs. Note by ACABQ. (Annex I:
Preliminary observations of Secretary-General; Annex II: JIU
report.)
A/8531/Add.1. Report of Fifth Committee (part II) (on budget
estimates for financial year 1972), paras. 138-145, and draft
resolution X, as orally suggested by Committee Chairman,
approved without vote by Fifth Committee on 6 December 1971,
meeting 1472.

RESOLUTION 2898(XXVI), as recommended by Fifth Committee,
A/8531/Add.1, adopted without vote by Assembly on 22
December 1971, meeting 2031.

The General Assembly
1. *Takes note* of the reports of the Secretary-General and
the Advisory Committee on Administrative and Budgetary Questions on the restructuring of the Department of Economic and
Social Affairs of the Secretariat, including the observations of the
Advisory Committee contained in paragraphs 8 to 11 of its report;
2. *Takes note also* of the report of the Joint Inspection Unit on
the Department of Economic and Social Affairs;
3. *Endorses* the suggestion made by the Advisory Committee
on Administrative and Budgetary Questions in paragraph 11 of its
report.

*Honorarium of Chairman of Advisory Committee
on Administrative and Budgetary Questions*

General Assembly—26th session
Fifth Committee, meetings 1442, 1443, 1489.
Plenary meeting 2031.

A/C.5/1365. Budget estimates for financial year 1972. Report of
Secretary-General.
A/8408/Add.3. Report of ACABQ.
A/8531/Add.1. Report of Fifth Committee, paras. 42-50, and draft
resolution I, prepared on basis of recommendation of Secretary-
General (A/C.5/1365, para. 8), approved by Fifth Committee on
29 October 1971, meeting 1443, by 47 votes to 14, with 17
abstentions.

RESOLUTION 2889(XXVI), as recommended by Fifth Committee,
A/8531/Add.1, adopted by Assembly on 22 December 1971,
meeting 2031, by recorded vote of 107 to 11, with 2 abstentions,
as follows:

In favour: Algeria, Argentina, Australia, Austria, Bahrain,
Belgium, Bhutan, Bolivia, Brazil, Burma, Burundi, Cameroon,
Canada, Ceylon, Chad, Chile, Colombia, Congo, Costa Rica,
Cyprus, Denmark, Dominican Republic, Ecuador, Egypt, El
Salvador, Equatorial Guinea, Ethiopia, Fiji, Finland, France,
Gambia, Ghana, Greece, Guatemala, Guinea, Guyana, Haiti,
Honduras, Iceland, India, Indonesia, Iran, Ireland, Israel, Italy,
Ivory Coast, Jamaica, Japan, Jordan, Kenya, Khmer Republic,
Kuwait, Laos, Lebanon, Lesotho, Liberia, Libyan Arab Republic,
Luxembourg, Madagascar, Malawi, Malaysia, Mali, Malta,
Mauritania, Mexico, Morocco, Nepal, Netherlands, New Zea-
land, Nicaragua, Niger, Nigeria, Norway, Pakistan, Panama,
Paraguay, Peru, Philippines, Portugal, Qatar, Rwanda, Sierra
Leone, Singapore, Somalia, South Africa, Spain, Sudan,
Swaziland, Sweden, Syrian Arab Republic, Thailand, Togo,
Trinidad and Tobago, Tunisia, Turkey, Uganda, United Arab
Emirates, United Kingdom, United Republic of Tanzania, United
States, Upper Volta, Uruguay, Venezuela, Yemen, Yugoslavia,
Zaire, Zambia.
Against: Bulgaria, Byelorussian SSR, Cuba, Czechoslovakia,
Hungary, Mongolia, People's Democratic Republic of Yemen,
Poland, Romania, Ukrainian SSR, USSR.
Abstaining: Afghanistan, Gabon.

The General Assembly,
Recalling its endorsement, at its 729th plenary meeting on 13
December 1957, of the recommendations made by the Fifth
Committee regarding the amount of the honorarium to be paid to
the Chairman of the Advisory Committee on Administrative and
Budgetary Questions, as well as its resolutions 2489(XXIII) and
2491(XXIII) of 21 December 1968 dealing with the payment of
honoraria and of subsistence allowances to members of organs
and subsidiary organs of the United Nations,
Having considered the report of the Secretary-General on the
honorarium of the Chairman of the Advisory Committee on
Administrative and Budgetary Questions and the related report of
the Advisory Committee,
1. *Decides* that, with effect from 1 January 1972, the
honorarium of the Chairman of the Advisory Committee on
Administrative and Budgetary Questions shall be $25,000 net per
annum, provided he is not actively engaged on behalf of his
Government or another body;
2. *Decides further* that the provisions of paragraph 1 (*b*) of
resolution 2491(XXIII) shall not apply to the Chairman of the
Advisory Committee on Administrative and Budgetary Questions if
he is entitled to the honorarium by virtue of paragraph 1 above.

A/8429. Resolutions adopted by General Assembly at its 26th
session, 21 September–22 December 1971. Other decisions,
p. 132 (item 76).

PART TWO

The inter-governmental organizations related to the United Nations

Chapter I

The International Atomic Energy Agency (IAEA)

The work of the International Atomic Energy
Agency (IAEA)[1] during 1971 was highlighted by the
convening of the Fourth International Conference
on the Peaceful Uses of Atomic Energy in
September and by the conclusion of nine safeguards agreements under the Treaty on the
Non-Proliferation of Nuclear Weapons.[2]

The Agency continued its other activities, which
included: establishing safety standards for nuclear
activities; applying safeguards to ensure that
nuclear materials were used for peaceful purposes
only; advising Governments on nuclear energy
programmes; awarding fellowships for students in
nuclear sciences; arranging the loan of equipment;
financing research; and acting as an intermediary
in supplying nuclear materials.

As at the end of 1971, the Agency had 102
member States, the same number as in 1970.

On 9 December 1971, the Board of Governors
of IAEA, by a vote of 13 to 6, with 5 abstentions,
adopted a resolution whereby it decided to
recognize the Government of the People's Republic of China as the only Government which had the
right to represent China in IAEA. (For further
details, see pp. 133 and 135.)

General conference

The fifteenth session of the IAEA General
Conference was held in Vienna, Austria, from 21
to 27 September 1971. José María Otero Navas-
cués, President of Spain's Junta de Energía
Nuclear, was elected President of the Conference.

Agency safeguards responsibilities

One of IAEA's major functions continued to be
the establishment and administration of safeguards to ensure that nuclear materials intended
for peaceful purposes were not diverted to
military purposes.

The Agency's safeguards programme involved
the following: reviewing the design of nuclear
plants; maintaining records of plant operations
and an inventory of nuclear material; examining
periodic reports supplied by Governments; and, if
necessary, sending inspectors to verify data.

The Treaty on the Non-Proliferation of Nuclear
Weapons, which came into force in 1970, called
upon each non-nuclear-weapon State party to the
Treaty to accept safeguards controls as set forth in
an agreement to be concluded with IAEA. The
implementation of the Treaty was expected to
entail expansion of the Agency's safeguards

activities and a shift from the application of
safeguards to nuclear material in individual
facilities to safeguards to nuclear material in entire
fuel cycles.

A model safeguards agreement was drawn up in
1971, and by the end of the year agreements had
been concluded with nine States: Austria, Bulgaria, Canada, Czechoslovakia, Finland, Hungary,
Iraq, Poland and Uruguay; discussions were
under way with a further 31 States.

Under both the new agreements and previously
concluded agreements relating to individual facilities, the Agency was applying safeguards to
nuclear materials in 11 nuclear power stations, 66
other reactors, 10 conversion-fabrication-fuel reprocessing plants and 85 other facilities.

Attention continued to be given to safeguards
research and development.

Technical assistance

The following sources were financing the
technical assistance programmes of IAEA: voluntary contributions from member States; funds
from the United Nations Development Programme (UNDP); and gifts in kind, such as
equipment, cost-free fellowships and cost-free
services of experts.

During 1971, some 52 countries received experts or equipment, or both. Some 323 fellowships
were awarded, and a dozen training courses, study
tours and seminars were arranged.

The Agency was co-operating with UNDP in the
implementation of three long-term programmes:
uranium exploration in Greece and Pakistan, and
nuclear research in agriculture in India.

Other activities in 1971

Environment

In co-operation with other international organizations, IAEA established basic safety standards and
recommendations regulating aspects of radiation
safety under both normal and emergency conditions. Thirty-six publications concerning these
standards had been issued by 1971, and IAEA
regulations for the safe transport of radioactive
materials by rail, road, sea and air had been
adopted as legal standards by many Governments.

The Agency's continued concern with environ-

---

[1]For further information on IAEA, see Y.U.N. for years 1953-1970.
[2]See Y.U.N., 1968, pp. 17-19, for text of Treaty.

mental pollution was emphasized during the Fourth International Conference on the Peaceful Uses of Atomic Energy, held in Geneva, Switzerland, from 6 to 16 September 1971.

First steps were taken towards setting up an international register of releases of radioactive materials to any sector of the environment which might go beyond national boundaries; work was completed on the determination of principles for limiting the introduction of radioactive wastes into the sea; and studies were continuing on the behaviour of radionuclides in the marine environment.

A panel meeting on the practical applications of the peaceful uses of nuclear explosions to industrial purposes was attended by participants from 25 member States and several international organizations.

Nuclear power

The Agency continued to provide advice and assistance to member States on the technical feasibility, design, technology and economics of power reactor systems. It also carried out studies of the economic aspects of nuclear power, including surveys of world energy needs and the future role of nuclear power. It was expected that by 1980, the world's nuclear electric capacity would have risen to 340,000 megawatts (electrical) (MW(e)), or about 15 per cent of all electric power generated at that time.

The Agency arranged four meetings on the development of fast breeder reactors, the main objective of the reactor development programmes of industrialized countries. Also during 1971, a meeting of the international working group on fast reactors was held to review the progress made in the field.

An Agency study group reviewed developments in nuclear desalting and the use of desalted water in agriculture and industry. A feasibility study of nuclear agro-industrial complexes was also being prepared.

The liaison group of the European Nuclear Energy Agency (ENEA) and IAEA on MHD (magnetohydrodynamic, or direct conversion of thermal to electrical energy) electrical power generation organized a fifth international conference on the subject and held several other meetings during the year.

The problems of financing nuclear power in developing countries also received special attention. The Agency initiated a market study to determine the demand for reactors below 500 MW (e).

Food and agriculture

In co-operation with the Food and Agriculture Organization of the United Nations (FAO), the Agency continued research on the use of radiation and radioisotopes in agriculture, including: plant improvement by induced mutation; eradication of destructive insects by the sterile-male technique; improvement of livestock nutrition and preparation of animal vaccines; the effect of insecticide residues; preservation of food by irradiation; and improvement of the use of nitrogen and phosphate fertilizer. A special report on this work, *Nuclear Techniques and the Green Revolution,* was prepared during 1971.

An international project for testing the wholesomeness of irradiated food was started during 1971; by the end of the year, organizations in 20 countries were taking part in the programme. The preliminary work on the project was done by ENEA and FAO, jointly with IAEA; the World Health Organization participated in an advisory capacity.

More than 200 agricultural projects, chiefly co-ordinated research programmes, were being supported in member States.

Life sciences and physical sciences

The IAEA programme in life sciences included medical applications of radioisotopes, radiation biology and dosimetry. Agency support was granted to 31 countries for research on applications of radioisotopes in endocrinology, immunology and nutrition, and to 32 countries for research in radiation biology. A manual on radiation sterilization of medical and biological materials was prepared.

More than 50 member States were participating in IAEA's world-wide postal dose comparison service, under which calibrated dosimeters prepared in an IAEA laboratory were distributed to hospitals and other institutions where they were used for calibrating cobalt or caesium sources applied in cancer treatment.

The Agency's programme in physics continued to concentrate on nuclear fission, fusion and neutron interactions, as well as on scientific problems on which research could be done in the developing countries. A number of international conferences and panels of experts were convened for these purposes. A co-ordinated research programme on the quality control of radiopharmaceuticals was started with institutes of several countries.

The Working Group on Nuclear Techniques in Hydrology, established in connexion with the International Hydrological Decade, for which the Agency served as technical secretariat, published a report on nuclear logging in hydrology.

The Agency's laboratories in Seibersdorf (Austria) and Monaco and the International Centre for Theoretical Physics in Trieste (Italy) continued their work.

Nuclear information

The International Nuclear Information System (INIS) employed computer techniques for the storage, correlation and retrieval of nuclear information and provided a world-wide catalogue of technical information relating to the peaceful uses of nuclear energy. As at the end of 1971, 40 countries and 11 international organizations were participating in the scheme.

Secretariat

As at the end of 1971, there were 1,102 staff members, drawn from 61 nationalities, employed by IAEA. Of these, 335 were in the professional and higher categories and 767 in the general service and maintenance and operative categories.

Budget

At its fifteenth (September 1971) session, the General Conference approved a budget for 1972 amounting to $16,561,000. It was decided to increase the 1972 target for voluntary contributions to the General Fund from $2.5 million to $3 million.

Annex I. MEMBERSHIP OF THE INTERNATIONAL ATOMIC ENERGY AGENCY AND CONTRIBUTIONS

(Membership as at 31 December 1971; contributions as set for 1971 and 1972)*

	Contribution for 1971		Contribution for 1972	
Member	Percentage	Net amount (in U.S. dollars)	Percentage†	Net amount (in U.S. dollars)
Afghanistan	0.04	5,221	0.03855	5,934
Albania	0.04	5,221	0.03855	5,934
Algeria	0.09	11,747	0.07833	12,056
Argentina	0.84	109,637	0.75066	115,541
Australia	1.38	180,117	1.34834	207,536
Austria	0.52	67,870	0.50311	77,439
Belgium	1.00	130,520	0.96597	148,682
Bolivia	0.04	5,221	0.03855	5,934
Brazil	0.81	105,721	0.71333	109,796
Bulgaria	0.16	20,883	0.15420	23,734
Burma	0.05	6,526	0.04819	7,417
Byelorussian SSR	0.46	60,039	0.45279	69,694
Cameroon	0.04	5,221	0.03855	5,934
Canada	2.73	356,320	2.81741	433,656
Ceylon	0.05	6,526	0.04819	7,417
Chile	0.21	27,409	0.17715	27,267
China	3.62	472,482	3.50559	539,580
Colombia	0.18	23,493	0.16506	25,406
Costa Rica	0.04	5,221	0.03855	5,934
Cuba	0.17	22,188	0.14701	22,627
Cyprus	0.04	5,221	0.03855	5,934
Czechoslovakia	0.83	108,332	0.82510	126,999
Denmark	0.56	73,091	0.56348	86,731
Dominican Republic	0.04	5,221	0.03855	5,934
Ecuador	0.04	5,221	0.03855	5,934
Egypt	0.18	23,493	0.15665	24,111
El Salvador	0.04	5,221	0.03855	5,934
Ethiopia	0.04	5,221	0.03855	5,934
Federal Republic of Germany	6.35	828,802	6.21843	957,140
Finland	0.44	57,429	0.41255	63,500
France	5.43	708,724	5.49395	845,629
Gabon	0.04	5,221	0.03855	5,934
Ghana	0.07	9,136	0.05905	9,089
Greece	0.26	33,935	0.25057	38,568
Guatemala	0.05	6,526	0.04819	7,417
Haiti	0.04	5,221	0.03855	5,934
Holy See	0.04	5,221	0.04026	6,196
Hungary	0.47	61,344	0.44273	68,145
Iceland	0.04	5,221	0.04026	6,196
India	1.57	204,916	1.37848	212,175
Indonesia	0.31	40,461	0.24828	38,215
Iran	0.20	26,104	0.19275	29,668

*Contributions for 1972 as set at the fifteenth session of the IAEA General Conference, held from 21 to 27 September 1971.

†In setting contributions for 1972 at its September 1971 session, the IAEA General Conference approved a more extended scale of percentage assessments for member States with respect to the financing of safeguards activities. Under the new assessments, 30 developed States paid more, and the developing members less, of the cost of safeguards activities.

Member	Contribution for 1971		Contribution for 1972	
	Percentage	*Net amount (in U.S. dollars)*	*Percentage†*	*Net amount (in U.S. dollars)*
Iraq	0.06	7,831	0.05782	8,900
Ireland	0.15	19,578	0.14087	21,682
Israel	0.18	23,493	0.18111	27,877
Italy	2.93	382,424	3.24002	498,704
Ivory Coast	0.04	5,221	0.03855	5,934
Jamaica	0.05	6,526	0.03978	6,123
Japan	3.42	446,378	4.94053	760,447
Jordan	0.04	5,221	0.03855	5,934
Kenya	0.04	5,221	0.03855	5,934
Khmer Republic	0.04	5,221	0.03855	5,934
Kuwait	0.06	7,831	0.07043	10,841
Lebanon	0.05	6,526	0.04819	7,417
Liberia	0.04	5,221	0.03855	5,934
Libyan Arab Republic	0.04	5,221	0.06037	9,292
Liechtenstein	0.04	5,221	0.04026	6,196
Luxembourg	0.05	6,526	0.05031	7,743
Madagascar	0.04	5,221	0.03855	5,934
Malaysia	0.10	13,052	0.08796	13,539
Mali	0.04	5,221	0.03855	5,934
Mexico	0.79	103,110	0.76977	118,483
Monaco	0.04	5,221	0.04026	6,196
Morocco	0.09	11,747	0.07833	12,056
Netherlands	1.05	137,046	1.07665	165,718
New Zealand	0.33	43,071	0.29180	44,914
Nicaragua‡	0.04	5,221	—	—
Niger	0.04	5,221	0.03855	5,934
Nigeria	0.13	16,967	0.10846	16,694
Norway	0.39	50,903	0.39242	60,402
Pakistan	0.33	43,071	0.30122	46,363
Panama	0.04	5,221	0.03855	5,934
Paraguay	0.04	5,221	0.03855	5,934
Peru	0.09	11,747	0.08674	13,351
Philippines	0.31	40,461	0.27352	42,100
Poland	1.33	173,592	1.23972	190,817
Portugal	0.14	18,273	0.14334	22,062
Republic of Korea	0.11	14,357	0.09760	15,022
Republic of Viet-Nam	0.06	7,831	0.05782	8,900
Romania	0.33	43,071	0.31804	48,953
Saudi Arabia	0.05	6,526	0.05660	8,712
Senegal	0.04	5,221	0.03855	5,934
Sierra Leone	0.04	5,221	0.03855	5,934
Singapore	0.05	6,526	0.04819	7,417
South Africa	0.47	61,344	0.46979	72,310
Spain	0.83	108,332	0.90086	138,660
Sudan	0.05	6,526	0.03978	6,123
Sweden	1.13	147,488	1.14708	176,559
Switzerland	0.78	101,806	0.76472	117,706
Syrian Arab Republic	0.04	5,221	0.03855	5,934
Thailand	0.12	15,662	0.11565	17,801
Tunisia	0.04	5,221	0.03855	5,934
Turkey	0.32	41,766	0.30840	47,469
Uganda	0.04	5,221	0.03855	5,934
Ukrainian SSR	1.75	228,410	1.71057	263,291
USSR	13.23	1,726,780	12.97015	1,996,366
United Kingdom	5.99	781,815	5.39333	830,141
United States	31.45	4,104,854	31.71600	4,881,726
Uruguay	0.08	10,442	0.06027	9,277
Venezuela	0.41	53,513	0.36149	55,640
Yugoslavia	0.36	46,987	0.33854	52,108
Zaire	0.05	6,526	0.03978	6,123
Zambia	0.04	5,221	0.03855	5,934
Total		13,052,000		15,392,000

‡Due to the withdrawal of Nicaragua from membership of IAEA on 14 December 1970, the amount of $5,221 was not assessed in accordance with the Agency's statute.

Annex II. OFFICERS AND OFFICES OF THE INTERNATIONAL ATOMIC ENERGY AGENCY

BOARD OF GOVERNORS
(For period October 1971–September 1972)

Argentina, Australia, Brazil, Canada, Ceylon, Chile, China, Colombia, Czechoslovakia, Egypt, France, Greece, India, Japan, Netherlands, Norway, Portugal, Romania, South Africa, Syrian Arab Republic, Thailand, USSR, United Kingdom, United States, Zaire

Chairman: C. W. van Boetzelaer van Asperen (Netherlands)
Vice-Chairmen: S. J. Walpita (Ceylon); J. Neumann (Czechoslovakia)

MAIN COMMITTEES OF BOARD OF GOVERNORS

ADMINISTRATIVE AND BUDGETARY COMMITTEE
Argentina, Australia, Brazil, Canada, Czechoslovakia, Egypt, France, Greece, India, Japan, Romania, South Africa, USSR, United Kingdom, United States, Zaire

TECHNICAL ASSISTANCE COMMITTEE
Argentina, Brazil, Canada, China, Colombia, Czechoslovakia, Egypt, France,

India, Japan, Norway, Romania, South Africa, USSR, United Kingdom, United States, Zaire

SCIENTIFIC ADVISORY COMMITTEE
M. A. El-Guebeily (Egypt), Bertrand Goldschmidt (France), W. B. Lewis (Canada), I. Malek (Czechoslovakia), S. Mitsui (Japan), L. C. Prado (Brazil), Isidor I. Rabi (United States), Homi N. Sethna (India), V. I. Spitsyn (USSR)

SENIOR SECRETARIAT
OFFICERS

Director-General: Sigvard Eklund
Deputy Director-General for Administration: John A. Hall
Deputy Director-General for Research and Isotopes: André Finkelstein

Deputy Director-General for Technical Assistance and Publications: Upendra Goswami
Deputy Director-General for Technical Operations: Yuri F. Chernilin
Inspector General for Safeguards and Inspection: Rudolf Rometsch

HEADQUARTERS

International Atomic Energy Agency
Kärntnerring 11-13
A-1010 Vienna, Austria
Cable Address: INATOM VIENNA
Telephone: 52 45 11
Telex: 12645

Chapter II

The International Labour Organisation (ILO)

During 1971, the International Labour Organisation (ILO)[1] pursued a broad range of programmes on such different fronts as employment promotion, the protection of workers against work accidents and occupational diseases, vocational training, management development, workers' education, social security, and the promotion of freedom of association, freedom from discrimination and other basic human rights.

At the end of 1971, ILO had 120 member States. (On 15 July 1969, Lesotho had given notice of its intent to withdraw from ILO membership. This withdrawal took effect on 15 July 1971.)

On 16 November 1971, the Governing Body of ILO adopted (by a vote of 36 to 3, with 8 abstentions) a decision to recognize the Government of the People's Republic of China as the representative Government of China. (See also p. 133.)

The International Labour Conference held its fifty-sixth session from 2 to 24 June 1971 in Geneva, Switzerland. The session was addressed by President Léopold Senghor of Senegal. Over 220 other speakers took part in the general debate, the theme of which concerned ways in which ILO could contribute to promoting freedom by fostering dialogue within and between nations.

The Conference adopted a Convention and a Recommendation concerning protection and facilities to be afforded to workers' representatives in the undertaking. It also adopted a Convention and a Recommendation on protection against hazards of benzene poisoning.

This brought the total number of standards adopted since ILO's foundation in 1919 to 136 Conventions and 144 Recommendations; 120 new ratifications were registered in 1971, bringing the total to 3,815.

In accordance with usual practice, the Confer-

[1]For further information on ILO's activities prior to 1971, see reports of Director-General to ILO Conference, Conference proceedings, and previous volumes of Y.U.N.

ence set up a tripartite (Governments-employers-workers) committee to examine the application by member States of ILO Conventions and Recommendations. The Committee also had before it a comprehensive study prepared by a committee of independent experts on the effect given to the Discrimination (Employment and Occupation) Convention and Recommendation.

The Conference also approved a number of resolutions. It called for action to combat *apartheid* and other forms of racial discrimination, to strengthen tripartism in ILO activities, to secure equal treatment for migrant workers, to extend social security coverage, to examine the social problems raised by multinational undertakings, and to study the relationship between international trade and employment.

The Seventh Asian Regional Conference of ILO was held at Teheran, Iran, from 4 to 15 December 1971. Government, employer and worker delegates from 20 Asian nations attended and agreed that efforts to expand employment should be pursued with increased vigour, with the support of the entire international community. The Conference declared that social and economic progress in Asia depended on the support of workers' and employers' organizations, and it urged more widespread ratification of international labour standards on freedom of association and on social policy.

During 1971, a number of ILO Committees met.

The African Advisory Committee made recommendations to improve the conditions of Africans working in countries other than their own, and for the promotion of balanced rural and urban development.

The Metal Trades Committee reviewed the social effects of changing conditions in the world's metal trades, ranging from electronics to shipbuilding. It recommended ways of easing the impact on workers of such changes and stressed the importance of suitable training arrangements.

The Building, Civil Engineering and Public Works Committee recommended measures to deal with problems faced by the industry in developing countries, as well as problems caused by the spread of prefabrication and other new technologies.

The first session of the Joint Committee on the Public Service laid the foundation for future activities of ILO affecting civil servants, including those concerned with protecting freedom of association.

The Committee on Work on Plantations advocated an end to discrimination against women plantation workers in their conditions of employment, as well as adequate training facilities for the young. The advantages of technological change, it declared, should be fairly distributed in the community and result in improved living and working conditions for plantation workers and their families.

The World Employment Programme

During 1971, ILO broadened its efforts under the World Employment Programme. The Programme, one of ILO's main contributions to the Second United Nations Development Decade, was intended to help promote national and international efforts to create productive employment.

An inter-agency mission sponsored by ILO visited Ceylon to help the Government prepare a long-term strategy for achieving a high level of employment. Another inter-agency team began work in Iran, and exploratory missions were sent to Madagascar and to Liberia.

In Latin America, ILO's regional employment team studied the manpower situation in Chile, Costa Rica, Jamaica and Peru. In Africa, a meeting for the exchange of experience on employment policies was held for government officials from six countries.

At ILO headquarters in Geneva, a meeting brought together directors of economic and social research institutes from some 20 countries to plan ways of co-ordinating their research on employment problems with that of ILO under its World Employment Programme. In addition, studies were initiated on ways of promoting employment through international trade.

Field activities

In 1971, there was further growth in ILO technical co-operation activities for the development of human resources and social institutions and the improvement of living and working conditions.

During the year, the agency spent more than $37.9 million on technical assistance, compared with $29.9 million in 1970 and $24.5 million in 1969.

These funds came from the following sources: the United Nations Development Programme (UNDP) pre-investment programme, $25.2 million; the UNDP technical assistance programme, $8.1 million; funds-in-trust (special financial contributions from Governments), $3 million; and the ILO regular budget, $1.7 million.

A major part of ILO's technical aid was provided for human resources development, including vocational training, productivity and management development, and employment planning and promotion.

Assistance also continued in the following fields: organization of co-operatives, social security, occupational safety and health, workers' education, vocational rehabilitation, rural development, labour relations and labour administration. The agency continued to co-ordinate the Andean

Indian Programme, a multi-agency project to assist the indigenous populations of South American countries, including new activities financed under the pre-investment programme of UNDP.

Sources of funds by various fields of activity are shown in the table below.

EXPENDITURES BY FIELD OF ACTIVITY AND SOURCE IN 1971
(in thousands of U.S. dollars)

Field of Activity	Source			
	ILO regular pro- gramme	UNDP tech- nical assis- tance	UNDP pre- invest- ment	Special pro- gramme
Statistics	33	167	—	7
Economic planning	—	—	—	58
Vocational train- ing	348	2,462	11,917	1,305
Management de- velopment	304	842	8,472	669
Manpower planning and organization	490	2,233	1,728	368
Social security	94	565	—	53
Occupational safety and health	16	308	342	92
General conditions of work	35	52	—	14
Maritime workers	3	7	393	—
Labour law and labour relations	33	90	—	26
Labour administra- tion	43	380	400	69
Workers' education	312	37	—	111
Co-operative, rural and related insti- tutions	58	896	1,900	182
Associate experts and others	13	30	—	88
Totals	1,782	8,069	25,152	3,042

The allocation of funds by region and type of assistance is shown below.

ALLOCATIONS BY REGION

Region	Expenditure (in millions of U.S. dollars)	Percentage
Africa	15.9	42.0
Americas	5.6	14.9
Asia	9.0	23.6
Europe	2.1	5.6
Middle East	2.3	6.1
Inter-regional	2.9	7.8

ALLOCATIONS BY TYPE OF ASSISTANCE

Type of Aid	Expenditure (in millions of U.S. dollars)	Percentage
Experts	26.6	70.03
Fellowships	5.0	13.15
Equipment, sub-contracts and miscellaneous	6.4	16.82

Training Centres and institutes

The ILO's International Institute for Labour Studies, Geneva, a centre for advanced study in the labour and social fields, continued to bring together persons from all parts of the world representing government departments, employers' organizations, trade unions, workers' education institutes and universities. In 1971, 94 participants from developing countries attended leadership training courses in labour and social policy. The Institute also held two symposia for the promotion of labour studies in Latin America and Africa, and two international symposia concerned with future trends in industrial relations and with workers' participation in management.

The International Centre for Advanced Technical and Vocational Training, established by ILO in 1963 at Turin, Italy, also continued to provide training in the latest techniques in management, technology and teaching methodology for key personnel, including managers, instructors, technicians and directors of training services, primarily from the developing regions of the world.

Thirty-three training programmes and 12 seminars, attended by more than 1,300 participants, were held during 1971 in the fields of technological, vocational, pedagogical and management training. Three programmes on financial and accounting management were organized for trade union officials from Latin America and Africa.

Research and publications

In 1971, publications of ILO included: Volume I, *Encyclopaedia of Occupational Health and Safety*; *Matching Employment Opportunities and Expectations: A Programme of Action for Ceylon*; *Agrarian Reform and Employment*; *Essays on Employment*; *Participation by Workers' and Employers' Organisations in Economic and Social Planning: A General Introduction*; *Agricultural Organisations and Economic and Social Development in Rural Areas*; *L'inspection du travail: sa mission, ses méthodes*; the twelfth edition of the trilingual *International Directory of Co-operative Organisations*; a set of safety regulations, in French, *Directives de sécurité pour la construction et l'installation des ascenseurs et monte-charge électriques*; and a programmed instruction textbook, also in French, *Création d'un marché*; reports on all the agenda items of the International Labour Conference and a two-part report by the Director-General; reports for the Seventh Asian Regional Conference; and the periodical publications: *International Labour Review*, *Official Bulletin*, *Legislative Series*, *Year Book of Labour Statistics* and the public information magazine ILO *Panorama*.

Secretariat

As at 31 December 1971, the total number of full-time staff under permanent, indefinite, fixed-term and short-term appointments at ILO headquarters and at area, branch and other offices stood at 3,044. Of these, 1,668 were in the professional and higher categories (drawn from about 100 nationalities) and 1,376 were in the general service and maintenance categories.

Of the professional and higher categories, 894 persons were assigned to technical assistance co-operation projects.

Budget

In June 1971, the International Labour Conference adopted a gross expenditure budget totalling US$71,503,000 for the 1972–1973 biennium. The main details of expenditure covered by the budget are shown below.

EXPENDITURES FOR 1972–1973

	Estimates (in U.S. dollars)		Estimates (in U.S. dollars)
Policy-making organs		Publications and public information	5,305,988
International Labour Conference	1,172,700	International Centre for Advanced Technical and Vocational Training	1,200,000
Governing Body	349,700	International Institute for Labour Studies	605,000
	1,522,400		53,782,921
General management	1,959,148		
		Service and support activities	
Programmes of activity		Legal services	346,896
Major regional meetings	657,280	Personnel and administrative services	7,967,712
Industrial activities	2,224,500	Occupation of the new building in 1973	565,000
Central research and planning	4,686,963	Financial and general services	3,673,044
Conditions of work and life	4,281,208		12,552,652
Employment planning and promotion department	4,147,490	Other budgetary provisions	1,480,816
			71,297,937
Human resources development	4,250,241		
Social institutions development	4,880,976	Deduct: Adjustment for staff turnover	—361,433
International labour standards	2,342,147		70,936,504
Central administration of technical co-operation and management of certain field programmes	3,473,271	Unforeseen expenditure	550,000
		Working Capital Fund	16,496
Management of field programmes in Africa	2,170,683	Total gross expenditure	71,503,000
Management of field programmes in the Americas	3,371,976	Miscellaneous income	
		Deduct: Receipts from UNDP	—1,829,000
Management of field programmes in Asia	3,034,368	Total net expenditure budget	69,674,000
Relations and conference services	7,150,830		

Annex I.   MEMBERSHIP OF INTERNATIONAL LABOUR ORGANISATION AND CONTRIBUTIONS

(Membership as at 31 December 1971; contributions as assessed for 1972)*

Member	Assessed contribution Percentage	Net amount (in U.S. dollars)	Member	Assessed contribution Percentage	Net amount (in U.S. dollars)	Member	Assessed contribution Percentage	Net amount (in U.S. dollars)
Afghanistan	0.07	24,386	China	3.17	1,104,333	Ghana	0.10	34,837
Algeria	0.12	41,804	Colombia	0.28	97,544	Greece	0.23	80,125
Argentina	1.26	438,946	Congo	0.07	24,386	Guatemala	0.07	24,386
Australia	1.83	637,517	Costa Rica	0.07	24,386	Guinea	0.07	24,386
Austria	0.44	153,283	Cuba	0.24	83,609	Guyana	0.07	24,386
Barbados	0.07	24,386	Cyprus	0.08	25,012	Haiti	0.07	24,386
Belgium	1.35	470,299	Czechoslovakia	0.92	320,500	Honduras	0.07	24,386
Bolivia	0.07	24,386	Dahomey	0.07	24,386	Hungary	0.42	146,315
Brazil	1.20	418,044	Denmark	0.70	243,859	Iceland	0.07	24,386
Bulgaria	0.19	66,190	Dominican Republic	0.07	24,386	India	2.39	808,218
Burma	0.07	24,386	Ecuador	0.07	24,386	Indonesia	0.42	146,315
Burundi	0.07	24,386	Egypt	0.27	94,060	Iran	0.27	94,060
Byelorussian SSR	0.45	156,766	El Salvador	0.07	24,386	Iraq	0.09	31,353
Cameroon	0.07	24,386	Ethiopia	0.07	24,386	Ireland	0.22	76,641
Canada	3.36	1,170,523	Federal Republic of Germany	5.34	1,860,296	Israel	0.16	55,739
Central African Republic	0.07	24,386	Finland	0.38	132,380	Italy	2.64	919,697
Ceylon	0.07	24,386	France	6.07	2,114,606	Ivory Coast	0.07	24,386
Chad	0.07	24,386	Gabon	0.07	24,386	Jamaica	0.07	24,386
Chile	0.30	104,511				Japan	3.16	1,100,849

Member	Assessed contribution Percentage	Net amount (in U.S. dollars)	Member	Assessed contribution Percentage	Net amount (in U.S. dollars)	Member	Assessed contribution Percentage	Net amount (in U.S. dollars)
Jordan	0.07	24,386	Niger	0.07	24,386	Syrian Arab Republic	0.07	24,386
Kenya	0.07	24,386	Nigeria	0.18	62,707	Thailand	0.18	62,707
Khmer Republic	0.07	24,386	Norway	0.51	177,669	Togo	0.07	24,386
Kuwait	0.09	31,353	Pakistan	0.50	174,185	Trinidad and Tobago	0.07	24,386
Laos	0.07	24,386	Panama	0.07	24,386	Tunisia	0.07	24,386
Lebanon	0.07	24,386	Paraguay	0.07	24,386	Turkey	0.49	170,701
Liberia	0.07	24,386	People's Democratic Republic of Yemen	0.07	24,386	Uganda	0.07	24,386
Libyan Arab Republic	0.08	27,870	Peru	0.13	45,288	Ukrainian SSR	1.51	526,039
Luxembourg	0.07	24,386	Philippines	0.37	128,897	USSR	10.45	3,640,466
Madagascar	0.07	24,386	Poland	1.24	438,946	United Kingdom	8.82	3,072,623
Malawi	0.07	24,386	Portugal	0.22	76,641	United Republic of Tanzania	0.07	24,386
Malaysia	0.15	52,255	Republic of Viet-Nam	0.09	31,353	United States	25.00	8,709,250
Mali	0.07	24,386	Romania	0.43	149,799	Upper Volta	0.07	24,386
Malta	0.07	24,386	Rwanda	0.07	24,386	Uruguay	0.10	34,837
Mauritania	0.07	24,386	Senegal	0.07	24,386	Venezuela	0.50	174,185
Mauritius	0.07	24,386	Sierra Leone	0.07	24,386	Yemen	0.07	24,386
Mexico	0.77	268,245	Singapore	0.07	24,386	Yugoslavia	0.40	139,348
Mongolia	0.07	24,386	Somalia	0.07	24,386	Zaire	0.07	24,386
Morocco	0.13	45,288	Spain	1.04	362,305	Zambia	0.07	24,386
Nepal	0.07	24,386	Sudan	0.07	24,386	Total		34,837.00
Netherlands	1.13	393,658	Sweden	1.58	550,424			
New Zealand	0.47	163,734	Switzerland	1.18	411,076			
Nicaragua	0.07	24,386						

*Contributions for 1972 as set at the fifty-sixth session of the International Labour Conference, held from 2 to 24 June 1971.

Annex II.   OFFICERS AND OFFICES OF THE INTERNATIONAL LABOUR ORGANISATION
(As at 31 December 1971)

MEMBERSHIP OF THE GOVERNING BODY OF THE INTERNATIONAL LABOUR OFFICE

Chairman: Umarjadi Nijotowijono (Indonesia)
Vice-Chairmen: Gullmar Bergenström (Sweden), Employers' Group; Joseph Morris (Canada), Workers' Group

REGULAR MEMBERS

Government members
Brazil, Canada,* Central African Republic, China,* Colombia, Czechoslovakia, Ecuador, Federal Republic of Germany,* France,* India,* Indonesia, Italy,* Japan,* Kenya, Libyan Arab Republic, Nigeria, Republic of Viet-Nam, Romania, Syrian Arab Republic, USSR,* United Kingdom,* United States,* Upper Volta, Uruguay

*Member holding non-elective seat as State of chief industrial importance.

Employers' Members
F. Bannerman-Menson (Ghana), Gullmar Bergenström (Sweden), E.-G. Erdmann (Federal Republic of Germany), H. Georget (Niger), M. Ghayour (Iran), D. Gonzales Blanco (Brazil), C.A.C. Henniker-Heaton (United Kingdom), M. Nasr (Lebanon), E. P. Neilan (United States), N. H. Tata (India), P. Waline (France), F. Yllanes Ramos (Mexico)

Workers' Members
M. Benseddik (Morocco), N. De Bock (Belgium), R. Faupl (United States), G. B. Fogam (Cameroon), M. Makhlouf (Tunisia), Joseph Morris (Canada), G. Muhr (Federal Republic of Germany), P. T. Pimenov (USSR), C. T. H. Plant (United Kingdom), A. Sánchez Madariaga (Mexico), I. Shioji (Japan), O. Sunde (Norway)

DEPUTY MEMBERS

Government deputy members
Algeria, Argentina, Belgium, Bulgaria, Chile, Congo, Denmark, Iran, Pakistan, Somalia, Uganda, Venezuela

Employers' deputy members
A. Abate (Ethiopia), D. Andriantsitohaina (Madagascar), A. Bastid (Ivory Coast), Sir Grant Ferrier (Australia), M. Ghali (Tunisia), M. Montt Balmaceda (Chile), D. A. R. Phiri (Zambia), F. K. Richan (Canada), F. M. Salvi (Italy), A. Verschueren (Belgium), A. Vitaic Jakasa (Argentina), K. F. Yoshimura (Japan)

Workers' deputy members
Abid Ali (India), B. Armato (Italy), A. Boltyah (Egypt), J. Gonzalez Navarro (Venezuela), F. Kikongi (Zaire), R. Louet (France), J. R. Mercado (Colombia), E. Moyal (Israel), S. Shita (Libyan Arab Republic), T. E. Skinner (New Zealand), B. Solomon (Ethiopia), G. Weissenberg (Austria)

SENIOR OFFICIALS OF INTERNATIONAL LABOUR OFFICE

Director-General: Wilfred Jenks
Deputy Directors-General: Abbas Ammar, Francis Blanchard

Assistant Directors-General: Bertil Bolin, Albert Tévoédjrè, Xavier Caballero Tomayo, Yujiro Ohno, Pavel N. Astapenko

HEADQUARTERS, REGIONAL, AREA, BRANCH AND LIAISON OFFICES

HEADQUARTERS
International Labour Office
CH-1211 Geneva 22
Switzerland
    Cable Address: INTERLAB GENEVE

REGIONAL OFFICES
International Labour Organisation Regional
    Office for Africa
P.O. Box 2788
Addis Ababa, Ethiopia
    Cable Address: INTERLAB ADDISABABA

International Labour Organisation Regional
  Office for Asia
P.O. Box 1759
Bangkok, Thailand
  Cable Address: INTERLAB BANGKOK

International Labour Organisation Regional
  Office for Latin America
Apartado postal 3638 and 5421
Lima, Peru
  Cable Address: INTERLAB LIMA

International Labour Organisation Regional
  Office, Middle East/Europe
CH-1211 Geneva 22
Switzerland
  Cable Address: INTERLAB GENEVE

AREA OFFICES
International Labour Organisation Area Office
Boîte postale 226
Alger-Gare, Algeria
  Cable Address: INTERLAB ALGER

International Labour Organisation Area Office
Boîte postale 4656
Beirut, Lebanon
  Cable Address: INTERLAB BEIRUT

International Labour Organisation Area Office
Avenida Julio A. Rocca No. 710, 3° piso
Buenos Aires, Argentina
  Cable Address: INTERLAB BUENOSAIRES

International Labour Organisation Area Office
9, Willcocks Street
Zamalek
Cairo, Egypt
  Cable Address: INTERLAB CAIRO

International Labour Organisation Area Office
Boîte postale 414
Dakar, Senegal
  Cable Address: INTERLAB DAKAR

International Labour Organisation Area Office
P. O. Box 9212
Dar es Salaam, United Republic of Tanzania
  Cable Address: INTERLAB DARESSALAAM

International Labour Organisation Area Office
P. O. Box 1047
Islamabad, Pakistan
  Cable Address: INTERLAB ISLAMABAD

International Labour Organisation Area Office
Gümüssuyu caddesi 96
Ayazpasa
Istanbul, Turkey
  Cable Address: INTERLAB ISTANBUL

International Labour Organisation Area Office
P. O. Box 2331
Lagos, Nigeria
  Cable Address: INTERLAB LAGOS

International Labour Organisation Area Office
P. O. Box 2181
Lusaka, Zambia
  Cable Address: INTERLAB LUSAKA

International Labour Organisation Area Office
P. O. Box 2965
Manila, Philippines
  Cable Address: INTERLAB MANILA

International Labour Organisation Area Office
Apartado postal 8636
Mexico 1, D.F., Mexico
  Cable Address: INTERLAB MEXICO D.F.

International Labour Organisation Area Office
Sardar patel Marg
Chanakyapuri
New Delhi 21, India
  Cable Address: INTERLAB NEWDELHI

International Labour Organisation Area Office
P. O. Box 1201
Port of Spain, Trinidad and Tobago
  Cable Address: INTERLAB PORTOFSPAIN

International Labour Organisation Area Office
Apartado postal 10170
San José, Costa Rica
  Cable Address: INTERLAB SANJOSE COSTARICA

International Labour Organisation Area Office
Boîte postale 13
Yaoundé, Cameroon
  Cable Address: INTERLAB YAOUNDE

BRANCH OFFICES
International Labour Office
Hohenzollernstrasse 21
D-53 Bonn–Bad Godesberg
Federal Republic of Germany
  Cable Address: INTERLAB BONN

International Labour Office
Sackville House
40, Piccadilly
London W.1, United Kingdom
  Cable Address: INTERLAB LONDON W.1

International Labour Office
Petrovka 15, Apt. 23
Moscow K. 9, USSR
  Cable Address: INTERLAB MOSCOW

International Labour Office
178, Queen Street
Ottawa, Ontario, KIP 5E1, Canada
  Cable Address: INTERLAB OTTAWA

International Labour Office
205, Boulevard Saint-Germain
F-75 Paris VIIe, France
  Cable Address: INTERLAB PARIS 044

International Labour Office
Caixa postal 607-ZC-00
Rio de Janeiro, Estado da Guanabara, Brazil
  Cable Address: INTERLAB RIODEJANEIRO

International Labour Office
Villa Aldobrandini
Via Panisperna 28
I-00184 Rome, Italy
  Cable Address: INTERLAB ROME

International Labour Office
World Trade Centre Building
5, Shiba-Hamamatsuchô, 3-Chôme
Minato-Ku, Tokyo 105, Japan
  Cable Address: INTERLAB TOKYO

International Labour Office
666 Eleventh Street, N.W.
Washington, D.C. 20001, U.S.A.
  Cable Address: INTERLAB WASHINGTON DC

LIAISON OFFICES
International Labour Organisation Liaison Office
  with the United Nations
345 East 46th Street
New York, N.Y. 10017, U.S.A.
  Cable Address: INTERLABOR NEWYORK

International Labour Organisation Liaison Office
  with the United Nations Economic
  Commission for Latin America
Casilla 2353
Santiago, Chile
  Cable Address: INTERLAB SANTIAGODECHILE

Chapter III

The Food and Agriculture Organization
of the United Nations (FAO)

During 1971, the main concern of the Food and Agriculture Organization of the United Nations (FAO)[1] continued to be the production of more and better food, but the Agency increasingly took into account such factors as social justice, land reform, employment opportunities, the quality of life in rural areas and environmental problems.

On 8 November 1971, at the sixteenth session of the FAO General Conference, the following six States were admitted to membership of FAO: Bahrain, Fiji, Maldives, Oman, Qatar and Swaziland. This brought the membership of FAO to 125.

At its fifty-seventh session, held from 1 to 4 November 1971, the Council of FAO was informed of a resolution adopted on 25 October 1971 by the United Nations General Assembly by which the Assembly decided to restore all rights to the People's Republic of China and to recognize the representatives of its Government as the only legitimate representatives of China to the United Nations, and to expel forthwith the representatives of Chiang Kai-shek from the place which they unlawfully occupied at the United Nations and in all the organizations related to it.

On 2 November 1971, the Council decided to authorize the Director-General to invite the People's Republic of China to seek formal membership in the organization and, if it so requested, to attend the sixteenth (November 1971) session of the FAO Conference. At that session of the Conference, the Director-General reported that he had taken action as authorized by the Council.

On 25 November 1971, by a vote of 68 to 0, with 3 abstentions, the Conference adopted a resolution by which it authorized the Director-General, when the People's Republic of China manifested the wish to resume its place in the organization, to take "all appropriate measures" to bring into effect the resumption by China of its place in the organization. (For further details, see pp. 133-34.)

World agricultural situation

The 1971 issue of FAO's annual publication *The State of Food and Agriculture* reported no change in the 1970 agricultural and food production of the developed market economies compared with the previous year. Total agricultural production in Eastern Europe was down 1 per cent in 1970, but the USSR showed a gain of 9 per cent.

Food production rose again in 1970 in the Far East but lagged behind population growth in Africa and the Near East and barely matched it in Latin America.

Estimates of world trade in agricultural products (excluding fishery and forestry products) indicated an increase of 13 per cent in the value of exports in 1970. The value of fishery exports rose by 16 per cent and of forestry exports by 6 per cent.

Activities in 1971

Field projects

Field activities accounted for approximately three quarters of total FAO expenditures from all sources during 1971. The major source of funds was the United Nations Development Programme (UNDP); more than $70 million was allocated under the Special Fund component of UNDP, and $14 million, on 700 small-scale projects, under the Technical Assistance component. Matching contributions were made by recipient countries.

A further $13.5 million was made available by Governments in trust funds for projects formulated and executed by FAO; other trust funds totalling $3.5 million paid for associate experts assigned to FAO work. The Freedom from Hunger Campaign contributed about $2.5 million to 130 FAO-executed projects.

The number of UNDP inter-agency projects involving FAO rose to 16 in 1971. There was also a marked expansion of joint projects with individual Governments. The number of projects operated by FAO and financed by bilateral agencies rose to 55 national and 30 inter-regional projects.

Research and policy guidance

Further progress was made in 1971 in developing various aspects of FAO's Perspective Study of World Agricultural Development (formerly known as the Indicative World Plan for Agricultural Development). The study involved examinations of policy alternatives relevant for government planning.

The establishment of a Consultative Group on International Agricultural Research was sponsored by FAO, UNDP and the International Bank for Reconstruction and Development. The Consultative Group, an informal association of aid agencies, donor countries and private foundations, was to organize financial support for agricultural research in developing countries.

---

[1]For further information on FAO's activities prior to 1971, see FAO Director-General's biennial reports on FAO *Programme of Work and Budget, Catalogue of FAO Publications,* and previous volumes of Y.U.N.

Cost of food production

The 34-nation Council of FAO, meeting in June 1971, discussed how to raise food production in developing countries through judicious use of technology and assistance. It was estimated that the cost of increasing food production to meet the demands of a growing population during the Second United Nations Development Decade would be about $185,000 million.

FAO Investment Centre

The FAO Investment Centre expanded its promotional activities for investment in agricultural development, strengthened its co-operative arrangements with banks and other financing agencies, and provided training in project preparation for government officials.

Lending for projects prepared under FAO's co-operative programme with the International Bank rose to $365 million in 23 countries during 1971. The projects were in fisheries, credit and land settlement, agricultural education, seed production and distribution and integrated rural development.

More than $84 million in credits were granted by the International Development Association for three projects in India aimed at increasing production of food grains and other crops.

The African Development Bank granted loans of $700,000 and $3 million, respectively, to a commercial farming project in Zambia and a livestock project in Algeria, both of which were prepared with the assistance of FAO.

Freedom from Hunger Campaign

The sub-title "Action for Development" was added to the title of the Freedom from Hunger Campaign in 1971 to emphasize its action-oriented nature.

The Campaign provided a co-ordinating point for the International Walk for Development, which was supported by tens of thousands of walkers in 51 countries.

National Freedom from Hunger committees and voluntary organizations contributed some $2.5 million and undertook 47 new projects, bringing the total number of projects executed by FAO under the Campaign during 1971 to 130. The projects, aimed at stimulating self-development, were intended to meet local needs and encourage local responsibility.

Industry Co-operative Programme

Through the Industry Co-operative Programme (ICP), financially supported by industry, FAO sought to interest potential investors in development activities. The organization provided machinery for the exchange of information and established contacts and co-ordinated action among inter-governmental agencies and public and private sectors.

At the end of 1971, some 80 companies were members of ICP.

Agricultural services

In 1971, the drive for higher yields and increased livestock production intensified the demand for FAO's services in the fields of agricultural engineering, production economics and farm management, and food and agricultural industries.

The organization offered advisory services on such problems as the mechanization and selection of farm equipment, storage problems, planning of farm buildings in tropical areas, and training programmes.

Integrated agricultural development projects such as those operating in the Euphrates River Basin and the Ghab (Syria) and Greater Musayyib (Iraq) regions were assisting new settlers to achieve better conditions and increased earnings.

Field activities in food processing included food development projects and commercial operations; FAO-assisted food research development centres were operating in Brazil, Malaysia, Nigeria, Peru, the Republic of Korea, Senegal, Sudan and Turkey.

Industry and the international community enabled the South American Farm Mechanization Centre in Buga, Colombia, to expand its training facilities. A grant of $70,000 was to support the establishment of training programmes for agricultural engineers and agronomists as teachers and extension workers. The Canadian International Development Association was contributing a further $35,000 in fellowships and equipment. Voluntary contributions under the Freedom from Hunger Campaign financed 100 fellowships for South American students.

Atomic energy in food and agriculture

The partnership of FAO and the International Atomic Energy Agency (IAEA) during 1971 was responsible for 56 projects and 200 research contracts and agreements. With major assistance from UNDP, national centres for nuclear research in agriculture were being set up in Brazil, Chile and India.

Results of inoculation of sheep in the Himalayan foot-hills with radiation-attenuated vaccines against lungworm were so promising that the Indian Government was planning large-scale application of this technique.

Mutant varieties of rice were being tested in Ceylon and the Philippines.

A panel met in Nairobi, Kenya, to examine the

effectiveness of radiation and isotopes in controlling parasitic and associated diseases in domestic animals.

A research programme on the use of nuclear techniques to raise plant protein content was launched with the co-operation and financial support of the Federal Republic of Germany. (For further information, see p. 684.)

Plant production and protection

In 1971, FAO supplied back-up support for some 600 plant specialists assigned to research, operational projects and training programmes in the field.

High-yielding spring wheat varieties from Mexico and a winter wheat from the USSR were selected for large-scale production in 23 countries of Africa, the Near East and Southern Europe. In Brazil, hybrids were produced between local wheats and Mexican varieties. In South-East Asia, the Near East and Africa, FAO helped to introduce new food legumes.

The number of field projects for seed production and distribution and quality control doubled during 1971.

Also, in 1971, FAO began a survey of plant genetic resources covering 93 countries in which more than 2 million samples had been located. The organization sponsored collecting expeditions to Latin America, the Mediterranean countries, Ethiopia and Nepal.

The Working Party on Pest Resistance to Pesticides recommended action to encourage industrial production of viruses "targeted" for individual pest species and to ensure avoidance of harmful effects of viruses on man, animals and the environment. Progress was made on the evaluation of pesticides to ensure that they met acceptable standards and did not contain contaminants.

Technicians from 11 African and Near and Middle Eastern countries were trained in modern plant-breeding techniques at a six-month course sponsored by FAO and the Swedish International Development Agency in India.

Animal and health production

The expansion of veterinary services in developing countries was a central element of FAO's animal health activities during 1971. Six projects, financed by allocations totalling $8 million from UNDP and by matching contributions from recipient countries, supported university and middle-grade courses in Afghanistan, Colombia, the Dominican Republic, Ethiopia, Kenya and Somalia.

Ten veterinary training courses were conducted and more than 100 veterinarians studied abroad on fellowships under FAO supervision. Five permanent post-graduate courses for veterinarians were sponsored in co-operation with the Danish and Swedish Governments.

The production and export of meat was actively encouraged to bolster the economies of many developing countries. A programme was started during the year to help FAO members to identify and develop promising areas for the production of exportable meat.

Twenty-two of the 135 field projects in animal health and production in 1971 concerned milk and milk products technology. Together with the United Nations Children's Fund (UNICEF), FAO supported the establishment of milk plant centres, mainly in Africa.

Land and water development

The Intergovernmental Working Group on Soils, which met at FAO headquarters in June 1971, warned of the danger of land degradation caused by the pressures of population and technology. The meeting stressed the imperative need for action on land use planning, soil conservation, water management, better disposal and recycling of waste, and legislation and education.

The identification of investment possibilities included a five-year pre-investment survey of the Naktong River Basin in the Republic of Korea, completed in 1971; and a four-year study of irrigation possibilities in the Terai Plain in Nepal. The First Regional Seminar on Systematic Evaluation of Land and Water Resources, held in Mexico City, Mexico, was attended by about 250 participants from 24 Central and South American countries.

The first two sheets—for South America—of the projected 18-sheet soil map of the world, a joint undertaking of FAO and the United Nations Educational, Scientific and Cultural Organization, were issued in 1971.

The FAO Fertilizer Programme celebrated its tenth anniversary in 1971. With the support of the fertilizer industry, donor Governments and non-governmental organizations, cash contributions increased from $275,000 in 1961 to $1.5 million in 1970, and the Programme was active in 22 countries.

Fisheries

The world fishery catch increased to 69.3 million tons in 1970—double what it was in 1960. However, the Director-General of FAO warned that intensive fishing was endangering some ocean stocks.

In 1971, FAO managed or participated in some 200 fishery projects manned by 380 experts in 60 countries and territories.

The Indian Ocean Fishery Commission, a 28-nation body responsible for the organization's first ocean-wide undertaking, approved plans for developing the potential of this marine area. Preparatory work was financed by UNDP. Member countries asked FAO to draw up proposals for organization along similar lines for the East Central Atlantic and for the South China Sea.

A $2.2 million fishery project was launched in Indonesia. The project included training in the use of modern fishing craft, marine engineering, fish processing and marketing and biology.

An FAO Committee for Inland Fisheries of Africa was established in 1971. The Committee was to promote and co-ordinate joint action intended to meet the continent's growing food needs, stimulate fisheries trade and defend the aquatic environment against pollution.

Steps were taken to institute fishery management and other measures in the heavily exploited waters of the East Central Atlantic, where catches had quadrupled since 1958.

The Convention on the Conservation of the Living Resources of the South-East Atlantic, for which FAO acted as depositary, came into force on 24 October 1971, following its ratification by the USSR and previous ratifications by Japan, Portugal and South Africa. The Convention provided for the establishment of an international commission to make recommendations on the rational use of the area's fisheries.

The organization issued the first maps of the illustrated atlas of the world's principal sea fisheries, to form part of FAO's contribution to the 1973 United Nations Conference on the Law of the Sea. The atlas was to comprise about 60 global and regional maps showing the location of the most commonly harvested fish resources.

Forestry

More than 140 specialists from developing and developed countries, meeting at FAO headquarters, agreed on the urgent need for comprehensive action to protect the world's forest resources, which were dwindling in the face of rising populations and mounting demand for forest products. Afforestation of new areas, improvement of tree species, expansion of man-made forests, better fire-protection and pest control were among the measures advocated.

Opportunities for economic expansion in developing countries with large reserves of untapped wood were discussed at an FAO consultation on demand, supply and trade in pulp and paper in May 1971.

Some 300 foresters, wood technologists, architects, builders, planners and bankers from all over the world attended a consultation in Van-

couver, Canada, on the use of wood in housing.

A large proportion of FAO's 1971 forestry activities and 16 of its field projects, financed under UNDP, were devoted to the promotion of training in forestry.

Protection and judicious exploitation of wildlife was also an important part of FAO's forestry programme. A conference on the conservation of the vicuña was held in Peru, in collaboration with the International Union for the Conservation of Nature and Natural Resources.

About $24 million was spent on field activities in forestry in 1971. Of this amount, UNDP projects accounted for over $12 million, and World Food Programme allocations for the equivalent of $11 million.

Nutrition

The organization continued to emphasize the importance of nutrition in national development planning.

A regional course on food policy and planning, sponsored by FAO, the World Health Organization (WHO) and UNICEF with the co-operation of the American University of Beirut, was held in Beirut, Lebanon, in 1971.

The South Pacific Community Training Centre in Fiji had, by the end of 1971, provided ten-month courses to some 300 women trainees from the 14 territories of the area.

In co-operation with the Latin American regional centre for nutrition, FAO sponsored a five-month training course for agronomists, home economists and teachers, which was attended by 32 fellows from 15 Latin American countries.

During 1971, 121 field projects were carried out and 23 fellowships were offered in nutrition. The national food and nutrition project in Zambia became fully operational in 1971.

Recognition of protein food development as an essential component of national development figured prominently in FAO's nutrition policy objectives. The Protein Advisory Group, sponsored jointly by FAO, WHO and UNICEF, reported that 20 per cent of all children under five years of age in developing countries showed signs of protein malnutrition.

A new protein-rich infant food was introduced in Turkey in October 1971, through a project jointly operated by FAO, UNICEF and WHO.

Codex Alimentarius

The FAO/WHO Codex Alimentarius Commission develops international food standards.

At the end of 1971, over 65 international food standards and six codes of hygienic practices had been adopted by the Commission. Approximately 400 food additives provisions had been examined by an FAO/WHO committee. The Commission's Code of Principles for Milk and Milk Products had been adopted by 71 countries, and its standards for the principal milk products had been accepted by some 65 countries. Membership of the Commission numbered 93 countries at the end of 1971.

Rural institutions

Agrarian reform and its concomitants, such as credit and marketing, co-operatives, and agricultural education and training continued to be given attention by FAO. The sixteenth FAO Conference endorsed a report which called agrarian reform an "urgent necessity" in much of the world. The report was drawn up by a special committee established by FAO in 1969.

Research institutes for agrarian reform were established in Ceylon, Chile and Peru, with UNDP and FAO support.

Permanent marketing development centres were set up in Iran, Kenya, Uganda and the United Republic of Tanzania with the help of UNDP and FAO. The centres' training curricula included applied research, methods of price stabilization and modern handling techniques.

The organization of agricultural research around major zones of a more or less uniform ecology continued during the year. In co-operation with the International Institute of Tropical Agriculture and the Ford Foundation, FAO arranged a conference in Nigeria (August 1971) to promote joint agricultural research in the humid tropical region of West Africa described as the "Guinean Zone."

Commodities and trade

Demand and production projections for selected commodities in 132 countries during the decade 1970-1980 were published in 1971. The projections indicated that if current trends continued, agricultural export earnings of the developing countries would increase very little, if at all, during the decade. The projections also indicated that the developing countries—excluding the Asian centrally planned economies—would produce only about one third of the world's agricultural output by 1980, although they contained nearly half the world's population.

The FAO Study Group on Rice unanimously agreed to recommend to Governments a set of guidelines for action on national rice production, trade and food-aid policies. The Study Group on Bananas established a standing committee to help banana-exporting countries formulate national production policies to achieve co-ordinated expansion of production.

The informal international quota arrangements for sisal and henequen, which had been evolved by the Consultative Committee on Hard Fibres and had been suspended during 1970, were reinstated in May 1971. The Consultative Committee on Tea recommended to Governments an informal arrangement of export quotas for 15 months to end in March 1972.

By 30 September 1971, 20 Governments and the European Economic Community had indicated their readiness to accept guidelines and procedures drawn up by the Committee on Commodity Problems early in 1971 for establishing market requirements under the FAO Principles of Surplus Disposal.

Economic analysis

The fifth agricultural planning course, held in Rome, Italy, was attended by 30 participants from 16 English- and 14 Spanish-speaking countries. A similar course was conducted in Uganda.

A planning team was set up by FAO to work with the Governments of Bolivia, Chile, Colombia, Ecuador and Peru (the Andean Group) to explore methods of developing an agricultural, livestock and forestry potential covering more than 300 million hectares.

Fourteen countries participated in a West African seminar for the promotion of economic co-operation and trade policies in agriculture, sponsored by FAO, the Economic Commission for Africa and the United Nations Conference on Trade and Development (UNCTAD).

Information systems and publications

The sixteenth FAO Conference decided to pursue efforts to set up an international information system for agricultural sciences and technology.

In 1971, FAO started a series of prototype training manuals for use in developing countries. The first group consisted of 23 booklets, published in Arabic, intended for village-level extension workers, farmers' groups and schools. The primers were originally issued in French by the Institut Africain pour le développement économique et social.

Continuing activities included a project in West Africa to develop rural broadcasting and group listening to agricultural programmes. Regular broadcasts on FAO activities through a network of radio stations in Latin America continued in 1971.

Publications and documents issued in 1971 included the following:

ANNUALS: *The State of Food and Agriculture 1971; Statistical Yearbooks* (on Animal Health, Fertilizers, Fisheries, Forest Products, Grain, Production and Trade).

PERIODICALS: *Ceres; Monthly Bulletin of Agricultural Economics and Statistics; Plant Protection Bul-*

letin; Unasylva; Food and Agricultural Legislation; Cocoa Statistics; Nutrition Newsletter.

OTHERS: *Agricultural Commodity Projections, 1970-1980; World Agriculture: The Last Quarter Century; Foreign Investment Laws in Agriculture; Pesticide Residues in Food; Fumigation for Insect Control; Handling of Food Grains; Milk Hygiene.*

FAO coin plan

Under the FAO international coin plan, launched in 1968, more than 40 countries had used their commemorative and circulating money to express "Food for All" goals. In 1971, coins were issued by Indonesia, Nepal, Panama, Poland, the Republic of Viet-Nam, Turkey, the United Republic of Tanzania, Yugoslavia and the East Caribbean Currency Authority.

Secretariat

As at the end of October 1971, the total number of staff employed by FAO on permanent, fixed-

term or short-term appointments stood at 6,468. Of the total, 3,706 were in the professional or higher categories. Of these, 1,287 (drawn from 93 nations) were in Headquarters, 142 in regional and country offices and 2,277 were experts working in field projects in some 110 countries. There were 2,762 in the general service and maintenance and operative categories, of which 2,174 were at Headquarters, and the rest in regional and country offices and in the field.

Budget

The sixteenth session of the FAO Conference, meeting in November 1971, approved a regular programme budget of nearly $86 million for the 1972-1973 biennium. This was 19.1 per cent more than the budget for the 1970-1971 biennium. However, only 1.6 per cent of the increase was earmarked for expanded FAO activities; the balance was to cover higher operating costs, due primarily to inflation.

Activities of the Food and Agriculture Organization in the field, 1971

Country or territory	Total UNDP	Trust funds	Other aid programmes[a]	Country or territory	Total UNDP	Trust funds	Other aid programmes[a]
Afghanistan	594,460	520,865	4,701	Ethiopia	1,745,262	56,679	252
Algeria	2,233,047	—	—	Fiji	430,318	—	906
Argentina	1,710,959	27,076	—	Gabon	646,315	—	—
Barbados	1	—	—	Gambia	24,215	—	—
Bolivia	925,529	—	6,920	Ghana	1,280,824	953	10,425
Botswana	495,387	4,880	—	Greece	970,656	—	—
Brazil	2,178,576	—	34,677	Guatemala	50,457	—	—
British Honduras	43,305	—	2,150	Guinea	966,489	—	—
Bulgaria	342,620	—	—	Guyana	89,383	—	—
Burma	218,713	—	14,566	Haiti	740,377	—	—
Brunei	5,192	—	—	Honduras	502,713	—	—
Burundi	1,017,596	—	12,554	Hungary	503,037	41,207	—
Cameroon	539,003	—	640	Iceland	6,299	—	—
Caribbean Territories	40,810	—	—	India	3,462,689	183,225	110,886
Central African Republic	751,678	—	—	Indonesia	1,077,022	50,960	51,171
				Iran	2,723,653	19,223	12,263
Ceylon	316,444	3,796	—	Iraq	2,091,226	—	1,045
Chad	234,956	—	42,364	Israel	214,063	—	—
Chile	1,173,427	262,254	—	Ivory Coast	813,040	44,961	6,578
China	286,660	—	—	Jamaica	657,683	13,952	—
Colombia	1,125,808	20,351	20,133	Jordan	1,264,317	—	—
Comoro Islands	32,360	—	—	Kenya	1,775,268	334,585	69,273
Congo	1,030,062	—	—	Khmer Republic	440,541	—	—
Cook Islands	413	—	—	Kuwait	45,708	41,309	—
Costa Rica	135,609	—	—	Laos	53,260	—	225
Cuba	450,565	19,741	—	Lebanon	872,090	132,727	—
Cyprus	686,696	—	—	Lesotho	399,137	86,739	—
Czechoslovakia	3,497	—	—	Liberia	717,506	—	21,395
Dahomey	994,585	3,380	241,300	Libyan Arab Republic	76,166	2,679	—
Dominican Republic	814,269	—	1,507	Madagascar	1,924,074	2,208	70,276
East African Community	6,873	—	—	Malawi	625,194	22,961	—
Ecuador	318,433	—	37,852	Malaysia	1,420,853	—	32,403
Egypt	1,344,689	—	—	Maldives	29,431	—	—
El Salvador	326,524	8,535	—	Mali	213,863	—	3,432
Equatorial Guinea	35,584	—	—	Malta	51,010	—	—
				Mauritania	778,225	—	—

Country or territory	Total UNDP	Trust funds	Other aid programmes[a]	Country or territory	Total UNDP	Trust funds	Other aid programmes[a]
Mauritius	446,381	—	6,265	Sudan	994,582	—	5,130
Mexico	1,047,564	—	4,586	Surinam	129,649	11,529	—
Mongolia	349,506	—	—	Swaziland	74,720	29,362	—
Morocco	1,431,261	—	—	Syrian Arab Republic	917,776	—	—
Nepal	1,269,020	—	12,128	Thailand	1,501,482	—	4,415
Netherlands Antilles	9,181	—	—	Togo	803,647	—	21,786
Nicaragua	574,748	7,769	—	Tonga	20,709	—	—
Niger	607,444	—	2,127	Trinidad and Tobago	168,620	5,219	—
Nigeria	1,701,421	47,328	38,632	Tunisia	1,679,724	119,775	—
Niue	2,442	—	—	Turkey	2,034,451	34,395	—
Pakistan	1,512,754	5,010	59,516	Uganda	623,477	26,476	8,737
Panama	548,973	—	—	United Republic of Tanzania	1,269,751	22,726	62,830
Papua New Guinea	22,517	—	—	Upper Volta	443,876	—	3,597
Paraguay	298,791	—	—	Uruguay	179,089	—	—
Peru	1,635,193	990	6,960	Venezuela	810,972	—	—
People's Democratic Republic of Yemen	794,533	—	—	Western Samoa	502,727	—	910
Philippines	1,601,263	—	6,431	Yemen	1,217,163	—	1,564
Poland	594,235	—	—	Yugoslavia	749,348	—	—
Qatar	60,151	—	—	Zaire	616,439	25,115	5,527
Republic of Korea	1,772,474	41,157	2,569	Zambia	1,461,211	288,370	—
Republic of Viet-Nam	238,903	—	672,937	Regional: Africa	4,100,505	492,650	3,390
Romania	660,555	—	—	Regional: Asia and the Far East	554,480	18,680	15,439
Rwanda	133,986	—	—	Regional: Latin America	2,627,290	191,516	26,881
Saudi Arabia	540,094	497,234	—	Regional: Middle East and Europe	220,234	136,610	—
Senegal	482,585	—	949	Regional: Southwest Pacific	250,561	—	23,169
Sierra Leone	244,137	—	—	Inter-regional	620,819	—	—
Singapore	652,710	—	—				
Solomon Islands	2,138	—	—				
Somalia	936,026	—	1,122				
Spain	669,398	—	—				

[a]Freedom from Hunger Campaign.

Annex I. MEMBERSHIP OF THE FOOD AND AGRICULTURE ORGANIZATION AND CONTRIBUTIONS

(Membership as at 31 December 1971; contributions as assessed for 1972)

Member	Contribution Percentage	Net amount (in U.S. dollars)	Member	Contribution Percentage	Net amount (in U.S. dollars)	Member	Contribution Percentage	Net amount (in U.S. dollars)
Afghanistan	0.04	15,864	Colombia	0.24	95,184	Greece	0.36	142,776
Algeria	0.11	43,626	Congo	0.04	15,864	Guatemala	0.06	23,796
Argentina	1.06	420,396	Costa Rica	0.04	15,864	Guinea	0.04	15,864
Australia	1.84	729,744	Cuba	0.20	79,320	Guyana	0.04	15,864
Austria	0.69	273,654	Cyprus	0.04	15,864	Haiti	0.04	15,864
Bahrain*†	0.04	15,864	Czechoslovakia	1.13	448,158	Honduras	0.04	15,864
Barbados	0.04	15,864	Dahomey	0.04	15,864	Hungary	0.60	237,960
Belgium	1.31	519,546	Denmark	0.78	309,348	Iceland	0.04	15,864
Bolivia	0.04	15,864	Dominican Republic	0.04	15,864	India	1.94	769,404
Botswana	0.04	15,864	Ecuador	0.04	15,864	Indonesia	0.35	138,810
Brazil	1.00	396,600	Egypt	0.23	91,218	Iran	0.28	111,048
Bulgaria	0.23	91,218	El Salvador	0.04	15,864	Iraq	0.09	35,694
Burma	0.06	23,796	Ethiopia	0.04	15,864	Ireland	0.19	75,354
Burundi	0.04	15,864	Federal Republic of Germany‡	8.52	3,379,032	Israel	0.25	99,150
Cameroon	0.04	15,864	Fiji†	0.04	15,864	Italy	4.43	1,756,938
Canada	3.86	1,530,876	Finland	0.56	222,096	Ivory Coast	0.04	15,864
Central African Republic	0.04	15,864	France	7.51	2,978,466	Jamaica	0.04	15,864
Ceylon	0.06	23,796	Gabon	0.04	15,864	Japan	6.76	2,681,016
Chad	0.04	15,864	Gambia	0.04	15,864	Jordan	0.04	15,864
Chile	0.25	99,150	Ghana	0.09	35,694	Kenya	0.04	15,864
						Khmer Republic	0.04	15,864

Member	Contribution Percentage	Net amount (in U.S. dollars)	Member	Contribution Percentage	Net amount (in U.S. dollars)	Member	Contribution Percentage	Net amount (in U.S. dollars)
Kuwait	0.10	39,660	Norway	0.54	214,164	Swaziland†	0.04	15,864
Laos	0.04	15,864	Oman†	0.04	15,864	Sweden	1.57	622,662
Lebanon	0.06	23,796	Pakistan	0.43	170,538	Switzerland	1.05	416,430
Lesotho	0.04	15,864	Panama	0.04	15,864	Syrian Arab Republic	0.04	15,864
Liberia	0.04	15,864	Paraguay	0.04	15,864	Thailand	0.16	63,456
Libyan Arab Republic	0.09	35,694	People's Democratic Republic of Yemen	0.04	15,864	Togo	0.04	15,864
Luxembourg	0.06	23,796	Peru	0.12	47,592	Trinidad and Tobago	0.04	15,864
Madagascar	0.04	15,864	Philippines	0.39	154,674	Tunisia	0.04	15,864
Malawi	0.04	15,864	Poland	1.77	701,982	Turkey	0.44	174,504
Malaysia	0.12	47,592	Portugal	0.20	79,320	Uganda	0.04	15,864
Maldives†	0.04	15,864	Qatar*†	0.04	15,864	United Kingdom	7.39	2,930,874
Mali	0.04	15,864	Republic of Korea‡	0.14	55,524	United Republic of Tanzania	0.04	15,864
Malta	0.04	15,864	Republic of Viet-Nam‡	0.09	35,694	United States	31.52	12,650,832
Mauritania	0.04	15,864	Romania	0.45	178,470	Upper Volta	0.04	15,864
Mauritius	0.04	15,864	Rwanda	0.04	15,864	Uruguay	0.09	35,694
Mexico	1.10	436,260	Saudi Arabia	0.09	35,694	Venezuela	0.51	202,266
Morocco	0.11	43,626	Senegal	0.04	15,864	Yemen	0.04	15,864
Nepal	0.04	15,864	Sierra Leone	0.04	15,864	Yugoslavia	0.48	190,368
Netherlands	1.48	586,968	Somalia	0.04	15,864	Zaire	0.04	15,864
New Zealand	0.40	158,640	Spain	1.30	515,580	Zambia	0.04	15,864
Nicaragua	0.04	15,864	Sudan	0.04	15,864	Total		39,810,000
Niger	0.04	15,864						
Nigeria	0.15	59,490						

*Associate member in the 1970–1971 scale of contributions.
†Member admitted at sixteenth session of the FAO Governing Conference, November 1971.
‡Not Members of the United Nations. Their contributions are based on the percentage rates at which they contribute to certain United Nations activities.

Annex II. MEMBERS OF THE COUNCIL OF THE FOOD AND AGRICULTURE ORGANIZATION

Independent Chairman: Michel Cépedè

Holding office until 31 December 1972: Chile, Egypt, France, India, New Zealand, Norway, Pakistan, Saudi Arabia, United Kingdom, United Republic of Tanzania, Upper Volta

Holding office until conclusion of seventeenth session of the Governing Conference, November 1973: Argentina, Ceylon, Federal Republic of Germany, Indonesia, Italy, Japan, Peru, Philippines, Romania, Togo, Zaire

Holding office until 31 December 1974: Brazil, Canada, Colombia, Hungary, Iran, Kenya, Morocco, Sierra Leone, Switzerland, Syrian Arab Republic, Venezuela, United States

Annex III. OFFICERS AND OFFICES OF THE FOOD AND AGRICULTURE ORGANIZATION

OFFICERS

OFFICE OF THE DIRECTOR-GENERAL
Director-General: Addeke H. Boerma
Deputy Director-General: Roy I. Jackson
Co-ordinator, Freedom from Hunger Campaign/Action for Development: Hans A. H. Dall

DEPARTMENTS
Assistant Director-General, Economic and Social Department: E. M. Ojala
Assistant Director-General, Development Department: P. Terver
Assistant Director-General, Agriculture Department: O. E. Fischnich
Assistant Director-General, Fisheries Department: F. E. Popper
Assistant Director-General, Administration and Finance Department: C. F. Pennison
Director, Office of General Affairs and Information: C. W. Broicher

REGIONAL REPRESENTATIVES OF THE DIRECTOR-GENERAL
Regional Representative of FAO for Africa: M. C. Mensah
Regional Representative of FAO for Asia and the Far East: Dioscoro L. Umali
Assistant Director-General for Near Eastern Affairs and Regional Representative for the Near East: M. A. Nour
Assistant Director-General for Latin American Affairs and Regional Representative for Latin America: Juan Felipe Yriart
Director, Liaison Office for North America: Howard R. Cottam
Director, Liaison Office with the United Nations: Charles H. Weitz

HEADQUARTERS AND REGIONAL OFFICES

HEADQUARTERS
Food and Agriculture Organization
Viale delle Terme di Caracalla
Rome, Italy
  Cable Address:
    FOODAGRI ROME

REGIONAL AND OTHER OFFICES
Food and Agriculture Organization Regional Office
for Asia and the Far East
Maliwan Mansion
Phra Atit Road
Bangkok 2, Thailand

Food and Agriculture Organization Regional Office
for Africa
United Nations Agency Building
North Maxwell Road
P.O. Box 1628
Accra, Ghana

Food and Agriculture Organization Liaison Office
for North America
1325 C Street, S.W.
Washington, D.C. 20437, U.S.A.

Food and Agriculture Organization Regional
  Office for Latin America
Oficina Regional de la FAO
Casilla 10095
Santiago, Chile

Food and Agriculture Organization Regional
  Office for the Near East
Box 2223, Agricultural Co-operative Bank
  Building
Sharia Sheikh El Rihan Street, Garden City
Cairo, Egypt

Food and Agriculture Organization Liaison
  Office with the United Nations
United Nations Headquarters, Room 2258
New York, N.Y. 10017, U.S.A.

Chapter IV

The United Nations Educational, Scientific and Cultural Organization (UNESCO)

The United Nations Educational, Scientific and Cultural Organization (UNESCO)[1] celebrated its twenty-fifth anniversary during 1971. The occasion was marked by ceremonies at the organization's headquarters in Paris, France, which were attended by the President of France and representatives of other heads of State.

During the year, UNESCO continued to promote international co-operation in the fields of education, science, culture and communication, with a particular view to the social development of peoples in the developing countries.

Membership of the organization stood at 125 full members and three associate members as at the end of 1971.

In a letter to the Director-General of UNESCO, dated 18 June 1971, the Portuguese Minister of Foreign Affairs announced that Portugal was withdrawing from UNESCO. In conformity with article II of the UNESCO Constitution, the withdrawal was to take effect as of 31 December in the year following that in which the notice was given.

On 29 October 1971, the Executive Board of UNESCO, by a vote of 25 to 2, with 5 abstentions, adopted a resolution whereby it decided that "from today onwards, the Government of the People's Republic of China is the only legitimate representative of China at UNESCO." (For further details, see also pp. 133, 134.)

Education

The purpose of UNESCO's activities in education was to aid in the transformation of the education needed to accelerate development in member States, education being recognized both as a human right and as an indispensable factor in the development of human resources.

The International Commission on the Development of Education was established during 1971 to assist Governments in working out national strategies for education. The Commission was under the chairmanship of Edgar Faure, former Premier and Minister of Education of France.

In 1971, for the first time, the rate of increase of school enrolments outstripped the rate of population increase. However, the enrolment increase was chiefly in primary schools, secondary schools not expanding fast enough to absorb their output. The efforts of UNESCO were therefore increasingly concentrated on the secondary school level, as well as on bringing about qualitative improvements in education.

In the academic year 1970-1971, some 257,000 Palestine refugee children were enrolled in the schools run jointly by UNESCO and the United Nations Relief and Works Agency for Palestine Refugees in the Near East (UNRWA); an additional 2,600 students were attending the jointly operated vocational centres and 1,600 were in teacher-training colleges. (For further details, see page 198.) African refugees, notably in Guinea, the United Republic of Tanzania and Zambia, were also aided. Plans for a $350,000 educational programme, chiefly in teacher training, were drawn up for consideration by the United Nations Development Programme (UNDP).

Teacher training was the focal point of UNESCO activities in secondary education. By 1971, 23 advanced teacher-training institutes in Africa alone had been created by UNESCO, with UNDP co-operation, and were turning out 4,000 qualified teachers a year. At the primary level, 84 projects were being carried out in collaboration with the United Nations Children's Fund (UNICEF); the emphasis was on rural schools. Other teacher-training projects aided by UNESCO included those in Afghanistan, Guatemala, Papua New Guinea, Saudi Arabia and Singapore.

In encouraging the adaptation of curricula to local needs and cultures, UNESCO gave support to educational research centres in Fiji, Iraq, the Ivory Coast, Madagascar and Spain.

[1]For further information on UNESCO's activities prior to 1971, see reports of UNESCO to the United Nations, reports of Director-General of UNESCO to General Conference, and previous volumes of Y.U.N.

New teaching techniques, including the use of audio-visual methods—films, radio, television and programmed instruction—were needed to solve the problems brought by educational expansion and to make the best use of schools and teachers. Expert assistance in this field was given by UNESCO to a number of member States during 1971. Co-operation was continued with the International Centre for Advanced Technical and Vocational Training in Turin, Italy, and technical and financial aid was given to the Latin American Institute for Educational Communications in Mexico City, Mexico. Projects for the development of educational radio and television in India and Tunisia were also aided.

To help meet the need for educational planning, as an integral part of over-all development planning, UNESCO created the International Institute for Educational Planning in Paris and assisted institutes in Beirut, Lebanon; Dakar, Senegal; New Delhi, India; and Santiago, Chile. This programme, carried out in co-operation with the International Bank for Reconstruction and Development and the International Development Association, involved the equivalent of some $200 million in aid.

By 1971, UNESCO had sent experts to 50 States to advise on functional literacy work and was carrying out projects in 12 countries under the Experimental World Literacy Programme.

Work continued on UNESCO's programme of youth activities. During the year, UNESCO completed a study of legislation on the rights and responsibilities of young people in 46 countries. The organization also collaborated with the International Council of Sport and Physical Education, the International Council on Health, Physical Education and Recreation and the International Federation of Sportive Medicine with the aim of promoting the concept of "sports for all."

Twenty-seven projects in the field of education for the handicapped were assisted by UNESCO during 1971; most of these were for the training of teachers of the physically handicapped and mentally retarded.

The organization participated in comprehensive reviews of family planning in Ceylon and Iran and sent consultative missions to nine other member States.

In collaboration with the United Nations Fund for Drug Abuse Control, UNESCO explored the possibilities for pilot projects in 22 countries to promote education, public information and research on national efforts to prevent drug abuse.

Natural sciences

The UNESCO programme in the natural sciences continued to try to meet the needs of both developed and developing member States and to keep pace with the principal trends of scientific activities.

One of UNESCO's main objectives—the furtherance of international scientific co-operation—is carried out mainly through Conferences of Ministers. A Latin American Conference of Ministers of Education and Science was held in Caracas, Venezuela, in December 1971.

Throughout 1971, contact was maintained with international scientific organizations, chiefly through the International Council of Scientific Unions and its individual member bodies, with particular reference to environmental and geological correlation programmes.

Also in 1971, member States approved the creation of a World Science Information System. It was expected that the system would be of significance for the developing member States, since access to scientific knowledge was one of the greatest obstacles to their development.

The International Centre for Theoretical Physics in Trieste, the Latin American Centre for Physics, and the Latin American Centre for Chemistry continued to receive assistance. Several meetings were held during the year to discuss the centres' status and financing, with special regard to the Trieste Centre and its future role in the fields of mathematics and physics.

Assistance was continued in the development of the life sciences and computer technology, through exchanges of information with and support for the International Brain Research Organization, the International Cell Research Organization and the International Computation Centre. Training courses in the life sciences were also conducted.

The inter-disciplinary research programme "Man and the Biosphere" continued in 1971. The programme's International Co-ordinating Council, meeting in November, decided that research should focus on the study of the structure and functioning of the biosphere and its ecological regions. The Council also agreed that there should be systematic observation research on the changes brought about by man in the biosphere and its resources, as well as on the effects of these changes upon the human species.

Preparations began in 1971 for the International Geological Correlation Programme. An international conference was held to devise plans for a programme of studies leading to better understanding of the geology of the earth and its mineral resources.

The International Hydrological Decade continued to be the basis of UNESCO's activities in hydrology.

The exploration and exploitation of the resources of the oceans acquired increasing urgency. In its marine sciences programme, UNESCO continued to promote physical, chemical, biological and geological studies in oceanography and to support the Intergovernmental Oceanographic Commission, which co-ordinated and facilitated scientific investigations of the oceans.

Culture

Following the 1970 Venice, Italy, conference on cultural development, UNESCO made preparations for a European conference on cultural policies to be held in Helsinki, Finland, in June 1972.

A meeting of experts was held in Amsterdam, the Netherlands, on the training of arts administrators and cultural activities organizers in Europe, and a clearing house for cultural development was established to help meet the needs of member States.

The operation to rescue the Philae monuments in Nubia, Egypt, moved into the active stage in June 1971 with the signing of a contract between Egyptian authorities and the firms carrying out the dismantling of the monuments, which were to be re-erected on nearby Agilkia Island. Work on reconstructing the monuments was to begin early in 1972. The four-year operation was scheduled to cost $13 million, of which the Egyptian Government was to provide one third.

The organization continued to co-operate with the Italian Government in the protection of Venice, the presentation of its treasures and the stimulation of its cultural life. Preparatory work for the restoration of Borobudur in Indonesia was also continued.

In the Middle East and the Khmer Republic, UNESCO continued the implementation of the Hague Convention on the Protection of Cultural Property in the Event of Armed Conflict. A preliminary draft recommendation and a draft convention were prepared on the protection of monuments, buildings and sites.

Forty-five works, chiefly in English and French, in the UNESCO series of translations of classical and contemporary authors were published during 1971. Five new sets of colour transparencies of works of art appeared, and the tenth travelling exhibition of reproductions, this one devoted to African arts, was prepared.

Studies of the Malay and Oceanic cultures were initiated during 1971.

The international scientific committee for the preparation of the *General History of Africa* held its first session in March-April 1971, to draw up the synopsis of the proposed eight-volume work; a detailed table of contents for the first three volumes was established in November.

A regional expert meeting was held in Dar es Salaam, United Republic of Tanzania, in December, on the promotion of African languages in Central and East Africa.

A symposium on "Culture and Science," held in Paris in September, was attended by some 20 participants and 13 observers. In observance of the International Year against Racism, a series of public lectures on "Race in Modern Society" was held in Paris in March. In Dar es Salaam, an international meeting of experts discussed the influence of colonialism on the artist.

Studies of problems arising from population increases and connected with development continued during the year.

A regional meeting of specialists was held in Singapore to discuss comparative models of national development. An international expert meeting on university teaching and research on problems of peace and conflict resolution, held in Manila, the Philippines, led to a set of guidelines for new teaching programmes on these problems. A regional meeting on the teaching of international law in Africa was held in Lagos, Nigeria.

Communication

The year 1971 was marked by increased technical assistance to member States for communication programmes: the assistance, totalling $2 million, as compared with $400,000 the previous year, indicated the increasing importance attached by States to this field. Emphasis was laid on developing a more scientific approach to the problems of instruction in the techniques and administration of the mass media. The first steps were taken to set up national radio and television production centres and regional centres for the development of communication.

A project was begun at Poona, India, to train 200 television specialists a year to meet the country's expanding needs in television and to provide a staff for the educational television satellite scheme, due to start in 1974. Experts began work at the Malaysian radio and television training centre, which was to be developed into a regional centre. Efforts were made towards the creation of a rural press to support development in French-speaking countries in Africa.

Among publications in the communications field during 1971 were *Radio and Television in Literacy, The Mass Media in a Violent World* and *The Role of Film in Development*.

Missions were sent to Afghanistan, the Dominican Republic, India, Indonesia, Iran, Japan, Nepal, the Philippines, the Republic of Korea and Thailand to identify communication needs for family planning programmes.

A major initiative during the year was the preparation of a preliminary draft of a declaration of principles on the use of space broadcasting. A major feasibility study on the regional use of a satellite in South America was carried out with the assistance of UNDP.

Missions were sent to East and West Africa to study ways of setting up African regional book-development centres, along the lines of those already established in Asia and Latin America. The regional centre in Karachi, Pakistan, continued to organize national courses in book production and staged a training course in Kuala Lumpur, Malaysia, for participants from 15 countries.

In preparation for International Book Year (1972), a draft "charter of the book," setting out principles to guide the treatment of the book at the national and international levels, was prepared and approved by international non-governmental organizations.

Work on documentation, libraries and archives included the initiation of a pilot project in mechanization of documentation services in Argentina and pre-project activities for the National Documentation Centre in Morocco, UNESCO's first UNDP Special Fund project in this field.

The Computerized Documentation Service was established at UNESCO headquarters, and work was begun on processing the organization's documents. Short-term training courses and seminars were organized in Europe, Africa and Latin America. A library school for the Caribbean was created in Jamaica, and an archivists' training section was established at the University of Dakar.

Secretariat

As at 31 December 1971, the total number of full-time staff employed by UNESCO on permanent, fixed-term and short-term appointments stood at 3,491. Of these, 1,814 were in the professional or higher categories (drawn from 107 nationalities), and 1,677 were in the general service and maintenance worker categories.

Of the professional staff, 1,049 were experts serving in the field; 410 of the general service and maintenance categories were also employed in the field.

Budget

The sixteenth General Conference of UNESCO, meeting in November 1970, had approved a budget of $89,898,560 for the two-year period 1971-1972. A further $69,422,000 was expected to come from UNDP for the organization's operational programmes.

Table I. Projects approved for 1971-1972 under participation programme of UNESCO

(By region and main field of aid)

Sector	Africa	Asia	Arab States	Europe	Latin America	Others	Total
Education	24	22	13	46	17	9	131
Natural Sciences	26	9	6	15	14	7	77
Social sciences, human sciences and culture	73	58	24	101	51	15	322
Communication	36	25	16	20	17	2	116
National commissions	41	26	23	36	19	2	147
Total	200	140	82	218	118	35	793

Table II. Assistance approved in 1971-1972 under the participation programme of UNESCO by country and main field of aid

(in U.S. dollars)

Country	Education	Natural sciences	Social sciences, human sciences and culture	Communication	National commissions	Total
Afghanistan	10,150	6,400	14,700	3,700	4,000	38,950
Albania	—	—	4,000	3,000	4,200	11,200
Argentina	8,500	6,000	21,000	5,000	1,000	41,500
Australia	7,250	2,000	18,700	—	—	27,950
Austria	6,000	—	20,500	3,000	—	29,500
Barbados	—	—	—	5,000	—	5,000
Bahrain	2,000	—	4,000	—	—	6,000
Belgium	4,500	—	23,500	3,000	—	31,000
Bolivia	3,000	1,350	6,300	—	1,420	12,070
Brazil	6,000	4,000	31,850	8,000	5,000	54,850
Bulgaria	—	8,000	5,350	—	8,200	21,550
Burma	—	—	4,000	—	—	4,000
Burundi	2,830	—	4,200	3,200	780	11,010

Country	Education	Natural sciences	Sector Social sciences, human sciences and culture	Commu- nication	National commissions	Total
Byelorussian SSR	3,700	—	7,600	1,400	9,000	21,700
Cameroon	9,350	—	8,400	10,000	1,000	28,750
Canada	4,000	7,500	17,500	—	3,000	32,000
Central African Republic	—	—	21,500	—	1,500	23,000
Ceylon	5,000	2,000	9,700	6,000	1,850	24,550
Chad	4,000	—	10,500	4,000	—	18,500
Chile	4,000	—	19,980	—	—	23,980
Colombia	500	3,700	18,000	2,000	—	24,200
Congo	6,950	3,800	8,650	9,700	3,850	32,950
Costa Rica	—	3,450	11,891	5,000	1,500	21,841
Cuba	21,000	17,100	5,000	17,100	5,000	65,200
Cyprus	3,200	—	13,000	—	1,500	17,700
Czechoslovakia	12,500	—	12,000	—	2,000	26,500
Dahomey	4,100	4,400	18,200	—	3,600	30,300
Denmark	11,700	—	9,000	—	—	20,700
Dominican Republic	3,700	—	6,000	—	1,000	10,700
Ecuador	2,000	—	2,000	—	—	4,000
Egypt	28,000	3,000	12,000	9,800	12,350	65,150
El Salvador	—	—	4,000	4,000	4,700	12,700
Ethiopia	3,700	3,700	23,200	11,750	3,260	45,610
Federal Republic of Germany	11,000	—	4,500	3,000	10,000	28,500
Finland	—	—	11,500	—	—	11,500
France	17,600	—	18,200	2,700	—	38,500
Gabon	4,000	—	4,200	3,000	5,050	16,250
Ghana	5,050	5,000	9,200	25,500	7,130	51,880
Greece	—	—	7,500	—	4,000	11,500
Guinea	6,700	—	2,200	—	—	8,900
Guyana	—	—	10,000	—	—	10,000
Haiti	—	—	5,000	—	—	5,000
Honduras	4,200	—	4,000	9,700	2,000	19,900
Hungary	7,100	2,350	16,250	8,700	3,700	38,100
Iceland	10,400	10,000	5,000	1,700	—	27,100
India	14,000	—	50,250	13,900	8,500	86,650
Indonesia	12,000	4,000	28,000	—	3,000	47,000
Iran	6,000	6,350	19,700	5,800	4,200	42,050
Iraq	—	3,500	3,700	16,000	2,820	26,020
Ireland	—	—	11,500	—	—	11,500
Israel	5,150	10,800	5,550	1,400	3,000	25,900
Italy	3,000	—	8,000	3,800	4,200	19,000
Ivory Coast	—	—	10,200	4,000	4,080	18,280
Jamaica	—	3,000	11,500	4,000	—	18,500
Japan	3,024	—	17,900	1,500	5,000	27,424
Jordan	—	—	7,000	3,200	1,500	11,700
Kenya	8,000	6,050	—	—	1,780	15,830
Khmer Republic	—	—	—	—	800	·800
Kuwait	8,000	—	2,000	—	1,000	11,000
Lebanon	3,200	—	3,000	—	—	6,200
Lesotho	—	3,000	—	—	1,500	4,500
Liberia	11,050	—	4,800	10,050	1,400	27,300
Libya	—	—	2,000	—	—	2,000
Madagascar	4,000	4,000	14,600	—	1,100	23,700
Malawi	—	—	9,050	5,000	—	14,050
Malaysia	4,100	—	3,000	22,950	1,500	31,550
Mali	2,000	3,400	15,000	7,700	1,320	29,420
Malta	3,350	—	4,400	—	2,500	10,250
Mauritania	—	—	—	3,000	—	3,000
Mauritius	8,000	6,000	—	5,050	1,900	20,950
Mexico	—	—	15,400	—	4,500	19,900
Mongolia	—	—	16,600	—	2,750	19,350
Morocco	—	—	4,600	—	2,420	7,020
Nepal	6,000	3,700	34,300	3,700	7,350	55,050

Country	Education	Natural sciences	Sector Social sciences, human sciences and culture	Communication	National commissions	Total
Netherlands Antilles	—	—	—	2,350	—	2,350
New Zealand	7,000	10,000	2,000	—	—	19,000
Nicaragua	1,500	—	—	1,500	—	3,000
Niger	—	—	27,900	—	3,000	30,900
Nigeria	3,000	9,500	53,800	7,000	2,500	75,800
Norway	1,400	—	11,500	—	—	12,900
Pakistan	—	—	12,800	6,000	600	19,400
Panama	—	5,050	21,150	—	—	26,200
Paraguay	—	—	10,000	—	1,980	11,980
People's Democratic Republic of Yemen	6,000	—	4,300	5,700	—	16,000
Peru	—	—	15,100	—	3,000	18,100
Philippines	3,850	3,800	13,800	2,800	3,500	27,750
Poland	10,000	—	17,000	5,300	2,500	34,800
Qatar	—	—	—	2,000	—	2,000
Republic of Korea	10,000	—	15,700	—	4,000	29,700
Republic of Viet-Nam	3,000	—	16,300	—	1,850	21,150
Romania	—	—	20,200	2,300	6,200	28,700
Rwanda	—	—	4,000	—	—	4,000
Saudi Arabia	2,350	—	—	—	—	2,350
Senegal	—	3,000	23,450	21,200	6,125	53,775
Sierra Leone	—	2,500	2,000	7,000	—	11,500
Singapore	—	—	7,700	6,100	—	13,800
Somalia	16,050	—	4,500	4,000	—	24,550
Spain	3,500	—	8,200	—	1,000	12,700
Sudan	4,000	7,250	14,800	17,800	5,000	48,850
Sweden	9,000	—	2,000	—	—	11,000
Switzerland	5,700	4,000	11,500	—	—	21,200
Syrian Arab Republic	5,700	1,000	12,950	3,000	5,000	27,650
Thailand	9,900	9,300	17,150	9,750	8,000	54,100
Togo	—	—	10,500	—	6,820	17,320
Trinidad and Tobago	—	6,350	4,500	8,700	1,500	21,050
Tunisia	4,700	—	22,000	4,000	—	30,700
Turkey	6,000	2,000	3,400	2,300	—	13,700
Uganda	5,000	8,000	4,200	—	2,500	19,700
Ukrainian SSR	3,700	11,100	7,000	—	10,050	31,850
United Kingdom	6,300	—	17,500	—	—	23,800
Upper Volta	4,000	—	8,400	4,000	2,000	18,400
Uruguay	6,000	12,000	3,000	—	—	21,000
United Republic of Tanzania	4,000	8,000	14,700	—	4,500	31,200
United States	20,000	—	3,614	10,000	—	33,614
USSR	19,800	11,100	17,400	9,000	—	57,300
Venezuela	—	—	12,000	2,100	1,000	15,100
Yemen	10,000	—	7,700	2,000	—	19,700
Yugoslavia	8,000	—	22,400	9,000	2,000	41,400
Zaire	10,350	—	15,900	3,000	2,500	31,750
Zambia	—	14,200	—	—	6,560	20,760

Annex I. MEMBERSHIP OF THE UNITED NATIONS EDUCATIONAL, SCIENTIFIC AND CULTURAL ORGANIZATION AND CONTRIBUTIONS

(Membership as at 31 December 1971; contributions as assessed for 1972)*

Member	Contribution Percentage	Amount (in U.S. dollars)	Member	Contribution Percentage	Amount (in U.S. dollars)	Member	Contribution Percentage	Amount (in U.S. dollars)
Afghanistan	0.04	16,260	Argentina	0.80	325,200	Barbados	0.04	16,260
Albania	0.04	16,260	Australia	1.39	565,035	Belgium	0.99	402,435
Algeria	0.08	32,520	Austria	0.52	211,380	Bolivia	0.04	16,260

Member	Contribution Percentage	Amount (in U.S. dollars)	Member	Contribution Percentage	Amount (in U.S. dollars)	Member	Contribution Percentage	Amount (in U.S. dollars)
Brazil	0.75	304,875	Ireland	0.14	56,910	Republic of Korea	0.10	40,650
Bulgaria	0.17	69,105	Israel	0.19	77,235	Republic of Viet-Nam	0.06	24,390
Burma	0.05	20,325	Italy	3.35	1,361,775	Romania	0.34	138,210
Burundi	0.04	16,260	Ivory Coast	0.04	16,260	Rwanda	0.04	16,260
Byelorussian SSR	0.47	191,055	Jamaica	0.04	16,260	Saudi Arabia	0.06	24,390
Cameroon	0.04	16,260	Japan	5.10	2,073,150	Senegal	0.04	16,260
Canada	2.91	1,182,915	Jordan	0.04	16,260	Sierra Leone	0.04	16,260
Central African Republic	0.04	16,260	Kenya	0.04	16,260	Singapore	0.05	20,325
Ceylon	0.05	20,325	Khmer Republic	0.04	16,260	Somalia	0.04	16,260
Chad	0.04	16,260	Kuwait	0.07	28,455	Spain	0.98	398,370
Chile	0.19	77,235	Laos	0.04	16,260	Sudan	0.04	16,260
China	2.50	1,016,250	Lebanon	0.05	20,325	Sweden	1.18	479,670
Colombia	0.18	73,170	Lesotho	0.04	16,260	Switzerland	0.79	321,135
Congo	0.04	16,260	Liberia	0.04	16,260	Syrian Arab Republic	0.04	16,260
Costa Rica	0.04	16,260	Libyan Arab Republic	0.06	24,390	Thailand	0.12	48,780
Cuba	0.15	60,975	Luxembourg	0.05	20,325	Togo	0.04	16,260
Cyprus	0.04	16,260	Madagascar	0.04	16,260	Trinidad and Tobago	0.04	16,260
Czechoslovakia	0.85	345,525	Malawi	0.04	16,260	Tunisia	0.04	16,260
Dahomey	0.04	16,260	Malaysia	0.09	36,585	Turkey	0.33	134,145
Denmark	0.58	235,770	Mali	0.04	16,260	Uganda	0.04	16,260
Dominican Republic	0.04	16,260	Malta	0.04	16,260	Ukrainian SSR	1.77	719,505
Ecuador	0.04	16,260	Mauritania	0.04	16,260	USSR	13.41	5,451,165
Egypt	0.17	69,105	Mauritius	0.04	16,260	United Kingdom	5.58	2,268,270
El Salvador	0.04	16,260	Mexico	0.83	337,395	United Republic of Tanzania	0.04	16,260
Ethiopia	0.04	16,260	Monaco	0.04	16,260	United States	29.80	12,113,700
Federal Republic of Germany	6.43	2,613,795	Mongolia	0.04	16,260	Upper Volta	0.04	16,260
Finland	0.42	170,730	Morocco	0.08	32,520	Uruguay	0.06	24,390
France	5.67	2,304,855	Nepal	0.04	16,260	Venezuela	0.39	158,535
Gabon	0.04	16,260	Netherlands	1.11	451,215	Yemen	0.04	16,260
Ghana	0.06	24,390	New Zealand	0.30	121,950	Yugoslavia	0.36	146,340
Greece	0.27	109,755	Nicaragua	0.04	16,260	Zaire	0.04	16,260
Guatemala	0.05	20,325	Niger	0.04	16,260	Zambia	0.04	16,260
Guinea	0.04	16,260	Nigeria	0.11	44,715	Total		40,650,000
Guyana	0.04	16,260	Norway	0.41	166,665			
Haiti	0.04	16,260	Pakistan	0.32	130,080			
Honduras	0.04	16,260	Panama	0.04	16,260			
Hungary	0.45	182,925	Paraguay	0.04	16,260	**Associate Member**		
Iceland	0.04	16,260	People's Democratic Republic of Yemen	0.04	16,260	Bahrain	0.02	8,130
India	1.46	593,490	Peru	0.09	36,585	British Eastern Caribbean Group	0.02	8,130
Indonesia	0.26	105,690	Philippines	0.29	117,885	Qatar	0.02	8,130
Iran	0.21	85,365	Poland	1.33	540.645	Total		24,390
Iraq	0.06	24,390	Portugal	0.15	60,975			

*Contributions as set at the sixteenth session of the UNESCO General Conference, held in November 1970.

Annex II. OFFICERS AND OFFICES OF THE UNITED NATIONS EDUCATIONAL, SCIENTIFIC AND CULTURAL ORGANIZATION

(As at 31 December 1971)

MEMBERS OF EXECUTIVE BOARD

Chairman: Prem Kirpal (India)
Vice-Chairmen: Bernard Dadie (Ivory Coast), Bernard de Hoog (Netherlands), Enrique Macaya-Lahmann (Costa Rica), Fuad Sarruf (Lebanon)

Members: Afghanistan, Algeria, Brazil, Canada, Ceylon, Colombia, Congo, Costa Rica, Czechoslovakia, Egypt, Ethiopia, Federal Republic of Germany, Finland, France, Ghana, Hungary, India, Ivory Coast, Jamaica, Japan, Lebanon, Mexico, Netherlands, Pakistan, Peru, Senegal, Spain, Switzerland, USSR, United Kingdom, United Republic of Tanzania, United States, Zaire, Zambia

PRINCIPAL OFFICERS OF THE SECRETARIAT

Director-General: René Maheu (France)
Deputy Director-General: John Fobes (United States)
Assistant Directors-General: Adriano Buzzati-Traverso (Italy), Vladimir Erofeev (USSR), Richard Hoggart (United Kingdom), Amadou Mahtar M'Bow (Senegal), Alberto Obligado (Argentina)

HEADQUARTERS AND OTHER OFFICES

HEADQUARTERS
UNESCO House
Place de Fontenoy
Paris 7e, France
    Cable Address: UNESCO PARIS

NEW YORK OFFICE
United Nations Educational, Scientific and Cultural Organization
United Nations Headquarters, Room 2201
New York, N.Y. 10017, U.S.A.
    Cable Address: UNESCORG NEWYORK

Chapter V

The World Health Organization (WHO)

The World Health Organization (WHO)[1] continued in 1971 to assist Governments in improving the health of their people, to provide a number of world-wide technical services and to promote international medical research.

In 1971, WHO had 131 member States: Gambia joined on 26 April, Oman on 28 May and Bahrain on 2 November.

On 11 November 1971, the Director-General of WHO informed all members of the organization by letter of the decision taken by the General Assembly on 25 October 1971 concerning the representation of China (by which the Assembly decided to restore all rights to the People's Republic of China and to recognize the representatives of its Government as the only legitimate representatives of China to the United Nations and to expel forthwith the representatives of Chiang Kai-shek from the place they unlawfully occupied at the United Nations and in all the organizations related to it.

In consequence of the Assembly's decision, that question would be proposed for inclusion in the provisional agenda of the twenty-fifth World Health Assembly (scheduled to open on 9 May 1972) and would be included in the agenda of the forty-ninth session of the Executive Board scheduled to open on 18 January 1972. (For further information, see pp. 133, 134.)

Official relations with seven additional non-governmental organizations were established in 1971 by the Executive Board, bringing to 92 the number of organizations having this status with WHO. The seven were: World Federation of Public Health Associations, International Standardization Organization, International Association of Medical Laboratory Technologists, International League against Epilepsy, International Association of Agricultural Medicine, International Solid Wastes and Public Cleansing Association, International Federation of Pharmaceutical Manufacturers Associations.

The twenty-fourth World Health Assembly, which met from 4 to 20 May 1971 in Geneva, Switzerland, adopted an effective working budget of $82 million for 1972.

In view of the continued spread of the seventh pandemic of cholera, the Assembly warned that this disease was a long-term socio-economic problem as well as a public health problem, and that the only possibility of making countries free of cholera was to improve water supplies, sanitation and personal hygiene.

During the session, the World Health Assembly also endorsed a long-term programme on the human environment and adopted the Fifth General Programme of Work for the organization, covering the period 1973-1977. This took into account changes of priorities in national and international health problems, and the new trends in WHO's work that had emerged in recent years—the strengthening of national health services, the development of health manpower, disease prevention and control, and environmental health.

Disease prevention

Cholera

In 1971, cholera was once again one of the dominant public health problems of the world. A major outbreak occurred in West Bengal, India, among refugees from East Pakistan. In addition to isolated and imported cases in a number of countries, 13 reported cholera for the first time. There were outbreaks in 39 countries during the year.

The number of cases reported to WHO was the highest since 1953: the world total on 10 December 1971 stood at 148,775 cases and 22,256 deaths since the beginning of the year, as against some 46,500 cases for the same period in 1970.

There was a sixfold increase in cases reported by African countries while the 1970 figures were doubled in Asian countries, Indonesia reporting

---

[1]For further information on WHO's activities prior to 1971, see *Official Records of the World Health Organization* and previous volumes of Y.U.N.

approximately 19,000 cases and India about 60,000, of which some 49,000 (with about 6,000 deaths) were in West Bengal refugee camps.

Assistance was provided by WHO in the form of equipment, expert advice and staff training. Intravenous rehydration fluid, antibiotics, vaccine, vaccination equipment, laboratory and diagnostic requirements were supplied to Governments. Several countries undertook production of rehydration fluid and cholera vaccine with WHO assistance.

Malaria

A review of malaria eradication programmes indicated that the number of persons freed from the risk of endemic malaria rose from 392 million in 1961 to 1,048 million in 1971. Over-all changes in the world malaria situation since 1970 were few, technical problems and serious operational difficulties having slowed down progress.

Of the estimated 1,844 million people living in the originally malarious areas of the world, 1,372 million had benefited from malaria eradication or from eradication programmes under way by September 1971. Eradication had not started in areas inhabited by 472 million people. Nevertheless, of these, 35 million were covered by control measures, while a further 161 million were being supplied with anti-malaria drugs by their Governments.

During 1971, research was continued on the biology of the malaria parasite, the epidemiology of malaria, the resistance of the parasite and the mosquito vector to drugs and the methodology of malaria eradication.

Smallpox

During 1971, the fifth year of the intensified programme of smallpox eradication, the area in which smallpox was known to be endemic decreased considerably. Brazil, most of Indonesia, and Zaire were thought to have been freed of the disease by the end of the year. The remaining endemic countries appeared to be Afghanistan, Ethiopia, India, Nepal, Pakistan and Sudan. Eradication programmes were in progress in each of them.

The annual total number of cases reported to WHO showed an increase for the first time since 1967, rising from a little more than 30,000 in 1970 to some 45,000 in 1971. This was principally due to the more complete reporting from Ethiopia as a consequence of the inception of an eradication programme there. Around 25,000 cases, or more than half the world total, were reported as having occurred in that country in 1971, compared to 722 cases reported in 1970. In the rest of the world, the smallpox incidence declined by more than 35 per cent, the fourth successive year in which a

decrease of this order of magnitude was observed.

Environmental health

A long-term programme on the human environment was approved by the twenty-fourth World Health Assembly with the following aims: to improve basic health and sanitation in all countries, especially developing countries; to enlarge knowledge of the adverse effect on health of pollutants; to stimulate the development of monitoring systems; to determine as rapidly as possible the permissible levels of pollutants and other adverse environmental influences; and to extend knowledge of factors affecting the environment by disseminating information, by research and by the training of personnel.

Family health

In 1970, WHO instituted a programme to focus attention on the health problems of the family as a whole and not merely on the needs of its individual members. In 1971, this aim was broadened to include nutrition, since the nutritional status of mothers and children, along with early control of infections and optimum management of pregnancies, was considered a priority requirement for the health of the whole family.

A significant development in the field of family health was the establishment of an expanded programme of research development and research training in human reproduction. It was increasingly recognized that the solution to many current problems lay in the better understanding of human reproductive processes and the development of safe, acceptable and effective methods of fertility regulation. This included the working out of a long-term research strategy on a world-wide basis.

Pledges amounting to $4.8 million were made to finance the expanded programme by the Governments of Denmark, Norway and Sweden; the International Development Research Centre; and the Ford Foundation.

The United Nations Fund for Population Activities continued to provide financial assistance for research and training. Advisory services continued to be made available to countries for the planning, implementation and evaluation of family planning services under WHO's regular programme.

In maternal and child health, WHO assisted 15 integrated family health projects in Africa that included nutrition, communicable disease control, and education and training. It also helped a variety of maternal and child-health, school-health and family-welfare projects in eight countries of the western Pacific, and 27 projects related to maternal and child health in South-East Asia.

A study made of pre-school children in 24

developing countries showed that between 4 and 44 per cent of children under five years suffered from protein-calorie malnutrition. A travelling seminar on protein problems, with particular reference to weaning foods, was held in September; it was jointly sponsored by the Food and Agriculture Organization (FAO) of the United Nations and WHO. The place of protein-rich mixtures in the prevention of protein-calorie nutrition, their formulation and testing, marketing and quality control were considered. Tests were carried out on new processed weaning foods in WHO centres in five countries.

Pharmacology and toxicology

A revised version of the *International Pharmacopoeia* was recommended by the WHO Expert Committee on Specifications for Pharmaceutical Preparations, meeting in April–May 1971, in view of the fact that recent advances and new concepts in pharmaceutical science had made it possible to ensure a greater measure of control over the quality of pharmaceutical preparations.

Incomplete knowledge of the type, frequency and severity of adverse reactions to drugs remained a major weakness of modern pharmacology. During 1971, WHO continued to advise and support national drug monitoring centres. Also during the year, the WHO project for international drug monitoring, initiated in 1968, entered its primary operational phase, with the active participation of national monitoring centres in 12 member States. By October, the files of the project contained almost 27,500 reports of suspected adverse reactions to more than 1,900 different drugs.

The self-administration of narcotic and non-narcotic dependence-producing drugs was rapidly becoming a major world health problem. Multiple drug use appeared to be on the increase. The twenty-fourth World Health Assembly approved an expansion of the organization's programme in this field and recommended that Governments be assisted in developing procedures for the co-ordination of their national programmes.

Education and training

The steadily increasing needs of member States for assistance in educating staff for health services were reflected in the award of a wide variety of fellowships in 1971, mainly for postgraduate studies. During the year, 5,774 individuals received assistance to travel for educational purposes: of these, 3,317 received fellowships, including 214 for undergraduate studies, and 2,457 for participation in meetings or other educational activities organized by WHO. Some 40,000 fellowships had been granted by WHO since 1948.

As in the past, WHO assisted institutions by providing teachers in medical and allied subjects for the training of professional and auxiliary health personnel.

The promotion of education and training continued to be an essential element of WHO's assistance in all programmes. In 1971, special emphasis was put on training for family planning, where the universal shortage of personnel continued to be a major obstacle to progress.

Secretariat

On 31 December 1971, the total number of full-time staff employed by WHO was 3,643. Of these, 1,885 were in the professional and higher categories (drawn from 98 member States), and 1,758 were in the general service category.

Budget

An effective working budget of $82,023,000 was adopted by the twenty-fourth World Health Assembly to finance the work of WHO in 1972. This figure represented an increase of 9.05 per cent over the 1971 budget, as revised by the Assembly.

Services and assistance rendered by WHO, by region, country and territory

(Estimated obligations for 1971, in U.S. dollars)

	Regular budget	Other sources	Total		Regular budget	Other sources	Total
AFRICA				Ghana	131,100	438,703	569,803
Botswana	25,400	12,713	38,113	Guinea	212,980	44,100	257,080
Burundi	190,135	84,858	274,993	Ivory Coast	40,310	291,912	332,222
Cameroon	149,630	643,246	792,876	Kenya	429,603	538,158	967,761
Central African Republic	71,670	173,182	244,852	Lesotho	59,645	—	59,645
Chad	132,850	36,000	168,850	Liberia	193,505	70,455	263,960
Comoro Archipelago	48,950	—	48,950	Madagascar	62,930	267,800	330,730
Congo	75,125	—	75,125	Malawi	101,990	71,671	173,661
Dahomey	207,950	29,944	237,894	Mali	188,930	98,623	287,553
Equatorial Guinea	145,770	—	145,770	Mauritania	146,330	—	146,330
Gabon	89,230	8,455	97,685	Mauritius	79,790	66,712	146,502
The Gambia	7,600	6,000	13,600	Niger	127,800	199,548	327,348

	Regular budget	Other sources	Total		Regular budget	Other sources	Total
Nigeria	702,512	650,015	1,352,527	Ceylon	486,450	668,477	1,154,927
Reunion	10,000	—	10,000	India	1,604,853	769,807	2,374,660
Rwanda	160,005	55,500	215,505	Indonesia	888,050	788,066	1,676,116
Senegal	253,500	1,014,499	1,267,999	Maldives	90,464	63,358	153,822
Seychelles	38,300	—	38,300	Mongolia	273,200	180,776	453,976
Sierra Leone	178,570	75,125	253,695	Nepal	512,154	282,433	794,587
St. Helena	4,000	—	4,000	Thailand	634,386	219,400	853,786
Swaziland	4,250	31,400	35,650	Inter-country programmes	886,640	521,173	1,407,813
Togo	316,915	60,645	377,560	Sub-total	5,720,348	3,742,470	9,462,818
Uganda	175,590	245,510	421,100				
United Republic of Tanzania	351,860	92,320	444,180	Regional Office	684,000	25,725	709,725
Upper Volta	171,650	98,700	270,350	Regional advisers	919,407	—	919,407
Zaire	945,749	247,301	1,193,050	WHO representatives	330,110	—	330,110
Zambia	192,075	37,192	229,267	Total	7,653,865	3,768,195	11,422,060
Inter-country programmes	2,058,210	293,061	2,351,271				
Sub-total	8,482,409	5,983,348	14,465,757	**EUROPE**			
				Albania	12,300	30,150	42,450
Regional Office	1,653,460	—	1,653,460	Algeria	292,600	982,944	1,275,544
Regional advisers	1,225,098	—	1,225,098	Austria	11,400	—	11,400
WHO representatives	886,453	—	886,453	Belgium	8,300	—	8,300
Total	12,247,420	5,983,348	18,230,768	Bulgaria	13,700	624,400	638,100
				Czechoslovakia	9,800	302,800	312,600
THE AMERICAS				Denmark	8,100	—	8,100
Argentina	269,541	1,194,133	1,463,674	Federal Republic of Germany	10,300	—	10,300
Barbados	—	129,900	129,900	Finland	10,300	—	10,300
Bolivia	75,420	379,455	454,875	France	10,300	—	10,300
Brazil	724,987	1,230,509	1,955,496	Greece	10,300	15,640	25,940
British Honduras	25,739	46,306	72,045	Hungary	21,600	115,350	136,950
Canada	15,800	—	15,800	Iceland	4,300	—	4,300
Chile	106,272	267,812	374,084	Ireland	9,400	—	9,400
Colombia	61,990	1,228,344	1,290,334	Italy	16,200	—	16,200
Costa Rica	83,249	197,101	280,350	Luxembourg	5,300	—	5,300
Cuba	116,600	356,376	472,976	Malta	3,300	187,909	191,209
Dominican Republic	101,629	335,493	437,122	Monaco	2,000	—	2,000
Ecuador	207,806	187,039	394,845	Morocco	269,000	302,370	571,370
El Salvador	114,391	169,679	284,070	Netherlands	9,400	—	9,400
French Antilles and Guiana	—	14,400	14,400	Norway	7,800	—	7,800
Guatemala	122,529	195,936	318,465	Poland	18,600	418,937	437,537
Guyana	103,452	109,294	212,746	Romania	19,600	365,050	384,650
Haiti	54,138	366,126	420,264	Spain	25,900	—	66,300
Honduras	107,576	119,058	226,634	Sweden	7,800	40,400	7,800
Jamaica	95,927	129,085	225,012	Switzerland	6,000	—	6,000
Mexico	211,850	448,334	660,184	Turkey	190,100	762,585	952,685
Netherlands Antilles	4,200	37,006	38,206	USSR	21,600	—	21,600
Nicaragua	154,395	108,911	263,306	United Kingdom	9,200	—	9,200
Panama	85,019	197,510	282,529	Yugoslavia	9,000	27,350	36,350
Paraguay	85,848	237,616	323,464	Inter-country programmes	657,670	27,800	685,470
Peru	144,708	250,875	395,583	Sub-total	1,711,170	4,203,685	5,914,855
Surinam	—	546,632	546,632				
Trinidad and Tobago	39,600	208,043	247,643	Regional Office	1,394,730	—	1,394,730
United States of America	28,400	25,200	53,600	Regional health officers	986,185	—	986,185
Uruguay	132,586	317,059	449,645	WHO representatives	148,700	—	148,700
Venezuela	194,098	427,964	622,062	Total	4,240,785	4,203,685	8,444,470
West Indies	88,051	208,888	296,939				
Inter-country programmes	1,773,870	10,604,374	12,378,244	**EASTERN MEDITERRANEAN**			
Sub-total	5,329,671	20,271,458	27,601,129	Afghanistan	753,877	496,685	1,250,562
				Bahrain	24,000	—	24,000
Regional Office	1,211,929	4,889,211	6,101,140	Cyprus	71,850	24,200	96,050
Regional advisers	830,129	—	830,129	Egypt	325,830	287,102	612,932
Zone Offices	19,458	892,112	911,570	Ethiopia	517,860	176,127	693,987
Total	7,391,187	26,052,781	33,443,968	French Territory of the Afars and the Issas	—	—	—
				Iran	296,193	431,427	727,620
SOUTH-EAST ASIA				Iraq	389,930	465,730	855,660
Burma	344,151	248,980	593,131				

	Regular budget	Other sources	Total		Regular budget	Other sources	Total
Israel	92,200	16,100	108,300	Guam	—	—	—
Jordan	173,153	114,100	287,253	Hong Kong	7,400	—	7,400
Kuwait	40,550	17,200	57,750	Japan	37,287	—	37,287
Lebanon	115,811	12,800	128,611	Khmer Republic	270,295	239,994	510,289
Libyan Arab Republic	122,640	447,470	570,110	Laos	242,659	219,572	462,231
Oman	10,000	—	10,000	Malaysia	643,564	33,800	677,364
Pakistan	894,638	412,120	1,306,758	New Hebrides	102,498	24,000	126,498
People's Democratic Republic of Yemen	227,440	276,755	504,195	New Zealand	6,400	—	6,400
Qatar	66,090	—	66,090	Niue	—	—	—
Saudi Arabia	237,850	93,626	331,476	Papua and New Guinea	83,142	—	83,142
Somalia	415,546	129,643	545,189	Philippines	284,281	263,965	548,246
Sudan	438,754	139,560	578,314	Republic of Korea	333,549	41,900	375,449
Syrian Arab Republic	318,870	367,295	686,165	Ryukyu Islands	58,641	—	58,641
Tunisia	264,700	190,936	455,636	Singapore	234,897	73,266	308,163
Yemen	395,054	433,640	828,694	Timor	—	—	—
Inter-country programmes	663,451	277,870	941,321	Tonga	43,725	17,608	61,333
Sub-total	6,856,287	4,810,386	11,666,673	Trust Territory of the Pacific Islands	62,101	—	62,101
				Viet-Nam	483,284	116,906	600,190
Regional Office	771,985	—	771,985	Wallis and Futuna	—	—	—
Regional advisers	673,925	16,589	690,514	Western Samoa	113,647	54,601	168,248
WHO representatives	370,293	—	370,293	Inter-country programmes	790,341	242,798	1,033,139
Total	8,672,490	4,826,975	13,499,465	Sub-total	4,159,858	1,696,591	5,856,449
WESTERN PACIFIC				Regional Office	715,727	—	715,727
American Samoa	7,250	—	7,250	Regional advisers	806,606	31,987	838,593
Australia	54,715	78,500	133,215	WHO representatives	314,830	—	314,830
British Solomon Islands Protectorate	5,870	—	5,870	Total	5,997,021	1,728,578	7,725,599
Brunei	234,086	230,848	464,934				
China	—	6,000	6,000	Inter-regional activities	1,129,541	1,707,490	2,837,031
Cook Islands	30,770	—	30,770	Assistance to research	5,070,648	596,554	5,667,202
Fiji	13,500	—	13,500	Collaboration with other organizations	889,714	244,800	1,134,514
French Polynesia	15,956	52,833	68,789	Total	7,089,903	2,548,844	9,638,747
Gilbert and Ellice Islands	—	—	—	Grand Total	53,292,671	49,112,406	102,405,077

Annex I. MEMBERSHIP OF THE WORLD HEALTH ORGANIZATION AND CONTRIBUTIONS

(Membership as at 31 December 1971; percentage assessments and contributions for 1972)

Member	Contribution Percentage Assessment	Amount* (in U.S. dollars)	Member	Contribution Percentage Assessment	Amount* (in U.S. dollars)	Member	Contribution Percentage Assessment	Amount* (in U.S. dollars)
Afghanistan	0.04	33,610	China	3.61	3,032,890	Greece	0.26	218,430
Albania	0.04	33,610	Colombia	0.17	142,820	Guatemala	0.05	42,000
Algeria	0.08	67,210	Congo	0.04	47,140	Guinea	0.04	33,610
Argentina	0.77	646,900	Costa Rica	0.04	33,610	Guyana	0.04	33,610
Australia	1.33	1,117,380	Cuba	0.14	117,620	Haiti	0.04	33,610
Austria	0.50	420,070	Cyprus	0.04	33,610	Honduras	0.04	33,610
Bahrain	0.02	16,800	Czechoslovakia	0.81	680,500	Hungary	0.43	361,260
Barbados	0.04	33,610	Dahomey	0.04	33,610	Iceland	0.04	33,610
Belgium	0.95	798,120	Denmark	0.56	470,470	India	1.40	1,176,190
Bolivia	0.04	33,610	Dominican Republic	0.04	33,610	Indonesia	0.25	210,030
Brazil	0.72	604,890	Ecuador	0.04	33,610	Iran	0.20	168,030
Bulgaria	0.16	134,420	Egypt	0.16	134,420	Iraq	0.06	50,400
Burma	0.05	42,000	El Salvador	0.04	33,610	Ireland	0.13	109,220
Burundi	0.04	33,610	Ethiopia	0.04	33,610	Israel	0.18	151,220
Byelorussian SSR	0.45	378,070	Federal Republic of Germany	6.14	5,158,440	Italy	3.20	2,688,430
Cameroon	0.04	33,610	Finland	0.41	344,460	Ivory Coast	0.04	33,610
Canada	2.78	2,335,570	France	5.42	4,580,540	Jamaica	0.04	33,610
Central African Republic	0.04	33,610	Gabon	0.04	33,610	Japan	4.88	4,099,870
Ceylon	0.05	42,000	Gambia	0.04	33,610	Jordan	0.04	33,610
Chad	0.04	33,610	Ghana	0.06	50,400	Kenya	0.04	33,610
Chile	0.18	151,220				Khmer Republic	0.04	33,610

Member	Contribution Percentage Assessment	Amount* (in U.S. dollars)	Member	Contribution Percentage Assessment	Amount* (in U.S. dollars)	Member	Contribution Percentage Assessment	Amount* (in U.S. dollars)
Kuwait	0.07	58,810	Norway	0.39	327,650	Syrian Arab Republic	0.04	33,610
Laos	0.04	33,610	Oman	0.04†	33,610†	Thailand	0.12	100,810
Lebanon	0.05	42,000	Pakistan	0.31	260,440	Togo	0.04	33,610
Lesotho	0.04	33,610	Panama	0.04	33,610	Trinidad and Tobago	0.04	33,610
Liberia	0.04	33,610	Paraguay	0.04	33,610	Tunisia	0.04	33,610
Libyan Arab Republic	0.06	50,400	People's Democratic Republic of Yemen	0.04	33,610	Turkey	0.32	271,230
Luxembourg	0.05	42,000	Peru	0.09	75,610	Uganda	0.04	35,020
Madagascar	0.04	33,610	Philippines	0.28	235,240	Ukrainian SSR	1.69	1,419,830
Malawi	0.04	33,610	Poland	1.27	1,066,970	USSR	12.80	10,753,730
Malaysia	0.09	75,610	Portugal	0.14	117,620	United Kingdom	5.33	4,477,910
Maldives	0.04	33,610	Republic of Korea	0.10	84,010	United Republic of Tanzania	0.04	33,210
Mali	0.04	33,610	Republic of Viet-Nam	0.06	50,400	United States	30.84	26,341,960
Malta	0.04	33,610	Romania	0.32	268,840	Upper Volta	0.04	33,610
Mauritania	0.04	33,610	Rwanda	0.04	33,610	Uruguay	0.06	50,400
Mauritius	0.04	33,610	Saudi Arabia	0.06	50,400	Venezuela	0.37	310,850
Mexico	0.79	663,700	Senegal	0.04	33,610	Western Samoa	0.04	33,610
Monaco	0.04	33,610	Sierra Leone	0.04	33,610	Yemen	0.04	33,610
Mongolia	0.04	33,610	Singapore	0.05	42,000	Yugoslavia	0.34	285,650
Morocco	0.08	67,210	Somalia	0.04	33,610	Zaire	0.04	33,610
Nepal	0.04	33,610	South Africa	0.49	411,670	Zambia	0.04	33,610
Netherlands	1.07	898,940	Spain	0.94	789,720	Total		84,472,970
New Zealand	0.29	243,640	Sudan	0.04	33,610			
Nicaragua	0.04	33,610	Sweden	1.13	949,350	**ASSOCIATE MEMBER**		
Niger	0.04	33,610	Switzerland	0.76	638,500			
Nigeria	0.11	92,410				Southern Rhodesia‡	0.02	16,800

*Adjusted to take account of the actual amounts paid to staff in reimbursement for tax levied by members on the WHO emoluments of their nationals.
†Provisional assessment for 1971–1972. The twenty-fourth World Health Assembly decided to assess Oman at this rate pending a decision by the twenty-fifth World Health Assembly.
‡Southern Rhodesia's associate membership is regarded as in suspense.

Annex II.   OFFICERS AND OFFICES OF THE WORLD HEALTH ORGANIZATION
(As at 31 December 1971)

PRESIDENT AND VICE-PRESIDENTS OF THE TWENTY-FOURTH WORLD HEALTH ASSEMBLY

President: Sir William Refshauge (Australia)
Vice-Presidents: Dr. S. Phong-Aksara (Thailand), A. N. Ansari (Pakistan), Dr. A. Todorov (Bulgaria), Dr. J. I. Diaz Granado (Colombia), B. M. Leseteli (Lesotho)

Chairman, Committee A: Dr. Abdul Razzak-Al-Adwani (Kuwait)
Chairman, Committee B: Dr. F. A. Bauhofer (Austria)

MEMBERS OF EXECUTIVE BOARD

Chairman: Dr. S. P. Ehrlich (United States)
Vice-Chairmen: Dr. V. P. Vassilopoulos (Cyprus), Dr. Ali Barraud (Upper Volta)
Rapporteurs: Dr. Hashim Abdul-Ghaffar (Saudi Arabia), Dr. A. Saenz Sanguinetti (Uruguay)

Members: Algeria, Austria, Bulgaria, Central African Republic, Cyprus, Denmark, Ecuador, Ethiopia, France, Italy, Japan, Kenya, Laos, Lesotho, Nepal, Nicaragua, Saudi Arabia, Syrian Arab Republic, Thailand, Trinidad and Tobago, USSR, United States, Upper Volta, Uruguay

SENIOR OFFICERS OF THE WORLD HEALTH ORGANIZATION SECRETARIAT

Director-General: Dr. M. G. Candau
Deputy Director-General: Dr. Pierre Dorolle
Assistant Directors-General: Dr. L. Bernard, Dr. H. Mahler, W. W. Furth, Dr. A. S. Pavlov, Dr. T. A. Lambo
Director, Regional Office for Africa: Dr. A. Quenum

Director, Regional Office for the Americas (Pan American Sanitary Bureau): Dr. A. Horwitz
Director, Regional Office for South-East Asia: Dr. V. T. H. Gunaratne
Director, Regional Office for Europe: Dr. L. Kaprio
Director, Regional Office for the Eastern Mediterranean: Dr. A. H. Taba
Director, Regional Office for the Western Pacific: Dr. F. J. Dy

HEADQUARTERS AND REGIONAL OFFICES

HEADQUARTERS
World Health Organization
Avenue Appia
1211 Geneva 27, Switzerland
    Cable Address: UNISANTE GENEVE

REGIONAL AND OTHER OFFICES
World Health Organization
Regional Office for Africa
P.O. Box No. 6
Brazzaville, Congo
    Cable Address: UNISANTE BRAZZAVILLE

World Health Organization
Regional Office for the Americas
Pan American Sanitary Bureau
525 23rd Street, N.W.
Washington, D.C. 20037, U.S.A.
    Cable Address: OFSANPAN WASHINGTON

World Health Organization
Regional Office for the Eastern Mediterranean
P.O. Box 1517
Alexandria, Egypt
    Cable Address: UNISANTE ALEXANDRIA

World Health Organization
Regional Office for Europe
8, Scherfigsvej
2100 Copenhagen 0, Denmark
    Cable Address: UNISANTE COPENHAGEN

World Health Organization
Regional Office for the Western Pacific
P.O. Box 2932
12115 Manila, Philippines
    Cable Address: UNISANTE MANILA

World Health Organization
Regional Office for South-East Asia
World Health House
Indraprastha Estate, Ring Road
New Delhi-1, India
    Cable Address: WORLDHELTH NEWDELHI

World Health Organization
United Nations Headquarters, Room 2235
New York, N.Y. 10017, U.S.A.
    Cable Address: UNISANTE NEWYORK

Chapter VI

The International Bank for Reconstruction and Development

In 1971, the activities of the International Bank for Reconstruction and Development[1] and those of its affiliates, the International Development Association (IDA) and the International Finance Corporation (IFC), together known as the World Bank Group, continued to operate in accordance with the five-year (1969–1973) programme of lending for economic development outlined in 1968.

Membership in the Bank increased by two to a total of 117 in 1971. Fiji joined on 28 May, Oman on 23 December.

In order to make its development financing more effective, the Bank gave increased attention in 1971 to the impact on economic development of such problems as unemployment, population pressures, malnutrition, threats to the environment and urbanization.

Lending for education and urban water supply and sewerage systems increased sharply, though the two sectors accounted for only a small proportion of total lending.

The Bank made its first loan specifically for a pollution control project in 1971. In addition, for the first time, the environmental effects of all projects were subjected to analysis as part of the Bank's regular appraisal procedure.

The Bank provided rehabilitation assistance in 1971 to Nigeria for a general programme of post-war rehabilitation and to Peru for post-earthquake aid in road building; it also provided assistance for projects in Pakistan after the cyclone of November 1970.

Lending operations

The Bank made loans amounting to $1,778.9 million to 37 countries in 1971. This new peak level of lending (loans for 1970 came to $1,615.1 million) brought the cumulative total of net commitments since the Bank's inception in 1946 to $16,262.1 million.

The following tables summarize the Bank's lending in 1971 by area and purpose.

BANK LOANS BY AREA
(in millions of U.S. dollars)

Area	Amount
Africa	254.9
Asia	356.1
Europe	378.6
Oceania	51.0
Western hemisphere	738.3

BANK LOANS BY PURPOSE
(in millions of U.S. dollars)

Purpose	Amount
Agriculture	175.7
Education	48.4
Transportation	618.9
Electric power	253.9
Telecommunications	96.2
Tourism	30.0
Water supply and sewerage	177.4
Population	3.0
Industry	290.0
Other	85.4

Agriculture

Bank lending for agricultural development expanded in 1971, totalling $175.7 million.

Increased attention was focused upon the need for deeper knowledge of agricultural development in all its aspects, including its relationship to such central questions as unemployment and maldistribution of income; for new and stronger institutional measures to apply knowledge; and for a rising level of capital assistance.

In 1971, the Bank made its first loan primarily for agricultural research, providing $12.7 million to help Spain finance the reorganization of

---

[1]For further information on the Bank's activities prior to 1971, see Bank's annual and supplementary reports for United Nations Economic and Social Council, and previous volumes of Y.U.N.

agricultural research and development activities for the entire country. The project included the establishment of six research centres, each oriented to a major commodity of national importance. One fourth of the loan funds provided technical assistance, including the international recruitment of research specialists and consultants and 200 overseas training fellowships for Spanish scientists.

A concerted international effort in support of agricultural research was launched jointly by the Bank, the Food and Agriculture Organization of the United Nations (FAO) and the United Nations Development Programme (UNDP), and under their sponsorship a Consultative Group on International Agricultural Research was established. Its members included 19 Governments, three private foundations, the International Development Research Centre of Canada, and the Development Assistance Committee of the Organisation for Economic Co-operation and Development (OECD).

The Consultative Group's purpose was to consider, on a continuing basis, the financial and technical requirements for international agricultural research and to organize the necessary financial support. At the Group's first meeting, the Bank announced that it would consider providing up to $3 million in grants in 1972 to assist activities supported by the Group, provided that needed funds could not be raised from other sources.

with the Bank, while help on specific projects was provided by UNDP and various bilateral agencies. Three of the projects approved during the year were identified or prepared with the help of UNESCO, and UNESCO staff members took part in 11 Bank missions for the preliminary identification of education projects. Staff members of FAO participated in five missions concerned with education projects related to agriculture.

LOANS FOR EDUCATION

Country	Amount (in millions of U.S. dollars)	Project
Brazil	8.4	Agricultural and industrial schools
Ireland	13.0	Post-primary schools, agriculture education centres, technical colleges
Jamaica	13.5	Secondary schools, teacher and vocational training facilities, educational television
Turkey	13.5	Vocational, technical and management training

Transport

Lending for transport accounted for the largest share of 1971 Bank lending. Twenty loans totalling $618.9 million were made to 17 countries for the development of ports, railways, pipelines, roads and harbours.

LOANS FOR AGRICULTURE

Country	Amount (in millions of U.S. dollars)	Project
Colombia	8.1	Livestock
Greece	25.0	Irrigation
Guatemala	4.0	Livestock
Ivory Coast	7.0	Oil palm and coconut development
Mexico	75.0	Livestock and agricultural credit
Nigeria	7.2	Agricultural development
Panama	3.4	Fisheries development
Philippines	14.3	Rice processing and storage
Spain	12.7	Agricultural assistance
Tunisia	5.0	Agricultural credit
Turkey	10.0	Fruit and vegetable development
Uruguay	4.0	Livestock

Education

The Bank made four loans for education in 1971, amounting to $48.4 million. Financing for education, a relatively new field for the Bank Group, expanded rapidly after 1968.

In lending for education, the Bank concentrated on secondary schooling, technical and vocational education and teacher training, as well as on educational technology and the development of a rational over-all structure in educational systems.

Both the United Nations Educational, Scientific and Cultural Organization (UNESCO) and FAO continued to assist with lending operations in the educational field under co-operative agreements

LOANS FOR TRANSPORT

Country	Amount (in millions of U.S. dollars)	Project
Argentina	84.0	Railway rehabilitation
	67.5	Highway expansion
Brazil	45.0	Santos Port improvement
	46.0	Railway improvements
China	15.0	Railway improvements
Fiji	11.8	Highway improvements
Finland	13.0	Expressway construction
Guinea	9.0	Port and railway expansion
Honduras	6.0	Port expansion
Israel	30.0	Highway expansion
Ivory Coast	20.5	Highway improvements
Malaysia	16.1	Port expansion in Sabah
New Zealand	16.0	Railway equipment
Panama	20.0	Airport expansion
Philippines	8.0	Mindanao road improvement, feasibility studies
Republic of Korea	54.5	Road programmes
Spain	90.0	Railway improvements
Tunisia	7.5*	Gas pipeline
	24.0	Highway improvements
Yugoslavia	35.0	Highway projects

*Also financed with $6.1 million loan from Kuwait.

Electric power

In 1971, Bank lending for electric power amounted to $253.9 million, raising the cumulative total to $5,046.9 million, the largest Bank commitment made in any sector.

LOANS FOR ELECTRIC POWER

Country or Territory	Amount (in millions of U.S. dollars)	Project
Brazil	70.0	700 MV (megavolts) hydroelectric plant, transmission facilities
China	55.0	500 MV reserve unit
Ireland	20.0	250 MV generating unit
Kenya	23.0*	60 MV transmission line
Liberia	4.7	Generating capacity increase, rehabilitation of distributing system
Papua New Guinea	23.1	45 MV hydroelectric power station
Thailand	27.0	310 MV generating unit
Turkey	24.0	Expansion of generating capacity, consolidation of power grid
	7.0	Power generation and transmission, staff training

*Jointly financed with a $14.3 million loan from Sweden.

Water supply

The Bank loaned more for the improvement and extension of water supply and sewerage systems in 1971 than in all its previous history—$177.4 million. The cumulative total was $308.4 million.

In lending for water supply and sewerage projects, the Bank Group continued to attempt to stimulate improvement in organization, engineering, management and financial practices, and, in the process, to help borrowers save by calling attention to design and analytical techniques that permitted improvements in project design and selection.

LOANS FOR WATER AND SEWERAGE

Country	Amount (in millions of U.S. dollars)	Project
Brazil	37.0	Water supply and pollution control
Colombia	88.0	Water supply expansion
	2.0	Water supply, sewerage facilities
Cyprus	3.5	Sewerage facilities
	1.9	Sewerage and drainage facilities
Yugoslavia	45.0	Water supply for industry, agriculture, communities and power generation

Telecommunications

In 1971, four Bank loans totalling $96.2 million were made for telecommunication projects.

LOANS FOR TELECOMMUNICATIONS

Country	Amount (in millions of U.S. dollars)	Project
Colombia	15.0	Trunk switching units, local exchange equipment
Iraq	27.5	Long distance and international services, subscriber trunk dialing
Malaysia	18.7	Telecommunication improvement
Venezuela	35.0	General expansion

Industry

By the end of 1971, the cumulative total of Bank lending for industry amounted to $2,556 million.

The bulk of the $290 million provided for this purpose during the year was channelled through development finance companies in member countries. Of the nine loans made in the year, seven, totalling $208 million, were made to such companies.

LOANS FOR INDUSTRY

Country	Amount (in millions of U.S. dollars)	Project
Botswana	32.0	Power, water, transport, township infrastructure for copper-nickel mining project
Brazil	50.0	Development of iron ore deposits
Colombia	40.0	Five development finance companies
Ecuador	8.0	Development finance company
Greece	25.0	Development finance company
India	60.0	Development finance company
Ireland	10.0	Development finance company
Morocco	35.0	Development finance company
Republic of Korea	30.0	Development finance company

Population

The Bank's assistance in the field of population planning in 1971 consisted of a $3 million loan in 1971 to Trinidad and Tobago for medical facilities, a family planning institute, nurse-midwife training centres and technical assistance.

Additional projects were in various stages of preparation, and missions were sent by the Bank to seven countries.

Tourism

In 1971, two loans for a total of $30 million were given to Yugoslavia for the development of tourism complexes.

By the end of 1971, a number of other projects were under consideration, surveys of the tourism sector had been carried out in 19 countries, and a programme of research was under way, including an international study of financial aspects of hotel operations.

Technical assistance

For pre-investment projects such as sector and feasibility studies, the Bank continued to encourage its members to seek financing from UNDP for which it often served as the executing agency. In addition, many of the Bank's loans contained allocations for training and other forms of technical assistance, and members were assisted in identifying and preparing projects through regular missions from headquarters and the work of resident staffs, such as those in Africa and Indonesia.

On behalf of UNDP, the Bank became executing agency in 1971 for 20 projects representing commitments of about $15.4 million. Of this total, $8.2 million was earmarked for transport studies in the following countries: Bolivia, Paraguay, the People's Democratic Republic of Yemen, Peru, the

Philippines, the Republic of Korea, Sierra Leone and Zaire.

The remaining $7.2 million was allocated for a study of urban transport and development in Bogotá, Colombia; a development planning project in Ethiopia; a survey of the sugar industry in Indonesia; plans for the development of tourism in Fiji and the Dominican Republic; a tourism study in Afghanistan; assistance to the Water and Power Development Authority of East Pakistan; telecommunication studies in Mali and Senegal; and a phosphate feasibility study in India.

Economic Development Institute

The Economic Development Institute was set up by the Bank in 1955 as a staff college for senior officials concerned with economic affairs in developing countries. By the end of 1971, it had graduated 1,405 fellows from courses in development and project evaluation.

In 1971, 191 persons participated in courses given by the Institute. Professional members of the Institute numbered 19.

Settlement of investment disputes

By the end of 1971, 62 States had ratified the Convention setting up the International Centre for Settlement of Investment Disputes (ICSID). Four additional Governments had signed but not yet ratified the Convention.

Development aid co-ordination

The Bank continued to encourage joint efforts by capital-exporting countries designed to co-ordinate the flow of development assistance through consortia (in India and Pakistan) and consultative groups (in Colombia, East Africa, Ethiopia, Ghana, Malaysia, Morocco, Nigeria, the Philippines, the Republic of Korea, Thailand, Tunisia and Zaire). The consultative groups in Ethiopia and Zaire were set up during the year, and the group for the Philippines met for the first time in 1971.

The Bank also participated in aid co-ordinating groups for Ceylon, Indonesia and Turkey, and provided staff support for the country-review exercises conducted by the Inter-American Committee on the Alliance for Progress and for groups convened by the Governments of Guyana and Honduras.

Close relations with specialized agencies of the United Nations, UNDP, the United Nations Industrial Development Organization and various regional banks were maintained.

Financial activities and resources

Bank borrowing

The Bank sold $1,586.9 million of its obligations in the international investment market during 1971. This included its first public issues in Japan, and borrowings in Belgium, Canada, the Federal Republic of Germany, Kuwait, the Netherlands, Switzerland, the United Kingdom and the United States.

The net increase in the Bank's funded debt was about $1,000 million, raising the total to about $6,000 million.

Bank income and reserves

The gross income of the Bank in 1971 was about $594 million, compared with $550 million in 1970. Expenses, which included about $343 million for interest on Bank borrowings, bond issuance and other financial costs, totalled $403 million, compared with the 1970 figure of $322 million. Net income in 1971 amounted to $190 million, compared with $228 million in 1970. Total reserves were about $1,500 million at year's end, made up of $1,200 million in the Supplemental Reserve and $300 million in the Special Reserve.

During the year, 21 countries increased their subscriptions to the Bank's capital. Thus by year's end, the Bank had a total subscribed capital of $24,000 million.

Secretariat

The acceleration of financing operations and a widening of activities required expansion of the Bank's staff which, by the end of 1971, numbered 2,952, drawn from 98 different nationalities. About half were in the professional and higher categories and about half were non-professionals.

STATEMENT OF INCOME AND EXPENSES
(For fiscal year ended 30 June 1971)

Income	Amount (in thousands of U.S. dollars)
Income from investments*	187,246
Income from loans:	
Interest	358,958
Commitment charges	24,310
Commissions	286
Service charges	21
Other income	7,015
Gross Income	577,836
Deduct—amount equivalent to commissions appropriated to Special Reserve	286
Gross Income less Reserve deduction	577,550
Expenses	
Administrative expenses†	56,394
Interest on borrowings	304,973
Bond issuance and other financial expenses	4,121
Discount on sale of loans	315
Gross Expenses	365,803
Net income	211.747

*Includes net capital gain (loss) of US$7,990,414—1971, (US$1,402,770)—1970 resulting from the sale of investments.

†All administrative expenses of the Bank and the International Development Association and a portion of the expenses of the International Finance

Corporation are paid by the Bank. A "Management Fee" is charged to the Association and a "Service and Support Fee" to the Corporation representing their respective share of the costs. The administrative expenses shown are net of the "Management Fee" (US$20,100,000—1971, US$15,800,000 —1970) and "Service and Support Fee" (US$1,749,000—1971). On 1 July 1970, the Bank commenced charging the "Service and Support Fee" which replaced a cost-sharing arrangement with the Bank covering certain categories of expenses.

Annex I. MEMBERS OF THE INTERNATIONAL BANK, SUBSCRIPTIONS AND VOTING POWER
(As at 31 December 1971)

Member	Subscription Amount (in millions of U.S. dollars)	Per Cent of Total	Voting power Number of Votes	Per Cent of Total	Member	Subscription Amount (in millions of U.S. dollars)	Per Cent of Total	Voting power Number of Votes	Per Cent of Total
Afghanistan	30.0	0.13	550	0.20	Israel	95.9	0.40	1,209	0.45*
Algeria	80.0	0.33	1,050	0.39	Italy	666.0	2.77	6,910	2.56
Argentina	373.3	1.61	3,983	1.53	Ivory Coast	20.0	0.08	450	0.17
Australia	533.0	2.07	5,580	2.22	Jamaica	44.6	0.19	696	0.26
Austria	230.4	0.96	2,554	0.95	Japan	1,023.0	4.25	10,480	3.88
Belgium	554.5	2.31	5,795	2.15	Jordan	16.3	0.07	413	0.15
Bolivia	21.0	0.09	460	0.18	Kenya	33.3	0.14	583	0.22
Botswana	3.2	0.01	282	0.10	Khmer Republic	20.3	0.09	453	0.17
Brazil	373.3	1.55	3,983	1.53	Kuwait	66.7	0.28	917	0.34
Burma	50.7	0.21	757	0.29	Laos	10.0	0.04	350	0.13
Burundi	15.0	0.06	400	0.15	Lebanon	9.0	0.04	340	0.13
Cameroon	20.0	0.08	450	0.17	Lesotho	3.2	0.01	282	0.10
Canada	792.0	3.29	8,170	3.03	Liberia	21.3	0.09	463	0.17
Central African Republic	10.0	0.04	350	0.13	Libyan Arab Republic	20.0	0.08	450	0.17
Ceylon	82.7	0.34	1,077	0.40	Luxembourg	20.0	0.08	450	0.17
Chad	10.0	0.04	350	0.13	Madagascar	20.0	0.08	450	0.17
Chile	93.3	0.39	1,183	0.44	Malawi	15.0	0.06	400	0.15
China	750.0	3.12	7,750	2.87	Malaysia	133.3	0.55	1,583	0.59
Colombia	93.3	0.39	1,183	0.44	Mali	17.3	0.07	423	0.16
Congo	10.0	0.04	350	0.13	Mauritania	10.0	0.04	350	0.13
Costa Rica	10.7	0.05	357	0.13	Mauritius	18.8	0.08	438	0.16
Cyprus	22.2	0.09	472	0.17	Mexico	228.0	0.95	2,530	0.94
Dahomey	10.0	0.04	350	0.13	Morocco	96.0	0.40	1,210	0.45
Denmark	221.1	0.92	2,461	0.91	Nepal	10.0	0.04	350	0.13
Dominican Republic	14.3	0.06	393	0.14	Netherlands	592.3	2.46	6,173	2.29
Ecuador	17.1	0.07	421	0.16	New Zealand	171.6	0.71	1,966	0.73
Egypt	142.1	0.59	1,671	0.62	Nicaragua	8.0	0.03	330	0.12
El Salvador	10.7	0.05	357	0.13	Niger	10.0	0.04	350	0.13
Equatorial Guinea	6.4	0.03	314	0.12	Nigeria	106.7	0.44	1,317	0.49
Ethiopia	11.4	0.05	364	0.13	Norway	160.0	0.67	1,850	0.69
Federal Republic of Germany	1,365.3	5.68	13,903	5.15	Oman	6.0	0.02	310	0.11
Fiji	11.1	0.05	361	0.13	Pakistan	200.0	0.83	2,250	0.83
Finland	133.3	0.55	1,583	0.59	Panama	17.6	0.07	426	0.16
France	1,050.0	4.37	10,750	3.98	Paraguay	6.0	0.02	310	0.11
Gabon	10.0	0.04	350	0.13	People's Democratic Republic of Yemen	23.5	0.10	485	0.18
Gambia	5.3	0.02	303	0.11	Peru	63.5	0.26	885	0.33
Ghana	73.4	0.31	984	0.36	Philippines	117.3	0.49	1,423	0.53
Greece	66.7	0.28	917	0.34	Portugal	80.0	0.33	1,050	0.39
Guatemala	12.3	0.05	373	0.14	Republic of Korea	53.3	0.22	783	0.29
Guinea	20.0	0.08	450	0.17	Republic of Viet-Nam	42.7	0.18	677	0.25
Guyana	16.0	0.07	410	0.15	Rwanda	15.0	0.06	400	0.15
Haiti	15.0	0.06	400	0.15	Saudi Arabia	114.3	0.48	1,393	0.52
Honduras	8.0	0.03	330	0.12	Senegal	33.3	0.14	583	0.22
Iceland	18.4	0.08	434	0.16	Sierra Leone	15.0	0.06	400	0.15
India	900.0	3.74	8,250	3.43	Singapore	32.0	0.13	570	0.21
Indonesia	220.0	0.92	2,450	0.91	Somalia	15.0	0.06	400	0.15
Iran	158.0	0.66	1,830	0.68	South Africa	213.3	0.89	2,383	0.88
Iraq	64.0	0.27	890	0.33	Spain	266.7	1.11	2,917	1.08
Ireland	85.3	0.36	1,103	0.41	Sudan	60.0	0.25	850	0.31

Member	Subscription		Voting power		Member	Subscription		Voting power	
	Amount (in millions of U.S. dollars)	Per Cent of Total	Number of Votes	Per Cent of Total		Amount (in millions of U.S. dollars)	Per Cent of Total	Number of Votes	Per Cent of Total
Swaziland	6.4	0.03	314	0.12	United States	6,350.0	26.41	63,750	23.64
Sweden	277.3	1.15	3,023	1.12	Upper Volta	10.0	.04	350	.13
Syrian Arab Republic	40.0	0.17	650	0.24	Uruguay	41.1	.17	661	.24
Thailand	114.3	0.48	1,393	0.52	Venezuela	197.2	.82	2,222	.82
Togo	15.0	0.06	400	0.15	Yemen	8.5	.04	335	.12
Trinidad and Tobago	46.7	0.19	717	0.26	Yugoslavia	106.7	.44	1,317	.49
Tunisia	37.3	0.16	623	0.23	Zaire	96.0	.40	1,210	.45
Turkey	115.0	0.48	1,400	0.52	Zambia	53.3	.22	783	.29
Uganda	33.3	0.14	583	0.22	Total	24,046.3		268,713	
United Kingdom	2,600.0	10.81	26,250	9.73					
United Republic of Tanzania	33.3	0.14	583	0.22					

Annex II. EXECUTIVE DIRECTORS AND ALTERNATES OF THE INTERNATIONAL BANK

(As at 31 December 1971)

Appointed Director	*Appointed Alternate*	*Casting the votes of*
Robert E. Wieczorowski	—	United States
D. J. Mitchell	K. M. Critchley	United Kindgom
Fritz Stedtfeld	Wolfgang H. Artopoeus	Federal Republic of Germany
Marc Viénot	Jean P. Carrière	France
Seitaro Hattori	Mansanari Sumi	Japan
S. R. Sen	M. R. Shroff	India

Elected Director	*Elected Alternate*	*Casting the votes of*
Khunying Suparb Yossundara (Thailand)	R. V. Navaratnam (Malaysia)	Burma, Ceylon, Laos, Malaysia, Nepal, Singapore, Thailand
Giorgio Rota (Italy)	Juan Moro (Spain)	Italy, Portugal, Spain
Claude M. Isbister (Canada)	Maurice Horgan (Ireland)	Canada, Guyana, Ireland, Jamaica
R. L. Knight (New Zealand)	M. A. Cranswick (Australia)	Australia, New Zealand, South Africa Africa
S. Osman Ali (Pakistan)	Mohammad Yeganeh (Iran)	Egypt, Iran, Iraq, Jordan, Kuwait, Lebanon, Oman, Pakistan, People's Democratic Republic of Yemen, Saudi Arabia, Syrian Arab Republic, Yemen
Reignson C. Chen (China)	Byong Hyun Shin (Republic of Korea)	China, Republic of Korea, Republic of Viet-Nam
Donatien Bihute (Burundi)	Bulcha Demeksa (Ethiopia)	Botswana, Burundi, Equatorial Guinea, Ethiopia, Gambia, Guinea, Kenya, Lesotho, Liberia, Malawi, Nigeria, Sierra Leone, Sudan, Swaziland, Trinidad and Tobago, Uganda, United Republic of Tanzania, Zambia
Alfred Pinnooy Kan (Netherlands)	Vladimir Ceric (Yugoslavia)	Cyprus, Israel, Netherlands, Yugoslavia
André van Campenhout (Belgium)	Viktor C. Wolf (Austria)	Austria, Belgium, Luxembourg, Turkey
Erik Tornqvist (Finland)	Carl I. Ohman (Sweden)	Denmark, Finland, Iceland, Norway, Sweden
Abderrahman Tazi (Morocco)	—	Afghanistan, Algeria, Ghana, Greece, Indonesia, Khmer Republic, Libyan Arab Republic, Morocco, Tunisia
Mohamed Nassim Kochman (Mauritania)	Benoit Boukar (Chad)	Cameroon, Central African Republic, Chad, Congo, Dahomey, Gabon, Ivory Coast, Madagascar, Mali, Mauritania, Mauritius, Niger, Rwanda, Senegal, Somalia, Togo, Upper Volta, Zaire
Adrián Lajous (Mexico)	Carlos Santistevan (Peru)	Costa Rica, El Salvador, Guatemala, Haiti, Honduras, Mexico, Nicaragua, Panama, Peru, Venezuela

Appointed Director	Appointed Alternate	Casting the votes of
Virgilio Barco (Colombia)	Placido L. Mapa, Jr. (Phillippines)	Brazil, Colombia, Dominican Republic, Ecuador, Philippines
Luis B. Mey (Argentina)	Oscar Vega-López (Bolivia)	Argentina, Bolivia, Chile, Paraguay, Uruguay

Annex III. PRINCIPAL OFFICERS AND OFFICES OF THE INTERNATIONAL BANK

(As at 31 December 1971)

PRINCIPAL OFFICERS*

President: Robert S. McNamara
Vice-President and Chairman, Loan Committee: J. Burke Knapp
Vice-President, Finance, and Director, Projects: S. Aldewereld
General Counsel: A. Broches
Director, Development Services Department: Richard H. Demuth
Economic Adviser to the President: Hollis B. Chenery
Vice-President: Sir Denis Rickett
Vice-President: Mohamed Shoaib

Treasurer: Eugene H. Rotberg
Controller: K. Georg Gabriel
Secretary: M. M. Mendels

*Officers and staff of the International Bank for Reconstruction and Development serve as officers and staff of the International Development Association.

HEADQUARTERS AND OTHER OFFICES

HEADQUARTERS
International Bank for Reconstruction and Development
1818 H Street, N.W.
Washington, D.C. 20433, U.S.A.
   Telephone: EXecutive 3-6360
   Cable Address: INTBAFRAD WASHINGTON

EUROPEAN OFFICE
International Bank for Reconstruction
   and Development
66 Avenue d'Iéna,
75116 Paris, France
   Telephone: 720-2510
   Cable Address: INTBAFRAD PARIS

TOKYO OFFICE
International Bank for Reconstruction and Development
Kokusai Building, Room 908
1-1, Marunouchi 3-Chôme
Chiyoda-Ku,
Tokyo 100, Japan
   Telephone: (03) 214-5001
   Cable Address: INTBAFRAD TOKYO

Chapter VII

The International Finance Corporation (IFC)

The International Finance Corporation (IFC)[1] was established in 1956 as an affiliate of the International Bank for Reconstruction and Development to assist developing member countries by helping them to promote the private sector of their economies.

The principal objectives of IFC are to provide risk capital for productive private enterprise, in association with private investors and management; to encourage the development of local capital markets; and to stimulate the international flow of private capital. It neither requires nor accepts guarantees by Governments in its operations.

Generally, IFC invests on a mixed equity and loan basis, with other investors providing the bulk of the funds required for any given project.

In 1971, IFC continued to make investments in the form of share subscriptions and long-term loans; to carry out stand-by and underwriting arrangements; and to provide financial and technical assistance to privately controlled devel-

opment finance companies. Paid-in share capital rose to $107.2 million in 1971.

Trinidad and Tobago joined IFC during 1971 (15 June), raising the total membership to 96 countries.

In 1971, the Corporation made 24 commitments, totalling US$107,709,069, in 16 countries: Argentina, Brazil, China, Indonesia, Iran, Lebanon, Mauritius, Mexico, Panama, the Philippines, the Republic of Korea, Senegal, Spain, Turkey, Venezuela and Yugoslavia. One regional investment was made in a development finance company in Africa. Other domestic and foreign financial institutions and private industrial firms made separate investments of approximately $566.1 million in projects IFC helped finance in 1971, raising the total capital mobilized by these projects to $673.8 million.

[1]For further information on IFC's activities prior to 1971, see IFC's annual reports to its Board of Directors and Board of Governors, summary proceedings of annual meetings of Board of Governors, and previous volumes of Y.U.N.

First commitments were made by IFC during the year in four countries—Indonesia, Lebanon, Mauritius and Panama—spreading the Corporation's investments to 47 countries.

By the end of 1971, IFC had made cumulative total commitments of $603.7 million over the previous 15 years. Commitments in Africa and the Middle East over that period totalled $98 million, or 16 per cent. Commitments in Asia totalled $191.6 million, or 32 per cent; and commitments in the western hemisphere totalled $232.7 million, or 39 per cent. The remaining 13 per cent represented investments in Europe and Australasia.

IFC COMMITMENTS IN 1971

Sector and Country	Amount (in millions of U.S. dollars)
Textiles and fibres	
China	2.6
Indonesia	2.5
	3.3
Iran	4.5
Lebanon	0.93
Mexico	12.0
Construction materials	
Argentina	5.5
Indonesia	13.15
Lebanon	1.2
Venezuela	2.0
Mining	
Philippines	15.0
Pulp and paper products	
Brazil	4.9
Spain	9.47
Turkey	0.05
Chemical products	
Brazil	6.0
Philippines	8.0
Other manufacturing	
Indonesia	3.17
Venezuela	1.0
Yugoslavia	9.0
Tourism	
Mauritius	0.6
Panama	1.47
Development finance companies	
Africa (regional)	0.5
Republic of Korea	0.7
Food and food processing	
Senegal	0.05

In 1971, an agreement was concluded providing for a loan of $5 million by the Netherlands to IFC, to be used by the Corporation in its investment operations. This was the first loan made by a member Government to IFC.

Since the funds available to IFC for equity investment were more limited than those available for lending, the Netherlands agreed to make its loan on terms that would allow the Corporation to use it for share investments.

The loan was for a term of 30 years, with an eight-year period of grace. The loan agreement provided that interest should be equal to the rate of dividend, if any, upon IFC's capital stock. (At that time, IFC had not declared dividends.)

The loan agreement also provided that any outstanding amount of the principal might be applied, at the option of the Netherlands, in subscribing to any additional shares of capital stock that might be issued by IFC.

Financial operations

The net income of IFC in 1971 was $6.4 million, and, as in previous years, was credited to the Reserve Against Losses. This brought the total Reserve Against Losses to $68.5 million at 31 December 1971. Total resources available to the Corporation rose to $606.2 million, compared with $549.2 million a year earlier.

Participation and portfolio sales

The Corporation sold or agreed to sell $19 million of loan and equity commitments in 1971, bringing the total at the end of the year to $164.7 million, including the acquisition by others of $30.6 million of securities covered by IFC stand-by and underwriting commitments.

Organization

The Capital Markets Department was established in IFC on 25 March 1971. Acting for IFC, the International Bank and the International Development Association, this department was to be responsible for providing assistance to developing member countries to improve their capital and money markets. An important function would be to help to build private capital market institutions in those countries which would contribute to the growth of domestic savings and to their efficient utilization through market mechanisms.

Secretariat

As at the end of 1971, IFC had a staff of 168, of whom 96 were professionals (drawn from 37 nationalities) and 72 were general service and special service staff.

STATEMENT OF INCOME AND EXPENSES
(For fiscal year ended 30 June 1971)

Income	Amount (in U.S. dollars)
Income from short-term securities and time deposits	675,161
Income from loan and equity investments and stand-by and underwriting commitments:	
Fixed interest	8,899,382

Income	Amount (in U.S. dollars)	Expenses	Amount (in U.S. dollars)
Additional interest	170,156	Administrative expenses	6,491,086
Commitment charges	816,161	Charges on borrowings	3,759,928
Dividends	3,908,959	Gross Expenses	10,251,014
Commissions	146,724		
Profit on sales of operational investments	1,766,166	Net Income (allocated to Reserve Against Losses)	6,171,061
Other income	39,366		
Gross Income	16,422,075		

ANNEX I. MEMBERS OF THE INTERNATIONAL FINANCE CORPORATION, SUBSCRIPTIONS AND VOTING POWER

(As at 31 December 1971)

Member	Subscription Amount (in thousands of U.S. dollars)	Per Cent of Total	Voting power Number of Votes	Per Cent of Total	Member	Subscription Amount (in thousands of U.S. dollars)	Per Cent of Total	Voting power Number of Votes	Per Cent of Total
Afghanistan	111	0.10	361	0.27	Japan	2,769	2.58	3,019	2.30
Argentina	1,662	1.55	1,912	1.46	Jordan	33	0.03	283	0.22
Australia	2,215	2.07	2,465	1.88	Kenya	184	0.17	434	0.33
Austria	554	0.52	804	0.61	Kuwait	369	0.34	619	0.47
Belgium	2,492	2.33	2,742	2.09	Lebanon	50	0.05	300	0.23
Bolivia	78	0.07	328	0.25	Liberia	83	0.08	333	0.25
Brazil	1,163	1.09	1,413	1.08	Libyan Arab Republic	55	0.05	305	0.23
Burma	166	0.16	416	0.32	Luxembourg	111	0.10	361	0.27
Canada	3,600	3.36	3,850	2.94	Madagascar	111	0.10	361	0.27
Ceylon	166	0.16	416	0.32	Malawi	83	0.08	333	0.25
Chile	388	0.36	638	0.49	Malaysia	277	0.26	527	0.40
China	4,154	3.88	4,404	3.36	Mauritania	55	0.05	305	0.23
Colombia	388	0.36	638	0.49	Mauritius	95	0.09	345	0.26
Costa Rica	22	0.02	272	0.21	Mexico	720	0.67	970	0.74
Cyprus	83	0.08	333	0.25	Morocco	388	0.36	638	0.49
Denmark	753	0.70	1,003	0.77	Nepal	55	0.05	305	0.23
Dominican Republic	22	0.02	272	0.21	Netherlands	3,046	2.84	3,296	2.51
Ecuador	35	0.03	285	0.22	New Zealand	923	0.86	1,173	0.89
Egypt	590	0.55	840	0.64	Nicaragua	9	0.01	259	0.20
El Salvador	11	0.01	261	0.20	Nigeria	369	0.34	619	0.47
Ethiopia	33	0.03	283	0.22	Norway	554	0.52	804	0.61
Federal Republic of Germany	3,655	3.41	3,905	2.98	Pakistan	1,108	1.03	1,358	1.04
Finland	421	0.39	671	0.51	Panama	2	.	252	0.19
France	5,815	5.43	6,065	4.62	Paraguay	16	0.02	266	0.20
Gabon	55	0.05	305	0.23	Peru	194	0.18	444	0.34
Ghana	166	0.16	416	0.32	Philippines	166	0.16	416	0.32
Greece	277	0.26	527	0.40	Portugal	443	0.41	693	0.53
Guatemala	22	0.02	272	0.21	Republic of Korea	139	0.13	389	0.30
Guyana	89	0.08	339	0.26	Republic of Viet-Nam	166	0.16	416	0.32
Haiti	22	0.02	272	0.21	Saudi Arabia	111	0.10	361	0.27
Honduras	11	0.01	261	0.20	Senegal	184	0.17	434	0.33
Iceland	11	0.01	261	0.20	Sierra Leone	83	0.08	333	0.25
India	4,431	4.14	4,681	3.57	Singapore	177	0.17	427	0.33
Indonesia	1,218	1.14	1,468	1.12	Somalia	83	0.08	333	0.25
Iran	372	0.35	622	0.47	South Africa	1,108	1.03	1,358	1.04
Iraq	67	0.06	317	0.24	Spain	1,108	1.03	1,358	1.04
Ireland	332	0.31	582	0.44	Sudan	111	0.10	361	0.27
Israel	50	0.05	300	0.23	Swaziland	35	0.03	285	0.22
Italy	1,994	1.86	2,244	1.71	Sweden	1,108	1.03	1,358	1.04
Ivory Coast	111	0.10	361	0.27	Syrian Arab Republic	72	0.07	322	0.25
Jamaica	148	0.14	398	0.30					

Member	Subscription Amount (in thousands of U.S. dollars)	Per Cent of Total	Voting power Number of Votes	Per Cent of Total	Member	Subscription Amount (in thousands of U.S. dollars)	Per Cent of Total	Voting power Number of Votes	Per Cent of Total
Thailand	139	0.13	389	0.30	United States	35,168	32.82	35,418	27.01
Togo	83	0.08	333	0.25	Uruguay	155	0.15	405	0.31
Trinidad and Tobago	148	0.14	398	0.30	Venezuela	116	0.11	366	0.28
Tunisia	133	0.12	383	0.29	Yemen	47	0.04	297	0.23
Turkey	476	0.44	726	0.55	Yugoslavia	591	0.55	841	0.64
Uganda	184	0.17	434	0.33	Zaire	332	0.31	582	0.44
United Kingdom	14,400	13.44	14,650	11.17	Zambia	295	0.28	545	0.42
United Republic of Tanzania	184	0.17	434	0.33	Total	107,157		131,157	

*Less than 0.005 per cent.

Annex II. EXECUTIVE DIRECTORS AND ALTERNATES OF THE INTERNATIONAL FINANCE CORPORATION

(As at 31 December 1971)

Appointed Director	*Appointed Alternate*	*Casting the votes of*
Robert E. Wieczorowski	—	United States
D. J. Mitchell	K. M. Critchley	United Kingdom
Marc Viénot	Jean P. Carrière	France
S. R. Sen	M. R. Shroff	India
Fritz Stedtfeld	Wolfgang H. Artopoeus	Federal Republic of Germany
Seitaro Hattori	Masanari Sumi	Japan

Elected Director	*Elected Alternate*	*Casting the votes of*
S. Osman Ali (Pakistan)	Mohammad Yeganeh (Iran)	Egypt, Iran, Iraq, Jordan, Kuwait, Lebanon, Pakistan, Saudi Arabia, Syrian Arab Republic, Yemen
Reignson C. Chen (China)	Byong Hyun Shin (Republic of Korea)	China, Republic of Korea, Republic of Viet-Nam
Claude M. Isbister (Canada)	Maurice Horgan (Ireland)	Canada, Guyana, Ireland, Jamaica
R. Lindsay Knight (New Zealand)	M. A. Cranswick (Australia)	Australia, New Zealand, South Africa
Donatien Bihute (Burundi)	Bulcha Demeksa (Ethiopia)	Ethiopia, Kenya, Liberia, Malawi, Nigeria, Sierra Leone, Sudan, Swaziland, Trinidad and Tobago, Uganda, United Republic of Tanzania, Zambia
Alfred Rinnooy Kan (Netherlands)	Branko Mijovic (Yugoslavia)	Cyprus, Israel, Netherlands, Yugoslavia
André van Campenhout (Belgium)	Viktor C. Wolf (Austria)	Austria, Belgium, Luxembourg, Turkey
Giorgio Rota (Italy)	Juan Moro (Spain)	Italy, Portugal, Spain
Abderrahman Tazi (Morocco)	Ghulam H. Jewayni (Afghanistan)	Afghanistan, Ghana, Greece, Indonesia, Libyan Arab Republic, Morocco, Tunisia
Erik Törnqvist (Finland)	Carl I. Ohman (Sweden)	Denmark, Finland, Iceland, Norway, Sweden
Adrián Lajous (Mexico)	Carlos Santistevan (Peru)	Costa Rica, El Salvador, Guatemala, Haiti, Honduras, Mexico, Nicaragua, Panama, Peru, Venezuela
Luis B. Mey (Argentina)	Oscar Vega-López (Bolivia)	Argentina, Bolivia, Chile, Paraguay, Uruguay
Mohamed Nassim Kochman (Mauritania)	Benoit Boukar (Chad)	Gabon, Ivory Coast, Madagascar, Mauritania, Mauritius, Senegal, Somalia, Togo, Zaire
Virgilio Barco (Colombia)	Placido L. Mapa, Jr. (Philippines)	Brazil, Colombia, Dominican Republic, Ecuador, Philippines
Khunying Suparb Yossundara (Thailand)	R. V. Navaratnam (Malaysia)	Burma, Ceylon, Malaysia, Nepal, Singapore, Thailand

Annex III. PRINCIPAL OFFICERS AND OFFICES OF INTERNATIONAL FINANCE CORPORATION
(As at 31 December 1971)

PRINCIPAL OFFICERS

President: Robert S. McNamara*
Executive Vice-President: William S. Gaud
Vice-President: Ladislaus von Hoffmann
General Counsel: R. B. J. Richards
Treasurer: Eugene H. Rotberg*
Controller: K. Georg Gabriel*
Secretary: M. M. Mendels*

Director, Programming and Budgeting Department: John H. Adler*
Director of Investments, Africa and Middle East: Albert Adomakoh
Director of Information and Public Affairs: William Clark*
Director of Personnel: R. A. Clarke*
Office of Portfolio Supervision: Douglas J. A. DuPre
Director, Capital Markets Department: David Gill
Director, Engineering Department: H. Geoffrey Hilton

Special Representative in Indonesia: Ronald K. Jones
Director, European Office: Arthur Karasz*
Director of Marketing: Henry Koch
Special Representative in Europe: Rolf T. Lundberg
Special Representative in the Far East: Naokado Nishihara
Director of Investments, Asia: Judhvir Parmar
Director of Investments, Central America, Australasia, Mexico and Europe:
      Neil J. Paterson
Economic Adviser: Moeen A. Qureshi
Director of Investments, South America: Rafael Talavera
Director of Administrative Services: James E. Twining*

*These officers and department heads hold the same positions in the
International Bank for Reconstruction and Development.

HEADQUARTERS AND OTHER OFFICES

HEADQUARTERS
International Finance Corporation
1818 H Street, N. W.
Washington, D.C. 20433, U.S.A.
    Telephone: EXecutive 3-6360
    Cable Address: CORINTFIN WASHINGTON

EUROPEAN OFFICE
International Finance Corporation
66 Avenue d'Iéna
75116 Paris, France
    Telephone: 720-2510
    Cable Address: CORINTFIN PARIS

TOKYO OFFICE
International Finance Corporation
1-10, 4-Chôme, Shinbashi, Manato-Ku
Tokyo, Japan
    Telephone: 431-5262
    Cable Address: SPCORINTFIN TOKYO

Chapter VIII

The International Development Association (IDA)

The International Development Association (IDA)[1] was founded in September 1960 as an affiliate of the International Bank for Reconstruction and Development. The purpose of IDA, like that of the Bank, is to promote economic development by supporting productive, high-priority projects in developing member countries.

The Association lends for the same kinds of projects as the Bank, using the same appraisal criteria and the same staff, but it obtains its funds from different sources and lends on different terms: the Bank borrows in the capital markets and lends on roughly conventional terms; most of IDA's resources are contributed by member Governments, enabling it to lend to the poorest countries on more flexible terms which bear less heavily on their balance of payments. Accordingly, IDA "credits" are free of interest, with a service charge of 3/4 of 1 per cent on funds disbursed. Credits are repayable over 50 years, with an initial period of grace of 10 years before repayment begins.

Unlike the Bank, which may lend to public or private entities with Government guarantees, IDA lends only to Governments. In the case of revenue-producing projects, IDA credits are re-

loaned by the Government on terms reflecting the local cost of capital. Thus, IDA's terms help Governments finance their economic development programmes without distorting the local credit structure.

In its 11 years of operations (at 31 December 1971), IDA's usable resources totalled almost $3,800 million. Contributions by Governments amounted to $2,354 million. In addition, the International Bank made available $595 million in grants out of its net earnings for the seven fiscal years beginning in 1964. Switzerland, which is not a member of IDA, made a $12 million interest-free 50-year loan. The cumulative net earnings of IDA totalled $44.9 million. Finally, 12 countries provided a total of $355 million in advance contributions towards a third general replenishment of IDA funds (see below).

Aside from initial subscriptions in usable form totalling $796 million, the bulk of IDA's funds for lending have been provided by its "Part I" (richer) members under a series of replenishment agreements. The first replenishment agreement took

[1] For information on IDA's activities prior to 1971, see IDA's annual reports to its Board of Governors and previous volumes of Y.U.N.

effect in 1964, the second in 1969.[2] The third agreement, concluded in 1970 subject to parliamentary or other official approval, provided for a virtual doubling of operations through contributions of about $800 million a year for three years by 18 Part I members.[3]

In addition, three "Part II" (developing) members pledged about $4 million a year, and Switzerland agreed to make a second loan equivalent to about $32 million.

It had been contemplated that first payments under the third replenishment agreement could be made in November 1971, since all of IDA's available resources had been committed by 30 June 1971. By the end of 1971, the agreement had not come into force and its effective date had been extended to 31 March 1972. Meanwhile, to permit the continuance of operations, 11 Part I countries and Yugoslavia, a Part II member, had come forward with advance contributions totalling $355 million. A grant of $110 million from the Bank's net income for fiscal 1971 brought the total of new funds to $465 million.

Participating members and their agreed annual contributions to the third replenishment are listed below. Except for Kuwait, which made its entire three-year allocation available, all advance contributions represented one-year payments. Iceland, formerly a Part II member, became a Part I member and a participant in the replenishment.

CONTRIBUTIONS IN 1971 UNDER REPLENISHMENT AGREEMENTS

Country	Amount (in U.S. dollar equivalents)
Australia*	16,000,000
Austria	5,440,000
Belgium	13,600,000
Canada*	50,000,000
Denmark*	8,800,000
Federal Republic of Germany*	78,000,000
Finland*	4,080,000
France	50,000,000
Iceland*	200,000
Italy	32,240,000
Japan*	48,000,000
Kuwait*	3,600,000
Luxembourg	400,000
Netherlands	22,520,000
Norway*	8,000,000
South Africa	1,000,000
Sweden*	34,000,000
United Kingdom*	103,680,000
United States	320,000,000

*Advance contribution made by 31 December 1971.

In addition, three Part II member countries agreed to contribute to the replenishment in the

following amounts over a nine-year period: Ireland—$4 million; Spain—$2.5 million; and Yugoslavia—$4.04 million.

Although it is a separate financial and legal entity, IDA is closely linked to the International Bank in its membership and administration. Any country that is a member of the Bank may join IDA, and each member country of IDA is represented by the same Governor and Executive Director who represent it for the Bank.

As at 31 December 1971, there were 107 IDA members, the same number as in the previous year.

Lending operations

As at 31 December 1971, IDA had made cumulative net commitments totalling $3,466.15 million, of which $580.15 million was committed in 1971. The tables below summarize IDA lending in 1971 by area and purpose.

IDA CREDITS BY AREA
(in millions of U.S. dollars)

Area	Amount
Africa	126.75
Asia	412.5
Europe	19.5
Western hemisphere	21.4

IDA CREDITS BY PURPOSE
(in millions of U.S. dollars)

Purpose	Amount
Agriculture	231.25
Education	50.1
Transportation	66.3
Electric power	87.7
Industry	30.0
Telecommunications	78.0
Water supply	3.0
Technical assistance	4.0
Population	4.8
Other	25.0

Agriculture

Most IDA credits and commitments in 1971 went into agriculture. Twenty-two credits amounting to $231.25 million to 13 countries were committed by IDA during the year.

CREDITS FOR AGRICULTURE

Country	Amount (in millions of U.S. dollars)	Purpose
Afghanistan	5.0	Irrigation
Bolivia	6.8	Improvement of livestock production

[2] See Y.U.N.,1963, pp. 639-40; Y.U.N., 1964, p. 535; Y.U.N., 1968, p. 991; and Y.U.N., 1969, p. 902.
[3] See Y.U.N., 1970, pp. 951-52.

Country	Amount (in millions of U.S. dollars)	Purpose
Dominican Republic	5.0	Dairy and beef production
Ethiopia	4.4	Agricultural credit
India	24.4	Farm credit
	35.0	Farm credit, tube-wells, electric pumps, tractor imports
	25.0	Farm credit, irrigation, farm mechanization
	5.0*	Construction of foodgrain storage and handling facilities
	39.0	Irrigation scheme
	6.0	Aerial spraying services
Indonesia	7.5	Rice seeds industry
	15.0	Rehabilitation and expansion of tea and cinchona production, transport improvement, worker housing, expansion of tea factories
Malawi	7.25	Comprehensive small farm development, credit
Mauritania	4.15	Livestock development
Mauritius	5.2	Small-holder tea development, credit
Republic of Korea	7.0	Dairy production, processing, marketing, research and demonstration planning
Senegal	1.35	Rural resettlement, ground nuts and cotton production
	3.7	Irrigation, rice storage facilities
Tunisia	3.0†	Improved production of wheat, dates and off-season vegetables
	2.0	Fisheries development
Turkey	4.5	Dairy production, training, studies, demonstration
	15.0‡	Production, handling, marketing, shipping of fruits and vegetables

*The Swedish Government was providing $5 million to help finance this project.

†The International Bank was lending $5 million to help finance this project.

‡The International Bank was lending $10 million to help finance this project.

Education

In 1971, IDA credits in the sector of education more than doubled over the previous year's figures—10 credits totalling $50.1 million, compared with four credits worth $21.7 million in 1970. Nine of the credits went to Africa; the other, a $4 million credit, went to the Dominican Republic to help finance curriculum reform in that country's secondary educational system.

CREDITS FOR EDUCATION

Country	Amount (in millions of U.S. dollars)	Project
Chad	2.2	Vocational, technical training
Congo	3.5	Teacher, technical training
Dominican Republic	4.0	Reform of secondary educational system
Ethiopia	9.5	Teacher, farmer and school-leaver training
Morocco	8.5	Educational research and teacher training
Senegal	2.0	Rehabilitation and expansion in industry and agriculture
Somalia	3.3	Farmer and teacher training, curriculum development
Uganda	7.3	Paramedical, rural and teacher training
United Republic of Tanzania	3.3	Farmer and worker training centres
Zaire	6.5	Teacher training and technical education

Transport

In 1971, eight credits in the transport sector, worth $66.3 million, were committed to eight countries.

CREDITS FOR TRANSPORT

Country	Amount (in millions of U.S. dollars)	Project
Cameroon	1.5	Port improvements
Congo	4.0	Highway maintenance
Indonesia	34.0	Highway improvement, regional development study
Jordan	6.0	Highway expansion
Niger	5.7	Road improvement
People's Democratic Republic of Yemen	1.6	Highway improvement
United Republic of Tanzania	6.5	Highway improvement
Zaire	7.0	River transport improvement

Electric power

Credits extended by IDA in the power sector totalled $87.7 million in 1971, more than double the previous year's figure.

The largest credit went to India: $75 million for line construction. Ghana received $7.1 million for system improvement and expansion, and El Salvador received $5.6 million for transmission facilities expansion.

Industry

Only two IDA credits were committed for the industrial sector (a sector traditionally assisted by conventional loans): $20 million to India to help increase its fertilizer production, and $10 million to Zaire for a second development finance company project.

Telecommunications

In 1971, IDA credits for the development of telecommunications increased almost threefold over the previous year, although only one credit—worth $78 million—was committed for the sector.

The recipient country was India, where the credit was to help finance expansion of the telephone system and improve the quality of long-distance services.

Water supply

One credit of $3 million was extended to Botswana by IDA for the development of water supply and sewerage facilities in Gaborone and Lobatse.

Technical assistance

One credit was provided by IDA for technical assistance in 1971: $4 million to Indonesia for pre-investment planning, feasibility and engineering studies, and consulting and advisory services. By the end of the year, the specific sub-projects for which the credit was to be used had not yet been determined. They were to be chosen in response to requests by the Indonesian Government, and in each case the Government was to contribute at least 15 per cent of the costs. The technical assistance credit was the third of its kind extended to Indonesia.

Population

One IDA credit for the financing of a population planning project in Tunisia was approved in 1971. That credit—of $4.8 million—was to finance a project to establish four maternity hospitals, two rural maternity centres and 29 maternal and child health centres where specially trained personnel would provide family planning services. The project also included the extension of a paramedical school in Tunis, including a post-graduate section.

Other credits

Early in 1971, IDA approved a credit of $25 million to assist Pakistan in rebuilding areas in East Pakistan devastated by the cyclone of November 1970, and in providing the population there with better protection against cyclones and floods.

Secretariat

The staff of IDA is the same as that for the International Bank for Reconstruction and Development. (See above, p. 717.)

STATEMENT OF INCOME AND EXPENSES
(For fiscal year ended 30 June 1971)

	Amount (in thousands of U.S. dollars)
Income	
Income from investments	13,245
Income from development credits	13,745
Gross Income	26,990
Expenses	
Management fee paid to International Bank for Reconstruction and Development	20,100
Deduct exchange adjustments	827
Gross Expenses	19,273
Net Income	7,717

Annex I. MEMBERS OF THE INTERNATIONAL DEVELOPMENT ASSOCIATION, SUBSCRIPTIONS AND VOTING POWER
(As at 31 December 1971)

Member	Subscription Amount (in millions of U.S. dollars)	Subscription Per Cent of Total	Voting power Number of Votes	Voting power Per Cent of Total	Member	Subscription Amount (in millions of U.S. dollars)	Subscription Per Cent of Total	Voting power Number of Votes	Voting power Per Cent of Total
"Part I" Countries					South Africa	10.09	0.99	2,518	0.98
Australia	20.18	1.99	4,536	1.77	Sweden	10.09	0.99	2,518	0.98
Austria	5.04	0.50	1,508	0.59	United Kingdom	131.14	12.90	26,728	10.41
Belgium	8.25	0.81	2,150	0.84	United States	320.29	31.51	64,558	25.14
Canada	37.83	3.72	8,066	3.14	Sub-total	751.45	73.93	159,789	62.22
Denmark	8.74	0.86	2,248	0.87					
Federal Republic of Germany	52.96	5.21	11,092	4.32	*"Part II" Countries*				
Finland	3.83	0.38	1,266	0.49	Afghanistan	1.01	0.10	702	0.27
France	52.96	5.21	11,092	4.32	Algeria	4.03	0.40	1,306	0.51
Iceland	0.10	0.01	520	0.20	Argentina	18.83	1.85	4,266	1.66
Italy	18.16	1.79	4,132	1.61	Bolivia	1.06	0.10	712	0.28
Japan	33.59	3.30	7,218	2.81	Botswana	0.16	0.02	532	0.21
Kuwait	3.36	0.33	1,172	0.46	Brazil	18.83	1.85	4,266	1.66
Luxembourg	0.38	0.04	575	0.22	Burma	2.02	0.20	904	0.35
Netherlands	27.74	2.73	6,048	2.35	Burundi	0.76	0.07	652	0.26
Norway	6.72	0.66	1,844	0.72	Cameroon	1.01	0.10	702	0.27

Member	Subscription Amount (in millions of U.S. dollars)	Per Cent of Total	Voting power Number of Votes	Per Cent of Total	Member	Subscription Amount (in millions of U.S. dollars)	Per Cent of Total	Voting power Number of Votes	Per Cent of Total
"Part II" Countries (continued)					Mali	0.87	0.09	674	0.26
Central African					Mauritania	0.50	0.05	600	0.23
Republic	0.50	0.05	600	0.23	Mauritius	0.86	0.08	672	0.26
Ceylon	3.03	0.30	1,106	0.43	Mexico	8.74	0.86	2,248	0.87
Chad	0.50	0.05	600	0.23	Morocco	3.53	0.35	1,206	0.47
Chile	3.53	0.35	1,206	0.47	Nepal	0.50	0.05	600	0.23
China	30.26	2.98	6,552	2.55	Nicaragua	0.30	0.03	560	0.22
Colombia	3.53	0.35	1,206	0.47	Niger	0.50	0.05	600	0.23
Congo	0.50	0.05	600	0.23	Nigeria	3.36	0.33	1,172	0.46
Costa Rica	0.20	0.02	540	0.21	Pakistan	10.09	0.99	2,518	0.98
Cyprus	0.76	0.07	652	0.26	Panama	0.02	*	504	0.20
Dahomey	0.50	0.05	600	0.23	Paraguay	0.30	0.03	560	0.22
Dominican	0.40	0.04	580	0.23	People's	1.18	0.12	736	0.29
Republic					Democratic				
Ecuador	0.65	0.06	630	0.25	Republic of				
Egypt	5.08	0.50	1,516	0.59	Yemen				
El Salvador	0.30	0.03	560	0.22	Peru	1.77	0.17	854	0.33
Ethiopia	0.50	0.05	600	0.23	Philippines	5.04	0.50	1,508	0.59
Gabon	0.50	0.05	600	0.23	Republic of	1.26	0.12	752	0.29
Gambia	0.27	0.03	553	0.22	Korea				
Ghana	2.36	0.23	972	0.38	Republic of	1.51	0.15	802	0.31
Greece	2.52	0.25	1,004	0.39	Viet-Nam				
Guatemala	0.40	0.04	580	0.23	Rwanda	0.76	0.07	652	0.26
Guinea	1.01	0.10	702	0.27	Saudi Arabia	3.70	0.36	1,240	0.48
Guyana	0.81	0.08	662	0.26	Senegal	1.68	0.17	836	0.32
Haiti	0.76	0.07	652	0.26	Sierra Leone	0.76	0.07	652	0.26
Honduras	0.30	0.03	560	0.22	Somalia	0.76	0.07	652	0.26
India	40.35	3.97	8,570	3.34	Spain	10.09	0.99	2,518	0.98
Indonesia	11.10	1.09	2,720	1.06	Sudan	1.01	0.10	702	0.27
Iran	4.54	0.45	1,408	0.55	Swaziland	0.32	0.03	564	0.22
Iraq	0.76	0.07	652	0.26	Syrian Arab	0.95	0.09	690	0.27
Ireland	3.03	0.30	1,106	0.43	Republic				
Israel	1.68	0.17	836	0.32	Thailand	3.03	0.30	1,106	0.43
Ivory Coast	1.01	0.10	702	0.27	Togo	0.76	0.07	652	0.26
Jordan	0.30	0.03	560	0.22	Tunisia	1.51	0.15	802	0.31
Kenya	1.68	0.17	836	0.32	Turkey	5.80	0.57	1,660	0.65
Khmer	1.02	0.10	704	0.28	Uganda	1.68	0.17	836	0.32
Republic					United	1.68	0.17	836	0.32
Laos	0.50	0.05	600	0.23	Republic of				
Lebanon	0.45	0.04	590	0.23	Tanzania				
Lesotho	0.16	0.02	532	0.21	Upper Volta	0.50	0.05	600	0.23
Liberia	0.76	0.07	652	0.26	Yemen	0.43	0.04	586	0.23
Libyan Arab	1.01	0.10	702	0.27	Yugoslavia	4.04	0.40	1,308	0.51
Republic					Zaire	3.02	0.30	1,104	0.43
Madagascar	1.01	0.10	702	0.27	Zambia	2.69	0.26	1,038	0.40
Malawi	0.76	0.07	652	0.26	Sub-total	265.02	26.07	97,003	37.78
Malaysia	2.52	0.25	1,004	0.39	Total	1,016.46†		256,792	

*Less than 0.005 per cent.
†Total rounded out separately from roundings for individual entries.

Annex II. EXECUTIVE DIRECTORS AND ALTERNATES OF THE INTERNATIONAL DEVELOPMENT ASSOCIATION

(As at 31 December 1971)

Appointed Director	Appointed Alternate	Casting the votes of
Robert E. Wieczorowski	—	United States
D. J. Mitchell	K. M. Critchley	United Kingdom
Fritz Stedtfeld	Wolfgang H. Artopoeus	Federal Republic of Germany

Appointed Director	Appointed Alternate	Casting the votes of
Marc Viénot	Jean P. Carrière	France
Seitaro Hattori	Masanari Sumi	Japan
S. R. Sen	M. R. Shroff	India
Elected Director	Elected Alternate	Casting the votes of
S. Osman Ali (Pakistan)	Mohammad Yeganeh (Iran)	Egypt, Iran, Iraq, Jordan, Kuwait, Lebanon, Pakistan, People's Democratic Republic of Yemen, Saudi Arabia, Syrian Arab Republic, Yemen
Giorgio Rota (Italy)	Juan Moro (Spain)	Italy, Spain
Claude M. Isbister (Canada)	Maurice Horgan (Ireland)	Canada, Guyana, Ireland
André van Campenhout (Belgium)	Viktor C. Wolf (Austria)	Austria, Belgium, Luxembourg, Turkey
R. Lindsay Knight (New Zealand)	M. A. Cranswick (Australia)	Australia, South Africa
Donatien Bihute (Burundi)	Bulcha Demeksa (Ethiopia)	Botswana, Burundi, Ethiopia, Gambia, Guinea, Kenya, Lesotho, Liberia, Malawi, Nigeria, Sierra Leone, Sudan, Swaziland, Uganda, United Republic of Tanzania, Zambia
Erik Törnqvist (Finland)	Carl I. Ohman (Sweden)	Denmark, Finland, Iceland, Norway, Sweden
Reignson C. Chen (China)	Byong Hyun Shin (Republic of Korea)	China, Republic of Korea, Republic of Viet-Nam
Alfred Rinnooy Kan (Netherlands)	Vladimir Ceric (Yugoslavia)	Cyprus, Israel, Netherlands, Yugoslavia
Abderrahman Tazi (Morocco)	—	Afghanistan, Algeria, Ghana, Greece, Indonesia, Khmer Republic, Libyan Arab Republic, Morocco, Tunisia
Adrián Lajous (Mexico)	Carlos Santistevan (Peru)	Costa Rica, El Salvador, Guatemala, Haiti, Honduras, Mexico, Nicaragua, Panama, Peru
Mohamed Nassim Kochman (Mauritania)	Benoît Boukar (Chad)	Cameroon, Central African Republic, Chad, Congo, Dahomey, Gabon, Ivory Coast, Madagascar, Mali, Mauritania, Mauritius, Niger, Rwanda, Senegal, Somalia, Togo, Upper Volta, Zaire
Virgilio Barco (Colombia)	Placido L. Mapa, Jr. (Philippines)	Brazil, Colombia, Dominican Republic, Ecuador, Philippines
Luis B. Mey (Argentina)	Oscar Vega-López (Bolivia)	Argentina, Bolivia, Chile, Paraguay
Khunying Suparb Yossundara (Thailand)	R. V. Navaratnam (Malaysia)	Burma, Ceylon, Laos, Malaysia, Nepal, Thailand

Annex III. PRINCIPAL OFFICERS AND OFFICES OF THE INTERNATIONAL DEVELOPMENT ASSOCIATION

(As at 31 December 1971)

PRINCIPAL OFFICERS*

President: Robert S. McNamara
Vice-President and Chairman, Loan Committee: J. Burke Knapp
Vice-President, Finance, and Director, Projects: S. Aldewereld
General Counsel: A. Broches
Director, Development Services Department: Richard H. Demuth
Economic Adviser to the President: Hollis B. Chenery
Vice-President: Sir Denis Rickett
Vice-President: Mohamed Shoaib

Treasurer: Eugene H. Rotberg
Controller: K. Georg Gabriel
Secretary: M. M. Mendels

*Officers and staff of the International Bank for Reconstruction and Development serve as officers and staff of the International Development Association.

HEADQUARTERS AND OTHER OFFICES

HEADQUARTERS
International Development Association
1818 H Street, N.W.
Washington, D.C. 20433, U.S.A.
 Telephone: EXecutive 3-6360
  Cable Address: INDEVAS WASHINGTON

EUROPEAN OFFICE
International Development Association
66 Avenue d'Iéna
75116 Paris, France
 Telephone: 720-2510
  Cable Address: INDEVAS PARIS

TOKYO OFFICE
International Development Association
Kokusai Building, Room 908
1-1, Marunouchi 3-Chôme, Chiyoda-Ku
Tokyo 100, Japan
 Telephone: (03) 214-5001
  Cable Address: INDEVAS TOKYO

Chapter IX

The International Monetary Fund

The background against which the activities of the International Monetary Fund[1] were conducted in 1971 included the continuing float of the Canadian dollar, which started in May 1970, and the announcement by the Federal Republic of Germany and the Netherlands, on 9 May 1971, that they would for the time being cease to maintain the exchange rates for their currencies within the established margins. On 15 August, the United States announced a number of economic and financial measures, including suspension of the United States dollar's convertibility. This suspension brought about a float of most major currencies, a situation involving uncertainty in trade and exchange relationships.

During the 1971 annual meeting of the Fund's Board of Governors, which took place from 27 September to 1 October, the Governors addressed themselves to the problems raised by these events and sought appropriate means to restore and strengthen the international monetary system.

By a resolution adopted on the closing day of the meeting, the Board of Governors called upon members to co-operate with each other in order to establish a satisfactory structure of exchange rates, maintained within suitable margins, and to facilitate resumption of the orderly conduct of Fund operations. They also requested the Executive Directors to report to them on necessary or desirable measures for the improvement or reform of the international monetary system.

Par values, central rates and wider margins

The Finance Ministers and Central Bank Governors of the Group of Ten (the industrial members of the Fund participating in its General Arrangements to Borrow) convened in Washington on 17 and 18 December 1971 and agreed on an inter-related set of measures designed to restore stability to international monetary arrangements and to provide for expanding international trade. Specifically, the Ministers and Governors reached a consensus on a new pattern of exchange-rate relationships between their currencies, and the United States agreed to propose to its Congress a suitable means for devaluing the dollar in terms of gold to $38 per ounce from the previous $35. The participants were unanimous in their view that discussions should be promptly undertaken, particularly within the framework of the Fund, to consider reform of the international monetary system over the longer term.

The Fund's Managing Director took part in the ministerial-level session and reported to the Ministers and Governors on the joint meeting of the Fund's Executive Directors and the Deputies of the Group of Ten, held on 16 December.

In the weeks that followed the 15 August announcement by the United States, the Managing Director of the Fund on several occasions called for an early return to a system of fixed parities through "contributions" by all major nations, and suggested that a small increase in the dollar price of gold would be helpful. In addition, the Executive Directors and staff of the Fund continued to give attention to various aspects of a reform of the international monetary system.

The Fund announced on 19 December that its Executive Directors had adopted a decision establishing a temporary régime under which a member might permit the exchange rates for its currency to move within margins of 2 1/4 per cent (instead of 1 per cent, as specified in the Articles of Agreement) on either side of the par value or the new exchange value of its currency resulting from the agreed realignment of exchange rates. The new exchange value for a currency resulting from realignment, if notified to the Fund only for the purpose of this temporary régime and not immediately proposed by the member as a new par value, was to be referred to as a central rate.

Before the end of the year, the Executive Directors approved new par values for the Bahamas, Botswana, Ghana, Kenya, Lesotho, the Netherlands' Surinam, South Africa, Swaziland, Uganda, the United Republic of Tanzania, Yugoslavia and Zambia. Par values maintained unchanged in terms of gold included those of: Australia, Barbados, Cyprus, Ethiopia, France, Gambia, Iraq, Ireland, Jamaica, Kuwait, the Libyan Arab Republic, Malawi, Malaysia, Morocco, New Zealand, Nigeria, Rwanda, Saudi Arabia, Sierra Leone, Singapore, Somalia, Spain, Tunisia, the United Kingdom and Hong Kong.

Members establishing central rates were Austria, Belgium, Burma, Denmark, the Dominican Republic, the Federal Republic of Germany, Finland, Greece, Guyana, Haiti, Honduras, Iceland, India, Israel, Italy, Japan, Jordan, Luxembourg, Malta, Mexico, the Netherlands, the Netherlands Antilles, Nicaragua, Norway, Panama, Portugal, Sweden, Turkey and Zaire.

---

[1]For further information on the Fund's activities prior to 1971, see annual reports of Executive Directors, summary proceedings of annual meetings of Board of Governors, schedules of par values, quarterly financial statements, and previous volumes of Y.U.N.

Special Drawing Rights

On 1 January 1971, Special Drawing Rights (SDRs) 2,949.2 million were allocated to 109 participants in the Fund's Special Drawing Account, based on a rate of 10.7 per cent of each member's quota as at 31 December 1970. By the end of 1971, the number of participants had risen to 113. Preparations were completed to allocate SDR 2,951.5 million on 1 January 1972, at a rate equal to 10.6 per cent of each participating member's quota as at 31 December 1971. Special Drawing Rights created by the three annual allocations of the first basic period would thus total about 9,300 million.

During 1971, transfers of SDRs totalled SDR 1,300 million compared with SDR 952.4 million during 1970. The main reason for the increase was the use by the United States of SDR 480 million to obtain balances of United States dollars from Belgium and the Netherlands by agreement with those countries.

The transfers of SDRs in which most participants using SDRs were involved during 1971 were transactions in which the users transferred SDRs to other participants, designated by the Fund to receive them, to obtain foreign exchange in return. Participants receiving currency from other participants in these transactions were expected to have a balance-of-payments need to do so, while the participants designated to provide currency were those whose balance of payments and reserve positions were judged to be sufficiently strong for them to be designated to provide foreign exchange.

During 1971, 28 participants used a total of SDR 362.2 million to acquire foreign exchange. Among the larger users in this category were Argentina (SDR 105 million), South Africa (SDR 60 million), Indonesia (SDR 25 million) and Iran (SDR 20 million).

Twenty-four participants, including both industrial and developing countries, were designated to provide foreign exchange in exchange for the SDRs which were used. The principal recipients of SDRs in these transactions were the United Kingdom (SDR 195 million), India (SDR 37 million), Italy (SDR 36 million), France (SDR 24 million) and the Federal Republic of Germany (SDR 23 million).

The total use of SDRs in these transactions with designation—SDR 362.2 million—compared with a total of SDR 291.2 million during 1970. As in 1970, there was some concentration on these transactions in the first quarter of the year immediately following the allocation of SDRs.

Participants are also able to use SDRs to make repurchases of outstanding drawings in the Fund's General Account and to pay charges arising from the use of Fund resources. During 1971, a total of SDR 323 million was transferred from participants to the General Account in this way, principally in repurchases. Of this total, SDR 167 million was used by the United Kingdom, SDR 33 million by India, SDR 16 million by Yugoslavia and SDR 15 million by Turkey.

During 1971, the Fund's General Account transferred a total of SDR 130 million to participants; in the course of the year, the Fund's holdings of SDRs rose by SDR 199 million to SDR 489 million as at 31 December 1971. Of the total SDRs transferred from the General Account, SDR 77 million was transferred to three participants —Canada, Finland and Italy—which exercised options granted by the Fund to receive SDRs in place of gold used to replenish the Fund's holdings of currencies.

Similar options to receive SDRs were granted to participants when the Fund paid a total of $37.4 million in remuneration on net creditor positions in the General Account and when the Fund made a distribution of net income totalling $12.5 million: 21 participants elected to receive a total of SDR 23 million in these operations.

As at 31 December 1971, there were 64 participants that had made net use of SDRs, so that their holdings were below the total amounts they had been allocated. Total net use by participants at the end of 1971 was SDR 1,503 million. The counterpart of this net use was reflected in the excess holdings (i.e. holdings above allocations) of SDR 1,014 million by 27 participants and the General Account's holdings of SDR 489 million.

The largest net users were the United States (SDR 484 million), the United Kingdom (SDR 119 million) and Argentina (SDR 103 million). The largest net recipients of SDRs were the Netherlands (SDR 408 million), Belgium (SDR 265 million) and Canada (SDR 130 million). Net receipts by Belgium and the Netherlands mainly reflected the voluntary acceptance of SDRs by these participants from the United States in exchange for balances of United States dollars.

Among the primary producing countries, 56 participants had made net use of SDR 890 million, while 17 participants held a total of SDR 47 million in excess of their allocation.

Drawings, repurchases and Fund holdings of member currencies

Total drawings on the Fund reached the equivalent of SDR 23,908.5 million at the end of 1971 against SDR 22,008.1 million a year earlier (figures included the Fund's repayments of earlier borrowings). Thirty-five of the Fund's 120 members made use of Fund resources in 1971. New drawings during the year amounted to SDR 1,900.3 million, compared to repayments by repurchase amounting to SDR 2,806.6 million. (See tables below.)

TABLE I. DRAWINGS AND REPAYMENTS BY REPURCHASE IN 1971
(in millions of SDRs)

Member	Drawings	Repurchases
Afghanistan	—	4.4
Argentina	5.2	—
Bolivia	4.5	4.0
Burma	6.5	5.0
Burundi	1.5	3.7
Central African Republic	1.3	—
Ceylon	14.0	23.4
Chile	77.5	39.5
China	59.9	—
Colombia	30.0	31.6
Costa Rica	6.0	0.3
Denmark	—	25.9
Dominican Republic	7.5	3.3
Ecuador	—	8.3
Egypt	32.0	11.5
El Salvador	9.0	5.3
France	—	983.8
Ghana	—	28.1
Guatemala	—	3.0
Guyana	4.0	—
Guinea	—	0.5
Haiti	—	3.7
Iceland	—	7.5
India	—	65.0
Indonesia	2.9	15.0
Israel	20.0	—
Jamaica	—	3.8
Jordan	4.5	—
Khmer Republic	6.3	—
Liberia	1.0	3.4
Mali	2.5	4.0
Malaysia	11.7	—
Mauritania	1.0	—
Morocco	8.3	35.8
Nicaragua	3.0	—
Pakistan	—	1.9
Panama	1.0	4.4
Peru	16.0	22.6
Philippines	35.0	14.0
Republic of Korea	7.5	—
Rwanda	—	3.0
Spain	—	48.8
Sudan	—	15.1
Syrian Arab Republic	—	4.8
Tunisia	2.5	10.0
Turkey	15.0	27.0
Uganda	16.5	0.8
United Kingdom	—	1,298.9
United States	1,362.0	—
Uruguay	9.5	10.6
Yugoslavia	96.3	25.2
Zambia	19.0	—

TABLE II. CURRENCIES DRAWN IN 1971
(in millions of SDRs)

Austrian schillings	10.0
Belgian francs	690.0
Canadian dollars	85.5
Deutsche mark	228.8
French francs	100.1
Irish pounds	5.0
Italian lire	60.9
Kuwaiti dinars	5.0
Netherlands guilders	672.0
Pounds sterling	27.9
Spanish pesetas	5.0
United States dollars	10.0

TABLE III. REPURCHASES BY CURRENCY OF REPURCHASE IN 1971
(in millions of SDRs)

Gold	478.6
Special Drawing Rights	301.5

Argentine pesos	15.0
Australian dollars	83.2
Austrian schillings	34.1
Belgian francs	430.9
Canadian dollars	351.3
Deutsche mark	63.0
French francs	44.5
Italian lire	0.3
Japanese yen	368.4
Kuwaiti dinars	5.0
Mexican pesos	30.1
Netherlands guilders	484.3
Norwegian kroner	44.7
Swedish kronor	39.8
United States dollars	38.3

By areas, 12 Latin American countries drew SDR 173.3 million during 1971, while repayments from Latin America (not necessarily from the same drawing countries) totalled SDR 140.3 million. Eleven member countries in Asia and the Middle East drew SDR 200.1 million; repayments from the same area were SDR 145 million. Nine African countries drew SDR 53.6 million, and repayments from Africa totalled SDR 104.3 million. Three industrial and developed countries drew SDR 1,473.3 million. Repayments from industrial and other developed countries totalled SDR 2,417.1 million.

Net drawings—representing the outstanding total of Fund resources in use by members—were SDR 3,663.9 million at 31 December 1971, down from the year's month-end peak of SDR 4,894.6 million reached in February.

Amounts available to members under stand-by arrangements at 31 December 1971 totalled SDR 217.8 million, against SDR 171.5 million a year earlier. (See table below.)

TABLE IV. FUND STAND-BY ARRANGEMENTS
(As at 31 December 1971, in millions of SDRs)

Member	Amount agreed	Amount drawn	Amount available
Brazil	50.0	—	50.0
Ceylon	24.5	14.0	10.5
Colombia	38.0	30.0	8.0
Guyana	4.0	2.2	1.8
Haiti	3.0	—	3.0
Honduras	15.0	—	15.0
Indonesia	50.0	—	50.0
Mali	4.5	2.5	2.0
Morocco	30.0	8.2	21.8
Panama	14.0	—	14.0
Philippines	45.0	35.0	10.0
Uganda	10.0	10.0	—
Yugoslavia	83.5	51.8	31.7
Total	371.5	153.7	217.8

The three largest drawings of the year were by the United States: SDR 250 million in January, SDR

250 million in June, and SDR 862 million in August.

Members that drew on the Fund's resources during 1971 were: Argentina, Bolivia, Burma, Burundi, the Central African Republic, Ceylon, Chile, China, Colombia, Costa Rica, the Dominican Republic, Egypt, El Salvador, Guyana, Indonesia, Israel, Jordan, the Khmer Republic, Liberia, Malaysia, Mali, Mauritania, Morocco, Nicaragua, Panama, Peru, the Philippines, the Republic of Korea, Tunisia, Turkey, Uganda, the United States, Uruguay, Yugoslavia and Zambia.

During 1971, the Fund used 12 member currencies in its support operations, six less than in 1970. The Fund sold in quantity Belgian francs, Canadian dollars, deutsche mark, French francs, Italian lire and Netherlands guilders.

Fund holdings of gold, currencies and SDRs totalled SDR 29,390.5 million at 31 December 1971, but holdings of some currencies were considerably below subscription levels as a result of Fund transactions. These included: Austrian schillings (47 per cent of quota), Belgian francs (8 per cent), deutsche mark (33 per cent), and Netherlands guilders (8 per cent).

Income and expenditures, gold transactions and borrowings

In September 1971, the Fund reported total expenditure under its General Account of $89.2 million and operational income of $135.6 million for fiscal 1971 (year ended 30 April 1971).

In the course of 1971, the Fund bought SDR 137.6 million of gold, all of it from South Africa under arrangements made at the end of 1969. The Fund sold SDR 385.5 million of gold during the year to replenish its holdings of members' currencies, bringing the total sold since the beginning of Fund operations to SDR 3,902 million.

In August, the Fund completed repayments of its outstanding debts under borrowing arrangements in repaying the equivalent of SDR 125 million under a bilateral borrowing arrangement with Japan and SDR 152 million of claims under the General Arrangements to Borrow. This was the first time since initial activation of the Arrangements in December 1964 that the Fund had no outstanding debt under the Arrangements. A total equivalent to SDR 2,155 million had been borrowed under the General Arrangements to Borrow from December 1964 to February 1970, to assist in financing large drawings by industrial countries.

Remuneration, distribution of net income

The Fund paid remuneration at the rate of 1.5 per cent per annum on members' creditor positions (i.e. the amount by which 75 per cent of a member's quota exceeded the average of the Fund's holdings of the member's currency) for the year ended 30 April 1971. The amount paid to 39 members totalled the equivalent of SDR 37.4 million, of which SDR 22.7 million was paid in gold and SDR 14.7 million in Special Drawing Rights. The Fund also decided to make a distribution of net income to members equal to a further 9.5 per cent on the same creditor positions. This distribution amounted to the equivalent of SDR 12.5 million of which members opted to receive SDR 8.3 million in Special Drawing Rights and SDR 4.2 million in their respective currencies.

Consultations and membership

The Fund continued its annual round of consultations with individual members on their balance of payments, foreign exchange practices and related problems, and provided technical assistance for a variety of fiscal, monetary, central banking and statistical problems.

Three countries became members of the Fund during 1971: Fiji (28 May), Oman (23 December), and Western Samoa (28 December), bringing the total membership to 120.

Publications

Publications issued by the Fund during 1971 included: *Annual Report; Annual Report on Exchange Restrictions; Summary Proceedings of Annual Meeting;* a monthly statistical bulletin, *International Financial Statistics,* published jointly with the International Bank for Reconstruction and Development; *Balance of Payments Yearbook; Staff Papers,* three times yearly; *Fund and Bank Review—Finance and Development,* published quarterly, jointly with the International Bank for Reconstruction and Development; and *International Financial News Survey,* a weekly.

Secretariat

On 31 December 1971, the total number of full-time staff employed by the Fund under permanent, fixed-term and short-term appointments stood at 1,253. Of these, 657 were in the professional and higher categories (drawn from 73 nationalities), and 596 were in the general service category.

Administrative budget

The Fund's Executive Board approved the following administrative budget for the fiscal year ended 30 April 1972:

	Amount (in U.S. dollars)
Board of Governors	760,000
Executive Directors	
Salaries	2,072,000
Other compensation and benefits	564,000

Executive Directors (continued)	Amount (in U.S. dollars)
Travel	495,000
Total	3,131,000

Staff	
Salaries	16,024,000
Other compensation and benefits	6,233,000
Travel	3,830,000
Total	26,087,000

Special Services to Member Countries	3,031,000

Other Administrative Expenses	
Communications	1,489,000
Office occupancy expenses	1,109,000
Books and printing	750,000
Supplies and equipment	719,000
Miscellaneous	774,000
Data processing services	650,000
Total	5,491,000
Grand Total	38,500,000

Fund Accounts

The Fund accounts (in millions of SDRs) as at 31 December 1971 were as follows:

Total Drawings	23,908.5
Net drawings	3,663.9
Total Quotas	28,807.8
Gold Account	
Gold with depositories	4,902.1
Investments	400.0
Total	5,302.1
Fund Holdings of Special Drawing Rights	488.8

Holdings of Selected Currencies and Percentage of Quotas

	Percentage	Amount (in million SDR equivalents)
Austrian schillings	47	127.6
Belgian francs	8	50.6
Canadian dollars	70	767.5
Deutsche mark	33	521.8
French francs	71	1,064.1
Italian lire	65	651.5
Japanese yen	59	710.1
Netherlands guilders	8	56.3
Pounds sterling	118	3,297.4
Swedish kronor	74	241.4
United States dollars	91	5,155.5

Annex I. MEMBERS OF THE INTERNATIONAL MONETARY FUND, QUOTAS AND VOTING POWER
(As at 31 December 1971)

Member	Quota			Voting power		
	Amount (in millions of SDRs)	General Account per cent of total	Special Drawing Account per cent of total	Number of votes*	General Account per cent of total	Special Drawing Account per cent of total
Afghanistan	37.00	0.13	0.13	620	0.19	0.20
Algeria	130.00	0.45	0.46	1,550	0.49	0.50
Argentina	440.00	1.53	1.55	4,650	1.46	1.49
Australia	665.00	2.31	2.34	6,900	2.17	2.21
Austria	270.00	0.94	0.95	2,950	0.93	0.94
Barbados	13.00	0.05	0.05	380	0.12	0.12
Belgium	650.00	2.26	2.29	6,750	2.12	2.16
Bolivia	37.00	0.13	0.13	620	0.19	0.20
Botswana	5.00	0.02	0.02	300	0.09	0.10
Brazil	440.00	1.53	1.55	4,650	1.46	1.49
Burma	60.00	0.21	0.21	850	0.27	0.27
Burundi	19.00	0.07	0.07	440	0.14	0.14
Cameroon	35.00	0.12	0.12	600	0.19	0.19
Canada	1,100.00	3.82	3.87	11,250	3.54	3.60
Central African Republic	13.00	0.05	0.05	380	0.12	0.12
Ceylon	98.00	0.34	0.35	1,230	0.39	0.39
Chad	13.00	0.05	0.05	380	0.12	0.12
Chile	158.00	0.55	0.56	1,830	0.58	0.59
China	550.00	1.91	1.94	5,750	1.81	1.84
Colombia	157.00	0.54	0.55	1,820	0.57	0.58
Congo	13.00	0.05	0.05	380	0.12	0.12
Costa Rica	32.00	0.11	0.11	570	0.18	0.18
Cyprus	26.00	0.09	0.09	510	0.16	0.16
Dahomey	13.00	0.05	0.05	380	0.12	0.12
Denmark	260.00	0.90	0.92	2,850	0.90	0.91
Dominican Republic	43.00	0.15	0.15	680	0.21	0.22

Member	Quota			Voting power		
	Amount (in millions of SDRs)	General Account per cent of total	Special Drawing Account per cent of total	Number of votes*	General Account per cent of total	Special Drawing Account per cent of total
Ecuador	33.00	0.11	0.12	580	0.18	0.19
Egypt	188.00	0.65	0.66	2,130	0.67	0.68
El Salvador	35.00	0.12	0.12	600	0.19	0.19
Equatorial Guinea	8.00	0.03	0.03	330	0.10	0.11
Ethiopia†	27.00	0.09	—	520	0.16	—
Federal Republic of Germany	1,600.00	5.55	5.63	16,250	5.11	5.21
Fiji	13.00	0.05	0.05	380	0.12	0.12
Finland	190.00	0.66	0.67	2,150	0.68	0.69
France	1,500.00	5.21	5.28	15,250	4.79	4.88
Gabon	15.00	0.05	0.05	400	0.13	0.13
Gambia	7.00	0.02	0.02	320	0.10	0.10
Ghana	87.00	0.30	0.31	1,120	0.35	0.36
Greece	138.00	0.48	0.49	1,630	0.51	0.52
Guatemala	36.00	0.12	0.13	610	0.19	0.20
Guinea	24.00	0.08	0.08	490	0.15	0.16
Guyana	20.00	0.07	0.07	450	0.14	0.14
Haiti	19.00	0.07	0.07	440	0.14	0.14
Honduras	25.00	0.09	0.09	500	0.16	0.16
Iceland	23.00	0.08	0.08	480	0.15	0.15
India	940.00	3.26	3.31	9,650	3.03	3.09
Indonesia	260.00	0.90	0.92	2,850	0.90	0.91
Iran	192.00	0.67	0.68	2,170	0.68	0.70
Iraq	109.00	0.38	0.38	1,340	0.42	0.43
Ireland	121.00	0.42	0.43	1,460	0.46	0.47
Israel	130.00	0.45	0.46	1,550	0.49	0.50
Italy	1,000.00	3.47	3.52	10,250	3.22	3.28
Ivory Coast	52.00	0.18	0.18	770	0.24	0.25
Jamaica	53.00	0.18	0.19	780	0.25	0.25
Japan	1,200.00	4.17	4.23	12,250	3.85	3.92
Jordan	23.00	0.08	0.08	480	0.15	0.15
Kenya	48.00	0.17	0.17	730	0.23	0.23
Khmer Republic	25.00	0.09	0.09	500	0.16	0.16
Kuwait†	65.00	0.23	—	900	0.28	—
Laos	13.00	0.05	0.05	380	0.12	0.12
Lebanon†	900	0.03	—	340	0.11	—
Lesotho	5.00	0.02	0.02	300	0.09	0.10
Liberia	29.00	0.10	0.10	540	0.17	0.17
Libyan Arab Republic†	24.00	0.08	—	490	0.15	—
Luxembourg	20.00	0.07	0.07	450	0.14	0.14
Madagascar	26.00	0.09	0.09	510	0.16	0.16
Malawi	15.00	0.05	0.05	400	0.13	0.13
Malaysia	186.00	0.65	0.66	2,110	0.66	0.68
Mali	22.00	0.08	0.08	470	0.15	0.15
Malta	16.00	0.06	0.06	410	0.13	0.13
Mauritania	13.00	0.05	0.05	380	0.12	0.12
Mauritius	22.00	0.08	0.08	470	0.15	0.15
Mexico	370.00	1.28	1.30	3,950	1.24	1.27
Morocco	113.00	0.39	0.40	1,380	0.43	0.44
Nepal	10.80	0.04	0.04	358	0.11	0.11
Netherlands	700.00	2.43	2.47	7,250	2.28	2.32
New Zealand	202.00	0.70	0.71	2,270	0.71	0.73
Nicaragua	27.00	0.09	0.10	520	0.16	0.17
Niger	13.00	0.05	0.05	380	0.12	0.12
Nigeria	135.00	0.47	0.48	1,600	0.50	0.51
Norway	240.00	0.83	0.85	2,650	0.83	0.85
Oman	7.00	0.02	0.02	320	0.10	0.10
Pakistan	235.00	0.82	0.83	2,600	0.82	0.84
Panama	36.00	0.12	0.13	610	0.19	0.20
Paraguay	19.00	0.07	0.07	440	0.14	0.14
People's Democratic Republic of Yemen	29.00	0.10	0.10	540	0.17	0.17

Member	Quota			Voting power		
	Amount (in millions of SDRs)	General Account per cent of total	Special Drawing Account per cent of total	Number of votes*	General Account per cent of total	Special Drawing Account per cent of total
Peru	123.00	0.43	0.43	1,480	0.47	0.47
Philippines	155.00	0.54	0.55	1,800	0.57	0.58
Portugal†	117.00	0.41	—	1,420	0.45	—
Republic of Korea	80.00	0.28	0.28	1,050	0.33	0.34
Republic of Viet-Nam	62.00	0.22	0.22	870	0.27	0.28
Rwanda	19.00	0.07	0.07	440	0.14	0.14
Saudi Arabia†	134.00	0.47	—	1,590	0.50	—
Senegal	34.00	0.12	0.12	590	0.19	0.19
Sierra Leone	25.00	0.09	0.09	500	0.16	0.16
Singapore†	37.00	0.13	—	620	0.19	—
Somalia	19.00	0.07	0.07	440	0.14	0.14
South Africa	320.00	1.11	1.13	3,450	1.08	1.11
Spain	395.00	1.37	1.39	4,200	1.32	1.35
Sudan	72.00	0.25	0.25	970	0.30	0.31
Swaziland	8.00	0.03	0.03	330	0.10	0.11
Sweden	325.00	1.13	1.14	3,500	1.10	1.12
Syrian Arab Republic	50.00	0.17	0.18	750	0.24	0.24
Thailand	134.00	0.47	0.47	1,590	0.50	0.51
Togo	15.00	0.05	0.05	400	0.13	0.13
Trinidad and Tobago	63.00	0.22	0.22	880	0.28	0.28
Tunisia	48.00	0.17	0.17	730	0.23	0.23
Turkey	151.00	0.52	0.53	1,760	0.55	0.56
Uganda	40.00	0.14	0.14	650	0.20	0.21
United Kingdom	2,800.00	9.72	9.86	28,250	8.88	9.05
United Republic of Tanzania	42.00	0.15	0.15	670	0.21	0.21
United States	6,700.00	23.26	23.60	67,250	21.14	21.54
Upper Volta	13.00	0.05	0.05	380	0.12	0.12
Uruguay	69.00	0.24	0.24	940	0.30	0.30
Venezuela	330.00	1.15	1.16	3,550	1.12	1.14
Western Samoa	2.00	0.01	0.01	270	0.08	0.09
Yemen	10.00	0.03	0.04	350	0.11	0.11
Yugoslavia	207.00	0.72	0.73	2,320	0.73	0.74
Zaire	113.00	0.39	0.40	1,380	0.43	0.44
Zambia	76.00	0.26	0.27	1,010	0.32	0.32
Totals General Account	28,807.80			318,078		
Special Drawing Account	28,394.80			312,198		

*Voting power varies on certain matters pertaining to the General Account with use of the Fund's resources in that Account. Only Governors appointed by members that are participants may cast their votes on matters pertaining to the Special Drawing Account.
†Not a participant in the Special Drawing Account.

Annex II. EXECUTIVE DIRECTORS AND ALTERNATES OF INTERNATIONAL MONETARY FUND
(As at 31 December 1971)

Appointed Director	Alternate	Casting the votes of
William B. Dale	Charles R. Harley	United States
Derek Mitchell	R. H. Gilchrist	United Kingdom
Guenther Schleiminger	Lore Fuenfgelt	Federal Republic of Germany
Marc Viénot	Claude Beaurain	France
Hideo Suzuki	Koichi Satow	Japan*
P. S. N. Prasad	S. S. Marathe	India

Elected Director	Alternate	Casting the votes of
Francesco Palamenghi-Crispi (Italy)	Carlos Bustelo (Spain)	Italy, Malta, Portugal, Spain

Elected Director	Alternate	Casting the votes of
Nazih Deif (Egypt)	Muhammad Al-Atrash (Syrian Arab Republic)	Afghanistan, Egypt, Iran, Iraq, Jordan, Kuwait, Lebanon, Pakistan, People's Democratic Republic of Yemen, Saudi Arabia, Somalia, Syrian Arab Republic, Yemen
Robert Bryce (Canada)	Donald Owen Mills (Jamaica)	Canada, Ireland, Jamaica
Lindsay B. Brand (Australia)	R. van S. Smit (South Africa)	Australia, Lesotho, New Zealand, South Africa, Swaziland
André van Campenhout (Belgium)	Heinrich G. Schneider (Austria)	Austria, Belgium, Luxembourg, Turkey
Erik Brofoss (Norway)	Sigurgeir Jonsson (Iceland)	Denmark, Finland, Iceland, Norway, Sweden
Pieter Lieftinck (Netherlands)	Tom de Vries (Netherlands)	Cyprus, Israel, Netherlands, Yugoslavia
Luis Ugueto (Venezuela)	Guillermo González (Costa Rica)	Costa Rica, El Salvador, Guatemala, Honduras, Mexico, Nicaragua, Venezuela
Byanti Kharmawan (Indonesia)	Costa P. Caranicas (Greece)	Algeria, Ghana, Greece, Indonesia, Khmer Republic, Libyan Arab Republic, Morocco, Tunisia
Alexandre Kafka (Brazil)	Basilio Martins (Brazil)	Brazil, Colombia, Dominican Republic, Guyana, Haiti, Panama, Peru
Maurice P. Omwony (Kenya)	S. B. Nicol-Cole (Sierra Leone)	Botswana, Burundi, Ethiopia, Gambia, Guinea, Kenya, Liberia, Malawi, Nigeria, Sierra Leone, Sudan, Trinidad and Tobago, Uganda, United Republic of Tanzania, Zambia
Peh Yuan Hsu (China)	Nguyen Huu Hanh (Republic of Viet-Nam)	China, Philippines, Republic of Korea, Republic of Viet-Nam
Carlos Massad (Chile)	Ricardo H. Arriazu (Argentina)	Argentina, Bolivia, Chile, Ecuador, Paraguay, Uruguay
Antoine W. Yaméogo (Upper Volta)	Léon M. Rajaobelina (Madagascar)	Cameroon, Central African Republic, Chad, Congo, Dahomey, Equatorial Guinea, Gabon, Ivory Coast, Madagascar, Mali, Mauritania, Mauritius, Niger, Rwanda, Senegal, Togo, Upper Volta, Zaire

*Burma, Ceylon, Laos, Malaysia, Nepal, Singapore and Thailand, which did not participate in the 1970 regular election of Executive Directors, designated the Executive Director appointed by Japan to look after their interests in the Fund. The votes of Barbados, Fiji, Oman and Western Samoa, which joined the Fund after the 1970 regular election of Executive Directors, are also not included.

Annex III. PRINCIPAL OFFICERS AND OFFICES OF INTERNATIONAL MONETARY FUND
(As at 31 December 1971)

PRINCIPAL OFFICERS

Managing Director: Pierre-Paul Schweitzer
Deputy Managing Director: Frank A. Southard, Jr.
The General Counsel: Joseph Gold
The Economic Counsellor: J. J. Polak
Director, Administration Department: Phillip Thorson
Director, African Department: Mamoudou Touré
Director, Asian Department: D. S. Savkar
Director, Central Banking Service: J. V. Mladek
Director, European Department: L. A. Whittome
Director, Exchange and Trade Relations Department: Ernest Sturc
Director, Fiscal Affairs Department: Richard Goode
Director, IMF Institute: F. A. G. Keesing
Director, Legal Department: Joseph Gold

*Acting Director, Middle Eastern Department:** John W. Gunter
Director, Research Department: J. J. Polak
Secretary, Secretary's Department: W. Lawrence Hebbard
Treasurer, Treasurer's Department: Walter O. Habermeir
Director, Western Hemisphere Department: Jorge Del Canto
Director, Bureau of Statistics: Earl Hicks
Director, Office in Europe (Paris): Jean-Paul Salle
Director, Office in Geneva: Edgar Jones
Chief Information Officer: Jay H. Reid
Internal Auditor: J. William Lowe
Special Representative to the United Nations: Gordon Williams

*Director (on leave): Anwar Ali

OFFICES

HEADQUARTERS
International Monetary Fund
19th and H Streets, N. W.
Washington, D. C. 20431, U.S.A.
Telephone: EXecutive 3-6362
Cable Address: INTERFUND WASHINGTON

OTHER OFFICES

International Monetary Fund
European Office
66 Avenue d'Iéna
Paris 16°, France
  Telephone: 720-2510
  Cable Address: INTERFUND PARIS

International Monetary Fund Representative
58, Rue de Moillebeau
1202 Geneva, Switzerland
  Telephone: 34-30-00
  Cable Address: INTERFUND GENEVA

International Monetary Fund Office
Room 2245 United Nations Headquarters
New York, N.Y. 10017, U.S.A.
  Telephone: 754-1234, Ext. 3097

Chapter X

The International Civil Aviation Organization (ICAO)

During 1971, total traffic on scheduled domestic and international services (passengers, freight and mail) of all airlines of the member States of the International Civil Aviation Organization (ICAO)[1] rose to 60,430 million tonne-kilometres, 6.6 per cent more than in 1970 and one of the lowest annual rates of growth ever for the industry. Even more than in 1970, negative economic factors, in particular in the industrialized States, had adverse effects on the development of scheduled traffic.

The number of passengers carried rose from 383 million in 1970 to 407 million in 1971 (an increase of 6.3 per cent), while the passenger traffic total was 494,000 million passenger-kilometres in 1971, 7.2 per cent more than the previous year. Air freight, which rose to 12,740 million tonne-kilometres, showed an increase of 6.7 per cent. On the other hand, air mail traffic, for the first time ever, actually declined: from 3,140 million tonne-kilometres in 1970 to 2,880 million tonne-kilometres in 1971 (a decrease of 8.3 per cent).

Despite the slackening in the growth rate of world air traffic in 1971 and, to a lesser extent, in 1970, the average annual growth rates for all traffic categories in the 10 years 1962-1971 remained higher than 10 per cent.

According to information available to ICAO, the number of passenger fatalities in accidents on scheduled air services in 1971 was 967 in 33 accidents, while accidents in non-scheduled air transport took a toll of 191 passenger lives (compared with 411 in 1970). In the light of available statistics, the 1971 fatality rate per 100 million passenger-kilometres for non-scheduled air transport appeared to be slightly lower than for scheduled air transport.

Although the over-all trend in airline safety remained fairly regular, it was to be noted that the traffic pattern and operating environment for jet aircraft generally were much more favourable from a safety point of view than for propeller aircraft.

Among the main issues before ICAO in 1971 were the proceedings in the ICAO Council concerning disagreements and a complaint which involved Pakistan and India. On 3 March 1971, Pakistan submitted to the Council an Application and a Complaint against India's prohibition of over-flights of Indian territory by Pakistan aircraft. India raised a preliminary objection against the jurisdiction of the Council in this matter, which was overruled by the Council on 29 July 1971. On 22 December 1971, India appealed the decision to the International Court of Justice. (For further details, see pp. 586-87.)

An extraordinary session of the ICAO Assembly was held at United Nations Headquarters, New York, on 11 and 12 March, at which it was decided to increase the number of seats in the ICAO Council from 27 to 30. A decision to increase the number of seats of the Air Navigation Commission from 12 to 15 was adopted by the Assembly in July in Vienna, Austria. Both decisions were subject to ratification by ICAO member States.

During 1971, membership of ICAO rose to 122 with the admission of Bahrain on 19 September and of Qatar on 5 October.

On 19 November 1971, the ICAO Council decided, "for the matters within its competence, to

[1] For further information on ICAO's activities prior to 1971, see Memorandum on ICAO; reports of ICAO Council to ICAO Assembly; ICAO budget estimates; ICAO Bulletin, July 1947, *et seq.*; and previous volumes of Y.U.N.

recognize the representatives of the Government of the People's Republic of China as the only legitimate representatives of China to the International Civil Aviation Organization." (See also pp. 133, 135.)

Legal matters

A number of legal questions were dealt with during 1971. These are described in the sections below. Also, ratifications of conventions adopted at conferences convened under the auspices of ICAO increased during the year.

International air law conventions

A diplomatic conference on the revision of the Warsaw Convention of 1929, as amended by the Hague Protocol of 1955, met at Guatemala City, Guatemala, from 9 February to 8 March 1971. The conference adopted a protocol to amend that instrument, substantially increasing the compensation for air passengers in case of injury or death. The Guatemala Protocol was signed on behalf of 21 States and was to enter into force after its ratification by 30 States.

Unlawful interference with international civil aviation

During 1971, ICAO was increasingly concerned with meeting the growing threat of violence against international civil aviation, including the unlawful seizure of aircraft.

Under ICAO auspices, a diplomatic conference on air law was convened in Montreal, Canada, from 8 to 23 September 1971. The conference, which was attended by representatives of 60 States, adopted the Convention for the Suppression of Unlawful Acts against the Safety of Civil Aviation. The Convention provided for legal measures to deter acts of sabotage, armed attacks and other forms of violence directed against civil aviation and its facilities, other than unlawful seizure of aircraft. It was signed on behalf of 31 States and was to enter into force following its ratification by 10 States.

The Convention for the Suppression of Unlawful Seizure of Aircraft entered into force on 14 October 1971, following its ratification by Bulgaria, Costa Rica, Gabon, Hungary, Israel, Japan, Norway, Sweden, Switzerland and the United States. The Convention, which had been concluded in December 1970, at The Hague, Netherlands, by a diplomatic conference convened under the auspices of ICAO, called for the detention of hijackers, their appropriately severe punishment in accordance with national law, or under specified conditions, the possibility of their extradition to States wherein the aircraft involved were registered.

At its eighteenth session, held in Vienna from 15

June to 8 July 1971, the ICAO Assembly adopted a resolution concerning additional technical measures to be taken for the protection of the security of international civil air transport. The Assembly also requested the ICAO Council to ensure that the subject of air transport security was given adequate attention by the Secretary-General of ICAO, and that the agenda of the appropriate meetings of the organization should include suitable items dealing with questions of security. Air security received the continuing attention of the Council.

During the year, ICAO also published a security manual designed to assist States in taking measures to prevent acts of unlawful interference with civil aviation, or to minimize their effect.

Air navigation

During 1971, the main efforts of ICAO in the air navigation field continued to be directed to the implementation and updating of ICAO Specifications and Regional Plans. The ICAO Specifications consisted of International Standards and Recommended Practices, contained in 15 Annexes to the Convention on International Civil Aviation, and Procedures for Air Navigation Services (PANS), contained in four PANS documents. The ICAO Regional Plans set forth air navigation facilities and services required in nine ICAO regions for international air navigation.

To promote uniform application of the ICAO Specifications, the organization prepared additional guidance material in the form of new technical manuals and amendments to the existing manuals. Assistance to States in implementing ICAO Regional Plans was offered principally through ICAO Regional Offices. The efforts of the Regional Offices were supplemented by special implementation projects, under which one or more experts were employed for temporary periods to advise States in various areas regarding the installation of new facilities and services and the operation of existing ones.

The Specifications in six Annexes and three PANS documents were amended during 1971. The ICAO Council adopted a new Annex setting forth specifications for the following: aircraft noise certification for future subsonic aircraft; noise measurement for monitoring purposes; noise exposure reference units for land use planning; and aircraft noise abatement operating procedures. The Regional Plans were kept up to date through amendments processed by correspondence and the recommendations of a regional air navigation meeting held in the ICAO European-Mediterranean Region.

Eight panel-type meetings of technical experts on air navigation were held during 1971. The panels provided the Air Navigation Commission of ICAO, through which the technical work of the organization was carried out, with expert advice on various international aviation problems. Also held was a meeting of a committee established by the ICAO Council to develop specifications for the certification of aircraft types not covered by the new Annex adopted in 1971 (see above).

Special attention was given to the following technical problems, among others: sonic boom, supersonic operations, all-weather operations, application of space techniques relating to aviation, aircraft separation, visual aids, rescue and fire fighting, airworthiness of aircraft, automated data interchange systems, improved aircraft infrastructure compatibility and the impact of civil aviation development on the human environment.

Air transport

The eighteenth ICAO Assembly adopted a number of resolutions with regard to the organization's air transport work programme. The Assembly decided to undertake a feasibility study regarding the initiation of a programme of recurrent studies of fares and rates in international air transport. The feasibility study was to cover passenger fares and freight rates on scheduled and non-scheduled air transport.

A study of the development of international air passenger travel in East and South Asia and the Pacific was completed, and work was begun on a study of the European region. (Earlier studies in the same series covered Africa, Latin America and the Middle East.)

The triennial *Review of the Economic Situation of Air Transport,* covering the decade 1960-1970, was issued. Also published was a manual on air traffic forecasting.

A number of decisions were taken with regard to the economics of route facilities and services and airport economics; it was decided to convene a conference on these subjects early in 1973.

The regular collection and reporting of statistics on non-scheduled commercial air transport, of both scheduled airlines and non-scheduled operators, was introduced in 1971.

The African Civil Aviation Commission, established in 1969 and for which ICAO provides secretariat services, held its first session in Dakar, Senegal, in February, 1971.

The European Civil Aviation Conference devoted much of its attention to questions relating to non-scheduled air transport. It also took several initiatives regarding the setting of new passenger fares and cargo rates for the North Atlantic.

Technical assistance

During 1971, ICAO provided technical assistance to a total of 87 States. In 38 of these States, there

were resident missions of one or more experts. Assistance was also provided in the form of equipment, fellowships and scholarships and short missions by experts.

Four new long-range projects for which ICAO was to be the executing agency were approved by the Governing Council of the United Nations Development Programme (UNDP). These involved a total UNDP earmarking of $2.838 million, against estimated Government contributions of the equivalent of $6.784 million. The four projects were for further assistance to the Civil Aviation Safety Centre, Beirut, Lebanon; for improvement in air traffic control, communications and navigation facilities for civil aviation in the Netherlands Antilles; for supplementary assistance to the Civil Aviation Training Centre in Nigeria; and for the development of the Civil Aviation and Meteorological Training School in Lusaka, Zambia.

In addition, ICAO continued to act as the executing agency for UNDP projects in Afghanistan, Bolivia, Brazil, Ecuador, Chile, Colombia, Iraq, Mexico, Nigeria, the People's Democratic Republic of Yemen, Peru and the East African Community.

A feasibility study on the development of Keflavik Airport in Iceland was initiated.

During 1971, expert services, fellowships and equipment were provided under funds-in-trust arrangements to Argentina, Iran, Lebanon, Morocco, Nigeria, Saudi Arabia and Tunisia. Under the Republic of Zaire Central Trust Fund, ICAO supplied expert assistance to Zaire.

Under an agreement between Sweden and ICAO, 10 Swedish experts were assigned to assist ICAO experts in the field.

The total of 562 fellowships and scholarships awarded in 1971 was the largest in ICAO's history—25 per cent more than the previous high of 446, achieved in 1968.

Secretariat

As at 31 December 1971, the total number of staff members employed in the ICAO secretariat was 613. Of these, 232 (drawn from 60 nationalities) were in the professional and higher categories, and 381 were in the general service category. In addition, there were 213 persons in the professional category employed by ICAO on UNDP projects in the field in 1971.

Budget

The appropriations voted by the ICAO Assembly in 1968 for the 1971 financial year totalled $8,514,359. Modifications were approved by the ICAO Council, and the adjustments made are reflected below:

	Original appropriations	Revised appropriations (in U.S. dollars)	Actual obligations		Original appropriations	Revised appropriations (in U.S. dollars)	Actual obligations
Meetings	293,550	293,550	290,396	Special Training Fund	100,000	100,000	100,000
Secretariat	7,178,995	8,252,995	8,178,373	Total	8,514,359	9,809,359	9,728,077
Services	816,044	1,016,044	1,014,720	Miscellaneous income			
Equipment	64,620	84,620	83,064	Estimated: 1,853,359 Actual: 1,911,846			
Other budgetary provisions	61,150	62,150	61,524				

Annex I. MEMBERSHIP OF THE INTERNATIONAL CIVIL AVIATION ORGANIZATION AND CONTRIBUTIONS

(Membership as at 31 December 1971; contributions as assessed for 1971)*

Member	Contribution Percentage	Net amount (in U.S. dollars)	Member	Contribution Percentage	Net amount (in U.S. dollars)	Member	Contribution Percentage	Net amount (in U.S. dollars)
Afghanistan	0.13	9,127	Haiti	0.13	9,127	People's Democratic Republic		
Algeria	0.15	10,532	Honduras	0.13	9,127	of Yemen	0.13	9,127
Argentina	0.93	65,296	Hungary	0.48	33,701	Peru	0.20	14,042
Australia	2.02	141,825	Iceland	0.13	9,127	Philippines	0.42	29,489
Austria	0.54	37,914	India	1.86	130,591	Poland	1.36	95,486
Bahrain†	0.13	2,282	Indonesia	0.37	25,978	Portugal	0.29	20,361
Barbados	0.13	9,127	Iran	0.26	18,255	Qatar‡	0.13	1,521
Belgium	1.25	87,763	Iraq	0.13	9,127	Republic of Korea	0.13	9,127
Bolivia	0.13	9,127	Ireland	0.31	21,766	Republic of Viet-Nam	0.13	9,127
Brazil	1.12	78,636	Israel	0.41	28,787	Romania	0.34	23,872
Bulgaria	0.18	12,638	Italy	3.90	273,819	Rwanda	0.13	9,127
Burma	0.13	9,127	Ivory Coast	0.13	9,127	Saudi Arabia	0.13	9,127
Burundi	0.13	9,127	Jamaica	0.13	9,127	Senegal	0.13	9,127
Cameroon	0.13	9,127	Japan	4.10	287,861	Sierra Leone	0.13	9,127
Canada	3.65	256,267	Jordan	0.13	9,127	Singapore	0.13	9,127
Central African Republic	0.13	9,127	Kenya	0.13	9,127	Somalia	0.13	9,127
Ceylon	0.13	9,127	Khmer Republic	0.13	9,127	South Africa	0.65	45,637
Chad	0.13	9,127	Kuwait	0.14	9,830	Spain	1.19	83,550
Chile	0.25	17,553	Laos	0.13	9,127	Sudan	0.13	9,127
China	0.67	47,041	Lebanon	0.22	15,447	Sweden	1.31	91,975
Colombia	0.33	23,170	Liberia	0.13	9,127	Switzerland	1.25	87,763
Congo	0.13	9,127	Libyan Arab Republic	0.13	9,127	Syrian Arab Republic	0.13	9,127
Costa Rica	0.13	9,127	Luxembourg	0.13	9,127	Thailand	0.18	12,638
Cuba	0.19	13,340	Madagascar	0.13	9,127	Togo	0.13	9,127
Cyprus	0.13	9,127	Malawi	0.13	9,127	Trinidad and Tobago	0.13	9,127
Czechoslovakia	0.82	57,573	Malaysia	0.13	9,127	Tunisia	0.13	9,127
Dahomey	0.13	9,127	Mali	0.13	9,127	Turkey	0.34	23,872
Denmark	0.70	49,147	Malta	0.13	9,127	Uganda	0.13	9,127
Dominican Republic	0.13	9,127	Mauritania	0.13	9,127	USSR	14.37	1,089,390
Ecuador	0.13	9,127	Mauritius	0.13	9,127	United Kingdom	8.09	567,999
Egypt	0.29	20,361	Mexico	1.01	70,913	United Republic of Tanzania	0.13	9,127
El Salvador	0.13	9,127	Morocco	0.13	9,127	United States	30.87	2,167,383
Ethiopia	0.13	9,127	Nepal	0.13	9,127	Upper Volta	0.13	9,127
Federal Republic of Germany	7.10	498,491	Netherlands	1.93	135,506	Uruguay	0.13	9,127
Finland	0.50	35,105	New Zealand	0.43	30,191	Venezuela	0.50	35,105
France	6.72	471,812	Nicaragua	0.13	9,127	Yemen	0.13	9,127
Gabon	0.13	9,127	Niger	0.13	9,127	Yugoslavia	0.40	28,084
Ghana	0.13	9,127	Nigeria	0.16	11,234	Zaire	0.13	9,127
Greece	0.39	27,382	Norway	0.54	37,914	Zambia	0.13	9,127
Guatemala	0.13	9,127	Pakistan	0.46	32,297	Total		8,166,148
Guinea	0.13	9,127	Panama	0.13	9,127			
Guyana	0.13	9,127	Paraguay	0.13	9,127			

*Contributions for 1971 as set by the ICAO Assembly in 1968.
†Contribution from 1 October 1971.
‡Contribution from 2 November 1971.

Annex II.   OFFICERS AND OFFICES OF THE INTERNATIONAL CIVIL AVIATION ORGANIZATION
(As at 31 December 1971)

ICAO COUNCIL

OFFICERS
President: Walter Binaghi (Argentina)
First Vice-President: A. Cucci (Italy)
Second Vice-President: Y.R. Malhotra (India)
Third Vice-President: H. K. El Meleigy (Egypt)
Secretary: Assad Kotaite, Secretary-General

MEMBERS
Argentina, Australia, Belgium, Brazil, Canada, Colombia, Congo, Czecho-slovakia, Egypt, Federal Republic of Germany, France, India, Indonesia, Italy, Japan, Lebanon, Mexico, Nicaragua, Nigeria, Norway, Senegal, Spain, Tunisia, Uganda, USSR, United Kingdom, United States

PRINCIPAL OFFICERS OF THE SECRETARIAT

Secretary-General: Assad Kotaite
Director, Navigation Bureau: W. J. Nemerever
Director, Air Transport Bureau: G. R. Besse

Director, Legal Bureau: P.K. Roy
Director, Technical Assistance Bureau: Jack Vivian
Chief, Public Information Office: T. M. Abrams

OFFICES

HEADQUARTERS
International Civil Aviation Organization
International Aviation Building
1080 University Street
Montreal 101, Canada
   Telephone: 866-2551
   Cable Address: ICAO MONTREAL

REGIONAL OFFICES

International Civil Aviation Organization
North American and Caribbean Office
Apartado Postal 5-377
Mexico 5, D.F., Mexico
   Telephone: 25-56-84, 14-96-56, 11-77-68
   Cable Address: ICAOREP MEXICO

International Civil Aviation Organization
Far East and Pacific Office
Sala Santitham
Rajadamoen Avenue, P.O. Box 614
Bangkok, Thailand
   Telephone: 815366
   Cable Address: ICAOREP BANGKOK

International Civil Aviation Organization
European Office
3 bis, villa Emile-Bergerat
92, Neuilly-sur-Seine (Hauts de Seine), France
   Telephone: 747-95-73
   Cable Address: ICAOREP PARIS

International Civil Aviation Organization
South American Office
Apartado 4127
Lima, Peru
   Telephone: 29-4525, 29-4524, 29-4523
   Cable Address: ICAOREP LIMA

International Civil Aviation Organization
Middle East and Eastern African Office
16 Hassan Sabri
Zamalek
Cairo, Egypt
   Telephone: 801806-7
   Cable Address: ICAOREP CAIRO

International Civil Aviation Organization
African Office
P.O. Box 2356
Dakar, Senegal
   Telephone: 260-71, 260-72
   Cable Address: ICAOREP DAKAR

Chapter XI
The Universal Postal Union (UPU)

The Universal Postal Union (UPU)[1] one of the oldest inter-governmental organizations, was established at Berne, Switzerland, in 1874.

During 1971, UPU continued its efforts to promote the organization and improvement of postal services and to further the development of international collaboration in this sphere. It also participated, as far as possible, in postal technical assistance requested by its member States.

In 1971, the membership of UPU increased from 143 to 145, with the admission of Fiji on 18 June and of Oman on 17 August.

Activities of UPU organs

Universal Postal Congress

The Universal Postal Congress, the supreme legislative authority of UPU, consists of representatives of all UPU member States and meets, as a rule, every five years. The sixteenth Congress was held in Tokyo, Japan, in 1969; the seventeenth

[1]For further information on UPU's activities prior to 1971, see L'Union postale universelle: sa fondation et son développement, 1874-1949—mémoire (Berne, Bureau international de l'Union, 1949), annual reports of UPU and previous volumes of Y.U.N.

Congress was scheduled to meet in Lausanne, Switzerland, in 1974. The Congress examines and revises the Acts of UPU on the basis of proposals submitted by member States, the Executive Council, and the Consultative Council for Postal Studies. The Acts of the 1969 Congress came into effect on 1 July 1971.

Executive Council

The 31-member UPU Executive Council, which meets annually, is responsible for ensuring the continuity of the work of UPU in the five-year interval between meetings of the UPU Congress. During its 1971 session, held at Berne from 27 May to 3 June 1971, the Council dealt with various administrative questions and with matters which had been referred to it by the 1969 Universal Postal Congress.

Among the questions examined by the Executive Council were: technical assistance programmes, especially vocational training in developing countries; international postal co-operation; UPU finances; relations with the United Nations and other international organizations; the possibility of expanding and developing relations between UPU and the Restricted Postal Unions; transit and transport costs of mail; the simplification of rate fixing and of conditions for acceptance of articles for letter post; simplification of customs treatment of postal items; postal relations in cases of dispute, conflict or war; modernization and simplification of the printed papers service; improvement of postal services for seafarers; maximizing the air conveyance of mail; security of air mail traffic; celebration of UPU Day (9 October) and of the UPU centenary in 1974, during the seventeenth Universal Postal Congress; and the organization of letter-writing competitions for young people.

Consultative Council for Postal Studies

The 30-member Consultative Council for Postal Studies was created to deal, in annual sessions, with technical, economic and technical co-operation problems of interest to the Postal Administrations of member States, in particular of the new and developing countries.

During its 1971 session, held in Berne from 27 September to 8 October, the Consultative Council reviewed the principal trends in the technical development of postal services; the use of modern methods and techniques in postal service; problems of the modernization of postal services in new countries; the development of human resources, in particular the training of postal employees; statistical methods for the assessment of postal traffic; and the role of postal savings accounts and financial services in the economic and social development of countries.

The Consultative Council undertook a study to establish the criteria to be taken into account and methods to be applied in determining the standard and form of services for the public, with a view to raising the quality of services provided to the population and the national economy. Postal market research was also undertaken with a view to enabling Postal Administrations to take timely action to cope with the constant increase in traffic.

Technical co-operation

The technical assistance activities of UPU during the Second United Nations Development Decade were aimed at enabling Postal Administrations to provide the following services: (1) to establish a post office for every area of 20 to 40 square kilometres, or 3,000 to 6,000 inhabitants; (2) to distribute first-class mail, under normal transport conditions, within a radius of 500 kilometres the day following mailing; (3) to establish financial services—savings banks, current postal accounts, et cetera—where they did not exist; and (4) to increase progressively to 30 per cent of the total the number of international postal parcels sent by air.

The following types of technical co-operation were provided by UPU in 1971: multilateral aid under both the Technical Assistance and Special Fund components of the United Nations Development Programme (UNDP); and assistance, mainly in the field of education, by the UPU Special Fund, established in 1967, and financed by voluntary contributions in cash or kind from UPU member countries. Bilateral technical assistance was provided by some Postal Administrations.

In 1971, 39 national and regional projects were carried out under the Technical Assistance component of UNDP, and eight projects were carried out under the Special Fund component (three of these in collaboration with the International Telecommunication Union).

Under these projects, 119 scholarships were granted in the following fields of study: organization of postal services; professional refresher courses; training of postal instructors and postal inspectors; organization and management of postal money order services; study of the use of postal vending machines; mechanization and automation of postal services.

An additional 33 scholarships were granted to students attending postal training courses given under two regional UNDP Special Fund projects.

Teaching aids were provided for several projects.

Three study courses in postal services were organized in Europe and Africa. The courses dealt with general problems of international postal service; dispatch and distribution of mail; and problems of the development of postal services. Some 70 high-ranking postal staff of various nationalities attended the courses.

Projects carried out under the UNDP Special Fund component were concerned mainly with the establishment and reorganization of national or regional vocational training centres; one project was aimed at the establishment of a postal savings bank and the extension of postal services.

Under these projects, 46 experts were sent on missions to various Postal Administrations.

An educational assistance programme was established in 1971 within the framework of the UPU Special Fund. It was financed from voluntary contributions from UPU member States in the amount of approximately 200,000 Swiss francs. With the agreement of the UPU Executive Council, the UPU International Bureau granted 12 scholarships for teacher training, 10 scholarships for an inter-regional seminar and six scholarships for specialized training; and it provided the sum of 81,000 Swiss francs to be used for the purchase of teaching aids.

Contributions in kind, in the form of furnishing material or granting scholarships, were also given within the framework of the Universal Postal Union Special Fund.

As in preceding years, UPU paid special attention to the training of postal instructors. In 1971, 21 students attended the courses given in London, United Kingdom, and in Paris, France.

Experts in postal development were sent on field assignments in Asia, Africa and Latin America. The experts studied the organization of postal services, postal training and future postal development. They also took part in UNDP Special Fund training projects and in the organization of seminars.

International Bureau of the Universal Postal Union

The International Bureau of the Universal Postal Union, operating at UPU headquarters in Berne, constitutes the secretariat of UPU and serves the Postal Administrations of member countries of UPU as an organ for liaison, information and consultation. The Bureau is headed by a Director-General and is under the general supervision of the Government of the Swiss Confederation.

In addition to collecting, collating, publishing and distributing information of every kind relating to the international postal service, the Bureau also conducts inquiries requested by Postal Administrations and acts as a clearing-house in the settlement of certain accounts between Postal Administrations.

As at 31 December 1971, the total number of permanent and temporary staff members of the International Bureau of UPU was 110, of whom 56

were in the professional and higher categories (drawn from 31 nationalities) and 54 in the general service category.

The staff of the translation units of the Bureau numbered 13 (8 in the professional and 5 in the general service category).

Budget

The Executive Council approved the UPU budget estimates for 1971, providing for gross expenditures of 9,488,000 Swiss francs (about US$2,470,000), and for 1972, calling for gross expenditures of 10,015,000 Swiss francs (about US$2,608,000).

The expenditures of UPU are borne in common by all member countries, which for the purpose of assessment are divided into seven classes. The following table shows the assessments for 1971 of the various classes.

Contribution			Assessments for 1971	
Class	Unit	Gold francs	Swiss francs	U.S. dollar equivalents*
1	25	144,481.91	192,775	50,201.82
2	20	115,855.35	154,220	40,161.45
3	15	86,689.15	115,665	30,121.09
4	10	57,792.77	77,110	20,080.73
5	5	28,896.38	38,555	10,040.36
6	3	17,337.83	23,133	6,024.22
7	1	5,779.28	7,711	2,008.07

*Calculated on the basis of 3.84 Swiss francs = US$1.

Note: See ANNEX below for listing of the particular class in which each member country is placed.

The Government of the Swiss Confederation supervises the expenditures of the International Bureau of the Universal Postal Union and advances the necessary funds.

INCOME AND EXPENDITURES IN 1971

Income

	Swiss francs
Contributions from member countries	7,348,583.00
Sale of publications	184,650.25
Other receipts	1,576,196.15
Total	9,109,429.40

Expenditures

Staff	6,197,970.48
General expenses	2,911,458.92
Total	9,109,429.40

Annex. MEMBERS OF THE UNIVERSAL POSTAL UNION, CLASS OF CONTRIBUTION, ORGANS, OFFICERS AND HEADQUARTERS

(As at 31 December 1971)

MEMBERS AND CLASS OF CONTRIBUTION

Member	Class of Contri-bution*	Member	Class of Contri-bution*	Member	Class of Contri-bution*	Member	Class of Contri-bution*	Member	Class of Contri-bution*	Member	Class of Contri-bution*
Afghanistan	6	Cyprus	7	India	1	Malta	7	Poland	3	Thailand	6
Albania	6	Czechoslovakia	3	Indonesia	3	Mauritania	7	Portugal	4	Togo	7
Algeria	7	Dahomey	7	Iran	5	Mauritius	7	Portuguese Pro-		Trinidad and	
Argentina	1	Denmark	4	Iraq	7	Mexico	3	vinces of East		Tobago	7
Australia	1	Dominican		Ireland	4	Monaco	7	Africa, Asia		Tunisia	5
Austria	5	Republic	6	Israel	6	Mongolia	7	and Oceania	4	Turkey	3
Barbados	7	Ecuador	6	Italy	1	Morocco	4	Portuguese Pro-		Uganda	7
Belgium	3	Egypt	3	Ivory Coast	7	Nauru	7	vinces of West		Ukrainian SSR	3
Bhutan	7	El Salvador	6	Jamaica	7	Nepal	6	Africa	4	USSR	1
Bolivia	6	Equatorial		Japan	1	Netherlands	3	Qatar	7	United Kingdom	1
Botswana	7	Guinea	7	Jordan	7	Netherlands		Romania	3	United Kingdom	
Brazil	1	Ethiopia	6	Kenya	7	Antilles and		Rwanda	7	Overseas	
Bulgaria	5	Fiji	7	Khmer Republic	7	Surinam	6	San Marino	7	Territories	5
Burma	6	Finland	4	Korea	4	New Zealand	1	Saudi Arabia	7	United Republic	
Burundi	7	France	1	Kuwait	7	Nicaragua	6	Senegal	6	of Tanzania	7
Byelorussian SSR	5	French Overseas		Laos	7	Niger	7	Sierra Leone	7	United States	1
Cameroon	7	Territories	6	Lebanon	7	Nigeria	5	Singapore	7	United States	
Canada	1	Gabon	7	Lesotho	7	Norway	4	Somalia	7	Territories	3
Central African		Germany	1	Liberia	7	Oman	7	South Africa	1	Upper Volta	7
Republic	7	Ghana	6	Libyan Arab		Pakistan	1	Spain	1	Uruguay	6
Ceylon	5	Greece	5	Republic	7	Panama	6	Spanish Territory		Vatican	7
Chad	7	Guatemala	6	Liechtenstein	7	Paraguay	6	of Africa	7	Venezuela	6
Chile	5	Guinea	6	Luxembourg	6	People's		Sudan	7	Viet-Nam	6
China	1	Guyana	7	Madagascar	6	Democratic		Swaziland	7	Yemen	7
Colombia	5	Haiti	6	Malaysia	6	Republic		Sweden	3	Yugoslavia	3
Congo	7	Honduras	6	Malawi	7	of Yemen	7	Switzerland	3	Zaire	6
Costa Rica	6	Hungary	4	Maldives	7	Peru	5	Syrian		Zambia	6
Cuba	6	Iceland	7	Mali	7	Philippines	7	Arab Republic	7		

*For amount of contributions from members, see listing of contributory shares in section on BUDGET above.
Note: Nomenclature of UPU differs from that of the United Nations.

EXECUTIVE COUNCIL

(Holding office until the Seventeenth (1974) Universal Postal Congress)

Chairman: Japan
Vice-Chairmen: Egypt, Netherlands, USSR, United States
Secretary-General: Michel Rahi (Egypt), Director-General of the International Bureau
Members: Austria, Australia, Bulgaria, Cameroon, Colombia, Congo, Egypt, Ethiopia, Finland, France, India, Indonesia, Iran, Italy, Japan, Lebanon, Morocco, Netherlands, Niger, Nigeria, Pakistan, Peru, Romania, Senegal, Thailand, Trinidad and Tobago, Tunisia, USSR, United States, Uruguay, Venezuela

CONSULTATIVE COUNCIL FOR POSTAL STUDIES

Chairman: Belgium
Vice-Chairmen: Argentina, Germany, Pakistan, Tunisia, USSR, United Kingdom
Members: Argentina, Australia, Belgium, Cameroon, China, Colombia, Czechoslovakia, Egypt, Germany, France, Hungary, India, Indonesia, Iran, Italy, Japan, Morocco, Netherlands, New Zealand, Nigeria, Norway, Pakistan, Poland, Switzerland, Thailand, Tunisia, USSR, United Kingdom, United States, Upper Volta

INTERNATIONAL BUREAU OF UPU

OFFICERS
Director-General: Michel Rahi
Deputy Director-General: Anthony H. Ridge
Assistant Directors-General: Zdenek Caha, Louis Lachaize

HEADQUARTERS
Bureau internationale de l'Union postale universelle
Weltpoststrasse 4
Berne, Switzerland
Postal Address: UPU, Case postale
3000 Berne 15, Switzerland
Cable Address: UPU BERNE

Chapter XII

The International Telecommunication Union (ITU)

In 1971, the membership of the International Telecommunication Union (ITU)[1] rose to 140 with the admission of Fiji on 5 May.

Administrative Council

The twenty-sixth session of the Administrative Council of ITU was held from 1 to 21 May 1971 at ITU headquarters in Geneva, Switzerland. In addition to dealing with administrative matters, the Council reviewed the preparations for future conferences of the Union and approved the text of a draft agreement between the Swiss Federal Council and ITU on the juridical status of the Union in Switzerland. The agreement was signed on 21 July 1971.

On 26 October 1971, the Secretary-General of the United Nations transmitted to the Secretary-General of ITU the text of a General Assembly resolution of 25 October 1971 by which the Assembly decided to restore all rights to the People's Republic of China, to recognize the representatives of its Government as the only legitimate representatives of China to the United Nations, and to expel forthwith the representatives of Chiang Kai-shek from the place which they unlawfully occupied at the United Nations and in all the organizations related to it. The Secretary-General, at the same time, drew attention to a General Assembly resolution of 14 December 1950 by which the Assembly recommended that the attitude adopted by the General Assembly on recognition by the United Nations of the representation of a Member State should be taken into account in other organs of the United Nations and in the specialized agencies.[2]

On 29 October 1971, the Secretary-General of ITU transmitted to the Chairman of the ITU Administrative Council the communication from the Secretary-General of the United Nations. Copies of the communication were also sent to all members of the Council, which was expected to consider the question in 1972. (See also pp. 133, 135.)

International consultative committees

Study groups of the two ITU international consultative committees—the International Radio Consultative Committee (CCIR) and the International Telegraph and Telephone Consultative Committee (CCITT)—held numerous meetings during the year.

A special joint meeting of CCIR study groups was held in Geneva from 3 February to 3 March to prepare for the Conference for Space Telecommunications.

Plan committees

Four Regional Plan Committees of ITU, covering the different areas of the world, were responsible for preparing plans setting out circuit and routing requirements for international telecommunications and for estimating the growth of international traffic. They also played an active part in the work of the World Plan Committee, which was concerned with inter-regional relations.

During 1971, the Regional Plan Committee for Africa met in Lagos, Nigeria, from 18 to 27 January, and the World Plan Committee met in Venice, Italy, from 11 to 22 October.

International Frequency Registration Board

Throughout 1971, the International Frequency Registration Board continued its work of keeping up to date the Master International Frequency Register, showing the frequencies assigned by countries to their radio stations. It also continued to prepare seasonal high-frequency broadcasting schedules and monthly summaries of monitoring information.

Conference for Space Telecommunications

The Radio Regulations were revised at the World Administrative Radio Conference for Space Telecommunications, held in Geneva from 7 June to 17 July 1971. The Conference was attended by representatives from 101 countries.

Technical co-operation

In 1971, under ITU's various programmes of technical co-operation in developing countries, 255 experts were on field missions, 448 fellows were undergoing training abroad, and equipment valued at $1,620,500 was delivered, mainly to telecommunication training centres. The total cost of this assistance amounted to $7,714,261.

The three main objectives of ITU's activity in the field of technical co-operation continued to be: (a) promoting the development of regional telecommunication networks in Africa, Asia and Latin America; (b) strengthening the telecommunication technical and administrative services in developing countries; and (c) developing the human resources required for telecommunication systems.

---

[1]For further information on ITU's activities prior to 1971, see annual and financial report by Secretary-General of ITU; Final Acts of International Telecommunication and Radio Conferences, Atlantic City, 1947, of Plenipotentiary Conference, Buenos Aires, 1952, of Plenipotentiary Conference, Geneva, 1959, and of Plenipotentiary Conference, Montreux, 1965; *Telecommunication Journal*; and previous volumes of Y.U.N.
[2]See Y.U.N., 1950, p. 435, text of resolution 396(V).

The Union continued its efforts to promote the establishment of international telecommunication networks on a pan-continental level in Africa, the Americas and Asia, in accordance with the objectives established by its World and Regional Plan Committees. To this end, studies and surveys were carried out by experts, engaged by the Union, working in collaboration with member administrations.

During 1971, considerable progress was made towards the establishment of the Central American telecommunication network, with the assistance of a team of ITU experts.

Work went forward on several pre-investment surveys, including the pre-investment study of an Asian regional network stretching from Iran to Indonesia. The field work portion of a pre-investment survey covering seven countries of Eastern Africa, carried out by consulting firms engaged by the Union, was almost completed. Contracts were signed with consultants for similar surveys in Central and Western Africa, and preparations were under way for a further contract covering eight countries in Western Africa.

The pre-investment study for an inter-American network in South America, carried out by the Inter-American Development Bank in association with ITU, was terminated.

Twenty-nine of the Union's field experts were engaged in study and survey work during 1971.

As in previous years, almost 65 per cent of the total field expenditure was utilized on training in order to meet the manpower demand in various sectors of telecommunications. During 1971, 143 experts were engaged in various phases of training.

Considerable assistance was also provided by ITU in the specialized fields of telephony, telegraphy, radio communications, frequency management, satellite communications, planning, organization, adminstration and management.

Publications

In 1971, the general secretariat of ITU issued a number of publications, some of them trilingual, others in separate English, French and Spanish editions. Among them were the following:

Financial Operating Report, 1970
Report on the Activities of the Union, 1970
Telecommunication Journal, 12 nos.
Operational Bulletin, Nos. 61-72
Table of International Telex Relations and Traffic, 1970
List of Point-to-Point Radio Telegraph Channels, 1970
List of Telegraph Offices, 23rd ed., 1971, and Supplements Nos. 1 and 2
List of International Telephone Routes, 11th ed., 1971
Telecommunication Statistics, 1970
List of Coast Stations, 4th ed., 1970, and Supplements Nos. 1 and 2

List of Ship Stations, 11th ed., 1971, and Supplement
List of Radiodetermination and Special Service Stations, 5th ed., 1970
Alphabetical List of Call Signs of Stations Used by the Maritime Mobile Service, 5th ed., 1970, and Supplements Nos. 3-5
Alphabetical List of Call Signs of Stations other than Amateur Stations, Experimental Stations and Stations of the Maritime Mobile Service, 4th ed., 1970, and Supplements Nos. 4-7
List of International Monitoring Stations, 3rd ed., 1971
Final Acts of the World Administrative Radio Conference for Space Telecommunications, Geneva 1971
General Plan for the Development of the Regional Network in the Region Europe and Mediterranean Basin, 1970–1974–1978
General Plan for the Development of the Regional Network in Africa, 1970–1974–1978
Handbook on Pressurization of Telecommunication Cables
Documents of the XIIth Plenary Assembly of the C.C.I.R., New Delhi 1970
IFRB Technical Standards, series M, 1971
International Frequency List, 6th ed., 1971, and Supplements Nos. 1 and 2
List of Fixed Stations Operating International Circuits, 6th ed., 1971, and supplements Nos. 1 and 2
List of Broadcasting Stations Operating in Bands below 5950 kc/s, 6th ed., 1971, and Supplement No. 1
List of Stations in the Space Service and in the Radio Astronomy Service, 3rd ed., 1971
IFRB Weekly Circulars, Parts I, II, III and IV, and Special, Nos. 940-990
Summaries of Monitoring Information received by the IFRB, Nos. 168-171
Tentative High Frequency Broadcasting Schedules, May 1971, September 1971, November 1971 and March 1972
High Frequency Broadcasting Schedules, September 1969, November 1969, March 1970 and June 1970
Seminar on Recent Progress in Telecommunication Techniques/Integration of Satellite Communication into the General Telecommunications Network, Geneva 1969

Secretariat

As at 31 December 1971, 516 officials (excluding staff on short-term contracts) were employed by ITU. Of these, 9 were elected officials, 177 were in the professional or higher categories and 330 were in the general service category. The staff was drawn from 44 countries.

Budget

The following revised budget for 1971 was adopted at the ITU Administrative Council session held in May 1971.

INCOME AND EXPENDITURES IN 1971

Income	Amount (in Swiss francs)
Contributions by members and private operating agencies	27,606,250
Contribution by UNDP for technical co-operation administrative expenses	4,447,300

Income	Amount (in Swiss francs)	Income	Amount (in Swiss francs)
Sale of publications	3,694,000	Technical co-operation	4,447,300
Miscellaneous	1,726,750	Publications	3,694,000
Total	37,474,300	Grand total	37,474,300

Expenditures	
Administrative Council	505,000
General secretariat	24,636,500
Mission expenses	128,000
Miscellaneous	35,000
Meetings	
International Consultative Committees	2,423,500
World Administrative Radio Conference for Space Telecommunications	1,545,000
Other expenses	60,000
Total general expenses	29,333,000

Each member of the ITU chooses the class of contribution in which it wishes to be included and pays in advance its annual contributory share to the budget calculated on the basis of the budgetary provision. The classes of contribution for the various members are listed in the ANNEX below. As at the end of 1971, the total of units was 479-1/2, the amount of the contributory unit being 58,200 Swiss francs (equivalent to US$14,265).

Annex. MEMBERSHIP OF THE INTERNATIONAL TELECOMMUNICATION UNION, CONTRIBUTIONS, OFFICERS AND HEADQUARTERS

(Membership as at 31 December 1971; contributions as assessed for 1972)

Member	Class	Contribution (In Swiss francs)	(Equivalent in U.S. dollars)	Member	Class	Contribution (In Swiss francs)	(Equivalent in U.S. dollars)
Afghanistan	½	29,100	7,132	Federal Republic of Germany	20	1,164,000	285,224
Albania	½	29,100	7,132	Fiji	½	29,100	7,132
Algeria	3	174,600	42,794	Finland	3	174,600	42,794
Argentina	15	873,000	213,971	France	30	1,746,000	427,941
Australia	18	1,047,600	256,765	French Overseas Territories	1	58,200	14,265
Austria	1	58,200	14,265	Gabon	½	29,100	7,132
Barbados	½	29,100	7,132	Ghana	1	58,200	14,265
Belgium	8	465,600	114,118	Greece	1	58,200	14,265
Bolivia	3	174,600	42,794	Guatemala	1	58,200	14,265
Botswana	½	29,100	7,132	Guinea	½	29,100	7,132
Brazil	5	291,000	71,324	Guyana	½	29,100	7,132
Bulgaria	1	58,200	14,265	Haiti	1	58,200	14,265
Burma	1	58,200	14,265	Honduras	½	29,100	7,132
Burundi	½	29,100	7,132	Hungary	1	58,200	14,265
Byelorussian SSR	1	58,200	14,265	Iceland	½	29,100	7,132
Cameroon	½	29,100	7,132	India	13	756,600	185,441
Canada	18	1,047,600	256,765	Indonesia	1	58,200	14,265
Central African Republic	½	29,100	7,132	Iran	1	58,200	14,265
Ceylon	1	58,200	14,265	Iraq	1	58,200	14,265
Chad	½	29,100	7,132	Ireland	3	174,600	42,794
Chile	3	174,600	42,794	Israel	1	58,200	14,265
China	15	873,000	213,971	Italy	10	582,000	142,647
Colombia	3	174,600	42,794	Ivory Coast	1	58,200	14,265
Congo	½	29,100	7,132	Jamaica	1	58,200	14,265
Costa Rica	½	29,100	7,132	Japan	20	1,164,000	285,224
Cuba	1	58,200	14,265	Jordan	½	29,100	7,132
Cyprus	½	29,100	7,132	Kenya	½	29,100	7,132
Czechoslovakia	3	174,600	42,794	Khmer Republic	1	58,200	14,265
Dahomey	½	29,100	7,132	Kuwait	1	58,200	14,265
Denmark	5	291,000	71,324	Laos	½	29,100	7,132
Dominican Republic	3	174,600	42,794	Lebanon	1	58,200	14,265
Ecuador	1	58,200	14,265	Lesotho	½	29,100	7,132
Egypt	5	291,000	71,324	Liberia	1	58,200	14,265
El Salvador	3	174,600	42,794	Libyan Arab Republic	½	29,100	7,132
Equatorial Guinea	½	29,100	7,132	Liechtenstein	½	29,100	7,132
Ethiopia	1	58,200	14,265	Luxembourg	½	29,100	7,132

Member	Class	Contribution (In Swiss francs)	(Equivalent in U.S. dollars)	Member	Class	Contribution (In Swiss francs)	(Equivalent in U.S. dollars)
Madagascar	1	58,200	14,265	Senegal	1	58,200	14,265
Malawi	½	29,100	7,132	Sierra Leone	½	29,100	7,132
Malaysia	3	174,600	42,794	Singapore	1	58,200	14,265
Maldives	½	29,100	7,132	Somalia	1	58,200	14,265
Mali	½	29,100	7,132	Spain	3	174,600	42,794
Malta	½	29,100	7,132	Spanish Province in Africa	1	58,200	14,265
Mauritius	½	29,100	7,132	South Africa	8	465,600	114,118
Mauritania	½	29,100	7,132	Sudan	1	58,200	14,265
Mexico	5	291,000	71,324	Swaziland	½	29,100	7,132
Monaco	½	29,100	7,132	Sweden	10	582,000	142,647
Mongolia	½	29,100	7,132	Switzerland	10	582,000	142,647
Morocco	1	58,200	14,265	Syrian Arab Republic	1	58,200	14,265
Nauru	½	29,100	7,132	Thailand	2	116,400	28,529
Nepal	½	29,100	7,132	Togo	½	29,100	7,132
Netherlands	8	465,600	114,118	Trinidad and Tobago	1	58,200	14,265
New Zealand	5	291,000	71,324	Tunisia	2	116,400	28,529
Nicaragua	1	58,200	14,265	Turkey	2	116,400	28,529
Niger	2	29,100	7,132	Uganda	½	29,100	7,132
Nigeria	2	116,400	28,529	Ukrainian SSR	3	174,600	42,794
Norway	5	291,000	71,324	USSR	30	1,746,000	427,941
Pakistan	3	174,600	42,794	United Kingdom	30	1,746,000	427,941
Panama	½	29,100	7,132	United Kingdom Overseas Territories	1	58,200	14,265
Paraguay	1	58,200	14,265	United Republic of Tanzania	½	29,100	7,132
People's Democratic Republic of Yemen	½	29,100	7,132	United States	30	1,746,000	427,941
Peru	2	116,400	28,529	United States Territories	25	1,455,000	356,618
Philippines	1	58,200	14,265	Upper Volta	½	29,100	7,132
Poland	3	174,600	42,724	Uruguay	1	58,200	14,265
Portugal	3	174,600	42,724	Vatican City State	½	29,100	7,132
Portuguese Overseas Provinces	3	174,600	42,794	Venezuela	3	174,600	42,794
Republic of Korea	1	58,200	14,265	Yemen	1	58,200	14,265
Republic of Viet-Nam	1	58,200	14,265	Yugoslavia	1	58,200	14,265
Rhodesia	1	58,200	14,265	Zaire	1	58,200	14,265
Romania	1	58,200	14,265	Zambia	1	58,200	14,265
Rwanda	½	29,100	7,132			27,848,700	6,825,379
Saudi Arabia	1	58,200	14,265				

Note: Nomenclature of ITU differs from that of the United Nations.

ADMINISTRATIVE COUNCIL, INTERNATIONAL FREQUENCY REGISTRATION BOARD AND PRINCIPAL OFFICERS

MEMBERS OF ITU ADMINISTRATIVE COUNCIL
Algeria, Argentina (Vice-Chairman), Australia, Brazil, Canada, China, Dahomey, Ethiopia, Federal Republic of Germany, France, India, Ireland, Italy, Japan, Lebanon, Madagascar, Mexico, Morocco, Nigeria, Pakistan, Poland, Saudi Arabia (Chairman), Switzerland, Uganda, USSR, United Kingdom, United States, Venezuela, Yugoslavia

PRINCIPAL OFFICERS OF THE UNION
Secretary-General: Mohamed Mili
Deputy-Secretary-General: Richard E. Butler

MEMBERS OF INTERNATIONAL FREQUENCY REGISTRATION BOARD (IFRB)
Chairman: Abderrazak Berrada (Morocco); *Vice-Chairman:* Fioravanti Dellamula (Argentina); Taro Nishizaki (Japan); Rene Petit (France); Vladimir Savantchuk (USSR), later replaced by Aleksandr Gromov (USSR)

OFFICERS OF INTERNATIONAL CONSULTATIVE COMMITTEES
Director, International Radio Consultative Committee (CCIR): Jack W. Herbstreit (United States)
Director, International Telegraph and Telephone Consultative Committee (CCITT): Jean Rouviere (France)

HEADQUARTERS

General Secretariat of the International Telecommunication Union
Place des Nations
1211 Geneva 20, Switzerland
Telephone: 34 70 00
Cable Address: BURINTERNA GENEVA
Telex: GENEVA 23000

Chapter XIII

The World Meteorological Organization (WMO)

The sixth World Meteorological Congress of the World Meteorological Organization (WMO)[1] was held in Geneva, Switzerland, from 5 to 30 April 1971. It reviewed the implementation of the World Weather Watch (WWW) Programme for 1968–1971 (see below), as well as the role played by the WMO Voluntary Assistance Programme, established in 1967 to assist members in implementing the WWW Programme. Special attention was also paid to WMO programmes in education, training and research and the interaction of man and his environment; and major decisions were taken on WMO activities, including those in ocean affairs and operational hydrology.

The Executive Committee of WMO held its twenty-third session from 3 to 6 May 1971 and discussed ways of implementing the decisions of the sixth WMO Congress.

The sixteenth International Meteorological Organization prize was awarded to Professor Jule G. Charney (United States) for his outstanding contributions to dynamical meteorology, furtherance of research in numerical methods of weather prediction and service to the cause of international co-operation.

Matters of a specialized technical nature were considered at sessions of the Commission for Aeronautical Meteorology and the Commission for Agricultural Meteorology, held in Geneva in October 1971.

Other meetings conducted by WMO in 1971 included six sessions of panels of experts established by the Executive Committee to deal with the following subjects: meteorology and economic development; oceanic meteorological research; the collection, storage and retrieval of research data; the International Hydrological Decade; tropical cyclones; and meteorological aspects of air pollution.

During 1971, Yemen became a WMO member State and the French territories of the Comoro Islands and of St. Pierre and Miquelon became separate member territories, thus raising the total membership of WMO to 136 members (123 member States and 13 member territories).

On 26 November 1971, the Secretary-General of WMO addressed a letter to all member States drawing their attention to the United Nations General Assembly's resolution of 25 October 1971 by which the Assembly decided to restore all rights to the People's Republic of China, to recognize the representatives of its Government as the only legitimate representatives of China to the United Nations, and to expel forthwith the representa-

tives of Chiang Kai-shek from the place which they unlawfully occupied at the United Nations and in all the organizations related to it. He also drew attention to a General Assembly resolution of 14 December 1950 by which the Assembly had recommended that the attitude adopted by the General Assembly on recognition by the United Nations of the representation of a Member State should be taken into account in other organs of the United Nations and in the specialized agencies.[2]

The Secretary-General of WMO further stated that, as a result of consultations with the President and members of the Executive Committee of WMO, it had been decided that the matter should be referred to the members of the organization, which by vote should decide upon the application of the United Nations decision within WMO. The voting was to be completed by not later than 24 February 1972.[3] (See also pp. 133, 135.)

Activities in 1971

World Weather Watch (WWW)

The primary aim of the World Weather Watch (WWW) was to make available to each member country the basic meteorological and environmental information it required in order to provide the most efficient and effective meteorological services, in both application and research. The World Weather Watch plan was reviewed by the sixth WMO Congress, which adopted a slightly amended plan for the period 1972–1975 for each of its major components: the global observing system, the global data processing system and the global telecommunication system.

Under the WWW programme, each member country was to be responsible for all meteorological activities within its territory. Activities in extraterritorial areas—such as observations from ships at sea, meteorological satellites and the meteorological observing network in the Antarctic—were being conducted by member countries on a voluntary basis.

The WWW programme was supported by the United Nations Development Programme (UNDP),

---

[1]For further information on the activities of WMO prior to 1971, see annual reports of WMO and previous volumes of Y. U. N.

[2]See Y.U.N., 1950, p. 435, text of resolution 396(V).

[3]The vote by correspondence was completed on 24 February 1972. Seventy WMO member States voted affirmatively as to the proposal that the United Nations General Assembly resolution on the representation of China should apply within WMO; 21 WMO member States voted negatively and there were eight abstentions. The total number of votes having exceeded that required for a quorum (62) and the number of affirmative votes (70) being greater than the two thirds majority of the votes cast "for" and "against," the proposal was adopted.

bilateral and multilateral arrangements and the WMO Voluntary Assistance Programme. The Voluntary Assistance Programme was supporting projects in 83 countries by providing equipment, expert services and long-term fellowships; the cost of those projects totalled about $14 million.

Education, training and research

Substantial progress was achieved in training meteorological personnel during 1971, in particular in developing countries. Assistance was provided to those countries through the organization of seminars, the establishment of regional meteorological training centres and the award of fellowships.

The main research effort of WMO, in collaboration with the International Council of Scientific Unions (ICSU), continued to be centred on the Global Atmospheric Research Programme (GARP). The aim of the programme was to reach a fuller understanding of the atmosphere's structure and behaviour. This world-wide scientific effort, involving both theoretical research and complex field experiments, was to enable the fundamental physical and mathematical bases of long-range weather prediction to be further developed and tested.

The first large experiment under the programme was to take place in the tropical part of the Atlantic. To organize the planning and detailed implementation of the tropical Atlantic experiment, the Executive Committees of WMO and ICSU established a Tropical Experiment Council and Tropical Experiment Board. The first sessions of these two new bodies were held during 1971.

Programme on the interaction of man and his environment

The WMO programme on the interaction of man and his environment included all activities aimed at applying meteorological knowledge to human activities, including agricultural meteorology, aeronautical meteorology, maritime meteorology and other oceanographic matters, human biometeorology, atmospheric and marine pollution and meteorological factors involved in industry and recreation.

In the field of agricultural meteorology, WMO intiated, in co-operation with the Food and Agriculture Organization of the United Nations (FAO), UNDP, the United Nations Educational, Scientific and Cultural Organization (UNESCO) and the World Health Organization (WHO), an interagency co-ordinating group on agricultural biometeorology. The objectives included the development and implementation of an agrometeorological programme for world food production. Agroclimatological surveys were completed in the Near East, in Africa south of the Sahara and in Eastern Africa. Similar surveys were planned in other areas, and related projects, including technical conferences, were being developed. In co-operation with UNDP, a global programme to study the climatic requirements of the new varieties of wheat and rice developed in the so-called green revolution was being initiated.

Through the Commission for Aeronautical Meteorology, acting in co-operation with expert bodies of the International Civil Aviation Organization (ICAO), universal regulations were updated for the supply of weather information for new classes of aircraft operations (in particular, supersonic transport) and for planning purposes.

Recognizing the interdependence of physical processes in the ocean and atmosphere, WMO took an active part in a number of international ocean research projects and in the planning and implementation of programmes for the acquisition of meteorological and oceanographic data and for the provision of oceanic meteorological services through its Commission for Maritime Meteorology. The Commission devoted considerable attention to sea ice problems.

Fields of interest common to WMO and other international organizations, such as the Integrated Global Ocean Station System (which was being developed as a joint programme between the Intergovernmental Oceanographic Commission and WMO), ocean atmosphere interaction, ocean circulation and pollution studies, were co-ordinated through joint working groups and mutual representation at meetings.

In co-operation with the Inter-Governmental Maritime Consultative Organization, FAO, UNESCO, WHO and the International Atomic Energy Agency, WMO sponsored a Joint Group of Experts on the Scientific Aspects of Marine Pollution which, among other things, developed programmes on oceanographic research aspects of marine pollution, including the monitoring aspects.

As a result of WMO studies of the meteorological aspects of air pollution, a global network of stations to measure background air pollution was established in July 1970. By 1971, 46 stations in 19 countries had been designated and were to start operating in the near future.

Close collaboration continued with the United Nations and other interested organizations in the field of hydrology and water resources development, in particular within the framework of the Second United Nations Development Decade which began in 1971. Of particular concern to WMO were the operational aspects of the collection and processing of data related to the land phase of the hydrological cycle, research and promotion of design of networks, standardization of instruments and methods of observation, hydrological forecasting, and the supply of meteorological and hydrological data for the design of projects.

The organization also continued to play a major role in the programme of the International Hydrological Decade.

The sixth WMO Congress took a number of decisions regarding the organization's programme in operational hydrology. Among other things, it established an advisory committee for operational hydrology services or equivalent agencies, to advise the WMO Congress and Executive Committee on policy matters concerning national hydrological services, and adopted a set of technical regulations for operational hydrology.

Technical co-operation

During 1971, technical assistance was provided to developing countries under UNDP and WMO's own assistance programme, principally the Voluntary Assistance Programme.

In 1971, WMO provided technical assistance to 80 countries under the Technical Assistance component of UNDP and funds-in-trust arrangements. Sixty experts served in 38 countries and territories, and 155 students from 58 countries and territories received training under fellowships. Approximately $1.5 million was spent on field projects during the year.

Of the 60 expert missions, 14 were devoted to meteorological training, 14 to the development of meteorological services, and 32 to special fields such as hydrometeorology or hydrology, meteorological instruments, agrometeorology, aeronautical meteorology and meteorological telecommunications. Seven of the missions involved the provision of operational experts.

With the continuation of 13 projects from previous years and the start of field operations in five projects, WMO projects in 1971 under the Special Fund component of UNDP showed a marked increase over previous years.

Implementation began of projects to strengthen and improve the national meteorological services in Tunisia and Cuba, and to establish an East African Institute for Meteorological Training and Research in Nairobi, Kenya, combining the meteorological department at the University of Nairobi and the Regional Meteorological Training Centre in Nairobi, which previously had been functioning separately. The second phase of a project to establish a Meteorological Institute for Research and Training in Cairo, Egypt, was approved for a three-year duration. Under a project for meteorological training in Latin America, 41 fellows from 14 countries commenced their studies in 1971.

Work also continued during the year on the following projects: improvement, expansion and development of meteorological, hydrometeorological or hydrological services in Afghanistan, Bolivia, Brazil, Colombia, Mongolia, the Carib-

bean and the Central American Isthmus; establishment of training and research institutions in Algeria, the Philippines and Zaire; development of flood forecasting and warning systems in China and on the Niger River in Mali and Guinea; and a project to conduct a hydrometeorological survey of the catchments of Lakes Victoria, Kyoga and Albert. The projects in Guinea, Mali, China and Zaire were completed during the year. Eighty-four experts and 88 fellowship holders participated in these projects. The total expenditure on the projects in 1971 was approximately $3 million.

Collaboration continued with ICAO in execution of the meteorological parts of the Special Fund projects for air navigation and aeronautical meteorological facilities at Baghdad (Iraq) and Aden (People's Democratic Republic of Yemen) airports.

In the implementation of the World Weather Watch, 204 projects benefiting 85 members were being implemented, 10 of which were completed in 1971. The projects included the provision of equipment and supplies and long-term fellowships for the training of meteorological personnel.

Under WMO programmes, 41 students studied under long-term fellowships in 1971. The fellowships, for durations of up to five years, were for studies leading to university degrees with specialization in meteorology.

Secretariat

As at 31 December 1971, the total number of full-time staff (excluding those on technical assistance projects) employed by WMO under permanent, fixed-term and short-term appointments stood at 271. Of these, 109 were in the professional and higher categories (drawn from 32 nationalities), and 162 were in the general service category. In addition, about 104 persons in the professional category were employed on technical assistance projects in the field.

Budget

The year 1971 was the fourth year of WMO's fifth financial period (1 January 1968–31 December 1971). The fifth WMO Congress (1967) set a maximum expenditure of $11,817,000 for this four-year period; it also authorized the executive Committee to incur additional expenditure resulting from any increases in secretariat staff salaries because of comparable changes in United Nations salaries and allowances, if such increases could not be met by economies within the approved budget.

At its October 1970 session, the WMO Executive Committee approved a budget of $3,605,577 for the year 1971. The 1971 budget for technical co-operation, financed entirely from overhead allocations from UNDP and other extrabudgetary sources, amounted to an additional $731,800.

The May 1971 session of the Executive Commit-

tee approved a budget of $3,962,400 for the year
1972, as detailed below.

Expenditures	Amount (in U.S. dollars)
Policy-making organs	114,750
Executive management	236,250
Programme of technical activities	2,549,600
Regional activities	166,000
Administrative and common services	702,300
Other budgetary provisions	193,500
Total	3,962,400

INCOME AND EXPENDITURES IN 1971

Revenue	Amount (in U.S. dollars)
Contributions	3,959,900
Miscellaneous income	2,500
Total	3,962,400

Annex.   MEMBERSHIP OF THE WORLD METEOROLOGICAL ORGANIZATION,
CONTRIBUTIONS, OFFICERS AND HEADQUARTERS
(Membership as at 31 December 1971; contributions as set for 1972)

MEMBERS AND CONTRIBUTIONS

State	Unit*	Contribution Net Amount (in U.S. dollars)	State	Unit*	Contribution Net Amount (in U.S. dollars)	State	Unit*	Contribution Net Amount (in U.S. dollars)
Afghanistan	1	3,443	Guinea	1	3,443	Paraguay	1	3,443
Albania	1	3,443	Guyana	1	3,443	People's Democratic Republic of Yemen	1	3,443
Algeria	1	3,443	Haiti	1	3,443	Peru	4	13,774
Argentina	15	51,651	Honduras	1	3,443	Philippines	6	20,660
Australia	20	68,868	Hungary	6	20,660	Poland	14	48,207
Austria	6	20,660	Iceland	1	3,443	Portugal	5	17,217
Barbados	1	3,443	India	26	89,528	Republic of Korea	2	6,887
Belgium	14	48,207	Indonesia	8	27,547	Republic of Viet-Nam	3	10,330
Bolivia	3	10,330	Iran	3	10,330	Romania	5	17,217
Botswana	1	3,443	Iraq	1	3,443	Rwanda	1	3,443
Brazil	15	51,651	Ireland	3	10,330	Saudi Arabia	1	3,443
Bulgaria	4	13,774	Israel	3	10,330	Senegal	1	3,443
Burma	3	10,330	Italy	26	89,528	Sierra Leone	1	3,443
Burundi	1	3,443	Ivory Coast	1	3,443	Singapore	1	3,443
Byelorussian SSR	6	20,660	Jamaica	1	3,443	Somalia	1	3,443
Cameroon	1	3,443	Japan	26	89,528	South Africa	10	34,434
Canada	30	103,302	Jordan	1	3,443	Spain	11	37,877
Central African Republic	1	3,443	Kenya	1	3,443	Sudan	2	6,887
Ceylon	3	10,330	Khmer Republic	1	3,443	Sweden	16	55,094
Chad	1	3,443	Kuwait	1	3,443	Switzerland	13	44,764
Chile	5	17,217	Laos	1	3,443	Syrian Arab Republic	2	6,887
China	43	148,066	Lebanon	1	3,443	Thailand	4	13,774
Colombia	4	13,774	Libyan Arab Republic	1	3,443	Togo	1	3,443
Congo	1	3,443	Luxembourg	1	3,443	Trinidad and Tobago	1	3,443
Costa Rica	1	3,443	Madagascar	1	3,443	Tunisia	1	3,443
Cuba	3	10,330	Malawi	1	3,443	Turkey	6	20,660
Cyprus	1	3,443	Malaysia	4	13,774	Uganda	1	3,443
Czechoslovakia	11	37,877	Mali	1	3,443	Ukrainian SSR	19	65,424
Dahomey	1	3,443	Mauritania	1	3,443	USSR	122	420,094
Denmark	8	27,547	Mauritius	1	3,443	United Kingdom	69	237,594
Dominican Republic	1	3,443	Mexico	10	34,434	United Republic of Tanzania	1	3,443
Ecuador	1	3,443	Mongolia	1	3,443	United States	274	943,489
Egypt	6	20,660	Morocco	2	6,887	Upper Volta	1	3,443
El Salvador	1	3,443	Nepal	1	3,443	Uruguay	4	13,774
Ethiopia	2	6,887	Netherlands	12	41,321	Venezuela	6	20,660
Federal Republic of Germany	53	182,500	New Zealand	6	20,660	Yemen	1	3,443
Finland	6	20,660	Nicaragua	1	3,443	Yugoslavia	6	20,660
France	52	179,056	Niger	1	3,443	Zaire	4	13,774
Gabon	1	3,443	Nigeria	3	10,330	Zambia	2	6,887
Ghana	2	6,887	Norway	7	24,104			
Greece	3	10,330	Pakistan	6	20,660			
Guatemala	1	3,443	Panama	1	3,443			

Territory	Unit*	Contribution Net amount (in U.S. dollars)	Territory	Unit*	Contribution Net Amount (in U.S. dollars)
Bahamas	1	3,443	St. Pierre and Miquelon	1	3,443
British Caribbean Territories	1	3,443	Southern Rhodesia	2	6,887
Comoro Islands	1	3,443	Surinam	1	3,443
French Polynesia	1	3,443	Total		3,959,900†‡
French Territory of the Afars and the Issas	1	3,443			
Hong Kong	1	3,443			
Netherlands Antilles	1	3,443			
New Caledonia	1	3,443			
Portuguese East Africa	2	6,887			
Portuguese West Africa	1	3,443			

Note: Nomenclature of WMO differs from that of the United Nations.

*Exact unit value is $3,443.39.
†Does not include figure for Yemen, which acceded to membership after adoption of 1972 budget information.
‡Total has been rounded.

MEMBERS OF WMO EXECUTIVE COMMITTEE*

President: M. F. Taha (Egypt)
First Vice-President: W. J. Gibbs (Australia)
Second Vice-President: J. Bessemoulin (France)
Third Vice-President: P. Koteswaram (India)

F. A. A. Acquaah (Ghana), B. Azmy (Morocco), E. Bobinski (Poland), S. Bravo Flores (Chile),† O. Coronel Parra (Venezuela), G. Echeverri Ossa (Colombia), G. Fea (Italy), E. K. Fedorov (USSR), B. J. Mason (United Kingdom), A. H. Navai (Iran),† J. R. H. Noble (Canada),† A. Nyberg (Sweden), K. Rajendram (Singapore),† M. Samiullah (Pakistan), M. Seck (Senegal),† R. Schneider (Switzerland),† E. Sussenberger (Federal Republic of Germany), K. Takahashi (Japan), S. Tewungwa (Kenya, Uganda, United Republic of Tanzania), R. M. White (United States)

*Members of the Executive Committee are elected in their personal capacities and do not represent Governments.
†*Ex officio* members of the Executive Committee—Presidents of Regional Associations.

SENIOR MEMBERS OF WMO SECRETARIAT

Secretary-General: D. A. Davies
Deputy Secretary-General: K. Langlo
Director, World Weather Watch Department: A. H. Glaser
Director, Education, Training and Research Department: E. M. Dobryshman
Director, Meteorological Applications Department: O. M. Ashford

Director, Technical Co-operation Department: K. Parthasarathy
Chief, Hydrology and Water Resources Department: J. Nemec
Chief, Administration and External Relations Department: R. L. Munteanu
Chief, Conferences, Publications and Public Information Department: J. M. Rubiato

PRESIDENTS OF REGIONAL ASSOCIATIONS AND TECHNICAL COMMISSIONS

REGIONAL ASSOCIATIONS
   I. Africa: M. Seck (Senegal)
  II. Asia: A. H. Navai (Iran)
 III. South America: S. Bravo Flores (Chile)
 IV. North and Central America: J. R. H. Noble (Canada)
  V. South West Pacific: K. Rajendram (Singapore)
 VI. Europe: R. Schneider (Switzerland)

TECHNICAL COMMISSIONS
Aeronautical Meteorology: P. Duverge (France)
Agicultural Meteorology: W. Baier (Canada)
Atmospheric Sciences: J. S. Sawyer (United Kingdom)
Basic Systems: N. Leonov (USSR)
Hydrology: E. G. Popov (USSR)
Instruments and Methods of Observation: V. D. Rockney (United States)
Maritime Meteorology: S. L. Tierney (Ireland)
Special Applications of Meteorology and Climatology: H. E. Landsberg (United States)

HEADQUARTERS

World Meteorological Organization
41, Avenue Giuseppe-Motta
1211 Geneva, Switzerland
Cable Address: METEOMOND GENEVA

Chapter XIV

The Inter-Governmental Maritime Consultative Organization (IMCO)

During 1971, the Inter-Governmental Maritime Consultative Organization (IMCO)[1] continued its efforts to facilitate co-operation and exchange of information among Governments on technical matters affecting international shipping and to achieve the highest practicable standards of maritime safety and efficient navigation, with special responsibility for safety of life at sea.

Among meetings under IMCO auspices during 1971 were the International Conference on Special Trade Passenger Ships and the Conference to Establish an International Compensation Fund for Oil Pollution Damage.

On 17 June 1971, Malaysia became a member of IMCO. As at the end of 1971, IMCO had 72 member States and one associate member State.

The organization was the depositary authority for the following international conventions, most of them the result of conferences called by IMCO as a corollary of its statutory functions:

International Convention for the Safety of Life at Sea, 1948;

International Convention for the Safety of Life at Sea, 1960;

International Convention for the Prevention of Pollution of the Sea by Oil, 1954, as amended in 1962;

Convention on Facilitation of International Maritime Traffic, 1965;

International Convention on Load Lines, 1966;

International Convention on Tonnage Measurement of Ships, 1969;

International Convention relating to Intervention on the High Seas in Cases of Oil Pollution Casualties, 1969;

International Convention on Civil Liability for Oil Pollution Damage, 1969;

Special Trade Passenger Ships Agreement, 1971;

Convention on the Establishment of an International Fund for Compensation for Oil Pollution Damage, 1971;

International Convention relating to Civil Liability in the Field of Maritime Carriage of Nuclear Material, 1971.

Activities in 1971

Safety of navigation

A number of traffic separation schemes, aimed at reducing the risk of collision in areas of high traffic density, were adopted by IMCO.

In October 1971, the seventh IMCO Assembly adopted an amendment to the International Convention for the Safety of Life at Sea, 1960; this provided for compulsory observance of the direction of traffic flow in such schemes.

Also, the seventh IMCO Assembly approved the establishment of a new sub-committee of the Maritime Safety Committee to deal exclusively with the task of framing international standards of training and certification for mariners.

Performance standards for navigational radar equipment, radio direction-finding systems, and echo-sounding equipment were adopted by the seventh Assembly. These standards, together with similar standards that were being prepared for such devices as gyro-compasses, radar reflectors and shipboard radio beacons, were eventually to be incorporated in a set of international performance standards for shipborne electronic aids to navigation.

Radio-communications

As part of the revision of the maritime distress system, the seventh IMCO Assembly adopted amendments to the International Convention for the Safety of Life at Sea, 1960, and it made recommendations to improve the existing radio-telephone and radio-telegraph facilities.

The organization was also preparing an organizational plan for an international maritime satellite system, to be used for both navigational and radio-communication purposes.

Search and rescue and life-saving applicances

The seventh Assembly of IMCO adopted a resolution concerning instructions on aspects of survival at sea, action to be taken on the arrival of rescue units at the scene of disaster, preparations for being taken in tow and rescue by helicopter. These instructions supplemented earlier IMCO recommendations.

[1]For further information on IMCO's activities prior to 1971, see annual reports of IMCO and previous volumes of Y.U.N.

Ship subdivision and stability

Recommendations on the intact stability of ships under 100 metres in length which carried deck cargoes, particularly timber, were adopted by the seventh IMCO Assembly, together with recommendations on simplified stability criteria for decked fishing vessels (to be used only where no drawing or stability calculations were available).

Ship design and equipment

Studies made by IMCO of oil tanker construction and equipment, from the viewpoint of preventing or limiting marine pollution by oil in the event of the vessel's stranding or collision, culminated in the proposal of amendments to the 1954 International Convention for the Prevention of Pollution of the Sea by Oil. The amendments, adopted by the seventh IMCO Assembly, dealt with requirements for the arrangement of tanks and for limiting their size. The hypothetical quantity of oil outflow in the event of a tanker collision was set at a maximum of 40,000 cubic metres; the requirements were to apply, in some cases, to tankers for which the building contract was placed on or after 1 January 1972, and, in all cases, to vessels delivered after 1 January 1977.

Bulk carriage of chemicals

A code for construction and equipment of ships carrying dangerous chemicals in bulk was also adopted by the IMCO Assembly.

The code defined three categories of vessel according to the specific environmental hazards of the intended cargo. Those carrying the most hazardous cargoes were required to be of double hull construction; reduced standards proportionate to the decreasing hazards of the cargo were prescribed for the other two categories.

The code was to be further developed to cover bulk carriers of hazardous compressed or liquefied gases.

Container transport

In preparation for the joint United Nations/IMCO Conference on International Container Traffic, scheduled for November 1972, IMCO prepared the initial text of a draft convention on the safety aspects of container traffic. In conjunction with the European Economic Community, the final text of a draft convention on the safe multimodal transport of containers was also being prepared;

the convention was to apply to both new and existing containers, excepting those especially designed for air transport.

Marine pollution

As part of the organization's anti-pollution programme, the IMCO Assembly approved and recommended the adoption of international specifications for oily-water separating equipment and oil content meters for installation in ships.

The Assembly also decided that the IMCO Conference on Marine Pollution—to be convened in 1973—should have as its main objective the complete elimination of intentional marine pollution by oil and other noxious pollutants, and the minimization of accidental spills; this objective was to be achieved by 1975, if possible, but in any event by the end of the decade.

The Convention on the Establishment of an International Fund for Compensation for Oil Pollution Damage was concluded at a conference convened by IMCO in Brussels, Belgium, in November-December 1971.

Technical co-operation

The technical co-operation programme of IMCO greatly intensified during 1971. Expert missions were sent and fellowships were awarded in the fields of maritime legislation, ship construction, maritime training and marine pollution.

A project for the development of a merchant marine school in Rio de Janeiro, Brazil, was continued.

Secretariat

As at 31 December 1971, the total number of full-time staff (excluding those on technical assistance projects) employed by IMCO under permanent, fixed-term and short-term appointments stood at 114. Of these, 42 were in the professional and higher categories (drawn from 20 nationalities) and 72 were in the general service category. In addition, some 22 persons in the professional category were employed on technical assistance projects in the field.

Budget

In October 1971, the seventh IMCO Assembly voted a budget of $3,996,600 for the two-year period 1972–1973.

Annex.   MEMBERSHIP OF THE INTER-GOVERNMENTAL MARITIME CONSULTATIVE
ORGANIZATION, CONTRIBUTIONS, OFFICERS AND HEADQUARTERS
(As at 31 December 1971)

MEMBERS AND CONTRIBUTIONS

Member	Net contribution for 1971 (in U.S. dollars)	Member	Net contribution for 1971 (in U.S. dollars)	Member	Net contribution for 1971 (in U.S. dollars)
Algeria	2,186	India	17,393	Peru	4,422
Argentina	10,114	Indonesia	6,121	Philippines	8,063
Australia	8,883	Iran	2,827	Poland	12,125
Barbados	2,007	Ireland	3,122	Republic of Korea	7,441
Belgium	8,805	Israel	6,575	Romania	4,185
Brazil	13,035	Italy	51,730	Saudi Arabia	2,314
Bulgaria	6,397	Ivory Coast	2,167	Senegal	2,057
Burma	2,326	Japan	177,053	Singapore	4,717
Cameroon	2,012	Khmer Republic	2,026	Spain	24,051
Canada	19,380	Kuwait	5,794	Sweden	33,536
China	11,472	Lebanon	3,167	Switzerland	3,256
Cuba	4,134	Liberia	215,381	Syrian Arab Republic	2,007
Czechoslovakia	2,570	Libyan Arab Republic	2,026	Trinidad and Tobago	2,135
Denmark	23,238	Madagascar	2,186	Tunisia	2,141
Dominican Republic	2,052	Malaysia	1,154	Turkey	6,466
Ecuador	2,288	Maldives	2,109	USSR	105,050
Egypt	3,525	Malta	2,224	United Kingdom	169,497
Federal Republic of Germany	54,505	Mauritania	2,007	United States	128,319
Finland	10,953	Mexico	4,441	Uruguay	2,903
France	45,386	Morocco	2,352	Yugoslavia	11,716
Ghana	3,064	Netherlands	35,369		
Greece	72,185	New Zealand	3,191	**Associate member**	
Haiti	2,000	Nigeria	2,634	Hong Kong	3,153
Honduras	2,385	Norway	125,984	Total	1,582,260
Hungary	2,199	Pakistan	5,627		
Iceland	2,763	Panama	38,182		

IMCO COUNCIL AND MARITIME SAFETY COMMITTEE

COUNCIL
Chairman: R. Y. Edwards (United States)

Algeria, Australia, Belgium, Brazil, Canada, Federal Republic of Germany,
France, Ghana, Greece, India, Italy, Japan, Netherlands, Norway, Poland,
USSR, United Kingdom, United States

MARITIME SAFETY COMMITTEE
Chairman: Jan Metz (Netherlands)

Argentina, Canada, Egypt, Federal Republic of Germany, France, Greece,
Italy, Japan, Netherlands, Norway, Pakistan, Spain, Sweden, USSR, United
Kingdom, United States

OFFICERS AND OFFICES

PRINCIPAL OFFICERS OF IMCO SECRETARIAT
Secretary-General: Colin Goad
Deputy Secretary-General: Jean Quéguiner
Secretary, Maritime Safety Committee: Alexander Saveliev

HEADQUARTERS
Inter-Governmental Maritime Consultative Organization
101-104, Piccadilly
London, W1V OAE, United Kingdom
Cable Address: INMARCOR LONDON

Chapter XV

The Interim Commission for the International Trade Organization (ICITO) and the General Agreement on Tariffs and Trade (GATT)

The United Nations Conference on Trade and Employment, held at Havana, Cuba, between November 1947 and March 1948, drew up a Charter, known as the Havana Charter, for an International Trade Organization (ITO) and established an Interim Commission for the International Trade Organization (ICITO).[1] As a result of the lack of acceptances of the Havana Charter, it became evident by the end of 1950 that the attempt to establish the International Trade Organization would be postponed indefinitely.

While the Charter for ITO was in the course of preparation, the members of the Preparatory Committee decided to proceed with tariff negotiations among themselves. They also drew up the General Agreement on Tariffs and Trade (GATT). The Agreement—a multilateral treaty embodying reciprocal rights and obligations—entered into force on 1 January 1948, there being 23 Contracting Parties to GATT at that time. Contracting Parties of GATT are estimated to carry on well over four fifths of all international trade.

During 1971, Romania (15 October) and Zaire (11 August) acceded to GATT, bringing the total number of Contracting Parties to 80. Sixteen countries that did not have full Contracting Party arrangements were also participating in the work of GATT.

The provisional accession of Tunisia was extended to 31 December 1973.

Further meetings were held of the working party which was created to examine Hungary's request for accession.

On 16 November 1971, at the twenty-seventh session of the Contracting Parties to GATT, the Chairman of the session drew attention to a United Nations General Assembly resolution of 25 October 1971 by which the Assembly decided to restore all rights to the People's Republic of China, to recognize the representatives of its Government as the only legitimate representatives of China to the United Nations, and to expel forthwith the representatives of Chiang Kai-shek from the place which they unlawfully occupied at the United Nations and in all the organizations related to it.

The Chairman recalled that in 1965, in reaching their decision to accede to the request from the Republic of China that it be represented by observers at sessions of the Contracting Parties, the Contracting Parties had agreed to follow decisions of the United Nations on essentially political matters. The Chairman added that it would be logical for the Contracting Parties to rely in this case on the decision taken by the United Nations and decide accordingly that the Republic of China should no longer have observer status at sessions of the Contracting Parties. After a short discussion, the Chairman noted that no request for a vote had been made and declared that there was a consensus for the adoption of the views expressed by him. (See also pp. 133, 135.)

In addition to the twenty-seventh regular session of the Contracting Parties held from 16 to 26 November 1971, a special informal high-level session took place from 28 to 30 April 1971. The purpose of the April session was to discuss the situation in international trade and to review progress under the GATT work programme established in 1967.

The regular, November session was held at the height of the monetary and trade crisis of the final months of 1971. Summing up the discussions at that session, the Chairman stated that the Contracting Parties had recognized that the situation presented opportunities as well as risks. They had reaffirmed their firm intention to continue to work together within the framework of GATT to overcome trade problems and differences, as well as their determination to give particular attention to the problems of developing countries.

They had agreed to pursue, through the GATT Programme for Trade Expansion, every opportunity of making further progress towards trade liberalization and to take such opportunities as might arise for the settlement of particular trade problems, especially those regarded as most dangerous and irritating. They had also agreed that it was their intention to pursue in GATT a new major initiative for dealing with the longer-term trade problems as soon as feasible.

The GATT Council of Representatives held nine meetings during 1971, and dealt with a wide range of problems, the more important of which are referred to below.

Work programme

At their twenty-fourth session, in November 1967, the Contracting Parties established a programme of work for the further expansion of trade in three main fields: industrial products,

[1]For further information, see previous volumes of Y. U. N.

agriculture, and the trade of the developing countries. The Committee on Trade in Industrial Products and the Agriculture Committee were established; the Committee on Trade and Development had been set up in 1965.

For industrial products, the programme required (*a*) an analysis of the tariff situation as it would be when all Kennedy Round concessions[2] had been fully implemented (i.e. from 1 January 1972); and (*b*) an inventory of non-tariff and para-tariff barriers affecting international trade.

For agriculture, the Programme called on the Agriculture Committee to explore possibilities for making progress in the attainment of the objectives of the General Agreement in the agricultural field.

With regard to the trade of developing countries, the programme called for action on a number of fronts, including advance implementation of the Kennedy Round reductions, examination of problems affecting trade in tropical products, the early removal of import restrictions on industrial products of particular interest to developing countries, and trade negotiations between developing countries.

Trade in industrial products

In the field of non-tariff barriers, work up to the end of 1970 had resulted in the establishment and examination of an inventory of some 800 notifications by Governments of barriers to trade that were being applied by other countries. The barriers had been divided into five main categories: government participation in trade; customs and administrative entry procedures; standards involving imports and domestic goods; specific limitations on imports and exports; and restraints on imports and exports through the price mechanism. A selected "illustrated list" of some 100 barriers had been examined in detail, with the aim of exploring possibilities for concrete action to reduce or remove them.

Early in 1971, the GATT Council of Representatives agreed to proceed to a new stage by working out, in detail, mutually acceptable solutions to the problems raised by certain specific non-tariff barriers. This work was being undertaken on an *ad referendum* basis, i.e. subject to approval by member Governments.

Initially, three types of barriers were studied: standards and their enforcement; problems of customs valuation; and quantitative restrictions, attention being directed initially to licensing. By late 1971, sufficient progress had been made to consider new barriers for action. These were export subsidies, import documentation (including consular formalities), and packaging and labelling. Possibilities of adding other topics to the work programme were to be explored continuous-

ly, and special attention was to be given throughout to the interests of developing countries.

The tariff study, an essential counterpart to the action on non-tariff barriers, involved the recording of data on trade. During 1970, the first tabulations had been prepared, analysing the tariff situation by areas and sectors of trade, by principal industrial categories, and in terms of differentials between tariffs on raw materials and finished products. These tabulations were published during 1971; they were to be kept up to date and extended in coverage. Work on the tariff study continued in 1971 with the systematic analysis and comparison of the structure of tariffs in each of 23 main product categories. The feasibility of measuring the effects of tariff changes on trade was also being examined.

Trade in agricultural products

Four working groups studied the principal problems of international trade in agricultural products, including imports, exports and production, with a view to finding mutually acceptable solutions. Early in 1971, the Council of Representatives considered a report by the Agriculture Committee on the progress of these studies. This showed that although the Committee had covered many suggested solutions, none commanded enough support to be acceptable. Discussions continued on the subject.

Trade of developing countries

The Committee on Trade and Development continued during 1971 to be responsible for ensuring that priority attention be given to the trade problems of developing countries. The Committee continued to stress the interest and concern of developing countries in other areas of GATT's operations, in particular, tariff and non-tariff barriers, the removal of import restrictions, and trade in tropical products. In this connexion, a special group, composed of the Chairmen of the Contracting Parties, the Council of Representatives and the Committee itself, was established.

This group of three was asked to formulate concrete proposals to overcome the trade problems of developing countries. Its proposals, put forward after consultation with developed countries, concentrated on the removal or reduction of quantitative restrictions on products of interest to developing countries; the removal of non-tariff barriers of particular concern to developing countries; action to assist trade in tropical products; and the problem of tariff escalation, particularly as it affected tropical products and vegetable oils. A number of the proposals were taken up by GATT;

[2]See Y. U. N., 1967, pp. 922-23 for information on the Kennedy Round negotiations.

in other cases, individual Governments of developed countries announced their intention of taking the action recommended.

In June 1971, GATT members voted to authorize the introduction by Governments of developed countries of generalized, non-discriminatory preferential treatment for products originating in developing countries. The authorization took the form of a ten-year waiver.

Approval was also given during 1971 for the introduction of preferences among developing countries. Sixteen developing countries, of which 14 were GATT members, were initially taking part in the scheme. They stated their intention of keeping under review the possibility of expanding the lists of concessions made to one another, and of facilitating the entry of other developing countries into the arrangements.

Import restrictions

Regular consultations were held in 1971 with countries maintaining import restrictions for balance-of-payments purposes. Also kept under consideration by GATT were schemes for import deposits or import surcharges maintained by a number of countries. Particularly close study was given to the import surcharges introduced by the United States (in August 1971) and by Denmark (in October 1971). In the case of the United States surcharge, the GATT Council of Representatives adopted the report of a working party which recognized the seriousness of the United States balance-of-payments situation, but which concluded that the measure was inappropriate and incompatible with the provisions of the General Agreement, to the extent that it raised customs duties beyond the bound maximum rate. The United States surcharge was removed in December 1971.

Similar conclusions were reached in the case of the Danish surcharge, in a working party report, with regard to the balance-of-payments situation and the incompatibility of the measure with GATT provisions; in this case it was noted that imports from developing countries, as far as these were covered by the Danish scheme for generalized preferences, would be exempted from the surcharge from January 1972 onwards. The Danish surcharge was to be phased out gradually and finally eliminated on 1 April 1973.

In 1971, the Council of Representatives decided to maintain in existence the Joint Working Group on Quantitative Import Restrictions, charged with the duty of carrying out regular reviews of all import restrictions.

Environmental measures and international trade

During 1971, the GATT secretariat submitted to Governments, and to the Secretary-General of the United Nations Conference on the Human Environment, a study on industrial pollution control and international trade. The study discussed some of the problems involved in reconciling national or international efforts to control pollution with the need to avoid introducing new barriers to trade.

A standing group was established in November 1971 to examine, upon request, any specific matters relevant to the trade policy aspects of measures to control pollution and protect the human environment.

Regional trading arrangements

As in 1970, a number of new trade arrangements were notified to GATT under the terms of article XXIV (which deals with customs unions and free trade areas) of the General Agreement. These were examined individually. Progress reports on earlier arrangements were also reviewed, as usual, in the GATT Council.

The examination or review of some of these arrangements, and especially those concluded between the European Economic Community and a number of countries, largely African or bordering the Mediterranean, revealed wide divergences of view with regard to their conformity to the General Agreement. In each case, the discussions were left open, and all countries retained their rights under the General Agreement.

To enable a more informed discussion of the place of such agreements in the multilateral trading system, GATT members agreed in November 1971 that the secretariat should gather statistics concerning the trade of member countries at most-favoured-nation and other rates.

Waivers from GATT obligations

A waiver was granted in March 1971 to authorize increases in margins of preference introduced for certain imports by Jamaica between 1947 and 1962. The decision overcame a technical difficulty that had arisen because Jamaica, in acceding to GATT in 1962, had done so by a procedure that required it accept 1947 as the base date for preferences.

During the year, the Council of Representatives as usual received reports on certain waivers granted at earlier sessions.

Training programme

During 1971, as in previous years, two five-month courses for officials from developing countries on international trade and commercial policy were held at GATT headquarters in Geneva, Switzerland. The officials held fellowships under the United Nations Development Programme. Thirty-two such courses had been held since 1955, and over 350 officials from 86 countries had participated.

Publications

In 1971, the GATT secretariat published *International Trade, 1970; Effective Tariff Protection; Industrial Pollution Control and International Trade; Japan's Economic Expansion and Foreign Trade 1955 to 1970; Status of Legal Instruments;* and a revised edition of *GATT: What It Is, What It Does.*

International Trade Centre

The International Trade Centre was established by GATT in 1964 in order to give direct help to developing countries in promoting their exports. In 1967, the United Nations Conference on Trade and Development (UNCTAD) and GATT decided to pool their resources and activities in this field, and, on 1 January 1968, the joint UNCTAD/GATT International Trade Centre came into operation.

In 1971, GATT financed half the budget of the Centre and provided it with considerable supporting services. The budget of the Centre for its regular work programme in 1972 was set at $2,001,600, of which the GATT share was to be $980,110. As at 31 December 1971, the personnel establishment of the Centre consisted of 118 posts: 50 in the professional and higher categories and 68 in the general service category; these figures

did not include a number of persons working for the Centre in connexion with particular projects.

(For a more detailed account of the work of the International Trade Centre in 1971, see pp. 286-87.)

Secretariat

As at 31 December 1971, the personnel establishment of the GATT secretariat (excluding the UNCTAD/GATT International Trade Centre) consisted of 199 posts; of these, 90 were in the professional and higher categories and 109 were in the general service category.

Financial arrangements

Governments parties to GATT participate financially in accordance with a scale of contributions assessed on the basis of the country's share in the total trade of the contracting parties and associated Governments. The scale of contributions for 1972 is given in Annex I below.

The GATT budget for 1971 was $4,024,000; for 1972 it was set at $4,738,200 (including GATT's share of $980,110 in the regular budget of the UNCTAD/GATT International Trade Centre).

Annex I. CONTRACTING PARTIES TO THE GENERAL AGREEMENT ON TARIFFS AND TRADE AND SCALE OF CONTRIBUTIONS FOR 1972
(As at 31 December 1971)

Contracting parties	Net contributions (in U.S. dollars)	Contracting parties	Net contributions (in U.S. dollars)	Contracting parties	Net contributions (in U.S. dollars)
Argentina	28,000	Guyana	5,330	Portugal	31,110
Australia	80,430	Haiti	5,330	Republic of Korea	21,780
Austria	48,880	Iceland	5,330	Romania	32,440
Barbados	5,330	India	37,330	Rwanda	5,330
Belgium	165,750	Indonesia	14,220	Senegal	5,330
Brazil	43,110	Ireland	20,890	Sierra Leone	5,330
Burma	5,330	Israel	18,220	South Africa	49,770
Burundi	5,330	Italy	220,410	Southern Rhodesia	5,780
Cameroon	5,330	Ivory Coast	7,110	Spain	55,990
Canada	259,510	Jamaica	6,220	Sweden	107,090
Central African Republic	5,330	Japan	288,400	Switzerland	91,100
Ceylon	6,670	Kenya	6,220	Togo	5,330
Chad	5,330	Kuwait	19,110	Trinidad and Tobago	8,890
Chile	16,890	Luxembourg	14,220	Turkey	12,440
Congo	5,330	Madagascar	5,330	Uganda	5,330
Cuba	15,110	Malawi	5,330	United Kingdom	390,160
Cyprus	5,330	Malaysia	25,330	United Republic of Tanzania	5,330
Czechoslovakia	63,550	Malta	5,330	United States	706,550
Dahomey	5,330	Mauritania	5,330	Upper Volta	5,330
Denmark	62,210	Mauritius	5,330	Uruguay	5,330
Dominican Republic	5,330	Netherlands	207,080	Yugoslavia	33,770
Egypt	12,890	New Zealand	20,890	Zaire	8,440
Federal Republic of Germany	493,250	Nicaragua	5,330		
Finland	36,880	Niger	5,330	**Associated**	
France	299,510	Nigeria	15,110	**Governments**	
Gabon	5,330	Norway	48,440	Khmer Republic	5,330
Gambia	5,330	Pakistan	16,000	Tunisia	5,330
Ghana	6,220	Peru	13,780	Total	4,443,700
Greece	19,550	Poland	60,440		

Annex II.   OFFICERS AND HEADQUARTERS
(As at 31 December 1971)

OFFICERS

OFFICERS OF THE CONTRACTING PARTIES*
Chairman of the Contracting Parties: Giorgio Smoquina (Italy)
Vice-Chairman: Héctor Gros-Espiell (Uruguay)
Chairman of the Council of Representatives: C. H. Archibald (Trinidad and Tobago)
Chairman of the Committee on Trade and Development: B. R. Patel (India)

*Elected at end of November 1971 session, to hold office until end of next session.

SENIOR OFFICERS OF THE SECRETARIAT
Director-General: Olivier Long
Assistant Director-General, Department of Trade Policy: G. Patterson
Assistant Director-General, Department of Trade and Development: M. G. Mathur
Assistant Director-General, Department of Conference Affairs and Administration: D. P. Taylor
Special Assistant to the Director-General: H. F. Reed

SENIOR OFFICERS OF THE UNCTAD/GATT INTERNATIONAL TRADE CENTRE

Director (Promotions): H. L. Jacobson   *Acting Director (Programmes):* V. E. Santiapillai

HEADQUARTERS

GATT Secretariat
Villa le Bocage
Palais des Nations
1211 Geneva 10, Switzerland
Cable Address: GATT GENEVA

Appendices

Appendix I

Roster of the United Nations

(As at 31 December 1971)

MEMBER	DATE OF ADMIS-SION TO U.N.	MEMBER	DATE OF ADMIS-SION TO U.N.	MEMBER	DATE OF ADMIS-SION TO U.N.
Afghanistan	19 Nov. 1946	Guatemala	21 Nov. 1945	Oman	7 Oct. 1971
Albania	14 Dec. 1955	Guinea	12 Dec. 1958	Pakistan	30 Sep. 1947
Algeria	8 Oct. 1962	Guyana	20 Sep. 1966	Panama	13 Nov. 1945
Argentina	24 Oct. 1945	Haiti	24 Oct. 1945	Paraguay	24 Oct. 1945
Australia	1 Nov. 1945	Honduras	17 Dec. 1945	People's Democratic	
Austria	14 Dec. 1955	Hungary	14 Dec. 1955	Republic of Yemen	14 Dec. 1967
Bahrain	21 Sep. 1971	Iceland	19 Nov. 1946	Peru	31 Oct. 1945
Barbados	9 Dec. 1966	India	30 Oct. 1945	Philippines	24 Oct. 1945
Belgium	27 Dec. 1945	Indonesia[4]	28 Sep. 1950	Poland	24 Oct. 1945
Bhutan	21 Sep. 1971	Iran	24 Oct. 1945	Portugal	14 Dec. 1955
Bolivia	14 Nov. 1945	Iraq	21 Dec. 1945	Qatar	21 Sep. 1971
Botswana	17 Oct. 1966	Ireland	14 Dec. 1955	Romania	14 Dec. 1955
Brazil	24 Oct. 1945	Israel	11 May 1949	Rwanda	18 Sep. 1962
Bulgaria	14 Dec. 1955	Italy	14 Dec. 1955	Saudi Arabia	24 Oct. 1945
Burma	19 Apr. 1948	Ivory Coast	20 Sep. 1960	Senegal	28 Sep. 1960
Burundi	18 Sep. 1962	Jamaica	18 Sep. 1962	Sierra Leone	27 Sep. 1961
Byelorussian SSR	24 Oct. 1945	Japan	18 Dec. 1956	Singapore[5]	21 Sep. 1965
Cameroon	20 Sep. 1960	Jordan	14 Dec. 1955	Somalia	20 Sep. 1960
Canada	9 Nov. 1945	Kenya	16 Dec. 1963	South Africa	7 Nov. 1945
Central African		Khmer Republic	14 Dec. 1955	Spain	14 Dec. 1955
Republic	20 Sep. 1960	Kuwait	14 May 1963	Sudan	12 Nov. 1956
Ceylon	14 Dec. 1955	Laos	14 Dec. 1955	Swaziland	24 Sep. 1968
Chad	20 Sep. 1960	Lebanon	24 Oct. 1945	Sweden	19 Nov. 1946
Chile	24 Oct. 1945	Lesotho	17 Oct. 1966	Syrian Arab	
China[1]	24 Oct. 1945	Liberia	2 Nov. 1945	Republic[3]	24 Oct. 1945
Colombia	5 Nov. 1945	Libyan Arab		Thailand	16 Dec. 1946
Congo[2]	20 Sep. 1960	Republic	14 Dec. 1955	Togo	20 Sep. 1960
Costa Rica	2 Nov. 1945	Luxembourg	24 Oct. 1945	Trinidad and Tobago	18 Sep. 1962
Cuba	24 Oct. 1945	Madagascar	20 Sep. 1960	Tunisia	12 Nov. 1956
Cyprus	20 Sep. 1960	Malawi	1 Dec. 1964	Turkey	24 Oct. 1945
Czechoslovakia	24 Oct. 1945	Malaysia[5]	17 Sep. 1957	Uganda	25 Oct. 1962
Dahomey	20 Sep. 1960	Maldives	21 Sep. 1965	Ukrainian SSR	24 Oct. 1945
Denmark	24 Oct. 1945	Mali	28 Sep. 1960	USSR	24 Oct. 1945
Dominican Republic	24 Oct. 1945	Malta	1 Dec. 1964	United Arab	
Ecuador	21 Dec. 1945	Mauritania	27 Oct. 1961	Emirates	9 Dec. 1971
Egypt[3]	24 Oct. 1945	Mauritius	24 Apr. 1968	United Kingdom	24 Oct. 1945
El Salvador	24 Oct. 1945	Mexico	7 Nov. 1945	United Republic	
Equatorial Guinea	12 Nov. 1968	Mongolia	27 Oct. 1961	of Tanzania[6]	14 Dec. 1961
Ethiopia	13 Nov. 1945	Morocco	12 Nov. 1956	United States	24 Oct. 1945
Fiji	13 Oct. 1970	Nepal	14 Dec. 1955	Upper Volta	20 Sep. 1960
Finland	14 Dec. 1955	Netherlands	10 Dec. 1945	Uruguay	18 Dec. 1945
France	24 Oct. 1945	New Zealand	24 Oct. 1945	Venezuela	15 Nov. 1945
Gabon	20 Sep. 1960	Nicaragua	24 Oct. 1945	Yemen	30 Sep. 1947
Gambia	21 Sep. 1965	Niger	20 Sep. 1960	Yugoslavia	24 Oct. 1945
Ghana	8 Mar. 1957	Nigeria	7 Oct. 1960	Zaire[7]	20 Sep. 1960
Greece	25 Oct. 1945	Norway	27 Nov. 1945	Zambia	1 Dec. 1964

[1]China is an original Member of the United Nations, the Charter having been signed and ratified on its behalf, on 26 June and 28 September 1945, respectively, by the Government of the Republic of China, which continued to represent China in the United Nations until 25 October 1971.

On 25 October 1971, the General Assembly of the United Nations adopted a resolution (2758(XXVI)), by which it recognized that "the representatives of the Government of the People's Republic of China are the only lawful representatives of China to the United Nations and that the People's Republic of China is one of the five permanent members of the Security Council," and decided "to restore all its rights to the People's Republic of China and to recognize the representatives of its Government as the only legitimate representatives of China to the United Nations, and to expel forthwith the representatives of Chiang Kai-shek from the place which they unlawfully occupy at the United Nations and in all the organizations related to it."

The United Nations had been notified on 18 November 1949 of the formation, on 1 October 1949, of the Central People's Government of the People's Republic of China. Proposals to effect a change in the representation of China in the United Nations subsequent to that time were not approved until the resolution cited above was adopted.

All entries recorded throughout this publication in respect of China refer to actions taken by the authorities representing China in the United Nations at the time of those actions.

(footnotes continued on next page)

(Footnotes—continued from preceding page)

[2]The People's Republic of the Congo changed its name to the Congo (People's Republic of) on 15 November 1971.

[3]Egypt and Syria, both of which became Members of the United Nations on 24 October 1945, joined together—following a plebiscite held in those countries on 21 February 1958—to form the United Arab Republic. On 13 October 1961, Syria, having resumed its status as an independent State, also resumed its separate membership in the United Nations, and the United Arab Republic continued as a Member of the United Nations.

The United Arab Republic changed its name to the Arab Republic of Egypt on 2 September 1971.

[4]In a letter dated 20 January 1965, Indonesia informed the Secretary-General that it had decided "at this stage and under the present circumstances" to withdraw from the United Nations. In a telegram dated 19 September 1966, Indonesia notified the Secretary-General of its decision "to resume full co-operation with the United Nations and to resume participation in its activities starting with the twenty-first session of the General Assembly." On 28 September 1966, the General Assembly took note of the decision of the Government of Indonesia and the President invited the representatives of that country to take their seats in the Assembly.

[5]On 16 September 1963, Sabah (North Borneo), Sarawak and Singapore joined with the Federation of Malaya (which became a United Nations Member on 17 September 1957) to form Malaysia. On 9 August 1965, Singapore became an independent State, and on 21 September 1965 it became a Member of the United Nations.

[6]Tanganyika was a Member of the United Nations from 14 December 1961, and Zanzibar was a Member from 16 December 1963. Following the ratification, on 26 April 1964, of Articles of Union between Tanganyika and Zanzibar, the United Republic of Tanganyika and Zanzibar continued as a single Member of the United Nations; on 1 November 1964, it changed its name to the United Republic of Tanzania.

[7]The Democratic Republic of the Congo changed its name to the Republic of Zaire on 27 October 1971.

Appendix II

The Charter of the United Nations and the Statute of the International Court of Justice

The Charter of the United Nations

NOTE: The Charter of the United Nations was signed on 26 June 1945, in San Francisco, at the conclusion of the United Nations Conference on International Organization, and came into force on 24 October 1945. The Statute of the International Court of Justice is an integral part of the Charter.

Amendments to Articles 23, 27 and 61 of the Charter were adopted by the General Assembly on 17 December 1963 and came into force on 31 August 1965. The amendment to Article 109, adopted by the General Assembly on 20 December 1965, came into force on 12 June 1968.

The amendment to Article 23 enlarges the membership of the Security Council from 11 to 15. The amended Article 27 provides that decisions of the Security Council on procedural matters shall be made by an affirmative vote of nine members (formerly seven) and on all other matters by an affirmative vote of nine members (formerly seven) including the concurring votes of the five permanent members of the Security Council.

The amendment to Article 61 enlarges the membership of the Economic and Social Council from 18 to 27.

The amendment to Article 109, which relates to the first paragraph of that Article, provides that a General Conference of Member States for the purpose of reviewing the Charter may be held at a date and place to be fixed by a two-thirds vote of the members of the General Assembly and by a vote of any nine members (formerly seven) of the Security Council. Paragraph 3 of Article 109, which deals with the consideration of a possible review conference during the tenth regular session of the General Assembly, has been retained in its original form in its reference to a "vote of any seven members of the Security Council," the paragraph having been acted upon in 1955 by the General Assembly, at its tenth regular session, and by the Security Council.

WE THE PEOPLES
OF THE UNITED NATIONS
DETERMINED

to save succeeding generations from the scourge of war, which twice in our life-time has brought untold sorrow to mankind, and

to reaffirm faith in fundamental human rights, in the dignity and worth of the human person, in the equal rights of men and women and of nations large and small, and

to establish conditions under which justice and respect for the obligations arising from treaties and other sources of international law can be maintained, and

to promote social progress and better standards of life in larger freedom,

AND FOR THESE ENDS

to practice tolerance and live together in peace with one another as good neighbours, and

to unite our strength to maintain international peace and security, and

to ensure, by the acceptance of principles and the institution of methods, that armed force shall not be used, save in the common interest, and

to employ international machinery for the promotion of the economic and social advancement of all peoples,

HAVE RESOLVED TO
COMBINE OUR EFFORTS TO
ACCOMPLISH THESE AIMS

Accordingly, our respective Governments, through representatives assembled in the city of San Francisco, who have exhibited their full powers found to be in good and due form, have agreed to the present Charter of the United Nations and do hereby establish an international organization to be known as the United Nations.

Chapter I
PURPOSES AND PRINCIPLES

Article 1
The Purposes of the United Nations are:

1. To maintain international peace and security, and to that end: to take effective collective measures for the prevention and removal of threats to the peace, and for the suppression of acts of aggression or other breaches of the peace, and to bring about by peaceful means, and in conformity with the principles of justice and international law, adjustment or settlement of international disputes or situations which might lead to a breach of the peace;

2. To develop friendly relations among nations based on respect for the principle of equal rights and self-determination of peoples, and to take other appropriate measures to strengthen universal peace;

3. To achieve international co-operation in solving international problems of an economic, social, cultural, or humanitarian character, and in promoting and encouraging respect for human rights and for fundamental freedoms for all without distinction as to race, sex, language, or religion; and

4. To be a centre for harmonizing the actions of nations in the attainment of these common ends.

Article 2
The Organization and its Members, in pursuit of the Purposes stated in Article 1, shall act in accordance with the following Principles.

1. The Organization is based on the principle of the sovereign equality of all its Members.

2. All Members, in order to ensure to all of them the rights and

benefits resulting from membership, shall fulfil in good faith the obligations assumed by them in accordance with the present Charter.

3. All Members shall settle their international disputes by peaceful means in such a manner that international peace and security, and justice, are not endangered.

4. All Members shall refrain in their international relations from the threat or use of force against the territorial integrity or political independence of any state, or in any other manner inconsistent with the Purposes of the United Nations.

5. All Members shall give the United Nations every assistance in any action it takes in accordance with the present Charter, and shall refrain from giving assistance to any state against which the United Nations is taking preventive or enforcement action.

6. The Organization shall ensure that states which are not Members of the United Nations act in accordance with these Principles so far as may be necessary for the maintenance of international peace and security.

7. Nothing contained in the present Charter shall authorize the United Nations to intervene in matters which are essentially within the domestic jurisdiction of any state or shall require the Members to submit such matters to settlement under the present Charter; but this principle shall not prejudice the application of enforcement measures under Chapter VII.

Chapter II
MEMBERSHIP

Article 3
The original Members of the United Nations shall be the states which, having participated in the United Nations Conference on International Organization at San Francisco, or having previously signed the Declaration by United Nations of 1 January 1942, sign the present Charter and ratify it in accordance with Article 110.

Article 4
1. Membership in the United Nations is open to all other peace-loving states which accept the obligations contained in the present Charter and, in the judgment of the Organization, are able and willing to carry out these obligations.

2. The admission of any such state to membership in the United Nations will be effected by a decision of the General Assembly upon the recommendation of the Security Council.

Article 5
A Member of the United Nations against which preventive or enforcement action has been taken by the Security Council may be suspended from the exercise of the rights and privileges of membership by the General Assembly upon the recommendation of the Security Council. The exercise of these rights and privileges may be restored by the Security Council.

Article 6
A Member of the United Nations which has persistently violated the Principles contained in the present Charter may be expelled from the Organization by the General Assembly upon the recommendation of the Security Council.

Chapter III
ORGANS

Article 7
1. There are established as the principal organs of the United Nations: a General Assembly, a Security Council, an Economic and Social Council, a Trusteeship Council, an International Court of Justice, and a Secretariat.

2. Such subsidiary organs as may be found necessary may be established in accordance with the present Charter.

Article 8
The United Nations shall place no restrictions on the eligibility of men and women to participate in any capacity and under conditions of equality in its principal and subsidiary organs.

Chapter IV
THE GENERAL ASSEMBLY

Composition

Article 9
1. The General Assembly shall consist of all the Members of the United Nations.

2. Each Member shall have not more than five representatives in the General Assembly.

Functions and powers

Article 10
The General Assembly may discuss any questions or any matters within the scope of the present Charter or relating to the powers and functions of any organs provided for in the present Charter, and, except as provided in Article 12, may make recommendations to the Members of the United Nations or to the Security Council or to both on any such questions or matters.

Article 11
1. The General Assembly may consider the general principles of co-operation in the maintenance of international peace and security, including the principles governing disarmament and the regulation of armaments, and may make recommendations with regard to such principles to the Members or to the Security Council or to both.

2. The General Assembly may discuss any questions relating to the maintenance of international peace and security brought before it by any Member of the United Nations, or by the Security Council, or by a state which is not a Member of the United Nations in accordance with Article 35, paragraph 2, and, except as provided in Article 12, may make recommendations with regard to any such questions to the state or states concerned or to the Security Council or to both. Any such question on which action is necessary shall be referred to the Security Council by the General Assembly either before or after discussion.

3. The General Assembly may call the attention of the Security Council to situations which are likely to endanger international peace and security.

4. The powers of the General Assembly set forth in this Article shall not limit the general scope of Article 10.

Article 12
1. While the Security Council is exercising in respect of any dispute or situation the functions assigned to it in the present Charter, the General Assembly shall not make any recommendation with regard to that dispute or situation unless the Security Council so requests.

2. The Secretary-General, with the consent of the Security Council, shall notify the General Assembly at each session of any matters relative to the maintenance of international peace and security which are being dealt with by the Security Council and shall similarly notify the General Assembly, or the Members of the United Nations if the General Assembly is not in session, immediately the Security Council ceases to deal with such matters.

Article 13
1. The General Assembly shall initiate studies and make recommendations for the purpose of:
   a. promoting international co-operation in the political field and encouraging the progressive development of international law and its codification;
   b. promoting international co-operation in the economic, social, cultural, educational, and health fields, and assisting in the realization of human rights and fundamental freedoms for all without distinction as to race, sex, language, or religion.

2. The further responsibilities, functions and powers of the General Assembly with respect to matters mentioned in paragraph 1(b) above are set forth in Chapters IX and X.

Article 14
Subject to the provisions of Article 12, the General Assembly may recommend measures for the peaceful adjustment of any

situation, regardless of origin, which it deems likely to impair the general welfare or friendly relations among nations, including situations resulting from a violation of the provisions of the present Charter setting forth the Purposes and Principles of the United Nations.

Article 15

1. The General Assembly shall receive and consider annual and special reports from the Security Council; these reports shall include an account of the measures that the Security Council has decided upon or taken to maintain international peace and security.

2. The General Assembly shall receive and consider reports from the other organs of the United Nations.

Article 16

The General Assembly shall perform such functions with respect to the international trusteeship system as are assigned to it under Chapters XII and XIII, including the approval of the trusteeship agreements for areas not designated as strategic.

Article 17

1. The General Assembly shall consider and approve the budget of the Organization.

2. The expenses of the Organization shall be borne by the Members as apportioned by the General Assembly.

3. The General Assembly shall consider and approve any financial and budgetary arrangements with specialized agencies referred to in Article 57 and shall examine the administrative budgets of such specialized agencies with a view to making recommendations to the agencies concerned.

Voting

Article 18

1. Each member of the General Assembly shall have one vote.

2. Decisions of the General Assembly on important questions shall be made by a two-thirds majority of the members present and voting. These questions shall include: recommendations with respect to the maintenance of international peace and security, the election of the non-permanent members of the Security Council, the election of the members of the Economic and Social Council, the election of members of the Trusteeship Council in accordance with paragraph 1(c) of Article 86, the admission of new Members to the United Nations, the suspension of the rights and privileges of membership, the expulsion of Members, questions relating to the operation of the trusteeship system, and budgetary questions.

3. Decisions on other questions, including the determination of additional categories of questions to be decided by a two-thirds majority, shall be made by a majority of the members present and voting.

Article 19

A Member of the United Nations which is in arrears in the payment of its financial contributions to the Organization shall have no vote in the General Assembly if the amount of its arrears equals or exceeds the amount of the contributions due from it for the preceding two full years. The General Assembly may, nevertheless, permit such a Member to vote if it is satisfied that the failure to pay is due to conditions beyond the control of the Member.

Procedure

Article 20

The General Assembly shall meet in regular annual sessions and in such special sessions as occasion may require. Special sessions shall be convoked by the Secretary-General at the request of the Security Council or of a majority of the Members of the United Nations.

Article 21

The General Assembly shall adopt its own rules of procedure. It shall elect its President for each session.

Article 22

The General Assembly may establish such subsidiary organs as it deems necessary for the performance of its functions.

Chapter V
THE SECURITY COUNCIL

Composition

Article 23[1]

1. The Security Council shall consist of fifteen Members of the United Nations. The Republic of China, France, the Union of Soviet Socialist Republics, the United Kingdom of Great Britain and Northern Ireland, and the United States of America shall be permanent members of the Security Council. The General Assembly shall elect ten other Members of the United Nations to be non-permanent members of the Security Council, due regard being specially paid, in the first instance to the contribution of Members of the United Nations to the maintenance of international peace and security and to the other purposes of the Organization, and also to equitable geographical distribution.

2. The non-permanent members of the Security Council shall be elected for a term of two years. In the first election of the non-permanent members after the increase of the membership of the Security Council from eleven to fifteen, two of the four additional members shall be chosen for a term of one year. A retiring member shall not be eligible for immediate re-election.

3. Each member of the Security Council shall have one representative.

Functions and powers

Article 24

1. In order to ensure prompt and effective action by the United Nations, its Members confer on the Security Council primary responsibility for the maintenance of international peace and security, and agree that in carrying out its duties under this responsibility the Security Council acts on their behalf.

2. In discharging these duties the Security Council shall act in accordance with the Purposes and Principles of the United Nations. The specific powers granted to the Security Council for the discharge of these duties are laid down in Chapters VI, VII, VIII, and XII.

3. The Security Council shall submit annual and, when necessary, special reports to the General Assembly for its consideration.

Article 25

The Members of the United Nations agree to accept and carry out the decisions of the Security Council in accordance with the present Charter.

Article 26

In order to promote the establishment and maintenance of international peace and security with the least diversion for

---

[1]Amended text of Article 23 which came into force on 31 August 1965.
(The text of Article 23 before it was amended read as follows:

1. The Security Council shall consist of eleven Members of the United Nations. The Republic of China, France, the Union of Soviet Socialist Republics, the United Kingdom of Great Britain and Northern Ireland, and the United States of America shall be permanent members of the Security Council. The General Assembly shall elect six other Members of the United Nations to be non-permanent members of the Security Council, due regard being specially paid, in the first instance to the contribution of Members of the United Nations to the maintenance of international peace and security and to the other purposes of the Organization, and also to equitable geographical distribution.

2. The non-permanent members of the Security Council shall be elected for a term of two years. In the first election of non-permanent members, however, three shall be chosen for a term of one year. A retiring member shall not be eligible for immediate re-election.

3. Each member of the Security Council shall have one representative.)

armaments of the world's human and economic resources, the Security Council shall be responsible for formulating, with the assistance of the Military Staff Committee referred to in Article 47, plans to be submitted to the Members of the United Nations for the establishment of a system for the regulation of armaments.

Voting

Article 27[2]

1. Each member of the Security Council shall have one vote.

2. Decisions of the Security Council on procedural matters shall be made by an affirmative vote of nine members.

3. Decisions of the Security Council on all other matters shall be made by an affirmative vote of nine members including the concurring votes of the permanent members; provided that, in decisions under Chapter VI, and under paragraph 3 of Article 52, a party to a dispute shall abstain from voting.

Procedure

Article 28

1. The Security Council shall be so organized as to be able to function continuously. Each member of the Security Council shall for this purpose be represented at all times at the seat of the Organization.

2. The Security Council shall hold periodic meetings at which each of its members may, if it so desires, be represented by a member of the government or by some other specially designated representative.

3. The Security Council may hold meetings at such places other than the seat of the Organization as in its judgment will best facilitate its work.

Article 29

The Security Council may establish such subsidiary organs as it deems necessary for the performance of its functions.

Article 30

The Security Council shall adopt its own rules of procedure, including the method of selecting its President.

Article 31

Any Member of the United Nations which is not a member of the Security Council may participate, without vote, in the discussion of any question brought before the Security Council whenever the latter considers that the interests of that Member are specially affected.

Article 32

Any Member of the United Nations which is not a member of the Security Council or any state which is not a Member of the United Nations, if it is a party to a dispute under consideration by the Security Council, shall be invited to participate, without vote, in the discussion relating to the dispute. The Security Council shall lay down such conditions as it deems just for the participation of a state which is not a Member of the United Nations.

Chapter VI
PACIFIC SETTLEMENT OF DISPUTES

Article 33

1. The parties to any dispute, the continuance of which is likely to endanger the maintenance of international peace and security, shall, first of all, seek a solution by negotiation, enquiry, mediation, conciliation, arbitration, judicial settlement, resort to regional agencies or arrangements, or other peaceful means of their own choice.

2. The Security Council shall, when it deems necessary, call upon the parties to settle their dispute by such means.

Article 34

The Security Council may investigate any dispute, or any situation which might lead to international friction or give rise to a dispute, in order to determine whether the continuance of the dispute or situation is likely to endanger the maintenance of international peace and security.

Article 35

1. Any Member of the United Nations may bring any dispute, or any situation of the nature referred to in Article 34, to the attention of the Security Council or of the General Assembly.

2. A state which is not a Member of the United Nations may bring to the attention of the Security Council or of the General Assembly any dispute to which it is a party if it accepts in advance, for the purposes of the dispute, the obligations of pacific settlement provided in the present Charter.

3. The proceedings of the General Assembly in respect of matters brought to its attention under this Article will be subject to the provisions of Articles 11 and 12.

Article 36

1. The Security Council may, at any stage of a dispute of the nature referred to in Article 33 or of a situation of like nature, recommend appropriate procedures or methods of adjustment.

2. The Security Council should take into consideration any procedures for the settlement of the dispute which have already been adopted by the parties.

3. In making recommendations under this Article the Security Council should also take into consideration that legal disputes should as a general rule be referred by the parties to the International Court of Justice in accordance with the provisions of the Statute of the Court.

Article 37

1. Should the parties to a dispute of the nature referred to in Article 33 fail to settle it by the means indicated in that Article, they shall refer it to the Security Council.

2. If the Security Council deems that the continuance of the dispute is in fact likely to endanger the maintenance of international peace and security, it shall decide whether to take action under Article 36 or to recommend such terms of settlement as it may consider appropriate.

Article 38

Without prejudice to the provisions of Articles 33 to 37, the Security Council may, if all the parties to any dispute so request, make recommendations to the parties with a view to a pacific settlement of the dispute.

Chapter VII
ACTION WITH RESPECT TO THREATS TO THE PEACE, BREACHES OF THE PEACE, AND ACTS OF AGGRESSION

Article 39

The Security Council shall determine the existence of any threat to the peace, breach of the peace, or act of aggression and shall make recommendations, or decide what measures shall be taken in accordance with Articles 41 and 42, to maintain or restore international peace and security.

Article 40

In order to prevent an aggravation of the situation, the Security Council may, before making the recommendations or deciding upon the measures provided for in Article 39, call upon the parties concerned to comply with such provisional measures as it deems

---

[2]Amended text of Article 27 which came into force on 31 August 1965.
(The text of Article 27 before it was amended read as follows:

   1. Each member of the Security Council shall have one vote.

   2. Decisions of the Security Council on procedural matters shall be made by an affirmative vote of seven members.

   3. Decisions of the Security Council on all other matters shall be made by an affirmative vote of seven members including the concurring votes of the permanent members; provided that, in decisions under Chapter VI, and under paragraph 3 of Article 52, a party to a dispute shall abstain from voting.)

necessary or desirable. Such provisional measures shall be without prejudice to the rights, claims, or position of the parties concerned. The Security Council shall duly take account of failure to comply with such provisional measures.

Article 41

The Security Council may decide what measures not involving the use of armed force are to be employed to give effect to its decisions, and it may call upon the Members of the United Nations to apply such measures. These may include complete or partial interruption of economic relations and of rail, sea, air, postal, telegraphic, radio, and other means of communication, and the severance of diplomatic relations.

Article 42

Should the Security Council consider that measures provided for in Article 41 would be inadequate or have proved to be inadequate, it may take such action by air, sea, or land forces as may be necessary to maintain or restore international peace and security. Such action may include demonstrations, blockade, and other operations by air, sea, or land forces of Members of the United Nations.

Article 43

1. All Members of the United Nations, in order to contribute to the maintenance of international peace and security, undertake to make available to the Security Council, on its call and in accordance with a special agreement or agreements, armed forces, assistance, and facilities, including rights of passage, necessary for the purpose of maintaining international peace and security.
2. Such agreement or agreements shall govern the numbers and types of forces, their degree of readiness and general location, and the nature of the facilities and assistance to be provided.
3. The agreement or agreements shall be negotiated as soon as possible on the initiative of the Security Council. They shall be concluded between the Security Council and Members or between the Security Council and groups of Members and shall be subject to ratification by the signatory states in accordance with their respective constitutional processes.

Article 44

When the Security Council has decided to use force it shall, before calling upon a Member not represented on it to provide armed forces in fulfilment of the obligations assumed under Article 43, invite that Member, if the Member so desires, to participate in the decisions of the Security Council concerning the employment of contingents of that Member's armed forces.

Article 45

In order to enable the United Nations to take urgent military measures, Members shall hold immediately available national air-force contingents for combined international enforcement action. The strength and degree of readiness of these contingents and plans for their combined action shall be determined, within the limits laid down in the special agreement or agreements referred to in Article 43, by the Security Council with the assistance of the Military Staff Committee.

Article 46

Plans for the application of armed force shall be made by the Security Council with the assistance of the Military Staff Committee.

Article 47

1. There shall be established a Military Staff Committee to advise and assist the Security Council on all questions relating to the Security Council's military requirements for the maintenance of international peace and security, the employment and command of forces placed at its disposal, the regulation of armaments, and possible disarmament.
2. The Military Staff Committee shall consist of the Chiefs of Staff of the permanent members of the Security Council or their representatives. Any Member of the United Nations not permanently represented on the Committee shall be invited by the Committee to be associated with it when the efficient discharge of the Committee's responsibilities requires the participation of that Member in its work.
3. The Military Staff Committee shall be responsible under the Security Council for, the strategic direction of any armed forces placed at the disposal of the Security Council. Questions relating to the command of such forces shall be worked out subsequently.
4. The Military Staff Committee, with the authorization of the Security Council and after consultation with appropriate regional agencies, may establish regional sub-committees.

Article 48

1. The action required to carry out the decisions of the Security Council for the maintenance of international peace and security shall be taken by all the Members of the United Nations or by some of them, as the Security Council may determine.
2. Such decisions shall be carried out by the Members of the United Nations directly and through their action in the appropriate international agencies of which they are members.

Article 49

The Members of the United Nations shall join in affording mutual assistance in carrying out the measures decided upon by the Security Council.

Article 50

If preventive or enforcement measures against any state are taken by the Security Council, any other state, whether a Member of the United Nations or not, which finds itself confronted with special economic problems arising from the carrying out of those measures shall have the right to consult the Security Council with regard to a solution of those problems.

Article 51

Nothing in the present Charter shall impair the inherent right of individual or collective self-defence if an armed attack occurs against a Member of the United Nations, until the Security Council has taken measures necessary to maintain international peace and security. Measures taken by Members in the exercise of this right of self-defence shall be immediately reported to the Security Council and shall not in any way affect the authority and responsibility of the Security Council under the present Charter to take at any time such action as it deems necessary in order to maintain or restore international peace and security.

Chapter VIII
REGIONAL ARRANGEMENTS

Article 52

1. Nothing in the present Charter precludes the existence of regional arrangements or agencies for dealing with such matters relating to the maintenance of international peace and security as are appropriate for regional action, provided that such arrangements or agencies and their activities are consistent with the Purposes and Principles of the United Nations.
2. The Members of the United Nations entering into such arrangements or constituting such agencies shall make every effort to achieve pacific settlement of local disputes through such regional arrangements or by such regional agencies before referring them to the Security Council.
3. The Security Council shall encourage the development of pacific settlement of local disputes through such regional arrangements or by such regional agencies either on the initiative of the states concerned or by reference from the Security Council.
4. This Article in no way impairs the application of Articles 34 and 35.

Article 53

1. The Security Council shall, where appropriate, utilize such regional arrangements or agencies for enforcement action under

its authority. But no enforcement action shall be taken under regional arrangements or by regional agencies without the authorization of the Security Council, with the exception of measures against any enemy state, as defined in paragraph 2 of this Article, provided for pursuant to Article 107 or in regional arrangements directed against renewal of aggressive policy on the part of any such state, until such time as the Organization may, on request of the Governments concerned, be charged with the responsibility for preventing further aggression by such a state.

2. The term enemy state as used in paragraph 1 of this Article applies to any state which during the Second World War has been an enemy of any signatory of the present Charter.

Article 54

The Security Council shall at all times be kept fully informed of activities undertaken or in contemplation under regional arrangements or by regional agencies for the maintenance of international peace and security.

Chapter IX
INTERNATIONAL ECONOMIC AND SOCIAL CO-OPERATION

Article 55

With a view to the creation of conditions of stability and well-being which are necessary for peaceful and friendly relations among nations based on respect for the principle of equal rights and self-determination of peoples, the United Nations shall promote:

a. higher standards of living, full employment, and conditions of economic and social progress and development;
b. solutions of international economic, social, health, and related problems; and international cultural and educational co-operation; and
c. universal respect for, and observance of, human rights and fundamental freedoms for all without distinction as to race, sex, language, or religion.

Article 56

All Members pledge themselves to take joint and separate action in co-operation with the Organization for the achievement of the purposes set forth in Article 55.

Article 57

1. The various specialized agencies, established by intergovernmental agreement and having wide international responsibilities, as defined in their basic instruments, in economic, social, cultural, educational, health, and related fields, shall be brought into relationship with the United Nations in accordance with the provisions of Article 63.

2. Such agencies thus brought into relationship with the United Nations are hereinafter referred to as specialized agencies.

Article 58

The Organization shall make recommendations for the co-ordination of the policies and activities of the specialized agencies.

Article 59

The Organization shall, where appropriate, initiate negotiations among the states concerned for the creation of any new specialized agencies required for the accomplishment of the purposes set forth in Article 55.

Article 60

Responsibility for the discharge of the functions of the Organization set forth in this Chapter shall be vested in the General Assembly and, under the authority of the General Assembly, in the Economic and Social Council, which shall have for this purpose the powers set forth in Chapter X.

Chapter X
THE ECONOMIC AND SOCIAL COUNCIL

Composition

Article 61[3]

1. The Economic and Social Council shall consist of twenty-seven Members of the United Nations elected by the General Assembly.

2. Subject to the provisions of paragraph 3, nine members of the Economic and Social Council shall be elected each year for a term of three years. A retiring member shall be eligible for immediate re-election.

3. At the first election after the increase in the membership of the Economic and Social Council from eighteen to twenty-seven members, in addition to the members elected in place of the six members whose term of office expires at the end of that year, nine additional members shall be elected. Of these nine additional members, the term of office of three members so elected shall expire at the end of one year, and of three other members at the end of two years, in accordance with arrangements made by the General Assembly.

4. Each member of the Economic and Social Council shall have one representative.

Functions and powers

Article 62

1. The Economic and Social Council may make or initiate studies and reports with respect to international economic, social, cultural, educational, health, and related matters and may make recommendations with respect to any such matters to the General Assembly, to the Members of the United Nations, and to the specialized agencies concerned.

2. It may make recommendations for the purpose of promoting respect for, and observance of, human rights and fundamental freedoms for all.

3. It may prepare draft conventions for submission to the General Assembly, with respect to matters falling within its competence.

4. It may call, in accordance with the rules prescribed by the United Nations, international conferences on matters falling within its competence.

Article 63

1. The Economic and Social Council may enter into agreements with any of the agencies referred to in Article 57, defining the terms on which the agency concerned shall be brought into relationship with the United Nations. Such agreements shall be subject to approval by the General Assembly.

2. It may co-ordinate the activities of the specialized agencies through consultation with and recommendations to such agencies and through recommendations to the General Assembly and to the Members of the United Nations.

Article 64

1. The Economic and Social Council may take appropriate steps to obtain regular reports from the specialized agencies. It may make arrangements with the Members of the United Nations

[3]Amended text of Article 61, which came into force on 31 August 1965. (The text of Article 61 before it was amended read as follows:

1. The Economic and Social Council shall consist of eighteen Members of the United Nations elected by the General Assembly.

2. Subject to the provisions of paragraph 3, six members of the Economic and Social Council shall be elected each year for a term of three years. A retiring member shall be eligible for immediate re-election.

3. At the first election, eighteen members of the Economic and Social Council shall be chosen. The term of office of six members so chosen shall expire at the end of one year, and of six other members at the end of two years, in accordance with arrangements made by the General Assembly.

4. Each member of the Economic and Social Council shall have one representative.)

and with the specialized agencies to obtain reports on the steps taken to give effect to its own recommendations and to recommendations on matters falling within its competence made by the General Assembly.

2. It may communicate its observations on these reports to the General Assembly.

Article 65

The Economic and Social Council may furnish information to the Security Council and shall assist the Security Council upon its request.

Article 66

1. The Economic and Social Council shall perform such functions as fall within its competence in connexion with the carrying out of the recommendations of the General Assembly.

2. It may, with the approval of the General Assembly, perform services at the request of Members of the United Nations and at the request of specialized agencies.

3. It shall perform such other functions as are specified elsewhere in the present Charter or as may be assigned to it by the General Assembly.

Voting

Article 67

1. Each member of the Economic and Social Council shall have one vote.

2. Decisions of the Economic and Social Council shall be made by a majority of the members present and voting.

Procedure

Article 68

The Economic and Social Council shall set up commissions in economic and social fields and for the promotion of human rights, and such other commissions as may be required for the performance of its functions.

Article 69

The Economic and Social Council shall invite any Member of the United Nations to participate, without vote, in its deliberations on any matter of particular concern to that Member.

Article 70

The Economic and Social Council may make arrangements for representatives of the specialized agencies to participate, without vote, in its deliberations and in those of the commissions established by it, and for its representatives to participate in the deliberations of the specialized agencies.

Article 71

The Economic and Social Council may make suitable arrangements for consultation with non-governmental organizations which are concerned with matters within its competence. Such arrangements may be made with international organizations and, where appropriate, with national organizations after consultation with the Member of the United Nations concerned.

Article 72

1. The Economic and Social Council shall adopt its own rules of procedure, including the method of selecting its President.

2. The Economic and Social Council shall meet as required in accordance with its rules, which shall include provision for the convening of meetings on the request of a majority of its members.

Chapter XI
DECLARATION REGARDING
NON-SELF-GOVERNING TERRITORIES

Article 73

Members of the United Nations which have or assume responsibilities for the administration of territories whose peoples have not yet attained a full measure of self-government recognize the principle that the interests of the inhabitants of these territories are paramount, and accept as a sacred trust the obligation to promote to the utmost, within the system of international peace and security established by the present Charter, the well-being of the inhabitants of these territories, and, to this end:

a. to ensure, with due respect for the culture of the peoples concerned, their political, economic, social, and educational advancement, their just treatment, and their protection against abuses;

b. to develop self-government, to take due account of the political aspirations of the peoples, and to assist them in the progressive development of their free political institutions, according to the particular circumstances of each territory and its peoples and their varying stages of advancement;

c. to further international peace and security;

d. to promote constructive measures of development, to encourage research, and to co-operate with one another and, when and where appropriate, with specialized international bodies with a view to the practical achievement of the social, economic, and scientific purposes set forth in this Article; and

e. to transmit regularly to the Secretary-General for information purposes, subject to such limitation as security and constitutional considerations may require, statistical and other information of a technical nature relating to economic, social, and educational conditions in the territories for which they are respectively responsible other than those territories to which Chapters XII and XIII apply.

Article 74

Members of the United Nations also agree that their policy in respect of the territories to which this Chapter applies, no less than in respect of their metropolitan areas, must be based on the general principle of good-neighbourliness, due account being taken of the interests and well-being of the rest of the world, in social, economic, and commercial matters.

Chapter XII
INTERNATIONAL TRUSTEESHIP SYSTEM

Article 75

The United Nations shall establish under its authority an international trusteeship system for the administration and supervision of such territories as may be placed thereunder by subsequent individual agreements. These territories are hereinafter referred to as trust territories.

Article 76

The basic objectives of the trusteeship system, in accordance with the Purposes of the United Nations laid down in Article 1 of the present Charter, shall be:

a. to further international peace and security;

b. to promote the political, economic, social, and educational advancement of the inhabitants of the trust territories, and their progressive development towards self-government or independence as may be appropriate to the particular circumstances of each territory and its peoples and the freely expressed wishes of the peoples concerned, and as may be provided by the terms of each trusteeship agreement;

c. to encourage respect for human rights and for fundamental freedoms for all without distinction as to race, sex, language, or religion, and to encourage recognition of the interdependence of the peoples of the world; and

d. to ensure equal treatment in social, economic, and commercial matters for all Members of the United Nations and their nationals, and also equal treatment for the latter in the administration of justice, without prejudice to the attainment of the foregoing objectives and subject to the provisions of Article 80.

Article 77

1. The trusteeship system shall apply to such territories in the following categories as may be placed thereunder by means of trusteeship agreements:

a. territories now held under mandate;
b. territories which may be detached from enemy states as a result of the Second World War; and
c. territories voluntarily placed under the system by states responsible for their administration.

2. It will be a matter for subsequent agreement as to which territories in the foregoing categories will be brought under the trusteeship system and upon what terms.

Article 78

The trusteeship system shall not apply to territories which have become Members of the United Nations, relationship among which shall be based on respect for the principle of sovereign equality.

Article 79

The terms of trusteeship for each territory to be placed under the trusteeship system, including any alteration or amendment, shall be agreed upon by the states directly concerned, including the mandatory power in the case of territories held under mandate by a Member of the United Nations, and shall be approved as provided for in Articles 83 and 85.

Article 80

1. Except as may be agreed upon in individual trusteeship agreements, made under Articles 77, 79, and 81, placing each territory under the trusteeship system, and until such agreements have been concluded, nothing in this Chapter shall be construed in or of itself to alter in any manner the rights whatsoever of any states or any peoples or the terms of existing international instruments to which Members of the United Nations may respectively be parties.

2. Paragraph 1 of this Article shall not be interpreted as giving grounds for delay or postponement of the negotiation and conclusion of agreements for placing mandated and other territories under the trusteeship system as provided for in Article 77.

Article 81

The trusteeship agreement shall in each case include the terms under which the trust territory will be administered and designate the authority which will exercise the administration of the trust territory. Such authority, hereinafter called the administering authority, may be one or more states or the Organization itself.

Article 82

There may be designated, in any trusteeship agreement, a strategic area or areas which may include part or all of the trust territory to which the agreement applies, without prejudice to any special agreement or agreements made under Article 43.

Article 83

1. All functions of the United Nations relating to strategic areas, including the approval of the terms of the trusteeship agreements and of their alteration or amendment, shall be exercised by the Security Council.

2. The basic objectives set forth in Article 76 shall be applicable to the people of each strategic area.

3. The Security Council shall, subject to the provisions of the trusteeship agreements and without prejudice to security considerations, avail itself of the assistance of the Trusteeship Council to perform those functions of the United Nations under the trusteeship system relating to political, economic, social, and educational matters in the strategic areas.

Article 84

It shall be the duty of the administering authority to ensure that the trust territory shall play its part in the maintenance of international peace and security. To this end the administering authority may make use of volunteer forces, facilities, and assistance from the trust territory in carrying out the obligations towards the Security Council undertaken in this regard by the administering authority, as well as for local defence and the maintenance of law and order within the trust territory.

Article 85

1. The functions of the United Nations with regard to trusteeship agreements for all areas not designated as strategic, including the approval of the terms of the trusteeship agreements and of their alteration or amendment, shall be exercised by the General Assembly.

2. The Trusteeship Council, operating under the authority of the General Assembly, shall assist the General Assembly in carrying out these functions.

Chapter XIII
THE TRUSTEESHIP COUNCIL

Composition

Article 86

1. The Trusteeship Council shall consist of the following Members of the United Nations:
a. those Members administering trust territories;
b. such of those Members mentioned by name in Article 23 as are not administering trust territories; and
c. as many other Members elected for three-year terms by the General Assembly as may be necessary to ensure that the total number of members of the Trusteeship Council is equally divided between those Members of the United Nations which administer trust territories and those which do not.

2. Each member of the Trusteeship Council shall designate one specially qualified person to represent it therein.

Functions and powers

Article 87

The General Assembly and, under its authority, the Trusteeship Council, in carrying out their functions, may:
a. consider reports submitted by the administering authority;
b. accept petitions and examine them in consultation with the administering authority;
c. provide for periodic visits to the respective trust territories at times agreed upon with the administering authority; and
d. take these and other actions in conformity with the terms of the trusteeship agreements.

Article 88

The Trusteeship Council shall formulate a questionnaire on the political, economic, social, and educational advancement of the inhabitants of each trust territory, and the administering authority for each trust territory within the competence of the General Assembly shall make an annual report to the General Assembly upon the basis of such questionnaire.

Voting

Article 89

1. Each member of the Trusteeship Council shall have one vote.
2. Decisions of the Trusteeship Council shall be made by a majority of the members present and voting.

Procedure

Article 90

1. The Trusteeship Council shall adopt its own rules of procedure, including the method of selecting its President.
2. The Trusteeship Council shall meet as required in accordance with its rules, which shall include provision for the convening of meetings on the request of a majority of its members.

Article 91

The Trusteeship Council shall, when appropriate, avail itself of the assistance of the Economic and Social Council and of the specialized agencies in regard to matters with which they are respectively concerned.

Chapter XIV
THE INTERNATIONAL COURT OF JUSTICE

Article 92

The International Court of Justice shall be the principal judicial organ of the United Nations. It shall function in accordance with the annexed Statute, which is based upon the Statute of the Permanent Court of International Justice and forms an integral part of the present Charter.

Article 93

1. All Members of the United Nations are *ipso facto* parties to the Statute of the International Court of Justice.

2. A state which is not a Member of the United Nations may become a party to the Statute of the International Court of Justice on conditions to be determined in each case by the General Assembly upon the recommendation of the Security Council.

Article 94

1. Each Member of the United Nations undertakes to comply with the decision of the International Court of Justice in any case to which it is a party.

2. If any party to a case fails to perform the obligations incumbent upon it under a judgment rendered by the Court, the other party may have recourse to the Security Council, which may, if it deems necessary, make recommendations or decide upon measures to be taken to give effect to the judgment.

Article 95

Nothing in the present Charter shall prevent Members of the United Nations from entrusting the solution of their differences to other tribunals by virtue of agreements already in existence or which may be concluded in the future.

Article 96

1. The General Assembly or the Security Council may request the International Court of Justice to give an advisory opinion on any legal question.

2. Other organs of the United Nations and specialized agencies, which may at any time be so authorized by the General Assembly, may also request advisory opinions of the Court on legal questions arising within the scope of their activities.

Chapter XV
THE SECRETARIAT

Article 97

The Secretariat shall comprise a Secretary-General and such staff as the Organization may require. The Secretary-General shall be appointed by the General Assembly upon the recommendation of the Security Council. He shall be the chief administrative officer of the Organization.

Article 98

The Secretary-General shall act in that capacity in all meetings of the General Assembly, of the Security Council, of the Economic and Social Council, and of the Trusteeship Council, and shall perform such other functions as are entrusted to him by these organs. The Secretary-General shall make an annual report to the General Assembly on the work of the Organization.

Article 99

The Secretary-General may bring to the attention of the Security Council any matter which in his opinion may threaten the maintenance of international peace and security.

Article 100

1. In the performance of their duties the Secretary-General and the staff shall not seek or receive instructions from any government or from any other authority external to the Organization. They shall refrain from any action which might reflect on their position as international officials responsible only to the Organization.

2. Each Member of the United Nations undertakes to respect the exclusively international character of the responsibilities of the Secretary-General and the staff and not to seek to influence them in the discharge of their responsibilities.

Article 101

1. The staff shall be appointed by the Secretary-General under regulations established by the General Assembly.

2. Appropriate staffs shall be permanently assigned to the Economic and Social Council, the Trusteeship Council, and, as required, to other organs of the United Nations. These staffs shall form a part of the Secretariat.

3. The paramount consideration in the employment of the staff and in the determination of the conditions of service shall be the necessity of securing the highest standards of efficiency, competence, and integrity. Due regard shall be paid to the importance of recruiting the staff on as wide a geographical basis as possible.

Chapter XVI
MISCELLANEOUS PROVISIONS

Article 102

1. Every treaty and every international agreement entered into by any Member of the United Nations after the present Charter comes into force as soon as possible be registered with the Secretariat and published by it.

2. No party to any such treaty or international agreement which has not been registered in accordance with the provisions of paragraph 1 of this Article may invoke that treaty or agreement before any organ of the United Nations.

Article 103

In the event of a conflict between the obligations of the Members of the United Nations under the present Charter and their obligations under any other international agreement, their obligations under the present Charter shall prevail.

Article 104

The Organization shall enjoy in the territory of each of its Members such legal capacity as may be necessary for the exercise of its functions and the fulfilment of its purposes.

Article 105

1. The Organization shall enjoy in the territory of each of its Members such privileges and immunities as are necessary for the fulfilment of its purposes.

2. Representatives of the Members of the United Nations and officials of the Organization shall similarly enjoy such privileges and immunities as are necessary for the independent exercise of their functions in connexion with the Organization.

3. The General Assembly may make recommendations with a view to determining the details of the application of paragraphs 1 and 2 of this Article or may propose conventions to the Members of the United Nations for this purpose.

Chapter XVII
TRANSITIONAL SECURITY ARRANGEMENTS

Article 106

Pending the coming into force of such special agreements referred to in Article 43 as in the opinion of the Security Council enable it to begin the exercise of its responsibilities under Article 42, the parties to the Four-Nation Declaration, signed at Moscow, 30 October 1943, and France, shall, in accordance with the provisions of paragraph 5 of that Declaration, consult with one another and as occasion requires with other Members of the United Nations with a view to such joint action on behalf of the Organization as may be necessary for the purpose of maintaining international peace and security.

Article 107

Nothing in the present Charter shall invalidate or preclude action, in relation to any state which during the Second World War has been an enemy of any signatory to the present Charter, taken or authorized as a result of that war by the Governments having responsibility for such action.

Chapter XVIII
AMENDMENTS

Article 108

Amendments to the present Charter shall come into force for all Members of the United Nations when they have been adopted by a vote of two thirds of the members of the General Assembly and ratified in accordance with their respective constitutional processes by two thirds of the Members of the United Nations, including all the permanent members of the Security Council.

Article 109[4]

1. A General Conference of the Members of the United Nations for the purpose of reviewing the present Charter may be held at a date and place to be fixed by a two-thirds vote of the members of the General Assembly and by a vote of any nine members of the Security Council. Each Member of the United Nations shall have one vote in the conference.

2. Any alteration of the present Charter recommended by a two-thirds vote of the conference shall take effect when ratified in accordance with their respective constitutional processes by two thirds of the Members of the United Nations including all the permanent members of the Security Council.

3. If such a conference has not been held before the tenth annual session of the General Assembly following the coming into force of the present Charter, the proposal to call such a conference shall be placed on the agenda of that session of the General Assembly, and the conference shall be held if so decided by a majority vote of the members of the General Assembly and by a vote of any seven members of the Security Council.

Chapter XIX
RATIFICATION AND SIGNATURE

Article 110

1. The present Charter shall be ratified by the signatory states in accordance with their respective constitutional processes.

2. The ratifications shall be deposited with the Government of the United States of America, which shall notify all the signatory states of each deposit as well as the Secretary-General of the Organization when he has been appointed.

3. The present Charter shall come into force upon the deposit of ratifications by the Republic of China, France, the Union of Soviet Socialist Republics, the United Kingdom of Great Britain and Northern Ireland, and the United States of America, and by a majority of the other signatory states. A protocol of the ratifications deposited shall thereupon be drawn up by the Government of the United States of America which shall communicate copies thereof to all the signatory states.

4. The states signatory to the present Charter which ratify it after it has come into force will become original Members of the United Nations on the date of the deposit of their respective ratifications.

Article 111

The present Charter, of which the Chinese, French, Russian, English, and Spanish texts are equally authentic, shall remain deposited in the archives of the Government of the United States of America. Duly certified copies thereof shall be transmitted by that Government to the Governments of the other signatory states.

IN FAITH WHEREOF the representatives of the Governments of the United Nations have signed the present Charter.

DONE at the city of San Francisco the twenty-sixth day of June, one thousand nine hundred and forty-five.

---

[4]Amended text of Article 109 which came into force on 12 June 1968.
(The text of Article 109 before it was amended read as follows:

1. A General Conference of the Members of the United Nations for the purpose of reviewing the present Charter may be held at a date and place to be fixed by a two-thirds vote of the members of the General Assembly and by a vote of any seven members of the Security Council. Each Member of the United Nations shall have one vote in the conference.

2. Any alteration of the present Charter recommended by a two-thirds vote of the conference shall take effect when ratified in accordance with their respective constitutional processes by two thirds of the Members of the United Nations including all the permanent members of the Security Council.

3. If such a conference has not been held before the tenth annual session of the General Assembly following the coming into force of the present Charter, the proposal to call such a conference shall be placed on the agenda of that session of the General Assembly, and the conference shall be held if so decided by a majority vote of the members of the General Assembly and by a vote of any seven members of the Security Council.)

The Statute of the International Court of Justice

Article 1

THE INTERNATIONAL COURT OF JUSTICE established by the Charter of the United Nations as the principal judicial organ of the United Nations shall be constituted and shall function in accordance with the provisions of the present Statute.

Chapter I
ORGANIZATION OF THE COURT

Article 2

The Court shall be composed of a body of independent judges, elected regardless of their nationality from among persons of high moral character, who possess the qualifications required in their respective countries for appointment to the highest judicial offices, or are jurisconsults of recognized competence in international law.

Article 3

1. The Court shall consist of fifteen members, no two of whom may be nationals of the same state.

2. A person who for the purposes of membership in the Court could be regarded as a national of more than one state shall be deemed to be a national of the one in which he ordinarily exercises civil and political rights.

Article 4

1. The members of the Court shall be elected by the General Assembly and by the Security Council from a list of persons nominated by the national groups in the Permanent Court of Arbitration, in accordance with the following provisions.

2. In the case of Members of the United Nations not represented in the Permanent Court of Arbitration, candidates shall be nominated by national groups appointed for this purpose by their governments under the same conditions as those prescribed for members of the Permanent Court of Arbitration by Article 44 of the Convention of The Hague of 1907 for the pacific settlement of international disputes.

3. The conditions under which a state which is a party to the present Statute but is not a Member of the United Nations may participate in electing the members of the Court shall, in the absence of a special agreement, be laid down by the General Assembly upon recommendation of the Security Council.

Article 5

1. At least three months before the date of the election, the Secretary-General of the United Nations shall address a written request to the members of the Permanent Court of Arbitration belonging to the states which are parties to the present Statute, and to the members of the national groups appointed under Article 4, paragraph 2, inviting them to undertake, within a given time, by

national groups, the nomination of persons in a position to accept the duties of a member of the Court.

2. No group may nominate more than four persons, not more than two of whom shall be of their own nationality. In no case may the number of candidates nominated by a group be more than double the number of seats to be filled.

Article 6

Before making these nominations, each national group is recommended to consult its highest court of justice, its legal faculties and schools of law, and its national academies and national sections of international academies devoted to the study of law.

Article 7

1. The Secretary-General shall prepare a list in alphabetical order of all the persons thus nominated. Save as provided in Article 12, paragraph 2, these shall be the only persons eligible.

2. The Secretary-General shall submit this list to the General Assembly and to the Security Council.

Article 8

The General Assembly and the Security Council shall proceed independently of one another to elect the members of the Court.

Article 9

At every election, the electors shall bear in mind not only that the persons to be elected should individually possess the qualifications required, but also that in the body as a whole the representation of the main forms of civilization and of the principal legal systems of the world should be assured.

Article 10

1. Those candidates who obtain an absolute majority of votes in the General Assembly and in the Security Council shall be considered as elected.

2. Any vote of the Security Council, whether for the election of judges or for the appointment of members of the conference envisaged in Article 12, shall be taken without any distinction between permanent and non-permanent members of the Security Council.

3. In the event of more than one national of the same state obtaining an absolute majority of the votes both of the General Assembly and of the Security Council, the eldest of these only shall be considered as elected.

Article 11

If, after the first meeting held for the purpose of the election, one or more seats remain to be filled, a second and, if necessary, a third meeting shall take place.

Article 12

1. If, after the third meeting, one or more seats still remain unfilled, a joint conference consisting of six members, three appointed by the General Assembly and three by the Security Council, may be formed at any time at the request of either the General Assembly or the Security Council, for the purpose of choosing by the vote of an absolute majority one name for each seat still vacant, to submit to the General Assembly and the Security Council for their respective acceptance.

2. If the joint conference is unanimously agreed upon any person who fulfils the required conditions, he may be included in its list, even though he was not included in the list of nominations referred to in Article 7.

3. If the joint conference is satisfied that it will not be successful in procuring an election, those members of the Court who have already been elected shall, within a period to be fixed by the Security Council, proceed to fill the vacant seats by selection from among those candidates who have obtained votes either in the General Assembly or in the Security Council.

4. In the event of an equality of votes among the judges, the eldest judge shall have a casting vote.

Article 13

1. The members of the Court shall be elected for nine years and may be re-elected; provided, however, that of the judges elected at the first election, the terms of five judges shall expire at the end of three years and the terms of five more judges shall expire at the end of six years.

2. The judges whose terms are to expire at the end of the above-mentioned initial periods of three and six years shall be chosen by lot to be drawn by the Secretary-General immediately after the first election has been completed.

3. The members of the Court shall continue to discharge their duties until their places have been filled. Though replaced, they shall finish any cases which they may have begun.

4. In the case of the resignation of a member of the Court, the resignation shall be addressed to the President of the Court for transmission to the Secretary-General. This last notification makes the place vacant.

Article 14

Vacancies shall be filled by the same method as that laid down for the first election, subject to the following provision: the Secretary-General shall, within one month of the occurrence of the vacancy, proceed to issue the invitations provided for in Article 5, and the date of the election shall be fixed by the Security Council.

Article 15

A member of the Court elected to replace a member whose term of office has not expired shall hold office for the remainder of his predecessor's term.

Article 16

1. No member of the Court may exercise any political or administrative function, or engage in any other occupation of a professional nature.

2. Any doubt on this point shall be settled by the decision of the Court.

Article 17

1. No member of the Court may act as agent, counsel, or advocate in any case.

2. No member may participate in the decision of any case in which he has previously taken part as agent, counsel, or advocate for one of the parties, or as a member of a national or international court, or of a commission of enquiry, or in any other capacity.

3. Any doubt on this point shall be settled by the decision of the Court.

Article 18

1. No member of the Court can be dismissed unless, in the unanimous opinion of the other members, he has ceased to fulfil the required conditions.

2. Formal notification thereof shall be made to the Secretary-General by the Registrar.

3. This notification makes the place vacant.

Article 19

The members of the Court, when engaged on the business of the Court, shall enjoy diplomatic privileges and immunities.

Article 20

Every member of the Court shall, before taking up his duties, make a solemn declaration in open court that he will exercise his powers impartially and conscientiously.

Article 21

1. The Court shall elect its President and Vice-President for three years; they may be re-elected.

2. The Court shall appoint its Registrar and may provide for the appointment of such other officers as may be necessary.

Article 22

1. The seat of the Court shall be established at The Hague. This, however, shall not prevent the Court from sitting and

exercising its functions elsewhere whenever the Court considers it desirable.

2. The President and the Registrar shall reside at the seat of the Court.

Article 23

1. The Court shall remain permanently in session, except during the judicial vacations, the dates and duration of which shall be fixed by the Court.

2. Members of the Court are entitled to periodic leave, the dates and duration of which shall be fixed by the Court, having in mind the distance between The Hague and the home of each judge.

3. Members of the Court shall be bound, unless they are on leave or prevented from attending by illness or other serious reasons duly explained to the President, to hold themselves permanently at the disposal of the Court.

Article 24

1. If, for some special reason, a member of the Court considers that he should not take part in the decision of a particular case, he shall so inform the President.

2. If the President considers that for some special reason one of the members of the Court should not sit in a particular case, he shall give him notice accordingly.

3. If in any such case the member of the Court and the President disagree, the matter shall be settled by the decision of the Court.

Article 25

1. The full Court shall sit except when it is expressly provided otherwise in the present Statute.

2. Subject to the condition that the number of judges available to constitute the Court is not thereby reduced below eleven, the Rules of the Court may provide for allowing one or more judges, according to circumstances and in rotation, to be dispensed from sitting.

3. A quorum of nine judges shall suffice to constitute the Court.

Article 26

1. The Court may from time to time form one or more chambers, composed of three or more judges as the Court may determine, for dealing with particular categories of cases; for example, labour cases and cases relating to transit and communications.

2. The Court may at any time form a chamber for dealing with a particular case. The number of judges to constitute such a chamber shall be determined by the Court with the approval of the parties.

3. Cases shall be heard and determined by the chambers provided for in this Article if the parties so request.

Article 27

A judgment given by any of the chambers provided for in Articles 26 and 29 shall be considered as rendered by the Court.

Article 28

The chambers provided for in Articles 26 and 29 may, with the consent of the parties, sit and exercise their functions elsewhere than at The Hague.

Article 29

With a view to the speedy dispatch of business, the Court shall form annually a chamber composed of five judges which, at the request of the parties, may hear and determine cases by summary procedure. In addition, two judges shall be selected for the purpose of replacing judges who find it impossible to sit.

Article 30

1. The Court shall frame rules for carrying out its functions. In particular, it shall lay down rules of procedure.

2. The Rules of the Court may provide for assessors to sit with the Court or with any of its chambers, without the right to vote.

Article 31

1. Judges of the nationality of each of the parties shall retain their right to sit in the case before the Court.

2. If the Court includes upon the Bench a judge of the nationality of one of the parties, any other party may choose a person to sit as judge. Such person shall be chosen preferably from among those persons who have been nominated as candidates as provided in Articles 4 and 5.

3. If the Court includes upon the Bench no judge of the nationality of the parties, each of these parties may proceed to choose a judge as provided in paragraph 2 of this Article.

4. The provisions of this Article shall apply to the case of Articles 26 and 29. In such cases, the President shall request one or, if necessary, two of the members of the Court forming the chamber to give place to the members of the Court of the nationality of the parties concerned, and, failing such, or if they are unable to be present, to the judges specially chosen by the parties.

5. Should there be several parties in the same interest, they shall, for the purpose of the preceding provisions, be reckoned as one party only. Any doubt upon this point shall be settled by the decision of the Court.

6. Judges chosen as laid down in paragraphs 2, 3, and 4 of this Article shall fulfil the conditions required by Articles 2, 17 (paragraph 2), 20, and 24 of the present Statute. They shall take part in the decision on terms of complete equality with their colleagues.

Article 32

1. Each member of the Court shall receive an annual salary.

2. The President shall receive a special annual allowance.

3. The Vice-President shall receive a special allowance for every day on which he acts as President.

4. The judges chosen under Article 31, other than members of the Court, shall receive compensation for each day on which they exercise their functions.

5. These salaries, allowances, and compensation shall be fixed by the General Assembly. They may not be decreased during the term of office.

6. The salary of the Registrar shall be fixed by the General Assembly on the proposal of the Court.

7. Regulations made by the General Assembly shall fix the conditions under which retirement pensions may be given to members of the Court and to the Registrar, and the conditions under which members of the Court and the Registrar shall have their travelling expenses refunded.

8. The above salaries, allowances, and compensation shall be free of all taxation.

Article 33

The expenses of the Court shall be borne by the United Nations in such a manner as shall be decided by the General Assembly.

Chapter II
COMPETENCE OF THE COURT

Article 34

1. Only states may be parties in cases before the Court.

2. The Court, subject to and in conformity with its Rules, may request of public international organizations information relevant to cases before it, and shall receive such information presented by such organizations on their own initiative.

3. Whenever the construction of the constituent instrument of a public international organization or of an international convention adopted thereunder is in question in a case before the Court, the Registrar shall so notify the public International organization concerned and shall communicate to it copies of all the written proceedings.

Article 35

1. The Court shall be open to the states parties to the present Statute.

2. The conditions under which the Court shall be open to other states shall, subject to the special provisions contained in treaties

in force, be laid down by the Security Council, but in no case shall such conditions place the parties in a position of inequality before the Court.

3. When a state which is not a Member of the United Nations is a party to a case, the Court shall fix the amount which that party is to contribute towards the expenses of the Court. This provision shall not apply if such state is bearing a share of the expenses of the Court.

Article 36

1. The jurisdiction of the Court comprises all cases which the parties refer to it and all matters specially provided for in the Charter of the United Nations or in treaties and conventions in force.

2. The states parties to the present Statute may at any time declare that they recognize as compulsory *ipso facto* and without special agreement, in relation to any other state accepting the same obligation, the jurisdiction of the Court in all legal disputes concerning:

a. the interpretation of a treaty;

b. any question of international law;

c. the existence of any fact which, if established, would constitute a breach of an international obligation;

d. the nature or extent of the reparation to be made for the breach of an international obligation.

3. The declarations referred to above may be made unconditionally or on condition of reciprocity on the part of several or certain states, or for a certain time.

4. Such declarations shall be deposited with the Secretary-General of the United Nations, who shall transmit copies thereof to the parties to the Statute and to the Registrar of the Court.

5. Declarations made under Article 36 of the Statute of the Permanent Court of International Justice and which are still in force shall be deemed, as between the parties to the present Statute, to be acceptances of the compulsory jurisdiction of the International Court of Justice for the period which they still have to run and in accordance with their terms.

6. In the event of a dispute as to whether the Court has jurisdiction, the matter shall be settled by the decision of the Court.

Article 37

Whenever a treaty or convention in force provides for reference of a matter to a tribunal to have been instituted by the League of Nations, or to the Permanent Court of International Justice, the matter shall, as between the parties to the present Statute, be referred to the International Court of Justice.

Article 38

1. The Court, whose function is to decide in accordance with international law such disputes as are submitted to it, shall apply:

a. international conventions, whether general or particular, establishing rules expressly recognized by the contesting states;

b. international custom, as evidence of a general practice accepted as law;

c. the general principles of law recognized by civilized nations;

d. subject to the provisions of Article 59, judicial decisions and the teachings of the most highly qualified publicists of the various nations, as subsidiary means for the determination of rules of law.

2. This provision shall not prejudice the power of the Court to decide a case *ex aequo et bono*, if the parties agree thereto.

Chapter III
PROCEDURE

Article 39

1. The official languages of the Court shall be French and English. If the parties agree that the case shall be conducted in French, the judgment shall be delivered in French. If the parties agree that the case shall be conducted in English, the judgment shall be delivered in English.

2. In the absence of an agreement as to which language shall be employed, each party may, in the pleadings, use the language which it prefers; the decision of the Court shall be given in French and English. In this case the Court shall at the same time determine which of the two texts shall be considered as authoritative.

3. The Court shall, at the request of any party, authorize a language other than French or English to be used by that party.

Article 40

1. Cases are brought before the Court, as the case may be, either by the notification of the special agreement or by a written application addressed to the Registrar. In either case the subject of the dispute and the parties shall be indicated.

2. The Registrar shall forthwith communicate the application to all concerned.

3. He shall also notify the Members of the United Nations through the Secretary-General, and also any other states entitled to appear before the Court.

Article 41

1. The Court shall have the power to indicate, if it considers that circumstances so require, any provisional measures which ought to be taken to preserve the respective rights of either party.

2. Pending the final decision, notice of the measures suggested shall forthwith be given to the parties and to the Security Council.

Article 42

1. The parties shall be represented by agents.

2. They may have the assistance of counsel or advocates before the Court.

3. The agents, counsel, and advocates of parties before the Court shall enjoy the privileges and immunities necessary to the independent exercise of their duties.

Article 43

1. The procedure shall consist of two parts: written and oral.

2. The written proceedings shall consist of the communication to the Court and to the parties of memorials, counter-memorials and, if necessary, replies; also all papers and documents in support.

3. These communications shall be made through the Registrar, in the order and within the time fixed by the Court.

4. A certified copy of every document produced by one party shall be communicated to the other party.

5. The oral proceedings shall consist of the hearing by the Court of witnesses, experts, agents, counsel, and advocates.

Article 44

1. For the service of all notices upon persons other than the agents, counsel, and advocates, the Court shall apply direct to the government of the state upon whose territory the notice has to be served.

2. The same provision shall apply whenever steps are to be taken to procure evidence on the spot.

Article 45

The hearing shall be under the control of the President or, if he is unable to preside, of the Vice-President; if neither is able to preside, the senior judge present shall preside.

Article 46

The hearing in Court shall be public, unless the Court shall decide otherwise, or unless the parties demand that the public be not admitted.

Article 47

1. Minutes shall be made at each hearing and signed by the Registrar and the President.

2. These minutes alone shall be authentic.

Article 48

The Court shall make orders for the conduct of the case, shall decide the form and time in which each party must conclude its arguments, and make all arrangements connected with the taking of evidence.

Article 49

The Court may, even before the hearing begins, call upon the agents to produce any document or to supply any explanations. Formal note shall be taken of any refusal.

Article 50

The Court may, at any time, entrust any individual, body, bureau, commission, or other organization that it may select, with the task of carrying out an enquiry or giving an expert opinion.

Article 51

During the hearing any relevant questions are to be put to the witnesses and experts under the conditions laid down by the Court in the rules of procedure referred to in Article 30.

Article 52

After the Court has received the proofs and evidence within the time specified for the purpose, it may refuse to accept any further oral or written evidence that one party may desire to present unless the other side consents.

Article 53

1. Whenever one of the parties does not appear before the Court, or fails to defend its case, the other party may call upon the Court to decide in favour of its claim.

2. The Court must, before doing so, satisfy itself, not only that it has jurisdiction in accordance with Articles 36 and 37, but also that the claim is well founded in fact and law.

Article 54

1. When, subject to the control of the Court, the agents, counsel, and advocates have completed their presentation of the case, the President shall declare the hearing closed.

2. The Court shall withdraw to consider the judgment.

3. The deliberations of the Court shall take place in private and remain secret.

Article 55

1. All questions shall be decided by a majority of the judges present.

2. In the event of an equality of votes, the President or the judge who acts in his place shall have a casting vote.

Article 56

1. The judgment shall state the reasons on which it is based.

2. It shall contain the names of the judges who have taken part in the decision.

Article 57

If the judgment does not represent in whole or in part the unanimous opinion of the judges, any judge shall be entitled to deliver a separate opinion.

Article 58

The judgment shall be signed by the President and by the Registrar. It shall be read in open court, due notice having been given to the agents.

Article 59

The decision of the Court has no binding force except between the parties and in respect of that particular case.

Article 60

The judgment is final and without appeal. In the event of dispute as to the meaning or scope of the judgment, the Court shall construe it upon the request of any party.

Article 61

1. An application for revision of a judgment may be made only when it is based upon the discovery of some fact of such a nature as to be a decisive factor, which fact was, when the judgment was given, unknown to the Court and also to the party claiming revision, always provided that such ignorance was not due to negligence.

2. The proceedings for revision shall be opened by a judgment of the Court expressly recording the existence of the new fact, recognizing that it has such a character as to lay the case open to revision, and declaring the application admissible on this ground.

3. The Court may require previous compliance with the terms of the judgment before it admits proceedings in revision.

4. The application for revision must be made at latest within six months of the discovery of the new fact.

5. No application for revision may be made after the lapse of ten years from the date of the judgment.

Article 62

1. Should a state consider that it has an interest of a legal nature which may be affected by the decision in the case, it may submit a request to the Court to be permitted to intervene.

2. It shall be for the Court to decide upon this request.

Article 63

1. Whenever the construction of a convention to which states other than those concerned in the case are parties is in question, the Registrar shall notify all such states forthwith.

2. Every state so notified has the right to intervene in the proceedings; but if it uses this right, the construction given by the judgment will be equally binding upon it.

Article 64

Unless otherwise decided by the Court, each party shall bear its own costs.

Chapter IV
ADVISORY OPINIONS

Article 65

1. The Court may give an advisory opinion on any legal question at the request of whatever body may be authorized by or in accordance with the Charter of the United Nations to make such a request.

2. Questions upon which the advisory opinion of the Court is asked shall be laid before the Court by means of a written request containing an exact statement of the question upon which an opinion is required, and accompanied by all documents likely to throw light upon the question.

Article 66

1. The Registrar shall forthwith give notice of the request for an advisory opinion to all states entitled to appear before the Court.

2. The Registrar shall also, by means of a special and direct communication, notify any state entitled to appear before the Court or international organization considered by the Court, or, should it not be sitting, by the President, as likely to be able to furnish information on the question, that the Court will be prepared to receive, within a time limit to be fixed by the President, written statements, or to hear, at a public sitting to be held for the purpose, oral statements relating to the question.

3. Should any such state entitled to appear before the Court have failed to receive the special communication referred to in paragraph 2 of this Article, such state may express a desire to submit a written statement or to be heard; and the Court will decide.

4. States and organizations having presented written or oral statements or both shall be permitted to comment on the statements made by other states or organizations in the form, to the extent, and within the time limits which the Court, or, should it not be sitting, the President, shall decide in each particular case. Accordingly, the Registrar shall in due time communicate any such written statements to states and organizations having submitted similar statements.

Article 67

The Court shall deliver its advisory opinions in open court, notice having been given to the Secretary-General and to the representatives of Members of the United Nations, of other states and of international organizations immediately concerned.

Article 68

In the exercise of its advisory functions the Court shall further be guided by the provisions of the present Statute which apply in contentious cases to the extent to which it recognizes them to be applicable.

Chapter V
AMENDMENT

Article 69

Amendments to the present Statute shall be effected by the same procedure as is provided by the Charter of the United Nations for amendments to that Charter, subject however to any provisions which the General Assembly upon recommendation of the Security Council may adopt concerning the participation of states which are parties to the present Statute but are not Members of the United Nations.

Article 70

The Court shall have power to propose such amendments to the present Statute as it may deem necessary, through written communications to the Secretary-General, for consideration in conformity with the provisions of Article 69.

Appendix III

The Structure of the United Nations

NOTE: Several United Nations Member States changed their official names in 1971. This altered their order of placement in alphabetical listings. The Members of United Nations bodies are given in this Appendix in the English alphabetical order of their names as registered with the Organization at 31 December 1971. Therefore, those Members that changed their names during the year are listed under their new names, even though meetings of the bodies in which they participated might have been held prior to the changes in their names. For the countries concerned, see Appendix I.

The General Assembly

The General Assembly is composed of all the Members of the United Nations.

Sessions in 1971
Twenty-sixth Session: 21 September–22 December 1971.

Officers
President, Twenty-sixth Session: Adam Malik (Indonesia).
Vice-Presidents, Twenty-sixth Session: Belgium, Burundi, China, Costa Rica, France, Greece, Hungary, Japan, People's Democratic Republic of Yemen, Peru, Sierra Leone, Sudan, USSR, United Kingdom, United States, Venezuela, Zambia.

The Assembly has four types of committees: (1) Main Committees; (2) procedural committees; (3) standing committees; (4) subsidiary and *ad hoc* bodies.

Main Committees

Seven Main Committees have been established under the rules of procedure of the General Assembly, as follows:

Political and Security Committee (including the regulation of armaments) (First Committee)
Special Political Committee
Economic and Financial Committee (Second Committee)
Social, Humanitarian and Cultural Committee (Third Committee)
Trusteeship Committee (including Non-Self-Governing Territories) (Fourth Committee)
Administrative and Budgetary Committee (Fifth Committee)
Legal Committee (Sixth Committee)

In addition to these seven Main Committees, the General Assembly may constitute other committees, on which all Members have the right to be represented.

Officers of the Main Committees, Twenty-sixth Session

FIRST COMMITTEE
Chairman: Milko Tarabanov (Bulgaria).
Vice-Chairman: Radha Ramphul (Mauritius).
Rapporteur: Giovanni Migliuolo (Italy).

SPECIAL POLITICAL COMMITTEE
Chairman: Cornelius C. Cremin (Ireland).
Vice-Chairman: V. S. Smirnov (Byelorussian SSR).
Rapporteur: Parviz Mohajer (Iran).

SECOND COMMITTEE
Chairman: Narciso G. Reyes (Philippines).
Vice-Chairman: Bernardo de Azevedo Brito (Brazil).
Rapporteur: Salih Mohamed Osman (Sudan).

THIRD COMMITTEE
Chairman: Mrs. Helvi Sipila (Finland).
Vice-Chairman: Yahya Mahmassani (Lebanon).
Rapporteur: Amre M. Moussa (Egypt).

FOURTH COMMITTEE
Chairman: Keith Johnson (Jamaica).
Vice-Chairman: Mrs. Brita Skottsberg-Ahman (Sweden).
Rapporteur: Yilma Tadesse (Ethiopia).

FIFTH COMMITTEE
Chairman: E. Olu Sanu (Nigeria).
Vice-Chairman: Gregor Woschnagg (Austria).
Rapporteur: Babooram Rambissoon (Trinidad and Tobago).

SIXTH COMMITTEE
Chairman: Zenon Rossides (Cyprus).
Vice-Chairman: Duke E. Pollard (Guyana).
Rapporteur: Alfons Klafkowski (Poland).

Procedural committees

There are two procedural committees of the Assembly: the General Committee and the Credentials Committee.

GENERAL COMMITTEE
The General Committee consists of the President of the General Assembly, as Chairman, the 17 Vice-Presidents and the Chairmen of the seven Main Committees.

CREDENTIALS COMMITTEE
The Credentials Committee consists of nine members appointed by the General Assembly on the proposal of the President.

Twenty-sixth Session
Australia, Colombia, France, Ireland (*Chairman*), Liberia, Mongolia, Somalia, USSR, United States.

Standing committees

The General Assembly has two standing committees: the Advisory Committee on Administrative and Budgetary Questions and the Committee on Contributions. Each consists of experts appointed in their individual capacities for a three-year term.

ADVISORY COMMITTEE ON ADMINISTRATIVE
AND BUDGETARY QUESTIONS
Members in 1971:
To serve until 31 December 1971: Mohamed Alwan (Iraq);* Mohsen S. Esfandiary (Iran); André Naudy (France); John I. M. Rhodes, *Chairman* (United Kingdom).
To serve until 31 December 1972: Albert F. Bender, Jr. (United States); Mario Majoli (Italy); V. K. Palamarchuk (USSR); José Piñera (Chile).

To serve until 31 December 1973: Paulo Lopes Corrêa (Brazil); Ahmed Tewfik Khalil (Egypt); C. S. M. Mselle (United Republic of Tanzania); Jozsef Tardos (Hungary).

*Appointed by the General Assembly on 11 October 1971 to fill the unexpired term of Salim A. Saleem (Iraq), who resigned with effect from 10 July 1971.

On 13 December 1971, the General Assembly decided to enlarge the Advisory Committee from 12 to 13 members, with effect from 1 January 1972, in order to include a member from China.

On 17 December 1971, the General Assembly reappointed the following for a three-year term ending on 31 December 1974 to fill the vacancies occurring on 31 December 1971: Mohamed Alwan (Iraq); Mohsen S. Esfandiary (Iran); André Naudy (France); John I. M. Rhodes (United Kingdom). The General Assembly also appointed Hsing Sung-yi (China) for a three-year term ending 31 December 1974 to fill the newly created seat on the Advisory Committee.

Members for 1972: Mohamed Alwan (Iraq); Albert F. Bender, Jr. (United States); Paulo Lopes Corrêa (Brazil); Mohsen S. Esfandiary (Iran); Hsing Sung-yi (China); Ahmed Tewfik Khalil (Egypt); Mario Majoli (Italy); C. S. M. Mselle (United Republic of Tanzania); André Naudy (France); V. K. Palamarchuk (USSR); José Piñera (Chile); John I. M. Rhodes (United Kingdom); Jozsef Tardos (Hungary).

COMMITTEE ON CONTRIBUTIONS

Members in 1971:

To serve until 31 December 1971: Mohamed Fakhreddine (Sudan); Théodore Idzumbuir (Zaire); John I. M. Rhodes (United Kingdom); David Silveira da Mota, Jr., Vice-Chairman (Brazil); Abele Zodda (Italy).

To serve until 31 December 1972: Amjad Ali, Chairman (Pakistan); Santiago Meyer Picón (Mexico); Maurice Viaud (France); A. V. Zakharov (USSR).

To serve until 31 December 1973: Seymour Maxwell Finger (United States);* Takeshi Naito (Japan); Stanislaw Raczkowski (Poland).

*On 13 December 1971, the General Assembly appointed David L. Stottlemyer (United States) to complete the term of office of Seymour Maxwell Finger (United States), who resigned with effect from 31 December 1971.

On 13 December 1971, the General Assembly appointed the following for three-year terms of office starting on 1 January 1972 to fill the vacancies occurring on 31 December 1971: Joseph Quao Cleland (Ghana); Abdulrahim A. Farah (Somalia); Angus J. Matheson (Canada); David Silveira da Mota, Jr. (Brazil); Miss K. Whalley (United Kingdom).

Members for 1972: Amjad Ali (Pakistan); Joseph Quao Cleland (Ghana); Abdulrahim A. Farah (Somalia); Angus J. Matheson (Canada); Santiago Meyer Picón (Mexico); Takeshi Naito (Japan); Stanislaw Raczkowski (Poland); David Silveira da Mota, Jr. (Brazil); David L. Stottlemyer (United States); Maurice Viaud (France); Miss K. Whalley (United Kingdom); A. V. Zakharov (USSR).

Subsidiary, Ad Hoc and Related Bodies

The following subsidiary, ad hoc and related bodies were either in existence or functioning in 1971, or else were established during the General Assembly's twenty-sixth session held from 21 September to 22 December 1971. Those bodies marked * were set up or began to function during 1971, and those marked † were discontinued in 1971.

Interim Committee of the General Assembly
Special Committee on Peace-keeping Operations
Working Group for a Study of Peace-keeping Measures
Disarmament Commission
Group of Experts on the Economic and Social Consequences of Disarmament
Group of Consultant Experts on the Economic and Social Consequences of the Arms Race and of Military Expenditures †
Committee on the Peaceful Uses of Outer Space
  Scientific and Technical Sub-Committee
  Legal Sub-Committee
  Working Group on Direct Broadcast Satellites
Committee on the Peaceful Uses of the Sea-bed and the Ocean Floor beyond the Limits of National Jurisdiction
  Sub-Committee I*
  Sub-Committee II*
  Sub-Committee III*
United Nations Scientific Advisory Committee
United Nations Scientific Committee on the Effects of Atomic Radiation
Panel for Inquiry and Conciliation
Peace Observation Commission
Collective Measures Committee
Panel of Military Experts
United Nations Commission for the Unification and Rehabilitation of Korea (UNCURK)
  Committee of UNCURK
United Nations Conciliation Commission for Palestine
United Nations Relief and Works Agency for Palestine Refugees in the Near East (UNRWA)
  Advisory Commission of UNRWA
  Working Group on the Financing of UNRWA*
Committee for the Twenty-fifth Anniversary of the United Nations†
Special Committee on the Situation with regard to the Implementation of the Declaration on the Granting of Independence to Colonial Countries and Peoples
  Sub-Committee on Petitions
  Working Group
  Sub-Committee I
  Sub-Committee II
  Sub-Committee III
Special Committee on Apartheid
  Sub-Committee on Petitions
  Sub-Committee on Information on Apartheid
  Working Group
Committee of Trustees of the United Nations Trust Fund for South Africa
United Nations Council for Namibia
  Standing Committee I
  Standing Committee II
  Ad Hoc Committee on the Question of Travel Documents
Sub-Committee on the Situation in Angola
Advisory Committee on the United Nations Educational and Training Programme for Southern Africa
United Nations Conference on Trade and Development (UNCTAD)
  Trade and Development Board
    Advisory Committee to the Board and to the Committee on Commodities
    Committee on Commodities
      Permanent Sub-Committee on Commodities
      Permanent Group on Synthetics and Substitutes
      Committee on Tungsten
    Committee on Manufactures
    Committee on Invisibles and Financing related to Trade
    Committee on Shipping
    Special Committee on Preferences
    Intergovernmental Group on Transfer of Technology
Joint Advisory Group on the UNCTAD/GATT International Trade Centre
United Nations Development Programme (UNDP)
United Nations Capital Development Fund
  Executive Board of the United Nations Capital Development Fund

Ad Hoc Committee on Co-operation between the United Nations Development Programme and the United Nations Industrial Development Organization*
United Nations Industrial Development Organization (UNIDO)
  Industrial Development Board
    Working Group on Programme and Co-ordination
Preparatory Committee for the United Nations Conference on the Human Environment
United Nations Institute for Training and Research (UNITAR)
  Board of Trustees
  Administrative and Training Committee
  Research Committee
  Panel of Experts on the Establishment of an International University
United Nations Children's Fund (UNICEF)
Committee on the Elimination of Racial Discrimination
Special Committee to Investigate Israeli Practices Affecting the Human Rights of the Population of the Occupied Territories
Special Committee to Select the Winners of the United Nations Human Rights Prize
Office of the United Nations High Commissioner for Refugees (UNHCR)
  Executive Committee of the Programme of the UNHCR
Ad Hoc Committee of the Whole Assembly
United Nations Joint Staff Pension Board
  Standing Committee of the Pension Board
  Committee of Actuaries
United Nations Staff Pension Committee
Investments Committee
Board of Auditors
Panel of External Auditors
Joint Inspection Unit
Special Committee for the Review of the United Nations Salary System
Special Committee on the Financial Situation of the United Nations*
Special Committee on the Rationalization of the Procedures and Organization of the General Assembly†
Consultative Panel on United Nations Information Policies and Programmes
United Nations Administrative Tribunal
Committee on Applications for Review of Administrative Tribunal Judgements
International Law Commission
Committee on Arrangements for a Conference for the Purpose of Reviewing the Charter
Special Committee on the Question of Defining Aggression
  Working Group
Commission on Permanent Sovereignty over Natural Resources
Advisory Committee on the United Nations Programme of Assistance in the Teaching, Study, Dissemination and Wider Appreciation of International Law
United Nations Commission on International Trade Law
  Working Group on Time-Limits and Limitations (Prescription) in the International Sale of Goods
  Working Group on the International Sale of Goods
  Working Group on International Legislation on Shipping*
Committee on Relations with the Host Country*

INTERIM COMMITTEE OF THE GENERAL ASSEMBLY
Each Member of the United Nations has the right to be represented on the Interim Committee.
The Committee did not meet in 1971.

SPECIAL COMMITTEE ON PEACE-KEEPING OPERATIONS
In 1971, the Special Committee on Peace-keeping Operations held meetings at United Nations Headquarters, New York, on 1 April, 6 May and 1 and 3 December.

Members in 1971: Afghanistan, Algeria, Argentina, Australia, Austria, Brazil, Canada, Czechoslovakia, Denmark, Egypt, El Salvador, Ethiopia, France, Hungary, India, Iraq, Italy, Japan, Mauritania, Mexico, Netherlands, Nigeria, Pakistan, Poland, Romania, Sierra Leone, Spain, Thailand, USSR, United Kingdom, United States, Venezuela, Yugoslavia.

Vice-Chairmen:* Yvon Beaulne (Canada), Zdenek Cernik (Czechoslovakia).
Rapporteur: Mahmoud Kassem (Egypt).

*On 1 April 1971, the Committee decided that, pending election of a chairman, the Committee should meet under the chairmanship of the two Vice-Chairmen, who would alternate in the Chair. A chairman was not elected in 1971.

Working Group for a Study of Peace-keeping Measures
Members in 1971:* Canada *(Vice-Chairman)*, Czechoslovakia *(Vice-Chairman)*, Egypt *(Rapporteur)*, France, USSR, United Kingdom, United States.

*The Chairman of the Special Committee on Peace-keeping Operations is also a member, *ex officio.*

DISARMAMENT COMMISSION
The Disarmament Commission consists of all the Members of the United Nations.
The Commission did not meet in 1971.

GROUP OF EXPERTS ON THE ECONOMIC AND SOCIAL CONSEQUENCES OF DISARMAMENT
In 1970, the General Assembly authorized the Secretary-General to establish the Group of Experts. It was to consist of not more than 10 members, to serve in their personal capacity.
The members of the Group of Experts were not appointed in 1971.

GROUP OF CONSULTANT EXPERTS ON THE ECONOMIC AND SOCIAL CONSEQUENCES OF THE ARMS RACE AND OF MILITARY EXPENDITURES
The Group of Consultant Experts consisted of 14 experts appointed by the Secretary-General to prepare a report on the economic and social consequences of the arms race and of military expenditures.
The Group held three sessions in 1971: the first between 16 and 19 February; the second between 20 May and 3 June; and the third from 23 August to 5 September 1971. The first two sessions were held at United Nations Headquarters, New York, and the third at Geneva, Switzerland.

The membership of the Group of Consultant Experts was as follows:
Gheorghe Dolgu (Romania); Willem F. Duisenberg (Netherlands); V. S. Emelyanov (USSR); Plácido García Reynoso (Mexico); Vojin Guzina (Yugoslavia); Douglas Le Pan (Canada); Ladislav Matejka (Czechoslovakia); Akira Matsui (Japan); Jacques Mayer (France); Maciej Perczynski (Poland); Mullath A. Vellodi (India); Henry C. Wallich (United States); Kifle Wodajo (Ethiopia); Lord Zuckerman (United Kingdom).

Chairman: Mangalam E. Chacko.

COMMITTEE ON THE PEACEFUL USES OF OUTER SPACE
The Committee held the second part of its fourteenth session from 1 to 10 September and the first part of its fifteenth session on 15 and 20 December 1971. All meetings were held at United Nations Headquarters, New York.

Members in 1971: Albania, Argentina, Australia, Austria, Belgium, Brazil, Bulgaria, Canada, Chad, Czechoslovakia, Egypt, France, Hungary, India, Iran, Italy, Japan, Lebanon, Mexico, Mongolia, Morocco, Poland, Romania, Sierra Leone, Sweden, USSR, United Kingdom, United States.

Chairman: Kurt Waldheim (Austria).
Vice-Chairman: Gheorghe Diaconescu (Romania).
Rapporteur: Celso Antônio de Souza e Silva (Brazil).

Scientific and Technical Sub-Committee

The Sub-Committee, a committee of the whole, held its eighth session at United Nations Headquarters, New York, from 6 to 15 July 1971.

Chairman: J. H. Carver (Australia).

The Sub-Committee has established a working group of the whole, the Working Group on Remote Sensing of the Earth by Satellites.

Legal Sub-Committee

The Sub-Committee, a committee of the whole, held its tenth session at Geneva, Switzerland, from 7 June to 2 July 1971.

Chairman: Eugeniusz Wyzner (Poland).

Working Group on Direct Broadcast Satellites

The Working Group did not meet in 1971.

COMMITTEE ON THE PEACEFUL USES OF THE SEA-BED AND THE OCEAN FLOOR BEYOND THE LIMITS OF NATIONAL JURISDICTION

The Committee held the following meetings in 1971: informal consultations in February and the first part of March; a first session between 12 and 26 March; a second session between 19 July and 27 August; and meetings on 14, 15 and 22 October 1971. The two sessions were held at Geneva, Switzerland, and the February, March and October meetings at United Nations Headquarters, New York.

In accordance with a decision of the General Assembly of 17 December 1970 to enlarge the Committee by 44 members (from 42 to 86), the Chairman of the Assembly's First (Political and Security) Committee announced, on 8 January 1971, the appointment of the following 43 new members, to which one more, from Eastern Europe, would be added at a later date:*
Afghanistan, Algeria, Bolivia, Byelorussian SSR, Colombia, Congo, Cyprus, Denmark, Ecuador, Ethiopia, Gabon, Ghana, Greece, Guatemala, Guinea, Guyana, Hungary, Indonesia, Iran, Iraq, Ivory Coast, Jamaica, Lebanon, Mali, Mauritius, Morocco, Nepal, Netherlands, New Zealand, Panama, Philippines, Senegal, Singapore, Somalia, Spain, Sweden, Tunisia, Turkey, Ukrainian SSR, Uruguay, Venezuela, Yemen, Zaire.

*As at 31 December 1971, the forty-fourth new member had not been appointed to the Committee.

In accordance with a decision of the General Assembly of 21 December 1971 to add to the membership of the Committee China and four other members (increasing its membership to 91), the Chairman of the First Committee on 22 December 1971 appointed the following: Fiji, Finland, Nicaragua, Zambia.

Members in 1971: Afghanistan, Algeria, Argentina, Australia, Austria, Belgium, Bolivia, Brazil, Bulgaria, Byelorussian SSR, Cameroon, Canada, Ceylon, Chile, China, Colombia, Congo, Cyprus, Czechoslovakia, Denmark, Ecuador, Egypt, El Salvador, Ethiopia, Fiji, Finland, France, Gabon, Ghana, Greece, Guatemala, Guinea, Guyana, Hungary, Iceland, India, Indonesia, Iran, Iraq, Italy, Ivory Coast, Jamaica, Japan, Kenya, Kuwait, Lebanon, Liberia, Libyan Arab Republic, Madagascar, Malaysia, Mali, Malta, Mauritania, Mauritius, Mexico, Morocco, Nepal, Netherlands, New Zealand, Nicaragua, Nigeria, Norway, Pakistan, Panama, Peru, Philippines, Poland, Romania, Senegal, Sierra Leone, Singapore, Somalia, Spain, Sudan, Sweden, Thailand, Trinidad and Tobago, Tunisia, Turkey, Ukrainian SSR, USSR, United Kingdom, United Republic of Tanzania, United

States, Uruguay, Venezuela, Yemen, Yugoslavia, Zaire, Zambia.

Chairman: Hamilton Shirley Amerasinghe (Ceylon).
Vice-Chairmen: Saoud Nasser Al-Sabah (Kuwait) (second session); Jens Evensen (Norway); Théodore Idzumbuir (Zaire) (first session); Soubhi J. Khanachet (Kuwait) (first session); A. Mandi (Zaire) (second session); Lazar Mojsov (Yugoslavia); Wlodzimierz Natorf (Poland); Radha Ramphul (Mauritius); P. V. J. Solomon (Trinidad and Tobago); Fernando Zegers (Chile).
Rapporteur: Charles V. Vella (Malta).

On 12 March 1971 the Committee established three sub-committees of the whole, replacing the Economic and Technical Sub-Committee and the Legal Sub-Committee. Sub-Committee I was to prepare draft treaty articles embodying the international régime for the area and resources of the sea-bed. Sub-Committee II was to prepare a comprehensive list of subjects and issues relating to the law of the sea. Sub-Committee III was to deal with the preservation of the marine environment.

Sub-Committee I

The Sub-Committee held two series of meetings in 1971, between 12 and 25 March, and between 20 July and 27 August, both at Geneva, Switzerland.

Chairman: E. E. Seaton (United Republic of Tanzania).
Vice-Chairmen: Gyorgy Fekete (Hungary); C. V. Ranganathan (India); Sergio M. Thompson-Flores (Brazil).
Rapporteur: Anton Prohaska (Austria).

Sub-Committee II

The Sub-Committee held two series of meetings in 1971, between 12 and 19 March, and between 22 July and 26 August, both at Geneva, Switzerland.

Chairman: Reynaldo Galindo Pohl (El Salvador).
Vice-Chairmen: Burleigh Holder (Liberia); Mohammad Ali Massoud-Ansari (Iran); Necmettin Tuncel (Turkey); Alexander Yankov (Bulgaria).
Rapporteur: Shaffie Abdel-Hamid (Egypt).

Sub-Committee III

The Sub-Committee held two series of meetings in 1971, between 12 and 25 March, and between 28 July and 27 August, both at Geneva, Switzerland.

Chairman: Alfred van der Essen (Belgium).
Vice-Chairmen: Augusto Espinosa Valderrama (Colombia); Mebratu Gebre-Kidan (Ethiopia).
Rapporteur: Takeo Iguchi (Japan).

UNITED NATIONS SCIENTIFIC ADVISORY COMMITTEE

The Committee held two meetings in 1971, one on 24 March at United Nations Headquarters, New York, and the other on 3 September at Geneva, Switzerland.

Members in 1971: Brazil, Canada, France, India, USSR, United Kingdom, United States.

UNITED NATIONS SCIENTIFIC COMMITTEE ON THE EFFECTS OF ATOMIC RADIATION

The United Nations Scientific Committee on the Effects of Atomic Radiation held its twenty-first session at United Nations Headquarters, New York, from 14 to 23 June 1971.

Members in 1971: Argentina, Australia, Belgium, Brazil, Canada, Czechoslovakia, Egypt, France, India, Japan, Mexico, Sweden, USSR, United Kingdom, United States.

Chairman: Bo Lindell (Sweden).
Vice-Chairman: F. H. Sobels (Belgium).
Rapporteur: L. R. Caldas (Brazil).

PANEL FOR INQUIRY AND CONCILIATION

The Panel for Inquiry and Conciliation was established by the General Assembly in 1949 (by resolution 268 D (III))[1] and consists of qualified persons, designated by United Nations Member States, to serve a term of five years.

The Panel did not meet in 1971.

PEACE OBSERVATION COMMISSION

Members in 1971: China, Czechoslovakia, France, Honduras, India, Iraq, Israel, New Zealand, Pakistan, Sweden, USSR, United Kingdom, United States, Uruguay.

On 18 December 1971, the General Assembly, on the suggestion of its President, who announced that China preferred not to serve, decided to reappoint the other 13 members of the Peace Observation Commission for 1972 and 1973.

The Commission did not meet in 1971.

COLLECTIVE MEASURES COMMITTEE

Members in 1971: Australia, Belgium, Brazil, Burma, Canada, Egypt, France, Mexico, Philippines, Turkey, United Kingdom, United States, Venezuela, Yugoslavia.

The Committee did not meet in 1971.

PANEL OF MILITARY EXPERTS

The General Assembly's "Uniting for Peace" resolution of 3 November 1950 (resolution 377(V))[2] called for the appointment of military experts to be available, on request, to United Nations Member States wishing to obtain technical advice on the organization, training and equipment of elements within their national armed forces which could be made available, in accordance with national constitutional processes, for service as a unit or units of the United Nations upon the recommendation of the Security Council or the General Assembly.

UNITED NATIONS COMMISSION FOR THE UNIFICATION AND REHABILITATION OF KOREA (UNCURK)

*Members in 1971:** Australia, Netherlands, Pakistan, Philippines, Thailand, Turkey.

*Chile withdrew from UNCURK on 14 November 1970, and the resulting vacancy was not filled during 1971.

Committee of UNCURK

Members in 1971: Australia, Netherlands, Philippines, Thailand, Turkey.

UNITED NATIONS CONCILIATION COMMISSION FOR PALESTINE

Members in 1971: France, Turkey, United States.

UNITED NATIONS RELIEF AND WORKS AGENCY FOR PALESTINE REFUGEES IN THE NEAR EAST (UNRWA)

Commissioner-General: Sir John Rennie.*

Deputy Commissioner-General: Sir John Rennie (until 15 May 1971).

*Appointed by the Secretary-General to succeed Laurence V. Michelmore, who resigned with effect from 15 May 1971.

Advisory Commission of UNRWA

The Advisory Commission held a meeting on 26 August 1971 at Beirut, Lebanon.

Members in 1971: Belgium, Egypt, France, Jordan, Lebanon, Syrian Arab Republic, Turkey, United Kingdom, United States.

Working Group on the Financing of UNRWA

Members in 1971: France, Ghana, Japan, Lebanon, Norway, Trinidad and Tobago, Turkey *(Chairman)*, United Kingdom, United States.

COMMITTEE FOR THE TWENTY-FIFTH ANNIVERSARY OF THE UNITED NATIONS

Members in 1971: Austria, Bulgaria *(Vice-Chairman)*, Byelorussian SSR, Canada, China, France, Ghana *(Chairman)*, Guatemala, Guinea, Guyana *(Vice-Chairman)*, India *(Vice-Chairman)*, Iran, Italy *(Rapporteur)*, Lebanon, Mauritania, Peru, Philippines, Somalia, Sweden, Togo, Trinidad and Tobago, Uganda, USSR, United Kingdom, United States.

SPECIAL COMMITTEE ON THE SITUATION WITH REGARD TO THE IMPLEMENTATION OF THE DECLARATION ON THE GRANTING OF INDEPENDENCE TO COLONIAL COUNTRIES AND PEOPLES

Members in 1971: Afghanistan, Bulgaria, Ecuador, Ethiopia, Fiji, India, Iran, Iraq, Ivory Coast, Madagascar, Mali, Poland, Sierra Leone, Sweden, Syrian Arab Republic, Trinidad and Tobago, Tunisia, USSR, United Kingdom,* United Republic of Tanzania, United States,* Venezuela, Yugoslavia.

*By letters of 11 January 1971, the United Kingdom and the United States informed the President of the General Assembly that they had decided to withdraw from membership of the Special Committee, with immediate effect.

Chairman: Germán Nava Carrillo (Venezuela).

Vice-Chairmen: Barouh Grinberg (Bulgaria), Rafic Jouejati (Syrian Arab Republic).

Rapporteur: Yilma Tadesse (Ethiopia).

On 20 December 1971, the President of the General Assembly nominated China, Indonesia and Czechoslovakia to fill three of the four existing vacancies on the Special Committee, with immediate effect.

The Special Committee has a Sub-Committee on Petitions and a Working Group. In addition, Sub-Committees I, II and III were maintained in 1971. Territories not referred to Sub-Committees I, II or III were taken up at plenary meetings of the Special Committee.

Sub-Committee on Petitions

Members in 1971: Ecuador *(Chairman)*, India, Madagascar, Mali, Poland, Syrian Arab Republic.

Working Group

In 1971, the Working Group of the Special Committee consisted of Ecuador, India, Madagascar, Sweden and the United Republic of Tanzania, and the officers of the Special Committee.*

*On 14 September 1971, the Special Committee decided that, in view of the departure from United Nations Headquarters of its Chairman (Venezuela) and Vice-Chairman (Bulgaria), Bulgaria and Venezuela should serve as members of the Working Group.

Sub-Committee I

Members in 1971: Mali, Sierra Leone, Syrian Arab Republic *(Chairman)*, Trinidad and Tobago, Tunisia, USSR, United Republic of Tanzania *(Rapporteur)*, Yugoslavia.

Sub-Committee II

Members in 1971: Afghanistan *(Chairman)*, Ethiopia, Fiji, India, Iraq, Poland.

Sub-Committee III

Members in 1971: Bulgaria, Iran *(Chairman)*, Ivory Coast, Madagascar, Sweden, Trinidad and Tobago *(Rapporteur)*.

SPECIAL COMMITTEE ON *APARTHEID**

Members in 1971: Algeria, Ghana, Guatemala, Guinea, Haiti, Hungary, India, Malaysia, Nepal, Nigeria, Philippines, Somalia,

[1]See Y.U.N., 1947-1948, p. 287.
[2]See Y.U.N., 1950, pp. 193-95.

Sudan, Syrian Arab Republic, Trinidad and Tobago, Ukrainian SSR.

Chairman: Abdulrahim A. Farah (Somalia).
Vice-Chairmen: M. D. Polyanichko (Ukrainian SSR); Raoul Siclait (Haiti).
Rapporteur: Uddhav Deo Bhatt (Nepal).

*On 8 December 1970, the General Assembly approved a recommendation of the Special Political Committee to shorten the title of the Committee. It was formerly called the "Special Committee on the Policies of *Apartheid* of the Government of the Republic of South Africa."

On 19 January 1971, the President of the General Assembly informed the Secretary-General that he had appointed Guatemala as the fifth of seven new members authorized by an Assembly decision of 8 December 1970 enlarging the Committee. Two of the seven authorized seats remained unfilled in 1971.

Sub-Committee on Petitions
Members in 1971: Algeria *(Chairman),* Guatemala, India, Nepal, Nigeria, Philippines, Somalia, Ukrainian SSR.

Sub-Committee on Information on *Apartheid*
Members in 1971: Ghana, Guinea, Haiti, Hungary, Malaysia *(Chairman),* Sudan, Syrian Arab Republic, Trinidad and Tobago.

Working Group
Members in 1971: Abdulrahim A. Farah, Chairman of the Special Committee (Somalia); M.D. Polyanichko, Vice-Chairman of the Special Committee (Ukrainian SSR); Raoul Siclait, Vice-Chairman of the Special Committee (Haiti); Uddhav Deo Bhatt, Rapporteur of the Special Committee (Nepal); Ahmed Oucif, Chairman of the Sub-Committee on Petitions (Algeria); Yeop Adlan-Rose, Chairman of the Sub-Committee on Information on *Apartheid* (Malaysia).

COMMITTEE OF TRUSTEES OF THE UNITED NATIONS
TRUST FUND FOR SOUTH AFRICA
Members in 1971: Chile, Morocco, Nigeria *(Vice-Chairman),* Pakistan, Sweden *(Chairman).*

UNITED NATIONS COUNCIL FOR NAMIBIA
The United Nations Council for Namibia* was established by the General Assembly on 19 May 1967. Its executive and administrative tasks are entrusted to a United Nations Commissioner for Namibia. The presidency of the Council rotates among members, in English alphabetical order, at four-month intervals.

*The Council, formerly known as the United Nations Council for South West Africa, was renamed the United Nations Council for Namibia in accordance with a General Assembly resolution of 12 June 1968 which, among other things, proclaimed that South West Africa was thenceforth to be known as Namibia.

Members in 1971: Chile, Colombia, Egypt, Guyana, India, Indonesia, Nigeria, Pakistan, Turkey, Yugoslavia, Zambia.

Acting United Nations Commissioner for Namibia: Agha Abdul Hamid.

The Council has established two standing committees. One deals with the planning of the Council's work, communications and publicity, and studies ways and means of enabling Namibians to participate in the Council's work. The second standing committee deals with administrative, legal and educational matters. All questions previously entrusted to various *ad hoc* bodies were transferred to those standing committees, with the exception of matters dealt with by the *Ad Hoc* Committee on the Question of Travel Documents.

Standing Committee I
Members in 1971: Colombia, India, Indonesia, Nigeria *(Chairman* from September 1971), Pakistan, Turkey *(Chairman* until September 1971).

Standing Committee II
Members in 1971: Chile, Egypt, Guyana, Yugoslavia, Zambia *(Chairman).*

Ad Hoc Committee on the Question of Travel Documents
Members in 1971: Egypt, Guyana *(Chairman),* India, Yugoslavia.

SUB-COMMITTEE ON THE SITUATION IN ANGOLA
Members: Bolivia, Dahomey, Finland, Malaysia, Sudan.

The Sub-Committee reported to both the General Assembly and the Security Council in 1961 and 1962. It adjourned *sine die* after consideration of its report to the General Assembly's seventeenth session in December 1962.

ADVISORY COMMITTEE ON THE UNITED NATIONS
EDUCATIONAL AND TRAINING PROGRAMME
FOR SOUTHERN AFRICA
Members in 1971: Canada, Denmark, India, United Republic of Tanzania, Venezuela, Zaire, Zambia *(Chairman).*

UNITED NATIONS CONFERENCE ON TRADE
AND DEVELOPMENT (UNCTAD)
The United Nations Conference on Trade and Development (UNCTAD) consists of those States which are Members of the United Nations or members of the specialized agencies or of the International Atomic Energy Agency.

TRADE AND DEVELOPMENT BOARD
The Trade and Development Board is a permanent organ of the United Nations Conference on Trade and Development, and consists of 55 members elected from the following four groups of States:

Group A. 22 of the following States: Afghanistan, Algeria, Botswana, Burma, Burundi, Cameroon, Central African Republic, Ceylon, Chad, China, Congo, Dahomey, Egypt, Equatorial Guinea,* Ethiopia, Fiji,* Gabon, Gambia, Ghana, Guinea, India, Indonesia, Iran, Iraq, Israel, Ivory Coast, Jordan, Kenya, Khmer Republic, Kuwait, Laos, Lebanon, Lesotho, Liberia, Libyan Arab Republic, Madagascar, Malawi, Malaysia, Maldives, Mali, Mauritania, Mauritius, Mongolia, Morocco, Nepal, Niger, Nigeria, Pakistan, People's Democratic Republic of Yemen, Philippines, Republic of Korea, Republic of Viet-Nam, Rwanda, Saudi Arabia, Senegal, Sierra Leone, Singapore, Somalia, South Africa, Sudan, Swaziland,* Syrian Arab Republic, Thailand, Togo, Tunisia, Uganda, United Republic of Tanzania, Upper Volta, Western Samoa, Yemen, Yugoslavia, Zaire, Zambia.
Group B. 18 of the following States: Australia, Austria, Belgium, Canada, Cyprus, Denmark, Federal Republic of Germany, Finland, France, Greece, Holy See, Iceland, Ireland, Italy, Japan, Liechtenstein, Luxembourg, Malta, Monaco, Netherlands, New Zealand, Norway, Portugal, San Marino, Spain, Sweden, Switzerland, Turkey, United Kingdom, United States.
Group C. 9 of the following States: Argentina, Barbados, Bolivia, Brazil, Chile, Colombia, Costa Rica, Cuba, Dominican Republic, Ecuador, El Salvador, Guatemala, Guyana, Haiti, Honduras, Jamaica, Mexico, Nicaragua, Panama, Paraguay, Peru, Trinidad and Tobago, Uruguay, Venezuela.
Group D. 6 of the following States: Albania, Bulgaria, Byelorussian SSR, Czechoslovakia, Hungary, Poland, Romania, Ukrainian SSR, USSR.

The members of the Board are elected at each regular session of the Conference and serve until the election of their successors.

The States listed with an asterisk (*) became members of UNCTAD after the second session of the Conference, held at New Delhi, India, from 1 February to 29 March 1968. On 11 September 1969, the Trade and Development Board decided that, for the purpose of elections to subsidiary bodies, Equatorial Guinea and Swaziland should be treated as if they were among the countries listed in Group A. On 3 March 1971, the Trade and Development Board took a similar decision concerning Fiji, which was admitted to membership in the United Nations on 13 October 1970.

Bahrain, Bhutan, Oman, Qatar and the United Arab Emirates became Members of the United Nations in 1971 during the General Assembly's twenty-sixth session, and consequently became members of UNCTAD. By the end of 1971, no decision had been taken about their listings for purposes of elections to UNCTAD's subsidiary bodies.

Sessions during 1971
During 1971, the Trade and Development Board held the following sessions:

Tenth Session (Second Part): 1 to 9 March 1971, at Geneva, Switzerland.
Tenth Session (Third Part): 24 May 1971, at Geneva, Switzerland.
Eleventh Session: 24 August to 21 September 1971, at Geneva, Switzerland.

Board Members in 1971
Group A: Afghanistan, Algeria, Chad, Ghana, India, Indonesia, Iran, Iraq, Ivory Coast, Madagascar, Malaysia, Mali, Nigeria, Pakistan, Philippines, Rwanda, Senegal, Somalia, Syrian Arab Republic, Tunisia, Uganda, Yugoslavia.
Group B: Australia, Austria, Belgium, Canada, Denmark, Federal Republic of Germany, Finland, France, Greece, Italy, Japan, Netherlands, New Zealand, Spain, Sweden, Switzerland, United Kingdom, United States.
Group C: Brazil, Chile, Colombia, Costa Rica, Guatemala, Jamaica, Mexico, Peru, Venezuela.
Group D: Bulgaria, Czechoslovakia, Hungary, Poland, Romania, USSR.

Officers of the Board in 1971
Tenth Session (Second and Third Parts)
President: Pierre A. Forthomme (Belgium).
Vice-Presidents: Anthony Hill (Jamaica); Frank G. Hooton (Canada); Peter S. Lai (Malaysia); Osmo Lares (Finland); Wlodzimierz Natorf (Poland); Amanullah Rassoul (Afghanistan); Armand Razafindrabe (Madagascar); Oswaldo De Rivero (Peru); F. Spinelli (Italy); Nicolay Stephanov (Bulgaria).
Rapporteur: Abdelaziz El-Ayadhi (Tunisia).

Eleventh Session
President: Hortencio J. Brillantes (Philippines).
Vice-Presidents: A. A. Adeyeye (Nigeria); Diego Garcés (Colombia); Umberto Garrone (Italy); Hideo Kitahara (Japan); Gunnar Ljungdahl (Sweden); Enrique López Herrarte (Guatemala); Bernard F. Meere (Australia); Bénié Nioupin (Ivory Coast); B. R. Patel (India); A. Petrescou (Romania).
Rapporteur: Andrey Lukanov (Bulgaria).

Bureau of the Trade and Development Board
The elected officers of the Trade and Development Board form the Bureau of the Board.

ADVISORY COMMITTEE TO THE BOARD AND TO THE COMMITTEE ON COMMODITIES
The Advisory Committee held its sixth session at Geneva, Switzerland, from 22 March to 2 April 1971.

Members in 1971 (to serve until 14 February 1972):
S. Osman Ali (Pakistan), elected by the Board as Chairman;
Samar Sen (India), nominated by FAO as a person specifically concerned with agricultural commodities;
Bénié Nioupin (Ivory Coast), nominated by the Contracting Parties to GATT;

and the following who were appointed by the Board on the recommendation of the Secretary-General of UNCTAD:

Tulio de Andrea (Peru), as a person particularly concerned with non-agricultural primary commodities;
Isaiah Frank (United States), as a person of wide experience in the problems confronting developing countries the economies of which are primarily dependent on the production and international marketing of primary commodities;
D. I. Kostyukhin (USSR), as a person particularly familiar with the problems of States trading in primary commodities;
Michel Cépède (France),* as a person with special knowledge and experience in the problems relating to primary commodities in major consuming countries.

*Appointed by the Board on 2 March 1971 to fill the vacancy left by the death of André Philip (France).

On 16 September 1971, the Trade and Development Board: took note of the renomination of Samar Sen (India) by the Director-General of FAO and of Bénié Nioupin (Ivory Coast) by the Contracting Parties to GATT; reappointed Michel Cépède (France), Isaiah Frank (United States) and D. I. Kostyukhin (USSR) members of the Advisory Committee; appointed Antonio Sánchez de Lozada Bustamante (Bolivia) as a member of the Committee as a person particularly concerned with non-agricultural primary commodities to replace Tulio de Andrea (Peru), whose term was to expire on 14 February 1972; and, as recommended by the Secretary-General of UNCTAD, re-elected S. Osman Ali (Pakistan) Chairman of the Committee—all for terms of office of three years expiring on 14 February 1975.

SUBSIDIARY ORGANS OF THE TRADE AND DEVELOPMENT BOARD
The following are the main standing or permanent subsidiaries of the Trade and Development Board:

Committee on Commodities
　　Permanent Sub-Committee on Commodities
　　Permanent Group on Synthetics and Substitutes
　　Committee on Tungsten
Committee on Manufactures
Committee on Invisibles and Financing related to Trade
Committee on Shipping
Special Committee on Preferences
Intergovernmental Group on Transfer of Technology

Committee on Commodities
The Committee on Commodities consists of 55 members, 22 drawn from "Group A" members of UNCTAD, 18 from "Group B" members, 9 from "Group C" and 6 from "Group D."

For the list of members constituting Groups A, B, C and D, see above, under TRADE AND DEVELOPMENT BOARD.

The Committee on Commodities held its sixth session at Geneva, Switzerland, from 5 to 16 July 1971.

Members in 1971:
To serve until 31 December 1971: Australia, Bolivia, Bulgaria, Egypt, Finland, France, Guatemala, Guinea, Iran, Iraq, Mali, Netherlands, Philippines, Poland, Senegal, Sweden, United States, Venezuela.
To serve until 31 December 1972: Brazil, Canada, Ceylon, Denmark, Ethiopia, Federal Republic of Germany, Ghana, Hungary, Indonesia, Ireland, Italy, Ivory Coast, Madagascar, Nigeria, Spain, Trinidad and Tobago, USSR, Uruguay.
To serve until 31 December 1973: Argentina, Austria, Belgium, Chad, Czechoslovakia, Ecuador, India, Japan, Kenya, Malaysia, Norway, Peru, Republic of Viet-Nam, Romania, Syrian Arab Republic, Thailand, Tunisia, Turkey, United Kingdom.

Chairman: Henri Janton (France).
Vice-Chairmen: Tibor Fabian (Hungary), Eero Kekomaki (Finland),

Enrique López Herrarte (Guatemala), Narongrid Snidvongs (Thailand), G. O. Niyi (Nigeria).
Rapporteur: Ghebrechidan Alula (Ethiopia).

On 17 September 1971, the Trade and Development Board decided to postpone until 1972 elections to fill vacancies which would occur in the Committee on Commodities when the terms of 18 members expired on 31 December 1971.

Permanent Sub-Committee on Commodities
Members in 1971: Argentina, Australia, Brazil, Cameroon, Canada, Ceylon, Colombia, Federal Republic of Germany, France, Ghana, India, Iran, Iraq, Italy, Japan, Madagascar, Mali, Nigeria, Philippines, Poland, Romania, Sweden, USSR, United Kingdom, United Republic of Tanzania, United States, Uruguay, Venezuela.

The Sub-Committee did not meet in 1971.

Permanent Group on Synthetics and Substitutes
The Permanent Group on Synthetics and Substitutes held its fifth session at Geneva, Switzerland, from 28 June to 3 July 1971.

Members in 1971: Argentina, Brazil, Canada, Ceylon, Chad, Federal Republic of Germany, France, Indonesia, Italy, Japan, Malaysia, Netherlands, Nigeria, Poland, Republic of Viet-Nam, Senegal, Sudan, Uganda, USSR, United Kingdom, United States.

Chairman: B. O. Awokoya (Nigeria).
Vice-Chairman/Rapporteur: A. Pathmarajah (Ceylon).

Committee on Tungsten
Members in 1971: Argentina, Australia, Austria, Belgium, Bolivia, Brazil, Canada, China, Cyprus, Federal Republic of Germany, France, Gabon, Italy, Japan, Mexico, Netherlands, Peru, Poland, Portugal, Republic of Korea, Romania, Rwanda, Spain, Sweden, Thailand, Turkey, USSR, United Kingdom, United States.

The Committee did not meet in 1971.

Committee on Manufactures
The Committee on Manufactures consists of 45 members, 18 drawn from "Group A" members of UNCTAD, 15 from "Group B" members, 7 from "Group C" and 5 from "Group D."
For the list of members constituting Groups A, B, C and D, see above, under TRADE AND DEVELOPMENT BOARD.

The Committee on Manufactures held its fifth session at Geneva, Switzerland, from 3 to 14 May 1971.

Members in 1971:
To serve until 31 December 1971: Afghanistan, Brazil, Bulgaria, Canada, Guinea, Italy, Malaysia, Nigeria, Poland, Senegal, Sweden, Switzerland, United Republic of Tanzania, United States, Uruguay.
To serve until 31 December 1972: Belgium, Chile, Egypt, El Salvador, Federal Republic of Germany, Hungary, Ivory Coast, Japan, Madagascar, Republic of Korea, Spain, Uganda, USSR, United Kingdom, Zaire.
To serve until 31 December 1973: Algeria, Austria, Colombia, Czechoslovakia, France, Greece, India, Iran, Mexico, Netherlands, Norway, Pakistan, Peru, Philippines, Saudi Arabia.

Chairman: Andrey Lukanov (Bulgaria).
Vice-Chairmen: Alberto Galeano (Colombia), Elmar Gamper (Austria), Sherif R. Loutfi (Egypt), Mohammad Mohsin (Pakistan), Hiroshi Ohki (Japan).
Rapporteur: Mustapha Kettab (Algeria).

On 17 September 1971, the Trade and Development Board decided to postpone until 1972 elections to fill vacancies which

would occur in the Committee on Manufactures when the terms of 15 members expired on 31 December 1971.

Committee on Invisibles and Financing related to Trade
The Committee on Invisibles and Financing related to Trade consists of 45 members, 18 drawn from "Group A" members of UNCTAD, 15 from "Group B" members, 7 from "Group C" and 5 from "Group D."
For the list of members constituting Groups A, B, C and D, see above, under TRADE AND DEVELOPMENT BOARD.

The Committee on Invisibles and Financing related to Trade held its fifth session at Geneva, Switzerland, from 1 to 14 December 1971.

Members in 1971:
To serve until 31 December 1971: Argentina, Canada, Egypt, Ethiopia, Federal Republic of Germany, Ghana, Hungary, Italy, Japan, Kuwait, Mali, Peru, Republic of Viet-Nam, Romania, Spain.
To serve until 31 December 1972: Belgium, Brazil, Chile, Czechoslovakia, Gabon, India, Netherlands, Poland, Republic of Korea, Sweden, Switzerland, Syrian Arab Republic, Uganda, United Kingdom, Zaire.
To serve until 31 December 1973: Australia, Ceylon, France, Guatemala, Kenya, Mexico, Nigeria, Norway, Pakistan, Tunisia, Turkey, USSR, United States, Venezuela, Yugoslavia.

Chairman: Paul Blanc (France).
Vice-Chairmen: Baudoin Richard Differding (Zaire); A. Pathmarajah (Ceylon); Paul Szigeti (Hungary); Hubert Wieland Alzamora (Peru); D. Wilson (Canada).
Rapporteur: Mohammad Mohsin (Pakistan).

On 17 September 1971, the Trade and Development Board decided to postpone until 1972 elections to fill vacancies which would occur in the Committee on Invisibles and Financing related to Trade when the terms of 15 members expired on 31 December 1971.

Committee on Shipping
The Committee on Shipping consists of 45 members, 18 drawn from "Group A" members of UNCTAD, 15 from "Group B" members, 7 from "Group C" and 5 from "Group D."
For the list of members constituting Groups A, B, C, and D, see above, under TRADE AND DEVELOPMENT BOARD.

The Committee on Shipping held the first part of its fifth session from 22 March to 3 April 1971, and the second part of its fifth session on 31 August 1971, both at Geneva, Switzerland.

Members in 1971:
To serve until 31 December 1971: Brazil, Chad, Czechoslovakia, Denmark, France, Ghana, India, Mexico, Netherlands, New Zealand, Norway, Republic of Korea, Senegal, Thailand, USSR.
To serve until 31 December 1972: Colombia, Ethiopia, Gabon, Greece, Hungary, Iran, Iraq, Italy, Pakistan, Philippines, Poland, Spain, Sweden, United States, Venezuela.
To serve until 31 December 1973: Argentina, Australia, Bulgaria, Canada, Chile, Egypt, Federal Republic of Germany, Indonesia, Ivory Coast, Japan, Madagascar, Nigeria, Panama, Uganda, United Kingdom.

Fifth Session
Chairman: Y. K. Quarley (Ghana) (first part); Diego Garcés (Colombia) (second part).
Vice-Chairmen: Diego Garcés (Colombia) (first part); A. Goldobenko (USSR); P. K. Kitonsa (Uganda); G. Krause (Federal Republic of Germany); M. H. Panggabean (Indonesia).
Rapporteur: Edmund J. Antoun (United States) (first part); Stig Brattstrom (Sweden) (second part).

On 17 September 1971, the Trade and Development Board decided to postpone until 1972 elections to fill vacancies which would occur in the Committee on Shipping when the terms of 15 members expired on 31 December 1971.

Special Committee on Preferences

The Special Committee on Preferences was established by the Second United Nations Conference on Trade and Development as a subsidiary organ of the Trade and Development Board and open to the participation of all States members of UNCTAD.

The Special Committee did not meet in 1971.

Intergovernmental Group on Transfer of Technology

The Intergovernmental Group on Transfer of Technology, established by the Trade and Development Board on 18 September 1970, consists of 45 members chosen on the basis of equitable geographical distribution and, as far as possible, at an expert level. Eighteen are drawn from "Group A" members of UNCTAD, 15 from "Group B" members, 7 from "Group C" and 5 from "Group D."

For the list of members constituting Groups A, B, C and D, see above, under TRADE AND DEVELOPMENT BOARD.

The work of the Intergovernmental Group was to be reviewed by the Board after the Group had held two substantive sessions. The terms of the members of the Group would expire after the Board's review.

The Intergovernmental Group held its first (organizational) session from 14 to 21 June 1971 at Geneva, Switzerland.

*Members in 1971:** Algeria, Argentina, Austria, Brazil, Bulgaria, Ceylon, Chile, Congo, Czechoslovakia, Ecuador, Egypt, El Salvador, Ethiopia, Federal Republic of Germany, Finland, France, Ghana, Greece, India, Indonesia, Iraq, Italy, Ivory Coast, Japan, Kenya, Madagascar, Netherlands, Nigeria, Pakistan, Panama, Philippines, Poland, Romania, Spain, Switzerland, Syrian Arab Republic, Tunisia, Turkey, USSR, United States, Venezuela, Yugoslavia.

*Three vacancies in the membership of the Intergovernmental Group were not filled in 1971.

Chairman: Ljubomir Sekulic (Yugoslavia).
Vice-Chairmen: Noury Chaouch (Tunisia); Pedro Daza (Chile); G. Krasnov (USSR); F. Ponti (Italy); J. R. Samaranayake (Ceylon).
Rapporteur: Rolf Moehler (Federal Republic of Germany).

JOINT ADVISORY GROUP ON THE UNCTAD/GATT INTERNATIONAL TRADE CENTRE

The Joint Advisory Group was established in accordance with an agreement between UNCTAD and the General Agreement on Tariffs and Trade (GATT)[3] effective on 1 January 1968, the date on which the UNCTAD/GATT International Trade Centre commenced operations.

Participation in the Joint Advisory Group is open to all UNCTAD members and all Contracting Parties to GATT.

The Joint Advisory Group held its fourth session at Geneva, Switzerland, from 12 to 16 January 1971.

UNITED NATIONS DEVELOPMENT PROGRAMME (UNDP)

The United Nations Development Programme (UNDP) was established by the General Assembly. Its Governing Council reports to both the Economic and Social Council and the General Assembly. (See below, under THE ECONOMIC AND SOCIAL COUNCIL.)

UNITED NATIONS CAPITAL DEVELOPMENT FUND

The United Nations Capital Development Fund was set up as an organ of the General Assembly to function as an autonomous organization within the United Nations framework, its policies and operations to be exercised by a 24-member Executive Board elected by the General Assembly from Members of the United Nations or members of the specialized agencies or of the International Atomic Energy Agency. The chief executive officer of the Fund, the Managing Director, exercises his functions under the general direction of the Executive Board. The Executive Board reports to the Assembly through the Economic and Social Council.

Executive Board of the United Nations Capital Development Fund

On 14 December 1971, the General Assembly reconfirmed its decision of 15 December 1967 that, on a provisional basis, the UNDP Governing Council should act as Executive Board of the United Nations Capital Development Fund until the Fund's institutional arrangements could be reviewed.

Managing Director

On 14 December 1971, the General Assembly reconfirmed its decision of 15 December 1967 that, on a provisional basis, the Administrator of UNDP be asked to act as Managing Director of the United Nations Capital Development Fund.

Managing Director: Paul G. Hoffman.

AD HOC COMMITTEE ON CO-OPERATION BETWEEN THE UNITED NATIONS DEVELOPMENT PROGRAMME AND THE UNITED NATIONS INDUSTRIAL DEVELOPMENT ORGANIZATION

The *Ad Hoc* Committee, established by the General Assembly on 16 December 1971, was composed of those Member States whose representatives were currently serving on the bureaux of the Governing Council of the United Nations Development Programme and the Industrial Development Board of the United Nations Industrial Development Organization.

The *Ad Hoc* Committee did not meet in 1971.

Members for 1972: Bulgaria, Costa Rica, Denmark, Ghana, Hungary, India, Italy, Mexico, Uganda.

UNITED NATIONS INDUSTRIAL DEVELOPMENT ORGANIZATION (UNIDO)

The United Nations Industrial Development Organization (UNIDO) was established by the General Assembly and functions as an autonomous organization within the United Nations. States eligible for election to the Industrial Development Board, its principal organ, are those which are Members of the United Nations or members of the specialized agencies or of the International Atomic Energy Agency.

Industrial Development Board

The Industrial Development Board, the principal organ of UNIDO, consists of 45 States elected by the General Assembly from among UNIDO's members, with due regard to the principle of equitable geographical distribution, to serve for a three-year term of office, one third of the terms expiring each year.

The Board reports annually to the General Assembly through the Economic and Social Council.

The Board's membership is drawn from the following four groups of States:

List A. 18 of the following States: Afghanistan, Algeria, Bahrain,* Bhutan,* Botswana, Burma, Burundi, Cameroon, Central African Republic, Ceylon, Chad, China, Congo, Dahomey, Egypt, Equatorial Guinea, Ethiopia, Fiji, Gabon, Gambia, Ghana, Guinea, India, Indonesia, Iran, Iraq, Israel, Ivory Coast, Jordan, Kenya, Khmer Republic, Kuwait, Laos, Lebanon, Lesotho, Liberia, Libyan Arab Republic, Madagascar, Malawi, Malaysia, Maldives, Mali, Mauritania, Mauritius, Mongolia, Morocco, Nepal, Niger, Nigeria, Oman,* Pakistan, People's Democratic Republic of Yemen, Philippines, Qatar,* Republic of Korea, Republic of Viet-Nam, Rwanda, Saudi Arabia, Senegal, Sierra Leone, Singapore, Somalia, South Africa, Sudan, Swaziland, Syrian Arab Republic, Thailand, Togo, Tunisia, Uganda, United

---

[3]For further information on GATT, see PART TWO, CHAPTER XV, of this volume.

Arab Emirates,* United Republic of Tanzania, Upper Volta, Western Samoa, Yemen, Yugoslavia, Zaire, Zambia.

List B. 15 of the following States: Australia, Austria, Belgium, Canada, Cyprus, Denmark, Federal Republic of Germany, Finland, France, Greece, Holy See, Iceland, Ireland, Italy, Japan, Liechtenstein, Luxembourg, Malta, Monaco, Netherlands, New Zealand, Norway, Portugal, San Marino, Spain, Sweden, Switzerland, Turkey, United Kingdom, United States.

List C. 7 of the following States: Argentina, Barbados, Bolivia, Brazil, Chile, Colombia, Costa Rica, Cuba, Dominican Republic, Ecuador, El Salvador, Guatemala, Guyana, Haiti, Honduras, Jamaica, Mexico, Nicaragua, Panama, Paraguay, Peru, Trinidad and Tobago, Uruguay, Venezuela.

List D. 5 of the following States: Albania, Bulgaria, Byelorussian SSR, Czechoslovakia, Hungary, Poland, Romania, Ukrainian SSR, USSR.

*On 16 December 1971, the General Assembly decided to include Bahrain, Bhutan, Oman, Qatar and the United Arab Emirates in List A of those States eligible for membership in the Board.

The Industrial Development Board held its fifth session at Vienna, Austria, from 24 to 28 May and 8 June 1971.

Board Members in 1971
To serve until 31 December 1971: Brazil, Chile, Cuba, Denmark, France, India, Iraq, Japan, Kuwait, Netherlands, Poland, Sudan, Thailand, United States, Upper Volta.
To serve until 31 December 1972: Federal Republic of Germany, Ghana, Hungary, Iran, Ivory Coast, Mali, Mexico, Norway, Pakistan, Philippines, Spain, Turkey, United Kingdom, Uruguay, Venezuela.
To serve until 31 December 1973: Algeria, Argentina, Austria, Belgium, Bulgaria, Costa Rica, Egypt, Indonesia, Italy, Kenya, Madagascar, Senegal, Sweden, Switzerland, USSR.

President: Kwaku B. Asante (Ghana).
Vice-Presidents: Massimo Casilli d'Aragona (Italy); V. C. Trivedi (India); Eric M. Zeilinger (Costa Rica).
Rapporteur: Erno Hars (Hungary).

Executive Director: Ibrahim Helmi Abdel-Rahman.

On 16 December 1971, the General Assembly elected, for a three-year term expiring on 31 December 1974, the following one third of the members of the Industrial Development Board to fill seats falling vacant at the end of 1971: Brazil, Cuba, Czechoslovakia, Denmark, France, India, Japan, Kuwait, Libyan Arab Republic, Malaysia, Netherlands, Peru, Thailand, United States, Upper Volta.

Board Members for 1972
List A: Algeria, Egypt, Ghana, India, Indonesia, Iran, Ivory Coast, Kenya, Kuwait, Libyan Arab Republic, Madagascar, Malaysia, Mali, Pakistan, Philippines, Senegal, Thailand, Upper Volta.
List B: Austria, Belgium, Denmark, Federal Republic of Germany, France, Italy, Japan, Netherlands, Norway, Spain, Sweden, Switzerland, Turkey, United Kingdom, United States.
List C: Argentina, Brazil, Costa Rica, Mexico, Peru, Uruguay, Venezuela.
List D: Bulgaria, Cuba,* Czechoslovakia, Hungary, USSR.

*At the elections to the Industrial Development Board held in 1966 and 1968, and again on 16 December 1971, the General Assembly decided, upon request, that Cuba be included on those particular occasions and in those particular cases among the States listed in part D of the Annex to the Assembly's resolution 2152(XXI) of 17 November 1966, which, *inter alia,* dealt with the composition of the Industrial Development Board.

Working Group on Programme and Co-ordination
The Working Group, open to all members of the Industrial Development Board, meets prior to each annual session of the Board to consider the documentation prepared for the Board session with a view to examining UNIDO's work programmes, assessing their financial implications and reviewing problems of co-ordination in the industrial development field.

The Working Group held its third session at Vienna, Austria, from 10 to 21 May 1971.

Chairman: Kwaku B. Asante (Ghana).
Vice-Chairmen: Massimo Casilli d'Aragona (Italy); V. C. Trivedi (India); Luis Weckmann Muñoz (Mexico).
Rapporteur: Erno Hars (Hungary).

PREPARATORY COMMITTEE FOR THE UNITED NATIONS CONFERENCE ON THE HUMAN ENVIRONMENT

The Preparatory Committee held its second session at Geneva, Switzerland, from 8 to 19 February 1971, and its third session at United Nations Headquarters, New York, from 13 to 24 September 1971.

The Committee consisted of highly qualified representatives nominated by the following 27 States: Argentina, Brazil, Canada, Costa Rica, Cyprus, Czechoslovakia, Egypt, France, Ghana, Guinea, India, Iran, Italy, Jamaica, Japan, Mauritius, Mexico, Netherlands, Nigeria, Singapore, Sweden, Togo, USSR, United Kingdom, United States, Yugoslavia, Zambia.

Chairman: Keith Johnson (Jamaica).
Vice-Chairmen: Fereydoun Hoveyda (Iran); Rastislav Lacko (Czechoslovakia); Vernon J. Mwaanga (Zambia).
Rapporteur: Ove Heyman (Sweden).

The Preparatory Committee established three sessional working groups in September 1971, corresponding to the proposed three main committees of the Conference: Working Group I, on the planning and management of human settlements for environmental quality, and on the educational, informational, social and cultural aspects of environmental issues; Working Group II, on the environmental aspects of natural resources management, and on development and environment; Working Group III, on the identification and control of pollutants and nuisances of broad international significance, and on the international organizational implications of action proposals.

The Preparatory Committee also established inter-governmental working groups on the following subjects: conservation; the Declaration on the Human Environment; marine pollution; monitoring or surveillance of the human environment; and soils.

UNITED NATIONS INSTITUTE FOR TRAINING AND RESEARCH (UNITAR)

The United Nations Institute for Training and Research (UNITAR) was established in accordance with a General Assembly resolution of 11 December 1963 and came into existence in 1965. The Executive Director of the Institute reports to the General Assembly and, as appropriate, to the Economic and Social Council.

Board of Trustees
The membership of UNITAR's Board of Trustees consists of: (a) those members appointed in their personal capacities by the Secretary-General in consultation with the Presidents of the General Assembly and the Economic and Social Council; and (b) *ex-officio* members.

The Board held its tenth session from 13 to 15 September 1971 at United Nations Headquarters, New York.

Members in 1971 (to serve three-year terms, until 14 March 1973): Ralph J. Bunche (Secretariat);* Henning Friis (Denmark); Shintaro Fukushima (Japan); Richard Gardner (United States); Mahmoud H. Hammad (Egypt); Hans A. Havemann (Federal Republic of Germany); Felipe Herrera, *Vice-Chairman* (Chile); John Holmes (Canada); N. Inozemtsev (USSR); Joseph Ki-Zerbo (Upper Volta); Jacques Kosciusko-Morizet (France);

Manfred Lachs (Poland); Jiri Nosek (Secretariat); G. Parthasarathi (India); Manuel Pérez Guerrero (Venezuela); Raymond Scheyven (Belgium); Mehdi Vakil (Iran); Kenneth Younger, *Chairman* (United Kingdom).

Ex-officio Members: The Secretary-General; the President of the General Assembly; the President of the Economic and Social Council; the Executive Director of UNITAR.

Executive Director: Chief S. O. Adebo.

*Retired in June 1971. The resulting vacancy was not filled in 1971.

Administrative and Training Committee
Members in 1971: Richard Gardner (United States); Mahmoud H. Hammad (Egypt); Jacques Kosciusko-Morizet (France); Manfred Lachs (Poland); Jiri Nosek (Secretariat); Manuel Pérez Guerrero (Venezuela); Raymond Scheyven (Belgium); Mehdi Vakil (Iran); Kenneth Younger, *Chairman* (United Kingdom).
Ex-officio Member: Chief S. O. Adebo, Executive Director.

Research Committee
Members in 1971: Henning Friis (Denmark); Shintaro Fukushima (Japan); Richard Gardner (United States); Hans A. Havemann (Federal Republic of Germany); Felipe Herrera, *Chairman* (Chile); John Holmes (Canada); N. Inozemtsev (USSR); Manfred Lachs (Poland); G. Parthasarathi (India); Manuel Perez Guerrero (Venezuela).
Ex-officio Member: Chief S. O. Adebo, Executive Director.

PANEL OF EXPERTS ON THE ESTABLISHMENT OF AN INTERNATIONAL UNIVERSITY

On 11 December 1970, the General Assembly authorized the Secretary-General to set up the Panel of Experts to consist of 10 experts nominated by Governments of United Nations Member States, designated by the President of the General Assembly, and five experts designated by the Secretary-General in consultation with the Director-General of the United Nations Educational, Scientific and Cultural Organization (UNESCO) and the Executive Director of the United Nations Institute for Training and Research (UNITAR).

The Panel of Experts held two series of meetings in 1971, one between 7 and 9 July, at Geneva, Switzerland, and a second between 3 and 5 November, at United Nations Headquarters, New York.

Members in 1971: Isao Amagi (Japan);† Sir William Mansfield Cooper (United Kingdom);† Andrew W. Cordier, *Chairman* (United States);* Mohamed Hassan El-Zayyat (Egypt);† Jacques Freymond (Switzerland);* Eduardo Hardoy (Argentina);† Felipe Herrera (Chile);* Davidson S. H. W. Nicol (Sierra Leone);† G. Parthasarathi, *Alternate Chairman* (India);† Victor Sahini, *Rapporteur* (Romania);* Abdus Salam (Pakistan);* Jean A. Sirinelli (France);† Seydou Madani Sy (Senegal);† Eugenio Rodrigues Vega (Costa Rica)† (until November 1971); Benjamin Núñez (Costa Rica)† (from November 1971); Stephan Verosta (Austria).†

*Designated by the Secretary-General.
†Designated by Governments of Member States.

On 16 December 1971, the General Assembly decided that the membership of the Panel of Experts should be increased to not more than 20 to allow for the nomination of five additional experts by the Director-General of UNESCO.

The additional experts were not nominated in 1971.

UNITED NATIONS CHILDREN'S FUND (UNICEF)

The United Nations Children's Fund, established by the General Assembly, reports through the Assembly to the Economic and Social Council. (See below, under THE ECONOMIC AND SOCIAL COUNCIL.)

COMMITTEE ON THE ELIMINATION OF RACIAL DISCRIMINATION

The Committee on the Elimination of Racial Discrimination was established under the terms of article 8 of the International Convention on the Elimination of All Forms of Racial Discrimination.[4] It consists of 18 experts elected by the States parties to the Convention to serve in their personal capacity, consideration being given to equitable geographical distribution and to the representation of the different forms of civilization and principal legal systems.

Members of the Committee were elected for four-year terms; however, the terms of nine of the members, chosen by lot by the Committee Chairman after the first election, were to expire at the end of two years to ensure rotation of one half of the members every two years.

The members' terms of office began on 19 January 1970, the date of the first meeting of the Committee.

The Committee held its third session from 12 to 23 April 1971, and its fourth session from 23 August to 10 September 1971. Both sessions were held at United Nations Headquarters, New York.

Members in 1971: Mahmoud Aboul-Nasr (Egypt); Alvin Robert Cornelius* (Pakistan); Rajeshwar Dayal,* *Chairman* (India); M. Z. Getmanets* (Ukrainian SSR); A. A. Haastrup, *Vice-Chairman* (Nigeria); José D. Ingles (Philippines); Sir Herbert Marchant (United Kingdom); Gonzalo Ortiz Martín,* *Vice-Chairman* (Costa Rica); Mrs. Doris Owusu-Addo (Ghana); Karl Josef Partsch (Federal Republic of Germany); Aleksander Peles* (Yugoslavia); Zbigniew Resich,* *Vice-Chairman* (Poland); Zenon Rossides* (Cyprus); Fayez Al Sayegh, *Rapporteur* (Kuwait); S. T. M. Sukati (Swaziland); N. K. Tarassov* (USSR); Jan Tomko* (Czechoslovakia); Luis Valencia Rodríguez (Ecuador).

*Chosen by lot by the Chairman at the Committee's first meeting, on 19 January 1970, to complete their term of office at the end of two years.

In accordance with article 12 of the International Convention on the Elimination of All Forms of Racial Discrimination, the Committee on the Elimination of Racial Discrimination has the authority to establish *ad hoc* conciliation commissions to settle controversies about violations.

SPECIAL COMMITTEE TO INVESTIGATE ISRAELI PRACTICES AFFECTING THE HUMAN RIGHTS OF THE POPULATION OF THE OCCUPIED TERRITORIES
Members in 1971: Ceylon (*Chairman*), Somalia, Yugoslavia

SPECIAL COMMITTEE TO SELECT THE WINNERS OF THE UNITED NATIONS HUMAN RIGHTS PRIZE

This Committee of *ex-officio* members was established pursuant to a decision of the General Assembly of 19 December 1966 recommending that a prize or prizes in the field of human rights should be awarded not more often than at five-year intervals. The first prizes were awarded on 9 December 1968 on the occasion of the celebration of the twentieth anniversary of the Universal Declaration of Human Rights.

The Special Committee did not meet in 1971.

Members: The President of the General Assembly; the President of the Economic and Social Council; the Chairman of the Commission on Human Rights; the Chairman of the Commission on the Status of Women; and the Chairman of the Sub-Commission on Prevention of Discrimination and Protection of Minorities.

OFFICE OF THE UNITED NATIONS HIGH COMMISSIONER FOR REFUGEES (UNHCR)
High Commissioner: Prince Sadruddin Aga Khan.

[4]See Y.U.N., 1965, pp. 440-46.

Executive Committee of the Programme of the UNHCR

The Executive Committee held its twenty-second session from 4 to 12 October 1971 at Geneva, Switzerland.

Members in 1971: Algeria, Australia, Austria, Belgium, Brazil, Canada, China, Colombia, Denmark, Federal Republic of Germany, France, Greece, Holy See, Iran, Israel, Italy, Lebanon, Madagascar, Netherlands, Nigeria, Norway, Sweden, Switzerland, Tunisia, Turkey, Uganda, United Kingdom, United Republic of Tanzania, United States, Venezuela, Yugoslavia.

Chairman: M. Loveday (Australia).
Vice-Chairman: Nuzhet Kandemir (Turkey).
Rapporteur: Miss G. Rheker (Federal Republic of Germany).

AD HOC COMMITTEE OF THE WHOLE ASSEMBLY

The *Ad Hoc* Committee of the Whole Assembly consists of all Members of the United Nations, under the chairmanship of the President of the session. It meets as soon as practicable after the opening of each regular session of the General Assembly to enable Governments to announce pledges of voluntary contributions to the programmes of the United Nations High Commissioner for Refugees and the United Nations Relief and Works Agency for Palestine Refugees in the Near East for the following year. States members of specialized agencies but not also United Nations Members are invited to attend to announce their pledges to these two refugee programmes.

UNITED NATIONS JOINT STAFF PENSION BOARD

The United Nations Joint Staff Pension Board is composed of 21 members, as follows:

Six appointed by the United Nations Staff Pension Committee (two from members elected by the General Assembly, two from those appointed by the Secretary-General, two from those elected by participants).

Fifteen appointed by Staff Pension Committees of the other member organizations of the Pension Fund (two each by the following: the International Labour Organisation; the Food and Agriculture Organization; the United Nations Educational, Scientific and Cultural Organization; the World Health Organization; the International Civil Aviation Organization; and the International Atomic Energy Agency; and one each by the following: the World Meteorological Organization; the Inter-Governmental Maritime Consultative Organization; and the International Telecommunication Union).

The Board held its sixteenth session from 19 to 30 July 1971 at Geneva, Switzerland.

Members of the Pension Board in 1971

United Nations
Representing the General Assembly: Representatives: Albert F. Bender, Jr.; Svenn Refshal. Alternate: Guillermo J. McGough.
Representing the Secretary-General: Representatives: Mohamed H. Gherab; Wilbur H. Ziehl. Alternate: Maurice Heenan.
Representing the Participants: Representatives: Alfred Landau; Mrs. Patricia K. Tsien, *First Vice-Chairman.* Alternate: A. J. Friedgut.

International Labour Organisation
Representing the Executive Head: Representative: C. J. Hislaire. Alternates: A. Aboughanem; P. M. C. Denby; J. Paleologos.
Representing the Participants: Representative: N. F. MacCabe, *Rapporteur.* Alternate: K. Doctor.

Food and Agriculture Organization
Representing the Executive Head: Representative: R. Piat, *Second Vice-Chairman.* Alternate: J. Greig.
Representing the Participants: Representative: T. Rivetta.

United Nations Educational, Scientific and Cultural Organization
Representing the Governing Body: Representatives: Rupert Prohme (first week); Rafik Said (second week).
Representing the Participants: Representative: Pierre Coeytaux. Alternate: W. Zyss.

World Health Organization
Representing the Governing Body: Representative: Dr. E. Aujaleu, *Chairman.*
Representing the Participants: Representative: Dr. J. Burton. Alternate: G. Dazin.

International Civil Aviation Organization
Representing the Governing Body: Representative: G. F. Scherer.
Representing the Executive Head: Representative: J. J. Rolian.

International Atomic Energy Agency
Representing the Governing Body: Representative: C. L. Lamb.
Representing the Executive Head: Representative: L. Alonso de Huarte.

World Meteorological Organization
Representing the Governing Body: Representative: H. Panzram.

Inter-Governmental Maritime Consultative Organization
Representing the Executive Head: Representative: Kaare Stangeland.

International Telecommunication Union
Representing the Participants: Representative: C. Glinz.

Standing Committee of the Pension Board
Members in 1971 (elected at the sixteenth session of the Board):

United Nations (Group I)
Representing the General Assembly: Representative: Guillermo J. McGough. Alternates: Svenn Refshal; Albert F. Bender, Jr.; Takeshi Naito.
Representing the Secretary-General: Representative: Wilbur H. Ziehl. Alternates: Maurice Heenan; David Miron; Clayton C. Timbrell.
Representing the Participants: Representative: Mrs. Patricia K. Tsien. Alternates: Alfred Landau; A. J. Friedgut; Marc Schreiber.

Specialized Agencies (Group II)
Representing the Governing Body: Representative: Dr. E. Aujaleu (WHO). Alternate: Dr. M. U. Henry (WHO).
Representing the Executive Head: Representative: M. Bardoux (ITU), *Vice-Chairman.* Alternate: L. Alonso de Huarte (IAEA).
Representing the Participants: Representative: K. Doctor (ILO). Alternates: N. F. MacCabe (ILO); V. T. Chivers (ILO).

Specialized Agencies (Group III)
Representing the Governing Body: Representative: Rafik Said (UNESCO). Alternate: Rupert Prohme (UNESCO), *Chairman.*
Representing the Executive Head: Representative: J. J. Rolian (ICAO). Alternate: W. H. Collins (ICAO).
Representing the Participants: Representative: W. K. Mudie (FAO). Alternates: I. L. Posner (FAO); V. de Silva (FAO).

Committee of Actuaries

The Joint Staff Pension Board's Committee of Actuaries is an independent expert group whose members are appointed by the Secretary-General on the recommendation of the United Nations Joint Staff Pension Board.

Members in 1971: Gonzalo Arroba (Ecuador); Robert J. Myers (United States); Francis Netter (France).

UNITED NATIONS STAFF PENSION COMMITTEE

The United Nations Staff Pension Committee consists of three members elected by the General Assembly, three appointed by the Secretary-General and three elected by the participants in the Fund. The term of office of the elected members is three years.

Members in 1971:

Appointed by Assembly (to serve until 31 December 1973): *Members:* Albert F. Bender, Jr. (United States); Guillermo J. McGough (Argentina); Miss K. Whalley (United Kingdom).*
Alternates: Harry L. Morris (Liberia); Takeshi Naito (Japan); Svenn Refshal (Norway).

Appointed by Secretary-General (to serve until further notice): *Members:* Wilbur H. Ziehl; Mohamed H. Gherab;† David B. Vaughan. *Alternates:* Maurice Heenan; David Miron; Clayton C. Timbrell.

Appointed by Participants (to serve until 31 December 1973): *Members:* A. J. Friedgut; Alfred Landau; Mrs. Patricia K. Tsien. *Alternates:* Angel A. García; Donald R. La Marr; Marc Schreiber.

*Appointed by the General Assembly on 11 October 1971 to replace John I. M. Rhodes, who resigned with effect from 22 September 1971, for the remainder of his term of office.
†Appointed by the Secretary-General on 2 April 1971 to replace Andrew A. Stark, who resigned with effect from 3 March 1971.

INVESTMENTS COMMITTEE

The members of the Investments Committee are appointed by the Secretary-General, usually for three-year terms, after consultation with the United Nations Joint Staff Pension Board and the General Assembly's Advisory Committee on Administrative and Budgetary Questions, subject to confirmation by the General Assembly.

In 1970, in order to ensure continuity of policy, the Investments Committee and the United Nations Joint Staff Pension Board recommended to the Secretary-General that the terms of the Committee members be staggered in such a way as to avoid their ending in the same year. Accordingly, on 11 December 1970, the General Assembly confirmed the reappointment by the Secretary-General of all the members of the Committee, effective 1 January 1971, with one-year, two-year and three-year terms as follows:

To serve until 31 December 1971: Eugene R. Black; Jacques Rueff.

To serve until 31 December 1972: Roger de Candolle; R. McAllister Lloyd, *Chairman.**

To serve until 31 December 1973: George A. Murphy; B. K. Nehru.

On 21 December 1971, the General Assembly confirmed the appointment by the Secretary-General of Eugene R. Black and David Montagu to serve three-year terms, beginning 1 January 1972.

*R. McAllister Lloyd resigned as at 31 December 1971, although he agreed to continue to serve as Chairman of the Committee on an *ad hoc* basis through 1972. On 21 December 1971, the General Assembly confirmed the appointment by the Secretary-General of Jean Guyot to serve for the remainder of R. McAllister Lloyd's term of office, from 1 January to 31 December 1972.

BOARD OF AUDITORS

The three members of the Board of Auditors are appointed by the General Assembly for three-year terms.

Members in 1971: Auditor-General of Canada; Auditor-General of Colombia; Comptroller and Auditor-General of Pakistan.

On 8 November 1971, the General Assembly reappointed the Auditor-General of Colombia for a three-year term beginning 1 July 1972.

PANEL OF EXTERNAL AUDITORS

The Panel of External Auditors consists of the members of the United Nations Board of Auditors and the appointed external auditors of the specialized agencies and the International Atomic Energy Agency.

JOINT INSPECTION UNIT

The membership of the Joint Inspection Unit consists of inspectors appointed by the Secretary-General after consultation with members of the Administrative Committee on Co-ordination. The inspectors are chosen for their special experience in national or international administrative and financial matters, with due regard to equitable geographical distribution.

Members in 1971: Maurice Bertrand (France), Lucio García del Solar (Argentina), Sreten Ilic (Yugoslavia), Chandra S. Jha (India), Robert M. Macy (United States), Joseph A. Sawe (United Republic of Tanzania), Sir Leonard Scopes (United Kingdom), A. F. Sokirkin (USSR).

SPECIAL COMMITTEE FOR THE REVIEW OF THE UNITED NATIONS SALARY SYSTEM

Established by the General Assembly on 17 December 1970, the Special Committee was composed of government experts of recognized standing and experience from 11 Member States nominated by the President of the General Assembly with due regard to geographical balance.

The Special Committee held meetings between 1 June and 24 August 1971.

Members in 1971: Zakari M. Bello (Nigeria); Masao Chiba (Japan); Zbigniew Dembowski (Poland) (1 to 10 June),* Jan Chowaniec (Poland) (from 5 July); Oscar R. Faura, *Vice-Chairman* (Peru); Arthur H. M. Hillis (United Kingdom); Dayton W. Hull (United States); K. A. Mariko, *Rapporteur* (Niger); Guillermo J. McGough (Argentina), Ricardo A. Ramayon (5 to 15 July); P. Robert-Duvilliers (France) (until 15 July), Michel Maler (France) (alternate) (from 15 July); S. K. Roy, *Chairman* (India); A. V. Zakharov (USSR).

*Temporarily replaced by Edward Sabik (Poland) and Zbigniew Dabrowski (Poland) (alternates) between 10 June and 5 July.

SPECIAL COMMITTEE ON THE FINANCIAL SITUATION OF THE UNITED NATIONS

The Special Committee was established by the General Assembly on 22 December 1971 to study all the facts, as well as existing and new suggestions for a solution to the serious financial situation of the United Nations, and to consider working out concrete proposals for presentation to the General Assembly in 1972.

Members in 1971: Brazil, Canada, China, France, Ghana, India, Japan, Kenya, Mexico, Nigeria, Norway, Poland, USSR, United Kingdom, United States.

The Special Committee did not meet in 1971.

SPECIAL COMMITTEE ON THE RATIONALIZATION OF THE PROCEDURES AND ORGANIZATION OF THE GENERAL ASSEMBLY

The Special Committee was composed of 31 Member States appointed by the President of the General Assembly on the basis of equitable geographical distribution.

Members in 1971: Afghanistan, Austria, Barbados, Bolivia, Brazil, Burundi, Cameroon, Canada, Chile, Denmark, Egypt, France, Greece, India, Japan, Lebanon, Liberia, Netherlands, Nigeria, Pakistan, Philippines, Poland, Romania, Senegal, Tunisia, USSR, United Kingdom, United States, Venezuela, Yugoslavia, Zambia.

Chairman: Otto R. Borch (Denmark).

Vice-Chairmen: Ibrahima Boye (Senegal), Eugeniusz Kulaga (Poland), Motoo Ogiso (Japan).
Rapporteur: Bernardo de Azevedo Brito (until 4 June 1971) (Brazil); Ronaldo Mota Sardenberg (from 4 June 1971) (Brazil).

CONSULTATIVE PANEL ON UNITED NATIONS INFORMATION POLICIES AND PROGRAMMES

Members in 1971: The Permanent Representatives of the following United Nations Member States: Czechoslovakia, France, India, Italy, Ivory Coast, Japan, Liberia, Peru, Sudan, USSR, United Kingdom, United States, Venezuela.

On 22 December 1971, the General Assembly requested the Secretary-General to review the composition of the Consultative Panel (originally set up following a General Assembly decision of 1 December 1959) to ensure that it reflected the current situation in the United Nations. (See pp. 654-58.)

Members for 1972: The Permanent Representatives of the following United Nations Member States: Canada, China, Colombia, Czechoslovakia, France, India, Italy, Ivory Coast, Japan, Jordan, Liberia, Netherlands, People's Democratic Republic of Yemen, Peru, Poland, Romania, Sudan, Sweden, Trinidad and Tobago, Tunisia, USSR, United Kingdom, United States, Venezuela, Yugoslavia, Zaire.

UNITED NATIONS ADMINISTRATIVE TRIBUNAL

Members in 1971:
To serve until 31 December 1971: Lord Crook (United Kingdom); Francis T. P. Plimpton (United States).
To serve until 31 December 1972: Francisco Forteza (Uruguay); Zenon Rossides (Cyprus).
To serve until 31 December 1973: Mrs. Paul Bastid (France); Vincent Mutuale (Zaire); R. Venkataraman (India).

On 8 November 1971, the General Assembly appointed Francis T. P. Plimpton (United States) and Sir Roger Bentham Stevens (United Kingdom) for a three-year term beginning 1 January 1972 to fill seats falling vacant at the end of 1971.

Members for 1972: Mrs. Paul Bastid (France); Francisco Forteza (Uruguay); Vincent Mutuale (Zaire); Francis T. P. Plimpton (United States); Zenon Rossides (Cyprus); Sir Roger Bentham Stevens (United Kingdom); R. Venkataraman (India).

COMMITTEE ON APPLICATIONS FOR REVIEW OF ADMINISTRATIVE TRIBUNAL JUDGEMENTS

The Committee held its resumed eighth session between 27 January and 12 February 1971 at United Nations Headquarters, New York.

Members (from 16 September 1970) (based on composition of the General Committee at the General Assembly's twenty-fifth session): Afghanistan, Bolivia, Brazil, Cameroon, Canada, Chad, China, Ecuador, France, Iraq, Jamaica, Kenya, Malta, Mauritius, Nepal, Norway, Philippines, Romania, Senegal, Ukrainian SSR, USSR, United Kingdom, United States, Venezuela, Zambia.

The Committee held its ninth session on 5 November 1971 at United Nations Headquarters, New York.

Members (from 21 September 1971) (based on composition of the General Committee at the General Assembly's twenty-sixth session): Belgium, Bulgaria, Burundi, China, Costa Rica, Cyprus, Finland, France, Greece, Hungary, Indonesia, Ireland, Jamaica, Japan, Nigeria, People's Democratic Republic of Yemen, Peru, Philippines, Sierra Leone, Sudan, USSR, United Kingdom, United States, Venezuela, Zambia.

INTERNATIONAL LAW COMMISSION

The International Law Commission consists of 25 persons of recognized competence in international law elected by the General Assembly in their individual capacities for a five-year term. Any vacancies occurring within the five-year period are filled by the Commission.
The Commission held its twenty-third session at Geneva, Switzerland, from 26 April to 30 July 1971.

Members in 1971: Roberto Ago, *First Vice-Chairman* (Italy); Fernando Albónico (Chile); Gonzalo Alcívar (Ecuador); Milan Bartos, *Second Vice-Chairman* (Yugoslavia); Mohammed Bedjaoui (Algeria); Jorge Castañeda (Mexico); Erik Castren (Finland); Abdullah El-Erian (Egypt); Taslim O. Elias (Nigeria); Constantin T. Eustathiades (Greece); Richard D. Kearney (United States); Mr. Nagendra Singh (India); Alfred Ramangasoavina (Madagascar); Paul Reuter (France); Shabtai Rosenne (Israel); José María Ruda (Argentina); José Sette Câmara, *Rapporteur* (Brazil); Abdul Hakim Tabibi (Afghanistan); Arnold J. P. Tammes (Netherlands); Doudou Thiam (Senegal); Senjin Tsuruoka, *Chairman* (Japan); N. A. Ushakov (USSR); Endre Ustor (Hungary); Sir Humphrey Waldock (United Kingdom); Mustafa Kamil Yasseen (Iraq).

On 17 November 1971, the General Assembly elected the following as members of the International Law Commission for a period of 5 years, commencing 1 January 1972:
Roberto Ago (Italy), Gonzalo Alcívar (Ecuador), Milan Bartos (Yugoslavia), Mohammed Bedjaoui (Algeria), Suat Bilge (Turkey), Jorge Castañeda (Mexico), Abdullah El-Erian (Egypt), Taslim O. Elias (Nigeria), Edvard Hambro (Norway), Richard D. Kearney (United States), Mr. Nagendra Singh (India), R. Q. Quentin-Baxter (New Zealand), Alfred Ramangasoavina (Madagascar), Paul Reuter (France), Zenon Rossides (Cyprus), José María Ruda (Argentina), José Sette Câmara (Brazil), Abdul Hakim Tabibi (Afghanistan), Arnold J. P. Tammes (Netherlands), Doudou Thiam (Senegal), Senjin Tsuruoka (Japan), N. A. Ushakov (USSR), Endre Ustor (Hungary), Sir Humphrey Waldock (United Kingdom), Mustafa Kamil Yasseen (Iraq).

COMMITTEE ON ARRANGEMENTS FOR A CONFERENCE FOR THE PURPOSE OF REVIEWING THE CHARTER

All Members of the United Nations are members of the Committee.
The Committee did not meet in 1971.

SPECIAL COMMITTEE ON THE QUESTION OF DEFINING AGGRESSION

The Special Committee is composed of 35 members appointed by the President of the General Assembly, taking into consideration the principle of equitable geographical representation and the necessity that the principal legal systems of the world be represented.
The Special Committee held a series of meetings from 1 February to 5 March 1971, at United Nations Headquarters, New York.

Members in 1971: Algeria, Australia, Bulgaria, Canada, Colombia, Cyprus, Czechoslovakia, Ecuador, Egypt, Finland, France, Ghana, Guyana, Haiti, Indonesia, Iran, Iraq, Italy, Japan, Madagascar, Mexico, Norway, Romania, Sierra Leone, Spain, Sudan, Syrian Arab Republic, Turkey, Uganda, USSR, United Kingdom, United States, Uruguay, Yugoslavia, Zaire.

Chairman: Augusto Legnani (Uruguay).
Vice-Chairmen: Matti Cawen (Finland), Ilja Hulinsky (Czechoslovakia), Vincent Mutuale (Zaire).
Rapporteur: Riyadh Al-Qaysi (Iraq).

Working Group
The Working Group, established in 1970 by the Special Committee, was re-established on 2 February 1971 to assist the Committee in formulating an agreed or generally accepted definition of aggression.

On 12 February 1971, the Special Committee decided that the membership of the Working Group would be: the Rapporteur of the Special Committee, and Cyprus, Ecuador, Egypt, France, Ghana, the USSR, the United Kingdom, the United States.

COMMISSION ON PERMANENT SOVEREIGNTY OVER NATURAL RESOURCES

Members in 1971: Afghanistan, Chile, Egypt, Guatemala, Netherlands, Philippines, Sweden, USSR, United States.

The Commission did not meet in 1971.

ADVISORY COMMITTEE ON THE UNITED NATIONS PROGRAMME OF ASSISTANCE IN THE TEACHING, STUDY, DISSEMINATION AND WIDER APPRECIATION OF INTERNATIONAL LAW

The Advisory Committee held its sixth session from 12 October to 8 November 1971, at United Nations Headquarters, New York.

Members in 1971: Belgium, Ecuador, France, Ghana, Hungary, Iraq, USSR, United Kingdom, United Republic of Tanzania, United States.

Chairman: Osei Tutu (Ghana).

On 18 December 1971, the General Assembly elected the following 13 members* to a four-year term of office beginning 1 January 1972: Barbados, Belgium, Cyprus, El Salvador, France, Ghana, Hungary, Iraq, Mali, USSR, United Kingdom, United Republic of Tanzania, United States.

*The General Assembly concurrently enlarged the Advisory Committee from 10 to 13 members.

UNITED NATIONS COMMISSION ON INTERNATIONAL TRADE LAW

The 29 States comprising the Commission's membership are elected by the General Assembly for six-year terms, in accordance with a formula providing equitable geographical representation and adequate representation of the principle economic and legal systems of the world. The terms of one half the members expire every three years.

The Commission held its fourth session from 29 March to 20 April 1971, at Geneva, Switzerland.

Members in 1971:

To serve until 31 December 1973: Argentina, Australia, Belgium, Brazil, Hungary, India, Iran, Kenya, Mexico, Romania, Spain, Syrian Arab Republic, Tunisia, United States, Zaire.

To serve until 31 December 1976: Austria, Chile, Egypt, France, Ghana, Guyana, Japan, Nigeria, Norway, Poland, Singapore, USSR, United Kingdom, United Republic of Tanzania.

Chairman: Mr. Nagendra Singh (India).
Vice-Chairmen: Joaquín Garrigues Díaz-Cañabate (Spain), Nehemias Gueiros (Brazil), Jerzy Jakubowski (Poland).
Rapporteur: Joseph D. Ogundere (Nigeria).

Working Group on Time-Limits and Limitations (Prescription) in the International Sale of Goods
The Working Group held its third session at United Nations Headquarters, New York, from 30 August to 10 September 1971.

Members in 1971: Argentina, Belgium (*Rapporteur*), Egypt, Japan, Norway (*Chairman*), Poland, United Kingdom.

Working Group on the International Sale of Goods
Members in 1971: Austria,* Brazil, France, Ghana, Hungary, India, Iran, Japan, Kenya, Mexico, Tunisia, USSR, United Kingdom, United States.

The Working Group did not meet in 1971.

*On 20 April 1971, Austria was appointed a member of the Working Group to replace Norway.

Working Group on International Legislation on Shipping
The Working Group held its second session from 22 to 26 March 1971, in Geneva, Switzerland.

Members in 1971: Chile, India, Egypt, USSR, United Kingdom, United States.

Chairman: Rafael Lasalvia (Chile).
Rapporteur: D. A. Kamat (India).

The Working Group was enlarged by the Commission at its fourth session, and met on 6 April. The members of the enlarged Working Group were: Argentina, Australia, Belgium, Brazil, Chile, Egypt, France, Ghana, Hungary, India, Japan, Nigeria, Norway, Poland, Singapore, Spain, USSR, United Kingdom, United Republic of Tanzania, United States, Zaire.

Chairman: Mr. Nagendra Singh (India).
Vice-Chairman: Gervasio Ramón Carlos Colombres (Argentina).

COMMITTEE ON RELATIONS WITH THE HOST COUNTRY

On 15 December 1971, the General Assembly established the Committee on Relations with the Host Country, which was to be composed of the host country and 14 Member States chosen by the President of the General Assembly, taking into consideration equitable geographical representation.

On 21 December 1971, the President of the General Assembly announced the appointment of the following as members of the Committee: Argentina, Bulgaria, Canada, China, Cyprus, France, Guyana, Iraq, Ivory Coast, Mali, Spain, USSR, United Kingdom, United Republic of Tanzania. The United States, as host country, is the fifteenth member of the Committee.

The Committee held one meeting in 1971, on 28 December.

Chairman: Zenon Rossides (Cyprus).

The Security Council

The Security Council consists of 15 Members of the United Nations in accordance with the provisions of Article 23 of the United Nations Charter as amended in 1965.

Members of the Council in 1971
Permanent Members: China, France, USSR, United Kingdom, United States.
Non-Permanent Members: Argentina, Belgium, Burundi, Italy, Japan, Nicaragua, Poland, Sierra Leone, Somalia, Syrian Arab Republic.

On 23 November 1971, the General Assembly elected Guinea, India, Panama, Sudan and Yugoslavia to serve for a two-year term ending 31 December 1973, to replace Burundi, Nicaragua, Poland, Sierra Leone and the Syrian Arab Republic, whose terms of office were due to expire on 31 December 1971.

Members of the Council for 1972
Permanent Members: China, France, USSR, United Kingdom, United States.

Non-Permanent Members:
  To serve until 31 December 1972: Argentina, Belgium, Italy, Japan, Somalia.
  To serve until 31 December 1973: Guinea, India, Panama, Sudan, Yugoslavia.

Presidents of the Council in 1971
The Presidency of the Council rotates monthly, according to the English alphabetical listing of its member States. The following served as Presidents during 1971:

Month	Member
January	United Kingdom
February	United States
March	Argentina
April	Belgium
May	Burundi
June	China
July	France
August	Italy
September	Japan
October	Nicaragua
November	Poland
December	Sierra Leone

Military Staff Committee

The Military Staff Committee met fortnightly throughout 1971. The first meeting was held on 14 January 1971 and the last on 30 December 1971.

The members consisted of army, navy and air force representatives of China, France, the USSR, the United Kingdom and the United States.

Disarmament Commission

The Commission reports to both the General Assembly and the Security Council. (See above, under THE GENERAL ASSEMBLY.)

Collective Measures Committee

The Committee reports to both the General Assembly and the Security Council. (See above, under THE GENERAL ASSEMBLY.)

Standing Committees

There are two standing committees of the Security Council: the Committee of Experts (established in 1946, to examine the provisional rules of procedure of the Council and any other matters entrusted to it by the Security Council); and the Committee on the Admission of New Members. Each is composed of representatives of all Council members.

Ad hoc bodies

UNITED NATIONS COMMISSION FOR INDONESIA
Members: Australia, Belgium, United States.

On 1 April 1961, the Commission adjourned *sine die.*

UNITED NATIONS TRUCE SUPERVISION ORGANIZATION
IN PALESTINE (UNTSO)
Chief of Staff: Major-General Ensio P. H. Siilasvuo.

UNITED NATIONS MIDDLE EAST MISSION (UNMEM):
SPECIAL REPRESENTATIVE OF THE SECRETARY-
GENERAL TO THE MIDDLE EAST
Gunnar V. Jarring.

UNITED NATIONS REPRESENTATIVE FOR INDIA
AND PAKISTAN (UNRIP)
Frank P. Graham.

UNITED NATIONS MILITARY OBSERVER GROUP
IN INDIA AND PAKISTAN (UNMOGIP)
Chief Military Observer: Lieutenant-General Luis Tassara González.

SUB-COMMITTEE ON THE SITUATION IN ANGOLA
The Sub-Committee reports to both the General Assembly and the Security Council. (See above, under THE GENERAL ASSEMBLY.) It adjourned *sine die* after consideration of its reports at the General Assembly's seventeenth session in December 1962.

SPECIAL COMMITTEE ON *APARTHEID*
The Committee reports to both the General Assembly and the Security Council. (See above, under THE GENERAL ASSEMBLY.)

UNITED NATIONS PEACE-KEEPING FORCE IN
CYPRUS (UNFICYP)
Commander: Major-General Dewan Prem Chand.
Special Representative of the Secretary-General in Cyprus: Bibiano F. Osorio-Tafall.

(For a list of United Nations Member States which have contributed personnel to the Force, see above, p. 216.)

COMMITTEE ESTABLISHED IN PURSUANCE OF
SECURITY COUNCIL RESOLUTION 253(1968)
(on sanctions for Southern Rhodesia)
The Committee consists of all the members of the Security Council. The chairmanship is rotated monthly in English alphabetical order according to the presidency of the Security Council.

AD HOC SUB-COMMITTEE ON NAMIBIA
*(established in pursuance of Security
Council resolution 283(1970))*
An *Ad Hoc* Sub-Committee established in pursuance of Security Council resolution 276(1970) was re-established on 29 July 1970 by resolution 283 to study further ways of implementing resolutions on Namibia and to study replies submitted by Governments in response to the recommendations adopted by the Security Council.
The *Ad Hoc* Sub-Committee consists of all the members of the Security Council.

Chairman: Nsanzé Térence (Burundi).

COMMITTEE OF EXPERTS ESTABLISHED BY THE
SECURITY COUNCIL AT ITS 1506TH MEETING
(on the question of micro-States)
The Committee consists of all the members of the Security Council. The chairmanship is rotated monthly in English alphabetical order.

1971 SPECIAL MISSION TO GUINEA
*(established by Security Council resolution 295(1971)
and consensus of 26 August 1971)*
Members: Argentina, Syrian Arab Republic.

1971 SPECIAL MISSION TO SENEGAL
*(established by Security Council
resolution 294(1971))*
Members: Belgium, Burundi, Japan, Nicaragua, Poland, Syrian Arab Republic.

The Economic and Social Council

The Economic and Social Council consists of 27 Members of the United Nations, elected by the General Assembly, each for a three-year term of office.

Members of the Council in 1971

To serve until 31 December 1971: Indonesia, Jamaica, Norway, Pakistan, Sudan, USSR, United Kingdom, Uruguay, Yugoslavia.
To serve until 31 December 1972: Brazil, Ceylon, France, Ghana, Greece, Italy, Kenya, Peru, Tunisia.
To serve until 31 December 1973: Haiti, Hungary, Lebanon, Madagascar, Malaysia, New Zealand, Niger, United States, Zaire.

On 23 November 1971, the General Assembly elected Bolivia, Burundi, Chile, China, Finland, Japan, Poland, the USSR and the United Kingdom for a three-year term ending on 31 December 1974, to replace the nine members whose terms of office were to expire on 31 December 1971.

Members of the Council for 1972

Bolivia, Brazil, Burundi, Ceylon, Chile, China, Finland, France, Ghana, Greece, Haiti, Hungary, Italy, Japan, Kenya, Lebanon, Madagascar, Malaysia, New Zealand, Niger, Peru, Poland, Tunisia, USSR, United Kingdom, United States, Zaire.

Sessions in 1971

Organizational Meetings for Fiftieth Session, held at United Nations Headquarters, New York, from 11 to 13 January 1971.
Fiftieth Session, held at United Nations Headquarters, New York, from 26 April to 21 May 1971.
Fifty-first Session, held at Geneva, Switzerland, from 5 to 30 July 1971, and resumed at United Nations Headquarters, New York, on 27-29 October, 23 and 30 November and 20 December 1971.

Officers of the Council in 1971

President: Rachid Driss (Tunisia).
Vice-Presidents: João Augusto de Araujo Castro (Brazil);* Costa P. Caranicas (Greece); Karoly Szarka (Hungary).

*On 5 July 1971, the Council elected Sérgio Armando Frazão (Brazil) as Vice-President to replace João Augusto de Araujo Castro, who had resigned.

SUBSIDIARY AND OTHER RELATED ORGANS

SUBSIDIARY ORGANS
Subsidiary organs reporting to the Economic and Social Council consist of functional commissions, regional economic commissions, standing committees and *ad hoc* committees. In addition, there are three sessional committees of the whole. An Administrative Committee on Co-ordination also reports to the Council. (For details, see below.)

OTHER RELATED BODIES
A number of other United Nations organs, though not established by the Economic and Social Council, report in various ways to the Council or through it to other bodies. (For details, see below.)

Sessional Committees

Each of the Economic and Social Council's sessional committees consists of all the members of the Council.

Sessional Committees in 1971
Economic Committee
Social Committee
Co-ordination Committee

Officers of the Sessional Committees in 1971
Economic Committee *Chairman:* Costa P. Caranicas (Greece).

Social Committee *Chairman:* Karoly Szarka (Hungary).
Co-ordination Committee *Chairman:* Sérgio Armando Frazão (Brazil).

On 30 July 1971, the Economic and Social Council recommended that the General Assembly amend the Charter in order to enlarge the Council's membership from 27 to 54. The Economic and Social Council concurrently decided to enlarge its sessional committees as from 1972, pending receipt of the necessary ratifications to the proposed Charter amendment.

On 20 December 1971, the General Assembly adopted an amendment to the Charter which would enlarge the membership of the Economic and Social Council to 54, and submitted the amendment for ratification by United Nations Member States.

Functional Commissions and Subsidiaries

The Economic and Social Council has six functional commissions and one sub-commission. Of these, the Population Commission, the Statistical Commission and the Commission on Narcotic Drugs, meet once every two years.

The Commission on Human Rights and its Sub-Commission on Prevention of Discrimination and Protection of Minorities meet annually.

On 8 August 1969, the Economic and Social Council decided that, starting in 1971, the Commission for Social Development and the Commission on the Status of Women,* which had hitherto met annually, were to meet biennially.

*By a resolution of 15 December 1969, the General Assembly urged the Economic and Social Council to reconsider its decision of 8 August 1969 so that the Commission on the Status of Women might continue to meet annually; on 31 July 1970, the Council reaffirmed its decision that the Commission should meet biennially with effect from 1 January 1971.

STATISTICAL COMMISSION
The Statistical Commission consists of 24 members, elected for four-year terms by the Economic and Social Council.

Members in 1971:
To serve until 31 December 1971: Australia, Cuba, Czechoslovakia, Egypt, Ghana, India, Indonesia, Ukrainian SSR.
To serve until 31 December 1972: Brazil, Denmark, France, Panama, Philippines, Poland, Thailand, United Kingdom.
To serve until 31 December 1973: Belgium, Ireland, Libyan Arab Republic, Morocco, Uganda, USSR, United States, Venezuela.

The Statistical Commission did not meet in 1971.
On 20 May 1971, the Economic and Social Council elected the following seven members for terms of office starting on 1 January 1972 to fill vacancies occurring on 31 December 1971: Czechoslovakia, Ghana, India, Kenya, Malaysia, Spain, Ukrainian SSR. The election of the eighth member was deferred until 1972.*

*On 7 January 1972, the Economic and Social Council elected Argentina as the eighth new member.

Members for 1972: Argentina, Belgium, Brazil, Czechoslovakia, Denmark, France, Ghana, India, Ireland, Kenya, Libyan Arab Republic, Malaysia, Morocco, Panama, Philippines, Poland, Spain, Thailand, Uganda, Ukrainian SSR, USSR, United Kingdom, United States, Venezuela.

POPULATION COMMISSION
The Population Commission consists of 27 members, elected for four-year terms by the Economic and Social Council.

Members in 1971:
To serve until 31 December 1971: Central African Republic, Egypt,

France, Ghana, Indonesia, Jamaica, Pakistan, Sweden, Ukrainian SSR.

To serve until 31 December 1972: Brazil, Czechoslovakia, Denmark, India, Kenya, New Zealand, Spain, Upper Volta, Venezuela.

To serve until 31 December 1973: Barbados, Gabon, Haiti, Iran, Japan, Tunisia, USSR, United Kingdom, United States.

The members and their chief representatives at the Commission's sixteenth session, held at Geneva, Switzerland, from 1 to 12 November 1971, were as follows:

Barbados: C. G. Alleyne. Brazil: J. L. Madeira; Eduardo Hermanny (alternate). Central African Republic: (not represented). Czechoslovakia: V. Wynnyczuk, *Vice-Chairman*; Jaroslav Stahl (alternate). Denmark: M. Boserup, *Rapporteur*. Egypt: Youssri Rizk (alternate). France: A. Sauvy; J. Bourgeois-Pichat (alternate). Gabon: Jean-Marie Aubame. Ghana: K. T. de Graft-Johnson, *Vice-Chairman*. Haiti: (not represented). India: A. Chandra Sekhar, *Chairman*. Indonesia: N. Iskandar. Iran: D. Behnam; Ebrahim Djahannema (alternate). Jamaica: G. W. Roberts, *Vice-Chairman*. Japan: T. Kuroda. Kenya: S. S. Heyer (alternate). New Zealand: J. P. Lewin. Pakistan: W. Ahmed; Tariq Osman Hyder (alternate). Spain: S. del Campo. Sweden: Mrs. U. Lindstrom; M. Tottie (alternate). Tunisia: Hassen Abbas, S. Annabi (alternates). Ukrainian SSR: V. F. Burlin. USSR: V. E. Ovsienko (alternate). United Kingdom: Miss J. Thompson; E. Grebenik (alternate). United States: W. H. Draper, Jr.; P. P. Claxton (alternate). Upper Volta: (not represented). Venezuela: B. Vildosola (alternate).

On 20 May 1971, the Economic and Social Council elected the following for terms of office starting on 1 January 1972 to fill vacancies occurring on 31 December 1971: Egypt, France, Ghana, Indonesia, Morocco, Peru, Philippines, Sweden, Ukrainian SSR.

Members for 1972: Barbados, Brazil, Czechoslovakia, Denmark, Egypt, France, Gabon, Ghana, Haiti, India, Indonesia, Iran, Japan, Kenya, Morocco, New Zealand, Peru, Philippines, Spain, Sweden, Tunisia, Ukrainian SSR, USSR, United Kingdom, United States, Upper Volta, Venezuela.

COMMISSION FOR SOCIAL DEVELOPMENT

The Commission for Social Development consists of 32 members, elected for four-year terms by the Economic and Social Council.

Members in 1971:

To serve until 31 December 1971: Byelorussian SSR, Congo, Cuba, France, Gabon, India, Lebanon, Netherlands, USSR, United States, Venezuela.

To serve until 31 December 1972: Canada, Chile, Czechoslovakia, Guatemala, Italy, Mauritania, Philippines, Sierra Leone, Sweden, Thailand.

To serve until 31 December 1974: Cameroon, Costa Rica, Cyprus, Egypt, Jamaica, Japan, Somalia, Spain, Tunisia, United Kingdom, Yugoslavia.

On 8 August 1969, the Economic and Social Council decided that, starting in 1971, the Commission for Social Development, which had hitherto met annually and whose members served three-year terms of office, would meet biennially, with its members serving four-year terms of office.

On 20 May 1971, the Economic and Social Council elected the following for terms of office starting on 1 January 1972 to fill vacancies occurring on 31 December 1971: Belgium, Dominican Republic, France, India, Indonesia, Ivory Coast, Nigeria, Ukrainian SSR, USSR, United States, Uruguay.

Members for 1972: Belgium, Cameroon, Canada, Chile, Costa Rica, Cyprus, Czechoslovakia, Dominican Republic, Egypt, France, Guatemala, India, Indonesia, Italy, Ivory Coast, Jamaica, Japan, Mauritania, Nigeria, Philippines, Sierra Leone, Somalia, Spain, Sweden, Thailand, Tunisia, Ukrainian SSR, USSR, United Kingdom, United States, Uruguay, Yugoslavia.

The members and their chief representatives at the Commission's twenty-second session, held at United Nations Headquarters, New York, from 1 to 22 March 1971, were as follows:

Byelorussian SSR: V. I. Luzgin, *Vice-Chairman*; P.I. Dolgovechny (alternate). Cameroon: Philippe Mataga; Souaibou Hayatou (alternate). Canada: John A. Macdonald, *Vice-Chairman*; Justin Ciale (alternate). Chile: Vicente Sánchez; Fernando Montaner (alternate). Congo: Philippe Gouamba. Costa Rica: José Luis Molina; Mrs. Emilia C. de Barish (alternate). Cuba: Ricardo Alarcón de Quesada. Cyprus: Mikis Demetriou Sparsis; Costas Papademas (alternate). Czechoslovakia: Josef Siktanc (alternate). Egypt: Ahmed Mohamed Khalifa, *Chairman*; Amre M. Moussa (alternate). France: Jacques Megret; Jean-Dominique Paolini (alternate). Gabon: Alfred Boucah. Guatemala: Mario Efraín Nájera-Farfán. India: Khaleeq Ahmed Naqvi; Ranjit Gupta, K. P. Saksena (alternates). Italy: Miss Maria A. Cao-Pinna. Jamaica: Hector Gibson, *Rapporteur*; H. Dale Anderson (alternate). Japan: Isamu Miyazaki; Kunio Katakura (alternate). Lebanon: Yahya Mahmassani (alternate). Mauritania: Abdou Ould Hachème. Netherlands: Mrs. D. Heroma-Meilink. Philippines: Leandro I. Verceles (alternate). Sierra Leone: Mrs. Rosalind O. Forde. Somalia: Hassan Kaid Abdulleh; Miss Fatima Issak Bihi (alternate). Spain: Manuel Alonso Olea; Alvaro Fernández-Villaverde (alternate). Sweden: Miss Lisa Mattson; H. Granqvist, Mrs. Madeleine Stroje-Wilkens (alternates). Thailand: Malai Huvanandana, *Vice-Chairman*; Thamnong Charurat (alternate). Tunisia: Mohamed Fourati (adviser). USSR: N. A. Kovalsky. United Kingdom: Duncan Fairn; A. R. G. Prosser (alternate). United States: Mrs. Jean Picker. Venezuela: Tulio Alvarado, Miss Franca Baroni (alternates). Yugoslavia: Mrs. Vida Tomsic; Naste Calovski (alternate).

**Advisory Committee of Experts
on the Prevention of Crime
and the Treatment of Offenders***

The Advisory Committee was composed of 10 members appointed by the Secretary-General to serve in their individual capacities as experts.

Members in 1971: Duncan Fairn (United Kingdom); Ahmed Mohamed Khalifa (Egypt); Thomas Adeoye Lambo, *Chairman* (Nigeria); Pietro Manca (Italy); H. G. Moeller, *Rapporteur* (United States); Norval Morris (Australia);† Atsushi Nagashima (Japan); Khaleeq Ahmed Naqvi (India); José A. Alves da Cruz Ríos (Brazil); B. A. Victorov (USSR).

†Did not attend.

The Advisory Committee held its fifth and final session at United Nations Headquarters, New York, from 19 to 26 July 1971.

*See below, p. 804, Committee on Crime Prevention and Control.

**Advisory Committee for the Research and
Training Programme in Regional Development**

The Advisory Committee did not meet in 1971.

COMMISSION ON HUMAN RIGHTS

The Commission on Human Rights consists of 32 members, elected for three-year terms by the Economic and Social Council.

Members in 1971:

To serve until 31 December 1971: Chile, Egypt, Finland, Iran, Mauritania, New Zealand, Senegal, Ukrainian SSR, United States, Uruguay, Yugoslavia.

To serve until 31 December 1972: Ghana, Guatemala, Iraq, Morocco, Netherlands, Peru, Poland, Turkey, United Kingdom, Zaire.

To serve until 31 December 1973: Austria, France, India, Lebanon, Mauritius, Mexico, Pakistan, Philippines, USSR, United Republic of Tanzania, Venezuela.

The members and their chief representatives attending the Commission's twenty-seventh session, held at Geneva, Switzerland, from 22 February to 26 March 1971, were as follows:

Austria: Felix Ermacora; Franz Ceska (alternate). Chile: Rafael Gumucio; Fernando Gamboa (alternate). Egypt: Hussein Khallaf; Abdel Raouf El Reedy, Youssri Rizk, Mrs. Mervat El Talawi, Sami Draz (alternates). Finland: Voitto Saario; Klaus Tornudd (alternate). France: Pierre Juvigny; Mrs. Nicole Questiaux (alternate). Ghana: Kofi Sekyiama (alternate). Guatemala: Carlos García-Bauer. India: Mrs. Leela Damodara Menon; A. S. Mani, P. M. S. Malik (alternates). Iran: Princess Ashraf Pahlavi; Parvis Radji (alternate). Iraq: Hisham Al-Shawi. Lebanon: Suleiman Sein; Mrs. Ruby Homsey (alternate). Mauritania: S. A. Ould Taya (alternate). Mauritius: Radha Ramphul. Mexico: Miss María Lavalle Urbina. Morocco: Ahmed Kettani, *Vice-Chairman*; Mohamed Al Arbi Khat (alternate). Netherlands: T. C. van Boven, *Vice-Chairman*; Miss F. Y. van der Wal (alternate). New Zealand: R. Q. Quentin-Baxter; B. W. P. Absolum (alternate). Pakistan: Abu Sayeed Chowdhury; Tariq Osman Hyder (alternate). Peru: Mario Alzamore Váldez; Luis Solari Tudela (alternate). Philippines: Narciso G. Reyes, *Rapporteur*; Virgilio C. Nañagas (alternate). Poland: Zbigniew Resich, *Vice-Chairman*; Jerzy Osiecki, Mrs. Helena Dobrzynska (alternates). Senegal: Ibrahima Boye. Turkey: Suat Bilge; Nuzhet Kandemir, Tugay Ulucevik, Miss Hulya Taylaner (alternates). Ukrainian SSR: I. Lukashuk (alternate). USSR: N. K. Tarassov; L. Verenikin (alternate). United Kingdom: Sir Keith Unwin; Miss Tessa A. Solesby (alternate). United Republic of Tanzania: Mahmud N. Rattansey. United States: Mrs. Rita E. Hauser; Warren E. Hewitt (alternate). Uruguay: Héctor Gros-Espiell; Sergio Pittaluga (alternate). Venezuela: Andrés Aguilar, *Chairman*; Pedro E. Coll (alternate). Yugoslavia: Branimir M. Jankovic; Milan Sahovic, Milan Ristic (alternates). Zaire: Nicolas Bofunga.

On 25 May 1971, the Economic and Social Council elected the following for terms of office starting on 1 January 1972 to fill vacancies occurring on 31 December 1971: Byelorussian SSR, Chile, Ecuador, Egypt, Iran, Italy, Nigeria, Norway, Romania, Senegal, United States.

Members for 1972: Austria, Byelorussian SSR, Chile, Ecuador, Egypt, France, Ghana, Guatemala, India, Iran, Iraq, Italy, Lebanon, Mauritius, Mexico, Morocco, Netherlands, Nigeria, Norway, Pakistan, Peru, Philippines, Poland, Romania, Senegal, Turkey, USSR, United Kingdom, United Republic of Tanzania, United States, Venezuela, Zaire.

Sub-Commission on Prevention
of Discrimination and
Protection of Minorities
The 26 members of the Sub-Commission are elected by the Commission on Human Rights from nominations of experts made by States Members of the United Nations in accordance with a scheme to ensure equitable geographical distribution. The members serve in their individual capacities as experts, rather than as governmental representatives, for three-year terms.

Members: Mohamed A. Abu Rannat (Sudan); Peter Calvocoressi (United Kingdom); Francesco Capotorti (Italy); Alvin Robert Cornelius (Pakistan); Aurel Cristescu (Romania);* Adib Daoudy (Syrian Arab Republic); Vicente Díaz Samayoa (Guatemala); I. J. D. Durlong (Nigeria); Clarence Clyde Ferguson, Jr. (United States); Miss Mary N. Gichuru (Kenya); Héctor Gros-Espiell (Uruguay); John P. Humphrey (Canada); Simon Ilako (Zaire); José D. Ingles (Philippines); Branimir M. Jankovic (Yugoslavia); Pierre Juvigny (France); Ahmed Kettani (Morocco); Ahmed Mohamed Khalifa (Egypt); Antonio Martínez Báez (Mexico); José R. Martínez Cobo (Ecuador); Erik Nettel (Austria); Paul Nikiema (Upper Volta); Nicodème Ruhashyankiki (Rwanda); Y. M. Rybakov (USSR); Hernán Santa Cruz (Chile); Waldo E. Waldron-Ramsey (Barbados).

*On 25 March 1971, Aurel Cristescu (Romania) was elected by the Commission on Human Rights to fill the vacancy left by the

resignation of Alexander Bolintineanu (Romania), for the remainder of the latter's term of office.

The Sub-Commission held its twenty-fourth session at United Nations Headquarters, New York, from 2 to 20 August 1971. The following members and alternates attended:

Mohamed A. Abu Rannat (Sudan). Peter Calvocoressi; Miss Tessa A. Solesby (alternate) (United Kingdom). Antonio Cassese (alternate) (Italy). Aurel Cristescu, *Vice-Chairman* (Romania). Adib Daoudy (Syrian Arab Republic). Juan Carlos Delprée-Crespo (alternate) (Guatemala). I. J. D. Durlong; Adamu Mohammed (alternate) (Nigeria). Clarence Clyde Ferguson, Jr.; John Carey, George Gowen (alternates) (United States). Miss Mary N. Gichuru, *Rapporteur* (Kenya). Héctor Gros-Espiell, *Chairman* (Uruguay). John P. Humphrey (Canada). Simon Ilako (Zaire). José D. Ingles; Cecilio R. Espejo (alternate) (Philippines). Branimir M. Jankovic (Yugoslavia). Pierre Juvigny (France). Ahmed Kettani (Morocco). Ahmed Mohamed Khalifa; Amre M. Moussa (alternate) (Egypt). Najmul Saguib Khan, Munir Akram (alternates) (Pakistan). Ricardo Lagos (alternate) (Chile). Antonio Martínez Baéz (Mexico). José R. Martínez Cobo (Ecuador). Erik Nettel, *Vice-Chairman* (Austria). Paul Nikiema (Upper Volta). Nicodème Ruhashyankiki (Rwanda). Y. M. Rybakov; N. I. Yevdokeev (alternate) (USSR).

Ad Hoc Committee on Periodic
Reports on Human Rights
The *Ad Hoc* Committee, a subsidiary of the Commission on Human Rights, held its 1971 meetings between 15 and 19 February at Geneva, Switzerland.

Members in 1971: France, Philippines (*Chairman/Rapporteur*), Poland, Senegal, USSR, United Kingdom, United States, Venezuela.

Ad Hoc Working Group of Experts
on the Treatment of Political
Prisoners in Southern Africa
(established by resolutions 2(XXIII) and 2(XXIV) adopted on 6 March 1967 and 16 February 1968, respectively, by the Commission on Human Rights)

The mandate of the Working Group included consideration of allegations of infringements of trade union rights in southern Africa.
The Working Group held meetings at United Nations Headquarters, New York, between 7 and 19 January 1971 and between 28 June and 6 July 1971.

Members in 1971: Ibrahima Boye, *Chairman/Rapporteur* (Senegal); Felix Ermacora (Austria); Branimir M. Jankovic, *Vice-Chairman* (Yugoslavia); N. N. Jha (India); Mahmud N. Rattansey (United Republic of Tanzania);* Luis Marchand Stens (Peru).

*Appointed on 25 March 1971 by the Chairman of the Commission on Human Rights to fill the vacancy left by the departure of Waldo E. Waldron-Ramsey (Barbados).

Special Working Group of Experts to Investigate
Allegations of Human Rights
Violations in Occupied Areas in the Middle East
(established by resolution 6(XXV) adopted on 4 March 1969 by the Commission on Human Rights)

The Special Working Group was established by the Commission on Human Rights to investigate allegations of violations by Israel of the 1949 Geneva Convention (relative to the protection of civilian persons in time of war) in territories occupied by Israel as a result of hostilities in the Middle East, and for that purpose to receive communications and to hear witnesses. It was composed of the members of the Commission's *Ad Hoc* Working Group of Experts on the treatment of political prisoners in South Africa (see above).

COMMISSION ON THE STATUS OF WOMEN
The Commission consists of 32 members, elected for four-year terms by the Economic and Social Council.

Members in 1971:
To serve until 31 December 1971: Chile, Costa Rica, France, Liberia, Malaysia, Morocco, Nicaragua, Norway, Philippines, Romania.
To serve until 31 December 1972: Austria, Belgium, Canada, Colombia, Egypt, Hungary, Iran, Iraq, Mauritania, Tunisia, Uruguay.
To serve until 31 December 1974: Byelorussian SSR, Central African Republic, Dominican Republic, Finland, Indonesia, Nigeria, Thailand, USSR, United Kingdom, United States, Zaire.

The Commission did not meet in 1971.

On 8 August 1969, the Economic and Social Council decided that, starting in 1971, the Commission on the Status of Women, which had hitherto met annually and whose members served three-year terms of office, would meet biennially, with its members serving four-year terms of office; the Council reaffirmed this decision on 31 July 1970.
On 20 May 1971, the Economic and Social Council elected the following for terms of office starting on 1 January 1972 to fill vacancies occurring on 31 December 1971: Costa Rica, France, Japan, Kenya, Liberia, Norway, Romania.
On 30 July 1971, the Council elected Argentina, Chile and Philippines for terms of office to fill the remaining vacancies occurring on 31 December 1971.

Members for 1972: Argentina, Austria, Belgium, Byelorussian SSR, Canada, Central African Republic, Chile, Colombia, Costa Rica, Dominican Republic, Egypt, Finland, France, Hungary, Indonesia, Iran, Iraq, Japan, Kenya, Liberia, Mauritania, Nigeria, Norway, Philippines, Romania, Thailand, Tunisia, USSR, United Kingdom, United States, Uruguay, Zaire.

COMMISSION ON NARCOTIC DRUGS
In 1971, the Commission on Narcotic Drugs consisted of 24 members elected by the Economic and Social Council from among the Members of the United Nations and of the specialized agencies and the parties to the Single Convention on Narcotic Drugs, 1961, with due regard to the adequate representation of (a) countries which are important producers of opium or coca leaves; (b) countries which are important in the manufacture of narcotic drugs; and (c) countries in which drug addiction or the illicit traffic in narcotic drugs constitutes an important problem.

Members in 1971:
To serve until 31 December 1971: Canada, Dominican Republic, France, Ghana, Peru, Switzerland, United States, Yugoslavia.
To serve until 31 December 1972: Egypt, Federal Republic of Germany, Hungary, India, Iran, Mexico, Pakistan, Sweden.
To serve until 31 December 1973: Brazil, Jamaica, Japan, Lebanon, Togo, Turkey, USSR, United Kingdom.

The members and their chief representatives at the Commission's twenty-fourth session, held from 27 September to 21 October 1971 at Geneva, Switzerland, were as follows:
Brazil: Dr. Deusdedit de Araújo; A. J. T. Gavazzoni Silva (alternate). Canada: Dr. R. A. Chapman; J. D. McCarthy, W. F. Craig (alternates). Dominican Republic: Dr. J. Patxot-Vallejo; F. Herrera-Roa, E. Paiewonsky (alternates). Egypt: Dr. W. Sadek; Dr. H. El Hakim, M. M. Abdel Razek (alternates). Federal Republic of Germany: Dr. H. Danner; Dr. Elsa von Kotzebue (alternate). France: C. Vaille; Mrs. G. Hirlemann (alternate). Ghana: T. E. C. Sagoe; E. Tchum (alternate). Hungary: Dr. Bela Bolcs, *Rapporteur*; Dr. I. Uranovicz, Dr. K. Agoston (alternates). India: B. S. Chawla. Iran: Dr. H. A. Azarakhch. Jamaica: A. H. Thompson; Miss F. M. Shilletto (alternate). Japan: Dr. T. Shimomura; A. Yamataka (alternate). Lebanon: Lieutenant-Colonel O. Osman; Mrs. Ruby Homsey (alternate). Mexico: Fernando Castro y Castro; J. Barona-Lobato, G. Calderon-Narvasz (alternates). Pakistan: K. A. Aziz Khan; A. Hussain (alternate). Peru: Hubert Wieland Alzamora; J. Alvarez-Calderón (alternate). Sweden: B. Rexed; Dr. S. Martens (alternate). Switzerland: J. P. Bertschinger; T. Kemény

(alternate). Togo: Dr. F. Johnson-Romuald, *Chairman*. Turkey: A. Coskun Kirca, *Second Vice-Chairman*; Dr. T. Alan, Resat Arim, Nuzhet Kandemir (alternates). USSR: E. Babian. United Kingdom: P. Beedle; C. G. Jefferey, F. Stewart, A. Hawkes (alternates). United States: J. E. Ingersoll, *First Vice-Chairman*; D. E. Miller, H. R. Wellman (alternates). Yugoslavia: D. Nikolic.

On 20 May 1971, the Economic and Social Council elected the following seven member States to four-year terms of office starting on 1 January 1972 to fill vacancies occurring on 31 December 1971: Canada, France, Nigeria, Peru, Switzerland, United States, Yugoslavia. On 30 July 1971, the Economic and Social Council elected Argentina to fill the eighth vacant seat.

Members for 1972: Argentina, Brazil, Canada, Egypt, Federal Republic of Germany, France, Hungary, India, Iran, Jamaica, Japan, Lebanon, Mexico, Nigeria, Pakistan, Peru, Sweden, Switzerland, Togo, Turkey, USSR, United Kingdom, United States, Yugoslavia.

Regional Economic Commissions
There are four regional economic commissions:

Economic Commission for Europe (ECE)
Economic Commission for Asia and the Far East (ECAFE)
Economic Commission for Latin America (ECLA)
Economic Commission for Africa (ECA)

ECONOMIC COMMISSION FOR EUROPE (ECE)
Members: Albania, Austria, Belgium, Bulgaria, Byelorussian SSR, Cyprus, Czechoslovakia, Denmark, Federal Republic of Germany, Finland, France, Greece, Hungary, Iceland, Ireland, Italy, Luxembourg, Malta, Netherlands, Norway, Poland, Portugal, Romania, Spain, Sweden, Switzerland,* Turkey, Ukrainian SSR, USSR, United Kingdom, United States, Yugoslavia.

*Switzerland was admitted to membership by a decision of the Economic and Social Council of 27 July 1971.

The Commission has established the following principal subsidiary bodies:
Committee on Agricultural Problems; Chemical Industry Committee; Coal Committee; Conference of European Statisticians; Committee on Electric Power; Committee on Gas; Committee on Housing, Building and Planning; Inland Transport Committee; Senior Advisers to ECE Governments on Environmental Problems; Senior Advisers to ECE Governments on Science and Technology; Senior Economic Advisers to ECE Governments; Steel Committee; Timber Committee; Committee on the Development of Trade; Committee on Water Problems.
Some of these committees have established subsidiary bodies, including standing sub-committees and working parties.
In addition, the Commission annually establishes a sessional committee to examine the reports of its principal subsidiary bodies before their discussion in plenary meetings.

The Commission held its twenty-sixth session from 19 to 30 April 1971 at Geneva, Switzerland.

Chairman: J. Kaufmann (Netherlands).
Vice-Chairman: M. Hruza (Czechoslovakia).
Rapporteur: D. J. Johnson (United Kingdom), B. S. Pojarsky (USSR).

ECONOMIC COMMISSION FOR ASIA AND THE FAR EAST (ECAFE)
Members: Afghanistan, Australia, Burma, Ceylon, China, France, India, Indonesia, Iran, Japan, Khmer Republic, Laos, Malaysia, Mongolia, Nauru,* Nepal, Netherlands, New Zealand, Pakistan, Philippines, Republic of Korea, Republic of Viet-Nam, Singapore, Thailand, Tonga,* USSR, United Kingdom, United States, Western Samoa.

Associate Members: British Solomon Islands Protectorate,* Brunei, Fiji, Hong Kong, Papua New Guinea.†

The Federal Republic of Germany and Switzerland, not Members of the United Nations, participate in a consultative capacity in the Commission's work.

*On 20 July 1971, Nauru and Tonga were admitted as members, and the British Solomon Islands Protectorate was admitted as an associate member.
†Formerly known as the Territory of Papua and the Trust Territory of New Guinea. The name was changed in accordance with a General Assembly decision of 20 December 1971.

The following are the main subsidiary bodies set up by the Commission: Committee on Industry and Natural Resources; Committee on Trade; Transport and Communications Committee; Committee for Co-ordination of Joint Prospecting for Mineral Resources in Asian Offshore Areas; Conference of Asian Economic Planners; Working Party on Social Development Conference of Asian Statisticians; Regional Conference on Water Resources Development; Asian Population Conference; Committee for the Co-ordination of Investigations of the Lower Mekong Basin; Governing Council, Asian Institute for Economic Development and Planning; Asian Highway Co-ordinating Committee; Asian Industrial Development Council; Council of Ministers for Asian Economic Co-operation; Asian Conference on Industrialization; Typhoon Committee.
Some of these bodies have established subsidiary bodies, including standing sub-committees and working parties.
The Commission established a sessional Committee of the Whole at its twenty-seventh session held in April 1971.

The Commission held its twenty-seventh session at Manila, Philippines, from 20 to 30 April 1971.

Chairman: Ernesto M. Maceda (Philippines).
Vice-Chairmen: Manuchehr Goodarzi (Iran); A. F. A. Hussain (Pakistan); M. Khir Johari (Malaysia); Adam Malik (Indonesia); L. N. Mishra (India); Abdul Hakim Tabibi (Afghanistan).

ECONOMIC COMMISSION FOR LATIN AMERICA (ECLA)

Members: Argentina, Barbados, Bolivia, Brazil, Canada, Chile, Colombia, Costa Rica, Cuba, Dominican Republic, Ecuador, El Salvador, France, Guatemala, Guyana, Haiti, Honduras, Jamaica, Mexico, Netherlands, Nicaragua, Panama, Paraguay, Peru, Trinidad and Tobago, United Kingdom, United States, Uruguay, Venezuela.
Associate Members: British Honduras (Belize), West Indies Associated States (collectively, as a single member: Antigua, Dominica, Grenada, St. Kitts-Nevis-Anguilla, St. Lucia and the territories of Montserrat and St. Vincent).

The Federal Republic of Germany and Switzerland, not Members of the United Nations, participate in a consultative capacity in the work of the Commission.

The Commission has established, as its main subsidiary bodies, the Trade Committee and the Central American Economic Co-operation Committee. These bodies have set up various sub-committees and working groups.
In addition, the Governing Council of the Latin American Institute for Economic and Social Planning, and the Governing Council of the Latin American Demographic Centre report to the Commission.

The Commission held its fourteenth session at Santiago, Chile, from 27 April to 8 May 1971.

Chairman: Pedro Vuskovic Bravo (Chile).
First Vice-Chairman: Arturo García (Peru).
Second Vice-Chairman: Carlos Manuel Castillo (Costa Rica).
Rapporteur: Juan V. Sourrouille (Argentina).

ECONOMIC COMMISSION FOR AFRICA (ECA)

Members: Algeria, Botswana, Burundi, Cameroon, Central African Republic, Chad, Congo, Dahomey, Egypt, Equatorial Guinea, Ethiopia, Gabon, Gambia, Ghana, Guinea, Ivory Coast, Kenya, Lesotho, Liberia, Libyan Arab Republic, Madagascar, Malawi, Mali, Mauritania, Mauritius, Morocco, Niger, Nigeria, Rwanda, Senegal, Sierra Leone, Somalia, South Africa,* Sudan, Swaziland, Togo, Tunisia, Uganda, United Republic of Tanzania, Upper Volta, Zaire, Zambia.
Associate Members: Non-Self-Governing Territories situated within the geographical area of the Commission, and States, other than Portugal, responsible for international relations in those territories (i.e. France, Spain and United Kingdom).

*On 30 July 1963, the Economic and Social Council decided that South Africa should not take part in the work of the Commission until conditions for constructive co-operation had been restored by a change in South Africa's racial policy.

The Federal Republic of Germany and Switzerland, not Members of the United Nations, participate in a consultative capacity in the work of the Commission.

On 13 February 1971, the Commission decided to abolish the seven working parties that had been established in 1965. These were the Working Parties on: Intra-African Trade; Monetary Management and Inter-African Payments; Industry and Natural Resources; Transport and Telecommunications; Agriculture; Economic Integration; and on Manpower and Training. The Technical Committee of Experts was to be organized into sub-committees to deal with matters in these various fields.
Other subsidiary bodies of ECA include the following: Conference of African Demographers; Conference of African Planners; Conference of African Statisticians; Governing Council of the African Institute for Economic Development and Planning; Committee on Staff Recruitment and Training; and Executive Committee.
On 13 February 1971, the Commission requested the Executive Secretary, in agreement with Cameroon, the Central African Republic, Kenya, Nigeria, Uganda and Zaire, to consider the establishment of a trans-African highway committee, which met in June 1971.
The Commission's regular biennial session is at the ministerial level and, from 1971, was known as the "Conference of Ministers."

The tenth session of the Commission (first meeting of the Conference of Ministers) was held at Tunis, Tunisia, from 8 to 13 February 1971.

Chairman: Tijani Chelly (Tunisia).
First Vice-Chairman: J. H. Mensah (Ghana).
Second Vice-Chairman: Henri-Paul Boundio (Central African Republic).
Rapporteur: Belai Abbai (Ethiopia).

Standing Committees

In 1971, the Economic and Social Council had the following Standing Committees:

Council Committee on Non-Governmental Organizations
Committee on Housing, Building and Planning
Committee for Programme and Co-ordination
Committee on Science and Technology for Development
Advisory Committee on the Application of Science and Technology to Development
Committee for Development Planning
Committee on Natural Resources
Committee on Crime Prevention and Control
Committee on Review and Appraisal

COUNCIL COMMITTEE ON NON-GOVERNMENTAL ORGANIZATIONS

The Committee is composed of 13 members of the Economic and Social Council elected annually on the basis of equitable geographical representation as follows: five members from African-Asian States; four from Western European and other States; two from Latin American States; and two from socialist States of Eastern Europe.

Members in 1971: France, Ghana, Hungary, Indonesia, Jamaica, Kenya, Norway, Pakistan, Sudan, USSR, United Kingdom, United States, Uruguay.

Chairman: Munir Akram (Pakistan).
Vice-Chairman/Rapporteur: Haakon B. Hjelde (Norway).

COMMITTEE ON HOUSING, BUILDING AND PLANNING

The Committee on Housing, Building and Planning consists of 27 members, elected by the Economic and Social Council on the basis of a pattern to ensure equitable geographical distribution. The Committee meets biennially, its members serving four-year terms of office.

The Committee held its seventh session at Geneva, Switzerland, from 18 to 29 October 1971.

Members in 1971:
To serve until 31 December 1971: Chile, France, Ghana, Italy, Kenya, Lebanon, Panama, USSR, United Kingdom.
To serve until 31 December 1972: Egypt, Guatemala, Hungary, Japan, Kuwait, Netherlands, United Republic of Tanzania, United States, Zaire.
To serve until 31 December 1973: Australia, Brazil, Bulgaria, Colombia, Finland, Libyan Arab Republic, Malaysia, Pakistan, Tunisia.

President: M. Hongo (Japan).
First Vice-President: W. Dam (Netherlands).
Second Vice-President: P. Grecov (Bulgaria).
Rapporteur: J. F. Nimmo (Australia).

On 20 May 1971, the Economic and Social Council elected the following nine countries to terms of office starting on 1 January 1972: Austria, Cameroon, France, India, Nigeria, Panama, Trinidad and Tobago, USSR, United Kingdom.

Members for 1972: Australia, Austria, Brazil, Bulgaria, Cameroon, Colombia, Egypt, Finland, France, Guatemala, Hungary, India, Japan, Kuwait, Libyan Arab Republic, Malaysia, Netherlands, Nigeria, Pakistan, Panama, Trinidad and Tobago, Tunisia, USSR, United Kingdom, United Republic of Tanzania, United States, Zaire.

COMMITTEE FOR PROGRAMME AND CO-ORDINATION

On 13 January 1970, the Economic and Social Council reconstituted the Committee for Programme and Co-ordination to consist of 21 States Members of the United Nations elected by the Council on the basis of equitable geographical distribution as follows: five from African States; five from Western European and other States; four from Asian States; four from Latin American States; and three from socialist States of Eastern Europe. Except for the initial period, the term of office for the members would be three years; for the initial three-year period, the term of office for members was determined by lot for one-year, two-year, or three-year terms.

The Committee for Programme and Co-ordination held its eighth session from 22 March to 8 April 1971 and its ninth session from 24 May to 14 June 1971. The first part of the Committee's tenth session was held from 13 to 17 September 1971, and the resumed tenth session was held between 5 and 17 November 1971. All meetings were held at United Nations Headquarters, New York.

Members in 1971:
To serve until 31 December 1971: Brazil, India, Japan, Philippines, Sierra Leone, Uganda, United Republic of Tanzania.
To serve until 31 December 1972: Bulgaria, Byelorussian SSR, Denmark, Guyana, Malta, Pakistan, United Kingdom.
To serve until 31 December 1973: Colombia, France, Nigeria, Sudan, Trinidad and Tobago, USSR, United States.

Chairman: Samar Sen (India).
Vice-Chairmen: Bernardo de Azevedo Brito (from 13 September 1971) (Brazil); Peter Hansen (from 8 November 1971) (Denmark); Arvid Pardo (until 13 September 1971) (Malta); N. M. S. Stoby (until 13 September 1971) (Guyana); Stefan Todorov (Bulgaria).
Rapporteur: Izzeldin Hamid (from 10 November 1971) (Sudan); C. S. M. Mselle (until 24 May 1971) (United Republic of Tanzania); Salih Mohamed Osman (24 May–10 November 1971).

On 20 May 1971, the Economic and Social Council elected the following for a three-year period starting on 1 January 1972 to fill vacancies occurring on 31 December 1971: Brazil, India, Indonesia, Japan, Kenya, Uganda, United Republic of Tanzania.

Members for 1972: Brazil, Bulgaria, Byelorussian SSR, Colombia, Denmark, France, Guyana, India, Indonesia, Japan, Kenya, Malta, Nigeria, Pakistan, Sudan, Trinidad and Tobago, Uganda, USSR, United Kingdom, United Republic of Tanzania, United States.

COMMITTEE ON SCIENCE AND TECHNOLOGY FOR DEVELOPMENT

The Economic and Social Council established this standing committee on 30 July 1971, to consist of 54 members elected in accordance with the geographical distribution of seats in the Council. The Committee is to provide policy guidance and make recommendations on matters relating to the application of science and technology, reporting through the Council to the General Assembly.

The members were not elected in 1971.

ADVISORY COMMITTEE ON THE APPLICATION OF SCIENCE AND TECHNOLOGY TO DEVELOPMENT

The Advisory Committee consists of 24 members appointed by the Economic and Social Council, on the nomination of the Secretary-General in consultation with Governments. Its mandate, which was to expire on 31 December 1971, was maintained by the Economic and Social Council by a decision of 30 July 1971.

The Advisory Committee held its fourteenth session from 16 to 25 February 1971 at United Nations Headquarters, New York, and its fifteenth session from 15 to 25 November 1971 at Geneva, Switzerland.

Members (to serve until 31 December 1971): Pierre Victor Auger (France). Lord Patrick Blackett (United Kingdom).† Daniel Bovet (Italy). Mourad Castel (Algeria).† Carlos Chagas (Brazil). Wilbert K. Chagula, *Vice-Chairman* (United Republic of Tanzania).† Josef Charvat (Czechoslovakia). J. M. Gvishiani (USSR).* Alexander Keynan (Israel). Thorkil Kristensen (Denmark). Thomas Adeoye Lambo (Nigeria).*† Sir Arthur Lewis (St. Lucia).* Leonard Mukendi (Zaire).† Stuart S. Peters (Canada). Oliverio Phillips (Colombia).* R. Sarwono Prawirohardjo (Indonesia).† Abdus Salam, *Chairman* (Pakistan). Irimie Staicu (Romania). M. S. Thacker (India). Victor L. Urquidi, *Vice-Chairman* (Mexico). Nicola Borissov Videnov (Bulgaria). Sir Ronald Walker (Australia). Carroll L. Wilson (United States). Mohammed Yeganeh (Iran).

*Did not attend the fourteenth session.
†Did not attend the fifteenth session.

On 20 December 1971, the Economic and Social Council decided to postpone until 1972 the appointment of new members to the Advisory Committee.

The Committee has established a number of ad hoc and functional working groups.

COMMITTEE FOR DEVELOPMENT PLANNING

The Committee for Development Planning is composed of 18 experts* representing different planning systems. They are appointed by the Economic and Social Council, from nominees of the Secretary-General, to serve in their personal capacities for a period of three years.

*On 30 July 1971, the Economic and Social Council decided to enlarge the Committee to 24 members, effective 1 January 1972.

The Committee held its seventh session at Geneva, Switzerland, from 22 March to 1 April 1971. Its members, whose terms were to expire on 31 December 1971, were as follows:
Gamani Corea (Ceylon). Nazih Deif (Egypt).* A. N. Efimov (USSR). Paul Kaya (Congo). J. A. Lacarte (Uruguay). John P. Lewis (United States). J. H. Mensah (Ghana). Saburo Okita (Japan). Josef Pajestka, *Rapporteur* (Poland). M. L. Qureshi, *Vice-Chairman* (Pakistan). K. N. Raj (India). W. B. Reddaway (United Kingdom).* Jean Ripert (France). Raúl Sáez (Chile).* Germánico Salgado (Ecuador). Jakov Sirotkovic (Yugoslavia).* Jan Tinbergen, *Chairman* (Netherlands). Zdenek Vergner (Czechoslovakia).*

*Did not attend the seventh session.

The 24 members of the enlarged Committee for Development Planning were not appointed in 1971.

COMMITTEE ON NATURAL RESOURCES

The Committee on Natural Resources was established by the Economic and Social Council on 27 July 1970, to be composed of 27 United Nations Member States elected by the Council on the basis of equitable geographical distribution. The membership was increased to 38 by the Council on 13 November 1970. For the initial period, 19 of the members were to serve for two years and 19 for four years, the term of office determined by drawing lots.

The Committee held its first session at United Nations Headquarters, New York, from 22 February to 10 March 1971.

Members in 1971:
To serve until 31 December 1972: Algeria, Austria, Bolivia, Brazil, Canada, Chile, Ghana, India, Jamaica, Japan, Malawi, Mali, Peru, Philippines, Romania, Sierra Leone, USSR, United Kingdom, Venezuela.
To serve until 31 December 1974: Argentina, Australia, Central African Republic, Egypt, France, Gabon, Guinea, Indonesia, Iran, Iraq, Italy, Kenya, Netherlands, Norway, Pakistan, Poland, Sweden, Turkey, Yugoslavia.

Chairman: Joseph Odero-Jowi (Kenya).
Vice-Chairmen: Guillermo J. Cano (Argentina); Leszek Kasprzyk (Poland); L. J. Mostertman (Netherlands).
Rapporteur: Ranjit Gupta (India).

On 30 July 1971, the Economic and Social Council increased the membership of the Committee from 38 to 54 members, effective 1 January 1972.
On 20 December 1971, the Council elected the following countries to the enlarged Committee:* Ceylon, Costa Rica, Greece, Hungary, Kuwait, Malaysia, Sudan, Trinidad and Tobago, Uganda, Ukrainian SSR, Zaire.

*The election of the five remaining members of the Committee was deferred to 1972. Also deferred was a decision on the terms of office of all 16 new members.

Members for 1972: Algeria, Argentina, Australia, Austria, Bolivia, Brazil, Canada, Central African Republic, Ceylon, Chile, Costa Rica, Egypt, France, Gabon, Ghana, Greece, Guinea, Hungary, India, Indonesia, Iran, Iraq, Italy, Jamaica, Japan, Kenya, Kuwait, Malawi, Malaysia, Mali, Netherlands, Norway, Pakistan, Peru, Philippines, Poland, Romania, Sierra Leone, Sudan, Sweden, Trinidad and Tobago, Turkey, Uganda, Ukrainian SSR, USSR, United Kingdom, Venezuela, Yugoslavia, Zaire.

COMMITTEE ON CRIME PREVENTION AND CONTROL

On 21 May 1971, the Economic and Social Council enlarged the membership of the Advisory Committee of Experts on the Prevention of Crime and the Treatment of Offenders from 10 to 15 members, who were to serve in their individual capacities as experts and be appointed for three-year terms by the Council on the recommendation of the Secretary-General. At the same time, the name of the Committee was changed to the Committee on Crime Prevention and Control.
On 20 December 1971, the Economic and Social Council appointed the following 13 members* to the Committee: Mrs. Sylvi Inkeri Anttila (Finland); Maurice Aydalot (France); Alphonse Boni (Ivory Coast); Norman A. Carlson (United States); William R. Cox (United Kingdom); Taslim O. Elias (Nigeria); Jozsef Godony (Hungary); Ahmed Mohamed Khalifa (Egypt); Pietro Manca (Italy); Khaleeq Ahmed Naqvi (India); Hamood'ur Rahman (Pakistan); José A. Alves da Cruz Ríos (Brazil); B. A. Victorov (USSR).

*On 6 January 1972, the Economic and Social Council appointed the two remaining members of the Committee: Atsushi Nagashima (Japan) and Jorge Arturo Montero Castro (Costa Rica).

COMMITTEE ON REVIEW AND APPRAISAL

The Economic and Social Council established the Committee on 30 July 1971, to consist of 54 members who were to be elected in accordance with the geographical distribution of seats in the Council. The Committee was set up to enable the Council to discharge responsibilities entrusted to it by the General Assembly, to assist the Assembly in the over-all review and appraisal of the Second United Nations Development Decade.
The members were not elected in 1971.

Administrative Committee on Co-ordination

The membership of the Administrative Committee on Co-ordination (ACC) includes, under the chairmanship of the Secretary-General of the United Nations, the executive heads of the following organizations: United Nations; International Labour Organisation; Food and Agriculture Organization; United Nations Educational, Scientific and Cultural Organization; World Health Organization; International Bank for Reconstruction and Development; International Monetary Fund; International Civil Aviation Organization; Universal Postal Union; International Telecommunication Union; World Meteorological Organization; Inter-Governmental Maritime Consultative Organization; and International Atomic Energy Agency.

Also taking part in the Committee's work as full members are the United Nations Under-Secretary-General for Economic and Social Affairs and the executive heads of the following bodies: United Nations Conference on Trade and Development; United Nations Industrial Development Organization; United Nations Development Programme; World Food Programme; United Nations Children's Fund; Office of the United Nations High Commissioner for Refugees; United Nations Relief and Works Agency for Palestine Refugees in the Near East; United Nations Institute for Training and Research; and the executive head of the secretariat of the Contracting Parties to the General Agreement on Tariffs and Trade.

The Secretary-General of the United Nations and the executive heads (or their representatives) of all member organizations and bodies attended meetings of ACC in 1971.

The Administrative Committee on Co-ordination has established a number of standing sub-committees and working groups.

Other Related Bodies

United Nations Development Programme (UNDP)
  Governing Council of UNDP
    Advisory Panel on Programme Policy
    Budgetary and Finance Committee
  Inter-Agency Consultative Board of UNDP (IACB)
United Nations Institute for Training and Research (UNITAR)
United Nations Children's Fund (UNICEF)
  Executive Board of UNICEF
    Programme Committee
    Committee on Administrative Budget
Office of the United Nations High Commissioner for Refugees (UNHCR)
International Narcotics Control Board
United Nations/FAO Intergovernmental Committee of the World Food Programme
United Nations Research Institute for Social Development (UNRISD)
  Board of Directors of UNRISD
Committee of Experts on the Transport of Dangerous Goods
  Group of Experts on Explosives
  Group of Rapporteurs on the Packing of Dangerous Goods

UNITED NATIONS DEVELOPMENT PROGRAMME (UNDP)

Governing Council of UNDP

In 1971, the Governing Council of the United Nations Development Programme (UNDP) consisted of 37 members elected by the Economic and Social Council from Members of the United Nations or members of the specialized agencies or the International Atomic Energy Agency.

Nineteen seats were allocated to developing countries of Africa, Asia and Latin America, and to Yugoslavia, to be filled as follows: seven from Africa, six from Asia and six from Latin America, it being understood that agreement had been reached among the developing countries to accommodate Yugoslavia.

Seventeen seats were allocated to economically more developed countries to be filled as follows: 14 from Western European and other countries, and three from Eastern Europe.

The terms of office of these 36 members were to run for three years, one third of them being elected each year.

The thirty-seventh seat on the Governing Council was to rotate, under the arrangement for 1971, among the groups of countries mentioned above in accordance with the following nine-year cycle:

First and second years: Western European and other countries.
Third, fourth and fifth years: Eastern European countries.
Sixth year: African countries.
Seventh year: Asian countries.
Eighth year: Latin American countries.
Ninth year: Western European and other countries.

The Governing Council held its eleventh session at United Nations Headquarters, New York, from 14 January to 2 February 1971. Its twelfth session was held at Santiago, Chile, from 7 to 23 June 1971.

Members in 1971:
To serve until 31 December 1971: Chile, Congo, Czechoslovakia, Federal Republic of Germany, Mauritania, Netherlands, Panama, Peru, Sweden, Switzerland, Syrian Arab Republic, United Republic of Tanzania.
To serve until 31 December 1972: Cameroon, Cuba, Denmark, India, Italy, Ivory Coast, Japan, Mexico, Philippines, USSR, United Kingdom, United States.
To serve until 31 December 1973: Australia, Belgium, Brazil, Canada, Central African Republic, France, Indonesia, Kuwait, Libyan Arab Republic, Norway, Pakistan, Romania, Uganda.

President: Hernán Santa Cruz (Chile).
First Vice-President: H. J. Hodder (Canada).
Second Vice-President: Siméon Ake (Ivory Coast).
Third Vice-President: Gheorghe Diaconescu (Romania).
Rapporteur: Leandro I. Verceles (Philippines).

On 21 May 1971, the Economic and Social Council elected the following, under the arrangement prevailing in 1971, for a three-year period starting on 1 January 1972 to fill vacancies occurring on 31 December 1971: Bulgaria, Ecuador, Ethiopia, Federal Republic of Germany, Finland, Iraq, Netherlands, Nigeria, Switzerland, Trinidad and Tobago, Uruguay, Yugoslavia.

On 14 December 1971, the General Assembly decided to enlarge the membership of the Governing Council as from 1 January 1972, by 11 members—i.e. from 37 to 48 members—to be elected from among Members of the United Nations or members of the specialized agencies or of the International Atomic Energy Agency, in accordance with the following conditions:

Twenty-seven seats were to be allocated to developing countries of Africa, Asia and Latin America, and Yugoslavia, to be filled as follows: 11 from African countries, 9 from Asian countries and Yugoslavia, and 7 from Latin American countries.

Twenty-one seats were to be allocated to economically more advanced countries, to be filled as follows: 17 from Western European and other countries, and 4 from Eastern European countries.

Accordingly, on 20 December 1971, the Economic and Social Council elected the following countries as members of the UNDP Governing Council to fill the new seats: Austria, Guatemala, Iran, Lebanon, Morocco, Poland, Sweden, Turkey, Upper Volta, Zaire, Zambia.

By drawing lots, it was determined that: Austria, Guatemala, Iran and Morocco would serve for one year, until 31 December 1972; Sweden, Zaire and Zambia would serve for two years, until 31 December 1973; and Lebanon, Poland, Turkey and Upper Volta would serve for three years, until 31 December 1974.

Members for 1972: Australia, Austria, Belgium, Brazil, Bulgaria, Cameroon, Canada, Central African Republic, Cuba, Denmark, Ecuador, Ethiopia, Federal Republic of Germany, Finland, France, Guatemala, India, Indonesia, Iran, Iraq, Italy, Ivory Coast, Japan, Kuwait, Lebanon, Libyan Arab Republic, Mexico, Morocco, Netherlands, Nigeria, Norway, Pakistan, Philippines, Poland, Romania, Sweden, Switzerland, Trinidad and Tobago, Turkey, Uganda, USSR, United Kingdom, United States, Upper Volta, Uruguay, Yugoslavia, Zaire, Zambia.

Administrator of UNDP: Paul G. Hoffman.*
Deputy Administrator of UNDP: C. V. Narasimhan.

*On 14 December 1971, the General Assembly confirmed the appointment of Rudolph A. Peterson as Administrator Designate of UNDP, with effect from 1 January 1972, and as Administrator for the period 15 January 1972 to 31 December 1975, upon the retirement of Paul G. Hoffman on 15 January 1972.

Advisory Panel on Programme Policy

On 30 September 1970, the Administrator of UNDP established the Advisory Panel consisting of eminent specialists to aid in designing policies to strengthen further the capacity of the United Nations development system.

Members: Lord Caradon (United Kingdom); Mohamed Diawara (Ivory Coast); Sir Arthur Lewis (St. Lucia); Edwin W. Martin (United States); Ernst Michanek (Sweden); Saburo Okita (Japan); I. G. Patel (India); Raúl Prebisch (Argentina); Yves

Roland-Billecart (France); S. A. Skachkov (USSR); Maurice F. Strong (Canada); B. J. Udink (Netherlands).

Chairman: David A. Morse (United States).

Ex-officio Members: Philippe de Seynes (United Nations Under-Secretary-General for Economic and Social Affairs); the Executive Secretaries of the regional economic commissions; and the Director of the United Nations Economic and Social Office at Beirut.

Budgetary and Finance Committee

This Committee was established as a Committee of the Whole by the Governing Council on 21 June 1971. It did not meet in 1971.

Inter-Agency Consultative Board of UNDP (IACB)

The Inter-Agency Consultative Board of UNDP consists of 15 members (the Secretary-General of the United Nations and the executive heads of the specialized agencies and the International Atomic Energy Agency, or their representatives), and the heads of the United Nations Conference on Trade and Development and the United Nations Industrial Development Organization. The Executive Directors of the United Nations Children's Fund and the World Food Programme and the United Nations High Commissioner for Refugees are invited to participate as appropriate.

The Board meets under the chairmanship of the Administrator or Deputy Administrator of UNDP; the member organizations carry out projects for UNDP, financed from voluntary contributions by Governments.

The organizations represented at the eleventh session of the Board, held on 29 March 1971 at Geneva, Switzerland, and the twelfth session, held on 20 October 1971 at United Nations Headquarters, New York, were:

United Nations; International Labour Organisation; Food and Agriculture Organization; United Nations Educational, Scientific and Cultural Organization; World Health Organization; International Bank for Reconstruction and Development; International Monetary Fund; International Civil Aviation Organization; Universal Postal Union; International Telecommunication Union; World Meteorological Organization; Inter-Governmental Maritime Consultative Organization; International Atomic Energy Agency; and the United Nations Conference on Trade and Development, the United Nations Industrial Development Organization, the United Nations Children's Fund, the Office of the United Nations High Commissioner for Refugees and the World Food Programme.

UNITED NATIONS INSTITUTE FOR TRAINING AND RESEARCH (UNITAR)

The United Nations Institute for Training and Research (UNITAR) was established in accordance with a General Assembly resolution of 11 December 1963 and came into existence in 1965. The Executive Director of the Institute reports to the General Assembly and, as appropriate, to the Economic and Social Council. (See above, under THE GENERAL ASSEMBLY.)

UNITED NATIONS CHILDREN'S FUND (UNICEF)

Executive Board of UNICEF

The Board consists of 30 members of the United Nations or of the specialized agencies, each elected by the Economic and Social Council for a three-year term.

Members in 1971:

To serve until 31 July 1971: Belgium, Brazil, Canada, Czechoslovakia, Federal Republic of Germany, India, Pakistan, Thailand, Tunisia, Venezuela.

To serve until 31 July 1972: Bulgaria, Chile, Indonesia, Nigeria, Philippines, Sierra Leone, Sweden, Switzerland, Turkey, United Kingdom.

To serve until 31 July 1973: China, Costa Rica, Egypt, France, Gabon, Italy, Malawi, Poland, USSR, United States.

In 1971, the Executive Board held a series of meetings between 13 and 29 April, and also held an organizational meeting (with its composition as at 1 August 1971) on 23 June, all at United Nations Headquarters, New York.

Chairman of Executive Board: Nils Thedin (Sweden).

On 20 May 1971, the Economic and Social Council elected the following members for a three-year period starting on 1 August 1971 to fill vacancies occurring on 31 July 1971: Algeria, Canada, Federal Republic of Germany, India, Norway, Pakistan, Romania, Thailand, Uruguay, Venezuela.

The Executive Board has established two committees: the Programme Committee and the Committee on Administrative Budget. In addition, UNICEF participates in a UNICEF/WHO Joint Committee on Health Policy, an FAO/UNICEF Joint Policy Committee and the Protein Advisory Group of the United Nations System.

Executive Director of UNICEF: Henry R. Labouisse.

Programme Committee

Effective 1 August 1970, the Programme Committee was constituted a Committee of the Whole.

Chairman: Hans Conzett (Switzerland).

Committee on Administrative Budget

Members (until 31 July 1971): Brazil, Bulgaria, Canada, Chile, France, India, Indonesia, Pakistan, Philippines, Sierra Leone, Switzerland, USSR, United Kingdom, United States.

Chairman: P. P. I. Vaidyanathan (India).

Members (from 1 August 1971): Bulgaria, Canada, Chile, France, India, Indonesia, Pakistan, Philippines, Sierra Leone, Switzerland, USSR, United Kingdom, United States, Uruguay.

Chairman: Bogoslav Juricic (Chile).

OFFICE OF THE UNITED NATIONS HIGH COMMISSIONER FOR REFUGEES

The Executive Committee of the Programme of the United Nations High Commissioner for Refugees reports through the Economic and Social Council to the General Assembly. (See above, under THE GENERAL ASSEMBLY.)

INTERNATIONAL NARCOTICS CONTROL BOARD

The International Narcotics Control Board was established under the terms of the Single Convention on Narcotic Drugs, 1961. The Economic and Social Council elects the Board's 11 members, 3 from candidates nominated by the World Health Organization (WHO) and 8 from Members of the United Nations or parties to the Single Convention, to serve in their individual capacity for a three-year term.

The Board held its eighth session from 17 May to 4 June 1971 and its ninth session from 25 October to 12 November 1971, both at Geneva, Switzerland.

Members in 1971:*

Elected from candidates submitted by WHO: A. Attisso, *Vice-President* (Togo); Marcel Granier-Doyeux, *Vice-President* (Venezuela); Sukru Kaymakcalan (Turkey).

Members elected from candidates submitted by Governments: Dr. N. K. Barcov (USSR); Dr. Fortunato Carranza (Peru); Sir Harry Greenfield, *President* (United Kingdom); Dr. Takanobu Itai (Japan); E. S. Krishnamoorthy (India); Pietro Di Mattei (Italy); Paul Reuter (France); Dr. Leon Steinig (United States).

*Elected on 14 May 1970 to serve for a term of three years from 2 March 1971.

UNITED NATIONS/FAO INTERGOVERNMENTAL COMMITTEE OF THE WORLD FOOD PROGRAMME

The 24-member Committee, the governing body of the World Food Programme, held its nineteenth session from 29 March to 6

April 1971, and its twentieth session from 18 to 22 October 1971, both at Rome, Italy.

Members in 1971:
To serve until 31 December 1971: Argentina,* Canada (*Chairman*),† Chile,† Denmark,* India (*Second Vice-Chairman*),† Niger,* Turkey (*First Vice-Chairman*),* United States.†
To serve until 31 December 1972: Egypt,* Ghana,† Indonesia,† Ireland,* Mexico,† Netherlands,† Pakistan,* Sweden.*
To serve until 31 December 1973: Australia,* Federal Republic of Germany,* France,† Kenya,* New Zealand,† Peru,* United Kingdom,* Uruguay.†

*Elected by the Economic and Social Council.
†Elected by the FAO Council.

On 20 May 1971, the Economic and Social Council elected the following for a three-year term starting on 1 January 1972 to fill vacancies occurring on 31 December 1971: Denmark, Hungary, Togo, Turkey.
On 26 November 1971, the FAO Council elected the following for a three-year term starting on 1 January 1972 to fill vacancies occurring on 31 December 1971: Canada, India, Trinidad and Tobago, United States.

Members for 1972: Australia,* Canada,† Denmark,* Egypt,* Federal Republic of Germany,† France,† Ghana,† Hungary,* India,† Indonesia,† Ireland,* Kenya,* Mexico,† Netherlands,† New Zealand,† Pakistan,* Peru,* Sweden,* Togo,* Trinidad and Tobago,† Turkey,* United Kingdom,* United States,† Uruguay.†

*Elected by the Economic and Social Council.
†Elected by the FAO Council.

Executive Director of the World Food Programme: Francisco Aquino.

UNITED NATIONS RESEARCH INSTITUTE
FOR SOCIAL DEVELOPMENT (UNRISD)

Board of Directors of UNRISD
In 1971, the Board of Directors consisted of:
The Chairman, appointed by the Secretary-General: Jan Tinbergen (Netherlands).
Seven members nominated by the Commission for Social Development and confirmed by the Economic and Social Council for three-year terms of office* as follows (to serve until 1 July 1972): Gonzalo Aguirre Beltrán (Mexico); Jacques Delors (France); Mohamed Ennaceur (Tunisia); Philip M. Hauser (United States); Akhter Hameed Khan (Pakistan); Gunnar Karl Myrdal (Sweden); Jan Szczepanski (Poland), *Vice-Chairman.*
Seven ex-officio members, consisting of: a representative of the Secretary-General; the Director of the Latin American Institute for Economic and Social Planning; the Director of the Asian Institute for Economic Development and Planning; the Director of the African Institute for Economic Development and Planning; the Director of UNRISD; the representatives of two of the following specialized agencies in annual rotation with the remaining two agencies as members and observers: International Labour Organisation and Food and Agriculture Organization (members); United Nations Educational, Scientific and Cultural Organization and World Health Organization (alternates).

*On 21 May 1971, the Economic and Social Council extended to four years the terms of office of the nominated members of the Board.

COMMITTEE OF EXPERTS ON THE TRANSPORT
OF DANGEROUS GOODS
Members (experts appointed by the following countries): Federal Republic of Germany, France, Italy, Japan, Norway, Poland, United Kingdom, United States.

The Committee did not meet in 1971.

On 22 May 1970, the Economic and Social Council decided that the membership of the Committee of Experts might be raised to 10 should additional Governments of Member States wish to make available, at the request of the Secretary-General and at their own expense, experts to serve on the Committee.

Group of Experts on Explosives
Members (experts appointed by the following countries): Federal Republic of Germany, France, United Kingdom, United States.

The Group of Experts held its eleventh session at Geneva, Switzerland, on 4 and 5 August 1971. Attending the session were: H. Barker (United Kingdom); A. Berry (United Kingdom); M. Boidart (France); W. Burns (United States); W. Byrd, *Chairman* (United States); R. Eaton (United Kingdom); K. Hannefeld (Federal Republic of Germany); E. Heinrich (Federal Republic of Germany); R. Herman (United States); H. Rittman (United States); R. Schwing (United States); W. Taylor (United States).
An expert from the Inter-Governmental Maritime Consultative Organization was also present.

**Group of Rapporteurs on the
Packing of Dangerous Goods**
Members (rapporteurs appointed by the following countries): Federal Republic of Germany, France, Italy (*Chairman*), United Kingdom, United States.

The Group of Rapporteurs held its eleventh session from 9 to 20 August 1971 at Geneva, Switzerland.

Ad Hoc Bodies
Commission on Permanent Sovereignty over Natural Resources
Preparatory Committee for the World Population Conference
Ad Hoc Working Group on the Question of a Declaration on International Economic Co-operation
Ad Hoc Group of Experts on Tax Treaties between Developed and Developing Countries

COMMISSION ON PERMANENT SOVEREIGNTY
OVER NATURAL RESOURCES
The Commission reports to both the General Assembly and the Economic and Social Council. (See above, under THE GENERAL ASSEMBLY.)

PREPARATORY COMMITTEE FOR THE WORLD
POPULATION CONFERENCE
On 3 April 1970, the Economic and Social Council authorized the Secretary-General to establish the Preparatory Committee to assist in formulating an agenda for the 1974 World Population Conference.

Representatives of the following organizations attended the first session of the Preparatory Committee, held at Geneva, Switzerland, from 22 to 26 February 1971: United Nations; International Labour Organisation; Food and Agriculture Organization; United Nations Educational, Scientific and Cultural Organization; World Health Organization; International Bank for Reconstruction and Development; United Nations Children's Fund; and United Nations Development Programme/United Nations Fund for Population Activities.

Chairman: Milos Macura (United Nations Secretariat).

Representatives of the following organizations attended the second session of the Preparatory Committee, held at Paris, France, from 16 to 22 June 1971: United Nations; International Labour Organisation; Food and Agriculture Organization; United Nations Educational, Scientific and Cultural Organization; World

Health Organization; and International Bank for Reconstruction and Development.

Chairman: Milos Macura (United Nations Secretariat).

AD HOC WORKING GROUP ON THE QUESTION OF A DECLARATION ON INTERNATIONAL ECONOMIC CO-OPERATION

Members: Australia, Brazil, Colombia, Ethiopia, France, India, Italy, Poland, USSR, United Kingdom, United States, Yugoslavia.

On 18 December 1968, the Economic and Social Council decided to postpone *sine die* the question of a meeting of the *Ad Hoc* Working Group.

AD HOC GROUP OF EXPERTS ON TAX TREATIES BETWEEN DEVELOPED AND DEVELOPING COUNTRIES

Members: Carlos C. Martínez Molteni (Argentina); Carlos Yacoman Godoy (Chile); Helmut Debatin (Federal Republic of Germany); Pierre Kerlan (France); A. N. E. Amissah (Ghana); R. D. Shah (India); Simcha Gafni (Israel); Torao Aoki (Japan); W. H. van den Berge (Netherlands); A. Sheel, *Rapporteur* (Norway); Qamarul Islam (Pakistan); Ambrosio M. Lina (Philippines); Hamzah Merghani, *Chairman* (Sudan); Kurt Lochner (Switzerland); Rachid Sfar (Tunisia); Adnan Baser Kafaoglu (Turkey); J. A. Johnstone (United Kingdom); Nathan Gordon (United States).

The *Ad Hoc* Group of Experts met between 25 October and 5 November 1971 at Geneva, Switzerland.

The Trusteeship Council

Article 86 of the United Nations Charter lays down that the Trusteeship Council shall consist of the following:

Members of the United Nations administering Trust Territories;

Permanent members of the Security Council which do not administer Trust Territories;

As many other members elected for a three-year term by the General Assembly as will ensure that the membership of the Council is equally divided between United Nations Members which administer Trust Territories and those which do not.*

*There were no elected members of the Trusteeship Council in 1971. New Zealand ceased to be a member of the Trusteeship Council upon the accession of Nauru to independence on 31 January 1968 and the United Kingdom changed its status from that of an administering member to that of a non-administering member. The remaining two members administering territories (Australia and the United States) thus became a minority on the Council. China, France, the USSR and the United Kingdom continued as members of the Trusteeship Council, in accordance with Article 86 of the Charter; thus the parity called for in that Article between administering and non-administering powers could no longer be maintained.

Members of the Council in 1971

Members Administering Trust Territories: Australia, United States.

Non-Administering Members: China, France, USSR, United Kingdom.

Sessions of the Council in 1971

The Trusteeship Council held its thirty-eighth session at United Nations Headquarters, New York, between 25 May and 18 June 1971.

Officers of the Council in 1971

President: David N. Lane (United Kingdom).

Vice-President: Christopher H. Phillips (United States) (until 27 May 1971); W. Tapley Bennett (United States) (from 28 May 1971).

VISITING MISSIONS

United Nations Visiting Mission to the Trust Territory of New Guinea, 1971

Members and Representatives: Paul Blanc (France); Adnan Raouf (Iraq);* C. E. Wyse (Sierra Leone);* Sir Denis Allen (United Kingdom), *Chairman.*

*Iraq and Sierra Leone, non-members of the Trusteeship Council, were designated by the President of the Council on the basis of consultations with the members of the Council, the Special Committee on the Situation with regard to the Implementation of the Declaration on the Granting of Independence to Colonial Countries and Peoples, and the Administering Power.

United Nations Visiting Mission to observe the elections to the Papua New Guinea House of Assembly in 1972

On 18 June 1971, the Trusteeship Council decided to dispatch a visiting mission to observe the elections to the Papua New Guinea House of Assembly in 1972, and invited the following to submit nominations for membership: Afghanistan,* United Kingdom, United States and Yugoslavia.*

*Afghanistan and Yugoslavia, non-members of the Trusteeship Council, were designated by the President of the Council on the basis of consultations with the members of the Council, the Special Committee on the Situation with regard to the Implementation of the Declaration on the Granting of Independence to Colonial Countries and Peoples, and the Administering Authority.

The International Court of Justice

JUDGES OF THE COURT

The International Court of Justice consists of 15 Judges elected for nine-year terms by the General Assembly and the Security Council, voting independently.

The following were the Judges of the Court serving in 1971, listed in order of precedence:

Judge	Country of Nationality	End of Term*
Sir Muhammad Zafrulla Khan, *President*	Pakistan	1973
Fouad Ammoun, *Vice-President*	Lebanon	1976
Sir Gerald Fitzmaurice	United Kingdom	1973
Luis Padilla Nervo	Mexico	1973

Judge	Country of Nationality	End of Term*
Isaac Forster	Senegal	1973
André Gros	France	1973
Cesar Bengzon	Philippines	1976
Sture Petren	Sweden	1976
Manfred Lachs	Poland	1976
Charles D. Onyeama	Nigeria	1976
Hardy C. Dillard	United States	1979
Louis Ignacio-Pinto	Dahomey	1979
Federico de Castro	Spain	1979
Platon D. Morozov	USSR	1979
Eduardo Jiménez de Aréchaga	Uruguay	1979

*Term expires on 5 February of year indicated.

Registrar: Stanislas Aquarone.
Deputy Registrar: William Tait.

CHAMBER OF SUMMARY PROCEDURE
(as elected by the Court on 22 January 1971)
Members: Sir Muhammad Zafrulla Khan, Fouad Ammoun, Luis Padilla Nervo, Cesar Bengzon, Manfred Lachs.
Substitute Members: Louis Ignacio-Pinto, Federico de Castro.

PARTIES TO THE COURT'S STATUTE
All Members of the United Nations are *ipso facto* parties to the Statute of the International Court of Justice. The following non-members have also become parties to the Court's Statute: Liechtenstein, San Marino, Switzerland.

In addition, the Court is open to the Federal Republic of Germany and the Republic of Viet-Nam, which have filed with the Registry of the Court declarations prescribed by the Security Council for that purpose.

STATES ACCEPTING THE COMPULSORY JURISDICTION OF THE COURT
Declarations made by the following States accepting the Court's compulsory jurisdiction (or made under the statute of the Permanent Court of International Justice and deemed to be an acceptance of the jurisdiction of the International Court) were in force at the end of 1971:

Australia, Austria, Belgium, Botswana, Canada, China, Colombia, Denmark, Dominican Republic, Egypt, El Salvador, Finland, France, Gambia, Haiti, Honduras, India, Israel, Japan, Kenya, Khmer Republic, Liberia, Liechtenstein, Luxembourg, Malawi, Malta, Mauritius, Mexico, Netherlands, New Zealand, Nicaragua, Nigeria, Norway, Pakistan, Panama, Philippines, Portugal, Somalia, Sudan, Swaziland, Sweden, Switzerland, Turkey, Uganda, United Kingdom, United States, Uruguay.

ORGANS AUTHORIZED TO REQUEST ADVISORY OPINIONS FROM THE COURT
Authorized by the United Nations Charter to request opinions on any legal question: General Assembly; Security Council.

Authorized by the General Assembly in accordance with the Charter to request opinions on legal questions arising within the scope of their activities: Economic and Social Council; Trusteeship Council; Interim Committee of the General Assembly; Committee on Applications for Review of Administrative Tribunal Judgements; International Atomic Energy Agency; International Labour Organisation; Food and Agriculture Organization; United Nations Educational, Scientific and Cultural Organization; World Health Organization; International Bank for Reconstruction and Development; International Finance Corporation; International Development Association; International Monetary Fund; International Civil Aviation Organization; International Telecommunication Union; World Meteorological Organization; Inter-Governmental Maritime Consultative Organization.

COMMITTEES OF THE COURT
The Court has established the following committees, all of which are standing committees except for the Committee for the Revision of the Rules of Court:

Budgetary and Administrative Committee
Members: Sir Muhammad Zafrulla Khan, Fouad Ammoun, Isaac Forster, Sture Petren, Hardy C. Dillard.

Committee on Relations
Members: Manfred Lachs, Charles D. Onyeama, Hardy C. Dillard.

Library Committee
Members: Sture Petren, Hardy C. Dillard, Louis Ignacio-Pinto.

Committee for the Revision of the Rules of Court
Members: Manfred Lachs, Louis Ignacio-Pinto, Platon D. Morozov, Eduardo Jiménez de Aréchaga.

Principal members of the United Nations Secretariat
(As at 31 December 1971)

Secretariat

Secretary-General: U Thant

Executive Office of the Secretary-General
Under-Secretary-General, Chef de Cabinet: C. V. Narasimhan
Under-Secretary-General in Charge of General Assembly Affairs: Constantin A. Stavropoulos

Office of the Under-Secretary-General for Special Political Affairs
Under-Secretary-General: Roberto E. Guyer

Office for Inter-Agency Affairs
Assistant Secretary-General: Ismat T. Kittani

Office of Legal Affairs
Under-Secretary-General, the Legal Counsel: Constantin A. Stavropoulos

Office of the Under-Secretary-General for Administration and Management
Under-Secretary-General: H. Keith Matthews

Office of the Controller
Assistant Secretary-General, Controller: Bruce R. Turner

Office of Personnel
Assistant Secretary-General, Director of Personnel: Mohamed Habib Gherab

Department of Political and Security Council Affairs
Under-Secretary-General: Leonid N. Kutakov

Department of Economic and Social Affairs
Under-Secretary-General: Philippe de Seynes
Assistant Secretary-General, Commissioner for Technical Co-operation: Victor Hoo
Assistant Secretary-General, Executive Secretary, Economic Commission for Europe: Janez I. Stanovnik
Assistant Secretary-General, Executive Secretary, Economic Commission for Asia and the Far East: U Nyun
Assistant Secretary-General, Executive Secretary, Economic Commission for Latin America: Carlos Quintana
Assistant Secretary-General, Executive Secretary, Economic Commission for Africa: Robert K. A. Gardiner

Department of Trusteeship and Non-Self-Governing Territories
Under-Secretary-General: Issoufou S. Djermakoye

Office of Public Information
Assistant Secretary-General: Agha Abdul Hamid

Office of Conference Services
Under-Secretary-General: Jiri Nosek

Office of General Services
Assistant Secretary-General: David B. Vaughan

United Nations Office at Geneva
Under-Secretary-General, Director-General of the United Nations Office at Geneva: Vittorio Winspeare Guicciardi

Subsidiary organs

United Nations Children's Fund (UNICEF)
Under-Secretary-General, Executive Director: Henry R. Labouisse

United Nations Military Observer Group in India and Pakistan (UNMOGIP)
Chief Military Observer: Lieutenant-General Luis Tassara González

United Nations Representative for India and Pakistan (UNRIP)
Representative: Frank P. Graham

United Nations Truce Supervision Organization in Palestine (UNTSO)
Chief of Staff: Major-General Ensio Siilasvuo

United Nations Relief and Works Agency for Palestine Refugees in the Near East (UNRWA)
Commissioner-General: Sir John Shaw Rennie

Office of the United Nations High Commissioner for Refugees (UNHCR)
High Commissioner: Prince Sadruddin Aga Khan

United Nations Development Programme (UNDP)
Administrator: Paul G. Hoffman
Deputy Administrator: C. V. Narasimhan
Assistant Administrator in charge of Bureau for Programme Co-ordination: Myer Cohen
Assistant Administrator and Director, Regional Bureau for Asia and the Far East: Rajendra Coomaraswamy
Assistant Administrator and Director, Regional Bureau for Africa: Michel Doo Kingue

Assistant Administrator and Director, Bureau for Programme Analysis and Policy Planning: Stephane Hessel
Assistant Administrator and Director, Regional Bureau for Europe, Mediterranean and Middle East: Sergije Makiedo
Executive Director, United Nations Fund for Population Activities (UNFPA): Rafael Salas
Assistant Administrator and Director, Regional Bureau for Latin America: Gabriel Valdes-Subercaseaux

United Nations Institute for Training and Research (UNITAR)
Under-Secretary-General, Executive Director: Chief S. O. Adebo

United Nations Conference on Trade and Development (UNCTAD)
Secretary-General: Manuel Pérez-Guerrero

United Nations Industrial Development Organization (UNIDO)
Under-Secretary-General, Executive Director: Ibrahim H. Abdel-Rahman

United Nations Peace-keeping Force in Cyprus (UNFICYP)
Commander: Major-General D. P. Chand
Special Representative of the Secretary-General in Cyprus: Bibiano F. Osorio-Tafall

United Nations Middle East Mission (UNMEM)
Under-Secretary-General, Special Representative: Gunnar V. Jarring

United Nations Conference on the Human Environment
Secretary-General: Maurice Strong

Conference of the Committee on Disarmament
Secretary-General's Special Representative: Ilka Pastinen

United Nations Fund for Drug Abuse Control
Personal Representative of the Secretary-General: Carl Schurmann

United Nations Relief Operation in Dacca (UNROD)
Headquarters Co-ordinator: Paul-Marc Henry

On 31 December 1971, the total number of staff, other than technical assistance experts, employed by the United Nations under probationary, permanent and fixed-term appointments stood at 11,014. Of these, 3,777 were in the professional and higher categories and 7,237 in the general service, manual workers and field service categories. There were 2,197 technical assistance experts employed by the United Nations as at 31 December 1971.

Appendix IV

United Nations Information Centres and Offices
(As at 1 May 1972)

ACCRA. United Nations Information Centre
Liberia and Maxwell Roads
(Post Office Box 2339)
Accra, Ghana

ADDIS ABABA. Information Service, United Nations Economic Commission for Africa
Africa Hall
(Post Office Box 3001)
Addis Ababa, Ethiopia

ALGIERS. United Nations Information Centre
19 Avenue Claude Debussy
(Post Office Box 803)
Algiers, Algeria

ASUNCION. Centro de Información de las Naciones Unidas
Calle Coronel Bogado 871
(Casilla de Correo 1107)
Asunción, Paraguay

ATHENS. United Nations Information Centre
36 Amalia Avenue
Athens 119, Greece

BAGHDAD. United Nations Information Centre
House No. 167/1 Abu Nouwas Street
(Post Office Box 2398 Alwiyah)
Baghdad, Iraq

BANGKOK. Information Service, United Nations Economic Commission for Asia and the Far East
Sala Santitham
Bangkok, Thailand

BEIRUT. United Nations Information Centre
Apt. No. 1, Fakhoury Building
Ardati Street
(Post Office Box 4656)
Beirut, Lebanon

BELGRADE. United Nations Information Centre
Svetozara Markovica 58
(Post Office Box 157)
Belgrade, Yugoslavia YU-11001

BOGOTA. Centro de Información de las Naciones Unidas
Calle 19, Número 7-30 (Séptimo Piso)
(Apartado Postal 6567)
Bogotá, Colombia

BUCHAREST. United Nations Information Centre
16 rue Aurel Vlaicu
Bucharest, Romania

BUENOS AIRES. Centro de Informacion de las Naciones Unidas
Marcelo T. de Alvear 684 (Tercer Piso)
Buenos Aires, Argentina

BUJUMBURA. Centre d'Information des Nations Unies
Avenue de la Poste et Place Jungers
(Boîte Postale 2160)
Bujumbura, Burundi

CAIRO. United Nations Information Centre
Sh. Osoris
Tagher Building (Garden City)
(Post Office Box 262)
Cairo, Egypt

COLOMBO. United Nations Information Centre
204 Buller's Road
(Post Office Box 1505)
Colombo 7, Ceylon

COPENHAGEN. United Nations Information Centre
37 H. C. Andersen's Boulevard
DK 1553 Copenhagen V, Denmark

DAKAR. Centre d'Information des Nations Unies
2 Avenue Roume
(Boîte Postale 154)
Dakar, Senegal

DAR ES SALAAM. United Nations Information Centre
Matasalamat Building
(Post Office Box 9224)
Dar es Salaam, United Republic of Tanzania

GENEVA. Information Service, United Nations European Office
Palais des Nations
1211 Geneva 10, Switzerland

ISLAMABAD. United Nations Information Centre
Bungalow No. 24
Ramna-6/3, 88th Street
(Post Office Box 1107)
Islamabad, Pakistan

KABUL. United Nations Information Centre
Shah Mahmoud Ghazi Watt
(Post Office Box 5)
Kabul, Afghanistan

KARACHI.* United Nations Information Centre
Havelock Road
(Post Office Box 349, G. P. O.)
Karachi 1, Pakistan

*Relocated to Islamabad effective 8 October 1971.

KATHMANDU. United Nations Information Centre
Lainchaur, Lazimpat
(Post Office Box 107)
Kathmandu, Nepal

KHARTOUM. United Nations Information Centre
House No. 9, Block 6.5.D.E.
Nejumi Street
(Post Office Box 1992)
Khartoum, Sudan

KINSHASA. Centre d'Information des Nations Unies
Building Deuxième République
Boulevard du 30 Juin
(Boîte Postale 7248)
Kinshasa, Zaire

LAGOS. United Nations Information Centre
17 Kingsway Road Ikoyi
(Post Office Box 1068)
Lagos, Nigeria

LA PAZ. Centro de Información de las Naciones Unidas
Avenida Arce No. 2419
(Apartado Postal 686)
La Paz, Bolivia

LIMA. Centro de Información de las Naciones Unidas
Avenida Arequipa 3330
San Isidro
(Apartado Postal 4480)
Lima, Peru

LOME. Centre d'Information des Nations Unies
Rue Albert Sarraut
Coin Avenue de Gaulle
(Boîte Postale 911)
Lomé, Togo

LONDON. United Nations Information Centre
14/15 Stratford Place
London W1N 9AF, England

MANILA. United Nations Information Centre
WHO Building
United Nations Avenue at Taft Avenue
(Post Office Box 2149)
Manila, Philippines

MEXICO CITY. Centro de Información de las Naciones Unidas
Hamburgo 63 (Tercer Piso)
Mexico 6, D.F., Mexico

MONROVIA. United Nations Information Centre
ULRC Building
(Post Office Box 274)
Monrovia, Liberia

MOSCOW. United Nations Information Centre
No. 4/16 Ulitsa, Lunacharskogo 1
Moscow, USSR

NEW DELHI. United Nations Information Centre
1 Barakhamba Road
New Delhi 1, India

PARIS. Centre d'Information des Nations Unies
1 Rue Miollis
75 Paris 15^e, France

PORT MORESBY. United Nations Information Centre
Hunter Street
Port Moresby, Papua New Guinea

PORT OF SPAIN. United Nations Information Centre
15 Keate Street
(Post Office Box 130)
Port of Spain, Trinidad and Tobago

PRAGUE. United Nations Information Centre
Panska 5
Praha 1, Czechoslovakia

RABAT. Centre d'Information des Nations Unies
Angle Avenue Urbain Blanc et rue de Nîmes
(Casier ONU)
Rabat, Morocco

RANGOON. United Nations Information Centre
132 University Avenue
Rangoon, Burma

RIO DE JANEIRO. United Nations Information Centre
Apt. 201
Cruz Lima Street, No. 19
Rio de Janeiro, Brazil

ROME. United Nations Information Centre
Palazzetto Venezia
Piazza San Marco 50
Rome, Italy

SAN SALVADOR. Centro de Información de las Naciones Unidas
Avenida Roosevelt 2818
(Apartado Postal 1114)
San Salvador, El Salvador

SANTIAGO. Information Service, United Nations Economic Commission for Latin America
Edificio Naciones Unidas
Avenida Dag Hammarskjold
Santiago, Chile

SYDNEY. United Nations Information Centre
London Assurance Building
20 Bridge Street
(Post Office Box R226)
Royal Exchange
Sydney 2000, Australia

TANANARIVE. Centre d'Information des Nations Unies
26 rue de Liège
(Boîte Postale 1348)
Tananarive, Madagascar

TEHERAN. United Nations Information Centre
Off Takhte Jamshid
12 Kh. Bandar Pahlavi
(Post Office Box 1555)
Teheran, Iran

TOKYO. United Nations Information Centre
New Ohtemachi Building, Room 411/412
2-1, Ohtemachi 2-chome
Chiyoda-ku
Tokyo, Japan

TUNIS. Centre d'Information des Nations Unies
61 Boulevard Bab Benat
(Boîte Postale 863)
Tunis, Tunisia

VIENNA. Information Service, United Nations Industrial Development Organization
Lerchenfelderstrasse 1
(Post Office Box 707)
A-1011, Vienna, Austria

WASHINGTON. United Nations Information Centre
Suite 714
1028 Connecticut Avenue, N.W.
Washington, D. C. 20006, United States

YAOUNDE. Centre d'Information des Nations Unies
(Boîte Postale 836)
Yaoundé, Cameroon

Indices

Abbreviations used in index

ACC	Administrative Committee on Co-ordination	prod.	product, production
act.	activities	prog.	programme
admin.	administration, administrative	pub.	publication
adv.	advisory	qn.	question
agri.	agricultural, agriculture	ratif.	ratification
art.	article	recomm.	recommendation
assoc.	associate	reg.	region, regional
Bank	International Bank for Reconstruction and Development	rel.	relations
		rep.	representation, representative
Bd.	Board	res.	resolution, resolutions
cap.	capital	rev.	revised, revision
CCD	Conference of the Committee on Disarmament	SC	Security Council
comm.	commission	sess.	session, sessions
Commr.	Commissioner	SF	special fund
conf.	conference	SG	Secretary-General
consid.	consideration	soc.	social
contrib.	contribution	sp.	special
conv.	convention	Sp. Ags.	specialized agencies
co-op.	co-operation	Sp. Cttee.	General Assembly's Special Committee on the Situation with regard to the Implementation of the Declaration on the Granting of Independence to Colonial Countries and Peoples
co-ord.	co-ordination		
cttee.	committee		
decl.	declaration		
del.	delegation	SSR	Soviet Socialist Republic
dev.	development	subs.	subscription
ECA	Economic Commission for Africa	subsid.	subsidiary
ECAFE	Economic Commission for Asia and the Far East	suppl.	supplemental, supplementary
ECE	Economic Commission for Europe	TA	technical assistance
ECLA	Economic Commission for Latin America	TC	Trusteeship Council
econ.	economic	TDB	Trade and Development Board (UNCTAD)
educ.	education, educational	telecomm.	telecommunication
ESC	Economic and Social Council	UK	United Kingdom of Great Britain and Northern Ireland
estab.	established, establishment		
exec.	executive	UN	United Nations
expend.	expenditure	UNCITRAL	United Nations Commission on International Trade Law
FAO	Food and Agriculture Organization of the United Nations		
		UNCTAD	United Nations Conference on Trade and Development
Fund	International Monetary Fund		
GA	General Assembly	UNCURK	United Nations Commission on the Unification and Rehabilitation of Korea
GATT	General Agreement on Tariffs and Trade		
Gov.	Governing, Governor	UNDP	United Nations Development Programme
govt.	government	UNDP/SF	Special Fund component of the United Nations Development Programme
hq.	headquarters		
IAEA	International Atomic Energy Agency	UNDP/TA	Technical Assistance component of the United Nations Development Programme
ICAO	International Civil Aviation Organization		
ICJ	International Court of Justice	UNESCO	United Nations Educational, Scientific and Cultural Organization
IDA	International Development Association		
IDB	Industrial Development Board (UNIDO)	UNFICYP	United Nations Peace-keeping Force in Cyprus
IFC	International Finance Corporation	UNHCR	United Nations High Commissioner for Refugees (Office of)
ILC	International Law Commission		
ILO	International Labour Organisation (Office)	UNICEF	United Nations Children's Fund
IMCO	Inter-Governmental Maritime Consultative Organization	UNIDO	United Nations Industrial Development Organization
indus.	industrial, industry	UNITAR	United Nations Institute for Training and Research
inf.	information	UNRISD	United Nations Research Institute for Social Development
inst.	institute		
int.	international	UNRWA	United Nations Relief and Works Agency for Palestine Refugees in the Near East
ITU	International Telecommunication Union		
JIU	Joint Inspection Unit	UNTSO	United Nations Truce Supervision Organization in Palestine
NGO	non-governmental organization		
NSGT	non-self-governing territory	UPU	Universal Postal Union
OAU	Organization of African Unity	US	United States of America
org.	organization	USSR	Union of Soviet Socialist Republics
part.	participation	WFP	World Food Programme
pet.	petition	WHO	World Health Organization
pop.	population	WMO	World Meteorological Organization
prep.	preparatory		

Subject index

and Under Water (Moscow, 1963), adherence to, 4, 22, 23, 25-26 (*res.*), CCD consid., 4-5, GA consid., 22, 23-24, 25-26 (*res.*)

sea-bed and ocean floor, *see* Sea-bed and ocean floor, peaceful uses of

Disasters, natural, 473-79; assistance, SG report on, ACC consid., 461; Disaster Relief Co-ordinator, appointment as Under-SG and functions, ESC consid., 474-75, 476-77 (*res.*), GA consid., 475, 477-79 (*res.*); emergency assistance, act. in 1971, ESC and GA consid., 473, 475-76 (*res.*), budget appropriation for 1972, 642, 647-48 (*res.*), Working Cap. Fund, allotments for 1971, 473, annual authorizations for, GA consid., 475, 477-79 (*res.*); fellowships, 258 (*table*); pre-disaster planning, fellowships for, 473; procedures for assistance, ESC and GA consid., 473-75, 476-79 (*res.*), SG report, 473-74; role of science and technology in reducing impact, report, 314; TA expenditures for projects, 258 (*table*); use of space radio-communications systems in relief operations (ITU), 474; *see also* Cyclones; Droughts; Earthquakes; Floods and flood control; Typhoons

Discrimination, prevention of, 394-416; against women plantation workers (ILO), 688; equality in admin. of justice, study, ESC consid., 412-13, 415, (*res.*), GA consid., 413, 415 (*res.*); evils of, seminar, 432; incitement to, measures against, ESC consid., 409-10 (*res.*), GA consid., 408-9, 409-10 (*res.*); in Employment and Occupation, Conv. and Recomm. (ILO), 688; inf. progs., reporting on, 396, 397-98 (*res.*); in political, econ., soc. and cultural spheres, study, ESC consid., 67, 405, 411-12, 413-14 (*res.*), GA consid., 67, 395, 396, 397-98 (*res.*), 412, 413 (*res.*); Int. Day for Elimination of Racial Discrimination (1970), observance, 65, 401-2; int. seminar on, 65; intolerance in all forms, int. seminar, 432; in Trust Territories, 500-1; measures against nazism and racial intolerance; ESC consid., 409-10 (*res.*), GA consid., 408-9, 409-10 (*res.*); religious intolerance, GA consid., 413, 415-16 (*res.*), 444 (*res.*); UN stamp, 671; *see also* Apartheid; *and relevant and related subjects*

Cttee. on Elimination of Racial Discrimination: GA subsid. body, 784, 792; members, 792; report, GA consid., 398, 400-1, 402-5 (*res.*); sess., 3d and 4th, 792, act., 400

elimination of all forms of: GA consid., 75-76, 107-8, 398-400, 402-4 (*res.*), 521; int. campaign against racial discrimination, message of GA President to Heads of State or Govt., 396, 398, 399-400, text, 402-4 (*res.*); mobilization of public opinion, ESC consid., 67, 395, 413-14 (*res.*), GA consid., 396, 398 (*res.*); NGOs act., 446; reports of ILO and UNESCO, 396, 397-98 (*res.*)

Int. Conv. on Elimination of All Forms of Racial Discrimination: implementation, GA consid., 107-8, 397-98 (*res.*), 398-400, 402-4 (*res.*), 521; ratif. or accession and parties to, 400, ESC consid., 395, 413-14 (*res.*), GA consid., 400-1, 404-5, (*res.*), 408, 410 (*res.*), SG report, 401

Int. Year for Action to Combat Racism and Racial Discrimination (1971), 395-96; campaign against *apartheid*, 65, 66, 68, ESC consid., 405, 407 (*res.*), GA consid., 398-400, 402-4 (*res.*), message of GA President to Heads of State or Govt., 396, 398, 399-400, text, 402-4 (*res.*); extension of to Decade, GA consid., 398-400, 402-4 (*res.*); observance, 65, 66, ESC consid., 395, 413-14 (*res.*), GA consid., 395-96, 397-98 (*res.*); SG report on measures and act., 395, 398 (*res.*); UNESCO act., 703

Sub-Comm. on Prevention of Discrimination and Protection of Minorities: act., 395, 398, 411, 412, 419, 434; ESC organ, 800; frequency of meeting, 799; members, 800; report, distribution of, 661; sess., 24th, members and reps., 800; studies, 67, 405, 411-12, 414-15 (*res.*), 434, 440-41 (*res.*)

Disease control: communicable, WHO act., 708-9; WHO act., 708

Disputes, peaceful settlement of: Conv. on Sp. Missions and Optional Protocol concerning Compulsory Settlement of Disputes, parties to, 625

Documentation: Latin American Centre for Econ. and Soc. Documentation (CLADES), estab., 341; UNESCO act., 704

Documentation, United Nations: budget appropriation, 1972, reduction in, 663-64 (*res.*); ESC comms. and subsid. bodies, form and content, ESC consid., 660-61, 663-64 (*res.*); JIU report on, GA consid., 661, 663-64 (*res.*); reduction in volume, ESC consid., 660-61, 662-63 (*res.*), GA consid., 661-62, 663-64 (*res.*)

Dominica: contrib. to UNICEF, 393; qns. *re* independence, GA consid., 541, 544 (*res.*); TA act. in, 370; WFP act. in, 269

Dominican Republic:
act. of in and for: Bank, 717; FAO, 695, 698; Fund, 733; IDA, 726; TA, 262, 356, 372, 378; UNDP/SF, 256; UNESCO, 703, 705; UNICEF, 392; UNIDO, 289; WHO, 711

admission to UN, date of, 765

contrib. to: FAO, 699; GATT, 761; IAEA, 685; ICAO, 741; ILO, 690; IMCO, 757; ITU, 748; UN, 653; UN Cap. Dev. Fund, 303; UNDP, 247; UNESCO, 707; UPU, 745; WFP, 267; WHO, 712; WMO, 753

GATT, Contracting Party to, 761

ICJ, acceptance of compulsory jurisdiction and party to Statute of, 809

member of and reps.: Bank, 718; ECLA, 802; ESC organ, 801; FAO, 699; Fund, 734; IAEA, 685; ICAO, 741; IDA, 728; IFC, 722; ILO, 690; IMCO, 757; ITU, 748; UNESCO, 707; UPU, 745; WHO, 712; WMO, 753

subs. to: Bank, 718; Fund, 734; IDA, 728; IFC, 722

Droughts: aid to victims, 266, 473, 476 (*res.*)

Drugs: monitoring service (WHO), 710; *see also* Narcotic drugs

Dubai: contrib. to UNHCR, 388, UNITAR, 480

Earthquakes: aid to victims, 473; Chile and Colombia, aid in reconstruction, ESC consid., 473, 475 (*res.*), WFP act., 266; Inter-reg. Seminar on Construction Resistant to, 370

East African Community: econ. co-op., 278; FAO act. in, 698; ICAO act. in, 740; UNIDO act. in, 290

Eastern Regional Organization for Public Administration, 449

Economic activities and programmes: co-ord. with econ. and human rights progs., harmonization of budgets and progs., ESC consid., 465-66 (*res.*), 674, SG report, 465; reports on work prog. performance, format and content of, 464-65, ESC consid., 465-66 (*res.*), GA consid., 641, SG report, 464; work prog., ESC consid., 467-68, 471 (*res.*)

Economic and Social Affairs, Department of: officers, 809; pattern of confs., JIU study, 661, GA consid., 678, 679 (*res.*); restructuring of for 2d Dev. Decade, GA consid., 678, 679 (*res.*)

Economic and Social Council:
ad hoc bodies, 807-8

comms. and subsids., 798-801; content of documentation, 660-61, 663-64 (*res.*)

Cttee. for Prog. and Co-ord. (CPC): act., 331 (*res.*), 456, 457, 458, 460-62, 464-65, 486, 659, 660, 674; ESC subsid. body, 802; joint sess. with ACC, 456, 457, 459 (*res.*), 460-61; members, 1971 and 1972, 803; officers, 803; reconstitution, 803; report, 456; sess., 8th-10th, 803

cttees.: sessional, act., 466, 468-69 (*res.*), Co-ord. Cttee., Econ. Cttee., Social Cttee., officers, 798, enlargement of, 466, 467, 468-69 (*res.*); standing, 802-4

co-ord. of progs. and act., 456-72; admin. and financial act., 462-64; annual reports of Sp. Ags., ESC consid., 458, 459-60 (*res.*); calendar of confs., 1972, ESC consid., 659, GA consid., 659, 660 (*res.*); econ., soc. and human rights progs., harmonization of budgets and progs., ESC consid., 465-66 (*res.*), 674, SG report, 465, reports on work prog. performance, format and content of, 464-65, ESC consid., 465-66 (*res.*), GA consid., 641, SG report, 464, work prog., ESC consid., 467-68, 471 (*res.*); econ., soc., scientific and technical act., ESC consid., 467, 470-71 (*res.*); prog. act., ESC consid., 456, 457-58 (*res.*); role of ACC, ESC consid., 456, 457-58 (*res.*); *see also* Administrative Committee on Co-ordination

econ. comms., reg., 801-2

ICJ, authorized to request adv. opinions from, 809

UNICEF Exec. Board, 806; UPU, 745; WHO, 712; WMO, 753

Sp. Ags., Conv. on, party to, 605

subs. to: Bank, 718; Fund, 735; IDA, 728; IFC, 722

see also Middle East, questions *re* situation in

Electric power: Bank loans for, 504, 714, 715-16, 717; ECE act., 333, 801; IAEA act., 684; IDA credits for, 725, 726; Mekong River Dev. Project, 338, 802

Electronic data-processing, *see* Computer use and programmes

Ellice Island, *see* Gilbert and Ellice Islands

El Salvador:

act. of in and for: FAO, 698; Fund, 732; 733; IDA, 726; TA, 262, 370, 378; UNDP/SF, 256; UNESCO, 705; UNICEF, 392; UNIDO, 289; WHO, 711

admission to UN, date of, 765

contrib. to: FAO, 699; IAEA, 685; ICAO, 741; ILO, 690; ITU, 748; UN, 653; UNDP, 247; UNESCO, 707; UPU, 745; WHO, 712; WMO, 753

ICJ, acceptance of compulsory jurisdiction and party to Statute of, 809

member of and reps.: Bank, 718; ECLA, 802; FAO, 699; Fund, 734; GA organs, 784, 785, 796; IAEA, 685; ICAO, 741; IDA, 728; IFC, 722; ILO, 690; ITU, 748; UNESCO, 707; UPU, 745; WHO, 712; WMO, 753

subs. to: Bank, 718; Fund, 735; IDA, 728; IFC, 722

Employment: Discrimination in, Conv. and Recomm. (ILO), 688; research insts., co-ord. of research (ILO), 688; women and girls, reg. conf. (ECA), 372; World Employment Prog. (ILO), 688

Energy resources: ECE act., 333; TA and UNDP/SF act., 323; *see also* Atomic energy, peaceful uses of; Electric power; Gas; International Atomic Energy Agency; Nuclear power; Water resources and supply

Engineers Joint Council, 450

Environment: ECE symposium, 334; IAEA act., 683-84; marine, uses of, ESC consid., 326, 329-30 (*res.*); national dev. plans (ECAFE), 337; Senior Advisers to ECE Govts. on Environmental Problems, 334, 801

Environment, human 307-13; biosphere, UNESCO act., 702; Group of 77 Dev. Countries, 292, 2d Ministerial Meeting, Decl. and Principles of Action Prog., 308, 311-12 (*res.*); in Strategy for 2d Dev. Decade, 308, 311-12 (*res.*); WMO act., 751-52; *see also* Pollution

UN Conf. on (1972), 307-13; ACC consid., 461; action plan and proposals, GA consid., 308-9, 312 (*res.*), 313 (*res.*); agenda for, 307, 309, 313 (*res.*); atomic radiation problems, 59, 60 (*res.*); decl. of draft, 307, 309, 313 (*res.*); ECLA part. in, 341; environmental policies of developing countries, effect of, UNCTAD study, proposal for, 309, 312 (*res.*); ESC consid., 307; GA consid., 307-10, 311-13 (*res.*); GATT measures *re* indus. pollution, 769; int. housing prog., 371;

participants, 309, 310, 313 (*res.*); Prep. Cttee. for, 784, members, 791, officers, 791, report, ESC consid., 307, GA consid., 307, 313 (*res.*), sess., 2d and 3d, 791, act., 307; rules of procedure, 307, 309, 313 (*res.*); SG, 810, report, GA consid., 307, 313 (*res.*); Working Groups, 791

Equatorial Guinea:

act. of in and for: FAO, 698; TA, 262; UNICEF, 392; WHO, 710

admission to UN, date of, 765

contrib. to: ITU, 748; UN, 653; UNDP, 247; UPU, 745

ICJ, party to Statute of, 809

member of and reps.: Bank, 718; ECA, 802; Fund, 734; ITU, 748; UPU, 745

subs. to: Bank, 718; Fund, 735

Ethiopia:

act. of in and for: Bank, 717; FAO, 695, 698; IDA, 726; TA, 262, 370; UNDP/SF, 256; UNESCO, 705; UNICEF, 392; UNIDO, 289, 290; WHO, 711

admission to UN, date of, 765

contrib. to: FAO, 699; IAEA, 685; ICAO, 741; ILO, 690; ITU, 748; UN, 653; UNDP, 247; UNESCO, 707; UNICEF, 393; UPU, 745; WHO, 712; WMO, 753

ICJ, party to Statute of, 809

member of and reps.: Bank, 718; ECA, 802; FAO, 699; Fund, 734; GA organs, 784, 785, 786; IAEA, 685; ICAO, 741; IDA, 728; IFC, 722; ILO, 690; ITU, 748; UNESCO, 707; UPU, Exec. Council, 745; WHO, 712, Exec. Bd., 713; WMO, 753

subs. to: Bank, 718; Fund, 735; IDA, 728; IFC, 722

Europe: air transport, Civil Aviation Conf., act., 740; Bank loans in, 714, 715, 716; Conf. of European Statisticians (ECE), 334, 801; cultural policies, UNESCO conf., 703; Econ. Comm., *see* Economic Commission for Europe; *Econ. Survey of in 1970* (ECE), 239; FAO act. in, 694, 695, 696, 697, 698-99 (*table*); IAEA act. in, 683, 684; ICAO act. in, 740; IDA credits to, 725, 726; IFC investment loans to, 720, 721; ILO act. in, 688; refugees in, 387; science and technology, reg. group, 314; Soc. Welfare Ministers, Conf., proposal for, ESC consid., 373; telecomm. reg. plan (ITU), 746, 747; UNDP reg. projects, 243, 244; UNESCO act. in, 701, 702, 703, 704, 704-7 (*table*); UNICEF act. in and allocations for aid, 389, 392 (*table*); UNIDO act. in, 288, 290; UPU act. in, 743, 744; WHO act. in, 711 (*table*)

European Alliance of Press Agencies, 450, 451

European Association for Animal Production, 451

European Association for Personnel Management, 451

European Bureau for Youth and Childhood, 451

European Centre for Overseas Industrial Development, 451

European Confederation of Agriculture, 451

European Confederation of Woodworking Industries, 451

European Economic Community (EEC), 697; association agreements (GATT), 760; contrib. to WFP, 267; rel. with ESC, 495; scheme of preferences, 275; sugar marketing, 274; UK entry into, effect on Papua New Guinea, 504-5; WFP aid, 268

European Federation of Associations of Engineers and Heads of Industrial Safety Services and Industrial Physicians, 451

European Federation of National Associations of Engineers, 451

European Insurance Committee, 449

European League for Economic Co-operation, 447, 448, 449

European Mechanical Handling Confederation, 451

European Nitrogen Produce Association, 451

European Nuclear Energy Agency (ENEA), 684

European Office of the United Nations, *see* United Nations Office at Geneva

European Society of Culture, 452

European Union of Coachbuilders, 452

European Writers' Community, 452

Experiment in International Living, 452

Experts: TA, *see under* Technical assistance for economic and social development, United Nations Development Programme/Technical Assistance component; total number, 244-45, 257, 258 (*table*); UNDP and TA, UN regular prog., project costs and numbers provided, by country, 261-65 (*table*); UNDP/SF, number, 257 (*table*), by field of activity, 258 (*table*), total number, 258 (*table*); UNDP /TA, by field of activity, 258 (*table*); *see also under specific subjects*

Falkland Islands (Islas Malvinas): NSGT, 577; qns. of sovereignty over, GA consid., 536, 545-46 (*res.*), Sp. Cttee. consid., 536

Family planning: ECAFE act., 338; IDA credits for, 727; meetings and seminars, 372; radio and television progs. (UNESCO), 703; social welfare aspects of, expert group, 356; UNESCO act., 702; UNICEF act., 390; WHO act., 709

Family welfare: advisers, 372; health, WHO act., 709-10; UNICEF act. and allocations, 390, 392 (*table*); *see also* Child welfare

Famines, *see* Droughts

Far East: Econ. Comm., *see* Economic Commission for Asia and the Far East; *Econ. Survey of Asia and the, 1970* (ECAFE), 336, 340; qns. relating to, 126-66; *see also* Asia

Federal Republic of Germany:

act. of in and for: Bank, 717; ILO, 692; TA, 262, 372; UNESCO, 705; WHO, 711

contrib. to: FAO, 699; GATT, 761; IAEA, 685; ICAO, 741; IDA, 725; ILO, 690; IMCO, 757; ITU, 748; UNDP, 247; UNESCO, 707; UNFICYP, 216;

Industrial development (*cont.*)
ing countries, SG report, ESC consid., 293-94; UNDP act., 244, ESC consid., 251, 254 (*res.*), 293-94
Industrial Development Board (IDB): documentation, control of, 663-64 (*res.*); Exec. Director, 791; GA organ, 784, 790; members, *1971* and *1972*, 791; officers, 791; report, ESC consid., 294, 297 (*res.*), GA consid., 294, 297 (*res.*); sess., 5th, 791, act., 293, 294; Working Group on Prog. and Co-ord., 784, 791, officers, 791, report, 293, sess., 3d, 791
UN Industrial Development Organization (UNIDO): act., 288-91; NGOs in consultative status with, 451, 452, 453, 454; part. in Strategy for 2d Dev. Decade, 225, 226, 227, 231 (*res.*), 291-92, GA consid., 293, 296 (*res.*); prog. and structure, 291-94, Sp. Int. Conf., 288, report and recomms., 291-92, ESC consid., 292, 295 (*res.*), GA consid., 292-93, 296-97 (*res.*), sess., 291; seminars and workshops, 290-91; technical co-op., 288-90, 292 (*see also* UNDP/SF act., UNDP/TA act.)
admin., co-ord., finances: budget, 292, appropriations for *1972*, 645, estimates for *1972*, 645, rev. appropriation for *1971*, 650; contribs., 295 (*table*), Pledging Conf., 294-95; co-op. with ECA, 341, FAO, 288, 317, 321 (*res.*), ILO, 288, 294, 317, 321 (*res.*), UNCTAD, 291, 293, 296 (*res.*), UNESCO, 290; co-op. with UNDP, 292, 293, 296 (*res.*), *Ad Hoc* Cttee. on, 784, eligibility of members, GA consid., 294, 297 (*res.*), members, 790; Exec. Director, 291, 292, 296-97 (*res.*), 352, 791, 810; GA organ, 784, 790; General Trust Fund, 288, 295; meetings with ACC, 804; members, 790-91; rep. to UNDP Inter-Agency Consultative Bd., 11th and 12th sess., 806; Sp. Indus. Services (SIS) Trust Fund Prog., 245, 246, 247, 288, 291, 292, 293, 296 (*res.*)
Industrialization, *see* Industrial development
Industry: African Ministers of, Conf. (ECA/OAU), 343; agri., co-op. prog. (FAO), 694; Bank loans for, 714, 716; ECA act., 343; ECAFE act., 337, 802; ECLA act., 341; GATT Cttee. on Trade in Indus. Prods., act., 759; Generalized System of Preferences, 291, 293, 296 (*res.*); IDA credits for, 725, 726; IFC investments in, 721; labour problems (ILO), 688; manufactures, UNCTAD act., 274-76; non-tariff barriers, UNCTAD consid., 275-76; product preferences for developing countries, Agreed Conclusions, 275, GA consid., 275, 282, 284 (*res.*); restrictive business practices, report, 276; UNDP/SF expends., 244, projects, 243, 244 (*table*); UNDP/TA expends., 244 (*table*), projects, 243, 244; UNIDO act., 290
UNCTAD Cttee. on Manufactures, 783; members and officers, 789; sess., 5th, 789, act., 274-75, 276

Information Centres, United Nations, 811-12 (*list*); staffing, 655
Information, freedom of: GA consid., 439, 444 (*res.*); periodic reports on, ESC consid., 439
Information, public: Centre for Econ. and Soc. Inf., reorg. of, 655, 657-58 (*res.*); Consultative Panel on UN Inf. Policies and Progs., composition, rev. of, 656, 657-58 (*res.*), 795, GA subsid. body, 784, members, 795, qn. of reactivation, 656, 657-58 (*res.*); UN policies and act., review and reappraisal, SG report, 654-55, GA consid., 655-58 (*res.*)
Office of (Hq.): Assistant SG, 809; pubs., 657; SG study, 654-55, GA consid., 655-58 (*res.*)
Inquiry and Conciliation, Panel for: GA subsid. body, 783; members and reps., 786
Inspection Unit, Joint, *see under* Finances of United Nations
Institute of International Law, 452
Institute of Man and Science, 452
Insurance: in developing countries, UNCTAD consid., 276
Inter-American Association of Broadcasters, 452
Inter-American Association of Sanitary Engineering, 452
Inter-American Federation of Public Relations Associations, 449
Inter-American Federation of Touring and Automobile Clubs, 451
Inter-American Planning Society, 449
Inter-American Press Association, 449
Inter-American Statistical Institute, 449
Inter-Governmental Committee for European Migration (ICEM), 386
Inter-governmental Council of Copper Exporting Countries (ECA), 345
Inter-Governmental Maritime Consultative Organization (IMCO), 755-57
act., 755-56; Assembly, 755-56; convs., deposits of, 755; technical co-op., 244, 756 (*see also under* UNDP/TA act.); *see also under relevant and related subjects*; Maritime questions
admin., co-ord., finances: budget, 756; contribs., 757 (*table*); co-op. with ECE, 334, FAO, 751, IAEA, 751, UNESCO, 751, WMO, 751, Council, members, 757; hq., 757; ICJ, authorized to request adv. opinions from, 809; Maritime Safety Cttee., members, 757; meetings with ACC, 804; members and assoc. member, 755, 759 (*table*); NGOs in consultative status with, 451, 452, 453, 454; officers and offices, 757; report, ESC consid., 458, 459-60 (*res.*); rep. to UNDP Inter-Agency Consultative Bd., 11th and 12th sess., 806; reps. on UN Joint Staff Pension Bd., 793; secretariat staff, 756; UN Joint Staff Pension Fund, part. in, 793
Intergovernmental Oceanographic Commission (UNESCO), 703; co-op. with WMO, 751
Inter-governmental organizations, non-UN: rel. with ESC, 494-95
Inter-governmental organizations related to United Nations, 683-762; UNDP Inter-

Agency Consultative Bd., rep. at 11th and 12th sess., 806; *see also* International Atomic Energy Agency; Specialized agencies; *names of individual agencies*
International Abolitionist Federation, 449
International Academy of Legal Medicine and of Social Medicine, 452
International Aeronautical Federation, 452
International Airline Navigators Council, 452
International Air Transport Association, 449
International Alliance of Women—Equal Rights, Equal Responsibilities, 449
International Association for Accident and Traffic Medicine, 452
International Association for Child Psychiatry and Allied Professions, 452
International Association for Earthquake Engineering, 452
International Association for Educational and Vocational Guidance, 452
International Association for Educational and Vocational Information, 452
International Association for Mass Communication Research, 452
International Association for Prevention of Blindness, 452
International Association for Religious Freedom, 452
International Association for Social Progress, 449
International Association for the Advancement of Educational Research, 452
International Association for the Exchange of Students for Technical Experience, 451
International Association for the Physical Sciences of the Ocean, 452
International Association for the Promotion and Protection of Private Foreign Investments, 449
International Association for Water Law (IAWL), 444, 448, 449
International Association of Agricultural Librarians and Documentalists, 452
International Association of Agricultural Medicine, 452, 708
International Association of Art Critics, 452
International Association of Art—Painting, Sculpture, Graphic Art, 452
International Association of Classification Societies, 452
International Association of Crafts and Small and Medium-sized Enterprises, 452
International Association of Democratic Lawyers, 449
International Association of Fish Meal Manufacturers, 452
International Association of Gerontology, 447, 451
International Association of Horticultural Producers, 452
International Association of Lawyers, 447, 449
International Association of Legal Science, 452
International Association of Lighthouse Authorities, 452
International Association of Literary Critics, 452

Manifesto on Southern Africa (Lusaka Manifesto), 69, 568, 569

Manpower: developing countries, outflow of trained personnel from ("Brain drain"), SG and UNITAR reports, ESC consid., 481-82; ECA act., 344; ILO act., 689

Manufacturers and manufacturing, see Industry

Maps: sea fisheries, world atlas (FAO), 696; soil, world (FAO/UNESCO), 695

Marine science, see Oceanography

Maritime questions: Conv. on Facilitation of Int. Maritime Traffic (1965), 755; electronic aids to navigation (IMCO), 755; Int. Convs. on Safety of Life at Sea, 755, 1971 amendment, 755; navigation safety, 755; radio communications, IMCO act., 755; workers, ILO act., 689; see also Inter-Governmental Maritime Consultative Organization; Ports; Shipping

Mass communication: UNESCO act., 702, 703-4 (table), 704-7 (table); see also Films; Journalism; Publishing; Radio broadcasting; Television broadcasting

Index of names